12⁹⁹

12⁹⁹

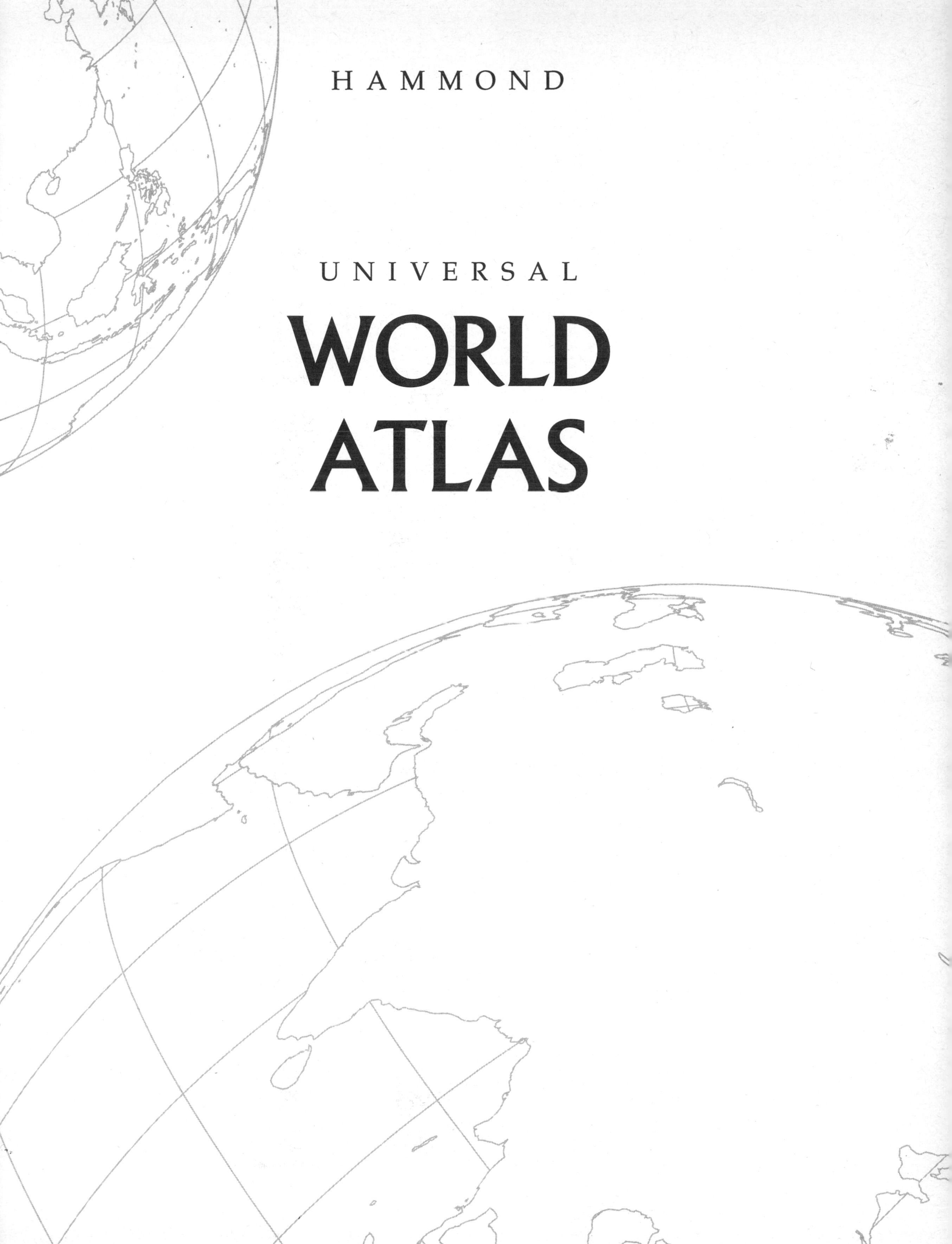

HAMMOND

UNIVERSAL

WORLD
ATLAS

Contents

Interpreting Maps

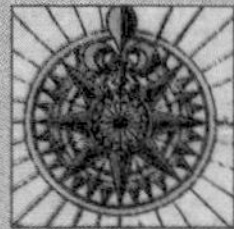

Designed to enhance your knowledge and enjoyment of the atlas, these pages explain map principles, scales, symbology and how to locate information quickly.

Geographic Comparisons

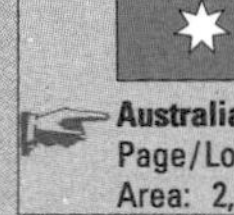

These eight pages contain flags and important facts about each independent country, plus dimensions of the earth's major mountains, longest rivers and largest lakes and islands.

Maps of the World

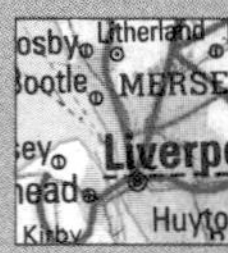

New maps, derived from a computer database, accurately present political detail while proprietary map projections show the most distortion-free views of the continents.

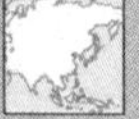

Europe and Northern Asia

Asia

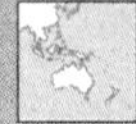

Pacific, Australia

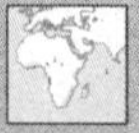

Africa, Antarctica

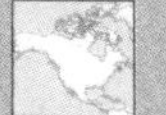

North America

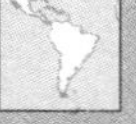

South America

Index

A 50,000-entry A to Z Index lists all places and geographic features in this atlas, complete with page numbers and easy-to-use alpha-numeric references.

ISBN 0-8437-1195-7

Map Projections

Simply stated, the map-maker's challenge is to project the earth's curved surface onto a flat plane. To achieve this elusive goal, cartographers have developed map projections — equations which govern this conversion of geographic data. This section explores some of the most widely used projections. It also introduces a new projection, the Hammond Optimal Conformal.

GENERAL PRINCIPLES AND TERMS

The earth rotates around its axis once a day. Its end points are the North and South poles; the line circling the earth midway between the poles is the equator. The arc from the equator to either pole is divided into 90 degrees of latitude. The equator represents 0° latitude. Circles of equal latitude, called parallels, are traditionally shown at every fifth or tenth degree.

The equator is divided into 360 degrees. Lines circling the globe from pole to pole through the degree points on the equator are called meridians, or great circles. All meridians are equal in length, but by international agreement the meridian passing through the Greenwich Observatory near London has been chosen as the prime meridian or 0° longitude. The distance in degrees from the prime meridian to any point east or west is its longitude.

While meridians are all equal in length, parallels become shorter as they approach the poles. Whereas one degree of latitude represents approximately 69 miles (112 km.) anywhere on the globe, a degree of longitude varies from 69 miles (112 km.) at the equator to zero at the poles. Each degree of latitude and longitude is divided into 60 minutes. One minute of latitude equals one nautical mile (1.15 land miles or 1.85 km.).

HOW TO FLATTEN A SPHERE: THE ART OF CONTROLLING DISTORTION

There is only one way to represent a sphere with absolute precision: on a globe. All attempts to project our planet's surface onto a plane unevenly stretch or tear the sphere as it flattens, inevitably distorting shapes, distances, area (sizes appear larger or smaller than actual size), angles or direction.

Since representing a sphere on a flat plane always creates distortion, only the parallels or the meridians (or some other set of lines) can maintain the same length as on a globe of corresponding scale. All other lines must be either too long or too short. Accordingly, the scale on a flat map cannot be true everywhere; there will always be different scales in different parts of a map. On world maps or very large areas, variations in scale may be extreme. Most maps seek to preserve either true area relationships (equal area projections) or true angles and shapes (conformal projections); some attempt to achieve overall balance.

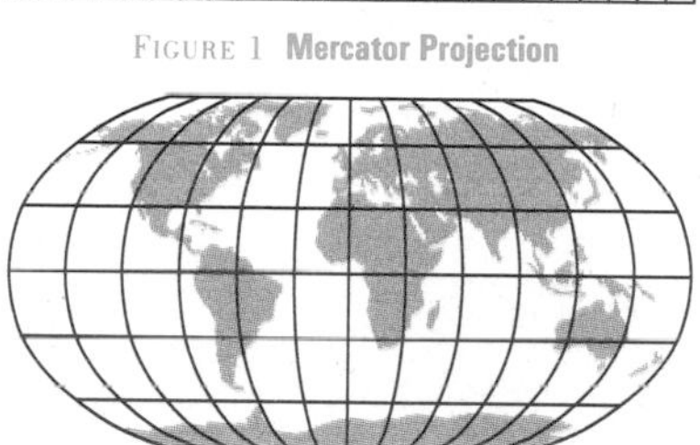

FIGURE 1 Mercator Projection

FIGURE 2 Robinson Projection

PROJECTIONS: SELECTED EXAMPLES

Mercator (Fig. 1): This projection is especially useful because all compass directions appear as straight lines, making it a valuable navigational tool. Moreover, every small region conforms to its shape on a globe — hence the name conformal. But because its meridians are evenly-spaced vertical lines which never converge (unlike the globe), the horizontal parallels must be drawn farther and farther apart at higher latitudes to maintain a correct relationship.

Only the equator is true to scale, and the size of areas in the higher latitudes is dramatically distorted.

Robinson (Fig. 2): To create the thematic maps in Global Relationships and the two-page world map in the Maps of the World section, the Robinson projection was used. It combines elements of both conformal and equal area projections to show the whole earth with relatively true shapes and reasonably equal areas.

Conic (Fig. 3): This projection has been used frequently for air navigation charts and to create most of the national and regional maps in this atlas. (See text in margin at left).

HAMMOND'S OPTIMAL CONFORMAL

As its name implies, this new conformal projection (Fig. 4) presents the optimal view of an area by reducing shifts in scale over an entire region to the minimum degree possible. While conformal maps generally preserve all small shapes, large shapes can become very distorted because of varying scales, causing considerable inaccuracy in distance measurements. The concept underlying the Optimal Conformal is that for any region on the globe, there is an ideal projection for which scale variation can be made as small as possible. Consequently, unlike other projections, the Optimal Conformal does not use one standard formula to construct a map. Each map is a unique projection — the optimal projection for that particular area.

After a cartographer defines the subject area, a sophisticated computer program evaluates the size and shape of the region, projecting the most distortion-free map possible. All of the continent maps in this atlas, except Antarctica, have been drawn using the Optimal projection.

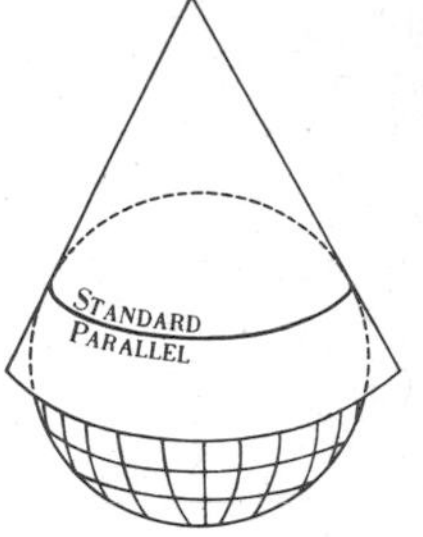

FIGURE 3
Conic Projection
The original idea of a conic projection is to cap the globe with a cone, and then project onto the cone from the planet's center the lines of latitude and longitude (the parallels and meridians). To produce a working map, the cone is simply cut open and laid flat. The conic projection used here is a modification of this idea. A cone can be made tangent to any standard parallel you choose. One popular version of a conic projection, the Lambert Conformal Conic, uses two standard parallels near the top and bottom of the map to further reduce errors of scale.

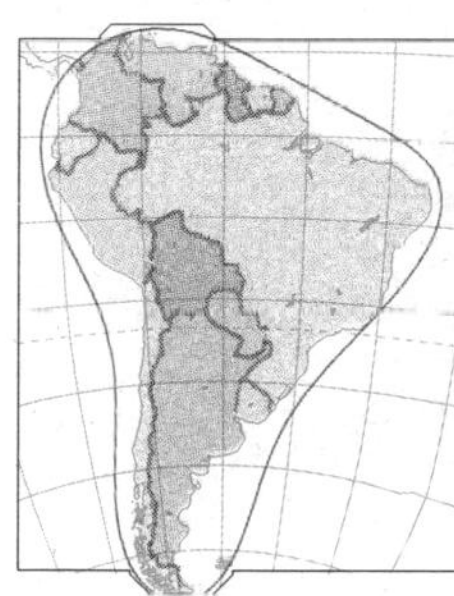

FIGURE 4
Hammond's Optimal Conformal Projection
Like all conformal maps, the Optimal projection preserves angles exactly and minimizes distortion in shapes. This projection is more successful than any previous projection at spreading curvature across the entire map, producing the most distortion-free map possible.

Using This Atlas

How to Locate Information Quickly
Our Maps of the World section is organized by continent. If you're looking for a major region of the world, consult the Contents on page two.

Australia
Page/Location: 70
Area: 2,966,136 sq
7,682,300 s
Population: 17,2
Capital: Canb
Largest

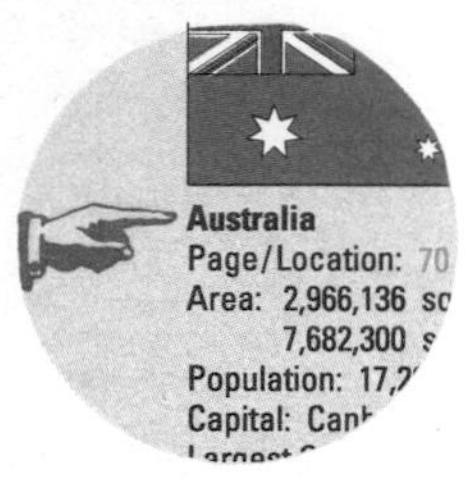

World Reference Guide
This concise guide lists the countries of the world alphabetically. If you're looking for the largest scale map of any country, you'll find a page and alpha-numeric reference at a glance, as well as information about each country, including its flag.

Merlimont, Fran
3/F4 **Mersch,** Luxembou
68/A3 **Mers-les-Bains,**
France
69/F4 **Mertert,** Luxembourg
69/F4 **Mertesdorf,** Germany
69/G6 **Mertzwiller,** France
68/B5 **Méru,** France
68/B2 **Merville,** France
69/F2 **Merzenich,** Germany
69/F5 **Merzig,** Germany
'F4 **Messancy,** Belc
'attat Belc

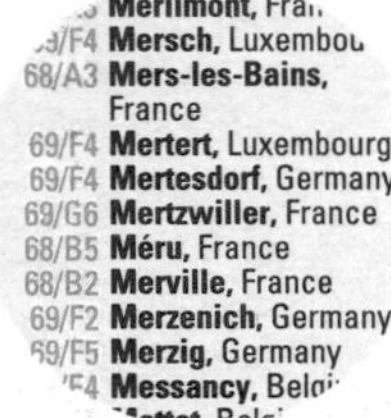

Master Index
When you're looking for a specific place or physical feature, your quickest route is the Master Index. This 50,000-entry alphabetical index lists both the page number and alpha-numeric reference for major places and features in Maps of the World.

This new atlas is created from a unique digital database, and its computer-generated maps represent a new phase in map-making technology.

How Computer-Generated Maps Are Made

To build a digital database capable of generating this world atlas, the latitude and longitude of every significant town, river, coastline, natural and political border, transportation network and peak elevation was researched and digitized. Hundreds of millions of data points describing every important geographic feature are organized into thousands of different map feature codes.

There are no maps in this unique system. Rather, it consists entirely of coded points, lines and polygons. To create a map, cartographers simply determine what specific information they wish to show, based upon considerations of scale, size, density and importance of different features.

New technology developed by mathematical physicist Mitchell Feigenbaum uses fractal geometry to describe and re-configure coastlines, borders and mountain ranges to fit a variety of map scales and projections. Dr. Feigenbaum has also created a computerized type placement program which allows thousands of map labels to be placed accurately in minutes. After these steps have been completed, the computer then draws the final map.

Each section of this atlas has been designed to be both easy and enjoyable to use. Familiarizing yourself with its organization will help you to benefit fully from its use.

World Flags and Reference Guide

This colorful section portrays each nation of the world, its flag, important geographical data, such as size, population and capital, and its location in the Maps of the World section.

Symbols Used on Maps of the World

First Order (National) Boundary	City and Urban Area Limits	Rome — First Order (National) Capital
First Order Water Boundary	Demilitarized Zone	Belfast — Second Order (Internal) Capital
First Order Disputed Boundary	National Park/Preserve/Scenic Area	Hull — Third Order (Internal) Capital
Second Order (Internal) Boundary	National Forest/Forest Reserve	Neighborhood
Second Order Water Boundary	National Wilderness/Grassland	Pass
Second Order Disputed Boundary	National Recreation Area/Monument	Ruins
Third Order (Internal) Boundary	National Seashore/Lakeshore	Falls
Undefined Boundary	National Wildlife/Wilderness Area	Rapids
International Date Line	Native Reservation/Reserve	Dam
Shoreline, River	Military/Government Reservation	Point Elevation
Intermittent River	Lake, Reservoir	Park
Canal/Aqueduct	Intermittent Lake	Wildlife Area
Continental Divide	Dry Lake	Point of Interest
Highways/Roads	Salt Pan	Well
Railroads	Desert/Sand Area	International Airport
Ferries	Swamp	Other Airport
Tunnels (Road, Railroad)	Lava Flow	Air Base
Ancient Walls	Glacier	Naval Base

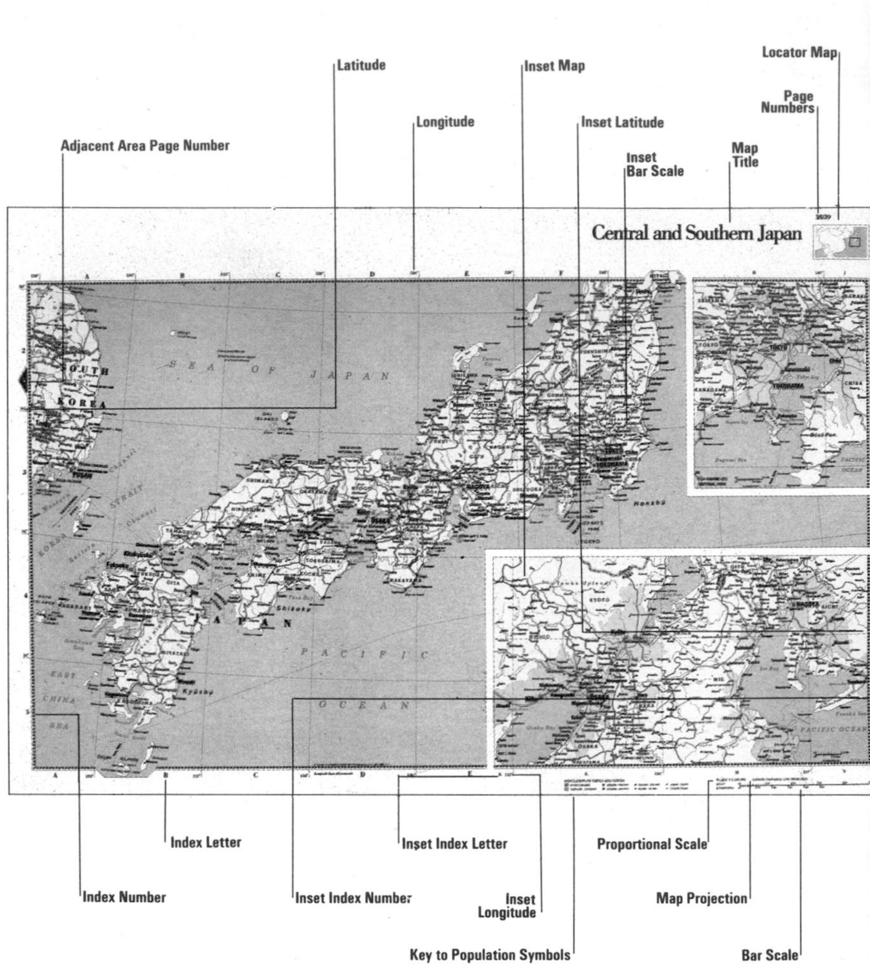

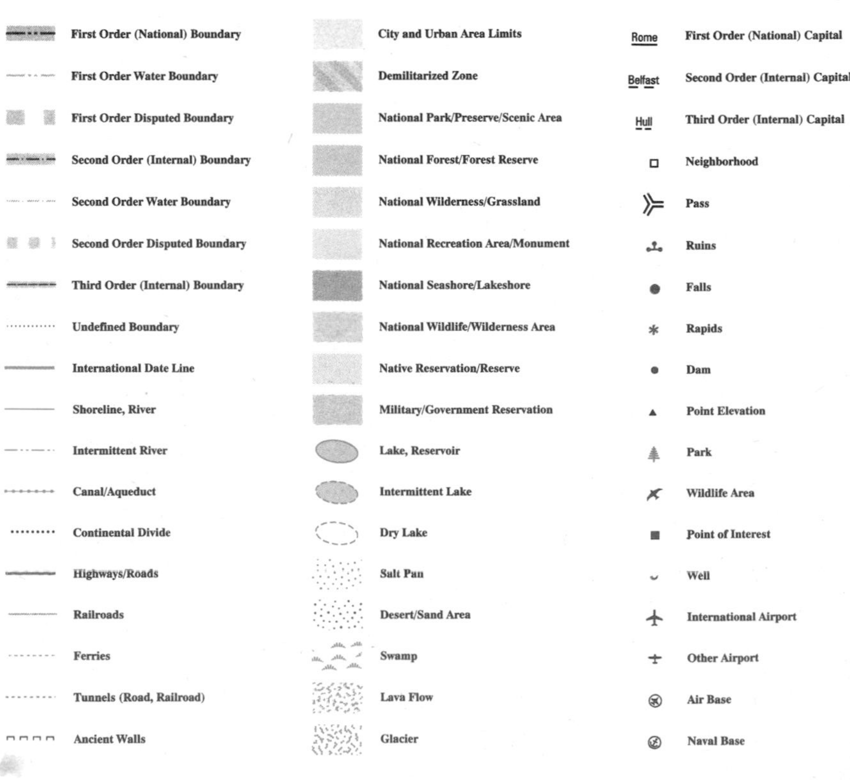

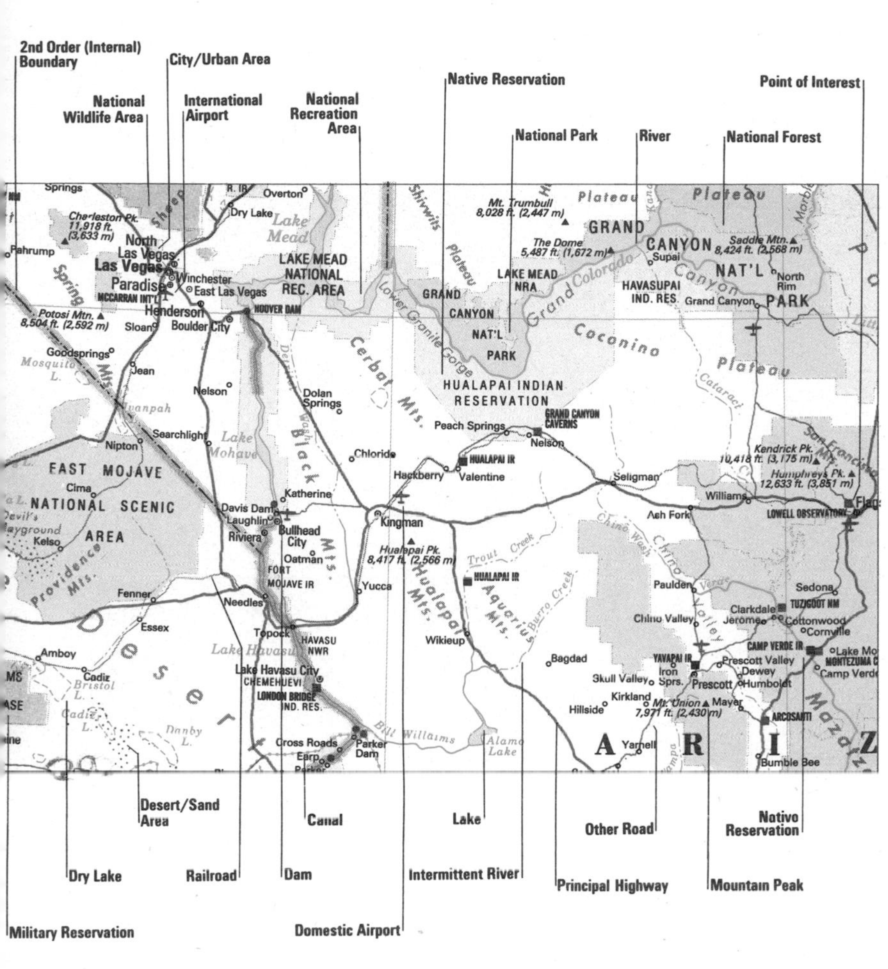

2nd Order (Internal) Boundary · City/Urban Area · National Wildlife Area · International Airport · National Recreation Area · Native Reservation · National Park · River · National Forest · Point of Interest

Desert/Sand Area · Canal · Lake · Other Road · Native Reservation

Dry Lake · Railroad · Dam · Intermittent River · Principal Highway · Mountain Peak

Military Reservation · Domestic Airport

WORLD STATISTICS

World Statistics lists the dimensions of the earth's principal mountains, islands, rivers and lakes, along with other useful geographic information.

MAPS OF THE WORLD

These detailed regional maps are arranged by continent, and introduced by a political map of that continent. The continent maps, which utilize Hammond's new Optimal Conformal projection, are distinguished by individual colors for each country to highlight political divisions.

On the regional maps, different colors and textures highlight distinctive features such as parks, forests, deserts and urban areas. These maps also provide considerable information concerning geographic features and political divisions.

MASTER INDEX

This is an A-Z listing of names found on the political maps. It also has its own abbreviation list which, along with other Index keys, appears on page 110.

MAP SCALES

A map's scale is the relationship of any length on the map to an identical length on the earth's surface. A scale of 1:3,000,000 means that one inch on the map represents 3,000,000 inches (47 miles, 76 km.) on the earth's surface. Thus, a 1:1,000,000 scale is larger than 1:3,000,000, just as 1/1 is larger than 1/3.

The most densely populated areas are shown at a scale of 1:1,170,000, while selected metropolitan areas are covered at either 1:587,000 or 1:1,170,000. Other populous areas are presented at 1:3,500,000 and 1:7,000,000, allowing you to accurately compare areas and distances of similar regions. Remaining regions are scaled at 1:10,500,000. The continent maps, as well as the United States, Canada, Russia, Pacific and World have smaller scales.

Boundary Policies
This atlas observes the boundary policies of the U.S. Department of State. Boundary disputes are customarily handled with a special symbol treatment, but de facto boundaries are favored if they seem to have any degree of permanence, in the belief that boundaries should reflect current geographic and political realities. The portrayal of independent nations in the atlas follows their recognition by the United Nations and/or the United States government.

Hammond also uses accepted conventional names for certain major foreign places. Usually, space permits the inclusion of the local form in parentheses. To make the maps more readily understandable to English-speaking readers, many foreign physical features are translated into more recognizable English forms.

A Word About Names
Our source for all foreign names and physical names in the United States is the decision lists of the U.S. Board of Geographic Names, which contain hundreds of thousands of place names. If a place is not listed, the Atlas follows the name form appearing on official foreign maps or in official gazetteers of the country concerned. For rendering domestic city, town and village names, this atlas follows the forms and spelling of the U.S. Postal Service.

PRINCIPAL MAP ABBREVIATIONS

ABOR. RSV.	ABORIGINAL RESERVE	IND. RES.	INDIAN RESERVATION	NWR	NATIONAL WILDLIFE
ADMIN.	ADMINISTRATION	INT'L	INTERNATIONAL		RESERVE
AFB	AIR FORCE BASE	IR	INDIAN RESERVATION	OBL.	OBLAST
AMM. DEP.	AMMUNITION DEPOT	ISTH.	ISTHMUS	OCC.	OCCUPIED
ARCH.	ARCHIPELAGO	JCT.	JUNCTION	OKR.	OKRUG
ARPT.	AIRPORT	L.	LAKE	PAR.	PARISH
AUT.	AUTONOMOUS	LAG.	LAGOON	PASSG.	PASSAGE
B.	BAY	LAKESH.	LAKESHORE	PEN.	PENINSULA
BFLD.	BATTLEFIELD	MEM.	MEMORIAL	PK.	PEAK
BK.	BROOK	MIL.	MILITARY	PLAT.	PLATEAU
BOR.	BOROUGH	MISS.	MISSILE	PN	PARK NATIONAL
BR.	BRANCH	MON.	MONUMENT	PREF.	PREFECTURE
C.	CAPE	MT.	MOUNT	PROM.	PROMONTORY
CAN.	CANAL	MTN.	MOUNTAIN	PROV.	PROVINCE
CAP.	CAPITAL	MTS.	MOUNTAINS	PRSV.	PRESERVE
C.G.	COAST GUARD	NAT.	NATURAL	PT.	POINT
CHAN.	CHANNEL	NAT'L	NATIONAL	R.	RIVER
CO.	COUNTY	NAV.	NAVAL	RA	RECREATION AREA
CR.	CREEK	NB	NATIONAL	RA.	RANGE
CTR.	CENTER		BATTLEFIELD	REC.	RECREATION(AL)
DEP.	DEPOT	NBP	NATIONAL	REF.	REFUGE
DEPR.	DEPRESSION		BATTLEFIELD PARK	REG.	REGION
DEPT.	DEPARTMENT	NBS	NATIONAL	REP.	REPUBLIC
DES.	DESERT		BATTLEFIELD SITE	RES.	RESERVOIR,
DIST.	DISTRICT	NHP	NATIONAL HISTORICAL		RESERVATION
DMZ	DEMILITARIZED ZONE		PARK	RVWY.	RIVERWAY
DPCY.	DEPENDENCY	NHPP	NATIONAL HISTORICAL	SA.	SIERRA
ENG.	ENGINEERING		PARK AND PRESERVE	SD.	SOUND
EST.	ESTUARY	NHS	NATIONAL HISTORIC	SEASH.	SEASHORE
FD.	FIORD, FJORD		SITE	SO.	SOUTHERN
FED.	FEDERAL	NL	NATIONAL LAKESHORE	SP	STATE PARK
FK.	FORK	NM	NATIONAL MONUMENT	SPR., SPRS.	SPRING, SPRINGS
FLD.	FIELD	NMEMP	NATIONAL MEMORIAL	ST.	STATE
FOR.	FOREST		PARK	STA.	STATION
FT.	FORT	NMILP	NATIONAL MILITARY	STM.	STREAM
G.	GULF		PARK	STR.	STRAIT
GOV.	GOVERNOR	NO.	NORTHERN	TERR.	TERRITORY
GOVT.	GOVERNMENT	NP	NATIONAL PARK	TUN.	TUNNEL
GD.	GRAND	NPP	NATIONAL PARK AND	TWP.	TOWNSHIP
GT.	GREAT		PRESERVE	VAL.	VALLEY
HAR.	HARBOR	NPRSV	NATIONAL PRESERVE	VILL.	VILLAGE
HD.	HEAD	NRA	NATIONAL	VOL.	VOLCANO
HIST.	HISTORIC(AL)		RECREATION AREA	WILD.	WILDLIFE,
HTS.	HEIGHTS	NRSV	NATIONAL RESERVE		WILDERNESS
I., IS.	ISLAND(S)	NS	NATIONAL SEASHORE	WTR.	WATER

World Flags and Reference Guide

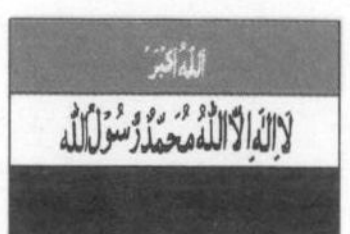

Afghanistan
Page/Location: 53/H2
Area: 250,775 sq. mi.
649,507 sq. km.
Population: 16,450,000
Capital: Kabul
Largest City: Kabul
Highest Point: Noshaq
Monetary Unit: afghani

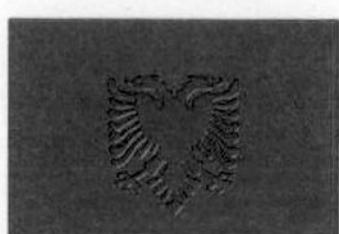

Albania
Page/Location: 39/F2
Area: 11,100 sq. mi.
28,749 sq. km.
Population: 3,335,000
Capital: Tiranë
Largest City: Tiranë
Highest Point: Korab
Monetary Unit: lek

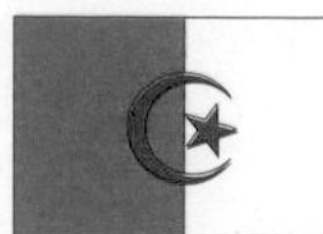

Algeria
Page/Location: 76/F2
Area: 919,591 sq. mi.
2,381,740 sq. km.
Population: 26,022,000
Capital: Algiers
Largest City: Algiers
Highest Point: Tahat
Monetary Unit: Algerian dinar

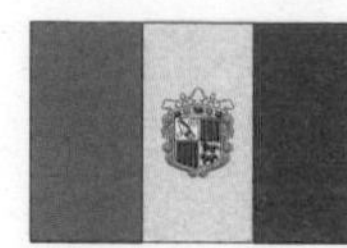

Andorra
Page/Location: 35/F1
Area: 188 sq. mi.
487 sq. km.
Population: 53,000
Capital: Andorra la Vella
Largest City: Andorra la Vella
Highest Point: Coma Pedrosa
Monetary Unit: Fr. franc, Sp. peseta

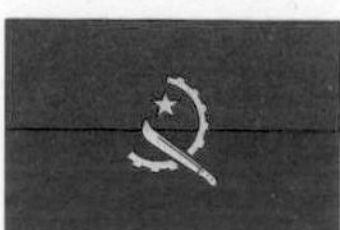

Angola
Page/Location: 82/C3
Area: 481,351 sq. mi.
1,246,700 sq. km.
Population: 8,668,000
Capital: Luanda
Largest City: Luanda
Highest Point: Morro de Môco
Monetary Unit: kwanza

Antigua and Barbuda
Page/Location: 104/F3
Area: 171 sq. mi.
443 sq. km.
Population: 64,000
Capital: St. John's
Largest City: St. John's
Highest Point: Boggy Peak
Monetary Unit: East Caribbean dollar

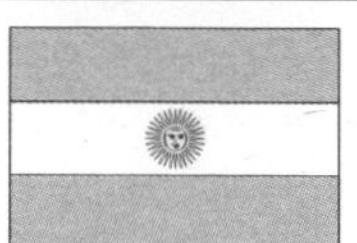

Argentina
Page/Location: 109/C4
Area: 1,072,070 sq. mi.
2,776,661 sq. km.
Population: 32,664,000
Capital: Buenos Aires
Largest City: Buenos Aires
Highest Point: Cerro Aconcagua
Monetary Unit: austral

Armenia
Page/Location: 45/H5
Area: 11,506 sq. mi.
29,800 sq. km.
Population: 3,283,000
Capital: Yerevan
Largest City: Yerevan
Highest Point: Alagez
Monetary Unit: Armenian ruble

Australia
Page/Location: 70
Area: 2,966,136 sq. mi.
7,682,300 sq. km.
Population: 17,288,000
Capital: Canberra
Largest City: Sydney
Highest Point: Mt. Kosciusko
Monetary Unit: Australian dollar

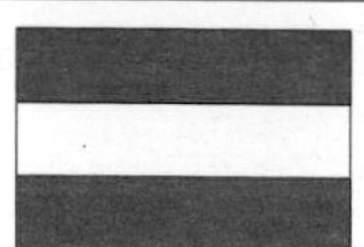

Austria
Page/Location: 33/L3
Area: 32,375 sq. mi.
83,851 sq. km.
Population: 7,666,000
Capital: Vienna
Largest City: Vienna
Highest Point: Grossglockner
Monetary Unit: schilling

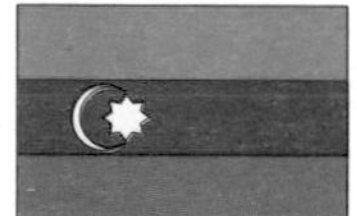

Azerbaijan
Page/Location: 45/H4
Area: 33,436 sq. mi.
86,600 sq. km.
Population: 7,029,000
Capital: Baku
Largest City: Baku
Highest Point: Bazardyuzyu
Monetary Unit: Azerbaijani ruble

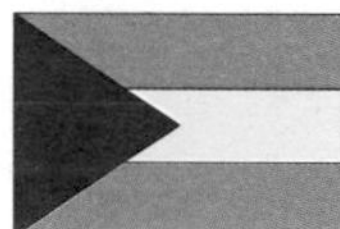

Bahamas
Page/Location: 104/B2
Area: 5,382 sq. mi.
13,939 sq. km.
Population: 252,000
Capital: Nassau
Largest City: Nassau
Highest Point: 207 ft. (63 m)
Monetary Unit: Bahamian dollar

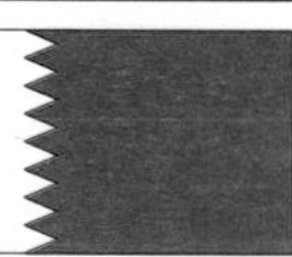

Bahrain
Page/Location: 52/F3
Area: 240 sq. mi.
622 sq. km.
Population: 537,000
Capital: Manama
Largest City: Manama
Highest Point: Jabal Dukhān
Monetary Unit: Bahraini dinar

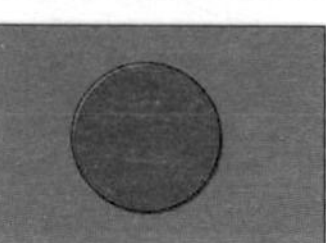

Bangladesh
Page/Location: 60/E3
Area: 55,126 sq. mi.
142,776 sq. km.
Population: 116,601,000
Capital: Dhaka
Largest City: Dhaka
Highest Point: Keokradong
Monetary Unit: taka

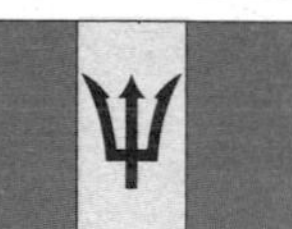

Barbados
Page/Location: 104/G4
Area: 166 sq. mi.
430 sq. km.
Population: 255,000
Capital: Bridgetown
Largest City: Bridgetown
Highest Point: Mt. Hillaby
Monetary Unit: Barbadian dollar

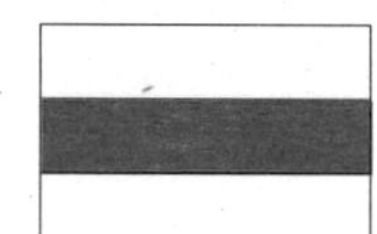

Belarus
Page/Location: 18/F3
Area: 80,154 sq. mi.
207,600 sq. km.
Population: 10,200,000
Capital: Minsk
Largest City: Minsk
Highest Point: Dzerzhinskaya
Monetary Unit: Belarusian ruble

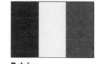

Belgium
Page/Location: 30/C2
Area: 11,781 sq. mi.
30,513 sq. km.
Population: 9,922,000
Capital: Brussels
Largest City: Brussels
Highest Point: Botrange
Monetary Unit: Belgian franc

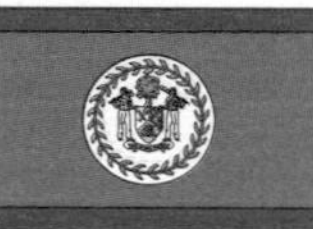

Belize
Page/Location: 102/D2
Area: 8,867 sq. mi.
22,966 sq. km.
Population: 228,000
Capital: Belmopan
Largest City: Belize City
Highest Point: Victoria Peak
Monetary Unit: Belize dollar

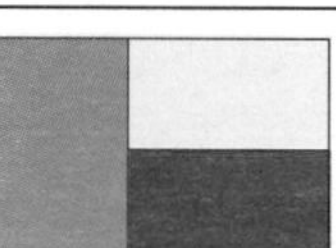

Benin
Page/Location: 79/F4
Area: 43,483 sq. mi.
112,620 sq. km.
Population: 4,832,000
Capital: Porto-Novo
Largest City: Cotonou
Highest Point: Nassoukou
Monetary Unit: CFA franc

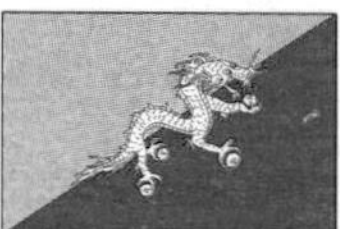

Bhutan
Page/Location: 62/E2
Area: 18,147 sq. mi.
47,000 sq. km.
Population: 1,598,000
Capital: Thimphu
Largest City: Thimphu
Highest Point: Kula Kangri
Monetary Unit: ngultrum

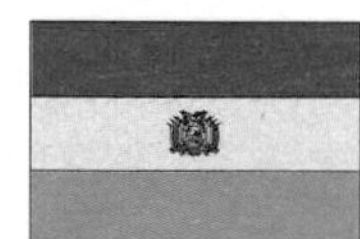

Bolivia
Page/Location: 106/F7
Area: 424,163 sq. mi.
1,098,582 sq. km.
Population: 7,157,000
Capital: La Paz; Sucre
Largest City: La Paz
Highest Point: Nevado Ancohuma
Monetary Unit: Bolivian peso

Bosnia and Hercegovina
Page/Location: 40/C3
Area: 19,940 sq. mi.
51,129 sq. km.
Population: 4,124,256
Capital: Sarajevo
Largest City: Sarajevo
Highest Point: Maglič
Monetary Unit: —

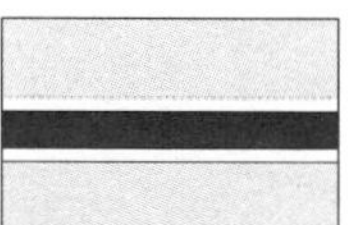

Botswana
Page/Location: 82/D5
Area: 224,764 sq. mi.
582,139 sq. km.
Population: 1,258,000
Capital: Gaborone
Largest City: Gaborone
Highest Point: Tsodilo Hills
Monetary Unit: pula

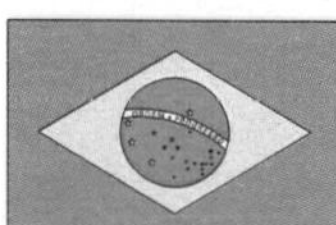

Brazil
Page/Location: 105/D3
Area: 3,284,426 sq. mi.
8,506,663 sq. km.
Population: 155,356,000
Capital: Brasília
Largest City: São Paulo
Highest Point: Pico da Neblina
Monetary Unit: cruzado

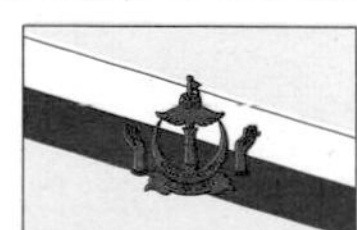

Brunei
Page/Location: 66/D2
Area: 2,226 sq. mi.
5,765 sq. km.
Population: 398,000
Capital: Bandar Seri Begawan
Largest City: Bandar Seri Begawan
Highest Point: Bukit Pagon
Monetary Unit: Brunei dollar

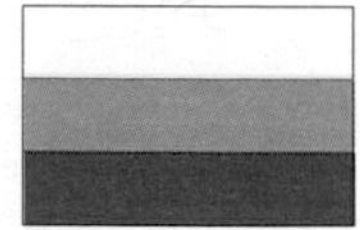

Bulgaria
Page/Location: 41/G4
Area: 42,823 sq. mi.
110,912 sq. km.
Population: 8,911,000
Capital: Sofia
Largest City: Sofia
Highest Point: Musala
Monetary Unit: lev

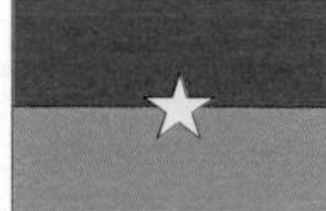

Burkina Faso
Page/Location: 79/E3
Area: 105,869 sq. mi.
274,200 sq. km.
Population: 9,360,000
Capital: Ouagadougou
Largest City: Ouagadougou
Highest Point: 2,405 ft. (733 m)
Monetary Unit: CFA franc

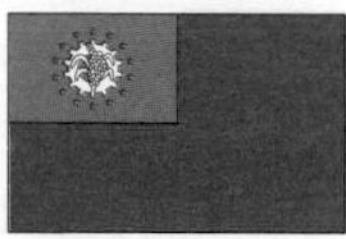

Burma
Page/Location: 63/G3
Area: 261,789 sq. mi.
678,034 sq. km.
Population: 42,112,000
Capital: Rangoon
Largest City: Rangoon
Highest Point: Hkakabo Razi
Monetary Unit: kyat

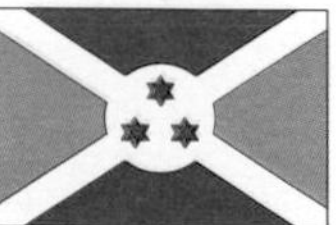

Burundi
Page/Location: 82/E1
Area: 10,747 sq. mi.
27,835 sq. km.
Population: 5,831,000
Capital: Bujumbura
Largest City: Bujumbura
Highest Point: 8,760 ft. (2,670 m)
Monetary Unit: Burundi franc

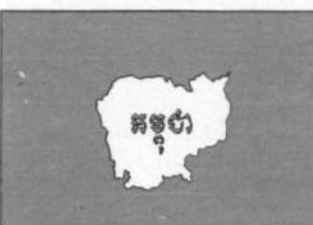

Cambodia
Page/Location: 65/D3
Area: 69,898 sq. mi.
181,036 sq. km.
Population: 7,146,000
Capital: Phnom Penh
Largest City: Phnom Penh
Highest Point: Phnum Aoral
Monetary Unit: riel

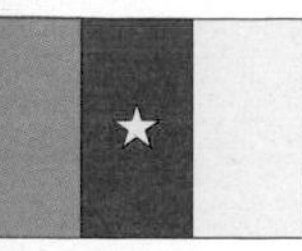

Cameroon
Page/Location: 76/H7
Area: 183,568 sq. mi.
475,441 sq. km.
Population: 11,390,000
Capital: Yaoundé
Largest City: Douala
Highest Point: Mt. Cameroon
Monetary Unit: CFA franc

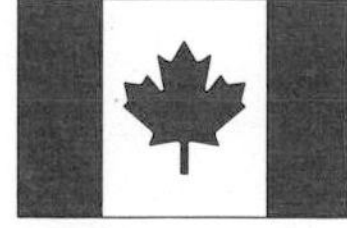

Canada
Page/Location: 86
Area: 3,851,787 sq. mi.
9,976,139 sq. km.
Population: 26,835,331
Capital: Ottawa
Largest City: Toronto
Highest Point: Mt. Logan
Monetary Unit: Canadian dollar

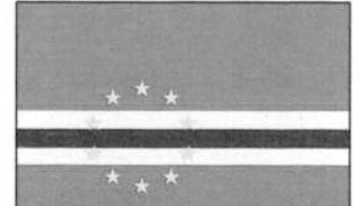

Cape Verde
Page/Location: 74/K9
Area: 1,557 sq. mi.
4,033 sq. km.
Population: 387,000
Capital: Praia
Largest City: Praia
Highest Point: 9,282 ft. (2,829 m)
Monetary Unit: Cape Verde escudo

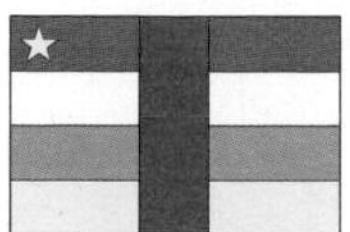

Central African Republic
Page/Location: 77/J6
Area: 242,000 sq. mi.
626,780 sq. km.
Population: 2,952,000
Capital: Bangui
Largest City: Bangui
Highest Point: Mt. Kayagangiri
Monetary Unit: CFA franc

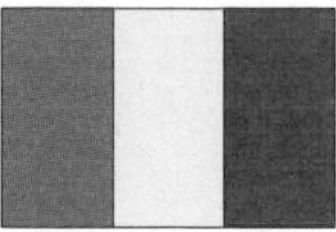

Chad
Page/Location: 77/J4
Area: 495,752 sq. mi.
1,283,998 sq. km.
Population: 5,122,000
Capital: N'Djamena
Largest City: N'Djamena
Highest Point: Emi Koussi
Monetary Unit: CFA franc

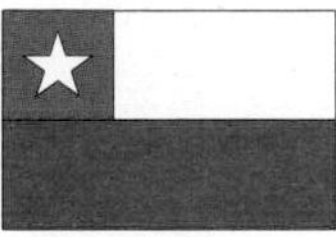

Chile
Page/Location: 109/B3
Area: 292,257 sq. mi.
756,946 sq. km.
Population: 13,287,000
Capital: Santiago
Largest City: Santiago
Highest Point: Nevado Ojos del Salado
Monetary Unit: Chilean peso

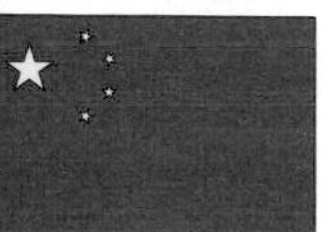

China
Page/Location: 48/J6
Area: 3,691,000 sq. mi.
9,559,690 sq. km.
Population: 1,151,487,000
Capital: Beijing
Largest City: Shanghai
Highest Point: Mt. Everest
Monetary Unit: yuan

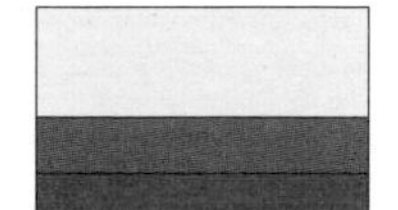

Colombia
Page/Location: 106/D3
Area: 439,513 sq. mi.
1,138,339 sq. km.
Population: 33,778,000
Capital: Bogotá
Largest City: Bogotá
Highest Point: Pico Cristóbal Colón
Monetary Unit: Colombian peso

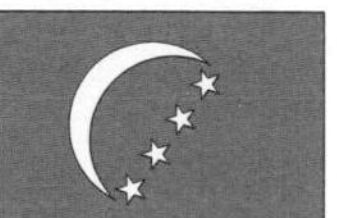

Comoros
Page/Location: 74/G6
Area: 719 sq. mi.
1,862 sq. km.
Population: 477,000
Capital: Moroni
Largest City: Moroni
Highest Point: Karthala
Monetary Unit: CFA franc

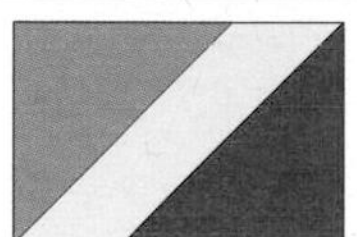

Congo
Page/Location: 74/D5
Area: 132,046 sq. mi.
342,000 sq. km.
Population: 2,309,000
Capital: Brazzaville
Largest City: Brazzaville
Highest Point: Lékéti Mts.
Monetary Unit: CFA franc

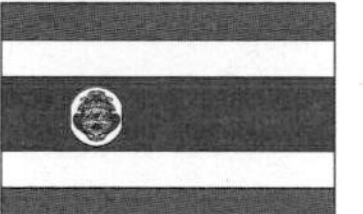

Costa Rica
Page/Location: 103/F4
Area: 19,575 sq. mi.
50,700 sq. km.
Population: 3,111,000
Capital: San José
Largest City: San José
Highest Point: Cerro Chirripó Grande
Monetary Unit: Costa Rican colón

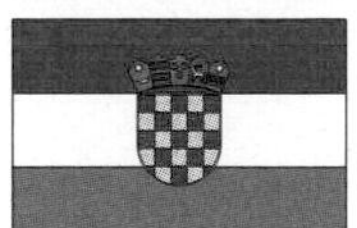

Croatia
Page/Location: 40/C3
Area: 22,050 sq. mi.
56,538 sq. km.
Population: 4,601,469
Capital: Zagreb
Largest City: Zagreb
Highest Point: Veliki Troglav
Monetary Unit: Croatian dinar

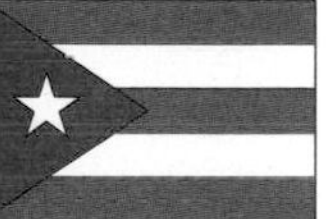

Cuba
Page/Location: 103/F1
Area: 44,206 sq. mi.
114,494 sq. km.
Population: 10,732,000
Capital: Havana
Largest City: Havana
Highest Point: Pico Turquino
Monetary Unit: Cuban peso

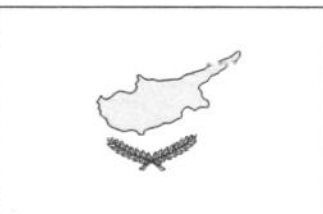

Cyprus
Page/Location: 49/C2
Area: 3,473 sq. mi.
8,995 sq. km.
Population: 709,000
Capital: Nicosia
Largest City: Nicosia
Highest Point: Olympus
Monetary Unit: Cypriot pound

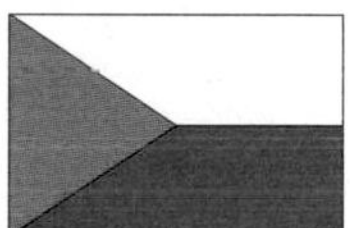

Czech Republic
Page/Location: 27/H4
Area: 30,449 sq. mi.
78,863 sq. km.
Population: 10,291,927
Capital: Prague
Largest City: Prague
Highest Point: Sněžka
Monetary Unit: Czech koruna

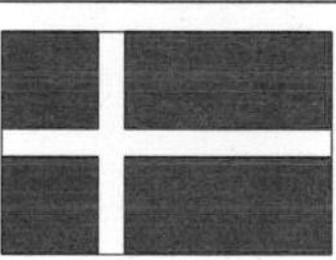

Denmark
Page/Location: 20/C5
Area: 16,629 sq. mi.
43,069 sq. km.
Population: 5,133,000
Capital: Copenhagen
Largest City: Copenhagen
Highest Point: Yding Skovhøj
Monetary Unit: krone

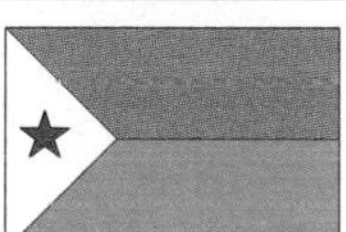

Djibouti
Page/Location: 77/P5
Area: 8,880 sq. mi.
23,000 sq. km.
Population: 346,000
Capital: Djibouti
Largest City: Djibouti
Highest Point: Moussa Ali
Monetary Unit: Djibouti franc

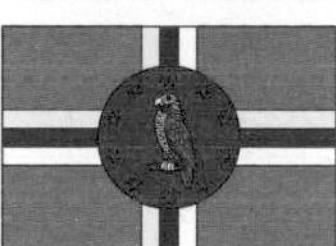

Dominica
Page/Location: 104/F4
Area: 290 sq. mi.
751 sq. km.
Population: 86,000
Capital: Roseau
Largest City: Roseau
Highest Point: Morne Diablotin
Monetary Unit: Dominican dollar

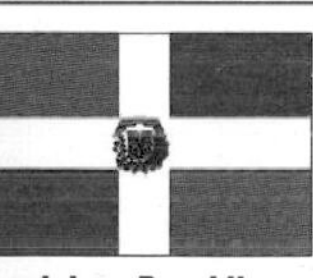

Dominican Republic
Page/Location: 104/D3
Area: 18,704 sq. mi.
48,443 sq. km.
Population: 7,385,000
Capital: Santo Domingo
Largest City: Santo Domingo
Highest Point: Pico Duarte
Monetary Unit: Dominican peso

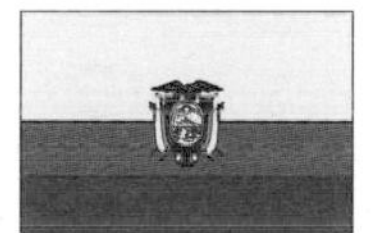

Ecuador
Page/Location: 106/C4
Area: 109,483 sq. mi.
283,591 sq. km.
Population: 10,752,000
Capital: Quito
Largest City: Guayaquil
Highest Point: Chimborazo
Monetary Unit: sucre

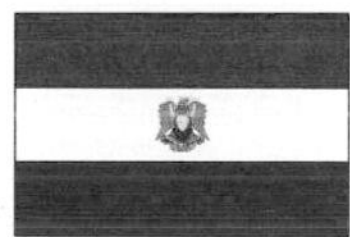

Egypt
Page/Location: 77/L2
Area: 386,659 sq. mi.
1,001,447 sq. km.
Population: 54,452,000
Capital: Cairo
Largest City: Cairo
Highest Point: Mt. Catherine
Monetary Unit: Egyptian pound

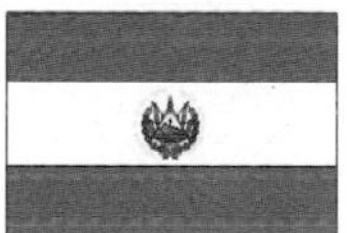

El Salvador
Page/Location: 102/D3
Area: 8,260 sq. mi.
21,393 sq. km.
Population: 5,419,000
Capital: San Salvador
Largest City: San Salvador
Highest Point: Santa Ana
Monetary Unit: Salvadoran colón

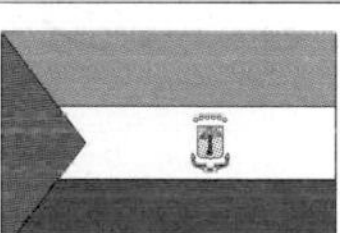

Equatorial Guinea
Page/Location: 76/G7
Area: 10,831 sq. mi.
28,052 sq. km.
Population: 379,000
Capital: Malabo
Largest City: Malabo
Highest Point: Pico de Santa Isabel
Monetary Unit: CFA franc

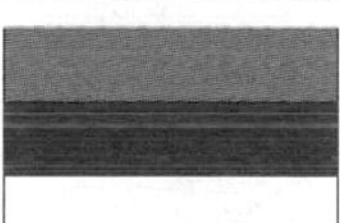

Estonia
Page/Location: 42/E4
Area: 17,413 sq. mi.
45,100 sq. km.
Population: 1,573,000
Capital: Tallinn
Largest City: Tallinn
Highest Point: Munamägi
Monetary Unit: kroon

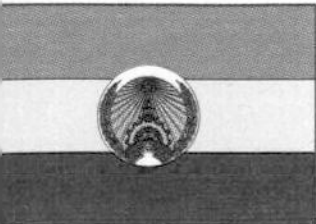

Ethiopia
Page/Location: 77/N6
Area: 471,776 sq. mi.
1,221,900 sq. km.
Population: 53,191,000
Capital: Addis Ababa
Largest City: Addis Ababa
Highest Point: Ras Dashen Terara
Monetary Unit: birr

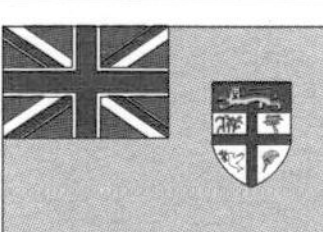

Fiji
Page/Location: 68/G6
Area: 7,055 sq. mi.
18,272 sq. km.
Population: 744,000
Capital: Suva
Largest City: Suva
Highest Point: Tomaniivi
Monetary Unit: Fijian dollar

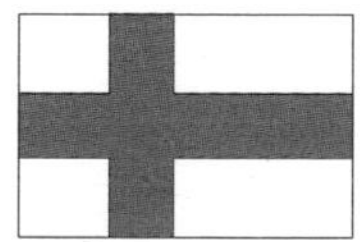

Finland
Page/Location: 20/H2
Area: 130,128 sq. mi.
337,032 sq. km.
Population: 4,991,000
Capital: Helsinki
Largest City: Helsinki
Highest Point: Kahperusvaara
Monetary Unit: markka

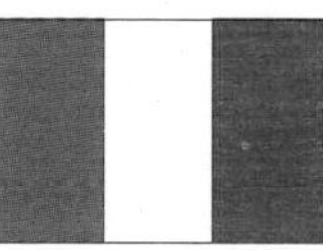

France
Page/Location: 32/D3
Area: 210,038 sq. mi.
543,998 sq. km.
Population: 56,596,000
Capital: Paris
Largest City: Paris
Highest Point: Mont Blanc
Monetary Unit: franc

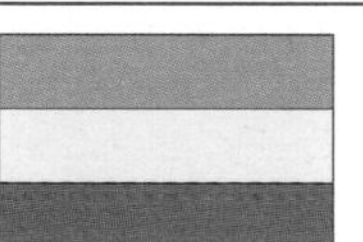

Gabon
Page/Location: 76/H7
Area: 103,346 sq. mi.
267,666 sq. km.
Population: 1,080,000
Capital: Libreville
Largest City: Libreville
Highest Point: Mt. Iboundji
Monetary Unit: CFA franc

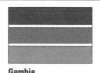

Gambia
Page/Location: 78/B3
Area: 4,127 sq. mi.
10,689 sq. km.
Population: 875,000
Capital: Banjul
Largest City: Banjul
Highest Point: 98 ft. (30 m)
Monetary Unit: dalasi

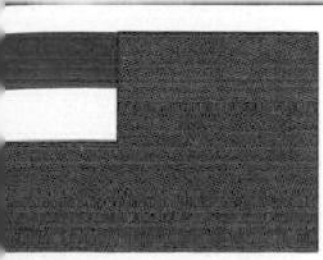

Georgia
Page/Location: 45/G4
Area: 26,911 sq. mi.
69,700 sq. km.
Population: 5,449,000
Capital: Tbilisi
Largest City: Tbilisi
Highest Point: Kazbek
Monetary Unit: Georgian ruble

Germany
Page/Location: 26/E3
Area: 137,753 sq. mi.
356,780 sq. km.
Population: 79,548,000
Capital: Berlin
Largest City: Berlin
Highest Point: Zugspitze
Monetary Unit: Deutsche mark

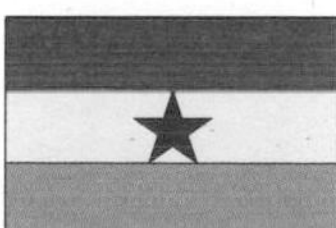

Ghana
Page/Location: 79/E4
Area: 92,099 sq. mi.
238,536 sq. km.
Population: 15,617,000
Capital: Accra
Largest City: Accra
Highest Point: Afadjoto
Monetary Unit: cedi

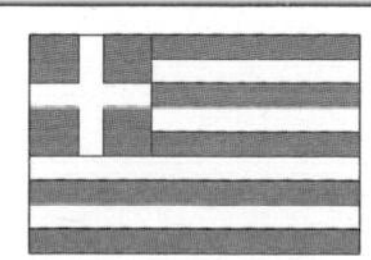

Greece
Page/Location: 39/G3
Area: 50,944 sq. mi.
131,945 sq. km.
Population: 10,043,000
Capital: Athens
Largest City: Athens
Highest Point: Mt. Olympus
Monetary Unit: drachma

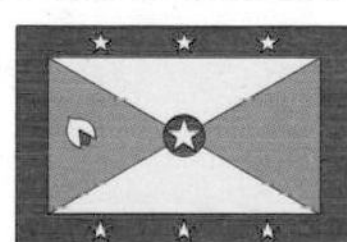

Grenada
Page/Location: 104/F5
Area: 133 sq. mi.
344 sq. km.
Population: 84,000
Capital: St. George's
Largest City: St. George's
Highest Point: Mt. St. Catherine
Monetary Unit: East Caribbean dollar

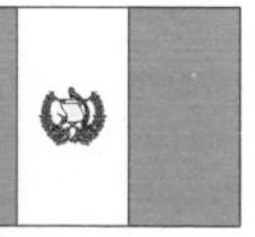

Guatemala
Page/Location: 102/D3
Area: 42,042 sq. mi.
108,889 sq. km.
Population: 9,266,000
Capital: Guatemala
Largest City: Guatemala
Highest Point: Tajumulco
Monetary Unit: quetzal

World Flags and Reference Guide

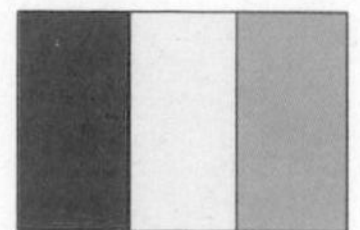

Guinea
Page/Location: 78/C4
Area: 94,925 sq. mi.
    245,856 sq. km.
Population: 7,456,000
Capital: Conakry
Largest City: Conakry
Highest Point: Mt. Nimba
Monetary Unit: syli

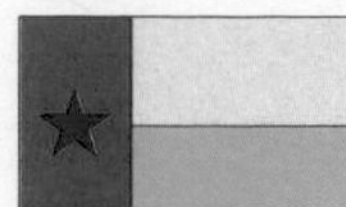

Guinea-Bissau
Page/Location: 78/B3
Area: 13,948 sq. mi.
    36,125 sq. km.
Population: 943,000
Capital: Bissau
Largest City: Bissau
Highest Point: 689 ft. (210 m)
Monetary Unit: Guinea-Bissau peso

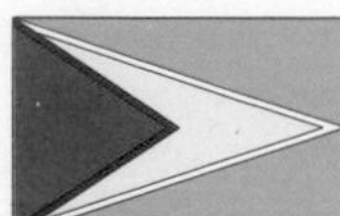

Guyana
Page/Location: 106/G2
Area: 83,000 sq. mi.
    214,970 sq. km.
Population: 1,024,000
Capital: Georgetown
Largest City: Georgetown
Highest Point: Mt. Roraima
Monetary Unit: Guyana dollar

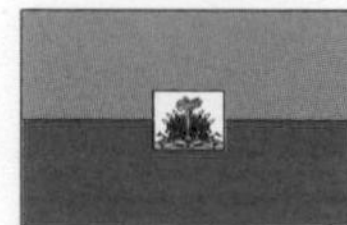

Haiti
Page/Location: 103/H2
Area: 10,694 sq. mi.
    27,697 sq. km.
Population: 6,287,000
Capital: Port-au-Prince
Largest City: Port-au-Prince
Highest Point: Pic la Selle
Monetary Unit: gourde

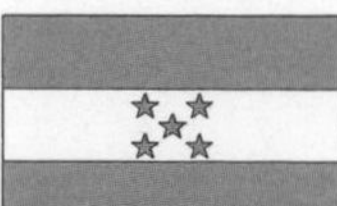

Honduras
Page/Location: 102/E3
Area: 43,277 sq. mi.
    112,087 sq. km.
Population: 4,949,000
Capital: Tegucigalpa
Largest City: Tegucigalpa
Highest Point: Cerro de las Minas
Monetary Unit: lempira

Hungary
Page/Location: 40/D2
Area: 35,919 sq. mi.
    93,030 sq. km.
Population: 10,558,000
Capital: Budapest
Largest City: Budapest
Highest Point: Kékes
Monetary Unit: forint

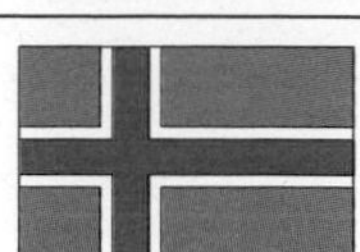

Iceland
Page/Location: 20/N7
Area: 39,768 sq. mi.
    103,000 sq. km.
Population: 260,000
Capital: Reykjavík
Largest City: Reykjavík
Highest Point: Hvannadalshnúkur
Monetary Unit: króna

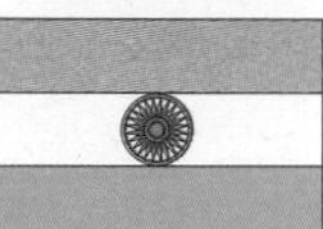

India
Page/Location: 62/C3
Area: 1,269,339 sq. mi.
    3,287,558 sq. km.
Population: 869,515,000
Capital: New Delhi
Largest City: Calcutta
Highest Point: Nanda Devi
Monetary Unit: Indian rupee

Indonesia
Page/Location: 67/E4
Area: 788,430 sq. mi.
    2, 042,034 sq. km.
Population: 195,600,000
Capital: Jakarta
Largest City: Jakarta
Highest Point: Puncak Jaya
Monetary Unit: rupiah

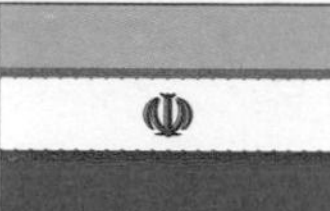

Iran
Page/Location: 51/H3
Area: 636,293 sq. mi.
    1,648,000 sq. km.
Population: 59,051,000
Capital: Tehran
Largest City: Tehran
Highest Point: Qolleh-ye Damāvand
Monetary Unit: Iranian rial

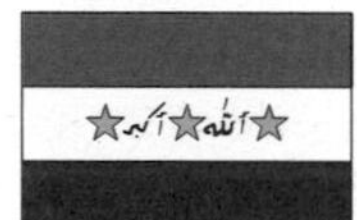

Iraq
Page/Location: 50/E3
Area: 172,476 sq. mi.
    446,713 sq. km.
Population: 19,525,000
Capital: Baghdad
Largest City: Baghdad
Highest Point: Haji Ibrahim
Monetary Unit: Iraqi dinar

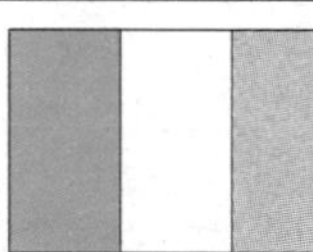

Ireland
Page/Location: 21/A4
Area: 27,136 sq. mi.
    70,282 sq. km.
Population: 3,489,000
Capital: Dublin
Largest City: Dublin
Highest Point: Carrantuohill
Monetary Unit: Irish pound

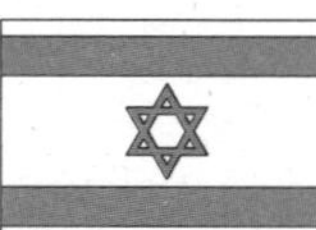

Israel
Page/Location: 49/D3
Area: 7,847 sq. mi.
    20,324 sq. km.
Population: 4,558,000
Capital: Jerusalem
Largest City: Tel Aviv-Yafo
Highest Point: Har Meron
Monetary Unit: shekel

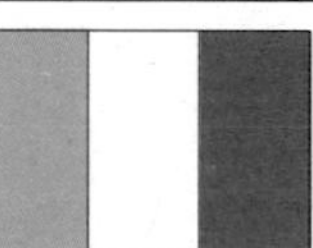

Italy
Page/Location: 18/E4
Area: 116,303 sq. mi.
    301,225 sq. km.
Population: 57,772,000
Capital: Rome
Largest City: Rome
Highest Point: Monte Rosa
Monetary Unit: lira

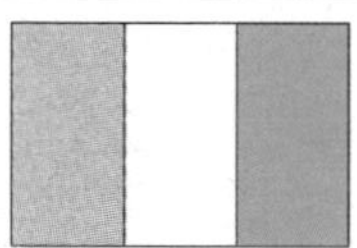

Ivory Coast
Page/Location: 78/D5
Area: 124,504 sq. mi.
    322,465 sq. km.
Population: 12,978,000
Capital: Yamoussoukro
Largest City: Abidjan
Highest Point: Mt. Nimba
Monetary Unit: CFA franc

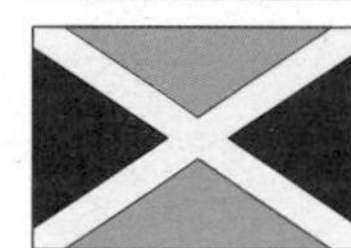

Jamaica
Page/Location: 103/G2
Area: 4,411 sq. mi.
    11,424 sq. km.
Population: 2,489,000
Capital: Kingston
Largest City: Kingston
Highest Point: Blue Mountain Pk.
Monetary Unit: Jamaican dollar

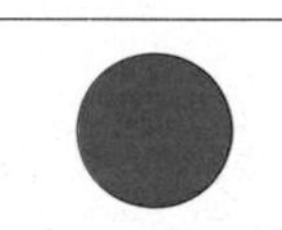

Japan
Page/Location: 55/M4
Area: 145,730 sq. mi.
    377,441 sq. km.
Population: 124,017,000
Capital: Tokyo
Largest City: Tokyo
Highest Point: Fujiyama
Monetary Unit: yen

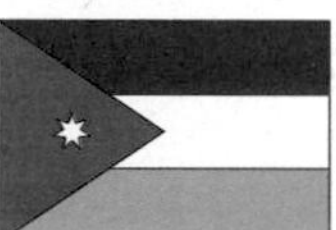

Jordan
Page/Location: 49/E4
Area: 35,000 sq. mi.
    90,650 sq. km.
Population: 3,413,000
Capital: Amman
Largest City: Amman
Highest Point: Jabal Ramm
Monetary Unit: Jordanian dinar

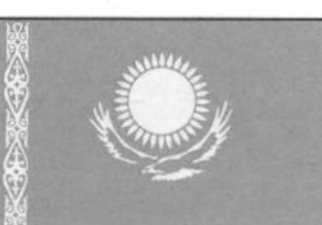

Kazakhstan
Page/Location: 46/G5
Area: 1,048,300 sq. mi.
    2,715,100 sq. km.
Population: 16,538,000
Capital: Alma-Ata
Largest City: Alma-Ata
Highest Point: Khan-Tengri
Monetary Unit: Kazakhstani ruble

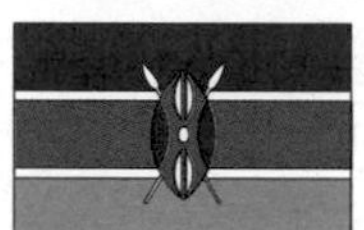

Kenya
Page/Location: 77/M7
Area: 224,960 sq. mi.
    582,646 sq. km.
Population: 25,242,000
Capital: Nairobi
Largest City: Nairobi
Highest Point: Mt. Kenya
Monetary Unit: Kenya shilling

Kiribati
Page/Location: 69/H5
Area: 291 sq. mi.
    754 sq. km.
Population: 71,000
Capital: Bairiki
Largest City: —
Highest Point: Banaba Island
Monetary Unit: Australian dollar

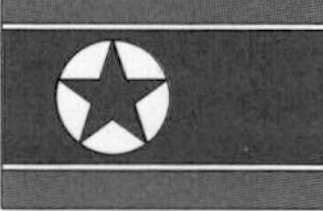

Korea, North
Page/Location: 58/D2
Area: 46,540 sq. mi.
    120,539 sq. km.
Population: 21,815,000
Capital: P'yŏngyang
Largest City: P'yŏngyang
Highest Point: Paektu-san
Monetary Unit: won

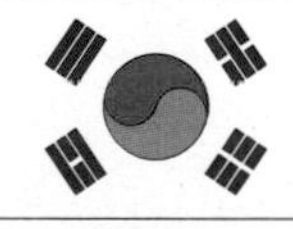

Korea, South
Page/Location: 58/D4
Area: 38,175 sq. mi.
    98,873 sq. km.
Population: 43,134,000
Capital: Seoul
Largest City: Seoul
Highest Point: Halla-san
Monetary Unit: won

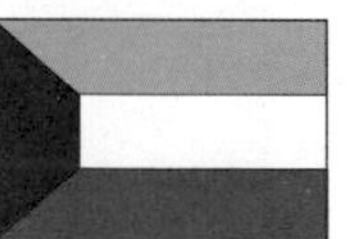

Kuwait
Page/Location: 51/F4
Area: 6,532 sq. mi.
    16,918 sq. km.
Population: 2,204,000
Capital: Al Kuwait
Largest City: Al Kuwait
Highest Point: 951 ft. (290 m)
Monetary Unit: Kuwaiti dinar

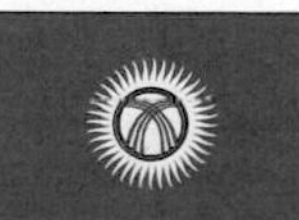

Kyrgyzstan
Page/Location: 46/H5
Area: 76,641 sq. mi.
    198,500 sq. km.
Population: 4,291,000
Capital: Bishkek
Largest City: Bishkek
Highest Point: Pik Pobedy
Monetary Unit: Kirghiz ruble

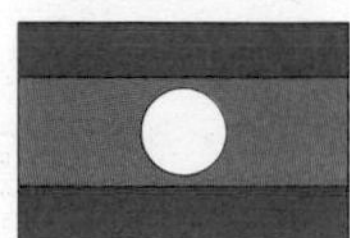

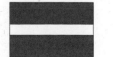

Laos
Page/Location: 65/C2
Area: 91,428 sq. mi.
    236,800 sq. km.
Population: 4,113,000
Capital: Vientiane
Largest City: Vientiane
Highest Point: Phou Bia
Monetary Unit: kip

Latvia
Page/Location: 42/E4
Area: 24,595 sq. mi.
    63,700 sq. km.
Population: 1,681,000
Capital: Riga
Largest City: Riga
Highest Point: Gaizina Kalns
Monetary Unit: Latvian ruble, lat

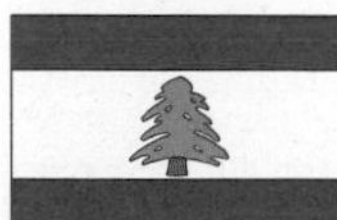

Lebanon
Page/Location: 49/D3
Area: 4,015 sq. mi.
    10,399 sq. km.
Population: 3,385,000
Capital: Beirut
Largest City: Beirut
Highest Point: Qurnat as Sawdā'
Monetary Unit: Lebanese pound

Lesotho
Page/Location: 80/E3
Area: 11,720 sq. mi.
    30,355 sq. km.
Population: 1,801,000
Capital: Maseru
Largest City: Maseru
Highest Point: Thabana-Ntlenyana
Monetary Unit: loti

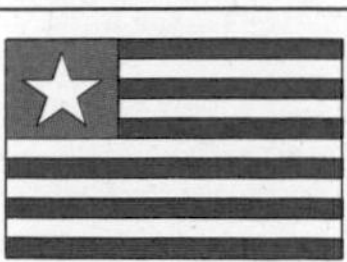

Liberia
Page/Location: 78/C4
Area: 43,000 sq. mi.
    111,370 sq. km.
Population: 2,730,000
Capital: Monrovia
Largest City: Monrovia
Highest Point: Mt. Wuteve
Monetary Unit: Liberian dollar

ya
ge/Location: 77/J2
ea: 679,358 sq. mi.
1,759,537 sq. km.
pulation: 4,353,000
pital: Tripoli
rgest City: Tripoli
ghest Point: Picco Bette
onetary Unit: Libyan dinar

Liechtenstein
Page/Location: 37/F3
Area: 61 sq. mi.
158 sq. km.
Population: 28,000
Capital: Vaduz
Largest City: Vaduz
Highest Point: Grauspitz
Monetary Unit: Swiss franc

Lithuania
Page/Location: 42/D5
Area: 25,174 sq. mi.
65,200 sq. km.
Population: 3,690,000
Capital: Vilnius
Largest City: Vilnius
Highest Point: Nevaišių
Monetary Unit: talonas

Luxembourg
Page/Location: 31/F4
Area: 999 sq. mi.
2,587 sq. km.
Population: 388,000
Capital: Luxembourg
Largest City: Luxembourg
Highest Point: Ardennes Plateau
Monetary Unit: Luxembourg franc

Macedonia
Page/Location: 39/G2
Area: 9,889 sq. mi.
25,713 sq. km.
Population: 1,909,136
Capital: Skopje
Largest City: Skopje
Highest Point: Korab
Monetary Unit: denar

Madagascar
Page/Location: 81/H8
Area: 226,657 sq. mi.
587,041 sq. km.
Population: 12,185,000
Capital: Antananarivo
Largest City: Antananarivo
Highest Point: Maromokotro
Monetary Unit: Madagascar franc

---

alawi
ge/Location: 82/F3
ea: 45,747 sq. mi.
118,485 sq. km.
pulation: 9,438,000
pital: Lilongwe
rgest City: Blantyre
ghest Point: Mulanje Mts.
onetary Unit: Malawi kwacha

Malaysia
Page/Location: 67/C2
Area: 128,308 sq. mi.
332,318 sq. km.
Population: 17,982,000
Capital: Kuala Lumpur
Largest City: Kuala Lumpur
Highest Point: Gunung Kinabalu
Monetary Unit: ringgit

Maldives
Page/Location: 48/G9
Area: 115 sq. mi.
298 sq. km.
Population: 226,000
Capital: Male
Largest City: Male
Highest Point: 20 ft. (6 m)
Monetary Unit: Maldivian rufiyaa

Mali
Page/Location: 76/E4
Area: 464,873 sq. mi.
1,204,021 sq. km.
Population: 8,339,000
Capital: Bamako
Largest City: Bamako
Highest Point: Hombori Tondo
Monetary Unit: CFA franc

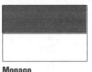

Malta
Page/Location: 38/D5
Area: 122 sq. mi.
316 sq. km.
Population: 356,000
Capital: Valletta
Largest City: Sliema
Highest Point: 830 ft. (253 m)
Monetary Unit: Maltese lira

Marshall Islands
Page/Location: 68/G3
Area: 70 sq. mi.
181 sq. km.
Population: 48,000
Capital: Majuro
Largest City: —
Highest Point: 20 ft. (6 m)
Monetary Unit: U.S. dollar

---

auritania
ge/Location: 76/C4
ea: 419,229 sq. mi.
1,085,803 sq. km.
pulation: 1,996,000
pital: Nouakchott
rgest City: Nouakchott
ghest Point: Kediet Ijill
onetary Unit: ouguiya

Mauritius
Page/Location: 81/S15
Area: 790 sq. mi.
2,046 sq. km.
Population: 1,081,000
Capital: Port Louis
Largest City: Port Louis
Highest Point: 2,713 ft. (827 m)
Monetary Unit: Mauritian rupee

Mexico
Page/Location: 84/G7
Area: 761,601 sq. mi.
1,972,546 sq. km.
Population: 90,007,000
Capital: Mexico City
Largest City: Mexico City
Highest Point: Citlaltépetl
Monetary Unit: Mexican peso

Micronesia
Page/Location: 68/D4
Area: 271 sq. mi.
702 sq. km.
Population: 108,000
Capital: Kolonia
Largest City: —
Highest Point: —
Monetary Unit: U.S. dollar

Moldova
Page/Location: 41/J2
Area: 13,012 sq. mi.
33,700 sq. km.
Population: 4,341,000
Capital: Kishinev
Largest City: Kishinev
Highest Point: 1,408 ft. (429 m)
Monetary Unit: Moldovan ruble

Monaco
Page/Location: 33/G5
Area: 368 acres
149 hectares
Population: 30,000
Capital: Monaco
Largest City: —
Highest Point: —
Monetary Unit: French franc

---

ongolia
ge/Location: 54/D2
ea: 606,163 sq. mi.
1,569,962 sq. km.
pulation: 2,247,000
pital: Ulaanbaatar
rgest City: Ulaanbaatar
ghest Point: Tavan Bogd Uul
onetary Unit: tughrik

Morocco
Page/Location: 76/C1
Area: 172,414 sq. mi.
446,550 sq. km.
Population: 26,182,000
Capital: Rabat
Largest City: Casablanca
Highest Point: Jebel Toubkal
Monetary Unit: dirham

Mozambique
Page/Location: 82/G4
Area: 303,769 sq. mi.
786,762 sq. km.
Population: 15,113,000
Capital: Maputo
Largest City: Maputo
Highest Point: Monte Binga
Monetary Unit: metical

Namibia
Page/Location: 82/C5
Area: 317,827 sq. mi.
823,172 sq. km.
Population: 1,521,000
Capital: Windhoek
Largest City: Windhoek
Highest Point: Brandberg
Monetary Unit: rand

Nauru
Page/Location: 68/F5
Area: 7.7 sq. mi.
20 sq. km.
Population: 9,000
Capital: Yaren (district)
Largest City: —
Highest Point: 230 ft. (70 m)
Monetary Unit: Australian dollar

Nepal
Page/Location: 62/D2
Area: 54,663 sq. mi.
141,557 sq. km.
Population: 19,612,000
Capital: Kathmandu
Largest City: Kathmandu
Highest Point: Mt. Everest
Monetary Unit: Nepalese rupee

---

therlands
ge/Location: 28/B5
ea: 15,892 sq. mi.
41,160 sq. km.
pulation: 15,022,000
pital: The Hague; Amsterdam
rgest City: Amsterdam
ghest Point: Vaalserberg
onetary Unit: guilder

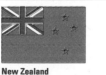

New Zealand
Page/Location: 71/Q10
Area: 103,736 sq. mi.
268,676 sq. km.
Population: 3,309,000
Capital: Wellington
Largest City: Auckland
Highest Point: Mt. Cook
Monetary Unit: New Zealand dollar

Nicaragua
Page/Location: 103/E3
Area: 45,698 sq. mi.
118,358 sq. km.
Population: 3,752,000
Capital: Managua
Largest City: Managua
Highest Point: Pico Mogotón
Monetary Unit: córdoba

Niger
Page/Location: 76/G4
Area: 489,189 sq. mi.
1,267,000 sq. km.
Population: 8,154,000
Capital: Niamey
Largest City: Niamey
Highest Point: Bagzane
Monetary Unit: CFA franc

Nigeria
Page/Location: 76/G6
Area: 357,000 sq. mi.
924,630 sq. km.
Population: 122,471,000
Capital: Abuja
Largest City: Lagos
Highest Point: Dimlang
Monetary Unit: naira

Norway
Page/Location: 20/C3
Area: 125,053 sq. mi.
323,887 sq. km.
Population: 4,273,000
Capital: Oslo
Largest City: Oslo
Highest Point: Glittertjnden
Monetary Unit: krone

---

an
ge/Location: 53/G4
ea: 120,000 sq. mi.
310,800 sq. km.
pulation: 1,534,000
pital: Muscat
rgest City: Muscat
ghest Point: Jabal ash Shām
onetary Unit: Omani rial

Pakistan
Page/Location: 53/H3
Area: 310,403 sq. mi.
803,944 sq. km.
Population: 117,490,000
Capital: Islamabad
Largest City: Karachi
Highest Point: K2 (Godwin Austen)
Monetary Unit: Pakistani rupee

Panama
Page/Location: 103/F4
Area: 29,761 sq. mi.
77,082 sq. km.
Population: 2,476,000
Capital: Panamá
Largest City: Panamá
Highest Point: Barú
Monetary Unit: balboa

Papua New Guinea
Page/Location: 68/D5
Area: 183,540 sq. mi.
475,369 sq. km.
Population: 3,913,000
Capital: Port Moresby
Largest City: Port Moresby
Highest Point: Mt. Wilhelm
Monetary Unit: kina

Paraguay
Page/Location: 105/D5
Area: 157,047 sq. mi.
406,752 sq. km.
Population: 4,799,000
Capital: Asunción
Largest City: Asunción
Highest Point: Sierra de Amambay
Monetary Unit: guaraní

Peru
Page/Location: 106/C5
Area: 496,222 sq. mi.
1,285,215 sq. km.
Population: 22,362,000
Capital: Lima
Largest City: Lima
Highest Point: Nevado Huascarán
Monetary Unit: nuevo sol

World Flags and Reference Guide

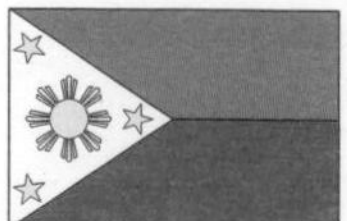

Philippines
Page/Location: 48/M8
Area: 115,707 sq. mi.
        299,681 sq. km.
Population: 65,759,000
Capital: Manila
Largest City: Manila
Highest Point: Mt. Apo
Monetary Unit: peso

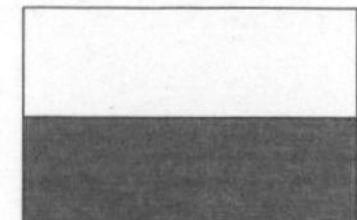

Poland
Page/Location: 27/K2
Area: 120,725 sq. mi.
        312,678 sq. km.
Population: 37,800,000
Capital: Warsaw
Largest City: Warsaw
Highest Point: Rysy
Monetary Unit: zloty

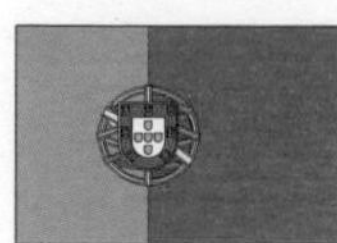

Portugal
Page/Location: 34/A3
Area: 35,549 sq. mi.
        92,072 sq. km.
Population: 10,388,000
Capital: Lisbon
Largest City: Lisbon
Highest Point: Serra da Estrela
Monetary Unit: escudo

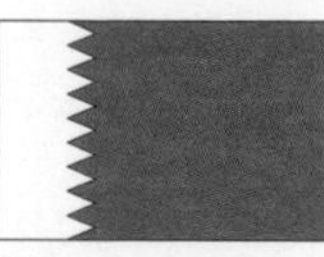

Qatar
Page/Location: 52/F3
Area: 4,247 sq. mi.
        11,000 sq. km.
Population: 518,000
Capital: Doha
Largest City: Doha
Highest Point: Dukhān Heights
Monetary Unit: Qatari riyal

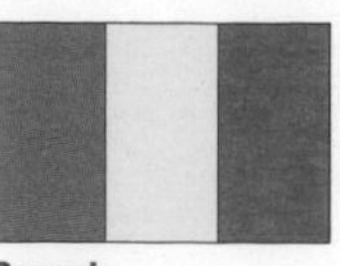

Romania
Page/Location: 41/F3
Area: 91,699 sq. mi.
        237,500 sq. km.
Population: 23,397,000
Capital: Bucharest
Largest City: Bucharest
Highest Point: Moldoveanul
Monetary Unit: leu

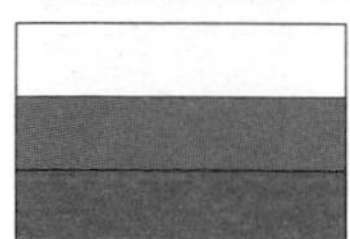

Russia
Page/Location: 46/H3
Area: 6,592,812 sq. mi.
        17,075,400 sq. km.
Population: 147,386,000
Capital: Moscow
Largest City: Moscow
Highest Point: El'brus
Monetary Unit: Russian ruble

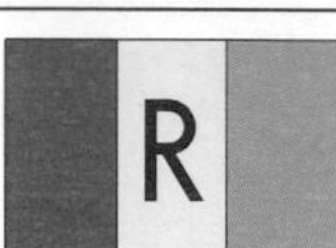

Rwanda
Page/Location: 82/E1
Area: 10,169 sq. mi.
        26,337 sq. km.
Population: 7,903,000
Capital: Kigali
Largest City: Kigali
Highest Point: Karisimbi
Monetary Unit: Rwanda franc

Saint Kitts and Nevis
Page/Location: 104/F3
Area: 104 sq. mi.
        269 sq. km.
Population: 40,000
Capital: Basseterre
Largest City: Basseterre
Highest Point: Mt. Misery
Monetary Unit: East Caribbean dollar

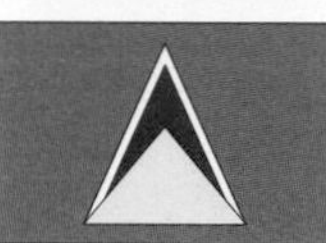

Saint Lucia
Page/Location: 104/F4
Area: 238 sq. mi.
        616 sq. km.
Population: 153,000
Capital: Castries
Largest City: Castries
Highest Point: Mt. Gimie
Monetary Unit: East Caribbean dollar

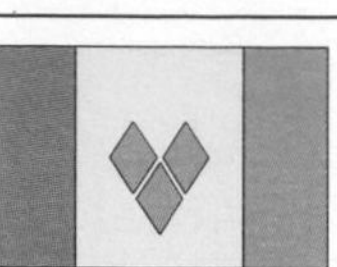

Saint Vincent and the Grenadines
Page/Location: 104/F4
Area: 150 sq. mi.
        388 sq. km.
Population: 114,000
Capital: Kingstown
Largest City: Kingstown
Highest Point: Soufrière
Monetary Unit: East Caribbean doll▮

San Marino
Page/Location: 33/K5
Area: 23.4 sq. mi.
        60.6 sq. km.
Population: 23,000
Capital: San Marino
Largest City: San Marino
Highest Point: Monte Titano
Monetary Unit: Italian lira

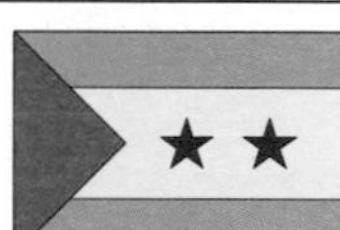

São Tomé and Príncipe
Page/Location: 76/G7
Area: 372 sq. mi.
        963 sq. km.
Population: 128,000
Capital: São Tomé
Largest City: São Tomé
Highest Point: Pico de São Tomé
Monetary Unit: dobra

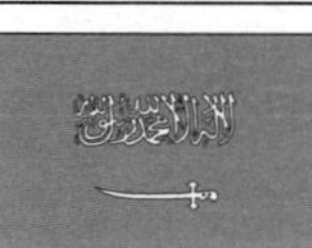

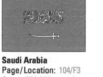

Saudi Arabia
Page/Location: 104/F3
Area: 829,995 sq. mi.
        2,149,687 sq. km.
Population: 17,870,000
Capital: Riyadh
Largest City: Riyadh
Highest Point: Jabal Sawdā'
Monetary Unit: Saudi riyal

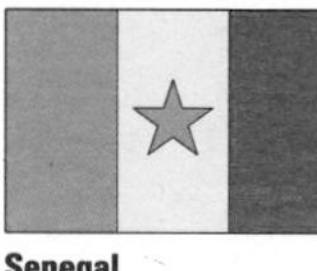

Senegal
Page/Location: 78/B3
Area: 75,954 sq. mi.
        196,720 sq. km.
Population: 7,953,000
Capital: Dakar
Largest City: Dakar
Highest Point: Fouta Djallon
Monetary Unit: CFA franc

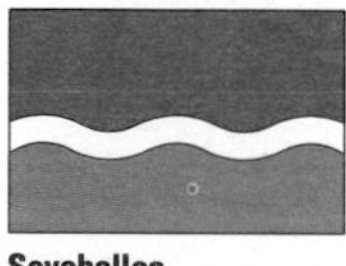

Seychelles
Page/Location: 74/H5
Area: 145 sq. mi.
        375 sq. km.
Population: 69,000
Capital: Victoria
Largest City: Victoria
Highest Point: Morne Seychellois
Monetary Unit: Seychellois rupee

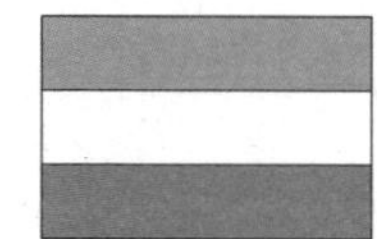

Sierra Leone
Page/Location: 78/B4
Area: 27,925 sq. mi.
        72,325 sq. km.
Population: 4,275,000
Capital: Freetown
Largest City: Freetown
Highest Point: Loma Mansa
Monetary Unit: leone

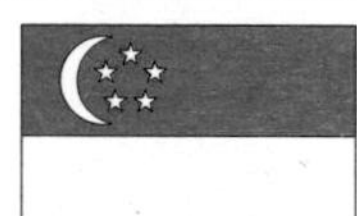

Singapore
Page/Location: 66/B3
Area: 226 sq. mi.
        585 sq. km.
Population: 2,756,000
Capital: Singapore
Largest City: Singapore
Highest Point: Bukit Timah
Monetary Unit: Singapore dollar

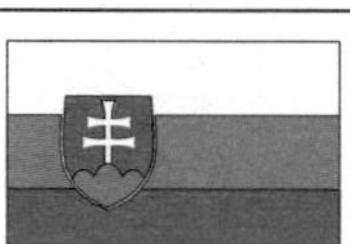

Slovakia
Page/Location: 27/K4
Area: 18,924 sq. mi.
        49,014 sq. km.
Population: 4,991,168
Capital: Bratislava
Largest City: Bratislava
Highest Point: Gerlachovský Štít
Monetary Unit: Slovak koruna

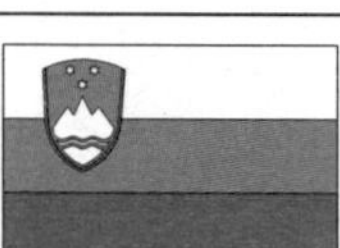

Slovenia
Page/Location: 40/B3
Area: 7,898 sq. mi.
        20,251 sq. km.
Population: 1,891,864
Capital: Ljubljana
Largest City: Ljubljana
Highest Point: Triglav
Monetary Unit: tolar

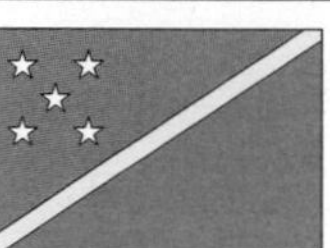

Solomon Islands
Page/Location: 68/E6
Area: 11,500 sq. mi.
        29,785 sq. km.
Population: 347,000
Capital: Honiara
Largest City: Honiara
Highest Point: Mt. Makarakomburu
Monetary Unit: Solomon Islands doll▮

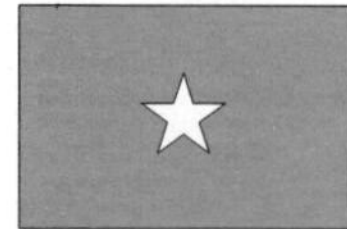

Somalia
Page/Location: 77/Q6
Area: 246,200 sq. mi.
        637,658 sq. km.
Population: 6,709,000
Capital: Mogadishu
Largest City: Mogadishu
Highest Point: Shimber Berris
Monetary Unit: Somali shilling

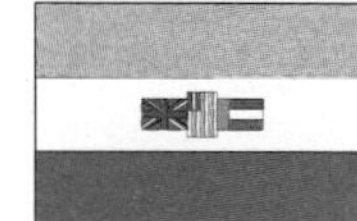

South Africa
Page/Location: 80/C3
Area: 455,318 sq. mi.
        1,179,274 sq. km.
Population: 40,601,000
Capital: Cape Town; Pretoria
Largest City: Johannesburg
Highest Point: Injasuti
Monetary Unit: rand

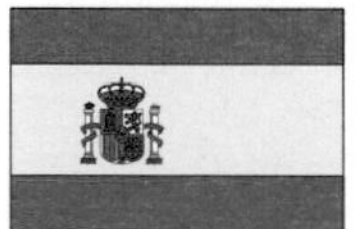

Spain
Page/Location: 34/C2
Area: 194,881 sq. mi.
        504,742 sq. km.
Population: 39,385,000
Capital: Madrid
Largest City: Madrid
Highest Point: Pico de Teide
Monetary Unit: peseta

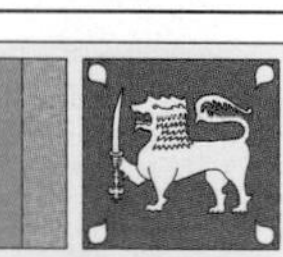

Sri Lanka
Page/Location: 62/D6
Area: 25,332 sq. mi.
        65,610 sq. km.
Population: 17,424,000
Capital: Colombo
Largest City: Colombo
Highest Point: Pidurutalagala
Monetary Unit: Sri Lanka rupee

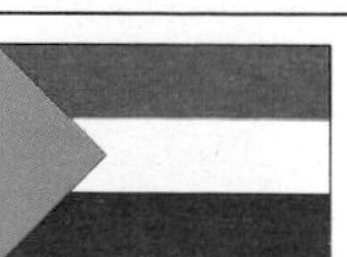

Sudan
Page/Location: 77/L5
Area: 967,494 sq. mi.
        2,505,809 sq. km.
Population: 27,220,000
Capital: Khartoum
Largest City: Omdurman
Highest Point: Jabal Marrah
Monetary Unit: Sudanese pound

Suriname
Page/Location: 107/G3
Area: 55,144 sq. mi.
        142,823 sq. km.
Population: 402,000
Capital: Paramaribo
Largest City: Paramaribo
Highest Point: Juliana Top
Monetary Unit: Suriname guilder

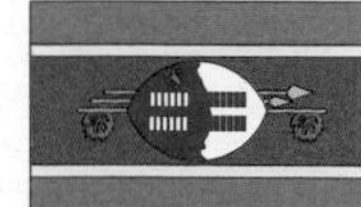

Swaziland
Page/Location: 81/E2
Area: 6,705 sq. mi.
        17,366 sq. km.
Population: 859,000
Capital: Mbabane
Largest City: Mbabane
Highest Point: Emlembe
Monetary Unit: lilangeni

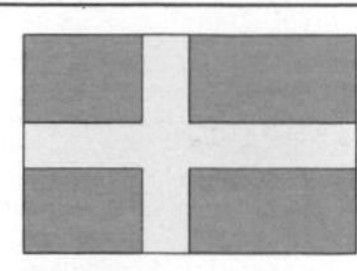

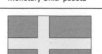

Sweden
Page/Location: 20/E3
Area: 173,665 sq. mi.
        449,792 sq. km.
Population: 8,564,000
Capital: Stockholm
Largest City: Stockholm
Highest Point: Kebnekaise
Monetary Unit: krona

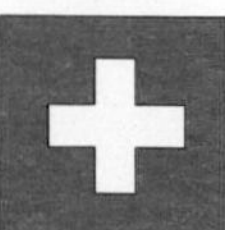

Switzerland
Page/Location: 36/D4
Area: 15,943 sq. mi.
        41,292 sq. km.
Population: 6,784,000
Capital: Bern
Largest City: Zürich
Highest Point: Dufourspitze
Monetary Unit: Swiss franc

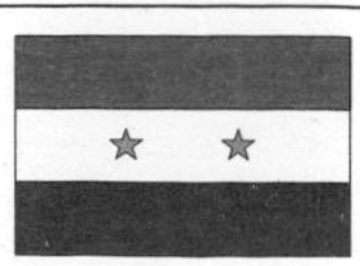

Syria
Page/Location: 50/D3
Area: 71,498 sq. mi.
        185,180 sq. km.
Population: 12,966,000
Capital: Damascus
Largest City: Damascus
Highest Point: Jabal ash Shaykh
Monetary Unit: Syrian pound

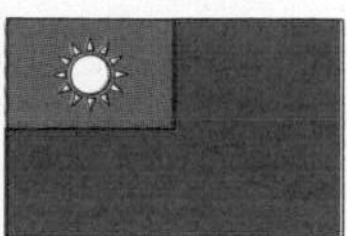

Taiwan
Page/Location: 61/J3
Area: 13,971 sq. mi.
36,185 sq. km.
Population: 16,609,961
Capital: Taipei
Largest City: Taipei
Highest Point: Yü Shan
Monetary Unit: new Taiwan dollar

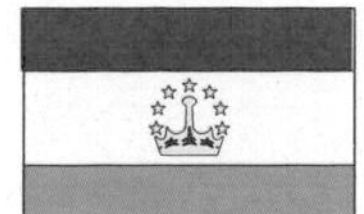

Tajikistan
Page/Location: 46/H6
Area: 55,251 sq. mi.
143,100 sq. km.
Population: 5,112,000
Capital: Dushanbe
Largest City: Dushanbe
Highest Point: Communism Peak
Monetary Unit: Tajik ruble

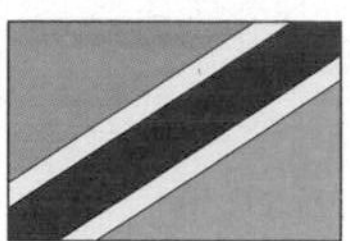

Tanzania
Page/Location: 82/F2
Area: 363,708 sq. mi.
942,003 sq. km.
Population: 26,869,000
Capital: Dar es Salaam
Largest City: Dar es Salaam
Highest Point: Kilimanjaro
Monetary Unit: Tanzanian shilling

Thailand
Page/Location: 65/C3
Area: 198,455 sq. mi.
513,998 sq. km.
Population: 56,814,000
Capital: Bangkok
Largest City: Bangkok
Highest Point: Doi Inthanon
Monetary Unit: baht

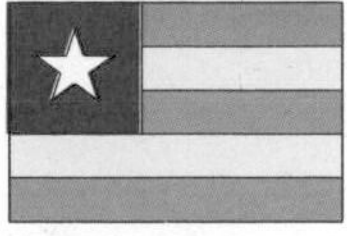

Togo
Page/Location: 79/F4
Area: 21,622 sq. mi.
56,000 sq. km.
Population: 3,811,000
Capital: Lomé
Largest City: Lomé
Highest Point: Mt. Agou
Monetary Unit: CFA franc

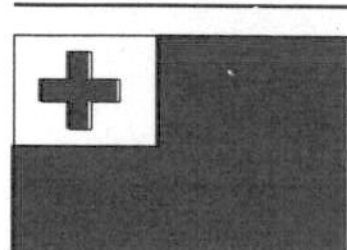

Tonga
Page/Location: 69/H7
Area: 270 sq. mi.
699 sq. km.
Population: 102,000
Capital: Nuku'alofa
Largest City: Nuku'alofa
Highest Point: Kao Island
Monetary Unit: pa'anga

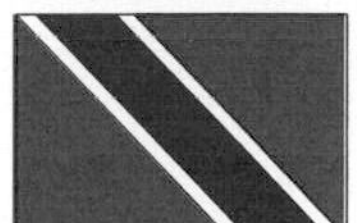

Trinidad and Tobago
Page/Location: 104/F5
Area: 1,980 sq. mi.
5,128 sq. km.
Population: 1,285,000
Capital: Port-of-Spain
Largest City: Port-of-Spain
Highest Point: El Cerro del Aripo
Monetary Unit: Trin. & Tobago dollar

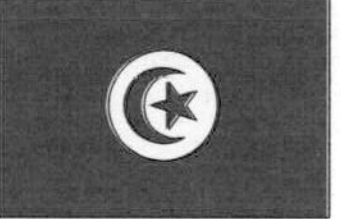

Tunisia
Page/Location: 76/G1
Area: 63,378 sq. mi.
164,149 sq. km.
Population: 8,276,000
Capital: Tunis
Largest City: Tunis
Highest Point: Jabal ash Sha'nabī
Monetary Unit: Tunisian dinar

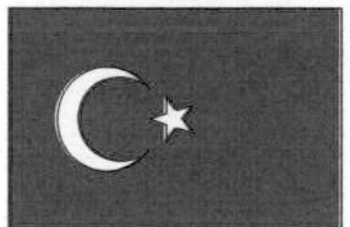

Turkey
Page/Location: 50/C2
Area: 300,946 sq. mi.
779,450 sq. km.
Population: 58,581,000
Capital: Ankara
Largest City: Istanbul
Highest Point: Mt. Ararat
Monetary Unit: Turkish lira

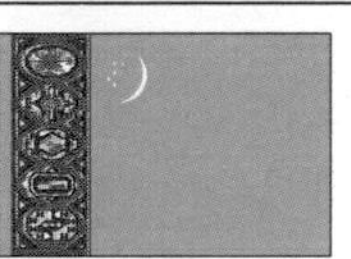

Turkmenistan
Page/Location: 46/F6
Area: 188,455 sq. mi.
488,100 sq. km.
Population: 3,534,000
Capital: Ashkhabad
Largest City: Ashkhabad
Highest Point: Rize
Monetary Unit: Turkmen ruble

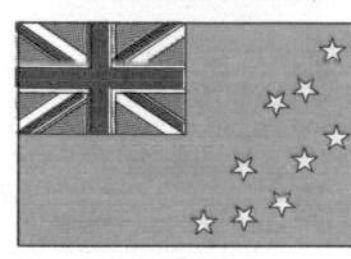

Tuvalu
Page/Location: 68/G5
Area: 9.8 sq. mi.
25.3 sq. km.
Population: 9,000
Capital: Fongafale
Largest City: —
Highest Point: 16 ft. (5 m)
Monetary Unit: Australian dollar

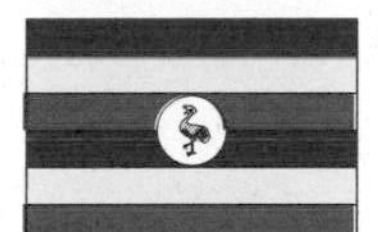

Uganda
Page/Location: 77/M7
Area: 91,076 sq. mi.
235,887 sq. km.
Population: 18,690,000
Capital: Kampala
Largest City: Kampala
Highest Point: Margherita Peak
Monetary Unit: Ugandan shilling

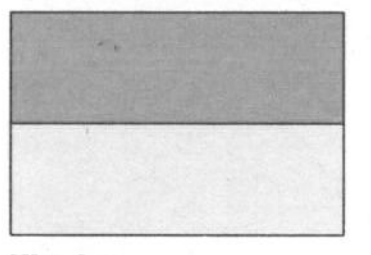

Ukraine
Page/Location: 44/D2
Area: 233,089 sq. mi.
603,700 sq. km.
Population: 51,704,000
Capital: Kiev
Largest City: Kiev
Highest Point: Goverla
Monetary Unit: Ukrainian ruble

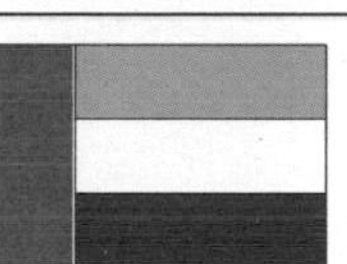

United Arab Emirates
Page/Location: 52/F4
Area: 32,278 sq. mi.
83,600 sq. km.
Population: 2,390,000
Capital: Abu Dhabi
Largest City: Dubayy
Highest Point: Hajar Mts.
Monetary Unit: dirham

United Kingdom
Page/Location: 21
Area: 94,399 sq. mi.
244,493 sq. km.
Population: 57,515,000
Capital: London
Largest City: London
Highest Point: Ben Nevis
Monetary Unit: pound sterling

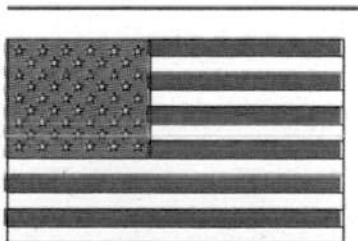

United States
Page/Location: 88
Area: 3,623,420 sq. mi.
9,384,658 sq. km.
Population: 252,502,000
Capital: Washington
Largest City: New York
Highest Point: Mt. McKinley
Monetary Unit: U.S. dollar

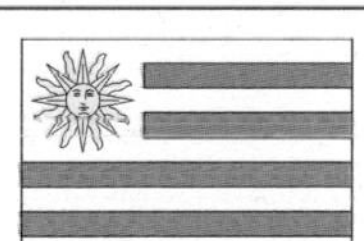

Uruguay
Page/Location: 109/E3
Area: 72,172 sq. mi.
186,925 sq. km.
Population: 3,121,000
Capital: Montevideo
Largest City: Montevideo
Highest Point: Cerro Catedral
Monetary Unit: Uruguayan peso

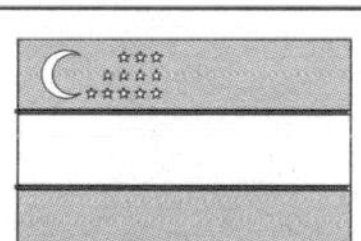

Uzbekistan
Page/Location: 46/G5
Area: 173,591 sq. mi.
449,600 sq. km.
Population: 19,906,000
Capital: Tashkent
Largest City: Tashkent
Highest Point: Khodzha-Pir'yakh
Monetary Unit: Uzbek ruble

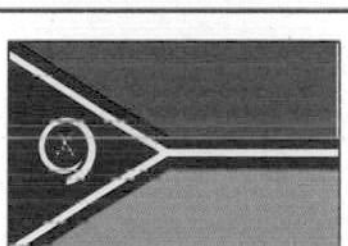

Vanuatu
Page/Location: 68/F6
Area: 5,700 sq. mi.
14,763 sq. km.
Population: 170,000
Capital: Vila
Largest City: Vila
Highest Point: Tabwemasana
Monetary Unit: vatu

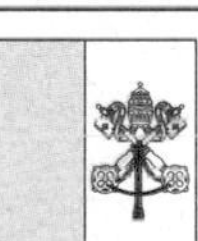

Vatican City
Page/Location: 38/C2
Area: 108.7 acres
44 hectares
Population: 1,000
Capital: —
Largest City: —
Highest Point: —
Monetary Unit: Italian lira

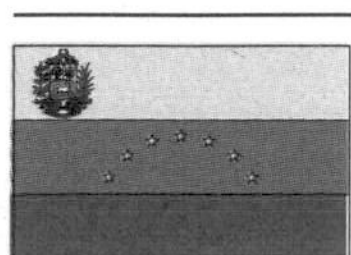

Venezuela
Page/Location: 106/E2
Area: 352,143 sq. mi.
912,050 sq. km.
Population: 20,189,000
Capital: Caracas
Largest City: Caracas
Highest Point: Pico Bolívar
Monetary Unit: bolívar

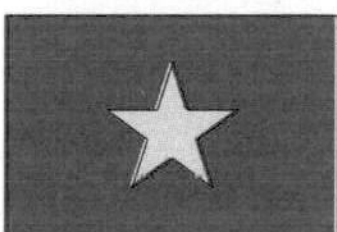

Vietnam
Page/Location: 65/D2
Area: 128,405 sq. mi.
332,569 sq. km.
Population: 67,568,000
Capital: Hanoi
Largest City: Ho Chi Minh City
Highest Point: Fan Si Pan
Monetary Unit: dong

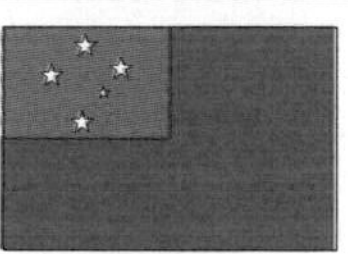

Western Samoa
Page/Location: 69/H6
Area: 1,133 sq. mi.
2,934 sq. km.
Population: 190,000
Capital: Apia
Largest City: Apia
Highest Point: Mt. Silisili
Monetary Unit: tala

Yemen
Page/Location: 52/E5
Area: 188,321 sq. mi.
487,752 sq. km.
Population: 10,063,000
Capital: Sanaa
Largest City: Aden
Highest Point: Nabī Shu'ayb
Monetary Unit: Yemeni rial

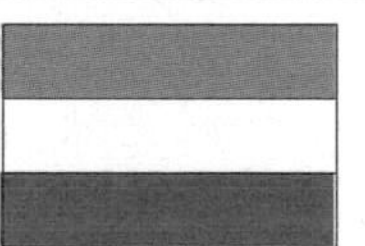

Yugoslavia
Page/Location: 40/E3
Area: 38,989 sq. mi.
102,173 sq. km.
Population: 11,371,275
Capital: Belgrade
Largest City: Belgrade
Highest Point: Đaravica
Monetary Unit: Yugoslav new dinar

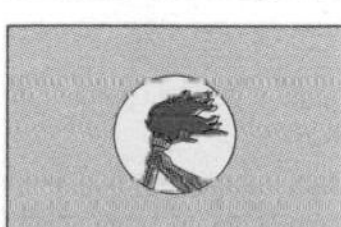

Zaire
Page/Location: 74/E5
Area: 905,063 sq. mi.
2,344,113 sq. km.
Population: 37,832,000
Capital: Kinshasa
Largest City: Kinshasa
Highest Point: Margherita Peak
Monetary Unit: zaire

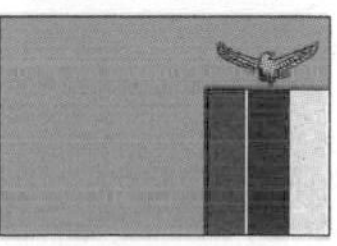

Zambia
Page/Location: 82/E3
Area: 290,586 sq. mi.
752,618 sq. km.
Population: 8,446,000
Capital: Lusaka
Largest City: Lusaka
Highest Point: Sunzu
Monetary Unit: Zambian kwacha

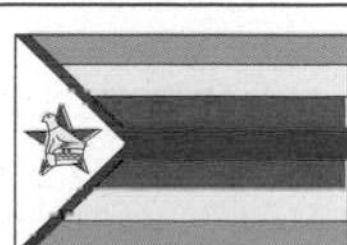

Zimbabwe
Page/Location: 82/E4
Area: 150,803 sq. mi.
390,580 sq. km.
Population: 10,720,000
Capital: Harare
Largest City: Harare
Highest Point: Inyangani
Monetary Unit: Zimbabwe dollar

World Statistics

ELEMENTS OF THE SOLAR SYSTEM

	Mean Distance from Sun: in Miles	in Kilometers	Period of Revolution around Sun	Period of Rotation on Axis	Equatorial Diameter in Miles	in Kilometers	Surface Gravity (Earth = 1)	Mass (Earth = 1)	Mean Density (Water = 1)	Number of Satellites
Mercury	35,990,000	57,900,000	87.97 days	59 days	3,032	4,880	0.38	0.055	5.5	0
Venus	67,240,000	108,200,000	224.70 days	243 days†	7,523	12,106	0.90	0.815	5.25	0
Earth	93,000,000	149,700,000	365.26 days	23h 56m	7,926	12,755	1.00	1.00	5.5	1
Mars	141,730,000	228,100,000	687.00 days	24h 37m	4,220	6,790	0.38	0.107	4.0	2
Jupiter	483,880,000	778,700,000	11.86 years	9h 50m	88,750	142,800	2.87	317.9	1.3	16
Saturn	887,130,000	1,427,700,000	29.46 years	10h 39m	74,580	120,020	1.32	95.2	0.7	23
Uranus	1,783,700,000	2,870,500,000	84.01 years	17h 24m†	31,600	50,900	0.93	14.6	1.3	15
Neptune	2,795,500,000	4,498,800,000	164.79 years	17h 50m	30,200	48,600	1.23	17.2	1.8	8
Pluto	3,667,900,000	5,902,800,000	247.70 years	6.39 days(?)	1,500	2,400	0.03(?)	0.01(?)	0.7(?)	1

† Retrograde motion

DIMENSIONS OF THE EARTH

	Area in: Sq. Miles	Sq. Kilometers
Superficial area	196,939,000	510,073,000
Land surface	57,506,000	148,941,000
Water surface	139,433,000	361,132,000

	Distance in: Miles	Kilometers
Equatorial circumference	24,902	40,075
Polar circumference	24,860	40,007
Equatorial diameter	7,926.4	12,756.4
Polar diameter	7,899.8	12,713.6
Equatorial radius	3,963.2	6,378.2
Polar radius	3,949.9	6,356.8

Volume of the Earth	2.6×10^{11} cubic miles	10.84×10^{11} cubic kilometers
Mass or weight	6.6×10^{21} short tons	6.0×10^{21} metric tons
Maximum distance from Sun	94,600,000 miles	152,000,000 kilometers
Minimum distance from Sun	91,300,000 miles	147,000,000 kilometers

OCEANS AND MAJOR SEAS

	Area in: Sq. Miles	Sq. Kms.	Greatest Depth in: Feet	Meters
Pacific Ocean	64,186,000	166,241,700	36,198	11,033
Atlantic Ocean	31,862,000	82,522,600	28,374	8,648
Indian Ocean	28,350,000	73,426,500	25,344	7,725
Arctic Ocean	5,427,000	14,056,000	17,880	5,450
Caribbean Sea	970,000	2,512,300	24,720	7,535
Mediterranean Sea	969,000	2,509,700	16,896	5,150
South China Sea	895,000	2,318,000	15,000	4,600
Bering Sea	875,000	2,266,250	15,800	4,800
Gulf of Mexico	600,000	1,554,000	12,300	3,750
Sea of Okhotsk	590,000	1,528,100	11,070	3,370
East China Sea	482,000	1,248,400	9,500	2,900
Yellow Sea	480,000	1,243,200	350	107
Sea of Japan	389,000	1,007,500	12,280	3,740
Hudson Bay	317,500	822,300	846	258
North Sea	222,000	575,000	2,200	670
Black Sea	185,000	479,150	7,365	2,245
Red Sea	169,000	437,700	7,200	2,195
Baltic Sea	163,000	422,170	1,506	459

THE CONTINENTS

	Area in: Sq. Miles	Sq. Kms.	Percent of World's Land
Asia	17,128,500	44,362,815	29.5
Africa	11,707,000	30,321,130	20.2
North America	9,363,000	24,250,170	16.2
South America	6,875,000	17,806,250	11.8
Antarctica	5,500,000	14,245,000	9.5
Europe	4,057,000	10,507,630	7.0
Australia	2,966,136	7,682,300	5.1

MAJOR SHIP CANALS

	Length in: Miles	Kms.	Minimum Depth in: Feet	Meters
Volga-Baltic, Russia	225	362	–	–
Baltic-White Sea, Russia	140	225	16	5
Suez, Egypt	100.76	162	42	13
Albert, Belgium	80	129	16.5	5
Moscow-Volga, Russia	80	129	18	6
Volga-Don, Russia	62	100	–	–
Göta, Sweden	54	87	10	3
Kiel (Nord-Ostsee), Germany	53.2	86	38	12
Panama Canal, Panama	50.72	82	41.6	13
Houston Ship, U.S.A.	50	81	36	11

LARGEST ISLANDS

	Area in: Sq. Miles	Sq. Kms.
Greenland	840,000	2,175,600
New Guinea	305,000	789,950
Borneo	290,000	751,100
Madagascar	226,400	586,376
Baffin, Canada	195,928	507,454
Sumatra, Indonesia	164,000	424,760
Honshu, Japan	88,000	227,920
Great Britain	84,400	218,896
Victoria, Canada	83,896	217,290
Ellesmere, Canada	75,767	196,236
Celebes, Indonesia	72,986	189,034
South I., New Zealand	58,393	151,238
Java, Indonesia	48,842	126,501
North I., New Zealand	44,187	114,444
Newfoundland, Canada	42,031	108,860
Cuba	40,533	104,981
Luzon, Philippines	40,420	104,688
Iceland	39,768	103,000
Mindanao, Philippines	36,537	94,631
Ireland	31,743	82,214
Sakhalin, Russia	29,500	76,405
Hispaniola, Haiti & Dom. Rep.	29,399	76,143

	Area in: Sq. Miles	Sq. Kms.
Hokkaido, Japan	28,983	75,066
Banks, Canada	27,038	70,028
Ceylon, Sri Lanka	25,332	65,610
Tasmania, Australia	24,600	63,710
Svalbard, Norway	23,957	62,049
Devon, Canada	21,331	55,247
Novaya Zemlya (north isl.), Russia	18,600	48,200
Marajó, Brazil	17,991	46,597
Tierra del Fuego, Chile & Argentina	17,900	46,360
Alexander, Antarctica	16,700	43,250
Axel Heiberg, Canada	16,671	43,178
Melville, Canada	16,274	42,150
Southhampton, Canada	15,913	41,215
New Britain, Papua New Guinea	14,100	36,519
Taiwan, China	13,836	35,835
Kyushu, Japan	13,770	35,664
Hainan, China	13,127	33,999
Prince of Wales, Canada	12,872	33,338
Spitsbergen, Norway	12,355	31,999
Vancouver, Canada	12,079	31,285
Timor, Indonesia	11,527	29,855
Sicily, Italy	9,926	25,708

	Area in: Sq. Miles	Sq. Kms.
Somerset, Canada	9,570	24,786
Sardinia, Italy	9,301	24,090
Shikoku, Japan	6,860	17,767
New Caledonia, France	6,530	16,913
Nordaustlandet, Norway	6,409	16,599
Samar, Philippines	5,050	13,080
Negros, Philippines	4,906	12,707
Palawan, Philippines	4,550	11,785
Panay, Philippines	4,446	11,515
Jamaica	4,232	10,961
Hawaii, United States	4,038	10,458
Viti Levu, Fiji	4,010	10,386
Cape Breton, Canada	3,981	10,311
Mindoro, Philippines	3,759	9,736
Kodiak, Alaska, U.S.A.	3,670	9,505
Cyprus	3,572	9,251
Puerto Rico, U.S.A.	3,435	8,897
Corsica, France	3,352	8,682
New Ireland, Papua New Guinea	3,340	8,651
Crete, Greece	3,218	8,335
Anticosti, Canada	3,066	7,941
Wrangel, Russia	2,819	7,301

PRINCIPAL MOUNTAINS

	Height in : Feet	Meters		Height in : Feet	Meters		Height in : Feet	Meters
verest, Nepal-China	29,028	8,848	Llullaillaco, Chile-Argentina	22,057	6,723	Blanc, France	15,771	4,807
2 (Godwin Austen), Pakistan-China	28,250	8,611	Nevada Ancohuma, Bolivia	21,489	6,550	Klyuchevskaya Sopka, Russia	15,584	4,750
Makalu, Nepal-China	27,789	8,470	Chimborazo, Ecuador	20,561	6,267	Fairweather, Br. Col., Canada	15,300	4,663
haulagiri, Nepal	26,810	8,172	McKinley, Alaska	20,320	6,194	Dufourspitze (Mte. Rosa), Italy-Switzerland	15,203	4,634
anga Parbat, Pakistan	26,660	8,126	Logan, Yukon, Canada	19,524	5,951	Ras Dashen, Ethiopia	15,157	4620
nnapurna, Nepal	26,504	8,078	Cotopaxi, Ecuador	19,347	5,897	Matterhorn, Switzerland	14,691	4,478
akaposhi, Pakistan	25,550	7,788	Kilimanjaro, Tanzania	19,340	5,895	Whitney, California, U.S.A.	14,494	4,418
ongur Shan, China	25,325	7,719	El Misti, Peru	19,101	5,822	Elbert, Colorado, U.S.A.	14,433	4,399
irich Mir, Pakistan	25,230	7,690	Pico Cristóbal Colón, Colombia	18,947	5,775	Rainier, Washington, U.S.A.	14,410	4,392
ongga Shan, China	24,790	7,556	Huila, Colombia	18,865	5,750	Shasta, California, U.S.A.	14,162	4,317
ommunism Peak, Tajikistan	24,590	7,495	Citlaltépetl (Orizaba), Mexico	18,701	5,700	Pikes Peak, Colorado, U.S.A.	14,110	4,301
obedy Peak, Kyrgyzstan	24,406	7,439	Damavand, Iran	18,606	5,671	Finsteraarhorn, Switzerland	14,022	4, 274
homo Lhari, Bhutan-China	23,997	7,314	El'brus, Russia	18,510	5,642	Mauna Kea, Hawaii, U.S.A.	13,796	4,205
Muztag, China	23,891	7,282	St. Elias, Alaska, U.S.A.-Yukon, Canada	18,008	5,489	Mauna Loa, Hawaii, U.S.A.	13,677	4,169
erro Aconcagua, Argentina	22,831	6,959	Dykh-tau, Russia	17,070	5,203	Jungfrau, Switzerland	13,642	4,158
jos del Salado, Chile-Argentina	22,572	6,880	Batian (Kenya), Kenya	17,058	5,199	Grossglockner, Austria	12,457	3,797
onete, Chile-Argentina	22,546	6,872	Ararat, Turkey	16,946	5,165	Fujiyama, Japan	12,389	3,776
upungato, Chile-Argentina	22,310	6,800	Vinson Massif, Antarctica	16,864	5,140	Cook, New Zealand	12,349	3,764
issis, Argentina	22,241	6,779	Margherita (Ruwenzori), Africa	16,795	5,119	Etna, Italy	10,902	3,323
Mercedario, Argentina	22,211	6,770	Kazbek, Georgia-Russia	16,550	5,047	Kosciusko, Australia	7,310	2,228
uascarán, Peru	22,205	6,768	Puncak Jaya, Indonesia	16,503	5,030	Mitchell, North Carolina, U.S.A.	6,684	2,037

LONGEST RIVERS

	Length in : Miles	Kms.		Length in : Miles	Kms.		Length in : Miles	Kms.
ile, Africa	4,145	6,671	Indus, Asia	1,800	2,897	Don, Russia	1,222	1,967
mazon, S. America	3,915	6,300	Danube, Europe	1,775	2,857	Red, U.S.A.	1,222	1,966
hang Jiang (Yangtze), China	3,900	6,276	Salween, Asia	1,770	2,849	Columbia, U.S.A.-Canada	1,214	1,953
Mississippi-Missouri-Red Rock, U.S.A.	3,741	6,019	Brahmaputra, Asia	1,700	2,736	Saskatchewan, Canada	1,205	1,939
b'-Irtysh-Black Irtysh, Russia-Kazakhstan	3,362	5,411	Euphrates, Asia	1,700	2,736	Peace-Finlay, Canada	1,195	1,923
enisey-Angara, Russia	3,100	4,989	Tocantins, Brazil	1,677	2,699	Tigris, Asia	1,181	1,901
uang He (Yellow), China	2,877	4,630	Xi (Si), China	1,650	2,601	Darling, Australia	1,160	1,867
mur-Shilka-Onon, Asia	2,744	4,416	Amudar'ya, Asia	1,616	2,601	Angara, Russia	1,135	1,827
na, Russia	2,734	4,400	Nelson-Saskatchewan, Canada	1,600	2,575	Sungari, Asia	1,130	1,819
ongo (Zaire), Africa	2,718	4,374	Orinoco, S. America	1,600	2,575	Pechora, Russia	1,124	1,809
ackenzie-Peace-Finlay,Canada	2,635	4,241	Zambezi, Africa	1,600	2,575	Snake, U.S.A.	1,038	1,670
ekong, Asia	2,610	4,200	Paraguay, S. America	1,584	2,549	Churchill, Canada	1,000	1,609
issouri-Red Rock, U.S.A.	2,564	4,125	Kolyma, Russia	1,562	2,514	Pilcomayo, S. America	1,000	1,609
iger, Africa	2,548	4,101	Ganges, Asia	1,550	2,494	Uruguay, S. America	994	1.600
araná-La Plata, S. America	2,450	3,943	Ural, Russia-Kazakhstan	1,509	2,428	Platte-N. Platte, U.S.A.	990	1,593
ississippi, U.S.A.	2,348	3,778	Japurá, S. America	1,500	2,414	Ohio, U.S.A.	981	1,578
urray-Darling, Australia	2,310	3,718	Arkansas, U.S.A.	1,450	2,334	Magdalena, Colombia	956	1,538
olga, Russia	2,194	3,531	Colorado, U.S.A.-Mexico	1,450	2,334	Pecos, U.S.A.	926	1,490
adeira, S. America	2,013	3,240	Negro, S. America	1,400	2,253	Oka, Russia	918	1,477
urus, S. America	1,995	3,211	Dnieper, Russia-Belarus-Ukraine	1,368	2,202	Canadian, U.S.A.	906	1,458
ukon, Alaska-Canada	1,979	3,185	Orange, Africa	1,350	2,173	Colorado, Texas, U.S.A.	894	1,439
t. Lawrence, Canada-U.S.A.	1,900	3,058	Irrawaddy, Burma	1,325	2,132	Dniester, Ukraine-Moldova	876	1,410
o Grande, Mexico-U.S.A.	1,885	3,034	Brazos, U.S.A.	1,309	2,107	Fraser, Canada	850	1,369
yrdar'ya-Naryn, Asia	1,859	2,992	Ohio-Allegheny, U.S.A.	1,306	2,102	Rhine, Europe	820	1,319
io Francisco, Brazil	1,811	2,914	Kama, Russia	1,252	2,031	Northern Dvina, Russia	809	1,302

PRINCIPAL NATURAL LAKES

	Area in: Sq. Miles	Sq. Kms.	Max. Depth in: Feet	Meters		Area in: Sq. Miles	Sq. Kms.	Max. Depth in: Feet	Meters
aspian Sea, Asia	143,243	370,999	3,264	995	Lake Eyre, Australia	3,500-0	9,000-0	–	–
ake Superior, U.S.A.-Canada	31,820	82,414	1,329	405	Lake Titicaca, Peru-Bolivia	3,200	8,288	1,000	305
ake Victoria, Africa	26,724	69,215	270	82	Lake Nicaragua, Nicaragua	3,100	8,029	230	70
ake Huron, U.S.A.-Canada	23,010	59,596	748	228	Lake Athabasca, Canada	3,064	7,936	400	122
ake Michigan, U.S.A.	22,400	58,016	923	281	Reindeer Lake, Canada	2,568	6,651	–	–
ral Sea, Kazakhstan-Uzbekistan	15,830	41,000	213	65	Lake Turkana (Rudolf), Africa	2,463	6,379	240	73
ake Tanganyika, Africa	12,650	32,764	4,700	1,433	Issyk-Kul', Kyrgyzstan	2,425	6,281	2,303	702
ake Baykal, Russia	12,162	31,500	5,316	1,620	Lake Torrens, Australia	2,230	5,776	–	–
reat Bear Lake, Canada	12,096	31,328	1,356	413	Vänern, Sweden	2,156	5,584	328	100
ake Nyasa (Malawi), Africa	11,555	29,928	2,320	707	Nettilling Lake, Canada	2,140	5,543	–	–
reat Slave Lake, Canada	11,031	28,570	2,015	614	Lake Winnipegosis, Canada	2,075	5,374	38	12
ake Erie, U.S.A.-Canada	9,940	25,745	210	64	Lake Mobutu Sese Seko (Albert), Africa	2,075	5,374	160	49
ake Winnipeg, Canada	9,417	24,390	60	18	Kariba Lake, Zambia-Zimbabwe	2,050	5,310	295	90
ake Ontario, U.S.A.-Canada	7,540	19,529	775	244	Lake Nipigon, Canada	1,872	4,848	540	165
ake Ladoga, Russia	7,104	18,399	738	225	Lake Mweru, Zaire-Zambia	1,800	4,662	60	18
ake Balkhash, Kazakhstan	7,027	18,200	87	27	Lake Manitoba, Canada	1,799	4,659	12	4
ake Maracaibo, Venezuela	5,120	13,261	100	31	Lake Taymyr, Russia	1,737	4,499	85	26
ake Chad, Africa	4,000 –	10,360 –			Lake Khanka, China-Russia	1,700	4,403	33	10
	10,000	25,900	25	8	Lake Kioga, Uganda	1,700	4,403	25	8
ake Onega, Russia	3,710	9,609	377	115	Lake of the Woods, U.S.A.-Canada	1,679	4,349	70	21J2

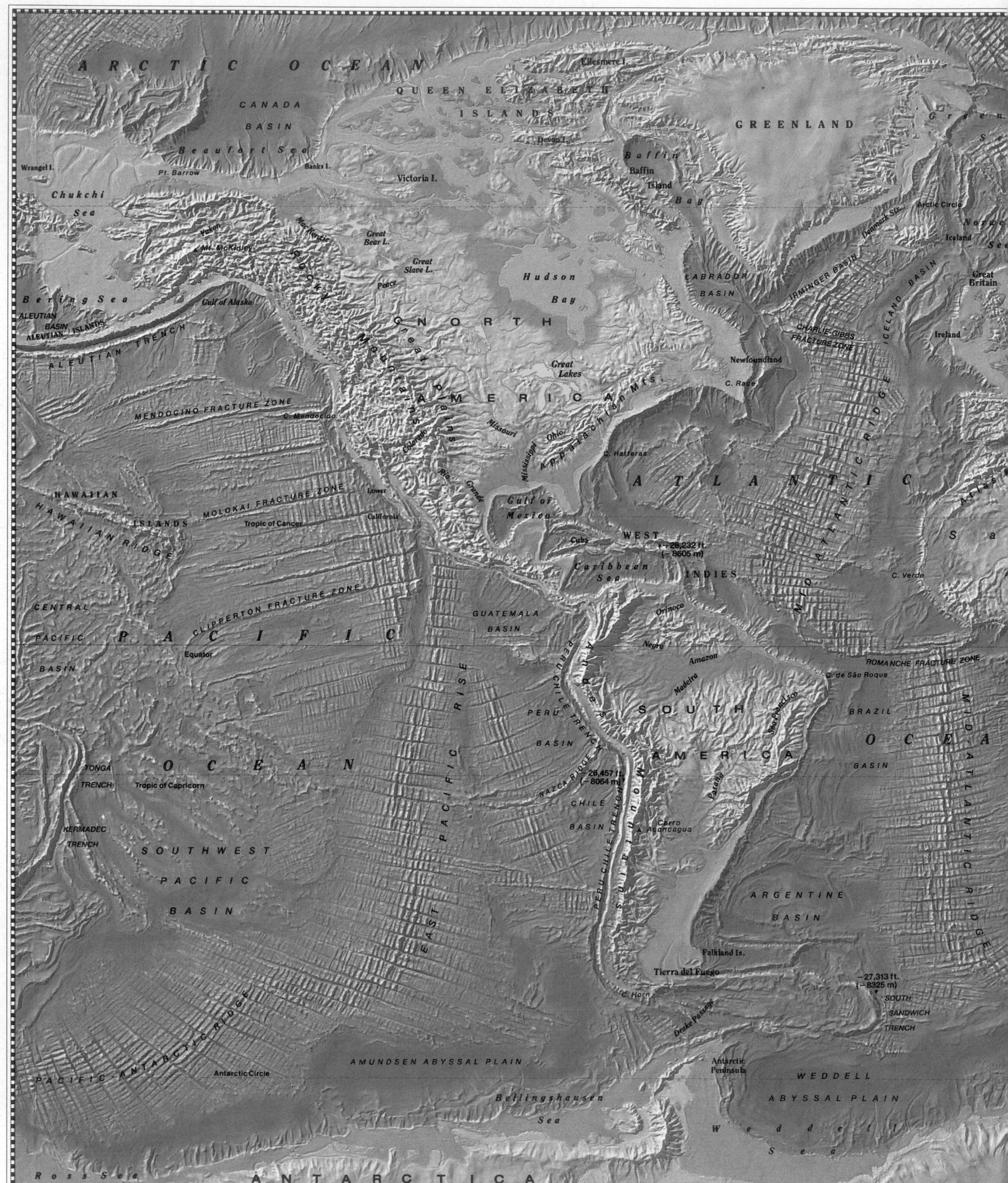

ARCTIC OCEAN
CANADA BASIN
Beaufort Sea
QUEEN ELIZABETH ISLANDS
Ellesmere I.
Devon I.
GREENLAND
Wrangel I.
Pt. Barrow
Banks I.
Victoria I.
Baffin Bay
Baffin Island
Chukchi Sea
Arctic Circle
Denmark St.
Iceland
Yukon
Mt. McKinley
Mackenzie
Great Bear L.
Great Slave L.
Peace
Rocky Mountains
Hudson Bay
LABRADOR BASIN
IRMINGER BASIN
ICELAND BASIN
Great Britain
Bering Sea
ALEUTIAN BASIN
ALEUTIAN ISLANDS
ALEUTIAN TRENCH
Gulf of Alaska
NORTH AMERICA
Great Plains
CHARLIE-GIBBS FRACTURE ZONE
Ireland
Newfoundland
C. Race
Great Lakes
Appalachian Mts.
MENDOCINO FRACTURE ZONE
C. Mendocino
Missouri
Ohio
Colorado
Mississippi
C. Hatteras
Rio Grande
ATLANTIC
MID-ATLANTIC RIDGE
HAWAIIAN ISLANDS
HAWAIIAN RIDGE
MOLOKAI FRACTURE ZONE
Lower California
Tropic of Cancer
Gulf of Mexico
Cuba
WEST INDIES
−28,232 ft. (−8605 m)
Caribbean Sea
C. Verde
CENTRAL PACIFIC BASIN
CLIPPERTON FRACTURE ZONE
GUATEMALA BASIN
Orinoco
PACIFIC
Equator
Negro
Amazon
ROMANCHE FRACTURE ZONE
C. de São Roque
Madeira
EAST PACIFIC RISE
PERU-CHILE TRENCH
Andes Mountains
PERU BASIN
SOUTH AMERICA
São Francisco
BRAZIL BASIN
OCEAN
TONGA TRENCH
Tropic of Capricorn
NAZCA RIDGE
−26,457 ft. (−8064 m)
Paraná
CHILE BASIN
Cerro Aconcagua
KERMADEC TRENCH
SOUTHWEST PACIFIC BASIN
ARGENTINE BASIN
Falkland Is.
Tierra del Fuego
−27,313 ft. (−8325 m)
C. Horn
SOUTH SANDWICH TRENCH
Drake Passage
PACIFIC-ANTARCTIC RIDGE
AMUNDSEN ABYSSAL PLAIN
Antarctic Circle
Antarctic Peninsula
WEDDELL ABYSSAL PLAIN
Bellingshausen Sea
Weddell Sea
Ross Sea
ANTARCTICA

A R C T I C   O C E A N

*17.861 ft.
(5490 m)

FRANZ JOSEF LAND   SEVERNAYA
                           ZEMLYA

SVALBARD   NEW SIBERIAN IS.

NOVAYA   L a p t e v   Wrangel I.
ZEMLYA   Kara
Norakap   Sea   S e a

Barents   B e r i n g
Sea   S i b e r i a   S e a
                                                                              ALEUTIAN
L. Ladoga   Ob.   Yenisey   Kamchatka   BASIN
Baltic Sea   Angara   Lena   Pen.   ALEUTIAN ISLANDS
Kolen   Sea
                    Irtish   Aldan   of
EUROPE   Ural Mountains   Lena   L. Baykal Okhotsk
Onieper   Volga   Amur   Sakhalin
Danube   Black Sea   Caspian Sea L. Balkhash   A S I A   NORTHWEST
Aral   Sea of
Mediterranean Sea   Euphrates   Sea   Gobi Honshu   JAPAN   PACIFIC
                                                        Japan   TRENCH   BASIN
            Red Sea   Indus   Kunlun   Huang East
Nile   Himalaya   Mt. Everest Chang China   P A C I F I C
Arabian   Ganges   Sea   Tropic of Cancer
Sea   ARABIAN   Chang   MARIANA
AFRICA   BASIN   Bay   Mekong   South   Taiwan
                  of   China   PHILIPPINE MARIANA IS.
C. Comorin Ceylon Bengal   Sea   Luzon BASIN TRENCH   MARSHALL IS. CENTRAL
CARLSBERG   Challenger Deep   PACIFIC
RIDGE   CEYLON   Mindanao 35,196 ft.
SOMALI   PLAIN   Borneo   (11,033 m)   BASIN
Victoria BASIN   CENTRAL   CAROLINE IS.
Kilimanjaro   MELANESIAN   Equator
          INDIAN   Sumatra   Java Celebes New Guinea BASIN
ANGOLA   RIDGE   24,143 ft.   O C E A N
Zambezi   (7450 m)
Madagascar   Coral   Fiji Is.
                  I N D I A N   Sea
                                  BROKEN   AUSTRALIA
CAPE OF   PLATEAU   Tropic of Capricorn
Good Hope Orange   O C E A N   C. Leeuwin   Tasman   North Cape
BASIN   Sea   North I.
AGULHAS RIDGE   SOUTHEAST INDIAN RIDGE   S. AUSTRALIA BASIN
                  KERGUELEN   Tasmania South I.
SOUTHWEST INDIAN RIDGE PLATEAU

                                                              SOUTHEAST INDIAN RIDGE
ENDERBY ABYSSAL PLAIN   AUSTRALIAN-ANTARCTIC BASIN

                                                    Antarctic Circle

                  Amery   C. Adare
                  Ice Shelf   Ross Sea

A N T A R C T I C A

© Copyright by HAMMOND INCORPORATED, Maplewood, N.J.

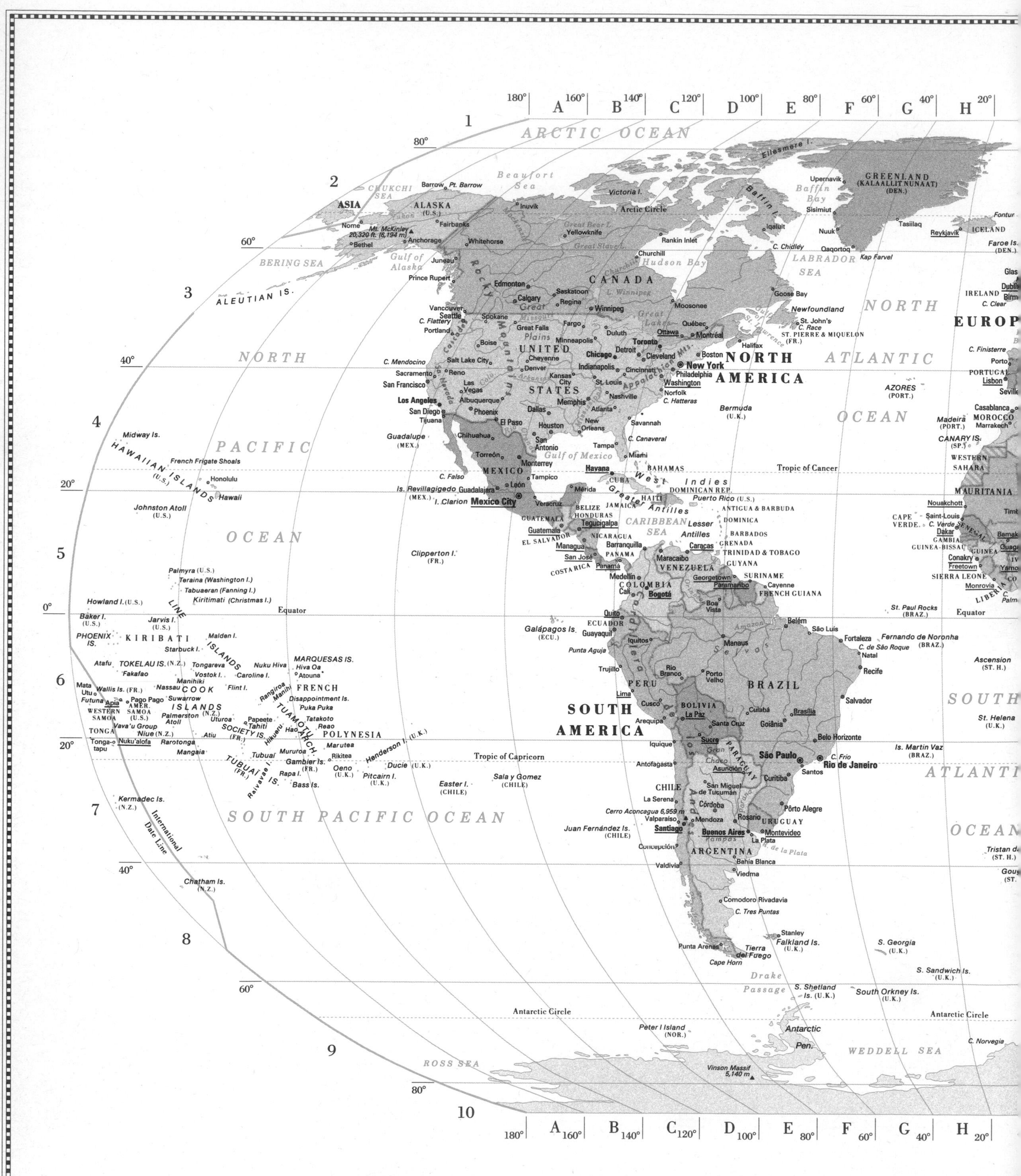

180°
A 160°
B 140°
C 120°
D 100°
E 80°
F 60°
G 40°
H 20°
1
2
3
4
5
6
7
8
9
10
80°
60°
40°
20°
0°
ARCTIC OCEAN
Beaufort Sea
CHUKCHI SEA
ASIA
Barrow
Pt. Barrow
ALASKA (U.S.)
Nome
Bethel
Fairbanks
Mt. McKinley 20,320 ft. (6,194 m)
Anchorage
BERING SEA
Gulf of Alaska
Juneau
Whitehorse
Inuvik
Victoria I.
Arctic Circle
Great Bear L.
Yellowknife
Great Slave L.
Rankin Inlet
Churchill
Hudson Bay
Ellesmere I.
Baffin I.
Baffin Bay
Upernavik
GREENLAND (KALAALLIT NUNAAT) (DEN.)
Sisimiut
Iqaluit
Nuuk
Tasiilaq
Qaqortoq
Kap Farvel
C. Chidley
LABRADOR SEA
Reykjavík
ICELAND
Faroe Is. (DEN.)
ALEUTIAN IS.
Prince Rupert
Edmonton
CANADA
Saskatoon
Calgary
Regina
L. Winnipeg
Winnipeg
Moosonee
Goose Bay
Newfoundland
Vancouver
Seattle
C. Flattery
Portland
Spokane
Great Plains
Great Falls
Fargo
Great Lakes
Québec
Montréal
Ottawa
St. John's
C. Race
ST. PIERRE & MIQUELON (FR.)
Halifax
Gulf of St. Lawrence
NORTH ATLANTIC
IRELAND
C. Clear
EUROP
Boise
UNITED
Minneapolis
Duluth
Toronto
Detroit
Boston
NORTH
Chicago
Cleveland
New York
Philadelphia
Washington
AMERICA
Norfolk
C. Hatteras
Salt Lake City
Cheyenne
Denver
Indianapolis
Cincinnati
C. Mendocino
Sacramento
Reno
San Francisco
Las Vegas
Kansas City
St. Louis
STATES
Nashville
Memphis
Atlanta
Los Angeles
San Diego
Tijuana
Albuquerque
Phoenix
Dallas
El Paso
Houston
New Orleans
San Antonio
Savannah
C. Canaveral
Tampa
Miami
Rocky Mountains
Appalachian Mts.
Bermuda (U.K.)
AZORES (PORT.)
C. Finisterre
Porto
PORTUGAL
Lisbon
Seville
Casablanca
MOROCCO
Madeira (PORT.)
Marrakech
CANARY IS. (SP.)
WESTERN SAHARA
OCEAN
NORTH
PACIFIC
Midway Is.
HAWAIIAN ISLANDS (U.S.)
French Frigate Shoals
Honolulu
Hawaii
Guadalupe (MEX.)
Chihuahua
Torreón
Monterrey
Gulf of Mexico
MEXICO
Tampico
C. Falso
Guadalajara
León
Is. Revillagigedo (MEX.)
I. Clarion
Mexico City
Veracruz
Mérida
Havana
CUBA
BAHAMAS
Tropic of Cancer
West Indies
DOMINICAN REP.
HAITI
Puerto Rico (U.S.)
Greater Antilles
JAMAICA
BELIZE
HONDURAS
Tegucigalpa
GUATEMALA
Guatemala
EL SALVADOR
NICARAGUA
Managua
San José
COSTA RICA
PANAMA
Panamá
CARIBBEAN SEA
Lesser Antilles
ANTIGUA & BARBUDA
DOMINICA
BARBADOS
GRENADA
TRINIDAD & TOBAGO
Caracas
Barranquilla
Maracaibo
VENEZUELA
GUYANA
Georgetown
SURINAME
Paramaribo
Cayenne
FRENCH GUIANA
Medellín
COLOMBIA
Cali
Bogotá
Boa Vista
Johnston Atoll (U.S.)
OCEAN
Clipperton I. (FR.)
CAPE VERDE
Nouakchott
MAURITANIA
Saint-Louis
C. Verde
Dakar
GAMBIA
GUINEA-BISSAU
GUINEA
Conakry
Freetown
SIERRA LEONE
Monrovia
LIBERIA
Palmyra (U.S.)
Teraina (Washington I.)
Tabuaeran (Fanning I.)
Kiritimati (Christmas I.)
LINE ISLANDS
Howland I. (U.S.)
Baker I. (U.S.)
Jarvis I. (U.S.)
Equator
PHOENIX IS.
KIRIBATI
Malden I.
Starbuck I.
Quito
ECUADOR
Guayaquil
Galápagos Is. (ECU.)
Belém
São Luís
Fortaleza
Fernando de Noronha (BRAZ.)
C. de São Roque
Natal
Recife
St. Paul Rocks (BRAZ.)
Equator
Iquitos
Manaus
Amazon
Punta Aguja
Trujillo
Rio Branco
Porto Velho
BRAZIL
Ascension (ST. H.)
Atafu
TOKELAU IS. (N.Z.)
Fakafao
Tongareva
Vostok I.
Manihiki
Nukuhiva
Hiva Oa
Atouna
MARQUESAS IS.
Caroline I.
Flint I.
Wallis Is. (FR.)
Futuna
Nassau
COOK ISLANDS (N.Z.)
Suwarrow
Pago Pago
AMER. SAMOA (U.S.)
Apia
WESTERN SAMOA
Palmerston Atoll
Vava'u Group
Niue (N.Z.)
TONGA
Nuku'alofa
Rarotonga
Mangaia
Aitu
Uturoa
Papeete
Tahiti
SOCIETY IS. (FR.)
FRENCH POLYNESIA
Rangiroa
Manihi
TUAMOTU ARCH.
Disappointment Is.
Puka Puka
Tatakoto
Reao
Hao
Hikueru
Tubuai
TUBUAI IS. (FR.)
Raivavae I.
Rapa I.
Bass Is.
Mururoa
Marutea
Gambier Is. (FR.)
Rikitea
Oeno (U.K.)
Pitcairn I. (U.K.)
Henderson I. (U.K.)
Ducie (U.K.)
Tropic of Capricorn
Easter I. (CHILE)
Sala y Gomez (CHILE)
Lima
PERU
Cusco
BOLIVIA
La Paz
Cuiabá
Brasília
Salvador
SOUTH AMERICA
Arequipa
Santa Cruz
Sucre
Goiânia
Belo Horizonte
Iquique
São Paulo
Rio de Janeiro
C. Frio
Santos
Antofagasta
PARAGUAY
Asunción
Curitiba
Gran Chaco
CHILE
San Miguel de Tucumán
La Serena
Córdoba
Pôrto Alegre
Cerro Aconcagua 6,959 m
Valparaíso
Mendoza
Rosario
URUGUAY
Santiago
Buenos Aires
Montevideo
La Plata
Juan Fernández Is. (CHILE)
Pampas
R. de la Plata
Concepción
ARGENTINA
Bahía Blanca
Valdivia
Viedma
Comodoro Rivadavia
C. Tres Puntas
Stanley
Falkland Is. (U.K.)
Punta Arenas
Tierra del Fuego
Cape Horn
S. Georgia (U.K.)
S. Sandwich Is. (U.K.)
SOUTH
St. Helena (U.K.)
Is. Martin Vaz (BRAZ.)
ATLANTI
OCEAN
Tristan da (ST. H.)
Kermadec Is. (N.Z.)
International Date Line
SOUTH PACIFIC OCEAN
Chatham Is. (N.Z.)
Drake Passage
S. Shetland Is. (U.K.)
South Orkney Is. (U.K.)
Antarctic Circle
Antarctic Circle
Peter I Island (NOR.)
Antarctic Pen.
WEDDELL SEA
C. Norvegia
ROSS SEA
Vinson Massif 5,140 m

World

ARCTIC OCEAN

FRANZ JOSEF LAND
(RUS.)

SVALBARD
(NOR.)

BARENTS
SEA

Novaya
Zemlya

Kara Sea

Severnaya Zemlya

New Siberian Is.

80°

Hammerfest North Cape
Tromsö Murmansk

Kiruna

Oulu

FINLAND

Archangel

Nar'yan-Mar

Vorkuta

Khatanga

Verkhoyansk

Arctic Circle

Anadyr

2

Umeå
Tampere Helsinki
Stockholm
Göteborg

St. Petersburg
Yaroslavl'

Syktyvkar

Salekhard

RUSSIA

Yenisey

Surgut

Siberia

Lena

Noril'sk

Lensk

Yakutsk

Bodaybo

60°

3

Okhotsk

BERING SEA

Kamchatka

Komsomol'sk-na-
Amure

Petropavlovsk-
Kamchatskiy
Mya Lopatka

Int'l Date Line

SWEDEN ESTONIA
Berlin
Moscow
Warsaw
Prague POLAND BELARUS
Vienna SLVK UKRAINE
Budapest ROMANIA
Belgrade BUL
Rome GREECE
Athens TURKEY
Istanbul Ankara

Nizhniy
Novgorod Perm'

Kazan'

Ufa

Chelyabinsk
Yekaterinburg

Omsk

Novosibirsk

Tomsk

Krasnoyarsk

Bratsk

Chita

Ulan-Ude

Irkutsk

L. Baikal

Blagoveshchensk

Qiqihar

Harbin

Khabarovsk

Sakhalin

SEA OF
OKHOTSK

KURIL IS.

Hokkaido

Sapporo

40°

4

Minsk

Kiev

Bucharest

Black Sea

GEORGIA
ARMENIA

Baku

Volgograd

Saratov

Samara
Orenburg

Magnitogorsk

Karaganda

Semipalatinsk

Balkhash

KAZAKHSTAN

Alma-Ata
Bishkek

MONGOLIA

Ulaanbaatar

Gobi

Choybalsan

Shenyang

Changchun

Vladivostok

N. KOREA

Pyŏngyang

S. KOREA

Sea of
Japan

Sendai

Hakodate

Honshu

JAPAN

NORTH

NIGER CHAD
Omdurman
Khartoum

SUDAN

ETHIOPIA

Addis Ababa

EGYPT

LIBYA

Cairo

ARABIA

SAUDI

Riyadh

OMAN

YEMEN

Sanaa

Aden

DJIBOUTI

SOMALIA

Mogadishu

INDIAN

OCEAN

POPULATION OF CITIES AND TOWNS

- OVER 5,000,000
- 2,000,000 - 4,999,999
- 500,000 - 1,999,999
- UNDER 500,000

SCALE 1:81,700,000   ROBINSON PROJECTION   STANDARD PARALLELS 38°N AND 38°S

MILES 0 ... 1000 ... 2000 ... 3000 ... 4000

KILOMETERS 0 ... 1000 ... 2000 ... 3000 ... 4000

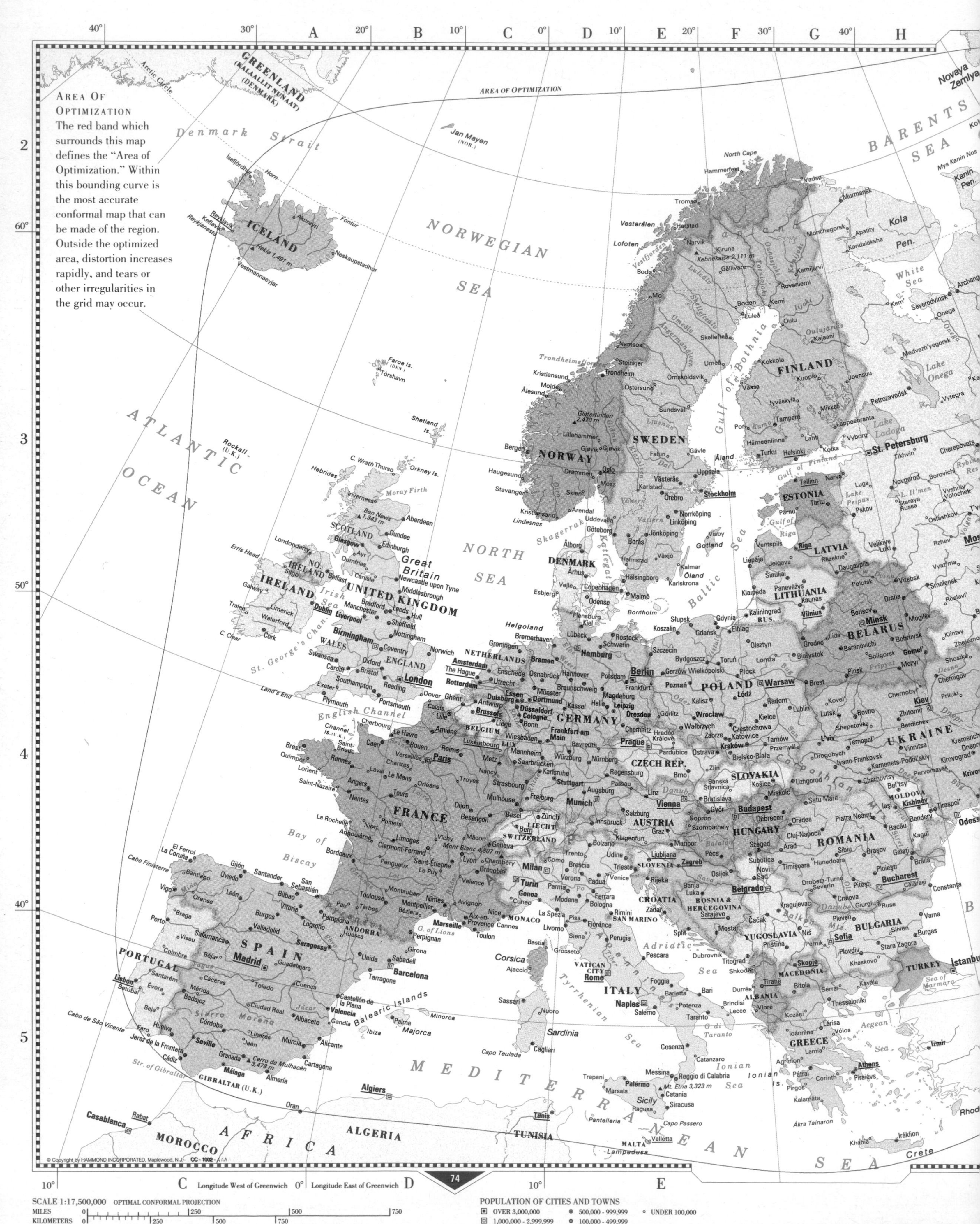

AREA OF
OPTIMIZATION
The red band which
surrounds this map
defines the "Area of
Optimization." Within
this bounding curve is
the most accurate
conformal map that can
be made of the region.
Outside the optimized
area, distortion increases
rapidly, and tears or
other irregularities in
the grid may occur.

SCALE 1:17,500,000   OPTIMAL CONFORMAL PROJECTION

MILES   0   250   500   750
KILOMETERS   0   250   500   750

POPULATION OF CITIES AND TOWNS

▣ OVER 3,000,000   ● 500,000 - 999,999   ○ UNDER 100,000
▢ 1,000,000 - 2,999,999   ● 100,000 - 499,999

◄ 74 ►

Europe

SCALE 1:587,000   LAMBERT CONFORMAL CONIC PROJECTION

Scandinavia and Finland, Iceland

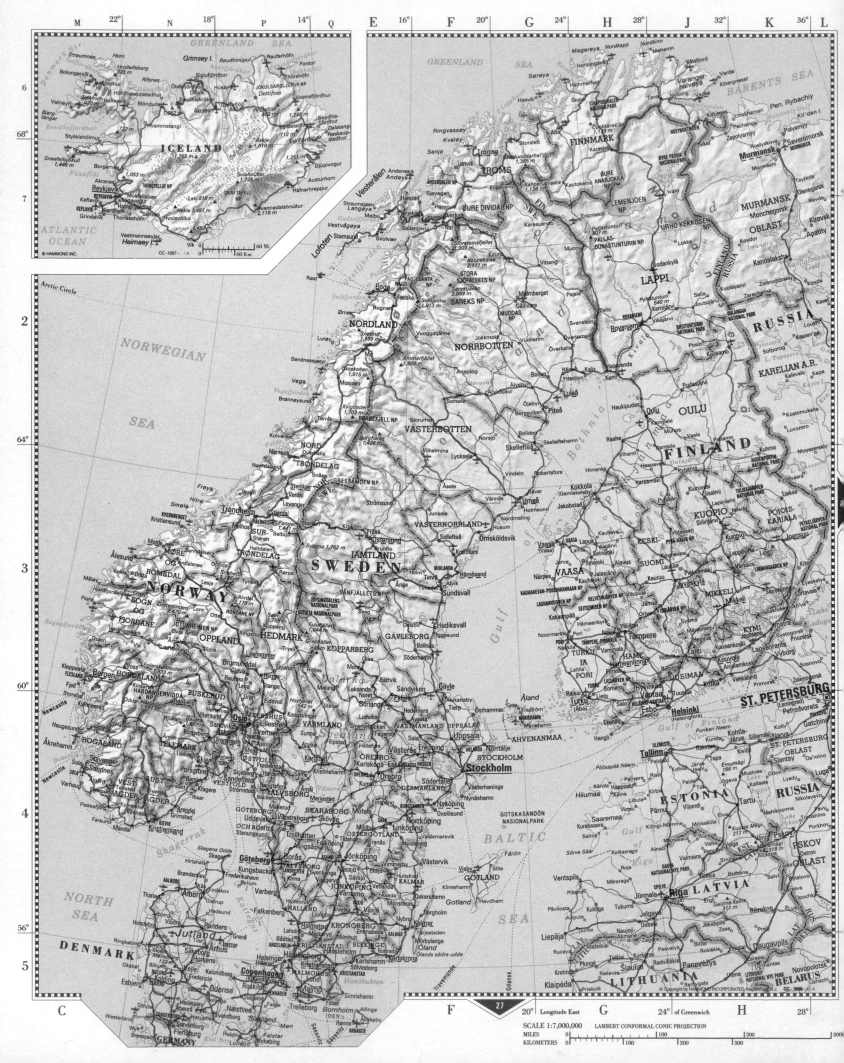

United Kingdom, Ireland

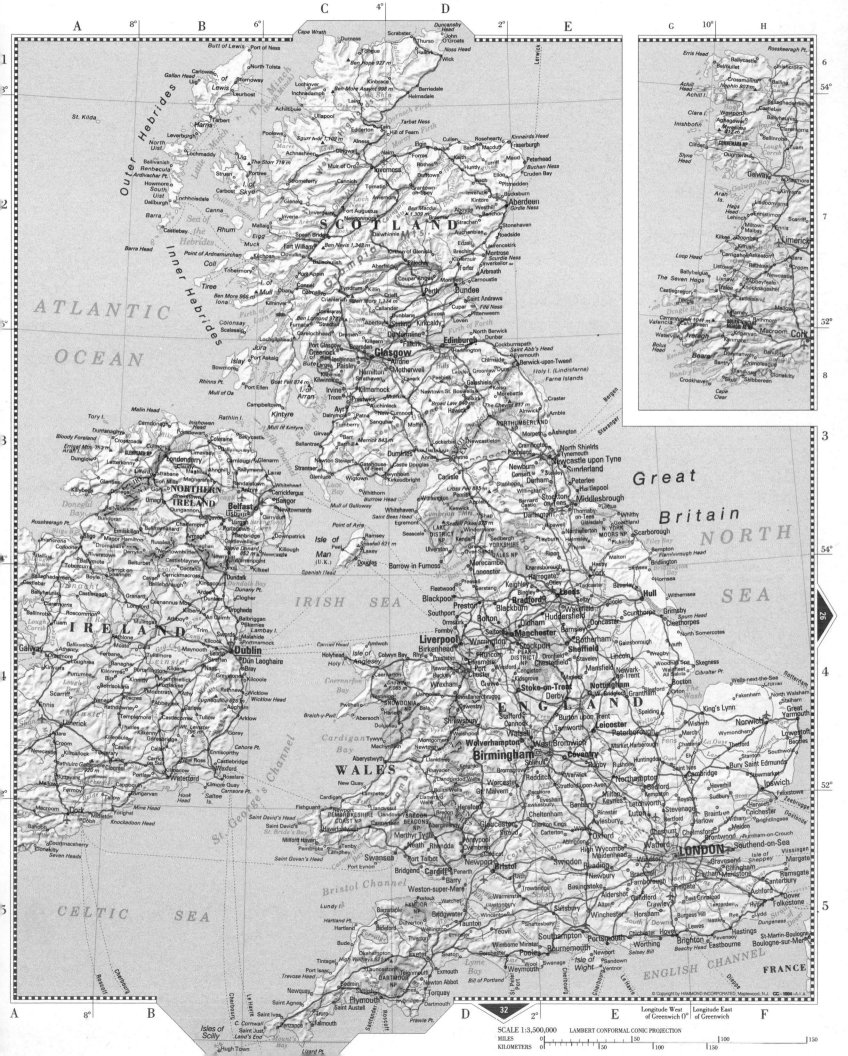

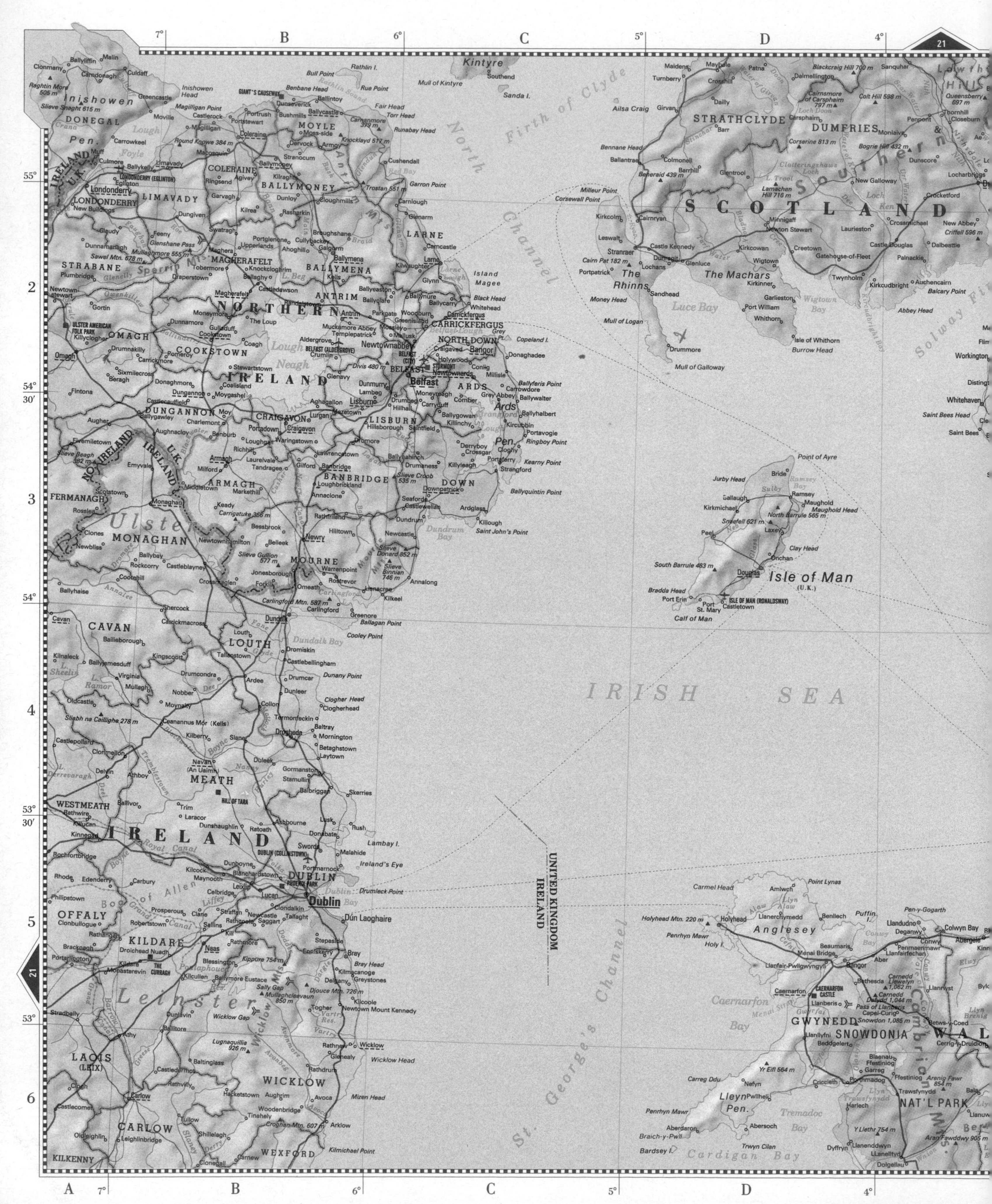
7°
B
6°
C
5°
D
4°
21
A
1
2
3
4
5
6
55°
54° 30′
54°
53° 30′
53°
NORTHERN IRELAND
IRELAND
SCOTLAND
IRISH SEA
Isle of Man
(U.K.)
North Channel
Firth of Clyde
St. George's Channel
UNITED KINGDOM
IRELAND
Ulster
Leinster
Southern Uplands
Kintyre
Mull of Kintyre
Southend
Sanda I.
Rathlin I.
Inishowen
DONEGAL
Malin
Ballyliffin
Clonmany
Carndonagh
Culdaff
Raghtin More 505 m
Slieve Snaght 615 m
Greencastle
Inishowen Head
Moville
Magilligan Point
Lough Foyle
Carrowkeel
Muff
Culmore
Londonderry
LONDONDERRY
LONDONDERRY (EGLINTON)
Eglinton
New Buildings
Limavady
LIMAVADY
Ballykelly
Round Knowe 384 m
Magilligan
Castlerock
Portstewart
Portrush
Coleraine
COLERAINE
Aghadowey
Ringsend
Garvagh
Dungiven
Feeny
Claudy
Dunnamanagh
Glenshane Pass
Sawel Mtn. 678 m
Mullaghmore 555 m
Sperrin Mts.
STRABANE
Plumbridge
Newtownstewart
Gortin
ULSTER AMERICAN FOLK PARK
Killyclogher
OMAGH
Omagh
Drumnakilly
Carrickmore
Sixmilecross
Beragh
Fintona
GIANT'S CAUSEWAY
Bushmills
Dunseverick
Benbane Head
Ballintoy
Ballycastle
Bull Point
Rue Point
Fair Head
Torr Head
Carnanmore 379 m
Runabay Head
MOYLE
Moss-side
Armoy
Knocklayd 517 m
Cushendall
Red Bay
Garron Point
Trostan 551 m
Antrim Mts.
Carnlough
Glenarm
BALLYMONEY
Ballymoney
Stranocum
Dervock
Dunloy
Cloughmills
Kilrea
Rasharkin
Swatragh
Maghera
MAGHERAFELT
Magherafelt
Tobermore
Draperstown
Portglenone
Upperlands
Ahoghill
Broughshane
Cullybackey
Galgorm
Ballymena
BALLYMENA
Kells
Knockcloghrim
Bellaghy
Castledawson
Randalstown
ANTRIM
Antrim
Lough Beg
LARNE
Larne
Carncastle
Kilwaughter
Glynn
Island Magee
Ballyeaston
Ballyclare
Ballynure
Ballycarry
Black Head
Whitehead
Parkgate
Woodburn
Carrickfergus
CARRICKFERGUS
Greenisland
Mossley
Mallusk
Newtownabbey
Muckamore Abbey
Templepatrick
Aldergrove
BELFAST (ALDERGROVE)
Crumlin
Lough Neagh
Moneymore
Gulladuff
Cookstown
COOKSTOWN
The Loup
Coagh
Dunnamore
Pomeroy
Stewartstown
Coalisland
Donaghmore
Dungannon
Moygashel
DUNGANNON
Castlecaulfield
Ballygawley
Augher
Moy
Charlemont
Aughnacloy
Benburb
Fivemiletown
Slieve Beagh 382 m
FERMANAGH
Scotstown
Rosslea
Clones
Newbliss
MONAGHAN
Monaghan
Emyvale
Ballybay
Rockcorry
Castleblayney
Cootehill
Ballyhaise
Annalee
Belfast Lough
BELFAST (CITY)
STORMONT
Belfast
Divis 480 m
Glenavy
Dunmurry
Lambeg
Lisburn
LISBURN
Aghagallon
Maze
Drumbeg
Hillhall
Carryduff
Moneyreagh
Lurgan
CRAIGAVON
Craigavon
Portadown
Waringstown
Loughgall
Richhill
Armagh
ARMAGH
Laurelvale
Tandragee
Markethill
Milford
Middletown
Keady
Carrigatuke 365 m
Monaghan
Bessbrook
Newtownhamilton
Belleek
Slieve Gullion 577 m
Crossmaglen
Jonesborough
Forkhill
Newry
Hillsborough
Saintfield
Dromore
Ballynahinch
Lawrencetown
Gilford
Banbridge
BANBRIDGE
Loughbrickland
Annaclone
Rathfriland
Hilltown
Slieve Croob 535 m
Drumaness
Seaforde
Castlewellan
Dundrum
Newcastle
Slieve Donard 852 m
Slieve Binnian 746 m
MOURNE
Mourne Mts.
Warrenpoint
Rostrevor
Omeath
Kilkeel
Annalong
Carlingford Lough
Carlingford Mtn. 587 m
Carlingford
Greenore
Dundrum Bay
NORTH DOWN
Bangor
Holywood
Craigavad
Newtownards
Conlig
Comber
ARDS
Ards Pen.
Ballygowan
Killinchy
Strangford Lough
Donaghadee
Copeland I.
Grey Point
Millisle
Carrowdore
Ballywalter
Ballyferis Point
Greyabbey
Ballyhalbert
Kircubbin
Portavogie
Ringboy Point
Cloghy
Derryboy
Crossgar
Killyleagh
Portaferry
Kearny Point
Strangford
DOWN
Downpatrick
Ballyquintin Point
Ardglass
Killough
Saint John's Point
Cavan
CAVAN
Bailieborough
Shercock
Carrickmacross
Kilnaleck
Lough Sheelin
Ballyjamesduff
Virginia
Lough Ramor
Mullagh
Oldcastle
Sliabh na Caillighe 278 m
Castlepollard
Clonmellon
Delvin
Lough Derravaragh
Athboy
WESTMEATH
Ballivor
Bathwire
Killucan
Kinnegad
Rochfortbridge
Rhode
Edenderry
Philipstown
OFFALY
Clonbullogue
Rathangan
Bracknagh
Portarlington
Kingscourt
Drumcondra
Nobber
Moynalty
Ceanannus Mór (Kells)
Kilberry
Navan (An Uaimh)
MEATH
HILL OF TARA
Trim
Laracor
Dunshaughlin
Ratoath
Ashbourne
Slane
Duleek
LOUTH
Louth
Dundalk
Dundalk Bay
Ballagan Point
Cooley Point
Tallanstown
Dromiskin
Castlebellingham
Dunany Point
Ardee
Drumcar
Dunleer
Clogher Head
Clogherhead
Collon
Termonfeckin
Drogheda
Baltray
Mornington
Betaghstown
Laytown
Gormanston
Stamullin
Balbriggan
Skerries
Lusk
Rush
Donabate
Lambay I.
Swords
Malahide
DUBLIN (COLLINSTOWN)
Portmarnock
Ireland's Eye
Kilcock
Dunboyne
Blanchardstown
DUBLIN
PHOENIX PARK
Dublin
Dublin Bay
Drumleck Point
Leixlip
Celbridge
Maynooth
Lucan
Clondalkin
Tallaght
Dún Laoghaire
Straffan
Newcastle
Saggart
Clane
Prosperous
Robertstown
Sallins
Rathcoole
Kill
Bog of Allen
Royal Canal
Grand Canal
Boyne
Liffey
Carbury
KILDARE
Kildare
Droichead Nuadh
Monasterevin
THE CURRAGH
Naas
Rathmore
Blessington
Poulaphouca
Kilcullen
Ballymore Eustace
Kippure 754 m
Stepaside
Enniskerry
Bray
Bray Head
Kilmacanoge
Delgany
Greystones
Djouce Mtn. 726 m
Sally Gap
Mullaghcleevaun 850 m
Kilcoole
Newtown Mount Kennedy
Wicklow Mts.
Wicklow Gap
Togher
Vartry Res.
Rathnew
Wicklow
Wicklow Head
Glenealy
Rathdrum
WICKLOW
Avoca
Mizen Head
Woodenbridge
Tinahely
Aughrim
Croghan Mtn. 607 m
Arklow
Kilmichael Point
Lugnaquillia 926 m
Dunlavin
Baltinglass
Ballitore
Athy
Stradbally
LAOIS (LEIX)
Castledermot
Rathvilly
Hacketstown
Tullow
Shillelagh
CARLOW
Carlow
Castlecomer
Old Leighlin
Leighlinbridge
Clonegall
Carnew
WEXFORD
KILKENNY
Slaney
Barrow
Maidens
Maybole
Patna
Turnberry
Crosshill
Dailly
Girvan
Ailsa Craig
Dalmellington
Blackcraig Hill 700 m
Sanquhar
Lowther Hills
Cairnsmore of Carsphairn 797 m
Loch Doon
Colt Hill 598 m
Queensberry 697 m
Thornhill
Closeburn
Penpont
Moniaive
STRATHCLYDE
DUMFRIES &
Barr
Carsphairn
Corserine 813 m
Bogrie Hill 432 m
Dunscore
Bennane Head
Ballantrae
Colmonell
Barrhill
Glentrool
Beneraid 439 m
Lamachan Hill 716 m
Clatteringshaws Loch
New Galloway
Lochar
Milleur Point
Corsewall Point
Kirkcolm
Cairnryan
Loch Ryan
Minnigaff
Newton Stewart
Crocketford
Crossmichael
New Abbey
Criffell 596 m
Laurieston
Leswalt
Stranraer
Castle Kennedy
Dunragit
Glenluce
Kirkcowan
Creetown
Gatehouse-of-Fleet
Castle Douglas
Dalbeattie
Palnackie
Cairn Pat 182 m
Portpatrick
Lochans
The Rhinns
The Machars
Wigtown
Kirkinner
Twynholm
Kirkcudbright
Auchencairn
Balcary Point
Sandhead
Garlieston
Wigtown Bay
Money Head
Luce Bay
Port William
Whithorn
Abbey Head
Mull of Logan
Isle of Whithorn
Burrow Head
Drummore
Mull of Galloway
Solway Firth
Workington
Whitehaven
Saint Bees Head
Saint Bees
Point of Ayre
Jurby Head
Bride
Ramsey Bay
Sulby
Ramsey
Ballaugh
Kirkmichael
Maughold
Maughold Head
Snaefell 621 m
North Barrule 565 m
Laxey
Peel
Clay Head
South Barrule 483 m
Onchan
Douglas
Bradda Head
Port Erin
Port St. Mary
ISLE OF MAN (RONALDSWAY)
Castletown
Calf of Man
Carmel Head
Amlwch
Point Lynas
Holyhead Mtn. 220 m
Holyhead
Holy I.
Penrhyn Mawr
Llanerchymedd
Benllech
Puffin I.
Anglesey
Pen-y-Gogarth
Llandudno
Colwyn Bay
Deganwy
Conwy
Abergele
Penmaenmawr
Llanfairfechan
Beaumaris
Menai Bridge
Llanfair-Pwllgwyngyll
Bangor
Aber
Bethesda
Carnedd Llewelyn 1,062 m
Carnedd Dafydd 1,044 m
Llanrwst
Caernarfon
CAERNARFON CASTLE
Menai Strait
Llanberis
Pass of Llanberis
Capel-Curig
Snowdon 1,085 m
Betws-y-Coed
Caernarfon Bay
GWYNEDD
SNOWDONIA
NAT'L PARK
WALES
Llanllyfni
Beddgelert
Cerrig-y-Druidion
Blaenau Ffestiniog
Garreg
Ffestiniog
Porthmadog
Criccieth
Arenig Fawr 854 m
Trawsfynydd
Harlech
Y Llethr 754 m
Cambrian Mts.
Aran Fawddwy 905 m
Llanenddwyn
Llanelltyd
Dolgellau
Yr Eifl 564 m
Carreg Ddu
Nefyn
Pwllheli
Lleyn Pen.
Tremadoc Bay
Penrhyn Mawr
Aberdaron
Abersoch
Braich-y-Pwll
Trwyn Cilan
Bardsey I.
Cardigan Bay
Dyffryn

Northeastern Ireland, Northern England and Wales

POPULATION OF CITIES AND TOWNS

◼ OVER 2,000,000	◉ 500,000 - 999,999
◻ 1,000,000 - 1,999,999	◉ 250,000 - 499,999

● 100,000 - 249,999	● 10,000 - 29,999	
● 30,000 - 99,999	• UNDER 10,000	

SCALE 1:1,170,000   LAMBERT CONFORMAL CONIC PROJECTION

MILES 0 ... 10 ... 20 ... 30 ... 40 ... 50

KILOMETERS 0 ... 10 ... 20 ... 30 ... 40 ... 50

Southern England and Wales

21

A 5° **B** 4° **C** 3° **D**

George's Channel

Cardigan Bay

GWYNEDD

SNOWDONIA NATIONAL PARK

POWYS

Teifiside

PEMBROKESHIRE

COAST

NAT'L

PARK

DYFED

W A L E S

SHROPSHIRE

HEREFORD

WORCESTER

BRECON

BEACONS

NAT'L

PARK

WEST

GLAMORGAN

MID

GLAMORGAN

Swansea

Gower Pen.

Swansea Bay

GWENT

ENGLAND

WALES

TINTERN ABBEY

Saint George's Channel

SOUTH

GLAMORGAN

Carüiff

CARDIFF-WALES

AVON

Bristol

Bath

Bristol Channel

Bridgwater Bay

SOMERSET

C E L T I C

S E A

Lundy I.

EXMOOR NAT'L

PARK

DEVON

DORSET

Lyme Bay

DARTMOOR

NAT'L

PARK

CORNWALL

Mount's Bay

Land's End

The Lizard

B 4° **C** 3° **D**

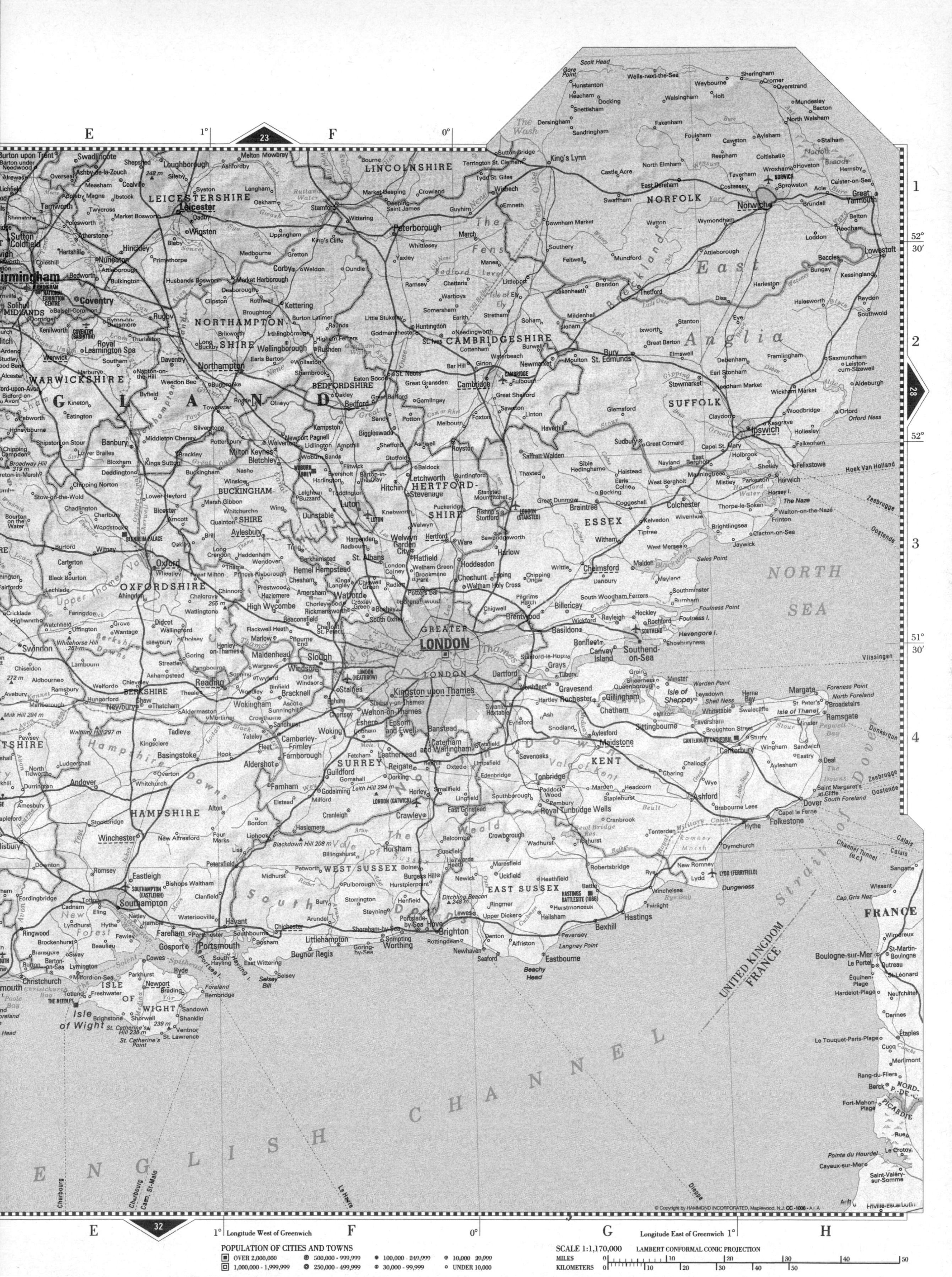

E
F
G
H
1°
0°
23
28
32
1
2
3
4
52° 30′
52°
51° 30′
51°
LINCOLNSHIRE
LEICESTERSHIRE
NORTHAMPTONSHIRE
WARWICKSHIRE
CAMBRIDGESHIRE
BEDFORDSHIRE
BUCKINGHAMSHIRE
HERTFORDSHIRE
OXFORDSHIRE
BERKSHIRE
HAMPSHIRE
SURREY
KENT
ESSEX
SUFFOLK
NORFOLK
WEST SUSSEX
EAST SUSSEX
ISLE OF WIGHT
ENGLAND
East Anglia
The Fens
The Wash
Breckland
GREATER LONDON
LONDON
Birmingham
Coventry
Leicester
Northampton
Peterborough
Cambridge
Norwich
Great Yarmouth
Lowestoft
Ipswich
Colchester
Chelmsford
Southend-on-Sea
Oxford
Reading
Luton
Bedford
Milton Keynes
Watford
Slough
Kingston upon Thames
Guildford
Maidstone
Canterbury
Dover
Folkestone
Brighton
Hastings
Eastbourne
Portsmouth
Southampton
Winchester
Swindon
King's Lynn
NORTH SEA
ENGLISH CHANNEL
Strait of Dover
FRANCE
UNITED KINGDOM
FRANCE
Calais
Boulogne-sur-Mer
Dunkerque
Oostende
Zeebrugge
Vlissingen
Hoek Van Holland
Dieppe
Le Havre
Cherbourg
NORD-PAS-DE-CALAIS
PICARDIE
© Copyright by HAMMOND INCORPORATED, Maplewood, N.J. CC-1006-A A
Longitude West of Greenwich
Longitude East of Greenwich
POPULATION OF CITIES AND TOWNS
OVER 2,000,000
1,000,000 - 1,999,999
500,000 - 999,999
250,000 - 499,999
100,000 - 249,999
30,000 - 99,999
10,000 - 29,999
UNDER 10,000
SCALE 1:1,170,000
LAMBERT CONFORMAL CONIC PROJECTION
MILES 0 10 20 30 40 50
KILOMETERS 0 10 20 30 40 50

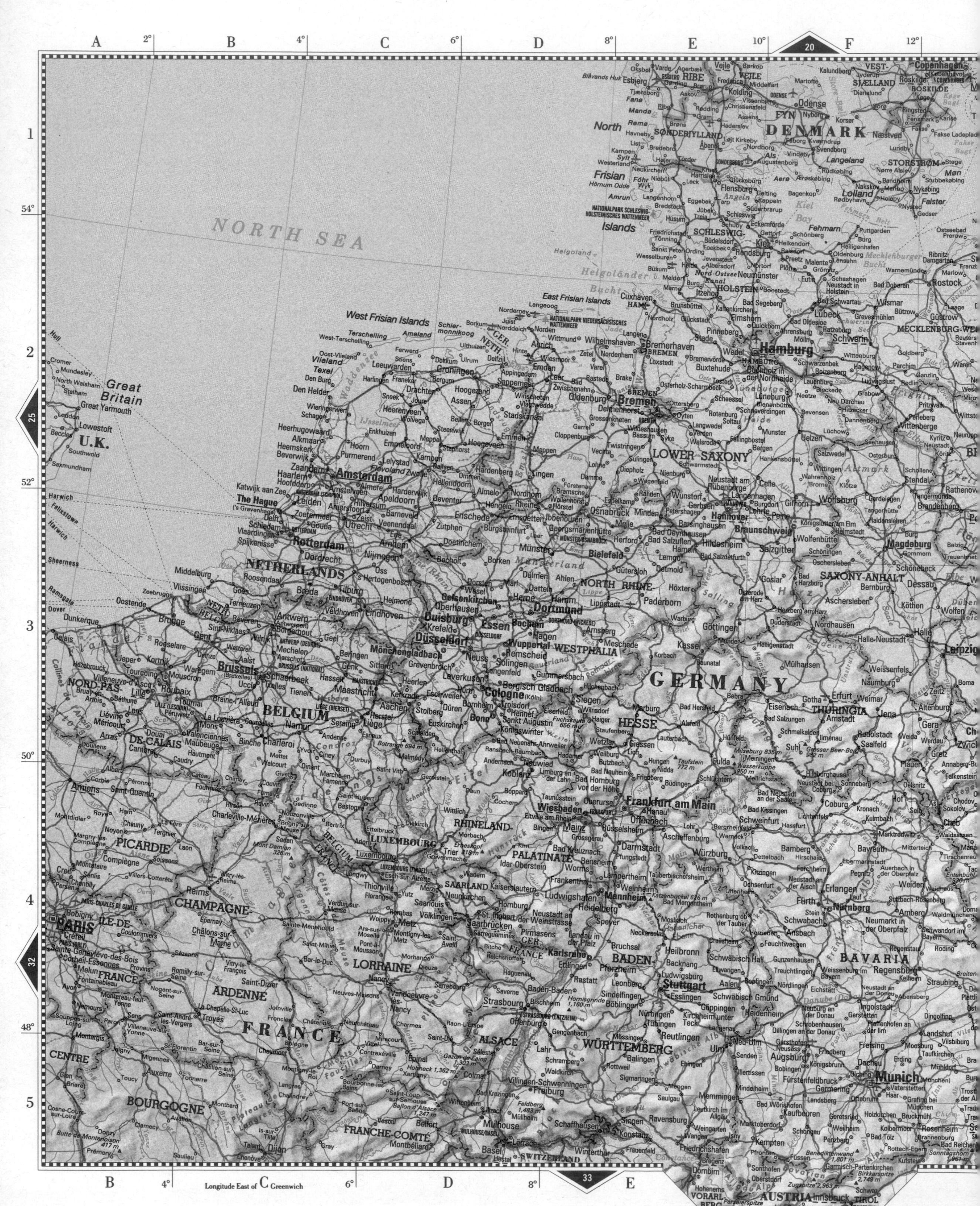

A
2°
B
4°
C
6°
D
8°
E
10°
F
12°
20
1
2
3
4
5
54°
52°
50°
48°
25
32
NORTH SEA
North
Frisian
Islands
West Frisian Islands
East Frisian Islands
Helgoländer
Bucht
Great
Britain
U.K.
DENMARK
Copenhagen
Odense
Esbjerg
Kiel
Hamburg
Bremen
Amsterdam
The Hague
Rotterdam
NETHERLANDS
BELGIUM
Brussels
LUXEMBOURG
Luxembourg
GERMANY
LOWER SAXONY
NORTH RHINE-
WESTPHALIA
HESSE
THURINGIA
SAXONY-ANHALT
RHINELAND-
PALATINATE
SAARLAND
BADEN-
WÜRTTEMBERG
BAVARIA
MECKLENBURG-WE
SCHLESWIG-
HOLSTEIN
Hannover
Braunschweig
Magdeburg
Dortmund
Essen
Duisburg
Düsseldorf
Cologne
Bonn
Frankfurt am Main
Wiesbaden
Mannheim
Karlsruhe
Stuttgart
Nürnberg
Munich
Leipzig
FRANCE
PARIS
NORD-PAS-
DE-CALAIS
PICARDIE
CHAMPAGNE-
ARDENNE
ILE-DE-
FRANCE
LORRAINE
ALSACE
CENTRE
BOURGOGNE
FRANCHE-COMTÉ
Strasbourg
SWITZERLAND
Basel
AUSTRIA
Innsbruck
TIROL
VORARL
BERG
B
4°
Longitude East of C Greenwich
6°
D
8°
33
E

North Central Europe

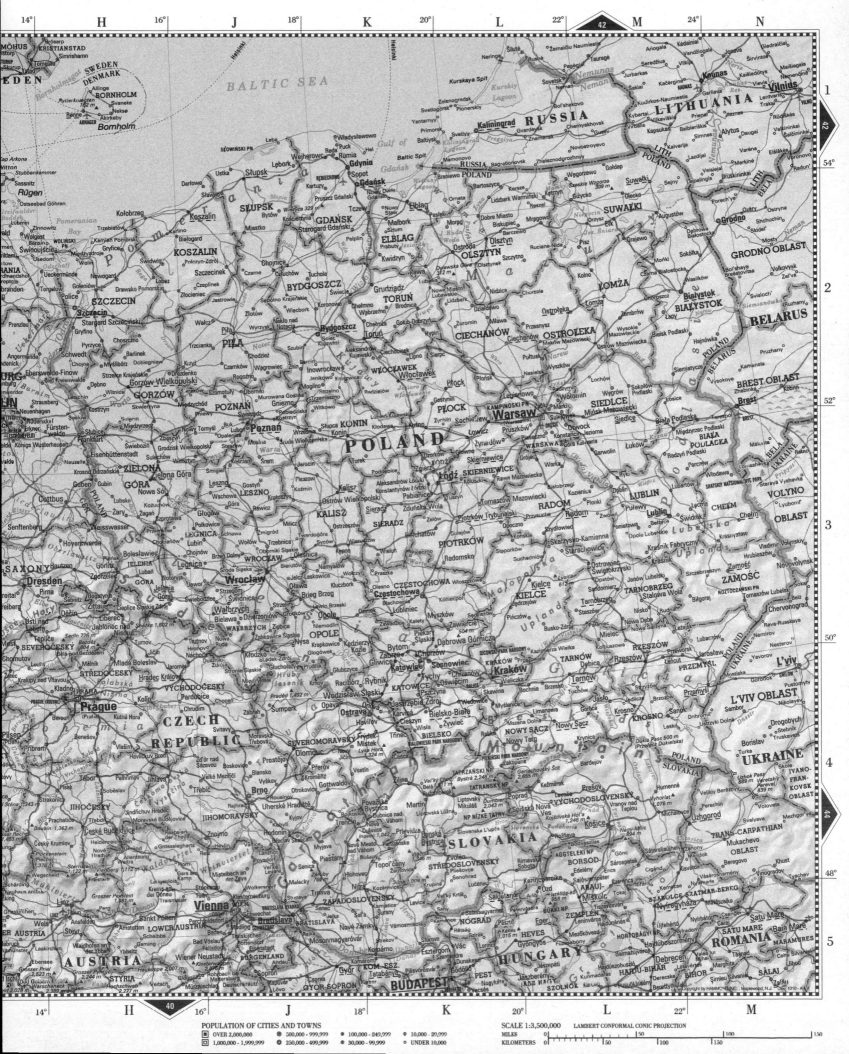

Netherlands, Northwestern Germany

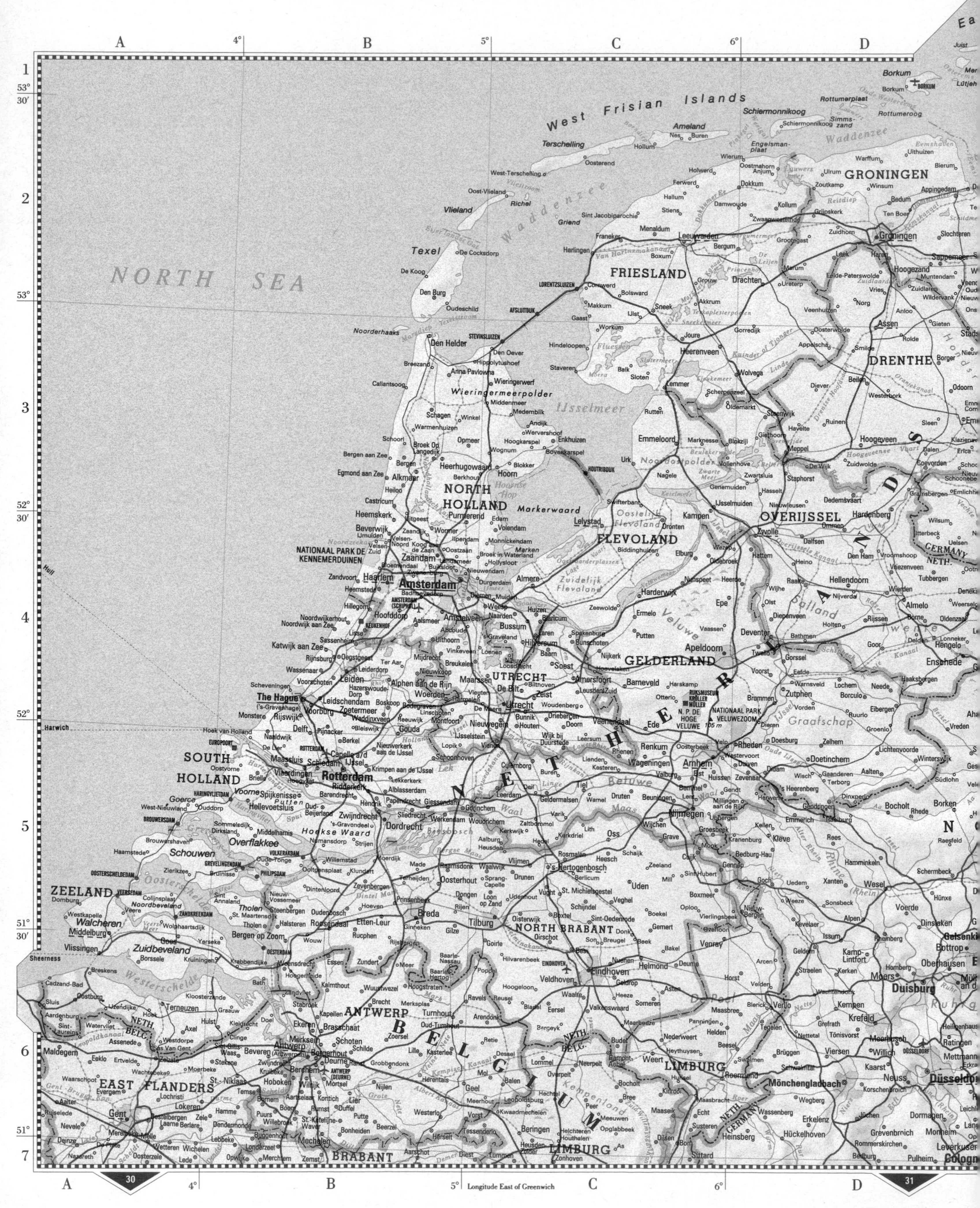

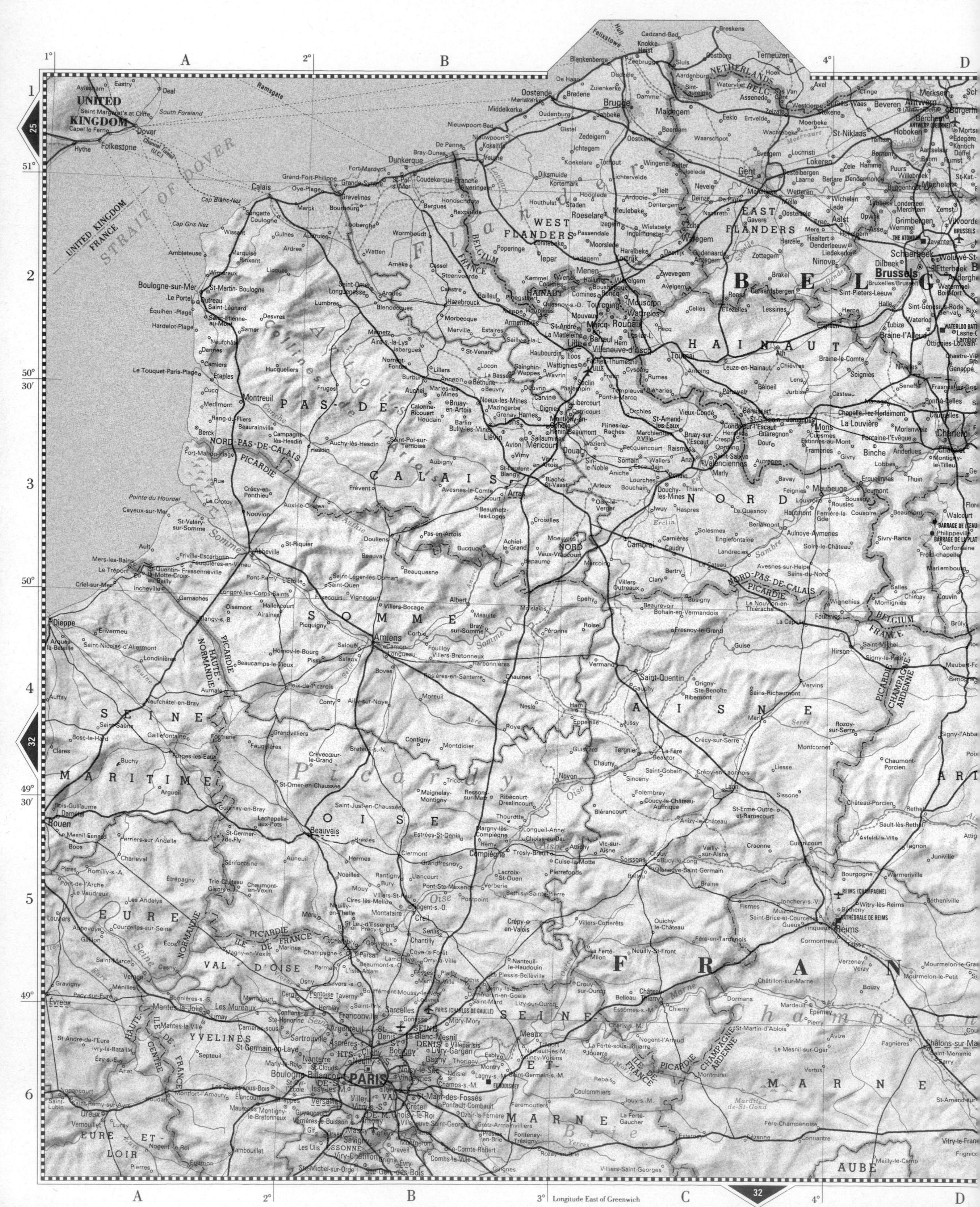

UNITED KINGDOM
STRAIT OF DOVER
UNITED KINGDOM
FRANCE
NETHERLANDS
BELG.
WEST FLANDERS
EAST FLANDERS
Flanders
BELGIUM
FRANCE
HAINAUT
BELG
Brussels
NORD-PAS-DE-CALAIS
PICARDIE
PAS-DE-CALAIS
Collines de l'Artois
NORD
SOMME
Picardy
AISNE
OISE
SEINE-MARITIME
HAUTE NORMANDIE
EURE
NORMANDIE
ILE DE FRANCE
VAL-D'OISE
YVELINES
PARIS
HTS.-DE-SEINE
SEINE-ST-DENIS
VAL-DE-MARNE
ESSONNE
SEINE-ET-MARNE
EURE-ET-LOIR
HAUTE-NORMANDIE
CENTRE
CHAMPAGNE-ARDENNE
MARNE
AUBE
FRANCE
Champagne
Brie
Calais
Dunkerque
Boulogne-sur-Mer
Lille
Amiens
Arras
Reims
Rouen
Beauvais
Compiègne
Soissons
Saint-Quentin
Laon
Dieppe
Abbeville
Valenciennes
Cambrai
Brugge
Gent
Oostende
Kortrijk
Mons
Charleroi
Antwerpen
Dover
Folkestone
Longitude East of Greenwich
1°
2°
3°
4°
51°
50° 30′
50°
49° 30′
49°
A
B
C
D
1
2
3
4
5
6
25
32

Belgium, Northern France, Western Germany

POPULATION OF CITIES AND TOWNS

■ OVER 2,000,000	● 500,000 - 999,999
□ 1,000,000 - 1,999,999	● 250,000 - 499,999
	● 100,000 - 249,999

● 30,000 - 99,999	● 10,000 - 29,999
	○ UNDER 10,000

SCALE 1:1,170,000   LAMBERT CONFORMAL CONIC PROJECTION

MILES

KILOMETERS

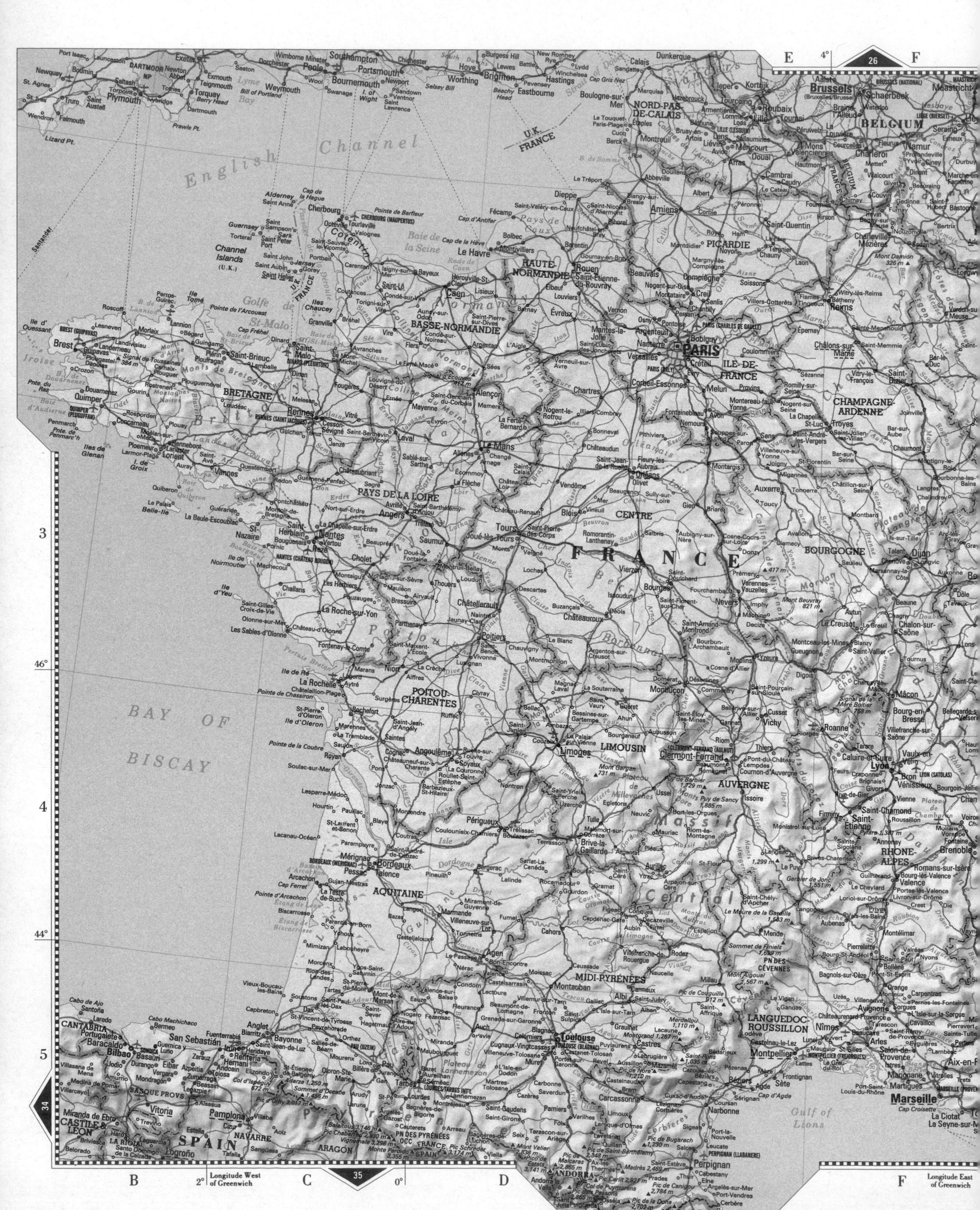

E
4°
26
F
English Channel
Strait of Dover
Channel Islands (U.K.)
Guernsey
Jersey
Alderney
Sark
U.K.
FRANCE
BELGIUM
Brussels
NORD-PAS-DE-CALAIS
PICARDIE
HAUTE-NORMANDIE
BASSE-NORMANDIE
BRETAGNE
PAYS DE LA LOIRE
ILE-DE-FRANCE
PARIS
CHAMPAGNE-ARDENNE
CENTRE
BOURGOGNE
POITOU-CHARENTES
LIMOUSIN
AUVERGNE
RHONE-ALPES
AQUITAINE
MIDI-PYRÉNÉES
LANGUEDOC-ROUSSILLON
FRANCE
Massif Central
BAY OF BISCAY
Gulf of Lions
Golfe de St-Malo
Baie de la Seine
Ile d' Ouessant
Belle-Ile
Ile de Noirmoutier
Ile d'Yeu
Ile de Ré
Ile d'Oleron
Lyon
Marseille
Toulouse
Bordeaux
Nantes
Rennes
Le Havre
Rouen
Lille
Orléans
Tours
Limoges
Clermont-Ferrand
Montpellier
Perpignan
Dijon
Reims
Amiens
Caen
Brest
Cherbourg
Plymouth
Southampton
Portsmouth
Brighton
Exeter
Bournemouth
Dunkerque
Calais
San Sebastián
Bilbao
Pamplona
Vitoria
Logroño
ANDORRA
SPAIN
CANTABRIA
BASQUE PROVS.
NAVARRE
ARAGÓN
CATALONIA
CASTILE & LEÓN
LA RIOJA
34
35
3
4
5
46°
44°
B
C
D
F
2°
0°
Longitude West of Greenwich
Longitude East of Greenwich

West Central Europe

POPULATION OF CITIES AND TOWNS

■ OVER 2,000,000   ● 500,000 900,000   ● 100,000 240,000   ○ 10,000 20,000

□ 1,000,000 - 1,999,999   ● 250,000 - 499,999   ● 30,000 99,999   ○ UNDER 10,000

SCALE 1:3,500,000   LAMBERT CONFORMAL CONIC PROJECTION

MILES 0   50   100   150

KILOMETERS 0   50   100   150

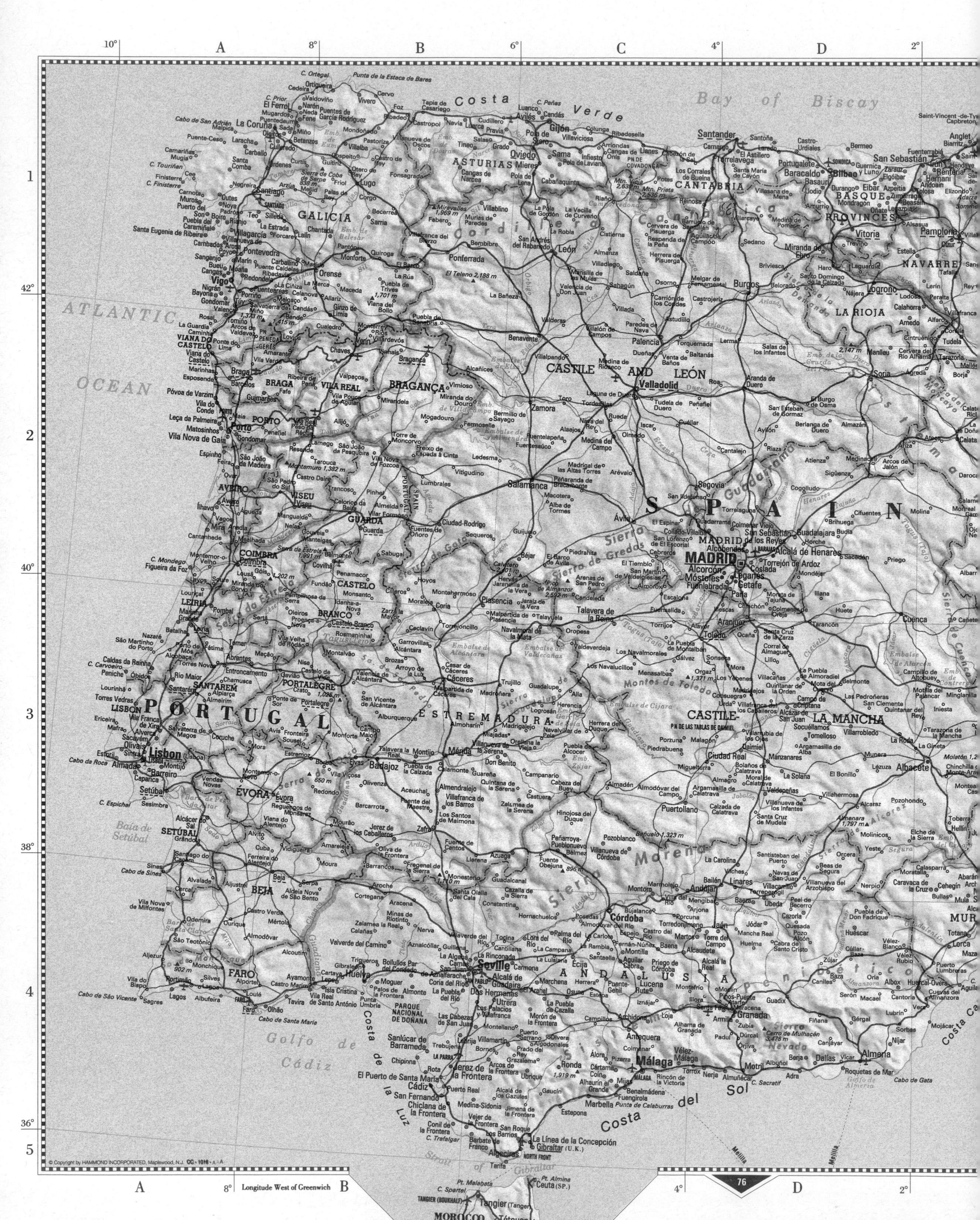

10°
A
8°
B
6°
C
4°
D
2°
1
2
3
4
5
42°
40°
38°
36°
Bay of Biscay
Costa Verde
ATLANTIC
OCEAN
Golfo de Cádiz
Costa de la Luz
Costa del Sol
Strait of Gibraltar
PORTUGAL
SPAIN
GALICIA
ASTURIAS
CANTABRIA
BASQUE PROVINCES
NAVARRE
LA RIOJA
CASTILE AND LEÓN
CASTILE-LA MANCHA
ESTREMADURA
ANDALUSIA
MADRID
Lisbon
Porto
Seville
Valladolid
Salamanca
Toledo
Córdoba
Granada
Málaga
Cádiz
Santander
Bilbao
San Sebastián
Pamplona
Vitoria
Burgos
León
Oviedo
Gijón
La Coruña
Vigo
Gibraltar (U.K.)
Tangier
Ceuta (SP.)
MOROCCO
Tétouan
Melilla
Sierra de Gredos
Sierra Morena
Sierra Nevada
Montes de Toledo
Cordillera Cantábrica
© Copyright by HAMMOND INCORPORATED, Maplewood, N.J.
Longitude West of Greenwich

Spain, Portugal

MADEIRA (PORT.)

AZORES (PORTUGAL)

CANARY ISLANDS (SPAIN)

POPULATION OF CITIES AND TOWNS

- OVER 2,000,000
- 1,000,000 - 1,999,999
- 500,000 - 999,999
- 250,000 - 499,999
- 100,000 - 249,999
- 30,000 - 99,999
- 10,000 - 29,999
- UNDER 10,000

SCALE 1:3,500,000 LAMBERT CONFORMAL CONIC PROJECTION

MILES 0 50 100 150

KILOMETERS 0 50 100 150

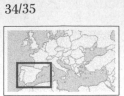

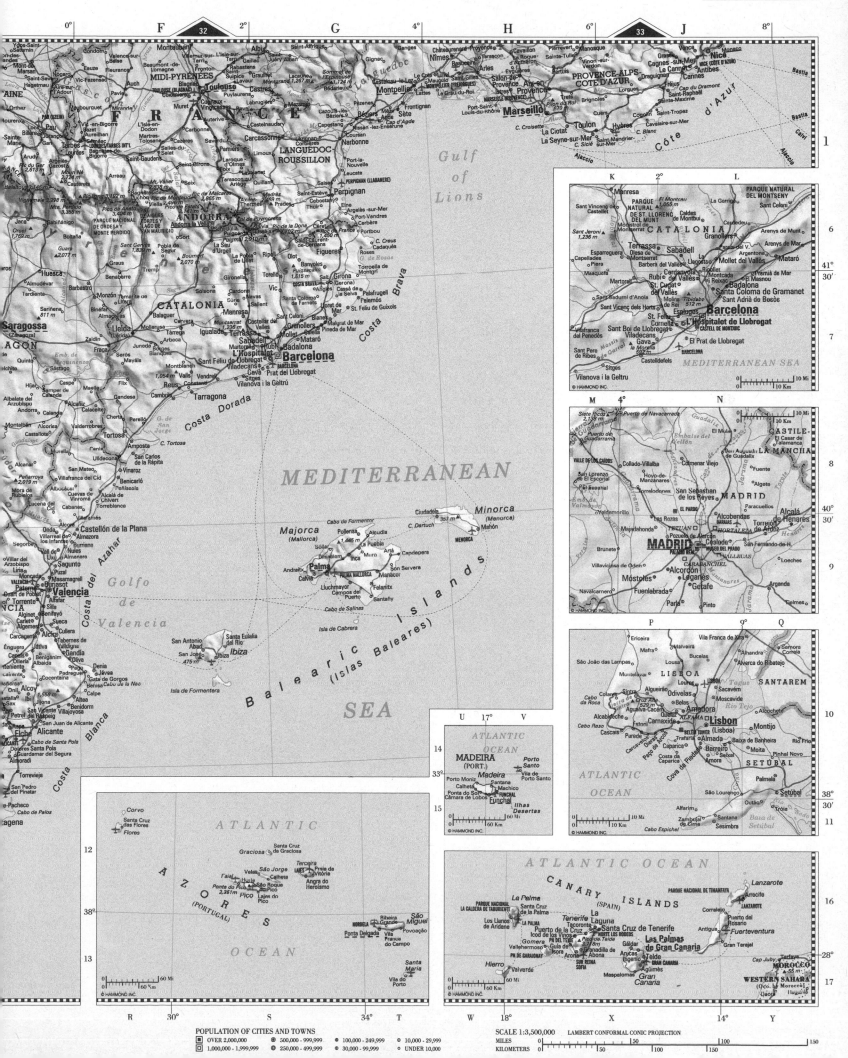

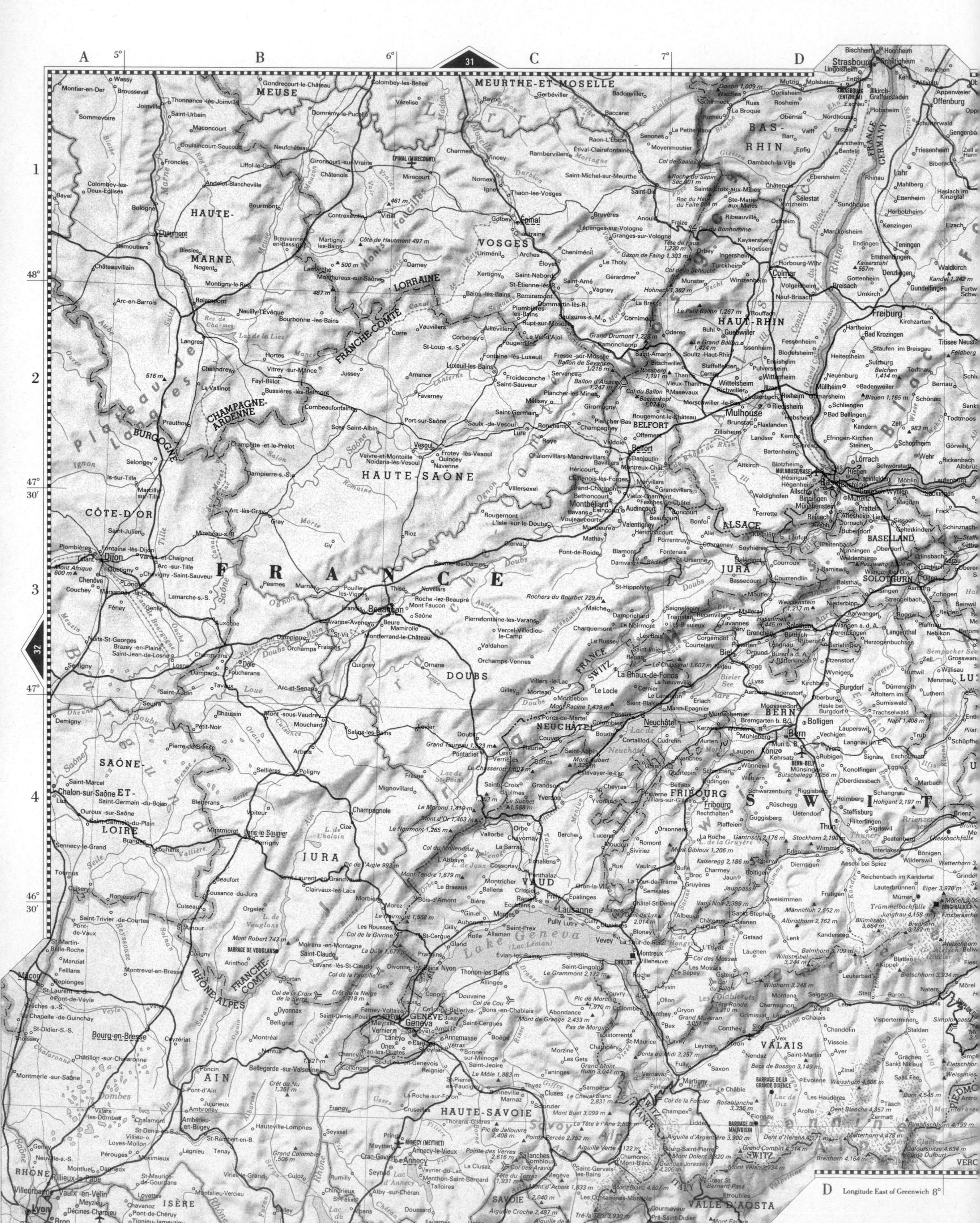

A
B
C
D
5°
6°
7°
8°
31
32
1
2
3
4
48°
47° 30′
47°
46° 30′
MEURTHE-ET-MOSELLE
MEUSE
BAS-RHIN
HAUT-RHIN
HAUTE-MARNE
VOSGES
LORRAINE
FRANCHE-COMTÉ
CHAMPAGNE-ARDENNE
BOURGOGNE
HAUTE-SAÔNE
CÔTE-D'OR
FRANCE
DOUBS
JURA
SAÔNE-ET-LOIRE
AIN
HAUTE-SAVOIE
SAVOIE
ISÈRE
RHÔNE
RHÔNE-ALPES
ALSACE
BASELLAND
SOLOTHURN
BERN
NEUCHÂTEL
FRIBOURG
VAUD
VALAIS
VALLE D'AOSTA
ITALY
GERMANY
FRANCE
SWITZ.
Strasbourg
Colmar
Mulhouse
Freiburg
Basel
Belfort
Besançon
Dijon
Épinal
Chaumont
Vesoul
Lons-le-Saunier
Bourg-en-Bresse
Mâcon
Lyon
Genève
Lausanne
Bern
Fribourg
Neuchâtel
Annecy
Lake Geneva
(Lac Léman)
Longitude East of Greenwich 8°

Central Alps Region

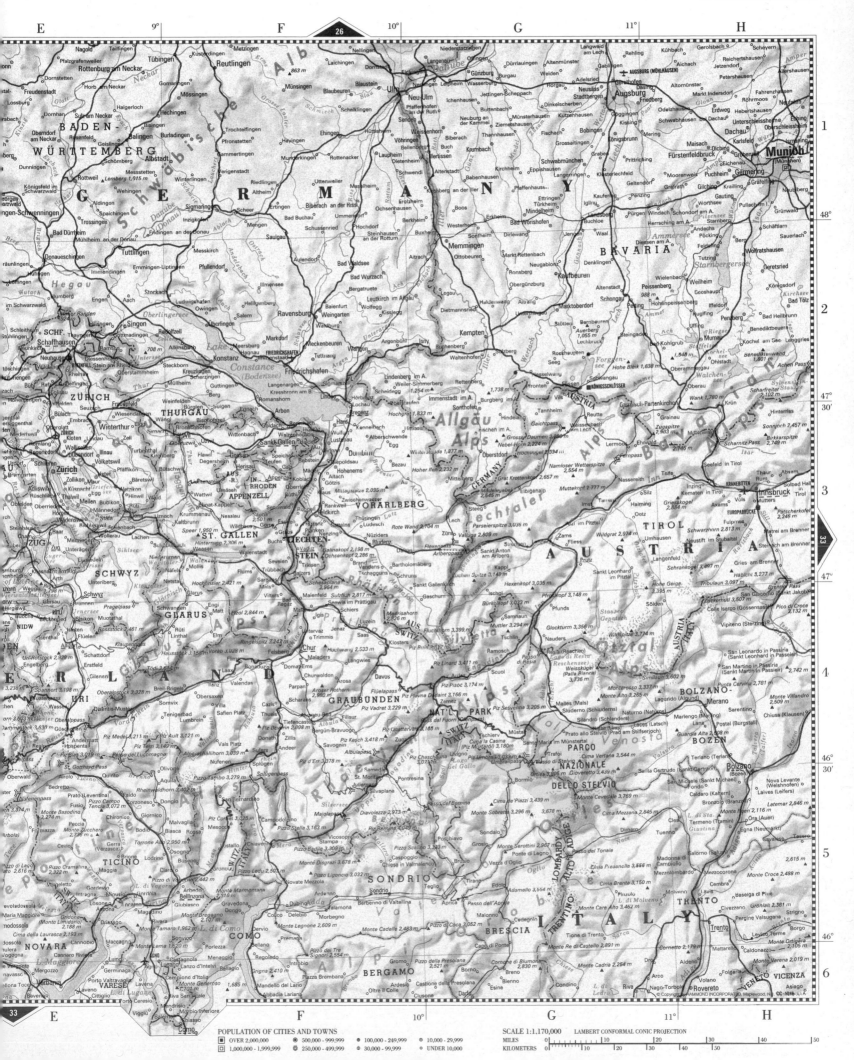

POPULATION OF CITIES AND TOWNS

■ OVER 2,000,000	● 500,000 - 999,999
□ 1,000,000 - 1,999,999	● 250,000 - 499,999

● 100,000 - 249,999	○ 10,000 - 29,999
● 30,000 - 99,999	· UNDER 10,000

SCALE 1:1,170,000   LAMBERT CONFORMAL CONIC PROJECTION

MILES 0   10   20   30   40   50

KILOMETERS 0   10   20   30   40   50

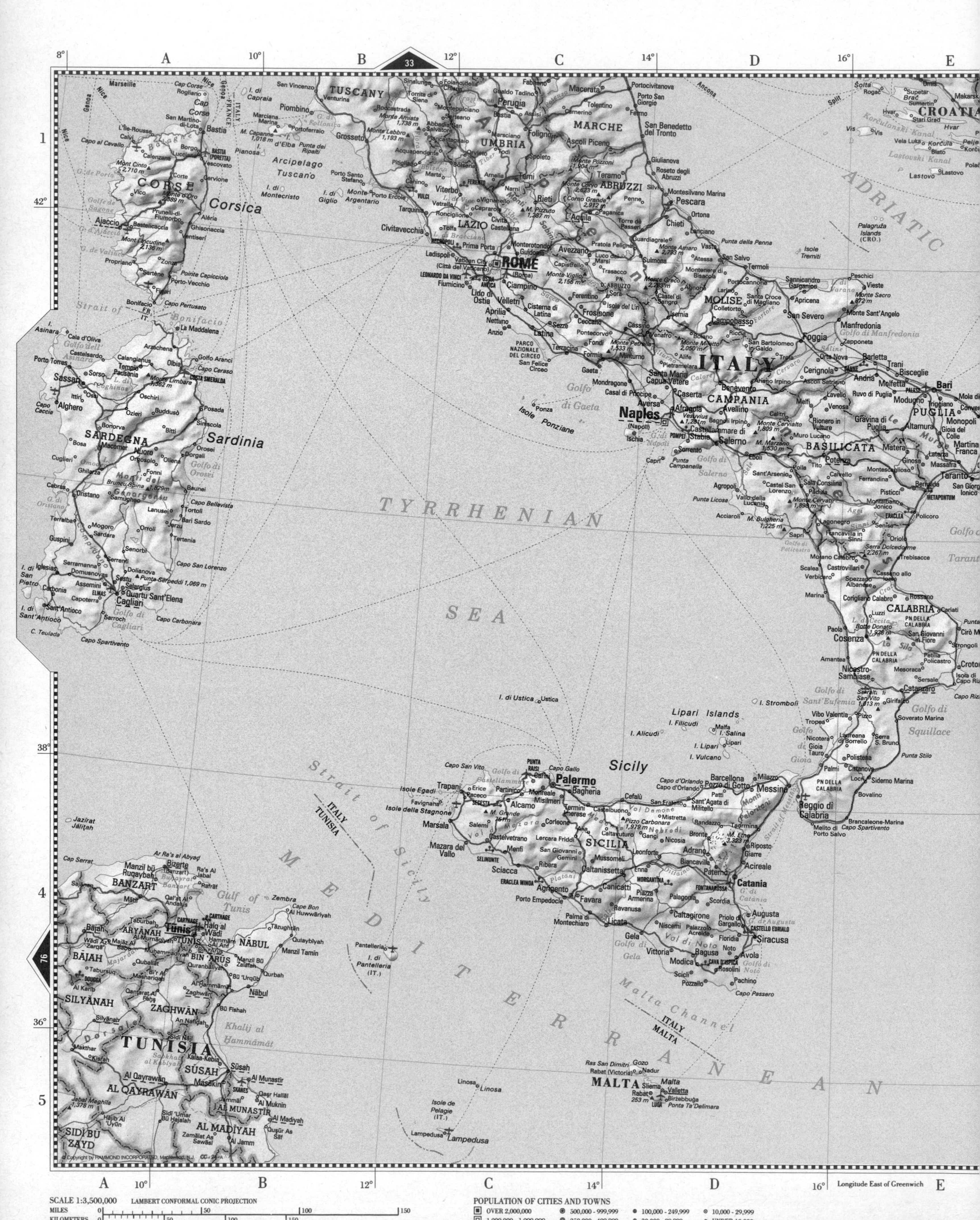

SCALE 1:3,500,000   LAMBERT CONFORMAL CONIC PROJECTION

POPULATION OF CITIES AND TOWNS

■ OVER 2,000,000   ● 500,000 - 999,999   ● 100,000 - 249,999   ● 10,000 - 29,999
□ 1,000,000 - 1,999,999   ● 250,000 - 499,999   ● 30,000 - 99,999   ○ UNDER 10,000

Longitude East of Greenwich

Southern Italy, Albania, Greece

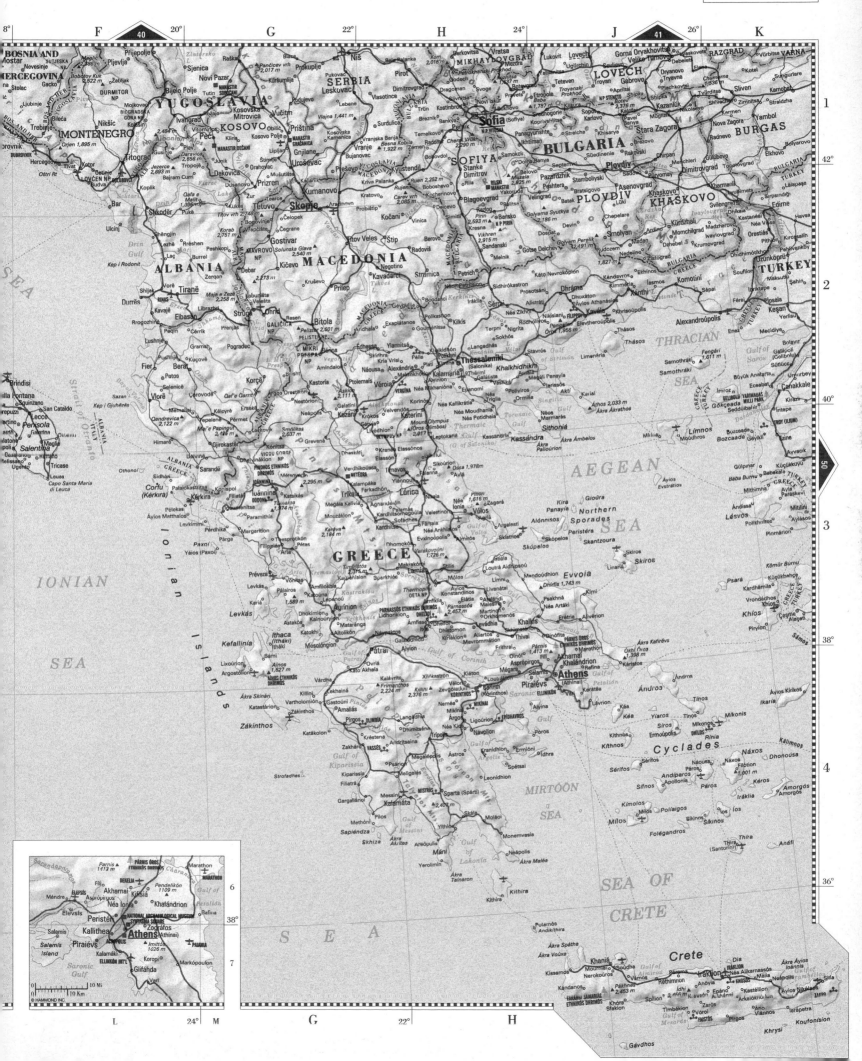

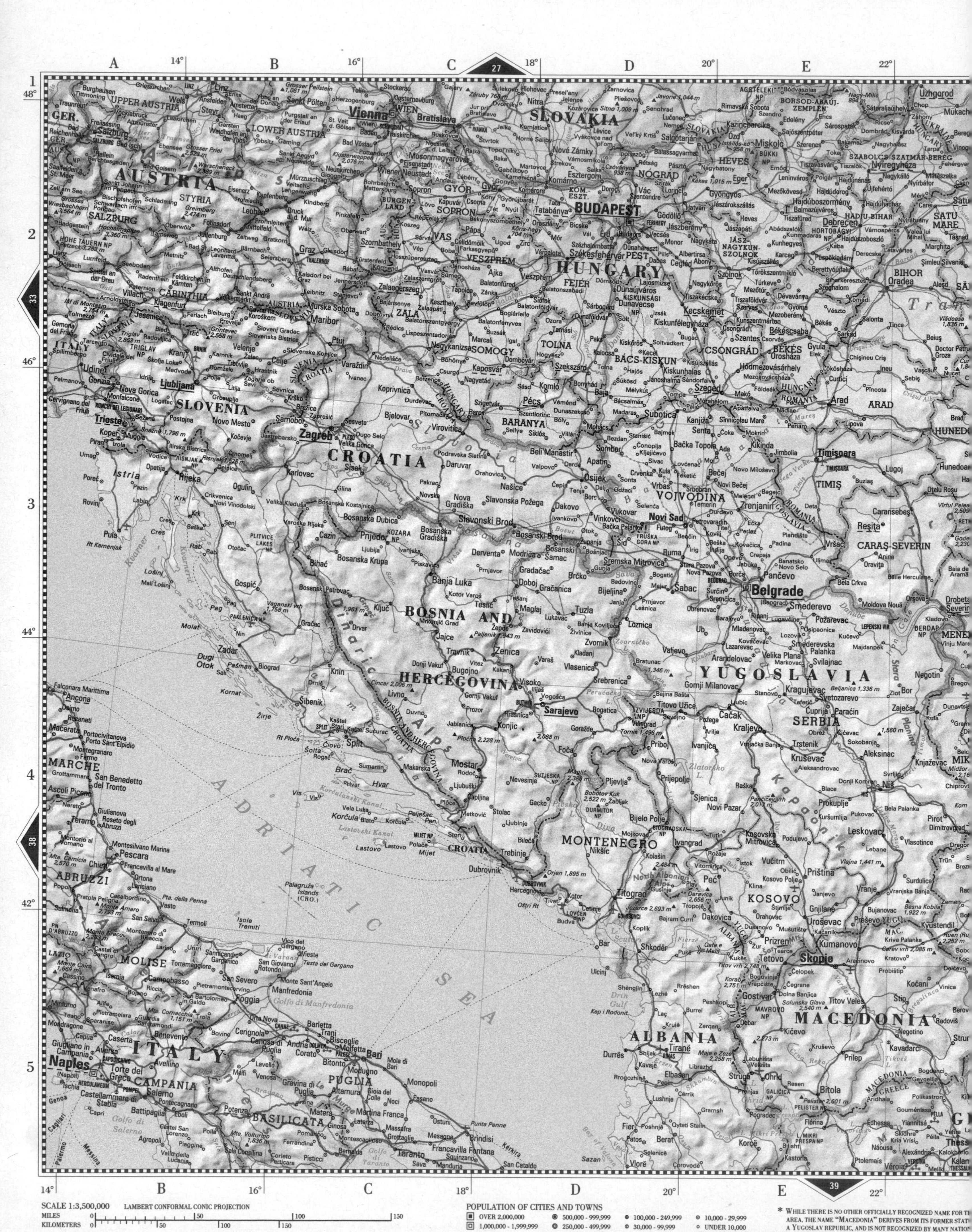

POPULATION OF CITIES AND TOWNS

| ▣ OVER 2,000,000 | ● 500,000 - 999,999 | ● 100,000 - 249,999 | ○ 10,000 - 29,999 |
| ▢ 1,000,000 - 1,999,999 | ● 250,000 - 499,999 | ● 30,000 - 99,999 | ○ UNDER 10,000 |

* WHILE THERE IS NO OTHER OFFICIALLY RECOGNIZED NAME FOR THE AREA, THE NAME "MACEDONIA" DERIVES FROM ITS FORMER STATUS AS A YUGOSLAV REPUBLIC, AND IS NOT RECOGNIZED BY MANY NATIONS

Hungary, Northern Balkan States

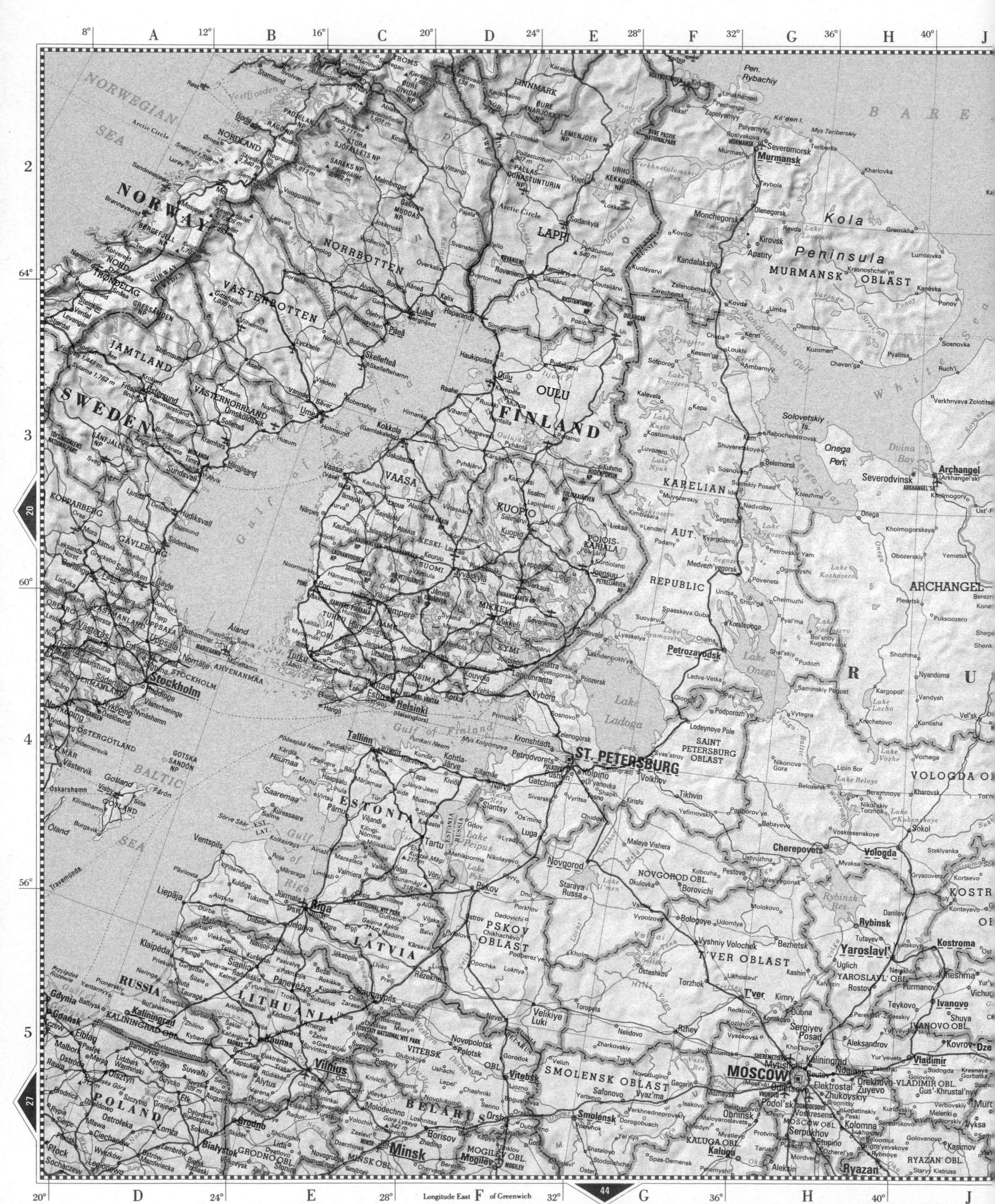

8° A 12° B 16° C 20° D 24° E 28° F 32° G 36° H 40° J
2
64°
3
60°
4
56°
5
20
27
NORWEGIAN SEA
Arctic Circle
NORWAY
SWEDEN
FINLAND
Gulf of Bothnia
NORRBOTTEN
VÄSTERBOTTEN
JAMTLAND
VÄSTERNORRLAND
GÄVLEBORG
KOPPARBERG
VÄSTMANLAND
UPPSALA
STOCKHOLM
SÖDERMANLAND
ÖSTERGÖTLAND
KALMAR
GOTLAND
NORDLAND
NORD TRØNDELAG
FINNMARK
TROMS
LAPPI
OULU
VAASA
KESKI-SUOMI
KUOPIO
POHJOIS-KARJALA
MIKKELI
HÄME
TURKU JA PORI
UUSIMAA
KYMI
AHVENANMAA
Åland
Bodø
Stockholm
Uppsala
Gävle
Sundsvall
Östersund
Umeå
Skellefteå
Luleå
Kiruna
Oulu
Vaasa
Kokkola
Tampere
Turku
Pori
Lahti
Kouvola
Kotka
Helsinki
(Helsingfors)
Jyväskylä
Kuopio
Joensuu
Mikkeli
Rovaniemi
Kemijärvi
Gulf of Finland
Tallinn
ESTONIA
Tartu
Pärnu
Narva
Gulf of Riga
Riga
LATVIA
Liepāja
Daugavpils
LITHUANIA
Vilnius
Kaunas
Klaipėda
Šiauliai
Panevėžys
RUSSIA
Kaliningrad
KALININGRAD OBL.
Gdańsk
Gdynia
POLAND
Olsztyn
Białystok
Grodno
Minsk
BELARUS
Vitebsk
Mogilev
Orsha
Borisov
Polotsk
GRODNO OBL.
MINSK OBL.
VITEBSK OBL.
MOGILEV OBL.
BALTIC SEA
ST. PETERSBURG
Lake Ladoga
Lake Onega
Lake Peipus
Petrozavodsk
KARELIAN AUT. REPUBLIC
Murmansk
MURMANSK OBLAST
Kola Peninsula
White Sea
BARENTS
Kandalaksha
Kandalaksha Gulf
Onega Bay
Onega Pen.
Dvina Bay
Archangel
(Arkhangel'sk)
Severodvinsk
ARCHANGEL
Belomorsk
Kem'
Solovetskiy Is.
Vologda
VOLOGDA O
Cherepovets
Rybinsk Res.
Rybinsk
Yaroslavl'
YAROSLAVL' OBL.
Kostroma
Ivanovo
IVANOVO OBL.
Vladimir
VLADIMIR OBL.
MOSCOW
(Moskva)
MOSCOW OBL.
Sergiyev Posad
Serpukhov
Kaluga
KALUGA OBL.
Ryazan
RYAZAN' OBL.
Smolensk
SMOLENSK OBLAST
T'VER OBLAST
T'ver
NOVGOROD OBL.
Novgorod
Pskov
PSKOV OBLAST
Velikiye Luki
SAINT PETERSBURG OBLAST
Valday Hills
Lake Il'men
Vyborg
Kronshtadt
Petrodvorets
Pen. Rybachiy
R U
Longitude East of Greenwich
20° D 24° E 28° F 32° G 36° H 40° J

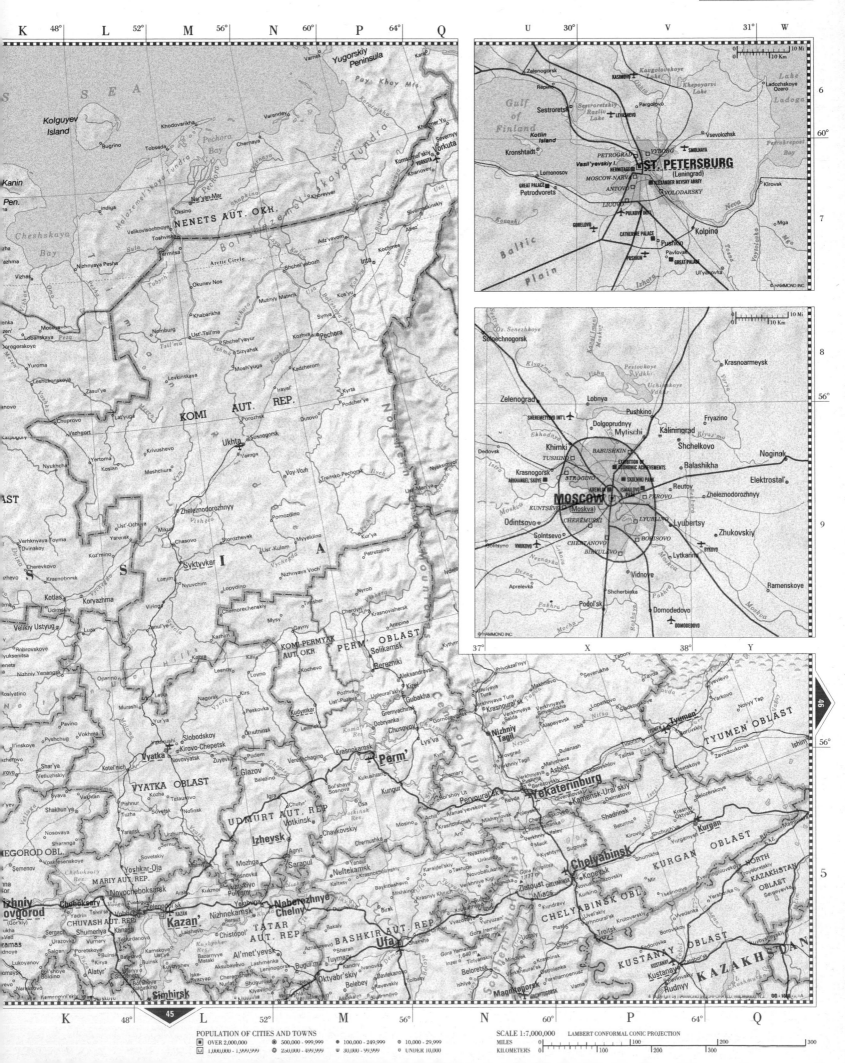

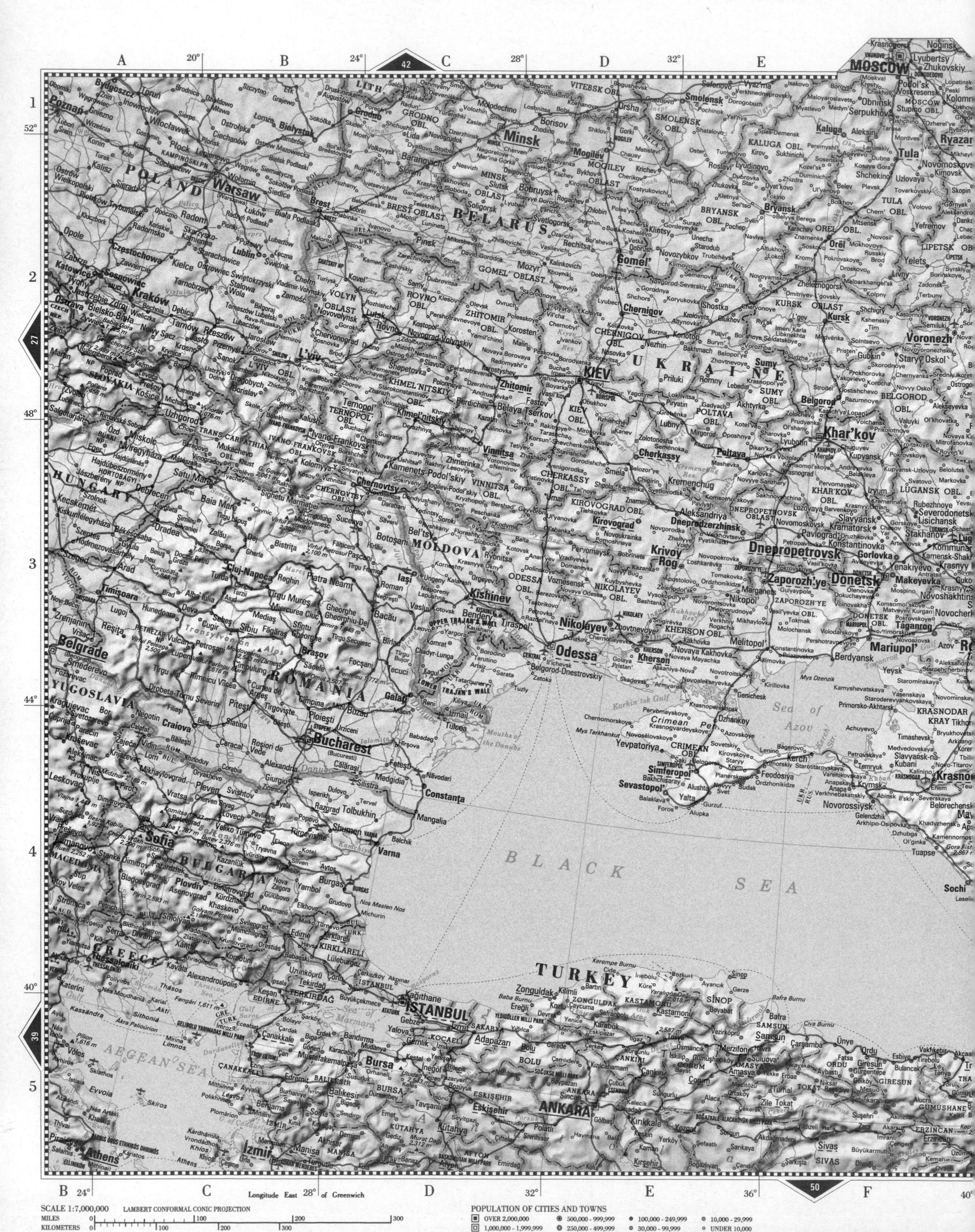

SCALE 1:7,000,000   LAMBERT CONFORMAL CONIC PROJECTION

Longitude East of Greenwich

MILES 0   100   200   300
KILOMETERS 0   100   200   300

POPULATION OF CITIES AND TOWNS

▣ OVER 2,000,000   ◉ 500,000 - 999,999   ● 100,000 - 249,999   ○ 10,000 - 29,999
▢ 1,000,000 - 1,999,999   ◎ 250,000 - 499,999   • 30,000 - 99,999   · UNDER 10,000

Southeastern Europe

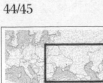

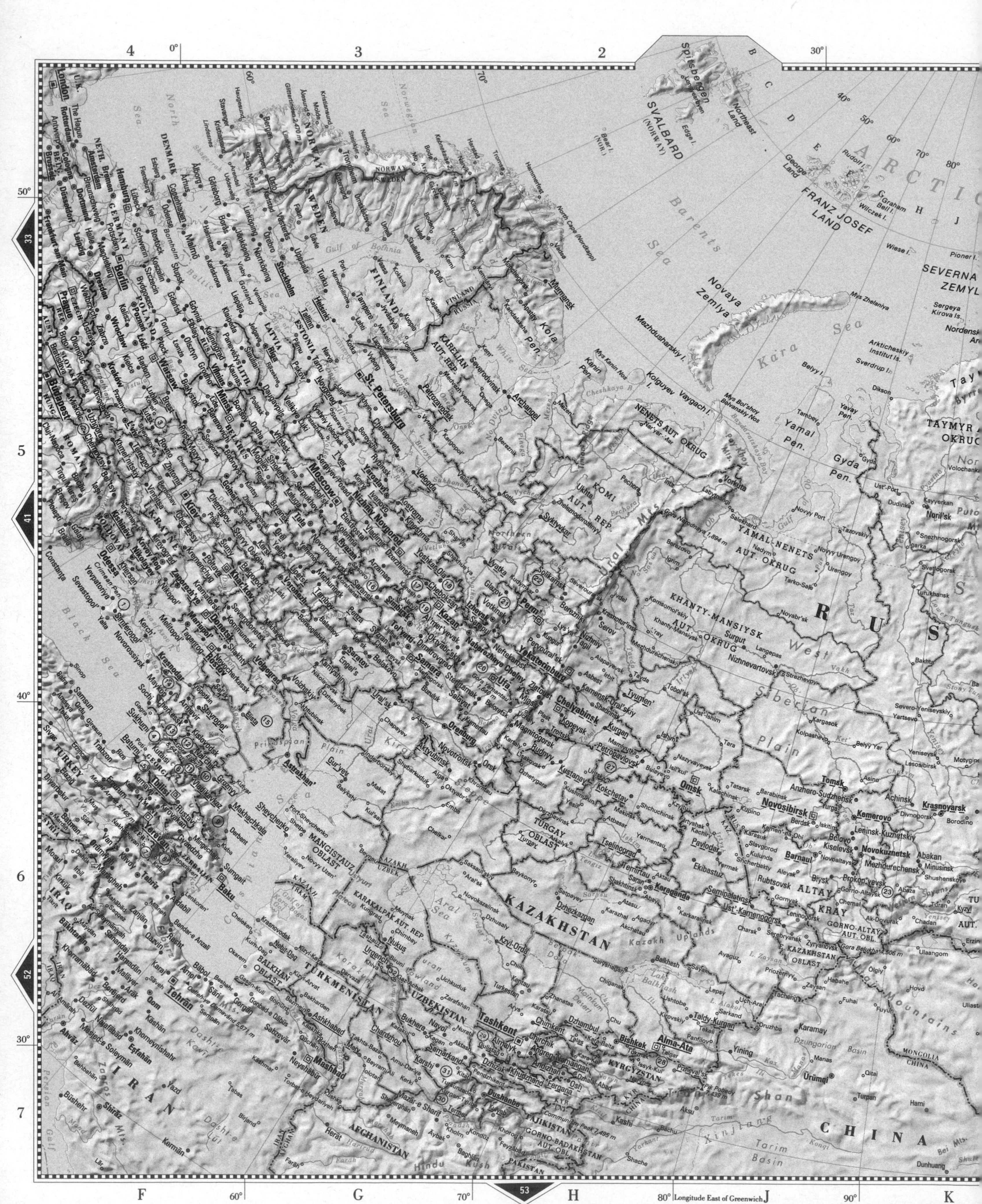

4
0°
3
2
30°
B
C
D
E
F
G
H
J
50°
40°
30°
5
6
7
33
41
52
53
60°
70°
80°
90°
K
Longitude East of Greenwich
SVALBARD
(NORWAY)
Spitsbergen
Northeast Land
FRANZ JOSEF LAND
SEVERNAYA ZEMLYA
Barents Sea
Kara Sea
Novaya Zemlya
NORWAY
SWEDEN
FINLAND
DENMARK
GERMANY
POLAND
ESTONIA
LATVIA
LITH.
BELARUS
RUSSIA
KAZAKHSTAN
TURKMENISTAN
UZBEKISTAN
KYRGYZSTAN
TAJIKISTAN
AFGHANISTAN
PAKISTAN
IRAN
IRAQ
TURKEY
CHINA
MONGOLIA
Black Sea
Caspian Sea
Aral Sea
Gulf of Bothnia
Baltic Sea
North Sea
Kola Pen.
Yamal Pen.
Gyda Pen.
West Siberian Plain
Kazakh Uplands
Ural Mts.
London
The Hague
Amsterdam
Hamburg
Berlin
Prague
Budapest
Copenhagen
Stockholm
Helsinki
Tallinn
Riga
Minsk
Warsaw
Kiev
Odessa
Moscow
St. Petersburg
Arkhangel'sk
Murmansk
Nizhniy Novgorod
Kazan'
Samara
Saratov
Volgograd
Rostov
Perm'
Yekaterinburg
Chelyabinsk
Ufa
Orenburg
Omsk
Novosibirsk
Tomsk
Kemerovo
Krasnoyarsk
Barnaul
Tbilisi
Yerevan
Baku
Tehrān
Ashkhabad
Tashkent
Dushanbe
Bishkek
Alma-Ata
Ürümqi
Mashhad
Shīrāz
Eşfahān

Russia and Neighboring Countries

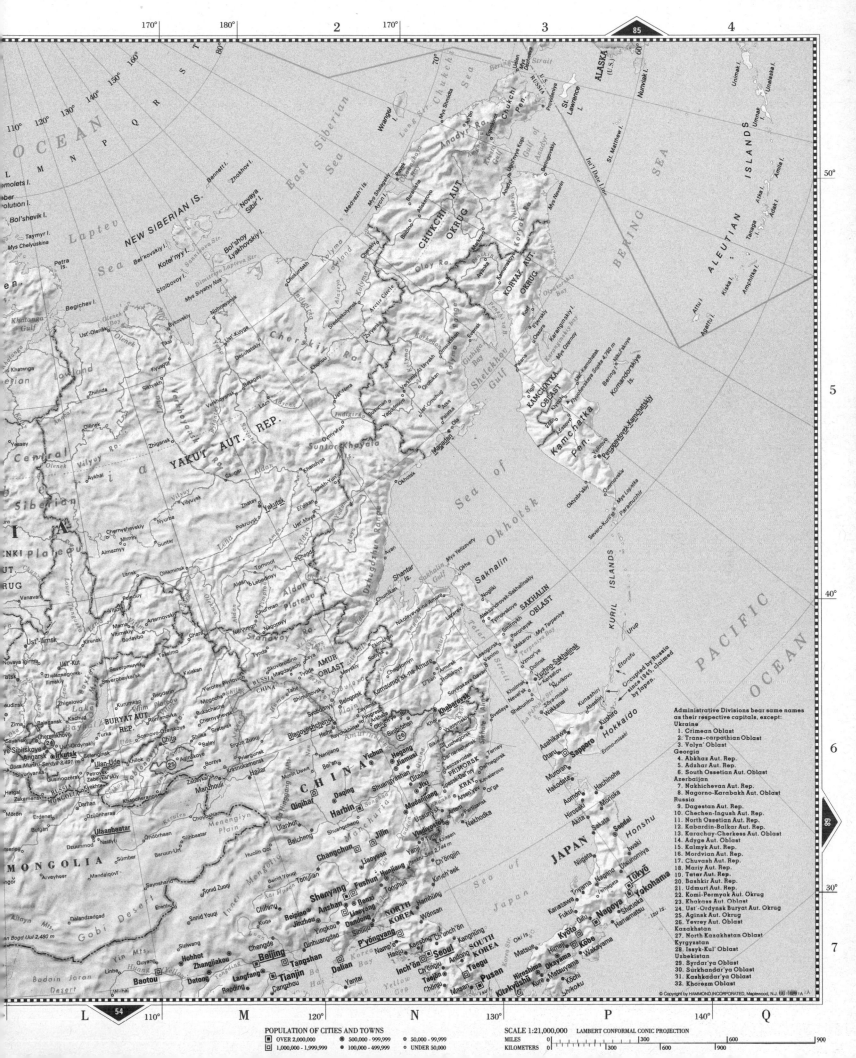

Administrative Divisions bear same names as their respective capitals, except:

Ukraine
1. Crimean Oblast
2. Trans-carpathian Oblast
3. Volyn' Oblast

Georgia
4. Abkhaz Aut. Rep.
5. Adzhar Aut. Rep.
6. South Ossetian Aut. Oblast

Azerbaijan
7. Nakhichevan Aut. Rep.
8. Nagorno-Karabakh Aut. Oblast

Russia
9. Dagestan Aut. Rep.
10. Chechen-Ingush Aut. Rep.
11. North Ossetian Aut. Rep.
12. Kabardin-Balkar Aut. Rep.
13. Karachay-Cherkess Aut. Oblast
14. Adyge Aut. Oblast
15. Kalmyk Aut. Rep.
16. Mordvian Aut. Rep.
17. Chuvash Aut. Rep.
18. Mariy Aut. Rep.
19. Tatar Aut. Rep.
20. Bashkir Aut. Rep.
21. Udmurt Aut. Rep.
22. Komi-Permyak Aut. Okrug
23. Khakass Aut. Oblast
24. Ust'-Ordynsk Buryat Aut. Okrug
25. Aginsk Aut. Okrug
26. Yevrey Aut. Oblast

Kazakhstan
27. North Kazakhstan Oblast

Kyrgyzstan
28. Issyk-Kul' Oblast

Uzbekistan
29. Syrdar'ya Oblast
30. Surkhandar'ya Oblast
31. Kashkadar'ya Oblast
32. Khorezm Oblast

© Copyright by HAMMOND INCORPORATED, Maplewood, N.J.

POPULATION OF CITIES AND TOWNS
OVER 2,000,000
1,000,000 - 1,999,999
500,000 - 999,999
100,000 - 499,999
50,000 - 99,999
UNDER 50,000

SCALE 1:21,000,000   LAMBERT CONFORMAL CONIC PROJECTION
MILES   0   300   600   900
KILOMETERS   0   300   600   900

Asia

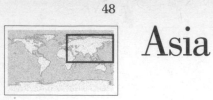

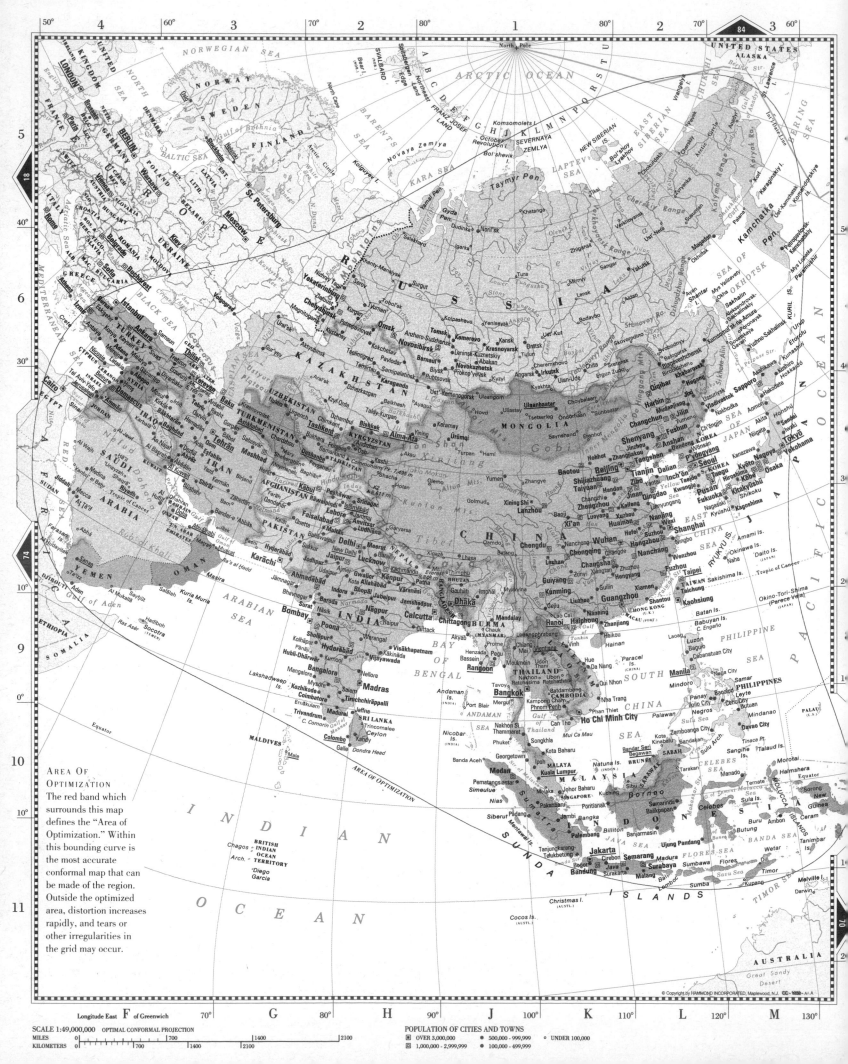

AREA OF
OPTIMIZATION
The red band which
surrounds this map
defines the "Area of
Optimization." Within
this bounding curve is
the most accurate
conformal map that can
be made of the region.
Outside the optimized
area, distortion increases
rapidly, and tears or
other irregularities in
the grid may occur.

Longitude East F of Greenwich

SCALE 1:49,000,000   OPTIMAL CONFORMAL PROJECTION

MILES 0   700   1400   2100
KILOMETERS 0   700   1400   2100

POPULATION OF CITIES AND TOWNS
☐ OVER 3,000,000   ● 500,000 - 999,999   ○ UNDER 100,000
☒ 1,000,000 - 2,999,999   ● 100,000 - 499,999

Eastern Mediterranean Region

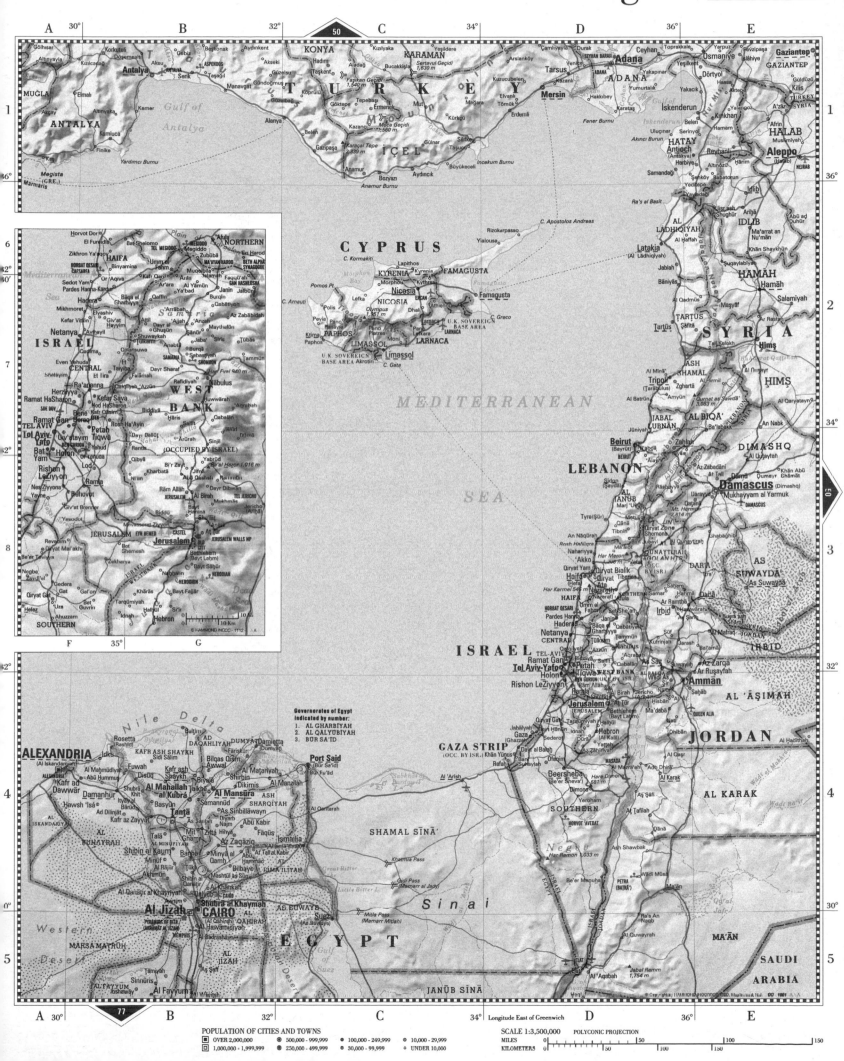

■ OVER 2,000,000	● 500,000 - 999,999	● 100,000 - 249,999	○ 10,000 - 29,999
□ 1,000,000 - 1,999,999	● 250,000 - 499,999	● 30,000 - 99,999	○ UNDER 10,000

SCALE 1:3,500,000   POLYCONIC PROJECTION

MILES

KILOMETERS

Longitude East of Greenwich

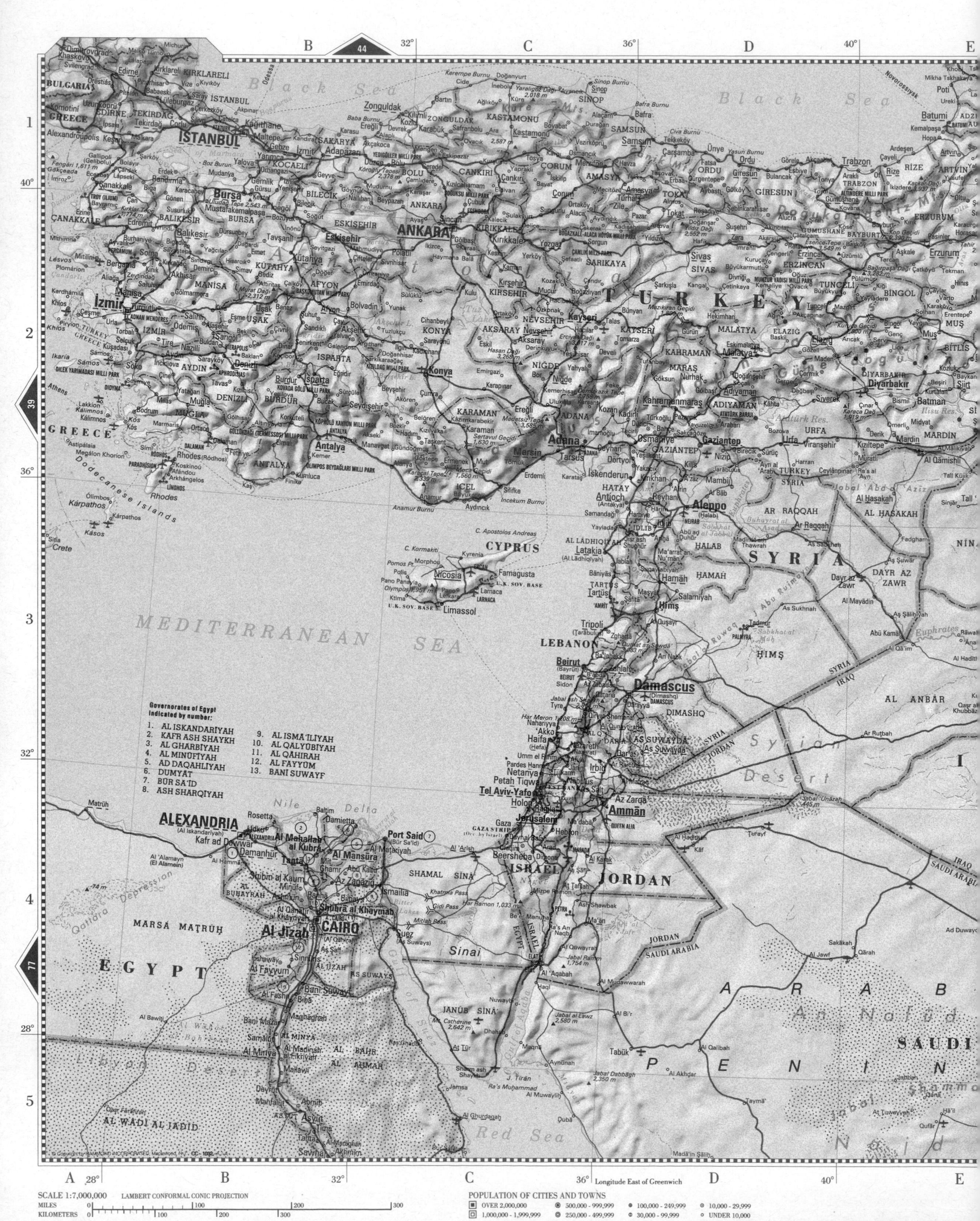

Black Sea
TURKEY
ISTANBUL
ANKARA
İzmir
Bursa
Konya
Adana
Antalya
Kayseri
Samsun
Trabzon
Erzurum
Diyarbakır
Gaziantep
Malatya
BULGARIA
GREECE
CYPRUS
Nicosia
Famagusta
Limassol
MEDITERRANEAN SEA
SYRIA
Aleppo
Latakia
Hamāh
Ḩimş
Damascus
LEBANON
Beirut
Tripoli
ISRAEL
Tel Aviv-Yafo
Haifa
Jerusalem
JORDAN
'Ammān
EGYPT
ALEXANDRIA
CAIRO
Al Jīzah
Port Said
Sinai
Red Sea
Gulf of Suez
Gulf of Aqaba
Dodecanese Islands
Rhodes
Crete
Libyan Desert
Qattara Depression
Syrian Desert
Euphrates
SAUDI ARABIA
An Nafūd
IRAQ
Governorates of Egypt indicated by number:
1. AL ISKANDARIYAH
2. KAFR ASH SHAYKH
3. AL GHARBIYAH
4. AL MINŪFIYAH
5. AD DAQAHLIYAH
6. DUMYĀT
7. BŪR SA'ĪD
8. ASH SHARQIYAH
9. AL ISMĀ'ĪLIYAH
10. AL QALYŪBIYAH
11. AL QĀHIRAH
12. AL FAYYŪM
13. BANĪ SUWAYF
Longitude East of Greenwich
SCALE 1:7,000,000
LAMBERT CONFORMAL CONIC PROJECTION
MILES 0 100 200 300
KILOMETERS 0 100 200 300
POPULATION OF CITIES AND TOWNS
OVER 2,000,000
1,000,000 - 1,999,999
500,000 - 999,999
250,000 - 499,999
100,000 - 249,999
30,000 - 99,999
10,000 - 29,999
UNDER 10,000

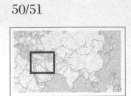

Inset map (Istanbul):

Black Sea

Durusu Lake · Durusu · Yeniköy · Kumköy

Çatalca · Boyalık · Arnavutköy · Kemerburgaz · Alemdar

Büyükçekmece · Büyük Lake · Kâğıthane · EYÜP MOSQUE · RUMELİ HİSAR · BEYLERBEYİ PALACE · Ömerli Res.

Küçükçekmece · BEYOĞLU · DOLMANCE PALACE · Samandıra

Gürpınar · YEDİKULE · BEŞIKTAŞ · TOPKAPI PALACE · ISTANBUL · ÜSKÜDAR · YILDIZ PARK · Sarıgazi

Avcılar · ATATÜRK INT'L · COVERED MARKET · KADIKÖY · Kurtköy

Heybeli Island · Büyükada Island · Pendik

Sea of Marmara · Aydınlı

0 10 Km   10 Mi

© HAMMOND INC.   CC-1113-A

Main map labels:

RUSSIA · KAZ. · OSSETIAN AUTOBL. · Tskhinvali · GEORGIA · Tbilisi · Rustavi · AZERBAIJAN · Sumgait · Baku · TURKMENISTAN · Ashkhabad

ARMENIA · Yerevan · Gyandzhe · Mingechaur · Shemakha · CASPIAN SEA · Krasnovodsk

AZER. · NAKHICHEVAN AUT. REP. · Mt. Ararat 5,165 m · Tabriz · Ardabil · GILAN · Bandar-e Anzali · Rasht · Lenkoran'

TURKEY · VAN · HAKKARI · Orümiyeh · Maragheh · Zanjan · ZANJAN · MAZANDARAN · Gorgan · Sabzevar · Neyshabur · Qüchan

IRBIL · Irbil · AT TA'MIN · Kirkük · AS SULAYMANIYAH · KORDESTAN · Sanandaj · Qazvin · TEHRAN · Karaj · TEHRĀN · SEMNĀN · Semnān · Dasht-e Kavir · KHORĀSĀN · Ferdows

Mosul · As Sulaymaniyah · BĀKHTARAN · HAMADĀN · Hamadān · MARKAZI · Qom · L. Namak

ŞALĀH AD DĪN · Sāmarrā · DIYĀLĀ · Bakhtaran · Malāyer · Arāk · Kāshān · ESFAHĀN

Al Fallūjah · Baghdad · BABYLON · Borūjerd · LORESTĀN · Khorramābād

Karbalā' · BĀBIL · Al Hillah · WĀSIT · ILAM · Andimeshk · Dezfūl · Najafābād · Esfahān · IRAN · YAZD · Yazd · Dasht-e Lūt · Kermān

An Najaf · AL QĀDISIYAH · Ad Dīwānīyah · MAYSĀN · Al 'Amārah · KHŪZESTĀN · Masjed-e Soleymān · CHAHĀR MAHALL & BAKHTIĀRĪ · Ahvāz

AN NAJAF · As Samāwah · DHĪ QĀR · An Nāsirīyah · Al Başrah · AL BAŞRAH · Abādān · KOHKĪLŪYEH & BOVIR AHMADI · FĀRS · KERMĀN

AL MUTHANNĀ · KUWAIT · Al Kuwait · As Sālimiyah · Hawalli · Shīrāz · PERSEPOLIS · Sirjān

SAUDI ARABIA · Persian Gulf · Bandar-e Büshehr · BÜSHEHR · HORMOZGĀN · Bandar-e Abbas · Qeshm

ARABIA · Persian Gulf · Strait of Hormuz · OMAN · Musandam Pen. · RAS AL KHAIMAH

Latitude/longitude: 44° · 48° · 52° · 29° · 41° · 36° · 32° · 28°

Grid: F · 45 · G · M · N · 6 · 7 · 2 · 3 · 53 · 4 · 5 · 52

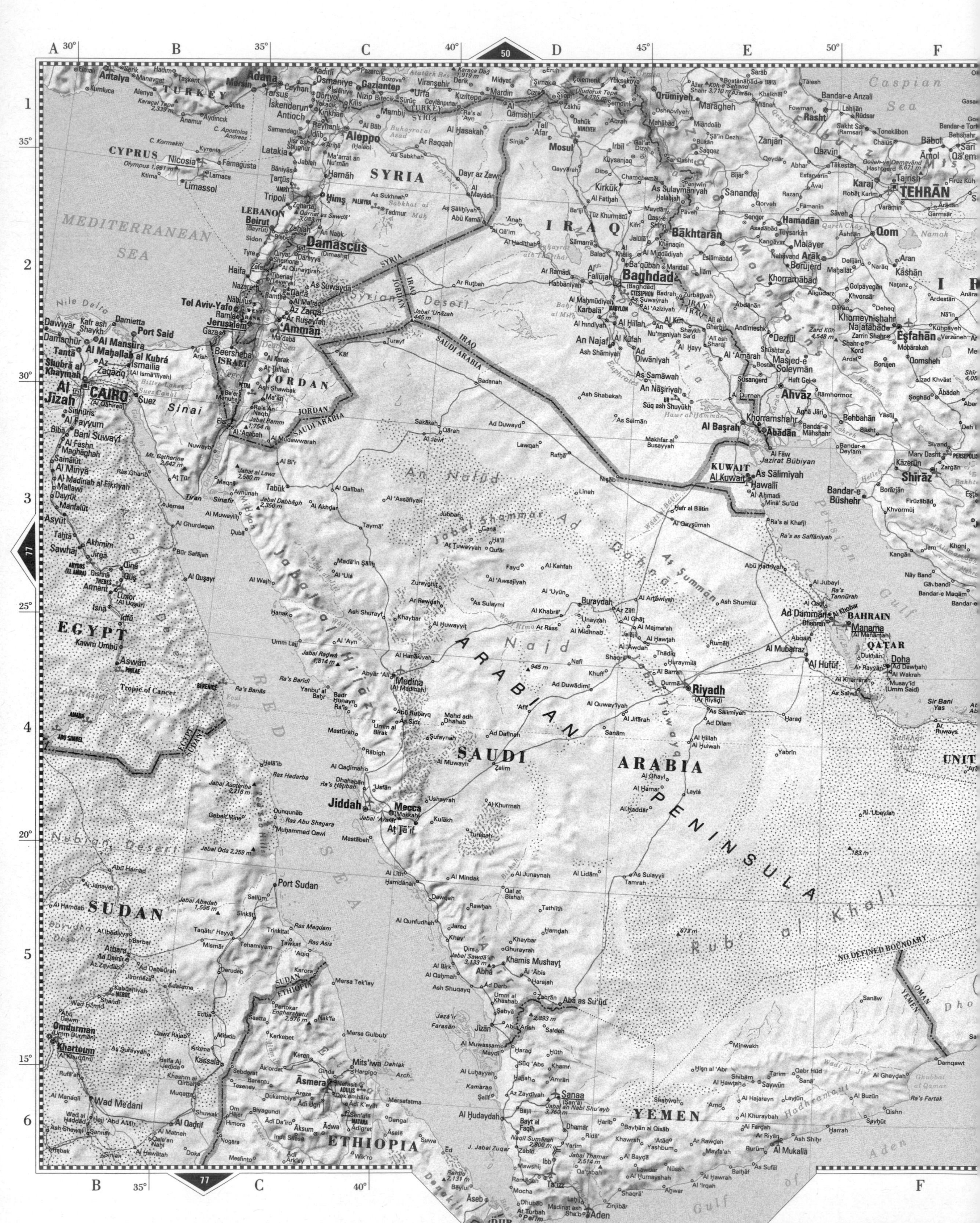

A
B
C
D
E
F
30°
35°
40°
45°
50°
20°
25°
15°
1
2
3
4
5
6
50
77
TURKEY
CYPRUS
SYRIA
IRAQ
JORDAN
ISRAEL
LEBANON
KUWAIT
BAHRAIN
QATAR
EGYPT
SUDAN
ETHIOPIA
YEMEN
OMAN
SAUDI ARABIA
ARABIAN PENINSULA
MEDITERRANEAN SEA
Caspian Sea
RED SEA
Persian Gulf
Gulf of Aden
Sinai
Syrian Desert
An Nafud
Ad Dahna
As Summan
Najd
Rub' al Khali
Nubian Desert
Tropic of Cancer
NO DEFINED BOUNDARY
Nile Delta
Bitter Lakes
Suez Canal
Adana
Antalya
Mersin
Tarsus
Gaziantep
Urfa
Mardin
Aleppo
Latakia
Nicosia
Famagusta
Limassol
Larnaca
Hims
Hamah
Tripoli
Beirut
Damascus
Haifa
Tel Aviv-Yafo
Jerusalem
Gaza
Beersheba
Amman
Az Zarqa'
Ma'an
Al 'Aqabah
Elat
Port Said
Ismailia
Suez
CAIRO
(Al Qahirah)
Al Jizah
Tanta
Damietta
Al Mansura
Al Fayyum
Bani Suwayf
Al Minya
Asyut
Sawhaj
Qina
Luxor
Aswan
Isna
Idfu
Al Ghurdaqah
Bur Safajah
Al Qusayr
Dayr az Zawr
Ar Raqqah
Tadmur
Abu Kamal
Mosul
Irbil
Kirkuk
As Sulaymaniyah
Baghdad
Karbala'
Al Hillah
An Najaf
Al Kut
Ad Diwaniyah
An Nasiriyah
Al 'Amarah
Al Basrah
Abadan
Khorramshahr
Al Kuwayt
Hawalli
As Salimiyah
Al Ahmadi
Qomishli
Orumiyeh
Maragheh
Tabriz
Zanjan
Qazvin
Rasht
Bandar-e Anzali
Karaj
TEHRAN
Qom
Hamadan
Bakhtaran
Sanandaj
Malayer
Arak
Borujerd
Khorramabad
Kashan
Esfahan
Najafabad
Dezful
Ahvaz
Shiraz
Bandar-e Bushehr
Kazerun
Tabuk
Al Jawf
Sakakah
'Ar'ar
Rafha'
Ha'il
Buraydah
Unayzah
Medina
(Al Madinah)
Yanbu' al Bahr
Jiddah
Mecca
(Makkah)
At Ta'if
Riyadh
(Ar Riyad)
Ad Dammam
Al Khobar
Al Jubayl
Al Hufuf
Manama
(Al Manamah)
Doha
(Ad Dawhah)
Al Wajh
Duba
Umm Lajj
Rabigh
Al Lith
Al Qunfudhah
Abha
Khamis Mushayt
Najran
Jizan
Sabya
Port Sudan
Sawakin
Atbara
Omdurman
Khartoum
Kassala
Wad Medani
Al Qadarif
Mits'iwa
Asmera
Aksum
Adigrat
Aseb
Sanaa
(San'a')
Al Hudaydah
Ta'izz
Ibb
Dhamar
Aden
Al Mukalla
Mocha
Jabal Ramm 1,754 m
Jabal al Lawz 2,580 m
Jabal Dabbagh 2,350 m
Jabal Radwa 1,814 m
Jabal Sawda' 3,133 m
Jabal an Nabi Shu'ayb 3,760 m
Olympus 1,951 m
Mt. Catherine 2,642 m

Southwestern Asia

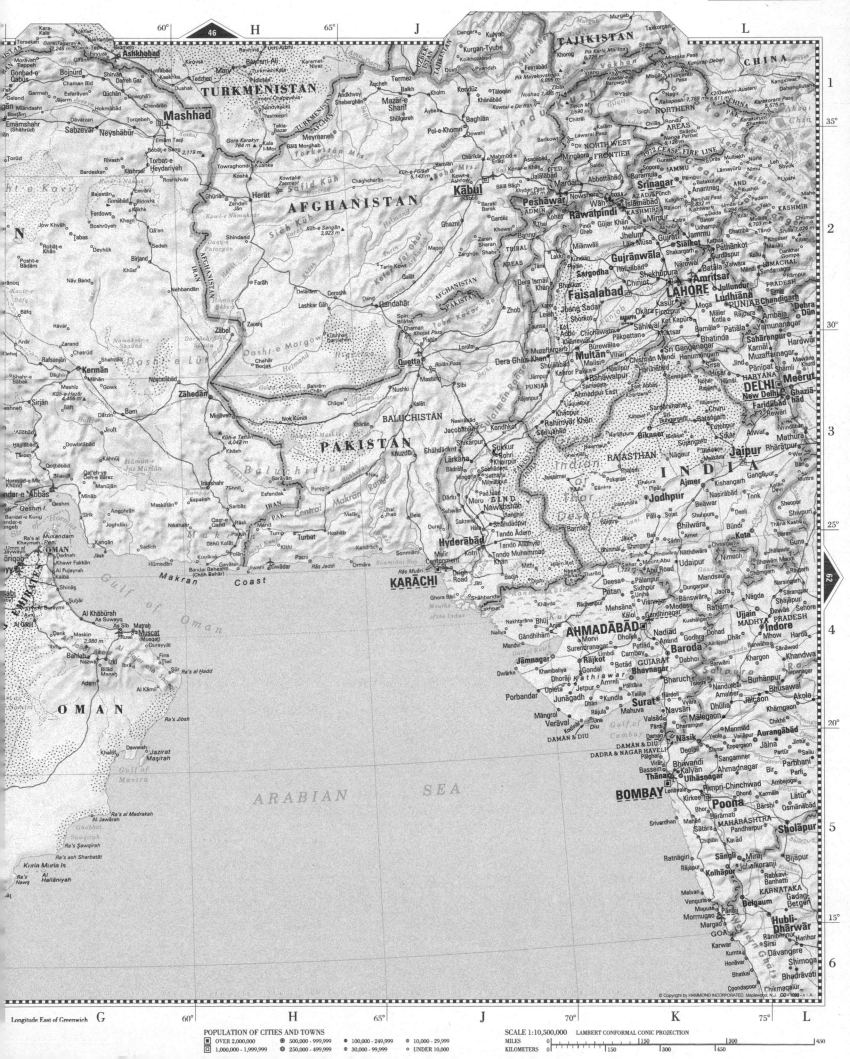

POPULATION OF CITIES AND TOWNS

■	OVER 2,000,000	●	500,000 - 999,999	●	100,000 - 249,999	●	10,000 - 29,999
◻	1,000,000 - 1,999,999	●	250,000 - 499,999	●	30,000 - 99,999	●	UNDER 10,000

SCALE 1:10,500,000   LAMBERT CONFORMAL CONIC PROJECTION

MILES 0 | 150 | 300 | 450
KILOMETERS 0 | 150 | 300 | 450

Longitude East of Greenwich

© Copyright by HAMMOND INCORPORATED, Maplewood, N.J.   CG-1090-A-A-A

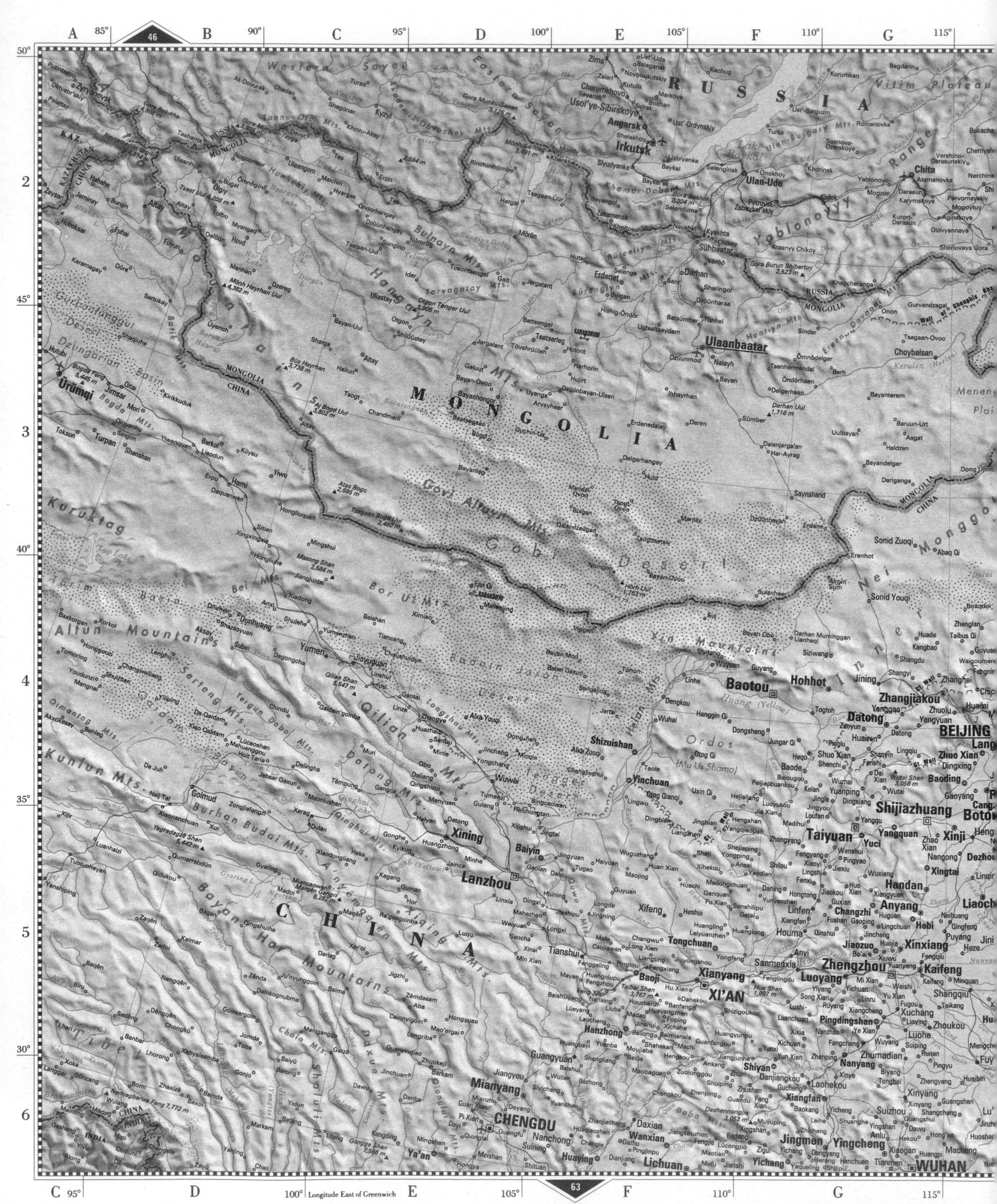

A 85° B 90° C 95° D 100° E 105° F 110° G 115°
46
50°
45°
40°
35°
30°
2
3
4
5
6
C 95° D 100° Longitude East of Greenwich E 105° F 110° G 115°
63
R U S S I A
M O N G O L I A
C H I N A
KAZAKHSTAN
INDIA
Western Sayan
Eastern Sayan
Tannu-Ola Mts.
Lake Baykal
Khamar-Daban Mts.
Yablonovyy Range
Vitim Plateau
Bulnayn Mts.
Hangayn Mts.
Tarvagatay Mts.
Mongol Altayn Nuruu
Gurbantünggüt Desert
Dzungarian Basin
Bogda Mts.
Kuruktag
Tarim Basin
Bei Mts.
Altun Mountains
Bor Ul Mts.
Govi Altayn Mts.
Gobi Desert
Badain Jaran Desert
Yin Mountains
Helan Mts.
Ordos
Tengger Desert
Qilian Mts.
Datong Mts.
Kunlun Mts.
Burhan Budai Mts.
Bayan Har Mountains
Tibet
Ulan-Ude
Irkutsk
Angarsk
Chita
Ulaanbaatar
Karakorum
Ürümqi
Turpan
Hami
Dunhuang
Yumen
Jiayuguan
Golmud
Xining
Lanzhou
Baiyin
Yinchuan
Shizuishan
Baotou
Hohhot
Zhangjiakou
Datong
BEIJING
Shijiazhuang
Taiyuan
Handan
Anyang
Xinxiang
Zhengzhou
Kaifeng
Luoyang
Xianyang
XI'AN
Baoji
Tianshui
Hanzhong
Tongchuan
Pingdingshan
Xiangfan
Shiyan
Mianyang
CHENGDU
Nanchong
Ya'an
Wanxian
Lichuan
Jingmen
Yingcheng
WUHAN
Huang (Yellow)
Wall of Chinggis Khan

Eastern Asia

POPULATION OF CITIES AND TOWNS

■ OVER 2,000,000	● 500,000 - 999,999
▣ 1,000,000 - 1,999,999	● 250,000 - 499,999

● 100,000 - 249,999	○ 10,000 - 29,999
● 30,000 - 99,999	○ UNDER 10,000

SCALE 1:10,500,000   LAMBERT CONFORMAL CONIC PROJECTION

MILES   0   150   300   450

KILOMETERS   0   150   150   450

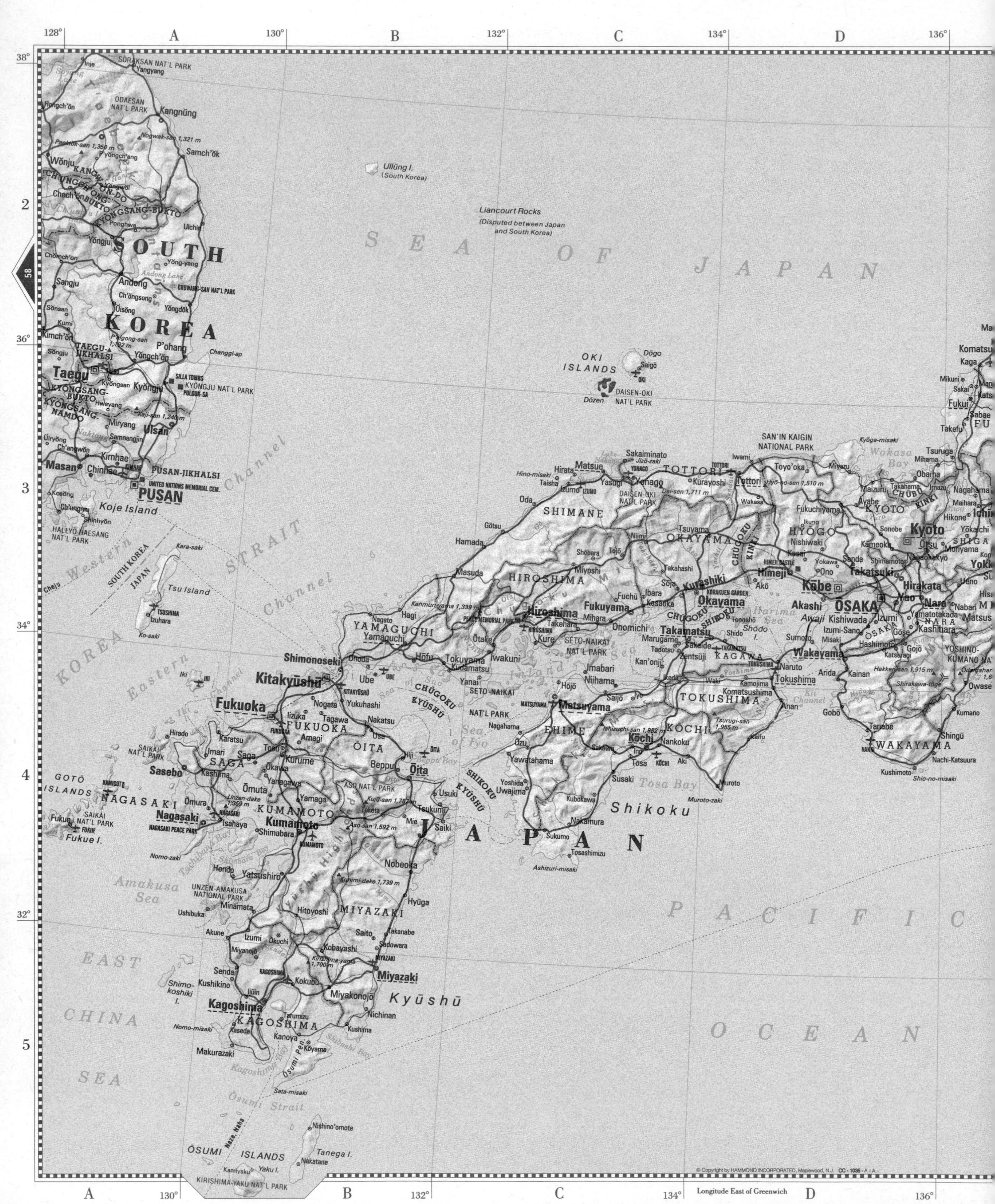
SEA OF JAPAN
SOUTH KOREA
JAPAN
PACIFIC OCEAN
EAST CHINA SEA
KOREA STRAIT
Shikoku
Kyūshū
Pusan
Taegu
Fukuoka
Kitakyūshū
Hiroshima
Okayama
Kōbe
Ōsaka
Kyoto
Nara
Wakayama
Matsuyama
Kōchi
Kumamoto
Nagasaki
Kagoshima
Miyazaki
Ōita
Takamatsu
Tokushima
Himeji
Tottori
Matsue
Shimonoseki
OKI ISLANDS
ŌSUMI ISLANDS
GOTŌ ISLANDS
Tsu Island
Ullŭng I. (South Korea)
Liancourt Rocks (Disputed between Japan and South Korea)
Longitude East of Greenwich
© Copyright by HAMMOND INCORPORATED, Maplewood, N.J.

Central and Southern Japan

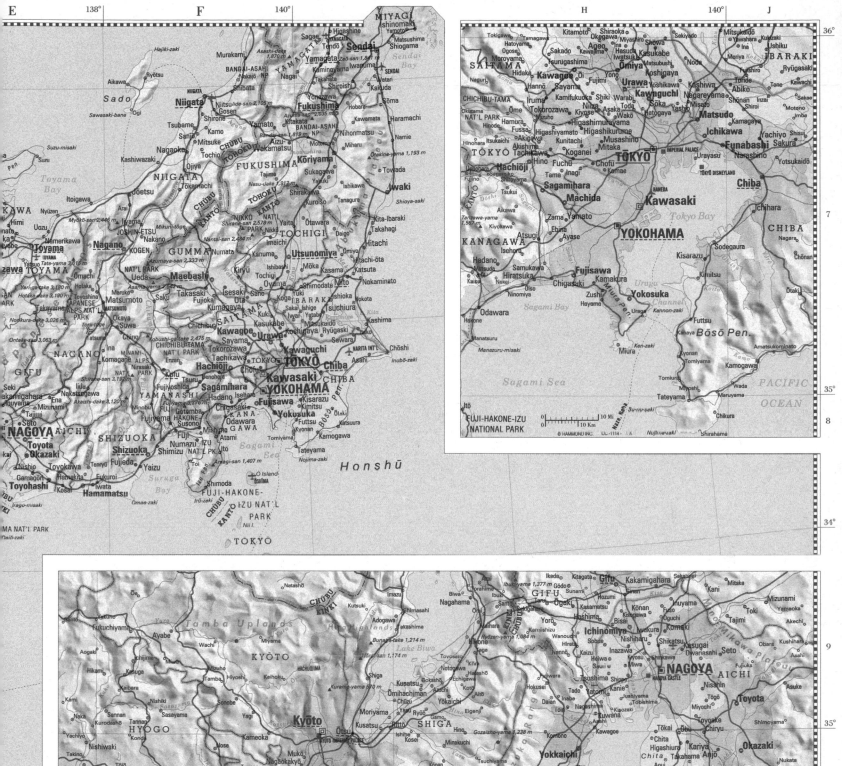

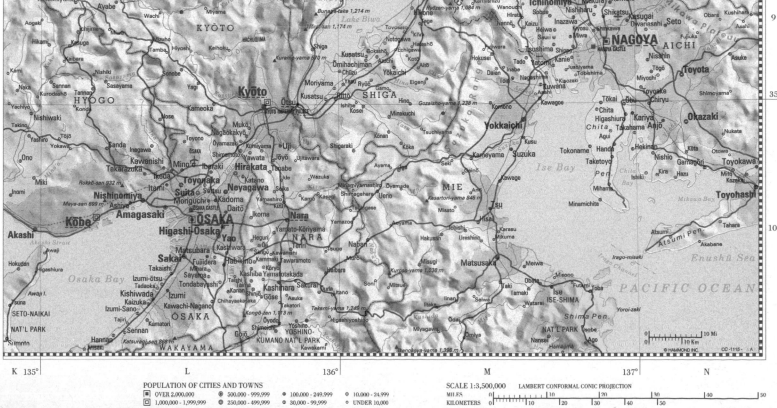

Korea

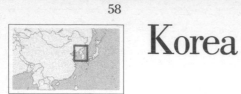

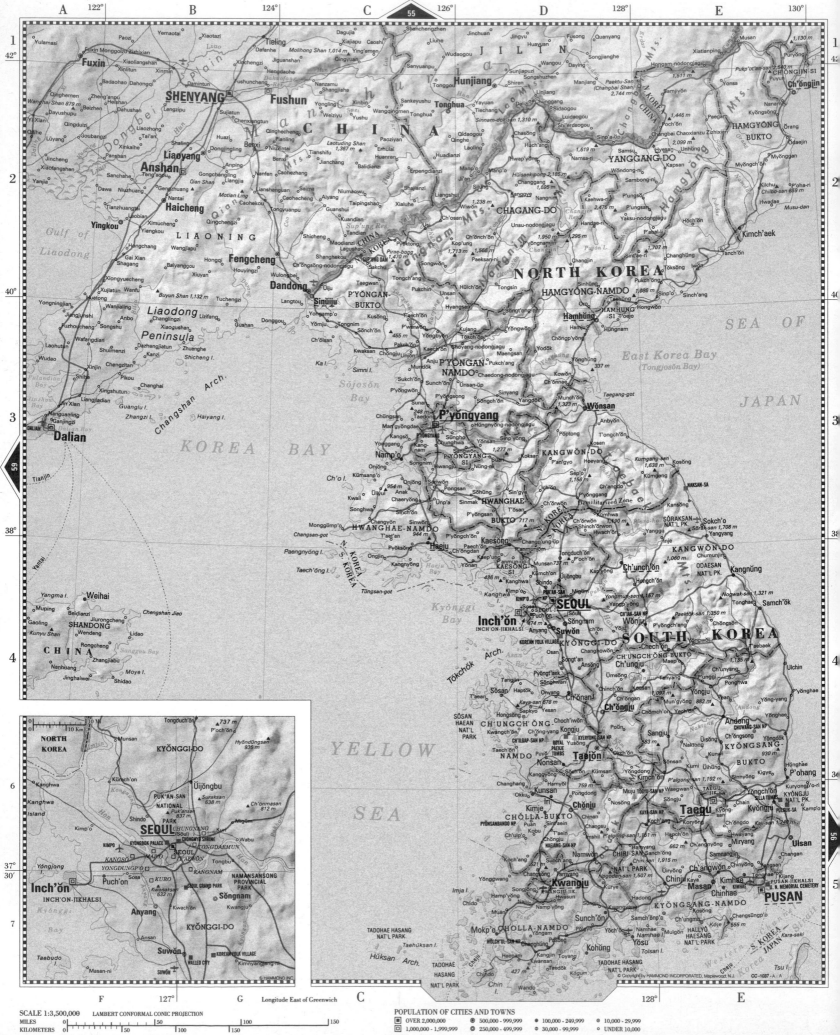

SCALE 1:3,500,000   LAMBERT CONFORMAL CONIC PROJECTION

MILES

KILOMETERS

POPULATION OF CITIES AND TOWNS

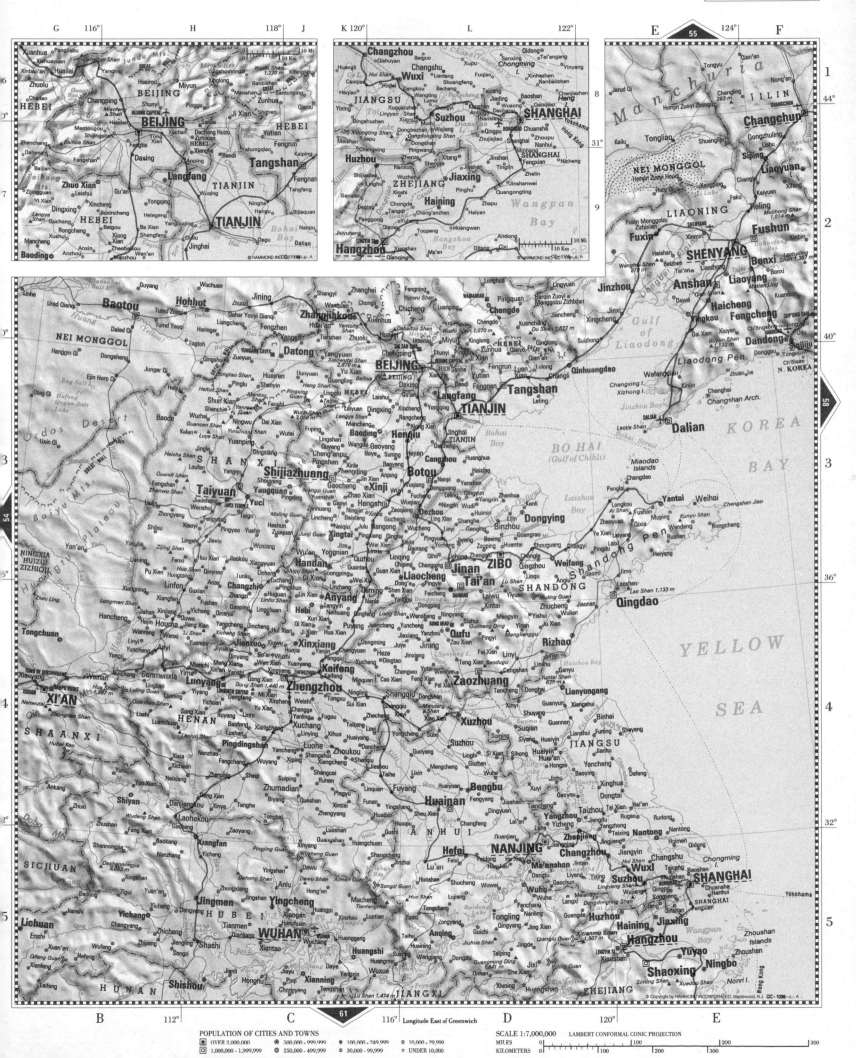

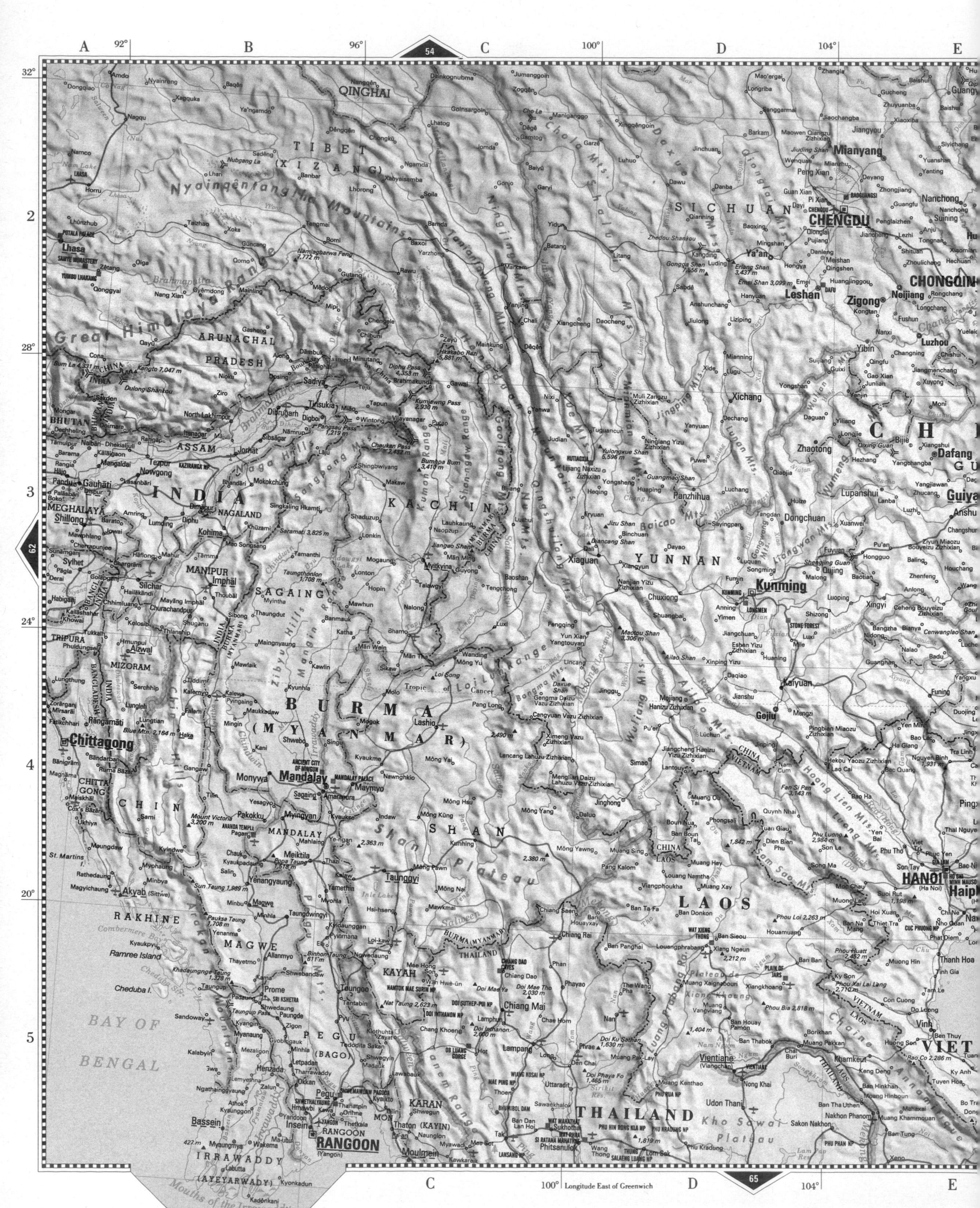

A
92°
B
96°
54
C
100°
D
104°
E
32°
28°
24°
20°
2
3
4
5
62
65
Longitude East of Greenwich
QINGHAI
TIBET
(XIZANG)
Nyainqêntanglha Mountains
Lhasa
Nagqu
Amdo
Nam Lake
Nubgang La
Lhari
Banbar
Lhorong
Soila
Xabyaisamba
Chongkü
Ngamda
Dêngqên
Nangqên
Dainkognubma
Jumanggoin
Zogqên
Golnsargoin
Lhatog
Jomda
Chola Mts.
Daxue Mts.
Markam
Batang
Litang
Yidun
Garzê
Luhuo
Dawu
Danba
Jinchuan
Barkam
Maowen Qiangzu Zizhixian
Mianyang
Deyang
Nanchong
SICHUAN
CHENGDU
Ya'an
Kangding
Gongga Shan 7,556 m
Emei Shan 3,099 m
Leshan
Zigong
Neijiang
CHONGQING
Luzhou
Yibin
Xichang
Jingping Mts.
Xide
Gongbujiang Mts.
Great Himalaya Range
Namjagbarwa Feng 7,772 m
Brahmaputra
Gyêmdong
Mainling
Nang Xian
Qonggyai
Zêtang
Mêdog
Bomi
Baxoi
Yarzhong
Rawu
Zayü
Hkakabo Razi 5,881 m
ARUNACHAL PRADESH
Kangto 7,047 m
BHUTAN
ASSAM
Dibrugarh
Tinsukia
Sadiya
Digboi
Itanagar
North Lakhimpur
Jorhat
Tezpur
Gauhati
Nowgong
MEGHALAYA
Shillong
Cherrapunjee
Sylhet
INDIA
NAGALAND
Kohima
Dimapur
Saramati 3,825 m
MANIPUR
Imphal
Silchar
SAGAING
KACHIN
Myitkyina
Bhamo
Katha
Shan-ngaw Range
Kumon Range
Gaoligong Mts.
Nu Mts.
Nujiang
Baoshan
Tengchong
Xiaguan
Dali
YUNNAN
Kunming
Chuxiong
Gejiu
Kaiyuan
Mengzi
Ailao Mts.
Wuliang Mts.
Jinghong
Simao
Lincang
Pu'er
TRIPURA
MIZORAM
Aizawl
BANGLADESH
Chittagong
Rangamati
CHIN
Blue Mtn. 2,164 m
Mount Victoria 3,200 m
BURMA (MYANMAR)
Tropic of Cancer
Lashio
Mandalay
Maymyo
Sagaing
Monywa
Pakokku
Myingyan
Meiktila
MANDALAY
SHAN
Shan Plateau
Taunggyi
Kengtung
Inle Lake
Salween
Irrawaddy
Chindwin
Akyab (Sittwe)
RAKHINE
Ramree Island
Cheduba I.
Arakan Mountains
MAGWE
Magwe
Prome
Pagan
Kayah
Loi-kaw
PEGU (BAGO)
Pegu
Toungoo
Pegu Mts.
KARAN
Thaton (KAYIN)
Moulmein
Mon
RANGOON
Bassein
IRRAWADDY (AYEYARWADY)
Mouths of the Irrawaddy
BAY OF BENGAL
Chiang Mai
Chiang Rai
Chiang Saen
Lampang
Phitsanulok
Sukhothai
THAILAND
Khorat Plateau
Tak
Mae Sot
LAOS
Luang Prabang
Vientiane (Viangchan)
Nong Khai
Udon Thani
Sakon Nakhon
Nakhon Phanom
Plateau de Xieng Khouang
Plain of Jars
Phou Bia 2,818 m
Mekong
CHINA
VIETNAM
Lao Cai
Fan Si Pan 3,143 m
Hoang Lien Mts.
Dien Bien Phu
Son La
HANOI (Ha Noi)
Haiphong
Thanh Hoa
Vinh
VIETNAM
Annamitique
Chaîne
Red (Hong)
Black (Da)
Phongsali
Muang Sing
Muang Xay
Louang Namtha
Ban Houayxay
Xiang Ngeun
Phou Loi 2,263 m
Doi Inthanon 2,590 m
Doi Luang
Dafang
Zhaotong
Guiyang
Lupanshui
Dongchuan
Panzhihua
Fuyuan
Qujing
Luoping
Xingyi
Yangtze

POPULATION OF CITIES AND TOWNS

■ OVER 2,000,000	● 500,000 - 999,999	○ 100,000 - 249,999	○ 10,000 - 29,999
⊡ 1,000,000 - 1,999,999	● 250,000 - 499,999	○ 30,000 - 99,999	○ UNDER 10,000

SCALE 1:7,000,000   LAMBERT CONFORMAL CONIC PROJECTION

MILES   0   100   200   300

KILOMETERS   0   100   200   300

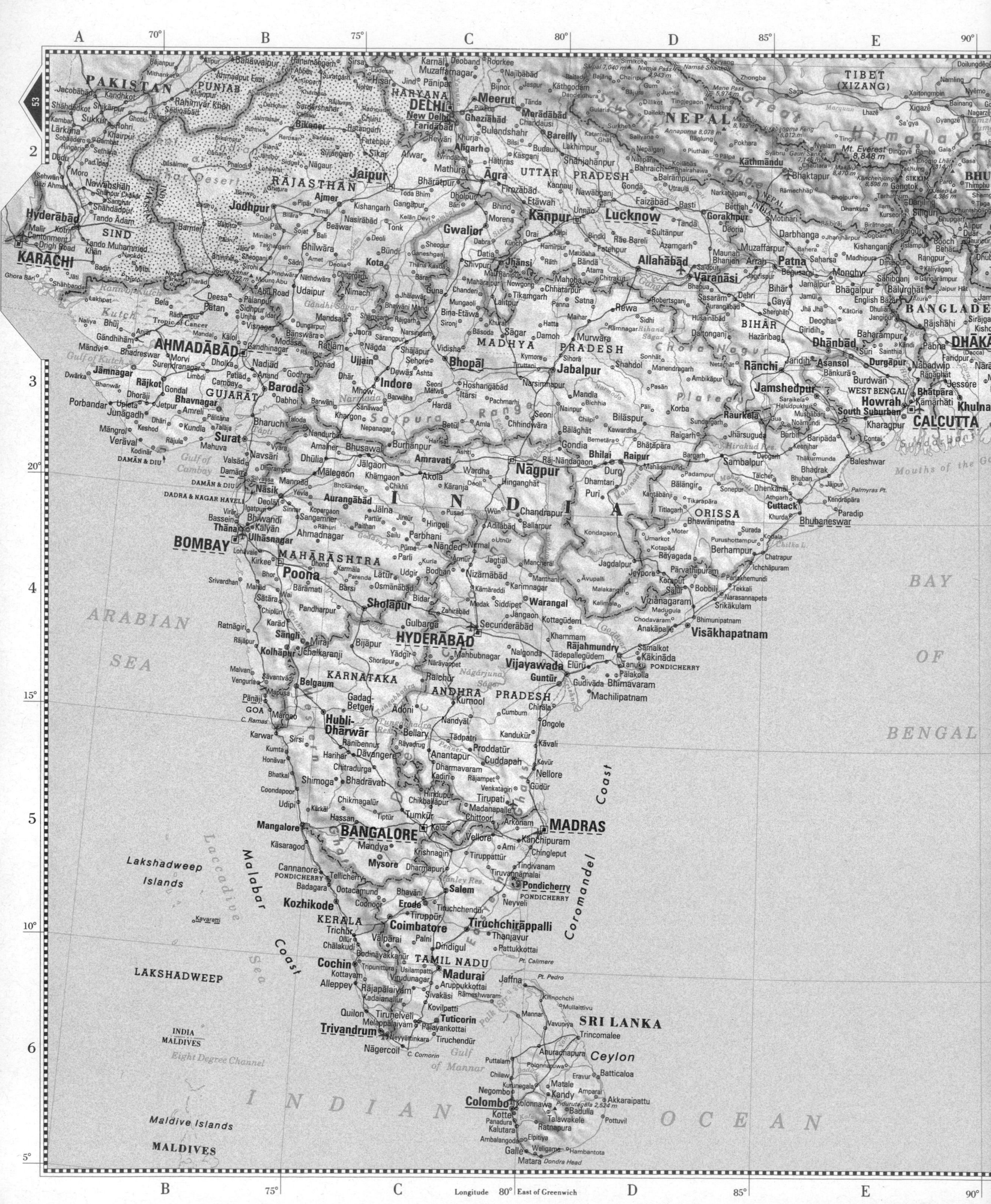

A
70°
B
75°
C
80°
D
85°
E
90°
53
2
3
4
5
6
20°
15°
10°
5°
PAKISTAN
PUNJAB
SIND
KARACHI
Hyderābād
Jacobābād
Sukkur
Bahāwalpur
Rahīmyār Khān
Thar Desert
RĀJASTHAN
Jodhpur
Jaipur
Ajmer
Bīkaner
Udaipur
Kota
Mount Abu
Rann of Kutch
Kutch
Bhuj
Tropic of Cancer
Gulf of Kutch
Jāmnagar
Rājkot
Porbandar
Bhavnagar
Junāgadh
Verāval
GUJARĀT
AHMADĀBĀD
Baroda
Surat
Bharuch
Gulf of Cambay
DAMĀN & DIU
Damān
DADRA & NAGAR HAVELI
Nāsik
Thāna
Kalyān
Ulhāsnagar
BOMBAY
MAHĀRĀSHTRA
Poona
Aurangābād
Ahmadnagar
Sholāpur
Kolhāpur
Sāngli
Ratnāgiri
Belgaum
Pānāji
GOA
Margao
Karwar
Hubli-Dhārwār
Dāvangere
Shimoga
Mangalore
Udipi
Hassan
Mysore
BANGALORE
KARNATAKA
Bellary
Raichūr
Gulbarga
Bijāpur
HYDERĀBĀD
Secunderābād
Warangal
ANDHRA PRADESH
Kurnool
Vijayawada
Guntūr
Machilipatnam
Rājahmundry
Kākināda
Visākhapatnam
Vizianagaram
Nellore
Tirupati
Chittoor
Vellore
MADRAS
Kānchipuram
Chingleput
Pondicherry
PONDICHERRY
Salem
Erode
Coimbatore
Tiruchchirāppalli
Thanjavur
Madurai
TAMIL NADU
Dindigul
Tuticorin
Tirunelveli
Nāgercoil
C. Comorin
KERALA
Kozhikode
Cannanore
Tellicherry
Trichūr
Cochin
Alleppey
Quilon
Trivandrum
Malabar Coast
Coromandel Coast
Eastern Ghats
Western Ghats
Lakshadweep Islands
Laccadive Sea
Kavaratti
LAKSHADWEEP
INDIA
MALDIVES
Eight Degree Channel
Maldive Islands
ARABIAN SEA
INDIAN OCEAN
BAY OF BENGAL
Gulf of Mannar
Palk Strait
Jaffna
SRI LANKA
Ceylon
Trincomalee
Anurādhapura
Batticaloa
Kandy
Colombo
Kotte
Ratnapura
Galle
Matara
Dondra Head
Pidurutalāgala 2,524 m
Adam's Bridge
Rāmeshwaram
Pt. Calimere
Pt. Pedro
DELHI
New Delhi
Meerut
Faridābād
Alīgarh
Āgra
Mathura
Gwalior
Jhānsi
Kānpur
Lucknow
Allahābād
Vārānasi
UTTAR PRADESH
HARYANA
Bareilly
Morādābād
Shāhjahānpur
Gorakhpur
Faizābād
MADHYA PRADESH
Bhopāl
Indore
Ujjain
Jabalpur
Sāgar
Ratlām
Narmada
Satpura Range
Burhānpur
Jalgaon
Dhūlia
Mālegaon
Akola
Amravati
Nāgpur
Chandrapur
Raipur
Bhilai
Durg
Bilāspur
Nānded
I N D I A
ORISSA
Cuttack
Bhubaneswar
Sambalpur
Raurkela
Berhampur
Chilka L.
Mahānadi
Godāvari
Krishna
BIHĀR
Patna
Gayā
Rānchi
Jamshedpur
Dhānbād
Chota Nagpur Plateau
Asansol
Durgāpur
WEST BENGAL
Howrah
CALCUTTA
South Suburban
Bhātpāra
Khulna
Jessore
BANGLADESH
DHĀKA
Rājshāhi
Mouths of the Ganges
Sundarbans
NEPAL
Kāthmāndu
Annapurna 8,078 m
Mt. Everest 8,848 m
Himalaya
SIKKIM
Gangtok
Dārjiling
Siliguri
BHUTAN
Thimphu
TIBET (XIZANG)
Great Himalaya Range
Siwalik Range
Ganga
Longitude 80° East of Greenwich

Southern Asia

Punjab Plain, Southern India

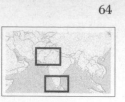

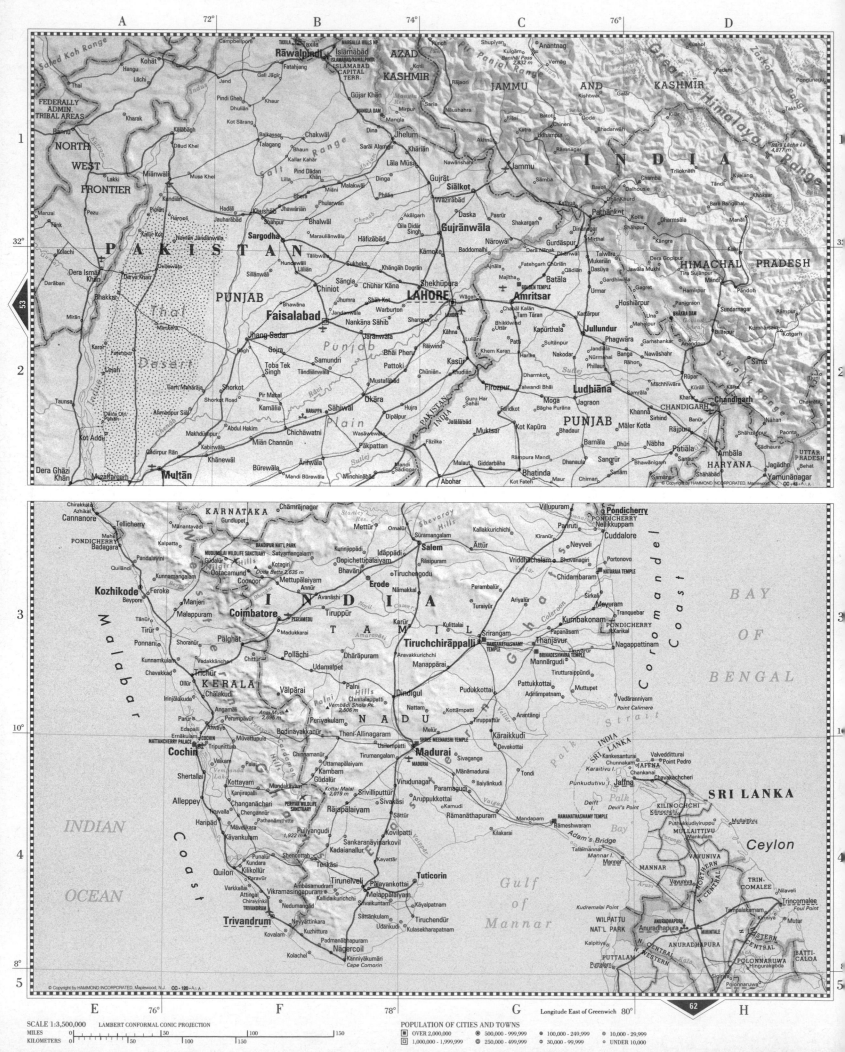

POPULATION OF CITIES AND TOWNS

Longitude East of Greenwich 80°

■ OVER 2,000,000	● 500,000 - 999,999	● 100,000 - 249,999	○ 10,000 - 29,999
□ 1,000,000 - 1,999,999	● 250,000 - 499,999	● 30,000 - 99,999	○ UNDER 10,000

Eastern Burma, Thailand, Indochina

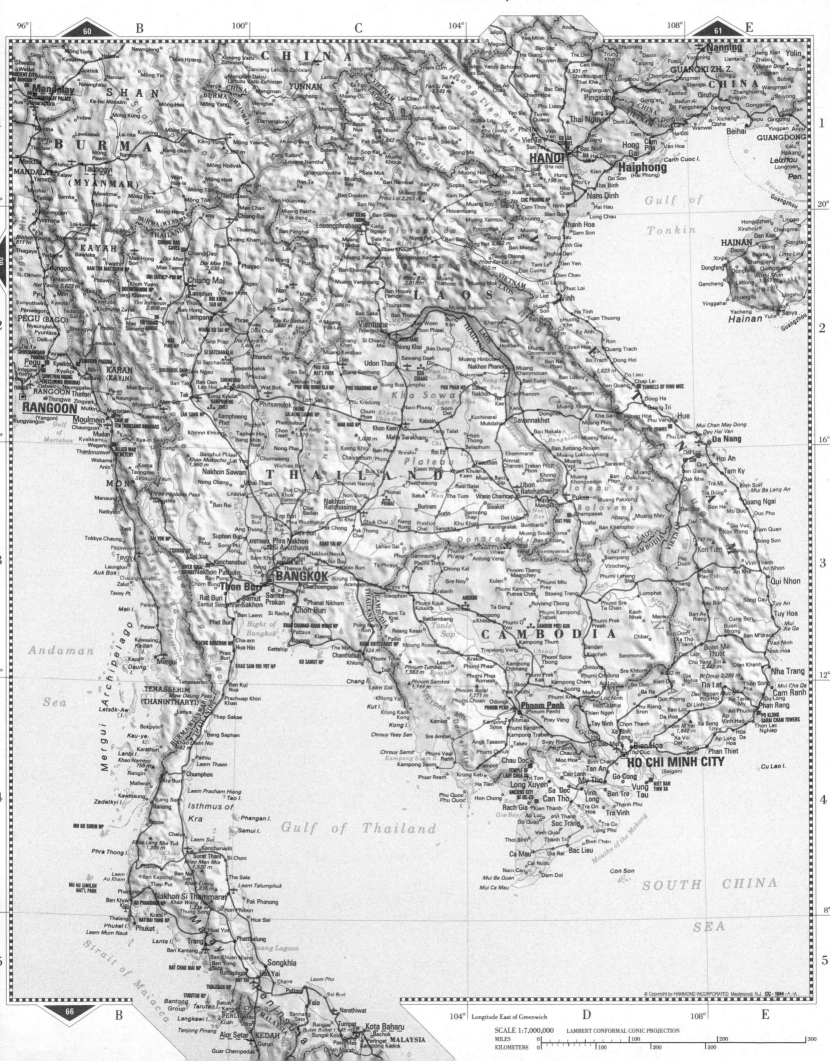

SCALE 1:7,000,000   LAMBERT CONFORMAL CONIC PROJECTION

© Copyright by HAMMOND INCORPORATED, Maplewood, N.J. CC-1044-A-A

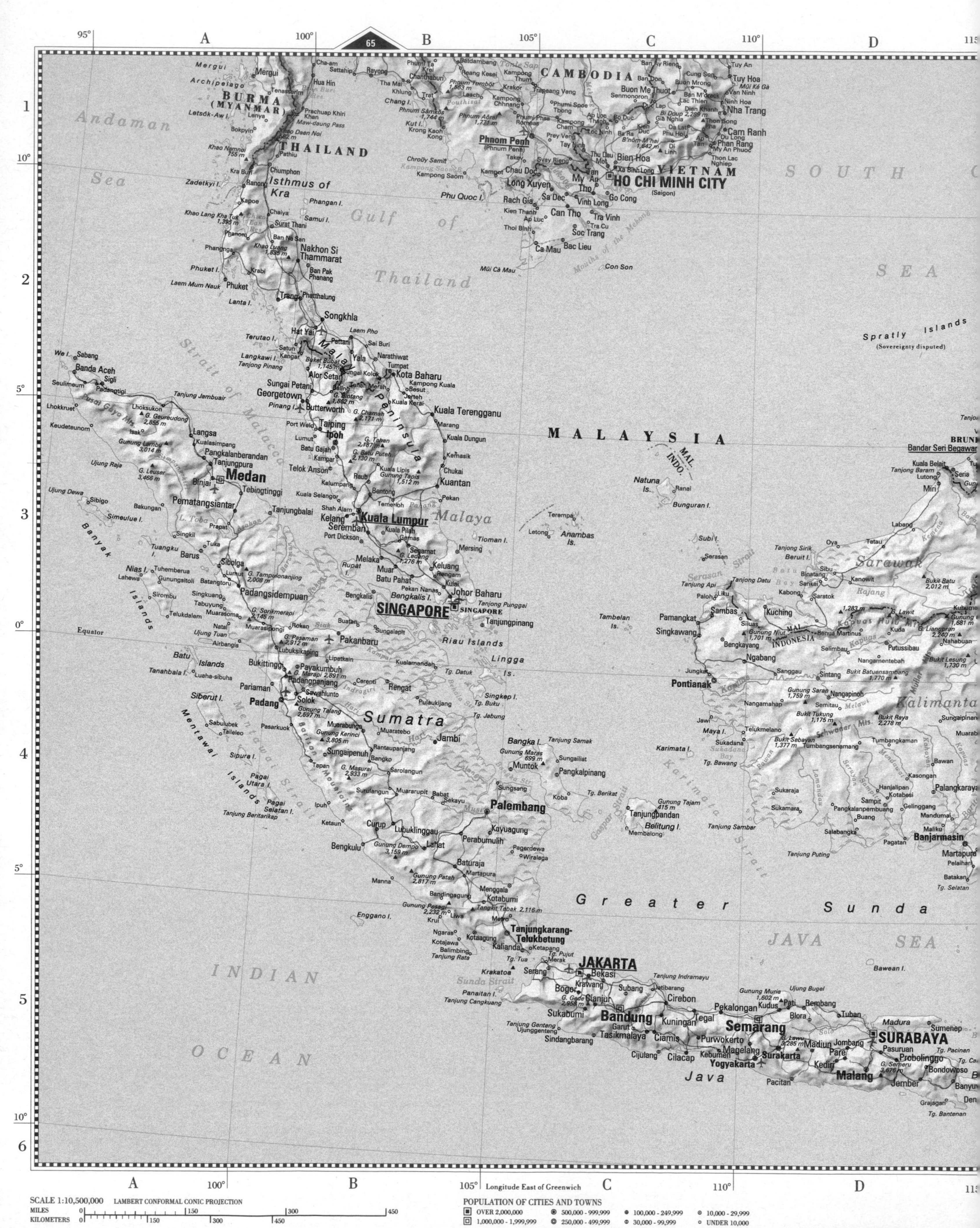
65
95°
A
100°
B
105°
C
110°
D
BURMA (MYANMAR)
THAILAND
CAMBODIA
VIETNAM
MALAYSIA
SINGAPORE
Mergui Archipelago
Mergui
Andaman Sea
Isthmus of Kra
Gulf of Thailand
Phnom Penh
(Phnum Penh)
HO CHI MINH CITY
(Saigon)
Nha Trang
Cam Ranh
Bien Hoa
Can Tho
Phu Quoc I.
Con Son
SOUTH CHINA SEA
Spratly Islands
(Sovereignty disputed)
Phuket
Songkhla
Hat Yai
Pattani
Kota Baharu
Alor Setar
Georgetown
Butterworth
Kuala Terengganu
Taiping
Ipoh
Malay Peninsula
Kuantan
Kuala Lumpur
Kelang
Seremban
Melaka
Johor Baharu
Strait of Malacca
Banda Aceh
Medan
Pematangsiantar
Tanjungbalai
Sibolga
Nias I.
Banyak Islands
Batu Islands
Padang
Bukittinggi
Pekanbaru
Riau Islands
Lingga Is.
Sumatra
Jambi
Mentawai Islands
Siberut I.
Bengkulu
Palembang
Bangka I.
Pangkalpinang
Belitung I.
Natuna Is.
Anambas Is.
Tambelan Is.
Sarawak
Kuching
Pontianak
Kalimantan
Banjarmasin
Bandar Seri Begawan
Miri
Karimata Strait
Gaspar Strait
Enggano I.
Tanjungkarang-Telukbetung
Sunda Strait
Krakatoa
JAKARTA
Bogor
Bandung
Cirebon
Semarang
Yogyakarta
Surakarta
Malang
SURABAYA
Madura
Java
JAVA SEA
Greater Sunda
INDIAN OCEAN
Equator
5°
10°
0°
1
2
3
4
5
6
Longitude East of Greenwich
SCALE 1:10,500,000 LAMBERT CONFORMAL CONIC PROJECTION
MILES 0 150 300 450
KILOMETERS 0 150 300 450
POPULATION OF CITIES AND TOWNS
OVER 2,000,000
1,000,000 - 1,999,999
500,000 - 999,999
250,000 - 499,999
100,000 - 249,999
30,000 - 99,999
10,000 - 29,999
UNDER 10,000

Southeastern Asia

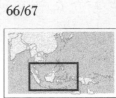

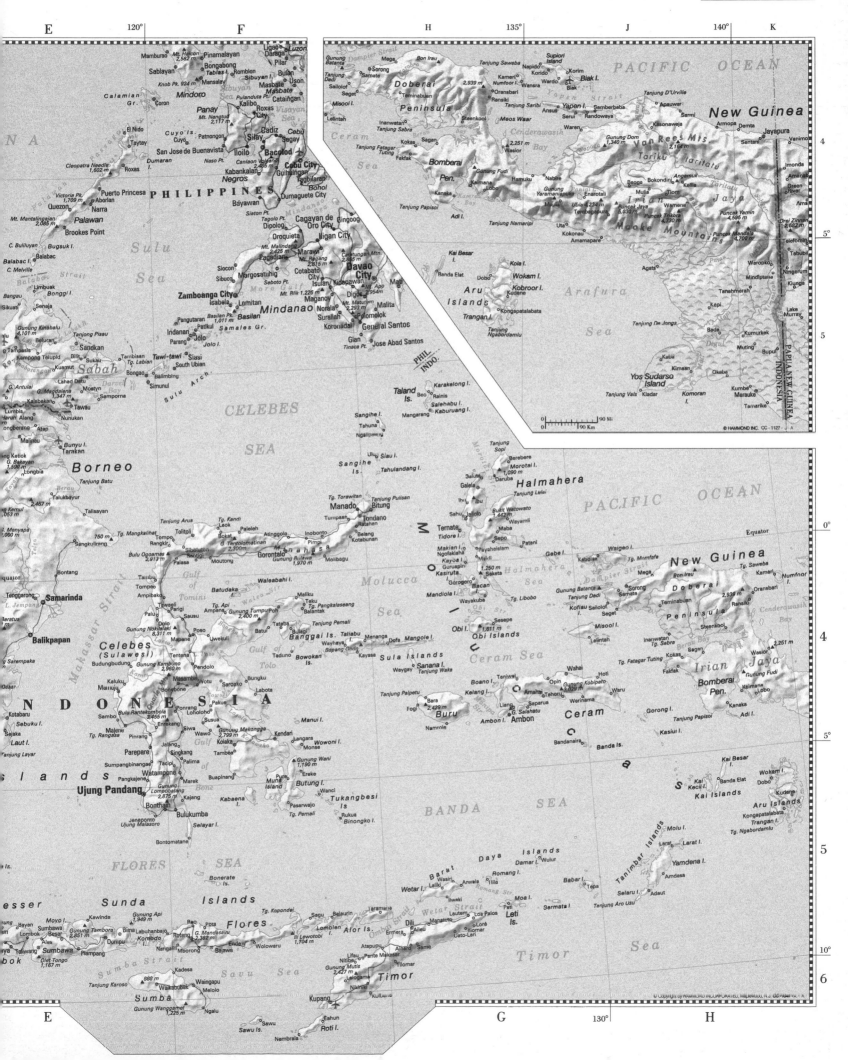

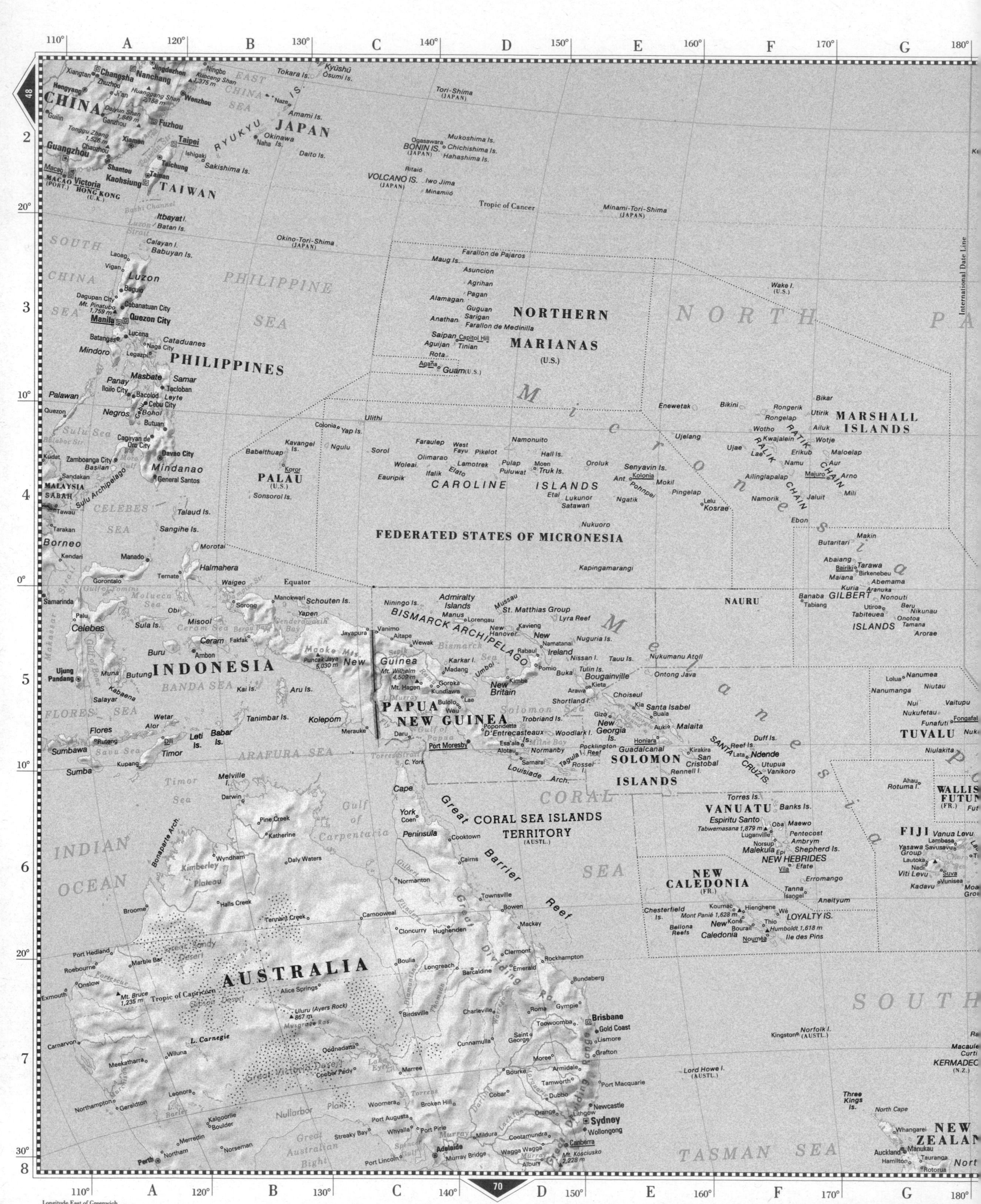

48

CHINA

Xiangtan Changsha Nanchang Jingdezhen Ningbo
Hengyang Chuzhou Ji'an Huangang Shan Wenzhou
Guilin Ganzhou Dayun Shan 1,375 m
Tongui Zhang 1,529 m Fuzhou
Guangzhou Xiamen
Macao Victoria Kaohsiung Taichung
MACAO Victoria Kaohsiung Taiwan
(PORT.) HONG KONG
(U.K.)

EAST CHINA SEA

Tokara Is. Kyūshū
Nara Ōsumi Is.
Amami Is.

JAPAN

RYUKYU IS.

Okinawa
Naha Is.
Ishigaki
Daito Is.
Sakishima Is.

Tori-Shima
(JAPAN)

Ogasawara Mukoshima Is.
BONIN IS. Chichishima Is.
(JAPAN) Hahashima Is.

Ritaiō
VOLCANO IS. Iwo Jima
(JAPAN) Minamiiō

Minami-Tori-Shima
(JAPAN)

Tropic of Cancer

SOUTH
CHINA
SEA

Bashi Channel

Itbayat I.
Batan Is.
Calayan I.
Babuyan Is.

Laoag
Vigan
Luzon
Baguio

Dagupan City
Mt. Pinatubo Cabanatuan City
1,759 m
Manila Quezon City
Lucena
Batangas Cataduanes
Negros City
Legazpi
Mindoro

PHILIPPINES

Masbate Samar
Panay
Iloilo City Tacloban
Bacolod Leyte
Cebu City
Negros Bohol
Butuan

Cagayan de
Oro City
Davao City

Mindanao

General Santos

Okino-Tori-Shima
(JAPAN)

PHILIPPINE
SEA

Farallon de Pajaros

Maug Is.
Asuncion
Agrihan
Pagan
Alamagan
Anathan Guguan
Sarigan
Farallon de Medinilla
Saipan Capitol Hill
Aguijan Tinian
Rota
Agaña Guam (U.S.)

NORTHERN

MARIANAS

(U.S.)

Micronesia

NORTH PA

International Date Line

Wake I.
(U.S.)

Enewetak Bikini Rongerik Bikar
Rongelap Utirik
Wotho Ailuk
Ujelang Kwajalein Wotje
Ujae Lae Erikub Maloelap
Namu Aur
Ant Kolonia Ailinglapalap Arno
Mokil Majuro
Pohnpei Jaluit Mili
Pingelap
Lelu Namorik
Kosrae Ebon

MARSHALL
ISLANDS

RATIK CHAIN
RALIK CHAIN

MALAYSIA
SABAH

Kudat
Zamboanga City Basilan
Sandakan
Sulu Archipelago
Tawau

CELEBES
SEA

Tarakan

Borneo
Kendari

Samarinda

Palu
Ujung
Pandang

Gulf of Tomini

Manado
Gorontalo

Ternate

Celebes

Molueca
Sea

Obi

Sula Is.

Morotai

Halmahera

Waigeo
Schouten Is.

Sorong

Misool Yapen
Ceram Berau Bay
Fakfak

Talaud Is.

Sangihe Is.

Ceram Sea

Equator

Colonia Yap Is.
Ulithi
Kavangel
Babelthuap Is.
Ngulu
Koror
PALAU Sorol
(U.S.)
Woleai
Sonsorol Is. Eauripik
Ifalik

Faraulep West
Fayu Pikelot
Olimarao
Lamotrek
Elato
Satawan

Namonuito

Hall Is.
Pulap Moen
Puluwat Truk Is.

Oroluk

Senyavin Is.
Ngatik
Etal Lukunor
Satawan

CAROLINE ISLANDS

Nukuoro

Mokil
Pingelap

FEDERATED STATES OF MICRONESIA

Kapingamarangi

NAURU

Makin
Butaritari

Abaiang Tarawa
Bairiki Birkenebeu
Maiana Abemama
Kuria Nonouti
Tabiang Onotoa Tamana
Tabiteuea Arorae

Banaba GILBERT

Nikunau
Beru

ISLANDS

INDONESIA

Buru

Ambon

Kai Is.

Aru Is.

BANDA SEA

Salayar

Kabaena

Butung

Muna

Maoke Mts.
Puncak Jaya
5,030 m

New Guinea
Jayapura
Vanimo
Wewak

Sepik

Ningino Is.
Manus
Lorengau

Admiralty
Islands

Mussau
St. Matthias Group
Lyra Reef

New
Hanover New
Kavieng Ireland

Karkar I.
Madang
Goroka
Mt. Hagen
Kundiawa

BISMARCK ARCHIPELAGO

Bismarck Sea

Rabaul

New
Britain

Buka

Nissan I.
Tauu Is.

Nuria Is.

Bougainville
Arawa Kieta

Nukumanu Atoll

Ontong Java

Melanesia

Lolua Nanumea
Nanumanga Niutau

Nui Vaitupu
Nukufetau Fongafal
Funafuti

TUVALU Nuk

FLORES
SEA

Flores

Ruteng

Sumbawa

Sumba

Wetar
Alor

Timor

Dili

Leti
Is.

Savu Sea

Babar
Is.

Tanimbar Is.

Kolepom

Merauke

Daru

PAPUA
NEW GUINEA

Bulolo Lae
Wau

Gulf of
Papua

L. Murray

Port Moresby

Popondetta
D'Entrecasteaux
Is.
Esa'ala
Alotau

Trobriand Is.

Samarai Woodlark I.

Normanby
Tagula Rossel I.

Louisiade Arch.

Umboi

Umboi

Solomon Sea

Kimbe

Gizo
New Shortland I.
Georgia Kia Santa Isabel
Buala
Aukii Malaita

Honiara

Guadalcanal

Choiseul

SOLOMON

ISLANDS

San
Cristobal
Rennell I.

SANTA
CRUZ IS.

Reef Is.
Lata
Ndende
Utupua
Vanikoro

Duff Is.

Niulakita

Ahau
Rotuma I.

WALLIS
FUTUN
(FR.) Fut

FIJI Vanua Levu
Lambasa
Yasawa Savusavu
Group
Lautoka
Nadi Suva
Viti Levu Vunisea
Kadavu

Sumba
Kupang

ARAFURA SEA

Torres Strait

C. York

Cape
York
Coen
Peninsula
Cooktown

Cairns

CORAL SEA ISLANDS
TERRITORY
(AUSTL.)

Great Barrier Reef

CORAL

SEA

Torres Is. Banks Is.

VANUATU
Espiritu Santo
Tabwemasana 1,879 m Maewo
Luganville Oba Pentecost
Norsup Ambrym
Malekula Epi Shepherd Is.
NEW HEBRIDES
Vila Efate

NEW
CALEDONIA
(FR.)

Erromango

Tanna
Isangel

Aneityum

Polynesia

INDIAN
OCEAN

Broome

Port Hedland
Roebourne
Onslow
Exmouth

Carnarvon

Northampton
Geraldton

Meekatharra

Wiluna

Darwin

Melville
I.

Pine Creek
Katherine

Wyndham

Kimberley
Plateau

Halls Creek

Timor
Sea

Bonaparte Arch.

Daly Waters

Gulf
of
Carpentaria

Normanton

Camooweal

Cloncurry Hughenden

Mt. Bruce
1,235 m

Marble Bar

Tropic of Capricorn

Wittenoom

Leonora

Kalgoorlie
Boulder
Norseman

Merredin
Perth
Northam

Great
Australian
Bight

Nullarbor Plain

Great Sandy
Desert

Gibson Desert

AUSTRALIA

Uluru (Ayers Rock)
867 m
Musgrave Ras.

Alice Springs

Great Victoria Desert

Coober Pedy

Oodnadatta

L. Carnegie

Barlee

Lake
Eyre

Streaky Bay

Port Lincoln

Whyalla
Port Pirie

Port Augusta

Adelaide
Murray Bridge

Boulia

Birdsville

Longreach
Barcaldine

Bourke

Broken Hill

Wilcannia

Cobar

Great Dividing Range

Townsville

Bowen
Mackay

Rockhampton
Emerald
Clermont

Bundaberg

Charleville Roma Gympie
Toowoomba Brisbane
Gold Coast
Cunnamulla Lismore
Saint
George Grafton

Armidale
Moree
Tamworth
Tenterfield Port Macquarie
Dubbo
Orange Lithgow
Newcastle
Sydney
Wollongong
Canberra
Wagga Wagga
Albury Mt. Kosciusko
2,228 m

Chesterfield
Is.

Bellona
Reefs

Mont Panié 1,628 m
Hienghene
Koumac We
Koné LOYALTY IS.
Bouraïl
New Thio Humboldt 1,618 m
Caledonia Ile des Pins
Nouméa

Kingston Norfolk I.
(AUSTL.)

Lord Howe I.
(AUSTL.)

Three
Kings
Is.

North Cape

SOUTH

TASMAN SEA

Macaule
Curti
KERMADEC
(N.Z.)

Whangarei NEW
ZEALAN
Auckland Manukau
Hamilton Tauranga
Rotorua

Central Pacific Ocean

POPULATION OF CITIES AND TOWNS
- OVER 3,000,000
- 1,000,000 - 2,999,999
- 500,000 - 999,999
- 100,000 - 499,999
- UNDER 100,000

SCALE 1:31,500,000 LAMBERT AZIMUTHAL EQUAL-AREA PROJECTION

MILES 0 400 800 1200

KILOMETERS 0 400 800 1200

Longitude West of Greenwich

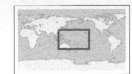

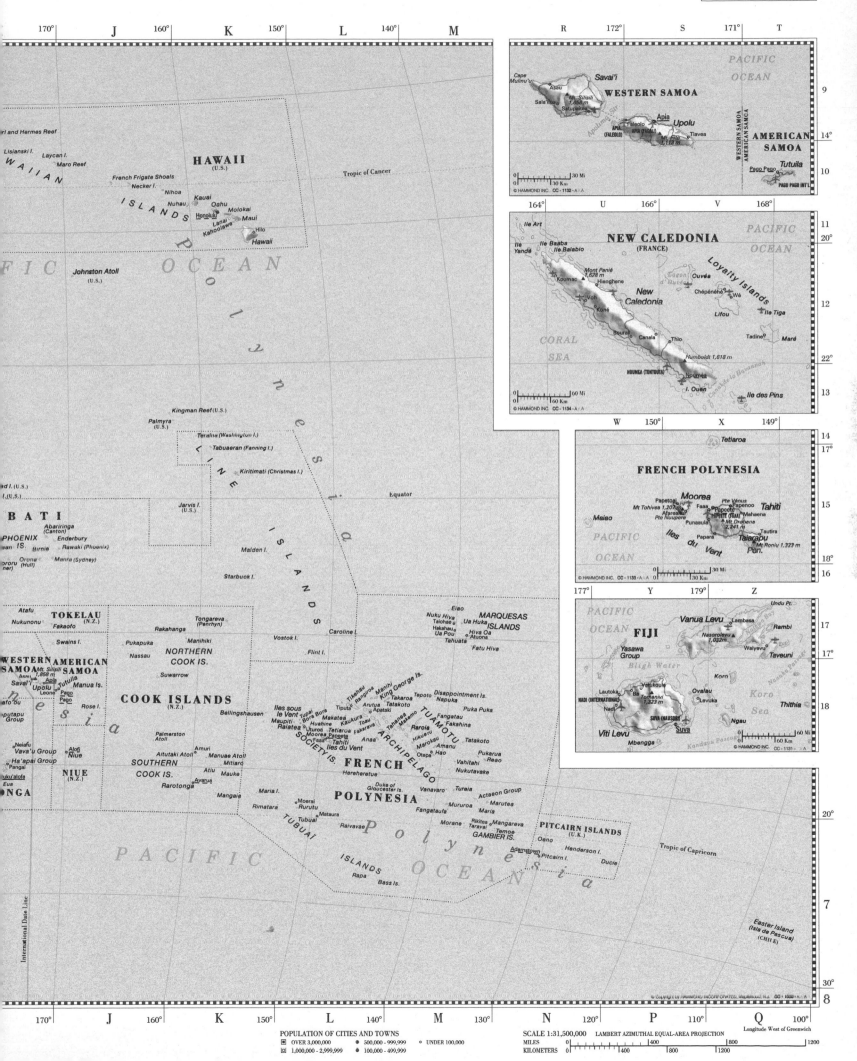

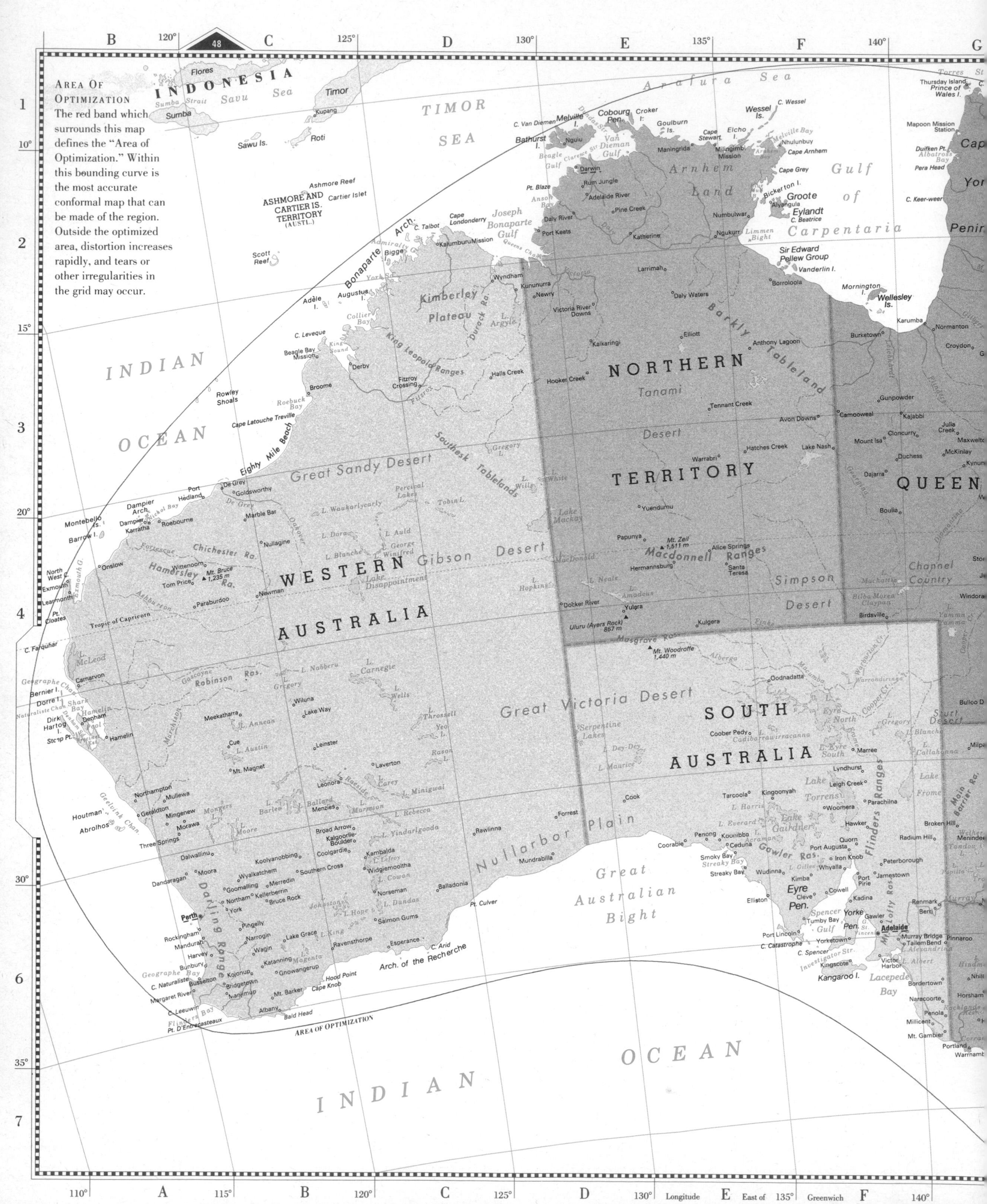

AREA OF
OPTIMIZATION
The red band which
surrounds this map
defines the "Area of
Optimization." Within
this bounding curve is
the most accurate
conformal map that can
be made of the region.
Outside the optimized
area, distortion increases
rapidly, and tears or
other irregularities in
the grid may occur.

INDONESIA
Flores
Sumba Strait Savu Sea
Timor
Kupang
Sawu Is. Roti

TIMOR
SEA

Arafura Sea

Thursday Island
Prince of
Wales I.
Torres Str.

ASHMORE AND
CARTIER IS.
TERRITORY
(AUSTL.)

Ashmore Reef Cartier Islet

Scott
Reef

C. Van Diemen Melville
I. Melville
Bathurst Ngulu Van
Beagle Clarence Dieman
Gulf Gulf
Darwin
Rum Jungle
Pt. Blaze Adelaide River
Anson Pine Creek
Bay
Daly River
Port Keats Katherine

Cobourg Croker
Pen. Goulburn
Cape Is. Elcho
Stewart Cape I.
Maningrida Milingimbi
Mission
Nhulunbuy
Cape Arnhem
Cape Grey

Wessel
Is. C. Wessel

Melville Bay

Mapoon Mission
Station

Duifken Pt. Cap
Albatross
Bay
Pera Head

Yor

C. Keer-weer

Gulf
of
Carpentaria

Pen

Cap

Bickerton I.
Groote
Alyangula Eylandt
C. Beatrice
Numbulwar
Ngukurr Limmen
Bight
Sir Edward
Pellew Group

INDIAN

Bonaparte Arch.

Admiralty
Bigge I.
York Sd.
Adèle Augustus
I. I.
Collier
Bay
Cape
C. Leveque Londonderry

Cape
Talbot
Kalumburu Mission

Wyndham
Kununurra
Newry

Kimberley Durack Ra.
Plateau
King Leopold Ranges L.
Argyle

Joseph
Bonaparte
Gulf
Queens Chan.

Victoria River
Downs
Kalkaringi

Daly Waters

Larrimah

Borroloola

Elliott

Vanderlin I.

Mornington

Wellesley
Is.

Karumba

Normanton

Croydon

OCEAN

Rowley
Shoals

Beagle Bay
Mission King
Sound
Derby

Broome

Fitzroy
Crossing Halls Creek

Cape Latouche Treville

Eighty Mile Beach

Southesk

Hooker Creek

Tanami

Anthony Lagoon

NORTHERN

Barkly Tableland

Burketown

Gunpowder

Gregory

Tablelands

Great Sandy Desert

De Grey
Port Goldsworthy
Hedland De Grey
Montebello Dampier Nickol Bay
Is. Arch. Roebourne
Barrow I. Dampier
Karratha Marble Bar
Roebourne Nullagine

Percival
Lakes
L. Waukarlycarly
L. Dora
L. Blanche
L. Auld
L. George
Winifred

Tobin L.

L.
Wills
L. White

Gregory TERRITORY

Desert

Warrabri

Tennant Creek

Avon Downs

Hatches Creek Lake Nash

Mt. Isa Cloncurry

Camooweal Kajabbi

Duchess

Dajarra

Julia
Creek
Maxwel

McKinlay

QUEEN

North
West C.
Exmouth
Learmonth Exmouth G.
Pt.
Cloates

Onslow
Hamersley
Tom Price Mt. Bruce
1,235 m Ra.
Paraburdoo

Chichester Ra.
Fortescue
Ashburton
Wittenoom
Newman

WESTERN

Tropic of Capricorn

Gibson Desert
Lake
Disappointment
L. Hopkins

L. Neale

L. Amadeus
Docker River Yulara

Macdonnell
Papunya Mt. Zeil
1,511 m
Hermannsburg Alice Springs
Santa
Teresa

Macdonald

L.
Mackay

Yuendumu

Boulia

Ranges

Simpson

Channel
Country

Muchotta

Bilpa Morea
Claypan

Windora

Simpson
Desert

AUSTRALIA

C. Farquhar

Uluru (Ayers Rock)
867 m
Kulgera

Mt. Woodroffe
1,440 m

Kugera

Birdsville

Yamma
Yamma

C. Cuvier

McLeod

Robinson Ras.
Gregory

L. Nabberu

Musgrave Ras.

Alberga

Warburton Cr.

Warrandirinna

L.

Bulloo

Oodnadatta

Geographe Chan.
Bernier I.
Dorre I. Shark
Hamelin Bay
Dirk Pool
Hartog Beagle
I. Hamelin
Steep Pt.

Carnarvon

Gascoyne

Meekatharra L. Annean

L. Carnegie

L.
Wells

L. Throssell
Yeo
L.

Great Victoria Desert

SOUTH

Serpentine
Lakes

Coober Pedy
Cadibarrawirracanna

Eyre
North L.

L. Gregory

Sturt
Desert

Milpa

L. Blanche

Naturaliste Chan.

Cue
L. Austin

Mt. Magnet

Wiluna
Lake Way

L. Rason
Carey

L. Maurice

Marree

Lyndhurst

L. Callabonna

L.
Frome

Houtman
Abrolhos

Greenough Chan.

Northampton
Mullewa
Geraldton Mingenew
Morawa
Three Springs
Dalwallinu
Dandaragan
Moora

Leonora
Leinster L. Raeside
Laverton Minigwal

Menzies
L. Rebecca

Barlee Ballard
Mongers L.
L.
Moore

Broad Arrow
Kalgoorlie-
Boulder
Koolyanobbing Coolgardie
Kambalda

Rawlinna

AUSTRALIA

Forrest

Cook

Tarcoola

Kingoonya

Lake
Torrens

Leigh Creek

Parachilna

Flinders Ranges

Radium Hill

Penong Koonibba
L. Harris
L. Everard

Woomera

Hawker

Broken Hill

Menindee

Tandou

Wyalkatchem
Goomalling Merredin
Northam Kellerberrin
Bruce Rock
Perth York
Rockingham
Mandurah Pingelly
Harvey Narrogin
Bunbury Wagin
Busselton Bridgetown
Margaret River Kojonup Gnowangerup

Southern Cross
L. Lefroy
Widgiemooltha
L. Cowan
Norseman
L. Dundas
Balladonia

Pt. Culver

Mundrabilla

Nullarbor Plain

Great

Australian

Bight

Ceduna
Coorabie Streaky Bay
Smoky Bay
Streaky Bay Wudinna
Elliston Kimba
Eyre
Pen.
Port Lincoln
Tumby Bay Cleve
C. Catastrophe Cowell
Kingscote

Koonibba Cleve
Iramana Kadina
Port Augusta Quorn
Iron Knob Peterborough
Whyalla Jamestown
L. Gilles
Kimba Port
Pirie
Cowell Yorke
Spencer Pen. Gawler
Gulf
Port Pirie
Yorketown Adelaide
Murray Bridge
Kangaroo I. C. Spencer Tailem Bend
Victor L. Albert
Investigator Str. Harbor
Lacepede L. Alexandrina
Bay

Renmark
Berri

Pinnaroo

Hindma

Murra

Bordertown

Hind

Naracoorte

Penola

Millicent

Portland

Mt. Gambier

Warrnambo

Darling Range

Wickepin

Lake Grace
L. King
Ravensthorpe

Esperance

C. Arid
Arch. of the Recherche

Geographe Bay
C. Naturaliste
C. Leeuwin
Flinders Bay
Pt. D'Entrecasteaux

Bunbury
Harvey
Nannup
Mt. Barker
Albany
Bald Head

Hood Point
Cape Knob

AREA OF OPTIMIZATION

OCEAN

INDIAN

OCEAN

Australia; New Zealand

45° H 150° J 155°

PAPUA NEW GUINEA
Louisiade Arch.
Misima I.
Tagula I.
Rossel I.
Pocklington Reef

Great Barrier Reef
Osprey Reef
Cape Melville
Cape Flattery
Cooktown
Bougainville Reef
CORAL
CORAL
SEA
ISLANDS
TERRITORY
(AUSTL.)
CORAL SEA
Willis Islets
Magdelaine Cays
Coringa Islets
Holmes Reefs
Flinders Reefs
Lihou Reef and Kays
Mellish Reef
Marion Reef
Mossman
Cairns
Mareeba
Gordonvale
Atherton
Bartle Frere 1,622 m
Innisfail
Ravenshoe
Hinchinbrook I.
Ingham
Palm Is.
Halifax Bay
Townsville
C. Bowling Green
Ayr
Home Hill
Bowen
Charters Towers
Whitsunday I.
Proserpine
Repulse Bay
Hughenden
Walkerston
Mackay
Sarina
Broad Sd. Chan.
Percy Isles
Capricorn Channel
Swain Reefs
Frederick Reef
Kenn Reef
Saumarez Reef
Bird Islet
West Islet
Wreck Reef
Cato I.
Drummond Ra.
Clermont
Ogmore
C. Manifold
Yeppoon
Rockhampton
Curtis I.
Longreach
Barcaldine
Alpha
Emerald
Blackwater
Gladstone
Blackall
Biloela
Moura
Monto
Bundaberg
Hervey Bay
Sandy Cape
Fraser I.
Maryborough
Warrego Ra.
Great Dividing Range
Augathella
Mundubbera
Charleville
Mitchell
Roma
Miles
Chinchilla
Gympie
Tewantin-Noosa
Caloundra
Cooladdi
Surat
Dalby
Moreton I.
Toowoomba
Brisbane
Darling Downs
Beaudesert
N. Stradbroke I.
Cunnamulla
Bollon
Saint George
Warwick
Gold Coast
Tweed Heads
Goondiwindi
Stanthorpe
Dirranbandi
Boomi
Casino
Lismore
Tenterfield
Moree
Brewarrina
Walgett
Inverell
Grafton
Glen Innes
Bourke
Narrabri
Armidale
Coffs Harbour
Great Dividing Range
NEW SOUTH WALES
Coonamble
Gunnedah
Tamworth
Kempsey
Cobar
Nyngan
Warren
Gilgandra
Port Macquarie
Narromine
Dubbo
Taree
Wellington
Mudgee
Singleton
Sugarloaf Pt.
Maitland
Port Stephens
Newcastle
Condobolin
Parkes
Orange
Hillston
Forbes
Bathurst
Lithgow
Katoomba
Sydney
West Wyalong
Cowra
Griffith
Young
Camden
Hay
Leeton
Temora
Cootamundra
Goulburn
Wollongong
Bomaderry
Narrandera
Wagga Wagga
Tumut
Canberra
Jervis Bay
AUSTRALIAN CAPITAL TERR.
Queanbeyan
AUSTL. CAP. TERR.
Finley
Echuca
Wodonga
Albury
Mt. Kosciusko 2,228 m
Cooma
Wangaratta
VICTORIA
Australian Alps
Bega
Melbourne
Orbost
C. Howe
Sale
Bairnsdale
Moe
Morwell
Traralgon
Wonthaggi
Corner Inlet
Wilsons Promontory
South East Pt.
Bass Strait
King I.
Furneaux Group
Flinders I.
Cape Barren I.
Banks Str.
Smithton
Wynyard
George Town
Eddystone Pt.
Ulverstone
Devonport
Launceston
Ossa 1,617 m
Queenstown
TASMANIA
New Norfolk
Great Oyster Bay
Hobart
Tasman Pen.
South West C.

Q 170° R 175° S

Three Kings Is.
North C.
C. Maria van Diemen
Te Kao
C. Kerikeri
C. Brett
Kaitaia
Kaikohe
Whangarei
Dargaville
Great Barrier I.
Kaipara Har.
Warkworth
Hauraki Gulf
Waitemata
Takapuna
Auckland
Manukau
Coromandel
Coromandel Peninsula
Thames
TASMAN SEA
North Island
Huntly
Hamilton
Te Aroha
Bay of Plenty
Mount Maunganui
Tauranga
Te Araroa
East C.
Te Awamutu
Cambridge
Whakatane
Hikurangi 1,754 m
Te Kuiti
Tokoroa
Rotorua
Kawerau
Murupara
Taupo
North Taranaki Bight
Lake Taupo
Gisborne
New Plymouth
Turangi
Mt Ngauruhoe 2,291 m
Wairoa
NEW ZEALAND
C. Egmont
Waitara
Stratford
Mahia Pen.
Mt Egmont 2,518 m
Mt Ruapehu 2,797 m
Hawke Bay
Hawera
Hastings
Napier
South Taranaki Bight
Havelock North
Wanganui
Dannevirke
Waipukurau
Ashhurst
C. Farewell
Tasman Bay
Palmerston North
Collingwood
Levin
Karamea Bight
Motueka
Paraparaumu
Masterton
Karamea
Porirua
Mt Owen 1,875 m
Nelson
Wellington
Upper Hutt
Lower Hutt
Blenheim
C. Palliser
Cook Strait
Westport
C. Foulwind
Murchison
Ward
Reefton
Mt Una 2,301 m
Clarence
Greymouth
Kaikoura
Lewis Pass
Hokitika
Otira
Waikari
Arthur's Pass
Pegasus Bay
Rangiora
Kaiapoi
Fox Glacier
Darfield
Christchurch
Mt Cook 3,764 m
Banks Pen.
Haast
Ashburton
Geraldine
South Island
Temuka
Mt Aspiring 3,027 m
Canterbury Bight
Twizel
Southern Alps
Timaru
Wanaka
Waimate
Queenstown
Cromwell
Oamaru
PACIFIC OCEAN
Alexandra
Te Anau
Palmerston
Lumsden
Mosgiel
West C.
Milton
Dunedin
Gore
Riverton
Balclutha
Invercargill
Bluff
Foveaux Strait
Mt Anglem 980 m
Oban
Stewart I.
South C.
Snares Is.

SCALE 1:10,500,000 LAMBERT CONFORMAL CONIC PROJECTION
MILES 0 150 300
KILOMETERS 0 150 300

9 35° 10 40° 11 45° 12

Norfolk I. (AUSTL.)
Kingston
Lord Howe I. (N.S. WALES)
PACIFIC OCEAN
TASMAN SEA
Three Kings Is.
North C.
NEW ZEALAND
North Island
Great Barrier I.
Auckland

5 30° 6 35° 7

J 155° K 160° L 165° M 170° N 175° P

POPULATION OF CITIES AND TOWNS
■ OVER 2,000,000
◉ 500,000 - 999,999
⊙ 50,000 - 99,999
□ 1,000,000 - 1,999,999
● 100,000 - 499,999
○ UNDER 50,000

SCALE 1:14,000,000 OPTIMAL CONFORMAL PROJECTION
MILES 0 200 400 600
KILOMETERS 0 200 400 600

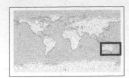

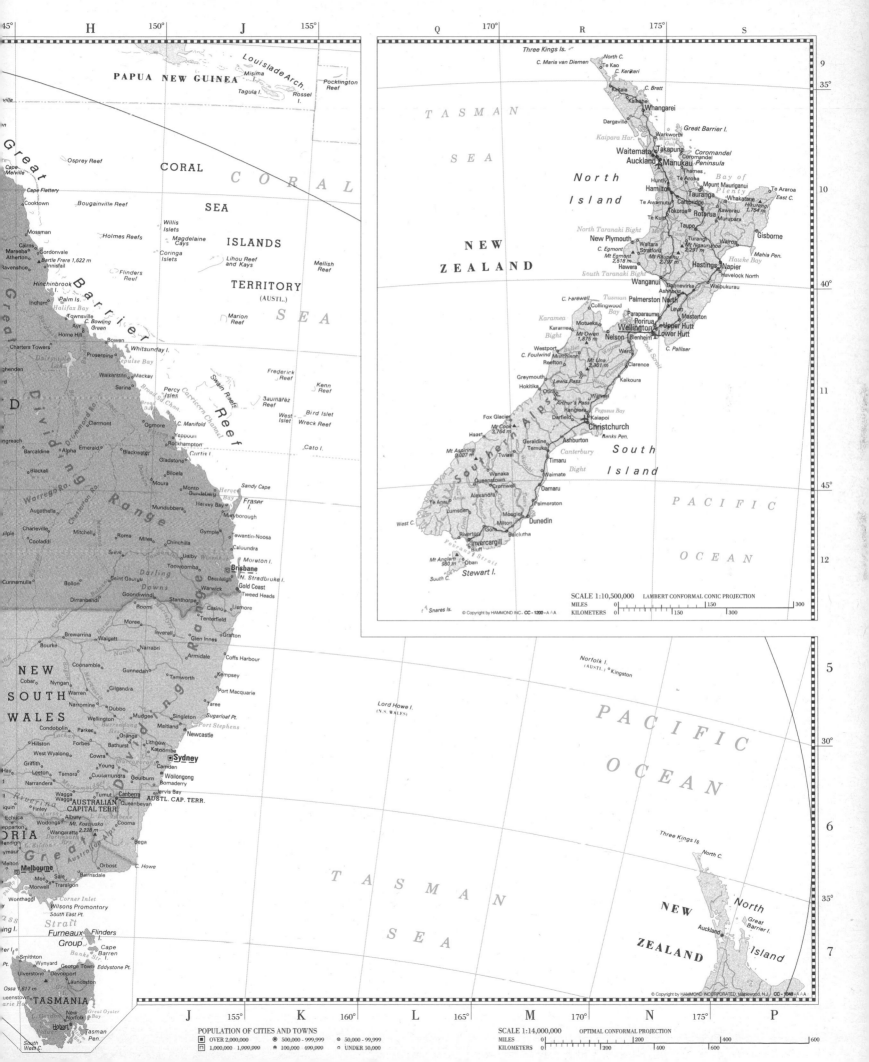

Northeastern Australia

CORAL SEA

CORAL SEA ISLANDS TERRITORY

Cape York Peninsula

Gulf of Carpentaria

QUEENSLAND

Great Barrier Reef

GREAT BARRIER REEF MARINE PARK

Great Dividing Range

Gregory Range

Grey Range

Warrego Range

Drummond Range

Leichhardt Range

Clarke Range

Selwyn Range

Beal Range

Forsyth Ra.

Darling Downs

Channel Country

Sturt Desert

Swain Reefs

Capricorn Channel

Tropic of Capricorn

Brisbane, Cairns, Townsville, Mackay, Rockhampton, Toowoomba, Gold Coast, Bundaberg, Maryborough, Gladstone, Charters Towers, Mount Isa, Cloncurry, Longreach, Winton, Charleville, Roma, Emerald, Hughenden, Cooktown, Normanton, Ipswich

SOUTH AUSTRALIA

NEW SOUTH WALES

Brisbane

Sydney

SCALE 1:7,000,000 LAMBERT CONFORMAL CONIC PROJECTION

MILES 0 100 200 300

KILOMETERS 0 100 200 300

Longitude East of Greenwich

POPULATION OF CITIES AND TOWNS

- OVER 2,000,000
- 1,000,000 - 1,999,999
- 500,000 - 999,999
- 250,000 - 499,999
- 100,000 - 249,999
- 30,000 - 99,999
- 10,000 - 29,999
- UNDER 10,000

70

73

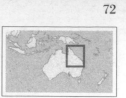

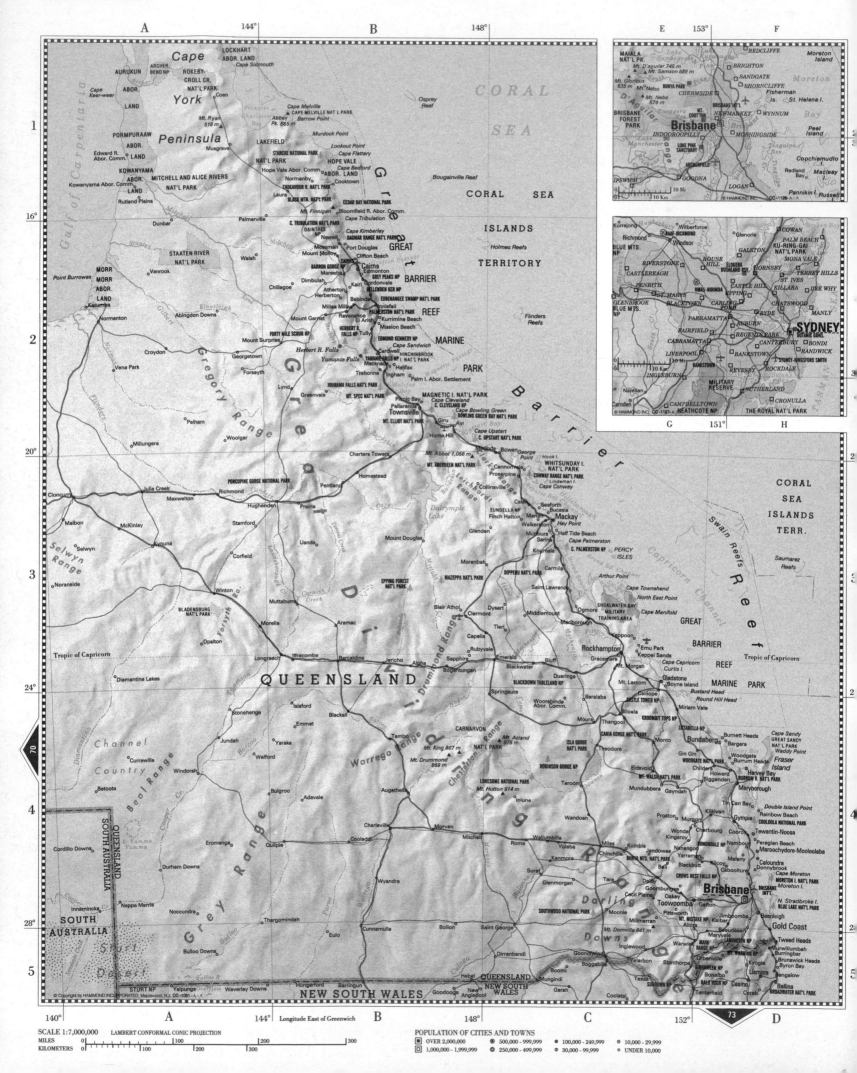

Southeastern Australia

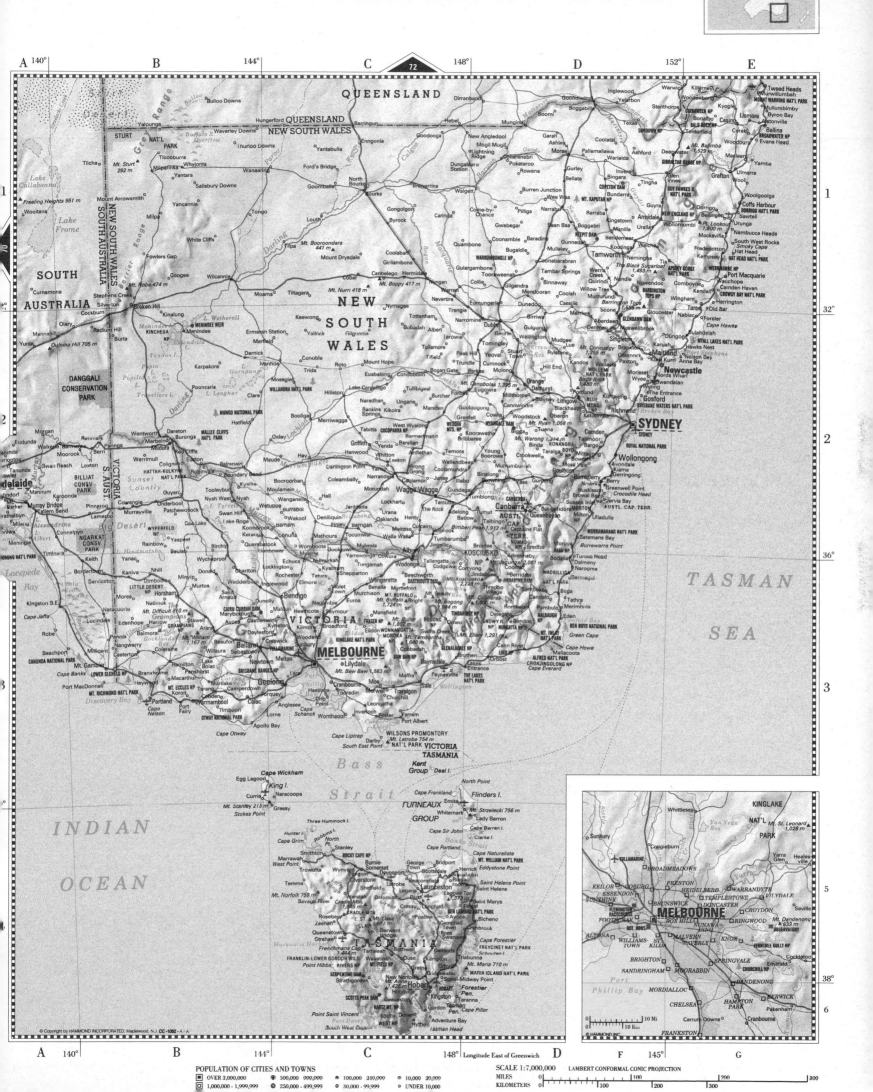

© Copyright by HAMMOND INCORPORATED, Maplewood, N.J. CC-1052-A-A

POPULATION OF CITIES AND TOWNS

■ OVER 2,000,000	● 500,000 900,000	● 100,000 240,000	○ 10,000 29,999
□ 1,000,000 - 1,999,999	● 250,000 - 499,999	● 30,000 - 99,999	○ UNDER 10,000

SCALE 1:7,000,000   LAMBERT CONFORMAL CONIC PROJECTION

MILES

KILOMETERS

Longitude East of Greenwich

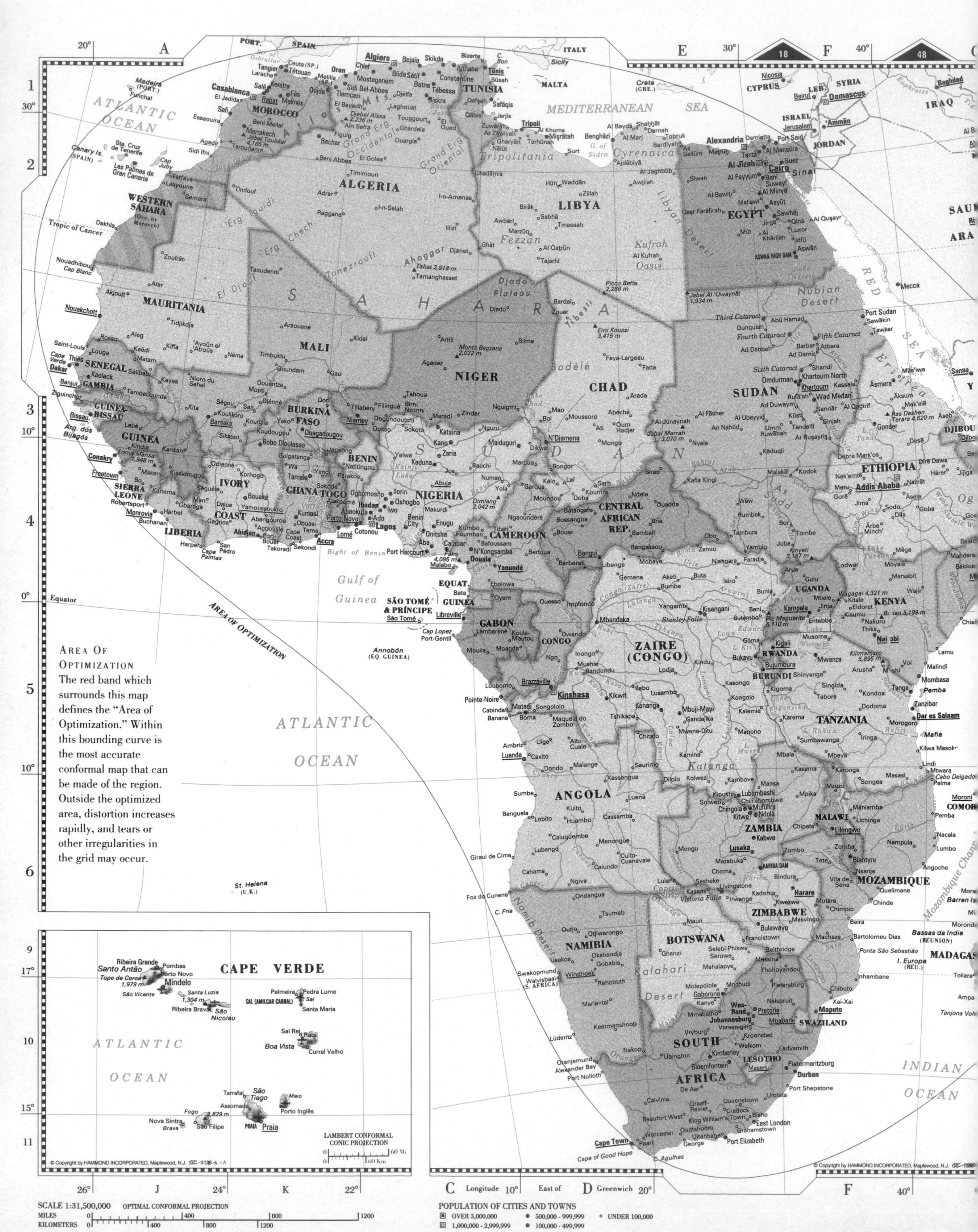

ATLANTIC OCEAN

MEDITERRANEAN SEA

PORT.   SPAIN

Madeira (PORT.)

Canary Is. (SPAIN)

Sta. Cruz de Tenerife
Las Palmas de Gran Canaria

Tropic of Cancer

MOROCCO

Casablanca

WESTERN SAHARA (Occ. by Morocco)

Nouadhibou
Cap Blanc

Nouakchott

MAURITANIA

ALGERIA

S   A   H   A   R   A

MALI

Timbuktu

SENEGAL
Dakar

GAMBIA
Banjul

GUINEA-BISSAU
Bissau

GUINEA
Conakry

SIERRA LEONE
Freetown

LIBERIA
Monrovia

IVORY COAST

NIGER

Agadez

BURKINA FASO
Ouagadougou

GHANA
Accra

TOGO
Lomé

BENIN

TUNISIA

Tripoli

LIBYA

Fezzan

CHAD

N'Djamena

NIGERIA
Lagos
Abuja

CAMEROON
Yaoundé
Douala

EQUAT. GUINEA
Malabo

SÃO TOMÉ & PRÍNCIPE
São Tomé

GABON
Libreville

Port-Gentil

CONGO
Brazzaville

Pointe-Noire

Cabinda

ZAIRE (CONGO)
Kinshasa

ITALY
Sicily

MALTA

Crete (GRE.)

CYPRUS
Nicosia

LEB. Beirut
SYRIA Damascus
ISRAEL Amman
Jerusalem **JORDAN**

IRAQ
Baghdad

EGYPT
Cairo
Alexandria

Aswan High Dam

Libyan Desert

Nubian Desert

Mecca

Port Sudan

SUDAN

Khartoum

ETHIOPIA
Addis Ababa

DJIBOUTI

CENTRAL AFRICAN REP.
Bangui

UGANDA
Kampala

KENYA
Nairobi

Lake Victoria

RWANDA
Kigali
BURUNDI
Bujumbura

Mt. Kilimanjaro 5,895 m

TANZANIA
Dar es Salaam
Dodoma
Zanzibar

Mombasa

ATLANTIC OCEAN

St. Helena (U.K.)

AREA OF OPTIMIZATION

Gulf of Guinea

Annobón (EQ. GUINEA)

Equator

Luanda

ANGOLA

Benguela

ZAMBIA
Lusaka

MALAWI
Lilongwe

MOZAMBIQUE

COMOROS
Moroni

ZIMBABWE
Harare

Victoria Falls

NAMIBIA
Windhoek

Namib Desert

BOTSWANA
Gaborone

Kalahari Desert

MADAGASCAR

I. Europa (REU.)

SOUTH AFRICA
Johannesburg
Pretoria

SWAZILAND
Mbabane
Maputo

LESOTHO
Maseru

Durban

INDIAN OCEAN

Cape Town
Cape of Good Hope
C. Agulhas

Port Elizabeth
East London

CAPE VERDE

Ribeira Grande
Santo Antão
Tope de Coroa 1,979 m
Mindelo
São Vicente
Santa Luzia
São Nicolau
Ribeira Brava

ATLANTIC OCEAN

Pombas
Porto Novo

Palmeira
SAL (AMILCAR CABRAL)
Sal
Santa Maria

Pedra Lume

Sal Rei
Rábil
Boa Vista
Curral Velho

Tarrafal
São Tiago
Assomada
PRAIA Praia
Porto Inglês

Maio

Nova Sintra
Brava
Fogo 2,829 m
São Filipe

SCALE 1:31,500,000   OPTIMAL CONFORMAL PROJECTION

MILES 0   400   800   1200
KILOMETERS 0   400   800

POPULATION OF CITIES AND TOWNS
- ▣ OVER 3,000,000
- ▣ 1,000,000 - 2,999,999
- ● 500,000 - 999,999
- ● 100,000 - 499,999
- ○ UNDER 100,000

Africa

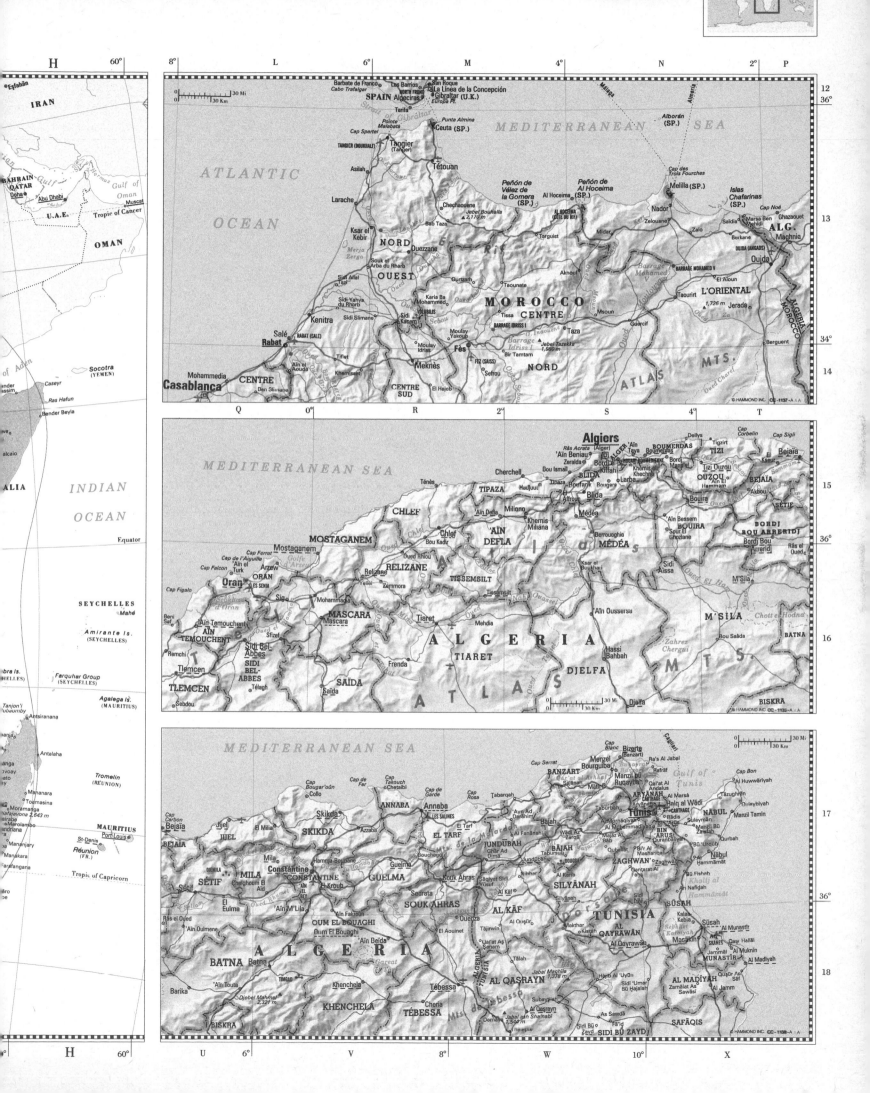

IRAN

BAHRAIN
QATAR
Doha
Abu Dhabi   U.A.E.   Muscat
                  Gulf of
                  Oman
                  OMAN
Tropic of Cancer

of Aden

Socotra
(YEMEN)

Ras Hafun

Bender Beyla

INDIAN

OCEAN

Equator

SEYCHELLES
Mahé

Amirante Is.
(SEYCHELLES)

Farquhar Group
(SEYCHELLES)

Agalega Is.
(MAURITIUS)

Tromelin
(RÉUNION)

MAURITIUS
Port Louis

Réunion
(FR.)

Tropic of Capricorn

Morocco map (top)

ATLANTIC OCEAN

MEDITERRANEAN SEA

SPAIN   Gibraltar (U.K.)   Europa Pt.

Cap Spartel   Ceuta (SP.)

Alborán (SP.)

TANGIER (BOUKHIAL)   Tangier (Tanger)

Tétouan

Asilah

Peñón de Vélez de la Gomera (SP.)
Al Hoceima   Peñón de Al Hoceima (SP.)
Melilla (SP.)
Islas Chafarinas (SP.)
Cap Noé

Larache

Nador

Ksar el Kebir   NORD   Ouezzane   Rif   ALG.   Maghnia

Chechaouene   Bab Taza   OUJDA (ANGADS)

Merja Zerga   OUEST   Oujda

Kenitra   Sidi Slimane   Volubilis   MOROCCO   CENTRE   Taourirt   L'ORIENTAL   Jerade

Salé   RABAT (SALE)   Rabat   Meknès   Fès   Taza   NORD   ATLAS MTS.

Casablanca   CENTRE   CENTRE SUD   Berguent

© HAMMOND INC.

Northern Algeria map (middle)

MEDITERRANEAN SEA

Algiers (Alger)   BOUMERDAS   TIZI   Cap Sigli

Cherchell   BLIDA   TIZI OUZOU   BEJAÏA   SÉTIF

CHLEF   'AÏN DEFLA   MÉDÉA   BOUIRA   BORDJ BOU ARRERIDJ

MOSTAGANEM   RELIZANE   TISSEMSILT   M'SILA

ORAN   MASCARA   Tiaret   ALGERIA   TIARET   DJELFA   BATNA

SIDI BEL-ABBES   SAÏDA   ATLAS   BISKRA

TLEMCEN

© HAMMOND INC.

Eastern Algeria / Tunisia map (bottom)

MEDITERRANEAN SEA

Gulf of Tunis   Cap Bon

BANZART   TUNIS   CARTHAGE   NABUL

BEJAÏA   SKIDA   ANNABA   EL TARF   JUNDUBAH   BAJAH   ZAGHWAN   SILYANAH   SÜSAH

SÉTIF   MILA   Constantine   GUELMA   SOUK AHRAS   AL KAF   TUNISIA   AL QAYRAWAN   MUNASTIR

BATNA   OUM EL BOUAGHI   AL QASRAYN   AL MADIYAH

ALGERIA   SIDI BU ZAYD   SAFAQIS

BISKRA   KHENCHELA   TÉBESSA

© HAMMOND INC.

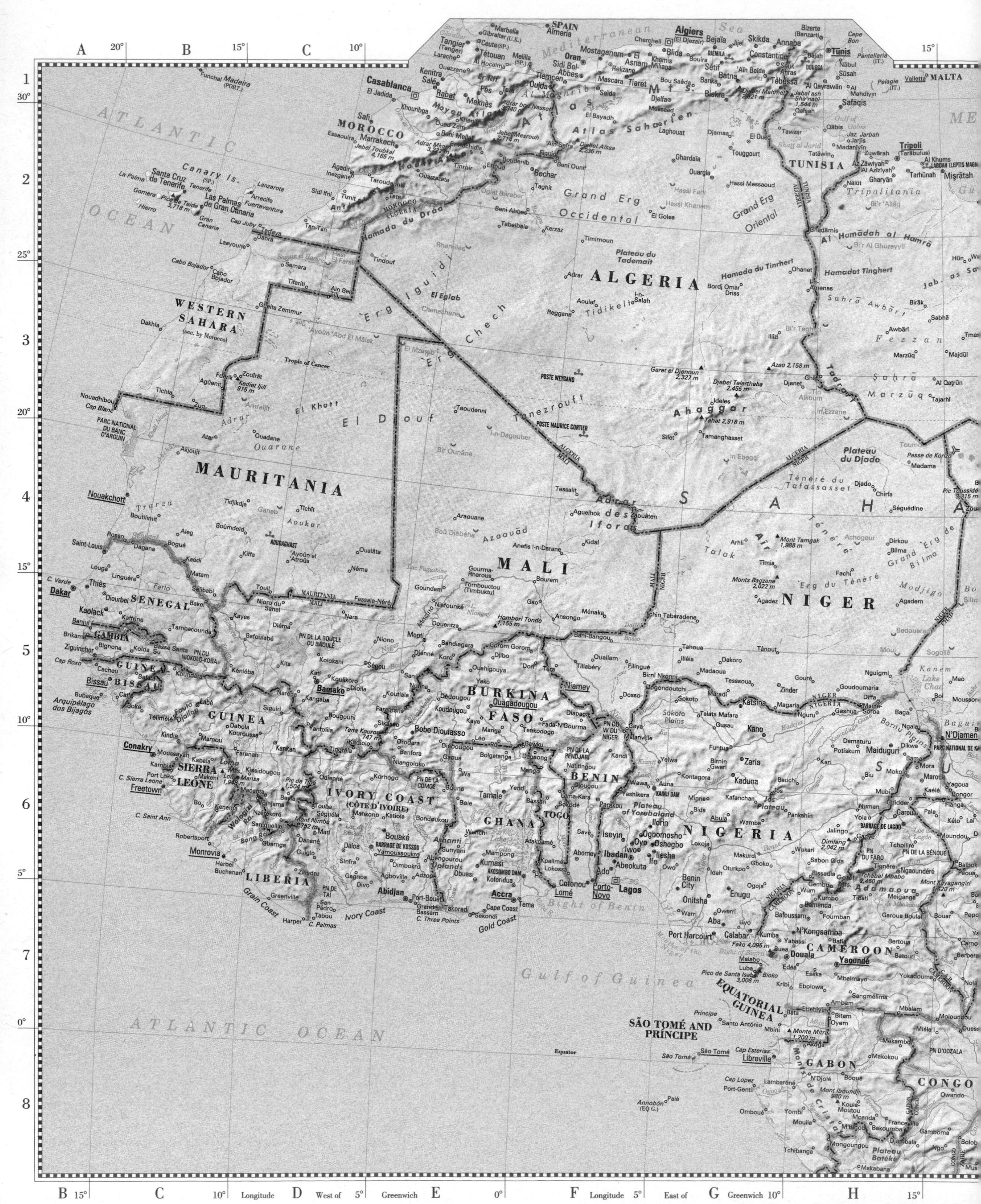

A
B
C
20°
15°
10°
15°
30°
25°
20°
15°
10°
5°
0°
1
2
3
4
5
6
7
8
ATLANTIC
OCEAN
ATLANTIC OCEAN
Mediterranean Sea
Gulf of Guinea
Bight of Benin
SPAIN
MALTA
MOROCCO
ALGERIA
TUNISIA
WESTERN SAHARA
(occ. by Morocco)
MAURITANIA
MALI
NIGER
SENEGAL
GAMBIA
GUINEA-BISSAU
GUINEA
SIERRA LEONE
LIBERIA
IVORY COAST
(CÔTE D'IVOIRE)
BURKINA FASO
GHANA
TOGO
BENIN
NIGERIA
CAMEROON
EQUATORIAL GUINEA
SÃO TOMÉ AND PRÍNCIPE
GABON
CONGO
Canary Is.
(SP.)
Madeira
(PORT.)
Atlas Saharien
Grand Erg Occidental
Grand Erg Oriental
Hamada du Drâa
Erg Iguidi
Erg Chech
El Djouf
Tanezrouft
Ahaggar
Adrar des Iforas
Tropic of Cancer
Equator
Casablanca
Rabat
Algiers
Tunis
Tripoli
Dakar
Banjul
Bissau
Conakry
Freetown
Monrovia
Bamako
Ouagadougou
Niamey
Accra
Lomé
Porto-Novo
Lagos
Abidjan
Yamoussoukro
Nouakchott
Yaoundé
Malabo
Libreville
São Tomé
Laayoune
Tombouctou
(Timbuktu)
Kano
Ibadan
B
15°
C
10°
Longitude
D
West of
5°
Greenwich
E
0°
F
Longitude
5°
East of
G
Greenwich
10°
H
15°

Northern Africa

POPULATION OF CITIES AND TOWNS

- OVER 2,000,000
- 1,000,000 - 1,999,999
- 500,000 - 999,999
- 100,000 - 499,999
- 50,000 - 99,999
- UNDER 50,000

SCALE 1:17,500,000 POLYCONIC PROJECTION

MILES 0 250 500 750

KILOMETERS 0 250 500 750

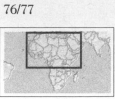

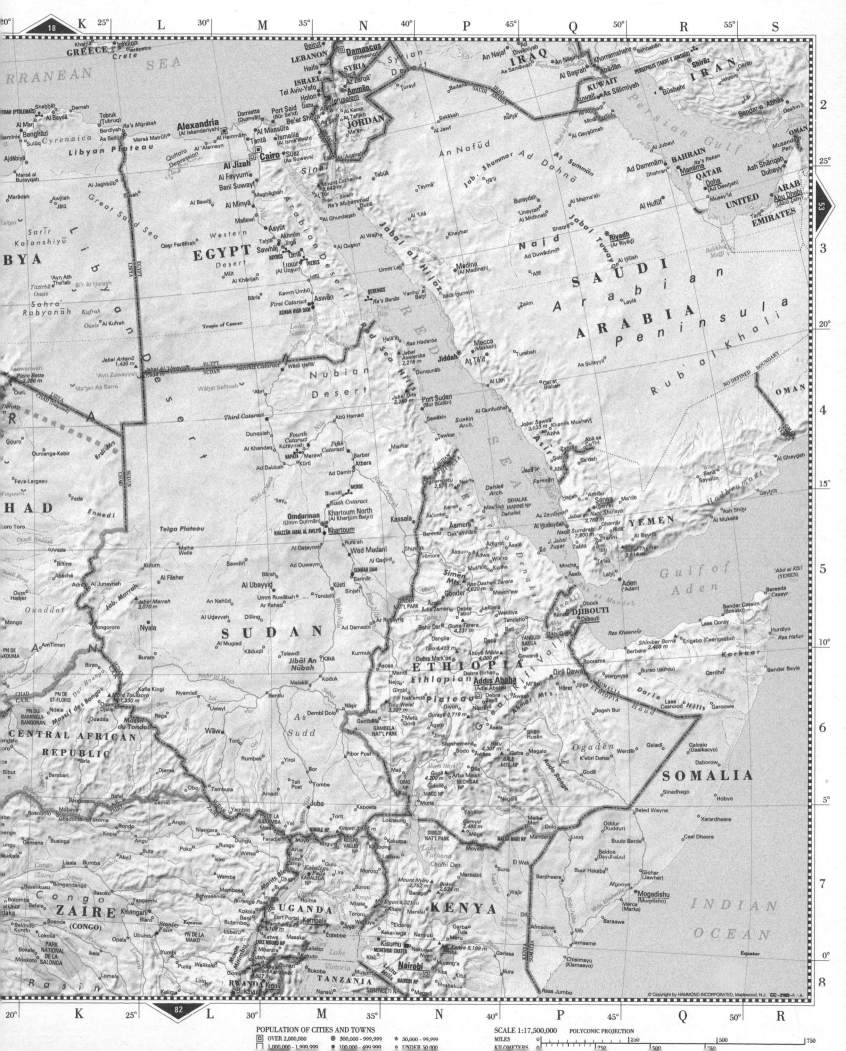

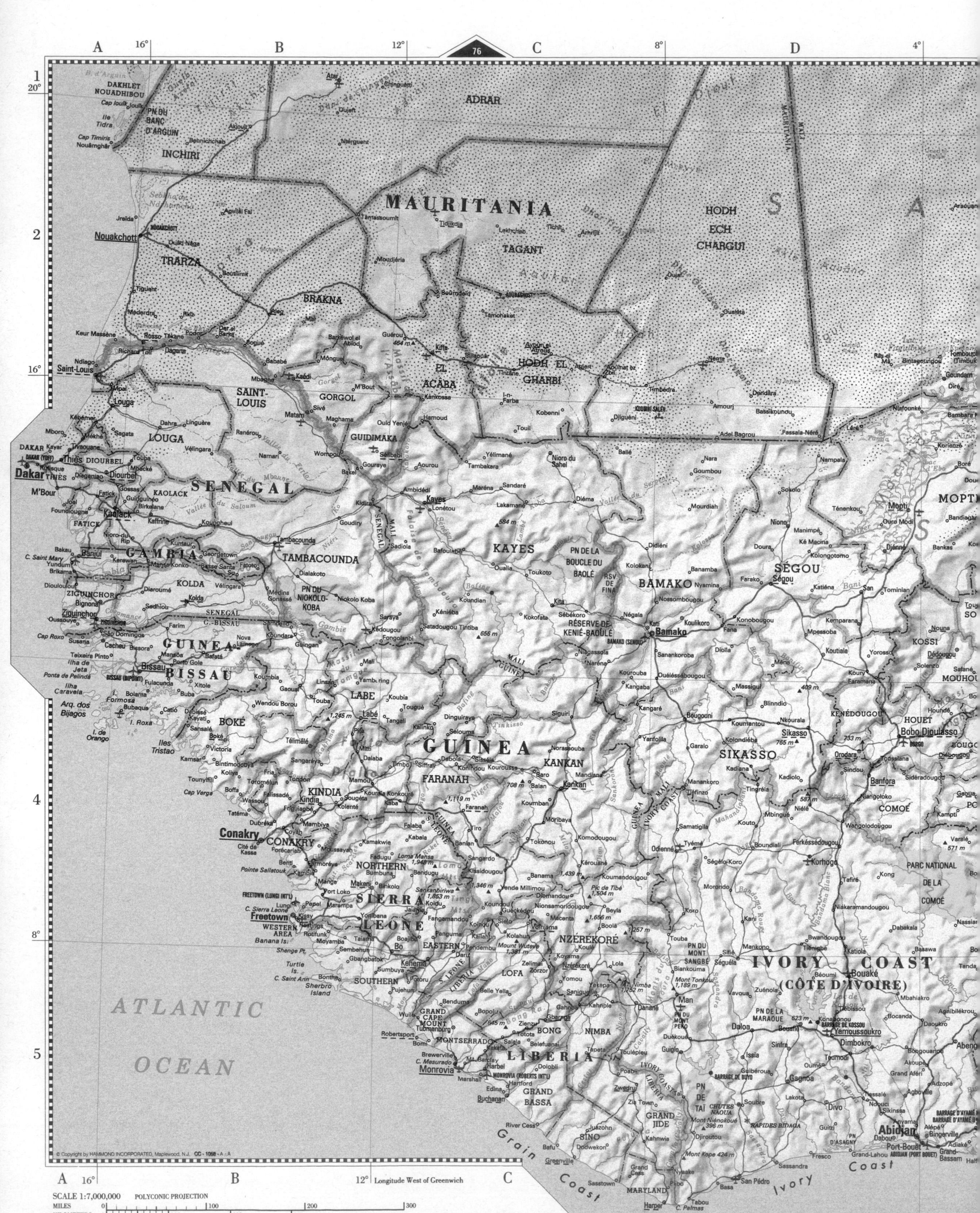

A
16°
B
12°
76
C
8°
D
4°
20°
16°
12°
8°
MAURITANIA
SENEGAL
GAMBIA
GUINEA-BISSAU
GUINEA
SIERRA LEONE
LIBERIA
IVORY COAST
(CÔTE D'IVOIRE)
ATLANTIC
OCEAN
Grain Coast
Ivory Coast
DAKHLET NOUADHIBOU
PN DU BANC D'ARGUIN
INCHIRI
ADRAR
TAGANT
HODH ECH CHARGUI
TRARZA
BRAKNA
GORGOL
GUIDIMAKA
HODH EL GHARBI
EL ACABA
SAINT-LOUIS
LOUGA
DIOURBEL
THIÈS
KAOLACK
FATICK
TAMBACOUNDA
KOLDA
ZIGUINCHOR
KAYES
PN DE LA BOUCLE DU BAOULÉ
BAMAKO
SÉGOU
SIKASSO
PN DU NIOKOLO-KOBA
BOKÉ
LABÉ
KINDIA
CONAKRY
FARANAH
KANKAN
NZÉRÉKORÉ
NORTHERN
EASTERN
SOUTHERN
WESTERN AREA
LOFA
BONG
NIMBA
GRAND CAPE MOUNT
MONTSERRADO
GRAND BASSA
GRAND JIDE
SINO
MARYLAND
PN DE TAÏ
PN DE LA MARAOUE
PN DU MONT SANGBÉ
KÉNÉDOUGOU
HOUET
COMOÉ
PARC NATIONAL DE LA COMOÉ
KOSSI
MOPTI
Nouakchott
Dakar
Banjul
Bissau
Conakry
Freetown
Monrovia
Bamako
Yamoussoukro
Abidjan
Saint-Louis
Thiès
Kaolack
Ziguinchor
Tambacounda
Kayes
Kankan
Labé
Kindia
Bo
Kenema
Buchanan
Robertsport
Man
Daloa
Bouaké
Korhogo
Ségou
Sikasso
Mopti
Bobo Dioulasso
Banfora
San Pédro
Harper
Atâr
Tidjikja
Kiffa
Néma
Kaédi
Rosso
Aleg
Boutilimit
Akjoujt
Nouâmghâr
Cap Timiris
Ile Tidra
Cap Vert
C. Saint Mary
Arq. dos Bijagos
Iles Tristao
Sherbro Island
C. Sierra Leone
C. Mesurado
C. Palmas
Mont Nimba 1,752 m
Loma Mansa 1,948 m
© Copyright by HAMMOND INCORPORATED, Maplewood, N.J.
Longitude West of Greenwich
SCALE 1:7,000,000
POLYCONIC PROJECTION
MILES
KILOMETERS
0
100
200
300

West Africa

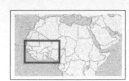

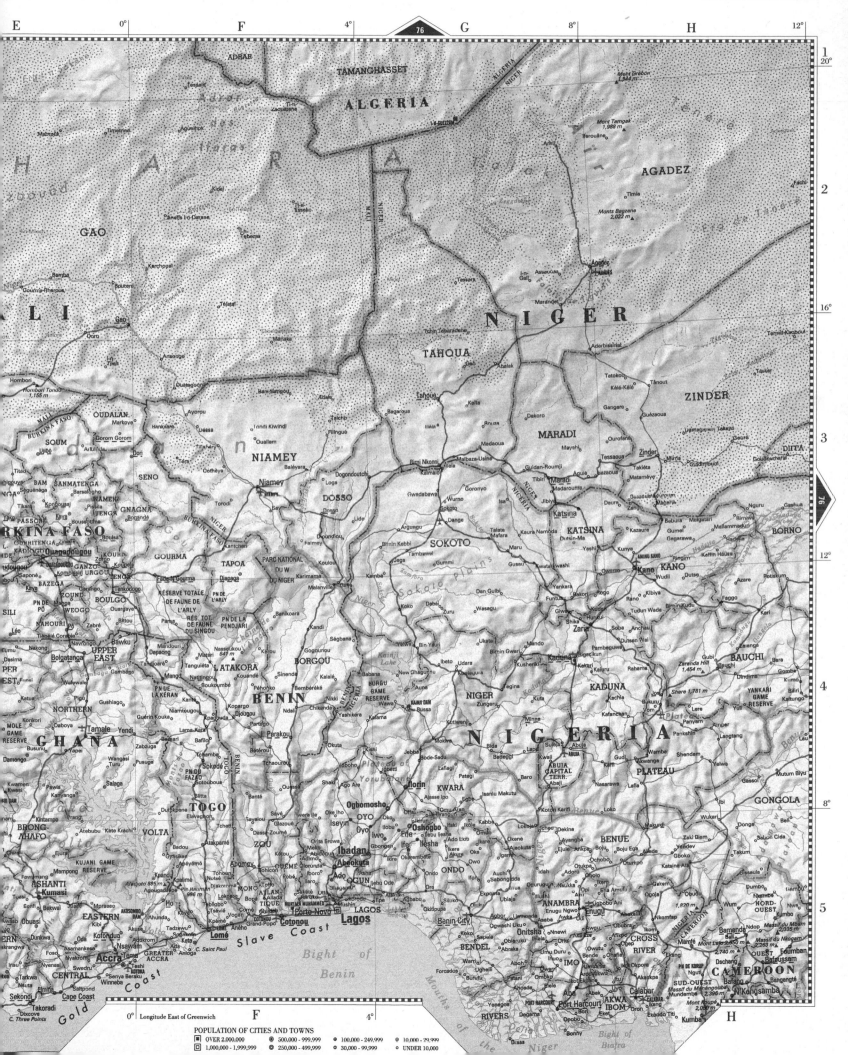

POPULATION OF CITIES AND TOWNS

■ OVER 2,000,000	● 500,000 - 999,999	● 100,000 - 249,999	● 10,000 - 29,999
□ 1,000,000 - 1,999,999	● 250,000 - 499,999	● 30,000 - 99,999	● UNDER 10,000

0° Longitude East of Greenwich

A 16° B 20° C 24° D 28°

24° 2 28° 3 32° 4

NAMIBIA

BOTSWANA

SOUTH AFRICA

CAPE PROVINCE

ORANGE FREE STATE

LESOTHO

BOPHUTHATSWANA

KGALAGADI

SOUTHERN

KWENENG

KGATLENG

TRANSKEI

CISKEI

ATLANTIC OCEAN

Kalahari Desert

GEMSBOK NATIONAL PARK

KALAHARI-GEMSBOK NP

MABUASEHUBE GAME RES.

NAMIB-NAUKLUFT PARK

Huib-Hoch Plateau

Namaqualand

Bushmanland

Great Karoo

Little Karoo

Orange

Gaborone

Mochudi

Molepolole

Kanye

Lobatse

Mafikeng

Mmabatho

Vryburg

Kimberley

Bloemfontein

Maseru

Welkom

Kroonstad

Klerksdorp

Potchefstroom

Johannesburg

Wes-Rand

Soweto

Pretoria

Germiston

Boksburg

Vereeniging

Upington

Keetmanshoop

Lüderitz

Kolmanskop

Mariental

Gibeon

Karasburg

Ariamsvlei

Nakop

Warmbad

Oranjemund

Alexander Bay

Port Nolloth

Springbok

Okiep

Kleinsee

Hondeklipbaai

Garies

Bitterfontein

Vanrhynsdorp

Vredendal

Calvinia

Nieuwoudtville

Williston

Carnarvon

Loxton

Fraserburg

Sutherland

Beaufort West

Victoria West

Richmond

Britstown

De Aar

Colesberg

Middelburg

Graaff-Reinet

Aberdeen

Cradock

Queenstown

East London

Grahamstown

Port Elizabeth

Uitenhage

Humansdorp

Jeffreys Bay

Knysna

George

Oudtshoorn

Mosselbaai

Riversdale

Heidelberg

Swellendam

Worcester

Paarl

Wellington

Stellenbosch

Cape Town

Bellville

Goodwood

Simonstown

Cape of Good Hope

C. Agulhas

Saldanha

Vredenburg

Clanwilliam

Citrusdal

Piketberg

Malmesbury

Dasseneiland

Lambert's Bay

St. Helena Bay

Table Bay

False Bay

Algoa Bay

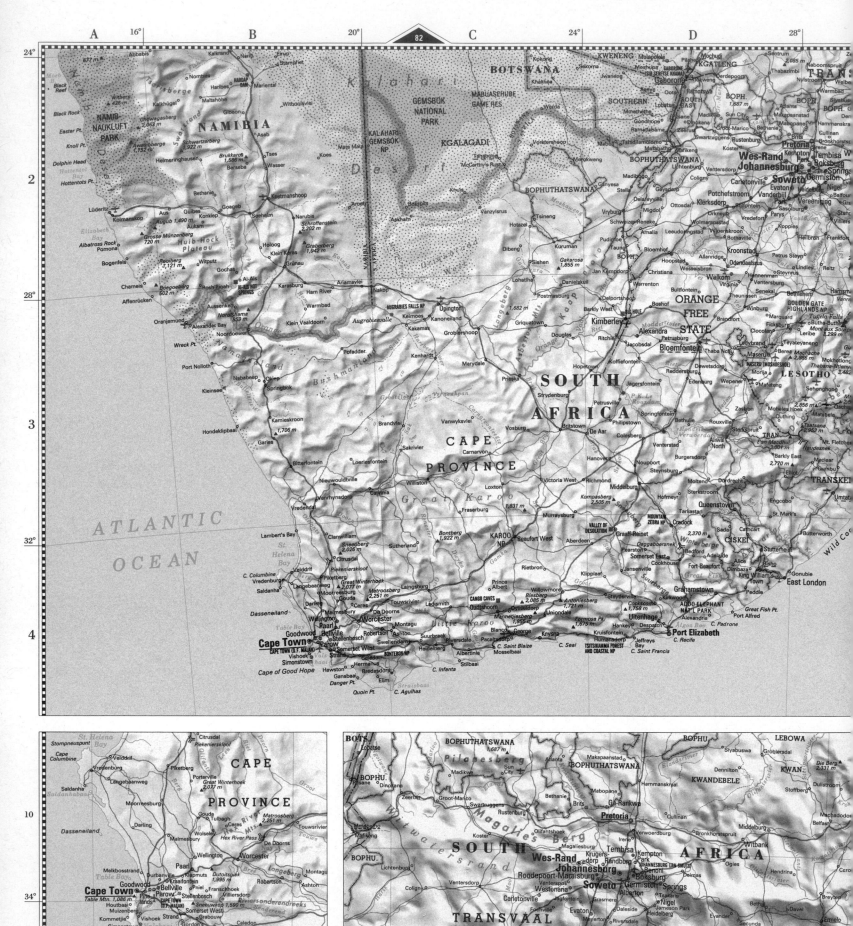

South Africa

POPULATION OF CITIES AND TOWNS

■ OVER 2,000,000	● 500,000 - 999,999	• 100,000 - 249,999	∘ 10,000 - 29,999
□ 1,000,000 - 1,999,999	○ 250,000 - 499,999	∘ 30,000 - 99,999	∘ UNDER 10,000

SCALE 1:7,000,000   LAMBERT CONFORMAL CONIC PROJECTION

MILES   0   100   200   300
KILOMETERS   0   100   200   300

© Copyright by HAMMOND INCORPORATED, Maplewood, N.J. CC-1065-A-A

© HAMMOND INC. CC-1140-A-A

© Copyright by HAMMOND INCORPORATED, Maplewood, N.J. CC-1143-A-A

82

Southern Africa

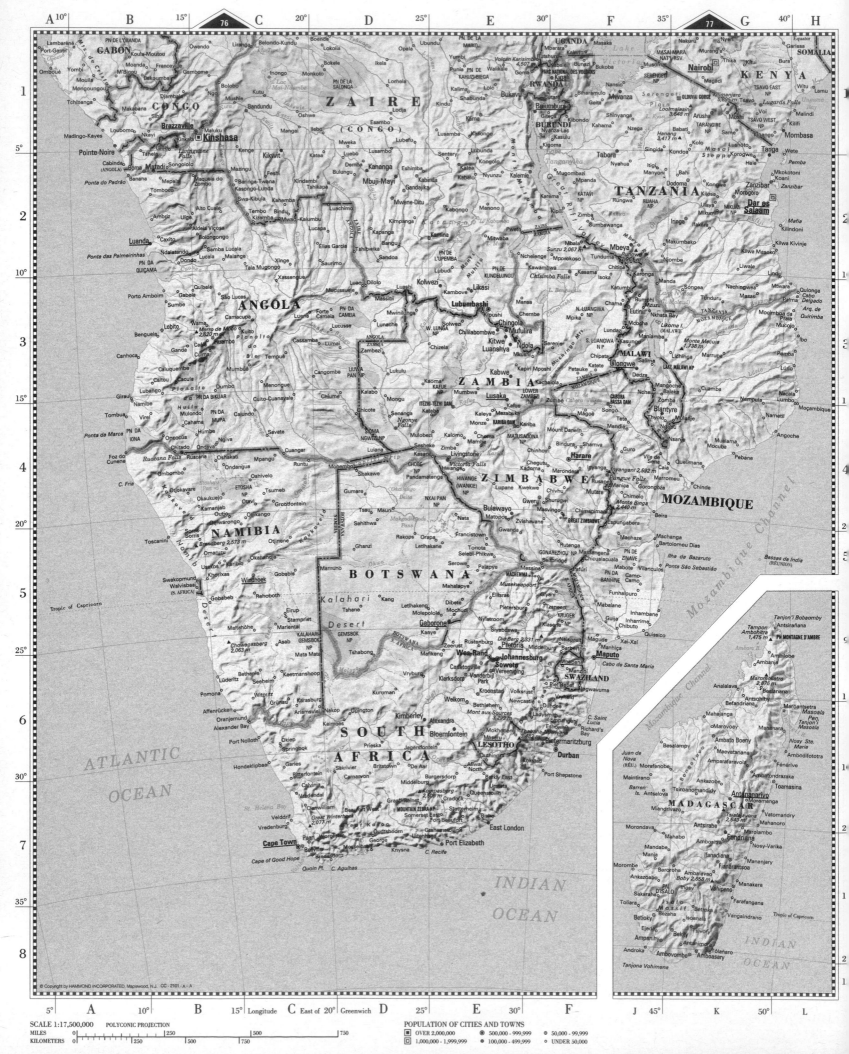

SCALE 1:17,500,000   POLYCONIC PROJECTION

POPULATION OF CITIES AND TOWNS

Antarctica

X 30° Y 15° Z 0° A 15° B 30° C

South Sandwich Is. (U.K.)
Bird I.
South Georgia (U.K.)
ATLANTIC OCEAN
Scotia Sea
Antarctic Circle
INDIAN OCEAN
South Orkney (U.K.) Is.
ORCADAS (ARG.)
SIGNY (U.K.)
Drake Passage
SANAE III (S. AFRICA)
GEORG VON NEUMAYER (GERMANY)
DAKSHIN GANGOTRI (INDIA)
NOVOLAZAREVSKAYA (RUSSIA)
Princess Astrid Coast
C. Norvegia
Riiser-Larsen Peninsula
Princess Martha Coast
New Schwabenland
Riiser-Larsen Ice Shelf
Princess Ragnhild Coast
Lützow-Holm Bay
SYOWA (JAPAN)
Queen Maud Land
Prince Harold Coast
Mt. Fukushima 2,360 m
MOLODEZHNAYA (RUSSIA)
Prince Olav Coast
Casey Bay
White I.
Amundsen Bay
C. Ann
South Shetland Is. (U.K.)
Elephant I.
BELLINGHAUSEN (RUSSIA)
Joinville I.
ARCTOWSKI (POLAND)
JUBANY (ARG.)
TTE. MARSH (CHILE)
ESPERANZA (ARG.)
VICECOMODORO MARAMBIO (ARG.)
GEN. B. O'HIGGINS (CHILE)
CAP. ARTURO PRAT (CHILE)
Weddell Sea
Lyddan I.
Caird Coast
MIZUHO (JAPAN)
3,212 m
2,532 m
PRIMAVERA (ARG.)
TENIENTE MATIENZO (ARG.)
Palmer Arch.
Antarctic
ALMIRANTE BROWN (ARG.)
PALMER (U.S.)
COMANDANTE FERRAZ (BRAZIL)
FARADAY (U.K.)
C. Alexander
Graham Land
HALLEY (U.K.)
NEW HALLEY (U.K.)
Coats Land
Luitpold Coast
3,498 m
3,318 m
2,311 m
C. Boothby
Edward VIII Bay
Enderby Land
Mawson Coast
MAWSON (AUSTL.)
Biscoe Is.
C. Agassiz
Hearst I.
Peninsula
Larsen Ice Shelf
GEN. BELGRANO II (ARG.)
GEN. BELGRANO III (ARG.)
80°
Mac. Robertson Land
Mt. Menzies 3,355 m
Adelaide I.
GEN. SAN MARTIN (ARG.)
ROTHERA (U.K.)
Kemp Pen.
FILCHNER (GERMANY)
Mt. Jackson 4,190 m
Palmer Land
Lassiter Coast
Smith Pen.
Filchner Ice Shelf
2,812 m
3,624 m
Fisher Glacier
Mt. Mecey 1,960 m
Marguerite Bay
Alexander I.
DRUZHNAYA II (RUSSIA)
694 m
C. Darnley
SOYUZ (RUSSIA)
Amery Ice Shelf
C. Vostok
Wilkins Sound
FOSSIL BLUFF (U.K.)
Orville Coast
Ronne Ice Shelf
SOBRAL (ARG.)
Lambert Glacier
Mackenzie Bay
Prydz Bay
Charcot I.
C. Byrd
Latady I.
Berlins Pt.
English Coast
Ronne Entr.
Dufek Massive
Pensacola Mts.
2,628 m
3,718 m
Ingrid Christiansen Coast
DAVIS (AUSTL.)
Spaatz I.
Smyley I.
2,190 m
POLE OF INACCESSABILITY
American Highland
Leopold and Astrid Coast
West Ice Shelf
Bryan Coast
SIPLE (U.S.)
South Polar Plateau
3,106 m
Bellingshausen Sea
Ellsworth Land
Vinson Massif 4,897 m
1,369 m
3,650 m
3,100 m
Wilhelm II Coast
SOUTH POLE
2,800 m
AMUNDSEN-SCOTT (U.S.)
3,832 m
Peter I Island (NORWAY)
Farwell I.
Eights Coast
Ellsworth Mts.
Transantarctic Mountains
90°
Davis Sea
Abbot Ice Shelf
1,745 m
3,269 m
MIRNYY (RUSSIA)
Queen Mary Coast
3,497 m
Walgreen Coast
Thurston I.
900 m
Marie Byrd Land
Pine I. Bay
2,801 m
2,896 m
VOSTOK (RUSSIA)
Masson I.
Denman Glacier
Shackleton Ice Shelf
C. Flying Fish
Burke I.
984 m
Horlick Ice Stream
Queen Maud Mts.
Beardmore Glacier
Blizzard Pk. 3,373 m
Mill I.
Bowman I.
Thwaites Iceberg Tongue
1,266 m
BYRD (U.S.)
Gould Coast
Mt. Kirkpatrick 4,528 m
2,593 m
Knox Coast
Martin Pen.
Rockefeller Plateau
1,245 m
Nimrod Glacier
Amundsen Sea
Bakutis Coast
Siple Coast
Shackleton Coast
2,407 m
2,854 m
DOME C (U.S.)
Vincennes Bay
Carney I.
Mt. Sidley 4,181 m
Ross Ice Shelf
Wilkes Land
2,192 m
CASEY (AUSTL.)
Budd Coast
Mt. Siple 3,100 m
Siple I.
C. Dart
Getz Ice Shelf
Sonders Coast
Byrd Glacier
Totten Glacier
C. Poinsett
Hobbs Coast
Roosevelt Island
Hillary Coast
RUSSKAYA (RUSSIA)
Edward VII Pen.
C. Colbeck
MCMURDO (U.S.)
VANDA (N.Z.)
2,479 m
Sabrina Coast
Moscow U. Ice Shelf
Sulzberger Ice Shelf
Sulzberger Bay
SCOTT (N.Z.)
C. Crozier
Ross I.
Mt. Erebus 3,794 m
Shapeless Mtn. 2,739 m
Franklin I.
Scott Coast
2,498 m
Banzare Coast
Frost Glacier
Voyeykov Ice Shelf
C. Goodenough
Ross Sea
Victoria Land
Mt. New Zealand 2,888 m
Porpoise Bay
2,220 m
Clarie Coast
Coulman I.
C. Hallett
Borchgrevink Coast
Ninnis Glacier
Mertz Glacier
Adélie Coast
Dibble Iceberg Tongue
LILLIE MARLEEN HÜTTE (GERMANY)
George V Coast
DUMONT D'URVILLE (FRANCE)
C. Adare
LENINGRADSKAYA (RUSSIA)
Mt. Blowaway 1,342 m
Cook Ice Shelf
C. Hudson
SOUTH MAGNETIC POLE
Balleny Is.
PACIFIC OCEAN
INDIAN OCEAN
60° 70° 45° 75° 105° 120° 135°
D E F G H J

Q Longitude West 150° of Greenwich P 165° N 180° M 165° L 150° Longitude East of Greenwich K

SCALE 1:28,000,000 POLAR STEREOGRAPHIC PROJECTION
MILES 0 300 600 900 1200
KILOMETERS 0 300 600 900 1200

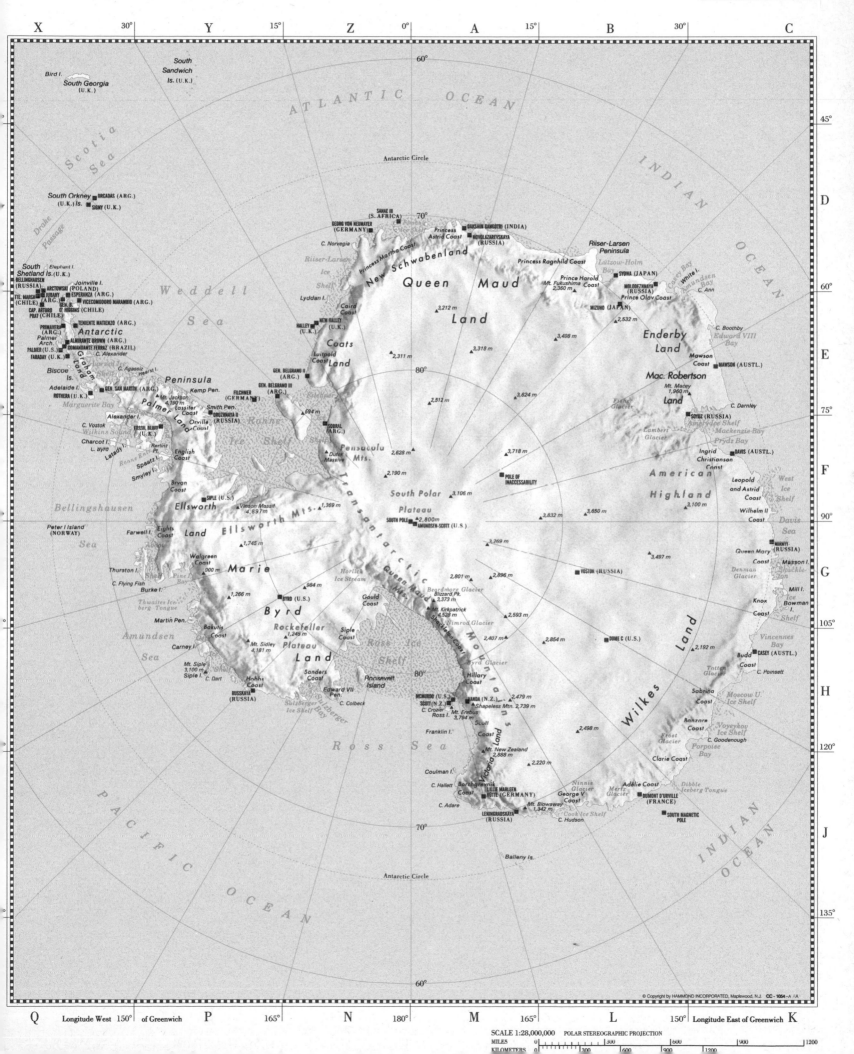

North America

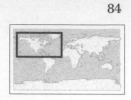

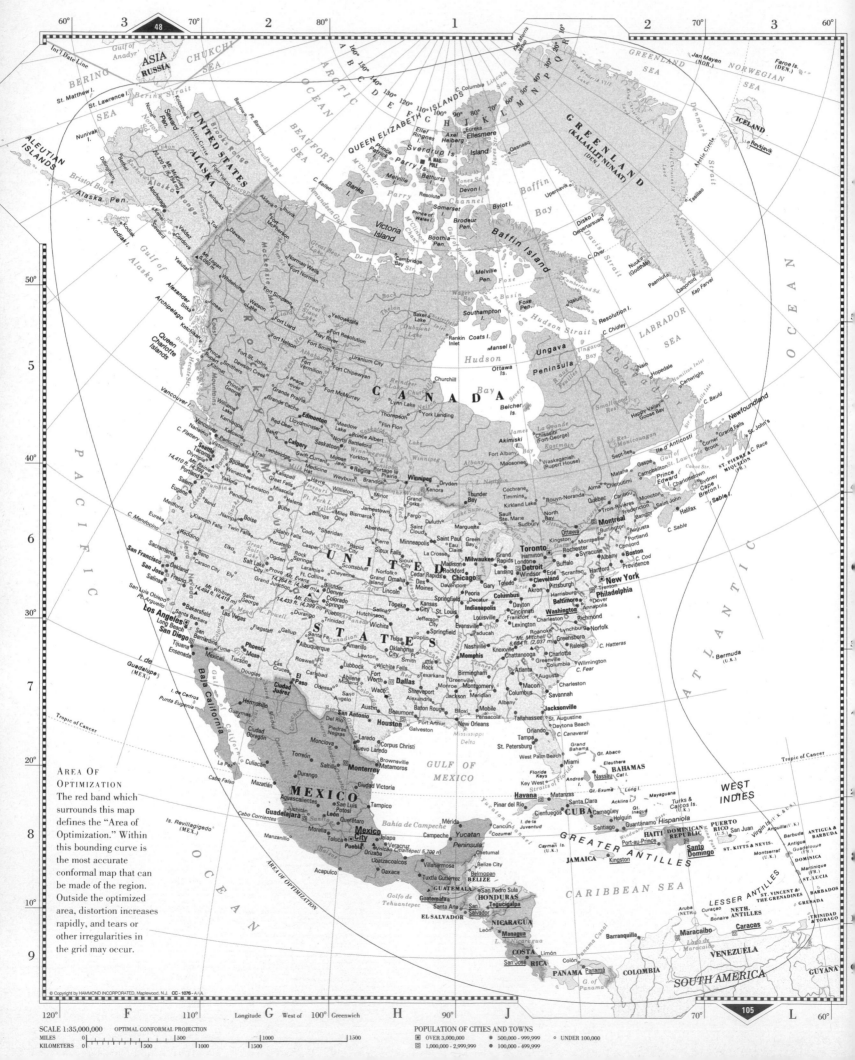

AREA OF OPTIMIZATION
The red band which surrounds this map defines the "Area of Optimization." Within this bounding curve is the most accurate conformal map that can be made of the region. Outside the optimized area, distortion increases rapidly, and tears or other irregularities in the grid may occur.

© Copyright by HAMMOND INCORPORATED, Maplewood, N.J.   CC-1076-A-IA

SCALE 1:35,000,000   OPTIMAL CONFORMAL PROJECTION

MILES   0   500   1000   1500
KILOMETERS   0   500   1000   1500

Longitude G West of 100° Greenwich

POPULATION OF CITIES AND TOWNS

■ OVER 3,000,000   ● 500,000 - 999,999   ○ UNDER 100,000
□ 1,000,000 - 2,999,999   ◐ 100,000 - 499,999

Alaska

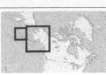
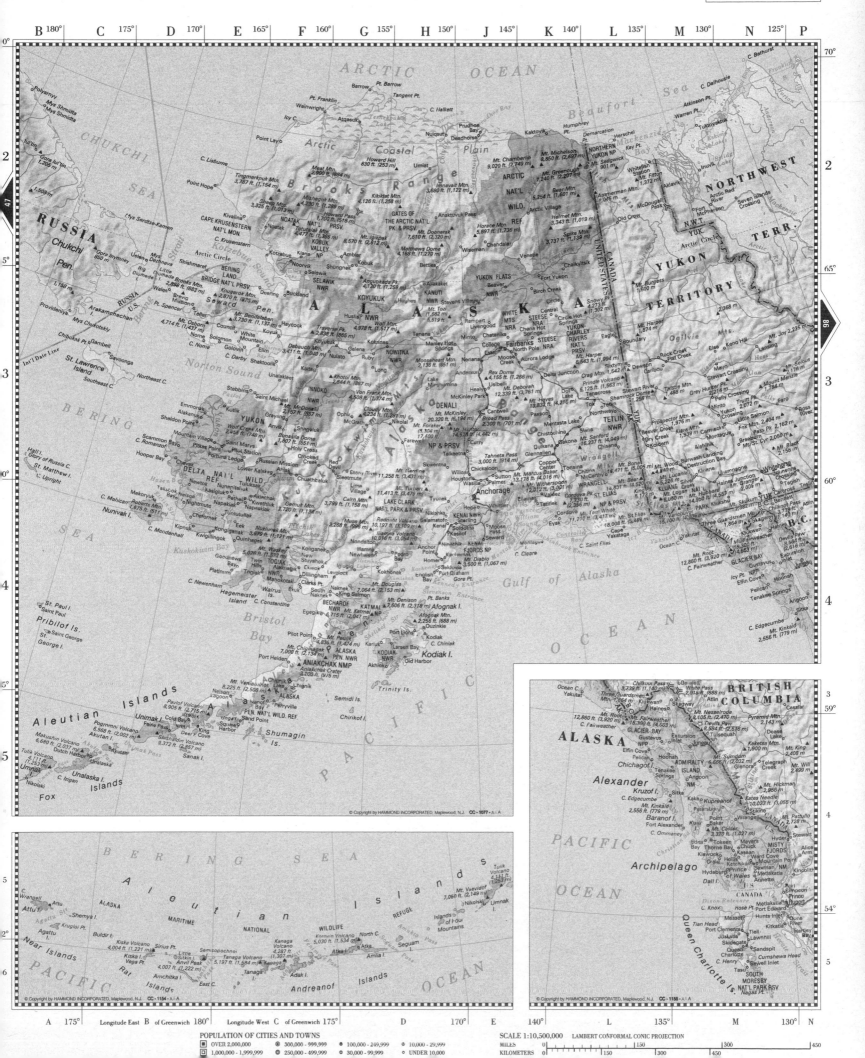

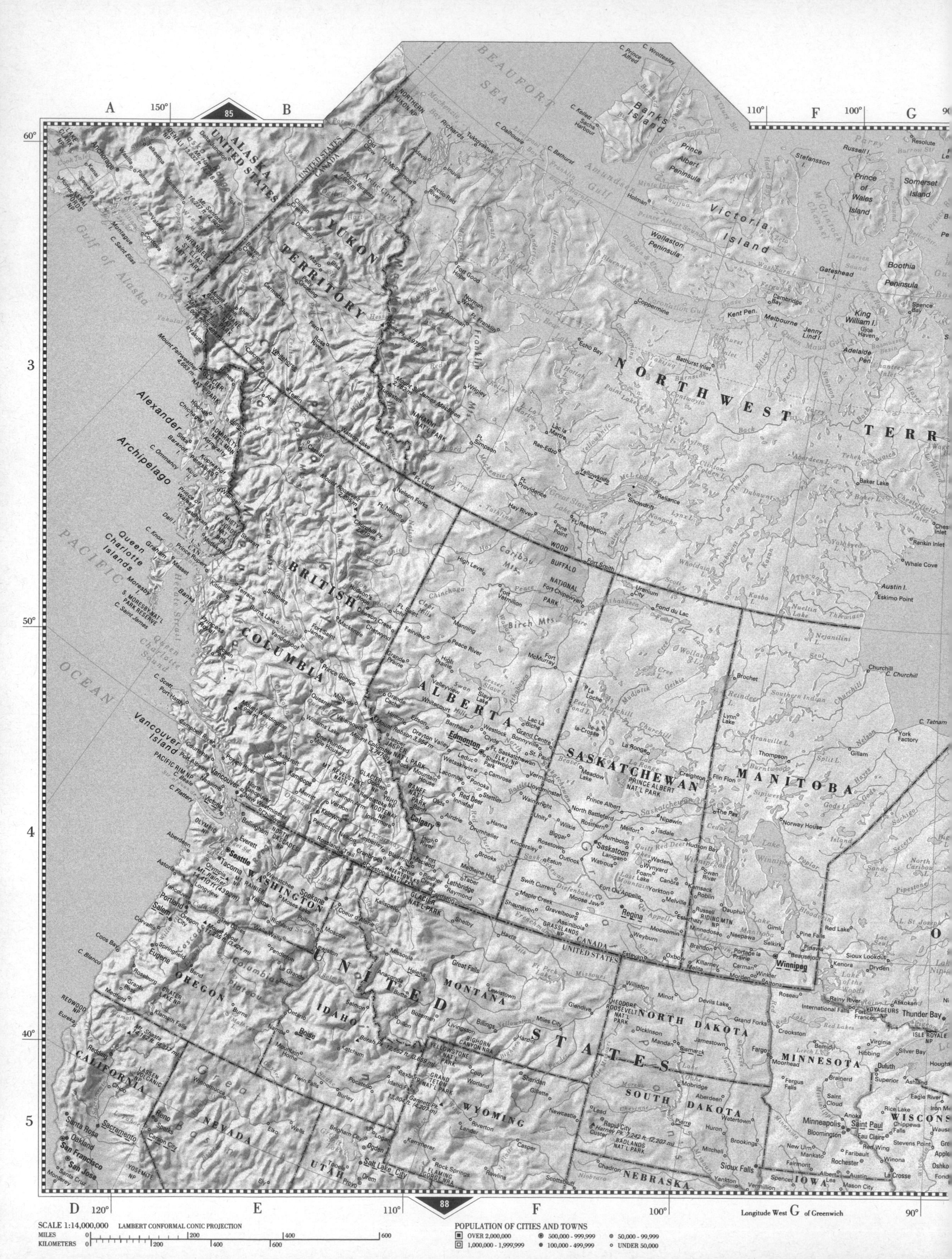

BEAUFORT SEA

C. Wrottesley
C. Prince Alfred
Sachs Harbour

Banks Island

Prince Albert Peninsula

Russell I.
Stefansson

Resolute

Somerset Island

UNITED STATES

Anchorage

Victoria Island

Prince of Wales Island

Boothia Peninsula

YUKON

TERRITORY

ARCTIC CIRCLE

Holman

Cambridge Bay

Melbourne I.

King William I.

Gjoa Haven

Gateshead

Adelaide Pen.

N O R T H W E S T

Coppermine

Kent Pen.

Echo Bay

Bathurst Inlet

UNITED STATES
CANADA

Ft. Norman

Ft. Franklin

Great Bear Lake

Reliance

Baker Lake

T E R R.

Wrigley

Rae-Edzo

Yellowknife

Snowdrift

Dubawnt L.

B R I T I S H

Ft. Simpson

Ft. Providence

Hay River

Ft. Resolution

Pine Point

WOOD

BUFFALO

Fort Smith

Austin I.

Eskimo Point

NAHANNI NAT'L PARK

Ft. Liard

Ft. Nelson

High Level

Caribou Mts.

NATIONAL

Nejanilini Lake

Whale Cove

Churchill

C. Churchill

A L E X A N D E R

Alexander Archipelago

Queen Charlotte Islands

Fort Vermilion

PARK

Fort Chipewyan

Uranium City

Fond du Lac

Churchill

PACIFIC

OCEAN

C O L U M B I A

Prince Rupert

Peace River

Manning

Fairview

Peace River

High Prairie

Grande Prairie

Valleyview

A L B E R T A

Whitecourt

Lac La Biche

La Loche

La Ronge

Brochet

Lynn Lake

Reindeer L.

Southern Indian L.

Vancouver Island

Terrace

Williams Lake

Quesnel

Prince George

Edson

Edmonton

Leduc

Camrose

St. Paul

Ft. Saskatchewan

Sherwood Park

Vermilion

Lloydminster

Meadow Lake

S A S K A T C H E W A N

Prince Albert

PRINCE ALBERT NAT'L PARK

Creighton

Flin Flon

M A N I T O B A

Thompson

Gillam

York Factory

C. Tatnam

JASPER NAT'L PARK

Red Deer

Innisfail

Wainwright

North Battleford

Nipawin

Tisdale

The Pas

BANFF NAT'L PARK

Calgary

Airdrie

Olds

Hanna

Drumheller

Kindersley

Biggar

Rosetown

Saskatoon

Humboldt

Wadena

Yorkton

Swan River

Dauphin

Norway House

KOOTENAY NAT'L PARK

Kamloops

Kelowna

Penticton

Cranbrook

Lethbridge

Medicine Hat

Brooks

Outlook

Lanigan

Canora

Kamsack

Roblin

Russell

Neepawa

Gods L.

Vancouver

New Westminster

Victoria

GLACIER NAT'L PARK

Swift Current

Maple Creek

Moose Jaw

Assiniboia

Gravelbourg

Regina

Qu'Appelle

Melville

Minnedosa

Brandon

Portage la Prairie

Winnipeg

Pine Falls

Kenora

Sioux Lookout

OLYMPIC NAT'L PARK

Seattle

Tacoma

Bellingham

Everett

WASHINGTON

Spokane

Shaunavon

GRASSLANDS NP

Weyburn

Estevan

Oxbow

Melita

Carman

Winkler

Morden

Roseau

Dryden

Lake of the Woods

Thunder Bay

ISLE ROYALE NP

Aberdeen

Olympia

MT. RAINIER

Yakima

Coeur d'Alene

Pullman

Moscow

CANADA
UNITED STATES

Estevan

Williston

Minot

Devils Lake

Grand Forks

International Falls

VOYAGEURS NAT'L PARK

Portland

Salem

Corvallis

OREGON

Bend

Pendleton

La Grande

Baker

Missoula

Helena

Great Falls

N O R T H   D A K O T A

Dickinson

Bismarck

Jamestown

Fargo

Crookston

Bemidji

M I N N E S O T A

Duluth

Superior

Ashland

Eugene

Springfield

Roseburg

Grants Pass

Medford

CRATER LAKE NP

Klamath Falls

REDWOOD NP

Eureka

Redding

LASSEN VOLCANIC NP

U N I T E D

M O N T A N A

Butte

Bozeman

Billings

BIGHORN CANYON NRA

Livingston

Miles City

Glendive

Newcastle

Lead

Rapid City

Mobridge

Aberdeen

Pierre

Huron

Watertown

Brookings

S O U T H   D A K O T A

Mitchell

Sioux Falls

Fergus Falls

Saint Cloud

Anoka

Minneapolis

Saint Paul

Eau Claire

W I S C O N

Chippewa Falls

Red Wing

I D A H O

S T A T E S

Salmon

W Y O M I N G

Sheridan

Gillette

Casper

New Ulm

Mankato

Faribault

Rochester

Winona

La Crosse

Santa Rosa

Oakland

San Francisco

San Jose

Santa Cruz

Monterey

C A L I F O R N I A

Sacramento

Reno

Sparks

Carson City

N E V A D A

YOSEMITE NP

Elko

Twin Falls

Pocatello

GRAND TETON NAT'L PARK

YELLOWSTONE NAT'L PARK

Riverton

Rawlins

Rock Springs

FLAMING GORGE NRA

BADLANDS NAT'L PARK

Chadron

N E B R A S K A

Scottsbluff

Spencer

Yankton

Vermillion

Sioux City

I O W A

Mason City

Salt Lake City

Provo

Ogden

Tooele

Brigham City

Ferron

Price

UTAH

SCALE 1:14,000,000   LAMBERT CONFORMAL CONIC PROJECTION

MILES 0   200   400   600

KILOMETERS 0   200   400   600

POPULATION OF CITIES AND TOWNS

■ OVER 2,000,000   ● 500,000 - 999,999   ● 50,000 - 99,999

□ 1,000,000 - 1,999,999   ● 100,000 - 499,999   ○ UNDER 50,000

Canada

H 80° J 70° K 60° L 50°

140° Q 120° R 100° S 80° T 60°

Map continued at right

ARCTIC OCEAN

Queen Elizabeth Islands

Sverdrup Islands

Parry Islands

Ellesmere Island

Axel Heiberg Island

Melville Island

Banks Island

Devon Island

NORTH MAGNETIC POLE

GREENLAND (KALAALLIT NUNAAT)

Viscount Melville Sd.

Map continued at left

Baffin Bay

Davis Strait

Baffin Island

GREENLAND (KALAALLIT NUNAAT) (DEN.)

AUYUITTUQ NATIONAL PARK

Arctic Circle

Cumberland Peninsula

Foxe Basin

Foxe Pen.

Southampton Island

Hudson Strait

Ungava Peninsula

Ungava Bay

Hudson Bay

LABRADOR SEA

NEWFOUNDLAND

Labrador

Smallwood Res.

QUÉBEC

James Bay

Gulf of St. Lawrence

Île d' Anticosti

Newfoundland

ST. PIERRE & MIQUELON (FR.)

Cabot Strait

PRINCE EDWARD ISLAND

NEW BRUNSWICK

NOVA SCOTIA

MAINE

VT. N.H.

NEW YORK

MASS.

Gulf of Maine

ATLANTIC OCEAN

Montréal

Ottawa

Québec

Toronto

Boston

Halifax

St. John's

Detroit

Cleveland

MICHIGAN

Lake Huron

Lake Ontario

6 7 80° 50° 4 40° 5

H J 70° K 60° L

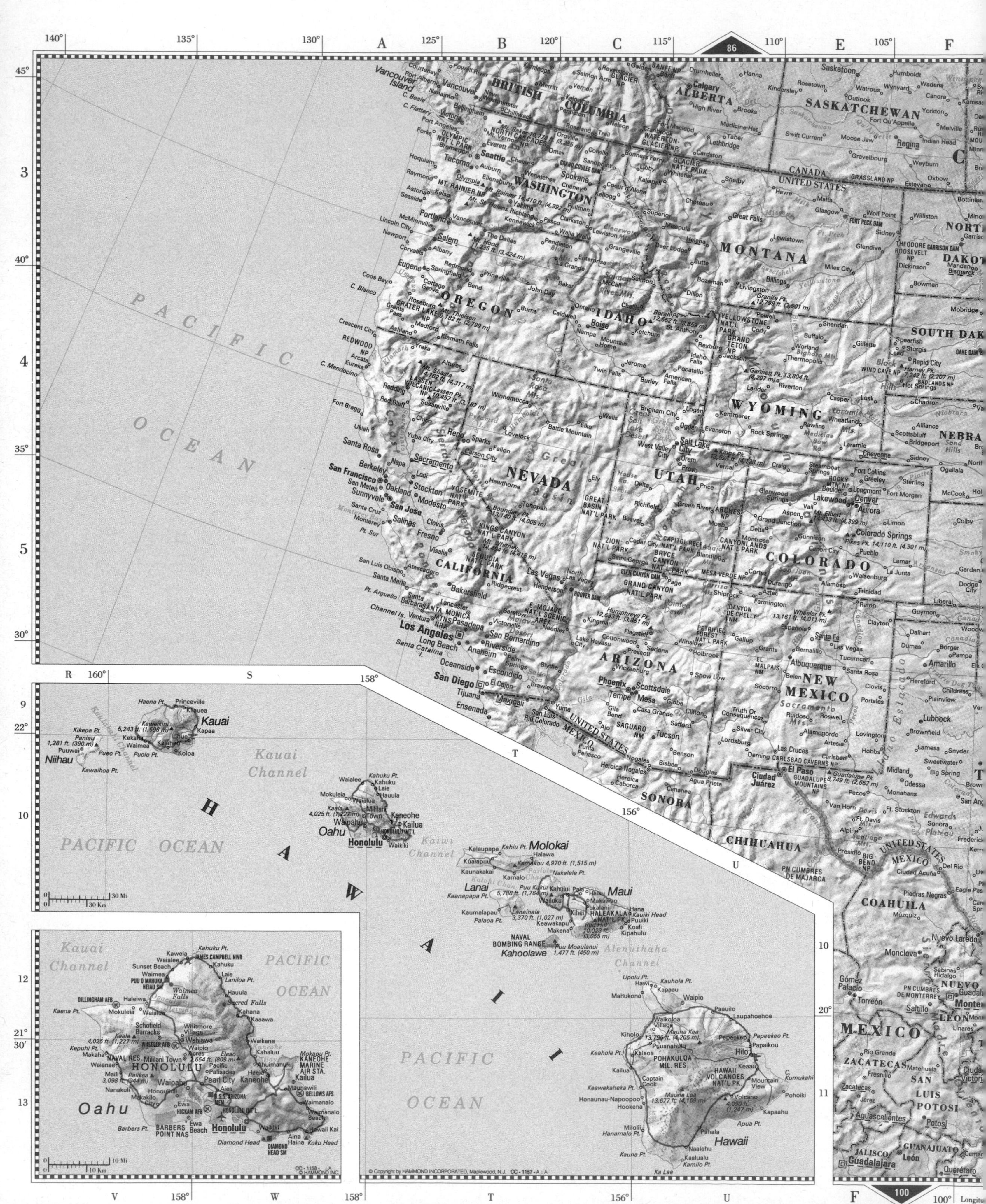

140°
135°
130°
A
125°
B
120°
C
115°
86
110°
E
105°
F
45°
3
40°
4
35°
5
30°
PACIFIC OCEAN
Vancouver Island
BRITISH COLUMBIA
ALBERTA
SASKATCHEWAN
Calgary
Regina
Saskatoon
Vancouver
Victoria
Seattle
Tacoma
Olympia
Spokane
WASHINGTON
Mt. Rainier 14,410 ft. (4,392 m)
OLYMPIC NAT'L PARK
NORTH CASCADES NP
CANADA
UNITED STATES
MONTANA
Great Falls
Helena
Missoula
Butte
Billings
Bozeman
Portland
Salem
Eugene
Medford
OREGON
CRATER LAKE NP
IDAHO
Boise
Pocatello
Idaho Falls
YELLOWSTONE NAT'L PARK
GRAND TETON NP
WYOMING
Casper
Cheyenne
Laramie
Rock Springs
NORTH DAKOTA
SOUTH DAKOTA
Rapid City
NEBRASKA
REDWOOD NP
Redding
Mt. Shasta
LASSEN VOLCANIC NP
Reno
Carson City
Sacramento
Santa Rosa
San Francisco
Oakland
San Jose
Stockton
Modesto
Fresno
YOSEMITE NAT'L PARK
KINGS CANYON NAT'L PARK
SEQUOIA NAT'L PARK
CALIFORNIA
Bakersfield
Santa Barbara
Los Angeles
Long Beach
Anaheim
Riverside
San Bernardino
San Diego
Tijuana
Ensenada
Mexicali
NEVADA
Las Vegas
Henderson
HOOVER DAM
GREAT BASIN NAT'L PARK
UTAH
Salt Lake City
Ogden
Provo
ZION NAT'L PARK
BRYCE CANYON NAT'L PARK
CAPITOL REEF NAT'L PARK
CANYONLANDS NAT'L PARK
ARCHES NP
COLORADO
Denver
Boulder
Colorado Springs
Pueblo
Grand Junction
Pikes Pk. 14,110 ft. (4,301 m)
ARIZONA
Phoenix
Scottsdale
Tempe
Mesa
Tucson
Flagstaff
GRAND CANYON NAT'L PARK
PETRIFIED FOREST NAT'L PARK
NEW MEXICO
Albuquerque
Santa Fe
Las Cruces
Roswell
CARLSBAD CAVERNS NP
El Paso
Ciudad Juárez
Amarillo
Lubbock
Midland
Odessa
SONORA
CHIHUAHUA
COAHUILA
NUEVO LEON
MEXICO
ZACATECAS
SAN LUIS POTOSI
JALISCO
GUANAJUATO
Guadalajara
León
Querétaro
Torreón
Monterrey
Saltillo
UNITED STATES
MEXICO
R
160°
S
158°
T
156°
U
9
22°
10
20°
11
HAWAII
Kauai
Niihau
Kauai Channel
Oahu
Honolulu
Molokai
Lanai
Maui
Kahoolawe
Hawaii
Hilo
Kailua
Kaiwi Channel
Alenuihaha Channel
HALEAKALA NAT'L PK.
HAWAII VOLCANOES NAT'L PK.
Mauna Kea 13,796 ft. (4,205 m)
Mauna Loa 13,677 ft. (4,169 m)
12
21° 30′
13
Kauai Channel
PACIFIC OCEAN
Oahu
HONOLULU
Pearl City
Kaneohe
Waipahu
Diamond Head
Koko Head
Kaena Pt.
Kahuku Pt.
Barbers Pt.
© Copyright by HAMMOND INCORPORATED, Maplewood, N.J. CC-1157-A
V
158°
W
158°
T
156°
U
F
100
100°

United States

POPULATION OF CITIES AND TOWNS

■ OVER 2,000,000	● 500,000 - 999,999	○ 50,000 - 99,999
▢ 1,000,000 - 1,999,999	● 100,000 - 499,999	○ UNDER 50,000

SCALE 1:14,000,000   LAMBERT CONFORMAL CONIC PROJECTION

MILES

KILOMETERS

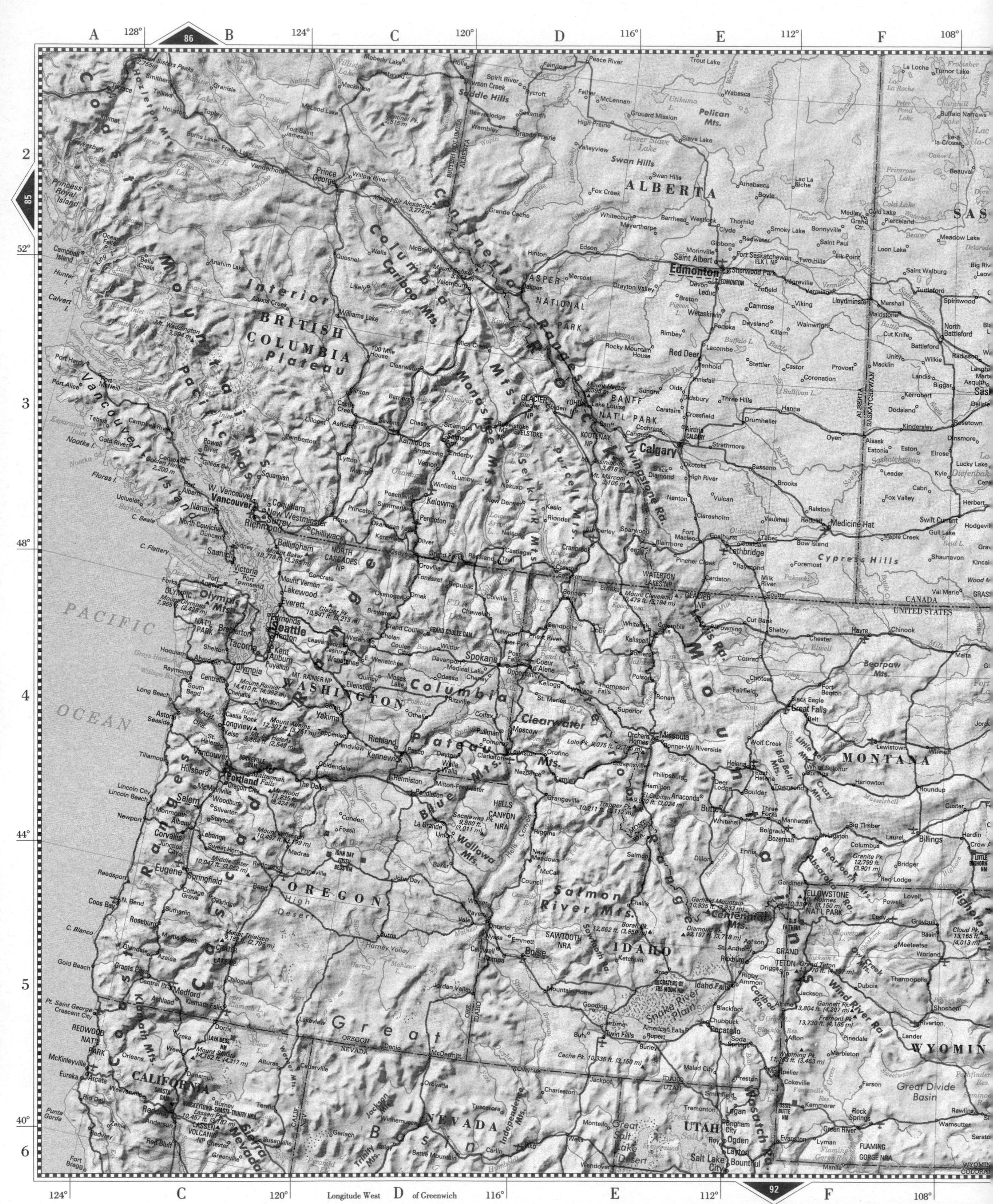

A
128°
86
B
124°
C
120°
D
116°
E
112°
F
108°
2
85
52°
3
48°
4
44°
5
40°
6
124°
C
120°
Longitude West
D
of Greenwich
116°
E
112°
92
F
108°
ALBERTA
Edmonton
Calgary
Lethbridge
Medicine Hat
Red Deer
BRITISH COLUMBIA
Interior Plateau
Prince George
Kamloops
Kelowna
Vancouver
Victoria
Vancouver Island
Coast Mountains
Columbia Mts.
Cariboo Mts.
Monashee Mts.
Selkirk Mts.
Purcell Mts.
JASPER NATIONAL PARK
BANFF NAT'L PARK
Lesser Slave Lake
Swan Hills
Pelican Mts.
Saddle Hills
Cypress Hills
CANADA
UNITED STATES
PACIFIC
OCEAN
WASHINGTON
Seattle
Tacoma
Olympia
Spokane
Yakima
Columbia Plateau
Olympic Mts.
OREGON
Portland
Salem
Eugene
Medford
Blue Mts.
Wallowa Mts.
High Desert
IDAHO
Boise
Pocatello
Idaho Falls
Clearwater Mts.
Salmon River Mts.
Sawtooth Ra.
Snake River Plain
MONTANA
Missoula
Helena
Butte
Great Falls
Billings
Bozeman
Bearpaw Mts.
Lewis Ra.
WYOMING
Great Divide Basin
Wind River Ra.
YELLOWSTONE NAT'L PARK
CALIFORNIA
Redding
Klamath Mts.
NEVADA
Great Basin
UTAH
Ogden
Salt Lake City
Great Salt Lake Desert
Wasatch Ra.
Cascade Range
Rocky Mountains

Southwestern Canada, Northwestern United States

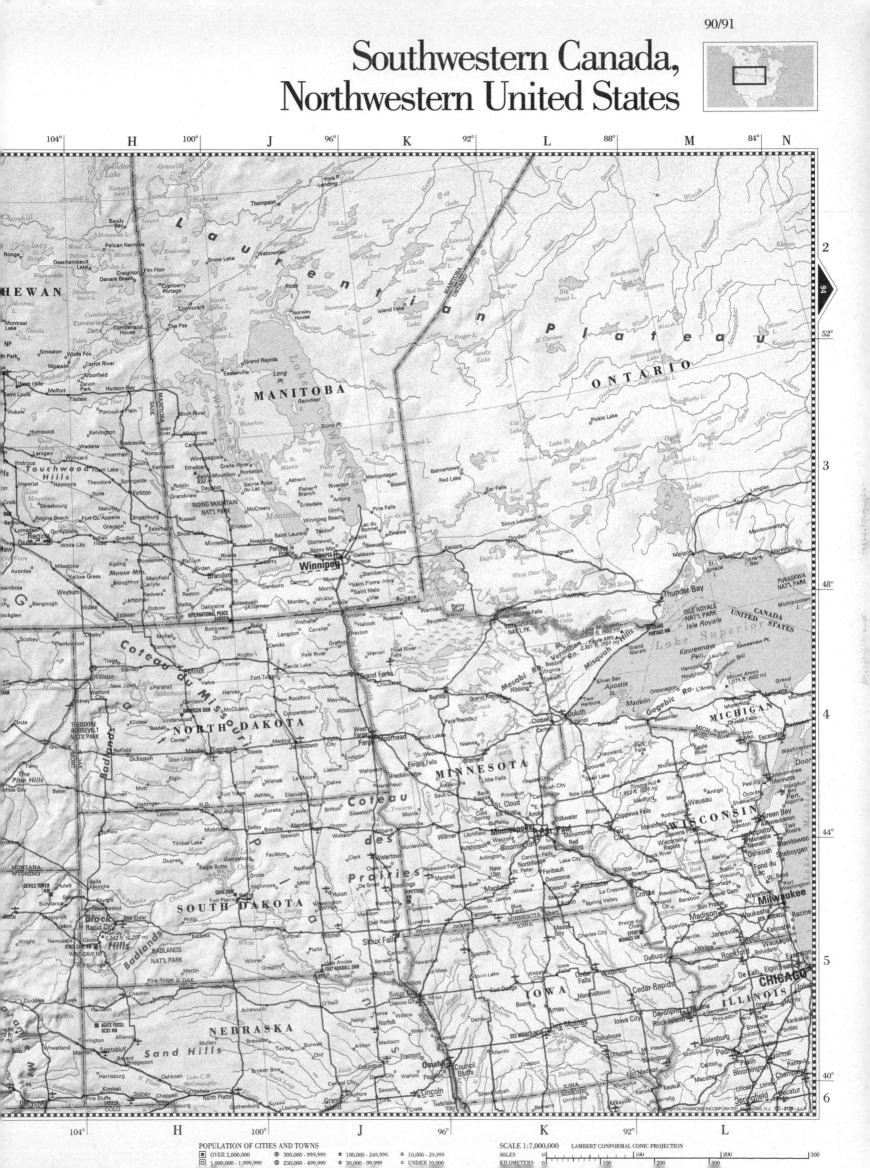

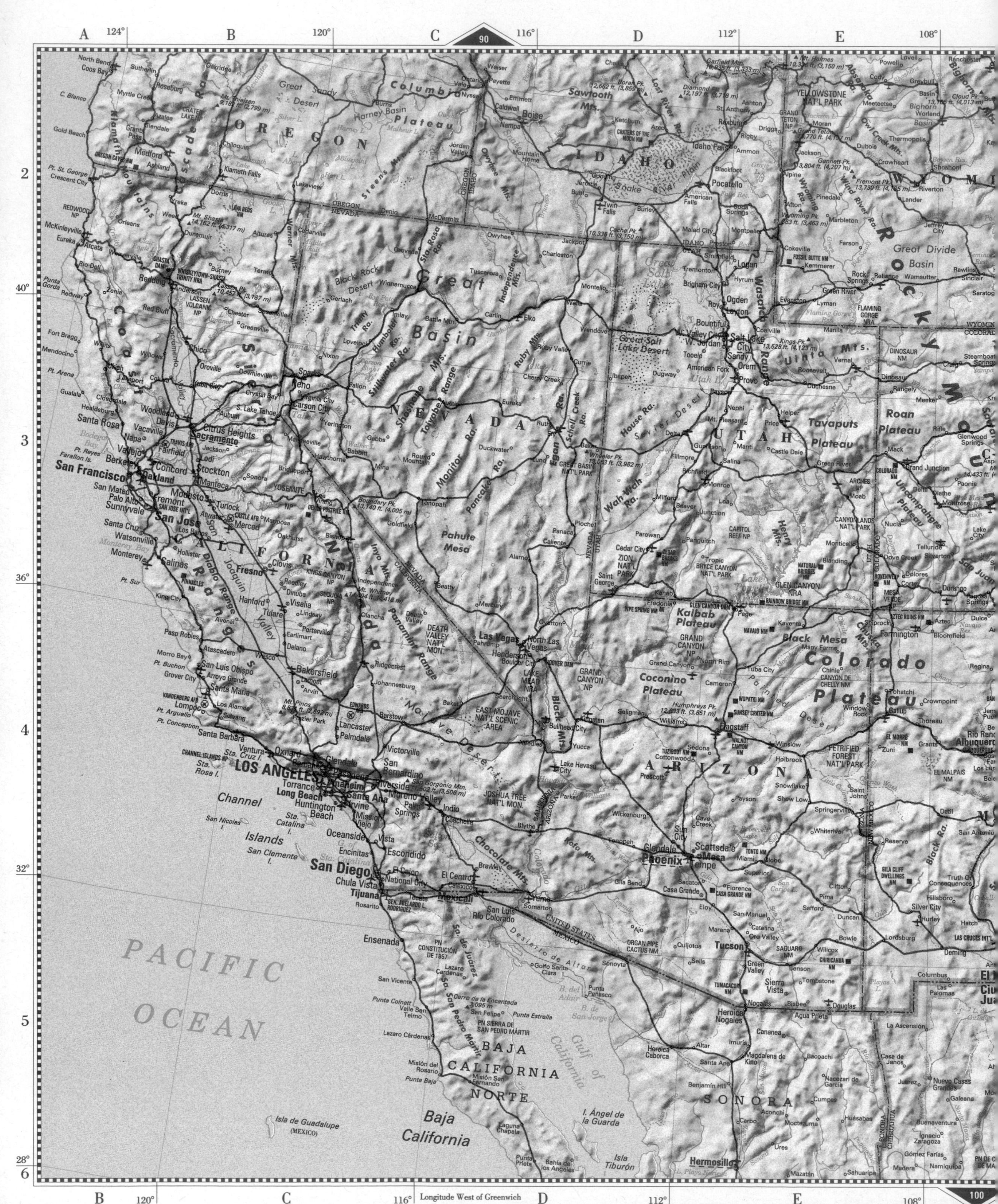

A
124°
B
120°
C
90
116°
D
112°
E
108°
2
3
4
5
6
40°
36°
32°
28°
OREGON
IDAHO
NEVADA
UTAH
CALIFORNIA
ARIZONA
WYOMI
BAJA CALIFORNIA NORTE
SONORA
PACIFIC OCEAN
Great Basin
Columbia Plateau
Harney Basin
Great Sandy Desert
Black Rock Desert
Snake River Plain
Sawtooth Mts.
Great Salt Lake Desert
Great Salt Lake
Sevier Desert
Wasatch Range
Uinta Mts.
Tavaputs Plateau
Roan Plateau
Great Divide Basin
Rocky Mountains
Colorado Plateau
Kaibab Plateau
Coconino Plateau
Painted Desert
Black Mesa
Mojave Desert
Sierra Nevada
Coast Ranges
Klamath Mountains
Cascade Range
Diablo Range
Joaquin Valley
Panamint Range
Pahute Mesa
Channel Islands
Gulf of California
Baja California
YELLOWSTONE NAT'L PARK
GRAND TETON NP
CRATERS OF THE MOON NM
CRATER LAKE NP
REDWOOD NP
LASSEN VOLCANIC NP
YOSEMITE NP
KINGS CANYON NP
SEQUOIA NP
DEATH VALLEY NAT'L MON.
EAST MOJAVE NAT'L SCENIC AREA
JOSHUA TREE NAT'L MON.
LAKE MEAD NRA
GRAND CANYON NP
ZION NAT'L PARK
BRYCE CANYON NAT'L PARK
CAPITOL REEF NP
CANYONLANDS NAT'L PARK
ARCHES NP
GLEN CANYON NRA
PETRIFIED FOREST NAT'L PARK
ORGAN PIPE CACTUS NM
GREAT BASIN NAT'L PARK
North Bend
Coos Bay
Medford
Ashland
Klamath Falls
Eureka
Arcata
Redding
Chico
Sacramento
Santa Rosa
San Francisco
Oakland
Stockton
Modesto
San Jose
Fresno
Monterey
Bakersfield
Santa Barbara
Lancaster
Palmdale
Victorville
San Bernardino
LOS ANGELES
Long Beach
Anaheim
Santa Ana
Riverside
Palm Springs
Oceanside
San Diego
Chula Vista
Tijuana
Mexicali
El Centro
Ensenada
Reno
Carson City
Las Vegas
Henderson
Boise
Nampa
Idaho Falls
Pocatello
Twin Falls
Logan
Ogden
Salt Lake City
Provo
Orem
Flagstaff
Phoenix
Scottsdale
Mesa
Tempe
Glendale
Tucson
Yuma
Nogales
Heroica Nogales
Hermosillo
Farmington
Gallup
Albuquerque
Isla de Guadalupe (MEXICO)
Longitude West of Greenwich
B
120°
C
116°
D
112°
E
108°
100

Southwestern United States

POPULATION OF CITIES AND TOWNS

- ▣ OVER 2,000,000
- ▢ 1,000,000 - 1,999,999
- ● 500,000 - 999,999
- ● 250,000 - 499,999
- ● 100,000 - 249,999
- ● 30,000 - 99,999
- ○ 10,000 - 29,999
- ○ UNDER 10,000

SCALE 1:7,000,000   LAMBERT CONFORMAL CONIC PROJECTION

MILES 0   100   200   300

KILOMETERS 0   100   200   300

© Copyright by HAMMOND INCORPORATED, Maplewood, N.J. CC-2110-A-A

Southeastern Canada, Northeastern United States

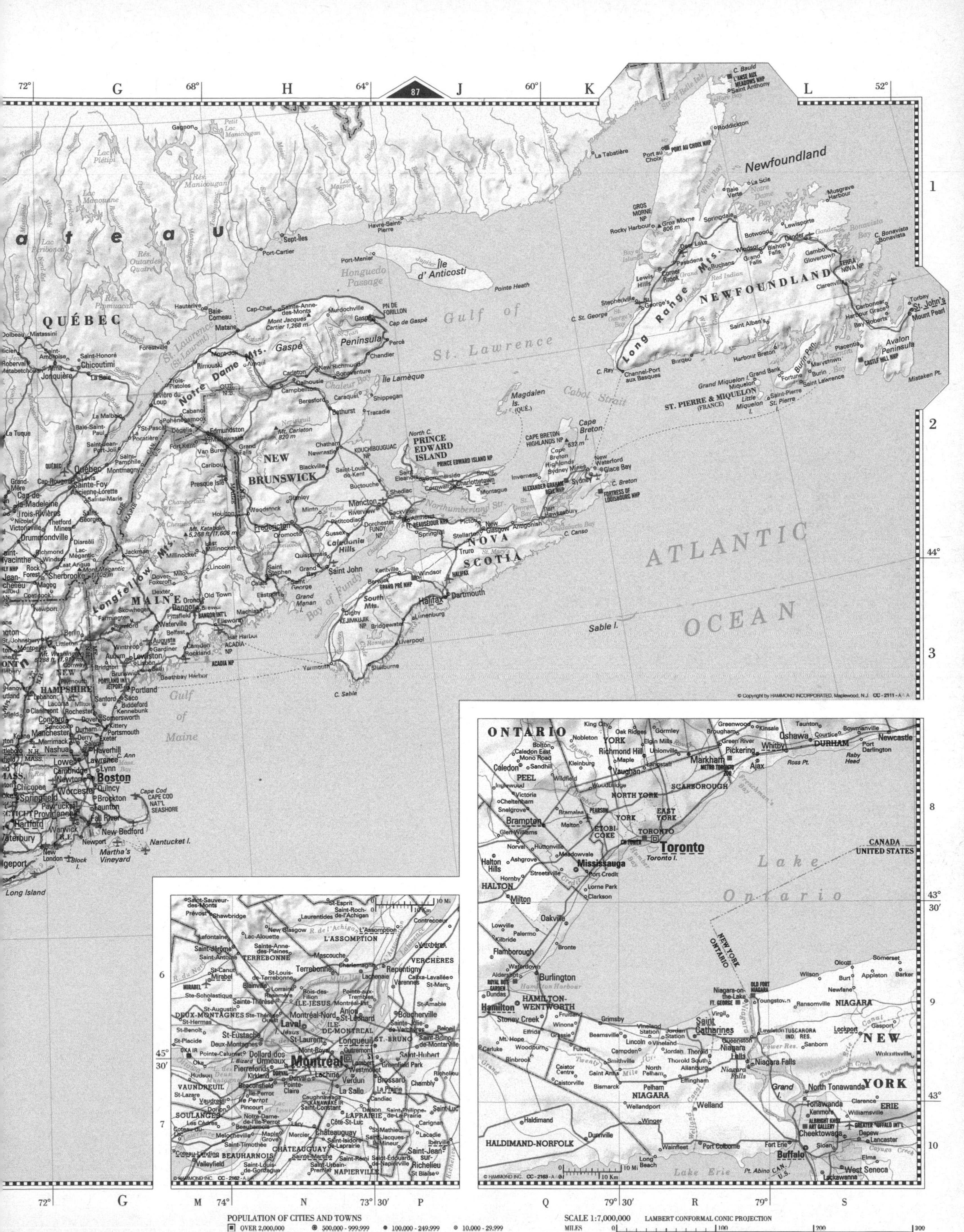

QUÉBEC

Newfoundland

NEWFOUNDLAND

Long Range Mts.

Gulf of St. Lawrence

Île d' Anticosti

Gaspé Peninsula

Notre Dame Mts.

NEW BRUNSWICK

PRINCE EDWARD ISLAND

NOVA SCOTIA

Cabot Strait

Magdalen Is. (QUÉ.)

ST. PIERRE & MIQUELON (FRANCE)

St. John's

Cape Breton

MAINE

NEW HAMPSHIRE

Longfellow Mts.

Bay of Fundy

Gulf of Maine

ATLANTIC OCEAN

Sable I.

MASS.

Boston

Cape Cod CAPE COD NAT'L SEASHORE

Nantucket I.

Martha's Vineyard

CONNECTICUT

R.I.

Long Island

Block I.

© Copyright by HAMMOND INCORPORATED, Maplewood, N.J. CC-2111-A·A

ONTARIO

YORK

PEEL

DURHAM

NORTH YORK

YORK

EAST YORK

METRO TORONTO

SCARBOROUGH

ETOBICOKE

TORONTO

Toronto

Brampton

Mississauga

HALTON

Milton

Toronto I.

Lake Ontario

CANADA
UNITED STATES

NEW YORK
ONTARIO

Oakville

Burlington

ROYAL BOT. GARDEN

Hamilton Harbour

HAMILTON-WENTWORTH

Hamilton

Stoney Creek

NIAGARA

Niagara-on-the-Lake

FT. GEORGE NHS

OLD FORT NIAGARA

Saint Catharines

NEW

Niagara Falls

Niagara Falls

YORK

ERIE

NIAGARA

HALDIMAND-NORFOLK

Buffalo

Lake Erie

© HAMMOND INC. CC-2163-A

ONTARIO

ILE-JESUS

Laval

ILE-DE-MONTREAL

Montreal

TERREBONNE

L'ASSOMPTION

VERCHÈRES

Longueuil

DEUX-MONTAGNES

VAUDREUIL

SOULANGES

BEAUHARNOIS

CHATEAUGUAY

LAPRAIRIE

NAPIERVILLE

© HAMMOND INC. CC-2162-A

A
108°
B
104°
C
93
100°
D
96°
E
2
3
4
5
6
36°
32°
28°
24°
92
100
104°
100°
Longitude West of Greenwich
96°
COLORADO
KANSAS
NEW MEXICO
OKLAHOMA
TEXAS
ARKANSAS
LOUISIANA
CHIHUAHUA
COAHUILA
NUEVO LEÓN
DURANGO
ZACATECAS
TAMULIPAS
MEXICO
Colorado Springs
Pueblo
Wichita
Kansas City
Topeka
Tulsa
Oklahoma City
Albuquerque
Santa Fe
Amarillo
Lubbock
El Paso
Ciudad Juárez
Fort Worth
Dallas
Arlington
Abilene
Odessa
Midland
San Angelo
Waco
Austin
San Antonio
Houston
Corpus Christi
Laredo
Nuevo Laredo
Shreveport
Chihuahua
Monterrey
Saltillo
Torreón
Gómez Palacio
Durango
Matamoros
Brownsville
Gulf Coastal Plain
Edwards Plateau
Llano Estacado
Cap Rock Escarpment
Great Plains
Ozark Plateau
Sierra Madre Oriental
Padre I.
Matagorda I.
Galveston I.

Southeastern United States

POPULATION OF CITIES AND TOWNS

- ■ OVER 2,000,000
- ◉ 500,000 - 999,999
- ● 100,000 - 249,999
- ○ 10,000 - 29,999
- ▣ 1,000,000 - 1,999,999
- ◎ 250,000 - 499,999
- ◦ 30,000 - 99,999
- · UNDER 10,000

SCALE 1:7,000,000   LAMBERT CONFORMAL CONIC PROJECTION

MILES 0   100   200   300
KILOMETERS 0 100 200 300

© Copyright by HAMMOND INCORPORATED, Maplewood, N.J. CG-2112-A-A

Los Angeles, New York-Philadelphia, Washington

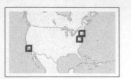

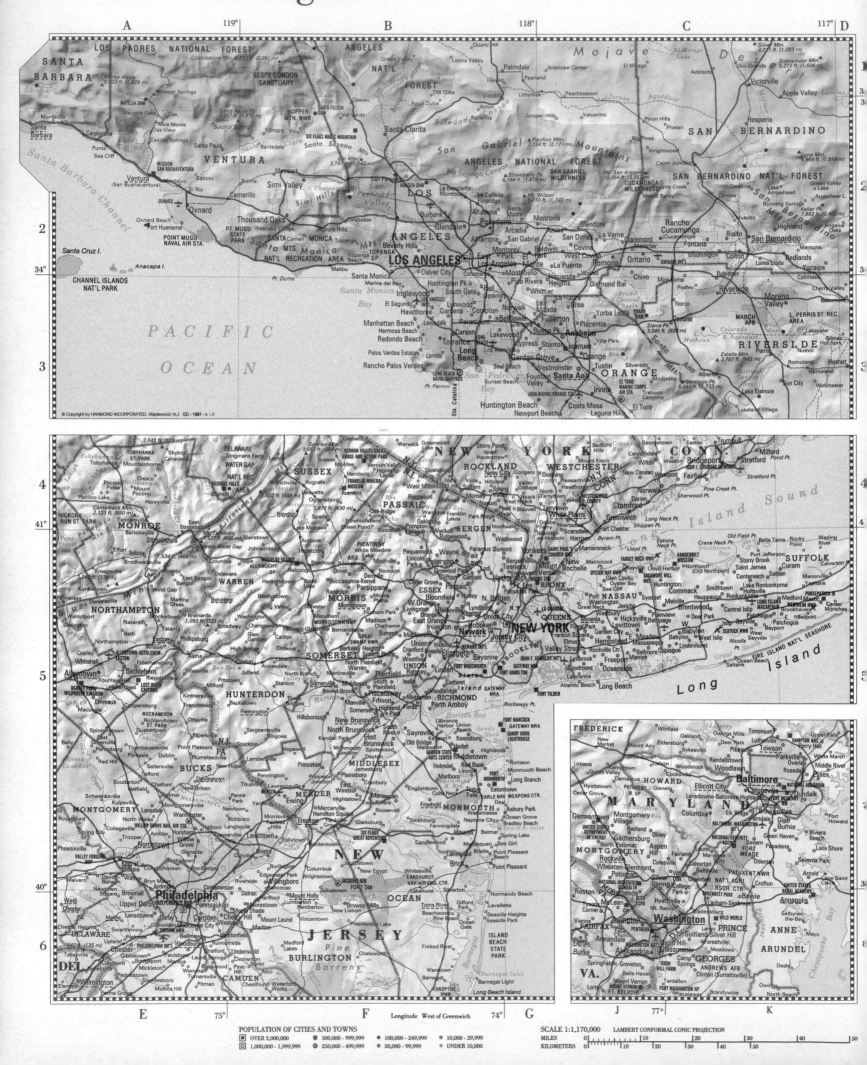

Longitude West of Greenwich

POPULATION OF CITIES AND TOWNS

- ■ OVER 2,000,000
- ▣ 1,000,000 - 1,999,999
- ● 500,000 - 999,999
- ● 250,000 - 499,999
- ● 100,000 - 249,999
- ● 30,000 - 99,999
- ● 10,000 - 29,999
- ● UNDER 10,000

SCALE 1:1,170,000   LAMBERT CONFORMAL CONIC PROJECTION

MILES 0   10   20   30   40

KILOMETERS 0   10   20   30   40   50

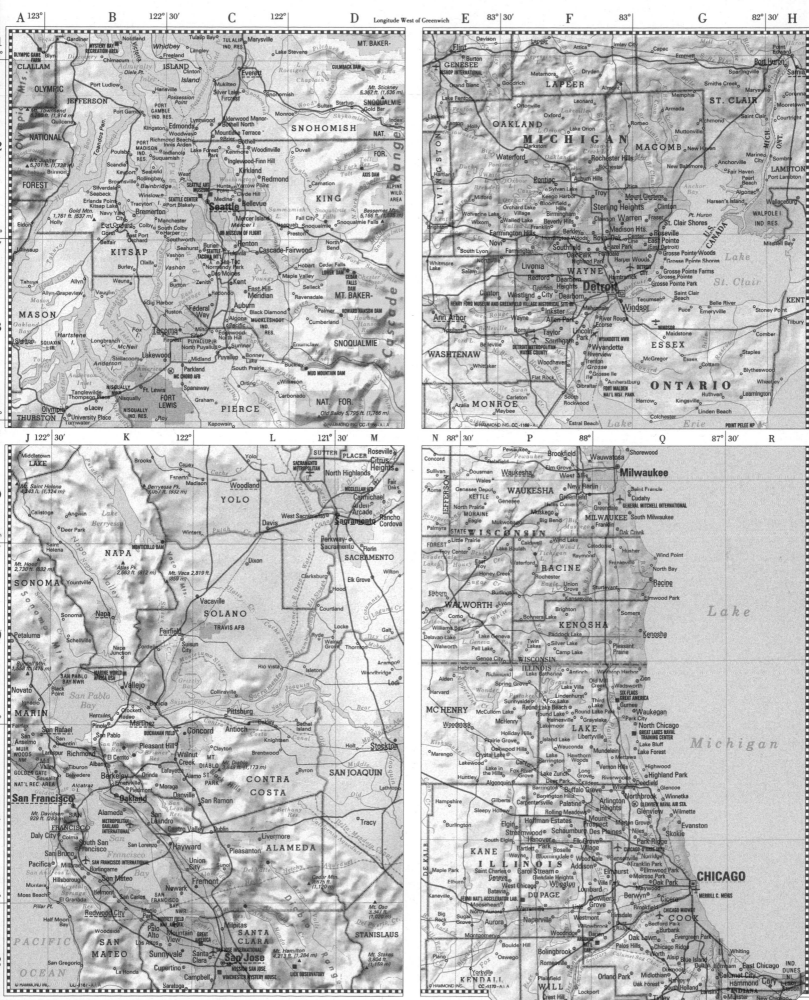

SCALE 1:1,170,000   LAMBERT CONFORMAL CONIC PROJECTION

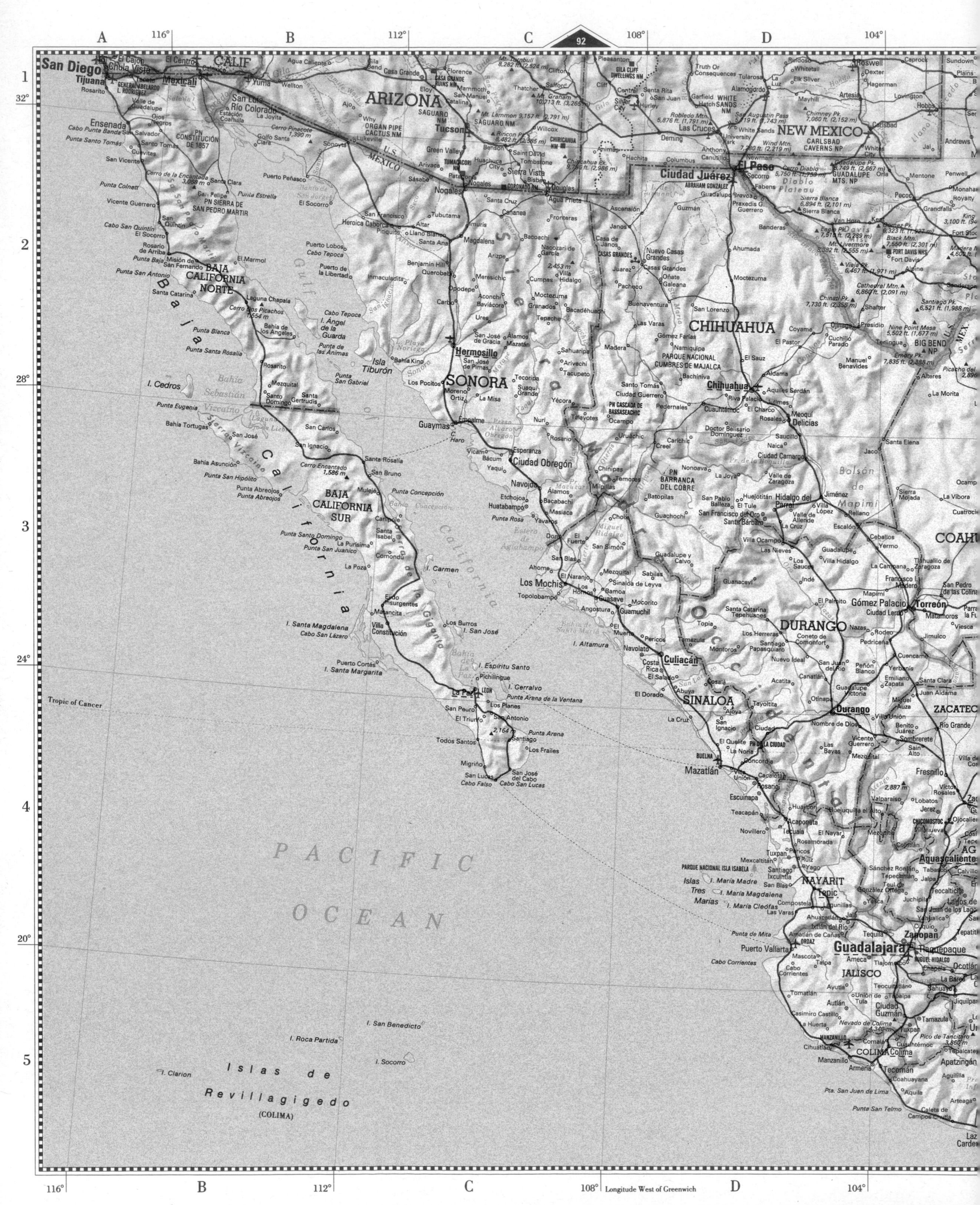

A   116°   B   112°   C   108°   D   104°

San Diego
Tijuana
El Cajon
Chula Vista
El Centro
Mexicali
CALIF
Rosarito
GENERAL ABELARDO L. RODRIGUEZ
Yuma
Wellton

32°

Ensenada
Cabo Punta Banda
San Salvador
San Luis Rio Colorado
San Luis
Coahuila
La Joyita
Why
Ajo
Gila
Bend
Casa Grande
ARIZONA
Florence
Eloy

Santo Tomás
Punta Santo Tomás
Ojos Negros
Valle de Guadalupe
PN CONSTITUCIÓN DE 1857
Golfo Santa Clara
Sonoyta
ORGAN PIPE CACTUS NM
Cerro Pinacate 1,390 m
Green Valley
Arivaca
Tucson

San Vicente
Cerro de la Encantada 3,098 m
Santa Clara
Puerto Peñasco
U.S.
MEXICO
Sásabe
Nogales
Nogales

Punta Colnett
San Felipe
Punta Estrella
El Socorro
Heroica Caborca
San Francisco
Tubutama
Imuris
Santa Cruz

Vicente Guerrero
Misión de Arriba
El Marmol
Puerto Lobos
Cabo Tepoca
Pitiquito
Altar
Magdalena
Santa Ana
Cananea
Fronteras

2

28°

Rosario
Punta Baja
Misión San Fernando
Santa Catarina
BAJA CALIFORNIA NORTE
Puerto de la Libertad
Inmaculadita
Querobabi
Benjamin Hill
2,453 m
Villa Hidalgo
Granados

Cabo San Quintín
El Socorro
Laguna Chapala
Cabo Tepoca
El Ángel de la Guarda
Punta de las Ánimas
Cabo San Gabriel
Opodepe
Aconchi
Baviácora
Moctezuma

Cerro Los Picachos 1,654 m
Bahía de los Ángeles
Isla Tiburón
Bahía Kino
San José de Pimas
Hermosillo
Ures
San José de Gracia
Álamos
Mazatán

Punta Blanca
Punta Santa Rosalia
Rosarito
Punta San Gabriel
Los Pocitos
SONORA
Tecoripa

I. Cedros
Bahía Sebastián Vizcaíno
Mezquital
Santo Domingo
Santa Gertrudis
Guaymas
Empalme
Moreno Ortiz
La Misa
Suaqui Grande
Arivechi
Tacupeto

Punta Eugenia
Bahía Tortugas
San José
Sierra Vizcaíno
Santa Rosalía
San Bruno
Guaymas
Haro
Vicam
Bácum
Esperanza
Rosario
Nuri
Yécora

3

Bahía Asunción
Punta San Hipólito
Punta Abreojos
Cerro Encantado 1,586 m
Santa Rosalía
Mulegé
Ciudad Obregón
Navojoa
Yaqui
Álamos
Chínipas
Témoris

BAJA CALIFORNIA SUR
Punta Concepción
Punta Rosa
Etchojoa
Bacabachi
Masiaca
Navojoa
Milpillas

Punta Santo Domingo
La Purísima
Santa Isabel
Comondú
Huatabampo
Yavaros
Choix
El Fuerte
San Simón
Guachochi
Batopilas

Punta San Juanico
La Poza
Campote
I. Carmen
San Blas
Los Mochis
Ahome
Topolobampo

24°

Ejido Insurgentes
Matancita
I. Santa Magdalena
Cabo San Lázaro
Villa Constitución
Los Burros
I. San José
El Naranjo
Los Hornos
Guasave
Guamúchil

Tropic of Cancer
Puerto Cortés
I. Santa Margarita
Bahía de La Paz
I. Espíritu Santo
Pichilingue
Angostura
Navolato
Culiacán
Costa Rica
El Salado

La Paz
LEÓN
Los Planes
Punta Arena de la Ventana
I. Cerralvo
El Dorado
SINALOA
Tayoltita

San Pedro
El Triunfo
San Antonio
Punta Arena
Santiago
Los Frailes
2,164 m
La Cruz
San Ignacio
Ciudad

4

Todos Santos
Migriño
San Lucas
Cabo Falso
San José del Cabo
Cabo San Lucas

PACIFIC

OCEAN

20°

I. San Benedicto

I. Roca Partida

I. Clarion
I. Socorro

Islas de

5

Revillagigedo

(COLIMA)

116°   B   112°   C   108°   Longitude West of Greenwich   D   104°

Northern and Central Mexico

SCALE 1:7,000,000   LAMBERT CONFORMAL CONIC PROJECTION

MILES   0   100   200   300

KILOMETERS 0   100   200   300

POPULATION OF CITIES AND TOWNS

☐ OVER 2,000,000   ◉ 500,000 - 999,999   ● 100,000 - 249,999   ○ 10,000 - 29,999
☐ 1,000,000 - 1,999,999   ◉ 250,000 - 499,999   ● 30,000 - 99,999   ○ UNDER 10,000

© Copyright by HAMMOND INCORPORATED, Maplewood, N.J. CC-1057-A-A

Southern Mexico, Central America, Western Caribbean

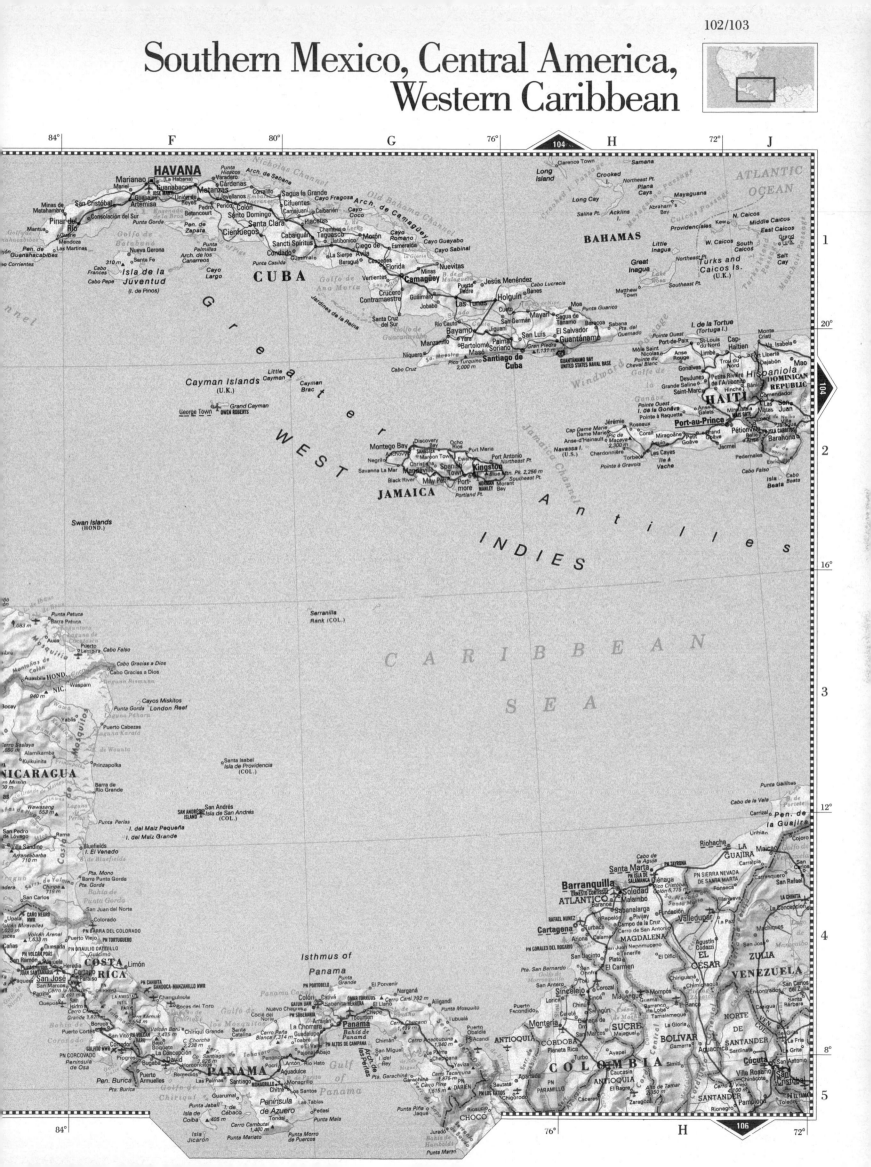

Eastern Caribbean, Bahamas

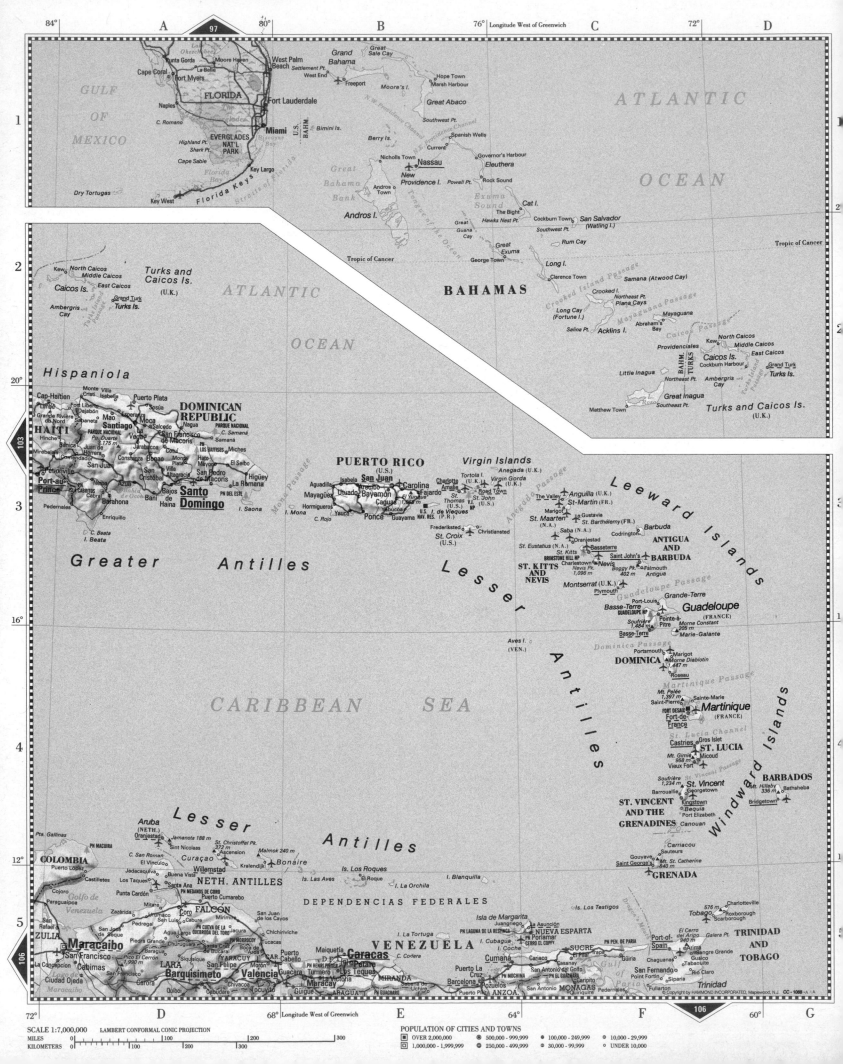

A 97 **B** 76° Longitude West of Greenwich **C** 72° **D**

84° **80°**

1

GULF OF MEXICO

FLORIDA

West Palm Beach
Fort Lauderdale
Miami
Biscayne Bay
Key Largo

EVERGLADES NAT'L PARK
Highland Pt.
Shark Pt.
Cape Sable
Florida Bay
Dry Tortugas
Key West
Florida Keys
Straits of Florida

Punta Gorda
Moore Haven
La Belle
Fort Myers
Cape Coral
Naples
C. Romano
Lake Okeechobee

U.S.
BAHM.
Bimini Is.

Grand Bahama
Great Sale Cay
West End
Freeport
Hope Town
Marsh Harbour
Great Abaco
Southwest Pt.
N.W. Providence Channel
N.E. Providence Channel

Berry Is.
Spanish Wells
Current
Governor's Harbour
Eleuthera
Nicholls Town
Nassau
New Providence I.
Powell Pt.
Rock Sound
Andros Town
Great Bahama Bank
Andros I.

ATLANTIC OCEAN

Cat I.
The Bight
Hawks Nest Pt.
Cockburn Town
San Salvador (Watling I.)
Southwest Pt.
Exuma Sound

2

Kew
North Caicos
Middle Caicos
East Caicos
Caicos Is.
Turks and Caicos Is. (U.K.)
Ambergris Cay
Grand Turk
Turks Is.

ATLANTIC OCEAN

Tropic of Cancer

BAHAMAS

Great Exuma
George Town
Long I.
Clarence Town
Crooked I. Passage
Rum Cay
Samana (Atwood Cay)
Crooked I.
Northeast Pt.
Plana Cays
Long Cay (Fortune I.)
Salina Pt.
Acklins I.
Mayaguana Passage
Abraham's Bay
Mayaguana

Tropic of Cancer

Providenciales
Kew
North Caicos
Middle Caicos
East Caicos
Caicos Is.
BAHM.
TURKS
Cockburn Harbour
Ambergris Cay
Grand Turk
Turks Is.
Little Inagua
Northeast Pt.
Caicos Passage

20°

Hispaniola

3

Cap-Haïtien
Monte Cristi
Villa Isabella
Puerto Plata
Sosúa
DOMINICAN REPUBLIC
Fort Liberté
Limbe
Dajabón
Moca
Nagua
Grande Rivière du Nord
Sabaneta
Mao
Salcedo
San Francisco de Macorís
PARQUE NACIONAL
C. Samaná
PN LOS HAITISES
Miches
Bánica
Juan de Herrera
Santiago
La Vega
Jarabacoa
Bonao
Cotuí
Hato Mayor
El Seibo
Mirebalais
Comendador
Constanza
Po. Duarte 3,175 m
Santo Domingo
Villa Altagracia
Higüey
HAITI
Hinche
San Juan
Azua
San Cristóbal
San Pedro de Macorís
La Romana
Pétionville
PN DEL ESTE
Port-au-Prince
ISLA CABRITOS
Cabral
Bani
Bajos de Haina
Santo Domingo
I. Saona
Pedernales
Neiba
Barahona
Bahía de Ocoa
Enriquillo
Mona Passage
I. Mona
C. Beata
I. Beata

PUERTO RICO (U.S.)
San Juan
Isabela
Aguadilla
Arecibo
Utuado
Bayamón
Carolina
Fajardo
El Yunque 1,065 m
Mayagüez
Hormigueros
Yauco
Caguas
I. de Vieques (U.S.)
Humacao
Ponce
Guayama
C. Rojo
U.S. NAV. RES. (P.R.)

Virgin Islands
Anegada (U.K.)
Tortola I. (U.K.)
Virgin Gorda
Charlotte Amalie
St. Thomas V.I. (U.S.)
Road Town
St. John (U.S.)
St. Croix (U.S.)
Frederiksted
Christiansted

Anguilla (U.K.)
The Valley
St-Martin (FR.)
Marigot
Marigot
St. Maarten (N.A.)
Gustavia
St. Barthélemy (FR.)
Oranjestad
Saba (N.A.)
St. Eustatius (N.A.)
St. Kitts
BRIMSTONE HILL NP
Basseterre
Charlestown
Nevis Pk. 1,096 m
Nevis
ST. KITTS AND NEVIS
Montserrat (U.K.)
Plymouth

Barbuda
Codrington
ANTIGUA AND BARBUDA
Saint John's
Boggy Pk. 402 m
Falmouth
Antigua

Leeward Islands
Anegada Passage

Greater Antilles

Lesser Antilles

16°

Port-Louis
Basse-Terre
GUADELOUPE NP
Soufrière 1,484 m
Basse-Terre
Grande-Terre
Guadeloupe (FRANCE)
Pointe-à-Pitre
Morne Constant 205 m
Marie-Galante

Guadeloupe Passage

Dominica Passage
Portsmouth
Marigot
Morne Diablotin 1,447 m
DOMINICA
Roseau

Martinique Passage
Mt. Pelée 1,397 m
Sainte-Marie
Saint-Pierre
FORT DESAIX
Martinique (FRANCE)
Fort-de-France

CARIBBEAN SEA

Aves I. (VEN.)

St. Lucia Channel
Castries
Gros Islet
ST. LUCIA
Mt. Gimie 958 m
Micoud
Vieux Fort

Lesser Antilles

4

Lesser Antilles

Aruba (NETH.)
Oranjestad
Jamanota 188 m
St. Christoffel Pk. 372 m
Sint Nicolaas
Ascension
Malmok 240 m
Curaçao
C. San Roman
El Vinculo
Jadacaquiva
Buena Vista
Willemstad
Bonaire
NETH. ANTILLES
Kralendijk

COLOMBIA
Pta. Gallinas
Puerto López
Castilletes
Cojoro
Paraguaipoa
Punta Cardón
Santa Ana
PN MEDANOS DE CORO
Puerto Cumarebo
Las Taques
PN MACUIRA
Golfo de Venezuela
San Rafael
ZULIA
Los Taques
Zarárida
Pedregal
Maicao
San Luis
San Francisco
Cabimas
San José de Seque
Piedra Grande
Agua Larga
QUEBRADA DEL TORO
Jacura
Coro
FALCON
Mirimire
San Juan de los Cayos
Chichiriviche
Maracaibo
Ciudad Ojeda
La Concepción
Lago de Maracaibo
Pico El Cerrón 1,990 m
Pedro
Bobures
San Felipe
Siquisique
LARA
Barquisimeto
San Francisco
Barinas
Carora
Quibor
Chivacoa
Morón
YARACUY
Duaca
Puerto Cabello
Valencia
Guacara
PN HENRI PITTER
Turmero
Maracay
La Victoria
AGUA
Güigue
PN GUACAMO

Is. Los Roques
El Roque
Is. Las Aves

DEPENDENCIAS FEDERALES

I. La Orchila
I. Blanquilla
I. La Tortuga
Isla de Margarita
PN LAGUNA DE LA RESTINGA
Juangriego
La Asunción
NUEVA ESPARTA
Porlamar
I. Cubagua
PN PEN. DE PARIA
I. Coche
CERRO EL COPEY

VENEZUELA
Maiquetía
Caracas
La Guaira
C. Codera
D.F.
Los Teques
MIRANDA
Petare
Cúa
PN GUATOPO
SUCRE
Cumaná
Cariaco
San Antonio del Golfo
Casanay
Cumanacoa
Guaca
Cariaquito
CARIPITO
Puerto La Cruz
Barcelona
Pozuelos
ANZOA.
Puerto Píritu
San Antonio
MONAGAS
PN MOCHIMA
Guiria
Pedernales

St. Vincent Passage
Soufrière 1,234 m
St. Vincent
Barrouallie
Georgetown
Kingstown
ST. VINCENT AND THE GRENADINES
Bequia
Port Elizabeth
Canouan
Carriacou
Sauteurs
Gouyave
Saint George's
Mt. St. Catherine 840 m
GRENADA

BARBADOS
Mt. Hillaby 336 m
Bathsheba
Bridgetown

Windward Islands

12°

Carriacou
Charlotteville
576 m
Tobago
Roxborough
Scarborough
Is. Los Testigos
Dragon's Mouth
Port-of-Spain
El Cerro del Aripo 940 m
Galera Pt.
TRINIDAD AND TOBAGO
Arima
Sangre Grande
Chaguanas
San Fernando
Point Fortin
Siparia
Trinidad
Rio Claro
Fullarton
Gulf of Paria
Guanoco
Tucupita

5

72° **D** **68°** Longitude West of Greenwich **E** **64°** **F** 106 **G** **60°**

© Copyright by HAMMOND INCORPORATED, Maplewood, N.J. CC-106B · A · A

SCALE 1:7,000,000 LAMBERT CONFORMAL CONIC PROJECTION
MILES 0 100 200 300
KILOMETERS 0 100 200 300

POPULATION OF CITIES AND TOWNS

■ OVER 2,000,000	● 500,000 - 999,999
▣ 1,000,000 - 1,999,999	● 250,000 - 499,999
● 100,000 - 249,999	● 10,000 - 29,999
● 30,000 - 99,999	○ UNDER 10,000

South America

AREA OF OPTIMIZATION
The red band which surrounds this map defines the "Area of Optimization." Within this bounding curve is the most accurate conformal map that can be made of the region. Outside the optimized area, distortion increases rapidly, and tears or other irregularities in the grid may occur.

POPULATION OF CITIES AND TOWNS
- OVER 3,000,000
- 1,000,000 - 2,999,999
- 500,000 - 999,999
- 100,000 - 499,999
- UNDER 100,000

SCALE 1:28,000,000   OPTIMAL CONFORMAL PROJECTION

Longitude West of Greenwich

© Copyright by HAMMOND INCORPORATED, Maplewood, N.J. CC-1069-A A A

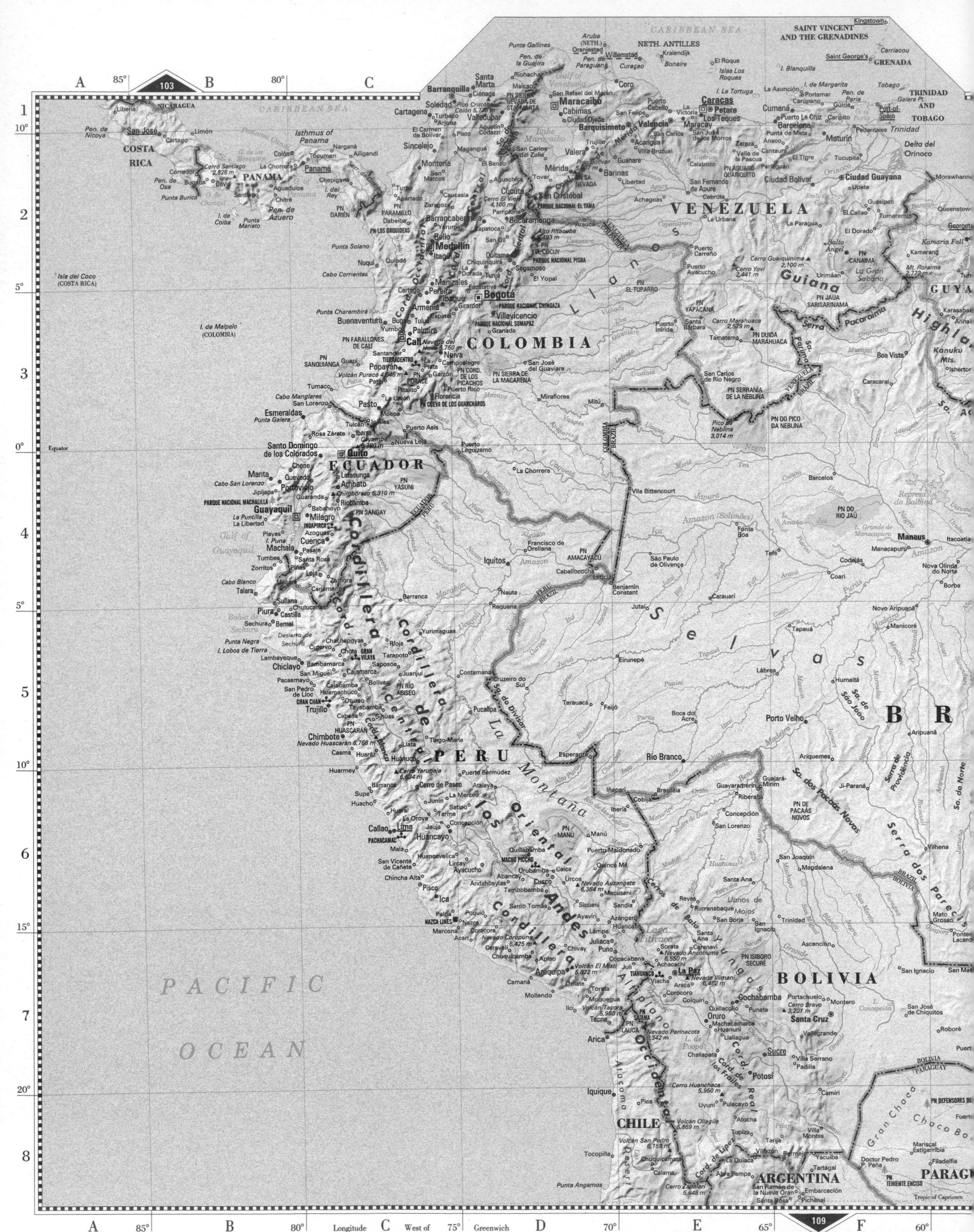

A
85°
103
B
80°
C
1
10°
2
5°
3
0°
4
5°
5
10°
6
15°
7
20°
8
CARIBBEAN SEA
PACIFIC
OCEAN
Equator
NICARAGUA
COSTA
RICA
San José
PANAMA
Panamá
Isthmus of
Panama
Colón
Limón
Pen. de
Nicoya
Pen. de
Azuero
I. de
Coiba
Isla del Coco
(COSTA RICA)
I. de Malpelo
(COLOMBIA)
Aruba
(NETH.)
Oranjestad
Willemstad
Curaçao
Kralendijk
Bonaire
NETH. ANTILLES
SAINT VINCENT
AND THE GRENADINES
Kingstown
Saint George's
GRENADA
TRINIDAD
AND
TOBAGO
Port-of-
Spain
Tobago
Trinidad
Delta del
Orinoco
Punta Gallinas
Pen. de
la Guajira
Pen. de
Paraguaná
Gulf of
Venezuela
Barranquilla
Santa
Marta
Cartagena
Soledad
Valledupar
Sincelejo
Montería
Maracaibo
Cabimas
Lago de
Maracaibo
Coro
Barquisimeto
Valencia
Caracas
Petare
Los Teques
Maracay
Cumaná
Barcelona
Maturín
Ciudad Bolívar
Ciudad Guayana
VENEZUELA
Mérida
Barinas
San Cristóbal
Cúcuta
Bucaramanga
Medellín
Itagüí
Bello
Manizales
Pereira
Armenia
Ibagué
Bogotá
Villavicencio
Buenaventura
Cali
Palmira
Neiva
Popayán
Pasto
Tumaco
COLOMBIA
Llanos
PN EL TUPARRO
Guiana
Highlands
Mt. Roraima
2,772 m
PN CANAIMA
Salto
Angel
Pico da
Neblina
3,014 m
PN DO PICO
DA NEBLINA
Esmeraldas
Quito
ECUADOR
Santo Domingo
de los Colorados
Manta
Portoviejo
Ambato
Chimborazo 6,310 m
Riobamba
Guayaquil
Milagro
Gulf of
Guayaquil
Cuenca
Machala
Loja
Talara
Sullana
Piura
Chiclayo
Cajamarca
Trujillo
Chimbote
Nevado Huascarán 6,768 m
Huacho
Callao
Lima
Huancayo
Ayacucho
Cusco
Machu Picchu
Ica
Nazca Lines
Arequipa
Mollendo
PERU
Cordillera
Occidental
Cordillera
Central
Cordillera
Oriental
Cordillera de los Andes
La Montaña
Iquitos
Pucallpa
Amazon
Marañón
Ucayali
Leticia
Manaus
Selvas
Rio Branco
Porto Velho
Lago
Titicaca
Puno
Juliaca
La Paz
Nevado Illimani
6,462 m
Oruro
Cochabamba
Santa Cruz
Sucre
Potosí
BOLIVIA
Altiplano
Arica
Iquique
Tocopilla
Calama
Desierto de Atacama
CHILE
ARGENTINA
PARAGUAY
Gran Chaco
Tropic of Capricorn
BRAZIL
A
85°
B
80°
Longitude
C
West of
75°
Greenwich
D
70°
E
65°
109
F
60°

Northern South America

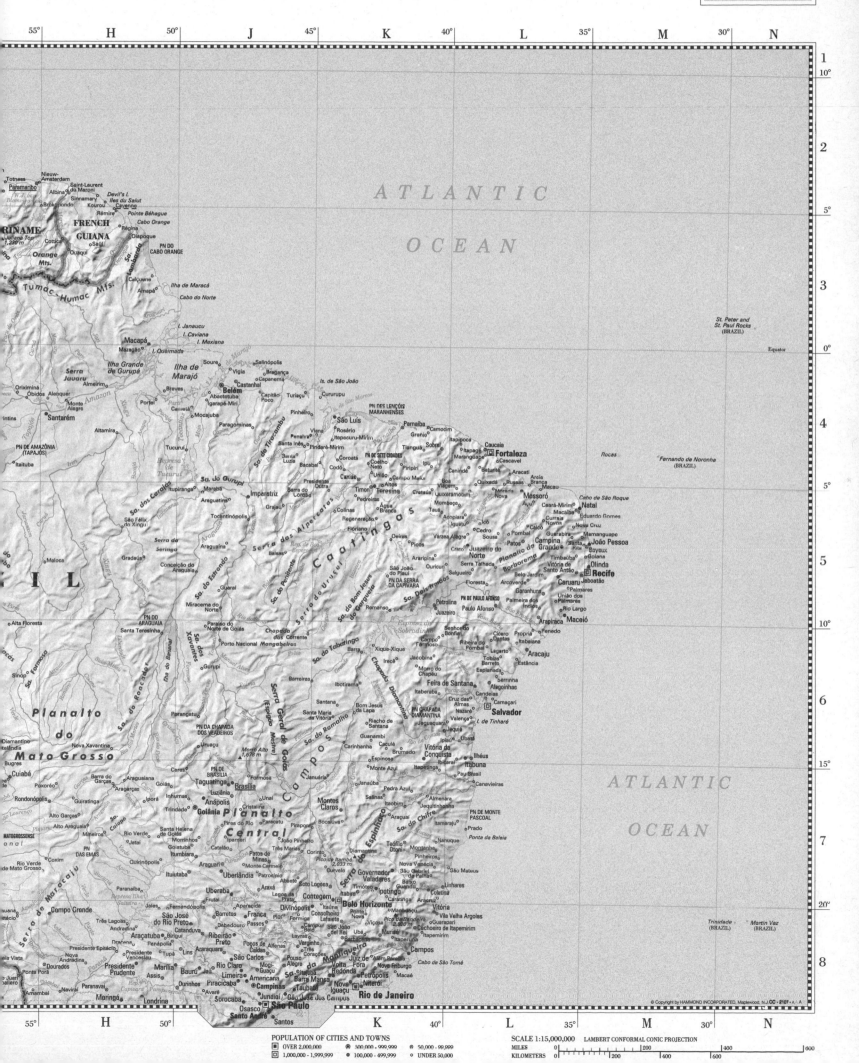

A T L A N T I C

O C E A N

Totness
Nieuw-
Amsterdam
Paramaribo
Albina
Saint-Laurent
du Maroni
Blommestein
Brokopondo
Sinnamary
Kourou
Devil's I.
Iles du Salut
SURINAME
Juliana Top
1,280 m
FRENCH
GUIANA
Cayenne
Rémire
Pointe Béhague
Orange
Mts.
Cotica
Régina
Oiapoque
Cabo Orange
PN DO
CABO ORANGE
Tumac-Humac Mts.
Calçoene
Amapá
Ilha de Maracá
Cabo do Norte

St. Peter and
St. Paul Rocks
(BRAZIL)

Oriximiná
Óbidos
Alenquer
Serra
Javaru
Ilha Grande
de Gurupá
Almeirim
I. Janaucu
I. Caviana
I. Mexiana
Equator
Equator

Macapá
Mazagão
I. Queimada
Monte
Alegre
Santarém
Breves
Portel
Soure
Salinópolis
Vigia
Capanema
Bragança
Is. de São João
PN DES LENÇÓIS
MARANHENSES
Ilha de
Marajó
Belém
Castanhal
Turiaçú
Cururupu
Fernando de Noronha
(BRAZIL)
Altamira
Abaetetuba
Igarapé-Miri
Mocajuba
Pinheiro
Parnaíba
Camocim
PN DE AMAZÔNIA
(TAPAJÓS)
Itaituba
Tucuruí
Paragominas
Viana
São Luís
Rosário
Itapecuru-Mirim
Granja
Itapipoca
Sobral
Caucaia
Santa Inês
Pindaré-Mirim
Santa
Luzia
Penalva
Bacabal
Coroatá
Viana
Codó
Ipu
Itapagé
Marangaupe
Fortaleza
Rocas
Cascavel
Santa
Rita

BRAZIL
Itupiranga
Marabá
Araguatins
Imperatriz
Barra do
Corda
Presidente
Dutra
União
Coelho
Neto
Caxias
Timon
Altos
Campo Maior
Teresina
Boa
Viagem
Quixeramobim
Mossoró
Cabo de São Roque
Natal
São Félix
do Xingu
Conceição do
Araguaia
Tocantinópolis
Grajaú
Colinas
Pedreiras
Regeneração
Floriano
Oeiras
Picos
Araripina
Crateús
Tauá
Acopiara
Icó
Cedro
Várzea Alegre
Juazeiro do
Norte
Crato
Serra Talhada
Sousa
Patos
Pombal
Calcó
Açu
Macau
Currais
Novos
Nova Cruz
Eduardo Gomes
Mamanguape
João Pessoa
Guarabira
Campina
Grande
Santa
Rita
Bayeux
Goiana
Olinda
Recife
Jaboatão
Araripe
Serra do
Espírito
Santo Antão
Vitória de
Santo Antão
Caruaru
Palmares
Gradaús
Miracema do
Norte
Paraíso do
Norte de Goiás
Balsas
São João
do Piauí
Ouricuri
Salgueiro
Floresta
Arcoverde
Belo Jardim
Garanhuns
União dos
Palmares
Rio Largo
Maceió
Alta Floresta
PN DO
ARAGUAIA
Santa Teresinha
Chapada
das Corrente
Mangabeiras
Remanso
Petrolina
Juazeiro
PN DE PAULO AFONSO
Palmeira dos
Índios
Arapiraca
Penedo
Senhor do
Bonfim
Campo
Formoso
Cícero
Dantas
Propriá
Diamantino
telândia
Nova Xavantina
PN DA CHAPADA
DOS VEADEIROS
Porto Nacional
Xique-Xique
Barra
Irecê
Jacobina
Ribeira do
Pombal
Tobias
Barreto
Itabaiana
Estância
Aracaju
Planalto
do
Bugres
Mato Grosso
Perangatu
Santana
Barreiras
Ibotirama
Morro do
Chapéu
Feira de Santana
Itaberaba
Serrinha
Esplanada
Alagoinhas
Cuiabá
Poxoréo
Barra do
Garças
Araguaiana
Goiás
Formosa
Santa Maria
da Vitória
Bom Jesus
da Lapa
PN CHAPADA
DIAMANTINA
Candeias
Camaçari
Salvador
Rondonópolis
Aragarças
Iporá
Inhumas
Luziânia
Brasília
Unaí
Januária
Guanambi
Carinhanha
Caculé
Riacho de
Santana
Jeguaquara
Ipiaú
Jequié
Ubatã
I. de Tinharé
Ilhéus
Itabuna
Alto Garças
Rio Verde
Ceres
PN DE
BRASÍLIA
Taguatinga
Cristalina
Anápolis
Formosa
Monte Azul
Espinosa
Brumado
Vitória da
Conquista
Ipiaú
Itapetinga
Pau Brasil
Canavieiras
MATOGROSSENSE
onal
Mineiros
Alto Araguaia
Santa Helena
de Goiás
Goiatuba
Itumbiara
Goiânia
Planalto
Central
Pires do Rio
Parcatu
Piracanjuba
João Pinheiro
Corinto
Montes
Claros
Salinas
Itaobim
Pedra Azul
Janaúba
Araçuaí
PN DE MONTE
PASCOAL
Almenara
Jequitinhonha
Prado
Ponta da Baleia
Rio Verde
de Mato Grosso
Coxim
PN
DAS EMAS
Catalão
Quirinópolis
Araguari
Patos de
Minas
Monte Carmelo
Três Marias
Curvelo
Diamantina
Pico do Itambé
2,033 m
Teófilo
Otoni
Montanha
Pinheiros
Nanuque
Mucuri
São Mateus
Paranaíba
Ituiutaba
Uberlândia
Prata
Araxá
Abaeté
Sete Lagoas
Itabira
Governador
Valadares
Baixo
Guandu
Caratinga
Aimorés
Colatina
Linhares
Três Lagoas
Andradina
Fernandópolis
Uberaba
Frutal
Aparecida
Barretos
França
Patrocínio
Conselheiro
Lafaiete
Divinópolis
Pouso
Formiga
Lagoa
da Prata
Ipatinga
Contagem
Belo Horizonte
Itabira
Ponte
Nova
Maguaçu
Vila Velha Argolas
Vitória
Cachoeiro de Itapemirim
Guarapari
São José
do Rio Preto
Catanduva
Barretos
Ribeirão
Preto
Passos
São João
del Rei
Viçosa
Uba
São Gabriel
da Palha
Itaperuna
Araçatuba
Birigui
Penápolis
Tupã
Araraquara
Poços de
Caldas
Varginha
Lavras
Três
Corações
Campos
Presidente Epitácio
Lins
Bauru
São Carlos
Rio Claro
Limeira
Mogi-
Guaçu
Pouso
Alegre
Juiz de
Fora
Alem Paraíba
Campos
Cabo de São Tomé
Presidente
Venceslau
Andradina
Marília
Assis
Piracicaba
Americana
Campinas
Sa. da Mantiqueira
Itajubá
Taubaté
Volta
Redonda
Barra Mansa
Nova
Friburgo
Macaé
Petrópolis
Presidente
Prudente
Dourados
Ourinhos
Jundiaí
São José dos Campos
Niterói
Maringá
Londrina
Sorocaba
São Paulo
Rio de Janeiro
Osasco
Santo André
Santos

A T L A N T I C

O C E A N

Trinidade
(BRAZIL)
Martin Vaz
(BRAZIL)

© Copyright by HAMMOND INCORPORATED, Maplewood, N.J CC - 2107 • A · A

Southeastern Brazil

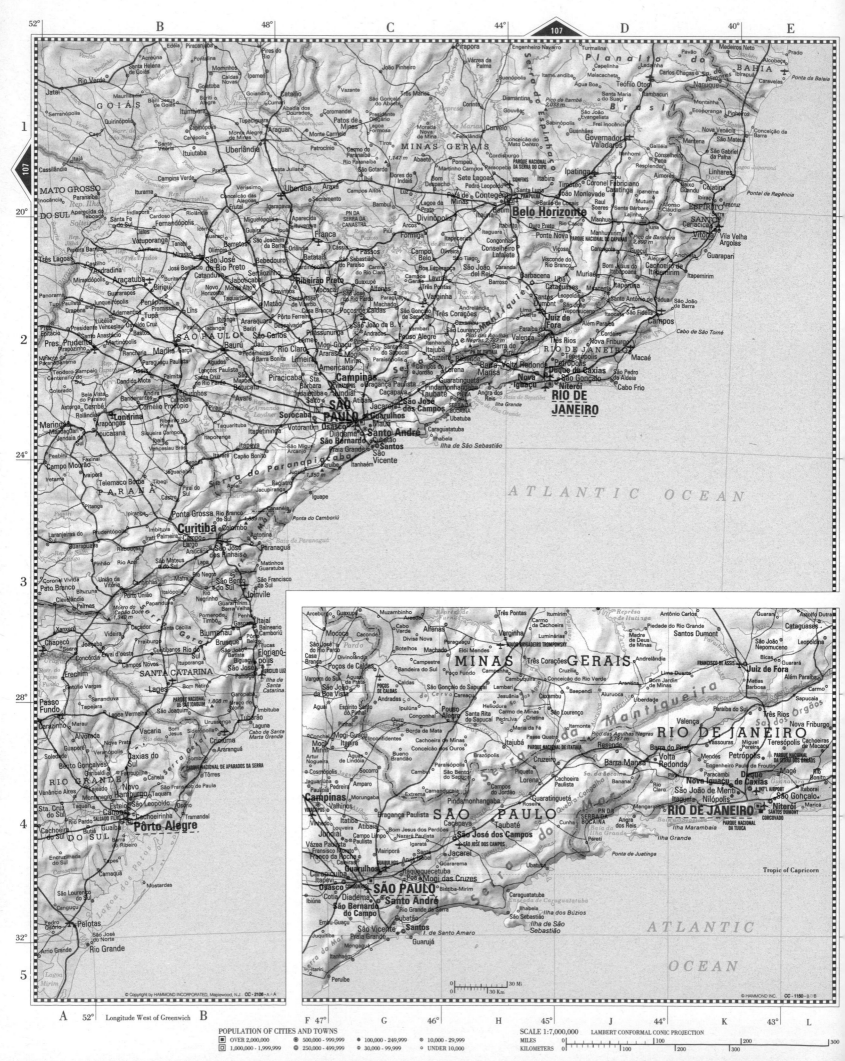

Longitude West of Greenwich

POPULATION OF CITIES AND TOWNS

■ OVER 2,000,000	● 500,000 - 999,999
□ 1,000,000 - 1,999,999	● 250,000 - 499,999
● 100,000 - 249,999	● 10,000 - 29,999
● 30,000 - 99,999	● UNDER 10,000

SCALE 1:7,000,000   LAMBERT CONFORMAL CONIC PROJECTION

MILES   0   100   200

KILOMETERS   0   100   200   300

Southern South America

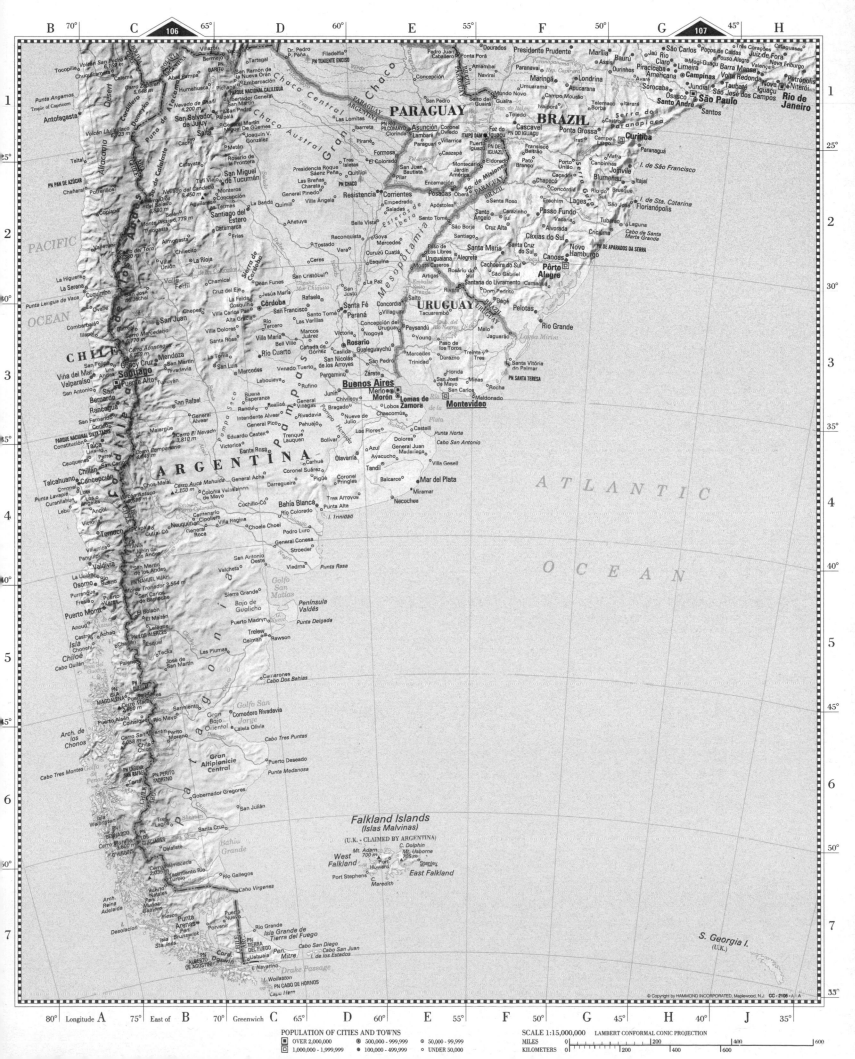

B 70° C 65° D 60° E 55° F 50° G 45° H

106   107

PACIFIC

OCEAN

CHILE

ARGENTINA

PARAGUAY

BRAZIL

URUGUAY

Asunción

Buenos Aires

Montevideo

São Paulo

Rio de Janeiro

Curitiba

Santiago

Córdoba

Rosario

Pôrto Alegre

A T L A N T I C

O C E A N

Falkland Islands
(Islas Malvinas)
(U.K. – CLAIMED BY ARGENTINA)

West
Falkland

East Falkland

Mt. Adam
700 m.

Mt. Usborne
705 m.

Port
Howard

Stanley

Port Stephens

S. Georgia I.
(U.K.)

© Copyright by HAMMOND INCORPORATED, Maplewood, N.J.   CC - 2105 - A - A

80° Longitude A 75° East of B 70° Greenwich C 65° D 60° E 55° F 50° G 45° H 40° J 35°

POPULATION OF CITIES AND TOWNS
☐ OVER 2,000,000
☐ 1,000,000 - 1,999,999
● 500,000 - 999,999
● 100,000 - 499,999
● 50,000 - 99,999
○ UNDER 50,000

SCALE 1:15,000,000   LAMBERT CONFORMAL CONIC PROJECTION
MILES   0   200   400   600
KILOMETERS   0   200   400

Index of the World

This index lists places and geographic features found in the atlas. Every name is followed by the country or area to which it belongs. Except for cities, towns, countries and cultural areas, all entries include a reference to feature type, such as province, river, island, peak, and so on. The page number and alpha-numeric code appear to the left of each listing. The code refers to the grid squares formed by the horizontal and vertical lines of latitude and longitude on each map. Following the letters from left to right, and the numbers from top to bottom, helps you to locate quickly the square containing the place or feature. Inset maps have their own alpha-numeric codes. Names that are accompanied by a point symbol are indexed to the symbol's location on the map. Other names are indexed to the initial letter of the name. The primary abbreviations used in this index are listed below.

Index Abbreviations

A A.F.B.	Air Force Base	
Afghan.	Afghanistan	
Ala.	Alabama	
Alg.	Algeria	
Alta.	Alberta	
Ant. & Barb.	Antigua & Barbuda	
Antarc.	Antarctica	
arch.	archipelago	
Arg.	Argentina	
Ariz.	Arizona	
Ark.	Arkansas	
Austr.	Australia	
aut.	autonomous	
B Bah.	Bahamas	
Bang.	Bangladesh	
Belg.	Belgium	
Bol.	Bolivia	
Bosn.	Bosnia & Hercegovina	
Bots.	Botswana	
Braz.	Brazil	
Br., Brit.	British	
Br. Col.	British Columbia	
Bulg.	Bulgaria	
Burk. Faso	Burkina Faso	
C Calif.	California	
Camb.	Cambodia	
Can.	Canada	
cap.	capital	
Cent. Afr. Rep.	Central African Republic	
chan.	channel	
Chan. Is.	Channel Islands	
Col.	Colombia	
Colo.	Colorado	
Conn.	Connecticut	
C. Rica	Costa Rica	
Czech Rep.	Czech Republic	
D DC	District of Columbia	
Del.	Delaware	
Dem.	Democratic	
Den.	Denmark	
depr.	depression	
des.	desert	
dist.	district	
Dom. Rep.	Dominican Republic	
E E.	East, Eastern	
Ecua.	Ecuador	
El Sal.	El Salvador	
Eng.	England	
Equat. Guin.	Equatorial Guinea	
est.	estuary	
Eth.	Ethiopia	

F Fed.	Federal, Federated
Fin.	Finland
Fla.	Florida
for.	forest
Fr.	France, French
Fr. Pol.	French Polynesia
Ft.	Fort
G Ga.	Georgia
Ger.	Germany
Greenl.	Greenland
Gt.	Great
Guad.	Guadeloupe
Guat.	Guatemala
Guy.	Guyana
H har., harb.	harbor
Hon.	Honduras
Hun.	Hungary
I Ill.	Illinois
Ind.	Indiana
Indon.	Indonesia
Int'l	International
Ire.	Ireland
isl., isls.	isle, island, islands
Isr.	Israel
isth.	isthmus
Iv. Coast	Ivory Coast
J Jam.	Jamaica
K Kans.	Kansas
Ky.	Kentucky
L La.	Louisiana
Leb.	Lebanon
Lux.	Luxembourg
M Madag.	Madagascar
Man.	Manitoba
Mass.	Massachusetts
Maur.	Mauritania
Md.	Maryland
Mex.	Mexico
Mich.	Michigan
Minn.	Minnesota
Miss.	Mississippi
Mo.	Missouri
Mong.	Mongolia
Mont.	Montana
Mor.	Morocco
Moz.	Mozambique
mt.	mount
mtn., mts.	mountain, mountains
N N,. No.	North, Northern
N. Amer.	North America

Nat'l Pk	National Park
N. Br.	New Brunswick
N.C.	North Carolina
N. Dak.	North Dakota
Nebr.	Nebraska
Neth.	Netherlands
Neth. Ant.	Netherlands Antilles
Nev.	Nevada
Newf.	Newfoundland
N.H.	New Hampshire
Nic.	Nicaragua
N. Ire.	Northern Ireland
N.J.	New Jersey
N. Korea	North Korea
N. Mex.	New Mexico
Nor.	Norway
N.S.	Nova Scotia
N.W.T.	Northwest Territories
N.Y.	New York
N.Z.	New Zealand
O Okla.	Oklahoma
Ont.	Ontario
Oreg.	Oregon
P Pa.	Pennsylvania
Pak.	Pakistan
Pan.	Panama
Papua N.G.	Papua New Guinea
Par.	Paraguay
P.E.I.	Prince Edward Island
pen.	peninsula
Phil.	Philippines
pk.	park
plat.	plateau
Pol.	Poland
Port.	Portugal, Portuguese
P. Rico	Puerto Rico
prom.	promontory
prov.	province, provincial
pt., pte.	point, pointe
Q Que.	Québec
R reg.	region
Rep.	Republic
res.	reservoir
R.I.	Rhode Island
riv.	river
Rom.	Romania
S S.	South, Southern
sa.	serra, sierra
S. Africa	South Africa
S. Amer.	South America

São T. & Pr.	São Tomé & Príncipe
Sask.	Saskatchewan
S.C.	South Carolina
Scot.	Scotland
S. Dak.	South Dakota
Sen.	Senegal
Sing.	Singapore
S. Korea	South Korea
S. Leone	Sierra Leone
Sol. Is.	Solomon Islands
Sp.	Spain, Spanish
St.	Saint, Sainte
str.	strait
St. Vinc. & Grens.	Saint Vincent & the Grenadines
Switz.	Switzerland
T Tanz.	Tanzania
Tenn.	Tennessee
Terr.	Territory
Thai.	Thailand
Trin. & Tob.	Trinidad & Tobago
Tun.	Tunisia
U U. A. E.	United Arab Emirates
U. K.	United Kingdom
Ukr.	Ukraine
Urug.	Uruguay
U. S.	United States
V Va.	Virginia
Ven. Venez.	Venezuela
V.I. (Br.)	Virgin Islands (British)
V.I. (U.S.)	Virgin Islands (U.S.)
Viet.	Vietnam
vol.	volcano
Vt,.	Vermont
W W.	West, Western
Wash.	Washington
W. Indies	West Indies
Wis.	Wisconsin
W. Samoa	Western Samoa
W. Va.	West Virginia
Wyo.	Wyoming
Y Yugo.	Yugoslavia
Z Zim.	Zimbabwe

111

Aa – Aksub

A

26/A3 **Aa** (riv.), Fr.
30/B2 **Aa** (riv.), Fr.
32/E1 **Aa** (riv.), Fr.
28/D5 **Aa** (riv.), Ger.
29/G5 **Aa** (riv.), Ger.
37/E3 **Aabach** (riv.), Swi.
37/E2 **Aach**, Ger.
37/F2 **Aach** (riv.), Ger.
26/D3 **Aachen**, Ger.
31/F2 **Aachen**, Ger.
33/G1 **Aachen**, Ger.
28/C5 **Aalburg**, Neth.
26/F4 **Aalen**, Ger.
33/J2 **Aalen**, Ger.
28/B4 **Aalsmeer**, Neth.
26/C3 **Aalst**, Belg.
30/D2 **Aalst**, Belg.
32/F1 **Aalst**, Belg.
28/D5 **Aalten**, Neth.
28/A6 **Aalter**, Belg.
30/C1 **Aalter**, Belg.
31/H3 **Aar** (riv.), Ger.
33/H3 **Aarau**, Swi.
36/E3 **Aarau**, Swi.
36/D3 **Aarberg**, Swi.
36/D3 **Aarburg**, Swi.
28/A6 **Aardenburg**, Neth.
30/C1 **Aardenburg**, Neth.
33/H3 **Aare** (riv.), Swi.
36/D3 **Aare** (riv.), Swi.
36/E3 **Aargau** (canton), Swi.
26/C3 **Aarschot**, Belg.
28/B7 **Aarschot**, Belg.
31/D2 **Aarschot**, Belg.
28/B6 **Aartselaar**, Belg.
30/D1 **Aartselaar**, Belg.
36/D3 **Aarwangen**, Swi.
54/E5 **Aba**, China
40/D2 **Aba**, Hun.
76/G6 **Aba**, Nga.
79/G5 **Aba**, Nga.
77/M7 **Aba**, Zaire
52/D5 **Abā as Su'ūd**, SAr.
77/P4 **Abā as Su'ūd**, SAr.
106/G5 **Abacaxis** (riv.), Braz.
52/C5 **Abadab** (peak), Sudan
48/D6 **Ābādān**, Iran
51/G4 **Ābādān**, Iran
52/E2 **Ābādān**, Iran
77/Q1 **Ābādān**, Iran
51/H4 **Ābādeh**, Iran
52/F2 **Ābādeh**, Iran
108/C1 **Abadia dos Dourados**, Braz.
40/E2 **Abádszalók**, Hun.
107/J7 **Abaeté**, Braz.
108/C1 **Abaeté**, Braz.
107/J4 **Abaetetuba**, Braz.
68/G4 **Abaiang** (atoll), Kiri.
88/D4 **Abajo** (mts.), Ut,US
46/K4 **Abakan**, Rus.
106/D6 **Abancay**, Peru
54/G3 **Abaq Qi**, China
34/E3 **Abarán**, Sp.
60/H6 **Abariringa (Canton)** (atoll), Kiri.
51/H4 **Abar Kūh**, Iran
52/F2 **Abar Kūh**, Iran
47/Q5 **Abashiri**, Japan
55/N3 **Abashiri**, Japan
101/E4 **Abasolo**, Mex.
46/H5 **Abay**, Kaz.
77/N6 **Ābaya Hayk'** (lake), Eth.
46/K4 **Abaza**, Rus.
37/F6 **Abbadia Lariana**, It.
33/J5 **Abbadia San Salvatore**, It.
38/B1 **Abbadia San Salvatore**, It.
30/A3 **Abbeville**, Fr.
32/D1 **Abbeville**, Fr.
89/H6 **Abbeville**, La,US
93/J5 **Abbeville**, La,US
96/E4 **Abbeville**, La,US
97/H3 **Abbeville**, SC,US
21/H7 **Abbeyfeale**, Ire.
22/E2 **Abbey Head** (pt.), Sc,UK
72/B3 **Abbot** (peak), Austl.
83/T **Abbot Ice Shelf**, Ant.
23/G6 **Abbots Bromley**, Eng,UK
24/D5 **Abbotsbury**, Eng,UK
19/M6 **Abbots Langley**, Eng,UK
53/K2 **Abbottābād**, Pak.
28/B4 **Abcoude**, Neth.
50/D2 **'Abd al 'Azīz, Jabal** (mts.), Syria
77/R5 **'Abd al Kūrī** (isl.), Yem.
52/E2 **Abdānān**, Iran
64/B2 **Abdul Hakīm**, Pak.
45/K1 **Abdulino**, Rus.
77/K5 **Abéché**, Chad
81/E2 **Abel Erasmuspas** (pass), SAfr.
68/G4 **Abemama** (atoll), Kiri.
76/E6 **Abengourou**, IvC.
78/E5 **Abengourou**, IvC.
20/D5 **Åbenrå**, Den.
26/E1 **Åbenrå**, Den.
26/F4 **Abens** (riv.), Ger.
33/J2 **Abens** (riv.), Ger.
26/F4 **Abensberg**, Ger.
76/F6 **Abeokuta**, Nga.
79/F5 **Abeokuta**, Nga.
22/D5 **Aber**, Wal,UK
24/B2 **Aberaeron**, Wal,UK
24/C1 **Aberangell**, Wal,UK
24/B2 **Aberarth**, UK
24/C3 **Abercarn**, Wal,UK
24/C3 **Aberdare**, Wal,UK
22/D6 **Aberdaron**, Wal,UK
73/D2 **Aberdeen**, Austl.
86/G2 **Aberdeen** (lake), NW,Can
80/D4 **Aberdeen**, SAfr.
18/C3 **Aberdeen**, Sc,UK
97/F3 **Aberdeen**, Ms,US
86/G4 **Aberdeen**, SD,US
89/G2 **Aberdeen**, SD,US
91/J4 **Aberdeen**, SD,US
86/D4 **Aberdeen**, Wa,US
90/C4 **Aberdeen**, Wa,US
24/B1 **Aberdyfi**, Wal,UK
24/C3 **Abergavenny**, Wal,UK
22/E5 **Abergele**, Wal,UK
24/B2 **Aberporth**, Wal,UK
22/D6 **Abersoch**, Wal,UK
24/C3 **Abersychan**, Wal,UK
92/B2 **Abert** (lake), Or,US
24/C3 **Abertillery**, Wal,UK
24/B2 **Aberystwyth**, Wal,UK
52/D5 **Abhā**, SAr.
77/P4 **Abhā**, SAr.
51/G2 **Abhar**, Iran
52/E1 **Abhar**, Iran
77/P5 **Abḩe Bad** (lake), Djib., Eth.
103/G4 **Abide, Serranía de** (range), Col.
76/F6 **Abidjan**, IvC.
78/D5 **Abidjan**, IvC.
57/J7 **Abiko**, Japan
93/H3 **Abilene**, Ks,US
96/D2 **Abilene**, Ks,US
101/F1 **Abilene**, Tx,US
88/G5 **Abilene**, Tx,US
93/H4 **Abilene**, Tx,US
96/D3 **Abilene**, Tx,US
25/E3 **Abingdon**, Eng,UK
94/D4 **Abingdon**, Va,US
97/H2 **Abingdon**, Va,US
95/R10 **Abino** (pt.), On,Can
93/F3 **Abiquiu**, NM,US
96/B2 **Abiquiu**, NM,US
42/C1 **Abisko**, Swe.
87/H4 **Abitibi** (lake), On,Can
87/H4 **Abitibi** (riv.), On,Can
94/D1 **Abitibi** (riv.), On,Can
94/E1 **Abitibi** (lake), On,Can
45/G4 **Abkhaz Aut. Rep.**, Geo.
37/F1 **Ablach** (riv.), Ger.
50/B5 **Abnūb**, Egypt
64/C2 **Abohar**, India
78/E5 **Aboisso**, IvC.
76/F6 **Abomey**, Ben.
79/F5 **Abomey**, Ben.
36/C5 **Abondance**, Fr.
40/E2 **Abony**, Hun.
67/E2 **Aborlan**, Phil.
20/G3 **Åbo (Turku)**, Fin.
42/D3 **Åbo (Turku)**, Fin.
61/J5 **Abra** (riv.), Phil.
94/C4 **Abraham Lincoln Birthplace Nat'l Hist. Site**, Ky,US
97/G2 **Abraham Lincoln Birthplace Nat'l Hist. Site**, Ky,US
103/H1 **Abraham's Bay**, Bahm.
104/C2 **Abraham's Bay**, Bahm.
34/A3 **Abrantes**, Port.
106/E8 **Abra Pampa**, Arg.
109/C1 **Abra Pampa**, Arg.
100/B3 **Abreojos, Punta** (pt.), Mex.
77/M3 **'Abrī**, Sudan
19/P7 **Abridge**, Eng,UK
40/F2 **Abrud**, Rom.
33/K5 **Abruzzi** (reg.), It.
38/C1 **Abruzzi** (reg.), It.
40/A4 **Abruzzi** (reg.), It.
38/C2 **Abruzzo Nat'l Park**, It.
40/A5 **Abruzzo Nat'l Park**, It.
33/J3 **Absam**, Aus.
37/H3 **Absam**, Aus.
90/F4 **Absaroka** (range), Mt, Wy,US
92/E1 **Absaroka** (range), Wy,US
50/D3 **Abū aḑ Ḑuhūr**, Syria
52/F4 **Abū al Abyaḑ** (isl.), UAE
51/G5 **Abū 'Alī** (isl.), SAr.
52/D5 **Abū 'Arīsh**, SAr
52/B5 **Abū Dawm**, Sudan
53/F4 **Abū Dhabi (Abū Ẓaby)** (cap.), UAE
52/E3 **Abū Ḩadrīyah**, SAr.
52/B5 **Abū Ḩamad**, Sudan
77/M4 **Abū Ḩamad**, Sudan
49/B4 **Abū Ḩammād**, Egypt
49/B4 **Abū Ḩummuş**, Egypt
76/G6 **Abuja** (cap.), Nga.
79/G4 **Abuja Cap. Terr.** (terr.), Nga.
49/B4 **Abū Kabīr**, Egypt
50/B4 **Abū Kabīr**, Egypt
50/E3 **Abū Kamāl**, Syria
52/D2 **Abū Kamāl**, Syria
57/G2 **Abukuma** (hills), Japan
57/G2 **Abukuma** (riv.), Japan
61/J5 **Abulug**, Phil.
106/E6 **Abunã** (riv.), Bol.
106/E5 **Abunã** (riv.), Braz.
49/G8 **Abū Qashsh**, WBnk.
53/K4 **Abu Road**, India
62/B3 **Abu Road**, India
52/C4 **Abū Rubayq**, SAr.
50/D3 **Abū Rujmayn, Jabal** (mts.), Syria
52/C4 **Abu Shagara** (cape), Sudan
52/B4 **Abu Simbel** (ruins), Egypt
77/N5 **Ābuyē Mēda** (peak), Eth.
53/F4 **Abū Ẓaby (Abu Dhabi)** (cap.), UAE
52/C4 **Abyār 'Alī**, SAr.
77/M2 **Abydos** (ruins), Egypt
52/B3 **Abydos (El Amra)** (ruins), Egypt
87/K4 **Acadia Nat'l Park**, Me,US
88/N3 **Acadia Nat'l Park**, Me,US
95/G2 **Acadia Nat'l Park**, Me,US
93/J5 **Acadian Village**, La,US
96/E4 **Acadian Village**, La,US
101/E4 **Acámbaro**, Mex.
99/M10 **Acampo**, Ca,US
103/G4 **Acandí**, Col.
100/D4 **Acaponeta**, Mex.
100/D4 **Acaponeta** (riv.), Mex.
101/E5 **Acapulco**, Mex.
102/B2 **Acapulco**, Mex.
84/H8 **Acapulco**, Mex.
106/G3 **Acarai** (mts.), Braz.
106/G5 **Acari** (riv.), Braz.
106/D7 **Acarí**, Peru
106/E2 **Acarigua**, Ven.
101/F5 **Acatlán**, Mex.
102/B2 **Acatlán**, Mex.
101/F5 **Acatlán de Pérez Figueroa**, Mex.
101/N8 **Acatlán de Pérez Figueroa**, Mex.
101/M8 **Acatzingo de Hidalgo**, Mex.
38/D2 **Acciaroli**, It.
76/E6 **Accra** (cap.), Gha.
79/E5 **Accra** (cap.), Gha.
23/F4 **Accrington**, Eng,UK
34/B3 **Aceuchal**, Sp.
37/H2 **Ach** (riv.), Ger.
106/E7 **Achacachi**, Bol.
106/E2 **Achaguas**, Ven.
109/B5 **Achao**, Chile
76/H4 **Achegour** (well), Niger
79/H2 **Achegour** (well), Niger
37/H2 **Achen** (pass), Ger.
55/K2 **Acheng**, China
19/S10 **Achères**, Fr.
31/H6 **Achern**, Ger.
30/B3 **Achicourt**, Fr.
30/B3 **Achiel-le-Grand**, Fr.
95/N6 **Achigan** (riv.), Qu,Can
21/G7 **Achill** (isl.), Ire.
21/G7 **Achill Head** (pt.), Ire.
78/D2 **Achmîm** (well), Mrta.
46/K4 **Achinsk**, Rus.
31/G3 **Acht, Hohe** (peak), Ger.
102/E3 **Achuapa**, Nic.
50/B2 **Acıpayam**, Turk.
38/D4 **Acireale**, It.
41/E1 **Ackerly**, Tx,US
103/H1 **Acklins** (isl.), Bahm.
104/C2 **Acklins** (isl.), Bahm.
84/K7 **Acklins** (isl.), Bahm.
89/M7 **Acklins** (isl.), Bahm.
23/G4 **Ackworth Moor Top**, Eng,UK
72/C4 **Acland** (peak), Austl.
25/H1 **Acle**, Eng,UK
105/B6 **Aconcagua** (peak), Arg.
109/B3 **Aconcagua** (peak), Arg.
100/C2 **Aconchi**, Mex.
92/E5 **Aconchi**, Mex
107/L5 **Acopiara**, Braz.
38/B1 **Acquapendente**, It.
33/H4 **Acqui Terme**, It.
70/F6 **Acraman** (lake), Austl.
108/B1 **Acreúna**, Braz.
39/L7 **Acropolis**, Gre.
69/M7 **Actaeon Group** (isls.), FrPol.
19/N7 **Acton**, Eng,UK
101/F5 **Actopan**, Mex.
101/L6 **Actopan**, Mex.
102/B2 **Actopan**, Mex.
107/L5 **Açu**, Braz.
101/P8 **Acula**, Mex.
102/F1 **Acumal**, Mex
93/G5 **Acuña**, Mex
96/C4 **Acuña**, Mex
79/F5 **Ada**, Gha.
94/D3 **Ada**, Oh,US
89/G5 **Ada**, Ok,US
93/H4 **Ada**, Ok,US
96/D3 **Ada**, Ok,US
40/E3 **Ada**, Yugo.
87/J1 **Adair** (cape), NW,Can
92/D5 **Adair** (bay), Mex
34/C2 **Adaja** (riv.), Sp.
47/U4 **Adak** (isl.), Ak,US
85/C6 **Adak** (isl.), Ak,US
85/C6 **Adak** (str.), Ak,US
109/D7 **Adam** (peak), Falk.
108/B2 **Adamantina**, Braz.
76/H6 **Adamaoua** (plat.), Camr.
37/G5 **Adamello** (peak), It.
73/D3 **Adaminaby**, Austl.
90/D3 **Adams** (lake), BC,Can
90/C4 **Adams** (peak), Wa,US
64/G4 **Adam's Bridge** (shoals), SrL.
69/M7 **Adamstown**, Pitc.
79/H5 **Adamwa** (plat.), Camr.
79/H5 **Adamwa** (plat.), Nga.
49/D1 **Adana**, Turk.
49/D1 **Adana** (prov.), Turk.
50/C2 **Adana**, Turk.
50/C2 **Adana** (prov.), Turk.
52/C1 **Adana**, Turk.
77/P5 **'Adan (Aden)**, Yem.
41/K5 **Adapazarı**, Turk.
44/D4 **Adapazarı**, Turk.
50/D1 **Adapazarı**, Turk.
52/B5 **Adarama**, Sudan
83/M **Adare** (cape), Ant.
21/H7 **Adare**, Ire.
32/C5 **Adarza** (mtn.), Fr.
34/E1 **Adarza** (mtn.), Fr.
33/H4 **Adda** (riv.), It.
37/F5 **Adda** (riv.), It.
77/M4 **Ad Dabbah**, Sudan
51/F5 **Ad Dahnā'** (des.), SAr.
52/D3 **Ad Dahnā'** (des.), SAr.
77/P2 **Ad Dahnā'** (des.), SAr.
77/M5 **Ad Damazin**, Sudan
52/B5 **Ad Dāmir**, Sudan
77/M4 **Ad Dāmir**, Sudan
52/F3 **Ad Dammām**, SAr.
77/R2 **Ad Dammām**, SAr.
49/B4 **Ad Daqahlīyah** (gov.), Egypt
50/B4 **Ad Daqahlīyah** (gov.), Egypt
52/F3 **Ad Dawḩah (Doha)** (cap.), Qatar
77/R2 **Ad Dawḩah (Doha)** (cap.), Qatar
51/E3 **Ad Dawr**, Iraq
49/B4 **Ad Dilinjāt**, Egypt
77/N6 **Addis Ababa** (cap.), Eth.
74/F4 **Addis Ababa (Ādis Ābeba)** (cap.), Eth.
99/Q16 **Addison**, Il,US
51/F4 **Ad Dīwānīyah**, Iraq
52/D2 **Ad Dīwānīyah**, Iraq
77/P1 **Ad Dīwānīyah**, Iraq
19/M7 **Addlestone**, Eng,UK
80/D4 **Addo Elephant Nat'l Park**, SAfr.
51/F3 **Ad Dujayl**, Iraq
77/P3 **Ad Duwādimī**, SAr.
52/D2 **Ad Duwayd**, SAr.
77/M5 **Ad Duwaym**, Sudan
83/V **Adelaide** (isl.), Ant.
68/C8 **Adelaide**, Austl.
70/F6 **Adelaide**, Austl.
86/G2 **Adelaide** (pen.), NW,Can
80/D4 **Adelaide**, SAfr.
70/E2 **Adelaide River**, Austl.
70/C3 **Adèle** (isl.), Austl.
29/G5 **Adelebsen**, Ger.
29/H3 **Adelheidsdorf**, Ger.
83/K **Adélie** (coast), Ant.
73/D2 **Adelong**, Austl.
37/G1 **Adelsried**, Ger.
77/Q5 **Aden** (gulf), Afr., Asia
48/D8 **Aden** (gulf), Asia
75/G3 **Aden** (gulf), Asia, Afr.
52/D6 **Aden**, Yem.
77/P5 **Aden**, Yem.
52/E6 **Aden** (gulf), Yemen
31/F3 **Adenau**, Ger.
29/H2 **Adendorf**, Ger.
49/D4 **Adh Dhirā'**, Jor.
67/H4 **Adi** (isl.), Indo.
52/C6 **Ādī Ārk'ay**, Eth.
52/C6 **Ādī Da'iro**, Eth.
33/J4 **Adige** (riv.), It.
37/H6 **Adige (Etsch)** (riv.), It.
51/E1 **Adigeni**, Geo.
52/C6 **Ādīgrat**, Eth
77/N5 **Ādīgrat**, Eth.
52/C6 **Ādī K'eyih**, Eth.
62/C4 **Adilābād**, India
51/E2 **Adilcevaz**, Turk.
79/E2 **Adiora** (well), Mali
64/G3 **Adirāmpatnam**, India
89/L3 **Adirondack** (mts.), NY,US
94/F2 **Adirondack** (mts.), NY,US
77/N6 **Ādīs Ābeba (Addis Ababa)** (cap.), Eth.
77/N5 **Ādīs Zemen**, Eth.
52/C6 **Ādī Ugrī**, Eth.
50/D2 **Adıyaman**, Turk.
50/D2 **Adıyaman** (prov.), Turk.
41/H2 **Adjud**, Rom.
101/F4 **Adjuntas** (res.), Mex.
23/F4 **Adlington**, Eng,UK
37/E3 **Adliswil**, Swi.
87/H1 **Admiralty** (inlet), NW,Can
86/C3 **Admirality** (isl.), Ak,US
86/C3 **Admiralty I. Nat'l Mon.**, Ak,US
70/D2 **Admiralty** (gulf), Austl.
68/D5 **Admiralty** (isls.), PNG
99/B2 **Admiralty** (inlet), Wa,US
85/M4 **Admiralty I. Nat'l Mem.**, Ak,US
57/L9 **Ado** (riv.), Japan
76/F6 **Ado**, Nga.
79/F5 **Ado**, Nga.
57/M9 **Adogawa**, Japan
62/C4 **Ādoni**, India
32/C5 **Adour** (riv.), Fr.
34/E1 **Adour** (riv.), Fr.
34/D4 **Adra**, Sp.
38/D4 **Adrano**, It.
76/E2 **Adrar**, Alg.
79/F1 **Adrar** (wilaya), Alg.
76/C3 **Adrar** (reg.), Mrta.
78/B1 **Adrar** (reg.), Mrta.
76/E1 **Adrar bou Nasser** (peak), Mor.
76/F4 **Adrar des Iforas** (mts.), Afr.
79/F1 **Adrar des Iforas** (mts.), Mali
77/K5 **Adré**, Chad
33/K4 **Adria**, It.
94/C3 **Adrian**, Mi,US
18/E4 **Adriatic** (sea), Eur.
33/K4 **Adriatic** (sea), Eur.
40/B4 **Adriatic** (sea), Eur.
100/C2 **Aduana del Sásabe**, Mex.
52/C5 **Adulis** (ruins), Eth.
25/F5 **Adur** (riv.), Eng,UK
52/C6 **Ādwa**, Eth.
77/N5 **Ādwa**, Eth.
23/G4 **Adwick le Street**, Eng,UK
47/P3 **Adycha** (riv.), Rus.
44/G3 **Adyge Aut. Rep.**, Rus.
45/G4 **Adzhar Aut. Rep.**, Geo.
50/E1 **Adzhar Aut. Rep.**, Geo.
76/E6 **Adzopé**, IvC.
43/N2 **Adz'va** (riv.), Rus.
18/F5 **Aegean** (sea), Eur.
39/J3 **Aegean** (sea), Gre.
44/B5 **Aegean** (sea), Gre., Turk.
26/F1 **Ærø** (isl.), Den.
24/B2 **Aeron** (riv.), Wal,UK
36/D3 **Aesch**, Swi.
36/D4 **Aeschi bei Spiez**, Swi.
22/E1 **Ae, Water of** (riv.), Sc,UK
79/F5 **Afadjoto** (peak), Gha.
51/F3 **'Afak**, Iraq
50/B2 **Afándou**, Gre.
69/X15 **Afareaitu**, FrPol.
49/F7 **Afek Nat'l Park**, Isr.
32/B3 **Aff** (riv.), Fr.
82/C6 **Affenrücken**, Namb.
36/D3 **Affoltern im Emmental**, Swi.
46/G6 **Afghanistan**
48/F6 **Afghanistan**
53/H2 **Afghanistan**
64/A1 **Afghanistan**
77/Q7 **Afgooye**, Som.
77/P3 **'Afīf**, SAr.
77/P7 **Afmadow**, Som.
85/H4 **Afognak** (isl.), Ak,US
85/H4 **Afognak** (mtn.), Ak,US
78/C2 **Afollé** (reg.), Mrta.
108/D2 **Afonso Cláudio**, Braz.
38/D2 **Afragola**, It.
16/J6 **Africa**
74/* **Africa**
99/K10 **Africa USA (Marine World)**, Ca,US
49/E1 **'Afrīn**, Syria
49/E1 **'Afrīn** (riv.), Syria
50/D2 **'Afrīn**, Syria
49/E1 **Afrin** (riv.), Turk.
36/A3 **Afrique** (mtn.), Fr.
50/D2 **Afşin**, Turk.
28/C2 **Afsluitdijk (IJsselmeer)** (dam), Neth.
29/F5 **Afte** (riv.), Ger.
90/F5 **Afton**, Wy,US
92/E2 **Afton**, Wy,US
49/D3 **'Afula**, Isr.
49/G6 **'Afula**, Isr.
50/C3 **'Afula**, Isr.
44/D5 **Afyon**, Turk.
50/B2 **Afyon**, Turk.
50/B2 **Afyon** (prov.), Turk.
76/H4 **Agadem**, Niger
76/G4 **Agadez**, Niger
79/G2 **Agadez**, Niger
79/H2 **Agadez** (dept.), Niger
76/D1 **Agadir**, Mor.
46/H5 **Agadyr'**, Kaz.
75/H6 **Agalega** (isls.), Mrts.
79/F2 **Agamor** (well), Mali
68/D3 **Agaña** (cap.), Guam
57/F2 **Agano** (riv.), Japan
77/N6 **Āgaro**, Eth.
63/F3 **Agartala**, India
83/V **Agassiz** (cape), Ant.
87/T6 **Agassiz** (ice field), NW,Can
107/H5 **Agate Fossil Beds Nat'l Mon.**, Nb,US
93/G2 **Agate Fossil Beds Nat'l Mon.**, Ne,US
67/J5 **Agats**, Indo.
47/T4 **Agattu** (isl.), Ak,US
85/A5 **Agattu** (isl.), Ak,US
85/A5 **Agattu** (str.), Ak,US
79/G5 **Agbor**, Nga.
76/E6 **Agboville**, IvC.
78/D5 **Agboville**, IvC.
45/H5 **Ağdam**, Azer.
51/F2 **Ağdam**, Azer.
51/F1 **Ağdash**, Azer.
32/E6 **Agde**, Fr.
35/G1 **Agde**, Fr.
32/E5 **Agde, Cap d'** (cape), Fr.
35/G1 **Agde, Cap d'** (cape), Fr.
51/F1 **Agdzhabedi**, Azer.
32/D4 **Agen**, Fr.
57/H7 **Ageo**, Japan
26/E1 **Agerbæk**, Den.
37/E3 **Agerisee** (lake), Swi.
29/E6 **Agger** (riv.), Ger.
31/G2 **Agger** (riv.), Ger.
27/L4 **Aggteleki Nat'l Park**, Hun.
40/E1 **Aggteleki Nat'l Park**, Hun.
22/B3 **Aghagallon**, NI,UK
21/H7 **Aghagower**, Ire.
51/G4 **Āghā Jārī**, Iran
52/E2 **Āghā Jārī**, Iran
100/C3 **Aglabampo** (lag.), Mex.
50/D2 **Ağın**, Turk.
47/M4 **Aginskoye**, Rus.
54/G1 **Aginskoye**, Rus.
22/B1 **Agivey**, NI,UK
50/C1 **Ağlıköy**, Turk.
32/E5 **Agly** (riv.), Fr.
39/G3 **Agnanderón**, Gre.
41/G3 **Agnita**, Rom.
37/E5 **Agno**, It.
37/E6 **Agno**, Swi.
38/D2 **Agnone**, It.
57/M10 **Ago**, Japan
33/H4 **Agogna** (riv.), It.
61/J5 **Agoo**, Phil.
33/K3 **Agordo**, It.
32/D5 **Agout** (riv.), Fr.
35/G1 **Agout** (riv.), Fr.
62/C2 **Āgra**, India
34/E2 **Agreda**, Sp.
38/E2 **Agri** (riv.), It.
45/G5 **Ağrı** (prov.), Turk.
51/E2 **Ağrı** (prov.), Turk.
39/H3 **Agriá**, Gre.
45/H5 **Ağrı (Ararat)** (peak), Turk.
38/C4 **Agrigento**, It.
68/D3 **Agrihan** (isl.), NMar.
18/F5 **Agrínion**, Gre.
39/G3 **Agrínion**, Gre.
38/D2 **Agropoli**, It.
40/B5 **Agropoli**, It.
43/M4 **Agryz**, Rus.
101/L6 **Agua Blanca Iturbide**, Mex.
108/D1 **Água Boa**, Braz.
107/K5 **Água Branca**, Braz.
100/B1 **Agua Caliente**, Az,US
103/H4 **Aguachica**, Col.
106/D2 **Aguachica**, Col.
104/E3 **Aguadilla**, PR
102/C2 **Agua Dulce**, Mex.
103/F4 **Aguadulce**, Pan.
106/B2 **Aguadulce**, Pan.
104/D5 **Agua Larga**, Ven.
35/P10 **Agualva-Cacém**, Port.
102/E3 **Aguan** (riv.), Hon.
95/J1 **Aguanus** (riv.), Qu,Can
108/B2 **Aguapeí** (riv.), Braz.
100/C2 **Agua Prieta**, Mex.
88/E5 **Agua Prieta**, Mex.
92/E5 **Agua Prieta**, Mex
106/E2 **Aguaro-Guariquito Nat'l Park**, Ven.
100/E4 **Aguascalientes**, Mex.
100/E4 **Aguascalientes** (state), Mex.
88/F7 **Aguascalientes**, Mex.
108/B1 **Aguavermelha** (res.), Braz.
108/B2 **Agudos**, Braz.
34/A2 **Agueda**, Port.
34/B2 **Agueda** (riv.), Sp.
76/F4 **Aguelhok**, Mali
76/C3 **Aguenit**, WSah.
57/M10 **Agui**, Japan
68/D3 **Aguijan** (isl.), NMar.
34/C4 **Aguilar**, Sp.
34/C1 **Aguilar de Campóo**, Sp.
109/C2 **Aguilares**, Arg.
34/E4 **Aguilas**, Sp.
100/E5 **Aguililla**, Mex.
35/X17 **Agüimes**, Canl.
105/A3 **Aguja** (pt.), Peru
74/E8 **Agulhas** (cape), SAfr.
80/C4 **Agulhas** (cape), SAfr.
80/M11 **Agulhas** (cape), SAfr.
82/D7 **Agulhas** (cape), SAfr.
67/E5 **Agung** (vol.), Indo.
103/H4 **Agustín Codazzi**, Col.
106/D1 **Agustín Codazzi**, Col.
74/C2 **Ahaggar** (mts.), Alg.
76/G3 **Ahaggar** (plat.), Alg.
51/F2 **Ahar**, Iran
28/E4 **Ahaus**, Ger.
31/F3 **Ahbach** (riv.), Ger.
50/C2 **Ahırlı**, Turk.
50/E2 **Ahlat**, Turk.
26/D3 **Ahlen**, Ger.
29/E5 **Ahlen**, Ger.
29/G2 **Ahlerstedt**, Ger.
53/K4 **Ahmadābād**, India
62/B3 **Ahmadābād**, India
53/K5 **Ahmadnagar**, India
62/B4 **Ahmadnagar**, India
53/K3 **Ahmadpur East**, Pak.
62/B2 **Ahmadpur East**, Pak.
64/A2 **Ahmadpur Siāl**, Pak.
77/P6 **Ahmar** (mts.), Eth.
22/B2 **Ahoghill**, NI,UK
100/C3 **Ahome**, Mex.
26/D3 **Ahr** (riv.), Ger.
31/F3 **Ahr** (riv.), Ger.
33/G1 **Ahr** (riv.), Ger.
49/B5 **Ahrāmāt al Jīzah (The Pyramids of Giza)**, Egypt
26/F2 **Ahrensburg**, Ger.
29/H1 **Ahrensburg**, Ger.
29/F5 **Ahse** (riv.), Ger.
101/K8 **Ahuacatitlán**, Mex.
100/D4 **Ahuacatlán**, Mex.
102/D3 **Ahuachapán**, ESal.
101/F5 **Ahuacuotzingo**, Mex.
102/B2 **Ahuacuotzingo**, Mex.
101/E4 **Ahualulco**, Mex.
88/W13 **Ahuimanu**, Hi,US
100/D2 **Ahumada**, Mex.
92/F5 **Ahumada**, Mex
96/B4 **Ahumada**, Mex
32/E3 **Ahun**, Fr.
49/F8 **Aḩuzzam**, Isr.
46/E6 **Ahvāz**, Iran
48/D6 **Ahvāz**, Iran
51/G4 **Ahvāz**, Iran
52/E2 **Ahvāz**, Iran
20/F4 **Ahvenanmaa** (prov.), Fin.
42/D4 **Ahvenanmaa** (prov.), Fin.
52/E6 **Aḩwar**, Yem.
58/C2 **Ai** (riv.), China
80/B2 **Ai-Ais Hot Springs**, Namb.
59/B2 **Aibag Gol** (riv.), China
37/H1 **Aichach**, Ger.
57/E3 **Aichi** (pref.), Japan
57/M9 **Aichi** (pref.), Japan
88/W13 **Aiea**, Hi,US
32/C3 **Aiffres**, Fr.
38/C3 **Aigle**, Swi.
31/D4 **Aiglemont**, Fr.
36/B4 **Aigle, Pic de l'** (peak), Fr.
32/E4 **Aigoual** (mtn.), Fr.
32/F4 **Aigues** (riv.), Fr.
35/F1 **Aigues Tortes y Lago de San Mauricio Nat'l Park**, Sp.
75/Q16 **Aiguille, Cap de l'** (cape), Alg.
57/F1 **Aikawa**, Japan
57/H7 **Aikawa**, Japan
89/K5 **Aiken**, SC,US
97/H3 **Aiken**, SC,US
60/D3 **Ailao** (mtn.), China
60/D4 **Ailao** (mts.), China
103/G4 **Ailigandí**, Pan.
106/C2 **Ailigandí**, Pan.
68/F4 **Ailinglapalap** (atoll), Mrsh.
36/C2 **Aillevillers-et-Lyaumont**, Fr.
30/B4 **Ailly-sur-Noye**, Fr.
22/C1 **Ailsa Craig** (isl.), Sc,UK
68/G3 **Ailuk** (atoll), Mrsh.
61/G2 **Aimen** (pass), China
59/C5 **Aimen Guan** (pass), China
109/C2 **Aimogasta**, Arg.
108/D1 **Aimorés**, Braz.
32/F4 **Ain** (riv.), Fr.
36/B5 **Ain** (dept.), Fr.
36/B5 **Ain** (riv.), Fr.
20/H4 **Ainaži**, Lat.
42/E4 **Ainaži**, Lat.
75/V18 **'Aïn Beïda**, Alg.
76/G1 **'Aïn Beïda**, Alg.
75/S15 **'Aïn Beniau**, Alg.
76/D2 **'Aïn Ben Tili**, Mrta.
75/S15 **'Aïn Bessem**, Alg.
75/R15 **'Aïn Defla**, Alg.
75/R15 **'Aïn Defla** (wilaya), Alg.
75/T15 **'Aïn El Hammam**, Alg.
75/Q16 **'Aïn el Turk**, Alg.
75/V17 **'Aïn Fakroun**, Alg.
75/V17 **'Aïn M'Lila**, Alg.
39/G3 **Aínos** (peak), Gre.
39/G3 **Ainos Nat'l Park**, Gre.
75/U18 **'Aïn Oulmene**, Alg.
75/S16 **'Aïn Oussersa**, Alg.
23/E4 **Ainsdale**, Eng,UK
76/E1 **'Aïn Sefra**, Alg.
91/J5 **Ainsworth**, Ne,US
93/H2 **Ainsworth**, Ne,US
75/S15 **'Aïn Taya**, Alg.
75/Q16 **'Aïn Temouchent**, Alg.
75/Q16 **'Aïn Temouchent** (wilaya), Alg.
75/U18 **'Aïn Touta**, Alg.
76/G4 **Aïr** (plat.), Niger
79/G2 **Aïr** (plat.), Niger
30/A4 **Airaines**, Fr.
86/E3 **Airdrie**, Ab,Can
90/E3 **Airdrie**, Ab,Can
21/D3 **Airdrie**, Sc,UK
30/D5 **Aire** (riv.), Fr.
32/F2 **Aire** (riv.), Fr.
23/G4 **Aire** (riv.), Eng,UK
30/B2 **Aire, Canal de** (can.), Fr.
23/E5 **Aire, Point of** (pt.), Wal,UK
32/C5 **Aire-sur-l'Adour**, Fr.
35/E1 **Aire-sur-l'Adour**, Fr.
30/B2 **Aire-sur-la-Lys**, Fr.
87/J2 **Air Force** (isl.), NW,Can
33/H3 **Airolo**, Swi.
37/E4 **Airolo**, Swi.
23/F3 **Airton**, Eng,UK
32/C3 **Airvault**, Fr.
33/J2 **Aisch** (riv.), Ger.
30/D3 **Aiseau-Presles**, Belg.
59/E3 **Ai Shan** (mtn.), China
85/L3 **Aishihik**, Yk,Can
31/E3 **Aisne** (riv.), Belg.
26/B4 **Aisne** (riv.), Fr.
30/C4 **Aisne** (dept.), Fr.
30/C5 **Aisne** (riv.), Fr.
32/E2 **Aisne** (riv.), Fr.
74/B1 **Aïssa** (peak), Alg.
76/E1 **Aïssa** (peak), Alg.
68/D5 **Aitape**, PNG
57/M9 **Aitō**, Japan
39/G3 **Aitolikón**, Gre.
37/G2 **Aitrach**, Ger.
37/G2 **Aitrang**, Ger.
69/J6 **Aitutaki** (atoll), CookIs.
41/F2 **Aiud**, Rom.
44/B3 **Aiud**, Rom.
18/D4 **Aix-en-Provence**, Fr.
32/F5 **Aix-en-Provence**, Fr.
35/H1 **Aix-en-Provence**, Fr.
32/F4 **Aix-les-Bains**, Fr.
39/H4 **Aíyina**, Gre.
39/H2 **Aíyínion**, Gre.
39/H3 **Aíyion**, Gre.
20/G4 **Aizpute**, Lat.
42/D4 **Aizpute**, Lat.
55/M4 **Aizu-Wakamatsu**, Japan
57/F2 **Aizu-Wakamatsu**, Japan
60/B4 **Aīzwal**, India
63/F3 **Aīzwal**, India
18/D4 **Ajaccio**, Fr.
38/A2 **Ajaccio**, Fr.
38/A2 **Ajaccio** (gulf), Fr.
101/F5 **Ajalpan**, Mex.
101/M8 **Ajalpan**, Mex.
102/B2 **Ajalpan**, Mex.
95/R8 **Ajax**, On,Can
54/D3 **Aj Bogd** (peak), Mong.
76/K1 **Ajdābiyā**, Libya
33/K4 **Ajdovščina**, Slov.
49/G7 **'Ajjah**, WBnk.
52/B5 **Aj Janayet**, Sudan
40/C2 **Ajka**, Hun.
53/K3 **Ajmer**, India
62/B2 **Ajmer**, India
100/B1 **Ajo**, Az,US
88/D5 **Ajo**, Az,US
92/D4 **Ajo**, Az,US
32/B5 **Ajo, Cabo de** (cape), Sp.
34/D1 **Ajo, Cabo de** (cape), Sp.
100/D3 **Ajoya**, Mex.
101/E5 **Ajuchitlán**, Mex.
101/Q10 **Ajusco** (mt.), Mex.
57/F1 **Aka** (riv.), Japan
57/N10 **Akabane**, Japan
54/C1 **Akademik Obruchev** (mts.), Rus.
57/F3 **Akaishi-dake** (mtn.), Japan
44/F5 **Akarsu**, Turk.
56/D3 **Akashi**, Japan
57/K10 **Akashi**, Japan
57/K10 **Akashi** (str.), Japan
75/T15 **Akbou**, Alg.
44/F4 **Akçaabat**, Turk.
50/D1 **Akçaabat**, Turk.
50/D2 **Akçadağ**, Turk.
50/D2 **Akçakale**, Turk.
41/K5 **Akçakoca**, Turk.
50/B1 **Akçakoca**, Turk.
49/A1 **Akçay**, Turk.
76/C3 **Akchâr** (reg.), Mrta.
78/B2 **Akchâr** (reg.), Mrta.
44/E5 **Akdağmadeni**, Turk.
50/C2 **Akdağmadeni**, Turk.
52/G4 **Akdar, Al Jabal** (mts.), Oman
46/K4 **Ak-Dovurak**, Rus.
54/C1 **Ak-Dovurak**, Rus.
57/N9 **Akechi**, Japan
20/D3 **Akershus** (co.), Nor.
77/K7 **Aketi**, Zaire
51/E1 **Akhalkalaki**, Geo.
45/G4 **Akhaltsikhe**, Geo.
51/E1 **Akhaltsikhe**, Geo.
39/H3 **Akharnaí**, Gre.
39/L6 **Akharnaí**, Gre.
39/G3 **Akhelóos** (riv.), Gre.
85/H4 **Akhiok**, Ak,US
44/C5 **Akhisar**, Turk.
50/A2 **Akhisar**, Turk.
51/F1 **Akhmeta**, Geo.
50/B5 **Akhmīm**, Egypt
52/B3 **Akhmīm**, Egypt
77/M2 **Akhmīm**, Egypt
53/K2 **Akhnūr**, India
51/G1 **Akhsu**, Azer.
41/H4 **Akhtopol**, Bul.
45/H3 **Akhtuba** (riv.), Rus.
19/H4 **Akhtubinsk**, Rus.
45/H2 **Akhtubinsk**, Rus.
46/E5 **Akhtubinsk**, Rus.
44/E2 **Akhtyrka**, Ukr.
56/C4 **Aki**, Japan
57/H7 **Aki** (riv.), Japan
85/F3 **Akiachak**, Ak,US
57/H7 **Akigawa**, Japan
84/J4 **Akimiski** (isl.), Can.
87/H3 **Akimiski** (isl.), NW,Can
49/D1 **Akıncı** (pt.), Turk.
44/F4 **Akıncılar**, Turk.
50/D1 **Akıncılar**, Turk.
20/E5 **Åkirkeby**, Den.
27/H1 **Åkirkeby**, Den.
57/H7 **Akishima**, Japan
47/Q6 **Akita**, Japan
55/N4 **Akita**, Japan
76/C4 **Akjoujt**, Mrta.
78/B2 **Akjoujt**, Mrta.
62/D6 **Akkaraipattu**, SrL.
49/D3 **'Akko**, Isr.
50/C3 **'Akko**, Isr.
28/C2 **Akkrum**, Neth.
84/D3 **Aklavik**, Can.
85/L2 **Aklavik**, NW,Can
86/C2 **Aklavik**, NW,Can
78/D2 **'Aklé 'Aouâna** (dune), Mali, Mrta.
56/D3 **Akō**, Japan
76/H7 **Akoga**, Gabon
53/L4 **Akola**, India
62/C3 **Akola**, India
52/C5 **Āk'ordat**, Eth.
77/N4 **Āk'ordat**, Eth.
50/C2 **Akören**, Turk.
76/F6 **Akosombo** (dam), Gha.
79/F5 **Akosombo** (dam), Gha.
87/K2 **Akpatok** (isl.), NW,Can
50/D2 **Akpazar**, Turk.
41/J5 **Akpınar**, Turk.
44/D4 **Akpınar**, Turk.
50/B1 **Akpınar**, Turk.
20/M7 **Akranes**, Ice.
39/J2 **Ákrathos, Ákra** (cape), Gre.
20/C4 **Åkrehamn**, Nor.
39/G4 **Akrítas, Ákra** (cape), Gre.
93/G2 **Akron**, Co,US
89/K3 **Akron**, Oh,US
94/D3 **Akron**, Oh,US
53/L1 **Aksai Chin** (reg.), China
45/K1 **Aksakovo**, Rus.
50/C2 **Aksaray**, Turk.
50/C2 **Aksaray** (prov.), Turk.
54/C4 **Aksay**, China
45/K2 **Aksay**, Kaz.
46/F4 **Aksay**, Kaz.
50/B2 **Akşehir**, Turk.
50/B2 **Akşehir** (lake), Turk.
49/B1 **Akseki**, Turk.
50/B2 **Akseki**, Turk.
46/J5 **Aksu**, China
49/B1 **Aksu** (riv.), Turk.
45/J1 **Aksubayevo**, Rus.

Āksum – Al Q

52/C6 **Āksum,** Eth.
77/N5 **Āksum,** Eth.
39/J2 **Aktí** (pen.), Gre.
44/C4 **Aktí** (pen.), Gre.
45/L2 **Aktyubinsk,** Kaz.
46/F4 **Aktyubinsk,** Kaz.
45/L3 **Aktyubinsk Obl.,** Kaz.
55/L5 **Akune,** Japan
56/B4 **Akune,** Japan
18/B2 **Akureyri,** Ice.
20/N6 **Akureyri,** Ice.
79/F5 **Akuse,** Gha.
85/E5 **Akutan,** Ak,US
85/E5 **Akutan** (isl.), Ak,US
85/E5 **Akutan** (passg.), Ak,US
79/G5 **Akwa Ibom** (state), Nga.
60/B4 **Akyab** (Sittwe), Burma
63/F3 **Akyab** (Sittwe), Burma
45/L2 **Ak"yar,** Rus.
41/K5 **Akyazı,** Turk.
20/D3 **Ål,** Nor.
54/B3 **Ala** (riv.), China
89/J5 **Alabama** (state), US
97/G3 **Alabama** (state), US
89/J5 **Alabama** (riv.), Al,US
97/G3 **Alabama Space and Rocket Center,** Al,US
97/G3 **Alabaster,** Al,US
44/E4 **Alaca,** Turk.
50/C1 **Alaca,** Turk.
50/D2 **Alaçam,** Turk.
50/C1 **Alaçam,** Turk.
97/H4 **Alachua,** Fl,US
103/F1 **Alacranes, Embalse** (res.), Cuba
49/C1 **Aladağ,** Turk.
34/C2 **Alaejos,** Sp.
45/H4 **Alagir,** Rus.
32/E4 **Alagnon** (riv.), Fr.
107/L6 **Alagoinhas,** Braz.
34/B2 **Alagón** (riv.), Sp.
35/E2 **Alagón,** Sp.
51/G4 **Al Aḥmadi,** Kuw.
77/Q2 **Al Aḥmadī,** Kuw.
20/G3 **Alajärvi,** Fin.
42/D3 **Alajärvi,** Fin.
103/E4 **Alajuela,** CR
85/F3 **Alakanuk,** Ak,US
52/C3 **Al Akhḍar,** SAr.
46/J5 **Alakol** (lake), Kaz.
49/D4 **Al 'Āl,** Jor.
50/B4 **Al 'Alamayn,** Egypt
77/L1 **Al 'Alamayn,** Egypt
107/G3 **Alalapadu,** Sur.
51/E2 **Al 'Amādīyah,** Iraq
68/D3 **Alamagan** (isl.), NMar.
46/E6 **Al 'Amārah,** Iraq
51/F4 **Al 'Amārah,** Iraq
52/E2 **Al 'Amārah,** Iraq
51/H5 **'Alāmarvdasht** (riv.), Iran
52/F3 **'Alāmarvdasht** (riv.), Iran
99/K11 **Alameda,** Ca,US
99/L11 **Alameda** (co.), Ca,US
99/L11 **Alameda** (cr.), Ca,US
101/F4 **Alamo,** Mex.
102/B1 **Alamo,** Mex.
92/D4 **Alamo** (lake), Az,US
99/K11 **Alamo,** Ca,US
92/D3 **Alamo,** Nv,US
100/D1 **Alamogordo,** NM,US
88/E5 **Alamogordo,** NM,US
93/E4 **Alamogordo,** NM,US
96/B3 **Alamogordo,** NM,US
100/C2 **Álamos,** Mex.
100/C3 **Álamos,** Mex.
88/E4 **Alamosa,** Co,US
93/F3 **Alamosa,** Co,US
96/B2 **Alamosa,** Co,US
50/E3 **Al Anbār** (gov.), Iraq
18/E2 **Åland** (isls.), Fin.
20/G3 **Åland** (isls.), Fin.
42/D3 **Åland** (isls.), Fin.
26/F2 **Åland** (riv.), Ger.
67/E3 **Alang,** Indo.
49/C1 **Alanya,** Turk.
50/C2 **Alanya,** Turk.
52/B1 **Alanya,** Turk.
81/J7 **Alaotra** (lake), Madg.
46/G4 **Alapayevsk,** Rus.
41/K5 **Alaplı,** Turk.
50/B1 **Alaplı,** Turk.
49/D5 **Al 'Aqabah,** Jor.
50/C4 **Al 'Aqabah,** Jor.
52/C3 **Al 'Aqabah,** Jor.
77/N2 **Al 'Aqabah,** Jor.
34/D3 **Alarcón** (res.), Sp.
50/C4 **Al 'Arīsh,** Egypt
52/B2 **Al 'Arīsh,** Egypt
50/B2 **Alaşehir,** Turk.
51/G3 **Alashtar,** Iran
49/E4 **Al 'Āsimah** (gov.), Jor.
47/V3 **Alaska,** US
84/B3 **Alaska** (range), US
84/B4 **Alaska** (range), US
84/B4 **Alaska** (pen.), US
84/C4 **Alaska** (gulf), US
85/F2 **Alaska,** US
85/L4 **Alaska,** US
86/B2 **Alaska** (state), US
85/F4 **Alaska** (pen.), Ak,US
85/H3 **Alaska Maritime Nat'l Wild. Ref.,** Ak,US
85/J4 **Alaska** (gulf), Ak,US
86/B3 **Alaska** (gulf), Ak,US
85/B5 **Alaska Maritime Nat'l Wild. Ref.,** Ak,US
85/G4 **Alaska Pen. Nat'l Wild. Ref.,** Ak,US
52/C3 **Al 'Assāfīyah,** SAr.
33/H5 **Alassio,** It.
19/H3 **Alatyr',** Rus.

43/K5 **Alatyr',** Rus.
45/H1 **Alatyr',** Rus.
46/E4 **Alatyr',** Rus.
45/H4 **Alaverdi,** Arm.
51/F1 **Alaverdi,** Arm.
20/G3 **Alavus,** Fin.
42/D3 **Alavus,** Fin.
33/H3 **Albula** (riv.), Swi.
37/F4 **Albula** (riv.), Swi.
34/B4 **Alaw, Llyn** (lake), Wal,UK
52/C3 **Al 'Ayn,** SAr.
34/C3 **Alayor,** Sp.
47/R3 **Alazeya** (riv.), Rus.
51/F3 **Al 'Azīzīyah,** Iraq
52/E2 **Al 'Azīzīyah,** Iraq
76/H1 **Al 'Azīzīyah,** Libya
36/H2 **Alb** (riv.), Ger.
33/H4 **Alba,** It.
41/F2 **Alba** (co.), Rom.
50/D2 **Al Bāb,** Syria
52/C1 **Al Bāb,** Syria
18/C5 **Albacete,** Sp.
34/E3 **Albacete,** Sp.
34/C2 **Alba de Tormes,** Sp.
49/B5 **Al Badrashayn,** Egypt
50/B4 **Al Baḥr al Aḥmar** (gov.), Egypt
35/E3 **Albaida,** Sp.
41/F2 **Alba Iulia,** Rom.
44/B3 **Alba Iulia,** Rom.
49/B4 **Al Bājūr,** Egypt
35/E2 **Albalate del Arzobispo,** Sp.
49/D3 **Al Balqā'** (gov.), Jor.
32/E5 **Alban,** Fr.
35/G1 **Alban,** Fr.
95/F1 **Albanel** (lake), Qu,Can
18/E4 **Albania**
39/F2 **Albania**
40/D5 **Albania**
70/B5 **Albania**
84/J4 **Albany,** Austl.
91/M3 **Albany** (riv.), Can.
87/H3 **Albany** (riv.), On,Can
99/K11 **Albany,** Ca,US
89/K5 **Albany,** Ga,US
97/G4 **Albany,** Ga,US
94/C4 **Albany,** Ky,US
87/J4 **Albany** (cap.), NY,US
89/M3 **Albany** (cap.), NY,US
94/F3 **Albany,** NY,US
88/B3 **Albany,** Or,US
90/C4 **Albany,** Or,US
38/B6 **Albarine** (riv.), Fr.
34/E2 **Albarracín,** Sp.
51/F4 **Al Başrah,** Iraq
51/E2 **Al Başrah** (gov.), Iraq
52/E2 **Al Başrah,** Iraq
77/Q1 **Al Başrah,** Iraq
80/A2 **Albatross** (bay), Austl.
80/A2 **Albatross** (pt.), Namb.
49/D2 **Al Batrūn,** Leb.
50/B4 **Al Bawīṭī,** Egypt
70/L2 **Al Bawīṭī,** Egypt
77/K1 **Al Baydā,** Libya
52/E6 **Al Baydā,** Yem.
77/Q5 **Al Baydā,** Yem.
36/E2 **Albbruck,** Ger.
97/H3 **Albemarle,** NC,US
33/H4 **Alben** (peak), It.
33/H4 **Albenga,** It.
38/B6 **Albens,** Fr.
34/C2 **Alberche** (riv.), Sp.
70/E5 **Alberga** (riv.), Austl.
98/C3 **Alberhill,** Ca,US
37/F3 **Alberschwende,** Aus.
26/E1 **Albersdorf,** Ger.
31/H5 **Albersweiler,** Ger.
70/F7 **Albert** (lake), Austl.
73/A2 **Albert** (inlet), Austl.
28/B6 **Albert** (can.), Belg.
31/E2 **Albert** (can.), Belg.
26/E4 **Albert,** Fr.
30/B4 **Albert,** Fr.
32/E2 **Albert,** Fr.
74/F4 **Albert** (lake), Ugan., Zaire
77/M7 **Albert** (lake), Ugan., Zaire
90/E2 **Alberta** (prov.), Can
86/E3 **Alberta** (prov.), Can.
88/D1 **Alberta** (prov.), Can.
40/D2 **Albertirsa,** Hun.
86/G4 **Albert Lea,** Mn,US
89/H3 **Albert Lea,** Mn,US
91/K5 **Albert Lea,** Mn,US
93/J2 **Albert Lea,** Mn,US
77/M7 **Albert Nile** (riv.), Ugan.
109/B7 **Alberto De Agostini Nat'l Park,** Chile
80/Q13 **Alberton,** SAfr.
33/G4 **Albertville,** Fr.
97/G3 **Albertville,** Al,US
31/F6 **Albestroff,** Fr.
36/D4 **Albeuve,** Swi.
32/E5 **Albi,** Fr.
35/G1 **Albi,** Fr.
107/H2 **Albina,** Sur.
33/H4 **Albino,** It.
94/C3 **Albion,** Mi,US
91/J5 **Albion,** Ne,US
93/H2 **Albion,** Ne,US
49/E2 **Al Biqā'** (gov.), Leb.
49/D3 **Al Biqā' (Bekaa)** (val.), Leb.
52/C3 **Al Bi'r,** SAr.
49/D4 **Al Bi'rah,** WBnk.
49/G8 **Al Bi'rah,** WBnk.
28/B5 **Alblasserdam,** Neth.
30/D3 **Albocácer,** Sp.
18/D3 **Ålborg,** Den.
20/D4 **Ålborg,** Den.
46/A4 **Ålborg,** Den.
34/A4 **Albox,** Sp.
95/S10 **Albright Knox Art Gallery,** NY,US
24/D1 **Albrighton,** Eng,UK
36/D5 **Albristhorn** (peak), Swi.

37/F1 **Albstadt,** Ger.
34/A4 **Albufeira,** Port.
49/B4 **Al Buḥayrah** (gov.), Egypt
50/B4 **Al Buḥayrah** (gov.), Egypt
33/H3 **Albula** (riv.), Swi.
37/F4 **Albulapass** (pass), Swi.
34/D4 **Albuñol,** Sp.
88/E4 **Albuquerque,** NM,US
92/H4 **Albuquerque,** NM,US
96/B3 **Albuquerque,** NM,US
34/B3 **Alburquerque,** Sp.
68/D8 **Albury,** Austl.
71/H7 **Albury,** Austl.
73/C3 **Albury,** Austl.
52/F5 **Al Buzūn,** Yem.
36/C6 **Alby-sur-Chéran,** Fr.
35/P10 **Alcabideche,** Port.
34/A3 **Alcácer do Sal,** Port.
35/F2 **Alcalá de Chivert,** Sp.
34/C4 **Alcalá de Guadaira,** Sp.
34/D2 **Alcalá de Henares,** Sp.
35/N9 **Alcalá de Henares,** Sp.
34/C4 **Alcalá de los Gazules,** Sp.
34/D4 **Alcalá la Real,** Sp.
38/C4 **Alcamo,** It.
35/E2 **Alcanadre** (riv.), Sp.
35/E2 **Alcanar,** Sp.
34/B2 **Alcañices,** Sp.
35/E2 **Alcañiz,** Sp.
34/B3 **Alcántara,** Sp.
34/B3 **Alcántara** (res.), Sp.
34/E4 **Alcantarilla,** Sp.
34/D3 **Alcaraz,** Sp.
34/D3 **Alcaraz** (range), Sp.
99/K11 **Alcatraz** (isl.), Ca,US
34/C4 **Alcaudete,** Sp.
34/D3 **Alcázar de San Juan,** Sp.
25/E2 **Alcester,** Eng,UK
35/E3 **Alcira,** Sp.
41/H5 **Alçıtepe,** Turk.
97/H3 **Alcoa,** Tn,US
108/E1 **Alcobaça,** Braz.
34/A3 **Alcobaça,** Port.
34/D2 **Alcobendas,** Sp.
35/N8 **Alcobendas,** Sp.
35/Q10 **Alcochete,** Port.
35/E2 **Alcora,** Sp.
34/D2 **Alcorcón,** Sp.
35/N9 **Alcorcón,** Sp.
35/E2 **Alcorisa,** Sp.
34/B4 **Alcoutim,** Port.
35/E3 **Alcoy,** Sp.
35/G3 **Alcudia,** Sp.
75/G5 **Aldabra** (isls.), Sey.
100/D2 **Aldama,** Mex.
101/F4 **Aldama,** Mex.
102/B1 **Aldama,** Mex.
96/B4 **Aldama,** Mex.
47/N4 **Aldan,** Rus.
47/N4 **Aldan** (plat.), Rus.
47/P3 **Aldan** (riv.), Rus.
48/N3 **Aldan** (riv.), Rus.
25/E4 **Aldbourne,** Eng,UK
23/H4 **Aldbrough,** Eng,UK
25/H2 **Alde** (riv.), Eng,UK
25/H2 **Aldeburgh,** Eng,UK
34/B4 **Aldeia Nova de São Bento,** Port.
82/B2 **Aldeia Viçosa,** Ang.
99/N15 **Alden,** Il,US
31/F2 **Aldenhoven,** Ger.
37/H6 **Aldeno,** It.
22/B2 **Aldergrove,** NI,UK
23/F5 **Alderley Edge,** Eng,UK
25/E4 **Aldermaston,** Eng,UK
32/B2 **Alderney** (isl.), ChI
95/Q9 **Aldershot,** On,Can
25/F4 **Aldershot,** Eng,UK
99/C2 **Alderwood Manor-Bothell North,** Wa,US
93/J5 **Aldine,** Tx,US
96/E4 **Aldine,** Tx,US
37/E1 **Aldingen,** Ger.
25/E1 **Aldridge,** Eng,UK
76/C4 **Aleg,** Mrta.
78/B2 **Aleg,** Mrta.
108/D2 **Alegre,** Braz.
109/E2 **Alegrete,** Braz.
105/A6 **Alejandro Selkirk** (isl.), Chile
85/G4 **Aleknagik,** Ak,US
44/E2 **Aleksandriya,** Ukr.
42/H4 **Aleksandrov,** Rus.
40/E4 **Aleksandrovac,** Yugo.
43/N4 **Aleksandrovsk,** Rus.
47/Q4 **Aleksandrovsk-Sakhalinskiy,** Rus.
75/P13 **Aleksandrovsk-Sakhalinskiy,** Rus.
55/N1 **Aleksandrovsk-Sakhalinskiy,** Rus.
27/K2 **Aleksandrów Kujawski,** Pol.
27/K3 **Aleksandrów Łódzki,** Pol.
44/F2 **Alekseyevka,** Rus.
42/H5 **Aleksin,** Rus.
44/F1 **Aleksin,** Rus.
40/E4 **Aleksinac,** Yugo.
34/A3 **Alenquer,** Port.
51/N6 **Alemdar,** Turk.
107/K8 **Além Paraíba,** Braz.
108/D2 **Além Paraíba,** Braz.
32/D2 **Alençon,** Fr.
107/H4 **Alenquer,** Braz.
88/T10 **Alenuihaha** (chan.), Hi,US
49/E1 **Aleppo (Ḥalab),** Syria
50/D2 **Aleppo (Ḥalab),** Syria
52/C1 **Aleppo (Ḥalab),** Syria
87/S6 **Alert** (pt.), NW,Can

40/F2 **Aleşd,** Rom.
33/H4 **Alessandria,** It.
20/D4 **Ålestrup,** Den.
18/D2 **Ålesund,** Nor.
20/C3 **Ålesund,** Nor.
46/A3 **Ålesund,** Nor.
36/D5 **Aletschhorn** (peak), Swi.
84/A4 **Aleutian** (isls.), US
47/T4 **Aleutian** (isls.), Ak,US
85/B5 **Aleutian** (isls.), Ak,US
85/E5 **Aleutian** (isls.), Ak,US
85/G4 **Aleutian** (range), Ak,US
83/V **Alexander** (cape), Ant.
83/V **Alexander** (isl.), Ant.
84/D4 **Alexander** (arch.), US
85/L4 **Alexander** (arch.), Ak,US
86/C3 **Alexander** (arch.), Ak,US
80/B3 **Alexander Bay,** SAfr.
82/C6 **Alexander Bay,** SAfr.
97/G3 **Alexander City,** Al,US
95/J2 **Alexander Graham Bell Nat'l Hist. Park,** Can
43/V7 **Alexander Nevsky Abbey,** Rus.
71/Q12 **Alexandra,** N.Z.
80/D3 **Alexandra,** SAfr.
82/D6 **Alexandra,** SAfr.
77/L1 **Alexandria,** Egypt
39/H2 **Alexándria,** Gre.
40/F5 **Alexándria,** Gre.
44/B4 **Alexándria,** Gre.
41/G4 **Alexandria,** Rom.
44/C4 **Alexandria,** Rom.
89/H5 **Alexandria,** La,US
93/H5 **Alexandria,** La,US
96/E4 **Alexandria,** La,US
89/G2 **Alexandria,** Mn,US
91/K4 **Alexandria,** Mn,US
89/L4 **Alexandria,** Va,US
94/F4 **Alexandria,** Va,US
97/J2 **Alexandria,** Va,US
98/J8 **Alexandria,** Va,US
49/A4 **Alexandria (Al Iskandarīyah),** Egypt
75/N13 **Alexandria (Al Iskandarīyah),** Egypt
70/F7 **Alexandrina** (lake), Austl.
73/A2 **Alexandrina** (lake), Austl.
39/J2 **Alexandroúpolis,** Gre.
41/G5 **Alexandroúpolis,** Gre.
44/C4 **Alexandroúpolis,** Gre.
50/A1 **Alexandroúpolis,** Gre.
90/C2 **Alexis Creek,** BC,Can
46/J4 **Aleysk,** Rus.
35/E3 **Alfafar,** Sp.
51/E3 **Al Fallūjah,** Iraq
52/D2 **Al Fallūjah,** Iraq
35/P10 **Alfama,** Port.
52/E6 **Al Fardah,** Yem.
35/P11 **Alfarim,** Port.
34/C1 **Alfaro,** Sp.
77/L5 **Al Fāsher,** Sudan
50/B4 **Al Fashn,** Egypt
52/B3 **Al Fashn,** Egypt
41/H4 **Alfatar,** Bul.
51/E3 **Al Fatḥah,** Iraq
52/D1 **Al Fatḥah,** Iraq
51/G4 **Al Fāw,** Iraq
52/E2 **Al Fāw,** Iraq
49/B5 **Al Fayyūm,** Egypt
49/B5 **Al Fayyūm** (gov.), Egypt
50/B4 **Al Fayyūm,** Egypt
50/B4 **Al Fayyūm** (gov.), Egypt
52/B3 **Al Fayyūm,** Egypt
77/M2 **Al Fayyūm,** Egypt
38/E3 **Alfeld,** Ger.
29/G5 **Alfeld,** Ger.
107/J8 **Alfenas,** Braz.
108/C2 **Alfenas,** Braz.
29/E4 **Alfhausen,** Ger.
39/G4 **Alfiós** (riv.), Gre.
23/J5 **Alford,** Eng,UK
73/D3 **Alfred Nat'l Park,** Austl.
23/G5 **Alfreton,** Eng,UK
25/E1 **Alfreton,** Eng,UK
25/G5 **Alfriston,** Eng,UK
31/G2 **Alfter,** Ger.
51/F4 **Al Fuhūd,** Iraq
52/E2 **Al Fuhūd,** Iraq
45/L2 **Alga,** Kaz.
46/F5 **Alga,** Kaz.
20/C4 **Ålgård,** Nor.
34/C4 **Algeciras,** Sp.
75/M12 **Algeciras,** Sp.
35/E3 **Algemesí,** Sp.
75/S15 **Alger** (wilaya), Alg.
75/S15 **Alger (Algiers)** (cap.), Alg.
74/B2 **Algeria**
75/P13 **Algeria**
75/R16 **Algeria**
75/V18 **Algeria**
76/F2 **Algeria**
79/F2 **Algeria**
29/G4 **Algermissen,** Ger.
35/N8 **Algete,** Sp.
49/B4 **Al Ghabīyah** (gov.), Egypt
51/F4 **Al Ghammās,** Iraq
50/B4 **Al Gharbī yah** (gov.), Egypt
77/R4 **Al Ghaydah,** Yem.
38/A2 **Alghero,** It.
50/C5 **Al Ghurdaqah,** Egypt
52/B3 **Al Ghurdaqah,** Egypt
77/M2 **Al Ghurdaqah,** Egypt
76/F1 **Algiers** (cap.), Alg.
75/S15 **Algiers (Alger)** (cap.), Alg.
92/E5 **Algiers** (riv.), Mex
39/H2 **Alistráti,** Gre.
39/J3 **Alivérion,** Gre.
80/D3 **Aliwal North,** SAfr.

34/C4 **Algodonales,** Sp.
91/M4 **Algoma,** Wi,US
94/C2 **Algoma,** Wi,US
99/C3 **Algoma,** Wa,US
99/G6 **Algonac,** Mi,US
99/P15 **Algonquin,** Il,US
35/P10 **Algueirão,** Port.
35/P10 **Algund (Lagundo),** It.
34/A4 **Aljezur,** Port.
49/B4 **Al Jīzah,** Egypt
49/B5 **Al Jīzah** (gov.), Egypt
50/D4 **Al Jīzah,** SAr.
51/E3 **Al Jīzah,** Egypt
50/B4 **Al Jīzah** (gov.), Egypt
52/B2 **Al Jīzah,** Egypt
53/G4 **Al Ḥajar ash Sharqī** (mts.), Oman
52/E5 **Al Hajarayn,** Yem.
53/G5 **Al Ḥallānīyah** (isl.), Oman
34/D4 **Alhama de Granada,** Sp.
34/E4 **Alhama de Murcia,** Sp.
49/D4 **Al Karak,** Jor.
50/C4 **Al Karak,** Jor.
52/C2 **Al Karak,** Jor.
77/N1 **Al Karak,** Jor.
98/D2 **Alhambra,** Ca,US
50/B4 **Al Hammām,** Egypt
77/L1 **Al Hammām,** Egypt
38/B4 **Al Ḥammāmāt,** Tun.
35/Q10 **Alhandra,** Port.
51/F4 **Al Hārithah,** Iraq
52/B3 **Al Karnak,** Egypt
31/E2 **Alken,** Belg.
50/E2 **Al Ḥasakah,** Syria
50/E2 **Al Ḥasakah** (prov.), Syria
53/G4 **Al Khāburah,** Oman
52/D1 **Al Ḥasakah,** Syria
34/C4 **Alhaurín el Grande,** Sp.
51/F3 **Al Khāliṣ,** Iraq
52/D2 **Al Khāliṣ,** Iraq
49/B5 **Al Ḥawāmidīyah,** Egypt
77/M4 **Al Khandaq,** Sudan
52/B6 **Al Hawātah,** Sudan
49/B4 **Al Khānkah,** Egypt
52/E6 **Al Hawrah,** Yem.
77/M2 **Al Khārijah,** Egypt
52/E5 **Al Ḥawṭah,** Yem.
77/M4 **Al Khartūm Baḥrī (Khartoum North),** Sudan
51/F3 **Al Ḥayy,** Iraq
52/E2 **Al Ḥayy,** Iraq
51/F4 **Al Khiḍr,** Iraq
51/F3 **Al Ḥillah,** Iraq
52/F3 **Al Khobar,** SAr.
52/D2 **Al Ḥillah,** Iraq
76/H1 **Al Khums,** Libya
77/O3 **Al Ḥillah,** SAr.
52/E5 **Al Khuraybah,** Yem.
51/F3 **Al Hindīyah,** Iraq
52/B5 **Al Khurṭūm (Khartoum)** (cap.), Sudan
52/D2 **Al Hindīyah,** Iraq
50/B4 **Al Maḥallah al Kubrá,** Egypt
49/E2 **Al Hirmil,** Leb.
52/B2 **Al Maḥallah al Kubrá,** Egypt
75/N13 **Al Hoceima,** Mor.
26/C2 **Alkmaar,** Neth.
47/T6 **Al Hoceima,** Mor.
28/B3 **Alkmaar,** Neth.
75/N13 **Al Hoceima** (isl.), Mor.
76/H3 **Alkoum** (well), Alg.
50/B4 **Al Ḥudaydah,** Yem.
51/F3 **Al Kūfah,** Iraq
77/P5 **Al Ḥudaydah,** Yem.
52/D2 **Al Kūfah,** Iraq
52/E1 **Al Ḥudaydah,** Yem.
77/K3 **Al Kufrah,** Libya
52/E3 **Al Ḥudaydah,** Yem.
38/B5 **Al Kuntillah,** Egypt (?)
52/E6 **Al Ḥumaymah,** Yem. (?)
51/F4 **Al Kūt,** Iraq
73/A2 **Alexandrina** (lake), Austl.
52/E2 **Al Kūt,** Iraq
38/B4 **Al Huwwārīyah,** Tun.
76/H1 **Al Kūt,** Iraq
48/D7 **Al Kuwait** (cap.), Kuw.
51/F4 **Al Maḥmūdīyah,** Iraq
51/F3 **Alia,** It.
51/F4 **Al Kuwait (Kuwait)** (cap.), Kuw.
52/D2 **Al Maḥmūdīyah,** Iraq
34/C3 **Alía,** Sp.
52/E3 **Al Kuwait (Kuwait)** (cap.), Kuw.
77/Q2 **Al Maḥmūdīyah,** Iraq
50/A2 **Aliağa,** Turk.
77/Q2 **Al Kuwayt (Kuwait)** (cap.), Kuw.
50/E2 **Al Mālikīyah,** Syria
39/G2 **Aliákmon** (riv.), Gre.
46/G5 **Almalyk,** Uzb.
39/G2 **Aliákmonos** (lake), Gre.
52/F3 **Al Manāmah (Manama)** (cap.), Bahr.
49/D2 **Al Lādhiqīyah** (dist.), Syria
77/R2 **Al Manāmah (Manama)** (cap.), Bahr.
51/F3 **'Alī al Gharbī,** Iraq
52/E2 **'Alī al Gharbī,** Iraq
50/C3 **Al Lādhiqīyah** (prov.), Syria
39/H3 **Aliártos,** Gre.
51/F3 **'Alī ash Sharqī,** Iraq
49/D2 **Al Lādhiqīyah (Latakia),** Syria
52/B6 **Al Manaqīl,** Sudan
52/E2 **'Alī ash Sharqī,** Iraq
93/G4 **Alibates Flint Quarries Nat'l Mon.,** Tx,US
50/C3 **Al Lādhiqīyah (Latakia),** Syria
92/B2 **Almanor** (lake), Ca,US
96/C4 **Alibates Flint Quarries Nat'l Mon.,** Tx,US
62/D2 **Allāhābād,** India
35/E3 **Almansa,** Sp.
41/H4 **Alibunar,** Yugo.
85/H2 **Allakaket,** Ak,US
90/F5 **Albany,** Wy,US
36/C5 **Allaman,** Swi.
50/B4 **Al Mansūra,** Egypt
91/G3 **Allan** (hills), Sk,Can
94/E3 **Alpine,** Wy,US
77/M1 **Al Mansūra,** Egypt
91/G3 **Allan,** Sk,Can
37/E1 **Alpirsbach,** Ger.
34/C1 **Almanza,** Sp.
93/G4 **Albany,** Wy,US (?)
49/B5 **Al Fayyūm** (gov.), Egypt

82/E7 **Aliwal North,** SAfr.
77/K2 **Al Jaghbūb,** Libya
38/B5 **Al Jamm,** Tun.
75/X18 **Al Jamm,** Tun.
49/D3 **Al Janūb** (gov.), Leb.
52/C3 **Al Jawf,** SAr.
77/N2 **Al Jawf,** SAr.
77/P3 **Al Jīzah,** SAr.
72/C5 **Allora,** Austl.
94/E2 **Allones,** Fr.
36/D2 **Allschwil,** Swi.
52/D5 **Al Luḥayyah,** Yem.
99/B3 **Allyn,** Wa,US
99/B3 **Allyn-Grapeview,** Wa,US
52/E4 **Al Mafraq,** Jor.
49/E3 **Al Mafraq,** Jor.
49/E3 **Al Mafraq,** Jor.
77/N3 **Al Madīnah (Medina),** SAr.
52/D5 **Al Madīnah al Fikrīyah,** Egypt
31/E2 **Alken,** Belg.
52/B3 **Al Madīnah al Fikrīyah,** Egypt
49/D4 **Al Khalīl (Hebron),** WBnk.
52/C4 **Al Madīnah (Medina),** SAr.
77/M4 **Al Khandaq,** Sudan
38/B4 **Al Murnāqiyah,** Tun.
77/M4 **Al Khartūm Baḥrī (Khartoum North),** Sudan
50/D1 **Almus,** Turk.
49/E3 **Al Mafraq,** Jor.
51/F3 **Al Musayyib,** Iraq
49/E3 **Al Mafraq,** Jor.
51/F4 **Al Muthanná** (gov.), Iraq
52/C2 **Al Mafraq,** Jor.
52/D5 **Al Muwassam,** SAr.
76/E1 **Al Maghrib** (reg.), Mor.
52/C3 **Al Muwayliḥ,** SAr.
69/J6 **Alofi,** Niue
68/H6 **Alofi** (isl.), Wall.
67/F5 **Alor** (isls.), Indo.
68/H5 **Alofi** (isl.), Wall.
50/B4 **Al Maḥallah al Kubrá,** Egypt
67/F5 **Alor** (isls.), Indo.
52/B2 **Al Maḥallah al Kubrá,** Egypt
68/B5 **Alor** (isls.), Indo.
52/B2 **Al Maḥallah al Kubrá,** Egypt
63/H6 **Alor Setar,** Malay.
75/X18 **Al Mahdīyah,** Tun.
65/C5 **Alor Setar,** Malay.
75/X18 **Al Mahdī yah** (gov.), Tun.
66/B2 **Alor Setar,** Malay.
51/F3 **Al Kūfah,** Iraq
68/E6 **Alotau,** PNG
52/D2 **Al Kūfah,** Iraq
28/E6 **Alpen,** Ger.
87/H4 **Alpena,** Mi,US
38/B5 **Al Mahdī yun,** Tun.
89/K2 **Alpena,** Mi,US
75/X18 **Al Mahdī yun,** Tun.
94/D2 **Alpena,** Mi,US
76/H1 **Al Mahdī yun,** Tun.
107/J5 **Alpercatas** (mts.), Braz.
48/D7 **Al Kuwait** (cap.), Kuw.
37/F4 **Alperschällihorn** (peak), Swi.
49/D2 **Al Mahmūdīyah,** Iraq
52/F3 **Al Manāmah (Manama)** (cap.), Bahr.
98/E5 **Alpha,** NJ,US
71/H4 **Alpha,** Austl.
28/B4 **Alphen aan de Rijn,** Neth.
34/A3 **Alpiarça,** Port.
100/E2 **Alpine,** Tx,US
88/F5 **Alpine,** Tx,US
90/F5 **Alpine,** Wy,US
99/D2 **Alpine Wild. Area,** Wa,US
37/E1 **Alpnach,** Swi.
37/E4 **Alpnach,** Swi.
34/C1 **Almanza,** Sp.
49/B4 **Al Manzilah,** Egypt
18/D4 **Alps** (mts.), Eur.
50/B4 **Al Manzilah,** Egypt
33/G4 **Alps** (mts.), Eur.
34/D4 **Almanzora** (riv.), Sp.
34/C2 **Almanzor, Pico de** (peak), Sp.
40/A2 **Alps** (range), Eur.
57/F3 **Alps-Minami Nat'l Park,** Japan
76/H1 **'Allāq** (well), Libya
50/B5 **Al Marāghah,** Egypt
77/M2 **Al Marāghah,** Egypt
76/K1 **Al Marj,** Libya
50/B2 **Alpu,** Turk.
77/M2 **Al 'Allāqi** (wadi), Egypt
52/B4 **Al 'Allāqi, Wādī al** (dry riv.), Egypt
107/J6 **Almas** (riv.), Braz.
53/G4 **Al Qābil,** Oman
50/D4 **Al Maṭarīyah,** Egypt
52/C4 **Al Qadīmah,** SAr.
38/E3 **Alice** (pt.), It.
50/C4 **Al Maṭarīyah,** Egypt
52/C4 **Al Qaḍrif,** Sudan
34/B1 **Allariz,** Sp.
50/C4 **Al Maṭarīyah,** Egypt
77/N5 **Al Qaḍrif,** Sudan
36/D3 **Alle,** Swi.
52/C6 **Al Matnah,** Sudan
94/C3 **Allegan,** Mi,US
51/E2 **Al Mawṣil (Mosul),** Iraq
51/F4 **Al Qādisīyah** (gov.), Iraq
89/K4 **Allegheny** (mts.), US
94/E4 **Allegheny** (mts.), US
50/E3 **Al Mayādin,** Syria
49/B4 **Al Qāhirah** (gov.), Egypt
97/H2 **Allegheny** (mts.), US
52/D1 **Al Mayādin,** Syria
34/D2 **Almazán,** Sp.
50/B4 **Al Qāhirah** (gov.), Egypt
94/E3 **Allegheny** (plat.), Pa,US
35/E3 **Almazora,** Sp.
94/E3 **Allegheny** (riv.), Pa,US
49/D4 **Al Mazra'ah,** Jor.
49/B4 **Al Qāhirah (Cairo)** (cap.), Egypt
26/E3 **Alme** (riv.), Ger.
29/F5 **Alme** (riv.), Ger.
50/B4 **Al Qāhirah (Cairo)** (cap.), Egypt
23/G5 **Alfreton,** Eng,UK (?)
31/G2 **Alfter,** Ger. (?)
38/D2 **Alife,** It.
34/A3 **Almeida,** Port.
52/B2 **Al Qāhirah (Cairo)** (cap.), Egypt
40/B5 **Alife,** It.
107/H4 **Almeirim,** Braz.
62/C2 **Alīgarh,** India
34/A3 **Almeirim,** Port.
77/M1 **Al Qāhirah (Cairo)** (cap.), Egypt
52/E2 **Alīgudarz,** Iran
97/H3 **Allendale,** SC,US
28/C4 **Almelo,** Neth.
34/B2 **Alijó,** Port.
101/E2 **Allende,** Mex.
28/D4 **Almelo,** Neth.
20/C4 **Ålgård,** Nor. (?)
96/C4 **Allende,** Mex
107/K7 **Almenara,** Braz.
34/C4 **Algeciras,** Sp. (?)
29/F6 **Allendorf,** Ger.
35/E3 **Almenara** (mtn.), Sp.
75/M12 **Algeciras,** Sp. (?)
62/E2 **Allpur Duār,** India
34/D3 **Almenara** (res.), Sp.
35/E3 **Algemesí,** Sp. (?)
19/N7 **All England Lawn Tennis Club,** Eng,UK
34/B3 **Almendralejo,** Sp.
75/S15 **Alger** (wilaya), Alg. (?)
52/E6 **Al 'Irqah,** Yem.
26/C2 **Almere,** Neth.
99/F7 **Allen Park,** Mi,US
28/C4 **Almere,** Neth.
49/A4 **Al Iskandarīyah** (gov.), Egypt
37/F2 **Allensbach,** Ger.
89/L3 **Allentown,** Pa,US
18/C5 **Almería,** Sp.
50/B4 **Al Iskandarīyah** (gov.), Egypt
94/F3 **Allentown,** Pa,US
34/D4 **Almería,** Sp.
51/F3 **Al Iskandarīyah,** Iraq
98/E5 **Allentown,** Pa,US
34/D4 **Almería** (gulf), Sp.
49/A4 **Al Iskandarīyah (Alexandria),** Egypt
98/E5 **Allentown-Bethlehem-Easton** (arpt.), Pa,US
19/J3 **Al'met'yevsk,** Rus.
50/B4 **Al Iskandarīyah (Alexandria),** Egypt
27/H4 **Allentsteig,** Aus.
43/M5 **Al'met'yevsk,** Rus.
77/L1 **Al Iskandarīyah (Alexandria),** Egypt
62/C6 **Alleppey,** India
46/F4 **Al'met'yevsk,** Rus.
49/B4 **Al Ismā'īlīyah** (gov.), Egypt
64/F4 **Alleppey,** India
26/F2 **Almḥult,** Swe.
29/G3 **Aller** (riv.), Ger.
77/P2 **Al Midhnab,** SAr.
49/D4 **Al Qaṣr,** Jor.
51/F4 **Al Ghammās,** Iraq (?)
50/C4 **Al Ismā'īlīyah** (gov.), Egypt
29/G3 **Aller** (riv.), Ger.
75/M13 **Almina** (pt.), Mor.
75/W18 **Al Qayrawān,** Tun.
50/B4 **Al Gharbī yah** (gov.), Egypt (?)
29/H4 **Allerkanal** (can.), Ger.
34/C4 **Almina** (pt.), Sp.
77/R4 **Al Ghaydah,** Yem. (?)
34/C4 **Al Ismā'īlīyah (Ismailia),** Egypt
49/B4 **Al Minūfīyah** (gov.), Egypt
77/M5 **Al Qataynah,** Sudan
38/A2 **Alghero,** It. (?)
37/H1 **Allershausen,** Ger.
50/B4 **Al Minūfīyah** (gov.), Egypt
76/H3 **Al Qubbah,** Libya
50/C5 **Al Ghurdaqah,** Egypt (?)
52/B2 **Al Ismā'īlīyah (Ismailia),** Egypt
37/H1 **Allgäu** (mts.), Aus., Ger.
38/A5 **Al Qulī'ah,** Tun.
52/B3 **Al Ghurdaqah,** Egypt (?)
50/B4 **Al Minyā** (gov.), Egypt
77/M1 **Al Ismā'īlīyah (Ismailia),** Egypt
26/F5 **Allgäu Alps** (mts.), Aus., Ger.
50/B4 **Al Minyā,** Egypt
77/M2 **Al Ghurdaqah,** Egypt (?)
33/J3 **Allgäu Alps** (mts.), Aus., Ger.
77/M2 **Al Minyā,** Egypt
76/F1 **Algiers** (cap.), Alg. (?)
52/C2 **Al Minyā,** Egypt
51/F3 **Al Miqdādīyah,** Iraq
75/X18 **Al Qayrawān,** Tun.
75/S15 **Algiers (Alger)** (cap.), Alg. (?)
88/F3 **Alliance,** Ne,US
52/D2 **Al Miqdādīyah,** Iraq
76/H1 **Al Qayrawān,** Tun.
92/E5 **Algiers** (riv.), Mex (?)
91/H5 **Alliance,** Ne,US
39/H3 **Almirós,** Gre.
52/E3 **Al Qayṣūmah,** SAr.
39/H2 **Alistráti,** Gre. (?)
93/G2 **Alliance,** Ne,US
44/B5 **Almirós,** Gre.
77/Q2 **Al Qayṣūmah,** SAr.

94/D3 **Alliance,** Oh,US
77/K2 **Al Jaghbūb,** Libya
65/B2 **Allied War Cemetery,** Burma
32/E3 **Allier** (riv.), Fr.
20/E5 **Allinge,** Den.
27/H1 **Allinge,** Den.
36/C5 **Allinges,** Fr.
34/B3 **Almoharín,** Sp.
19/U11 **Almont** (riv.), Fr.
99/F6 **Almont,** Mi,US
94/E2 **Almonte,** On,Can
34/B4 **Almonte,** Sp.
36/D2 **Allschwil,** Swi.
52/D5 **Al Luḥayyah,** Yem.
108/D1 **Almores** (range), Braz.
34/C2 **Almorox,** Sp.
52/E3 **Al Mubarraz,** SAr.
50/C4 **Al Mudawwarah,** SAr.
52/C3 **Al Mudawwarah,** SAr.
35/E1 **Almudévar,** Sp.
87/J4 **Alma,** Qu,Can
94/C3 **Alma,** Mi,US
77/L5 **Al Muglad,** Sudan
93/H2 **Alma,** Ne,US
38/B4 **Al Muḥammadīyah,** Tun.
96/D1 **Alma,** Ne,US
52/E6 **Al Mukallā,** Yem.
46/H5 **Alma-Ata** (cap.), Kaz.
77/Q5 **Al Mukallā,** Yem.
34/A3 **Almada,** Port.
38/B5 **Al Muknīn,** Tun.
35/P10 **Almada,** Port.
75/X18 **Al Muknīn,** Tun.
34/C3 **Almadén,** Sp.
38/B5 **Al Munastīr** (gov.), Tun.
52/B3 **Al Madīnah al Fikrīyah,** Egypt
75/X18 **Al Munastīr,** Tun.
52/B3 **Al Madīnah al Fikrīyah,** Egypt
75/X18 **Al Munastīr** (gov.), Tun.
52/C4 **Al Madīnah (Medina),** SAr.
34/D4 **Almuñécar,** Sp.
77/N3 **Al Madīnah (Medina),** SAr.
38/B4 **Al Murnāqiyah,** Tun.
50/D1 **Almus,** Turk.
49/E3 **Al Mafraq,** Jor.
51/F3 **Al Musayyib,** Iraq
49/E3 **Al Mafraq,** Jor.
51/F4 **Al Muthanná** (gov.), Iraq
52/C2 **Al Mafraq,** Jor.
52/D5 **Al Muwassam,** SAr.
76/E1 **Al Maghrib** (reg.), Mor.
52/C3 **Al Muwayliḥ,** SAr.
69/J6 **Alofi,** Niue
68/H6 **Alofi** (isl.), Wall.
54/C6 **Along,** India
60/B2 **Along,** India
63/G2 **Along,** India
39/H3 **Alónnisos** (isl.), Gre.
67/F5 **Alor** (isls.), Indo.
68/B5 **Alor** (isls.), Indo.
63/H6 **Alor Setar,** Malay.
65/C5 **Alor Setar,** Malay.
66/B2 **Alor Setar,** Malay.
68/E6 **Alotau,** PNG
28/E6 **Alpen,** Ger.
87/H4 **Alpena,** Mi,US
89/K2 **Alpena,** Mi,US
94/D2 **Alpena,** Mi,US
107/J5 **Alpercatas** (mts.), Braz.
37/F4 **Alperschällihorn** (peak), Swi.
98/E5 **Alpha,** NJ,US
71/H4 **Alpha,** Austl.
28/B4 **Alphen aan de Rijn,** Neth.
34/A3 **Alpiarça,** Port.
100/E2 **Alpine,** Tx,US
88/F5 **Alpine,** Tx,US
90/F5 **Alpine,** Wy,US
94/E3 **Alpine,** Wy,US
37/E1 **Alpirsbach,** Ger.
37/E4 **Alpnach,** Swi.
37/F4 **Alpnach,** Port.
18/D4 **Alps** (mts.), Eur.
33/G4 **Alps** (mts.), Eur.
34/C2 **Almanzor, Pico de** (peak), Sp.
40/A2 **Alps** (range), Eur.
57/F3 **Alps-Minami Nat'l Park,** Japan
50/B2 **Alpu,** Turk.
53/G4 **Al Qābil,** Oman
52/C4 **Al Qadīmah,** SAr.
52/C4 **Al Qaḍrif,** Sudan
77/N5 **Al Qaḍrif,** Sudan
51/F4 **Al Qādisīyah** (gov.), Iraq
49/B4 **Al Qāhirah** (gov.), Egypt
50/B4 **Al Qāhirah** (gov.), Egypt
49/B4 **Al Qāhirah (Cairo)** (cap.), Egypt
50/B4 **Al Qāhirah (Cairo)** (cap.), Egypt
52/B2 **Al Qāhirah (Cairo)** (cap.), Egypt
77/M1 **Al Qāhirah (Cairo)** (cap.), Egypt
50/E3 **Al Qā'im,** Iraq
52/D2 **Al Qā'im,** Iraq
52/C3 **Al Qal'bah,** SAr.
49/B4 **Al Qalyūbī yah** (gov.), Egypt
50/B4 **Al Qalyūbī yah** (gov.), Egypt
50/E2 **Al Qāmishlī,** Syria
52/D1 **Al Qāmishlī,** Syria
49/B4 **Al Qanāṭir al Khayrī yah,** Egypt
50/B4 **Al Qanāṭir al Khayrī yah,** Egypt
49/C4 **Al Qantarah,** Egypt
50/D3 **Al Qaryatayn,** Syria
49/D4 **Al Qasr,** Jor.
75/W18 **Al Qayrawān** (gov.), Tun.
77/M5 **Al Qataynah,** Sudan
76/H3 **Al Qubbah,** Libya
38/A5 **Al Qulī'ah,** Tun.
77/M5 **Al Qataynah,** Sudan
76/H3 **Al Qubbah,** Libya
38/A5 **Al Qulī'ah,** Tun.
75/X18 **Al Qayrawān,** Tun.
76/H1 **Al Qayrawān,** Tun.
52/E3 **Al Qayṣūmah,** SAr.
77/Q2 **Al Qayṣūmah,** SAr.

39/J5 **Almiroú** (gulf), Gre.
34/A4 **Almodôvar,** Port.
34/C3 **Almodôvar del Campo,** Sp.
34/C4 **Almodóvar del Río,** Sp.
34/B3 **Almoharín,** Sp.
19/U11 **Almont** (riv.), Fr.
99/F6 **Almont,** Mi,US
94/E2 **Almonte,** On,Can
34/B4 **Almonte,** Sp.
36/D2 **Allschwil,** Swi.
52/D5 **Al Luḥayyah,** Yem.
108/D1 **Almores** (range), Braz.
34/C2 **Almorox,** Sp.
52/E3 **Al Mubarraz,** SAr.
50/C4 **Al Mudawwarah,** SAr.
52/C3 **Al Mudawwarah,** SAr.
35/E1 **Almudévar,** Sp.
77/L5 **Al Muglad,** Sudan
38/B4 **Al Muḥammadīyah,** Tun.
52/E6 **Al Mukallā,** Yem.
77/Q5 **Al Mukallā,** Yem.
38/B5 **Al Muknīn,** Tun.
75/X18 **Al Muknīn,** Tun.
38/B5 **Al Munastīr** (gov.), Tun.
75/X18 **Al Munastīr,** Tun.
75/X18 **Al Munastīr** (gov.), Tun.
34/D4 **Almuñécar,** Sp.
38/B4 **Al Murnāqiyah,** Tun.
50/D1 **Almus,** Turk.
51/F3 **Al Musayyib,** Iraq
51/F4 **Al Muthanná** (gov.), Iraq
52/D5 **Al Muwassam,** SAr.
52/C3 **Al Muwayliḥ,** SAr.
69/J6 **Alofi,** Niue
68/H6 **Alofi** (isl.), Wall.
67/F5 **Alor** (isls.), Indo.
68/B5 **Alor** (isls.), Indo.
63/H6 **Alor Setar,** Malay.
65/C5 **Alor Setar,** Malay.
66/B2 **Alor Setar,** Malay.
68/E6 **Alotau,** PNG
28/E6 **Alpen,** Ger.
87/H4 **Alpena,** Mi,US
89/K2 **Alpena,** Mi,US
94/D2 **Alpena,** Mi,US
107/J5 **Alpercatas** (mts.), Braz.
37/F4 **Alperschällihorn** (peak), Swi.
98/E5 **Alpha,** NJ,US
71/H4 **Alpha,** Austl.
28/B4 **Alphen aan de Rijn,** Neth.
34/A3 **Alpiarça,** Port.
100/E2 **Alpine,** Tx,US
88/F5 **Alpine,** Tx,US
90/F5 **Alpine,** Wy,US
94/E3 **Alpine,** Wy,US
37/E1 **Alpirsbach,** Ger.
37/E4 **Alpnach,** Swi.
18/D4 **Alps** (mts.), Eur.
33/G4 **Alps** (mts.), Eur.
40/A2 **Alps** (range), Eur.
57/F3 **Alps-Minami Nat'l Park,** Japan
50/B2 **Alpu,** Turk.
53/G4 **Al Qābil,** Oman
52/C4 **Al Qadīmah,** SAr.
52/C4 **Al Qaḍrif,** Sudan
77/N5 **Al Qaḍrif,** Sudan
51/F4 **Al Qādisīyah** (gov.), Iraq
49/B4 **Al Qāhirah** (gov.), Egypt
50/B4 **Al Qāhirah** (gov.), Egypt
49/B4 **Al Qāhirah (Cairo)** (cap.), Egypt
50/B4 **Al Qāhirah (Cairo)** (cap.), Egypt
52/B2 **Al Qāhirah (Cairo)** (cap.), Egypt
77/M1 **Al Qāhirah (Cairo)** (cap.), Egypt
50/E3 **Al Qā'im,** Iraq
52/D2 **Al Qā'im,** Iraq
52/C3 **Al Qal'bah,** SAr.
49/B4 **Al Qalyūbī yah** (gov.), Egypt
50/B4 **Al Qalyūbī yah** (gov.), Egypt
50/E2 **Al Qāmishlī,** Syria
52/D1 **Al Qāmishlī,** Syria
49/B4 **Al Qanāṭir al Khayrī yah,** Egypt
50/B4 **Al Qanāṭir al Khayrī yah,** Egypt
49/C4 **Al Qantarah,** Egypt
50/D3 **Al Qaryatayn,** Syria
49/D4 **Al Qasr,** Jor.
75/W18 **Al Qayrawān** (gov.), Tun.
77/M5 **Al Qataynah,** Sudan
76/H3 **Al Qubbah,** Libya
38/A5 **Al Qulī'ah,** Tun.
75/X18 **Al Qayrawān,** Tun.
76/H1 **Al Qayrawān,** Tun.
52/E3 **Al Qayṣūmah,** SAr.
77/Q2 **Al Qayṣūmah,** SAr.

113

Alq – Ansai

51/E2 Alqōsh, Iraq
49/D3 Al Qunayţirah (dist.), Syria
50/C3 Al Qunayţirah, Syria
50/C3 Al Qunaytirah (prov.), Syria
52/C2 Al Qunayţirah, Syria
77/P4 Al Qunfudhah, SAr.
51/F4 Al Qurnah, Iraq
52/E2 Al Qurnah, Iraq
52/B3 Al Quşayr, Egypt
77/M2 Al Quşayr, Egypt
49/E2 Al Quşayr, Syria
50/D3 Al Quşayr, Syria
49/E3 Al Quţayfah, Syria
49/D5 Al Quwayrah, Jor.
50/C4 Al Quwayrah, Jor.
23/G6 Alrewas, Eng,UK
25/E1 Alrewas, Eng,UK
26/F1 Als (isl.), Den.
26/D4 Alsace (reg.), Fr.
31/G6 Alsace (reg.), Fr.
33/G2 Alsace (reg.), Fr.
36/D2 Alsace (hist. reg.), Fr.
36/D3 Alsace (reg.), Fr.
26/D5 Alsace, Ballon d' (mtn.), Fr.
23/F5 Alsager, Eng,UK
90/F3 Alsask, Sk,Can
32/B5 Alsasua, Sp.
34/D1 Alsasua, Sp.
31/F2 Alsdorf, Ger.
31/G4 Alsenz, Ger.
31/G4 Alsenz (riv.), Ger.
26/E3 Alsfeld, Ger.
33/H1 Alsfeld, Ger.
99/Q16 Alsip, Il,US
40/E1 Alsózsolca, Hun.
29/H1 Alster (riv.), Ger.
31/F5 Alsting, Fr.
23/F2 Alston, Eng,UK
73/E1 Alstonville, Austl.
23/F4 Alt (riv.), Eng,UK
20/G1 Alta, Nor.
109/C2 Altacama (des.), Chile
37/F3 Altach, Aus.
98/B2 Altadena, Ca,US
107/G6 Alta Floresta, Braz.
109/D3 Alta Gracia, Arg.
46/J5 Altai (mts.), Asia
54/B1 Altai (mts.), Asia
48/H5 Altai (mts.), Mong.
107/I14 Altamira, Braz.
101/F4 Altamira, Mex.
102/B1 Altamira, Mex.
97/H4 Altamonte Springs, Fl,US
38/E2 Altamura, It.
40/C5 Altamura, It.
100/C3 Altamura (isl.), Mex.
100/C2 Altar, Mex.
92/D4 Altar (des.), Mex
92/E5 Altar, Mex
102/D2 Altar de los Sacrificios (ruins), Guat.
54/B2 Altay, China
46/K5 Altay, Mong.
54/B2 Altay, Mong.
54/C3 Altay, Mong.
54/D2 Altay, Mong.
46/J4 Altay Kray, Rus.
33/H3 Altdorf, Swi.
37/E4 Altdorf, Swi.
33/J2 Altdorf bei Nürnberg, Ger.
35/E3 Altea, Sp.
29/E6 Altena, Ger.
31/G2 Altenahr, Ger.
29/F5 Altenau (riv.), Ger.
29/H5 Altenau, Ger.
29/F5 Altenbeken, Ger.
26/G3 Altenburg, Ger.
31/G4 Altenglan, Ger.
29/H6 Altengottern, Ger.
31/G2 Altenkirchen, Ger.
37/G1 Altenmünster, Ger.
37/G1 Altenstadt, Ger.
37/G2 Altenstadt, Ger.
27/G2 Altentreptow, Ger.
101/F5 Altepexi, Mex.
101/M8 Altepexi, Mex.
102/B2 Altepexi, Mex.
34/B3 Alter do Chão, Port.
28/D5 Alter Rhein (riv.), Ger.
29/G1 Altes Land (reg.), Ger.
37/F1 Altheim, Ger.
33/L3 Althofen, Aus.
40/B2 Althofen, Aus.
23/H4 Althorpe, Eng,UK
50/D1 Altındere Milli Park, Turk.
49/E1 Altınözü, Turk.
44/D5 Altıntaş, Turk.
50/B2 Altıntaş, Turk.
49/A1 Altınyayla, Turk.
50/B2 Altınyayla, Turk.
106/E7 Altiplano (plain), Bol., Chile
105/C4 Altiplano (plat.), Bol., Peru
36/D2 Altkirch, Fr.
26/F2 Altmark (reg.), Ger.
33/J2 Altmühl (riv.), Ger.
27/G5 Altmünster, Aus.
33/K3 Altmünster, Aus.
40/A2 Altmünster, Aus.
107/J6 Alto (peak), Braz.
33/J5 Alto (peak), It.
107/H7 Alto Araguaia, Braz.
82/C2 Alto Cuale, Ang.
103/H5 Alto de Tamar (peak), Col.
107/H7 Alto Garças, Braz.
101/N7 Alto Lucero, Mex.
37/G4 Alto, Monte (peak), It.
37/H1 Altomünster, Ger.
25/F4 Alton, Eng,UK
89/H4 Alton, Il,US
93/K3 Alton, Il,US
94/B4 Alton, Il,US
97/F2 Alton, Il,US
73/F5 Altona, Austl.
86/G4 Altona, Mb,Can
91/J3 Altona, Mb,Can
89/L3 Altoona, Pa,US
94/E3 Altoona, Pa,US
106/D6 Alto Purús (riv.), Peru
107/K5 Altos, Braz.
103/G4 Altos de Campana Nat'l Park, Pan.
101/F5 Altotonga, Mex.
101/M7 Altotonga, Mex.
102/B2 Altotonga, Mex.
23/F5 Altrincham, Eng,UK
48/H6 Altun (mts.), China
54/C4 Altun (mts.), China
101/H5 Altun Ha (ruins), Belz.
102/D2 Altun Ha (ruins), Belz.
88/B3 Alturas, Ca,US
90/C5 Alturas, Ca,US
92/B2 Alturas, Ca,US
88/G5 Altus, Ok,US
93/H4 Altus, Ok,US
93/H4 Altus (A.F.B.), Ok,US
93/H4 Altus (res.), Ok,US
96/D3 Altus, Ok,US
96/D3 Altus (A.F.B.), Ok,US
77/M5 Al Ubayyiḑ, Sudan
44/F4 Alucra, Turk.
50/F1 Alucra, Turk.
77/L5 Al Udayyah, Sudan
20/H4 Alūksne, Lat.
42/E4 Alūksne, Lat.
52/C3 Al 'Ulá, SAr.
77/N2 Al 'Ulá, SAr.
22/E5 Alun (riv.), Wal,UK
52/B3 Al Uqşur (Luxor), Egypt
77/M2 Al Uqşur (Luxor), Egypt
53/F5 Ālūs, Iraq
44/E3 Alushta, Ukr.
74/E2 Al 'Uwaynāt (peak), Sudan
77/L3 Al 'Uwaynāt (peak), Sudan
51/F4 Al 'Uzayr, Iraq
93/H3 Alva, Ok,US
96/D2 Alva, Ok,US
34/A4 Alvalade, Port.
101/G5 Alvarado, Mex.
101/P8 Alvarado, Mex.
102/C2 Alvarado, Mex.
100/C3 Alvaro Obregón (res.), Mex.
20/D3 Alvdal, Nor.
25/E2 Alvechurch, Eng,UK
34/A3 Alverca, Port.
35/P10 Alverca do Ribatejo, Port.
30/B1 Alveringem, Belg.
20/E4 Alvesta, Swe.
24/D4 Alveston, Eng,UK
20/F3 Alvik, Swe.
42/C3 Alvik, Swe.
93/J5 Alvin, Tx,US
96/E4 Alvin, Tx,US
34/B3 Alvito, Port.
20/F3 Älvkarleby, Swe.
108/A4 Alvorada, Braz.
109/F2 Alvorada, Braz.
101/F1 Alvord, Tx,US
20/E4 Älvsborg (co.), Swe.
20/G2 Älvsbyn, Swe.
42/D2 Älvsbyn, Swe.
50/B5 Al Wādī al Jadīd (gov.), Egypt
50/B4 Al Wāḩāt al Baḩrīyah (oasis), Egypt
52/C3 Al Wajh, SAr.
77/N2 Al Wajh, SAr.
53/L3 Alwar, India
62/C2 Alwar, India
49/B5 Al Wāsiţah, Egypt
64/F3 Alwaye, India
54/E4 Alxa Youqi, China
54/F4 Alxa Zuoqi, China
49/G7 Al Yāmūn, WBnk.
70/F2 Alyangula, Austl.
51/G2 Alyat, Azer.
27/N1 Alytus, Lith.
42/E5 Alytus, Lith.
40/A1 Alz (riv.), Aus.
26/G4 Alz (riv.), Ger.
33/K2 Alz (riv.), Ger.
33/H4 Alzano Lombardo, It.
31/F4 Alzette (riv.), Lux.
31/H4 Alzey, Ger.
106/D4 Amacayacú Nat'l Park, Col.
101/K8 Amacuzac (riv.), Mex.
102/B2 Amacuzac (riv.), Mex.
52/B4 Amada (ruins), Egypt
70/E4 Amadeus (lake), Austl.
77/M6 Amadi, Sudan
87/J2 Amadjuak (lake), NW,Can
34/A3 Amadora, Port.
35/P10 Amadora, Port.
55/M5 Amagasaki, Japan
57/L10 Amagasaki, Japan
56/B4 Amagi, Japan
57/F3 Amagi-san (mtn.), Japan
67/G4 Amahai, Indo.
101/L6 Amajac (riv.), Mex.
102/B1 Amajac (riv.), Mex.
55/K5 Amakusa (sea), Japan
56/A4 Amakusa (sea), Japan
20/E4 Åmål, Swe.
54/G1 Amalat (riv.), Rus.
39/G4 Amaliás, Gre.
53/L4 Amalner, India
62/C3 Amalner, India
107/G8 Amambaí, Braz.
107/H8 Amambaí (riv.), Braz.
109/E1 Amambaí, Braz.
48/N7 Amami (isls.), Japan
68/B2 Amami (isls.), Japan
106/F4 Amaña (lake), Braz.
36/C2 Amance, Fr.
38/E3 Amantea, It.
69/L6 Amanu (atoll), FrPol.
34/A2 Amarante, Port.
60/C4 Amarapura, Burma
63/G3 Amarapura, Burma
65/B1 Amarapura, Burma
64/F3 Amarāvati (riv.), India
34/B3 Amareleja, Port.
92/C3 Amargosa (dry riv.), Ca, Nv,US
84/G6 Amarillo, US
88/F4 Amarillo, Tx,US
93/G4 Amarillo, Tx,US
96/C3 Amarillo, Tx,US
38/D1 Amaro (peak), It.
40/B4 Amaro (peak), It.
41/L5 Amasra, Turk.
44/E4 Amasya, Turk.
44/E4 Amasya (prov.), Turk.
46/D5 Amasya, Turk.
50/C1 Amasya, Turk.
50/C1 Amasya (prov.), Turk.
100/D4 Amatlán de Cañas, Mex.
57/J7 Amatsukominato, Japan
31/E2 Amay, Belg.
101/L8 Amayuca, Mex.
105/D3 Amazon (riv.), SAm.
107/H4 Amazon (riv.), SAm.
107/G4 Amazônia (Tapajós) Nat'l Park, Braz.
53/L5 Ambajogai, India
62/C4 Ambajogai, India
53/L2 Ambāla, India
64/D2 Ambāla, India
62/D6 Ambalangoda, SrL.
81/H8 Ambalavao, Madg.
76/H7 Ambam, Camr.
75/G6 Ambanja, Madg.
81/J6 Ambanja, Madg.
81/H6 Ambaro (bay), Madg.
82/R9 Ambaro (bay), Madg.
64/F4 Ambāsamudram, India
106/C4 Ambato, Ecu.
75/G6 Ambato Boeny, Madg.
81/H7 Ambato Boeny, Madg.
81/H8 Ambatofinandrahana, Madg.
81/H7 Ambatolampy, Madg.
81/H7 Ambatomainty, Madg.
81/H7 Ambatomanoina, Madg.
81/J7 Ambatondrazaka, Madg.
32/D4 Ambazac, Fr.
39/H4 Ambelos, Ákra (cape), Gre.
26/F4 Amberg, Ger.
33/J2 Amberg, Ger.
23/G5 Ambergate, Eng,UK
102/E2 Ambergris (cay), Belz.
104/C2 Ambergris (cay), Trks.
36/B6 Ambérieu-en-Bugey, Fr.
31/E3 Amberloup, Belg.
62/D3 Ambikāpur, India
36/C5 Ambilly, Fr.
81/J6 Ambilobe, Madg.
81/J7 Ambinaninony, Madg.
81/J6 Ambinanitelo, Madg.
23/G1 Amble, Eng,UK
85/G2 Ambler, Ak,US
98/E5 Ambler, Pa,US
23/F3 Ambleside, Eng,UK
30/A2 Ambleteuse, Fr.
26/C3 Amblève (riv.), Belg.
31/F3 Amblève, Belg.
31/F3 Amblève (riv.), Belg.
32/F1 Amblève (riv.), Belg.
81/H8 Amboasary, Madg.
81/J7 Ambodifototra, Madg.
81/H7 Ambohidratrimo, Madg.
81/J7 Ambohijanahary, Madg.
81/H8 Ambohimahasoa, Madg.
81/H8 Ambohinihaonana, Madg.
81/J7 Ambohitsilaozana, Madg.
48/M10 Ambon, Indo.
67/G4 Ambon, Indo.
67/G4 Ambon (isl.), Indo.
68/B5 Ambon, Indo.
81/H9 Ambondro, Madg.
75/G7 Ambositra, Madg.
81/H8 Ambositra, Madg.
75/G7 Ambovombe, Madg.
81/H9 Ambovombe, Madg.
82/B2 Ambriz, Ang.
30/B5 Ambronay, Fr.
68/F6 Ambrym (isl.), Van.
47/T4 Amchitka (isl.), Ak,US
85/B6 Amchitka (isl.), Ak,US
85/B6 Amchitka (passg.), Ak,US
52/E5 'Amd, Yem.
60/A1 Amdo, China
101/K6 Amealco, Mex.
100/D4 Ameca, Mex.
101/L7 Amecameca de Juárez, Mex.
101/R10 Amecameca de Juárez, Mex.
31/F3 Amel, Belg.
26/C2 Ameland (isl.), Neth.
28/C2 Ameland (isl.), Neth.
38/C1 Amelia, It.
29/H2 Amelinghausen, Ger.
28/B5 Amer (chan.), Neth.
83/F American (highland), Ant.
99/M9 American (riv.), Ca,US
99/B3 American (lake), Wa,US
107/J8 Americana, Braz.
108/C2 Americana, Braz.
109/G1 Americana, Braz.
88/D3 American Falls, Id,US
90/E5 American Falls, Id,US
92/D2 American Falls, Id,US
92/D2 American Falls (res.), Id,US
92/E2 American Fork, Ut,US
92/B3 American, North Fork (riv.), Ca,US
69/T9 American Samoa
69/J6 American Samoa (terr.), US
92/B3 American, South Fork (riv.), Ca,US
89/K5 Americus, Ga,US
97/G3 Americus, Ga,US
33/L3 Ameringkogel (peak), Aus.
26/C2 Amersfoort, Neth.
28/C4 Amersfoort, Neth.
80/Q13 Amersfoort, SAfr.
25/F3 Amersham, Eng,UK
83/E Amery Ice Shelf, Ant.
89/H3 Ames, Ia,US
91/K5 Ames, Ia,US
93/J2 Ames, Ia,US
25/E4 Amesbury, Eng,UK
53/K3 Amet, India
39/H3 Amfíklia, Gre.
39/G3 Amfilokhía, Gre.
39/H3 Ámfissa, Gre.
47/N3 Amga (riv.), Rus.
47/T3 Amguema (riv.), Rus.
47/P4 Amgun' (riv.), Rus.
55/M1 Amgun' (riv.), Rus.
63/G4 Amherst, Burma
87/K4 Amherst, NS,Can
89/P2 Amherst, NS,Can
95/H2 Amherst, NS,Can
99/F7 Amherstburg, On,Can
33/J5 Amiata (peak), It.
38/B1 Amiata (peak), It.
18/D4 Amiens, Fr.
26/B4 Amiens, Fr.
30/B4 Amiens, Fr.
32/E2 Amiens, Fr.
49/E1 Amik (lake), Turk.
50/D2 Amik (lake), Turk.
47/U4 Amila (isl.), Ak,US
74/K10 Amilcar Cabral (Sal) (int'l arpt.), CpV.
39/G2 Amíndaion, Gre.
40/E5 Amíndaion, Gre.
75/H5 Amirante (isls.), Sey.
91/H2 Amisk (lake), Sk,Can
93/G5 Amistad (res.), Mex, US
101/E2 Amistad (int'l res.), US
101/E2 Amistad (dam), Tx,US
93/G5 Amistad Nat'l Rec. Area, Tx,US
93/K5 Amite (riv.), La,US
62/C3 Amla, India
85/D6 Amlia (isl.), Ak,US
22/D5 Amlwch, Wal,UK
49/D4 'Ammān (cap.), Jor.
50/C4 'Ammān (cap.), Jor.
52/C2 'Ammān (cap.), Jor.
77/N1 'Ammān (cap.), Jor.
24/C3 Amman (riv.), Wal,UK
24/C3 Ammanford, Wal,UK
20/E2 Ammarfjället (peak), Swe.
42/B2 Ammarfjället (peak), Swe.
37/H2 Ammer (riv.), Ger.
85/K2 Ammerman (mtn.), Yk,Can
33/J2 Ammersee (lake), Ger.
37/H2 Ammersee (lake), Ger.
90/F5 Ammon, Id,US
92/E2 Ammon, Id,US
65/D3 Amnat Charoen, Thai.
31/F5 Amnéville, Fr.
60/D4 Amo (riv.), China
46/F6 Āmol, Iran
51/H2 Āmol, Iran
52/F1 Āmol, Iran
35/P10 Amora, Port.
39/J4 Amorgós, Gre.
39/J4 Amorgós (isl.), Gre.
97/F3 Amory, Ms,US
87/J4 Amos, Qu,Can
94/E1 Amos, Qu,Can
20/C4 Åmot, Nor.
81/J6 Ampanefena, Madg.
81/J8 Ampangalana (can.), Madg.
81/H9 Ampanihy, Madg.
81/J7 Amparafaravola, Madg.
62/D6 Amparai, SrL.
81/J6 Ampasindava (bay), Madg.
37/H1 Amper (riv.), Ger.
61/G5 Amphitrite Group (isls.), China
81/H7 Ampitatafika, Madg.
35/F2 Amposta, Sp.
25/F2 Ampthill, Eng,UK
95/H1 Amqui, Qu,Can
52/D5 'Amrān, Yem.
77/P4 'Amrān, Yem.
62/C3 Amravati, India
53/K4 Amreli, India
62/B3 Amreli, India
63/F2 Amring, India
50/C3 'Amrīt (ruins), Syria
52/C2 'Amrīt (ruins), Syria
53/K2 Amritsar, India
64/C2 Amritsar, India
26/E1 Amrun (isl.), Ger.
28/B4 Amstel (riv.), Neth.
26/C2 Amstelveen, Neth.
28/B4 Amstelveen, Neth.
17/N7 Amsterdam (isl.), Fr.
18/D3 Amsterdam (cap.), Neth.
26/C2 Amsterdam (cap.), Neth.
28/B4 Amsterdam (cap.), Neth.
46/A4 Amsterdam (cap.), Neth.
94/F3 Amsterdam, NY,US
28/C5 Amsterdam-Rijnkanaal (can.), Neth.
27/H4 Amstetten, Aus.
33/L2 Amstetten, Aus.
40/B1 Amstetten, Aus.
77/K5 AmTiman, Chad
48/F5 Amudar'ya (riv.), Asia
53/J1 Amu Darya (riv.), Trkm.
46/G5 Amudar'ya (riv.), Uzb.,Trkm.
45/L4 Amu Darya (riv.), Uzb.
85/D5 Amukta (passg.), Ak,US
87/S7 Amund Rignes (isl.), NW,Can
83/D Amundsen (bay), Ant.
83/S Amundsen (sea), Ant.
84/E2 Amundsen (gulf), Can.
86/D1 Amundsen (gulf), NW,Can
83/A Amundsen-Scott, Ant.
47/P4 Amur (riv.), Rus.
48/N4 Amur (riv.), China.,Rus.
55/M1 Amur (Heilong) (riv.), Rus.
69/K6 Amuri, CookIs.
47/N4 Amur Obl., Rus.
32/B5 Amurrio, Sp.
34/D1 Amurrio, Sp.
47/P4 Amursk, Rus.
55/M1 Amursk, Rus.
52/B5 'Amur, Wādī (dry riv.), Sudan
49/D2 Amyūn, Leb.
69/LG Anaa (atoll), FrPol.
47/L3 Anabar (riv.), Rus.
49/G7 'Anabtā, WBnk.
103/G4 Anachucuna (mtn.), Pan.
106/F2 Anaco, Ven.
86/E4 Anaconda, Mt,US
90/E4 Anaconda-Deer Lodge County, Mt,US
89/G4 Anadarko, Ok,US
93/H4 Anadarko, Ok,US
96/D3 Anadarko, Ok,US
47/T3 Anadyr', Rus.
47/T3 Anadyr' (range), Rus.
47/U3 Anadyr' (gulf), Rus.
48/S3 Anadyr' (riv.), Rus.
48/T3 Anadyr' (gulf), Rus.
39/J4 Anáfi (isl.), Gre.
50/E3 'Ānah, Iraq
52/D2 'Ānah, Iraq
88/C5 Anaheim, Ca,US
92/C4 Anaheim, Ca,US
98/C3 Anaheim, Ca,US
90/B2 Anahim Lake, BC,Can
101/E3 Anáhuac, Mex.
96/C5 Anáhuac, Mex
93/J5 Anahuac, Tx,US
96/E4 Anahuac, Tx,US
64/F3 Anai Mudi (mtn.), India
58/C3 Anak, NKor.
62/D4 Anakāpalle, India
85/H2 Anaktuvuk Pass, Ak,US
75/G6 Analalava, Madg.
81/H6 Analalava, Madg.
81/J7 Analamaitso (plat.), Madg.
81/H7 Analvory, Madg.
103/G1 Ana María (gulf), Cuba
66/C3 Anambas (isls.), Indo.
79/G5 Anambra (state), Nga.
49/C1 Anamur, Turk.
49/C1 Anamur (pt.), Turk.
50/C2 Anamur, Turk.
50/C2 Anamur (pt.), Turk.
52/B1 Anamur, Turk.
55/L5 Anan, Japan
56/D4 Anan, Japan
53/K4 Anand, India
62/B3 Anand, India
60/B4 Ananda Temple, Burma
62/C5 Anantapur, India
53/L2 Anantnag, India
64/C1 Anantnag, India
41/J2 Anan'yev, Ukr.
44/F3 Anapa, Rus.
107/J7 Anápolis, Braz.
107/H4 Anapu (riv.), Braz.
51/H4 Anār, Iran
53/G2 Anār, Iran
51/H3 Anārak, Iran
52/F2 Anārak, Iran
107/G8 Anastácio, Braz.
49/G8 'Anātā, WBnk.
68/D3 Anathan (isl.), NMar.
44/D5 Anatolia (reg.), Turk.
50/B2 Anatolia (reg.), Turk.
109/D2 Añatuya, Arg.
106/F3 Anauá (riv.), Braz.
95/Q9 Ancaster, On,Can
108/D2 Anchieta, Braz.
99/G6 Anchor (bay), Mi,US
85/J3 Anchorage, Ak,US
86/B2 Anchorage, Ak,US
85/H4 Anchor Point, Ak,US
99/G6 Anchorville, Mi,US
103/G2 Anchovy, Jam.
95/G2 Ancienne-Lorette, Qu,Can
105/C4 Ancohuma (peak), Bol.
106/E7 Ancohuma (peak), Bol.
33/K5 Ancona, It.
40/A4 Ancona, It.
109/B5 Ancud, Chile
109/B5 Ancud (gulf), Chile
55/K2 Anda, China
106/D6 Andahuaylas, Peru
81/J7 Andaingo Gara, Madg.
20/C3 Åndalsnes, Nor.
34/C4 Andalusia (aut. comm.), Sp.
89/J5 Andalusia, Al,US
97/G4 Andalusia, Al,US
48/J8 Andaman (sea), Asia
63/F5 Andaman (sea), Asia
65/B3 Andaman (sea), Burma
48/H8 Andaman (isls.), India
63/F5 Andaman (isls.), India
66/A1 Andaman (sea), Indo., Thai.
63/F5 Andaman & Nicobar Islands (terr.), India
81/J6 Andapa, Madg.
27/J5 Andau, Aus.
40/C2 Andau, Aus.
37/H2 Andechs, Ger.
37/F4 Andeer, Swi.
37/E2 Andelfingen, Swi.
30/A4 Andelle (riv.), Fr.
36/B1 Andelot-Blancheville, Fr.
37/F2 Andelsbach (riv.), Ger.
81/H8 Andemaka, Madg.
20/F1 Andenes, Nor.
26/C3 Andenne, Belg.
31/E3 Andenne, Belg.
32/F1 Andenne, Belg.
20/F1 Anderdalen Nat'l Park, Nor.
30/D3 Anderlues, Belg.
37/E4 Andermatt, Swi.
26/D3 Andernach, Ger.
31/G3 Andernach, Ger.
85/N2 Anderson (riv.), NW,Can
86/D2 Anderson (riv.), NW,Can
85/J3 Anderson, Ak,US
90/C5 Anderson, Ca,US
92/B2 Anderson, Ca,US
89/J3 Anderson, In,US
94/C3 Anderson, In,US
97/G1 Anderson, In,US
89/K5 Anderson, SC,US
97/H3 Anderson, SC,US
93/J5 Anderson, Tx,US
96/E4 Anderson, Tx,US
99/B3 Anderson (inlet), Wa,US
99/B3 Anderson (isl.), Wa,US
97/G3 Andersonville Nat'l Hist. Site, Ga,US
105/C4 Andes (mts.), SAm.
106/D6 Andes (range), SAm.
109/C2 Andes (mts.), SAm.
81/J7 Andevoranto, Madg.
20/F1 Andfjorden (fjord), Nor.
62/C4 Andhra Pradesh (state), India
28/C3 Andijk, Neth.
39/H5 Andikíthira (isl.), Gre.
81/J7 Andilamena, Madg.
51/G3 Andīmeshk, Iran
52/E2 Andīmeshk, Iran
39/J4 Andíparos (isl.), Gre.
100/D2 Andira, Braz.
39/J3 Ándissa, Gre.
46/H5 Andizhan, Uzb.
32/B5 Andoain, Sp.
34/D1 Andoain, Sp.
47/N6 Andong, SKor.
54/K4 Andong, SKor.
56/A2 Andong, SKor.
56/A2 Andong (lake), SKor.
58/E4 Andong, SKor.
58/E4 Andong (lake), SKor.
18/D4 Andorra
32/D5 Andorra
35/F1 Andorra
35/E2 Andorra, Sp.
32/D5 Andorra la Vella (cap.), And.
35/F1 Andorra la Vella (cap.), And.
25/E4 Andover, Eng,UK
20/E1 Andøya (isl.), Nor.
108/C2 Andradas, Braz.
107/H8 Andradina, Braz.
108/B2 Andradina, Braz.
35/G3 Andraitx, Sp.
81/H7 Andramasina, Madg.
81/H8 Andranolava, Madg.
81/H7 Andranomavo (riv.), Madg.
81/G8 Andranopasy, Madg.
85/C6 Andreanof (isls.), Ak,US
108/C2 Andrelândia, Braz.
19/S10 Andrésy, Fr.
100/E1 Andrews, Tx,US
93/G4 Andrews, Tx,US
96/C3 Andrews, Tx,US
98/K8 Andrews A.F.B., Md,US
38/E1 Andria, It.
40/C5 Andria, It.
81/H8 Andringitra (mts.), Madg.
39/G4 Andrítsaina, Gre.
81/H9 Androka, Madg.
81/J6 Androntany (cape), Madg.
94/G2 Androscoggin (riv.), Me, NH,US
104/B1 Andros (isl.), Bahm.
84/K7 Andros (isl.), Bahm.
89/L7 Andros (isl.), Bahm.
39/J4 Ándros, Gre.
39/J4 Ándros (isl.), Gre.
34/C3 Andújar, Sp.
76/F4 Anefis I-n-Darane, Mali
104/E3 Anegada (isl.), BVI
103/F5 Anegada (pt.), Pan.
104/E3 Anegada (passg.), West Indies
79/F5 Aného, Togo
68/G7 Aneityum (isl.), Van.
30/A6 Anet, Fr.
35/F1 Aneto, Pico de (peak), Sp.
63/K2 Anfu, China
64/F3 Angamāli, India
106/D8 Angamos (pt.), Chile
109/B1 Angamos (pt.), Chile
47/K4 Angara (riv.), Rus.
48/J4 Angara (riv.), Rus.
54/E1 Angara (riv.), Rus.
47/L4 Angarsk, Rus.
54/E1 Angarsk, Rus.
20/E3 Ånge, Swe.
42/B3 Ånge, Swe.
29/E5 Angel (riv.), Ger.
106/F2 Ángel (fall, falls), Ven.
100/B2 Ángel de la Guarda (isl.), Mex.
92/D5 Ángel de la Guarda (isl.), Mex
26/E1 Angeln (reg.), Ger.
99/F6 Angelus (lake), Mi,US
67/J4 Angemuk (mtn.), Indo.
18/E2 Ångermanälven (riv.), Swe.
20/E2 Ångermanälven (riv.), Swe.
27/H2 Angermünde, Ger.
18/C4 Angers, Fr.
32/C3 Angers, Fr.
65/C3 Angkor (ruins), Camb.
65/D4 Angk Tasaom, Camb.
71/Q12 Anglem (peak), N.Z.
35/G2 Anglès, Sp.
73/C3 Anglesea, Austl.
22/D5 Anglesey (isl.), Wal,UK
32/C5 Anglet, Fr.
34/E1 Anglet, Fr.
89/G6 Angleton, Tx,US
93/J5 Angleton, Tx,US
96/E4 Angleton, Tx,US
32/D3 Anglin (riv.), Fr.
60/D5 Ang Nam Ngum (lake), Laos
63/H4 Ang Nam Ngum (lake), Laos
65/C2 Ang Nam Ngum (lake), Laos
77/L7 Ango, Zaire
82/G4 Angoche, Moz.
53/G3 Angohrān, Iran
109/B4 Angol, Chile
74/D6 Angola
82/C3 Angola
93/J3 Angola, In,US
85/M4 Angoon, Ak,US
100/C3 Angostura, Mex.
102/C2 Angostura (res.), Mex.
18/D4 Angoulême, Fr.
32/D4 Angoulême, Fr.
35/S12 Angra do Heroísmo, Azor.
108/C2 Angra dos Reis, Braz.
46/H5 Angren, Uzb.
63/H5 Ang Thong, Thai.
65/C3 Ang Thong, Thai.
77/K7 Angu, Zaire
104/F3 Anguilla (isl.), UK
84/L8 Anguilla (isl.), UK
85/G2 Angutikada (peak), Ak,US
99/K9 Angwin, Ca,US
107/H8 Anhanduí (riv.), Braz.
31/D3 Anhée, Belg.
101/E3 Anhelo, Mex.
61/F2 Anhua, China
63/K2 Anhua, China
59/D4 Anhui (prov.), China
61/H1 Anhui (prov.), China
85/G3 Aniak, Ak,US
85/G4 Aniakchak (crater), Ak,US
85/G4 Aniakchak Nat'l Mem. Park, Ak,US
30/C3 Aniche, Fr.
92/F3 Animas (riv.), Co, NM,US
100/C2 Animas, NM,US
100/B2 Ánimas, Punta de las (pt.), Mex
49/G7 'Ānīn, WBnk.
40/E3 Anina, Rom.
55/N2 Aniva (cape), Rus.
55/N2 Aniva (sea), Rus.
30/C5 Anizy-le-Château, Fr.
20/H3 Anjalankoski, Fin.
53/K4 Anjār, India
62/B3 Anjār, India
57/N10 Anjō, Japan
95/N6 Anjou, Qu,Can
32/C3 Anjou (hist. reg.), Fr.
81/H6 Anjouan (isl.), Com.
81/H7 Anjozorobe, Madg.
54/F5 Anju, China
58/C3 Anju, NKor.
54/F5 Ankang, China
41/K5 Ankara (prov.), Turk.
44/E4 Ankara (prov.), Turk.
44/E5 Ankara (cap.), Turk.
50/C1 Ankara (prov.), Turk.
50/C2 Ankara (cap.), Turk.
81/H7 Ankaratra, massif (plat.), Madg.
81/H7 Ankavandra, Madg.
81/H8 Ankazoabo, Madg.
81/H7 Ankazobe, Madg.
81/H6 Ankerika, Madg.
63/J5 An Khe, Viet.
65/E3 An Khe, Viet.
81/G8 Ankililioka, Madg.
81/H8 Ankilizato, Madg.
27/G2 Anklam, Ger.
29/E3 Ankum, Ger.
60/E2 Anlong, China
63/J2 Anlong Bouyeizu Miaozu Zizhixian, China
65/D3 Anlong Veng, Camb.
28/D2 Anloo, Neth.
54/G5 Anlu, China
59/C5 Anlu, China
61/G2 Anlu, China
83/D Ann (cape), Ant.
87/J4 Ann (cape), Ma,US
89/M3 Ann (cape), Ma,US
95/G3 Ann (cape), Ma,US
94/E4 Anna (lake), Va,US
75/V17 Annaba, Alg.
75/V17 Annaba (gov.), Alg.
76/G1 Annaba, Alg.
73/E2 Anna Bay, Austl.
26/G3 Annaberg-Buchholz, Ger.
33/K1 Annaberg-Buchholz, Ger.
49/E2 An Nabk, Syria
50/D3 An Nabk, Syria
52/C2 An Nabk, Syria
22/B3 Annaclone, NI,UK
38/B4 An Nafīḑah, Tun.
50/D4 An Nafūd (des.), SAr.
52/C3 An Nafūd (des.), SAr.
77/P2 An Nafūd (des.), SAr.
77/L5 An Nahūd, Sudan
106/G3 Annai, Guy.
51/E4 An Najaf (gov.), Iraq
51/F4 An Najaf, Iraq
52/D2 An Najaf, Iraq
77/P1 An Najaf, Iraq
21/B3 Annalee (riv.), Ire.
22/A3 Annalee (riv.), Ire.
22/C3 Annalong, NI,UK
60/E5 Annamitique (mts.), Laos, Viet.
65/D2 Annamitique (mts.), Laos, Viet.
63/J4 Annamitique, Chaine (chain), Viet.,Laos
23/E1 Annan (riv.), Sc,UK
23/E2 Annan, Sc,UK
98/J8 Annandale, Va,US
28/B3 Anna Pavlowna, Neth.
89/L4 Annapolis (cap.), Md,US
94/E4 Annapolis, Md,US
97/J2 Annapolis, Md,US
98/K8 Annapolis (cap.), Md,US
62/D2 Annapurna (mtn.), Nepal
52/C3 An Naqb, Ra's, Jor.
87/H4 Ann Arbor, Mi,US
89/K3 Ann Arbor, Mi,US
94/D3 Ann Arbor, Mi,US
99/E7 Ann Arbor, Mi,US
51/F4 An Nāşirīyah, Iraq
52/E2 An Nāşirīyah, Iraq
77/Q1 An Nāşirīyah, Iraq
73/C4 Anne (peak), Austl.
70/B5 Annean (lake), Austl.
98/K8 Anne Arundel (co.), Md,US
33/G4 Annecy, Fr.
36/C6 Annecy, Fr.
36/C6 Annecy (lake), Fr.
38/C8 Annecy-le-Vieux, Fr.
36/C5 Annemasse, Fr.
19/U10 Annet-sur-Marne, Fr.
85/M4 Annette, Ak,US
30/B2 Annezin, Fr.
63/J5 An Nhon, Viet.
65/E3 An Nhon, Viet.
60/D3 Anning, China
60/D3 Anning (riv.), China
89/J5 Anniston, Al,US
97/G3 Anniston, Al,US
74/C5 Annobón (isl.), EqG.
76/F8 Annobón (isl.), EqG.
32/F4 Annonay, Fr.
51/F3 An Nu'manīyah, Iraq
52/E2 An Nu'manīyah, Iraq
64/F3 Annūr, India
31/G5 Annweiler, Ger.
57/M10 Anō, Japan
35/K7 Anoia (riv.), Sp.
86/G4 Anoka, Mn,US
91/K4 Anoka, Mn,US
81/J7 Anosibe an' Ala, Madg.
36/C1 Anould, Fr.
79/G2 Anou-Zeggarene (wadi), Niger
39/J5 Áno Viánnos, Gre.
39/J5 Anóyia, Gre.
39/J5 An Phuoc, Viet.
65/E4 An Phuoc, Viet.
66/C1 An Phuoc, Viet.
59/C3 Anping, China
59/H7 Anping, China
59/D5 Anqing, China
61/H2 Anqing, China
59/D3 Anqiu, China
63/K2 Anren, China
29/F5 Anröchte, Ger.
31/E2 Ans, Belg.
54/F4 Ansai, China

Ansai – Asadā

59/B3 Ansai, China
58/F7 Ansan, SKor.
26/F4 Ansbach, Ger.
33/J2 Ansbach, Ger.
103/H2 Anse-à-Galets, Haiti
103/H2 Anse-d'Hainault, Haiti
103/H2 Anse Rouge, Haiti
27/H4 Ansfelden, Aus.
33/L2 Ansfelden, Aus.
40/B1 Ansfelden, Aus.
47/N5 Anshan, China
55/J3 Anshan, China
58/B2 Anshan, China
59/E2 Anshan, China
60/E3 Anshun, China
63/J2 Anshun, China
70/D2 Anson (bay), Austl.
101/F1 Anson, Tx,US
93/H4 Anson, Tx,US
96/D3 Anson, Tx,US
55/K4 Ansŏng, SKor.
58/D4 Ansŏng, SKor.
76/F4 Ansongo, Mali
79/F3 Ansongo, Mali
68/E4 Ant (atoll), Micr.
25/H1 Ant (riv.), Eng,UK
49/E1 Antakya (Antioch), Turk.
50/D2 Antakya (Antioch), Turk.
75/H6 Antalaha, Madg.
81/J6 Antalaha, Madg.
49/A1 Antalya (prov.), Turk.
49/B1 Antalya, Turk.
49/B1 Antalya (gulf), Turk.
50/B2 Antalya, Turk.
50/B2 Antalya (prov.), Turk.
52/B1 Antalya, Turk.
75/G6 Antananarivo (cap.), Madg.
81/H7 Antananarivo (cap.), Madg.
81/H7 Antananarivo (prov.), Madg.
81/H7 Antanifotsy, Madg.
81/G8 Antanimieva, Madg.
81/H9 Antanimora, Madg.
83/W Antarctic (pen.), Ant.
16/J9 Antarctica
83/* Antarctica
83/Z Antarctic Circle, Ant.
108/B4 Antas (riv.), Braz.
30/D5 Ante (riv.), Fr.
34/C4 Antequera, Sp.
93/H3 Anthony, Ks,US
96/D2 Anthony, Ks,US
100/D1 Anthony, NM,US
92/F4 Anthony, NM,US
96/B3 Anthony, NM,US
70/F3 Anthony Lagoon, Austl.
76/D2 Anti-Atlas (mts.), Mor.
33/G5 Antibes, Fr.
35/J1 Antibes, Fr.
84/L5 Anticosti (isl.), Can.
87/K4 Anticosti (isl.), Qu,Can
95/J1 Anticosti (isl.), Qu,Can
32/D2 Antifer, Cap d' (cape), Fr.
89/J2 Antigo, Wi,US
91/L4 Antigo, Wi,US
94/B2 Antigo, Wi,US
87/K4 Antigonish, NS,Can
89/P2 Antigonish, NS,Can
95/J2 Antigonish, NS,Can
104/F3 Antigua (isl.), Anti.
84/L8 Antigua (isl.), Anti.
35/X16 Antigua, Canl.
84/M8 Antigua & Barbuda
104/F3 Antigua and Barbuda
102/D3 Antigua Guatemala, Guat.
101/F4 Antiguo Morelos, Mex.
102/B1 Antiguo Morelos, Mex.
49/D3 Anti-Lebanon (mts.), Leb.
52/C1 Antioch, Turk.
99/L10 Antioch, Ca,US
99/P15 Antioch, Il,US
49/E1 Antioch (Antakya), Turk.
50/D2 Antioch (Antakya), Turk.
103/H5 Antioquia (dept.), Col.
17/T8 Antipodes (isls.), NZ
93/J4 Antlers, Ok,US
96/E3 Antlers, Ok,US
109/B1 Antofagasta, Chile
30/C2 Antoing, Belg.
81/H8 Antokonosy Manambondro, Madg.
103/F4 Antón, Pan.
81/J6 Antongil (bay), Madg.
82/K10 Antongil (bay), Madg.
81/H6 Antonibe, Madg.
80/C4 Antoniesberg (peak), SAfr.
108/B3 Antonina, Braz.
101/Q10 Antonio Alzate (lake), Mex.
93/F3 Antonito, Co,US
96/B2 Antonito, Co,US
101/P7 Antón Lizardo, Mex.
101/P7 Anton Lizardo (pt.), Mex.
101/G5 Anton Lizardo, Punta (pt.), Mex.
102/C2 Anton Lizardo, Punta (pt.), Mex.
41/H4 Antonovo, Bul.
19/S10 Antony, Fr.
30/B6 Antony, Fr.
43/V7 Antovo, Rus.
22/B1 Antrim (mts.), NI,UK
22/B2 Antrim, NI,UK
22/B2 Antrim (dist.), NI,UK
36/E5 Antronapiana, It.
81/H7 Antsalova, Madg.
81/J6 Antsambalahy, Madg.
81/J8 Antsenavolo, Madg.
75/G6 Antsirabe, Madg.
81/H7 Antsirabe, Madg.
75/G6 Antsiranana, Madg.
81/J6 Antsiranana, Madg.
81/J6 Antsiranana (prov.), Madg.
81/H6 Antsohihy, Madg.
109/B4 Antuco (vol.), Chile
67/E3 Antulai (mtn.), Malay.
18/D3 Antwerp, Belg.
28/B6 Antwerp (prov.), Belg.
31/E1 Antwerp (prov.), Belg.
46/A4 Antwerp, Belg.
26/C3 Antwerp (Antwerpen), Belg.
28/B6 Antwerp (Antwerpen), Belg.
30/D1 Antwerp (Antwerpen), Belg.
26/C3 Antwerpen (Antwerp), Belg.
28/B6 Antwerpen (Antwerp), Belg.
30/D1 Antwerpen (Antwerp), Belg.
22/B4 An Uaimh, Ire.
62/B2 Anūpgarh, India
62/D6 Anuradhapura, SrL.
64/H4 Anuradhapura, SrL.
64/H4 Anuradhapura (dist.), SrL.
64/H4 Anuradhapura (ruins), SrL.
85/F3 Anvik, Ak,US
85/B6 Anvil (vol.), Ak,US
54/D3 Anxi, China
61/H3 Anxi, China
54/G4 Anyang, China
59/C3 Anyang, China
58/D4 Anyang, SKor.
58/F7 Anyang, SKor.
58/F7 Anyang (riv.), SKor.
54/D4 A'nyêmaqê (mts.), China
54/D4 A'nyêmaqên (mts.), China
54/G4 Anyi, China
59/B4 Anyi, China
61/G3 Anyuan, China
55/M2 Anyuy (riv.), Rus.
36/E6 Anza (riv.), It.
49/G7 'Anzah, WBnk.
59/C3 Anze, China
30/C2 Anzegem, Belg.
46/J4 Anzhero-Sudzhensk, Rus.
30/C3 Anzin, Fr.
38/C2 Anzio, It.
104/E5 Anzoátegui (state), Ven.
57/L9 Aogaki, Japan
32/C5 Aoiz, Sp.
34/E1 Aoiz, Sp.
63/G6 Ao Kham (pt.), Thai.
65/B4 Ao Kham (pt.), Thai.
47/Q5 Aomori, Japan
55/N3 Aomori, Japan
39/G2 Aóos (riv.), Gre.
65/B4 Ao Phangnga Nat'l Park, Thai.
63/H5 Aoral (peak), Camb.
65/D3 Aoral (peak), Camb.
66/B1 Aoral (peak), Camb.
33/G4 Aosta, It.
76/C4 Aoudaghast (ruins), Mrta.
78/C2 Aoudaghost (ruins), Mrta.
77/K5 Aouk (riv.), CAfr., Chad
76/D4 Aoukar (reg.), Mrta.
78/C2 Aoukar (reg.), Mrta.
76/F2 Aoulef, Alg.
57/M10 Aoyama, Japan
76/J3 Aozou, Chad
96/B4 Apache (mts.), Tx,US
89/K6 Apalachicola, Fl,US
97/G4 Apalachicola, Fl,US
101/L7 Apan, Mex.
107/J8 Aparecida, Braz.
108/C2 Aparecida, Braz.
108/B2 Aparecida do Taboado, Braz.
61/J5 Aparri, Phil.
103/G5 Apartado, Col.
106/C2 Apartado, Col.
69/L6 Apataki, FrPol.
40/D3 Apatin, Yugo.
18/G2 Apatity, Rus.
20/K2 Apatity, Rus.
42/G2 Apatity, Rus.
46/D3 Apatity, Rus.
100/E5 Apatzingán, Mex.
101/K7 Apaxco de Ocampo, Mex.
101/F5 Apaxtla, Mex.
102/B2 Apaxtla de Castrejon, Mex.
65/D4 Ap Binh Chau, Viet.
42/E4 Ape, Lat.
26/C2 Apeldoorn, Neth.
28/C4 Apeldoorn, Neth.
28/D4 Apeldoornsch (can.), Neth.
29/G4 Apelern, Ger.
29/E2 Apen, Ger.
18/E4 Apennines (mts.), It.
33/J5 Apennines (range), It.
38/C1 Apennines (range), It.
40/B5 Apennines (range), It.
29/G2 Apensen, Ger.
50/B2 Aphrodisias (ruins), Turk.
66/C3 Api (cape), Indo.
67/E5 Api (peak), Indo.
67/F4 Api (cape), Indo.
69/H6 Apia (cap.), WSam.
69/S9 Apia (cap.), WSam.
107/G6 Apiacás (mts.), Braz.
108/B3 Apiaí, Braz.
101/F5 Apizaco, Mex.
101/L7 Apizaco, Mex.
106/D7 Aplao, Peru
65/D4 Ap Loc Thanh, Viet.
66/C1 Ap Loc Thanh, Viet.
65/E4 Ap Long Hoa, Viet.
63/J6 Ap Luc, Viet.
65/D4 Ap Luc, Viet.
66/C2 Ap Luc, Viet.
67/G2 Apo (mtn.), Phil.
101/E3 Apodaca, Mex.
69/R9 Apolima (str.), WSam.
73/B3 Apollo Bay, Austl.
39/J4 Apollonia, Gre.
107/H7 Apore (riv.), Braz.
108/B1 Aporé (riv.), Braz.
102/E3 Aposentillo (pt.), Nic.
91/L4 Apostle (isls.), Wi,US
94/B2 Apostle (isls.), Wi,US
109/E2 Apóstoles, Arg.
49/D2 Apostolos Andreas (cape), Cyp.
50/C3 Apostolos Andreas (cape), Cyp.
52/B1 Apostolos Andreas (cape), Cyp.
41/L2 Apostolovo, Ukr.
84/J6 Appalachian (mts.), US
89/K4 Appalachian (mts.), US
94/E4 Appalachian (mts.), US
97/H3 Appalachian (mts.), US
29/G1 Appen, Ger.
31/G6 Appenweier, Ger.
36/D1 Appenweier, Ger.
37/F3 Appenzell, Swi.
26/D2 Appingedam, Neth.
28/D2 Appingedam, Neth.
23/F2 Appleby, Eng,UK
25/E1 Appleby Magna, Eng,UK
95/S9 Appleton, NY,US
86/H4 Appleton, Wi,US
89/J3 Appleton, Wi,US
91/L4 Appleton, Wi,US
94/B2 Appleton, Wi,US
98/C1 Apple Valley, Ca,US
43/X9 Aprelevka, Rus.
37/G5 Aprica, It.
37/G5 Aprica, Passo dell' (pass), It.
38/D2 Apricena, It.
39/J1 Apriltsi, Bul.
41/G4 Apriltsi, Bul.
44/F3 Apsheronsk, Rus.
73/E1 Apsley Gorge Nat'l Park, Austl.
65/E4 Ap Tan My, Viet.
66/D2 Ap Tan My, Viet.
88/U11 Apua (pt.), Hi,US
33/J4 Apuane (mts.), It.
108/B2 Apucarana, Braz.
109/F1 Apucarana, Braz.
106/E2 Apure (riv.), Ven.
105/B4 Apurímac (riv.), Peru
106/D6 Apurímac (riv.), Peru
65/E4 Ap Vinh Hao, Viet.
49/D5 Aqaba (gulf), Afr., Asia
48/C7 Aqaba (gulf), Asia
77/N2 Aqaba (gulf), Asia
50/C4 Aqaba (gulf), Egypt, SAr.
52/B3 Aqaba (gulf), Egypt, SAr.
52/C5 'Aqīq, Sudan
53/F1 Aq Qal'eh, Iran
49/D3 'Aqrabah, WBnk.
49/G7 'Aqrabah, WBnk.
51/E2 'Aqrah, Iraq
52/D1 'Aqrah, Iraq
100/E3 Aquanaval (riv.), Mex.
107/G8 Aquidauana, Braz.
107/G8 Aquidauana (riv.), Braz.
100/E5 Aquila, Mex.
37/E5 Aquila, Swi.
100/D2 Aquiles Serdán, Mex.
96/B4 Aquiles Serdán, Mex
103/H2 Aquin, Haiti
32/C4 Aquitaine (reg.), Fr.
35/E1 Aquitaine (reg.), Fr.
54/D4 Ar (riv.), China
57/F3 Ara (riv.), Japan
57/H7 Ara (riv.), Japan
50/C1 Ara, Turk.
77/L5 'Arab (riv.), Sudan
97/G3 Arab, Al,US
50/B4 'Arabah (dry riv.), Egypt
50/D2 Araban, Turk.
48/F8 Arabian (sea), Asia
52/D3 Arabian (pen.), Asia
53/H5 Arabian (sea), Asia
77/P3 Arabian (pen.), Asia
49/B5 Arabian (des.), Egypt
50/C5 Arabian (des.), Egypt
52/B3 Arabian (des.), Egypt
77/M2 Arabian (des.), Egypt
50/D4 Arabian (pen.), SAr.
49/E3 'Arab, Jabal al (mts.), Syria
44/E4 Araç (riv.), Turk.
106/E7 Araca, Bol.
107/L6 Aracaju, Braz.
107/L4 Aracati, Braz.
107/H8 Araçatuba, Braz.
108/B2 Araçatuba, Braz.
34/B4 Aracena, Sp.
39/G1 Aračinovo, Macd.
40/E4 Aračinovo, Macd.
107/K7 Aracruz, Braz.
108/D1 Aracruz, Braz.
107/K7 Araçuaí, Braz.
50/C4 'Arad, Isr.
77/N1 'Arad, Isr.
18/F4 Arad, Rom.
40/E2 Arad, Rom.
40/E2 Arad (co.), Rom.
44/B3 Arad, Rom.
77/K4 Arada, Chad
51/H3 Ārādān, Iran
52/F1 Ārādān, Iran
52/D4 'Arafāt, Jabal (mtn.), SAr.
68/C5 Arafura (sea)
70/E2 Arafura (sea), Austl.
67/J5 Arafura (sea), Indo.
107/H7 Aragarças, Braz.
45/H4 Aragats, Gora (peak), Arm.
32/C5 Aragon (aut. comm.), Sp.
32/C5 Aragón (riv.), Sp.
34/E1 Aragón (riv.), Sp.
35/E2 Aragon (aut. comm.), Sp.
104/E5 Aragua (state), Ven.
105/E3 Araguaia (riv.), Braz.
107/J5 Araguaia (riv.), Braz.
107/H7 Araguaiana, Braz.
107/H5 Araguaia Nat'l Park, Braz.
107/J5 Araguaína, Braz.
107/H3 Araguari (riv.), Braz.
107/J7 Araguari, Braz.
107/J7 Araguari (riv.), Braz.
108/B1 Araguari, Braz.
108/C1 Araguari (Velhas) (riv.), Braz.
107/J5 Araguatins, Braz.
57/F2 Arai, Japan
46/E6 Arāk, Iran
48/D6 Arāk, Iran
51/G3 Arāk, Iran
52/E2 Arāk, Iran
85/D3 Arakamchechan (isl.), Rus.
60/B4 Arakan (mts.), Burma
63/F3 Arakan (mts.), Burma
39/G3 Árakhthos (riv.), Gre.
50/E1 Araklı, Turk.
19/H5 Araks (riv.), Eur., Asia
46/G5 Aral (sea), Uzb.,Kaz.
45/L3 Aral (sea), Kaz., Uzb.
48/E5 Aral (sea), Kaz., Uzb.
45/H5 Aralık, Turk.
51/F2 Aralık, Turk.
46/G5 Aral'sk, Kaz.
45/H2 Aralsor (lake), Kaz.
72/B3 Aramac, Austl.
101/F3 Aramberri, Mex.
51/G3 Ārān, Iran
52/F2 Ārān, Iran
21/A3 Aran (isl.), Ire.
21/H7 Aran (isls.), Ire.
34/D2 Aranda de Duero, Sp.
100/E4 Arandas, Mex.
40/E3 Arandelovac, Yugo.
34/D2 Aranjuez, Sp.
22/E6 Aran Mawddwy (mtn.), Wal,UK
89/G6 Aransas Pass, Tx,US
96/D5 Aransas Pass, Tx,US
64/G3 Arantāngi, India
68/G4 Aranuka (atoll), Kiri.
76/E4 Araouane, Mali
107/L5 Arapiraca, Braz.
50/D2 Arapkir, Turk.
108/B2 Arapongas, Braz.
49/G7 'Ar'ara, Isr.
108/B4 Araranguá, Braz.
107/J8 Araraquara, Braz.
108/B2 Araraquara, Braz.
108/C2 Araras, Braz.
70/G7 Ararat, Austl.
73/B3 Ararat, Austl.
46/E6 Ararat (mtn.), Turk.
51/F2 Ararat (mt.), Turk.
45/H5 Ararat (Ağri) (peak), Turk.
48/D6 Ararat, Mount (peak), Turk.
107/K5 Araripina, Braz.
45/H5 Aras (riv.), Asia
46/E6 Aras (riv.), Asia
50/F2 Aras (riv.), Asia
78/C2 Aratane (well), Mrta.
106/F4 Arauá (riv.), Braz.
106/D2 Arauca, Col.
105/C2 Arauca (riv.), Ven.
108/B3 Araucária, Braz.
36/C6 Aravis, Col des (pass), Fr.
68/E5 Arawa, PNG
107/J7 Araxá, Braz.
108/C1 Araxá, Braz.
77/N6 Ārba Minch', Eth.
35/F2 Arbeca, Sp.
32/F3 Arbois, Fr.
36/B4 Arbois, Fr.
36/C6 Arbois, Mont d' (mtn.), Fr.
37/E5 Arbola, Punta d' (peak), It.
37/F2 Arbon, Swi.
21/D2 Arborath, Sc,UK
91/H2 Arborfield, Sk,Can
91/J3 Arborg, Mb,Can
32/F5 Arc (riv.), Fr.
33/G4 Arc (riv.), Fr.
35/H1 Arc (riv.), Fr.
32/C4 Arcachon, Fr.
32/C4 Arcachon (lag.), Fr.
32/C4 Arcachon, Pointe d' (pt.), Fr.
97/H5 Arcadia, Fl,US
88/B3 Arcata, Ca,US
90/B5 Arcata, Ca,US
92/A2 Arcata, Ca,US
19/S10 Arc de Triomphe, Fr.
36/B2 Arc-en-Barrois, Fr.
36/B3 Arc-et-Senans, Fr.
18/H2 Archangel, Rus.
42/J2 Archangel (Arkhangel'sk), Rus.
46/E3 Archangel (Arkhangel'sk), Rus.
42/H3 Archangel Obl., Rus.
34/E3 Archena, Sp.
72/A1 Archer (riv.), Austl.
72/A1 Archer Bend Nat'l Park, Austl.
93/H4 Archer City, Tx,US
96/D3 Archer City, Tx,US
36/C1 Arches, Fr.
88/E4 Arches Nat'l Park, Ut,US
92/E3 Arches Nat'l Park, Ut,US
34/C4 Archidona, Sp.
32/F3 Arc-lès-Gray, Fr.
36/B3 Arc-lès-Gray, Fr.
33/J4 Arco, It.
37/G6 Arco, It.
90/E5 Arco, Id,US
92/D2 Arco, Id,US
108/C2 Arcos, Braz.
34/D2 Arcos de Jalón, Sp.
34/C4 Arcos de la Frontera, Sp.
34/A2 Arcos de Valdevez, Port.
107/L5 Arcoverde, Braz.
36/B3 Arc-sur-Tille, Fr.
16/A1 Arctic (ocean)
46/F1 Arctic (ocean)
85/G1 Arctic (ocean)
87/Q7 Arctic (ocean)
85/F2 Arctic (coast. pl.), Ak,US
87/H1 Arctic Bay, NW,Can
85/J2 Arctic Nat'l Wild. Ref., Ak,US
85/M2 Arctic Red (riv.), NW,Can
85/M2 Arctic Red River, NW,Can
86/C2 Arctic Red River, NW,Can
85/J2 Arctic Village, Ak,US
39/J2 Arda (riv.), Bul.
41/G5 Arda (riv.), Bul.
44/C4 Arda (riv.), Bul.
46/E6 Ardabīl, Iran
48/D6 Ardabīl, Iran
51/G2 Ardabīl, Iran
45/G4 Ardahan, Turk.
51/E1 Ardahan, Turk.
51/H3 Ardakān, Iran
52/F2 Ardakān, Iran
51/G4 Ardal, Iran
52/F2 Ardal, Iran
20/C3 Årdalstangen, Nor.
45/G4 Ardanuç, Turk.
50/E1 Ardanuç, Turk.
45/G1 Ardatov, Rus.
23/E6 Arddleen, Wal,UK
32/F4 Ardèche (riv.), Fr.
22/B4 Ardee, Ire.
98/E6 Arden, De,US
99/M9 Arden-Arcade, Ca,US
26/C3 Ardennes (for.), Belg.
30/D3 Ardennes (for.), Belg.
32/F1 Ardennes (for.), Belg., Fr.
30/D4 Ardennes (dept.), Fr.
31/D4 Ardennes, Canal des (can.), Fr.
37/F5 Ardenno, It.
45/G4 Ardeşen, Turk.
50/E1 Ardeşen, Turk.
37/F6 Ardesio, It.
51/H3 Ardestān, Iran
52/F2 Ardestān, Iran
37/G4 Ardez, Swi.
22/C3 Ardglass, NI,UK
34/B3 Ardila (riv.), Sp.
39/J2 Ardino, Bul.
41/G5 Ardino, Bul.
73/C2 Ardlethan, Austl.
89/G5 Ardmore, Ok,US
93/H4 Ardmore, Ok,US
96/D3 Ardmore, Ok,US
98/E5 Ardmore, Pa,US
36/D5 Ardon, Swi.
30/C2 Ardooie, Belg.
30/A2 Ardres, Fr.
22/C2 Ards (dist.), NI,UK
22/C3 Ards (pen.), NI,UK
20/E3 Åre, Swe.
42/B3 Åre, Swe.
104/E3 Arecibo, PR
107/L4 Areia Branca, Braz.
92/B3 Arena (pt.), Ca,US
100/C3 Arena de la Ventana, Punta (pt.), Mex.
103/E4 Arenal (vol.), CR
107/G6 Arenápolis, Braz.
100/C4 Arena, Punta (pt.), Mex.
34/C2 Arenas de San Pedro, Sp.
18/D3 Arendal, Nor.
20/D4 Arendal, Nor.
46/A4 Arendal, Nor.
28/C6 Arendonk, Belg.
22/E6 Arenig Fawr (mtn.), Wal,UK
35/L6 Arenys de Mar, Sp.
35/L6 Arenys de Munt, Sp.
39/H4 Areópolis, Gre.
106/D7 Arequipa, Peru
34/C2 Arévalo, Sp.
52/C6 Āreza, Eth.
33/J5 Arezzo, It.
51/H3 Arfa' Deh, Iran
32/C5 Arga (riv.), Sp.
39/H3 Argalastí, Gre.
34/D3 Argamasilla de Alba, Sp.
34/C3 Argamasilla de Calatrava, Sp.
35/N9 Arganda, Sp.
32/C5 Argelès-Gazost, Fr.
35/E1 Argelès-Gazost, Fr.
32/E5 Argelès-sur-Mer, Fr.
35/G1 Argelès-sur-Mer, Fr.
37/F2 Argen (riv.), Ger.
37/F2 Argenbühl, Ger.
33/G5 Argens (riv.), Fr.
35/H1 Argens (riv.), Fr.
32/C2 Argentan, Fr.
38/B1 Argentario (mt.), It.
32/D4 Argentat, Fr.
33/G4 Argentera (peak), It.
19/S10 Argenteuil, Fr.
30/B6 Argenteuil, Fr.
32/E2 Argenteuil, Fr.
36/D6 Argentière, Aiguille d' (peak), Swi.
105/C4 Argentina
106/F8 Argentina
109/C4 Argentina
35/L6 Argentona, Sp.
32/D3 Argenton-sur-Creusot, Fr.
41/G3 Argeş (co.), Rom.
41/G3 Argeş (riv.), Rom.
44/C3 Argeş (riv.), Rom.
53/J2 Arghandab (riv.), Afg.
39/H4 Argolis (gulf), Gre.
26/C4 Argonne (for.), Fr.
31/E5 Argonne (for.), Fr.
32/F2 Argonne (for.), Fr.
99/Q16 Argonne Nat'l Lab., Il,US
39/H4 Árgos, Gre.
39/G2 Árgos Orestikón, Gre.
39/G3 Argostólion, Gre.
30/A4 Argueil, Fr.
84/E6 Arguello (pt.), Ca,US
88/B5 Arguello (pt.), Ca,US
92/B4 Arguello (pt.), Ca,US
78/A1 Arguin (bay), Mrta.
55/H1 Argun (riv.), Rus.
48/L4 Argun (riv.), China.,Rus.
47/M4 Argun (riv.), Rus., China
54/B2 Argut (riv.), Rus.
50/D2 Arguvan, Turk.
70/D3 Argyle (lake), Austl.
76/G4 Arhli, Niger
55/J3 Ar Horqin Qi, China
76/C3 Arhreijît (well), Mrta.
18/E3 Århus, Den.
20/D4 Århus, Den.
46/B4 Århus, Den.
82/C6 Ariamsvlei, Namb.
38/D2 Ariano Irpino, It.
34/C1 Arianza (riv.), Sp.
106/D7 Arica, Chile
70/C6 Arid (cape), Austl.
56/D3 Arida, Japan
39/H2 Aridhaía, Gre.
40/F5 Aridhaía, Gre.
32/D5 Ariège (riv.), Fr.
35/F1 Ariège (riv.), Fr.
41/K5 Arifiye, Turk.
64/B2 Ārifwāla, Pak.
49/E2 Arīḩā, Syria
50/D3 Arīḩā, Syria
52/C1 Arīḩā, Syria
49/D4 Arīḩā (Jericho), WBnk.
49/G8 Arīḩā (Jericho), WBnk.
40/E4 Arilje, Yugo.
104/F5 Arima, Trin.
107/G6 Arinos (riv.), Braz.
36/B5 Arinthod, Fr.
27/M1 Ariogala, Lith.
42/D5 Ariogala, Lith.
105/D3 Aripuanã (riv.), Braz.
106/F5 Aripuanã, Braz.
106/F5 Aripuanã (riv.), Braz.
106/F5 Ariquemes, Braz.
72/B2 Arish, Austl.
50/C4 'Arīsh (dry riv.), Egypt
49/C4 'Arīsh, Wādī al (riv.), Egypt
100/C2 Arivaca, Az,US
100/C2 Arivechi, Mex.
81/H7 Arivonimamo, Madg.
64/G3 Ariyalūr, India
34/D2 Ariza, Sp.
35/F1 Arize (riv.), Fr.
100/B1 Arizona (state), US
88/D5 Arizona (state), US
92/D4 Arizona (state), US
100/C2 Arizpe, Mex.
20/F2 Arjeplog, Swe.
42/C2 Arjeplog, Swe.
103/H4 Arjona, Col.
106/C1 Arjona, Col.
34/C4 Arjona, Sp.
89/H5 Arkadelphia, Ar,US
93/J4 Arkadelphia, Ar,US
96/E3 Arkadelphia, Ar,US
39/J5 Arkalokhórion, Gre.
46/G4 Arkalyk, Kaz.
84/H6 Arkansas (riv.), US
89/H4 Arkansas (riv.), US
89/H4 Arkansas (state), US
93/J4 Arkansas (state), US
96/E3 Arkansas (state), US
97/F3 Arkansas City, Ar,US
93/H3 Arkansas City, Ks,US
96/D2 Arkansas City, Ks,US
77/K3 Arkanū (peak), Libya
50/B2 Arkhángelos, Gre.
42/J2 Arkhangel'sk (Archangel), Rus.
46/E3 Arkhangel'sk (Archangel), Rus.
43/X9 Arkhangel'skoye, Rus.
47/P5 Arkhara, Rus.
22/B6 Arklow, Ire.
27/G1 Arkona, Kap (cape), Ger.
62/C5 Arkonam, India
23/G4 Arksey, Eng,UK
46/H2 Arkticheskiy Institut (isls.), Rus.
34/C1 Arlanza (riv.), Sp.
34/C1 Arlazón (riv.), Sp.
37/G3 Arlbergpass (pass), Aus.
32/F5 Arles, Fr.
35/H1 Arles, Fr.
36/D3 Arlesheim, Swi.
30/C3 Arleux, Fr.
97/G4 Arlington, Ga,US
91/K4 Arlington, Mn,US
101/F1 Arlington, Tx,US
89/G5 Arlington, Tx,US
93/H4 Arlington, Tx,US
96/D3 Arlington, Tx,US
94/E4 Arlington, Va,US
97/J2 Arlington, Va,US
98/J8 Arlington, Va,US
94/C3 Arlington Heights, Il,US
99/Q15 Arlington Heights, Il,US
27/L4 Arló, Hun.
26/C4 Arlon, Belg.
31/E4 Arlon, Belg.
32/F2 Arlon, Belg.
36/C6 Arly (riv.), Fr.
79/F4 Arly Nat'l Park, Burk.
79/F4 Arly Res., Ben.
99/G6 Armada, Mi,US
101/E4 Armadillo, Mex.
22/B3 Armagh, NI,UK
22/B3 Armagh (dist.), NI,UK
32/F3 Armançon (riv.), Fr.
108/B2 Armando Laydner (res.), Braz.
52/B3 Armant, Egypt
19/H4 Armavir, Rus.
45/G3 Armavir, Rus.
46/E5 Armavir, Rus.
33/G5 Arme, Cap d' (cape), Fr.
35/J1 Arme, Cap d' (cape), Fr.
19/H4 Armenia
45/H5 Armenia
46/E5 Armenia
51/F1 Armenia
106/C3 Armenia, Col.
30/B2 Armentières, Fr.
32/E1 Armentières, Fr.
100/E5 Armería, Mex.
68/E8 Armidale, Austl.
71/J6 Armidale, Austl.
73/D1 Armidale, Austl.
34/D4 Armilla, Sp.
22/B1 Armoy, NI,UK
90/D3 Armstrong, Can
23/G4 Armthorpe, Eng,UK
62/C4 Ārmūr, India
32/D3 Arnage, Fr.
39/H2 Arnaía, Gre.
41/F5 Arnaía, Gre.
87/J3 Arnaud (riv.), Qu,Can
49/C2 Arnauti (cape), Cyp.
51/M6 Arnavutköy, Turk.
25/E3 Arncott, Eng,UK
34/D1 Arnedo, Sp.
30/B2 Arnèke, Fr.
93/H3 Arnett, Ok,US
96/D2 Arnett, Ok,US
70/F2 Arnhem (bay), Austl.
70/F2 Arnhem (cape), Austl.
26/C3 Arnhem, Neth.
28/C5 Arnhem, Neth.
70/E2 Arnhem Land (reg.), Austl.
62/C5 Arni, India
33/J5 Arno (riv.), It.
68/G4 Arno (atoll), Mrsh.
23/G5 Arnold, Eng,UK
33/K3 Arnoldstein, Aus.
40/A2 Arnoldstein, Aus.
32/E3 Arnon (riv.), Fr.
19/T10 Arnouville-lès-Gonesse, Fr.
94/E2 Arnprior, On,Can
26/E3 Arnsberg, Ger.
29/F6 Arnsberg, Ger.
23/F3 Arnside, Eng,UK
26/F3 Arnstadt, Ger.
33/J1 Arnstadt, Ger.
80/B2 Aroab, Namb.
34/B4 Aroche, Sp.
36/D6 Arolla, Swi.
29/G6 Arolsen, Ger.
52/C5 Aroma, Sudan
32/E3 Aron (riv.), Fr.
35/X16 Arona, Canl.
30/B4 Aronde (riv.), Fr.
68/G5 Arorae (atoll), Kiri.
33/H3 Arosa, Swi.
37/F4 Arosa, Swi.
37/F4 Aroser Rothorn (peak), Swi.
26/F1 Ærøskøbing, Den.
67/H5 Aro Usu (cape), Indo.
45/G4 Arpaçay, Turk.
51/E1 Arpaçay, Turk.
19/S11 Arpajon, Fr.
32/E4 Arpajon-sur-Cere, Fr.
30/B2 Arques, Fr.
30/A4 Arques-la-Bataille, Fr.
49/G7 'Arrābah, WBnk.
62/D2 Arrah, India
77/M5 Ar Rahad, Sudan
51/E3 Ar Raḩḩālīyah, Iraq
107/H6 Arraias (riv.), Braz.
103/G4 Arraiján, Pan.
23/H4 Arram, Eng,UK
51/E3 Ar Ramādī, Iraq
52/D2 Ar Ramādī, Iraq
49/E3 Ar Ramthā, Jor.
50/D3 Ar Ramthā, Jor.
52/C2 Ar Ramthā, Jor.
21/C3 Arran (isl.), Sc,UK
103/E4 Arrancabarba (mtn.), Nic.
50/D2 Ar Raqqah (prov.), Syria
50/D3 Ar Raqqah, Syria
52/C1 Ar Raqqah, Syria
26/B3 Arras, Fr.
30/B3 Arras, Fr.
32/E1 Arras, Fr.
38/A4 Ar Ra's al Abyaḑ (cape), Tun.
49/E2 Ar Rastan, Syria
35/F1 Arrats (riv.), Fr.
52/E6 Ar Rawḑah, Yem.
32/D5 Arreau, Fr.
35/F1 Arreau, Fr.
35/Y16 Arrecife, Canl.
76/C2 Arrecife, Sp.
32/B2 Arrée (mts.), Fr.
102/C2 Arriaga, Mex.
51/F4 Ar Rifā'ī, Iraq
108/A5 Arrio Grande, Braz.
34/C1 Arriondas, Sp.
52/E4 Ar Riyāḑ (Riyadh) (cap.), SAr.
77/Q3 Ar Riyāḑ (Riyadh) (cap.), SAr.
52/E6 Ar Riyān, Yem.
34/B3 Arronches, Port.
32/F3 Arroux (riv.), Fr.
34/B3 Arroyo de la Luz, Sp.
92/B4 Arroyo Grande, Ca,US
51/F4 Ar Rumaythah, Iraq
49/E3 Ar Ruşayfah, Jor.
52/C2 Ar Ruşayfah, Jor.
77/M5 Ar Ruşayriş, Sudan
50/E3 Ar Ruţbah, Iraq
52/D2 Ar Ruţbah, Iraq
52/F4 Ar Ruways, SAr.
47/P5 Arsen'yev, Rus.
55/L3 Arsen'yev, Rus.
26/F1 Årslev, Den.
26/D4 Ars-sur-Moselle, Fr.
31/F5 Ars-sur-Moselle, Fr.
32/G2 Ars-sur-Moselle, Fr.
69/T11 Art (isl.), NCal.
39/G3 Árta, Gre.
39/G3 Árta (gulf), Gre.
35/G3 Artá, Sp.
100/E5 Arteaga, Mex.
101/E3 Arteaga, Mex.
34/A1 Arteijo, Sp.
47/P5 Artem, Rus.
55/L3 Artem, Rus.
103/F1 Artemisa, Cuba
51/G1 Artëm-Ostrov, Azer.
100/D1 Artesia, NM,US
88/F5 Artesia, NM,US
93/F4 Artesia, NM,US
96/B3 Artesia, NM,US
37/E3 Arth, Swi.
72/C3 Arthur (pt.), Austl.
71/R11 Arthur's (pass), N.Z.
109/E3 Artigas, Uru.
51/E1 Artik, Arm.
26/A3 Artois (reg.), Fr.
30/A2 Artois (reg.), Fr.
32/E1 Artois (reg.), Fr.
30/B2 Artois, Collines de (hills), Fr.
26/A3 Artois, Collines de l' (hills), Fr.
32/E1 Artois, Collines de l' (hills), Fr.
44/F4 Artova, Turk.
50/D1 Artova, Turk.
41/J3 Artsiz, Ukr.
45/G4 Artvin, Turk.
45/G4 Artvin (prov.), Turk.
50/E1 Artvin, Turk.
50/E1 Artvin (prov.), Turk.
67/H5 Aru (isls.), Indo.
68/C5 Aru (isls.), Indo.
77/M7 Arua, Ugan.
104/D4 Aruba (isl.), Neth.
105/B1 Aruba (isl.), Neth.
106/D1 Aruba (isl.), Neth.
84/K8 Aruba (isl.), Neth.
35/X16 Arucas, Canl.
32/C5 Arudy, Fr.
35/E1 Arudy, Fr.
25/F5 Arun (riv.), Eng,UK
60/B2 Arunachal Pradesh (state), India
63/F2 Arunachal Pradesh (state), India
25/F5 Arundel, Eng,UK
62/C6 Aruppukkottai, India
64/G4 Aruppukkottai, India
49/G7 'Arūrā, WBnk.
67/F3 Arus (cape), Indo.
82/G1 Arusha, Tanz.
69/L6 Arutua (atoll), FrPol.
64/H4 Aruvi (riv.), SrL.
74/E4 Aruwimi (riv.), Zaire
77/L7 Aruwimi (riv.), Zaire
47/L5 Arvayheer, Mong.
54/E2 Arvayheer, Mong.
36/C6 Arve (riv.), Fr.
20/F2 Arvidsjaur, Swe.
42/C2 Arvidsjaur, Swe.
20/E4 Arvika, Swe.
92/C4 Arvin, Ca,US
91/L4 Arvon (peak), Mi,US
94/B2 Arvon (peak), Mi,US
38/A4 Aryānah (gov.), Tun.
75/X17 Aryānah (gov.), Tun.
46/G5 Arys', Kaz.
32/B3 Arz (riv.), Fr.
38/A2 Arzachena, It.
19/H3 Arzamas, Rus.
43/J5 Arzamas, Rus.
45/G1 Arzamas, Rus.
46/E4 Arzamas, Rus.
31/G3 Arzbach, Ger.
75/Q16 Arzew, Alg.
31/F3 Arzfeld, Ger.
37/G3 Arzl im Pitztal, Aus.
34/A1 Arzúa, Sp.
28/C6 As, Belg.
31/E1 As, Belg.
26/G3 Aš, Czh.
33/K1 Aš, Czh.
20/D4 Ås, Nor.
82/C6 Asab, Namb.
51/G3 Asadābād, Iran
52/E2 Asadābād, Iran

78/D5 Asagny Nat'l Park, IvC.
66/A3 Asahan (riv.), Indo.
56/C3 Asahi (riv.), Japan
57/G3 Asahi, Japan
57/M9 Asahi, Japan
57/N9 Asahi, Japan
57/F1 Asahi-Bandai Nat'l Park, Japan
57/G2 Asahi-Bandai Nat'l Park, Japan
55/N3 Asahi-dake (mtn.), Japan
47/Q5 Asahikawa, Japan
55/N3 Asahikawa, Japan
57/H7 Asaka, Japan
57/M9 Asake (riv.), Japan
52/D6 Āsalē, Eth.
77/P5 Āsalē, Eth.
57/F2 Asama-yama (mtn.), Japan
58/D4 Asan (bay), SKor.
62/E3 Asansol, India
69/R9 Asau, WSam.
76/J3 Asawanwah (well), Libya
31/G2 Asbach, Ger.
43/P4 Asbest, Rus.
46/G4 Asbest, Rus.
80/C3 Asbestos (mts.), SAfr.
98/F5 Asbury Park, NJ,US
106/F7 Ascención, Bol.
101/J5 Ascención (bay), Mex.
102/E2 Ascención (bay), Mex.
26/E4 Aschaffenburg, Ger.
29/E5 Ascheberg, Ger.
29/E2 Aschendorf, Ger.
26/F3 Aschersleben, Ger.
38/A1 Asco (riv.), Fr.
33/K5 Ascoli Piceno, It.
38/C1 Ascoli Piceno, It.
40/A4 Ascoli Piceno, It.
38/D2 Ascoli Satriano, It.
37/E5 Ascona, Swi.
25/F4 Ascot, Eng,UK
52/D6 Āseb, Eth.
77/P5 Āseb, Eth.
20/E4 Åseda, Swe.
77/N6 Āsela, Eth.
20/F2 Åsele, Swe.
42/C2 Åsele, Swe.
29/G2 Asendorf, Ger.
29/G3 Asendorf, Ger.
39/J1 Asenovgrad, Bul.
41/G4 Asenovgrad, Bul.
44/C4 Asenovgrad, Bul.
30/D5 Asfeld-la-Ville, Fr.
54/G2 Asgat, Mong.
25/G4 Ash, Eng,UK
25/E4 Ashampstead, Eng,UK
79/F5 Ashanti (reg.), Gha.
79/E5 Ashanti (uplands), Gha.
22/B6 Ashbourne, Ire.
23/G5 Ashbourne, Eng,UK
70/D4 Ashburton (riv.), Austl.
71/R11 Ashburton, N.Z.
24/C5 Ashburton, Eng,UK
25/E1 Ashby (can.), Eng,UK
23/G6 Ashby-de-la-Zouch, Eng,UK
25/E1 Ashby de la Zouch, Eng,UK
24/D3 Ashchurch, Eng,UK
86/D3 Ashcroft, BC,Can
90/C3 Ashcroft, BC,Can
97/J3 Asheboro, NC,US
91/J3 Ashern, Mb,Can
101/F2 Asherton, Tx,US
89/K4 Asheville, NC,US
97/H3 Asheville, NC,US
91/M2 Asheweig (riv.), On,Can
73/D1 Ashford, Austl.
19/M7 Ashford, Eng,UK
25/G4 Ashford, Eng,UK
23/H6 Ashfordby, Eng,UK
25/F1 Ashfordby, Eng,UK
95/Q8 Ashgrove, On,Can
71/S11 Ashhurst, N.Z.
23/G1 Ashington, Eng,UK
57/L10 Ashiya, Japan
55/L5 Ashizuri-misaki (cape), Japan
56/C4 Ashizuri-misaki (cape), Japan
75/W17 Ashkal (lake), Tun.
46/F6 Ashkhabad (cap.), Trkm.
51/J2 Ashkhabad (cap.), Trkm.
53/G1 Ashkhabad (cap.), Trkm.
93/H3 Ashland, Ks,US
96/D2 Ashland, Ks,US
89/K4 Ashland, Ky,US
94/D4 Ashland, Ky,US
97/H2 Ashland, Ky,US
94/D3 Ashland, Oh,US
88/B3 Ashland, Or,US
90/C5 Ashland, Or,US
92/B2 Ashland, Or,US
86/G4 Ashland, Wi,US
89/H2 Ashland, Wi,US
91/L4 Ashland, Wi,US
94/B2 Ashland, Wi,US
91/J4 Ashley, ND,US
19/M6 Ashley Green, Eng,UK
70/C2 Ashmore (reef), Austl.
70/C2 Ashmore and Cartier Is. (terr.), Austl.
49/B4 Ashmūn, Egypt
50/B4 Ashmūn, Egypt
50/E4 Ash Shabakah, Iraq
52/D2 Ash Shabakah, Iraq
49/E2 Ash Shamāl (gov.), Leb.
51/F4 Ash Shāmīyah, Iraq
52/D2 Ash Shāmīyah, Iraq
53/G3 Ash Shāriqah, UAE
77/S2 Ash Shāriqah, UAE
51/E3 Ash Sharqāt, Iraq
49/B4 Ash Sharqīyah (gov.), Egypt
50/B4 Ash Sharqīyah (gov.), Egypt
51/F4 Ash Shaṭrah, Iraq
52/B6 Ash Shawal, Sudan
49/D4 Ash Shawbak, Jor.
50/C4 Ash Shawbak, Jor.
52/C2 Ash Shawbak, Jor.
52/E6 Ash Shiḥr, Yem.
77/Q5 Ash Shiḥr, Yem.
52/C3 Ash Shurayf, SAr.
62/C3 Ashta, India
89/K3 Ashtabula, Oh,US
94/D3 Ashtabula, Oh,US
19/N8 Ashtead, Eng,UK
52/F2 Āshtīān, Iran
80/M10 Ashton, SAfr.
90/F4 Ashton, Id,US
92/E1 Ashton, Id,US
23/F5 Ashton-in-Makerfield, Eng,UK
23/F5 Ashton-under-Lyne, Eng,UK
91/L4 Ashwaubenon, Wi,US
94/B2 Ashwaubenon, Wi,US
25/F2 Ashwell, Eng,UK
17/N3 Asia
48/* Asia
37/H6 Asiago, It.
75/L13 Asilah, Mor.
38/A2 Asinara (gulf), It.
38/A2 Asinara (isl.), It.
46/J4 Asino, Rus.
52/D5 'Asīr (mts.), SAr., Yemen
77/P4 'Asīr (mts.), SAr., Yemen
52/C5 Asis (cape), Sudan
45/G5 Aşkale, Turk.
50/E2 Aşkale, Turk.
23/E3 Askam in Furness, Eng,UK
21/H7 Askeaton, Ire.
20/D4 Asker, Nor.
23/G4 Askern, Eng,UK
20/D4 Askim, Nor.
39/G2 Áskion (peak), Gre.
20/P6 Askja (crater), Ice.
26/E1 Askov, Den.
52/C5 Āsmera, Eth.
77/N4 Āsmera, Eth.
19/T9 Asnières-sur-Oise, Fr.
19/S10 Asnières-sur-Seine, Fr.
30/B6 Asnières-sur-Seine, Fr.
56/B4 Aso Nat'l Park, Japan
77/M5 Āsosa, Eth.
56/B4 Aso-san (mtn.), Japan
52/C4 Asoteriba (peak), Sudan
77/N3 Asoteriba (peak), Sudan
23/E2 Aspatria, Eng,UK
35/E3 Aspe, Sp.
88/E4 Aspen, Co,US
92/F3 Aspen, Co,US
96/B2 Aspen, Co,US
49/B1 Aspendos (ruins), Turk.
90/J7 Aspen Hill, Md,US
93/G4 Aspermont, Tx,US
96/C3 Aspermont, Tx,US
35/F1 Aspin, Col d' (pass), Fr.
71/Q11 Aspiring (peak), N.Z.
39/H3 Asprópirgos, Gre.
39/L6 Asprópirgos, Gre.
90/G2 Asquith, Sk,Can
78/C2 'Assâba, Massif de l' (reg.), Mrta.
50/D3 As Sabkhah, Syria
52/C1 As Sabkhah, Syria
51/F3 As Sa'dīyah, Iraq
49/B5 Aş Şaff, Egypt
50/B4 Aş Şaff, Egypt
49/D4 Aş Şāfī, Jor.
50/C4 Aş Şāfī, Jor.
77/N1 Aş Şāfī, Jor.
52/D2 Aş Şāliḥīyah, Syria
51/G4 As Sālimīyah, Kuw.
52/E3 As Sālimīyah, Kuw.
77/Q2 As Sālimīyah, Kuw.
52/E4 As Sālimīyah, SAr.
77/L1 As Sallūm, Egypt
51/F3 As Salmān, Iraq
52/D2 As Salmān, Iraq
49/D3 As Salṭ, Jor.
50/C3 As Salṭ, Jor.
60/B3 Assam (state), India
63/F2 Assam (state), India
51/F4 As Samāwah, Iraq
52/E2 As Samāwah, Iraq
77/Q1 As Samāwah, Iraq
49/B4 As Santah, Egypt
49/D3 Aş Şarīḥ, Jor.
30/D2 Asse, Belg.
38/A3 Assemini, It.
26/D2 Assen, Neth.
28/D2 Assen, Neth.
28/A6 Assenede, Belg.
30/C1 Assenede, Belg.
26/E1 Assens, Den.
31/E3 Assesse, Belg.
76/J1 As Sidr, Libya
52/C4 As Sidr, SAr.
49/B4 As Sinbillāwayn, Egypt
86/F4 Assiniboia, Sk,Can
91/G3 Assiniboia, Sk,Can
90/E3 Assiniboine (peak), Can.
91/J3 Assiniboine (riv.), Mb,Can
86/F3 Assiniboine (riv.), Mb,Can
94/F1 Assinika (lake), Qu,Can
107/H8 Assis, Braz.
108/B2 Assis, Braz.
109/F1 Assis, Braz.
38/C1 Assisi, It.
74/K10 Assomada, CpV.
35/G1 Assou (riv.), Fr.
77/M6 As Sudd (reg.), Sudan
52/E6 As Sufāl, Yem.
52/B5 Aş Şufayyah, Sudan
52/C2 As Sukhnah, Syria
46/E6 As Sulaymānīyah, Iraq
51/F3 As Sulaymānīyah, Iraq
51/F3 As Sulaymānīyah (gov.), Iraq
52/E1 As Sulaymānīyah, Iraq
77/Q3 As Sulayyil, SAr.
51/F5 Aş Şummān (mts.), SAr.
52/E3 Aş Şummān (mts.), SAr.
77/Q2 Aş Şummān (mts.), SAr.
49/E3 As Suwaydā', Syria
49/E3 As Suwaydā' (dist.), Syria
50/D3 As Suwaydā', Syria
50/D3 As Suwaydā' (prov.), Syria
52/C2 As Suwaydā', Syria
51/F3 Aş Şuwayrah, Iraq
52/D2 Aş Şuwayrah, Iraq
49/C4 As Suways (gov.), Egypt
50/B4 As Suways (gov.), Egypt
49/C5 As Suways (Suez), Egypt
50/C4 As Suways (Suez), Egypt
77/M2 As Suways (Suez), Egypt
39/G3 Astakós, Gre.
28/C6 Asten, Neth.
33/H4 Asti, It.
50/A2 Astipálaia, Gre.
25/E2 Aston, Eng,UK
24/D2 Aston on Clun, Eng,UK
108/B2 Astorga, Braz.
86/D4 Astoria, Or,US
88/B2 Astoria, Or,US
90/C4 Astoria, Or,US
19/H4 Astrakhan', Rus
45/J3 Astrakhan', Rus.
46/E5 Astrakhan', Rus.
45/H3 Astrakhan Obl., Rus.
39/H4 Ástros, Gre.
34/C1 Astudillo, Sp.
34/B1 Asturias (aut. comm.), Sp.
25/E2 Astwood Bank, Eng,UK
57/L10 Asuka, Japan
57/N9 Asuke, Japan
68/D3 Asuncion (isl.), NMar.
109/E2 Asunción (cap.), Par.
102/C2 Asunción Ixtaltepec, Mex.
101/F5 Asunción Nochixtlán, Mex.
77/M7 Aswa (riv.), Ugan.
52/B4 Aswān, Egypt
77/M3 Aswān, Egypt
74/F2 Aswan High (dam), Egypt
77/M3 Aswan High (dam), Egypt
50/B5 Asyūţ, Egypt
50/B5 Asyūţ (gov.), Egypt
52/B3 Asyūţ, Egypt
77/M2 Asyūţ, Egypt
50/B2 Atabey, Turk.
109/C1 Atacama (plat.), Arg.
105/C5 Atacama (des.), Chile
106/E8 Atacama (des.), Chile
79/F4 Atacora (range), Ben.
69/H5 Atafu (atoll), Tok.
76/F6 Atakpamé, Togo
79/F5 Atakpamé, Togo
43/B5 Atalándi, Gre.
44/B5 Atalándi, Gre.
106/D6 Atalaya, Peru
57/F3 Atami, Japan
67/E3 Atap, Indo.
52/E6 'Ataq, Yem.
76/C3 Atar, Mrta.
78/B1 Atar, Mrta.
34/D4 Atarfe, Sp.
101/E4 Atarjea, Mex.
102/A1 Atarjea, Mex.
62/D2 Atarra, India
54/D3 Atas Bogd (peak), Mong.
88/B4 Atascadero, Ca,US
92/B4 Atascadero, Ca,US
46/H5 Atasu, Kaz.
50/D2 Atatürk (dam), Turk.
50/D2 Atatürk (res.), Turk.
52/C1 Atatürk (res.), Turk.
74/F3 Atbara (riv.), Eth., Sudan
77/N5 Atbara (riv.), Eth., Sudan
52/B5 Atbara, Sudan
77/M4 Atbara, Sudan
77/M4 Atbarah (riv.), Sudan
52/B5 'Atbarah, Nahr (riv.), Sudan
46/G4 Atbasar, Kaz.
93/K5 Atchafalaya (bay), La,US
93/K5 Atchafalaya (riv.), La,US
93/J3 Atchison, Ks,US
96/E2 Atchison, Ks,US
98/F6 Atco, NJ,US
79/E5 Atebubu, Gha.
34/E2 Ateca, Sp.
20/G1 Ateelva (riv.), Nor.
100/D4 Atengo (riv.), Mex.
38/C1 Aterno (riv.), It.
38/D1 Atessa, It.
30/C2 Ath, Belg.
84/F4 Athabasca (lake), Can.
84/F4 Athabasca (riv.), Can.
90/E2 Athabasca (riv.), Ab,Can
86/E3 Athabasca (riv.), Ab,Can
90/E2 Athabasca, Ab,Can
86/F3 Athabasca (lake), Ab,Sk,Can
91/H2 Athapapuskow (lake), Mb,Can
76/K1 Athār Ţulmaythah (Ptolemaïs) (ruins), Libya
22/B4 Athboy, Ire.
21/A4 Athenry, Ire.
18/F5 Athens (cap.), Gre.
97/G3 Athens, Al,US
89/K5 Athens, Ga,US
97/H3 Athens, Ga,US
89/K4 Athens, Oh,US
94/D4 Athens, Oh,US
97/H2 Athens, Oh,US
89/K4 Athens, Tn,US
97/G3 Athens, Tn,US
101/G1 Athens, Tx,US
93/J4 Athens, Tx,US
96/E3 Athens, Tx,US
39/H4 Athens (Athínai) (cap.), Gre.
39/L7 Athens (Athínai) (cap.), Gre.
25/E1 Atherstone, Eng,UK
71/H3 Atherton, Austl.
72/B2 Atherton, Austl.
23/F4 Atherton, Eng,UK
39/H4 Athínai (Athens) (cap.), Gre.
39/L7 Athínai (Athens) (cap.), Gre.
19/T10 Athis-Mons, Fr.
21/B4 Athlone, Ire.
60/B5 Athok, Burma
63/G4 Athok, Burma
39/J2 Áthos (peak), Gre.
22/B6 Athy, Ire.
76/J5 Ati, Chad
108/C2 Atibaia, Braz.
34/D2 Atienza, Sp.
86/G4 Atikokan, On,Can
89/H2 Atikokan, On,Can
91/L3 Atikokan, On,Can
94/B1 Atikokan, On,Can
102/D3 Atitlán (lake), Guat.
69/K7 Atiu (isl.), Cookls.
47/U4 Atka (isl.), Ak,US
85/C5 Atka (isl.), Ak,US
85/D5 Atka, Ak,US
45/H2 Atkarsk, Rus.
85/M2 Atkinson (pt.), NW,Can
101/F5 Atlacomulco de Fabela, Mex.
101/K7 Atlacomulco de Fabela, Mex.
80/P12 Atlanta, SAfr.
84/J6 Atlanta, US
89/K5 Atlanta (cap.), Ga,US
97/G3 Atlanta, Ga,US
93/J4 Atlanta, Tx,US
96/E3 Atlanta, Tx,US
104/C1 Atlantic (ocean)
104/D2 Atlantic (ocean)
16/G3 Atlantic (ocean)
83/X Atlantic (ocean), Ant.
18/A3 Atlantic (ocean), Eur.
91/K5 Atlantic, Ia,US
93/J2 Atlantic, Ia,US
89/M4 Atlantic City, NJ,US
94/F4 Atlantic City, NJ,US
103/H4 Atlántico (dept.), Col.
79/F5 Atlantique (prov.), Ben.
76/E2 Atlas (mts.), Afr.
75/R16 Atlas (mts.), Alg.
74/B1 Atlas (mts.), Alg., Mor.
75/N14 Atlas (mts.), Mor.
99/K10 Atlas (peak), Ca,US
76/E1 Atlas Saharien (mts.), Alg., Mor.
101/M7 Atlazayanca, Mex.
85/M4 Atlin, BC,Can
85/M4 Atlin (lake), BC,Can
86/C3 Atlin, BC,Can
101/F5 Atlixco, Mex.
101/L8 Atlixco, Mex.
102/B2 Atlixco, Mex.
97/G4 Atmore, Al,US
106/E8 Atocha, Bol.
30/D2 Atomium, The, Belg.
101/L6 Atotonilco el Grande, Mex.
76/B3 Atoui (dry riv.), Mrta.
102/B2 Atoyac (riv.), Mex.
85/G1 Atqasuk, Ak,US
46/F6 Atrak (riv.), Iran
51/J2 Atrak (riv.), Iran
53/G1 Atrak (riv.), Iran
106/C2 Atrato (riv.), Col.
57/H7 Atsugi, Japan
57/N10 Atsumi, Japan
57/N10 Atsumi (pen.), Japan
49/D4 Aţ Ţafīlah, Jor.
50/C4 Aţ Ţafīlah, Jor.
52/C2 Aţ Ţafīlah, Jor.
77/N1 Aţ Ţafīlah, Jor.
52/D4 Aţ Ţā'if, SAr.
77/P3 Aţ Ţā'if, SAr.
36/C4 Attalens, Swi.
49/E3 At Tall, Syria
97/G3 Attalla, Al,US
49/B4 At Tall al Kabīr, Egypt
51/E3 At Ta'mīm (gov.), Iraq
63/J5 Attapu, Laos
65/D3 Attapu, Laos
107/M2 Attawapiskat (riv.), On,Can
87/H3 Attawapiskat (riv.), On,Can
29/E6 Attendorn, Ger.
31/G1 Attendorn, Ger.
33/K3 Attersee (lake), Aus.
40/A2 Attersee (lake), Aus.
31/E4 Attert, Belg.
99/F5 Attica, Mi,US
30/C5 Attichy, Fr.
30/D5 Attigny, Fr.
49/G7 'Attīl, WBnk.
64/F4 Attingal, India
25/E2 Attleborough, Eng,UK
25/H2 Attleborough, Eng,UK
47/T4 Attu (isl.), Ak,US
85/A5 Attu (isl.), Ak,US
50/C4 Aţ Ţūr, Egypt
52/B3 Aţ Ţūr, Egypt
77/M2 Aţ Ţūr, Egypt
64/G3 Āttūr, India
49/D4 Aţ Ţūr, WBnk.
49/G8 Aţ Ţūr, WBnk.
52/D6 At Turbah, Yem.
52/D3 Aţ Ţuwayyah, SAr.
109/C4 Atuel (riv.), Arg.
69/M5 Atuona, FrPol.
20/F4 Åtvidaberg, Swe.
42/C4 Åtvidaberg, Swe.
92/B3 Atwater, Ca,US
93/G3 Atwood, Ks,US
96/C2 Atwood, Ks,US
103/H1 Atwood (Samana) (cay), Bahm.
104/C2 Atwood (Samana) (cay), Bahm.
101/Q10 Atzcapotzalco, Mex.
37/F3 Au, Swi.
31/E4 Aubange, Belg.
26/C4 Aube (riv.), Fr.
30/D6 Aube (dept.), Fr.
32/F2 Aube (riv.), Fr.
36/A2 Aube (riv.), Fr.
32/F4 Aubenas, Fr.
36/C4 Aubert, Mont (peak), Swi.
19/T10 Aubervilliers, Fr.
30/C6 Aubetin (riv.), Fr.
30/C5 Aubette (riv.), Fr.
30/A5 Aubevoye, Fr.
30/B3 Aubigny, Fr.
32/E3 Aubigny-sur-Nère, Fr.
32/E4 Aubin, Fr.
36/C5 Aubonne, Swi.
31/E5 Auboué, Fr.
32/E4 Aubrac (mts.), Fr.
31/D3 Aubrives, Fr.
72/B8 Auburn, Austl.
89/J5 Auburn, Al,US
97/G3 Auburn, Al,US
92/B3 Auburn, Ca,US
94/C3 Auburn, In,US
89/M3 Auburn, Me,US
95/G2 Auburn, Me,US
93/J2 Auburn, Ne,US
87/J4 Auburn, NY,US
94/E3 Auburn, NY,US
88/B2 Auburn, Wa,US
90/C4 Auburn, Wa,US
99/C3 Auburn, Wa,US
99/F6 Auburn Hills, Mi,US
32/E4 Aubusson, Fr.
109/C4 Aucá Mahuida (peak), Arg.
32/D5 Auch, Fr.
35/F1 Auch, Fr.
30/B3 Auchel, Fr.
22/E2 Auchencairn, Sc,UK
30/B3 Auchy-lès-Hesdin, Fr.
17/S8 Auckland (isls.), NZ
68/G8 Auckland, N.Z.
71/R10 Auckland, N.Z.
32/E5 Aude (riv.), Fr.
30/D2 Auderghem, Belg.
36/C3 Audeux (riv.), Fr.
32/A3 Audierne (bay), Fr.
36/C3 Audincourt, Fr.
23/F6 Audlem, Eng,UK
23/F5 Audley, Eng,UK
77/P6 Audo (range), Eth.
30/B2 Audruicq, Fr.
31/E5 Audun-le-Roman, Fr.
31/E5 Audun-le-Tiche, Fr.
26/G3 Aue, Ger.
29/E2 Aue (riv.), Ger.
29/F3 Aue (riv.), Ger.
33/K1 Aue, Ger.
33/K1 Auerbach, Ger.
26/F4 Auerbach in der Oberpfalz, Ger.
33/J2 Auerbach in der Oberpfalz, Ger.
37/G2 Auerberg (mtn.), Ger.
37/H5 Auer (Ora), It.
30/A4 Auffay, Fr.
71/H5 Augathella, Austl.
72/B4 Augathella, Austl.
22/A3 Augher, NI,UK
22/B3 Aughnacloy, NI,UK
22/B6 Aughrim, Ire.
80/C3 Augrabies Falls Nat'l Park, SAfr.
80/C3 Augrabiesvalle (falls), SAfr.
18/E4 Augsburg, Ger.
26/F4 Augsburg, Ger.
33/J2 Augsburg, Ger.
37/G1 Augsburg, Ger.
80/A2 Augub (peak), Namb.
103/H4 Augusta (pt.), Col.
38/D4 Augusta, It.
38/D4 Augusta (gulf), It.
89/K5 Augusta, Ga,US
97/H3 Augusta, Ga,US
87/K4 Augusta (cap.), Me,US
89/N3 Augusta (cap.), Me,US
95/G2 Augusta, Me,US
98/F4 Augusta, NJ,US
29/F5 Augustdorf, Ger.
26/E1 Augustenborg, Den.
27/M2 Augustów, Pol.
42/D5 Augustów, Pol.
44/B1 Augustów, Pol.
70/C3 Augustus (isl.), Austl.
65/B3 Auk Bok (isl.), Burma
68/F5 Auki, Sol.
70/C4 Auld (lake), Austl.
35/M9 Aulencia (riv.), Sp.
37/F2 Aulendorf, Ger.
19/T10 Aulnay-sous-Bois, Fr.
32/B2 Aulne (riv.), Fr.
30/C3 Aulnoye-Aymeries, Fr.
25/H6 Ault, Fr.
30/A3 Ault, Fr.
37/F4 Ault, Piz (peak), Swi.
30/A4 Aumale, Fr.
31/E5 Aumetz, Fr.
29/H1 Aumühle, Ger.
76/F5 Auna, Nga.
32/C2 Aunay-sur-Odon, Fr.
30/B5 Aunette (riv.), Fr.
30/B5 Auneuil, Fr.
80/B2 Auob (dry riv.), Namb.
80/C2 Auobrivier (dry riv.), SAfr.
68/G4 Aur (atoll), Mrsh.
53/L5 Aurangābād, India
62/C4 Aurangābād, India
62/D3 Aurangābād, India
32/B3 Auray, Fr.
32/D5 Aureilhan, Fr.
35/F1 Aureilhan, Fr.
26/D2 Aurich, Ger.
29/E2 Aurich, Ger.
108/B2 Auriflama, Braz.
32/E4 Aurillac, Fr.
88/F4 Aurora, Co,US
93/F3 Aurora, Co,US
89/J3 Aurora, Il,US
93/K2 Aurora, Il,US
94/B3 Aurora, Il,US
99/P16 Aurora, Il,US
93/J3 Aurora, Mo,US
96/E2 Aurora, Mo,US
91/J5 Aurora, Ne,US
93/H2 Aurora, Ne,US
85/J3 Aurora Lodge, Ak,US
72/A1 Aurukun Abor. Land, Austl.
80/B2 Aus, Namb.
94/C2 Au Sable (riv.), Mi,US
27/K3 Auschwitz (Oświęcim), Pol.
37/F3 Ausserrhoden (demi-canton), Swi.
32/E5 Aussillon, Fr.
20/C4 Aust-Agder (co.), Nor.
70/B5 Austin (lake), Austl.
86/G2 Austin (isl.), NW,Can
86/G4 Austin, Mn,US
89/H3 Austin, Mn,US
91/K5 Austin, Mn,US
93/J2 Austin, Mn,US
92/C3 Austin, Nv,US
101/F2 Austin, Tx,US
89/G5 Austin (cap.), Tx,US
93/H5 Austin, Tx,US
96/D4 Austin, Tx,US
17/R7 Australia
68/D7 Australia
70/* Australia
71/H7 Australian Alps (mts.), Austl.
73/C3 Australian Alps (mts.), Austl.
71/H7 Australian Cap. Terr., Austl.
73/D3 Australian Cap. Terr., Austl.
18/E4 Austria
26/F5 Austria
27/H5 Austria
33/L3 Austria
37/G3 Austria
40/A2 Austria
46/B5 Austria
20/P7 Austurhorn (pt.), Ice.
35/F1 Auterive, Fr.
26/B3 Authie (riv.), Fr.
30/B3 Authie (riv.), Fr.
100/D5 Autlán, Mex.
30/B5 Automne (riv.), Fr.
30/C3 Autreppe, Belg.
32/F3 Autun, Fr.
32/E4 Auvergne (reg.), Fr.
19/S9 Auvers-sur-Oise, Fr.
30/B5 Auvers-sur-Oise, Fr.
32/D4 Auvézère (riv.), Fr.
26/B5 Auxerre, Fr.
32/E3 Auxerre, Fr.
30/B3 Auxi-le-Château, Fr.
32/F3 Auxonne, Fr.
36/B3 Auxonne, Fr.
94/D2 Aux Sables (riv.), On,Can
87/K2 Auyuittuq Nat'l Park, NW,Can
106/D6 Auzangate (peak), Peru
51/G3 Āvaj, Iran
52/E1 Āvaj, Iran
26/B5 Avallon, Fr.
32/E3 Avallon, Fr.
87/L4 Avalon (pen.), Nf,Can
95/K2 Avalon (pen.), Nf,Can
64/F3 Avanāshi, India
36/B3 Avanne-Aveney, Fr.
107/J8 Avaré, Braz.
108/B2 Avaré, Braz.
109/G1 Avaré, Braz.
69/K7 Avarua, N.Z.
51/M7 Avcilar, Turk.
25/E4 Avebury, Eng,UK
25/E4 Avebury Stone Circle (ruins), UK
34/A2 Aveiro, Port.
34/A2 Aveiro (dist.), Port.
19/P7 Aveley, Eng,UK
30/C2 Avelgem, Belg.
38/D2 Avellino, It.
40/B5 Avellino, It.
30/A4 Avelon (riv.), Fr.
92/B3 Avenal, Ca,US
36/D4 Avenches, Swi.
30/A6 Aver (riv.), Fr.
38/D2 Aversa, It.
40/B5 Aversa, It.
104/E4 Aves (isl.), Ven.
30/B3 Avesnes-le-Comte, Fr.
30/C3 Avesnes-sur-Helpe, Fr.
20/F3 Avesta, Swe.
42/C3 Avesta, Swe.
32/D4 Aveyron (riv.), Fr.
38/C1 Avezzano, It.
18/D4 Avignon, Fr.
32/F5 Avignon, Fr.
49/F7 Aviḥayil, Isr.
34/C2 Ávila de los Caballeros, Sp.
34/C1 Avilés, Sp.
30/B3 Avion, Fr.
32/E1 Avion, Fr.
34/B3 Avis, Port.
37/H5 Avisio (riv.), It.
34/B3 Aviz, Port.
30/D6 Avize, Fr.
73/B3 Avoca, Austl.
73/C4 Avoca, Austl.
22/B6 Avoca, Ire.
22/B6 Avoca (riv.), Ire.
38/D4 Avola, It.
26/B4 Avon, Fr.
32/E2 Avon, Fr.
24/C6 Avon (riv.), Eng,UK
24/D4 Avon (co.), Eng,UK
24/D4 Avon (riv.), Eng,UK
25/E2 Avon (riv.), Eng,UK
25/E5 Avon (riv.), Eng,UK
22/B6 Avonbeg (riv.), Ire.
73/D2 Avondale, Austl.
70/F4 Avon Downs, Austl.
91/G3 Avonlea, Sk,Can
22/B6 Avonmore (riv.), Ire.
24/D4 Avonmouth, Eng,UK
32/C2 Avranches, Fr.
26/B4 Avre (riv.), Fr.
30/B4 Avre (riv.), Fr.
32/C2 Avre (riv.), Fr.
32/D2 Avre (riv.), Fr.
32/E2 Avre (riv.), Fr.
32/C3 Avrillé, Fr.
51/G2 Avrora, Azer.
56/D3 Awaji (isl.), Japan
57/L10 Awaji, Japan
49/E3 A'waj, Nahr al (riv.), Syria
31/E2 Awans, Belg.
77/N6 Āwasa, Eth.
77/P6 Āwash, Eth.
77/P5 Āwash Wenz (riv.), Eth.
80/A2 Awasibberge (peak), Namb.
79/E5 Awaso, Gha.
76/H2 Awbārī, Libya
77/K2 Awjilah, Libya
49/B4 Awsīm, Egypt
37/H3 Axams, Aus.
20/P6 Axarfjördhur (bay), Ice.
24/D4 Axbridge, Eng,UK
24/D4 Axe (riv.), Eng,UK
24/D5 Axe (riv.), Eng,UK
28/A6 Axel, Neth.
30/C1 Axel, Neth.
84/H2 Axel Heiberg (isl.), Can.
87/S7 Axel Heiberg (isl.), NW,Can
79/E5 Axim, Gha.
39/H2 Axios (riv.), Gre.
99/D2 Axis (dam), Wa,US
32/D5 Ax-les-Thermes, Fr.
35/F1 Ax-les-Thermes, Fr.
24/D5 Axminster, Eng,UK
101/L8 Axochiapan, Mex.
30/D5 Ay, Fr.
43/N5 Ay (riv.), Rus.
56/D3 Ayabe, Japan
57/L9 Ayabe, Japan
109/E4 Ayacucho, Arg.
106/D6 Ayacucho, Peru
46/J5 Ayaguz, Kaz.
57/M10 Ayama, Japan
78/E5 Ayamé I, Barrage d' (dam), IvC.
78/E5 Ayamé II, Barrage d' (dam), IvC.
34/B4 Ayamonte, Sp.
44/E4 Ayancık, Turk.
50/C1 Ayancık, Turk.
103/H4 Ayapel, Col.
103/H5 Ayapel, Serranía (range), Col.
50/C1 Ayaş, Turk.
57/H7 Ayase, Japan
106/D6 Ayaviri, Peru
46/G6 Aybak, Afg.
53/J1 Aybak, Afg.
49/G7 'Aybāl, Jabal (Har Eval) (mtn.), WBnk.
44/F4 Aybastı, Turk.
50/D1 Aybastı, Turk.
50/A2 Aydın, Turk.
50/B2 Aydın (prov.), Turk.
49/C1 Aydıncık, Turk.
50/C1 Aydıncık, Turk.
50/C2 Aydıncık, Turk.
52/B1 Aydıncık, Turk.
51/N7 Aydinli, Turk.
50/E1 Aydıntepe, Turk.
36/D5 Ayer, Swi.
68/C7 Ayers Rock (Uluru) (peak), Austl.
70/E5 Ayers Rock (Uluru) (peak), Austl.
60/B5 Ayeyarwady (Irrawaddy) (div.), Burma
39/H3 Ayiá, Gre.
44/B5 Ayiá, Gre.
39/K3 Ayía Paraskeví, Gre.
50/A2 Ayía Paraskeví, Gre.
39/K3 Ayiásos, Gre.
39/J2 Áyios Athanásios, Gre.
41/G5 Áyios Athanásios, Gre.
39/J3 Áyios Evstrátios (isl.), Gre.
39/J5 Áyios Ioánnis, Ákra (cape), Gre.
39/K4 Áyios Kírikos, Gre.
39/H3 Áyios Konstandínos, Gre.
39/F3 Áyios Matthaíos, Gre.
39/J5 Áyios Nikólaos, Gre.
25/F3 Aylesbury, Eng,UK
25/G4 Aylesford, Eng,UK
25/H4 Aylesham, Eng,UK
30/A1 Aylesham, Eng,UK
34/D2 Ayllón, Sp.
86/F2 Aylmer (lake), NW,Can
25/H1 Aylsham, Eng,UK
50/D2 'Ayn al 'Arab, Syria
77/K2 'Ayn Ath Tha'lab, Libya
52/D1 'Ayn, Ra's al, Syria
52/C3 'Aynūnah, SAr.
77/K3 'Ayn Zuwayyah (well), Libya
47/S3 Ayon (isl.), Rus.
35/E3 Ayora, Sp.
101/F5 Ayotzintepec, Mex.
102/B2 Ayotzintepec, Mex.
76/D3 'Ayoûn 'Abd el Mâlek (well), Mrta.
76/D4 'Ayoûn el 'Atroûs, Mrta.
71/H3 Ayr, Austl.
72/B2 Ayr, Austl.
18/C3 Ayr, Sc,UK
21/C3 Ayr, Sc,UK
50/C2 Ayrancı, Turk.
22/D3 Ayre, Point of (pt.), Eng,UK
23/H3 Ayton, Eng,UK
41/H4 Aytos, Bul.
44/C4 Aytos, Bul.
32/C3 Aytré, Fr.
100/D4 Ayutla, Mex.
102/B2 Ayutla, Mex.
65/C3 Ayutthaya (ruins), Thai.
39/K3 Ayvacık, Turk.
50/A2 Ayvacık, Turk.
44/C5 Ayvalık, Turk.
50/A2 Ayvalık, Turk.
31/E3 Aywaille, Belg.
84/B1 Azad Kashmir (terr.), Pak.
35/F3 Azahar (coast), Sp.
57/M9 Azaj, Japan
90/C5 Azalea, Or,US
92/B2 Azalea, Or,US
99/E7 Azalia, Mi,US
62/D2 Azamgarh, India
106/D6 Azángaro, Peru
76/G2 Azao (peak), Alg.
76/E4 Azaouâd (des.), Mali
79/E2 Azaouad (reg.), Mali
79/G2 Azaouak, Vallée de l' (wadi), Mali, Niger
51/F2 Āzarān, Iran
52/E1 Āzarān, Iran
51/F2 Āzarbāyjān-e Bākhtarī (gov.), Iran
51/F2 Āzarbāyjān-e Khāvarī (gov.), Iran
52/E1 Āzar Shahr, Iran
49/E1 A'zāz, Syria
50/D2 A'zāz, Syria
19/H4 Azerbaijan
45/H4 Azerbaijan
46/E5 Azerbaijan
51/F1 Azerbaijan
53/K1 Azerbaijan
77/N5 Āzezo, Eth.
50/D2 'Azīz, Jabal 'Abd al (mts.), Syria
34/B4 Aznalcóllar, Sp.
106/C4 Azogues, Ecu.
35/R12 Azores (aut. reg.), Port.
35/R12 Azores (isls.), Port.
44/F3 Azov, Rus.
46/D5 Azov (sea), Ukr.,Rus.
44/E3 Azov (sea), Rus., Ukr.
19/G4 Azov (sea), Rus,UKr.
102/B2 Azoyú, Mex.
32/B5 Azpeitia, Sp.
34/D1 Azpeitia, Sp.
88/E4 Aztec, NM,US
92/F3 Aztec, NM,US
96/B2 Aztec, NM,US
92/E3 Aztec Ruins Nat'l Mon., NM,US
104/D3 Azua, DRep.
34/C3 Azuaga, Sp.
35/E2 Azuara, Sp.
57/M9 Azuchi, Japan
103/F5 Azuero (pen.), Pan.
106/B2 Azuero (pen.), Pan.
109/E4 Azul, Arg.
102/D2 Azul (riv.), Belz.
103/E4 Azul (mtn.), CR
102/D2 Azul (riv.), Guat., Mex.
101/H5 Azul (riv.), NAm.
57/G2 Azuma-san (mtn.), Japan
57/F2 Azumaya-san (mtn.), Japan
33/G5 Azur, Côte d' (coast), Fr.

35/J1 Azur, Côte d' (coast), Fr.
75/V17 Azzaba, Alg.
49/G7 Az Zabābidah, WBnk.
49/E3 Az Zabadānī, Syria
50/D3 Az Zabadānī, Syria
49/D4 Az Zāhirīyah, WBnk.
77/R2 Az Zahrān (Dhahran), SAr.
33/K4 Azzano Decimo, It.
49/B4 Az Zaqāzīq, Egypt
50/B4 Az Zaqāzīq, Egypt
52/B2 Az Zaqāzīq, Egypt
49/E3 Az Zarqā', Jor.
50/D3 Az Zarqā', Jor.
52/C2 Az Zarqā', Jor.
77/N1 Az Zarqā', Jor.
76/H1 Az Zāwiyah, Libya
52/B5 Az Zaydāb, Sudan
52/D5 Az Zaydīyah, Yem.
77/P4 Az Zaydīyah, Yem.
51/F4 Az Zubayr, Iraq
49/D3 'Azzūn, WBnk.
49/G7 'Azzūn, WBnk.

B

54/F5 Ba (riv.), China
61/E2 Ba (riv.), China
69/Y18 Ba, Fiji
63/J5 Ba (riv.), Viet.
65/E3 Ba (riv.), Viet.
69/U11 Baaba (isl.), NCal.
49/G8 Ba'al Hazor (mtn.), WBnk.
49/G8 Ba'al Hazor (Tall 'Asūr) (mtn.), WBnk.
33/H3 Baar, Swi.
37/E3 Baar, Swi.
74/G4 Baarawe, Som.
28/B6 Baarle-Hertog, Belg.
28/B6 Baarle-Nassau, Neth.
28/C4 Baarn, Neth.
54/D2 Baatsagaan, Mong.
53/J2 Baba (mts.), Afg.
39/H1 Baba (peak), Bul.
41/F4 Baba (peak), Bul.
44/B4 Baba (peak), Bul.
39/K3 Baba (pt.), Turk.
41/K5 Baba (pt.), Turk.
50/B1 Baba (pt.), Turk.
44/D4 Baba Burnu (pt.), Turk.
41/J3 Babadag, Rom.
44/D3 Babadag, Rom.
41/H5 Babaeski, Turk.
44/C4 Babaeski, Turk.
50/A1 Babaeski, Turk.
106/C4 Babahoyo, Ecu.
50/A2 Babakale, Turk.
67/G5 Babar (isl.), Indo.
68/B5 Babar (isls.), Indo.
82/G1 Babati, Tanz.
24/C5 Babbacombe (bay), Eng,UK
91/L4 Babbitt, Mn,US
94/B2 Babbitt, Mn,US
92/C3 Babbitt, Nv,US
50/C3 B'abdā, Leb.
52/C2 B'abdā, Leb.
52/D6 Bab el Mandeb (str.), Afr., Asia
68/C4 Babelthuap (isl.), Palau
37/G1 Babenhausen, Ger.
44/A2 Babia Gora (peak), Pol.
60/D4 Babian (riv.), China
63/H3 Babian (riv.), China
51/F3 Bābil (gov.), Iraq
72/B2 Babinda, Austl.
90/B2 Babine (lake), BC,Can
86/D3 Babine (riv.), BC,Can
46/F6 Bābol, Iran
48/E6 Bābol, Iran
51/H2 Bābol, Iran
52/F1 Bābol, Iran
51/H2 Bābol Sar, Iran
43/X9 Babushkin, Rus.
48/M8 Babuyan (isls.), Phil.
61/J5 Babuyan (isls.), Phil.
68/B3 Babuyan (isls.), Phil.
51/F3 Babylon (ruins), Iraq
52/D2 Babylon (ruins), Iraq
98/G5 Babylon, NY,US
107/K4 Bacabal, Braz.
100/C2 Bacadéhuachi, Mex.
107/H4 Bacajá (riv.), Braz.
101/H5 Bacalar, Mex.
102/D2 Bacalar, Mex.
102/D2 Bacalar (lag.), Mex.
67/G4 Bacan (isl.), Indo.
61/J5 Bacarra, Phil.
18/F4 Bacău, Rom.
41/H2 Bacău, Rom.
41/H2 Bacău (co.), Rom.
44/C3 Bacău, Rom.
46/C5 Bacău, Rom.
63/J3 Bac Can, Viet.
65/D1 Bac Can, Viet.
36/C1 Baccarat, Fr.
65/D1 Bac Giang, Viet.
31/G3 Bacharach, Ger.
100/D2 Bachíniva, Mex.
65/C5 Bachok, Malay.
46/H6 Bachu, China
84/G3 Back (riv.), Can.
86/G2 Back (riv.), NW,Can
94/E2 Back (lake), On,Can
98/K7 Back (riv.), Md,US
40/D3 Bačka (reg.), Yugo.
40/D3 Bačka Palanka, Yugo.
40/D3 Bačka Topola, Yugo.
20/E4 Bäckefors, Swe.
26/E4 Backnang, Ger.
33/H2 Backnang, Ger.
24/D4 Backwell, Eng,UK
63/J6 Bac Lieu, Viet.
65/D4 Bac Lieu, Viet.
66/C2 Bac Lieu, Viet.
60/E4 Bac Ninh, Viet.
63/J3 Bac Ninh, Viet.
65/D1 Bac Ninh, Viet.
100/C2 Bacoachi, Mex.
92/E5 Bacoachi, Mex
67/F1 Bacolod, Phil.
68/B3 Bacolod, Phil.
60/E4 Bac Quang, Viet.
63/H3 Bac Quang, Viet.
65/D1 Bac Quang, Viet.
40/D2 Bácsalmás, Hun.
40/D2 Bács-Kiskun (co.), Hun.
25/H1 Bacton, Eng,UK
100/C3 Bácum, Mex.
23/F4 Bacup, Eng,UK
91/H4 Bad (riv.), SD,US
62/C5 Badagara, India
64/E3 Badagara, India
54/E3 Badain Jarah (des.), China
47/L5 Badain Jaran (des.), China
18/C5 Badajoz, Sp.
34/B3 Badajoz, Sp.
35/G2 Badalona, Sp.
35/L7 Badalona, Sp.
77/P1 Badanah, SAr.
89/K3 Bad Axe, Mi,US
94/D3 Bad Axe, Mi,US
36/D2 Bad Bellingen, Ger.
29/E3 Badbergen, Ger.
31/H5 Bad Bergzabern, Ger.
29/F6 Bad Berleburg, Ger.
31/G2 Bad Breisig, Ger.
37/F1 Bad Buchau, Ger.
31/H3 Bad Camberg, Ger.
29/H4 Baddeckenstedt, Ger.
26/F1 Bad Doberan, Ger.
64/C2 Baddomalhi, Pak.
29/G5 Bad Driburg, Ger.
31/H5 Bad Dürkheim, Ger.
37/E1 Bad Dürrheim, Ger.
67/J5 Bade, Indo.
31/G3 Bad Ems, Ger.
27/J4 Baden, Aus.
33/M2 Baden, Aus.
40/C1 Baden, Aus.
37/E3 Baden, Swi.
26/E4 Baden-Baden, Ger.
33/H2 Baden-Baden, Ger.
36/D2 Badenweiler, Ger.
26/E4 Baden-Württemberg (state), Ger.
31/H6 Baden-Württemberg (state), Ger.
33/H2 Baden-Württemberg (state), Ger.
37/E1 Baden-Württemberg (state), Ger.
29/F4 Bad Essen, Ger.
27/H2 Bad Freienwalde, Ger.
29/H5 Bad Gandersheim, Ger.
33/K3 Badgastein, Aus.
40/A2 Badgastein, Aus.
27/G5 Bad Goisern, Aus.
33/K3 Bad Goisern, Aus.
40/A2 Bad Goisern, Aus.
29/H5 Bad Grund, Ger.
26/F3 Bad Harzburg, Ger.
29/H5 Bad Harzburg, Ger.
37/H2 Bad Heilbrunn, Ger.
26/E3 Bad Hersfeld, Ger.
33/H1 Bad Hersfeld, Ger.
33/K3 Bad Hofgastein, Aus.
40/A2 Bad Hofgastein, Aus.
26/E3 Bad Homburg vor der Höhe, Ger.
33/H1 Bad Homburg vor der Höhe, Ger.
31/G2 Bad Honnef, Ger.
31/G2 Bad Hönningen, Ger.
37/F5 Badile, Pizzo (peak), It.
53/J4 Badīn, Pak.
62/A3 Badīn, Pak.
27/G5 Bad Ischl, Aus.
33/K3 Bad Ischl, Aus.
40/A2 Bad Ischl, Aus.
29/G5 Bad Karlshafen, Ger.
26/F3 Bad Kissingen, Ger.
37/H2 Bad Kohlgrub, Ger.
26/D4 Bad Kreuznach, Ger.
31/G4 Bad Kreuznach, Ger.
33/G2 Bad Kreuznach, Ger.
26/D5 Bad Krozingen, Ger.
33/G3 Bad Krozingen, Ger.
36/D2 Bad Krozingen, Ger.
91/H4 Badlands (uplands), ND,US
91/H5 Badlands (hills), SD,US
91/H5 Badlands Nat'l Park, SD,US
86/F4 Badlands Nat'l Park, SD,US
88/F2 Badlands Nat'l Park, SD,US
93/G2 Badlands Nat'l Park, SD,US
29/H6 Bad Langensalza, Ger.
29/H5 Bad Lauterberg, Ger.
29/F3 Bad Lippspringe, Ger.
31/G2 Bad Marienberg, Ger.
26/E4 Bad Mergentheim, Ger.
33/H2 Bad Mergentheim, Ger.
29/G4 Bad Munder am Deister, Ger.
31/F2 Bad Münstereifel, Ger.
26/E3 Bad Nauheim, Ger.
33/H1 Bad Nauheim, Ger.
29/G4 Bad Nenndorf, Ger.
26/D3 Bad Neuenahr-Ahrweiler, Ger.
31/G2 Bad Neuenahr-Ahrweiler, Ger.
33/G1 Bad Neuenahr-Ahrweiler, Ger.
26/F3 Bad Neustadt an der Saale, Ger.
33/J1 Bad Neustadt an der Saale, Ger.
26/E2 Bad Oeynhausen, Ger.
29/F4 Bad Oeynhausen, Ger.
26/F2 Bad Oldesloe, Ger.
54/G5 Badong, China
59/B5 Badong, China
61/F2 Badong, China
36/C1 Badonviller, Fr.
40/D3 Badovinci, Yugo.
37/E1 Bad Peterstal-Griesbach, Ger.
29/G5 Bad Pyrmont, Ger.
37/F3 Bad Ragaz, Swi.
51/F3 Badrah, Iraq
52/E2 Badrah, Iraq
53/J3 Bādrāh, Pak.
26/G5 Bad Reichenhall, Ger.
33/K3 Bad Reichenhall, Ger.
40/A2 Bad Reichenhall, Ger.
52/C4 Badr Hunayn, SAr.
77/N3 Badr Hunayn, SAr.
29/H5 Bad Sachsa, Ger.
26/F2 Bad Salzdetfurth, Ger.
29/H4 Bad Salzdetfurth, Ger.
26/E2 Bad Salzuflen, Ger.
29/F4 Bad Salzuflen, Ger.
26/F3 Bad Salzungen, Ger.
33/L3 Bad Sankt-Leonhard im Lavanttal, Aus.
40/B2 Bad Sankt-Leonhard im Lavanttal, Aus.
29/F5 Bad Sassendorf, Ger.
31/H3 Bad Schwalbach, Ger.
26/F2 Bad Schwartau, Ger.
26/F2 Bad Segeberg, Ger.
29/G6 Bad Sooden-Allendorf, Ger.
26/F5 Bad Tölz, Ger.
33/J3 Bad Tölz, Ger.
37/H2 Bad Tölz, Ger.
62/D6 Badulla, SrL.
27/J5 Bad Vöslau, Aus.
33/M3 Bad Vöslau, Aus.
40/C2 Bad Vöslau, Aus.
37/F2 Bad Waldsee, Ger.
29/G6 Bad Wildungen, Ger.
26/F4 Bad Wörishofen, Ger.
37/G1 Bad Wörishofen, Ger.
37/F2 Bad Wurzach, Ger.
26/E2 Bad Zwischenahn, Ger.
29/E2 Bad Zwischenahn, Ger.
34/C4 Baena, Sp.
36/C2 Baerenkopf (mtn.), Fr.
31/F2 Baesweiler, Ger.
34/D4 Baeza, Sp.
79/H5 Bafang, Camr.
76/C5 Bafatá, GBis.
84/K2 Baffin (isl.), Can.
34/L2 Baffin (bay), Can.
87/H1 Baffin (isl.), NW,Can
87/T7 Baffin (bay), NW,Can
87/K1 Baffin (bay), Can.,Den.
101/F3 Baffin (bay), Tx,US
76/H7 Bafia, Camr.
78/D4 Bafing (riv.), Gui., IvC.
76/C5 Bafing (riv.), Gui., Mali
78/C3 Bafing (riv.), Gui., Mali
76/C5 Bafoulabé, Mali
78/C3 Bafoulabé, Mali
76/H6 Bafoussam, Camr.
79/H5 Bafoussam, Camr.
51/H4 Bāfq, Iran
53/G2 Bāfq, Iran
44/E4 Bafra, Turk.
46/D5 Bafra, Turk.
50/C1 Bafra, Turk.
50/D1 Bafra (cape), Turk.
44/E4 Bafra Burnu (cape), Turk.
78/B2 Bafrechié (well), Mrta.
51/J4 Bāft, Iran
53/G3 Bāft, Iran
77/L7 Bafwasende, Zaire
59/B3 Bag (salt lake), China
76/H5 Baga, Nga.
103/E4 Bagaces, CR
67/G2 Baganga, Phil.
79/G3 Bagaroua, Niger
47/M4 Bagdarin, Rus.
109/F3 Bagé, Braz.
26/F1 Bagenkop, Den.
24/B4 Baggy (pt.), UK
64/B2 Bāgh, Pak.
51/F3 Baghdad (cap.), Iraq
51/F3 Baghdad (gov.), Iraq
52/D2 Baghdād (Baghdad) (cap.), Iraq
52/D2 Baghdad (Baghdād) (cap.), Iraq
38/C3 Bagheria, It.
53/G2 Bāghīn, Iran
46/G6 Baghlān, Afg.
53/J1 Baghlān, Afg.
51/J5 Bāghū, Iran
50/E2 Bağırpaşa (peak), Turk.
24/C3 Baglan, Wal,UK
91/K4 Bagley, Mn,US
32/D5 Bagnères-de-Bigorre, Fr.
35/F1 Bagnères-de-Bigorre, Fr.
32/D5 Bagnères-de-Luchon, Fr.
35/F1 Bagnères-de-Luchon, Fr.
19/S10 Bagneux, Fr.
19/T10 Bagnolet, Fr.
38/D2 Bagnoli Irpino, It.
32/F4 Bagnols-sur-Cèze, Fr.
76/D6 Bagoe (riv.), IvC., Mali
78/D3 Bagoe (riv.), IvC., Mali
60/B5 Bago (Pegu) (div.), Burma
65/B2 Bago (Pegu) (div.), Burma
27/L1 Bagrationovsk, Rus.
61/J5 Baguio, Phil.
68/B3 Baguio, Phil.
76/J5 Baguirmi (reg.), Chad
74/C3 Bagzane (peak), Niger
76/G4 Bagzane (peak), Niger
79/H2 Bagzane (peak), Niger
103/H1 Bahamas
104/B2 Bahamas
84/K7 Bahamas
89/L6 Bahamas
62/E3 Baharampur, India
53/K3 Bahāwalpur, Pak.
62/B2 Bahāwalpur, Pak.
50/D2 Bahçe, Turk.
51/E2 Bahçesaray, Turk.
82/G2 Bahi, Tanz.
108/E1 Bahia (state), Braz.
109/D4 Bahía Blanca, Arg.
92/D5 Bahía de los Angeles, Mex
62/D3 Bahía Honda, Cuba
102/E2 Bahía, Islas de la (isls.), Hon.
100/C2 Bahía Kino, Mex.
100/B3 Bahía Tortugas, Mex.
77/N5 Bahir Dar, Eth.
53/G4 Bahlah, Oman
62/D2 Bahraich, India
48/E7 Bahrain
52/F3 Bahrain
77/R2 Bahrain
52/F3 Bahrain (gulf), Bahr., SAr.
74/E3 Bahr al Arab (riv.), Sudan
51/E3 Bahr al Milh (lake), Iraq
52/D2 Bahr al Milh (lake), Iraq
74/D4 Bahr Aouk (riv.), CAfr., Chad
54/H3 Bai (riv.), China
59/C2 Bai (riv.), China
59/C4 Bai (riv.), China
40/F3 Baia de Aramă, Rom.
27/M5 Baia Mare, Rom.
41/F2 Baia Mare, Rom.
44/B3 Baia Mare, Rom.
41/F2 Baia Sprie, Rom.
76/J6 Baïbokoum, Chad
60/D3 Baicao (mts.), China
47/N5 Baicheng, China
55/J2 Baicheng, China
41/G3 Băicoi, Rom.
77/P7 Baidoa, Som.
59/D5 Baidong (lake), China
87/K4 Baie-Comeau, Qu,Can
95/G1 Baie-Comeau, Qu,Can
87/J3 Baie-du-Poste, Qu,Can
89/M1 Baie-du-Poste, Qu,Can
37/F2 Baienfurt, Ger.
37/E1 Baiersbronn, Ger.
87/J4 Baie-Saint-Paul, Qu,Can
89/M2 Baie-Saint-Paul, Qu,Can
95/G2 Baie-Saint-Paul, Qu,Can
87/L4 Baie Verte, Nf,Can
95/K1 Baie Verte, Nf,Can
57/G2 Baigou (riv.), China
59/C3 Baihua Shan (mtn.), China
59/G7 Baihua Shan (mtn.), China
51/E3 Ba'īji, Iraq
52/D2 Ba'īji, Iraq
23/G4 Baildon, Eng,UK
40/F3 Băile Herculane, Rom.
34/D3 Bailén, Sp.
41/G3 Băile Olănești, Rom.
41/F3 Băilești, Rom.
44/B3 Băilești, Rom.
41/G2 Băile Tușnad, Rom.
22/B4 Bailieborough, Ire.
30/B2 Bailleul, Fr.
54/E5 Bailong (riv.), China
59/C4 Bailu (riv.), China
54/E5 Baima, China
23/H5 Bain (riv.), Eng,UK
62/E2 Bainang, China
97/G4 Bainbridge, Ga,US
99/B2 Bainbridge (isl.), Wa,US
36/C2 Bains-les-Bains, Fr.
55/K2 Baiquan, China
85/F3 Baird (inlet), Ak,US
101/F1 Baird, Tx,US
93/H4 Baird, Tx,US
96/D3 Baird, Tx,US
71/H7 Bairnsdale, Austl.
73/C3 Bairnsdale, Austl.
49/E4 Bā'ir, Wādī (riv.), Jor.
32/D5 Baïse (riv.), Fr.
35/F1 Baïse (riv.), Fr.
61/F5 Baisha, China
63/J4 Baisha, China
65/E2 Baisha, China
61/H3 Baishi (peak), China
54/F5 Baishui, China
61/H3 Baisong (pass), China
62/D2 Baitadi, Nepal
63/J4 Bai Thuong, Viet.
65/D2 Bai Thuong, Viet.
35/P10 Baixa de Banheira, Port.
59/C3 Baixiang, China
107/K7 Baixo Guandu, Braz.
108/D1 Baixo Guandu, Braz.
54/E4 Baiyin, China
54/D5 Baiyü, China
59/B3 Baiyu (mts.), China
61/G3 Baiyun (mtn.), China
40/D2 Baja, Hun.
100/B2 Baja California (pen.), Mex.
84/F6 Baja California (pen.), Mex.
92/D5 Baja California (pen.), Mex
100/B2 Baja California Norte (state), Mex.
88/C5 Baja California Norte (state), Mex.
92/D5 Baja California Norte (state), Mex
100/B3 Baja California Sur (state), Mex.
38/A4 Bājah, Tun.
38/A4 Bājah (gov.), Tun.
75/W17 Bājah, Tun.
75/W17 Bājah (gov.), Tun.
76/G1 Bājah, Tun.
101/E3 Baján, Mex.
33/M3 Bajánsenye, Hun.
100/B2 Baja, Punta (pt.), Mex.
67/F5 Bajawa, Indo.
51/J3 Bajestān, Iran
53/G2 Bajestān, Iran
52/D5 Bājil, Yem.
40/D4 Bajina Bašta, Yugo.
73/E1 Bajmba (peak), Austl.
40/D3 Bajmok, Yugo.
103/F4 Bajo Boquete, Pan.
104/D3 Bajos de Haina, DRep.
40/E4 Bajram Curri, Alb.
67/E3 Bakayan (peak), Indo.
76/C5 Bakel, Sen.
78/B3 Bakel, Sen.
86/G2 Baker (lake), NW,Can
69/H4 Baker (isl.), PacUS
92/C4 Baker, Ca,US
91/G4 Baker, Mt,US
92/D3 Baker, Nv,US
86/E4 Baker, Or,US
88/C3 Baker, Or,US
90/D4 Baker, Or,US
88/B2 Baker (mt.), Wa,US
90/C3 Baker (peak), Wa,US
84/H3 Baker Lake, Can.
86/G2 Baker Lake, NW,Can
84/F6 Bakersfield, US
88/C4 Bakersfield, Ca,US
92/C4 Bakersfield, Ca,US
23/G5 Bakewell, Eng,UK
46/F6 Bakharden, Trkm.
53/G1 Bakharden, Trkm.
44/E3 Bakhchisaray, Ukr.
44/E2 Bakhmach, Ukr.
46/E6 Bākhtarān, Iran
48/D6 Bākhtarān, Iran
51/F3 Bākhtarān, Iran
51/F3 Bākhtarān (gov.), Iran
52/E2 Bākhtarān, Iran
51/H4 Bakhtegān (lake), Iran
52/F3 Bakhtegān (lake), Iran
51/G4 Bakhtīārī and Chahār Mahāll (gov.), Iran
20/P6 Bakkaflói (bay), Ice.
50/B2 Baklan, Turk.
76/H8 Bakoumba, Gabon
82/B1 Bakoumba, Gabon
78/C4 Bakoye (riv.), Gui., Mali
19/H4 Baku (cap.), Azer.
45/J4 Baku (cap.), Azer.
46/E5 Baku (cap.), Azer.
51/G1 Baku (cap.), Azer.
83/S Bakutis (coast), Ant.
106/E6 Bala (mts.), Bol.
44/E5 Balâ, Turk.
50/C2 Balâ, Turk.
22/E6 Bala, Wal,UK
67/E2 Balabac (str.), Malay., Phil.
68/A4 Balabac (str.), Malay., Phil.
67/E2 Balabac, Phil.
67/E2 Balabac (isl.), Phil.
49/E3 Ba'labakk, Leb.
50/D3 Ba'labakk, Leb.
69/U12 Balabio (isl.), NCal.
51/F3 Balad, Iraq
52/D2 Balad, Iraq
47/L4 Balagansk, Rus.
62/D3 Bālāghāt, India
38/A1 Balagne (range), Fr.
35/F2 Balaguer, Sp.
32/C5 Balaïtous (mtn.), Fr.
35/E1 Balaïtous (mtn.), Fr.
82/F3 Balaka, Malw.
51/G1 Balakhany, Azer.
43/J4 Balakhna, Rus.
19/H3 Balakovo, Rus.
45/H1 Balakovo, Rus.
46/E4 Balakovo, Rus.
49/E3 Bal'amā, Jor.
53/H1 Bālā Morghab, Afg.
41/G2 Bălan, Rom.
101/H5 Balancán, Mex.
102/D2 Balancán, Mex.
63/J4 Ba Lang An (cape), Viet.
65/E3 Ba Lang An (cape), Viet.
62/D3 Bālāngīr, India
61/J5 Balaoan, Phil.
43/X9 Balashikha, Rus.
19/H3 Balashov, Rus.
45/G2 Balashov, Rus.
46/E4 Balashov, Rus.
27/K4 Balassagyarmat, Hun.
40/D1 Balassagyarmat, Hun.
18/E4 Balaton (lake), Hun.
40/C2 Balaton (lake), Hun.
40/C2 Balatonfüred, Hun.
40/C2 Balatonszentgyörgy, Hun.
27/M1 Balbieriškis, Lith.
105/D3 Balbina (res.), Braz.
106/F4 Balbina (res.), Braz.
22/B4 Balbriggan, Ire.
109/E4 Balcarce, Arg.
22/E2 Balcary (pt.), Sc,UK
41/J4 Balchik, Bul.
44/D4 Balchik, Bul.
71/Q12 Balclutha, N.Z.
25/F4 Balcombe, Eng,UK
101/E2 Balcones (plat.), Tx,US
93/G5 Balcones Escarpment (upland), Tx,US
96/D4 Balcones Escarpment (plat.), Tx,US
70/B7 Bald (pt.), Austl.
97/H2 Bald (peak), Va,US
25/F3 Baldock, Eng,UK
72/D5 Bald Rock Nat'l Park, Austl.
73/E1 Bald Rock Nat'l Park, Austl.
98/C2 Baldwin Park, Ca,US
91/H3 Baldy (peak), Can
102/D2 Baldy Beacon (mtn.), Belz.
35/F3 Baleares (Balearic) (isls.), Sp.
18/D5 Balearic (isls.), Sp.
35/F3 Balearic (Baleares) (isls.), Sp.
87/K3 Baleine (riv.), Qu,Can
87/J3 Baleine, Grande Rivière de la (riv.), Qu,Can
87/J3 Baleine, Petite Rivière de la (riv.), Qu,Can
77/N6 Bale Mountains Nat'l Park, Eth.
28/C6 Balen, Belg.
31/E1 Balen, Belg.
37/F6 Balerna, Swi.
62/E3 Baleshwar, India
47/M4 Baley, Rus.
54/H1 Baley, Rus.
80/Q13 Balfour, SAfr.
52/E6 Balhāf, Yem.
53/K3 Bali, India
62/B2 Bali, India
48/L10 Bali (isl.), Indo.
66/D5 Bali (isl.), Indo.
66/D5 Bali (sea), Indo.
67/J4 Baliem (riv.), Indo.
44/C5 Balıkesir, Turk.
44/C5 Balıkesir (prov.), Turk.
50/A2 Balıkesir, Turk.
50/A2 Balıkesir (prov.), Turk.
67/E4 Balikpapan, Indo.
67/E2 Balimbing, Phil.
63/H6 Baling, Malay.
66/B2 Baling, Malay.
26/E4 Balingen, Ger.
33/H2 Balingen, Ger.
37/E1 Balingen, Ger.
28/C3 Balk, Neth.
39/H1 Balkan (mts.), Bul.
41/F4 Balkan (range), Bul.
44/C4 Balkan (mts.), Bul.
18/F4 Balkan (mts.), Eur.
45/K4 Balkhan Obl., Trkm.
46/F6 Balkhan Obl., Trkm.
51/H2 Balkhan Obl., Trkm.
46/H5 Balkhash, Kaz.
46/H5 Balkhash (lake), Kaz.
48/G5 Balkhash (lake), Kaz.
70/C6 Balladonia, Austl.
22/B4 Ballagan (pt.), Ire.
21/A4 Ballaghaderreen, Ire.
20/F1 Ballangen, Nor.
42/C1 Ballangen, Nor.
22/C1 Ballantrae, Sc,UK
71/G7 Ballarat, Austl.
73/B3 Ballarat, Austl.
70/C5 Ballard (lake), Austl.
62/C4 Ballarpur, India
22/D3 Ballaugh, IM,UK
36/C4 Ballens, Swi.
83/L Balleny (isls.), Ant.
72/D5 Ballina, Austl.
73/E1 Ballina, Austl.
21/A3 Ballina, Ire.
21/A4 Ballinasloe, Ire.
22/B2 Ballinderry (riv.), NI,UK
101/F2 Ballinger, Tx,US
93/H5 Ballinger, Tx,US
96/D4 Ballinger, Tx,US
21/A4 Ballinrobe, Ire.
22/B1 Ballintoy, NI,UK
22/B6 Ballitore, Ire.
22/B4 Ballivor, Ire.
36/C2 Ballon, Col du (pass), Fr.
33/G3 Ballon d'Alsace (mtn.), Fr.
36/C2 Ballon d'Alsace (mtn.), Fr.
36/C2 Ballon de Sevance (mtn.), Fr.
98/E5 Bally, Pa,US
22/B3 Ballybay, Ire.
22/C2 Ballycarry, NI,UK
21/H6 Ballycastle, Ire.
22/B1 Ballycastle, NI,UK
22/B2 Ballyclare, NI,UK
22/C2 Ballyeaston, NI,UK
22/A3 Ballygawley, NI,UK
22/C3 Ballygowan, NI,UK
22/A3 Ballyhaise, Ire.
22/C3 Ballyhalbert, NI,UK
21/A4 Ballyhaunis, Ire.
21/H7 Ballyheigue, Ire.
22/A4 Ballyjamesduff, Ire.
22/A1 Ballykelly, NI,UK
22/A1 Ballyliffin, Ire.
22/B2 Ballymena, NI,UK
22/B2 Ballymena (dist.), NI,UK
22/B1 Ballymoney, NI,UK
22/B1 Ballymoney (dist.), NI,UK
22/B5 Ballymore Eustace, Ire.
21/A3 Ballymote, Ire.
22/C3 Ballynahinch, NI,UK
22/C2 Ballynure, NI,UK
22/C3 Ballyquintin (pt.), NI,UK
21/A3 Ballyshannon, Ire.
22/C2 Ballywalter, NI,UK
109/B7 Balmaceda (peak), Chile
27/L5 Balmazújváros, Hun.
40/E2 Balmazújváros, Hun.
91/K3 Balmertown, On,Can
36/D5 Balmhorn (peak), Swi.
73/B3 Balmoral, Austl.
108/B3 Balneario Camboriú, Braz.
101/E2 Balneario de los Novillos Nat'l Park, Mex.
71/H5 Balonne (riv.), Austl.
72/C4 Balonne (riv.), Austl.
53/K3 Bālotra, India
62/B2 Bālotra, India
54/G4 Balougou, China
59/B3 Balougou, China
62/D2 Balrāmpur, India
71/G6 Balranald, Austl.
73/B2 Balranald, Austl.
41/G3 Balş, Rom.
44/C3 Balş, Rom.
25/E2 Balsall Common, Eng,UK
107/J5 Balsas, Braz.
107/J5 Balsas (riv.), Braz.
100/E5 Balsas (riv.), Mex.
102/B2 Balsas (riv.), Mex.
84/G8 Balsas (riv.), Mex.
101/M6 Balsas de Agua, Mex.
36/D3 Balsthal, Swi.
41/J2 Balta, Ukr.
34/C2 Baltanás, Sp.
18/E3 Baltic (sea), Eur.
20/F4 Baltic (sea), Eur.
27/J1 Baltic (sea), Eur.
42/C4 Baltic (sea), Eur.
46/B4 Baltic (sea), Eur.
27/K1 Baltic (spit), Pol., Rus.
43/U7 Baltic (plain), Rus.
49/B4 Baltīm, Egypt
50/B4 Baltīm, Egypt
89/L4 Baltimore, Md,US
94/E4 Baltimore, Md,US
97/J2 Baltimore, Md,US
98/K7 Baltimore, Md,US
98/K7 Baltimore Highlands-Lansdowne, Md,US
98/K7 Baltimore-Washington (int'l arpt.), Md,US
22/B6 Baltinglass, Ire.
27/K1 Baltiysk, Rus.
42/C5 Baltiysk, Rus.
22/B4 Baltray, Ire.
29/E1 Baltrum (isl.), Ger.
53/H3 Baluchistan (reg.), Iran, Pak.
62/E2 Bālurghāt, India
29/E6 Balve, Ger.
20/H4 Balvi, Lat.
42/E4 Balvi, Lat.
50/A2 Balya, Turk.
45/J3 Balykshi, Kaz.
46/F5 Balykshi, Kaz.
37/F3 Balzers, Lcht.
79/E3 Bam (prov.), Burk.
48/E7 Bam, Iran
51/J4 Bam, Iran
53/G3 Bam, Iran
76/H5 Bama, Nga.
91/K3 Bamaji (lake), On,Can
94/A1 Bamaji (lake), On,Can
76/D5 Bamako (cap.), Mali
78/D3 Bamako (cap.), Mali
78/D3 Bamako (reg.), Mali
61/E3 Bama Yaozu Zizhixian, China
63/J3 Bama Yaozu Zizhixian, China
78/E2 Bamba, Mali
79/E2 Bamba, Mali
106/C5 Bambamarca, Peru
103/E3 Bambana (riv.), Nic.
77/K6 Bambari, CAfr.
26/F4 Bamberg, Ger.
33/J2 Bamberg, Ger.
97/H3 Bamberg, SC,US
23/F4 Bamber Bridge, Eng,UK
20/D4 Bamble, Nor.
108/C2 Bambuí, Braz.
54/D5 Bamda, China
76/H6 Bamenda, Camr.
79/H5 Bamenda, Camr.
53/J2 Bāmīān, Afg.
61/G3 Bamian (mtn.), China
77/K6 Bamingui-Bangoran Nat'l Park, CAfr.
100/C3 Bamoa, Mex.
24/C5 Bampton, Eng,UK
53/H3 Bampūr (riv.), Iran
68/F5 Banaba (isl.), Kiri.
78/D3 Banamba, Mali
78/B4 Banana (isls.), SLeo.
82/B2 Banana, Zaire
107/H6 Bananal, Braz.
53/L3 Banās (riv.), India
62/B2 Banās (riv.), India
52/C4 Banās, Ra's (pt.), Egypt
40/E3 Banat (reg.), Yugo.
40/E3 Banatsko Novo Selo, Yugo.
63/J5 Ban Ay Rieng, Viet.
66/C1 Ban Ay Rieng, Viet.
44/D5 Banaz, Turk.
50/B2 Banaz, Turk.
60/D5 Ban Ban, Laos
63/H4 Ban Ban, Laos
54/D5 Banbar, China
60/B2 Banbar, China
60/D4 Ban Boun Tai, Laos
63/H3 Ban Boun Tai, Laos
65/C1 Ban Boun Tai, Laos
22/B3 Banbridge, NI,UK
22/B3 Banbridge (dist.), NI,UK
25/E2 Banbury, Eng,UK
76/B3 Banc D'Arguin Nat'l Park, Mrta.
78/B2 Banc d'Arguin Nat'l Park, Mrta.
65/C2 Ban Chiang (ruins), Thai.
103/F4 Banco (pt.), CR
94/E2 Bancroft, On,Can
62/D2 Bāndā, India
48/M10 Banda (sea), Indo.
67/G5 Banda (sea), Indo.
67/H4 Banda (isls.), Indo.
68/B5 Banda (sea), Indo.
66/A2 Banda Aceh, Indo.
57/F1 Bandai-Asahi Nat'l Park, Japan
57/G2 Bandai-Asahi Nat'l Park, Japan
57/G2 Bandai-san (mtn.), Japan
76/D6 Bandama (riv.), IvC.
78/D5 Bandama (riv.), IvC.
78/D4 Bandama Blanc (riv.), IvC.
78/D4 Bandama Rouge (riv.), IvC.
60/C5 Ban Dan Lan Hoi, Thai.
53/H3 Bandar Beheshtī (Chāh Behār), Iran
48/E7 Bandar-e 'Abbās, Iran
51/J5 Bandar-e 'Abbās, Iran
53/G3 Bandar-e 'Abbās, Iran
77/S2 Bandar-e 'Abbās, Iran
46/E6 Bandar-e Anzalī, Iran
51/G2 Bandar-e Anzalī, Iran
52/E1 Bandar-e Anzalī, Iran
51/G4 Bandar-e Būshehr, Iran
52/F3 Bandar-e Būshehr, Iran
52/F3 Bandar-e Chārak, Iran
51/G4 Bandar-e Deylam, Iran
52/F2 Bandar-e Deylam, Iran
53/F3 Bandar-e Kong, Iran
51/H5 Bandar-e Lengeh, Iran
53/F3 Bandar-e Lengeh, Iran
51/G4 Bandar-e Māhshahr, Iran
52/E2 Bandar-e Māhshahr, Iran
52/F3 Bandar-e Maqām, Iran
51/H4 Bandar-e Rīg, Iran
51/H2 Bandar-e Torkeman, Iran
52/F1 Bandar-e Torkeman, Iran
66/D3 Bandar Seri Begawan (cap.), Bru.
34/B1 Bande, Sp.
108/B2 Bandeirantes, Braz.
105/E5 Bandeira, Pico da (peak), Braz.
92/F4 Bandelier Nat'l Mon., NM,US
101/F2 Bandera, Tx,US
93/H5 Bandera, Tx,US
96/D4 Bandera, Tx,US
100/D2 Banderas, Mex.
101/N7 Banderilla, Mex.
26/F1 Bandholm, Den.
76/E5 Bandiagara, Mali
78/E3 Bandiagara, Mali
64/F3 Bandipur Nat'l Park, India
41/H5 Bandırma, Turk.
41/J5 Bandırma (gulf), Turk.
44/C4 Bandırma, Turk.
50/A1 Bandırma, Turk.
21/A5 Bandon, Ire.
21/A5 Bandon (riv.), Ire.
63/J5 Ban Don, Viet.
60/D4 Ban Donkon, Laos
63/H3 Ban Donkon, Laos
82/C1 Bandundu, Zaire
66/C5 Bandung, Indo.
35/E3 Bañeres, Sp.
103/H1 Banes, Cuba
84/F4 Banff, Can.
86/E3 Banff, Ab,Can

88/C1 Banff, Ab,Can
90/E3 Banff, Ab,Can
90/E3 Banff Nat'l Park, Ab, BC,Can
86/E3 Banff Nat'l Park, Ab,Can
88/C1 Banff Nat'l Park, Ab, BC,Can.
76/E5 Banfora, Burk.
78/D4 Banfora, Burk.
64/C2 Banga, India
62/C5 Bangalore, India
72/D5 Bangalow, Austl.
79/H5 Bangangté, Camr.
61/J5 Bangar, Phil.
77/K7 Bangassou, CAfr.
67/E2 Bangau (cape), Malay.
67/F4 Banggai (isls.), Indo.
65/D2 Banghiang (riv.), Laos
48/K10 Bangka (isl.), Indo.
66/B4 Bangka (str.), Indo.
66/C4 Bangka (isl.), Indo.
63/G5 Bangkok (bay), Thai.
65/C3 Bangkok (bight), Thai.
63/H5 Bangkok (Krung Thep) (cap.), Thai.
65/C3 Bangkok (Krung Thep) (cap.), Thai.
60/B4 Bangladesh
62/E3 Bangladesh
48/H7 Bangladesh, Asia
65/C5 Bang Lang (res.), Thai.
60/C4 Bangma (mts.), China
22/C2 Bangor, NI,UK
22/D5 Bangor, Wal,UK
87/K4 Bangor, Me,US
89/N3 Bangor, Me,US
95/G2 Bangor, Me,US
98/E5 Bangor, Pa,US
23/F6 Bangor-is-y-Coed, Wal,UK
82/D2 Bangu, Zaire
61/J5 Bangued, Phil.
77/J7 Bangui (cap.), CAfr.
63/H3 Bangzha, China
49/B4 Banhā, Egypt
50/B4 Banhā, Egypt
82/F5 Banhine Nat'l Park, Moz.
60/E5 Ban Hinkhan, Laos
60/D5 Ban Houay Pamon, Laos
63/H4 Ban Houay Pamon, Laos
60/D4 Ban Houayxay, Laos
63/H3 Ban Houayxay, Laos
65/C1 Ban Houayxay, Laos
104/D3 Baní, DRep.
76/D5 Bani (riv.), Mali
78/D3 Bani (riv.), Mali
76/F4 Bani-Bangou, Niger
103/J2 Bánica, DRep.
104/D3 Bánica, DRep.
78/D3 Banifing (riv.), Burk., Mali
60/A4 Bānigrām, Bang.
53/L2 Banihāl (pass), India
50/B4 Banī Mazār, Egypt
49/D4 Banī Suhaylah, Gaza
50/B4 Banī Suwayf, Egypt
50/B4 Banī Suwayf (gov.), Egypt
52/B3 Banī Suwayf, Egypt
77/M2 Banī Suwayf, Egypt
49/D2 Bāniyās, Syria
50/C3 Bāniyās, Syria
52/C1 Bāniyās, Syria
40/D3 Banja Koviljača, Yugo.
18/E4 Banja Luka, Bosn.
40/C3 Banja Luka, Bosn.
66/D4 Banjarmasin, Indo.
76/B5 Banjul (cap.), Gam.
78/A3 Banjul (cap.), Gam.
51/G2 Bank, Azer.
65/B5 Ban Kantang, Thai.
78/E3 Bankas, Mali
63/J4 Ban Kengkok, Laos
65/D3 Ban Khampho, Laos
65/C5 Ban Khuan Niang, Thai.
71/H8 Banks (str.), Austl.
73/B3 Banks (cape), Austl.
73/C4 Banks (str.), Austl.
84/E2 Banks (isl.), Can.
86/C3 Banks (isl.), BC,Can
86/D1 Banks (isl.), NW,Can
87/Q7 Banks (isl.), NW,Can
71/R11 Banks (pen.), NZ
85/H4 Banks (pt.), Ak,US
90/D4 Banks (lake), Wa,US
68/F6 Banks (isls.), Van.
72/H8 Bankstown, Austl.
62/E3 Bānkura, India
39/H1 Bankya, Bul.
65/D1 Banli, China
65/D2 Ban Loboy, Laos
63/J5 Ban Mdrack, Viet.
65/E3 Ban Mdrack, Viet.
66/C1 Ban Mdrack, Viet.
65/D2 Ban Mong, Viet.
65/D2 Ban Muangsen, Laos
22/B2 Bann (riv.), NI,UK
60/E4 Ban Na Mang, Laos
63/H3 Ban Nambak, Laos
65/D2 Ban Nape, Laos
63/H3 Ban Na Pho, Laos
63/G6 Ban Na San, Thai.
66/A2 Ban Na San, Thai.
53/K2 Bannu, Pak.
64/A1 Bannu, Pak.
40/D3 Banovići, Bosn.
65/C4 Ban Pak Phanang, Thai.
66/B2 Ban Pak Phanang, Thai.
60/D5 Ban Panghai, Laos
63/H4 Ban Panghai, Laos
63/H4 Ban Phai, Thai.
65/D3 Ban Phon, Laos
59/B4 Banpo (ruins), China
63/G4 Ban Rai, Thai.
60/D5 Ban Sieou, Laos
63/H4 Ban Sieou, Laos
65/C2 Ban Sieou, Laos
27/H2 Bansin, Ger.
27/K4 Banská Bystrica, Slvk.
18/E4 Banská Štiavnica, Slvk.
39/H2 Bansko, Bul.
41/F5 Bansko, Bul.
19/N8 Banstead, Eng,UK
25/F4 Banstead, Eng,UK
53/K4 Bānswāra, India
62/B3 Bānswāra, India
60/D4 Ban Ta Fa, Laos
63/H3 Ban Ta Fa, Laos
66/D5 Bantenan (cape), Indo.
60/D5 Ban Thabok, Laos
65/C2 Ban Thabok, Laos
65/B5 Bantong Group (isls.), Thai.
21/G8 Bantry (bay), Ire.
21/H8 Bantry, Ire.
60/E5 Ban Tung, Laos
63/H4 Ban Tung, Laos
34/C3 Bañuelo (mtn.), Sp.
65/D3 Ban Xebang-Nouan, Laos
66/A3 Banyak (isls.), Indo.
35/G1 Banyoles, Sp.
66/D5 Banyuwangi, Indo.
83/J Banzare (coast), Ant.
38/A4 Banzart (gov.), Tun.
75/W17 Banzart (gov.), Tun.
75/W17 Banzart (lake), Tun.
38/A4 Banzart (Bizerte), Tun.
75/W17 Banzart (Bizerte), Tun.
76/G1 Banzart (Bizerte), Tun.
38/A4 Banzart, Buḩayrat (lake), Tun.
54/G4 Baode, China
59/B3 Baode, China
59/D3 Baodi, China
59/H7 Baodi, China
47/M6 Baoding, China
54/H4 Baoding, China
59/C3 Baoding, China
59/G7 Baoding, China
59/D4 Baodugu (mtn.), China
59/C4 Baofeng, China
60/E2 Baoguangsi, China
60/E4 Bao Ha, Viet.
63/H3 Bao Ha, Viet.
65/D1 Bao Ha, Viet.
54/F5 Baoji, China
63/J2 Baojing, China
54/G5 Baokang, China
59/B5 Baokang, China
61/F2 Baokang, China
60/E4 Bao Lac, Viet.
63/J3 Bao Lac, Viet.
65/D1 Bao Lac, Viet.
65/D4 Bao Loc, Viet.
103/J2 Baoruco, Sierra de (range), DRep
59/E5 Baoshan, China
59/L8 Baoshan, China
60/C3 Baoshan, China
61/J2 Baoshan, China
63/G2 Baoshan, China
47/M5 Baotou, China
54/G3 Baotou, China
59/B2 Baotou, China
78/D4 Baoulé (riv.), IvC., Mali
76/D5 Baoulé (riv.), Mali
76/D5 Baoulé (riv.), Mali
60/D2 Baoxing, China
59/D4 Baoying, China
62/D4 Bāpatla, India
30/B3 Bapaume, Fr.
98/E5 Baptistown, NJ,US
49/D3 Bāqa el Gharbiyya, Isr.
49/G7 Bāqa el Gharbiyya, Isr.
54/C5 Baqên, China
60/B1 Baqên, China
65/D4 Ba Quan (cape), Viet.
51/F3 Ba'qūbah, Iraq
53/F3 Ba'qūbah, Iraq
26/C4 Bar (riv.), Fr.
30/D5 Bar (riv.), Fr.
32/F2 Bar (riv.), Fr.
39/F1 Bar, Yugo.
40/D4 Bar, Yugo.
27/G1 Bara, Swe.
65/D4 Ba Ra, Viet.
66/C1 Ba Ra, Viet.
77/P7 Baraawe, Som.
66/E4 Barabai, Indo.
46/H4 Barabinsk, Rus.
89/J3 Baraboo, Wi,US
91/L5 Baraboo, Wi,US
93/K2 Baraboo, Wi,US
94/B3 Baraboo, Wi,US
32/B5 Baracaldo, Sp.
34/D1 Baracaldo, Sp.
103/H1 Baracoa, Cuba
49/E3 Baradá (riv.), Syria
73/D1 Baradine, Austl.
77/N7 Baragoi, Kenya
103/G1 Baraguá, Cuba
104/D5 Baragua, Ven.
104/D3 Barahona, DRep.
40/E3 Barajevo, Yugo.
60/B3 Barāk (riv.), India
72/C4 Baralaba, Austl.
64/D1 Bārā Lācha La (pass), India
66/D3 Baram (cape), Malay.
66/D3 Baram (riv.), Malay.
106/G2 Barama (riv.), Guy.
60/A3 Barama, India
53/K5 Bārāmati, India
62/B4 Bārāmati, India
53/K2 Baramula, India
44/D1 Baran', Bela.
53/L3 Bāran, India
62/C2 Bāran, India
103/H4 Baranoa, Col.
85/L4 Baranof (isl.), Ak,US
86/C3 Baranof (isl.), Ak,US
18/F3 Baranovichi, Bela.
44/C1 Baranovichi, Bela.
46/C4 Baranovichi, Bela.
40/C3 Baranya (co.), Hun.
108/D1 Barão de Cocais, Braz.
41/G2 Baraolt, Rom.
31/E3 Baraque de Fraiture (hill), Belg.
67/G5 Barat Daya (isls.), Indo.
107/K8 Barbacena, Braz.
108/D2 Barbacena, Braz.
104/G4 Barbados
84/L8 Barbados
52/B5 Barbar, Sudan
77/M4 Barbar, Sudan
35/F1 Barbastro, Sp.
34/C4 Barbate de Franco, Sp.
75/M12 Barbate de Franco, Sp.
87/T6 Barbeau (peak), NW,Can
35/L6 Barbera del Valles, Sp.
88/V13 Barbers (pt.), Hi,US
88/V13 Barbers Point Nav. Air Sta., Hi,US
81/E2 Barberton, SAfr.
82/F6 Barberton, SAfr.
94/D3 Barberton, Oh,US
32/C4 Barbezieux-Saint-Hilaire, Fr.
62/E3 Barbil, India
23/F3 Barbon, Eng,UK
94/D4 Barbourville, Ky,US
97/H2 Barbourville, Ky,US
104/F3 Barbuda (isl.), Anti.
84/L8 Barbuda (isl.), Anti.
68/D7 Barcaldine, Austl.
71/H4 Barcaldine, Austl.
72/B3 Barcaldine, Austl.
34/B3 Barcarrota, Sp.
40/F2 Barcău (riv.), Rom.
38/D3 Barcellona Pozzo di Gotto, It.
18/D4 Barcelona, Sp.
35/G2 Barcelona, Sp
35/L7 Barcelona, Sp.
104/E5 Barcelona, Ven.
106/F1 Barcelona, Ven.
106/F4 Barcelos, Braz.
34/A2 Barcelos, Port.
27/J2 Barcin, Pol.
71/G4 Barcoo (riv.), Austl.
72/A4 Barcoo (riv.), Austl.
40/C3 Barcs, Hun.
27/L2 Barczewo, Pol.
70/J3 Bardaï, Chad
49/C4 Bardawīl, Sabkhat al (lag.), Egypt
27/L4 Bardejov, Slvk.
44/B2 Bardejov, Slvk.
53/G1 Bardeskan, Iran
77/P7 Bardheere, Som.
77/L1 Bardīyah, Libya
23/H5 Bardney, Eng,UK
53/K4 Bārdoli, India
62/B3 Bārdoli, India
22/D6 Bardsey (isl.), Wal,UK
94/C4 Bardstown, Ky,US
97/G2 Bardstown, Ky,US
77/R5 Bareeda, Som.
62/C2 Bareilly, India
73/C2 Barellan, Austl.
28/B5 Barendrecht, Neth.
32/D2 Barentin, Fr.
20/K1 Barents (sea), Nor., Rus.
18/G1 Barents (sea), Rus.
42/H1 Barents (sea), Rus.
46/D2 Barents (sea), Nor.,Rus.
52/C5 Barentu, Eth.
77/N4 Barentu, Eth.
37/E3 Bäretswil, Swi.
32/C2 Barfleur, Pointe de (pt.), Fr.
72/D4 Bargara, Austl.
62/D3 Bargarh, India
29/H1 Bargfeld-Stegen, Ger.
73/D2 Bargo, Austl.
24/C3 Bargoed, Wal,UK
29/H1 Bargteheide, Ger.
54/F1 Barguzin (riv.), Rus.
62/D2 Barhaj, India
73/C2 Barham, Austl.
89/N3 Bar Harbor, Me,US
95/G2 Bar Harbor, Me,US
25/G2 Bar Hill, Eng,UK
53/L3 Bāri, India
62/C2 Bāri, India
18/E4 Bari, It.
38/E2 Bari, It.
40/C5 Bari, It.
52/C4 Barīdī, Ra's (pt.), SAr.
75/U18 Barika, Alg.
76/G1 Barika, Alg.
102/D3 Barillas, Guat.
106/D2 Barinas, Ven.
82/C2 Baringa-Twana, Zaire
62/E3 Baripāda, India
108/B2 Bariri, Braz.
77/M3 Bārīs, Egypt
62/F3 Barisāl, Bang.
66/B4 Barisan (mts.), Indo.
38/A3 Bari Sardo, It.
66/D4 Barito (riv.), Indo.
109/C1 Baritu Nat'l Park, Arg.
99/N13 Bark (riv.), Wi,US
54/E5 Barkam, China
95/S9 Barker, NY,US
19/P7 Barking & Dagenham (bor.), Eng,UK
90/B3 Barkley (sound), BC,Can
94/C4 Barkley (lake), Ky,US
70/E3 Barkly (tablelands), Austl.
80/D3 Barkly East, SAfr.
82/E7 Barkly East, SAfr.
54/C3 Barkol, China
23/F6 Barlaston, Eng,UK
23/G4 Barlby, Eng,UK
26/C4 Bar-le-Duc, Fr.
31/E6 Bar-le-Duc, Fr.
32/F2 Bar-le-Duc, Fr.
68/A7 Barlee (lake), Austl.
70/B5 Barlee (lake), Austl.
18/E4 Barletta, It.
38/E2 Barletta, It.
40/C5 Barletta, It.
30/B3 Barlin, Fr.
27/H2 Barlinek, Pol.
73/C2 Barmedman, Austl.
109/E2 Barmejo (riv.), Arg.
53/K3 Barmer, India
62/B2 Barmer, India
73/B2 Barmera, Austl.
24/B1 Barmouth, Wal,UK
29/G1 Barmstedt, Ger.
53/L2 Barnāla, India
64/C2 Barnāla, India
23/G2 Barnard Castle, Eng,UK
46/J4 Barnaul, Rus.
40/B2 Bärnbach, Aus.
98/F6 Barnegat, NJ,US
98/F6 Barnegat (bay), NJ,US
98/F6 Barnegat (inlet), NJ,US
98/F6 Barnegat Light, NJ,US
19/N7 Barnet, Eng,UK
19/N7 Barnet (bor.), Eng,UK
26/C2 Barneveld, Neth.
28/C4 Barneveld, Neth.
101/E2 Barnhart, Tx,US
27/G2 Barnim (reg.), Ger.
23/F4 Barnoldswick, Eng,UK
23/G4 Barnsley, Eng,UK
24/B4 Barnstaple, Eng,UK
24/B4 Barnstaple (Bideford) (bay), Eng,UK
29/F3 Barnstorf, Ger.
24/E2 Barnt Green, Eng,UK
29/G5 Barntrup, Ger.
97/H3 Barnwell, SC,US
53/K4 Baroda, India
62/B3 Baroda, India
53/K1 Barowghīl (Khybor) (pass), Afg.
62/F2 Barpeta, India
104/D5 Barquisimeto, Ven.
106/E1 Barquisimeto, Ven.
36/D1 Barr, Fr.
22/D1 Barr, Sc,UK
107/K6 Barra, Braz.
73/D1 Barraba, Austl.
108/B2 Barra Bonita, Braz.
108/B2 Barra Bonita (res.), Braz.
103/F4 Barra del Colorado Nat'l Park, CR
107/G7 Barra do Bugres, Braz.
107/J5 Barra do Corda, Braz.
107/H7 Barra do Garças, Braz.
108/D2 Barra do Piraí, Braz.
108/B4 Barra do Ribeiro, Braz.
76/D6 Barrage de Kossou (dam), IvC.
76/H6 Barrage de Lagdo (dam), Camr.
82/F4 Barragem de Cahora Bassa (dam), Moz.
107/K8 Barra Mansa, Braz.
108/C2 Barra Mansa, Braz.
109/H1 Barra Mansa, Braz.
106/C4 Barranca, Peru
106/C6 Barranca, Peru
106/D2 Barrancabermeja, Col.
100/D3 Barranca del Cobre Nat'l Park, Mex.
103/H4 Barranco de Loba, Col.
34/B3 Barrancos, Port.
103/H4 Barranquilla, Col.
106/D1 Barranquilla, Col.
103/F4 Barra Punta Gorda, Nic.
108/B3 Barra Velha, Braz.
109/C3 Barreal, Arg.
107/K6 Barreiras, Braz.
34/A3 Barreiro, Port.
35/P10 Barreiro, Port.
74/G7 Barren (isls.), Madg.
82/J10 Barren (isls.), Madg.
81/G7 Barren, Nosy (isls.), Madg.
107/J8 Barretos, Braz.
108/B2 Barretos, Braz.
86/E3 Barrhead, Ab,Can
90/E2 Barrhead, Ab,Can
22/D1 Barrhill, Sc,UK
87/J4 Barrie, On,Can
89/L3 Barrie, On,Can
94/E2 Barrie, On,Can
73/B1 Barrier (range), Austl.
90/C3 Barrière, Can
99/P15 Barrington, Il,US
99/P15 Barrington Hills, Il,US
73/D1 Barrington Tops (peak), Austl.
73/D1 Barrington Tops Nat'l Park, Austl.
72/B5 Barringun, Austl.
72/B2 Barron Gorge Nat'l Park, Austl.
108/D2 Barroso, Braz.
104/F4 Barrouallie, StV.
70/A4 Barrow (isl.), Austl.
72/B1 Barrow (pt.), Austl.
86/G1 Barrow (str.), NW,Can
87/S7 Barrow (str.), NW,Can
22/A5 Barrow (riv.), Ire.
84/B2 Barrow (pt.), US
85/G1 Barrow, Ak,US
85/G1 Barrow (pt.), Ak,US
23/H6 Barrowby, Eng,UK
23/F4 Barrowford, Eng,UK
23/E3 Barrow-in-Furness, Eng,UK
34/C1 Barruelo de Santullán, Sp.
24/C4 Barry, Wal,UK
45/L4 Barsakel'mes (salt pan), Uzb.
53/L5 Bārshi, India
62/C4 Bārsi, India
26/E2 Barsinghausen, Ger.
29/G4 Barsinghausen, Ger.
29/E2 Barssel, Ger.
88/C5 Barstow, Ca,US
92/C4 Barstow, Ca,US
100/E2 Barstow, Tx,US
32/F2 Bar-sur-Aube, Fr.
26/C4 Bar-sur-Seine, Fr.
32/F2 Bar-sur-Seine, Fr.
36/D2 Bartenheim, Fr.
26/G1 Barth, Ger.
37/F3 Bartholomäberg, Aus.
106/G2 Bartica, Guy.
41/L5 Bartın, Turk.
44/E4 Bartın, Turk.
50/C1 Bartın, Turk.
71/H3 Bartle Frere (peak), Austl.
89/G4 Bartlesville, Ok,US
93/J3 Bartlesville, Ok,US
96/E2 Bartlesville, Ok,US
99/P16 Bartlett, Il,US
101/F2 Bartlett, Tx,US
103/G1 Bartolomé Masó, Cuba
82/G5 Bartolomeu Dias, Moz.
25/F3 Barton in the Clay, Eng,UK
25/E5 Barton on Sea, Eng,UK
98/E4 Bartonsville, Pa,US
23/G6 Barton under Needwood, Eng,UK
25/E1 Barton under Needwood, Eng,UK
23/H4 Barton upon Humber, Eng,UK
27/L1 Bartoszyce, Pol.
42/D5 Bartoszyce, Pol
27/G2 Bartow, Ger.
97/H5 Bartow, Fl,US
103/F4 Barú (vol.), Pan.
66/B3 Barumun (riv.), Indo.
66/A3 Barus, Indo.
54/C2 Baruun Huuray (reg.), Mong.
47/M5 Baruun-Urt, Mong.
54/G2 Baruun-Urt, Mong.
53/L4 Barwāha, India
62/C3 Barwāha, India
53/K4 Barwāni, India
62/B3 Barwāni, India
71/H5 Barwon (riv.), Austl.
73/D1 Barwon (riv.), Austl.
27/J3 Barycz (riv.), Pol.
45/H1 Barysh, Rus.
77/J7 Basankusu, Zaire
32/B5 Basauri, Sp.
34/D1 Basauri, Sp.
31/E4 Bascharage, Lux.
23/F6 Baschurch, Eng,UK
24/D1 Baschurch, Eng,UK
18/D4 Basel, Swi.
26/D5 Basel, Swi.
33/G3 Basel, Swi.
36/D2 Basel, Swi.
37/H5 Baselga di Pinè, It.
36/D3 Baselland (canton), Swi.
38/E2 Basento (riv.), It.
80/E3 Bashee (riv.), SAfr.
68/B2 Bashi (chan.)
61/J4 Bashi (chan.), Phil., Tai.
55/B1 Bashkaus (riv.), Rus.
43/M5 Bashkir Aut. Rep., Rus.
45/L1 Bashkir Aut. Rep., Rus.
51/G4 Bāsht, Iran
52/F2 Bāsht, Iran
41/L2 Bashtanka, Ukr.
67/F2 Basilan (isl.), Phil.
67/F2 Basilan (peak), Phil.
68/B4 Basilan (isl.), Phil.
25/G3 Basildon, Eng,UK
38/D2 Basilicata (reg.), It.
40/B5 Basilicata (reg.), It.
62/C3 Bāsim, India
90/F4 Basin, Wy,US
92/E1 Basin, Wy,US
19/M8 Basingstoke (can.), Eng,UK
25/E4 Basingstoke, Eng,UK
49/D2 Basīt, Ra's al (pt.), Syria
33/L4 Baška, Cro.
51/F2 Başkale, Turk.
94/F2 Baskatong (res.), Qu,Can
50/D2 Baskil, Turk.
44/D5 Başkomutan Milli Park, Turk.
50/B2 Başkomutan Nat'l Park, Turk.
50/B2 Başmakçı, Turk.
62/C3 Basoda, India
37/E5 Basodino, Monte (peak), It.
77/K7 Basoko, Zaire
32/B5 Basque Provinces (aut. comm.), Sp.
34/D1 Basque Provinces (aut. comm.), Sp.
30/G6 Bas-Rhin (dept.), Fr.
36/D1 Bas-Rhin (dept.), Fr.
71/G7 Bass (str.), Austl.
73/C3 Bass (strait), Austl.
69/L7 Bass (isls.), FrPol.
39/G4 Bassae (ruins), Gre.
90/E3 Bassano, Ab,Can
33/J4 Bassano del Grappa, It.
76/F6 Bassari, Togo
74/G7 Bassas da India (isl.), Reun.
82/H5 Bassas da India (isl.), Reun.
36/D3 Bassecourt, Swi.
60/B5 Bassein, Burma
60/B5 Bassein (riv.), Burma
63/F4 Bassein, Burma
63/F4 Bassein (riv.), Burma
53/K5 Bassein, India
62/B4 Bassein, India
31/E2 Bassenge, Belg.
31/G3 Bassenheim, Ger.
32/C2 Basse-Normandie (reg.), Fr.
22/E2 Bassenthwaite (lake), Eng,UK
76/C5 Basse Santa Su, Gam.
78/B3 Basse Santa Su, Gam.
104/F3 Basse-Terre, Guad.
104/F3 Basse-Terre (isl.), Guad.
104/F3 Basseterre (cap.), StK.
26/E2 Bassum, Ger.
29/F3 Bassum, Ger.
94/B1 Basswood (lake), On,Can, Mn,US
20/E4 Båstad, Swe.
51/H5 Bastak, Iran
52/F3 Bastak, Iran
51/H2 Basṭām, Iran
53/G1 Basṭām, Iran
38/A2 Bastelicaccia, Fr
62/D2 Bastī, India
18/D4 Bastia, Fr.
38/A1 Bastia, Fr.
33/K5 Bastia, It.
38/C1 Bastia, It.
26/C4 Bastogne, Belg.
31/E3 Bastogne, Belg.
32/F2 Bastogne, Belg.
108/B2 Bastos, Braz.
89/H5 Bastrop, La,US
93/K4 Bastrop, La,US
96/F3 Bastrop, La,US
101/F2 Bastrop, Tx,US
93/H6 Bastrop, Tx,US
96/D4 Bastrop, Tx,US
49/B4 Basyūn, Egypt
76/G7 Bata, EqG.
103/F1 Batabanó (gulf), Cuba
61/J5 Batac, Phil.
47/P3 Batagay, Rus.
39/J2 Batak, Bul.
41/G5 Batak, Bul.
53/L2 Batāla, India
64/C2 Batāla, India
34/A3 Batalha, Port.
48/M7 Batan (isls.), Phil.
68/B2 Batan (isls.), Phil.
54/D6 Batang, China
60/C2 Batang, China
77/J6 Batangafo, CAfr.
68/B3 Batangas, Phil.
67/H4 Batanta (mtn.), Indo.
108/C2 Batatais, Braz.
99/P16 Batavia, Il,US
94/E3 Batavia, NY,US
44/F3 Bataysk, Rus.
48/K8 Batdambang, Camb.
63/H5 Batdambang, Camb.
72/H9 Bate (bay), Austl.
76/H8 Batéké (plat.), Congo
73/D2 Batemans Bay, Austl.
97/H3 Batesburg, SC,US
93/K4 Batesville, Ar,US
97/F3 Batesville, Ar,US
93/K4 Batesville, Ms,US
97/F3 Batesville, Ms,US
24/D4 Bath, Eng,UK
89/N3 Bath, Me,US
95/G3 Bath, Me,US
94/E3 Bath, NY,US
98/E5 Bath, Pa,US
28/D4 Bathmen, Neth.
70/D2 Bathurst (isl.), Austl.
71/H6 Bathurst, Austl.
73/D2 Bathurst, Austl.
84/G2 Bathurst (isl.), Can.
87/K4 Bathurst, NB,Can
89/N2 Bathurst, NB,Can
95/H2 Bathurst, NB,Can
85/N1 Bathurst (cape), NW,Can
86/D1 Bathurst (cape), NW,Can
86/F2 Bathurst (inlet), NW,Can
87/R7 Bathurst (isl.), NW,Can
86/F2 Bathurst Inlet, NW,Can
77/P5 Batī, Eth.
74/F5 Batian (peak), Kenya
77/N8 Batian (peak), Kenya
54/C2 Batik (mts.), China
77/Q2 Bāṭin (wadi), Asia
52/E3 Bāṭin, Wādī al (dry riv.), SAr.
51/H3 Bāṭlāq-e Gāv Khūnī (marsh), Iran
23/G4 Batley, Eng,UK
73/D2 Batlow, Austl.
46/E6 Batman, Turk.
50/E2 Batman, Turk.
75/T16 Batna (wilaya), Alg.
75/U18 Batna (gov.), Alg.
75/V18 Batna, Alg.
76/G1 Batna, Alg.
40/E3 Batočina, Yugo.
89/H5 Baton Rouge (cap.), La,US
93/K5 Baton Rouge, La,US
96/F4 Baton Rouge, La,US
100/D3 Batopilas, Mex.
53/L2 Batoti, India
76/H7 Batouri, Camr.
49/D4 Baṭrā' (Petra) (ruins), Jor.
20/J1 Båtsfjord, Nor.
49/G6 Bat Shelomo, Isr.
95/F2 Batsican (riv.), Qu,Can
98/F6 Batsto (riv.), NJ,US
54/F2 Batsümber, Mong.
29/F6 Battenberg, Ger.
36/D3 Bätterkinden, Swi.
23/G3 Battersby, Eng,UK
19/N7 Battersea, Eng,UK
62/D6 Batticaloa, SrL.
64/H4 Batticaloa (dist.), SrL.
40/B5 Battipaglia, It.
90/F2 Battle (riv.), Ab, Sk,Can
86/E3 Battle (riv.), Ab,Can
25/G5 Battle, Eng,UK
32/D1 Battle, Eng,UK
90/F3 Battle (cr.), Mt,US
89/J3 Battle Creek, Mi,US
94/C3 Battle Creek, Mi,US
90/F2 Battleford, Sk,Can
88/C3 Battle Mountain, Nv,US
90/D5 Battle Mountain, Nv,US
92/C2 Battle Mountain, Nv,US
40/E2 Battonya, Hun.
54/E2 Battsengel, Mong.
77/N6 Batu (peak), Eth.
66/A4 Batu (isls.), Indo.
67/E3 Batu (cape), Indo.
66/D3 Batu (bay), Malay.
66/D3 Batu (peak), Malay.
67/F4 Batudaka (isl.), Indo.
66/D3 Batuensambang (peak), Indo.
66/B3 Batu Gajah, Malay.
19/H4 Batumi, Geo.
45/G4 Batumi, Geo.
46/E5 Batumi, Geo.
50/E1 Batumi, Geo.
88/B3 Batu Pahat, Malay.
66/B3 Batu Puteh (peak), Malay.
66/B4 Baturaja, Indo.
107/L4 Baturité, Braz.
49/D7 Bat Yam, Isr.
76/G5 Bauchi, Nga.
79/H4 Bauchi (state), Nga.
91/K3 Baudette, Mn,US
103/G5 Baudo, Serranía de (range), Col.
38/A2 Baunei, It
107/J8 Baurú, Braz.
108/B2 Baurú, Braz.
109/G1 Baurú, Braz.
27/H3 Bautzen, Ger.
36/C3 Bavans, Fr.
26/F4 Bavaria (state), Ger.
33/J2 Bavaria (state), Ger.
37/G2 Bavaria (state), Ger.
26/F5 Bavarian Alps (mts.), Aus., Ger.
33/J3 Bavarian Alps (mts.), Aus., Ger.
37/H3 Bavarian Alps (mts.), Aus., Ger.
30/C3 Bavay, Fr.
37/E6 Baveno, It.
100/C2 Baviácora, Mex.
36/C2 Bavilliers, Fr.
100/C2 Bavispe (riv.), Mex.
92/E5 Bavispe (riv.), Mex
45/K1 Bavly, Rus.
66/C4 Bawang (cape), Indo.
73/C3 Baw Baw (peak), Austl.
73/C3 Baw Baw Nat'l Park, Austl.
66/D5 Bawean (isl.), Indo.
76/E5 Bawku, Gha.
79/E4 Bawku, Gha.
63/J2 Ba Xian, China
54/D5 Baxoi, China
60/C2 Baxoi, China
63/G1 Baxoi, China
103/G1 Bayamo, Cuba
104/E3 Bayamón, PR
55/K2 Bayan, China
54/F2 Bayan, Mong.
54/G2 Bayandelger, Mong.
54/D5 Bayan Har (mts.), China
47/L5 Bayanhongor, Mong.
54/E2 Bayanhongor, Mong.
54/E3 Bayanleg, Mong.
103/G4 Bayano (res.), Pan.
54/E2 Bayan-Ovoo, Mong.
54/F3 Bayan-Ovoo, Mong.
54/G2 Bayanterem, Mong.
54/D2 Bayan-Uul, Mong.
91/H5 Bayard, Ne,US
93/G2 Bayard, Ne,US
44/E4 Bayat, Turk.
50/C1 Bayat, Turk.
67/F2 Bayawan, Phil.
31/G3 Baybach (riv.), Ger.
44/F4 Bayburt (prov.), Turk.
44/G4 Bayburt, Turk.
50/E1 Bayburt, Turk.
50/E1 Bayburt (prov.), Turk.
87/H4 Bay City, Mi,US
89/K3 Bay City, Mi,US
94/D3 Bay City, Mi,US
101/G2 Bay City, Tx,US
89/G6 Bay City, Tx,US
93/J5 Bay City, Tx,US
96/E4 Bay City, Tx,US
46/G2 Baydaratskaya (bay), Rus.
77/P7 Baydhabo (Baidoa), Som.
54/D2 Baydrag (riv.), Mong.
36/A1 Bayel, Fr.
33/K2 Bayerischer Wald Nat'l Park, Ger.
107/M5 Bayeux, Braz.
32/C2 Bayeux, Fr.
52/E6 Bayḩān al Qişāb, Yem.
50/A2 Bayındır, Turk.
47/L4 Baykal (lake), Rus.
47/L4 Baykal (mts.), Rus.
48/L4 Baykal (lake), Rus.
54/F1 Baykal (lake), Rus.
50/E2 Baykan, Turk.
97/G4 Bay Minette, Al,US
61/J5 Bayombong, Phil.
36/C1 Bayon, Fr.
34/A1 Bayona, Sp.
97/H4 Bayonet Point, Fl,US
32/C5 Bayonne, Fr.
34/E1 Bayonne, Fr.
98/F5 Bayonne, NJ,US
46/G6 Bayram-Ali, Trkm.
53/H1 Bayram-Ali, Trkm.
41/H5 Bayramıç, Turk.
44/C4 Bayramıç, Turk.
50/A1 Bayramıç, Turk.
18/E4 Bayreuth, Ger.
26/F4 Bayreuth, Ger.
33/J2 Bayreuth, Ger.
95/L2 Bay Roberts, Nf,Can
49/D3 Bayrūt (Beirut) (cap.), Leb.
50/C3 Bayrūt (Beirut) (cap.), Leb.
52/C2 Bayrūt (Beirut) (cap.), Leb.
77/N1 Bayrūt (Beirut) (cap.), Leb.
94/E2 Bays (lake), On,Can
97/F4 Bay Saint Louis, Ms,US
35/E1 Bayse (riv.), Fr.
24/D1 Bayston Hill, Eng,UK
52/D6 Bayt al Faqīh, Yem.
49/G8 Bayt Fajjār, WBnk.
49/G8 Bayt Ḩanīnā, WBnk.
52/C2 Bayt Ḩanīnā, WBnk.
49/D4 Bayt Ḩānūn, Gaza
49/D4 Bayt Laḩm (Bethlehem), WBnk.
49/G8 Bayt Laḩm (Bethlehem), WBnk.
93/J5 Baytown, Tx,US
96/E4 Baytown, Tx,US
49/G8 Bayt Sāḩūr, WBnk.
52/B5 Bayudha (des.), Sudan
34/D4 Baza, Sp.
51/F1 Bazardyuzyu (peak), Rus.
45/H4 Bazardyuzyu, Gora (peak), Rus.
45/J1 Bazarnyye Mataki, Rus.
82/G5 Bazaruto (isl.), Moz.
32/C4 Bazas, Fr.
79/E4 Bazèga (prov.), Burk.
32/D5 Bazet, Fr.
35/F1 Bazet, Fr.
54/F5 Bazhong, China
60/E2 Bazhong, China
94/F2 Bazin (riv.), Qu,Can
73/B3 Beachport, Austl.
98/F6 Beachwood, NJ,US
25/G5 Beachy Head (pt.), Eng,UK
32/D1 Beachy Head (pt.), Eng,UK
24/C2 Beacon (hill), Wal,UK
73/C4 Beaconsfield, Austl.
95/N7 Beaconsfield, Qu,Can
25/F3 Beaconsfield, Eng,UK
24/B5 Beaford, Eng,UK
70/E2 Beagle (gulf), Austl.
70/C3 Beagle Bay Mission, Austl.
72/A4 Beal (mts.), Austl.
81/J6 Bealanana, Madg.
90/B3 Beale (cape), Can
86/D4 Beale (cape), BC,Can
88/A2 Beale (cape), BC,Can.
93/G4 Beals (creek), Tx,US
24/D5 Beaminster, Eng,UK
81/H9 Beampingaratra (ridge), Madg.
95/R9 Beamsville, On,Can
91/K2 Bear (lake), Mb,Can
90/F5 Bear (lake), Id, Ut,US
90/F5 Bear (riv.), Id, Ut,US
92/E2 Bear (lake), Id, Ut,US
46/C2 Bear (isl.), Nor.
92/E2 Bear (riv.), US
85/K2 Bear (mtn.), Ak,US
85/K3 Bear (mt.), Ak,US

118

Bear – Betha

99/M10 Bear (cr.), Ca,US
88/C3 Bear (lake), Id, Ut,US
21/H8 Beara (pen.), Ire.
83/M Beardmore (glac.), Ant.
90/F3 Bearpaw (mts.), Mt,US
21/C3 Bearsden, Sc,UK
90/F4 Beartooth (mts.), Mt, Wy,US
93/K5 Bear Town, Ms,US
97/F4 Bear Town, Ms,US
64/D2 Beās (riv.), India
32/B5 Beasain, Sp.
34/D1 Beasain, Sp.
34/D3 Beas de Segura, Sp.
103/J2 Beata (cape), DRep.
103/J2 Beata (isl.), DRep.
104/D3 Beata (cape), DRep.
104/D3 Beata (isl.), DRep.
36/D4 Beatenberg, Swi.
70/F2 Beatrice (cape), Austl.
89/G3 Beatrice, Ne,US
93/H2 Beatrice, Ne,US
96/D1 Beatrice, Ne,US
22/E1 Beattock, Sc,UK
92/C3 Beatty, Nv,US
32/F5 Beaucaire, Fr.
35/H1 Beaucaire, Fr.
30/A4 Beaucamps-le-Vieux, Fr.
19/S9 Beauchamp, Fr.
36/C3 Beaucourt, Fr.
72/D4 Beaudesert, Austl.
73/B3 Beaufort, Austl.
84/C2 Beaufort (sea), Can., US
85/K1 Beaufort (sea), Can., US
36/B4 Beaufort, Fr.
31/F4 Beaufort, Lux.
86/C1 Beaufort (sea), Can,US
89/K5 Beaufort, SC,US
97/H3 Beaufort, SC,US
80/C4 Beaufort West, SAfr.
82/D7 Beaufort West, SAfr.
32/D3 Beaugency, Fr.
95/N7 Beauharnois, Qu,Can
95/N7 Beauharnois (co.), Qu,Can
32/F4 Beaujolais (mts.), Fr.
25/E5 Beaulieu, Eng,UK
22/D5 Beaumaris, Wal,UK
32/F3 Beaume, Fr.
30/B3 Beaumetz-les-Loges, Fr.
30/D3 Beaumont, Belg.
32/E4 Beaumont, Fr.
89/H5 Beaumont, Tx,US
93/J5 Beaumont, Tx,US
96/E4 Beaumont, Tx,US
32/D5 Beaumont-de-Lomagne, Fr.
35/F1 Beaumont-de-Lomagne, Fr.
19/S9 Beaumont-sur-Oise, Fr.
30/B5 Beaumont-sur-Oise, Fr.
32/F3 Beaune, Fr.
32/C3 Beaupréau, Fr.
30/B3 Beauquesne, Fr.
31/D3 Beauraing, Belg.
32/F1 Beauraing, Belg.
30/A3 Beaurainville, Fr.
30/C3 Beaurevoir, Fr.
86/G3 Beauséjour, Mb,Can
91/J3 Beauséjour, Mb,Can
30/C4 Beautor, Fr.
30/B5 Beauvais, Fr.
32/E2 Beauvais, Fr.
90/G2 Beauval, Sk,Can
30/B3 Beauval, Fr.
90/F2 Beaver (riv.), Ab,Can
86/F3 Beaver (riv.), Sk,Can
86/D2 Beaver (riv.), Yk,Can
85/J2 Beaver, Ak,US
94/C2 Beaver (isl.), Mi,US
93/G3 Beaver, Ok,US
96/C2 Beaver, Ok,US
88/D4 Beaver, Ut,US
92/D3 Beaver, Ut,US
85/K3 Beaver Creek, Yk,Can
86/B2 Beaver Creek, Yk,Can
91/L5 Beaver Dam, Wi,US
93/K2 Beaver Dam, Wi,US
94/B3 Beaver Dam, Wi,US
90/E4 Beaverhead (riv.), Mt,US
90/D2 Beaverlodge, Ab,Can
91/L2 Beaver Stone (riv.), On,Can
53/K3 Beāwar, India
62/B2 Beāwar, India
107/J8 Bebedouro, Braz.
108/B2 Bebedouro, Braz.
75/G3 Beb el Mandeb (str.), Afr., Asia
23/E5 Bebington, Eng,UK
26/E3 Bebra, Ger.
29/G7 Bebra, Ger.
101/H4 Becal, Mex.
102/D1 Becal, Mex.
101/H5 Becanchén, Mex.
102/D1 Becanchén, Mex.
25/H2 Beccles, Eng,UK
26/A2 Beccles, Eng.,UK
40/E3 Bečej, Yugo.
34/B1 Becerreá, Sp.
76/E1 Bechar, Alg.
85/G4 Becharof (lake), Ak,US
85/G4 Becharof Nat'l Wild. Ref., Ak,US
31/G5 Bechhofen, Ger.
29/G2 Beckdorf, Ger.
19/N7 Beckenham, Eng,UK
37/E4 Beckenried, Swi.
31/F5 Beckingen, Ger.
23/H5 Beckingham, Eng,UK
89/K4 Beckley, WV,US
94/D4 Beckley, WV,US
97/H2 Beckley, WV,US
29/F5 Beckum, Ger.
41/G2 Beclean, Rom.
36/D5 Becs de Bosson (peak), Swi.
23/G3 Bedale, Eng,UK
32/E5 Bédarieux, Fr.
35/G1 Bédarieux, Fr.
28/D7 Bedburg, Ger.
31/F1 Bedburg, Ger.
28/D5 Bedburg-Hau, Ger.
24/C3 Beddau, Wal,UK
22/D5 Beddgelert, Wal,UK
72/B1 Bedford (cape), Austl.
95/F2 Bedford, Qu,Can
25/F2 Bedford, Eng,UK
89/J4 Bedford, In,US
94/C4 Bedford, In,US
97/G2 Bedford, In,US
94/E4 Bedford, Va,US
97/J2 Bedford, Va,US
98/G4 Bedford Hills, NY,US
25/G2 Bedford Level (reg.), Eng,UK
99/Q16 Bedford Park, Il,US
25/F2 Bedfordshire (co.), Eng,UK
23/G1 Bedlington, Eng,UK
19/M6 Bedmond, Eng,UK
76/H4 Bedouaram (well), Niger
37/E5 Bedretto, Swi.
28/D2 Bedum, Neth.
24/C3 Bedwas, Wal,UK
25/E2 Bedworth, Eng,UK
73/C3 Beechworth, Austl.
31/E2 Beek, Neth.
29/F5 Beelen, Ger.
71/J5 Beenleigh, Austl.
72/D4 Beenleigh, Austl.
24/C5 Beer, Eng,UK
24/C5 Beer Head (pt.), Eng,UK
50/C4 Be'er Menuḥa, Isr.
52/C2 Be'er Menuḥa, Isr.
30/C1 Beernem, Belg.
50/C4 Beersheba, Isr.
52/B2 Beersheba, Isr.
49/D4 Beersheba (Be'er Sheva'), Isr.
77/M1 Be'er Sheva', Isr.
49/D4 Be'er Sheva' (Beersheba), Isr.
49/F8 Be'er Toviyya, Isr.
28/B6 Beerzel, Belg.
31/D1 Beerzel, Belg.
28/D6 Beesel, Neth.
31/F1 Beesel, Neth.
23/G6 Beeston, Eng,UK
101/F2 Beeville, Tx,US
89/G6 Beeville, Tx,US
96/D4 Beeville, Tx,US
77/K7 Befale, Zaire
81/J6 Befandriana, Madg.
71/H7 Bega, Austl.
73/D3 Bega, Austl.
29/F5 Bega (riv.), Ger.
62/C3 Begamganj, India
32/B2 Bégard, Fr.
45/K4 Begarslan (peak), Trkm.
40/E3 Bega Veche (riv.), Rom.
40/E3 Begejci, Yugo.
47/M2 Begichev (isl.), Rus.
22/B2 Beg, Lough (lake), NI,UK
20/D3 Begna (riv.), Nor.
44/D1 Begoml', Bela.
62/E2 Begusarai, India
107/H3 Béhague (pt.), FrG.
66/B4 Behala (str.), Indo.
46/F6 Behbahān, Iran
51/G4 Behbahān, Iran
52/F2 Behbahān, Iran
77/R1 Behbahān, Iran
31/F5 Behren-lès-Forbach, Fr.
51/H2 Behshahr, Iran
52/F1 Behshahr, Iran
46/K5 Bei (mts.), China
54/C3 Bei (mts.), China
54/E4 Bei (riv.), China
59/B5 Bei (riv.), China
61/F2 Bei (riv.), China
61/G3 Bei (riv.), China
61/H2 Bei (mtn.), China
47/N5 Bei'an, China
55/K2 Bei'an, China
54/F5 Beiba, China
54/D4 Beida (riv.), China
61/J3 Beigantang (isl.), Tai.
61/F4 Beihai, China
63/J3 Beihai, China
65/E1 Beihai, China
47/M6 Beijing (cap.), China
54/H4 Beijing (cap.), China
53/C3 Beijing (mun.), China
59/D3 Beijing (cap.), China
59/H6 Beijing (prov.), China
59/H7 Beijing (cap.), China
26/D2 Beilen, Neth.
28/D3 Beilen, Neth.
61/H4 Beiliu, China
63/K3 Beiliu, China
54/C5 Beilu (riv.), China
61/E4 Beilun (pass), China
65/D1 Beilun (pass), China
36/E3 Beinwil am See, Swi.
47/N5 Beipiao, China
55/J3 Beipiao, China
59/E2 Beipiao, China
82/F4 Beira, Moz.
63/K2 Beirong, China
59/C4 Beiru (riv.), China
77/N1 Beirut (cap.), Leb.
49/D3 Beirut (Bayrūt) (cap.), Leb.
50/C3 Beirut (Bayrūt) (cap.), Leb.
52/C2 Beirut (Bayrūt) (cap.), Leb.
54/D3 Beishan, China
82/E5 Beitbridge, Zim.
40/F2 Beiuș, Rom.
44/B3 Beiuș, Rom.
58/A2 Beizhen, China
59/E2 Beizhen, China
18/C5 Beja, Port.
34/A4 Beja (dist.), Port.
34/B3 Beja, Port.
75/T15 Bejaïa, Alg.
75/T15 Bejaïa (wilaya), Alg.
75/U17 Bejaïa, Alg.
75/U17 Bejaïa (gov.), Alg.
76/G1 Bejaïa, Alg.
18/C4 Béjar, Sp.
34/C2 Béjar, Sp.
53/J3 Bejhi (riv.), Pak.
49/D3 Bekaa (Al Biqā') (val.), Leb.
66/C5 Bekasi, Indo.
51/H1 Bekdash, Trkm.
40/E2 Békés, Hun.
40/E2 Békés (co.), Hun.
40/E2 Békéscsaba, Hun.
44/B3 Békéscsaba, Hun.
50/B2 Bekilli, Turk.
81/H8 Bekily, Madg.
79/E5 Bekwai, Gha.
62/B3 Bela, India
53/J3 Bela, Pak.
27/K4 Belá, Slvk.
40/E3 Bela Crkva, Yugo.
39/H1 Bela Palanka, Yugo.
40/F4 Bela Palanka, Yugo.
27/H3 Bělá pod Bezdězem, Czh.
33/L1 Bělá pod Bezdězem, Czh.
18/F3 Belarus
20/H5 Belarus
27/N2 Belarus
42/F5 Belarus
44/C1 Belarus
46/C4 Belarus
35/P10 Belas, Port.
107/G8 Bela Vista, Braz.
81/F2 Bela Vista, Moz.
108/B2 Bela Vista do Paraiso, Braz.
43/M5 Belaya (riv.), Rus.
45/L1 Belaya (riv.), Rus.
46/F4 Belaya (riv.), Rus.
45/G2 Belaya Kalitva, Rus.
41/L2 Belaya Krinitsa, Ukr.
44/D2 Belaya Tserkov', Ukr.
27/K3 Beł chatów, Pol.
36/D2 Belchen (peak), Ger.
84/J4 Belcher (isls.), Can.
87/H3 Belcher (isls.), NW,Can
87/S7 Belcher (chan.), NW,Can
35/E2 Belchite, Sp.
91/J3 Belcourt, ND,US
43/M5 Belebey, Rus.
45/K1 Belebey, Rus.
77/Q7 Beled Weyne, Som.
107/J4 Belém, Braz.
35/P10 Belem Tower, Port.
109/C2 Belén, Arg.
49/E1 Belen, Turk.
50/D2 Belen, Turk.
88/E5 Belen, NM,US
92/F4 Belen, NM,US
96/B3 Belen, NM,US
41/G4 Belene, Bul.
34/B1 Belesar (res.), Sp.
77/N5 Beles Wenz (riv.), Eth.
44/F1 Belev, Rus.
99/B2 Belfair, Wa,US
80/Q12 Belfast, SAfr.
18/C3 Belfast, NI,UK
22/C2 Belfast (cap.), NI,UK
22/C2 Belfast (dist.), NI,UK
95/G2 Belfast, Me,US
22/C2 Belfast Lough (inlet), NI,UK
36/D4 Belfaux, Swi.
91/H4 Belfield, ND,US
26/D5 Belfort, Fr.
33/G3 Belfort, Fr.
36/C2 Belfort, Fr.
36/C2 Belfort (dept.), Fr.
53/K5 Belgaum, India
62/B4 Belgaum, India
18/D3 Belgium
26/C3 Belgium
28/B6 Belgium
30/D3 Belgium
31/D3 Belgium
32/F1 Belgium
46/A4 Belgium
19/G3 Belgorod, Rus.
44/F2 Belgorod, Rus.
46/D4 Belgorod, Rus.
41/K2 Belgorod-Dnestrovskiy, Ukr.
44/D3 Belgorod-Dnestrovskiy, Ukr.
44/F2 Belgorod Obl., Rus.
90/F4 Belgrade, Mt,US
18/F4 Belgrade (cap.), Yugo.
40/E3 Belgrade (Beograd) (cap.), Yugo.
44/B3 Belgrade (Beograde) (cap.), Yugo.
39/G1 Beli Drim (riv.), Yugo.
40/E4 Beli Drim (riv.), Yugo.
51/G1 Belidzhi, Rus.
40/D3 Beli Manastir, Cro.
40/F4 Beli Timok (riv.), Yugo.
39/H2 Belitsa, Bul.
41/F5 Belitsa, Bul.
66/C4 Belitung (isl.), Indo.
101/H5 Belize
102/D2 Belize
84/J8 Belize
102/D2 Belize (riv.), Belz.
101/H5 Belize City, Belz.
102/D2 Belize City, Belz.
40/E3 Beljanica (peak), Yugo.
47/P2 Bel'kovskiy (isl.), Rus.
72/C4 Bell, Austl.
87/H2 Bell (pen.), NW,Can
87/J4 Bell (riv.), Qu,Can
94/E1 Bell (riv.), Qu,Can
98/B3 Bell, Ca,US
31/G3 Bell, Ger.
32/D3 Bellac, Fr.
90/B2 Bella Coola, BC,Can
22/B2 Bellaghy, NI,UK
37/F6 Bellagio, It.
37/F5 Bellano, It.
62/C4 Bellary, India
109/E2 Bella Vista, Arg.
38/A3 Bellavista (cape), It.
99/G6 Belle (riv.), Mi,US
99/G7 Belle (riv.), Mi,US
103/H2 Belle-Anse, Haiti
30/C5 Belleau, Fr.
22/B3 Belleek, NI,UK
94/D3 Bellefontaine, Oh,US
98/E6 Bellefonte, De,US
91/G4 Belle Fourche (riv.), SD, Wy,US
91/H4 Belle Fourche, SD,US
93/G1 Belle Fourche, SD,US
32/F3 Bellegarde-sur-Valserine, Fr.
36/B5 Bellegarde-sur-Valserine, Fr.
89/K6 Belle Glade, Fl,US
97/H5 Belle Glade, Fl,US
98/J8 Belle Haven, Va,US
32/B3 Belle-Ile (isl.), Fr.
84/M4 Belle Isle (str.), Can.
87/L3 Belle Isle (str.), Nf,Can
95/K1 Belle Isle (str.), Nf, Qu,Can
37/G1 Bellenberg, Ger.
72/B2 Bellenden Ker Nat'l Park, Austl.
32/E3 Bellerive-sur-Allier, Fr.
30/C5 Belleu, Fr.
87/J4 Belleville, On,Can
94/E2 Belleville, On,Can
89/J4 Belleville, Il,US
93/K3 Belleville, Il,US
94/B4 Belleville, Il,US
97/F2 Belleville, Il,US
93/H3 Belleville, Ks,US
96/D2 Belleville, Ks,US
99/E7 Belleville (lake), Mi,US
99/F7 Belleville, Mi,US
31/E5 Belleville-sur-Meuse, Fr.
99/C2 Bellevue, Wa,US
36/B6 Belley, Fr.
98/B3 Bellflower, Ca,US
36/B5 Bellignat, Fr.
20/D5 Bellinge, Den.
73/E1 Bellingen, Austl.
23/F1 Bellingham, Eng,UK
86/D4 Bellingham, Wa,US
88/B2 Bellingham, Wa,US
90/C3 Bellingham, Wa,US
97/F4 Bellingrath Gardens, Al,US
83/U Bellingshausen (sea), Ant.
69/K6 Bellingshausen (isl.), FrPol.
29/E2 Bellingwolde, Neth.
33/H3 Bellinzona, Swi.
37/F5 Bellinzona, Swi.
98/E6 Bellmawr, NJ,US
101/F2 Bellmead, Tx,US
106/C2 Bello, Col.
68/F7 Bellona (reefs), NCal.
86/G1 Bellot (str.), NW,Can
88/W13 Bellows A.F.B., Hi,US
98/H5 Bellport, NY,US
33/K3 Belluno, It.
109/D3 Bell Ville, Arg.
80/B4 Bellville, SAfr.
80/L10 Bellville, SAfr.
82/C7 Bellville, SAfr.
101/F2 Bellville, Tx,US
93/H5 Bellville, Tx,US
96/D4 Bellville, Tx,US
36/E5 Bellwald, Swi.
29/F4 Belm, Ger.
34/C3 Bélmez, Sp.
99/K11 Belmont, Ca,US
34/B2 Belmonte, Port.
34/D3 Belmonte, Sp.
101/H5 Belmopan (cap.), Belz.
102/D2 Belmopan (cap.), Belz.
21/H6 Belmullet, Ire.
30/C2 Beloeil, Belg.
95/P6 Beloeil, Qu,Can
47/N4 Belogorsk, Rus.
55/K1 Belogorsk, Rus.
40/F4 Belogradchik, Bul.
81/H9 Beloha, Madg.
107/K7 Belo Horizonte, Braz.
108/D1 Belo Horizonte, Braz.
93/H3 Beloit, Ks,US
96/D2 Beloit, Ks,US
89/J3 Beloit, Wi,US
91/L5 Beloit, Wi,US
93/K2 Beloit, Wi,US
94/B3 Beloit, Wi,US
107/L5 Belo Jardim, Braz.
42/G2 Belomorsk, Rus.
77/J8 Belondo-Kundu, Zaire
82/C1 Belondo-Kundu, Zaire
32/B5 Belorado, Sp.
34/D1 Belorado, Sp.
44/F3 Belorechensk, Rus.
19/J3 Beloretsk, Rus.
43/N5 Beloretsk, Rus.
45/L1 Beloretsk, Rus.
46/F4 Beloretsk, Rus.
40/E4 Beloševac, Yugo.
41/H4 Beloslav, Bul.
81/H7 Belo-Tsiribihina, Madg.
39/J1 Belovo, Bul.
41/G4 Belovo, Bul.
46/J4 Belovo, Rus.
42/H3 Beloye (lake), Rus.
46/D3 Beloye (lake), Rus.
23/G5 Belper, Eng,UK
23/G1 Belsay, Eng,UK
90/F4 Belt, Mt,US
28/D3 Belterwijde (lake), Neth.
31/G3 Beltheim, Ger.
25/H1 Belton, Eng,UK
93/H5 Belton, Tx,US
96/D4 Belton, Tx,US
98/K7 Beltsville, Md,US
18/F4 Bel'tsy, Mol.
41/H2 Bel'tsy, Mol.
44/C3 Bel'tsy, Mol.
46/C5 Bel'tsy, Mol.
98/E5 Beltzville (lake), Pa,US
46/J5 Belukha (peak), Rus.
54/B2 Belukha (peak), Rus.
67/E2 Beluran, Malay.
99/K11 Belvedere, Ca,US
91/L5 Belvidere, Il,US
94/B3 Belvidere, Il,US
98/E5 Belvidere, NJ,US
71/H4 Belyando (riv.), Austl.
72/B3 Belyando (riv.), Austl.
41/K2 Belyayevka, Ukr.
46/G2 Belyy (isl.), Rus.
27/N3 Belz, Ukr.
26/G2 Belzig, Ger.
27/M3 Bełżyce, Pol.
81/H7 Bemaraha (plat.), Madg.
81/H7 Bemarivo (riv.), Madg.
34/B1 Bembibre, Sp.
73/D3 Bemboka, Austl.
25/E5 Bembridge, Eng,UK
86/G4 Bemidji, Mn,US
89/H2 Bemidji, Mn,US
91/K4 Bemidji, Mn,US
28/C5 Bemmel, Neth.
23/H3 Bempton, Eng,UK
35/F1 Benabarre, Sp.
73/C3 Benalla, Austl.
34/C4 Benalmádena, Sp.
34/C2 Benavente, Sp.
96/D5 Benavides, Tx,US
22/B1 Benbane Head (pt.), NI,UK
73/D3 Ben Boyd Nat'l Park, Austl.
22/B3 Benburb, NI,UK
86/D4 Bend, Or,US
88/B3 Bend, Or,US
90/C4 Bend, Or,US
101/F2 Bend, Tx,US
79/G5 Bendel (state), Nga.
85/F2 Bendeleben (mt.), Ak,US
73/D1 Bendemeer, Austl.
77/R6 Bender Beyla, Som.
77/Q5 Bender Cassim, Som.
18/F4 Bendery, Mol.
41/J2 Bendery, Mol.
44/D3 Bendery, Mol.
71/G7 Bendigo, Austl.
73/C3 Bendigo, Austl.
49/F7 Bene Beraq, Isr.
87/L3 Benedict (mtn.), Nf,Can
37/H2 Benediktbeuern, Ger.
26/F5 Benediktenwand (peak), Ger.
37/H2 Benediktenwand (peak), Ger.
22/D1 Beneraid (hill), Sc,UK
27/H4 Benešov, Czh.
33/L2 Benešov, Czh.
38/D2 Benevento, It.
40/B5 Benevento, It.
36/D1 Benfeld, Fr.
25/G3 Benfleet, Eng,UK
48/H8 Bengal (bay), Asia
62/E4 Bengal (bay), Asia
64/H3 Bengal (bay), Asia
60/B5 Bengal (bay), Burma
55/H5 Bengbu, China
59/D4 Bengbu, China
77/K1 Benghāzī, Libya
65/D3 Ben Giang, Viet.
66/B3 Bengkalis, Indo.
66/B3 Bengkalis (isl.), Indo.
56/C3 Bengkayang, Indo.
66/B4 Bengkulu, Indo.
91/G3 Bengough, Sk,Can
20/E4 Bengtsfors, Swe.
82/B3 Benguela, Ang.
82/F3 Bengweulu (lake), Zam.
105/C4 Beni (riv.), Bol.
106/E6 Beni (riv.), Bol.
77/L7 Beni, Zaire
76/E1 Beni Abbes, Alg.
35/F2 Benicarló, Sp.
99/K10 Benicia, Ca,US
35/E3 Benidorm, Sp.
35/E3 Benifayó, Sp.
35/E3 Benigánim, Sp.
76/D1 Beni Mellal, Mor.
74/C3 Benin
76/F5 Benin
79/F4 Benin
76/F6 Benin (bight), Afr.
79/F5 Benin (bight), Ben., Nga.
74/C4 Benin, Bight of (bay), Afr.
76/G6 Benin City, Nga.
79/G5 Benin City, Nga.
76/E1 Beni Ounif, Alg.
35/F3 Benisa, Sp.
100/E4 Benito Juárez, Mex.
93/H4 Benjamin, Tx,US
96/D3 Benjamin, Tx,US
106/D4 Benjamin Constant, Braz.
100/C2 Benjamín Hill, Mex.
92/E5 Benjamín Hill, Mex
93/G2 Benkelman, Ne,US
22/D5 Benllech, Wal,UK
73/C4 Ben Lomond Nat'l Park, Austl.
22/C1 Bennane Head (pt.), Sc,UK
47/R2 Bennett (isl.), Rus.
97/J3 Bennettsville, SC,US
18/C3 Ben Nevis (mtn.), Sc,UK
95/F3 Bennington, Vt,US
80/Q13 Benoni, SAfr.
81/J6 Be, Nosy (isl.), Madg.
82/K9 Be, Nosy (isl.), Madg.
76/H6 Bénoue Nat'l Park, Camr.
61/E5 Ben Quang, Viet.
63/J4 Ben Quang, Viet.
65/D2 Ben Quang, Viet.
99/Q16 Bensenville, Il,US
26/E4 Bensheim, Ger.
33/H2 Bensheim, Ger.
100/C2 Benson, Az,US
88/D5 Benson, Az,US
92/E5 Benson, Az,US
91/K4 Benson, Mn,US
23/F3 Bentham, Eng,UK
29/E4 Bentheim, Ger.
60/E5 Ben Thuy, Viet.
77/L6 Bentiu, Sudan
23/G4 Bentley, Eng,UK
108/B4 Bento Gonçalves, Braz.
93/J4 Benton, Ar,US
96/E3 Benton, Ar,US
94/B4 Benton, Il,US
97/F2 Benton, Il,US
94/B4 Benton, Ky,US
97/F2 Benton, Ky,US
66/B3 Bentong, Malay.
94/C3 Benton Harbor, Mi,US
93/J3 Bentonville, Ar,US
96/E2 Bentonville, Ar,US
63/J5 Ben Tre, Viet.
65/D4 Ben Tre, Viet.
76/G6 Benue (riv.), Nga.
79/G4 Benue (riv.), Nga.
79/G5 Benue (state), Nga.
47/N5 Benxi, China
55/J3 Benxi, China
58/B2 Benxi, China
58/C2 Benxi, China
59/E2 Benxi, China
67/G3 Beo, Indo.
40/D3 Beočin, Yugo.
40/E3 Beograd (Belgrade) (cap.), Yugo.
44/B3 Beograd (Belgrade) (cap.), Yugo.
55/L5 Beppu, Japan
56/B4 Beppu, Japan
56/B4 Beppu (bay), Japan
104/F4 Bequia (isl.), StV.
76/E1 Beraber (well), Alg.
22/A2 Beragh, NI,UK
39/F2 Berat, Alb.
40/D5 Berat, Alb.
67/E4 Beratus (peak), Indo.
67/E3 Berau (riv.), Indo.
67/H4 Berau (bay), Indo.
68/C5 Berau (bay), Indo.
37/F5 Berbenno di Valtellina, It.
77/Q5 Berbera, Som.
76/J7 Berberati, CAfr.
106/G2 Berbice (riv.), Guy.
28/B6 Berchem, Belg.
30/D1 Berchem, Belg.
36/C4 Bercher, Swi.
33/K3 Berchtesgaden, Ger.
40/A2 Berchtesgaden, Ger.
33/K3 Berchtesgaden Nat'l Park, Ger.
25/H6 Berck, Fr.
30/A3 Berck, Fr.
32/D1 Berck, Fr.
18/F4 Berdichev, Ukr.
44/D2 Berdichev, Ukr.
46/C5 Berdichev, Ukr.
31/F4 Berdorf, Lux.
46/J4 Berdsk, Rus.
19/G4 Berdyansk, Ukr.
44/F3 Berdyansk, Ukr.
94/C4 Berea, Ky,US
97/G2 Berea, Ky,US
41/G1 Beregomet, Ukr.
27/M4 Beregovo, Ukr.
40/F1 Beregovo, Ukr.
44/B2 Beregovo, Ukr.
81/H8 Bereketa, Madg.
79/E5 Berekum, Gha.
52/C4 Berenice (ruins), Egypt
77/N3 Berenice (ruins), Egypt
24/D5 Bere Regis, Eng,UK
95/H2 Beresford, Can
91/J5 Beresford, SD,US
93/H2 Beresford, SD,US
41/H2 Bereşti, Rom.
40/E2 Berettyó (riv.), Hun.
27/L5 Berettyóújfalu, Hun.
40/E2 Berettyóújfalu, Hun.
81/H7 Berevo, Madg.
42/F5 Berezina (riv.), Bela.
44/D1 Berezina (riv.), Bela.
44/D1 Berezino, Bela.
18/H2 Bereznik, Rus.
46/E3 Bereznik, Rus.
19/J3 Berezniki, Rus.
43/N4 Berezniki, Rus.
46/F4 Berezniki, Rus.
41/K2 Berezovka, Ukr.
46/G3 Berezovo, Rus.
31/H6 Berg, Ger.
37/H2 Berg, Ger.
31/F4 Berg, Lux.
80/B4 Berg (riv.), SAfr.
80/L10 Berg (riv.), SAfr.
37/F2 Berg, Swi.
44/C5 Bergama, Turk.
50/A2 Bergama, Turk.
37/F6 Bergamasque Alps (mts.), It.
33/H4 Bergamo, It.
37/F6 Bergamo (prov.), It.
37/F2 Bergatruete, Ger.
26/E2 Bergen, Ger.
27/G1 Bergen, Ger.
29/G3 Bergen, Ger.
28/B3 Bergen, Neth.
98/F5 Bergen (co.), NJ,US
18/D2 Bergen, Nor.
20/C3 Bergen, Nor.
46/A3 Bergen, Nor.
29/G3 Bergen-Belsen, Ger.
98/F5 Bergenfield, NJ,US
28/B6 Bergen op Zoom, Neth.
32/D4 Bergerac, Fr.
28/C6 Bergeyk, Neth.
31/F2 Bergheim, Ger.
26/D3 Bergisch Gladbach, Ger.
29/E6 Bergisch Gladbach, Ger.
31/G2 Bergisch Gladbach, Ger.
29/E5 Bergkamen, Ger.
42/D2 Bergnäset, Swe.
29/E6 Bergneustadt, Ger.
31/G1 Bergneustadt, Ger.
26/F4 Bergrheinfeld, Ger.
93/H5 Bergstrom (A.F.B.), Tx,US
96/D4 Bergstrom (A.F.B.), Tx,US
20/G2 Bergsviken, Swe.
42/D2 Bergsviken, Swe.
75/N13 Berguent, Mor.
30/B2 Bergues, Fr.
26/D2 Bergum, Neth.
28/C2 Bergum, Neth.
28/D2 Bergumermeer (lake), Neth.
37/F4 Bergün-Bravuogn, Swi.
54/G2 Berh, Mong.
62/D4 Berhampur, India
66/C4 Berikat (cape), Indo.
84/A2 Bering (str.), NAm., Asia
84/A3 Bering (sea), NAm., Asia
47/S4 Bering (isl.), Rus.
47/V3 Bering (str.), US.,Rus.
85/D3 Bering (sea), Rus., Ak,US
85/E3 Bering (str.), Rus., Ak,US
26/C3 Beringen, Belg.
28/C6 Beringen, Belg.
31/E1 Beringen, Belg.
85/E2 Bering Land Bridge Nat'l Prsv., Ak,US
41/L2 Berislav, Ukr.
66/B4 Beritarikap (cape), Indo.
34/D4 Berja, Sp.
26/D3 Berkel (riv.), Ger.
28/D4 Berkel (riv.), Ger.
28/B5 Berkel, Neth.
24/D3 Berkeley, Eng,UK
88/B4 Berkeley, Ca,US
92/B3 Berkeley, Ca,US
99/K11 Berkeley, Ca,US
19/M6 Berkhamsted, Eng,UK
25/F3 Berkhamsted, Eng,UK
37/G1 Berkheim, Ger.
28/C3 Berkhout, Neth.
99/F6 Berkley, Mi,US
83/W Berkner (isl.), Ant.
39/H1 Berkovitsa, Bul.
41/F4 Berkovitsa, Bul.
19/M7 Berkshire (co.), Eng,UK
25/E4 Berkshire (co.), Eng,UK
25/E4 Berkshire Downs (uplands), Eng,UK
30/C3 Berlaimont, Fr.
34/D2 Berlanga de Duero, Sp.
28/B6 Berlare, Belg.
30/C1 Berlare, Belg.
28/C5 Berlicum, Neth.
18/E3 Berlin (cap.), Ger.
27/G2 Berlin (cap.), Ger.
46/B4 Berlin (cap.), Ger.
87/J4 Berlin, NH,US
89/M3 Berlin, NH,US
95/G2 Berlin, NH,US
98/F6 Berlin, NJ,US
91/L5 Berlin, Wi,US
94/B3 Berlin, Wi,US
83/V Berlioz (pt.), Ant.
73/D3 Bermagui, Austl.
105/C5 Bermejo (riv.), Arg.
106/F8 Bermejo, Bol.
109/D1 Bermejo, Bol.
32/B5 Bermeo, Sp.
34/D1 Bermeo, Sp.
34/B2 Bermillo de Sayago, Sp.
89/N5 Bermuda (isl.), Berm.
84/L6 Bermuda (isl.), UK
18/D4 Bern (cap.), Swi.
33/G3 Bern (cap.), Swi.
36/D3 Bern (canton), Swi.
36/D4 Bern (cap.), Swi.
106/B5 Bernal, Peru
38/E2 Bernalda, It.
40/C5 Bernalda, It.
88/E4 Bernalillo, NM,US
92/F4 Bernalillo, NM,US
96/B3 Bernalillo, NM,US
86/D1 Bernard (riv.), NW,Can
109/B6 Bernardo O'Higgins Nat'l Park, Chile
36/E2 Bernau, Ger.
32/D2 Bernay, Fr.
37/G2 Bernbeuren, Ger.
26/F3 Bernburg, Ger.
29/F2 Berne (riv.), Ger.
33/G3 Bernese Alps (range), Swi.
36/D5 Bernese Alps (mts.), Swi.
19/S9 Bernes-sur-Oise, Fr.
70/A4 Bernier (isl.), Austl.
86/G1 Bernier (bay), NW,Can
37/F5 Bernina (mts.), It., Swi.
33/H3 Bernina (peak), Swi.
37/G5 Bernina, Passo del (pass), Swi.
37/F5 Bernina, Piz (peak), Swi.
30/C3 Bernissart, Belg.
31/G4 Bernkastel-Kues, Ger.
36/E3 Beromünster, Swi.
81/H8 Beroroha, Madg.
27/H4 Beroun, Czh.
33/L2 Beroun, Czh.
27/G4 Berounka (riv.), Czh.
33/K2 Berounka (riv.), Czh.
39/H2 Berovo, Macd.
40/F5 Berovo, Macd.
32/F5 Berre (lag.), Fr.
70/G6 Berri, Austl.
73/B2 Berri, Austl.
73/D3 Berridale, Austl.
24/C1 Berriew, Wal,UK
73/C2 Berrigan, Austl.
102/C2 Berriozábal, Mex.
75/S15 Berrouaghia, Alg.
73/D2 Berry, Austl.
104/B1 Berry (isls.), Bahm.
32/D3 Berry (hist. reg.), Fr.
99/K9 Berryessa (lake), Ca,US
99/K9 Berryessa (peak), Ca,US
24/C6 Berry Head (pt.), UK
32/B1 Berry Head (pt.), UK
93/J3 Berryville, Ar,US
96/E2 Berryville, Ar,US
29/E3 Bersenbrück, Ger.
41/J1 Bershad', Ukr.
31/E3 Bertogne, Belg.
76/H7 Bertoua, Camr.
26/C4 Bertrix, Belg.
31/E4 Bertrix, Belg.
32/F2 Bertrix, Belg.
30/C3 Bertry, Fr.
68/G5 Beru (atoll), Kiri.
66/D3 Beruit (isl.), Malay.
73/G5 Berwick, Austl.
95/H2 Berwick, Can
94/E3 Berwick, Pa,US
21/D3 Berwick-upon-Tweed, Eng.,UK
22/E6 Berwyn (mts.), Wal,UK
99/Q16 Berwyn, Il,US
98/E5 Berwyn-Devon, Pa,US
40/C2 Berzence, Hun.
32/E4 Bès (riv.), Fr.
81/H7 Besalampy, Madg.
18/D4 Besançon, Fr.
32/G3 Besançon, Fr.
36/C3 Besançon, Fr.
67/E4 Besar (peak), Indo.
32/E3 Besbre (riv.), Fr.
46/F6 Beshahr, Iran
53/F3 Beshneh, Iran
50/E2 Beşiri, Turk.
40/E3 Beška, Yugo.
27/K4 Beskids (mts.), Pol.
45/H4 Beslan, Rus.
39/H1 Besna Kobila (peak), Yugo.
40/F4 Besna Kobila (peak), Yugo.
44/B4 Besna Kobila (peak), Yugo.
91/G3 Besnard (lake), Sk,Can
50/D2 Besni, Turk.
23/G4 Bessacarr, Eng,UK
19/S9 Bessancourt, Fr.
41/J2 Bessarabia (reg.), Mol.
22/B3 Bessbrook, NI,UK
89/J5 Bessemer, Al,US
97/G3 Bessemer, Al,US
91/L4 Bessemer, Mi,US
94/B2 Bessemer, Mi,US
99/D2 Bessemer (mtn.), Wa,US
45/K3 Besshoky, Gora (peak), Kaz.
32/D3 Bessines-sur-Gartempe, Fr.
28/C6 Best, Neth.
101/E2 Best, Tx,US
29/F6 Bestwig, Ger.
22/B4 Betaghstown, Ire.
81/H7 Betanantanana, Madg.
34/A1 Betanzos, Sp.
75/M14 Beth (riv.), Mor.
81/E2 Bethal, SAfr.
49/G6 Beth Alpha Synagogue Nat'l Park, Isr.
80/B2 Bethanie, Namb.
82/C6 Bethanie, Namb.
80/P12 Bethanie, SAfr.
99/L11 Bethany (res.), Ca,US
93/J2 Bethany, Mo,US
96/E1 Bethany, Mo,US

84/A3 **Bethel,** US
85/F3 **Bethel,** Ak,US
99/L10 **Bethel Island,** Ca,US
30/D5 **Bétheniville,** Fr.
30/D5 **Bétheny,** Fr.
32/F2 **Bétheny,** Fr.
22/D5 **Bethesda,** Wal,UK
94/E4 **Bethesda,** Md,US
97/J2 **Bethesda,** Md,US
98/J8 **Bethesda,** Md,US
30/B5 **Béthisy-Sainte-Pierre,** Fr.
80/E3 **Bethlehem,** SAfr.
82/E6 **Bethlehem,** SAfr.
94/F3 **Bethlehem,** Pa,US
98/E5 **Bethlehem,** Pa,US
98/E5 **Bethlehem-Allentown-Easton** (arpt.), Pa,US
49/D4 **Bethlehem** (Bayt Laḩm), WBnk.
49/G8 **Bethlehem** (Bayt Laḩm), WBnk.
36/C2 **Bethoncourt,** Fr.
98/G5 **Bethpage,** NY,US
80/D3 **Bethulie,** SAfr.
91/G3 **Bethune,** Sk,Can
26/B3 **Béthune,** Fr.
30/A4 **Béthune** (riv.), Fr.
30/B2 **Béthune,** Fr.
32/D2 **Béthune** (riv.), Fr.
32/E1 **Béthune,** Fr.
108/C1 **Betim,** Braz.
81/H8 **Betioky,** Madg.
72/A4 **Betoota,** Austl.
46/G5 **Betpak-Dala** (des.), Kaz.
81/H8 **Betroka,** Madg.
31/G6 **Betschdorf,** Fr.
49/D3 **Bet She'an,** Isr.
49/F8 **Bet Shemesh,** Isr.
87/J3 **Betsiamites** (riv.), Qu,Can
95/G1 **Betsiamites** (riv.), Qu,Can
81/H7 **Betsiboka** (riv.), Madg.
31/D6 **Bettancourt-la-Ferrée,** Fr.
74/D2 **Bette** (peak), Libya
77/J3 **Bette** (peak), Libya
31/F4 **Bettembourg,** Lux.
62/D2 **Bettiah,** India
36/D3 **Bettlach,** Swi.
85/H2 **Bettles,** Ak,US
62/C3 **Betūl,** India
28/C5 **Betuwe** (reg.), Neth.
22/E5 **Betws-y-Coed,** Wal,UK
31/G2 **Betzdorf,** Ger.
91/H4 **Beulah,** ND,US
99/P14 **Beulah** (lake), Wi,US
28/D3 **Beulakerwijde** (lake), Neth.
25/G4 **Beult** (riv.), Eng,UK
28/C5 **Beuningen,** Neth.
36/C3 **Beure,** Fr.
32/D3 **Beuvron** (riv.), Fr.
19/U10 **Beuvronne** (riv.), Fr.
30/B2 **Beuvry,** Fr.
26/F2 **Bevensen,** Ger.
29/H2 **Bevensen,** Ger.
29/E4 **Bever** (riv.), Ger.
26/C3 **Beveren,** Belg.
28/B6 **Beveren,** Belg.
30/D1 **Beveren,** Belg.
37/F4 **Beverin, Piz** (peak), Swi.
23/H4 **Beverley,** Eng,UK
90/B2 **Beverly Hills,** Ca,US
99/F6 **Beverly Hills,** Mi,US
29/F2 **Beverstedt,** Ger.
29/G5 **Beverungen,** Ger.
26/C2 **Beverwijk,** Neth.
28/B4 **Beverwijk,** Neth.
23/F1 **Bewcastle,** Eng,UK
24/D2 **Bewdley,** Eng,UK
25/G4 **Bewl Bridge** (res.), Eng,UK
33/G3 **Bex,** Swi.
36/D5 **Bex,** Swi.
31/G5 **Bexbach,** Ger.
25/G5 **Bexhill,** Eng,UK
19/P7 **Bexley** (bor.), Eng,UK
41/J5 **Beykoz,** Turk.
76/D6 **Beyla,** Gui.
51/N6 **Beylerbeyi Palace,** Turk.
52/D6 **Bēylul,** Eth.
31/E2 **Beyne-Heusay,** Belg.
46/F5 **Beyneu,** Kaz.
51/M6 **Beyoğlu,** Turk.
41/K5 **Beypazarı,** Turk.
44/D4 **Beypazarı,** Turk.
50/B1 **Beypazarı,** Turk.
64/E3 **Beypore,** India
64/F3 **Beypore** (riv.), India
50/B2 **Beyşehir,** Turk.
50/B2 **Beyşehir** (lake), Turk.
81/H8 **Bezaha,** Madg.
40/D3 **Bezdan,** Yugo.
27/H3 **Bezděz** (peak), Czh.
33/L1 **Bezděz** (peak), Czh.
42/H4 **Bezhetsk,** Rus.
51/F1 **Bezhta,** Rus.
18/D4 **Béziers,** Fr.
32/E5 **Béziers,** Fr.
35/G1 **Béziers,** Fr.
46/F6 **Bezmein,** Trkm.
53/G1 **Bezmein,** Trkm.
62/D2 **Bhabua,** India
64/C2 **Bhadaur,** India
62/E3 **Bhadrak,** India
53/L6 **Bhadrāvati,** India
62/C5 **Bhadrāvati,** India
62/A3 **Bhadreswar,** India
62/E2 **Bhāgalpur,** India
64/B2 **Bhāi Pheru,** Pak.
53/K2 **Bhakkar,** Pak.
64/A2 **Bhakkar,** Pak.
64/D2 **Bhākra** (dam), India
62/E2 **Bhaktapur,** Nepal
64/B1 **Bhalwāl,** Pak.
60/C3 **Bhamo,** Burma
63/G3 **Bhamo,** Burma
53/L3 **Bhārātpur,** India
62/C2 **Bhārātpur,** India
60/B3 **Bhareli** (riv.), India
53/K4 **Bharuch,** India
62/B3 **Bharuch,** India
62/D3 **Bhātāpāra,** India
53/K2 **Bhatinda,** India
64/C2 **Bhatinda,** India
53/K6 **Bhatkal,** India
62/B5 **Bhatkal,** India
62/E3 **Bhātpāra,** India
62/C5 **Bhavāni,** India
64/F3 **Bhavāni,** India
64/F3 **Bhavāni** (riv.), India
53/K4 **Bhavnagar,** India
62/B3 **Bhavnagar,** India
64/B2 **Bhawāna,** Pak.
53/L4 **Bhawāni Mandi,** India
62/C3 **Bhawāni Mandi,** India
62/D4 **Bhawānipatna,** India
64/B1 **Bhera,** Pak.
62/D3 **Bhilai,** India
53/K3 **Bhīlwāra,** India
62/B2 **Bhīlwāra,** India
53/L5 **Bhīma** (riv.), India
62/C4 **Bhīma** (riv.), India
62/D4 **Bhīmavaram,** India
62/D4 **Bhimunipatnam,** India
62/C2 **Bhind,** India
53/K4 **Bhīnmāl,** India
62/B3 **Bhīnmāl,** India
53/K5 **Bhiwandi,** India
62/B4 **Bhiwandi,** India
62/E2 **Bhojpur,** Nepal
62/C3 **Bhopāl,** India
53/K5 **Bhor,** India
62/B4 **Bhor,** India
62/E3 **Bhuban,** India
62/E3 **Bhubaneswar,** India
53/J4 **Bhūj,** India
62/A3 **Bhūj,** India
60/C5 **Bhumibol** (dam), Thai.
65/B2 **Bhumibol** (dam), Thai.
53/L4 **Bhusawal,** India
62/C3 **Bhusawal,** India
48/H7 **Bhutan**
60/A3 **Bhutan**
62/E2 **Bhutan**
64/G3 **Bhuvanagiri,** India
54/D5 **Bi** (riv.), China
106/E4 **Biá** (riv.), Braz.
78/E5 **Bia** (riv.), Gui., IvC.
30/B3 **Biache-Saint-Vaast,** Fr.
74/C4 **Biafra** (gulf), Afr.
76/G7 **Biafra** (bight), Afr.
79/G5 **Biafra** (bight), Nga.
67/J4 **Biak** (isl.), Indo.
27/M2 **Biała Podlaska,** Pol.
27/M3 **Biała Podlaska** (prov.), Pol.
44/B1 **Biała Podlaska,** Pol.
27/L3 **Białobrzegi,** Pol.
27/J2 **Białogard,** Pol.
27/K4 **Białowieski Nat'l Park,** Pol.
18/F3 **Białystok,** Pol.
27/M2 **Białystok,** Pol.
27/M2 **Białystok** (prov.), Pol.
42/D5 **Białystok,** Pol.
44/B1 **Białystok,** Pol.
46/C4 **Białystok,** Pol.
33/J3 **Bianca** (peak), It.
38/D4 **Biancavilla,** It.
77/L7 **Biaro,** Zaire
32/C5 **Biarritz,** Fr.
34/E1 **Biarritz,** Fr.
33/H3 **Biasca,** Swi.
37/E5 **Biasca,** Swi.
50/B4 **Bibā,** Egypt
52/B3 **Bibā,** Egypt
36/E1 **Biberach,** Ger.
37/G1 **Biberach,** Ger.
37/F1 **Biberach an der Riss,** Ger.
36/D3 **Biberist,** Swi.
60/A3 **Bibiyana** (riv.), Bang., India
41/H2 **Bicaz,** Rom.
25/E3 **Bicester,** Eng,UK
73/D4 **Bicheno,** Austl.
70/F2 **Bickerton** (isl.), Austl.
40/D2 **Bicske,** Hun.
76/G6 **Bida,** Nga.
78/D5 **Bidaga** (rapids), IvC.
62/C4 **Bīdar,** India
95/G3 **Biddeford,** Me,US
49/D3 **Biddiyā,** WBnk.
49/G7 **Biddiyā,** WBnk.
49/G8 **Biddū,** WBnk.
23/F5 **Biddulph,** Eng,UK
24/B4 **Bideford,** Eng,UK
24/B4 **Bideford** (Barnstaple) (bay), Eng,UK
25/E2 **Bidford on Avon,** Eng,UK
51/J3 **Bīdokht,** Iran
53/G2 **Bīdokht,** Iran
65/E3 **Bi Doup** (peak), Viet.
66/C1 **Bi Doup** (peak), Viet.
35/E1 **Bidouze** (riv.), Fr.
82/B4 **Bíe** (plat.), Ang.
27/M2 **Biebzra** (riv.), Pol.
33/G3 **Biel,** Swi.
36/D3 **Biel,** Swi.
27/J3 **Bielawa,** Pol.
26/E2 **Bielefeld,** Ger.
29/F4 **Bielefeld,** Ger.
87/J1 **Bieler** (lake), NW,Can
36/D3 **Bieler** (lake), Swi.
27/K4 **Bielsko** (prov.), Pol.
18/E4 **Bielsko-Biała,** Pol.
27/K4 **Bielsko-Biała,** Pol.
44/A2 **Bielsko-Biała,** Pol.
27/M2 **Bielsk Podlaski,** Pol.
42/D5 **Bielsk Podlaski,** Pol.
44/B1 **Bielsk Podlaski,** Pol.
26/F2 **Bienenbüttel,** Ger.
29/H2 **Bienenbüttel,** Ger.
63/J5 **Bien Hoa,** Viet.
65/D4 **Bien Hoa,** Viet.
66/C1 **Bien Hoa,** Viet.
36/B5 **Bienne** (riv.), Fr.
37/G6 **Bienno,** It.
63/J3 **Bien Son,** Viet.
65/D1 **Bien Son,** Viet.
87/J3 **Bienville** (lake), Qu,Can
36/C4 **Bière,** Swi.
28/D2 **Bierum,** Neth.
27/J3 **Bierutów,** Pol.
28/B5 **Biesbosch** (reg.), Neth.
36/B1 **Biesles,** Fr.
28/D5 **Biesme** (riv.), Fr.
33/G3 **Bietschhorn** (peak), Swi.
36/D5 **Bietschhorn** (peak), Swi.
31/E4 **Bièvre,** Belg.
19/S10 **Bièvre** (riv.), Fr.
19/S10 **Bièvres,** Fr.
38/D2 **Biferno** (riv.), It.
73/B2 **Big** (des.), Austl.
86/D1 **Big** (riv.), NW,Can
87/J2 **Big** (isl.), NW,Can
99/E6 **Big** (lake), Mi,US
41/H5 **Biga,** Turk.
44/C4 **Biga,** Turk.
50/A1 **Biga,** Turk.
44/D5 **Bigadiç,** Turk.
50/B2 **Bigadiç,** Turk.
106/F4 **Big Belt** (mts.), Mt,US
99/P14 **Big Bend,** Wi,US
100/E2 **Big Bend Nat'l Park,** Tx,US
88/F6 **Big Bend Nat'l Park,** Tx,US
93/G5 **Big Bend Nat'l Park,** Tx,US
96/C4 **Big Bend Nat'l Park,** Tx,US
93/K4 **Big Black** (riv.), Ms,US
24/C6 **Bigbury** (bay), Eng,UK
85/D2 **Big Diomede** (isl.), Rus.
91/K4 **Big Fork** (riv.), Mn,US
86/F3 **Biggar,** Sk,Can
90/G2 **Biggar,** Sk,Can
31/G1 **Biggasee** (lake), Ger.
70/D2 **Bigge** (isl.), Austl.
29/E6 **Bigge** (riv.), Ger.
31/G2 **Bigge** (riv.), Ger.
72/D4 **Biggenden,** Austl.
29/E6 **Biggesee** (res.), Ger.
19/P8 **Biggin Hill,** Eng,UK
25/F2 **Biggleswade,** Eng,UK
80/D3 **Big Hole,** SAfr.
90/E4 **Big Hole** (riv.), Mt,US
90/F4 **Bighorn** (lake), Mt, Wy,US
90/G4 **Bighorn** (mts.), Mt, Wy,US
90/G4 **Bighorn** (riv.), Mt, Wy,US
88/E3 **Bighorn** (riv.), Mt, Wy,US
88/E3 **Bighorn** (mts.), Wy,US
92/E1 **Bighorn** (basin), Wy,US
92/F1 **Bighorn** (mts.), Wy,US
92/F1 **Bighorn** (riv.), Wy,US
86/F4 **Bighorn** (riv.), Mt,Wy,US
86/F4 **Bighorn Canyon Nat'l Rec. Area,** Mt,US
104/C1 **Bight, The,** Bahm.
93/G5 **Big Lake,** Tx,US
96/C4 **Big Lake,** Tx,US
92/D2 **Big Lost** (riv.), Id,US
99/P14 **Big Muskego** (lake), Wi,US
76/B5 **Bignona,** Sen.
78/A3 **Bignona,** Sen.
94/C3 **Big Rapids,** Mi,US
90/G2 **Big River,** Sk,Can
99/N16 **Big Rock,** Il,US
99/N16 **Big Rock** (cr.), Il,US
92/E2 **Big Sandy** (riv.), Wy,US
91/J5 **Big Sioux** (riv.), Ia, SD,US
101/E1 **Big Spring,** Tx,US
88/F5 **Big Spring,** Tx,US
93/G4 **Big Spring,** Tx,US
96/C3 **Big Spring,** Tx,US
91/J4 **Big Stone** (lake), Mn, SD,US
94/D4 **Big Stone Gap,** Va,US
97/H2 **Big Stone Gap,** Va,US
90/F4 **Big Timber,** Mt,US
91/L2 **Big Trout** (lake), On,Can
86/H3 **Big Trout** (lake), On,Can
108/B3 **Biguaçu,** Braz.
92/D2 **Big Wood** (riv.), Id,US
33/L4 **Bihać,** Yugo.
40/B3 **Bihać,** Yugo.
62/D3 **Bihār** (state), India
62/E2 **Bihār,** India
82/F1 **Biharamulo,** Tanz.
40/E2 **Biharkeresztes,** Hun.
27/M5 **Bihor** (co.), Rom.
40/F2 **Bihor** (co.), Rom.
30/A4 **Bihorel,** Fr.
32/D2 **Bihorel,** Fr.
74/A3 **Bijagós** (arch.), GBis.
76/B5 **Bijagos** (isls.), GBis.
78/A4 **Bijagos** (isls.), GBis.
53/L5 **Bijāpur,** India
62/C4 **Bijāpur,** India
51/F3 **Bījār,** Iran
52/E1 **Bījār,** Iran
40/D3 **Bijeljina,** Bosn.
39/F1 **Bijelo Polje,** Yugo.
40/D4 **Bijelo Polje,** Yugo.
61/H3 **Bijia** (mtn.), China
60/C3 **Bijiang,** China
63/G2 **Bijiang,** China
55/H4 **Bijiaquan,** China
60/E3 **Bijie,** China
63/J2 **Bijie,** China
62/C2 **Bijnor,** India
53/K3 **Bikampur,** India
53/K3 **Bīkaner,** India
62/B2 **Bīkaner,** India
68/G3 **Bikar** (atoll), Mrsh.
47/P5 **Bikin,** Rus.
55/L2 **Bikin,** Rus.
55/M2 **Bikin** (riv.), Rus.
68/F3 **Bikini** (atoll), Mrsh.
82/C4 **Bikuar Nat'l Park,** Moz.
62/D3 **Bilāspur,** India
63/G5 **Bilaukraung** (range), Burma
65/B3 **Bilauktaung** (range), Burma, Thai.
70/G5 **Bilba Morea Claypan** (lake), Austl.
18/C4 **Bilbao,** Sp.
32/B5 **Bilbao,** Sp.
34/D1 **Bilbao,** Sp.
49/B4 **Bilbays,** Egypt
50/B4 **Bilbays,** Egypt
39/F1 **Bileća,** Bosn.
40/D4 **Bileća,** Bosn.
41/K5 **Bilecik** (prov.), Turk.
44/D4 **Bilecik,** Turk.
50/B1 **Bilecik,** Turk.
50/B1 **Bilecik** (prov.), Turk.
27/M3 **Biłgoraj,** Pol.
44/B2 **Biłgoraj,** Pol.
47/S3 **Bilibino,** Rus.
60/C5 **Bilin,** Burma
63/G4 **Bilin,** Burma
65/B2 **Bilin,** Burma
65/B2 **Bilin** (riv.), Burma
40/E5 **Bilisht,** Alb.
67/E2 **Bilit,** Malay.
58/B3 **Biliu** (riv.), China
91/G5 **Bill,** Wy,US
93/F2 **Bill,** Wy,US
73/C2 **Billabong** (cr.), Austl.
29/H1 **Bille** (riv.), Ger.
29/E5 **Billerbeck,** Ger.
32/C6 **Billère,** Fr.
35/E1 **Billère,** Fr.
25/G3 **Billericay,** Eng,UK
73/B2 **Billiat Consv. Park,** Austl.
23/F5 **Billinge,** Eng,UK
23/G2 **Billingham,** Eng,UK
86/F4 **Billings,** Mt,US
88/E2 **Billings,** Mt,US
90/F4 **Billings,** Mt,US
25/F4 **Billingshurst,** Eng,UK
48/K10 **Billiton** (isl.), Indo.
20/D5 **Billund,** Den.
92/D4 **Bill Williams** (riv.), Az,US
76/H4 **Bilma,** Niger
71/J4 **Biloela,** Austl.
72/C4 **Biloela,** Austl.
89/J5 **Biloxi,** Ms,US
97/F4 **Biloxi,** Ms,US
49/B4 **Bilqas Qism Awwal,** Egypt
50/B4 **Bilqās Qism Awwal,** Egypt
62/C2 **Bilsi,** India
77/K5 **Biltine,** Chad
31/E2 **Bilzen,** Belg.
67/E5 **Bima,** Indo.
73/D2 **Bimberi** (peak), Austl.
77/J7 **Bimbo,** CAfr.
104/B1 **Bimini** (isls.), Bahm.
62/C3 **Bina-Etāwa,** India
38/B4 **Bin 'Arūs** (gov.), Tun.
75/X17 **Bin 'Arus** (gov.), Tun.
95/Q9 **Binbrook,** On,Can
23/H5 **Binbrook,** Eng,UK
26/C3 **Binche,** Belg.
30/D3 **Binche,** Belg.
60/D3 **Binchuan,** China
63/H2 **Binchuan,** China
54/G2 **Binder,** Mong.
62/D2 **Bindki,** India
82/C2 **Bindu,** Zaire
82/F4 **Bindura,** Zim.
35/F2 **Binéfar,** Sp.
25/F4 **Binfield,** Eng,UK
82/F4 **Binga** (mtn.), Moz.
73/D1 **Bingara,** Austl.
26/D4 **Bingen,** Ger.
31/G4 **Bingen,** Ger.
33/G2 **Bingen,** Ger.
78/E5 **Bingerville,** IvC.
23/H6 **Bingham,** Eng,UK
89/L3 **Binghamton,** NY,US
94/F3 **Binghamton,** NY,US
23/G4 **Bingley,** Eng,UK
50/E2 **Bingöl,** Turk.
50/E2 **Bingöl** (prov.), Turk.
55/H5 **Binhai,** China
59/D4 **Binhai,** China
65/D4 **Binh Chanh,** Viet.
65/D4 **Binh Chau,** Viet.
60/B5 **Binhon** (peak), Burma
63/G4 **Binhon** (peak), Burma
65/A2 **Binhon** (peak), Burma
65/E3 **Binh Son,** Viet.
35/G3 **Binisalem,** Sp.
66/A3 **Binjai,** Indo.
73/D1 **Binnaway,** Austl.
36/D2 **Binningen,** Swi.
67/F5 **Binongko** (isl.), Indo.
66/B2 **Bintang** (peak), Malay.
49/F6 **Binyamina,** Isr.
61/F4 **Binyang,** China
63/J3 **Binyang,** China
55/H4 **Binzhou,** China
59/D3 **Binzhou,** China
109/B4 **Bio-Bio** (riv.), Chile
33/L5 **Biograd,** Cro.
40/B4 **Biograd,** Cro.
39/F1 **Biogradska Gora Nat'l Park,** Yugo
40/D4 **Biogradska Nat'l Park,** Yugo.
76/G7 **Bioko** (isl.), EqG.
29/E3 **Bippen,** Ger.
53/L5 **Bīr,** India
62/C4 **Bīr,** India
47/P5 **Bira,** Rus.
76/H2 **Birāk,** Libya
76/H2 **Bi'r al Ghuzayyil** (well), Libya
77/K2 **Bi'r al Ḩarash** (well), Libya
38/A4 **Bi'r Al Mashariqah,** Tun.
103/G1 **Birama** (pt.), Cuba
77/K5 **Birao,** CAfr.
62/E2 **Birātnagar,** Nepal
86/E3 **Birch** (range), Ab,Can
85/J2 **Birch Creek,** Ak,US
91/G2 **Birch Hills,** Sk,Can
73/B2 **Birchip,** Austl.
91/H2 **Birch River,** Mb,Can
83/X **Bird** (isl.), Ant.
71/K4 **Bird Islet** (isl.), Austl.
73/D2 **Birds Rock** (peak), Austl.
68/C7 **Birdsville,** Austl.
70/F5 **Birdsville,** Austl.
50/D2 **Birecik,** Turk.
52/C1 **Birecik,** Turk.
107/H8 **Birigui,** Braz.
108/B2 **Birigui,** Braz.
46/F6 **Bīrjand,** Iran
48/E6 **Birjand,** Iran
53/G2 **Bīrjand,** Iran
49/B5 **Birkat Qārūn** (lake), Egypt
68/G4 **Birkenebeu,** Kiri.
31/G4 **Birkenfeld,** Ger.
23/E5 **Birkenhead,** Eng,UK
31/G2 **Birken-Honigsessen,** Ger.
27/G2 **Birkenwerder,** Ger.
26/F5 **Birkkarspitze** (peak), Aus.
33/J3 **Birkkarspitze** (peak), Aus.
37/H3 **Birkkarspitze** (peak), Aus.
41/H2 **Bîrlad,** Rom.
41/H2 **Bîrlad** (riv.), Rom.
44/C3 **Bîrlad,** Rom.
44/C3 **Bîrlad** (riv.), Rom.
18/C3 **Birmingham,** Eng,UK
25/E2 **Birmingham,** Eng,UK
89/J5 **Birmingham,** Al,US
97/G3 **Birmingham,** Al,US
99/F6 **Birmingham,** Mi,US
33/K3 **Birnhorn** (peak), Aus.
69/H5 **Birnie** (isl.), Kiri.
76/G5 **Birnin Gwari,** Nga.
76/G5 **Birni Nkonni,** Niger
79/G3 **Birni Nkonni,** Niger
47/P5 **Birobidzhan,** Rus.
55/L2 **Birobidzhan,** Rus.
76/E3 **Bîr Ounâne** (well), Mali
36/D3 **Birs** (riv.), Swi.
33/G3 **Birse** (riv.), Swi.
36/D3 **Birse** (riv.), Swi.
36/D2 **Birsfelden,** Swi.
43/M5 **Birsk,** Rus.
42/E5 **Birštonas,** Lith.
54/C5 **Biru,** China
43/X9 **Biryulëvo,** Rus.
20/H4 **Biržai,** Lith.
42/E4 **Biržai,** Lith.
49/G8 **Bi'r Zayt,** WBnk.
38/D5 **Birżebbuġa,** Malta
41/F4 **Bis** (lake), Rom.
57/M9 **Bisai,** Japan
100/C2 **Bisbee,** Az,US
88/E5 **Bisbee,** Az,US
92/E5 **Bisbee,** Az,US
32/C4 **Biscarrosse,** Fr.
32/C4 **Biscarrosse** (lag.), Fr.
32/B4 **Biscay** (bay), Eur.
18/C4 **Biscay** (bay), Fr.
34/C1 **Biscay** (bay), Fr., Sp.
104/A1 **Biscayne** (bay), Fl,US
89/L6 **Biscayne Nat'l Park,** Fl,US
97/H5 **Biscayne Nat'l Park,** Fl,US
38/E2 **Bisceglie,** It.
40/C5 **Bisceglie,** It.
26/D4 **Bischheim,** Fr.
33/G2 **Bischheim,** Fr.
36/D1 **Bischheim,** Fr.
33/K3 **Bischofshofen,** Aus.
40/A2 **Bischofshofen,** Aus.
37/F3 **Bischofszell,** Swi.
31/G6 **Bischwiller,** Fr.
83/V **Biscoe** (isls.), Ant.
52/D4 **Bīshah** (dry riv.), SAr.
46/H5 **Bishkek** (cap.), Kyr.
82/E7 **Bisho,** SAfr.
92/C3 **Bishop,** Ca,US
23/G2 **Bishop Auckland,** Eng,UK
24/D2 **Bishops Castle,** Eng,UK
24/D3 **Bishops Cleeve,** Eng,UK
95/L1 **Bishop's Falls,** Nf,Can
25/G3 **Bishop's Stortford,** Eng,UK
25/E5 **Bishops Waltham,** Eng,UK
23/H4 **Bishop Wilton,** Eng,UK
37/E1 **Bisingen,** Ger.
75/T16 **Biskra** (wilaya), Alg.
75/U18 **Biskra** (gov.), Alg.
76/G1 **Biskra,** Alg.
27/L2 **Biskupiec,** Pol.
95/Q9 **Bismarck,** On,Can
68/D5 **Bismarck** (arch.), PNG
68/D5 **Bismarck** (sea), PNG
84/G5 **Bismarck,** US
86/F4 **Bismarck** (cap.), ND,US
88/F2 **Bismarck** (cap.), ND,US
91/H4 **Bismarck,** ND,US
50/E2 **Bismil,** Turk.
103/F3 **Bismuna** (lag.), Nic.
42/C3 **Bispgarden,** Swe.
29/H2 **Bispingen,** Ger.
76/B5 **Bissau** (cap.), GBis.
78/B4 **Bissau** (cap.), GBis.
76/H6 **Bissaula,** Nga.
29/F4 **Bissendorf,** Ger.
91/K3 **Bissett,** Mb,Can
41/G2 **Bistriţa,** Rom.
44/C3 **Bistriţa,** Rom.
41/G2 **Bistriţa-Năsăud** (co.), Rom.
106/E2 **Bita** (riv.), Col.
76/H7 **Bitam,** Gabon
31/F4 **Bitburg,** Ger.
26/D4 **Bitche,** Fr.
31/G5 **Bitche,** Fr.
33/G2 **Bitche,** Fr.
76/J5 **Bitkin,** Chad
50/E2 **Bitlis,** Turk.
50/E2 **Bitlis** (prov.), Turk.
18/F4 **Bitola,** Macd.
39/G2 **Bitola,** Macd.
40/E5 **Bitola,** Macd.
40/C5 **Bitonto,** It.
41/G2 **Bitriţa** (riv.), Rom.
36/D2 **Bitschwiller,** Fr.
50/C4 **Bitter** (lakes), Egypt
52/B2 **Bitter** (lakes), Egypt
82/C7 **Bitterfontein,** SAfr.
90/E4 **Bitteroot** (range), Id, Mt,US
88/C2 **Bitterroot** (range), Id, Mt,US
38/A2 **Bitti,** It.
67/G3 **Bitung,** Indo.
108/B3 **Bituruna,** Braz.
76/H5 **Biu,** Nga.
56/E3 **Biwa** (lake), Japan
57/M9 **Biwa,** Japan
57/M9 **Biwa** (lake), Japan
93/J4 **Bixby,** Ok,US
96/E3 **Bixby,** Ok,US
52/C6 **Biyagundi,** Eth.
49/B4 **Biyalā,** Egypt
54/G5 **Biyang,** China
59/C4 **Biyang,** China
46/J4 **Biysk,** Rus.
95/N7 **Bizard** (isl.), Qu,Can
76/G1 **Bizerte,** Tun.
38/A4 **Bizerte** (Banzart), Tun.
75/W17 **Bizerte** (Banzart), Tun.
20/M6 **Bjargtangar** (pt.), Ice.
26/G1 **Bjärred,** Swe.
40/C3 **Bjelovar,** Cro.
87/S7 **Bjorne** (pen.), NW,Can
20/D3 **Bjugn,** Nor.
25/E1 **Blaby,** Eng,UK
39/G1 **Blace,** Yugo.
40/E4 **Blace,** Yugo.
27/K3 **Blachownia,** Pol.
93/K3 **Black** (riv.), Ar, Mo,US
48/C5 **Black** (sea), Asia
46/D5 **Black** (sea), Eur.,Asia
91/L2 **Black** (riv.), On,Can
91/L3 **Black** (bay), On,Can
94/B1 **Black** (bay), On,Can
85/M3 **Black** (mtn.), Yk,Can
65/C1 **Black** (riv.), China
18/G4 **Black** (sea), Eur.
41/K3 **Black** (sea), Eur.
44/D4 **Black** (sea), Eur.
26/D5 **Black** (for.), Ger.
33/H2 **Black** (for.), Ger.
36/D2 **Black** (for.), Ger.
80/A2 **Black** (pt.), Namb.
92/G1 **Black** (hills), SD, Wy,US
50/B1 **Black** (sea), Turk.
51/N6 **Black** (sea), Turk.
24/A6 **Black** (pt.), Eng,UK
24/C3 **Black** (mtn.), Wal,UK
24/C3 **Black** (mts.), Wal,UK
88/F3 **Black** (mts.), US
92/D4 **Black** (mts.), Az,US
92/E4 **Black** (riv.), Az,US
99/L11 **Black** (hills), Ca,US
99/G5 **Black** (riv.), Mi,US
94/B4 **Black** (riv.), Mo,US
92/F4 **Black** (range), NM,US
94/F3 **Black** (riv.), NY,US
107/H5 **Black** (hills), SD,US
100/E2 **Black** (mtn.), Tx,US
101/E2 **Black** (mtn.), Tx,US
91/L4 **Black** (riv.), Wi,US
63/H3 **Black** (riv.), Viet.
71/H4 **Blackall,** Austl.
72/B4 **Blackall,** Austl.
99/P16 **Blackberry** (cr.), Il,US
25/E3 **Black Bourton,** Eng,UK
23/F4 **Blackburn,** Eng,UK
72/D4 **Blackbutt,** Austl.
22/D1 **Blackcraig** (hill), Sc,UK
60/E4 **Black** (Da) (riv.), Viet.
65/C1 **Black** (Da) (riv.), Viet.
90/E3 **Black Diamond,** Ab,Can
99/C3 **Black Diamond,** Wa,US
24/C5 **Blackdown** (hills), Eng,UK
25/F4 **Blackdown** (hill), Eng,UK
72/C3 **Blackdown Tableland Nat'l Park,** Austl.
90/F4 **Black Eagle,** Mt,US
90/F5 **Blackfoot** (res.), Id,US
90/E5 **Blackfoot,** Id,US
92/D2 **Blackfoot,** Id,US
23/G2 **Blackhall Rocks,** Eng,UK
22/C2 **Black Head** (pt.), NI,UK
73/D2 **Blackheath,** Austl.
92/E3 **Black Mesa** (upland), Az,US
24/B6 **Blackmoor** (upland), Eng,UK
19/P6 **Blackmore,** Eng,UK
72/B1 **Black Mountain Nat'l Park,** Austl.
99/J10 **Black Point,** Ca,US
23/E4 **Blackpool,** Eng,UK
80/A2 **Black Reef** (pt.), Namb.
103/G2 **Black River,** Jam.
91/L4 **Black River Falls,** Wi,US
94/B2 **Black River Falls,** Wi,US
92/C2 **Black Rock** (des.), Nv,US
23/F4 **Blackrod,** Eng,UK
89/K4 **Blacksburg,** Va,US
94/D4 **Blacksburg,** Va,US
97/H2 **Blacksburg,** Va,US
41/J2 **Black Sea** (lowland), Ukr.
94/E4 **Blackstone,** Va,US
97/J2 **Blackstone,** Va,US
73/D1 **Black Sugarloaf** (peak), Austl.
72/G8 **Blacktown,** Austl.
95/H2 **Blackville,** NB,Can
74/B4 **Black Volta** (riv.), Afr.
76/E5 **Black Volta** (riv.), Afr.
78/E4 **Black Volta** (riv.), Afr.
71/H4 **Blackwater,** Austl.
72/C3 **Blackwater,** Austl.
21/A4 **Blackwater** (riv.), Ire.
22/B4 **Blackwater** (riv.), Ire.
25/G3 **Blackwater** (riv.), Eng,UK
22/B3 **Blackwater** (riv.), NI,UK
93/H3 **Blackwell,** Ok,US
96/D2 **Blackwell,** Ok,US
101/E1 **Blackwell,** Tx,US
24/C3 **Blackwood,** Wal,UK
98/E6 **Blackwood,** NJ,US
98/K8 **Bladensburg,** Md,US
72/A3 **Bladensburg Nat'l Park,** Austl.
22/D2 **Bladnoch** (riv.), Sc,UK
22/E6 **Blaenau-Ffestiniog,** Wal,UK
24/C3 **Blaenavon,** Wal,UK
32/D5 **Blagnac,** Fr.
35/F1 **Blagnac,** Fr.
31/E4 **Blagny,** Fr.
39/H1 **Blagoevgrad,** Bul.
41/F4 **Blagoevgrad,** Bul.
44/B4 **Blagoevgrad,** Bul.
47/N4 **Blagoveshchensk,** Rus.
55/K1 **Blagoveshchensk,** Rus.
90/G2 **Blaine Lake,** Sk,Can
95/N6 **Blainville,** Qu,Can
91/J5 **Blair,** Ne,US
93/H2 **Blair,** Ne,US
86/E4 **Blairmore,** Ab,Can
90/E3 **Blairmore,** Ab,Can
30/A6 **Blaise** (riv.), Fr.
32/F2 **Blaise** (riv.), Fr.
36/A1 **Blaise** (riv.), Fr.
41/F2 **Blaj,** Rom.
97/G4 **Blakely,** Ga,US
36/C3 **Blamont,** Fr.
18/D4 **Blanc** (mtn.), Fr.
33/G4 **Blanc** (mtn.), Fr.
35/J1 **Blanc** (cape), Fr.
74/A2 **Blanc** (cape), Mrta.
76/B3 **Blanc** (cape), Mrta.
105/C6 **Blanca** (bay), Arg.
106/C5 **Blanca** (range), Peru
34/E3 **Blanca,** Sp.
35/E4 **Blanca** (coast), Sp.
93/F4 **Blanca** (peak), NM,US
96/B3 **Blanca** (peak), NM,US
100/D2 **Blanca** (peak), Tx,US
100/B2 **Blanca, Punta** (pt.), Mex.
22/B5 **Blanchardstown,** Ire.
70/C4 **Blanche** (lake), Austl.
70/G5 **Blanche** (lake), Austl.
36/C6 **Blanc, Mont** (mtn.), Fr.
30/A2 **Blanc Nez** (cape), Fr.
103/E4 **Blanco** (cape), CR
106/B4 **Blanco** (cape), Peru
86/D4 **Blanco** (cape), Or,US
88/B3 **Blanco** (cape), Or,US
90/B5 **Blanco** (cape), Or,US
92/A2 **Blanco** (cape), Or,US
93/H5 **Blanco** (riv.), Tx,US
24/D5 **Blandford Forum,** Eng,UK
88/E4 **Blanding,** Ut,US
92/E3 **Blanding,** Ut,US
35/G2 **Blanes,** Sp.
35/G1 **Blanes, Serre de** (mtn.), Fr.
30/A4 **Blangy-sur-Bresle,** Fr.
32/D2 **Blangy-sur-Bresle,** Fr.
27/G4 **Blanice** (riv.), Czh.
30/C1 **Blankenberge,** Belg.
31/F3 **Blankenheim,** Ger.
101/F2 **Blanket,** Tx,US
104/E5 **Blanquilla** (isl.), Ven.
106/F1 **Blanquilla** (isl.), Ven.
27/J4 **Blansko,** Czh.
33/M2 **Blansko,** Czh.
82/G4 **Blantyre,** Malw.
32/F3 **Blanzy,** Fr.
28/C4 **Blaricum,** Neth.
37/E4 **Blas, Piz** (peak), Swi.
38/E1 **Blato,** Cro.
40/C4 **Blato,** Cro.
36/D5 **Blatten,** Swi.
37/F1 **Blau** (riv.), Ger.
37/F1 **Blaubeuren,** Ger.
36/D2 **Blauen** (peak), Ger.
37/F1 **Blaustein,** Ger.
98/G4 **Blauvelt,** NY,US
26/E1 **Blåvands Huk** (pt.), Den.
32/B2 **Blavet** (riv.), Fr.
32/C4 **Blaye,** Fr.
73/D2 **Blayney,** Austl.
70/D2 **Blaze** (pt.), Austl.
26/F2 **Bleckede,** Ger.
29/H2 **Bleckede,** Ger.
33/L3 **Bled,** Slov.
40/B2 **Bled,** Slov.
31/E2 **Blégny,** Belg.
30/C2 **Bléharies,** Belg.
40/B2 **Bleiburg,** Aus.
29/H6 **Bleicherode,** Ger.
37/G2 **Bleick, Hohe** (peak), Ger.
28/B4 **Bleiswijk,** Neth.
20/E4 **Blekinge** (co.), Swe.
30/B2 **Blendecques,** Fr.
29/G3 **Blender,** Ger.
71/R11 **Blenheim,** N.Z.
25/E3 **Blenheim Palace,** Eng,UK
31/F6 **Blénod-lès-Pont-à-Mousson,** Fr.
33/G4 **Bléone** (riv.), Fr.
30/C4 **Blérancourt,** Fr.
80/C4 **Blesberg** (peak), SAfr.
22/B5 **Blessington,** Ire.
19/N8 **Bletchingley,** Eng,UK
25/F2 **Bletchley,** Eng,UK
36/B4 **Bletterans,** Fr.
25/E3 **Blewbury,** Eng,UK
75/S15 **Blida,** Alg.
75/S15 **Blida** (wilaya), Alg.
76/F1 **Blida,** Alg.
23/G5 **Blidworth,** Eng,UK
31/G5 **Blies** (riv.), Fr.
31/G5 **Blies** (riv.), Ger.
31/G5 **Bliesbruck,** Fr.
31/G5 **Blieskastel,** Ger.
69/Y18 **Bligh Water** (sound), Fiji
67/F2 **Blik** (mt.), Phil.
37/E5 **Blinnenhorn** (peak), Swi.
23/G6 **Blithfield** (res.), Eng,UK
83/L **Blizzard** (peak), Ant.
95/G3 **Block** (isl.), RI,US
36/D2 **Blodelsheim,** Fr.
28/B4 **Bloemendaal,** Neth.
80/D3 **Bloemfontein,** SAfr.
82/E6 **Bloemfontein,** SAfr.
80/D2 **Bloemhofdam** (res.), SAfr.
32/D3 **Blois,** Fr.
28/C3 **Blokker,** Neth.
29/E1 **Blomberg,** Ger.
29/G5 **Blomberg,** Ger.
36/C5 **Blonay,** Swi.
20/N6 **Blönduós,** Ice.
86/G3 **Bloodvein** (riv.), Mb,Can
91/J3 **Bloodvein** (riv.), Mb, On,Can
21/A3 **Bloody Foreland** (pt.), Ire.
91/L4 **Bloomer,** Wi,US
94/B2 **Bloomer,** Wi,US
98/F5 **Bloomfield,** NJ,US
92/F3 **Bloomfield,** NM,US
96/B2 **Bloomfield,** NM,US
99/F6 **Bloomfield Hills,** Mi,US
72/B1 **Bloomfield River Abor. Community,** Austl.
99/P16 **Bloomingdale,** Il,US
89/J3 **Bloomington,** Il,US
91/L5 **Bloomington,** Il,US
93/K2 **Bloomington,** Il,US
94/B3 **Bloomington,** Il,US
89/J4 **Bloomington,** In,US
94/C4 **Bloomington,** In,US
97/G2 **Bloomington,** In,US
86/G4 **Bloomington,** Mn,US
91/K4 **Bloomington,** Mn,US
94/E3 **Bloomsburg,** Pa,US
98/E5 **Bloomsbury,** NJ,US
66/D5 **Blora,** Indo.
36/D2 **Blotzheim,** Fr.
80/L10 **Bloubergstrand,** SAfr.
97/G4 **Blountstown,** Fl,US
83/L **Blowaway** (peak), Ant.
25/E3 **Bloxham,** Eng,UK
24/E1 **Bloxwich,** Eng,UK
33/K1 **Blšanka** (riv.), Czh.
33/H3 **Bludenz,** Aus.
37/F3 **Bludenz,** Aus.
60/B4 **Blue** (mtn.), India
63/F3 **Blue** (mtn.), India
90/D4 **Blue** (mts.), Or, Wa,US
88/C2 **Blue** (mts.), Or,US
98/E5 **Blue** (mtn.), Pa,US
91/K5 **Blue Earth,** Mn,US
93/J2 **Blue Earth,** Mn,US
94/D4 **Bluefield,** Va,US
97/H2 **Bluefield,** Va,US
89/K4 **Bluefield,** WV,US

120

Bluef – Boval

94/D4 Bluefield, WV,US
97/H2 Bluefield, WV,US
103/F4 Bluefields, Nic.
103/F4 Bluefields (bay), Nic.
99/Q16 Blue Island, Il,US
92/C2 Bluejoint (lake), Or,US
72/D4 Blue Lake Nat'l Park, Austl.
92/F3 Blue Mesa (res.), Co,US
103/G2 Blue Mountain (peak), Jam.
72/G8 Blue Mountains Nat'l Park, Austl.
73/D2 Blue Mountains Nat'l Park, Austl.
70/F2 Blue Mud (bay), Austl.
74/F3 Blue Nile (riv.), Eth., Sudan
77/M5 Blue Nile (riv.), Eth., Sudan
52/B5 Blue Nile (riv.), Sudan
86/E2 Bluenose (lake), NW,Can
97/H2 Blue Ridge (mts.), NC, Va,US
97/G3 Blue Ridge, Ga,US
72/C3 Bluff, Austl.
71/Q12 Bluff, N.Z.
94/C3 Bluffton, In,US
37/E2 Blumberg, Ger.
108/B3 Blumenau, Braz.
109/G2 Blumenau, Braz.
36/D5 Blümlisalp (peak), Swi.
37/G6 Blumone, Cornone di (peak), It.
99/A1 Blyn, Wa,US
23/G1 Blyth, Eng,UK
23/G1 Blyth (riv.), Eng,UK
23/G5 Blyth, Eng,UK
25/H2 Blyth (riv.), Eng,UK
23/F6 Blythe (riv.), Eng,UK
88/D5 Blythe, Ca,US
92/D4 Blythe, Ca,US
23/F6 Blythe Bridge, Eng,UK
89/J4 Blytheville, Ar,US
93/K4 Blytheville, Ar,US
94/B5 Blytheville, Ar,US
97/F3 Blytheville, Ar,US
63/J5 Bnom Mhai (peak), Viet.
65/D4 B'nom M'hai (peak), Viet.
66/C1 Bnom Mhai (peak), Viet.
76/C6 Bo, SLeo.
78/C5 Bo, SLeo.
102/E3 Boaco, Nic.
107/J5 Boa Esperança (res.), Braz.
108/C2 Boa Esperança, Braz.
54/G4 Bo'ai, China
59/C4 Bo'ai, China
67/G4 Boano (isl.), Indo.
87/H2 Boas (riv.), NW,Can
107/L5 Boa Viagem, Braz.
106/F3 Boa Vista, Braz.
74/K10 Boa Vista (isl.), CpV.
97/G3 Boaz, Al,US
61/F4 Bobai, China
63/J3 Bobai, China
65/E1 Bobai, China
75/G6 Bobaomby (cape), Madg.
81/J5 Bobaomby (cape), Madg.
62/D4 Bobbili, India
26/B4 Bobigny, Fr.
30/B6 Bobigny, Fr.
32/E2 Bobigny, Fr.
26/F4 Bobingen, Ger.
37/G1 Bobingen, Ger.
26/E4 Böblingen, Ger.
33/H2 Böblingen, Ger.
76/E5 Bobo Dioulasso, Burk.
78/D4 Bobo Dioulasso, Burk.
39/H1 Boboshevo, Bul.
40/F4 Boboshevo, Bul.
39/F1 Bobotov Kuk (peak), Yugo.
40/D4 Bobotov Kuk (peak), Yugo.
39/H1 Bobovdol, Bul.
40/F4 Bobovdol, Bul.
44/D1 Bobr, Bela.
27/H3 Bóbr (riv.), Pol.
41/L1 Bobrinets, Ukr.
44/G2 Bobrov, Rus.
18/F3 Bobruysk, Bela.
44/D1 Bobruysk, Bela.
46/C4 Bobruysk, Bela.
81/H8 Boby (peak), Madg.
104/D5 Boca de Aroa, Ven.
103/H4 Boca del Grita, Ven.
101/F5 Boca del Río, Mex.
101/N7 Boca del Río, Mex.
102/B2 Boca del Río, Mex.
106/E5 Boca do Acre, Braz.
35/E3 Bocairente, Sp.
107/K7 Bocaiúva, Braz.
89/K6 Boca Raton, Fl,US
97/H5 Boca Raton, Fl,US
103/E3 Bocay (riv.), Nic.
102/C2 Bochil, Mex.
27/L4 Bochnia, Pol.
44/B2 Bochnia, Pol.
28/C6 Bocholt, Belg.
31/E1 Bocholt, Belg.
26/D3 Bocholt, Ger.
28/D5 Bocholt, Ger.
26/D3 Bochum, Ger.
29/E6 Bochum, Ger.
29/H4 Bockenem, Ger.
31/H4 Bockenheim an der Weinstrasse, Ger.
29/F2 Bockhorn, Ger.
25/G3 Bocking, Eng,UK
31/D3 Bocq (riv.), Belg.
76/J7 Boda, CAfr.
73/D3 Bodalla, Austl.
47/M4 Bodaybo, Rus.
26/F3 Bode (riv.), Ger.
92/B3 Bodega (bay), Ca,US
28/B4 Bodegraven, Neth.
74/D3 Bodélé (depr.), Chad
76/J4 Bodélé (reg.), Chad
18/F2 Boden, Swe.
20/G2 Boden, Swe.
42/D2 Boden, Swe.
46/C3 Boden, Swe.
37/F2 Bodensee (Constance) (lake), Eur.
33/H3 Bodensee (Constance) (lake), Ger., Swi.
29/H3 Bodenteich, Ger.
62/C4 Bodhan, India
62/C5 Bodināyakkanūr, India
64/F3 Bodināyakkanūr, India
33/H3 Bodio, Swi.
37/E5 Bodio, Swi.
24/B6 Bodmin, Eng,UK
32/A1 Bodmin, Eng,UK
24/B5 Bodmin Moor (upland), Eng,UK
18/E2 Bodø, Nor.
20/E2 Bodø, Nor.
42/B2 Bodø, Nor.
46/B3 Bodø, Nor.
54/C2 Bodonchiyn (riv.), Mong.
27/L4 Bodrog (riv.), Hun.
40/E1 Bodrog (riv.), Hun.
50/A2 Bodrum, Turk.
65/D4 Bo Duc, Viet.
66/C1 Bo Duc, Viet.
27/L4 Bódvaszilas, Hun.
40/E1 Bódvaszilas, Hun.
36/C5 Boëge, Fr.
80/A2 Boegoeberg (peak), Namb.
28/C5 Boekel, Neth.
77/K8 Boende, Zaire
82/D1 Boende, Zaire
101/F2 Boerne, Tx,US
93/K4 Boeuf (riv.), Ar, La,US
89/J5 Bogalusa, La,US
97/F4 Bogalusa, La,US
71/H6 Bogan (riv.), Austl.
73/C1 Bogan (riv.), Austl.
79/E3 Bogandé, Burk.
40/D3 Bogatić, Yugo.
27/H3 Bogatynia, Pol.
44/E4 Boğazkale-Alacahöyük Milli Park, Turk.
50/C1 Boğazkale-Alacahöyük Nat'l Park, Turk.
44/E5 Boğazlıyan, Turk.
50/C2 Boğazlıyan, Turk.
54/E2 Bogd, Mong.
54/B3 Bogda (mts.), China
54/B3 Bogda (peak), China
39/H2 Bogdanci, Macd.
40/F5 Bogdanci, Macd.
51/E1 Bogdanovka, Geo.
42/C1 Bogen, Nor.
72/C5 Boggabilla, Austl.
73/D1 Boggabilla, Austl.
73/D1 Boggabri, Austl.
104/F3 Boggy (peak), Anti.
25/F5 Bognor Regis, Eng,UK
26/C4 Bogny-sur-Meuse, Fr.
31/D4 Bogny-sur-Meuse, Fr.
32/F2 Bogny-sur-Meuse, Fr.
73/C3 Bogong (peak), Austl.
73/C3 Bogong Nat'l Park, Austl.
66/C5 Bogor, Indo.
106/D3 Bogotá (cap.), Col.
39/G2 Bogovinje, Macd.
40/E5 Bogovinje, Macd.
62/E3 Bogra, Bang.
22/E1 Bogrie (hill), Sc,UK
76/C4 Bogué, Mrta.
78/B2 Bogué, Mrta.
44/D1 Bogushëvsk, Bela.
47/M6 Bo Hai (gulf), China
55/H4 Bo Hai (gulf), China
59/D3 Bohai (bay), China
59/E3 Bohai (str.), China
59/H7 Bohai (bay), China
59/D3 Bo Hai (Chihli) (gulf), China
30/C4 Bohain-en-Vermandois, Fr.
27/G4 Bohemia (reg.), Czh.
33/K1 Bohemia (reg.), Czh.
26/G4 Bohemian (for.), Ger.
33/K2 Bohemian (for.), Czh., Ger.
26/G4 Bohemian (for.), Ger.
29/G3 Böhme (riv.), Ger.
29/F4 Bohmte, Ger.
99/P14 Bohners Lake, Wi,US
67/F2 Bohol (isl.), Phil.
68/B4 Bohol (isl.), Phil.
40/C2 Böhönye, Hun.
60/E5 Bo Ho Su, Viet.
63/J4 Bo Ho Su, Viet.
38/D2 Boiano, It.
60/B4 Boinu (riv.), Burma, India
34/A1 Boiro, Sp.
108/B1 Bois (riv.), Braz.
36/C4 Bois-d'Amont, Fr.
19/S10 Bois-d'Arcy, Fr.
95/N6 Bois-des-Filion, Qu,Can
90/E5 Boise (riv.), Id,US
86/E4 Boise (cap.), Id,US
88/C3 Boise (cap.), Id,US
90/D5 Boise, Id,US
92/C2 Boise, Id,US
92/D2 Boise (riv.), Id,US
93/G3 Boise City, Ok,US
96/C2 Boise City, Ok,US
30/A5 Bois-Guillaume, Fr.
91/H3 Boissevain, Mb,Can
19/S9 Boissy-l'Aillerie, Fr.
19/T10 Boissy-Saint-Léger, Fr.
26/F2 Boizenburg, Ger.
29/H2 Boizenburg, Ger.
76/C2 Bojador (cape), WSah.
40/B5 Bojano, It.
61/J5 Bojeador (cape), Phil.
27/J4 Bojkovice, Czh.
46/F6 Bojnūrd, Iran
51/J2 Bojnūrd, Iran
53/G1 Bojnūrd, Iran
62/E3 Bokaro Steel City, India
76/C5 Boké, Gui.
78/B4 Boké (comm.), Gui.
77/K8 Bokele, Zaire
82/D1 Bokele, Zaire
20/C4 Boknafjorden (fjord), Nor.
60/A3 Boko, India
77/N7 Bokol (peak), Kenya
76/J5 Bokoro, Chad
63/G5 Bokpyin, Burma
65/B4 Bokpyin, Burma
66/A1 Bokpyin, Burma
80/E2 Boksburg, SAfr.
80/Q13 Boksburg, SAfr.
97/H5 Bok Tower Gardens, Fl,US
76/H5 Bol, Chad
78/B4 Bolama, GBis.
53/J3 Bolān (pass), Pak.
100/E4 Bolaños, Mex.
34/D3 Bolaños de Calatrava, Sp.
39/K2 Bolayır, Turk.
41/H5 Bolayır, Turk.
44/C4 Bolayır, Turk.
50/A1 Bolayır, Turk.
32/D2 Bolbec, Fr.
41/H3 Boldeşti-Scăeni, Rom.
23/G2 Boldon, Eng,UK
76/E6 Bole, Gha.
79/E4 Bole, Gha.
27/H3 Bolesławiec, Pol.
76/E5 Bolgatanga, Gha.
79/E4 Bolgatanga, Gha.
41/J3 Bolgrad, Ukr.
55/L2 Boli, China
20/G2 Boliden, Swe.
42/D2 Boliden, Swe.
61/H5 Bolinao, Phil.
99/P16 Bolingbrook, Il,US
109/D4 Bolívar, Arg.
103/H4 Bolívar (dept.), Col.
106/C5 Bolívar, Peru
93/J3 Bolivar, Mo,US
96/E2 Bolivar, Mo,US
94/B5 Bolivar, Tn,US
97/F3 Bolivar, Tn,US
105/B2 Bolívar (peak), Ven.
106/D2 Bolívar (peak), Ven.
105/C4 Bolivia
106/F7 Bolivia
31/F4 Bollendorf, Ger.
32/F4 Bollène, Fr.
33/G3 Bolligen, Swi.
36/D4 Bolligen, Swi.
23/F5 Bollin (riv.), Eng,UK
23/F5 Bollington, Eng,UK
20/F3 Bollnäs, Swe.
42/C3 Bollnäs, Swe.
71/H5 Bollon, Austl.
34/B4 Bollullos Par del Condado, Sp.
25/F5 Bolney, Eng,UK
51/F1 Bolnisi, Geo.
76/J8 Bolobo, Zaire
82/C1 Bolobo, Zaire
18/E4 Bologna, It.
33/J4 Bologna, It.
26/C4 Bologne, Fr.
36/B1 Bologne, Fr.
42/G4 Bologoye, Rus.
77/J7 Bolomba, Zaire
55/M2 Bolon' (lake), Rus.
102/D2 Bolonchén de Rejón, Mex.
82/C2 Bolongongo, Ang.
65/D3 Bolovens (plat.), Laos
38/B1 Bolsena, It.
38/B1 Bolsena (lake), It.
27/L1 Bol'shakovo, Rus.
42/D5 Bol'shakovo, Rus.
44/C1 Bol'shaya Breëstovitsa, Bela.
45/K2 Bol'shaya Khobda (riv.), Kaz., Rus.
45/K1 Bol'shaya Kinel' (riv.), Rus.
43/P2 Bol'shaya Rogovaya (riv.), Rus.
43/N2 Bol'shaya Synya (riv.), Rus.
55/L2 Bol'shaya Ussurka (riv.), Rus.
47/L2 Bol'shevik (isl.), Rus.
48/H2 Bol'shevik (isl.), Rus.
43/M2 Bol'shezemel'skaya (tundra), Rus.
46/F2 Bol'shoy Bolvanskiy Nos (pt.), Rus.
45/H1 Bol'shoye Boldino, Rus.
45/H1 Bol'shoye Nagatkino, Rus.
45/H2 Bol'shoy Irgiz (riv.), Rus.
48/P2 Bol'shoy Lyakhov (isl.), Rus.
47/Q2 Bol'shoy Lyakhovskiy (isl.), Rus.
45/J2 Bol'shoy Uzen' (riv.), Kaz., Rus.
54/D1 Bol'shoy Yenisey (riv.), Rus.
23/G5 Bolsover, Eng,UK
28/C2 Bolsward, Neth.
35/F1 Boltaña, Sp.
24/C6 Bolt Head (pt.), UK
36/D4 Boltigen, Swi.
95/Q8 Bolton, On,Can
23/F4 Bolton, Eng,UK
23/G4 Bolton Abbey, Eng,UK
41/K5 Bolu, Turk.
41/K5 Bolu (prov.), Turk.
44/D4 Bolu, Turk.
44/D4 Bolu (prov.), Turk.
50/B1 Bolu, Turk.
50/B1 Bolu (prov.), Turk.
20/M6 Bolungavík, Ice.
21/G8 Bolus Head (pt.), Ire.
50/B2 Bolvadin, Turk.
39/K1 Bolyarovo, Bul.
41/H4 Bolyarovo, Bul.
18/E4 Bolzano, It.
33/J3 Bolzano, It.
37/H4 Bolzano-Bozen (prov.), It.
37/H5 Bolzano (Bozen), It.
82/B2 Boma, Zaire
71/J6 Bomaderry, Austl.
73/D2 Bomaderry, Austl.
73/D3 Bombala, Austl.
53/K5 Bombay, India
62/B4 Bombay, India
67/H4 Bomberai (pen.), Indo.
108/C1 Bom Despacho, Braz.
54/D6 Bomi, China
60/B2 Bomi, China
63/G2 Bomi, China
108/B4 Bom Jesus, Braz.
107/K6 Bom Jesus da Lapa, Braz.
108/B1 Bom Jesus de Goiás, Braz.
107/K5 Bom Jesus do Gurgueia (mts.), Braz.
108/D2 Bom Jesus do Itabapoana, Braz.
29/G3 Bomlitz, Ger.
108/B3 Bom Retiro, Braz.
74/E4 Bomu (riv.), CAfr., Zaire
77/L6 Bomu (riv.), Zaire
38/B4 Bon (cape), Tun.
85/K3 Bona (mt.), Ak,US
37/F4 Bonaduz, Swi.
104/D5 Bonaire (isl.), NAnt.
106/E1 Bonaire (isl.), NAnt.
84/L8 Bonaire (isl.), NAnt.
72/D5 Bonalbo, Austl.
73/E1 Bonalbo, Austl.
102/D2 Bonampak (ruins), Mex.
104/D3 Bonao, DRep.
68/B6 Bonaparte (arch.), Austl.
70/C2 Bonaparte (arch.), Austl.
85/F3 Bonasila (mtn.), Ak,US
95/H1 Bonaventure, Qu,Can
95/H1 Bonaventure (riv.), Qu,Can
95/L1 Bonavista (cape), Can
87/L4 Bonavista, Nf,Can
95/L1 Bonavista, Nf,Can
95/L1 Bonavista (bay), Nf,Can
36/D3 Boncourt, Swi.
33/J4 Bondeno, It.
72/H8 Bondi, Austl.
77/K7 Bondo, Zaire
76/E6 Bondoukou, IvC.
78/E4 Bondoukou, IvC.
66/D5 Bondowoso, Indo.
48/M10 Bone (gulf), Indo.
67/F4 Bone (gulf), Indo.
68/B5 Bone (gulf), Indo.
29/E5 Bönen, Ger.
32/D4 Bon-Encontre, Fr.
67/F5 Bonerate (isls.), Indo.
36/D3 Bonfol, Swi.
76/C6 Bong (range), Libr.
78/C5 Bong (co.), Libr.
78/C5 Bong (range), Libr.
67/F1 Bongabong, Phil.
77/K7 Bongandanga, Zaire
67/E2 Bongao, Phil.
67/E3 Bonggaw, Phil.
66/E2 Bonggi (isl.), Malay.
67/F4 Bongka (riv.), Indo.
81/H7 Bongolava (uplands), Madg.
82/K10 Bongolava (upland), Madg.
76/J5 Bongor, Chad
77/K6 Bongos (mts.), CAfr.
65/E3 Bong Son, Viet.
93/H4 Bonham, Tx,US
96/D3 Bonham, Tx,US
28/B6 Bonheiden, Belg.
30/D1 Bonheiden, Belg.
36/D1 Bonhomme, Col du (pass), Fr.
38/A2 Bonifacio, Fr.
38/A2 Bonifacio (str.), Fr., It.
97/G4 Bonifay, Fl,US
36/D4 Bönigen, Swi.
68/D2 Bonin (isls.), Japan
97/H5 Bonita Springs, Fl,US
102/E3 Bonito (peak), Hon.
18/D3 Bonn, Ger.
26/D3 Bonn, Ger.
31/G2 Bonn, Ger.
33/G1 Bonn, Ger.
37/E2 Bonndorf im Schwarzwald, Ger.
19/S11 Bonnelles, Fr.
88/C2 Bonners Ferry, Id,US
90/D3 Bonners Ferry, Id,US
90/E4 Bonner-West Riverside, Mt,US
36/C5 Bonne-sur-Ménoge, Fr.
107/K3 Bonnet (lake), Mb,Can
19/T10 Bonneuil-sur-Marne, Fr.
32/D2 Bonneval, Fr.
33/G3 Bonneville, Fr.
36/C5 Bonneville, Fr.
90/C4 Bonneville (dam), Or, Wa,US
99/C3 Bonney Lake, Wa,US
30/A5 Bonnières-sur-Seine, Fr.
86/E3 Bonnyville, Ab,Can
90/F2 Bonnyville, Ab,Can
38/A2 Bonorva, It.
36/C5 Bons-en-Chablais, Fr.
80/C4 Bontberg (peak), SAfr.
80/C4 Bontebok Nat'l Park, SAfr.
67/E5 Bonthain, Indo.
78/B5 Bonthe, SLeo.
61/J5 Bontoc, Phil.
40/D2 Bonyhád, Hun.
83/J Bonzare (coast), Ant.
28/B6 Boom, Belg.
30/D1 Boom, Belg.
71/H5 Boomi, Austl.
72/C5 Boomi, Austl.
91/K5 Boone, Ia,US
93/J2 Boone, Ia,US
94/D4 Boone, NC,US
97/H2 Boone, NC,US
97/F3 Booneville, Ms,US
54/D2 Bööntsagaan (lake), Mong.
94/C4 Boonville, In,US
97/G2 Boonville, In,US
77/P6 Boorama, Som.
73/C1 Booroondara (peak), Austl.
73/D2 Boorowa, Austl.
30/A5 Boos, Fr.
37/G1 Boos, Ger.
26/F1 Boostedt, Ger.
95/G3 Boothbay Harbor, Me,US
83/D Boothby (cape), Ant.
84/H2 Boothia (pen.), Can.
84/J2 Boothia (gulf), Can.
86/G1 Boothia (gulf), NW,Can
86/G1 Boothia (pen.), NW,Can
23/E5 Bootle, Eng,UK
76/H8 Booué, Gabon
26/F4 Bopfingen, Ger.
80/D2 Bophuthatswana (aut. rep.), SAfr.
80/P12 Bophuthatswana (aut. rep.), SAfr.
26/D3 Boppard, Ger.
31/G3 Boppard, Ger.
33/G1 Boppard, Ger.
73/C1 Boppy (peak), Austl.
100/D3 Boquilla (res.), Mex.
93/G5 Boquillas del Carmen, Mex
96/C4 Boquillas del Carmen, Mex
77/N7 Bor (dry riv.), Kenya
43/K4 Bor, Rus.
77/M6 Bor, Sudan
50/C2 Bor, Turk.
40/F3 Bor, Yugo.
44/B3 Bor, Yugo.
69/K6 Bora Bora (isl.), FrPol.
86/E4 Borah (peak), Id,US
88/D3 Borah (peak), Id,US
90/E4 Borah (peak), Id,US
92/D1 Borah (peak), Id,US
18/E3 Borås, Swe.
20/E4 Borås, Swe.
46/B4 Borås, Swe.
51/G4 Borāzjān, Iran
52/F3 Borāzjān, Iran
106/G4 Borba, Braz.
34/B3 Borba, Port.
32/D3 Borbonnais (hist. reg.), Fr.
107/L5 Borborema (plat.), Braz.
40/E3 Borča, Yugo.
29/F5 Borchen, Ger.
83/M Borchgrevink (coast), Ant.
45/G4 Borçka, Turk.
28/D4 Borculo, Neth.
18/C4 Bordeaux, Fr.
32/C4 Bordeaux, Fr.
87/H2 Borden (pen.), NW,Can
87/R7 Borden (isl.), NW,Can
23/F1 Borders (reg.), Sc,UK
70/G7 Bordertown, Austl.
73/B3 Bordertown, Austl.
75/T15 Bordj Bou Arreridj, Alg.
75/T15 Bordj Bou Arreridj (wilaya), Alg.
75/S15 Bordj el Kiffan, Alg.
75/S15 Bordj Menaïel, Alg.
76/G2 Bordj Omar Driss, Alg.
25/F4 Bordon, Eng,UK
19/N7 Borehamwood, Eng,UK
25/F3 Borehamwood, Eng,UK
20/N7 Borgarnes, Ice.
20/E2 Børgefjell Nat'l Park, Nor.
42/B2 Børgefjell Nat'l Park, Nor.
29/G5 Borgentreich, Ger.
29/E3 Börger, Ger.
26/D2 Borger, Neth.
28/D3 Borger, Neth.
88/F4 Borger, Tx,US
93/G4 Borger, Tx,US
96/C3 Borger, Tx,US
26/C3 Borgerhout, Belg.
28/B6 Borgerhout, Belg.
30/D1 Borgerhout, Belg.
35/F2 Borges Blanques, Sp.
20/F4 Borgholm, Swe.
29/F4 Borgholzhausen, Ger.
29/E4 Borghorst, Ger.
31/E2 Borgloon, Belg.
36/D5 Borgne (riv.), Swi.
38/A1 Borgo, Fr.
37/H5 Borgo, It.
33/G4 Borgo San Dalmazzo, It.
79/F4 Borgou (prov.), Ben.
33/H4 Borgo Val di Taro, It.
79/F4 Borgu Game Rsv., Nga.
27/M4 Borislav, Ukr.
44/B2 Borislav, Ukr.
19/H3 Borisoglebsk, Rus.
45/G2 Borisoglebsk, Rus.
46/E4 Borisoglebsk, Rus.
18/F3 Borisov, Bela.
42/F5 Borisov, Bela.
44/D1 Borisov, Bela.
46/C4 Borisov, Bela.
43/X9 Borisovo, Rus.
81/H6 Boriziny, Madg.
34/E2 Borja, Sp.
26/D3 Borken, Ger.
28/D5 Borken, Ger.
29/G6 Borken, Ger.
26/E1 Børkop, Den.
26/D2 Borkum, Ger.
28/D1 Borkum, Ger.
28/D1 Borkum (isl.), Ger.
20/E3 Borlänge, Swe.
42/B3 Borlänge, Swe.
33/H4 Bormida (riv.), It.
37/G5 Bormio, It.
28/C6 Born, Neth.
31/E1 Born, Neth.
26/G3 Borna, Ger.
28/C2 Borndiep (chan.), Neth.
36/C6 Borne (riv.), Fr.
28/D4 Borne, Neth.
30/B5 Bornel, Fr.
28/B6 Bornem, Belg.
30/D1 Bornem, Belg.
48/L9 Borneo (isl.), Asia
66/E3 Borneo (isl.), Asia
68/A4 Borneo (isl.), Asia
26/D3 Bornheim, Ger.
31/F2 Bornheim, Ger.
18/E3 Bornholm (isl.), Den.
20/E5 Bornholm (isl.), Den.
27/H1 Bornholm (co.), Den.
27/H1 Bornholm (isl.), Den.
46/B4 Bornholm (isl.), Den.
27/H1 Bornholmsgat (chan.), Swe.
37/G6 Borno, It.
79/H3 Borno (state), Nga.
34/C4 Bornos, Sp.
29/H2 Börnsen, Ger.
76/H5 Bornu (plains), Nga.
77/L6 Boro (riv.), Sudan
41/J2 Borodino, Ukr.
23/G3 Boroughbridge, Eng,UK
18/G3 Borovichi, Rus.
42/G4 Borovichi, Rus.
46/D4 Borovichi, Rus.
41/G4 Borovo, Bul.
40/D3 Borovo, Cro.
21/A4 Borrisokane, Ire.
70/F3 Borroloola, Austl.
41/F2 Borşa, Rom.
44/B3 Borşa, Rom.
41/G2 Borsec, Rom.
55/H1 Borshchovochnyy (mts.), Rus.
27/L4 Borsod-Abaúj-Zemplén (co.), Hun.
40/E1 Borsod-Abaúj-Zemplén (co.), Hun.
28/A6 Borssele, Neth.
29/F3 Borstel, Ger.
24/B2 Borth, Wal,UK
32/E4 Bort-les-Orgues, Fr.
103/F4 Boruca, CR
51/G3 Borūjen, Iran
52/F2 Borūjen, Iran
46/E6 Borūjerd, Iran
51/G3 Borūjerd, Iran
52/E2 Borūjerd, Iran
46/K5 Bor Ul (mts.), China
54/D3 Bor Ul (mts.), China
47/M4 Borzya, Rus.
54/H1 Borzya, Rus.
38/A2 Bosa, It.
40/C3 Bosanska Dubica, Bosn.
40/C3 Bosanska Gradiška, Bosn.
40/C3 Bosanska Kostajnica, Bosn.
40/C3 Bosanska Krupa, Bosn.
40/D3 Bosanski Brod, Bosn.
40/C3 Bosanski Petrovac, Bosn.
40/D3 Bosanski Šamac, Bosn.
77/Q5 Bosaso (Bender Cassim), Som.
24/B5 Boscastle, Eng,UK
30/A4 Bosc-le-Hard, Fr.
60/E4 Bose, China
63/J3 Bose, China
25/F5 Bosham, Eng,UK
53/G2 Boshrūyeh, Iran
28/B4 Boskoop, Neth.
27/J4 Boskovice, Czh.
33/M2 Boskovice, Czh.
40/D3 Bosna (riv.), Bosn.
18/E4 Bosnia & Hercegovina
33/L4 Bosnia and Hercegovina
39/E1 Bosnia and Hercegovina
40/C3 Bosnia and Hercegovina
40/D3 Bošnjaci, Cro.
57/G3 Bōsō (pen.), Japan
57/H7 Bōsō (pen.), Japan
77/J7 Bosobolo, Zaire
41/J5 Bosporus (strait), Turk.
44/D4 Bosporus (str.), Turk.
50/B1 Bosporus (str.), Turk.
51/N6 Bosporus (str.), Turk.
92/F4 Bosque Farms, NM,US
96/B3 Bosque Farms, NM,US
76/J6 Bossangoa, CAfr.
93/J4 Bossier City, La,US
96/E3 Bossier City, La,US
51/G4 Bostān, Iran
52/E2 Bostān, Iran
51/F2 Bostānābād-e Bālā, Iran
52/E1 Bostānābād-e Bālā, Iran
23/H6 Boston, Eng,UK
93/J4 Boston (mts.), Ar,US
96/E3 Boston (mts.), Ar,US
87/J4 Boston (cap.), Ma,US
89/M3 Boston (cap.), Ma,US
96/E3 Boston, Tx,US
40/D3 Bosut (riv.), Cro.
37/E3 Boswil, Swi.
53/K4 Botād, India
62/B3 Botād, India
72/H8 Botanic Gardens, Austl.
73/F5 Botanic Gardens, Austl.
72/H8 Botany (bay), Austl.
97/H3 Boteler (peak), NC,US
81/F2 Botelerpunt (pt.), SAfr.
39/J1 Botev (peak), Bul.
44/C4 Botev (peak), Bul.
39/H1 Botevgrad, Bul.
41/F4 Botevgrad, Bul.
44/B4 Botevgrad, Bul.
81/E2 Bothaspas (pass), SAfr.
29/G2 Bothel, Ger.
23/E2 Bothel, Eng,UK
99/C2 Bothell, Wa,US
99/C2 Bothell North-Alderwood Manor, Wa,US
24/D5 Bothenhampton, Eng,UK
18/E2 Bothnia (gulf), Eur.
46/B3 Bothnia (gulf), Swe.,Fin.
20/F3 Bothnia (gulf), Fin.,Swe.
42/C3 Bothnia (gulf), Fin., Swe.
73/C4 Bothwell, Austl.
41/H2 Botoşani, Rom.
41/H2 Botoşani (co.), Rom.
44/C3 Botoşani, Rom.
54/H4 Botou, China
59/D3 Botou, China
60/E5 Bo Trach, Viet.
63/J4 Bo Trach, Viet.
65/D2 Bo Trach, Viet.
26/D3 Botrange (mtn.), Belg.
31/F3 Botrange (mtn.), Belg.
32/G1 Botrange (mtn.), Belg.
80/L11 Botrivier, SAfr.
74/E7 Botswana
80/C2 Botswana
80/N12 Botswana
82/D5 Botswana
38/E3 Botte Donato (peak), It.
23/H4 Bottesford, Eng,UK
23/H6 Bottesford, Eng,UK
88/F2 Bottineau, ND,US
91/H3 Bottineau, ND,US
28/D5 Bottrop, Ger.
108/B2 Botucatu, Braz.
95/L1 Botwood, Nf,Can
78/D4 Bou (riv.), IvC.
78/D5 Bouaflé, IvC.
76/D6 Bouaké, IvC.
78/D5 Bouaké, IvC.
76/J6 Bouar, CAfr.
27/G4 Boubín (peak), Czh.
33/K2 Boubín (peak), Czh.
77/J6 Bouca, CAfr.
30/C3 Bouchain, Fr.
75/V17 Bouchegouf, Alg.
95/P6 Boucherville, Qu,Can
76/D5 Boucle du Baoulé Nat'l Park, Mali
78/C3 Boucle du Baoulé Nat'l Park, Mali
76/E1 Boudenib, Mor.
76/E4 Boû Djébéha (well), Mali
79/E2 Boû Djébéha (well), Mali
36/C4 Boudry, Swi.
75/S15 Boufarik, Alg.
19/S9 Bouffémont, Fr.
30/B5 Bouffémont, Fr.
71/H3 Bougainville (reef), Austl.
72/B1 Bougainville (reef), Austl.
68/E5 Bougainville (isl.), PNG
75/S15 Bougara, Alg.
75/V17 Bougar'oûn (cape), Alg.
76/D5 Bougouni, Mali
78/D4 Bougouni, Mali
78/E4 Bougouriba (prov.), Burk.
32/C3 Bouguenais, Fr.
75/M13 Bouhalla (peak), Mor.
75/V17 Bou Hamdane (riv.), Alg.
31/E4 Bouillon, Belg.
75/S15 Bouira, Alg.
75/S15 Bouira (wilaya), Alg.
76/F1 Bouira, Alg.
75/S15 Bou Ismaïl, Alg.
75/R15 Bou Kadir, Alg.
31/E4 Boulaide, Lux.
31/F5 Boulay-Moselle, Fr.
32/D4 Boulazac, Fr.
68/B8 Boulder, Austl.
88/E3 Boulder, Co,US
93/F2 Boulder, Co,US
90/E4 Boulder, Mt,US
92/D4 Boulder City, Nv,US
99/P16 Boulder Hill, Il,US
79/E4 Boulgo (prov.), Burk.
68/C7 Boulia, Austl.
70/F4 Boulia, Austl.
31/E5 Bouligny, Fr.
79/E3 Boulkiemde (prov.), Burk.
32/C3 Boulogne (riv.), Fr.
19/S10 Boulogne-Billancourt, Fr.
30/B6 Boulogne-Billancourt, Fr.
25/H5 Boulogne sur Mer, Fr.
30/A2 Boulogne-sur-Mer, Fr.
32/D1 Boulogne-sur-Mer, Fr.
23/F4 Boulsworth (hill), Eng,UK
76/C4 Boûmdeïd, Mrta.
75/S15 Boumerdas, Alg.
75/S15 Boumerdas (wilaya), Alg.
35/F1 Boumort (mtn.), Sp.
76/E6 Bouna, IvC.
78/E4 Bouna, IvC.
85/K3 Boundary, Yk,Can
88/C4 Boundary (peak), Nv,US
92/C3 Boundary (peak), Nv,US
73/B2 Boundary Bend, Austl.
78/D4 Boundiali, IvC.
60/D4 Boun Nua, Laos
63/H3 Boun Nua, Laos
65/C1 Boun Nua, Laos
90/F5 Bountiful, Ut,US
92/E2 Bountiful, Ut,US
17/T8 Bounty (isls.), NZ
69/U12 Bourail, NCal.
36/C3 Bourbet, Rochers du (mtn.), Fr.
32/E3 Bourbon-L'Archambault, Fr.
91/M5 Bourbonnais, Il,US
94/C3 Bourbonnais, Il,US
26/C5 Bourbonne-les-Bains, Fr.
32/F3 Bourbonne-les-Bains, Fr.
36/B2 Bourbonne-les-Bains, Fr.
30/B2 Bourbourg, Fr.
75/L14 Bou Regreg (riv.), Mor.
76/E4 Bourem, Mali
79/E2 Bourem, Mali
79/F2 Bouressa (wadi), Mali
32/D4 Bourganeuf, Fr.
32/F3 Bourg-en-Bresse, Fr.
36/B5 Bourg-en-Bresse, Fr.
32/E3 Bourges, Fr.
36/B6 Bourget (lake), Fr.
32/F4 Bourg-lès-Valence, Fr.
32/B3 Bourgneuf (bay), Fr.
26/B5 Bourgogne (reg.), Fr.
30/D5 Bourgogne, Fr.
32/E3 Bourgogne (reg.), Fr.
36/B3 Bourgogne (can.), Fr.
32/F4 Bourgoin-Jallieu, Fr.
32/F4 Bourg-Saint-Andéol, Fr.
33/G4 Bourg-Saint-Maurice, Fr.
36/D6 Bourg-Saint-Pierre, Swi.
68/D8 Bourke, Austl.
71/H6 Bourke, Austl.
73/C1 Bourke, Austl.
36/B1 Bourmont, Fr.
19/M8 Bourne (riv.), Eng,UK
23/H6 Bourne, Eng,UK
25/E4 Bourne (riv.), Eng,UK
25/F1 Bourne, Eng,UK
25/F3 Bourne End, Eng,UK
25/E5 Bournemouth, Eng,UK
32/C1 Bournemouth, Eng,UK
25/E2 Bournville, Eng,UK
21/H7 Bourn-Vincent Mem. Nat'l Park, Ire.
31/F4 Bourscheid, Lux.
29/E3 Bourtanger Moor (reg.), Ger.
25/E3 Bourton on the Water, Eng,UK
76/F1 Bou Saâda, Alg.
30/C2 Bousbecque, Fr.
75/T15 Bou Sellam (riv.), Alg.
75/U17 Bou Sellam (riv.), Alg.
76/J5 Bousso, Chad
30/D3 Boussois, Fr.
76/C4 Boutilimit, Mrta.
78/B2 Boutilimit, Mrta.
17/K8 Bouvet (isl.), Nor.
31/F6 Bouxières-aux-Dames, Fr.
31/G6 Bouxwiller, Fr.
31/F5 Bouzonville, Fr.
30/C5 Boucy, Fr.
38/E3 Bovalino, It.

121

Boven – Buffa

29/G5 **Bovenden**, Ger.
28/D3 **Bovenwijde** (lake), Neth.
30/B4 **Boves**, Fr.
24/C5 **Bovey Tracey**, Eng,UK
9/M6 **Bovingdon**, Eng,UK
40/B5 **Bovino**, It.
51/G4 **Bovīr Aḩmadi and Kohkīlūyeh** (gov.), Iran
33/J4 **Bovolone**, It.
90/E3 **Bow** (riv.), Ab,Can
86/E3 **Bow** (riv.), Ab,Can
91/J4 **Bowdle**, SD,US
23/F5 **Bowdon**, Eng,UK
68/D7 **Bowen**, Austl.
71/H4 **Bowen**, Austl.
72/C3 **Bowen**, Austl.
28/C5 **Bowen Merwede** (can.), Neth.
23/G3 **Bowes**, Eng,UK
92/E4 **Bowie**, Az,US
98/K8 **Bowie**, Md,US
90/F3 **Bow Island**, Ab,Can
71/H3 **Bowling Green** (cape), Austl.
72/B2 **Bowling Green** (cape), Austl.
89/J4 **Bowling Green**, Ky,US
94/C4 **Bowling Green**, Ky,US
97/G2 **Bowling Green**, Ky,US
93/K3 **Bowling Green**, Mo,US
94/B4 **Bowling Green**, Mo,US
97/F2 **Bowling Green**, Mo,US
94/D3 **Bowling Green**, Oh,US
72/B2 **Bowling Green Bay Nat'l Park**, Austl.
83/G **Bowman** (isl.), Ant.
87/J2 **Bowman** (bay), NW,Can
88/F2 **Bowman**, ND,US
91/H4 **Bowman**, ND,US
95/S8 **Bowmanville**, Nf,Can
23/E2 **Bowness-on-Solway**, Eng,UK
67/F4 **Bowokan** (isls.), Indo.
73/D2 **Bowral**, Austl.
30/C2 **Bowron** (riv.), BC,Can
91/H4 **Box Elder**, SD,US
73/C3 **Box Hill**, Austl.
73/C5 **Box Hill**, Austl.
59/D3 **Boxing**, China
28/C5 **Boxmeer**, Neth.
28/C5 **Boxtel**, Neth.
44/E4 **Boyabat**, Turk.
50/C1 **Boyabat**, Turk.
1/M6 **Boyalik**, Turk.
41/F4 **Boychinovtsi**, Bul.
73/D2 **Boyd Konongra Nat'l Park**, Austl.
59/C3 **Boye**, China
91/K5 **Boyer** (riv.), Ia,US
90/E2 **Boyle**, Ab,Can
21/A4 **Boyle**, Ire.
22/B4 **Boyne** (riv.), Ire.
94/C2 **Boyne City**, Mi,US
72/C3 **Boyne Island**, Austl.
97/H5 **Boynton Beach**, Fl,US
90/F5 **Boysen** (res.), Wy,US
92/F2 **Boysen** (res.), Wy,US
50/B1 **Boz** (pt.), Turk.
39/J3 **Bozcaada** (isl.), Turk.
39/K3 **Bozcaada**, Turk.
50/B2 **Bozdoğan**, Turk.
36/E4 **Bozeman**, Mt,US
88/D2 **Bozeman**, Mt,US
90/F4 **Bozeman**, Mt,US
37/H5 **Bozen** (Bolzano), It.
50/C2 **Bozkir**, Turk.
44/E4 **Bozkurt**, Turk.
76/J6 **Bozoum**, CAfr.
40/D2 **Bozova**, Turk.
52/C1 **Bozova**, Turk.
44/D5 **Bozüyük**, Turk.
50/B2 **Bozüyük**, Turk.
49/C1 **Bozyazı**, Turk.
43/G4 **Bra**, It.
28/B7 **Brabant** (prov.), Belg.
30/D2 **Brabant** (prov.), Belg.
25/G4 **Brabourne Lees**, Eng,UK
38/E1 **Brač** (isl.), Cro.
40/C4 **Brač** (isl.), Cro.
38/B1 **Bracciano** (lake), It.
84/E2 **Bracebridge**, On,Can
2/B3 **Bräcke**, Swe.
29/H2 **Brackel**, Ger.
3/G5 **Brackettville**, Tx,US
96/C4 **Brackettville**, Tx,US
25/E2 **Brackley**, Eng,UK
2/A5 **Bracknagh**, Ire.
25/F4 **Bracknell**, Eng,UK
8/B4 **Braço do Norte**, Braz.
40/F2 **Brad**, Rom.
4/B3 **Brad**, Rom.
8/D2 **Bradano** (riv.), It.
0/B5 **Bradano** (riv.), It.
2/D3 **Bradda Head** (pt.), IM,UK
9/K6 **Bradenton**, Fl,US
7/H5 **Bradenton**, Fl,US
8/C3 **Bradford**, Eng,UK
3/G4 **Bradford**, Eng,UK
89/L3 **Bradford**, Pa,US
94/E3 **Bradford**, Pa,US
4/D4 **Bradford on Avon**, Eng,UK
5/E5 **Brading**, Eng,UK
4/C5 **Bradninch**, Eng,UK
3/H5 **Brady**, Tx,US
6/D4 **Brady**, Tx,US
45/L3 **Braeburn**, Yk,Can
8/C4 **Braga**, Port.
4/A2 **Braga**, Port.
4/A2 **Braga** (dist.), Port.
109/D4 **Bragado**, Arg.
107/J4 **Bragança**, Braz.
34/B2 **Bragança**, Port.
34/B2 **Bragança** (dist.), Port.
108/C2 **Bragança Paulista**, Braz.
63/G2 **Brahmakund**, India
48/J7 **Brahmaputra** (riv.), Asia
63/F2 **Brahmaputra** (riv.), Asia
22/D6 **Braich-y-Pwll** (pt.), Wal,UK
24/B1 **Braich y Pwll** (pt.), Wal,UK
22/B2 **Braid** (riv.), NI,UK
18/F4 **Brăila**, Rom.
41/H3 **Brăila**, Rom.
41/H3 **Brăila** (co.), Rom.
46/C5 **Brăila**, Rom.
98/E5 **Brainards**, NJ,US
30/C5 **Braine**, Fr.
26/C3 **Braine-l'Alleud**, Belg.
30/D2 **Braine-l'Alleud**, Belg.
32/F1 **Braine-l'Alleud**, Belg.
30/D2 **Braine-le-Comte**, Belg.
86/G4 **Brainerd**, Mn,US
89/H2 **Brainerd**, Mn,US
91/K4 **Brainerd**, Mn,US
25/G3 **Braintree**, Eng,UK
80/C3 **Brak** (riv.), SAfr.
26/E2 **Brake**, Ger.
29/F2 **Brake**, Ger.
30/C2 **Brakel**, Belg.
29/G5 **Brakel**, Ger.
78/B2 **Brakna** (reg.), Mrta.
32/E5 **Bram**, Fr.
95/Q8 **Bramalea**, On,Can
23/G4 **Bramhope**, Eng,UK
94/E3 **Brampton**, On,Can
95/Q8 **Brampton**, On,Can
23/F2 **Brampton**, Eng,UK
26/E2 **Bramsche**, Ger.
29/E4 **Bramsche**, Ger.
29/F2 **Bramstedt**, Ger.
38/E4 **Brancaleone-Marina**, It.
98/F4 **Branchville**, NJ,US
105/C2 **Branco** (riv.), Braz.
106/F4 **Branco** (riv.), Braz.
82/B5 **Brandberg** (peak), Namb.
26/G2 **Brandenburg**, Ger.
26/G2 **Brandenburg** (state), Ger.
23/H4 **Brandesburton**, Eng,UK
86/G4 **Brandon**, Mb,Can
88/G2 **Brandon**, Mb,Can
91/J3 **Brandon**, Mb,Can
23/G2 **Brandon**, Eng,UK
25/G2 **Brandon**, Eng,UK
97/H5 **Brandon**, Fl,US
97/F3 **Brandon**, Ms,US
00/C3 **Brandvlei**, SAfr.
98/K8 **Brandywine**, Md,US
30/B4 **Branges**, Fr.
27/K1 **Braniewo**, Pol.
42/C5 **Braniewo**, Pol.
20/G5 **Brannenburg**, Ger.
25/E5 **Bransgore**, Eng,UK
73/C4 **Branxholm**, Austl.
37/H5 **Branzoll** (Bronzolo), It.
95/J2 **Bras d'or** (lake), NS,Can
106/E6 **Brasiléia**, Braz.
107/J7 **Brasília** (cap.), Braz.
107/J7 **Brasília Nat'l Park**, Braz.
18/F4 **Brașov**, Rom.
41/G3 **Brașov**, Rom.
41/G3 **Brașov** (co.), Rom.
44/C3 **Brașov**, Rom.
46/C5 **Brașov**, Rom.
28/B6 **Brasschaat**, Belg.
97/H3 **Brasstown Bald** (peak), Ga,US
18/E4 **Bratislava** (cap.), Slvk.
27/J4 **Bratislava** (cap.), Slvk.
27/J4 **Bratislava** (reg.), Slvk.
33/M2 **Bratislava** (cap.), Slvk.
46/B5 **Bratislava** (cap.), Slvk.
39/J1 **Bratsigovo**, Bul.
41/G4 **Bratsigovo**, Bul.
47/L4 **Bratsk**, Rus.
41/K2 **Bratskoye**, Ukr.
95/F3 **Brattleboro**, Vt,US
40/D3 **Bratunac**, Bosn.
31/G3 **Braubach**, Ger.
103/F4 **Braulio Carrillo Nat'l Park**, CR
26/G4 **Braunau am Inn**, Aus.
33/K2 **Braunau am Inn**, Aus.
29/H5 **Braunlage**, Ger.
37/E2 **Bräunlingen**, Ger.
18/E3 **Braunschweig**, Ger.
26/F2 **Braunschweig**, Ger.
46/B4 **Braunschweig**, Ger.
29/H4 **Braunschweig** (Brunswick), Ger.
24/B4 **Braunton**, Eng,UK
74/J11 **Brava** (isl.), CpV.
35/G2 **Brava** (coast), Sp.
108/F7 **Bravo** (peak), Bol.
103/H4 **Bravo** (riv.), Ven.
93/F5 **Bravo del Norte** (riv.), Mex
101/E2 **Bravo del Norte, Rio** (riv.), Mex.
93/F5 **Bravo del Norte, Río** (riv.), Mex
88/C5 **Brawley**, Ca,US
92/D4 **Brawley**, Ca,US
87/J2 **Bray** (isl.), NW,Can
22/B5 **Bray**, Ire.
30/B1 **Bray-Dunes**, Fr.
32/D3 **Braye** (riv.), Fr.
22/B5 **Bray Head** (pt.), Ire.
30/B4 **Bray-sur-Somme**, Fr.
36/B3 **Brazey-en-Plaine**, Fr.
105/D3 **Brazil**
106/F5 **Brazil**
109/E1 **Brazil**
94/C4 **Brazil**, In,US
97/G2 **Brazil**, In,US
105/E4 **Brazilian** (plat.), Braz.
84/H6 **Brazos** (riv.), US
101/F2 **Brazos** (riv.), Tx,US
89/G5 **Brazos** (riv.), Tx,US
93/J5 **Brazos** (riv.), Tx,US
93/H4 **Brazos, Clear Fork** (riv.), Tx,US
93/G4 **Brazos, Double Mountain Fork** (riv.), Tx,US
82/C1 **Brazzaville** (cap.), Congo
40/D3 **Brčko**, Bosn.
26/J2 **Brda** (riv.), Pol.
27/G4 **Brdy** (mts.), Czh.
33/K2 **Brdy** (mts.), Czh.
98/C3 **Brea**, Ca,US
24/D3 **Bream**, Eng,UK
41/G3 **Breaza**, Rom.
30/B4 **Brêche** (riv.), Fr.
31/H3 **Brechen**, Ger.
28/B6 **Brecht**, Belg.
91/J4 **Breckenridge**, Mn,US
101/F1 **Breckenridge**, Tx,US
29/E6 **Breckerfeld**, Ger.
25/G2 **Breckland** (phys. reg.), Eng,UK
27/J4 **Břeclav**, Czh.
33/M2 **Břeclav**, Czh.
24/C3 **Brecon**, Wal,UK
24/C3 **Brecon Beacons** (mts.), Wal,UK
24/C3 **Brecon Beacons Nat'l Park**, Wal,UK
26/C3 **Breda**, Neth.
28/B5 **Breda**, Neth.
80/C4 **Bredasdorp**, SAfr.
80/M11 **Bredasdorp**, SAfr.
82/D7 **Bredasdorp**, SAfr.
26/E1 **Bredebro**, Den.
30/B1 **Bredene**, Belg.
20/D5 **Bredstedt**, Ger.
26/E1 **Bredstedt**, Ger.
28/C6 **Bree**, Belg.
31/E1 **Bree**, Belg.
80/B4 **Breë** (riv.), SAfr.
80/L10 **Breë** (riv.), SAfr.
26/E5 **Breg** (riv.), Ger.
37/E1 **Breg** (riv.), Ger.
37/F5 **Bregagno, Monte** (peak), It.
40/F5 **Bregalnica** (riv.), Macd.
39/H2 **Bregalnica** (riv.), Macd.
26/E5 **Bregenz**, Aus.
33/H3 **Bregenz**, Aus.
37/F2 **Bregenz**, Aus.
37/F3 **Bregenzer Ache** (riv.), Aus.
40/F3 **Bregovo**, Bul.
32/C2 **Bréhal**, Fr.
20/M6 **Breidhafjördhur** (bay), Ice.
37/F4 **Breil-Brigels**, Swi.
36/D1 **Breisach**, Ger.
26/G4 **Breitenauriegel** (peak), Ger.
36/D3 **Breitenbach**, Swi.
29/H6 **Breitenworbis**, Ger.
36/D6 **Breithorn** (peak), It., Swi.
36/D5 **Breithorn** (peak), Swi.
37/F6 **Brembo** (riv.), It.
18/D3 **Bremen**, Ger.
26/E2 **Bremen**, Ger.
26/E2 **Bremen** (state), Ger.
29/F2 **Bremen**, Ger.
29/F2 **Bremen** (state), Ger.
46/A4 **Bremen**, Ger.
72/E7 **Bremer** (riv.), Austl.
18/D3 **Bremerhaven**, Ger.
26/E2 **Bremerhaven**, Ger.
29/F1 **Bremerhaven**, Ger.
88/B2 **Bremerton**, Wa,US
90/C4 **Bremerton**, Wa,US
99/B2 **Bremerton**, Wa,US
26/E2 **Bremervörde**, Ger.
29/G2 **Bremervörde**, Ger.
37/E3 **Bremgarten**, Swi.
36/D4 **Bremgarten bei Bern**, Swi.
99/E6 **Brendel** (lake), Mi,US
24/C4 **Brendon** (hills), Eng,UK
101/F2 **Brenham**, Tx,US
89/G5 **Brenham**, Tx,US
93/H5 **Brenham**, Tx,US
96/D4 **Brenham**, Tx,US
22/E5 **Brenig, Llyn** (lake), Wal,UK
26/C5 **Brenne** (riv.), Fr.
32/F3 **Brenne** (riv.), Fr.
36/B4 **Brenne** (riv.), Fr.
37/H4 **Brenner** (pass), Aus.
33/J3 **Brenner** (Brennerpass) (pass), Aus.
33/J3 **Brennerpass** (Brenner) (pass), Aus.
37/E4 **Brenno** (riv.), Swi.
37/G6 **Breno**, It.
19/N7 **Brent** (bor.), Eng,UK
19/N7 **Brent** (res.), Eng,UK
19/N7 **Brent** (riv.), Eng,UK
33/J4 **Brenta** (riv.), It.
37/H5 **Brenta** (riv.), It.
37/G5 **Brenta, Cima** (peak), It.
19/P7 **Brentwood**, Eng,UK
25/G3 **Brentwood**, Eng,UK
99/L11 **Brentwood**, Ca,US
98/G5 **Brentwood**, NY,US
18/E4 **Brescia**, It.
33/J4 **Brescia**, It.
37/G5 **Brescia** (prov.), It.
30/C1 **Breskens**, Neth.
30/A4 **Bresle** (riv.), Fr.
30/B5 **Bresles**, Fr.
33/J3 **Bressanone**, It.
32/C3 **Bressuire**, Fr.
18/F3 **Brest**, Bela.
27/M2 **Brest**, Bela.
44/B1 **Brest**, Bela.
46/C4 **Brest**, Bela.
18/C4 **Brest**, Fr.
32/A2 **Brest**, Fr.
44/C1 **Brest Obl.**, Bela.
27/M2 **Brest Oblast**, Bela.
32/B2 **Bretagne** (mts.), Fr.
32/B2 **Bretagne** (reg.), Fr.
81/R15 **Bretagne** (pt.), Reun.
30/B4 **Breteuil-sur-Noye**, Fr.
19/S11 **Brétigny-sur-Orge**, Fr.
95/K2 **Breton** (cape), Can
90/E2 **Breton**, Ab,Can
71/R10 **Brett** (cape), N.Z.
31/G4 **Bretzenheim**, Ger.
19/S11 **Breuillet**, Fr.
28/B4 **Breukelen**, Neth.
29/G6 **Breuna**, Ger.
36/B1 **Breuvannes-en-Bassigny**, Fr.
107/H4 **Breves**, Braz.
85/E2 **Brevig Mission**, Ak,US
87/K2 **Brevoort** (isl.), NW,Can
71/H5 **Brewarrina**, Austl.
73/C1 **Brewarrina**, Austl.
95/G2 **Brewer**, Me,US
24/D1 **Brewood**, Eng,UK
91/J5 **Brewster**, Ne,US
93/H2 **Brewster**, Ne,US
90/D3 **Brewster**, Wa,US
97/G4 **Brewton**, Al,US
81/E2 **Breyten**, SAfr.
33/L4 **Brežice**, Slov.
40/B3 **Brežice**, Slov.
39/H1 **Breznik**, Bul.
40/F4 **Breznik**, Bul.
41/G3 **Brezoi**, Rom.
39/J1 **Brezovo**, Bul.
41/G4 **Brezovo**, Bul.
77/K6 **Bria**, CAfr.
33/G4 **Briançon**, Fr.
24/C2 **Brianne, Lyn** (res.), Wal,UK
26/B5 **Briare**, Fr.
32/E3 **Briare**, Fr.
98/F5 **Brick**, NJ,US
19/M6 **Bricket Wood**, Eng,UK
21/A4 **Bride** (riv.), Ire.
22/D3 **Bride**, IM,UK
93/J5 **Bridge City**, Tx,US
96/E4 **Bridge City**, Tx,US
24/C4 **Bridgend**, Wal,UK
92/C3 **Bridgeport**, Ca,US
89/M3 **Bridgeport**, Ct,US
95/F3 **Bridgeport**, Ct,US
98/G4 **Bridgeport**, Ct,US
88/F3 **Bridgeport**, Ne,US
91/H5 **Bridgeport**, Ne,US
93/G2 **Bridgeport**, Ne,US
98/E6 **Bridgeport**, NJ,US
94/D4 **Bridgeport**, WV,US
97/H2 **Bridgeport**, WV,US
90/F4 **Bridger**, Mt,US
70/B6 **Bridgetown**, Austl.
104/G4 **Bridgetown** (cap.), Bar.
73/C4 **Bridgewater**, Austl.
87/K4 **Bridgewater**, NS,Can
89/P3 **Bridgewater**, NS,Can
95/H2 **Bridgewater**, NS,Can
94/E4 **Bridgewater**, Va,US
97/J2 **Bridgewater**, Va,US
24/D1 **Bridgnorth**, Eng,UK
95/G2 **Bridgton**, Me,US
24/D4 **Bridgwater**, Eng,UK
24/C4 **Bridgwater** (bay), England.,UK
23/H3 **Bridlington**, Eng,UK
23/H3 **Bridlington** (bay), Eng,UK
73/C4 **Bridport**, Austl.
24/D5 **Bridport**, Eng,UK
19/U10 **Brie** (reg.), Fr.
26/B4 **Brie** (reg.), Fr.
19/T10 **Brie-Comte-Robert**, Fr.
30/B6 **Brie-Comte-Robert**, Fr.
27/J3 **Brieg Brzeg**, Pol.
28/B5 **Brielle**, Neth.
33/H3 **Brienz**, Swi.
36/E4 **Brienz**, Swi.
36/D4 **Brienzersee** (lake), Swi.
99/C2 **Brier**, Wa,US
23/F4 **Brierfield**, Eng,UK
31/E5 **Briey**, Fr.
33/G3 **Brig**, Swi.
37/E1 **Brigach** (riv.), Ger.
23/H4 **Brigg**, Eng,UK
33/G3 **Brig-Glis**, Swi.
36/D5 **Brig-Glis**, Swi.
86/E4 **Brigham City**, Ut,US
88/D3 **Brigham City**, Ut,US
90/E5 **Brigham City**, Ut,US
92/D2 **Brigham City**, Ut,US
23/G4 **Brighouse**, Eng,UK
25/E5 **Brighstone**, Eng,UK
73/C3 **Bright**, Austl.
25/H3 **Brightlingsea**, Eng,UK
72/F6 **Brighton**, Austl.
73/F5 **Brighton**, Austl.
25/F5 **Brighton**, Eng,UK
32/C1 **Brighton**, Eng,UK
93/F3 **Brighton**, Co,US
99/E6 **Brighton**, Mi,US
99/P14 **Brighton**, Wi,US
32/F4 **Brignais**, Fr.
32/G5 **Brignoles**, Fr.
35/J1 **Brignoles**, Fr.
64/G3 **Brihadeshwara Temple**, India
34/D2 **Brihuega**, Sp.
19/S11 **Briis-sous-Forges**, Fr.
76/B5 **Brikama**, Gam.
78/A3 **Brikama**, Gam.
25/E3 **Brill**, Eng,UK
107/H8 **Brillante** (riv.), Braz.
29/F6 **Brilon**, Ger.
23/G5 **Brimington**, Eng,UK
104/F3 **Brimstone Hill Nat'l Park**, StK.
18/E4 **Brindisi**, It.
39/E2 **Brindisi**, It.
40/C5 **Brindisi**, It.
24/E3 **Brinkworth**, Eng,UK
99/B2 **Brinnon**, Wa,US
34/A1 **Brion**, Sp.
37/E5 **Brione**, Swi.
99/K11 **Briones** (res.), Ca,US
68/E7 **Brisbane**, Austl.
71/J5 **Brisbane**, Austl.
72/D4 **Brisbane**, Austl.
72/E6 **Brisbane**, Austl.
72/F6 **Brisbane** (int'l airpt.), Austl.
72/F6 **Brisbane** (riv.), Austl.
72/E6 **Brisbane For. Park**, Austl.
73/C3 **Brisbane Ranges Nat'l Park**, Austl.
73/D2 **Brisbane Waters Nat'l Park**, Austl.
37/E5 **Brissago**, Swi.
24/B4 **Bristol** (chan.), U. K.
18/C3 **Bristol**, Eng,UK
24/D4 **Bristol**, Eng,UK
84/A3 **Bristol** (bay), US
85/F4 **Bristol** (bay), Ak,US
98/F5 **Bristol**, Pa,US
89/K4 **Bristol**, Tn,US
94/D4 **Bristol**, Tn,US
97/H2 **Bristol**, Tn,US
93/H4 **Bristow**, Ok,US
96/D3 **Bristow**, Ok,US
85/K2 **British** (mts.), Yk,Can, Ak,US
90/C3 **British Columbia** (prov.), Can
85/M4 **British Columbia** (prov.), Can.
86/D3 **British Columbia** (prov.), Can.
88/B1 **British Columbia** (prov.), Can.
87/S8 **British Empire** (range), NW,Can
48/G10 **British Indian Ocean Terr.**
19/N7 **British Museum**, Eng,UK
80/D2 **Brits**, SAfr.
80/P12 **Brits**, SAfr.
80/C3 **Britstown**, SAfr.
82/D7 **Britstown**, SAfr.
32/B2 **Brittany** (reg.), Fr.
91/J4 **Britton**, SD,US
32/D4 **Brive-la-Gaillarde**, Fr.
32/E4 **Brives-Charensac**, Fr.
32/B5 **Briviesca**, Sp.
34/D1 **Briviesca**, Sp.
24/C6 **Brixham**, Eng,UK
25/F2 **Brixworth**, Eng,UK
18/E4 **Brno**, Czh.
27/J4 **Brno**, Czh.
33/M2 **Brno**, Czh.
46/B5 **Brno**, Czh.
71/H4 **Broad** (sound), Austl.
72/C3 **Broad** (sound), Austl.
85/J3 **Broad** (pass), Ak,US
70/C6 **Broad Arrow**, Austl.
94/E1 **Broadback** (riv.), Qu,Can
73/C3 **Broadford**, Austl.
73/F5 **Broadmeadows**, Austl.
71/H4 **Broad Sound** (chan.), Austl.
72/C3 **Broad Sound** (chan.), Austl.
25/H4 **Broadstairs**, Eng,UK
25/E5 **Broadstone**, Eng,UK
91/G4 **Broadus**, Mt,US
72/D5 **Broadwater Nat'l Park**, Austl.
73/E1 **Broadwater Nat'l Park**, Austl.
25/E2 **Broadway**, Eng,UK
25/E2 **Broadway** (hill), Eng,UK
98/E5 **Broadway**, NJ,US
24/D5 **Broadwindsor**, Eng,UK
103/F1 **Broa, Ensenada de la** (bay), Cuba
36/D4 **Broc**, Swi.
86/F3 **Brochet**, Mb,Can
87/R7 **Brock** (isl.), NW,Can
29/H5 **Brocken** (peak), Ger.
25/E5 **Brockenhurst**, Eng,UK
95/G3 **Brockton**, Ma,US
87/J4 **Brockville**, On,Can
94/F2 **Brockville**, On,Can
84/J2 **Brodeur** (pen.), Can.
86/G1 **Brodeur** (pen.), NW,Can
98/E4 **Brodhead** (cr.), Pa,US
98/E5 **Brodheadsville**, Pa,US
27/K2 **Brodnica**, Pol.
42/C5 **Brodnica**, Pol.
44/A1 **Brodnica**, Pol.
28/C4 **Broek in Waterland**, Neth.
28/B3 **Broek Op Langedijk**, Neth.
72/H8 **Broken** (bay), Austl.
73/D2 **Broken** (bay), Austl.
93/J3 **Broken Arrow**, Ok,US
96/E2 **Broken Arrow**, Ok,US
88/G3 **Broken Bow**, Ne,US
91/J5 **Broken Bow**, Ne,US
93/H2 **Broken Bow**, Ne,US
93/J4 **Broken Bow**, Ok,US
93/J4 **Broken Bow** (lake), Ok,US
96/E3 **Broken Bow**, Ok,US
68/D8 **Broken Hill**, Austl.
70/G6 **Broken Hill**, Austl.
73/B1 **Broken Hill**, Austl.
96/B3 **Brokeoff** (mts.), NM,US
107/G2 **Brokopondo**, Sur.
26/F2 **Brome**, Ger.
19/P7 **Bromley**, Eng,UK
19/P7 **Bromley** (bor.), Eng,UK
19/P7 **Bromley Common**, Eng,UK
24/D2 **Bromsgrove**, Eng,UK
29/F6 **Bromskirchen**, Ger.
24/D2 **Bromyard**, Eng,UK
32/F4 **Bron**, Fr.
36/A6 **Bron**, Fr.
20/D4 **Brønderslev**, Den.
79/E5 **Brong-Ahafo** (reg.), Gha.
33/H4 **Broni**, It.
80/Q12 **Bronkhorstspruit**, SAfr.
24/C3 **Bronllys**, Wal,UK
20/E2 **Brønnøysund**, Nor.
42/B2 **Brønnøysund**, Nor.
26/E1 **Brøns**, Den.
37/F3 **Bronschhofen**, Swi.
95/Q9 **Bronte**, On,Can
38/D4 **Bronte**, It.
101/E2 **Bronte**, Tx,US
98/G5 **Bronx** (co.), NY,US
37/H5 **Bronzolo** (Branzoll), It.
67/E2 **Brookes Point**, Phil.
99/Q16 **Brookfield**, Il,US
93/J3 **Brookfield**, Mo,US
96/E2 **Brookfield**, Mo,US
99/P13 **Brookfield**, Wi,US
89/H5 **Brookhaven**, Ms,US
93/K5 **Brookhaven**, Ms,US
97/F4 **Brookhaven**, Ms,US
98/H5 **Brookhaven**, NY,US
86/G4 **Brookings**, SD,US
89/G3 **Brookings**, SD,US
91/J4 **Brookings**, SD,US
93/H1 **Brookings**, SD,US
98/G5 **Brooklyn** (Kings) (co.), NY,US
98/K7 **Brooklyn Park**, Md,US
19/N6 **Brookmans Park**, Eng,UK
25/F3 **Brookmans Park**, Eng,UK
86/E3 **Brooks**, Ab,Can
88/D1 **Brooks**, Ab,Can
90/F3 **Brooks**, Ab,Can
84/B3 **Brooks** (range), US
85/E2 **Brooks** (mtn.), Ak,US
85/F2 **Brooks** (range), Ak,US
99/K9 **Brooks**, Ca,US
93/H5 **Brooks** (A.F.B.), Tx,US
96/D4 **Brooks** (A.F.B.), Tx,US
97/H4 **Brooksville**, Fl,US
98/E6 **Broomall**, Pa,US
68/B6 **Broome**, Austl.
70/C3 **Broome**, Austl.
26/E1 **Brørup**, Den.
27/H1 **Brösarp**, Swe.
95/P7 **Brossard**, Qu,Can
23/H2 **Brotton**, Eng,UK
23/F2 **Brough**, Eng,UK
95/R8 **Brougham**, On,Can
22/B2 **Broughshane**, NI,UK
25/F2 **Broughton**, Eng,UK
23/E3 **Broughton in Furness**, Eng,UK
87/K2 **Broughton Island**, NW,Can
25/G4 **Broughton Street**, Eng,UK
36/A1 **Brousseval**, Fr.
28/A5 **Brouwersdam** (dam), Neth.
28/A5 **Brouwershaven**, Neth.
24/D2 **Brown Clee** (hill), Eng,UK
100/E1 **Brownfield**, Tx,US
88/F5 **Brownfield**, Tx,US
93/G4 **Brownfield**, Tx,US
96/C3 **Brownfield**, Tx,US
25/E1 **Brownhills**, Eng,UK
90/E3 **Browning**, Mt,US
25/E5 **Brownsea** (isl.), Eng,UK
98/F6 **Browns Mills**, NJ,US
94/B5 **Brownsville**, Tn,US
97/F3 **Brownsville**, Tn,US
101/F3 **Brownsville**, Tx,US
89/G6 **Brownsville**, Tx,US
96/D5 **Brownsville**, Tx,US
99/B2 **Brownsville**, Wa,US
24/B5 **Brown Willy** (hill), UK
101/F2 **Brownwood**, Tx,US
88/G5 **Brownwood**, Tx,US
93/H5 **Brownwood**, Tx,US
96/D4 **Brownwood**, Tx,US
19/N6 **Broxbourne**, Eng,UK
36/C4 **Broye** (riv.), Swi.
34/B3 **Brozas**, Sp.
26/B3 **Bruay-en-Artois**, Fr.
30/B3 **Bruay-en-Artois**, Fr.
32/E1 **Bruay-en-Artois**, Fr.
30/C3 **Bruay-sur-l'Escaut**, Fr.
68/A7 **Bruce** (peak), Austl.
70/B4 **Bruce** (peak), Austl.
94/D2 **Bruce** (pen.), On,Can
70/B6 **Bruce Rock**, Austl.
33/G2 **Bruche** (riv.), Fr.
36/G1 **Bruche** (riv.), Fr.
29/G3 **Bruchhausen-Vilsen**, Ger.
31/G5 **Bruchmühlbach-Miesau**, Ger.
26/E4 **Bruchsal**, Ger.
33/H2 **Bruchsal**, Ger.
29/G5 **Brucht** (riv.), Ger.
33/K3 **Bruck an der Grossglockner-strasse**, Aus.
33/M2 **Bruck an der Leitha**, Aus.
40/C1 **Bruck an der Leitha**, Aus.
33/L3 **Bruck an der Mur**, Aus.
40/B2 **Bruck an der Mur**, Aus.
26/F5 **Bruckmühl**, Ger.
24/D4 **Brue** (riv.), Eng,UK
30/C1 **Bruges** (Brugge), Belg.
36/D3 **Brügg**, Swi.
26/B3 **Brugge**, Belg.
30/C1 **Brugge** (Bruges), Belg.
28/D6 **Brüggen**, Ger.
31/F1 **Brüggen**, Ger.
31/F2 **Brühl**, Ger.
28/B5 **Bruinisse**, Neth.
80/B2 **Brukkaros** (peak), Namb.
107/K6 **Brumado**, Braz.
31/G6 **Brumath**, Fr.
28/D4 **Brummen**, Neth.
20/D3 **Brumunddal**, Nor.
38/A2 **Bruncu Spina** (peak), It.
25/H1 **Brundall**, Eng,UK
30/D4 **Brune** (riv.), Fr.
92/D2 **Bruneau** (riv.), Id, Nv,US
106/E5 **Bruneau** (riv.), Id,US
48/L9 **Brunei**
66/D2 **Brunei**
35/M9 **Brunete**, Sp.
20/E3 **Brunflo**, Swe.
42/B3 **Brunflo**, Swe.
33/J3 **Brunico**, It.
36/E4 **Brünigpass** (pass), Swi.
37/E4 **Brunnen**, Swi.
19/T10 **Brunoy**, Fr.
26/E2 **Brunsbüttel**, Ger.
29/G1 **Brunsbüttel**, Ger.
31/E2 **Brunssum**, Neth.
36/D2 **Brunstatt**, Fr.
73/F5 **Brunswick**, Austl.
109/B7 **Brunswick** (pen.), Chile
89/K5 **Brunswick**, Ga,US
97/H4 **Brunswick**, Ga,US
95/G3 **Brunswick**, Me,US
94/D3 **Brunswick**, Oh,US
29/H4 **Brunswick** (Braunschweig), Ger.
72/D5 **Brunswick Heads**, Austl.
103/E3 **Brus** (lag.), Hon.
40/F4 **Brusartsi**, Bul.
37/G5 **Brusio**, Swi.
108/B3 **Brusque**, Braz.
109/G2 **Brusque**, Braz.
18/D3 **Brussels** (cap.), Belg.
46/A4 **Brussels** (cap.), Belg.
26/C3 **Brussels** (Bruxelles) (cap.), Belg.
30/D2 **Brussels** (Bruxelles) (cap.), Belg.
32/F1 **Brussels** (Bruxelles/Brussel) (cap.), Belg.
73/C3 **Bruthen**, Austl.
24/D4 **Bruton**, Eng,UK
26/C3 **Bruxelles** (Brussels) (cap.), Belg.
30/D2 **Bruxelles** (Brussels) (cap.), Belg.
32/F1 **Bruxelles** (Brussels/Brussel) (cap.), Belg.
36/C1 **Bruyères**, Fr.
19/S11 **Bruyères-le-Châtel**, Fr.
19/S9 **Bruyères-sur-Oise**, Fr.
32/C2 **Bruz**, Fr.
83/U **Bryan** (coast), Ant.
94/C3 **Bryan**, Oh,US
101/F2 **Bryan**, Tx,US
89/G5 **Bryan**, Tx,US
93/H5 **Bryan**, Tx,US
96/D4 **Bryan**, Tx,US
18/G3 **Bryansk**, Rus.
44/E1 **Bryansk**, Rus.
46/D4 **Bryansk**, Rus.
44/E1 **Bryansk Obl.**, Rus.
88/D4 **Bryce Canyon Nat'l Park**, Ut,US
92/D3 **Bryce Canyon Nat'l Park**, Ut,US
23/E5 **Brymbo**, Wal,UK
24/C2 **Bryn Brawd** (mtn.), Wal,UK
24/C3 **Brynithel**, Wal,UK
24/C3 **Brynmawr**, Wal,UK
98/E5 **Bryn Mawr**, Pa,US
27/J3 **Brzeg Dolny**, Pol.
27/L4 **Brzesko**, Pol.
27/M4 **Brzozów**, Pol.
63/H4 **Bua Chum**, Thai.
68/E5 **Buala**, Sol.
65/C3 **Bua Yai**, Thai.
78/B4 **Buba**, GBis.
76/B5 **Bubaque**, GBis.
78/B4 **Bubaque**, GBis.
36/D3 **Bubendorf**, Swi.
37/E3 **Bubikon**, Swi.
51/G4 **Būbiyān** (isl.), Kuw.
52/E3 **Būbiyān** (isl.), Kuw.
19/S10 **Buc**, Fr.
50/B2 **Bucak**, Turk.
103/H5 **Bucaramanga**, Col.
106/D2 **Bucaramanga**, Col.
72/C3 **Bucasia**, Austl.
35/P10 **Bucelas**, Port.
37/G1 **Buch**, Ger.
87/J1 **Buchan** (gulf), NW,Can
76/C6 **Buchanan**, Libr.
78/C5 **Buchanan**, Libr.
93/H5 **Buchanan** (lake), Tx,US
95/K1 **Buchans**, Nf,Can
18/F4 **Bucharest** (cap.), Rom.
41/H3 **Bucharest** (București) (cap.), Rom.
44/C3 **Bucharest** (București) (cap.), Rom.
37/G2 **Buchenberg**, Ger.
31/G3 **Buchholz**, Ger.
26/E2 **Buchholz in der Nordheide**, Ger.
29/G2 **Buchholz in der Nordheide**, Ger.
37/G1 **Buchloe**, Ger.
92/B4 **Buchon** (pt.), Ca,US
37/F3 **Buchs**, Swi.
30/A4 **Buchy**, Fr.
23/F3 **Buckden Pike** (mtn.), Eng,UK
29/G4 **Bückeburg**, Ger.
24/C6 **Buckfastleigh**, Eng,UK
94/D4 **Buckhannon**, WV,US
97/H2 **Buckhannon**, WV,US
19/P7 **Buckhurst Hill**, Eng,UK
94/F2 **Buckingham**, Qu,Can
25/F3 **Buckingham**, Eng,UK
19/N7 **Buckingham Palace**, Eng,UK
19/M7 **Buckinghamshire** (co.), Eng,UK
25/F3 **Buckinghamshire** (co.), Eng,UK
85/F2 **Buckland**, Ak,US
23/E5 **Buckley**, Wal,UK
99/C3 **Buckley**, Wa,US
24/D2 **Bucknell**, Eng,UK
98/E5 **Bucks** (co.), Pa,US
30/B3 **Bucquoy**, Fr.
95/H2 **Buctouche**, NB,Can
101/H4 **Buctzotz**, Mex.
102/D1 **Buctzotz**, Mex.
41/H3 **București** (Bucharest) (cap.), Rom.
44/C3 **București** (Bucharest) (cap.), Rom.
30/C5 **Bucy-le-Long**, Fr.
94/D3 **Bucyrus**, Oh,US
40/D2 **Budaörs**, Hun.
18/E4 **Budapest** (cap.), Hun.
27/K5 **Budapest** (cap.), Hun.
27/K5 **Budapest** (co.), Hun.
40/D2 **Budapest** (cap.), Hun.
46/B5 **Budapest** (cap.), Hun.
62/C2 **Budaun**, India
83/H **Budd** (coast), Ant.
99/B3 **Budd** (inlet), Wa,US
38/A2 **Buddusò**, It.
24/B5 **Bude**, Eng,UK
24/B5 **Bude** (bay), Eng,UK
28/C6 **Budel**, Neth.
31/E1 **Budel**, Neth.
26/E1 **Büdelsdorf**, Ger.
34/D2 **Budia**, Sp.
26/E3 **Büdingen**, Ger.
33/H1 **Büdingen**, Ger.
77/J7 **Budjala**, Zaire
24/C5 **Budleigh Salterton**, Eng,UK
39/F1 **Budva**, Yugo.
40/D4 **Budva**, Yugo.
41/J2 **Budzhak** (reg.), Mol., Ukr.
76/G7 **Buea**, Camr.
32/F4 **Büech** (riv.), Fr.
109/C3 **Buena Esperanza**, Arg.
98/C3 **Buena Park**, Ca,US
106/C3 **Buenaventura**, Col.
100/D2 **Buenaventura**, Mex.
92/F5 **Buenaventura**, Mex
100/E5 **Buenavista**, Mex.
93/F3 **Buena Vista**, Co,US
96/B2 **Buena Vista**, Co,US
94/E4 **Buena Vista**, Va,US
97/J2 **Buena Vista**, Va,US
104/D5 **Buena Vista**, Ven.
108/C1 **Buenópolis**, Braz.
109/B6 **Buenos Aires** (lake), Arg.
109/E3 **Buenos Aires** (cap.), Arg.
105/B7 **Buenos Aires** (lake), Arg., Chile
36/C5 **Buet** (mtn.), Fr.
34/A1 **Bueu**, Sp.
73/C3 **Buffalo** (peak), Austl.
90/E2 **Buffalo** (lake), Ab,Can
81/E2 **Buffalo** (riv.), SAfr.
93/J4 **Buffalo** (riv.), Ar,US
91/K4 **Buffalo**, Mn,US
93/J3 **Buffalo**, Mo,US
96/E2 **Buffalo**, Mo,US
87/J4 **Buffalo**, NY,US
89/L3 **Buffalo**, NY,US
94/E3 **Buffalo**, NY,US
95/S10 **Buffalo**, NY,US

122

Buffa – Camb

93/H3 Buffalo, Ok,US
96/D2 Buffalo, Ok,US
91/H4 Buffalo, SD,US
88/E3 Buffalo, Wy,US
90/G4 Buffalo, Wy,US
92/F1 Buffalo, Wy,US
101/F1 Buffalo Gap, Tx,US
99/Q15 Buffalo Grove, Il,US
90/F2 Buffalo Narrows, Sk,Can
73/B1 Buffalo Riv. Overflow (swamp), Austl.
80/B3 Buffelsrivier (dry riv.), SAfr.
38/B4 Bū Fīshah, Tun.
97/G3 Buford, Ga,US
41/G3 Buftea, Rom.
44/B1 Bug (riv.), Bela., Pol.
27/M2 Bug (riv.), Pol.
42/D5 Bug (riv.), Pol.
46/C4 Bug (riv.), Pol.
18/F3 Bug (riv.), Pol., Ukr.
18/G4 Bug (riv.), Ukr.
41/K2 Bug (estuary), Ukr.
44/B2 Bug (riv.), Ukr.
106/C3 Buga, Col.
103/F4 Bugaba, Pan.
106/B2 Bugaba, Pan.
40/D2 Bugac, Hun.
32/E5 Bugarach, Pic de (peak), Fr.
35/G1 Bugarach, Pic de (peak), Fr.
54/C2 Bugat, Mong.
25/E2 Bugbrooke, Eng,UK
51/H2 Bugdayly, Trkm.
66/D5 Bugel (pt.), Indo.
28/B6 Buggenhout, Belg.
30/D1 Buggenhout, Belg.
40/C3 Bugojno, Bosn.
67/E2 Bugsuk (isl.), Phil.
43/M5 Bugul'ma, Rus.
45/K1 Bugul'ma, Rus.
45/K1 Buguruslan, Rus.
54/D4 Buh (riv.), China
50/D2 Buhayrat al Asad (lake), Syria
52/C1 Buhayrat al Asad (lake), Syria
50/B4 Buhayrat al Manzilah (lake), Egypt
51/E3 Buḩayrat ath Tharthār (lake), Iraq
52/D2 Buḩayrat ath Tharthār (lake), Iraq
36/D2 Buhl, Fr.
37/E2 Bühl, Ger.
90/E5 Buhl, Id,US
92/D2 Buhl, Id,US
41/H2 Buhuşi, Rom.
79/E4 Bui (dam), Gha.
79/E4 Bui Gorge (res.), Gha.
24/C2 Builth Wells, Wal,UK
37/G4 Buin, Piz (peak), Swi.
45/J1 Buinsk, Rus.
34/C4 Bujalance, Sp.
39/G1 Bujanovac, Yugo.
40/E4 Bujanovac, Yugo.
41/H3 Bujor, Rom.
82/E1 Bujumbura (cap.), Buru.
27/J2 Buk, Pol.
68/E5 Buka (isl.), PNG
47/M4 Bukachacha, Rus.
54/H1 Bukachacha, Rus.
51/F2 Būkān, Iran
52/E1 Būkān, Iran
77/L8 Bukavu, Zaire
82/E1 Bukavu, Zaire
65/C5 Buket Bubat (peak), Malay.
46/G6 Bukhara, Uzb.
39/H1 Bukhovo, Bul.
41/F4 Bukhovo, Bul.
54/A2 Bukhtarma (riv.), Kaz.
66/B4 Bukittinggi, Indo.
27/L4 Bükki Nat'l Park, Hun.
40/E1 Bükki Nat'l Park, Hun.
44/B2 Bükki Nat'l Park, Hun.
77/M8 Bukoba, Tanz.
82/F1 Bukoba, Tanz.
66/B4 Buku (cape), Indo.
37/E2 Bülach, Swi.
73/E2 Bulahdelah, Austl.
67/F1 Bulan, Phil.
44/F4 Bulancak, Turk.
50/D1 Bulancak, Turk.
62/C2 Bulandshahr, India
50/E2 Bulanık, Turk.
67/F3 Bulawa (peak), Indo.
82/E5 Bulawayo, Zim.
50/B2 Buldan, Turk.
85/B5 Buldir (isl.), Ak,US
47/L5 Bulgan, Mong.
54/C2 Bulgan, Mong.
54/C2 Bulgan (riv.), Mong.
18/F4 Bulgaria
39/J1 Bulgaria
41/G4 Bulgaria
44/C4 Bulgaria
50/A1 Bulgaria
41/H4 Bülgarovo, Bul.
38/D2 Bulgheria (peak), It.
67/E2 Buliluyan (cape), Phil.
72/F7 Bulimba (cr.), Austl.
25/E2 Bulkington, Eng,UK
90/B2 Bulkley (riv.), BC,Can
22/B1 Bull (pt.), NI,UK
31/F3 Bullange, Belg.
34/E3 Bullas, Sp.
36/D4 Bulle, Swi.
73/C3 Buller (peak), Austl.
97/D4 Bullhead City, Az,US
31/F3 Büllingen, Belg.
19/R11 Bullion, Fr.
71/G5 Bulloo (riv.), Austl.
72/A5 Bulloo (riv.), Austl.
73/B1 Bulloo (riv.), Austl.
70/G5 Bulloo Downs, Austl.
73/B1 Bulloo Downs, Austl.
72/A5 Bulloo Riv. Overflow (swamp), Austl.
30/B3 Bully-les-Mines, Fr.
54/D2 Bulnayn (mts.), Mong.
68/D5 Bulolo, PNG
19/Q7 Bulphan, Eng,UK
67/F5 Bulukumba, Indo.
82/D2 Bulungu, Zaire
77/K7 Bumba, Zaire
60/C3 Bumhpa (peak), Burma
60/A3 Bum La (pass), India
77/N7 Buna, Kenya
57/L9 Bunaga-take (peak), Japan
77/M8 Bunazi, Tanz.
82/F1 Bunazi, Tanz.
70/B6 Bunbury, Austl.
68/E7 Bundaberg, Austl.
71/J4 Bundaberg, Austl.
72/D4 Bundaberg, Austl.
73/D1 Bundarra, Austl.
29/E2 Bunde, Ger.
29/F4 Bünde, Ger.
53/L3 Būndi, India
62/C2 Būndi, India
21/A3 Bundoran, Ire.
25/H2 Bungay, Eng,UK
73/D2 Bungendore, Austl.
66/C3 Bunguran (isl.), Indo.
77/M7 Bunia, Zaire
97/H4 Bunnell, Fl,US
28/C4 Bunnik, Neth.
35/E3 Buñol, Sp.
28/C4 Bunschoten, Neth.
25/F3 Buntingford, Eng,UK
72/C4 Bunya Mountains Nat'l Park, Austl.
50/C2 Bünyan, Turk.
72/E6 Bunya Park, Austl.
67/E3 Bunyu (isl.), Indo.
37/E4 Buochs, Swi.
33/J5 Buonconvento, It.
63/J5 Buon Me Thuot, Viet.
65/E3 Buon Me Thuot, Viet.
66/C1 Buon Me Thuot, Viet.
63/J5 Buon Mrong, Viet.
65/E3 Buon Mrong, Viet.
66/C1 Buon Mrong, Viet.
67/K5 Bupul, Indo.
77/N8 Bura, Kenya
82/G1 Bura, Kenya
77/L5 Buram, Sudan
77/M7 Buranga (pass), Ugan.
77/Q6 Burao, Som.
97/F4 Buras-Triumph, La,US
52/D3 Buraydah, SAr.
77/P2 Buraydah, SAr.
37/E2 Burbach, Ger.
92/C4 Burbank, Ca,US
99/Q16 Burbank, Il,US
30/B2 Burbure, Fr.
77/Q6 Burco (Burao), Som.
71/H3 Burdekin (riv.), Austl.
72/B3 Burdekin (riv.), Austl.
99/J10 Burdell (mtn.), Ca,US
50/B2 Burdur, Turk.
50/B2 Burdur (lake), Turk.
50/B2 Burdur (prov.), Turk.
62/E3 Burdwān, India
25/H1 Bure (riv.), Eng,UK
29/F5 Büren, Ger.
28/C5 Buren, Neth.
36/D3 Büren an der Aare, Swi.
54/E2 Bürengiyn (mts.), Mong.
19/S10 Bures-sur-Yvette, Fr.
53/K2 Būrewāla, Pak.
64/B2 Būrewāla, Pak.
47/P4 Bureya (riv.), Rus.
55/L1 Bureya (mts.), Rus.
55/L1 Bureya (riv.), Rus.
25/E3 Burford, Eng,UK
26/E2 Burg, Ger.
26/F1 Burg, Ger.
26/F2 Burg, Ger.
18/F4 Burgas, Bul.
39/K1 Burgas (prov.), Bul.
41/H4 Burgas, Bul.
41/H4 Burgas (bay), Bul.
41/H4 Burgas (reg.), Bul.
44/C4 Burgas, Bul.
37/G1 Burgau, Ger.
97/J3 Burgaw, NC,US
37/G2 Burgberg im Allgäu, Ger.
31/G3 Burgbrohl, Ger.
26/F2 Burgdorf, Ger.
29/H4 Burgdorf, Ger.
36/D3 Burgdorf, Swi.
27/J5 Burgenland (prov.), Aus.
33/M3 Burgenland (prov.), Aus.
40/C2 Burgenland (prov.), Aus.
95/K2 Burgeo, Nf,Can
80/D3 Burgersdorp, SAfr.
82/E7 Burgersdorp, SAfr.
86/C2 Burgess (mtn.), NW,Can
85/L2 Burgess (mtn.), Yk,Can
25/F5 Burgess Hill, Eng,UK
32/C1 Burgess Hill, Eng,UK
20/E2 Burgfjället (peak), Swe.
26/G4 Burghausen, Ger.
40/A1 Burghausen, Ger.
23/J5 Burgh le Marsh, Eng,UK
37/F2 Bürglen, Swi.
33/K2 Burglengenfeld, Ger.
101/F3 Burgos, Mex.
18/C4 Burgos, Sp.
34/D1 Burgos, Sp.
37/H4 Burgstall (Postal), It.
26/D2 Burgsteinfurt, Ger.
29/E4 Burgsteinfurt, Ger.
42/C4 Burgsvik, Swe.
32/F3 Burgundy (reg.), Fr.
36/A3 Burgundy (hist. reg.), Fr.
29/G3 Burgwedel, Ger.
54/D4 Burhan Budai (mts.), China
44/C5 Burhaniye, Turk.
50/A2 Burhaniye, Turk.
53/L4 Burhānpur, India
62/C3 Burhānpur, India
60/B3 Burhi Dihing (riv.), India
103/F4 Burica (pen.), CR, Pan.
103/F4 Burica (pt.), Pan.
106/B2 Burica (pt.), Pan.
99/C3 Burien, Wa,US
87/L4 Burin (pen.), Nf,Can
95/K2 Burin (pen.), Nf,Can
95/L2 Burin, Nf,Can
63/H5 Buriram, Thai.
65/C3 Buriram, Thai.
108/B2 Buritama, Braz.
108/B1 Buriti Alegre, Braz.
108/C1 Buritizeiro, Braz.
35/E3 Burjasot, Sp.
93/H4 Burkburnett, Tx,US
96/D3 Burkburnett, Tx,US
83/S Burke (isl.), Ant.
98/J8 Burke, Va,US
106/B2 Burke Channel (inlet), BC,Can
37/G4 Bürkelkopf (peak), Aus.
70/F3 Burketown, Austl.
74/B3 Burkina Faso
76/E5 Burkina Faso
79/E3 Burkina Faso
37/F1 Burladingen, Ger.
86/E4 Burley, Id,US
88/D3 Burley, Id,US
90/E5 Burley, Id,US
92/D2 Burley, Id,US
99/B3 Burley, Wa,US
99/K11 Burlingame, Ca,US
94/E3 Burlington, On,Can
95/Q9 Burlington, On,Can
93/G3 Burlington, Co,US
96/C2 Burlington, Co,US
89/H3 Burlington, Ia,US
91/L5 Burlington, Ia,US
93/K2 Burlington, Ia,US
94/B3 Burlington, Ia,US
99/N15 Burlington, Il,US
93/J3 Burlington, Ks,US
96/E2 Burlington, Ks,US
97/J2 Burlington, NC,US
98/F6 Burlington (co.), NJ,US
87/J4 Burlington, Vt,US
89/M3 Burlington, Vt,US
95/F2 Burlington, Vt,US
93/K2 Burlington, Wi,US
94/B3 Burlington, Wi,US
99/P14 Burlington, Wi,US
48/J7 Burma (Myanmar)
60/B4 Burma (Myanmar)
63/G3 Burma (Myanmar)
65/B1 Burma (Myanmar)
66/A1 Burma (Myanmar)
41/K3 Burnas (lake), Ukr.
101/F2 Burnet, Tx,US
93/H5 Burnet, Tx,US
96/D4 Burnet, Tx,US
72/D4 Burnett Heads, Austl.
90/C5 Burney, Ca,US
92/B2 Burney, Ca,US
99/Q16 Burnham, Il,US
25/G3 Burnham on Crouch, Eng,UK
24/D4 Burnham on Sea, UK
73/C4 Burnie-Somerset, Austl.
23/F4 Burnley, Eng,UK
86/E4 Burns, Or,US
88/C3 Burns, Or,US
90/D5 Burns, Or,US
92/C2 Burns, Or,US
86/E2 Burnside (riv.), NW,Can
86/D3 Burns Lake, BC,Can
90/B2 Burns Lake, BC,Can
91/J2 Burntwood (riv.), Mb,Can
86/G3 Burntwood (riv.), Mb,Can
25/E1 Burntwood, Eng,UK
73/B2 Buronga, Austl.
49/G7 Burqā, WBnk.
54/B2 Burqin, China
54/B2 Burqin (riv.), China
49/G7 Burqīn, WBnk.
71/H6 Burragorang (lake), Austl.
39/G2 Burrel, Alb.
40/E5 Burrel, Alb.
71/H6 Burrendong (res.), Austl.
73/D2 Burrendong (res.), Austl.
72/D3 Burrewarra (pt.), Austl.
35/E3 Burriana, Sp.
72/D5 Burringbar, Austl.
73/D2 Burrinjuck (res.), Austl.
96/C4 Burro (mts.), Mex
100/E2 Burro, Serranías del (mts.), Mex.
72/A2 Burrowes (pt.), Austl.
22/D2 Burrow Head (pt.), Sc,UK
99/Q16 Burr Ridge, Il,US
72/D4 Burrum Heads, Austl.
72/D4 Burrum River Nat'l Park, Austl.
24/B3 Burry (inlet), Wal,UK
24/B3 Burry Port, Wal,UK
41/J5 Bursa (prov.), Turk.
44/D4 Bursa, Turk.
44/D5 Bursa (prov.), Turk.
50/B1 Bursa, Turk.
50/B2 Bursa (prov.), Turk.
50/C5 Būr Safājah, Egypt
52/B3 Būr Safājah, Egypt
49/C4 Būr Sa'īd (gov.), Egypt
50/C4 Būr Sa'īd (gov.), Egypt
49/C4 Būr Sa'īd (Port Said), Egypt
50/C4 Būr Sa'īd (Port Said), Egypt
77/M1 Būr Sa'īd (Port Said), Egypt
29/E6 Burscheid, Ger.
31/G1 Burscheid, Ger.
23/F4 Burscough Bridge, Eng,UK
77/N4 Būr Sūdān (Port Sudan), Sudan
95/S9 Burt, NY,US
37/G1 Burtenbach, Ger.
25/E5 Burton, Eng,UK
99/E6 Burton, Mi,US
99/C3 Burton, Wa,US
25/F2 Burton Latimer, Eng,UK
23/G6 Burton upon Trent, Eng,UK
25/E1 Burton upon Trent, Eng,UK
48/M10 Buru (isl.), Indo.
67/G4 Buru (isl.), Indo.
68/B5 Buru (isl.), Indo.
49/B4 Burullus, Buḩayrat al (lag.), Egypt
52/E6 Burūm, Yem.
67/F1 Buruncan (pt.), Phil.
74/E5 Burundi
82/E1 Burundi
54/F2 Burun Shibertuy (peak), Rus.
85/L3 Burwash Landing, Yk,Can
25/G2 Burwell, Eng,UK
91/J5 Burwell, Ne,US
93/H2 Burwell, Ne,US
30/B5 Bury, Fr.
23/F4 Bury, Eng,UK
25/F5 Bury, Eng,UK
47/M4 Buryat Aut. Rep., Rus.
45/J3 Burynshyk (pt.), Kaz.
25/G2 Bury Saint Edmunds, Eng,UK
33/H4 Busalla, It.
97/H4 Busch Gardens, Fl,US
31/G5 Busenberg, Ger.
37/F5 Buseno, Swi.
22/B1 Bush (riv.), NI,UK
54/C2 Būs Hayrhan (peak), Mong.
46/F7 Būshehr, Iran
48/E7 Būshehr, Iran
51/G4 Būshehr, Iran
51/G4 Būshehr (gov.), Iran
77/R2 Būshehr, Iran
19/M7 Bushey, Eng,UK
25/F3 Bushey, Eng,UK
98/E4 Bush Kill (riv.), Pa,US
98/E4 Bushkill, Pa,US
98/E4 Bushkill (falls), Pa,US
80/B3 Bushmanland (reg.), SAfr.
22/B1 Bushmills, NI,UK
30/C3 Busigny, Fr.
77/K7 Businga, Zaire
20/D3 Buskerud (co.), Nor.
27/L3 Busko-Zdrój, Pol.
70/B6 Busselton, Austl.
77/L6 Busseri (riv.), Sudan
36/B2 Bussières-lès-Belmont, Fr.
28/C4 Bussum, Neth.
101/E3 Bustamante, Mex.
101/F4 Bustamante, Mex.
96/C5 Bustamante, Mex
72/C4 Bustard (pt.), Austl.
41/G3 Buşteni, Rom.
33/H4 Busto Arsizio, It.
26/E1 Büsum, Ger.
77/K7 Buta, Zaire
82/E1 Butare, Rwa.
68/G4 Butaritari (atoll), Kiri.
90/B3 Bute (inlet), BC,Can
54/E2 Büteeliyn (mts.), Mong.
77/L7 Butembo, Zaire
31/F3 Bütgenbach, Belg.
108/B4 Butiá, Braz.
89/L3 Butler, Pa,US
94/E3 Butler, Pa,US
67/F5 Buton (isl.), Indo.
19/S9 Butry-sur-Oise, Fr.
36/D4 Bütschelegg (peak), Swi.
37/F3 Bütschwil, Swi.
84/F5 Butte, US
86/E4 Butte, Mt,US
88/D2 Butte, Mt,US
66/B2 Butterworth, Malay.
36/C4 Buttes, Swi.
90/E4 Butte-Silver Bow County, Mt,US
21/A4 Buttevant, Ire.
68/B4 Butuan, Phil.
48/M10 Butung (isl.), Indo.
68/B5 Butung (isl.), Phil.
45/G2 Buturlinovka, Rus.
26/E3 Butzbach, Ger.
33/H1 Butzbach, Ger.
26/F2 Bützow, Ger.
77/Q7 Buulo Berde, Som.
77/P7 Buur Hakaba, Som.
38/B4 Bū 'Urqūb, Tun.
37/G2 Buxheim, Ger.
26/E2 Buxtehude, Ger.
29/G2 Buxtehude, Ger.
23/G5 Buxton, Eng,UK
42/J4 Buy, Rus.
45/H4 Buynaksk, Rus.
78/D5 Buyo, Barrage de (dam), IvC.
55/H2 Buyr (lake), Mong.
60/D4 Buyuan (riv.), China
51/N7 Büyükada (isl.), Turk.
39/K2 Büyük Anafarta, Turk.
44/F5 Büyükarmutlu, Turk.
41/J5 Büyükçekmece, Turk.
44/D4 Büyükçekmece, Turk.
51/M6 Büyükçekmece (lake), Turk.
50/C2 Büyükeceli, Turk.
58/B2 Buyun (peak), China
59/E2 Buyun Shan (peak), China
45/J3 Buzachi (pen.), Kaz.
32/D3 Buzançais, Fr.
31/D5 Buzancy, Fr.
41/H3 Buzău, Rom.
41/H3 Buzău (co.), Rom.
41/H3 Buzău (riv.), Rom.
44/C3 Buzău, Rom.
44/C3 Buzău (riv.), Rom.
40/E3 Buziaş, Rom.
19/J3 Buzuluk, Rus.
45/K1 Buzuluk, Rus.
46/F4 Buzuluk, Rus.
41/G4 Byala, Bul.
41/H4 Byala, Bul.
44/C4 Byala, Bul.
41/F4 Byala Slatina, Bul.
87/R7 Byam Martin (chan.), NW,Can
87/R7 Byam Martin (isl.), NW,Can
18/E3 Bydgoszcz, Pol.
27/J2 Bydgoszcz, Pol.
27/J2 Bydgoszcz (prov.), Pol.
44/A1 Bydgoszcz, Pol.
46/B4 Bydgoszcz, Pol.
25/E2 Byfield, Eng,UK
19/M8 Byfleet, Eng,UK
44/D1 Bykhov, Bela.
22/E5 Bylchau, Wal,UK
84/K2 Bylot (isl.), Can.
87/J1 Bylot (isl.), NW,Can
51/F2 Byoyuk-Kirs (peak), Azer.
98/G4 Byram (riv.), NY, Ct,US
83/L Byrd (glac.), Ant.
83/U Byrd (cape), Ant.
99/L11 Byron, Ca,US
72/D5 Byron Bay, Austl.
73/E1 Byron Bay, Austl.
46/K2 Byrranga (mts.), Rus.
20/D4 Byrum, Den.
27/K4 Bystrá (peak), Slvk.
47/N3 Bytantay (riv.), Rus.
27/K3 Bytom, Pol.
27/J1 Bytów, Pol.
51/M6 Byükçekemece, Turk.

C

63/J4 Ca (riv.), Viet.
65/D2 Ca (riv.), Viet.
82/C3 Caála, Ang.
105/E3 Caatingas (reg.), Braz.
107/K5 Caatingas (reg.), Braz.
109/E2 Caazapá, Par.
103/G1 Cabaiguán, Cuba
92/F4 Caballo (res.), NM,US
106/D4 Caballococha, Peru
106/C5 Cabana, Peru
34/C1 Cabañaquinta, Sp.
68/B3 Cabanatuan City, Phil.
24/C2 Caban Coch (res.), Wal,UK
35/F2 Cabanes, Sp.
95/G2 Cabano, Qu,Can
32/E5 Cabestany, Fr.
35/G1 Cabestany, Fr.
34/C3 Cabeza del Buey, Sp.
34/C1 Cabezón de la Sal, Sp.
104/D5 Cabimas, Ven.
106/D1 Cabimas, Ven.
82/B2 Cabinda, Ang.
76/C2 Cabo Bojador, WSah.
109/C8 Cabo de Hornos (Cape Horn) (cape), Chile
109/C7 Cabo de Hornos Nat'l Park, Chile
82/F6 Cabo de Santa Maria (cape), Moz.
108/B4 Cabo de Santa Marta Grande (cape), Braz.
109/G2 Cabo de Santa Marta Grande (cape), Braz.
107/L5 Cabo de São Roque (cape), Braz.
107/K8 Cabo de São Tomé (cape), Braz.
108/D2 Cabo de São Tomé (cape), Braz.
107/J3 Cabo do Norte (cape), Braz.
108/D2 Cabo Frio, Braz.
103/F3 Cabo Gracias a Dios, Nic.
87/J4 Cabonga (res.), Qu,Can
94/E2 Cabonga (res.), Qu,Can
72/D4 Caboolture, Austl.
107/H3 Cabo Orange Nat'l Park, Braz.
82/F4 Cabora Bassa (lake), Moz.
84/L5 Cabot (str.), Can.
87/K4 Cabot (str.), Can.
89/P2 Cabot (str.), Nf, PE,Can
95/J2 Cabot (str.), Nf, NS,Can
34/C4 Cabra, Sp.
34/D4 Cabra de Santo Cristo, Sp.
104/D3 Cabral, DRep.
72/G8 Cabramatta, Austl.
38/A3 Cabras, It.
35/G3 Cabrera (isl.), Sp.
90/F3 Cabri, Sk,Can
34/E3 Cabriel (riv.), Sp.
106/E2 Cabruta, Ven.
104/D5 Cabudare, Ven.
61/J5 Cabugao, Phil.
104/D5 Cabure, Ven.
108/B3 Caçador, Braz.
109/F2 Caçador, Braz.
18/F4 Čačak, Yugo.
40/E4 Čačak, Yugo.
100/D4 Cacalotán, Mex.
108/C2 Caçapava, Braz.
38/A2 Caccia (cape), It.
106/G7 Cáceres, Braz.
103/H5 Cáceres, Col.
18/C5 Cáceres, Sp.
34/B3 Cáceres, Sp.
19/S10 Cachan, Fr.
92/B3 Cache (creek), Ca,US
99/L10 Cache (slough), Ca,US
99/L9 Cache (cr.), Ca,US
90/E5 Cache (peak), Id,US
92/D2 Cache (peak), Id,US
90/C3 Cache Creek, BC,Can
76/B5 Cacheu, GBis.
78/A3 Cacheu, GBis.
109/C2 Cachí, Arg.
107/G5 Cachimbo (mts.), Braz.
108/A4 Cachoeira do Sul, Braz.
109/F3 Cachoeira do Sul, Braz.
108/B4 Cachoeirinha, Braz.
107/K8 Cachoeiro de Itapemirim, Braz.
108/D2 Cachoeiro de Itapemirim, Braz.
108/B1 Caçu, Braz.
82/B3 Cacula, Ang.
107/K6 Caculé, Braz.
35/G1 Cadaques, Sp.
27/K4 Čadca, Slvk.
96/E3 Caddo (mts.), Ar,US
37/F5 Cadelle, Monte (peak), It.
29/G1 Cadenberge, Ger.
24/C1 Cader Idris (mtn.), UK
70/E5 Cadibarrawirracanna (lake), Austl.
89/J3 Cadillac, Mi,US
94/C2 Cadillac, Mi,US
67/F1 Cadiz, Phil.
18/C5 Cádiz, Sp.
34/B4 Cádiz, Sp.
34/B4 Cádiz (gulf), Sp.
94/C4 Cadiz, Ky,US
97/G2 Cadiz, Ky,US
25/E5 Cadnam, Eng,UK
37/G6 Cadria, Monte (peak), It.
30/C1 Cadzand-Bad, Neth.
18/C4 Caen, Fr.
32/C2 Caen, Fr.
32/C2 Caen (har.), Fr.
24/D3 Caerleon, Wal,UK
22/D5 Caernafon Castle, Wal,UK
22/D5 Caernarfon, Wal,UK
22/D5 Caernarfon (bay), Wal,UK
24/C3 Caerphilly, Wal,UK
24/C1 Caersws, Wal,UK
49/F6 Caesarea Nat'l Park, Isr.
30/B2 Caëstre, Fr.
109/C2 Cafayate, Arg.
67/F2 Cagayancillo, Phil.
67/F2 Cagayan de Oro City, Phil.
68/B4 Cagayan de Oro City, Phil.
18/D5 Cagliari, It.
38/A3 Cagliari, It.
38/A3 Cagliari (gulf), It.
33/G5 Cagnes-sur-Mer, Fr.
35/J1 Cagnes-sur-Mer, Fr.
106/D3 Caguán (riv.), Col.
104/E3 Caguas, PR
82/B4 Cahama, Ang.
21/G8 Cahirsiveen, Ire.
32/D4 Cahors, Fr.
103/F4 Cahuita (pt.), CR
103/F4 Cahuita Nat'l Park, CR
108/B4 Cai (riv.), Braz.
82/G4 Caia, Moz.
107/H7 Caiapó (mts.), Braz.
107/H7 Caiapó (riv.), Braz.
103/G1 Caibarién, Cuba
107/L5 Caicó, Braz.
103/H1 Caicos (passg.), Bahm., Trks.
104/C2 Caicos (passg.), Bahm.,Trks.
104/C2 Caicos (isls.), Trks.
30/A4 Cailly (riv.), Fr.
65/D4 Cai Nuoc, Viet.
33/J4 Caio (peak), It.
83/Y Caird (coast), Ant.
85/G3 Cairn (mtn.), Ak,US
73/B3 Cairn Curran (dam), Austl.
22/C2 Cairn Pat (hill), Sc,UK
22/C2 Cairnryan, Sc,UK
68/D6 Cairns, Austl.
71/H3 Cairns, Austl.
72/B2 Cairns, Austl.
22/D1 Cairnsmore of Carsphairn (mtn.), Sc,UK
77/M1 Cairo (cap.), Egypt
40/A5 Cairo (peak), It.
97/G4 Cairo, Ga,US
89/J4 Cairo, Il,US
93/K3 Cairo, Il,US
94/B4 Cairo, Il,US
97/F2 Cairo, Il,US
49/B4 Cairo (Al Qāhirah) (cap.), Egypt
50/B4 Cairo (Al Qāhirah) (cap.), Egypt
52/B2 Cairo (Al Qāhirah) (cap.), Egypt
25/H1 Caister on Sea, Eng,UK
23/H5 Caistor, Eng,UK
95/Q9 Caistor Centre, On,Can
95/Q9 Caistorville, On,Can
82/B3 Caitou, Ang.
82/C4 Caiundo, Ang.
59/C5 Caizi (lake), China
106/C5 Cajabamba, Peru
106/C5 Cajamarca, Peru
103/E1 Cajón (pt.), Cuba
50/B2 Çal, Turk.
76/G7 Calabar, Nga.
79/H5 Calabar, Nga.
106/E2 Calabozo, Ven.
38/E3 Calabria (reg.), It.
38/D3 Calabria Nat'l Park, It.
38/E3 Calabria Nat'l Park, It.
34/C4 Calaburras, Punta de (pt.), Sp.
35/F2 Calaceite, Sp.
38/A2 Cala d'Oliva, It.
40/F4 Calafat, Rom.
44/B4 Calafat, Rom.
109/B7 Calafate, Arg.
34/E1 Calahorra, Sp.
18/D3 Calais, Fr.
26/A3 Calais, Fr.
30/A2 Calais, Fr.
32/D1 Calais, Fr.
87/K4 Calais, Me,US
89/N2 Calais, Me,US
95/H2 Calais, Me,US
30/A2 Calais, Canal de (can.), Fr.
109/C2 Calalaste (mts.), Arg.
106/E8 Calama, Chile
109/C1 Calama, Chile
103/H4 Calamar, Col.
67/E1 Calamian (isls.), Phil.
34/E2 Calamocha, Sp.
34/B3 Calamonte, Sp.
40/F3 Călan, Rom.
34/B4 Calañas, Sp.
35/E2 Calanda, Sp.
38/A2 Calangianus, It.
18/F4 Călăraşi, Rom.
41/H3 Călăraşi, Rom.
41/H3 Călăraşi (co.), Rom.
44/C3 Călăraşi, Rom.
34/E3 Calasparra, Sp.
34/E2 Calatayud, Sp.
34/E2 Calatorao, Sp.
99/L12 Calaveras (res.), Ca,US
61/J5 Calayan, Phil.
61/J5 Calayan (isl.), Phil.
68/B3 Calayan (isl.), Phil.
29/H4 Calberlah, Ger.
106/D6 Calca, Peru
93/J5 Calcasieu (riv.), La,US
94/F2 Calcium, NY,US
107/H3 Calçoene, Braz.
62/E3 Calcutta, India
33/J3 Caldaro (Kaltern), It.
37/H5 Caldaro (Kaltern), It.
34/A3 Caldas da Rainha, Port.
108/B1 Caldas Novas, Braz.
23/E2 Caldbeck, Eng,UK
29/G6 Calden, Ger.
23/G4 Calder (riv.), Eng,UK
85/M4 Calder (mt.), Ak,US
101/H5 Calderitas, Mex.
35/L6 Caldes de Montbui, Sp.
23/F2 Caldew (riv.), Eng,UK
24/D3 Caldicot, Wal,UK
45/G5 Çaldıran, Turk.
51/E2 Çaldıran, Turk.
37/H6 Caldonazzo, It.
88/C3 Caldwell, Id,US
90/D5 Caldwell, Id,US
92/C2 Caldwell, Id,US
101/F2 Caldwell, Tx,US
93/H5 Caldwell, Tx,US
96/D4 Caldwell, Tx,US
99/P14 Caldwell, Wi,US
24/B3 Caldy (isl.), Wal,UK
80/D3 Caledon (riv.), Les., SAfr.
80/B4 Caledon, SAfr.
80/L11 Caledon, SAfr.
95/Q8 Caledon East, On,Can
95/H2 Caledonia (hills), NB,Can
99/Q14 Caledonia, Wi,US
35/G2 Calella, Sp.
72/C3 Calen, Austl.
38/A1 Calenzana, Fr.
103/H1 Caleta (pt.), Cuba
109/C6 Caleta Olivia, Arg.
100/B1 Calexico, Ca,US
92/D4 Calexico, Ca,US
23/F3 Calf, The (mtn.), Eng,UK
90/E3 Calgary, Ab,Can
86/E3 Calgary, Ab,Can
35/U15 Calheta, Madr.
35/S12 Calheta, Azor.
97/G3 Calhoun, Ga,US
94/C4 Calhoun, Ky,US
97/G2 Calhoun, Ky,US
106/C3 Cali, Col.
34/E4 Calida, Costa (coas Sp.
92/D3 Caliente, Nv,US
100/B2 California (gulf), M
84/F7 California (gulf), M
92/D5 California (gulf), M
100/B1 California (state), U
90/C5 California (state), U
86/D4 California (state), U
88/C4 California (state), U
92/B3 California (state), U
99/L11 California (aquedu Ca,US
94/E4 California, Md,US
97/J2 California, Md,US
93/J3 California, Mo,US
96/E2 California, Mo,US
109/D1 Calilegua Nat'l Par Arg.
41/G3 Călimăneşti, Rom.
62/C5 Calimere (pt.), India
64/G3 Calimere (pt.), India
99/J9 Calistoga, Ca,US
38/D2 Calitri, It.
95/P6 Calixa-Lavallée, Qu,Can
101/H4 Calkiní, Mex.
102/D1 Calkiní, Mex.
50/B2 Çalköy, Turk.
73/A1 Callabonna (lake), Austl.
70/G5 Callahonna (lake), Austl.
28/B3 Callantsoog, Neth.
106/C6 Callao, Peru
97/G4 Callaway, Fl,US
35/J1 Calle-Rousse, Poin de (pt.), Fr.
24/B6 Callington, Eng,UK
72/C4 Calliope, Austl.
35/E3 Callosa de Ensarri Sp.
35/E3 Callosa de Segura, Sp.
101/F4 Calnali, Mex.
102/B1 Calnali, Mex.
24/D4 Calne, Eng,UK
30/B3 Calonne-Ricouart, Fr.
38/D2 Calore (riv.), It.
40/B5 Calore (riv.), It.
101/H4 Calotmul, Mex.
102/D1 Calotmul, Mex.
71/J5 Caloundra, Austl.
72/D4 Caloundra, Austl.
35/F3 Calpe, Sp.
101/L7 Calpulálpan, Mex.
24/B6 Calstock, Eng,UK
38/D4 Caltagirone, It.
38/D4 Caltanissetta, It.
38/C4 Caltavuturo, It.
32/F4 Caluire-et-Cuire, F
99/Q16 Calumet (riv.), Il,US
99/Q16 Calumet City, Il,US
99/Q16 Calumet Sag (chan Il,US
82/B3 Caluquembe, Ang.
33/G4 Caluso, It.
38/D2 Calvello, It.
90/A3 Calvert (isl.), BC,Ca
101/F2 Calvert, Tx,US
23/G5 Calverton, Eng,UK
98/K7 Calverton, Md,US
98/H5 Calverton, NY,US
38/A1 Calvi, Fr.
35/G3 Calviá, Sp.
100/E4 Calvillo, Mex.
80/B3 Calvinia, SAfr.
82/C7 Calvinia, SAfr.
34/C2 Calvitero (mtn.), Sp.
34/D3 Calzada de Calatra
25/G2 Cam (riv.), Eng,UK
107/L6 Camaçari, Braz.
100/E3 Camacho, Mex.
82/C3 Camacupa, Ang.
103/G1 Camagüey, Cuba
103/G1 Camagüey (arch.), Cuba
89/L7 Camagüey, Cuba
33/J5 Camaiore, It.
103/G1 Camajuaní, Cuba
106/D7 Camaná, Peru
108/A4 Camaquã (riv.), Bra
108/B4 Camaquã, Braz.
109/F3 Camaquã, Braz.
35/V15 Câmara de Lobos, Madr.
33/G5 Camarat (cape), Fr.
35/J1 Camarat (cape), Fr.
88/G7 Camargo, Mex.
34/D1 Camargo, Sp.
98/A2 Camarillo, Ca,US
34/A1 Camariñas, Sp.
103/E3 Camarón (cape), H
109/C5 Camarones, Arg.
34/B4 Camas, Sp.
48/K9 Ca Mau (cape), Vie
63/H6 Ca Mau (cape), Vie
63/J6 Ca Mau, Viet.
65/D4 Ca Mau, Viet.
65/D4 Ca Mau (cape), Vie
66/B2 Ca Mau (cape), Vie
66/C2 Ca Mau, Viet.
102/D3 Camayagua (mts.), Hon.
34/A1 Cambados, Sp.
108/B2 Cambará, Braz.
53/K4 Cambay, India
53/K4 Cambay (gulf), Indi
62/B3 Cambay, India
62/B3 Cambay (gulf), Indi
108/B2 Cambé, Braz.
25/F4 Camberley Frimley, Eng,UK
19/N7 Camberwell, Eng,U
48/K8 Cambodia
63/H5 Cambodia
65/D3 Cambodia
66/B1 Cambodia
24/A6 Camborne, Eng,UK
26/B3 Cambrai, Fr.

123

Camb – Casim

30/C3 **Cambrai**, Fr.
32/E1 **Cambrai**, Fr.
22/D5 **Cambrian** (mts.), Wal,UK
24/C2 **Cambrian** (mts.), Wal,UK
94/D3 **Cambridge**, On,Can
1/S10 **Cambridge**, N.Z.
25/G2 **Cambridge**, Eng,UK
95/G3 **Cambridge**, Ma,US
94/E4 **Cambridge**, Md,US
97/J2 **Cambridge**, Md,US
91/K4 **Cambridge**, Mn,US
94/A2 **Cambridge**, Mn,US
94/D3 **Cambridge**, Oh,US
84/G3 **Cambridge Bay**, Can.
86/F2 **Cambridge Bay**, NW,Can
25/G2 **Cambridgeshire** (co.), Eng,UK
35/F2 **Cambrils**, Sp.
03/F5 **Cambutal** (mtn.), Pan.
71/J6 **Camden**, Austl.
72/G9 **Camden**, Austl.
73/D2 **Camden**, Austl.
19/N7 **Camden** (bor.), Eng,UK
97/G4 **Camden**, Al,US
93/J4 **Camden**, Ar,US
96/E3 **Camden**, Ar,US
95/G2 **Camden**, Me,US
94/F4 **Camden**, NJ,US
98/E6 **Camden**, NJ,US
98/F6 **Camden** (co.), NJ,US
97/H3 **Camden**, SC,US
73/E1 **Camden Haven**, Austl.
93/J3 **Camdenton**, Mo,US
96/E2 **Camdenton**, Mo,US
82/D3 **Cameia Nat'l Park**, Ang.
24/B6 **Camel** (riv.), Eng,UK
98/E4 **Camelback** (mtn.), Pa,US
24/B5 **Camelford**, Eng,UK
33/K5 **Camerino**, It.
38/C1 **Camerino**, It.
87/R7 **Cameron** (isl.), NW,Can
92/E4 **Cameron**, Az,US
93/J5 **Cameron**, La,US
96/E4 **Cameron**, La,US
93/J3 **Cameron**, Mo,US
96/E2 **Cameron**, Mo,US
01/F2 **Cameron**, Tx,US
93/H5 **Cameron**, Tx,US
96/D4 **Cameron**, Tx,US
74/D4 **Cameroon**
76/H7 **Cameroon**
79/H5 **Cameroon**
07/J4 **Cametá**, Braz.
40/A4 **Camicia** (peak), It.
30/A2 **Camiers**, Fr.
97/G4 **Camilla**, Ga,US
34/A2 **Caminha**, Port.
06/F8 **Camiri**, Bol.
44/E4 **Çamlıdere**, Turk.
50/C1 **Çamlıdere**, Turk.
50/C2 **Çamlık Milli Park**, Turk.
49/D1 **Çamlıyayla**, Turk.
03/E3 **Camoapa**, Nic.
82/F5 **Camo-Camo**, Moz.
07/K4 **Camocim**, Braz.
30/B4 **Camon**, Fr.
68/C6 **Camooweal**, Austl.
70/F3 **Camooweal**, Austl.
63/F6 **Camorta** (isl.), India
30/A3 **Campagne**, Fr.
09/B4 **Campanario** (peak), Arg.
34/C3 **Campanario**, Sp.
38/D2 **Campanella** (cape), It.
38/D2 **Campania** (reg.), It.
40/B5 **Campania** (reg.), It.
17/T8 **Campbell** (isl.), NZ
99/L12 **Campbell**, Ca,US
90/A2 **Campbell Island**, BC,Can
86/D3 **Campbell River**, BC,Can
90/B3 **Campbell River**, BC,Can
94/C4 **Campbellsville**, Ky,US
97/G2 **Campbellsville**, Ky,US
89/N2 **Campbellton**, Can.
95/H2 **Campbellton**, Can
87/K4 **Campbellton**, NB,Can
72/G9 **Campbelltown**, Austl.
73/C4 **Campbell Town**, Austl.
95/Q9 **Campbellville**, On,Can
95/R9 **Campden**, On,Can
01/G4 **Campeche** (bay), Mex.
01/H5 **Campeche**, Mex.
01/H5 **Campeche** (state), Mex.
02/C1 **Campeche** (bay), Mex.
02/D2 **Campeche**, Mex.
02/D2 **Campeche** (state), Mex.
84/H7 **Campeche** (bay), Mex.
01/P7 **Campeche, Bahía** (bay), Mex.
73/B3 **Camperdown**, Austl.
91/H3 **Camperville**, Mb,Can
61/E4 **Cam Pha**, Viet.
65/D1 **Cam Pha**, Viet.
38/A3 **Campidano** (range), It.
34/E3 **Campillo de Altobuey**, Sp.
34/C4 **Campillos**, Sp.
07/L5 **Campina Grande**, Braz.
07/J8 **Campinas**, Braz.
08/C2 **Campinas**, Braz.
109/G1 **Campinas**, Braz.
108/B1 **Campina Verde**, Braz.
37/E6 **Campione d'Italia**, It.
99/P14 **Camp Lake**, Wi,US
106/C3 **Campoalegre**, Col.
38/D2 **Campobasso**, It.
40/B5 **Campobasso**, It.
107/J8 **Campo Belo**, Braz.
108/C2 **Campo Belo**, Braz.
34/D3 **Campo de Criptana**, Sp.
103/H4 **Campo de la Cruz**, Col.
37/F5 **Campodolcino**, It.
107/K6 **Campo Formoso**, Braz.
107/H8 **Campo Grande**, Braz.
109/G2 **Campo Largo**, Braz.
107/K4 **Campo Maior**, Braz.
34/B3 **Campo Maior**, Port.
33/H4 **Campomorone**, It.
108/A3 **Campo Mourão**, Braz.
109/F1 **Campo Mourão**, Braz.
34/C1 **Camporredondo** (res.), Sp.
105/D5 **Campos** (reg.), Braz.
107/J7 **Campos** (reg.), Braz.
107/K8 **Campos**, Braz.
108/D2 **Campos**, Braz.
108/C1 **Campos Altos**, Braz.
35/G3 **Campos del Puerto**, Sp.
108/C2 **Campos do Jordão**, Braz.
108/C2 **Campos Gerais**, Braz.
108/B3 **Campos Novos**, Braz.
37/E5 **Campo Tencia, Pizzo** (peak), Swi.
98/K8 **Camp Springs**, Md,US
93/J5 **Campti**, La,US
96/E4 **Campti**, La,US
63/J5 **Cam Ranh**, Viet.
65/E4 **Cam Ranh**, Viet.
66/C1 **Cam Ranh**, Viet.
86/E3 **Camrose**, Ab,Can
90/E2 **Camrose**, Ab,Can
65/D1 **Cam Thuy**, Viet.
41/H5 **Çan**, Turk.
44/C4 **Çan**, Turk.
50/A1 **Çan**, Turk.
84/G4 **Canada**
86/* **Canada**
86/E2 **Canada**
89/F2 **Canada**
109/D3 **Cañada de Gómez**, Arg.
98/E4 **Canadensis**, Pa,US
84/G6 **Canadian** (riv.), US
88/F4 **Canadian** (riv.), US
93/G4 **Canadian**, Tx,US
96/C3 **Canadian**, Tx,US
106/F2 **Canaima Nat'l Park**, Ven.
39/K2 **Çanakkale**, Turk.
41/H5 **Çanakkale**, Turk.
41/H5 **Çanakkale** (prov.), Turk
44/C4 **Çanakkale**, Turk.
44/C5 **Çanakkale** (prov.), Turk.
50/A1 **Çanakkale**, Turk.
50/A2 **Çanakkale** (prov.), Turk.
69/U12 **Canala**, NCal.
35/E3 **Canals**, Sp.
94/E3 **Canandaigua**, NY,US
100/C2 **Cananea**, Mex.
88/D5 **Cananea**, Mex.
92/E5 **Cananea**, Mex
108/C3 **Cananéia**, Braz.
108/B1 **Canápolis**, Braz.
99/G7 **Canard** (riv.), On,Can
103/F1 **Canarreos** (arch.), Cuba
35/X16 **Canary** (isls.), Sp.
74/A2 **Canary** (isls.), Sp.
76/B2 **Canary** (isls.), Sp.
35/X16 **Canary Islands** (aut. comm.), Sp.
103/E4 **Cañas**, CR
100/D3 **Canatlán**, Mex.
84/J7 **Canaveral** (cape), US
89/K6 **Canaveral** (cape), Fl,US
97/H4 **Canaveral** (cape), Fl,US
107/L7 **Canavieiras**, Braz.
68/D8 **Canberra** (cap.), Austl.
71/H7 **Canberra** (cap.), Austl.
73/D2 **Canberra** (cap.), Austl.
25/H6 **Canche** (riv.), Fr.
30/A3 **Canche** (riv.), Fr.
32/E1 **Canche** (riv.), Fr.
102/E1 **Cancún**, Mex.
84/J7 **Cancún**, Mex.
44/C5 **Çandarli** (gulf), Turk.
50/A2 **Çandarlı** (gulf), Turk.
34/C1 **Candás**, Sp.
107/L6 **Candeias**, Braz.
101/H5 **Candelaria**, Mex.
101/H5 **Candelaria** (riv.), Mex.
102/D2 **Candelaria**, Mex.
102/D2 **Candelaria** (riv.), Mex.
34/C2 **Candeleda**, Sp.
73/D3 **Candelo**, Austl.
95/N7 **Candiac**, Qu,Can
108/B2 **Candido Mota**, Braz.
66/D5 **Canding** (cape), Indo.
44/E5 **Çandır**, Turk.
50/C2 **Çandır**, Turk.
91/G2 **Candle** (lake), Sk,Can
91/J3 **Cando**, ND,US
61/J5 **Candon**, Phil.
108/B4 **Canela**, Braz.
33/H4 **Canelli**, It.
101/E3 **Caneros**, Mex.
34/E2 **Cañete**, Sp.
34/A1 **Cangas**, Sp.
34/B1 **Cangas de Narcea**, Sp.
34/C1 **Cangas de Onís**, Sp.
66/C5 **Cangkuang** (cape), Indo.
80/C4 **Cango Caves**, SAfr.
82/D3 **Cangombe**, Ang.
55/J1 **Cangshan**, China
59/D4 **Cangshan**, China
108/A4 **Canguçu**, Braz.
63/K3 **Cangwu**, China
60/C4 **Cangyuan** (Cangyuan Vazu Zizhixian), China
63/G3 **Cangyuan** (Cangyuan Vazu Zizhixian), China
60/C4 **Cangyuan Vazu Zizhixian** (Cangyuan), China
63/G3 **Cangyuan Vazu Zizhixian** (Cangyuan), China
47/M6 **Cangzhou**, China
55/H4 **Cangzhou**, China
59/D3 **Cangzhou**, China
65/D1 **Canh Cuoc** (isl.), Viet.
82/B3 **Canhoca**, Ang.
72/C4 **Cania Gorge Nat'l Park**, Austl.
87/K3 **Caniapiscau** (lake), Qu,Can
87/K3 **Caniapiscau** (riv.), Qu,Can
38/C4 **Canicatti**, It.
32/E5 **Canigou, Pic de** (peak), Fr.
35/G1 **Canigou, Pic de** (peak), Fr.
50/C1 **Canik** (mts.), Turk.
34/D4 **Caniles**, Sp.
107/K5 **Canindé** (riv.), Braz.
107/L4 **Canindé**, Braz.
38/B1 **Canino**, It.
34/D4 **Canjáyar**, Sp.
44/E4 **Çankırı**, Turk.
44/E4 **Çankırı** (prov.), Turk.
50/C1 **Çankırı**, Turk.
50/C1 **Çankiri** (prov.), Turk.
67/F1 **Canlaon** (vol.), Phil.
90/E3 **Canmore**, Ab,Can
62/C5 **Cannanore**, India
64/E3 **Cannanore**, India
38/E2 **Canne** (ruins), It.
40/C5 **Canne** (ruins), It.
31/F5 **Canner** (riv.), Fr.
37/E5 **Cannero Riviera**, It.
18/D4 **Cannes**, Fr.
33/G5 **Cannes**, Fr.
35/J1 **Cannes**, Fr.
37/E5 **Cannobio**, It.
24/D1 **Cannock**, Eng,UK
93/G4 **Cannon** (A.F.B.), NM,US
96/C3 **Cannon** (A.F.B.), NM,US
107/H4 **Cannonball** (riv.), ND,US
98/G4 **Cannondale**, Ct,US
91/K4 **Cannon Falls**, Mn,US
72/C3 **Cannonvale**, Austl.
73/D3 **Cann River**, Austl.
108/B3 **Canoas** (riv.), Braz.
108/B4 **Canoas**, Braz.
109/F2 **Canoas**, Braz.
73/D2 **Canobolas** (peak), Austl.
90/F2 **Canoe** (lake), Sk,Can
108/B3 **Canoinhas**, Braz.
109/F2 **Canoinhas**, Braz.
23/F1 **Canonbie**, Sc,UK
88/E4 **Canon City**, Co,US
93/F3 **Canon City**, Co,US
96/B2 **Canon City**, Co,US
102/C2 **Cañon del Sumidero Nat'l Park**, Mex.
101/M8 **Cañon de Río Blanco Nat'l Park**, Mex.
103/E4 **Caño Negro Nat'l Wild. Ref.**, CR
86/F3 **Canora**, Sk,Can
88/F1 **Canora**, Sk,Can
91/H3 **Canora**, Sk,Can
40/C5 **Canosa di Puglia**, It.
104/F4 **Canouan** (isl.), StV.
73/D2 **Canowindra**, Austl.
89/P2 **Canso** (cape), Can.
95/J2 **Canso** (cape), Can.
87/K4 **Canso** (cape), NS,Can
32/B5 **Cantabria** (aut. comm.), Sp.
34/C1 **Cantabria** (aut. comm.), Sp.
32/E4 **Cantal** (plat.), Fr.
34/D2 **Cantalejo**, Sp.
34/A2 **Cantanhede**, Port.
106/F2 **Cantaura**, Ven.
72/H8 **Canterbury**, Austl.
71/R11 **Canterbury** (bight), NZ
25/H4 **Canterbury**, Eng,UK
25/H4 **Canterbury Cathedral**, Eng,UK
48/K8 **Can Tho**, Viet.
63/J5 **Can Tho**, Viet.
65/D4 **Can Tho**, Viet.
66/C1 **Can Tho**, Viet.
34/C4 **Cantillana**, Sp.
91/L5 **Canton**, Il,US
93/K2 **Canton**, Il,US
94/B3 **Canton**, Il,US
99/E7 **Canton**, Mi,US
97/F3 **Canton**, Ms,US
94/F2 **Canton**, NY,US
89/K3 **Canton**, Oh,US
94/D3 **Canton**, Oh,US
93/H3 **Canton**, Ok,US
96/D2 **Canton**, Ok,US
91/J5 **Canton**, SD,US
93/H2 **Canton**, SD,US
93/J4 **Canton**, Tx,US
96/E3 **Canton**, Tx,US
69/H5 **Canton** (Abariringa) (atoll), Kiri.
61/G4 **Canton** (Guangzhou), China
34/D4 **Cantoria**, Sp.
33/H4 **Cantù**, It.
85/J3 **Cantwell**, Ak,US
73/B3 **Canunda Nat'l Park**, Austl.
100/D2 **Canutillo**, Tx,US
25/G3 **Canvey Island**, Eng,UK
90/G2 **Canwood**, Sk,Can
93/G4 **Canyon**, Tx,US
96/C3 **Canyon**, Tx,US
88/E4 **Canyon de Chelly Nat'l Mon.**, Az,US
92/E3 **Canyon de Chelly Nat'l Mon.**, Az,US
88/E4 **Canyonlands Nat'l Park**, Ut,US
92/E3 **Canyonlands Nat'l Park**, Ut,US
58/C2 **Cao** (riv.), China
60/E4 **Cao Bang**, Viet.
63/J3 **Cao Bang**, Viet.
65/D1 **Cao Bang**, Viet.
61/E3 **Caodu** (riv.), China
61/J2 **Cao'e** (riv.), China
65/D4 **Cao Lanh**, Viet.
59/C4 **Cao Xian**, China
99/G5 **Capac**, Mi,US
106/E2 **Capanaparo** (riv.), Ven.
107/J4 **Capanema**, Braz.
38/B1 **Capanne** (peak), It.
33/J5 **Capannori**, It.
108/B3 **Capão Bonito**, Braz.
34/A3 **Caparica**, Port.
35/P10 **Caparica**, Port.
99/K9 **Capay**, Ca,US
32/C5 **Capbreton**, Fr.
34/E1 **Capbreton**, Fr.
87/K4 **Cap-Chat**, Qu,Can
89/N2 **Cap-Chat**, Qu,Can
95/H1 **Cap-Chat**, Qu,Can
95/H1 **Cap de Gaspé** (cape), Can
95/F2 **Cap-de-la-Madeleine**, Qu,Can
32/E4 **Capdenac-Gare**, Fr.
35/G3 **Capdepera**, Sp.
72/B3 **Cape** (riv.), Austl.
80/C3 **Cape** (prov.), SAfr.
80/L10 **Cape** (prov.), SAfr.
71/H8 **Cape Barren** (isl.), Austl.
73/D4 **Cape Barren** (isl.), Austl.
76/H1 **Cape Bon** (cape), Tun.
84/L5 **Cape Breton** (isl.), Can.
87/K4 **Cape Breton** (isl.), NS,Can
89/Q2 **Cape Breton** (isl.), NS,Can
95/J2 **Cape Breton** (highlands), NS,Can
95/J2 **Cape Breton** (isl.), NS,Can
87/K4 **Cape Breton Highlands**, NS,Can
89/Q2 **Cape Breton Highlands Nat'l Park**, NS,Can
95/J2 **Cape Breton Highlands Nat'l Park**, NS,Can
72/B2 **Cape Cleveland Nat'l Park**, Austl.
76/E6 **Cape Coast**, Gha.
79/E5 **Cape Coast**, Gha.
95/G3 **Cape Cod Nat'l Seashore**, Ma,US
104/A1 **Cape Coral**, Fl,US
89/K6 **Cape Coral**, Fl,US
97/H5 **Cape Coral**, Fl,US
87/J2 **Cape Dorset**, NW,Can
89/J4 **Cape Girardeau**, Mo,US
93/K3 **Cape Girardeau**, Mo,US
94/B4 **Cape Girardeau**, Mo,US
97/F2 **Cape Girardeau**, Mo,US
97/K3 **Cape Hatteras Nat'l Seashore**, NC,US
109/C8 **Cape Horn** (cape), Chile
85/E2 **Cape Krusenstern Nat'l Mon.**, Ak,US
19/Q8 **Capel**, Eng,UK
22/E5 **Capel-Curig**, Wal,UK
108/D1 **Capelinha**, Braz.
72/C3 **Capella**, Austl.
35/K6 **Capellades**, Sp.
25/H4 **Capel le Ferne**, Eng,UK
30/A1 **Capel le Ferne**, Eng,UK
97/J3 **Cape Lookout Nat'l Seashore**, NC,US
25/H2 **Capel Saint Mary**, Eng,UK
72/B1 **Cape Melville Nat'l Park**, Austl.
82/C7 **Cape of Good Hope** (cape), SAfr.
72/C3 **Cape Palmerston Nat'l Park**, Austl.
98/K7 **Cape Saint Claire**, Md,US
32/E5 **Capestang**, Fr.
35/G1 **Capestang**, Fr.
80/B4 **Cape Town** (cap.), SAfr.
80/L10 **Cape Town** (cap.), SAfr.
82/C7 **Cape Town** (cap.), SAfr.
72/B2 **Cape Tribulation Nat'l Park**, Austl.
72/B2 **Cape Upstart Nat'l Park**, Austl.
74/K9 **Cape Verde**
85/K3 **Cape Yakataga**, Ak,US
68/D6 **Cape York** (pen.), Austl.
70/G2 **Cape York** (pen.), Austl.
72/A1 **Cape York** (pen.), Austl.
103/H2 **Cap-Haïtien**, Haiti
104/C3 **Cap-Haïtien**, Haiti
38/A2 **Capicciola** (pt.), Fr.
107/J4 **Capim** (riv.), Braz.
108/B1 **Capinópolis**, Braz.
108/B2 **Capirara** (res.), Braz.
109/F1 **Capirara** (res.), Braz.
38/C2 **Capistrello**, It.
96/B3 **Capitan** (mts.), NM,US
107/J4 **Capitão Poco**, Braz.
68/D3 **Capitol Hill**, NMar.
88/D4 **Capitol Reef Nat'l Park**, Ut,US
92/E3 **Capitol Reef Nat'l Park**, Ut,US
107/H8 **Capivara** (res.), Braz.
39/E1 **Čapljina**, Bosn.
40/C4 **Čapljina**, Bosn.
38/D3 **Capo d'Orlando**, It.
38/A3 **Capoterra**, It.
38/A1 **Capraia** (isl.), It.
38/C1 **Caprarola**, It.
94/D2 **Capreol**, On,Can
38/D2 **Capri**, It.
40/B5 **Capri**, It.
71/J4 **Capricorn** (chan.), Austl.
72/C3 **Capricorn** (cape), Austl.
72/C3 **Capricorn** (chan.), Austl.
74/E6 **Caprivi Strip** (reg.), Namb.
82/D4 **Caprivi Strip** (reg.), Namb.
100/E1 **Caprock**, NM,US
96/C3 **Cap Rock Escarpment** (cliffs), Tx,US
96/C3 **Caprock, The** (cliffs), NM,US
95/G2 **Cap-Rouge**, Qu,Can
33/G5 **Cap Roux, Pointe du** (pt.), Fr.
35/J1 **Cap Roux, Pointe du** (pt.), Fr.
88/U11 **Captain Cook**, Hi,US
73/D2 **Captains Flat**, Austl.
40/B5 **Capua**, It.
101/K7 **Capulhuac de Mirafuentes**, Mex.
93/G3 **Capulin Volcano Nat'l Mon.**, NM,US
96/C2 **Capulin Volcano Nat'l Mon.**, NM,US
105/B3 **Caquetá** (riv.), Col.
106/D4 **Caquetá** (riv.), Col.
35/N9 **Carabanchel** (nrbhd.), Sp.
104/D5 **Carabobo** (state), Ven.
41/G3 **Caracal**, Rom.
44/C3 **Caracal**, Rom.
106/F3 **Caracaraí**, Braz.
104/E5 **Caracas** (cap.), Ven.
106/E1 **Caracas** (cap.), Ven.
24/B5 **Caradon** (hill), Eng,UK
108/C2 **Caraguatatuba**, Braz.
107/H5 **Carajás** (mts.), Braz.
106/E7 **Caranavi**, Bol.
108/D2 **Carandaí**, Braz.
108/D2 **Carangola**, Braz.
40/F3 **Caransebeş**, Rom.
38/D2 **Carapelle** (riv.), It.
95/H2 **Caraquet**, NB,Can
40/E3 **Caraş-Severin** (co.), Rom.
103/F3 **Caratasca** (lag.), Hon.
107/K7 **Caratinga**, Braz.
108/D1 **Caratinga**, Braz.
106/E4 **Carauari**, Braz.
34/E3 **Caravaca de la Cruz**, Sp.
78/A4 **Caravela** (isl.), GBis.
108/E1 **Caravelas**, Braz.
106/D7 **Caravelí**, Peru
109/F2 **Carazinho**, Braz.
34/A1 **Carballino**, Sp.
34/A1 **Carballo**, Sp.
91/J3 **Carberry**, Mb,Can
100/C2 **Carbo**, Mex.
92/E5 **Carbo**, Mex
75/U17 **Carbon** (cape), Alg.
99/C3 **Carbon** (riv.), Wa,US
99/C3 **Carbonado**, Wa,US
38/A3 **Carbonara** (cape), It.
38/D4 **Carbonara, Pizzo** (peak), It.
89/J4 **Carbondale**, Il,US
93/K3 **Carbondale**, Il,US
94/B4 **Carbondale**, Il,US
97/F2 **Carbondale**, Il,US
94/F3 **Carbondale**, Pa,US
95/L2 **Carbonear**, Nf,Can
38/A3 **Carbonia**, It.
32/D5 **Carbonne**, Fr.
35/F1 **Carbonne**, Fr.
22/B5 **Carbury**, Ire.
35/E3 **Carcagente**, Sp.
32/E5 **Carcassonne**, Fr.
35/G1 **Carcassonne**, Fr.
35/P10 **Carcavelos**, Port.
34/E3 **Carche** (mtn.), Sp.
85/M3 **Carcross**, Yk,Can
86/C2 **Carcross**, Yt,Can
41/H5 **Çardak**, Turk.
44/C4 **Çardak**, Turk.
50/A1 **Çardak**, Turk.
64/F4 **Cardamon** (hills), India
35/L6 **Cardedeu**, Sp.
103/F1 **Cárdenas**, Cuba
101/F4 **Cárdenas**, Mex.
101/G5 **Cárdenas**, Mex.
102/B1 **Cárdenas**, Mex.
102/C2 **Cárdenas**, Mex.
18/C3 **Cardiff**, Wal,UK
24/C4 **Cardiff** (cap.), Wal,UK
22/D6 **Cardigan** (bay), Wal,UK
24/B1 **Cardigan** (bay), Wal,UK
24/B2 **Cardigan**, Wal,UK
35/F2 **Cardona**, Sp.
108/B2 **Cardoso**, Braz.
86/E4 **Cardston**, Ab,Can
88/D2 **Cardston**, Ab,Can
90/E3 **Cardston**, Ab,Can
72/B2 **Cardwell**, Austl.
37/G5 **Care Alto, Monte** (peak), It.
27/M5 **Carei**, Rom.
40/F2 **Carei**, Rom.
44/B3 **Carei**, Rom.
32/C2 **Carentan**, Fr.
39/H1 **Carev vrh** (peak), Macd.
40/F4 **Carev vrh** (peak), Macd.
70/C5 **Carey** (lake), Austl.
32/B2 **Carhaix-Plouguer**, Fr.
109/D4 **Carhué**, Arg.
108/D2 **Cariacica**, Braz.
104/F5 **Cariaco**, Ven.
106/C4 **Cariamanga**, Ecu.
38/E3 **Cariati**, It.
103/G3 **Caribbean** (sea)
106/E1 **Caribbean** (sea)
89/K7 **Caribbean** (sea)
84/K8 **Caribbean** (sea)
104/D4 **Caribbean** (sea), West Indies
90/C2 **Cariboo** (mts.), BC,Can
86/E3 **Caribou** (mts.), Ab,Can
91/L3 **Caribou** (lake), On,Can
91/M3 **Caribou** (lake), On,Can
94/B1 **Caribou** (lake), On,Can
85/L3 **Caribou**, Yk,Can
84/L5 **Caribou**, US
90/F5 **Caribou** (range), Id,US
87/K4 **Caribou**, Me,US
89/N2 **Caribou**, Me,US
95/G2 **Caribou**, Me,US
100/D3 **Carichic**, Mex.
95/P7 **Carignan**, Qu,Can
31/E4 **Carignan**, Fr.
34/E2 **Cariñena**, Sp.
107/K6 **Carinhanha**, Braz.
38/C3 **Carini**, It.
33/K3 **Carinthia** (prov.), Aus.
40/B2 **Carinthia** (prov.), Aus.
104/F5 **Caripito**, Ven.
106/F1 **Caripito**, Ven.
35/E3 **Carlet**, Sp.
95/H1 **Carleton**, Can
95/H2 **Carleton** (peak), Can
87/K4 **Carleton** (mtn.), NB,Can
95/H2 **Carleton** (riv.), NS,Can
99/F7 **Carleton**, Mi,US
94/E2 **Carleton Place**, On,Can
80/D2 **Carletonville**, SAfr.
80/P13 **Carletonville**, SAfr.
82/E6 **Carletonville**, SAfr.
90/D5 **Carlin**, Nv,US
92/C2 **Carlin**, Nv,US
31/F5 **Carling**, Fr.
72/H8 **Carlingford**, Austl.
22/B3 **Carlingford**, Ire.
22/B3 **Carlingford** (mtn.), Ire.
22/B3 **Carlingford Lough** (inlet), Ire.
93/K3 **Carlinville**, Il,US
94/B4 **Carlinville**, Il,US
97/F2 **Carlinville**, Il,US
95/Q9 **Carlisle**, On,Can
18/C3 **Carlisle**, Eng,UK
23/F2 **Carlisle**, Eng,UK
94/E3 **Carlisle**, Pa,US
32/D5 **Carlit** (peak), Fr.
35/F1 **Carlit** (peak), Fr.
108/D1 **Carlos Chagas**, Braz.
103/G1 **Carlos M. De Céspedes**, Cuba
22/B6 **Carlow**, Ire.
22/B6 **Carlow** (co.), Ire.
84/G6 **Carlsbad**, US
88/F5 **Carlsbad**, NM,US
93/F4 **Carlsbad**, NM,US
96/B3 **Carlsbad**, NM,US
101/E2 **Carlsbad**, Tx,US
101/D1 **Carlsbad Caverns Nat'l Park**, NM,US
88/E5 **Carlsbad Caverns Nat'l Park**, NM,US
93/F4 **Carlsbad Caverns Nat'l Park**, NM,US
96/B3 **Carlsbad Caverns Nat'l Park**, NM,US
31/H5 **Carlsberg**, Ger.
23/G6 **Carlton**, Eng,UK
91/K4 **Carlton**, Mn,US
94/A2 **Carlton**, Mn,US
95/Q9 **Carluke**, On,Can
91/H3 **Carlyle**, Sk,Can
93/K3 **Carlyle** (lake), Il,US
85/L3 **Carmacks**, Yk,Can
86/C2 **Carmacks**, Yt,Can
33/G4 **Carmagnola**, It.
86/G4 **Carman**, Mb,Can
91/J3 **Carman**, Mb,Can
24/B3 **Carmarthen**, Wal,UK
24/B3 **Carmarthen** (bay), Wal,UK
32/E4 **Carmaux**, Fr.
49/D3 **Carmel** (mtn.), Isr.
94/C4 **Carmel**, In,US
97/G2 **Carmel**, In,US
22/D5 **Carmel Head** (pt.), Wal,UK
101/H5 **Carmelita**, Guat.
49/D3 **Carmel, Mount** (Har Karmel) (mtn.), Isr.
100/C3 **Carmen** (isl.), Mex.
101/E3 **Carmen**, Mex.
102/D2 **Carmen** (isl.), Mex.
92/E5 **Carmen** (riv.), Mex
94/B4 **Carmi**, Il,US
97/F2 **Carmi**, Il,US
99/M9 **Carmichael**, Ca,US
108/C1 **Carmo do Paranaíba**, Braz.
108/C2 **Carmo do Rio Claro**, Braz.
34/C4 **Carmona**, Sp.
22/B1 **Carnanmore** (mtn.), NI,UK
68/A7 **Carnarvon**, Austl.
70/A4 **Carnarvon**, Austl.
80/C3 **Carnarvon**, SAfr.
82/D7 **Carnarvon**, SAfr.
80/C3 **Carnarvonleegte** (dry riv.), SAfr.
72/B4 **Carnarvon Nat'l Park**, Austl.
99/D2 **Carnation**, Wa,US
35/P10 **Carnaxide**, Port.
22/C2 **Carncastle**, NI,UK
22/A1 **Carndonagh**, Ire.
91/H3 **Carnduff**, Sk,Can
22/D5 **Carnedd Dafydd** (mtn.), Wal,UK
22/E5 **Carnedd Llewelyn** (mtn.), Wal,UK
68/B7 **Carnegie** (lake), Austl.
70/C5 **Carnegie** (lake), Austl.
22/B6 **Carnew**, Ire.
83/S **Carney** (isl.), Ant.
23/F3 **Carnforth**, Eng,UK
30/C3 **Carnières**, Fr.
22/B2 **Carnlough**, NI,UK
76/J7 **Carnot**, CAfr.
34/A1 **Carnota**, Sp.
21/B4 **Carnsore** (pt.), Ire.
86/D2 **Carnwath** (riv.), NW,Can
94/D3 **Caro**, Mi,US
104/E3 **Carolina**, PR
80/Q13 **Carolina**, SAfr.
97/J3 **Carolina Beach**, NC,US
69/K5 **Caroline** (isl.), Kiri.
68/D4 **Caroline** (isls.), Micr.
99/P16 **Carol Stream**, Il,US
105/C2 **Caroni** (riv.), Ven.
104/D5 **Carora**, Ven.
36/C5 **Carouge**, Swi.
18/F4 **Carpathian** (mts.), Eur.
27/J4 **Carpathian** (mts.), Eur.
44/B2 **Carpathian** (mts.), Eur.
46/C5 **Carpathian** (mts.), Eur.
40/F1 **Carpathian** (mts.), Rom.
33/J4 **Carpenedolo**, It.
68/C6 **Carpentaria** (gulf), Austl.
70/F2 **Carpentaria** (gulf), Austl.
72/A2 **Carpentaria** (gulf), Austl.
99/P15 **Carpentersville**, Il,US
32/F4 **Carpentras**, Fr.
33/J4 **Carpi**, It.
98/A2 **Carpinteria**, Ca,US
99/B3 **Carr** (inlet), Wa,US
97/G4 **Carrabelle**, Fl,US
103/H4 **Carraipía**, Col.
102/C2 **Carranza**, Mex.
33/J4 **Carrara**, It.
103/J4 **Carrasquero**, Ven.
22/D6 **Carreg Ddu** (pt.), Wal,UK
104/F4 **Carriacou** (isl.), Gren.
106/F1 **Carriacou** (isl.), StV.
22/C2 **Carrickfergus**, NI,UK
22/C2 **Carrickfergus** (dist.), NI,UK
22/B4 **Carrickmacross**, Ire.
22/A2 **Carrickmore**, NI,UK
21/A4 **Carrick on Shannon**, Ire.
19/S10 **Carrières-sous-Poissy**, Fr.
30/B6 **Carrières-sous-Poissy**, Fr.
21/H7 **Carrigaholt**, Ire.
22/B3 **Carrigatuke** (mtn.), NI,UK
89/G2 **Carrington**, ND,US
91/J4 **Carrington**, ND,US
34/C1 **Carrión** (riv.), Sp.
34/C1 **Carrión de los Condes**, Sp.
103/H3 **Carrizal**, Col.
88/E4 **Carrizo** (mts.), Az,US
88/G6 **Carrizo Springs**, Tx,US
96/D4 **Carrizo Springs**, Tx,US
92/E4 **Carrizo Wash** (dry riv.), Az, NM,US
93/F4 **Carrizozo**, NM,US
96/B3 **Carrizozo**, NM,US
97/G3 **Carrollton**, Ga,US
94/C4 **Carrollton**, Ky,US
97/G2 **Carrollton**, Ky,US
93/J3 **Carrollton**, Mo,US
96/E2 **Carrollton**, Mo,US
91/H2 **Carrot** (riv.), Sk,Can
91/H2 **Carrot River**, Sk,Can
22/C2 **Carrowdore**, NI,UK
73/G6 **Carrum Downs**, Austl.
22/C2 **Carryduff**, NI,UK
44/F4 **Çarşamba**, Turk.
50/D1 **Çarşamba**, Turk.
98/B3 **Carson**, Ca,US
92/C3 **Carson** (riv.), Nv,US
92/C3 **Carson** (sink), Nv,US
86/E5 **Carson City** (cap.), Nv,US
88/C4 **Carson City** (cap.), Nv,US
92/C3 **Carson City**, Nv,US
22/D1 **Carsphairn**, Sc,UK
90/E3 **Carstairs**, Ab,Can
96/D3 **Carswell** (A.F.B.), Tx,US
103/H4 **Cartagena**, Col.
106/C1 **Cartagena**, Col.
18/C5 **Cartagena**, Sp.
35/E4 **Cartagena**, Sp.
106/C3 **Cartago**, Col.
103/F4 **Cartago**, CR
106/B2 **Cartago**, CR
34/C4 **Cártama**, Sp.
34/A3 **Cartaxo**, Port.
34/B4 **Cartaya**, Sp.
72/A1 **Carter** (peak), Austl.
97/G3 **Cartersville**, Ga,US
25/E3 **Carterton**, Eng,UK
38/B4 **Carthage** (ruins), Tun.
93/J3 **Carthage**, Mo,US
96/F2 **Carthage**, Mo,US
97/F3 **Carthage**, Ms,US
94/C4 **Carthage**, Tn,US
97/G2 **Carthage**, Tn,US
101/G1 **Carthage**, Tx,US
89/H5 **Carthage**, Tx,US
93/J4 **Carthage**, Tx,US
96/E3 **Carthage**, Tx,US
103/G4 **Cartí** (mtn.), Pan.
70/C2 **Cartier Islet** (isl.), Austl.
91/J3 **Cartwright**, Can
87/L3 **Cartwright**, Nf,Can
107/L5 **Caruaru**, Braz.
106/F1 **Carúpano**, Ven.
93/K3 **Caruthersville**, Mo,US
94/B4 **Caruthersville**, Mo,US
97/F2 **Caruthersville**, Mo,US
30/B2 **Carvin**, Fr.
34/A3 **Carvoeiro** (cape), Port.
99/P15 **Cary**, Il,US
97/J3 **Cary**, NC,US
75/L14 **Casablanca**, Mor.
76/D1 **Casablanca**, Mor.
108/C2 **Casa Branca**, Braz.
100/C2 **Casa de Janos**, Mex.
92/E5 **Casa de Janos**, Mex
100/C1 **Casa Grande**, Az,US
88/D5 **Casa Grande**, Az,US
92/E4 **Casa Grande**, Az,US
92/E4 **Casa Grande Nat'l Mon.**, Az,US
100/C1 **Casa Grande Ruins Nat'l Mon.**, Az,US
40/B4 **Casalbordino**, It.
38/D2 **Casal di Principe**, It.
33/J4 **Casalecchio di Reno**, It.
33/H4 **Casale Monferrato**, It.
78/A3 **Casamance** (riv.), Sen.
106/D2 **Casanare** (riv.), Col., Ven.
104/F5 **Casanay**, Ven.
39/F3 **Casarano**, It.
34/B3 **Casar de Cáceres**, Sp.
101/F4 **Casas**, Mex.
100/C2 **Casas Grandes** (ruins), Mex.
100/D2 **Casas Grandes**, Mex.
92/E5 **Casas Grandes** (dry riv.), Mex
34/E3 **Casas-Ibáñez**, Sp.
100/C2 **Cascada de Bassaseachic Nat'l Park**, Mex.
90/C5 **Cascade** (range), Can., US
84/C5 **Cascade** (range), US
88/B3 **Cascade** (range), US
92/B2 **Cascade** (range), US
90/D4 **Cascade** (res.), Id,US
99/D3 **Cascade** (range), Wa,US
86/D4 **Cascade** (range), Or,Wa,US
99/C3 **Cascade-Fairwood**, Wa,US
81/R15 **Cascades** (pt.), Reun.
35/P10 **Cascais**, Port.
95/H1 **Cascapédia** (riv.), Qu,Can
107/L4 **Cascavel**, Braz.
109/F1 **Cascavel**, Braz.
33/J5 **Cascina-Navacchio**, It.
99/B3 **Case** (inlet), Wa,US
38/D2 **Caserta**, It.
40/B5 **Caserta**, It.
83/D **Casey** (bay), Ant.
83/H **Casey**, Ant.
75/H3 **Caseyr** (cape), Som.
77/R5 **Caseyr** (cape), Som.
90/C4 **Cashmere**, Wa,US
103/H4 **Casigua**, Ven.
109/D3 **Casilda**, Arg.
103/F1 **Casilda** (pt.), Cuba
100/D5 **Casimiro Castillo**, Mex.

124

Casin – Chant

37/G4 Casina, Cima la (Piz Murtaröl) (peak), It.
71/J5 Casino, Austl.
72/D5 Casino, Austl.
73/E1 Casino, Austl.
106/C5 Casma, Peru
35/E2 Caspe, Sp.
86/F4 Casper, Wy,US
88/E3 Casper, Wy,US
91/G5 Casper, Wy,US
93/F2 Casper, Wy,US
46/F6 Caspian (sea)
48/E5 Caspian (sea)
51/G1 Caspian (sea)
45/J4 Caspian (sea)
19/H4 Caspian (sea)
52/F1 Caspian (sea)
37/F5 Caspoggio, It.
99/F6 Cass (lake), Mi,US
35/G2 Cassà de la Selva, Sp.
82/D3 Cassai (riv.), Ang.
82/D3 Cassamba, Ang.
38/E3 Cassano allo Ionio, It.
94/D3 Cass City, Mi,US
30/B2 Cassel, Fr.
108/C2 Cássia, Braz.
85/N4 Cassiar, BC,Can
86/C3 Cassiar (range), BC,Can
86/D3 Cassiar, BC,Can
108/B1 Cassilândia, Braz.
38/C2 Cassino, It.
40/A5 Cassino, It.
93/J3 Cassville, Mo,US
96/E2 Cassville, Mo,US
33/J5 Castagneto Carducci, It.
37/E5 Castagnola, Swi.
98/B1 Castaic (lake), Ca,US
35/E3 Castalla, Sp.
32/D5 Castanet-Tolosan, Fr.
107/J4 Castanhal, Braz.
102/E3 Castañones (pt.), Nic.
101/E3 Castaños, Mex.
96/C5 Castaños, Mex
38/D4 Castelbuono, It.
33/K5 Castel del Piano
38/D2 Castel di Sangro, It.
40/B5 Castel di Sangro, It.
33/K5 Castelfidardo, It.
32/D4 Casteljaloux, Fr.
38/C3 Castellammare (gulf), It.
38/D2 Castellammare di Stabia, It.
40/B5 Castellammare di Stabia, It.
33/G4 Castellamonte, It.
35/G2 Castellar del Vallès, Sp.
35/K7 Castelldefels, Sp.
35/L7 Castell de Montjuic, Sp.
109/E4 Castelli, Arg.
38/D4 Castello Eurialo (ruins), It.
18/C5 Castellón de la Plana, Sp.
35/E3 Castellón de la Plana, Sp.
35/E2 Castellote, Sp.
49/G8 Castel Nat'l Park, Isr.
32/D5 Castelnaudary, Fr.
35/F1 Castelnaudary, Fr.
32/E5 Castelnau-le-Lez, Fr.
35/G1 Castelnau-le-Lez, Fr.
33/J4 Castelnovo ne'Monti, It.
34/B2 Castelo Branco (dist.), Port.
34/B3 Castelo Branco, Port.
34/B3 Castelo de Vide, Port.
38/D2 Castel San Lorenzo, It.
40/B5 Castel San Lorenzo, It.
38/A2 Castelsardo, It.
32/D4 Castelsarrasin, Fr.
38/C4 Castelvetrano, It.
73/B3 Casterton, Austl.
33/J5 Castiglion Fiorentino, It.
32/B5 Castile and Leon (aut. comm.), Sp.
35/N8 Castile-La Mancha (aut. comm.), Sp.
108/B2 Castilho, Braz.
106/B5 Castilla, Peru
34/C2 Castille and León (aut. comm.), Sp.
34/D3 Castille-La Mancha (aut. comm.), Sp.
104/D5 Castilletes, Col.
102/D3 Castillo de San Felipe, Guat.
97/H4 Castillo de San Marcos Nat'l Mon., Fl,US
37/G6 Castione della Presolana, It.
92/B3 Castle (A.F.B.), Ca,US
25/G1 Castle Acre, Eng,UK
21/A4 Castlebar, Ire.
22/B4 Castlebellingham, Ire.
22/B3 Castleblayney, Ire.
24/D4 Castle Cary, Eng,UK
22/B3 Castlecaulfield, NI,UK
24/D4 Castle Combe, Eng,UK
22/A6 Castlecomer, Ire.
92/E3 Castle Dale, Ut,US
22/B2 Castledawson, NI,UK
22/B6 Castledermot, Ire.
23/G6 Castle Donnington, Eng,UK
25/E1 Castle Donnington, Eng,UK
22/E2 Castle Douglas, Sc,UK
23/G4 Castleford, Eng,UK
90/D3 Castlegar, BC,Can
21/G7 Castlegregory, Ire.
72/H8 Castle Hill, Austl.
95/L2 Castle Hill Nat'l Hist. Park, Can
21/H7 Castleisland, Ire.
22/D2 Castle Kennedy, Sc,UK
73/C3 Castlemaine, Austl.
22/A4 Castlepollard, Ire.
72/G8 Castlereagh, Austl.
21/A4 Castlereagh, Ire.
22/B1 Castlerock, NI,UK
93/F3 Castle Rock, Co,US
96/B2 Castle Rock, Co,US
90/C4 Castle Rock, Wa,US
91/L5 Castle Rock (lake), Wi,US
72/C4 Castle Tower Nat'l Park, Austl.
22/D3 Castletown, IM,UK
22/C3 Castlewellan, NI,UK
90/F2 Castor, Ab,Can
76/D6 Castos (riv.), Libr.
32/E5 Castres, Fr.
35/G1 Castres, Fr.
28/B3 Castricum, Neth.
104/F4 Castries (cap.), StL.
108/B3 Castro, Braz.
109/G1 Castro, Braz.
109/B5 Castro, Chile
34/B2 Castro Daire, Port.
34/C4 Castro del Río, Sp.
34/B1 Castro de Rey, Sp.
34/C1 Castrojeriz, Sp.
34/B4 Castro Marim, Port.
34/B1 Castropol, Sp.
29/E5 Castrop-Rauxel, Ger.
34/D1 Castro-Urdiales, Sp.
99/K11 Castro Valley, Ca,US
34/A4 Castro Verde, Port.
38/E3 Castrovillari, It.
34/C3 Castuera, Sp.
104/C1 Cat (isl.), Bahm.
84/K7 Cat (isl.), Bahm.
89/L7 Cat (isl.), Bahm.
91/K3 Cat (lake), On,Can
102/E3 Catacamas, Hon.
68/B3 Catanduanes (isl.), Phil.
108/D2 Cataguases, Braz.
109/H1 Cataguases, Braz.
67/F1 Catañgan, Phil.
51/E2 Çatak, Turk.
41/K5 Çatalağzı, Turk.
107/J7 Catalão, Braz.
108/C1 Catalão, Braz.
41/J5 Çatalca, Turk.
50/B1 Çatalca, Turk.
51/M6 Çatalca, Turk.
100/C1 Catalina, Az,US
92/E4 Catalina, Az,US
32/D5 Catalonia (aut. comm.), Sp.
35/F2 Catalonia (aut. comm.), Sp.
35/K6 Catalonia (aut. comm.), Sp.
109/C2 Catamarca, Arg.
107/J8 Catanduva, Braz.
108/B2 Catanduva, Braz.
18/E5 Catania, It.
38/D4 Catania, It.
38/D4 Catania (gulf), It.
18/E5 Catanzaro, It.
38/E3 Catanzaro, It.
67/F1 Catarman, Indo.
35/E3 Catarroja, Sp.
70/E7 Catastrophe (cape), Austl.
67/F2 Catatungan (mtn.), Phil.
61/E4 Cat Ba (isl.), Viet.
61/E4 Cat Ba Nat'l Park, Viet.
102/C2 Catemaco (lake), Mex.
19/N8 Caterham, Eng,UK
25/F4 Caterham and Warlingham, Eng,UK
100/E2 Cathedral (mtn.), Tx,US
50/C4 Catherine (mt.), Egypt
52/B3 Catherine, Mount (Katrīnah, Jabal) (mtn.), Egypt
43/V7 Catherine Palace, Rus.
76/B5 Catió, GBis.
103/G4 Cativá, Pan.
50/E2 Çatköyü, Turk.
94/D4 Catlettsburg, Ky,US
97/H2 Catlettsburg, Ky,US
71/K4 Cato (isl.), Austl.
89/J7 Catoche (cape), Mex.
101/J4 Catoche, Cabo (cape), Mex.
102/E1 Catoche, Cabo (cape), Mex.
84/J7 Catoche, Cabo (cape), Mex.
101/E4 Catorce, Mex.
33/K5 Catria (peak), It.
106/F3 Catrimani (riv.), Braz.
24/D2 Catshill, Eng,UK
94/F3 Catskill (mts.), NY,US
31/F5 Cattenom, Fr.
23/G3 Catterick, Eng,UK
103/H4 Cauca (riv.), Col.
105/B2 Cauca (riv.), Col.
106/C2 Cauca (riv.), Col.
107/L4 Caucaia, Braz.
103/H5 Caucasia, Col.
106/C2 Caucasia, Col.
46/E5 Caucasus (mts.), Asia
51/F1 Caucasus (mts.), Azer., Rus.
19/H4 Caucasus (mts.), Eur.
45/G4 Caucasus (mts.), Eur.
35/E3 Caudete, Sp.
26/B3 Caudry, Fr.
30/C3 Caudry, Fr.
32/E1 Caudry, Fr.
95/N7 Caughnawaga, Qu,Can
23/F1 Cauldcleuch (mtn.), Sc,UK
109/B4 Cauquenes, Chile
32/D4 Caussade, Fr.
32/C5 Cauterets, Fr.
35/E1 Cauterets, Fr.
103/G1 Cauto (riv.), Cuba
64/F3 Cauvery (riv.), India
38/D4 Cava d'Ispica (ruins), It.
34/B2 Cávado (riv.), Port.
32/F5 Cavaillon, Fr.
35/H1 Cavaillon, Fr.
33/G5 Cavalaire-sur-Mer, Fr.
35/J1 Cavalaire-sur-Mer, Fr.
37/H5 Cavalese, It.
91/J3 Cavalier, ND,US
76/D6 Cavalla (riv.), IvC., Libr.
78/D5 Cavalla (riv.), Libr.
38/A1 Cavallo, Capo al (cape), Fr.
78/C5 Cavally (Cavalla) (riv.), IvC.
22/A4 Cavan, Ire.
22/A4 Cavan (co.), Ire.
92/E4 Cave Creek, Az,US
107/J3 Caviana, Braz.
41/F2 Cavnic, Rom.
44/B3 Cavnic, Rom.
73/B2 Cawndilla (lake), Austl.
23/G4 Cawood, Eng,UK
25/H1 Cawston, Eng,UK
108/C2 Caxambu, Braz.
107/K4 Caxias, Braz.
108/B4 Caxias do Sul, Braz.
109/F2 Caxias do Sul, Braz.
102/E2 Caxinas (pt.), Hon.
82/B2 Caxito, Ang.
50/B2 Çay, Turk.
51/N6 Çayağzi (riv.), Turk.
106/C3 Cayambe (vol.), Ecu.
97/H3 Cayce, SC,US
41/L5 Çaycuma, Turk.
44/E4 Çaycuma, Turk.
45/G4 Çayeli, Turk.
50/E1 Çayeli, Turk.
107/H3 Cayenne (cap.), FrG.
25/H6 Cayeux-sur-Mer, Fr.
30/A3 Cayeux-sur-Mer, Fr.
103/F2 Cayman (isls.), Cay.
89/L8 Cayman (isls.), Cay.
103/G2 Cayman Brac (isl.), Cay.
103/F2 Cayman Islands (dpcy.), UK
84/J8 Cayman Islands (dpcy.), UK
95/S10 Cayuga (cr.), NY,US
34/C4 Cazalla de la Sierra, Sp.
32/D5 Cazères, Fr.
35/F1 Cazères, Fr.
33/L4 Cazin, Bosn.
40/B3 Cazin, Bosn.
37/F4 Cazis, Swi.
102/B1 Cazones (riv.), Mex.
34/D4 Cazorla, Sp.
32/E5 Cazouls-lès-Béziers, Fr.
35/G1 Cazouls-lès-Béziers, Fr.
34/C1 Cea (riv.), Sp.
22/B4 Ceanannus Mór, Ire.
107/L5 Ceará-Mirim, Braz.
103/F5 Cébaco (isl.), Pan.
100/D3 Ceballos, Mex.
96/B5 Ceballos, Mex
34/C2 Cebreros, Sp.
67/F1 Cebu (isl.), Phil.
68/B4 Cebu (isl.), Phil.
67/F1 Cebu City, Phil.
68/B3 Cebu City, Phil.
38/C2 Ceccano, It.
81/E2 Cecil Macks (pass), Swaz.
72/C4 Cecil Plains, Austl.
33/J5 Cecina, It.
38/E3 Cecita (lake), It.
34/B3 Ceclavín, Sp.
91/H2 Cedar (lake), Mb,Can
86/F3 Cedar (lake), Mb,Can
94/E2 Cedar (lake), On,Can
99/L11 Cedar (mtn.), Ca,US
91/L5 Cedar (riv.), Ia,US
89/H3 Cedar (riv.), Ia,US
93/K2 Cedar (riv.), Ia,US
94/A3 Cedar (riv.), Ia,US
98/F6 Cedar (cr.), NJ,US
99/C3 Cedar (riv.), Wa,US
72/B1 Cedar Bay Nat'l Park, Austl.
92/D3 Cedar Breaks Nat'l Mon., Ut,US
88/D4 Cedar City, Ut,US
92/D3 Cedar City, Ut,US
101/F1 Cedar Cr. (res.), Tx,US
93/H4 Cedar Creek (res.), Tx,US
91/K5 Cedar Falls, Ia,US
93/J2 Cedar Falls, Ia,US
99/D3 Cedar Falls, Wa,US
99/D3 Cedar Falls (dam), Wa,US
98/J7 Cedar Grove, Md,US
97/H4 Cedar Key, Fl,US
84/H5 Cedar Rapids, US
89/H3 Cedar Rapids, Ia,US
91/L5 Cedar Rapids, Ia,US
93/K2 Cedar Rapids, Ia,US
94/B3 Cedar Rapids, Ia,US
97/G3 Cedartown, Ga,US
90/C5 Cedarville, Ca,US
92/B2 Cedarville, Ca,US
37/G5 Cedegolo, It.
34/A1 Cedeira, Sp.
101/E4 Cedral, Mex.
107/L5 Cedro, Braz.
100/B2 Cedros (isl.), Mex.
84/F7 Cedros (isl.), Mex.
70/E6 Ceduna, Austl.
34/A1 Cee, Sp.
77/Q7 Ceel Dheere, Som.
77/Q5 Ceerigaabo (Erigabo), Som.
38/D3 Cefalù, It.
22/D5 Cefni (riv.), Wal,UK
23/E6 Cefn-mawr, Wal,UK
34/C2 Cega (riv.), Sp.
40/D2 Cegléd, Hun.
39/G2 Čegrane, Macd.
40/E5 Čegrane, Macd.
34/E3 Cehegín, Sp.
60/E3 Ceheng Bouyeizu Zizhixian, China
63/J3 Ceheng Bouyeizu Zizhixian, China
27/M5 Cehu Silvaniei, Rom.
41/F2 Cehu Silvaniei, Rom.
23/E6 Ceiriog (riv.), Wal,UK
44/E4 Çekerek, Turk.
44/F4 Çekerek (riv.), Turk.
50/C1 Çekerek, Turk.
34/B1 Celanova, Sp.
102/E1 Celarain, Punta (pt.), Mex.
101/E4 Celaya, Mex.
22/B5 Celbridge, Ire.
68/B4 Celebes (sea)
48/M9 Celebes (sea), Asia
48/L10 Celebes (isl.), Indo.
67/F3 Celebes (sea), Indo.
68/A5 Celebes (isl.), Indo.
67/E4 Celebes (Sulawesi) (isl.), Indo.
36/C5 Céligny, Swi.
50/D2 Çelikhan, Turk.
94/C3 Celina, Oh,US
101/F1 Celina, Tx,US
33/L3 Celje, Slov.
40/B2 Celje, Slov.
34/E2 Cella, Sp.
40/C2 Celldömölk, Hun.
26/B4 Celle (riv.), Fr.
32/E2 Celle (riv.), Fr.
26/F2 Celle, Ger.
29/H3 Celle, Ger.
30/C2 Celles, Belg.
31/E3 Celles, Belg.
39/G2 Čelopek, Macd.
40/E5 Čelopek, Macd.
34/B2 Celorico da Beira, Port.
21/A5 Celtic (sea)
24/A4 Celtic (sea)
24/B2 Cemaes Head (pt.), Wal,UK
66/D3 Cemaru (peak), Indo.
37/H5 Cembra, It.
34/E3 Cenajo (res.), Sp.
67/H4 Cenderawasih (bay), Indo.
68/C5 Cenderawasih (bay), Indo.
44/F5 Çengerli, Turk.
63/J2 Cengong, China
35/F2 Cenia, Sp.
109/C4 Centenario, Arg.
108/B2 Centenario do Sul, Braz.
92/D4 Centennial (wash), Az,US
90/E4 Centennial (mts.), Id,US
91/H4 Center, ND,US
93/J5 Center, Tx,US
96/E4 Center, Tx,US
99/F7 Center Line, Mi,US
98/H5 Center Moriches, NY,US
97/G3 Center Point, Al,US
98/G5 Centereach, NY,US
94/C5 Centerville, Tn,US
97/G3 Centerville, Tn,US
93/J5 Centerville, Tx,US
96/E4 Centerville, Tx,US
33/J4 Cento, It.
79/E5 Central (reg.), Gha.
49/D3 Central (dist.), Isr.
49/F7 Central (dist.), Isr.
85/K2 Central, Ak,US
100/C1 Central, NM,US
74/D4 Central African Republic
77/J6 Central African Republic
90/G3 Central Butte, Sk,Can
91/J5 Central City, Ne,US
93/H2 Central City, Ne,US
103/H5 Central, Cordillera (range), Col.
106/C5 Central, Cordillera (range), SAm.
93/K3 Centralia, Il,US
94/B4 Centralia, Il,US
97/F2 Centralia, Il,US
88/B2 Centralia, Wa,US
90/C4 Centralia, Wa,US
98/J8 Central Intelligence Agency, Va,US
53/H3 Central Makrān (range), Pak.
32/E4 Central, Massif (plat.), Fr.
107/J7 Central, Planalto (plat.), Braz.
90/C5 Central Point, Or,US
47/L3 Central Siberian (plat.), Rus.
43/N4 Central Ural (mts.), Rus.
26/B5 Centre (reg.), Fr.
30/A6 Centre (reg.), Fr.
32/D3 Centre (reg.), Fr.
75/L14 Centre (reg.), Mor.
75/M13 Centre Nord (reg.), Mor.
75/M14 Centre Sud (reg.), Mor.
97/G3 Centreville, Al,US
60/E3 Cenwanglao (mtn.), China
63/K3 Cenxi, China
32/D4 Céou (riv.), Fr.
40/D3 Čepin, Cro.
48/N10 Ceram (isl.), Indo.
67/G4 Ceram (isl.), Indo.
67/G4 Ceram (sea), Indo.
67/H4 Ceram (sea), Indo.
68/B5 Ceram (isl.), Indo.
68/B5 Ceram (sea), Indo.
38/A2 Ceraso (cape), It.
32/E5 Cerbère, Fr.
35/G1 Cerbère, Fr.
34/A4 Cercal, Port.
38/C4 Cerda, It.
35/L7 Cerdanyola del Vallès, Sp.
32/D4 Cère (riv.), Fr.
33/J4 Cerea, It.
109/D2 Ceres, Arg.
107/J7 Ceres, Braz.
80/B4 Ceres, SAfr.
80/L10 Ceres, SAfr.
35/G1 Céret, Fr.
103/H4 Cereté, Col.
30/D3 Cerfontaine, Belg.
19/S9 Cergy, Fr.
30/B5 Cergy, Fr.
38/D2 Cerignola, It.
40/B5 Cerignola, It.
44/E4 Çerkeş, Turk.
50/C1 Çerkeş, Turk.
41/J5 Çerkezköy, Turk.
44/D4 Çerkezköy, Turk.
50/B1 Çerkezköy, Turk.
50/D2 Çermik, Turk.
41/J3 Cernavodă, Rom.
36/D2 Cernay, Fr.
19/R10 Cernay-la-Ville, Fr.
24/D5 Cerne Abbas, Eng,UK
36/C3 Cernier, Swi.
100/C3 Cerralvo (isl.), Mex.
101/F3 Cerralvo, Mex.
96/D5 Cerralvo, Mex.
22/E5 Cerrig-y-Druidion, Wal,UK
39/F2 Cërrik, Alb.
40/D5 Cërrik, Alb.
101/E4 Cerritos, Mex.
102/A1 Cerritos, Mex.
101/F4 Cerro Azul, Mex.
102/B1 Cerro Azul, Mex.
109/C4 Cerro Colorados (res.), Arg.
92/D5 Cerro de la Encantada (peak), Mex
101/E4 Cerro de las Campanas Nat'l Park, Mex.
109/C2 Cerro del Toro (peak), Arg.
106/C6 Cerro de Pasco, Peru
103/H4 Cerro de San Antonio, Col.
104/F5 Cerro El Copey Nat'l Park, Ven.
38/D2 Cervaro (riv.), It.
40/B5 Cervaro (riv.), It.
38/D2 Cervati (peak), It.
35/F2 Cervera, Sp.
34/E1 Cervera del Río Alhama, Sp.
34/C1 Cervera de Pisuerga, Sp.
33/K4 Cervia, It.
38/D2 Cervialto (peak), It.
33/K4 Cervignano del Friuli, It.
40/A3 Cervignano del Friuli, It.
37/H4 Cervina, Punta (peak), It.
38/A1 Cervione, Fr.
34/B1 Cervo, Sp.
103/H4 César (riv.), Col.
33/K4 Cesena, It.
33/K4 Cesenatico, It.
20/H4 Cēsis, Lat.
42/E4 Cēsis, Lat.
27/H4 České Budějovice, Czh.
33/L2 České Budějovice, Czh.
27/H4 Českomoravská Vysočina (upland), Czh.
33/L2 Českomoravská Vysočina (mts.), Czh.
27/H4 Český Krumlov, Czh.
33/L2 Český Krumlov, Czh.
40/C3 Česma (riv.), Cro.
39/K3 Çeşme, Turk.
44/C5 Çeşme, Turk.
50/A2 Çeşme, Turk.
103/G1 Céspedes, Cuba
19/T11 Cesson, Fr.
32/C2 Cesson-Sévigné, Fr.
78/C5 Cestos (riv.), Libr.
40/C4 Cetina (riv), Cro.
39/F1 Cetinje, Yugo.
40/D4 Cetinje, Yugo.
50/D2 Çetinkaya, Turk.
34/D2 Ceurda del Pozo (res.), Sp.
34/C5 Ceuta, Sp.
75/M13 Ceuta, Sp.
76/D1 Ceuta, Sp.
37/G5 Cevedale, Monte (peak), It.
32/E5 Cévennes (mts.), Fr.
32/E4 Cévennes Nat'l Park, Fr.
37/E5 Cevio, Swi.
49/D1 Ceyhan, Turk.
49/D1 Ceyhan (riv.), Turk.
50/C2 Ceyhan, Turk.
52/C1 Ceyhan, Turk.
50/E2 Ceylânpınar, Turk.
52/D1 Ceylânpınar, Turk.
48/H9 Ceylon (isl.), SrL.
62/D6 Ceylon (isl.), SrL.
64/H4 Ceylon (isl.), SrL.
36/B5 Ceyzériat, Fr.
32/F4 Cèze (riv.), Fr.
63/G5 Cha-am, Thai.
66/A1 Cha-am, Thai.
32/C5 Chabarrou (peak), Fr.
35/E1 Chabarrou (peak), Fr.
101/H5 Chablé, Mex.
102/D2 Chablé, Mex.
106/C5 Chachapoyas, Peru
63/H5 Chachoengsao, Thai.
65/C3 Chachoengsao, Thai.
92/F3 Chaco (dry riv.), NM,US
96/B3 Chaco (mesa), NM,US
109/D2 Chaco Austral (plain), Arg.
106/G8 Chaco Boreal (reg.), Par.
109/D1 Chaco Central (plain), Arg.
109/E2 Chaco Nat'l Park, Arg.
102/D3 Chacujal (ruins), Guat.
74/D3 Chad
77/J4 Chad
74/D3 Chad (lake), Afr.
76/H5 Chad (lake), Afr.
63/J5 Cha Da (cape), Viet.
65/E4 Cha Da (cape), Viet.
46/K4 Chadan, Rus.
54/C1 Chadan, Rus.
25/E3 Chadlington, Eng,UK
86/F4 Chadron, Ne,US
88/F3 Chadron, Ne,US
91/H5 Chadron, Ne,US
93/G2 Chadron, Ne,US
41/J2 Chadyr-Lunga, Mol.
44/D3 Chadyr-Lunga, Mol.
60/C5 Chae Hom, Thai.
63/G4 Chae Hom, Thai.
75/N13 Chafarinas (isls.), Sp.
58/D2 Chagang-do (prov.), NKor.
47/P4 Chagda, Rus.
32/F3 Chagny, Fr.
48/G10 Chagos (arch.), BrIn.
104/F5 Chaguanas, Trin.
51/G4 Chahār Maḩāll and Bakhtīārī (gov.), Iran
53/H3 Chāh Behār (Bandar Beheshtī), Iran
102/C2 Chahuites, Mex.
63/H4 Chai Badan, Thai.
63/H4 Chai Buri, Thai.
58/E5 Chain, SKor.
63/H4 Chainat, Thai.
65/C3 Chainat, Thai.
109/B5 Chaitén, Chile
63/G6 Chaiya, Thai.
66/A2 Chaiya, Thai.
63/H4 Chaiyaphum, Thai.
65/C3 Chaiyaphum, Thai.
64/B1 Chakwāl, Pak.
36/B4 Chalain (lake), Fr.
36/D5 Chalais, Swi.
62/C5 Chālakudi, India
64/F3 Chālakudi, India
36/B5 Chalamont, Fr.
36/A5 Chalaronne (riv.), Fr.
102/D3 Chalatenango, ESal.
77/N7 Chalbi (des.), Kenya
102/C2 Chalchijapan, Mex.
55/H2 Chalchyn (riv.), Mong.
101/R10 Chalco, Mex.
101/F5 Chalco de Díaz Covarrubias, Mex.
101/L7 Chalco de Díaz Covarrubias, Mex.
89/N2 Chaleur (bay), Nb, Qu,Can
87/K4 Chaleur (bay), Qu,NB,Can
95/H2 Chaleur (bay), NB, Qu,Can
98/E5 Chalfont, Pa,US
19/M7 Chalfont Saint Giles, Eng,UK
19/M7 Chalfont Saint Peter, Eng,UK
25/F3 Chalfont Saint Peter, Eng,UK
25/E3 Chalgrove, Eng,UK
54/D6 Chali, China
63/G2 Chali, China
19/U10 Chalifert (can.), Fr.
26/C5 Chalindrey, Fr.
32/F3 Chalindrey, Fr.
36/B2 Chalindrey, Fr.
96/C4 Chalk (mts.), Tx,US
101/F1 Chalk Mountain, Tx,US
85/K2 Chalkyitsik, Ak,US
32/C3 Challans, Fr.
106/E7 Challapata, Bol.
87/S6 Challenger (mts.), NW,Can
31/D5 Challerange, Fr.
88/D3 Challis, Id,US
90/E4 Challis, Id,US
92/D1 Challis, Id,US
25/G4 Challock, Eng,UK
26/C4 Châlons-sur-Marne, Fr.
30/D6 Châlons-sur-Marne, Fr.
32/F2 Châlons-sur-Marne, Fr.
32/F3 Chalon-sur-Saône, Fr.
36/A4 Chalon-sur-Saône, Fr.
36/C2 Châlonvillars-Mandrevillars, Fr.
51/G2 Chālūs, Iran
52/F1 Chālūs, Iran
26/G4 Cham, Ger.
33/K2 Cham, Ger.
37/E3 Cham, Swi.
92/F3 Chama (riv.), Co, NM,US
82/F3 Chama, Zam.
66/B2 Chamah (peak), Malay.
53/J2 Chaman, Pak.
53/G1 Chaman Bīd, Iran
53/L2 Chamba, India
64/D1 Chamba, India
53/L3 Chambal (riv.), India
62/C2 Chambal (riv.), India
32/F4 Chambaran (plat.), Fr.
95/G2 Chamberlain (lake), Me,US
91/J5 Chamberlain, SD,US
93/H2 Chamberlain, SD,US
85/K2 Chamberlin (mt.), Ak,US
94/E4 Chambersburg, Pa,US
18/D4 Chambéry, Fr.
32/F4 Chambéry, Fr.
82/F3 Chambeshi (riv.), Zam.
95/P7 Chambly, Qu,Can
19/S9 Chambly, Fr.
30/B5 Chambly, Fr.
19/S10 Chambourcy, Fr.
51/F3 Chamchamāl, Iraq
52/D1 Chamchamāl, Iraq
103/G4 Chame (pt.), Pan.
32/F4 Chamechaude (mtn.), Fr.
109/C3 Chamical, Arg.
33/G4 Chamonix-Mont-Blanc, Fr.
36/C6 Chamonix-Mont-Blanc, Fr.
85/L3 Champagne, Yk,Can
26/C4 Champagne (reg.), Fr.
30/C6 Champagne (reg.), Fr.
32/F2 Champagne (reg.), Fr.
26/B4 Champagne-Ardenne (reg.), Fr.
32/F2 Champagne-Ardenne (reg.), Fr.
36/B2 Champagne-Ardenne (reg.), Fr.
30/D4 Champagne-Ardennes (reg.), Fr.
19/S9 Champagne-sur-Oise, Fr.
30/B5 Champagne-sur-Oise, Fr.
36/C2 Champagney, Fr.
36/B4 Champagnole, Fr.
89/J3 Champaign, Il,US
91/L5 Champaign, Il,US
93/K2 Champaign, Il,US
94/B3 Champaign, Il,US
97/F1 Champaign, Il,US
63/J5 Champasak, Laos
65/D3 Champasak, Laos
36/C5 Champéry, Swi.
31/F6 Champigneulles, Fr.
19/T10 Champigny-sur-Marne, Fr.
94/F2 Champlain (lake), Can., US
89/M3 Champlain (lake), NY, Vt,US
87/J4 Champlain (lake), NY,Vt,US
36/B2 Champlitte-et-le-Prélot, Fr.
101/H5 Champotón, Mex.
101/H5 Champotón (riv.), Mex.
102/D2 Champotón, Mex.
102/D2 Champotón (riv.), Mex.
30/B6 Champs-sur-Marne, Fr.
36/B3 Champvans, Fr.
64/F3 Chāmrājnagar, India
34/A3 Chamusca, Port.
109/B2 Chañaral, Chile
34/B4 Chança (riv.), Port.
101/E4 Chancaquero, Mex.
106/C5 Chan Chan, Peru
36/B5 Chancy, Swi.
85/J2 Chandalar, Ak,US
85/J2 Chandalar (riv.), Ak,US
85/J2 Chandalar, East Fork (riv.), Ak,US
62/C2 Chandausi, India
62/C3 Chanderi, India
53/L2 Chandigarh, India
64/D2 Chandigarh, India
64/D2 Chandigarh (terr.), India
87/K4 Chandler, Qu,Can
89/P2 Chandler, Qu,Can
95/H1 Chandler, Qu,Can
85/H2 Chandler (riv.), Ak,US
96/D3 Chandler, Ok,US
106/D6 Chandless (riv.), Braz.
54/D2 Chandmanī, Mong.
36/D5 Chandolin, Swi.
62/C4 Chandrapur, India
48/L6 Chang (riv.), China
54/F5 Chang (riv.), China
55/J5 Chang (riv.), China
59/C5 Chang (lake), China
59/B8 Chang (riv.), China
61/G2 Chang (lake), China
63/H5 Chang (isl.), Thai.
65/C3 Chang (isl.), Thai.
66/B1 Chang (isl.), Thai.
58/E5 Changan, SKor.
64/F4 Changanācheri, India
61/J2 Chang'anzhen, China
55/K3 Changbai (peak), China
58/D2 Changbai (mts.), China
58/E2 Changbai (peak), China
55/K3 Changbai (mts.), China, NKor.
58/E2 Changbai Chaoxian Zizhixian, China
47/N5 Changchun, China
55/K3 Changchun, China
59/F2 Changchun, China
59/D5 Changdang (lake), China
55/J4 Changdao, China
59/E3 Changdao, China
61/F2 Changde, China
32/D3 Changé, Fr.
59/D4 Changfeng, China
61/H1 Changfeng, China
59/C4 Changge, China
55/K4 Changgi-ap (cape), SKor.
56/A2 Changgi-ap (cape), SKor.
55/J4 Changhai, China
58/B3 Changhai, China
59/E3 Changhai, China
58/D4 Changhang, SKor.
58/D4 Changhowŏn, SKor.
61/J3 Changhua, Tai.
55/K3 Changhŭng, NKor.
55/K5 Changhŭng, SKor.
58/D5 Changhŭng, SKor.
61/F5 Changjiang, China
63/J4 Changjiang, China
65/E2 Changjiang, China
61/G2 Changjiang Zhongxiayou (plain), China
58/D2 Changjin (lake), NK
58/D2 Changjin (res.), NK
60/C5 Chang Khoeng, Tha
63/G4 Chang Khoeng, Tha
54/F5 Changle, China
59/D3 Changle, China
59/D3 Changli, China
55/J4 Changling, China
59/E1 Changling, China
55/J4 Changlingzi, China
65/C5 Changlun, Malay.
60/E2 Changning, China
63/G3 Changning, China
63/H2 Changning, China
58/E5 Ch'angnyŏng, SKor
59/D2 Changping, China
59/H6 Changping, China
59/D3 Changqing, China
55/J4 Changsan-got (cap NKor.
58/C3 Changsan-got (cap NKor.
61/G2 Changsha, China
63/K2 Changsha, China
68/A2 Changsha, China
55/J4 Changshan (arch.), China
58/B3 Changshan (arch.), China
59/E3 Changshan (arch.), China
55/J5 Changshu, China
59/E5 Changshu, China
59/L8 Changshu, China
61/J2 Changshu, China
60/E3 Changshun, China
63/J2 Changshun, China
55/K4 Changsŏng, SKor.
58/D5 Changsŏng, SKor.
58/D5 Changsu, SKor.
55/J3 Changtu, China
59/F2 Changtu, China
103/F4 Changuinola, Pan.
56/A3 Ch'angwŏn, SKor.
58/E5 Ch'angwŏn, SKor.
54/F4 Changwu, China
59/E3 Changxing (isl.), China
59/K8 Changxing, China
59/B5 Changyang, China
61/F2 Changyang, China
59/D5 Chang (Yangtze) (ri China
61/H2 Chang (Yangtze) (ri China
59/D3 Changyi, China
58/C3 Changyŏn, NKor.
59/C4 Changyuan, China
54/G4 Changzhi, China
59/C3 Changzhi, China
55/H5 Changzhou, China
59/D5 Changzhou, China
59/K8 Changzhou, China
61/H2 Changzhou, China
64/G4 Chankanai, SrL.
63/J4 Chan May Dong (cape), Viet.
65/E2 Chan May Dong (cape), Viet.
18/C4 Channel (isls.), UK
32/B4 Channel (isls.), UK
25/H4 Channel (tunnel), U Fr.
88/B5 Channel (isls.), Ca,
92/C4 Channel (isls.), Ca,
70/G4 Channel Country (plain), Austl.
72/A4 Channel Country (plain), Austl.
32/B2 Channel Islands, U
92/B4 Channel Islands N Park, Ca,US
92/C4 Channel Islands N Park, Ca,US
87/L4 Channel-Port aux Basques, Nf,Can
89/Q2 Channel-Port aux Basques, Nf,Can
95/K2 Channel-Port aux Basques, Nf,Can
30/A2 Channel Tunnel (U.C.), U.K., Fr.
93/G4 Channing, Tx,US
96/C3 Channing, Tx,US
34/B1 Chantada, Sp.
19/S10 Chanteloup-les-Vignes, Fr.

63/H5 **Chanthaburi,** Thai.
65/C3 **Chanthaburi,** Thai.
66/B1 **Chanthaburi,** Thai.
26/B4 **Chantilly,** Fr.
30/B5 **Chantilly,** Fr.
32/E2 **Chantilly,** Paris
36/C1 **Chantraine,** Fr.
86/G2 **Chantrey** (inlet), NW,Can
93/J3 **Chanute,** Ks,US
96/E2 **Chanute,** Ks,US
55/H3 **Chao** (riv.), China
59/D2 **Chao** (riv.), China
59/D5 **Chao** (lake), China
59/H6 **Chao** (riv.), China
61/H2 **Chao** (lake), China
55/H4 **Chaobai** (riv.), China
65/C3 **Chao Phraya** (riv.), Thai.
55/J2 **Chaor** (riv.), China
55/J3 **Chaoyang,** China
61/H4 **Chaoyang,** China
61/H4 **Chaozhou,** China
68/A2 **Chaozhou,** China
107/K6 **Chapada Diamantina Nat'l Park,** Braz.
107/J6 **Chapada dos Veadeiros Nat'l Park,** Braz.
94/F1 **Chapais,** Qu,Can
100/E4 **Chapala,** Mex.
100/E4 **Chapala** (lake), Mex.
46/F4 **Chapayev,** Kaz.
19/H3 **Chapayevsk,** Rus.
45/J1 **Chapayevsk,** Rus.
46/E4 **Chapayevsk,** Rus.
108/A3 **Chapecó,** Braz.
109/F2 **Chapecó,** Braz.
23/G5 **Chapel en le Frith,** Eng,UK
23/F2 **Chapelfell Top** (mtn.), Eng,UK
97/J3 **Chapel Hill,** NC,US
30/D3 **Chapelle-Lez-Herlaimont,** Belg.
23/J5 **Chapel Saint Leonards,** Eng,UK
23/G5 **Chapeltown,** Eng,UK
99/D2 **Chaplain** (lake), Wa,US
61/E5 **Chap Le,** Viet.
65/D2 **Chap Le,** Viet.
87/H4 **Chapleau,** On,Can
89/K2 **Chapleau,** On,Can
94/D2 **Chapleau,** On,Can
93/G3 **Chaplin,** Sk,Can
91/H5 **Chappell,** Ne,US
93/G2 **Chappell,** Ne,US
101/Q10 **Chapultepec Park,** Mex.
47/M4 **Chara** (riv.), Rus.
106/C3 **Charambirá** (pt.), Col.
39/L6 **Charandra** (riv.), Gre.
109/D2 **Charata,** Arg.
101/E4 **Charcas,** Mex.
83/U **Charcot** (isl.), Ant.
24/D5 **Chard,** Eng,UK
103/H2 **Chardonnière,** Haiti
46/G6 **Chardzhou,** Trkm.
75/N14 **Charef, Oued** (riv.), Mor.
32/C4 **Charente** (riv.), Fr.
19/T10 **Charenton-le-Pont,** Fr.
51/F1 **Charentsavan,** Arm.
63/F3 **Chargrām,** Bang.
74/D3 **Chari** (riv.), Chad
76/J5 **Chari** (riv.), Chad
53/J1 **Chārīkār,** Afg.
25/G4 **Charing,** Eng,UK
91/K5 **Chariton** (riv.), Ia, Mo,US
25/E3 **Charlbury,** Eng,UK
95/P6 **Charlemagne,** Qu,Can
22/B3 **Charlemont,** NI,UK
26/C3 **Charleroi,** Belg.
30/D3 **Charleroi,** Belg.
32/F1 **Charleroi,** Belg.
30/D2 **Charleroi à Bruxelles, Canal de** (can.), Belg.
87/J2 **Charles** (isl.), NW,Can
94/F4 **Charles** (cape), Va,US
97/K2 **Charles** (cape), Va,US
89/H3 **Charles City,** Ia,US
91/K5 **Charles City,** Ia,US
93/J2 **Charles City,** Ia,US
19/T9 **Charles de Gaulle** (Paris) (int'l arpt.), Fr.
94/B4 **Charleston,** Il,US
97/F2 **Charleston,** Il,US
93/K3 **Charleston,** Mo,US
94/B4 **Charleston,** Mo,US
97/F2 **Charleston,** Mo,US
93/K4 **Charleston,** Ms,US
97/F3 **Charleston,** Ms,US
90/E5 **Charleston,** Nv,US
92/D2 **Charleston,** Nv,US
89/L5 **Charleston,** SC,US
97/H3 **Charleston** (A.F.B.), SC,US
97/J3 **Charleston,** SC,US
89/K4 **Charleston** (cape), WV,US
94/D4 **Charleston,** WV,US
97/H2 **Charleston,** WV,US
104/F3 **Charlestown,** StK.
30/A5 **Charleval,** Fr.
68/D7 **Charleville,** Austl.
71/H5 **Charleville,** Austl.
72/B4 **Charleville,** Austl.
26/C4 **Charleville-Mézières,** Fr.
31/D4 **Charleville-Mézières,** Fr.
32/F2 **Charleville-Mézières,** Fr.
94/C2 **Charlevoix,** Mi,US
85/K2 **Charley-Yukon Rivers Nat'l Prsv.,** Ak,US
90/B2 **Charlotte** (lake), BC,Can
94/C3 **Charlotte,** Mi,US
89/K4 **Charlotte,** NC,US
97/H3 **Charlotte,** NC,US
104/E3 **Charlotte Amalie,** USVI
89/L4 **Charlottesville,** Va,US
94/E4 **Charlottesville,** Va,US
97/J2 **Charlottesville,** Va,US
87/K4 **Charlottetown** (cap.), PE,Can
89/P2 **Charlottetown** (cap.), PE,Can
73/B3 **Charlton,** Austl.
87/H3 **Charlton** (isl.), NW,Can
24/D3 **Charlton Kings,** Eng,UK
19/N8 **Charlwood,** Eng,UK
30/C6 **Charly-sur-Marne,** Fr.
26/D4 **Charmes,** Fr.
33/G2 **Charmes,** Fr.
36/B2 **Charmes** (res.), Fr.
36/C1 **Charmes,** Fr.
36/D4 **Charmey,** Swi.
32/F3 **Charnay-lès-Mâcon,** Fr.
31/E5 **Charny-sur-Meuse,** Fr.
32/F3 **Charolais** (mts.), Fr.
36/C3 **Charquemont,** Fr.
19/R9 **Chars,** Fr.
46/J5 **Charsk,** Kaz.
68/D7 **Charters Towers,** Austl.
71/H4 **Charters Towers,** Austl.
72/B3 **Charters Towers,** Austl.
18/D4 **Chartres,** Fr.
32/D2 **Chartres,** Fr.
37/G4 **Chaschauna, Piz** (peak), Swi.
109/E4 **Chascomús,** Arg.
90/D3 **Chase,** BC,Can
58/D2 **Chasŏng,** NKor.
32/F4 **Chassezac** (riv.), Fr.
32/C3 **Chassiron, Pointe de** (pt.), Fr.
30/D2 **Chastre-Villeroux-Blanmont,** Belg.
85/J2 **Chatanika,** Ak,US
32/C3 **Châteaubriant,** Fr.
35/H1 **Château d'If,** Fr.
36/D5 **Château-d'Oex,** Swi.
32/C3 **Château-d'Olonne,** Fr.
32/D3 **Château-du-Loir,** Fr.
32/D2 **Châteaudun,** Fr.
95/N7 **Châteauguay,** Qu,Can
95/N7 **Châteauguay** (co.), Qu,Can
32/C4 **Châteauneuf-sur-Charente,** Fr.
30/D4 **Château-Porcien,** Fr.
32/F5 **Châteaurenard-Provence,** Fr.
35/H1 **Châteaurenard-Provence,** Fr.
32/D3 **Château-Renault,** Fr.
32/D3 **Châteauroux,** Fr.
31/F6 **Château-Salins,** Fr.
30/C5 **Château-Thierry,** Fr.
36/A1 **Châteauvillain,** Fr.
32/C3 **Châtelaillon-Plage,** Fr.
30/D3 **Châtelet,** Belg.
32/D3 **Châtellerault,** Fr.
36/C4 **Châtel-Saint-Denis,** Swi.
19/S10 **Châtenay-Malabry,** Fr.
26/C4 **Châtenois,** Fr.
36/B1 **Châtenois,** Fr.
36/D1 **Châtenois,** Fr.
36/C2 **Châtenois-les-Forges,** Fr.
93/J2 **Chatfield,** Mn,US
94/A3 **Chatfield,** Mn,US
87/K4 **Chatham,** NB,Can
89/N2 **Chatham,** NB,Can
98/F5 **Chatham,** NJ,US
94/D3 **Chatham,** On,Can
16/A7 **Chatham** (isls.), NZ
25/G4 **Chatham,** Eng,UK
19/S10 **Châtillon,** Fr.
33/G4 **Châtillon,** It.
36/A5 **Châtillon-sur-Chalaronne,** Fr.
30/C5 **Châtillon-sur-Marne,** Fr.
26/C5 **Châtillon-sur-Seine,** Fr.
32/F3 **Châtillon-sur-Seine,** Fr.
19/S10 **Chatou,** Fr.
62/D4 **Chatrapur,** India
53/G2 **Chatrūd,** Iran
72/H8 **Chatswood,** Austl.
97/G3 **Chatsworth,** Ga,US
98/F6 **Chatsworth,** NJ,US
97/G4 **Chattahoochee,** Fl,US
84/J6 **Chattanooga,** US
89/J4 **Chattanooga,** Tn,US
97/G3 **Chattanooga,** Tn,US
25/G2 **Chatteris,** Eng,UK
32/C2 **Chaucey** (isls.), Fr.
31/E2 **Chaudfontaine,** Belg.
95/G2 **Chaudière** (riv.), Qu,Can
63/J5 **Chau Doc,** Viet.
65/D4 **Chau Doc,** Viet.
66/C1 **Chau Doc,** Viet.
60/B4 **Chauk,** Burma
63/F3 **Chauk,** Burma
60/C3 **Chaukan** (pass), India
63/G2 **Chaukan** (pass), India
30/B4 **Chaulnes,** Fr.
19/U10 **Chaumes-en-Brie,** Fr.
26/C4 **Chaumont,** Fr.
32/F2 **Chaumont,** Fr.
36/B1 **Chaumont,** Fr.
30/A5 **Chaumont-en-Vexin,** Fr.
30/D4 **Chaumont-Porcien,** Fr.
47/T3 **Chaunskaya** (bay), Rus.
26/B4 **Chauny,** Fr.
30/C4 **Chauny,** Fr.
32/E2 **Chauny,** Fr.
36/B4 **Chaussin,** Fr.
94/E3 **Chautauqua** (lake), NY,US
32/D3 **Chauvigny,** Fr.
64/H4 **Chavakachcheri,** SrL.
64/F3 **Chavakkad,** India
36/B6 **Chavanoz,** Fr.
34/B2 **Chaves,** Port.
36/C4 **Chavornay,** Swi.
65/D1 **Chay** (riv.), Viet.
106/E7 **Chayana** (riv.), Bol.
43/M4 **Chaykovskiy,** Rus.
23/G6 **Cheadle,** Eng,UK
97/G3 **Cheaha** (peak), Al,US
26/G3 **Cheb,** Czh.
33/K1 **Cheb,** Czh.
19/H3 **Cheboksary,** Rus.
43/K4 **Cheboksary,** Rus.
43/K4 **Cheboksary** (res.), Rus.
46/E4 **Cheboksary,** Rus.
89/K2 **Cheboygan,** Mi,US
94/C2 **Cheboygan,** Mi,US
75/M13 **Chechaouene,** Mor.
41/J1 **Chechel'nik,** Ukr.
45/H4 **Chechen'** (isl.), Rus.
45/H4 **Chechen-Ingush Aut. Rep.,** Rus.
74/B2 **Chech, 'Erg** (des.), Afr.
55/K4 **Chech'ŏn,** SKor.
56/A2 **Chech'ŏn,** SKor.
58/E4 **Chech'ŏn,** SKor.
93/J4 **Checotah,** Ok,US
96/E3 **Checotah,** Ok,US
95/J2 **Chedabucto** (bay), NS,Can
24/D4 **Cheddar,** Eng,UK
60/B5 **Cheduba** (isl.), Burma
60/B5 **Cheduba** (str.), Burma
63/F4 **Cheduba** (isl.), Burma
94/E3 **Cheektowaga,** NY,US
95/S10 **Cheektowaga,** NY,US
94/D1 **Cheepash** (riv.), On,Can
94/D1 **Cheepay** (riv.), On,Can
85/F3 **Chefornak,** Ak,US
47/P4 **Chegdomyn,** Rus.
55/L1 **Chegdomyn,** Rus.
82/F4 **Chegutu,** Zim.
90/C4 **Chehalis,** Wa,US
33/G5 **Cheiron, Cime du** (peak), Fr.
55/K6 **Choju,** SKor.
55/K5 **Cheju** (isl.), SKor.
55/K5 **Cheju** (str.), SKor.
55/N2 **Chekhov,** Rus.
90/C4 **Chelan** (lake), Wa,US
88/B2 **Chelan,** Wa,US
90/C4 **Chelan,** Wa,US
46/F6 **Cheleken,** Trkm.
51/H2 **Cheleken,** Trkm.
23/F5 **Chelford,** Eng,UK
75/V17 **Chelghoum El Aïd,** Alg.
45/L3 **Chelkar,** Kaz.
46/F5 **Chelkar,** Kaz.
19/T10 **Chelles,** Fr.
27/M3 **Chełm,** Pol.
27/M3 **Chełm** (prov.), Pol.
44/B2 **Chełm,** Pol.
25/G3 **Chelmer** (riv.), Eng,UK
27/K2 **Chełmno,** Pol.
25/G3 **Chelmsford,** Eng,UK
27/K2 **Chełmża,** Pol.
73/G6 **Chelsea,** Austl.
19/N7 **Chelsea,** Eng,UK
19/N7 **Chelsea & Kensington** (bor.), Eng,UK
95/Q8 **Cheltenham,** On,Can
24/D3 **Cheltenham,** Eng,UK
35/E3 **Chelva,** Sp.
43/P5 **Chelyabinsk,** Rus.
46/G4 **Chelyabinsk,** Rus.
43/P5 **Chelyabinsk Obl.,** Rus.
45/L1 **Chelyabinsk Obl.,** Rus.
47/L2 **Chelyuskina** (cape), Rus.
46/J4 **Chemal,** Rus.
101/J4 **Chemax,** Mex.
102/E1 **Chemax,** Mex.
82/E3 **Chembe,** Zam.
18/E3 **Chemnitz,** Ger.
26/G3 **Chemnitz,** Ger.
61/F3 **Chen** (riv.), China
64/A2 **Chenāb** (riv.), India
53/K2 **Chenāb** (riv.), Pak.
64/A2 **Chenāb** (riv.), Pak.
76/E2 **Chenachane** (well), Alg.
85/J2 **Chena Hot Springs,** Ak,US
102/C2 **Chenalhó,** Mex.
53/G1 **Chenārān,** Iran
55/H2 **Chen Baraq Qi,** China
102/D2 **Chencoh,** Mex.
88/C2 **Cheney,** Wa,US
90/D4 **Cheney,** Wa,US
60/D3 **Cheng** (lake), China
64/F4 **Chengannūr,** India
59/C3 **Cheng'anpu,** China
61/F3 **Chengbu Miaozu Zizhixian,** China
63/K2 **Chengbu Miaozu Zizhixian,** China
47/M5 **Chengde,** China
55/H3 **Chengde,** China
59/D2 **Chengde,** China
54/E5 **Chengdu,** China
60/E2 **Chengdu,** China
54/D6 **Chengele,** India
63/G2 **Chengele,** India
54/F5 **Chengkou,** China
61/F2 **Chengkou,** China
61/F5 **Chengmai,** China
63/J4 **Chengmai,** China
65/E2 **Chengmai,** China
55/J4 **Chengshan** (cape), China
58/B4 **Chengshan** (cape), China
59/E3 **Chengshan Jiao** (cape), China
59/C4 **Chengwu,** China
36/C1 **Cheniménil,** Fr.
19/T10 **Chennevières-sur-Marne,** Fr.
26/C5 **Chenòve,** Fr.
32/F3 **Chenòve,** Fr.
36/A3 **Chenòve,** Fr.
63/K2 **Chenxi,** China
61/G3 **Chenzhou,** China
63/K2 **Chenzhou,** China
39/J2 **Chepelare,** Bul.
41/G5 **Chepelare,** Bul.
69/V12 **Chépénéhé,** NCal.
109/C3 **Chepes,** Arg.
103/G4 **Chepigana,** Pan.
106/C2 **Chepigana,** Pan.
103/G4 **Chepo,** Pan.
24/D3 **Chepstow,** Wal,UK
43/M4 **Cheptsa** (riv.), Rus.
32/D3 **Cher** (riv), Fr.
36/C6 **Chéran** (riv.), Fr.
97/J3 **Cheraw,** SC,US
72/C4 **Cherbourg,** Austl.
18/C4 **Cherbourg,** Fr.
32/C2 **Cherbourg,** Fr.
75/S15 **Cherchell,** Alg.
76/F1 **Cherchell,** Alg.
47/L4 **Cheremkhovo,** Rus.
54/E1 **Cheremkhovo,** Rus.
45/J1 **Cheremshan,** Rus.
43/X9 **Cherëmuski,** Rus.
18/G3 **Cherepovets,** Rus.
42/H4 **Cherepovets,** Rus.
46/D4 **Cherepovets,** Rus.
75/V17 **Cherf** (riv.), Alg.
75/S16 **Chergui** (lake), Alg.
75/V18 **Cheria,** Alg.
44/E2 **Cherkassy,** Ukr.
46/D5 **Cherkassy,** Ukr.
44/D2 **Cherkassy Obl.,** Ukr.
19/H4 **Cherkessk,** Rus.
45/G3 **Cherkessk,** Rus.
46/E5 **Cherkessk,** Rus.
36/D5 **Chermignon,** Swi.
72/E6 **Chermside,** Austl.
43/M2 **Chernaya** (riv.), Rus.
18/G3 **Chernigov,** Ukr.
44/D2 **Chernigov,** Ukr.
46/D4 **Chernigov,** Ukr.
44/D2 **Chernigov Obl.,** Ukr.
41/H4 **Cherni Lom** (riv.), Bul.
39/H1 **Cherni Vrŭkh** (peak), Bul.
41/F4 **Cherni Vrŭkh** (peak), Bul.
44/B4 **Cherni Vrŭkh** (peak), Bul.
41/L2 **Chernobayevka,** Ukr.
18/G3 **Chernobyl',** Ukr.
46/D4 **Chernobyl',** Ukr.
41/L3 **Chernomorskoye,** Ukr.
18/F4 **Chernovtsy,** Ukr.
41/G1 **Chernovtsy,** Ukr.
44/C2 **Chernovtsy,** Ukr.
46/C5 **Chernovtsy,** Ukr.
41/G1 **Chernovtsy Obl.,** Ukr.
44/C2 **Chernovtsy Obl.,** Ukr.
43/N4 **Chernushka,** Rus.
27/L1 **Chernyakhovsk,** Rus.
47/M4 **Chernyshevsk,** Rus.
54/H1 **Chernyshevsk,** Rus.
93/H3 **Cherokee,** Ok,US
96/D2 **Cherokee,** Ok,US
60/A3 **Cherrapunjee,** India
63/F2 **Cherrapunjee,** India
92/D3 **Cherry Creek,** Nv,US
88/E6 **Cherry Hill,** NJ,US
47/Q3 **Cherskiy** (range), Rus.
48/P3 **Cherskiy** (range), Rus.
43/X9 **Chertanovo,** Rus.
19/M7 **Chertsey,** Eng,UK
25/F4 **Chertsey,** Eng,UK
44/D1 **Cherven',** Bela.
41/G4 **Cherven Bryag,** Bul.
44/C4 **Cherven Bryag,** Bul.
27/N3 **Chervonograd,** Ukr.
44/C2 **Chervonograd,** Ukr.
25/E3 **Cherwell** (riv.), Eng,UK
94/C3 **Chesaning,** Mi,US
94/E4 **Chesapeake** (bay), Md, Va,US
89/L4 **Chesapeake** (bay), US
98/K8 **Chesapeake** (bay), US
25/F3 **Chesham,** Eng,UK
23/F5 **Cheshire** (co.), Eng,UK
23/F5 **Cheshire** (plain), Eng,UK
18/H2 **Cheshskaya** (bay), Rus.
43/K2 **Cheshskaya** (bay), Rus.
46/E3 **Cheshskaya** (bay), Rus.
19/N6 **Cheshunt,** Eng,UK
25/F3 **Cheshunt,** Eng,UK
98/F6 **Chesilhurst,** NJ,US
23/F5 **Chester,** Eng,UK
90/C5 **Chester,** Ca,US
92/B2 **Chester,** Ca,US
90/F3 **Chester,** Mt,US
94/F4 **Chester,** Pa,US
98/E6 **Chester,** Pa,US
98/E6 **Chester** (cr.), Pa,US
97/H3 **Chester,** SC,US
84/H3 **Chesterfield** (inlet), Can.
86/G2 **Chesterfield** (inlet), NW,Can
68/E7 **Chesterfield** (isls.), NCal.
23/G5 **Chesterfield,** Eng,UK
86/G2 **Chesterfield Inlet,** NW,Can
81/H7 **Chesterfield, Nosy** (isl.), Madg.
98/E6 **Chester Heights,** Pa,US
23/G2 **Chester-le-Street,** Eng,UK
99/D3 **Chester Morse** (lake), Wa,US
71/H5 **Chesterton** (range), Austl.
72/B3 **Chesterton** (range), Austl.
95/G2 **Chesuncook** (lake), Me,US
101/H5 **Chetumal** (bay), Belz.
102/D2 **Chetumal** (bay), Belz., Mex.
101/H5 **Chetumal,** Mex.
101/H5 **Chetumal** (bay), Mex.
102/D2 **Chetumal,** Mex.
86/D3 **Chetwynd,** BC,Can
90/C2 **Chetwynd,** BC,Can
85/E3 **Chevak,** Ak,US
103/H2 **Cheval Blanc, Pointe du** (pt.), Haiti
36/B3 **Chevigny-Saint-Sauveur,** Fr.
19/T10 **Chevilly-Larue,** Fr.
23/F1 **Cheviot** (hills), Eng,Sc,UK
19/S10 **Chevreuse,** Fr.
19/T10 **Chevry-Cossigny,** Fr.
24/D4 **Chew** (riv.), Eng,UK
90/D3 **Chewelah,** Wa,US
24/D4 **Chew Valley** (lake), Eng,UK
36/C5 **Chexbres,** Swi.
91/H4 **Cheyenne** (riv.), SD, Wy,US
84/G5 **Cheyenne** (riv.), US
93/H4 **Cheyenne,** Ok,US
96/D3 **Cheyenne,** Ok,US
86/F4 **Cheyenne** (riv.), SD,US
88/F3 **Cheyenne** (cap.), Wy,US
91/G5 **Cheyenne,** Wy,US
93/F2 **Cheyenne,** Wy,US
93/G3 **Cheyenne Wells,** Co,US
96/C2 **Cheyenne Wells,** Co,US
36/C4 **Cheyres,** Swi.
53/K3 **Chhaīn,** India
62/C3 **Chhatarpur,** India
62/C3 **Chhindwāra,** India
65/D3 **Chhlong,** Camb.
59/D4 **Chi** (riv.), China
61/H1 **Chi** (riv.), China
63/H4 **Chi** (riv.), Thai.
65/C2 **Chi** (riv.), Thai.
58/E4 **Ch'iak-san Nat'l Park,** SKor.
33/J5 **Chianciano Terme,** It.
60/C5 **Chiang Dao,** Thai.
63/G4 **Chiang Dao,** Thai.
65/B2 **Chiang Dao** (caves), Thai.
60/C5 **Chiang Dao Caves,** Thai.
63/H4 **Chiang Khan,** Thai.
60/C5 **Chiang Mai,** Thai.
63/G4 **Chiang Mai,** Thai.
65/B2 **Chiang Mai,** Thai.
60/C5 **Chiang Rai,** Thai.
63/G4 **Chiang Rai,** Thai.
65/B2 **Chiang Rai,** Thai.
60/D4 **Chiang Saen,** Thai.
63/H3 **Chiang Saen,** Thai.
38/C1 **Chiani** (riv.), It.
101/G5 **Chiapas** (state), Mex.
102/C2 **Chiapas** (state), Mex.
37/F6 **Chiasso,** Swi.
45/G4 **Chiatura,** Geo.
51/E1 **Chiatura,** Geo.
33/H4 **Chiavari,** It.
33/H3 **Chiavenna,** It.
37/F5 **Chiavenna,** It.
61/J4 **Chiayi,** Tai.
55/N4 **Chiba,** Japan
57/G3 **Chiba,** Japan
57/G3 **Chiba** (pref.), Japan
57/J7 **Chiba,** Japan
57/J7 **Chiba** (pref.), Japan
87/J4 **Chibougamau,** Qu,Can
89/M2 **Chibougamau,** Qu,Can
94/F1 **Chibougamau,** Qu,Can
94/F1 **Chibougamau** (lake), Qu,Can
94/F1 **Chibougamau** (riv.), Qu,Can
85/D3 **Chibukak** (pt.), Ak,US
54/D6 **Chibuni,** India
63/G2 **Chibuni,** India
82/F5 **Chibuto,** Moz.
89/J3 **Chicago,** Il,US
91/M5 **Chicago,** Il,US
93/L2 **Chicago,** Il,US
94/C3 **Chicago,** Il,US
99/Q16 **Chicago,** Il,US
99/Q16 **Chicago Heights,** Il,US
99/Q16 **Chicago, North Branch** (riv.), Il,US
99/Q16 **Chicago Ridge,** Il,US
99/Q16 **Chicago Sanitary & Ship** (can.), Il,US
85/L4 **Chichagof** (isl.), Ak,US
86/C3 **Chichagof** (isl.), Ak,US
53/K2 **Chīchāwatni,** Pak.
64/B2 **Chīchāwatni,** Pak.
54/H3 **Chicheng,** China
59/C2 **Chicheng,** China
101/H4 **Chichén Itzá** (ruins), Mex.
102/D1 **Chichén Itzá** (ruins), Mex.
70/B4 **Chichester** (range), Austl.
25/F5 **Chichester,** Eng,UK
32/C1 **Chichester,** Eng,UK
57/F3 **Chichibu,** Japan
57/F3 **Chichibu-Tama Nat'l Park,** Japan
57/H7 **Chichibu-Tama Nat'l Park,** Japan
102/D3 **Chichicastenango,** Guat.
102/E3 **Chichigalpa,** Nic.
104/D5 **Chichiriviche,** Ven.
68/D2 **Chichishima** (isls.), Japan
85/J3 **Chickaloon,** Ak,US
89/G4 **Chickasha,** Ok,US
93/H4 **Chickasha,** Ok,US
96/D3 **Chickasha,** Ok,US
24/D5 **Chickerell,** Eng,UK
34/B4 **Chiclana de la Frontera,** Sp.
106/C5 **Chiclayo,** Peru
105/C7 **Chico** (riv.), Arg.
109/C6 **Chico** (riv.), Arg.
86/D5 **Chico,** Ca,US
88/B4 **Chico,** Ca,US
92/B3 **Chico,** Ca,US
81/F2 **Chicomo,** Moz.
100/E4 **Chicomostoc** (ruins), Mex.
102/C3 **Chicomuselo,** Mex.
95/F3 **Chicopee,** Ma,US
82/D4 **Chicote,** Ang.
87/J4 **Chicoutimi,** Qu,Can
89/M2 **Chicoutimi,** Qu,Can
95/G1 **Chicoutimi,** Qu,Can
82/F5 **Chicualacuala,** Moz.
64/G3 **Chidambaram,** India
19/P8 **Chiddingstone,** Eng,UK
81/F2 **Chidenguele,** Moz.
84/L3 **Chidley** (cape), Can.
87/K2 **Chidley** (cape), Nf,Can
58/D5 **Chido,** SKor.
97/H4 **Chiefland,** Fl,US
63/J3 **Chiem Hoa,** Viet.
65/D1 **Chiem Hoa,** Viet.
26/G5 **Chiemsee** (lake), Ger.
33/K3 **Chiemsee** (lake), Ger.
38/C1 **Chienti** (riv.), It.
63/G6 **Chieo Lan** (res.), Thai.
65/B4 **Chieo Lan** (res.), Thai.
66/A2 **Chieo Lan** (res.), Thai.
30/C5 **Chierry,** Fr.
31/E5 **Chiers** (riv.), Fr.
37/F5 **Chiesa in Valmalenco,** It.
33/J3 **Chiese** (riv.), It.
37/G6 **Chiese** (riv.), It.
38/D1 **Chieti,** It.
40/B4 **Chieti,** It.
101/F5 **Chietla,** Mex.
101/L8 **Chietla,** Mex.
102/B2 **Chietla,** Mex.
25/E4 **Chieveley,** Eng,UK
30/C2 **Chièvres,** Belg.
47/M5 **Chifeng,** China
55/H3 **Chifeng,** China
107/K7 **Chifre** (mts.), Braz.
46/H5 **Chiganak,** Kaz.
57/F3 **Chigasaki,** Japan
57/H7 **Chigasaki,** Japan
85/G4 **Chiginagak** (mt.), Ak,US
101/L7 **Chignahuapan,** Mex.
95/H2 **Chignecto** (bay), NS,Can
85/G4 **Chignik,** Ak,US
85/G4 **Chignik Lake,** Ak,US
103/G5 **Chigorodó,** Col.
19/P7 **Chigwell,** Eng,UK
25/G3 **Chigwell,** Eng,UK
57/L10 **Chihayaakasaka,** Japan
55/H4 **Chihli** (gulf), China
59/D3 **Chihli** (Bo Hai) (gulf), China
100/D2 **Chihuahua,** Mex.
100/D2 **Chihuahua** (state), Mex.
88/E6 **Chihuahua** (state), Mex.
92/F5 **Chihuahua** (state), Mex
96/B4 **Chihuahua,** Mex
62/C5 **Chikballāpur,** India
53/L4 **Chikhli,** India
62/C3 **Chikhli,** India
101/H4 **Chikindzonot,** Mex.
102/D1 **Chikindzonot,** Mex.
53/L6 **Chikmagalūr,** India
62/C5 **Chikmagalūr,** India
47/L4 **Chikoy** (riv.), Rus.
54/G1 **Chikoy** (riv.), Rus.
56/B4 **Chikugo** (riv.), Japan
57/F2 **Chikuma** (riv.), Japan
57/H8 **Chikura,** Japan
61/J3 **Chilaichu** (mtn.), Tai.
62/D4 **Chilakalūrupet,** India
102/B2 **Chilapa,** Mex.
101/F5 **Chilapa de Alvarez,** Mex.
62/C6 **Chilaw,** SrL.
58/E2 **Chilbo-san** (mtn.), NKor.
101/M7 **Chilchotla,** Mex.
90/C3 **Chilcotin** (riv.), BC,Can
86/D3 **Chilcotin** (riv.), BC,Can
97/G3 **Childersburg,** Al,US
88/F5 **Childress,** Tx,US
93/G4 **Childress,** Tx,US
96/C3 **Childress,** Tx,US
105/B6 **Chile**
106/E8 **Chile**
109/B3 **Chile**
109/B6 **Chile Chico,** Chile
109/C2 **Chilecito,** Arg.
58/D4 **Ch'ilgap-san Nat'l Park,** SKor.
82/E3 **Chililabombwe,** Zam.
62/E4 **Chilka** (lake), India
90/C3 **Chilko** (lake), BC,Can
86/D3 **Chilko** (lake), BC,Can
85/L4 **Chilkoot** (pass), BC,Can, Ak,US
109/B4 **Chillán,** Chile
91/L5 **Chillicothe,** Il,US
93/K2 **Chillicothe,** Il,US
94/B3 **Chillicothe,** Il,US
89/H4 **Chillicothe,** Mo,US
93/J3 **Chillicothe,** Mo,US
96/E2 **Chillicothe,** Mo,US
89/K4 **Chillicothe,** Oh,US
94/D4 **Chillicothe,** Oh,US
97/H2 **Chillicothe,** Oh,US
86/D4 **Chilliwack,** BC,Can
88/B2 **Chilliwack,** BC,Can
90/C3 **Chilliwack,** BC,Can
36/C5 **Chillon,** Swi.
19/S10 **Chilly-Mazarin,** Fr.
105/B7 **Chiloé** (isl.), Chile
109/A5 **Chiloé** (isl.), Chile
102/C2 **Chilón,** Mex.
90/C5 **Chiloquin,** Or,US
92/B2 **Chiloquin,** Or,US
101/F5 **Chilpancingo,** Mex.
102/B2 **Chilpancingo,** Mex.
25/F3 **Chiltern** (hills), Eng,UK
82/G4 **Chilwa** (lake), Malw.
99/B1 **Chimacum,** Wa,US
102/D3 **Chimaltenango,** Guat.
103/G4 **Chimán,** Pan.
82/F4 **Chimanimani,** Zim.
26/C3 **Chimay,** Belg.
30/D3 **Chimay,** Belg.
32/F1 **Chimay,** Belg.
46/F5 **Chimbay,** Uzb.
105/B3 **Chimborazo** (vol.), Ecu.
106/C4 **Chimborazo** (vol.), Ecu.
106/C5 **Chimbote,** Peru
103/H4 **Chimichaqua,** Col.
46/G5 **Chimkent,** Kaz.
100/D1 **Chimney** (peak), NM,US
82/F4 **Chimoio,** Moz.
60/B4 **Chin** (hills), Burma
60/B4 **Chin** (state), Burma
63/F3 **Chin** (state), Burma
55/K5 **Chin** (isl.), SKor.
58/D5 **Chin** (isl.), SKor.
46/J5 **China**
48/J6 **China**
53/L1 **China**
54/D5 **China**
58/A4 **China**
59/C2 **China**
60/E3 **China**
63/H2 **China**
65/E1 **China**
68/A2 **China**
101/F3 **Chiná,** Mex
101/H5 **Chiná,** Mex.
102/D2 **Chiná,** Mex.
58/D5 **Chinan,** SKor.
102/E3 **Chinandega,** Nic.
100/D2 **Chinati** (peak), Tx,US
96/B4 **Chinati** (mts.), Tx,US
106/C6 **Chincha Alta,** Peru
86/E3 **Chinchaga** (riv.), Ab,Can
71/J5 **Chinchilla,** Austl.
34/E3 **Chinchilla de Monte-Aragón,** Sp.
58/D4 **Chinch'ŏn,** SKor.
34/D2 **Chinchón,** Sp.
102/E2 **Chinchorro, Banco** (reef), Mex.
94/F4 **Chincoteague,** Va,US
97/K2 **Chincoteague,** Va,US
82/G4 **Chinde,** Moz.
58/D5 **Chindo,** SKor.
36/B6 **Chindrieux,** Fr.
54/D4 **Chindu,** China
60/B4 **Chindwin** (riv.), Burma
63/F3 **Chindwin** (riv.), Burma
60/E4 **Chi Ne,** Viet.
106/D3 **Chingaza Nat'l Park,** Col.
19/P7 **Chingford,** Eng,UK
62/C5 **Chingleput,** India
82/E3 **Chingola,** Zam.
78/B1 **Chinguetti, Dhar de** (hills), Mrta.
55/K4 **Chinhae,** SKor.
56/A3 **Chinhae,** SKor.
58/E5 **Chinhae,** SKor.
82/F4 **Chinhoyi,** Zim.
85/H4 **Chiniak** (cape), Ak,US
53/K2 **Chiniot,** Pak.
64/B2 **Chiniot,** Pak.
100/C3 **Chinipas,** Mex.
65/D3 **Chinit** (riv.), Camb.
58/E5 **Chinju,** SKor.
77/K6 **Chinko** (riv.), CAfr.
92/E3 **Chinle** (dry riv.), Az, Ut,US
92/E3 **Chinle,** Az,US
64/F3 **Chinnalappatti,** India
64/F4 **Chinnamanūr,** India
25/F3 **Chinnor,** Eng,UK
57/F3 **Chino,** Japan
90/F3 **Chinook,** Mt,US
103/H4 **Chinú,** Col.
31/E4 **Chiny,** Belg.
58/E5 **Chinyŏng,** SKor.
82/F3 **Chipata,** Zam.
59/D3 **Chiping,** China
34/B4 **Chipiona,** Sp.
97/G4 **Chipley,** Fl,US
53/K5 **Chiplūn,** India
62/B4 **Chiplūn,** India
24/D4 **Chippenham,** Eng,UK
91/K4 **Chippewa** (riv.), Mn,US
91/L4 **Chippewa** (riv.), Wi,US
94/B2 **Chippewa** (riv.), Wi,US
86/G4 **Chippewa Falls,** Wi,US
91/L4 **Chippewa Falls,** Wi,US
94/B2 **Chippewa Falls,** Wi,US
25/E2 **Chipping Campden,** Eng,UK
25/E3 **Chipping Norton,** Eng,UK
19/P6 **Chipping Ongar,** Eng,UK
25/G3 **Chipping Ongar,** Eng,UK
24/D3 **Chipping Sodbury,** Eng,UK
40/F4 **Chiprovtsi,** Bul.
19/N8 **Chipstead,** Eng,UK
95/H2 **Chiputneticook** (lakes), NB,Can, Me,US
102/D3 **Chiquimula,** Guat.
102/D3 **Chiquimulilla,** Guat.
106/D2 **Chiquinquirá,** Col.
105/C6 **Chiquita, Mar** (lake), Arg.
105/A3 **Chira** (riv.), Peru
62/C5 **Chirakkal,** India
62/D4 **Chīrāla,** India
46/G5 **Chirchik,** Uzb.
76/H5 **Chirfa,** Niger
100/C2 **Chiricahua** (peak), Az,US
92/E4 **Chiricahua Nat'l Mon.,** Az,US
103/H4 **Chiriguaná,** Col.
85/G4 **Chirikof** (isl.), Ak,US
103/E4 **Chiripa** (mtn.), Nic.
103/F4 **Chiriquí** (gulf), Pan.
103/F4 **Chiriquí** (lag.), Pan.
106/B2 **Chiriquí** (gulf), Pan.
58/D5 **Chiri-san** (mt.), SKor.
58/D5 **Chiri-san Nat'l Park,** SKor.
23/E6 **Chirk,** Eng,UK
21/D3 **Chirnside,** Sc,UK
37/E5 **Chironico,** Swi.
39/J1 **Chirpan,** Bul.
41/G4 **Chirpan,** Bul.
103/F4 **Chirripó Grande** (mtn.), CR
103/F4 **Chirripó Nat'l Park,** CR
57/N10 **Chiryu,** Japan
85/K3 **Chisana,** Ak,US
87/J3 **Chisasibi** (Fort-George), Qu,Can
25/E3 **Chiseldon,** Eng,UK
94/A2 **Chisholm,** Mn,US
53/K3 **Chishtiān Mandi,** Pak.
60/E3 **Chishui** (riv.), China
77/P8 **Chisimayu,** Som.
82/F3 **Chisimba** (fall, falls), Zam.
40/E2 **Chişineu Criş,** Rom.
85/K3 **Chistochina,** Ak,US
43/L5 **Chistopol',** Rus.
19/M6 **Chiswell Green,** Eng,UK
25/F3 **Chiswell Green,** Eng,UK
19/N7 **Chiswick,** Eng,UK
57/M10 **Chita,** Japan
57/M10 **Chita** (bay), Japan
57/M10 **Chita** (pen.), Japan
47/M4 **Chita,** Rus.
54/G1 **Chita,** Rus.
82/B4 **Chitado,** Ang.
85/K3 **Chitina,** Ak,US
82/F2 **Chitipa,** Malw.
53/K4 **Chitorgarh,** India
62/B3 **Chitorgarh,** India
55/N3 **Chitose,** Japan
62/C5 **Chitradurga,** India
62/D2 **Chitrakut,** India
103/F5 **Chitré,** Pan.
106/B2 **Chitré,** Pan.
60/A4 **Chittagong,** Bang.
60/B4 **Chittagong** (div.), Bang.
63/F3 **Chittagong,** Bang.
62/C5 **Chittoor,** India
64/F3 **Chittūr,** India
82/D4 **Chiume,** Ang.
37/H4 **Chiusa** (Klausen), It.
33/J5 **Chiusi,** It.
104/D5 **Chivacoa,** Ven.
33/G4 **Chivasso,** It.
108/D7 **Chivay,** Peru
82/F4 **Chivhu,** Zim.
109/D3 **Chivilcoy,** Arg.
102/D3 **Chixoy** (riv.), Guat., Mex.
82/E3 **Chizela,** Zam.
74/C1 **Chlef,** Alg.
75/R15 **Chlef,** Alg.
75/R15 **Chlef** (riv.), Alg.
75/R15 **Chlef** (wilaya), Alg.
60/C2 **Cho** (pass), China
58/C3 **Ch'o** (isl.), NKor.
65/D3 **Choam Khsant,** Camb.

127

Colom – Crate

36/C4 Colombier, Swi.
08/B3 Colombo, Braz.
62/C6 Colombo (cap.), SrL.
32/D5 Colomiers, Fr.
35/F1 Colomiers, Fr.
02/D3 Colomoncagua, Hon.
03/F1 Colón, Cuba
03/E3 Colón (mts.), Hon.
01/E4 Colón, Mex.
02/A1 Colón, Mex.
03/G4 Colón, Pan.
06/C2 Colón, Pan.
68/C4 Colonia, Micro.
00/B1 Colonia Coahuila, Mex.
09/C4 Colonia Veinticinco de Mayo, Arg.
05/C6 Colorado (riv.), Arg.
09/D4 Colorado (riv.), Arg.
08/B2 Colorado, Braz.
00/B1 Colorado (riv.), Mex., US
02/D4 Colorado (riv.), Mex., US
84/F6 Colorado (riv.), US
84/E6 Colorado (riv.), US
88/D5 Colorado (riv.), US
88/E4 Colorado (state), US
92/E3 Colorado (plat.), US
92/F3 Colorado (state), US
01/F2 Colorado (riv.), Tx,US
88/F5 Colorado (riv.), Tx,US
93/H5 Colorado (riv.), Tx,US
93/F3 Colorado City, Co,US
96/B2 Colorado City, Co,US
01/E1 Colorado City, Tx,US
93/G4 Colorado City, Tx,US
96/C3 Colorado City, Tx,US
92/E3 Colorado Nat'l Mon., Co,US
98/C3 Colorado River (aqueduct), Ca,US
09/C2 Colorados (marsh), Arg.
88/F4 Colorado Springs, Co,US
93/F3 Colorado Springs, Co,US
96/B2 Colorado Springs, Co,US
00/E4 Colotlán, Mex.
02/B2 Colotlipa, Mex.
06/E7 Colquiri, Bol.
02/D2 Colson (pt.), Belz.
90/G4 Colstrip, Mt,US
22/D1 Colt (hill), Sc,UK
25/H1 Coltishall, Eng,UK
05/D4 Coluene (riv.), Braz.
34/K1 Columbia (cape), Can.
86/E3 Columbia (mtn.), Ab,Can
06/C2 Columbia (mts.), BC,Can
86/E3 Columbia (riv.), BC,Can
07/T6 Columbia (cape), NW,Can
90/C4 Columbia (riv.), Can., US
90/D4 Columbia (plat.), US
36/D4 Columbia (riv.), Can., US
38/B1 Columbia (riv.), Can., US
92/C2 Columbia (plat.), US
34/C4 Columbia, Ky,US
37/G2 Columbia, Ky,US
93/J4 Columbia, La,US
96/E3 Columbia, La,US
94/E4 Columbia, Md,US
97/J2 Columbia, Md,US
38/K7 Columbia, Md,US
39/H4 Columbia, Mo,US
93/J3 Columbia, Mo,US
96/E2 Columbia, Mo,US
97/F4 Columbia, Ms,US
95/E3 Columbia, NJ,US
86/E4 Columbia (plat.), US
89/K5 Columbia (cap.), SC,US
97/H3 Columbia, SC,US
98/J4 Columbia, Tn,US
34/C5 Columbia, Tn,US
37/G3 Columbia, Tn,US
90/E3 Columbia Falls, Mt,US
30/B4 Columbine (cape), SAfr.
39/K5 Columbus, Ga,US
37/G3 Columbus, Ga,US
39/J4 Columbus, In,US
34/C4 Columbus, In,US
37/G2 Columbus, In,US
39/J5 Columbus, Ms,US
97/F3 Columbus, Ms,US
97/F3 Columbus (A.F.B.), Ms,US
90/F4 Columbus, Mt,US
93/G3 Columbus, Ne,US
91/J5 Columbus, Ne,US
93/H2 Columbus, Ne,US
00/D2 Columbus, NM,US
92/F5 Columbus, NM,US
96/B4 Columbus, NM,US
39/K4 Columbus (cap.), Oh,US
34/D4 Columbus, Oh,US
37/H2 Columbus, Oh,US
01/F2 Columbus, Tx,US
93/H5 Columbus, Tx,US
36/D4 Columbus, Tx,US
36/C1 Colunga, Sp.
92/B3 Colusa, Ca,US
86/D2 Colville (lake), NW,Can
35/H2 Colville (riv.), Ak,US
35/C2 Colville, Wa,US
90/D3 Colville, Wa,US
99/B3 Colvos (passage), Wa,US
24/D2 Colwall, Eng,UK
24/C4 Colwinston, Wal,UK
22/E5 Colwyn Bay, Wal,UK
33/K4 Comacchio, It.
33/K4 Comacchio, Valli di (lag.), It.
63/F2 Comai, China
100/E5 Comala, Mex.
101/G5 Comalcalco, Mex.
102/C2 Comalcalco, Mex.
93/H5 Comanche, Tx,US
96/D4 Comanche, Tx,US
41/H2 Comănești, Rom.
41/G3 Comarnic, Rom.
102/E3 Comayagua, Hon.
109/B3 Combarbalá, Chile
36/B2 Combeaufontaine, Fr.
24/B4 Combe Martin, Eng,UK
99/G7 Comber, On,Can
22/C2 Comber, NI,UK
60/B5 Combermere (bay), Burma
31/E3 Comblain-au-Pont, Belg.
36/C6 Combloux, Fr.
19/T11 Combs-la-Ville, Fr.
30/B6 Combs-la-Ville, Fr.
103/J2 Comendador, DRep.
104/D3 Comendador, DRep.
72/C4 Comet (riv.), Austl.
63/F3 Comilla, Bang.
30/B2 Comines, Belg.
30/C2 Comines, Fr.
102/C2 Comitán, Mex.
98/G5 Commack, NY,US
32/E3 Commentry, Fr.
31/E6 Commercy, Fr.
87/H2 Committee (bay), NW,Can
48/G6 Communism (peak), Taj.
46/H6 Communism (peak), Taj.
18/D4 Como, It.
33/H3 Como (lake), It.
33/H4 Como, It.
37/F5 Como (lake), It.
37/F5 Como (prov.), It.
37/F6 Como, It.
99/P14 Como, Wi,US
99/P14 Como (lake), Wi,US
109/C6 Comodoro Rivadavia, Arg.
78/D4 Comoé (prov.), Burk.
76/E6 Comoe Nat'l Park, IvC.
78/E4 Comoé Nat'l Park, IvC.
100/C3 Comondú, Mex.
48/G9 Comorin (cape), India
62/C6 Comorin (cape), India
64/F4 Comorin (cape), India
74/G6 Comoros
81/G5 Comoros
90/B3 Comox, BC,Can
26/B4 Compiègne, Fr.
30/B5 Compiègne, Fr.
32/E2 Compiègne, Fr.
100/D4 Compostela, Mex.
98/B3 Compton, Ca,US
93/G5 Comstock, Tx,US
96/C4 Comstock, Tx,US
60/A3 Cona, China
63/F2 Cona, China
60/A2 Co Nag (lake), China
76/C8 Conakry (cap.), Gui.
78/B4 Conakry (cap.), Gui.
78/B4 Conakry (comm.), Gui.
32/B3 Concarneau, Fr.
108/E1 Conceição da Barra, Braz.
108/B1 Conceicão das Alagoas, Braz.
107/J5 Conceição do Araguaia, Braz.
108/D1 Conceicão do Mato Dentro, Braz.
109/C2 Concepción, Arg.
106/E6 Concepción, Bol.
106/F7 Concepción (lake), Bol.
109/B4 Concepción, Chile
100/C3 Concepción (bay), Mex.
107/G8 Concepción, Par.
109/E1 Concepción, Par.
106/C6 Concepción, Peru
101/E3 Concepción del Oro, Mex.
109/E3 Concepción del Uruguay, Arg.
100/C3 Concepción, Punta (pt.), Mex.
92/B4 Conception (pt.), Ca,US
19/U10 Conches, Fr.
93/G5 Concho (riv.), Tx,US
100/D2 Conchos (riv.), Mex.
84/G7 Conchos (riv.), Mex.
93/F5 Conchos (riv.), Mex
92/B3 Concord, Ca,US
99/K11 Concord, Ca,US
97/H3 Concord, NC,US
87/J4 Concord (cap.), NH,US
89/M3 Concord (cap.), NH,US
95/G3 Concord (cap.), NH,US
99/N13 Concord, Wi,US
109/E3 Concordia, Arg.
108/A3 Concórdia, Braz.
109/F2 Concórdia, Braz.
100/D4 Concordia, Mex.
93/H3 Concordia, Ks,US
96/D2 Concordia, Ks,US
90/C3 Concrete, Wa,US
102/D3 Concuen (riv.), Guat.
60/E5 Con Cuong, Viet.
65/D2 Con Cuong, Viet.
103/G1 Condado, Cuba
71/J5 Condamine (riv.), Austl.
30/C3 Condé-sur-L'Escaut, Fr.
32/C2 Condé-sur-Noireau, Fr.
32/C2 Condé-sur-Vire, Fr.
37/G6 Condino, It.
71/H6 Condobolin, Austl.
73/C2 Condobolin, Austl.
32/D5 Condom, Fr.
35/F1 Condom, Fr.
72/C4 Condomine (riv.), Austl.
90/C4 Condon, Or,US
26/C3 Condroz (plat.), Belg.
31/D3 Condroz (upland), Belg.
32/F1 Condroz (upland), Belg.
33/K4 Conegliano, It.
96/B2 Conejos, Co,US
100/D3 Coneto de Comonfort, Mex.
31/E5 Conflans-en-Jarnisy, Fr.
19/S10 Conflans-Sainte-Honorine, Fr.
98/G4 Congers, NY,US
61/G4 Conghua, China
63/K3 Conghua, China
61/F3 Congjiang, China
63/J2 Congjiang, China
23/F5 Congleton, Eng,UK
74/D5 Congo
76/J8 Congo
82/B1 Congo
74/D5 Congo (riv.), Afr.
77/K7 Congo (basin), Afr.
82/C1 Congo (riv.), Afr.
76/J8 Congo (riv.), Congo, Zaire
108/D2 Congonhas, Braz.
74/E5 Congo (Zaire)
34/B4 Conil de la Frontera, Sp.
23/H5 Coningsby, Eng,UK
23/G5 Conisbrough, Eng,UK
23/E3 Coniston, Eng,UK
23/E3 Coniston Water (lake), Eng,UK
22/C2 Conlig, NI,UK
87/J1 Conn (lake), NW,Can
21/A4 Connacht (prov.), Ire.
23/E5 Connah's Quay, Wal,UK
30/C6 Connantre, Fr.
94/D3 Conneaut, Oh,US
87/J4 Connecticut (state), US
89/M3 Connecticut (state), US
95/F3 Connecticut (state), US
95/G2 Connecticut (riv.), US
98/G4 Connecticut (state), US
94/E3 Connellsville, Pa,US
21/H7 Connemara Nat'l Park, Ire.
94/C4 Connersville, In,US
97/G2 Connersville, In,US
21/A3 Conn, Lough (lake), Ire.
72/D4 Conondale Nat'l Park, Austl.
40/D3 Čonoplja, Yugo.
32/E4 Conques, Fr.
90/F3 Conrad, Mt,US
89/G5 Conroe, Tx,US
93/J5 Conroe, Tx,US
96/E4 Conroe, Tx,US
31/F4 Consdorf, Lux.
107/K8 Conselheiro Lafaiete, Braz.
108/D2 Conselheiro Lafaiete, Braz.
108/D1 Conselheiro Pena, Braz.
23/G2 Consett, Eng,UK
98/E5 Conshohocken, Pa,US
103/F1 Consolación del Sur, Cuba
63/J6 Con Son (isl.), Viet.
65/D4 Con Son (isl.), Viet.
66/C2 Con Son (isl.), Viet.
26/E5 Constance (lake), Eur.
37/F2 Constance (Bodensee) (lake), Eur.
33/H3 Constance (Bodensee) (lake), Swi., Ger.
104/F4 Constant (mtn.), Guad.
18/F4 Constanța, Rom.
41/J3 Constanța, Rom.
41/J3 Constanța (co.), Rom.
44/D3 Constanța, Rom.
46/C5 Constanța, Rom.
35/F2 Constantí, Sp.
34/C4 Constantina, Sp.
75/V17 Constantine, Alg.
75/V17 Constantine (gov.), Alg.
76/G1 Constantine, Alg.
85/G4 Constantine (cape), Ak,US
104/D3 Constanza, DRep.
109/B4 Constitución, Chile
100/B2 Constitución de 1857 Nat'l Park, Mex.
92/C5 Constitución de 1857 Nat'l Park, Mex
34/D3 Consuegra, Sp.
62/E3 Contai, India
106/D5 Contamana, Peru
33/K4 Contarina, It.
107/K6 Contas (riv.), Braz.
107/K7 Contegem, Braz.
108/C1 Contegem, Braz.
33/G5 Contes, Fr.
33/G3 Conthey, Swi.
36/D5 Conthey, Swi.
30/B4 Contigny, Fr.
106/C2 Continental (ranges), Ab, BC,Can
102/E1 Contoy (isl.), Mex.
99/L11 Contra Costa (can.), Ca,US
99/L11 Contra Costa (co.), Ca,US
95/P6 Contrecoeur, Qu,Can
34/E3 Contreras (res.), Sp.
26/C4 Contrexéville, Fr.
36/B1 Contrexéville, Fr.
85/J3 Controller (bay), Ak,US
31/G5 Contwig, Ger.
86/E2 Contwoyto (lake), NW,Can
30/B4 Conty, Fr.
38/E2 Conversano, It.
72/C3 Conway (cape), Austl.
89/H4 Conway, Ar,US
93/J4 Conway, Ar,US
96/E3 Conway, Ar,US
95/G3 Conway, NH,US
97/J3 Conway, SC,US
72/C3 Conway Range Nat'l Park, Austl.
22/E5 Conway, Vale of (val.), Wal,UK
22/D5 Conwy (bay), Wal,UK
22/E5 Conwy, Wal,UK
22/E5 Conwy (riv.), Wal,UK
68/C7 Coober Pedy, Austl.
70/E5 Coober Pedy, Austl.
62/E2 Cooch Behār, India
72/F7 Coochiemudlo (isl.), Austl.
70/E6 Cook, Austl.
71/R11 Cook (peak), N.Z.
71/R11 Cook (strait), N.Z.
85/H3 Cook (inlet), Ak,US
86/A2 Cook (inlet), Ak,US
99/Q16 Cook (co.), Il,US
94/C4 Cookeville, Tn,US
97/G2 Cookeville, Tn,US
83/L Cook Ice Shelf, Ant.
69/J6 Cook Islands (terr.), N.Z.
22/B2 Cookstown, NI,UK
22/B2 Cookstown (dist.), NI,UK
98/J7 Cooksville, Md,US
68/D6 Cooktown, Austl.
71/H3 Cooktown, Austl.
72/B1 Cooktown, Austl.
73/B3 Coola Coola (swamp), Austl.
71/H5 Cooladdi, Austl.
73/D1 Coolah, Austl.
73/C2 Coolamon, Austl.
73/C1 Coolangatta, Austl.
72/C5 Coolatai, Austl.
22/B4 Cooley (pt.), Ire.
70/C6 Coolgardie, Austl.
101/F2 Coolidge, Tx,US
72/D4 Cooloola Nat'l Park, Austl.
71/H7 Cooma, Austl.
73/D3 Cooma, Austl.
99/N15 Coon (cr.), Il,US
99/G6 Coon (cr.), Mi,US
73/D1 Coonabarabran, Austl.
73/A2 Coonalpyn, Austl.
71/H6 Coonamble, Austl.
73/D1 Coonamble, Austl.
53/K6 Coondapoor, India
62/B5 Coondapoor, India
99/G6 Coon, East Branch (cr.), Mi,US
62/C5 Coonoor, India
64/F3 Coonoor, India
70/G5 Cooper (cr.), Austl.
72/A4 Cooper (cr.), Austl.
101/G1 Cooper, Tx,US
93/J4 Cooper, Tx,US
96/E3 Cooper, Tx,US
98/E5 Coopersburg, Pa,US
91/J4 Cooperstown, ND,US
70/E6 Coorabie, Austl.
73/A3 Coorong Nat'l Park, Austl.
72/D4 Cooroy, Austl.
86/D4 Coos Bay, Or,US
88/B3 Coos Bay, Or,US
90/B5 Coos Bay, Or,US
92/A2 Coos Bay, Or,US
68/D8 Cootamundra, Austl.
71/H6 Cootamundra, Austl.
73/D2 Cootamundra, Austl.
22/A3 Cootehill, Ire.
106/E7 Copacabana, Bol.
102/C2 Copainalá, Mex.
102/B2 Copala, Mex.
101/F5 Copalillo, Mex.
102/B2 Copalillo, Mex.
102/D3 Copán (ruins), Hon.
34/E4 Cope (cape), Sp.
22/C2 Copeland (isl.), NI,UK
18/E3 Copenhagen (cap.), Den.
46/B4 Copenhagen (cap.), Den.
20/E5 Copenhagen (København) (cap.), Den.
26/G1 Copenhagen (København) (cap.), Den.
39/F2 Copertino, It.
73/D1 Copeton (dam), Austl.
109/B2 Copiapó, Chile
98/E5 Coplay, Pa,US
33/J4 Copparo, It.
29/G4 Coppenbrügge, Ger.
86/B2 Copper (riv.), Ak,US
93/H5 Copperas Cove, Tx,US
96/D4 Copperas Cove, Tx,US
85/J3 Copper Center, Ak,US
86/E2 Coppermine, NW,Can
86/E2 Coppermine (riv.), NW,Can
36/C5 Coppet, Swi.
23/F4 Coppull, Eng,UK
41/G2 Copșa Mică, Rom.
23/F1 Coquet (riv.), Eng,UK
23/G1 Coquet Dale (val.), Eng,UK
109/B2 Coquimbo, Chile
41/G4 Corabia, Rom.
44/C4 Corabia, Rom.
106/D7 Coracora, Peru
103/H2 Corail, Haiti
72/D5 Coraki, Austl.
73/E1 Coraki, Austl.
68/E6 Coral (sea)
69/U10 Coral (sea)
71/K2 Coral (sea)
72/C1 Coral (sea)
103/H4 Corales del Rosario Nat'l Park, Col.
97/H5 Coral Gables, Fl,US
87/H2 Coral Harbour, NW,Can
68/D6 Coral Sea Is. (terr.), Austl.
71/J2 Coral Sea Is. (terr.), Austl.
72/B1 Coral Sea Is. (terr.), Austl.
72/H3 Coral Sea Is. (terr.), Austl.
97/H5 Coral Springs, Fl,US
98/H5 Coram, NY,US
40/C5 Corato, It.
19/T11 Corbeil-Essonnes, Fr.
26/B4 Corbeil-Essonnes, Fr.
32/E2 Corbeil-Essonnes, Fr.
75/T15 Corbelin (cape), Alg.
36/C2 Corbenay, Fr.
37/F5 Corbet, Piz (peak), Swi.
26/B4 Corbie, Fr.
30/B4 Corbie, Fr.
32/E2 Corbie, Fr.
32/E5 Corbieres (mts.), Fr.
89/K4 Corbin, Ky,US
94/C4 Corbin, Ky,US
97/G2 Corbin, Ky,US
23/F2 Corbridge, Eng,UK
25/F2 Corby, Eng,UK
105/B7 Corcovado (gulf), Chile
103/F4 Corcovado Nat'l Park, CR
108/D2 Cordeiro, Braz.
89/K5 Cordele, Ga,US
97/H4 Cordele, Ga,US
99/K10 Cordelia, Ca,US
93/H4 Cordell (New Cordell), Ok,US
96/D3 Cordell (New Cordell), Ok,US
33/K4 Cordenons, It.
106/D3 Cordillera de los Picachos Nat'l Park, Col.
72/A4 Cordillo Downs, Austl.
108/C1 Cordisburgo, Braz.
109/D3 Córdoba, Arg.
109/D3 Córdoba (mts.), Arg.
103/G4 Córdoba (dept.), Col.
101/F5 Córdoba, Mex.
101/N8 Córdoba, Mex.
102/B2 Córdoba, Mex.
18/C5 Córdoba, Sp.
34/C4 Córdoba, Sp.
84/C3 Cordova, US
85/J3 Cordova, Ak,US
85/J3 Cordova (peak), Ak,US
86/B2 Cordova, Ak,US
34/E1 Corella, Sp.
106/G3 Corentyne (riv.), Guy., Sur.
70/G4 Corfield, Austl.
39/F3 Corfu (Kérkira) (isl.), Gre.
36/D3 Corgémont, Swi.
34/B1 Corgo, Sp.
34/B3 Coria, Sp.
34/B4 Coria del Río, Sp.
73/D2 Coricudgy (peak), Austl.
38/E3 Corigliano Calabro, It.
71/J3 Coringa Islets (isls.), Austl.
18/F5 Corinth, Gre.
39/H4 Corinth (ruins), Gre.
89/J5 Corinth, Ms,US
97/F3 Corinth, Ms,US
39/H4 Corinth (Kórinthos), Gre.
107/K7 Corinto, Braz.
108/C1 Corinto, Braz.
102/E3 Corinto, Nic.
34/A1 Coristanco, Sp.
18/C3 Cork, Ire.
21/A5 Cork, Ire.
38/C4 Corleone, It.
40/C5 Corleto Perticara, It.
41/H5 Çorlu, Turk.
44/C4 Çorlu, Turk.
50/A1 Çorlu, Turk.
30/D5 Cormontreuil, Fr.
91/H2 Cormorant (lake), Mb,Can
91/H2 Cormorant, Mb,Can
40/B5 Cornacchia (peak), It.
29/G6 Cornberg, Ger.
24/C1 Corndon (hill), UK
108/B2 Cornélio Procópio, Braz.
87/K2 Cornelius Grinnel (bay), NW,Can
35/L7 Cornella, Sp.
71/H7 Corner (inlet), Austl.
73/C3 Corner (inlet), Austl.
87/L4 Corner Brook, Nf,Can
95/K1 Corner Brook, Nf,Can
37/H6 Cornetto (peak), It.
36/C2 Cornimont, Fr.
89/L3 Corning, NY,US
94/E3 Corning, NY,US
72/B3 Cornish (cr.), Austl.
33/J4 Corno alle Scale (peak), It.
95/J2 Cornwall, Can
87/S7 Cornwall (isl.), NW,Can
87/J4 Cornwall, On,Can
94/F2 Cornwall, On,Can
24/B6 Cornwall (co.), Eng,UK
87/S7 Cornwallis (isl.), NW,Can
104/D5 Coro, Ven.
106/E1 Coro, Ven.
74/J9 Coroa (mtn.), CpV.
107/K4 Coroatá, Braz.
106/E7 Corocoro, Bol.
108/C1 Coromandel, Braz.
62/D5 Coromandel (coast), India
71/S10 Coromandel, N.Z.
71/S10 Coromandel (pen.), NZ
64/H3 Coromandel Coast (reg.), India
67/F1 Coron, Phil.
98/C3 Corona, Ca,US
93/F4 Corona, NM,US
96/B3 Corona, NM,US
103/E4 Coronado (bay), CR
100/C2 Coronado Nat'l Mon., Az,US
90/F2 Coronation, Ab,Can
86/E2 Coronation (gulf), NW,Can
109/B4 Coronel, Chile
108/D1 Coronel Fabriciano, Braz.
109/E2 Coronel Oviedo, Par.
109/D4 Coronel Pringles, Arg.
109/D4 Coronel Suárez, Arg.
108/A3 Coronel Vivida, Braz.
106/D7 Coropuna (peak), Peru
40/E5 Corovodë, Alb.
102/D2 Corozal, Belz.
103/H4 Corozal, Col.
101/F4 Corozal, Mex.
101/H5 Corozal Town, Belz.
84/H7 Corpus Christi, US
101/F3 Corpus Christi, Tx,US
89/G6 Corpus Christi, Tx,US
96/D5 Corpus Christi, Tx,US
34/D3 Corral de Almaguer, Sp.
35/Y16 Corralejo, Canl.
103/F1 Corralillo, Cuba
70/G7 Corrangamite (lake), Austl.
73/B3 Corrangamite (lake), Austl.
36/C2 Corre, Fr.
103/F4 Corredor, CR
106/B2 Corredor, CR
107/J6 Corrente, Braz.
108/B1 Corrente (riv.), Braz.
81/F2 Correntes, Cabo das (cape), Moz.
21/H7 Corrib, Lough (lake), Ire.
109/E2 Corrientes, Arg.
105/B2 Corrientes (pt.), Col.
106/C2 Corrientes (pt.), Col.
103/E1 Corrientes (cape), Cuba
106/C4 Corrientes (riv.), Ecu., Peru
88/E7 Corrientes (cape), Mex.
100/D4 Corrientes, Cabo (cape), Mex.
84/G7 Corrientes, Cabo (cape), Mex.
24/C1 Corris, Wal,UK
73/C3 Corryong, Austl.
33/H5 Corse (cape), Fr.
33/H5 Corse (reg.), Fr.
38/A1 Corse (cape), Fr.
38/A1 Corse (reg.), Fr.
22/D1 Corserine (mtn.), Sc,UK
22/C1 Corsewall (pt.), Sc,UK
24/D4 Corsham, Eng,UK
18/D4 Corsica (isl.), Fr.
33/H5 Corsica (isl.), Fr.
38/A1 Corsica (isl.), Fr.
101/F1 Corsicana, Tx,US
89/G5 Corsicana, Tx,US
93/H4 Corsicana, Tx,US
96/D3 Corsicana, Tx,US
36/C4 Cortaillod, Swi.
38/A1 Corte, Fr.
34/B4 Cortegana, Sp.
88/E4 Cortez, Co,US
92/E3 Cortez, Co,US
96/A2 Cortez, Co,US
33/K3 Cortina d'Ampezzo, It.
89/L3 Cortland, NY,US
94/E3 Cortland, NY,US
78/B4 Corubal (riv.), GBis.
34/A3 Coruche, Port.
45/G4 Çoruh (riv.), Turk.
44/E4 Çorum, Turk.
44/E4 Çorum (prov.), Turk.
50/C1 Çorum, Turk.
50/C1 Çorum (prov.), Turk.
106/G7 Corumbá, Braz.
107/J7 Corumbá (riv.), Braz.
108/B1 Corumbá (riv.), Braz.
86/D4 Corvallis, Or,US
88/B3 Corvallis, Or,US
90/C4 Corvallis, Or,US
92/B1 Corvallis, Or,US
24/D2 Corve (riv.), Eng,UK
35/R12 Corvo (isl.), Azor.
38/C1 Corvo (peak), It.
23/E6 Corwen, Wal,UK
37/E5 Corzoneso, Swi.
100/D3 Cosalá, Mex.
101/G5 Cosamaloapan, Mex.
102/C2 Cosamaloapan, Mex.
101/P8 Cosamaloapan de Carpio, Mex.
101/N7 Cosautlán de Carvajal, Mex.
101/M7 Coscomatepec de Bravo, Mex.
18/E5 Cosenza, It.
38/E3 Cosenza, It.
94/D3 Coshocton, Oh,US
102/E3 Cosigüina (pt.), Nic.
100/E4 Cosío, Mex.
34/D2 Coslada, Sp.
35/N9 Coslada, Sp.
26/B5 Cosne-Cours-sur-Loire, Fr.
32/E3 Cosne-Cours-sur-Loire, Fr.
32/E3 Cosne d'Allier, Fr.
101/N8 Cosolapa, Mex.
101/G5 Cosoleacaque, Mex.
102/C2 Cosoleacaque, Mex.
34/B1 Cospeito, Sp.
109/D3 Cosquín, Arg.
32/D3 Cosson (riv.), Fr.
36/C4 Cossonay, Swi.
35/P10 Costa da Caparica, Port.
35/C4 Costa del Sol (reg.), Sp.
35/P10 Costa do Sol (reg.), Port.
98/C3 Costa Mesa, Ca,US
103/F4 Costa Rica
106/B2 Costa Rica
84/J8 Costa Rica
100/D3 Costa Rica, Mex.
25/H1 Costessey, Eng,UK
41/G3 Costești, Rom.
99/M10 Cosumnes (riv.), Ca,US
67/F2 Cotabato City, Phil.
103/H4 Cotatumbo (riv.), Col., Ven.
95/M7 Coteau-du-Lac, Qu,Can
95/M7 Coteau-Landing, Qu,Can
33/G5 Côte-d'Azur (coast), Fr.
78/D5 Côte d'Ivoire (Ivory Coast)
32/F3 Côte d'Or (uplands), Fr.
30/A3 Côte-d'Or (dept.), Fr.
32/C2 Cotentin (pen.), Fr.
95/N7 Côte-Saint-Luc, Qu,Can
24/B3 Cothi (riv.), Wal,UK
76/F6 Cotonou, Ben.
79/F5 Cotonou, Ben.
24/D4 Cotswolds (hills), Eng,UK
88/B3 Cottage Grove, Or,US
90/C5 Cottage Grove, Or,US
99/G7 Cottam, On,Can
27/H3 Cottbus, Ger.
25/G2 Cottenham, Eng,UK
33/G4 Cottian Alps (range), Fr., It.
107/H3 Cottica, Sur.
88/D5 Cottonwood, Az,US
92/D4 Cottonwood, Az,US
93/F5 Cottonwood (dry riv.), Tx,US
104/D3 Cotuí, DRep.
101/F2 Cotulla, Tx,US
96/D4 Cotulla, Tx,US
19/U10 Coubert, Fr.
32/C4 Coubre, Pointe de la (pt.), Fr.
36/A3 Couchey, Fr.
36/C5 Cou, Col de (pass), Fr.
30/C5 Coucy-le-Château-Auffrique, Fr.
30/B1 Coudekerque-Branche, Fr.
32/E5 Couguille, Pic de (peak), Fr.
35/G1 Couguille, Pic de (peak), Fr.
32/D2 Coulaines, Fr.
90/D4 Coulee City, Wa,US
83/M Coulman (isl.), Ant.
30/A2 Coulogne, Fr.
26/B4 Coulommiers, Fr.
30/C6 Coulommiers, Fr.
32/E2 Coulommiers, Fr.
94/E2 Coulonge (riv.), Qu,Can
32/D4 Coulounieix-Chamiers, Fr.
19/N8 Coulsdon, Eng,UK
85/F3 Council, Ak,US
90/D4 Council, Id,US
89/G3 Council Bluffs, Ia,US
91/K5 Council Bluffs, Ia,US
93/J2 Council Bluffs, Ia,US
93/H3 Council Grove, Ks,US
96/D2 Council Grove, Ks,US
19/U10 Coupvray, Fr.
105/D2 Courantyne (riv.), Guy.
19/S10 Courbevoie, Fr.
26/C3 Courcelles, Belg.
30/D3 Courcelles, Belg.
32/F1 Courcelles, Belg.
31/F5 Courcelles-Chaussy, Fr.
30/A5 Courcelles-sur-Seine, Fr.
19/T11 Courcouronnes, Fr.
36/D3 Courgenay, Swi.
36/C6 Courmayeur, It.
32/E4 Cournon-d'Auvergne, Fr.
36/D3 Courrendlin, Swi.
36/D3 Courroux, Swi.
32/E5 Coursan, Fr.
35/G1 Coursan, Fr.
36/D3 Courtelary, Swi.
86/D4 Courtenay, BC,Can
88/B2 Courtenay, BC,Can
36/D4 Courtepin, Swi.
95/S8 Courtice, On,Can
30/D6 Courtisols, Fr.
99/L10 Courtland, Ca,US
21/A5 Courtmacsherry, Ire.
30/C2 Courtrai (Kortrijk), Belg.
19/T10 Courtry, Fr.
36/B4 Cousance-du-Jura, Fr.
30/D3 Cousolre, Fr.
32/C2 Coutances, Fr.
32/C4 Coutras, Fr.
90/F3 Coutts, Ab,Can
36/C4 Couvet, Swi
26/C3 Couvin, Belg.
30/D3 Couvin, Belg.
32/F1 Couvin, Belg.
32/D4 Couzeix, Fr.
35/P10 Cova da Piedade, Port.
34/C1 Covadonga Nat'l Park, Sp.
40/G3 Covasna (co.), Rom.
41/H3 Covasna, Rom.
18/C3 Coventry, Eng,UK
25/E1 Coventry (co.), Eng,UK
25/E2 Coventry, Eng,UK
51/M7 Covered Market, Turk.
34/B2 Covilhã, Port.
98/C2 Covina, Ca,US
97/H3 Covington, Ga,US
94/C4 Covington, Ky,US
97/G2 Covington, Ky,US
93/K4 Covington, Tn,US
94/B5 Covington, Tn,US
97/F3 Covington, Tn,US
94/E4 Covington, Va,US
97/J2 Covington, Va,US
70/C6 Cowan (lake), Austl.
72/H8 Cowan, Austl.
24/C4 Cowbridge, Wal,UK
70/F6 Cowell, Austl.
25/E5 Cowes, Eng,UK
23/F2 Cow Green (res.), Eng,UK
90/C4 Cowlitz (riv.), Wa,US
97/H3 Cowpens Nat'l Bfld., SC,US
71/H6 Cowra, Austl.
73/D2 Cowra, Austl.
101/F5 Coxcotlán, Mex.
102/B2 Coxcotlán, Mex.
23/G2 Coxhoe, Eng,UK
107/H7 Coxim, Braz.
63/F3 Cox's Bāzār, Bang.
100/D2 Coyame, Mex.
93/F5 Coyame, Mex
96/B4 Coyame, Mex
19/T9 Coye-la-Forêt, Fr.
30/B5 Coye-la-Forêt, Fr.
101/Q10 Coyoacán, Mex.
92/D5 Coyote (riv.), Mex
99/L12 Coyote (cr.), Ca,US
101/K7 Coyotepec, Mex.
101/E5 Coyuca, Mex.
102/A2 Coyuca de Benítez, Mex.
101/M6 Coyutla, Mex.
91/J5 Cozad, Ne,US
93/H2 Cozad, Ne,US
102/E1 Cozumel, Mex.
102/E1 Cozumel (isl.), Mex.
84/J7 Cozumel (isl.), Mex.
89/J7 Cozumel (isl.), Mex.
73/C4 Cradle (peak), Austl.
73/C4 Cradle Mountain-Lake St. Clair Nat'l Park, Austl.
80/D4 Cradock, SAfr.
82/E7 Cradock, SAfr.
85/K3 Crag (mtn.), Yk,Can
23/G3 Crag (hill), Eng,UK
85/M4 Craig, Ak,US
88/E3 Craig, Co,US
92/F2 Craig, Co,US
22/C2 Craigavad, NI,UK
22/B3 Craigavon, NI,UK
22/B3 Craigavon (dist.), NI,UK
73/F5 Craigieburn, Austl.
91/G3 Craik, Sk,Can
26/F4 Crailsheim, Ger.
33/J2 Crailsheim, Ger.
18/F4 Craiova, Rom.
41/F3 Craiova, Rom.
44/B3 Craiova, Rom.
37/E5 Cramalina, Pizzo (peak), Swi.
23/G1 Cramlington, Eng,UK
22/A1 Crana (riv.), Ire.
91/H2 Cranberry Portage, Mb,Can
24/D5 Cranborne Chase (for.), Eng,UK
73/C3 Cranbourne, Austl.
73/G6 Cranbourne, Austl.
86/E4 Cranbrook, BC,Can
88/C2 Cranbrook, BC,Can
90/E3 Cranbrook, BC,Can
25/G4 Cranbrook, Eng,UK
93/G5 Crane, Tx,US
96/C4 Crane, Tx,US
91/J3 Crane River, Mb,Can
36/C6 Cran-Gevrier, Fr.
25/F4 Cranleigh, Eng,UK
30/C5 Craonne, Fr.
32/F4 Craponne, Fr.
41/F2 Crasna (riv.), Rom.
92/B2 Crater (lake), Or,US
90/C5 Crater Lake Nat'l Park, Or,US
86/D4 Crater Lake Nat'l Park, Or,US

Crate – Danne

88/B3 Crater Lake Nat'l Park, Or,US
92/B2 Crater Lake Nat'l Park, Or,US
90/E5 Craters of the Moon Nat'l Mon., Id,US
92/D2 Craters of the Moon Nat'l Mon., Id,US
107/K5 Crateús, Braz.
38/E3 Crati (riv.), It.
107/L5 Crato, Braz.
34/B3 Crato, Port.
108/C2 Cravinhos, Braz.
94/C3 Crawfordsville, In,US
97/G1 Crawfordsville, In,US
97/G4 Crawfordville, Fl,US
25/F4 Crawley, Eng,UK
19/P7 Cray (riv.), Eng,UK
19/P7 Crayford, Eng,UK
90/F4 Crazy (mts.), Mt,US
36/A5 Crêches-sur-Saône, Fr.
30/A3 Crécy-en-Ponthieu, Fr.
30/C4 Crécy-sur-Serre, Fr.
24/D2 Credenhill, Eng,UK
95/Q8 Credit (riv.), On,Can
24/C5 Crediton, Eng,UK
86/F3 Cree (lake), Sk,Can
86/F3 Cree (riv.), Sk,Can
22/D2 Cree (riv.), Sc,UK
100/D3 Creel, Mex.
22/D2 Creetown, Sc,UK
19/U10 Crégy-lès-Meaux, Fr.
31/F5 Créhange, Fr.
86/F3 Creighton, Sk,Can
91/H2 Creighton, Sk,Can
26/B4 Creil, Fr.
30/B5 Creil, Fr.
32/E2 Creil, Fr.
33/H4 Crema, It.
36/B6 Crémieu, Fr.
29/H4 Cremlingen, Ger.
33/J4 Cremona, It.
40/E3 Crepaja, Yugo.
30/C4 Crépy-en-Laonnois, Fr.
30/B5 Crépy-en-Valois, Fr.
33/L4 Cres, Cro.
33/L4 Cres (isl.), Cro.
40/B3 Cres (isl.), Cro.
88/B3 Crescent City, Ca,US
90/B5 Crescent City, Ca,US
92/A2 Crescent City, Ca,US
61/F5 Crescent Group (isls.), China
98/E4 Cresco, Pa,US
30/C3 Crespin, Fr.
73/C4 Cressy, Austl.
32/F4 Crest, Fr.
99/P16 Crest Hill, Il,US
90/D3 Creston, Can
86/E4 Creston, BC,Can
91/K5 Creston, Ia,US
93/J2 Creston, Ia,US
97/G4 Crestview, Fl,US
23/G5 Creswell, Eng,UK
73/B3 Creswick, Austl.
36/B5 Crêt de la Neige (mtn.), Fr.
36/B5 Crêt du Nu (mtn.), Fr.
18/F5 Crete (isl.), Gre.
39/J5 Crete (isl.), Gre.
39/J5 Crete (sea), Gre.
50/A3 Crete (isl.), Gre.
77/L1 Crete (isl.), Gre.
91/J5 Crete, Ne,US
93/H2 Crete, Ne,US
19/T10 Créteil, Fr.
26/B4 Créteil, Fr.
30/B6 Créteil, Fr.
32/E2 Créteil, Fr.
35/G1 Creus (cape), Sp.
32/D3 Creuse (riv.), Fr.
31/F5 Creutzwald-la-Croix, Fr.
29/H6 Creuzburg, Ger.
33/J4 Crevalcore, It.
30/B4 Crèvecœur-le-Grand, Fr.
35/E3 Crevillente, Sp.
37/E5 Crevoladossola, It.
23/F5 Crewe, Eng,UK
24/D5 Crewkerne, Eng,UK
73/C3 Crib Point, Austl.
22/D6 Criccieth, Wal,UK
108/B4 Criciúma, Braz.
109/G2 Criciúma, Braz.
24/C3 Crickhowell, Wal,UK
25/E3 Cricklade, Eng,UK
30/A3 Criel-sur-Mer, Fr.
22/E2 Criffell (hill), Eng,UK
33/L4 Crikvenica, Cro.
40/B3 Crikvenica, Cro.
19/G4 Crimea (pen.), Ukr.
46/D5 Crimean (pen.), Ukr.
41/L3 Crimean (pen.), Ukr.
44/E3 Crimean (pen.), Ukr.
41/L3 Crimean Obl., Ukr.
44/E3 Crimean Obl., Ukr.
36/C4 Crissier, Swi.
76/H7 Cristal (mts.), Gabon
82/B1 Cristal (mts.), Gabon
107/J7 Cristalina, Braz.
103/H4 Cristóbal Colón (peak), Col.
105/B1 Cristóbal Colón (peak), Col.
106/D1 Cristóbal Colón (peak), Col.
40/F2 Criştul Alb (riv.), Rom.
41/G2 Cristuru Secuiesc, Rom.
40/E2 Crişul Negru (riv.), Rom.
107/H6 Crixás-Açu (riv.), Braz.
39/G2 Crna Reka (riv.), Macd.
40/E5 Crna Reka (riv.), Macd.
33/L4 Črnomelj, Slov.
40/B3 Črnomelj, Slov.
73/D3 Croajingolong Nat'l Park, Austl.
18/E4 Croatia
33/L4 Croatia
38/E1 Croatia
40/C3 Croatia
37/H5 Croce, Monte (peak), It.
37/H4 Croce, Pico di (peak), It.
95/F2 Croche (riv.), Qu,Can
36/C6 Croche, Aiguille (peak), Fr.
66/E3 Crocker (range), Malay.
22/E1 Crocketford, Sc,UK
99/K10 Crockett, Ca,US
89/G5 Crockett, Tx,US
93/J5 Crockett, Tx,US
96/E4 Crockett, Tx,US
73/D2 Crocodile (pt.), Austl.
37/E5 Crodo, It.
98/K7 Crofton, Md,US
24/B3 Crofty, Wal,UK
24/A2 Croghan (mtn.), Ire.
32/F5 Croisette (cape), Fr.
35/H1 Croisette (cape), Fr.
30/B3 Croisilles, Fr.
19/T10 Croissy-Beaubourg, Fr.
91/L3 Croix (lake), Can., US
94/B1 Croix (lake), On,Can, Mn,US
36/B5 Croix de la Serra, Col de la (pass), Fr.
70/E2 Croker (isl.), Austl.
25/H1 Cromer, Eng,UK
26/A2 Cromer, Eng.,UK
71/Q12 Cromwell, N.Z.
65/E3 Crong A Na (riv.), Viet.
72/H9 Cronulla, Austl.
23/G2 Crook, Eng,UK
103/H1 Crooked (isl.), Bahm.
104/C2 Crooked (isl.), Bahm.
85/G3 Crooked Creek, Ak,US
103/H1 Crooked Island (passg.), Bahm.
104/C2 Crooked Island (passg.), Bahm.
21/H8 Crookhaven, Ire.
86/G4 Crookston, Mn,US
91/J4 Crookston, Mn,US
73/D2 Crookwell, Austl.
21/A4 Croom, Ire.
23/E5 Crosby, Eng,UK
91/H3 Crosby, ND,US
93/G4 Crosbyton, Tx,US
96/C3 Crosbyton, Tx,US
19/T10 Crosne, Fr.
79/H5 Cross (riv.), Camr., Nga.
91/J2 Cross (lake), Mb,Can
97/H4 Cross City, Fl,US
93/K4 Crossett, Ar,US
96/F3 Crossett, Ar,US
23/F2 Cross Fell (mtn.), Eng,UK
90/E3 Crossfield, Ab,Can
22/C3 Crossgar, NI,UK
24/C2 Crossgates, Wal,UK
22/D1 Crosshill, Sc,UK
24/C3 Crosskeys, Wal,UK
22/B3 Crossmaglen, NI,UK
22/E2 Crossmichael, Sc,UK
21/H6 Crossmolina, Ire.
101/F1 Cross Plains, Tx,US
79/H5 Cross River (state), Nga.
98/G4 Cross River (res.), NY,US
21/A3 Crossroads, Ire.
97/G3 Crossville, Tn,US
23/F4 Croston, Eng,UK
38/E3 Crotone, It.
25/G3 Crouch (riv.), Eng,UK
30/C5 Crouy, Fr.
30/C5 Crouy-sur-Ourq, Fr.
90/G4 Crow Agency, Mt,US
25/G4 Crowborough, Eng,UK
73/E1 Crowdy Bay Nat'l Park, Austl.
94/E2 Crowe (riv.), On,Can
90/F5 Crowheart, Wy,US
92/E2 Crowheart, Wy,US
25/F1 Crowland, Eng,UK
23/H4 Crowle, Eng,UK
93/J5 Crowley, La,US
96/E4 Crowley, La,US
97/F3 Crowley's (ridge), Ar,US
91/K4 Crow, North Fork (riv.), Mn,US
94/C3 Crown Point, In,US
92/E4 Crownpoint, NM,US
96/A3 Crownpoint, NM,US
87/H1 Crown Prince Frederik (isl.), NW,Can
72/D4 Crows Nest Falls Nat'l Park, Austl.
25/F4 Crowthorne, Eng,UK
19/M7 Croxley Green, Eng,UK
25/F3 Croxley Green, Eng,UK
70/G3 Croydon, Austl.
72/A2 Croydon, Austl.
73/G5 Croydon, Austl.
19/N7 Croydon, Eng,UK
19/N7 Croydon (bor.), Eng,UK
17/M8 Crozet (isls.), Fr.
83/M Crozier (cape), Ant.
32/A2 Crozon, Fr.
103/G1 Crucero Contramaestre, Cuba
101/F3 Cruillas, Mex.
22/B2 Crumlin, NI,UK
23/E2 Crummock Water (lake), Eng,UK
36/C5 Cruseilles, Fr.
31/E5 Crusnes (riv.), Fr.
103/G2 Cruz (cape), Cuba
109/F2 Cruz Alta, Braz.
35/P10 Cruz Alta (mtn.), Port.
107/L6 Cruz das Almas, Braz.
109/D3 Cruz del Eje, Arg.
108/C2 Cruzeiro, Braz.
106/D5 Cruzeiro do Sul, Braz.
40/D3 Crvenka, Yugo.
23/E5 Cryn-y-Brain (mtn.), Wal,UK
92/C3 Crystal Bay, Nv,US
96/D4 Crystal City, Tx,US
91/L4 Crystal Falls, Mi,US
94/B2 Crystal Falls, Mi,US
99/P15 Crystal Lake, Il,US
99/K11 Crystal Springs (res.), Ca,US
27/M5 Csenger, Hun.
40/F2 Csenger, Hun.
33/M3 Csepreg, Hun.
40/E2 Csongrád, Hun.
40/E2 Csongrád (co.), Hun.
27/J5 Csorna, Hun.
40/C2 Csorna, Hun.
40/E2 Csorvás, Hun.
40/D2 Csóványos (peak), Hun.
40/C2 Csurgó, Hun.
51/F3 Ctesiphon (ruins), Iraq
52/D2 Ctesiphon (ruins), Iraq
102/B2 Cuajinicuilapa, Mex.
34/B2 Cualedro, Sp.
82/G3 Cuamba, Moz.
82/D4 Cuando (riv.), Ang.
82/C4 Cuangar, Ang.
82/C2 Cuango (riv.), Ang.
74/D5 Cuanza (riv.), Ang.
82/B2 Cuanza (riv.), Ang.
35/E3 Cuart de Poblet, Sp.
100/E3 Cuatrociénagas, Mex.
96/C5 Cuatrociénagas de Carranza, Mex
100/D2 Cuauhtémoc, Mex.
100/E5 Cuauhtémoc, Mex.
96/B4 Cuauhtémoc, Mex
101/L6 Cuautepec de Hinojosa, Mex.
101/K7 Cuautitlán, Mex.
101/Q9 Cuautitlán, Mex.
101/Q9 Cuautitlan (riv.), Mex.
101/L8 Cuautla, Mex.
102/B2 Cuautla, Mex.
101/F5 Cuautla Morelos, Mex.
103/F1 Cuba
84/K7 Cuba
89/K7 Cuba
34/B3 Cuba, Port.
93/K3 Cuba, Mo,US
97/F2 Cuba, Mo,US
104/E5 Cubagua (isl.), Ven.
82/C4 Cubango (riv.), Ang.
74/D6 Cubango (riv.), Ang., Namb.
108/C2 Cubatão, Braz.
44/E4 Çubuk, Turk.
50/C1 Çubuk, Turk.
109/D4 Cuchillo-Có, Arg.
100/D2 Cuchillo Parado, Mex.
106/E2 Cuchivero (riv.), Ven.
102/D3 Cuchumatanes, Sierra los (range), Guat.
25/F4 Cuckfield, Eng,UK
25/G5 Cuckmere (riv.), Eng,UK
60/E4 Cuc Phuong Nat'l Park, Viet.
65/D1 Cuc Phuong Nat'l Park, Viet.
25/H6 Cucq, Fr.
30/A3 Cucq, Fr.
32/D1 Cucq, Fr.
103/H5 Cúcuta, Col.
106/D2 Cúcuta, Col.
102/D3 Cucuyagua, Hon.
99/Q14 Cudahy, Wi,US
62/C5 Cuddalore, India
64/G3 Cuddalore, India
62/C5 Cuddapah, India
23/F5 Cuddington, Eng,UK
73/C3 Cudgewa, Austl.
34/B1 Cudillero, Sp.
36/D4 Cudrefin, Swi.
23/G4 Cudworth, Eng,UK
70/B5 Cue, Austl.
34/C2 Cuéllar, Sp.
106/C4 Cuenca, Ecu.
18/C4 Cuenca, Sp.
34/D2 Cuenca, Sp.
34/E2 Cuenca (range), Sp.
100/E3 Cuencamé, Mex.
101/E5 Cueramo, Mex.
101/F5 Cuernavaca, Mex.
101/K8 Cuernavaca, Mex.
102/B2 Cuernavaca, Mex.
101/F2 Cuero, Tx,US
93/H5 Cuero, Tx,US
96/D4 Cuero, Tx,US
32/G5 Cuers, Fr.
35/J1 Cuers, Fr.
103/H1 Cueto, Cuba
104/D5 Cueva de la Quebrada del Toro Nat'l Park, Ven.
106/C3 Cueva de los Guarcharos Nat'l Park, Col.
34/E4 Cuevas del Almanzora, Sp.
35/F2 Cuevas de Vinromá, Sp.
100/A2 Cuevitas, Mex.
19/N6 Cuffley, Eng,UK
41/F3 Cugir, Rom.
44/B3 Cugir, Rom.
38/A2 Cuglieri, It.
32/D5 Cugnaux-Vingtcasses, Fr.
35/F1 Cugnaux-Vingtcasses, Fr.
107/G7 Cuiabá, Braz.
107/G7 Cuiabá (riv.), Braz.
28/C5 Cuijk, Neth.
102/D3 Cuilapa, Guat.
102/C3 Cuilco (riv.), Guat., Mex.
82/C2 Cuilo (riv.), Ang.
82/C3 Cuima, Ang.
36/B4 Cuisance (riv.), Fr.
36/B5 Cuiseaux, Fr.
30/C5 Cuise-la-Motte, Fr.
36/B4 Cuisery, Fr.
101/N8 Cuitlahuac, Mex.
82/C4 Cuito (riv.), Ang.
82/C4 Cuito-Cuanavale, Ang.
106/F4 Cuiuni (riv.), Braz.
61/G3 Cuiwei (mtn.), China
101/Q10 Cujimalpa, Mex.
50/C2 Çukur, Turk.
51/E2 Çukurca, Turk.
65/E4 Cu Lao (isl.), Viet.
73/C2 Culcairn, Austl.
22/A1 Culdaff, Ire.
22/A1 Culdaff (riv.), Ire.
28/C5 Culemborg, Neth.
107/H6 Culene (riv.), Braz.
71/H5 Culgoa (riv.), Austl.
73/C1 Culgoa (riv.), Austl.
100/D3 Culiacán, Mex.
69/Q2 Culiacán, Mex.
34/D4 Cúllar Baza, Sp.
35/E3 Cullera, Sp.
34/A1 Culleredo, Sp.
80/Q12 Cullinan, SAfr.
89/J5 Cullman, Al,US
97/G3 Cullman, Al,US
24/C5 Cullompton, Eng,UK
36/C5 Cully, Swi.
22/B2 Cullybackey, NI,UK
99/D2 Culmback (dam), Wa,US
22/A1 Culmore, NI,UK
72/B5 Culoga (riv.), Austl.
36/B6 Culoz, Fr.
94/E4 Culpeper, Va,US
97/J2 Culpeper, Va,US
70/C6 Culver (pt.), Austl.
98/B2 Culver City, Ca,US
98/F4 Culvers (lake), NJ,US
104/E5 Cumaná, Ven.
106/F1 Cumaná, Ven.
108/B1 Cumari, Braz.
84/L3 Cumberland (sound), Can.
87/K2 Cumberland (pen.), NW,Can
87/K2 Cumberland (sound), NW,Can
91/H2 Cumberland (delta), Sk,Can
91/H2 Cumberland (lake), Sk,Can
97/G3 Cumberland (plat.), US
97/H4 Cumberland (isl.), Ga,US
94/C4 Cumberland (lake), Ky,US
94/C4 Cumberland (riv.), Ky,US
97/G2 Cumberland (fall, falls), Ky,US
89/J4 Cumberland (riv.), Ky, Tn,US
89/L4 Cumberland, Md,US
94/E4 Cumberland, Md,US
97/J2 Cumberland, Md,US
99/D3 Cumberland, Wa,US
94/D4 Cumberland Gap Nat'l Hist. Park, Tn,US
97/H2 Cumberland Gap Nat'l Hist. Park, Tn,US
91/H2 Cumberland House, Sk,Can
101/G5 Cumbres Bastonal, Cerro (mt.), Mex.
102/C2 Cumbres Bastonal, Cerro (mtn.), Mex.
100/D2 Cumbres de Majalca Nat'l Park, Mex.
92/F5 Cumbres de Majalca Nat'l Park, Mex.
96/A4 Cumbres de Majalca Nat'l Park, Mex
88/E6 Cumbres de Majarca Nat'l Park, Mex.
101/E3 Cumbres de Monterrey Nat'l Park, Mex.
88/F6 Cumbres de Monterrey Nat'l Park, Mex.
96/C5 Cumbres de Monterrey Nat'l Park, Mex
23/F2 Cumbria (co.), Eng,UK
23/E3 Cumbrian (mts.), Eng,UK
62/C4 Cumbum, India
73/D2 Cumnock, Austl.
100/C2 Cumpas, Mex.
92/E5 Cumpas, Mex
50/C2 Çumra, Turk.
85/M5 Cumshewa (pt.), BC,Can
101/G5 Cunduacán, Mex.
102/C2 Cunduacán, Mex.
82/B4 Cunene (riv.), Ang.
74/D6 Cunene (riv.), Ang., Namb.
18/D4 Cuneo, It.
33/G4 Cuneo, It.
63/J5 Cung Son, Viet.
65/E3 Cung Son, Viet.
66/C1 Cung Son, Viet.
68/D7 Cunnamulla, Austl.
71/H5 Cunnamulla, Austl.
72/B5 Cunnamulla, Austl.
20/H1 Čuokkaraš'ša (peak), Nor.
33/G4 Cuorgnè, It.
99/K12 Cupertino, Ca,US
33/K5 Cupra Marittima, It.
40/E4 Ćuprija, Yugo.
44/B4 Ćuprija, Yugo.
100/E4 Cuquío, Mex.
104/D5 Curaçao (isl.), NAnt.
106/E1 Curaçao (isl.), NAnt.
84/L8 Curaçao (isl.), NAnt.
109/B4 Curanilahue, Chile
106/C4 Curaray (riv.), Ecu., Peru
102/E3 Curaren, Hon.
40/F2 Curcubăta (peak), Rom.
44/B3 Curcubăta (peak), Rom.
26/B5 Cure (riv.), Fr.
32/E3 Cure (riv.), Fr.
81/S15 Curepipe, Mrts.
109/B3 Curicó, Chile
108/B3 Curitiba, Braz.
109/G2 Curitiba, Braz.
108/B3 Curitibanos, Braz.
73/A1 Curnamona, Austl.
22/B5 Curragh, The, Ire.
107/L5 Currais Novos, Braz.
74/K10 Curral Velho, CpV.
93/K3 Current (riv.), Ar, Mo,US
73/B3 Currie, Austl.
92/D2 Currie, Nv,US
85/H3 Curry, Ak,US
41/G3 Curtea de Argeş, Rom.
44/C3 Curtea de Argeş, Rom.
40/E2 Curtici, Rom.
71/J4 Curtis (isl.), Austl.
72/C3 Curtis (isl.), Austl.
68/H8 Curtis (isl.), N.Z.
34/A1 Curtis, Sp.
107/G4 Curuá (riv.), Braz.
107/H5 Curuá (riv.), Braz.
106/D5 Curuçú (riv.), Braz.
103/E4 Curú Nat'l Wild. Ref., CR
66/B4 Curup, Indo.
107/K4 Cururupu, Braz.
109/E2 Curuzú Cuatiá, Arg.
107/K7 Curvelo, Braz.
108/C1 Curvelo, Braz.
89/J2 Curwood (mt.), Mi,US
91/L4 Curwood (peak), Mi,US
106/D6 Cusco, Peru
22/B1 Cushendall, NI,UK
22/B3 Cusher (riv.), NI,UK
93/H4 Cushing, Ok,US
96/D3 Cushing, Ok,US
32/E3 Cusset, Fr.
97/G3 Cusseta, Ga,US
90/G4 Custer, Mt,US
86/F4 Custer, SD,US
91/H5 Custer, SD,US
93/G2 Custer, SD,US
31/F6 Custines, Fr.
24/C5 Cut (hill), Eng,UK
90/E3 Cut Bank, Mt,US
106/C5 Cutervo, Peru
97/G4 Cuthbert, Ga,US
90/F2 Cut Knife, Sk,Can
109/C4 Cutral-Có, Arg.
62/E3 Cuttack, India
32/E5 Cuxac-d'Aude, Fr.
35/G1 Cuxac-d'Aude, Fr.
26/E2 Cuxhaven, Ger.
29/F1 Cuxhaven, Ger.
92/C4 Cuyama (riv.), Ca,US
67/F1 Cuyo, Phil.
67/F1 Cuyo (isls.), Phil.
106/F2 Cuyuni (riv.), Guy., Ven.
24/C3 Cwm, Wal,UK
24/C3 Cwmafan, Wal,UK
24/C3 Cwmbran, Wal,UK
91/H5 C.W. McConaughy (lake), Nb,US
39/J4 Cyclades (isls.), Gre.
94/C4 Cynthiana, Ky,US
97/G2 Cynthiana, Ky,US
24/B3 Cynwyl Elfed, Wal,UK
90/F3 Cypress (hills), Ab, Sk,Can
48/C6 Cyprus
49/C2 Cyprus
50/C3 Cyprus
52/B1 Cyprus
74/E1 Cyrenaica (reg.), Libya
77/K1 Cyrenaica (reg.), Libya
30/C2 Cysoing, Fr.
24/B3 Cywyn (riv.), Wal,UK
27/J2 Czaplinek, Pol.
27/M2 Czarna Białostocka, Pol.
27/J2 Czarne, Pol.
27/J2 Czarnków, Pol.
18/E4 Czech Republic
27/H4 Czech Republic
33/L2 Czech Republic
44/A2 Czech Republic
46/B5 Czech Republic
18/E3 Częstochowa, Pol.
27/K3 Częstochowa, Pol.
27/K3 Czestochowa (prov.), Pol.
44/A2 Częstochowa, Pol.
27/J2 Człuchów, Pol.

D

54/D5 Da (riv.), China
60/C2 Da (riv.), China
61/J2 Da (riv.), China
31/G2 Daaden, Ger.
55/J2 Da'an, China
54/F5 Daba (mts.), China
59/B4 Daba (mts.), China
61/F2 Daba (mts.), China
78/D4 Dabakala, IvC.
40/D2 Dabas, Hun.
50/C5 Dabbāgh, Jabal (mtn.), SAr.
52/C3 Dabbāgh, Jabal (mtn.), SAr.
106/C2 Dabeiba, Col.
53/K4 Dabhoi, India
62/B3 Dabhoi, India
61/G2 Dabie (mts.), China
60/E4 Da (Black) (riv.), Viet.
65/D1 Da (Black) (riv.), Viet.
31/G6 Dabo, Fr.
99/B2 Dabob (bay), Wa,US
76/C5 Dabola, Gui.
77/Q6 Daborow, Som.
78/D5 Dabou, IvC.
79/E4 Daboya, Gha.
62/C2 Dabra, India
27/M2 Dąbrowa Białostocka, Pol.
42/D5 Dąbrowa Białostocka, Pol.
27/K3 Dąbrowa Górnicza, Pol.
59/H7 Dachang Huizu Zizhixian, China
26/F4 Dachau, Ger.
33/J2 Dachau, Ger.
37/H1 Dachau, Ger.
65/D3 Dac Sut, Viet.
63/J5 Dac To, Viet.
65/D3 Dac To, Viet.
97/H4 Dade City, Fl,US
67/H4 Dadi (cape), Indo.
62/B4 Dadra & Nagar Haveli (terr.), India
54/E5 Dadu (riv.), China
60/D2 Dadu (riv.), China
53/J3 Dādu, Pak.
62/A2 Dādu, Pak.
62/D6 Daduru (riv.), SrL.
63/G5 Daen Noi (peak), Thai.
65/B4 Daen Noi (peak), Thai.
66/A1 Daen Noi (peak), Thai.
60/E3 Dafang, China
63/J2 Dafang, China
59/E4 Dafeng, China
60/D2 Dafu, China
61/H2 Dafu, China
76/B4 Dagana, Sen.
78/B2 Dagana, Sen.
45/H3 Dagestan Aut. Rep., Rus.
51/G1 Dagestanskiye Ogni, Rus.
80/D4 Daggaboersnek (pass), SAfr.
72/B2 Dagmar Range Nat'l Park, Austl.
36/B6 Dagneux, Fr.
60/D3 Daguan, China
63/H2 Daguan, China
72/E6 D'Aguilar (mtn.), Austl.
72/E6 D'Aguilar (range), Austl.
55/K2 Daguokui (peak), China
68/B3 Dagupan City, Phil.
59/C2 Dahaituo Shan (mtn.), China
59/G6 Dahaituo Shan (mtn.), China
48/D7 Dahana (des.), SAr.
53/K5 Dāhānu, India
62/B4 Dāhānu, India
62/A2 Daharki, Pak.
59/B2 Dahei (riv.), China
55/K2 Daheiding (peak), China
47/N5 Da Hinggang (mts.), China
48/M5 Da Hinggang (mts.), China
55/J2 Da Hinggang (mts.), China
52/D5 Dahlak (arch.), Eth.
77/N4 Dahlak (arch.), Eth.
31/F3 Dahlem, Ger.
29/H2 Dahlenburg, Ger.
97/H3 Dahlonega, Ga,US
27/G3 Dahme (riv.), Ger.
31/G5 Dahn, Ger.
65/D4 Da Hoa, Viet.
59/C5 Dahong (mtn.), China
61/G2 Dahong (mtn.), China
53/L1 Dahongliutan, China
46/E6 Dahūk, Iraq
51/E2 Dahūk, Iraq
51/E2 Dahūk (gov.), Iraq
52/D1 Dahūk, Iraq
58/C2 Dahuofang (res.), China
59/F2 Dahuofang (res.), China
59/C2 Dai (lake), China
61/J2 Dai (isl.), China
57/M9 Daian, Japan
59/D3 Daicheng, China
57/G2 Daigo, Japan
62/D2 Dailekh, Nepal
22/D1 Dailly, Sc,UK
63/J4 Dai Loc, Viet.
65/E3 Dai Loc, Viet.
59/D3 Daimiao, China
34/D3 Daimiel, Sp.
93/J4 Daingerfield, Tx,US
96/E3 Daingerfield, Tx,US
54/D5 Dainkognubma, China
72/B2 Daintree Nat'l Park, Austl.
57/E3 Daiō-zaki (pt.), Japan
103/H2 Daiquirí, Cuba
64/A2 Dāira Dīn Panāh, Pak.
55/L4 Dai-sen (mtn.), Japan
56/C3 Dai-sen (mtn.), Japan
56/C2 Daisen-Oki Nat'l Park, Japan
56/C3 Daisen-Oki Nat'l Park, Japan
48/N7 Daito (isls.), Japan
57/L10 Daitō, Japan
68/C2 Daito (isls.), Japan
54/G4 Dai Xian, China
59/C3 Dai Xian, China
61/H3 Daiyun (peak), China
61/J3 Daiyun (peak), China
103/J2 Dajabón, DRep.
104/D3 Dajabón, DRep.
70/F4 Dajarra, Austl.
76/B5 Dakar (cap.), Sen.
78/A3 Dakar (cap.), Sen.
78/A3 Dakar (reg.), Sen.
76/B3 Dakhla, WSah.
78/A1 Dakhlet Nouadhibou (reg.), Mrta.
63/J4 Dak Nhe, Viet.
65/D3 Dak Nhe, Viet.
76/G5 Dakoro, Niger
79/G3 Dakoro, Niger
91/J5 Dakota City, Ne,US
93/H2 Dakota City, Ne,US
39/G1 Dakovica, Yugo.
40/E4 Dakovica, Yugo.
40/D3 Dakovo, Yugo.
83/A Dakshin Gangotri, Ant.
18/E2 Dal (riv.), Swe.
46/B3 Dal (riv.), Swe.
59/B2 Dalad Qi, China
54/H3 Dalai (salt lake), China
50/B2 Dalaman, Turk.
47/L5 Dalandzadgad, Mong.
54/E3 Dalandzadgad, Mong.
54/F2 Dalanjargalan, Mong.
20/E3 Dalarna (reg.), Swe.
63/J5 Da Lat, Viet.
65/E4 Da Lat, Viet.
66/C1 Da Lat, Viet.
20/Q6 Dalatangi (pt.), Ice.
22/E2 Dalbeattie, Sc,UK
71/J5 Dalby, Austl.
72/C4 Dalby, Austl.
28/D3 Dalen, Neth.
26/D2 Dalfsen, Neth.
28/D4 Dalfsen, Neth.
88/F4 Dalhart, Tx,US
93/G3 Dalhart, Tx,US
96/C2 Dalhart, Tx,US
95/H1 Dalhousie, NB,Can
85/N1 Dalhousie (cape), NW,Can
86/D1 Dalhousie (cape), NW,Can
54/F4 Dali (riv.), China
59/B3 Dali (riv.), China
59/B4 Dali, China
60/D3 Dali, China
63/H2 Dali, China
47/N6 Dalian, China
55/J4 Dalian, China
58/A3 Dalian, China
58/A3 Dalian (bay), China
59/E3 Dalian, China
34/D4 Dalías, Sp.
51/F2 Dalidag (peak), Azer.
55/H3 Daling (riv.), China
58/A2 Daling (riv.), China
59/D2 Daling (riv.), China
40/D3 Dalj, Cro.
85/J4 Dall (lake), Ak,US
85/M4 Dall (isl.), Ak,US
86/C3 Dall (isl.), Ak,US
101/F1 Dallas, Tx,US
89/G5 Dallas, Tx,US
93/H4 Dallas, Tx,US
96/D3 Dallas, Tx,US
86/D4 Dalles, The, Or,US
88/B2 Dalles, The, Or,US
76/F4 Dallol Basso (wadi), Mali, Niger
79/F3 Dallol Bosso (wadi), Mali, Niger
40/C4 Dalmatia (reg.), Cro.
22/D1 Dalmellington, Sc,UK
73/D3 Dalmeny, Austl.
47/P5 Dal'negorsk, Rus.
55/M3 Dal'negorsk, Rus.
47/P5 Dal'nerechensk, Rus.
55/L2 Dal'nerechensk, Rus.
76/D6 Daloa, IvC.
78/D5 Daloa, IvC.
71/H4 Dalrymple (lake), Austl.
72/B3 Dalrymple (lake), Austl.
89/K5 Dalton, Ga,US
97/G3 Dalton, Ga,US
62/D3 Daltonganj, India
23/E3 Dalton-in-Furness, Eng,UK
61/G4 Daluo (peak), China
65/C1 Daluo, China
20/N6 Dalvík, Ice.
70/B6 Dalwallinu, Austl.
70/E2 Daly (riv.), Austl.
86/H2 Daly (bay), NW,Can
99/K11 Daly City, Ca,US
70/E2 Daly River, Austl.
68/C6 Daly Waters, Austl.
70/E3 Daly Waters, Austl.
51/J5 Damāgheh-ye Kūh (pt.), Iran
53/K4 Daman, India
62/B3 Damān, India
62/B3 Damān & Diu (terr.), India
49/B4 Damanhūr, Egypt
50/B4 Damanhūr, Egypt
52/B2 Damanhūr, Egypt
61/H2 Damao (mtn.), Chin
67/G5 Damar (isl.), Indo.
77/N1 Damascus (cap.), Syria
98/J7 Damascus, Md,US
49/E3 Damascus (Dimash (cap.), Syria
50/D3 Damascus (Dimash (cap.), Syria
52/C2 Damascus (Dimash (cap.), Syria
76/H5 Damaturu, Nga.
46/F6 Damavānd (mtn.), Iran
51/H3 Damāvand, Iran
51/H3 Damāvand (mtn.), Iran
52/F1 Damavānd (mtn.), Iran
36/D1 Dambach-la-Ville,
54/D6 Dāmbuk, India
63/G2 Dāmbuk, India
65/D4 Dam Doi, Viet.
103/H2 Dame Marie, Haiti
103/H2 Dame Marie (cape Haiti
25/E5 Damerham, Eng,UK
51/H2 Dāmghān, Iran
53/F1 Dāmghān, Iran
50/B4 Damietta, Egypt
52/B2 Damietta, Egypt
77/M1 Damietta, Egypt
49/B4 Damietta (Dumyāṭ), Egypt
59/C3 Daming, China
61/F4 Daming (mtn.), Chir
26/C4 Damion (mtn.), Fr.
31/D4 Damion (mtn.), Fr.
32/F2 Damion (mtn.), Fr.
19/U9 Dammartin-en-Goë Fr.
30/B5 Dammartin-en-Goë Fr.
37/E4 Dammastock (peak Swi.
30/C1 Damme, Belg.
26/E2 Damme, Ger.
29/F3 Damme, Ger.
62/C3 Damoh, India
79/E4 Damongo, Gha.
36/B3 Damparis, Fr.
70/B4 Dampier, Austl.
70/B4 Dampier (arch.), Austl.
67/H4 Dampier (str.), Indo
68/C5 Dampier (str.), Indo
19/R10 Dampierre, Fr.
36/B3 Dampierre, Fr.
36/B2 Dampierre-sur-Sa Fr.
36/C3 Damprichard, Fr.
65/C4 Damrei (mts.), Cam
28/D2 Damsterdiep (riv.), Neth.
61/H3 Damuzhi (mtn.), Ch
36/C3 Damvant, Swi.
31/E5 Damvillers, Fr.
54/H5 Dan (riv.), China
59/B4 Dan (riv.), China
49/D4 Dānā, Jor.
77/P5 Danakil (reg.), Djib
76/D6 Danané, IvC.
78/C5 Danané, IvC.
48/K8 Da Nang, Viet.
63/J4 Da Nang, Viet.
65/E2 Da Nang, Viet.
54/E5 Danba, China
60/D2 Danba, China
25/G3 Danbury, Eng,UK
59/D4 Dancheng, China
70/B6 Dandaragan, Austl.
73/G5 Dandenong, Austl.
73/G5 Dandenong (cr.), Austl.
73/G5 Dandenong (mt.), Austl.
47/N5 Dandong, China
55/J3 Dandong, China
58/C2 Dandong, China
59/F2 Dandong, China
23/F5 Dane (riv.), Eng,UK
54/D4 Dang (riv.), China
52/D6 Dangal, Eth.
53/J1 Dangara, Taj.
80/B4 Danger (pt.), SAfr.
80/L11 Danger (pt.), SAfr.
73/B2 Danggali Consv. Park, Austl.
77/N5 Dangila, Eth.
60/A3 Dangme (riv.), Bhu
59/D4 Dangshan, China
55/H5 Dangtu, China
59/D5 Dangtu, China
61/H2 Dangtu, China
54/G5 Dangyang, China
59/B5 Dangyang, China
61/F2 Dangyang, China
98/E5 Danielsville, Pa,U
42/J4 Danilov, Rus.
54/G4 Daning, China
59/B3 Daning, China
54/G5 Danjiangkou, Chir
55/G5 Danjiangkou (res.), China
59/B4 Danjiangkou, Chir
59/B4 Danjiangkou (res. China
61/F1 Danjiangkou, Chir
36/C2 Danjoutin, Fr.
44/F1 Dankov, Rus.
62/D2 Danleng, China
102/E3 Danlí, Hon.
26/F2 Dannenberg, Ger.
25/H5 Dannes, Fr.
30/A2 Dannes, Fr.
71/S11 Dannevirke, N.Z.

63/H4 Dan Sai, Thai.
18/F4 Danube (riv.), Eur.
27/K5 Danube (riv.), Eur.
33/L2 Danube (riv.), Eur.
41/J3 Danube (riv.), Eur.
44/D3 Danube (riv.), Eur.
41/J3 Danube (delta), Rom.
41/H3 Danube, Borcea Branch (riv.), Rom.
41/J3 Danube, Mouths of the, Rom.
41/J3 Danube, Sfîntu Gheorghe Br. (riv.), Rom.
41/J3 Danube, Sulina Branch (riv.), Rom.
99/L11 Danville, Ca,US
89/J3 Danville, Il,US
94/C3 Danville, Il,US
97/G1 Danville, Il,US
89/K4 Danville, Ky,US
94/C4 Danville, Ky,US
97/G2 Danville, Ky,US
94/E3 Danville, Pa,US
89/L4 Danville, Va,US
94/E4 Danville, Va,US
97/J2 Danville, Va,US
61/F5 Dan Xian, China
63/J4 Dan Xian, China
65/E2 Dan Xian, China
63/H2 Daocheng, China
77/N1 Daora, WSah.
61/F3 Dao Xian, China
63/K2 Dao Xian, China
61/E2 Daozhen, China
63/J2 Daozhen, China
76/F5 Dapaong, Togo
79/F4 Dapaong, Togo
97/G4 Daphne, Al,US
63/H3 Daqiao, China
47/N5 Daqing, China
55/K2 Daqing, China
59/H7 Daqing (riv.), China
53/H2 Daqq-e Patargān (lake), Afg.
53/H2 Daqq-e Patargān (lake), Iran
61/J2 Daqu (isl.), China
49/E3 Dar'ā, Syria
49/E3 Dar'ā (dist.), Syria
50/C3 Dar'ā (prov.), Syria
50/D3 Dar'ā, Syria
52/C2 Dar'ā, Syria
77/N1 Dar'ā, Syria
51/H4 Dārāb, Iran
53/F3 Dārāb, Iran
77/R2 Dārāb, Iran
41/H1 Darabani, Rom.
44/C2 Darabani, Rom.
67/F1 Daraga, Phil.
51/G3 Dārān, Iran
52/F2 Dārān, Iran
39/G1 Đaravica (peak), Yugo.
40/E1 Đaravica (peak), Yugo.
40/C3 Dārayyā, Syria
50/D3 Dārayyā, Syria
52/C2 Dārayyā, Syria
62/E2 Darbhanga, India
85/F3 Darby (cape), Ak,US
98/E6 Darby, Pa,US
40/D3 Darda, Cro.
39/J3 Dardanelles (str.), Turk.
41/H5 Dardanelles (str.), Turk.
44/C5 Dardanelles (str.), Turk.
50/A2 Dardanelles (str.), Turk.
73/G5 Darebin (cr.), Austl.
50/D2 Darende, Turk.
19/P8 Darent (riv.), Eng,UK
82/G2 Dar es Salaam (cap.), Tanz.
73/B2 Dareton, Austl.
1/R11 Darfield, N.Z.
33/J4 Darfo, It.
37/G6 Darfo, It.
1/R10 Dargaville, N.Z.
22/B5 Dargle (riv.), Ire.
47/L5 Darhan, Mong.
54/F2 Darhan, Mong.
54/F2 Darhan (peak), Mong.
77/Q6 Darie (hills), Som.
06/C2 Darién (range), Col., Pan.
98/G4 Darien, Ct,US
97/H4 Darien, Ga,US
9/Q16 Darien, Il,US
03/G5 Darién Nat'l Park, Pan.
06/C2 Darién Nat'l Park, Pan.
03/G4 Darién, Serranía de (range), Col., Pan.
54/G2 Dariganga, Mong.
04/D3 Darién (range), Pan.
62/E2 Darjiling, India
25/D5 Darlag, China
68/D8 Darling (riv.), Austl.
70/B6 Darling (range), Austl.
71/G6 Darling (riv.), Austl.
73/B2 Darling (riv.), Austl.
0/L10 Darling, SAfr.
71/J5 Darling Downs (upland), Austl.
72/C4 Darling Downs (ridge), Austl.
23/G2 Darlington, Eng,UK
89/L5 Darlington, SC,US
97/J3 Darlington, SC,US
73/C2 Darlington Point, Austl.
27/J1 Darłowo, Pol.
26/E4 Darmstadt, Ger.
33/H2 Darmstadt, Ger.
77/K1 Darnah, Libya
/W10 Darnāya, Tun.
30/A5 Darnétal, Fr.
26/D4 Darney, Fr.
32/G2 Darney, Fr.
36/C1 Darney, Fr.
83/E Darnley (cape), Ant.
86/D2 Darnley (bay), NW,Can
34/E2 Daroca, Sp.
23/G1 Darras Hall, Eng,UK
109/D4 Darregueira, Arg.
51/J2 Darreh Gaz, Iran
53/G1 Darreh Gaz, Iran
77/K6 Dar Rounga (reg.), CAfr.
83/R Dart (cape), Ant.
24/C6 Dart (riv.), Eng,UK
19/P7 Dartford, Eng,UK
25/G4 Dartford, Eng,UK
24/C6 Dartington, Eng,UK
24/B5 Dartmoor (upland), Eng,UK
24/C5 Dartmoor Nat'l Park, Eng,UK
32/A1 Dartmoor Nat'l Park, Eng,UK
71/H7 Dartmouth (res.), Austl.
73/C3 Dartmouth (dam), Austl.
73/C3 Dartmouth (res.), Austl.
87/K4 Dartmouth, NS,Can
89/P3 Dartmouth, NS,Can
95/J2 Dartmouth, NS,Can
24/C6 Dartmouth, Eng,UK
32/B1 Dartmouth, Eng,UK
23/G4 Darton, Eng,UK
35/G3 Dartuch (cape), Sp.
68/D5 Daru, PNG
40/C3 Daruvar, Cro.
46/F5 Darvaza, Trkm.
67/F3 Darvel (bay), Malay.
23/F4 Darwen, Eng,UK
68/C6 Darwin, Austl.
70/E2 Darwin, Austl.
109/B7 Darwin (mts.), Chile
53/H2 Daryācheh-ye Sīstān (lake), Iran
64/A2 Darya Khan, Pak.
53/G3 Dārzīn, Iran
55/H3 Dashengtang (peak), China
54/G5 Dashennongjia (peak), China
59/B5 Dashennongjia (peak), China
61/F2 Dashennongjia (peak), China
74/F3 Dashen, Ras (peak), Eth.
51/F1 Dashkesan, Azer.
46/F6 Dasht-e Kavīr (salt des.), Iran
51/H3 Dasht-e Kavīr (des.), Iran
53/F2 Dasht-e Kavīr (des.), Iran
46/F6 Dasht-e Lūt (des.), Iran
51/J4 Dasht-e Lūt (des.), Iran
53/G2 Dasht-e Lūt (des.), Iran
53/H2 Dasht-e Mārgow (des.), Afg.
63/H3 Dasht Kaur (riv.), Pak.
37/H1 Dasing, Ger.
64/C1 Daska, Pak.
29/G5 Dassel, Ger.
29/H2 Dassendorf, Ger.
80/B4 Dasseneiland (isl.), SAfr.
80/K10 Dasseneiland (isl.), SAfr.
64/C2 Dasūya, India
19/M7 Datchet, Eng,UK
65/D4 Dat Do, Viet.
62/C2 Datia, India
61/F4 Datian (peak), China
92/F4 Datil, NM,US
96/B3 Datil, NM,US
47/M5 Datong, China
54/D4 Datong (mts.), China
54/D4 Datong (riv.), China
54/E4 Datong, China
54/G3 Datong, China
59/C2 Datong, China
26/D3 Datteln, Ger.
29/E5 Datteln, Ger.
66/C3 Datu (cape), Malay.
66/B3 Datuk (cape), Indo.
27/N1 Daugai, Lith.
20/H4 Daugava (riv.), Lat.
42/E4 Daugava (riv.), Lat.
18/F3 Daugavpils, Lat.
20/H5 Daugavpils, Lat.
42/E5 Daugavpils, Lat.
46/C4 Daugavpils, Lat.
26/D3 Daun, Ger.
31/F3 Daun, Ger.
33/G1 Daun, Ger.
65/B3 Daung (isl.), Burma
91/J3 Dauphin (lake), Mb,Can
86/F3 Dauphin, Mb,Can
88/F1 Dauphin, Mb,Can
91/H3 Dauphin, Mb,Can
32/F4 Dauphiné (hist. reg.), Fr.
32/F4 Dauphiné (mts.), Fr.
53/L6 Dāvangere, India
62/C5 Dāvangere, India
67/G2 Davao City, Phil.
68/B4 Davao City, Phil.
53/G1 Dāvarzan, Iran
80/Q13 Davel, SAfr.
89/H3 Davenport, Ia,US
91/L5 Davenport, Ia,US
93/K2 Davenport, Ia,US
94/B3 Davenport, Ia,US
90/D4 Davenport, Wa,US
25/E2 Daventry, Eng,UK
31/E3 Daverdisse, Belg.
87/T6 Davgaard-Jensen (reg.), Grld.
103/F4 David, Pan.
106/B2 David, Pan.
91/J5 David City, Ne,US
93/H2 David City, Ne,US
91/G3 Davidson, Sk,Can
99/K11 Davidson (mt.), Ca,US
83/F Davis, Ant.
83/F Davis (sea), Ant.
87/L2 Davis (str.), NW,Can, Den.
84/M3 Davis (str.), NAm.
92/B3 Davis, Ca,US
99/L9 Davis, Ca,US
99/E7 Davis (cr.), Mi,US
94/E4 Davis (peak), Pa,US
100/D2 Davis (mts.), Tx,US
88/F5 Davis (mts.), Tx,US
93/F5 Davis (mts.), Tx,US
96/B4 Davis (mts.), Tx,US
99/E5 Davison, Mi,US
43/M5 Davlekanovo, Rus.
45/K1 Davlekanovo, Rus.
78/D5 Davo (riv.), IvC.
33/H3 Davos, Swi.
37/F4 Davos, Swi.
54/C1 Davst, Mong.
58/B2 Dawa, China
59/E2 Dawa, China
61/H3 Dawang (mtn.), China
77/N7 Dawa Wenz (riv.), Afr.
54/H4 Dawen (riv.), China
59/D4 Dawen (riv.), China
24/C5 Dawlish, Eng,UK
71/H4 Dawson (riv.), Austl.
72/C4 Dawson (riv.), Austl.
85/L3 Dawson, Yk,Can
86/C2 Dawson, Yk,Can
97/G4 Dawson, Ga,US
84/E4 Dawson Creek, Can.
86/D3 Dawson Creek, BC,Can
90/C2 Dawson Creek, BC,Can
54/E5 Dawu, China
54/G5 Dawu, China
59/C5 Dawu, China
60/D2 Dawu, China
61/G2 Dawu, China
61/G2 Dawu (mtn.), China
59/C5 Dawu Shan (mtn.), China
52/G4 Dawwah, Oman
32/C5 Dax, Fr.
35/E1 Dax, Fr.
54/F5 Daxian, China
61/E2 Daxian, China
63/J3 Daxin, China
65/D1 Daxin, China
59/D3 Daxing, China
59/H7 Daxing, China
54/E5 Daxue (riv.), China
60/C4 Daxue (peak), China
60/D2 Daxue (mts.), China
58/B2 Dayang (riv.), China
60/D3 Dayao, China
63/H2 Dayao, China
59/C5 Daye, China
61/G2 Daye, China
54/E5 Dayi, China
60/D2 Dayi, China
60/C3 Daying (riv.), China
63/G3 Daying (riv.), China
73/C3 Daylesford, Austl.
61/F2 Dayong, China
49/D4 Dayr al Balaḩ, Gaza
50/C4 Dayr al Balaḩ, Gaza
49/G7 Dayr al Ghuşūn, WBnk.
50/E3 Dayr Az Zawr (prov.), Syria
50/E3 Dayr az Zawr, Syria
52/D1 Dayr az Zawr, Syria
49/G7 Dayr Ballūţ, WBnk.
49/D4 Dayr Dibwān, WBnk.
49/G8 Dayr Dibwān, WBnk.
49/G7 Dayr Sharaf, WBnk.
50/B5 Dayrūţ, Egypt
52/B3 Dayrūţ, Egypt
90/E2 Daysland, Ab,Can
84/J6 Dayton, US
89/K4 Dayton, Oh,US
94/C4 Dayton, Oh,US
97/G2 Dayton, Oh,US
97/G3 Dayton, Tn,US
90/D4 Dayton, Wa,US
84/J7 Daytona Beach, US
89/K6 Daytona Beach, Fl,US
97/H4 Daytona Beach, Fl,US
61/G3 Dayu, China
61/J3 Dayu (isl.), China
63/K2 Dayu, China
61/G4 Dayunwu (mtn.), China
54/F5 Dazhu, China
61/E2 Dazhu, China
80/D3 De Aar, SAfr.
82/D7 De Aar, SAfr.
49/D4 Dead (sea), Isr., Jor.
50/C4 Dead (sea), Isr., Jor.
52/C2 Dead (sea), Isr., Jor.
49/G8 Dead (sea), WBnk.
85/J1 Deadhorse, Ak,US
91/H4 Deadwood, SD,US
93/G1 Deadwood, SD,US
73/C3 Deal (isl.), Austl.
25/H4 Deal, Eng,UK
30/A1 Deal, Eng,UK
98/K8 Deale, Md,US
90/B2 Dean (riv.), BC,Can
90/B2 Dean Channel (inlet), BC,Can
24/D3 Dean, Forest of (for.), Eng,UK
103/D3 Deán Funes, Arg.
99/F7 Dearborn, Mi,US
99/F7 Dearborn Heights, Mi,US
23/G4 Dearne, Eng,UK
23/G4 Dearne (riv.), Eng,UK
84/F3 Dease (str.), Can.
85/N4 Dease (riv.), BC,Can
86/D3 Dease (riv.), BC,Can
86/F2 Dease (str.), NW,Can
85/M4 Dease Lake, BC,Can
92/C3 Death Valley, Ca,US
92/C3 Death Valley Nat'l Mon., Ca, Nv,US
51/F1 Deavgay (peak), Rus.
39/G2 Debar, Macd.
40/E5 Debar, Macd.
85/G3 Debauch (mtn.), Ak,US
39/J1 Debelets, Bul.
41/G4 Debelets, Bul.
25/H2 Deben (riv.), Eng,UK
25/H2 Debenham, Eng,UK
27/L3 Dębica, Pol.
44/B2 Dębica, Pol.
28/C4 De Bilt, Neth.
27/L3 Dęblin, Pol.
27/H2 Dębno, Pol.
85/J3 Deborah (mt.), Ak,US
77/N6 Debre Birhan, Eth.
18/F4 Debrecen, Hun.
27/L5 Debrecen, Hun.
40/E2 Debrecen, Hun.
44/B3 Debrecen, Hun.
77/N5 Debre Mark'os, Eth.
77/N5 Debre Tabor, Eth.
77/N6 Debre Zeyit, Eth.
89/J5 Decatur, Al,US
97/G3 Decatur, Al,US
97/G3 Decatur, Ga,US
89/J4 Decatur, Il,US
91/L6 Decatur, Il,US
93/K3 Decatur, Il,US
94/B4 Decatur, Il,US
97/F2 Decatur, Il,US
94/C3 Decatur, In,US
101/F1 Decatur, Tx,US
93/H4 Decatur, Tx,US
96/D3 Decatur, Tx,US
32/E4 Decazeville, Fr.
62/C5 Deccan (plat.), India
60/D3 Dechang, China
60/A3 Dechheling, Bhu.
27/H3 Děčín, Czh.
36/A6 Décines-Charpieu, Fr.
32/E3 Decize, Fr.
25/E3 Deddington, Eng,UK
28/D3 Dedemsvaart, Neth.
80/L10 De Doorns, SAfr.
76/E5 Dédougou, Burk.
78/E3 Dédougou, Burk.
43/X9 Dedovsk, Rus.
55/K2 Dedu, China
82/F3 Dedza, Malw.
22/B4 Dee (riv.), Ire.
21/D2 Dee (riv.), Sc,UK
22/D1 Dee (riv.), Sc,UK
23/E5 Dee (riv.), Wal,UK
22/A4 Deel (riv.), Ire.
25/F1 Deeping Saint James, Eng,UK
87/J4 Deep River, On,Can
89/L2 Deep River, On,Can
94/E2 Deep River, On,Can
73/D1 Deepwater, Austl.
86/F6 Deer (isl.), Ak,US
99/Q15 Deerfield, Il,US
85/F2 Deering, Ak,US
95/K1 Deer Lake, Can
30/C2 Deerlijk, Belg.
88/D2 Deer Lodge, Mt,US
90/E4 Deer Lodge, Mt,US
99/K9 Deer Park, Ca,US
99/P15 Deer Park, Il,US
98/K7 Deer Park, Md,US
98/G5 Deer Park, NY,US
90/D4 Deer Park, Wa,US
53/K4 Deesa, India
62/B3 Deesa, India
72/H8 Dee Why, Austl.
77/Q6 Deex Nugaaleed (dry river), Som.
106/F8 Defensores del Chaco Nat'l Park, Par.
94/C3 Defiance, Oh,US
97/G4 De Funiak Springs, Fl,US
22/E5 Deganwy, Wal,UK
77/P6 Degeh Bur, Eth.
95/G2 Dégelis, Qu,Can
37/F3 Degersheim, Swi.
26/G4 Deggendorf, Ger.
33/K2 Deggendorf, Ger.
70/B4 De Grey, Austl.
70/B4 De Grey (riv.), Austl.
30/C1 De Haan, Belg.
73/F2 Dehaj, Iran
77/P4 Dehalak (isl.), Eth.
77/P4 Dehalak Marine Nat'l Park, Eth.
51/H4 Deh Bīd, Iran
52/F2 Deh Bīd, Iran
51/G4 Dehdez, Iran
51/G3 Deheq, Iran
52/F2 Deheq, Iran
52/F2 Deh-e Shīr, Iran
53/L2 Dehra Dūn, India
62/D3 Dehri, India
61/H3 Dehua, China
55/K3 Dehui, China
31/H5 Deidesheim, Ger.
29/G1 Deinste, Ger.
26/B3 Deinze, Belg.
28/A7 Deinze, Belg.
30/C2 Deinze, Belg.
29/G4 Deister (mts.), Ger.
41/F2 Dej, Rom.
44/B3 Dej, Rom.
61/F2 Dejiang, China
63/J2 Dejiang, China
67/J5 De Jongs (cape), Indo.
91/L5 De Kalb, Il,US
93/K2 De Kalb, Il,US
94/B3 De Kalb, Il,US
99/N16 De Kalb (co.), Il,US
52/C5 Dek'emhāre, Eth.
77/N4 Dek'emhāre, Eth.
100/D4 De la Ciudad Nat'l Park, Mex.
99/P13 Delafield, Wi,US
89/K6 De Land, Fl,US
97/H4 De Land, Fl,US
92/C4 Delano, Ca,US
53/H2 Delārām, Afg.
90/G2 Delarode (lake), Sk,Can
94/B3 Delavan, Wi,US
99/N14 Delavan, Wi,US
99/N14 Delavan (lake), Wi,US
99/N14 Delavan Lake, Wi,US
94/F4 Delaware (bay), De, NJ,US
89/L4 Delaware (state), US
94/F3 Delaware (riv.), US
94/F4 Delaware (state), US
98/E5 Delaware (riv.), US
98/E5 Delaware, NJ,US
94/D3 Delaware, Oh,US
98/E6 Delaware (co.), Pa,US
98/E5 Delaware Water Gap (pass), Pa,US
98/F4 Delaware Water Gap Nat'l Rec. Area, NJ, Pa,US
29/F5 Delbrück, Ger.
39/H2 Delčevo, Macd.
40/F5 Delčevo, Macd.
28/D4 Delden, Neth.
57/F5 Delebio, It.
73/D3 Delegate, Austl.
28/D2 De Leijen (lake), Neth.
33/G3 Delémont, Swi.
36/D3 Delémont, Swi.
26/C3 Delft, Neth.
28/B5 Delft, Neth.
64/E4 Delft (isl.), SrL.
26/D2 Delfzijl, Neth.
28/D2 Delfzijl, Neth.
109/D5 Delgada (pt.), Arg.
74/G6 Delgado (cape), Moz.
82/H3 Delgado (cape), Moz.
22/B5 Delgany, Ire.
54/D2 Delger (riv.), Mong.
54/F2 Delgerhaan, Mong.
54/E2 Delgerhangay, Mong.
53/L3 Delhi, India
62/C2 Delhi, India
44/E5 Delice, Turk.
44/E5 Delice (riv.), Turk.
50/C2 Delice, Turk.
100/D2 Delicias, Mex.
103/H5 Delicias, Ven.
28/B6 De Lier, Neth.
51/G3 Delījān, Iran
52/F2 Delījān, Iran
38/D5 Delimara, Ponta Ta' (pt.), Malta
90/G3 Delisle, Can
29/G5 Delligsen, Ger.
91/J5 Dell Rapids, SD,US
93/H2 Dell Rapids, SD,US
80/Q13 Delmas, SAfr.
31/F6 Delme, Fr.
29/F3 Delme (riv.), Ger.
26/E2 Delmenhorst, Ger.
29/F2 Delmenhorst, Ger.
33/L4 Delnice, Cro.
40/B3 Delnice, Cro.
93/F3 Del Norte, Co,US
96/B2 Del Norte, Co,US
73/C4 Deloraine, Austl.
91/H3 Deloraine, Mb,Can
39/J4 Delos (ruins), Gre.
109/A6 de los Chonos (isls.), Chile
39/H3 Delphi (ruins), Gre.
94/C3 Delphos, Oh,US
99/M12 Del Puerto (cr.), Ca,US
97/H5 Delray Beach, Fl,US
101/E2 Del Rio, Tx,US
88/F6 Del Rio, Tx,US
93/G5 Del Rio, Tx,US
96/C4 Del Rio, Tx,US
20/F3 Delsbo, Swe.
42/C3 Delsbo, Swe.
95/N7 Delson, Qu,Can
88/E4 Delta, Co,US
92/E3 Delta, Co,US
96/A2 Delta, Co,US
88/D4 Delta, Ut,US
92/D3 Delta, Ut,US
85/J3 Delta Junction, Ak,US
86/B2 Delta Junction, Ak,US
99/M11 Delta-Mendota (can.), Ca,US
97/H4 Deltona, Fl,US
54/C2 Delüün, Mong.
99/L11 Del Valle (lake), Ca,US
22/A4 Delvin, Ire.
39/G3 Delvinë, Alb.
41/G1 Delyatin, Ukr.
43/M5 Dëma (riv.), Rus.
45/K1 Dëma (riv.), Rus.
34/D1 Demanda (range), Sp.
85/K2 Demarcation (pt.), Ak,US
82/D2 Demba, Zaire
77/M6 Dembī Dolo, Eth.
26/C3 Demer (riv.), Belg.
28/B7 Demer (riv.), Belg.
36/A4 Demigny, Fr.
100/D1 Deming, NM,US
88/E5 Deming, NM,US
92/F4 Deming, NM,US
96/B3 Deming, NM,US
106/F3 Demini (riv.), Braz.
44/D5 Demirci, Turk.
50/B2 Demirci, Turk.
50/C2 Demirkazık (peak), Turk.
50/C2 Demirkent, Turk.
41/H5 Demirköy, Turk.
26/G2 Demmin, Ger.
38/D4 Demone (val.), It.
97/G3 Demopolis, Al,US
66/B4 Dempo (peak), Indo.
30/C3 Denain, Fr.
52/C5 Denakil (reg.), Eth.
77/P5 Denakil (reg.), Eth.
86/B2 Denali Nat'l Park, Ak,US
85/H3 Denali Nat'l Park & Prsv., Ak,US
91/H2 Denare Beach, Sk,Can
23/E5 Denbigh, Wal,UK
26/C2 Den Burg, Neth.
28/B2 Den Burg, Neth.
23/G4 Denby Dale, Eng,UK
60/D5 Den Chai, Thai.
63/H4 Den Chai, Thai.
26/B3 Dender (riv.), Belg.
28/B7 Dender (riv.), Belg.
30/D2 Dender (riv.), Belg.
32/E1 Dender (riv.), Belg.
30/D2 Denderleeuw, Belg.
28/B6 Dendermonde, Belg.
30/D1 Dendermonde, Belg.
28/D4 Denekamp, Neth.
59/C4 Dengfeng, China
54/F3 Dengkou, China
54/D5 Dêngqên, China
61/G3 Dengta, China
59/C4 Deng Xian, China
61/G1 Deng Xian, China
70/A5 Denham, Austl.
70/A5 Denham (sound), Austl.
28/D4 Den Ham, Neth.
19/M7 Denham, Eng,UK
26/C2 Den Helder, Neth.
28/B3 Den Helder, Neth.
23/G4 Denholme, Eng,UK
35/F3 Denia, Sp.
71/G7 Deniliquin, Austl.
73/C2 Deniliquin, Austl.
90/D5 Denio, Nv,US
92/C2 Denio, Nv,US
85/H4 Denison (mt.), Ak,US
89/G3 Denison, Ia,US
91/K5 Denison, Ia,US
93/J2 Denison, Ia,US
89/G5 Denison, Tx,US
93/H4 Denison, Tx,US
96/D3 Denison, Tx,US
50/B2 Denizli, Turk.
50/B2 Denizli (prov.), Turk.
37/G2 Denklingen, Ger.
83/G Denman (glac.), Ant.
73/D2 Denman, Austl.
18/D3 Denmark
20/C5 Denmark
26/F1 Denmark
46/A4 Denmark
18/A2 Denmark (str.),
20/M6 Denmark (str.)
84/Q3 Denmark (str.)
80/Q12 Dennilton, SAfr.
28/C3 Den Oever, Neth.
66/E5 Denpasar, Indo.
36/D5 Dent Blanche (peak), Swi.
36/C4 Dent de Lys (peak), Swi.
36/D6 Dent d'Hérens (peak), It., Swi.
30/C2 Dentergem, Belg.
23/F5 Denton, Eng,UK
25/G5 Denton, Eng,UK
101/F1 Denton, Tx,US
89/G5 Denton, Tx,US
93/H4 Denton, Tx,US
96/D3 Denton, Tx,US
70/A6 D'Entrecasteaux (pt.), Austl.
68/D5 D'Entrecasteaux (isls.), PNG
36/C5 Dents du Midi (peak), It., Swi.
88/F4 Denver (cap.), Co,US
93/F3 Denver (cap.), Co,US
98/F5 Denville, NJ,US
36/D1 Denzlingen, Ger.
62/C2 Deoband, India
62/D3 Deogarh, India
62/E3 Deoghar, India
53/K5 Deolāli, India
62/B4 Deolāli, India
53/L3 Deoli, India
62/C2 Deoli, India
32/D3 Déols, Fr.
62/D2 Deoria, India
30/B1 De Panne, Belg.
28/C6 De Peel (reg.), Neth.
109/A6 de Penas (gulf), Chile
104/E5 Dependencias Federales (terr.), Ven.
95/S10 Depew, NY,US
28/A7 De Pinte, Belg.
30/C2 De Pinte, Belg.
19/N7 Deptford, Eng,UK
63/G2 Dêqên, China
59/L9 Deqing, China
77/P7 Dera (dry riv.), Som.
53/K2 Dera Ghāzi Khān, Pak.
64/A2 Dera Ghāzi Khān, Pak.
60/A3 Derai, Bang.
53/K2 Dera Ismāīl Khān, Pak.
64/A2 Dera Ismāīl Khān, Pak.
19/H4 Derbent, Rus.
45/J4 Derbent, Rus.
46/E5 Derbent, Rus.
51/G1 Derbent, Rus.
70/C3 Derby, Austl.
23/G6 Derby, Eng,UK
93/H3 Derby, Ks,US
96/D2 Derby, Ks,US
23/G6 Derbyshire (co.), Eng,UK
41/F3 Đerdap Nat'l Park, Yugo.
27/L5 Derecske, Hun.
40/E2 Derecske, Hun.
51/M6 Dereköy (riv.), Turk.
54/F2 Deren, Mong.
36/D3 Derendingen, Swi.
21/A4 Derg, Lough (lake), Ire.
89/H5 De Ridder, La,US
93/J5 De Ridder, La,US
96/E4 De Ridder, La,US
50/E2 Derik, Turk.
52/D1 Derik, Turk.
50/C2 Derinkuyu, Turk.
31/G2 Dernau, Ger.
32/B2 Déroute (passg.), Fr., Chl,UK
22/A4 Derravaragh, Lough (lake), Ire.
22/B6 Derry (riv.), Ire.
95/G3 Derry, NH,US
22/C3 Derryboy, NI,UK
21/B3 Derrylin, NI,UK
25/G1 Dersingham, Eng,UK
52/C5 Derudeb, Sudan
40/C3 Derventa, Bosn.
37/F5 Dervio, It.
22/B1 Dervock, NI,UK
73/C4 Derwent (riv.), Austl.
23/E2 Derwent (riv.), Eng,UK
23/F2 Derwent (res.), Eng,UK
23/G5 Derwent (riv.), Eng,UK
23/H4 Derwent (riv.), Eng,UK
22/E2 Derwent Water (lake), Eng,UK
46/G4 Derzhavinsk, Kaz.
106/E7 Desaguadero (riv.), Bol.
101/Q9 Desagüe, Gran Canal de (canal), Mex.
25/F2 Desborough, Eng,UK
108/C2 Descalvado, Braz.
102/E4 Descartes (pt.), CR
32/D3 Descartes, Fr.
91/H2 Deschambault (lake), Sk,Can
91/H2 Deschambault Lake, Sk,Can
90/C4 Deschutes (riv.), Or,US
86/D4 Deschutes (riv.), Or,US
92/B2 Deschutes (riv.), Or,US
103/H2 Desdunes, Haiti
77/N5 Desē, Eth.
105/C7 Deseado (riv.), Arg.
109/C6 Deseado (riv.), Arg.
35/V15 Desertas (isl.), Madr.
32/F3 Désertines, Fr.
59/B4 Deshengpu, China
61/F1 Deshengpu, China
101/Q10 Desierto de Los Leones Nat'l Park, Mex.
91/J4 De Smet, SD,US
93/H1 De Smet, SD,US
91/K5 Des Moines (riv.), Ia, Mo,US
89/H3 Des Moines (cap.), Ia,US
91/K5 Des Moines (cap.), Ia,US
93/J2 Des Moines (cap.), Ia,US
93/J2 Des Moines (riv.), Ia,US
89/H3 Des Moines (riv.), Ia, Mn,US
99/C3 Des Moines, Wa,US
43/X9 Desna (riv.), Rus.
44/E1 Desna (riv.), Rus.
18/G3 Desna (riv.), Ukr.
44/D2 Desna (riv.), Ukr.
46/D4 Desna (riv.), Rus.,Ukr.
109/A7 Desolacíon (isl.), Chile
80/D4 Desolation, Valley of (val.), SAfr.
93/K3 De Soto, Mo,US
94/B4 De Soto, Mo,US
97/F2 De Soto, Mo,US
101/F1 DeSoto, Tx,US
80/D4 Despatch, SAfr.
99/P16 Des Plaines (riv.), Il,US
99/Q15 Des Plaines, Il,US
26/G3 Dessau, Ger.
28/C6 Dessel, Belg.
31/E1 Dessel, Belg.
36/C3 Dessoubre (riv.), Fr.
28/A6 Destelbergen, Belg.
30/C1 Destelbergen, Belg.
85/L3 Destruction Bay, Yk,Can
38/A2 Desulo, It.
30/A2 Desvres, Fr.
40/E3 Deta, Rom.
29/E2 Detern, Ger.
26/E3 Detmold, Ger.
29/F5 Detmold, Ger.
99/F7 Detroit (riv.), On,Can, Mi,US
87/H4 Detroit, Mi,US
89/K3 Detroit, Mi,US
94/D3 Detroit, Mi,US
99/F7 Detroit, Mi,US
89/G2 Detroit Lakes, Mn,US
91/K4 Detroit Lakes, Mn,US
26/F4 Dettelbach, Ger.
20/P6 Dettifoss (falls), Ice.
31/G6 Dettwiller, Fr.
73/D2 Deua Nat'l Park, Austl.
19/S10 Deuil-la-Barre, Fr.
30/B2 Deûle (riv.), Fr.
28/B6 Deurne, Belg.
28/C6 Deurne, Neth.
29/H2 Deutsch Evern, Ger.
27/J5 Deutschkreutz, Aus.
33/M3 Deutschkreutz, Aus.
33/L3 Deutschlandsberg, Aus.
40/B2 Deutschlandsberg, Aus.
95/M6 Deux-Montagnes (co.), Qu,Can
95/M7 Deux Montagnes (lake), Qu,Can
95/N6 Deux-Montagnes, Qu,Can
40/F3 Deva, Rom.
44/B3 Deva, Rom.
64/G4 Devakottai, India
40/E2 Dévaványa, Hun.
50/E2 Devegeçidi (dam), Turk.
50/C2 Develi, Turk.
26/D2 Deventer, Neth.
28/D4 Deventer, Neth.
31/D4 Deville, Fr.
107/H2 Devil's (isl.), FrG.
64/H4 Devil's (pt.), SrL.
101/E2 Devils (riv.), Tx,US
93/G5 Devils (riv.), Tx,US
86/G4 Devils Lake, ND,US
89/G2 Devils Lake, ND,US
91/J3 Devils Lake, ND,US
85/M4 Devils Paw (mtn.), BC,Can, Ak,US
92/C3 Devils Postpile Nat'l Mon., Ca,US
91/G4 Devils Tower Nat'l Mon., Wy,US
93/F1 Devils Tower Nat'l Mon., Wy,US
39/J2 Devin, Bul.
41/G5 Devin, Bul.
101/F2 Devine, Tx,US
93/H5 Devine, Tx,US
96/D4 Devine, Tx,US
25/E4 Devizes, Eng,UK
41/H4 Devnya, Bul.
39/G2 Devoll (riv.), Alb.
40/E5 Devoll (riv.), Alb.
84/J2 Devon (isl.), Can.
90/E2 Devon, Ab,Can
87/H1 Devon (isl.), NW,Can
87/S7 Devon (isl.), NW,Can
24/C5 Devon (co.), Eng,UK
98/E5 Devon-Berwyn, Pa,US
71/H8 Devonport, Austl.
73/C4 Devonport, Austl.
41/K5 Devrek, Turk.
44/D4 Devrek, Turk.
44/D4 Devrek (riv.), Turk.
50/D1 Devrek, Turk.
41/K5 Devrek Çayl (riv.), Turk.
44/E4 Devrez (riv.), Turk.
66/A3 Dewa (pt.), Indo.
53/L4 Dewās, India
62/C3 Dewās, India
96/E2 Dewey, Ok,US
28/D3 De Wijk, Neth.
93/K4 De Witt, Ar,US
96/F3 De Witt, Ar,US
93/H2 De Witt, Ne,US
23/G4 Dewsbury, Eng,UK
95/G2 Dexter, Me,US
100/D1 Dexter, NM,US
54/E5 Deyang, China
60/E2 Deyang, China
70/D5 Dey-Dey (lake), Austl.
53/G2 Deyhūk, Iran
46/E6 Dez (riv.), Iran
51/G3 Dez (riv.), Iran
52/E2 Dez (riv.), Iran
46/E6 Dezfūl, Iran
48/D6 Dezfūl, Iran
51/G3 Dezfūl, Iran
52/E2 Dezfūl, Iran
85/E2 Dezhneva, Mys (pt.), Rus.
54/H4 Dezhou, China
59/D3 Dezhou, China
50/C4 Dhahab, Egypt
77/P4 Dhahran, SAr.
77/R2 Dhahran, SAr.
62/F3 Dhākā (Dacca) (cap.), Bang.
60/B4 Dhaleswari (riv.), India
49/C2 Dhali, Cyp.
52/D6 Dhamār, Yem.
77/P5 Dhamār, Yem.
62/D3 Dhamtari, India
64/C2 Dhanaula, India
62/E3 Dhānbād, India
62/E2 Dhankuta, Nepal
53/L4 Dhar, India
62/C3 Dhār, India
53/K4 Dharampur, India
62/B3 Dharampur, India
64/F3 Dhārāpuram, India
53/K4 Dhāri, India
62/B3 Dhāri, India
64/C2 Dhāriwāl, India
62/C5 Dharmapuri, India
62/C5 Dharmavaram, India
64/D1 Dharmsāla, India
62/D2 Dhaulāgiri (peak), Nepal
39/H3 Dhelfoí, Gre.
39/G3 Dhelvinákion, Gre.
62/E3 Dhenkānāl, India
39/G3 Dheskáti, Gre.
36/A4 Dheune (riv.), Fr.
49/D4 Dhībān, Jor.
39/K2 Dhidhimótikhon, Gre.
41/H5 Dhidhimótikhon, Gre.
39/K2 Dhíkaia, Gre.

Dhíka – Drigh

21/H8 **Drimoleague**, Ire.
39/F1 **Drin** (riv.), Alb.
39/F2 **Drin** (gulf), Alb.
40/D5 **Drin** (gulf), Alb.
40/E5 **Drin** (riv.), Alb.
40/D3 **Drina** (riv.), Yugo.
40/E5 **Drin i zi** (riv.), Alb.
40/C4 **Drniš**, Cro.
37/G6 **Dro**, It.
18/F4 **Drobeta-Turnu Severin**, Rom.
40/F3 **Drobeta-Turnu Severin**, Rom.
44/B3 **Drobeta-Turnu Severin**, Rom.
29/G1 **Drochtersen**, Ger.
22/B4 **Drogheda**, Ire.
18/F4 **Drogobych**, Ukr.
27/M4 **Drogobych**, Ukr.
40/B2 **Drogobych**, Ukr.
46/C5 **Drogobych**, Ukr.
22/B5 **Droichead Nuadh**, Ire.
24/D2 **Droitwich**, Eng,UK
31/G6 **Drolingen**, Fr.
29/E6 **Drolshagen**, Ger.
31/G1 **Drolshagen**, Ger.
21/A3 **Dromahaire**, Ire.
32/F4 **Drôme** (riv.), Fr.
22/B4 **Dromiskin**, Ire.
22/A3 **Dromore** (riv.), Ire.
22/B3 **Dromore**, NI,UK
33/G4 **Dronero**, It.
23/G5 **Dronfield**, Eng,UK
32/D4 **Dronne** (riv.), Fr.
28/C3 **Dronten**, Neth.
32/D4 **Dropt** (riv.), Fr.
30/A6 **Drouette** (riv.), Fr.
94/C1 **Drowning** (riv.), On,Can
22/C3 **Drumaness**, NI,UK
22/C2 **Drumbeg**, NI,UK
22/B4 **Drumcar**, Ire.
22/B4 **Drumcondra**, Ire.
86/E3 **Drumheller**, Ab,Can
88/D1 **Drumheller**, Ab,Can
90/E3 **Drumheller**, Ab,Can
22/B5 **Drumleck** (pt.), Ire.
71/H4 **Drummond** (range), Austl.
72/B4 **Drummond** (peak), Austl.
72/B4 **Drummond** (range), Austl.
87/J4 **Drummondville**, Qu,Can
89/M2 **Drummondville**, Qu,Can
95/F2 **Drummondville**, Qu,Can
22/D2 **Drummore**, Sc,UK
22/A2 **Drumnakilly**, NI,UK
28/C5 **Drunen**, Neth.
23/G1 **Druridge** (bay), Eng,UK
31/G6 **Drusenheim**, Fr.
27/M1 **Druskininkai**, Lith.
42/D5 **Druskininkai**, Lith.
44/B1 **Druskininkai**, Lith.
28/C5 **Druten**, Neth.
46/J5 **Druzhba**, Kaz.
40/C3 **Drvar**, Bosn.
27/K2 **Drwęca** (riv.), Pol.
9/M10 **Dry** (cr.), Ca,US
99/M9 **Dry** (cr.), Ca,US
39/J1 **Dryanovo**, Bul.
41/G4 **Dryanovo**, Bul.
85/K3 **Dry Creek**, Yk,Can
86/G4 **Dryden**, On,Can
89/H2 **Dryden**, On,Can
91/K3 **Dryden**, On,Can
94/A1 **Dryden**, On,Can
99/F6 **Dryden**, Mi,US
93/G5 **Dryden**, Tx,US
96/C4 **Dryden**, Tx,US
24/C2 **Drygarn Fawr** (mtn.), Wal,UK
04/A1 **Dry Tortugas** (keys), Fl,US
79/H5 **Dschang**, Camr.
54/G5 **Du** (riv.), China
59/B4 **Du** (riv.), China
61/F2 **Du** (riv.), China
24/B3 **Duad** (riv.), Wal,UK
72/C3 **Duaringa**, Austl.
04/D3 **Duarte** (peak), DRep.
42/C3 **Dubā**, SAr.
77/N2 **Dubā**, SAr.
48/H3 **Dubawnt** (lake), Can.
86/F2 **Dubawnt** (lake), NW,Can
86/F2 **Dubawnt** (riv.), NW,Can
53/G3 **Dubayy**, UAE
77/S2 **Dubayy**, UAE
68/D8 **Dubbo**, Austl.
71/H6 **Dubbo**, Austl.
73/D2 **Dubbo**, Austl.
37/E3 **Dübendorf**, Swi.
26/G3 **Dübener Heide** (for.), Ger.
37/F5 **Dubino**, It.
18/C3 **Dublin** (cap.), Ire.
22/B5 **Dublin** (bay), Ire.
22/B5 **Dublin** (cap.), Ire.
22/B5 **Dublin** (co.), Ire.
99/L11 **Dublin**, Ca,US
89/K5 **Dublin**, Ga,US
97/H3 **Dublin**, Ga,US
96/E5 **Dublin**, Pa,US
101/F1 **Dublin**, Tx,US
42/H4 **Dubna**, Rus.
44/F1 **Dubna**, Rus.
27/K4 **Dubnica nad Váhom**, Slvk.
44/C2 **Dubno**, Ukr.
94/E3 **Du Bois**, Pa,US
90/F5 **Dubois**, Wy,US
92/E2 **Dubois**, Wy,US
41/J2 **Dubossary** (res.), Mol.
18/E4 **Dubrovnik**, Cro.
39/F1 **Dubrovnik**, Cro.
40/D4 **Dubrovnik**, Cro.
89/H3 **Dubuque**, Ia,US
91/L5 **Dubuque**, Ia,US
93/K2 **Dubuque**, Ia,US
94/B3 **Dubuque**, Ia,US
92/E2 **Duchesne**, Ut,US
92/E2 **Duchesne** (riv.), Ut,US
70/F4 **Duchess**, Austl.
69/N7 **Ducie** (atoll), Pitc.
99/E6 **Duck** (lake), Mi,US
94/C5 **Duck** (riv.), Tn,US
99/A2 **Duckabush** (riv.), Wa,US
91/G2 **Duck Lake**, Sk,Can
92/D3 **Duckwater**, Nv,US
63/J5 **Duc Lap**, Viet.
65/D3 **Duc Lap**, Viet.
66/C1 **Duc Pho**, Viet.
63/J5 **Duc Pho**, Viet.
65/E3 **Duc Pho**, Viet.
65/D4 **Duc Phong**, Viet.
23/E3 **Dudden** (riv.), Eng,UK
31/F5 **Dudelange**, Lux.
26/F3 **Duderstadt**, Ger.
29/H5 **Duderstadt**, Ger.
36/D4 **Düdingen**, Swi.
46/J3 **Dudinka**, Rus.
24/D2 **Dudley**, Eng,UK
34/C2 **Dueñas**, Sp.
34/C2 **Duero** (riv.), Sp.
83/W **Dufek Massive** (mtn.), Ant.
68/F5 **Duff** (isl.), Sol.
28/B6 **Duffel**, Belg.
30/D1 **Duffel**, Belg.
23/G6 **Duffield**, Eng,UK
36/D6 **Dufour, Punta** (Dufourspitze) (peak), It., Swi.
33/G4 **Dufourspitze** (peak), Swi.
36/D6 **Dufourspitze** (Punta Dufour) (peak), It., Swi.
52/C6 **Dukambīya**, Eth.
69/L7 **Duke of Gloucester** (isls.), FrPol.
27/L4 **Dukielska, Przełęcz** (Dukla) (pass), Pol.
27/L4 **Dukla** (Przełęcz Dukielska) (pass), Pol.
42/E5 **Dūkštas**, Lith.
54/D4 **Dulan**, China
109/D2 **Dulce** (riv.), Arg.
103/F4 **Dulce** (gulf), CR
92/F3 **Dulce**, NM,US
96/B2 **Dulce**, NM,US
103/E3 **Dulce Nombre de Culmí**, Hon.
22/B4 **Duleek**, Ire.
41/H4 **Dŭlgopol**, Bul.
61/F3 **Duliu** (riv.), China
63/J2 **Duliu** (riv.), China
64/A2 **Dullewāla**, Pak.
80/Q12 **Dullstroom**, SAfr.
26/D3 **Dülmen**, Ger.
29/E5 **Dülmen**, Ger.
60/B3 **Dulong** (pass), China
63/J5 **Du Long**, Viet.
66/C1 **Du Long**, Viet.
41/H4 **Dulovo**, Bul.
44/C4 **Dulovo**, Bul.
86/G4 **Duluth**, Mn,US
89/H2 **Duluth**, Mn,US
91/K4 **Duluth**, Mn,US
94/A2 **Duluth**, Mn,US
24/C4 **Dulverton**, Eng,UK
49/E3 **Dūmā**, Syria
49/G7 **Dūmā**, WBnk.
67/F2 **Dumaguete City**, Phil.
67/F1 **Dumaran** (isl.), Phil.
73/D1 **Dumaresq** (riv.), Austl.
93/K4 **Dumas**, Ar,US
96/F3 **Dumas**, Ar,US
88/F4 **Dumas**, Tx,US
93/G4 **Dumas**, Tx,US
96/C3 **Dumas**, Tx,US
27/K4 **Ďumbier** (peak), Slvk.
82/C3 **Dumbo**, Ang.
41/G2 **Dumbrăveni**, Rom.
18/C3 **Dumfries**, Sc,UK
22/E1 **Dumfries**, Sc,UK
22/D1 **Dumfries & Galloway** (reg.), Sc,UK
45/G4 **Dumlu**, Turk.
29/F3 **Dümmer** (lake), Ger.
87/J4 **Dumoine** (lake), Qu,Can
94/F2 **Dumoine** (lake), Qu,Can
94/E2 **Dumoine** (riv.), Qu,Can
83/K **Dumont d'Urville**, Ant.
49/B4 **Dumyāţ** (gov.), Egypt
50/B4 **Dumyāţ** (gov.), Egypt
49/B4 **Dumyāţ** (Damietta), Egypt
77/M1 **Dumyāţ** (Damietta), Egypt
27/K5 **Duna** (Danube) (riv.), Hun.
40/D2 **Dunaföldvár**, Hun.
40/D2 **Dunaharaszti**, Hun.
27/K5 **Dunaj** (Danube) (riv.), Slvk.
27/L4 **Dunajec** (riv.), Pol.
27/K5 **Dunakeszi**, Hun.
22/B4 **Dunany** (pt.), Ire.
40/D2 **Dunaszekcso**, Hun.
40/D2 **Dunaújváros**, Hun.
40/D2 **Dunavecse**, Hun.
40/F4 **Dunavtsi**, Bul.
21/D2 **Dunbar**, Sc,UK
22/B5 **Dunboyne**, Ire.
90/C3 **Duncan**, BC,Can
92/E4 **Duncan**, Az,US
89/G5 **Duncan**, Ok,US
93/H4 **Duncan**, Ok,US
96/D3 **Duncan**, Ok,US
93/H4 **Duncanville**, Tx,US
96/D3 **Duncanville**, Tx,US
22/B3 **Dundalk**, Ire.
22/B4 **Dundalk** (bay), Ire.
98/K7 **Dundalk**, Md,US
70/C6 **Dundas** (lake), Austl.
70/E2 **Dundas** (str.), Austl.
87/R7 **Dundas** (pen.), NW,Can
95/Q9 **Dundas**, On,Can
81/E3 **Dundee**, SAfr.
82/F6 **Dundee**, SAfr.
18/C3 **Dundee**, Sc,UK
99/E8 **Dundee**, Mi,US
22/C3 **Dundrum**, NI,UK
22/C3 **Dundrum** (bay), NI,UK
90/G3 **Dundurn**, Sk,Can
71/R12 **Dunedin**, N.Z.
97/H4 **Dunedin**, Fl,US
73/D2 **Dunedoo**, Austl.
21/D2 **Dunfermline**, Sc,UK
22/B2 **Dungannon**, NI,UK
22/B3 **Dungannon** (dist.), NI,UK
53/K4 **Dungarpur**, India
62/B3 **Dungarpur**, India
21/B4 **Dungarvan**, Ire.
25/G5 **Dungeness** (pt.), Eng,UK
22/B2 **Dungiven**, NI,UK
21/A3 **Dunglow**, Ire.
73/D2 **Dungog**, Austl.
77/L7 **Dungu**, Zaire
55/K3 **Dunhua**, China
46/K5 **Dunhuang**, China
54/C3 **Dunhuang**, China
26/B3 **Dunkerque**, Fr.
30/B1 **Dunkerque** (Dunkirk), Fr.
32/E1 **Dunkerque** (Dunkirk), Fr.
24/C4 **Dunkery** (hill), Eng,UK
30/B1 **Dunkirk** (Dunkerque), Fr.
32/E1 **Dunkirk** (Dunkerque), Fr.
79/E5 **Dunkwa**, Gha.
22/B5 **Dún Laoghaire**, Ire.
22/B5 **Dunlavin**, Ire.
22/B4 **Dunleer**, Ire.
22/B2 **Dunloy**, NI,UK
21/H8 **Dunmanway**, Ire.
22/B2 **Dunmurry**, NI,UK
97/J3 **Dunn**, NC,US
22/A2 **Dunnamanagh**, NI,UK
22/B2 **Dunnamore**, NI,UK
36/D3 **Dünnern** (riv.), Swi.
37/E1 **Dunningen**, Ger.
23/H4 **Dunnington**, Eng,UK
80/Q13 **Dunnottar**, SAfr.
95/Q10 **Dunnville**, On,Can
73/B3 **Dunolly**, Austl.
77/M4 **Dunqulah**, Sudan
77/N3 **Dunqunāb**, Sudan
22/D2 **Dunragit**, Sc,UK
22/E1 **Dunscore**, Sc,UK
91/H3 **Dunseith**, ND,US
22/B1 **Dunseverick**, NI,UK
22/B5 **Dunshaughlin**, Ire.
90/C5 **Dunsmuir**, Ca,US
92/B2 **Dunsmuir**, Ca,US
25/F3 **Dunstable**, Eng,UK
31/E5 **Dun-sur-Meuse**, Fr.
55/J1 **Duobukur** (riv.), China
63/J3 **Duojing**, China
54/H3 **Duolun**, China
99/P16 **Du Page** (co.), Il,US
99/P16 **Du Page** (riv.), Il,US
99/P16 **Du Page, East Branch** (riv.), Il,US
91/H4 **Dupree**, SD,US
108/D2 **Duque de Caxias**, Braz.
89/J4 **Du Quoin**, Il,US
93/K3 **Du Quoin**, Il,US
94/B4 **Du Quoin**, Il,US
97/F2 **Du Quoin**, Il,US
49/D4 **Dūrā**, WBnk.
70/D3 **Durack** (range), Austl.
50/C1 **Durağan**, Turk.
32/F5 **Durance** (riv.), Fr.
100/D3 **Durango**, Mex.
100/D3 **Durango** (state), Mex.
84/G7 **Durango**, Mex.
32/B5 **Durango**, Sp.
34/D1 **Durango**, Sp.
88/F4 **Durango**, Co,US
92/F3 **Durango**, Co,US
96/B2 **Durango**, Co,US
96/B5 **Durango de Victoria**, Mex.
89/G5 **Durant**, Ok,US
93/H4 **Durant**, Ok,US
96/D3 **Durant**, Ok,US
109/E3 **Durazno**, Uru.
81/E3 **Durban**, SAfr.
82/F8 **Durban**, SAfr.
80/L10 **Durbanville**, SAfr.
20/G4 **Durbe**, Lat.
42/D4 **Durbe**, Lat.
36/C1 **Durbion** (riv.), Fr.
26/C3 **Durbuy**, Belg.
31/E3 **Durbuy**, Belg.
32/F1 **Durbuy**, Belg.
34/D4 **Dúrcal**, Sp.
40/C2 **Đurđevac**, Cro.
40/E3 **Đurđevo**, Yugo.
26/D3 **Düren**, Ger.
31/F2 **Düren**, Ger.
33/G1 **Düren**, Ger.
62/D3 **Durg**, India
62/E3 **Durgāpur**, India
95/S8 **Durham** (co.), On,Can
23/F2 **Durham** (co.), Eng,UK
23/G2 **Durham**, Eng,UK
89/L4 **Durham**, NC,US
97/J3 **Durham**, NC,US
95/G3 **Durham**, NH,US
25/E5 **Durlston Head** (pt.), UK
28/B6 **Durme** (riv.), Belg.
30/D1 **Durme** (riv.), Belg.
39/F1 **Durmitor Nat'l Park**, Yugo.
40/D4 **Durmitor Nat'l Park**, Yugo.
36/D3 **Dürrenroth**, Swi.
18/E4 **Durrës**, Alb.
39/F2 **Durrës**, Alb.
40/D5 **Durrës**, Alb.
25/E4 **Durrington**, Eng,UK
37/G1 **Dürrlauingen**, Ger.
24/D3 **Dursley**, Eng,UK
44/D5 **Dursunbey**, Turk.
50/B2 **Dursunbey**, Turk.
51/M6 **Durusu**, Turk.
51/M6 **Durusu** (lake), Turk.
67/J4 **D'Urville** (cape), Indo.
39/G1 **Dusanovo**, Yugo.
40/E4 **Dusanovo**, Yugo.
91/M3 **Dusey** (riv.), On,Can
94/C1 **Dusey** (riv.), On,Can
59/D2 **Du Shan** (peak), China
61/E3 **Dushan**, China
63/J2 **Dushan**, China
46/G6 **Dushanbe** (cap.), Taj.
51/F1 **Dusheti**, Geo.
61/E3 **Dushui** (riv.), China
18/D3 **Düsseldorf**, Ger.
26/D3 **Düsseldorf**, Ger.
28/D6 **Düsseldorf**, Ger.
31/F1 **Düsseldorf**, Ger.
46/A4 **Düsseldorf**, Ger.
27/J3 **Duszniki-Zdrój**, Pol.
33/M1 **Duszniki-Zdrój**, Pol.
23/H4 **Dutch** (riv.), Eng,UK
85/E5 **Dutch Harbor**, Ak,US
29/F4 **Düte** (riv.), Ger.
80/L10 **Dutoitspiek** (peak), SAfr.
99/D2 **Duvall**, Wa,US
40/C4 **Duvno**, Bosn.
63/J3 **Duyang**, China
61/E3 **Duyun**, China
63/J2 **Duyun**, China
41/K5 **Düzce**, Turk.
50/B1 **Düzce**, Turk.
50/D2 **Düziçi**, Turk.
41/G4 **Dve Mogili**, Bul.
42/H2 **Dvina** (bay), Rus.
43/J3 **Dvina, Northern** (riv.), Rus.
42/F5 **Dvina, Western** (riv.), Bel., Rus.
53/J4 **Dwārka**, India
62/A3 **Dwarka**, India
90/D4 **Dworshak** (res.), Id,US
22/D6 **Dwyfor** (riv.), Wal,UK
80/C4 **Dwyka** (riv.), SAfr.
44/E1 **Dyat'kovo**, Rus.
42/E5 **Dyatlovo**, Bela.
84/L3 **Dyer** (cape), Can.
87/K2 **Dyer** (cape), NW,Can
94/C3 **Dyer**, In,US
93/K3 **Dyersburg**, Tn,US
94/B4 **Dyersburg**, Tn,US
97/F2 **Dyersburg**, Tn,US
93/H4 **Dyess** (A.F.B.), Tx,US
96/D3 **Dyess** (A.F.B.), Tx,US
24/B3 **Dyfed** (co.), Wal,UK
22/D6 **Dyffryn**, Wal,UK
24/C1 **Dyfi** (riv.), Wal,UK
27/J4 **Dyje** (riv.), Czh.
33/L2 **Dyje** (riv.), Czh.
45/G4 **Dykh-tau, Gora** (peak), Rus.
26/C3 **Dyle** (riv.), Belg.
30/D2 **Dyle** (Dijle) (riv.), Belg.
27/K2 **Dylewska** (peak), Pol.
42/C5 **Dylewska Gora** (peak), Pol.
25/G4 **Dymchurch**, Eng,UK
72/C3 **Dysart**, Austl.
51/F1 **Dyul'tydag** (peak), Rus.
45/H4 **Dyul'tydag, Gora** (peak), Rus.
81/H6 **Dzaoudzi** (cap.), May.
54/C2 **Dzavhan** (riv.), Mong.
44/F3 **Dzenzik, Mys** (pt.), Ukr.
54/C2 **Dzereg**, Mong.
42/E5 **Dzerzhinsk**, Bela.
44/C1 **Dzerzhinsk**, Bela.
19/H3 **Dzerzhinsk**, Rus.
42/J4 **Dzerzhinsk**, Rus.
46/E4 **Dzerzhinsk**, Rus.
46/H5 **Dzhalal-Abad**, Kyr.
46/H5 **Dzhambul**, Kaz.
51/H1 **Dzhanga**, Trkm.
44/E3 **Dzhankoy**, Ukr.
46/E5 **Dzhanybek**, Kaz.
41/L2 **Dzharylgach** (gulf), Ukr.
39/J2 **Dzhebel**, Bul.
41/G5 **Dzhebel**, Bul.
51/F2 **Dzhebrail**, Azer.
45/M1 **Dzhetygara**, Kaz.
46/G4 **Dzhetygara**, Kaz.
46/G5 **Dzhezkazgan**, Kaz.
46/G5 **Dzhizak**, Uzb.
47/P4 **Dzhugdzhur** (range), Rus.
48/N4 **Dzhugdzhur** (range), Rus.
51/F2 **Dzhul'fa**, Azer.
27/L2 **Działdowo**, Pol.
42/D5 **Działdowo**, Pol.
44/B1 **Działdowo**, Pol.
101/H5 **Dzibalchén**, Mex.
102/D2 **Dzibalchén**, Mex.
101/H4 **Dzibilchaltún** (ruins), Mex.
102/D1 **Dzibilchaltún** (ruins), Mex.
101/H4 **Dzidzantún**, Mex.
102/D1 **Dzidzantún**, Mex.
27/J3 **Dzierżoniów**, Pol.
101/H4 **Dzitbalché**, Mex.
102/D1 **Dzitbalché**, Mex.
46/J5 **Dzungarian** (basin), China
54/B3 **Dzungarian** (basin), China
54/G3 **Dzüünbayan**, Mong.
54/E2 **Dzüünbayan-Ulaan**, Mong.
54/D2 **Dzüünhangay**, Mong.
47/L5 **Dzüünharaa**, Mong.
54/F2 **Dzüünharaa**, Mong.
47/L5 **Dzuunmod**, Mong.
54/F2 **Dzuunmod**, Mong.

E

93/G3 **Eads**, Co,US
96/C2 **Eads**, Co,US
87/L3 **Eagle** (riv.), Nf,Can
91/K3 **Eagle** (lake), On,Can
94/A1 **Eagle** (lake), On,Can
90/F3 **Eagle** (riv.), Sk,Can
85/K3 **Eagle**, Ak,US
90/C5 **Eagle** (lake), Ca,US
92/B2 **Eagle** (lake), Ca,US
92/F3 **Eagle**, Co,US
89/H2 **Eagle** (mtn.), Mn,US
91/L4 **Eagle** (peak), Mn,US
94/B2 **Eagle** (peak), Mn,US
100/D2 **Eagle** (peak), Tx,US
99/P14 **Eagle**, Wi,US
99/P14 **Eagle** (lake), Wi,US
91/H4 **Eagle Butte**, SD,US
101/E2 **Eagle Pass**, Tx,US
88/F6 **Eagle Pass**, Tx,US
96/C4 **Eagle Pass**, Tx,US
86/H4 **Eagle River**, Wi,US
91/L4 **Eagle River**, Wi,US
94/B2 **Eagle River**, Wi,US
23/E1 **Eaglesfield**, Sc,UK
19/M7 **Ealing** (bor.), Eng,UK
23/F4 **Earby**, Eng,UK
91/K3 **Ear Falls**, On,Can
94/A1 **Ear Falls**, On,Can
25/G2 **Earith**, Eng,UK
92/C4 **Earlimart**, Ca,US
25/F2 **Earls Barton**, Eng,UK
25/G3 **Earls Colne**, Eng,UK
25/H2 **Earl Stonham**, Eng,UK
93/H5 **Early**, Tx,US
96/D4 **Early**, Tx,US
23/G2 **Easington**, Eng,UK
23/G3 **Easingwold**, Eng,UK
97/H3 **Easley**, SC,US
71/S10 **East** (cape), N.Z.
85/B6 **East** (cape), Ak,US
99/C3 **East** (passg.), Wa,US
25/G2 **East Anglia** (reg.), Eng,UK
95/G2 **East Angus**, Qu,Can
98/E5 **East Bangor**, Pa,US
19/N7 **East Barnet**, Eng,UK
25/H3 **East Bergholt**, Eng,UK
91/K4 **East Bethel**, Mn,US
94/A2 **East Bethel**, Mn,US
25/G5 **Eastbourne**, Eng,UK
32/D1 **Eastbourne**, Eng,UK
98/F5 **East Brunswick**, NJ,US
103/J1 **East Caicos** (isl.), Trks.
104/D2 **East Caicos** (isl.), Trks.
23/G1 **East Chevington**, Eng,UK
99/R16 **East Chicago**, In,US
68/B2 **East China** (sea)
48/M6 **East China** (sea)
55/K5 **East China** (sea)
61/J3 **East China** (sea)
56/A5 **East China** (sea)
19/M8 **East Clandon**, Eng,UK
24/B3 **East Cleddau** (riv.), Wal,UK
24/C5 **East Dart** (riv.), Eng,UK
25/G1 **East Dereham**, Eng,UK
99/G7 **East Detroit** (East Pointe), Mi,US
99/G7 **East Detroit** (East Pointe), Mi,US
69/Q7 **Easter** (isl.), Chile
80/A2 **Easter** (pt.), Namb.
79/E5 **Eastern** (reg.), Gha.
78/C4 **Eastern** (prov.), SLeo.
64/H4 **Eastern** (prov.), Srl.
23/H4 **Eastern** (plain), Eng,UK
56/A4 **Eastern Channel** (str.), Japan
82/C5 **Eastern Ghats** (mts.), India
64/F4 **Eastern Ghats** (uplands), India
46/K4 **Eastern Sayans** (mts.), Rus.
54/D1 **Eastern Sayans** (mts.), Rus.
91/J2 **Easterville**, Mb,Can
105/D7 **East Falkland** (isl.), Falk.
109/E7 **East Falkland** (isl.), Falk.
28/A6 **East Flanders** (prov.), Belg.
30/C2 **East Flanders** (prov.), Belg.
26/D2 **East Frisian** (isls.), Ger.
29/E1 **East Frisian** (isls.), Ger.
25/F1 **East Glen** (riv.), Eng,UK
98/E5 **East Greenville**, Pa,US
25/F4 **East Grinstead**, Eng,UK
90/F4 **East Helena**, Mt,US
99/C2 **East Hill-Meridian**, Wa,US
19/M8 **East Horsley**, Eng,UK
94/C2 **East Jordan**, Mi,US
46/J5 **East Kazakhstan Obl.**, Kaz.
55/K4 **East Korea** (bay), NKor.
58/D3 **East Korea** (Tongjosŏn) (bay), NKor.
101/F1 **Eastland**, Tx,US
93/H4 **Eastland**, Tx,US
96/D3 **Eastland**, Tx,US
94/C3 **East Lansing**, Mi,US
23/G6 **East Leake**, Eng,UK
25/E5 **Eastleigh**, Eng,UK
94/D3 **East Liverpool**, Oh,US
80/D4 **East London**, SAfr.
82/E7 **East London**, SAfr.
98/B2 **East Los Angeles**, Ca,US
84/K4 **Eastmain** (riv.), Can.
87/J3 **Eastmain** (riv.), Qu,Can
94/F1 **Eastmain** (riv.), Qu,Can
97/H3 **Eastman**, Ga,US
95/G2 **East Millinocket**, Me,US
88/C4 **East Mojave Nat'l Scenic Area**, Ca,US
92/D4 **East Mojave Nat'l Scenic Area**, Ca,US
19/M7 **East Molesey**, Eng,UK
91/K5 **East Nishnabotna** (riv.), Ia,US
24/D5 **Easton**, Eng,UK
98/G4 **Easton**, Ct,US
94/F3 **Easton**, Pa,US
98/E5 **Easton**, Pa,US
98/E5 **Easton-Bethlehem-Allentown** (arpt.), Pa,US
98/F5 **East Orange**, NJ,US
98/H5 **East Patchogue**, NY,US
97/G3 **East Point**, Ga,US
99/G7 **East Pointe** (East Detroit), Mi,US
89/N3 **Eastport**, Me,US
95/H2 **Eastport**, Me,US
99/B2 **East Port Orchard**, Wa,US
23/H5 **East Retford**, Eng,UK
23/E2 **Eastriggs**, Sc,UK
25/H4 **Eastry**, Eng,UK
30/A1 **Eastry**, Eng,UK
94/B4 **East Saint Louis**, Il,US
97/F2 **East Saint Louis**, Il,US
47/S2 **East Siberian** (sea), Rus.
48/Q2 **East Siberian** (sea), Rus.
98/E5 **East Stroudsburg**, Pa,US
25/G5 **East Sussex** (co.), Eng,UK
94/D2 **East Tawas**, Mi,US
24/B4 **East the Water**, Eng,UK
99/P14 **East Troy**, Wi,US
90/C4 **East Wenatchee**, Wa,US
25/F5 **East Wittering**, Eng,UK
23/G6 **Eastwood**, Eng,UK
95/R8 **East York**, On,Can
25/E2 **Eatington**, Eng,UK
93/F2 **Eaton**, Co,US
90/F3 **Eatonia**, Sk,Can
25/F2 **Eaton Socon**, Eng,UK
98/F5 **Eatontown**, NJ,US
23/H5 **Eau** (riv.), Eng,UK
19/S10 **Eaubonne**, Fr.
87/J3 **Eau Claire** (lake), Qu,Can
86/G4 **Eau Claire**, Wi,US
89/H3 **Eau Claire**, Wi,US
91/L4 **Eau Claire**, Wi,US
94/B2 **Eau Claire**, Wi,US
30/A4 **Eaulne** (riv.), Fr.
68/D4 **Eauripik** (atoll), Micr.
32/D5 **Eauze**, Fr.
35/F1 **Eauze**, Fr.
25/F4 **Ebble** (riv.), Eng,UK
24/C3 **Ebbw Vale**, Wal,UK
76/H7 **Ebebiyín**, EqG.
76/G3 **Ebeggi** (well), Alg
29/H6 **Ebeleben**, Ger.
27/G5 **Ebensee**, Aus.
33/K3 **Ebensee**, Aus.
40/A2 **Ebensee**, Aus.
29/H5 **Ebergötzen**, Ger.
26/F4 **Ebermannstadt**, Ger.
31/G4 **Ebersberg**, Ger.
36/D1 **Ebersheim**, Fr.
27/G2 **Eberswalde-Finow**, Ger.
55/N3 **Ebetsu**, Japan
63/H2 **Ebian**, China
57/H7 **Ebina**, Japan
37/F3 **Ebnat-Kappel**, Swi.
78/D3 **Ebo** (lake), Mali
38/D2 **Eboli**, It.
40/B5 **Eboli**, It.
76/H7 **Ebolowa**, Camr.
68/F4 **Ebon** (atoll), Mrsh.
18/C4 **Ebro** (riv.), Sp.
32/B5 **Ebro** (riv.), Sp.
35/F2 **Ebro** (riv.), Sp.
29/H2 **Ebstorf**, Ger.
101/Q9 **Ecatepec**, Mex.
101/F5 **Ecatepec de Morelos**, Mex.
101/K7 **Ecatepec de Morelos**, Mex.
102/B2 **Ecatepec de Morelos**, Mex.
23/E1 **Ecclefechan**, Sc,UK
23/F5 **Eccles**, Eng,UK
23/F6 **Eccleshall**, Eng,UK
39/K2 **Eceabat**, Turk.
41/H5 **Eceabat**, Turk.
44/C4 **Eceabat**, Turk.
50/A1 **Eceabat**, Turk.
36/C4 **Echallens**, Swi.
103/F4 **Echandi** (mtn.), CR
79/H3 **Eché Fadadinga** (wadi), Niger
61/G2 **Echeng**, China
57/M9 **Echigawa**, Japan
37/H1 **Eching**, Ger.
32/F4 **Echirolles**, Fr.
45/H4 **Echmiadzin**, Arm.
51/F1 **Echmiadzin**, Arm.
98/F4 **Echo** (lake), NJ,US
86/E2 **Echo Bay**, NW,Can
91/L2 **Echoing** (riv.), Mb, On,Can
28/C6 **Echt**, Neth.
31/E1 **Echt**, Neth.
31/F4 **Echternach**, Lux.
71/H7 **Echuca**, Austl.
73/C3 **Echuca**, Austl.
34/C4 **Ecija**, Sp.
40/E3 **Ečka**, Yugo.
26/E1 **Eckernförde**, Ger.
23/G5 **Eckington**, Eng,UK
24/D2 **Eckington**, Eng,UK
87/H1 **Eclipse** (sound), NW,Can
32/D3 **Écommoy**, Fr.
108/D1 **Ecoporanga**, Braz.
99/F7 **Ecorse**, Mi,US
99/F7 **Ecorse** (riv.), Mi,US
30/A5 **Écos**, Fr.
19/T9 **Écouen**, Fr.
32/D2 **Écouves, Signal d'** (peak), Fr.
33/G4 **Écrins Nat'l Park**, Fr.
31/E6 **Écrouves**, Fr.
105/B3 **Ecuador**
106/C4 **Ecuador**
36/C4 **Ecublens**, Swi.
52/D6 **Ed**, Eth.
77/P5 **Ed**, Eth.
50/A2 **Edcemit** (gulf), Turk.
71/H7 **Eddystone** (pt.), Austl.
73/D4 **Eddystone** (pt.), Austl.
24/B6 **Eddystone** (rocks), Eng,UK
26/C2 **Ede**, Neth.
28/C4 **Ede**, Neth.
79/G5 **Ede**, Nga.
76/H7 **Edéa**, Camr.
30/D1 **Edegem**, Belg.
108/B1 **Edéia**, Braz.
27/L4 **Edelény**, Hun.
40/E1 **Edelény**, Hun.
29/H4 **Edemissen**, Ger.
73/D3 **Eden**, Austl.
23/F2 **Eden** (riv.), Eng,UK
94/E4 **Eden**, NC,US
97/J2 **Eden**, NC,US
19/P8 **Edenbridge**, Eng,UK
25/G4 **Edenbridge**, Eng,UK
80/D3 **Edenburg**, SAfr.
81/E3 **Edendale**, SAfr.
22/A5 **Edenderry**, Ire.
73/B3 **Edenhope**, Austl.
31/H5 **Edenkoben**, Ger.
23/F2 **Edenside** (val.), Eng,UK
97/J2 **Edenton**, NC,US
26/E3 **Eder** (riv.), Ger.
29/F6 **Eder** (riv.), Ger.
29/G6 **Eder** (riv.), Ger.
31/H1 **Eder** (riv.), Ger.
29/F6 **Eder-Stausee** (res.), Ger.
29/E2 **Edewecht**, Ger.
25/E2 **Edgbaston**, Eng,UK
46/C2 **Edge** (isl.), Sval.
85/L4 **Edgecumbe** (cape), Ak,US
87/K2 **Edgell** (isl.), NW,Can
91/G5 **Edgerton**, Wy,US
93/F2 **Edgerton**, Wy,US
99/C3 **Edgewood-North Hill**, Wa,US
23/F6 **Edgmond**, Eng,UK
24/D1 **Edgmond**, Eng,UK
19/N7 **Edgware**, Eng,UK
39/H2 **Édhessa**, Gre.
40/F5 **Édhessa**, Gre.
94/D3 **Edinboro**, Pa,US
101/F3 **Edinburg**, Tx,US
96/D5 **Edinburg**, Tx,US
18/C3 **Edinburgh**, Sc,UK
39/K2 **Edirne**, Turk
41/H5 **Edirne**, Turk.
41/H5 **Edirne** (prov.), Turk.
44/C4 **Edirne**, Turk.
44/C4 **Edirne** (prov.), Turk.
50/A1 **Edirne**, Turk.
50/A1 **Edirne** (prov.), Turkey
98/F5 **Edison**, NJ,US
97/H3 **Edisto Island**, SC,US
79/F2 **Edjérir** (wadi), Mali
90/C4 **Edmonds**, Wa,US
99/C2 **Edmonds**, Wa,US
90/E2 **Edmonton** (cap.), Ab,Can
86/E3 **Edmonton** (cap.), Ab,Can
19/N7 **Edmonton**, Eng,UK
91/K2 **Edmund** (lake), Mb,Can
72/B2 **Edmund Kennedy Nat'l Park**, Austl.
87/K4 **Edmundston**, NB,Can
89/N2 **Edmundston**, NB,Can
95/G2 **Edmundston**, NB,Can
101/F2 **Edna**, Tx,US
93/H5 **Edna**, Tx,US
96/D4 **Edna**, Tx,US
85/M4 **Edna Bay**, Ak,US
57/H7 **Edo** (riv.), Japan
37/G5 **Edolo**, It.
44/C5 **Edremit**, Turk.
44/C5 **Edremit** (gulf), Turk.
50/A2 **Edremit**, Turk.
86/E3 **Edson**, Ab,Can
90/D2 **Edson**, Ab,Can
109/D4 **Eduardo Castex**, Arg.
107/L5 **Eduardo Gomes**, Braz.
74/E5 **Edward** (lake), Ugan., Zaire
77/L8 **Edward** (lake), Ugan., Zaire
82/E1 **Edward** (lake), Ugan., Zaire
72/A1 **Edward River Abor. Community**, Austl.
93/K2 **Edwards** (riv.), Il,US
101/E2 **Edwards** (plat.), Tx,US
88/F5 **Edwards** (plat.), Tx,US
93/G5 **Edwards** (plat.), Tx,US
96/C4 **Edwards** (plat.), Tx,US
92/C4 **Edwards A.F.B.**, Ca,US
93/K3 **Edwardsville**, Il,US
94/B4 **Edwardsville**, Il,US
97/F2 **Edwardsville**, Il,US
83/P **Edward VII** (pen.), Ant.
83/D **Edward VIII** (bay), Ant.
101/H5 **Edzná** (ruins), Mex.
102/D2 **Edzná** (ruins), Mex.
85/F3 **Eek**, Ak,US
28/A6 **Eeklo**, Belg.
30/C1 **Eeklo**, Belg.
90/C6 **Eel** (riv.), Ca,US
92/B3 **Eel** (riv.), Ca,US
28/D2 **Eelde-Paterswolde**, Neth.
28/C4 **Eem** (riv.), Neth.
26/D2 **Eems** (Ems) (riv.), Ger., Neth.
28/D2 **Eems** (Ems) (riv.), Ger., Neth.
28/D2 **Eemshaven** (harb.), Neth.
28/D2 **Eemskanaal** (can.), Neth.
28/C6 **Eersel**, Neth.
68/F6 **Efate** (isl.), Van.
91/L5 **Effigy Mounds Nat'l Mon.**, Ia,US
94/A3 **Effigy Mounds Nat'l Mon.**, Ia,US
95/H9 **Effingham**, Un,Can
19/M8 **Effingham**, Eng,UK
94/B4 **Effingham**, Il,US
97/F2 **Effingham**, Il,US
98/E5 **Effort**, Pa,US
50/C1 **Eflâni**, Turk.
41/J3 **Eforie**, Rom.
36/D2 **Efringen-Kirchen**, Ger.
24/C1 **Efyrnwy, Llyn** (lake), Wal,UK
22/E6 **Efyrnwy, Llyn** (lake), Wal,UK
38/C3 **Egadi** (isls.), It.
92/D3 **Egan** (range), Nv,US
85/G4 **Egegik**, Ak,US
26/G3 **Eger** (riv.), Ger.
33/K1 **Eger** (riv.), Ger.
27/L5 **Eger**, Hun.
40/E2 **Eger**, Hun.
44/B3 **Eger**, Hun.
20/C4 **Egersund**, Nor.
29/H2 **Egestorf**, Ger.
37/F3 **Egg**, Aus.
37/E3 **Egg**, Swi.
26/E1 **Eggebek**, Ger.
29/F5 **Eggegebirge** (ridge), Ger.
33/L2 **Eggenburg**, Aus.
36/D4 **Eggiwil**, Swi.
23/G3 **Egglescliffe**, Eng,UK
23/G2 **Eggleston**, Eng,UK
19/M7 **Egham**, Eng,UK
25/F4 **Egham**, Eng,UK
31/D2 **Éghezée**, Belg.
20/P6 **Egilsstadhir**, Ice.
54/E1 **Egiyn** (riv.), Mong.
32/E4 **Egletons**, Fr.
87/R7 **Eglinton** (isl.), NW,Can
22/A1 **Eglinton**, NI,UK
37/E2 **Eglisau**, Swi.
24/C4 **Eglwys Brewis**, Wal,UK
19/S11 **Égly**, Fr.
28/B3 **Egmond aan Zee**, Neth.
71/R10 **Egmont** (cape), N.Z.
71/R10 **Egmont** (peak), N.Z.
37/F2 **Egnach**, Swi.
37/H5 **Egna** (Neumarkt), It.
22/E3 **Egremont**, Eng,UK
50/B2 **Eğridir**, Turk.
50/B2 **Eğridir** (lake), Turk.
49/C5 **Egypt**
50/A4 **Egypt**
52/B4 **Egypt**
74/E2 **Egypt**
77/L2 **Egypt**
56/C4 **Ehime** (pref.), Japan
26/E4 **Ehingen**, Ger.
33/H2 **Ehingen**, Ger.
37/F1 **Ehingen**, Ger.
36/D1 **Ehn** (riv.), Fr.
33/H1 **Ehringshausen**, Ger.

132

Ehrwa – Esche

37/G3 **Ehrwald**, Aus.
69/L5 **Eiao** (isl.), FrPol.
32/B5 **Eibar**, Sp.
34/D1 **Eibar**, Sp.
28/D4 **Eibergen**, Neth.
31/G6 **Eichel** (riv.), Fr.
37/H1 **Eichenau**, Ger.
26/F4 **Eichstätt**, Ger.
33/J2 **Eichstätt**, Ger.
29/H3 **Eicklingen**, Ger.
72/C4 **Eidsvold**, Austl.
20/D3 **Eidsvoll**, Nor.
26/D4 **Eifel** (plat.), Ger.
31/F3 **Eifel** (plat.), Ger.
33/G1 **Eifel** (plat.), Ger.
19/S10 **Eiffel Tower**, Fr.
57/M9 **Eigenji**, Japan
36/D4 **Eiger** (peak), Swi.
62/B6 **Eight Degree** (chan.), India,Mald.
83/T **Eights** (coast), Ant.
70/C3 **Eighty Mile** (beach), Austl.
28/B2 **Eijerlandsee Gat** (chan.), Neth.
31/E2 **Eijsden**, Neth.
71/H7 **Eildon** (lake), Austl.
73/C3 **Eildon**, Austl.
73/C3 **Eildon** (lake), Austl.
72/A2 **Einasleigh** (riv.), Austl.
29/G5 **Einbeck**, Ger.
26/C3 **Eindhoven**, Neth.
28/C6 **Eindhoven**, Neth.
37/E3 **Einsiedeln**, Swi.
31/F6 **Einville-au-Jard**, Fr.
106/E5 **Eirunepé**, Braz.
82/C5 **Eirup**, Namb.
37/H4 **Eisack** (Isarco) (riv.), It.
31/E4 **Eisch** (riv.), Lux.
26/F3 **Eisenach**, Ger.
29/H7 **Eisenach**, Ger.
31/H4 **Eisenberg**, Ger.
33/L3 **Eisenerz**, Aus.
40/B2 **Eisenerz**, Aus.
27/H2 **Eisenhüttenstadt**, Ger.
27/J5 **Eisenstadt**, Aus.
33/M3 **Eisenstadt**, Aus.
40/C2 **Eisenstadt**, Aus.
26/D3 **Eiserfeld**, Ger.
31/G2 **Eiserfeld**, Ger.
27/N1 **Eišiškės**, Lith.
42/E5 **Eišiškės**, Lith.
44/C1 **Eišiškės**, Lith.
31/G3 **Eitelborn**, Ger.
29/F3 **Eiter** (riv.), Ger.
31/G2 **Eitorf**, Ger.
35/E1 **Ejea de los Caballeros**, Sp.
59/B3 **Ejin Horo Qi**, China
54/E3 **Ejin Qi**, China
102/B2 **Ejutla**, Mex.
20/G4 **Ekenäs**, Fin.
42/D4 **Ekenäs**, Fin.
28/B6 **Ekeren**, Belg.
39/J2 **Ekhínos**, Gre.
41/G5 **Ekhínos**, Gre.
46/H4 **Ekibastuz**, Kaz.
47/P4 **Ekimchan**, Rus.
20/E4 **Eksjö**, Swe.
91/M2 **Ekwan** (riv.), On,Can
87/H3 **Ekwan** (riv.), On,Can
85/G4 **Ekwok**, Ak,US
63/G4 **Ela**, Burma
65/B2 **Ela**, Burma
78/C2 **El 'Acâba** (reg.), Mrta.
75/S15 **El Affroun**, Alg.
96/B5 **El Águila**, Mex
52/B3 **El Amra** (Abydos) (ruins), Egypt
24/C2 **Elan** (riv.), Wal,UK
19/R10 **Élancourt**, Fr.
30/A6 **Élancourt**, Fr.
80/D2 **Elands** (riv.), SAfr.
80/P12 **Elands** (riv.), SAfr.
80/Q12 **Elandsrivier** (riv.), SAfr.
75/V18 **El Aouinet**, Alg.
34/C4 **El Arahal**, Sp.
78/D2 **El Arhlaf** (well), Mrta.
72/B2 **El Arish**, Austl.
76/F1 **El Asnam**, Alg.
39/H3 **Elassón**, Gre.
34/D1 **El Astillero**, Sp.
49/D5 **Elat**, Isr.
50/C4 **Elat**, Isr.
52/B3 **Elat**, Isr.
77/M2 **Elat**, Isr.
39/H3 **Elátia**, Gre.
68/D4 **Elato** (atoll), Micr.
46/D6 **Elazığ**, Turk.
50/D2 **Elazığ**, Turk.
50/D2 **Elazığ** (prov.), Turk.
33/J5 **Elba** (isl.), It.
38/B1 **Elba** (isl.), It.
97/G4 **Elba**, Al,US
103/H5 **El Bagre**, Col.
47/P4 **El'ban**, Rus.
103/H4 **El Banco**, Col.
106/D2 **El Banco**, Col.
34/B1 **El Barco**, Sp.
34/C2 **El Barco de Ávila**, Sp.
101/F3 **El Barretal**, Mex.
39/G2 **Elbasan**, Alb.
40/E5 **Elbasan**, Alb.
76/F1 **El Bayadh**, Alg.
31/G2 **Elbbach** (riv.), Ger.
46/B4 **Elbe** (riv.), Ger.
18/D3 **Elbe** (riv.), Ger.
26/E2 **Elbe** (riv.), Ger.
29/F1 **Elbe** (riv.), Ger.
29/G6 **Elbe** (riv.), Ger.
33/L1 **Elbe** (Labe) (riv.), Czh.
92/F3 **Elbert** (peak), Co,US
96/B2 **Elbert** (peak), Co,US
97/H3 **Elberton**, Ga,US
29/H2 **Elbe-Seitenkanal** (can.), Ger.
32/D2 **Elbeuf**, Fr.
50/D2 **Elbistan**, Turk.
18/E3 **Elblag**, Pol.
27/K1 **Elblag**, Pol.
27/K2 **Elblag** (prov.), Pol.
42/C5 **Elblag**, Pol.
46/B4 **Elblag**, Pol.
109/B5 **El Bolsón**, Arg.
34/D3 **El Bonillo**, Sp.
90/G3 **Elbow**, Sk,Can
46/E5 **El'brus** (peak), Rus.
19/H4 **El'brus, Gora** (peak), Rus.
45/G4 **El'brus, Gora** (peak), Rus.
28/C4 **Elburg**, Neth.
34/D2 **El Burgo de Osma**, Sp.
99/P16 **Elburn**, Il,US
46/E6 **Elburz** (mts.), Iran
51/G2 **Elburz** (mts.), Iran
52/E1 **Elburz** (mts.), Iran
102/E3 **El Cajón** (res.), Hon.
100/A1 **El Cajon**, Ca,US
88/C5 **El Cajon**, Ca,US
92/C4 **El Cajon**, Ca,US
106/F2 **El Callao**, Ven.
101/F2 **El Campo**, Tx,US
93/H5 **El Campo**, Tx,US
96/D4 **El Campo**, Tx,US
90/E4 **El Capitan** (peak), Mt,US
103/H4 **El Carmen**, Col.
106/C2 **El Carmen de Bolívar**, Col.
35/N8 **El Casar de Talamanca**, Sp.
101/H5 **El Cayo**, Belz.
100/B1 **El Centro**, Ca,US
92/D4 **El Centro**, Ca,US
103/J2 **El Cercado**, DRep.
99/K11 **El Cerrito**, Ca,US
104/F5 **El Cerro del Aripo** (mtn.), Trin.
104/D5 **El Cerrón** (peak), Ven.
103/H4 **El César** (dept.), Col.
100/D2 **El Charco**, Mex.
35/E3 **Elche**, Sp.
34/D3 **Elche de la Sierra**, Sp.
101/F4 **El Chico Nat'l Park**, Mex.
101/L6 **El Chico Nat'l Park**, Mex.
102/B1 **El Chico Nat'l Park**, Mex.
37/G1 **Elchingen**, Ger.
70/F2 **Elcho** (isl.), Austl.
106/D2 **El Cocuy Nat'l Park**, Col.
109/E2 **El Colorado**, Arg.
102/D2 **El Corozal**, Mex.
99/B3 **Eld** (inlet), Wa,US
35/E3 **Elda**, Sp.
26/G2 **Elde** (riv.), Ger.
98/K7 **Eldersburg**, Md,US
103/H4 **El Difícil**, Col.
50/C1 **Eldivan**, Turk.
76/F1 **El Djezair** (Algiers) (cap.), Alg.
74/B2 **El Djouf** (des.), Afr.
76/D3 **El Djouf** (des.), Afr.
78/C1 **El Djouf** (des.), Mrta.
99/A2 **Eldon**, Wa,US
109/F2 **Eldorado**, Arg.
100/D3 **El Dorado**, Mex.
89/H5 **El Dorado**, Ar,US
93/J4 **El Dorado**, Ar,US
96/E3 **El Dorado**, Ar,US
93/H3 **El Dorado**, Ks,US
96/D2 **El Dorado**, Ks,US
101/E2 **Eldorado**, Tx,US
93/G5 **Eldorado**, Tx,US
96/C4 **Eldorado**, Tx,US
106/F2 **El Dorado**, Ven.
77/N7 **Eldoret**, Kenya
88/W13 **Eleao** (peak), Hi,US
99/C4 **Electron**, Wa,US
76/D2 **El Eglab** (plat.), Alg.
40/E2 **Elek**, Hun.
42/E5 **Eléktrénai**, Lith.
19/G3 **Elektrostal'**, Rus.
42/H5 **Elektrostal'**, Rus.
43/Y9 **Elektrostal'**, Rus.
46/D4 **Elektrostal'**, Rus.
39/J1 **Elena**, Bul.
41/G4 **Elena**, Bul.
44/C4 **Elena**, Bul.
83/W **Elephant** (isl.), Ant.
100/D1 **Elephant Butte**, NM,US
35/M8 **El Escorial**, Sp.
45/G5 **Eleşkirt**, Turk.
51/E2 **Eleşkirt**, Turk.
34/C2 **El Espinar**, Sp.
75/U17 **El Eulma**, Alg.
104/B1 **Eleuthera** (isl.), Bahm.
84/K7 **Eleuthera** (isl.), Bahm.
93/K3 **Eleven Point** (riv.), Ar, Mo,US
39/L6 **Elevsís**, Gre.
41/F6 **Elevsís**, Gre.
44/B5 **Elevsís**, Gre.
39/J2 **Elevtheroúpolis**, Gre.
18/C4 **El Ferrol**, Sp.
34/A1 **El Ferrol**, Sp.
85/L4 **Elfin Cove**, Ak,US
95/Q9 **Elfrida**, On,Can
100/C3 **El Fuerte**, Mex.
49/F6 **El Fureidīs**, Isr.
37/E3 **Elgg**, Swi.
89/J3 **Elgin**, Il,US
93/K2 **Elgin**, Il,US
94/B3 **Elgin**, Il,US
99/P15 **Elgin**, Il,US
91/H4 **Elgin**, ND,US
21/D2 **Elgin**, Sc,UK
101/F2 **Elgin**, Tx,US
93/H5 **Elgin**, Tx,US
96/D4 **Elgin**, Tx,US
95/R8 **Elgin Mills**, On,Can
34/D1 **Elgóibar**, Sp.
76/F1 **El Golea**, Alg.
102/D3 **El Golfete** (lake), Guat.
99/K11 **El Granada**, Ca,US
104/F5 **El Guachara Nat'l Park**, Ven.
75/T16 **El Ham** (riv.), Alg.
101/F4 **El Higo**, Mex.
102/B1 **El Higo**, Mex.
82/D2 **Elias Garcia**, Ang.
93/G4 **Elida**, NM,US
96/C3 **Elida**, NM,US
80/L11 **Elim**, SAfr.
85/F3 **Elim**, Ak,US
96/C4 **El Indio**, Tx,US
25/E5 **Eling**, Eng,UK
19/H4 **Elista**, Rus.
45/H3 **Elista**, Rus.
46/E5 **Elista**, Rus.
80/A2 **Elizabeth** (bay), Namb.
98/F5 **Elizabeth**, NJ,US
89/L4 **Elizabeth City**, NC,US
97/J2 **Elizabeth City**, NC,US
94/D4 **Elizabethton**, Tn,US
97/H2 **Elizabethton**, Tn,US
94/C4 **Elizabethtown**, Ky,US
97/G2 **Elizabethtown**, Ky,US
32/C5 **Elizondo**, Sp.
76/D1 **El Jadida**, Mor.
27/M2 **Ełk**, Pol.
42/D5 **Ełk**, Pol.
44/B1 **Ełk**, Pol.
99/L10 **Elk** (slough), Ca,US
96/B2 **Elk** (mts.), Co,US
88/G4 **Elk City**, Ok,US
93/H4 **Elk City**, Ok,US
96/D3 **Elk City**, Ok,US
31/G2 **Elkenroth**, Ger.
99/M10 **Elk Grove**, Ca,US
99/Q15 **Elk Grove Village**, Il,US
94/C3 **Elkhart**, In,US
93/G3 **Elkhart**, Ks,US
96/C2 **Elkhart**, Ks,US
76/D3 **El Khatt** (escarp.), Mrta.
78/C2 **El Khatt** (depr.), Mrta.
91/H3 **Elkhorn**, Mb,Can
91/J5 **Elkhorn** (riv.), Nb,US
89/G3 **Elkhorn** (riv.), Ne,US
94/B3 **Elkhorn**, Wi,US
99/N14 **Elkhorn**, Wi,US
39/K1 **Elkhovo**, Bul.
41/H4 **Elkhovo**, Bul.
44/C4 **Elkhovo**, Bul.
94/D4 **Elkin**, NC,US
97/H2 **Elkin**, NC,US
89/L4 **Elkins**, WV,US
94/E4 **Elkins**, WV,US
97/J2 **Elkins**, WV,US
90/E2 **Elk Island Nat'l Park**, Ab,Can
86/E3 **Elk Island Nat'l Park**, Ab,Can
86/E4 **Elko**, Nv,US
88/C3 **Elko**, Nv,US
90/E5 **Elko**, Nv,US
92/D2 **Elko**, Nv,US
90/F2 **Elk Point**, Ab,Can
94/C2 **Elk Rapids**, Mi,US
98/K7 **Elk Ridge**, Md,US
91/K4 **Elk River**, Mn,US
75/V17 **El Kroub**, Alg.
75/T15 **El Kseur**, Alg.
85/J3 **Ellamar**, Ak,US
23/G4 **Elland**, Eng,UK
31/F2 **Elle** (riv.), Ger.
84/G2 **Ellef Ringnes** (isl.), Can.
87/R7 **Ellef Ringnes** (isl.), NW,Can
23/E2 **Ellen** (riv.), Eng,UK
91/J4 **Ellendale**, ND,US
88/B2 **Ellensburg**, Wa,US
90/C4 **Ellensburg**, Wa,US
29/H5 **Eller** (riv.), Ger.
31/G4 **Ellerbach** (riv.), Ger.
73/D3 **Ellery** (peak), Austl.
84/J2 **Ellesmere** (isl.), Can.
87/T6 **Ellesmere** (isl.), NW,Can
87/T6 **Ellesmere Island Nat'l Park**, NW,Can
23/F5 **Ellesmere Port**, Eng,UK
30/C2 **Ellezelles**, Belg.
86/F2 **Ellice** (riv.), NW,Can
94/E4 **Ellicott City**, Md,US
98/K7 **Ellicott City**, Md,US
80/D3 **Elliot**, SAfr.
87/H4 **Elliot Lake**, On,Can
89/K2 **Elliot Lake**, On,Can
94/D2 **Elliot Lake**, On,Can
70/E3 **Elliott**, Austl.
97/J2 **Elliott** (peak), Va,US
82/E5 **Ellisras**, SAfr.
70/E6 **Elliston**, Austl.
103/G4 **El Llano**, Pan.
23/H4 **Elloughton**, Eng,UK
29/H5 **Ellrich**, Ger.
83/T **Ellsworth** (mts.), Ant.
93/H3 **Ellsworth**, Ks,US
96/D2 **Ellsworth**, Ks,US
89/N3 **Ellsworth**, Me,US
95/G2 **Ellsworth**, Me,US
94/A2 **Ellsworth**, Wi,US
83/U **Ellsworth Land** (reg.), Ant.
26/F4 **Ellwangen**, Ger.
33/J2 **Ellwangen**, Ger.
37/F4 **Elm**, Swi.
95/S10 **Elma**, NY,US
44/E5 **Elmadağ**, Turk.
50/C2 **Elmadağ**, Turk.
109/B5 **El Maitén**, Arg.
49/A1 **Elmalı**, Turk.
50/B2 **Elmalı**, Turk.
52/A1 **Elmalı**, Turk.
88/E5 **El Malpais Nat'l Mon.**, NM,US
92/F4 **El Malpais Nat'l Mon.**, NM,US
96/B3 **El Malpais Nat'l Mon.**, NM,US
100/B2 **El Marmol**, Mex.
35/L7 **El Masnou**, Sp.
99/P13 **Elm Grove**, Wi,US
99/Q16 **Elmhurst**, Il,US
75/V17 **El Milia**, Alg.
79/E5 **Elmina**, Gha.
89/L3 **Elmira**, NY,US
94/E3 **Elmira**, NY,US
105/B4 **El Misti** (vol.), Peru
106/D7 **El Misti** (vol.), Peru
35/N8 **El Molar**, Sp.
35/L6 **El Montcau** (peak), Sp.
98/B2 **El Monte**, Ca,US
73/C3 **Elmore**, Austl.
92/E4 **El Morro Nat'l Mon.**, NM,US
96/A3 **El Morro Nat'l Mon.**, NM,US
78/C2 **El Mreyyé** (reg.), Mrta.
26/E2 **Elmshorn**, Ger.
29/G1 **Elmshorn**, Ger.
31/G5 **Elmstein**, Ger.
25/G2 **Elmswell**, Eng,UK
100/C3 **El Muerto**, Mex.
99/Q16 **Elmwood Park**, Il,US
99/Q14 **Elmwood Park**, Wi,US
76/D3 **El Mzereb** (well), Mali
100/D4 **El Nayar**, Mex.
32/E5 **Elne**, Fr.
35/G1 **Elne**, Fr.
102/E3 **El Negrito**, Hon.
109/C4 **El Nevado** (peak), Arg.
67/E1 **El Nido**, Phil.
32/A2 **Elorn** (riv.), Fr.
76/G1 **El Oued**, Alg.
72/H8 **Elouera Bushland Rsv.**, Austl.
100/C1 **Eloy**, Az,US
92/E4 **Eloy**, Az,US
36/C1 **Éloyes**, Fr.
101/N8 **El Palmar**, Mex.
102/E3 **El Paraíso**, Hon.
35/N8 **El Pardo**, Sp.
100/D2 **El Paso**, Tx,US
88/E5 **El Paso**, Tx,US
92/F5 **El Paso**, Tx,US
96/B4 **El Paso**, Tx,US
100/D2 **El Pastor**, Mex.
101/E3 **El Pequeño**, Mex.
104/F5 **El Pilar**, Ven.
62/D6 **Elpitiya**, SrL.
93/F5 **El Porvenir**, Mex
96/B4 **El Porvenir**, Mex
101/E3 **El Potosí**, Mex.
102/A1 **El Potosí Nat'l Park**, Mex.
35/G2 **El Prat de Llobregat**, Sp.
35/L7 **El Prat de Llobregat**, Sp.
102/D3 **El Progreso**, Guat.
102/E3 **El Progreso**, Hon.
34/B4 **El Puerto de Santa María**, Sp.
100/D4 **El Quelite**, Mex.
101/E2 **El Remolino**, Mex.
93/H4 **El Reno**, Ok,US
96/D3 **El Reno**, Ok,US
103/F4 **El Roble**, Pan.
104/E5 **El Roque**, Ven.
106/E1 **El Roque**, Ven.
90/F3 **Elrose**, Sk,Can
85/L3 **Elsa**, Yk,Can
86/C2 **Elsa**, Yk,Can
33/J5 **Elsa** (riv.), It.
34/B2 **Elsa** (res.), Sp.
34/C1 **Elsa** (riv.), Sp.
101/F3 **El Sabinal Nat'l Park**, Mex.
100/D3 **El Salado**, Mex.
101/E3 **El Salado**, Mex.
103/D3 **El Salvador**
84/H8 **El Salvador**
103/H1 **El Salvador**, Cuba
101/E3 **El Salvador**, Mex.
100/D2 **El Sauz**, Mex.
29/G2 **Elsdorf**, Ger.
31/F2 **Elsdorf**, Ger.
29/F4 **Else** (riv.), Ger.
104/D3 **El Seibo**, DRep.
29/F2 **Elsfleth**, Ger.
98/C3 **Elsinore** (lake), Ca,US
98/E6 **Elsmere**, De,US
28/C5 **Elst**, Neth.
25/F4 **Elstead**, Eng,UK
101/F4 **El Tajín** (ruins), Mex.
101/M6 **El Tajín** (ruins), Mex.
102/B1 **El Tajín** (ruins), Mex.
106/D2 **El Tama Nat'l Park**, Ven.
75/V17 **El Tarf** (gov.), Alg.
75/W17 **El Tarf**, Alg.
34/B1 **El Teleno** (mtn.), Sp.
101/F3 **El Temascal**, Mex.
101/L7 **El Tepotzteco Nat'l Park**, Mex.
19/P7 **Eltham**, Eng,UK
34/C2 **El Tiemblo**, Sp.
106/F2 **El Tigre**, Ven.
45/H2 **El'ton** (lake), Rus.
98/C3 **El Toro**, Ca,US
98/C3 **El Toro Marine Corps Air Station**, Ca,US
96/B4 **El Trece**, Mex
100/C4 **El Triunfo**, Mex.
100/D3 **El Tule**, Mex.
106/E3 **El Tuparro Nat'l Park**, Col.
26/E3 **Eltville am Rhein**, Ger.
31/H3 **Eltville am Rhein**, Ger.
33/H1 **Eltville am Rhein**, Ger.
62/D4 **Elūrū**, India
20/H4 **Elva**, Est.
42/E4 **Elva**, Est.
103/F4 **El Valle**, Pan.
34/B3 **Elvas**, Port.
103/F4 **El Venado** (isl.), Nic.
20/D3 **Elverum**, Nor.
103/H5 **El Viejo** (peak), Col.
90/D2 **El Viejo** (peak), Col.
102/E3 **El Viejo**, Nic.
104/D4 **El Vínculo**, Ven.
77/P7 **El Wak**, Kenya
90/F3 **Elwell** (lake), Mt,US
94/C3 **Elwood**, In,US
22/E5 **Elwy** (riv.), Wal,UK
25/G2 **Ely**, Eng,UK
91/L4 **Ely**, Mn,US
94/B2 **Ely**, Mn,US
86/E5 **Ely**, Nv,US
88/D4 **Ely**, Nv,US
92/D3 **Ely**, Nv,US
49/F7 **Elyashiv**, Isr.
25/G2 **Ely, Isle of** (phys. reg.), Eng,UK
106/D2 **El Yopal**, Col.
94/D3 **Elyria**, Oh,US
104/E3 **El Yunque** (mtn.), PR
31/H3 **Elz**, Ger.
36/D1 **Elz** (riv.), Ger.
36/E1 **Elzach**, Ger.
31/G3 **Elzbach** (riv.), Ger.
29/G4 **Elze**, Ger.
51/H2 **Emāmshahr**, Iran
53/F1 **Emāmshahr**, Iran
107/H7 **Emas Nat'l Park**, Braz.
45/K3 **Emba** (riv.), Kaz.
45/L2 **Emba**, Kaz.
46/F5 **Emba**, Kaz.
46/F5 **Emba** (riv.), Kaz.
106/F8 **Embarcación**, Arg.
109/D1 **Embarcación**, Arg.
106/D5 **Embira** (riv.), Braz.
108/C1 **Emborcaçao** (res.), Braz.
37/E3 **Embrach**, Swi.
33/G4 **Embrun**, Fr.
29/H2 **Embsen**, Ger.
77/N8 **Embu**, Kenya
26/D2 **Emden**, Ger.
29/E2 **Emden**, Ger.
60/D2 **Emei**, China
60/D2 **Emei** (peak), China
63/H2 **Emei**, China
68/D7 **Emerald**, Austl.
71/H4 **Emerald**, Austl.
72/C3 **Emerald**, Austl.
73/G5 **Emerald**, Austl.
91/J3 **Emerson**, Mb,Can
99/K11 **Emeryville**, Ca,US
44/D5 **Emet**, Turk.
50/B2 **Emet**, Turk.
101/H5 **Emiliano Zapata**, Mex.
102/D2 **Emiliano Zapata**, Mex.
33/J4 **Emilia-Romagna** (reg.), It.
93/K3 **Eminence**, Mo,US
97/F2 **Eminence**, Mo,US
41/H4 **Emine, Nos** (cape), Bul.
44/D5 **Emirdağ**, Turk.
50/B2 **Emirdağ**, Turk.
50/C2 **Emirgazi**, Turk.
81/E2 **Emlembe** (peak), Swaz.
28/D3 **Emlichheim**, Ger.
20/E4 **Emmaboda**, Swe.
98/E5 **Emmaus**, Pa,US
36/D4 **Emme** (riv.), Swi.
26/C2 **Emmeloord**, Neth.
28/C3 **Emmeloord**, Neth.
26/D2 **Emmen**, Neth.
28/D3 **Emmen**, Neth.
37/E3 **Emmenbrücke**, Swi.
33/G2 **Emmendingen**, Ger.
36/D1 **Emmendingen**, Ger.
36/D3 **Emmental** (val.), Swi.
29/G5 **Emmer** (riv.), Ger.
29/E5 **Emmerbach** (riv.), Ger.
28/D5 **Emmerich**, Ger.
90/D5 **Emmett**, Id,US
92/C2 **Emmett**, Id,US
99/G6 **Emmett**, Mi,US
37/E2 **Emmingen-Liptingen**, Ger.
85/F3 **Emmonak**, Ak,US
25/G1 **Emneth**, Eng,UK
100/E2 **Emory** (peak), Tx,US
93/J4 **Emory**, Tx,US
96/E3 **Emory**, Tx,US
36/C5 **Emosson** (lake), Swi.
100/C3 **Empalme**, Mex.
81/E3 **Empangeni**, SAfr.
82/F6 **Empangeni**, SAfr.
109/E2 **Empedrado**, Arg.
89/G4 **Emporia**, Ks,US
93/H3 **Emporia**, Ks,US
96/D2 **Emporia**, Ks,US
94/E4 **Emporia**, Va,US
97/J2 **Emporia**, Va,US
51/J3 **'Emrānī**, Iran
53/G2 **'Emrānī**, Iran
29/E4 **Emsbüren**, Ger.
26/D2 **Emsdetten**, Ger.
29/E4 **Emsdetten**, Ger.
26/D2 **Ems** (Eems) (riv.), Ger., Neth.
28/D2 **Ems** (Eems) (riv.), Ger., Neth.
29/E2 **Ems-Jade** (can.), Ger.
26/D2 **Emsland** (reg.), Ger.
29/E3 **Emsland** (reg.), Ger.
29/F3 **Emstek**, Ger.
20/H4 **Emumägi** (hill), Est.
72/C3 **Emu Park**, Austl.
55/J1 **Emur** (riv.), China
22/B3 **Emyvale**, Ire.
57/E3 **Ena**, Japan
90/G5 **Encampment**, Wy,US
100/B2 **Encantada, Cerro de la** (mtn.), Mex.
100/B3 **Encantado, Cerro** (mt.), Mex.
100/E4 **Encarnación**, Mex.
109/E2 **Encarnación**, Par.
78/E5 **Enchi**, Gha.
92/C4 **Encinitas**, Ca,US
103/H4 **Encontrados**, Ven.
73/A2 **Encounter** (bay), Austl.
108/A4 **Encruzilhada do Sul**, Braz.
27/L4 **Encs**, Hun.
40/E1 **Encs**, Hun.
67/F5 **Ende**, Indo.
72/B1 **Endeavour River Nat'l Park**, Austl.
69/H5 **Enderbury** (atoll), Kiri.
90/D3 **Enderby**, BC,Can.
83/D **Enderby Land** (reg.), Ant.
91/J4 **Enderlin**, ND,US
94/E3 **Endicott**, NY,US
36/D1 **Endingen**, Ger.
106/D6 **Ene** (riv.), Peru
68/F3 **Enewetak** (atoll), Mrsh.
39/K2 **Enez**, Turk.
41/H5 **Enez**, Turk.
19/N7 **Enfield**, Eng,UK
19/N7 **Enfield** (bor.), Eng,UK
48/M8 **Engaño** (cape), Phil.
37/E4 **Engelberg**, Swi.
19/H3 **Engel's**, Rus.
45/H2 **Engel's**, Rus.
46/E4 **Engel's**, Rus.
31/G2 **Engelskirchen**, Ger.
28/D2 **Engelsmanplaat** (isl.), Neth.
37/E2 **Engen**, Ger.
108/D1 **Engenheiro Navarro**, Braz.
29/F4 **Enger**, Ger.
33/L2 **Engerwitzdorf**, Aus.
66/B5 **Enggano** (isl.), Indo.
52/C5 **Enghershatu** (peak), Eth.
77/N4 **Enghershatu** (peak), Eth.
30/D2 **Enghien**, Belg.
37/F4 **Engi**, Swi.
24/D2 **England**, UK
18/C3 **England**, UK
30/C3 **Englefontaine**, Fr.
94/E2 **Englehart**, On,Can.
98/G5 **Englewood**, NJ,US
25/E6 **English** (chan.)
83/V **English** (coast), Ant.
91/K3 **English** (riv.), On,Can.
18/C4 **English** (chan.), Eur.
32/B2 **English** (chan.)
85/H4 **English Bay**, Ak,US
62/E3 **English Bāzār**, India
35/E3 **Énguera**, Sp.
49/G6 **'En Ḩarod**, Isr.
89/G4 **Enid**, Ok,US
93/H3 **Enid**, Ok,US
96/D2 **Enid**, Ok,US
31/G5 **Enkenbach-Alsenborn**, Ger.
26/C2 **Enkhuizen**, Neth.
28/C3 **Enkhuizen**, Neth.
31/G4 **Enkirch**, Ger.
20/F4 **Enköping**, Swe.
42/C4 **Enköping**, Swe.
38/D4 **Enna**, It.
77/K4 **Ennedi** (plat.), Chad
29/E6 **Ennepe** (riv.), Ger.
29/E6 **Ennepetal**, Ger.
19/S9 **Ennery**, Fr.
29/F5 **Enningerloh**, Ger.
21/A4 **Ennis**, Ire.
90/F4 **Ennis**, Mt,US
93/H4 **Ennis**, Tx,US
96/D3 **Ennis**, Tx,US
22/B5 **Enniskerry**, Ire.
21/B3 **Enniskillen**, NI,UK
21/H7 **Ennistimon**, Ire.
27/H4 **Enns**, Aus.
27/H5 **Enns** (riv.), Aus.
33/L3 **Enns** (riv.), Aus.
40/A2 **Enns** (riv.), Aus.
40/B1 **Enns**, Aus.
72/E6 **Enoggera** (res.), Austl.
20/G1 **Enontekiö**, Fin.
42/D1 **Enontekiö**, Fin.
61/G4 **Enping**, China
63/K3 **Enping**, China
103/J2 **Enriquillo**, DRep.
104/D3 **Enriquillo**, DRep.
18/D3 **Enschede**, Neth.
26/D2 **Enschede**, Neth.
28/D4 **Enschede**, Neth.
29/E6 **Ense**, Ger.
100/A2 **Ensenada**, Mex.
88/C5 **Ensenada**, Mex.
92/C5 **Ensenada**, Mex
59/B5 **Enshi**, China
61/F2 **Enshi**, China
36/D2 **Ensisheim**, Fr.
77/M7 **Entebbe**, Ugan.
26/G4 **Entenbühl** (peak), Ger.
33/K2 **Entenbühl** (peak), Ger.
89/J5 **Enterprise**, Al,US
97/G4 **Enterprise**, Al,US
88/C2 **Enterprise**, Or,US
36/E4 **Entlebuch**, Swi.
73/D2 **Entrance, The**, Austl.
102/E3 **Entre Ríos, Cordillera** (range), Hon.
34/A3 **Entroncamento**, Port.
36/D1 **Entzheim**, Fr.
76/G6 **Enugu**, Nga.
79/G5 **Enugu**, Nga.
99/D3 **Enumclaw**, Wa,US
57/N10 **Enushū** (sea), Japan
30/A4 **Envermeu**, Fr.
54/F5 **Enyang**, China
26/E4 **Enz** (riv.), Ger.
33/H2 **Enz** (riv.), Ger.
57/F3 **Enzan**, Japan
31/F4 **Enzbach** (riv.), Ger.
36/C4 **Epalinges**, Swi.
39/J5 **Epáno Arkhánai**, Gre.
39/H2 **Epanomí**, Gre.
28/C4 **Epe**, Neth.
30/C3 **Epehy**, Fr.
26/B4 **Épernay**, Fr.
30/C5 **Épernay**, Fr.
32/E2 **Épernay**, Fr.
30/A6 **Épernon**, Fr.
36/D1 **Epfig**, Fr.
68/F6 **Epi** (isl.), Van.
39/H4 **Epidaurus** (ruins), Gre.
26/D4 **Épinal**, Fr.
33/G2 **Épinal**, Fr.
36/C1 **Épinal**, Fr.
19/S10 **Épinay-sur-Orge**, Fr.
19/S10 **Épinay-sur-Seine**, Fr.
39/G3 **Epirus** (reg.), Gre.
49/C2 **Episkopi**, Cyp.
31/F5 **Eppelborn**, Ger.
31/G5 **Eppenbrunn**, Ger.
30/C4 **Eppeville**, Fr.
72/H8 **Epping**, Austl.
19/P6 **Epping**, Eng,UK
25/G3 **Epping**, Eng,UK
19/P7 **Epping Forest** (plain), Eng,UK
72/B3 **Epping Forest Nat'l Park**, Austl.
37/G1 **Eppishausen**, Ger.
19/N8 **Epsom**, Eng,UK
25/F4 **Epsom and Ewell**, Eng,UK
30/A4 **Epte** (riv.), Fr.
23/H4 **Epworth**, Eng,UK
74/C4 **Equatorial Guinea**
76/G7 **Equatorial Guinea**
25/H5 **Équihen Plage**, Fr.
30/A2 **Équihen-Plage**, Fr.
60/C3 **Er** (lake), China
63/H2 **Er** (lake), China
38/E2 **Eraclea** (ruins), It.
38/C4 **Eraclea Minoa** (ruins), It.
19/S9 **Éragny**, Fr.
102/D3 **Erandique**, Hon.
62/D6 **Eravur**, SrL.
65/B3 **Erawan Nat'l Park**, Thai.
33/H4 **Erba**, It.
44/F4 **Erbaa**, Turk.
50/D1 **Erbaa**, Turk.
26/D4 **Erbeskopf** (peak), Ger.
33/G2 **Erbeskopf** (peak), Ger.
51/E2 **Erçek**, Turk.
51/E2 **Erçek** (lake), Turk.
51/E2 **Erciş**, Turk.
50/C2 **Erciyes** (peak), Turk.
30/C3 **Erclin** (riv.), Fr.
40/D2 **Érd**, Hun.
55/K3 **Erdao** (riv.), China
58/E1 **Erdao** (riv.), China
41/H5 **Erdek**, Turk.
41/H5 **Erdek** (gulf), Turk.
44/C4 **Erdek**, Turk.
50/A1 **Erdek**, Turk.
49/D1 **Erdemli**, Turk.
50/C2 **Erdemli**, Turk.
54/G3 **Erdene**, Mong.
54/E2 **Erdenedalay**, Mong.
47/L5 **Erdenet**, Mong.
54/E2 **Erdenet**, Mong.
77/K4 **Erdi-Ma** (plat.), Chad
26/F4 **Erding**, Ger.
33/J2 **Erding**, Ger.
32/C3 **Erdre** (riv.), Fr.
37/H1 **Erdweg**, Ger.
83/M **Erebus** (vol.), Ant.
108/A3 **Erechim**, Braz.
109/F2 **Erechim**, Braz.
54/G2 **Ereen Davaanī** (mts.), Mong.
41/K5 **Ereğli**, Turk.
44/D4 **Ereğli**, Turk.
50/B1 **Ereğli**, Turk.
50/C2 **Ereğli**, Turk.
47/M5 **Erenhot**, China
54/G3 **Erenhot**, China
41/K5 **Erenler**, Turk.
50/B1 **Erenler**, Turk.
107/G4 **Erepecu** (lake), Braz.
34/C2 **Eresma** (riv.), Sp.
39/H3 **Erétria**, Gre.
31/E3 **Érezée**, Belg.
76/E1 **Erfoud**, Mor.
26/D3 **Erft** (riv.), Ger.
28/D6 **Erft** (riv.), Ger.
31/F1 **Erft** (riv.), Ger.
31/F2 **Erftstadt**, Ger.
26/F3 **Erfurt**, Ger.
50/D2 **Ergani**, Turk.
76/D3 **'Erg Chech** (des.), Afr.
76/H4 **'Erg du Ténéré** (des.), Niger
41/H5 **Ergene Nehri** (riv.), Turk.
76/D2 **'Erg Iguidi** (des.), Afr.
20/H4 **Ērgļi**, Lat.
42/E4 **Ērgļi**, Lat.
76/J5 **Erguig** (riv.), Chad
55/H1 **Ergun** (riv.), China, Rus.
55/J1 **Ergun Youqi**, China
47/N4 **Ergun Zuoqi**, China
55/J1 **Ergun Zuoqi**, China
52/C5 **Eriba**, Sudan
38/C3 **Erice**, It.
34/A3 **Ericeira**, Port.
35/P10 **Ericeira**, Port.
90/D3 **Erickson**, Can.
91/J3 **Erickson**, Can.
95/R10 **Erie** (lake), On,Can.
99/G8 **Erie** (lake), Can., US
87/H4 **Erie** (lake), Can.,US
95/R10 **Erie** (lake), NY,US
95/S10 **Erie** (co.), NY,US
95/S9 **Erie** (can.), NY,US
87/H4 **Erie**, Pa,US
89/K3 **Erie**, Pa,US
94/D3 **Erie**, Pa,US
84/J5 **Erie** (lake), US, Can
89/K3 **Erie** (lake), US, Can
94/D3 **Erie** (lake), US, Can
77/Q5 **Erigabo**, Som.
91/J3 **Eriksdale**, Mb,Can.
68/F4 **Erikub** (atoll), Mrsh
39/G4 **Erímanthos** (peak), Gre.
47/Q5 **Erimo-misaki** (cape Japan
55/N3 **Erimo-misaki** (cape Japan
39/H3 **Erithraí**, Gre.
52/C5 **Eritrea** (reg.), Eth.
74/F3 **Eritrea** (reg.), Eth.
77/N4 **Eritrea** (reg.), Eth.
28/D6 **Erkelenz**, Ger.
31/F1 **Erkelenz**, Ger.
37/G1 **Erkheim**, Ger.
27/G2 **Erkner**, Ger.
28/D6 **Erkrath**, Ger.
31/F1 **Erkrath**, Ger.
36/D3 **Erlach**, Swi.
99/B2 **Erlands Point-Kitsa Lake**, Wa,US
60/D2 **Erlang** (peak), Chin
26/F4 **Erlangen**, Ger.
33/J2 **Erlangen**, Ger.
36/D4 **Erlenbach**, Swi.
36/D3 **Erlinsbach**, Swi.
59/F2 **Erlongshan** (res.), China
24/C6 **Erme** (riv.), Eng,UK
28/C4 **Ermelo**, Neth.
80/Q13 **Ermelo**, SAfr.
81/E2 **Ermelo**, SAfr.
49/C1 **Ermenek**, Turk.
49/C1 **Ermenek** (riv.), Turk
50/C2 **Ermenek**, Turk.
19/U9 **Ermenonville**, Fr.
39/H4 **Ermióni**, Gre.
19/S10 **Ermont**, Fr.
39/J4 **Ermoúpolis**, Gre.
37/F1 **Erms** (riv.), Ger.
31/H2 **Erndtebrück**, Ger.
32/C2 **Ernée**, Fr.
32/C2 **Ernée** (riv.), Fr.
21/B3 **Erne, Lower** (lake), NI,UK
62/C5 **Erode**, India
64/F3 **Erode**, India
37/G1 **Erolzheim**, Ger.
73/D2 **Erowal Bay**, Austl.
31/G2 **Erpel**, Ger.
30/D3 **Erquelinnes**, Belg.
76/E1 **Er Rachidīa**, Mor.
75/M13 **Er Rif** (mts.), Mor.
76/D1 **Er Rif** (mts.), Mor.
21/A3 **Errigal** (mtn.), Ire.
18/C3 **Erris Head** (pt.), Ire
21/G6 **Erris Head** (pt.), Ire
68/F6 **Erromango** (isl.), Va
37/F4 **Err, Piz d'** (peak), S
29/H4 **Erse** (riv.), Ger.
36/D1 **Erstein**, Fr.
37/E4 **Erstfeld**, Swi.
37/F1 **Ertingen**, Ger.
54/B2 **Ertix** (riv.), China
28/A6 **Ertvelde**, Belg.
50/E2 **Eruh**, Turk.
52/D1 **Eruh**, Turk.
108/B3 **Erval d'oeste**, Braz
94/D4 **Erwin**, Tn,US
29/F5 **Erwitte**, Ger.
60/C3 **Eryuan**, China
63/G2 **Eryuan**, China
26/G3 **Erzegebirge** (Krušn Hory) (mts.), Czh., G
39/F2 **Erzen** (riv.), Alb.
40/D5 **Erzen** (riv.), Alb.
33/K1 **Erzgebirge** (Krušné Hory) (mts.), Czh., G
46/K4 **Erzin**, Rus.
54/D1 **Erzin**, Rus.
44/F5 **Erzincan**, Turk.
44/F5 **Erzincan** (prov.), Tu
46/D6 **Erzincan**, Turk.
50/D2 **Erzincan**, Turk.
50/D2 **Erzincan** (prov.), Tu
45/G4 **Erzurum** (prov.), Tu
45/G5 **Erzurum**, Turk.
46/E6 **Erzurum**, Turk.
50/E1 **Erzurum** (prov.), Tu
50/E2 **Erzurum**, Turk.
68/D5 **Esa'ala**, PNG
82/D1 **Esambo**, Zaire
55/N3 **Esashi**, Japan
44/F4 **Esbiye**, Turk.
50/D1 **Esbiye**, Turk.
18/D3 **Esbjerg**, Den.
20/D5 **Esbjerg**, Den.
26/E1 **Esbjerg**, Den.
46/A4 **Esbjerg**, Den.
19/U10 **Esbly**, Fr.
30/B6 **Esbly**, Fr.
20/H3 **Esbo** (Espoo), Fin.
42/E3 **Esbo** (Espoo), Fin.
92/E3 **Escalante** (riv.), Ut,
100/D3 **Escalón**, Mex.
96/B5 **Escalón**, Mex
34/C2 **Escalona**, Sp.
87/H4 **Escanaba**, Mi,US
89/J2 **Escanaba**, Mi,US
91/M4 **Escanaba**, Mi,US
94/C2 **Escanaba**, Mi,US
30/C3 **Escaudain**, Fr.
26/B3 **Escaut** (riv.), Belg.,
30/C3 **Escaut** (riv.), Belg.,
32/E1 **Escaut** (riv.), Fr., Be
31/E6 **Esch** (riv.), Fr.
37/E1 **Eschach** (riv.), Ger.
37/G2 **Eschach** (riv.), Ger.
36/D1 **Eschau**, Fr.
29/H3 **Eschede**, Ger.
37/F3 **Eschen**, Lcht.
29/G5 **Eschershausen**, Ge

0/B5 Esches (riv.), Fr.
6/D4 Escholzmatt, Swi.
6/C4 Esch-sur-Alzette, Lux.
1/E5 Esch-sur-Alzette, Lux.
2/F2 Esch-sur-Alzette, Lux.
1/E4 Esch-sur-Sure, Lux.
9/H6 Eschwege, Ger.
6/D3 Eschweiler, Ger.
1/F2 Eschweiler, Ger.
8/C5 Escondido, Ca,US
2/C4 Escondido, Ca,US
0/D4 Escuinapa, Mex.
2/D3 Escuintla, Guat.
2/C3 Escuintla, Mex.
9/G6 Esdraelon, Plain of (plain), Isr.
6/H7 Eséka, Camr.
0/D2 Esence (peak), Turk.
9/E1 Esens, Ger.
5/F1 Esera (riv.), Sp.
6/F6 Eşfahān, Iran
8/E6 Eşfahān, Iran
1/G3 Eşfahān, Iran
1/H3 Eşfahān (gov.), Iran
2/F2 Eşfahān, Iran
3/H3 Esfandak, Iran
3/G1 Esfarāyen, Iran
2/E1 Esfarvarīn, Iran
4/C1 Esgair Ddu (mtn.), UK
3/G2 Esh, Eng,UK
0/D3 Eshan Yizu Zizhixian, China
3/H3 Eshan Yizu Zizhixian, China
9/M7 Esher, Eng,UK
5/F4 Esher, Eng,UK
2/D2 Eshimba, Zaire
1/E3 Eshowe, SAfr.
2/F6 Eshowe, SAfr.
3/G2 Esh Winning, Eng,UK
7/G6 Esine, It.
3/E2 Esk (riv.), Eng,UK
3/H3 Esk (riv.), Eng,UK
3/F1 Eskdale (val.), Sc,UK
0/Q6 Eskifjördhur, Ice.
0/C2 Eskil, Turk.
0/F4 Eskilstuna, Swe.
2/C4 Eskilstuna, Swe.
0/D2 Eskimalatya, Turk.
5/M2 Eskimo (lakes), NW,Can.
6/C2 Eskimo (lakes), NW,Can.
6/G2 Eskimo Point, NW,Can.
4/E4 Eskipazar, Turk.
0/C1 Eskipazar, Turk.
4/D5 Eskişehir, Turk.
4/D5 Eskişehir (prov.), Turk.
0/B2 Eskişehir, Turk.
0/B2 Eskişehir (prov.), Turk.
4/C1 Esla (riv.), Sp.
1/F3 Eslāmābād, Iran
2/E2 Eslāmābād, Iran
9/F6 Eslohe, Ger.
0/B2 Eşme, Turk.
3/G1 Esmeralda, Cuba
6/C3 Esmeraldas, Ecu.
5/C3 Esneux, Belg.
6/C3 Esneux, Belg.
1/E2 Esneux, Belg.
2/E4 Espalion, Fr.
9/K2 Espanola, On,Can.
0/K2 Espanola, On,Can.
8/E4 Española, NM,US
7/F4 Española, NM,US
6/B3 Española, NM,US
5/K6 Esparreguera, Sp.
2/E3 Esparta, Hon.
9/K9 Esparto, Ca,US
4/C4 Espejo, Sp.
6/E2 Espelkamp, Ger.
9/F4 Espelkamp, Ger.
0/C6 Esperance, Austl.
6/B3 Esperanza (inlet), BC,Can.
4/D3 Esperanza, DRep.
0/C3 Esperanza, Mex.
1/M8 Esperanza, Mex.
0/D5 Esperanza, Peru
4/A3 Espichel (cape), Port.
5/P11 Espichel (cape), Port.
6/D3 Espinal, Col.
1/M6 Espinal, Mex.
7/K7 Espinhaço (mts.), Braz.
8/D1 Espinhaço (range), Braz.
4/A2 Espinho, Port.
7/K6 Espinosa, Braz.
8/D1 Espirito Santo (state), Braz.
0/C3 Espíritu Santo (isl.), Mex.
2/E2 Espíritu Santo (bay), Mex.
8/F6 Espiritu Santo (isl.), Van.
1/H4 Espita, Mex.
2/D1 Espita, Mex.
7/L6 Esplanada, Braz.
5/E2 Espluga de Francolí, Sp.
5/L7 Espluges, Sp.
0/H3 Espoo (Esbo), Fin.
2/E3 Espoo (Esbo), Fin.
4/A2 Esposende, Port.
2/F5 Espungabera, Moz.
9/B5 Esquel, Arg.
9/E3 Esquina, Arg.
6/D1 Essaouira, Mor.
9/G5 Esse (riv.), Ger.
8/B6 Essen, Belg.
8/D3 Essen, Ger.
6/D3 Essen, Ger.
6/E3 Essen, Ger.
9/E3 Essen, Ger.
5/E3 Essendon, Austl.
1/H4 Essenheim, Ger.
5/D2 Essequibo (riv.), Guy.
106/G2 Essequibo (riv.), Guy.
99/G7 Essex, On,Can.
98/F5 Essex (co.), NJ,US
99/G7 Essex (co.), On,Can.
19/P6 Essex (co.), Eng,UK
25/G3 Essex (co.), Eng,UK
98/K7 Essex, Md,US
26/E4 Esslingen, Ger.
33/H2 Esslingen, Ger.
30/C5 Essômes-sur-Marne, Fr.
19/S11 Essonne (dept.), Fr.
19/T11 Essonne (riv.), Fr.
30/B6 Essonne (dept.), Fr.
32/E2 Essonne (riv.), Fr.
36/C1 Est (can.), Fr.
100/B1 Estación Coatiuila, Mex.
109/D7 Estados (isl.), Arg.
51/H4 Eşţahbān, Iran
52/F3 Eşţahbān, Iran
30/B2 Estaires, Fr.
107/L6 Estância, Braz.
102/C2 Estancia Macaya, Mex.
101/F4 Estancia Tamuín, Mex.
102/B1 Estancia Tamuín, Mex.
32/D5 Estats, Pico de (peak), Sp.
35/F1 Estats, Pico de (peak), Sp.
36/C4 Estavayer-le-Lac, Swi.
31/E5 Est, Canal de l' (can.), Fr.
81/E3 Estcourt, SAfr.
26/E2 Este (riv.), Ger.
29/G2 Este (riv.), Ger.
33/J4 Este, It.
108/B4 Esteio, Braz.
102/E3 Estelí, Nic.
32/B5 Estella, Sp.
34/D1 Estella, Sp.
98/C3 Estelle (mtn.), Ca,US
104/D3 Este Nat'l Park, DRep.
34/C4 Estepa, Sp.
34/C4 Estepona, Sp.
85/J3 Ester, Ak,US
86/F3 Esterhazy, Sk,Can.
91/H3 Esterhazy, Sk,Can.
78/G7 Esterias (cape), Gabon
30/C6 Esternay, Fr.
33/G5 Estéron (riv.), Fr.
29/E3 Esterwegen, Ger.
86/F4 Estevan, Sk,Can.
88/F2 Estevan, Sk,Can.
91/H3 Estevan, Sk,Can.
30/D3 Estinnes-Au-Mont, Belg.
86/F3 Eston, Sk,Can.
90/F3 Eston, Sk,Can.
23/G2 Eston, Eng,UK
18/F3 Estonia
20/H4 Estonia
42/E4 Estonia
46/C4 Estonia
34/A3 Estoril, Port.
35/P10 Estoril, Port.
99/F8 Estral Beach, Mi,US
30/B5 Estrées-Saint-Denis, Fr.
34/A3 Estrela (range), Port.
34/A3 Estrela, Serra da (range), Port.
34/B2 Estrela, Serra da (mtn.), Port.
100/B2 Estrella, Punta (pt.), Mex.
34/B3 Estremadura (aut. comm.), Sp.
34/B3 Estremoz, Port.
107/J5 Estrondo (mts.), Braz.
27/K5 Esztergom, Hun.
40/D2 Esztergom, Hun.
31/E5 Etain, Fr.
68/E4 Etal (atoll), Micr.
31/E4 Etalle, Belg.
25/H5 Etaples, Fr.
30/A2 Etaples, Fr.
32/D1 Etaples, Fr.
62/C2 Etāwah, India
100/C3 Etchojoa, Mex.
91/H3 Ethelbert, Mb,Can.
53/C6 Ethiopia
74/F4 Ethiopia
77/N5 Ethiopia
77/N6 Ethiopian (plat.), Eth.
57/M9 Eti (riv.), Japan
19/T11 Etiolles, Fr.
36/C1 Etival-Clairefontaine, Fr.
38/D4 Etna, Monte (Mount Etna) (vol.), It.
18/E5 Etna, Mount (vol.), It.
38/D4 Etna, Mount (Monte Etna) (vol.), It.
95/Q8 Etobicoke, On,Can.
85/E3 Etolin (str.), Ak,US
47/Q5 Etorofu (isl.), Rus.
48/P5 Etorofu (isl.), Rus.
55/P2 Etorofu (isl.), Rus.
82/C4 Etosha Nat'l Park, Namb.
82/C4 Etosha Pan (salt pan), Namb.
30/A5 Étrépagny, Fr.
39/J1 Etropole, Bul.
41/G4 Etropole, Bul.
36/D6 Etroubles, It.
37/G4 Etsch (Adige) (riv.), It.
57/F2 Etsu-Joshin Kogen Nat'l Park, Japan
49/F7 Et Taiyiba, Isr.
26/D4 Ettelbruck, Lux.
31/F4 Ettelbruck, Lux.
32/G2 Ettelbruck, Lux.
36/D1 Ettenheim, Ger.
28/B5 Etten-Leur, Neth.
30/D2 Etterbeek, Belg.
49/F7 Et Tīra, Isr.
26/E4 Ettlingen, Ger.
33/H2 Ettlingen, Ger.
23/E1 Ettrick Pen (mtn.), Sc,UK
37/G1 Ettringen, Ger.
30/A3 Eu, Fr.
32/D1 Eu, Fr.
69/H7 Eua (isl.), Tonga
72/B2 Eubenangee Swamp Nat'l Park, Austl.
89/K3 Euclid, Oh,US
94/D3 Euclid, Oh,US
71/H7 Eucumbene (lake), Austl.
93/K4 Eudora, Ar,US
97/F3 Eudora, Ar,US
73/A2 Eudunda, Austl.
89/J5 Eufaula, Al,US
97/G4 Eufaula, Al,US
89/G4 Eufaula (lake), Ok,US
93/J4 Eufaula, Ok,US
96/E3 Eufaula, Ok,US
86/D4 Eugene, Or,US
88/B3 Eugene, Or,US
90/C4 Eugene, Or,US
100/B3 Eugenia, Punta (pt.), Mex.
84/F7 Eugenia, Punta (pt.), Mex.
73/D2 Eugowra, Austl.
34/B1 Eume (lake), Sp.
72/C3 Eungella Nat'l Park, Austl.
93/J5 Eunice, La,US
96/E4 Eunice, La,US
93/G4 Eunice, NM,US
96/C3 Eunice, NM,US
31/F2 Eupen, Belg.
48/D6 Euphrates (riv.), Asia
51/F4 Euphrates (riv.), Asia
52/D2 Euphrates (riv.), Asia
77/Q1 Euphrates (riv.), Asia
30/A5 Eure (dept.), Fr.
30/A5 Eure (riv.), Fr.
32/D2 Eure (riv.), Fr.
30/A6 Eure-et-Loir (dept.), Fr.
87/S6 Eureka, NW,Can.
87/S7 Eureka (sound), NW,Can.
86/D4 Eureka, Ca,US
88/B3 Eureka, Ca,US
90/B5 Eureka, Ca,US
92/A2 Eureka, Ca,US
90/E3 Eureka, Mt,US
92/D3 Eureka, Nv,US
91/J4 Eureka, SD,US
73/C3 Euroa, Austl.
30/B6 Eurodisney, Fr.
36/C1 Euron (riv.), Fr.
75/M12 Europa (pt.), Gib.
74/F7 Europa (isl.), Reun.
82/G5 Europa (isl.), Reun.
37/H3 Europabrücke, Aus.
16/J3 Europe
18/* Europe
28/B5 Europoort, Neth.
26/D3 Euskirchen, Ger.
31/F2 Euskirchen, Ger.
33/G1 Euskirchen, Ger.
97/H4 Eustis, Fl,US
73/B2 Euston, Austl.
26/F1 Eutin, Ger.
82/F3 Eutini, Malw.
90/B2 Eutsuk (lake), BC,Can
31/E6 Euville, Fr.
23/F4 Euxton, Eng,UK
94/E1 Évain, Qu,Can.
80/Q13 Evander, SAfr.
87/H2 Evans (str.), NW,Can.
94/E1 Evans (lake), Qu,Can.
84/G6 Evans (mt.), US
93/F2 Evans, Co,US
93/F3 Evans (peak), Co,US
73/E1 Evans Head, Austl.
91/M5 Evanston, Il,US
93/L2 Evanston, Il,US
94/C3 Evanston, Il,US
99/Q15 Evanston, Il,US
88/D3 Evanston, Wy,US
90/F5 Evanston, Wy,US
92/E2 Evanston, Wy,US
84/J6 Evansville, US
89/J4 Evansville, In,US
94/C4 Evansville, In,US
97/G2 Evansville, In,US
93/F2 Evansville, Wy,US
90/E5 Evaporation (basin), Ut,US
94/C3 Evart, Mi,US
80/D2 Evaton, SAfr.
80/P13 Evaton, SAfr.
51/H5 Evaz, Iran
52/F3 Evaz, Iran
91/K4 Eveleth, Mn,US
94/A2 Eveleth, Mn,US
47/L3 Evenki Aut. Okr., Rus.
25/E3 Evenlode (riv.), Eng,UK
20/F1 Evenskjer, Nor.
42/C1 Evenskjer, Nor.
49/F7 Even Yehuda, Isr.
70/F6 Everard (lake), Austl.
73/D3 Everard (cape), Austl.
24/D4 Evercreech, Eng,UK
48/H7 Everest, Mount (mtn.), China, Nepal
62/E2 Everest, Mount (mtn.), China, Nepal
86/D4 Everett, Wa,US
88/B2 Everett, Wa,US
90/C4 Everett, Wa,US
99/C2 Everett, Wa,US
28/A6 Evergem, Belg.
30/C1 Evergem, Belg.
104/A1 Everglades Nat'l Park, Fl,US
89/K6 Everglades Nat'l Park, Fl,US
97/H5 Everglades Nat'l Park, Fl,US
104/A1 Everglades, The (swamp), Fl,US
97/G4 Evergreen, Al,US
99/Q16 Evergreen Park, Il,US
25/F3 Eversholt, Eng,UK
29/E5 Everswinkel, Ger.
25/E2 Evesham, Eng,UK
36/C5 Évian-les-Bains, Fr.
39/G3 Évinos (riv.), Gre.
36/D5 Evolène, Swi.
18/C5 Évora, Port.
34/A3 Évora (dist.), Port.
34/B3 Évora, Port.
30/A5 Évreux, Fr.
32/D2 Évreux, Fr.
32/C2 Évron, Fr.
39/H4 Evrótas (riv.), Gre.
19/T11 Évry, Fr.
30/B6 Évry, Fr.
32/E2 Évry, Fr.
39/H3 Évvoia (gulf), Gre.
39/H3 Évvoia (isl.), Gre.
44/B5 Évvoia (gulf), Gre.
44/B5 Évvoia (isl.), Gre.
39/H3 Evxinoúpolis, Gre.
88/V13 Ewa, Hi,US
88/V13 Ewa Beach, Hi,US
103/G2 Ewarton, Jam.
19/N7 Ewell, Eng,UK
55/H2 Ewenkizu Zizhiqi, China
39/H2 Exaplátanos, Gre.
93/J3 Excelsior Springs, Mo,US
96/E2 Excelsior Springs, Mo,US
85/L4 Excursion Inlet, Ak,US
24/C5 Exe (riv.), Eng,UK
18/C3 Exeter, Eng,UK
24/C5 Exeter, Eng,UK
32/B1 Exeter, Eng,UK
95/G3 Exeter, NH,US
43/X9 Exhibition of Economic Achievements, Rus.
36/C3 Exincourt, Fr.
24/C5 Exminster, Eng,UK
24/C4 Exmoor (upland), Eng,UK
24/C4 Exmoor Nat'l Park, Eng,UK
94/F5 Exmore, Va,US
97/K2 Exmore, Va,US
68/A7 Exmouth, Austl.
70/A4 Exmouth, Austl.
70/A4 Exmouth (gulf), Austl.
24/C5 Exmouth, Eng,UK
32/B1 Exmouth, Eng,UK
87/L4 Exploits (riv.), Nf,Can.
104/B1 Exuma (sound), Bahm.
37/F1 Eyach (riv.), Ger.
85/J3 Eyak, Ak,US
23/G5 Eyam, Eng,UK
82/F1 Eyasi (lake), Tanz.
25/F1 Eye (brook), Eng,UK
25/H2 Eye, Eng,UK
32/F5 Eyguières, Fr.
35/H1 Eyguières, Fr.
49/G8 Eyn Hemed Nat'l Park, Isr.
19/P7 Eynsford, Eng,UK
25/G4 Eynsford, Eng,UK
70/F6 Eyre (pen.), Austl.
83/C7 Eyre (lake), Austl.
70/F5 Eyre North (lake), Austl.
70/F5 Eyre South (lake), Austl.
51/M6 Eyüp, Turk.
51/M6 Eyüp Mosque, Turk.
19/T9 Ézanville, Fr.
102/B1 Ezequiel Montes, Mex.
39/K3 Ezine, Turk.
44/C5 Ezine, Turk.
50/A2 Ezine, Turk.
30/A6 Ézy-sur-Eure, Fr.
76/H3 Ezzane (well), Alg.

F

69/L6 Faaa, FrPol.
69/X15 Faaa, FrPol.
100/D2 Fabens, Tx,US
93/F5 Fabens, Tx,US
96/B4 Fabens, Tx,US
34/B1 Fabero, Sp.
26/F1 Fåborg, Den.
33/K5 Fabriano, It.
38/C1 Fabriano, It.
106/D3 Facatativá, Col.
30/C2 Faches-Thumesnil, Fr.
76/H4 Fachi, Niger
77/K4 Fada, Chad
76/F5 Fada-N'Gourma, Burk.
79/F3 Fada-N'Gourma, Burk.
33/J4 Faenza, It.
77/J6 Fafa (riv.), CAfr.
34/A2 Fafe, Port.
77/P6 Fafen Shet' (riv.), Eth.
41/G3 Făgăraş, Rom.
44/C3 Făgăraş, Rom.
20/E4 Fagersta, Swe.
42/B4 Fagersta, Swe.
30/D6 Fagnières, Fr.
76/D4 Faguibine (lake), Mali
78/D2 Faguibine (lake), Mali
76/F1 Fahl (well), Alg.
37/H1 Fahrenzhausen, Ger.
35/S12 Faial (isl.), Azor.
33/H3 Faido, Swi.
37/E5 Faido, Swi.
23/F4 Failsworth, Eng,UK
31/E6 Fains-Véel, Fr.
84/C3 Fairbanks, US
85/J3 Fairbanks, Ak,US
99/J11 Fairfax, Ca,US
98/J8 Fairfax, Va,US
98/J8 Fairfax (co.), Va,US
99/C3 Fairfax, Wa,US
72/G8 Fairfield, Austl.
92/B3 Fairfield, Ca,US
99/K10 Fairfield, Ca,US
98/G4 Fairfield, Ct,US
90/F4 Fairfield, Mt,US
94/C4 Fairfield, Oh,US
97/G2 Fairfield, Oh,US
101/F2 Fairfield, Tx,US
93/H5 Fairfield, Tx,US
96/D4 Fairfield, Tx,US
25/E3 Fairford, Eng,UK
99/G6 Fair Haven, Mi,US
95/F3 Fair Haven, Vt,US
22/B1 Fair Head (pt.), NI,UK
98/K7 Fairland, Md,US
98/F5 Fair Lawn, NJ,US
25/G5 Fairlight, Eng,UK
86/G4 Fairmont, Mn,US
89/H3 Fairmont, Mn,US
91/K5 Fairmont, Mn,US
93/J2 Fairmont, Mn,US
89/K4 Fairmont, WV,US
94/D4 Fairmont, WV,US
97/H2 Fairmont, WV,US
99/M9 Fair Oaks, Ca,US
96/B2 Fairplay, Co,US
86/E3 Fairview, Ab,Can.
90/D1 Fairview, Ab,Can.
93/H3 Fairview, Ok,US
96/D2 Fairview, Ok,US
86/C3 Fairweather (mtn.), Yk,Can.
85/L4 Fairweather (cape), Ak,US
85/L4 Fairweather (mt.), BC,Can, Ak,US
99/C3 Fairwood-Cascade, Wa,US
53/K2 Faisalabad, Pak.
64/B2 Faisalabad, Pak.
39/J5 Faistós (ruins), Gre.
62/D2 Faizābād, India
104/E3 Fajardo, PR
69/M6 Fakahina (isl.), FrPol.
69/H5 Fakaofo (atoll), Tok.
69/L6 Fakarava (atoll), FrPol.
25/G1 Fakenham, Eng,UK
68/C5 Fakfak, Indo.
74/C4 Fako (peak), Camr.
76/G7 Fako (peak), Camr.
20/E5 Fakse, Den.
26/G1 Fakse, Den.
26/G1 Fakse Bugt (bay), Den.
26/G1 Fakse Ladeplads, Den.
55/J3 Faku, China
24/B6 Fal (riv.), Eng,UK
78/C3 Falaise de Tambaoura (escarp.), Mali
79/G2 Falaise de Tiguidit (escarp.), Niger
60/B4 Falam, Burma
49/G7 Falāmah, WBnk.
39/H3 Fálanna, Gre.
75/Q16 Falcon (cape), Alg.
101/F3 Falcon (int'l res.), US
101/F3 Falcon (dam), Tx,US
104/D5 Falcón (state), Ven.
33/K5 Falconara Marittima, It.
40/A4 Falconara Marittima, It.
78/C3 Falémé (riv.), Afr.
76/C5 Falémé (riv.), Mali, Sen.
69/S9 Faleolo, WSam.
101/F3 Falfurrias, Tx,US
96/D5 Falfurrias, Tx,US
90/D2 Falher, Ab,Can
20/E4 Falkenberg, Swe.
25/H2 Falkenham, Eng,UK
26/G3 Falkenstein, Ger.
33/K1 Falkenstein, Ger.
21/D3 Falkirk, Sc,UK
105/D8 Falkland (isls.), UK
109/D7 Falkland (isls.), UK
20/E4 Falköping, Swe.
99/D2 Fall City, Wa,US
36/D6 Fallere, Monte (peak), It.
26/E2 Fallingbostel, Ger.
29/G3 Fallingbostel, Ger.
88/C4 Fallon, Nv,US
92/C3 Fallon, Nv,US
95/G3 Fall River, Ma,US
98/J8 Falls Church, Va,US
93/J2 Falls City, Ne,US
96/E1 Falls City, Ne,US
104/F3 Falmouth, Anti.
24/A6 Falmouth, Eng,UK
24/A6 Falmouth (bay), Eng,UK
32/A1 Falmouth, Eng,UK
85/F5 False Pass, Ak,US
88/E7 Falso (cape), Mex.
103/J2 Falso, Cabo (cape), DRep.
103/F3 Falso, Cabo (cape), Hon.
100/C4 Falso, Cabo (cape), Mex.
84/G7 Falso, Cabo (cape), Mex.
20/E5 Falster (isl.), Den.
26/G1 Falster (isl.), Den.
41/H2 Fălticeni, Rom.
44/C3 Fălticeni, Rom.
18/E2 Falun, Swe.
20/E3 Falun, Swe.
42/B3 Falun, Swe.
46/B3 Falun, Swe.
49/C2 Famagusta, Cyp.
49/C2 Famagusta (bay), Cyp.
49/C2 Famagusta (dist.), Cyp.
50/C3 Famagusta, Cyp.
52/B1 Famagusta, Cyp.
52/E1 Fāmanīn, Iran
26/D4 Fameck, Fr.
31/F5 Fameck, Fr.
33/G2 Fameck, Fr.
31/E3 Famenne (reg.), Belg.
59/D5 Fanchang, China
61/H2 Fanchang, China
75/G7 Fandriana, Madg.
81/H8 Fandriana, Madg.
22/B4 Fane (riv.), Ire.
69/L6 Fangatau (isl.), FrPol.
69/L7 Fangataufa (isl.), FrPol.
54/G5 Fangcheng, China
59/C4 Fangcheng, China
61/F4 Fangcheng, China
65/E1 Fangcheng , China
63/J3 Fangcheng Gezu Zizhixian, China
61/E2 Fangdou (mts.), China
59/B3 Fangshan, China
54/G5 Fang Xian, China
59/B4 Fang Xian, China
61/F1 Fang Xian, China
61/F3 Fanjing (peak), China
63/J2 Fanjing (peak), China
69/K4 Fanning (Tabuaeran) (atoll), Kiri.
26/E1 Fanø (isl.), Den.
33/K5 Fano, It.
54/G4 Fanshi, China
59/C3 Fanshi, China
60/D4 Fan Si Pan (peak), Viet.
63/H3 Fan Si Pan (peak), Viet.
65/C1 Fan Si Pan (peak), Viet.
49/G7 Faqqū'ah, WBnk.
49/B4 Fāqūs, Egypt
77/L7 Faradje, Zaire
75/G7 Faradofay, Madg.
81/H9 Faradofay, Madg.
52/F2 Farādonbeh, Iran
75/G7 Farafangana, Madg.
81/H8 Farafangana, Madg.
46/G6 Farāh, Afg.
46/G6 Farāh (riv.), Afg.
53/H2 Farāh (riv.), Afg.
49/G7 Fa'rah, Wādī (dry riv.), WBnk.
92/B3 Farallon (isls.), Ca,US
68/D3 Farallon de Medinilla (isl.), NMar.
68/D2 Farallon de Pajaros (isl.), NMar.
106/C3 Farallones de Cali Nat'l Park, Col.
76/E5 Faramana, Burk.
76/C5 Faranah, Gui.
78/C4 Faranah (comm.), Gui.
81/H8 Faraony (riv.), Madg.
48/C8 Farasan (isls.), SAr.
52/D5 Farasān (isls.), SAr.
68/D4 Faraulep (atoll), Micr.
30/D3 Farciennes, Belg.
30/C6 Faremoutiers, Fr.
71/R11 Farewell (cape), N.Z.
85/H3 Farewell, Ak,US
86/G4 Fargo, ND,US
89/G2 Fargo, ND,US
91/J4 Fargo, ND,US
86/G4 Faribault, Mn,US
89/H3 Faribault, Mn,US
91/K4 Faribault, Mn,US
53/L3 Farīdābād, India
62/C2 Farīdābād, India
64/C2 Farīdkot, India
62/E3 Farīdpur, Bang.
25/E3 Faringdon, Eng,UK
49/B4 Fāriskūr, Egypt
20/F4 Färjestaden, Swe.
39/H3 Farkadhón, Gre.
95/G2 Farmington, Me,US
99/F7 Farmington, Mi,US
93/K3 Farmington, Mo,US
94/D4 Farmington, Mo,US
97/F2 Farmington, Mo,US
88/E4 Farmington, NM,US
92/E3 Farmington, NM,US
96/A2 Farmington, NM,US
99/F7 Farmington Hills, Mi,US
94/E4 Farmville, Va,US
97/J2 Farmville, Va,US
25/F4 Farnborough, Eng,UK
25/F4 Farnham, Eng,UK
19/P7 Farningham, Eng,UK
23/F4 Farnworth, Eng,UK
86/C2 Faro, Yk,Can
18/C5 Faro, Port.
34/A4 Faro (dist.), Port.
34/B4 Faro, Port.
18/C2 Faroe (isls.), Den.
20/F4 Fårön (isl.), Swe.
42/C4 Fårön (isl.), Swe.
76/H6 Faro Nat'l Park, Camr.
70/A4 Farquhar (cape), Austl.
75/H5 Farquhar (isls.), Sey.
51/H4 Farrāshband, Iran
108/B4 Farroupilha, Braz.
62/C2 Farrukhābād, India
51/H4 Fars (gov.), Iran
39/H3 Fársala, Gre.
90/F5 Farson, Wy,US
92/E2 Farson, Wy,US
20/C4 Farsund, Nor.
52/F5 Fartak, Ra's (pt.), Yem.
84/N4 Farvel (cape), Grld.
83/T Farwell (isl.), Ant.
93/G4 Farwell, Tx,US
96/C3 Farwell, Tx,US
51/H4 Fasā, Iran
52/F3 Fasa, Iran
38/E2 Fasano, It.
40/C5 Fasano, It.
49/C1 Faşıkan (pass), Turk.
76/D4 Fassala-Néré, Mrta.
29/H3 Fassberg, Ger.
44/D2 Fastov, Ukr.
67/H4 Fatagar Tuting (cape), Indo.
64/B1 Fatahjang, Pak.
53/K3 Fatehpur, India
62/B2 Fatehpur, India
62/D2 Fatehpur, India
78/A3 Fatick (reg.), Sen.
60/A4 Fatikchhari, Bang.
34/A3 Fátima, Port.
52/C4 Fāţimah (dry riv.), SAr.
44/F4 Fatsa, Turk.
50/D1 Fatsa, Turk.
69/M6 Fatu Hiva (isl.), FrPol.
36/C5 Faucille, Col de la (pass), Fr.
26/C5 Faucilles (mts.), Fr.
32/F2 Faucilles (mts.), Fr.
36/B1 Faucilles (mts.), Fr.
22/A2 Faughan (riv.), NI,UK
91/J4 Faulkton, SD,US
31/F5 Faulquemont, Fr.
41/H3 Făurei, Rom.
20/E2 Fauske, Nor.
42/B2 Fauske, Nor.
31/E4 Fauvillers, Belg.
33/K5 Favalto (peak), It.
38/C4 Favara, It.
36/D1 Fave (riv.), Fr.
36/C6 Faverges, Fr.
36/C2 Faverney, Fr.
25/G4 Faversham, Eng,UK
38/C4 Favignana, It.
25/E5 Fawley, Eng,UK
107/L2 Fawn (riv.), On,Can
86/H3 Fawn (riv.), On,Can
20/M7 Faxaflói (bay), Ice.
108/B2 Faxinal, Braz.
77/J4 Faya-Largeau, Chad
52/D3 Fayd, SAr.
97/G3 Fayette, Al,US
93/J3 Fayette, Mo,US
96/E2 Fayette, Mo,US
93/K5 Fayette, Ms,US
97/F4 Fayette, Ms,US
89/H4 Fayetteville, Ar,US
93/J3 Fayetteville, Ar,US
96/E2 Fayetteville, Ar,US
97/G3 Fayetteville, Ga,US
89/L4 Fayetteville, NC,US
97/J3 Fayetteville, NC,US
97/G3 Fayetteville, Tn,US
36/B2 Fayl-Billot, Fr.
79/F4 Fazao (mts.), Gha., Togo
79/F4 Fazao Nat'l Park, Togo
86/E4 F.D.R. (Franklin D. Roosevelt) (res.), Wa,US
21/H7 Feale (riv.), Ire.
84/K6 Fear (cape), US
89/L5 Fear (cape), NC,US
97/J3 Fear (cape), NC,US
92/B3 Feather (riv.), Ca,US
23/G4 Featherstone, Eng,UK
32/D2 Fécamp, Fr.
36/D1 Fecht (riv.), Fr.
64/A1 Fed. Admin. Tribal Areas (terr.), Pak.
99/C3 Federal Way, Wa,US
68/D4 Federated States of Micronesia
22/A2 Feeny, NI,UK
40/F2 Fehérgyarmat, Hun.
26/F1 Fehmarn (isl.), Ger.
26/F1 Fehmarn Belt (str.), Den., Ger.
59/D4 Fei (riv.), China
108/D2 Feia (lake), Braz.
59/D3 Feicheng, China
59/D5 Feidong, China
61/H2 Feidong, China
30/C3 Feignies, Fr.
59/D4 Fei Huang (riv.), China
106/D5 Feijó, Braz.
36/A5 Feillans, Fr.
34/A2 Feira, Port.
107/L6 Feira de Santana, Braz.
33/L3 Feistritz (riv.), Aus.
40/B2 Feistritz (riv.), Aus.
55/H5 Feixi, China
59/D5 Feixi, China
61/H2 Feixi, China
55/H4 Fei Xian, China
59/D4 Fei Xian, China
40/D2 Fejér (co.), Hun.
50/C2 Feke, Turk.
40/D3 Feketić, Yugo.
35/G3 Felanitx, Sp.
37/H2 Feldafing, Ger.
26/E5 Feldberg (peak), Ger.
33/H3 Feldberg (peak), Ger.
36/E2 Feldberg (peak), Ger.
33/H3 Feldkirch, Aus.
37/F3 Feldkirch, Aus.
33/L3 Feldkirchen bei Graz, Aus.
33/L3 Feldkirchen in Kärnten, Aus.
40/B2 Feldkirchen in Kärnten, Aus.
102/D2 Felipe Carillo Puerto, Mex.
27/J5 Felixdorf, Aus.
108/C1 Felixlândia, Braz.
25/H3 Felixstowe, Eng,UK
93/F5 Félix U. Gómez, Mex
96/B4 Félix U. Gómez, Mex
31/F4 Fell, Ger.
23/G2 Felling, Eng,UK
29/G6 Felsberg, Ger.
37/F4 Felsberg, Swi.
19/M7 Feltham, Eng,UK
25/G2 Feltwell, Eng,UK
33/K5 Fema (peak), It.
54/G4 Fen (riv.), China
54/G5 Fen (riv.), China
59/C4 Fen (riv.), China
36/B3 Fénay, Fr.
34/A1 Fene, Sp.
49/D1 Fener (pt.), Turk.
31/G6 Fénétrange, Fr.
39/J2 Fengári (peak), Gre.
41/G5 Fengári (peak), Gre.
44/C4 Fengári (peak), Gre.
50/A1 Fengári (peak), Gre.
55/J3 Fengcheng, China
58/C2 Fengcheng, China
59/F2 Fengcheng, China
61/G3 Fengchuihudie (peak), China
61/G2 Fengding (mtn.), China
63/J2 Fenghuang, China
54/F5 Fengjie, China
59/B5 Fengjie, China
61/F2 Fengjie, China
59/D5 Fengle (riv.), China
59/D3 Fengnan, China
59/J7 Fengnan, China
54/H3 Fengning, China
59/D2 Fengning, China
60/C3 Fengqing, China
63/G3 Fengqing, China
54/G4 Fengqiu, China
59/C4 Fengqiu, China
59/D3 Fengrun, China
59/J7 Fengrun, China
55/H3 Fengshan, China
63/J3 Fengshan, China
61/G3 Fengshuba (res.), China
55/J1 Fengshui (peak), China
59/H7 Fengtai, China
59/D4 Feng Xian, China
59/E5 Fengxian, China
59/L9 Fengxian, China
61/J2 Fengxian, China
54/G4 Fengyang, China
59/B3 Fengyang, China
59/D4 Fengyang, China
59/C2 Fengzhen, China
85/C5 Fenimore (passg.), Ak,US
81/J7 Fenoarivo Atsinanana, Madg.
61/H3 Fenshui (pass), China
61/H4 Fenshui Guan (pass), China
23/H6 Fens, The (reg.), Eng,UK
25/G2 Fens, The (phys. reg.), Eng,UK
94/D3 Fenton, Mi,US
99/E6 Fenton, Mi,US
99/E6 Fenton (lake), Mi,US
54/G4 Fenxi, China
59/B3 Fenxi, China
44/E3 Feodosiya, Ukr.
39/K2 Férai, Gre.
41/H5 Férai, Gre.
75/V17 Fer, Cap de (cape), Alg.
27/G2 Ferdinandshof, Ger.
51/J3 Ferdows, Iran
53/G2 Ferdows, Iran
30/C6 Fère-Champenoise, Fr.
30/C5 Fère-en-Tardenois, Fr.
38/C2 Ferentino, It.
38/C1 Ferento (ruins), It.
46/H5 Fergana, Uzb.
86/G4 Fergus Falls, Mn,US
89/G2 Fergus Falls, Mn,US
91/J4 Fergus Falls, Mn,US
86/F2 Ferguson (lake), NW,Can
78/D4 Ferkéssédougou, IvC.
33/L3 Ferlach, Aus.
40/B2 Ferlach, Aus.
76/C4 Ferlo (grsld.), Sen.
78/B3 Ferlo, Vallée du (wadi), Sen.
22/A3 Fermanagh (dist.), NI,UK
98/B3 Fermin (pt.), Ca,US
99/P16 Fermi Nat'l Accelerator Lab., Il,US
33/K5 Fermo, It.
38/C1 Fermo, It.
40/A4 Fermo, It.
34/B2 Fermoselle, Sp.
21/A4 Fermoy, Ire.
101/F4 Fernández, Mex.
97/H4 Fernandina Beach, Fl,US
105/F3 Fernando de Noronha (isl.), Braz.
107/M4 Fernando de Noronha, Braz.
107/H8 Fernandópolis, Braz.
108/B2 Fernandópolis, Braz.
34/C4 Fernán-Núñez, Sp.
98/K7 Ferndale, Md,US
99/F7 Ferndale, Mi,US
25/E5 Ferndown, Eng,UK
38/C5 Ferney-Voltaire, Fr.
86/E4 Fernie, BC,Can
90/E3 Fernie, BC,Can
37/G3 Fernpass (pass), Aus.
73/G5 Ferntree Gully Nat'l Park, Austl.
64/C3 Feroke, India
38/E2 Ferrandina, It.
40/C5 Ferrandina, It.
18/E4 Ferrara, It.
33/J4 Ferrara, It.
34/A3 Ferreira do Alentejo, Port.
32/C4 Ferret (cape), Fr.
36/D3 Ferrette, Fr.

134
Ferri – Frech

93/K5 **Ferriday**, La,US
96/F4 **Ferriday**, La,US
30/D3 **Ferrière-la-Grande**, Fr.
31/E3 **Ferrières**, Belg.
23/G2 **Ferryhill**, Eng,UK
24/B3 **Ferryside**, Wal,UK
45/L1 **Fershampenuaz**, Rus.
33/M3 **Fertő** (Neusiedler See) (lake), Aus., Hun.
26/C2 **Ferwerd**, Neth.
28/C2 **Ferwerd**, Neth.
75/M13 **Fès**, Mor.
76/E1 **Fès**, Mor.
36/C2 **Fesches-le-Châtel**, Fr.
82/C2 **Feshi**, Zaire
36/D2 **Fessenheim**, Fr.
93/K3 **Festus**, Mo,US
94/B4 **Festus**, Mo,US
97/F2 **Festus**, Mo,US
19/M8 **Fetcham**, Eng,UK
25/F4 **Fetcham**, Eng,UK
41/H3 **Feteşti**, Rom.
44/C3 **Feteşti**, Rom.
50/B2 **Fethiye**, Turk.
19/R10 **Feucherolles**, Fr.
33/J2 **Feucht**, Ger.
26/F4 **Feuchtwangen**, Ger.
87/J3 **Feuilles** (lake), Qu,Can
87/J3 **Feuilles** (riv.), Qu,Can
84/K4 **Feuilles, Rivière aux** (riv.), Can.
30/A4 **Feuquières**, Fr.
30/A3 **Feuquières-en-Vimeu**, Fr.
32/F4 **Feurs**, Fr.
49/E1 **Fevzipaşa**, Turk.
46/H6 **Feyẕābād**, Afg.
53/K1 **Feyẕābād**, Afg.
74/D2 **Fezzan** (reg.), Libya
76/H2 **Fezzan** (reg.), Libya
22/E6 **Ffestiniog**, Wal,UK
75/G7 **Fianarantsoa**, Madg.
81/H8 **Fianarantsoa**, Madg.
81/H8 **Fianarantsoa** (prov.), Madg.
76/J6 **Fianga**, Chad
26/F3 **Fichtelgebirge** (mts.), Ger.
33/J1 **Fichtelgebirge** (range), Ger.
80/D3 **Ficksburg**, SAfr.
33/J4 **Fidenza**, It.
78/C4 **Fié** (riv.), Gui., Mali
41/G3 **Fieni**, Rom.
39/F2 **Fier**, Alb.
40/D5 **Fier**, Alb.
36/B6 **Fier** (riv.), Fr.
39/G1 **Fierzë** (lake), Alb.
40/D4 **Fierzë** (lake), Alb.
36/E5 **Fiesch**, Swi.
99/E5 **Fife**, Wa,US
77/M4 **Fifth** (fall, falls), Sudan
74/F3 **Fifth Cataract** (falls), Sudan
75/Q16 **Figalo** (cape), Alg.
38/A2 **Figari**, Fr.
32/E4 **Figeac**, Fr.
34/A2 **Figueira da Foz**, Port.
35/G1 **Figueres**, Sp.
76/E1 **Figuig**, Mor.
81/G8 **Fiherenana** (riv.), Madg.
68/G6 **Fiji**
69/Y17 **Fiji**
106/F8 **Filadelfia**, Par.
109/D1 **Filadelfia**, Par.
83/X **Filchner Ice Shelf**, Ant.
23/H3 **Filey**, Eng,UK
23/H3 **Filey** (bay), Eng,UK
39/H3 **Filí**, Gre.
39/J6 **Filí**, Gre.
41/F3 **Filiaşi**, Rom.
44/B3 **Filiaşi**, Rom.
39/G3 **Filiatái**, Gre.
39/G4 **Filiatrá**, Gre.
38/D3 **Filicudi** (isl.), It.
36/C6 **Filière** (riv.), Fr.
76/F5 **Filingué**, Niger
79/F3 **Filingué**, Niger
39/G3 **Filippiás**, Gre.
39/J2 **Filippoi** (ruins), Gre.
41/G5 **Filippoi** (ruins), Gre.
20/E4 **Filipstad**, Swe.
37/F4 **Filisur**, Swi.
92/D3 **Fillmore**, Ut,US
69/S9 **Filo** (peak), WSam.
101/H5 **Filomena Mata**, Mex.
102/D2 **Filomena Mata**, Mex.
39/J4 **Filótion**, Gre.
29/E2 **Filsum**, Ger.
24/D3 **Filton**, Eng,UK
83/Z **Fimbul Ice Shelf**, Ant.
76/J8 **Fimi** (riv.), Zaire
33/H4 **Finale Ligure**, It.
34/D4 **Fiñana**, Sp.
78/C3 **Fina Rsv.**, Mali
72/C3 **Finch Hatton**, Austl.
19/N7 **Finchley**, Eng,UK
89/K3 **Findlay**, Oh,US
94/D3 **Findlay**, Oh,US
98/E5 **Finesville**, NJ,US
73/D4 **Fingal**, Austl.
91/K2 **Finger** (lake), On,Can
94/E3 **Finger** (lakes), NY,US
36/C5 **Finhaut**, Swi.
32/E4 **Finiels, Sommet de** (peak), Fr.
49/B1 **Finike**, Turk.
50/B2 **Finike**, Turk.
18/C4 **Finisterre** (cape), Sp.
34/A1 **Finisterre**, Sp.
34/A1 **Finisterre** (cape), Sp.
70/F5 **Finke** (riv.), Austl.
33/K3 **Finkenstein**, Aus.
18/F2 **Finland**
20/H2 **Finland**
42/E2 **Finland**
46/C3 **Finland**
18/F3 **Finland** (gulf), Eur.
20/H4 **Finland** (gulf), Eur.
42/E4 **Finland** (gulf), Eur.
43/U6 **Finland** (gulf), Eur.
46/C4 **Finland** (gulf), Eur.
86/D3 **Finlay** (riv.), BC,Can
96/B4 **Finlay** (mts.), Tx,US
71/H7 **Finley**, Austl.
73/C2 **Finley**, Austl.
29/E6 **Finnentrop**, Ger.
31/G1 **Finnentrop**, Ger.
99/C2 **Finn Hill-Inglewood**, Wa,US
72/B1 **Finnigan** (peak), Austl.
20/G1 **Finnmark** (co.), Nor.
42/D1 **Finnmark** (co.), Nor.
20/E4 **Finspång**, Swe.
42/B4 **Finspång**, Swe.
36/E4 **Finsteraarhorn** (peak), Swi.
20/F3 **Finström**, Fin.
42/C3 **Finström**, Fin.
29/G2 **Fintel**, Ger.
22/A3 **Fintona**, NI,UK
33/J5 **Fiora** (riv.), It.
38/B1 **Fiora** (riv.), It.
33/H4 **Fiorenzuola d'Arda**, It.
81/H7 **Firavahana**, Madg.
99/B3 **Fircrest**, Wa,US
99/C2 **Fircrest-Silver Lake**, Wa,US
98/G5 **Fire Island Nat'l Seashore**, NY,US
33/J5 **Firenze** (Florence), It.
32/E4 **Firmi**, Fr.
32/F4 **Firminy**, Fr.
62/C2 **Firozābād**, India
53/K2 **Firozpur**, India
64/C2 **Firozpur**, India
77/M3 **First Cataract** (fall, falls), Egypt
51/H4 **Fīrūzābād**, Iran
52/F3 **Fīrūzābād**, Iran
51/H3 **Fīrūz Kūh**, Iran
52/F1 **Fīrūz Kūh**, Iran
53/G1 **Firyuza**, Trkm.
37/G1 **Fischach**, Ger.
33/L3 **Fischbacher** (mts.), Aus.
37/G3 **Fischen im Allgäu**, Ger.
80/B2 **Fish** (riv.), Namb.
82/C5 **Fish** (riv.), Namb.
80/C3 **Fish** (riv.), SAfr.
23/G2 **Fishburn**, Eng,UK
83/E **Fisher** (glac.), Ant.
91/J3 **Fisher** (bay), Mb,Can
87/H2 **Fisher** (str.), NW,Can
91/J3 **Fisher Branch**, Mb,Can
72/F6 **Fisherman** (isl.), Austl.
24/B3 **Fishguard**, Wal,UK
44/F4 **Fisht, Gora** (peak), Rus.
23/J6 **Fishtoft**, Eng,UK
30/C5 **Fismes**, Fr.
32/E2 **Fismes**, Fr.
69/S8 **Fito** (peak), WSam.
85/L2 **Fitton** (mtn.), Yk,Can
97/H4 **Fitzgerald**, Ga,US
90/B3 **Fitz Hugo** (sound), BC,Can
70/D3 **Fitzroy** (riv.), Austl.
71/H4 **Fitzroy** (riv.), Austl.
72/C3 **Fitzroy** (riv.), Austl.
70/D3 **Fitzroy Crossing**, Austl.
87/R7 **Fitzwilliam** (str.), NW,Can
38/C2 **Fiumicino**, It.
22/A3 **Fivemiletown**, NI,UK
51/F2 **Fizuli**, Azer.
20/C3 **Fjell**, Nor.
31/F5 **Flack**, Fr.
25/F3 **Flackwell Heath**, Eng,UK
93/G3 **Flagler**, Co,US
96/C2 **Flagler**, Co,US
97/H4 **Flagler Beach**, Fl,US
88/D4 **Flagstaff**, Az,US
92/E4 **Flagstaff**, Az,US
91/L4 **Flambeau**, Wi,US
94/B2 **Flambeau** (riv.), Wi,US
95/Q9 **Flamborough**, On,Can
23/H3 **Flamborough**, Eng,UK
23/H3 **Flamborough Head** (pt.), Eng,UK
26/G2 **Fläming** (hills), Ger.
90/F5 **Flaming Gorge** (res.), Ut, Wy,US
92/E2 **Flaming Gorge** (res.), Ut, Wy,US
86/F4 **Flaming Gorge Nat'l Rec. Area**, Ut, Wy,US
90/F5 **Flaming Gorge Nat'l Rec. Area**, Ut, Wy,US
92/E2 **Flaming Gorge Nat'l Rec. Area**, Ut, Wy,US
91/K2 **Flanagan** (riv.), On,Can
30/B2 **Flanders** (reg.), Belg.
26/B3 **Flanders** (reg.), Belg., Fr.
32/E1 **Flanders** (reg.), Belg., Fr.
30/B2 **Flanders** (reg.), Fr.
91/J4 **Flandreau**, SD,US
93/H1 **Flandreau**, SD,US
85/L3 **Flat Creek**, Yk,Can
90/E4 **Flathead** (lake), Mt,US
90/E4 **Flathead** (riv.), Mt,US
90/E4 **Flathead, South Fork** (riv.), Mt,US
24/C4 **Flat Holm** (isl.), Eng,UK
93/K3 **Flat River**, Mo,US
94/B4 **Flat River**, Mo,US
97/F2 **Flat River**, Mo,US
99/F7 **Flat Rock**, Mi,US
71/H2 **Flattery** (cape), Austl.
72/B1 **Flattery** (cape), Austl.
84/E5 **Flattery** (cape), US
86/D4 **Flattery** (cape), Wa,US
88/B2 **Flattery** (cape), Wa,US
90/B3 **Flattery** (cape), Wa,US
37/F3 **Flawil**, Swi.
36/D2 **Flaxlanden**, Fr.
25/F4 **Fleet**, Eng,UK
23/E4 **Fleetwood**, Eng,UK
20/C4 **Flekkefjord**, Nor.
73/F5 **Flemington Racecourse**, Austl.
18/D3 **Flensburg**, Ger.
20/D5 **Flensburg**, Ger.
26/E1 **Flensburg**, Ger.
46/A4 **Flensburg**, Ger.
31/E2 **Fleron**, Belg.
32/C2 **Flers**, Fr.
36/D5 **Fletschhorn** (peak), Swi.
32/D5 **Fleurance**, Fr.
35/F1 **Fleurance**, Fr.
36/C4 **Fleurier**, Swi.
30/D3 **Fleurus**, Belg.
32/F1 **Fleurus**, Belg.
32/D3 **Fleury-les-Aubrais**, Fr.
26/C2 **Flevoland** (polders), Neth.
28/C4 **Flevoland** (prov.), Neth.
37/G3 **Flexenpass** (pass), Aus.
37/G3 **Fliess**, Aus.
22/E2 **Flimby**, Eng,UK
37/F4 **Flims**, Swi.
68/D6 **Flinders** (riv.), Austl.
70/A6 **Flinders** (bay), Austl.
70/F6 **Flinders** (ranges), Austl.
70/G3 **Flinders** (riv.), Austl.
71/H3 **Flinders** (reef), Austl.
71/H7 **Flinders** (isl.), Austl.
72/A2 **Flinders** (riv.), Austl.
72/C2 **Flinders** (reefs), Austl.
73/D3 **Flinders** (isl.), Austl.
91/J3 **Flindt** (riv.), On,Can
30/C3 **Flines-lez-Raches**, Fr.
91/H2 **Flin Flon**, Can
86/F3 **Flin Flon**, Mb,Can
87/J2 **Flint** (lake), NW,Can
69/K6 **Flint** (isl.), Kiri.
22/E5 **Flint**, Wal,UK
89/K5 **Flint** (riv.), Ga,US
93/H3 **Flint** (hills), Ks,US
96/D2 **Flint** (hills), Ks,US
87/H4 **Flint**, Mi,US
89/K3 **Flint**, Mi,US
94/D3 **Flint**, Mi,US
99/E5 **Flint**, Mi,US
99/F6 **Flint, South Branch** (riv.), Mi,US
25/F3 **Flitwick**, Eng,UK
35/F2 **Flix**, Sp.
30/B3 **Flixecourt**, Fr.
31/D4 **Flize**, Fr.
101/Q10 **Floating Gardens**, Mex.
29/F1 **Flögelner See** (lake), Ger.
27/G3 **Flöha** (riv.), Ger.
31/D4 **Floing**, Fr.
31/H4 **Flonheim**, Ger.
94/B4 **Flora**, Il,US
97/F2 **Flora**, Il,US
98/G5 **Floral Park**, NY,US
26/D4 **Florange**, Fr.
31/F5 **Florange**, Fr.
32/G2 **Florange**, Fr.
31/D3 **Floreffe**, Belg.
18/E4 **Florence**, It.
89/J5 **Florence**, Al,US
97/G3 **Florence**, Al,US
100/C1 **Florence**, Az,US
92/E4 **Florence**, Az,US
93/F3 **Florence**, Co,US
96/B2 **Florence**, Co,US
89/L5 **Florence**, SC,US
97/J3 **Florence**, SC,US
33/J5 **Florence** (Firenze), It.
106/C3 **Florencia**, Col.
30/D3 **Florennes**, Belg.
31/E4 **Florenville**, Belg.
35/R12 **Flores** (isl.), Azor.
90/B3 **Flores** (isl.), BC,Can
102/D2 **Flores**, Guat.
48/L10 **Flores** (isl.), Indo.
48/M10 **Flores** (isl.), Indo.
67/E5 **Flores** (sea), Indo.
67/F5 **Flores** (isl.), Indo.
68/A5 **Flores** (sea), Indo.
68/B5 **Flores** (isl.), Indo.
44/D3 **Floreshty**, Mol.
107/L5 **Floresta**, Braz.
101/F2 **Floresville**, Tx,US
93/H5 **Floresville**, Tx,US
96/D4 **Floresville**, Tx,US
107/K5 **Floriano**, Braz.
108/B3 **Florianópolis**, Braz.
109/G2 **Florianópolis**, Braz.
103/G1 **Florida**, Cuba
102/D3 **Florida**, Hon.
84/J7 **Florida** (str.), NAm.
109/E3 **Florida**, Uru.
104/A1 **Florida** (state), US
89/K6 **Florida** (state), US
97/H4 **Florida** (state), US
104/A1 **Florida** (bay), Fl,US
104/A1 **Florida** (keys), Fl,US
104/A1 **Florida** (str.), Fl,US
89/K7 **Florida** (str.), US, Cuba
84/J7 **Florida Keys** (isls.), US
89/K7 **Florida Keys** (isls.), Fl,US
97/H5 **Florida Keys** (isls.), Fl,US
38/D4 **Floridia**, It.
99/M10 **Florin**, Ca,US
39/G2 **Flórina**, Gre.
40/E5 **Flórina**, Gre.
93/K3 **Florissant**, Mo,US
94/B4 **Florissant**, Mo,US
97/F2 **Florissant**, Mo,US
20/C3 **Florø**, Nor.
93/G4 **Floydada**, Tx,US
96/C3 **Floydada**, Tx,US
37/G4 **Fluchthorn** (peak), Aus.
37/F4 **Flüelapass** (pass), Swi.
37/E4 **Flüelen**, Swi.
28/C3 **Fluessen** (lake), Neth.
38/A3 **Flumendosa** (riv.), It.
37/F3 **Flums**, Swi.
94/D3 **Flushing**, Mi,US
28/A6 **Flushing** (Vlissingen), Neth.
68/D5 **Fly** (riv.), PNG
83/T **Flying Fish** (cape), Ant.
20/P6 **Fnjóská** (riv.), Ice.
86/F3 **Foam Lake**, Sk,Can
91/H3 **Foam Lake**, Sk,Can
40/D4 **Foča**, Bosn.
26/E1 **Fockbek**, Ger.
41/H3 **Focşani**, Rom.
44/C3 **Focşani**, Rom.
63/K3 **Fogang**, China
18/E4 **Foggia**, It.
38/D2 **Foggia**, It.
40/B5 **Foggia**, It.
74/J10 **Fogo** (isl.), CpV.
33/L3 **Fohnsdorf**, Aus.
40/B2 **Fohnsdorf**, Aus.
26/E1 **Föhr** (isl.), Ger.
31/F4 **Föhren**, Ger.
38/B1 **Foiano della Chiana**, It.
32/D5 **Foix**, Fr.
35/F1 **Foix**, Fr.
20/C3 **Folarskardnuten** (peak), Nor.
20/D2 **Folda** (fjord), Nor.
20/E2 **Folda** (fjord), Nor.
42/B2 **Folda** (fjord), Nor.
40/E2 **Földeák**, Hun.
39/J4 **Folégandros** (isl.), Gre.
30/C4 **Folembray**, Fr.
87/J2 **Foley** (isl.), NW,Can
37/H6 **Folgaria**, It.
33/K5 **Foligno**, It.
38/C1 **Foligno**, It.
25/H4 **Folkestone**, Eng,UK
30/A1 **Folkestone**, Eng,UK
97/H4 **Folkston**, Ga,US
33/J5 **Follonica** (gulf), It.
38/B1 **Follonica** (gulf), It.
31/F5 **Folschviller**, Fr.
81/G6 **Fomboni**, Com.
86/F3 **Fond du Lac** (riv.), Sk,Can
86/H4 **Fond du Lac**, Wi,US
89/J3 **Fond du Lac**, Wi,US
91/L5 **Fond du Lac**, Wi,US
94/B3 **Fond du Lac**, Wi,US
38/C2 **Fondi**, It.
37/H5 **Fondo**, It.
20/D3 **Fongen** (peak), Nor.
42/A3 **Fongen** (peak), Nor.
38/A2 **Fonni**, It.
34/B1 **Fonsagrada**, Sp.
103/H4 **Fonseca**, Col.
102/E3 **Fonseca** (gulf), NAm.
32/F4 **Fontaine**, Fr.
26/B4 **Fontainebleau**, Fr.
32/E2 **Fontainebleau**, Fr.
36/A3 **Fontaine-lès-Dijon**, Fr.
36/C2 **Fontaine-lès-Luxeuil**, Fr.
30/D3 **Fontaine-L'Evêque**, Belg.
98/C2 **Fontana**, Ca,US
106/E4 **Fonte Boa**, Braz.
36/D3 **Fontenais**, Swi.
32/C3 **Fontenay-le-Comte**, Fr.
19/S10 **Fontenay-le-Fleury**, Fr.
19/S11 **Fontenay-les-Briis**, Fr.
19/T10 **Fontenay-sous-Bois**, Fr.
19/U10 **Fontenay-Trésigny**, Fr.
30/B6 **Fontenay-Trésigny**, Fr.
90/F5 **Fontenelle** (res.), Wy,US
31/F5 **Fontoy**, Fr.
33/G4 **Font Sancte, Pic de la** (peak), Fr.
18/B2 **Fontur** (pt.), Ice.
20/P6 **Fontur** (pt.), Ice.
73/F5 **Footscray**, Austl.
54/F5 **Foping**, China
85/H3 **Foraker** (mt.), Ak,US
31/F5 **Forbach**, Fr.
71/H6 **Forbes**, Austl.
73/D2 **Forbes**, Austl.
34/A1 **Forcarey**, Sp.
26/F4 **Forchheim**, Ger.
33/J2 **Forchheim**, Ger.
36/D5 **Forclaz, Col de la** (pass), Swi.
99/E7 **Ford** (lake), Mi,US
25/E5 **Fordingbridge**, Eng,UK
89/H5 **Fordyce**, Ar,US
93/J4 **Fordyce**, Ar,US
96/E3 **Fordyce**, Ar,US
25/E5 **Foreland** (pt.), UK
24/C4 **Foreland** (pt.), Eng,UK
90/F3 **Foremost**, Ab,Can
25/H4 **Foreness** (pt.), UK
97/F3 **Forest**, Ms,US
73/D4 **Forestier** (cape), Austl.
95/G1 **Forestville**, Qu,Can
98/K8 **Forestville**, Md,US
32/E4 **Forez** (mts.), Fr.
19/S11 **Forges-les-Bains**, Fr.
30/A4 **Forges-les-Eaux**, Fr.
37/G2 **Forggensee** (lake), Ger.
87/K4 **Forillon Nat'l Park**, Qu,Can
95/H1 **Forillon Nat'l Park**, Qu,Can
98/F6 **Forked River**, NJ,US
22/B3 **Forkill**, NI,UK
88/B2 **Forks**, Wa,US
90/B4 **Forks**, Wa,US
33/K4 **Forlì**, It.
23/E4 **Formby**, Eng,UK
23/E4 **Formby** (pt.), Eng,UK
35/F3 **Formentera** (isl.), Sp.
35/G3 **Formentor, Cabo de** (cape), Sp.
30/A4 **Formerie**, Fr.
38/C2 **Formia**, It.
107/J8 **Formiga**, Braz.
108/C2 **Formiga**, Braz.
109/E2 **Formosa**, Arg.
107/G6 **Formosa** (mts.), Braz.
107/J7 **Formosa**, Braz.
78/A4 **Formosa** (isl.), GBis.
80/C4 **Formosa** (peak), SAfr.
107/J6 **Formoso** (riv.), Braz.
33/J5 **Fornacelle**, It.
70/D6 **Forrest**, Austl.
89/H4 **Forrest City**, Ar,US
93/K4 **Forrest City**, Ar,US
97/F3 **Forrest City**, Ar,US
71/G3 **Forsayth**, Austl.
20/G3 **Forssa**, Fin.
42/D3 **Forssa**, Fin.
72/A3 **Forsyth** (range), Austl.
97/H3 **Forsyth**, Ga,US
90/G4 **Forsyth**, Mt,US
53/K3 **Fort Abbās**, Pak.
62/B2 **Fort Abbās**, Pak.
84/J4 **Fort Albany**, Can.
107/L4 **Fortaleza**, Braz.
80/D4 **Fort Beaufort**, SAfr.
82/E7 **Fort Beaufort**, SAfr.
95/H2 **Fort Beauséjour Nat'l Hist. Park**, Can
98/J8 **Fort Belvoir** (mil. res.), Va,US
90/F4 **Fort Benton**, Mt,US
88/B4 **Fort Bragg**, Ca,US
92/B3 **Fort Bragg**, Ca,US
95/F2 **Fort Chambly Nat'l Hist. Park**, Can
84/F4 **Fort Chipewyan**, Can.
86/E3 **Fort Chipewyan**, Ab,Can
93/H4 **Fort Cobb** (res.), Ok,US
84/G5 **Fort Collins**, US
88/E3 **Fort Collins**, Co,US
93/F2 **Fort Collins**, Co,US
100/E2 **Fort Davis**, Tx,US
88/F5 **Fort Davis**, Tx,US
93/G5 **Fort Davis**, Tx,US
96/C4 **Fort Davis**, Tx,US
100/E2 **Fort Davis Nat'l Hist. Site**, Tx,US
31/E5 **Fort de Douaumont**, Fr.
104/F4 **Fort-de-France**, Mart.
104/F4 **Fort Desaix**, Mart.
31/E5 **Fort de Vaux**, Fr.
98/F5 **Fort Dix Mil. Res.**, NJ,US
89/H3 **Fort Dodge**, Ia,US
91/K5 **Fort Dodge**, Ia,US
93/J2 **Fort Dodge**, Ia,US
82/D3 **Forte Cameia**, Ang.
95/S10 **Fort Erie**, On,Can
68/A7 **Fortescue** (riv.), Austl.
70/B4 **Fortescue** (riv.), Austl.
86/G4 **Fort Frances**, On,Can
89/H2 **Fort Frances**, On,Can
91/K3 **Fort Frances**, On,Can
94/A1 **Fort Frances**, On,Can
86/D2 **Fort Franklin**, NW,Can
97/F4 **Fort Gaines**, Al,US
101/F2 **Fort Gates**, Tx,US
95/R9 **Fort George**, On,Can
84/K4 **Fort-George** (Chisasibi), Can.
87/J3 **Fort-George** (Chisasibi), Qu,Can
93/J4 **Fort Gibson**, Ok,US
96/E3 **Fort Gibson**, Ok,US
86/D2 **Fort Good Hope**, NW,Can
76/C3 **Fort-Gouraud**, Mrta.
21/D2 **Forth, Firth of** (bay), Sc,UK
98/K7 **Fort Howard**, Md,US
101/N8 **Fortín de las Flores**, Mex.
95/G2 **Fort Kent**, Me,US
104/A1 **Fort Lauderdale**, Fl,US
89/K6 **Fort Lauderdale**, Fl,US
97/H5 **Fort Lauderdale**, Fl,US
99/B3 **Fort Lewis**, Wa,US
84/E3 **Fort Liard**, Can.
86/D2 **Fort Liard**, NW,Can
103/J2 **Fort Liberté**, Haiti
104/D3 **Fort Liberté**, Haiti
93/F2 **Fort Lupton**, Co,US
86/E4 **Fort Macleod**, Ab,Can
88/D2 **Fort Macleod**, Ab,Can
90/E3 **Fort Macleod**, Ab,Can
91/L5 **Fort Madison**, Ia,US
93/K2 **Fort Madison**, Ia,US
94/B3 **Fort Madison**, Ia,US
25/H6 **Fort Mahon Plage**, Fr.
30/A3 **Fort-Mahon-Plage**, Fr.
99/F7 **Fort Malden Nat'l Hist. Park**, On.,Can
30/B1 **Fort-Mardyck**, Fr.
97/H4 **Fort Matanzas Nat'l Mon.**, Fl,US
98/K7 **Fort McHenry Nat'l Mon. & Hist. Site**, Md,US
84/F4 **Fort McMurray**, Can.
86/E3 **Fort McMurray**, Ab,Can
85/M2 **Fort McPherson**, NW,Can
86/C2 **Fort McPherson**, NW,Can
98/K7 **Fort Meade** (mil. res.), Md,US
94/C2 **Fort Michilimackinac**, Mi,US
98/F5 **Fort Monmouth** mil. res., NJ,US
88/F3 **Fort Morgan**, Co,US
93/G2 **Fort Morgan**, Co,US
97/J3 **Fort Moultrie**, SC,US
104/A1 **Fort Myers**, Fl,US
89/K6 **Fort Myers**, Fl,US
97/H5 **Fort Myers**, Fl,US
86/D3 **Fort Nelson**, BC,Can
86/D3 **Fort Nelson** (riv.), BC,Can
84/E3 **Fort Norman**, Can.
86/D2 **Fort Norman**, NW,Can
23/F4 **Forton**, Eng,UK
38/D2 **Fortore** (riv.), It.
97/G3 **Fort Payne**, Al,US
106/G4 **Fort Peck** (lake), Mt,US
86/F4 **Fort Peck** (lake), Mt,US
88/E2 **Fort Peck** (dam), Mt,US
88/E2 **Fort Peck** (lake), Mt,US
91/G4 **Fort Peck** (dam), Mt,US
89/K6 **Fort Pierce**, Fl,US
97/H5 **Fort Pierce**, Fl,US
91/H4 **Fort Pierre**, SD,US
93/G1 **Fort Pierre**, SD,US
77/M7 **Fort Portal**, Ugan.
86/E2 **Fort Providence**, NW,Can
86/F3 **Fort Qu'Appelle**, Sk,Can
88/F1 **Fort Qu'Appelle**, Sk,Can
91/H3 **Fort Qu'Appelle**, Sk,Can
97/K3 **Fort Raleigh Nat'l Hist. Site**, NC,US
89/G3 **Fort Randall** (dam), SD,US
91/J5 **Fort Randall** (dam), SD,US
93/H2 **Fort Randall** (dam), SD,US
84/F3 **Fort Resolution**, Can.
86/E2 **Fort Resolution**, NW,Can
95/J2 **Fortress of Louisbourg Nat'l Hist. Park**, Can
86/D3 **Fort Saint James**, BC,Can
90/B2 **Fort Saint James**, BC,Can
84/E4 **Fort Saint John**, Can.
86/D3 **Fort Saint John**, BC,Can
86/E3 **Fort Saskatchewan**, Ab,Can
90/E2 **Fort Saskatchewan**, Ab,Can
89/H4 **Fort Scott**, Ks,US
93/J3 **Fort Scott**, Ks,US
96/E2 **Fort Scott**, Ks,US
45/J3 **Fort-Shevchenko**, Kaz.
46/F5 **Fort-Shevchenko**, Kaz.
84/E3 **Fort Simpson**, Can.
86/D2 **Fort Simpson**, NW,Can
84/F3 **Fort Smith**, Can.
86/E2 **Fort Smith**, NW,Can
89/H4 **Fort Smith**, Ar,US
93/J4 **Fort Smith**, Ar,US
96/E3 **Fort Smith**, Ar,US
100/E2 **Fort Stockton**, Tx,US
88/F5 **Fort Stockton**, Tx,US
93/G5 **Fort Stockton**, Tx,US
96/C4 **Fort Stockton**, Tx,US
93/F4 **Fort Sumner**, NM,US
96/B3 **Fort Sumner**, NM,US
91/J4 **Fort Totten**, ND,US
95/L2 **Fortune**, Nf,Can
95/L2 **Fortune** (bay), Nf,Can
104/C2 **Fortune** (Long Cay) (cay), Bahm.
24/D5 **Fortuneswell**, Eng,UK
93/F4 **Fort Union Nat'l Mon.**, NM,US
84/F4 **Fort Vermilion**, Can.
86/E3 **Fort Vermilion**, Ab,Can
89/J5 **Fort Walton Beach**, Fl,US
97/G4 **Fort Walton Beach**, Fl,US
98/J8 **Fort Washington Park**, Md,US
89/J3 **Fort Wayne**, In,US
94/C3 **Fort Wayne**, In,US
94/F2 **Fort Wellington Nat'l Hist. Park**, Can
21/C2 **Fort William**, Sc,UK
101/F1 **Fort Worth**, Tx,US
89/G5 **Fort Worth**, Tx,US
93/H4 **Fort Worth**, Tx,US
96/D3 **Fort Worth**, Tx,US
91/H4 **Fort Yates**, ND,US
72/B2 **Forty Mile Scrub Nat'l Park**, Austl.
84/C3 **Fort Yukon**, Ak,US
85/J2 **Fort Yukon**, Ak,US
51/H5 **Forūr** (isl.), Iran
61/G4 **Foshan**, China
63/K3 **Foshan**, China
87/S7 **Fosheim** (pen.), NW,Can
23/G3 **Foss** (riv.), Eng,UK
33/G4 **Fossano**, It.
19/T9 **Fosses**, Fr.
30/B5 **Fosses**, Fr.
31/D3 **Fosses-la-Ville**, Belg.
90/C4 **Fossil**, Or,US
90/F5 **Fossil Butte Nat'l Mon.**, Wy,US
92/E2 **Fossil Butte Nat'l Mon.**, Wy,US
73/C3 **Foster**, Austl.
94/D3 **Fostoria**, Oh,US
36/B3 **Foucherans**, Fr.
31/E6 **Foug**, Fr.
32/C2 **Fougères**, Fr.
36/C2 **Fougerolles**, Fr.
30/B4 **Fouilloy**, Fr.
77/N3 **Foul** (bay), Egypt, Sudan
64/H4 **Foul** (pt.), SrL.
25/G3 **Foulness** (pt.), UK
23/H4 **Foulness** (riv.), Eng,UK
25/G3 **Foulness** (isl.), Eng,UK
25/H1 **Foulsham**, Eng,UK
76/H6 **Foumban**, Camr.
79/H5 **Foumban**, Camr.
93/F3 **Fountain**, Co,US
96/B2 **Fountain**, Co,US
98/E5 **Fountain Hill**, Pa,US
23/G3 **Fountains Abbey**, Eng,UK
98/C3 **Fountain Valley**, Ca,US
32/E3 **Fourchambault**, Fr.
93/J4 **Fourche la Fave** (riv.), Ar,US
25/E4 **Four Marks**, Eng,UK
26/C4 **Fourmies**, Fr.
30/D4 **Fourmies**, Fr.
32/F2 **Fourmies**, Fr.
85/D5 **Four Mountains** (isls.), Ak,US
81/R15 **Fournaise, Piton de la** (peak), Reun.
77/M4 **Fourth** (fall, falls), Sudan
74/F3 **Fourth Cataract** (falls), Sudan
78/B4 **Fouta Djallon** (reg.), Gha.
76/C5 **Fouta Djallon** (reg.), Ghana
71/Q12 **Foveaux** (strait), NZ
24/B6 **Fowey**, Eng,UK
24/B6 **Fowey** (riv.), Eng,UK
73/B1 **Fowlers Gap**, Austl.
51/G2 **Fowman**, Iran
52/E1 **Fowman**, Iran
85/M3 **Fox** (mtn.), Yk,Can
93/K2 **Fox** (riv.), Il, Wi,US
85/E5 **Fox** (isls.), Ak,US
94/B3 **Fox** (riv.), Il,US
99/P15 **Fox** (lake), Il,US
99/P16 **Fox** (riv.), Il,Wi,US
99/B3 **Fox** (isl.), Wa,US
90/D2 **Fox Creek**, Ab,Can
84/J3 **Foxe** (chan.), Can.
84/K3 **Foxe** (pen.), Can.
87/H2 **Foxe** (chan.), NW,Can
87/J2 **Foxe** (pen.), NW,Can
84/J3 **Foxe Basin** (sound), NW,Can
87/J2 **Foxe Basin** (sound), NW,Can
71/R11 **Fox Glacier**, N.Z.
99/P15 **Fox Lake**, Il,US
99/P15 **Fox River Grove**, Il,US
25/G2 **Foxton**, Eng,UK
90/F3 **Fox Valley**, Sk,Can
22/A2 **Foyle** (riv.), NI,UK
22/A1 **Foyle, Lough** (inlet), NI,UK
34/B1 **Foz**, Sp.
82/B4 **Foz do Cunene**, Ang.
109/F2 **Foz do Iguaçu**, Braz.
35/F2 **Fraga**, Sp.
103/G1 **Fragoso** (cay), Cuba
108/B3 **Fraiburgo**, Braz.
106/E7 **Frailes** (range), Bol.
36/B3 **Fraisans**, Fr.
36/D1 **Fraize**, Fr.
30/C3 **Frameries**, Belg.
25/H2 **Framlingham**, Eng,UK
107/J8 **Franca**, Braz.
108/C2 **Franca**, Braz.
40/B4 **Francavilla al Mare**, It.
39/E2 **Francavilla Fontana**, It.
40/C5 **Francavilla Fontana**, It.
38/E2 **Francavilla in Sinni**, It.
18/D4 **France**
26/C4 **France**
30/C5 **France**
32/D5 **France**
35/F1 **France**
36/B3 **France**
38/A1 **France**
19/T9 **France, Pays de** (plain), Fr.
86/C2 **Frances** (lake), Yk,Can
103/E1 **Francés** (cape), Cuba
76/H8 **Franceville**, Gabo
82/B1 **Franceville**, Gabo
26/C5 **Franche-Comté** (r Fr.
33/G3 **Franche-Comté** (r Fr.
36/B2 **Franche-Comté** (r Fr.
36/C3 **Franche-Comté** (h reg.), Fr.
91/J5 **Francis Case** (lak SD,US
106/D4 **Francisco de Orellana**, Peru
101/H5 **Francisco Escárce** Mex.
102/D2 **Francisco Escárce** Mex.
100/E3 **Francisco I. Made** Mex.
82/E5 **Francistown**, Bots
90/B2 **Francois** (lake), BC,Can
19/S10 **Franconville**, Fr.
30/B6 **Franconville**, Fr.
26/C2 **Franeker**, Neth.
28/C2 **Franeker**, Neth.
36/B5 **Frangy**, Fr.
29/F6 **Frankenau**, Ger.
29/F6 **Frankenberg-Eder** Ger.
26/F4 **Frankenhöhe** (mts Ger.
33/J2 **Frankenhohe** (mts Ger.
94/D3 **Frankenmuth**, Mi,
26/E4 **Frankenthal**, Ger.
94/C3 **Frankfort**, In,US
97/G1 **Frankfort**, In,US
89/K4 **Frankfort** (cap.), Ky,US
94/C4 **Frankfort**, Ky,US
97/G2 **Frankfort**, Ky,US
18/E3 **Frankfurt**, Ger.
27/H2 **Frankfurt**, Ger.
18/D3 **Frankfurt am Mai** Ger.
26/E3 **Frankfurt am Mai** Ger.
33/H1 **Frankfurt am Mai** Ger.
46/A4 **Frankfurt am Mai** Ger.
26/F4 **Fränkische Alb** (m Ger.
33/J2 **Fränkische Alb** (range), Ger.
26/E3 **Fränkische Saale** (riv.), Ger.
33/H1 **Fränkische Saale** (riv.), Ger.
26/F4 **Fränkische Schwe** (reg.), Ger.
33/J2 **Fränkische Schwe** (reg.), Ger.
73/C3 **Frankland** (cape), Austl.
83/M **Franklin** (isl.), Ant.
85/N1 **Franklin** (bay), NW,Can
86/D1 **Franklin** (bay), NW,Can
86/D2 **Franklin** (mts.), NW,Can
85/G1 **Franklin** (pt.), Ak,U
94/C4 **Franklin**, In,US
97/G2 **Franklin**, In,US
94/C4 **Franklin**, Ky,US
97/G2 **Franklin**, Ky,US
99/F6 **Franklin**, Mi,US
97/H3 **Franklin**, NC,US
98/F4 **Franklin**, NJ,US
89/J4 **Franklin**, Tn,US
94/C5 **Franklin**, Tn,US
97/G3 **Franklin**, Tn,US
93/H5 **Franklin**, Tx,US
96/D4 **Franklin**, Tx,US
94/E4 **Franklin**, Va,US
97/J2 **Franklin**, Va,US
99/P14 **Franklin**, Wi,US
94/E4 **Franklin**, WV,US
97/J2 **Franklin**, WV,US
90/D3 **Franklin D. Roose** (lake), Wa,US
86/E4 **Franklin D. Roose** (F.D.R.) (res.), Wa,
98/F4 **Franklin Lakes**, NJ,US
73/C4 **Franklin-Lower Gordon Wild River Nat'l Park**, Austl.
98/F4 **Franklin Mineral Museum**, NJ,US
99/Q16 **Franklin Park**, Il,U
99/Q14 **Franksville**, Wi,US
36/B3 **Franois**, Fr.
80/L10 **Franschhoek**, SAfr
109/F2 **Fransisco Beltrão**, Braz.
42/C3 **Fränsta**, Swe.
26/G1 **Franzburg**, Ger.
46/F2 **Franz Josef Land** (arch.), Rus.
71/J5 **Fraser** (isl.), Austl.
72/D4 **Fraser** (isl.), Austl.
90/B2 **Fraser** (lake), BC,C
90/C3 **Fraser** (riv.), BC,Ca
86/D3 **Fraser** (riv.), BC,Ca
88/B1 **Fraser** (riv.), BC,Ca
99/G6 **Fraser**, Mi,US
21/E2 **Fraserburgh**, Sc,U
90/B2 **Fraser Lake**, BC,C
73/C3 **Fraser Nat'l Park**, Austl.
36/C4 **Frasne**, Fr.
37/F3 **Frastanz**, Aus.
26/E5 **Frauenfeld**, Swi.
33/H3 **Frauenfeld**, Swi.
37/E2 **Frauenfeld**, Swi.
33/M3 **Frauenkirchen**, Au
92/C4 **Frazier Park**, Ca,U
31/F2 **Frechen**, Ger.

135

Freci – Gboko

70/A5 Frecinet (estuary), Austl.
31/H5 Freckenfeld, Ger.
80/E3 Fred (mt.), SAfr.
20/D5 Fredericia, Den.
26/E1 Fredericia, Den.
71/J4 Frederick (reef), Austl.
94/E4 Frederick, Md,US
97/J2 Frederick, Md,US
98/J7 Frederick (co.), Md,US
93/H4 Frederick, Ok,US
96/D3 Frederick, Ok,US
101/F2 Fredericksburg, Tx,US
88/G5 Fredericksburg, Tx,US
93/H5 Fredericksburg, Tx,US
96/D4 Fredericksburg, Tx,US
89/L4 Fredericksburg, Va,US
94/E4 Fredericksburg, Va,US
97/J2 Fredericksburg, Va,US
73/E1 Frederickton, Austl.
87/K4 Fredericton (cap.), NB,Can
89/N2 Fredericton (cap.), NB,Can
95/H2 Fredericton, (cap.), NB,Can
20/D4 Frederikshavn, Den.
104/E3 Frederiksted, USVI
92/D3 Fredonia, Az,US
93/J3 Fredonia, Ks,US
96/E2 Fredonia, Ks,US
94/E3 Fredonia, NY,US
20/D4 Fredrikstad, Nor.
93/H3 Freedom, Ok,US
96/D2 Freedom, Ok,US
98/F5 Freehold, NJ,US
99/B1 Freeland, Wa,US
73/A1 Freeling Heights (peak), Austl.
98/E5 Freemansburg, Pa,US
104/B1 Freeport, Bahm.
91/L5 Freeport, Il,US
93/K2 Freeport, Il,US
94/B3 Freeport, Il,US
98/G5 Freeport, NY,US
98/G6 Freeport, Tx,US
93/J5 Freeport, Tx,US
96/E4 Freeport, Tx,US
96/D5 Freer, Tx,US
76/C6 Freetown (cap.), SLeo.
78/B4 Freetown (cap.), SLeo.
34/B3 Fregenal de la Sierra, Sp.
32/B2 Fréhel (cape), Fr.
26/G3 Freib (riv.), Ger.
27/G3 Freiberg, Ger.
26/G3 Freiberger Mulde (riv.), Ger.
18/D4 Freiburg, Ger.
26/D5 Freiburg, Ger.
29/G1 Freiburg, Ger.
33/G3 Freiburg, Ger.
36/D2 Freiburg, Ger.
37/E3 Freienbach, Swi.
108/D1 Frei Inocêncio, Braz.
40/A2 Freilassing, Ger.
31/G4 Freisen, Ger.
26/F4 Freising, Ger.
33/J2 Freising, Ger.
27/H4 Freistadt, Aus.
33/L2 Freistadt, Aus.
27/G3 Freital, Ger.
34/B2 Freixo de Espada à Cinta, Port.
33/G5 Fréjus, Fr.
35/J1 Fréjus, Fr.
68/A8 Fremantle, Austl.
24/B4 Fremington, Eng,UK
93/D2 Fremont, Ca,US
99/L11 Fremont, Ca,US
94/C3 Fremont, Mi,US
89/G3 Fremont, Ne,US
91/J5 Fremont, Ne,US
93/H2 Fremont, Ne,US
94/D3 Fremont, Oh,US
92/E3 Fremont (riv.), Ut,US
90/F5 Fremont (peak), Wy,US
92/E2 Fremont (peak), Wy,US
94/D2 French (riv.), On,Can
98/E5 French (cr.), Pa,US
69/J2 French Frigate (shoals), Hi.,US
107/H3 French Guiana (dpcy.), Fr.
105/D2 French Guiana (dpcy.), Fr.
86/F4 Frenchman (riv.), Sk,Can
106/G3 Frenchman (riv.), Can., US
95/R8 Frenchman's (bay), On,Can
73/C4 Frenchmans Cap (peak), Austl.
69/L6 French Polynesia (terr.), Fr.
9/W15 French Polynesia (terr.), Fr.
98/E5 Frenchtown, NJ,US
76/R16 Frenda, Alg.
19/S9 Frépillon, Fr.
29/E4 Freren, Ger.
107/H5 Fresco (riv.), Braz.
78/D5 Fresco, IvC.
25/E5 Freshwater, Eng,UK
109/B5 Fresia, Chile
19/S10 Fresnes, Fr.
31/E5 Fresnes-en-Woëvre, Fr.
100/E4 Fresnillo, Mex.
88/F7 Fresnillo, Mex.
88/C4 Fresno, Ca,US
92/C3 Fresno, Ca,US
30/C4 Fresnoy-le-Grand, Fr.
30/A3 Fressenneville, Fr.
36/C2 Fresse-sur-Moselle, Fr.
30/C2 Fretin, Fr.
31/G2 Freudenberg, Ger.
31/F4 Freudenburg, Ger.
37/E1 Freudenstadt, Ger.
30/B3 Frévent, Fr.
73/D4 Freycinet Nat'l Park, Austl.
31/F5 Freyming-Merlebach, Fr.
27/G4 Freyung, Ger.
33/K2 Freyung, Ger.
74/D6 Fria (cape), Namb.
82/B4 Fria (cape), Namb.
109/C2 Frías, Arg.
33/G3 Fribourg, Swi.
36/D4 Fribourg, Swi.
36/D4 Fribourg (canton), Swi.
36/E2 Frick, Swi.
37/E1 Fridingen an der Donau, Ger.
26/E3 Friedberg, Ger.
26/F4 Friedberg, Ger.
33/H1 Friedberg, Ger.
37/G1 Friedberg, Ger.
29/E2 Friedeburg, Ger.
33/H1 Friedrichsdorf, Ger.
26/E5 Friedrichshafen, Ger.
33/H3 Friedrichshafen, Ger.
37/F2 Friedrichshafen, Ger.
26/E1 Friedrichstadt, Ger.
31/G5 Friedrichsthal, Ger.
29/G7 Frielendorf, Ger.
31/G2 Friesenhagen, Ger.
33/G2 Friesenheim, Ger.
36/D1 Friesenheim, Ger.
28/C2 Friesland (prov.), Neth.
29/E2 Friesoythe, Ger.
30/D6 Frignicourt, Fr.
25/F4 Frimley, Eng,UK
25/H3 Frinton, Eng,UK
101/F2 Frio (riv.), Tx,US
93/H5 Frio (riv.), Tx,US
34/B1 Friol, Sp.
31/F4 Frisange, Lux.
29/G6 Fritzlar, Ger.
33/K3 Friuli-Venezia Giulia (reg.), It.
25/H6 Friville-Escarbotin, Fr.
30/A3 Friville-Escarbotin, Fr.
22/E2 Frizington, Eng,UK
87/K2 Frobisher (bay), NW,Can
90/F1 Frobisher (lake), Sk,Can
23/F5 Frodsham, Eng,UK
20/D3 Frohavet (bay), Nor.
33/L3 Frohnleiten, Aus.
40/B2 Frohnleiten, Aus.
30/D3 Froidchapelle, Belg.
36/C2 Froideconche, Fr.
45/G2 Frolovo, Rus.
70/F5 Frome (riv.), Austl.
70/G6 Frome (lake), Austl.
73/B1 Frome (lake), Austl.
24/D2 Frome (riv.), Eng,UK
24/D5 Frome, Eng,UK
24/D5 Frome (riv.), Eng,UK
26/C4 Froncles, Fr.
36/B1 Froncles, Fr.
93/F2 Front (range), Co,US
34/B3 Fronteira, Port.
101/E3 Frontera, Mex.
101/G5 Frontera, Mex.
102/C2 Frontera, Mex.
102/C3 Frontera Comalapa, Mex.
100/C2 Fronteras, Mex.
32/E5 Frontignan, Fr.
35/G1 Frontignan, Fr.
32/D5 Fronton, Fr.
35/F1 Fronton, Fr.
94/E4 Front Royal, Va,US
97/J2 Front Royal, Va,US
38/C2 Frosinone, It.
20/E3 Frösö, Swe.
42/B3 Frösö, Swe.
83/J Frost (glac.), Ant.
36/C2 Frotey-lès-Vesoul, Fr.
31/F6 Frouard, Fr.
20/D3 Frøya (isl.), Nor.
87/H2 Frozen (str.), NW,Can
30/B2 Fruges, Fr.
95/Q9 Fruitland, On,Can
41/J2 Frunzovka, Ukr.
40/D3 Fruška Gora Nat'l Park, Yugo.
107/J8 Frutal, Braz.
108/B2 Frutal, Braz.
36/D4 Frutigen, Swi.
43/Y9 Fryazino, Rus.
27/K4 Frýdek-Místek, Czh.
54/E5 Fu (riv.), China
54/G5 Fu (riv.), China
59/C5 Fu (riv.), China
60/E1 Fu (riv.), China
61/H2 Fu (riv.), China
61/H3 Fu'an, China
59/D3 Fucheng, China
26/E3 Fuchskaute (peak), Ger.
33/H1 Fuchskaute (peak), Ger.
31/H2 Fuchskauten (peak), Ger.
56/C3 Fuchū, Japan
57/H7 Fuchū, Japan
59/D5 Fuchun (riv.), China
67/H4 Fudi (mtn.), Indo.
61/J3 Fuding, China
34/C4 Fuengirola, Sp.
34/D2 Fuenlabrada, Sp.
35/N9 Fuenlabrada, Sp.
34/C2 Fuensalida, Sp.
35/N8 Fuente, Sp.
35/E4 Fuente-Álamo, Sp.
34/B3 Fuente de Cantos, Sp.
34/B3 Fuente del Maestre, Sp.
34/C2 Fuentelapeña, Sp.
34/C3 Fuente Obejuna, Sp.
32/C5 Fuenterrabía, Sp.
34/E1 Fuenterrabía, Sp.
34/C2 Fuentesaúco, Sp.
34/C4 Fuentes de Andalucía, Sp.
34/B2 Fuentes de Oñoro, Sp.
100/C3 Fuerte (riv.), Mex.
106/G8 Fuerte Olimpo, Par.
35/Y16 Fuerteventura (isl.), Canl., Sp.
76/C2 Fuerteventura (isl.), Canl., Sp.
63/G2 Fugong, China
54/G5 Fugou, China
59/C4 Fugou, China
46/J5 Fuhai, China
54/B2 Fuhai, China
26/F3 Fuhne (riv.), Ger.
29/H4 Fuhse (riv.), Ger.
55/M4 Fuji, Japan
57/F3 Fuji, Japan
57/F3 Fuji (riv.), Japan
61/H3 Fujian (prov.), China
57/F3 Fujieda, Japan
57/F3 Fuji-Hakone-Izu Nat'l Park, Japan
57/H8 Fuji-Hakone-Izu Nat'l Park, Japan
57/L10 Fujiidera, Japan
57/H7 Fujimi, Japan
57/H7 Fujino, Japan
57/F3 Fujinomiya, Japan
57/F2 Fujioka, Japan
57/N9 Fujioka, Japan
57/F3 Fujisawa, Japan
57/H7 Fujisawa, Japan
57/J7 Fujishiro, Japan
57/M9 Fujiwara, Japan
57/F3 Fujiyama (mtn.), Japan
57/F3 Fujiyoshida, Japan
56/D3 Fukuchiyama, Japan
57/L9 Fukuchiyama, Japan
55/K5 Fukue (isl.), Japan
56/A4 Fukue, Japan
56/A4 Fukue (isl.), Japan
47/P6 Fukui, Japan
55/M4 Fukui, Japan
56/E2 Fukui, Japan
56/E3 Fukui (pref.), Japan
55/L5 Fukuoka, Japan
56/B4 Fukuoka, Japan
56/B4 Fukuoka (pref.), Japan
57/E3 Fukuroi, Japan
83/C Fukushima (peak), Ant.
55/N4 Fukushima, Japan
57/F2 Fukushima, Japan
57/F2 Fukushima (pref.), Japan
56/C3 Fukuyama, Japan
53/J2 Fūlādī (mtn.), Afg.
25/G2 Fulbourn, Eng,UK
26/E3 Fulda, Ger.
26/E3 Fulda (riv.), Ger.
29/G6 Fulda (riv.), Ger.
33/H1 Fulda, Ger.
23/G4 Fulford, Eng,UK
61/E2 Fuling, China
98/C3 Fullerton, Ca,US
98/E5 Fullerton (Whitehall), Pa,US
33/G3 Fully, Swi.
36/D5 Fully, Swi.
37/H3 Fulpmes, Aus.
95/Q9 Fulton, On,Can
94/B4 Fulton, Ky,US
97/F2 Fulton, Ky,US
93/K3 Fulton, Mo,US
96/F2 Fulton, Mo,US
94/E3 Fulton, NY,US
20/E3 Fulufjället (peak), Swe.
23/F4 Fulwood, Eng,UK
26/C4 Fumay, Fr.
31/D4 Fumay, Fr.
32/F2 Fumay, Fr.
32/D4 Fumel, Fr.
60/D3 Fumin, China
63/H2 Fumin, China
57/H7 Funabashi, Japan
68/G5 Funafuti (atoll), Tuv.
59/C4 Funan, China
35/V15 Funchal (cap.), Madr.
76/B1 Funchal (cap.), Madr.
103/H4 Fundación, Col.
34/B2 Fundão, Port.
89/N3 Fundy (bay), NB, NS,Can
95/H2 Fundy (bay), NB, NS,Can
87/K4 Fundy (bay), NB,NS,Can
87/K4 Fundy Nat'l Park, NB,Can
95/H2 Fundy Nat'l Park, NB,Can
82/F5 Funhalouro, Moz.
55/H5 Funing, China
59/D4 Funing, China
60/E4 Funing, China
63/J3 Funing, China
76/G5 Funtua, Nga.
37/G4 Fuorn (Ofenpass) (pass), Swi.
59/C3 Fuping, China
63/J2 Fuquan, China
58/C2 Fur (riv.), China
36/B6 Furan (riv.), Fr.
42/J4 Furmanov, Rus.
105/E5 Furnas (res.), Braz.
107/J8 Furnas (res.), Braz.
108/C2 Furnas (res.), Braz.
71/H7 Furneaux Group (isls.), Austl.
73/C4 Furneaux Group (isls.), Austl.
26/D2 Fürstenau, Ger.
29/E3 Fürstenau, Ger.
40/C2 Fürstenfeld, Aus.
26/F4 Fürstenfeldbruck, Ger.
33/J2 Fürstenfeldbruck, Ger.
37/H1 Fürstenfeldbruck, Ger.
27/H2 Fürstenwalde, Ger.
26/F4 Fürth, Ger.
33/J2 Fürth, Ger.
33/K2 Furth im Wald, Ger.
36/E1 Furtwangen im Schwarzwald, Ger.
55/N4 Furukawa, Japan
87/H2 Fury and Hecla (str.), NW,Can
54/G4 Fushan, China
55/J4 Fushan, China
59/B4 Fushan, China
59/E3 Fushan, China
47/N5 Fushun, China
55/J3 Fushun, China
58/B2 Fushun, China
59/E2 Fushun, China
60/E2 Fushun, China
63/J2 Fushun, China
37/E5 Fusio, Swi.
57/M9 Fuso, Japan
55/K3 Fusong, China
58/D1 Fusong, China
57/H7 Fussa, Japan
26/F5 Füssen, Ger.
33/J3 Füssen, Ger.
37/G2 Füssen, Ger.
63/J3 Fusui, China
65/D1 Fusui, China
57/M10 Futami, Japan
40/D3 Futog, Yugo.
57/F3 Futtsu, Japan
57/H7 Futtsu, Japan
68/H6 Futuna (isl.), Wall.
49/B4 Fuwah, Egypt
54/F4 Fu Xian, China
59/B3 Fu Xian, China
60/D3 Fuxian (lake), China
63/H3 Fuxian (lake), China
55/J3 Fuxin, China
58/A1 Fuxin, China
59/E2 Fuxin, China
58/A1 Fuxin Monggolzu Zizhixian, China
59/F2 Fuxin Monggolzu Zizhixian, China
54/H5 Fuyang, China
59/C4 Fuyang, China
61/F3 Fuyi (riv.), China
55/J2 Fuyu, China
60/E3 Fuyuan, China
63/H2 Fuyuan, China
46/J5 Fuyun, China
54/B2 Fuyun, China
27/L5 Füzesabony, Hun.
61/H3 Fuzhou, China
68/A2 Fuzhou, China
19/P6 Fyfield, Eng,UK
20/D5 Fyn (isl.), Den.
26/F1 Fyn (co.), Den.

G

77/Q6 Gaalkacyo (Galcaio), Som.
28/D5 Gaanderen, Neth.
28/C2 Gaast, Neth.
32/C5 Gabas (riv.), Fr.
35/E1 Gabas (riv.), Fr.
92/C3 Gabbs, Nv,US
82/B3 Gabela, Ang.
76/H1 Gabes (gulf), Tun.
37/G1 Gablingen, Ger.
74/D4 Gabon
76/H7 Gabon
82/B1 Gabon
80/D2 Gaborone (cap.), Bots.
82/E5 Gaborone (cap.), Bots.
39/J1 Gabrovo, Bul.
41/G4 Gabrovo, Bul.
39/F1 Gacko, Bosn.
40/D4 Gacko, Bosn.
53/L5 Gadag-Betgeri, India
62/C4 Gadag-Betgeri, India
37/E4 Gadmen, Swi.
51/F2 Gadrut, Azer.
89/J5 Gadsden, Al,US
97/G3 Gadsden, Al,US
41/G3 Găeşti, Rom.
44/C3 Găeşti, Rom.
38/C2 Gaeta, It.
38/C2 Gaeta (gulf), It.
97/H3 Gaffney, SC,US
42/G5 Gagarin, Rus.
76/D6 Gagnoa, IvC.
78/D5 Gagnoa, IvC.
87/K3 Gagnon, Qu,Can
95/G1 Gagnon, Qu,Can
19/T10 Gagny, Fr.
30/B6 Gagny, Fr.
19/H4 Gagra, Geo.
44/G4 Gagra, Geo.
46/E5 Gagra, Geo.
37/G3 Gaichtpass (pass), Aus.
33/K3 Gail (riv.), Aus.
40/A2 Gail (riv.), Aus.
32/D5 Gaillac, Fr.
35/F1 Gaillac, Fr.
30/A4 Gaillefontaine, Fr.
30/A5 Gaillon, Fr.
33/K3 Gailtaler Alps (mts.), Aus.
109/C5 Gaiman, Arg.
89/K6 Gainesville, Fl,US
97/H4 Gainesville, Fl,US
89/K5 Gainesville, Ga,US
97/H3 Gainesville, Ga,US
93/J3 Gainesville, Mo,US
96/E2 Gainesville, Mo,US
89/G5 Gainesville, Tx,US
93/H4 Gainesville, Tx,US
96/D3 Gainesville, Tx,US
23/G2 Gainford, Eng,UK
23/H5 Gainsborough, Eng,UK
70/F6 Gairdner (lake), Austl.
37/F3 Gais, Swi.
98/J7 Gaithersburg, Md,US
58/B2 Gai Xian, China
59/E2 Gai Xian, China
20/H4 Gaizina (peak), Lat.
42/E4 Gaizina Kalns (peak), Lat.
33/M2 Gajary, Slvk.
80/C2 Gakarosa (peak), SAfr.
85/J3 Gakona, Ak,US
51/H2 Galand, Iran
53/G1 Galand, Iran
34/D2 Galapagar, Sp.
53/L2 Galār, India
21/D3 Galashiels, Sc,UK
18/F4 Galați, Rom.
41/H3 Galați (co.), Rom.
41/J3 Galați, Rom.
44/D3 Galați, Rom.
46/C5 Galați, Rom.
39/F2 Galatina, It.
39/G2 Galatiní, Gre.
39/H2 Galátista, Gre.
39/F2 Galatone, It.
94/D4 Galax, Va,US
97/H2 Galax, Va,US
39/H3 Galaxídhiou, Gre.
77/Q6 Galcaio, Som.
35/X16 Gáldar, Canl.
100/D2 Galeana, Mex.
101/E3 Galeana, Mex.
92/F5 Galeana, Mex
67/G3 Galela, Indo.
85/G3 Galena, Ak,US
91/L5 Galena, Il,US
93/K2 Galena, Il,US
94/B3 Galena, Il,US
105/A2 Galera (pt.), Ecu.
106/B3 Galera (pt.), Ecu.
104/F5 Galera (pt.), Trin.
106/F1 Galera (pt.), Trin.
89/H3 Galesburg, Il,US
91/L5 Galesburg, Il,US
93/K2 Galesburg, Il,US
94/B3 Galesburg, Il,US
21/H7 Galey (riv.), Ire.
22/B2 Galgorm, NI,UK
42/J4 Galich, Rus.
27/L3 Galicia (reg.), Pol., Ukr.
34/A1 Galicia (aut. comm.), Sp.
39/G2 Galičica Nat'l Park, Macd.
40/E5 Galičica Nat'l Park, Macd.
53/G1 Gālīkash, Iran
49/D3 Galilee, Sea of (Tiberias) (lake), Isr.
108/D1 Galiléia, Braz.
37/F3 Galinakopf (peak), Aus.
94/D3 Galion, Oh,US
94/C4 Gallatin, Tn,US
97/G2 Gallatin, Tn,US
62/D6 Galle, SrL.
109/B7 Gallegos (riv.), Arg.
103/J3 Gallinas (pt.), Col.
104/D4 Gallinas (pt.), Col.
105/B1 Gallinas (pt.), Col.
106/D1 Gallinas (pt.), Col.
96/B3 Gallinas (mts.), NM,US
39/E2 Gallipoli, It.
41/H5 Gallipoli (pen.), Turk.
39/K2 Gallipoli (Gelibolu), Turk.
41/H5 Gallipoli (Gelibolu), Turk.
50/A1 Gallipoli (Gelibolu), Turk.
94/D4 Gallipolis, Oh,US
97/H2 Gallipolis, Oh,US
18/F2 Gällivare, Swe.
20/G2 Gällivare, Swe.
42/D2 Gällivare, Swe.
46/C3 Gällivare, Swe.
33/L2 Gallneukirchen, Aus.
37/G4 Gallo (lake), It.
30/C3 Gallo (cape), It.
22/D2 Galloway, Mull of (pt.), Sc,UK
88/E4 Gallup, NM,US
92/E4 Gallup, NM,US
96/A3 Gallup, NM,US
34/E2 Gallur, Sp.
19/R10 Gally (riv.), Fr.
49/F8 Gal'on, Isr.
72/H8 Galston, Austl.
54/D2 Galt, Mong.
99/M10 Galt, Ca,US
21/A4 Galtymore (mtn.), Ire.
54/E2 Galuut, Mong.
89/H6 Galveston, Tx,US
93/J5 Galveston, Tx,US
93/J5 Galveston (bay), Tx,US
93/J5 Galveston (isl.), Tx,US
96/E4 Galveston, Tx,US
96/E4 Galveston (isl.), Tx,US
34/C3 Gálvez, Sp.
18/C3 Galway, Ire.
21/A4 Galway, Ire.
21/H7 Galway (bay), Ire.
60/E4 Gam (riv.), Viet.
63/J3 Gam (riv.), Viet.
65/D1 Gam (riv.), Viet.
30/A4 Gamaches, Fr.
80/C2 Gamagara (dry riv.), SAfr.
57/E3 Gamagōri, Japan
57/N10 Gamagōri, Japan
103/H4 Gamarra, Col.
62/E2 Gamba, China
79/E4 Gambaga, Gha.
79/E4 Gambaga Scarp (escarp.), Gha., Togo
62/A2 Gambat, Pak.
77/M6 Gambēla, Eth.
77/M6 Gambela Nat'l Park, Eth.
85/D3 Gambell, Ak,US
74/A3 Gambia
76/B5 Gambia
78/B3 Gambia
74/A3 Gambia (riv.), Afr.
76/C5 Gambia (riv.), Afr.
78/A3 Gambia (Gambie) (riv.), Afr.
78/B3 Gambie (Gambia) (riv.), Afr.
69/M7 Gambier (isls.), FrPol.
95/L1 Gambo, Nf,Can
76/J8 Gamboma, Congo
82/C1 Gamboma, Congo
27/H5 Gaming, Aus.
40/B2 Gaming, Aus.
80/C4 Gamka (riv.), SAfr.
80/B3 Gamkab (dry riv.), Namb.
20/G3 Gamlakarleby (Kokkola), Fin.
42/D3 Gamlakarleby (Kokkola), Fin.
25/F2 Gamlingay, Eng,UK
42/D2 Gammelstad, Swe.
37/F1 Gammertingen, Ger.
57/M9 Gamo, Japan
27/G5 Gamsfeld (peak), Aus.
77/N7 Gamud (peak), Eth.
55/J1 Gan (riv.), China
61/G2 Gan (riv.), China
32/C5 Gan, Fr.
35/E1 Gan, Fr.
94/E2 Gananoque, On,Can
51/G4 Ganāveh, Iran
82/B3 Ganda, Ang.
82/D2 Gandajika, Zaire
87/L4 Gander, Nf,Can
95/L1 Gander, Nf,Can
95/L1 Gander (lake), Nf,Can
29/F2 Ganderkesee, Ger.
35/F2 Gandesa, Sp.
53/K4 Gāndhi (res.), India
53/J4 Gāndhidhām, India
62/B3 Gāndhīdhām, India
53/K4 Gandhinagar, India
62/B3 Gandhinagar, India
62/B3 Gāndhi Sāgar (res.), India
18/C5 Gandia, Sp.
35/E3 Gandia, Sp.
103/F4 Gandoca-Manzanillo Nat'l Wild. Ref., CR
76/C4 Ganeb (well), Mrta.
53/L3 Gangāpur, India
62/C2 Gangāpur, India
62/E3 Gangārāmpur, India
60/B4 Gangaw, Burma
63/F3 Gangaw, Burma
54/E4 Gangca, China
31/F2 Gangelt, Ger.
32/E5 Ganges, Fr.
35/G1 Ganges, Fr.
62/E3 Ganges (riv.), India
48/H7 Ganges (riv.), India, Nepal
62/E3 Ganges, Mouths of the (delta), Bang.,India
38/D4 Gangi, It.
62/E2 Gangtok, India
49/G7 Gan Hashlosha Nat'l Park, Isr.
63/H2 Ganluo, China
55/J2 Gannan, China
32/E3 Gannat, Fr.
86/F4 Gannett (peak), Wy,US
88/E3 Gannett (peak), Wy,US
90/F5 Gannett (peak), Wy,US
92/E2 Gannett (peak), Wy,US
54/F4 Ganquan, China
59/B3 Ganquan, China
80/L11 Gansbaai, SAfr.
36/D4 Gantrisch (peak), Swi.
76/H6 Ganye, Nga.
59/D4 Ganyu, China
61/G3 Ganzhou, China
68/A2 Ganzhou, China
26/G2 Ganzlin, Ger.
79/E3 Ganzourgou (prov.), Burk.
61/G3 Gao (mtn.), China
76/E4 Gao, Mali
79/E2 Gao, Mali
79/F2 Gao (reg.), Mali
61/G2 Gao'an, China
59/C3 Gaocheng, China
55/H5 Gaochun, China
59/D5 Gaochun, China
61/H2 Gaochun, China
54/E4 Gaolan, China
61/G4 Gaolan (isl.), China
60/C3 Gaoligong (mts.), China
59/D3 Gaomi, China
63/K2 Gaomutang, China
54/C4 Gaoping, China
59/C4 Gaoping, China
55/H4 Gaoqing, China
59/D3 Gaoqing, China
63/K2 Gaoqitou, China
54/D4 Gaotai, China
59/D3 Gaotang, China
76/E5 Gaoua, Burk.
78/E4 Gaoua, Burk.
54/H4 Gaoyang, China
59/C3 Gaoyang, China
59/C3 Gaoyi, China
55/H5 Gaoyou (lake), China
59/D4 Gaoyou, China
59/D4 Gaoyou (lake), China
61/F4 Gaozhou, China
63/K3 Gaozhou, China
33/G4 Gap, Fr.
73/B1 Gap, The, Austl.
54/D5 Gar (riv.), China
103/G4 Garachiné, Pan.
103/G4 Garachiné (pt.), Pan.
72/C5 Garah, Austl.
62/E3 Garai (riv.), Bang.
35/X16 Garajonay Nat'l Park, Canl.
77/L7 Garamba Nat'l Park, Zaire
107/L5 Garanhuns, Braz.
77/N7 Garba Tula, Kenya
26/E2 Garbsen, Ger.
108/B2 Garça, Braz.
107/H7 Garças (riv.), Braz.
19/S10 Garches, Fr.
34/C3 Garcia de Sota (res.), Sp.
32/F5 Gard (riv.), Fr.
33/J4 Garda (lake), It.
51/F1 Gardabani, Geo.
75/V17 Garde, Cap de (cape), Alg.
26/F2 Gardelegen, Ger.
98/B3 Gardena, Ca,US
97/H3 Garden City, Ga,US
88/F4 Garden City, Ks,US
93/G3 Garden City, Ks,US
96/C2 Garden City, Ks,US
99/F7 Garden City, Mi,US
98/G5 Garden City, NY,US
90/A2 Gardener Canal (inlet), BC,Can
98/C3 Garden Grove, Ca,US
53/J2 Gardēz, Afg.
95/G2 Gardiner, Me,US
90/F4 Gardiner, Mt,US
99/B1 Gardiner, Wa,US
69/H5 Gardner (Nikumaroro) (atoll), Kiri.
76/G2 Garet el Djenoun (peak), Alg.
90/E4 Garfield (peak), Mt,US
92/D1 Garfield (peak), Mt,US
100/D1 Garfield, NM,US
23/G4 Garforth, Eng,UK
39/G4 Gargaliánoi, Gre.
32/D4 Gargan (mtn.), Fr.
19/T10 Garges-lès-Gonesse, Fr.
23/F4 Gargrave, Eng,UK
42/D5 Gargždai, Lith.
62/C3 Garhākotā, India
64/A2 Garh Mahārāja, Pak.
108/B4 Garibaldi, Braz.
80/B3 Garies, SAfr.
82/C7 Garies, SAfr.
77/N8 Garissa, Kenya
82/G1 Garissa, Kenya
101/F1 Garland, Tx,US
93/H4 Garland, Tx,US
96/D3 Garland, Tx,US
27/M1 Garliava, Lith.
22/D2 Garlieston, Sc,UK
53/G1 Garmeh, Iran
26/F5 Garmisch-Partenkirchen, Ger.
33/J3 Garmisch-Partenkirchen, Ger.
37/H3 Garmisch-Partenkirchen, Ger.
51/H3 Garmsār, Iran
52/F1 Garmsār, Iran
93/H3 Garnett, Ks,US
96/E2 Garnett, Ks,US
73/B2 Garnpung (lake), Austl.
18/C4 Garonne (riv.), Fr.
32/D4 Garonne (riv.), Fr.
77/Q6 Garoowe, Som.
108/B4 Garopaba, Braz.
79/E2 Garou (lake), Mali
76/H6 Garoua, Camr.
76/H6 Garoua Boulaï, Camr.
35/K7 Garraf (range), Sp.
22/D6 Garreg, Wal,UK
26/E2 Garrel, Ger.
29/F3 Garrel, Ger.
88/F2 Garrison, ND,US
88/F2 Garrison (dam), ND,US
91/H4 Garrison, ND,US
91/H4 Garrison (dam), ND,US
22/C1 Garron (pt.), NI,UK
34/B3 Garrovillas, Sp.
86/F2 Garry (lake), NW,Can
87/H2 Garry (bay), NW,Can
27/H4 Gars am Kamp, Aus.
33/L2 Gars am Kamp, Aus.
23/F4 Garstang, Eng,UK
33/L2 Garsten, Aus.
40/B1 Garsten, Aus.
29/H6 Garte (riv.), Ger.
32/D3 Gartempe (riv.), Fr.
24/C2 Garth, Wal,UK
66/C5 Garut, Indo.
22/B2 Garvagh, NI,UK
27/L3 Garwolin, Pol.
89/J3 Gary, In,US
94/C3 Gary, In,US
99/R16 Gary, In,US
54/C5 Garzê, China
60/D2 Garzê, China
106/C3 Garzón, Col.
20/P6 Gæsafjöll (peak), Ice.
46/F6 Gasan-Kuli, Trkm.
52/F1 Gasan-Kuli, Trkm.
94/C3 Gas City, In,US
32/C5 Gascony (reg.), Fr.
35/E1 Gascony (hist. prov.), Fr.
70/B5 Gascoyne (riv.), Austl.
54/C6 Gasheng, India
63/F2 Gasheng, India
76/H5 Gashua, Nga.
30/A5 Gasny, Fr.
108/B3 Gaspar, Braz.
66/C4 Gaspar (riv.), Indo.
87/K4 Gaspé, Qu,Can
87/K4 Gaspé (pen.), Qu,Can
89/N2 Gaspé (pen.), Qu,Can
89/P2 Gaspé, Qu,Can
95/H1 Gaspé, Qu,Can
95/H1 Gaspé (pen.), Qu,Can
95/S9 Gasport, NY,US
89/K4 Gastonia, NC,US
97/H3 Gastonia, NC,US
39/G4 Gastoúni, Gre.
49/F8 Gat, Isr.
49/C2 Gata (cape), Cyp.
34/B2 Gata (range), Sp.
34/D4 Gata, Cabo de (cape), Sp.
35/F3 Gata de Gorgos, Sp.
20/J4 Gatchina, Rus.
42/F4 Gatchina, Rus.
22/D2 Gatehouse-of-Fleet, Sc,UK
86/F1 Gateshead (isl.), NW,Can
23/G2 Gateshead, Eng,UK
85/H2 Gates of the Arctic Nat'l Pk. & Prsv., Ak,US
93/H5 Gatesville, Tx,US
96/D4 Gatesville, Tx,US
98/F5 Gateway Nat'l Rec. Area, NJ,NY, US
32/C3 Gâtine (hills), Fr.
87/J4 Gatineau (riv.), Qu,Can
94/F2 Gatineau, Qu,Can
94/F2 Gatineau (riv.), Qu,Can
33/M2 Gattendorf, Aus.
72/D4 Gatton, Austl.
103/G4 Gatun (dam), Pan.
103/G4 Gatún (lake), Pan.
19/N8 Gatwick (London) (int'l arpt.), Eng,UK
31/H4 Gau Algesheim, Ger.
31/H4 Gau-Bickelheim, Ger.
30/C4 Gauchy, Fr.
34/C4 Gaucín, Sp.
60/A3 Gauhāti, India
63/F2 Gauhāti, India
23/G2 Gaunless (riv.), Eng,UK
31/H4 Gau Odernheim, Ger.
62/E2 Gauripur, India
62/F2 Gauri Sankar (mtn.), Nepal
20/D4 Gausta (peak), Nor.
37/H1 Gauting, Ger.
20/H4 Gauya Nat'l Park, Lat.
42/E4 Gauya Nat'l Park, Lat.
35/G2 Gavà, Sp.
35/K7 Gavà, Sp.
52/F3 Gāvbandī, Iran
39/J5 Gávdhos (isl.), Gre.
34/E1 Gave de Pau (riv.), Fr.
30/C2 Gavere, Belg.
34/B3 Gavião, Port.
18/E2 Gävle, Swe.
20/F3 Gävle, Swe.
42/C3 Gävle, Swe.
46/B3 Gävle, Swe.
20/E3 Gävleborg (co.), Swe.
42/C3 Gävleborg (co.), Swe.
63/G2 Gawai, Burma
27/J4 Gaweinstal, Aus.
70/F6 Gawler, Austl.
70/F6 Gawler (ranges), Austl.
73/A2 Gawler, Austl.
54/D3 Gaxun (lake), China
45/L2 Gay, Rus.
94/D4 Gay (peak), WV,US
97/H2 Gay (peak), WV,US
55/K3 Gaya (riv.), China
62/E3 Gaya, India
76/F5 Gaya, Niger
79/F4 Gaya, Niger
94/C2 Gaylord, Mi,US
72/C4 Gayndah, Austl.
44/D2 Gaysin, Ukr.
41/J1 Gayvoron, Ukr.
50/C4 Gaza, Gaza
52/B2 Gaza, Gaza
77/M1 Gaza, Gaza
81/F2 Gaza (prov.), Moz.
49/D4 Gaza (Ghazzah), Gaza
49/D4 Gaza Strip (occ. zone)
50/C4 Gaza Strip (occ. zone)
49/E1 Gaziantep, Turk.
49/E1 Gaziantep (prov.), Turk.
50/D2 Gaziantep, Turk.
50/D2 Gaziantep (prov.), Turk.
52/C1 Gaziantep, Turk.
55/H1 Gazimur (riv.), Rus.
49/C1 Gazipaşa, Turk.
26/D4 Gazon de Faing (peak), Fr.
33/G2 Gazon de Faing (peak), Fr.
36/D1 Gazon de Faing (peak), Fr.
77/K7 Gbadolite, Zaire
76/D6 Gbarnga, Libr.
78/C5 Gbarnga, Libr.
76/G6 Gboko, Nga.

136

Gdańsk – Gonda

18/E3 Gdańsk, Pol.
27/K1 Gdańsk, Pol.
27/K1 Gdańsk (prov.), Pol.
42/C5 Gdańsk, Pol.
46/B4 Gdańsk, Pol.
27/K1 Gdańsk (gulf), Pol., Rus.
42/C5 Gdańsk (gulf), Pol., Rus.
20/H4 Gdov, Rus.
42/E4 Gdov, Rus.
18/E3 Gdynia, Pol.
27/K1 Gdynia, Pol.
42/C5 Gdynia, Pol.
46/B4 Gdynia, Pol.
59/D5 Ge (lake), China
59/K8 Ge (lake), China
33/J1 Gebaberg (peak), Ger.
67/G3 Gebe (isl.), Indo.
52/C4 Gebeit Mine, Sudan
31/G2 Gebhardshain, Ger.
41/J5 Gebze, Turk.
44/D4 Gebze, Turk.
50/B1 Gebze, Turk.
66/C5 Gede (peak), Indo.
49/F8 Gedera, Isr.
26/C4 Gedinne, Belg.
31/D4 Gedinne, Belg.
32/F2 Gedinne, Belg.
44/D5 Gediz, Turk.
50/A2 Gediz (riv.), Turk.
50/B2 Gediz, Turk.
26/F1 Gedser, Den.
26/C3 Geel, Belg.
28/C6 Geel, Belg.
31/E1 Geel, Belg.
71/G7 Geelong, Austl.
73/C3 Geelong, Austl.
70/A5 Geelvink (chan.), Austl.
29/E3 Geeste, Ger.
29/F2 Geeste (riv.), Ger.
29/H2 Geesthacht, Ger.
73/C4 Geeveston, Austl.
29/F3 Gehrde, Ger.
29/G4 Gehrden, Ger.
24/C2 Geifas (mtn.), Wal,UK
37/G3 Geige, Hohe (peak), Aus.
86/F3 Geikie (riv.), Sk,Can
31/F2 Geilenkirchen, Ger.
57/M10 Geinō, Japan
31/G4 Geisenheim, Ger.
37/E1 Geislingen, Ger.
33/H2 Geislingen an der Steige, Ger.
82/F1 Geita, Tanz.
60/D4 Gejiu, China
63/H3 Gejiu, China
77/L6 Gel (riv.), Sudan
38/D4 Gela, It.
38/D4 Gela (gulf), It.
77/Q6 Geladī, Eth.
37/E5 Gelato (mtn.), It.
28/C4 Gelderland (prov.), Neth.
28/C5 Geldermalsen, Neth.
28/D5 Geldern, Ger.
28/C6 Geldrop, Neth.
31/E2 Geleen, Neth.
50/B2 Gelendost, Turk.
44/F3 Gelendzhik, Rus.
39/K2 Gelibolu (Gallipoli), Turk.
41/H5 Gelibolu (Gallipoli), Turk.
50/A1 Gelibolu (Gallipoli), Turk.
41/H5 Gelibolu Yarımadas Milli Park, Turk.
44/C4 Gelibolu Yarımadas Milli Park, Turk.
39/K2 Gelibolu Yarımadas Nat'l Park, Turk.
51/E2 Gelincik (peak), Turk.
24/C3 Gelligaer, Wal,UK
26/D3 Gelsenkirchen, Ger.
28/E5 Gelsenkirchen, Ger.
37/H1 Geltendorf, Ger.
36/D3 Gelterkinden, Swi.
26/E1 Gelting, Ger.
66/B3 Gemas, Malay.
31/D2 Gembloux, Belg.
76/H6 Gembu, Nga.
77/J7 Gemena, Zaire
28/C5 Gemert, Neth.
41/J5 Gemlik, Turk.
41/J5 Gemlik (gulf), Turk.
44/D4 Gemlik, Turk.
50/B1 Gemlik, Turk.
33/K3 Gemona del Friuli, It.
40/A2 Gemona del Friuli, It.
80/C2 Gemsbok-Kalahari Nat'l Park, SAfr.
80/C2 Gemsbok Nat'l Park, Bots.
82/D6 Gemsbok Nat'l Park, Bots.
85/G3 Gemuk (mtn.), Ak,US
55/J1 Gen (riv.), China
77/N6 Genalē Wenz (riv.), Eth.
30/D2 Genappe, Belg.
38/A3 Genargentu (mts.), It.
36/A6 Genay, Fr.
50/E2 Genç, Turk.
28/D5 Gendringen, Neth.
28/C5 Gendt, Neth.
28/D3 Genemuiden, Neth.
109/D4 General Acha, Arg.
109/C3 General Alvear, Arg.
101/F3 General Bravo, Mex.
101/E3 General Cepeda, Mex.
109/D5 General Conesa, Arg.
101/F5 General Juan Alvarez, Mex.
102/B2 General Juan Álvarez Nat'l Park, Mex.
109/E4 General Juan Madariaga, Arg.
109/C1 General Martín Miguel De Güemes, Arg.
109/D4 General Pico, Arg.
109/D2 General Pinedo, Arg.
67/G2 General Santos, Phil.
68/B4 General Santos, Phil.
101/F3 General Terán, Mex.
41/J4 General-Toshevo, Bul.
109/D4 General Villegas, Arg.
37/F6 Generoso, Monte (peak), Swi.
99/E6 Genesee (co.), Mi,US
94/E3 Genesee (riv.), NY,US
99/P14 Genesee, Wi,US
99/P14 Genesee Depot, Wi,US
91/L5 Geneseo, Il,US
94/E3 Geneseo, NY,US
36/C5 Geneva (Léman) (lake), Fr., Swi.
18/D4 Geneva, Swi.
97/G4 Geneva, Al,US
99/P16 Geneva, Il,US
93/H2 Geneva, Ne,US
89/L3 Geneva, NY,US
94/E3 Geneva, NY,US
99/P14 Geneva (lake), Wi,US
33/G3 Geneva (Genève), Swi.
36/C5 Geneva (Genève), Swi.
33/G3 Geneva (Léman) (lake), Fr., Swi.
36/C5 Genève (canton), Swi.
33/G3 Genève (Geneva), Swi.
36/C5 Genève (Geneva), Swi.
61/E3 Gengding (mtn.), China
26/E4 Gengenbach, Ger.
33/H2 Gengenbach, Ger.
36/E1 Gengenbach, Ger.
60/C4 Gengma Daizu Vazu Zizhixian, China
44/E3 Genichesk, Ukr.
34/C4 Genil (riv.), Sp.
26/C3 Genk, Belg.
31/E2 Genk, Belg.
36/B3 Genlis, Fr.
37/G2 Gennach (riv.), Ger.
28/C5 Gennep, Neth.
19/S10 Gennevilliers, Fr.
18/D4 Genoa, It.
99/P15 Genoa City, Wi,US
33/H4 Genoa (Genova), It.
33/H4 Genova (gulf), It.
33/H4 Genova (Genoa), It.
31/G4 Gensingen, Ger.
26/B3 Gent, Belg.
28/A6 Gent-Brugge (can.), Belg.
30/C1 Gent-Brugge (can.), Belg.
66/C5 Genteng (cape), Indo.
28/A6 Gent (Ghent), Belg.
30/C1 Gent (Ghent), Belg.
70/A4 Geographe (chan.), Austl.
70/A6 Geographe (bay), Austl.
51/F1 Geokchay, Azer.
53/G1 Geok-Tepe, Trkm.
70/C4 George (lake), Austl.
72/C3 George (pt.), Austl.
73/D2 George (lake), Austl.
84/L4 George (riv.), Can.
87/K3 George (riv.), Qu,Can
80/C4 George, SAfr.
82/D7 George, SAfr.
46/E1 George Land (isl.), Rus.
72/G9 Georges (riv.), Austl.
70/G3 Georgetown, Austl.
71/H8 George Town, Austl.
72/A2 Georgetown, Austl.
73/C4 George Town, Austl.
95/Q8 Georgetown, On,Can
103/F2 George Town, Cay.
78/B3 Georgetown, Gam.
106/G2 Georgetown (cap.), Guy.
66/B2 Georgetown, Malay.
104/F4 Georgetown, StV.
98/G4 Georgetown, Ct,US
97/H4 Georgetown, Ga,US
94/C4 Georgetown, Ky,US
97/G2 Georgetown, Ky,US
89/L5 Georgetown, SC,US
97/J3 Georgetown, SC,US
101/F2 Georgetown, Tx,US
93/H5 Georgetown, Tx,US
96/D4 Georgetown, Tx,US
83/L George V (coast), Ant.
83/V George VI (sound), Ant.
101/F2 George West, Tx,US
96/D4 George West, Tx,US
19/H4 Georgia
45/G4 Georgia
46/E5 Georgia
51/E1 Georgia
90/B3 Georgia (str.), Can., US
89/K5 Georgia (state), US
97/G3 Georgia (state), US
87/H4 Georgian (bay), On,Can
94/D2 Georgian (bay), On,Can
89/K2 Georgian (bay), US, Can.
94/D2 Georgian Bay Islands Nat'l Park, Can
70/F4 Georgina (riv.), Austl.
41/H4 Georgi Traykov, Bul.
26/E2 Georgsmarienhütte, Ger.
29/F4 Georgsmarienhütte, Ger.
26/G3 Gera, Ger.
30/C2 Geraardsbergen, Belg.
108/B3 Geral (range), Braz.
107/J6 Geral de Goiás (Espigão Mestre) (mts.), Braz.
71/R11 Geraldine, N.Z.
68/A7 Geraldton, Austl.
70/A5 Geraldton, Austl.
87/H4 Geraldton, On,Can
89/J2 Geraldton, On,Can
91/M3 Geraldton, On,Can
94/C1 Geraldton, On,Can
36/C1 Gérardmer, Fr.
36/C1 Gerbéviller, Fr.
32/F4 Gerbier de Jonc (mtn.), Fr.
29/H3 Gerdau (riv.), Ger.
85/H3 Gerdine (mt.), Ak,US
41/L5 Gerede, Turk.
44/E4 Gerede, Turk.
50/C1 Gerede, Turk.
53/H2 Gereshk, Afg.
26/F5 Geretsried, Ger.
33/J3 Geretsried, Ger.
37/H2 Geretsried, Ger.
34/D4 Gérgal, Sp.
50/D2 Gerger, Turk.
90/D5 Gerlach, Nv,US
92/C2 Gerlach, Nv,US
27/L4 Gerlachovský Štít (peak), Slvk.
44/B2 Gerlachovský Štít (peak), Slvk.
36/D3 Gerlafingen, Swi.
98/J7 Germantown, Md,US
97/F3 Germantown, Tn,US
18/D3 Germany
20/D5 Germany
26/E3 Germany
29/E3 Germany
31/F3 Germany
33/H2 Germany
37/E1 Germany
40/A2 Germany
46/A4 Germany
26/F4 Germering, Ger.
33/J2 Germering, Ger.
37/H1 Germering, Ger.
37/E6 Germinaga, It.
80/E2 Germiston, SAfr.
80/Q13 Germiston, SAfr.
37/H1 Gerolsbach, Ger.
26/D3 Gerolstein, Ger.
31/F3 Gerolstein, Ger.
33/G1 Gerolstein, Ger.
35/G2 Gerona (Girona), Sp.
35/E1 Ger, Pic du (peak), Fr.
30/D3 Gerpinnes, Belg.
19/M7 Gerrards Cross, Eng,UK
37/E5 Gerra (Verzasca), Swi.
73/D2 Gerringong, Austl.
32/D5 Gers (riv.), Fr.
37/E4 Gersau, Swi.
31/G5 Gersheim, Ger.
26/F4 Gerstetten, Ger.
36/D1 Gerstheim, Fr.
26/F4 Gersthofen, Ger.
37/G1 Gersthofen, Ger.
29/H7 Gerstungen, Ger.
44/E4 Gerze, Turk.
50/C1 Gerze, Turk.
28/E5 Gescher, Ger.
29/F5 Geseke, Ger.
31/D4 Gespunsart, Fr.
77/P6 Gestro Wenz (riv.), Eth.
31/E3 Gesves, Belg.
20/F3 Geta, Fin.
34/D2 Getafe, Sp.
35/N9 Getafe, Sp.
54/G4 Getai, China
59/B5 Getai, China
31/E2 Gete (riv.), Belg.
26/E1 Gettorf, Ger.
92/E4 Gettysburg, Pa,US
91/J4 Gettysburg, SD,US
108/A3 Getúlio Vargas, Braz.
83/S Getz Ice Shelf, Ant.
31/E2 Geul (riv.), Belg.
31/E2 Geul (riv.), Neth.
66/A3 Geureudong (peak), Indo.
73/D2 Geurie, Austl.
51/E2 Gevaş, Turk.
29/E6 Gevelsberg, Ger.
39/H2 Gevgelija, Macd.
40/F5 Gevgelija, Macd.
44/B4 Gevgelija, Macd.
77/P5 Gewanē, Eth.
37/C5 Gex, Fr.
81/H6 Geyser (reef), Madg.
41/K5 Geyve, Turk.
50/B1 Geyve, Turk.
76/G1 Ghadāmis, Libya
64/D2 Ghaggar (riv.), India
74/B4 Ghana
76/E6 Ghana
79/E4 Ghana
82/D5 Ghanzi, Bots.
76/F1 Ghardaïa, Alg.
52/B3 Gharib, Ra's, Egypt
76/H1 Gharyān, Libya
76/H3 Ghāt, Libya
76/J5 Ghazal (riv.), Chad
75/P13 Ghazaouet, Alg.
53/L3 Ghaziābād, India
62/C2 Ghaziābād, India
53/J2 Ghaznī, Afg.
49/D4 Ghazzah (Gaza), Gaza
77/M1 Ghazzah (Gaza), Gaza
54/G2 Ghengis Khan Wall (ruins), Mong.
18/D3 Ghent, Belg.
28/A6 Ghent (Gent), Belg.
30/C1 Ghent (Gent), Belg.
41/H2 Gheorghe Gheorghiu-Dej, Rom.
44/C3 Gheorghe Gheorghiu-Dej, Rom.
41/G2 Gheorgheni, Rom.
41/F2 Gherla, Rom.
44/B3 Gherla, Rom.
53/K3 Gheura, India
38/A2 Ghilarza, It.
38/A1 Ghisonaccia, Fr.
101/F2 Gholson, Tx,US
62/A3 Ghora Bāri, Pak.
62/A3 Ghotki, Pak.
53/H2 Ghūrīān, Afg.
63/J5 Gia Nghia, Viet.
65/D4 Gia Nghia, Viet.
66/C1 Gia Nghia, Viet.
80/E3 Giant's Castle (peak), SAfr.
22/B1 Giant's Causeway, NI,UK
38/D4 Giarre, It.
65/E3 Gia Vuc, Viet.
90/E2 Gibbons, Ab,Can
98/E6 Gibbstown, NJ,US
36/D4 Gibloux, Mont (peak), Swi.
34/B4 Gibraleón, Sp.
18/C5 Gibraltar (str.)
74/B1 Gibraltar (str.)
76/D1 Gibraltar (str.)
95/R8 Gibraltar (pt.), On,Can
75/M12 Gibraltar, Gib.
76/D1 Gibraltar, Gib.
34/B4 Gibraltar (str.)
75/M13 Gibraltar (str.)
18/C5 Gibraltar (dpcy.), UK
34/C4 Gibraltar (dpcy.), UK
99/F7 Gibraltar, Mi,US
73/E1 Gibraltar Range Nat'l Park, Austl.
68/B7 Gibson (des.), Austl.
70/D4 Gibson (des.), Austl.
64/C2 Giddarbāha, India
101/F2 Giddings, Tx,US
93/H5 Giddings, Tx,US
96/D4 Giddings, Tx,US
49/C4 Gidi (Mamarr al Jady) (pass), Egypt
77/N6 Gidollē, Eth.
29/H5 Gieboldehausen, Ger.
27/N1 Giedraičiai, Lith.
42/E5 Giedraičiai, Lith.
26/B5 Gien, Fr.
32/E3 Gien, Fr.
33/J2 Giengen an der Brenz, Ger.
32/F4 Gier (riv.), Fr.
36/E4 Giessbachfälle (falls), Swi.
36/D1 Giessen (riv.), Fr.
26/E3 Giessen, Ger.
33/H1 Giessen, Ger.
28/B5 Giessendam, Neth.
28/D2 Gieten, Neth.
30/B6 Gif, Fr.
45/L5 Gīfān, Iran
51/J2 Gīfān, Iran
53/G1 Gīfān, Iran
87/H1 Gifford (riv.), NW,Can
97/H5 Gifford, Fl,US
36/C5 Giffre (riv.), Fr.
26/F2 Gifhorn, Ger.
29/H4 Gifhorn, Ger.
19/S10 Gif-sur-Yvette, Fr.
47/P6 Gifu, Japan
55/M4 Gifu, Japan
57/E3 Gifu, Japan
57/E3 Gifu (pref.), Japan
57/M9 Gifu, Japan
57/M9 Gifu (pref.), Japan
100/C3 Giganta, Sierra de la (mts.), Mex.
102/E4 Gigante (pt.), Nic.
23/F3 Giggleswick, Eng,UK
99/B3 Gig Harbor, Wa,US
38/B1 Giglio (isl.), It.
35/G1 Gignac, Fr.
18/C4 Gijón, Sp.
34/C1 Gijón, Sp.
92/D4 Gila (riv.), Az, NM,US
100/B1 Gila (riv.), Az., NM,US
88/D5 Gila (riv.), Az, NM,US
100/B1 Gila Bend, Az,US
88/D5 Gila Bend, Az,US
92/D4 Gila Bend, Az,US
100/C1 Gila Cliff Dwellings Nat'l Mon., NM,US
92/E4 Gila Cliff Dwellings Nat'l Mon., NM,US
51/G2 Gīlān (gov.), Iran
23/H4 Gilberdyke Newport, Eng,UK
68/D6 Gilbert (riv.), Austl.
70/G3 Gilbert (riv.), Austl.
72/A2 Gilbert (riv.), Austl.
68/G5 Gilbert (isls.), Kiri.
94/A2 Gilbert, Mn,US
99/P15 Gilberts, Il,US
37/H1 Gilching, Ger.
24/C3 Gilfach Goch, Wal,UK
22/B3 Gilford, NI,UK
98/F6 Gilford Park, NJ,US
71/H6 Gilgandra, Austl.
73/D1 Gilgandra, Austl.
70/F6 Gilles (lake), Austl.
86/F4 Gillette, Wy,US
88/E3 Gillette, Wy,US
91/G4 Gillette, Wy,US
93/F1 Gillette, Wy,US
36/C3 Gilley, Fr.
90/B3 Gillies Bay, BC,Can
24/D4 Gillingham, Eng,UK
25/G4 Gillingham, Eng,UK
36/C5 Gilly, Swi.
93/J4 Gilmer, Tx,US
96/E3 Gilmer, Tx,US
53/K1 Gilgit (riv.), Pak.
55/K1 Gilyuy (riv.), Rus.
28/B5 Gilze, Neth.
77/N6 Gīmbī, Eth.
36/C4 Gimel, Swi.
104/F4 Gimie (mtn.), StL.
86/G3 Gimli, Mb,Can
89/G1 Gimli, Mb,Can
91/J3 Gimli, Mb,Can
35/F1 Gimone (riv.), Fr.
57/M9 Ginan, Japan
52/C5 Gīnda, Eth.
31/E2 Gingelom, Belg.
72/C4 Gin Gin, Austl.
67/G2 Gingoog, Phil.
27/G1 Gingst, Ger.
38/E2 Ginosa, It.
40/C5 Ginosa, It.
34/B1 Ginzo de Limia, Sp.
77/Q7 Giohar, Som.
38/D3 Gioia (gulf), It.
38/E2 Gioia del Colle, It.
40/C5 Gioia del Colle, It.
38/D3 Gioia Tauro, It.
33/H3 Giornico, Swi.
37/E5 Giornico, Swi.
39/J3 Gioūra (isl.), Gre.
37/G4 Gioveretto (peak), It.
25/G2 Gipping (riv.), Eng,UK
106/D3 Girardot, Col.
82/B4 Giraul, Ang.
74/D6 Giraul de Cima, Ang.
31/E5 Giraumont, Fr.
44/F4 Giresun, Turk.
44/F4 Giresun (prov.), Turk.
46/D5 Giresun, Turk.
50/D1 Giresun, Turk.
50/D1 Giresun (prov.), Turk.
62/E3 Girīdīh, India
38/E3 Girifalco, It.
19/N7 Girling (res.), Eng,UK
36/C2 Giromagny, Fr.
18/D4 Girona, Sp.
35/G2 Girona (Gerona), Sp.
36/B1 Gironcourt-sur-Vraine, Fr.
32/C4 Gironde (riv.), Fr.
35/F1 Gironella, Sp.
72/C5 Girraween Nat'l Park, Austl.
73/D1 Girraween Nat'l Park, Austl.
25/G2 Girton, Eng,UK
72/B2 Giru, Austl.
22/D1 Girvan, Sc,UK
22/D1 Girvan, Water of (riv.), Sc,UK
71/S10 Gisborne, N.Z.
30/A5 Gisors, Fr.
30/B1 Gistel, Belg.
20/D4 Gistrup, Den.
82/E1 Gitega, Buru.
42/B2 Gittsfjället (peak), Swe.
33/H3 Giubiasco, Swi.
37/F5 Giubiasco, Swi.
40/B5 Giugliano in Campania, It.
33/K5 Giulianova, It.
38/C1 Giulianova, It.
40/A4 Giulianova, It.
18/F4 Giurgiu, Rom.
41/G3 Giurgiu (co.), Rom.
41/G4 Giurgiu, Rom.
44/C4 Giurgiu, Rom.
49/F7 Giv'atayim, Isr.
49/F8 Giv'at Brenner, Isr.
49/F7 Giv'at Ḥayyim, Isr.
26/C3 Givet, Fr.
31/D3 Givet, Fr.
32/F1 Givet, Fr.
32/F4 Givors, Fr.
36/C5 Givrine, Col de la (pass), Swi.
31/D6 Givry-en-Argonne, Fr.
82/F5 Giyani, SAfr.
77/N6 Giyon, Eth.
49/B5 Giza, The Pyramids of (Ahrāmāt al Jīzah), Egypt
47/R3 Gizhiga (bay), Rus.
68/E5 Gizo, Sol.
27/L1 Giżycko, Pol.
42/D5 Giżycko, Pol.
20/D4 Gjerstad, Nor.
39/G2 Gjirokastër, Alb.
86/G2 Gjoa Haven, NW,Can
18/E2 Gjøvik, Nor.
20/D3 Gjøvik, Nor.
46/B3 Gjøvik, Nor.
39/F2 Gjuhëzës, Kep i (cape), Alb.
31/E2 Glabbeek, Belg.
87/L4 Glace Bay, NS,Can
95/K2 Glace Bay, NS,Can
90/D3 Glacier, BC,Can
90/C3 Glacier (peak), Wa,US
86/C3 Glacier Bay Nat'l Park, Ak,US
85/L4 Glacier Bay Nat'l Park & Prsv., Ak,US
90/D3 Glacier Nat'l Park, BC,Can
86/E3 Glacier Nat'l Park, BC,Can
88/C1 Glacier Nat'l Park, BC,Can
90/E3 Glacier Nat'l Park, Mt,US
86/E4 Glacier Nat'l Park, Mt,US
88/D2 Glacier Nat'l Park, Mt,US
28/D5 Gladbeck, Ger.
71/J4 Gladstone, Austl.
72/C3 Gladstone, Austl.
91/M4 Gladstone, Mi,US
94/C2 Gladstone, Mi,US
94/C3 Gladwin, Mi,US
23/H3 Glaisdale, Eng,UK
18/E2 Glåma (riv.), Nor.
20/D3 Glåma (riv.), Nor.
46/B3 Glåma (riv.), Nor.
26/D4 Glan (riv.), Ger.
31/G4 Glan (riv.), Ger.
33/G2 Glan (riv.), Ger.
67/G2 Glan, Phil.
24/C3 Glanamman, Wal,UK
30/D4 Gland (riv.), Fr.
33/G3 Gland, Swi.
36/C5 Gland, Swi.
21/H8 Glandore, Ire.
29/F4 Glandorf, Ger.
37/E3 Glärnisch (range), Swi.
33/H3 Glarus, Swi.
37/E4 Glarus (mts.), Swi.
37/F3 Glarus, Swi.
37/F4 Glarus (canton), Swi.
33/H3 Glarus Alps (range), Swi.
24/C2 Glasbury, Wal,UK
18/C3 Glasgow, Sc,UK
94/C4 Glasgow, Ky,US
97/G2 Glasgow, Ky,US
88/E2 Glasgow, Mt,US
90/G3 Glasgow, Mt,US
22/D6 Glaslyn (riv.), Wal,UK
22/D3 Glass (riv.), IM,UK
96/D2 Glass (mts.), Ok,US
96/C4 Glass (mts.), Tx,US
98/K8 Glassmanor-Oxon Hill, Md,US
24/D4 Glastonbury, Eng,UK
37/E2 Glatt (riv.), Swi.
37/E2 Glattfelden, Swi.
41/H4 Glavinitsa, Bul.
19/J3 Glazov, Rus.
43/M4 Glazov, Rus.
46/F4 Glazov, Rus.
40/B2 Gleisdorf, Aus.
25/G2 Glemsford, Eng,UK
23/H6 Glen (riv.), Eng,UK
25/F1 Glen (riv.), Eng,UK
73/C3 Glenaladale Nat'l Park, Austl.
94/E4 Glen Allen, Va,US
97/J2 Glen Allen, Va,US
32/A3 Glénan (isls.), Fr.
22/C2 Glenarm, NI,UK
22/C2 Glenarm (riv.), NI,UK
22/B2 Glenavy, NI,UK
73/D2 Glenbawn (dam), Austl.
91/J3 Glenboro, Mb,Can
72/G8 Glenbrook, Austl.
98/K7 Glen Burnie, Md,US
88/D4 Glen Canyon (dam), Az,US
92/E3 Glen Canyon (dam), Az,US
92/E3 Glen Canyon Nat'l Rec. Area, Az, Ut,US
22/E1 Glencaple, Sc,UK
81/E3 Glencoe, SAfr.
99/Q15 Glencoe, Il,US
98/G5 Glen Cove, NY,US
92/D4 Glendale, Az,US
92/C4 Glendale, Ca,US
90/C5 Glendale, Or,US
92/B2 Glendale, Or,US
99/P16 Glendale Heights, Il,US
72/C3 Glenden, Austl.
86/F4 Glendive, Mt,US
88/F2 Glendive, Mt,US
91/G4 Glendive, Mt,US
90/G5 Glendo (res.), Wy,US
98/C2 Glendora, Ca,US
22/B1 Glendun (riv.), NI,UK
22/B6 Glenealy, Ire.
98/J8 Glen Echo (park), Md,US
73/B3 Glenelg (riv.), Austl.
98/K7 Glenelg, Md,US
22/A2 Glenelly (riv.), NI,UK
71/J5 Glen Innes, Austl.
73/D1 Glen Innes, Austl.
22/D2 Glenluce, Sc,UK
85/J3 Glennallen, Ak,US
86/B2 Glennallen, Ak,US
98/E6 Glenolden, Pa,US
85/M4 Glenora, BC,Can
72/H8 Glenorie, Austl.
93/H4 Glenpool, Ok,US
96/D3 Glenpool, Ok,US
101/F1 Glen Rose, Tx,US
93/H4 Glen Rose, Tx,US
96/D3 Glen Rose, Tx,US
87/J4 Glens Falls, NY,US
89/M3 Glens Falls, NY,US
94/F3 Glens Falls, NY,US
22/B2 Glenshane (pass), NI,UK
98/E5 Glenside, Pa,US
21/A3 Glenties, Ire.
22/D1 Glentrool, Sc,UK
91/H4 Glen Ullin, ND,US
99/Q15 Glenview, Il,US
99/Q15 Glenview Nav. Air Sta., Il,US
95/Q8 Glen Williams, On,Can
98/F4 Glenwood, NJ,US
88/E4 Glenwood Springs, Co,US
92/F3 Glenwood Springs, Co,US
39/L7 Glifáda, Gre.
33/M4 Glina, Cro.
40/C3 Glina, Cro.
29/H1 Glinde, Ger.
18/D2 Glittertinden (peak), Nor.
20/D3 Glittertinden (peak), Nor.
46/A3 Glittertinden (peak), Nor.
27/K3 Gliwice, Pol.
88/D5 Globe, Az,US
92/E4 Globe, Az,US
37/G4 Glockturm (peak), Aus.
27/H5 Gloggnitz, Aus.
40/B2 Gloggnitz, Aus.
27/J3 Głogów, Pol.
27/J3 Głogówek, Pol.
37/H1 Glonn (riv.), Ger.
103/G1 Gloria (bay), Cuba
81/H5 Glorieuses, Iles (isls.), Reun.
72/E6 Glorious (mtn.), Austl.
85/D3 Glory of Russia (cape), Ak,US
23/G5 Glossop, Eng,UK
73/D2 Gloucester, Austl.
94/F2 Gloucester, On,Can
24/D3 Gloucester, Eng,UK
98/E6 Gloucester City, NJ,US
24/D3 Gloucestershire (co.), Eng,UK
24/D3 Gloucester, Vale of (vall.), Eng,UK
102/E2 Glovers (reef), Belz.
95/L1 Glovertown, Nf,Can
27/K3 Głowno, Pol.
27/J3 Głubczyce, Pol.
27/J3 Głuchołazy, Pol.
26/E1 Glücksburg, Ger.
26/E2 Glückstadt, Ger.
29/G1 Glückstadt, Ger.
44/E2 Glukhov, Ukr.
41/G1 Glybokaya, Ukr.
22/B4 Glyde (riv.), Ire.
24/C3 Glyncorrwg, Wal,UK
22/C2 Glynn, NI,UK
24/C3 Glyn Neath, Wal,UK
27/H4 Gmünd, Aus.
79/E3 Gnagna (prov.), Burk.
29/G2 Gnarrenburg, Ger.
27/J2 Gniezno, Pol.
44/A1 Gniezno, Pol.
39/G1 Gnjilane, Yugo.
40/E4 Gnjilane, Yugo.
23/F6 Gnosall, Eng,UK
24/D1 Gnosall, Eng,UK
70/B6 Gnowangerup, Austl.
56/C3 Gō (riv.), Japan
62/B4 Goa (state), India
62/F2 Goālpāra, India
23/H3 Goathland, Eng,UK
77/N6 Goba, Eth.
81/F2 Goba, Moz.
82/C5 Gobabeb, Namb.
82/C5 Gobabis, Namb.
109/B6 Gobernador Gregores, Arg.
54/E3 Gobi (des.), China, Mong.
47/L5 Gobi (des.), Mong.
48/K5 Gobi (des.), Mong.
55/M5 Gobō, Japan
56/D4 Gobō, Japan
23/E6 Gobowen, Eng,UK
28/D5 Goch, Ger.
63/J5 Go Cong, Viet.
65/D4 Go Cong, Viet.
66/C1 Go Cong, Viet.
25/F4 Godalming, Eng,UK
65/D4 Go Dau Ha, Viet.
48/G8 Godāvari (riv.), India
53/L5 Godāvari (riv.), India
62/D4 Godāvari (riv.), India
77/P6 Godē, Eth.
40/F3 Godeanu (peak), Rom.
39/H1 Godech, Bul.
94/D3 Goderich, On,Can
53/K4 Godhra, India
62/B3 Godhra, India
101/F1 Godley, Tx,US
25/F2 Godmanchester, Eng,UK
67/F4 Godo (mtn.), Indo.
57/M9 Gōdo, Japan
27/K5 Gödöllő, Hun.
40/D2 Gödöllő, Hun.
24/A6 Godolphin Cross, Eng,UK
109/C3 Godoy Cruz, Arg.
91/K2 Gods (lake), Mb,Can
91/K2 Gods (riv.), Mb,Can
86/G3 Gods (lake), Mb,Can
86/G3 Gods (riv.), Mb,Can
87/H2 Gods Mercy (bay), NW,Can
19/N8 Godstone, Eng,UK
84/M3 Godthåb (Nuuk), Grld.
53/L1 Godwin Austen (K2) (peak), China, Pak.
48/G6 Godwin Austen (K2) (mtn.), China, Pak.
94/E1 Goéland (lake), Qu,Can
28/A5 Goerce, Neth.
26/B3 Goes, Neth.
28/A6 Goes, Neth.
91/L4 Gogebic (range), Mi,US
94/B2 Gogebic (range), Mi,US
37/G1 Göggingen, Ger.
62/D2 Gogra (riv.), India
29/G3 Gohbach (riv.), Ger.
107/M5 Goiana, Braz.
108/B1 Goiandira, Braz.
107/J7 Goiânia, Braz.
107/H7 Goiás, Braz.
108/B1 Goiás (state), Braz.
107/J7 Goiatuba, Braz.
108/B1 Goiatuba, Braz.
54/D5 Goinsargoin, China
28/C5 Goirle, Neth.
34/A2 Góis, Port.
56/D3 Gojō, Japan
57/L10 Gojō, Japan
64/B2 Gojra, Pak.
44/E4 Gök (riv.), Turk.
56/B4 Gokase (riv.), Japan
57/M9 Gokashō, Japan
39/J2 Gökçeada (isl.), Turk.
41/G5 Gökçeada (isl.), Turk.
50/A1 Gökçeada (isl.), Turk.
41/K5 Gökçebey, Turk.
49/C1 Göksu (riv.), Turk.
50/D2 Göksu (riv.), Turk.
50/D2 Göksun, Turk.
50/C2 Göktepe, Turk.
20/D3 Gol, Nor.
49/D3 Golan Heights (reg Syria
60/B3 Golāpganj, Bang.
41/L2 Golaya Pristan', Uk
44/E5 Gölbaşı, Turk.
50/C2 Gölbaşı, Turk.
50/D2 Gölbaşı, Turk.
36/C1 Golbey, Fr.
23/F5 Golborne, Eng,UK
41/J5 Gölcük, Turk.
50/B1 Gölcük, Turk.
99/B2 Gold (mtn.), Wa,US
37/F3 Goldach, Swi.
27/M1 Gołdap, Pol.
99/D2 Gold Bar, Wa,US
90/B5 Gold Beach, Or,US
92/A2 Gold Beach, Or,US
26/G2 Goldberg, Ger.
76/E7 Gold Coast (reg.), A
68/E7 Gold Coast, Austl.
71/J5 Gold Coast, Austl.
72/D4 Gold Coast, Austl.
79/E5 Gold Coast (reg.), Gha.
86/E3 Golden, BC,Can
88/C1 Golden, BC,Can
90/D3 Golden, BC,Can
93/F3 Golden, Co,US
90/C4 Goldendale, Wa,US
26/F3 Goldene Aue (reg.), Ger.
99/J11 Golden Gate (chan Ca,US
80/E3 Golden Gate Highlands Nat'l Pa SAfr.
99/J11 Golden Gate Nat'l Rec. Area, Ca,US
90/B3 Golden Hinde (pea Can
29/F3 Goldenstedt, Ger.
64/C2 Golden Temple, In
92/C3 Goldfield, Nv,US
90/B3 Gold River, BC,Can
89/L4 Goldsboro, NC,US
97/J3 Goldsboro, NC,US
70/B4 Goldsworthy, Austl
93/H5 Goldthwaite, Tx,US
96/D4 Goldthwaite, Tx,US
45/G4 Göle, Turk.
50/E1 Göle, Turk.
27/H2 Goleniów, Pol.
103/F4 Golfito Nat'l Wild. Ref., CR
38/A2 Golfo Aranci, It.
100/B2 Golfo Santa Clara, Mex.
92/D5 Golfo Santa Clara, Mex
73/B2 Gol Gol, Austl.
49/A1 Gölhisar, Turk.
50/B2 Gölhisar, Turk.
101/F2 Goliad, Tx,US
93/H5 Goliad, Tx,US
96/D4 Goliad, Tx,US
43/X9 Golitsyno, Rus.
44/F4 Gölköy, Turk.
50/D1 Gölköy, Turk.
31/H4 Göllheim, Ger.
50/A2 Gölmarmara, Turk.
54/C4 Golmud, China
45/G1 Golovanovo, Rus.
85/F3 Golovin, Ak,US
51/G3 Golpāyegān, Iran
52/F2 Golpāyegān, Iran
41/K5 Gölpazarı, Turk.
50/B1 Gölpazarı, Turk.
33/M3 Gols, Aus.
27/K2 Golub-Dobrzyń, Po
41/H4 Golyama Kamchiya (riv.), Bul.
39/J2 Golyama Syutkya (peak), Bul.
41/G5 Golyama Syutkya (peak), Bul.
39/J2 Golyam Perelik (peak), Bul.
41/G5 Golyam Perelik (peak), Bul.
44/C4 Golyam Perelik (peak), Bul.
77/L8 Goma, Zaire
82/E1 Goma, Zaire
37/F1 Gomaringen, Ger.
18/G3 Gomel', Bela.
44/D1 Gomel', Bela.
46/D4 Gomel', Bela.
44/C2 Gomel' Obl., Bela.
35/X16 Gomera (isl.), Canl. Sp.
76/B2 Gomera (isl.), Canl. Sp.
19/S10 Gometz-le-Châtel,
100/D2 Gomez (peak), Tx,U
100/D2 Gómez Farías, Mex
101/E3 Gómez Farías, Mex
101/F4 Gómez Farías, Mex
92/F5 Gómez Farías, Mex
100/E3 Gómez Palacio, Me
88/F6 Gómez Palacio, Me
96/C5 Gómez Palacio, Me
51/H2 Gomīshān, Iran
52/F1 Gomīshān, Iran
26/F2 Gommern, Ger.
36/E5 Goms (val.), Swi.
37/F3 Goms, Swi.
25/F4 Gomshall, Eng,UK
51/J3 Gonābād, Iran
53/G2 Gonābād, Iran
103/J2 Gonaïves, Haiti
82/F5 Gonarezhou Nat'l Park, Zim.
103/H2 Gonâve (gulf), Haiti
103/H2 Gonâve (isl.), Haiti
89/M8 Gonâve (gulf), Haiti
46/F6 Gonbad-e Qābūs, I
51/H2 Gonbad-e Qābūs, I
53/G1 Gonbad-e Qābūs, I
27/L4 Gönc, Hun.
40/E1 Gönc, Hun.
62/D2 Gondā, India

53/K4 **Gondal**, India
52/B3 **Gondal**, India
77/N5 **Gonder**, Eth.
52/D3 **Gondia**, India
34/A2 **Gondomar**, Port.
34/A1 **Gondomar**, Sp.
36/B1 **Gondrecourt-le-Château**, Fr.
31/E6 **Gondreville**, Fr.
41/H5 **Gönen**, Turk.
44/C4 **Gönen**, Turk.
50/A1 **Gönen**, Turk.
9/T10 **Gonesse**, Fr.
30/B6 **Gonesse**, Fr.
61/F3 **Gong'an**, China
63/K3 **Gong'an**, China
65/D1 **Gong'an**, China
63/F2 **Gongbo'gyamda**, China
65/E1 **Gongche**, China
54/E6 **Gongga** (peak), China
50/D2 **Gongga** (peak), China
53/H2 **Gongga** (peak), China
62/F2 **Gonggar**, China
63/E1 **Gongguan**, China
54/E4 **Gonghe**, China
76/G6 **Gongola** (riv.), Nga.
79/H6 **Gongola** (riv.), Nga.
79/H4 **Gongola** (state), Nga.
73/C1 **Gongolgon**, Austl.
53/G2 **Gongshan Drungzu Nuzu Zizhixian**, China
60/D3 **Gongwang** (mts.), China
59/C4 **Gong Xian**, China
63/H2 **Gong Xian**, China
55/J3 **Gongzhuling**, China
59/F2 **Gongzhuling**, China
54/D5 **Gonjo**, China
60/C2 **Gonjo**, China
39/H3 **Gónnoi**, Gre.
40/C2 **Gönyü**, Hun.
01/F2 **Gonzales**, Tx,US
93/H5 **Gonzales**, Tx,US
86/D4 **Gonzales**, Tx,US
01/F4 **González**, Mex.
02/B1 **González**, Mex.
83/J **Goodenough** (cape), Ant.
93/G5 **Goodfellow** (A.F.B.), Tx,US
96/C4 **Goodfellow** (A.F.B.), Tx,US
80/D2 **Goodhope**, Bots.
80/B4 **Good Hope** (cape), SAfr.
0/L11 **Good Hope** (cape), SAfr.
74/D8 **Good Hope, Cape of** (cape), SAfr.
90/E5 **Gooding**, Id,US
92/D2 **Gooding**, Id,US
93/G3 **Goodland**, Ks,US
96/C2 **Goodland**, Ks,US
72/E7 **Goodna**, Austl.
85/F4 **Goodnews Bay**, Ak,US
72/B5 **Goodooga**, Austl.
73/C1 **Goodooga**, Austl.
99/E6 **Goodrich**, Mi,US
24/B3 **Goodwick**, Wal,UK
80/B4 **Goodwood**, SAfr.
0/L10 **Goodwood**, SAfr.
28/C4 **Gooimeer** (lake), Neth.
23/H4 **Goole**, Eng,UK
73/C2 **Goolgowi**, Austl.
73/D2 **Gooloogong**, Austl.
73/A2 **Goolwa**, Austl.
70/B6 **Goomalling**, Austl.
72/C4 **Goombungee**, Austl.
71/J5 **Goondiwindi**, Austl.
72/C5 **Goondiwindi**, Austl.
73/D1 **Goondiwindi**, Austl.
28/D4 **Goor**, Neth.
91/H2 **Goose** (lake), Mb,Can
90/C5 **Goose** (lake), Ca, Or,US
92/B2 **Goose** (lake), Ca, Or,US
88/B3 **Goose** (lake), Ca, Or,US
84/L4 **Goose Bay-Happy Valley**, Can.
23/F5 **Goostrey**, Eng,UK
64/F3 **Gopichettipālaiyam**, India
26/E4 **Göppingen**, Ger.
33/H2 **Göppingen**, Ger.
65/D4 **Go Quao**, Viet.
27/J3 **Góra**, Pol.
51/F2 **Goradiz**, Azer.
27/L3 **Góra Kalwaria**, Pol.
62/D2 **Gorakhpur**, India
40/D4 **Goražde**, Bosn.
03/F1 **Gorda** (pt.), Cuba
03/F3 **Gorda** (pt.), Nic.
03/F3 **Gorda** (pt.), Nic.
04/E4 **Gorda** (pt.), Nic.
90/B5 **Gorda** (pt.), Ca,US
92/A2 **Gorda** (pt.), Ca,US
50/B2 **Gördes**, Turk.
37/E5 **Gordevio**, Swi.
26/E1 **Gørding**, Den.
37/E5 **Gordola**, Swi.
71/H8 **Gordon** (lake), Austl.
73/C4 **Gordon** (lake), Austl.
80/L11 **Gordon's Bay**, SAfr.
71/H3 **Gordonvale**, Austl.
72/B2 **Gordonvale**, Austl.
76/J6 **Goré**, Chad
77/N6 **Gorē**, Eth.
1/Q12 **Gore**, N.Z.
25/G1 **Gore** (pt.), UK
85/H4 **Gore** (pt.), Ak,US
50/D1 **Görele**, Turk.
32/B2 **Gorey**, Chl,UK
46/F6 **Gorgān**, Iran
48/E6 **Gorgān**, Iran
51/H2 **Gorgān**, Iran
51/H2 **Gorgān** (riv.), Iran
53/F1 **Gorgān**, Iran
31/F4 **Gorge du Loup**, Lux.
35/J1 **Gorges du Verdon**, Fr.
78/B2 **Gorgol** (riv.), Mrta.
78/B3 **Gorgol** (reg.), Mrta.
45/H4 **Gori**, Geo.
51/F1 **Gori**, Geo.
28/B5 **Gorinchem**, Neth.
25/E3 **Goring**, Eng,UK
25/F5 **Goring by Sea**, Eng,UK
51/F2 **Goris**, Arm.
33/K4 **Gorizia**, It.
40/A3 **Gorizia**, It.
41/F3 **Gorj** (co.), Rom.
42/F5 **Gorki**, Bela.
44/D1 **Gorki**, Bela.
42/J4 **Gor'kiy** (res.), Rus.
43/K4 **Gor'kiy** (Nizhniy Novgorod), Rus.
27/L4 **Gorlice**, Pol.
18/E3 **Görlitz**, Ger.
27/H3 **Görlitz**, Ger.
24/C2 **Gorllwyn** (mtn.), Wal,UK
19/G4 **Gorlovka**, Ukr.
44/F2 **Gorlovka**, Ukr.
101/F1 **Gorman**, Tx,US
22/B4 **Gormanston**, Ire.
95/R8 **Gormley**, On,Can
39/J1 **Gorna Oryakhovitsa**, Bul.
41/G4 **Gorna Oryakhovitsa**, Bul.
36/D6 **Gorner** (glac.), It., Swi.
40/E3 **Gornji Milanovac**, Yugo.
40/C4 **Gornji Vakuf**, Bosn.
46/J4 **Gorno-Altay Aut. Obl.**, Rus.
46/J4 **Gorno-Altaysk**, Rus.
46/H6 **Gorno-Badakhstan Aut. Obl.**, Taj.
46/J4 **Gornyak**, Rus.
43/J4 **Gorodets**, Rus.
42/F5 **Gorodok**, Bela.
27/M4 **Gorodok**, Ukr.
68/D5 **Goroka**, PNG
76/E5 **Gorom Gorom**, Burk.
67/H4 **Gorong** (isl.), Indo.
82/F4 **Gorongoza**, Moz.
67/F3 **Gorontalo**, Indo.
68/B4 **Gorontalo**, Indo.
24/B3 **Gorseinon**, Wal,UK
28/D4 **Gorssel**, Neth.
99/B2 **Gorst**, Wa,US
22/A2 **Gortin**, NI,UK
36/C2 **Görwihl**, Ger.
44/C2 **Goryn'** (riv.), Bela., Ukr.
33/K5 **Gorzano** (peak), It.
27/H2 **Gorzów** (prov.), Pol.
18/E3 **Gorzów Wielkopolski**, Pol.
27/H2 **Gorzów Wielkopolski**, Pol.
37/E4 **Göschenen**, Swi.
56/D3 **Gōse**, Japan
57/L10 **Gose**, Japan
57/F2 **Gosen**, Japan
23/G2 **Gosforth**, Eng,UK
55/N3 **Goshogawara**, Japan
26/F3 **Goslar**, Ger.
29/H5 **Goslar**, Ger.
33/L4 **Gospić**, Cro.
40/B3 **Gospić**, Cro.
25/E5 **Gosport**, Eng,UK
37/F3 **Gossau**, Swi.
37/H4 **Gossensass** (Colle Isarco), It.
31/G5 **Gossersweiler-Stein**, Ger.
39/G2 **Gostivar**, Macd.
40/E5 **Gostivar**, Macd.
27/J3 **Gostyń**, Pol.
27/K2 **Gostynin**, Pol.
41/A1 **Gostynin**, Pol.
18/E3 **Göteborg**, Swe.
20/D4 **Göteborg**, Swe.
46/B4 **Göteborg**, Swe.
20/D4 **Göteborg och Bohus** (co.), Swe.
76/H6 **Gotel** (mts.), Camr., Nga.
57/F3 **Gotemba**, Japan
26/F3 **Gotha**, Ger.
29/H7 **Gotha**, Ger.
91/H5 **Gothenburg**, Ne,US
93/G2 **Gothenburg**, Ne,US
18/E3 **Gotland** (isl.), Swe.
20/F4 **Gotland** (co.), Swe.
20/F4 **Gotland** (isl.), Swe.
42/C4 **Gotland** (co.), Swe.
42/C4 **Gotland** (isl.), Swe.
46/B4 **Gotland** (isl.), Swe.
55/K5 **Gotō** (isls.), Japan
56/A4 **Gotō** (isls.), Japan
39/H2 **Gotse Delchev**, Bul.
41/F5 **Gotse Delchev**, Bul.
20/F4 **Gotska Sandön Nat'l Park**, Swe.
42/C4 **Gotska Sandön Nat'l Park**, Swe.
56/C3 **Gōtsu**, Japan
36/D1 **Gottenheim**, Ger.
26/E3 **Göttingen**, Ger.
29/G5 **Göttingen**, Ger.
37/E2 **Gottmadingen**, Ger.
26/C2 **Gouda**, Neth.
28/B4 **Gouda**, Neth.
80/L10 **Gouda**, SAfr.
76/H5 **Goudoumaria**, Niger
16/J8 **Gough** (isl.), StH.
87/J4 **Gouin** (res.), Qu,Can
94/F1 **Gouin** (res.), Qu,Can
94/C2 **Goulais** (riv.), On,Can
70/E2 **Goulburn** (isls.), Austl.
71/H6 **Goulburn**, Austl.
73/D2 **Goulburn**, Austl.
73/D2 **Goulburn** (riv.), Austl.
83/P **Gould** (coast), Ant.
93/K4 **Gould**, Ar,US
96/F3 **Gould**, Ar,US
60/E3 **Goulou** (peak), China
61/F4 **Goulou** (mts.), China
39/H2 **Gouménissa**, Gre.
40/F5 **Gouménissa**, Gre.
76/E4 **Goundam**, Mali
78/E2 **Goundam**, Mali
32/D4 **Gourdon**, Fr.
76/H5 **Gouré**, Niger
79/H3 **Gouré**, Niger
32/B2 **Gourin**, Fr.
80/C4 **Gourits** (riv.), SAfr.
79/F3 **Gourma** (prov.), Burk.
79/F3 **Gourma** (reg.), Burk.
76/E4 **GourmaRharous**, Mali
79/E2 **Gourma-Rharous**, Mali
30/A5 **Gournay-en-Bray**, Fr.
32/D2 **Gournay-en-Bray**, Fr.
77/J4 **Gouro**, Chad
19/T9 **Goussainville**, Fr.
108/D1 **Gouvêa**, Braz.
34/B2 **Gouveia**, Port.
30/B5 **Gouvieux**, Fr.
31/E3 **Gouvy**, Belg.
104/F4 **Gouyave**, Gren.
41/G1 **Goverla** (peak), Ukr.
44/C2 **Goverla** (peak), Ukr.
107/K7 **Governador Valadares**, Braz.
108/D1 **Governador Valadares**, Braz.
47/K5 **Govĭ Altayn** (mts.), Mong.
54/D3 **Govĭ Altayn** (mts.), Mong.
64/D2 **Govind Sāgar** (res.), India
53/H3 **Gowd-e-Zereh** (lake), Afg.
24/B3 **Gower** (pen.), Wal,UK
53/G3 **Gowk**, Iran
23/H4 **Goxhill**, Eng,UK
109/E2 **Goya**, Arg.
41/K5 **Göynük**, Turk.
50/B1 **Göynük**, Turk.
23/F5 **Goyt** (riv.), Eng,UK
57/M9 **Gozaisho-yama** (peak), Japan
38/D4 **Gozo** (isl.), Malta
80/D4 **Graaff-Reinet**, SAfr.
82/D7 **Graaff-Reinet**, SAfr.
28/D4 **Graafschap** (reg.), Neth.
37/G1 **Graben**, Ger.
80/B2 **Grabenberg** (peak), Namb.
80/L11 **Grabouw**, SAfr.
26/F2 **Grabow**, Ger.
37/F3 **Grabs**, Swi.
33/L4 **Gračac**, Cro.
40/B3 **Gračac**, Cro.
40/D3 **Gračanica**, Bosn.
72/C3 **Gracemere**, Austl.
97/G4 **Graceville**, Fl,US
36/D5 **Grächen**, Swi.
102/D3 **Gracias**, Hon.
103/F3 **Gracias a Dios** (cape), Nic.
35/S12 **Graciosa** (isl.), Azor.
40/D3 **Gradačac**, Bosn.
107/H5 **Gradaús**, Braz.
34/B1 **Grado**, Sp.
37/H1 **Gräfelfing**, Ger.
25/F2 **Grafham Water** (lake), Eng,UK
26/F4 **Grafing bei München**, Ger.
37/H1 **Grafrath**, Ger.
68/E7 **Grafton**, Austl.
71/J5 **Grafton**, Austl.
72/B2 **Grafton** (pass.), Austl.
73/E1 **Grafton**, Austl.
91/J3 **Grafton**, ND,US
94/D4 **Grafton**, WV,US
97/H2 **Grafton**, WV,US
86/C3 **Graham** (isl.), BC,Can
87/S7 **Graham** (isl.), NW,Can
100/C1 **Graham** (mt.), Az,US
101/F1 **Graham**, Tx,US
93/H4 **Graham**, Tx,US
96/D3 **Graham**, Tx,US
99/C3 **Graham**, Wa,US
46/G1 **Graham Bell** (isl.), Rus.
83/V **Graham Land** (reg.), Ant.
80/D4 **Grahamstown**, SAfr.
82/E7 **Grahamstown**, SAfr.
33/G4 **Graian Alps** (range), Fr., It.
25/G4 **Grain**, Eng,UK
37/H3 **Grainau**, Ger.
76/C6 **Grain Coast** (reg.), Afr.
78/C5 **Grain Coast** (reg.), Libr.
107/J4 **Grajau** (riv.), Braz.
107/J5 **Grajaú**, Braz.
27/M2 **Grajewo**, Pol.
42/D5 **Grajewo**, Pol.
44/B1 **Grajewo**, Pol.
26/E1 **Gram**, Den.
40/F4 **Gramada**, Bul.
32/D4 **Gramat**, Fr.
32/D4 **Gramat** (plat.), Fr.
21/C2 **Grampian** (mts.), Sc,UK
73/B3 **Grampians Nat'l Park**, Austl.
73/B3 **Grampians, The** (mts.), Austl.
28/D3 **Gramsbergen**, Neth.
40/E5 **Gramsh**, Alb.
20/D3 **Gran**, Nor.
106/D3 **Granada**, Col.
102/E4 **Granada**, Nic.
18/C5 **Granada**, Sp.
34/D4 **Granada**, Sp.
35/X16 **Granadilla de Abona**, Canl.
100/C2 **Granados**, Mex.
109/C6 **Gran Altiplanicie Central** (plat.), Arg.
101/F1 **Granbury**, Tx,US
93/H4 **Granbury**, Tx,US
96/D3 **Granbury**, Tx,US
93/F2 **Granby**, Co,US
35/X17 **Gran Canaria** (isl.), Canl., Sp.
76/B2 **Gran Canaria** (isl.), Canl., Sp.
109/D2 **Gran Chaco** (plain), Arg., Par.
106/F8 **Gran Chaco** (reg.), Par.
105/C5 **Gran Chaco** (reg.), SAm.
95/H2 **Grand** (lake), NB,Can
87/L4 **Grand** (lake), Nf,Can
95/K1 **Grand** (lake), Nf,Can
95/Q9 **Grand** (riv.), On,Can
95/S9 **Grand** (isl.), On,Can
87/J3 **Grand** (riv.), Qu,Can
54/H4 **Grand** (can.), China
59/D4 **Grand** (can.), China
59/L9 **Grand** (can.), China
22/B5 **Grand** (can.), Ire.
93/J5 **Grand** (lake), La,US
91/M4 **Grand** (isl.), Mi,US
94/C2 **Grand** (isl.), Mi,US
95/S9 **Grand** (isl.), NY,US
91/H4 **Grand** (riv.), SD,US
36/D2 **Grand Alsace** (can.), Fr.
104/B1 **Grand Bahama** (isl.), Bahm.
84/K7 **Grand Bahama** (isl.), Bahm.
89/L6 **Grand Bahama** (isl.), Bahm.
87/L4 **Grand Bank**, Nf,Can
95/L2 **Grand Bank**, Nf,Can
78/C5 **Grand Bassa** (co.), Libr.
76/E6 **Grand-Bassam**, IvC.
78/E5 **Grand-Bassam**, IvC.
95/H2 **Grand Bay**, NB,Can
99/E6 **Grand Blanc**, Mi,US
92/D3 **Grand Canyon**, Az,US
88/D4 **Grand Canyon Nat'l Park**, Az,US
92/D3 **Grand Canyon Nat'l Park**, Az,US
78/C5 **Grand Cape Mount** (co.), Libr.
103/F2 **Grand Cayman** (isl.), Cay.
86/E3 **Grand Centre**, Ab,Can
90/F2 **Grand Centre**, Ab,Can
36/C2 **Grand-Charmont**, Fr.
36/D6 **Grand Colombier** (mtn.), Fr.
36/D6 **Grand Combin** (peak), Swi.
88/C2 **Grand Coulee** (dam), Wa,US
90/D4 **Grand Coulee**, Wa,US
90/D4 **Grand Coulee** (dam), Wa,US
36/C4 **Grandcour**, Swi.
36/C2 **Grand Drumont** (mtn.), Fr.
105/C7 **Grande** (bay), Arg.
109/C1 **Grande** (riv.), Arg.
109/C7 **Grande** (bay), Arg.
106/F7 **Grande** (riv.), Bol.
105/E5 **Grande** (riv.), Braz.
107/J7 **Grande** (riv.), Braz.
107/K6 **Grande** (riv.), Braz.
108/C2 **Grande** (isl.), Braz.
108/C2 **Grande** (riv.), Braz.
101/Q9 **Grande** (riv.), Mex.
103/G4 **Grande** (pt.), Pan.
84/F4 **Grande Cache**, Can.
86/E3 **Grande Cache**, Ab,Can
90/D2 **Grande Cache**, Ab,Can
81/G5 **Grande Comore** (isl.), Com.
38/C1 **Grande, Corno** (peak), It.
107/H4 **Grande de Gurupá**, Braz.
106/F4 **Grande de Manacapuru** (lake), Braz.
103/E3 **Grande de Matagalpa** (riv.), Nic.
36/D5 **Grande Dixence, Barrage de la** (dam), Swi.
38/C4 **Grande, Monte** (peak), It.
84/F4 **Grande Prairie**, Can.
86/E3 **Grande Prairie**, Ab,Can
90/D2 **Grande Prairie**, Ab,Can
76/H4 **Grand 'Erg de Bilma** (des.), Niger
74/C1 **Grand Erg Occidental** (des.), Alg.
76/E1 **Grand Erg Occidental** (des.), Alg.
74/C1 **Grand Erg Oriental** (des.), Alg.
76/G1 **Grand Erg Oriental** (des.), Alg.
84/G7 **Grande, Rio** (riv.), US, Mex.
104/C3 **Grande Rivière du Nord**, Haiti
103/H2 **Grande Saline**, Haiti
36/D6 **Grandes Jorasses** (peak), It.
30/B1 **Grande-Synthe**, Fr.
104/F3 **Grande-Terre** (isl.), Guad.
87/K4 **Grand Falls**, NB,Can
89/N2 **Grand Falls**, NB,Can
87/L4 **Grand Falls**, Nf,Can
100/E2 **Grandfalls**, Tx,US
86/G4 **Grand Forks**, ND,US
89/G2 **Grand Forks**, ND,US
91/J4 **Grand Forks**, ND,US
30/B2 **Grand-Fort-Philippe**, Fr.
30/B5 **Grandfresnoy**, Fr.
103/H2 **Grand Goâve**, Haiti
94/C3 **Grand Haven**, Mi,US
89/G3 **Grand Island**, Ne,US
91/J5 **Grand Island**, Ne,US
93/H2 **Grand Island**, Ne,US
97/F4 **Grand Isle**, La,US
78/D5 **Grand Jide** (co.), Libr.
88/E4 **Grand Junction**, Co,US
92/E3 **Grand Junction**, Co,US
96/A2 **Grand Junction**, Co,US
78/D5 **Grand-Lahou**, IvC.
93/J3 **Grand L. O'The Cherokees** (lake), Ok,US
95/H2 **Grand Manan** (isl.), NB,Can
89/H2 **Grand Marais**, Mn,US
91/L4 **Grand Marais**, Mn,US
94/B2 **Grand Marais**, Mn,US
30/C6 **Grand Marin** (riv.), Fr.
95/F2 **Grand-Mère**, Can
95/K2 **Grand Miquelon** (isl.), StP,Fr
33/G3 **Grand Mont Ruan** (mtn.), Fr.
36/C5 **Grand Mont Ruan** (mtn.), Fr.
36/D5 **Grand Muveran** (peak), Swi.
34/A3 **Grândola**, Port.
91/L4 **Grand Portage Nat'l Mon.**, Mn,US
94/B2 **Grand Portage Nat'l Mon.**, Mn,US
31/D5 **Grandpré**, Fr.
95/H2 **Grand Pré Nat'l Hist. Park**, Can
91/J2 **Grand Rapids**, Mb,Can
89/J3 **Grand Rapids**, Mi,US
94/C3 **Grand Rapids**, Mi,US
89/H2 **Grand Rapids**, Mn,US
91/K4 **Grand Rapids**, Mn,US
94/A2 **Grand Rapids**, Mn,US
32/F5 **Grand Rhône** (riv.), Fr.
36/C4 **Grandson**, Swi.
36/C4 **Grand Taureau** (mtn.), Fr.
90/F5 **Grand Teton** (peak), Wy,US
92/E2 **Grand Teton** (peak), Wy,US
90/F5 **Grand Teton Nat'l Park**, Wy,US
88/E4 **Grand Teton Nat'l Park**, Wy,US
88/D3 **Grand Teton Nat'l Park**, Wy,US
92/E1 **Grand Teton Nat'l Park**, Wy,US
104/D2 **Grand Turk**, Trks.
19/M6 **Grand Union** (can.), Eng,UK
25/F2 **Grand Union** (can.), Eng,UK
91/H3 **Grandview**, Mb,Can
101/F1 **Grandview**, Tx,US
90/D4 **Grandview**, Wa,US
36/C2 **Grandvillars**, Fr.
30/A4 **Grandvilliers**, Fr.
20/E3 **Granfjället** (peak), Swe.
23/F3 **Grange**, Eng,UK
36/C5 **Grange, Mont de** (mtn.), Fr.
85/L3 **Granger** (mtn.), Yk,Can
36/C1 **Granges-sur-Vologne**, Fr.
88/C2 **Grangeville**, Id,US
90/D4 **Grangeville**, Id,US
90/B2 **Granisle**, BC,Can
88/E2 **Granite** (peak), Mt,US
90/F4 **Granite** (peak), Mt,US
94/B4 **Granite City**, Il,US
97/F2 **Granite City**, Il,US
107/K4 **Granja**, Braz.
35/G2 **Granollers**, Sp.
35/L6 **Granollers**, Sp.
33/G4 **Gran Paradiso Nat'l Park**, It.
103/H2 **Gran Piedra** (hill), Cuba
33/J3 **Gran Pilastro** (peak), It.
35/Y16 **Gran Tarajal**, Canl.
23/H6 **Grantham**, Eng,UK
88/E4 **Grants**, NM,US
92/F4 **Grants**, NM,US
96/B3 **Grants**, NM,US
91/K4 **Grantsburg**, Wi,US
94/A2 **Grantsburg**, Wi,US
86/D4 **Grants Pass**, Or,US
88/B3 **Grants Pass**, Or,US
90/C5 **Grants Pass**, Or,US
92/B2 **Grants Pass**, Or,US
106/C5 **Gran Vilaya**, Peru
91/H1 **Granville** (lake), Mb,Can
86/F3 **Granville** (lake), Mb,Can
32/C2 **Granville**, Fr.
99/B3 **Grapeview**, Wa,US
99/B3 **Grapeview-Allyn**, Wa,US
29/F2 **Grasberg**, Ger.
23/E3 **Grasmere**, Eng,UK
99/P15 **Grass** (lake), Il,US
33/G5 **Grasse**, Fr.
35/J1 **Grasse**, Fr.
95/Q9 **Grassie**, On,Can
23/G3 **Grassington**, Eng,UK
88/D2 **Grassland Nat'l Park**, Sk,Can
90/G3 **Grasslands Nat'l Park**, Sk,Can
86/F4 **Grasslands Nat'l Park**, Sk,Can
73/C4 **Grassy**, Austl.
40/B2 **Gratkorn**, Aus.
37/F4 **Graubünden** (canton), Swi.
32/E5 **Graulhet**, Fr.
35/G1 **Graulhet**, Fr.
35/F1 **Graus**, Sp.
28/C5 **Grave**, Neth.
37/F5 **Gravedona**, It.
86/F4 **Gravelbourg**, Sk,Can
88/E2 **Gravelbourg**, Sk,Can
90/G3 **Gravelbourg**, Sk,Can
30/B2 **Gravelines**, Fr.
37/E6 **Gravellona Toce**, It.
94/E2 **Gravenhurst**, On,Can
19/Q7 **Gravesend**, Eng,UK
25/G4 **Gravesend**, Eng,UK
30/A5 **Gravigny**, Fr.
38/E2 **Gravina di Puglia**, It.
40/C5 **Gravina di Puglia**, It.
103/H2 **Gravois, Pointe à** (pt.), Haiti
26/C5 **Gray**, Fr.
32/F3 **Gray**, Fr.
36/B3 **Gray**, Fr.
85/F3 **Grayling**, Ak,US
94/C2 **Grayling**, Mi,US
19/P7 **Grays**, Eng,UK
25/G4 **Grays**, Eng,UK
106/F5 **Grays** (lake), Id,US
92/E2 **Grays** (lake), Id,US
90/B4 **Grays** (har.), Wa,US
99/P15 **Grayslake**, Il,US
91/H3 **Grayson**, Sk,Can
18/E4 **Graz**, Aus.
33/L3 **Graz**, Aus.
40/B2 **Graz**, Aus.
34/C4 **Grazalema**, Sp.
71/H8 **Great** (lake), Austl.
73/C4 **Great** (lake), Austl.
91/G3 **Great** (plains), Can., US
90/D5 **Great** (basin), US
92/C2 **Great** (basin), US
86/F3 **Great** (plains), Can,US
86/E4 **Great** (basin), Nv,US
88/C4 **Great** (basin), Nv,US
104/B1 **Great Abaco** (isl.), Bahm.
84/K7 **Great Abaco** (isl.), Bahm.
89/L6 **Great Abaco** (isl.), Bahm.
27/L5 **Great Alföld** (plain), Hun.
40/D2 **Great Alföld** (plain), Hun.
99/L12 **Great America**, Ca,US
99/Q15 **Great America** (Six Flags), Il,US
68/B8 **Great Australian** (bight), Austl.
70/D6 **Great Australian** (bight), Austl.
104/B1 **Great Bahama** (bank), Bahm.
25/F2 **Great Barford**, Eng,UK
68/D6 **Great Barrier** (reef), Austl.
70/H2 **Great Barrier** (reef), Austl.
72/B1 **Great Barrier** (reef), Austl.
71/S10 **Great Barrier** (isl.), NZ
72/B2 **Great Barrier Reef Marine Park**, Austl.
25/G2 **Great Barton**, Eng,UK
88/D4 **Great Basin Nat'l Park**, Nv,US
92/D3 **Great Basin Nat'l Park**, Nv,US
84/E3 **Great Bear** (lake), Can.
86/D2 **Great Bear** (lake), NW,Can
89/G4 **Great Bend**, Ks,US
93/H3 **Great Bend**, Ks,US
96/D2 **Great Bend**, Ks,US
49/C4 **Great Bitter** (lake), Egypt
19/M8 **Great Bookham**, Eng,UK
80/C3 **Great Brak** (riv.), SAfr.
18/C3 **Great Britain** (isl.), UK
26/B2 **Great Britain** (isl.), UK
25/G2 **Great Cornard**, Eng,UK
92/E2 **Great Divide** (basin), Wy,US
90/F5 **Great Divide** (basin), Wy,US
68/D6 **Great Dividing** (range), Austl.
68/D8 **Great Dividing** (range), Austl.
71/H7 **Great Dividing** (range), Austl.
72/B2 **Great Dividing** (range), Austl.
73/C2 **Great Dividing** (range), Austl.
23/H4 **Great Driffield**, Eng,UK
25/G3 **Great Dunmow**, Eng,UK
79/F5 **Greater Accra** (reg.), Gha.
84/K8 **Greater Antilles** (isls.), NAm.
104/C3 **Greater Antilles** (isls.), West Indies
103/F1 **Greater Antilles** (isls.), W. Indies
45/L3 **Greater Barsuki** (des.), Kaz.
19/P7 **Greater London** (co.), Eng,UK
25/F3 **Greater London** (co.), Eng,UK
23/F5 **Greater Manchester** (co.), Eng,UK
66/C4 **Greater Sunda** (isls.), Indo.
104/C2 **Great Exuma** (isl.), Bahm.
84/K7 **Great Exuma** (isl.), Bahm.
86/E4 **Great Falls**, Mt,US
88/D2 **Great Falls**, Mt,US
90/F4 **Great Falls**, Mt,US
80/D4 **Great Fish** (pt.), SAfr.
80/D4 **Great Fish** (riv.), SAfr.
25/F2 **Great Gransden**, Eng,UK
104/B1 **Great Guana** (cay), Bahm.
23/G2 **Greatham**, Eng,UK
23/F4 **Great Harwood**, Eng,UK
53/L2 **Great Himalaya** (range), Asia
62/D2 **Great Himalaya** (range), Asia
64/D1 **Great Himalaya** (range), Asia
60/A2 **Great Himalaya** (range), China
103/H1 **Great Inagua** (isl.), Bahm.
104/C2 **Great Inagua** (isl.), Bahm.
84/K7 **Great Inagua** (isl.), Bahm.
89/M7 **Great Inagua** (isl.), Bahm.
53/K3 **Great Indian** (des.), India, Pak.
62/A2 **Great Indian** (des.), India,Pak.
80/C3 **Great Karoo** (reg.), SAfr.
82/D7 **Great Karoo** (reg.), SAfr.
80/D4 **Great Kei** (riv.), SAfr.
99/Q15 **Great Lakes Naval Training Center**, Il,US
24/D2 **Great Malvern**, Eng,UK
25/E3 **Great Milton**, Eng,UK
24/B5 **Great Mis Tor** (hill), Eng,UK
63/F6 **Great Nicobar** (isl.), India
25/G1 **Great Ouse** (riv.), Eng,UK
71/H8 **Great Oyster** (bay), Austl.
73/C4 **Great Oyster** (bay), Austl.
43/U7 **Great Palace**, Rus.
43/V7 **Great Palace**, Rus.
93/G2 **Great Plains** (reg.), NAm
77/N6 **Great Rift** (valley), Afr.
82/F2 **Great Rift** (val.), Afr.
82/F2 **Great Ruaha** (riv.), Tanz.
36/D6 **Great Saint Bernard** (pass), It., Swi.
104/B1 **Great Sale** (cay), Bahm.
84/E6 **Great Salt** (lake), US
88/D3 **Great Salt** (lake), US
90/E5 **Great Salt** (lake), Ut,US
86/E4 **Great Salt** (lake), Ut,US
92/D2 **Great Salt** (lake), Ut,US
88/D3 **Great Salt Lake** (des.), US
90/E5 **Great Salt Lake** (des.), Ut,US
92/D2 **Great Salt Lake** (des.), Ut,US
93/F3 **Great Sand Dunes Nat'l Mon.**, Co,US
77/K2 **Great Sand Sea** (des.), Egypt, Libya
68/B7 **Great Sandy** (des.), Austl.
70/C4 **Great Sandy** (des.), Austl.
92/B2 **Great Sandy** (des.), Or,US
72/D4 **Great Sandy Nat'l Park**, Austl.
78/B4 **Great Scarcies** (riv.), Gui., SLeo.
25/G2 **Great Shelford**, Eng,UK
23/F3 **Great Shunner Fell** (mtn.), Eng,UK
84/F3 **Great Slave** (lake), Can.
86/E2 **Great Slave** (lake), NW,Can
97/H3 **Great Smoky Mts. Nat'l Park**, NC, Tn,US
89/K4 **Great Smoky Mts. Nat'l Park**, NC, Tn,US
98/G5 **Great South** (bay), NY,US
25/G4 **Great Stour** (riv.), Eng,UK
98/F5 **Great Swamp Nat'l Wildlife Ref.**, NJ,US
65/B3 **Great Tenasserim** (riv.), Burma
24/B5 **Great Torrington**, Eng,UK
68/B7 **Great Victoria** (des.), Austl.
70/D5 **Great Victoria** (des.), Austl.
54/F4 **Great Wall** (ruins), China
54/G3 **Great Wall** (ruins), China
59/B3 **Great Wall** (ruins), China
59/H6 **Great Wall** (ruins), China
19/P7 **Great Warley**, Eng,UK
73/C4 **Great Western Tiers** (mts.), Austl.
80/B4 **Great Winterhoek** (peak), SAfr.
80/L10 **Great Winterhoek** (peak), SAfr.
82/C7 **Great Winterhoek** (peak), SAfr.
24/D2 **Great Witley**, Eng,UK
25/H1 **Great Yarmouth**, Eng,UK
26/A2 **Great Yarmouth**, Eng.,UK
51/E2 **Great Zab** (riv.), Iraq
82/F5 **Great Zimbabwe** (ruins), Zim.
29/G6 **Grebenstein**, Ger.
79/H2 **Grébon** (peak), Niger
49/D2 **Greco** (cape), Cyp.
38/D2 **Greco** (peak), It.
40/A5 **Greco** (peak), It.
34/C2 **Gredos** (range), Sp.
18/F5 **Greece**
39/G3 **Greece**
40/F5 **Greece**
44/B4 **Greece**
50/A1 **Greece**
77/K1 **Greece**
88/F3 **Greeley**, Co,US
93/F2 **Greeley**, Co,US
87/S6 **Greely** (fjord), NW,Can
73/D3 **Green** (cape), Austl.
91/M4 **Green** (bay), Mi, Wi,US
88/D4 **Green** (riv.), US
92/E3 **Green** (riv.), US
94/C4 **Green** (riv.), Ky,US
95/G3 **Green** (mts.), Vt,US
99/D3 **Green** (riv.), Wa,US
86/E4 **Green** (riv.), Wy,US
90/F5 **Green** (riv.), Ut, Wy,US
86/H4 **Green Bay**, Wi,US
89/J3 **Green Bay**, Wi,US
91/L4 **Green Bay**, Wi,US
94/B2 **Green Bay**, Wi,US
98/K7 **Greenbelt**, Md,US
98/K8 **Greenbelt Park**, Md,US
22/B1 **Greencastle**, Ire.
94/C4 **Greencastle**, In,US
97/G2 **Greencastle**, In,US
97/H4 **Green Cove Springs**, Fl,US
99/Q14 **Greendale**, Wi,US
94/D4 **Greeneville**, Tn,US
97/H2 **Greeneville**, Tn,US
94/C4 **Greenfield**, In,US
97/G2 **Greenfield**, In,US
95/F3 **Greenfield**, Ma,US
99/P14 **Greenfield**, Wi,US
95/P7 **Greenfield Park**, Qu,Can
98/K7 **Green Haven**, Md,US
22/C2 **Greenisland**, NI,UK
20/N6 **Greenland** (sea), Ice.
84/R2 **Greenland** (sea), NAm.
84/N2 **Greenland** (Kalaallit Nunaat)
87/T7 **Greenland** (Kalaallit Nunaat)
18/A2 **Greenland** (Kalaallit Nunaat) (dpcy.), Den.
87/L1 **Greenland** (Kalaallit Nunaat) (dpcy.), Den.
87/T7 **Greenland** (Kalaallit Nunaat) (dpcy.), Den.
21/C3 **Greenock**, Sc,UK
22/B3 **Greenore**, Ire.
85/K2 **Greenough** (mt.), Ak,US
98/F4 **Green Pond**, NJ,US
95/R8 **Green River**, On,Can
88/D4 **Green River**, Ut,US
92/E3 **Green River**, Ut,US
90/F5 **Green River**, Wy,US
92/E2 **Green River**, Wy,US
84/K6 **Greensboro**, US
97/G3 **Greensboro**, Al,US
89/L4 **Greensboro**, NC,US
97/J2 **Greensboro**, NC,US
94/C4 **Greensburg**, In,US
94/E3 **Greensburg**, Pa,US
95/Q9 **Greensville**, On,Can
72/B2 **Greenvale**, Austl.
100/C2 **Green Valley**, Az,US
92/E5 **Green Valley**, Az,US
98/J7 **Green Valley**, Md,US
76/D7 **Greenville**, Libr.
78/C5 **Greenville**, Libr.
97/G4 **Greenville**, Al,US
90/C5 **Greenville**, Ca,US
92/B2 **Greenville**, Ca,US
94/C4 **Greenville**, Ky,US
97/G2 **Greenville**, Ky,US
94/C3 **Greenville**, Mi,US
89/H5 **Greenville**, Ms,US
93/K4 **Greenville**, Ms,US
97/F3 **Greenville**, Ms,US
89/L4 **Greenville**, NC,US
97/J3 **Greenville**, NC,US
94/C3 **Greenville**, Oh,US

97/G1 Greenville, Oh,US
89/K5 Greenville, SC,US
97/H3 Greenville, SC,US
101/F1 Greenville, Tx,US
89/G5 Greenville, Tx,US
93/H4 Greenville, Tx,US
96/D3 Greenville, Tx,US
99/D3 Greenwater (riv.), Wa,US
73/D2 Greenwell Point, Austl.
19/P7 Greenwich (bor.), Eng,UK
98/G4 Greenwich, Ct,US
19/P7 Greenwich Observatory, Eng,UK
95/R8 Greenwood, On,Can
89/H5 Greenwood, Ms,US
93/K4 Greenwood, Ms,US
97/F3 Greenwood, Ms,US
98/F4 Greenwood (lake), NJ, NY,US
89/K5 Greenwood, SC,US
97/H3 Greenwood, SC,US
98/F4 Greenwood Lake, NY,US
93/J4 Greers Ferry (lake), Ar,US
22/B6 Greese (riv.), Ire.
28/D6 Grefrath, Ger.
106/D5 Gregório (riv.), Braz.
70/C5 Gregory (lake), Austl.
70/D4 Gregory (lake), Austl.
70/F5 Gregory (lake), Austl.
70/G3 Gregory (range), Austl.
72/A2 Gregory (range), Austl.
91/J5 Gregory, SD,US
93/H2 Gregory, SD,US
27/G1 Greifswald, Ger.
27/G1 Greifswalder Bodden (bay), Ger.
40/B2 Greimberg (peak), Aus.
26/G3 Greiz, Ger.
33/K1 Greiz, Ger.
43/N4 Gremyachinsk, Rus.
20/D4 Grenå, Den.
104/F5 Grenada
106/F1 Grenada
84/L8 Grenada
89/J5 Grenada, Ms,US
93/K4 Grenada, Ms,US
97/F3 Grenada, Ms,US
32/D5 Grenade-sur-Garonne, Fr.
35/F1 Grenade-sur-Garonne, Fr.
30/B3 Grenay, Fr.
33/G3 Grenchen, Swi.
36/D3 Grenchen, Swi.
73/D2 Grenfell, Austl.
91/H3 Grenfell, Sk,Can
18/D4 Grenoble, Fr.
32/F4 Grenoble, Fr.
70/G2 Grenville (cape), Austl.
36/D2 Grenzach-Wyhlen, Ger.
20/E2 Gressåmoen Nat'l Park, Nor.
42/B2 Gressåmoen Nat'l Park, Nor.
23/E2 Greta (riv.), Eng,UK
23/F3 Greta (riv.), Eng,UK
91/J3 Gretna, Mb,Can
23/E2 Gretna, Sc,UK
97/F4 Gretna, La,US
25/F1 Gretton, Eng,UK
19/U10 Gretz-Armainvilliers, Fr.
30/B6 Gretz-Armainvilliers, Fr.
28/B5 Grevelingendam (dam), Neth.
29/E4 Greven, Ger.
39/G2 Grevená, Gre.
26/D3 Grevenbroich, Ger.
28/D6 Grevenbroich, Ger.
31/F1 Grevenbroich, Ger.
26/D4 Grevenmacher, Lux.
31/F4 Grevenmacher, Lux.
31/F4 Grevenmacher (dist.), Lux.
33/G2 Grevenmacher, Lux.
26/F2 Grevesmühlen, Ger.
28/A5 Grevlingen (chan.), Neth.
70/F2 Grey (cape), Austl.
70/G5 Grey (range), Austl.
72/A5 Grey (range), Austl.
73/B1 Grey (range), Austl.
95/K2 Grey (riv.), Nf,Can
22/C2 Grey (pt.), NI,UK
22/C2 Grey Abbey, NI,UK
90/F4 Greybull, Wy,US
92/E1 Greybull, Wy,US
85/L3 Grey Hunter (peak), Yk,Can
80/Q13 Greylingstad, SAfr.
71/R11 Greymouth, N.Z.
72/B2 Grey Peaks Nat'l Park, Austl.
23/F2 Greystoke, Eng,UK
22/B5 Greystones, Ire.
81/E3 Greytown, SAfr.
31/D2 Grez-Doiceau, Belg.
24/B6 Gribbin (pt.), Eng,UK
37/E5 Gridone (Monte Limidario) (peak), It.
37/E3 Griefensee (lake), Swi.
28/C2 Griend (isl.), Neth.
37/H3 Gries am Brenner, Aus.
27/G4 Grieskirchen, Aus.
40/A1 Grieskirchen, Aus.
37/H3 Griesskogel (peak), Aus.
89/K5 Griffin, Ga,US
97/G3 Griffin, Ga,US
71/H6 Griffith, Austl.
73/C2 Griffith, Austl.
99/R16 Griffith, In,US
37/F6 Grigna (peak), It.
19/T11 Grigny, Fr.
30/B6 Grigny, Fr.
44/F1 Grigor'yevskoye, Rus.
102/C2 Grijalva (riv.), Mex.
28/D2 Grijpskerk, Neth.
73/C4 Grim (cape), Austl.
30/D2 Grimbergen, Belg.
36/D5 Grimisuat, Swi.
24/D2 Grimley, Eng,UK
26/G1 Grimmen, Ger.
95/Q9 Grimsby, On,Can
23/H4 Grimsby, Eng,UK
37/E4 Grimselpass (pass), Swi.
20/N6 Grimsey (isl.), Ice.
20/D4 Grimstad, Nor.
20/M7 Grindavík, Ice.
33/H3 Grindelwald, Swi.
36/E4 Grindelwald, Swi.
87/S7 Grinnel (pen.), NW,Can
33/L3 Grintavec (peak), Slov.
40/B2 Grintavec (peak), Slov.
80/E3 Griqualand East (reg.), SAfr.
80/C2 Griqualand West (reg.), SAfr.
80/C3 Griquatown, SAfr.
87/S7 Grise Fiord, NW,Can
25/H5 Gris Nez (cape), Fr.
30/A2 Gris Nez (cape), Fr.
32/D1 Gris Nez (cape), Fr.
19/U10 Grisy-Suisnes, Fr.
99/K10 Grizzly (bay), Ca,US
109/B6 Grl. Carrera (lake), Chile
40/C3 Grmeč (mtn.), Bosn.
28/B6 Grobbendonk, Belg.
31/D1 Grobbendonk, Belg.
37/H1 Gröbenzell, Ger.
80/Q12 Groblersdal, SAfr.
27/J3 Grodków, Pol.
18/F3 Grodno, Bela.
27/M2 Grodno, Bela.
42/D5 Grodno, Bela.
44/B1 Grodno, Bela.
46/C4 Grodno, Bela.
42/E5 Grodno Obl., Bela.
44/C1 Grodno Obl., Bela.
27/M2 Grodno Oblast, Bela.
27/J2 Grodzisk Wielkopolski, Pol.
28/D4 Groenlo, Neth.
101/F2 Groesbeck, Tx,US
93/H5 Groesbeck, Tx,US
96/D4 Groesbeck, Tx,US
28/C5 Groesbeek, Neth.
32/B3 Groix (isl.), Fr.
27/L3 Grójec, Pol.
26/F1 Grömitz, Ger.
37/F6 Gromo, It.
28/E4 Gronau, Ger.
29/G4 Gronau, Ger.
18/D3 Groningen, Neth.
26/D2 Groningen, Neth.
28/D2 Groningen, Neth.
28/D2 Groningen (prov.), Neth.
33/J3 Gronlait (peak), It.
37/H5 Gronlait (peak), It.
37/F5 Grono, Swi.
80/C4 Groot (riv.), SAfr.
80/M10 Groot (riv.), SAfr.
82/D7 Groot (riv.), SAfr.
80/Q13 Grootdraaidam (res.), SAfr.
70/F2 Groote Eylandt (isl.), Austl.
28/D2 Grootegast, Neth.
82/C4 Grootfontein, Namb.
80/D2 Groot-Marico (riv.), SAfr.
80/P12 Groot-Marico, SAfr.
80/P12 Groot-Marico (riv.), SAfr.
80/C3 Grootvloer (salt pan), SAfr.
31/G5 Grosbliederstroff, Fr.
33/J3 Grosio, It.
37/G5 Grosio, It.
104/F4 Gros Islet, StL.
95/K1 Gros Morne (peak), Can
87/L4 Gros Morne (mtn.), Nf,Can
87/L4 Gros Morne Nat'l Park, Nf,Can
95/K1 Gros Morne Nat'l Park, Nf,Can
32/F3 Grosne (riv.), Fr.
37/G1 Grossaitingen, Ger.
29/G6 Grossalmerode, Ger.
29/E3 Grosse Aa (riv.), Ger.
99/F7 Grosse Ile, Mi,US
99/F7 Grosse Ile (isl.), Mi,US
37/F1 Grosse Lauter (riv.), Ger.
80/A2 Grosse Münzenberg (peak), Namb.
29/H6 Grossengottern, Ger.
31/G2 Grosse Nister (riv.), Ger.
26/E2 Grossenkneten, Ger.
29/F3 Grossenkneten, Ger.
33/M2 Gross-Enzersdorf, Aus.
99/G7 Grosse Pointe, Mi,US
99/G7 Grosse Pointe Farms, Mi,US
99/G7 Grosse Pointe Park, Mi,US
99/G7 Grosse Pointe Shores, Mi,US
99/G7 Grosse Pointe Woods, Mi,US
36/D5 Grosser Aletsch (glac.), Swi.
33/K2 Grosser Arber (peak), Ger.
29/G3 Grosser Aue (riv.), Ger.
26/F3 Grosser Beer-Berg (peak), Ger.
33/J1 Grosser Beer-Berg (peak), Ger.
33/L3 Grosser Bösenstein (peak), Aus.
37/G3 Grosser Daumen (peak), Ger.
29/F1 Grosser Knechtsand (isl.), Ger.
27/H4 Grosser Peilstein (peak), Aus.
40/B1 Grosser Peilstein (peak), Aus.
27/H5 Grosser Priel (peak), Aus.
33/L3 Grosser Priel (peak), Aus.
40/B2 Grosser Priel (peak), Aus.
27/H5 Grosser Pyhrgas (peak), Aus.
27/G4 Grosser Rachel (peak), Ger.
33/K2 Grosser Rachel (peak), Ger.
29/E2 Grosses Meer (lake), Ger.
40/A2 Grosses Wiesbachhorn (peak), Aus.
18/E4 Grosseto, It.
33/J5 Grosseto, It.
38/B1 Grosseto, It.
26/E4 Grossgerau, Ger.
33/H2 Grossgerau, Ger.
33/K3 Grossglockner (peak), Aus.
29/H1 Grosshansdorf, Ger.
31/G3 Grossmaischeid, Ger.
33/H5 Grosso (cape), Fr.
29/H3 Gross Oesingen, Ger.
31/F5 Grossrosseln, Ger.
27/H4 Grosssiegharts, Aus.
36/E3 Grosswangen, Swi.
40/B3 Grosuplje, Slov.
31/E2 Grote Gete (riv.), Belg.
28/B6 Grote Nete (riv.), Belg.
31/D1 Grote Nete (riv.), Belg.
91/J4 Groton, SD,US
38/E2 Grottaglie, It.
40/C5 Grottaglie, It.
40/A4 Grottammare, It.
31/E3 Grotte de Han, Belg.
35/E1 Grottes de Bétharram, Fr.
75/L14 Grou (riv.), Mor.
90/D2 Grouard Mission, Ab,Can
94/D1 Groundhog (riv.), On,Can
28/C2 Grouw, Neth.
25/E3 Grove, Eng,UK
98/K7 Grove (pt.), Md,US
93/J3 Grove, Ok,US
96/E2 Grove, Ok,US
92/B4 Grover City, Ca,US
93/J5 Groves, Tx,US
96/E4 Groves, Tx,US
98/J8 Groveton, Va,US
19/H4 Groznyy, Rus.
45/H4 Groznyy, Rus.
46/E5 Groznyy, Rus.
41/H4 Grudovo, Bul.
44/C4 Grudovo, Bul.
27/K2 Grudziądz, Pol.
82/C6 Grünau, Namb.
23/E2 Grune (pt.), Eng,UK
31/H4 Grünstadt, Ger.
37/H1 Grünwald, Ger.
36/D4 Gruyère (lake), Swi.
36/D4 Gruyères, Swi.
44/F1 Gryazi, Rus.
42/B3 Grycksbo, Swe.
27/H2 Gryfice, Pol.
27/H2 Gryfino, Pol.
36/D5 Gryon, Swi.
36/D5 Gsteig, Swi.
61/H3 Gu (mtn.), China
103/G1 Guacanayabo (gulf), Cuba
104/E5 Guacara, Ven.
104/E5 Guacharo Nat'l Park, Ven.
100/D3 Guachochi, Mex.
103/F4 Guácimo, CR
108/D2 Guaçuí, Braz.
100/E4 Guadalajara, Mex.
88/F7 Guadalajara, Mex.
18/C4 Guadalajara, Sp.
34/D2 Guadalajara, Sp.
68/E6 Guadalcanal (isl.), Sol.
34/C3 Guadalcanal, Sp.
34/E4 Guadalentín (riv.), Sp.
34/D3 Guadalimlar (riv.), Sp.
35/N8 Guadalix (riv.), Sp.
35/E2 Guadalope (riv.), Sp.
34/D4 Guadalquivir (riv.), Sp.
100/D3 Guadalupe, Mex.
100/E4 Guadalupe, Mex.
101/E3 Guadalupe, Mex.
101/F3 Guadalupe, Mex.
101/Q9 Guadalupe (res.), Mex.
84/E7 Guadalupe (isl.), Mex.
92/C5 Guadalupe (isl.), Mex
96/C5 Guadalupe, Mex
96/B3 Guadalupe (mts.), NM, Tx,US
103/G4 Guadalupe, Pan.
34/C3 Guadalupe, Sp.
34/C3 Guadalupe (range), Sp.
100/D2 Guadalupe (peak), Tx,US
101/F2 Guadalupe (riv.), Tx,US
88/F5 Guadalupe (peak), Tx,US
93/F5 Guadalupe (peak), Tx,US
93/H5 Guadalupe (riv.), Tx,US
96/B4 Guadalupe (peak), Tx,US
100/D2 Guadalupe Bravos, Mex.
101/D2 Guadalupe Mountains Nat'l Park, Tx,US
93/F5 Guadalupe Mountains Nat'l Park, Tx,US
88/E5 Guadalupe Mts. Nat'l Park, Tx,US
96/B4 Guadalupe Mts. Nat'l Park, Tx,US
100/D3 Guadalupe Victoria, Mex.
101/M7 Guadalupe Victoria, Mex.
100/D3 Guadalupe y Calvo, Mex.
34/C2 Guadarrama, Sp.
34/C2 Guadarrama (range), Sp.
34/C3 Guadarrama (riv.), Sp.
35/M8 Guadarrama (mts.), Sp.
35/M8 Guadarrama (pass), Sp.
35/N8 Guadarrama (riv.), Sp.
104/F3 Guadeloupe (dept.), Fr.
84/L8 Guadeloupe (isl.), Fr.
104/F3 Guadeloupe (passg.), West Indies
104/F3 Guadeloupe Nat'l Park, Guad.
101/Q9 Guadelupe, Basilica of, Mex.
34/B4 Guadiana (riv.), Sp., Port.
34/D4 Guadiana Menor (riv.), Sp.
34/D4 Guadix, Sp.
109/B5 Guafo (chan.), Chile
108/B4 Guaíba, Braz.
108/B4 Guaíba (riv.), Braz.
103/G1 Guaicanamar, Cuba
103/G1 Guáimaro, Cuba
106/E3 Guainiá (riv.), Col.
106/F2 Guaiquinima (peak), Ven.
108/D2 Guaíra, Braz.
109/F1 Guaíra, Braz.
106/E6 Guajará-Mirim, Braz.
103/H4 Guajira (pen.), Col.
105/B1 Guajira (pen.), Col.
106/D1 Guajira (pen.), Col.
102/E3 Gualaco, Hon.
92/B3 Gualala, Ca,US
102/D3 Gualán, Guat.
33/K5 Gualdo Tadino, It.
38/C1 Gualdo Tadino, It.
109/E3 Gualeguaychú, Arg.
109/C5 Gualicho (val.), Arg.
68/D3 Guam (isl.), PacUS
103/H4 Guamal, Col.
100/D3 Guamuchil, Mex.
59/D3 Gu'an, China
59/H7 Gu'an, China
103/F1 Guanabacoa, Cuba
100/D3 Guanacevi, Mex.
103/E1 Guanahacabibes (gulf), Cuba
103/E1 Guanahacabibes (pen.), Cuba
102/E2 Guanaja, Hon.
102/E2 Guanaja (isl.), Hon.
103/F1 Guanajay, Cuba
101/E4 Guanajuato, Mex.
101/E4 Guanajuato (state), Mex.
102/A1 Guanajuato (state), Mex.
88/F7 Guanajuato (state), Mex.
107/K6 Guanambi, Braz.
106/E2 Guanare, Ven.
106/E2 Guanare (riv.), Ven.
59/C3 Guancen Shan (mtn.), China
59/B3 Guandi Shan (mtn.), China
54/G5 Guandu, China
59/B5 Guandu, China
103/E1 Guane, Cuba
61/H3 Guangchang, China
59/D5 Guangde, China
61/H2 Guangde, China
61/G3 Guangdong (prov.), China
63/K3 Guangdong (prov.), China
65/E1 Guangdong (prov.), China
54/E5 Guangfu, China
59/C3 Guangling, China
58/B3 Guanglu (isl.), China
60/D3 Guangmao (mtn.), China
61/H2 Guangming (peak), China
59/D5 Guangming Ding (peak), China
60/E3 Guangnan, China
63/J3 Guangnan, China
59/C3 Guangping, China
61/H3 Guangping, China
59/D3 Guangrao, China
54/G5 Guangshan, China
59/C4 Guangshan, China
61/G1 Guangshan, China
54/G5 Guangshui, China
61/F4 Guangxi Zhuangzu Zizhiqu (aut. reg.), China
63/J3 Guangxi Zhuangzu Zizhiqu (aut. reg.), China
65/D1 Guangxi Zhuangzu Zizhiqu (aut. reg.), China
54/F5 Guangyuan, China
60/E1 Guangyuan, China
61/H3 Guangze, China
63/K3 Guangzhou, China
68/A2 Guangzhou, China
61/G4 Guangzhou (Canton), China
108/D1 Guanhães, Braz.
61/F2 Guanmian (mts.), China
55/H5 Guannan, China
59/D4 Guannan, China
103/H1 Guantánamo, Cuba
89/L7 Guantánamo, Cuba
103/H2 Guantánamo Bay U.S. Nav. Base, Cuba
59/C3 Guantao, China
59/G6 Guanting (res.), China
54/E5 Guan Xian, China
59/C3 Guan Xian, China
60/D2 Guan Xian, China
55/H5 Guanyun, China
59/D4 Guanyun, China
106/C3 Guapí, Col.
105/C4 Guaporé (riv.), Braz.
106/F6 Guaporé (riv.), Braz.
108/B4 Guaporé, Braz.
35/E1 Guara (peak), Sp.
107/L5 Guarabira, Braz.
108/B2 Guaraci, Braz.
107/J5 Guaraí, Braz.
108/B3 Guaramirim, Braz.
106/C4 Guaranda, Ecu.
107/K8 Guarapari, Braz.
108/D2 Guarapari, Braz.
108/B3 Guarapuava, Braz.
108/B2 Guararapes, Braz.
108/C2 Guaratinguetá, Braz.
108/B3 Guaratuba, Braz.
65/C5 Guar Chempedak, Malay.
34/B2 Guarda, Port.
34/B2 Guarda (dist.), Port.
35/E3 Guardamar del Segura, Sp.
37/H4 Guardia Alta (peak), It.
38/D1 Guardiagrele, It.
38/D2 Guardia Sanframondi, It.
40/B5 Guardia Sanframondi, It.
34/B3 Guareña, Sp.
103/H1 Guarico (pt.), Cuba
106/E2 Guárico (res.), Ven.
108/C2 Guarulhos, Braz.
103/F5 Guarumal, Pan.
100/C3 Guasave, Mex.
103/G1 Guasimal, Cuba
106/F2 Guasipati, Ven.
101/H5 Guatemala
103/D3 Guatemala
84/H8 Guatemala
102/D3 Guatemala (cap.), Guat.
84/H8 Guatemala (cap.), Guat.
105/C2 Guaviare (riv.), Col.
108/C2 Guaxupé, Braz.
103/G1 Guayabo (cay), Cuba
101/F4 Guayalejo (riv.), Mex.
104/E3 Guayama, PR
102/E3 Guayape (riv.), Hon.
105/A3 Guayaquil (gulf), Ecu.
106/B4 Guayaquil (gulf), Ecu.
106/C4 Guayaquil, Ecu.
106/E6 Guayaramerín, Bol.
100/C3 Guaymas, Mex.
69/P2 Guaymas, Mex.
43/N4 Gubakha, Rus.
27/H3 Guben, Ger.
27/H3 Gubin, Pol.
44/F2 Gubkin, Rus.
54/G5 Gucheng, China
59/B4 Gucheng, China
59/C3 Gucheng, China
59/G7 Gucheng, China
61/F1 Gucheng, China
54/E2 Guchin-Us, Mong.
64/F3 Güdalür, India
64/F4 Güdalür, India
35/E2 Gúdar (range), Sp.
29/G6 Gudensberg, Ger.
45/H4 Gudermes, Rus.
62/D4 Gudivāda, India
61/G4 Gudou (peak), China
29/H1 Gudow, Ger.
41/L5 Güdül, Turk.
50/C1 Güdül, Turk.
62/C5 Gūdūr, India
36/D2 Guebwiller, Fr.
32/B5 Guecho, Sp.
34/D1 Guecho, Sp.
78/B1 Guelb Azefal (mts.), Mrta.
75/V17 Guelma, Alg.
75/V17 Guelma (gov.), Alg.
89/K3 Guelph, On,Can
94/D3 Guelph, On,Can
76/C2 Guelta Zemmur, WSah.
32/C3 Guémené-Penfao, Fr.
101/F4 Güémez, Mex.
31/F5 Guénange, Fr.
32/B3 Guérande, Fr.
32/D3 Guéret, Fr.
32/B5 Guernica y Luno, Sp.
34/D1 Guernjica y Luno, Sp.
32/B2 Guernsey (isl.), Chl
101/E5 Guerrero (state), Mex.
101/K8 Guerrero (state), Mex.
102/B2 Guerrero (state), Mex.
32/F3 Gueugnon, Fr.
30/C5 Gueux, Fr.
79/H3 Guézaoua, Niger
77/N6 Gugē (peak), Eth.
36/D4 Guggisberg, Swi.
68/D3 Guguan (isl.), NMar.
61/F4 Gui (riv.), China
35/X16 Guía de Isora, Sp.
105/C2 Guiana (plat.), SAm.
106/F2 Guiana Highlands (mts.), SAm.
32/C3 Guichen, Fr.
55/H5 Guichi, China
59/D5 Guichi, China
61/H2 Guichi, China
102/C2 Guichicovi, Mex.
76/H6 Guidder, Camr.
78/B3 Guidimaka (reg.), Mrta.
63/J2 Guiding, China
63/K2 Guidong, China
38/C2 Guidonia, It.
76/D6 Guiglo, IvC.
78/D5 Guiglo, IvC.
19/U11 Guignes, Fr.
30/B6 Guignes, Fr.
30/C5 Guignicourt, Fr.
104/E5 Güigüe, Ven.
67/F1 Guihulñgan, Phil.
81/F2 Guija, Moz.
82/F5 Guija, Moz.
34/C2 Guijuelo, Sp.
19/M8 Guildford, Eng,UK
25/F4 Guildford, Eng,UK
32/F4 Guilherand, Fr.
63/K2 Guilin, China
63/K2 Guilin, China
68/A2 Guilin, China
87/J3 Guillaume-Delisle (lake), Qu,Can
34/B4 Guillena, Sp.
24/C1 Guilsfield, Wal,UK
34/A2 Guimarães, Port.
59/D4 Guimeng Ding (mtn.), China
54/E4 Guinan, China
74/A3 Guinea
76/C5 Guinea
78/C4 Guinea
74/C4 Guinea (gulf), Afr.
76/F7 Guinea (gulf), Afr.
74/A3 Guinea-Bissau
76/C5 Guinea-Bissau
78/B3 Guinea-Bissau
30/A2 Guînes, Fr.
32/B2 Guingamp, Fr.
102/E4 Guiones (pt.), CR
32/A2 Guipavas, Fr.
63/K3 Guiping, China
107/H7 Guiratinga, Braz.
104/F5 Güiria, Ven.
106/F1 Güiria, Ven.
23/G2 Guisborough, Eng,UK
30/C4 Guiscard, Fr.
30/C4 Guise, Fr.
23/G4 Guiseley, Eng,UK
34/B1 Guitiriz, Sp.
61/H2 Guixi, China
63/H2 Guixi, China
61/F4 Gui Xian, China
63/J3 Gui Xian, China
60/E3 Guiyang, China
61/G3 Guiyang, China
63/J2 Guiyang, China
63/K2 Guiyang, China
60/E3 Guizhou (prov.), China
63/J2 Guizhou (prov.), China
32/C4 Gujan-Mestras, Fr.
62/B3 Gujarāt (state), India
53/K2 Gūjar Khān, Pak.
64/B1 Gūjar Khān, Pak.
53/K2 Gujrānwāla, Pak.
64/C1 Gujrānwāla, Pak.
53/K2 Gujrāt, Pak.
64/C1 Gujrāt, Pak.
44/F2 Gukovo, Rus.
54/E4 Gulang, China
73/D1 Gulargambone, Austl.
62/C4 Gulbarga, India
20/H4 Gulbene, Lat.
42/E4 Gulbene, Lat.
31/G3 Guldenbach (riv.), Ger.
20/C3 Gulen, Nor.
101/F5 Gulf Coastal (plain), Tx,US
96/D5 Gulf Coastal Plain (plain), Tx,US
97/F4 Gulf Islands Nat'l Seashore, US
89/J5 Gulfport, Ms,US
97/F4 Gulfport, Ms,US
97/G4 Gulf Shores, Al,US
73/D2 Gulgong, Austl.
46/G5 Gulistan, Uzb.
55/J2 Guliya (peak), China
85/J3 Gulkana, Ak,US
22/B2 Gulladuff, NI,UK
90/F3 Gull Lake, Can
50/B2 Güllükdağı Nat'l Park, (Termessos) Turk.
49/C1 Gülnar, Turk.
50/C2 Gülnar, Turk.
31/E2 Gulpen, Neth.
50/A2 Gülpınar, Turk.
50/C2 Gülşehir, Turk.
77/M7 Gulu, Ugan.
39/J1 Gülübovo, Bul.
41/G4 Gülübovo, Bul.
44/C4 Gülübovo, Bul.
41/G4 Gulyantsi, Bul.
64/A2 Gumal (riv.), Pak.
82/D4 Gumare, Bots.
31/G6 Gumbrechtshoffen, Fr.
57/F2 Gumma (pref.), Japan
26/D3 Gummersbach, Ger.
29/E6 Gummersbach, Ger.
31/G1 Gummersbach, Ger.
44/E4 Gümüşhacıköy, Turk.
44/F4 Gümüşhane, Turk.
44/F4 Gümüshane (prov.), Turk.
50/D1 Gümüşhane, Turk.
50/D1 Gümüşhane (prov.), Turk.
77/N5 Guna (peak), Eth.
53/L4 Guna, India
62/C3 Guna, India
73/C2 Gunbower, Austl.
54/C6 Güncang, China
63/F2 Güncang, China
73/D2 Gundagai, Austl.
36/D1 Gundelfingen, Ger.
31/H4 Gundersheim, Ger.
31/G6 Gundershoffen, Fr.
64/F3 Gundlupet, India
49/C1 Gündoğmuş, Turk.
50/C2 Gündoğmuş, Turk.
50/B2 Güney, Turk.
50/D2 Güneydogu Toroslar (mts.), Turk.
51/F1 Gunib, Rus.
91/J2 Gunisao (lake), Mb,Can
91/J2 Gunisao (riv.), Mb,Can
40/C3 Gunja, Cro.
71/J6 Gunnedah, Austl.
73/D1 Gunnedah, Austl.
73/D2 Gunning, Austl.
88/E4 Gunnison, Co,US
92/F3 Gunnison, Co,US
92/F3 Gunnison (riv.), Co,US
96/B2 Gunnison, Co,US
92/E3 Gunnison, Ut,US
70/F3 Gunpowder, Austl.
97/G3 Guntersville, Al,US
97/G3 Guntersville (dam), Al,US
62/D4 Guntūr, India
26/F4 Günz (riv.), Ger.
33/J2 Günz (riv.), Ger.
37/G1 Günz (riv.), Ger.
37/G1 Günzburg, Ger.
26/F4 Gunzenhausen, Ger.
33/J2 Gunzenhausen, Ger.
54/H5 Guo (riv.), China
59/C4 Guo (riv.), China
59/D4 Guoyang, China
77/N6 Guragē (peak), Eth.
41/G2 Gura Humorului, Rom.
109/F2 Gural (mts.), Braz.
54/B2 Gurbantünggut (des.), China
53/L2 Gurdāspur, India
64/C1 Gurdāspur, India
51/F1 Gurdzhaani, Geo.
44/F4 Gürgentepe, Turk.
50/D1 Gürgentepe, Turk.
107/K6 Gurgueia (riv.), Braz.
105/C2 Guri (res.), Ven.
106/F2 Guri (res.), Ven.
33/L3 Gurk (riv.), Aus.
40/B2 Gurk (riv.), Aus.
41/G4 Gurkovo, Bul.
33/K3 Gurkthaler (mts.), Aus.
99/Q15 Gurnee, Il,US
82/F4 Guro, Moz.
50/E2 Güroymak, Turk.
51/E2 Gürpınar, Turk.
51/M7 Gürpinar, Turk.
41/J5 Gürsu, Turk.
50/B1 Gürsu, Turk.
65/C5 Gurun, Malay.
50/D2 Gürün, Turk.
107/J4 Gurupi (mts.), Braz.
107/J4 Gurupi (riv.), Braz.
107/J6 Gurupi, Braz.
53/K4 Guru Sikhar (mtn.), India
62/B3 Guru Sikhar (mtn.), India
54/G2 Gurvandzagal, Mong.
45/J3 Gur'yev, Kaz.
46/F5 Gur'yev, Kaz.
45/J3 Gur'yev Obl., Kaz.
76/G5 Gusau, Nga.
27/M1 Gusev, Rus.
59/C4 Gushi, China
61/G1 Gushi, China
39/F1 Gusinje, Yugo.
40/D4 Gusinje, Yugo.
42/J5 Gus'-Khrustal'nyy, Rus.
38/A3 Guspini, It.
101/Q10 Gustavo A. Marrero, Mex.
85/L4 Gustavus, Ak,US
31/F4 Gusterath, Ger.
101/F2 Gustine, Tx,US
26/G2 Güstrow, Ger.
63/G2 Gutang, China
26/E3 Gütersloh, Ger.
29/F5 Gütersloh, Ger.
93/H4 Guthrie, Ok,US
96/D3 Guthrie, Ok,US
93/G4 Guthrie, Tx,US
96/C3 Guthrie, Tx,US
101/F4 Gutiérrez Zamora, Mex.
101/M6 Gutiérrez Zamora, Mex.
37/E4 Guttannen, Swi.
37/F2 Guttingen, Swi.
20/E3 Gutulia Nat'l Park, Nor.
29/G6 Guxhagen, Ger.
54/G4 Guxian, China
59/B3 Guxian, China
105/D2 Guyana
106/G3 Guyana
19/S10 Guyancourt, Fr.
30/B6 Guyancourt, Fr.
47/M5 Guyang, China
54/G3 Guyang, China
59/B2 Guyang, China
32/C4 Guyenne (reg.), Fr.
73/E1 Guy Fawkes River Nat'l Park, Austl.
25/G1 Guyhirn, Eng,UK
88/F4 Guymon, Ok,US
93/G3 Guymon, Ok,US
96/C2 Guymon, Ok,US
73/D1 Guyra, Austl.
54/F4 Guyuan, China
54/H3 Guyuan, China
63/J2 Guzhang, China
55/H5 Guzhen, China
59/D4 Guzhen, China
100/D2 Guzmán, Mex.
100/D2 Guzman (lake), Me
92/F5 Guzmán (lake), Me
27/L1 Gvardeysk, Rus.
53/H3 Gwādar, Pak.
62/C2 Gwalior, India
82/E5 Gwanda, Zim.
73/D2 Gwandalan, Austl.
25/F1 Gwash (riv.), Eng,U
24/C2 Gwaunceste (mtn.), Wal,UK
93/J3 G. W. Carver Nat'l Mon., Mo,US
27/J2 Gwda (riv.), Pol.
24/A6 Gweek, Eng,UK
24/D3 Gwent (co.), Wal,U
23/E5 Gwersyllt, Wal,UK
82/E4 Gweru, Zim.
73/D1 Gwydir (riv.), Austl.
22/D5 Gwynedd (co.), Wal,UK
24/B1 Gwynedd (co.), Wal,UK
36/B3 Gy, Fr.
63/F2 Gyaca, China
45/H4 Gyandzhe, Azer.
46/E5 Gyandzhe, Azer.
51/F1 Gyandzhe, Azer.
62/E2 Gyangzê, China
55/D5 Gyaring (lake), Chin
79/E5 Gyasikan, Gha.
46/H2 Gyda (pen.), Rus.
48/G2 Gyda (pen.), Rus.
29/G2 Gyhum, Ger.
68/E7 Gympie, Austl.
71/J5 Gympie, Austl.
72/D4 Gympie, Austl.
60/B5 Gyobingauk, Burma
63/G4 Gyobingauk, Burma
40/E2 Gyoma, Hun.
27/K5 Gyöngyös, Hun.
40/D2 Gyöngyös, Hun.
40/D2 Gyonk, Hun.
18/E4 Győr, Hun.
27/J5 Győr, Hun.
40/C2 Győr, Hun.
27/J5 Györ-Sopron (co.), Hun.
40/C2 Győr-Sopron (co.), Hun.
40/E2 Gyula, Hun.
44/B3 Gyula, Hun.

H

30/D2 Haacht, Belg.
33/L2 Haag, Aus.
40/B1 Haag, Aus.
28/D4 Haaksbergen, Neth.
30/D2 Haaltert, Belg.
28/A5 Haamstede, Neth.
28/E6 Haan, Ger.
31/G1 Haan, Ger.
69/H6 Ha'apai Group (isls.), Tonga
20/H2 Haapavesi, Fin.
42/E2 Haapavesi, Fin.
20/G4 Haapsalu, Est.
42/D4 Haapsalu, Est.
26/F4 Haar, Ger.
33/J2 Haar, Ger.
31/G5 Haardt (mts.), Ger.
33/G2 Haardt (mts.), Ger.
26/C2 Haarlem, Neth.
28/B4 Haarlem, Neth.
71/Q11 Haast, N.Z.
53/J3 Hab (riv.), Pak.
46/J5 Habahe, China
54/B2 Habahe, China
31/E4 Habay, Belg.
51/E3 Habbānīyah, Iraq
52/D2 Habbānīyah, Iraq
37/H3 Habicht (peak), Aus
60/A3 Habiganj, Bang.
63/F3 Habiganj, Bang.
57/L10 Habikino, Japan
55/N3 Haboro, Japan
36/D2 Habsheim, Fr.
29/F3 Hache (riv.), Ger.
31/G2 Hachenburg, Ger.
55/N5 Hachijō (isl.), Japan
47/Q5 Hachinohe, Japan
57/F3 Hachiōji, Japan
57/H7 Hachiōji, Japan
100/C2 Hachita, NM,US
50/C2 Hacıbektaş, Turk.
98/C3 Hacienda Heights, Ca,US
50/C2 Hacılar, Turk.
98/F5 Hackensack, NJ,US
22/B6 Hacketstown, Ire.
19/N7 Hackney (bor.), Eng,UK
61/E4 Ha Coi, Viet.
63/J3 Ha Coi, Viet.
65/D1 Ha Coi, Viet.
64/B1 Hadāli, Pak.
26/E3 Hadamar, Ger.
31/H3 Hadamar, Ger.
33/H1 Hadamar, Ger.
57/F3 Hadano, Japan
57/H7 Hadano, Japan
52/C4 Hadarba (cape), Sudan

7/N3 **Hadarba** (cape), Sudan
7/J4 **Haddad** (wadi), Chad
25/F3 **Haddenham**, Eng,UK
8/E6 **Haddonfield**, NJ,US
8/E6 **Haddon** (Westmont), NJ,US
3/G4 **Ḩadd, Ra's al** (pt.), Oman
6/G5 **Hadejia** (riv.), Nga.
9/H3 **Hadejia** (riv.), Nga.
29/F1 **Hadelner** (can.), Ger.
9/D3 **Hadera**, Isr.
49/F7 **Ḩadera**, Isr.
0/D5 **Haderslev**, Den.
26/E1 **Haderslev**, Den.
52/E5 **Hadhramaut** (reg.), Yemen
7/Q4 **Hadhramaut** (reg.), Yemen
9/C1 **Hadım**, Turk.
0/C2 **Hadım**, Turk.
2/B1 **Hadım**, Turk.
/S15 **Hadjout**, Alg.
40/E2 **Hadjú-Bihar** (co.), Hun.
36/F1 **Hadley** (bay), NW,Can
9/Q8 **Hadlow**, Eng,UK
23/F1 **Hadrian's Wall** (ruins), Eng,UK
20/E1 **Hadselfjorden** (fjord), Nor.
0/D4 **Hadsund**, Den.
7/N6 **Haeju**, NKor.
35/K4 **Haeju**, NKor.
8/C3 **Haeju**, NKor.
8/C4 **Haeju** (bay), NKor.
8/S9 **Haena** (pt.), Hi,US
8/D5 **Haenam**, SKor.
44/F5 **Hafik**, Turk.
0/D2 **Hafik**, Turk.
3/K2 **Hāfizābād**, Pak.
4/B1 **Hāfizābād**, Pak.
0/B3 **Hāflong**, India
53/F2 **Hāflong**, India
0/N7 **Hafnarfjördhur**, Ice.
20/P7 **Hafnarhreppur**, Ice.
52/E3 **Ḩafr al Bāţin**, SAr.
1/G4 **Ḩaft Gel**, Iran
52/E2 **Haft Gel**, Iran
7/R5 **Hafun** (pt.), Som.
5/H3 **Hafun, Ras** (pt.), Som.
35/F4 **Hagemeister** (isl.), Ak,US
26/D3 **Hagen**, Ger.
29/E6 **Hagen**, Ger.
29/E4 **Hagen am Teutoburger Wald**, Ger.
29/F2 **Hagen im Bremischen**, Ger.
26/F2 **Hagenow**, Ger.
0/D1 **Hagerman**, NM,US
33/F4 **Hagerman**, NM,US
46/B3 **Hagerman**, NM,US
38/L4 **Hagerstown**, Md,US
34/E4 **Hagerstown**, Md,US
32/C5 **Hagetmau**, Fr.
35/F1 **Hagetmau**, Fr
6/B3 **Hagi**, Japan
50/E4 **Ha Giang**, Viet.
3/H3 **Ha Giang**, Viet.
5/D1 **Ha Giang**, Viet.
24/D2 **Hagley**, Eng,UK
37/F2 **Hagnau am Bodensee**, Ger.
31/F5 **Hagondange**, Fr.
21/H7 **Hags Head** (pt.), Ire.
31/G2 **Hague**, Sk,Can
32/C2 **Hague, Cap de la** (cape), Fr.
26/D4 **Haguenau**, Fr.
1/G6 **Haguenau**, Fr.
33/G2 **Haguenau**, Fr.
32/D2 **Hahashima** (isl.), Jap.
26/F3 **Hahle** (riv.), Ger.
29/H6 **Hahle** (riv.), Ger.
3/A2 **Hahndorf**, Austl.
31/G3 **Hahnenbach** (riv.), Ger.
31/H3 **Hahnstätten**, Ger.
69/D3 **Hai** (riv.), China
69/H7 **Hai** (riv.), China
55/J5 **Hai'an**, China
59/E4 **Hai'an**, China
7/L10 **Haibara**, Japan
58/J3 **Haicheng**, China
58/B2 **Haicheng**, China
59/E2 **Haicheng**, China
51/D1 **Hai Duong**, Viet.
49/D3 **Haifa**, Isr.
49/D3 **Haifa** (dist.), Isr.
49/F6 **Haifa** (dist.), Isr.
52/B2 **Haifa**, Isr.
7/N1 **Haifa**, Isr.
64/F1 **Haifeng**, China
26/E3 **Haiger**, Ger.
31/H2 **Haiger**, Ger.
31/H1 **Haiger**, Ger.
37/E1 **Haigerloch**, Ger.
50/E4 **Hai Hau**, Viet.
55/D1 **Hai Hau**, Viet.
53/K3 **Haikang**, China
55/E1 **Haikang**, China
61/F4 **Haikou**, China
53/K3 **Haikou**, China
8/T10 **Haiku-Pauwela**, HI,US
52/D3 **Ḩā'il**, SAr.
77/P2 **Ḩā'il**, SAr.
63/K3 **Hailākāndi**, India
7/M5 **Hailar**, China
55/H2 **Hailar**, China
55/J2 **Hailar** (riv.), China
37/J4 **Haileybury**, On,Can
94/E2 **Haileybury**, On,Can
61/F4 **Hailing** (isl.), China
25/G5 **Hailsham**, Eng,UK
55/K2 **Hailun**, China
55/J5 **Haimen**, China
59/E5 **Haimen**, China
61/J2 **Haimen**, China
26/F5 **Haiming**, Aus.
37/G3 **Haiming**, Aus.
29/F6 **Haina**, Ger.
48/L8 **Hainan** (isl.), China
61/F4 **Hainan** (str.), China
61/F5 **Hainan** (isl.), China
61/F5 **Hainan** (prov.), China
63/J4 **Hainan** (prov.), China
63/K4 **Hainan** (isl.), China
65/E1 **Hainan** (str.), China
65/E2 **Hainan** (isl.), China
65/E2 **Hainan** (prov.), China
30/B2 **Hainaut** (prov.), Belg.
33/H1 **Hainburg**, Ger.
85/L4 **Haines**, Ak,US
86/C3 **Haines**, Ak,US
97/H4 **Haines City**, Fl,US
85/L3 **Haines Junction**, Yk,Can
99/P15 **Hainesville**, Il,US
26/F3 **Hainich** (mts.), Ger.
29/H6 **Hainich** (mts.), Ger.
55/J5 **Haining**, China
59/L9 **Haining**, China
61/J2 **Haining**, China
60/E4 **Hai Phong** (Haiphong), Viet.
60/E4 **Haiphong** (Hai Phong), Viet.
63/J3 **Hai Phong** (Haiphong), Viet.
63/J3 **Haiphong** (Haiphong), Viet.
65/D1 **Hai Phong** (Haiphong), Viet.
65/D1 **Haiphong** (Hai Phong), Viet.
61/H3 **Haitan** (isl.), China
103/H2 **Haiti**
104/C3 **Haiti**
84/K8 **Haiti**
89/M8 **Haiti**
65/E2 **Hai Van** (pass), Viet.
63/K3 **Haixia** (str.), China
55/H4 **Haixing**, China
59/D3 **Haixing**, China
54/E4 **Haiyan**, China
63/K3 **Haiyan**, China
55/J4 **Haiyang**, China
58/B3 **Haiyang** (isl.), China
59/E3 **Haiyang**, China
54/F4 **Haiyuan**, China
59/D4 **Haizhou** (bay), China
27/L5 **Hajdú-Bihar** (co.), Hun.
27/L5 **Hajdúböszormény**, Hun.
40/E2 **Hajdúböszormény**, Hun.
44/B3 **Hajdúböszormény**, Hun.
40/E2 **Hajdúdorog**, Hun.
40/E2 **Hajdúhadház**, Hun.
40/E2 **Hajdúnánás**, Hun.
27/L5 **Hajdúnánás**, Hun.
44/B3 **Hajdúnánás**, Hun.
27/L5 **Hajdúszoboszló**, Hun.
40/E2 **Hajdúszoboszló**, Hun.
38/A5 **Hājīb Al 'Uyūn**, Tun
57/F1 **Hajiki-zaki** (pt.), Japan
52/B6 **Ḩajj 'Abd Allāh**, Sudan
52/D5 **Ḩajjah**, Yem.
77/P4 **Ḩajjah**, Yem.
53/G3 **Ḩājjīābād**, Iran
27/M2 **Hajnówka**, Pol.
60/A3 **Hājo**, India
63/F2 **Hājo**, India
40/D2 **Hajós**, Hun.
63/F3 **Haka**, Burma
69/L5 **Hakahau**, Fr.Pol.
51/E2 **Hakkâri** (prov.), Turk.
56/D3 **Hakken-san** (mtn.), Japan
47/O5 **Hakodate**, Japan
55/N3 **Hakodate**, Japan
57/H8 **Hakone**, Japan
57/H8 **Hakone-Fuji-Izu Nat'l Park**, Japan
57/E2 **Hakui**, Japan
57/E2 **Haku-san** (mtn.), Japan
57/M10 **Hakusan**, Japan
57/E2 **Hakusan Nat'l Park**, Japan
53/J3 **Hāla**, Pak.
62/A2 **Hāla**, Pak.
49/E1 **Ḩalab** (prov.), Syria
50/D3 **Ḩalab** (prov.), Syria
49/E1 **Ḩalab** (Aleppo), Syria
50/D2 **Ḩalab** (Aleppo), Syria
52/C1 **Ḩalab** (Aleppo), Syria
51/F3 **Ḩalabjah**, Iraq
52/E1 **Ḩalabjah**, Iraq
101/M6 **Halachó**, Mex.
52/C4 **Ḩalā'ib**, Sudan
77/N3 **Ḩalā'ib**, Sudan
67/F1 **Halcon** (mt.), Phil.
20/D4 **Halden**, Nor.
26/F2 **Haldensleben**, Ger.
37/G2 **Haldenwang**, Ger.
95/Q10 **Haldimand**, On,Can
54/G2 **Haldzan**, Mong.
82/G2 **Hale**, Tanz.
23/F5 **Hale**, Eng,UK
88/T10 **Haleakala Nat'l Park**, HI,US
88/V12 **Haleiwa**, Hi,US
31/E2 **Halen**, Belg.
99/P14 **Hales Corners**, Wi,US
24/D2 **Halesowen**, Eng,UK
25/H2 **Halesworth**, Eng,UK
97/G3 **Haleyville**, Al,US
52/C5 **Halfa Aj Jadīda**, Sudan
78/E5 **Half Assini**, Gha.
99/K12 **Half Moon Bay**, Ca,US
72/C3 **Half Tide Beach**, Austl.
49/D4 **Ḩalḩūl**, WBnk.
49/G8 **Ḩalḩūl**, WBnk.
94/E2 **Haliburton** (hills), On,Can
71/H3 **Halifax** (bay), Austl.
72/B2 **Halifax**, Austl.
72/B2 **Halifax** (bay), Austl.
87/K4 **Halifax** (cap.), NS,Can
89/P3 **Halifax** (cap.), NS,Can
95/J2 **Halifax**, (cap.), NS,Can
23/G4 **Halifax**, Eng,UK
51/J4 **Halīl** (riv.), Iran
53/G3 **Halīl** (riv.), Iran
39/K3 **Halileli**, Turk.
54/D2 **Haliun**, Mong.
85/H1 **Halkett** (cape), Ak,US
73/C2 **Hall**, Austl.
87/K2 **Hall** (pen.), NW,Can
68/E4 **Hall** (isls.), Micr.
85/D3 **Hall** (isl.), Ak,US
20/E4 **Halland** (co.), Swe.
55/K5 **Halla-san** (mtn.), SKor.
87/H2 **Hall Beach**, NW,Can
30/D2 **Halle**, Belg.
18/E3 **Halle**, Ger.
26/F3 **Halle**, Ger.
29/F4 **Halle**, Ger.
46/B4 **Halle**, Ger.
20/E4 **Hällefors**, Swe.
26/G5 **Hallein**, Aus.
33/K3 **Hallein**, Aus.
40/A2 **Hallein**, Aus.
29/F6 **Hallenberg**, Ger.
30/A4 **Hallencourt**, Fr.
26/F3 **Halle-Neustadt**, Ger.
83/M **Hallett** (cape), Ant.
101/F2 **Hallettsville**, Tx,US
93/H5 **Hallettsville**, Tx,US
96/D4 **Hallettsville**, Tx,US
91/J3 **Hallock**, Mn,US
68/B6 **Halls Creek**, Austl.
70/D3 **Halls Creek**, Austl.
26/B4 **Hallu** (riv.), Fr.
30/B3 **Hallue** (riv.), Fr.
30/C2 **Halluin**, Fr.
36/E3 **Hallwilersee** (lake), Swi.
56/A3 **Hallyŏ Haesang Nat'l Park**, SKor.
58/E5 **Hallyŏ Haesang Nat'l Park**, SKor.
48/M9 **Halmahera** (isl.), Indo.
67/G3 **Halmahera** (isl.), Indo.
67/G4 **Halmahera** (sea), Indo.
68/B4 **Halmahera** (isl.), Indo.
18/E3 **Halmstad**, Swe.
20/E4 **Halmstad**, Swe.
46/B4 **Halmstad**, Swe.
30/D4 **Ḩalq al Wādī**, Tun.
75/X17 **Ḩalq al Wādī**, Tun.
18/E3 **Hälsingborg**, Swe.
20/E4 **Hälsingborg**, Swe.
25/G3 **Halstead**, Eng,UK
20/D5 **Halsteren**, Neth.
54/C4 **Haltang** (riv.), China
20/D3 **Haltdalen**, Nor.
23/H4 **Haltemprice**, Eng,UK
29/E5 **Haltern**, Ger.
95/Q8 **Halton** (co.), On,Can
95/Q8 **Halton Hills**, On,Can
23/F2 **Haltwhistle**, Eng,UK
29/E6 **Halver**, Ger.
31/G1 **Halver**, Ger.
29/E3 **Halverder Aa** (riv.), Ger.
26/B4 **Ham**, Fr.
30/C4 **Ham**, Fr.
32/E2 **Ham**, Fr.
56/C3 **Hamada**, Japan
46/E6 **Hamadān**, Iran
48/D6 **Hamadān**, Iran
51/G3 **Hamadān**, Iran
51/G3 **Hamadān** (gov.), Iran
52/E2 **Hamadān**, Iran
49/E2 **Ḩamāh**, Syria
49/E2 **Ḩamāh** (prov.), Syria
50/D3 **Ḩamāh**, Syria
50/D3 **Ḩamāh** (prov.), Syria
52/C1 **Ḩamāh**, Syria
57/M10 **Hamajima**, Japan
57/E3 **Hamakita**, Japan
47/P6 **Hamamatsu**, Japan
57/E3 **Hamamatsu**, Japan
20/D3 **Hamar**, Nor.
62/D6 **Hambantota**, SrL.
29/F2 **Hambergen**, Ger.
25/E5 **Hamble**, Eng,UK
23/G3 **Hambleton** (hills), Eng,UK
29/G3 **Hambühren**, Ger.
18/D3 **Hamburg**, Ger.
26/E2 **Hamburg**, Ger.
26/E2 **Hamburg** (state), Ger.
29/G1 **Hamburg**, Ger.
29/H1 **Hamburg** (state), Ger.
46/A4 **Hamburg**, Ger.
93/K4 **Hamburg**, Ar,US
96/F3 **Hamburg**, Ar,US
98/F4 **Hamburg**, NJ,US
94/E3 **Hamburg**, NY,US
77/N2 **Ḩamḑ** (wadi), SAr.
52/C3 **Ḩamḑ, Wādī al** (dry riv.), SAr.
20/G3 **Häme** (prov.), Fin.
42/E3 **Häme** (prov.), Fin.
42/D3 **Hämeenkyrö**, Fin.
18/F2 **Hämeenlinna**, Fin.
20/H3 **Hämeenlinna**, Fin.
42/E3 **Hämeenlinna**, Fin.
46/C3 **Hämeenlinna**, Fin.
70/A5 **Hamelin Pool**, Austl.
70/A5 **Hamelin Pool** (bay), Austl.
26/E2 **Hameln**, Ger.
29/G4 **Hameln**, Ger.
70/B4 **Hamersley** (range), Austl.
25/H3 **Hamford Water** (inlet), Eng,UK
55/K3 **Hamgyŏng** (mts.), NKor.
58/E2 **Hamgyŏng** (mts.), NKor.
58/D2 **Hamgyŏng-Namdo** (prov.), NKor.
47/N6 **Hamhŭng**, NKor.
55/K4 **Hamhŭng**, NKor.
58/D3 **Hamhŭng**, NKor.
58/D3 **Hamhŭng-Si** (prov.), NKor.
46/K5 **Hami**, China
54/C3 **Hami**, China
70/G7 **Hamilton**, Austl.
73/B3 **Hamilton**, Austl.
84/M4 **Hamilton** (inlet), Can.
87/L3 **Hamilton** (inlet), Nf,Can
87/J4 **Hamilton**, On,Can
89/L3 **Hamilton**, On,Can
94/E3 **Hamilton**, On,Can
95/Q9 **Hamilton**, On,Can
95/Q9 **Hamilton** (har.), On,Can
68/G8 **Hamilton**, N.Z.
71/S10 **Hamilton**, N.Z.
21/C3 **Hamilton**, Sc,UK
97/G3 **Hamilton**, Al,US
99/L12 **Hamilton** (mt.), Ca,US
90/E4 **Hamilton**, Mt,US
89/K4 **Hamilton**, Oh,US
94/C4 **Hamilton**, Oh,US
97/G2 **Hamilton**, Oh,US
101/F2 **Hamilton**, Tx,US
93/H5 **Hamilton**, Tx,US
96/D4 **Hamilton**, Tx,US
62/D2 **Hamīrpur**, India
64/D2 **Hamīrpur**, India
55/K4 **Hamju**, NKor.
101/E1 **Hamlin**, Tx,US
26/D3 **Hamm**, Ger.
29/E5 **Hamm**, Ger.
31/G2 **Hamm**, Ger.
75/V17 **Hamma-Bouziane**, Alg.
38/B4 **Ḩammāmāt** (gulf), Tun.
75/X17 **Ḩammāmāt** (gulf), Tun.
75/Q16 **Hammam, Oued el** (riv.), Alg.
80/Q12 **Hammanskraal**, SAfr.
42/C3 **Hammarstrand**, Swe.
28/B6 **Hamme**, Belg.
30/D1 **Hamme**, Belg.
29/F2 **Hamme** (riv.), Ger.
18/F1 **Hammerfest**, Nor.
20/G1 **Hammerfest**, Nor.
46/C2 **Hammerfest**, Nor.
19/N7 **Hammersmith & Fulham** (bor.), Eng,UK
28/D5 **Hamminkeln**, Ger.
94/C3 **Hammond**, In,US
99/R16 **Hammond**, In,US
97/F4 **Hammond**, La,US
10/N6 **Hammond Street**, Eng,UK
20/F1 **Hamnvik**, Nor.
42/C1 **Hamnvik**, Nor.
31/E3 **Hamois**, Belg.
28/C6 **Hamont-Achel**, Belg.
31/E1 **Hamont-Achel**, Belg.
25/E4 **Hampshire** (co.), Eng,UK
99/N15 **Hampshire**, Il,US
25/E4 **Hampshire Downs** (hills), Eng,UK
19/N7 **Hampstead**, Eng,UK
94/E4 **Hampton**, Va,US
97/J2 **Hampton**, Va,US
19/M7 **Hampton Court**, Eng,UK
98/K7 **Hampton Nat'l Hist. Site**, Md,US
73/G6 **Hampton Park**, Austl.
58/D5 **Hamp'yŏng**, SKor.
76/H1 **Ḩamrā** (upland), Libya
31/F5 **Ham-sous-Varsberg**, Fr.
99/F7 **Hamtramck**, Mi,US
57/H7 **Hamura**, Japan
58/D5 **Hamyang**, SKor.
58/D4 **Hamyŏl**, SKor.
58/E2 **Hamyŏng-Bukto** (prov.), NKor.
48/L6 **Han** (riv.), China
54/G5 **Han** (riv.), China
59/C5 **Han** (riv.), China
61/G2 **Han** (riv.), China
55/K4 **Han** (riv.), SKor.
56/A2 **Han** (riv.), SKor.
58/D4 **Han** (riv.), SKor.
58/C4 **Han** (riv.), SKor.
88/U10 **Hana**, Hi,US
52/C3 **Ḩanak**, SAr.
45/G4 **Ḩanak**, Turk.
51/E1 **Hanak**, Turk.
55/N4 **Hanamaki**, Japan
88/U11 **Hanamalo** (pt.), Hi,US
55/M5 **Hanamatsu**, Japan
82/G1 **Hanang** (peak), Tanz.
26/E3 **Hanau**, Ger.
54/G5 **Hanchuan**, China
59/C5 **Hanchuan**, China
91/L4 **Hancock**, Mi,US
94/B2 **Hancock**, Mi,US
57/M10 **Handa**, Japan
55/K3 **Handae-ri**, NKor.
54/G4 **Handan**, China
59/C3 **Handan**, China
29/G2 **Handeloh**, Ger.
25/E1 **Handsworth**, Eng,UK
92/C3 **Hanford**, Ca,US
48/K5 **Hangayn** (mts.), Mong.
54/D2 **Hangayn** (mts.), Mong.
54/F4 **Hanggin Qi**, China
59/B3 **Hanggin Qi**, China
24/C5 **Hangingstone** (hill), Eng,UK
80/L11 **Hangklip** (cape), SAfr.
20/G4 **Hangö**, Fin.
42/D4 **Hangö**, Fin.
64/A1 **Hangu**, Pak.
59/L9 **Hangzhou**, China
59/L9 **Hangzhou** (bay), China
61/J2 **Hangzhou**, China
54/C2 **Hanhöhiy** (mts.), Mong.
50/E2 **Hani**, Turk.
26/F2 **Hankensbüttel**, Ger.
29/H3 **Hankensbüttel**, Ger.
91/J4 **Hankinson**, ND,US
91/G3 **Hanley**, Sk,Can
86/E3 **Hanna**, Ab,Can
88/D1 **Hanna**, Ab,Can
90/F3 **Hanna**, Ab,Can
90/G5 **Hanna**, Wy,US
92/F2 **Hanna**, Wy,US
57/L10 **Hannan**, Japan
89/H4 **Hannibal**, Mo,US
93/K3 **Hannibal**, Mo,US
94/B4 **Hannibal**, Mo,US
97/F2 **Hannibal**, Mo,US
57/H7 **Hannō**, Japan
18/D3 **Hannover**, Ger.
26/E2 **Hannover**, Ger.
29/G4 **Hannover**, Ger.
31/E2 **Hannut**, Belg.
20/E5 **Hanöbukten** (bay), Swe.
63/J3 **Ha Noi** (Hanoi) (cap.), Viet.
63/J3 **Hanoi** (Ha Noi) (cap.), Viet.
94/D2 **Hanover**, On,Can
95/F3 **Hanover**, NH,US
99/P16 **Hanover Park**, Il,US
59/D5 **Hanshan**, China
61/H2 **Hanshan**, China
62/C2 **Hānsi**, India
53/L3 **Hānsi**, India
29/H2 **Hanstedt**, Ger.
99/B2 **Hansville**, Wa,US
87/J2 **Hantzsch** (riv.), NW,Can
53/K3 **Hanumāngarh**, India
62/B2 **Hanumāngarh**, India
54/E2 **Hanuy** (riv.), Mong.
73/C2 **Hanwood**, Austl.
60/D2 **Hanyuan**, China
63/H2 **Hanyuan**, China
54/F5 **Hanzhong**, China
69/L6 **Hao** (atoll), FrPol.
20/H2 **Haparanda**, Swe.
42/E2 **Haparanda**, Swe.
58/E5 **Hapch'ŏn**, SKor.
84/L4 **Happy Valley-Goose Bay**, Can.
87/K3 **Happy Valley-Goose Bay**, Nf,Can
58/D4 **Hapt'ŏk**, SKor.
50/C4 **Ḩaql**, SAr.
54/D4 **Har** (lake), China
64/C2 **Har** (lake), Mong.
54/F2 **Haraa** (riv.), Mong.
52/D5 **Ḩaraḑ**, Yem.
55/N4 **Haramachi**, Japan
57/G2 **Haramachi**, Japan
53/K2 **Harappa** (ruins), Pak.
64/B2 **Harappa** (ruins), Pak.
82/F4 **Harare** (cap.), Zim.
54/F2 **Har-Ayag**, Mong.
54/F2 **Har-Ayrag**, Mong.
76/C6 **Harbel**, Libr.
78/C5 **Harbel**, Libr.
47/N5 **Harbin**, China
55/K2 **Harbin**, China
49/E1 **Harbiye**, Turk.
50/D2 **Harbiye**, Turk.
30/B4 **Harbonnières**, Fr.
95/L2 **Harbour Breton**, Nf,Can
87/L4 **Harbour Grace**, Nf,Can
95/L2 **Harbour Grace**, Nf,Can
25/E2 **Harbury**, Eng,UK
37/F3 **Hard**, Aus.
53/L4 **Hardā**, India
62/C3 **Hardā**, India
20/C3 **Hardangervidda Nat'l Park**, Nor.
80/B2 **Hardap** (dam), Namb.
29/H3 **Hardau** (riv.), Ger.
29/G5 **Hardegsen**, Ger.
25/H5 **Hardelot Plage**, Fr.
26/D2 **Hardenberg**, Neth.
28/D3 **Hardenberg**, Neth.
26/C2 **Harderwijk**, Neth.
28/C4 **Harderwijk**, Neth.
86/F4 **Hardin**, Mt,US
90/G4 **Hardin**, Mt,US
53/L3 **Hardwār**, India
95/L1 **Hare** (bay), Nf,Can
30/C2 **Harelbeke**, Belg.
29/E3 **Haren**, Ger.
28/D2 **Haren**, Neth.
77/P6 **Hārer**, Eth.
49/G7 **Har Eval** (Jabal 'Aybāl) (mtn.), WBnk.
31/G4 **Hargesheim**, Ger.
77/P6 **Hargeysa**, Som.
41/G2 **Harghita** (co.), Rom.
41/G2 **Harghita** (peak), Rom.
52/C5 **Hargīgo**, Eth.
54/E2 **Harhorin**, Mong.
66/B4 **Hari** (riv.), Indo.
52/E6 **Ḩarīb**, Yem.
62/C5 **Harihar**, India
49/E1 **Ḩārim**, Syria
50/D2 **Ḩārim**, Syria
56/D3 **Harima** (sound), Japan
49/D3 **Ḩarīmā**, Jor.
19/N7 **Haringey** (bor.), Eng,UK
28/B5 **Haringvliet** (chan.), Neth.
28/B5 **Haringvlietdam** (dam), Neth.
64/F4 **Haripād**, India
46/G6 **Harīrūd** (riv.), Afg.
53/H2 **Harīrūd** (riv.), Afg.
48/F6 **Harīrūd** (riv.), Asia
49/G7 **Ḩāris**, WBnk.
94/D4 **Harlan**, Ky,US
97/H2 **Harlan**, Ky,US
22/D6 **Harlech**, Wal,UK
25/H2 **Harleston**, Eng,UK
26/C2 **Harlingen**, Neth.
28/C2 **Harlingen**, Neth.
101/F3 **Harlingen**, Tx,US
96/D5 **Harlingen**, Tx,US
25/F3 **Harlington**, Eng,UK
19/P6 **Harlow**, Eng,UK
25/G3 **Harlow**, Eng,UK
90/F4 **Harlowton**, Mt,US
28/B4 **Harmelen**, Neth.
30/B3 **Harnes**, Fr.
90/D5 **Harney** (lake), Or,US
90/D5 **Harney** (val.), Or,US
92/C2 **Harney** (basin), Or,US
92/C2 **Harney** (lake), Or,US
86/F4 **Harney** (peak), SD,US
88/F3 **Harney** (peak), SD,US
91/H5 **Harney** (peak), SD,US
93/G2 **Harney** (peak), SD,US
64/A1 **Harnoli**, Pak.
20/F3 **Härnösand**, Swe.
42/C3 **Härnösand**, Swe.
32/B5 **Haro**, Sp.
34/D1 **Haro**, Sp.
100/C3 **Haro, Cabo** (pt.), Mex.
25/F3 **Harpenden**, Eng,UK
85/L3 **Harper** (mtn.), Yk,Can
76/D7 **Harper**, Libr.
78/D5 **Harper**, Libr.
85/K3 **Harper** (mt.), Ak,US
96/D2 **Harper**, Ks,US
99/B2 **Harper**, Wa,US
94/E4 **Harpers Ferry Nat'l Hist. Park**, WV,US
97/J2 **Harpers Ferry Nat'l Hist. Park**, WV,US
99/G7 **Harper Woods**, Mi,US
29/F3 **Harpstedt**, Ger.
55/H3 **Harqin Qi**, China
59/D2 **Harqin Zuoyi Monggolzu Zizhixian**, China
52/F6 **Ḩarrah**, Yem.
50/D2 **Ḩarran**, Turk.
87/J4 **Harricana** (riv.), Qu,Can
94/E1 **Harricana** (riv.), Qu,Can
94/C5 **Harriman**, Tn,US
97/G3 **Harriman**, Tn,US
73/E1 **Harrington**, Austl.
21/B2 **Harris** (isl.), Sc,UK
70/F6 **Harris** (lake), Austl.
94/B4 **Harrisburg**, Il,US
97/F2 **Harrisburg**, Il,US
91/J5 **Harrisburg**, Ne,US
93/G2 **Harrisburg**, Ne,US
89/L3 **Harrisburg** (cap.), Pa,US
94/E3 **Harrisburg** (cap.), Pa,US
26/E1 **Harrislee**, Ger.
80/E3 **Harrismith**, SAfr.
90/C3 **Harrison** (lake), BC,Can
87/L3 **Harrison** (cape), Nf,Can
85/H1 **Harrison** (bay), Ak,US
89/H4 **Harrison**, Ar,US
93/J3 **Harrison**, Ar,US
96/E2 **Harrison**, Ar,US
91/H5 **Harrison**, Ne,US
93/G2 **Harrison**, Ne,US
89/L4 **Harrisonburg**, Va,US
94/E4 **Harrisonburg**, Va,US
97/J2 **Harrisonburg**, Va,US
94/C4 **Harrodsburg**, Ky,US
97/G2 **Harrodsburg**, Ky,US
23/G4 **Harrogate**, Eng,UK
99/G7 **Harrow**, On,Can
19/M7 **Harrow** (bor.), Eng,UK
19/N7 **Harrow**, Eng,UK
29/G2 **Harsefeld**, Ger.
29/F5 **Harsewinkel**, Ger.
18/E2 **Harstad**, Nor.
20/F1 **Harstad**, Nor.
46/B3 **Harstad**, Nor.
86/C2 **Hart** (riv.), Yk,Can
94/C3 **Hart**, Mi,US
92/C2 **Hart** (lake), Or,US
80/C3 **Hartbeesrivier** (dry riv.), SAfr.
20/C3 **Hårteigen** (peak), Nor.
28/B5 **Hartelkanaal** (can.), Neth.
89/M3 **Hartford** (cap.), Ct,US
95/F3 **Hartford** (cap.), Ct,US
98/F6 **Hartford**, NJ,US
94/C3 **Hartford City**, In,US
36/D2 **Hartheim**, Ger.
93/H2 **Hartington**, Ne,US
24/B4 **Hartland** (pt.), UK
24/B5 **Hartland**, Eng,UK
99/E6 **Hartland**, Mi,US
24/D2 **Hartlebury**, Eng,UK
23/G2 **Hartlepool**, Eng,UK
25/F3 **Hartley**, Eng,UK
25/G4 **Hartley**, Eng,UK
91/H3 **Hartney**, Mb,Can
80/D3 **Harts** (riv.), SAfr.
80/N13 **Harts** (riv.), SAfr.
98/G4 **Hartsdale**, NY,US
97/G3 **Hartselle**, Al,US
25/E1 **Hartshill**, Eng,UK
99/B3 **Hartstene** (isl.), Wa,US
97/H3 **Hartwell**, Ga,US
73/C4 **Hartz Mountain Nat'l Park**, Austl.
31/G6 **Hartzviller**, Fr.
67/E3 **Harun** (peak), Indo.
53/K3 **Hārūnābād**, Pak.
54/C2 **Har Us** (lake), Mong.
54/D2 **Har-Us** (riv.), Mong.
53/H2 **Hārūt** (riv.), Afg.
99/N15 **Harvard**, Il,US
70/B6 **Harvey**, Austl.
99/Q16 **Harvey**, Il,US
91/J4 **Harvey**, ND,US
25/H3 **Harwich**, Eng,UK
23/G5 **Harworth**, Eng,UK
62/C2 **Haryana** (state), India
64/D2 **Haryana** (state), India
26/F3 **Harz** (mts.), Ger.
29/H5 **Harz** (mts.), Ger.
50/C2 **Hasan** (peak), Turk.
50/E2 **Hasankeyf**, Turk.
26/D2 **Hase** (riv.), Ger.
29/E3 **Hase** (riv.), Ger.
29/E3 **Haselünne**, Ger.
36/D3 **Hasenmatt** (mtn.), Swi.
57/M9 **Hashima**, Japan
56/D3 **Hashimoto**, Japan
52/F1 **Hashtgerd**, Iran
76/D2 **Hasi el Farsía** (well), WSah.
53/K3 **Hāsilpur**, Pak.
101/F1 **Haskell**, Tx,US
93/H4 **Haskell**, Tx,US
96/D3 **Haskell**, Tx,US
36/E1 **Haslach im Kinzigtal**, Ger.
36/D3 **Hasle bei Burgdorf**, Swi.
25/F4 **Haslemere**, Eng,UK
99/F6 **Hasler** (cr.), Mi,US
23/F4 **Haslingden**, Eng,UK
23/F5 **Haslington**, Eng,UK
29/G1 **Hasloh**, Ger.
30/C3 **Haspres**, Fr.
49/E1 **Hassa**, Turk.
62/C5 **Hassan**, India
87/S7 **Hassel** (sound), NW,Can
29/G3 **Hassel**, Ger.
26/C3 **Hasselt**, Belg.
31/E2 **Hasselt**, Belg.
28/D3 **Hasselt**, Neth.
26/F3 **Hassfurt**, Ger.
33/J1 **Hassfurt**, Ger.
75/S16 **Hassi Bahbah**, Alg.
76/G1 **Hassi Messaoud**, Alg.
20/E4 **Hässleholm**, Swe.
29/G4 **Haste**, Ger.
73/C3 **Hastings**, Austl.
71/S10 **Hastings**, N.Z.
25/G5 **Hastings**, Eng,UK
32/D1 **Hastings**, Eng,UK
94/C3 **Hastings**, Mi,US
91/K4 **Hastings**, Mn,US
94/A2 **Hastings**, Mn,US
89/G3 **Hastings**, Ne,US
93/H2 **Hastings**, Ne,US
25/G5 **Hastings Battlesite**, Eng,UK
00/C4 **Hastings on Hudson**, NY,US
57/H7 **Hasuda**, Japan
20/G1 **Hasvik**, Nor.
75/W10 **Ḩaţab** (riv.), Tun.
57/M9 **Hatashō**, Japan
49/E1 **Hatay** (prov.), Turk.
50/C2 **Hatay** (prov.), Turk.
98/E5 **Hatboro**, Pa,US
100/D1 **Hatch**, NM,US
92/F4 **Hatch**, NM,US
96/B3 **Hatch**, NM,US
65/B5 **Hat Chao Mai Nat'l Park**, Thai.
70/F4 **Hatches Creek**, Austl.
40/F3 **Haţeg**, Rom.
19/N6 **Hatfield**, Eng,UK
25/F3 **Hatfield**, Eng,UK
98/E5 **Hatfield**, Pa,US
47/L5 **Hatgal**, Mong.
54/E1 **Hatgal**, Mong.
73/E1 **Hat Head**, Austl.
73/E1 **Hat Head Nat'l Park**, Austl.
23/G5 **Hathersage**, Eng,UK
62/C2 **Hāthras**, India
52/C4 **Ḩāţibah, Ra's** (pt.), SAr.
65/D4 **Ha Tien**, Viet.
65/D2 **Ha Tinh**, Viet.
65/B5 **Hat Nai Yang Nat'l Park**, Thai.
57/H7 **Hatogaya**, Japan
104/D3 **Hato Mayor**, DRep.
57/H7 **Hatoyama**, Japan
62/C3 **Hatta**, India
73/B2 **Hattah-Kulkyne Nat'l Park**, Austl.
28/D4 **Hattem**, Neth.
31/G6 **Hatten**, Fr.
29/F2 **Hatten**, Ger.
84/K6 **Hatteras** (cape), US
89/L4 **Hatteras** (cape), NC,US
97/K3 **Hatteras**, NC,US
97/K3 **Hatteras** (cape), NC,US
89/J5 **Hattiesburg**, Ms,US
97/F4 **Hattiesburg**, Ms,US
101/H5 **Hattieville**, Belz.
102/D2 **Hattieville**, Belz.
29/E6 **Hattingen**, Ger.
23/G6 **Hatton**, Eng,UK
40/D2 **Hatvan**, Hun.
63/H6 **Hat Yai**, Thai.
65/C5 **Hat Yai**, Thai.
66/B2 **Hat Yai**, Thai.
29/F6 **Hatzfeld**, Ger.
63/J5 **Hau Bon**, Viet.
65/E3 **Hau Bon**, Viet.
30/B2 **Haubourdin**, Fr.
77/Q6 **Haud** (reg.), Eth., Som.
18/D3 **Haugesund**, Nor.
20/C4 **Haugesund**, Nor.
46/A4 **Haugesund**, Nor.
65/D4 **Hau Giang** (riv.), Viet.
20/C4 **Haukeligrend**, Nor.
20/H2 **Haukipudas**, Fin.
42/E2 **Haukipudas**, Fin.
26/E3 **Haune** (riv.), Ger.
71/S10 **Hauraki** (gulf), NZ
36/E1 **Hausach**, Ger.
35/E1 **Hauskoa** (mtn.), Fr.
37/F4 **Hausstock** (peak), Swi.
76/D1 **Haut Atlas** (mts.), Mor.
36/B1 **Haute-Marne** (dept.), Fr.
30/A4 **Haute-Normandie** (reg.), Fr.
32/D2 **Haute-Normandie** (reg.), Fr.
87/K4 **Hauterive**, Qu,Can
89/N2 **Hauterive**, Qu,Can
95/G1 **Hauterive**, Qu,Can
36/B2 **Haute-Saône** (dept.), Fr.
36/C5 **Haute-Savoie** (dept.), Fr.
31/E3 **Hautes Fagnes** (uplands), Belg.
32/F4 **Hauteville-Lompnes**, Fr.
36/B6 **Hauteville-Lompnes**, Fr.
26/B3 **Hautmont**, Fr.
30/C3 **Hautmont**, Fr.
32/E1 **Hautmont**, Fr.
36/B1 **Hautmont, Côte de** (hill), Fr.
36/D2 **Haut-Rhin** (dept.), Fr.
19/S10 **Hauts-de-Seine** (dept.), Fr.
30/B6 **Hauts-de-Seine** (dept.), Fr.
88/T10 **Hauula**, Hi,US
88/W12 **Hauula**, Hi,US
89/K7 **Havana** (cap.), Cuba
103/F1 **Havana** (La Habana) (cap.), Cuba
69/V13 **Havannah** (chan.), NCal.
25/F5 **Havant**, Eng,UK
92/D4 **Havasu** (lake), Az, Ca,US
20/F4 **Havdhem**, Swe.
27/G2 **Havel** (riv.), Ger.
31/E3 **Havelange**, Belg.
26/G2 **Havelland** (reg.), Ger.
97/J3 **Havelock**, NC,US
71/S10 **Havelock North**, N.Z.
28/D3 **Havelte**, Neth.
25/G3 **Havengore** (isl.), Eng,UK
24/B3 **Haverfordwest**, Wal,UK
25/G2 **Haverhill**, Eng,UK
95/G3 **Haverhill**, Ma,US
19/P7 **Havering** (bor.), Eng,UK
27/K4 **Havířov**, Czh.
29/E5 **Havixbeck**, Ger.
27/H4 **Havlíčkův Brod**, Czh.
33/L2 **Havlíčkův Brod**, Czh.
26/E1 **Havneby**, Den.
86/F4 **Havre**, Mt,US
88/E2 **Havre**, Mt,US
90/F3 **Havre**, Mt,US
87/K3 **Havre-Saint-Pierre**, Qu,Can
95/J1 **Havre-Saint-Pierre**, Qu,Can
39/K2 **Havsa**, Turk.
41/H5 **Havsa**, Turk.
44/C4 **Havsa**, Turk.
44/E4 **Havza**, Turk.
50/C1 **Havza**, Turk.
69/K2 **Hawaii** (state), US
69/K3 **Hawaii** (isl.), Hi.,US
88/U11 **Hawaii** (isl.), Hi,US
69/H2 **Hawaiian** (isls.), Hi.,US
88/U11 **Hawaii Volcanoes Nat'l Park**, Hi,US
51/G4 **Ḩawallī**, Kuw.
52/E3 **Ḩawallī**, Kuw.
23/E5 **Hawarden**, Wal,UK
91/J5 **Hawarden**, Ia,US
93/H2 **Hawarden**, Ia,US
71/R10 **Hawera**, N.Z.
23/F3 **Hawes**, Eng,UK
23/F2 **Haweswater** (res.), Eng,UK
88/U10 **Hawi**, Hi,US
73/E2 **Hawke** (cape), Austl.
71/S10 **Hawke** (bay), NZ
70/F6 **Hawker**, Austl.
72/G8 **Hawkesbury** (riv.), Austl.
90/A2 **Hawkesbury** (isl.), BC,Can
87/J4 **Hawkesbury**, On,Can
94/F2 **Hawkesbury**, On,Can
73/E2 **Hawks Nest**, Austl.
104/C1 **Hawks Nest** (pt.), Bahm.
51/F4 **Hawr al Ḩammār** (lake), Iraq
52/E2 **Hawr al Ḩammār** (lake), Iraq
49/B4 **Ḩawsh 'Īsá**, Egypt
80/B4 **Hawston**, SAfr.
80/L11 **Hawston**, SAfr.
98/B3 **Hawthorne**, Ca,US
88/C4 **Hawthorne**, Nv,US
92/C3 **Hawthorne**, Nv,US
98/G4 **Hawthorne**, NY,US
99/P15 **Hawthorn Woods**, Il,US
49/D3 **Ḩawwārah**, Jor.

140

Haxby – Hoher

23/G3 Haxby, Eng,UK
71/G6 Hay, Austl.
72/C3 Hay (pt.), Austl.
73/C2 Hay, Austl.
84/F4 Hay (riv.), Can.
86/E3 Hay (riv.), Ab,Can
57/H7 Hayama, Japan
31/F5 Hayange, Fr.
32/G2 Hayange, Fr.
31/D3 Haybes, Fr.
85/F2 Haycock, Ak,US
23/F5 Haydock, Eng,UK
23/F2 Haydon Bridge, Eng,UK
91/K2 Hayes (riv.), Mb,Can
86/G3 Hayes (riv.), Mb,Can
86/G2 Hayes (riv.), NW,Can
87/T7 Hayes (pen.), Grld.
19/M7 Hayes, Eng,UK
85/J3 Hayes (mt.), Ak,US
86/B2 Hayes (mt.), Ak,US
37/F1 Hayingen, Ger.
24/A6 Hayle, Eng,UK
24/A6 Hayle (riv.), Eng,UK
25/F5 Hayling (isl.), Eng,UK
44/E5 Haymana, Turk.
50/C2 Haymana, Turk.
93/J4 Haynesville, La,US
96/E3 Haynesville, La,US
24/C2 Hay on Wye, Wal,UK
41/H5 Hayrabolu, Turk.
50/A1 Hayrabolu, Turk.
84/F3 Hay River, Can.
86/E2 Hay River, NW,Can
88/G4 Hays, Ks,US
93/H3 Hays, Ks,US
96/D2 Hays, Ks,US
93/H3 Haysville, Ks,US
96/D2 Haysville, Ks,US
99/K11 Hayward, Ca,US
91/L4 Hayward, Wi,US
94/B2 Hayward, Wi,US
25/F5 Haywards Heath, Eng,UK
51/J4 Hazār (mtn.), Iran
53/G3 Hazār (mtn.), Iran
89/K4 Hazard, Ky,US
94/D4 Hazard, Ky,US
97/H2 Hazard, Ky,US
62/E3 Hazāribag, India
26/B3 Hazebrouck, Fr.
30/B2 Hazebrouck, Fr.
32/E1 Hazebrouck, Fr.
23/F5 Hazel Grove, Eng,UK
99/F7 Hazel Park, Mi,US
87/R7 Hazen (str.), NW,Can
85/E3 Hazen (bay), Ak,US
28/B4 Hazerswoude-Dorp, Neth.
93/K5 Hazlehurst, Ms,US
97/F4 Hazlehurst, Ms,US
25/F3 Hazlemere, Eng,UK
90/B2 Hazleton (mts.), BC,Can
94/F3 Hazleton, Pa,US
57/N10 Hazu, Japan
61/F4 He (riv.), China
61/G3 He (riv.), China
63/K3 He (riv.), China
25/G1 Heacham, Eng,UK
25/G4 Headcorn, Eng,UK
23/G4 Headingley, Eng,UK
92/B3 Healdsburg, Ca,US
73/G5 Healesville, Austl.
85/J3 Healy, Ak,US
23/G6 Heanor, Eng,UK
101/F2 Hearne, Tx,US
93/H5 Hearne, Tx,US
96/D4 Hearne, Tx,US
83/V Hearst (isl.), Ant.
87/H4 Hearst, On,Can
89/K2 Hearst, On,Can
94/D1 Hearst, On,Can
91/H4 Heart (riv.), ND,US
95/J1 Heath (pt.), Can
87/K4 Heath (pt.), Qu,Can
73/C3 Heathcote, Austl.
72/G9 Heathcote Nat'l Park, Austl.
25/G5 Heathfield, Eng,UK
19/M7 Heathrow (London) (int'l arpt.), Eng,UK
101/F3 Hebbronville, Tx,US
96/D5 Hebbronville, Tx,US
23/F4 Hebden Bridge, Eng,UK
59/D2 Hebei (prov.), China
59/G6 Hebei (prov.), China
73/C1 Hebel, Austl.
93/J4 Heber Springs, Ar,US
96/E3 Heber Springs, Ar,US
37/H1 Hebertshausen, Ger.
54/G4 Hebi, China
59/C4 Hebi, China
18/C3 Hebrides (isls.), Sc,UK
21/B2 Hebrides (sea), Sc,UK
21/A2 Hebrides, Outer (isls.), Sc,UK
99/P15 Hebron, Il,US
93/H2 Hebron, Ne,US
96/D1 Hebron, Ne,US
49/G8 Hebron, WBnk.
50/C4 Hebron, WBnk.
49/D4 Hebron (Al Khalīl), WBnk.
84/D4 Hecate (str.), Can.
85/M5 Hecate (str.), BC,Can
86/C3 Hecate (str.), BC,Can
101/H4 Hecelchakán, Mex.
102/D1 Hecelchakán, Mex.
61/F3 Hechi, China
63/J3 Hechi, China
37/E1 Hechingen, Ger.
28/C6 Hechtel, Belg.
31/E1 Hechtel, Belg.
29/G1 Hechthausen, Ger.
60/E2 Hechuan, China
23/H6 Heckington, Eng,UK
91/J4 Hecla, SD,US
87/R7 Hecla and Griper (bay), NW,Can
90/D3 Hector (peak), Can
28/C5 Hedel, Neth.
20/E3 Hedemora, Swe.
42/B3 Hedemora, Swe.
61/F4 Hedi (res.), China
20/D3 Hedmark (co.), Nor.
23/H4 Hedon, Eng,UK
29/E3 Heede, Ger.
88/W13 Heeia, Hi,US
29/E4 Heek, Ger.
26/C2 Heemskerk, Neth.
28/B3 Heemskerk, Neth.
28/B4 Heemstede, Neth.
28/D4 Heerde, Neth.
26/C2 Heerenveen, Neth.
28/C3 Heerenveen, Neth.
26/C2 Heerhugowaard, Neth.
28/B3 Heerhugowaard, Neth.
26/C3 Heerlen, Neth.
31/E2 Heerlen, Neth.
31/E2 Heers, Belg.
28/C5 Heesch, Neth.
29/G2 Heeslingen, Ger.
28/C6 Heeze, Neth.
50/C3 Ḥefa, Isr.
49/D3 Ḥefa (Haifa), Isr.
77/N1 Ḥefa (Haifa), Isr.
55/H5 Hefei, China
59/D5 Hefei, China
61/H2 Hefei, China
59/B5 Hefeng Tujiazu Zizhixian, China
61/F2 Hefeng Tujiazu Zizhixian, China
47/P5 Hegang, China
55/L2 Hegang, China
26/E5 Hegau (reg.), Ger.
33/H3 Hegau (reg.), Ger.
37/E2 Hegau (reg.), Ger.
36/D2 Hégenheim, Fr.
57/L10 Heguri, Japan
54/D4 Hei (riv.), China
59/B3 Heicha Shan (mtn.), China
26/E1 Heide, Ger.
73/G5 Heidelberg, Austl.
26/E4 Heidelberg, Ger.
33/H2 Heidelberg, Ger.
80/E2 Heidelberg, SAfr.
80/Q13 Heidelberg, SAfr.
81/E2 Heidelberg, SAfr.
97/F4 Heidelberg, Ms,US
28/D5 Heiden, Ger.
37/F3 Heiden, Swi.
26/F4 Heidenheim, Ger.
33/J2 Heidenheim, Ger.
27/H4 Heidenreichstein, Aus.
33/L2 Heidenreichstein, Aus.
31/E4 Heiderscheid, Lux.
47/N4 Heihe, China
55/K1 Heihe, China
26/F1 Heikendorf, Ger.
80/D2 Heilbron, SAfr.
80/P13 Heilbron, SAfr.
26/E4 Heilbronn, Ger.
33/H2 Heilbronn, Ger.
37/F2 Heiligenberg, Ger.
33/K3 Heiligenblut, Aus.
26/F1 Heiligenhafen, Ger.
28/D6 Heiligenhaus, Ger.
26/F3 Heiligenstadt, Ger.
29/H6 Heiligenstadt, Ger.
47/N5 Heilong (Amur) (riv.), China
55/L2 Heilong (Amur) (riv.), China
28/B3 Heiloo, Neth.
20/N7 Heimaey (isl.), Ice.
88/V12 Heimano (stream), Hi,US
31/F2 Heimbach, Ger.
36/D4 Heimberg, Swi.
28/D4 Heino, Neth.
20/H3 Heinola, Fin.
42/E3 Heinola, Fin.
28/D6 Heinsberg, Ger.
31/F1 Heinsberg, Ger.
55/J3 Heishan, China
58/B2 Heishan, China
59/E2 Heishan, China
36/D2 Heitersheim, Ger.
59/C3 Heituo Shan (mtn.), China
57/M9 Heiwa, Japan
59/D3 Hejian, China
59/B4 Hejin, China
50/D2 Hekimhan, Turk.
57/M10 Hekinan, Japan
18/B2 Hekla (vol.), Ice.
20/N7 Hekla (vol.), Ice.
60/D4 Hekou, China
63/H3 Hekou, China
65/C1 Hekou Yaozu Zizhixian, China
27/K1 Hel, Pol.
54/F4 Helan (mts.), China
29/H6 Helbe (riv.), Ger.
28/C6 Helchteren, Belg.
28/D3 Helden, Neth.
93/K4 Helena, Ar,US
97/F3 Helena, Ar,US
86/E4 Helena (cap.), Mt,US
88/D2 Helena (cap.), Mt,US
90/E4 Helena, Mt,US
49/F8 Ḥelez, Isr.
26/D1 Helgoländer Bucht (bay), Ger.
29/F1 Helgoländer Bucht (bay), Ger.
51/G4 Ḥelleh (riv.), Iran
52/F3 Ḥelleh (riv.), Iran
26/D2 Hellendoorn, Neth.
28/D4 Hellendoorn, Neth.
26/D3 Hellenthal, Ger.
31/F3 Hellenthal, Ger.
33/G1 Hellenthal, Ger.
98/E5 Hellertown, Pa,US
28/B5 Hellevoetsluis, Neth.
34/E3 Hellín, Sp.
90/D4 Hells (canyon), Id, Or,US
90/D4 Hells Canyon Nat'l Rec. Area, Id, Or,US
48/F7 Helmand (riv.), Afg.
53/H2 Helmand (riv.), Afg.
26/F3 Helme (riv.), Ger.
29/H5 Helme (riv.), Ger.
85/K2 Helmet (mtn.), Ak,US
26/C3 Helmond, Neth.
28/C6 Helmond, Neth.
23/G3 Helmsley, Eng,UK
26/F2 Helmstedt, Ger.
55/K3 Helong, China
92/E3 Helper, Ut,US
23/F5 Helsby, Eng,UK
36/E5 Helsenhorn (peak), Swi.
20/H3 Helsingfors (Helsinki), Fin.
42/E3 Helsingfors (Helsinki) (cap.), Fin.
20/E4 Helsingør, Den.
18/F2 Helsinki (cap.), Fin.
20/H3 Helsinki (cap.), Fin.
46/C3 Helsinki (cap.), Fin.
42/E3 Helsinki (Helsingfors) (cap.), Fin.
24/A6 Helston, Eng,UK
20/G3 Helvetinjärven Nat'l Park, Fin.
42/D3 Helvetinjärven Nat'l Park, Fin.
30/B2 Hem (riv.), Fr.
30/C2 Hem, Fr.
19/M6 Hemel Hempstead, Eng,UK
25/F3 Hemel Hempstead, Eng,UK
29/E6 Hemer, Ger.
98/D3 Hemet, Ca,US
29/G4 Hemmingen, Ger.
29/G1 Hemmoor, Ger.
93/J5 Hemphill, Tx,US
96/E4 Hemphill, Tx,US
98/G5 Hempstead, NY,US
101/F2 Hempstead, Tx,US
25/H1 Hemsby, Eng,UK
23/G4 Hemsworth, Eng,UK
59/B4 Henan (prov.), China
61/G1 Henan (prov.), China
34/D2 Henares (riv.), Sp.
35/N9 Henares (riv.), Sp.
32/C5 Hendaye, Fr.
34/E1 Hendaye, Fr.
41/K5 Hendek, Turk.
69/N7 Henderson (isl.), Pitc.
94/C4 Henderson, Ky,US
97/G2 Henderson, Ky,US
94/E4 Henderson, NC,US
97/J2 Henderson, NC,US
88/D4 Henderson, Nv,US
92/D3 Henderson, Nv,US
94/B5 Henderson, Tn,US
97/F3 Henderson, Tn,US
93/J4 Henderson, Tx,US
96/E3 Henderson, Tx,US
99/B3 Henderson (bay), Wa,US
97/H3 Hendersonville, NC,US
94/C4 Hendersonville, Tn,US
97/G2 Hendersonville, Tn,US
19/N7 Hendon, Eng,UK
28/B5 Hendrik-Ido-Ambacht, Neth.
80/D3 Hendrik Verwoerdam (res.), SAfr.
80/Q13 Hendrina, SAfr.
25/F5 Henfield, Eng,UK
59/L8 Heng (isl.), China
60/D3 Heng (riv.), China
61/G3 Heng (peak), China
63/K2 Hengdong, China
60/C2 Hengduan (mts.), China
63/G2 Hengduan (mts.), China
26/D2 Hengelo, Neth.
28/D4 Hengelo, Neth.
54/F5 Hengkou, China
59/B4 Hengkou, China
54/F4 Hengshan, China
59/B3 Hengshan, China
59/C3 Heng Shan (mtn.), China
63/K2 Hengshan, China
54/H4 Hengshui, China
59/C3 Hengshui, China
61/F4 Heng Xian, China
63/J3 Heng Xian, China
65/E1 Heng Xian, China
61/G3 Hengyang, China
63/K2 Hengyang, China
68/A2 Hengyang, China
30/B3 Hénin-Beaumont, Fr.
25/F3 Henley on Thames, Eng,UK
94/F4 Henlopen (cape), De,US
97/K2 Henlopen (cape), De,US
25/E2 Henly in Arden, Eng,UK
32/B3 Hennebont, Fr.
26/D3 Hennef, Ger.
31/G2 Hennef, Ger.
31/E2 Henri-Chapelle, Belg.
93/H4 Henrietta, Tx,US
96/D3 Henrietta, Tx,US
87/H3 Henrietta Maria (cape), On,Can
104/E5 Henri Pittier Nat'l Park, Ven.
85/M5 Henry (cape), BC,Can
92/E3 Henry (mts.), Ut,US
93/J4 Henryetta, Ok,US
96/E3 Henryetta, Ok,US
99/F7 Henry Ford Museum & Greenfield Vill., Mi,US
98/E4 Henryville, Pa,US
30/C3 Hensies, Belg.
54/F2 Hentiyn (mts.), Mong.
73/C2 Henty, Austl.
60/B5 Henzada, Burma
63/G4 Henzada, Burma
61/F4 Hepu, China
63/J3 Hepu, China
65/E1 Hepu, China
60/D3 Heqing, China
63/H2 Heqing, China
54/G4 Hequ, China
59/B3 Hequ, China
20/N6 Heradhsvötn (riv.), Ice.
46/G6 Herāt, Afg.
53/H2 Herāt, Afg.
35/G1 Hérault (riv.), Fr.
72/B2 Herbert (riv.), Austl.
90/G3 Herbert, Sk,Can
72/B2 Herberton, Austl.
72/B2 Herbert River (falls), Austl.
72/B2 Herbert River Falls Nat'l Park, Austl.
31/E4 Herbeumont, Belg.
19/S10 Herblay, Fr.
30/B6 Herblay, Fr.
36/D1 Herbolzheim, Ger.
39/F1 Hercegnovi, Yugo.
40/D4 Hercegnovi, Yugo.
40/B5 Herculaneum (ruins), It.
99/K10 Hercules, Ca,US
29/E6 Herdecke, Ger.
31/G2 Herdorf, Ger.
103/E4 Heredia, CR
24/D2 Hereford, Eng,UK
88/F5 Hereford, Tx,US
93/G4 Hereford, Tx,US
96/C3 Hereford, Tx,US
24/D2 Hereford & Worcester (co.), Eng,UK
69/L6 Hereheretue (isl.), FrPol.
41/J5 Hereke, Turk.
34/C3 Herencia, Sp.
28/B6 Herentals, Belg.
31/D1 Herentals, Belg.
26/E2 Herford, Ger.
29/F4 Herford, Ger.
37/E4 Hergiswil, Swi.
36/C2 Héricourt, Fr.
36/C3 Hérimoncourt, Fr.
93/H3 Herington, Ks,US
96/D2 Herington, Ks,US
33/H3 Herisau, Swi.
37/F3 Herisau, Swi.
31/E2 Herk (riv.), Belg.
31/E2 Herk-de-Stad, Belg.
54/G2 Herlen (riv.), Mong.
29/H6 Herleshausen, Ger.
97/F2 Hermann, Mo,US
70/E4 Hermannsburg, Austl.
29/H3 Hermannsburg, Ger.
20/C3 Hermansverk, Nor.
80/B4 Hermanus, SAfr.
80/L11 Hermanus, SAfr.
31/G5 Hermersberg, Ger.
30/B5 Hermes, Fr.
31/F4 Hermeskeil, Ger.
90/D4 Hermiston, Or,US
43/V7 Hermitage, Rus.
49/D3 Hermon (mtn.), Leb.
49/D3 Hermon (mtn.), Syria
100/C2 Hermosillo, Mex.
69/P2 Hermosillo, Mex.
92/E5 Hermosillo, Mex
100/E4 Hernández, Mex.
93/K4 Hernando, Ms,US
97/F3 Hernando, Ms,US
32/C5 Hernani, Sp.
34/E1 Hernani, Sp.
30/D2 Herne, Belg.
26/D3 Herne, Ger.
29/E5 Herne, Ger.
25/H4 Herne Bay, Eng,UK
20/D4 Herning, Den.
49/G8 Herodian (ruins), WBnk.
49/G8 Herodion Nat'l Park, WBnk.
100/B2 Heroica Caborca, Mex.
88/D5 Heroica Caborca, Mex.
92/D5 Heroica Caborca, Mex
100/C2 Heroica Nogales, Mex.
88/D5 Heroica Nogales, Mex.
92/E5 Heroica Nogales, Mex
54/G5 Herong, China
32/C2 Herouville-Saint-Clair, Fr.
34/C4 Herrera, Sp.
34/C3 Herrera del Duque, Sp.
34/C1 Herrera de Pisuerga, Sp.
101/J5 Herrero, Punta (pt.), Mex.
102/E2 Herrero, Punta (pt.), Mex.
26/F4 Herrieden, Ger.
31/G6 Herrlisheim, Fr.
37/H2 Herrsching am Ammersee, Ger.
32/D5 Hers (riv.), Fr.
31/G2 Herschbach, Ger.
29/E6 Herscheid, Ger.
31/G1 Herscheid, Ger.
85/L2 Herschel, Yk,Can
28/B6 Herselt, Belg.
31/D1 Herselt, Belg.
26/C3 Herstal, Belg.
31/E2 Herstal, Belg.
25/G5 Herstmonceux, Eng,UK
29/E5 Herten, Ger.
25/F3 Hertford, Eng,UK
97/J2 Hertford, NC,US
19/N6 Hertfordshire (co.), Eng,UK
25/F3 Hertfordshire (co.), Eng,UK
34/C2 Hervás, Sp.
31/E2 Herve, Belg.
71/J4 Hervey (bay), Austl.
72/D4 Hervey (bay), Austl.
71/J5 Hervey Bay, Austl.
72/D4 Hervey Bay, Austl.
26/F3 Herzberg am Harz, Ger.
29/H5 Herzberg am Harz, Ger.
29/F5 Herzebrock-Clarholz, Ger.
30/C2 Herzele, Belg.
49/F7 Herzliyya, Isr.
33/J2 Herzogenaurach, Ger.
36/D3 Herzogenbuchsee, Swi.
40/B1 Herzogenburg, Aus.
31/F2 Herzogenrath, Ger.
31/D3 Hesbay (plat.), Belg.
26/C3 Hesbaye (plat.), Belg.
32/F1 Hesbaye (plat.), Belg.
30/B3 Hesdin, Fr.
29/E2 Hesel, Ger.
61/F4 Heshan, China
63/J3 Heshan, China
54/F4 Heshui, China
63/K3 Heshui, China
59/C3 Heshun, China
36/D2 Hésingue, Fr.
31/F4 Hesperange, Lux.
85/M3 Hess (riv.), Yk,Can
86/C2 Hess (riv.), Yk,Can
26/E3 Hesse (state), Ger.
29/G6 Hesse (state), Ger.
31/H3 Hesse (state), Ger.
33/H1 Hesse (state), Ger.
29/F5 Hessel (riv.), Ger.
29/H4 Hessen, Ger.
29/G6 Hessisch Lichtenau, Ger.
29/G4 Hessisch Oldendorf, Ger.
23/H4 Hessle, Eng,UK
23/E5 Heswall, Eng,UK
99/L11 Hetch Hetchy (aqueduct), Ca,US
31/H4 Hettenleidelheim, Ger.
91/H4 Hettinger, ND,US
23/G2 Hetton-le-Hole, Eng,UK
31/F4 Hetzerath, Ger.
29/E5 Heubach (riv.), Ger.
27/H5 Heukuppe (peak), Aus.
28/C5 Heusden, Neth.
28/C6 Heusden-Zolder, Belg.
31/E1 Heusden-Zolder, Belg.
31/F5 Heusweiler, Ger.
32/D2 Hève, Cap de la (cape), Fr.
27/L5 Heves (co.), Hun.
40/E1 Heves (co.), Hun.
40/E2 Heves, Hun.
33/M2 Hevlín, Czh.
98/F4 Hewitt, NJ,US
37/G3 Hexenkopf (peak), Aus.
23/F2 Hexham, Eng,UK
59/D5 He Xian, China
61/H2 He Xian, China
55/H3 Hexigten, China
55/H3 Hexigten Qi, China
80/L10 Hex River (mts.), SAfr.
80/L10 Hex River (pass), SAfr.
51/N7 Heybeli (isl.), Turk.
23/F3 Heysham, Eng,UK
28/C6 Heythuysen, Neth.
31/E1 Heythuysen, Neth.
73/B3 Heywood, Austl.
23/F4 Heywood, Eng,UK
54/H4 Heze, China
59/C4 Heze, China
60/E3 Hezhang, China
63/H2 Hezhang, China
89/K6 Hialeah, Fl,US
97/H5 Hialeah, Fl,US
93/J3 Hiawatha, Ks,US
96/E2 Hiawatha, Ks,US
86/G4 Hibbing, Mn,US
89/H2 Hibbing, Mn,US
91/K4 Hibbing, Mn,US
94/A2 Hibbing, Mn,US
73/C4 Hibbs (pt.), Austl.
103/F1 Hicacos (pt.), Cuba
88/W13 Hickam A.F.B., Hi,US
85/M4 Hickman (mtn.), BC,Can
94/B4 Hickman, Ky,US
97/F2 Hickman, Ky,US
99/Q16 Hickory (cr.), Il,US
89/K4 Hickory, NC,US
97/H3 Hickory, NC,US
98/E4 Hickory Run St. Park, Pa,US
98/G5 Hicksville, NY,US
101/F2 Hico, Tx,US
57/E3 Hida (riv.), Japan
56/D4 Hidaka (riv.), Japan
57/H7 Hidaka, Japan
101/E3 Hidalgo, Mex.
101/F3 Hidalgo, Mex.
101/F4 Hidalgo (state), Mex.
101/K6 Hidalgo (state), Mex.
102/B1 Hidalgo (state), Mex.
96/B5 Hidalgo del Parral, Mex
29/F4 Hiddenhausen, Ger.
69/U12 Hienghene, NCal.
50/B2 Hierapolis (ruins), Turk.
35/W17 Hierro (isl.), Canl., Sp.
76/B2 Hierro (isl.), Canl., Sp.
29/E2 Hieve (lake), Ger.
57/H7 Higashikurume, Japan
57/H7 Higashimurayama, Japan
57/G1 Higashine, Japan
57/L10 Higashi-Ōsaka, Japan
57/K10 Higashiura, Japan
57/M10 Higashiura, Japan
57/H7 Higashiyamato, Japan
57/L10 Higashiyoshino, Japan
90/C5 High (des.), Or,US
25/F2 Higham Ferrers, Eng,UK
24/D4 Highbridge, Eng,UK
93/J5 High Island, Tx,US
96/E4 High Island, Tx,US
104/A1 Highland (pt.), Fl,US
99/R16 Highland, In,US
98/F4 Highland Lakes, NJ,US
99/Q15 Highland Park, Il,US
99/F7 Highland Park, Mi,US
86/E3 High Level, Ab,Can
24/D2 Highley, Eng,UK
91/J4 Highmore, SD,US
93/H1 Highmore, SD,US
89/K4 High Point, NC,US
97/H3 High Point, NC,US
98/F4 High Point (pk.), NJ,US
86/E3 High Prairie, Ab,Can
90/D2 High Prairie, Ab,Can
86/E3 High River, Ab,Can
88/D1 High River, Ab,Can
90/E3 High River, Ab,Can
91/H2 Highrock (lake), Mb,Can
23/F3 High Street (mtn.), Eng,UK
23/E4 Hightown, Eng,UK
24/B5 High Willhays (hill), Eng,UK
99/Q15 Highwood, Il,US
25/E3 Highworth, Eng,UK
25/F3 High Wycombe, Eng,UK
104/D3 Higüey, DRep.
49/B4 Hihyā, Egypt
20/J3 Hiidenportin Nat'l Park, Fin.
42/F3 Hiidenportin Nat'l Park, Fin.
20/G4 Hiiumaa (isl.), Est.
42/D4 Hiiumaa (isl.), Est.
35/E2 Híjar, Sp.
77/N2 Hijāz (mts.), SAr.
52/C3 Hijāz, Jabal al (mts.), SAr.
56/B4 Hiji, Japan
57/L9 Hikami, Japan
56/E3 Hikone, Japan
57/M9 Hikone, Japan
69/L6 Hikueru (atoll), FrPol.
71/S10 Hikurangi (peak), N.Z.
26/E3 Hilchenbach, Ger.
31/H2 Hilchenbach, Ger.
26/F3 Hildburghausen, Ger.
33/J1 Hildburghausen, Ger.
28/D6 Hilden, Ger.
31/F1 Hilden, Ger.
26/E2 Hildesheim, Ger.
29/G4 Hildesheim, Ger.
29/G3 Hilgermissen, Ger.
104/G4 Hillaby (mtn.), Bar.
83/L Hillary (coast), Ant.
93/H3 Hill City, Ks,US
96/D2 Hill City, Ks,US
98/F4 Hillcrest, NY,US
29/F4 Hille, Ger.
28/B4 Hillegom, Neth.
20/E5 Hillerød, Den.
31/F3 Hillesheim, Ger.
22/B2 Hillhall, NI,UK
19/M7 Hillingdon (bor.), Eng,UK
91/J4 Hillsboro, ND,US
92/F4 Hillsboro, NM,US
96/B3 Hillsboro, NM,US
94/D4 Hillsboro, Oh,US
97/H2 Hillsboro, Oh,US
90/C4 Hillsboro, Or,US
101/F1 Hillsboro, Tx,US
89/G5 Hillsboro, Tx,US
93/H4 Hillsboro, Tx,US
96/D3 Hillsboro, Tx,US
72/C3 Hillsborough (chan.), Austl.
22/B3 Hillsborough, NI,UK
99/K11 Hillsborough, Ca,US
94/C3 Hillsdale, Mi,US
71/H6 Hillston, Austl.
73/C2 Hillston, Austl.
22/B3 Hilltown, NI,UK
69/K3 Hilo, Hi,US
88/U11 Hilo, Hi,US
23/E3 Hilpsford (pt.), Eng,UK
36/D4 Hilterfingen, Swi.
97/H3 Hilton Head (isl.), SC,US
97/H3 Hilton Head Island, SC,US
28/C6 Hilvarenbeek, Neth.
26/C2 Hilversum, Neth.
28/C4 Hilversum, Neth.
37/E2 Hilzingen, Ger.
64/D2 Himachal Pradesh (state), India
48/G6 Himalaya (mts.), Asia
53/L2 Himalaya, Great (range), Asia
62/D2 Himalaya, Great (range), Asia
60/A2 Himalaya, Great (range), China
20/G2 Himanka, Fin.
42/D2 Himanka, Fin.
47/P6 Himeji, Japan
56/D3 Himeji, Japan
56/D3 Himeji Castle, Japan
57/E2 Himi, Japan
29/G1 Himmelpforten, Ger.
52/C6 Himora, Eth.
77/N5 Himora, Eth.
49/E2 Ḥimṣ, Syria
49/E2 Ḥimṣ (prov.), Syria
50/D3 Ḥimṣ, Syria
50/D3 Ḥimṣ (prov.), Syria
52/C2 Ḥimṣ, Syria
103/H2 Hinche, Haiti
104/C3 Hinche, Haiti
71/H3 Hinchinbrook (isl.), Austl.
85/J3 Hinchinbrook (chan.), Ak,US
72/B2 Hinchinbrook I. Nat'l Park, Austl.
25/E1 Hinckley, Eng,UK
37/G3 Hindelang, Ger.
28/C3 Hindeloopen, Neth.
23/H2 Hinderwell, Eng,UK
23/F4 Hindley, Eng,UK
70/G7 Hindmarsh (lake), Austl.
73/B2 Hindmarsh (lake), Austl.
53/J1 Hindu Kush (mts.), Afg., Pak.
46/G6 Hindu Kush (mts.), Asia
48/F6 Hindu Kush (mts.), Asia
62/C5 Hindupur, India
97/H4 Hinesville, Ga,US
62/C3 Hinganghāt, India
53/J3 Hingol (riv.), Pak.
62/C4 Hingoli, India
53/J3 Hingorja, Pak.
62/A2 Hingorja, Pak.
45/G5 Hınıs, Turk.
50/E2 Hınıs, Turk.
57/H7 Hino, Japan
57/M9 Hino, Japan
57/M9 Hino (riv.), Japan
57/H7 Hinode, Japan
57/H7 Hinohara, Japan
34/C3 Hinojosa del Duque, Sp.
56/C3 Hino-misaki (cape), Japan
99/Q16 Hinsdale, Il,US
23/F6 Hinstock, Eng,UK
26/D2 Hinte, Ger.
29/E2 Hinte, Ger.
37/F4 Hinterrhein (riv.), Swi.
37/F3 Hinterrugg (peak), Swi.
31/G5 Hinterweidenthal, Ger.
86/E3 Hinton, Ab,Can
90/D2 Hinton, Ab,Can
94/D4 Hinton, WV,US
97/H2 Hinton, WV,US
37/E3 Hinwil, Swi.
28/B3 Hippolytushoef, Neth.
23/G3 Hipswell, Eng,UK
57/L9 Hira (mts.), Japan
56/A4 Hirado, Japan
56/D3 Hirakata, Japan
57/L10 Hirakata, Japan
62/D3 Hirakud (res.), India
56/C3 Hirata, Japan
57/M9 Hirata, Japan
57/H7 Hiratsuka, Japan
50/C2 Hirfanlı (dam), Turk.
41/H2 Hîrlău, Rom.
44/C3 Hîrlău, Rom.
47/Q5 Hirosaki, Japan
55/N3 Hirosaki, Japan
47/P6 Hiroshima, Japan
55/L5 Hiroshima, Japan
56/C3 Hiroshima, Japan
56/C3 Hiroshima (pref.), Japan
26/F4 Hirschaid, Ger.
33/J2 Hirschau, Ger.
26/C4 Hirson, Fr.
30/D4 Hirson, Fr.
32/F2 Hirson, Fr.
41/H3 Hîrşova, Rom.
44/C3 Hîrşova, Rom.
20/D4 Hirtshals, Den.
24/C3 Hirwaun, Wal,UK
56/E3 Hisai, Japan
57/M10 Hisai, Japan
53/L3 Hisār, India
62/C2 Hisār, India
49/D4 Ḥisbān, Jor.
54/E2 Hishig-Öndör, Mong.
52/E5 Ḥişn al 'Abr, Yem.
89/M7 Hispaniola (isl.)
103/H2 Hispaniola (isl.), DRep., Haiti
104/C2 Hispaniola (isl.), DRep., Haiti
84/K7 Hispaniola (isl.), Haiti, DRep.
51/E3 Hīt, Iraq
55/N4 Hitachi, Japan
57/G2 Hitachi, Japan
57/G2 Hitachi-ōta, Japan
25/F3 Hitchin, Eng,UK
55/L5 Hitoyoshi, Japan
56/B4 Hitoyoshi, Japan
20/C3 Hitra (isl.), Nor.
26/F2 Hitzacker, Ger.
37/E3 Hitzkirch, Swi.
69/M5 Hiva Oa (isl.), FrPol.
57/L9 Hiyoshi, Japan
50/E2 Hizan, Turk.
42/B2 Hjartfjellet (peak), Nor.
65/B1 Hka (riv.), Burma
60/C2 Hkakabo (peak), Burma
63/G2 Hkakabo (peak), Burma
27/J4 Hlohovec, Slvk.
40/C1 Hlohovec, Slvk.
72/G8 Hmas-Nirimba, Au
60/C5 Hmawbi, Burma
63/G4 Hmawbi, Burma
76/F6 Ho, Gha.
79/F5 Ho, Gha.
65/D1 Hoa Bin, Viet.
65/E4 Hoa Da, Viet.
60/D4 Hoang Lien (mts.), Viet.
65/C1 Hoang Lien (mts.), Viet.
87/K2 Hoare (bay), NW,C
57/G2 Hobara, Japan
71/H8 Hobart, Austl.
73/C4 Hobart, Austl.
93/H4 Hobart, Ok,US
96/D3 Hobart, Ok,US
99/D3 Hobart, Wa,US
83/Q Hobbs (coast), Ant
88/F5 Hobbs, NM,US
93/G4 Hobbs, NM,US
96/C3 Hobbs, NM,US
28/B6 Hoboken, Belg.
30/D1 Hoboken, Belg.
98/F5 Hoboken, NJ,US
54/B2 Hoboksar, China
77/Q6 Hobyo, Som.
40/A2 Hochalmspitze (peak), Aus.
37/F1 Hochdorf, Ger.
31/G6 Hochfelden, Fr.
37/F3 Hochfinsler (peak) Swi.
37/G3 Hochgrat (peak), G
63/J5 Ho Chi Minh City (Saigon), Viet.
65/D4 Ho Chi Minh City (Saigon), Viet.
66/C1 Ho Chi Minh City (Saigon), Viet.
60/E4 Ho Chi Minh Mausoleum, Viet.
33/K3 Hochkönig (peak), Aus.
58/D2 Hŏch'ŏn (riv.), NKo
27/H5 Hochschwab (pea Aus.
33/L3 Hochschwab (pea Aus.
31/G3 Hochsimmer (peak Ger.
31/G5 Hochspeyer, Ger.
37/F3 Höchst, Aus.
31/G4 Hochstetten-Dhau Ger.
37/G3 Hochvogel (peak), Aus.
37/F4 Hochwang (peak), Swi.
25/G3 Hockley, Eng,UK
23/F4 Hodder (riv.), Eng,U
19/N6 Hoddesdon, Eng,UK
25/G3 Hoddesdon, Eng,U
29/G3 Hodenhagen, Ger.
90/G3 Hodgeville, Sk,Car
78/C2 Hodh (reg.), Mrta.
49/F7 Hod HaSharon, Isr
78/D2 Hodh ech Chargui (reg.), Mrta.
78/C2 Hodh El Gharbi (re Mrta.
40/E2 Hódmezovásárhely Hun.
44/B3 Hódmezovásárhely Hun.
75/T16 Hodna, Chott el (sa lake), Alg.
23/F6 Hodnet, Eng,UK
27/J4 Hodonín, Czh.
31/E2 Hoegnel (riv.), Belg
30/C1 Hoek, Neth.
28/B5 Hoekse Waard (polder), Neth.
31/G6 Hoenheim, Fr.
33/G2 Hoenheim, Fr.
36/D1 Hoenheim, Fr.
31/E2 Hoensbroek, Neth.
31/G6 Hoerdt, Fr.
31/E2 Hoeselt, Belg.
28/C4 Hoevelaken, Neth.
28/B5 Hoeven, Neth.
26/F3 Hof, Ger.
33/J1 Hof, Ger.
20/N6 Höfdhakaupstadhu Ice.
99/P15 Hoffman Estates, Il,US
29/G6 Hofgeismar, Ger.
59/B3 Hofong Qagan (sal lake), China
20/P6 Hofsá (riv.), Ice.
20/N7 Hofsjökull (glac.),
56/B3 Hōfu, Japan
28/C4 Hoge Veluwe Nat'l Park, Neth.
40/D2 Hogyész, Hun.
29/G6 Hohegrass (peak), Ger.
26/E5 Hohenems, Aus.
33/H3 Hohenems, Aus.
37/F3 Hohenems, Aus.
29/H4 Hohenhameln, Ger
26/E4 Hohenloher (plain) Ger.
33/H2 Hohenloher Ebene (plain), Ger.
37/H2 Hohenpeissenberg Ger.
33/K3 Hoher Dachstein (peak), Aus.

37/G3 Hoher Ifen (peak), Aus., Ger.
37/E2 Hoher Randen (peak), Ger.
33/K3 Hohe Tauern (mts.), Aus.
33/K3 Hohe Tauern Nat'l Park, Aus.
41/A2 Hohe Tauern Nat'l Park, Aus.
36/D4 Hohgant (peak), Swi.
47/M5 Hohhot, China
54/G3 Hohhot, China
59/B2 Hohhot, China
31/G2 Höhn, Ger.
26/D4 Hohneck (mtn.), Fr.
33/G2 Hohneck (mtn.), Fr.
36/D1 Hohneck (mtn.), Fr.
29/H2 Hohnstorf, Ger.
31/C3 Höhr-Grenzhausen, Ger.
63/J4 Hoi An, Viet.
65/E3 Hoi An, Viet.
77/M7 Hoima, Ugan.
96/D2 Hoisington, Ks,US
60/E4 Hoi Xuan, Viet.
65/D1 Hoi Xuan, Viet.
26/F1 Højby, Den.
26/E1 Højer, Den.
56/C4 Hōjō, Japan
71/R11 Hokitika, N.Z.
47/Q5 Hokkaidō (isl.), Japan
48/P5 Hokkaidō (isl.), Japan
55/N3 Hokkaidō (isl.), Japan
53/G1 Ḩokmābād, Iran
57/G2 Hokota, Japan
57/K10 Hokudan, Japan
57/M9 Hokusei, Japan
23/J6 Holbeach, Eng,UK
73/C2 Holbrook, Austl.
25/H3 Holbrook, Eng,UK
88/D5 Holbrook, Az,US
92/E4 Holbrook, Az,US
93/H4 Holdenville, Ok,US
96/D3 Holdenville, Ok,US
23/H4 Holderness (pen.), Eng,UK
29/F3 Holdorf, Ger.
88/G3 Holdrege, Ne,US
93/F2 Holdrege, Ne,US
20/D5 Holeby, Den.
26/F1 Holeby, Den.
103/G1 Holguín, Cuba
89/L7 Holguín, Cuba
99/P15 Holiday Hills, Il,US
85/G3 Holitna (riv.), Ak,US
20/E3 Höljes, Swe.
89/J3 Holland, Mi,US
94/C3 Holland, Mi,US
93/K4 Hollandale, Ms,US
97/F3 Hollandale, Ms,US
28/B4 Hollandse IJssel (riv.), Neth.
29/G2 Hollenstedt, Ger.
25/H2 Hollesley, Eng,UK
85/M4 Hollis, Ak,US
93/H4 Hollis, Ok,US
96/D3 Hollis, Ok,US
98/B3 Hollister, Ca,US
31/E2 Hollogne-aux-Pierres, Belg.
20/H3 Hollola, Fin.
42/E3 Hollola, Fin.
93/F4 Holloman (A.F.B.), NM,US
96/B3 Holloman (A.F.B.), NM,US
99/E6 Holly, Mi,US
99/B2 Holly, Wa,US
97/F3 Holly Springs, Ms,US
89/K6 Hollywood, Fl,US
97/H5 Hollywood, Fl,US
29/G1 Holm, Ger.
20/F3 Holm, Swe.
86/E1 Holman, NW,Can
20/N6 Hólmavík, Ice.
71/H3 Holmes (reefs), Austl.
72/C2 Holmes (reefs), Austl.
90/F4 Holmes (peak), Wy,US
92/E1 Holmes (peak), Wy,US
23/F5 Holmes Chapel, Eng,UK
19/N8 Holmesdale (val.), Eng,UK
23/H4 Holme upon Spalding Moor, Eng,UK
23/G4 Holmfirth, Eng,UK
83/C Holm-Lützow (bay), Ant.
20/F3 Holmsjön (lake), Swe.
20/G3 Holmsund, Swe.
42/D3 Holmsund, Swe.
49/D3 Ḩolon, Isr.
49/F7 Ḩolon, Isr.
50/C3 Ḩolon, Isr.
77/M1 Ḩolon, Isr.
20/D4 Holstebro, Den.
24/B5 Holsworthy, Eng,UK
25/H1 Holt, Eng,UK
99/M11 Holt, Ca,US
28/D4 Holten, Neth.
29/E2 Holtland, Ger.
93/J3 Holton, Ks,US
96/E2 Holton, Ks,US
22/D5 Holy (isl.), Wal,UK
85/G3 Holy Cross, Ak,US
22/D5 Holyhead, Wal,UK
22/D5 Holyhead (mtn.), Wal,UK
93/G2 Holyoke, Co,US
95/F3 Holyoke, Ma,US
23/E5 Holywell, Wal,UK
22/C2 Holywood, NI,UK
26/F5 Holzkirchen, Ger.
29/G5 Holzminden, Ger.
29/E6 Holzwickede, Ger.
80/B3 Hom (dry riv.), Namb.
28/D6 Homberg, Ger.
29/G6 Homberg, Ger.
76/E4 Hombori Tondo (peak), Mali
79/E3 Hombori Tondo (peak), Mali
31/F5 Hombourg-Haut, Fr.
26/D4 Homburg, Ger.
31/G5 Homburg, Ger.
33/G2 Homburg, Ger.
87/K2 Home (bay), NW,Can
31/E5 Homécourt, Fr.
71/H3 Home Hill, Austl.
72/B2 Home Hill, Austl.
98/C3 Homeland, Ca,US
85/H4 Homer, Ak,US
86/A3 Homer, Ak,US
93/J4 Homer, La,US
96/E3 Homer, La,US
89/K6 Homestead, Fl,US
97/H5 Homestead, Fl,US
97/H5 Homestead (A.F.B.), Fl,US
97/G3 Homewood, Al,US
99/Q16 Homewood, Il,US
52/C5 Homib (dry riv.), Eth.
101/H4 Homún, Mex.
102/D1 Homún, Mex.
88/U11 Honaunau-Napoopoo, Hi,US
53/K6 Honāvar, India
62/B5 Honāvar, India
65/D4 Hon Chong, Viet.
24/C3 Honddu (riv.), Wal,UK
82/C7 Hondeklipbaai, SAfr.
101/H5 Hondo (riv.), Belz., Mex.
102/D2 Hondo (riv.), Belz., Mex.
56/B4 Hondo, Japan
99/L12 Hondo (arroyo), Ca,US
100/D1 Hondo (riv.), NM,US
93/F4 Hondo (dry riv.), NM,US
101/F2 Hondo, Tx,US
93/H5 Hondo, Tx,US
96/D4 Hondo, Tx,US
101/Q9 Hondo de Tepotzotlán (riv.), Mex.
30/B2 Hondschoote, Fr.
26/D2 Hondsrug (reg.), Neth.
28/D3 Hondsrug (reg.), Neth.
103/E3 Honduras
84/J8 Honduras
102/D2 Honduras (gulf), NAm.
20/D3 Hønefoss, Nor.
101/L6 Honey, Mex.
106/C5 Honey (lake), Ca,US
92/B2 Honey (lake), Ca,US
99/P14 Honey (cr.), Wi,US
25/F2 Honeybourne, Eng,UK
99/P14 Honey Creek, Wi,US
59/C4 Hong (riv.), China
59/C5 Hong (lake), China
61/G2 Hong (lake), China
55/K3 Hongam-nodongjagu, NKor.
54/G5 Hong'an, China
59/C5 Hong'an, China
61/G2 Hong'an, China
58/D4 Hongch'ŏn, SKor.
63/J2 Hongdu (riv.), China
63/J3 Hongdu, China
61/E4 Hong Gai, Viet.
63/J3 Hong Gai, Viet
65/D1 Hong Gai, Viet.
63/H2 Hongguo, China
59/C5 Honghu, China
61/G2 Honghu, China
61/F3 Hongjiang, China
63/J2 Hongjiang, China
63/K3 Hong Kong (dpcy.), U.K.
48/L7 Hong Kong (dpcy.), U.K.
61/G4 Hong Kong (dpcy.), U.K.
68/A2 Hong Kong (dpcy.), U.K.
54/F4 Hongliu (riv.), China
59/B3 Hongliu (riv.), China
61/H2 Hongmiao (mtn.), China
60/E4 Hong (Red) (riv.), Viet.
65/C1 Hong (Red) (riv.), Viet.
36/D5 Hongrin (lake), Swi.
61/H3 Hongshan (mtn.), China
61/E4 Hongshui (riv.), China
63/J3 Hongshui (riv.), China
58/D4 Hongsŏng, SKor.
59/C3 Hongtao Shan (mtn.), China
54/G4 Hongtong, China
59/B3 Hongtong, China
87/K4 Honguedo (str.), Qu,Can
95/H1 Honguedo (passg.), Qu,Can
58/D2 Hongwŏn, NKor.
54/E6 Hongya, China
60/D2 Hongya, China
59/B5 Hongyan, China
61/F2 Hongyan, China
54/E5 Hongyuan, China
55/H5 Hongze (lake), China
59/D4 Hongze, China
59/D4 Hongze (lake), China
68/E5 Honiara (cap.), Sol.
24/C5 Honiton, Eng,UK
20/H1 Honningsvåg, Nor.
69/K2 Honokaa, Hi,US
88/T10 Honolulu (cap.), Hi,US
88/V13 Honolulu (co.), Hi,US
88/W13 Honolulu (cap.), Hi,US
88/V13 Honouliuli, Hi,US
65/D4 Hon Quan, Viet.
47/Q6 Honshu (isl.), Japan
48/P6 Honshū (isl.), Japan
55/M5 Honshu (isl.), Japan
57/E3 Honshu (isl.), Japan
70/B6 Hood (pt.), Austl.
99/J10 Hood (mt.), Ca,US
99/L10 Hood, Ca,US
86/D4 Hood (mtn.), Or,US
88/B2 Hood (mtn.), Or,US
90/C4 Hood (peak), Or,US
99/B2 Hood Canal (inlet), Wa,US
90/C4 Hood Canal (inlet), Wa,US
26/C2 Hoofddorp, Neth.
28/B4 Hoofddorp, Neth.
28/C6 Hoogeloon, Neth.
28/B6 Hoogerheide, Neth.
26/D2 Hoogeveen, Neth.
28/D3 Hoogeveen, Neth.
28/D3 Hoogeveense Vaart (can.), Neth.
26/D2 Hoogezand, Neth.
28/D2 Hoogezand, Neth.
62/E3 Hooghly-Chinsura, India
28/C3 Hoogkarspel, Neth.
30/C2 Hooglede, Belg.
28/B6 Hoogstraten, Belg.
72/C3 Hook (isl.), Austl.
25/F4 Hook, Eng,UK
88/U11 Hookena, Hi,US
70/E3 Hooker Creek, Austl.
21/B4 Hook Head (pt.), Ire.
85/L4 Hoonah, Ak,US
86/C3 Hoonah, Ak,US
85/E3 Hooper Bay, Ak,US
94/C3 Hoopeston, Il,US
26/C2 Hoorn, Neth.
28/C3 Hoorn, Neth.
28/C3 Hoornse Hop (bay), Neth.
88/D4 Hoover (dam), Az,US
92/D3 Hoover (dam), Az,US
45/G4 Hopa, Turk.
50/E1 Hopa, Turk.
70/C6 Hope (lake), Austl.
90/C3 Hope, BC,Can
23/E5 Hope, Wal,UK
85/J3 Hope, Ak,US
89/H5 Hope, Ar,US
93/J4 Hope, Ar,US
96/E3 Hope, Ar,US
87/K3 Hopedale, Nf,Can
101/H5 Hopelchén, Mex.
102/D2 Hopelchén, Mex.
87/K2 Hopes Advance (cape), Qu,Can
24/C6 Hope's Nose (pt.), Eng,UK
80/D3 Hopetown, SAfr.
24/D2 Hope under Dinmore, Eng,UK
72/B1 Hope Vale Abor. Community, Austl.
72/B1 Hope Vale Abor. Land, Austl.
94/E4 Hopewell, Va,US
97/J2 Hopewell, Va,US
63/G3 Hopin, Burma
70/D4 Hopkins (lake), Austl.
73/B3 Hopkins (riv.), Austl.
89/J4 Hopkinsville, Ky,US
94/C4 Hopkinsville, Ky,US
97/G2 Hopkinsville, Ky,US
29/F6 Hoppecke (riv.), Ger.
31/G4 Hoppstädten-Weiersbach, Ger.
29/E4 Hopsten, Ger.
88/B2 Hoquiam, Wa,US
90/C4 Hoquiam, Wa,US
85/J2 Horace (mtn.), Ak,US
57/L9 Hōrai-san (peak), Japan
45/G4 Horasan, Turk.
50/E1 Horasan, Turk.
37/E1 Horb am Neckar, Ger.
49/D3 Ḩorbat Qesari (ruins), Isr.
49/F6 Ḩorbat Qesari (ruins), Isr.
36/D1 Horbourg Wihr, Fr.
37/F2 Hörbranz, Aus.
23/G4 Horbury, Eng,UK
34/D2 Horche, Sp.
103/F4 Horconcitos, Pan.
20/C3 Hordaland (co.), Nor.
23/G2 Horden, Eng,UK
41/G3 Horezu, Rom.
37/G1 Horgau, Ger.
37/E3 Horgen, Swi.
54/F3 Hörh (peak), Mong.
59/B2 Horinger, China
19/N8 Horley, Eng,UK
25/F4 Horley, Eng,UK
83/R Horlick Ice Stream, Ant.
104/E3 Hormigüeros, PR
51/H5 Hormozgān (gov.), Iran
53/F3 Hormūd-e Mīr Khūnd, Iran
53/G3 Hormuz (str.), Asia
51/H5 Hormuz (str.), Iran, Oman
27/I14 Horn, Aus.
33/L2 Horn, Aus.
105/C8 Horn (cape), Chile
18/A2 Horn (pt.), Ice.
20/M6 Horn (pt.), Ice.
34/C4 Hornachuelos, Sp.
27/L4 Hornád (riv.), Slvk
20/E2 Hornavan (lake), Swe.
31/G5 Hornbach, Ger.
29/F5 Horn-Bad Meinberg, Ger.
37/E1 Hornberg, Ger.
95/Q8 Hornby, On,Can
23/H5 Horncastle, Eng,UK
19/P7 Hornchurch, Eng,UK
29/G2 Horneburg, Ger
94/E3 Hornell, NY,US
94/C1 Hornepayne, On,Can
26/E4 Hornisgrinde (peak), Ger.
31/H6 Hornisgrinde (peak), Ger.
30/A4 Hornoy-le-Bourg, Fr.
72/H8 Hornsby, Austl.
23/H4 Hornsea, Eng,UK
26/E1 Hornum Odde (cape), Ger.
55/N3 Horoshiri-dake (mtn.), Japan
55/J2 Horqin Youyi Zhongqi, China
59/E1 Horqin Youyi Zhongqi, China
59/E2 Horqin Zuoyi Houqi, China
59/E1 Horqin Zuoyi Zhongqi, China
24/B6 Horrabridge, Eng,UK
94/C4 Horse Cave, Ky,US
97/G2 Horse Cave, Ky,US
90/C2 Horsefly (lake), BC,Can
20/D5 Horsens, Den.
25/H3 Horsey (isl.), Eng,UK
23/G4 Horsforth, Eng,UK
70/G7 Horsham, Austl.
73/B3 Horsham, Austl.
25/F4 Horsham, Eng,UK
98/E5 Horsham, Pa,US
28/D6 Horst, Neth.
26/D2 Hörstel, Ger.
29/E4 Hörstel, Ger.
29/E4 Horstmar, Ger.
35/S12 Horta, Azor.
35/N9 Hortaleza (nbrhd.), Sp.
36/B2 Hortes, Fr.
27/L5 Hortobágyi Nat'l Park, Hun.
40/E2 Hortobágyi Nat'l Park, Hun.
44/B3 Hortobágyi Nat'l Park, Hun.
85/N2 Horton (riv.), NW,Can
86/D2 Horton (riv.), NW,Can
19/P7 Horton Kirby, Eng,UK
20/D5 Høruphav, Den.
49/D4 Ḩorvot 'Avedat (ruins), Isr.
49/F6 Ḩorvot Dor, Isr.
49/D4 Ḩorvot Mezada (Masada) (ruins), Isr.
50/C4 Ḩorvot Mezada (Masada) (ruins), Isr.
37/E3 Horw, Swi.
23/F4 Horwich, Eng,UK
94/D2 Horwood (lake), On,Can
62/C3 Hoshangābād, India
64/C2 Hoshiārpur, India
31/F3 Hosingen, Lux.
37/E4 Hospental, Swi.
62/C4 Hospet, India
60/C5 Hot, Thai.
57/E2 Hotaka, Japan
57/E2 Hotaka-dake (mtn.), Japan
54/E2 Hotont, Mong.
88/F3 Hot Springs, SD,US
91/H5 Hot Springs, SD,US
93/G2 Hot Springs, SD,US
93/J4 Hot Springs National Park, Ar,US
96/F3 Hot Springs National Park, Ar,US
89/H5 Hot Springs Nat'l Park, Ar,US
93/J4 Hot Springs Nat'l Park, Ar,US
96/E3 Hot Springs Nat'l Park, Ar,US
93/J4 Hot Springs Village, Ar,US
96/E3 Hot Springs Village, Ar,US
86/E2 Hottah (lake), NW,Can
80/A2 Hottentot (bay), Namb.
80/A2 Hottentots (pt.), Namb.
31/E3 Hotton, Belg.
54/F5 Hou (riv.), China
61/E2 Hou (riv.), China
60/D4 Houamuang, Laos
63/J2 Houchang, China
30/B3 Houdain, Fr.
30/A6 Houdan, Fr.
78/D4 Houet (prov.), Burk.
31/E3 Houffalize, Belg.
86/H4 Houghton, Mi,US
89/J2 Houghton, Mi,US
91/L4 Houghton, Mi,US
94/B2 Houghton, Mi,US
94/C2 Houghton Lake, Mi,US
23/G2 Houghton-le-Spring, Eng,UK
19/S10 Houilles, Fr.
87/K4 Houlton, Me,US
89/N2 Houlton, Me,US
95/H2 Houlton, Me,US
54/G4 Houma, China
59/B4 Houma, China
89/H6 Houma, La,US
93/K5 Houma, La,US
97/F4 Houma, La,US
19/M7 Hounslow (bor.), Eng,UK
30/B2 Houplines, Fr.
25/H6 Hourdel (pt.), Fr.
30/A3 Hourdel, Pointe du (pt.), Fr.
32/C4 Hourtin, Fr.
88/D4 House (range), Ut,US
92/D3 House (range), Ut,US
23/F1 Housesteads Roman Fort, Eng,UK
36/D1 Houssen, Fr.
90/B2 Houston, BC,Can
85/J3 Houston, Ak,US
93/K3 Houston, Mo,US
96/F2 Houston, Mo,US
97/F3 Houston, Ms,US
89/G6 Houston, Tx,US
93/J5 Houston, Tx,US
96/E4 Houston, Tx,US
80/L11 Houtbaai, SAfr.
28/C4 Houten, Neth.
28/C6 Houthalen, Belg.
30/B2 Houthulst, Belg.
70/A5 Houtman Abrolhos (isls.), Austl.
28/C3 Houtribdijk (dam), Neth.
31/E3 Houyet, Belg.
46/K5 Hovd, Mong.
48/J5 Hovd, Mong.
54/C2 Hovd, Mong.
25/F5 Hove, Eng,UK
32/C1 Hove, Eng,UK
29/F5 Hövelhof, Ger.
92/E3 Hovenweep Nat'l Mon., Co,US
25/H1 Hoveton, Eng,UK
20/E3 Hovfjället (peak), Swe.
23/H3 Hovingham, Eng,UK
54/E1 Hövsgöl (lake), Mong.
72/D4 Howard, Austl.
85/G2 Howard (pass), Ak,US
85/H2 Howard (hill), Ak,US
98/K7 Howard (co.), Md,US
99/D3 Howard Hanson (dam), Wa,US
99/D3 Howard Hanson (res.), Wa,US
23/H4 Howden, Eng,UK
71/H7 Howe (cape), Austl.
73/D3 Howe (cape), Austl.
94/D3 Howell, Mi,US
81/E3 Howick, SAfr.
69/H4 Howland (isl.), PacUS
62/E3 Howrah, India
26/E3 Höxter, Ger.
29/G3 Hoya, Ger.
27/H3 Hoyerswerda, Ger.
23/E5 Hoylake, Eng,UK
23/G5 Hoyland Nether, Eng,UK
35/N8 Hoyo-de-Manzanares, Sp.
34/B2 Hoyos, Sp.
31/E3 Hoyoux (riv.), Belg.
54/E2 Hoyt Tamir (riv.), Mong.
57/M9 Hozumi, Japan
18/E3 Hradec Králové, Czh.
27/H3 Hradec Králové, Czh.
33/L1 Hradec Králové, Czh.
40/D4 Hrasnica, Bosn.
33/L3 Hrastnik, Slov.
40/B2 Hrastnik, Slov.
20/M6 Hrolleifsborg (peak), Ice.
27/K4 Hron (riv.), Slvk
40/D1 Hron (riv.), Slvk.
44/A2 Hron (riv.), Slvk.
27/J3 Hronov, Czh.
33/M1 Hronov, Czh.
27/M3 Hrubieszów, Pol.
27/J3 Hrubý Jeseník (mts.), Czh.
33/M1 Hrubý Jeseník (mts.), Czh.
20/P6 Hrútafjöll (peak), Ice.
63/G3 Hsi-hseng, Burma
65/B1 Hsi-hseng, Burma
61/J4 Hsiukulan (mtn.), Tai.
61/J3 Hsüeh (peak), Tai.
54/G5 Hua (peak), China
54/F4 Huachi, China
106/C6 Huacho, Peru
55/L2 Huachuan, China
100/C2 Huachuca City, Az,US
54/G3 Huade, China
55/K3 Huadian, China
61/J2 Huading (mtn.), China
63/G5 Hua Hin, Thai.
65/B3 Hua Hin, Thai.
66/A1 Hua Hin, Thai.
69/K6 Huahine (isl.), FrPol.
59/C4 Huai (riv.), China
55/H5 Huai'an, China
59/C2 Huai'an, China
59/D4 Huai'an, China
54/H5 Huaibei, China
54/H5 Huaibin, China
59/C4 Huaibin, China
61/G1 Huaibin, China
61/F3 Huaihua, China
63/J2 Huaihua, China
61/G4 Huaiji, China
63/K3 Huaiji, China
54/H3 Huailai, China
59/C2 Huailai, China
59/G6 Huailai, China
55/H5 Huainan, China
59/D4 Huainan, China
59/D5 Huaining, China
61/H2 Huaining, China
54/G4 Huairen, China
59/C3 Huairen, China
59/D2 Huairou, China
59/H6 Huairou, China
59/C4 Huaiyang, China
55/H5 Huaiyin, China
59/D4 Huaiyin, China
59/D4 Huaiyuan, China
100/D4 Huajicori, Mex.
101/F5 Huajuapan de León, Mex.
102/B2 Huajuapan de León, Mex.
105/B3 Huallaga (riv.), Peru
106/C5 Huallaga (riv.), Peru
106/C5 Huamachuco, Peru
101/F5 Huamantla, Mex.
101/M7 Huamantla, Mex.
82/C3 Huambo, Ang.
102/C2 Huamelula, Mex.
101/F5 Huamuxtitlán, Mex.
102/B2 Huamuxtitlán, Mex.
59/C5 Huan (riv.), China
61/G2 Huan (riv.), China
55/L2 Huanan, China
106/E7 Huancané, Peru
106/C6 Huancavelica, Peru
106/C6 Huancayo, Peru
106/E8 Huanchaca (peak), Bol.
48/L6 Huang (riv.), China
55/H4 Huang (riv.), China
59/D4 Huang (riv.), China
60/D5 Huang (riv.), Laos, Thai.
65/C2 Huang (riv.), Laos, Thai.
54/F5 Huangbayi, China
59/C4 Huangchuan, China
61/G1 Huangchuan, China
59/C5 Huanggang, China
61/G2 Huanggang, China
61/H3 Huanggang (peak), China
68/A2 Huanggang (peak), China
55/H4 Huanghua, China
59/D3 Huanghua, China
61/H3 Huangjinkenggang (mtn.), China
54/F4 Huangling, China
59/B4 Huangling, China
63/J4 Huangliu, China
65/E2 Huangliu, China
54/F4 Huanglong, China
59/B4 Huanglong, China
59/B4 Huanglongtan, China
61/F1 Huanglongtan, China
61/H3 Huangmao (peak), China
59/C5 Huangmei, China
61/G2 Huangmei, China
54/G5 Huangpi, China
59/C5 Huangpi, China
61/G2 Huangpi, China
63/J2 Huangping, China
59/C2 Huangqi (lake), China
59/D5 Huangshan, China
61/H2 Huangshan, China
59/C5 Huangshi, China
61/G2 Huangshi, China
59/C5 Huangtang (lake), China
59/B4 Huangtu (plat.), China
47/L5 Huang (Yellow) (riv.), China
59/D3 Huang (Yellow) (riv.), China
54/G5 Huangyunpu, China
59/B4 Huangyunpu, China
54/E4 Huangzhong, China
63/H3 Huaning, China
63/J3 Huanjiang, China
55/K3 Huanren, China
58/C2 Huanren, China
59/D3 Huantai, China
106/C5 Huánuco, Peru
106/E7 Huanuni, Bol.
54/F4 Huan Xian, China
103/E3 Huapí (mts.), Nic.
101/F5 Huaquechula, Mex.
102/B2 Huaquechula, Mex.
106/C6 Huaral, Peru
106/C5 Huaráz, Peru
106/C6 Huarmey, Peru
92/E5 Huásabas, Mex
105/B3 Huascarán (peak), Peru
106/C5 Huascarán (peak), Peru
106/C5 Huascarán Nat'l Park, Peru
59/B4 Hua Shan (peak), China
61/G3 Huashi (mts.), China
100/C3 Huatabampo, Mex.
106/E6 Huatunas (lake), Bol.
102/B2 Huatusco, Mex.
101/F5 Huatuxco, Mex.
101/F4 Huauchinango, Mex.
101/L6 Huauchinango, Mex.
102/B2 Huautla, Mex.
101/F5 Huautla de Jiménez, Mex.
59/C4 Hua Xian, China
54/F5 Huaying, China
60/E2 Huaying, China
61/G2 Huayuan, China
63/J2 Huayuan, China
63/K3 Huazhou, China
85/L3 Hubbard (mt.), Ak,US, Yk,Can
93/H4 Hubbard Creek (res.), Tx,US
59/C5 Hubei (prov.), China
61/F2 Hubei (prov.), China
59/B4 Hubei Kou (pass), China
53/L5 Hubli-Dhārwār, India
62/C4 Hubli-Dhārwār, India
58/D2 Huch'ang, NKor.
28/D6 Hückelhoven, Ger.
31/F1 Hückelhoven, Ger.
29/E6 Hückeswagen, Ger.
31/G1 Hückeswagen, Ger.
23/G5 Hucknall Torkard, Eng,UK
30/A2 Hucqueliers, Fr.
23/G4 Huddersfield, Eng,UK
42/C4 Huddinge, Swe.
29/F2 Hude, Ger.
20/F3 Hudiksvall, Swe.
42/C3 Hudiksvall, Swe.
83/L Hudson (cape), Ant.
84/J3 Hudson (bay), Can.
84/K3 Hudson (str.), Can.
87/H2 Hudson (bay), Can.
95/M7 Hudson, Qu,Can
87/J2 Hudson (str.), NW,Qu,Can
98/F5 Hudson (co.), NJ,US
98/G4 Hudson (riv.), NJ, NY,US
87/J4 Hudson (riv.), NJ, NY,US
94/F3 Hudson, NY,US
94/F3 Hudson (riv.), NJ, NY,US
86/F3 Hudson Bay, Sk,Can
91/H2 Hudson Bay, Sk,Can
86/D3 Hudson's Hope, BC,Can
48/K8 Hue, Viet.
63/J4 Hue, Viet.
65/D2 Hue, Viet.
40/F2 Huedin, Rom.
102/D3 Huehuetenango, Guat.
101/L6 Huehuetla, Mex.
101/L8 Huehuetlán el Chico, Mex.
100/D3 Huejotitán, Mex.
101/L7 Huejotzingo, Mex.
100/E4 Huejuquilla el Alto, Mex.
101/F4 Huejutla, Mex.
102/B1 Huejutla, Mex.
34/D4 Huelma, Sp.
18/C5 Huelva, Sp.
34/B3 Huelva (riv.), Sp.
34/B4 Huelva, Sp.
34/E4 Huercal-Overa, Sp.
18/C4 Huesca, Sp.
35/E1 Huesca, Sp.
34/D4 Huéscar, Sp.
101/E5 Huetamo, Mex.
34/D2 Huete, Sp.
102/C2 Hueyapan de Ocampo, Mex.
37/E2 Hüfingen, Ger.
68/D7 Hughenden, Austl.
71/G4 Hughenden, Austl.
72/B3 Hughenden, Austl.
85/H2 Hughes, Ak,US
21/B5 Hugh Town, Eng,UK
37/H2 Huglfing, Ger.
62/E3 Hugli (riv.), India
93/G3 Hugo, Co,US
96/C2 Hugo, Co,US
93/J4 Hugo, Ok,US
96/E3 Hugo, Ok,US
93/G3 Hugoton, Ks,US
96/C2 Hugoton, Ks,US
54/G4 Huguan, China
59/C3 Huguan, China
54/H2 Hui (riv.), China
61/J2 Hui (mtn.), China
80/B2 Huib-Hock (plat.), Namb.
101/K6 Huichapan, Mex.
58/D2 Hŭich'ŏn, NKor.
82/B4 Huíla (plat.), Ang.
105/B2 Huila, Nevado del (peak), Col.
63/H2 Huili, China
101/G5 Huimanguillo, Mex.
102/C2 Huimanguillo, Mex
59/D3 Huimin, China
55/K3 Huinan, China
54/F4 Huining, China
58/D2 Hŭisaek-pong (mtn.), NKor.
59/E5 Hui Shan (mtn.), China
59/L8 Hui Shan (mtn.), China
63/J2 Huishui, China
32/D2 Huisne (riv.), Fr.
28/C5 Huissen, Neth.
63/J2 Huitong, China
42/D3 Huittinen, Fin.
101/M7 Huitzilan, Mex.
101/F5 Huitzuco, Mex.
102/B2 Huitzuco, Mex.
101/K8 Huitzuco de los Figueroa, Mex.
59/C4 Hui Xian, China
102/C3 Huixtla, Mex.
60/D3 Huize, China
63/H2 Huize, China
28/C4 Huizen, Neth.
61/G4 Huizhou, China
63/K3 Huizhou, China
54/E2 Hujirt, Mong.
64/B2 Hujra, Pak.
55/J5 Hŭksan (arch.), SKor.
58/C5 Hŭksan (arch.), SKor.
54/K2 Hulan (riv.), China
55/K2 Hulan, China
54/F2 Huld, Mong.
91/G4 Hulett, Wy,US
93/F1 Hulett, Wy,US
87/J4 Hull, Qu,Can
89/L2 Hull, Qu,Can
94/F2 Hull, Qu,Can
18/C3 Hull, Eng,UK
23/H4 Hull, Eng,UK
23/H4 Hull (riv.), Eng,UK
29/F4 Hüllhorst, Ger.
69/H5 Hull (Orona) (isl.), Kiri.
28/B6 Hulst, Neth.
20/E4 Hultsfred, Swe.
54/F4 Hulu (riv.), China
59/B3 Hulu (riv.), China
54/H2 Hulun (lake), China
47/N4 Huma (riv.), China
55/K1 Huma, China
55/K1 Huma (riv.), China
109/C1 Humahuaca, Arg.
106/F5 Humaitá, Braz.
80/D4 Humansdorp, SAfr
82/B4 Humbe, Ang.
95/K2 Humber (riv.), Nf,Can
95/Q8 Humber (riv.), On,Can
95/R8 Humber (bay), On,Can
23/H4 Humber (riv.), Eng,UK
23/H4 Humberside (co.), Eng,UK
23/H4 Humberston, Eng,UK
93/J5 Humble, Tx,US
96/E4 Humble, Tx,US
100/E1 Humble City, NM,US
86/F3 Humboldt, Sk,Can
88/E1 Humboldt, Sk,Can
91/G2 Humboldt, Sk,Can
103/G5 Humboldt (bay), Col.
68/F7 Humboldt (peak), NCal.
69/V12 Humboldt (peak), NCal.
90/D5 Humboldt (riv.), Nv,US
86/E4 Humboldt (riv.), Nv,US
88/C3 Humboldt (riv.), Nv,US
92/C2 Humboldt (range), Nv,US
92/D2 Humboldt (riv.), Nv,US
94/B5 Humboldt, Tn,US
97/F3 Humboldt, Tn,US
73/C2 Hume (lake), Austl.
27/L4 Humenné, Slvk.
44/B2 Humenné, Slvk.
109/D4 Humida (plain), Arg.
85/K2 Humphrey (pt.), Ak,US
88/D4 Humphreys (peak), Az,US
92/E4 Humphreys (peak), Az,US
23/F1 Humshaugh, Eng,UK
54/G3 Hun (riv.), China
55/J3 Hun (riv.), China
55/K3 Hun (riv.), China
58/C2 Hun (riv.), China
58/D2 Hun (riv.), China
59/B2 Hun (riv.), China
59/F1 Hun (riv.), China
76/J2 Hūn, Libya
20/N6 Húnaflói (bay), Ice.
59/B5 Hunan (prov.), China
61/F2 Hunan (prov.), China
63/K2 Hunan (prov.), China
55/L3 Hunchun, China
31/G3 Hundsangen, Ger.
10/F4 Hunedoara, Rom.
40/F2 Hunedoara (co.), Rom.
40/F3 Hunedoara, Rom.
44/B3 Hunedoara, Rom.
37/E3 Hünenberg, Swi.
26/E3 Hünfeld, Ger.
33/H1 Hünfeld, Ger.
18/E4 Hungary
27/K5 Hungary
33/M3 Hungary
40/D2 Hungary
44/A3 Hungary
46/C5 Hungary
26/E3 Hungen, Ger.
33/H1 Hungen, Ger.
72/B5 Hungerford, Austl.
25/E4 Hungerford, Eng,UK
55/K4 Hŭngnam, NKor.
58/D3 Hŭngnam, NKor.
54/C2 Hüngüy (riv.), Mong.
65/D1 Hung Yen, Viet.
47/N5 Hunjiang, China
55/K3 Hunjiang, China
58/D2 Hunjiang, China
23/H3 Hunmanby, Eng,UK
28/C6 Hunsel, Neth.
31/E1 Hunsel, Neth.
31/G1 Hunspatch, Fr.
26/D4 Hunsrück (mts.), Ger.
31/G4 Hunsrück (mts.), Ger.
33/G2 Hunsrück (plat.), Ger.
25/G1 Hunstanton, Eng,UK
26/E2 Hunte (riv.), Ger.
29/F2 Hunte (riv.), Ger.
71/G8 Hunter (isl.), Austl.
73/C4 Hunter (isl.), Austl.
73/D2 Hunter (riv.), Austl.
90/A3 Hunter (isl.), BC,Can
85/H3 Hunter (mt.), Ak,US
94/C4 Huntingburg, In,US
97/G2 Huntingburg, In,US
25/F2 Huntingdon, Eng,UK
23/G4 Huntington, Eng,UK
94/C3 Huntington, In,US
98/G5 Huntington, NY,US
89/K4 Huntington, WV,US
94/D4 Huntington, WV,US
97/H2 Huntington, WV,US
92/C4 Huntington Beach, Ca,US
98/C3 Huntington Beach, Ca,US
98/B3 Huntington Park, Ca,US
99/F7 Huntington Woods, Mi,US
99/P15 Huntley, Il,US
71/S10 Huntly, N.Z.
85/M4 Hunts Inlet, BC,Can
99/C2 Hunts Point, Wa,US
87/J4 Huntsville, On,Can
89/L2 Huntsville, On,Can
94/E2 Huntsville, On,Can
89/J5 Huntsville, Al,US
97/G3 Huntsville, Al,US
93/J5 Huntsville, Tx,US
96/E4 Huntsville, Tx,US
101/H4 Hunucmá, Mex.
102/D1 Hunucmá, Mex.
28/D5 Hünxe, Ger.
59/C3 Hunyuan, China
61/H2 Huo (mtn.), China
54/G4 Huojia, China
59/C4 Huojia, China
47/M5 Huolin Gol, China
55/H2 Huolin Gol, China
65/D2 Huong Hoa, Viet.
63/J4 Huong Khe, Viet.
60/E5 Huong Son, Viet.
63/J4 Huong Son, Viet.
65/D2 Huong Son, Viet.
63/J4 Huong Thuy, Viet.
59/D4 Huoqiu, China
61/H1 Huoqiu, China
54/H5 Huoshan, China
59/B3 Huo Shan (peak), China

59/D5 Huo Shan (mtn.), China
59/D5 Huoshan, China
61/H2 Huoshan, China
54/G4 Huo Xian, China
59/B3 Huo Xian, China
77/R5 Hurdiyo, Som.
19/S11 Hurepoix (hist. reg.), Fr.
55/J3 Hure Qi, China
59/E2 Hure Qi, China
100/C1 Hurley, NM,US
92/E4 Hurley, NM,US
89/K3 Huron (lake), On,Can,Mi,US
94/D2 Huron (lake), On,Can, Mi,US
99/H5 Huron (lake), On,Can, Mi,US
99/F7 Huron (riv.), Mi,US
99/G6 Huron (pt.), Mi,US
86/G4 Huron, SD,US
89/G3 Huron, SD,US
91/J4 Huron, SD,US
93/H1 Huron, SD,US
94/D4 Hurricane, WV,US
25/F5 Hurstpierpoint, Eng,UK
30/D4 Hurtaut (riv.), Fr.
26/D3 Hürth, Ger.
31/F2 Hürth, Ger.
23/G3 Hurworth, Eng,UK
62/D3 Husainābād, India
20/P6 Húsavík, Ice.
25/E2 Husbands Bosworth, Eng,UK
99/Q14 Husher, Wi,US
41/J2 Huşi, Rom.
73/D2 Huskisson, Austl.
85/G2 Huslia, Ak,US
31/E5 Hussigny-Godbrange, Fr.
26/E1 Husum, Ger.
20/F3 Husum, Swe.
42/C3 Husum, Swe.
54/E2 Hutag, Mong.
89/G4 Hutchinson, Ks,US
93/H3 Hutchinson, Ks,US
96/D2 Hutchinson, Ks,US
91/K4 Hutchinson, Mn,US
52/D5 Ḩūth, Yem.
60/D3 Hutiaoxia, China
37/F1 Hüttisheim, Ger.
23/J5 Huttoft, Eng,UK
72/C4 Hutton (peak), Austl.
19/Q7 Hutton, Eng,UK
23/H4 Hutton Cranswick, Eng,UK
23/G3 Hutton Rudby, Eng,UK
95/Q8 Huttonville, On,Can
36/D3 Huttwil, Swi.
54/B3 Hutubi, China
59/C3 Hutuo (riv.), China
35/H1 Huveane (riv.), Fr.
49/G7 Ḩuwwārah, WBnk.
54/F5 Hu Xian, China
59/B4 Hu Xian, China
31/E2 Huy, Belg.
23/F5 Huyton-with-Roby, Eng,UK
51/G4 Hūzgān, Iran
55/J5 Huzhou, China
59/E5 Huzhou, China
59/F4 Huzhou, China
61/J2 Huzhou, China
20/N6 Hvammstangi, Ice.
20/P7 Hvannadalshnúkur (peak), Ice.
38/E1 Hvar, Cro.
38/E1 Hvar (isl.), Cro.
40/C4 Hvar (isl.), Cro.
20/N7 Hvítá (riv.), Ice.
20/N7 Hvolsvöllur, Ice.
82/E4 Hwange, Zim.
82/E4 Hwange Nat'l Park, (Wankie) Zim.
58/D3 Hwanghae-Bukto (prov.), NKor.
58/C3 Hwanghae-Namdo (prov.), NKor.
58/C3 Hwangju, NKor.
58/D3 Hwangju (riv.), NKor.
58/D5 Hwasun, SKor.
56/A3 Hwayang, SKor.
58/E5 Hwayang, SKor.
54/C2 Hyargas, Mong.
54/C2 Hyargas (lake), Mong.
98/J7 Hyattstown, Md,US
98/K8 Hyattsville, Md,US
85/M4 Hydaburg, Ak,US
23/F5 Hyde, Eng,UK
19/N7 Hyde Park, Eng,UK
85/M4 Hyder, Ak,US
62/C4 Hyderābād, India
48/G8 Hyderābād, India
53/J3 Hyderābād, Pak.
62/A2 Hyderābād, Pak.
33/G5 Hyères, Fr.
33/G5 Hyères (isls.), Fr.
35/J1 Hyères, Fr.
55/K3 Hyesan, NKor.
86/D2 Hyland (riv.), Yk,Can
20/E4 Hyltebruk, Swe.
94/D4 Hylton (hill), Ky,US
97/H2 Hylton (hill), Ky,US
56/D3 Hyōgo (pref.), Japan
57/L9 Hyōgo (pref.), Japan
58/G6 Hyŏndŭngsan (mt.), SKor.
56/D3 Hyō-no-sen (mtn.), Japan
92/E2 Hyrum, Ut,US
25/E5 Hythe, Eng,UK
25/H4 Hythe, Eng,UK
30/A1 Hythe, Eng,UK
56/B4 Hyūga, Japan
20/H3 Hyvinkää, Fin.
42/E3 Hyvinkää, Fin.

I

108/B2 Iacanga, Braz.
106/E6 Iaco (riv.), Braz.
40/A2 Iâf di Montasio (peak), It.
41/H3 Ialomiţa (co.), Rom.
41/H3 Ialomiţa (riv.), Rom.
44/C3 Ialomiţa (riv.), Rom.
108/D1 Iapu, Braz.
18/F4 Iaşi, Rom.
41/H2 Iaşi, Rom.
41/H2 Iaşi (co.), Rom.
44/C3 Iaşi, Rom.
46/C5 Iaşi, Rom.
39/J2 Iasmos, Gre.
41/G5 Iasmos, Gre.
76/F6 Ibadan, Nga.
79/F5 Ibadan, Nga.
106/C3 Ibagué, Col.
108/B2 Ibaiti, Braz.
103/E3 Ibans (lag.), Hon.
92/D2 Ibapah, Ut,US
39/G1 Ibar (riv.), Yugo.
40/E4 Ibar (riv.), Yugo.
56/C3 Ibara, Japan
57/F2 Ibaraki (pref.), Japan
57/J7 Ibaraki (pref.), Japan
57/L10 Ibaraki, Japan
106/C3 Ibarra, Ecu.
109/E2 Ibarreta, Arg.
52/D6 Ibb, Yem.
77/P5 Ibb, Yem.
77/L6 Ibba (riv.), Sudan
26/D2 Ibbenbüren, Ger.
29/E4 Ibbenbüren, Ger.
79/F2 Ibdekhene (wadi), Mali
109/E2 Ibera (marsh), Arg.
106/E6 Iberia, Peru
34/D2 Ibérica (range), Sp.
95/P7 Iberville, Qu,Can
55/M4 Ibi (riv.), Japan
56/E3 Ibi (riv.), Japan
57/M9 Ibi (riv.), Japan
35/E3 Ibi, Sp.
108/C1 Ibiá, Braz.
107/L6 Ibicaraí, Braz.
108/D1 Ibiraçu, Braz.
108/D1 Ibirapuã, Braz.
108/B2 Ibitinga, Braz.
18/D5 Ibiza (isl.), Sp.
35/F3 Ibiza, Sp.
35/F3 Ibiza (isl.), Sp.
56/D3 Ibo (riv.), Japan
82/H3 Ibo, Moz.
107/K6 Ibotirama, Braz.
76/H8 Iboundji (peak), Gabon
27/L4 Ibrány, Hun.
39/K2 Ibriktepe, Turk.
49/B5 Ibshawāy, Egypt
50/B4 Ibshawāy, Egypt
25/E1 Ibstock, Eng,UK
67/G3 Ibu (mtn.), Indo.
57/M9 Ibuki, Japan
57/M9 Ibuki-yama (peak), Japan
105/C3 Içá (riv.), Braz.
106/E4 Iça (riv.), Braz.
106/C6 Ica, Peru
106/E3 Içana (riv.), Braz.
49/C1 İçel (prov.), Turk.
50/C2 Icel (prov.), Turk.
18/A2 Iceland
20/N7 Iceland
108/B2 Icém, Braz.
53/K5 Ichalkaranji, India
62/B4 Ichalkaranji, India
62/D4 Ichchāpuram, India
37/G1 Ichenhausen, Ger.
57/J7 Ichihara, Japan
57/L9 Ichijima, Japan
57/H7 Ichikawa, Japan
56/E3 Ichinomiya, Japan
57/M9 Ichinomiya, Japan
55/N4 Ichinoseki, Japan
57/M10 Ichishi, Japan
58/D4 Ich'ŏn, SKor.
30/C1 Ichtegem, Belg.
107/L5 Icó, Braz.
35/X16 Icod de los Vinos, Canl.
85/F1 Icy (cape), Ak,US
85/K4 Icy (bay), Ak,US
85/L4 Icy (pt.), Ak,US
85/L4 Icy (str.), Ak,US
86/B3 Icy (bay), Ak,US
93/J4 Idabel, Ok,US
96/E3 Idabel, Ok,US
76/G6 Idah, Nga.
90/E5 Idaho (state), US
86/E4 Idaho (state), US
88/C3 Idaho (state), US
92/D2 Idaho (state), US
86/E4 Idaho Falls, Id,US
88/D3 Idaho Falls, Id,US
90/E5 Idaho Falls, Id,US
92/D2 Idaho Falls, Id,US
34/B3 Idanha-a-Nova, Port.
64/F3 Idāppādi, India
62/B3 Idar, India
31/G4 Idarkopf (peak), Ger.
26/D4 Idar-Oberstein, Ger.
31/G4 Idar-Oberstein, Ger.
33/G2 Idar-Oberstein, Ger.
57/L10 Ide, Japan
76/G3 Ideles, Alg.
54/D2 Ider, Mong.
54/D2 Ider (riv.), Mong.
52/B4 Idfū, Egypt
77/M3 Idfū, Egypt
39/J5 Ídhi (peak), Gre.
39/H4 Ídhra, Gre.
50/E2 Idil, Turk.
49/B4 Idkū, Egypt
50/B4 Idkū, Egypt
23/H5 Idle (riv.), Eng,UK
49/E2 Idlib, Syria
49/E2 Idlib (prov.), Syria
50/C3 Idlib (prov.), Syria
50/D3 Idlib, Syria
52/C1 Idlib, Syria
49/D4 Idnah, WBnk.
49/F8 Idnah, WBnk.
33/L4 Idrija, Slov.
40/B3 Idrija, Slov.
75/M13 Idriss I (dam), Mor.
75/M13 Idriss I (res.), Mor.
31/H3 Idstein, Ger.
26/B3 Ieper, Belg.
30/B2 Ieper (Ypres), Belg.
32/E1 Ieper (Ypres), Belg.
39/J5 Ierápetra, Gre.
77/L1 Ierápetra, Gre.
39/H2 Ierissós, Gre.
82/G2 Ifakara, Tanz.
68/D4 Ifalik (isl.), Micr.
81/H8 Ifanadiana, Madg.
76/F6 Ife, Nga.
79/G5 Ife, Nga.
37/G3 Ifen, Hoher (peak), Aus., Ger.
37/H2 Iffeldorf, Ger.
31/H6 Iffezheim, Ger.
57/M10 Iga, Japan
57/M10 Iga (riv.), Japan
40/C2 Igal, Hun.
108/C2 Igarapava, Braz.
107/J4 Igarapé-Miri, Braz.
46/J3 Igarka, Rus.
62/B4 Igatpuri, India
45/H5 Iğdır, Turk.
51/F2 Iğdır, Turk.
31/F4 Igel, Ger.
20/F3 Iggesund, Swe.
42/C3 Iggesund, Swe.
19/P8 Ightham, Eng,UK
85/H2 Igikpak (mt.), Ak,US
37/F4 Igis, Swi.
85/G4 Igiugig, Ak,US
38/A3 Iglesias, It.
37/G1 Igling, Ger.
87/H2 Igloolik, NW,Can
91/L3 Ignace, On,Can
94/B1 Ignace, On,Can
102/C2 Ignacio Ramírez, Mex.
92/F5 Ignacio Zaragoza, Mex
42/E5 Ignalina, Lith.
41/J5 İğneada (cape), Turk.
36/C1 Igney, Fr.
36/A2 Ignon (riv.), Fr.
19/S10 Igny, Fr.
98/G4 Igor I. Sikorsky Mem. (arpt.), Ct,US
39/G3 Igoumenítsa, Gre.
43/M4 Igra, Rus.
105/D5 Iguaçu (riv.), Braz.
109/E2 Iguaçu (riv.), Braz.
109/F2 Iguaçu Nat'l Park, Braz.
102/B2 Iguala, Mex.
35/F2 Igualada, Sp.
101/F5 Iguala de la Independencia, Mex.
101/K8 Iguala de la Independencia, Mex.
109/E2 Iguapa (riv.), Braz.
108/C3 Iguape, Braz.
107/L5 Iguatu, Braz.
105/D5 Iguazú Falls, Braz.
109/F2 Iguazu Nat'l Park, Arg.
74/B2 Iguidi, 'Erg (des.), Afr.
54/F2 Ihhayrhan, Mong.
81/H8 Ihosy, Madg.
81/G8 Ihotry (lake), Madg.
50/B2 İhsaniye, Turk.
20/H2 Ii, Fin.
42/E2 Ii, Fin.
46/C3 Ii (riv.), Fin.
57/E3 Iida, Japan
57/F2 Iide-san (mtn.), Japan
18/F2 Iijoki (riv.), Fin.
42/E2 Iijoki (riv.), Fin.
57/M10 Iinan, Japan
20/H3 Iisalmi, Fin.
42/E3 Iisalmi, Fin.
57/M10 Iitaka, Japan
42/E3 Iitti, Fin.
57/F2 Iiyama, Japan
55/L5 Iizuka, Japan
56/B4 Iizuka, Japan
76/C3 Ijill (peak), Mrta.
28/C4 IJmeer (bay), Neth.
28/B4 IJmuiden, Neth.
78/B2 Ijnaoun (well), Mrta.
20/H2 Ijoki (riv.), Fin.
28/C4 IJssel (riv.), Neth.
26/C2 IJsselmeer (lake), Neth.
28/C2 IJsselmeer (dam), Neth.
28/C3 IJsselmeer (lake), Neth.
28/C3 IJsselmuiden, Neth.
28/C4 IJsselstein, Neth.
109/F2 Ijuí, Braz.
56/B5 Ijūin, Japan
26/B3 Ijzer (riv.), Belg.
30/B2 Ijzer (riv.), Belg.
43/M5 Ik (riv.), Rus.
45/K1 Ik (riv.), Rus.
81/H7 Ikahavo (plat.), Madg.
39/J4 Ikaría (isl.), Gre.
50/A2 Ikaría (isl.), Gre.
56/C3 Ikeda, Japan
57/L10 Ikeda, Japan
57/M9 Ikeda, Japan
77/K8 Ikela, Zaire
82/D1 Ikela, Zaire
57/M10 Ikenokoya-yama (peak), Japan
39/H1 Ikhtiman, Bul.
41/F4 Ikhtiman, Bul.
56/A4 Iki (chan.), Japan
56/A4 Iki (isl.), Japan
50/C2 İkizce, Turk.
50/E1 İkizdere, Turk.
57/L10 Ikoma, Japan
81/H8 Ikongo, Madg.
81/H7 Ikopa (riv.), Madg.
56/D3 Ikuno, Japan
64/G4 Ilaiyānkudi, India
51/F3 Īlām, Iran
51/F3 Īlām (gov.), Iran
52/E2 Īlām, Iran
62/E2 Ilam, Nepal
37/F4 Ilanz, Swi.
27/K2 Iława, Pol.
42/C5 Iława, Pol.
77/M4 'Ilay, Sudan
24/D4 Ilchester, Eng,UK
91/G2 Ile-a-la-Crosse (lake), Sk,Can
86/F3 Île-à-la-Crosse, Sk,Can
90/G2 Île-à-la-Crosse, Sk,Can
82/D1 Ilebo, Zaire
19/T9 Ile-de-France (reg.), Fr.
26/B4 Ile-de-France (reg.), Fr.
30/A5 Ile-de-France (reg.), Fr.
32/E2 Ile-de-France (reg.), Fr.
95/N6 Ile-de-Montréal (co.), Qu,Can
95/N6 Ile-Jésus (co.), Qu,Can
45/L4 Ilek (riv.), Kaz.
45/K2 Ilek (riv.), Rus.
95/N7 Ile-Perrot, Qu,Can
78/E5 Iles Ehotilés Nat'l Park, IvC.
76/F6 Ilesha, Nga.
79/G5 Ilesha, Nga.
36/D4 Ilfis (riv.), Swi.
19/P7 Ilford, Eng,UK
72/B3 Ilfracombe, Austl.
24/B4 Ilfracombe, Eng,UK
44/E4 Ilgaz, Turk.
50/C1 Ilgazdağı Nat'l Park, Turk.
50/B2 Ilgın, Turk.
108/C2 Ilhabela, Braz.
108/C2 Ilha Grande (bay), Braz.
107/H7 Ilha Salteira (res.), Braz.
108/B1 Ilha Solteira (res.), Braz.
34/A2 Ílhavo, Port.
107/L6 Ilhéus, Braz.
46/H5 Ili (riv.), China, Kaz.
48/G5 Ili (riv.), China, Kaz.
85/G4 Iliamna (lake), Ak,US
85/H3 Iliamna (vol.), Ak,US
85/H4 Iliamna, Ak,US
44/F5 İliç, Turk.
50/D2 İliç, Turk.
45/G5 Ilıca, Turk.
50/E2 Ilıca, Turk.
44/D3 Il'ichevsk, Ukr.
67/F2 Iligan City, Phil.
40/D4 Ilijaš, Bosn.
33/L4 Ilirska Bistrica, Slov.
40/B3 Ilirska Bistrica, Slov.
50/E2 Ilisu (res.), Turk.
41/H6 Ilium (Troy) (ruins), Turk.
44/C5 Ilium (Troy) (ruins), Turk.
50/A2 Ilium (Troy) (ruins), Turk.
23/G6 Ilkeston, Eng,UK
23/G4 Ilkley, Eng,UK
33/H3 Ill (riv.), Aus.
37/F3 Ill (riv.), Aus.
33/G2 Ill (riv.), Fr.
36/D1 Ill (riv.), Fr.
34/D2 Illana, Sp.
109/B3 Illapel, Chile
51/F2 Il'lchëvsk, Azer.
76/G5 Illéla, Niger
79/G3 Illéla, Niger
33/J3 Iller (riv.), Ger.
37/G1 Iller (riv.), Ger.
26/F4 Illertissen, Ger.
37/G1 Illertissen, Ger.
34/D2 Illescas, Sp.
32/D2 Illiers-Combray, Fr.
106/E7 Illimani (peak), Bol.
31/G5 Illingen, Ger.
91/L5 Illinois (state), US
89/H4 Illinois (state), US
93/K3 Illinois (state), US
94/B4 Illinois (state), US
99/P16 Illinois (riv.), Il,US
91/L5 Illinois (riv.), Il,US
89/H3 Illinois (riv.), Il,US
94/B3 Illinois (riv.), Il,US
76/G2 Illizi, Alg.
36/D1 Illkirch-Graffenstaden, Fr.
37/F2 Illmensee, Ger.
37/E3 Illnau, Swi.
24/A6 Illogan, Eng,UK
34/D4 Illora, Sp.
26/D5 Illzach, Fr.
33/G3 Illzach, Fr.
36/D2 Illzach, Fr.
26/F3 Ilm (riv.), Ger.
26/F4 Ilm (riv.), Ger.
33/J2 Ilm (riv.), Ger.
20/G3 Ilmajoki, Fin.
42/D3 Ilmajoki, Fin.
29/G5 Ilme (riv.), Ger.
18/G3 Il'men (lake), Rus.
42/F4 Il'men' (lake), Rus.
46/D4 Il'men (lake), Rus.
26/F3 Ilmenau, Ger.
29/H2 Ilmenau (riv.), Ger.
33/J1 Ilmenau, Ger.
24/D5 Ilminster, Eng,UK
106/D7 Ilo, Peru
67/F1 Iloilo City, Phil.
68/B3 Iloilo City, Phil.
76/F6 Ilorin, Nga.
79/G4 Ilorin, Nga.
45/H2 Ilovlya (riv.), Rus.
28/B4 Ilpendam, Neth.
29/H4 Ilse (riv.), Ger.
29/H4 Ilsede, Ger.
29/H5 Ilsenburg, Ger.
41/H5 Ilyas (pt.), Turk.
43/N3 Ilych (riv.), Rus.
27/G4 Ilz (riv.), Ger.
33/K2 Ilz (riv.), Ger.
56/C3 Imabari, Japan
57/F2 Imaichi, Japan
81/H8 Imaloto (riv.), Madg.
50/C2 Imamoğlu, Turk.
20/J2 Imandra (lake), Rus.
42/F2 Imandra (lake), Rus.
56/A4 Imari, Japan
20/J3 Imatra, Fin.
42/F3 Imatra, Fin.
56/E3 Imazu, Japan
57/M9 Imazu, Japan
57/J7 Imba, Japan
108/B4 Imbituba, Braz.
108/B3 Imbituva, Braz.
43/X8 Imeni Moskvy (can.), Rus.
81/J7 Imerimandroso, Madg.
77/P6 Īmī, Eth.
45/J5 Imishli, Azer.
51/G2 Imishli, Azer.
39/L7 Imittós (mt.), Gre.
58/C5 Imja (isl.), SKor.
55/K4 Imjin (riv.), NKor.
58/D3 Imjin (riv.), NKor.
58/F6 Imjin (riv.), SKor.
90/D5 Imlay, Nv,US
92/C2 Imlay, Nv,US
99/F5 Imlay City, Mi,US
37/E2 Immendingen, Ger.
29/G6 Immenhausen, Ger.
37/F2 Immenstaad am Bodensee, Ger.
33/J3 Immenstadt im Allgäu, Ger.
37/G2 Immenstadt im Allgäu, Ger.
23/H4 Immingham, Eng,UK
97/H5 Immokalee, Fl,US
85/J2 Imnavait (mtn.), Ak,US
79/G5 Imo (state), Nga.
33/J4 Imola, It.
107/J5 Imperatriz, Braz.
33/H5 Imperia, It.
91/G3 Imperial, Sk,Can
93/G2 Imperial, Ne,US
57/H7 Imperial Palace, Japan
76/J7 Impfondo, Congo
60/B3 Imphāl, India
63/F3 Imphāl, India
32/E3 Imphy, Fr.
41/J5 İmralı (isl.), Turk.
44/F5 İmranlı, Turk.
50/D2 İmranlı, Turk.
39/J2 İmroz, Turk.
41/G5 İmroz, Turk.
44/C4 İmroz, Turk.
50/A1 İmroz, Turk.
58/D5 Imshil, SKor.
26/F5 Imst, Aus.
33/J3 Imst, Aus.
37/G3 Imst, Aus.
100/C2 Imuris, Mex.
92/E5 Imuris, Mex
57/E3 Ina, Japan
57/H7 Ina, Japan
57/J7 Ina, Japan
57/L10 Ina (riv.), Japan
27/H2 Ina (riv.), Pol.
57/M9 Inabe, Japan
57/M9 Inagawa, Japan
57/H7 Inagi, Japan
76/G2 I-n-Amenas, Alg.
57/K10 Inami, Japan
75/M13 Inaouene (riv.), Mor.
106/E6 Iñapari, Peru
20/H1 Inari (lake), Fin.
42/E1 Inari (lake), Fin.
41/G2 Inău (peak), Rom.
57/G2 Inawashiro (lake), Japan
57/M9 Inazawa, Japan
35/G3 Inca, Sp.
49/C1 Incekum (pt.), Turk.
50/C2 Incekum (pt.), Turk.
79/F2 I-n-Chaouâg (wadi), Mali
30/A3 Incheville, Fr.
21/C3 Inchinnan, Sc,UK
78/B2 Inchiri (reg.), Mrta.
47/N6 Inch'ŏn, SKor.
55/K4 Inch'ŏn, SKor.
58/D4 Inch'ŏn, SKor.
58/F7 Inch'ŏn, SKor.
58/D4 Inch'ŏn-Jikhalsi, SKor.
58/F7 Inch'ŏn-Jikhalsi (prov.), SKor.
50/A2 İncirliova, Turk.
81/F2 Inciumi (riv.), Moz.
38/A2 Incudine, Mont I' (mtn.), Fr.
76/E3 I-n-Dagouber (well), Mali
108/C1 Indaiá (riv.), Braz.
108/C2 Indaiatuba, Braz.
20/E3 Indalsälven (riv.), Swe.
67/F2 Indanan, Phil.
52/C6 Inda Silasē, Eth.
63/G3 Indaw, Burma
65/B1 Indaw, Burma
60/B3 Indawgyi (lake), Burma
31/F2 Inde (riv.), Ger.
100/D3 Indé, Mex.
31/F2 Inden, Ger.
102/D2 Independence, Belz.
92/C3 Independence, Ca,US
93/J3 Independence, Ks,US
96/E2 Independence, Ks,US
89/H4 Independence, Mo,US
93/J3 Independence, Mo,US
96/E2 Independence, Mo,US
106/D5 Independence (mts.), Nv,US
92/C2 Independence (mts.), Nv,US
98/E6 Independence Nat'l Hist. Park, Pa,US
45/J2 Inder (lake), Kaz.
46/F5 Inderborskiy, Kaz.
99/D2 Index, Wa,US
48/G7 India
53/K3 India
54/C6 India
60/B3 India
62/C3 India
64/C1 India
66/A3 India
64/F3 India
17/N6 Indian (ocean)
66/A5 Indian (ocean)
68/A6 Indian (ocean)
77/Q7 Indian (ocean)
81/F3 Indian (ocean)
81/J9 Indian (ocean)
81/R14 Indian (ocean)
82/E8 Indian (ocean)
83/C Indian (ocean), Ant.
89/J4 Indiana (state), US
94/C3 Indiana (state), US
99/R16 Indiana (state), US
94/E3 Indiana, Pa,US
99/R16 Indiana Dunes Nat'l Lakesh., In,US
89/J4 Indianapolis (cap.), In,US
94/C4 Indianapolis (cap.), In,US
97/G2 Indianapolis (cap.), In,US
88/F1 Indian Head, Sk,Can
91/H3 Indian Head, Sk,Can
93/K4 Indianola, Ms,US
97/F3 Indianola, Ms,US
99/B2 Indianola, Wa,US
97/H5 Indiantown, Fl,US
108/B1 Indiaporã, Braz.
47/Q3 Indigirka (riv.), Rus.
48/P3 Indigirka (riv.), Rus.
40/E3 Inđija, Yugo.
92/C4 Indio, Ca,US
63/H4 Indochina (reg.), Asia
65/C1 Indochina (reg.), Asia
48/K10 Indonesia
68/B5 Indonesia
67/E4 Indonesia
72/E6 Indooroopilly, Austl.
53/L4 Indore, India
62/C3 Indore, India
66/B4 Indragiri (riv.), Indo.
66/C5 Indramayu (cape), Indo.
62/D4 Indrāvati (riv.), India
32/D3 Indre (riv.), Fr.
32/D3 Indrois (riv.), Fr.
48/F7 Indus (riv.), Asia
53/L2 Indus (riv.), India
64/A2 Indus (riv.), India
53/J4 Indus (riv.), Pak.
62/A2 Indus (riv.), Pak.
64/A2 Indus (riv.), Pak.
53/J4 Indus, Mouths of the (delta), Pak.
44/E4 İnebolu, Turk.
50/C1 İnebolu, Turk.
79/E1 I-n-Echaï (well), Mali
44/D4 İnegöl, Turk.
50/B1 İnegöl, Turk.
40/E2 Ineu, Rom.
44/B3 Ineu, Rom.
76/D1 Inezgane, Mor.
80/C4 Infanta (cape), SAfr.
100/E5 Infiernillo (res.), Mex.
34/C1 Infiesto, Sp.
79/G2 I-n-Gall, Niger
106/C4 Ingapirca, Ecu.
19/Q7 Ingatestone, Eng,UK
30/C2 Ingelmunster, Belg.
35/X17 Ingenio, Canl.
36/D1 Ingersheim, Fr.
71/H3 Ingham, Austl.
72/B2 Ingham, Austl.
72/G8 Ingleburn, Austl.
31/H4 Ingleheim, Ger.
23/G2 Ingleton, Eng,UK
72/C5 Inglewood, Austl.
73/B3 Inglewood, Austl.
73/D1 Inglewood, Austl.
92/B3 Inglewood, Ca,US
95/Q8 Inglewood, On,Can
99/Q7 Inglewood-Finn Hill, Wa,US
97/H4 Inglis, Fl,US
47/M4 Ingoda (riv.), Rus.
54/G1 Ingoda (riv.), Rus.
23/J5 Ingoldmells, Eng,UK
26/F4 Ingolstadt, Ger.
33/J2 Ingolstadt, Ger.
19/Q7 Ingrave, Eng,UK
83/E Ingrid Christianson (coast), Ant.
79/G2 I-n-Guezzâm, Alg.
41/L2 Ingulets, Ukr.
44/E3 Ingulets (riv.), Ukr.
45/G4 Inguri (riv.), Geo.
81/E2 Ingwavuma, SAfr.
82/F6 Ingwavuma, SAfr.
31/G6 Ingwiller, Fr.
81/F2 Inhambane (prov.), Moz.
82/G5 Inhambane, Moz.
81/F2 Inharrime, Moz.
82/G5 Inharrime, Moz.
107/J7 Inhumas, Braz.
34/E3 Iniesta, Sp.
21/G7 Inishbofin (isl.), Ire.
21/A3 Inishcrone, Ire.
22/A1 Inishowen (pen.), Ire.
22/B1 Inishowen Head (pt.), Ire.
56/A1 Inje, SKor.
58/E3 Inje, SKor.
72/C4 Injune, Austl.
99/F7 Inkster, Mi,US
56/C3 Inland (sea), Japan
60/C4 Inle (lake), Burma
63/G3 Inle (lake), Burma
100/C2 Inmaculadita, Mex.
79/E1 I-n-Milach (well), Mali
26/G4 Inn (riv.), Aus.
37/G3 Inn (riv.), Aus.
33/K2 Inn (riv.), Eur.
26/G4 Inn (riv.), Ger.
26/F5 Inn (riv.), Swi.
72/A4 Innamincka, Austl.
102/D2 Inner (chan.), Belz.
21/B2 Inner Hebrides (isls.), Sc,UK
37/F3 Innerhoden (demi-canton), Swi.
47/M5 Inner Mongolia (reg.), China
48/L5 Inner Mongolia (reg.), China
54/G3 Inner Mongolia (reg.), China
29/H4 Innerste (riv.), Ger.
37/E4 Innertkirchen, Swi.
33/K3 Innichen (San Candido), It.
71/H3 Innisfail, Austl.
72/B2 Innisfail, Austl.
86/E3 Innisfail, Ab,Can
90/E2 Innisfail, Ab,Can
85/G3 Innoko (riv.), Ak,US
85/G3 Innoko Nat'l Wild. Ref., Ak,US
18/E4 Innsbruck, Aus.
26/F5 Innsbruck, Aus.
33/J3 Innsbruck, Aus.
37/H3 Innsbruck, Aus.
24/B5 Inny (riv.), Eng,UK
56/C4 Ino, Japan
108/B1 Inocência, Braz.
77/J8 Inongo, Zaire
82/C1 Inongo, Zaire
45/D4 İnönü, Turk.
50/B2 İnönü, Turk.
27/K4 Inovec (peak), Slvk.
27/K2 Inowrocław, Pol.
42/D5 Inowrocław, Pol.
44/E1 I-n-Sâkâne, Erg (des.), Mali
76/F2 I-n-Salah, Alg.
60/C5 Insein, Burma
63/G4 Insein, Burma
90/A2 Inside (passg.), BC,Can
19/K2 Inta, Rus.
43/P2 Inta, Rus.
46/G3 Inta, Rus.
79/F2 I-n-Tassik (well), Mali
109/D4 Intendente Alvear, Arg.
39/K3 İntepe, Turk.
41/H6 İntepe, Turk.
90/B2 Interior (plat.), BC,Can
33/G3 Interlaken, Swi.
36/D4 Interlaken, Swi.
86/G4 International Falls, Mn,US
89/H2 International Falls, Mn,US
91/K3 International Falls, Mn,US
94/A1 International Falls, Mn,US
91/H3 International Peace Garden, Can,US
60/C5 Inthanon (peak), Thai.
63/G4 Inthanon (peak), Thai.
65/B2 Inthanon (peak), Thai.
102/E3 Intipucá, ESal.
41/H3 Întorsura Buzăului, Rom.
37/E5 Intragna, Swi.
37/F6 Introbio, It.
55/N4 Inubō-zaki (pt.), Japan
57/G3 Inubō-zaki (pt.), Japan
87/J3 Inukjuak, Qu,Can
84/D3 Inuvik, Can.
85/M2 Inuvik, NW,Can
86/C2 Inuvik, NW,Can
57/E3 Inuyama, Japan
57/M9 Inuyama, Japan
71/Q12 Invercargill, N.Z.
73/D1 Inverell, Austl.
71/J5 Inverell, Austl.
73/C3 Inverloch, Austl.
91/H3 Invermay, Sk, Can
86/E3 Invermere, BC,Can
87/K4 Inverness, NS,Can
18/C3 Inverness, Sc,UK
97/G3 Inverness, Al,US
97/H4 Inverness, Fl,US
70/F7 Investigator (str.), Austl.
82/F4 Inyanga, Zim.
82/F4 Inyangani (peak), Zim.
85/D2 Inymney, Gora (mt.), Rus.
92/C3 Inyo (mts.), Ca,US
45/H1 Inza, Rus.
57/J7 Inzai, Japan
45/L1 Inzer, Rus.
37/F1 Inzigkofen, Ger.
37/H3 Inzing, Aus.
18/F5 Ioánnina, Gre.
39/G3 Ioánnina, Gre.
93/J3 Iola, Ks,US
96/E2 Iola, Ks,US
46/G6 Iolotan', Trkm.
53/H1 Iolotan', Trkm.
82/B4 Iona Nat'l Park, Ang.
94/C3 Ionia, Mi,US
18/E5 Ionian (sea), Eur.
18/E5 Ionian (isls.), Gre.
39/F3 Ionian (isls.), Gre.
39/F3 Ionian (sea), Gre., I
39/J4 Ios, Gre.
39/J4 Ios (isl.), Gre.
78/A2 Iouîk (cape), Mrta.
91/K5 Iowa (state), US
86/G4 Iowa (state), US
89/H3 Iowa (state), US
93/J2 Iowa (state), US
91/L5 Iowa (riv.), Ia,US
93/K2 Iowa (riv.), Ia,US
94/A3 Iowa (riv.), Ia,US
89/H3 Iowa City, Ia,US
91/L5 Iowa City, Ia,US
93/K2 Iowa City, Ia,US
94/B3 Iowa City, Ia,US
89/H3 Iowa Falls, Ia,US
91/K5 Iowa Falls, Ia,US
93/J2 Iowa Falls, Ia,US
107/J7 Ipameri, Braz.
108/B1 Ipameri, Braz.
108/D1 Ipanema, Braz.
107/K7 Ipatinga, Braz.
108/D1 Ipatinga, Braz.
27/K4 Ipel' (riv.), Czh.
40/D1 Ipel' (Ipoly) (riv.), Sl
106/C3 Ipiales, Col.
107/L6 Ipiaú, Braz.
108/B3 Ipiranga, Braz.
66/B3 Ipoh, Malay.
27/K4 Ipoly (riv.), Hun.
40/D1 Ipoly (Ipel') (riv.), Sl
107/H7 Iporá, Braz.
39/K2 İpsala, Turk.
41/H5 İpsala, Turk.
44/C4 İpsala, Turk.
50/A1 İpsala, Turk.
72/E7 Ipswich, Austl.
25/H2 Ipswich, Eng,UK
91/J4 Ipswich, SD,US
107/K4 Ipu, Braz.
108/B2 Ipuã, Braz.
84/L3 Iqaluit, Can.
87/K2 Iqaluit, NW,Can
106/D8 Iquique, Chile
106/D4 Iquitos, Peru
57/M10 Irago (chan.), Japa
57/E3 Irago-misaki (cape
57/N10 Irago-misaki (cape Japan
39/H2 Iráklia, Gre.
39/J4 Iráklia (isl.), Gre.
41/F5 Iráklia, Gre.
18/F5 Iráklion, Gre.
39/J5 Iráklion, Gre.
77/L1 Iráklion, Gre.
45/H5 Iran
46/F6 Iran
48/E6 Iran
51/H3 Iran
52/F2 Iran
77/R2 Iran
66/D3 Iran (mts.), Indo., Malay.
53/H3 Irānshahr, Iran
104/F5 Irapa, Ven.
101/E4 Irapuato, Mex.
46/E6 Iraq
48/D6 Iraq
50/E3 Iraq
52/D2 Iraq
77/P1 Iraq
108/B3 Irati, Braz.
109/F2 Irati, Braz.
67/H4 Irau (mtn.), Indo.
49/D3 Irbid, Jor.
49/E3 Irbid (gov.), Jor.
50/C3 Irbid, Jor.
46/E6 Irbīl, Iraq
51/E3 Irbīl (gov.), Iraq
51/F2 Irbīl, Iraq
52/D1 Irbīl, Iraq
46/G4 Irbit, Rus.
107/K6 Irecê, Braz.
18/C3 Ireland
21/A4 Ireland
22/B5 Ireland's Eye (isl.), Ire.
43/N5 Iremel', Gora (peak Rus.
80/Q12 Irene, SAfr.
108/A3 Iretama, Braz.
24/C2 Irfon (riv.), Wal,UK
79/G2 Irhazer Oua-n-Aga (wadi), Niger
55/K4 Iri, SKor.
58/D5 Iri, SKor.
67/H4 Irian Jaya (reg.), In
40/D3 Irig, Yugo.
78/D2 Irigui (reg.), Mali, Mrta.
45/L2 Iriklinskiy (res.), R
82/G2 Iringa, Tanz.
64/F3 Irinjālakuda, India
107/H4 Iriri (riv.), Braz.
22/C4 Irish (sea)
18/C3 Irish (sea)
54/E1 Irkut (riv.), Rus.
47/L4 Irkutsk, Rus.
54/E1 Irkutsk, Rus.
23/F5 Irlam, Eng,UK
32/A2 Iroise (bay), Fr.
24/D1 Iron Bridge, Eng,U
40/F3 Iron Gate (gorge), Rom.
70/F6 Iron Knob, Austl.
86/H4 Iron Mountain, Mi,
89/J2 Iron Mountain, Mi,
91/L4 Iron Mountain, Mi,
94/B2 Iron Mountain, Mi,
91/L4 Iron River, Mi,US
94/B2 Iron River, Mi,US
94/D4 Ironton, Oh,US
97/H2 Ironton, Oh,US
89/H2 Ironwood, Mi,US
91/L4 Ironwood, Mi,US
94/B2 Ironwood, Mi,US
87/H4 Iroquois Falls, On,C

89/K2 Iroquois Falls, On,Can
94/D1 Iroquois Falls, On,Can
44/E1 Irput' (riv.), Bela.
44/F1 Irput' (riv.), Rus.
60/B5 Irrawaddy (riv.),
63/F4 Irrawaddy (div.),
 Burma
63/G4 Irrawaddy (riv.),
 Burma
48/J7 Irrawaddy (riv.),
 Burma.,China
60/B5 Irrawaddy
 (Ayeyarwady) (div.),
 Burma
60/B5 Irrawaddy, Mouths of
 the (delta), Burma
63/F4 Irrawaddy, Mouths of
 the (delta),
 Burma,India
31/F4 Irrel, Ger.
31/F4 Irsch, Ger.
31/F3 Irsen (riv.), Ger.
40/C5 Irsina, It.
23/E4 Irt (riv.), Eng,UK
23/F1 Irthing (riv.), Eng,UK
25/F2 Irthlingborough,
 Eng,UK
46/G4 Irtysh (riv.), Rus.,Kaz.
48/G4 Irtysh (riv.), Kaz., Rus.
46/H4 Irtyshsk, Kaz.
57/H4 Iruma, Japan
77/L7 Irumu, Zaire
32/C5 Irún, Sp.
34/E1 Irún, Sp.
92/C4 Irvine, Ca,US
98/C3 Irvine, Ca,US
101/F1 Irving, Tx,US
93/H4 Irving, Tx,US
96/D3 Irving, Tx,US
98/F5 Irvington, NJ, US
71/H4 Isaac (riv.), Austl.
72/C3 Isaac (riv.), Austl.
67/F2 Isabela, Phil.
104/E3 Isabela, PR
102/E3 Isabela, Cordillera
 (range), Nic.
87/K2 Isabella (bay),
 NW,Can
41/J3 Isaccea, Rom.
87/R7 Isachsen (cape),
 NW,Can
20/M6 Isafjardhardjúp
 (fjord), Ice.
18/A2 Isafjördhur, Ice.
20/M6 Isafjördhur, Ice.
56/B4 Isahaya, Japan
56/B4 Isahaya, Japan
32/J11 Isalo Massif (upland),
 Madg.
81/H8 Isalo Nat'l Park,
 Madg.
81/H8 Isalo Ruiniform,
 Massif (plat.), Madg.
01/C3 Isandhlwana
 Battlesite, SAfr.
37/H1 Isar (riv.), Aus., Ger.
33/K2 Isar (riv.), Ger.
33/K2 Isar (riv.), Ger.
33/J7 Isarco (riv.), It
37/H4 Isarco (Eisack) (riv.),
 It.
30/B2 Isbergues, Fr.
34/C2 Iscar, Sp.
38/C2 Ischia, It.
40/A5 Ischia, It.
29/H3 Ise (riv.), Ger.
56/E3 Ise (bay), Japan
7/M10 Ise, Japan
7/M10 Ise (bay), Japan
25/F2 Ise, Eng,UK
57/H7 Isehara, Japan
57/H7 Isehara, Japan
33/K2 Isen (riv.), Ger.
37/E4 Isenthal, Swi.
33/J4 Iseo (lake), It.
32/F4 Isère (riv.), Fr.
32/F4 Isère (dept.), Fr.
30/B6 Isère (riv.), Fr.
29/E6 Iserlohn, Ger.
38/D2 Isernia, It.
40/B5 Isernia, It.
57/E3 Ise-Shima Nat'l Park,
 Japan
7/M10 Ise-Shima Nat'l Park,
 Japan
43/Q4 Iset' (riv.), Rus.
76/F6 Iseyin, Nga.
79/F5 Iseyin, Nga.
06/G3 Isherton, Guy.
57/L10 Ishi (riv.), Japan
57/F2 Ishibashi, Japan
57/M9 Ishibe, Japan
68/B2 Ishigaki, Japan
57/E2 Ishige, Japan
57/E2 Ishikawa (pref.),
 Japan
57/E2 Ishikawa, Japan
57/N10 Ishiki, Japan
43/G5 Ishim (riv.), Kaz.
46/H4 Ishim (riv.), Rus.,Kaz.
43/H5 Ishim (riv.), Kaz., Rus.
43/R4 Ishim, Rus.
45/L1 Ishimbay, Rus.
55/N4 Ishinomaki, Japan
57/G1 Ishinomaki, Japan
57/G1 Ishioka, Japan
56/C4 Ishizuchi-san (mtn.),
 Japan
45/L4 Ishlya, Rus.
93/J2 Ishpeming, Mi,US
91/M4 Ishpeming, Mi,US
94/C2 Ishpeming, Mi,US
106/E7 Isiboro Securé Nat'l
 Park, Bol.
32/C2 Isigny-sur-Mer, Fr.
46/H4 Isil'kul', Rus.
77/L7 Isiro, Zaire

72/B4 Isisford, Austl.
49/D1 Iskenderun (gulf),
 Turk.
49/E1 Iskenderun, Turk.
50/D2 Iskenderun, Turk.
52/C1 Iskenderun, Turk.
45/J3 Iske-Ryazyap, Rus.
44/E4 Iskilip, Turk.
50/C1 Iskilip, Turk.
39/H1 Iskür (res.), Bul.
39/H1 Iskür (riv.), Bul.
41/F4 Iskür (lake), Bul.
41/G4 Iskür (riv.), Bul.
101/G5 Isla, Mex.
102/C2 Isla, Mex.
101/H5 Isla Aguada, Mex.
102/D2 Isla Aguada, Mex.
103/J2 Isla Cabritos Nat'l
 Park, DRep.
104/D3 Isla Cabritos Nat'l
 Park, DRep.
34/B4 Isla Cristina, Sp.
72/C4 Isla Gorge Nat'l Park,
 Austl.
49/E1 Islâhiye, Turk.
50/D2 Islâhiye, Turk.
52/C1 Islâhiye, Turk.
101/J4 Isla Holbox, Mex.
100/D4 Isla Holbox, Mex.
100/D4 Isla Isabela Nat'l
 Park, Mex.
53/K4 Islâmâbâd (cap.),
 Pak.
64/D3 Islâmâbâd (cap.),
 Pak.
64/B3 Islamabad Cap. Terr.
 (terr.), Pak.
109/B5 Isla Magdalena Nat'l
 Park, Chile
53/K4 Islâm Kot, Pak.
97/H5 Islamorada, Fl,US
62/E2 Islâmpur, India
102/E1 Isla Mujeres, Mex.
91/K2 Island (lake), Mb,Can
86/G3 Island (lake), Mb,Can
99/C2 Island (co.), Wa,US
98/F6 Island Beach St.
 Park, NJ,US
91/K2 Island Lake, Can
99/P15 Island Lake, Il,US
18/E4 Island, Ca,US
33/H4 Islington (bor.),
 Eng,UK
95/K1 Islands (bay), Nf,Can
21/D3 Islay (isl.), Sc,UK
32/D4 Isle (riv.), Fr.
25/G2 Isleham, Eng,UK
22/D2 Isle of Whithorn,
 Sc,UK
91/L4 Isle Royale (isl.),
 Mi,US
94/B1 Isle Royale (isl.),
 Mi,US
91/L3 Isle Royale Nat'l
 Park, Mi,US
86/G4 Isle Royale Nat'l
 Park, Mi,US
89/J2 Isle Royale Nat'l
 Park, Mi,US
94/B2 Isle Royale Nat'l
 Park, Mi,US
99/L10 Isleton, Ca,US
19/N7 Islington (bor.),
 Eng,UK
98/G3 Islip, NY,US
50/C4 Ismailia, Egypt
77/M1 Ismailia, Egypt
49/C4 Ismailia (Al
 Ismâ'îlîyah), Egypt
52/B2 Ismailia (Al
 Ismâ'îlîyah), Egypt
51/G1 Ismailly, Azer.
43/X9 Ismailovo Park, Rus.
37/H1 Ismaning, Ger.
52/B3 Isnâ, Egypt
26/F5 Isny, Ger.
33/J3 Isny, Ger.
37/G2 Isny, Ger.
81/H8 Isoanala, Madg.
57/M10 Isobe, Japan
20/H3 Isojärven Nat'l Park,
 Fin.
42/E3 Isojärven Nat'l Park,
 Fin.
42/D3 Isojoki, Fin.
82/F3 Isoka, Zam.
38/C2 Isola del Liri, It.
38/E3 Isola di Capo Rizzuto,
 It.
50/B2 Isparta, Turk.
32/C5 Isparta (prov.), Turk.
34/E1 Ispéguy, Col d' (pass),
 Fr.
41/H4 Isperikh, Bul.
44/C4 Isperikh, Bul.
45/G4 Ispir, Turk.
50/E1 Ispir, Turk.
48/C6 Israel
49/C3 Israel
49/F7 Israel
50/C4 Israel
52/B2 Israel
77/M1 Israel
99/C2 Issaquah, Wa,US
99/C2 Issaquah (cr.), Wa,US
28/D5 Issel (riv.), Ger.
28/D5 Isselburg, Ger.
26/D5 Issenheim, Fr.
70/D5 Issia, IvC.
32/E4 Issoire, Fr.
32/D3 Issoudun, Fr.
38/A2 Issum, Ger.
32/C4 Is-sur-Tille, Fr.
32/F3 Is-sur-Tille, Fr.
36/B2 Is-sur Tille, Fr.
30/B6 Issy-les-Moulineaux,
 Fr.
27/L4 Istállós-kö (peak),
 Hun.
40/D4 Istállós-kö (peak),
 Hun.
91/H3 Istanbul, Turk.
18/F4 Istanbul, Turk.
10/J5 Istanbul, Turk.
44/C4 Istanbul, Turk.
108/B3 Istanbul, Braz.
108/B1 Itumbiara (res.),
 Braz.
91/H3 Ituna, Sk,Can
18/F4 Istanbul, Turk.
108/B3 Ituporanga, Braz.
108/B1 Iturama, Braz.
33/K4 Izola, Slov.

41/J5 Istanbul (prov.), Turk.
44/D4 Istanbul, Turk.
44/D4 Istanbul (prov.), Turk.
50/B1 Istanbul, Turk.
50/B1 Istanbul (prov.), Turk.
51/N6 Istanbul (cap.), Turk.
39/H3 Istiaía, Gre.
44/B5 Istiaía, Gre.
39/G1 Istok, Yugo.
40/E4 Istok, Yugo.
43/X9 Istra (riv.), Rus.
41/H5 Istranca (mts.), Turk.
32/F5 Istres, Fr.
35/H1 Istres, Fr.
40/A3 Istria (pen.), Cro.
33/K4 Istria (pen.), Cro.,
 Slov.
67/F2 Isulan, Phil.
107/K6 Itaberaba, Braz.
107/K7 Itabira, Braz.
108/D1 Itabira, Braz.
108/D2 Itabirito, Braz.
107/L6 Itabuna, Braz.
107/H5 Itacaiunas (riv.),
 Braz.
106/G4 Itacoatiara, Braz.
106/D5 Itacuai (riv.), Braz.
58/G6 It'aewön, SKor.
108/C2 Itaguara, Braz.
106/C2 Itaguí, Col.
108/B2 Itaí, Braz.
108/B3 Itaiópolis, Braz.
108/B2 Itaipu (res.), Braz.
105/D5 Itaipu (res.), Braz.,
 Par.
109/E1 Itaipu (res.), Par.
109/F2 Itaipú (dam), Par.
107/G4 Itaituba, Braz.
108/B1 Itajá, Braz.
108/B3 Itajaí (riv.), Braz.
108/B3 Itajaí, Braz.
109/G2 Itajaí, Braz.
107/J8 Itajubá, Braz.
108/D2 Itajubá, Braz.
57/G3 Itako, Japan
18/E4 Italy
33/H4 Italy
37/G5 Italy
38/D2 Italy
40/A5 Italy
101/F1 Italy, Tx,US
107/L7 Itamaraju, Braz.
108/D1 Itamarandiba, Braz.
108/D1 Itambacuri, Braz.
57/L10 Itami, Japan
60/B3 Itanagar, India
63/F2 Itanagar, India
108/D2 Itanhaém, Braz.
108/C2 Itanhandu, Braz.
108/D1 Itanhém (riv.), Braz.
108/D1 Itaobim, Braz.
107/K7 Itaobim, Braz.
100/D2 Itaocara, Braz.
107/L4 Itapagé, Braz.
108/C2 Itapecerica, Braz.
107/K4 Itapecuru-Mirim,
 Braz.
107/K8 Itapemirim, Braz.
108/D2 Itapemirim, Braz.
107/K8 Itaperuna, Braz.
108/D2 Itaperuna, Braz.
107/K7 Itapetinga, Braz.
108/B2 Itapetininga, Braz.
108/B2 Itapeva, Braz.
107/K5 Itapicuru (riv.), Braz.
107/L6 Itapicuru (riv.), Braz.
107/L4 Itapipoca, Braz.
108/B2 Itaporanga, Braz.
108/B3 Itararé, Braz.
109/G1 Itararé, Braz.
62/C3 Itârsi, India
108/C2 Itatinga, Braz.
107/K5 Itaueira (riv.), Braz.
108/C2 Itaúna, Braz.
107/K8 Itaúna, Braz.
55/N3 Itayanagi, Japan
61/J4 Itbayat, Phil.
G1/J4 Itbayat (isl.), Phil.
68/B2 Itbayat (isl.), Phil.
25/E4 Itchen (riv.), Eng,UK
39/H3 Itéa, Gre.
77/K7 Itembiri (riv.), Zaire
105/C4 Iténez (riv.), Bol.
106/F6 Iténez (riv.), Bol.
82/E4 Itezhi-Tezhi (dam),
 Zam.
89/L3 Ithaca, NY,US
94/E3 Ithaca, NY,US
29/G5 Ith Hils (ridge), Ger.
24/C2 Ithon (riv.), Wal,UK
82/F2 Itigi, Tanz.
57/F3 Itô, Japan
57/H8 Itô, Japan
57/E2 Itoigawa, Japan
30/A5 Iton (riv.), Fr.
32/D2 Iton (riv.), Fr.
101/Q10 Ixtapalapa, Mex.
101/K8 Ixtapan de la Sal,
 Mex.
100/D4 Ixtlán del Río, Mex.
25/G2 Ixworth, Eng,UK
54/D1 Iya (riv.), Rus.
56/C4 Iyo, Japan
56/C4 Iyo (sea), Japan
102/D3 Izabal (lake), Guat.
51/H4 İzad Khvâst, Iran
52/F2 İzad Khvâst, Iran
101/J4 Izamal, Mex.
102/D1 Izamal, Mex.
45/H4 Izberbash, Rus.
30/C2 Izegem, Belg.
85/F4 Izembek Nat'l Wild.
 Ref., Ak,US
19/J3 Izhevsk, Rus.
43/M4 Izhevsk, Rus.
46/F4 Izhevsk, Rus.
43/M2 Izhma (riv.), Rus.
43/V7 Izhora (riv.), Rus.
85/E5 Izigan (cape), Ak,US
53/G4 Izki', Oman
41/J3 Izmail, Ukr.
44/D3 Izmail, Ukr.
44/C3 İzmir, Turk.
50/A2 İzmir, Turk.
50/A2 İzmir (prov.), Turk.
44/C3 İzmir (prov.), Turk.
44/C3 İzmit, Turk.
50/B1 İzmit, Turk.
41/J5 İzmit (gulf), Turk.
50/B1 İzmit, Turk.
34/D4 Iznájar, Sp.
34/C4 Iznalloz, Sp.
41/H5 İznik (lake), Turk.
41/J5 İznik, Turk.
50/B1 İznik, Turk.
33/K4 Izola, Slov.

108/C2 Ituverava, Braz.
106/E5 Ituxi (riv.), Braz.
49/B4 Ityay al Bârûd, Egypt
26/F3 Itz (riv.), Ger.
26/E2 Itzehoe, Ger.
85/C2 Iul'tin, Gora (mt.),
 Rus.
108/D2 Iuna, Braz.
108/B3 Ivaiporã, Braz.
109/F1 Ivaiporã, Braz.
20/H1 Ivalo, Fin.
20/H1 Ivalojoki (riv.), Fin.
42/E1 Ivalojoki (riv.), Fin.
33/M2 Ivančice, Czh.
33/M3 Ivanec, Cro.
40/C2 Ivanec, Cro.
39/F1 Ivangrad, Yugo.
40/D4 Ivangrad, Yugo.
71/G6 Ivanhoe, Austl.
73/C2 Ivanhoe, Austl.
94/D1 Ivanhoe (riv.), On,Can
40/C4 Ivanjica, Yugo.
40/C3 Ivanjska, Bosn.
40/D3 Ivankovo, Cro.
85/G4 Ivanof Bay, Ak,US
18/F4 Ivano-Frankovsk, Ukr.
44/C2 Ivano-Frankovsk, Ukr.
41/G1 Ivano-Frankovsk Obl.,
 Ukr.
44/C2 Ivano-Frankovsk Obl.,
 Ukr.
27/M4 Ivano-Frankovsk
 Oblast, Ukr.
19/H3 Ivanovo, Rus.
42/J4 Ivanovo, Rus.
46/E4 Ivanovo, Rus.
43/J4 Ivanovo Obl., Rus.
39/J2 Ivaylovgrad (res.),
 Bul.
39/K2 Ivaylovgrad, Bul.
41/H5 Ivaylovgrad, Bul.
43/P3 Ivdel, Rus.
46/G3 Ivdel, Rus.
19/M7 Iver, Eng,UK
21/G8 Iveragh (pen.), Ire.
19/M7 Iver Heath, Eng,UK
76/H7 Ivindo (riv.), Gabon
81/H8 Ivohibe, Madg.
81/J7 Ivondro (riv.), Madg.
30/C1 Ivrea, It.
74/B4 Ivory Coast
76/D6 Ivory Coast
76/D7 Ivory Coast (reg.), Afr.
78/D5 Ivory Coast (reg.), IvC.
78/D5 Ivory Coast (Côte
 d'Ivoire)
33/G4 Ivrea, It.
44/C5 İvrindi, Turk.
50/A2 İvrindi, Turk.
30/A6 Ivry-la-Bataille, Fr.
30/B6 Ivry-sur-Seine, Fr.
87/J2 Ivujivik, Qu,Can
24/C6 Ivybridge, Eng,UK
32/B1 Ivybridge, Eng,UK
57/F2 Iwai, Japan
47/Q6 Iwaki, Japan
55/N4 Iwaki, Japan
57/G1 Iwaki, Japan
55/L5 Iwakuni, Japan
56/C3 Iwakuni, Japan
57/M9 Iwakura, Japan
56/D3 Iwamizawa, Japan
57/G1 Iwanuma, Japan
57/E3 Iwata, Japan
55/N4 Iwate-san (mtn.),
 Japan
57/H7 Iwatsuki, Japan
76/F6 Iwo, Nga.
79/G5 Iwo, Nga.
68/D2 Iwo Jima (isl.), Japan
58/E2 Iwön, NKor.
30/C3 Iwuy, Fr.
102/D3 Ixcán (riv.), Guat.,
 Mex.
26/C3 Ixelles, Belg.
101/F4 Ixmiquilpan, Mex.
101/K6 Ixmiquilpan, Mex.
102/B1 Ixmiquilpan, Mex.
101/L7 Ixtacihuatl-
 Popotzteco Nat'l
 Park, Mex.
101/Q10 Ixtapalapa, Mex.
101/K8 Ixtapan de la Sal,
 Mex.

40/A3 Izola, Slov.
102/E3 Izopo (pt.), Hon.
49/E3 Izra', Syria
50/D3 Izra', Syria
40/D2 Izsák, Hun.
47/P6 Izu (isls.), Japan
55/M5 Izu (isls.), Japan
55/M5 Izu (pen.), Japan
101/F5 Izúcar de
 Matamoros, Mex.
101/L8 Izúcar de
 Matamoros, Mex.
102/B2 Izúcar de
 Matamoros, Mex.
57/H8 Izu-Fuji-Hakone Nat'l
 Park, Japan
56/A3 Izuhara, Japan
56/M3 Izumi, Japan
56/D3 Izumi, Japan
57/L10 Izumi, Japan
56/D3 Izumi-ôtsu, Japan
56/D3 Izumi-Sano, Japan
57/L10 Izumi-Sano, Japan
55/L4 Izumo, Japan
56/C3 Izumo, Japan
44/F2 Izyum, Ukr.

J

49/G7 Jaba', WBnk.
77/P4 Jabal an Nabî
 Shu'ayb (peak), Yem.
76/G1 Jabal ash Sha'nabî
 (peak), Tun.
103/F5 Jabalí (pt.), Pan.
77/M2 Jabal Kâtrînâ
 (Mount Catherine)
 (peak), Egypt
49/D2 Jabal Lubnân (gov.),
 Leb.
51/J2 Jabalón (riv.), Sp.
62/C3 Jabalpur, India
77/P4 Jabal Sawdâ' (peak),
 SAr.
77/Q5 Jabal Thamar (peak),
 Yem.
49/D4 Jabâlyah, Gaza
30/C1 Jabbeke, Belg.
50/D3 Jabbûl, Sabkhat al
 (lake), Syria
96/C3 Jabiru, Syria
100/D4 Jabjabah, Wâdî (dry
 riv.), Sudan
49/E3 Jablah, Syria
50/D3 Jablah, Syria
52/C1 Jablah, Syria
39/G2 Jablanica (mts.), Alb.
27/H3 Jablonec nad Nisou,
 Czh.
108/D2 Jaboticabal, Braz.
40/E3 Jabuka, Yugo.
66/B4 Jabung (cape), Indo.
35/E1 Jaca, Sp.
108/D3 Jacareí, Braz.
77/Q5 Jaceel (riv.), Som.
95/G2 Jackman, Me,US
90/E5 Jackpot, Nv,US
92/E2 Jackpot, Nv,US
101/F1 Jacksboro, Tx,US
96/D3 Jacksboro, Tx,US
89/J4 Jackson, Al,US
97/G4 Jackson, Al,US
92/B3 Jackson, Ca,US
89/K3 Jackson, Mi,US
94/C3 Jackson, Mi,US
91/K5 Jackson, Mn,US
93/J2 Jackson, Mn,US
93/K3 Jackson, Mo,US
94/B4 Jackson, Mo,US
89/H5 Jackson (cap.),
 Ms,US
93/K4 Jackson (cap.),
 Ms,US
97/F3 Jackson (cap.),
 Ms,US
90/D3 Jackson (mts.),
 Nv,US
90/D4 Jackson, Oh,US
97/H2 Jackson, Oh,US
89/J4 Jackson, Tn,US
94/B5 Jackson, Tn,US
97/F3 Jackson, Tn,US
90/F4 Jackson (lake),
 Wy,US
88/D3 Jackson, Wy,US
90/F5 Jackson, Wy,US
92/E2 Jackson, Wy,US
92/E2 Jackson (lake),
 Wy,US
89/K5 Jacksonville, Al,US
93/K3 Jacksonville, Ar,US
96/F3 Jacksonville, Ar,US
89/K5 Jacksonville, Fl,US
97/H4 Jacksonville, Fl,US
93/K3 Jacksonville, Il,US
94/B4 Jacksonville, Il,US
97/F2 Jacksonville, Il,US
97/J5 Jacksonville, NC,US
97/J5 Jacksonville, NC,US
101/N7 Jacksonville, Tx,US
89/J5 Jacksonville, Tx,US
89/K5 Jacksonville Beach,
 Fl,US
97/H4 Jacksonville Beach,
 Fl,US
103/H2 Jacmel, Haiti
100/D3 Jaco, Mex.
101/J5 Jacobābād, Pak.
62/A2 Jacobābād, Pak.
107/K6 Jacobina, Braz.
100/E5 Jacona de Plancarte,
 Mex.
95/H1 Jacques Cartier
 (peak), Can
87/K4 Jacques Cartier
 (riv.), Qu,Can
89/N2 Jacques Cartier
 (mtn.), Qu,Can

95/G2 Jacques-Cartier (riv.),
 Qu,Can
107/L6 Jacui (riv.), Braz.
107/L6 Jacuipe (riv.), Braz.
108/C3 Jacupiranga, Braz.
104/D5 Jacura, Ven.
104/D5 Jadacaquiva, Ven.
53/H3 Jaddi (pt.), Pak.
26/E2 Jade (bay), Ger.
29/F2 Jade, Ger.
29/F2 Jade (riv.), Ger.
27/F2 Jadebusen (bay), Ger.
18/C5 Jaén, Sp.
34/D4 Jaén, Sp.
64/F4 Jaffna, SrL.
64/D2 Jaffna, SrL.
73/A3 Jaffa (cape), Austl.
62/D6 Jaffna, SrL.
53/K4 Jagdalpur, India
62/D4 Jagdalpur, India
60/D3 Jagdïspur, India
62/D4 Jagdïspur, India
80/D3 Jagersfontein, SAfr.
82/E6 Jagersfontein, SAfr.
64/C2 Jagraon, India
33/J2 Jagst (riv.), Ger.
62/C4 Jagtïâl, India
109/F3 Jaguarão, Braz.
42/B3 Jaguariaíva, Braz.
108/B3 Jaguariaíva, Braz.
107/L5 Jaguaribe (riv.), Braz.
73/D3 Jagungal (peak),
 Austl.
42/E3 Janakkala, Fin.
107/K7 Janaúba, Braz.
103/F5 Jatibonico, Cuba
35/E3 Játiva, Sp.
54/E4 Jaincha, China
53/L3 Jaipur, India
62/C2 Jaipur, India
53/K3 Jaisalmer, India
53/K3 Jaisalmer, India
51/J2 Jâjarm, Iran
53/G1 Jâjarm, Iran
94/B3 Janesville, Wi,US
40/C3 Jajce, Bosn.
53/K3 Jâjpur, India
66/C5 Jakarta (cap.), Indo.
42/D3 Jakobstad, Fin.
27/K2 Janikowo, Pol.
49/D4 Janîn, WBnk.
49/G7 Janîn, WBnk.
40/G7 Jal, NM,US
100/E1 Jal, NM,US
94/G7 Janîn, WBnk.
50/C3 Janîn, WBnk.
40/D3 Janjevo, Yugo.
1/M7 Jan Mayen (isl.), Nor.
18/C1 Jan Mayen (isl.), Nor.
100/M7 Jalacingo, Mex.
55/J2 Jalaid Qi, China
64/C2 Jalâlâbâd, Afg.
40/D2 Jánoshalma, Hun.
49/G6 Jalamah, WBnk.
101/F5 Jalapa, Guat.
101/N7 Jalapa, Mex.
50/C4 Janûb Sînâ' (gov.),
 Egypt
102/A2 Jalapa, Mex.
102/B2 Jalapa, Mex.
32/C2 Janzé, Fr.
20/G3 Jalasjärvi, Fin.
42/D3 Jalasjärvi, Fin.
62/C3 Jaora, India
101/E1 Jayton, Tx,US
77/Q5 Jaceel (riv.), Som.
95/G2 Jackman, Me,US
108/B2 Jales, Braz.
55/M4 Japan
56/A4 Japan
58/E5 Japan
96/C3 Japan
55/M4 Japan
25/H3 Jaywick, Eng,UK
52/D4 Jazâ'ir Farasân (isls.),
 SAr.
47/P6 Japan (sea), Asia
48/N5 Japan (sea), Asia
55/L3 Japan (sea), Asia
27/L4 Jedlicze, Pol.
100/D4 Jalisco (state), Mex.
55/L3 Japan (sea), Asia
38/A4 Jâlïtah, Jazî rat (isl.),
 Tun.
55/M4 Japanese Alps (mts.),
 Japan
36/C6 Jallouvre. Pic de
 (peak), Fr.
57/E3 Japanese Alps
 (range), Japan
57/E2 Japanese Alps Nat'l
 Park, Japan
53/L5 Jâlna, India
62/C4 Jâlna, India
93/J3 Jefferson, Tx,US
34/E2 Jalon (riv.), Sp.
53/K3 Jalor, India
53/K3 Jâlor, India
62/B3 Jâlor, India
103/G5 Jaqué, Pan.
104/D3 Jarabacoa, DRep.
50/D2 Jarâbulus, Syria
34/C2 Jaraíz de la Vera, Sp.
102/C2 Jalpa de Méndez,
 Mex.
35/N9 Jarama (riv.), Sp.
62/E2 Jalpaiguri, India
34/C2 Jarandilla de la Vera,
 Sp.
101/F4 Jalpan, Mex.
102/B1 Jalpan, Mex.
64/D2 Jorânwâla, Pak.
49/D3 Jarash, Pol.
102/C2 Jaltepec (riv.), Mex.
76/H1 Jarbah (isl.), Tun.
101/G5 Jáltipan, Mex.
102/C2 Jáltipan, Mex.
77/K2 Jâlû, Libya
103/G1 Jardines de la Reina
 (arch.), Cuba
49/G7 Jâlûd, WBnk.
68/F4 Jaluit (atoll), Mrsh.
108/B2 Jardinópolis, Braz.
51/F3 Jalûlâ', Iraq
54/D2 Jargalant, Mong.
51/H5 Jam, Iran
105/D2 Jari (riv.), Braz.
107/H3 Jari (riv.), Braz.
62/E2 Jarídih, India
76/H1 Jarjîs, Tun.
77/P7 Jamaame, Som.
76/H1 Jarjîs, Tun.
79/H4 Jamaare (riv.), Nga.
27/G2 Jarmen, Ger.
31/E5 Jarny, Fr.
46/C2 Jelgava, Lat.
27/J3 Jarocin, Pol.
84/K8 Jamaica
103/H2 Jamaica (chan.),
 Haiti, Jam.
27/H3 Jaroměř, Czh.
33/L1 Jaroměř, Czh.
44/B2 Jarosław, Pol.
62/E2 Jamâlpur, Bang.
27/M3 Jarosław, Pol.
62/E2 Jamâlpur, India
23/G2 Jarrow, Eng,UK
104/D4 Jamanota (peak), Aru.
107/G5 Jamanxim (riv.), Braz.
21/J5 Jars (plain), Laos
101/N7 Jamapa, Mex.
55/J3 Jarud Qi, China
66/B4 Jambi, Indo.
59/E1 Jarud Qi, China
67/K4 Jempang (riv.), Indo.
66/B4 Jambuair (pt.), Indo.
20/H4 Järva-Jaani, Est.
31/F8 Jarville-la-
 Malgrange, Fr.
89/K1 James (lake), On,Can
69/J5 Jarvis (isl.), PacUS
100/E3 Jaco, Mex.
94/D1 James (bay), Can
91/J4 James (riv.), ND,
 SD,US
53/G2 Jâsk, Iran
62/D2 Jacobābād, Pak.
91/J4 James (riv.), ND,
 SD,US
27/K3 Jasło, Pol.
44/D2 Jasło, Pol.
93/H2 James (riv.), ND,
 SD,US
90/D2 Jasper, Ab,Can
87/H3 James (bay), On,
 Qu,Can
89/J5 Jasper, Al,US
86/G1 James (riv.), ND,
 SD,US
97/H4 Jasper, Fl,US
89/N2 James (riv.), ND,
 SD,US
89/J5 Jasper, Ga,US
97/G2 Jasper, In,US

94/E4 James (riv.), Va,US
 Qu,Can
88/V12 James Campbell
 Nat'l Wild. Ref., Hi,US
80/Q13 Jameson Park, SAfr.
86/G1 James Ross (str.),
 NW,Can
70/F6 Jamestown, Austl.
86/G2 Jamestown, ND,US
89/G2 Jamestown, ND,US
91/J4 Jamestown, ND,US
87/J4 Jamestown, NY,US
89/L3 Jamestown, NY,US
89/L3 Jamestown, NY,US
94/C4 Jamestown, Tn,US
97/J2 Jamestown, Tn,US
102/B2 Jamiltepec, Mex.
38/B5 Jammâl, Tun.
53/K2 Jammu, India
64/C1 Jammu, India
64/C1 Jammu and Kashmîr
 (state), India
53/K4 Jâmnagar, India
53/K3 Jâmpur, Pak.
20/H3 Jämsä, Fin.
42/E3 Jämsä, Fin.
107/H5 Jamshedpur, India
62/E3 Jamshedpur, India
20/E3 Jämtland (co.), Swe.
42/B3 Jämtland (co.), Swe.
62/E3 Jamûi, India
91/H2 Jan (lake), Sk,Can
42/E3 Janakkala, Fin.
107/K7 Janaúba, Braz.
107/J8 Janaucu (isl.), Braz.
108/B2 Jandaia do Sul, Braz.
43/J4 Jandaq, Iran
51/H3 Jandaq, Iran
53/F2 Jandaq, Iran
72/C4 Jandowae, Austl.
34/C4 Jándula (riv.), Sp.
109/G1 Jaú, Braz.
91/L5 Janesville, Wi,US
93/K2 Janesville, Wi,US
94/B3 Janesville, Wi,US
49/D2 Janîn, WBnk.
49/G7 Janîn, WBnk.
50/C3 Janîn, WBnk.
40/D3 Janjevo, Yugo.
48/K10 Java (sea), Indo.
48/K10 Java (sea), Indo.
66/C5 Java (sea), Indo.
66/D5 Java (sea), Indo.
106/D5 Javari (riv.), Braz.
18/C1 Jan Mayen (isl.), Nor.
100/C2 Janos, Mex.
40/D2 Jánoshalma, Hun.
40/C2 Jánosháza, Hun.
27/M3 Janów Lubelski, Pol.
107/K7 Januária, Braz.
49/C5 Janûb Sînâ' (gov.),
 Egypt
50/C4 Janûb Sînâ' (gov.),
 Egypt
67/K4 Jaya (peak), Indo.
67/K4 Jayapura, Indo.
68/D5 Jayapura, Indo.
101/E1 Jayton, Tx,US
55/M4 Japan
56/A4 Japan
25/H3 Jaywick, Eng,UK
52/D4 Jazâ'ir Farasân (isls.),
 SAr.
58/E5 Japan
77/P4 Jazâ'ir Farasân
 (arch.), SAr.
47/P6 Japan (sea), Asia
20/D4 Jebjerg, Den.
48/N5 Japan (sea), Asia
27/L4 Jedlicze, Pol.
27/L5 Japan (sea), Asia
27/J3 Jędrzejów, Pol.
55/M4 Japan (sea), Asia
26/F7 Jeetze (riv.), Ger.
55/M4 Japanese Alps (mts.),
 Japan
86/E4 Jefferson (riv.), Mt,US
57/E3 Japanese Alps
 (range), Japan
90/C4 Jefferson (peak),
 Or,US
57/E2 Japanese Alps Nat'l
 Park, Japan
93/H4 Jefferson, Tx,US
105/C2 Japurá (riv.), Braz.
106/E4 Japurá (riv.), Braz.
99/B2 Jefferson (co.),
 Wi,US
103/G5 Jaqué, Pan.
104/D3 Jarabacoa, DRep.
99/N14 Jefferson (co.), Wi,US
50/D2 Jarâbulus, Syria
89/H4 Jefferson City (cap.),
 Mo,US
34/C2 Jaraíz de la Vera, Sp.
34/C2 Jaramillo, Arg.
93/K3 Jefferson City, Mo,US
35/N9 Jarama (riv.), Sp.
96/F2 Jefferson City, Mo,US
34/C2 Jarandilla de la Vera,
 Sp.
94/C4 Jeffersonville, In,US
101/F4 Jalpan, Mex.
97/G2 Jeffersonville, In,US
64/D2 Jorânwâla, Pak.
90/G5 Jeffrey City, Wy,US
49/D3 Jarash, Pol.
92/F2 Jeffrey City, Wy,US
76/H1 Jarbah (isl.), Tun.
36/D2 Jegenstorf, Swi.
109/E2 Jardín América, Arg.
27/J3 Jēkabpils, Lat.
77/K2 Jâlû, Libya
42/E4 Jēkabpils, Lat.
103/G1 Jardines de la Reina
 (arch.), Cuba
27/J3 Jelcz-Laskowice,
 Pol.
108/B2 Jardinópolis, Braz.
27/H3 Jelenia Góra, Pol.
54/D2 Jargalant, Mong.
27/H3 Jelenia Góra (prov.),
 Pol.
105/D2 Jari (riv.), Braz.
62/E2 Jelep (pass), China
107/H3 Jari (riv.), Braz.
18/F3 Jelgava, Lat.
62/E2 Jarídih, India
20/G4 Jelgava, Lat.
76/H1 Jarjîs, Tun.
42/D4 Jelgava, Lat.
27/G2 Jarmen, Ger.
46/C4 Jelgava, Lat.
31/E5 Jarny, Fr.
40/C1 Jelka, Slvk.
27/J3 Jarocin, Pol.
30/C3 Jemappes, Belg.
27/H3 Jaroměř, Czh.
66/D5 Jember, Indo.
33/L1 Jaroměř, Czh.
92/F4 Jemez Pueblo,
 NM,US
44/B2 Jarosław, Pol.
27/M3 Jarosław, Pol.
96/B3 Jemez Pueblo,
 NM,US
23/G2 Jarrow, Eng,UK
54/E2 Jeminay, China
55/J3 Jarud Qi, China
67/K4 Jempang (riv.), Indo.
59/E1 Jarud Qi, China
50/C5 Jemsa, Egypt
20/H4 Järva-Jaani, Est.
52/B3 Jemsa, Egypt
42/E4 Järva-Jaani, Est.
31/F8 Jarville-la-
 Malgrange, Fr.
93/J3 Jena, La,US
69/J5 Jarvis (isl.), PacUS
96/F3 Jena, La,US
51/J3 Jâsk, Iran
33/J3 Jenbach, Aus.
27/K3 Jasło, Pol.
27/G6 Jeneponto, Indo.
44/B2 Jasło, Pol.
37/G2 Jengen, Ger.
90/D2 Jasper, Ab,Can
98/E5 Jenkintown, Pa,US
86/E3 Jasper, Ab,Can
40/D3 Jennersdorf, Aus.
89/J5 Jasper, Al,US
93/J3 Jennings, La,US
97/G3 Jasper, Al,US
96/F2 Jennings, La,US
89/J5 Jasper, Fl,US
86/F2 Jenny Lind (isl.),
 NW,Can
97/H4 Jasper, Fl,US
87/H2 Jens Muck (isl.),
 NW,Can
97/G2 Jasper, In,US

89/H5 Jasper, Tx,US
96/E4 Jasper, Tx,US
90/D2 Jasper Nat'l Park, Ab,
 BC,Can
86/E3 Jasper Nat'l Park,
 Ab,Can
62/E2 Jaspur, India
33/L4 Jastrebarsko, Cro.
40/B3 Jastrebarsko, Cro.
27/J2 Jastrowie, Pol.
44/A2 Jastrzębie Zdroj, Pol.
27/L5 Jászapáti, Hun.
27/L5 Jászapáti, Hun.
40/D2 Jászárokszállás, Hun.
27/K5 Jászberény, Hun.
40/A3 Jászberény, Hun.
40/E2 Jászladány, Hun.
27/L5 Jász-Nagykun-
 Szolnok (co.), Hun.
40/E2 Jász-Nagykun-
 Szolnok (co.), Hun.
107/M7 Jataí, Braz.
108/B1 Jataí, Braz.
106/G4 Jatapu (riv.), Braz.
102/D2 Jatate (riv.), Mex.
53/J4 Jâti, Pak.
62/A3 Jâti, Pak.
103/G1 Jatibonico, Cuba
35/E3 Játiva, Sp.
106/F4 Jaú (riv.), Braz.
107/J8 Jaú, Braz.
108/B2 Jaú, Braz.
109/G1 Jaú, Braz.
106/E4 Jauaperi (riv.), Braz.
107/H4 Jauaru (mts.), Braz.
106/F3 Jaua Sarisariñama
 Nat'l Park, Ven.
64/B1 Jauharābād, Pak.
106/C6 Jauja, Peru
101/F4 Jaumave, Mex.
32/D3 Jaunay-Clan, Fr.
33/G3 Jaunpass (pass), Swi.
36/D4 Jaunpass (pass), Swi.
48/K10 Java (isl.), Indo.
48/K10 Java (isl.), Indo.
66/C5 Java (sea), Indo.
66/D5 Java (sea), Indo.
66/C5 Java (sea), Indo.
106/D5 Javari (riv.), Braz.
35/F3 Jávea, Sp.
40/D1 Javorio (peak), Slvk.
77/Q7 Jawhar (Giohar),
 Som.
27/J3 Jawor, Pol.
67/K4 Jaya (peak), Indo.
67/K4 Jayapura, Indo.
68/D5 Jayapura, Indo.
101/E1 Jayton, Tx,US
93/G4 Jayton, Tx,US
96/C3 Jayton, Tx,US
25/H3 Jaywick, Eng,UK
52/D4 Jazâ'ir Farasân (isls.),
 SAr.
77/P4 Jazâ'ir Farasân
 (arch.), SAr.
20/D4 Jebjerg, Den.
27/L4 Jedlicze, Pol.
27/J3 Jędrzejów, Pol.
88/D2 Jefferson (riv.), Mt,US
86/E4 Jefferson (riv.), Mt,US
90/C4 Jefferson (peak),
 Or,US
93/H4 Jefferson, Tx,US
99/B2 Jefferson (co.),
 Wi,US
99/N14 Jefferson (co.), Wi,US
89/H4 Jefferson City (cap.),
 Mo,US
93/K3 Jefferson City, Mo,US
96/F2 Jefferson City, Mo,US
94/C4 Jeffersonville, In,US
97/G2 Jeffersonville, In,US
90/G5 Jeffrey City, Wy,US
90/G5 Jeffrey City, Wy,US
36/D2 Jegenstorf, Swi.
49/D2 Jēkabpils, Lat.
42/E4 Jēkabpils, Lat.
27/J3 Jelcz-Laskowice,
 Pol.
27/H3 Jelenia Góra, Pol.
27/H3 Jelenia Góra (prov.),
 Pol.
62/E2 Jelep (pass), China
18/F3 Jelgava, Lat.
20/G4 Jelgava, Lat.
42/D4 Jelgava, Lat.
46/C4 Jelgava, Lat.
40/C1 Jelka, Slvk.
30/C3 Jemappes, Belg.
66/D5 Jember, Indo.
92/F4 Jemez Pueblo,
 NM,US
96/B3 Jemez Pueblo,
 NM,US
54/E2 Jeminay, China
67/K4 Jempang (riv.), Indo.
50/C5 Jemsa, Egypt
52/B3 Jemsa, Egypt
28/F3 Jena, Ger.
93/J3 Jena, La,US
96/F3 Jena, La,US
37/J4 Jenaz, Swi.
27/G6 Jeneponto, Indo.
37/G2 Jengen, Ger.
98/E5 Jenkintown, Pa,US
40/D3 Jennersdorf, Aus.
93/J3 Jennings, La,US
96/F2 Jennings, La,US
86/F2 Jenny Lind (isl.),
 NW,Can
87/H2 Jens Muck (isl.),
 NW,Can

Jequi – Kaise

107/K6 Jequié, Braz.
105/E4 Jequitinhonha (riv.), Braz.
107/K7 Jequitinhonha, Braz.
107/K7 Jequitinhonha (riv.), Braz.
75/N13 Jerada, Mor.
101/E4 Jerécuaro, Mex.
103/H2 Jérémie, Haiti
100/E4 Jerez, Mex.
88/F7 Jerez, Mex.
18/C5 Jerez de la Frontera, Sp.
34/B4 Jerez de la Frontera, Sp.
34/B3 Jerez de los Caballeros, Sp.
72/B3 Jericho, Austl.
49/D4 Jericho (Arīḩā), WBnk.
49/G8 Jericho (Arīḩā), WBnk.
73/C2 Jerilderie, Austl.
101/F1 Jermyn, Tx,US
88/D3 Jerome, Id,US
90/E5 Jerome, Id,US
92/D2 Jerome, Id,US
32/B2 Jersey (isl.), Chl,UK
98/F5 Jersey City, NJ,US
93/K3 Jerseyville, Il,US
94/B4 Jerseyville, Il,US
97/F2 Jerseyville, Il,US
63/H6 Jerteh, Malay.
49/D4 Jerusalem (dist.), Isr.
49/F8 Jerusalem (dist.), Isr.
49/G8 Jerusalem (cap.), Isr.
50/C4 Jerusalem (cap.), Isr.
52/B2 Jerusalem (cap.), Isr.
77/N1 Jerusalem (cap.), Isr.
49/G8 Jerusalem Walls Nat'l Park, Isr.
49/D4 Jerusalem (Yerushalayim) (cap.), Isr.
90/C3 Jervis (inlet), BC,Can
71/J7 Jervis Bay, Austl.
73/D2 Jervis Bay, Austl.
38/A3 Jerzu, It.
29/G6 Jesberg, Ger.
33/L3 Jesenice, Slov.
40/B2 Jesenice, Slov.
33/K5 Jesi, It.
62/E3 Jessore, Bang.
89/K5 Jesup, Ga,US
97/H4 Jesup, Ga,US
95/N6 Jésus (isl.), Qu,Can
101/G5 Jesús Carranza, Mex.
109/D3 Jesús María, Arg.
103/J1 Jesús Menéndez, Cuba
78/A4 Jeta (isl.), GBis.
93/H3 Jetmore, Ks,US
96/D2 Jetmore, Ks,US
53/K4 Jetpur, India
62/B3 Jetpur, India
37/G1 Jettingen-Scheppach, Ger.
37/H1 Jetzendorf, Ger.
30/D3 Jeumont, Fr.
26/E1 Jevenstedt, Ger.
29/E1 Jever, Ger.
91/G5 Jewel Cave Nat'l Mon., SD,US
93/G2 Jewel Cave Nat'l Mon., SD,US
62/D4 Jeypore, India
39/F1 Jezerce (peak), Alb.
40/D4 Jezerce (peak), Alb.
27/G4 Jezerní Stěna (peak), Czh.
27/K2 Jeziorák (lake), Pol.
62/E3 Jhā Jhā, India
53/L4 Jhālawār, India
62/C3 Jhālawār, India
53/K2 Jhang Sadar, Pak.
64/B2 Jhang Sadar, Pak.
62/C2 Jhānsi, India
62/D3 Jhārsuguda, India
64/B1 Jhawāriān, Pak.
64/B1 Jhelum (riv.), India
53/K2 Jhelum, Pak.
53/K2 Jhelum (riv.), Pak.
64/B1 Jhelum, Pak.
64/B1 Jhelum (riv.), Pak.
64/B2 Jhumra, Pak.
54/D5 Ji (riv.), China
60/B1 Ji (riv.), China
59/L8 Jiading, China
62/E3 Jiāganj, India
63/K2 Jiahe, China
48/K6 Jialing (riv.), China
54/F5 Jialing (riv.), China
54/H5 Jialu (riv.), China
59/C4 Jialu (riv.), China
47/P5 Jiamusi, China
55/L2 Jiamusi, China
61/F4 Jian (riv.), China
61/G3 Ji'an, China
61/H3 Jian (riv.), China
68/A2 Ji'an, China
55/H3 Jianchang, China
59/D2 Jianchang, China
60/E2 Jiancheng, China
61/F4 Jiancheng, China
65/E1 Jianq (riv.), China
63/J2 Jiang'an, China
60/C3 Jiangao (mtn.), China
60/D4 Jiangcheng Hanizu Yizu Zizhixian, China
65/C1 Jiangcheng Hanizu Yizu Zizhixian, China
63/H3 Jiangcheng Hanizu Yizu Zizhixian (Jiangcheng), China
63/H3 Jiangcheng (Jiangcheng Hanizu Yizu Zizhixian), China
60/D3 Jiangchuan, China
63/H3 Jiangchuan, China
59/D4 Jiangdu, China
61/H1 Jiangdu, China
61/F3 Jianghua Yaozu Zizhixian, China
63/K3 Jianghua Yaozu Zizhixian, China
60/E2 Jiangjin, China
63/J2 Jiangjin, China
55/J4 Jiangjunshi, China
54/F5 Jiangkouzhen, China
59/C5 Jiangling, China
61/G2 Jiangling, China
61/G4 Jiangmen, China
63/K3 Jiangmen, China
59/D5 Jiangning, China
61/H2 Jiangning, China
59/D4 Jiangsu (prov.), China
59/L8 Jiangsu (prov.), China
61/J2 Jiangsu (prov.), China
59/D5 Jiangxi (prov.), China
61/G3 Jiangxi (prov.), China
59/B4 Jiang Xian, China
59/E5 Jiangyin, China
61/J2 Jiangyin, China
61/F3 Jiangyong, China
63/K2 Jiangyong, China
54/E5 Jiangyou, China
60/E2 Jiangyou, China
63/J2 Jianhe, China
59/D4 Jianhu, China
59/C5 Jianli, China
61/G2 Jianli, China
61/H3 Jian'ou, China
55/H3 Jianping, China
54/F5 Jianshi, China
59/B5 Jianshi, China
61/F2 Jianshi, China
60/D4 Jianshui, China
63/H3 Jianshui, China
61/H3 Jianyang, China
59/C3 Jiaocheng, China
55/K3 Jiaohe, China
61/J2 Jiaojiang, China
54/G4 Jiaokou, China
59/C3 Jiaokou, China
59/C3 Jiaolai (riv.), China
55/H4 Jiaonan, China
59/D4 Jiaonan, China
54/G4 Jiaozuo, China
59/C4 Jiaozuo, China
55/H5 Jiashan, China
59/D4 Jiashan, China
59/L9 Jiashan, China
54/G4 Jia Xian, China
59/B3 Jia Xian, China
59/D4 Jiaxiang, China
55/J5 Jiaxing, China
59/L9 Jiaxing, China
61/J2 Jiaxing, China
55/L2 Jiayin, China
59/C5 Jiayu, China
61/G2 Jiayu, China
54/D4 Jiayuguan, China
27/M5 Jibou, Rom.
41/F2 Jibou, Rom.
53/G4 Jibsh, Ra's (pt.), Oman
101/N8 Jicaro, Mex.
103/F5 Jicarón (isl.), Pan.
27/H3 Jičín, Czh.
33/L1 Jičín, Czh.
101/F5 Jico, Mex.
101/N7 Jico, Mex.
102/B2 Jico, Mex.
52/C4 Jiddah, SAr.
77/N3 Jiddah, SAr.
55/L2 Jidong, China
59/C4 Jieshou, China
54/G4 Jiexiu, China
59/B3 Jiexiu, China
61/H4 Jieyang, China
27/N1 Jieznas, Lith.
49/G8 Jifnā, WBnk.
103/G1 Jiguaní, Cuba
54/E5 Jigzhi, China
27/H4 Jihlava, Czh.
33/L2 Jihlava, Czh.
33/L2 Jihlava (riv.), Czh.
27/H4 Jihočeský (reg.), Czh.
33/L2 Jihočeský (reg.), Czh.
27/J4 Jihomoravský (reg.), Czh.
33/M2 Jihomoravský (reg.), Czh.
75/U17 Jijel, Alg.
75/U17 Jijel (gov.), Alg.
76/G1 Jijel, Alg.
41/H2 Jijia (riv.), Rom.
44/C3 Jijia (riv.), Rom.
77/P6 Jijiga, Eth.
35/E3 Jijona, Sp.
108/B2 Jilhá (res.), Braz.
27/J4 Jilhava (riv.), Czh.
54/B2 Jili (lake), China
77/P7 Jilib, Som.
47/N5 Jilin, China
55/K3 Jilin, China
58/D1 Jilin (prov.), China
59/F1 Jilin (prov.), China
55/J1 Jiliu (riv.), China
35/E2 Jiloca (riv.), Sp.
101/F5 Jilotepec de Abasolo, Mex.
101/K7 Jilotepec de Abasolo, Mex.
102/B2 Jilotepec de Abasolo, Mex.
77/N6 Jīma, Eth.
103/J2 Jimaní, DRep.
40/E3 Jimbolia, Rom.
72/D4 Jimboomba, Austl.
34/C4 Jimena de la Frontera, Sp.
100/D3 Jiménez, Mex.
101/E2 Jiménez, Mex.
96/B5 Jiménez, Mex
52/B5 Jimmēza, Sudan
59/E3 Jimo, China
54/B3 Jimsar, China
100/E3 Jimulco, Mex.
61/G2 Jin (riv.), China
61/H3 Jin (riv.), China
63/K2 Jin (riv.), China
55/H4 Jinan, China
59/D3 Jinan, China
54/E4 Jinchang, China
54/G4 Jincheng, China
59/C4 Jincheng, China
54/E5 Jinchuan, China
55/K3 Jinchuan, China
60/D2 Jinchuan, China
59/C3 Jinci Temple, China
53/L3 Jīnd, India
62/C2 Jīnd, India
73/D3 Jindabyne, Austl.
73/D3 Jindabyne (dam), Austl.
27/H4 Jindřichuv Hradec, Czh.
33/L2 Jindřichuv Hradec, Czh.
61/E2 Jinfo (mtn.), China
54/F5 Jing (riv.), China
59/B4 Jing (riv.), China
54/F4 Jingbian, China
59/B3 Jingbian, China
59/D5 Jingde, China
61/H2 Jingde, China
61/H2 Jingdezhen, China
68/A2 Jingdezhen, China
63/H3 Jingdong, China
61/G3 Jinggangshan, China
63/K2 Jinggangshan, China
63/H3 Jinggu, China
54/H4 Jinghai, China
59/D3 Jinghai, China
59/H7 Jinghai, China
61/H4 Jinghai, China
55/J4 Jinghaiwei, China
60/D4 Jinghong, China
63/H3 Jinghong, China
65/C1 Jinghong, China
59/E4 Jingjiang, China
61/J1 Jingjiang, China
54/G4 Jingle, China
59/B3 Jingle, China
54/G5 Jingmen, China
59/C5 Jingmen, China
61/G2 Jingmen, China
54/F4 Jingning, China
60/D3 Jingping (mts.), China
59/C5 Jingshan, China
61/G2 Jingshan, China
60/E4 Jingxi, China
63/J3 Jingxi, China
65/D1 Jingxi, China
55/H5 Jing Xian, China
59/D5 Jing Xian, China
61/F3 Jing Xian, China
61/H2 Jing Xian, China
63/J2 Jing Xian, China
55/K3 Jingyu, China
58/D1 Jingyu, China
54/E4 Jingyuan, China
59/D4 Jinhu, China
61/H2 Jinhua, China
54/G3 Jining, China
54/H4 Jining, China
59/C2 Jining, China
59/D4 Jining, China
77/M7 Jinja, Ugan.
63/H2 Jinkouhe, China
61/H3 Jinmen (isl.), China
102/E3 Jinotega, Nic.
102/E4 Jinotepe, Nic.
61/D4 Jinping, China
61/F3 Jinping, China
63/J2 Jinping, China
65/C1 Jinping, China
54/F5 Jinqian (riv.), China
59/B4 Jinqian (riv.), China
48/J7 Jinsha (riv.), China
54/D5 Jinsha (riv.), China
60/D3 Jinsha (riv.), China
63/G2 Jinsha (riv.), China
63/J2 Jinsha, China
55/J5 Jinshan, China
59/L9 Jinshan, China
61/J2 Jinshan, China
61/J2 Jinshanwei, China
60/D3 Jinsha (Yangtze) (riv.), China
63/K2 Jinshi, China
59/D5 Jintan, China
61/H2 Jintan, China
53/L5 Jintūr, India
62/C4 Jintūr, India
55/J3 Jinxi, China
59/E2 Jinxi, China
61/H3 Jinxi, China
59/C3 Jin Xian, China
59/D4 Jinxiang, China
63/K3 Jinxiu Yaozu Zizhixian, China
61/J2 Jinyun, China
54/H5 Jinzhai, China
59/C5 Jinzhai, China
61/G2 Jinzhai, China
47/N5 Jinzhou, China
55/J3 Jinzhou, China
58/A3 Jinzhou (bay), China
59/E2 Jinzhou, China
59/E3 Jinzhou (bay), China
106/F5 Jiparaná (riv.), Braz.
106/F6 Ji-Paraná, Braz.
106/B4 Jipijapa, Ecu.
100/E5 Jiquilpan de Juárez, Mex.
101/Q9 Jiquipilco, Mex.
52/B3 Jirgā, Egypt
77/M2 Jirgā, Egypt
53/G3 Jīroft, Iran
59/B4 Jishan, China
61/F2 Jishou, China
63/J2 Jishou, China
49/E2 Jisr ash Shughūr, Syria
50/D3 Jisr ash Shughūr, Syria
52/C1 Jisr ash Shughūr, Syria
65/C5 Jitra, Malay.
41/F4 Jiu (riv.), Rom.
44/B3 Jiu (riv.), Rom.
60/D2 Jiuding (mtn.), China
61/G2 Jiugong (mts.), China
61/H2 Jiuhua (mtn.), China
59/D5 Jiuhua Shan (mtn.), China
59/C5 Jiujiang, China
61/G2 Jiujiang, China
61/G2 Jiuling (mts.), China
60/D2 Jiulong, China
63/H2 Jiulong, China
55/K3 Jiutai, China
61/E3 Jiuwan (mts.), China
47/P5 Jixi, China
55/L2 Jixi, China
61/H2 Jixi, China
55/H3 Ji Xian, China
55/L2 Jixian, China
59/C4 Ji Xian, China
59/D2 Ji Xian, China
59/H6 Ji Xian, China
59/D3 Jiyang, China
59/C4 Jiyuan, China
52/D5 Jīzān, SAr.
77/P4 Jīzān, SAr.
59/C3 Jize, China
27/H3 Jizera (riv.), Czh.
33/L1 Jizera (riv.), Czh.
52/C3 Jizl, Wādī al (dry riv.), SAr.
56/C3 Jizō-zaki (pt.), Japan
60/D3 Jizu (mtn.), China
52/F5 Jiz', Wādī al (dry riv.), Yem.
108/B3 Joaçaba, Braz.
101/N8 Joachín, Mex.
108/D1 João Monlevade, Braz.
107/M5 João Pessoa, Braz.
107/J7 João Pinheiro, Braz.
108/C1 João Pinheiro, Braz.
109/D2 Joaquín V. González, Arg.
103/G1 Jobabo, Cuba
102/E3 Jocón, Hon.
34/D4 Jódar, Sp.
53/K3 Jodhpur, India
62/B2 Jodhpur, India
31/D2 Jodoigne, Belg.
18/F2 Joensuu, Fin.
20/J3 Joensuu, Fin.
42/F3 Joensuu, Fin.
46/C3 Joensuu, Fin.
55/M4 Jōetsu, Japan
57/F2 Jōetsu, Japan
31/F5 Joeuf, Fr.
20/H4 Jōgeva, Est.
42/E4 Jōgeva, Est.
53/G3 Joghdān, Iran
80/E2 Johannesburg, SAfr.
80/Q13 Johannesburg, SAfr.
82/E6 Johannesburg, SAfr.
92/C4 Johannesburg, Ca,US
90/C4 John Day (riv.), Or,US
86/D4 John Day (riv.), Or,US
88/B3 John Day (riv.), Or,US
88/C3 John Day, Or,US
90/D4 John Day, Or,US
90/C4 John Day Fossil Beds Nat'l Mon., Or,US
90/D4 John Day, Middle Fork (riv.), Or,US
90/D4 John Day, North Fork (riv.), Or,US
94/E4 John H. Kerr (dam), Va,US
97/J2 John H. Kerr (dam), Va,US
95/S9 Johnson (cr.), NY,US
89/K4 Johnson City, Tn,US
94/D4 Johnson City, Tn,US
97/H2 Johnson City, Tn,US
101/F2 Johnson City, Tx,US
93/H5 Johnson City, Tx,US
96/D4 Johnson City, Tx,US
93/G3 Johnson (Johnson City), Ks,US
96/C2 Johnson (Johnson City), Ks,US
85/M3 Johnsons Crossing, Yk,Can
70/C6 Johnston (lake), Austl.
69/J3 Johnston (atoll), PacUS
24/B3 Johnston, Wal,UK
89/L3 Johnstown, Pa,US
94/E3 Johnstown, Pa,US
98/C3 John Wayne/Orange Co. (int'l arpt.), Ca,US
66/B3 Johor Baharu, Malay.
26/B5 Joigny, Fr.
32/E3 Joigny, Fr.
108/B3 Joinvile, Braz.
109/G2 Joinvile, Braz.
83/W Joinville (isl.), Ant.
26/C4 Joinville, Fr.
32/F2 Joinville, Fr.
36/B1 Joinville, Fr.
101/F5 Jojutla, Mex.
102/B2 Jojutla, Mex.
101/K8 Jojutla de Juárez, Mex.
77/M6 Jokau, Sudan
20/F2 Jokkmokk, Swe.
42/C2 Jokkmokk, Swe.
20/P6 Jökulsargljufur Nat'l Park, Ice.
89/J3 Joliet, Il,US
91/L5 Joliet, Il,US
93/K2 Joliet, Il,US
94/B3 Joliet, Il,US
99/P16 Joliet, Il,US
87/J4 Joliette, Qu,Can
89/M2 Joliette, Qu,Can
94/F2 Joliette, Qu,Can
101/F2 Jollyville, Tx,US
93/H5 Jollyville, Tx,US
96/D4 Jollyville, Tx,US
67/F2 Jolo, Phil.
67/F2 Jolo (isl.), Phil.
66/D5 Jombang, Indo.
54/D5 Jomda, China
60/C2 Jomda, China
33/H3 Jona, Swi.
37/E3 Jona, Swi.
101/L8 Jonacatepec
27/N1 Jonava, Lith.
42/E5 Jonava, Lith.
30/C5 Jonchery-sur-Vesle, Fr.
84/J2 Jones (sound), Can.
87/S7 Jones (sound), NW,Can
89/H4 Jonesboro, Ar,US
93/K4 Jonesboro, Ar,US
97/F3 Jonesboro, Ar,US
89/H5 Jonesboro, La,US
93/J4 Jonesboro, La,US
96/E3 Jonesboro, La,US
26/D2 Jonesborough, NI,UK
18/E3 Jönköping, Swe.
20/E4 Jönköping, Swe.
20/E4 Jönköping (co.), Swe.
46/B4 Jönköping, Swe.
87/J4 Jonquière, Qu,Can
89/M2 Jonquière, Qu,Can
95/G1 Jonquière, Qu,Can
101/G5 Jonuta, Mex.
102/C2 Jonuta, Mex.
32/C4 Jonzac, Fr.
84/H6 Joplin, US
89/H4 Joplin, Mo,US
93/J3 Joplin, Mo,US
96/E2 Joplin, Mo,US
98/K7 Joppatowne (Joppa), Md,US
48/C6 Jordan
49/E4 Jordan
50/D4 Jordan
52/C2 Jordan
77/N1 Jordan
49/D4 Jordan (riv.), Asia
95/R9 Jordan, On,Can
52/C2 Jordan (riv.), Jor.
90/G4 Jordan, Mt,US
92/E2 Jordan (riv.), Ut,US
95/R9 Jordan Station, On,Can
90/D5 Jordan Valley, Or,US
92/C2 Jordan Valley, Or,US
60/B3 Jorhāt, India
63/F2 Jorhāt, India
29/G1 Jork, Ger.
96/B3 Jornada del Muerto (val.), NM,US
76/G6 Jos, Nga.
76/G6 Jos (plat.), Nga.
79/H4 Jos (plat.), Nga.
67/G2 Jose Abad Santos, Phil.
108/B2 José Bonifacio, Braz.
101/N7 José Cardel, Mex.
109/B5 José de San Martín, Arg.
70/D2 Joseph Bonaparte (gulf), Austl.
57/F2 Joshin-Etsu Kogen Nat'l Park, Japan
92/D4 Joshua Tree Nat'l Mon., Ca,US
20/C3 Jotunheimen Nat'l Park, Nor.
32/C2 Jouanne (riv.), Fr.
30/C6 Jouarre, Fr.
32/D3 Joué-lès-Tours, Fr.
72/B2 Jourama Falls Nat'l Park, Austl.
101/F2 Jourdanton, Tx,US
93/H5 Jourdanton, Tx,US
96/D4 Jourdanton, Tx,US
26/C2 Joure, Neth.
28/C3 Joure, Neth.
20/J3 Joutseno, Fin.
42/F3 Joutseno, Fin.
42/E2 Joutsijärvi, Fin.
36/C4 Joux (lake), Fr.
19/S10 Jouy-en-Josas, Fr.
19/S9 Jouy-le-Moutier, Fr.
30/C6 Jouy-sur-Morin, Fr.
103/F1 Jovellanos, Cuba
51/J2 Joveyn (riv.), Iran
52/G1 Joveyn (riv.), Iran
60/B3 Jowai, India
63/F2 Jowai, India
53/H1 Jow Khvāh, Iran
85/M3 Joy (mtn.), Yk,Can
57/L10 Jōyō, Japan
78/A2 Jreïda, Mrta.
54/G5 Ju (riv.), China
59/B5 Ju (riv.), China
61/F2 Ju (riv.), China
100/E3 Juan Aldama, Mex.
59/C4 Juancheng, China
90/B3 Juan de Fuca (str.), Can., US
86/D4 Juan de Fuca (strait), BC,Can, Wa,US
104/D3 Juan de Herrera, DRep.
81/G7 Juan de Nova, Reun.
82/J10 Juan de Nova (isl.), Reun.
105/A6 Juan Fernández (isls.), Chile
104/F5 Juangriego, Ven.
106/C5 Juanjuí, Peru
100/C2 Juarez, Mex.
101/E3 Juárez, Mex.
92/D5 Juárez (range), Mex
92/E5 Juarez, Mex
107/K5 Juazeiro, Braz.
107/K5 Juazeiro do Norte, Braz.
77/M7 Juba, Sudan
77/P7 Jubba (riv.), Som.
52/D3 Jubbah, SAr.
74/G4 Jubba, Webi (riv.), Eth., Som.
26/E1 Jübek, Ger.
35/Y17 Juby (cape), Mor.
74/A2 Juby (cape), Mor.
76/C2 Juby (cape), Mor.
18/C5 Júcar (riv.), Sp.
34/D3 Júcar (riv.), Sp.
28/D6 Jüchen, Ger.
31/F1 Jüchen, Ger.
100/E4 Juchipila, Mex.
101/N7 Juchique de Ferrer, Mex.
102/C2 Juchitán, Mex.
49/G8 Judaea (reg.), WBnk.
103/E4 Judas (pt.), CR
33/L3 Judenburg, Aus.
40/B2 Judenburg, Aus.
90/F4 Judith (riv.), Mt,US
61/F3 Juicai (mtn.), China
103/E3 Juigalpa, Nic.
19/U9 Juilly, Fr.
61/H2 Juilong (mtn.), China
32/E2 Juine (riv.), Fr.
26/D2 Juist, Ger.
28/D1 Juist (isl.), Ger.
28/E1 Juist, Ger.
107/K8 Juiz de Fora, Braz.
108/D2 Juiz de Fora, Braz.
109/H1 Juiz de Fora, Braz.
36/B5 Jujurieux, Fr.
91/H5 Julesburg, Co,US
93/G2 Julesburg, Co,US
106/E7 Juli, Peru
106/D7 Juliaca, Peru
70/G4 Julia Creek, Austl.
72/A3 Julia Creek, Austl.
33/K3 Julian Alps (mts.), It., Slov.
31/F2 Jülich, Ger.
37/F5 Julierpass (pass)
100/D2 Julimes, Mex.
53/L2 Jullundur, India
64/C2 Jullundur, India
59/C3 Julu, China
54/H4 Juma (riv.), China
59/C3 Juma (riv.), China
59/G7 Juma (riv.), China
34/E3 Jumilla, Sp.
75/W17 Jūmīn (riv.), Tun.
62/D2 Jumla, Nepal
29/E2 Jümme (riv.), Ger.
61/G2 Jun (mtn.), China
53/K4 Junāgadh, India
62/B3 Junāgadh, India
55/H4 Junan, China
59/D4 Junan, China
88/G5 Junction, Tx,US
93/H5 Junction, Tx,US
96/D4 Junction, Tx,US
92/D3 Junction, Ut,US
89/G4 Junction City, Ks,US
93/H3 Junction City, Ks,US
96/D2 Junction City, Ks,US
90/C4 Junction City, Or,US
70/G4 Jundah, Austl.
107/J8 Jundiaí, Braz.
108/C2 Jundiaí, Braz.
109/G1 Jundiaí, Braz.
59/H6 Jundu (mts.), China
75/W17 Jundūbah, Tun.
75/W17 Jundūbah (gov.), Tun.
85/M4 Juneau (cap.), Ak,US
86/C3 Juneau (cap.), Ak,US
35/F2 Juneda, Sp.
73/C2 Junee, Austl.
54/G4 Jungar Qi, China
59/B2 Jungar Qi, China
33/G3 Jungfrau (peak), Swi.
36/D4 Jungfrau (peak), Swi.
36/D4 Jungfraujoch, Swi.
31/F4 Junglinster, Lux.
94/E3 Juniata (riv.), Pa,US
39/G1 Junik, Yugo.
40/E4 Junik, Yugo.
109/D3 Junín, Arg.
106/C6 Junín, Peru
109/B4 Junín de los Andes, Arg.
30/D5 Juniville, Fr.
59/C3 Junji Guan (pass), China
60/E2 Junlian, China
63/H2 Junlian, China
97/H5 Juno Beach, Fl,US
108/B2 Junqueirópolis, Braz.
20/F3 Junsele, Swe.
42/C3 Junsele, Swe.
108/E1 Juparaná (lake), Braz.
95/J1 Jupiter (riv.), Qu,Can
97/H5 Jupiter, Fl,US
99/A2 Jupiter (mt.), Wa,US
108/C3 Juquiá, Braz.
77/L6 Jur (riv.), Sudan
21/C3 Jura (isl.), Sc,UK
36/C4 Jura (mts.), Eur.
32/F3 Jura (mts.), Fr.
36/B4 Jura (dept.), Fr.
36/D3 Jura (canton), Swi.
103/G5 Juradó, Col.
32/C5 Jurançon, Fr.
35/E1 Jurançon, Fr.
27/M1 Jurbarkas, Lith.
42/D5 Jurbarkas, Lith.
30/C2 Jurbise, Belg.
22/D3 Jurby Head (pt.), IM,UK
20/G4 Jūrmala, Lat.
42/D4 Jūrmala, Lat.
40/C1 Jur pri Bratislave, Slvk.
105/C3 Juruá (riv.), Braz.
106/E4 Juruá (riv.), Braz.
105/D4 Juruena (riv.), Braz.
106/G6 Juruena (riv.), Braz.
107/G4 Juruti, Braz.
20/G3 Jurva, Fin.
42/D3 Jurva, Fin.
63/J3 Jushi, China
57/M9 Jushiyama, Japan
85/M5 Juskatla, BC,Can
36/B2 Jussey, Fr.
30/C4 Jussy, Fr.
36/C5 Jussy, Swi.
106/E4 Jutaí (riv.), Braz.
106/E5 Jutaí, Braz.
102/D3 Jutiapa, Guat.
102/E3 Juticalpa, Hon.
20/D4 Jutland (pen.), Den.
20/H3 Juva, Fin.
42/E3 Juva, Fin.
103/F1 Juventud (isl.), Cuba
84/J7 Juventud (isl.), Cuba
89/K7 Juventud (isl.), Cuba
19/T10 Juvisy-sur-Orge, Fr.
55/H4 Ju Xian, China
59/D4 Ju Xian, China
59/D4 Juye, China
59/C5 Juzhang (riv.), China
40/E4 Južna Morava (riv.), Yugo.
80/D2 Jwaneng, Bots.
26/F1 Jyderup, Den.
18/F2 Jyväskylä, Fin.
20/H3 Jyväskylä, Fin.
42/E3 Jyväskylä, Fin.
46/C3 Jyväskylä, Fin.

K

53/L1 K2 (Godwin Austen) (peak), China, Pak.
48/G6 K2 (Godwin Austen) (mtn.), China, Pak.
76/F5 Ka (riv.), Nga.
58/C3 Ka (isl.), NKor.
88/W12 Kaaawa, Hi,US
77/M7 Kaabong, Ugan.
46/F6 Kaakhka, Trkm.
88/S10 Kaala (peak), Hi,US
88/V12 Kaala (peak), Hi,US
80/C3 Kaap (plat.), SAfr.
42/D3 Kaarina, Fin.
28/D6 Kaarst, Ger.
31/F1 Kaarst, Ger.
40/E2 Kaba, Hun.
67/J5 Kaba, Indo.
67/F5 Kabaena (isl.), Indo.
68/B5 Kabaena (isl.), Indo.
101/H4 Kabah (ruins), Mex.
102/D1 Kabah (ruins), Mex.
76/C6 Kabala, SLeo.
78/C4 Kabala, SLeo.
77/L8 Kabale, Ugan.
82/E1 Kabale, Ugan.
77/M7 Kabalega (fall, falls), Ugan.
77/M7 Kabalega Nat'l Park, Ugan.
82/E2 Kabalo, Zaire
82/E2 Kabamba (lake), Zaire
67/F2 Kabankalan, Phil.
45/G4 Kabardin-Balkar Aut. Rep., Rus.
64/F3 Kabbani (riv.), India
94/C1 Kabinakagani (lake), On,Can
82/D2 Kabinda, Zaire
75/V17 Kabir (riv.), Alg.
50/F3 Kabīr Kūh (mts.), Syria
64/A2 Kabīrwāla, Pak.
38/A5 Kabīyah (lag.), Tun.
41/H4 Kableshkovo, Bul.
53/J2 Kābol (Kābul) (cap.), Afg.
82/D3 Kabompo (riv.), Zam.
82/E2 Kabongo, Zaire
48/F6 Kābul (cap.), Afg.
53/J2 Kabul (riv.), Afg.
53/J2 Kābul (Kābol) (cap.), Afg.
67/G3 Kaburuang (isl.), Indo.
52/B5 Kabūshīyah, Sudan
82/E3 Kabwe, Zam.
39/G1 Kačanik, Yugo.
40/E4 Kačanik, Yugo.
27/M1 Kačergine, Lith.
42/D5 Kačergine, Lith.
82/F3 Kachalola, Zam.
85/H4 Kachemak, Ak,US
85/H4 Kachemak (bay), Ak,US
60/C3 Kachin (state), Burma
63/G2 Kachin (state), Burma
46/H4 Kachiry, Kaz.
47/L4 Kachug, Rus.
51/F1 Kaçkar (peak), Turk.
62/C6 Kadaianallur, India
64/F4 Kadaianallur, India
63/G5 Kadan (isl.), Burma
65/B3 Kadan (isl.), Burma
27/G3 Kadaň, Czh.
33/K1 Kadaň, Czh.
68/G6 Kadavu (isl.), Fiji
76/J7 Kadeï (riv.), CAfr., Congo
41/H5 Kadıköy, Turk.
51/N7 Kadıköy, Turk.
70/F6 Kadina, Austl.
50/C2 Kadınhanı, Turk.
79/E3 Kadiogo (prov.), Burk.
76/D5 Kadiolo, Mali
78/D4 Kadiolo, Mali
62/C5 Kadiri, India
50/D2 Kadirli, Turk.
52/C1 Kadirli, Turk.
50/C2 Kadışehri, Turk.
91/H5 Kadoka, SD,US
93/G2 Kadoka, SD,US
57/L10 Kadoma, Japan
82/E4 Kadoma, Zim.
63/G4 Kadōnkani, Burma
76/G5 Kaduna, Nga.
76/G5 Kaduna (riv.), Nga.
79/G4 Kaduna, Nga.
79/G4 Kaduna (riv.), Nga.
79/G4 Kaduna (state), Nga.
77/L5 Kāduqli, Sudan
58/C3 Kaech'ŏn, NKor.
76/C4 Kaédi, Mrta.
78/B2 Kaédi, Mrta.
76/H5 Kaélé, Camr.
88/V12 Kaena (pt.), Hi,US
65/C2 Kaeng Khlo, Thai.
65/B3 Kaeng Krachan Nat'l Park, Thai.
47/N6 Kaesŏng, NKor.
55/K4 Kaesŏng, NKor.
58/D3 Kaesŏng, NKor.
58/D4 Kaesŏng-Si, NKor.
52/C2 Kāf, SAr.
19/H5 Kafan, Arm.
45/H5 Kafan, Arm.
46/E6 Kafan, Arm.
51/F2 Kafan, Arm.
76/G6 Kafanchan, Nga.
53/J2 Kafar Jar Ghar (mts.), Afg.
80/D4 Kaffraria (reg.), SAfr.
76/B5 Kaffrine, Sen.
78/B3 Kaffrine, Sen.
77/K6 Kafia Kingi, Sudan
39/J3 Kafirévs, Akra (cape), Gre.
49/B4 Kafr ad Dawwār, Egypt
50/B4 Kafr ad Dawwār, Egypt
52/B2 Kafr ad Dawwār, Egypt
49/B4 Kafr Ash Shaykh (gov.), Egypt
49/B4 Kafr ash Shaykh, Egypt
50/B4 Kafr ash Shaykh (gov.), Egypt
52/B2 Kafr ash Shaykh, Egypt
49/B4 Kafr az Zayyāt, Egypt
49/G7 Kafr Qari', Isr.
49/F7 Kafr Qāsim, Isr.
82/E4 Kafue, Zam.
82/E4 Kafue (riv.), Zam.
82/E4 Kafue Nat'l Park, Zam.
56/E2 Kaga, Japan
76/J6 Kaga Bandoro, CAfr.
46/G6 Kagan, Uzb.
56/D3 Kagawa (pref.), Japan
41/J5 Kağıthane, Turk.
44/D4 Kağıthane, Turk.
50/B1 Kağıthane, Turk.
51/M6 Kâğithane, Turk.
51/M6 Kâğithane (riv.), Turk.
45/G4 Kağızman, Turk.
51/E1 Kağızman, Turk.
55/L5 Kagoshima, Japan
56/B5 Kagoshima, Japan
56/B5 Kagoshima (bay), Japan
56/B5 Kagoshima (pref.), Japan
18/F4 Kagul, Mol.
41/J3 Kagul, Mol.
44/D3 Kagul, Mol.
88/W13 Kahaluu, Hi,US
82/F1 Kahama, Tanz.
88/W12 Kahana, Hi,US
66/D4 Kahayan (riv.), Indo.
82/C2 Kahemba, Zaire
88/T10 Kahiu (pt.), Hi,US
54/D1 Kahmsara (riv.), Rus.
64/C2 Kāhna, Pak.
53/G3 Kahnūj, Iran
91/L5 Kahoka, Mo,US
93/K2 Kahoka, Mo,US
96/F1 Kahoka, Mo,US
69/K2 Kahoolawe (isl.), Hi.,US
88/T10 Kahoolawe (isl.), Hi,US
20/G1 Kahperusvaara (peak), Fin.
42/D1 Kahperusvaara (peak), Fin.
50/D2 Kahraman Maraş (prov.), Turk.
50/D2 Kahramanmaraş, Turk.
53/K3 Kahror Pakka, Pak.
50/D2 Kâhta, Turk.
88/T10 Kahuku, Hi,US
88/T10 Kahuku (pt.), Hi,US
88/W12 Kahuku, Hi,US
88/W12 Kahuku (pt.), Hi,US
88/T10 Kahului, Hi,US
82/E1 Kahuzi-Biega Nat'l Park, Zaire
67/H5 Kai (isls.), Indo.
68/C5 Kai (isls.), Indo.
71/R11 Kaiapoi, N.Z.
92/D3 Kaibab (plat.), Az,US
57/L9 Kaibara, Japan
67/H5 Kai Besar (isl.), Indo.
54/G5 Kaifeng, China
59/C4 Kaifeng, China
56/D4 Kaifu, Japan
61/E2 Kaijiang, China
67/H5 Kai Kecil (isl.), Indo.
71/R10 Kaikohe, N.Z.
71/R11 Kaikoura, N.Z.
60/B3 Kailāshahar, India
61/E3 Kaili, China
63/J2 Kaili, China
55/J3 Kailu, China
59/E2 Kailu, China
88/T10 Kailua, Hi,US
88/U11 Kailua, Hi,US
88/W13 Kailua, Hi,US
20/G4 Käina, Est.
80/B2 Kainab (dry riv.), Namb.
40/B2 Kainach (riv.), Aus.
56/D3 Kainan, Japan
74/C4 Kainji (lake), Nga.
76/F6 Kainji (dam), Nga.
79/G4 Kainji (dam), Nga.
79/G4 Kainji (lake), Nga.
39/G3 Kainoúryion, Gre.
71/R10 Kaipara (harbor), N.Z.
72/B2 Kairi, Austl.
57/H7 Kaisei, Japan
36/D4 Kaiseregg (peak), Swi.
31/G3 Kaisersesch, Ger.
26/D4 Kaiserslautern, Ger.
31/G5 Kaiserslautern, Ger.
33/G2 Kaiserslautern, Ger.

145

Kaise – Kaufm

36/D1 Kaiserstuhl (peak), Ger.
27/N1 Kaišiadorys, Lith.
71/R10 Kaitaia, N.Z.
88/T10 Kaiwi (chan.), Hi,US
63/J2 Kaiyang, China
55/J3 Kaiyuan, China
59/F2 Kaiyuan, China
60/D4 Kaiyuan, China
63/H3 Kaiyuan, China
57/M9 Kaizu, Japan
57/L10 Kaizuka, Japan
18/F2 Kajaani, Fin.
46/C3 Kajaani, Fin.
70/G4 Kajabbi, Austl.
56/A3 Kaji-san (mtn.), SKor.
58/E5 Kaji-san (mtn.), SKor.
77/M5 Kākā, Sudan
20/G3 Kakaanpää, Fin.
77/M7 Kakamega, Kenya
57/E3 Kakamigahara, Japan
57/M9 Kakamigahara, Japan
40/D3 Kakanj, Bosn.
85/M4 Kake, Ak,US
85/M4 Kaketsa (mtn.), BC,Can
51/J3 Kākhk, Iran
53/G2 Kākhk, Iran
41/L2 Kakhovka, Ukr.
44/E3 Kakhovka, Ukr.
44/E3 Kakhovka (res.), Ukr.
62/D4 Kākināda, India
57/L9 Kako (riv.), Japan
78/B4 Kakrima (riv.), Gui.
85/K1 Kaktovik, Ak,US
57/G2 Kakuda, Japan
77/M7 Kakuma, Kenya
77/M8 Kakuto, Ugan.
82/F1 Kakuto, Ugan.
64/H4 Kala (riv.), SrL.
38/D5 Kalaa-Kebia, Tun.
75/X18 Kalaa-Kebia, Tun.
84/N2 Kalaallit Nunaat (Greenland)
87/L1 Kalaallit Nunaat (Greenland), Den.
64/A1 Kalābāgh, Pak.
67/E3 Kalabakan, Malay.
82/D3 Kalabo, Zam.
63/F4 Kalabyin, Burma
45/G2 Kalach, Rus.
46/H4 Kalachinsk, Rus.
45/G2 Kalach-na-Donu, Rus.
63/F3 Kaladan (riv.), Burma
88/U11 Ka Lae (cape), Hi,US
82/D5 Kalahari (des.), Afr.
80/B2 Kalahari (des.), Afr.
74/E7 Kalahari (des.), Bots.
80/C2 Kalahari-Gemsbok Nat'l Park, SAfr.
82/C6 Kalahari-Gemsbok Nat'l Park, SAfr.
88/S10 Kalaheo, Hi,US
60/A3 Kālāigaon, India
39/L7 Kalamáki, Gre.
39/H2 Kalamariá, Gre.
40/F5 Kalamariá, Gre.
18/F5 Kalamata, Gre.
39/H4 Kalamáta, Gre.
89/J3 Kalamazoo, Mi,US
94/C3 Kalamazoo, Mi,US
39/G3 Kalampáka, Gre.
41/L2 Kalanchak, Ukr.
88/U11 Kalaoa, Hi,US
44/D3 Kalarash, Mol.
53/K3 Kālasar, India
63/H4 Kalasin, Thai.
65/C2 Kalasin, Thai.
53/J3 Kalāt, Pak.
88/T10 Kalaupapa, Hi,US
39/H3 Kalávrita, Gre.
63/G3 Kalaw, Burma
65/B1 Kalaw, Burma
72/D4 Kalbar, Austl.
75/X18 Kalbīyah (lake), Tun.
20/N7 Kaldakvísl (riv.), Ice.
50/B2 Kale, Turk.
44/E4 Kalecik, Turk.
50/C1 Kalecik, Turk.
29/H5 Kalefeld, Ger.
82/E2 Kalemie, Zaire
60/D4 Kalemyo, Burma
63/F3 Kalemyo, Burma
51/J2 Kāl-e Shūr (riv.), Iran
27/K3 Kalety, Pol.
20/J2 Kalevala, Rus.
60/B4 Kalewa, Burma
63/F3 Kalewa, Burma
82/E4 Kaleya, Zam.
68/B4 Kalgoorlie, Austl.
70/C6 Kalgoorlie-Boulder, Austl.
41/J4 Kaliakra, Nos (pt.), Bul.
66/C5 Kalianda, Indo.
67/F1 Kalibo, Phil.
77/L8 Kalima, Zaire
82/E1 Kalima, Zaire
66/D4 Kalimantan (reg.), Indo.
50/A2 Kálimnos, Gre.
50/A2 Kálimnos (isl.), Gre.
18/F3 Kaliningrad, Rus.
27/K1 Kaliningrad (lag.), Rus.
27/L1 Kaliningrad, Rus.
42/D5 Kaliningrad, Rus.
42/H5 Kaliningrad, Rus.
43/X9 Kaliningrad, Rus.
46/C4 Kaliningrad, Rus.
42/D5 Kaliningrad Obl., Rus.
45/H2 Kalininsk, Rus.
44/D1 Kalinkovichi, Bela.
77/M8 Kalisizo, Ugan.
86/E4 Kalispell, Mt,US
88/D2 Kalispell, Mt,US
90/E3 Kalispell, Mt,US
18/E3 Kalisz, Pol.
27/J3 Kalisz (prov.), Pol.
27/K3 Kalisz, Pol.
44/A2 Kalisz, Pol.
46/B4 Kalisz, Pol.
20/G2 Kalix, Swe.
42/D2 Kalix, Swe.
20/G2 Kalixälv (riv.), Swe.
42/D2 Kalixälv (riv.), Swe.
62/E2 Kāliyāganj, India
70/E3 Kalkaringi, Austl.
94/C2 Kalkaska, Mi,US
64/G3 Kallakkurichichi, India
20/H4 Kallaste, Est.
42/E4 Kallaste, Est.
64/F4 Kallidaikurichchi, India
39/L7 Kallithea, Gre.
20/E3 Kallsjön (lake), Swe.
18/E3 Kalmar, Swe.
20/E4 Kalmar (co.), Swe.
20/F4 Kalmar, Swe.
42/C4 Kalmar (co.), Swe.
46/B4 Kalmar, Swe.
28/B6 Kalmthout, Belg.
45/H3 Kalmyk Aut. Rep., Rus.
40/D2 Kalocsa, Hun.
39/J1 Kalofer, Bul.
88/T10 Kalohi (chan.), Hi,US
40/F5 Kalokhórion, Gre.
53/K4 Kālol, India
62/B3 Kālol, India
82/E4 Kalomo, Zam.
62/C2 Kālpi, India
64/G4 Kalpitiya, SrL.
33/L3 Kalsdorf bei Graz, Aus.
40/B2 Kalsdorf bei Graz, Aus.
85/G3 Kaltag, Ak,US
37/F3 Kaltbrunn, Swi.
26/E1 Kaltenkirchen, Ger.
33/F4 Kaltern (Caldaro), It.
37/H5 Kaltern (Caldaro), It.
62/D6 Kalu (riv.), SrL.
18/G3 Kaluga, Rus.
42/H5 Kaluga, Rus.
44/F1 Kaluga, Rus.
46/D4 Kaluga, Rus.
42/G5 Kaluga Obl., Rus.
44/E1 Kaluga Obl., Rus.
70/D2 Kalumburu Mission, Austl.
20/D5 Kalundborg, Den.
27/F1 Kalundborg, Den.
64/A1 Kalūr Kot, Pak.
44/C2 Kalush, Ukr.
62/C6 Kalutara, SrL.
27/M1 Kalvarija, Lith.
42/D5 Kalvarija, Lith.
53/K5 Kalyān, India
62/B4 Kalyān, India
60/B5 Kama, Burma
63/G4 Kama, Burma
19/J3 Kama (riv.), Rus.
43/M4 Kama (res.), Rus.
43/M5 Kama (riv.), Rus.
46/F3 Kama (riv.), Rus.
82/E1 Kama, Zaire
57/J7 Kamagaya, Japan
55/N4 Kamaishi, Japan
88/T10 Kamakou (peak), Hi,US
57/H7 Kamakura, Japan
64/B2 Kamālia, Pak.
88/T10 Kamalo, Hi,US
44/E5 Kaman, Turk.
50/C2 Kaman, Turk.
78/E2 Kamango (lake), Mali
82/B4 Kamanjab, Namb.
52/D5 Kamaran (isl.), Yemen
106/F2 Kamarang, Guy.
62/C4 Kāmāreddi, India
62/E3 Kāmārhāti, India
106/G2 Kamaria (fall, falls), Guy.
70/C6 Kambalda, Austl.
64/F4 Kambam, India
62/A2 Kambar, Pak.
76/C6 Kambia, SLeo.
78/B4 Kambia, SLeo.
82/E3 Kambove, Zaire
67/F4 Kambuno (peak), Indo.
47/R4 Kamchatka (pen.), Rus.
48/Q4 Kamchatka (pen.), Rus.
47/R4 Kamchatka Obl., Rus.
41/H4 Kamchiya (riv.), Bul.
44/C4 Kamchiya (riv.), Bul.
29/E5 Kamen, Ger.
18/F4 Kamenets-Podol'skiy, Ukr.
44/C2 Kamenets-Podol'skiy, Ukr.
33/K4 Kamenjak, Rt (cape), Cro.
40/A3 Kamenjak, Rt (cape), Cro.
44/D2 Kamenka, Mol.
45/H1 Kamenka, Rus.
55/M3 Kamenka, Rus.
46/J4 Kamen'-na-Obi, Rus.
41/H4 Kameno, Bul.
44/G2 Kamensk-Shakhtinskiy, Rus.
43/P4 Kamensk-Ural'skiy, Rus.
46/G4 Kamensk-Ural'skiy, Rus.
56/D3 Kameoka, Japan
57/L9 Kameoka, Japan
57/M10 Kameyama, Japan
57/K9 Kami, Japan
90/D4 Kamiah, Id,US
27/H2 Kamień Pomorski, Pol.
57/H7 Kamifukuoka, Japan
55/N3 Kamiisco, Japan
57/M9 Kamiishizu, Japan
88/U11 Kamilo (pt.), Hi,US
82/E2 Kamina, Zaire
57/G1 Kaminoyama, Japan
85/H4 Kamishak (bay), Ak,US
55/L5 Kamiyaku, Japan
56/B5 Kamiyaku, Japan
86/D3 Kamloops, BC,Can
88/B1 Kamloops, BC,Can
90/C3 Kamloops, BC,Can
65/C4 Kamlot, Camb.
57/L10 Kammaki, Japan
33/L3 Kamnik, Slov.
40/B2 Kamnik, Slov.
51/F1 Kamo, Arm.
57/F2 Kamo, Japan
57/J7 Kamo (riv.), Japan
57/L10 Kamo, Japan
57/G3 Kamogawa, Japan
57/J7 Kamogawa, Japan
56/D3 Kamojima, Japan
64/C2 Kāmoke, Pak.
27/H4 Kamp (riv.), Aus.
33/L2 Kamp (riv.), Aus.
77/M7 Kampala (cap.), Ugan.
67/G2 Kampalili (mt.), Phil.
66/B3 Kampar (riv.), Indo.
66/B3 Kampar, Malay.
31/G3 Kamp-Bornhofen, Ger.
26/E1 Kampen, Ger.
26/C2 Kampen, Neth.
28/C3 Kampen, Neth.
65/B2 Kamphaeng Phet, Thai.
65/B2 Kamphaeng Phet (ruins), Thai.
27/L2 Kampinoski Nat'l Park, Pol.
44/B1 Kampinoski Nat'l Park, Pol.
28/D6 Kamp-Lintfort, Ger.
58/E5 Kamp'o, SKor.
48/K8 Kampong Cham, Camb.
63/J5 Kampong Cham, Camb.
65/D4 Kampong Cham, Camb.
66/C1 Kampong Cham, Camb.
63/H5 Kampong Chhnang, Camb.
65/D3 Kampong Chhnang, Camb.
66/B1 Kampong Chhnang, Camb.
65/D3 Kampong Khleang, Camb.
63/H6 Kampong Kuala Besut, Malay.
66/B2 Kampong Kuala Besut, Malay.
65/C5 Kampong Raja, Malay.
63/H5 Kampong Saom, Camb.
65/C4 Kampong Saom, Camb.
65/C4 Kampong Saom (bay), Camb.
66/B1 Kampong Saom, Camb.
66/B1 Kampong Saom (bay), Camb.
65/D4 Kampong Spoe, Camb.
67/E2 Kampong Telupid, Malay.
63/H5 Kampong Thum, Camb.
65/D3 Kampong Thum, Camb.
66/B1 Kampong Thum, Camb.
65/D4 Kampong Trabek, Camb.
63/H5 Kampot, Camb.
65/D4 Kampot, Camb.
66/B1 Kampot, Camb.
67/H4 Kamrau (bay), Indo.
86/F3 Kamsack, Sk,Can
88/F1 Kamsack, Sk,Can
91/H3 Kamsack, Sk,Can
91/H1 Kamuchawie (lake), Sk,Can
103/F4 Kámuk (mtn.), CR
19/H3 Kamyshin, Rus.
45/H2 Kamyshin, Rus.
46/E4 Kamyshin, Rus.
87/J3 Kanaaupscow (riv.), Qu,Can
92/D3 Kanab (riv.), Az, Ut,US
92/D3 Kanab, Ut,US
85/C6 Kanaga (isl.), Ak,US
85/C6 Kanaga (vol.), Ak,US
57/F3 Kanagawa (pref.), Japan
57/H7 Kanagawa (pref.), Japan
87/K3 Kanairiktok (riv.), Nf,Can
57/L10 Kanan, Japan
82/D2 Kananga, Zaire
19/H3 Kanash, Rus.
43/K5 Kanash, Rus.
46/E4 Kanash, Rus.
95/N7 Kanawake Ind. Res., Qu,Can
94/D4 Kanawha (riv.), WV,US
47/P6 Kanazawa, Japan
55/M4 Kanazawa, Japan
57/E2 Kanazawa, Japan
63/G3 Kanbalu, Burma
63/G5 Kanchanaburi, Thai.
65/B3 Kanchanaburi, Thai.
62/E2 Kānchenjunga (mtn.), Nepal
62/C5 Kānchīpuram, India
18/G2 Kandalaksha, Rus.
20/K2 Kandalaksha, Rus.
20/K2 Kandalaksha (gulf), Rus.
42/G2 Kandalaksha, Rus.
42/G2 Kandalaksha (gulf), Rus.
46/D3 Kandalaksha, Rus.
39/H5 Kándanos, Gre.
69/Y18 Kandavu Passage (chan.), Fiji
31/H5 Kandel, Ger.
36/E1 Kandel (peak), Ger.
36/D4 Kander (riv.), Swi.
36/D2 Kandern, Ger.
36/D5 Kandersteg, Swi.
53/J3 Kandhkot, Pak.
62/A2 Kandhkot, Pak.
76/F5 Kandi, Ben.
62/E3 Kāndi, India
67/F3 Kandi (cape), Indo.
41/K5 Kandıra, Turk.
50/B1 Kandıra, Turk.
73/D2 Kandos, Austl.
45/K1 Kandry, Rus.
62/C4 Kandukūr, India
62/D6 Kandy, SrL.
87/T7 Kane (bay), NW,Can
99/P16 Kane (co.), Il,US
76/H5 Kanem (reg.), Chad
88/T10 Kaneohe, Hi,US
88/W13 Kaneohe, Hi,US
88/W13 Kaneohe (bay), Hi,US
88/W13 Kaneohe Marine Air Sta., Hi,US
99/N16 Kaneville, Il,US
82/D5 Kang, Bots.
76/D5 Kangaba, Mali
78/C4 Kangaba, Mali
50/D2 Kangal, Turk.
51/H5 Kangān, Iran
52/F3 Kangān, Iran
53/G3 Kangān, Iran
63/H6 Kangar, Malay.
65/C5 Kangar, Malay.
66/B2 Kangar, Malay.
70/F7 Kangaroo (isl.), Austl.
42/E3 Kangasala, Fin.
51/F3 Kangāvar, Iran
52/E2 Kangāvar, Iran
54/G3 Kangbao, China
54/E5 Kangding, China
60/D2 Kangding, China
67/E5 Kangean (isls.), Indo.
55/K3 Kanggye, NKor.
58/D2 Kanggye, NKor.
58/D4 Kanggyŏng, SKor.
58/D4 Kanghwa, SKor.
58/D4 Kanghwa (isl.), SKor.
58/F6 Kanghwa, SKor.
58/F6 Kanghwa (isl.), SKor.
87/K3 Kangiqsualujjuaq, Qu,Can
87/J2 Kangiqsujuaq, Qu,Can
87/J2 Kangirsuk, Qu,Can
58/D5 Kangjin, SKor.
62/E2 Kangmar, China
55/K4 Kangnam, NKor.
58/C2 Kangnam (mts.), NKor.
58/G6 Kangnam, SKor.
47/N6 Kangnŭng, SKor.
55/K4 Kangnŭng, SKor.
56/A2 Kangnŭng, SKor.
58/F4 Kangnŭng, SKor.
55/J3 Kangping, China
59/E2 Kangping, China
58/F6 Kangsŏ, SKor.
60/B3 Kangto (peak), China
63/F2 Kangto (peak), China
58/D3 Kangwŏn-Do (prov.), NKor.
56/A2 Kangwon-do (prov.), SKor.
58/E4 Kangwŏn-Do (prov.), SKor.
53/L1 Kangxiwar, China
62/C3 Kanhān (riv.), India
60/B4 Kani, Burma
57/N9 Kani, Japan
57/M9 Kanie, Japan
18/H2 Kanin (pen.), Rus.
43/K2 Kanin (pen.), Rus.
46/E3 Kanin (pen.), Rus.
18/H2 Kanin Nos (pt.), Rus.
46/E3 Kanin Nos (pt.), Rus.
73/B3 Kaniva, Austl.
64/F4 Kanjirapalli, India
40/E2 Kanjiža, Yugo.
94/C3 Kankakee (riv.), Il, In,US
89/J3 Kankakee, Il,US
91/M5 Kankakee, Il,US
93/L2 Kankakee, Il,US
94/C3 Kankakee, Il,US
76/D5 Kankan, Gui.
78/C4 Kankan, Gui.
78/C4 Kankan (comm.), Gui.
62/D3 Kānker, India
64/H4 Kankesanturai, SrL.
56/C3 Kanmuri-yama (mtn.), Japan
97/H3 Kannapolis, NC,US
62/C2 Kannauj, India
64/F4 Kanniyākumāri, India
57/H7 Kannon-zaki (pt.), Japan
20/G3 Kannus, Fin.
42/D3 Kannus, Fin.
76/G5 Kano, Nga.
79/H3 Kano (state), Nga.
79/H4 Kano, Nga.
56/C3 Kan'onji, Japan
56/B5 Kanoya, Japan
62/D2 Kānpur, India
89/G4 Kansas (state), US
93/H3 Kansas (state), US
89/G4 Kansas (riv.), Ks,US
93/H3 Kansas (riv.), Ks,US
89/H4 Kansas City, Ks,US
93/J3 Kansas City, Ks,US
96/E2 Kansas City, Ks,US
89/H4 Kansas City, Mo,US
93/J3 Kansas City, Mo,US
96/E2 Kansas City, Mo,US
99/P14 Kansasville, Wi,US
46/K4 Kansk, Rus.
58/E3 Kansŏng, SKor.
62/D3 Kantābānji, India
57/F2 Kantō (prov.), Japan
57/H7 Kantō (prov.), Japan
101/J4 Kantunilkín, Mex.
102/E1 Kantunilkín, Mex.
106/G3 Kanuku (mts.), Guy.
57/F2 Kanuma, Japan
85/H2 Kanuti Nat'l Wild. Ref., Ak,US
80/D2 Kanye, Bots.
82/E5 Kanye, Bots.
65/D3 Kaoh Nhek, Camb.
48/M7 Kaohsiung, Tai.
61/J4 Kaohsiung, Tai.
68/B2 Kaohsiung, Tai.
82/B4 Kaokoveld (reg.), Namb.
76/B5 Kaolack, Sen.
78/A3 Kaolack, Sen.
78/B3 Kaolack (reg.), Sen.
41/H4 Kaolinovo, Bul.
82/D3 Kaoma, Zam.
88/S9 Kapaa, Hi,US
88/U11 Kapaahu, Hi,US
88/U10 Kapaau, Hi,US
82/D2 Kapanga, Zaire
39/G1 Kapaonik (upland), Yugo.
40/E4 Kapaonik (upland), Yugo.
28/B6 Kapellen, Belg.
33/L3 Kapfenberg, Aus.
40/B2 Kapfenberg, Aus.
41/H5 Kapidaği (pen.), Turk.
68/E4 Kapingamarangi (isl.), Micr.
82/E3 Kapiri Mposhi, Zam.
91/M2 Kapiskau (riv.), On,Can
87/H3 Kapiskau (riv.), On,Can
63/G6 Kapoe, Thai.
66/A2 Kapoe, Thai.
77/M7 Kapoeta, Sudan
40/C2 Kapos (riv.), Hun.
40/C2 Kaposvár, Hun.
99/C4 Kapowsin, Wa,US
31/H6 Kappelrodeck, Ger.
37/G3 Kappl, Aus.
58/E2 Kapsan, NKor.
27/M1 Kapsukas, Lith.
42/D5 Kapsukas, Lith.
66/C4 Kapuas (riv.), Indo.
66/D4 Kapuas (riv.), Indo.
66/D3 Kapuas Hulu (mts.), Indo., Malay.
73/A2 Kapunda, Austl.
64/C2 Kapūrthala, India
87/H4 Kapuskasing, On,Can
89/K2 Kapuskasing, On,Can
94/D1 Kapuskasing, On,Can
94/D1 Kapuskasing (riv.), On,Can
27/J5 Kapuvár, Hun.
33/M3 Kapuvár, Hun.
40/C2 Kapuvár, Hun.
51/F2 Kapydzhik (peak), Azer.
45/H5 Kapydzhik, Gora (peak), Azer.
58/D4 Kap'yŏng, SKor.
19/J1 Kara (sea), Rus.
43/Q1 Kara (riv.), Rus.
46/G2 Kara (sea), Rus.
48/F2 Kara (sea), Rus.
46/H5 Kara-Balta, Kyr.
45/K4 Kara-Bogaz-Gol (gulf), Trkm.
46/F5 Kara-Bogaz-Gol (gulf), Trkm.
51/H1 Kara-Bogaz-Gol, Trkm.
51/H1 Kara-Bogaz-Gol (gulf), Trkm.
67/H4 Karabra (riv.), Indo.
44/E4 Karabük, Turk.
50/C1 Karabük, Turk.
50/D2 Karaca (peak), Turk.
52/C1 Karaca (peak), Turk.
44/D4 Karacabey, Turk.
50/B1 Karacabey, Turk.
49/C1 Karaçal (peak), Turk.
50/C2 Karaçal (peak), Turk.
52/B1 Karaçal (peak), Turk.
45/G4 Karachay-Cherkass Aut. Obl., Rus.
44/E1 Karachev, Rus.
53/J4 Karāchi, Pak.
62/A3 Karāchi, Pak.
53/K5 Karād, India
62/B4 Karād, India
46/H5 Karaganda, Kaz.
48/R4 Karaginskiy (isl.), Rus.
62/C5 Kāraikkudi, India
64/G3 Kāraikkudi, India
50/C2 Karaisalı, Turk.
64/G4 Karaitivu (isl.), SrL.
46/F6 Karaj, Iran
51/G3 Karaj, Iran
52/F1 Karaj, Iran
51/J2 Kara-Kala, Trkm.
53/G1 Kara-Kala, Trkm.
45/L3 Karakalpak Aut. Rep., Uzb.
46/F5 Karakalpak Aut. Rep., Uzb.
53/L1 Karakax (riv.), China
50/D2 Karakaya (dam), Turk.
67/G3 Karakelong (isl.), Indo.
54/E3 Karakhoto (ruins), China
50/E2 Karakoçan, Turk.
53/L1 Karakoram (pass), India
53/K1 Karakoran (range), Pak., India
78/C3 Karakoro (riv.), Mali, Mrta.
53/L1 Karakorum (pass), China
53/L1 Karakorum (range), India, Pak.
54/E2 Karakorum (ruins), Mong.
45/G5 Karaköse, Turk.
51/E2 Karaköse, Turk.
46/H5 Kara-Kul', Kyr.
45/L5 Karakumy (des.), Trkm.
46/F5 Karakumy (des.), Trkm.
45/K4 Karakyon, Gora (peak), Trkm.
53/H1 Karakyr (peak), Trkm.
67/E4 Karam (riv.), Indo.
49/C1 Karaman (prov.), Turk.
50/C2 Karaman, Turk.
50/C2 Karaman (prov.), Turk.
50/B2 Karamanlı, Turk.
46/J5 Karamay, China
71/R11 Karamea, N.Z.
71/R11 Karamea (bight), NZ
41/J5 Karamürsel, Turk.
63/G4 Karan (state), Burma
67/E5 Karangasem, Indo.
47/S4 Karanginskiy (bay), Rus.
47/S4 Karanginskiy (isl.), Rus.
62/C3 Kāranja, India
60/C5 Karan (Kayin) (state), Burma
65/B2 Karan (Kayin) (state), Burma
50/C2 Karapınar, Turk.
106/G3 Karasabai, Guy.
56/A3 Kara-saki (pt.), Japan
58/E5 Kara-saki (pt.), Japan
50/C1 Karaşar, Turk.
80/B3 Karasburg, Namb.
82/C6 Karasburg, Namb.
20/H1 Karasjok, Nor.
42/E1 Karasjok, Nor.
57/M10 Karasu, Japan
41/K5 Karasu, Turk.
50/B1 Karasu, Turk.
46/H4 Karasuk, Rus.
103/F3 Karatá (lag.), Nic.
49/D1 Karataş, Turk.
50/C2 Karataş, Turk.
46/H5 Karatau, Kaz.
56/A4 Karatsu, Japan
39/G3 Karáva (peak), Gre.
44/F4 Karayaka, Turk.
45/G5 Karayazı, Turk.
50/E2 Karayazı, Turk.
46/H5 Karazhal, Kaz.
51/E3 Karbalā' (gov.), Iraq
51/F3 Karbalā', Iraq
52/D2 Karbalā', Iraq
27/L5 Karcag, Hun.
40/E2 Karcag, Hun.
39/K3 Kardhámila, Gre.
44/C5 Kardhámila, Gre.
50/A2 Kardhámila, Gre.
39/G3 Kardhitsa, Gre.
39/G3 Kardhitsomagoúla, Gre.
20/G4 Kärdla, Est.
42/D4 Kärdla, Est.
20/J2 Karelian Aut. Rep., Rus.
42/G2 Karelian Aut. Rep., Rus.
46/D3 Karelian Aut. Rep., Rus.
82/F2 Karema, Tanz.
54/H1 Karenga (riv.), Rus.
20/G1 Karesuando, Swe.
42/D1 Karesuando, Swe.
50/C1 Kargı, Turk.
18/G2 Kargopol', Rus.
46/D3 Kargopol', Rus.
76/H5 Kari, Nga.
39/G3 Kariá, Gre.
39/J2 Kariai, Gre.
44/C4 Kariai, Gre.
74/E6 Kariba (lake), Afr.
74/E6 Kariba (dam), Zam.
82/E4 Kariba (dam), Zam.
82/E4 Kariba (lake), Zam., Zim.
82/E4 Kariba, Zim.
82/D5 Karibib, Namb.
64/G3 Karikal, India
66/C4 Karimata (isl.), Indo.
66/C4 Karimata (str.), Indo.
62/C4 Karīmnagar, India
26/G1 Karise, Den.
77/L8 Karisimbi (vol.), Rwa.
82/E1 Karisimbi (vol.), Rwa.
39/J3 Káristos, Gre.
45/C5 Káristos, Gre.
57/M10 Kariya, Japan
77/Q6 Karkaar (mts.), Som.
62/B5 Kārkāl, India
68/D5 Karkar (isl.), PNG
44/E3 Karkinitsk (gulf), Ukr.
53/K1 Karla Marksa (peak), Taj.
27/H1 Karlino, Pol.
50/E2 Karlıova, Turk.
33/L4 Karlovac, Slov.
40/B3 Karlovac, Slov.
39/J1 Karlovo, Bul.
41/G4 Karlovo, Bul.
44/C4 Karlovo, Bul.
26/G3 Karlovy Vary, Czh.
33/K1 Karlovy Vary, Czh.
37/H1 Karlsfeld, Ger.
20/E4 Karlshamn, Swe.
20/E4 Karlskoga, Swe.
18/E3 Karlskrona, Swe.
20/E4 Karlskrona, Swe.
46/B4 Karlskrona, Swe.
18/D4 Karlsruhe, Ger.
26/E4 Karlsruhe, Ger.
33/H2 Karlsruhe, Ger.
18/E3 Karlstad, Swe.
20/E4 Karlstad, Swe.
46/B4 Karlstad, Swe.
85/H4 Karluk, Ak,US
53/L5 Karmāla, India
62/C4 Karmāla, India
49/D3 Karmel, Har (Mount Carmel) (mtn.), Isr.
53/L3 Karnāl, India
62/C2 Karnāl, India
62/C4 Karnataka (state), India
64/F3 Karnataka (state), India
101/F2 Karnes City, Tx,US
93/H5 Karnes City, Tx,US
96/D4 Karnes City, Tx,US
39/K1 Karnobat, Bul.
41/H4 Karnobat, Bul.
40/A2 Kärnten (prov.), Aus.
80/C4 Karoo Nat'l Park, SAfr.
73/A2 Karoonda, Austl.
53/K2 Karor, Pak.
64/A2 Karor, Pak.
52/C5 Karora, Sudan
67/E5 Karoso (cape), Indo.
50/A3 Kárpathos, Gre.
50/A3 Kárpathos (isl.), Gre.
41/G1 Karpatskiy Nat'l Park, Ukr.
39/G3 Karpenísion, Gre.
70/B4 Karratha, Austl.
80/M11 Kars (riv.), SAfr.
45/G4 Kars, Turk.
45/G4 Kars (prov.), Turk.
45/G4 Kars (riv.), Turk.
46/E5 Kars, Turk.
50/E1 Kars (prov.), Turk.
51/E1 Kars, Turk.
20/H3 Kärsämäki, Fin.
42/E3 Kärsämäki, Fin.
20/H4 Kärsava, Lat.
42/E4 Kärsava, Lat.
46/G6 Karshi, Uzb.
45/M1 Kartaly, Rus.
46/G4 Kartaly, Rus.
64/C2 Kartārpur, India
41/L3 Kartinitsk (gulf), Ukr.
27/K1 Kartuzy, Pol.
73/D2 Karuah, Austl.
70/G3 Karumba, Austl.
72/A2 Karumba, Austl.
46/E6 Kārūn (riv.), Iran
51/G4 Kārūn (riv.), Iran
52/E2 Kārūn (riv.), Iran
64/G3 Karūr, India
27/K4 Karviná, Czh.
53/K6 Karwar, India
62/B5 Karwar, India
20/D4 Kås, Den.
49/A1 Kaş, Turk.
50/B2 Kaş, Turk.
85/M4 Kasaan, Ak,US
91/L2 Kasabonika (lake), On,Can
57/L10 Kasagi, Japan
62/E3 Kāsai (riv.), India
56/D3 Kasai, Japan
74/D5 Kasai (riv.), Zaire
82/C1 Kasai (riv.), Zaire
57/G2 Kasama, Japan
82/F3 Kasama, Zam.
57/M9 Kasamatsu, Japan
82/E4 Kasane, Bots.
56/C3 Kasaoka, Japan
62/C5 Kāsaragod, India
57/M10 Kasartori-yama (peak), Japan
86/F2 Kasba (lake), NW,Can
56/B5 Kaseda, Japan
62/C2 Kāsganj, India
53/H1 Kashaf (riv.), Iran
46/F6 Kāshān, Iran
51/G3 Kāshān, Iran
52/F2 Kāshān, Iran
46/H6 Kashi, China
57/L10 Kashiba, Japan
56/D3 Kashihara, Japan
57/L10 Kashihara, Japan
56/B4 Kashima, Japan
57/G3 Kashima, Japan
42/H4 Kashin, Rus.
57/H7 Kashiwa, Japan
57/L10 Kashiwara, Japan
57/F2 Kashiwazaki, Japan
46/F6 Kāshmar, Iran
51/J3 Kāshmar, Iran
53/G1 Kāshmar, Iran
64/C1 Kashmīr, Jammu and (state), India
62/A2 Kashmor, Pak.
53/J1 Kashof (riv.), Iran
85/F3 Kasigluk, Ak,US
85/H3 Kasilof, Ak,US
42/J5 Kasimov, Rus.
45/G1 Kasimov, Rus.
67/G4 Kasiruta (isl.), Indo.
67/H4 Kasiui (isl.), Indo.
93/K3 Kaskaskia (riv.), Il,US
94/B4 Kaskaskia (riv.), Il,US
90/D3 Kaslo, BC,Can
82/E1 Kasongo, Zaire
82/C2 Kasongo-Lunda, Zaire
50/A3 Kásos (isl.), Gre.
51/F1 Kaspi, Geo.
41/H4 Kaspichan, Bul.
45/H4 Kaspiysk, Rus.
52/C5 Kassala, Sudan
77/N4 Kassala, Sudan
39/H3 Kassándra (pen.), Gre.
44/B4 Kassándra (pen.), Gre.
39/H2 Kassándria, Gre.
18/D3 Kassel, Ger.
26/E3 Kassel, Ger.
29/G6 Kassel, Ger.
91/K4 Kasson, Mn,US
44/E4 Kastamonu, Turk.
44/E4 Kastamonu (prov.), Turk.
50/C1 Kastamonu, Turk.
50/C1 Kastamonu (prov.), Turk.
39/K2 Kastanéai, Gre.
41/H5 Kastanéai, Gre.
31/G3 Kastellaun, Ger.
39/J5 Kastéllion, Gre.
40/C4 Kaštel Stari, Cro.
40/C4 Kaštel Sućurac, Cro.
28/B6 Kasterlee, Belg.
31/D1 Kasterlee, Belg.
39/G2 Kastoría, Gre.
40/E5 Kastoría, Gre.
39/G3 Kastrakíou (lake), Gre.
57/L9 Kasuga, Japan
57/E3 Kasugai, Japan
57/M9 Kasugai, Japan
57/F3 Kasukabe, Japan
57/H7 Kasukabe, Japan
82/F1 Kasulu, Tanz.
57/G2 Kasumiga (lake), Japan
82/F3 Kasungu, Malw.
53/K2 Kasūr, Pak.
64/C2 Kasūr, Pak.
82/E4 Kataba, Zam.
87/K4 Katahdin (mt.), Me,US
89/N2 Katahdin (mt.), Me,US
95/G2 Katahdin (peak), Me,US
39/G4 Katákolon, Gre.
74/E5 Katanga (reg.), Zaire
82/E2 Katanga (reg.), Zaire
70/B6 Katanning, Austl.
57/L10 Katano, Japan
39/G4 Katastárion, Gre.
82/F2 Katavi Nat'l Park, Tanz.
63/F6 Katchall (isl.), India
82/D2 Katea, Zaire
82/E2 Katea, Zaire
39/H2 Kateríni, Gre.
44/B4 Kateríni, Gre.
85/M4 Kates Needle (mtn.), Ak,US
82/F3 Katete, Zam.
60/C3 Katha, Burma
63/G3 Katha, Burma
68/C6 Katherine, Austl.
70/E2 Katherine, Austl.
62/C2 Kāthgodām, India
53/K4 Kathiawar (pen.), India
62/E2 Kāthmāndu (cap.), Nepal
53/L2 Kathua, India
64/C1 Kathua, India
76/D5 Kati, Mali
78/C3 Kati, Mali
76/D6 Katiola, IvC.
78/D4 Katiola, IvC.
29/H5 Katlenburg-Lindau, Ger.
85/H4 Katmai (vol.), Ak,US
85/G4 Katmai Nat'l Park & Prsv., Ak,US
39/G3 Káto Akhaía, Gre.
39/G3 Katokhí, Gre.
39/H2 Káto Nevrokópion, Gre.
41/F5 Káto Nevrokópion, Gre.
39/G3 Katoúna, Gre.
18/E3 Katowice, Pol.
27/K3 Katowice, Pol.
27/K3 Katowice (prov.), Pol.
44/A2 Katowice, Pol.
53/K2 Katra, India
64/C1 Katra, India
52/B3 Katrīnah, Jabal (Mount Catherine) (mtn.), Egypt
39/G3 Katsikás, Gre.
76/G5 Katsina, Nga.
79/G3 Katsina, Nga.
79/G3 Katsina (state), Nga.
79/H5 Katsina Ala (riv.), Camr.
79/H5 Katsina Ala (riv.), Nga.
57/L9 Katsura (riv.), Japan
56/D3 Katsuragi, Japan
57/L10 Katsuragi-san (peak), Japan
55/N4 Katsuta, Japan
57/G2 Katsuta, Japan
57/G3 Katsuura, Japan
56/E2 Katsuyama, Japan
94/E1 Kattawagami (riv.), On,Can
20/D4 Kattegat (str.), Den.,Swe.
18/E3 Kattegat (str.), Eur.
82/F3 Katumbi, Malw.
54/B1 Katun' (riv.), Rus.
77/L8 Katwe, Ugan.
26/C2 Katwijk aan Zee, Neth.
28/B4 Katwijk aan Zee, Neth.
26/E4 Katzenbuckel (peak), Ger.
33/H2 Katzenbuckel (peak), Ger.
31/G3 Katzenelnbogen, Ger.
31/F3 Katzwinkel, Ger.
69/K2 Kauai (isl.), Hi,US
88/S10 Kauai (chan.), Hi,US
88/S9 Kauai (isl.), Hi,US
88/V12 Kauai (chan.), Hi,US
26/F5 Kaufbeuren, Ger.
33/J3 Kaufbeuren, Ger.
37/G2 Kaufbeuren, Ger.
37/G1 Kaufering, Ger.
101/F1 Kaufman, Tx,US

146

Kaufm – Kilre

96/D3 Kaufman, Tx,US
29/G6 Kaufungen, Ger.
20/G3 Kauhajoki, Fin.
42/D3 Kauhajoki, Fin.
20/G3 Kauhanevan-Pohjankankaan Nat'l Park, Fin.
42/D3 Kauhanevan-Pohjankankaan Nat'l Park, Fin.
20/G3 Kauhava, Fin.
42/D3 Kauhava, Fin.
88/U10 Kauhola (pt.), Hi,US
88/U10 Kauiki Head (pt.), Hi,US
82/C5 Kaukaveld (mts.), Namb.
69/L6 Kaukura (atoll), FrPol.
88/R9 Kaulakahi (chan.), Hi,US
88/U11 Kauna (pt.), Hi,US
88/T10 Kaunakakai, Hi,US
18/F3 Kaunas, Lith.
27/M1 Kaunas, Lith.
27/N1 Kaunas (res.), Lith.
42/D5 Kaunas, Lith.
46/C4 Kaunas, Lith.
44/D3 Kaushany, Mol.
20/G1 Kautokeino, Nor.
42/D1 Kautokeino, Nor.
65/B4 Kau-ye (isl.), Burma
39/H2 Kavadarci, Macd.
40/F5 Kavadarci, Macd.
39/F2 Kavajë, Alb.
40/D5 Kavajë, Alb.
18/F4 Kavála, Gre.
39/J2 Kavála, Gre.
41/G5 Kavála, Gre.
44/C4 Kavála, Gre.
47/P5 Kavalerovo, Rus.
55/M3 Kavalerovo, Rus.
62/C5 Kāvali, India
68/C4 Kavangel (isls.), Palau
62/B5 Kavaratti, India
41/J4 Kavarna, Bul.
43/V6 Kavgolovskoye (lake), Rus.
68/E5 Kavieng, PNG
51/H4 Kavīr-e Bāfq (salt depr.), Iran
53/G2 Kavīr-e Bāfq (salt dep.), Iran
51/J3 Kavīr-e Namak (salt depr.), Iran
53/G2 Kavīr-e Namak (salt dep.), Iran
57/J7 Kawachi, Japan
57/L10 Kawachi-Nagano, Japan
57/M10 Kawage, Japan
57/F3 Kawagoe, Japan
57/H7 Kawagoe, Japan
57/M9 Kawagoe, Japan
57/F3 Kawaguchi, Japan
57/H7 Kawaguchi, Japan
88/R10 Kawaihoa (pt.), Hi,US
88/S9 Kawaikini (peak), Hi,US
57/H7 Kawajima, Japan
57/L10 Kawakami, Japan
57/G2 Kawamata, Japan
82/E4 Kawambwa, Zam.
57/L10 Kawanishi, Japan
62/D3 Kawardha, India
94/E2 Kawartha (lakes), On,Can
55/M4 Kawasaki, Japan
57/F3 Kawasaki, Japan
57/H7 Kawasaki, Japan
57/M9 Kawashima, Japan
88/V12 Kawela Bay (Kawela), Hi,US
88/V12 Kawela (Kawela Bay), Hi,US
71/S10 Kawerau, N.Z.
65/B2 Kawkareik, Burma
60/B4 Kawlin, Burma
63/G3 Kawlin, Burma
52/B4 Kawm Umbū, Egypt
77/M3 Kawm Umbū, Egypt
65/B4 Kawthaung, Burma
46/J5 Kax (riv.), China
85/L2 Kay (pt.), Yk,Can
76/E5 Kaya, Burk.
79/E4 Kaya, Burk.
58/E5 Kaya, SKor.
76/J6 Kayagangiri (peak), CAfr.
60/C5 Kayah (state), Burma
63/G4 Kayah (state), Burma
65/B2 Kayah (state), Burma
64/G4 Kāyalpatnam, India
48/L9 Kayan (riv.), Indo.
67/E3 Kayan (riv.), Indo.
78/B3 Kayanga (riv.), Sen.
64/F4 Kāyankulam, India
58/D4 Kaya-san (mtn.), SKor.
58/E5 Kaya-san Nat'l Park, SKor.
90/G5 Kaycee, Wy,US
92/F2 Kaycee, Wy,US
92/E3 Kayenta, Az,US
76/C5 Kayes, Mali
78/C3 Kayes, Mali
78/C3 Kayes (reg.), Mali
60/C5 Kayin (Karan) (state), Burma
65/B2 Kayin (Karan) (state), Burma
31/F5 Kayl, Lux.
41/J5 Kaynarca, Turk.
67/G3 Kayoa (isl.), Indo.
50/E2 Kayser (dam), Turk.
50/C2 Kayseri, Turk.
50/C2 Kayseri (prov.), Turk.
36/D1 Kaysersberg, Fr.
66/B4 Kayuagung, Indo.
51/F1 Kazakh, Azer.
46/H5 Kazakh (uplands), Kaz.
43/Q5 Kazakhstan
45/J2 Kazakhstan
46/G5 Kazakhstan
48/E5 Kazakhstan
51/H1 Kazakhstan
54/A2 Kazakhstan
86/F2 Kazan (riv.), NW,Can
19/H3 Kazan', Rus.
43/L5 Kazan', Rus.
46/E4 Kazan', Rus.
41/L2 Kazanka, Ukr.
49/D1 Kazanlı, Turk.
39/J1 Kazanlŭk, Bul.
41/G4 Kazanlŭk, Bul.
44/C4 Kazanlŭk, Bul.
44/D2 Kazatin, Ukr.
45/H4 Kazbek (peak), Geo.
51/G4 Kāzerūn, Iran
52/F3 Kāzerūn, Iran
51/G1 Kazi-Magomed, Azer.
27/L3 Kazimierza Wielka, Pol.
50/C2 Kâzımkarabekir, Turk.
27/L4 Kazincbarcika, Hun.
40/E1 Kazincbarcika, Hun.
60/B3 Kaziranga Nat'l Park, India
55/N3 Kazuno, Japan
39/J4 Kéa, Gre.
39/J4 Kéa (isl.), Gre.
88/U11 Keaau, Hi,US
22/B3 Keady, NI,UK
88/T11 Keahole (pt.), Hi,US
88/T10 Keanapapa (pt.), Hi,US
98/F5 Keansburg, NJ,US
88/G3 Kearney, Ne,US
93/H2 Kearney, Ne,US
22/C3 Kearny (pt.), NI,UK
99/E6 Kearsley (cr.), Mi,US
88/U11 Keawekaheka (pt.), Hi,US
50/D2 Keban, Turk.
50/D2 Keban (dam), Turk.
18/E2 Kebnekaise (peak), Swe.
20/F2 Kebnekaise (peak), Swe.
42/C2 Kebnekaise (peak), Swe.
46/B3 Kebnekaise (peak), Swe.
77/P6 K'ebri Dehar, Eth.
66/C5 Kebumen, Indo.
40/D2 Kecel, Hun.
50/B2 Keçiborlu, Turk.
40/D2 Kecskemét, Hun.
44/A3 Kecskemét, Hun.
51/F1 Kedabek, Azer.
65/C5 Kedah (state), Malay.
27/M1 Kėdainiai, Lith.
42/D5 Kėdainiai, Lith.
31/F5 Kédange-sur Canner, Fr.
66/D5 Kediri, Indo.
55/K2 Kedong, China
78/B3 Kédougou, Sen.
27/K3 Kędzierzyn-Koźle, Pol.
99/F6 Keego Harbor, Mi,US
86/D2 Keele (riv.), NW,Can
86/C2 Keele (peak), Yk,Can
61/J3 Keelung, Tai.
95/F3 Keene, NH,US
73/D1 Keepit (dam), Austl.
70/G2 Keer-weer (cape), Austl.
72/A1 Keer-weer (cape), Austl.
80/B2 Keetmanshoop, Namb.
82/C6 Keetmanshoop, Namb.
39/G3 Kefallinía (isl.), Gre.
49/F7 Kefar Sava, Isr.
49/F7 Kefar Vitkin, Isr.
18/A2 Keflavík, Ice.
20/M7 Keflavík, Ice.
52/C6 K'eftya, Eth.
63/J5 Ke Ga (cape), Viet.
66/C1 Ke Ga (cape), Viet.
62/D6 Kegalla, SrL.
23/G6 Kegworth, Eng,UK
31/G6 Kehl, Ger.
36/D1 Kehl, Ger.
42/E4 Kehra, Est.
36/D4 Kehrsatz, Swi.
23/G4 Keighley, Eng,UK
57/L9 Keihoku, Japan
73/F5 Keilor, Austl.
80/C3 Keimoes, SAfr.
82/D6 Keimoes, SAfr.
77/J6 Kéita (riv.), Chad
73/B3 Keith, Austl.
87/K4 Kejimkujik Nat'l Park, NS,Can
89/N3 Kejimkujik Nat'l Park, NS,Can
95/H2 Kejimkujik Nat'l Park, NS,Can
88/S10 Kekaha, Hi,US
27/K5 Kékes (peak), Hun.
40/D2 Kékes (peak), Hun.
54/G4 Kelan, China
59/B3 Kelan, China
53/L3 Kelān Devī, India
67/G4 Kelang (isl.), Indo.
66/B3 Kelang, Malay.
31/F3 Kelberg, Ger.
79/H3 Kélé-Kélé, Niger
44/D5 Keles, Turk.
26/F4 Kelheim, Ger.
33/J2 Kelheim, Ger.
44/F4 Kelkit, Turk.
50/D1 Kelkit, Turk.
50/D1 Kelkit (riv.), Turk.
31/F4 Kell, Ger.
86/D2 Keller (lake), NW,Can
70/B6 Kellerberrin, Austl.
84/E2 Kellett (cape), Can.
86/D1 Kellett (cape), NW,Can
88/C2 Kellogg, Id,US
90/D4 Kellogg, Id,US
22/B2 Kells, NI,UK
93/H5 Kelly (A.F.B.), Tx,US
96/D4 Kelly (A.F.B.), Tx,US
42/D5 Kelmė, Lith.
41/H1 Kel'mentsy, Ukr.
76/J6 Kélo, Chad
84/F5 Kelowna, Can.
86/E4 Kelowna, BC,Can
88/C2 Kelowna, BC,Can
90/D3 Kelowna, BC,Can
23/F5 Kelsall, Eng,UK
24/A6 Kelsey Head (pt.), UK
88/B2 Kelso, Wa,US
90/C4 Kelso, Wa,US
63/K3 Kelu, China
65/E1 Kelu, China
66/B3 Keluang, Malay.
25/G3 Kelvedon, Eng,UK
91/H2 Kelvington, Sk,Can
18/G2 Kem', Rus.
20/K2 Kem' (riv.), Rus.
42/G2 Kem', Rus.
42/G2 Kem' (riv.), Rus.
46/D3 Kem', Rus.
46/D3 Kem' (riv.), Rus.
78/D3 Ké Macina, Mali
44/F5 Kemah, Turk.
50/D2 Kemah, Turk.
50/D2 Kemaliye, Turk.
45/G4 Kemalpaşa, Turk.
50/E1 Kemalpaşa, Turk.
66/B3 Kemasik, Malay.
37/H3 Kematen in Tirol, Aus.
24/D3 Kemble, Eng,UK
36/D2 Kembs, Fr.
27/L4 Kemecse, Hun.
40/E1 Kemecse, Hun.
66/D3 Kemena (riv.), Malay.
49/B1 Kemer, Turk.
50/B2 Kemer, Turk.
51/M6 Kemerburgaz, Turk.
50/C2 Kemerhisar, Turk.
46/J4 Kemerovo, Rus.
18/F2 Kemi, Fin.
20/H2 Kemi, Fin.
46/C3 Kemi, Fin.
20/H2 Kemijaärvi, Fin.
18/F2 Kemijärvi, Fin.
42/E2 Kemijärvi, Fin.
46/C3 Kemijärvi, Fin.
18/F2 Kemijoki (riv.), Fin.
20/H2 Kemijoki (riv.), Fin.
42/E2 Kemijoki (riv.), Fin.
30/B2 Kemmel, Belg.
86/E4 Kemmerer, Wy,US
88/D3 Kemmerer, Wy,US
90/F5 Kemmerer, Wy,US
92/E2 Kemmerer, Wy,US
83/W Kemp (pen.), Ant.
93/H4 Kemp (lake), Tx,US
20/H2 Kempele, Fin.
42/E2 Kempele, Fin.
28/D6 Kempen, Ger.
31/G3 Kempenich, Ger.
26/C3 Kempenland (reg.), Belg.
28/C6 Kempenland (reg.), Belg.
31/E1 Kempenland (reg.), Belg.
28/B6 Kempisch (can.), Belg.
31/E1 Kempisch (can.), Belg.
71/J6 Kempsey, Austl.
73/E1 Kempsey, Austl.
25/F2 Kempston, Eng,UK
94/F2 Kempt (lake), Qu,Can
26/F5 Kempten, Ger.
33/J3 Kempten, Ger.
37/G2 Kempten, Ger.
73/C4 Kempton, Austl.
80/E2 Kempton Park, SAfr.
80/Q13 Kempton Park, SAfr.
98/J7 Kemptown, Md,US
67/E3 Kemul (peak), Indo.
85/H3 Kenai, Ak,US
86/A2 Kenai, Ak,US
85/J3 Kenai Fjords Nat'l Park, Ak,US
86/A3 Kenai Fords Nat'l Park, Ak,US
85/H3 Kenai Nat'l Wild. Ref., Ak,US
75/V18 Kenchela (gov.), Alg.
23/F3 Kendal, Eng,UK
73/E1 Kendall, Austl.
97/H5 Kendall, Fl,US
99/P16 Kendall (co.), Il,US
94/C3 Kendallville, In,US
67/F4 Kendari, Indo.
68/A4 Kendari, Indo.
39/J2 Kéndavros, Gre.
41/G5 Kéndavros, Gre.
28/D5 Kendel (riv.), Neth., Ger.
62/E3 Kendrāpāra, India
78/D4 Kénédougou (prov.), Burk.
76/C6 Kenema, SLeo.
78/C5 Kenema, SLeo.
60/E5 Keng Deng, Laos
63/J4 Keng Deng, Laos
82/C1 Kenge, Zaire
65/B1 Kēng Tung, Burma
80/C3 Kenhardt, SAfr.
76/C5 Kéniéba, Mali
78/C3 Kéniéba, Mali
78/C3 Kenié-Baoulé Rsv., Mali
25/E2 Kenilworth, Eng,UK
75/L13 Kenitra, Mor.
76/D1 Kenitra, Mor.
59/D3 Kenli, China
22/D1 Ken, Loch (lake), Sc,UK
21/G8 Kenmare (riv.), Ire.
21/H8 Kenmare, Ire.
91/H3 Kenmare, ND,US
95/S10 Kenmore, NY,US
99/C2 Kenmore, Wa,US
71/K4 Kenn (reef), Austl.
31/F4 Kenn, Ger.
95/G2 Kennebec (riv.), Me,US
95/G3 Kennebunk, Me,US
87/T6 Kennedy (chan.), NW,Can
85/H4 Kennedy (str.), Ak,US
37/F3 Kennelbach, Aus.
28/B4 Kennemerduinen Nat'l Park, Neth.
97/F4 Kenner, La,US
25/E4 Kennet (riv.), Eng,UK
24/D4 Kennet and Avon (can.), Eng,UK
93/K3 Kennett, Mo,US
94/B4 Kennett, Mo,US
97/F2 Kennett, Mo,US
88/C2 Kennewick, Wa,US
90/D4 Kennewick, Wa,US
91/M3 Kenogami (riv.), On,Can
87/H3 Kenogami (riv.), On,Can
94/C1 Kenogami (riv.), On,Can
85/L3 Keno Hill, Yk,Can
86/G4 Kenora, On,Can
89/H2 Kenora, On,Can
91/K3 Kenora, On,Can
94/A1 Kenora, On,Can
89/J3 Kenosha, Wi,US
91/M5 Kenosha, Wi,US
93/L2 Kenosha, Wi,US
94/C3 Kenosha, Wi,US
99/P14 Kenosha (co.), Wi,US
99/Q14 Kenosha, Wi,US
19/N7 Kensington & Chelsea (bor.), Eng,UK
86/F2 Kent (pen.), NW,Can
99/H7 Kent (co.), On,Can
19/P8 Kent (co.), Eng,UK
19/P8 Kent (val.), Eng,UK
23/F3 Kent (riv.), Eng,UK
25/G4 Kent (co.), Eng,UK
99/E6 Kent (lake), Mi,US
94/D3 Kent, Oh,US
100/D2 Kent, Tx,US
99/C3 Kent, Wa,US
46/G5 Kentau, Kaz.
73/C3 Kent Group (isls.), Austl.
61/J4 Kenting Nat'l Park, Tai.
94/D3 Kenton, Oh,US
89/J4 Kentucky (state), US
93/K3 Kentucky (state), US
94/C4 Kentucky (state), US
89/J4 Kentucky (lake), Ky,US
94/B4 Kentucky (lake), Ky,US
94/C4 Kentucky (riv.), Ky,US
25/G4 Kent, Vale of (val.), Eng,UK
87/K4 Kentville, NS,Can
95/H2 Kentville, NS,Can
22/D1 Ken, Water of (riv.), Sc,UK
74/F4 Kenya
77/N7 Kenya
82/G1 Kenya
57/H7 Ken-zaki (pt.), Japan
36/D1 Kenzingen, Ger.
89/H3 Keokuk, Ia,US
91/L5 Keokuk, Ia,US
93/K2 Keokuk, Ia,US
94/B3 Keokuk, Ia,US
97/F1 Keokuk, Ia,US
62/E3 Keonjhar, India
20/K2 Kepa, Rus.
67/J5 Kepi, Indo.
27/J3 Kępno, Pol.
72/C3 Keppel Sands, Austl.
50/B2 Kepsut, Turk.
62/C5 Kerala (state), India
64/F3 Kerala (state), India
73/B2 Kerang, Austl.
79/F4 Kéran Nat'l Park, Togo
39/H4 Keratéa, Gre.
44/F3 Kerch' (str.), Rus., Ukr.
19/G4 Kerch', Ukr.
44/F3 Kerch', Ukr.
46/D5 Kerch', Ukr.
90/D3 Keremeos, BC,Can
50/C1 Kerempe (pt.), Turk.
44/E4 Kerempe Burnu (pt.), Turk.
52/C5 Keren, Eth.
77/N4 Keren, Eth.
101/F1 Kerens, Tx,US
20/K2 Keret', Rus.
20/K2 Keret' (lake), Rus.
42/G2 Keret' (lake), Rus.
17/N8 Kerguélen (isl.), Fr.
71/R9 Kerikeri (cape), N.Z.
66/B4 Kerinci (peak), Indo.
28/C5 Kerkdriel, Neth.
52/C5 Kerkebet, Eth.
28/D6 Kerken, Ger.
46/G6 Kerki, Trkm.
39/H2 Kerkínis (lake), Gre.
41/F5 Kerkínis (lake), Gre.
39/F3 Kérkira, Gre.
39/F3 Kérkira (Corfu) (isl.), Gre.
26/D3 Kerkrade, Neth.
31/F2 Kerkrade, Neth.
28/C5 Kerkwijk, Neth.
68/G8 Kermadec (isls.), N.Z.
46/F6 Kermān, Iran
48/E6 Kermān, Iran
51/J4 Kermān, Iran
51/J4 Kermān (gov.), Iran
53/G2 Kermān, Iran
39/K1 Kermen, Bul.
41/H4 Kermen, Bul.
93/G5 Kermit, Tx,US
96/C4 Kermit, Tx,US
92/C4 Kern (riv.), Ca,US
33/H3 Kerns, Swi.
37/E4 Kerns, Swi.
92/C4 Kern, South Fork (riv.), Ca,US
39/J4 Kéros (isl.), Gre.
93/J4 Kerr (lake), Ok,US
94/E4 Kerr (res.), Va,US
90/F3 Kerrobert, Sk,Can
101/F2 Kerrville, Tx,US
88/G5 Kerrville, Tx,US
93/H5 Kerrville, Tx,US
96/D4 Kerrville, Tx,US
24/C2 Kerry, Wal,UK
75/N13 Kert (riv.), Mor.
47/M5 Kerulen (riv.), Mong.,China
54/G2 Kerulen (riv.), Mong.
48/L5 Kerulen (riv.), China.,Mong.
76/E2 Kerzaz, Alg.
31/H4 Kerzenheim, Ger.
36/D4 Kerzers, Swi.
94/D1 Kesagami (riv.), On,Can
39/K2 Keşan, Turk.
41/H5 Keşan, Turk.
44/C4 Keşan, Turk.
50/A1 Keşan, Turk.
37/F4 Kesch, Piz (peak), Swi.
55/N4 Kesen'numa, Japan
25/H2 Kesgrave, Eng,UK
55/K2 Keshan, China
62/B3 Keshod, India
44/E5 Keskin, Turk.
50/C2 Keskin, Turk.
20/H3 Keski-Suomi (prov.), Fin.
42/E3 Keski-Suomi (prov.), Fin.
25/H2 Kessingland, Eng,UK
44/D4 Kestel, Turk.
50/B1 Kestel, Turk.
20/J2 Kesten'ga, Rus.
28/C5 Kesteren, Neth.
23/E2 Keswick, Eng,UK
40/C2 Keszthely, Hun.
46/J4 Ket' (riv.), Rus.
79/F5 Keta, Gha.
42/K3 Keta (riv.), Rus.
85/M4 Ketchikan, Ak,US
86/C3 Ketchikan, Ak,US
86/E4 Ketchum, Id,US
88/D3 Ketchum, Id,US
90/E5 Ketchum, Id,US
92/D2 Ketchum, Id,US
79/E5 Kete Krachi, Gha.
28/C3 Ketelmeer (lake), Neth.
27/L1 Kętrzyn, Pol.
42/D5 Kętrzyn, Pol.
25/F2 Kettering, Eng,UK
94/C4 Kettering, Oh,US
97/G2 Kettering, Oh,US
90/D3 Kettle (riv.), Can., US
91/K4 Kettle (riv.), Mn,US
99/P14 Kettle Moraine St. Park, Wi,US
23/F3 Kettlewell, Eng,UK
28/B4 Keukenhof, Neth.
20/H3 Keuruu, Fin.
42/E3 Keuruu, Fin.
28/D5 Kevelaer, Ger.
103/H1 Kew, Trks.
94/C2 Kewaunee, Wi,US
91/L4 Keweenaw (bay), Mi,US
91/L4 Keweenaw (pen.), Mi,US
89/J2 Keweenaw (pt.), Mi,US
91/M4 Keweenaw (pt.), Mi,US
94/B2 Keweenaw (bay), Mi,US
94/B2 Keweenaw (pen.), Mi,US
94/C2 Keweenaw (pt.), Mi,US
19/N7 Kew Gardens, Eng,UK
104/A1 Key Largo, Fl,US
89/K6 Key Largo, Fl,US
97/H5 Key Largo, Fl,US
24/D4 Keynsham, Eng,UK
99/B2 Keyport, Wa,US
94/E4 Keyser, WV,US
97/J2 Keyser, WV,US
84/J7 Key West, Fl,US
104/A1 Key West, Fl,US
89/K7 Key West, Fl,US
97/H5 Key West, Fl,US
23/G6 Keyworth, Eng,UK
27/L4 Kežmarok, Slvk.
44/B2 Kežmarok, Slvk.
80/C2 Kgalagadi (dist.), Bots.
80/D2 Kgatleng (dist.), Bots.
77/Q5 Khaanziir (cape), Som.
47/P5 Khabarovsk, Rus.
55/M2 Khabarovsk, Rus.
45/J4 Khachmas, Azer.
51/G1 Khachmas, Azer.
60/B5 Khadaungnge (peak), Burma
52/E3 Khafjī, Ra's al, SAr.
62/D2 Khairābād, India
53/J3 Khairpur, Pak.
62/A2 Khairpur, Pak.
80/C2 Khakhea, Bots.
39/H3 Khalándrion, Gre.
39/L6 Khalándrion, Gre.
51/G2 Khalkhāl, Iran
52/E1 Khalkhāl, Iran
39/H2 Khalkhidhikhi (pen.), Gre.
39/H2 Khalkidhón, Gre.
39/H3 Khalkís, Gre.
44/B5 Khalkís, Gre.
54/E1 Khamar-Daban (mts.), Rus.
62/D3 Khamaria, India
53/J4 Khambaliya, India
53/L4 Khāmgaon, India
62/C3 Khāmgaon, India
52/D5 Khamīs Mushayţ, SAr.
77/P4 Khamīs Mushayţ, SAr.
60/E5 Khamkeut, Laos
63/H4 Khamkeut, Laos
62/D4 Khammam, India
52/D5 Khamr, Yem.
53/J1 Khānābād, Afg.
51/F3 Khānaqīn, Iraq
52/E2 Khānaqīn, Iraq
53/L4 Khandwa, India
62/C3 Khandwa, India
76/F1 Khanem (well), Alg.
53/K2 Khānewāl, Pak.
64/A2 Khānewāl, Pak.
64/B2 Khāngāh Dogrān, Pak.
18/F5 Khaniá, Gre.
39/J5 Khaniá, Gre.
77/K1 Khaniá, Gre.
48/N5 Khanka (lake), China, Rus.
47/P5 Khanka (lake), Rus.
55/L3 Khanka (lake), Rus.
54/E1 Khankh, Mong.
64/D2 Khanna, India
53/K3 Khānpur, Pak.
62/B2 Khānpur, Pak.
46/G3 Khanty-Mansiysk, Rus.
46/G3 Khanty-Mansiysk Aut. Okr., Rus.
49/D4 Khān Yūnus, Gaza
50/C4 Khān Yūnus, Gaza
65/C3 Khao Chamao-Khao Wong Nat'l Park, Thai.
65/C3 Khao Khitchakut Nat'l Park, Thai.
63/G5 Khao Laem (res.), Thai.
65/B3 Khao Laem (res.), Thai.
65/B3 Khao Sam Roi Yot Nat'l Park, Thai.
65/C3 Khao Wong-Khao Chamao Nat'l Park, Thai.
65/C3 Khao Yai Nat'l Park, Thai.
47/M5 Khapcheranga, Rus.
62/E3 Kharagpur, India
64/A1 Kharak, Pak.
53/J3 Khārān, Pak.
53/F2 Kharānoq, Iran
64/D2 Kharar, India
49/D4 Kharās, WBnk.
49/G8 Kharās, WBnk.
53/K3 Kharbara, India
49/G8 Kharbatā, WBnk.
53/L4 Khargon, India
62/C3 Khargon, India
64/B1 Khāriān, Pak.
51/G4 Khārk (isl.), Iran
19/G4 Khar'kov, Ukr.
44/F2 Khar'kov, Ukr.
46/D5 Khar'kov, Ukr.
44/F2 Khar'kov Obl., Ukr.
39/J2 Kharmanli, Bul.
41/G5 Kharmanli, Bul.
44/C4 Kharmanli, Bul.
42/J4 Kharovsk, Rus.
75/M13 Kharrour (riv.), Mor.
77/M4 Khartoum (cap.), Sudan
52/B5 Khartoum (Al Khurţūm) (cap.), Sudan
77/M4 Khartoum North, Sudan
77/M4 Khartūm (Khartoum) (cap.), Sudan
47/P5 Khasan, Rus.
45/H4 Khasavyurt, Rus.
53/H2 Khāsh (riv.), Afg.
53/H3 Khāsh, Iran
52/C6 Khashm al Qirbah, Sudan
45/G4 Khashuri, Geo.
51/E1 Khashuri, Geo.
18/F4 Khaskovo, Bul.
39/J2 Khaskovo, Bul.
39/J2 Khaskovo (prov.), Bul.
41/G5 Khaskovo, Bul.
41/G5 Khaskovo (reg.), Bul.
44/C4 Khaskovo, Bul.
50/A1 Khaskovo, Bul.
47/L2 Khatanga (gulf), Rus.
47/L2 Khatanga (riv.), Rus.
49/C4 Khatmia (pass), Egypt
50/C4 Khatmia (pass), Egypt
64/B1 Khaur, Pak.
52/C3 Khaybar, SAr.
52/D5 Khaybar, SAr.
77/N2 Khaybar, SAr.
53/G3 Khaymah, Ra's al, UAE
51/F3 Khazzān Darbandīkhān (res.), Iraq
51/F3 Khazzān Dūkān (res.), Iraq
77/M4 Khazzān Jabal Al Awliyā (dam), Sudan
75/S15 Khemis el Khechna, Alg.
75/S15 Khemis Miliana, Alg.
76/F1 Khemis Miliana, Alg.
63/J4 Khemmarat, Thai.
75/V18 Khenchela, Alg.
76/D1 Khenifra, Mor.
43/V6 Khepoyarvi (lake), Rus.
51/G4 Khersān (riv.), Iran
52/F2 Khersān (riv.), Iran
18/G4 Kherson, Ukr.
41/L2 Kherson, Ukr.
44/E3 Kherson, Ukr.
46/D5 Kherson, Ukr.
41/L2 Kherson Obl., Ukr.
44/E3 Kherson Obl., Ukr.
63/J4 Khe Sanh, Viet.
53/G2 Khezrī, Iran
47/M4 Khilok, Rus.
54/F1 Khilok (riv.), Rus.
54/G1 Khilok, Rus.
43/X9 Khimki, Rus.
39/J3 Khíos (isl.), Gre.
39/K3 Khíos, Gre.
44/C5 Khíos, Gre.
44/C5 Khíos (isl.), Gre.
50/A2 Khíos, Gre.
50/A2 Khíos (isl.), Gre.
39/J1 Khisarya, Bul.
41/G4 Khisarya, Bul.
46/G5 Khiva, Uzb.
41/H4 Khlebarovo, Bul.
63/H5 Khlung, Thai.
66/B1 Khlung, Thai.
44/C2 Khmel'nitsiy Obl., Ukr.
44/C2 Khmel'nitskiy, Ukr.
46/C5 Khmel'nitskiy, Ukr.
50/E1 Khobi, Geo.
53/J2 Khojak (pass), Pak.
65/C3 Khok Samrong, Thai.
53/L2 Khoksar, India
46/G6 Kholm, Afg.
53/J1 Kholm, Afg.
47/Q5 Kholmsk, Rus.
55/N2 Kholmsk, Rus.
51/G2 Khomām, Iran
46/F6 Khomeynī shahr, Iran
51/G3 Khomeynī shahr, Iran
52/F2 Khomeynī shahr, Iran
52/F3 Khonj, Iran
63/H4 Khon Kaen, Thai.
65/C2 Khon Kaen, Thai.
19/H3 Khoper (riv.), Rus.
45/G2 Khopër (riv.), Rus.
46/E4 Khōper (riv.), Rus.
47/P5 Khor, Rus.
47/P5 Khor (riv.), Rus.
55/M2 Khor (riv.), Rus.
51/J3 Khorāsān (gov.), Iran
39/J5 Khóra Sfakíon, Gre.
50/A2 Khoríon, Gre.
82/C5 Khorixas, Namb.
46/H6 Khorog, Taj.
53/K1 Khorog, Taj.
46/E6 Khorramābād, Iran
51/G3 Khorramābād, Iran
52/E2 Khorramābād, Iran
51/G4 Khorramshahr, Iran
52/E2 Khorramshahr, Iran
77/Q1 Khorramshahr, Iran
60/D5 Kho Sawai (plat.), Thai.
63/H4 Kho Sawai (plat.), Thai.
65/C2 Kho Sawai (plat.), Thai.
41/H1 Khotin, Ukr.
85/G3 Khotol (mtn.), Ak,US
76/D1 Khouribga, Mor.
54/C1 Khovu-Aksy, Rus.
60/A3 Khowai, India
63/F3 Khowai, India
53/J2 Khowst, Afg.
39/J2 Khrisoúpolis, Gre.
41/G5 Khrisoúpolis, Gre.
44/C4 Khrisoúpolis, Gre.
45/L2 Khromtau, Kaz.
46/F4 Khromtau, Kaz.
39/J5 Khrysí (isl.), Gre.
65/C2 Khuan Ubon Ratana (res.), Thai.
51/F1 Khuchni, Rus.
51/G1 Khudat, Azer.
64/C2 Khudiān, Pak.
46/G5 Khudzhand, Taj.
80/C2 Khuis, Bots.
63/H5 Khu Khan, Thai.
62/E3 Khulna, Bang.
50/E1 Khulo, Geo.
51/L1 Khūnjerāb (pass), Pak.
62/C3 Khurai, India
62/E3 Khurda, India
62/C2 Khurja, India
53/G2 Khūsf, Iran
64/B1 Khushāb, Pak.
27/M4 Khust, Ukr.
41/F1 Khust, Ukr.
44/B2 Khust, Ukr.
53/J3 Khuzdār, Pak.
51/G4 Khūzestān (gov.), Iran
51/G4 Khūzestan, Jolgeh-ye (plain), Iran
55/L3 Khvalynka, Rus.
51/G3 Khvonsār, Iran
52/F2 Khvonsār, Iran
51/H3 Khvor, Iran
53/G2 Khvor, Iran
52/F3 Khvormūj, Iran
46/E6 Khvoy, Iran
51/F2 Khvoy, Iran
64/A1 Khyber (pass), Pak.
53/K2 Khyber (Barowghīl) (pass), Afg., Pak.
68/E5 Kia, Sol.
73/D2 Kiama, Austl.
96/E3 Kiamichi (mts.), Ok,US
85/F2 Kiana, Ak,US
76/F5 Kianji (lake), Nga.
23/G2 Kibblesworth, Eng,UK
20/J1 Kibergneset (pt.), Nor.
82/G1 Kibo (peak), Tanz.
82/F1 Kibondo, Tanz.
41/K5 Kıbrısçık, Turk.
39/G2 Kičevo, Macd.
40/E5 Kičevo, Macd.
76/F4 Kidal, Mali
79/F2 Kidal, Mali
67/G2 Kidapawan, Phil.
24/D2 Kidderminster, Eng,UK
77/M7 Kidepo Valley Nat'l Park, Ugan.
23/F5 Kidsgrove, Eng,UK
24/B3 Kidwelly, Wal,UK
20/D5 Kiel (bay), Den.,Ger.
18/E3 Kiel, Ger.
26/F1 Kiel, Ger.
26/F1 Kiel (bay), Ger.
46/B4 Kiel, Ger.
18/F3 Kielce, Pol.
27/L3 Kielce, Pol.
27/L3 Kielce (prov.), Pol.
44/B2 Kielce, Pol.
46/C4 Kielce, Pol.
23/F1 Kielder, Eng,UK
23/F1 Kielder (res.), Eng,U
65/D1 Kien An, Viet.
63/J5 Kien Duc, Viet.
65/D4 Kien Duc, Viet.
66/C1 Kien Duc, Viet.
63/J6 Kien Thanh, Viet.
65/D4 Kien Thanh, Viet.
66/C2 Kien Thanh, Viet.
29/E6 Kierspe, Ger.
31/G1 Kierspe, Ger.
68/E5 Kieta, PNG
18/G3 Kiev (cap.), Ukr.
46/D4 Kiev (cap.), Ukr.
44/D2 Kiev (Kiyev) (cap.), Ukr.
44/D2 Kiev Obl., Ukr.
76/G4 Kiffa, Mrta.
78/C2 Kiffa, Mrta.
39/L6 Kifisiá, Gre.
51/F3 Kifrī, Iraq
52/D2 Kifrī, Iraq
77/M8 Kigali (cap.), Rwa.
82/F1 Kigali (cap.), Rwa.
50/E2 Kiğı, Turk.
82/E1 Kigoma, Tanz.
58/E4 Kigye, SKor.
88/T10 Kihei, Hi,US
88/U11 Kiholo, Hi,US
56/D4 Kii (chan.), Japan
56/D4 Kii (mts.), Japan
58/E5 Kijang, SKor.
88/R9 Kikepa (pt.), Hi,US
85/H2 Kikiktat (mtn.), Ak,U
40/E3 Kikinda, Yugo.
82/C2 Kikwit, Zaire
64/G4 Kīlakarai, India
102/E3 Kilambe (mtn.), Nic.
53/L2 Kilār, India
88/S9 Kilauea, Hi,US
22/B4 Kilberry, Ire.
95/Q9 Kilbride, On,Can
58/E2 Kilchu, NKor.
22/B5 Kilcock, Ire.
22/B5 Kilcoole, Ire.
72/D4 Kilcoy, Austl.
22/B5 Kilcullen, Ire.
22/B5 Kildare, Ire.
22/B5 Kildare (co.), Ire.
99/P15 Kildeer, Il,US
20/K1 Kil'den (isl.), Rus.
42/G1 Kil'den (isl.), Rus.
21/H8 Kilgarvan, Ire.
93/J4 Kilgore, Tx,US
96/E3 Kilgore, Tx,US
23/H3 Kilham, Eng,UK
87/R7 Kilian (isl.), NW,Car
82/G1 Kilifi, Kenya
64/F4 Kilikollūr, India
41/K5 Kilimli, Turk.
44/D4 Kilimli, Turk.
50/B1 Kilimli, Turk.
82/G2 Kilindoni, Tanz.
20/H4 Kilingi-Nõmme, Est
42/E4 Kilingi-Nõmme, Est
62/D6 Kilinochchi, SrL.
64/H4 Kilinochchi (dist.), SrL.
49/E1 Kilis, Turk.
50/D2 Kilis, Turk.
52/C1 Kilis, Turk.
41/J3 Kiliya, Ukr.
44/D3 Kiliya, Ukr.
21/H7 Kilkee, Ire.
22/B3 Kilkeel, NI,UK
22/A6 Kilkenny (co.), Ire.
21/B4 Kilkenny, Ire.
39/H2 Kilkís, Gre.
40/F5 Kilkís, Gre.
44/B4 Kilkís, Gre.
72/D4 Kilkivan, Austl.
22/B5 Kill, Ire.
90/F2 Killam, Can
23/G5 Killamarsh, Eng,UK
72/H8 Killara, Austl.
73/E1 Killarney, Austl.
93/J1 Killarney, Can
86/G4 Killarney, Mb,Can
21/H7 Killarney, Ire.
91/H4 Killdeer, ND,US
89/G5 Killeen, Tx,US
93/H5 Killeen, Tx,US
96/D4 Killeen, Tx,US
22/C3 Killinchy, NI,UK
87/K2 Killinek (isl.), NW,C
39/G4 Killíni, Gre.
39/H4 Killíni (peak), Gre.
22/C3 Killough, NI,UK
21/A3 Killucan, Ire.
21/A3 Killybegs, Ire.
22/A2 Killyclogher, NI,UK
22/A3 Killyleagh, NI,UK
22/B5 Kilmacanoge, Ire.
21/A4 Kilmallock, Ire.
21/C3 Kilmarnock, Sc,UK
24/B5 Kilmar Tor (hill), Eng,UK
22/B6 Kilmichael (pt.), Ire
73/C3 Kilmore, Austl.
22/A4 Kilnaleck, Ire.
82/G2 Kilosa, Tanz.
22/B1 Kilraghts, NI,UK
22/B2 Kilrea, NI,UK

21/H7 **Kilrush**, Ire.
82/G2 **Kilwa Kivinje**, Tanz.
82/G2 **Kilwa Masoko**, Tanz.
22/C2 **Kilwaughter**, NI,UK
67/J5 **Kimaan**, Indo.
70/F6 **Kimba**, Austl.
91/H5 **Kimball**, Ne,US
91/J5 **Kimball**, SD,US
93/H2 **Kimball**, SD,US
68/E5 **Kimbe**, PNG
68/B6 **Kimberley** (plat.), Austl.
70/D3 **Kimberley** (plat.), Austl.
72/B2 **Kimberley** (cape), Austl.
86/E4 **Kimberley**, BC,Can
90/E3 **Kimberley**, BC,Can
80/D3 **Kimberley**, SAfr.
82/D6 **Kimberley**, SAfr.
47/N5 **Kimch'aek**, NKor.
55/K3 **Kimch'aek**, NKor.
58/E2 **Kimch'aek**, NKor.
56/A2 **Kimch'ŏn**, SKor.
58/E4 **Kimch'ŏn**, SKor.
55/K4 **Kimhae**, SKor.
56/A3 **Kimhae**, SKor.
58/E5 **Kimhae**, SKor.
39/J3 **Kími**, Gre.
39/H2 **Kímina**, Gre.
57/F3 **Kimitsu**, Japan
57/H7 **Kimitsu**, Japan
55/K4 **Kimje**, SKor.
58/D5 **Kimje**, SKor.
39/J2 **Kimméria**, Gre.
41/G5 **Kimméria**, Gre.
58/G7 **Kimnyangjang-ni**, SKor.
39/J4 **Kímolos** (isl.), Gre.
42/F3 **Kimovaara**, Rus.
44/F1 **Kimovsk**, Rus.
82/D2 **Kimpanga**, Zaire
58/D4 **Kimp'o**, SKor.
58/F6 **Kimp'o**, SKor.
18/G3 **Kimry**, Rus.
42/H4 **Kimry**, Rus.
46/D4 **Kimry**, Rus.
67/E2 **Kinabalu** (peak), Malay.
82/G1 **Kinango**, Kenya
67/E2 **Kinatangan** (riv.), Malay.
90/D2 **Kinbasket** (lake), BC,Can
90/G3 **Kincaid**, Sk,Can
94/D2 **Kincardine**, On,Can
73/B2 **Kinchega Nat'l Park**, Austl.
82/D2 **Kindambi**, Zaire
33/L3 **Kindberg**, Aus.
40/B2 **Kindberg**, Aus.
23/G5 **Kinder Scout** (mtn.), Eng,UK
86/F3 **Kindersley**, Sk,Can
88/E1 **Kindersley**, Sk,Can
90/F3 **Kindersley**, Sk,Can
70/C5 **Kindia**, Gui.
78/B4 **Kindia**, Gui.
78/B4 **Kindia** (comm.), Gui.
31/G5 **Kindsbach**, Ger.
82/E1 **Kindu**, Zaire
45/J1 **Kinel'**, Rus.
19/H3 **Kineshma**, Rus.
42/J4 **Kineshma**, Rus.
46/E4 **Kineshma**, Rus.
25/E2 **Kineton**, Eng,UK
70/B6 **King** (lake), Austl.
70/C3 **King** (sound), Austl.
71/G7 **King** (isl.), Austl.
72/B4 **King** (peak), Austl.
73/C3 **King** (isl.), Austl.
90/B2 **King** (isl.), BC,Can
85/N4 **King** (mtn.), BC,Can
85/J3 **King** (peak), Yk,Can
100/E2 **King** (mtn.), Tx,US
99/D2 **King** (co.), Wa,US
72/C4 **Kingaroy**, Austl.
87/R7 **King Christian** (isl.), NW,Can
84/P3 **King Christian IX Land** (reg.), Grld.
84/Q2 **King Christian X Land** (reg.), Grld.
95/Q8 **King City**, On,Can
92/B3 **King City**, Ca,US
85/F4 **King Cove**, Ak,US
93/H4 **Kingfisher**, Ok,US
96/D3 **Kingfisher**, Ok,US
84/N3 **King Frederik VI Coast** (reg.), Grld.
84/Q2 **King Frederik VIII Land** (reg.), Grld.
69/L6 **King George** (isl.), FrPol.
94/E4 **King George**, Va,US
97/J2 **King George**, Va,US
19/N7 **King George's** (res.), Eng,UK
73/C3 **Kinglake Nat'l Park**, Austl.
73/G5 **Kinglake Nat'l Park**, Austl.
70/D3 **King Leopold** (ranges), Austl.
69/J4 **Kingman** (reef), PacUS
88/D4 **Kingman**, Az,US
92/D4 **Kingman**, Az,US
93/H3 **Kingman**, Ks,US
96/D2 **Kingman**, Ks,US
98/E5 **King of Prussia**, Pa,US
70/F6 **Kingoonyah**, Austl.
92/C3 **Kings** (riv.), Ca,US
88/D3 **Kings** (peak), Ut,US
92/E2 **Kings** (peak), Ut,US
85/G4 **King Salmon**, Ak,US
24/C6 **Kingsbridge**, Eng,UK
88/C4 **Kings Canyon Nat'l Park**, Ca,US
92/C3 **Kings Canyon Nat'l Park**, Ca,US
25/E4 **Kingsclere**, Eng,UK
25/F1 **King's Cliffe**, Eng,UK
70/F7 **Kingscote**, Austl.
22/B4 **Kingscourt**, Ire.
94/B2 **Kingsford**, Mi,US
24/D2 **Kingsland**, Eng,UK
19/M6 **Kings Langley**, Eng,UK
25/F3 **Kings Langley**, Eng,UK
25/G1 **King's Lynn**, Eng,UK
89/K4 **Kingsport**, Tn,US
94/D4 **Kingsport**, Tn,US
97/H2 **Kingsport**, Tn,US
25/E2 **Kings Sutton**, Eng,UK
24/C5 **Kingsteignton**, Eng,UK
71/M5 **Kingston**, Austl.
73/C4 **Kingston**, Austl.
94/E2 **Kingston**, Can
87/J4 **Kingston**, On,Can
89/L3 **Kingston**, On,Can
103/G2 **Kingston** (cap.), Jam.
68/F7 **Kingston**, Norfl.
89/M3 **Kingston**, NY,US
94/F3 **Kingston**, NY,US
99/C2 **Kingston**, Wa,US
73/A3 **Kingston S.E.**, Austl.
19/N7 **Kingston upon Thames** (bor.), Eng,UK
25/F4 **Kingston upon Thames**, Eng,UK
104/F4 **Kingstown** (cap.), StV.
106/F1 **Kingstown** (cap.), StV.
97/J3 **Kingstree**, SC,US
99/G7 **Kingsville**, On,Can
101/F3 **Kingsville**, Tx,US
89/G6 **Kingsville**, Tx,US
96/D5 **Kingsville**, Tx,US
24/D2 **Kingswinford**, Eng,UK
24/D4 **Kingswood**, Eng,UK
49/D3 **King Ṭalāl** (dam), Jor.
24/C2 **Kington**, Eng,UK
86/G2 **King William** (isl.), NW,Can
80/D4 **King William's Town**, SAfr.
44/C5 **Kınık**, Turk.
50/A2 **Kınık**, Turk.
85/L4 **Kinkaid** (mt.), Ak,US
82/B1 **Kinkala**, Congo
56/D3 **Kinki** (prov.), Japan
57/M9 **Kinki** (prov.), Japan
78/B4 **Kinkon, Chutes de** (falls), Gui.
22/E5 **Kinmel**, Wal,UK
20/E4 **Kinna**, Swe.
21/E2 **Kinnairds Head** (pt.), Sc,UK
22/A5 **Kinnegad**, Ire.
49/F8 **Kinneret-Negev Conduit**, Isr.
64/H4 **Kinniya**, SrL.
56/D3 **Kino** (riv.), Japan
94/D1 **Kinojé** (riv.), On,Can
28/C6 **Kinrooi**, Belg.
31/E1 **Kinrooi**, Belg.
95/R8 **Kinsale**, On,Can
20/C3 **Kinsarvik**, Nor.
82/C1 **Kinshasa** (cap.), Zaire
93/H3 **Kinsley**, Ks,US
96/D2 **Kinsley**, Ks,US
89/L4 **Kinston**, NC,US
97/J3 **Kinston**, NC,US
79/E4 **Kintampo**, Gha.
98/E5 **Kintnersville**, Pa,US
22/C1 **Kintyre** (pen.), Sc,UK
22/C1 **Kintyre, Mull of** (pt.), Sc,UK
36/D1 **Kintzheim**, Fr.
57/F2 **Kinu** (riv.), Japan
57/H7 **Kinu** (riv.), Japan
21/A4 **Kinvarra**, Ire.
74/F4 **Kinyeti** (peak), Sudan
77/M7 **Kinyeti** (peak), Sudan
26/E3 **Kinzig** (riv.), Ger.
37/E1 **Kinzig** (riv.), Ger.
88/T10 **Kipahulu**, Hi,US
39/G4 **Kiparissía**, Gre.
39/G4 **Kiparissía** (gulf), Gre.
94/E2 **Kipawa** (lake), Qu,Can
82/F2 **Kipili**, Tanz.
91/H3 **Kipling**, Sk,Can
85/F4 **Kipnuk**, Ak,US
36/D5 **Kippel**, Swi.
22/B5 **Kippure** (mtn.), Ire.
82/E3 **Kipushi**, Zaire
57/N10 **Kira**, Japan
39/H3 **Kira Panayía** (isl.), Gre.
39/K2 **Kirazlı**, Turk.
41/H5 **Kirazlı**, Turk.
20/G4 **Kirbla**, Est.
31/G4 **Kirchberg**, Ger.
36/D3 **Kirchberg**, Swi.
37/G1 **Kirchberg an der Iller**, Ger.
29/F3 **Kirchdorf**, Ger.
37/G1 **Kirchheim**, Ger.
31/H4 **Kirchheimbolanden**, Ger.
26/E4 **Kirchheim unter Teck**, Ger.
29/F6 **Kirchhundem**, Ger.
31/H1 **Kirchhundem**, Ger.
29/F4 **Kirchlengern**, Ger.
29/G3 **Kirchlinteln**, Ger.
37/H2 **Kirchsee** (lake), Ger.
36/D2 **Kirchzarten**, Ger.
22/C3 **Kircubbin**, NI,UK
22/D2 **Kircudbright** (bay), Sc,UK
47/L4 **Kirensk**, Rus.
46/F5 **Kirgiz Steppe** (grsld.), Kaz.,Rus.
39/H3 **Kiriákion**, Gre.
68/H5 **Kiribati**
45/G4 **Kırık**, Turk.
49/E1 **Kırıkhan**, Turk.
50/D2 **Kırıkhan**, Turk.
52/C1 **Kırıkhan**, Turk.
44/E5 **Kırıkkale**, Turk.
50/C2 **Kırıkkale**, Turk.
50/C2 **Kirikkale** (prov.), Turk.
54/C3 **Kirikkuduk**, China
42/G4 **Kirishi**, Rus.
56/B5 **Kirishima-Yaku Nat'l Park**, Japan
56/B5 **Kirishima-yama** (mtn.), Japan
69/K4 **Kiritimati** (Christmas) (atoll), Kiri.
44/C5 **Kırkağaç**, Turk.
50/A2 **Kırkağaç**, Turk.
23/G4 **Kirkburton**, Eng,UK
23/F5 **Kirkby**, Eng,UK
23/G5 **Kirkby in Ashfield**, Eng,UK
23/F3 **Kirkby Lonsdale**, Eng,UK
23/H3 **Kirkbymoorside**, Eng,UK
23/F3 **Kirkby Stephen**, Eng,UK
21/D2 **Kirkcaldy**, Sc,UK
22/C2 **Kirkcolm**, Sc,UK
22/D2 **Kirkcowan**, Sc,UK
22/D2 **Kirkcudbright**, Sc,UK
53/K5 **Kirkee**, India
62/B4 **Kirkee**, India
20/J1 **Kirkenes**, Nor.
42/F1 **Kirkenes**, Nor.
23/F4 **Kirkham**, Eng,UK
22/D2 **Kirkinner**, Sc,UK
95/N7 **Kirkland**, Qu,Can
99/C2 **Kirkland**, Wa,US
84/J5 **Kirkland Lake**, Can.
87/H4 **Kirkland Lake**, On,Can
89/K2 **Kirkland Lake**, On,Can
94/D1 **Kirkland Lake**, On,Can
50/A2 **Kırklar** (peak), Turk.
41/H5 **Kırklareli**, Turk.
41/H5 **Kırklareli** (prov.), Turk.
44/C4 **Kırklareli**, Turk.
44/C4 **Kırklareli** (prov.), Turk.
50/A1 **Kırklareli**, Turk.
50/A1 **Kırklareli** (prov.), Turk.
86/D3 **Kirkmichael**, IM,UK
41/L2 **Kirkovgrad Obl.**, Ukr.
83/M **Kirkpatrick** (mt.), Ant.
23/F3 **Kirkstone** (pass), Eng,UK
89/H3 **Kirksville**, Mo,US
91/K5 **Kirksville**, Mo,US
93/J2 **Kirksville**, Mo,US
96/E1 **Kirksville**, Mo,US
46/E6 **Kirkūk**, Iraq
51/F3 **Kirkūk**, Iraq
52/D1 **Kirkūk**, Iraq
80/D4 **Kirkwood**, SAfr.
26/D4 **Kirn**, Ger.
31/G4 **Kirn**, Ger.
33/G2 **Kirn**, Ger.
44/E1 **Kirov**, Rus.
19/H4 **Kirovakan**, Arm.
45/H4 **Kirovakan**, Arm.
46/E5 **Kirovakan**, Arm.
51/F1 **Kirovakan**, Arm.
43/L4 **Kirovo-Chepetsk**, Rus.
18/G4 **Kirovograd**, Ukr.
44/E2 **Kirovograd**, Ukr.
46/D5 **Kirovograd**, Ukr.
44/D2 **Kirovograd Obl.**, Ukr.
20/K2 **Kirovsk**, Rus.
42/G2 **Kirovsk**, Rus.
43/W7 **Kirovsk**, Rus.
55/L2 **Kirovskiy**, Rus.
31/H5 **Kirrweiler**, Ger.
19/H3 **Kirsanov**, Rus.
45/G1 **Kirsanov**, Rus.
44/E5 **Kırşehir**, Turk.
50/C2 **Kırşehir**, Turk.
50/C2 **Kirsehir** (prov.), Turk.
23/H6 **Kirton**, Eng,UK
23/H5 **Kirton in Lindsey**, Eng,UK
18/F2 **Kiruna**, Swe.
20/G2 **Kiruna**, Swe.
42/D2 **Kiruna**, Swe.
46/C3 **Kiruna**, Swe.
57/F2 **Kiryū**, Japan
20/E4 **Kisa**, Swe.
77/L7 **Kisangani**, Zaire
57/F3 **Kisarazu**, Japan
57/H7 **Kisarazu**, Japan
27/K5 **Kisbér**, Hun.
46/J4 **Kiselevsk**, Rus.
51/H5 **Kīsh** (isl.), Iran
52/F3 **Kīsh**, Iran
62/E2 **Kishanganj**, India
53/K3 **Kishangarh**, India
62/B2 **Kishangarh**, India
18/F4 **Kishinëv** (cap.), Mol.
41/J2 **Kishinëv** (cap.), Mol.
44/D3 **Kishinëv** (cap.), Mol.
46/C5 **Kishinëv** (cap.), Mol.
56/D3 **Kishiwada**, Japan
57/L10 **Kishiwada**, Japan
62/F3 **Kishorganj**, Bang.
53/L2 **Kishtwar**, India
64/C1 **Kishtwar**, India
99/N15 **Kishwaukee** (riv.), Il,US
77/M8 **Kisii**, Kenya
47/T4 **Kiska** (isl.), Ak,US
85/B5 **Kiska** (vol.), Ak,US
85/B6 **Kiska** (isl.), Ak,US
90/C2 **Kiskatinaw** (riv.), BC,Can
91/J2 **Kiskitto** (lake), Mb,Can
40/D2 **Kiskőrös**, Hun.
40/D2 **Kiskunfélegyháza**, Hun.
44/A3 **Kiskunfélegyháza**, Hun.
40/D2 **Kiskunhalas**, Hun.
40/D2 **Kiskunmajsa**, Hun.
40/D2 **Kiskunsági Nat'l Park**, Hun.
19/H4 **Kislovodsk**, Rus.
45/G4 **Kislovodsk**, Rus.
46/E5 **Kislovodsk**, Rus.
77/P8 **Kismaayo** (Chisimayu), Som.
57/E3 **Kiso** (riv.), Japan
57/M9 **Kiso** (riv.), Japan
57/M9 **Kisogawa**, Japan
57/M9 **Kisozaki**, Japan
38/A5 **Kisrah**, Tun.
39/H5 **Kíssamos**, Gre.
78/C6 **Kissidougou**, Gui.
97/H4 **Kissimmee**, Fl,US
37/G1 **Kissing**, Ger.
107/H2 **Kississing** (lake), Mb,Can
37/F2 **Kisslegg**, Ger.
40/E2 **Kisújszállás**, Hun.
77/M8 **Kisumu**, Kenya
27/M4 **Kisvárda**, Hun.
40/F1 **Kisvárda**, Hun.
57/G2 **Kita** (inlet), Japan
76/D5 **Kita**, Mali
78/C3 **Kita**, Mali
57/M9 **Kitagata**, Japan
55/N4 **Kita-Ibaraki**, Japan
57/G2 **Kita-Ibaraki**, Japan
57/F2 **Kitakata**, Japan
47/P6 **Kitakyūshū**, Japan
55/L5 **Kitakyūshū**, Japan
56/B4 **Kitakyūshū**, Japan
77/N7 **Kitale**, Kenya
55/N2 **Kitami** (mts.), Japan
55/N3 **Kitami**, Japan
57/H6 **Kitamoto**, Japan
87/H4 **Kitchener**, On,Can
89/K3 **Kitchener**, On,Can
94/D3 **Kitchener**, On,Can
20/J3 **Kitee**, Fin.
42/F3 **Kitee**, Fin.
77/M7 **Kitgum**, Ugan.
39/H4 **Kíthira**, Gre.
39/H4 **Kíthira** (isl.), Gre.
39/J4 **Kíthnos**, Gre.
39/J4 **Kíthnos** (isl.), Gre.
39/J4 **Kíthnos** (isls.), Gre.
86/D3 **Kitimat**, BC,Can
90/A2 **Kitimat**, BC,Can
90/A2 **Kitimat Arm** (inlet), BC,Can
99/B3 **Kitsap** (co.), Wa,US
99/B2 **Kitsap Lake-Erlands Point**, Wa,US
41/G1 **Kitsman'**, Ukr.
98/E4 **Kittatinny** (mts.), NJ, Pa,US
95/G3 **Kittery**, Me,US
77/N8 **Kitui**, Kenya
82/C1 **Kitui**, Kenya
82/E3 **Kitwe**, Zam.
33/K3 **Kitzbühel**, Aus.
26/F4 **Kitzingen**, Ger.
33/J2 **Kitzingen**, Ger.
67/K5 **Kiunga**, PNG
20/H3 **Kiuruvesi**, Fin.
42/E3 **Kiuruvesi**, Fin.
85/F2 **Kivalina**, Ak,US
20/H2 **Kivalo** (mts.), Fin.
42/E2 **Kivalo** (mts.), Fin.
20/H4 **Kiviöli**, Est.
42/E4 **Kiviõli**, Est.
74/E5 **Kivu** (lake), Afr.
77/L8 **Kivu** (lake), Rwa., Zaire
82/E1 **Kivu** (lake), Rwa., Zaire
44/D2 **Kiyev** (res.), Ukr.
44/D2 **Kiyev** (Kiev) (cap.), Ukr.
41/J5 **Kıyıköy**, Turk.
50/B1 **Kıyıköy**, Turk.
57/H7 **Kiyokawa**, Japan
57/H7 **Kiyose**, Japan
57/M9 **Kiyosu**, Japan
82/C2 **Kizamba**, Zaire
19/J3 **Kizel**, Rus.
43/N4 **Kizel**, Rus.
46/H6 **Kizil** (riv.), China
44/E4 **Kızılcahamam**, Turk.
50/C1 **Kızılcahamam**, Turk.
50/B2 **Kızıldag Nat'l Park**, Turk.
50/B2 **Kızılhisar**, Turk.
44/E4 **Kızılırmak** (riv.), Turk.
44/F5 **Kızılırmak** (riv.), Turk.
50/C1 **Kızılırmak** (riv.), Turk.
50/C2 **Kızılören**, Turk.
50/E2 **Kızıltepe**, Turk.
52/D1 **Kızıltepe**, Turk.
50/C2 **Kızılyaka**, Turk.
19/H4 **Kizlyar**, Rus.
45/H4 **Kizlyar**, Rus.
46/E5 **Kizlyar**, Rus.
56/E3 **Kizu** (riv.), Japan
57/L10 **Kizu**, Japan
57/L10 **Kizu** (riv.), Japan
45/L5 **Kizyl-Arvat**, Trkm.
46/F6 **Kizyl-Arvat**, Trkm.
51/J2 **Kizyl-Arvat**, Trkm.
46/F6 **Kizyl-Kaya**, Trkm.
42/C1 **Kjerkestinden** (peak), Nor.
20/E2 **Kjølen** (mts.), Nor.,Swe.
42/B2 **Kjølen** (Kölen) (mts.), Nor.
42/C2 **Kjølen** (Kölen) (mts.), Swe.
40/D3 **Kladanj**, Bosn.
67/J5 **Kladar**, Indo.
27/H3 **Kladno**, Czh.
33/L1 **Kladno**, Czh.
40/F3 **Kladovo**, Yugo.
18/E4 **Klagenfurt**, Aus.
33/L3 **Klagenfurt**, Aus.
40/B2 **Klagenfurt**, Aus.
18/F3 **Klaipėda**, Lith.
20/G5 **Klaipėda**, Lith.
42/D5 **Klaipėda**, Lith.
46/C4 **Klaipėda**, Lith.
106/C5 **Klamath** (mts.), Ca, Or,US
106/C5 **Klamath** (riv.), Ca, Or,US
92/A2 **Klamath** (mts.), Ca, Or,US
92/B2 **Klamath** (riv.), Ca, Or,US
86/D4 **Klamath** (riv.), Ca,Or,US
88/B3 **Klamath** (riv.), Ca, Or,US
86/D4 **Klamath Falls**, Or,US
88/B3 **Klamath Falls**, Or,US
90/C5 **Klamath Falls**, Or,US
92/B2 **Klamath Falls**, Or,US
46/B3 **Klar** (riv.), Swe.
18/E2 **Klaralven** (riv.), Swe.
20/E3 **Klaralven** (riv.), Swe.
82/F5 **Klaserie**, SAfr.
27/G4 **Klatovy**, Czh.
37/F3 **Klaus**, Aus.
37/H4 **Klausen** (Chiusa), It.
37/E4 **Klausenpass** (pass), Swi.
85/M4 **Klawock**, Ak,US
85/L3 **Klaza** (mtn.), Yk,Can
28/E3 **Klazienaveen**, Neth.
31/G5 **Kleinblittersdorf**, Ger.
95/Q8 **Kleinburg**, On,Can
27/G3 **Kleine Elster** (riv.), Ger.
36/F4 **Kleine Emme** (riv.), Swi.
31/E2 **Kleine Gete** (riv.), Belg.
28/B6 **Kleine Nete** (riv.), Belg.
31/D1 **Kleine Nete** (riv.), Belg.
36/D3 **Kleinlützel**, Swi.
80/L11 **Kleinmond**, SAfr.
80/Q12 **Kleinolifants** (riv.), SAfr.
20/C3 **Kleppestø**, Nor.
80/D2 **Klerksdorp**, SAfr.
80/P13 **Klerksdorp**, SAfr.
82/E6 **Klerksdorp**, SAfr.
28/D5 **Kleve**, Ger.
39/G1 **Klina**, Yugo.
40/E4 **Klina**, Yugo.
31/H5 **Klingenmünster**, Ger.
20/F4 **Klintehamn**, Swe.
42/C4 **Klintehamn**, Swe.
18/G3 **Klintsy**, Rus.
44/E1 **Klintsy**, Rus.
46/D4 **Klintsy**, Rus.
80/E2 **Klip** (riv.), SAfr.
80/Q13 **Klip** (riv.), SAfr.
39/J1 **Klisura**, Bul.
41/G4 **Klisura**, Bul.
40/D3 **Kljajićevo**, Yugo.
40/C3 **Ključ**, Bosn.
27/K2 **Kłodawa**, Pol.
27/J3 **Kłodzko**, Pol.
33/M1 **Kłodzko**, Pol.
37/E3 **Klöntalersee** (lake), Swi.
29/F3 **Klosterbach** (riv.), Ger.
37/G1 **Klosterlechfeld**, Ger.
27/J4 **Klosterneuburg**, Aus.
33/M2 **Klosterneuburg**, Aus.
40/C1 **Klosterneuburg**, Aus.
37/F4 **Klosters**, Swi.
27/H5 **Klosterwappen** (peak), Aus.
33/L3 **Klosterwappen** (peak), Aus.
40/B2 **Klosterwappen** (peak), Aus.
37/E3 **Kloten**, Swi.
65/B2 **Klothuhta Zayat**, Burma
26/F2 **Klötze**, Ger.
85/L3 **Kluane**, Yk,Can
86/C2 **Kluane**, Yk,Can
85/K3 **Kluane Nat'l Park**, Yk,Can
86/C2 **Kluane Nat'l Park**, Yk,Can
27/K3 **Kluczbork**, Pol.
85/L3 **Klukshu**, Yk,Can
85/L4 **Klukwan**, Ak,US
28/B5 **Klundert**, Neth.
29/E3 **Klüstenkanal** (can.), Ger.
45/K1 **Klyavlino**, Rus.
42/J4 **Klyaz'ma** (riv.), Rus.
43/X8 **Klyaz'ma** (riv.), Rus.
47/S4 **Klyuchevskaya** (peak), Rus.
23/G3 **Knaresborough**, Eng,UK
25/F3 **Knebworth**, Eng,UK
107/K2 **Knee** (lake), Mb,Can
41/G4 **Knezha**, Bul.
106/B3 **Knight** (inlet), BC,Can
24/C2 **Knighton**, Wal,UK
99/L11 **Knightsen**, Ca,US
40/C3 **Knin**, Cro.
33/L3 **Knittelfeld**, Aus.
40/B2 **Knittelfeld**, Aus.
40/F4 **Knjaževac**, Yugo.
44/B4 **Knjaževac**, Yugo.
70/B6 **Knob** (cape), Austl.
67/F1 **Knob** (peak), Phil.
22/B2 **Knockcloghrim**, NI,UK
22/B1 **Knocklayd** (mtn.), NI,UK
21/H7 **Knocknagashel**, Ire.
30/C1 **Knokke-Heist**, Belg.
80/A2 **Knoll** (pt.), Namb.
39/J5 **Knosós** (Knossos) (ruins), Gre.
39/J5 **Knossos** (Knosós) (ruins), Gre.
101/E1 **Knott**, Tx,US
23/F4 **Knott End**, Eng,UK
23/G4 **Knottingley**, Eng,UK
83/G **Knox** (coast), Ant.
73/G5 **Knox**, Austl.
85/M4 **Knox** (cape), BC,Can
86/C3 **Knox** (cape), BC,Can
101/F1 **Knox City**, Tx,US
84/J6 **Knoxville**, US
89/K4 **Knoxville**, Tn,US
94/D5 **Knoxville**, Tn,US
97/H3 **Knoxville**, Tn,US
23/F5 **Knutsford**, Eng,UK
80/C4 **Knysna**, SAfr.
82/D7 **Knysna**, SAfr.
55/M2 **Ko** (peak), Rus.
88/T10 **Koali**, Hi,US
82/G2 **Koani**, Tanz.
55/L5 **Kobayashi**, Japan
56/B5 **Kobayashi**, Japan
47/P6 **Kōbe**, Japan
55/M5 **Kōbe**, Japan
56/D3 **Kōbe**, Japan
57/L10 **Kōbe**, Japan
20/E5 **København** (Copenhagen) (cap.), Den.
26/G1 **København** (Copenhagen) (cap.), Den.
31/G3 **Kobern-Gondorf**, Ger.
67/G4 **Kobipato** (peak), Indo.
37/F3 **Koblach**, Aus.
26/D3 **Koblenz**, Ger.
31/G3 **Koblenz**, Ger.
33/G1 **Koblenz**, Ger.
37/E2 **Koblenz**, Swi.
27/N2 **Kobrin**, Bela.
44/C1 **Kobrin**, Bela.
67/H5 **Kobroor** (isl.), Indo.
85/G2 **Kobuk**, Ak,US
85/G2 **Kobuk** (riv.), Ak,US
85/G2 **Kobuk Valley Nat'l Park**, Ak,US
57/F3 **Kobushi-ga-take** (mtn.), Japan
33/M2 **Kobylí**, Czh.
41/J5 **Kocaeli** (prov.), Turk.
44/D4 **Kocaeli** (prov.), Turk.
50/B1 **Kocaeli** (prov.), Turk.
50/D2 **Koçalı**, Turk.
39/H2 **Kočani**, Macd.
40/F5 **Kočani**, Macd.
44/B4 **Kočani**, Macd.
33/L4 **Kočevje**, Slov.
40/B3 **Kočevje**, Slov.
87/J2 **Koch** (isl.), NW,Can
55/K4 **Koch'ang**, SKor.
58/D5 **Koch'ang**, SKor.
37/H2 **Kochel am See**, Ger.
37/H2 **Kochelsee** (lake), Ger.
33/H2 **Kocher** (riv.), Ger.
30/H1 **Kocherinovo**, Bul.
40/F4 **Kocherinovo**, Bul.
47/P6 **Kōchi**, Japan
55/L5 **Kōchi**, Japan
56/C4 **Kōchi**, Japan
56/C4 **Kōchi** (pref.), Japan
85/H4 **Kodiak**, Ak,US
85/H4 **Kodiak** (isl.), Ak,US
85/H4 **Kodiak Nat'l Wild. Ref.**, Ak,US
53/K4 **Kodinār**, India
62/B3 **Kodinār**, India
77/M6 **Kodok**, Sudan
41/H2 **Kodry** (hills), Mol.
44/D2 **Kodyma**, Ukr.
30/B1 **Koekelare**, Belg.
62/D3 **Koel** (riv.), India
31/F5 **Koenigsmacker**, Fr.
80/B2 **Koes**, Namb.
58/D4 **Koesan**, SKor.
92/D4 **Kofa** (mts.), Az,US
41/H5 **Kofçaz**, Turk.
80/D3 **Koffiefontein**, SAfr.
67/G4 **Kofiau** (isl.), Indo.
76/E6 **Koforidua**, Gha.
79/E5 **Koforidua**, Gha.
57/F3 **Kōfu**, Japan
57/F2 **Koga**, Japan
57/H7 **Koganei**, Japan
26/G1 **Køge**, Den.
26/G1 **Køge Bugt** (bay), Den.
76/C5 **Kogon** (riv.), Gui.
78/B4 **Kogon** (riv.), Gui.
58/D5 **Kōgum** (isl.), SKor.
53/K2 **Kohāt**, Pak.
64/A1 **Kohāt**, Pak.
20/H4 **Kohila**, Est.
42/E4 **Kohila**, Est.
60/B3 **Kohīma**, India
63/F2 **Kohīma**, India
51/G4 **Kohkīlūyeh and Bovīr Aḥmadī** (gov.), Iran
20/H4 **Kohtla-Järve**, Est.
42/E4 **Kohtla-Järve**, Est.
55/K5 **Kohŭng**, SKor.
58/D5 **Kohŭng**, SKor.
101/H5 **Kohunlich** (ruins), Mex.
102/D2 **Kohunlich** (ruins), Mex.
80/A2 **Koichab** (dry riv.), Namb.
85/K3 **Koidern**, Yk,Can
41/F5 **Koímisis**, Gre.
57/H7 **Koito** (riv.), Japan
56/A3 **Koje** (isl.), SKor.
58/E5 **Kōje** (isl.), SKor.
70/B6 **Kojonup**, Austl.
27/L4 **Kojšovská Hol'a** (peak), Slvk.
65/B1 **Kok** (riv.), Burma
57/M10 **Kōka**, Japan
57/J7 **Kokai** (riv.), Japan
46/G4 **Kokchetav**, Kaz.
85/H4 **Kokhonak**, Ak,US
18/F2 **Kokkola**, Fin.
46/C3 **Kokkola**, Fin.
20/G3 **Kokkola** (Gamlakarleby), Fin.
42/D3 **Kokkola** (Gamlakarleby), Fin.
79/G4 **Koko**, Nga.
79/G5 **Koko**, Nga.
78/C3 **Kokofata**, Mali
88/W13 **Koko Head** (crater), Hi,US
77/L7 **Kokola**, Zaire
89/J3 **Kokomo**, In,US
94/C3 **Kokomo**, In,US
80/C2 **Kokong**, Bots.
62/F2 **Kokrajhar**, India
85/H3 **Kokrines**, Ak,US
58/D3 **Koksan**, NKor.
30/B1 **Koksijde**, Belg.
87/K3 **Koksoak** (riv.), Qu,Can
80/E3 **Kokstad**, SAfr.
82/E7 **Kokstad**, SAfr.
56/B5 **Kokubu**, Japan
67/H5 **Kola** (isl.), Indo.
18/G2 **Kola** (pen.), Rus.
42/G1 **Kola** (riv.), Rus.
42/H1 **Kola** (pen.), Rus.
46/D3 **Kola** (pen.), Rus.
64/F4 **Kolachel**, India
67/F4 **Kolaka**, Indo.
62/C5 **Kolār**, India
39/F1 **Kolašin**, Yugo.
40/D4 **Kolašin**, Yugo.
26/G5 **Kolbermoor**, Ger.
27/L3 **Kolbuszowa**, Pol.
76/C5 **Kolda**, Sen.
78/B3 **Kolda**, Sen.
78/B3 **Kolda** (reg.), Sen.
20/D5 **Kolding**, Den.
26/E1 **Kolding**, Den.
20/E2 **Kolen** (Kjølen) (mts.), Nor.,Swe.
42/C2 **Kölen** (Kjølen) (mts.), Swe.
68/C5 **Kolepom** (isl.), Indo.
42/F4 **Kolgompya** (cape), Rus.
18/H2 **Kolguyev** (isl.), Rus.
43/K1 **Kolguyev** (isl.), Rus.
46/F3 **Kolguyev** (isl.), Rus.
53/K5 **Kolhāpur**, India
62/B4 **Kolhāpur**, India
78/B3 **Koliba** (riv.), Gui.
85/G4 **Koliganek**, Ak,US
27/H3 **Kolín**, Czh.
33/L1 **Kolín**, Czh.
20/G4 **Kolkasrags** (pt.), Lat.
42/D4 **Kolkasrags** (pt.), Lat.
28/D2 **Kollum**, Neth.
26/D3 **Köln** (Cologne), Ger.
28/D7 **Köln** (Cologne), Ger.
31/F2 **Köln** (Cologne), Ger.
33/G1 **Köln** (Cologne), Ger.
27/L2 **Kolno**, Pol.
44/A1 **Koło**, Pol.
82/G1 **Kolo**, Tanz.
88/S10 **Koloa**, Hi,US
27/H1 **Kołobrzeg**, Pol.
76/D5 **Kolokani**, Mali
78/C3 **Kolokani**, Mali
19/G3 **Kolomna**, Rus.
42/H5 **Kolomna**, Rus.
44/F1 **Kolomna**, Rus.
46/D4 **Kolomna**, Rus.
41/G1 **Kolomyya**, Ukr.
44/C2 **Kolomyya**, Ukr.
78/D4 **Kolondiéba**, Mali
62/C6 **Kolonnawa**, SrL.
78/D3 **Kolossa** (riv.), Mali
46/J4 **Kolpashevo**, Rus.
42/F4 **Kolpino**, Rus.
43/V7 **Kolpino**, Rus.
40/E3 **Kolubara** (riv.), Yugo
27/K3 **Koluszki**, Pol.
43/N2 **Kolva** (riv.), Rus.
20/D2 **Kolvereid**, Nor.
42/A2 **Kolvereid**, Nor.
82/E3 **Kolwezi**, Zaire
47/R2 **Kolyma** (lowland), Rus.
47/R3 **Kolyma** (range), Rus.
47/R3 **Kolyma** (riv.), Rus.
48/Q3 **Kolyma** (range), Rus.
48/Q3 **Kolyma** (riv.), Rus.
39/H1 **Kom** (peak), Bul.
40/F4 **Kom** (peak), Bul.
57/H7 **Koma** (riv.), Japan
40/E2 **Komádi**, Hun.
76/H5 **Komadugu Gana** (riv.), Nga.
79/H4 **Komadugu Gana** (riv.), Nga.
79/H3 **Komadugu Yobé** (riv.), Nga.
57/H7 **Komae**, Japan
57/E3 **Komagane**, Japan
57/M9 **Komaki**, Japan
47/S4 **Komandorskiye** (isls.), Rus.
48/R4 **Komandorskiye** (isls.), Rus.
27/K5 **Komárno**, Slvk.
40/D2 **Komárno**, Slvk.
27/K5 **Komárom**, Hun.
40/D2 **Komárom**, Hun.
27/K5 **Komárom-Esztergom** (co.), Hun.
40/D2 **Komárom-Esztergom** (co.), Hun.
80/R12 **Komatirivier** (riv.), SAfr.
55/M4 **Komatsu**, Japan
56/E2 **Komatsu**, Japan
56/D4 **Komatsushima**, Japan
43/L2 **Komi Aut. Rep.**, Rus.
46/F3 **Komi Aut. Rep.**, Rus.
43/M3 **Komi-Permyak Aut. Okr.**, Rus.
40/D1 **Komjatice**, Slvk.
40/D2 **Komló**, Hun.
19/G4 **Kommunarsk**, Ukr.
44/F2 **Kommunarsk**, Ukr.
46/D5 **Kommunarsk**, Ukr.
67/E5 **Komodo** (isl.), Indo.
67/E5 **Komodo Island Nat'l Park**, Indo.
76/E6 **Komoé** (riv.), IvC.
78/E5 **Komoé** (riv.), IvC.
56/E3 **Komono**, Japan
57/M9 **Komono**, Japan
67/J5 **Komoran** (isl.), Indo.
39/J2 **Komotiní**, Gre.
41/G5 **Komotiní**, Gre.
44/C4 **Komotiní**, Gre.
50/A1 **Komotiní**, Gre.
80/D3 **Kompasberg** (peak), SAfr.
82/D7 **Kompasberg** (peak), SAfr.
41/J2 **Komrat**, Mol.
44/D3 **Komrat**, Mol.
47/L1 **Komsomolets** (isl.), Rus.
48/H1 **Komsomolets** (isl.), Rus.
43/P2 **Komsomol'skiy**, Rus.
45/H1 **Komsomol'skiy**, Rus.
46/G3 **Komsomol'skiy**, Rus.
47/P4 **Komsomol'sk-na-Amure**, Rus.
55/M1 **Komsomol'sk-na-Amure**, Rus.
39/K3 **Kömür** (pt.), Turk.
50/A2 **Kömür** (pt.), Turk.
42/H4 **Konakovo**, Rus.
57/M10 **Kōnan**, Japan
57/M9 **Kōnan**, Japan
73/D2 **Konangra-Boyd Nat'l Park**, Austl.
67/F4 **Konaweha** (riv.), Indo.
57/L10 **Konda**, Japan
54/G1 **Konda** (riv.), Rus.
82/G1 **Kondoa**, Tanz.
42/G3 **Kondopoga**, Rus.
46/G6 **Kondūz**, Afg.
53/J1 **Kondūz**, Afg.
69/U12 **Koné**, NCal.
65/C4 **Kong** (isl.), Camb.
78/D4 **Kong**, IvC.
65/D3 **Kong** (riv.), Laos
85/F4 **Kongiganak**, Ak,US
55/K4 **Kongju**, SKor.
58/D4 **Kongju**, SKor.
59/D4 **Kong Miao**, China
58/F6 **Kongnŭng** (riv.), SKor.
82/E2 **Kongolo**, Zaire
57/L10 **Kongō-zan** (peak), Japan
20/D4 **Kongsberg**, Nor.
20/E3 **Kongsvinger**, Nor.
82/G2 **Kongwa**, Tanz.
27/K3 **Koniecpol**, Pol.
26/F4 **Königsbrunn**, Ger.
37/G1 **Königsbrunn**, Ger.
37/G2 **Königsschlösser**, Ger.
37/H2 **Königsdorf**, Ger.
37/E1 **Königsfeld im Schwarzwald**, Ger.
26/F2 **Königslutter am Elm**, Ger.
29/H4 **Königslutter am Elm**, Ger.
26/D3 **Königswinter**, Ger.
31/G2 **Königswinter**, Ger.
27/G2 **Königs Wusterhausen**, Ger.
27/K2 **Konin**, Pol.
27/K2 **Konin** (prov.), Pol.
44/A1 **Konin**, Pol.
39/G2 **Kónitsa**, Gre.
33/G3 **Köniz**, Swi.
36/D4 **Köniz**, Swi.
40/C4 **Konjic**, Bosn.
80/B2 **Konkiep** (dry riv.), Namb.
78/B4 **Konkouré** (riv.), Gui.
20/H3 **Konnevesi**, Fin.
42/E3 **Konnevesi**, Fin.
36/D4 **Konolfingen**, Swi.
44/E2 **Konotop**, Ukr.
46/J5 **Konqi** (riv.), China
54/B3 **Konqi** (riv.), China
27/L3 **Końskie**, Pol.
44/B2 **Końskie**, Pol.
27/L2 **Konstancin-Jeziorna**, Pol.
44/F2 **Konstantinovka**, Ukr.
27/K3 **Konstantynów Łódzki**, Pol.
26/E5 **Konstanz**, Ger.
33/H3 **Konstanz**, Ger.
37/F2 **Konstanz**, Ger.
76/G5 **Kontagora**, Nga.
28/B6 **Kontich**, Belg.
30/D1 **Kontich**, Belg.
20/J3 **Kontiolahti**, Fin.
42/F3 **Kontiolahti**, Fin.
63/J5 **Kon Tum**, Viet.
65/E3 **Kon Tum**, Viet.
49/C1 **Konya** (prov.), Turk.
50/C2 **Konya**, Turk.
50/C2 **Konya** (prov.), Turk.
31/F4 **Konz**, Ger.
90/E3 **Koocanusa** (lake), Can., US
70/B6 **Koolyanobbing**, Austl.
73/C2 **Koondrook**, Austl.
70/E6 **Koonibba**, Austl.
73/D2 **Koorawatha**, Austl.
90/D3 **Kootenai** (riv.), Id, Mt,US
90/D3 **Kootenay** (lake), BC,Can
86/E3 **Kootenay** (lake), BC,Can
90/D3 **Kootenay Nat'l Park**, BC,Can
86/E3 **Kootenay Nat'l Park**, BC,Can
73/D1 **Kootingal**, Austl.

148

Kop – Kutai

50/E1 Kop (pass), Turk.
53/K5 Kopargaon, India
62/B4 Kopargaon, India
20/N7 Kópavogur, Ice.
78/D5 Kope (peak), IvC.
27/G2 Köpenick, Ger.
33/K4 Koper, Slov.
40/A3 Koper, Slov.
43/P5 Kopeysk, Rus.
46/G4 Kopeysk, Rus.
44/G4 Kop Geçidi (pass), Turk.
77/K7 Kopia, Zaire
60/B3 Kopili (riv.), India
42/C4 Köping, Swe.
40/D4 Koplik, Alb.
67/F5 Kopondei (cape), Indo.
20/D3 Koppang, Nor.
20/E3 Kopparberg (co.), Swe.
42/B3 Kopparberg (co.), Swe.
55/M2 Koppi (riv.), Rus.
80/P13 Koppies, SAfr.
40/C2 Koprivnica, Cro.
39/J1 Koprivshtitsa, Bul.
41/G4 Koprivshtitsa, Bul.
49/B1 Köprü (riv.), Turk.
50/B2 Köprülü Kanyon Nat'l Park, Turk.
44/D1 Kopys', Bela.
51/H4 Kor (riv.), Iran
52/F2 Kor (riv.), Iran
57/M9 Kōra, Japan
39/G2 Korab (peak), Alb.
40/E5 Korab (peak), Alb.
56/C3 Korakuen Garden, Japan
87/K3 Koraluk (riv.), Nf,Can
33/L4 Korana (riv.), Bosn., Cro.
62/D4 Koraput, India
62/D3 Korba, India
26/E3 Korbach, Ger.
29/F6 Korbach, Ger.
39/G2 Korçë, Alb.
40/E5 Korçë, Alb.
38/E1 Korčula, Cro.
38/E1 Korčula (isl.), Cro.
40/C4 Korčula (isl.), Cro.
38/E1 Korčulanski (chan.), Cro.
40/C4 Korčulanski (chan.), Cro.
31/F4 Kordel, Ger.
51/F3 Kordestān (gov.), Iran
51/H2 Kord Küy, Iran
52/F1 Kord Küy, Iran
47/N6 Korea (bay), NKor.,China
55/J4 Korea (bay), China, NKor.
58/B3 Korea (bay), China, NKor.
55/K5 Korea (str.), Japan, SKor.
56/A4 Korea (str.), Japan, SKor.
58/E5 Korea (str.), Japan, SKor.
47/P6 Korea (str.), SKor., Japan
58/D4 Korean Folk Village, SKor.
58/G7 Korean Folk Village, SKor.
58/D4 Korea, North
58/D4 Korea, South
44/F3 Korenovsk, Rus.
50/D1 Korgan, Turk.
76/D6 Korhogo, IvC.
78/D4 Korhogo, IvC.
39/H2 Korinós, Gre.
39/H4 Kórinthos (Corinth), Gre.
40/C2 Kőris-hegy (peak), Hun.
55/N4 Kōriyama, Japan
57/G2 Kōriyama, Japan
47/R3 Korkodon (riv.), Rus.
49/B1 Korkuteli, Turk.
50/B2 Korkuteli, Turk.
49/C2 Kormakiti (cape), Cyp.
50/C3 Kormakiti (cape), Cyp.
52/B1 Kormakiti (cape), Cyp.
33/M3 Körmend, Hun.
40/B4 Kornat (isl.), Cro.
29/H6 Körner, Ger.
44/D3 Korneshty, Mol.
33/M2 Korneuburg, Aus.
33/L5 Kornot (isl.), Cro.
68/G6 Koro (sea), Fiji
69/Z18 Koro (isl.), Fiji
69/Z18 Koro (sea), Fiji
76/E5 Koro, Mali
41/K5 Köroğlu (peak), Turk.
50/B1 Köroğlu (peak), Turk.
82/G2 Korogwe, Tanz.
73/B3 Koroit, Austl.
67/G2 Koronadal, Phil.
39/H2 Korónia (lake), Gre.
41/F5 Korónia (lake), Gre.
27/J2 Koronowo, Pol.
39/L7 Koropí, Gre.
68/C4 Koror, Palau
40/E2 Körös (riv.), Hun.
44/D2 Korosten', Ukr.
44/D2 Korostyshev, Ukr.
43/P1 Korotaikha (riv.), Rus.
76/J4 Koro Toro, Chad
85/D5 Korovin (vol.), Ak,US
47/Q5 Korsakov, Rus.
55/N2 Korsakov, Rus.
28/D6 Korschenbroich, Ger.
31/F1 Korschenbroich, Ger.
26/F1 Korsør, Den.
27/L1 Korsze, Pol.
30/C1 Kortemark, Belg.
31/E2 Kortenaken, Belg.
30/D2 Kortenberg, Belg.
31/E2 Kortessem, Belg.
26/B3 Kortrijk, Belg.
32/E1 Kortrijk, Belg.
30/C2 Kortrijk (Courtrai), Belg.
79/H5 Korup Nat'l Park, Camr.
47/T3 Koryak (range), Rus.
48/R3 Koryak (range), Rus.
47/S3 Koryak Aut. Okr., Rus.
43/K3 Koryazhma, Rus.
57/L10 Kōryō, Japan
58/E5 Koryŏng, SKor.
50/A2 Kos, Gre.
50/A2 Kós (isl.), Gre.
57/E3 Kosai, Japan
56/A3 Ko-saki (pt.), Japan
65/C3 Ko Samut Nat'l Park, Thai.
27/J2 Kościan, Pol.
27/J1 Kościerzyna, Pol.
68/D8 Kosciusko (peak), Austl.
71/H7 Kosciusko (peak), Austl.
73/D3 Kosciusko (peak), Austl.
97/F3 Kosciusko, Ms,US
73/D3 Kosciusko Nat'l Park, Austl.
50/D1 Köse, Turk.
57/M10 Kosei, Japan
57/F3 Koshigaya, Japan
57/H7 Koshigaya, Japan
53/H2 Koshk, Afg.
62/E2 Kosi (riv.), India
18/F4 Košice, Slvk.
27/L4 Košice, Slvk.
44/B2 Košice, Slvk.
46/C5 Košice, Slvk.
50/B2 Koskinoú, Gre.
55/K4 Kosŏng, NKor.
58/E3 Kosŏng, NKor.
56/A3 Kosŏng, SKor.
58/E5 Kosŏng, SKor.
41/G1 Kosov, Ukr.
39/G1 Kosovo (aut. reg.), Yugo.
40/E4 Kosovo (aut. reg.), Yugo.
39/G1 Kosovo Polje, Yugo.
40/E4 Kosovo Polje, Yugo.
39/G1 Kosovska Kamenica, Yugo.
39/G1 Kosovska Mitrovica, Yugo.
40/E4 Kosovska Mitrovica, Yugo.
68/F4 Kosrae (isl.), Micr.
78/D3 Kossi (prov.), Burk.
76/D6 Kossou (lake), IvC.
78/D5 Kossou (lake), IvC.
78/D5 Kossou, Barrage de (dam), IvC.
80/P12 Koster, SAfr.
39/H1 Kostinbrod, Bul.
41/F4 Kostinbrod, Bul.
20/J2 Kostomuksha, Kaz.
44/C2 Kostopol', Ukr.
19/H3 Kostroma, Rus.
42/J4 Kostroma, Rus.
42/J4 Kostroma (riv.), Rus.
46/E4 Kostroma, Rus.
42/J4 Kostroma Obl., Rus.
27/H2 Kostrzyn, Pol.
27/J2 Kostrzyn, Pol.
43/N4 Kos'va (riv.), Rus.
43/N2 Kos'yu (riv.), Rus.
18/E3 Koszalin, Pol.
27/H2 Koszalin (prov.), Pol.
27/J1 Koszalin, Pol.
46/B4 Koszalin, Pol.
40/C2 Koszeg, Hun.
48/G7 Kota, India
53/L3 Kota, India
62/C2 Kota, India
57/N10 Kōta, Japan
66/B5 Kotaagung, Indo.
63/H6 Kota Baharu, Malay.
65/C5 Kota Baharu, Malay.
66/B2 Kota Baharu, Malay.
67/E4 Kotabaru, Indo.
66/C4 Kotabumi, Indo.
53/K2 Kot Addu, Pak.
64/A2 Kot Addu, Pak.
64/F3 Kotagiri, India
67/E2 Kota Kinabalu, Malay.
39/K1 Kotel, Bul.
41/H4 Kotel, Bul.
44/C4 Kotel, Bul.
43/L4 Kotel'nich, Rus.
45/G3 Kotel'nikovo, Rus.
47/P2 Kotel'nyy (isl.), Rus.
53/L2 Kotgarh, India
26/F3 Köthen, Ger.
18/F2 Kotka, Fin.
20/H3 Kotka, Fin.
46/C3 Kotka, Fin.
53/K2 Kot Kapūra, India
64/C2 Kot Kapūra, India
19/H2 Kotlas, Rus.
43/K3 Kotlas, Rus.
46/E3 Kotlas, Rus.
85/F3 Kotlik, Ak,US
43/U6 Kotlin (isl.), Rus.
20/J4 Kotly, Rus.
57/M9 Kotō, Japan
39/F1 Kotor, Yugo.
40/D4 Kotor, Yugo.
40/C3 Kotor Varoš, Bosn.
45/H2 Kotovo, Rus.
44/D3 Kotovsk, Mol.
45/G1 Kotovsk, Rus.
41/J2 Kotovsk, Ukr.
53/J3 Kotri, Pak.
62/A2 Kotri, Pak.
62/D4 Kottagūdem, India
64/F4 Kottai Malai (mtn.), India
62/C6 Kottayam, India
64/F4 Kottayam, India
62/C6 Kotte, SrL.
77/K6 Kotto (riv.), CAfr.
47/L3 Kotuy (riv.), Rus.
48/K3 Kotuy (riv.), Rus.
85/E2 Kotzebue (sound), Ak,US
85/F2 Kotzebue, Ak,US
87/K4 Kouchibouguac Nat'l Park, NB,Can
95/H2 Kouchibouguac Nat'l Park, NB,Can
76/E5 Koudougou, Burk.
79/E3 Koudougou, Burk.
39/J5 Koufonísion (isl.), Gre.
85/E2 Kougarok (mtn.), Ak,US
87/J2 Koukdjuak (riv.), NW,Can
76/H8 Koula-Moutou, Gabon
82/B1 Koula-Moutou, Gabon
76/D5 Koulikoro, Mali
78/D3 Koulikoro, Mali
78/B3 Koulountou (riv.), Gui., Sen.
69/U12 Koumac, NCal.
78/D3 Koumbi Saleh (ruins), Mrta.
76/J6 Koumra, Chad
76/C5 Koundara, Gui.
78/B3 Koundara, Gui.
93/J5 Kountze, Tx,US
96/E4 Kountze, Tx,US
79/H5 Koupé (peak), Camr.
79/E3 Koupela, Burk.
79/E3 Kouritenga (prov.), Burk.
107/H2 Kourou, FrG.
76/D5 Kouroussa, Gui.
74/D3 Koussi (peak), Chad
76/J4 Koussi (peak), Chad
76/D5 Koutiala, Mali
78/D3 Koutiala, Mali
20/H3 Kouvola, Fin.
42/E3 Kouvola, Fin.
40/E3 Kovačevac, Yugo.
40/E3 Kovačica, Yugo.
50/B2 Kovada Gölü Nat'l Park, Turk.
64/F4 Kovalam, India
43/U7 Kovashi (riv.), Rus.
20/K3 Kovda, Rus.
20/J2 Kovdor, Rus.
20/J2 Kovdozero (lake), Rus.
42/F2 Kovdozero (lake), Rus.
18/F3 Kovel', Ukr.
44/C2 Kovel', Ukr.
46/C4 Kovel', Ukr.
40/E3 Kovilj, Yugo.
62/C6 Kovilpatti, India
64/F4 Kovilpatti, India
42/J4 Kovrov, Rus.
62/C5 Kovūr, India
45/G1 Kovylkino, Rus.
72/A1 Kowanyama Abor. Community, Austl.
72/A1 Kowanyama Abor. Land, Austl.
53/J1 Kowkcheh (riv.), Afg.
53/H2 Kowl-e Namaksār (lake), Afg., Iran
61/G4 Kowloon, HK
55/K4 Kowŏn, NKor.
56/B5 Kōyama, Japan
41/G4 Koynare, Bul.
85/F3 Koyuk, Ak,US
85/G3 Koyukuk, Ak,US
85/H2 Koyukuk (riv.), Ak,US
85/G2 Koyukuk Nat'l Wild. Ref., Ak,US
85/H2 Koyukuk, North Fork (riv.), Ak,US
85/H2 Koyukuk, South Fork (riv.), Ak,US
57/N10 Kozakai, Japan
50/C2 Kozaklı, Turk.
50/C2 Kozan, Turk.
18/F4 Kozáni, Gre.
39/G2 Kozáni, Gre.
40/C3 Kozara Nat'l Park, Bosn.
27/K4 Kozárovice, Slvk.
40/D1 Kozárovice, Slvk.
48/G8 Kozhikode, India
62/C5 Kozhikode, India
64/E3 Kozhikode, India
42/H3 Kozhozero (lake), Rus.
43/M2 Kozhva (riv.), Rus.
27/L3 Kozienice, Pol.
41/F4 Kozloduy, Bul.
44/B4 Kozloduy, Bul.
41/K5 Kozlu, Turk.
44/D4 Kozlu, Turk.
50/B1 Kozlu, Turk.
50/E2 Kozluk, Turk.
27/J3 Koźmin, Pol.
39/H1 Koznitsa (peak), Bul.
41/F4 Koznitsa (peak), Bul.
44/B4 Koznitsa (peak), Bul.
27/H3 Kożuchów, Pol.
76/F6 Kpalimé, Togo
79/F5 Kpalimé, Togo
79/F5 Kpandu, Gha.
79/F5 Kpémé, Togo
63/G6 Kra (isth.), Burma,Thai.
65/B4 Kra (isth.), Burma, Thai.
66/A2 Kra (isth.), Thai.
80/D3 Kraai (riv.), SAfr.
80/L10 Kraaifontein, SAfr.
63/G6 Krabi, Thai.
65/B4 Krabi, Thai.
66/A2 Krabi, Thai.
63/G5 Kra Buri, Thai.
66/A1 Kra Buri, Thai.
63/J5 Kracheh, Camb.
65/D3 Kracheh, Camb.
20/D4 Kragerø, Nor.
18/F4 Kragujevac, Yugo.
40/E3 Kragujevac, Yugo.
44/B3 Kragujevac, Yugo.
33/H2 Kraichgau (reg.), Ger.
37/H1 Krailling, Ger.
66/C5 Krakatoa (vol.), Indo.
63/H5 Krakor, Camb.
65/D3 Krakor, Camb.
66/B1 Krakor, Camb.
18/E3 Kraków, Pol.
27/K3 Kraków, Pol.
27/K3 Kraków (prov.), Pol.
44/A2 Kraków, Pol.
46/B4 Kraków, Pol.
63/H5 Kralanh, Camb.
65/C3 Kralanh, Camb.
104/D4 Kralendijk, Bonaire, NAnt.
106/E1 Kralendijk, Bonaire, NAnt.
40/E4 Kraljevo, Yugo.
27/H3 Kralupy nad Vltavou, Czh.
33/L1 Kralupy nad Vltavou, Czh.
19/G4 Kramatorsk, Ukr.
44/F2 Kramatorsk, Ukr.
46/D5 Kramatorsk, Ukr.
20/F3 Kramfors, Swe.
42/C3 Kramfors, Swe.
28/B5 Krammer (chan.), Neth.
39/G3 Kranéa Elassónos, Gre.
28/D5 Kranenburg, Ger.
39/H4 Kranídhion, Gre.
33/L3 Kranj, Slov.
40/B2 Kranj, Slov.
27/J3 Krapkowice, Pol.
42/E5 Krāslava, Lat.
27/M3 Kraśnik, Pol.
27/M3 Kraśnik Fabryczny, Pol.
45/L1 Krasninsk, Rus.
43/Y8 Krasnoarmeysk, Rus.
45/H2 Krasnoarmeysk, Rus.
19/G4 Krasnodar, Rus.
44/F3 Krasnodar, Rus.
46/D5 Krasnodar, Rus.
44/F3 Krasnodar Kray, Rus.
43/X9 Krasnogorsk, Rus.
44/F1 Krasnogorsk, Rus.
44/E2 Krasnograd, Ukr.
47/M4 Krasnokamensk, Rus.
55/H1 Krasnokamensk, Rus.
43/M4 Krasnokamsk, Rus.
45/H2 Krasnoslobodsk, Rus.
46/G4 Krasnotur'insk, Rus.
43/P4 Krasnoural'sk, Rus.
45/K5 Krasnovodsk, Trkm.
46/F6 Krasnovodsk, Trkm.
51/H2 Krasnovodsk, Trkm.
46/K4 Krasnoyarsk, Rus.
27/M3 Krasnystaw, Pol.
41/J2 Krasnyy Okny, Ukr.
45/H2 Krasnyy Kut, Rus.
44/F2 Krasnyy Luch, Ukr.
44/G3 Krasnyy Sulin, Rus.
39/H1 Kratovo, Macd.
40/F4 Kratovo, Macd.
63/H5 Kravanh (mts.), Camb.
65/C4 Kravanh (mts.), Camb.
66/C5 Krawang, Indo.
26/D3 Krefeld, Ger.
28/D6 Krefeld, Ger.
29/G5 Kreiensen, Ger.
39/G3 Kremastón (lake), Gre.
18/G4 Kremenchug, Ukr.
44/E2 Kremenchug, Ukr.
44/E2 Kremenchug (res.), Ukr.
46/D5 Kremenchug, Ukr.
43/X9 Kremlin, Rus.
92/F2 Kremmling, Co,US
29/G1 Krempe, Ger.
27/H4 Krems an der Donau, Aus.
33/L2 Krems an der Donau, Aus.
33/L2 Kremsmünster, Aus.
98/E5 Kresgeville, Pa,US
39/H2 Kresna, Bul.
41/F5 Kresna, Bul.
37/F2 Kressbronn am Bodensee, Ger.
47/T3 Kresta (gulf), Rus.
39/G4 Kréstena, Gre.
44/F1 Kresty, Rus.
20/G5 Kretinga, Lith.
31/F2 Kreuzau, Ger.
37/F2 Kreuzlingen, Swi.
31/G2 Kreuztal, Ger.
39/H2 Kría Vrísi, Gre.
40/F5 Kría Vrísi, Gre.
76/G7 Kribi, Camr.
44/D1 Krichev, Bela.
33/L3 Krieglach, Aus.
37/E3 Kriens, Swi.
55/N2 Kril'on (cape), Rus.
28/B5 Krimpen aan de IJssel, Neth.
41/G5 Kriníthes, Gre.
48/G8 Krishna (riv.), India
53/L5 Krishna (riv.), India
62/D4 Krishna (riv.), India
62/C5 Krishnagiri, India
18/D3 Kristiansand, Nor.
20/C4 Kristiansand, Nor.
46/A4 Kristiansand, Nor.
20/E4 Kristianstad, Swe.
20/E4 Kristianstad (co.), Swe.
27/H1 Kristianstad (co.), Swe.
18/D2 Kristiansund, Nor.
20/C3 Kristiansund, Nor.
46/A3 Kristiansund, Nor.
20/E4 Kristinehamn, Swe.
39/H1 Kriva Palanka, Macd.
40/F4 Kriva Palanka, Macd.
42/E5 Krivichi, Bela.
41/K2 Krivoye Ozero, Ukr.
18/G4 Krivoy Rog, Ukr.
41/L2 Krivoy Rog, Ukr.
44/E3 Krivoy Rog, Ukr.
46/D5 Krivoy Rog, Ukr.
33/L4 Krk, Cro.
33/L4 Krk (isl.), Cro.
40/B3 Krk, Cro.
40/B3 Krk (isl.), Cro.
40/C3 Krka (riv.), Cro.
27/J3 Krnov, Czh.
80/Q12 Krokodil (riv.), SAfr.
81/E2 Krokodil (riv.), SAfr.
80/D2 Krokodilrivier (riv.), SAfr.
80/P12 Krokodilrivier (riv.), SAfr.
20/E3 Krokom, Swe.
42/B3 Krokom, Swe.
39/G2 Krókos, Gre.
28/C4 Kröller Müller Rijksmuseum (State Museum), Neth.
44/E2 Krolevets, Ukr.
27/J4 Kroměříž, Czh.
26/F3 Kronach, Ger.
33/J1 Kronach, Ger.
63/H5 Krong Kaoh Kong, Camb.
65/C4 Krong Kaoh Kong, Camb.
66/B1 Krong Kaoh Kong, Camb.
65/D4 Krong Keb, Camb.
20/E4 Kronoberg (co.), Swe.
42/F4 Kronshtadt, Rus.
43/U7 Kronshtadt, Rus.
72/C4 Kroombit Tops Nat'l Park, Austl.
80/D2 Kroonstad, SAfr.
82/E6 Kroonstad, SAfr.
19/H4 Kropotkin, Rus.
45/G3 Kropotkin, Rus.
46/E5 Kropotkin, Rus.
27/L4 Krosno, Pol.
27/L4 Krosno (prov.), Pol.
44/B2 Krosno, Pol.
27/H2 Krosno Odrzańskie, Pol.
27/J3 Krotoszyn, Pol.
45/J1 Krotovka, Rus.
37/G3 Krottenkopf, Grat (peak), Aus.
39/J5 Krousón, Gre.
31/G4 Kröv, Ger.
33/L4 Krško, Slov.
40/B3 Krško, Slov.
29/G1 Kruckau (riv.), Ger.
81/E2 Kruger Nat'l Park SAfr., SAfr.
82/F5 Kruger Nat'l Park, SAfr.
80/P13 Krugersdorp, SAfr.
43/N5 Kruglitsa, Gora (peak), Rus.
85/A5 Krugloi (pt.), Ak,US
28/B6 Kruibeke, Belg.
40/D5 Krujë, Alb.
37/G1 Krumbach, Ger.
37/F3 Krummenau, Swi.
39/J2 Krumovgrad, Bul.
41/G5 Krumovgrad, Bul.
44/C4 Krumovgrad, Bul.
37/H3 Krün, Ger.
63/H5 Krung Thep (Bangkok) (cap.), Thai.
65/C3 Krung Thep (Bangkok) (cap.), Thai.
27/K4 Krupina, Slvk.
26/E1 Kruså, Den.
85/F2 Krusenstern (cape), Ak,US
40/E4 Kruševac, Yugo.
44/B4 Kruševac, Yugo.
39/G2 Kruševo, Macd.
40/E5 Kruševo, Macd.
26/G3 Krušné Hory (Erzgebirge), Czh.
33/K1 Krušné Hory (Erzgebirge) (mts.), Czh., Ger.
27/K2 Kruszwica, Pol.
85/L4 Kruzof (isl.), Ak,US
44/F3 Krymsk, Rus.
27/L4 Krynica, Pol.
44/B2 Krynica, Pol.
41/J1 Kryzhopol', Ukr.
27/M3 Krzna (riv.), Pol.
27/J2 Krzyż, Pol.
75/M13 Ksar el Kebir, Mor.
50/C3 Ktima, Cyp.
52/B2 Ktima, Cyp.
65/B5 Kuah, Malay.
54/H5 Kuai (riv.), China
59/D4 Kuai (riv.), China
66/D3 Kuala Belait, Bru.
66/B3 Kuala Dungun, Malay.
63/H6 Kuala Kerai, Malay.
66/B2 Kuala Kerai, Malay.
66/B3 Kuala Lipis, Malay.
66/B3 Kuala Lumpur (cap.), Malay.
66/B3 Kuala Pilah, Malay.
88/T10 Kualapuu, Hi,US
66/B3 Kuala Selangor, Malay.
63/H6 Kuala Terengganu, Malay.
66/B2 Kuala Terengganu, Malay.
67/E2 Kuamut, Malay.
61/J4 Kuan (peak), Tai.
55/H3 Kuancheng, China
59/D2 Kuancheng, China
58/C2 Kuandian, China
59/F2 Kuandian, China
66/B3 Kuantan, Malay.
19/H4 Kuba, Azer.
45/J4 Kuba, Azer.
46/E5 Kuba, Azer.
51/G1 Kuba, Azer.
19/G4 Kuban (riv.), Rus.
44/E3 Kuban' (riv.), Rus.
46/D5 Kuban' (riv.), Rus.
50/E3 Kubaysah, Iraq
42/H4 Kubenskoye (lake), Rus.
56/C4 Kubokawa, Japan
41/H4 Kubrat, Bul.
40/E3 Kučevo, Yugo.
37/G3 Kuchen (peak), Aus.
66/D3 Kuching, Malay.
27/G5 Kuchl, Aus.
33/K3 Kuchl, Aus.
39/F2 Kuçovë, Alb.
51/M6 Küçükçekmece (lake), Turk.
56/B4 Kudamatsu, Japan
68/A4 Kudat, Malay.
27/M1 Kudirkos-Naumiestis, Lith.
64/G4 Kudremalai (pt.), SrL.
66/D5 Kudus, Indo.
19/J3 Kudymkar, Rus.
43/M4 Kudymkar, Rus.
46/F4 Kudymkar, Rus.
74/E2 Kufrah (oasis), Libya
77/K3 Kufrah (oasis), Libya
49/D3 Kufrinjah, Jor.
26/G5 Kufstein, Aus.
33/K3 Kufstein, Aus.
37/H1 Kühbach, Ger.
20/J2 Kuhmo, Fin.
42/F2 Kuhmo, Fin.
51/H3 Kūhpāyeh, Iran
52/F2 Kūhpāyeh, Iran
28/D3 Kuinder of Tjonger (riv.), Neth.
61/F4 Kuishan (mtn.), China
65/E1 Kuishan (mtn.), China
82/C3 Kuito, Ang.
85/M4 Kuiu (isl.), Ak,US
86/C3 Kuiu (isl.), Ak,US
55/K4 Kujang, NKor.
79/E5 Kujani Game Rsv., Gha.
27/K2 Kujawy (reg.), Pol.
55/N3 Kuji, Japan
56/B4 Kujū-san (mtn.), Japan
103/E3 Kukalaya (riv.), Nic.
60/C3 Kuke (riv.), China
39/G1 Kukës, Alb.
40/E4 Kukës, Alb.
57/F2 Kuki, Japan
57/J7 Kukizaki, Japan
51/H5 Kūl (riv.), Iran
53/G3 Kūl (riv.), Iran
40/F4 Kula, Bul.
44/D5 Kula, Turk.
50/B2 Kula, Turk.
40/D3 Kula, Yugo.
64/A2 Kulachi, Pak.
66/B3 Kulai, Malay.
45/J3 Kulaly (isl.), Kaz.
45/K4 Kulandag (mts.), Trkm.
64/G4 Kulasekharapatnam, India
50/E1 Kulashi, Geo.
20/G4 Kuldīga, Lat.
42/D4 Kuldīga, Lat.
42/J5 Kulebaki, Rus.
65/D3 Kulen, Camb.
53/L2 Kulgām, India
70/E5 Kulgera, Austl.
64/G3 Kulittalai, India
73/B2 Kulkyne-Hattah Nat'l Park, Austl.
53/L2 Kullu, India
26/F3 Kulmbach, Ger.
33/J1 Kulmbach, Ger.
43/J2 Kuloy (riv.), Rus.
98/E5 Kulpsville, Pa,US
45/K3 Kul'sary, Kaz.
46/F5 Kul'sary, Kaz.
64/D2 Kulu, India
44/E5 Kulu, Turk.
50/C2 Kulu, Turk.
46/H4 Kulunda, Rus.
46/G6 Kulyab, Taj.
53/J1 Kulyab, Taj.
58/D4 Kŭm (riv.), SKor.
19/H4 Kuma (riv.), Rus.
45/H3 Kuma (riv.), Rus.
46/E5 Kuma (riv.), Rus.
57/F2 Kumagaya, Japan
55/L5 Kumamoto, Japan
56/B4 Kumamoto, Japan
56/B4 Kumamoto (pref.), Japan
56/D4 Kumano (riv.), Japan
56/E4 Kumano, Japan
39/G1 Kumanovo, Macd.
40/E4 Kumanovo, Macd.
44/B4 Kumanovo, Macd.
56/E3 Kumano-Yoshino Nat'l Park, Japan
76/E6 Kumasi, Gha.
79/E5 Kumasi, Gha.
57/L10 Kumatori, Japan
19/H4 Kumayri, Arm.
45/G4 Kumayri, Arm.
46/E5 Kumayri, Arm.
51/E1 Kumayri, Arm.
76/G7 Kumba, Camr.
79/H5 Kumba, Camr.
64/G3 Kumbakonam, India
67/K5 Kumbe, Indo.
72/C4 Kumbia, Austl.
76/H6 Kumbo, Camr.
79/H5 Kumbo, Camr.
58/D4 Kŭmch'on, SKor.
58/F6 Kŭmch'on, SKor.
45/K5 Kum-Dag, Trkm.
46/F6 Kum-Dag, Trkm.
19/J3 Kumertau, Rus.
45/K1 Kumertau, Rus.
46/F4 Kumertau, Rus.
58/E3 Kumgang-san (mtn.), NKor.
58/E5 Kŭmho (riv.), SKor.
56/A2 Kumi, SKor.
58/E4 Kumi, SKor.
57/L10 Kumiyama, Japan
60/C3 Kumjawng (pass), India
39/K3 Kumkale, Turk.
41/H6 Kumkale, Turk.
41/J5 Kumköy, Turk.
51/N6 Kumköy, Turk.
20/E4 Kumla, Swe.
42/B4 Kumla, Swe.
49/B1 Kumluca, Turk.
50/B2 Kumluca, Turk.
52/B1 Kumluca, Turk.
18/F2 Kumo (riv.), Fin.
60/C3 Kumon (range), Burma
63/G2 Kumon (range), Burma
58/D4 Kŭmsan, SKor.
55/K4 Kŭmsanp'o, NKor.
53/K6 Kumta, India
62/B5 Kumta, India
88/U11 Kumukahi (cape), Hi,US
67/K5 Kumurkek, Indo.
47/Q5 Kunashiri (isl.), Rus.
48/P5 Kunashiri (isl.), Rus.
55/P3 Kunashiri (isl.), Rus.
62/C2 Kūnch, India
20/H4 Kunda, Est.
42/E4 Kunda, Est.
64/F4 Kundara, India
82/E3 Kundelungu Nat'l Park, Zaire
53/K2 Kundiān, Pak.
64/A1 Kundiān, Pak.
68/D5 Kundiawa, PNG
53/K4 Kundla, India
62/B3 Kundla, India
46/F5 Kungrad, Uzb.
20/E4 Kungsbacka, Swe.
77/J7 Kungu, Zaire
19/J3 Kungur, Rus.
43/N4 Kungur, Rus.
46/F4 Kungur, Rus.
40/E2 Kunhegyes, Hun.
65/B1 Kunhing, Burma
56/B4 Kunimi-dake (mtn.), Japan
66/C5 Kuningan, Indo.
57/H7 Kunitachi, Japan
53/L1 Kunjirap (pass), China
98/E5 Kunkletown, Pa,US
48/H6 Kunlun (mts.), China
54/C4 Kunlun (mts.), China
61/F4 Kunlun (pass), China
27/L5 Kunmadaras, Hun.
40/E2 Kunmadaras, Hun.
60/D3 Kunming, China
63/H2 Kunming, China
64/E3 Kunnamangalam, India
64/F3 Kunnamkulam, India
55/K4 Kunsan, SKor.
58/D5 Kunsan, SKor.
59/E5 Kunshan, China
59/L8 Kunshan, China
61/J2 Kunshan, China
40/E2 Kunszentmárton, Hun.
43/X9 Kuntsëvo, Rus.
53/L3 Kunu (riv.), India
70/D3 Kununurra, Austl.
58/E4 Kunwi, SKor.
58/A4 Kunyu (mtn.), China
59/E3 Kunyu Shan (mtn.), China
61/J2 Kuocang (peak), China
68/B2 Kuocang (peak), China
20/J2 Kuolayarvi, Rus.
18/F2 Kuopio, Fin.
20/H3 Kuopio, Fin.
20/H3 Kuopio (prov.), Fin.
42/E3 Kuopio, Fin.
42/E3 Kuopio (prov.), Fin.
40/C3 Kuopio, Fin.
40/B3 Kupa (riv.), Cro., Slov.
33/L4 Kupa (riv.), Cro., Slov.
67/F6 Kupang, Indo.
68/B6 Kupang, Indo.
46/H4 Kupino, Rus.
42/E5 Kupiškis, Lith.
85/M4 Kupreanof (isl.), Ak,US
86/C3 Kupreanof (isl.), Ak,US
44/F2 Kupyansk, Ukr.
47/M5 Kuqa, China
55/L1 Kur (riv.), Rus.
46/E6 Kura (riv.), Azer., Geo.
51/F1 Kura (riv.), Azer., Geo.
45/J5 Kura (riv.), Azer., Geo.
51/F1 Kurakh, Rus.
64/D2 Kūrālī, India
57/L9 Kurama-yama (peak), Japan
55/L5 Kurashiki, Japan
56/C3 Kurashiki, Japan
77/M4 Kuraymah, Sudan
56/C3 Kurayoshi, Japan
46/E6 Kurdistan (reg.), Asia
51/E2 Kurdistan (reg.), Asia
52/D1 Kurdistan (reg.), Asia
39/J2 Kŭrdzhali, Bul.
39/J2 Kŭrdzhali (res.), Bul.
41/G5 Kŭrdzhali, Bul.
44/C4 Kŭrdzhali, Bul.
50/A1 Kŭrdzhali, Bul.
47/P6 Kure, Japan
56/C3 Kure, Japan
44/E4 Küre, Turk.
50/C1 Küre, Turk.
50/C1 Küre (mts.), Turk.
68/H2 Kure (isl.), Hi.,US
20/G4 Kuressaare, Est.
42/D4 Kuressaare, Est.
46/K3 Kureyka (riv.), Rus.
43/Q5 Kurgan, Rus.
46/G4 Kurgan, Rus.
43/Q5 Kurgan Obl., Rus.
46/G6 Kurgan-Tyube, Taj.
53/J1 Kurgan-Tyube, Taj.
58/G6 Kuri, SKor.
68/G4 Kuria (isl.), Kiri.
48/E8 Kuria Muria (isls.), Oman
52/G5 Kuria Muria (isls.), Oman
47/Q5 Kuril (isls.), Rus.
48/Q5 Kuril (isls.), Rus.
72/H8 Ku-Ring-Gai Nat'l Park, Austl.
64/F3 Kurinjippādi, India
103/E3 Kurinwas (riv.), Nic
77/M5 Kurmuk, Sudan
62/C4 Kurnool, India
58/F7 Kuro, SKor.
57/K9 Kurodashō, Japan
55/N4 Kuroiso, Japan
57/G2 Kuroiso, Japan
57/M10 Kuroso-yama (peak Japan
72/G8 Kurrajong, Austl.
73/D2 Kurrajong, Austl.
53/K2 Kurram (riv.), Pak.
64/A1 Kurram (riv.), Pak.
72/B2 Kurrimine Beach, Austl.
20/G5 Kuršėnai, Lith.
42/D5 Kuršėnai, Lith.
62/E2 Kurseong, India
19/G3 Kursk, Rus.
44/F2 Kursk, Rus.
46/D4 Kursk, Rus.
27/L1 Kurskaya (spit), Lith Rus.
27/L1 Kurskiy (lag.), Rus.
44/E2 Kursk Obl., Rus.
39/G1 Kuršumlija, Yugo.
40/E4 Kuršumlija, Yugo.
44/E4 Kurşunlu, Turk.
50/C1 Kurşunlu, Turk.
50/E2 Kurtalan, Turk.
29/E6 Kürten, Ger.
31/G1 Kürten, Ger.
77/M4 Kurtī, Sudan
51/N7 Kurtköy, Turk.
77/L6 Kuru (riv.), Sudan
50/E2 Kuruca (pass), Turk
46/G4 Kuruçay (riv.), Turk.
54/B3 Kuruktag (mts.), Ch
80/C2 Kuruman, SAfr.
82/D6 Kuruman, SAfr.
80/C2 Kurumanrivier (dry riv.), SAfr.
55/L5 Kurume, Japan
56/B4 Kurume, Japan
47/M4 Kurumkan, Rus.
62/D6 Kurunegala, SrL.
72/E6 Kurwongbah (lake) Austl.
58/D5 Kurye, SKor.
58/C3 Kuryong (riv.), NKor
50/A2 Kuşadası, Turk.
77/M7 Kusania (lake), Uga
51/G1 Kusary, Azer.
60/D5 Ku Sathan (peak), Thai.
63/H4 Ku Sathan (peak), Thai.
65/C2 Ku Sathan (peak), Thai.
57/L9 Kusatsu, Japan
57/M9 Kusatsu, Japan
50/B1 Kuş Cenneti Nat'l Park, Turk.
31/G4 Kusel, Ger.
57/M10 Kushida (riv.), Japa
57/N9 Kushihara, Japan
56/B5 Kushikino, Japan
56/B5 Kushima, Japan
56/D4 Kushimoto, Japan
47/Q5 Kushiro, Japan
55/N3 Kushiro, Japan
46/G6 Kushka, Trkm.
43/Q5 Kushmurun (lake), Kaz.
53/L2 Kushol, India
54/F4 Kushui (riv.), China
45/J2 Kushum (riv.), Kaz.
85/F3 Kuskokwim (riv.), Ak,US
85/F4 Kuskokwim (bay), Ak,US
85/G3 Kuskokwim (mts.), Ak,US
85/H3 Kuskokwim, North Fork (riv.), Ak,US
85/H3 Kuskokwim, South Fork (riv.), Ak,US
37/E3 Küsnacht, Swi.
58/C3 Kusŏng, NKor.
37/E3 Küssnacht am Rigi, Swi.
43/P5 Kustanay, Kaz.
45/M1 Kustanay, Kaz.
46/G4 Kustanay, Kaz.
43/P5 Kustanay Obl., Kaz.
45/M2 Kustanay Obl., Kaz.
37/F1 Kusterdingen, Ger.
77/M5 Kūstī, Sudan
57/M10 Kusu, Japan
63/H5 Kut (isl.), Thai.
65/C4 Kut (isl.), Thai.
66/B1 Kut (isl.), Thai.
41/K5 Kütahya, Turk.
44/D5 Kütahya (prov.), Tu
50/B2 Kütahya, Turk.
50/B2 Kütahya (prov.), Tu
19/H4 Kutaisi, Geo.
45/G4 Kutaisi, Geo.
46/E5 Kutaisi, Geo.

51/E1 Kutaisi, Geo.
53/J4 Kutch (gulf), India
53/K4 Kutch (reg.), India
62/A3 Kutch (gulf), India
62/A3 Kutch (reg.), India
62/A3 Kutch, Rann of (swamp), India
53/J4 Kutch, Rann of (swamp), India, Pak.
29/G2 Kutenholz, Ger.
27/H4 Kutná Hora, Czh.
33/L2 Kutná Hora, Czh.
27/K2 Kutno, Pol.
44/A1 Kutno, Pol.
57/L9 Kutsuki, Japan
36/E3 Küttigen, Swi.
76/J8 Kutu, Zaire
82/C1 Kutu, Zaire
77/K5 Kutum, Sudan
37/G1 Kutzenhausen, Ger.
86/E1 Kuujjua (riv.), NW,Can
87/K3 Kuujjuaq (Fort-Chimo), Qu,Can
87/J3 Kuujjuarapik, Qu,Can
51/H1 Kuuli-Mayak, Trkm.
20/J2 Kuusamo, Fin.
20/H3 Kuusankoski, Fin.
42/E3 Kuusankoski, Fin.
20/H4 Kuutse (hill), Est.
42/E4 Kuutse Mägi (hill), Est.
45/L2 Kuvandyk, Rus.
48/D7 Kuwait
52/E3 Kuwait
77/Q2 Kuwait
77/Q2 Kuwait (cap.), Kuw.
52/E3 Kuwait (Al Kuwait) (cap.), Kuw.
62/D2 Kuwānā (riv.), India
56/E3 Kuwana, Japan
57/M9 Kuwana, Japan
19/H3 Kuybyshev (res.), Rus.
43/L5 Kuybyshev (res.), Rus.
45/H1 Kuybyshev (res.), Rus.
45/J1 Kuybyshev, Rus.
46/E4 Kuybyshev (res.), Rus.
41/K2 Kuybyshevka, Ukr.
54/G4 Kuye (riv.), China
59/B3 Kuye (riv.), China
51/F2 Küysanjaq, Iraq
52/D1 Küysanjaq, Iraq
20/J2 Kuyto (lake), Rus.
42/F2 Kuyto (lake), Rus.
64/F4 Kuzhittura, India
85/E2 Kuzitrin (riv.), Ak,US
45/H1 Kuznetsk, Rus.
20/F1 Kvaløy (isl.), Nor.
51/F1 Kvareli, Geo.
40/B3 Kvarerić (chan.), Cro.
26/F1 Kværndrup, Den.
33/L4 Kvarner (gulf), Cro.
40/B3 Kvarner (gulf), Cro.
33/L4 Kvarnerić (gulf), Cro.
20/F2 Kvigtinden (peak), Nor.
42/B2 Kvigtinden (peak), Nor.
20/C4 Kvinesdal, Nor.
20/C4 Kvinnherad, Nor.
74/D5 Kwa (riv.), Zaire
82/C1 Kwa (riv.), Zaire
28/C6 Kwaadmechelen, Belg.
58/F7 Kwach'ŏn, SKor.
65/B3 Kwai, River (bridge), Thai.
68/F4 Kwajelein (atoll), Mrsh.
0/Q12 Kwandebele (homeland), SAfr.
58/D4 Kwangch'ŏn, SKor.
55/K4 Kwangju, SKor.
58/D5 Kwangju, SKor.
58/F7 Kwangju, SKor.
58/D5 Kwangju-Jikhalsi, SKor.
74/D5 Kwango (riv.), Ang., Zaire
82/C1 Kwango (riv.), Zaire
58/F7 Kwangsan (mt.), SKor.
58/D5 Kwangyang, SKor.
58/D5 Kwansan, SKor.
79/G4 Kwara (state), Nga.
94/D1 Kwataboahegan (riv.), On,Can
82/E4 Kwekwe, Zim.
80/D2 Kweneng (dist.), Bots.
85/F3 Kwethluk, Ak,US
27/K2 Kwidzyn, Pol.
85/F4 Kwigillingok, Ak,US
77/N5 Kwīha, Eth.
82/C1 Kwili (riv.), Zaire
74/D5 Kwilu (riv.), Zaire
76/J6 Kyabé, Chad
73/C3 Kyabram, Austl.
63/G4 Kyaikkami, Burma
65/B2 Kyaikkami, Burma
65/B2 Kyaiktiyo Pagoda, Burma
60/C5 Kyaikto, Burma
63/G4 Kyaikto, Burma
65/B2 Kyaikto, Burma
63/G4 Kya-in Seikkyi, Burma
47/L4 Kyakhta, Rus.
54/F1 Kyakhta, Rus.
60/B5 Kyangin, Burma
63/G4 Kyangin, Burma
60/E5 Ky Anh, Viet.
63/J4 Ky Anh, Viet.
65/D2 Ky Anh, Viet.
60/C4 Kyaukme, Burma
65/B1 Kyaukme, Burma
60/B4 Kyaukpadaung, Burma
63/G3 Kyaukpadaung, Burma
60/B5 Kyaukpyu, Burma
63/F4 Kyaukpyu, Burma
60/C4 Kyaukse, Burma
63/G3 Kyaukse, Burma
65/B1 Kyaukse, Burma
63/G4 Kyaunggon, Burma
27/M1 Kybartai, Lith.
42/D5 Kybartai, Lith.
58/D4 Kyeryong-san Nat'l Park, SKor.
65/B2 Kyidaunggan, Burma
63/F3 Kyindwe, Burma
27/J4 Kyjov, Czh.
90/F3 Kyle, Sk,Can
26/D3 Kyll (riv.), Ger.
31/F3 Kyll (riv.), Ger.
33/G2 Kyll (riv.), Ger.
31/F3 Kyllburg, Ger.
25/F2 Kym (riv.), Eng,UK
20/H3 Kymi (prov.), Fin.
42/E3 Kymi (prov.), Fin.
62/C3 Kymore, India
73/C3 Kyneton, Austl.
70/G4 Kynuna, Austl.
77/M7 Kyoga (lake), Ugan.
55/M4 Kyōga-misaki (cape), Japan
56/D3 Kyōga-misaki (cape), Japan
72/D5 Kyogle, Austl.
73/E1 Kyogle, Austl.
57/F3 Kyonan, Japan
57/H7 Kyonan, Japan
58/G7 Kyŏngan (riv.), SKor.
58/F6 Kyongbok Palace, SKor.
58/C4 Kyŏnggi (bay), SKor.
58/F7 Kyŏnggi (bay), SKor.
58/D4 Kyŏnggi-Do (prov.), SKor.
58/F6 Kyŏnggi-Do (prov.), SKor.
55/K4 Kyŏngju, SKor.
56/A3 Kyŏngju, SKor.
56/A3 Kyŏngju Nat'l Park, SKor.
58/E5 Kyŏngju Nat'l Park, SKor.
56/A3 Kyŏngsan, SKor.
58/E5 Kyŏngsan, SKor.
56/A2 Kyŏngsang-bukto (prov.), SKor.
58/E4 Kyŏngsang-Bukto (prov.), SKor.
56/A3 Kyŏngsang-namdo (prov.), SKor.
58/E5 Kyŏngsang-Namdo (prov.), SKor.
63/G4 Kyönkadun, Burma
47/P6 Kyōto, Japan
55/M4 Kyōto, Japan
56/D3 Kyōto, Japan
56/D3 Kyōto (pref.), Japan
57/L9 Kyōto, Japan
57/L9 Kyōto (pref.), Japan
57/L10 Kyōto Imperial Palace, Japan
49/C2 Kyrenia, Cyp.
49/C2 Kyrenia (dist.), Cyp.
50/C3 Kyrenia, Cyp.
52/B1 Kyrenia, Cyp.
46/H5 Kyrgyzstan
48/G5 Kyrgyzstan
26/G2 Kyritz, Ger.
60/E5 Ky Son, Viet.
63/H4 Ky Son, Viet.
49/C2 Kythrea, Cyp.
48/M6 Kyūshū (isl.), Japan
55/L5 Kyūshū (isl.), Japan
58/B4 Kyūshū (mts.), Japan
56/B4 Kyūshū (prov.), Japan
56/B5 Kyūshū (isl.), Japan
68/C1 Kyūshū (isl.), Japan
39/H1 Kyustendil, Bul.
40/F4 Kyustendil, Bul.
63/F4 Kywebwe, Burma
46/K4 Kyzyl, Rus.
54/C1 Kyzyl, Rus.
46/G5 Kyzylkum (des.), Kaz.,Uzb.
46/G5 Kzyl-Orda, Kaz.

L

91/L4 L'Anse, Mi,US
94/B2 L'Anse, Mi,US
30/B5 L'Isle-Adam, Fr.
33/M2 Laa an der Thaya, Aus.
26/G2 Laage, Ger.
103/H4 La Aguja, Cabo de (pt.), Col.
27/G5 Laakirchen, Aus.
33/K3 Laakirchen, Aus.
40/A2 Laakirchen, Aus.
34/B4 La Algaba, Sp.
34/E2 La Almunia de Doña Godina, Sp.
103/F4 La Amistad Int'l Park, CR
101/N7 La Antigua Veracruz, Mex.
28/A6 Laarne, Belg.
30/C1 Laarne, Belg.
77/Q6 Laas Caanood, Som.
100/D2 La Ascensión, Mex.
92/F5 La Ascensión, Mex
37/G4 Laas (Lasa), It.
77/Q5 Laas Qoray, Som.
104/F5 La Asunción, Ven.
106/F1 La Asunción, Ven.
29/G4 Laatzen, Ger.
37/F4 Laax, Swi.
76/C2 Laayoune, WSah.
100/E2 La Babia, Mex.
96/C4 La Babia, Mex.
95/G1 La Baie, Qu,Can
34/A1 La Baña, Sp.
109/D2 La Banda, Arg.
34/C1 La Bañeza, Sp.
100/E4 La Barca, Mex.
30/B2 La Bassée, Fr.
32/B3 La Baule-Escoublac, Fr.
36/C4 L'Abbaye, Swi.
38/B1 Labbro (peak), It.
76/H1 Labdah (Leptis Magna) (ruins), Libya
33/L1 Labe (riv.), Czh.
76/C5 Labé, Gui.
78/B4 Labé, Gui.
78/B4 Labé (comm.), Gui.
27/H3 Labe (Elbe) (riv.), Czh.
104/A1 La Belle, Fl,US
97/H5 La Belle, Fl,US
67/E2 Labian (cape), Malay.
33/L4 Labin, Cro.
40/B3 Labin, Cro.
45/G3 Labinsk, Rus.
35/G2 La Bisbal, Sp.
101/H4 Labná (ruins), Mex.
102/D1 Labná (ruins), Mex.
27/L4 Laborec (riv.), Slvk.
32/C4 Labouheyre, Fr.
109/D3 Laboulaye, Arg.
84/L4 Labrador (reg.), Can.
87/K3 Labrador (reg.), Nf,Can
84/M4 Labrador (sea), Can., Grld.
87/L3 Labrador (sea), Can., Grld.
87/K3 Labrador City, Nf,Can
106/F5 Lábrea, Braz.
36/C2 La Bresse, Fr.
36/D1 La Broque, Fr.
32/E5 Labrugière, Fr.
35/G1 Labrugière, Fr.
31/E5 Labry, Fr.
67/E2 Labuk (bay), Malay.
67/E2 Labuk (riv.), Malay.
39/G2 Labuništa, Macd.
40/E5 Labuništa, Macd.
63/F4 Labutta, Burma
39/F2 Laç, Alb.
40/D5 Laç, Alb.
95/P7 Lacadie, Qu,Can
35/X16 La Caldera de Taburiente Nat'l Park, Canl.
95/N6 Lac-Alouette, Qu,Can
100/E3 La Campana, Mex.
34/C4 La Campana, Sp.
32/C4 Lacanau-Océan, Fr.
102/D2 Lacantum (riv.), Mex.
30/C4 La Capelle-en-Thiérache, Fr.
34/C4 La Carlota, Sp.
34/D3 La Carolina, Sp.
101/Q9 La Catedral (mt.), Mex.
32/E5 Lacaune, Fr.
35/G1 Lacaune, Fr.
62/B5 Laccadive (sea), India
91/J3 Lac du Bonnet, Mb,Can
102/F3 La Ceiba, Hon.
19/S10 La Celle-Saint-Cloud, Fr.
70/F7 Lacepede (bay), Austl.
73/A3 Lacepede (bay), Austl.
99/B3 Lacey, Wa,US
42/H3 Lacha (lake), Rus.
71/H6 Lachan (riv.), Austl.
30/A5 Lachapelle-aux-Pots, Fr.
36/A5 La Chapelle-de-Guinchay, Fr.
26/C4 La Chapelle-Saint-Luc, Fr.
32/F2 La Chapelle-St-Luc, Fr.
32/C3 La Chapelle-sur-Erdre, Fr.
36/C3 La Chaux-de-Fonds, Swi.
37/E3 Lachen, Swi.
95/N6 Lachenaie, Qu,Can
29/H3 Lachendorf, Ger.
64/A1 Lāchi, Pak.
51/F2 Lachin, Azer.
95/N7 Lachine, Qu,Can
68/D8 Lachlan (riv.), Austl.
73/C2 Lachlan (riv.), Austl.
106/D4 La Chorrera, Col.
103/G4 La Chorrera, Pan.
106/C2 La Chorrera, Pan.
29/H3 Lachte (riv.), Ger.
93/F4 La Cienega, NM,US
96/B3 La Cienega, NM,US
34/A1 La Ciñiza, Sp.
32/F5 La Ciotat, Fr.
35/H1 La Ciotat, Fr.
95/S10 Lackawanna, NY,US
86/E3 Lac La Biche, Ab,Can
90/F2 Lac La Biche, Ab,Can
86/E2 Lac la Martre, NW,Can
36/C6 La Clusaz, Fr.
95/G2 Lac-Mégantic, Qu,Can
61/J5 Lacob ti-Duyong (mt.), Phil.
24/D4 Lacock, Eng,UK
101/F3 La Coma, Mex.
88/E3 Lacombe, Ab,Can
90/E2 Lacombe, Ab,Can
101/Q9 La Concepción (res.), Mex.
102/E4 La Concepción, Nic.
103/F4 La Concepción, Pan.
103/J4 La Concepción, Ven.
104/D5 La Concepción, Ven.
102/C2 La Concordia, Mex.
87/J4 Laconia, NH,US
89/M3 Laconia, NH,US
95/G3 Laconia, NH,US
18/C4 La Coruña, Sp.
34/A1 La Coruña, Sp.
19/T10 La Courneuve, Fr.
32/D4 La Couronne, Fr.
32/C3 La Crèche, Fr.
91/L5 La Crescent, Mn,US
94/B3 La Crescent, Mn,US
30/B5 Lacroix-Saint-Ouen, Fr.
86/G4 La Crosse, Wi,US
89/H3 La Crosse, Wi,US
91/L5 La Crosse, Wi,US
93/K2 La Crosse, Ks,US
94/B3 La Crosse, Wi,US
102/E4 La Cruz, CR
100/D3 La Cruz, Mex.
100/D4 La Cruz, Mex.
63/J3 Lac Son, Viet.
65/D1 Lac Son, Viet.
66/C1 Lac Thien, Viet.
108/D1 Ladainha, Braz.
53/L2 Ladakh (mts.), Pak., India
29/E4 Ladbergen, Ger.
73/B3 Laddon (riv.), Austl.
27/J3 Lądek-Zdrój, Pol.
33/M1 Lądek-Zdrój, Pol.
38/C2 Ladispoli, It.
18/G2 Ladoga (lake), Rus.
20/J3 Ladoga (lake), Rus.
42/F3 Ladoga (lake), Rus.
43/W6 Ladoga (lake), Rus.
46/D3 Ladoga (lake), Rus.
36/C5 La Dôle (peak), Swi.
106/D2 La Dorada, Col.
43/W6 Ladozhskoye Ozero, Rus.
103/G1 Ladrillo (pt.), Cuba
23/G5 Ladybower (res.), Eng,UK
80/D3 Ladybrand, SAfr.
65/D4 Lady Chua Xu, Temple of, Viet.
81/E3 Ladysmith, SAfr.
82/E6 Ladysmith, SAfr.
91/L4 Ladysmith, Wi,US
94/B2 Ladysmith, Wi,US
68/F4 Lae (atoll), Mrsh.
68/D5 Lae, PNG
26/D2 Laer, Ger.
29/E4 Laer, Ger.
101/F3 La Escondida, Mex.
102/D3 La Esperanza, Hon.
102/E3 La Esperanza, Sierra (range), Hon.
34/B1 La Estaca de Bares, Punta de (cape), Sp.
34/A1 La Estrada, Sp.
109/D3 La Falda, Arg.
99/K11 Lafayette, Ca,US
97/G3 La Fayette, Ga,US
89/J3 Lafayette, In,US
94/C3 Lafayette, In,US
89/H5 Lafayette, La,US
93/J5 Lafayette, La,US
96/E4 Lafayette, La,US
98/F4 Lafayette, NJ,US
26/B4 La Fère, Fr.
30/C4 La Fère, Fr.
32/F2 La Fère, Fr.
32/D2 La Ferté-Bernard, Fr.
30/C6 La Ferté-Gaucher, Fr.
32/C2 La Ferté-Macé, Fr.
30/C5 La Ferté-Milon, Fr.
30/C6 La Ferté-sous-Jouarre, Fr.
94/E1 Laflamme (riv.), Qu,Can
32/C3 La Flèche, Fr.
33/L3 Lafnitz (riv.), Aus.
40/C2 Lafnitz (riv.), Aus.
95/M6 Lafontaine, Qu,Can
103/H4 La Fría, Ven.
63/F6 Lāfūl, India
22/B3 Lagan (riv.), NI,UK
19/S10 La Garenne-Colombes, Fr.
96/B2 La Garita (mts.), Co,US
35/L6 La Garriga, Sp.
107/L6 Lagarto, Braz.
61/J5 Lagawe, Phil.
76/H6 Lagdo (riv.), Camr.
29/F5 Lage, Ger.
108/B3 Lages, Braz.
109/F2 Lages, Braz.
28/C4 Lage Vaart (can.), Neth.
76/F1 Laghouat, Alg.
34/E3 La Gineta, Sp.
103/H4 La Gloria, Col.
36/B6 Lagnieu, Fr.
19/U9 Lagny-le-Sec, Fr.
30/B5 Lagny-le-Sec, Fr.
19/U10 Lagny-sur-Marne, Fr.
30/B6 Lagny-sur-Marne, Fr.
34/A4 Lagoa, Port.
107/J8 Lagoa da Prata, Braz.
108/C2 Lagoa da Prata, Braz.
108/C1 Lagoa Formosa, Braz.
108/B4 Lagoa Vermelha, Braz.
102/D3 Lago de Atitlán Nat'l Park, Guat.
51/F1 Lagodekhi, Geo.
37/E5 Lago Gelato, Pizzo di (peak), It.
38/D2 Lagonegro, It.
32/C3 Lagord, Fr.
76/F6 Lagos, Nga.
79/F5 Lagos, Nga.
79/F5 Lagos (state), Nga.
34/A4 Lagos, Port.
100/E4 Lagos de Moreno, Mex.
84/K4 La Grande (riv.), Can.
86/E4 La Grande, Or,US
88/C2 La Grande, Or,US
90/D4 La Grande, Or,US
33/G4 La Grande Ruine (mtn.), Fr.
89/J5 La Grange, Ga,US
97/G3 La Grange, Ga,US
94/C4 La Grange, Ky,US
97/G2 La Grange, Ky,US
101/F2 La Grange, Tx,US
93/H5 La Grange, Tx,US
96/D4 La Grange, Tx,US
106/F2 La Gran Sabana (plain), Ven.
103/J4 La Grita, Ven.
103/H4 La Guajira (dept.), Col.
32/B5 Laguardia, Sp.
34/A2 La Guardia, Sp.
34/D1 Laguardia, Sp.
108/B4 Laguna, Braz.
109/G2 Laguna, Braz.
99/M10 Laguna (cr.), Ca,US
92/D5 Laguna Chapala, Mex
34/C2 Laguna de Duero, Sp.
104/E5 Laguna de la Restinga Nat'l Park, Ven.
98/C3 Laguna Hills, Ca,US
109/B6 Laguna San Rafael Nat'l Park, Chile
102/B2 Lagunas de Chacahua Nat'l Park, Mex.
37/H4 Lagundo (Algund), It.
100/D4 Lagunillas, Mex.
101/F4 Lagunillas, Mex.
102/B1 Lagunillas, Mex.
103/E3 Laguntara (lag.), Hon.
103/F1 La Habana (Havana) (cap.), Cuba
98/C3 La Habra, Ca,US
67/E2 Lahad Datu, Malay.
66/B4 Lahat, Indo.
95/H2 La Have (riv.), NS,Can
109/B2 La Higuera, Chile
52/D6 Laḥij, Yem.
77/P5 Laḥij, Yem.
51/G2 Lāhījān, Iran
52/F1 Lāhījān, Iran
26/E3 Lahn (riv.), Ger.
31/G3 Lahn (riv.), Ger.
33/H1 Lahn (riv.), Ger.
31/G3 Lahnstein, Ger.
20/E4 Laholm, Swe.
99/K12 La Honda, Ca,US
53/K2 Lahore, Pak.
64/C2 Lahore, Pak.
26/D4 Lahr, Ger.
33/G2 Lahr, Ger.
36/D1 Lahr, Ger.
18/F2 Lahti, Fin.
20/H3 Lahti, Fin.
42/E3 Lahti, Fin.
46/C3 Lahti, Fin.
101/E5 La Huacana, Mex.
100/D5 La Huerta, Mex.
76/J6 Laï, Chad
59/D4 Lai'an, China
61/H1 Lai'an, China
63/J3 Laibin, China
63/H3 Lai Chau, Viet.
65/C1 Lai Chau, Viet.
37/F1 Laichingen, Ger.
88/T10 Laie, Hi,US
88/W12 Laie, Hi,US
59/B5 Laifeng Tujiazu Zizhixian, China
61/F2 Laifeng Tujiazu Zizhixian, China
32/D2 L'Aigle, Fr.
20/G3 Laihia, Fin.
42/D3 Laihia, Fin.
20/G1 Lainioälven (riv.), Swe.
42/D1 Lainioälven (riv.), Swe.
59/C3 Laishui, China
59/G7 Laishui, China
42/C2 Laisvall, Swe.
20/G3 Laitila, Fin.
42/D3 Laitila, Fin.
33/J3 Laives (Leifers), It.
37/H5 Laives (Leifers), It.
55/H4 Laiwu, China
59/D3 Laiwu, China
59/E3 Laixi, China
55/J4 Laiyang, China
59/E3 Laiyang, China
59/C3 Laiyuan, China
59/D3 Laizhou (bay), China
108/B4 Lajeado, Braz.
35/S12 Lajes do Pico, Azor.
108/D2 Lajinha, Braz.
40/D2 Lajosmizse, Hun.
100/D3 La Joya, Mex.
100/B1 La Joyita, Mex.
63/G2 Lāju, India
88/F4 La Junta, Co,US
93/G3 La Junta, Co,US
96/C2 La Junta, Co,US
99/J9 Lake (co.), Ca,US
99/P15 Lake (co.), Il,US
99/R16 Lake (co.), In,US
91/J5 Lake Andes, SD,US
93/H2 Lake Andes, SD,US
98/C2 Lake Arrowhead, Co,US
102/D3 Lake Atitlán Nat'l Park, Guat.
99/P15 Lake Barrington, Il,US
99/P14 Lake Beulah, Wi,US
99/Q15 Lake Bluff, Il,US
73/B2 Lake Boga, Austl.
73/C2 Lake Cargelligo, Austl.
99/P15 Lake Catherine, Il,US
93/J5 Lake Charles, La,US
96/E4 Lake Charles, La,US
92/F3 Lake City, Co,US
96/B2 Lake City, Co,US
89/K5 Lake City, Fl,US
97/H4 Lake City, Fl,US
91/K4 Lake City, Mn,US
94/A2 Lake City, Mn,US
86/A2 Lake Clark Nat'l Park, Ak,US
85/H3 Lake Clark Nat'l Park & Prsv., Ak,US
23/E2 Lake District Nat'l Park, Eng,UK
98/C3 Lake Elsinore, Ca,US
99/E6 Lake Fenton, Mi,US
72/B1 Lakefield Nat'l Park, Austl.
99/Q15 Lake Forest, Il,US
99/C2 Lake Forest Park, Wa,US
99/P14 Lake Geneva, Wi,US
70/B6 Lake Grace, Austl.
87/K2 Lake Harbour, NW,Can
88/D5 Lake Havasu City, Az,US
92/D4 Lake Havasu City, Az,US
99/P15 Lake in the Hills, Il,US
93/J5 Lake Jackson, Tx,US
96/E4 Lake Jackson, Tx,US
89/K6 Lakeland, Fl,US
97/H4 Lakeland, Fl,US
98/C3 Lakeland Village, Ca,US
90/D3 Lake Louise, Ab,Can
82/F3 Lake Malawi Nat'l Park, Malw.
77/M8 Lake Mburo Nat'l Park, Ugan.
92/D4 Lake Mead Nat'l Rec. Area, Az, Nv,US
39/G2 Lake Mikri Prespa Nat'l Park, Gre.
40/E5 Lake Mikri Prespa Nat'l Park, Gre.
85/H3 Lake Minchumina, Ak,US
98/F4 Lake Mohawk, NJ,US
99/P15 Lakemoor, Il,US
67/K5 Lake Murray, PNG
70/F4 Lake Nash, Austl.
25/G2 Lakenheath, Eng,UK
93/J3 Lake of the Ozarks (lake), Mo,US
89/H2 Lake of the Woods (lake), Can, US
86/G4 Lake of the Woods (lake), Can.,US
84/H5 Lake of the Woods (lake), US, Can.
99/F6 Lake Orion, Mi,US
98/C3 Lake Perris St. Rec. Area, Ca,US
92/B3 Lakeport, Ca,US
93/K4 Lake Providence, La,US
96/F3 Lake Providence, La,US
98/G5 Lake Ronkonkoma, NY,US
73/C4 Lake Saint Clair-Cradle Mountain Nat'l Park, Austl.
73/D3 Lakes Entrance, Austl.
20/H1 Lakesfjorden (fjord), Nor.
98/K7 Lake Shore, Md,US
94/E4 Lakeside, Va,US
97/J2 Lakeside, Va,US
73/C3 Lakes Nat'l Park, The, Austl.
99/R16 Lake Station, In,US
99/C1 Lake Stevens, Wa,US
98/C3 Lakeview, Ca,US
90/C5 Lakeview, Or,US
92/B2 Lakeview, Or,US
99/P15 Lake Villa, Il,US
99/F6 Lakeville (lake), Mi,US
97/H5 Lake Wales, Fl,US
70/C5 Lake Way, Austl.
101/F2 Lakeway, Tx,US
98/B3 Lakewood, Ca,US
88/E4 Lakewood, Co,US
93/F3 Lakewood, Co,US
99/P15 Lakewood, Il,US
98/F5 Lakewood, NJ,US
90/C3 Lakewood, Wa,US
97/H5 Lake Worth, Fl,US
99/P15 Lake Zurich, Il,US
20/J3 Lakhdenpokh'ya, Rus.
62/D2 Lakhīmpur, India
53/J4 Lakhpat, India
20/N7 Laki (vol.), Ice.
53/K2 Lakki, Pak.
64/A1 Lakki, Pak.
39/H4 Lakonía (gulf), Gre.
48/F8 Lakshadweep (isls.), India
62/B5 Lakshadweep (isls.), India
62/B6 Lakshadweep (terr.), India
35/X16 La Laguna, Canl.
101/F4 La Laja, Mex.
102/B1 La Laja, Mex.
53/K2 Lāla Mūsa, Pak.
64/B1 Lāla Mūsa, Pak.
81/H8 Lalana (riv.), Madg.
66/B4 Lalang (riv.), Indo.
39/K2 Lâlapaşa, Turk.
41/H5 Lâlapaşa, Turk.
50/A1 Lâlapaşa, Turk.
62/E3 Lālgola, India
64/B2 Lāliān, Pak.
77/N5 Lalībela, Eth.
106/B4 La Libertad, Ecu.
102/D2 La Libertad, Guat.
102/E3 La Libertad, Hon.
55/K3 Lalin (riv.), China
34/A1 Lalín, Sp.
32/D4 Lalinde, Fr.
18/C5 La Línea de la Concepción, Sp.
34/C4 La Línea de la Concepción, Sp.
75/M12 La Línea de la Concepción, Sp.
62/C3 Lalitpur, India
35/L6 La Llagosta, Sp.
86/F3 La Loche, Sk,Can
90/F1 La Loche, Sk,Can
26/C3 La Louvière, Belg.
30/D3 La Louvière, Belg.
32/F1 La Louvière, Belg.
34/C4 La Luisiana, Sp.
100/D1 La Luz, NM,US
34/B4 La Luz, Costa de (coast), Sp.
22/D1 Lamachan (mtn.), Sc,UK
32/E3 La Machine, Fr.
38/A2 La Maddalena, It.
30/C2 La Madeleine, Fr.
101/E3 Lamadrid, Mex.
96/C5 Lamadrid, Mex
76/F6 Lama-Kara, Togo
79/F4 Lama-Kara, Togo
95/G2 La Malbaie, Qu,Can
101/H5 Lamanai (ruins), Belz.
102/D2 Lamanai (ruins), Belz.
66/D4 Lamandau (riv.), Indo.
88/F4 Lamar, Co,US
93/G3 Lamar, Co,US
96/C2 Lamar, Co,US
36/B1 Lamarche, Fr.
36/B3 Lamarche-sur-Saône, Fr.
86/E2 La Martre (lake), NW,Can
102/E3 La Masica, Hon.
32/B2 Lamballe, Fr.
109/E2 Lambaré, Par.
76/H8 Lambaréné, Gabon
82/B1 Lambaréné, Gabon
108/C2 Lambari, Braz.
68/G6 Lambasa, Fiji
69/Z17 Lambasa, Fiji
22/B5 Lambay (isl.), Ire.
106/C5 Lambayeque, Peru
22/B3 Lambeg, NI,UK
78/C3 Lambé Koba (riv.), Mali
83/E Lambert (glac.), Ant.
80/B4 Lambert's Bay, SAfr.
94/D3 Lambertville, Mi,US
32/F5 Lambesc, Fr.
19/N7 Lambeth (bor.), Eng,UK
25/E3 Lambourn, Eng,UK
31/H5 Lambrecht, Ger.
99/H6 Lambton (co.), On,Can
34/B2 Lamego, Port.
95/H2 Lamèque (isl.), NB,Can
34/B1 La Merca, Sp.
106/C6 La Merced, Peru
32/F3 La Mère Boitier, Signal de (mtn.), Fr.
73/B2 Lameroo, Austl.
101/F3 La Mesa, Mex.
100/E1 Lamesa, Tx,US
88/F5 Lamesa, Tx,US
93/G4 Lamesa, Tx,US
96/C3 Lamesa, Tx,US
18/F5 Lamía, Gre.
39/H3 Lamía, Gre.
72/D5 Lamington Nat'l Park, Austl.
100/C2 La Misa, Mex.
67/F2 Lamitan, Phil.
94/B3 La Moine (riv.), Il,US
33/J4 Lamone (riv.), It.
92/C4 Lamont, Ca,US
105/B3 La Montaña (reg.), Peru
106/D5 La Montaña (reg.), Peru
35/K7 La Morella (peak), Sp.
100/E2 La Morita, Mex.
19/T9 Lamorlaye, Fr.
30/B5 Lamorlaye, Fr.
68/D4 Lamotrek (isl.), Micr.
91/J4 LaMoure, ND,US
106/D7 Lampa, Peru
60/C5 Lampang, Thai.
63/G4 Lampang, Thai.
65/B2 Lampang, Thai.
60/D5 Lam Pao (res.), Thai.
65/C2 Lam Pao (res.), Thai.
101/F2 Lampasas (riv.), Tx,US
89/G5 Lampasas, Tx,US
93/H5 Lampasas, Tx,US
96/D4 Lampasas, Tx,US
96/C5 Lampazos de Naranjo, Mex
18/E5 Lampedusa (isl.), It.
38/C5 Lampedusa, It.
38/C5 Lampedusa (isl.), It.
26/E4 Lampertheim, Ger.
33/H2 Lampertheim, Ger.
24/B2 Lampeter, Wal,UK
24/B3 Lamphey, Wal,UK
60/C5 Lamphun, Thai.
63/G4 Lamphun, Thai.
65/B2 Lamphun, Thai.
91/H3 Lampman, Sk,Can
29/G1 Lamstedt, Ger.
82/H1 Lamu, Kenya
103/F4 La Muerte, Cerro (mtn.), CR
32/F4 La Mure, Fr.
61/J4 Lan (isl.), Tai.
33/J3 Lana, It.
37/H4 Lana, It.
69/K2 Lanai (isl.), Hi.,US
88/T10 Lanai (isl.), Hi,US
88/T10 Lanaihale (peak), Hi,US
31/E2 Lanaken, Belg.
35/F3 la Nao, Cabo de (cape), Sp.
102/C2 Lana, Río de la (riv.), Mex.
63/G5 Lanbi (isl.), Burma
65/B4 Lanbi (isl.), Burma
54/D5 Lancang (riv.), China
60/C4 Lancang Lahuzu Zizhixian, China
65/B1 Lancang Lahuzu Zizhixian, China
63/G3 Lancang Lahuzu Zizhixian (Lancang), China
63/G3 Lancang (Lancang Lahuzu Zizhixian), China
23/F4 Lancashire (co.), Eng,UK
23/F4 Lancashire (plain), Eng,UK
87/H1 Lancaster (sound), NW,Can
87/S7 Lancaster (sound), NW,Can
23/F3 Lancaster, Eng,UK
88/C5 Lancaster, Ca,US
92/C4 Lancaster, Ca,US
95/S10 Lancaster, NY,US
89/K4 Lancaster, Oh,US
94/D4 Lancaster, Oh,US
97/H2 Lancaster, Oh,US
89/L3 Lancaster, Pa,US
94/E3 Lancaster, Pa,US
97/H3 Lancaster, SC,US
91/L5 Lancaster, Wi,US
93/K2 Lancaster, Wi,US
94/B3 Lancaster, Wi,US
23/G2 Lanchester, Eng,UK
50/E1 Lanchkhuti, Geo.
38/D1 Lanciano, It.
40/B4 Lanciano, It.
27/M3 Łańcut, Pol.
36/C5 Lancy, Swi.
26/G4 Landau an der Isar, Ger.
33/K2 Landau an der Isar, Ger.
26/E4 Landau in der Pfalz, Ger.
31/H5 Landau in der Pfalz, Ger.
33/H2 Landau in der Pfalz, Ger.
33/J3 Landeck, Aus.
37/G3 Landeck, Aus.
31/E2 Landen, Belg.
86/F4 Lander, Wy,US
88/E3 Lander, Wy,US
90/F5 Lander, Wy,US
92/E2 Lander, Wy,US
32/A2 Landerneau, Fr.
32/C4 Landes (reg.), Fr.
29/G3 Landesbergen, Ger.
32/B3 Landes de Lanvaux (reg.), Fr.
90/F2 Landis, Sk,Can
32/A2 Landivisiau, Fr.
29/G1 Land Kehdingen (reg.), Ger.
30/C3 Landrecies, Fr.
26/F4 Landsberg, Ger.
37/G1 Landsberg, Ger.
72/B3 Landsborough (cr.), Austl.
18/C3 Land's End (pt.), Eng,UK
24/A6 Land's End (pt.), Eng,UK
36/D2 Landser, Fr.
26/G4 Landshut, Ger.
33/K2 Landshut, Ger.
28/B4 Landsmeer, Neth.
31/G5 Landstuhl, Ger.
23/F2 Lanercost, Eng,UK
32/B3 Lanester, Fr.
97/G3 Lanett, Al,US
36/D3 La Neuveville, Swi.
61/J2 Lang (mtn.), China
39/H2 Langadhás, Gre.
40/F5 Langadhás, Gre.
91/J3 Langdon, ND,US
32/E4 Langeac, Fr.
80/L10 Langebaanweg, SAfr.
80/C3 Langeberg (mts.), SAfr.
80/L10 Langeberg (mts.), SAfr.
26/F1 Langeland (isl.), Den.
29/H5 Langelsheim, Ger.
26/E2 Langen, Ger.
29/F1 Langen, Ger.
33/H2 Langen, Ger.
37/F2 Langenargen, Ger.
26/F4 Langenau, Ger.
37/G1 Langenau, Ger.
29/E6 Langenberg, Ger.
91/H3 Langenburg, Sk,Can
26/D3 Langenfeld, Ger.
28/D6 Langenfeld, Ger.
31/F1 Langenfeld, Ger.
26/E2 Langenhagen, Ger.
29/G4 Langenhagen, Ger.
26/E1 Langenhorn, Ger.
27/H4 Langenlois, Aus.
33/G3 Langenthal, Swi.
36/D3 Langenthal, Swi.
33/L3 Langenwang, Aus.
40/B2 Langenwang, Aus.
26/D2 Langeoog, Ger.
29/E1 Langeoog, Ger.
29/E1 Langeoog (isl.), Ger.
37/G1 Langerringen, Ger.
36/D3 Langeten (riv.), Swi.
47/M6 Langfang, China
54/H4 Langfang, China
59/D3 Langfang, China
59/H7 Langfang, China
90/G2 Langham, Sk,Can
25/F1 Langham, Eng,UK
23/F1 Langholm, Sc,UK
20/N7 Langjökull (glac.), Ice.
65/B5 Langkawi (isl.), Malay.

66/A2 **Langkawi** (isl.), Malay.
63/G6 **Langkawi** (isl.), Thai.
63/G6 **Lang Kha Tuk** (peak), Thai.
65/B4 **Lang Kha Tuk** (peak), Thai.
66/A2 **Lang Kha Tuk** (peak), Thai.
19/M7 **Langley**, Eng,UK
99/C1 **Langley**, Wa,US
36/D4 **Langnau im Emmental**, Swi.
25/G5 **Langney** (pt.), UK
32/E4 **Langogne**, Fr.
32/C4 **Langon**, Fr.
20/E1 **Langøya** (isl.), Nor.
26/C5 **Langres**, Fr.
26/C5 **Langres** (plat.), Fr.
32/F3 **Langres**, Fr.
32/F3 **Langres** (plat.), Fr.
36/B2 **Langres**, Fr.
36/B2 **Langres** (plat.), Fr.
36/B2 **Langres, Plateau de** (plat.), Fr.
66/A3 **Langsa**, Indo.
60/E4 **Lang Son**, Viet.
63/J3 **Lang Son**, Viet.
65/D1 **Lang Son**, Viet.
95/R8 **Langstaff**, On,Can
65/B4 **Lang Suan**, Thai.
101/E2 **Langtry**, Tx,US
93/G5 **Langtry**, Tx,US
96/C4 **Langtry**, Tx,US
32/E5 **Languedoc** (reg.), Fr.
35/G1 **Languedoc** (hist. prov.), Fr.
32/E5 **Languedoc-Roussillon** (reg.), Fr.
32/G5 **Languedoc-Roussillon** (reg.), Fr.
35/G1 **Languedoc-Roussillon** (reg.), Fr.
26/E2 **Langwedel**, Ger.
29/G3 **Langwedel**, Ger.
37/G1 **Langweid am Lech**, Ger.
37/F4 **Langwies**, Swi.
59/D5 **Langxi**, China
61/H2 **Langxi**, China
59/C3 **Langya Shan** (mtn.), China
59/G7 **Langya Shan** (mtn.), China
98/K8 **Lanham-Seabrook**, Md,US
86/F3 **Lanigan**, Sk,Can
91/G3 **Lanigan**, Sk,Can
88/W12 **Laniloa** (pt.), Hi,US
109/B4 **Lanin Nat'l Park**, Arg.
32/D5 **Lannemezan**, Fr.
32/D5 **Lannemezan** (plat.), Fr.
24/A6 **Lanner**, Eng,UK
32/B2 **Lannion**, Fr.
32/B2 **Lannion** (bay), Fr.
100/D4 **La Noria**, Mex.
19/S11 **La Norville**, Fr.
60/C5 **Lansang Nat'l Park**, Thai.
65/B2 **Lan Sang Nat'l Park**, Thai.
98/E5 **Lansdale**, Pa,US
98/E6 **Lansdowne**, Pa,US
98/K7 **Lansdowne-Baltimore Highlands**, Md,US
95/L1 **L'Anse aux Meadows Nat'l Hist. Park**, Can
98/E5 **Lansford**, Pa,US
61/G3 **Lanshan**, China
63/K2 **Lanshan**, China
85/M3 **Lansing**, Yk,Can
99/Q16 **Lansing**, Il,US
87/H4 **Lansing** (cap.), Mi,US
89/K3 **Lansing** (cap.), Mi,US
94/C3 **Lansing** (cap.), Mi,US
63/G6 **Lanta** (isl.), Thai.
65/B5 **Lanta** (isl.), Thai.
66/A2 **Lanta** (isl.), Thai.
36/C2 **Lanterne** (riv.), Fr.
60/D4 **Lantouy**, Laos
38/A3 **Lanusei**, It.
55/K2 **Lanxi**, China
61/H2 **Lanxi**, China
35/Y16 **Lanzarote** (isl.), Canl., Sp.
76/C2 **Lanzarote** (isl.), Canl., Sp.
54/E4 **Lanzhou**, China
58/D2 **Lao** (mts.), China
61/G2 **Lao** (riv.), China
61/J5 **Laoag**, Phil.
68/B3 **Laoag**, Phil.
48/K7 **Lao Cai**, Viet.
60/E4 **Lao Cai**, Viet.
65/C1 **Lao Cai**, Viet.
61/G2 **Laodao** (riv.), China
55/H3 **Laoha** (riv.), China
54/G5 **Laohekou**, China
59/B4 **Laohekou**, China
61/F1 **Laohekou**, China
22/A6 **Laois** (Leix) (co.), Ire.
59/B4 **Laojun Shan** (mtn.), China
26/B4 **Laon**, Fr.
30/C4 **Laon**, Fr.
32/E2 **Laon**, Fr.
104/E5 **La Orchila** (isl.), Ven.
106/C6 **La Oroya**, Peru
48/K8 **Laos**
60/D4 **Laos**
63/H3 **Laos**
65/C2 **Laos**
55/J4 **Lao Shan** (peak), China
59/E3 **Lao Shan** (peak), China
59/E3 **Laoshan**, China
55/J4 **Laotie Shan** (mtn.), China
59/E3 **Laotie Shan** (mtn.), China
55/J3 **Laotuding** (peak), China
58/C2 **Laotuding Shan** (peak), China
59/F2 **Laotuding Shan** (peak), China
75/M13 **Laou** (riv.), Mor.
35/G1 **Laouzas, Barrage de** (dam), Fr.
108/B3 **Lapa**, Braz.
79/G4 **Lapai**, Nga.
101/E2 **La Palestina**, Mex.
35/X16 **La Palma** (isl.), Canl., Sp.
76/B2 **La Palma** (isl.), Canl., Sp.
100/D3 **La Palma**, Mex.
103/G4 **La Palma**, Pan.
106/F2 **La Paragua**, Ven.
109/E3 **La Paz**, Arg.
106/E7 **La Paz** (cap.), Bol.
103/H4 **La Paz**, Col.
102/E3 **La Paz**, Hon.
100/C3 **La Paz**, Mex.
100/C3 **La Paz** (bay), Mex.
69/P2 **La Paz**, Mex.
88/D7 **La Paz**, Mex.
94/F2 **La Pêche**, Qu,Can
42/F3 **Lapeenranta**, Fin.
94/D3 **Lapeer**, Mi,US
99/F5 **Lapeer**, Mi,US
99/F6 **Lapeer** (co.), Mi,US
103/F4 **La Peña**, Pan.
96/B4 **La Perla**, Mex
47/Q5 **La Pérouse** (str.), Japan.,Rus.
48/P5 **La Perouse** (str.), Japan.,Rus.
55/N2 **La Pérousse** (str.), Japan, Rus.
36/D1 **La Petite-Raon**, Fr.
20/H3 **Lapinlahti**, Fin.
42/E3 **Lapinlahti**, Fin.
49/C2 **Lapithos**, Cyp.
18/F2 **Lapland** (reg.), Eur.
20/F1 **Lapland** (reg.), Eur.
42/C1 **Lapland** (reg.), Eur.
46/C3 **Lapland** (reg.), Eur.
106/C3 **La Plata**, Col.
96/B2 **La Plata** (peak), Co,US
94/E4 **La Plata**, Md,US
97/J2 **La Plata**, Md,US
30/D3 **La Plate Taile, Barrage de** (dam), Belg.
35/F1 **La Pobla de Lillet**, Sp.
49/C2 **La Pocatière**, Qu,Can
34/C1 **La Pola de Gordón**, Sp.
94/C3 **La Porte**, In,US
55/N1 **Lapotina** (mtn.), Rus.
40/E3 **Lapovo**, Yugo.
100/B3 **La Poza**, Mex.
18/F2 **Lappeenranta**, Fin.
20/J3 **Lappeenranta**, Fin.
46/C3 **Lappeenranta**, Fin.
33/K2 **Lappersdorf**, Ger.
20/H2 **Lappi** (prov.), Fin.
42/E2 **Lappi** (prov.), Fin.
95/N7 **La Prairie**, Qu,Can
95/N7 **Laprarie** (co.), Qu,Can
101/F2 **La Pryor**, Tx,US
93/H5 **La Pryor**, Tx,US
96/D4 **La Pryor**, Tx,US
50/A1 **Lâpseki**, Turk.
47/N2 **Laptev** (sea), Rus.
48/L2 **Laptev** (sea), Rus.
20/G3 **Lapua**, Fin.
42/D3 **Lapua**, Fin.
35/G3 **La Puebla**, Sp.
34/D3 **La Puebla de Almoradiel**, Sp.
34/C4 **La Puebla de Cazalla**, Sp.
34/B4 **La Puebla del Río**, Sp.
34/C3 **La Puebla de Montalbán**, Sp.
106/B4 **La Puntilla** (pt.), Ecu.
100/B3 **La Purísima**, Mex.
44/D3 **Lapushna**, Mol.
27/M2 **Łapy**, Pol.
106/E8 **La Quiaca**, Arg.
38/C1 **L'Aquila**, It.
46/F7 **Lār**, Iran
51/H5 **Lār**, Iran
53/F3 **Lār**, Iran
77/R2 **Lār**, Iran
73/C3 **Lara**, Austl.
104/D5 **Lara** (state), Ven.
34/A1 **Laracha**, Sp.
75/L13 **Larache**, Mor.
76/D1 **Larache**, Mor.
22/B4 **Laracor**, Ire.
32/F4 **Laragne-Montéglin**, Fr.
51/J5 **Lārak** (isl.), Iran
34/C4 **La Rambla**, Sp.
90/G5 **Laramie** (riv.), Co, Wy,US
88/E3 **Laramie**, Wy,US
88/E3 **Laramie** (mts.), Wy,US
91/G5 **Laramie**, Wy,US
91/G5 **Laramie** (peak), Wy,US
93/F2 **Laramie**, Wy,US
93/F2 **Laramie** (mts.), Wy,US
93/F2 **Laramie** (peak), Wy,US
90/G5 **Laramie** (mts.), Wy, US
108/A3 **Laranjeiras do Sul**, Braz.
67/H5 **Larat** (isl.), Indo.
75/S15 **Larba**, Alg.
32/B2 **L'Arcouest, Pointe de** (pt.), Fr.
20/C3 **Lærdalsøyri**, Nor.
90/A2 **Laredo** (sound), BC,Can
32/B5 **Laredo**, Sp.
34/D1 **Laredo**, Sp.
101/F3 **Laredo**, Tx,US
88/G6 **Laredo**, Tx,US
96/D5 **Laredo**, Tx,US
28/C4 **Laren**, Neth.
103/F1 **Largo** (cay), Cuba
97/H5 **Largo**, Fl,US
98/K8 **Largo**, Md,US
36/D2 **Largue** (riv.), Fr.
34/E1 **La Rhune** (mtn.), Fr.
67/F4 **Lariang** (riv.), Indo.
34/C4 **La Rinconada**, Sp.
38/D2 **Larino**, It.
40/B5 **Larino**, It.
109/C2 **La Rioja**, Arg.
32/B5 **La Rioja** (aut. comm.), Sp.
34/D1 **La Rioja** (aut. comm.), Sp.
18/F5 **Lárisa**, Gre.
39/H3 **Lárisa**, Gre.
25/G2 **Lark** (riv.), Eng,UK
53/J3 **Lārkāna**, Pak.
62/A2 **Lārkāna**, Pak.
25/E4 **Larkhill**, Eng,UK
99/J11 **Larkspur**, Ca,US
32/B3 **Larmor-Plage**, Fr.
49/C2 **Larnaca**, Cyp.
49/C2 **Larnaca** (dist.), Cyp.
50/C3 **Larnaca**, Cyp.
52/B2 **Larnaca**, Cyp.
22/C2 **Larne**, NI,UK
22/C2 **Larne** (dist.), NI,UK
93/H3 **Larned**, Ks,US
96/D2 **Larned**, Ks,US
22/C2 **Larne Lough** (inlet), NI,UK
34/C1 **La Robla**, Sp.
90/F1 **La Roche** (lake), Sk,Can
36/D4 **La Roche**, Swi.
31/E3 **La Roche-en-Ardenne**, Belg.
18/C4 **La Rochelle**, Fr.
32/C3 **La Rochelle**, Fr.
33/G3 **La Roche-sur-Foron**, Fr.
36/C5 **La Roche-sur-Foron**, Fr.
32/C3 **La Roche-sur-Yon**, Fr.
31/F4 **Larochette**, Lux.
34/D3 **La Roda**, Sp.
104/D3 **La Romana**, DRep.
86/F3 **La Ronge**, Sk,Can
86/F3 **La Ronge** (lake), Sk,Can
91/G2 **La Ronge**, Sk,Can
35/H1 **La Roque-d'Anthéron**, Fr.
32/D5 **Laroque-d'Olmes**, Fr.
35/F1 **Laroque-d'Olmes**, Fr.
97/F4 **Larose**, La,US
101/E2 **La Rosita**, Mex.
102/C2 **Larrainzar**, Mex.
102/E3 **Larreynaga**, Nic.
70/E3 **Larrimah**, Austl.
86/G1 **Larsen** (sound), NW,Can
85/H4 **Larsen Bay**, Ak,US
83/V **Larsen Ice Shelf**, Ant.
34/B1 **La Rúa**, Sp.
32/C5 **Laruns**, Fr.
95/N7 **La Salle**, Qu,Can
94/B3 **La Salle**, Il,US
93/G3 **Las Animas**, Co,US
96/C2 **Las Animas**, Co,US
36/C4 **La Sarraz**, Swi.
87/J4 **La Sarre**, Qu,Can
89/L2 **La Sarre**, Qu,Can
94/E1 **La Sarre**, Qu,Can
33/G5 **La Sauvette** (mtn.), Fr.
35/J1 **La Sauvette** (mtn.), Fr.
104/E5 **Las Aves** (isl.), Ven.
109/D2 **Las Breñas**, Arg.
34/C4 **Las Cabezas de San Juan**, Sp.
101/E3 **Las Carboneras**, Mex.
101/G5 **Las Choapas**, Mex.
95/L1 **La Scie**, Nf,Can
100/D1 **Las Cruces**, NM,US
88/E5 **Las Cruces**, NM,US
92/F4 **Las Cruces**, NM,US
96/B3 **Las Cruces**, NM,US
109/B2 **La Serena**, Chile
35/F1 **La Seu d'Urgell**, Sp.
96/C4 **Las Eutimias**, Mex
32/F5 **La Seyne-sur-Mer**, Fr.
35/H1 **La Seyne-sur-Mer**, Fr.
109/E4 **Las Flores**, Arg.
60/C4 **Lashio**, Burma
63/G3 **Lashio**, Burma
53/H2 **Lashkar Gāh**, Afg.
45/J1 **Lashmanka**, Rus.
103/G1 **La Sierpe**, Cuba
38/E3 **La Sila** (mts.), It.
109/D1 **Las Lomitas**, Arg.
102/D2 **Las Margaritas**, Mex.
103/E1 **Las Martinas**, Cuba
103/J2 **Las Matas de Farfán**, DRep.
30/D2 **Lasne-Chapelle-Saint-Lambert**, Belg.
100/D3 **Las Nieves**, Mex.
96/B5 **Las Nieves**, Mex
34/D3 **La Solana**, Sp.
67/F4 **Lasolo** (riv.), Indo.
32/D3 **La Souterraine**, Fr.
103/F4 **Las Palmas**, Pan.
35/X16 **Las Palmas de Gran Canaria**, Canl.,Sp.
76/B2 **Las Palmas de Gran Canaria**, Canl.,Sp.
92/F5 **Las Palomas**, Mex
96/B4 **Las Palomas**, Mex
34/D3 **Las Pedroñeras**, Sp.
18/D4 **La Spezia**, It.
33/H4 **La Spezia**, It.
109/C5 **Las Plumas**, Arg.
35/N9 **Las Rozas**, Sp.
88/B3 **Lassen** (peak), Ca,US
90/C5 **Lassen** (peak), Ca,US
92/B2 **Lassen** (peak), Ca,US
90/C5 **Lassen Volcanic Nat'l Park**, Ca,US
86/D4 **Lassen Volcanic Nat'l Park**, Ca,US
88/B3 **Lassen Volcanic Nat'l Park**, Ca,US
92/B2 **Lassen Volcanic Nat'l Park**, Ca,US
83/V **Lassiter** (coast), Ant.
95/N6 **L'Assomption** (co.), Qu,Can
95/P6 **L'Assomption**, Qu,Can
95/P6 **L'Assomption** (riv.), Qu,Can
103/F5 **Las Tablas**, Pan.
34/D3 **Las Tablas de Daimiel Nat'l Park** , Sp.
109/D2 **Las Termas**, Arg.
91/G3 **Last Mountain** (lake), Sk,Can
86/F3 **Last Mountain** (lake), Sk,Can
38/E1 **Lastovo**, Cro.
38/E1 **Lastovo** (isl.), Cro.
40/C4 **Lastovo** (isl.), Cro.
38/E1 **Lastovski** (chan.), Cro.
40/C4 **Lastovski** (chan.), Cro.
29/E3 **Lastrup**, Ger.
103/G1 **Las Tunas**, Cuba
100/C2 **Las Varas**, Mex.
100/D4 **Las Varas**, Mex.
109/D3 **Las Varillas**, Arg.
88/E4 **Las Vegas**, NM,US
93/F4 **Las Vegas**, NM,US
96/B3 **Las Vegas**, NM,US
88/C4 **Las Vegas**, Nv,US
92/D3 **Las Vegas**, Nv,US
87/L3 **La Tabatière**, Qu,Can
95/K1 **La Tabatière**, Qu,Can
106/C4 **Latacunga**, Ecu.
83/U **Latady** (isl.), Ant.
52/C1 **Latakia**, Syria
49/D2 **Latakia** (Al Lādhiqīyah), Syria
50/C3 **Latakia** (Al Lādhiqīyah), Syria
79/F4 **L'Atakora** (prov.), Ben.
37/H5 **Latemar** (peak), It.
38/E2 **Laterza**, It.
40/C5 **Laterza**, It.
32/C4 **La Teste-de-Buch**, Fr.
36/C6 **La Tête à l'Ane** (peak), Fr.
32/C3 **Lathan** (riv.), Fr.
99/M11 **Lathrop**, Ca,US
102/E3 **La Tigra Nat'l Park**, Hon.
19/M7 **Latimer**, Eng,UK
38/C2 **Latina**, It.
109/C3 **La Toma**, Arg.
27/L4 **Latorica** (riv.), Slvk.
104/E5 **La Tortuga** (isl.), Ven.
106/E1 **La Tortuga** (isl.), Ven.
70/B3 **Latouche Treville** (cape), Austl.
36/C5 **La Tour-de-Peilz**, Swi.
36/D4 **La Tour-de-Trême**, Swi.
32/C4 **La Tremblade**, Fr.
61/J5 **La Trinidad**, Phil.
102/C2 **La Trinitaria**, Mex.
73/C3 **Latrobe** (peak), Austl.
73/C3 **Latrobe** (riv.), Austl.
73/C4 **Latrobe**, Austl.
37/G4 **Latsch** (Laces), It.
32/E5 **Lattes**, Fr.
35/G1 **Lattes**, Fr.
87/J4 **La Tuque**, Qu,Can
89/M2 **La Tuque**, Qu,Can
95/F2 **La Tuque**, Qu,Can
53/L5 **Lātūr**, India
62/C4 **Lātūr**, India
18/F3 **Latvia**
20/H4 **Latvia**
42/E4 **Latvia**
46/C4 **Latvia**
106/E7 **Lauca Nat'l Park**, Chile
33/G3 **Lauch** (riv.), Fr.
37/F1 **Lauchert** (riv.), Ger.
99/N14 **Lauderdale** (lakes), Wi,US
29/G2 **Lauenbrück**, Ger.
26/F2 **Lauenburg**, Ger.
29/H2 **Lauenburg**, Ger.
36/D5 **Lauenen**, Swi.
26/F4 **Lauf**, Ger.
33/J2 **Lauf**, Ger.
36/D3 **Laufen**, Swi.
36/E2 **Laufenburg**, Swi.
24/B3 **Laugharne**, Wal,UK
93/G5 **Laughlin** (A.F.B.), Tx,US
96/C4 **Laughlin** (A.F.B.), Tx,US
68/H6 **Lau Group** (isls.), Fiji
20/G3 **Lauhanvuoren Nat'l Park**, Fin.
42/D3 **Lauhanvuoren Nat'l Park**, Fin.
63/G2 **Lauhkaung**, Burma
20/H3 **Laukaa**, Fin.
42/E3 **Laukaa**, Fin.
71/H8 **Launceston**, Austl.
73/C4 **Launceston**, Austl.
24/B5 **Launceston**, Eng,UK
32/A1 **Launceston**, Eng,UK
19/U9 **Launette** (riv.), Fr.
109/B5 **La Unión**, Chile
106/C3 **La Unión**, Col.
102/E3 **La Unión**, ESal.
101/E5 **La Unión**, Mex.
35/E4 **La Unión**, Sp.
88/U11 **Laupahoehoe**, Hi,US
36/D4 **Laupen**, Swi.
36/D4 **Lauperswil**, Swi.
37/F1 **Laupheim**, Ger.
71/G3 **Laura**, Austl.
37/E5 **Laurasca, Cima della** (peak), It.
106/E2 **La Urbana**, Ven.
38/E3 **Laureana di Borrello**, It.
98/K7 **Laurel**, Md,US
89/J5 **Laurel**, Ms,US
97/F4 **Laurel**, Ms,US
90/F4 **Laurel**, Mt,US
98/E6 **Laurel Springs**, NJ,US
22/B3 **Laurelvale**, NI,UK
97/H3 **Laurens**, SC,US
91/H2 **Laurentian** (plat.), Can
94/C1 **Laurentian** (plat.), Can
95/N6 **Laurentides**, Qu,Can
22/D2 **Laurieston**, Sc,UK
89/L5 **Laurinburg**, NC,US
97/J3 **Laurinburg**, NC,US
91/L4 **Laurium**, Mi,US
94/B2 **Laurium**, Mi,US
33/G3 **Lausanne**, Swi.
36/C4 **Lausanne**, Swi.
67/E4 **Laut** (isl.), Indo.
31/G5 **Lauter** (riv.), Fr.
33/H2 **Lauter** (riv.), Fr.
26/D4 **Lauter** (riv.), Ger.
31/G5 **Lauter** (riv.), Ger.
33/H2 **Lauter** (riv.), Ger.
26/E3 **Lauterbach**, Ger.
33/H1 **Lauterbach**, Ger.
31/H6 **Lauterbourg**, Fr.
36/D4 **Lauterbrunnen**, Swi.
31/G4 **Lauterecken**, Ger.
68/G6 **Lautoka**, Fiji
69/Y18 **Lautoka**, Fiji
28/D2 **Lauwers** (chan.), Neth.
28/D2 **Lauwersmeer** (lake), Neth.
90/C5 **Lava Beds Nat'l Mon.**, Ca,US
92/B2 **Lava Beds Nat'l Mon.**, Ca,US
87/J4 **Laval**, Qu,Can
89/M2 **Laval**, Qu,Can
94/F2 **Laval**, Qu,Can
95/N6 **Laval**, Qu,Can
18/C4 **Laval**, Fr.
32/C2 **Laval**, Fr.
98/F6 **Lavallette**, NJ,US
36/B2 **La Vallinot**, Fr.
51/H5 **Lāvān** (isl.), Iran
36/B5 **Lavans-lès-Saint-Claude**, Fr.
33/L3 **Lavant** (riv.), Aus.
109/B4 **Lavapié** (pt.), Chile
35/F1 **Lavaur**, Fr.
34/C1 **La Vecilla de Curveño**, Sp.
104/D3 **La Vega**, DRep.
103/H3 **La Vela, Cabo de** (pt.), Col.
32/D5 **Lavelanet**, Fr.
35/F1 **Lavelanet**, Fr.
38/D2 **Lavello**, It.
40/B5 **Lavello**, It.
37/E6 **Lavena**, It.
37/E6 **Laveno**, It.
100/C3 **La Ventana**, Mex.
19/R10 **La Verrière**, Fr.
70/C5 **Laverton**, Austl.
36/D5 **Lavey**, Swi.
100/E3 **La Víbora**, Mex.
96/C5 **La Víbora**, Mex
104/E5 **La Victoria**, Ven.
106/E1 **La Victoria**, Ven.
33/J3 **Lavis**, It.
37/H5 **Lavis**, It.
34/A2 **Lavos**, Port.
107/K8 **Lavras**, Braz.
108/C2 **Lavras**, Braz.
39/J4 **Lávrion**, Gre.
63/G4 **Lawabauk**, Burma
65/B2 **Lawabauk**, Burma
31/G6 **La Wantzenau**, Fr.
53/K1 **Lawarai** (pass), Pak.
52/E6 **Lawdar**, Yem.
66/D3 **Lawit** (mtn.), Indo.
63/H6 **Lawit** (peak), Malay.
85/M5 **Lawnhill**, BC,Can
52/D3 **Lawqah**, SAr.
78/E4 **Lawra**, Gha.
89/G4 **Lawrence**, Ks,US
93/J3 **Lawrence**, Ks,US
96/E2 **Lawrence**, Ks,US
95/G3 **Lawrence**, Ma,US
94/C4 **Lawrenceburg**, In,US
97/G2 **Lawrenceburg**, In,US
97/G2 **Lawrenceburg**, Ky,US
97/G3 **Lawrenceburg**, Tn,US
22/B3 **Lawrencetown**, NI,UK
97/H3 **Lawrenceville**, Ga,US
89/G5 **Lawton**, Ok,US
93/H4 **Lawton**, Ok,US
96/D3 **Lawton**, Ok,US
66/D5 **Lawu** (peak), Indo.
50/C4 **Lawz, Jabal al** (mtn.), SAr.
52/C3 **Lawz, Jabal al** (mtn.), SAr.
22/D3 **Laxey**, IM,UK
31/F6 **Laxou**, Fr.
32/C3 **Lay** (riv.), Fr.
43/N2 **Laya** (riv.), Rus.
67/E4 **Layar** (cape), Indo.
69/H2 **Laycan** (isl.), Hi.,US
52/E5 **Layjūn**, Yem.
52/E4 **Laylá**, SAr.
77/Q3 **Laylá**, SAr.
51/F3 **Laylān**, Iraq
32/C3 **Layon** (riv.), Fr.
31/F6 **Lay-Saint-Christophe**, Fr.
98/F4 **Layton**, NJ,US
90/F5 **Layton**, Ut,US
92/E2 **Layton**, Ut,US
22/B4 **Laytown**, Ire.
40/E3 **Lazarevac**, Yugo.
100/E5 **Lazaro Cardenas**, Mex.
92/D5 **Lazaro Cardenas**, Mex
27/M1 **Lazdijai**, Lith.
33/J5 **Lazio** (reg.), It.
38/C1 **Lazio** (reg.), It.
40/A5 **Lazio** (reg.), It.
23/F2 **Lazonby**, Eng,UK
41/J2 **Lazovsk**, Mol.
25/F3 **Lea** (riv.), Eng,UK
63/H5 **Leach**, Camb.
65/C3 **Leach**, Camb.
66/B1 **Leach**, Camb.
25/E3 **Leach** (riv.), Eng,UK
86/F4 **Lead**, SD,US
88/F3 **Lead**, SD,US
91/H4 **Lead**, SD,US
93/G1 **Lead**, SD,US
23/H5 **Leadenham**, Eng,UK
90/F3 **Leader**, Sk,Can
24/D2 **Leadon** (riv.), Eng,UK
96/B2 **Leadville**, Co,US
73/B2 **Leaghur** (lake), Austl.
93/J5 **League City**, Tx,US
96/E4 **League City**, Tx,US
101/F2 **Leakey**, Tx,US
93/H5 **Leakey**, Tx,US
96/D4 **Leakey**, Tx,US
19/N7 **Lea** (Lee) (riv.), Eng,UK
25/E2 **Leam** (riv.), Eng,UK
94/D3 **Leamington**, On,Can
99/G7 **Leamington**, On,Can
61/H2 **Le'an** (riv.), China
70/A4 **Learmonth**, Austl.
19/N8 **Leatherhead**, Eng,UK
25/F4 **Leatherhead**, Eng,UK
30/D3 **L'Eau d'Heure** (riv.), Belg.
30/D3 **L'Eau d'Heure, Barrage de** (dam), Belg.
93/J3 **Leavenworth**, Ks,US
96/E2 **Leavenworth**, Ks,US
90/C4 **Leavenworth**, Wa,US
27/J1 **Łeba**, Pol.
31/F5 **Lebach**, Ger.
39/G1 **Lebane**, Yugo.
40/E4 **Lebane**, Yugo.
48/C6 **Lebanon**
49/D3 **Lebanon**
50/C3 **Lebanon**
52/B2 **Lebanon**
77/M1 **Lebanon**
49/D3 **Lebanon** (mts.), Leb.
94/C3 **Lebanon**, In,US
97/G1 **Lebanon**, In,US
94/C4 **Lebanon**, Ky,US
97/G2 **Lebanon**, Ky,US
93/J3 **Lebanon**, Mo,US
96/E2 **Lebanon**, Mo,US
89/M3 **Lebanon**, NH,US
95/F3 **Lebanon**, NH,US
90/C4 **Lebanon**, Or,US
89/L3 **Lebanon**, Pa,US
94/E3 **Lebanon**, Pa,US
94/C4 **Lebanon**, Tn,US
97/G2 **Lebanon**, Tn,US
94/D4 **Lebanon**, Va,US
97/H2 **Lebanon**, Va,US
31/F5 **Le Ban-Saint-Martin**, Fr.
28/B6 **Lebbeke**, Belg.
30/D2 **Lebbeke**, Belg.
44/E2 **Lebedin**, Ukr.
94/E1 **Lebel-sur-Quévillon**, Qu,Can
75/M13 **Lebene** (riv.), Mor.
32/D3 **Le Blanc**, Fr.
19/T10 **Le Blanc-Mesnil**, Fr.
30/B6 **Le Blanc-Mesnil**, Fr.
81/E2 **Lebombo** (mts.), Moz., SAfr.
27/J1 **Lębork**, Pol.
19/T10 **Le Bourget** (Paris) (arpt.), Fr.
80/Q12 **Lebowa** (homeland), SAfr.
33/G3 **Le Brassus**, Swi.
36/C4 **Le Brassus**, Swi.
32/F3 **Le Breuil**, Fr.
34/B4 **Lebrija**, Sp.
109/B4 **Lebu**, Chile
34/A2 **Leça da Palmeira**, Port.
33/G5 **Le Cannet**, Fr.
35/J1 **Le Cannet**, Fr.
26/B3 **Le Cateau**, Fr.
30/C3 **Le Cateau**, Fr.
32/E1 **Le Cateau**, Fr.
18/E4 **Lecce**, It.
39/F2 **Lecce**, It.
33/H4 **Lecco**, It.
37/G3 **Lech** (riv.), Aus.
33/J2 **Lech** (riv.), Aus., Ger.
26/F5 **Lech** (riv.), Ger.
37/G1 **Lech** (riv.), Ger.
33/G3 **Le Châble**, Swi.
36/D5 **Le Châble**, Swi.
63/K2 **Lechang**, China
36/D3 **Le Chasseral** (peak), Swi.
36/C4 **Le Chasseron** (peak), Swi.
37/G2 **Lechbruck**, Ger.
103/G1 **Leche** (lag.), Cuba
19/S10 **Le Chesnay**, Fr.
31/D4 **Le Chesne**, Fr.
36/C5 **Le Cheval Blanc** (mtn.), Fr.
32/F4 **Le Cheylard**, Fr.
25/E3 **Lechlade**, Eng,UK
37/G3 **Lechtaler Alps** (mts.), Aus.
26/E1 **Leck**, Ger.
33/J5 **Le Cornate** (peak), It.
35/G1 **Le Crès**, Fr.
32/F3 **Le Creusot**, Fr.
25/H6 **Le Crotoy**, Fr.
30/A3 **Le Crotoy**, Fr.
32/D5 **Lectoure**, Fr.
27/M3 **Łęczna**, Pol.
44/B2 **Łęczna**, Pol.
29/E2 **Leda** (riv.), Ger.
66/B3 **Ledang** (peak), Malay.
24/D2 **Ledbury**, Eng,UK
28/A7 **Lede**, Belg.
30/C2 **Lede**, Belg.
30/C2 **Ledegem**, Belg.
34/C2 **Ledesma**, Sp.
61/F5 **Ledong**, China
63/J4 **Ledong**, China
65/E2 **Ledong**, China
37/G6 **Ledro** (lake), It.
86/E3 **Leduc**, Ab,Can
90/E2 **Leduc**, Ab,Can
37/F5 **Ledu, Pizzo** (peak), It.
21/A5 **Lee** (riv.), Ire.
91/K4 **Leech** (lake), Mn,US
86/G4 **Leech** (lake), Mn,US
89/G2 **Leech** (lake), Mn,US
18/C3 **Leeds**, Eng,UK
23/G4 **Leeds**, Eng,UK
23/G4 **Leeds and Liverpool** (can.), Eng,UK
28/D2 **Leek**, Neth.
23/F5 **Leek**, Eng,UK
19/N7 **Lee** (Lea) (riv.), Eng,UK
26/D2 **Leer**, Ger.
29/E2 **Leer**, Ger.
28/C5 **Leerdam**, Neth.
28/C4 **Leersum**, Neth.
97/H4 **Leesburg**, Fl,US
94/E4 **Leesburg**, Va,US
97/J2 **Leesburg**, Va,US
29/G3 **Leese**, Ger.
93/J5 **Leesville**, La,US
96/E4 **Leesville**, La,US
71/H6 **Leeton**, Austl.
73/C2 **Leeton**, Austl.
80/L10 **Leeu** (riv.), SAfr.
80/P13 **Leeudoringstad**, SAfr.
26/C2 **Leeuwarden**, Neth.
28/C2 **Leeuwarden**, Neth.
70/B6 **Leeuwin** (cape), Austl.
92/C3 **Lee Vining**, Ca,US
104/F3 **Leeward Islands** (isls.), West Indies
32/B2 **Leff** (riv.), Fr.
49/C2 **Lefka**, Cyp.
79/H5 **Lefo** (peak), Camr.
70/C6 **Lefroy** (lake), Austl.
73/C4 **Legana**, Austl.
34/D2 **Leganés**, Sp.
35/N9 **Leganés**, Sp.
37/G2 **Legau**, Ger.
68/B3 **Legazpi**, Phil.
32/B5 **Legazpia**, Sp.
34/D1 **Legazpia**, Sp.
73/C4 **Legges Tor** (peak), Austl.
27/L2 **Legionowo**, Pol.
42/D5 **Legionowo**, Pol.
44/B1 **Legionowo**, Pol.
31/E4 **Léglise**, Belg.
33/J4 **Legnago**, It.
33/H4 **Legnano**, It.
27/H3 **Legnica** (prov.), Pol.
27/J3 **Legnica**, Pol.
37/F5 **Legnone, Monte** (peak), It.
36/C5 **Le Grammont** (peak), Swi.
36/D2 **Le Grand Ballon** (mtn.), Fr.
32/F5 **Le Grau-du-Roi**, Fr.
35/H1 **Le Grau-du-Roi**, Fr.
53/L2 **Leh**, India
18/D4 **Le Havre**, Fr.
32/D2 **Le Havre**, Fr.
98/E5 **Lehigh** (riv.), Pa,US
97/H5 **Lehigh Acres**, Fl,US
21/H7 **Lehinch**, Ire.
26/E2 **Lehrte**, Ger.
29/G4 **Lehrte**, Ger.
61/G3 **Lei** (riv.), China
63/K2 **Lei** (riv.), China
53/K2 **Leiah**, Pak.
64/A2 **Leiah**, Pak.
33/L3 **Leibnitz**, Aus.
40/B2 **Leibnitz**, Aus.
63/H2 **Leibo**, China
25/E1 **Leicester**, Eng,UK
23/H6 **Leicestershire** (co.), Eng,UK
25/E1 **Leicestershire** (co.), Eng,UK
70/F3 **Leichhardt** (riv.), Austl.
72/B3 **Leichhardt** (mts.), Austl.
28/E6 **Leichlingen**, Ger.
31/G1 **Leichlingen**, Ger.
26/C2 **Leiden**, Neth.
28/B4 **Leiden**, Neth.
28/B4 **Leiderdorp**, Neth.
28/B4 **Leidschendam**, Neth.
28/A7 **Leie** (riv.), Belg.
33/J3 **Leifers** (Laives), It.
37/H5 **Leifers** (Laives), It.
19/N8 **Leigh**, Eng,UK
19/P8 **Leigh**, Eng,UK
23/F5 **Leigh**, Eng,UK
70/F6 **Leigh Creek**, Austl.
22/B6 **Leighlinbridge**, Ire.
25/F3 **Leighton Buzzard**, Eng,UK
61/F3 **Leigong** (mtn.), Chir
54/G5 **Leihe**, China
26/E3 **Leine** (riv.), Ger.
29/G5 **Leine** (riv.), Ger.
29/H6 **Leinefelde**, Ger.
70/C5 **Leinster**, Austl.
21/B4 **Leinster** (mt.), Ire.
22/B5 **Leinster** (reg.), Ire.
24/D2 **Leintwardine**, Eng,
37/G1 **Leipheim**, Ger.
18/E3 **Leipzig**, Ger.
26/G3 **Leipzig**, Ger.
46/B4 **Leipzig**, Ger.
30/C2 **Leir** (riv.), Belg.
34/A3 **Leiria**, Port.
34/A3 **Leiria** (dist.), Port.
25/H2 **Leiston cum Sizewell**, Eng,UK
94/C4 **Leitchfield**, Ky,US
97/G2 **Leitchfield**, Ky,US
25/F4 **Leith** (hill), Eng,UK
27/J5 **Leitha** (riv.), Aus.
40/C2 **Leitha** (riv.), Aus.
22/A6 **Leix** (Laois) (co.), Ir
22/B5 **Leixlip**, Ire.
61/G3 **Leiyang**, China
63/K2 **Leiyang**, China
54/F4 **Leiyuanzhen**, China
59/B4 **Leiyuanzhen**, China
61/F4 **Leizhou** (pen.), Chir
63/J3 **Leizhou** (pen.), Chir
65/E1 **Leizhou** (pen.), Chir
27/M1 **Lejpalingis**, Lith.
28/B5 **Lek** (riv.), Neth.
39/G4 **Lekhainá**, Gre.
28/B5 **Lekkerkerk**, Neth.
79/G5 **Lekki** (lag.), Nga.
20/E3 **Leksands-Noret**, Swe.
42/B3 **Leksands-Noret**, Swe.
20/J3 **Leksozero** (lake), R
42/F3 **Leksozero** (lake), R
67/G3 **Lelai** (cape), Indo.
97/F3 **Leland**, Ms,US
36/D3 **Le Landeron**, Swi.
33/G5 **Le Lavandou**, Fr.
109/B5 **Leleque**, Arg.
55/H4 **Leling**, China
59/D3 **Leling**, China
36/C3 **Le Locle**, Swi.
68/F4 **Lelu**, Micro.
33/G5 **Le Luc**, Fr.
35/J1 **Le Luc**, Fr.
26/C2 **Lelystad**, Neth.
28/C3 **Lelystad**, Neth.
37/E5 **Lema, Monte** (peak), It.
33/G3 **Léman** (Geneva) (lake), Fr., Swi.
36/C5 **Léman** (Geneva) (isls.), Fr., Swi.
18/D4 **Le Mans**, Fr.
32/D3 **Le Mans**, Fr.
91/J5 **Le Mars**, Ia,US
93/H2 **Le Mars**, Ia,US
31/G5 **Lembach**, Fr.
31/G5 **Lemberg**, Ger.
37/E1 **Lemberg** (peak), Ge
66/A3 **Lembu** (peak), Indo
108/C2 **Leme**, Braz.
19/T11 **Le Mée-sur-Seine**, F
20/H1 **Lemenjoen Nat'l Park**, Fin.
42/E1 **Lemenjoen Nat'l Park**, Fin.
30/A5 **Le Mesnil-Esnard**, F
19/S10 **Le Mesnil-le-Roi**, F
19/R10 **Le Mesnil-Saint-Denis**, Fr.
30/D6 **Le Mesnil-sur-Oge** Fr.
26/E2 **Lemgo**, Ger.
29/F4 **Lemgo**, Ger.
28/C3 **Lemmer**, Neth.
100/C1 **Lemmon** (mt.), Az,U
91/H4 **Lemmon**, SD,US
36/C5 **Le Môle** (mtn.), Fr.
36/C4 **Le Morond** (mtn.), F
32/E4 **Le Moure de la Gardille** (mtn.), Fr.
102/D3 **Lempa** (riv.), NAm.
32/E4 **Lempdes**, Fr.
60/B4 **Lemro** (riv.), Burma
38/E2 **Le Murge** (upland), It.
40/C5 **Le Murge** (upland), It.
43/P2 **Lemva** (riv.), Rus.
29/F2 **Lemwerder**, Ger.
20/D3 **Lena**, Nor.
47/N3 **Lena** (riv.), Rus.
48/M3 **Lena** (riv.), Rus.
54/F1 **Lena** (riv.), Rus.
107/K4 **Lençóis Maranhenses Nat' Park**, Braz.
108/B2 **Lençóis Paulista**, Braz.
20/J3 **Lendery**, Rus.
33/J4 **Lendinara**, It.
29/H4 **Lengede**, Ger.
29/F4 **Lengerich**, Ger.
37/H2 **Lenggries**, Ger.
36/D3 **Lengnau**, Swi.
61/F3 **Lengshuijiang**, Chi
63/K2 **Lengshuijiang**, Chi
61/F3 **Lengshuitan**, China
63/K2 **Lengshuitan**, China
109/B3 **Lengua de Vaca** (p Chile
20/J4 **Leningrad** (Saint Petersburg), Rus.
42/F4 **Leningrad** (Saint Petersburg), Rus.
43/V7 **Leningrad** (Saint Petersburg), Rus.
83/L **Leningradskaya**, A
46/J4 **Leninogorsk**, Kaz.
43/M5 **Leninogorsk**, Rus.
45/K1 **Leninogorsk**, Rus.

151

Lenin – Little

46/J4 **Leninsk-Kuznetskiy,** Rus.
27/L5 **Leninváros,** Hun.
40/E2 **Leninváros,** Hun.
36/D5 **Lenk,** Swi.
19/H5 **Lenkoran',** Azer.
45/J5 **Lenkoran',** Azer.
46/E6 **Lenkoran',** Azer.
51/G2 **Lenkoran',** Azer.
26/E3 **Lenne** (riv.), Ger.
29/E6 **Lenne** (riv.), Ger.
29/F6 **Lennestadt,** Ger.
31/H1 **Lennestadt,** Ger.
97/H3 **Lenoir,** NC,US
97/G3 **Lenoir City,** Tn,US
36/C4 **Le Noirmont** (mtn.), Fr.
36/C3 **Le Noirmont,** Swi.
36/C5 **Le Noirmont** (peak), Swi.
30/C3 **Le Nouvion-en-Thiérache,** Fr.
30/C2 **Lens,** Belg.
26/B3 **Lens,** Fr.
30/B3 **Lens,** Fr.
32/E1 **Lens,** Fr.
35/D5 **Lens,** Swi.
26/F1 **Lensahn,** Ger.
47/M3 **Lensk,** Rus.
27/N1 **Lentvaris,** Lith.
20/F1 **Lenvik,** Nor.
63/G5 **Lenya,** Burma
66/A1 **Lenya,** Burma
36/E3 **Lenzburg,** Swi.
36/E2 **Lenzkirch,** Ger.
76/E5 **Léo,** Burk.
79/E4 **Léo,** Burk.
33/K3 **Leoben,** Aus.
33/L3 **Leoben,** Aus.
40/A2 **Leoben,** Aus.
40/B2 **Leoben,** Aus.
30/B2 **Leoberghe,** Fr.
91/J4 **Leola,** SD,US
24/D2 **Leominster,** Eng,UK
32/C4 **Léon** (lag.), Fr.
101/E4 **León,** Mex.
88/F7 **León,** Mex.
102/E3 **León,** Nic.
18/C4 **León,** Sp.
34/C1 **León,** Sp.
93/H5 **Leon** (riv.), Tx,US
99/F6 **Leonard,** Mi,US
101/F1 **Leonard,** Tx,US
26/E4 **Leonberg,** Ger.
33/L2 **Leonding,** Aus.
36/E5 **Leone, Monte** (peak), It.
38/D4 **Leonforte,** It.
73/C3 **Leongatha,** Austl.
39/H4 **Leonídhion,** Gre.
68/B7 **Leonora,** Austl.
70/C5 **Leonora,** Austl.
101/F2 **Leon Valley,** Tx,US
83/F **Leopold and Astrid** (coast), Ant.
108/D2 **Leopoldina,** Braz.
28/A6 **Leopoldkanaal** (can.), Belg.
30/C1 **Leopoldkanaal** (can.), Belg.
28/C6 **Leopoldsburg,** Belg.
31/E1 **Leopoldsburg,** Belg.
29/F4 **Leopoldshöhe,** Ger.
93/G3 **Leoti,** Ks,US
96/C2 **Leoti,** Ks,US
90/G2 **Leoville,** Sk,Can
44/D3 **Leovo,** Mol.
102/D3 **Lepaera,** Hon.
32/B3 **Le Palais,** Fr.
32/D4 **Le Palais-sur-Vienne,** Fr.
36/C1 **Lépanges-sur-Vologne,** Fr.
32/D4 **Le Passage,** Fr.
34/B4 **Lepe,** Sp.
19/S10 **Le Pecq,** Fr.
39/G3 **Lepenoú,** Gre.
40/F3 **Lepenski Vir,** Yugo.
36/D2 **Le Petit Ballon** (mtn.), Fr.
61/H2 **Leping,** China
19/U9 **Le Plessis-Belleville,** Fr.
30/B5 **Le Plessis-Belleville,** Fr.
19/T10 **Le Plessis-Trévise,** Fr.
33/H3 **Lepontine Alps** (range), It., Swi.
37/E5 **Lepontine Alps** (mts.), It., Swi.
81/R15 **Le Port,** Reun.
25/H5 **Le Portel,** Fr.
30/A2 **Le Portel,** Fr.
20/H3 **Leppävirta,** Fin.
42/E3 **Leppävirta,** Fin.
46/H5 **Lepsy,** Kaz.
39/H2 **Leptokariá,** Gre.
35/F1 **Le Puech** (mtn.), Fr.
18/D4 **Le Puy,** Fr.
32/F4 **Le Puy,** Fr.
30/C3 **Le Quesnoy,** Fr.
78/D4 **Léraba** (riv.), Burk., IvC.
19/T10 **Le Raincy,** Fr.
38/C4 **Lercara Friddi,** It.
101/P8 **Lerdo de Tejada,** Mex.
80/E3 **Lerlbe,** Les.
33/H4 **Lerici,** It.
35/F2 **Lérida** (Lleida), Sp.
51/G2 **Lerik,** Azer.
34/E1 **Lerín,** Sp.
101/H5 **Lerma,** Mex.
101/K7 **Lerma** (riv.), Mex.
101/Q10 **Lerma** (riv.), Mex.
102/A2 **Lerma** (riv.), Mex.
102/D2 **Lerma,** Mex.
34/D1 **Lerma,** Sp.
31/E6 **Lérouville,** Fr.
80/D3 **Le Roux dam, P. K.** (res.), SAfr.
36/C3 **Le Russey,** Fr.
95/N7 **Léry,** Qu,Can
30/A5 **Les Andelys,** Fr.
36/C3 **Les Bois,** Swi.
36/D3 **Les Breuleux,** Swi.
103/H2 **Les Cayes,** Haiti
95/M7 **Les Cèdres,** Qu,Can
19/R10 **Les Clayes-sous-Bois,** Fr.
30/A6 **Les Clayes-sous-Bois,** Fr.
36/C6 **Les Contamines-Montjoie,** Fr.
36/D5 **Les Diablerets** (range), Swi.
36/D5 **Le Sépey,** Swi.
36/D5 **Les Gets,** Fr.
60/D2 **Leshan,** China
63/H2 **Leshan,** China
31/D4 **Les Hautes-Rivières,** Fr.
32/C3 **Les Herbiers,** Fr.
19/T10 **Lésigny,** Fr.
31/E5 **Les Islettes,** Fr.
20/D3 **Lesja,** Nor.
27/M4 **Lesko,** Pol.
39/G1 **Leskovac,** Yugo.
40/E4 **Leskovac,** Yugo.
44/B4 **Leskovac,** Yugo.
19/T10 **Les Lilas,** Fr.
19/S10 **Les Molières,** Fr.
30/A6 **Les Mureaux,** Fr.
32/A2 **Lesneven,** Fr.
40/D3 **Lešnica,** Yugo.
47/Q5 **Lesogorsk,** Rus.
74/E7 **Lesotho**
81/D3 **Lesotho**
82/E6 **Lesotho**
47/P5 **Lesozavodsk,** Rus.
55/L2 **Lesozavodsk,** Rus.
32/C4 **Lesparre-Médoc,** Fr.
35/G1 **L'Espinouse, Sommet de** (peak), Fr.
36/C4 **Les Ponts-de-Martel,** Swi.
32/G3 **Les Rousses,** Fr.
36/C5 **Les Rousses,** Fr.
32/C3 **Les Sables-d'Olonne,** Fr.
26/C4 **Lesse** (riv.), Belg.
31/E4 **Lesse** (riv.), Belg.
20/E4 **Lessebo,** Swe.
84/L8 **Lesser Antilles** (isls.), NAm.
104/E3 **Lesser Antilles** (isls.), West Indies
45/G4 **Lesser Kavkaz** (mts.), Eur.
51/E1 **Lesser Kavkaz** (mts.), Eur.
90/D2 **Lesser Slave** (lake), Ab,Can
86/E3 **Lesser Slave** (lake), Ab,Can
67/E5 **Lesser Sunda** (isls.), Indo.
30/C2 **Lessines,** Belg.
33/G3 **Le Suchet** (peak), Swi.
36/C4 **Le Suchet** (peak), Swi.
30/B6 **Les Ulis,** Fr.
66/D3 **Lesung** (peak), Indo.
36/C4 **Les Verrières,** Swi.
39/J3 **Lésvos** (isl.), Gre.
44/C5 **Lésvos** (isl.), Gre.
50/A2 **Lésvos** (isl.), Gre.
22/C2 **Leswalt,** Sc,UK
27/J3 **Leszno,** Pol.
27/J3 **Leszno** (prov.), Pol.
81/R15 **Le Tampon,** Reun.
19/S10 **L'Étang-la-Ville,** Fr.
27/L5 **Létavértes,** Hun.
25/F3 **Letchworth,** Eng,UK
90/E3 **Lethbridge,** Ab,Can
86/E4 **Lethbridge,** Ab,Can
88/D2 **Lethbridge,** Ab,Can
29/F2 **Lethe** (riv.), Ger.
36/C1 **Le Tholy,** Fr.
67/G5 **Leti** (isls.), Indo.
68/B5 **Leti** (isls.), Indo.
106/E4 **Leticia,** Col.
59/D3 **Leting,** China
82/E5 **Letlhakane,** Bots.
82/D5 **Letlhakeng,** Bots.
41/G4 **Letnitsa,** Bul.
30/B3 **L'Étoile,** Fr.
25/H5 **Le Touquet-Paris-Plage,** Fr.
30/A2 **Le Touquet-Paris-Plage,** Fr.
32/D1 **Le Touquet-Paris-Plage,** Fr.
60/B5 **Letpadan,** Burma
63/G4 **Letpadan,** Burma
30/A3 **Le Tréport,** Fr.
32/D1 **Le Tréport,** Fr.
27/H2 **Letschin,** Ger.
65/B4 **Letsôk-Aw** (isl.), Burma
66/A1 **Letsôk-Aw** (isl.), Burma
21/B3 **Letterkenny,** Ire.
32/E5 **Leucate,** Fr.
35/G1 **Leucate,** Fr.
36/D5 **Leuk,** Swi.
36/D5 **Leukerbad,** Swi.
28/C4 **Leusden-Zuid,** Neth.
66/A3 **Leuser** (peak), Indo.
26/F5 **Leutkirch im Allgäu,** Ger.
33/J3 **Leutkirch im Allgäu,** Ger.
37/G2 **Leutkirch im Allgäu,** Ger.
31/D2 **Leuven** (Louvain), Belg.
30/C2 **Leuze-en-Hainaut,** Belg.
39/H3 **Levádhia,** Gre.
36/C2 **Le Val-d'Ajol,** Fr.
19/S10 **Levallois-Perret,** Fr.
20/D3 **Levanger,** Nor.
42/A3 **Levanger,** Nor.
30/A5 **Le Vaudreuil,** Fr.
88/F5 **Levelland,** Tx,US
93/G4 **Levelland,** Tx,US
96/C3 **Levelland,** Tx,US
85/G4 **Levelock,** Ak,US
81/F2 **Leven** (pt.), SAfr.
23/F3 **Leven** (riv.), Eng,UK
23/G3 **Leven** (riv.), Eng,UK
23/H4 **Leven,** Eng,UK
37/E5 **Leventina** (Prato), It.
70/C3 **Leveque** (cape), Austl.
26/D3 **Leverkusen,** Ger.
28/D6 **Leverkusen,** Ger.
31/F1 **Leverkusen,** Ger.
19/S10 **Le Vésinet,** Fr.
27/K4 **Levice,** Slvk.
40/D1 **Levice,** Slvk.
37/H5 **Levico Terme,** It.
36/C4 **Levier,** Fr.
32/E5 **Le Vigan,** Fr.
71/S11 **Levin,** N.Z.
87/J4 **Lévis,** Qu,Can
95/G2 **Lévis,** Qu,Can
19/R10 **Lévis-Saint-Nom,** Fr.
98/G5 **Levittown,** NY,US
94/F3 **Levittown,** Pa,US
39/G3 **Levkás,** Gre.
39/G3 **Levkás** (isl.), Gre.
39/G3 **Levkímmi,** Gre.
27/L4 **Levoča,** Slvk.
44/B2 **Levoča,** Slvk.
41/G4 **Levski,** Bul.
68/G6 **Levuka,** Fiji
69/Y18 **Levuka,** Fiji
25/G5 **Lewes,** Eng,UK
32/D1 **Lewes,** Eng,UK
27/J3 **Lewin Brzeski,** Pol.
95/K1 **Lewis** (hills), Nf,Can
21/B1 **Lewis** (isl.), Sc,UK
71/R11 **Lewis** (pass), N.Z.
90/E3 **Lewis** (range), Mt,US
90/C4 **Lewis** (riv.), Wa,US
91/J5 **Lewis & Clark** (lake), Nb, SD,US
97/G3 **Lewisburg,** Tn,US
94/D4 **Lewisburg,** WV,US
97/H2 **Lewisburg,** WV,US
19/N7 **Lewisham** (bor.), Eng,UK
95/L1 **Lewisporte,** Nf,Can
86/E4 **Lewiston,** Id,US
88/C2 **Lewiston,** Id,US
90/D4 **Lewiston,** Id,US
87/J4 **Lewiston,** Me,US
95/G2 **Lewiston,** Me,US
95/R9 **Lewiston,** NY,US
86/F4 **Lewistown,** Mt,US
88/E2 **Lewistown,** Mt,US
90/F4 **Lewistown,** Mt,US
94/E3 **Lewistown,** Pa,US
67/F5 **Lewotobi** (peak), Indo.
89/K4 **Lexington,** Ky,US
94/C4 **Lexington,** Ky,US
97/G2 **Lexington,** Ky,US
97/H3 **Lexington,** NC,US
88/G3 **Lexington,** Ne,US
91/J5 **Lexington,** Ne,US
93/H2 **Lexington,** Ne,US
97/H3 **Lexington,** SC,US
94/B5 **Lexington,** Tn,US
97/F3 **Lexington,** Tn,US
89/L4 **Lexington,** Va,US
94/E4 **Lexington,** Va,US
97/J2 **Lexington,** Va,US
94/E4 **Lexington Park,** Md,US
97/J2 **Lexington Park,** Md,US
23/G3 **Leyburn,** Eng,UK
60/E3 **Leye,** China
63/J3 **Leye,** China
23/F4 **Leyland,** Eng,UK
36/D5 **Leysin,** Swi.
48/M8 **Leyte** (isl.), Phil.
68/B3 **Leyte** (isl.), Phil.
19/N7 **Leyton,** Eng,UK
36/D5 **Leytron,** Swi.
32/F4 **Lez** (riv.), Fr.
35/F1 **Lez** (riv.), Fr.
27/M3 **Leżajsk,** Pol.
39/F2 **Lezhë,** Alb.
40/D5 **Lezhë,** Alb.
60/E2 **Lezhi,** China
32/E5 **Lézignan-Corbières,** Fr.
35/G1 **Lézignan-Corbières,** Fr.
34/D3 **Lezuza,** Sp.
44/E2 **L'gov,** Rus.
54/C5 **Lhari,** China
60/B2 **Lhari,** China
60/A2 **Lhasa,** China
60/A2 **Lhasa** (riv.), China
62/F2 **Lhasa,** China
62/E2 **Lhazê,** China
54/D5 **Lhorong,** China
60/C2 **Lhorong,** China
35/G2 **L'Hospitalet,** Sp.
35/L7 **L'Hospitalet de Llobregat,** Sp.
62/F2 **Lhozhag,** China
63/G2 **Lhünzê,** China
59/B5 **Li** (riv.), China
59/C4 **Li** (riv.), China
61/F2 **Li** (riv.), China
61/F3 **Li** (riv.), China
63/K2 **Li** (riv.), China
60/E3 **Lian** (riv.), China
61/G3 **Lian** (riv.), China
61/H3 **Liancheng,** China
30/B5 **Liancourt,** Fr.
56/B2 **Liancourt** (rocks), Japan, SKor.
59/C2 **Liangcheng,** China
66/D3 **Liangpran** (peak), Indo.
59/D4 **Liang Shan** (mtn.), China
60/D3 **Liangwan** (mts.), Laos
54/F4 **Liangzhen,** China
59/B3 **Liangzhen,** China
59/C5 **Liangzi** (lake), China
61/G2 **Liangzi** (lake), China
61/G4 **Lianhua** (mts.), China
63/K2 **Lianhua,** China
61/H3 **Lianjiang,** China
63/K3 **Lianjiang,** China
61/G3 **Liannan Yaozu Zizhixian,** China
55/H5 **Lianshui,** China
59/D4 **Lianshui,** China
61/G3 **Lian Xian,** China
63/K3 **Lian Xian,** China
61/G2 **Lianyun** (peak), China
55/H5 **Lianyungang,** China
59/D4 **Lianyungang,** China
48/M5 **Liao** (riv.), China
55/J3 **Liao** (riv.), China
58/A2 **Liao** (riv.), China
59/E2 **Liao** (riv.), China
54/H4 **Liaocheng,** China
59/C3 **Liaocheng,** China
55/J3 **Liaodong** (gulf), China
58/A2 **Liaodong** (gulf), China
58/B3 **Liaodong** (pen.), China
59/E2 **Liaodong** (gulf), China
59/E3 **Liaodong** (pen.), China
58/B2 **Liaoning** (prov.), China
59/E2 **Liaoning** (prov.), China
47/N5 **Liaoyang,** China
55/J3 **Liaoyang,** China
58/B2 **Liaoyang,** China
59/E2 **Liaoyang,** China
47/N5 **Liaoyuan,** China
55/K3 **Liaoyuan,** China
59/F2 **Liaoyuan,** China
58/B2 **Liaozhong,** China
59/E2 **Liaozhong,** China
53/K3 **Liāquatpur,** Pak.
62/B2 **Liāquatpur,** Pak.
84/E3 **Liard** (riv.), Can.
86/D2 **Liard** (riv.), NW,Can
88/C2 **Libby,** Mt,US
90/E3 **Libby,** Mt,US
77/J7 **Libenge,** Zaire
88/F4 **Liberal,** Ks,US
93/G3 **Liberal,** Ks,US
96/C2 **Liberal,** Ks,US
30/C3 **Libercourt,** Fr.
107/H6 **Liberdade** (riv.), Braz.
27/H3 **Liberec,** Czh.
74/B4 **Liberia**
76/D6 **Liberia**
78/C5 **Liberia**
103/E4 **Liberia,** CR
106/A1 **Liberia,** CR
101/H5 **Libertad,** Belz.
102/D2 **Libertad,** Belz.
106/E2 **Libertad,** Ven.
109/D1 **Libertador General San Martín,** Arg.
94/C4 **Liberty,** Ky,US
97/G2 **Liberty,** Ky,US
98/K7 **Liberty** (res.), Md,US
96/E2 **Liberty,** Mo,US
93/K5 **Liberty,** Ms,US
97/F4 **Liberty,** Ms,US
93/J5 **Liberty,** Tx,US
96/E4 **Liberty,** Tx,US
99/Q15 **Libertyville,** Il,US
31/E4 **Libin,** Belg.
61/E3 **Libo,** China
63/J2 **Libo,** China
67/G4 **Libobo** (cape), Indo.
27/G3 **Liboc** (riv.), Czh.
33/K1 **Liboc** (riv.), Czh.
40/E5 **Librazhd,** Alb.
101/M7 **Libres,** Mex.
76/G7 **Libreville** (cap.), Gabon
63/K3 **Libu,** China
74/D2 **Libya**
77/J2 **Libya**
77/K2 **Libyan** (des.), Afr.
74/E2 **Libyan** (des.), Afr.
77/K1 **Libyan** (plat.), Libya
38/C4 **Licata,** It.
50/E2 **Lice,** Turk.
26/E3 **Lich,** Ger.
33/H1 **Lich,** Ger.
59/C3 **Licheng,** China
59/D3 **Licheng,** China
25/E1 **Lichfield,** Eng,UK
82/G3 **Lichinga,** Moz.
29/F5 **Lichtenau,** Ger.
31/H6 **Lichtenau,** Ger.
80/P13 **Lichtenburg,** SAfr.
26/F3 **Lichtenfels,** Ger.
33/J1 **Lichtenfels,** Ger.
37/F3 **Lichtensteig,** Swi.
28/D5 **Lichtenvoorde,** Neth.
30/C1 **Lichtervelde,** Belg.
54/F5 **Lichuan,** China
59/B5 **Lichuan,** China
61/F2 **Lichuan,** China
61/H3 **Lichuan,** China
94/C4 **Licking** (riv.), Ky,US
99/L12 **Lick Observatory,** Ca,US
38/D2 **Licosa** (cape), It.
30/A2 **Licques,** Fr.
18/F3 **Lida,** Bela.
42/E5 **Lida,** Bela.
44/C1 **Lida,** Bela.
46/C4 **Lida,** Bela.
23/F1 **Liddell Water** (riv.), Sc,UK
36/D6 **Liddes,** Swi.
87/R7 **Liddon** (gulf), NW,Can
39/H3 **Lidhorikion,** Gre.
25/F2 **Lidlington,** Eng,UK
33/K4 **Lido,** It.
38/C2 **Lido di Ostia,** It.
27/K2 **Lidzbark,** Pol.
27/L1 **Lidzbark Warmiński,** Pol.
42/D5 **Lidzbark Warmiński,** Pol.
80/E2 **Liebenbergsvlei** (riv.), SAfr.
100/B3 **Liebre** (bay), Mex.
18/D4 **Liechtenstein**
32/H3 **Liechtenstein**
33/H3 **Liechtenstein**
37/F3 **Liechtenstein**
30/D2 **Liedekerke,** Belg.
18/D3 **Liège,** Belg.
26/C3 **Liège,** Belg.
31/E2 **Liège,** Belg.
31/E3 **Liège** (prov.), Belg.
32/F1 **Liège,** Belg.
20/J3 **Lieksa,** Fin.
42/F3 **Lieksa,** Fin.
28/C5 **Lienden,** Neth.
29/E4 **Lienen,** Ger.
33/K3 **Lienz,** Aus.
40/A2 **Lienz,** Aus.
18/F3 **Liepāja,** Lat.
20/G4 **Liepāja,** Lat.
42/D4 **Liepāja,** Lat.
46/C4 **Liepāja,** Lat.
28/B6 **Lier,** Belg.
30/D1 **Lier,** Belg.
31/E3 **Lierneux,** Belg.
32/E1 **Lies** (riv.), Belg.
31/F3 **Lieser** (riv.), Ger.
20/G3 **Liesjärven Nat'l Park,** Fin.
42/D3 **Liesjärven Nat'l Park,** Fin.
30/C4 **Liesse,** Fr.
26/D5 **Liestal,** Swi.
33/G3 **Liestal,** Swi.
36/D3 **Liestal,** Swi.
20/G3 **Lieto,** Fin.
42/D3 **Lieto,** Fin.
26/B3 **Liévin,** Fr.
30/B3 **Liévin,** Fr.
32/E1 **Liévin,** Fr.
94/F2 **Lièvre** (riv.), Qu,Can
36/B2 **Liez** (lake), Fr.
27/H5 **Liezen,** Aus.
33/L3 **Liezen,** Aus.
22/B5 **Liffey** (riv.), Ire.
36/B1 **Liffol-le-Grand,** Fr.
69/V12 **Lifou** (isl.), NCal.
24/B5 **Lifton,** Eng,UK
67/F1 **Ligao,** Phil.
73/C1 **Lightning Ridge,** Austl.
31/E6 **Ligny-en-Barrois,** Fr.
37/F5 **Ligoncio, Pizzo** (peak), It.
39/H4 **Ligoúrion,** Gre.
43/V7 **Ligovo,** Rus.
33/H4 **Ligure Appenino** (range), It.
33/H4 **Liguria** (reg.), It.
33/H5 **Ligurian** (sea), Eur.
71/J3 **Lihou** (reef), Austl.
88/S10 **Lihue,** Hi,US
20/G4 **Lihula,** Est.
42/D4 **Lihula,** Est.
63/H2 **Lijiang** (Lijiang Naxizu Zizhixian), China
60/D3 **Lijiang Naxizu Zizhixian,** China
63/H2 **Lijiang Naxizu Zizhixian** (Lijiang), China
59/D3 **Lijin,** China
61/H2 **Liju** (mtn.), China
82/E3 **Likasi,** Zaire
90/C2 **Likely,** BC,Can
82/F3 **Likoma** (isl.), Malw.
76/J8 **Likouala** (riv.), Congo
43/X9 **Likova** (riv.), Rus.
38/A1 **L'Île-Rousse,** Fr.
19/T10 **L'Île-Saint-Denis,** Fr.
29/F2 **Lilienthal,** Ger.
63/K2 **Liling,** China
28/B6 **Lille,** Belg.
31/D1 **Lille,** Belg.
18/D3 **Lille,** Fr.
26/B3 **Lille,** Fr.
30/C2 **Lille,** Fr.
32/E1 **Lille,** Fr.
18/E2 **Lillehammer,** Nor.
20/D3 **Lillehammer,** Nor.
46/B3 **Lillehammer,** Nor.
30/B2 **Lillers,** Fr.
20/D4 **Lillestrøm,** Nor.
83/L **Lille Marleen Hütte,** Ant.
99/A3 **Lilliwaup,** Wa,US
34/D3 **Lillo,** Sp.
90/C3 **Lillooet** (riv.), BC,Can
86/D3 **Lillooet,** BC,Can
90/C3 **Lillooet,** BC,Can
82/F3 **Lilongwe** (cap.), Malw.
73/C3 **Lilydale,** Austl.
73/G5 **Lilydale,** Austl.
39/F1 **Lim** (riv.), Yugo.
40/D4 **Lim** (riv.), Yugo.
105/C6 **Lima** (cap.), Peru
34/A2 **Lima** (riv.), Port.
91/L4 **Lima** (peak), Mn,US
94/B2 **Lima** (peak), Mn,US
89/K3 **Lima,** Oh,US
94/C3 **Lima,** Oh,US
37/E5 **Limadario, Monte** (Gridone) (peak), It.
108/D2 **Lima Duarte,** Braz.
27/L4 **Limanowa,** Pol.
49/C2 **Limassol,** Cyp.
49/C2 **Limassol** (dist.), Cyp.
50/C3 **Limassol,** Cyp.
52/B2 **Limassol,** Cyp.
22/A2 **Limavady** (dist.), NI,UK
22/B1 **Limavady,** NI,UK
105/B7 **Limay** (riv.), Arg.
109/C4 **Limay** (riv.), Arg.
30/A6 **Limay,** Fr.
38/A2 **Limbara** (peak), It.
42/E4 **Limbaži,** Lat.
53/K4 **Limbdi,** India
62/B3 **Limbdi,** India
103/H2 **Limbé,** Haiti
104/C3 **Limbé,** Haiti
31/E2 **Limbourg,** Belg.
67/E2 **Limbuak,** Malay.
28/C6 **Limburg** (prov.), Belg.
31/E2 **Limburg** (prov.), Belg.
28/C6 **Limburg** (prov.), Neth.
31/E1 **Limburg** (prov.), Neth.
26/E3 **Limburg an der Lahn,** Ger.
31/H3 **Limburg an der Lahn,** Ger.
33/H1 **Limburg an der Lahn,** Ger.
95/Q8 **Limehouse,** On,Can
19/T10 **Limeil-Brévannes,** Fr.
107/J8 **Limeira,** Braz.
108/C2 **Limeira,** Braz.
109/G1 **Limeira,** Braz.
39/J2 **Limenária,** Gre.
41/G5 **Limenária,** Gre.
18/C3 **Limerick,** Ire.
21/A4 **Limerick,** Ire.
85/G3 **Lime Village,** Ak,US
34/B2 **Limia** (riv.), Sp.
70/F2 **Limmen** (bight), Austl.
39/H3 **Límni,** Gre.
39/J3 **Límnos** (isl.), Gre.
44/C5 **Límnos** (isl.), Gre.
18/D4 **Limoges,** Fr.
32/D4 **Limoges,** Fr.
32/D4 **Limogne** (plat.), Fr.
103/F4 **Limón,** CR
106/B2 **Limón,** CR
103/E3 **Limón,** Hon.
88/F4 **Limon,** Co,US
93/G3 **Limon,** Co,US
96/C2 **Limon,** Co,US
19/S11 **Limours,** Fr.
32/D4 **Limousin** (mts.), Fr.
32/D4 **Limousin** (reg.), Fr.
32/E5 **Limoux,** Fr.
35/G1 **Limoux,** Fr.
74/F7 **Limpopo** (riv.), Afr.
82/F5 **Limpopo** (riv.), Afr.
81/F2 **Limpopo** (riv.), Africa
19/P8 **Limpsfield,** Eng,UK
25/G4 **Limpsfield,** Eng,UK
61/F5 **Limu** (mtn.), China
65/E2 **Limu** (mtn.), China
52/D3 **Līnah,** SAr.
20/J1 **Linakhamari,** Rus.
37/G4 **Linard, Piz** (peak), Swi.
109/B4 **Linares,** Chile
101/F3 **Linares,** Mex.
88/G7 **Linares,** Mex.
96/D5 **Linares,** Mex
18/C5 **Linares,** Sp.
34/D3 **Linares,** Sp.
39/J3 **Linariá,** Gre.
60/D4 **Lincang,** China
63/H3 **Lincang,** China
59/C3 **Lincheng,** China
61/H3 **Linchuan,** China
95/R9 **Lincoln,** On,Can
84/L1 **Lincoln** (sea), Can., Grld.
87/T6 **Lincoln** (sea),Can, Grld.
23/H5 **Lincoln,** Eng,UK
91/L5 **Lincoln,** Il,US
93/K2 **Lincoln,** Il,US
94/B3 **Lincoln,** Il,US
97/F1 **Lincoln,** Il,US
95/G2 **Lincoln,** Me,US
89/G3 **Lincoln** (cap.), Ne,US
91/J5 **Lincoln** (cap.), Ne,US
93/H2 **Lincoln** (cap.), Ne,US
90/B4 **Lincoln Beach,** Or,US
88/B3 **Lincoln City,** Or,US
90/B4 **Lincoln City,** Or,US
25/F1 **Lincoln Heath** (woodl.), Eng,UK
99/F7 **Lincoln Park,** Mi,US
23/H5 **Lincolnshire** (co.), Eng,UK
25/F1 **Lincolnshire** (co.), Eng,UK
23/H5 **Lincolnshire Wolds** (hills), Eng,UK
97/H3 **Lincolnton,** NC,US
38/A2 **L'Incudine, Mont** (mtn.), Fr.
37/F2 **Lindau,** Ger.
37/F3 **Lindau,** Swi.
28/D3 **Linde** (riv.), Neth.
72/C3 **Lindeman** (isl.), Austl.
106/G2 **Linden,** Guy.
38/D3 **Linden,** Al,US
99/E6 **Linden,** Mi,US
98/F5 **Linden,** NJ,US
99/G7 **Linden Beach,** On,Can
33/H3 **Lindenberg im Allgäu,** Ger.
37/F2 **Lindenberg im Allgäu,** Ger.
99/P15 **Lindenhurst,** Il,US
98/F6 **Lindenwold,** NJ,US
29/E3 **Lindern,** Ger.
42/B4 **Lindesberg,** Swe
18/D3 **Lindesnes** (cape), Nor.
46/A4 **Lindesnes** (cape), Nor.
50/B2 **Lindhos** (ruins), Gre.
82/G3 **Lindi,** Tanz.
55/J2 **Lindian,** China
29/E6 **Lindlar,** Ger.
31/G1 **Lindlar,** Ger.
73/D3 **Lind Nat'l Park,** Austl.
94/E2 **Lindsay,** On,Can
92/C3 **Lindsay,** Ca,US
96/D2 **Lindsborg,** Ks,US
69/K4 **Line** (isls.), Kiri
54/G4 **Linfen,** China
59/B3 **Linfen,** China
61/F5 **Lingao,** China
63/J4 **Lingao,** China
65/E2 **Lingao,** China
59/B4 **Lingbao,** China
55/H5 **Lingbi,** China
59/D4 **Lingbi,** China
54/G4 **Lingchuan,** China
59/C4 **Lingchuan,** China
63/K2 **Lingchuan,** China
28/C5 **Linge** (riv.), Neth.
26/D2 **Lingen,** Ger.
29/E3 **Lingen,** Ger.
19/N8 **Lingfield,** Eng,UK
25/F4 **Lingfield,** Eng,UK
66/B3 **Lingga** (isls.), Indo.
31/G6 **Lingolsheim,** Fr.
36/D1 **Lingolsheim,** Fr.
54/G4 **Lingqiu,** China
59/C3 **Lingqiu,** China
59/C3 **Lingshan,** China
61/F4 **Lingshan,** China
63/J3 **Lingshan,** China
65/E1 **Lingshan,** China
54/G4 **Lingshi,** China
59/B3 **Lingshi,** China
61/F5 **Lingshui,** China
63/J4 **Lingshui,** China
65/E2 **Lingshui,** China
76/B4 **Linguère,** Sen.
78/B3 **Linguère,** Sen.
54/H4 **Ling Xian,** China
59/D3 **Ling Xian,** China
63/K2 **Ling Xian,** China
59/E5 **Lingyang Shan** (mtn.), China
59/L8 **Lingyen Shan** (mtn.), China
59/E5 **Lingyin Si,** China
59/L9 **Lingyin Si,** China
61/J2 **Lingyin Si,** China
59/D2 **Lingyuan,** China
63/J3 **Lingyun,** China
55/J1 **Linhai,** China
61/J2 **Linhai,** China
107/K7 **Linhares,** Braz.
108/D1 **Linhares,** Braz.
47/L5 **Linhe,** China
54/F3 **Linhe,** China
59/A2 **Linhe,** China
18/F3 **Linköping,** Swe.
20/E4 **Linköping,** Swe.
46/B4 **Linköping,** Swe.
59/C3 **Linliu Shan** (mtn.), China
37/E3 **Linmat** (riv.), Swi.
101/F3 **Linn,** Tx,US
20/J3 **Linnansaaren Nat'l Park,** Fin.
42/F3 **Linnansaaren Nat'l Park,** Fin.
24/A3 **Linney Head** (pt.), Wal,UK
31/F2 **Linnich,** Ger.
38/C5 **Linosa** (isl.), It.
54/H4 **Linqing,** China
59/C3 **Linqing,** China
59/D3 **Linqu,** China
59/C4 **Linquan,** China
54/G5 **Linru,** China
59/C4 **Linru,** China
107/J8 **Lins,** Braz.
108/B2 **Lins,** Braz.
28/B4 **Linschoten,** Neth.
59/D4 **Linshu,** China
103/G2 **Linstead,** Jam.
81/H9 **Linta** (riv.), Madg.
37/E4 **Linth** (riv.), Swi.
37/F4 **Linthal,** Swi.
25/G2 **Linton,** Eng,UK
94/C4 **Linton,** In,US
97/G2 **Linton,** In,US
91/H4 **Linton,** ND,US
23/H5 **Linwood,** Eng,UK
62/K2 **Linwu,** China
59/C3 **Linxi,** China
59/C3 **Lin Xian,** China
55/H4 **Linyi,** China
59/B4 **Linyi,** China
59/D3 **Linyi,** China
59/D4 **Linyi,** China
54/G5 **Linying,** China
59/C4 **Linying,** China
18/E4 **Linz,** Aus.
27/H4 **Linz,** Aus.
33/L2 **Linz,** Aus.
40/B1 **Linz,** Aus.
31/G2 **Linz am Rhein,** Ger.
54/E4 **Linze,** China
59/C3 **Linzhang,** China
18/D4 **Lions** (gulf), Fr.
32/E5 **Lions** (gulf), Fr.
35/G1 **Lions** (gulf), Fr.
38/D3 **Lipari,** It.
38/D3 **Lipari** (isl.), It.
38/D3 **Lipari** (isls.), It.
20/J3 **Liperi,** Fin.
42/F3 **Liperi,** Fin.
19/G3 **Lipetsk,** Rus.
44/F1 **Lipetsk,** Rus.
46/D4 **Lipetsk,** Rus.
44/F1 **Lipetsk Obl.,** Rus.
106/E8 **Lípez** (range), Bol.
106/E8 **Lípez** (riv.), Bol.
25/F4 **Liphook,** Eng,UK
61/F3 **Liping,** China
63/J2 **Liping,** China
39/G1 **Lipljan,** Yugo.
40/E4 **Lipljan,** Yugo.
27/K2 **Lipno,** Pol.
33/L2 **Lipno, Údolní nádrž** (res.), Czh.
40/E2 **Lipova,** Rom.
26/D3 **Lippe** (riv.), Ger.
26/E3 **Lippe** (riv.), Ger.
28/E5 **Lippe** (riv.), Ger.
29/F5 **Lippetal,** Ger.
26/E3 **Lippstadt,** Ger.
29/F5 **Lippstadt,** Ger.
27/K4 **Liptovský Mikuláš,** Slvk.
73/C3 **Liptrap** (cape), Austl.
61/F3 **Lipu,** China
63/K3 **Lipu,** China
77/M7 **Lira,** Ugan.
76/J8 **Liranga,** Congo
82/C1 **Liranga,** Congo
106/D6 **Lircay,** Peru
38/C2 **Liri** (riv.), It.
35/E3 **Liria,** Sp.
37/F5 **Liro** (riv.), It.
46/G4 **Lisakovsk,** Kaz.
77/K7 **Lisala,** Zaire
35/P10 **Lisboa** (dist.), Port.
34/A3 **Lisboa** (Lisbon) (cap.), Port.
35/P10 **Lisboa** (Lisbon) (cap.), Port.
18/C5 **Lisbon** (cap.), Port.
34/A3 **Lisbon** (Lisboa) (cap.), Port.
35/P10 **Lisbon** (Lisboa) (cap.), Port.
34/A3 **Lisbon** (dist.), Port.
98/J7 **Lisbon,** Md,US
95/G2 **Lisbon,** Me,US
91/J4 **Lisbon,** ND,US
22/B2 **Lisburn,** NI,UK
22/B3 **Lisburn** (dist.), NI,UK
85/E2 **Lisburne** (cape), Ak,US
21/H7 **Lisdoonvarna,** Ire.
59/B4 **Li Shan** (mtn.), China
60/D3 **Lishe** (riv.), China
63/H2 **Lishe** (riv.), China
55/J3 **Lishu,** China
59/F2 **Lishu,** China
61/H2 **Lishui,** China
69/H2 **Lisianski** (isl.), Hi.,US
44/F2 **Lisichansk,** Ukr.
32/D2 **Lisieux,** Fr.
24/B6 **Liskeard,** Eng,UK
19/G3 **Liski,** Rus.
46/D4 **Liski,** Rus.
99/P16 **Lisle,** Il,US
19/S9 **L'Isle-Adam,** Fr.
32/D5 **L'Isle-en-Dodon,** Fr.
35/F1 **L'Isle-en-Dodon,** Fr.
32/F5 **L'Isle-sur-la-Sorgue,** Fr
36/C3 **L'Isle-sur-le-Doubs,** Fr.
32/D5 **L'Isle-sur-Tarn,** Fr.
35/F1 **L'Isle-sur-Tarn,** Fr.
68/E7 **Lismore,** Austl.
71/J5 **Lismore,** Austl.
72/D5 **Lismore,** Austl.
73/E1 **Lismore,** Austl.
22/B3 **Lisnacree,** NI,UK
40/C2 **Lispeszentadorján,** Hun.
25/F4 **Liss,** Eng,UK
28/B4 **Lisse,** Neth.
19/T11 **Lisses,** Fr.
26/E1 **List,** Ger.
29/E6 **Lister** (riv.), Ger.
94/D3 **Listowel,** On,Can
21/H7 **Listowel,** Ire.
54/E6 **Litang,** China
60/D2 **Litang,** China
60/D2 **Litang** (riv.), China
63/H2 **Litang** (riv.), China
49/D3 **Līţānī** (riv.), Leb.
93/K3 **Litchfield,** Il,US
94/B4 **Litchfield,** Il,US
97/F2 **Litchfield,** Il,US
91/K4 **Litchfield,** Mn,US
28/C5 **Lith,** Neth.
23/F5 **Litherland,** Eng,UK
68/E8 **Lithgow,** Austl.
71/J6 **Lithgow,** Austl.
73/D2 **Lithgow,** Austl.
18/F3 **Lithuania**
20/G5 **Lithuania**
27/M1 **Lithuania**
42/D5 **Lithuania**
44/C1 **Lithuania**
46/C4 **Lithuania**
33/L3 **Litija,** Slov.
40/B2 **Litija,** Slov.
20/H5 **Litovskiy Nat'l Park,** Lith.
42/E5 **Litovskiy Nat'l Park,** Lith.
72/D4 **Littabella Nat'l Park,** Austl.
37/E3 **Littau,** Swi.
93/J4 **Little** (riv.), La,US
93/J4 **Little** (riv.), Ok,US
93/H5 **Little** (riv.), Tx,US
94/D1 **Little Abitibi** (riv.), On,Can
27/J5 **Little Alföld** (plain), Hun.
63/F5 **Little Andaman** (isl.), India
90/F4 **Little Belt** (mts.), Mt,US
19/N6 **Little Berkhamstead,** Eng,UK
90/G4 **Little Bighorn Nat'l Mon.,** Mt,US
49/C4 **Little Bitter** (lake), Egypt
23/F4 **Littleborough,** Eng,UK
99/Q16 **Little Calumet** (riv.), Il,US
103/F2 **Little Cayman** (isl.), Cay.
19/M7 **Little Chalfont,** Eng,UK
92/E4 **Little Colorado** (riv.), Az,US
91/M3 **Little Current** (riv.), On,Can
94/C1 **Little Current** (riv.), On,Can
94/D2 **Little Current,** On,Can
24/C5 **Little Dart** (riv.), Eng,UK
73/B3 **Little Desert Nat'l Park,** Austl.

Little – Lubac

85/E2 Little Diomede (isl.), Ak,US
91/K4 Little Falls, Mn,US
93/G4 Littlefield, Tx,US
96/C3 Littlefield, Tx,US
91/K4 Little Fork (riv.), Mn,US
25/F5 Littlehampton, Eng,UK
103/H1 Little Inagua (isl.), Bahm.
104/C2 Little Inagua (isl.), Bahm.
80/C4 Little Karoo (reg.), SAfr.
21/B2 Little Minch (sound), Sc,UK
95/K2 Little Miquelon (isl.), StP,Fr
91/H4 Little Missouri (riv.), ND, SD,US
93/J4 Little Missouri (riv.), Ar,US
63/F6 Little Nicobar (isl.), India
25/G2 Little Ouse (riv.), Eng,UK
98/K7 Little Patuxent (riv.), Md,US
25/G2 Littleport, Eng,UK
99/N14 Little Prairie, Wi,US
93/J4 Little Red (riv.), Ar,US
89/H5 Little Rock (cap.), Ar,US
93/J4 Little Rock (cap.), Ar,US
96/E3 Little Rock (cap.), Ar,US
99/N16 Little Rock (cr.), Il,US
102/D2 Little Rocky (pt.), Belz.
85/L3 Little Salmon, Yk,Can
78/B4 Little Scarcies (riv.), Gui., SLeo.
91/K5 Little Sioux (riv.), Ia,US
89/G3 Little Sioux (riv.), Ia,US
85/B5 Little Sitkin (isl.), Ak,US
90/D2 Little Smoky (riv.), Ab,Can
92/E2 Little Snake (riv.), Co, Wy,US
25/G4 Little Stour (riv.), Eng,UK
25/F2 Little Stukeley, Eng,UK
95/G2 Littleton, NH,US
93/K3 Little Wabash (riv.), Il,US
94/B4 Little Wabash (riv.), Il,US
90/E5 Little Wood (riv.), Id,US
51/E3 Little Zab (riv.), Iraq
47/N5 Liu (riv.), China
55/J3 Liu (riv.), China
55/K3 Liu (riv.), China
58/C1 Liu (riv.), China
59/E2 Liu (riv.), China
59/E5 Liu (riv.), China
61/F4 Liu (riv.), China
63/J3 Liu (riv.), China
54/F5 Liuba, China
63/J3 Liucheng, China
55/K3 Liuhe, China
58/C1 Liuhe, China
61/J2 Liuheng (isl.), China
59/B3 Liulin, China
82/D3 Liuwa Pan Nat'l Park, Zam.
61/G4 Liuxi (riv.), China
61/G2 Liuyang (riv.), China
63/K2 Liuyang, China
61/F3 Liuzhou, China
63/J3 Liuzhou, China
39/H2 Livádhion, Gre.
39/H3 Livanátai, Gre.
42/E4 Līvāni, Lat.
85/J2 Livengood, Ak,US
97/H4 Live Oak, Fl,US
31/F6 Liverdun, Fr.
99/L11 Livermore, Ca,US
100/D2 Livermore (mt.), Tx,US
93/F5 Livermore (peak), Tx,US
96/B4 Livermore (peak), Tx,US
72/G8 Liverpool, Austl.
87/K4 Liverpool, NS,Can
89/P3 Liverpool, NS,Can
95/H2 Liverpool, NS,Can
85/M2 Liverpool (bay), NW,Can
86/C1 Liverpool (bay), NW,Can
87/J1 Liverpool (cape), NW,Can
18/C3 Liverpool, Eng,UK
23/E5 Liverpool (bay), Eng,UK
23/F5 Liverpool, Eng,UK
23/H2 Liverton, Eng,UK
33/J3 Livigno, It.
37/G4 Livigno, It.
102/D3 Livingston, Guat.
99/E6 Livingston (co.), Mi,US
86/E4 Livingston, Mt,US
88/D2 Livingston, Mt,US
90/F4 Livingston, Mt,US
89/H5 Livingston, Tx,US
93/J5 Livingston, Tx,US
93/J5 Livingston (lake), Tx,US
96/E4 Livingston, Tx,US
90/E3 Livingstone (range), Ab,Can
82/E4 Livingstone, Zam.
82/B1 Livingstone Falls (fall, falls), Congo
40/C4 Livno, Bosn.
44/F1 Livny, Rus.
20/H2 Livojoki (riv.), Fin.
42/E2 Livojoki (riv.), Fin.
94/D3 Livonia, Mi,US
99/F7 Livonia, Mi,US
18/E4 Livorno, It.
33/J5 Livorno, It.
32/F4 Livron-sur-Drôme, Fr.
30/B6 Livry-Gargan, Fr.
82/G2 Liwale, Tanz.
61/F2 Li Xian, China
59/D4 Lixin, China
61/H3 Lixin, China
21/H7 Lixnaw, Ire.
39/G3 Lixoúrion, Gre.
59/D5 Liyang, China
61/H2 Liyang, China
24/A7 Lizard (pt.), Eng,UK
21/C5 Lizard (pt.), Eng,UK
24/A7 Lizard, Eng,UK
32/A2 Lizard (pt.), Eng,UK
24/A6 Lizard, The (pen.), Eng,UK
30/C5 Lizy-sur-Ourcq, Fr.
40/E4 Ljubic, Yugo.
40/C3 Ljubija, Bosn.
39/F1 Ljubinje, Bosn.
40/D4 Ljubinje, Bosn.
18/E4 Ljubljana (cap.), Slov.
33/L3 Ljubljana (cap.), Slov.
40/B2 Ljubljana (cap.), Slov.
38/E1 Ljubuški, Cro.
40/C4 Ljubuški, Cro.
20/F3 Ljungan (riv.), Swe.
42/C3 Ljungan (riv.), Swe.
20/E4 Ljungby, Swe.
42/C3 Ljusdal, Swe.
18/E2 Ljusnan (riv.), Swe.
20/E3 Ljusnan (riv.), Swe.
42/B3 Ljusnan (riv.), Swe.
106/E7 Llallagua, Bol.
24/B2 Llanarth, Wal,UK
22/D5 Llanberis, Wal,UK
22/D5 Llanberis, Pass of (pass), Wal,UK
24/C3 Llandeilo, Wal,UK
24/D3 Llandogo, Wal,UK
24/C3 Llandovery, Wal,UK
22/E6 Llandrillo, Wal,UK
24/C2 Llandrindod Wells, Wal,UK
22/E5 Llandudno, Wal,UK
24/C3 Llandybie, Wal,UK
24/B2 Llandyssul, Wal,UK
24/B3 Llanelli, Wal,UK
22/E6 LLanelltyd, Wal,UK
24/C1 Llanelltyd, Wal,UK
22/D6 Llanenddwyn, Wal,UK
22/D5 Llanerchymedd, Wal,UK
34/C1 Llanes, Sp.
24/C1 Llanfair Caereinion, Wal,UK
22/E5 Llanfairfechan, Wal,UK
22/D5 Llanfair-Pwllgwyngyll, Wal,UK
23/E6 Llanfyllin, Wal,UK
24/C1 Llanfyllin, Wal,UK
24/C2 Llangammarch Wells, Wal,UK
24/C3 Llangattock, Wal,UK
23/E6 Llangollen, Wal,UK
24/C2 Llangurig, Wal,UK
24/C2 Llanidloes, Wal,UK
22/D5 Llanllyfni, Wal,UK
24/B3 Llannon, Wal,UK
101/F2 Llano, Tx,US
93/H5 Llano, Tx,US
93/H5 Llano (riv.), Tx,US
96/D4 Llano, Tx,US
100/C2 Llano Blanco, Mex.
92/G4 Llano Estacado (plain), NM, Tx,US
96/C3 Llano Estacado (plain), NM, Tx,US
88/F5 Llano Estacado (reg.), MN, Tx,US
100/E1 Llano Estacado (plain), NM, Tx,US
24/B2 Llanon, Wal,UK
105/C2 Llanos (plain), Col., Ven.
106/D3 Llanos (plain), Col., Ven.
23/E5 Llanrhaeadr, Wal,UK
24/B2 Llanrhystyd, Wal,UK
24/A3 Llanrian, Wal,UK
22/E5 Llanrwst, Wal,UK
24/C3 Llanthony, Wal,UK
24/C3 Llantrisant, Wal,UK
24/C4 Llantwit Major, Wal,UK
22/E6 Llanuwchllyn, Wal,UK
24/C1 Llanwnog, Wal,UK
24/C2 Llanwrtyd Wells, Wal,UK
106/C5 Llata, Peru
23/E5 Llay, Wal,UK
24/C2 Lledrod, Wal,UK
18/D4 Lleida, Sp.
35/F2 Lleida (Lérida), Sp.
101/F4 Llera de Canales, Mex.
34/B3 Llerena, Sp.
22/D6 Lleyn (pen.), Wal,UK
35/F1 Llivia, Sp.
35/F1 Llobregat (riv.), Sp.
35/K6 Llobregat (riv.), Sp.
32/B5 Llodio, Sp.
34/D1 Llodio, Sp.
35/G2 Lloret de Mar, Sp.
86/F3 Lloydminster, Ab, Sk,Can
90/F2 Lloydminster, Ab, Sk,Can
95/K1 Lloyds (riv.), Nf,Can
35/G3 Lluchmayor, Sp.
105/C5 Llullaillaco (vol.), Chile
109/C1 Llullaillaco (vol.), Chile
24/C3 Llynfi (riv.), Wal,UK
60/E4 Lo (riv.), Viet.
65/D1 Lo (riv.), Viet.
105/C5 Loa (riv.), Chile
106/E8 Loa (riv.), Chile
109/C1 Loa (riv.), Chile
92/E3 Loa, Ut,US
33/H4 Loano, It.
35/N8 Loaoya (can.), Sp.
100/E4 Lobatos, Mex.
80/D2 Lobatse, Bots.
80/N12 Lobatse, Bots.
30/D3 Lobbes, Belg.
82/B3 Lobito, Ang.
43/X8 Lobnya, Rus.
78/D5 Lobo (riv.), IvC.
109/E4 Lobos, Arg.
106/B5 Lobos de Tierra (isl.), Peru
33/H3 Locarno, Swi.
37/E5 Locarno, Swi.
22/D2 Lochans, Sc,UK
22/E1 Locharbriggs, Sc,UK
37/F2 Lochau, Aus.
28/D4 Lochem, Neth.
32/D3 Loches, Fr.
22/E1 Lochmaben, Sc,UK
27/L2 Łochów, Pol.
28/A6 Lochristi, Belg.
30/C1 Lochristi, Belg.
99/L10 Locke, Ca,US
23/E1 Lockerbie, Sc,UK
73/C2 Lockhart, Austl.
101/F2 Lockhart, Tx,US
93/H5 Lockhart, Tx,US
96/D4 Lockhart, Tx,US
72/A1 Lockhart Abor. Land, Austl.
94/E3 Lock Haven, Pa,US
73/C3 Lockington, Austl.
26/F2 Locknitz (riv.), Ger.
99/P16 Lockport, Il,US
94/E3 Lockport, NY,US
95/S9 Lockport, NY,US
19/N7 Lockwood (res.), Eng,UK
65/D4 Loc Ninh, Viet.
66/C1 Loc Ninh, Viet.
30/B2 Locon, Fr.
38/E3 Locri, It.
49/F8 Lod, Isr.
71/G7 Loddon (riv.), Austl.
25/E4 Loddon (riv.), Eng,UK
25/H1 Loddon, Eng,UK
26/A2 Loddon, Eng.,UK
32/E5 Lodève, Fr.
42/G3 Lodeynoye Pole, Rus.
90/F3 Lodge (cr.), Mt,US
90/G5 Lodgepole (riv.), Nb, Wy,US
33/H4 Lodi, It.
88/B4 Lodi, Ca,US
92/B3 Lodi, Ca,US
99/M10 Lodi, Ca,US
82/D1 Lodja, Zaire
34/D1 Lodosa, Sp.
37/E5 Lodrino, Swi.
77/N7 Lodwar, Kenya
18/E3 Łódź, Pol.
27/K3 Łódź, Pol.
27/K3 Łódź (prov.), Pol.
46/B4 Łódź, Pol.
35/N9 Loeches, Sp.
63/H4 Loei, Thai.
65/C2 Loei, Thai.
28/C4 Loenen, Neth.
78/C5 Lofa (co.), Libr.
78/C5 Lofa (riv.), Libr.
37/E2 Löffingen, Ger.
18/E2 Lofoten (isls.), Nor.
20/D2 Lofoten (isls.), Nor.
23/H2 Loftus, Eng,UK
73/C4 Lofty (range), Austl.
72/F7 Logan, Austl.
84/C3 Logan (mtn.), Can.
85/K3 Logan (mtn.), Yk,Can
86/B2 Logan (mtn.), Yk,Can
93/G4 Logan, NM,US
96/C3 Logan, NM,US
94/D4 Logan, Oh,US
97/H2 Logan, Oh,US
86/E4 Logan, Ut,US
88/D3 Logan, Ut,US
90/F5 Logan, Ut,US
92/E2 Logan, Ut,US
94/D4 Logan, WV,US
97/H2 Logan, WV,US
22/D2 Logan, Mull of (pt.), Sc,UK
89/J3 Logansport, In,US
94/C3 Logansport, In,US
33/L4 Logatec, Slov.
40/B3 Logatec, Slov.
74/D3 Logone (riv.), Camr., Chad
76/J6 Logone (riv.), Camr., Chad
18/C4 Logroño, Sp.
32/B5 Logroño, Sp.
34/D1 Logroño, Sp.
34/C3 Logrosán, Sp.
29/G6 Lohfelden, Ger.
42/E3 Lohja, Fin.
31/G2 Lohmar, Ger.
26/E2 Lohne, Ger.
29/F3 Lohne, Ger.
29/F4 Löhne, Ger.
26/E4 Lohr, Ger.
33/H2 Lohr, Ger.
63/G4 Loi-kaw, Burma
65/B2 Loi-kaw, Burma
60/C4 Loi Lun (range), Burma, China
63/G3 Loi Lun (range), Burma, China
26/B5 Loing (riv.), Fr.
32/E2 Loing (riv.), Fr.
32/C3 Loir (riv.), Fr.
18/D4 Loire (riv.), Fr.
26/B5 Loire (riv.), Fr.
32/C3 Loire (riv.), Fr.
31/E5 Loisin (riv.), Fr.
60/C4 Loi Song (mtn.), Burma
77/N8 Loita (hills), Kenya
106/C4 Loja, Ecu.
34/C4 Loja, Sp.
26/E1 Løjt Kirkeby, Den.
51/G1 Lokbatan, Azer.
28/B6 Lokeren, Belg.
30/D1 Lokeren, Belg.
77/N7 Lokitaung, Kenya
42/E2 Lokka, Fin.
42/F4 Loknya, Rus.
76/G6 Lokoja, Nga.
77/K8 Lokolia, Zaire
82/D1 Lokolia, Zaire
77/K8 Lokolo (riv.), Zaire
81/H8 Lokomby, Madg.
77/J8 Lokoro (riv.), Zaire
40/E2 Lökösháza, Hun.
76/F6 Lokossa, Ben.
87/K2 Loks (isl.), NW,Can
77/L6 Lol (riv.), Sudan
20/D5 Lolland (isl.), Den.
26/F1 Lolland (isl.), Den.
90/E4 Lolo (peak), Mt,US
77/L8 Lolo, Zaire
82/E1 Lolo, Zaire
101/F4 Lolotla, Mex.
68/G5 Lolua, Tuv.
41/F4 Lom, Bul.
44/B4 Lom, Bul.
20/D3 Lom, Nor.
76/C6 Loma (mts.), Gui., SLeo.
78/C4 Loma (mts.), Gui., SLeo.
101/G5 Loma Bonita, Mex.
102/C2 Loma Bonita, Mex.
74/A4 Loma Mansa (peak), SLeo.
76/C6 Loma Mansa (peak), SLeo.
78/C4 Loma Mansa (peak), SLeo.
74/E5 Lomami (riv.), Zaire
77/K8 Lomami (riv.), Zaire
82/D1 Lomami (riv.), Zaire
101/F4 Lomas del Real, Mex.
102/B1 Lomas del Real, Mex.
109/E3 Lomas de Zamora, Arg.
99/P16 Lombard, Il,US
107/H3 Lombarda (mts.), Braz.
33/J4 Lombardy (reg.), It.
37/G5 Lombardy (reg.), It.
67/F5 Lomblen (isl.), Indo.
48/L10 Lombok (isl.), Indo.
67/E5 Lombok (isl.), Indo.
76/F6 Lomé (cap.), Togo
79/F5 Lomé (cap.), Togo
77/K8 Lomela, Zaire
77/K8 Lomela (riv.), Zaire
82/D1 Lomela, Zaire
32/E1 Lomme, Fr.
28/C6 Lommel, Belg.
31/E1 Lommel, Belg.
21/C2 Lomond (lake), Sc,UK
43/U7 Lomonosov, Rus.
67/E5 Lompobatang (peak), Indo.
92/B4 Lompoc, Ca,US
60/D5 Lom Sak, Thai.
63/H4 Lom Sak, Thai.
65/C2 Lom Sak, Thai.
18/F3 Łomża, Pol.
27/M2 Łomża, Pol.
27/M2 Łomża (prov.), Pol.
42/D5 Łomża, Pol.
44/B1 Łomża, Pol.
46/C4 Łomża, Pol.
53/K5 Lonāvale, India
62/B4 Lonāvale, India
28/B7 Londerzeel, Belg.
30/D2 Londerzeel, Belg.
30/A4 Londinières, Fr.
87/H4 London, On,Can
89/K3 London, On,Can
94/D3 London, On,Can
103/F3 London (reef), Nic.
18/C3 London (cap.), Eng,UK
19/N7 London (cap.), Eng,UK
25/F3 London (cap.), Eng,UK
94/C4 London, Ky,US
97/G2 London, Ky,US
19/N7 London, City of (bor.), Eng,UK
19/N6 London Colney, Eng,UK
25/F3 London Colney, Eng,UK
70/D2 Londonderry (cape), Austl.
18/C3 Londonderry, NI,UK
22/A2 Londonderry, NI,UK
22/A2 Londonderry (dist.), NI,UK
19/N8 London (Gatwick) (int'l arpt.), Eng,UK
19/M7 London (Heathrow) (int'l arpt.), Eng,UK
107/H8 Londrina, Braz.
108/B2 Londrina, Braz.
109/F1 Londrina, Braz.
93/H4 Lone Grove, Ok,US
96/D3 Lone Grove, Ok,US
72/E7 Lone Pine Sanct, Austl.
72/C4 Lonesome Nat'l Park, Austl.
103/H1 Long (cay), Bahm.
103/H1 Long (isl.), Bahm.
104/C2 Long (cay), Bahm.
104/C2 Long (isl.), Bahm.
84/K7 Long (isl.), Bahm.
89/L7 Long (cay), Bahm.
91/J2 Long (pt.), Mb,Can
91/M3 Long (lake), On,Can
94/C1 Long (lake), On,Can
61/F3 Long (riv.), China
35/F1 Long (peak), Fr.
47/T2 Long (str.), Rus.
60/C5 Long, Thai.
24/C1 Long (mtn.), Wal,UK
85/G3 Long, Ak,US
95/F3 Long (isl.), NY,US
98/G5 Long (isl.), NY,US
63/J3 Long'an, China
95/R10 Long Beach, On,Can
88/C5 Long Beach, Ca,US
92/C4 Long Beach, Ca,US
98/F6 Long Beach (isl.), NJ,US
98/G5 Long Beach, NY,US
90/B4 Long Beach, Wa,US
23/G1 Longbenton, Eng,UK
67/E3 Longberang, Indo.
97/H5 Longboat Key, Fl,US
89/M3 Long Branch, NJ,US
94/F3 Long Branch, NJ,US
99/B3 Longbranch, Wa,US
25/E2 Long Buckby, Eng,UK
60/E2 Longchang, China
63/J2 Longchang, China
60/E4 Long Chau, Viet.
63/J3 Long Chau, Viet.
65/D1 Long Chau, Viet.
60/C3 Longchuan (riv.), Burma, China
61/G3 Longchuan, China
63/G3 Longchuan, China
25/F3 Long Crendon, Eng,UK
54/F4 Longde, China
19/N7 Long Ditton, Eng,UK
23/G6 Long Eaton, Eng,UK
31/E5 Longeau (riv.), Fr.
31/E6 Longeville-en-Barrois, Fr.
31/F5 Longeville-lès-Metz, Fr.
31/F5 Longeville-lès-Saint-Avold, Fr.
95/G2 Longfellow (mts.), Me,US
19/P7 Longfield, Eng,UK
73/C4 Longford, Austl.
99/Q15 Long Grove, Il,US
63/K4 Longgun, China
59/D2 Longhua, China
61/F3 Longhua (pass), China
61/F3 Longhui, China
63/K2 Longhui, China
98/G5 Long Island (sound), NY,US
55/J2 Longjiang, China
19/S10 Longjumeau, Fr.
59/E3 Longkou, China
91/M3 Longlac, On,Can
94/C1 Longlac, On,Can
24/D4 Longleat House, Eng,UK
63/J2 Longli, China
59/C4 Longmen, China
60/D3 Longmen, China
63/K3 Longmen, China
65/E1 Longmen, China
59/B4 Longmen Shan (mtn.), China
59/C4 Longmen Shiyao (caves), China
88/E3 Longmont, Co,US
93/F2 Longmont, Co,US
24/D1 Long Mynd, The (hill), Eng,UK
61/G3 Longnan, China
98/G4 Long Neck (pt.), Ct,US
23/G5 Longnor, Eng,UK
65/D4 Long Phu, Viet.
19/S11 Longpont-sur-Orge, Fr.
30/A3 Longpré-les-Corps-Saints, Fr.
61/H2 Longquan, China
95/K2 Long Range (mts.), Nf,Can
68/D7 Longreach, Austl.
71/G4 Longreach, Austl.
72/B3 Longreach, Austl.
54/E5 Longriba, China
23/F4 Longridge, Eng,UK
61/F2 Longshan, China
54/E4 Longshou (mts.), China
23/J6 Long Sutton, Eng,UK
65/E1 Longtan, China
23/F2 Longtown, Eng,UK
30/B4 Longueau, Fr.
30/B5 Longueil-Annel, Fr.
30/B2 Longuenesse, Fr.
95/N6 Longueuil, Qu,Can
31/E5 Longuyon, Fr.
32/F3 Longvic, Fr.
36/B3 Longvic, Fr.
89/H5 Longview, Tx,US
93/J4 Longview, Tx,US
96/E3 Longview, Tx,US
86/D4 Longview, Wa,US
90/C4 Longview, Wa,US
26/C4 Longwy, Fr.
31/E4 Longwy, Fr.
32/F2 Longwy, Fr.
54/E4 Longxi, China
63/J5 Long Xuyen, Viet.
65/D4 Long Xuyen, Viet.
66/C1 Long Xuyen, Viet.
61/H3 Longyan, China
61/H2 Longyou, China
65/D1 Longzhou, China
29/E3 Löningen, Ger.
63/G2 Lonkin, Burma
32/C5 Lons, Fr.
35/E1 Lons, Fr.
32/F3 Lons-le-Saunier, Fr.
36/B4 Lons-le-Saunier, Fr.
63/G2 Lonton, Burma
31/E2 Lontzen, Belg.
36/D5 Lonza (riv.), Swi.
24/B6 Looe, Eng,UK
24/B6 Looe (isl.), Eng,UK
72/B1 Lookout (pt.), Austl.
97/J3 Lookout (cape), NC,US
82/G1 Loolmalasin (peak), Tanz.
90/F2 Loon Lake, Can
28/C5 Loon op Zand, Neth.
21/H7 Loop Head (pt.), Ire.
30/C2 Loos, Fr.
32/E1 Loos, Fr.
54/C3 Lop (lake), China
42/H5 Lopatinskiy, Rus.
48/Q4 Lopatka (cape), Rus.
47/R4 Lopatka, Mys (cape), Rus.
63/H5 Lop Buri, Thai.
65/C3 Lop Buri, Thai.
74/C5 Lopez (cape), Gabon
76/G8 Lopez (cape), Gabon
28/B5 Lopik, Neth.
77/K7 Lopori (riv.), Zaire
20/G1 Lopphavet (bay), Nor.
53/J3 Lora (riv.), Pak.
34/C4 Lora del Río, Sp.
53/J3 Lora, Hāmūn-i- (lake), Pak.
89/K3 Lorain, Oh,US
94/D3 Lorain, Oh,US
101/E1 Loraine, Tx,US
53/J2 Loralai, Pak.
35/E4 Lorca, Sp.
31/G3 Lorch, Ger.
68/E8 Lord Howe (isl.), Austl.
71/K6 Lord Howe (isl.), Austl.
88/E5 Lordsburg, NM,US
92/E4 Lordsburg, NM,US
31/G3 Lorelei (cliff), Ger.
108/C2 Lorena, Braz.
68/D5 Lorengau, PNG
67/J5 Lorentz (riv.), Indo.
28/C2 Lorentzsluizen (dam), Neth.
51/G3 Lorestān (gov.), Iran
91/J3 Lorette, Mb,Can
33/G5 Lorgues, Fr.
35/J1 Lorgues, Fr.
77/N7 Lorian (swamp), Kenya
103/H4 Lorica, Col.
18/C4 Lorient, Fr.
32/B3 Lorient, Fr.
75/N13 L'Oriental (reg.), Mor.
86/G2 Lorillard (riv.), NW,Can
27/K5 Lorinci, Hun.
40/D2 Lorinci, Hun.
32/F4 Loriol-sur-Drôme, Fr.
21/B2 Lorn, Firth of (bay), Sc,UK
73/B3 Lorne, Austl.
95/Q8 Lorne Park, On,Can
31/G6 Lorquin, Fr.
26/D5 Lörrach, Ger.
33/G3 Lörrach, Ger.
36/D2 Lörrach, Ger.
31/F6 Lorrain (plat.), Fr.
33/G2 Lorrain (plat.), Fr.
36/C1 Lorraine (hist. reg.), Fr.
95/N6 Lorraine, Qu,Can
26/C4 Lorraine (reg.), Fr.
31/F5 Lorraine (reg.), Fr.
33/G2 Lorraine (reg.), Fr.
36/C1 Lorraine (reg.), Fr.
23/E2 Lorton, Eng,UK
98/J8 Lorton, Va,US
29/E3 Lorup, Ger.
92/B4 Los Alamos, Ca,US
93/F4 Los Alamos, NM,US
96/B3 Los Alamos, NM,US
109/B5 Los Alerces Nat'l Park, Arg.
99/K12 Los Altos, Ca,US
102/D3 Los Amates, Guat.
109/B3 Los Andes, Chile
109/B4 Los Ángeles, Chile
88/C5 Los Angeles, Ca,US
92/C4 Los Angeles, Ca,US
98/B2 Los Angeles (riv.), Ca,US
102/B1 Los Aztecas, Mex.
92/B3 Los Banos, Ca,US
34/C4 Los Barrios, Sp.
75/M12 Los Barrios, Sp.
105/B7 Los Chonos (arch.), Chile
34/C1 Los Corrales de Buelna, Sp.
100/C4 Los Frailes, Mex.
109/B6 Los Glaciares Nat'l Park, Arg.
104/D3 Los Haitises Nat'l Park, DRep.
31/F4 Losheim, Ger.
100/D3 Los Herreras, Mex.
44/D1 Loshnitsa, Bela.
100/C3 Los Hornos, Mex.
27/M2 Łosice, Pol.
103/F1 Los Indios (can.), Cuba
33/L4 Lošinj (isl.), Cro.
40/B3 Lošinj (isl.), Cro.
103/G5 Los Katios Nat'l Park, Col.
35/X16 Los Llanos de Aridane, Canl.
92/F4 Los Lunas, NM,US
96/B3 Los Lunas, NM,US
101/F4 Los Mármoles Nat'l Park, Mex.
102/B1 Los Mármoles Nat'l Park, Mex.
100/C3 Los Mochis, Mex.
34/C3 Los Navalmorales, Sp.
34/C3 Los Navalucillos, Sp.
36/B3 Losne, Fr.
37/E5 Losone, Swi.
106/C2 Los Orquideas Nat'l Park, Col.
34/C4 Los Palacios y Villafranca, Sp.
100/C4 Los Planes, Mex.
100/C2 Los Pocitos, Mex.
100/E5 Los Reyes, Mex.
101/Q10 Los Reyes, Mex.
104/E5 Los Roques (isls.), Ven.
106/E1 Los Roques (isls.), Ven.
103/F5 Los Santos, Pan.
34/B3 Los Santos de Maimona, Sp.
100/D3 Los Sauces, Mex.
37/E1 Lossburg, Ger.
28/E4 Losser, Neth.
37/F5 Lostallo, Swi.
104/D5 Los Taques, Ven.
104/E5 Los Teques, Ven.
106/E1 Los Teques, Ven.
104/F5 Los Testigos (isls.), Ven.
92/D1 Lost River (range), Id,US
98/E5 Lost River Caverns, Pa,US
24/B6 Lostwithiel, Eng,UK
34/D3 Los Yébenes, Sp.
18/D4 Lot (riv.), Fr.
32/D4 Lot (riv.), Fr.
109/B4 Lota, Chile
53/G1 Lotfābād, Trkm.
29/E4 Lotte, Ger.
59/B5 Lou (riv.), China
61/F2 Lou (riv.), China
60/D4 Louang Namtha, Laos
63/H3 Louang Namtha, Laos
65/C1 Louang Namtha, Laos
60/D5 Louangphrabang, Laos
63/H4 Louangphrabang, Laos
65/C2 Louangphrabang, Laos
82/B1 Loubomo, Congo
33/K1 Loučná (peak), Czh.
32/B2 Loudéac, Fr.
61/F3 Loudi, China
63/K2 Loudi, China
32/D3 Loudun, Fr.
32/F3 Loue (riv.), Fr.
36/B3 Loue (riv.), Fr.
54/G4 Loufan, China
59/B3 Loufan, China
76/B4 Louga, Sen.
78/A3 Louga, Sen.
78/B3 Louga (reg.), Sen.
23/G6 Loughborough, Eng,UK
25/E1 Loughborough, Eng,UK
22/B3 Loughbrickland, NI,UK
87/R7 Lougheed (isl.), NW,Can
22/B3 Loughgall, NI,UK
21/A4 Loughrea, Ire.
19/P7 Loughton, Eng,UK
36/B4 Louhans, Fr.
94/E4 Louisa, Va,US
97/J2 Louisa, Va,US
68/E6 Louisiade (arch.), PNG
89/H5 Louisiana (state), US
93/J5 Louisiana (state), US
96/E4 Louisiana (state), US
89/J4 Louisville, Ky,US
94/C4 Louisville, Ky,US
97/G2 Louisville, Ky,US
97/F3 Louisville, Ms,US
87/J3 Louis XIV (pt.), Qu,Can
20/K2 Loukhi, Rus.
75/M13 Loukkos (riv.), Mor.
34/A4 Loulé, Port.
27/G3 Louny, Czh.
33/K1 Louny, Czh.
91/J5 Loup (riv.), Nb,US
22/B2 Loup, The, NI,UK
30/C3 Lourches, Fr.
19/U10 L'Ourcq (can.), Fr.
32/C5 Lourdes, Fr.
35/E1 Lourdes, Fr.
35/P10 Loures, Port.
34/A3 Louriçal, Port.
34/A3 Lourinhã, Port.
34/A2 Lousã, Port.
35/P10 Lousa, Port.
61/E2 Loushan (pass), China
22/B4 Louth, Ire.
22/B4 Louth (co.), Ire.
23/H5 Louth, Eng,UK
39/H3 Loutrá Aidhipsoú, Gre.
39/H4 Loutrákion, Gre.
35/E1 Louts (riv.), Fr.
31/D2 Louvain (Leuven), Belg.
30/A5 Louviers, Fr.
32/D2 Louviers, Fr.
32/C2 Louvigné-du-Désert, Fr.
19/T9 Louvres, Fr.
30/B5 Louvres, Fr.
30/C3 Louvroil, Fr.
30/B2 Lovaart (can.), Belg.
42/F4 Lovat' (riv.), Bela., Rus.
40/D3 Lovćenac, Yugo.
39/F1 Lovćen Nat'l Park, Yugo.
40/D4 Lovćen Nat'l Park, Yugo.
39/J1 Lovech, Bul.
39/J1 Lovech (prov.), Bul.
41/G4 Lovech, Bul.
41/G4 Lovech (reg.), Bul.
44/C4 Lovech, Bul.
93/F2 Loveland, Co,US
90/F4 Lovell, Wy,US
92/E1 Lovell, Wy,US
88/C3 Lovelock, Nv,US
92/C2 Lovelock, Nv,US
33/J4 Lovere, It.
93/F4 Loving, NM,US
96/B3 Loving, NM,US
100/E1 Lovington, NM,US
88/F5 Lovington, NM,US
93/G4 Lovington, NM,US
96/C3 Lovington, NM,US
34/A2 Lovios, Sp.
27/J5 Lövő, Hun.
33/M3 Lövő, Hun.
40/C2 Lövő, Hun.
42/G2 Lovozero (lake), Rus
87/H2 Low (cape), NW,Ca
74/E5 Lowa (riv.), Zaire
77/L8 Lowa (riv.), Zaire
101/E2 Lowake, Tx,US
23/H6 Lowdham, Eng,UK
87/J4 Lowell, Ma,US
95/G3 Lowell, Ma,US
80/B2 Löwen (dry riv.), Namb.
99/D3 Lower (dam), Wa,U
106/D3 Lower Arrow (lake), BC,Can
27/H4 Lower Austria (prov, Aus.
33/L2 Lower Austria (prov, Aus.
40/B2 Lower Austria (prov, Aus.
25/E2 Lower Brailes, Eng,UK
37/G4 Lower Engadine (val.), Swi.
73/B3 Lower Glenelg Nat' Park, Austl.
73/C4 Lower Gordon-Franklin Wild River Nat'l Park, Austl.
25/E3 Lower Heyford, Eng,UK
71/R11 Lower Hutt, N.Z.
85/F3 Lower Kalskag, Ak,US
19/P6 Lower Nazeing, Eng,UK
91/K4 Lower Red (lake), Mn,US
99/E7 Lower Rouge (riv.), Mi,US
26/E2 Lower Saxony (stat, Ger.
29/G3 Lower Saxony (stat, Ger.
41/J3 Lower Trajan's (wa, Mol.
44/D3 Lower Trajan's (wa, Mol., Ukr.
46/K3 Lower Tunguska (riv.), Rus.
48/J3 Lower Tunguska (riv.), Rus.
82/E4 Lower Zambezi Nat Park, Zam.
25/H2 Lowestoft, Eng,UK
26/A2 Lowestoft, Eng.,UK
82/E1 Lowi (riv.), Zaire
27/K2 Łowicz, Pol.
22/E1 Lowther (hills), Sc,U
95/Q9 Lowville, On,Can
102/B3 Loxicha, Mex.
26/E2 Loxstedt, Ger.
29/F2 Loxstedt, Ger.
73/B2 Loxton, Austl.
68/F7 Loyalty (isls.), NCal
69/V12 Loyalty (isls.), NCal
36/B6 Loyettes, Fr.
40/D3 Loznica, Yugo.
41/H4 Loznitsa, Bul.
44/F2 Lozovaya, Ukr.
40/E3 Lozovik, Yugo.
59/C5 Lu (riv.), China
61/G2 Lu (peak), China
61/G2 Lu (riv.), China
61/J4 Lü (isl.), Tai.
82/D2 Luachimo, Ang.
74/E5 Lualaba (riv.), Zaire
77/L8 Lualaba (riv.), Zaire
82/E1 Lualaba (riv.), Zaire
59/J6 Luam (riv.), China
88/T10 Lua Makika (crater, Hi,US
47/M5 Luan (riv.), China
54/H5 Lu'an, China
55/H3 Luan (riv.), China
59/D2 Luan (riv.), China
59/D5 Lu'an, China
61/H2 Lu'an, China
103/G2 Luana (pt.), Jam.
54/G5 Luanchuan, China
59/B4 Luanchuan, China
34/C1 Luanco, Sp.
82/B2 Luanda (cap.), Ang.
63/G6 Luang (peak), Thai.
63/H6 Luang (lag.), Thai.
65/B4 Luang (peak), Thai.
65/C5 Luang (lag.), Thai.
66/A2 Luang (peak), Thai.
60/D5 Luang Prabang (range), Laos
65/C2 Luang Prabang (range), Laos
82/F3 Luangwa (riv.), Zan
59/D2 Luanping, China
82/E3 Luanshya, Zam.
55/H4 Luan Xian, China
59/D3 Luan Xian, China
82/D3 Luao, Ang.
34/B1 Luarca, Sp.
82/D3 Luashi, Zaire
76/G7 Luba, EqG.
102/D2 Lubaantun (ruins), Belz.
27/M3 Lubaczów, Pol.

153

Lubac – Mahār

44/B2 **Lubaczów**, Pol.
27/H3 **Lubań**, Pol.
82/B3 **Lubango**, Ang.
27/M3 **Lubartów**, Pol.
44/B2 **Lubartów**, Pol.
27/K2 **Lubawa**, Pol.
29/F4 **Lübbecke**, Ger.
31/D2 **Lubbeek**, Belg.
88/F5 **Lubbock**, Tx,US
93/G4 **Lubbock**, Tx,US
96/C3 **Lubbock**, Tx,US
18/E3 **Lübeck**, Ger.
26/F2 **Lübeck**, Ger.
46/B4 **Lübeck**, Ger.
82/D1 **Lubefu**, Zaire
27/M3 **Lubelska** (upland), Pol.
77/L8 **Lubero**, Zaire
27/K2 **Lubień Kujawski**, Pol.
27/J3 **Lubin**, Pol.
18/F3 **Lublin**, Pol.
27/M3 **Lublin**, Pol.
27/M3 **Lublin** (prov.), Pol.
44/B2 **Lublin**, Pol.
46/C4 **Lublin**, Pol.
27/K3 **Lubliniec**, Pol.
27/G1 **Lubmin**, Ger.
44/E2 **Lubny**, Ukr.
27/J2 **Luboń**, Pol.
44/A1 **Luboń**, Pol.
34/D4 **Lubrín**, Sp.
27/H3 **Lubsko**, Pol.
82/E2 **Lubudi**, Zaire
66/B4 **Lubuklinggau**, Indo.
66/B3 **Lubuksikaping**, Indo.
82/E3 **Lubumbashi**, Zaire
82/E2 **Lubunda**, Zaire
82/C2 **Lucala**, Ang.
22/B5 **Lucan**, Ire.
65/D1 **Luc An Chau**, Viet.
85/K3 **Lucania** (mt.), Yk,Can
82/D2 **Lucapa**, Ang.
33/J5 **Lucca**, It.
38/A1 **Lucciana**, Fr.
22/D2 **Luce** (bay), Sc,UK
97/F4 **Lucedale**, Ms,US
108/B2 **Lucélia**, Braz.
68/B3 **Lucena**, Phil.
34/C4 **Lucena**, Sp.
35/E2 **Lucena del Cid**, Sp.
27/K4 **Lučenec**, Slvk.
40/D1 **Lučenec**, Slvk.
44/A2 **Lučenec**, Slvk.
36/C4 **Lucens**, Swi.
33/H3 **Lucerne** (lake), Swi.
33/H3 **Lucerne** (Luzern), Swi.
37/E3 **Lucerne** (Luzern), Swi.
37/E3 **Lucerne** (Vierwaldstättensee) (lake), Swi.
47/P5 **Luchegorsk**, Rus.
59/C3 **Lucheng**, China
28/F2 **Lüchow**, Ger.
63/K3 **Luchuan**, China
73/B3 **Lucindale**, Austl.
27/G2 **Luckenwalde**, Ger.
62/D2 **Lucknow**, India
90/G3 **Lucky Lake**, Sk,Can
38/C2 **Luco dei Marsi**, It.
37/E4 **Lucomagno, Passo del** (pass), It., Swi.
103/H1 **Lucrecia** (cape), Cuba
82/D3 **Lucusse**, Ang.
39/K1 **Luda Kamchiya** (riv.), Bul.
41/H4 **Luda Kamchiya** (riv.), Bul.
29/E6 **Lüdenscheid**, Ger.
31/G1 **Lüdenscheid**, Ger.
80/A2 **Lüderitz**, Namb.
82/C6 **Lüderitz**, Namb.
37/F3 **Ludesch**, Aus.
25/E4 **Ludgershall**, Eng,UK
53/L2 **Ludhiāna**, India
64/C2 **Ludhiāna**, India
63/H2 **Ludian**, China
60/D2 **Luding**, China
29/E5 **Ludinghausen**, Ger.
87/H4 **Ludington**, Mi,US
89/J3 **Ludington**, Mi,US
94/C3 **Ludington**, Mi,US
24/D2 **Ludlow**, Eng,UK
41/H4 **Ludogorie** (reg.), Bul.
41/G2 **Luduş**, Rom.
20/E3 **Ludvika**, Swe.
42/B3 **Ludvika**, Swe.
26/E4 **Ludwigsburg**, Ger.
33/H2 **Ludwigsburg**, Ger.
27/G2 **Ludwigsfelde**, Ger.
26/E4 **Ludwigshafen**, Ger.
33/H2 **Ludwigshafen**, Ger.
37/F2 **Ludwigshafen**, Ger.
26/F2 **Ludwigslust**, Ger.
20/H4 **Ludza**, Lat.
42/E4 **Ludza**, Lat.
82/D2 **Luebo**, Zaire
82/C3 **Luena**, Ang.
61/G4 **Lufeng**, China
89/H5 **Lufkin**, Tx,US
93/J5 **Lufkin**, Tx,US
96/E4 **Lufkin**, Tx,US
18/F3 **Luga**, Rus.
20/J4 **Luga**, Rus.
42/F4 **Luga**, Rus.
46/C4 **Luga**, Rus.
37/E6 **Lugano** (lake), It., Swi.
33/H3 **Lugano**, Swi.
37/E6 **Lugano**, Swi.
19/G4 **Lugansk**, Ukr.
44/F2 **Lugansk**, Ukr.
44/F2 **Lugansk Obl.**, Ukr.
68/F6 **Luganville**, Van.
82/G1 **Lugards** (fall, falls), Kenya
40/E3 **Lugavčina**, Yugo.
29/G5 **Lügde**, Ger.
82/G3 **Lugenda** (riv.), Moz.
24/D2 **Lugg** (riv.), Eng,UK
22/B6 **Lugnaquillia** (mtn.), Ire.
34/B1 **Lugo**, Sp.
40/E3 **Lugoj**, Rom.
44/B3 **Lugoj**, Rom.
36/C5 **Lugrin**, Fr.
63/H2 **Lugu**, China
59/D4 **Luhe**, China
29/H2 **Lühe** (riv.), Ger.
60/C3 **Luhit** (riv.), India
60/D2 **Luhuo**, China
82/D4 **Luiana**, Ang.
33/H4 **Luino**, It.
37/E6 **Luino**, It.
100/E4 **Luis Moya**, Mex.
83/X **Luitpold** (coast), Ant.
55/H5 **Lujiang**, China
59/D5 **Lujiang**, China
61/H2 **Lujiang**, China
33/M3 **Lukácsháza**, Hun.
40/D3 **Lukavac**, Bosn.
82/C1 **Lukenie** (riv.), Zaire
100/B2 **Lukeville**, Az,US
42/H5 **Lukhovitsy**, Rus.
39/J2 **Lŭki**, Bul.
41/G5 **Lŭki**, Bul.
63/K2 **Lukoupu**, China
39/J1 **Lukovit**, Bul.
41/G4 **Lukovit**, Bul.
27/M3 **Łuków**, Pol.
44/B2 **Łuków**, Pol.
82/D3 **Lukulu**, Zam.
68/E4 **Lukunor** (atoll), Micr.
18/F2 **Luleå**, Swe.
20/G2 **Luleå**, Swe.
42/D2 **Luleå**, Swe.
46/C3 **Luleå**, Swe.
18/E2 **Luleälv** (riv.), Swe.
20/G2 **Luleälv** (riv.), Swe.
42/D2 **Luleälv** (riv.), Swe.
41/H5 **Lüleburgaz**, Turk.
44/C4 **Lüleburgaz**, Turk.
50/A1 **Lüleburgaz**, Turk.
63/H2 **Luliang**, China
59/B4 **Luling Guan** (pass), China
59/D3 **Lulong**, China
74/E4 **Lulonga** (riv.), Zaire
68/G5 **Lulua**, Tuv.
74/E5 **Lulua** (riv.), Zaire
82/D2 **Lulua** (riv.), Zaire
82/D3 **Lumai**, Ang.
89/L5 **Lumberton**, NC,US
97/J3 **Lumberton**, NC,US
98/F6 **Lumberton**, NJ,US
93/J5 **Lumberton**, Tx,US
96/E4 **Lumberton**, Tx,US
67/E3 **Lumbis**, Indo.
82/H4 **Lumbo**, Moz.
34/B2 **Lumbrales**, Sp.
37/F4 **Lumbrein**, Swi.
30/B2 **Lumbres**, Fr.
90/D3 **Lumby**, BC,Can
60/B3 **Lumding**, India
63/F2 **Lumding**, India
28/C7 **Lummen**, Belg.
31/E2 **Lummen**, Belg.
63/J5 **Lumphat**, Camb.
65/D3 **Lumphat**, Camb.
91/G3 **Lumsden**, Can
71/Q12 **Lumsden**, N.Z.
66/B3 **Lumut**, Malay.
82/D3 **Lunache**, Ang.
60/D3 **Lunan** (mts.), China
20/E5 **Lund**, Swe.
27/G1 **Lund**, Swe.
92/D3 **Lund**, Nv,US
82/F3 **Lundazi**, Zam.
26/F1 **Lundby**, Den.
20/D4 **Lunde**, Nor.
82/F5 **Lundi** (riv.), Zim.
24/B4 **Lundy** (isl.), Eng,UK
29/F2 **Lune** (riv.), Ger.
23/F2 **Lune** (riv.), Eng,UK
23/F3 **Lune** (riv.), Eng,UK
26/F2 **Lüneburg**, Ger.
29/H2 **Lüneburg**, Ger.
26/E2 **Lüneburger Heide** (reg.), Ger.
29/G2 **Lüneburger Heide** (reg.), Ger.
32/F5 **Lunel**, Fr.
35/H1 **Lunel**, Fr.
29/E5 **Lünen**, Ger.
95/H2 **Lunenburg**, NS,Can
29/F2 **Lunestedt**, Ger.
82/E3 **Lunga** (riv.), Zam.
36/E4 **Lungern**, Swi.
78/B4 **Lungi**, SLeo.
60/B4 **Lunglei**, India
63/F3 **Lunglei**, India
60/A4 **Lungthung**, India
82/D3 **Lungue-Bungo** (riv.), Ang.
53/K3 **Luni** (riv.), India
62/B3 **Luni** (riv.), India
29/E4 **Lünne**, Ger.
54/F4 **Luo** (riv.), China
54/G5 **Luo** (riv.), China
59/B3 **Luo** (riv.), China
59/B4 **Luo** (riv.), China
55/L2 **Luobei**, China
61/H3 **Luobo** (mtn.), China
61/F3 **Luocheng**, China
63/J3 **Luocheng**, China
60/E3 **Luodian**, China
63/J2 **Luodian**, China
61/F4 **Luoding**, China
63/K3 **Luoding**, China
61/G4 **Luofu** (peak), China
61/H3 **Luohan** (mtn.), China
54/G5 **Luohe**, China
59/C4 **Luohe**, China
59/D4 **Luoma** (lake), China
60/E4 **Luong** (mts.), Viet.
65/C1 **Luong** (mts.), Viet.
59/B4 **Luoning**, China
60/E3 **Luoping**, China
61/F3 **Luoqing** (riv.), China
59/C4 **Luoshan**, China
61/G1 **Luoshan**, China
61/F2 **Luoshuikan**, China
59/C5 **Luotian**, China
61/G2 **Luotian**, China
54/G5 **Luoyang**, China
59/C4 **Luoyang**, China
54/G4 **Luoyukou**, China
59/B3 **Luoyukou**, China
82/B1 **Luozi**, Zaire
82/E4 **Lupane**, Zim.
60/E3 **Lupanshui**, China
63/H2 **Lupanshui**, China
41/F3 **Lupeni**, Rom.
44/B3 **Lupeni**, Rom.
54/E5 **Luqu**, China
60/D3 **Luquan**, China
63/H2 **Luquan**, China
53/J2 **Lūrah** (riv.), Afg.
30/A6 **Luray**, Fr.
94/E4 **Luray**, Va,US
97/J2 **Luray**, Va,US
36/C2 **Lure**, Fr.
22/B3 **Lurgan**, NI,UK
33/H5 **Luri**, Fr.
74/F6 **Lúrio** (riv.), Moz.
82/G3 **Lúrio** (riv.), Moz.
82/H3 **Lúrio**, Moz.
40/A2 **Lurnfeld**, Aus.
20/E2 **Lurøy**, Nor.
42/B2 **Lurøy**, Nor.
82/E4 **Lusaka** (cap.), Zam.
82/E1 **Lusamba**, Zaire
82/D1 **Lusambo**, Zaire
59/C4 **Lushan**, China
59/C5 **Lu Shan** (peak), China
59/D3 **Lu Shan** (mtn.), China
54/G5 **Lushi**, China
59/B4 **Lushi**, China
39/F2 **Lushnje**, Alb.
40/D5 **Lushnje**, Alb.
82/G1 **Lushoto**, Tanz.
60/C3 **Lushui**, China
63/G2 **Lushui**, China
32/D3 **Lusignan**, Fr.
22/B4 **Lusk**, Ire.
88/F3 **Lusk**, Wy,US
91/G5 **Lusk**, Wy,US
93/F2 **Lusk**, Wy,US
37/F3 **Lustenau**, Aus.
77/J7 **Lutanga** (riv.), Zaire
36/D3 **Luthern**, Swi.
98/K7 **Lutherville**, Md,US
28/D1 **Lütjehorn** (isl.), Ger.
25/F3 **Luton**, Eng,UK
66/D3 **Lutong**, Malay.
36/C5 **Lutry**, Swi.
18/F3 **Lutsk**, Ukr.
44/C2 **Lutsk**, Ukr.
46/C4 **Lutsk**, Ukr.
29/F5 **Lutter** (riv.), Ger.
36/D2 **Lutterbach**, Fr.
37/F3 **Lutz** (riv.), Aus.
83/C **Lützow-Holm** (bay), Ant.
77/P7 **Luuq**, Som.
91/J5 **Luverne**, Mn,US
93/H2 **Luverne**, Mn,US
20/J2 **Luvozero**, Rus.
82/G2 **Luwega** (riv.), Tanz.
38/A4 **Lux**, Fr.
18/D4 **Luxembourg**
26/C4 **Luxembourg**
31/E4 **Luxembourg**
32/F2 **Luxembourg**
31/E4 **Luxembourg** (prov.), Belg.
18/D4 **Luxembourg** (cap.), Lux.
26/D4 **Luxembourg** (cap.), Lux.
31/F4 **Luxembourg** (cap.), Lux.
31/F4 **Luxembourg** (dist.), Lux.
33/G2 **Luxembourg** (cap.), Lux.
36/C2 **Luxeuil-les-Bains**, Fr.
60/C3 **Luxi**, China
60/D3 **Luxi**, China
63/G3 **Luxi**, China
63/H3 **Luxi**, China
63/K2 **Luxi**, China
63/J2 **Lu Xian**, China
77/M2 **Luxor**, Egypt
52/B3 **Luxor** (Al Uqşur), Egypt
32/C5 **Luy** (riv.), Fr.
35/E1 **Luy** (riv.), Fr.
59/B3 **Luya Shan** (mtn.), China
59/C4 **Luyi**, China
108/C1 **Luz**, Braz.
43/L3 **Luza** (riv.), Rus.
37/F4 **Luzein**, Swi.
36/E3 **Luzern** (canton), Swi.
33/H3 **Luzern** (Lucerne), Swi.
37/E3 **Luzern** (Lucerne), Swi.
63/J3 **Luzhai**, China
60/D3 **Lüzhi** (riv.), China
60/E3 **Luzhi**, China
63/J2 **Luzhi**, China
60/E2 **Luzhou**, China
63/J2 **Lužhou**, China
107/J7 **Luziânia**, Braz.
27/H4 **Lužnice** (riv.), Czh.
33/L2 **Lužnice** (riv.), Czh.
68/B2 **Luzon** (str.)
48/M8 **Luzon** (isl.), Phil.
61/H5 **Luzon** (isl.), Phil.
67/F1 **Luzon** (isl.), Phil.
68/B3 **Luzon** (isl.), Phil.
38/E3 **Luzzi**, It.
108/B3 **Ivaí** (riv.), Braz.
18/F4 **L'viv**, Ukr.
27/N4 **L'viv**, Ukr.
44/C2 **L'viv**, Ukr.
46/C5 **L'viv**, Ukr.
44/B2 **L'viv Obl.**, Ukr.
27/M4 **L'viv Oblast**, Ukr.
65/C1 **Lwi** (riv.), Burma
20/J4 **Lyady**, Rus.
43/P3 **Lyapin** (riv.), Rus.
20/J3 **Lyaskelya**, Rus.
39/J1 **Lyaskovets**, Bul.
41/G4 **Lyaskovets**, Bul.
20/F2 **Lycksele**, Swe.
42/C2 **Lycksele**, Swe.
25/G5 **Lydd**, Eng,UK
32/D1 **Lydd**, Eng,UK
83/Y **Lyddan** (isl.), Ant.
81/E2 **Lydenburg**, SAfr.
24/D3 **Lydney**, Eng,UK
90/F5 **Lyman**, Wy,US
92/E2 **Lyman**, Wy,US
24/C5 **Lyme** (bay), Eng,UK
32/B1 **Lyme** (bay), Eng,UK
24/D5 **Lyme Regis**, Eng,UK
25/E5 **Lymington**, Eng,UK
23/F5 **Lymm**, Eng,UK
27/L1 **Łyna** (riv.), Pol.
22/D5 **Lynas** (pt.), Wal,UK
89/L4 **Lynchburg**, Va,US
94/E4 **Lynchburg**, Va,US
97/J2 **Lynchburg**, Va,US
72/A2 **Lynd** (riv.), Austl.
70/F6 **Lyndhurst**, Austl.
25/E5 **Lyndhurst**, Eng,UK
101/F2 **Lyndon B. Johnson Nat'l Hist. Park**, Tx,US
23/F1 **Lyne** (riv.), Eng,UK
20/G1 **Lyngen** (fjord), Nor.
89/M3 **Lynn**, Ma,US
95/G3 **Lynn**, Ma,US
97/G4 **Lynn Haven**, Fl,US
86/F3 **Lynn Lake**, Mb,Can
99/C2 **Lynnwood**, Wa,US
24/C4 **Lynton**, Eng,UK
86/F2 **Lynx** (lake), NW,Can
18/D4 **Lyon**, Fr.
32/F4 **Lyon**, Fr.
36/A6 **Lyon**, Fr.
93/H3 **Lyons**, Ks,US
96/D2 **Lyons**, Ks,US
99/P14 **Lyons**, Wi,US
24/C4 **Lype** (hill), Eng,UK
68/E5 **Lyra** (reef), PNG
32/E1 **Lys** (riv.), Belg., Fr.
30/B2 **Lys** (riv.), Fr.
27/K4 **Lysá** (peak), Czh.
42/E5 **Lysaya, Gora** (hill), Bela.
27/L3 **Łysica** (peak), Pol.
30/C2 **Lys-lez-Lannoy**, Fr.
36/D3 **Lyss**, Swi.
19/J3 **Lys'va**, Rus.
43/N4 **Lys'va**, Rus.
46/F4 **Lys'va**, Rus.
24/D5 **Lytchett Matravers**, Eng,UK
23/E4 **Lytham Saint Anne's**, Eng,UK
43/X9 **Lytkarino**, Rus.
101/F2 **Lytle**, Tx,US
90/C3 **Lytton**, BC,Can
43/X9 **Lyubertsy**, Rus.
44/F1 **Lyubertsy**, Rus.
39/K2 **Lyubimets**, Bul.
41/H5 **Lyubimets**, Bul.
43/X9 **Lyublino**, Rus.
27/N3 **Lyuboml'**, Ukr.
44/E2 **Lyubotin**, Ukr.
44/E1 **Lyudinovo**, Rus.
24/C3 **Lywd** (riv.), Wal,UK

M

65/C1 **Ma** (riv.), Laos, Viet.
60/E4 **Ma** (riv.), Laos, Viet.
49/D3 **Ma'alot**, Isr.
52/C2 **Ma'alot**, Isr.
49/D4 **Ma'ān**, Jor.
49/E5 **Ma'ān** (gov.), Jor.
50/C4 **Ma'ān**, Jor.
52/C2 **Ma'ān**, Jor.
77/N1 **Ma'ān**, Jor.
42/F2 **Maanselkä** (mts.), Fin.
20/H1 **Maanselklä** (mts.), Fin.
59/D5 **Ma'anshan**, China
61/H2 **Ma'anshan**, China
28/C6 **Maarheeze**, Neth.
49/E2 **Ma'arrat an Nu'mān**, Syria
50/D3 **Ma'arrat an Nu'mān**, Syria
52/C1 **Ma'arrat an Nu'mān**, Syria
28/C4 **Maarssen**, Neth.
31/E1 **Maas** (riv.), Belg.
32/F1 **Maas** (riv.), Belg., Neth.
26/D3 **Maas** (riv.), Belg., Neth.
28/C5 **Maas** (riv.), Neth.
31/E1 **Maas** (riv.), Neth.
28/C6 **Maasbracht**, Neth.
31/E1 **Maasbracht**, Neth.
28/D6 **Maasbree**, Neth.
28/C6 **Maaseik**, Belg.
31/E1 **Maaseik**, Belg.
67/G1 **Maasin**, Phil.
31/E2 **Maasmechelen**, Belg.
28/B5 **Maassluis**, Neth.
26/C3 **Maastricht**, Neth.
31/E2 **Maastricht**, Neth.
32/F1 **Maastricht**, Neth.
49/G6 **Ma'ayan Harod Nat'l Park**, Isr.
82/F5 **Mabalane**, Moz.
63/H2 **Mabian**, China
23/J5 **Mablethorpe**, Eng,UK
80/Q12 **Mabopane**, SAfr.
82/F6 **Maboto**, Moz.
80/C2 **Mabuasehube Game Rsv.**, Bots.
80/D2 **Mabuli**, Bots.
109/B6 **Macá** (peak), Chile
107/K8 **Macaé**, Braz.
108/D2 **Macaé**, Braz.
34/D4 **Macael**, Sp.
107/L5 **Macaíba**, Braz.
34/B3 **Mação**, Port.
63/K3 **Macao** (Macau) (cap.), Macau
68/A2 **Macao** (Macau) (cap.), Macau
48/L7 **Macao** (Macau) (terr.), Port.
68/A2 **Macao** (Macau) (terr.), Port.
107/H3 **Macapá**, Braz.
106/C4 **Macará**, Ecu.
73/B3 **Macarthur**, Austl.
107/L5 **Macau**, Braz.
61/G4 **Macau** (cap.), Macau
61/G4 **Macau** (dpcy.), Port.
63/K3 **Macau** (dpcy.), Port.
63/K3 **Macau** (Macao) (cap.), Macau
68/A2 **Macau** (Macao) (cap.), Macau
48/L7 **Macau** (Macao) (terr.), Port.
68/A2 **Macau** (Macao) (terr.), Port.
68/H7 **Macauley** (isl.), N.Z.
106/D3 **Macaya** (riv.), Col.
103/H2 **Macaya, Pic de** (peak), Haiti
37/E5 **Maccagno**, It.
97/H4 **Macclenny**, Fl,US
23/F5 **Macclesfield**, Eng,UK
23/F5 **Macclesfield** (can.), Eng,UK
80/D3 **Macdhui** (peak), SAfr.
97/H5 **MacDill** (A.F.B.), Fl,US
70/D4 **MacDonald** (lake), Austl.
70/E4 **Macdonnell** (ranges), Austl.
21/D2 **Macdui, Ben** (peak), Sc,UK
34/B1 **Maceda**, Sp.
18/F4 **Macedonia**
39/G2 **Macedonia**
40/E5 **Macedonia**
44/B4 **Macedonia**
39/G2 **Macedonia** (reg.), Gre.
40/F5 **Macedonia** (reg.), Gre.
107/L5 **Maceió**, Braz.
76/D6 **Macenta**, Gui.
33/K5 **Macerata**, It.
38/C1 **Macerata**, It.
40/A4 **Macerata**, It.
83/E **Macey** (peak), Ant.
106/E7 **Machacamarca**, Bol.
80/D3 **Machache** (peak), Les.
108/C2 **Machado**, Braz.
103/H4 **Machado, Ciénaga de** (lake), Col.
80/Q12 **Machadodorp**, SAfr.
77/N8 **Machakos**, Kenya
100/C4 **Machala**, Ecu.
106/B4 **Machalilla Nat'l Park**, Ecu.
82/F5 **Machanga**, Moz.
102/D2 **Machaquilá** (riv.), Guat.
22/D2 **Machars, The** (pen.), Sc,UK
70/G5 **Machattie** (lake), Austl.
82/F5 **Machaze**, Moz.
32/C3 **Machecoul**, Fr.
82/E5 **Machemma** (ruins), SAfr.
24/C3 **Machen**, Wal,UK
54/H5 **Macheng**, China
59/C5 **Macheng**, China
61/G2 **Macheng**, China
95/H2 **Machias**, Me,US
32/B5 **Machichaco** (cape), Sp.
34/D1 **Machichaco** (cape), Sp.
35/V15 **Machico** Madr.,Port.
57/H7 **Machida**, Japan
62/D4 **Machilipatnam**, India
103/H4 **Machiques**, Ven.
93/F4 **Macho** (dry riv.), NM,US
106/D6 **Machu Picchu**, (ruins),Peru
106/F6 **Machupo** (riv.), Bol.
24/C1 **Machynlleth**, Wal,UK
81/F2 **Macia**, Moz.
41/J3 **Măcin**, Rom.
44/D3 **Măcin**, Rom.
76/E4 **Macina** (depr.), Mali
78/D3 **Macina** (reg.), Mali
71/J5 **Macintyre** (riv.), Austl.
73/D1 **Macintyre** (riv.), Austl.
92/E3 **Mack**, Co,US
68/D7 **Mackay**, Austl.
70/D4 **Mackay** (lake), Austl.
71/H4 **Mackay**, Austl.
72/C3 **Mackay**, Austl.
83/E **MacKenzie** (bay), Ant.
72/C3 **Mackenzie** (riv.), Austl.
84/D3 **Mackenzie** (mts.), Can.
84/E3 **Mackenzie** (riv.), Can.
86/D3 **Mackenzie**, BC,Can
90/C2 **Mackenzie**, BC,Can
85/N2 **Mackenzie** (riv.), NW,Can
86/C2 **Mackenzie** (mts.), NW,Can
86/D2 **Mackenzie** (riv.), NW,Can
85/L2 **Mackenzie** (bay), NW,Can, Yk,Can
87/C2 **Mackenzie** (bay), NW,Yk,Can
87/R7 **Mackenzie King** (isl.), NW,Can
94/C2 **Mackinac Island**, Mi,US
94/C2 **Mackinaw City**, Mi,US
90/F2 **Macklin**, Sk,Can
72/B2 **Macknade**, Austl.
73/E1 **Macksville**, Austl.
73/E1 **Maclean**, Austl.
80/E3 **Maclear**, SAfr.
72/F7 **Macleay** (isl.), Austl.
85/L3 **Macmillan** (riv.), Yk,Can
89/H3 **Macomb**, Il,US
91/L5 **Macomb**, Il,US
93/K2 **Macomb**, Il,US
94/B3 **Macomb**, Il,US
99/G6 **Macomb** (co.), Mi,US
38/A2 **Macomer**, It.
93/K4 **Macon** (riv.), Ar, La,US
18/D4 **Mâcon**, Fr.
32/F3 **Mâcon**, Fr.
36/A5 **Mâcon**, Fr.
89/K5 **Macon**, Ga,US
97/H3 **Macon**, Ga,US
99/E7 **Macon** (cr.), Mi,US
93/J3 **Macon**, Mo,US
96/E2 **Macon**, Mo,US
99/E7 **Macon, North Branch** (cr.), Mi,US
22/B1 **Macosquin**, NI,UK
34/C2 **Macotera**, Sp.
17/R8 **Macquarie** (isl.), Austl.
71/H6 **Macquarie** (riv.), Austl.
73/C1 **Macquarie** (riv.), Austl.
73/C4 **Macquarie** (har.), Austl.
73/C4 **Macquarie** (riv.), Austl.
71/G8 **Macquarie** (har.), Austl.
83/D **Mac-Robertson Land** (reg.), Ant.
21/A5 **Macroom**, Ire.
102/D3 **Macuelizo**, Hon.
106/F5 **Macuim** (riv.), Braz.
104/D4 **Macuira Nat'l Park**, Col.
70/F5 **Macumba** (riv.), Austl.
98/E5 **Macungie**, Pa,US
106/D6 **Macusani**, Peru
101/G5 **Macuspana**, Mex.
102/C2 **Macuspana**, Mex.
100/C3 **Macuzari** (res.), Mex.
90/C5 **Mad** (riv.), Ca,US
49/D4 **Ma'dabā**, Jor.
50/C4 **Ma'dabā**, Jor.
52/C2 **Ma'dabā**, Jor.
74/G7 **Madagascar**
81/J10 **Madagascar**
82/K10 **Madagascar**
52/C3 **Madā'in Şāliḩ**, SAr.
76/H3 **Madama**, Niger
39/J2 **Madan**, Bul.
41/G5 **Madan**, Bul.
44/C4 **Madan**, Bul.
62/C5 **Madanapalle**, India
68/D5 **Madang**, PNG
76/H1 **Madanīyīn**, Tun.
76/G5 **Madaoua**, Niger
79/G3 **Madaoua**, Niger
40/D2 **Madaras**, Hun.
62/F3 **Mādārīpur**, Bang.
60/C5 **Madauk**, Burma
63/G4 **Madauk**, Burma
94/E2 **Madawaska** (riv.), On,Can
95/G2 **Madawaska**, Me,US
103/G4 **Madden** (dam), Pan.
35/U15 **Madeira** (isl.)
105/C3 **Madeira** (riv.), Braz.
106/F5 **Madeira** (riv.), Braz.
35/U14 **Madeira** (aut. reg.), Port.
35/U14 **Madeira** (isl.), Port.
74/A1 **Madeira** (isl.), Port.
76/B1 **Madeira** (isl.), Port.
37/G3 **Mädelegabel** (peak), Aus., Ger.
91/L4 **Madelin** (isl.), Wi,US
50/D2 **Maden**, Turk.
37/F3 **Mäder**, Aus.
100/C2 **Madera**, Mex.
92/E5 **Madera**, Mex
103/E4 **Madera** (vol.), Nic.
100/E2 **Madera** (mtn.), Tx,US
62/E2 **Madhipura**, India
62/C3 **Madhya Pradesh** (state), India
106/E6 **Madidi** (riv.), Bol.
80/P12 **Madikwe**, SAfr.
93/H4 **Madill**, Ok,US
96/D3 **Madill**, Ok,US
52/D6 **Madīnat ash Sha'b**, Yem.
82/B1 **Madingo-Kayes**, Congo
97/G3 **Madison**, Al,US
99/L9 **Madison**, Ca,US
97/H4 **Madison**, Fl,US
94/C4 **Madison**, In,US
97/G2 **Madison**, In,US
97/F3 **Madison**, Ms,US
90/F4 **Madison** (riv.), Mt,US
88/D2 **Madison** (riv.), Mt,US
91/J5 **Madison**, Ne,US
93/H2 **Madison**, Ne,US
98/F5 **Madison**, NJ,US
91/J4 **Madison**, SD,US
93/H1 **Madison**, SD,US
89/J3 **Madison** (cap.), Wi,US
91/L5 **Madison** (cap.), Wi,US
93/K2 **Madison** (cap.), Wi,US
94/B3 **Madison** (cap.), Wi,US
94/D4 **Madison**, WV,US
97/H2 **Madison**, WV,US
99/F6 **Madison Heights**, Mi,US
94/C4 **Madisonville**, Ky,US
97/G2 **Madisonville**, Ky,US
101/G2 **Madisonville**, Tx,US
93/J5 **Madisonville**, Tx,US
96/E4 **Madisonville**, Tx,US
66/D5 **Madiun**, Indo.
54/D5 **Madoi**, China
26/D4 **Madon** (riv.), Fr.
33/G2 **Madon** (riv.), Fr.
36/C1 **Madon** (riv.), Fr.
42/E4 **Madona**, Lat.
38/C4 **Madonie Nebrodi** (mts.), It.
37/G5 **Madonna di Campiglio**, It.
53/G5 **Madrakah, Ra's al** (pt.), Oman
62/D5 **Madras**, India
90/C4 **Madras**, Or,US
101/F3 **Madre** (bay), Mex.
101/F3 **Madre** (lag.), Tx,US
105/C4 **Madre de Dios** (riv.), Bol., Peru
101/E5 **Madre del Sur, Sierra** (mts.), Mex.
102/B2 **Madre del Sur, Sierra** (mts.), Mex.
100/C2 **Madre Occidental, Sierra** (mts.), Mex.
84/G7 **Madre Occidental, Sierra** (mts.), Mex.
88/F6 **Madre Oriental** (mts.), Mex.
96/C5 **Madre Oriental** (mts.), Mex
101/E3 **Madre Oriental, Sierra** (mts.), Mex.
101/L6 **Madre Oriental, Sierra** (mts.), Mex.
102/B1 **Madre Oriental, Sierra** (mts.), Mex.
84/G7 **Madre Oriental, Sierra** (mts.), Mex.
32/E5 **Madrès** (mtn.), Fr.
35/G1 **Madrès** (mtn.), Fr.
102/C3 **Madre, Sierra** (mts.), Mex.
18/C4 **Madrid** (cap.), Sp.
34/C2 **Madrid** (aut. comm.), Sp.
34/D2 **Madrid** (cap.), Sp.
35/N8 **Madrid** (aut. comm.), Sp.
35/N9 **Madrid** (cap.), Sp.
34/D3 **Madridejos**, Sp.
34/C2 **Madrigal de las Altas Torres**, Sp.
34/C3 **Madrigalejo**, Sp.
37/F4 **Madrisahorn** (peak), Swi.
34/C3 **Madroñera**, Sp.
62/D4 **Madugula**, India
64/F3 **Madukkkarai**, India
48/L10 **Madura** (isl.), Indo.
62/C6 **Madurai**, India
64/G4 **Madurai**, India
39/J2 **Madzharovo**, Bul.
41/G5 **Madzharovo**, Bul.
55/M4 **Maebashi**, Japan
57/F2 **Maebashi**, Japan
65/C2 **Mae Charim**, Thai.
60/C5 **Mae Hong Son**, Thai.
63/G4 **Mae Hong Son**, Thai.
65/B2 **Mae Hong Son**, Thai.
35/F2 **Maella**, Sp.
60/C5 **Mae Ping Nat'l Park**, Thai.
65/B2 **Mae Ping Nat'l Park**, Thai.
58/E4 **Maep'o**, SKor.
60/C5 **Mae Sot**, Thai.
63/G4 **Mae Sot**, Thai.
24/C3 **Maesteg**, Wal,UK
103/G2 **Maestra, Sierra** (range), Cuba
60/C5 **Mae Tho** (peak), Thai.
63/G4 **Mae Tho** (peak), Thai.
65/B2 **Mae Tho** (peak), Thai.
81/H7 **Maevatanana**, Madg.
68/F6 **Maewo** (isl.), Van.
60/C5 **Mae Ya** (mtn.), Thai.
65/B2 **Mae Ya** (mtn.), Thai.
80/D3 **Mafeteng**, Les.
73/C3 **Maffra**, Austl.
75/G5 **Mafia** (isl.), Tanz.
82/H2 **Mafia** (isl.), Tanz.
80/D2 **Mafikeng**, SAfr.
80/N12 **Mafikeng**, SAfr.
82/E6 **Mafikeng**, SAfr.
78/C4 **Mafou** (riv.), Gui.
108/B3 **Mafra**, Braz.
109/G2 **Mafra**, Braz.
34/A3 **Mafra**, Port.
35/P10 **Mafra**, Port.
47/R4 **Magadan**, Rus.
77/N8 **Magadi**, Kenya
82/G1 **Magadi**, Kenya
37/E5 **Magadino**, Swi.
80/P12 **Magalies Berg** (range), SAfr.
103/H4 **Magangué**, Col.
106/D2 **Magangué**, Col.
67/F2 **Maganoy**, Phil.
76/G5 **Magaria**, Niger
79/H3 **Magaria**, Niger
93/J4 **Magazine** (peak), Ar,US
96/E3 **Magazine** (peak), Ar,US
47/N4 **Magdagachi**, Rus.
55/K1 **Magdagachi**, Rus.
87/K4 **Magdalen** (isls.), Qu,Can
89/P2 **Magdalen** (isls.), Qu,Can
95/J2 **Magdalen** (isls.), Qu,Can
106/F6 **Magdalena**, Bol.
103/H4 **Magdalena** (dept.), Col.
103/H4 **Magdalena** (riv.), Col.
105/B2 **Magdalena** (riv.), Col.
106/D2 **Magdalena** (riv.), Col.
67/E3 **Magdalena** (peak), Malay.
100/C2 **Magdalena**, Mex.
100/E4 **Magdalena**, Mex.
92/E5 **Magdalena de Kino**, Mex
18/E3 **Magdeburg**, Ger.
26/F2 **Magdeburg**, Ger.
48/B4 **Magdeburg**, Ger.
26/F2 **Magdeburger Börde** (plain), Ger.
71/J3 **Magdelaine** (cays), Austl.
36/D2 **Magden**, Swi.
97/F4 **Magee**, Ms,US
22/C2 **Magee, Island** (pen.), NI,UK
66/C5 **Magelang**, Indo.
105/B8 **Magellan** (str.), Arg., Chile
109/C7 **Magellan** (str.), Chile
70/B6 **Magenta** (lake), Austl.
30/C5 **Magenta**, Fr.
20/H1 **Magerøya** (isl.), Nor.
37/E5 **Maggia**, Swi.
37/E5 **Maggia** (riv.), Swi.
33/H4 **Maggiorasca** (peak), It.
33/K5 **Maggiore** (peak), It.
33/H4 **Maggiore** (lake), It., Swi.
37/E6 **Maggiore** (lake), It., Swi.
50/B4 **Maghāghah**, Egypt
52/B3 **Maghāghah**, Egypt
77/M2 **Maghāghah**, Egypt
22/B2 **Maghera**, NI,UK
22/B2 **Magherafelt**, NI,UK
22/B2 **Magherafelt** (dist.), NI,UK
75/W18 **Maghīla** (peak), Tun.
38/A5 **Maghīla, Jabal** (peak), Tun.
75/P13 **Maghnia**, Alg.
23/F4 **Maghull**, Eng,UK
22/B1 **Magilligan**, NI,UK
22/B1 **Magilligan** (pt.), NI,UK
40/D3 **Maglaj**, Bosn.
39/F1 **Maglić** (peak), Yugo.
40/D4 **Maglić** (peak), Yugo.
39/F2 **Maglie**, It.
32/D3 **Magnac Laval**, Fr.
60/A4 **Magnāma**, Bang.
94/D2 **Magnetawan** (riv.), On,Can
72/B2 **Magnetic** (pass.), Austl.
72/B2 **Magnetic I. Nat'l Park**, Austl.
43/N5 **Magnitogorsk**, Rus.
45/L1 **Magnitogorsk**, Rus.
46/F4 **Magnitogorsk**, Rus.
89/H5 **Magnolia**, Ar,US
93/J4 **Magnolia**, Ar,US
96/E3 **Magnolia**, Ar,US
30/A5 **Magny-en-Vexin**, Fr.
19/S10 **Magny-les-Hameaux**, Fr.
82/F4 **Mágoè**, Moz.
95/F2 **Magog**, Qu,Can
77/N6 **Mago Nat'l Park**, Eth.
24/D3 **Magor**, Wal,UK
95/H1 **Magpie** (lake), Qu,Can
95/H1 **Magpie** (riv.), Qu,Can
95/H1 **Magpie Ouest** (riv.), Qu,Can
65/D1 **Maguan**, China
81/F2 **Magude**, Moz.
82/F6 **Magude**, Moz.
74/E4 **Maguerite** (peak), Zaire
77/L7 **Maguerite** (peak), Zaire
60/B4 **Magwe**, Burma
60/B5 **Magwe** (div.), Burma
63/F3 **Magwe**, Burma
63/F4 **Magwe** (div.), Burma
63/F3 **Magyichaung**, Burma
46/E6 **Mahābād**, Iran
51/F2 **Mahābād**, Iran
52/E1 **Mahābād**, Iran
81/H7 **Mahaboboka**, Madg.
53/K5 **Mahād**, India
62/B4 **Mahād**, India
69/X15 **Mahaena**, FrPol.
106/G2 **Mahaica**, Guy.
81/H6 **Mahajamba** (bay), Madg.
81/H7 **Mahajamba** (riv.), Madg.
75/G6 **Mahajanga**, Madg.
81/H6 **Mahajanga** (prov.), Madg.
81/H7 **Mahajilo** (riv.), Madg.
67/E3 **Mahakam** (riv.), Indo.
82/E5 **Mahalapye**, Bots.
51/G3 **Maḩallāt**, Iran
52/F2 **Maḩallāt**, Iran
51/J4 **Māhān**, Iran
53/G2 **Māhān**, Iran
62/D3 **Mahānadī** (riv.), India
78/D4 **Mahandiabani** (riv.), IvC.
81/J7 **Mahanoro**, Madg.
62/C2 **Mahārajpur**, India

154

Mahār – Maral

62/B4 **Mahārāshtra** (state), India
62/D3 **Mahāsamund**, India
63/H4 **Maha Sarakham**, Thai.
65/C2 **Maha Sarakham**, Thai.
81/H7 **Mahavavy** (riv.), Madg.
64/H4 **Mahaweli** (riv.), SrL.
60/E5 **Mahaxai**, Laos
63/J4 **Mahaxai**, Laos
81/H8 **Mahazoarivo**, Madg.
81/H7 **Mahazoma**, Madg.
62/C4 **Mahbubnagar**, India
53/L2 **Mahe**, India
64/E3 **Mahe**, India
75/H5 **Mahé** (isl.), Sey.
81/S15 **Mahébourg**, Mrts.
71/S10 **Mahia** (pen.), NZ
81/H7 **Mahitsy**, Madg.
60/B4 **Mahlaing**, Burma
63/G3 **Mahlaing**, Burma
36/D1 **Mahlberg**, Ger.
90/D5 **Mahleur** (lake), Or,US
90/D5 **Mahleur** (riv.), Or,US
75/V18 **Mahmel** (peak), Alg.
76/G1 **Mahmel** (peak), Alg.
44/D5 **Mahmudiye**, Turk.
50/B2 **Mahmudiye**, Turk.
62/C2 **Mahoba**, India
35/H3 **Mahón**, Sp.
88/U10 **Mahukona**, Hi,US
53/K4 **Mahuva**, India
62/B3 **Mahuva**, India
98/F4 **Mahwah**, NJ,US
34/A2 **Maia**, Port.
72/E6 **Maiala Nat'l Park**, Austl.
35/F2 **Maials**, Sp.
68/G4 **Maiana** (atoll), Kiri.
69/W15 **Maiao** (isl.), FrPol.
103/H4 **Maicao**, Col.
106/D1 **Maicao**, Col.
36/C3 **Maîche**, Fr.
107/H3 **Maicuru** (riv.), Braz.
25/F3 **Maidenhead**, Eng,UK
24/D5 **Maiden Newton**, Eng,UK
22/D1 **Maidens**, Sc,UK
99/G7 **Maidstone**, On,Can
25/G4 **Maidstone**, Eng,UK
76/H5 **Maiduguri**, Nga.
37/F3 **Maienfeld**, Swi.
30/B4 **Maignelay-Montigny**, Fr.
21/A4 **Maigue** (riv.), Ire.
62/D3 **Maihar**, India
56/E3 **Maihara**, Japan
57/M9 **Maihara**, Japan
77/L8 **Maiko Nat'l Park**, Zaire
82/E1 **Maiko Nat'l Park**, Zaire
88/V13 **Maili**, Hi,US
30/D6 **Mailly-le-Camp**, Fr.
53/K3 **Mailsi**, Pak.
26/E4 **Main** (riv.), Ger.
33/H2 **Main** (riv.), Ger.
22/B2 **Main** (riv.), NI,UK
70/G6 **Main Barrier** (range), Austl.
19/U11 **Maincy**, Fr.
77/J8 **Mai-Ndombe** (lake), Zaire
82/C1 **Mai-Ndombe** (lake), Zaire
87/K4 **Maine** (gulf), Can., US
95/G3 **Maine** (gulf), Can., US
32/C2 **Maine** (hills), Fr.
21/H7 **Maine** (riv.), Ire.
87/K4 **Maine** (state), US
89/N2 **Maine** (state), US
95/G2 **Maine** (state), US
76/H5 **Maïné-Soroa**, Niger
57/G3 **Maingnyaung**, Burma
54/C6 **Mainling**, China
60/B2 **Mainling**, China
63/F2 **Mainling**, China
72/C5 **Main Range Nat'l Park**, Austl.
81/H7 **Maintirano**, Madg.
26/E4 **Mainz**, Ger.
31/H3 **Mainz**, Ger.
33/H2 **Mainz**, Ger.
74/K10 **Maio** (isl.), CpV.
104/E5 **Maiquetía**, Ven.
33/G4 **Maira** (riv.), It.
37/H1 **Maisach**, Ger.
27/N1 **Maišiagala**, Lith.
19/T10 **Maisons-Alfort**, Fr.
19/S10 **Maisons-Laffitte**, Fr.
71/J6 **Maitland**, Austl.
73/D2 **Maitland**, Austl.
94/D3 **Maitland** (riv.), On,Can
103/F3 **Maiz Grande** (isl.), Nic.
63/F2 **Maizhokunggar**, China
31/F5 **Maizières-lès-Metz**, Fr.
103/F3 **Maiz Pequeña** (isl.), Nic.
56/D3 **Maizuru**, Japan
35/N9 **Majadahonda**, Sp.
39/G2 **Maja e Zezë** (peak), Alb.
40/E5 **Maja e Zezë** (peak), Alb.
103/H4 **Majagual**, Col.
75/W17 **Majardah** (mts.), Alg., Tun.
38/A4 **Majardah** (riv.), Tun.
75/W17 **Majardah** (riv.), Tun.
38/A4 **Majāz Al Bāb**, Tun.
40/E3 **Majdanpek**, Yugo.
76/J2 **Majdūl**, Libya
67/E4 **Majene**, Indo.
77/N6 **Majī**, Eth.
59/D3 **Majia** (riv.), China
37/F5 **Majolapass** (pass), Swi.
18/D5 **Majorca** (isl.), Sp.
35/G3 **Majorca** (Mallorca) (isl.), Sp.
40/D3 **Majur**, Yugo.
68/G4 **Majuro** (atoll), Mrsh.
76/H8 **Makabana**, Congo
82/B1 **Makabana**, Congo
88/V13 **Makaha**, Hi,US
88/V13 **Makakilo City**, Hi,US
62/E2 **Makālu** (mtn.), Nepal
80/Q12 **Makapaanstad**, SAfr.
88/W13 **Makapuu** (pt.), Hi,US
47/Q5 **Makarov**, Rus.
55/N2 **Makarov**, Rus.
38/E1 **Makarska**, Cro.
40/C4 **Makarska**, Cro.
48/L10 **Makassar** (str.), Indo.
66/E4 **Makassar** (str.), Indo.
68/A5 **Makassar** (str.), Indo.
46/F5 **Makat**, Kaz.
69/L6 **Makatea** (isl.), FrPol.
63/G2 **Makaw**, Burma
88/T10 **Makawao**, Hi,US
81/H8 **Makay** (massif), Madg.
69/L6 **Makemo** (atoll), FrPol.
88/T10 **Makena**, Hi,US
76/C6 **Makeni**, SLeo.
78/B4 **Makeni**, SLeo.
19/G4 **Makeyevka**, Ukr.
44/F2 **Makeyevka**, Ukr.
82/D5 **Makgadikgadi Pans** (salt pans), Bots.
19/H4 **Makhachkala**, Rus.
45/H4 **Makhachkala**, Rus.
46/E5 **Makhachkala**, Rus.
64/B2 **Makhdūmpur**, Pak.
51/F4 **Makhfar al Busayyah**, Iraq
52/E2 **Makhfar al Busayyah**, Iraq
51/E3 **Makhmūr**, Iraq
50/D4 **Makhrūq** (dry riv.), Jor.
49/E4 **Makhrūq, Wādī al** (riv.), Jor.
67/G3 **Makian** (isl.), Indo.
68/G4 **Makin** (atoll), Kiri.
46/H4 **Makinsk**, Kaz.
52/C4 **Makkah** (Mecca), SAr.
77/N3 **Makkah** (Mecca), SAr.
87/L3 **Makkovik**, Nf,Can
40/E2 **Makó**, Hun.
76/H7 **Makokou**, Gabon
27/L2 **Maków Mazowiecki**, Pol.
39/H3 **Makrakómi**, Gre.
53/G4 **Makran** (coast), Iran, Pak.
53/H3 **Makran** (reg.), Iran, Pak.
53/K3 **Makrāna**, India
39/H2 **Makrokhórion**, Gre.
39/K2 **Maksutlu**, Turk.
38/A5 **Makthar**, Tun.
45/H5 **Mākū**, Iran
51/F2 **Mākū**, Iran
82/F2 **Makumbako**, Tanz.
55/L5 **Makurazaki**, Japan
56/B5 **Makurazaki**, Japan
76/G6 **Makurdi**, Nga.
85/E5 **Makushin** (vol.), Ak,US
102/E4 **Mala** (pt.), CR
103/G5 **Mala** (pt.), Pan.
106/C6 **Mala**, Peru
23/F4 **Mala**, Swe.
62/B5 **Malabar** (coast), India
64/E3 **Malabar Coast** (reg.), India
34/C5 **Malabata** (pt.), Mor.
75/M13 **Malabata** (pt.), Mor.
76/G7 **Malabo** (cap.), EqG.
108/D1 **Malacacheta**, Braz.
48/J9 **Malacca** (str.), Asia
63/G6 **Malacca** (str.), Asia
66/A2 **Malacca** (str.), Indo.
65/B5 **Malacca** (str.), Malay., Thai.
27/J4 **Malacky**, Slvk.
90/E5 **Malad City**, Id,US
92/D2 **Malad City**, Id,US
37/F4 **Maladers**, Swi.
18/C5 **Málaga**, Sp.
34/C4 **Málaga**, Sp.
34/D3 **Malagón**, Sp.
103/G1 **Malagueta** (bay), Cuba
22/B5 **Malahide**, Ire.
81/H8 **Malaimbandy**, Madg.
68/F5 **Malaita** (isl.), Sol.
77/M6 **Malakāl**, Sudan
62/D4 **Malakangiri**, India
64/B1 **Malakwāl**, Pak.
103/H4 **Malambo**, Col.
66/D5 **Malang**, Indo.
82/C2 **Malange**, Ang.
37/F4 **Malans**, Swi.
76/F5 **Malanville**, Ben.
64/F3 **Malappuram**, India
109/C4 **Malargüe**, Arg.
94/E1 **Malartic**, Qu,Can
67/E5 **Malasoro** (pt.), Indo.
50/D2 **Malatya**, Turk.
50/D2 **Malatya** (prov.), Turk.
64/C2 **Malaut**, India
74/F6 **Malawi**
82/F3 **Malawi**
65/B5 **Malay** (pen.), Malay., Thai.
66/B2 **Malay** (pen.), Malay., Thai.
63/G6 **Malay** (pen.), Malay., Thai.
48/K9 **Malaya** (reg.), Malay.
66/B3 **Malaya** (reg.), Malay.
42/G4 **Malaya Vishera**, Rus.
46/E6 **Malāyer**, Iran
51/G3 **Malāyer**, Iran
52/E2 **Malāyer**, Iran
48/K9 **Malaysia**
63/H6 **Malaysia**
66/C2 **Malaysia**
68/A4 **Malaysia**
43/L2 **Malazemel'skaya** (tundra), Rus.
50/E2 **Malazgirt**, Turk.
95/G2 **Malbaie** (riv.), Qu,Can
79/G3 **Malbaza-Usine**, Niger
27/K1 **Malbork**, Pol.
42/C5 **Malbork**, Pol.
32/D5 **Malcaras, Pic de** (peak), Fr.
35/F1 **Malcaras, Pic de** (peak), Fr.
26/G2 **Malchin**, Ger.
54/C2 **Malchin**, Mong.
28/A6 **Maldegem**, Belg.
30/C1 **Maldegem**, Belg.
69/K5 **Malden** (isl.), Kiri.
93/K3 **Malden**, Mo,US
94/B4 **Malden**, Mo,US
97/F2 **Malden**, Mo,US
62/B6 **Maldive** (isls.), Mald.
48/F9 **Maldives**
62/B6 **Maldives**
73/C3 **Maldon**, Austl.
25/G3 **Maldon**, Eng,UK
109/F3 **Maldonado**, Uru.
39/H4 **Maléa, Ákra** (cape), Gre.
53/K4 **Mālegaon**, India
62/B3 **Mālegaon**, India
68/F6 **Malekula** (isl.), Van.
32/D4 **Malemort-sur-Corrèze**, Fr.
26/F1 **Malente**, Ger.
72/D4 **Maleny**, Austl.
53/L2 **Māler Kotla**, India
64/C2 **Māler Kotla**, India
39/H3 **Malesína**, Gre.
38/D3 **Malfa**, It.
45/H4 **Malgobek**, Rus.
35/G2 **Malgrat de Mar**, Sp.
77/L4 **Malha Wells**, Sudan
86/E4 **Malheur** (lake), Or,US
92/C2 **Malheur** (lake), Or,US
81/S14 **Malheureux** (cape), Mrts.
74/B3 **Mali**
76/E4 **Mali**
78/E2 **Mali**
60/C3 **Mali** (riv.), Burma
63/G2 **Mali** (riv.), Burma
65/B3 **Mali** (isl.), Burma
39/J5 **Mália**, Gre.
54/F4 **Malian** (riv.), China
98/B2 **Malibu**, Ca,US
77/L4 **Malik** (wadi), Sudan
33/L4 **Mali Lošinj**, Cro.
40/B3 **Mali Lošinj**, Cro.
22/A1 **Malin**, Ire.
44/D2 **Malin**, Ukr.
67/E3 **Malinau**, Indo.
67/F2 **Malindang** (mt.), Phil.
82/H1 **Malindi**, Kenya
30/D1 **Malines** (Mechelen), Belg.
59/C3 **Maling Guan** (pass), China
21/B3 **Malin Head** (pt.), Ire.
81/H8 **Malio** (riv.), Madg.
65/D1 **Malipo**, China
53/J4 **Malīr Cantonment**, Pak.
62/A3 **Malīr Cantonment**, Pak.
67/G2 **Malita**, Phil.
77/P7 **Malka Mari Nat'l Park**, Kenya
41/H5 **Malkara**, Turk.
50/A1 **Malkara**, Turk.
41/H5 **Malko Tŭrnovo**, Bul.
44/C4 **Malko Tŭrnovo**, Bul.
50/A1 **Malko Tŭrnovo**, Bul.
73/D3 **Mallacoota**, Austl.
76/H3 **Mallammaduri**, Nga.
75/W17 **Mallāq, Wādī** (riv.), Tun.
50/B5 **Mallawī**, Egypt
52/B3 **Mallawī**, Egypt
77/M2 **Mallawī**, Egypt
73/B2 **Mallee Cliffs Nat'l Park**, Austl.
34/E2 **Mallén**, Sp.
36/D3 **Malleray**, Swi.
37/F5 **Mallero** (riv.), It.
37/G4 **Malles** (Mals), It.
35/G3 **Mallorca** (Majorca) (isl.), Sp.
21/A4 **Mallow**, Ire.
20/G2 **Malmberget**, Swe.
42/D2 **Malmberget**, Swe.
26/D3 **Malmédy**, Belg.
31/F3 **Malmédy**, Belg.
32/G1 **Malmédy**, Belg.
80/B4 **Malmesbury**, SAfr.
80/L10 **Malmesbury**, SAfr.
24/D3 **Malmesbury**, Eng,UK
18/E3 **Malmö**, Swe.
20/E5 **Malmö**, Swe.
26/G1 **Malmö**, Swe.
20/E5 **Malmöhus** (co.), Swe.
27/G1 **Malmöhus** (co.), Swe.
104/D4 **Malmok** (peak), NAnt.
43/L4 **Malmyzh**, Rus.
107/H5 **Maloca**, Braz.
68/G4 **Maloelap** (atoll), Mrsh.
94/F2 **Malone**, NY,US
60/D3 **Malong**, China
63/H2 **Malong**, China
37/G5 **Malonno**, It.
27/L3 **Małopolska** (upland), Pol.
44/C2 **Malorita**, Bela.
20/C3 **Måløy**, Nor.
44/F1 **Maloyaroslavets**, Rus.
34/B3 **Malpartida de Cáceres**, Sp.
34/B3 **Malpartida de Plasencia**, Sp.
23/F5 **Malpas**, Eng,UK
105/A2 **Malpelo** (isl.), Col.
106/B3 **Malpelo** (isl.), Col.
34/A1 **Malpica**, Sp.
27/H4 **Malše** (riv.), Czh.
37/G4 **Mals** (Malles), It.
18/E5 **Malta**
38/D5 **Malta**
76/J1 **Malta**
38/D4 **Malta** (chan.)
38/D5 **Malta** (isl.), Malta
88/E2 **Malta**, Mt,US
90/G3 **Malta**, Mt,US
80/B2 **Maltahöhe**, Namb.
82/C5 **Maltahöhe**, Namb.
23/G2 **Maltby**, Eng,UK
23/G5 **Maltby**, Eng,UK
50/B1 **Maltepe**, Turk.
36/E3 **Malters**, Swi.
95/Q8 **Malton**, On,Can
23/H3 **Malton**, Eng,UK
82/C1 **Maluku**, Zaire
20/E3 **Malung**, Swe.
37/E5 **Malvaglia**, Swi.
53/K5 **Malvan**, India
62/B4 **Malvan**, India
35/P10 **Malveira**, Port.
73/G5 **Malvern**, Austl.
93/J4 **Malvern**, Ar,US
96/E3 **Malvern**, Ar,US
98/E5 **Malvern**, Pa,US
24/D2 **Malvern** (Great Malvern), Eng,UK
109/D7 **Malvinas** (Falkland) (isls.), UK
45/J2 **Malyy Uzen'** (riv.), Kaz.
54/D1 **Malyy Yenisey** (riv.), Rus.
31/F6 **Malzéville**, Fr.
107/L5 **Mamanguape**, Braz.
49/C4 **Mamarr al Jady** (Gidi) (pass), Egypt
49/C4 **Mamarr Mitlah** (Mitla) (pass), Egypt
50/C4 **Mamarr Mitlah** (Mitla) (pass), Egypt
82/E4 **Mamba**, Zam.
77/L7 **Mambasa**, Zaire
67/J4 **Mamberamo** (riv.), Indo.
76/J6 **Mambéré** (riv.), CAfr.
50/D2 **Mambij**, Syria
52/C1 **Mambij**, Syria
67/F1 **Mamburao**, Phil.
51/G1 **Mamedkala**, Rus.
31/F4 **Mamer**, Lux.
32/D2 **Mamers**, Fr.
30/B2 **Mametz**, Fr.
79/H5 **Mamfé**, Camr.
36/C3 **Mamirolle**, Fr.
46/G4 **Mamlyutka**, Kaz.
100/C1 **Mammoth**, Az,US
89/J4 **Mammoth Cave Nat'l Park**, Ky,US
94/C4 **Mammoth Cave Nat'l Park**, Ky,US
97/G2 **Mammoth Cave Nat'l Park**, Ky,US
93/K3 **Mammoth Spring**, Ar,US
97/F2 **Mammoth Spring**, Ar,US
27/K1 **Mamonovo**, Rus.
105/C4 **Mamoré** (riv.), Bol.
76/C5 **Mamou**, Gui.
81/H7 **Mampikony**, Madg.
76/E6 **Mampong**, Gha.
79/E5 **Mampong**, Gha.
27/L1 **Mamry** (lake), Pol.
67/E4 **Mamuju**, Indo.
82/D5 **Mamuno**, Bots.
107/G4 **Mamuri** (riv.), Braz.
59/C5 **Man** (riv.), China
76/D6 **Man**, IvC.
78/D5 **Man**, IvC.
102/D3 **Manabique, Punta de** (pt.), Hon.
106/F4 **Manacapuru**, Braz.
24/A6 **Manacle** (pt.), UK
35/G3 **Manacor**, Sp.
67/F3 **Manado**, Indo.
68/B4 **Manado**, Indo.
102/E3 **Managua** (cap.), Nic.
102/E3 **Managua** (lake), Nic.
81/J7 **Manakambahiny**, Madg.
75/G7 **Manakara**, Madg.
81/J8 **Manakara**, Madg.
52/D5 **Manākhah**, Yem.
53/L2 **Manāli**, India
77/R2 **Manama** (cap.), Bahr.
52/F3 **Manama** (Al Manāmah) (cap.), Bahr.
64/G4 **Mānāmadurai**, India
81/H7 **Manambaho** (riv.), Madg.
81/H7 **Manambolo** (riv.), Madg.
81/H8 **Manantanana** (riv.), Madg.
75/G6 **Mananara**, Madg.
81/H8 **Mananara** (riv.), Madg.
81/J7 **Mananara**, Madg.
81/J7 **Mananara** (riv.), Madg.
75/G7 **Mananjary**, Madg.
81/H8 **Mananjary** (riv.), Madg.
81/J8 **Mananjary**, Madg.
64/G3 **Manappārai**, India
46/J5 **Manas**, China
46/J5 **Manas** (riv.), China
62/D2 **Manāslu** (mtn.), Nepal
93/F3 **Manassa**, Co,US
96/B2 **Manassa**, Co,US
94/E4 **Manassas**, Va,US
97/J2 **Manassas**, Va,US
39/G1 **Manastir Dečani**, Yugo.
39/G1 **Manastir Gračanica**, Yugo.
39/G1 **Manastir Sopoćani**, Yugo.
57/H7 **Manatsuru**, Japan
63/G4 **Manaung**, Burma
106/F4 **Manaus**, Braz.
49/B1 **Manavgat**, Turk.
50/B2 **Manavgat**, Turk.
52/B1 **Manavgat**, Turk.
91/H2 **Manawan** (lake), Sk,Can
57/H7 **Manazuru-misaki** (cape), Japan
22/D3 **Man, Calf of** (isl.), IM,UK
36/B2 **Mance** (riv.), Fr.
34/D4 **Mancha Real**, Sp.
59/C3 **Mancheng**, China
59/G7 **Mancheng**, China
62/C4 **Mancherāl**, India
72/E6 **Manchester** (lake), Austl.
18/C3 **Manchester**, Eng,UK
23/F5 **Manchester**, Eng,UK
94/D4 **Manchester**, Ky,US
87/J4 **Manchester**, NH,US
89/M3 **Manchester**, NH,US
95/G3 **Manchester**, NH,US
97/G3 **Manchester**, Tn,US
99/B2 **Manchester**, Wa,US
47/N5 **Manchuria** (reg.), China
55/J3 **Manchuria** (reg.), China
58/B2 **Manchuria** (reg.), China
59/E1 **Manchuria** (reg.), China
31/E5 **Mancieulles**, Fr.
46/F7 **Mand** (riv.), Iran
51/H4 **Mand** (riv.), Iran
52/F3 **Mand** (riv.), Iran
82/F3 **Manda**, Tanz.
81/H8 **Mandabe**, Madg.
108/B2 **Mandaguari**, Braz.
20/C4 **Mandal**, Nor.
67/K4 **Mandala** (peak), Indo.
60/B4 **Mandalay** (div.), Burma
60/C4 **Mandalay**, Burma
63/G3 **Mandalay**, Burma
63/G3 **Mandalay** (div.), Burma
65/A1 **Mandalay** (div.), Burma
65/B1 **Mandalay**, Burma
60/C4 **Mandalay Palace**, Burma
65/B1 **Mandalay Palace**, Burma
47/L5 **Mandalgovĭ**, Mong.
51/F3 **Mandalī**, Iraq
52/E2 **Mandalī**, Iraq
54/E3 **Mandal-Ovoo**, Mong.
86/F4 **Mandan**, ND,US
88/F2 **Mandan**, ND,US
91/H4 **Mandan**, ND,US
77/J6 **Manda Nat'l Park**, Chad
59/D4 **Mandang Shan** (mtn.), China
67/F5 **Mandasavu** (peak), Indo.
77/P5 **Mandeb** (str.), Afr., Asia
33/H4 **Mandello del Lario**, It.
37/F6 **Mandello del Lario**, It.
77/P7 **Mandera**, Kenya
31/F3 **Manderscheid**, Ger.
36/C3 **Mandeure**, Fr.
103/G2 **Mandeville**, Jam.
53/L2 **Mandi**, India
64/D2 **Mandi**, India
82/F4 **Mandié**, Moz.
67/G4 **Mandiola** (isl.), Indo.
64/B2 **Mandi Sādiqganj**, Pak.
62/D3 **Mandla**, India
26/E1 **Mandø** (isl.), Den.
27/M4 **Mándok**, Hun.
40/F1 **Mándok**, Hun.
81/H7 **Mandoto**, Madg.
39/H3 **Mandoúdhion**, Gre.
39/L6 **Mándra**, Gre.
81/H9 **Mandrare** (riv.), Madg.
81/J6 **Mandritsara**, Madg.
53/L4 **Mandsaur**, India
62/C3 **Mandsaur**, India
70/B6 **Mandurah**, Austl.
39/E2 **Manduria**, It.
40/C5 **Manduria**, It.
62/A3 **Māndvi**, India
62/C5 **Mandya**, India
62/D2 **Mane** (pass), Nepal
25/G2 **Manea**, Eng,UK
62/D3 **Manendragarh**, India
79/H5 **Manengouba, Massif du** (peak), Camr.
33/J4 **Manerbio**, It.
50/B5 **Manfalūt**, Egypt
52/B3 **Manfalūt**, Egypt
38/D2 **Manfredonia**, It.
38/E2 **Manfredonia** (gulf), It.
40/B5 **Manfredonia**, It.
40/C5 **Manfredonia** (gulf), It.
59/B4 **Mang** (riv.), China
76/E5 **Manga**, Burk.
107/J6 **Mangabeiras** (mts.), Braz.
82/C1 **Mangai**, Zaire
69/K7 **Mangaia** (isl.), CookIs.
60/B3 **Mangaldai**, India
63/F2 **Mangaldai**, India
41/J4 **Mangalia**, Rom.
44/D4 **Mangalia**, Rom.
62/B5 **Mangalore**, India
67/G3 **Mangarang**, Indo.
69/M7 **Mangareva** (isl.), FrPol.
61/E3 **Mangchang**, China
60/B4 **Mangin** (range), Burma
45/K4 **Mangistauz Obl.**, Kaz.
46/F5 **Mangistauz Obl.**, Kaz.
67/E3 **Mangkalihat** (cape), Indo.
53/K2 **Mangla**, Pak.
64/B1 **Mangla**, Pak.
64/B1 **Mangla** (dam), Pak.
64/B1 **Mangla** (res.), Pak.
106/C3 **Manglares** (pt.), Col.
76/F5 **Mango**, Togo
79/F4 **Mango**, Togo
82/G3 **Mangoche**, Malw.
74/G7 **Mangoky** (riv.), Madg.
81/H8 **Mangoky** (riv.), Madg.
82/J11 **Mangoky** (riv.), Madg.
67/G4 **Mangole** (isl.), Indo.
81/J7 **Mangoro** (riv.), Madg.
24/D4 **Mangotsfield**, Eng,UK
53/K4 **Māngrol**, India
62/B3 **Māngrol**, India
34/B2 **Mangualde**, Port.
93/H4 **Mangum**, Ok,US
96/D3 **Mangum**, Ok,US
45/J3 **Mangyshlak** (pen.), Kaz.
45/K4 **Mangyshlak** (plat.), Kaz.
54/C2 **Manhan**, Mong.
89/G4 **Manhattan**, Ks,US
93/H3 **Manhattan**, Ks,US
96/D2 **Manhattan**, Ks,US
90/F4 **Manhattan**, Mt,US
98/B3 **Manhattan Beach**, Ca,US
31/E3 **Manhay**, Belg.
81/F2 **Manhiça**, Moz.
82/F6 **Manhiça**, Moz.
107/K8 **Manhuaçu**, Braz.
108/D2 **Manhuaçu**, Braz.
108/D2 **Manhumirim**, Braz.
39/H4 **Máni** (pen.), Gre.
81/H7 **Mania** (riv.), Madg.
82/G3 **Maniamba**, Moz.
82/F4 **Manica**, Moz.
106/F5 **Manicoré**, Braz.
106/F5 **Manicoré** (riv.), Braz.
84/L4 **Manicouagan** (res.), Can.
87/K3 **Manicouagan** (res.), Qu,Can
87/K3 **Manicouagan** (riv.), Qu,Can
95/G1 **Manicouagan** (riv.), Qu,Can
95/G1 **Manicougan** (res.), Qu,Can
95/H1 **Manicougan** (lake), Qu,Can
71/J4 **Manifold** (cape), Austl.
72/C3 **Manifold** (cape), Austl.
54/D5 **Maniganggo**, China
91/J3 **Manigotagan**, Mb,Can
69/L6 **Manihi** (isl.), FrPol.
69/J6 **Manihiki** (atoll), CookIs.
90/F5 **Manila**, Ut,US
92/E2 **Manila**, Ut,US
68/B3 **Manila City** (cap.), Phil.
73/D1 **Manilla**, Austl.
81/J7 **Maningory** (riv.), Madg.
70/E2 **Maningrida**, Austl.
67/G4 **Manipa** (str.), Indo.
60/B3 **Manipur** (state), India
63/F3 **Manipur** (state), India
44/C5 **Manisa**, Turk.
44/D5 **Manisa** (prov.), Turk.
50/A2 **Manisa**, Turk.
50/B2 **Manisa** (prov.), Turk.
22/D3 **Man, Isle of** (isl.), UK
89/J3 **Manistee**, Mi,US
94/C2 **Manistee**, Mi,US
94/C2 **Manistee** (riv.), Mi,US
89/J2 **Manistique**, Mi,US
94/C2 **Manistique**, Mi,US
91/J2 **Manitoba** (prov.), Can
84/G4 **Manitoba** (lake), Can.
86/G3 **Manitoba** (prov.), Can.
89/G1 **Manitoba** (prov.), Can.
91/J3 **Manitoba** (lake), Mb,Can
86/G3 **Manitoba** (lake), Mb,Can
89/G1 **Manitoba** (lake), Mb,Can
95/H1 **Manitou** (riv.), Qu,Can
87/H4 **Manitoulin** (isl.), On,Can
94/D2 **Manitoulin** (isl.), On,Can
96/B2 **Manitou Springs**, Co,US
91/M3 **Manitouwadge**, On,Can
94/C1 **Manitouwadge**, On,Can
87/H4 **Manitowoc**, Wi,US
89/J3 **Manitowoc**, Wi,US
91/M4 **Manitowoc**, Wi,US
94/C2 **Manitowoc**, Wi,US
94/F2 **Maniwaki**, Qu,Can
106/C2 **Manizales**, Col.
81/H8 **Manja**, Madg.
81/F2 **Manjacaze**, Moz.
81/J7 **Manjakandriana**, Madg.
64/F3 **Manjeri**, India
70/B6 **Manjimup**, Austl.
62/C4 **Manjlegaon**, India
53/L5 **Mānjra** (riv.), India
62/C4 **Mānjra** (riv.), India
86/G4 **Mankato**, Mn,US
89/H3 **Mankato**, Mn,US
91/K4 **Mankato**, Mn,US
93/J1 **Mankato**, Mn,US
76/D6 **Mankono**, IvC.
78/D4 **Mankono**, IvC.
64/H4 **Mankulam**, SrL.
54/F3 **Manlay**, Mong.
85/H2 **Manley Hot Springs**, Ak,US
34/D2 **Manlleu**, Sp.
72/H8 **Manly**, Austl.
53/K4 **Manmād**, India
62/B3 **Manmād**, India
61/J5 **Manmanoc** (mt.), Phil.
65/B4 **Man Mia** (peak), Thai.
63/G2 **Mān Ming**, Burma
73/B2 **Mannahill**, Austl.
62/C6 **Mannar**, SrL.
64/G4 **Mannar**, SrL.
64/H4 **Mannar** (dist.), SrL.
48/G9 **Mannar** (gulf), India.,SrL.
64/G4 **Mannar** (gulf), India, SrL.
62/C6 **Mannar** (gulf), India, SrL.
64/G4 **Mannar** (gulf), India, SrL.
64/G4 **Mannar** (isl.), SrL.
62/C5 **Mannārgudi**, India
64/G3 **Mannārgudi**, India
37/E3 **Männedorf**, Swi.
40/C2 **Mannersdorf an der Rabnitz**, Aus.
80/C4 **Mannetjiesberg** (peak), SAfr.
18/D4 **Mannheim**, Ger.
26/E4 **Mannheim**, Ger.
33/H2 **Mannheim**, Ger.
86/E3 **Manning**, Ab,Can
87/Q7 **Manning** (cape), NW,Can
97/H3 **Manning**, SC,US
25/H3 **Manningtree**, Eng,UK
36/D4 **Männlifluh** (peak), Swi.
38/A2 **Mannu** (riv.), It.
38/A3 **Mannu** (riv.), It.
73/A2 **Mannum**, Austl.
76/C6 **Mano** (riv.), Libr., SLeo.
78/C5 **Mano** (riv.), Libr., SLeo.
85/G4 **Manokotak**, Ak,US
81/G8 **Manombo**, Madg.
82/E2 **Manono**, Zaire
21/A3 **Manor Hamilton**, Ire.
98/H5 **Manorville**, NY,US
32/F5 **Manosque**, Fr.
35/H1 **Manosque**, Fr.
95/G1 **Manouane** (lake), Qu,Can
95/G1 **Manouane** (riv.), Qu,Can
69/H5 **Manra** (Sydney) (atoll), Kiri.
35/F2 **Manresa**, Sp.
35/K6 **Manresa**, Sp.
82/E3 **Mansa**, Zam.
78/B3 **Mansa Konko**, Gam.
67/F1 **Mansalay**, Phil.
84/J3 **Mansel** (isl.), Can.
87/H2 **Mansel** (isl.), NW,Can
73/C3 **Mansfield**, Austl.
23/G5 **Mansfield**, Eng,UK
93/J4 **Mansfield**, La,US
96/E3 **Mansfield**, La,US
89/K3 **Mansfield**, Oh,US
94/D3 **Mansfield**, Oh,US
23/G5 **Mansfield Woodhouse**, Eng,UK
34/C1 **Mansilla de las Mulas**, Sp.
106/B4 **Manta**, Ecu.
67/E2 **Mantalingajan** (mt.), Phil.
106/C6 **Mantaro** (riv.), Peru
92/B3 **Manteca**, Ca,US
34/B2 **Manteigas**, Port.
108/D1 **Mantena**, Braz.
30/A6 **Mantes-la-Jolie**, Fr.
32/D2 **Mantes-la-Jolie**, Fr.
30/A6 **Mantes-la-Ville**, Fr.
62/C4 **Manthani**, India
92/E3 **Manti**, Ut,US
107/K8 **Mantiqueira** (mts.), Braz.
108/C2 **Mantiqueira** (range), Braz.
59/C3 **Mantou Shan** (mtn.), China
33/J4 **Mantova**, It.
103/E1 **Mantua**, Cuba
98/E6 **Mantua**, NJ,US
43/K4 **Manturovo**, Rus.
20/H3 **Mäntyharju**, Fin.
42/E3 **Mäntyharju**, Fin.
106/D6 **Manú**, Peru
106/E6 **Manú** (riv.), Peru
69/J6 **Manua** (isls.), ASam.
69/K6 **Manuae** (atoll), CookIs.
88/W13 **Manuawili**, Hi,US
107/J6 **Manuel Alves** (riv.) Braz.
100/D2 **Manuel Benavides**, Mex.
93/F5 **Manuel Benavides**, Mex
96/B4 **Manuel Benavides**, Mex
67/F4 **Manui** (isl.), Indo.
53/G3 **Manūjān**, Iran
66/C5 **Manuk** (riv.), Indo.
68/G8 **Manukau**, N.Z.
71/R10 **Manukau**, N.Z.
106/D6 **Manú Nat'l Park**, Peru
106/E6 **Manuripe** (riv.), Bol
68/D5 **Manus** (isl.), PNG
98/F5 **Manville** NJ, US
93/J5 **Many**, La,US
96/E4 **Many**, La,US
45/G3 **Manych** (riv.), Rus.
46/E5 **Manych** (riv.), Rus.
45/G3 **Manych-Gudilo** (lake), Rus.
92/E3 **Many Farms**, Az,US
82/F2 **Manyoni**, Tanz.
34/D3 **Manzanares**, Sp.
35/N8 **Manzanares** (riv.),
35/N9 **Manzanares** (riv.),
103/G1 **Manzanillo**, Cuba
100/D5 **Manzanillo**, Mex.
103/F4 **Manzanillo-Gandoca Nat'l Wild. Ref.**, CR
96/B3 **Manzano** (mts.), NM,US
47/M5 **Manzhouli**, China
55/H2 **Manzhouli**, China
36/A5 **Manziat**, Fr.
49/B4 **Manzilah, Buḥayrat al** (lag.), Egypt
38/A4 **Manzil bū Ruqaybah**, Tun.
75/W17 **Manzil bū Ruqaybah**, Tun.
38/B4 **Manzil Bū Zalafah**, Tun.
38/B4 **Manzil Tamīn**, Tun
75/X17 **Manzil Tamīn**, Tun
81/E2 **Manzini**, Swaz.
82/F6 **Manzini**, Swaz.
76/J5 **Mao**, Chad
103/J2 **Mao**, DRep.
104/D3 **Mao**, DRep.
54/F5 **Maobaguan**, China
54/E5 **Mao'ergai**, China
67/J4 **Maoke** (mts.), Indo
68/C5 **Maoke** (mts.), Indo
61/F4 **Maoming**, China
63/K3 **Maoming**, China
60/D3 **Maotou** (peak), Chi
102/C3 **Mapastepec**, Mex.
67/J5 **Mapi** (riv.), Indo.
100/D3 **Mapimí** (depr.), Me
100/E3 **Mapimí**, Mex.
96/B5 **Mapimí** (depr.), Me
95/Q8 **Maple**, On,Can
91/K5 **Maple** (riv.), Ia,US
91/J4 **Maple** (riv.), ND,US
86/F4 **Maple Creek**, Sk,C
90/F3 **Maple Creek**, Sk,C
95/N7 **Maple Grove**, Qu,C
99/N16 **Maple Park**, Il,US
98/F6 **Maple Shade**, NJ,U
99/C3 **Maple Valley**, Wa,
98/F5 **Maplewood**, NJ,U
58/F6 **Map'o**, SKor.
70/G2 **Mapoon Mission S** Austl.
106/G4 **Mapuera** (riv.), Bra
53/K5 **Mapusa**, India
62/B4 **Mapusa**, India
81/F2 **Maputo** (prov.), Mo
82/F6 **Maputo** (cap.), Moz.
81/F2 **Maputo, Rio** (riv.), Moz.
52/C5 **Maqdam** (cape), Sudan
52/B3 **Maqnā**, SAr.
53/J2 **Maqor**, Afg.
82/C2 **Maquela do Zombo** Ang.
93/K2 **Maquoketa** (riv.), Ia,US
105/E5 **Mar** (range), Braz.
108/B3 **Mar** (range), Braz.
54/E5 **Mar** (riv.), China
60/D1 **Mar** (riv.), China
107/J5 **Marabá**, Braz.
107/J3 **Maracá** (isl.), Braz.
103/J4 **Maracaibo**, Ven.
103/J4 **Maracaibo** (lake), Ven.
104/D5 **Maracaibo**, Ven.
104/D5 **Maracaibo** (lake), Ven.
105/B2 **Maracaibo** (lake), Ven.
106/D1 **Maracaibo**, Ven.
106/D2 **Maracaibo** (lake), Ven.
107/H7 **Maracaju** (mts.), Braz.
104/E5 **Maracay**, Ven.
106/E1 **Maracay**, Ven.
34/D4 **Maracena**, Sp.
76/J2 **Marādah**, Libya
76/G5 **Maradi**, Niger
79/G3 **Maradi**, Niger
79/G3 **Maradi** (dept.), Nig
46/E6 **Marāgheh**, Iran
51/F2 **Marāgheh**, Iran
52/E1 **Marāgheh**, Iran
106/E3 **Marahuaca** (peak),
61/J5 **Maraira** (pt.), Phil.
105/D3 **Marajó** (isl.), Braz.
105/E3 **Marajó** (bay), Braz
107/J4 **Marajó**, Braz.
107/J4 **Marajó** (bay), Braz
77/N7 **Maralal**, Kenya
51/E1 **Maralik**, Arm.

155

Mara – McDon

7/M5 **Maramures** (co.), Rom.
41/F2 **Maramureş** (co.), Rom.
92/E4 **Marana**, Az,US
51/F2 **Marand**, Iran
66/B2 **Marang**, Malay.
07/L4 **Maranguape**, Braz.
07/J6 **Maranhão** (riv.), Braz.
71/H5 **Maranoa** (riv.), Austl.
72/C4 **Maranoa** (riv.), Austl.
05/B3 **Marañón** (riv.), Peru
06/C4 **Marañón** (riv.), Peru
32/C3 **Marans**, Fr.
78/D5 **Maraoue Nat'l Park**, IvC.
66/B4 **Marapi** (peak), Indo.
66/C4 **Maras** (peak), Indo.
41/H3 **Mărăşeşti**, Rom.
37/H4 **Marathon**, On,Can
89/J2 **Marathon**, On,Can
1/M3 **Marathon**, On,Can
94/C1 **Marathon**, On,Can
39/H3 **Marathón**, Gre.
39/L6 **Marathon**, Gre.
97/H5 **Marathon**, Fl,US
93/G5 **Marathon**, Tx,US
96/C4 **Marathon**, Tx,US
08/A4 **Marau**, Braz.
64/B1 **Marauliānwāla**, Pak.
93/G5 **Maravillas** (creek), Tx,US
67/F2 **Marawi**, Phil.
7/M4 **Marawī**, Sudan
24/A6 **Marazion**, Eng,UK
36/D4 **Marbach**, Swi.
31/F6 **Marbache**, Fr.
34/C4 **Marbella**, Sp.
76/E1 **Marbella**, Sp.
68/A7 **Marble Bar**, Austl.
70/B4 **Marble Bar**, Austl.
90/F5 **Marbleton**, Wy,US
92/E2 **Marbleton**, Wy,US
26/E3 **Marburg**, Ger.
33/H1 **Marburg**, Ger.
40/C2 **Marcali**, Hun.
25/G1 **March**, Eng,UK
98/C3 **March A.F.B.**, Ca,US
32/D3 **Marche** (mts.), Fr.
33/K5 **Marche** (reg.), It.
38/C1 **Marche** (reg.), It.
40/A4 **Marche** (reg.), It.
26/C3 **Marche-en-Famenne**, Belg.
31/E3 **Marche-en-Famenne**, Belg.
32/F1 **Marche-en-Famenne**, Belg.
34/C4 **Marchena**, Sp.
30/C3 **Marchiennes-Ville**, Fr.
31/E3 **Marchin**, Belg.
05/C6 **Mar Chiquita** (lake), Arg.
9/D3 **Mar Chiquita** (lake), Arg.
8/B1 **Marciana Marina**, It.
6/B3 **Marcilly-sur-Tille**, Fr.
0/A2 **Marck**, Fr.
6/D1 **Marckolsheim**, Fr.
7/H5 **Marco**, Fl,US
0/C3 **Marcoing**, Fr.
6/C7 **Marcona**, Peru
0/E3 **Marconi** (peak), Can
9/D3 **Marcos Juárez**, Arg.
0/C2 **Marcq-en-Baroeul**, Fr.
5/J3 **Marcus Baker** (mt.), Ak,US
4/F2 **Marcy** (peak), NY,US
1/F1 **Mardakert**, Azer.
3/K2 **Mardān**, Pak.
9/E4 **Mar del Plata**, Arg.
5/G4 **Marden**, Eng,UK
0/C5 **Mardeuil**, Fr.
6/E6 **Mardin**, Turk.
0/E2 **Mardin**, Turk.
0/E2 **Mardin** (prov.), Turk.
2/D1 **Mardin**, Turk.
W12 **Maré** (isl.), NCal.
1/H3 **Mareeba**, Austl.
2/B2 **Mareeba**, Austl.
3/H5 **Mareham le Fen**, Eng,UK
/N15 **Marengo**, Il,US
2/C4 **Marennes**, Fr.
5/G5 **Maresfield**, Eng,UK
3/F5 **Marfa**, Tx,US
6/B4 **Marfa**, Tx,US
4/B1 **Margalla Hills Nat'l Park**, Pak.
4/C3 **Margam**, Wal,UK
4/E3 **Marganets**, Ukr.
3/K5 **Margao**, India
2/B4 **Margao**, India
0/B6 **Margaret River**, Austl.
4/E5 **Margarita** (isl.), Ven.
6/F1 **Margarita** (isl.), Ven.
9/G3 **Margarítion**, Gre.
1/E3 **Margate**, SAfr.
5/H4 **Margate**, Eng,UK
2/E4 **Margeride** (mts.), Fr.
7/L7 **Margherita** (peak), Ugan.
/M5 **Marghita**, Rom.
0/F2 **Marghita**, Rom.
4/B3 **Marghita**, Rom.
6/B4 **Margny-lès-Compiègne**, Fr.
0/B5 **Margny-lès-Compiègne**, Fr.
2/E2 **Margny-lès-Compiègne**, Fr.
7/F2 **Margosatubig**, Phil.
1/E2 **Margraten**, Neth.
83/V **Marguerite** (bay), Ant.
3/D4 **Maria** (peak), Austl.
9/K7 **Maria** (isl.), FrPol.
0/D4 **María Cleófas** (isl.), Mex.
3/D4 **Maria Island Nat'l Park**, Austl.
100/D4 **María Madre** (isl.), Mex.
100/D4 **María Magdalena** (isl.), Mex.
72/C3 **Marian**, Austl.
103/F1 **Marianao**, Cuba
93/K4 **Marianna**, Ar,US
97/F3 **Marianna**, Ar,US
89/J5 **Marianna**, Fl,US
97/G4 **Marianna**, Fl,US
26/G4 **Mariánské Lázně**, Czh.
33/K2 **Mariánské Lázně**, Czh.
90/F3 **Marias** (riv.), Mt,US
103/F5 **Mariato** (pt.), Pan.
106/B2 **Mariato** (pt.), Pan.
77/Q4 **Ma'rib**, Yem.
26/F1 **Maribo**, Den.
18/E4 **Maribor**, Slov.
33/L3 **Maribor**, Slov.
40/B2 **Maribor**, Slov.
106/E4 **Marié** (riv.), Braz.
83/S **Marie Byrd Land** (reg.), Ant.
104/F4 **Marie-Galante** (isl.), Guad.
20/F3 **Mariehamn**, Fin.
42/C3 **Mariehamn**, Fin.
103/F1 **Mariel**, Cuba
29/E1 **Marienhafe**, Ger.
29/E6 **Marienheide**, Ger.
31/G1 **Marienheide**, Ger.
80/B2 **Mariental**, Namb.
82/C5 **Mariental**, Namb.
20/E4 **Mariestad**, Swe.
89/K5 **Marietta**, Ga,US
97/G3 **Marietta**, Ga,US
94/D4 **Marietta**, Oh,US
97/H2 **Marietta**, Oh,US
93/H4 **Marietta**, Ok,US
96/D3 **Marietta**, Ok,US
32/F5 **Marignane**, Fr.
104/F4 **Marigot**, Dom.
107/J8 **Marília**, Braz.
108/B2 **Marília**, Braz.
109/G1 **Marília**, Braz.
34/A1 **Marín**, Sp.
99/J10 **Marin** (co.), Ca,US
38/D2 **Marina**, It.
99/G6 **Marine City**, Mi,US
36/D3 **Marin-Epagnier**, Swi.
19/R9 **Marines**, Fr.
30/A5 **Marines**, Fr.
87/H4 **Marinette**, Wi,US
89/J2 **Marinette**, Wi,US
91/M4 **Marinette**, Wi,US
94/C2 **Marinette**, Wi,US
99/K10 **Marine World Africa USA**, Ca,US
107/H8 **Maringá**, Braz.
108/B2 **Maringá**, Braz.
109/F1 **Maringá**, Braz.
34/A3 **Marinha Grande**, Port.
34/A2 **Marinhas**, Port.
71/J3 **Marion** (reef), Austl.
97/G3 **Marion**, Al,US
89/J4 **Marion**, Il,US
93/K3 **Marion**, Il,US
94/B4 **Marion**, Il,US
97/F2 **Marion**, Il,US
94/C3 **Marion**, In,US
94/B4 **Marion**, Ky,US
97/F2 **Marion**, Ky,US
94/C2 **Marion**, Mi,US
89/K3 **Marion**, Oh,US
94/D3 **Marion**, Oh,US
89/K5 **Marion** (lake), SC,US
94/D4 **Marion**, Va,US
97/H2 **Marion**, Va,US
92/C3 **Mariposa**, Ca,US
106/F8 **Mariscal Estigarribia**, Par.
33/G4 **Maritime Alps** (range), Fr., It.
41/G4 **Maritsa** (riv.), Bul.
44/C4 **Maritsa** (riv.), Bul., Turk.
41/H5 **Maritsa** (riv.), Gre.
39/K2 **Maritsa** (riv.), Gre., Turk.
41/H5 **Maritsa** (riv.), Turk.
19/G4 **Mariupol'**, Ukr.
44/F3 **Mariupol'**, Ukr.
46/D5 **Mariupol'**, Ukr.
43/K4 **Mariy Aut. Rep.**, Rus.
42/E4 **Märjamaa**, Est.
49/D3 **Marj 'Uyūn**, Leb.
50/C3 **Marj 'Uyūn**, Leb.
28/B6 **Mark** (riv.), Belg.
54/B2 **Markakol** (lake), Kaz.
54/D6 **Markam**, China
60/C2 **Markam**, China
63/G2 **Markam**, China
77/P7 **Marka** (Merca), Som.
20/E4 **Markaryd**, Swe.
51/G3 **Markazī** (gov.), Iran
37/F2 **Markdorf**, Ger.
28/C4 **Marken** (isl.), Neth.
28/C4 **Markerwaard** (polder), Neth.
25/E1 **Market Bosworth**, Eng,UK
25/F1 **Market Deeping**, Eng,UK
23/F6 **Market Drayton**, Eng,UK
25/F2 **Market Harborough**, Eng,UK
22/B3 **Markethill**, NI,UK
23/H5 **Market Rasen**, Eng,UK
23/H4 **Market Weighton**, Eng,UK
87/J2 **Markham** (bay), NW,Can
94/E3 **Markham**, On,Can
95/N8 **Markham**, On,Can
27/L2 **Marki**, Pol.
92/C3 **Markleeville**, Ca,US
39/L7 **Markópoulon**, Gre.
40/E3 **Markovac**, Yugo.
45/H2 **Marks**, Rus.
93/J5 **Marksville**, La,US
96/E4 **Marksville**, La,US
37/H1 **Markt Indersdorf**, Ger.
26/F5 **Marktoberdorf**, Ger.
37/G2 **Marktoberdorf**, Ger.
26/G4 **Marktredwitz**, Ger.
33/K2 **Marktredwitz**, Ger.
37/G2 **Markt Rettenbach**, Ger.
93/J3 **Mark Twain** (lake), Mo,US
26/D3 **Marl**, Ger.
29/E5 **Marl**, Ger.
25/E4 **Marlborough**, Eng,UK
30/C4 **Marle**, Fr.
37/H4 **Marlengo** (Marling), It.
31/G6 **Marlenheim**, Fr.
30/B3 **Marles-les-Mines**, Fr.
37/H4 **Marling** (Marlengo), It.
26/G1 **Marlow**, Ger.
25/F3 **Marlow**, Eng,UK
98/F6 **Marlton**, NJ,US
30/C3 **Marly**, Fr.
19/T9 **Marly-la-Ville**, Fr.
30/B5 **Marly-la-Ville**, Fr.
19/S10 **Marly-le-Roi**, Fr.
30/B6 **Marly-le-Roi**, Fr.
31/F5 **Marly-sur-Seille**, Fr.
32/D4 **Marmande**, Fr.
19/F4 **Marmara** (sea), Turk.
41/H5 **Marmara**, Turk.
41/H5 **Marmara** (isl.), Turk.
41/J5 **Marmara** (sea), Turk.
44/C4 **Marmara** (sea), Turk.
50/A1 **Marmara** (sea), Turk.
51/M7 **Marmara** (sea), Turk.
41/H5 **Marmaraereğlisi**, Turk.
50/B2 **Marmaris**, Turk.
106/F5 **Marmelos** (riv.), Braz.
70/C5 **Marmion** (lake), Austl.
91/K3 **Marmion** (lake), On,Can
94/A1 **Marmion** (lake), On,Can
33/J3 **Marmolada** (peak), It.
34/C3 **Marmolejo**, Sp.
37/F5 **Marmontana, Monte** (peak), It.
31/G6 **Marmoutier**, Fr.
36/B3 **Marnay**, Fr.
36/C5 **Marnaz**, Fr.
19/U10 **Marne** (riv.), Fr.
26/B4 **Marne** (riv.), Fr.
30/C5 **Marne** (riv.), Fr.
30/C6 **Marne** (dept.), Fr.
32/E2 **Marne** (riv.), Fr.
36/B1 **Marne** (riv.), Fr.
26/E2 **Marne**, Ger.
36/B3 **Marne à la Saône** (can.), Fr.
31/D6 **Marne au Rhin, Canal de la** (can.), Fr.
24/D5 **Marnhull**, Eng,UK
76/J6 **Maro**, Chad
69/H2 **Maro** (reef), Hi.,US
81/J6 **Maroantsetra**, Madg.
69/L6 **Marokau** (atoll), FrPol.
75/G7 **Marolambo**, Madg.
81/J8 **Marolambo**, Madg.
19/S11 **Marolles-en-Hurepoix**, Fr.
81/J6 **Maromokotro** (peak), Madg.
82/F4 **Marondera**, Zim.
105/D2 **Maroni** (riv.), FrG., Sur.
107/H3 **Maroni** (riv.), FrG., Sur.
72/D4 **Maroochydore-Mooloolaba**, Austl.
103/G2 **Maroon Town**, Jam.
33/K5 **Marotta**, It.
76/H5 **Maroua**, Camr.
75/G6 **Marovoay**, Madg.
81/H7 **Marovoay**, Madg.
31/G5 **Marpingen**, Ger.
23/F5 **Marple**, Eng,UK
54/D5 **Marqên Gangri** (peak), China
62/E2 **Marquan** (riv.), China
68/D8 **Marquarie** (riv.), Austl.
69/M5 **Marquesas** (isls.), FrPol.
87/H4 **Marquette**, Mi,US
89/J2 **Marquette**, Mi,US
91/M4 **Marquette**, Mi,US
94/C2 **Marquette**, Mi,US
30/A2 **Marquise**, Fr.
32/D1 **Marquise**, Fr.
81/F2 **Marracuene**, Moz.
74/E3 **Marrah** (peak), Sudan
77/K5 **Marrah** (mts.), Sudan
77/K5 **Marrah** (peak), Sudan
76/D1 **Marrakech**, Mor.
68/C7 **Marree**, Austl.
70/F5 **Marree**, Austl.
82/G4 **Marromeu**, Moz.
82/G3 **Marrupa**, Moz.
76/J1 **Marsá al Burayqah**, Libya
77/N7 **Marsabit**, Kenya
18/E5 **Marsala**, It.
38/C4 **Marsala**, It.
49/B5 **Marsá Maţrūḩ** (gov.), Egypt
50/A4 **Marsá Matrūh**, Egypt
50/D4 **Marsá Maţrūḩ** (gov.), Egypt
77/L1 **Marsá Matrūh**, Egypt
19/U10 **Marsange** (riv.), Fr.
32/F3 **Marsannay-la-Côte**, Fr.
36/A3 **Marsannay-la-Côte**, Fr.
29/F6 **Marsberg**, Ger.
33/K5 **Marsciano**, It.
38/C1 **Marsciano**, It.
23/G4 **Marsden**, Eng,UK
28/B3 **Marsdiep** (chan.), Neth.
18/D4 **Marseille**, Fr.
32/F5 **Marseille**, Fr.
35/H1 **Marseille**, Fr.
93/K5 **Marsh** (isl.), La,US
96/E4 **Marsh** (isl.), La,US
99/F7 **Marsh** (cr.), Mi,US
90/F2 **Marshall**, Sk,Can
89/G3 **Marshall**, Mn,US
91/K4 **Marshall**, Mn,US
93/J3 **Marshall**, Mo,US
96/E2 **Marshall**, Mo,US
93/J4 **Marshall**, Tx,US
96/E3 **Marshall**, Tx,US
68/G3 **Marshall Islands**
89/H3 **Marshalltown**, Ia,US
91/K5 **Marshalltown**, Ia,US
93/J2 **Marshalltown**, Ia,US
93/J3 **Marshfield**, Mo,US
96/E2 **Marshfield**, Mo,US
89/H3 **Marshfield**, Wi,US
91/L4 **Marshfield**, Wi,US
94/B2 **Marshfield**, Wi,US
25/E3 **Marsh Gibbon**, Eng,UK
23/G2 **Marske-by-the-Sea**, Eng,UK
38/B1 **Marta**, It.
63/G4 **Martaban**, Burma
65/B2 **Martaban**, Burma
65/B2 **Martaban** (gulf), Burma
31/E4 **Martelange**, Belg.
90/G2 **Martensville**, Sk,Can
29/G3 **Martfeld**, Ger.
95/G3 **Martha's Vineyard** (isl.), Ma,US
33/G3 **Martigny**, Swi.
36/D5 **Martigny**, Swi.
36/B1 **Martigny-les-Bains**, Fr.
32/F5 **Martigues**, Fr.
83/S **Martin** (pen.), Ant.
27/K4 **Martin**, Slvk.
44/A2 **Martin**, Slvk.
91/H5 **Martin**, SD,US
93/G2 **Martin**, SD,US
94/B4 **Martin**, Tn,US
97/F2 **Martin**, Tn,US
38/E2 **Martina Franca**, It.
40/C5 **Martina Franca**, It.
101/F4 **Martínez**, Mex.
102/B1 **Martínez**, Mex.
99/K10 **Martinez**, Ca,US
97/H3 **Martinez**, Ga,US
101/M6 **Martínez de la Torre**, Mex.
108/C1 **Martinho Campos**, Braz.
104/F4 **Martinique** (passg.), Dom., Mart.
104/F4 **Martinique** (isl.), Fr.
84/L8 **Martinique** (isl.), Fr.
39/H3 **Martínon**, Gre.
108/B2 **Martinópolis**, Braz.
94/E4 **Martinsburg**, WV,US
97/J2 **Martinsburg**, WV,US
98/E5 **Martins Creek**, Pa,US
94/C4 **Martinsville**, In,US
97/G2 **Martinsville**, In,US
89/L4 **Martinsville**, Va,US
94/E4 **Martinsville**, Va,US
97/J2 **Martinsville**, Va,US
107/N8 **Martin Vaz** (isls.), Braz.
16/H7 **Martin Vaz** (isls.), Braz.
24/D2 **Martley**, Eng,UK
24/D5 **Martock**, Eng,UK
26/F1 **Martofte**, Den.
35/F2 **Martorell**, Sp.
35/K7 **Martorell**, Sp.
34/D4 **Martos**, Sp.
94/F1 **Martre** (riv.), Qu,Can
32/D5 **Martres-Tolosane**, Fr.
35/F1 **Martres-Tolosane**, Fr.
91/J5 **Marty**, SD,US
93/H2 **Marty**, SD,US
56/C3 **Marugame**, Japan
57/F2 **Maruko**, Japan
28/D2 **Marum**, Neth.
56/E2 **Maruoka**, Japan
69/M7 **Marutea** (atoll), FrPol.
57/H7 **Maruyama**, Japan
51/H4 **Marv Dasht**, Iran
52/F3 **Marv Dasht**, Iran
72/D4 **Mary** (riv.), Austl.
46/G6 **Mary**, Trkm.
53/H1 **Mary**, Trkm.
71/G7 **Maryborough**, Austl.
71/J5 **Maryborough**, Austl.
72/D4 **Maryborough**, Austl.
73/B3 **Maryborough**, Austl.
97/G4 **Mary Esther**, Fl,US
91/H3 **Maryfield**, Sk,Can
78/C5 **Maryland** (co.), Libr.
89/L4 **Maryland** (state), US
94/E4 **Maryland** (state), US
98/K7 **Maryland** (state), US
98/K7 **Maryland City**, Md,US
22/E2 **Maryport**, Eng,UK
87/L4 **Marystown**, Nf,Can
95/L2 **Marystown**, Nf,Can
93/H3 **Marysville**, Ks,US
96/D2 **Marysville**, Ks,US
99/H6 **Marysville**, Mi,US
99/C1 **Marysville**, Wa,US
93/J2 **Maryville**, Mo,US
96/E1 **Maryville**, Mo,US
97/H3 **Maryville**, Tn,US
38/D2 **Marzano** (peak), It.
103/G5 **Marzo** (pt.), Col.
101/F3 **Marzo, 18 de**, Mex.
76/H2 **Marzūq**, Libya
50/C4 **Masada** (ruins), Isr.
49/D4 **Masada** (Horvot Mezada) (ruins), Isr.
82/G1 **Masai Steppe** (grsld.), Tanz.
77/M8 **Masaka**, Ugan.
82/F1 **Masaka**, Ugan.
38/B5 **Masākin**, Tun.
75/X18 **Masākin**, Tun.
51/G2 **Masally**, Azer.
35/E3 **Masamagrell**, Sp.
67/F4 **Masamba**, Indo.
47/N6 **Masan**, SKor.
55/K4 **Masan**, SKor.
56/A3 **Masan**, SKor.
58/E5 **Masan**, SKor.
58/F7 **Masan-ni**, SKor.
82/G3 **Masasi**, Tanz.
102/E4 **Masaya**, Nic.
67/F1 **Masbate**, Phil.
67/G1 **Masbate** (isl.), Phil.
68/B3 **Masbate** (isl.), Phil.
75/R16 **Mascara**, Alg.
75/R16 **Mascara** (wilaya), Alg.
76/F1 **Mascara**, Alg.
81/S15 **Mascarene** (isls.), Mrts., Reun.
100/D4 **Mascota**, Mex.
95/N6 **Mascouche**, Qu,Can
37/F1 **Maselheim**, Ger.
80/D3 **Maseru** (cap.), Les.
82/E6 **Maseru** (cap.), Les.
36/D2 **Masevaux**, Fr.
48/E6 **Mashad**, Iran
23/G3 **Masham**, Eng,UK
63/J3 **Mashan**, China
46/F6 **Mashhad**, Iran
53/G1 **Mashhad**, Iran
53/G3 **Mashīz**, Iran
53/H3 **Māshkel, Hāmūn-i-** (lake), Pak.
53/H3 **Māshkīd** (riv.), Iran
51/G1 **Mashtaga**, Azer.
49/B4 **Mashtūl as Sūq**, Egypt
100/C3 **Masiaca**, Mex.
34/A1 **Maside**, Sp.
77/Q4 **Masīlah** (wadi), Yemen
45/L1 **Masim** (peak), Rus.
53/G5 **Masira** (gulf), Oman
48/E7 **Maşīrah** (isl.), Oman
53/G4 **Maşīrah** (isl.), Oman
51/F2 **Masis**, Arm.
46/E6 **Masjed-e Soleymān**, Iran
51/G4 **Masjed-e Soleymān**, Iran
52/E2 **Masjed-e Soleymān**, Iran
102/D2 **Maskall**, Belz.
21/H7 **Mask, Lough** (lake), Ire.
81/J6 **Masoala** (cape), Madg.
81/J6 **Masoala** (pen.), Madg.
82/L10 **Masoala** (pen.), Madg.
81/H7 **Masoarivo**, Madg.
94/C3 **Mason**, Mi,US
101/F2 **Mason**, Tx,US
93/H5 **Mason**, Tx,US
96/D4 **Mason**, Tx,US
99/A3 **Mason** (co.), Wa,US
99/A3 **Mason** (lake), Wa,US
86/G4 **Mason City**, Ia,US
89/H3 **Mason City**, Ia,US
91/K5 **Mason City**, Ia,US
93/J2 **Mason City**, Ia,US
33/H4 **Masone**, It.
35/X17 **Maspalomas**, Canl.
35/K6 **Masquefa**, Sp.
33/J4 **Massa**, It.
87/J4 **Massachusetts** (state), US
89/M3 **Massachusetts** (state), US
95/F3 **Massachusetts** (state), US
95/G3 **Massachusetts** (bay), Ma,US
38/E2 **Massafra**, It.
40/C5 **Massafra**, It.
33/J5 **Massa Marittima**, It.
33/K5 **Massa Martana**, It.
82/F5 **Massangena**, Moz.
87/J4 **Massena**, NY,US
89/M3 **Massena**, NY,US
94/F2 **Massena**, NY,US
85/M5 **Masset**, BC,Can
86/C3 **Masset**, BC,Can
87/S7 **Massey** (sound), NW,Can
82/D3 **Massibi**, Ang.
32/E4 **Massif Central** (plat.), Fr.
94/D3 **Massillon**, Oh,US
83/G **Masson** (isl.), Ant.
19/S10 **Massy**, Fr.
30/B6 **Massy**, Fr.
52/C4 **Mastābah**, SAr.
71/S11 **Masterton**, N.Z.
28/B5 **Mastgat** (chan.), Neth.
98/H5 **Mastic**, NY,US
53/J3 **Mastung**, Pak.
52/C4 **Mastūrah**, SAr.
56/B3 **Masuda**, Japan
66/B4 **Masurai** (peak), Indo.
82/F5 **Masvingo**, Zim.
49/E2 **Maşyāf**, Syria
50/D3 **Maşyāf**, Syria
39/F2 **Mat** (riv.), Alb.
82/B2 **Matadi**, Zaire
93/G4 **Matador**, Tx,US
90/C3 **Matador**, Tx,US
102/E3 **Matagalpa**, Nic.
103/E3 **Matagalpa, Rio Grande de** (riv.), Nic.
94/E1 **Matagami** (lake), Qu,Can
101/F2 **Matagorda** (bay), Tx,US
101/F2 **Matagorda** (isl.), Tx,US
93/H5 **Matagorda** (bay), Tx,US
96/D4 **Matagorda** (isl.), Tx,US
62/D6 **Matale**, SrL.
76/C4 **Matam**, Sen.
78/B3 **Matam**, Sen.
82/D6 **Mata Mata**, SAfr.
100/F3 **Matamoros**, Mex.
101/E3 **Matamoros**, Mex.
84/H7 **Matamoros**, Mex.
96/C5 **Matamoros**, Mex
96/D5 **Matamoros**, Mex
77/K3 **Ma'ţan as Sarra** (well), Libya
100/C3 **Matancita**, Mex.
84/L5 **Matane**, Can.
87/K4 **Matane**, Qu,Can
89/N2 **Matane**, Qu,Can
95/H1 **Matane**, Qu,Can
95/H1 **Matane** (riv.), Qu,Can
103/F1 **Matanzas**, Cuba
89/K7 **Matanzas**, Cuba
108/B2 **Matão**, Braz.
100/C2 **Matape** (riv.), Mex.
95/H1 **Matapedia** (riv.), Qu,Can
52/C6 **Matara** (ruins), Egypt
52/C6 **Matara**, Eth.
62/D6 **Matara**, SrL.
67/E5 **Mataram**, Indo.
39/G3 **Mataránga**, Gre.
35/G2 **Mataró**, Sp.
35/L6 **Mataró**, Sp.
80/E3 **Matatiele**, SAfr.
69/L7 **Mataura**, FrPol.
68/H6 **Mata Utu**, Wall.
101/E4 **Matehuala**, Mex.
88/F7 **Matehuala**, Mex.
38/E2 **Matera**, It.
40/C5 **Matera**, It.
27/M5 **Mátészalka**, Hun.
40/F2 **Mátészalka**, Hun.
44/B2 **Mátészalka**, Hun.
36/C3 **Mathay**, Fr.
98/C3 **Mathews** (lake), Ca,US
101/F2 **Mathis**, Tx,US
96/D4 **Mathis**, Tx,US
73/C2 **Mathoura**, Austl.
53/L3 **Mathurā**, India
62/C2 **Mathurā**, India
67/G2 **Mati**, Phil.
102/C2 **Matías Romero**, Mex.
103/E3 **Matíguas**, Nic.
108/B3 **Matinhos**, Braz.
38/A4 **Mātir**, Tun.
75/W17 **Mātir**, Tun.
23/G5 **Matlock**, Eng,UK
105/D4 **Mato Grosso** (plat.), Braz.
106/G7 **Mato Grosso**, Braz.
107/J7 **Mato Grosso** (plat.), Braz.
108/A1 **Mato Grosso do Sul** (state), Braz.
81/F2 **Matolo-Rio**, Moz.
82/E5 **Matopos**, Zim.
34/A2 **Matosinhos**, Port.
53/G4 **Maţraḩ**, Oman
33/K3 **Matrei in Osttirol**, Aus.
80/B4 **Matroosberg** (peak), SAfr.
80/L10 **Matroosberg** (peak), SAfr.
50/A4 **Maţrūḩ**, Egypt
74/E1 **Maţrūḩ**, Egypt
81/H8 **Matsiatra** (riv.), Madg.
57/L10 **Matsubara**, Japan
57/H7 **Matsubushi**, Japan
57/H7 **Matsuda**, Japan
57/H7 **Matsudo**, Japan
47/P6 **Matsue**, Japan
55/L4 **Matsue**, Japan
56/C3 **Matsue**, Japan
55/N3 **Matsumae**, Japan
57/E2 **Matsumoto**, Japan
56/E3 **Matsusaka**, Japan
57/M10 **Matsusaka**, Japan
57/G1 **Matsushima**, Japan
56/E2 **Matsutō**, Japan
47/P6 **Matsuyama**, Japan
55/L5 **Matsuyama**, Japan
56/C4 **Matsuyama**, Japan
37/F4 **Matt**, Swi.
94/D1 **Mattagami** (riv.), On,Can
64/F4 **Mattancherry Palace**, India
37/H6 **Mattarello**, It.
94/E2 **Mattawa**, On,Can
36/D6 **Matterhorn** (peak), It., Swi.
33/G4 **Matterhorn** (peak), Swi.
30/D5 **Mattertal** (val.), Swi.
99/Q16 **Matteson**, Il,US
85/H2 **Matthews** (mtn.), Ak,US
103/H1 **Matthew Town**, Bahm.
36/E5 **Mattmarksee** (lake), Swi.
56/E2 **Mattō**, Japan
22/B4 **Mattock** (riv.), Ire.
89/J4 **Mattoon**, Il,US
93/K3 **Mattoon**, Il,US
94/B4 **Mattoon**, Il,US
97/F2 **Mattoon**, Il,US
106/F2 **Maturín**, Ven.
82/E4 **Matusadona Nat'l Park**, Zim.
67/G2 **Matutum** (mt.), Phil.
106/G3 **Maú** (riv.), Braz., Guy.
108/C2 **Mauá**, Braz.
30/D4 **Maubert-Fontaine**, Fr.
26/B3 **Maubeuge**, Fr.
30/C3 **Maubeuge**, Fr.
60/B5 **Ma-ubin**, Burma
63/G4 **Ma-ubin**, Burma
32/D5 **Maubourguet**, Fr.
35/F1 **Maubourguet**, Fr.
62/D2 **Maudaha**, India
81/F2 **Mau-é-Ele**, Moz.
106/G4 **Maués**, Braz.
106/G4 **Maués Açu** (riv.), Braz.
68/D3 **Maug** (isls.), NMar.
22/D3 **Maughold**, IM,UK
22/D3 **Maughold Head** (pt.), IM,UK
32/F5 **Mauguio**, Fr.
35/H1 **Mauguio**, Fr.
69/K2 **Maui** (isl.), Hi.,US
88/T10 **Maui** (isl.), Hi,US
69/K7 **Mauke** (isl.), CookIs.
30/A6 **Mauldre** (riv.), Fr.
32/C3 **Mauléon**, Fr.
94/C3 **Maumee** (riv.), In, Oh,US
82/D4 **Maun**, Bots.
62/D2 **Maunah Bhanjan**, India
88/U11 **Mauna Kea** (peak), Hi,US
88/U11 **Mauna Loa** (peak), Hi,US
60/B4 **Maungdaw**, Burma
63/F3 **Maungdaw**, Burma
69/K6 **Maupiti** (isl.), FrPol.
37/E3 **Maur**, Swi.
62/C2 **Mau Rānīpur**, India
19/S10 **Maurecourt**, Fr.
30/A6 **Maurepas**, Fr.
32/E4 **Mauriac**, Fr.
70/E5 **Maurice** (lake), Austl.
76/F3 **Maurice Cortier** (ruins), Alg.
87/J4 **Mauricie Nat'l Park**, Qu,Can
89/M2 **Mauricie Nat'l Park**, Qu,Can
95/F2 **Mauricie Nat'l Park**, Qu,Can
33/G4 **Maurienne** (val.), Fr.
108/B1 **Maurilândia**, Braz.
74/A3 **Mauritania**
76/C4 **Mauritania**
78/B2 **Mauritania**
75/H6 **Mauritius**
81/S15 **Mauritius**
91/L5 **Mauston**, Wi,US
94/B3 **Mauston**, Wi,US
36/D6 **Mauvoisin, Barrage de** (dam), Swi.
64/F4 **Māvelikara**, India
39/H3 **Mavrommátion**, Gre.
39/G2 **Mavrovo Nat'l Park**, Macd.
40/E5 **Mavrovo Nat'l Park**, Macd.
53/L3 **Mawāna Khurd**, India
63/G5 **Maw Daung** (pass), Thai.
65/B4 **Maw Daung** (pass), Thai.
66/A1 **Maw-daung** (pass), Thai.
63/J2 **Mawei**, China
63/G3 **Mawhun**, Burma
63/G3 **Mawkmai**, Burma
65/B1 **Mawkmai**, Burma
60/B4 **Mawlaik**, Burma
63/F3 **Mawlaik**, Burma
60/A3 **Mawphlang**, India
52/D6 **Mawshij**, Yem.
83/D **Mawson** (coast), Ant.
83/E **Mawson**, Ant.
101/H4 **Maxcanú**, Mex.
102/D1 **Maxcanú**, Mex.
31/F6 **Maxéville**, Fr.
70/G4 **Maxwelton**, Austl.
89/M4 **May** (cape), NJ,US
94/F4 **May** (cape), NJ,US
97/K2 **May** (cape), NJ,US
102/D2 **Maya** (mts.), Belz., Guat.
66/C4 **Maya** (isl.), Indo.
47/P4 **Maya** (riv.), Rus.
48/N4 **Maya** (riv.), Rus.
103/H1 **Mayaguana** (isl.), Bahm.
103/H1 **Mayaguana** (passg.), Bahm.
104/C2 **Mayaguana** (isl.), Bahm.
104/C2 **Mayaguana** (passg.), Bahm.
84/K7 **Mayaguana** (isl.), Bahm.
89/M7 **Mayaguana** (isl.), Bahm.
104/E3 **Mayagüez**, PR
51/E1 **Mayakovskiy**, Geo.
53/K1 **Mayakovskogo** (peak), Taj.
63/J2 **Mayang**, China
103/H1 **Mayarí**, Cuba
57/L10 **Maya-san** (peak), Japan
99/E7 **Maybee**, Mi,US
22/D1 **Maybole**, Sc,UK
77/N5 **Maych'ew**, Eth.
46/E6 **Maydān**, Iraq
51/F3 **Maydān**, Iraq
52/E2 **Maydān**, Iraq
52/D5 **Maydī**, Yem.
31/G3 **Mayen**, Ger.
32/C2 **Mayenne**, Fr.
32/C3 **Mayenne** (riv.), Fr.
90/E2 **Mayerthorpe**, Ab,Can
52/E6 **Mayfa'ah**, Yem.
89/J4 **Mayfield**, Ky,US
94/B4 **Mayfield**, Ky,US
97/F2 **Mayfield**, Ky,US
100/D1 **Mayhill**, NM,US
19/H4 **Maykop**, Rus.
44/G3 **Maykop**, Rus.
46/E5 **Maykop**, Rus.
25/G3 **Mayland**, Eng,UK
60/C4 **Maymyo**, Burma
63/G3 **Maymyo**, Burma
22/B5 **Maynooth**, Ire.
109/B6 **Mayo** (riv.), Arg.
85/L3 **Mayo**, Yk,Can
86/C2 **Mayo**, Yk,Can
100/C3 **Mayo** (riv.), Mex.
98/K8 **Mayo**, Md,US
34/D1 **Mayor** (cape), Sp.
74/G6 **Mayotte** (isl.), Fr.
81/H6 **Mayotte** (terr.), Fr.
61/J5 **Mayoyao**, Phil.
103/G2 **May Pen**, Jam.
51/F4 **Maysān** (gov.), Iraq
47/N4 **Mayskiy**, Rus.
55/K1 **Mayskiy**, Rus.
89/K4 **Maysville**, Ky,US
94/D4 **Maysville**, Ky,US
97/H2 **Maysville**, Ky,US
49/G7 **Maythalūn**, WBnk.
64/G3 **Mayuram**, India
91/J4 **Mayville**, ND,US
99/Q16 **Maywood**, Il,US
82/E4 **Mazabuka**, Zam.
107/H4 **Mazagão**, Braz.
32/E5 **Mazamet**, Fr.
35/G1 **Mazamet**, Fr.
51/H2 **Māzandarān** (gov.), Iran
101/E3 **Mazapil**, Mex.
38/C4 **Mazara** (val.), It.
38/C4 **Mazara del Vallo**, It.
46/G6 **Mazār-e Sharīf**, Afg.
53/J1 **Mazār-e Sharīf**, Afg.
34/A1 **Mazaricos**, Sp.
34/E4 **Mazarrón**, Sp.
106/G2 **Mazaruni** (riv.), Guy.
100/C2 **Mazatán**, Mex.
92/E5 **Mazatán**, Mex
102/D3 **Mazatenango**, Guat.
100/D4 **Mazatlán**, Mex.
69/Q2 **Mazatlán**, Mex.
20/G4 **Mažeikiai**, Lith.
42/D4 **Mažeikiai**, Lith.
72/B3 **Mazeppa Nat'l Park**, Austl.
22/B3 **Mazetown**, NI,UK
50/D2 **Mazgirt**, Turk.
50/D2 **Mazıkıran** (pass), Turk.
30/B3 **Mazingarbe**, Fr.
82/C2 **Mazingu**, Zaire
54/D3 **Mazong** (peak), China
20/H4 **Mazsalaca**, Lat.
42/E4 **Mazsalaca**, Lat.
27/L2 **Mazury** (reg.), Pol.
81/E2 **Mbabane** (cap.), Swaz.
82/F6 **Mbabane** (cap.), Swaz.
76/H6 **Mbabo** (peak), Camr.
76/J7 **Mbaïki**, CAfr.
77/H6 **Mbakaou** (lake), Camr.
82/F2 **Mbala**, Zam.
76/H7 **Mbalam**, Camr.
77/M7 **Mbale**, Ugan.
76/H7 **Mbalmayo**, Camr.
79/H5 **Mbam** (riv.), Camr.
79/H5 **Mbam, Massif du** (peak), Camr.
77/J7 **Mbandaka**, Zaire
77/M8 **Mbarara**, Ugan.
82/F1 **Mbarara**, Ugan.
77/J7 **Mbata**, CAfr.
69/Y18 **Mbengga** (isl.), Fiji
82/F2 **Mbeya**, Tanz.
82/F2 **Mbeya** (range), Tanz.
76/H8 **M'Bigou**, Gabon
82/B1 **M'Bigou**, Gabon
76/G7 **Mbini**, EqG.
76/H7 **Mbini** (riv.), EqG.
77/L6 **Mbomou** (riv.), CAfr.
78/B3 **Mboune, Vallée du** (wadi), Sen.
78/A3 **M'Bour**, Sen.
82/D2 **Mbuji-Mayi**, Zaire
98/F4 **McAfee**, NJ,US
89/G5 **McAlester**, Ok,US
93/J4 **McAlester**, Ok,US
96/E3 **McAlester**, Ok,US
101/F3 **McAllen**, Tx,US
89/G6 **McAllen**, Tx,US
96/D5 **McAllen**, Tx,US
86/D3 **McBride**, BC,Can
90/C2 **McBride**, BC,Can
88/C3 **McCall**, Id,US
90/D4 **McCall**, Id,US
93/G5 **McCamey**, Tx,US
96/C4 **McCamey**, Tx,US
85/K3 **McCarthy**, Ak,US
99/C3 **McChord A.F.B.**, Wa,US
99/M9 **McClellan A.F.B.**, Ca,US
91/H4 **McClusky**, ND,US
89/H5 **McComb**, Ms,US
93/K5 **McComb**, Ms,US
97/F4 **McComb**, Ms,US
93/H3 **McConnell** (A.F.B.), Ks,US
96/D2 **McConnell** (A.F.B.), Ks,US
88/F3 **McCook**, Ne,US
93/G2 **McCook**, Ne,US
97/H3 **McCormick**, SC,US
91/J3 **McCreary**, Mb,Can
99/P15 **McCullom Lake**, Il,US
90/D5 **McDermitt**, Nv,US
92/C2 **McDermitt**, Nv,US
17/N0 **McDonald** (isls.), Austl.
85/F3 **McDonald** (mt.), Ak,US

85/L2 **McDougall** (pass), Yk,Can, NW,Can
93/K4 **McGehee**, Ar,US
96/F3 **McGehee**, Ar,US
85/G3 **McGrath**, Ak,US
90/C2 **McGregor** (riv.), BC,Can
99/G7 **McGregor**, On,Can
98/F5 **McGuire AFB**, NJ,US
99/N15 **McHenry** (co.), Il,US
99/P15 **McHenry**, Il,US
69/H5 **McKean** (atoll), Kiri.
87/K2 **McKeand** (riv.), NW,Can
89/L3 **McKeesport**, Pa,US
94/E3 **McKeesport**, Pa,US
94/B4 **McKenzie**, Tn,US
97/F2 **McKenzie**, Tn,US
70/G4 **McKinlay**, Austl.
72/A3 **McKinlay**, Austl.
84/B3 **McKinley** (mt.), Ak,US
85/H3 **McKinley** (mt.), Ak,US
85/J3 **McKinley Park**, Ak,US
90/B5 **McKinleyville**, Ca,US
92/A2 **McKinleyville**, Ca,US
101/F1 **McKinney**, Tx,US
93/H4 **McKinney**, Tx,US
96/D3 **McKinney**, Tx,US
91/H4 **McLaughlin**, SD,US
98/J8 **McLean**, Va,US
90/D2 **McLennan**, Ab,Can
70/A4 **McLeod** (lake), Austl.
90/D2 **McLeod** (riv.), Ab,Can
86/E2 **McLeod** (bay), NW,Can
90/C2 **McLeod Lake**, BC,Can
84/G2 **M'Clintock** (chan.), Can.
86/F1 **M'Clintock** (chan.), NW,Can
84/E2 **M'Clure** (str.), Can.
86/E1 **M'Clure** (str.), NW,Can
87/Q7 **M'Clure** (str.), NW,Can
88/B2 **McMinnville**, Or,US
90/C4 **McMinnville**, Or,US
89/J4 **McMinnville**, Tn,US
94/C5 **McMinnville**, Tn,US
97/G3 **McMinnville**, Tn,US
83/M **McMurdo**, Ant.
99/B3 **McNeil** (isl.), Wa,US
82/F3 **Mcocha**, Malw.
93/H3 **McPherson**, Ks,US
96/D2 **McPherson**, Ks,US
54/E5 **Mê** (riv.), China
92/D3 **Mead** (lake), Az, Nv,US
84/F6 **Mead** (lake), US
85/G2 **Meade** (riv.), Ak,US
100/E1 **Meadow**, Tx,US
84/G4 **Meadow Lake**, Can.
86/F3 **Meadow Lake**, Sk,Can
90/F2 **Meadow Lake**, Sk,Can
95/Q8 **Meadowvale**, On,Can
92/D3 **Meadow Valley** (riv.), Nv,US
93/K5 **Meadville**, Ms,US
97/F4 **Meadville**, Ms,US
94/D3 **Meadville**, Pa,US
34/A2 **Mealhada**, Port.
107/J5 **Mearim** (riv.), Braz.
25/E1 **Measham**, Eng,UK
85/F2 **Meat** (mt.), Ak,US
22/B4 **Meath** (co.), Ire.
91/G2 **Meath Park**, Sk,Can
30/B4 **Méaulte**, Fr.
19/U10 **Meaux**, Fr.
30/B6 **Meaux**, Fr.
101/M6 **Mecapalapa**, Mex.
77/N3 **Mecca**, SAr.
52/C4 **Mecca** (Makkah), SAr.
26/C3 **Mechelen**, Belg.
28/B6 **Mechelen**, Belg.
30/D1 **Mechelen** (Malines), Belg.
39/K2 **Mecidiye**, Turk.
41/H5 **Mecidiye**, Turk.
44/E4 **Mecitözü**, Turk.
50/C1 **Mecitözü**, Turk.
37/F2 **Meckenbeuren**, Ger.
31/G2 **Meckenheim**, Ger.
26/F1 **Mecklenburger Bucht** (bay), Ger.
26/F2 **Mecklenburg-Western Pomerania** (state), Ger.
29/H2 **Mecklenburg-Western Pomerania** (state), Ger.
82/G3 **Mecuia** (peak), Moz.
62/C4 **Medak**, India
66/A3 **Medan**, Indo.
109/C6 **Medanosa** (pt.), Arg.
104/D5 **Medanos de Coro Nat'l Park**, Ven.
25/F1 **Medbourne**, Eng,UK
75/S15 **Médéa**, Alg.
75/S15 **Médéa** (wilaya), Alg.
29/F6 **Medebach**, Ger.
108/D1 **Medeiros Neto**, Braz.
106/C2 **Medellín**, Col.
37/E4 **Medel, Piz** (peak), Swi.
28/C3 **Medemblik**, Neth.
23/G5 **Meden** (riv.), Eng,UK
35/J1 **Mèdes, Cap de** (cape), Fr.
50/C2 **Medetsiz** (peak), Turk.
98/H5 **Medford**, NY,US
86/D4 **Medford**, Or,US
88/B3 **Medford**, Or,US
90/C5 **Medford**, Or,US
92/B2 **Medford**, Or,US
91/L4 **Medford**, Wi,US
94/B2 **Medford**, Wi,US
98/F6 **Medford Lakes**, NJ,US
41/J3 **Medgidia**, Rom.
44/D3 **Medgidia**, Rom.
98/E6 **Media**, Pa,US
41/G2 **Mediaş**, Rom.
44/C3 **Mediaş**, Rom.
90/D4 **Medical Lake**, Wa,US
88/E3 **Medicine Bow** (range), Wy,US
91/G5 **Medicine Bow**, Wy,US
92/F2 **Medicine Bow** (range), Wy,US
93/F2 **Medicine Bow**, Wy,US
86/E3 **Medicine Hat**, Ab,Can
88/D1 **Medicine Hat**, Ab,Can
90/F3 **Medicine Hat**, Ab,Can
77/N3 **Medina**, SAr.
25/E5 **Medina** (riv.), Eng,UK
91/J4 **Medina**, ND,US
94/D3 **Medina**, Oh,US
93/H5 **Medina**, Tx,US
99/C2 **Medina**, Wa,US
52/C4 **Medina** (Al Madīnah), SAr.
34/D2 **Medinaceli**, Sp.
34/C2 **Medina del Campo**, Sp.
32/B5 **Medina de Pomar**, Sp.
34/D1 **Medina de Pomar**, Sp.
34/C2 **Medina de Rioseco**, Sp.
34/C4 **Medina-Sidonia**, Sp.
18/D5 **Mediterranean** (sea)
76/J1 **Mediterranean** (sea)
74/D1 **Mediterranean** (sea)
49/B2 **Mediterranean** (sea), Afr., Asia
48/A6 **Mediterranean** (sea)
52/B2 **Mediterranean** (sea)
35/F2 **Mediterranean** (sea)
38/B4 **Mediterranean** (sea)
90/F2 **Medley**, Ab,Can
45/L2 **Mednogorsk**, Rus.
54/D6 **Mêdog**, China
63/G2 **Mêdog**, China
46/E4 **Medveditsa** (riv.), Rus.
45/H2 **Medveditsa, Gora** (mt.), Rus.
47/S2 **Medvezh'i** (isls.), Rus.
18/G2 **Medvezh'yegorsk**, Rus.
42/G3 **Medvezh'yegorsk**, Rus.
46/D3 **Medvezh'yegorsk**, Rus.
33/L3 **Medvode**, Slov.
40/B2 **Medvode**, Slov.
19/P8 **Medway** (riv.), Eng,UK
25/G4 **Medway** (riv.), Eng,UK
44/E1 **Medyn'**, Rus.
68/A7 **Meekatharra**, Austl.
70/B5 **Meekatharra**, Austl.
92/F2 **Meeker**, Co,US
29/G3 **Meerbach** (riv.), Ger.
28/D6 **Meerbusch**, Ger.
28/C6 **Meerhout**, Belg.
31/E1 **Meerhout**, Belg.
37/F2 **Meersburg**, Ger.
31/E2 **Meerssen**, Neth.
53/L3 **Meerut**, India
62/C2 **Meerut**, India
23/F6 **Meese** (riv.), Eng,UK
25/E1 **Meese** (riv.), Eng,UK
90/F4 **Meeteetse**, Wy,US
92/E1 **Meeteetse**, Wy,US
28/C6 **Meeuwen**, Belg.
77/N7 **Mēga**, Eth.
39/G3 **Megála Kalívia**, Gre.
39/H2 **Megáli Panayía**, Gre.
77/P6 **Megalo**, Eth.
50/A2 **Megálon Khoríon**, Gre.
39/H4 **Megalópolis**, Gre.
95/G2 **Megantic** (peak), Can
39/H3 **Mégara**, Gre.
36/C6 **Megève**, Fr.
60/A3 **Meghalaya** (state), India
63/F2 **Meghalaya** (state), India
49/G6 **Megiddo**, Isr.
49/G6 **Megiddo** (ruins), Isr.
94/E1 **Mégiscane** (lake), Qu,Can
94/E1 **Mégiscane** (riv.), Qu,Can
49/A1 **Megista** (isl.), Gre.
31/E2 **Mehaigne** (riv.), Belg.
20/H1 **Mehamn**, Nor.
75/R16 **Mehdia**, Alg.
29/G1 **Mehe** (riv.), Ger.
20/H4 **Mehikoorma**, Est.
42/E4 **Mehikoorma**, Est.
62/C3 **Mehkar**, India
31/G5 **Mehlingen**, Ger.
51/H5 **Mehrān** (riv.), Iran
53/F3 **Mehrān** (riv.), Iran
31/F4 **Mehring**, Ger.
51/H4 **Mehrīz**, Iran
52/F2 **Mehrīz**, Iran
53/K4 **Mehsāna**, India
62/B3 **Mehsāna**, India
61/G3 **Mei** (riv.), China
61/G4 **Mei** (riv.), China
108/B1 **Meia Ponte** (riv.), Braz.
76/H6 **Meiganga**, Camr.
87/R6 **Meighen** (isl.), NW,Can
63/H2 **Meigu**, China
55/K3 **Meihekou**, China
60/B4 **Meiktila**, Burma
63/G3 **Meiktila**, Burma
65/A1 **Meiktila**, Burma
37/E3 **Meilen**, Swi.
29/H4 **Meine**, Ger.
29/H4 **Meinersen**, Ger.
29/E6 **Meinerzhagen**, Ger.
31/G1 **Meinerzhagen**, Ger.
26/F3 **Meiningen**, Ger.
33/J1 **Meiningen**, Ger.
33/H3 **Meiringen**, Swi.
36/E4 **Meiringen**, Swi.
31/G4 **Meisenheim**, Ger.
54/E5 **Meishan**, China
59/C5 **Meishan** (res.), China
59/D5 **Meishan**, China
59/K8 **Meishan**, China
60/D2 **Meishan**, China
27/G3 **Meissen**, Ger.
29/G6 **Meissner** (peak), Ger.
57/M10 **Meiwa**, Japan
31/E4 **Meix-devant-Virton**, Belg.
61/H3 **Meizhou**, China
76/H7 **Mekambo**, Gabon
77/N5 **Mek'elē**, Eth.
75/M14 **Meknès**, Mor.
76/D1 **Meknès**, Mor.
48/K8 **Mekong** (riv.), Asia
63/J5 **Mekong** (riv.), Asia
65/D4 **Mekong** (riv.), Asia
55/D5 **Mekong** (riv.), Asia
60/E5 **Mekong** (riv.), Asia
67/F4 **Mekongga** (peak), Indo.
60/D4 **Mekong** (Lancang) (riv.), China
63/J6 **Mekong, Mouths of** the (delta), Viet.
65/D4 **Mekong, Mouths of** the (delta), Viet.
66/C2 **Mekong, Mouths of** the (delta), Viet.
85/E3 **Mekoryuk**, Ak,US
66/B3 **Melaka**, Malay.
68/E5 **Melanesia** (reg.)
62/C6 **Melappālaiyam**, India
64/F4 **Melappālaiyam**, India
66/D4 **Melawi** (riv.), Indo.
29/H2 **Melbeck**, Ger.
25/G2 **Melbourn**, Eng,UK
71/H7 **Melbourne**, Austl.
73/C3 **Melbourne**, Austl.
73/F5 **Melbourne**, Austl.
86/F2 **Melbourne** (isl.), NW,Can
23/G6 **Melbourne**, Eng,UK
89/K6 **Melbourne**, Fl,US
97/H4 **Melbourne**, Fl,US
102/D2 **Melchor de Mencos**, Guat.
101/E3 **Melchor Múzquiz**, Mex.
96/C5 **Melchor Múzquiz**, Mex
24/D5 **Melcombe Regis**, Eng,UK
26/E1 **Meldorf**, Ger.
40/E3 **Melenci**, Yugo.
42/J5 **Melenki**, Rus.
45/G1 **Melenki**, Rus.
32/C2 **Melesse**, Fr.
45/K1 **Meleuz**, Rus.
87/J3 **Mélèzes** (riv.), Qu,Can
37/E5 **Melezza** (riv.), It.
76/J5 **Melfi**, Chad
38/D2 **Melfi**, It.
40/B5 **Melfi**, It.
86/F3 **Melfort**, Sk,Can
91/G2 **Melfort**, Sk,Can
34/C1 **Melgar de Fernamental**, Sp.
20/D3 **Melhus**, Nor.
39/G4 **Meligalás**, Gre.
40/F5 **Meliki**, Gre.
75/N13 **Melilla**, Sp.
76/E1 **Melilla**, Sp.
36/C2 **Mélisey**, Fr.
39/F3 **Melissano**, It.
86/F4 **Melita**, Mb,Can
91/H3 **Melita**, Mb,Can
38/D4 **Melito di Porto Salvo**, It.
19/G4 **Melitopol'**, Ukr.
44/E3 **Melitopol'**, Ukr.
46/D5 **Melitopol'**, Ukr.
33/L2 **Melk**, Aus.
77/P7 **Melka Meri**, Eth.
80/L10 **Melkbosstrand**, SAfr.
24/D4 **Melksham**, Eng,UK
28/A6 **Melle**, Belg.
30/C2 **Melle**, Belg.
26/E2 **Melle**, Ger.
29/F4 **Melle**, Ger.
75/W17 **Mellègue** (riv.), Alg.
20/E4 **Mellerud**, Swe.
34/B1 **Mellid**, Sp.
23/F3 **Melling**, Eng,UK
37/E3 **Mellingen**, Swi.
71/K3 **Mellish** (reef), Austl.
26/F3 **Mellrichstadt**, Ger.
33/J1 **Mellrichstadt**, Ger.
29/F1 **Mellum** (isl.), Ger.
39/H2 **Melnik**, Bul.
41/F5 **Melnik**, Bul.
27/H3 **Mělník**, Czh.
33/L1 **Mělník**, Czh.
109/F3 **Melo**, Uru.
95/N7 **Melocheville**, Qu,Can
99/Q16 **Melrose Park**, Il,US
37/F3 **Mels**, Swi.
29/G6 **Melsungen**, Ger.
23/G4 **Meltham**, Eng,UK
71/G7 **Melton**, Austl.
73/C3 **Melton**, Austl.
23/H6 **Melton Mowbray**, Eng,UK
25/F1 **Melton Mowbray**, Eng,UK
19/T11 **Melun**, Fr.
26/B4 **Melun**, Fr.
32/E2 **Melun**, Fr.
64/G3 **Melūr**, India
68/B6 **Melville** (isl.), Austl.
70/E2 **Melville** (isl.), Austl.
70/F2 **Melville** (bay), Austl.
71/G2 **Melville** (cape), Austl.
72/B1 **Melville** (cape), Austl.
84/F2 **Melville** (isl.), Can.
84/J3 **Melville** (pen.), Can.
87/L3 **Melville** (lake), Nf,Can
87/H2 **Melville** (pen.), NW,Can
87/R7 **Melville** (isl.), NW,Can
86/F3 **Melville**, Sk,Can
88/F1 **Melville**, Sk,Can
91/H3 **Melville**, Sk,Can
67/E2 **Melville** (cape), Phil.
101/F2 **Melvin**, Tx,US
99/F7 **Melvindale**, Mi,US
40/D2 **Mélykút**, Hun.
28/D1 **Memmert** (isl.), Ger.
26/F5 **Memmingen**, Ger.
33/J3 **Memmingen**, Ger.
37/G2 **Memmingen**, Ger.
65/D4 **Memot**, Camb.
49/B5 **Memphis** (ruins), Egypt
99/G6 **Memphis**, Mi,US
91/K5 **Memphis**, Mo,US
93/J2 **Memphis**, Mo,US
89/H4 **Memphis**, Tn,US
93/K4 **Memphis**, Tn,US
94/B5 **Memphis**, Tn,US
97/F3 **Memphis**, Tn,US
93/G4 **Memphis**, Tx,US
96/C3 **Memphis**, Tx,US
93/J4 **Mena**, Ar,US
96/E3 **Mena**, Ar,US
37/F5 **Menaggio**, It.
22/D5 **Menai** (str.), Wal,UK
22/D5 **Menai Bridge**, Wal,UK
76/F4 **Ménaka**, Mali
79/F3 **Ménaka**, Mali
28/C2 **Menaldum**, Neth.
81/H9 **Menarandra** (riv.), Madg.
93/H5 **Menard**, Tx,US
96/D4 **Menard**, Tx,US
34/C3 **Menasalbas**, Sp.
91/L4 **Menasha**, Wi,US
94/B2 **Menasha**, Wi,US
81/H7 **Menavava** (riv.), Madg.
66/D4 **Mendawai** (riv.), Indo.
32/E4 **Mende**, Fr.
29/E6 **Menden**, Ger.
85/E4 **Mendenhall** (cape), Ak,US
101/F3 **Méndez**, Mex.
77/N6 **Mendī**, Eth.
31/G3 **Mendig**, Ger.
24/D4 **Mendip** (hills), Eng,UK
84/E5 **Mendocino** (cape), US
88/B3 **Mendocino** (cape), Ca,US
92/B3 **Mendocino**, Ca,US
73/D1 **Mendooran**, Austl.
99/M11 **Mendota-Delta** (can.), Ca,US
109/C3 **Mendoza**, Arg.
103/E1 **Mendoza**, Cuba
81/H9 **Mendrare** (riv.), Madg.
37/E6 **Mendrisio**, Swi.
40/F3 **Menedinţi** (co.), Rom.
44/C5 **Menemen**, Turk.
50/A2 **Menemen**, Turk.
30/C2 **Menen**, Belg.
77/N8 **Menengai Crater**, Kenya
47/M5 **Menengiyn** (plain), Mong.
54/H2 **Menengiyn** (plain), Mong.
38/C4 **Menfi**, It.
54/H5 **Mengcheng**, China
59/D4 **Mengcheng**, China
26/E4 **Mengen**, Ger.
37/F1 **Mengen**, Ger.
41/L5 **Mengen**, Turk.
44/E4 **Mengen**, Turk.
50/C1 **Mengen**, Turk.
31/H2 **Mengerskirchen**, Ger.
33/L3 **Mengeš**, Slov.
66/C4 **Menggala**, Indo.
63/H3 **Menghai**, China
65/C1 **Menghai**, China
34/D4 **Mengibar**, Sp.
63/H3 **Mengla**, China
65/C1 **Mengla**, China
60/C4 **Menglian Daizu Lahuzu Vazu Zizhixian**, China
63/G3 **Menglian Daizu Lahuzu Vazu Zizhixian**, China
65/B1 **Menglian Daizu Lahuzu Vazu Zizhixian**, China
59/D4 **Mengliangu** (mtn.), China
61/F3 **Mengshan**, China
63/K3 **Mengshan**, China
59/C4 **Meng Xian**, China
55/H4 **Mengyin**, China
59/D4 **Mengyin**, China
60/D4 **Mengzi**, China
63/H3 **Mengzi**, China
30/A5 **Ménilles**, Fr.
70/G6 **Menindee**, Austl.
73/B2 **Menindee**, Austl.
73/B2 **Menindee** (dam), Austl.
73/B2 **Menindee** (lake), Austl.
73/A2 **Meningie**, Austl.
99/K12 **Menlo Park**, Ca,US
19/T11 **Mennecy**, Fr.
91/M4 **Menominee**, Mi,US
94/C2 **Menominee**, Mi,US
94/B3 **Menomonee Falls**, Wi,US
91/L4 **Menomonie**, Wi,US
94/B2 **Menomonie**, Wi,US
82/C3 **Menongue**, Ang.
35/H3 **Menorca** (Minorca) (isl.), Sp.
85/K3 **Mentasta Lake**, Ak,US
48/J10 **Mentawai** (isls.), Indo.
66/A4 **Mentawai** (isls.), Indo.
66/A4 **Mentawai** (str.), Indo.
29/H6 **Menteroda**, Ger.
36/C6 **Menthon-Saint-Bernard**, Fr.
100/E2 **Mentone**, Tx,US
93/G5 **Mentone**, Tx,US
96/C4 **Mentone**, Tx,US
94/D3 **Mentor**, Oh,US
36/C4 **Mentue** (riv.), Swi.
19/R9 **Menucourt**, Fr.
30/A5 **Menucourt**, Fr.
67/E3 **Menyapa** (peak), Indo.
54/E4 **Menyuan**, China
75/W17 **Menzel Bourguiba**, Tun.
85/M3 **Menzie** (mtn.), Yk,Can
70/C5 **Menzies**, Austl.
36/E3 **Menziken**, Swi.
37/E3 **Menzingen**, Swi.
36/E3 **Menznau**, Swi.
25/E5 **Meon** (riv.), Eng,UK
19/Q7 **Meopham**, Eng,UK
100/D2 **Meoquí**, Mex.
96/B4 **Meoquí**, Mex.
67/H4 **Meos Waar** (isl.), Indo.
82/B2 **Mepala**, Ang.
45/G4 **Mepistskaro** (peak), Geo.
26/D2 **Meppel**, Neth.
28/D3 **Meppel**, Neth.
26/D2 **Meppen**, Ger.
29/E3 **Meppen**, Ger.
35/E2 **Mequinenzo** (res.), Sp.
32/D3 **Mer**, Fr.
37/F5 **Mera** (riv.), It., Swi.
93/K3 **Meramec** (riv.), Mo,US
33/J3 **Merano**, It.
37/H4 **Merano**, It.
66/D4 **Meratus** (mts.), Indo.
67/K5 **Merauke**, Indo.
68/D5 **Merauke**, Indo.
73/B2 **Merbein**, Austl.
77/P7 **Merca**, Som.
33/G4 **Mercantour Nat'l Park**, Fr.
92/B3 **Merced**, Ca,US
92/C3 **Merced** (riv.), Ca,US
109/B3 **Mercedario** (peak), Arg.
109/C3 **Mercedes**, Arg.
109/E2 **Mercedes**, Arg.
109/E3 **Mercedes**, Uru.
99/C2 **Mercer** (isl.), Wa,US
99/C2 **Mercer Island**, Wa,US
28/B7 **Merchtem**, Belg.
30/D2 **Merchtem**, Belg.
95/N7 **Mercier**, Qu,Can
90/D2 **Mercoal**, Ab,Can
92/D3 **Mercury**, Nv,US
87/K2 **Mercy** (cape), Yk,Can
31/E5 **Mercy-le-Bas**, Fr.
32/E5 **Merdellou** (mtn.), Fr.
35/G1 **Merdellou** (mtn.), Fr.
24/D4 **Mere**, Eng,UK
109/D7 **Meredith** (cape), Falk.
44/F2 **Merefa**, Ukr.
28/A6 **Merelbeke**, Belg.
30/C2 **Merelbeke**, Belg.
31/H2 **Merenberg**, Ger.
100/C2 **Meresichic**, Mex.
65/D3 **Mereuch**, Camb.
19/Q8 **Mereworth**, Eng,UK
55/J2 **Mergel** (riv.), China
37/E6 **Mergozzo**, It.
63/G5 **Mergui**, Burma
63/G5 **Mergui** (arch.), Burma
65/B3 **Mergui**, Burma
65/B4 **Mergui** (arch.), Burma
66/A1 **Mergui**, Burma
66/A1 **Mergui** (arch.), Burma
41/H5 **Meriç**, Turk.
39/J1 **Merichleri**, Bul.
41/G4 **Merichleri**, Bul.
26/B3 **Méricourt**, Fr.
30/B3 **Méricourt**, Fr.
32/E1 **Méricourt**, Fr.
101/H4 **Mérida**, Mex.
102/D1 **Mérida**, Mex.
89/J7 **Mérida**, Mex.
18/C5 **Mérida**, Sp.
34/B3 **Mérida**, Sp.
106/D2 **Mérida**, Ven.
106/D2 **Mérida** (range), Ven.
89/J5 **Meridian**, Ms,US
97/F3 **Meridian**, Ms,US
101/F2 **Meridian**, Tx,US
93/H5 **Meridian**, Tx,US
96/D4 **Meridian**, Tx,US
99/C2 **Meridian-East Hill**, Wa,US
32/C4 **Mérignac**, Fr.
73/D3 **Merimbula**, Austl.
72/C3 **Merinda**, Austl.
37/G1 **Mering**, Ger.
40/F2 **Mérk**, Hun.
101/E1 **Merkel**, Tx,US
27/N1 **Merkinė**, Lith.
28/B6 **Merksem**, Belg.
30/D1 **Merksem**, Belg.
28/B6 **Merksplas**, Belg.
25/H6 **Merlimont**, Fr.
30/A3 **Merlimont**, Fr.
109/E3 **Merlo**, Arg.
52/B5 **Meroe** (ruins), Sudan
77/M4 **Meroe** (ruins), Sudan
49/D3 **Meron, Har** (mtn.), Isr.
50/C3 **Meron, Har** (mt.), Isr.
68/A8 **Merredin**, Austl.
70/B6 **Merredin**, Austl.
73/F5 **Merri** (cr.), Austl.
98/G5 **Merrick**, NY,US
91/L4 **Merrill**, Wi,US
94/B2 **Merrill**, Wi,US
98/E5 **Merrill Creek** (res.), NJ,US
95/G3 **Merrimack**, NH,US
24/D5 **Merriott**, Eng,UK
86/D3 **Merritt**, BC,Can
88/B1 **Merritt**, BC,Can
90/C3 **Merritt**, BC,Can
97/H4 **Merritt Island**, Fl,US
73/D2 **Merriwa**, Austl.
52/D6 **Mersa Fatma**, Eth.
52/C5 **Mersa Gulbub**, Eth.
52/C5 **Mersa Tek'lay**, Eth.
31/F4 **Mersch**, Lux.
23/F5 **Mersey** (riv.), Eng,UK
23/F5 **Merseyside** (co.), Eng,UK
49/D1 **Mersin**, Turk.
50/C2 **Mersin**, Turk.
52/B1 **Mersin**, Turk.
66/B3 **Mersing**, Malay.
30/A3 **Mers-les-Bains**, Fr.
20/G4 **Mērsrags**, Lat.
42/D4 **Mērsrags**, Lat.
19/N8 **Merstham**, Eng,UK
31/F5 **Merten**, Fr.
31/F4 **Mertert**, Lux.
31/F4 **Mertesdorf**, Ger.
24/C3 **Merthyr Tydfil**, Wal,UK
34/B4 **Mértola**, Port.
19/N7 **Merton** (bor.), Eng,UK
83/K **Mertz** (glac.), Ant.
93/G5 **Mertzon**, Tx,US
96/C4 **Mertzon**, Tx,US
31/G6 **Mertzwiller**, Fr.
30/B5 **Méru**, Fr.
77/N7 **Meru**, Kenya
30/B2 **Merville**, Fr.
28/C5 **Merwedekanaal** (can.), Neth.
19/S9 **Méry-sur-Oise**, Fr.
29/E4 **Merzen**, Ger.
31/F2 **Merzenich**, Ger.
44/E4 **Merzifon**, Turk.
50/C1 **Merzifon**, Turk.
26/D4 **Merzig**, Ger.
31/F5 **Merzig**, Ger.
33/G2 **Merzig**, Ger.
85/G3 **Mesa** (mtn.), Ak,US
88/D5 **Mesa**, Az,US
92/E4 **Mesa**, Az,US
91/K4 **Mesabi** (range), Mn,US
94/A2 **Mesabi** (range), Mn,US
39/E2 **Mesagne**, It.
40/C5 **Mesagne**, It.
39/J5 **Mesarás** (gulf), Gre.
88/E4 **Mesa Verde Nat'l Park**, Co,US
92/E3 **Mesa Verde Nat'l Park**, Co,US
96/A2 **Mesa Verde Nat'l Park**, Co,US
96/C3 **Mescalero** (ridge), NM,US
26/E3 **Meschede**, Ger.
29/F6 **Meschede**, Ger.
33/H4 **Mesco, Punta di** (pt.), It.
52/C6 **Mesfinto**, Eth.
94/F1 **Mesgouez** (lake), Qu,Can
100/D1 **Mesilla**, NM,US
37/F5 **Mesocco**, Swi.
39/G3 **Mesolóngion**, Gre.
81/J8 **Mesomeloka**, Madg.
109/E3 **Mesopotamia** (reg.), Arg.
51/E3 **Mesopotamia** (reg.), Iraq
52/D2 **Mesopotamia** (reg.), Iraq
38/E3 **Mesoraca**, It.
89/G5 **Mesquite**, Tx,US
93/H4 **Mesquite**, Tx,US
96/D3 **Mesquite**, Tx,US
76/E1 **Mesrouh** (peak), Mor.
76/F1 **Messaad**, Alg.
31/E4 **Messancy**, Belg.
18/E5 **Messina**, It.
38/D3 **Messina**, It.
38/D4 **Messina** (str.), It.
82/F5 **Messina**, SAfr.
39/H4 **Messíni**, Gre.
39/H4 **Messíni** (gulf), Gre.
37/F2 **Messkirch**, Ger.
37/E1 **Messstetten**, Ger.
19/U10 **Messy**, Fr.
39/H2 **Mesta** (riv.), Bul.
41/F5 **Mesta** (riv.), Bul.
33/K4 **Mestre**, It.
44/F4 **Mesudiye**, Turk.
78/C5 **Mesurado** (cape), Libr.
105/C2 **Meta** (riv.), Col., Ven.
95/G1 **Metabetchouan**, Qu,Can
95/G1 **Métabetchouane** (riv.), Qu,Can
87/K2 **Meta Incognita** (pen.), NW,Can
89/H6 **Metairie**, La,US
97/F4 **Metairie**, La,US
99/F6 **Metamora**, Mi,US
109/D2 **Metán**, Arg.
38/E3 **Metapontum** (ruins), It.
33/K5 **Metauro** (riv), It.
29/E4 **Metelen**, Ger.
39/G3 **Metéora**, Gre.
101/K7 **Metepec**, Mex.
101/L8 **Metepec**, Mex.
102/B2 **Metepec**, Mex
23/H5 **Metheringham**, Eng,UK
39/G4 **Methóni**, Gre.
39/E1 **Metković**, Cro.
40/C4 **Metković**, Cro.
86/C3 **Metlakatla**, Ak,US
85/M4 **Metlakatla**, BC,Can, Ak,US
102/B2 **Metlatonoc**
40/B2 **Metnitz**, Aus.
94/B4 **Metropolis**, Il,US
97/F2 **Metropolis**, Il,US
95/R8 **Metro Toronto Zoo**, On,Can
39/G3 **Métsovon**, Gre.
99/Q15 **Mettawa**, Il,US
26/C3 **Mettet**, Belg.
31/D3 **Mettet**, Belg.
32/F1 **Mettet**, Belg.
29/E4 **Mettingen**, Ger.
31/F5 **Mettlach**, Ger.
28/D6 **Mettmann**, Ger.
31/F1 **Mettmann**, Ger.
64/F3 **Mettupālaiyam**, India
64/F3 **Mettūr**, India
77/N6 **Metu**, Eth.
49/D3 **Metulla**, Isr.
18/D4 **Metz**, Fr.
26/D4 **Metz**, Fr.
31/F5 **Metz**, Fr.
33/G2 **Metz**, Fr.
37/F1 **Metzingen**, Ger.
101/F4 **Metztitlán**, Mex.
101/L6 **Metztitlán**, Mex.
102/B1 **Metztitlán**, Mex.
19/S10 **Meudon**, Fr.
31/G3 **Meudt**, Ger.
30/C2 **Meulebeke**, Belg.
36/C1 **Meurthe** (riv.), Fr.
31/E6 **Meurthe-et-Moselle** (dept.), Fr.
36/C1 **Meurthe-et-Moselle** (dept.), Fr.
31/E3 **Meuse** (riv.), Belg.
32/F1 **Meuse** (riv.), Belg., Fr.
26/C4 **Meuse** (riv.), Fr.
30/E6 **Meuse** (dept.), Fr.
31/E6 **Meuse** (riv.), Fr.
32/F2 **Meuse** (uplands), Fr.
36/B1 **Meuse** (dept.), Fr.
36/B1 **Meuse** (riv.), Fr.
26/C4 **Meuse, Côtes de** (mts.), Fr.
31/E5 **Meuse, Cotes de** (uplands), Fr.
36/A3 **Meuzin** (riv.), Fr.
49/G8 **Mevasseret Ziyyon**, Isr.
23/G5 **Mexborough**, Eng,UK
100/D4 **Mexcaltitán**, Mex.
93/H5 **Mexia**, Tx,US
96/D4 **Mexia**, Tx,US
107/J3 **Mexiana**, Braz.
100/B1 **Mexicali**, Mex.
88/C5 **Mexicali**, Mex.
92/D4 **Mexicali**, Mex
102/B2 **Mexico**
102/C1 **Mexico** (gulf)
84/G7 **Mexico**
88/F7 **Mexico**
101/G3 **Mexico** (gulf)
101/N6 **Mexico** (gulf)
84/H7 **Mexico** (gulf), NAm.
93/J5 **Mexico** (gulf), NAm
101/G3 **Mexico** (gulf)
89/H6 **Mexico** (gulf)
101/K7 **México** (state), Mex.
101/E5 **Mexico** (state), Mex.
101/Q9 **México** (state), Mex.
102/A2 **Mexico** (state), Mex.
89/H4 **Mexico**, Mo,US
93/K3 **Mexico**, Mo,US
96/F2 **Mexico**, Mo,US
101/F5 **Mexico City** (cap.), Mex.
101/K7 **Mexico City** (cap.), Mex.
101/Q10 **Mexico City** (cap.), Mex.
102/B2 **Mexico City** (cap.), Mex.
36/B6 **Meximieux**, Fr.
51/H3 **Meybod**, Iran
52/F2 **Meybod**, Iran
51/H4 **Meydān-e Gel** (lake), Iran
85/M4 **Meyers Chuck**, Ak,US
80/Q13 **Meyerton**, SAfr.
46/G6 **Meymaneh**, Afg.
53/H1 **Meymaneh**, Afg.
36/C5 **Meyrin**, Swi.
36/C6 **Meythet**, Fr.
36/B6 **Meyzieu**, Fr.
63/G4 **Mezaligon**, Burma
39/H1 **Mezdra**, Bul.
41/F4 **Mezdra**, Bul.
32/E5 **Mèze**, Fr.
35/G1 **Mèze**, Fr.
18/H2 **Mezen'**, Rus.
19/H2 **Mezen'** (riv.), Rus.
42/J2 **Mezen'** (bay), Rus.
42/K2 **Mezen'** (riv.), Rus.
46/E3 **Mezen'**, Rus.
46/E3 **Mezen'** (riv.), Rus.
46/J4 **Mezhdurechensk**, Rus.
46/E2 **Mezhdusharskiy** (i Rus.
27/M4 **Mezhgor'ye**, Ukr.
41/F1 **Mezhgor'ye**, Ukr.
40/E2 **Mezoberény**, Hun.
40/E2 **Mezokovácsháza**, Hun.
27/L5 **Mezőkövesd**, Hun
40/E2 **Mezőkövesd**, Hun
40/E2 **Mezőtúr**, Hun.
100/D4 **Mezquital**, Mex.
100/E4 **Mezquitic**, Mex.
37/G5 **Mezzana, Cima** (peak), It.
37/H5 **Mezzocorona**, It.
33/J3 **Mezzolombardo**, It
37/H5 **Mezzolombardo**, It
43/W7 **Mga**, Rus.
43/W7 **Mga** (riv.), Rus.
53/L4 **Mhow**, India
62/C3 **Mhow**, India
59/D3 **Mi** (riv.), China
102/B2 **Miahuatlán**, Mex.
34/C3 **Miajadas**, Sp.
92/E4 **Miami**, Az,US
104/A1 **Miami**, Fl,US
89/K6 **Miami**, Fl,US
97/H5 **Miami**, Fl,US
89/H4 **Miami**, Ok,US
93/J3 **Miami**, Ok,US
96/E2 **Miami**, Ok,US
89/K6 **Miami Beach**, Fl,U
97/H5 **Miami Beach**, Fl,U
64/B2 **Miān Channūn**, Pa
59/B4 **Mianchi**, China
53/G1 **Mīāndasht**, Iran
51/F2 **Mīāndoāb**, Iran
52/E1 **Mīāndoāb**, Iran
81/H7 **Miandrivazo**, Mad
46/E6 **Mīāneh**, Iran
51/F2 **Mīāneh**, Iran
52/E1 **Mīāneh**, Iran
64/B1 **Miāni**, Pak.
60/D2 **Mianmian** (mts.), China
60/D2 **Mianning**, China
63/H2 **Mianning**, China
98/G4 **Mianus** (riv.), Ct,U
53/K2 **Miānwāli**, Pak.
64/A1 **Miānwāli**, Pak.
54/E5 **Mianyang**, China
60/E2 **Mianyang**, China
54/E5 **Mianzhu**, China
60/E2 **Mianzhu**, China
59/E3 **Miaodao** (isls.), Ch
61/F3 **Miao'er** (peak), Ch
59/H6 **Miaofeng Shan** (mtn.), China
81/H7 **Miarinarivo**, Mad
81/G8 **Miary**, Madg.
43/P5 **Miass**, Rus.
43/Q5 **Miass** (riv.), Rus.
46/G4 **Miass**, Rus.
27/J2 **Miastko**, Pol.
90/D2 **Mica Creek**, BC,C
27/L4 **Michalovce**, Slvk.
44/B2 **Michalovce**, Slvk.
85/K2 **Michelson** (mt.), Ak,US
104/D3 **Miches**, DRep.
91/L4 **Michigan** (state),
91/M5 **Michigan** (lake), U
87/H4 **Michigan** (lake), U
87/H4 **Michigan** (state),
89/J2 **Michigan** (state),
89/J3 **Michigan** (lake), U
93/L2 **Michigan** (lake), U
94/C2 **Michigan** (riv.), US
94/C2 **Michigan** (state),
99/F6 **Michigan** (state),
99/R15 **Michigan** (lake), U
84/J5 **Michigan** (lake), U Can.
94/C3 **Michigan City**, In,
91/M4 **Michipicoten** (isl.) On,Can
94/C2 **Michipicoten** (isl.) On,Can
101/E5 **Michoacan** (state Mex.
41/H4 **Michurin**, Bul.
44/C4 **Michurin**, Bul.
50/A1 **Michurin**, Bul.
19/H3 **Michurinsk**, Rus.
45/G1 **Michurinsk**, Rus.
46/E4 **Michurinsk**, Rus.
23/F2 **Mickle Fell** (mtn.) Eng,UK
23/F2 **Mickleton**, Eng,UK
98/E6 **Mickleton**, NJ,US
103/E3 **Mico** (riv.), Nic.
104/F4 **Micoud**, StL.
68/E3 **Micronesia** (reg.)
68/D4 **Micronesia, Federated States**
79/G2 **Midal** (well), Nige
91/H3 **Midale**, Sk,Can
26/B3 **Middelburg**, Neth
28/A6 **Middelburg**, Neth
80/D3 **Middelburg**, SAfr.
80/Q12 **Middelburg**, SAfr.
81/E2 **Middelburg**, SAfr.
82/E6 **Middelburg**, SAfr.
82/E7 **Middelburg**, SAfr.
26/E1 **Middelfart**, Den.
28/B5 **Middelharnis**, Ne
30/B1 **Middelkerke**, Bel
99/M11 **Middle** (riv.), Ca,U
92/C2 **Middle Alkali** (lak Ca,US
63/F5 **Middle Andaman** (isl.), India
95/F2 **Middlebury**, Vt,US
103/J1 **Middle Caicos** (is Trks.
104/D2 **Middle Caicos** (is Trks.
23/G3 **Middleham**, Eng,U
91/J5 **Middle Loup** (riv.), Nb,US

72/C3 **Middlemount**, Austl.
98/K7 **Middle River**, Md,US
99/F7 **Middle Rouge** (riv.), Mi,US
89/K4 **Middlesboro**, Ky,US
94/D4 **Middlesboro**, Ky,US
97/H2 **Middlesboro**, Ky,US
18/C3 **Middlesbrough**, Eng,UK
23/G2 **Middlesbrough**, Eng,UK
25/F4 **Middlesex** (reg.), Eng,UK
90/C4 **Middle Sister** (peak), Or,US
23/F4 **Middleton**, Eng,UK
25/E2 **Middleton Cheney**, Eng,UK
23/F2 **Middleton-in-Teesdale**, Eng,UK
22/B3 **Middletown**, NI,UK
98/F5 **Middletown**, NJ,US
99/J9 **Middletown**, Ca,US
23/F5 **Middlewich**, Eng,UK
24/C3 **Mid Glamorgan** (co.), Wal,UK
25/F5 **Midhurst**, Eng,UK
32/D5 **Midi** (can.), Fr.
35/G1 **Midi** (can.), Fr.
32/D4 **Midi-Pyrénées** (reg.), Fr.
35/F1 **Midi-Pyrénées** (reg.), Fr.
94/E2 **Midland**, On,Can
89/K3 **Midland**, Mi,US
94/C3 **Midland**, Mi,US
100/E2 **Midland**, Tx,US
88/F5 **Midland**, Tx,US
93/G5 **Midland**, Tx,US
96/C4 **Midland**, Tx,US
99/C3 **Midland**, Wa,US
21/A5 **Midleton**, Ire.
99/Q16 **Midlothian**, Il,US
29/F1 **Midlum**, Ger.
70/G6 **Midona** (lake), Austl.
81/H8 **Midongy Atsimo**, Madg.
32/C5 **Midou** (riv.), Fr.
24/D4 **Midsomer Norton**, Eng,UK
63/H2 **Midu**, China
68/H2 **Midway** (isls.), PacUS
73/C4 **Midway Point-Sorell**, Austl.
93/H4 **Midwest City**, Ok,US
96/D3 **Midwest City**, Ok,US
50/C5 **Midyan** (reg.), SAr.
52/C3 **Midyan** (reg.), SAr.
50/E2 **Midyat**, Turk.
52/D1 **Midyat**, Turk.
44/B4 **Midzhur** (peak), Bul.
40/F4 **Midžor** (peak), Yugo.
56/B4 **Mie**, Japan
56/E3 **Mie** (pref.), Japan
57/M10 **Mie** (pref.), Japan
27/H2 **Międzychód**, Pol.
27/J3 **Międzylesie**, Pol.
33/M1 **Międzylesie**, Pol.
27/M3 **Międzyrzec Podlaski**, Pol.
27/H2 **Międzyrzecz**, Pol.
27/H2 **Międzyzdroje**, Pol.
31/G3 **Miehlen**, Ger.
27/L3 **Mielec**, Pol.
76/J7 **Miéle I**, Congo
101/F3 **Mier**, Mex.
41/G2 **Miercurea Ciuc**, Rom.
44/C3 **Miercurea Ciuc**, Rom.
34/C1 **Mieres**, Sp.
33/J3 **Miesbach**, Ger.
77/P6 **Mī'ēso**, Eth.
26/B5 **Migennes**, Fr.
32/E3 **Migennes**, Fr.
36/C4 **Mignovillard**, Fr.
101/N8 **Miguel Aleman** (res.), Mex.
102/B2 **Miguel Alemán** (res.), Mex.
100/E3 **Miguel Auza**, Mex.
100/C3 **Miguel Hidalgo** (res.), Mex.
101/Q10 **Miguel Hidalgo**, Mex.
108/B2 **Miguelópolis**, Braz.
34/D3 **Miguelturra**, Sp.
58/D4 **Migŭm**, SKor.
58/G6 **Migŭm**, SKor.
50/B2 **Mihalıççık**, Turk.
56/D3 **Mihama**, Japan
57/M10 **Mihama**, Japan
56/C3 **Mihara**, Japan
57/L10 **Mihara**, Japan
57/G2 **Miharu**, Japan
64/H4 **Mihintale** (ruins), SrL.
29/H6 **Mihla**, Ger.
53/J3 **Mihrābpur**, Pak.
35/E2 **Mijares** (riv.), Sp.
34/C4 **Mijas**, Sp.
28/B4 **Mijdrecht**, Neth.
57/N10 **Mikawa** (bay), Japan
57/N9 **Mikawa-Mino** (mts.), Japan
50/E1 **Mikha Tskhakaya**, Geo.
39/H1 **Mikhaylovgrad** (prov.), Bul.
40/F4 **Mikhaylovgrad** (reg.), Bul.
41/F4 **Mikhaylovgrad**, Bul.
44/B4 **Mikhaylovgrad**, Bul.
19/H3 **Mikhaylovka**, Rus.
45/G2 **Mikhaylovka**, Rus.
46/E4 **Mikhaylovka**, Rus.
49/F7 **Mikhmoret**, Isr.
57/K10 **Miki**, Japan
39/H4 **Mikínai**, Gre.
18/F2 **Mikkeli**, Fin.
20/H3 **Mikkeli**, Fin.
20/H3 **Mikkeli** (prov.), Fin.
42/E3 **Mikkeli**, Fin.
42/E3 **Mikkeli** (prov.), Fin.
46/C3 **Mikkeli**, Fin.
39/J4 **Míkonos**, Gre.
39/J4 **Míkonos** (isl.), Gre.
39/G2 **Mikri Prespa** (lake), Gre.
40/E5 **Mikrí Prespa** (lake), Gre.
57/M10 **Mikuma**, Japan
82/G2 **Mikumi**, Tanz.
82/G2 **Mikumi Nat'l Park**, Tanz.
56/E2 **Mikuni**, Japan
57/F2 **Mikuni-tōge** (pass), Japan
75/U17 **Mila** (gov.), Alg.
75/V17 **Mila**, Alg.
106/C4 **Milagro**, Ecu.
18/D4 **Milan**, It.
33/H4 **Milan** (Milano), It.
73/A2 **Milang**, Austl.
33/H4 **Milano** (Milan), It.
50/A2 **Milas**, Turk.
38/D3 **Milazzo**, It.
24/D5 **Milborne Port**, Eng,UK
25/G2 **Mildenhall**, Eng,UK
68/D8 **Mildura**, Austl.
70/G6 **Mildura**, Austl.
73/B2 **Mildura**, Austl.
60/D3 **Mile**, China
63/H3 **Mile**, China
71/J5 **Miles**, Austl.
72/C4 **Miles**, Austl.
93/G5 **Miles**, Tx,US
96/C4 **Miles**, Tx,US
86/F4 **Miles City**, Mt,US
88/E2 **Miles City**, Mt,US
91/G4 **Miles City**, Mt,US
33/K1 **Milešovka** (peak), Czh.
91/G3 **Milestone**, Sk,Can
38/D2 **Miletto** (peak), It.
25/F4 **Milford**, Eng,UK
22/B3 **Milford**, NI,UK
98/G4 **Milford**, Ct,US
99/E6 **Milford**, Mi,US
92/D3 **Milford**, Ut,US
24/A3 **Milford Haven**, Wal,UK
24/A3 **Milford Haven** (inlet), Wal,UK
25/E5 **Milford on Sea**, Eng,UK
68/G4 **Mili** (atoll), Mrsh.
75/S15 **Miliana**, Alg.
27/J3 **Milicz**, Pol.
88/S10 **Mililani Town**, Hi,US
88/V13 **Mililani Town**, Hi,US
70/E2 **Milingimbi Mission**, Austl.
72/G9 **Military Rsv.**, Austl.
90/F3 **Milk** (riv.), Can., US
25/E4 **Milk** (hill), Eng,UK
88/E2 **Milk** (riv.), Ab,Can, Mt,,US
86/F4 **Milk** (riv.), Can,US
84/F5 **Milk** (riv.), US, Can.
90/E3 **Milk River**, Ab,Can
83/G **Mill** (isl.), Ant.
87/J2 **Mill** (isl.), NW,Can
99/G5 **Mill** (cr.), Mi,US
72/B2 **Millaa Millaa**, Austl.
32/E4 **Millau**, Fr.
99/K11 **Millbrae**, Ca,US
24/B6 **Millbrook**, Eng,UK
89/K5 **Milledgeville**, Ga,US
97/H3 **Milledgeville**, Ga,US
95/N6 **Mille Iles** (riv.), Qu,Can
91/L3 **Mille Lacs** (lake), On,Can
94/B1 **Mille Lacs** (lake), On,Can
91/K4 **Mille Lacs** (lake), Mn,US
89/H2 **Mille Lacs** (lake), Mn,US
91/J4 **Miller**, SD,US
93/H1 **Miller**, SD,US
45/G2 **Millerovo**, Rus.
97/G3 **Millers Ferry** (dam), Al,US
22/C1 **Milleur** (pt.), Sc,UK
32/D4 **Millevaches** (plat.), Fr.
95/Q9 **Millgrove**, On,Can
70/G7 **Millicent**, Austl.
73/B3 **Millicent**, Austl.
95/R8 **Milliken**, On,Can
28/D5 **Millingen aan de Rijn**, Neth.
87/K4 **Millinocket**, Me,US
89/N2 **Millinocket**, Me,US
95/G2 **Millinocket**, Me,US
22/C2 **Millisle**, NI,UK
72/C4 **Millmerran**, Austl.
23/E3 **Millom**, Eng,UK
91/G5 **Mills**, Wy,US
23/F3 **Millthrop**, Eng,UK
99/J11 **Mill Valley**, Ca,US
68/E5 **Milne** (bay), PNG
23/F4 **Milnrow**, Eng,UK
70/C4 **Milo** (riv.), Gui.
95/G2 **Milo**, Me,US
88/U11 **Milolii**, Hi,US
39/J4 **Mílos**, Gre.
39/J4 **Mílos** (isl.), Gre.
101/Q10 **Milpa Alta**, Mex.
70/G5 **Milparinka**, Austl.
99/L12 **Milpitas**, Ca,US
26/E3 **Milseburg** (peak), Ger.
33/H1 **Milseburg** (peak), Ger.
73/D2 **Milton**, Austl.
95/Q8 **Milton**, On,Can
71/Q12 **Milton**, N.Z.
23/F2 **Milton**, Eng,UK
25/G4 **Milton**, Eng,UK
97/G4 **Milton**, Fl,US
96/G3 **Milton**, NH,US
99/C3 **Milton**, Wa,US
90/D4 **Milton-Freewater**, Or,US
95/Q8 **Milton Heights**, On,Can
25/F2 **Milton Keynes**, Eng,UK
21/H7 **Miltown Malbay**, Ire.
61/G2 **Miluo** (riv.), China
24/C4 **Milverton**, Eng,UK
89/J3 **Milwaukee**, Wi,US
91/M5 **Milwaukee**, Wi,US
93/L2 **Milwaukee**, Wi,US
94/C3 **Milwaukee**, Wi,US
99/Q13 **Milwaukee**, Wi,US
99/Q14 **Milwaukee** (co.), Wi,US
56/B4 **Mimi** (riv.), Japan
32/C4 **Mimizan**, Fr.
54/E5 **Min** (riv.), China
60/D2 **Min** (riv.), China
61/H3 **Min** (riv.), China
63/H2 **Min** (riv.), China
75/R16 **Mīna** (riv.), Alg.
101/E3 **Mina**, Mex.
92/C3 **Mina**, Nv,US
51/J5 **Mīnāb**, Iran
53/G3 **Mīnāb**, Iran
67/F3 **Minahasa** (pen.), Indo.
57/M10 **Minakuchi**, Japan
56/B4 **Minamata**, Japan
57/F3 **Minami-Alps Nat'l Park**, Japan
57/M10 **Minamichita**, Japan
68/D2 **Minamiiō** (isl.), Japan
68/E2 **Minami-Tori-Shima** (isl.), Japan
57/L10 **Minamiyamashiro**, Japan
103/G1 **Minas**, Cuba
109/E3 **Minas**, Uru.
103/F1 **Minas de Matahambre**, Cuba
34/B4 **Minas de Ríotinto**, Sp.
108/C1 **Minas Gerais** (state), Braz.
52/E3 **Mīnā' Su'ūd**, Kuw.
77/Q2 **Mīnā' Sa'ūd**, Kuw.
101/G5 **Minatitlán**, Mex.
102/C2 **Minatitlán**, Mex.
60/B4 **Minbu**, Burma
63/F3 **Minbu**, Burma
60/B4 **Minbya**, Burma
63/F3 **Minbya**, Burma
64/B2 **Minchinābād**, Pak.
24/D3 **Minchinhampton**, Eng,UK
21/B2 **Minch, The** (sound), Sc,UK
48/M8 **Mindanao** (isl.), Phil.
67/F2 **Mindanao** (isl.), Phil.
67/F2 **Mindanao** (sea), Phil.
68/B4 **Mindanao** (isl.), Phil.
26/F4 **Mindel** (riv.), Ger.
33/J2 **Mindel** (riv.), Ger.
37/G1 **Mindel** (riv.), Ger.
26/F4 **Mindelheim**, Ger.
37/G1 **Mindelheim**, Ger.
74/J10 **Mindelo**, CpV.
26/E2 **Minden**, Ger.
29/F4 **Minden**, Ger.
89/H5 **Minden**, La,US
93/J4 **Minden**, La,US
96/E3 **Minden**, La,US
93/H2 **Minden**, Ne,US
67/K5 **Mindiptana**, Indo.
48/L8 **Mindoro** (isl.), Phil.
67/F1 **Mindoro** (isl.), Phil.
68/A3 **Mindoro** (isl.), Phil.
45/L1 **Mindyak**, Rus.
24/C4 **Minehead**, Eng,UK
98/G5 **Mineola**, NY,US
107/H7 **Mineiros**, Braz.
101/L6 **Mineral del Monte**, Mex.
45/G3 **Mineral'nye Vody**, Rus.
101/F1 **Mineral Wells**, Tx,US
93/H4 **Mineral Wells**, Tx,US
96/D3 **Mineral Wells**, Tx,US
33/H5 **Minerbio** (pt.), Fr.
31/H5 **Minfeld**, Ger.
59/C3 **Ming** (riv.), China
61/E4 **Ming** (riv.), China
63/J3 **Ming** (riv.), China
95/J1 **Mingan** (riv.), Qu,Can
53/K2 **Mingāora**, Pak.
19/H4 **Mingechaur**, Azer.
45/H4 **Mingechaur**, Azer.
45/H4 **Mingechaur** (res.), Azer.
46/E5 **Mingechaur**, Azer.
51/F1 **Mingechaur**, Azer.
51/F1 **Mingechaur** (res.), Azer.
70/B5 **Mingenew**, Austl.
60/B4 **Mingin**, Burma
34/E3 **Minglanilla**, Sp.
54/E5 **Mingshan**, China
60/D2 **Mingshan**, China
55/K2 **Mingshui**, China
60/B4 **Mingun, Ancient City of** (ruins), Burma
65/A1 **Mingun, Ancient City of** (ruins), Burma
54/E4 **Minhe**, China
63/G4 **Minhla**, Burma
34/B1 **Minho** (riv.), Sp.
70/C5 **Minigwal** (lake), Austl.
91/L3 **Miniss** (lake), On,Can
91/H2 **Minitonas**, Mb,Can
54/E4 **Minle**, China
76/G6 **Minna**, Nga.
84/H5 **Minneapolis**, US
86/G4 **Minneapolis**, Mn,US
89/H3 **Minneapolis**, Mn,US
91/K4 **Minneapolis**, Mn,US
86/G3 **Minnedosa**, Mb,Can
88/G1 **Minnedosa**, Mb,Can
91/J3 **Minnedosa**, Mb,Can
91/K4 **Minnesota** (state), US
86/G4 **Minnesota** (state), US
89/G2 **Minnesota** (state), US
93/J2 **Minnesota** (state), US
91/K4 **Minnesota** (riv.), Mn,US
86/G4 **Minnesota** (riv.), Mn,US
22/D2 **Minnigaff**, Sc,UK
94/B1 **Minnis** (lake), On,Can
91/L3 **Minnitaki** (lake), On,Can
94/A1 **Minnitaki** (lake), On,Can
57/E3 **Mino**, Japan
34/A1 **Miño**, Sp.
18/C4 **Miño** (riv.), Port.,Sp.
57/F3 **Minobu**, Japan
57/N9 **Mino-Mikawa** (mts.), Japan
57/L10 **Mino'o**, Japan
57/L10 **Mino'o** (riv.), Japan
18/D5 **Minorca** (isl.), Sp.
35/G3 **Minorca** (Menorca) (isl.), Sp.
86/F4 **Minot**, ND,US
88/F2 **Minot**, ND,US
91/H3 **Minot**, ND,US
54/E4 **Minqin**, China
61/H3 **Minqing**, China
54/H5 **Minquan**, China
59/C4 **Minquan**, China
29/F1 **Minsener Oog** (isl.), Ger.
18/F3 **Minsk** (cap.), Bela.
42/E5 **Minsk** (cap.), Bela.
44/C1 **Minsk** (cap.), Bela.
46/C4 **Minsk** (cap.), Bela.
27/L2 **Mińsk Mazowiecki**, Pol.
42/E5 **Minsk Obl.**, Bela.
44/C1 **Minsk Obl.**, Bela.
25/G4 **Minster**, Eng,UK
53/K1 **Mintaka** (pass), China
95/H2 **Minto**, Can
86/E1 **Minto** (inlet), NW,Can
85/L3 **Minto**, Yk,Can
85/J2 **Minto**, Ak,US
38/C2 **Minturno**, It.
40/A5 **Minturno**, It.
49/B4 **Minūf**, Egypt
50/B4 **Minūf**, Egypt
46/K4 **Minusinsk**, Rus.
37/E5 **Minusio**, Swi.
63/G2 **Minutang**, India
54/E5 **Min Xian**, China
49/B4 **Minyā al Qamḩ**, Egypt
73/B3 **Minyip**, Austl.
42/E5 **Miory**, Bela.
54/D6 **Mipi**, India
63/G2 **Mipi**, India
95/K2 **Miquelon**, StP
106/C3 **Mira** (riv.), Col., Ecu.
34/A2 **Mira**, Port.
34/A4 **Mira** (riv.), Port.
95/M6 **Mirabel**, Qu,Can
108/D2 **Miracema**, Braz.
107/J5 **Miracema do Norte**, Braz.
106/D3 **Miraflores**, Col.
103/H2 **Miragoâne**, Haiti
53/K5 **Miraj**, India
62/B4 **Miraj**, India
109/E4 **Miramar**, Arg.
39/J5 **Mirambéllou** (gulf), Gre.
32/D4 **Miramont-de-Guyenne**, Fr.
107/G8 **Miranda** (riv.), Braz.
104/E5 **Miranda** (state), Ven.
32/B5 **Miranda de Ebro**, Sp.
34/D1 **Miranda de Ebro**, Sp.
34/A2 **Miranda do Corvo**, Port.
34/B2 **Miranda do Douro**, Port.
32/D5 **Mirande**, Fr.
35/F1 **Mirande**, Fr.
34/B2 **Mirandela**, Port.
33/J4 **Mirandola**, It.
108/B2 **Mirandópolis**, Braz.
108/B2 **Mirante do Paranapanema**, Braz.
108/B2 **Mirassol**, Braz.
103/E4 **Miravalles** (vol.), CR
34/B1 **Miravalles** (mtn.), Sp.
51/F1 **Mir-Bashir**, Azer.
103/H2 **Mirebalais**, Haiti
104/C3 **Mirebalais**, Haiti
36/B3 **Mirebeau-sur-Bèze**, Fr.
26/D4 **Mirecourt**, Fr.
33/G2 **Mirecourt**, Fr.
36/C1 **Mirecourt**, Fr.
23/G4 **Mirfield**, Eng,UK
44/E2 **Mirgorod**, Ukr.
66/D3 **Miri**, Malay.
72/C4 **Miriam Vale**, Austl.
108/A5 **Mirim** (lake), Braz.
109/E3 **Mirim** (lake), Braz., Uru.
104/D5 **Mirimire**, Ven.
39/J3 **Mírina**, Gre.
44/C5 **Mírina**, Gre.
53/H3 **Mirjāveh**, Iran
83/G **Mirnyy**, Ant.
47/M3 **Mirnyy**, Rus.
91/H2 **Mirond** (lake), Sk,Can
26/G2 **Mirow**, Ger.
53/K2 **Mīrpur**, Pak.
98/F6 **Mirror** (lake), NJ,US
60/A4 **Mīrsarāi**, Bang.
39/H4 **Mirtóön** (sea), Gre.
56/A3 **Miryang**, SKor.
58/E5 **Miryang**, SKor.
51/F1 **Mirzaani**, Geo.
62/D2 **Mirzāpur**, India
77/M7 **Misa**, Zaire
56/D3 **Misaki**, Japan
57/L10 **Misaki**, Japan
101/F5 **Misantla**, Mex.
101/N7 **Misantla**, Mex.
102/B2 **Misantla**, Mex.
57/H7 **Misato**, Japan
57/M10 **Misato**, Japan
55/L2 **Mishan**, China
94/C3 **Mishawaka**, In,US
85/F2 **Misheguk** (mtn.), Ak,US
57/F3 **Mishima**, Japan
38/C3 **Misilmeri**, It.
92/D5 **Misión del Rosario**, Mex
100/B2 **Misión de San Fernando**, Mex.
109/F2 **Misiones** (mts.), Arg.
92/D5 **Misión San Fernando**, Mex
103/F3 **Miskitos** (cay), Nic.
18/F4 **Miskolc**, Hun.
27/L4 **Miskolc**, Hun.
40/E1 **Miskolc**, Hun.
44/B2 **Miskolc**, Hun.
46/C5 **Miskolc**, Hun.
52/C5 **Mismār**, Sudan
77/N4 **Mismār**, Sudan
57/M10 **Misono**, Japan
67/H4 **Misool** (isl.), Indo.
91/L4 **Misquah** (hills), Mn,US
94/B2 **Misquah** (hills), Mn,US
76/J1 **Mişrātah**, Libya
77/L1 **Mişrātah** (pt.), Libya
87/H3 **Missinaibi** (riv.), On,Can
94/D1 **Missinaibi** (lake), On,Can
94/D1 **Missinaibi** (riv.), On,Can
96/D5 **Mission**, Tx,US
72/B2 **Mission Beach**, Austl.
92/C4 **Mission Viejo**, Ca,US
91/M2 **Missisa** (lake), On,Can
94/E1 **Missisicabi** (riv.), On,Can
87/J4 **Mississauga**, On,Can
94/E3 **Mississauga**, On,Can
95/Q8 **Mississauga**, On,Can
91/L5 **Mississippi** (riv.), US
84/H6 **Mississippi** (riv.), US
84/J7 **Mississippi** (delta), US
89/H5 **Mississippi** (riv.), US
89/H5 **Mississippi** (state), US
89/J6 **Mississippi** (delta), US
93/K4 **Mississippi** (state), US
93/K5 **Mississippi** (riv.), US
94/B4 **Mississippi** (riv.), US
97/F3 **Mississippi** (state), US
86/G4 **Mississippi** (riv.), US
68/C5 **Missol** (isl.), Indo.
86/E4 **Missoula**, Mt,US
88/D2 **Missoula**, Mt,US
90/E4 **Missoula**, Mt,US
90/K5 **Missouri** (riv.), US
84/H5 **Missouri** (riv.), US
86/G4 **Missouri** (riv.), US
89/G3 **Missouri** (riv.), US
89/H4 **Missouri** (state), US
93/J3 **Missouri** (state), US
93/J5 **Missouri City**, Tx,US
96/E4 **Missouri City**, Tx,US
91/H3 **Missouri, Coteau du** (upland), Can., US
72/B3 **Mistake** (cr.), Austl.
95/L2 **Mistaken** (pt.), Can
95/F1 **Mistassibi** (riv.), Qu,Can
95/G1 **Mistassibi Nord Est** (riv.), Qu,Can
87/J3 **Mistassini** (lake), Qu,Can
87/J4 **Mistassini**, Qu,Can
94/F1 **Mistassini**, Qu,Can
94/F1 **Mistassini** (lake), Qu,Can
95/F1 **Mistassini**, Qu,Can
95/F1 **Mistassini** (riv.), Qu,Can
27/J4 **Mistelbach an der Zaya**, Aus.
33/M2 **Mistelbach an der Zaya**, Aus.
25/H3 **Mistley**, Eng,UK
39/H4 **Mistrás** (ruins), Gre.
38/D4 **Mistretta**, It.
85/M4 **Misty Fjords Nat'l Mem.**, Ak,US
86/C3 **Misty Fjords Nat'l Mon.**, Ak,US
57/M10 **Misugi**, Japan
57/H7 **Mitaka**, Japan
57/N9 **Mitake**, Japan
100/D4 **Mita, Punta de** (pt.), Mex.
104/D5 **Mitare**, Ven.
52/C5 **Mitatib**, Sudan
24/D3 **Mitcheldean**, Eng,UK
70/G3 **Mitchell** (riv.), Austl.
71/H5 **Mitchell**, Austl.
72/A1 **Mitchell** (riv.), Austl.
72/D4 **Mitchell**, Austl.
89/K4 **Mitchell** (mt.), NC,US
97/H3 **Mitchell** (peak), NC,US
91/H5 **Mitchell**, Ne,US
93/G2 **Mitchell**, Ne,US
86/G4 **Mitchell**, SD,US
89/G3 **Mitchell**, SD,US
91/J5 **Mitchell**, SD,US
93/H2 **Mitchell**, SD,US
72/A1 **Mitchell & Alice Rivers Nat'l Park**, Austl.
49/B4 **Mīt Ghamr**, Egypt
50/B4 **Mīt Ghamr**, Egypt
62/B2 **Mithankot**, Pak.
53/J4 **Mithi**, Pak.
62/A3 **Mithi**, Pak.
39/K3 **Míthimna**, Gre.
44/C5 **Míthimna**, Gre.
50/A2 **Míthimna**, Gre.
69/K6 **Mitiaro** (isl.), Cookls.
39/K3 **Mitilíni**, Gre.
44/C5 **Mitilíni**, Gre.
50/A2 **Mitilíni**, Gre.
102/B2 **Mitla** (ruins), Mex.
50/C4 **Mitlah** (pass), Egypt
49/C4 **Mitla** (Mamarr Mitlah) (pass), Egypt
55/N4 **Mito**, Japan
57/G2 **Mito**, Japan
57/N10 **Mito**, Japan
76/G7 **Mitra** (peak), EqG.
109/C7 **Mitre** (pen.), Arg.
100/E2 **Mitre** (peak), Tx,US
19/T10 **Mitry-Mory**, Fr.
30/B6 **Mitry-Mory**, Fr
81/G5 **Mitsamiouli**, Com.
81/H7 **Mitsinjo**, Madg.
81/J6 **Mitsio, Nosy** (isl.), Madg.
77/N4 **Mits'iwa**, Eth.
57/M10 **Mitsue**, Japan
57/F2 **Mitsukaidō**, Japan
57/H6 **Mitsukaidō**, Japan
57/F2 **Mitsuke**, Japan
73/D2 **Mittagong**, Austl.
37/F3 **Mittagspitze** (peak), Aus.
33/J3 **Mittelberg**, Aus.
37/G3 **Mittelberg**, Aus.
29/F4 **Mittelland Kanal** (can.), Ger.
29/E3 **Mittelradde** (riv.), Ger.
37/H3 **Mittenwald**, Ger.
33/K3 **Mittersill**, Aus.
26/G4 **Mitterteich**, Ger.
26/G3 **Mittweida**, Ger.
106/D3 **Mitú**, Col.
82/E2 **Mitumba** (mts.), Zaire
82/E2 **Mitwaba**, Zaire
57/H7 **Miura**, Japan
57/H7 **Miura** (pen.), Japan
57/L9 **Miwa**, Japan
57/M9 **Miwa**, Japan
102/D3 **Mixco Viejo** (ruins), Guat.
54/G5 **Mi Xian**, China
59/C4 **Mi Xian**, China
101/F4 **Mixquiahuala**, Mex.
101/K6 **Mixquiahuala**, Mex.
102/B1 **Mixquiahuala**, Mex.
102/B2 **Mixteco** (riv.), Mex.
57/M10 **Miya** (riv.), Japan
57/M10 **Miyagawa**, Japan
57/G1 **Miyagi** (pref.), Japan
55/N4 **Miyako**, Japan
55/L5 **Miyakonojō**, Japan
56/B5 **Miyakonojō**, Japan
57/L9 **Miyama**, Japan
56/B5 **Miyanojō**, Japan
57/H6 **Miyashiro**, Japan
55/L5 **Miyazaki**, Japan
56/B4 **Miyazaki** (pref.), Japan
56/B5 **Miyazaki**, Japan
56/D3 **Miyazu**, Japan
63/H2 **Miyi**, China
56/C3 **Miyoshi**, Japan
57/H7 **Miyoshi**, Japan
57/N9 **Miyoshi**, Japan
54/H3 **Miyun**, China
59/D2 **Miyun**, China
59/D2 **Miyun** (res.), China
59/H6 **Miyun**, China
67/H6 **Miyun** (res.), China
22/B6 **Mizen Head** (pt.), Ire.
41/H3 **Mizil**, Rom.
44/C3 **Mizil**, Rom.
41/F4 **Miziya**, Bul.
60/B4 **Mizoram** (state), India
63/F3 **Mizoram** (state), India
50/C4 **Mizpe Ramon**, Isr.
57/H7 **Mizuho**, Japan
57/L9 **Mizuho**, Japan
57/E3 **Mizunami**, Japan
57/N9 **Mizunami**, Japan
20/E4 **Mjölby**, Swe.
20/D3 **Mjøsa** (lake), Nor.
82/G2 **Mkokotoni**, Tanz.
76/D1 **Mkorn** (peak), Mor.
82/E3 **Mkushi**, Zam.
81/F2 **Mkuze** (riv.), SAfr.
27/H3 **Mladá Boleslav**, Czh.
33/L1 **Mladá Boleslav**, Czh.
40/E3 **Mladenovac**, Yugo.
27/L2 **Mława**, Pol.
42/D5 **Mława**, Pol.
44/B1 **Mława**, Pol.
38/E1 **Mljet** (isl.), Cro.
40/C4 **Mljet** (isl.), Cro.
40/C4 **Mljet Nat'l Park**, Cro.
80/N12 **Mmabatho**, SAfr.
80/D2 **Mmathethe**, Bots.
18/E2 **Mo**, Nor.
20/E2 **Mo**, Nor.
42/B2 **Mo**, Nor.
46/B3 **Mo**, Nor.
103/H1 **Moa**, Cuba
67/G5 **Moa** (isl.), Indo.
78/C5 **Moa** (riv.), Libr., SLeo.
88/E4 **Moab**, Ut,US
92/E3 **Moab**, Ut,US
96/A2 **Moab**, Ut,US
68/H6 **Moala Group** (isls.), Fiji
73/C1 **Moama**, Austl.
73/C3 **Moama**, Austl.
81/F2 **Moamba**, Moz.
34/A1 **Moaña**, Sp.
76/H8 **Moanda**, Gabon
82/B1 **Moanda**, Gabon
51/G3 **Mobārakeh**, Iran
52/F2 **Mobārakeh**, Iran
77/K7 **Mobaye**, CAfr.
89/H4 **Moberly**, Mo,US
93/J3 **Moberly**, Mo,US
96/E2 **Moberly**, Mo,US
90/C2 **Moberly Lake**, BC,Can
89/J5 **Mobile**, Al,US
97/F4 **Mobile**, Al,US
86/F4 **Mobridge**, SD,US
88/F2 **Mobridge**, SD,US
91/H4 **Mobridge**, SD,US
104/D3 **Moca**, DRep.
49/C1 **Moca** (pass), Turk.
50/C2 **Moca** (pass), Turk.
107/J4 **Mocajuba**, Braz.
82/H4 **Moçambique**, Moz.
82/B4 **Moçâmedes**, Ang.
60/E4 **Moc Chau**, Viet.
43/X9 **Mocha** (riv.), Rus.
52/D6 **Mocha**, Yem.
77/P5 **Mocha**, Yem.
104/E5 **Mochima Nat'l Park**, Ven.
65/D4 **Moc Hoa**, Viet.
80/D2 **Mochudi**, Bots.
82/E5 **Mochudi**, Bots.
82/H3 **Mocímboa da Praia**, Moz.
34/D4 **Moclín**, Sp.
106/C3 **Mocoa**, Col.
108/C2 **Mococa**, Braz.
100/D3 **Mocorito**, Mex.
100/C2 **Moctezuma**, Mex.
101/E4 **Moctezuma**, Mex.
92/E5 **Moctezuma**, Mex
92/F5 **Moctezuma**, Mex
96/B4 **Moctezuma**, Mex
82/G4 **Mocuba**, Moz.
53/K4 **Modāsa**, India
62/B3 **Modāsa**, India
24/C6 **Modbury**, Eng,UK
80/D3 **Modderrivier** (riv.), SAfr.
18/E4 **Modena**, It.
33/J4 **Modena**, It.
33/G2 **Moder** (riv.), Fr.
31/G6 **Moder** (riv.), Ger.
88/B4 **Modesto**, Ca,US
92/B3 **Modesto**, Ca,US
38/D4 **Modica**, It.
98/C3 **Modjeska**, Ca,US
76/H4 **Modjigo** (reg.), Niger
27/J4 **Mödling**, Aus.
33/M2 **Mödling**, Aus.
40/D3 **Modriča**, Bosn.
63/J5 **Mo Duc**, Viet.
65/E3 **Mo Duc**, Viet.
38/E2 **Modugno**, It.
40/C5 **Modugno**, It.
71/H7 **Moe**, Austl.
73/C3 **Moe**, Austl.
80/A2 **Moeb** (bay), Namb.
32/B3 **Moëlan-sur-Mer**, Fr.
23/E5 **Moel Fammau** (mtn.), Wal,UK
23/E6 **Moel Fferna** (mtn.), Wal,UK
24/C1 **Moelfre** (mtn.), UK
24/C2 **Moel Hywel** (mtn.), Wal,UK
23/E6 **Moel Sych** (mtn.), Wal,UK
24/C2 **Moel y Llyn** (mtn.), UK
68/E4 **Moen**, Micr.
92/E3 **Moenkopi** (dry riv.), Az,US
69/K7 **Moerai**, FrPol.
28/A6 **Moerbeke**, Belg.
30/C1 **Moerbeke**, Belg.
28/D6 **Moers**, Ger.
28/A6 **Moervaart** (can.), Belg.
30/C1 **Moervaart** (can.), Belg.
37/F5 **Moesa** (riv.), Swi.
22/E1 **Moffat**, Sc,UK
99/K12 **Moffett Field Nav. Air Sta.**, Ca,US
53/L2 **Moga**, India
64/C2 **Moga**, India
77/Q7 **Mogadishu** (cap.), Som.
34/B2 **Mogadouro**, Port.
57/G2 **Mogami** (riv.), Japan
60/C3 **Mogaung**, Burma
63/G2 **Mogaung**, Burma
35/L6 **Mogent** (riv.), Sp.
107/J8 **Mogi-Guaçu**, Braz.
108/C2 **Mogi-Guaçu**, Braz.
109/G1 **Mogi-Guaçu**, Braz.
18/G3 **Mogilëv**, Bela.
42/F5 **Mogilëv**, Bela.
44/D1 **Mogilëv**, Bela.
46/D4 **Mogilëv**, Bela.
42/F5 **Mogilëv Obl.**, Bela.
44/D1 **Mogilev Obl.**, Bela.
41/H1 **Mogilev-Podol'skiy**, Ukr.
44/C2 **Mogilev-Podol'skiy**, Ukr.
27/J2 **Mogilno**, Pol.
108/C2 **Mogi-Mirim**, Braz.
47/M4 **Mogocha**, Rus.
55/H1 **Mogocha**, Rus.
60/C4 **Mogok**, Burma
63/G3 **Mogok**, Burma
38/A3 **Mogoro**, It.
102/E3 **Mogotón** (peak), Nic.
34/B4 **Moguer**, Sp.
40/D3 **Mohács**, Hun.
80/D3 **Mohales Hoek**, Les.
91/H3 **Mohall**, ND,US
75/N13 **Mohamed V** (dam), Mor.
75/N13 **Mohamed V** (res.), Mor.
75/R16 **Mohammadia**, Alg.
75/L14 **Mohammedia**, Mor.
98/F4 **Mohawk** (lake), NJ,US
87/J4 **Mohawk** (riv.), NY,US
94/F3 **Mohawk** (riv.), NY,US
81/G6 **Mohéli** (isl.), Com.
82/D4 **Mohembo**, Bots.
85/E3 **Mohican** (cape), Ak,US
36/D2 **Möhlin**, Swi.
29/F6 **Möhne** (riv.), Ger.
29/F6 **Möhnestausee** (res.), Ger.
41/H2 **Moineşti**, Rom.
46/H5 **Moinkum** (des.), Kaz.
79/E5 **Moinsi** (hills), Gha.
94/E2 **Moira** (riv.), On,Can
32/F4 **Moirans**, Fr.
36/B5 **Moirans-en-Montagne**, Fr.
20/H4 **Mõisaküla**, Est.
42/E4 **Mõisaküla**, Est.
87/K3 **Moisie** (riv.), Qu,Can
95/H1 **Moisie** (riv.), Qu,Can
30/B4 **Moislains**, Fr.
32/D4 **Moissac**, Fr.
35/Q10 **Moita**, Port.
34/E4 **Mojácar**, Sp.
88/C5 **Mojave** (des.), Ca,US
92/C4 **Mojave** (des.), Ca,US
92/C4 **Mojave** (dry riv.), Ca,US
60/D4 **Mojiang Hanizu Zizhixian**, China
63/H3 **Mojiang Hanizu Zizhixian**, China
91/L3 **Mojikit** (lake), On,Can
39/F1 **Mojkovac**, Yugo.
40/D4 **Mojkovac**, Yugo.
106/E6 **Mojos** (plain), Bol.
107/J4 **Moju** (riv.), Braz.
57/F2 **Mōka**, Japan
88/W13 **Mokapu** (pt.), Hi,US
92/B3 **Mokelumne** (riv.), Ca,US
99/M10 **Mokelumne** (riv.), Ca,US
99/M11 **Mokelumne** (aqueduct), Ca,US
99/Q16 **Mokena**, Il,US
82/E6 **Mokhotlong**, Les.
68/F4 **Mokil** (atoll), Micr.
63/G4 **Mokochu** (peak), Thai.
65/B3 **Mokochu** (peak), Thai.
60/B3 **Mokokchūng**, India
63/F2 **Mokokchūng**, India
76/H5 **Mokolo**, Camr.
55/K5 **Mokp'o**, SKor.
58/D5 **Mokp'o**, SKor.
40/E3 **Mokrin**, Yugo.
45/G1 **Moksha** (riv.), Rus.
88/S10 **Mokuleia**, Hi,US
88/V12 **Mokuleia**, Hi,US
28/C6 **Mol**, Belg.
31/E1 **Mol**, Belg.
40/E3 **Mol**, Yugo.
38/E2 **Mola di Bari**, It.
40/C5 **Mola di Bari**, It.
39/H4 **Moláoi**, Gre.
102/E1 **Molas, Punta** (pt.), Mex.
40/B3 **Molat** (isl.), Cro.
34/E3 **Molatón** (mtn.), Sp.
29/E3 **Molbergen**, Ger.
23/E5 **Mold**, Wal,UK
41/H2 **Moldavia** (reg.), Rom.
41/G2 **Moldavian Carpathians** (range), Rom.
18/D2 **Molde**, Nor.
20/C3 **Molde**, Nor.
46/A3 **Molde**, Nor.
18/F4 **Moldova**
41/H2 **Moldova**
44/C3 **Moldova**
46/C5 **Moldova**
41/H2 **Moldova** (riv.), Rom.
40/E3 **Moldova Nouă**, Rom.
41/G3 **Moldoveanu** (peak), Rom.
44/C3 **Moldoveanu** (peak), Rom.
19/M7 **Mole** (riv.), Eng,UK
24/C5 **Mole** (riv.), Eng,UK
24/F4 **Mole** (riv.), Eng,UK
103/H2 **Môle, Cap du** (cape), Haiti
79/E4 **Mole Game Rsv.**, Gha.
80/D2 **Molepolole**, Bots.
82/E5 **Molepolole**, Bots.
103/H2 **Môle Saint Nicolas**, Haiti
38/E2 **Molfetta**, It.
40/C5 **Molfetta**, It.
58/C1 **Molihong** (peak), China
59/F2 **Molihong Shan** (peak), China
34/E2 **Molina**, Sp.
34/E3 **Molina de Segura**, Sp.
91/L5 **Moline**, Il,US
93/K2 **Moline**, Il,US
94/B3 **Moline**, Il,US
34/D3 **Molinicos**, Sp.
101/L7 **Molino de Flores Nat'l Park**, Mex.
38/D2 **Molise** (reg.), It.
40/B5 **Molise** (reg.), It.
33/K3 **Möll** (riv.), Aus.
20/D5 **Møllebjerg** (peak), Den.
106/D7 **Mollendo**, Peru
36/C4 **Mollendruz, Col du** (pass), Swi.
35/F2 **Mollerussa**, Sp.
35/G2 **Mollet**, Sp.
35/L6 **Mollet del Vallès**, Sp.
35/L7 **Mollins de Rei**, Sp.
37/F3 **Mollis**, Swi.
26/F2 **Mölln**, Ger.
63/G3 **Molo**, Burma
42/E5 **Molodechno**, Bela.
44/C1 **Molodechno**, Bela.

83/D Molodezhnaya, Ant.
42/H4 Mologa (riv.), Rus.
69/K2 Molokai (isl.), Hi.,US
88/T10 Molokai (isl.), Hi,US
43/L4 Moloma (riv.), Rus.
73/D2 Molong, Austl.
80/C2 Molopo (dry riv.), Bots.
74/E7 Molopo (dry riv.), Bots., SAfr.
82/D6 Molopo (riv.), Bots., SAfr.
80/C2 Moloporivier (dry riv.), SAfr.
39/H3 Mólos, Gre.
76/J7 Moloundou, Camr.
36/D1 Molsheim, Fr.
91/J2 Molson (lake), Mb,Can
80/D3 Molteno, SAfr.
67/H5 Molu (isl.), Indo.
48/M10 Molucca (sea), Indo.
48/M9 Molucca (isls.), Indo.
67/G4 Molucca (sea), Indo.
68/B5 Molucca (sea), Indo.
67/G3 Moluccas (isls.), Indo.
37/G5 Molveno, It.
37/G5 Molveno (lake), It.
107/L5 Mombaça, Braz.
82/G1 Mombasa, Kenya
55/N3 Mombetsu, Japan
39/J2 Momchilgrad, Bul.
41/G5 Momchilgrad, Bul.
44/C4 Momchilgrad, Bul.
50/A1 Momchilgrad, Bul.
67/H4 Momfafa (cape), Indo.
30/D3 Momignies, Belg.
103/H4 Mompós, Col.
60/B4 Mon (riv.), Burma
60/C5 Mon (state), Burma
63/F3 Mon (riv.), Burma
63/G4 Mon (state), Burma
65/B3 Mon (state), Burma
20/E5 Møn (isl.), Den.
26/G1 Møn (isl.), Den.
104/D3 Mona (passg.), DRep., PR
84/L8 Mona (chan.), NAm.
104/E3 Mona (isl.), PR
18/D4 Monaco
33/G5 Monaco
35/J1 Monaco
33/G5 Monaco (cap.), Mona.
35/J1 Monaco (cap.), Mona.
104/F5 Monagas (state), Ven.
22/A3 Monaghan (co.), Ire.
22/B3 Monaghan, Ire.
103/F4 Monagrillo (ruins), Pan.
103/F5 Monagrillo, Pan.
100/E2 Monahans, Tx,US
88/F5 Monahans, Tx,US
93/G5 Monahans, Tx,US
96/C4 Monahans, Tx,US
90/D3 Monashee (mts.), BC,Can
22/A5 Monasterevin, Ire.
72/H8 Mona Vale, Austl.
35/E3 Moncada, Sp.
33/G4 Moncalieri, It.
34/D2 Moncayo (range), Sp.
36/E4 Mönch (peak), Swi.
18/G2 Monchegorsk, Rus.
20/K2 Monchegorsk, Rus.
42/G2 Monchegorsk, Rus.
46/D3 Monchegorsk, Rus.
26/D3 Mönchengladbach, Ger.
28/D6 Mönchengladbach, Ger.
31/F1 Mönchengladbach, Ger.
34/A4 Monchique, Port.
34/A4 Monchique (range), Port.
97/H3 Moncks Corner, SC,US
101/E3 Monclova, Mex.
88/F6 Monclova, Mex.
96/C5 Monclova, Mex
87/K4 Moncton, NB,Can
89/P2 Moncton, NB,Can
95/H2 Moncton, NB,Can
34/A2 Mondego (cape), Port.
34/A2 Mondego (riv.), Port.
34/D2 Mondéjar, Sp.
34/B1 Mondoñedo, Sp.
31/F5 Mondorf-les-Bains, Lux.
33/G4 Mondovì, It.
32/B5 Mondragón, Sp.
34/D1 Mondragón, Sp.
38/C2 Mondragone, It.
40/A5 Mondragone, It.
39/H4 Monemvasía, Gre.
34/B3 Monesterio, Sp.
93/J3 Monett, Mo,US
96/E2 Monett, Mo,US
22/C2 Money Head (pt.), Sc,UK
22/B2 Moneymore, NI,UK
22/C2 Moneyreagh, NI,UK
33/K4 Monfalcone, It.
40/A3 Monfalcone, It.
33/H4 Monferrato (reg.), It.
34/B3 Monforte, Port.
34/B1 Monforte, Sp.
60/A3 Mongar, Bhu.
61/E4 Mong Cai, Viet.
63/J3 Mong Cai, Viet.
65/D1 Mong Cai, Viet.
70/B5 Mongers (lake), Austl.
63/B3 Möng Hsu, Burma
65/B1 Möng Hsu, Burma
62/E2 Monghyr, India
63/G3 Möng Küng, Burma
65/B1 Möng Küng, Burma
63/G3 Möng Long, Burma
63/G3 Möng Nai, Burma
77/J5 Mongo, Chad
78/C4 Mongo (riv.), Gui., SLeo.
47/L5 Mongolia
48/J5 Mongolia
54/D2 Mongolia
77/K5 Mongororo, Chad
76/H8 Mongoungou, Gabon
82/B1 Mongoungou, Gabon
63/G3 Möng Pawn, Burma
65/B1 Möng Pawn, Burma
82/D4 Mongu, Zam.
63/G3 Möng Yai, Burma
65/B1 Möng Yai, Burma
63/G3 Möng Yang, Burma
65/B1 Möng Yang, Burma
65/C1 Möng Yawng, Burma
28/D6 Monheim, Ger.
31/F1 Monheim, Ger.
54/C2 Mönh Hayrhan (peak), Mong.
54/E1 Mönh Sarĭdag (peak), Mong.
22/E1 Moniaive, Sc,UK
35/K6 Monistrol de Montserrat, Sp.
32/F4 Monistrol-sur-Loire, Fr.
92/C3 Monitor (range), Nv,US
102/D2 Monkey River, Belz.
27/M2 Mońki, Pol.
77/K8 Monkoto, Zaire
82/D1 Monkoto, Zaire
24/D3 Monmouth, Eng,UK
91/L5 Monmouth, Il,US
93/K2 Monmouth, Il,US
94/B3 Monmouth, Il,US
90/C4 Monmouth, Or,US
24/D2 Monmow (riv.), UK
28/C4 Monnickendam, Neth.
79/F5 Mono (prov.), Ben.
76/F6 Mono (riv.), Ben., Togo
103/F4 Mono (pt.), Nic.
79/F5 Mono (riv.),,Togo
92/C3 Mono (lake), Ca,US
38/E2 Monopoli, It.
40/C5 Monopoli, It.
40/D2 Monor, Hun.
95/Q8 Mono Road, On,Can
35/E3 Monóvar, Sp.
34/E2 Monreal del Campo, Sp.
38/C3 Monreale, It.
97/H3 Monroe, Ga,US
89/H5 Monroe, La,US
93/J4 Monroe, La,US
96/E3 Monroe, La,US
94/D3 Monroe, Mi,US
99/E7 Monroe (co.), Mi,US
97/H3 Monroe, NC,US
98/E4 Monroe (co.), Pa,US
92/D3 Monroe, Ut,US
99/D2 Monroe, Wa,US
91/L5 Monroe, Wi,US
93/K2 Monroe, Wi,US
94/B3 Monroe, Wi,US
97/G4 Monroeville, Al,US
98/C2 Monrovia, Ca,US
76/C6 Monrovia (cap.), Libr.
78/C5 Monrovia (cap.), Libr.
26/B3 Mons, Belg.
30/C3 Mons, Belg.
32/E1 Mons, Belg.
34/B2 Monsanto, Port.
31/F2 Monschau, Ger.
33/J4 Monselice, It.
98/F4 Monsey, NY,US
31/H4 Monsheim, Ger.
28/B4 Monster, Neth.
20/F4 Mönsteras, Swe.
31/G3 Montabaur, Ger.
37/F3 Montafon (val.), Aus.
81/J6 Montagne d'Ambre Nat'l Park, Madg.
19/U9 Montagny-Sainte-Félicité, Fr.
80/C4 Montagu, SAfr.
80/M10 Montagu, SAfr.
95/J2 Montague, PEI,Can
85/L3 Montague, Yk,Can
85/J4 Montague (isl.), Ak,US
85/J4 Montague (str.), Ak,US
86/B2 Montague (isl.), Ak,US
93/H4 Montague, Tx,US
96/D3 Montague, Tx,US
32/C3 Montaigu, Fr.
35/E2 Montalbán, Sp.
38/E2 Montalbano Jonico, It.
36/B6 Montalieu-Vercieu, Fr.
34/B3 Montalvão, Port.
36/D5 Montana, Swi.
90/F4 Montana (state), US
86/E4 Montana (state), US
88/D2 Montana (state), US
105/B3 Montaña, La (reg.), Peru
34/B3 Montánchez, Sp.
107/K7 Montanha, Braz.
108/D1 Montanha, Braz.
99/J11 Montara, Ca,US
34/A3 Montargil, Port.
26/B5 Montargis, Fr.
32/E3 Montargis, Fr.
26/B4 Montataire, Fr.
30/B5 Montataire, Fr.
32/E2 Montataire, Fr.
18/D4 Montauban, Fr.
32/D4 Montauban, Fr.
35/F1 Montauban, Fr.
35/F1 Montaud, Pic de (peak), Fr.
82/E6 Mont aux Sources (peak), Les.
26/C5 Montbard, Fr.
32/F3 Montbard, Fr.
26/D5 Montbéliard, Fr.
33/G3 Montbéliard, Fr.
36/C2 Montbéliard, Fr.
35/F2 Montblanc, Sp.
35/L7 Montcada i Reixac, Sp.
32/F3 Montceau-les-Mines, Fr.
30/D4 Montcornet, Fr.
32/C5 Mont-de-Marsan, Fr.
35/E1 Mont-de-Marsan, Fr.
26/B4 Montdidier, Fr.
30/B4 Montdidier, Fr.
32/E2 Montdidier, Fr.
102/B2 Monte Albán (ruins), Mex.
107/H4 Monte Alegre, Braz.
34/E3 Montealegre del Castillo, Sp.
108/B1 Monte Alegre de Minas, Braz.
108/B2 Monte Alto, Braz.
107/K7 Monte Azul, Braz.
70/A4 Montebello (isls.), Austl.
109/F2 Montecarlo, Arg.
35/J1 Monte-Carlo, Mona.
107/J7 Monte Carmelo, Braz.
108/C1 Monte Carmelo, Braz.
109/E3 Monte Caseros, Arg.
103/J2 Monte Cristi, DRep.
104/D3 Monte Cristi, DRep.
38/B1 Montecristo (isl.), It.
102/D3 Montecristo Nat'l Park, ESal.
102/E3 Monte el Chile (mtn.), Hon.
34/C4 Montefrío, Sp.
103/G2 Montego Bay, Jam.
40/A4 Montegranaro, It.
34/B2 Montehermoso, Sp.
35/P10 Montelavar, Port.
32/F4 Montélimar, Fr.
34/C4 Montellano, Sp.
90/E5 Montello, Nv,US
92/D2 Montello, Nv,US
101/F3 Montemorelos, Mex.
88/G6 Montemorelos, Mex.
96/D5 Montemorelos, Mex.
34/A3 Montemor-o-Novo, Port.
34/A2 Montemor-o-Velho, Port.
34/A2 Montemuro (mtn.), Port.
32/C4 Montendre, Fr.
108/B4 Montenegro, Braz.
39/F1 Montenegro (rep.), Yugo.
40/D4 Montenegro (rep.), Yugo.
38/D2 Montenero di Bisaccia, It.
40/B5 Montenero di Bisaccia, It.
26/B5 Montenoison, Butte de (mtn.), Fr.
107/L7 Monte Pascoal Nat'l Park, Braz.
104/D3 Monte Plata, DRep.
33/J5 Montepulciano, It.
38/B1 Montepulciano, It.
26/B4 Montereau-faut-Yonne, Fr.
32/E2 Montereau-faut-Yonne, Fr.
86/D5 Monterey, Ca,US
88/B4 Monterey, Ca,US
88/B4 Monterey (bay), Ca,US
92/B3 Monterey, Ca,US
92/B3 Monterey (bay), Ca,US
103/H4 Montería, Col.
106/C2 Montería, Col.
106/F7 Montero, Bol.
109/C2 Monteros, Arg.
36/D6 Monte Rosa (mtn.), It., Swi.
37/G4 Monterosso (peak), It.
38/C1 Monterotondo, It.
101/E3 Monterrey, Mex.
88/F6 Monterrey, Mex.
96/C5 Monterrey, Mex.
34/B2 Monterrey, Sp.
38/D2 Monte Sant'Angelo, It.
40/B5 Monte Sant'Angelo, It.
38/E2 Montescaglioso, It.
40/C5 Montescaglioso, It.
107/K7 Montes Claros, Braz.
38/D1 Montesilvano Marina, It.
40/B4 Montesilvano Marina, It.
19/S10 Montesson, Fr.
32/F4 Monteux, Fr.
109/E3 Montevideo (cap.), Uru.
89/G3 Montevideo, Mn,US
91/K4 Montevideo, Mn,US
19/U10 Montévrain, Fr.
99/L10 Montezuma (slough), Ca,US
31/E5 Montfaucon, Fr.
36/C3 Mont Faucon, Fr.
19/T10 Montfermeil, Fr.
36/B3 Montferrand-le-Château, Fr.
28/B4 Montfoort, Neth.
30/A6 Montfort-l'Amaury, Fr.
19/T10 Montgeron, Fr.
30/B6 Montgeron, Fr.
24/C1 Montgomery, Wal,UK
89/J5 Montgomery (cap.), Al,US
97/G3 Montgomery (cap.), Al,US
99/P16 Montgomery, Il,US
98/J7 Montgomery (co.), Md,US
98/E5 Montgomery (co.), Pa,US
94/D4 Montgomery, WV,US
97/H2 Montgomery, WV,US
98/J7 Montgomery Village, Md,US
98/E5 Montgomeryville, Pa,US
32/E5 Montgrand (mtn.), Fr.
35/G1 Montgrand (mtn.), Fr.
31/D4 Monthermé, Fr.
33/G3 Monthey, Swi.
36/C5 Monthey, Swi.
36/B1 Monthureux-sur-Saône, Fr.
19/U9 Monthyon, Fr.
93/K4 Monticello, Ar,US
96/F3 Monticello, Ar,US
99/K9 Monticello (dam), Ca,US
97/H4 Monticello, Fl,US
94/C3 Monticello, In,US
94/C4 Monticello, Ky,US
97/G2 Monticello, Ky,US
91/L5 Monticello, Mo,US
93/K2 Monticello, Mo,US
96/F1 Monticello, Mo,US
92/E3 Monticello, Ut,US
96/A2 Monticello, Ut,US
94/E4 Monticello, Va,US
97/J2 Monticello, Va,US
36/A1 Montier-en-Der, Fr.
30/B3 Montigny-en-Gohelle, Fr.
19/S10 Montigny-le-Bretonneux, Fr.
30/B6 Montigny-le-Bretonneux, Fr.
26/C4 Montigny-le-Roi, Fr.
32/F2 Montigny-le-Roi, Fr.
36/B1 Montigny-le-Roi, Fr.
19/S10 Montigny-lès-Cormeilles, Fr.
26/D4 Montigny-les-Metz, Fr.
31/F5 Montigny-lès-Metz, Fr.
33/G2 Montigny-lès-Metz, Fr.
30/D3 Montigny-le-Tilleul, Belg.
34/A3 Montijo, Port.
35/Q10 Montijo, Port.
34/B3 Montijo, Sp.
34/C4 Montilla, Sp.
32/D2 Montivilliers, Fr.
87/K4 Mont-Joli, Qu,Can
89/N2 Mont-Joli, Qu,Can
95/G1 Mont-Joli, Qu,Can
87/J4 Mont-Laurier, Qu,Can
89/L2 Mont-Laurier, Qu,Can
94/F2 Mont-Laurier, Qu,Can
36/C3 Montlebon, Fr.
19/S11 Montlhéry, Fr.
32/E3 Montluçon, Fr.
36/B6 Montluel, Fr.
95/G2 Montmagny, Qu,Can
31/E4 Montmédy, Fr.
36/A5 Montmerle-sur-Saône, Fr.
30/C6 Montmirail, Fr.
19/S10 Montmorency, Fr.
32/D3 Montmorillon, Fr.
36/B4 Montmorot, Fr.
71/J4 Monto, Austl.
72/C4 Monto, Austl.
32/B3 Montoir-de-Bretagne, Fr.
31/F5 Montois-la-Montagne, Fr.
33/K5 Montorio al Vomano, It.
40/A4 Montorio al Vomano, It.
34/C3 Montoro, Sp.
100/D3 Montoros, Mex.
78/D5 Mont Peko Nat'l Park, IvC.
103/G2 Montpelier, Jam.
90/F5 Montpelier, Id,US
92/E2 Montpelier, Id,US
87/J4 Montpelier (cap.), Vt,US
89/M3 Montpelier (cap.), Vt,US
95/F2 Montpelier, (cap.), Vt,US
18/D4 Montpellier, Fr.
32/E5 Montpellier, Fr.
35/G1 Montpellier, Fr.
84/K5 Montréal, Can.
94/C2 Montreal (riv.), On,Can
87/J4 Montréal, Qu,Can
89/M2 Montréal, Qu,Can
94/F2 Montréal, Qu,Can
95/N7 Montréal, Qu,Can
91/G2 Montreal (lake), Sk,Can
36/B5 Montréal, Fr.
95/N6 Montréal-Est, Qu,Can
91/G2 Montreal Lake, Sk,Can
95/N6 Montréal-Nord, Qu,Can
32/D5 Montréjeau, Fr.
19/T10 Montreuil, Fr.
30/A3 Montreuil, Fr.
32/D1 Montreuil, Fr.
33/G3 Montreux, Swi.
36/C5 Montreux, Swi.
36/C2 Montreux-Château, Fr.
36/B5 Montrevel-en-Bresse, Fr.
36/C4 Montricher, Swi.
88/E4 Montrose, Co,US
92/F3 Montrose, Co,US
96/B2 Montrose, Co,US
21/D2 Montrose, Sc,UK
19/S10 Montrouge, Fr.
95/N6 Mont-Royal, Qu,Can
32/C3 Montreuil-Bellay, Fr.
19/U10 Montry, Fr.
30/B6 Montry, Fr.
32/D3 Monts, Fr.
95/P6 Mont-Saint-Hilaire, Qu,Can
94/F2 Mont-Saint-Michel, Qu,Can
32/C2 Mont-Saint-Michel, Fr.
32/C2 Mont-Saint-Michel (bay), Fr.
78/D4 Mont Sangbé Nat'l Park, IvC.
77/M7 Monts Bleu (mts.), Ugan., Zaire
35/L6 Montseny Nat'l Park, Sp.
78/C5 Montserrado (co.), Libr.
35/F2 Montserrat (mtn.), Sp.
104/F3 Montserrat (isl.), UK
84/L8 Montserrat (isl.), UK
77/L8 Monts Mitimbu (mts.), Zaire
19/S9 Montsoult, Fr.
36/B4 Mont-sous-Vaudrey, Fr.
31/E4 Mont-St-Martin, Fr.
93/G4 Monument Draw (creek), NM, Tx,US
60/B4 Monywa, Burma
63/G3 Monywa, Burma
33/H4 Monza, It.
82/E4 Monze, Zam.
31/G4 Monzingen, Ger.
35/F2 Monzón, Sp.
80/P13 Mool (riv.), SAfr.
72/D4 Mooloolaba-Maroochydore, Austl.
70/B6 Moora, Austl.
73/G5 Moorabbin, Austl.
91/G4 Moorcroft, Wy,US
93/F1 Moorcroft, Wy,US
70/B5 Moore (lake), Austl.
95/R8 Moore (pt.), On,Can
93/H4 Moore, Ok,US
96/D3 Moore, Ok,US
69/K6 Moorea (isl.), FrPol.
69/X15 Moorea (isl.), FrPol.
104/A1 Moore Haven, Fl,US
97/H5 Moore Haven, Fl,US
37/H1 Moorenweis, Ger.
104/B1 Moore's (isl.), Bahm.
98/F6 Moorestown, NJ,US
97/H3 Mooresville, NC,US
99/H6 Mooretown, On,Can
86/G4 Moorhead, Mn,US
89/G2 Moorhead, Mn,US
91/J4 Moorhead, Mn,US
73/B2 Moorook, Austl.
80/B4 Moorreesburg, SAfr.
80/L10 Moorreesburg, SAfr.
30/C2 Moorslede, Belg.
26/F4 Moosburg, Ger.
33/J2 Moosburg, Ger.
94/D1 Moose (riv.), On,Can
91/H3 Moose (mt.), Sk,Can
85/J3 Moose Creek, Ak,US
94/D1 Moose Factory, On,Can
89/N2 Moosehead (lake), Me,US
95/G2 Moosehead (lake), Me,US
85/H3 Mooseheart (mtn.), Ak,US
99/P16 Mooseheart, Il,US
86/F3 Moose Jaw, Sk,Can
88/E1 Moose Jaw, Sk,Can
91/G3 Moose Jaw, Sk,Can
85/J3 Moose Pass, Ak,US
86/F3 Moosomin, Sk,Can
91/H3 Moosomin, Sk,Can
87/H3 Moosonee, On,Can
89/K1 Moosonee, On,Can
94/D1 Moosonee, On,Can
36/D3 Moosseedorf, Swi.
76/E5 Mopti, Mali
78/D3 Mopti, Mali
78/E3 Mopti (reg.), Mali
106/D7 Moquegua, Peru
40/D2 Mór, Hun.
76/H5 Mora, Camr.
34/A3 Mora, Port.
34/D3 Mora, Sp.
20/E3 Mora, Swe.
42/B3 Mora, Swe.
93/F4 Mora, NM,US
96/B3 Mora, NM,US
39/F1 Morača (riv.), Yugo.
62/C2 Morādābād, India
107/L5 Morada Nova, Braz.
108/C1 Morada Nova de Mina, Braz.
35/E2 Mora de Rubielos, Sp.
81/H7 Morafenobe, Madg.
27/K2 Morąg, Pol.
42/C5 Morąg, Pol.
40/D2 Mórahalom, Hun.
19/R10 Morainvilliers, Fr.
34/D3 Moral de Calatrava, Sp.
109/B5 Moraleda (chan.), Chile
34/B2 Moraleja, Sp.
102/D3 Morales, Guat.
75/G6 Moramanga, Madg.
81/J7 Moramanga, Madg.
92/E2 Moran, Wy,US
72/C3 Moranbah, Austl.
69/M7 Morane (isl.), FrPol.
19/T10 Morangis, Fr.
38/E3 Morano Calabro, It.
103/G2 Morant Bay, Jam.
36/D4 Morat (lake), Swi.
34/D2 Morata de Tajuña, Sp.
34/E3 Moratalla, Sp.
27/J4 Morava (riv.), Czh.
33/M2 Morava (riv.), Czh.
39/G1 Morava (riv.), Yugo.
53/G1 Morāveh Tappeh, Iran
27/J4 Moravia (reg.), Czh.
33/M2 Moravia (reg.), Czh.
27/J4 Moravská Třebová, Czh.
33/M2 Moravská Třebová, Czh.
27/H4 Moravské Budějovice, Czh.
33/L2 Moravské Budějovice, Czh.
70/B5 Morawa, Austl.
106/G2 Morawhanna, Guy.
18/C3 Moray (firth), Sc,UK
26/D4 Morbach, Ger.
31/G4 Morbach, Ger.
33/G2 Morbach, Ger.
30/B2 Morbecque, Fr.
33/H3 Morbegno, It.
37/F5 Morbegno, It.
36/C4 Morbier, Fr.
37/F6 Morbio Inferiore, Swi.
20/F4 Mörbylånga, Swe.
32/C4 Morcenx, Fr.
35/E1 Morcenx, Fr.
36/C5 Morclan, Pic de (mtn.), Fr.
36/C5 Morclan, Pic de (peak), Fr.
86/G4 Morden, Mb,Can
91/J3 Morden, Mb,Can
19/N7 Morden, Eng,UK
73/G6 Mordialloc, Austl.
44/F1 Mordves, Rus.
45/G1 Mordvian Aut. Rep., Rus.
91/H4 Moreau (riv.), SD,US
86/F4 Moreau (riv.), SD,US
23/E3 Morecambe (bay), Eng,UK
23/F3 Morecambe, Eng,UK
68/D7 Moree, Austl.
71/H5 Moree, Austl.
73/D1 Moree, Austl.
94/D4 Morehead, Ky,US
97/H2 Morehead, Ky,US
97/J3 Morehead City, NC,US
36/E5 Mörel, Swi.
101/E5 Morelia, Mex.
71/G4 Morella, Austl.
35/E2 Morella, Sp.
101/E2 Morelos, Mex.
101/K8 Morelos (state), Mex.
101/Q10 Morelos (state), Mex.
102/B2 Morelos (state), Mex.
62/C2 Morena, India
18/C5 Morena (mts.), Sp.
34/C3 Morena (range), Sp.
41/G3 Moreni, Rom.
92/C4 Moreno Valley, Ca,US
98/C3 Moreno Valley, Ca,US
20/C3 Møre og Romsdal (co.), Nor.
86/C3 Moresby (isl.), BC,Can
71/J5 Moreton (isl.), Austl.
72/D4 Moreton (cape), Austl.
72/D4 Moreton (isl.), Austl.
72/F6 Moreton (bay), Austl.
72/F6 Moreton (isl.), Austl.
19/P6 Moreton, Eng,UK
24/C5 Moretonhampstead, Eng,UK
72/D4 Moreton I. Nat'l Park, Austl.
25/E3 Moreton in Marsh, Eng,UK
30/B4 Moreuil, Fr.
43/N2 Moreyu (riv.), Rus.
32/G3 Morez, Fr.
36/C4 Morez, Fr.
72/A2 Morgan, Austl.
89/H6 Morgan City, La,US
93/K5 Morgan City, La,US
97/F4 Morgan City, La,US
94/C4 Morganfield, Ky,US
97/G2 Morganfield, Ky,US
38/D4 Morgantina (ruins), It.
97/H3 Morganton, NC,US
94/C4 Morgantown, Ky,US
97/G2 Morgantown, Ky,US
89/L4 Morgantown, WV,US
94/E4 Morgantown, WV,US
97/J2 Morgantown, WV,US
32/E3 Morge (riv.), Fr.
80/Q13 Morgenzon, SAfr.
33/G3 Morges, Swi.
36/C4 Morges, Swi.
36/D6 Morgex, It.
46/G6 Morghāb (riv.), Afg.
53/H1 Morghāb (riv.), Afg.
36/C5 Morgins, Pas de (pass), Fr., Swi.
26/D4 Morhange, Fr.
31/F6 Morhange, Fr.
33/G2 Morhange, Fr.
54/C3 Mori, China
33/J4 Mori, It.
93/F4 Moriarty, NM,US
96/B3 Moriarty, NM,US
90/B2 Morice (lake), BC,Can
57/L10 Moriguchi, Japan
47/N5 Morin Dawa, China
55/J2 Morin Dawa, China
29/G5 Moringen, Ger.
90/E2 Morinville, Ab,Can
47/Q6 Morioka, Japan
55/N4 Morioka, Japan
73/D2 Morisset, Austl.
57/H7 Moriya, Japan
56/D3 Moriyama, Japan
57/L9 Moriyama, Japan
32/B2 Morlaix, Fr.
30/D3 Morlanwelz, Belg.
23/G4 Morley, Eng,UK
53/K5 Mormugao, India
62/B4 Mormugao, India
72/F6 Morningside, Austl.
70/F3 Mornington (isl.), Austl.
22/B4 Mornington, Ire.
53/J3 Moro, Pak.
62/A2 Moro, Pak.
67/F2 Moro (gulf), Phil.
68/B4 Moro (gulf), Phil.
34/B5 Morocco
35/Y17 Morocco
74/B1 Morocco
75/M13 Morocco
76/C1 Morocco
102/E3 Morocelí, Hon.
82/G2 Morogoro, Tanz.
73/C3 Moroka-Wonnangatta Nat'l Park, Austl.
101/E4 Moroleón, Mex.
81/G8 Morombe, Madg.
109/E3 Morón, Arg.
103/G1 Morón, Cuba
47/L5 Mörön, Mong.
54/E2 Mörön, Mong.
104/D5 Morón, Ven.
106/C4 Morona (riv.), Ecu., Peru
81/H8 Morondara (riv.), Madg.
81/H8 Morondava, Madg.
34/C4 Morón de la Frontera, Sp.
81/G5 Moroni (cap.), Com.
48/M9 Morotai (isl.), Indo.
67/G3 Morotai (isl.), Indo.
67/G3 Morotai (str.), Indo.
68/B4 Morotai (isl.), Indo.
77/M7 Moroto, Ugan.
57/H7 Moroyama, Japan
45/G2 Morozovsk, Rus.
23/G1 Morpeth, Eng,UK
49/C2 Morphou, Cyp.
49/C2 Morphou (bay), Cyp.
50/C3 Morphou, Cyp.
28/C3 Morra (lake), Neth.
91/H5 Morrill, Ne,US
93/G2 Morrill, Ne,US
107/J7 Morrinhos, Braz.
108/B1 Morrinhos, Braz.
91/J3 Morris, Mb,Can
98/F5 Morris (co.), NJ,US
91/L5 Morris, Il,US
93/K2 Morris, Il,US
94/B3 Morris, Il,US
91/K4 Morris, Mn,US
84/P1 Morris Jesup (cape), Grld.
24/C3 Morriston, Wal,UK
98/F5 Morristown, NJ,US
94/D4 Morristown, Tn,US
97/H2 Morristown, Tn,US
98/F5 Morristown Nat'l Hist. Park, NJ,US
72/A2 Morr Morr Abor. Land, Austl.
92/B4 Morro Bay, Ca,US
104/D5 Morrocoy Nat'l Park, Ven.
82/C3 Morro de Môco (peak), Ang.
103/F5 Morro de Puercos (pt.), Pan.
108/B3 Morro do Capão Doce (hill), Braz.
107/K6 Morro do Chapéu, Braz.
101/F5 Morro, Punta del (pt.), Mex.
101/N7 Morro, Punta del (pt.), Mex.
102/B2 Morro, Punta del (pt.), Mex.
103/G4 Morrosquillo (gulf), Col.
19/T11 Morsang-sur-Orge, Fr.
31/F5 Morsbach, Fr.
31/G2 Morsbach, Ger.
36/D2 Morschwiller-le-Bas, Fr.
19/H3 Morshansk, Rus.
45/G1 Morshansk, Rus.
46/E4 Morshansk, Rus.
45/J3 Morskoy (isl.), Kaz.
29/G3 Morsum, Ger.
36/C1 Mortagne (riv.), Fr.
32/C3 Mortagne-sur-Sèvre, Fr.
36/B3 Morte (riv.), Fr.
24/B4 Morte (pt.), UK
36/C3 Morteau, Fr.
107/H6 Mortes (riv.), Braz.
25/E4 Mortimer, Eng,UK
24/D2 Mortimers Cross, Eng,UK
73/B5 Mortlake, Austl.
94/B3 Morton, Il,US
90/C4 Morton, Wa,US
99/Q15 Morton Grove, Il,US
73/D2 Morton Nat'l Park, Austl.
28/B6 Mortsel, Belg.
30/D1 Mortsel, Belg.
73/D2 Moruya, Austl.
32/E3 Morvan (plat.), Fr.
72/B4 Morven, Austl.
53/K4 Morvi, India
62/B3 Morvi, India
36/C2 Morvillars, Fr.
71/H7 Morwell, Austl.
73/C3 Morwell, Austl.
36/C5 Morzine, Fr.
34/A1 Mos, Sp.
26/E4 Mosbach, Ger.
33/H2 Mosbach, Ger.
35/P10 Moscavide, Port.
18/G3 Moscow (cap.), Rus
42/G5 Moscow (upland), Rus.
46/D4 Moscow (cap.), Ru
86/E4 Moscow, Id,US
90/D4 Moscow, Id,US
42/H5 Moscow (Moskva) (cap.), Rus.
43/X9 Moscow (Moskva) (cap.), Rus.
44/F1 Moscow (Moskva) (cap.), Rus.
43/V7 Moscow-Narva, Ru
42/H5 Moscow Obl., Rus.
44/F1 Moscow Obl., Rus.
83/H Moscow Univ. Ice Shelf, Ant.
26/D3 Mosel (riv.), Ger.
31/F4 Mosel (riv.), Ger.
33/G1 Mosel (riv.), Ger.
80/C2 Moselebe (dry riv.), Bots.
26/D4 Moselle (riv.), Fr.
30/F5 Moselle (dept.), Fr.
31/F5 Moselle (riv.), Fr.
33/G2 Moselle (riv.), Fr.
36/C1 Moselle (riv.), Fr.
36/C2 Moselotte (riv.), Fr.
86/E4 Moses Lake, Wa,U
88/C2 Moses Lake, Wa,U
90/D4 Moses Lake, Wa,U
20/N7 Mosfellsbær, Ice.
71/R12 Mosgiel, N.Z.
80/C2 Moshaweng (dry ri SAfr.
82/G1 Moshi, Tanz.
80/D2 Moshupa, Bots.
27/J2 Mosina, Pol.
20/E2 Mosjøen, Nor.
42/B2 Mosjøen, Nor.
42/G5 Moskva (riv.), Rus.
43/Y9 Moskva (riv.), Rus.
42/H5 Moskva (Moscow) (cap.), Rus.
43/X9 Moskva (Moscow) (cap.), Rus.
44/F1 Moskva (Moscow) (cap.), Rus.
27/J5 Mosonmagyaróvár, Hun.
40/C2 Mosonmagyaróvár, Hun.
93/G4 Mosquero, NM,US
96/C3 Mosquero, NM,US
103/E3 Mosquitia (reg.), H
103/G4 Mosquito (pt.), Pan.
103/F4 Mosquitos (gulf), Pa
106/B2 Mosquitos (gulf), Pa
103/E4 Mosquitos, Costa d (reg.), Nic.
18/E3 Moss, Nor.
20/D4 Moss, Nor.
46/B4 Moss, Nor.
99/K11 Moss Beach, Ca,US
82/D7 Mosselbaai, SAfr.
36/D5 Mosses, Col des (pass), Swi.
78/E4 Mossi Highlands (upland), Burk.
26/E4 Mössingen, Ger.
33/H2 Mössingen, Ger.
37/F1 Mössingen, Ger.
23/F4 Mossley, Eng,UK
22/C2 Mossley, NI,UK
71/H3 Mossman, Austl.
72/B2 Mossman, Austl.
107/L5 Mossoró, Braz.
97/F4 Moss Point, Ms,US
22/B1 Moss-side, NI,UK
73/D2 Moss Vale, Austl.
27/G3 Most, Czh.
33/K1 Most, Czh.
75/R15 Mostaganem (wilaya), Alg.
75/R16 Mostaganem, Alg.
76/F1 Mostaganem, Alg.
18/E4 Mostar, Bosn.
39/E1 Mostar, Bosn.
40/C4 Mostar, Bosn.
108/B4 Mostardas, Braz.
27/M4 Mostiska, Ukr.
34/D2 Móstoles, Sp.
35/N9 Móstoles, Sp.
42/E5 Mosty, Bela.
44/C1 Mosty, Bela.
67/E3 Mostyn, Malay.
23/E5 Mostyn, Wal,UK
46/E6 Mosul, Iraq
52/D1 Mosul, Iraq
51/E2 Mosul (Al Mawşil), Iraq
34/D3 Mota del Cuervo, S
102/D3 Motagua (riv.), Guat
20/E4 Motala, Swe.
102/D2 Mother (pt.), Belz.
21/C3 Motherwell, Sc,UK
58/B2 Motian (mtn.), China
59/E2 Motian Ling (mtn.), China
62/D2 Motīhāri, India
34/E3 Motilla del Palanca Sp.
57/G2 Motomiya, Japan
57/J7 Motono, Japan
20/K1 Motovskiy (gulf), Ru
102/C3 Motozintla de Mendoza, Mex.
34/D4 Motril, Sp.
91/H4 Mott, ND,US
71/R11 Motueka, N.Z.
101/H4 Motul de Felipe Carrillo Puerto, Me
102/D1 Motul de Felipe Carrillo Puerto, Me
46/K4 Motygino, Rus.
36/B4 Mouchard, Fr.
103/J1 Mouchoir (passg.), Trks.
39/J3 Moúdhros, Gre.
36/C4 Moudon, Swi.

159

Mougr – Nagor

78/B2 Mougris (well), Mrta.
78/E3 Mouhoun (prov.), Burk.
76/H8 Mouila, Gabon
82/B1 Mouila, Gabon
76/H4 Moul (well), Niger
73/C2 Moulamein, Austl.
73/C2 Moulamein (riv.), Austl.
23/F5 Mouldsworth, Eng,UK
32/E3 Moulins, Fr.
60/C5 Moulmein, Burma
63/G4 Moulmein, Burma
65/B2 Moulmein, Burma
75/N13 Moulouya (riv.), Mor.
76/E1 Moulouya (riv.), Mor.
25/G2 Moulton, Eng,UK
89/K5 Moultrie, Ga,US
97/H4 Moultrie, Ga,US
93/J3 Mound City, Ks,US
96/E2 Mound City, Ks,US
76/J6 Moundou, Chad
94/D4 Moundsville, WV,US
97/H2 Moundsville, WV,US
65/C3 Moung Roessei, Camb.
65/D3 Mounlapamok, Laos
35/E1 Moun Né (mtn.), Fr.
72/B3 Mount Aberdeen Nat'l Park, Austl.
53/K4 Mount Abu, India
62/B3 Mount Abu, India
86/D2 Mountain (riv.), NW,Can
24/C3 Mountain Ash, Wal,UK
97/G3 Mountain Brook, Al,US
93/J3 Mountain Grove, Mo,US
96/E2 Mountain Grove, Mo,US
89/H4 Mountain Home, Ar,US
93/J3 Mountain Home, Ar,US
96/E2 Mountain Home, Ar,US
86/E4 Mountain Home, Id,US
88/C3 Mountain Home, Id,US
90/E5 Mountain Home, Id,US
92/D2 Mountain Home, Id,US
98/E4 Mountainhome, Pa,US
85/M4 Mountain Point, Ak,US
93/J4 Mountain View, Ar,US
96/E3 Mountain View, Ar,US
99/K12 Mountain View, Ca,US
88/U11 Mountain View, Hi,US
85/F3 Mountain Village, Ak,US
80/D4 Mountain Zebra Nat'l Park, SAfr.
82/E7 Mountain Zebra Nat'l Park, SAfr.
98/J7 Mount Airy, Md,US
94/D4 Mount Airy, NC,US
97/H2 Mount Airy, NC,US
99/D3 Mount Baker-Snoqualmie Nat'l For., Wa,US
70/B6 Mount Barker, Austl.
73/A2 Mount Barker, Austl.
72/C5 Mount Barney Nat'l Park, Austl.
73/C3 Mount Beauty, Austl.
73/C3 Mount Buffalo Nat'l Park, Austl.
94/C4 Mount Carmel, Il,US
97/G2 Mount Carmel, Il,US
77/M2 Mount Catherine (peak), Egypt
99/G6 Mount Clemens, Mi,US
72/E6 Mount Coot'tha, Austl.
82/F4 Mount Darwin, Zim.
99/L11 Mount Diablo St. Park, Ca,US
73/B3 Mount Eccles Nat'l Park, Austl.
72/B2 Mount Elliot Nat'l Park, Austl.
73/B3 Mount Emu (cr.), Austl.
73/C4 Mount Field Nat'l Park, Austl.
70/G7 Mount Gambier, Austl.
73/B3 Mount Gambier, Austl.
72/B2 Mount Garnet, Austl.
68/D5 Mount Hagen, PNG
98/F6 Mount Holly, NJ,US
95/Q9 Mount Hope, On,Can
73/D3 Mount Imlay Nat'l Park, Austl.
70/F4 Mount Isa, Austl.
73/D1 Mount Kaputar Nat'l Park, Austl.
98/G4 Mount Kisco, NY,US
99/C2 Mountlake Terrace, Wa,US
72/C3 Mount Larcom, Austl.
98/F6 Mount Laurel, NJ,US
70/F6 Mount Lofty (ranges), Austl.
70/B5 Mount Magnet, Austl.
71/S10 Mount Maunganui, N.Z.
72/D4 Mount Mistake Nat'l Park, Austl.
72/C3 Mount Morgan, Austl.
94/D3 Mount Morris, Mi,US
72/E6 Mount Nebo, Austl.
19/Q7 Mountnessing, Eng,UK
97/J3 Mount Olive, NC,US
39/H3 Mount Parnes Nat'l Park, Gre.
44/B5 Mount Parnes Nat'l Park, Gre.
95/L2 Mount Pearl, Nf,Can
91/L5 Mount Pleasant, Ia,US
93/K2 Mount Pleasant, Ia,US
94/B3 Mount Pleasant, Ia,US
89/K3 Mount Pleasant, Mi,US
94/C3 Mount Pleasant, Mi,US
101/G1 Mount Pleasant, Tx,US
93/J4 Mount Pleasant, Tx,US
96/E3 Mount Pleasant, Tx,US
92/E3 Mount Pleasant, Ut,US
98/E4 Mount Pocono, Pa,US
99/Q15 Mount Prospect, Il,US
98/K8 Mount Rainier, Md,US
90/C4 Mount Rainier Nat'l Park, Wa,US
86/D4 Mount Rainier Nat'l Park, Wa,US
88/B2 Mount Rainier Nat'l Park, Wa,US
90/D3 Mount Revelstoke Nat'l Park, BC,Can
86/E3 Mount Revelstoke Nat'l Park, BC,Can
73/B3 Mount Richmond Nat'l Park, Austl.
93/G2 Mount Rushmore Nat'l Mem., SD,US
24/A6 Mount's (bay), Eng,UK
72/B2 Mount Spec Nat'l Park, Austl.
94/D4 Mount Sterling, Ky,US
97/H2 Mount Sterling, Ky,US
89/J4 Mount Vernon, Il,US
93/K3 Mount Vernon, Il,US
94/B4 Mount Vernon, Il,US
97/F2 Mount Vernon, Il,US
94/C4 Mount Vernon, In,US
97/G2 Mount Vernon, In,US
98/G5 Mount Vernon, NY,US
94/D3 Mount Vernon, Oh,US
98/J8 Mount Vernon, Va,US
88/B2 Mount Vernon, Wa,US
90/C3 Mount Vernon, Wa,US
72/C4 Mount Walsh Nat'l Park, Austl.
72/D5 Mount Warning Nat'l Park, Austl.
73/E1 Mount Warning Nat'l Park, Austl.
73/D4 Mount William Nat'l Park, Austl.
71/J4 Moura, Austl.
72/C4 Moura, Austl.
34/B3 Moura, Port.
34/B3 Mourão, Port.
32/C5 Mourenx, Fr.
35/E1 Mourenx, Fr.
30/D5 Mourmelon-le-Grand, Fr.
30/D5 Mourmelon-le-Petit, Fr.
22/B3 Mourne (dist.), NI,UK
22/B3 Mourne (mts.), NI,UK
39/J5 Mourniai, Gre.
26/B3 Mouscron, Belg.
30/C2 Mouscron, Belg.
70/C6 Moussayah, Gui.
76/J6 Moussoro, Chad
19/T9 Moussy-le-Neuf, Fr.
30/B5 Moussy-le-Neuf, Fr.
44/D3 Mouths of the Danube (delta), Rom.
76/G7 Mouths of the Niger (delta), Nga.
36/D3 Moutier, Swi.
33/G4 Moûtiers, Fr.
30/C2 Mouvaux, Fr.
30/B5 Mouy, Fr.
39/G3 Mouzákion, Gre.
31/E4 Mouzon, Fr.
36/B1 Mouzon (riv.), Fr.
22/A1 Moville, Ire.
22/B3 Moy, NI,UK
77/N7 Moyalē, Eth.
78/B4 Moyamba, SLeo.
58/B4 Moye (isl.), China
76/D1 Moyen Atlas (mts.), Mor.
36/C1 Moyenmoutier, Fr.
31/F5 Moyeuvre-Grande, Fr.
22/B2 Moygashel, NI,UK
22/B1 Moyle (dist.), NI,UK
22/B4 Moynalty, Ire.
67/E5 Moyo (isl.), Indo.
77/M7 Moyo, Ugan.
102/D3 Moyuta, Guat.
74/F6 Mozambique
81/F2 Mozambique
82/G4 Mozambique
74/G6 Mozambique (chan.), Afr.
81/G6 Mozambique (chan.), Afr.
82/G5 Mozambique (chan.), Afr.
42/H5 Mozhaysk, Rus.
43/M4 Mozhga, Rus.
18/F3 Mozyr', Bela.
44/D1 Mozyr', Bela.
46/C4 Mozyr', Bela.
82/F2 Mpanda, Tanz.
82/C4 Mpangu, Namb.
82/F3 Mpika, Zam.
82/F2 Mporokoso, Zam.
79/E5 Mpraeso, Gha.
27/L2 Mrągowo, Pol.
40/C3 Mrkonjić Grad, Bosn.
75/T16 M'Sila, Alg.
75/T16 M'sila (riv.), Alg.
75/T16 M'sila (wilaya), Alg.
75/N13 Msoun (riv.), Mor.
42/G4 Msta (riv.), Rus.
42/F5 Mstislavl', Bela.
27/L4 Mszana Dolna, Pol.
44/F1 Mtsensk, Rus.
82/H3 Mtwara, Tanz.
60/B4 Mu (riv.), Burma
82/G4 Mualama, Moz.
58/D5 Muan, SKor.
65/D2 Muang Gnommarat, Laos
60/D4 Muang Hay, Laos
63/H3 Muang Hay, Laos
60/E5 Muang Hinboun, Laos
63/H4 Muang Hinboun, Laos
65/D2 Muang Hinboun, Laos
60/D5 Muang Kenthao, Laos
63/H4 Muang Kenthao, Laos
65/C2 Muang Kenthao, Laos
60/E5 Muang Khammouan, Laos
63/H4 Muang Khammouan, Laos
65/D2 Muang Khammouan, Laos
63/J5 Muang Khong, Laos
65/D3 Muang Khong, Laos
65/D3 Muang Khongxedon, Laos
63/J4 Muang Lakhonpheng, Laos
65/D3 Muang Lakhonpheng, Laos
60/D4 Muang Ou Tai, Laos
63/H3 Muang Ou Tai, Laos
60/D5 Muang Pak-Lay, Laos
63/H4 Muang Pak-Lay, Laos
65/C2 Muang Pak-Lay, Laos
60/D5 Muang Pakxan, Laos
63/H4 Muang Pakxan, Laos
60/D4 Muang Sing, Laos
63/H3 Muang Sing, Laos
65/C1 Muang Sing, Laos
65/D1 Muang Sing, Laos
65/C2 Muang Thathom, Laos
60/D5 Muang Vangviang, Laos
63/H4 Muang Vangviang, Laos
65/C2 Muang Vangviang, Laos
60/D5 Muang Xaignabouri, Laos
63/H4 Muang Xaignabouri, Laos
65/C2 Muang Xaignabouri, Laos
65/D2 Muang Xamteu, Laos
60/D4 Muang Xay, Laos
63/H3 Muang Xay, Laos
65/C1 Muang Xay, Laos
65/D2 Muang Xepon, Laos
66/B3 Muar, Malay.
66/B4 Muarabungo, Indo.
53/J4 Muāri (pt.), Pak.
76/H5 Mubi, Nga.
106/F3 Mucajaí (riv.), Braz.
31/G2 Much, Ger.
82/F3 Muchinga (mts.), Zam.
24/D1 Much Wenlock, Eng,UK
22/B2 Muckamore Abbey, NI,UK
99/C3 Muckleshoot Ind. Res., Wa,US
82/H3 Mucojo, Moz.
102/E3 Mucupina (mtn.), Hon.
50/C2 Mucur, Turk.
107/K7 Mucuri (riv.), Braz.
108/D1 Mucuri (riv.), Braz.
82/D3 Mucussueje, Ang.
47/N5 Mudanjiang, China
55/K3 Mudanjiang, China
41/J5 Mudanya, Turk.
44/D4 Mudanya, Turk.
50/B1 Mudanya, Turk.
47/N5 Muddan (riv.), China
55/K2 Muddan (riv.), China
20/F2 Muddas Nat'l Park, Swe.
42/D2 Muddas Nat'l Park, Swe.
92/E3 Muddy (riv.), Ut,US
93/H4 Muddy Boggy (creek), Ok,US
29/H3 Müden, Ger.
31/G2 Mudersbach, Ger.
71/H6 Mudgee, Austl.
73/D2 Mudgee, Austl.
90/G1 Mudjatik (riv.), Sk,Can
86/F3 Mudjatik (riv.), Sk,Can
99/D3 Mud Mountain (dam), Wa,US
99/D3 Mud Mountain (lake), Wa,US
63/G4 Mudon, Burma
65/B2 Mudon, Burma
64/F3 Mudumalai Wild. Sanct., India
41/K5 Mudurnu, Turk.
50/B1 Mudurnu, Turk.
49/G7 Mufjir, Nahr (dry riv.), WBnk.
54/F5 Mufu, China
61/G2 Mufu (peak), China
82/E3 Mufulira, Zam.
34/A1 Mugardos, Sp.
34/A3 Muge, Port.
33/K4 Muggia, It.
40/A3 Muggia, It.
34/A1 Mugia, Sp.
49/A1 Muğla (prov.), Turk.
50/B2 Muğla, Turk.
50/B2 Muğla (prov.), Turk.
39/J1 Müglizh, Bul.
41/G4 Müglizh, Bul.
45/L2 Mugodzharskoye (mts.), Kaz.
82/F2 Mugombazi, Tanz.
52/C4 Muḩammad Qawl, Sudan
82/E3 Muhila (mts.), Zaire
26/G4 Mühldorf, Ger.
36/D4 Mühleberg, Swi.
29/H6 Mühlhausen, Ger.
37/E1 Mühlheim an der Donau, Ger.
27/G4 Mühlviertel (reg.), Aus.
33/K2 Mühlviertel (reg.), Aus.
20/H2 Muhos, Fin.
42/E2 Muhos, Fin.
50/D3 Muḩ, Sabkhat al (riv.), Syria
52/C2 Muḩ, Sabkhat al (lake), Syria
42/D4 Muhu (isl.), Est.
28/C4 Muiden, Neth.
99/J11 Muir Woods Nat'l Mon., Ca,US
30/C5 Muizon, Fr.
55/K4 Muju, SKor.
58/D5 Muju, SKor.
27/M4 Mukachevo, Ukr
40/F1 Mukachevo, Ukr.
44/B2 Mukachevo, Ukr.
63/H4 Mukdahan, Thai.
64/C2 Mukeriān, India
91/M2 Muketei (riv.), On,Can
49/E3 Mukhayyam al Yarmūk, Syria
49/G8 Mukhmās, WBnk.
51/G1 Mukhtadir, Azer.
99/C2 Mukilteo, Wa,US
57/L10 Mukō, Japan
68/D2 Mukoshima (isls.), Japan
65/B4 Mu Ko Similan Nat'l Park, Thai.
65/B4 Mu Ko Surin Nat'l Park, Thai.
53/K2 Muktsar, India
64/C2 Muktsar, India
99/P14 Mukwonago, Wi,US
31/E3 Mula, Sp.
55/K2 Mulan, China
82/G4 Mulanje, Malw.
102/C2 Mulato, Mex.
85/C4 Mulchatna (riv.), Ak,US
26/G3 Mulde (riv.), Ger.
83/D Mule (pt.), Ant.
100/B3 Mulejé, Mex.
93/G4 Muleshoe, Tx,US
96/C3 Muleshoe, Tx,US
18/C5 Mulhacén, Cerro de (mtn.), Sp.
34/D4 Mulhacén, Cerro de (mtn.), Sp.
26/F3 Mülhausen, Ger.
28/D6 Mülheim an der Ruhr, Ger.
18/D4 Mulhouse, Fr.
26/D5 Mulhouse, Fr.
33/G3 Mulhouse, Fr.
36/D2 Mulhouse, Fr.
67/J5 Muli (riv.), Indo.
55/L2 Muling (riv.), China
59/D3 Muling (pass), China
69/R9 Mulinu'u (cape), WSam.
60/D3 Muli Zangzu Zizhixian, China
63/H2 Muli Zangzu Zizhixian, China
53/L2 Mulkila (mtn.), India
21/C2 Mull (isl.), Sc,UK
22/B4 Mullagh, Ire.
22/B5 Mullaghcleevaun (mtn.), Ire.
22/B2 Mullaghmore (mtn.), NI,UK
62/D6 Mullaittivu, SrL.
64/H4 Mullaittivu, SrL.
64/H4 Mullaittivu (dist.), SrL.
91/H5 Mullen, Ne,US
93/G2 Mullen, Ne,US
66/D4 Muller (mts.), Indo.
70/B5 Mullewa, Austl.
26/D5 Müllheim, Ger.
33/G3 Müllheim, Ger.
36/D2 Müllheim, Ger.
37/F2 Müllheim, Swi.
98/E6 Mullica Hill, NJ,US
101/F2 Mullin, Tx,US
97/J3 Mullins, SC,US
24/A6 Mullion, Eng,UK
73/E1 Mullumbimby, Austl.
82/E4 Mulobezi, Zam.
82/C4 Mulondo, Ang.
53/K2 Multān, Pak.
64/A2 Multān, Pak.
90/C3 Multnomah (falls), Or,US
66/D3 Mulu (peak), Malay.
73/C2 Mulwala, Austl.
82/C3 Mumbué, Ang.
82/E3 Mumbwa, Zam.
63/G6 Mum Nauk (pt.), Thai.
65/B5 Mum Nauk (pt.), Thai.
66/A2 Mum Nauk (pt.), Thai.
63/H4 Mun (riv.), Thai.
65/C3 Mun (riv.), Thai.
67/F4 Muna (isl.), Indo.
68/B5 Muna (isl.), Indo.
101/H4 Muna, Mex.
20/H4 Munamägi (hill), Est.
42/E4 Munamägi (hill), Est.
26/F4 München (Munich), Ger.
33/J2 München (Munich), Ger.
37/H1 München (Munich), Ger.
36/D2 Münchenstein, Swi.
31/G5 Münchweiler an der Rodalb, Ger.
89/J3 Muncie, In,US
94/C3 Muncie, In,US
97/G1 Muncie, In,US
64/F4 Mundakāyam, India
101/F1 Munday, Tx,US
99/P15 Mundelein, Il,US
79/H5 Mundemba, Camr.
26/E3 Munden, Ger.
29/G6 Münden, Ger.
37/F1 Munderkingen, Ger.
25/H1 Mundesley, Eng,UK
26/A2 Mundesley, Eng.,UK
25/G2 Mundford, Eng,UK
55/K4 Mundŏk, NKor.
109/F1 Mundo Novo, Braz.
70/D6 Mundrabilla, Austl.
71/J5 Mundubbera, Austl.
34/D3 Munera, Sp.
62/C3 Mungaolī, India
72/C5 Mungindi, Austl.
73/B2 Mungo Nat'l Park, Austl.
54/C1 Mungun-Tayga (peak), Rus.
58/E4 Mun'gyŏng, SKor.
18/E4 Munich, Ger.
26/F4 Munich (München), Ger.
33/J2 Munich (München), Ger.
37/H1 Munich (München), Ger.
89/J2 Munising, Mi,US
91/M4 Munising, Mi,US
94/C2 Munising, Mi,US
47/L4 Munku-Sardyk (peak), Rus.
54/D1 Munku-Sasan (peak), Rus.
109/B7 Muñoz Gamero (pen.), Chile
58/D4 Munsan, SKor.
58/F6 Munsan, SKor.
37/F1 Münsingen, Ger.
36/D4 Münsingen, Swi.
30/D1 Munster, Fr.
18/D3 Münster, Ger.
26/D3 Münster, Ger.
26/F2 Munster, Ger.
29/E5 Münster, Ger.
29/H3 Munster, Ger.
21/A4 Munster (prov.), Ire.
37/E5 Münster, Swi.
99/Q16 Munster, In,US
37/G1 Münsterhausen, Ger.
26/D3 Münsterland (reg.), Ger.
29/E4 Münsterland (reg.), Ger.
31/G3 Münstermaifeld, Ger.
41/F2 Muntele Mare (peak), Rom.
28/D2 Muntendam, Neth.
66/C4 Muntok, Indo.
36/D3 Müntschemier, Swi.
50/D2 Munzur Vadisi Nat'l Park, Turk.
60/E5 Muong Hin, Viet.
65/D1 Muong Khuong, Viet.
60/F4 Muong Lat, Viet
63/H3 Muong Lat, Viet.
20/G2 Muonio, Fin.
42/D2 Muonio, Fin.
20/G1 Muonioälv (riv.), Swe.
42/D1 Muonioälv (Muoniojoki) (riv.), Swe.
20/G1 Muoniojoki (riv.), Fin.
42/D1 Muoniojoki (Muonioälv) (riv.), Fin.
37/E4 Muotathal, Swi.
82/C4 Mupa Nat'l Park, Ang.
58/A4 Muping, China
59/E3 Muping, China
52/C6 Muqatta', Sudan
77/Q7 Muqdisho (Mogadishu) (cap.), Som.
49/G6 Muqeibila, Isr.
33/L3 Mur (riv.), Aus.
40/B2 Mur (riv.), Aus.
40/C2 Mura (riv.), Slvk.
51/E2 Muradiye, Turk.
57/F1 Murakami, Japan
109/B6 Murallón (peak), Arg
77/N8 Murang'a, Kenya
82/G1 Murang'a, Kenya
50/B2 Murat (peak), Turk.
44/D5 Murat Daği (peak), Turk.
41/H5 Muratlı, Turk.
50/E2 Muratlı, Turk.
68/A7 Murchison (riv.), Austl.
70/B5 Murchison (riv.), Austl.
73/C3 Murchison, Austl.
71/R11 Murchison, N.Z.
18/C5 Murcia, Sp.
34/E4 Murcia (aut. comm.), Sp.
35/E4 Murcia, Sp.
95/H1 Murdochville, Qu,Can
72/B1 Murdock (pt.), Austl.
41/G2 Mureş (co.), Rom.
41/G2 Mureş (riv.), Rom.
44/B3 Mureş (riv.), Rom.
32/D5 Muret, Fr.
35/F1 Muret, Fr.
93/J4 Murfreesboro, Ar,US
96/E3 Murfreesboro, Ar,US
89/J4 Murfreesboro, Tn,US
94/C5 Murfreesboro, Tn,US
97/G3 Murfreesboro, Tn,US
31/H6 Murg (riv.), Ger.
53/K1 Murgab, Taj.
46/G6 Murgab (riv.), Trkm.
53/H1 Murgab (riv.), Trkm.
72/C4 Murgon, Austl.
37/E3 Muri, Swi.
66/D5 Muria (peak), Indo.
107/K8 Muriaé, Braz.
108/D2 Muriaé, Braz.
53/G3 Mūrī ān, Hāmūn-e Jaz (lake), Iran
34/B1 Murias de Paredes, Sp.
33/G3 Muribei Bern, Swi.
36/D4 Muri bei Bern, Swi.
26/G2 Müritz See (lake), Ger.
77/N6 Murle, Eth.
18/G2 Murmansk, Rus.
20/K1 Murmansk, Rus.
42/G1 Murmansk, Rus.
46/D3 Murmansk, Rus.
20/J1 Murmansk Obl., Rus.
42/G2 Murmansk Obl., Rus.
20/K1 Murmashi, Rus.
37/H2 Murnau, Ger.
57/M10 Muro, Japan
35/G3 Muro, Sp.
38/D2 Muro Lucano, It.
42/J5 Murom, Rus.
47/Q5 Muroran, Japan
55/N3 Muroran, Japan
34/A1 Muros, Sp.
55/L5 Muroto, Japan
56/D4 Muroto, Japan
55/L5 Muroto-zaki (pt.), Japan
56/D4 Muroto-zaki (pt.), Japan
27/J2 Murowana Goślina, Pol.
97/G3 Murphy, NC,US
93/K3 Murphysboro, Il,US
94/B4 Murphysboro, Il,US
97/F2 Murphysboro, Il,US
102/E3 Murra, Nic.
73/D2 Murramarang Nat'l Park, Austl.
68/D8 Murray (riv.), Austl.
70/G6 Murray (riv.), Austl.
73/A2 Murray (riv.), Austl.
60/D5 Murray (lake), PNG
94/B4 Murray, Ky,US
97/F2 Murray, Ky,US
68/C8 Murray Bridge, Austl
70/F7 Murray Bridge, Austl.
73/A2 Murray Bridge, Austl.
73/B2 Murrayville, Austl.
71/H6 Murrumbidgee (riv.), Austl.
73/C2 Murrumbidgee (riv.), Austl.
73/D2 Murrumburrah, Austl.
73/D1 Murrurundi, Austl.
33/M3 Murska Sobota, Slov.
40/C2 Murska Sobota, Slov.
37/G4 Murtaröl, Piz (Cima la Casina) (peak), Swi.
36/D4 Murten, Swi.
73/B3 Murtoa, Austl.
23/G2 Murton, Eng,UK
66/E3 Murud (peak), Malay.
71/S10 Murupara, N.Z.
69/M7 Mururoa (isl.), FrPol.
62/D3 Murwāra, India
72/D5 Murwillumbah, Austl.
73/E1 Murwillumbah, Austl.
27/H5 Mürz (riv.), Aus.
27/H5 Mürzzuschlag, Aus.
33/L3 Mürzzuschlag, Aus.
40/B2 Mürzzuschlag, Aus.
46/E6 Muş, Turk.
50/E2 Muş, Turk.
50/E2 Muş (prov.), Turk.
39/H1 Musala (peak), Bul.
41/F4 Musala (peak), Bul.
18/E1 Musan, NKor.
51/H5 Musandam (pen.), Oman
53/G3 Musandam (pen.), Oman
77/S2 Musandam (pen.), Oman
57/H7 Musashino, Japan
77/R3 Musayʻīd, Qatar
53/G4 Muscat (Musqaţ) (cap.), Oman
98/E5 Musconetcong (riv.), NJ,US
82/E5 Musekwapoort (pass), SAfr.
35/N9 Museo del Prado, Sp.
99/C2 Museum of Flight, Wa,US
68/C7 Musgrave (ranges), Austl.
70/E5 Musgrave (ranges), Austl.
95/L1 Musgrave Harbour, Nf,Can
62/E3 Mushābani, India
49/G8 Mushāsh, Wādī (dry riv.), WBnk.
101/E1 Mushaway (peak), Tx,US
76/J8 Mushie, Zaire
82/C1 Mushie, Zaire
66/B4 Musi (riv.), Indo.
99/P14 Muskego, Wi,US
87/H4 Muskegon, Mi,US
87/H4 Muskegon (riv.), Mi,US
89/J3 Muskegon, Mi,US
94/C3 Muskegon, Mi,US
94/C3 Muskegon (riv.), Mi,US
94/D4 Muskingum (riv.), Oh,US
89/G4 Muskogee, Ok,US
93/J4 Muskogee, Ok,US
96/E3 Muskogee, Ok,US
94/E2 Muskoka (lake), On,Can
77/M8 Musoma, Tanz.
82/F1 Musoma, Tanz.
53/G4 Musqaţ (Muscat) (cap.), Oman
95/J1 Musquaro (riv.), Qu,Can
68/D5 Mussau (isl.), PNG
106/F4 Musselshell (riv.), Mt,US
88/E2 Musselshell (riv.), Mt,US
38/C4 Mussomeli, It.
31/E4 Musson, Belg.
64/B2 Mustafābād, Pak.
44/D4 Mustafakemalpaşa, Turk.
50/B1 Mustafakemalpaşa, Turk.
37/G4 Müstair, Swi.
62/D2 Mustāng, Nepal
93/H4 Mustang, Ok,US
96/D3 Mustang, Ok,US
33/K2 Můstek (peak), Czh.
20/H4 Mustvee, Est.
42/E4 Mustvee, Est.
55/K3 Musu-dan (pt.), NKor.
58/E2 Musu-dan (pt.), NKor.
103/E3 Musún (mtn.), Nic.
39/G1 Mušutište, Yugo.
40/E4 Mušutište, Yugo.
73/D2 Muswellbrook, Austl.
77/L2 Mūt, Egypt
49/C1 Mut, Turk.
50/C2 Mut, Turk.
82/F4 Mutare, Zim.
67/K5 Muting, Indo.
67/F5 Mutis (peak), Indo.
50/E2 Mutki, Turk.
81/H6 Mutsamudu, Com.
55/N3 Mutsu, Japan
50/B2 Muttalip, Turk.
37/G3 Muttekopf (peak), Aus.
36/D2 Muttenz, Swi.
37/G4 Muttler (peak), Swi.
99/G6 Muttonville, Mi,US
64/G3 Muttupet, India
108/D1 Mutum, Braz.
64/H4 Mutur, SrL.
36/D1 Mutzig, Fr.
61/F4 Mūvattupula, India
20/J3 Muyezerskiy, Rus.
45/L4 Muynak, Uzb.
46/F5 Muynak, Uzb.
54/G5 Muyuping, China
53/K2 Muzaffargarh, Pak.
64/A2 Muzaffargarh, Pak.
53/L3 Muzaffarnagar, India
62/C2 Muzaffarnagar, India
62/E2 Muzaffarpur, India
100/E3 Múzquiz, Mex.
82/C2 Mwadi-Kalumbu, Zaire
82/F1 Mwanza, Tanz.
21/H7 Mweelrea (mtn.), Ire.
82/D1 Mweka, Zaire
82/D2 Mwene-Ditu, Zaire
74/E5 Mweru (lake), Zaire, Zam.
82/E2 Mweru (lake), Zaire, Zam.
82/D3 Mwinilunga, Zam.
72/E2 Myall Lakes Nat'l Park, Austl.
60/B5 Myanaung, Burma
63/G4 Myanaung, Burma
54/C2 Myangad, Mong.
48/J7 Myanmar (Burma)
60/B4 Myanmar (Burma)
63/G3 Myanmar (Burma)
65/B1 Myanmar (Burma)
66/A1 Myanmar (Burma)
44/E1 Myatlevo, Rus.
60/B5 Myaungmya, Burma
63/F4 Myaungmya, Burma
63/G4 Myawadi, Burma
65/B2 Myawadi, Burma
39/H4 Mycenae (ruins), Gre.
63/F5 Myebon, Burma
60/B4 Myingyan, Burma
63/G3 Myingyan, Burma
60/B4 Myintha, Burma
60/C4 Myitinge (riv.), Burma
60/C3 Myitkyina, Burma
63/G2 Myitkyina, Burma
60/B4 Myittha (riv.), Burma
27/J4 Myjava, Slvk.
42/D3 Mynämäki, Fin.
24/C2 Mynydd Eppynt (mts.), Wal,UK
24/B2 Mynydd Pencarreg (mtn.), Wal,UK
60/B4 Myohaung, Burma
63/F3 Myohaung, Burma
65/B1 Myohla, Burma
57/F2 Myōkō-san (mtn.), Japan
58/E2 Myŏngch'ŏn, NKor.
89/L5 Myrtle Beach, SC,US
97/J3 Myrtle Beach, SC,US
97/J3 Myrtle Beach (A.F.B.), SC,US
90/C5 Myrtle Creek, Or,US
92/B2 Myrtle Creek, Or,US
73/C3 Myrtleford, Austl.
20/D4 Mysen, Nor.
27/K4 Myślenice, Pol.
27/H2 Myślibórz, Pol.
65/E3 My Son (ruins), Viet.
62/C5 Mysore, India
99/B1 Mystery Bay Rec. Area, Wa,US
27/K3 Myszków, Pol.
63/J5 My Tho, Viet.
65/D4 My Tho, Viet.
66/C1 My Tho, Viet.
43/X9 Mytishchi, Rus.
42/H5 Mytishchi, Rus.
51/F1 Myusyuslyu, Azer.
33/K2 Mže (riv.), Czh.
82/F3 Mzuzu, Malw.

N

65/C1 Na (riv.), Viet.
33/J2 Naab (riv.), Ger.
28/B5 Naaldwijk, Neth.
88/U11 Naalehu, Hi,US
28/C4 Naarden, Neth.
22/B5 Naas, Ire.
80/B3 Nababeep, SAfr.
62/E3 Nabadwīp, India
102/E1 Nabalam, Mex.
56/E3 Nabari, Japan
57/M10 Nabari, Japan
57/M10 Nabari (riv.), Japan
70/C5 Nabberu (lake), Austl.
19/J3 Naberezhnye Chelny, Rus.
43/M5 Naberezhnye Chelny, Rus.
46/F4 Naberezhnye Chelny, Rus.
64/D2 Nābha, India
73/E2 Nabiac, Austl.
52/D5 Nabī Shu'ayb, Jabal an (mtn.), Yem.
95/J1 Nabisipi (riv.), Qu,Can
38/B4 Nābul, Tun.
38/B4 Nābul (gov.), Tun.
75/X17 Nābul, Tun.
75/X17 Nabul (gov.), Tun.
76/H1 Nābul, Tun.
49/D3 Nābulus, WBnk.
49/G7 Nābulus, WBnk.
50/C3 Nābulus, WBnk.
52/C2 Nābulus, WBnk.
82/H3 Nacala, Moz.
102/E3 Nacaome, Hon.
56/D4 Nachi-Katsuura, Japan
82/G3 Nachingwea, Tanz.
27/J3 Náchod, Czh.
33/M1 Náchod, Czh.
29/E6 Nachrodt-Wiblingwerde, Ger.
89/H5 Nacogdoches, Tx,US
93/J5 Nacogdoches, Tx,US
96/E4 Nacogdoches, Tx,US
100/C2 Nacozari de García, Mex.
92/E5 Nacozari de García, Mex
24/D4 Nadder (riv.), Eng,UK
68/G6 Nadi, Fiji
69/Y18 Nadi, Fiji
53/K4 Nadiād, India
62/B3 Nadiād, India
40/E2 Nădlac, Rom.
75/N13 Nador, Mor.
38/D4 Nadur, Malta
58/D5 Naejang-san Nat'l Park, SKor.
37/F3 Näfels, Swi.
23/H3 Nafferton, Eng,UK
51/F1 Naftalan, Azer.
53/J3 Nag, Pak.
60/B3 Naga (hills), India
68/B3 Naga City, Phil.
56/C4 Nagahama, Japan
56/E3 Nagahama, Japan
57/M9 Nagahama, Japan
57/G1 Nagai, Japan
60/B3 Nāgāland (state), India
63/F2 Nāgāland (state), India
73/C3 Nagambie, Austl.
47/P6 Nagano, Japan
55/M4 Nagano, Japan
57/E3 Nagano (pref.), Japan
57/F2 Nagano, Japan
55/M4 Nagaoka, Japan
57/F2 Nagaoka, Japan
56/D3 Nagaokakyō, Japan
57/L10 Nagaokakyō, Japan
64/G3 Nagappattinam, India
57/E3 Nagara (riv.), Japan
57/J7 Nagara, Japan
57/H7 Nagareyama, Japan
62/B4 Nagar Haveli, Dadrak (terr.), India
62/C4 Nāgārjuna Sāgar (res.), India
53/K4 Nagar Pārkar, Pak.
62/F2 Nagarzê, China
85/M5 Nagas (pt.), BC,Can
55/K5 Nagasaki, Japan
56/A4 Nagasaki, Japan
56/A4 Nagasaki (pref.), Japan
56/A4 Nagasaki Peace Park, Japan
57/M9 Nagashima, Japan
56/B3 Nagato, Japan
53/K3 Nāgaur, India
62/B2 Nāgaur, India
53/L4 Nāgda, India
62/C3 Nāgda, India
62/C6 Nāgercoil, India
64/F4 Nāgercoil, India
37/E1 Nagold, Ger.
45/H5 Nagorno-Karabakh Aut. Obl., Azer.

Nagor – Ness

21/C2 Ness, Loch (lake), Sc,UK
26/F3 Nesse (riv.), Ger.
29/H6 Nesse (riv.), Ger.
85/M4 Nesselrode (mt.), Ak,US
37/G2 Nesselwang, Ger.
37/F3 Nesslau, Swi.
44/B2 Nesterov, Ukr.
23/E5 Neston, Eng,UK
39/G2 Nestórion, Gre.
39/J2 Néstos (riv.), Gre.
41/G5 Néstos (riv.), Gre.
49/F8 Nes Ziyyona, Isr.
49/D3 Netanya, Isr.
49/F7 Netanya, Isr.
50/C3 Netanya, Isr.
98/F5 Netcong, NJ,US
106/E1 Neth. Antilles
29/G5 Nethe (riv.), Ger.
24/D3 Netherend, Eng,UK
18/D3 Netherlands
26/C3 Netherlands
28/B5 Netherlands
33/E4 Netherlands
46/A4 Netherlands
84/L8 Netherlands Antilles
104/D5 Netherlands Antilles (isls.), Neth.
25/E5 Netley, Eng,UK
38/E3 Neto (riv.), It.
31/H2 Netphen, Ger.
37/F3 Netstal, Swi.
28/D6 Nette (riv.), Ger.
29/H5 Nette (riv.), Ger.
31/G3 Nettebach (riv.), Ger.
31/F3 Nettersheim, Ger.
28/D6 Nettetal, Ger.
87/J2 Nettilling (lake), NW,Can
23/H5 Nettleham, Eng,UK
38/C2 Nettuno, It.
101/L7 Netzahualcóyotl, Mex.
101/Q10 Netzahualcóyotl, Mex.
37/H1 Neubiberg, Ger.
27/G2 Neubrandenburg, Ger.
31/H6 Neuburg, Ger.
26/F4 Neuburg an der Donau, Ger.
37/G1 Neuburg an der Kammel, Ger.
33/G3 Neuchâtel, Swi.
33/G3 Neuchâtel (lake), Swi.
36/C4 Neuchâtel, Swi.
36/C4 Neuchâtel (canton), Swi.
36/C4 Neuchâtel (lake), Swi.
26/F2 Neu Darchau, Ger.
29/H2 Neu Darchau, Ger.
36/D2 Neuenburg am Rhein, Ger.
27/G2 Neuenhagen, Ger.
28/D4 Neuenhaus, Ger.
29/E4 Neuenkirchen, Ger.
29/F3 Neuenkirchen, Ger.
29/E6 Neuenrade, Ger.
31/F3 Neuerburg, Ger.
37/H1 Neufahrn bei Freising, Ger.
36/D1 Neuf-Brisach, Fr.
31/E4 Neufchâteau, Belg.
26/C4 Neufchâteau, Fr.
32/F2 Neufchâteau, Fr.
36/B1 Neufchâteau, Fr.
25/H5 Neufchâtel, Fr.
30/A4 Neufchâtel-en-Bray, Fr.
32/D2 Neufchâtel-en-Bray, Fr.
31/D4 Neufmanil, Fr.
27/G4 Neuhaus am Inn, Ger.
31/G3 Neuhäusel, Ger.
37/E2 Neuhausen am Rheinfall, Swi.
30/B5 Neuilly-en-Thelle, Fr.
36/B2 Neuilly-l'Évêque, Fr.
30/C5 Neuilly-Saint-Front, Fr.
19/T10 Neuilly-sur-Marne, Fr.
19/S10 Neuilly-sur-Seine, Fr.
30/B6 Neuilly-sur-Seine, Fr.
26/E1 Neukirchen, Ger.
37/H5 Neumarkt (Egna), It.
26/F4 Neumarkt in der Oberpfalz, Ger.
33/J2 Neumarkt in der Oberpfalz, Ger.
26/E1 Neumünster, Ger.
37/E2 Neunkirch, Swi.
33/M3 Neunkirchen, Aus.
40/C2 Neunkirchen, Aus.
26/D4 Neunkirchen, Ger.
31/G5 Neunkirchen, Ger.
31/H2 Neunkirchen, Ger.
33/G2 Neunkirchen, Ger.
31/G2 Neunkirchen-Seelscheid, Ger.
109/C4 Neuquén, Arg.
109/C4 Neuquén (riv.), Arg.
26/G2 Neuruppin, Ger.
28/F4 Neusäss, Ger.
37/G1 Neusäss, Ger.
40/C2 Neusiedl am See, Aus.
27/J5 Neusiedler (lake), Aus.
40/C2 Neusiedler See (lake), Aus.
33/M3 Neusiedler See (Fertő) (lake), Aus., Hun.
26/D3 Neuss, Ger.
28/D6 Neuss, Ger.
31/F1 Neuss, Ger.
26/G2 Neustadt, Ger.
26/E2 Neustadt am Rübenberge, Ger.
29/G4 Neustadt am Rübenberge, Ger.
26/F4 Neustadt an der Aisch, Ger.
26/F4 Neustadt an der Donau, Ger.
33/J2 Neustadt an der Donau, Ger.
26/E4 Neustadt an der Weinstrasse, Ger.
31/H5 Neustadt an der Weinstrasse, Ger.
33/H2 Neustadt an der Weinstrasse, Ger.
26/F3 Neustadt bei Coburg, Ger.
33/J1 Neustadt bei Coburg, Ger.
26/F1 Neustadt in Holstein, Ger.
33/J3 Neustift im Stubaital, Aus.
37/H3 Neustift im Stubaital, Aus.
26/G2 Neustrelitz, Ger.
26/F4 Neu-Ulm, Ger.
33/J2 Neu-Ulm, Ger.
37/G1 Neu-Ulm, Ger.
26/D4 Neuves-Maisons, Fr.
32/G2 Neuves-Maisons, Fr.
32/E4 Neuvic, Fr.
36/A6 Neuville-sur-Saône, Fr.
29/F1 Neuwerk (isl.), Ger.
26/D3 Neuwied, Ger.
31/G3 Neuwied, Ger.
33/G1 Neuwied, Ger.
27/H2 Neuzelle, Ger.
43/V7 Neva (riv.), Rus.
90/C5 Nevada (range), Ca, Nv,US
34/D4 Nevada (mts.), Sp.
90/D5 Nevada (state), US
86/E4 Nevada (state), US
88/C4 Nevada (state), US
92/C3 Nevada (state), US
93/J3 Nevada, Mo,US
96/E2 Nevada, Mo,US
109/C1 Nevado de Chañi (peak), Arg.
100/E5 Nevado de Colima (peak), Mex.
109/C2 Nevado del Candado (peak), Arg.
106/C3 Nevado del Huila (peak), Col.
102/B2 Nevado de Toluca (peak), Mex.
101/K7 Nevado de Toluca Nat'l Park, Mex.
42/F4 Nevel', Rus.
28/A6 Nevele, Belg.
30/C1 Nevele, Belg.
47/Q5 Nevel'sk, Rus.
55/N2 Nevel'sk, Rus.
32/E3 Nevers, Fr.
39/F1 Nevesinje, Bosn.
40/D4 Nevesinje, Bosn.
45/G3 Nevinnomyssk, Rus.
104/F3 Nevis (isl.), StK.
104/F3 Nevis (peak), StK.
50/C2 Nevşehir, Turk.
50/C2 Nevsehir (prov.), Turk.
106/G3 New (riv.), Guy.
25/E5 New (for.), Eng,UK
94/D4 New (riv.), WV,US
22/E2 New Abbey, Sc,UK
94/C4 New Albany, In,US
97/G2 New Albany, In,US
97/F3 New Albany, Ms,US
25/E4 New Alfresford, Eng,UK
107/G2 New Amsterdam, Guy.
23/H5 New Ancholme (riv.), Eng,UK
72/B5 New Angledool, Austl.
99/K11 Newark, Ca,US
89/M3 Newark, NJ,US
94/F3 Newark, NJ,US
89/K3 Newark, Oh,US
94/D3 Newark, Oh,US
97/H1 Newark, Oh,US
23/H5 Newark-on-Trent, Eng,UK
99/G6 New Baltimore, Mi,US
89/M3 New Bedford, Ma,US
95/G3 New Bedford, Ma,US
99/P14 New Berlin, Wi,US
89/L4 New Bern, NC,US
97/J3 New Bern, NC,US
94/C2 Newberry, Mi,US
97/H3 Newberry, SC,US
23/G1 Newbiggin-by-the-Sea, Eng,UK
22/A3 Newbliss, Ire.
101/F2 New Braunfels, Tx,US
89/G6 New Braunfels, Tx,US
93/H5 New Braunfels, Tx,US
96/D4 New Braunfels, Tx,US
24/C2 Newbridge on Wye, Wal,UK
68/D5 New Britain (isl.), PNG
95/F3 New Britain, Ct,US
98/E5 New Britain, Pa,US
87/K4 New Brunswick (prov.), Can.
89/N2 New Brunswick (prov.), Can.
95/H2 New Brunswick (prov.), Can.
98/F5 New Brunswick, NJ,US
22/A2 New Buildings, NI,UK
23/G2 Newburn, Eng,UK
25/E4 Newbury, Eng,UK
23/F3 Newby Bridge, Eng,UK
68/F6 New Caledonia (terr.), Fr.
68/F7 New Caledonia (isl.), Fr.
69/U11 New Caledonia (terr.), Fr.
69/U12 New Caledonia (isl.), NCal.
98/G4 New Canaan, Ct,US
68/E8 Newcastle, Austl.
71/J6 Newcastle, Austl.
73/D2 Newcastle, Austl.
95/S8 Newcastle, On,Can
21/A4 Newcastle, Ire.
22/B5 Newcastle, Ire.
81/E2 Newcastle, SAfr.
82/E6 Newcastle, SAfr.
22/C3 Newcastle, NI,UK
94/C4 New Castle, In,US
97/G2 New Castle, In,US
94/D3 New Castle, Pa,US
101/F1 Newcastle, Tx,US
86/F4 Newcastle, Wy,US
91/G5 Newcastle, Wy,US
93/F2 Newcastle, Wy,US
24/B2 Newcastle Emlyn, Wal,UK
23/F1 Newcastleton, Sc,UK
23/F5 Newcastle-under-Lyme, Eng,UK
18/C3 Newcastle upon Tyne, Eng,UK
23/G2 Newcastle upon Tyne, Eng,UK
99/R16 New Chicago, In,US
98/G4 New City, NY,US
53/L3 New Delhi (cap.), India
62/C2 New Delhi (cap.), India
90/D3 New Denver, BC,Can
19/N8 Newdigate, Eng,UK
31/F4 Newel, Ger.
72/B2 Newell, Austl.
73/E1 New England Nat'l Park, Austl.
85/F4 Newenham (cape), Ak,US
24/D3 Newent, Eng,UK
95/S9 Newfane, NY,US
84/M5 Newfoundland (isl.), Can.
87/K3 Newfoundland (prov.), Can.
89/Q2 Newfoundland (prov.), Can.
87/L4 Newfoundland (isl.), Nf,Can
95/L1 Newfoundland (isl.), Nf,Can
98/F4 Newfoundland, NJ,US
22/D1 New Galloway, Sc,UK
68/F5 New Georgia (isls.), Sol.
68/E5 New Georgia (sound), Sol.
95/J2 New Glasgow, Can
87/K4 New Glasgow, NS,Can
89/P2 New Glasgow, NS,Can
95/N6 New Glasgow, Qu,Can
48/N10 New Guinea (isl.), Indo., PNG
67/H4 New Guinea (isl.), Indo., PNG
68/C5 New Guinea (isl.), Indo., PNG
67/J4 New Guinea (isl.), Indo., PNG
85/H4 Newhalen, Ak,US
19/P7 Newham (bor.), Eng,UK
87/J4 New Hampshire (state), US
89/M3 New Hampshire (state), US
95/G3 New Hampshire (state), US
68/D5 New Hanover (isl.), PNG
25/F5 Newhaven, Eng,UK
89/M3 New Haven, Ct,US
94/F3 New Haven, Ct,US
99/G6 New Haven, Mi,US
68/F6 New Hebrides (isls.), Van.
89/H5 New Iberia, La,US
93/K5 New Iberia, La,US
96/F4 New Iberia, La,US
25/G5 Newick, Eng,UK
68/E5 New Ireland (isl.), PNG
89/M3 New Jersey (state), US
94/F3 New Jersey (state), US
94/E3 New Kensington, Pa,US
96/D2 Newkirk, Ok,US
99/Q16 New Lenox, Il,US
98/F6 New Lisbon, NJ,US
87/J4 New Liskeard, On,Can
89/L2 New Liskeard, On,Can
94/E2 New Liskeard, On,Can
89/M3 New London, Ct,US
95/F3 New London, Ct,US
91/L4 New London, Wi,US
94/B2 New London, Wi,US
24/A6 Newlyn, Eng,UK
93/K3 New Madrid, Mo,US
94/B4 New Madrid, Mo,US
97/F2 New Madrid, Mo,US
70/B4 Newman, Austl.
72/F6 Newmarket, Austl.
94/E2 Newmarket, On,Can
25/G2 Newmarket, Eng,UK
98/J7 New Market, Md,US
94/D4 New Martinsville, WV,US
97/H2 New Martinsville, WV,US
90/D4 New Meadows, Id,US
100/D1 New Mexico (state), US
88/E5 New Mexico (state), US
92/F4 New Mexico (state), US
23/F5 New Mills, Eng,UK
89/K5 Newnan, Ga,US
97/G3 Newnan, Ga,US
24/D3 Newnham, Eng,UK
71/H8 New Norfolk, Austl.
73/C4 New Norfolk, Austl.
89/H6 New Orleans, La,US
97/F4 New Orleans, La,US
94/D3 New Philadelphia, Oh,US
71/R10 New Plymouth, N.Z.
24/B2 Newport, Wal,UK
23/F6 Newport, Eng,UK
24/D1 Newport, Eng,UK
25/E5 Newport, Eng,UK
32/C1 Newport, Eng,UK
24/D3 Newport, Wal,UK
93/K4 Newport, Ar,US
97/F3 Newport, Ar,US
94/C4 Newport, Ky,US
97/G2 Newport, Ky,US
88/B3 Newport, Or,US
90/B4 Newport, Or,US
95/G3 Newport, RI,US
94/D5 Newport, Tn,US
89/M3 Newport, Vt,US
95/F2 Newport, Vt,US
90/D3 Newport, Wa,US
98/C3 Newport Beach, Ca,US
89/L4 Newport News, Va,US
94/E4 Newport News, Va,US
97/J2 Newport News, Va,US
25/F2 Newport Pagnell, Eng,UK
97/H4 New Port Richey, Fl,US
104/B1 New Providence (isl.), Bahm.
89/L6 New Providence (isl.), Bahm.
24/A6 Newquay, Eng,UK
32/A1 Newquay, Eng,UK
24/B2 New Quay, Wal,UK
24/C2 New Radnor, Wal,UK
95/H1 New Richmond, Qu,Can
98/G5 New Rochelle, NY,US
91/J4 New Rockford, ND,US
25/G5 New Romney, Eng,UK
32/D1 New Romney, Eng,UK
23/G5 New Rossington, Eng,UK
70/D3 Newry, Austl.
22/B3 Newry, NI,UK
22/B3 Newry (can.), NI,UK
83/Z New Schwabenland (reg.), Ant.
47/P2 New Siberian (isls.), Rus.
48/N2 New Siberian (isls.), Rus.
97/H4 New Smyrna Beach, Fl,US
71/H6 New South Wales (state), Austl.
72/B5 New South Wales (state), Austl.
73/C2 New South Wales (state), Austl.
85/G4 New Stuyahok, Ak,US
85/F3 Newtok, Ak,US
24/D2 Newton, Eng,UK
23/E1 Newton, Sc,UK
93/H3 Newton, Ks,US
96/D2 Newton, Ks,US
95/G3 Newton, Ma,US
98/F4 Newton, NJ,US
93/J5 Newton, Tx,US
96/E4 Newton, Tx,US
24/C5 Newton Abbot, Eng,UK
32/B1 Newton Abbot, Eng,UK
23/G2 Newton Aycliffe, Eng,UK
24/B6 Newton Ferrers, Eng,UK
23/F5 Newton-le-Willows, Eng,UK
23/G1 Newton on the Moor, Eng,UK
22/D2 Newton Stewart, Sc,UK
73/B3 Newtown, Austl.
24/C1 Newtown, Wal,UK
91/H4 New Town, ND,US
22/C2 Newtownabbey, NI,UK
22/C2 Newtownards, NI,UK
22/B3 Newtownhamilton, NI,UK
22/B5 Newtown Mount Kennedy, Ire.
98/E6 Newtown Square, Pa,US
22/A2 Newtownstewart, NI,UK
24/C3 New Tredegar, Wal,UK
86/G4 New Ulm, Mn,US
89/H3 New Ulm, Mn,US
91/K4 New Ulm, Mn,US
95/J2 New Waterford, NS,Can
86/D4 New Westminster, BC,Can
88/B2 New Westminster, BC,Can
87/J4 New York (state), US
89/L3 New York (state), US
94/F3 New York (state), US
95/S9 New York (state), US
89/M3 New York, NY,US
94/F3 New York, NY,US
68/G8 New Zealand
71/Q10 New Zealand
83/L New Zealand (peak), Ant.
57/L10 Neyagawa, Japan
24/B3 Neyland, Wal,UK
51/H4 Neyrīz, Iran
53/F3 Neyrīz, Iran
46/F6 Neyshābūr, Iran
51/J2 Neyshābūr, Iran
53/G1 Neyshābūr, Iran
43/P4 Neyva (riv.), Rus.
62/C5 Neyveli, India
64/G3 Neyveli, India
62/C6 Neyyāttinkara, India
64/F4 Neyyāttinkara, India
44/D2 Nezhin, Ukr.
43/X9 Neznayka (riv.), Rus.
90/D4 Nezperce, Id,US
94/D1 N. French (riv.), On,Can
66/C3 Ngabang, Indo.
67/H5 Ngabordamlu (cape), Indo.
82/F4 Ngabu, Malw.
76/H5 Ngala, Nga.
67/G3 Ngalipaeng, Indo.
63/G4 Ngao, Thai.
76/H6 Ngaoundéré, Camr.
73/B2 Ngarkat Consv. Park, Austl.
68/E4 Ngatik (isl.), Micr.
69/Z18 Ngau (isl.), Fiji
71/S10 Ngauruhoe (vol.), N.Z.
63/J4 Nghia Dan, Viet.
65/D2 Nghia Dan, Viet.
65/D1 Nghia Lo, Viet.
82/C4 Ngiva, Ang.
76/J8 Ngo, Congo
82/C1 Ngo, Congo
65/E4 Ngoan Muc (pass), Viet.
63/J4 Ngoc Linh (peak), Viet.
82/D4 Ngonye (fall, falls), Zam.
55/D5 Ngoring (lake), China
80/N12 Ngotwane (riv.), SAfr.
76/H8 Ngounié (riv.), Gabon
76/H5 Nguigmi, Niger
70/E2 Nguiu, Austl.
70/E2 Ngukurr, Austl.
68/C4 Ngulu (atoll), Micr.
60/D5 Ngum (riv.), Laos
65/C2 Ngum (riv.), Laos
76/H5 Nguru, Nga.
60/E4 Nguyen Binh, Viet.
63/J3 Nguyen Binh, Viet.
65/D1 Nguyen Binh, Viet.
65/B2 Ngwedaung, Burma
81/E2 Ngwenya (peak), Swaz.
105/D3 Nhamundá (riv.), Braz.
106/G4 Nhamundá (riv.), Braz.
63/J5 Nha Trang, Viet.
65/E3 Nha Trang, Viet.
66/C1 Nha Trang, Viet.
70/G7 Nhill, Austl.
73/B3 Nhill, Austl.
60/E4 Nho Quan, Viet.
63/J3 Nho Quan, Viet.
70/F2 Nhulunbuy, Austl.
76/E4 Niafounké, Mali
78/E3 Niafounké, Mali
95/R9 Niagara (co.), On,Can
95/R9 Niagara (riv.), Can, US
95/R9 Niagara (falls), NY,US
95/S9 Niagara (co.), NY,US
94/E3 Niagara Falls, On,Can
95/R9 Niagara Falls, On,Can
89/L3 Niagara Falls, NY,US
94/E3 Niagara Falls, NY,US
95/R9 Niagara Falls, NY,US
95/R9 Niagara-on-the-Lake, On,Can
76/F5 Niamey (cap.), Niger
79/F3 Niamey (cap.), Niger
79/F3 Niamey (dept.), Niger
78/C4 Niandan (riv.), Gui.
77/L7 Niangara, Zaire
76/E4 Niangay (lake), Mali
78/E3 Niangay (lake), Mali
76/E5 Niangoloko, Burk.
59/C3 Niangzi Guan (pass), China
48/J9 Nias (isl.), Indo.
66/A3 Nias (isl.), Indo.
103/E3 Nicaragua
106/B1 Nicaragua
84/J8 Nicaragua
103/E4 Nicaragua (lake), Nic.
84/J8 Nicaragua (lake), Nic.
38/E3 Nicastro-Sambiase, It.
18/D4 Nice, Fr.
33/G5 Nice, Fr.
35/J1 Nice, Fr.
97/G4 Niceville, Fl,US
56/B5 Nichinan, Japan
103/F1 Nicholas (chan.), Bahm., Cuba
70/B4 Nickol (bay), Austl.
48/J9 Nicobar (isls.), India
63/F6 Nicobar (isls.), India
63/F6 Nicobar, Car (isl.), India
95/F2 Nicolet, Qu,Can
49/C2 Nicosia (cap.), Cyp.
49/C2 Nicosia (dist.), Cyp.
50/C3 Nicosia (cap.), Cyp.
52/B1 Nicosia (cap.), Cyp.
38/D4 Nicosia, It.
38/D3 Nicotera, It.
103/E4 Nicoya, CR
103/E4 Nicoya (gulf), CR
103/E4 Nicoya (pen.), CR
106/A1 Nicoya (pen.), CR
36/D3 Nidau, Swi.
23/G4 Nidd (riv.), Eng,UK
26/E3 Nidda, Ger.
26/E3 Nidda (riv.), Ger.
33/H1 Nidda, Ger.
31/F2 Nideggen, Ger.
31/G6 Niderviller, Fr.
63/H3 Nidong, China
37/E4 Nidwalden (demi-canton), Swi.
27/L2 Nidzica, Pol.
26/E1 Niebüll, Ger.
33/G2 Nied (riv.), Fr.
31/F5 Nied (riv.), Ger.
29/G6 Niedenstein, Ger.
31/F4 Niederanven, Lux.
36/D3 Niederbipp, Swi.
31/G6 Niederbronn-les-Bains, Fr.
33/K3 Niedere Tauern (mts.), Aus.
31/G2 Niederfischbach, Ger.
37/E3 Niederhasli, Swi.
27/G3 Niederlausitz (reg.), Ger.
31/H4 Nieder-Olm, Ger.
26/D2 Niedersächsisches Wattenmeer Nat'l Park, Ger.
29/E1 Niedersächsisches Wattenmeer Nat'l Park, Ger.
37/G1 Niederstotzingen, Ger.
37/F3 Niederurnen, Swi.
40/B1 Niederösterreich (prov.), Aus.
31/F2 Niederzier, Ger.
31/G3 Niederzissen, Ger.
27/L2 Niegocin (lake), Pol.
29/G5 Nieheim, Ger.
27/J3 Niemodlin, Pol.
26/E2 Nienburg, Ger.
29/G3 Nienburg, Ger.
78/D5 Niénokoué (peak), IvC.
30/B2 Nieppe, Fr.
78/B3 Niéri Ko (riv.), Sen.
28/D5 Niers (riv.), Ger.
31/F1 Niers (riv.), Ger.
65/D4 Niet Ban Tinh Xa, Viet.
107/G2 Nieuw-Amsterdam, Sur.
28/D5 Nieuw-Bergen, Neth.
28/C4 Nieuwegein, Neth.
28/D2 Nieuwe Pekela, Neth.
28/B5 Nieuwerkerk aan de IJssel, Neth.
29/E2 Nieuweschans, Neth.
28/B4 Nieuwkoop, Neth.
28/D3 Nieuwleusen, Neth.
28/C4 Nieuw-Loosdrecht, Neth.
107/G2 Nieuw-Nickerie, Sur.
30/B1 Nieuwpoort, Belg.
28/D3 Nieuw-Schoonebeek, Neth.
28/B5 Nieuw-Vossemeer, Neth.
50/C2 Niğde, Turk.
50/C2 Niğde (prov.), Turk.
80/E2 Nigel, SAfr.
80/Q13 Nigel, SAfr.
74/C3 Niger
76/G4 Niger
79/G2 Niger
74/C4 Niger (riv.), Afr.
76/G6 Niger (riv.), Afr.
79/G5 Niger (riv.), Afr.
79/G4 Niger (state), Nga.
74/C4 Nigeria
76/G6 Nigeria
79/G4 Nigeria
79/G5 Niger, Mouths of the (delta), Nga.
94/D1 Nighthawk (lake), On,Can
85/F3 Nightmute, Ak,US
34/A1 Nigrán, Sp.
39/H2 Nigrita, Gre.
41/F5 Nigrita, Gre.
69/J2 Nihoa (isl.), Hi.,US
57/G2 Nihonmatsu, Japan
57/F3 Nii (isl.), Japan
47/P6 Niigata, Japan
55/M4 Niigata, Japan
57/F2 Niigata, Japan
57/F2 Niigata (pref.), Japan
55/L5 Niihama, Japan
56/C4 Niihama, Japan
88/R10 Niihau (isl.), Hi,US
56/C3 Niimi, Japan
55/M4 Niitsu, Japan
57/F2 Niitsu, Japan
57/H7 Niiza, Japan
34/D4 Nijar, Sp.
28/C4 Nijkerk, Neth.
28/B6 Nijlen, Belg.
30/D1 Nijlen, Belg.
26/C3 Nijmegen, Neth.
28/C5 Nijmegen, Neth.
39/H3 Níkaia, Gre.
20/J1 Nikel', Rus.
42/F1 Nikel', Rus.
85/H3 Nikishka, Ak,US
39/J2 Nikísiani, Gre.
41/G5 Nikísiani, Gre.
57/F2 Nikkō, Japan
57/F2 Nikkō Nat'l Park, Japan
33/L3 Niklasdorf, Aus.
39/J1 Nikolaevo, Bul.
41/G4 Nikolaevo, Bul.
85/H3 Nikolai, Ak,US
18/G4 Nikolayev, Ukr.
27/M4 Nikolayev, Ukr.
41/L2 Nikolayev, Ukr.
44/E3 Nikolayev, Ukr.
46/D5 Nikolayev, Ukr.
41/K2 Nikolayevka, Ukr.
20/J4 Nikolayevo, Rus.
41/K2 Nikolayev Obl., Ukr.
44/D3 Nikolayev Obl., Ukr.
46/E4 Nikolayevsk, Rus.
47/Q4 Nikolayevsk-na-Amure, Rus.
45/H1 Nikol'sk, Rus.
85/E5 Nikolski, Ak,US
47/S4 Nikol'skoye, Rus.
41/G4 Nikopol, Bul.
19/G4 Nikopol', Ukr.
44/E3 Nikopol', Ukr.
46/D5 Nikopol', Ukr.
44/F4 Niksar, Turk.
50/D1 Niksar, Turk.
53/H3 Nīkshahr, Iran
39/F1 Nikšic, Yugo.
40/D4 Nikšic, Yugo.
69/H5 Nikumaroro (Gardner) (atoll), Kiri.
68/G5 Nikunau (isl.), Kiri.
49/B5 Nile (riv.), Afr.
74/F2 Nile (riv.), Afr.
77/M2 Nile (riv.), Afr.
49/B4 Nile (delta), Egypt
50/B4 Nile (delta), Egypt
52/B2 Nile (delta), Egypt
49/B4 Nile, Damietta Branch (riv.), Egypt
49/B4 Nile, Rosetta Branch (riv.), Egypt
99/Q15 Niles, Il,US
94/C3 Niles, Mi,US
94/D3 Niles, Oh,US
64/F3 Nilgiri (hills), India
49/G8 Nīlīn, WBnk.
20/J3 Nilsiä, Fin.
42/F3 Nilsiä, Fin.
31/F5 Nilvange, Fr.
53/K4 Nīmach, India
62/B3 Nīmach, India
55/L1 Niman (riv.), Rus.
76/D6 Nimba (peak), IvC.
78/C5 Nimba (peak), IvC.
78/C5 Nimba (co.), Libr.
18/D4 Nîmes, Fr.
32/F5 Nîmes, Fr.
35/H1 Nîmes, Fr.
83/L Nimrod (glac.), Ant.
31/F4 Nimsbach (riv.), Ger.
77/M7 Nimule Nat'l Park, Sudan
33/L4 Nin, Cro.
40/B3 Nin, Cro.
50/E3 Nīnawá (gov.), Iraq
100/E2 Nine Point (mesa), Tx,US
51/E2 Nineveh (ruins), Iraq
52/D1 Nineveh (ruins), Iraq
55/K3 Ning'an, China
61/J2 Ningbo, China
68/B2 Ningbo, China
67/K5 Ningerum, PNG
61/G3 Ninggang, China
63/K2 Ninggang, China
54/H4 Ningjin, China
59/C3 Ningjin, China
59/D3 Ningjin, China
60/C2 Ningjing (mts.), China
60/D3 Ninglang Yizu Zizhixian, China
63/H2 Ninglang Yizu Zizhixian, China
59/C4 Ningling, China
61/E4 Ningmeng, China
63/J3 Ningming, China
65/D1 Ningming, China
59/C3 Ningwu, China
59/B3 Ningxia Huizu Zizhiqu (aut. reg.), China
59/D4 Ningyang, China
63/K2 Ningyuan, China
65/D1 Ninh Binh, Viet.
63/J5 Ninh Hoa, Viet.
65/E3 Ninh Hoa, Viet.
66/C1 Ninh Hoa, Viet.
85/H3 Ninilchik, Ak,US
68/D5 Niningo (isl.), PNG
83/K Ninnis (glac.), Ant.
57/H7 Ninomiya, Japan
30/D2 Ninove, Belg.
91/J5 Niobrara (riv.), Ne,US
86/F4 Niobrara (riv.), Ne,US
88/F3 Niobrara (riv.), Ne,US
76/C5 Niokolo-Koba Nat'l Park, Sen.
78/B3 Niokolo-Koba Nat'l Park, Sen.
63/F2 Nioku, India
76/D5 Niono, Mali
78/D3 Niono, Mali
78/B3 Nioro-du-Rip, Sen.
76/D4 Nioro du Sahel, Mali
78/C3 Nioro du Sahel, Mali
18/C4 Niort, Fr.
32/C3 Niort, Fr.
86/F3 Nipawin, Sk,Can
91/H2 Nipawin, Sk,Can
103/H1 Nipe (bay), Cuba
91/M3 Nipigon (lake), Can
84/J4 Nipigon (lake), Can.
86/H4 Nipigon, On,Can
86/H4 Nipigon (lake), On,Can
89/J2 Nipigon, On,Can
89/J2 Nipigon (lake), On,Can
91/L3 Nipigon, On,Can
94/B1 Nipigon, On,Can
94/B1 Nipigon (lake), On,Can
87/J4 Nipissing (lake), On,Can
94/E2 Nipissing (lake), On,Can
99/P15 Nippersink (cr.), Il,US
103/G1 Niquero, Cuba
57/F3 Nirasaki, Japan
72/H8 Nirimba-Hmas, Austl.
62/C4 Nirmal, India
18/F4 Niš, Yugo.
39/G1 Niš, Yugo.
40/E4 Niš, Yugo.
44/B4 Niš, Yugo.
34/B3 Nisa, Port.
52/D3 Nişāb, SAr.
39/H1 Nišava (riv.), Yugo.
38/D4 Niscemi, It.
57/M9 Nishiharu, Japan
56/C3 Nishiki (riv.), Japan
57/L9 Nishiki, Japan
57/L10 Nishinomiya, Japan
55/L5 Nishino'omote, Japan
56/B5 Nishino'omote, Japan
57/E3 Nishio, Japan
57/N10 Nishio, Japan
56/D3 Nishiwaki, Japan
57/K10 Nishiwaki, Japan
27/M3 Nisko, Pol.
41/J2 Nisporeny, Mol.
99/B3 Nisqually, Wa,US
99/B3 Nisqually (riv.), Wa,US
99/B3 Nisqually Ind. Res., Wa,US
99/B3 Nisqually Nat'l Wild. Ref., Wa,US
99/B3 Nisqually Reach (str.), Wa,US
68/E5 Nissan (isl.), PNG
35/G1 Nissan-lez-Enserune, Fr.
57/N9 Nisshin, Japan
91/K4 Nisswa, Mn,US
107/K8 Niterói, Braz.
108/D2 Niterói, Braz.
109/H1 Niterói, Braz.
22/E1 Nith (riv.), Sc,UK
22/E1 Nithsdale (val.), Sc,UK
27/K4 Nitra, Slvk.
27/K4 Nitra (riv.), Slvk.
40/D1 Nitra, Slvk.
43/P4 Nitsa (riv.), Rus.
31/F4 Nittel, Ger.
69/H6 Niuafo'ou (isl.), Tonga
69/H6 Niuatoputapu Group (isls.), Tonga
69/J6 Niue (isl.), N.Z.
69/J7 Niue (terr.), N.Z.
68/G6 Niulakita (isl.), Tuv.
60/D3 Niulan (riv.), China
63/H2 Niulan (riv.), China
66/C3 Niut (peak), Indo.
68/G5 Niutao (isl.), Tuv.
61/H2 Niutou (mtn.), China
61/J2 Niutou (isl.), China
30/D2 Nivelles, Belg.
32/E3 Nivernais (hills), Fr.
91/J3 Niverville, Mb,Can
92/C3 Nixon, Nv,US
56/C4 Niyodo (riv.), Japan
34/B3 Niza, Port.
62/C4 Nizāmābād, India
43/K4 Nizhegorod Obl., Rus.
45/G1 Nizhegorod Obl., Rus.
43/M4 Nizhnekama (res.), Rus.
43/L5 Nizhnekamsk, Rus.
47/K4 Nizhneudinsk, Rus.
46/H3 Nizhnevartovsk, Rus.
45/G1 Nizhniy Lomov, Rus.
19/H3 Nizhniy Novgorod, Rus.
46/E4 Nizhniy Novgorod, Rus.
43/K4 Nizhniy Novgorod (Gor'kiy), Rus.
43/N4 Nizhniy Tagil, Rus.
46/F4 Nizhniy Tagil, Rus.
50/D2 Nizip, Turk.
52/C1 Nizip, Turk.
27/K4 Nízke Tatry Nat'l Park, Slvk.
20/M7 Njardhvík, Ice.
82/F2 Njombe, Tanz.
79/H5 Nkambe, Camr.
82/B1 Nkayi, Congo
82/F3 Nkhata Bay, Malw.
79/H5 Nkogam, Massif du (peak), Camr.
76/G7 N'Kongsamba, Camr.
79/H5 N'Kongsamba, Camr.
60/C3 Nmai (riv.), Burma
63/G2 Nmai (riv.), Burma
30/B5 Noailles, Fr.
62/F3 Noākhāli, Bang.
62/E3 Noāmundi, India
85/F2 Noatak, Ak,US
85/F2 Noatak (riv.), Ak,US
85/F2 Noatak Nat'l Prsv., Ak,US
22/B4 Nobber, Ire.
56/B4 Nobeoka, Japan
93/H4 Noble, Ok,US
96/D3 Noble, Ok,US
94/C3 Noblesville, In,US
97/G1 Noblesville, In,US
95/Q8 Nobleton, On,Can
55/N3 Noboribetsu, Japan
37/G5 Noce (riv.), It.

162

Nochi – Nylst

102/B2 Nochixtlán, Mex.
40/C5 Noci, It.
98/E5 Nockamixon St. Park, Pa,US
57/H7 Noda, Japan
75/P13 Noé (cape), Alg.
30/B3 Noeux-les-Mines, Fr.
101/M8 Nogales, Mex.
100/C2 Nogales, Az,US
88/D5 Nogales, Az,US
92/E5 Nogales, Az,US
52/C6 Nogara, Eth.
32/C5 Nogaro, Fr.
35/E1 Nogaro, Fr.
56/B4 Nogata, Japan
36/B1 Nogent, Fr.
30/C6 Nogent-l'Artaud, Fr.
30/A6 Nogent-le-Roi, Fr.
32/D2 Nogent-le-Rotrou, Fr.
19/T10 Nogent-sur-Marne, Fr.
30/B5 Nogent-sur-Oise, Fr.
32/E2 Nogent-sur-Oise, Fr.
26/B4 Nogent-sur-Seine, Fr.
32/E2 Nogent-sur-Seine, Fr.
42/H5 Noginsk, Rus.
43/Y9 Noginsk, Rus.
44/F1 Noginsk, Rus.
72/B4 Nogoa (riv.), Austl.
58/D5 Nogodan-san (mtn.), SKor.
54/C2 Nogoonuur, Mong.
109/E3 Nogoyá, Arg.
27/K5 Nógrád (co.), Hun.
40/D2 Nógrád (co.), Hun.
35/F1 Noguera Pallarosa (riv.), Sp.
56/A2 Nogwak-san (mtn.), SKor.
58/E4 Nogwak-san (mtn.), SKor.
53/K3 Nohar, India
62/B2 Nohar, India
31/G4 Nohfelden, Ger.
102/E2 Nohkú, Punta (pt.), Mex.
55/K5 Nohwa, SKor.
60/E5 Noi (riv.), Laos
65/D2 Noi (riv.), Laos
63/J5 Noi (riv.), Viet.
36/C2 Noidans-lès-Vesoul, Fr.
94/E2 Noire (riv.), Qu,Can
32/B2 Noires (mts.), Fr.
32/B3 Noirmoutier (isl.), Fr.
30/B6 Noisiel, Fr.
19/T10 Noisy-le-Grand, Fr.
19/S10 Noisy-le-Roi, Fr.
30/B6 Noisy-le-Sec, Fr.
57/F3 Nojima-zaki (pt.), Japan
57/H8 Nojima-zaki (pt.), Japan
20/G3 Nokia, Fin.
42/D3 Nokia, Fin.
67/F4 Nokilalaki (peak), Indo.
53/H3 Nok Kundi, Pak.
76/J7 Nola, CAfr.
101/F2 Nolanville, Tx,US
73/D2 Nomadgi Nat'l Park, Austl.
100/D4 Nombre de Dios, Mex.
102/E3 Nombre de Dios, Cordillera (range), Hon.
85/E3 Nome, Ak,US
85/F3 Nome (cape), Ak,US
31/F6 Noméný, Fr.
36/C1 Nomexy, Fr.
56/B5 Nomo-misaki (cape), Japan
56/A4 Nomo-zaki (pt.), Japan
54/D2 Nömrög, Mong.
86/F2 Nonacho (lake), NW,Can
30/A6 Nonancourt, Fr.
85/H4 Nondalton, Ak,US
33/G4 None, It.
30/B5 Nonette (riv.), Fr.
55/K3 Nong'an, China
59/F1 Nong'an, China
65/D2 Nong Han (res.), Thai.
65/C2 Nong Het, Laos
60/D5 Nong Khai, Thai.
63/H4 Nong Khai, Thai.
65/C2 Nong Khai, Thai.
65/C2 Nong Pet, Laos
31/F4 Nonnweiler, Ger.
100/D3 Nonoava, Mex.
68/G5 Nonouti (atoll), Kiri.
59/E5 Nonri (isl.), China
55/K4 Nonsan, SKor.
58/D4 Nonsan, SKor.
63/H4 Non Sung, Thai.
32/D4 Nontron, Fr.
28/A5 Noordbeveland (isl.), Neth.
28/B3 Noorderhaaks (isl.), Neth.
28/B3 Noordhollandsch (can.), Neth.
28/C3 Noordostpolder (polder), Neth.
28/B4 Noordwijk aan Zee, Neth.
28/B4 Noordwijkerhout, Neth.
28/B4 Noordzeekanaal (can.), Neth.
20/G3 Noormarkku, Fin.
42/D3 Noormarkku, Fin.
85/F2 Noorvik, Ak,US
72/D4 Noosa-Tewantin, Austl.
90/B3 Nootka (isl.), BC,Can
90/B3 Nootka (sound), BC,Can
55/L1 Nora (riv.), Rus.
42/B4 Nora, Swe.
67/F2 Norala, Phil.
84/K5 Noranda-Rouyn, Can.
33/K5 Norcia, It.
98/C3 Norco, Ca,US
95/M6 Nord (riv.), Qu,Can
30/C3 Nord (dept.), Fr.
26/E1 Nordborg, Den.
30/B3 Nord, Canal du (can.), Fr.
26/D2 Norddeich, Ger.
29/E1 Norddeich, Ger.
26/D2 Norden, Ger.
29/E1 Norden, Ger.
26/E2 Nordenham, Ger.
29/F2 Nordenham, Ger.
46/K2 Nordenskjöld (arch.), Rus.
26/D2 Norderney, Ger.
29/E1 Norderney, Ger.
29/E1 Norderney (isl.), Ger.
29/G1 Norderstedt, Ger.
20/C3 Nordfjordeid, Nor.
26/F3 Nordhausen, Ger.
26/E2 Nordholz, Ger.
29/F1 Nordholz, Ger.
26/D2 Nordhorn, Ger.
29/E4 Nordhorn, Ger.
36/D1 Nordhouse, Fr.
20/H1 Nordkapp (cape), Nor.
46/C2 Nordkapp (North) (cape), Nor.
20/H1 Nordkinn (pt.), Nor.
29/E5 Nordkirchen, Ger.
20/E2 Nordland (co.), Nor.
42/B2 Nordland (co.), Nor.
99/B1 Nordland, Wa,US
26/F4 Nördlingen, Ger.
20/F3 Nordmaling, Swe.
42/C3 Nordmaling, Swe.
26/E1 Nord-Ostee (canal), Ger.
29/G1 Nord-Ostee (can.), Ger.
79/H5 Nord-Ouest (prov.), Camr.
75/M13 Nord Ouest (reg.), Mor.
25/H6 Nord Pas de Calais (reg.), Fr.
26/A3 Nord-Pas-de-Calais (reg.), Fr.
30/A3 Nord-Pas-de-Calais (reg.), Fr.
32/D1 Nord-Pas-de-Calais (reg.), Fr.
29/E3 Nord-Radde (riv.), Ger.
29/E3 Nord-Sud (can.), Ger.
73/D2 Nords Wharf, Austl.
20/E2 Nord-Trøndelag (co.), Nor.
42/A2 Nord-Trøndelag (co.), Nor.
29/E4 Nordwalde, Ger.
21/B4 Nore (riv.), Ire.
32/E5 Nore, Pic de (peak), Fr.
35/G1 Nore, Pic de (peak), Fr.
68/F7 Norfolk (isl.), Austl.
71/M5 Norfolk (isl.), Austl.
73/C4 Norfolk (peak), Austl.
23/J6 Norfolk (co.), Eng,UK
25/G1 Norfolk (co.), Eng,UK
89/G3 Norfolk, Ne,US
91/J5 Norfolk, Ne,US
93/H2 Norfolk, Ne,US
89/L4 Norfolk, Va,US
94/E4 Norfolk, Va,US
97/J2 Norfolk, Va,US
25/H1 Norfolk Broads (swamp), Eng,UK
93/J3 Norfork (lake), Ar, Mo,US
28/D2 Norg, Neth.
57/E2 Norikura-dake (mtn.), Japan
46/J3 Noril'sk, Rus.
93/K2 Normal, Il,US
94/B3 Normal, Il,US
72/A2 Norman (riv.), Austl.
89/G4 Norman, Ok,US
93/H4 Norman, Ok,US
96/D3 Norman, Ok,US
68/E6 Normanby (isl.), PNG
32/C2 Normandie (hills), Fr.
32/C2 Normandy (reg.), Fr.
99/C3 Normandy Park, Wa,US
68/D6 Normanton, Austl.
70/G3 Normanton, Austl.
72/A2 Normanton, Austl.
23/G4 Normanton, Eng,UK
86/D2 Norman Wells, NW,Can
80/B3 Norotshama (peak), Namb.
91/H3 Norquay, Sk,Can
20/F2 Norrbotten (co.), Swe.
42/C2 Norrbotten (co.), Swe.
34/B1 Norrea (riv.), Sp.
26/F1 Nørre Alslev, Den.
30/B2 Norrent-Fontes, Fr.
99/Q16 Norridge, Il,US
94/F3 Norristown, Pa,US
98/E5 Norristown, Pa,US
18/E3 Norrköping, Swe.
20/F4 Norrköping, Swe.
42/C4 Norrköping, Swe.
46/B4 Norrköping, Swe.
20/F2 Norrland (reg.), Swe.
42/C2 Norrland (reg.), Swe.
20/F4 Norrtälje, Swe.
42/C4 Norrtälje, Swe.
68/B8 Norseman, Austl.
70/C6 Norseman, Austl.
20/F2 Norsjö, Swe.
42/C2 Norsjö, Swe.
109/E4 Norte (pt.), Arg.
106/G6 Norte (mts.), Braz.
103/H4 Norte de Santander (dept.), Col.
107/G6 Nortelândia, Braz.
29/G5 Nörten-Hardenberg, Ger.
22/C1 North (chan.)
73/C3 North (pt.), Austl.
73/C4 North (pt.), Austl.
95/J2 North (cape), Can
94/D2 North (chan.), On,Can
87/K4 North (cape), PE,Can
89/P2 North (cape), PEI,Can
18/D3 North (sea), Eur.
20/C4 North (sea), Eur.
26/B1 North (sea), Eur.
46/A4 North (sea), Eur.
68/G8 North (cape), N.Z.
68/G8 North (isl.), N.Z.
71/N6 North (cape), N.Z.
71/R10 North (isl.), N.Z.
71/R9 North (cape), N.Z.
85/D5 North (cape), Ak,US
85/F3 North (peak), Ak,US
40/D4 North Albanian Alps (mts.), Alb., Yugo.
39/F1 North Albanian Alps (range), Yugo.
23/G3 Northallerton, Eng,UK
68/A8 Northam, Austl.
70/B6 Northam, Austl.
24/B4 Northam, Eng,UK
16/F3 North America
84/* North America
68/A7 Northampton, Austl.
70/A5 Northampton, Austl.
25/E2 Northampton (uplands), Eng,UK
25/F2 Northampton, Eng,UK
94/F3 Northampton, Ma,US
98/E5 Northampton, Pa,US
98/E5 Northampton (co.), Pa,US
25/F2 Northamptonshire (co.), Eng,UK
63/F5 North Andaman (isl.), India
87/K3 North Aulatsivik (isl.), Nf,Can
99/P16 North Aurora, Il,US
19/N6 Northaw, Eng,UK
22/D3 North Barrule (mtn.), IM,UK
84/G4 North Battleford, Can.
86/F3 North Battleford, Sk,Can
90/F2 North Battleford, Sk,Can
87/J4 North Bay, On,Can
89/L2 North Bay, On,Can
94/E2 North Bay, On,Can
99/Q14 North Bay, Wi,US
98/K8 North Beach, Md,US
90/B5 North Bend, Or,US
92/A2 North Bend, Or,US
99/D3 North Bend, Wa,US
98/F5 North Bergen, NJ,US
28/C5 North Brabant (prov.), Neth.
99/Q15 Northbrook, Il,US
103/J1 North Caicos (isl.), Trks.
104/D2 North Caicos (isl.), Trks.
88/F4 North Canadian (riv.), Ok,US
18/F1 North Cape (cape), Nor.
91/L2 North Caribou (lake), On,Can
86/G3 North Caribou (lake), On,Can
89/K4 North Carolina (state), US
97/H3 North Carolina (state), US
90/C3 North Cascades Nat'l Park, Wa,US
86/D4 North Cascades Nat'l Park, Wa,US
88/B2 North Cascades Nat'l Park, Wa,US
64/H4 North Central (prov.), SrL.
101/F1 North Central (plain), Tx,US
89/L5 North Charleston, SC,US
97/J3 North Charleston, SC,US
99/Q15 North Chicago, Il,US
23/H5 North Collingham, Eng,UK
90/C3 North Cowichan, BC,Can
91/H4 North Dakota (state), US
86/F4 North Dakota (state), US
88/F2 North Dakota (state), US
24/D5 North Dorset Downs (uplands), Eng,UK
22/C2 North Down (dist.), NI,UK
19/N8 North Downs (plat.), UK
25/F4 North Downs (hills), Eng,UK
72/C3 North East (pt.), Austl.
103/H1 Northeast (pt.), Bahm.
104/C2 Northeast (pt.), Bahm.
103/G2 Northeast (pt.), Jam.
85/E3 Northeast (cape), Ak,US
94/E3 North East, Pa,US
46/C2 Northeast Land (isl.), Sval.
104/B1 North East Providence (chan.), Bahm.
29/G5 Northeim, Ger.
25/G1 North Elmham, Eng,UK
79/E4 Northern (reg.), Gha.
49/D3 Northern (dist.), Isr.
49/G6 Northern (dist.), Isr.
78/B4 Northern (prov.), SLeo.
64/H4 Northern (prov.), SrL.
69/J6 Northern Cook (isls.), Cookls.
18/H2 Northern Dvina (riv.), Rus.
43/K3 Northern Dvina (riv.), Rus.
46/E3 Northern Dvina (riv.), Rus.
18/C3 Northern Ireland, UK
94/B1 Northern Light (lake), On,Can, Mn,US
68/D3 Northern Marianas, US
46/G3 Northern Sos'va (riv.), Rus.
39/J3 Northern Sporades (isls.), Gre.
70/E3 Northern Territory (state), Austl.
43/N3 Northern Ural (mts.), Rus.
43/K4 Northern Uval (hills), Rus.
46/E4 Northern Uvals (upland), Rus.
85/K2 Northern Yukon Nat'l Park, Yk,Can
86/C2 Northern Yukon Nat'l Park, Yk,Can
91/K4 Northfield, Mn,US
19/P7 Northfleet, Eng,UK
25/G4 Northfleet, Eng,UK
25/H4 North Foreland (pt.), UK
97/H5 North Fort Myers, Fl,US
26/E1 North Frisian (isls.), Den., Ger.
95/F2 North Hero, Vt,US
99/M9 North Highlands, Ca,US
99/C3 North Hill-Edgewood, Wa,US
28/B3 North Holland (prov.), Neth.
23/H5 North Hykeham, Eng,UK
43/Q5 North Kazakhstan Obl., Rus.
47/N5 North Korea
48/M5 North Korea
55/K3 North Korea
58/D4 North Korea
58/F6 North Korea
59/F3 North Korea
60/B3 North Lakhimpur, India
63/F2 North Lakhimpur, India
88/C4 North Las Vegas, Nv,US
92/D3 North Las Vegas, Nv,US
89/H5 North Little Rock, Ar,US
93/J4 North Little Rock, Ar,US
96/E3 North Little Rock, Ar,US
91/H5 North Loup (riv.), Nb,US
82/F3 North Luangwa Nat'l Park, Zam.
84/G2 North Magnetic Pole, NAm.
91/J2 North Moose (lake), Mb,Can
97/J3 North Myrtle Beach, SC,US
46/C2 North (Nordkapp) (cape), Nor.
45/G4 North Ossetian Aut. Rep., Rus.
68/F3 North Pacific (ocean)
95/R9 North Pelham, On,Can
24/C4 North Petherton, Eng,UK
72/E6 North Pine (riv.), Austl.
88/F3 North Platte, Ne,US
91/H5 North Platte, Ne,US
93/G2 North Platte, Ne,US
88/F3 North Platte (riv.), US
86/F4 North Platte (riv.), US
91/H5 North Platte (riv.), US
85/J3 North Pole, Ak,US
97/G3 Northport, Al,US
98/J7 North Potomac, Md,US
99/P14 North Prairie, Wi,US
99/C3 North Puyallup, Wa,US
91/K5 North Raccoon (riv.), Ia,US
26/E3 North Rhine-Westphalia (state), Ger.
29/E5 North Rhine-Westphalia (state), Ger.
31/F1 North Rhine-Westphalia (state), Ger.
33/G1 North Rhine-Westphalia (state), Ger.
92/D3 North Rim, Az,US
86/E3 North Saskatchewan (riv.), Ab, Sk,Can
23/G2 North Shields, Eng,UK
46/K2 North Siberian (plain), Rus.
23/J5 North Somercotes, Eng,UK
71/J5 North Stradbroke (isl.), Austl.
72/D4 North Stradbroke (isl.), Austl.
71/R10 North Taranaki (bight), NZ
98/G4 North Tarrytown, NY,US
23/H5 North Thoresby, Eng,UK
25/E4 North Tidworth, Eng,UK
95/S9 North Tonawanda, NY,US
23/F1 North Tyne (riv.), Eng,UK
21/B2 North Uist (isl.), Sc,UK
95/J2 Northumberland (str.), Can
89/P2 Northumberland (str.), NB, PE,Can
23/F1 Northumberland (co.), Eng,UK
23/F1 Northumberland Nat'l Park, Eng,UK
92/B2 North Umpqua (riv.), Or,US
98/G4 Northvale, NJ,US
86/D4 North Vancouver, BC,Can
99/F7 Northville, Mi,US
98/E5 North Wales, Pa,US
25/H1 North Walsham, Eng,UK
26/A2 North Walsham, Eng.,UK
85/K3 Northway, Ak,US
19/P6 North Weald Bassett, Eng,UK
70/A4 North West (cape), Austl.
103/G2 Northwest (pt.), Jam.
64/H4 North Western (prov.), SrL.
64/A1 North West Frontier (prov.), Pak.
21/C2 North West Highlands (upland), Sc,UK
104/B1 North West Providence (chan.), Bahm.
85/M2 Northwest Territories (terr.), Can.
86/E2 Northwest Territories (prov.), Can.
23/H5 North Wheatley, Eng,UK
23/F5 Northwich, Eng,UK
23/G5 North Wingfield, Eng,UK
91/J4 Northwood, ND,US
95/R8 North York, On,Can
23/H3 North York Moors Nat'l Park, Eng,UK
23/G3 North Yorkshire (co.), Eng,UK
84/A3 Norton (sound), US
85/E3 Norton (sound), Ak,US
85/F3 Norton (bay), Ak,US
88/G4 Norton, Ks,US
93/H3 Norton, Ks,US
96/D2 Norton, Ks,US
94/D4 Norton, Va,US
97/H2 Norton, Va,US
23/F6 Norton Bridge, Eng,UK
94/C3 Norton Shores, Mi,US
26/E1 Nortorf, Ger.
32/C3 Nort-sur-Erdre, Fr.
95/Q8 Norval, On,Can
83/Z Norvegia (cape), Ant.
31/F2 Nörvenich, Ger.
94/F3 Norwalk, Ct,US
98/G4 Norwalk, Ct,US
94/D3 Norwalk, Oh,US
18/D2 Norway
20/C3 Norway
42/B2 Norway
46/A3 Norway
86/G3 Norway House, Mb,Can
91/J2 Norway House, Mb,Can
87/S7 Norwegian (bay), NW,Can
18/C2 Norwegian (sea)
20/C2 Norwegian (sea)
42/A2 Norwegian (sea)
46/A3 Norwegian (sea)
18/D3 Norwich, Eng,UK
25/H1 Norwich, Eng,UK
94/F3 Norwich, NY,US
57/L10 Nose, Japan
53/K1 Noshaq (mtn.), Pak.
55/N3 Noshiro, Japan
41/H4 Nos Maslen Nos (pt.), Bul.
44/C4 Nos Maslen Nos (pt.), Bul.
66/E2 Nosong (cape), Malay.
80/C2 Nosop (dry riv.), Bots.
44/D2 Nosovka, Ukr.
53/G3 Noşratābād, Iran
80/B2 Nossob (dry riv.), Namb.
80/C2 Nossobrivier (dry riv.), SAfr.
81/J8 Nosy-Varika, Madg.
27/J2 Notec (riv.), Pol.
38/D4 Noto, It.
38/D4 Noto (gulf), It.
38/D4 Noto (val.), It.
57/E2 Noto (pen.), Japan
38/D4 Noto Antica (ruins), It.
57/M9 Notogawa, Japan
87/L4 Notre Dame (bay), Nf,Can
95/L1 Notre Dame (bay), Nf,Can
87/J4 Notre Dame (mts.), Qu,Can
95/G1 Notre Dame (mts.), Qu,Can
19/T10 Notre Dame, Fr.
95/N7 Notre-Dame-de-l'Ile-Perrot, Qu,Can
87/J3 Nottaway (riv.), Qu,Can
94/E1 Nottaway (riv.), Qu,Can
87/H2 Nottingham (isl.), NW,Can
18/C3 Nottingham, Eng,UK
23/G6 Nottingham, Eng,UK
23/H5 Nottinghamshire (co.), Eng,UK
29/E5 Nottuln, Ger.
74/A2 Nouadhibou, Mrta.
76/B4 Nouakchott (cap.), Mrta.
78/B2 Nouakchott (cap.), Mrta.
35/F1 Noue (riv.), Fr.
68/F7 Nouméa, NCal.
69/V13 Nouméa (cap.), NCal.
76/E5 Nouna, Burk.
80/D3 Noupoort, SAfr.
30/A3 Nouvion, Fr.
31/D4 Nouvion-sur-Meuse, Fr.
26/C4 Nouzonville, Fr.
31/D4 Nouzonville, Fr.
32/F2 Nouzonville, Fr.
107/H8 Nova Andradina, Braz.
41/F3 Novaci, Rom.
107/L5 Nova Cruz, Braz.
27/K4 Nová Dubnica, Slvk.
107/K8 Nova Friburgo, Braz.
108/D2 Nova Friburgo, Braz.
109/H1 Nova Friburgo, Braz.
33/K4 Nova Gorica, Slov.
40/A3 Nova Gorica, Slov.
40/C3 Nova Gradiška, Cro.
107/K8 Nova Iguaçu, Braz.
108/D2 Nova Iguaçu, Braz.
109/H1 Nova Iguaçu, Braz.
37/H5 Nova Levante (Welshnofen), It.
106/G4 Nova Olinda do Norte, Braz.
40/E3 Nova Pazova, Yugo.
108/B4 Nova Prata, Braz.
33/H4 Novara, It.
37/E5 Novara (prov.), It.
87/K4 Nova Scotia (prov.), Can.
89/P3 Nova Scotia (prov.), Can.
95/J2 Nova Scotia (prov.), Can
74/J11 Nova Sintra, CpV.
37/F5 Novate Mezzola, It.
99/J10 Novato, Ca,US
40/D4 Nova Varoš, Yugo.
107/K7 Nova Venécia, Braz.
108/D1 Nova Venécia, Braz.
107/H6 Nova Xavantina, Braz.
41/J3 Novaya Ivanovka, Ukr.
41/L2 Novaya Kakhovka, Ukr.
44/E3 Novaya Kakhovka, Ukr.
41/L2 Novaya Mayachka, Ukr.
41/K2 Novaya Odessa, Ukr.
47/R2 Novaya Sibir' (isl.), Rus.
18/H1 Novaya Zemlya (isl.), Rus.
46/E2 Novaya Zemlya (arch.), Rus.
39/K1 Nova Zagora, Bul.
41/H4 Nova Zagora, Bul.
44/C4 Nova Zagora, Bul.
27/H4 Nové Hrady, Czh.
33/L2 Nové Hrady, Czh.
35/E3 Novelda, Sp.
27/J4 Nové Mesto nad Váhom, Slvk.
27/K5 Nové Zámky, Slvk.
40/D2 Nové Zámky, Slvk.
18/G3 Novgorod, Rus.
42/F4 Novgorod, Rus.
46/D4 Novgorod, Rus.
42/G4 Novgorod Obl., Rus.
99/F7 Novi, Mi,US
40/E3 Novi Banovci, Yugo.
40/E3 Novi Bečej, Yugo.
44/B3 Novi Bečej, Yugo.
39/H1 Novi Iskŭr, Bul.
41/F4 Novi Iskŭr, Bul.
47/Q5 Novikovo, Rus.
33/H4 Novi Ligure, It.
36/C3 Novillars, Fr.
100/D4 Novillero, Mex.
41/H4 Novi Pazar, Bul.
39/G1 Novi Pazar, Yugo.
40/E4 Novi Pazar, Yugo.
18/E4 Novi Sad, Yugo.
40/D3 Novi Sad, Yugo.
33/L4 Novi Vinodolski, Cro.
40/B3 Novi Vinodolski, Cro.
45/G2 Novoanninskiy, Rus.
106/F5 Novo Aripuanã, Braz.
43/K4 Novocheboksarsk, Rus.
19/H4 Novocherkassk, Rus.
44/G3 Novocherkassk, Rus.
46/E5 Novocherkassk, Rus.
44/C2 Novograd-Volynskiy, Ukr.
42/E5 Novogrudok, Bela.
44/C1 Novogrudok, Bela.
108/B4 Novo Hamburgo, Braz.
109/F2 Novo Hamburgo, Braz.
108/B2 Novo Horizonte, Braz.
46/G5 Novokazalinsk, Kaz.
45/J1 Novokuybyshevsk, Rus.
46/J4 Novokuznetsk, Rus.
83/A Novolazarevskaya, Ant.
44/D1 Novolukoml', Bela.
33/L4 Novo Mesto, Slov.
40/B3 Novo Mesto, Slov.
40/E3 Novo Miloševo, Yugo.
19/G3 Novomoskovsk, Rus.
44/F1 Novomoskovsk, Rus.
46/D4 Novomoskovsk, Rus.
44/E3 Novomoskovsk, Ukr.
20/J5 Novopolotsk, Bela.
42/F5 Novopolotsk, Bela.
19/G4 Novorossiysk, Rus.
43/F3 Novorossiysk, Rus.
46/D5 Novorossiysk, Rus.
41/H1 Novoselitsa, Ukr.
44/F3 Novoshakhtinsk, Rus.
46/J4 Novosibirsk, Rus.
27/L1 Novostroyevo, Rus.
19/J3 Novotroitsk, Rus.
45/L2 Novotroitsk, Rus.
46/F4 Novotroitsk, Rus.
44/D2 Novoukrainka, Ukr.
27/N3 Novovolynsk, Ukr.
44/C2 Novovolynsk, Ukr.
43/L4 Novovyatsk, Rus.
44/D1 Novozybkov, Rus.
40/C3 Novska, Cro.
27/K4 Nový Jičín, Czh.
41/L2 Novyy Bug, Ukr.
45/K4 Novyy Uzen', Kaz.
46/F5 Novyy Uzen', Kaz.
27/L3 Nowa Dęba, Pol.
27/J3 Nowa Ruda, Pol.
27/M3 Nowa Sarzyna, Pol.
27/H3 Nowa Sól, Pol.
93/J3 Nowata, Ok,US
96/E2 Nowata, Ok,US
27/K2 Nowe, Pol.
27/K2 Nowe Miasto Lubawskie, Pol.
60/B3 Nowgong, India
62/C2 Nowgong, India
63/F2 Nowgong, India
85/H3 Nowitna (riv.), Ak,US
85/H3 Nowitna Nat'l Wild. Ref., Ak,US
27/H2 Nowogard, Pol.
92/F1 Nowood (riv.), Wy,US
53/K2 Nowshera, Pak.
27/K1 Nowy Dwór Gdański, Pol.
27/L4 Nowy Sącz, Pol.
27/L4 Nowy Sacz (prov.), Pol.
44/B2 Nowy Sącz, Pol.
27/K1 Nowy Staw, Pol.
27/L4 Nowy Targ, Pol.
27/J2 Nowy Tomyśl, Pol.
34/A1 Noya, Sp.
30/B5 Noye (riv.), Fr.
64/F3 Noyil (riv.), India
26/B4 Noyon, Fr.
30/C4 Noyon, Fr.
32/E2 Noyon, Fr.
82/G4 Nsanje, Malw.
79/E5 Nsawam, Gha.
63/G2 Nsopzup, Burma
79/E5 Nsuta, Gha.
54/D5 Nu (riv.), China
63/G2 Nu (mts.), China
77/M5 Nūbah (mts.), Sudan
60/B2 Nubgang (pass), China
52/B4 Nubian (des.), Sudan
74/F2 Nubian (des.), Sudan
77/M3 Nubian (des.), Sudan
40/F2 Nucet, Rom.
92/E3 Nucla, Co,US
96/A2 Nucla, Co,US
101/F3 Nueces (riv.), Tx,US
95/H5 Nueces (riv.), Tx,US
86/G2 Nueltin (lake), NW,Can
28/C6 Nuenen, Neth.
59/E2 Nü'er (riv.), China
101/F3 Nueva Ciudad Guerrero, Mex.
102/D2 Nueva Coahuila Nat'l Cap. Park, Mex.
102/D3 Nueva Concepción, Guat.
104/F5 Nueva Esparta (state), Ven.
103/F1 Nueva Gerona, Cuba
106/C3 Nueva Loja, Ecu.
102/D3 Nueva Ocotepéque, Hon.
101/N8 Nueva Patria, Mex.
101/E3 Nueva Rosita, Mex.
96/C5 Nueva Rosita, Mex
109/D4 Nueve de Julio, Arg.
103/G1 Nuevitas, Cuba
109/D5 Nuevo (gulf), Arg.
98/C3 Nuevo, Ca,US
100/D2 Nuevo Casas Grandes, Mex.
92/F5 Nuevo Casas Grandes, Mex
103/F4 Nuevo Chagres, Pan.
100/D3 Nuevo Ideal, Mex.
101/F3 Nuevo Laredo, Mex.
88/G6 Nuevo Laredo, Mex.
96/D5 Nuevo Laredo, Mex
101/F3 Nuevo León (state), Mex.
88/F6 Nuevo Leon (state), Mex.
37/F4 Nufenen, Swi.
37/E5 Nufenenpass (pass), Swi.
68/E5 Nuguria (isls.), PN
69/J2 Nuhau (isl.), Hi.,US
29/F6 Nuhne (riv.), Ger.
68/G5 Nui (atoll), Tuv.
85/H1 Nuiqsut, Ak,US
36/A3 Nuits-Saint-Georg
Fr.
57/N10 Nukata, Japan
85/F4 Nuklunek (mtn.), Ak,US
69/H7 Nuku'alofa (cap.), Tonga
68/G5 Nukufetau (atoll), T
69/L5 Nuku Hiva (isl.), Fr
68/H5 Nukulaelae (isl.), T
68/F5 Nukumanu (atoll), PNG
69/H5 Nukunonu (atoll), T
68/E4 Nukuoro (isl.), Mic
46/F5 Nukus, Uzb.
69/M6 Nukutavake (isl.),
FrPol.
69/M6 Nukutavake (isl.),
85/G3 Nulato, Ak,US
35/E3 Nules, Sp.
70/C4 Nullagine, Austl.
68/B8 Nullarbor (plain), Austl.
70/D6 Nullarbor (plain), Austl.
76/H6 Numan, Nga.
28/B5 Numansdorp, Neth
57/F2 Numata, Japan
57/F3 Numazu, Japan
31/G2 Nümbrecht, Ger.
70/F2 Numbulwar, Austl.
67/H4 Numfoor (isl.), Indo
73/C3 Numurkah, Austl.
85/F3 Nunapitchuk, Ak,U
73/G5 Nunawading, Aust
73/D1 Nundle, Austl.
25/E1 Nuneaton, Eng,UK
73/D3 Nungatta Nat'l Par
Austl.
85/E4 Nunivak (isl.), Ak,U
36/D3 Nunningen, Swi.
28/C4 Nunspeet, Neth.
23/G2 Nunthorpe, Eng,UK
67/E3 Nunukan, Indo.
47/V4 Nunivak (isl.), Ak,U
55/J1 Nuomin (riv.), Chin
78/C5 Nuon (riv.), IvC., Li
18/D4 Nuoro, It.
38/A2 Nuoro, It.
106/C2 Nuquí, Col.
49/E1 Nur (mts.), Turk.
31/F3 Nürburgring, Ger.
50/D2 Nurhak, Turk.
100/C2 Nuri, Mex.
73/A2 Nuriootpa, Austl.
45/J1 Nurlat, Rus.
18/E4 Nürnberg, Ger.
26/F4 Nürnberg, Ger.
33/J2 Nürnberg, Ger.
73/C1 Nurri (peak), Austl
26/E4 Nürtingen, Ger.
33/H2 Nürtingen, Ger.
52/E6 Nüsah, Yem.
60/C2 Nu (Salween) (riv.), China
50/D2 Nusaybin, Turk.
85/G4 Nushagak (riv.), Ak,US
53/J3 Nushki, Pak.
31/E2 Nuth, Neth.
84/M3 Nuuk (Godthåb), G
69/X15 Nuupere (pt.), FrPo
50/C4 Nuwaybi', Egypt
52/B3 Nuwaybi', Egypt
80/L10 Nuy (riv.), SAfr.
33/H3 Nüziders, Aus.
37/F3 Nüziders, Aus.
95/L1 N.W. Gander (riv.), Nf,Can
82/E4 Nxai Pan Nat'l Par
Bots.
98/G4 Nyack, NY,US
73/B2 Nyah, Austl.
82/F2 Nyahua, Tanz.
73/B2 Nyah West, Austl.
60/B2 Nyainqêntanglha (mts.), China
60/B1 Nyainrong, China
77/K5 Nyala, Sudan
62/E2 Nyalam, China
77/L6 Nyamlell, Sudan
42/J3 Nyandoma, Rus.
60/B2 Nyang (riv.), China
82/E1 Nyanza-Lac, Buru.
74/F6 Nyasa (lake), Afr.
82/F3 Nyasa (Malawi) (lake), Afr.
26/F1 Nyborg, Den.
20/J1 Nyborg, Nor.
20/E4 Nybro, Swe.
62/F2 Nyêmo, China
77/N8 Nyeri, Kenya
82/G1 Nyeri, Kenya
54/E5 Nyikog (riv.), China
60/D1 Nyikog (riv.), China
40/F2 Nyírábrány, Hun.
27/L5 Nyíradony, Hun.
27/M5 Nyírbátor, Hun.
40/F2 Nyírbátor, Hun.
27/L5 Nyíregyháza, Hun.
40/E2 Nyíregyháza, Hun.
44/B3 Nyíregyháza, Hun.
27/M4 Nyírmada, Hun.
40/F1 Nyírmada, Hun.
77/N7 Nyiru (peak), Keny
20/D5 Nykøbing, Den.
26/F1 Nykøbing, Den.
20/F4 Nyköping, Swe.
42/C4 Nyköping, Swe.
80/E2 Nylstroom, SAfr.

163

Nylst – Ŏrang

82/E5 Nylstroom, SAfr.
20/F4 Nynäshamn, Swe.
42/C4 Nynäshamn, Swe.
71/H6 Nyngan, Austl.
73/C1 Nyngan, Austl.
33/G3 Nyon, Swi.
36/C5 Nyon, Swi.
32/F4 Nyons, Fr.
27/G4 Nýřany, Czh.
33/K2 Nýřany, Czh.
27/J3 Nysa, Pol.
90/D5 Nyssa, Or,US
92/C2 Nyssa, Or,US
26/F1 Nysted, Den.
55/M4 Nyūdo-zaki (pt.), Japan
42/F2 Nyuk (lake), Rus.
82/E2 Nyunzu, Zaire
57/E2 Nyūzen, Japan
82/F1 Nzega, Tanz.
76/D6 Nzérékoré, Gui.
78/C4 Nzérékoré (comm.), Gui.
78/C5 Nzérékoré, Gui.
76/E6 Nzi (riv.), IvC.
78/D5 Nzi (riv.), IvC.

O

55/M5 Ō (isl.), Japan
57/F3 Ō (isl.), Japan
25/E1 Oadby, Eng,UK
91/H4 Oahe (lake), ND, SD,US
86/F4 Oahe (res.), ND,SD,US
88/F3 Oahe (dam), SD,US
91/H4 Oahe (dam), SD,US
93/G1 Oahe (dam), SD,US
69/K2 Oahu (isl.), Hi,US
8/S10 Oahu (isl.), Hi,US
8/V13 Oahu (isl.), Hi,US
91/J3 Oakbank, Mb,Can
9/Q14 Oak Creek, Wi,US
91/J4 Oakes, ND,US
72/C4 Oakey, Austl.
9/Q16 Oak Forest, Il,US
25/F1 Oakham, Eng,UK
94/D4 Oak Hill, WV,US
97/H2 Oak Hill, WV,US
92/C3 Oakhurst, Ca,US
86/D5 Oakland, Ca,US
88/B4 Oakland, Ca,US
92/B3 Oakland, Ca,US
9/K11 Oakland, Ca,US
98/K7 Oakland, Md,US
99/F6 Oakland (co.), Mi,US
99/F6 Oakland (lake), Mi,US
98/F4 Oakland, NJ,US
99/A3 Oakland (bay), Wa,US
73/C2 Oaklands, Austl.
9/Q16 Oak Lawn, Il,US
25/E3 Oakley, Eng,UK
25/F2 Oakley, Eng,UK
0/L11 Oakley, Ca,US
93/G3 Oakley, Ks,US
90/C2 Oakley, Ks,US
70/C4 Oakover (riv.), Austl.
9/Q16 Oak Park, Il,US
99/F6 Oak Park, Mi,US
98/F4 Oak Ridge, NJ,US
90/C5 Oakridge, Or,US
92/B2 Oakridge, Or,US
89/K4 Oak Ridge, Tn,US
94/C4 Oak Ridge, Tn,US
97/G2 Oak Ridge, Tn,US
95/R8 Oak Ridges, On,Can
24/D3 Oaksey, Eng,UK
95/Q9 Oakville, On,Can
9/P15 Oakwood Hills, Il,US
1/R12 Oamaru, N.Z.
73/C4 Oatlands, Austl.
01/F5 Oaxaca (state), Mex.
01/N8 Oaxaca (state), Mex.
02/B2 Oaxaca, Mex.
02/B2 Oaxaca (state), Mex.
84/H8 Oaxaca, Mex.
46/G3 Ob' (riv.), Rus.
46/H3 Ob' (gulf), Rus.
48/T3 Ob' (riv.), Rus.
48/G3 Ob' (gulf), Rus.
68/F6 Oba (isl.), Van.
94/D2 Obabika (lake), On,Can
56/D3 Obama, Japan
79/H5 Oban (hills), Camr., Nga.
1/Q12 Oban, N.Z.
57/N9 Obara, Japan
94/D1 Obasatika (riv.), On,Can
7/M10 Obata, Japan
20/H5 Obeliai, Lith.
42/E5 Obeliai, Lith.
09/E2 Oberá, Arg.
37/E4 Oberalppass (pass), Swi.
37/E4 Oberalpstock (peak), Swi.
37/H2 Oberammergau, Ger.
37/H2 Oberau, Ger.
31/G6 Oberbetschdorf, Fr.
36/D3 Oberburg, Swi.
36/D4 Oberdiessbach, Swi.
36/D3 Oberdorf, Swi.
29/H6 Oberdorla, Ger.
36/E3 Oberentfelden, Swi.
37/E3 Oberglatt, Swi.
37/G2 Obergünzburg, Ger.
26/D3 Oberhausen, Ger.
28/D8 Oberhausen, Ger.
31/H6 Oberkirch, Ger.
36/E1 Oberkirch, Ger.
27/H3 Oberlausitz (reg.), Ger.
93/G3 Oberlin, Ks,US
96/C2 Oberlin, Ks,US
36/D1 Obernai, Fr.
33/H2 Oberndorf am Neckar, Ger.
37/E1 Oberndorf am Neckar, Ger.
29/G4 Obernkirchen, Ger.
31/H4 Ober-Olm, Ger.
73/D2 Oberon, Austl.
37/E3 Oberrieden, Swi.
37/F3 Oberriet, Swi.
37/F4 Obersaxen, Swi.
37/H1 Oberschleissheim, Ger.
37/E3 Obersiggenthal, Swi.
37/E2 Oberstammheim, Swi.
37/G2 Oberstaufen, Ger.
26/F5 Oberstdorf, Ger.
37/G3 Oberstdorf, Ger.
31/G4 Oberthal, Ger.
26/E3 Oberursel, Ger.
37/F3 Oberuzwil, Swi.
37/E4 Oberwald, Swi.
40/C2 Oberwart, Aus.
31/G3 Oberwesel, Ger.
36/D4 Oberwil, Swi.
33/L3 Oberwölz, Aus.
40/B2 Oberwölz, Aus.
37/E3 Obfelden, Swi.
67/G4 Obi (isl.), Indo.
67/G4 Obi (isls.), Indo.
67/G4 Obi (str.), Indo.
68/B5 Obi (isl.), Indo.
107/G4 Óbidos, Braz.
34/A3 Óbidos, Port.
55/N3 Obihiro, Japan
39/G1 Obilić, Yugo.
40/E4 Obilić, Yugo.
57/J7 Obitsu (riv.), Japan
60/C5 Ob Luang Gorge, Thai.
65/B2 Ob Luang Gorge, Thai.
47/P5 Obluch'ye, Rus.
55/L2 Obluch'ye, Rus.
42/H5 Obninsk, Rus.
44/F1 Obninsk, Rus.
77/L6 Obo, CAfr.
77/P5 Obock, Djib.
27/J2 Oborniki, Pol.
44/A1 Oborniki, Pol.
27/J3 Oborniki Śląskie, Pol.
27/J2 Obra (riv.), Pol.
40/E3 Obrenovac, Yugo.
40/E4 Obrež, Yugo.
57/M10 Ōbu, Japan
76/E6 Obuasi, Gha.
79/E5 Obuasi, Gha.
37/E4 Obwalden (demi-canton), Swi.
41/H4 Obzor, Bul.
89/K6 Ocala, Fl,US
97/H4 Ocala, Fl,US
100/C2 Ocampo, Mex.
100/E3 Ocampo, Mex.
101/F4 Ocampo, Mex.
34/D3 Ocaña, Sp.
32/C5 Occabe, Sommet d' (peak), Fr.
34/E1 Occabe, Sommet d' (peak), Fr.
106/E7 Occidental, Cordillera (range), SAm.
85/L4 Ocean (cape), Ak,US
98/F6 Ocean (co.), NJ,US
89/L4 Ocean City, Md,US
94/F4 Ocean City, Md,US
97/K2 Ocean City, Md,US
86/D3 Ocean Falls, BC,Can
90/B2 Ocean Falls, BC,Can
98/F6 Ocean Gate, NJ,US
88/C5 Oceanside, Ca,US
92/C4 Oceanside, Ca,US
98/G5 Oceanside, NY,US
65/D4 Oc-Eo, Ancient City of (ruins), Viet.
41/K2 Ochakov, Ukr.
45/G4 Ochamchira, Geo.
55/P3 Ochiishi-misaki (cape), Japan
103/G2 Ocho Rios, Jam
26/F4 Ochsenfurt, Ger.
37/F1 Ochsenhausen, Ger.
37/F3 Ochsenkopf (peak), Aus.
31/G3 Ochtendung, Ger.
29/E4 Ochtrup, Ger.
29/F2 Ochtum (riv.), Ger.
25/E3 Ock (riv.), Eng,UK
42/C3 Ockelbo, Swe.
31/G4 Ockenheim, Ger.
41/F2 Ocna Mureş, Rom.
41/G3 Ocna Sibiului, Rom.
41/G3 Ocnele Mari, Rom.
89/J3 Oconto, Wi,US
91/M4 Oconto, Wi,US
94/C2 Oconto, Wi,US
104/D3 Ocos (bay), DRep.
102/C2 Ocosingo, Mex.
102/E3 Ocotal, Nic.
102/B2 Ocotlán de Morelos, Mex.
97/K3 Ocracoke, NC,US
32/C2 Octeville, Fr.
47/L1 October Revolution (isl.), Rus.
48/H2 October Revolution (isl.), Rus.
79/E5 Oda, Gha.
56/C3 Oda, Japan
52/C4 Oda (peak), Sudan
77/N3 Oda (peak), Sudan
20/P7 Ódádhahraun (lava flow), Ice.
58/E4 Odaesan Nat'l Park, SKor.
56/A2 Odaesan Nat'l Park, SKor.
57/M10 Ōdai, Japan
56/E3 Ōdaigahara-san (mtn.), Japan
55/N3 Odate, Japan
57/F3 Odawara, Japan
57/H7 Odawara, Japan
20/C3 Odda, Nor.
77/P7 Oddur, Som.
29/F6 Odeborn (riv.), Ger.
37/H1 Odelzhausen, Ger.
34/A4 Odemira, Port.
50/A2 Ödemiş, Turk.
80/D2 Odendaalsrus, SAfr.
18/E3 Odense, Den.
20/D5 Odense, Den.
26/F1 Odense, Den.
46/B4 Odense, Den.
29/E6 Odenthal, Ger.
31/G1 Odenthal, Ger.
98/K7 Odenton, Md,US
18/E3 Oder (riv.), Eur.
27/H2 Oder (riv.), Ger.
29/H5 Oder (riv.), Ger.
46/B4 Oder (riv.), Ger.,Pol.
36/C2 Oderen, Fr.
27/H2 Oderhaff (lag.), Ger.
27/H2 Oderhaff (lag.), Pol.
33/K4 Oderzo, It.
18/G4 Odessa, Ukr.
41/K2 Odessa, Ukr.
44/D3 Odessa, Ukr.
46/D5 Odessa, Ukr.
100/E2 Odessa, Tx,US
101/E2 Odessa, Tx,US
88/F5 Odessa, Tx,US
93/G5 Odessa, Tx,US
96/C4 Odessa, Tx,US
90/D4 Odessa, Wa,US
41/J2 Odessa Obl., Ukr.
41/K2 Odessa Obl., Ukr.
44/D3 Odessa Obl., Ukr.
32/B2 Odet (riv.), Fr.
76/D6 Odienné, IvC.
78/D4 Odienné, IvC.
42/H5 Odintsovo, Rus.
43/X9 Odintsovo, Rus.
35/P10 Odivelas, Port.
41/H3 Odobeşti, Rom.
32/C2 Odon (riv.), Fr.
65/D4 Odongk, Camb.
28/D3 Odoorn, Neth.
41/G2 Odorheiu Secuiesc, Rom.
27/H2 Odra (Oder) (riv.), Pol.
40/D3 Odžaci, Yugo.
76/J7 Odzala Nat'l Park, Congo
57/L9 Ōe, Japan
28/B4 Oegstgeest, Neth.
107/K5 Oeiras, Braz.
29/F5 Oelde, Ger.
26/G3 Oelsnitz, Ger.
33/K1 Oelsnitz, Ger.
69/M7 Oeno (atoll), Pitc.
36/D3 Oensingen, Swi.
29/E5 Oer-Erkenschwick, Ger.
31/E4 Oesling (mts.), Lux.
28/B6 Oesterdam (dam), Neth.
31/H4 Oestrich-Winkel, Ger.
33/H2 Oestrich-Winkel, Ger.
39/H3 Oeta Nat'l Park, Gre.
50/E1 Of, Turk.
38/D2 Ofanto (riv.), It.
41/B5 Ofanto (riv.), It.
40/D4 Ofaqim, Isr.
50/C4 Ofaqim, Isr.
37/E5 Ofenhorn (Punta d' Arbola) (peak), Swi.
37/G4 Ofenpass (Pass dal Fuorn) (pass), Swi.
22/A5 Offaly (co.), Ire.
36/C2 Offemont, Fr.
26/E3 Offenbach, Ger.
33/H1 Offenbach, Ger.
26/D4 Offenburg, Ger.
33/G2 Offenburg, Ger.
36/D1 Offenburg, Ger.
37/G1 Offingen, Ger.
33/G3 Oftringen, Swi.
55/M4 Oga, Japan
74/G4 Ogaden (reg.), Eth.
77/P6 Ogaden (reg.), Eth.
56/E3 Ōgaki, Japan
57/M9 Ōgaki, Japan
88/F3 Ogallala, Ne,US
91/H5 Ogallala, Ne,US
93/G2 Ogallala, Ne,US
68/D2 Ogasawara, Japan
76/F6 Ogbomosho, Nga.
79/G4 Ogbomosho, Nga.
86/E4 Ogden, Ut,US
88/D3 Ogden, Ut,US
90/F5 Ogden, Ut,US
92/E2 Ogden, Ut,US
98/F4 Ogdensburg, NJ,US
87/J4 Ogdensburg, NY,US
89/L3 Ogdensburg, NY,US
94/F2 Ogdensburg, NY,US
57/F2 Ogi, Japan
87/H4 Ogidaki (mtn.), Can.
94/D2 Ogidaki (peak), Can
80/Q13 Ogies, SAfr.
85/L3 Ogilvie (mts.), Yk,Can
86/C2 Ogilvie (mts.), Yk,Can
86/C2 Ogilvie (riv.), Yk,Can
51/H2 Oglanly, Trkm.
101/F2 Oglesby, Tx,US
33/J4 Oglio (riv.), It.
37/G5 Oglio (riv.), It.
71/H4 Ogmore, Austl.
24/C4 Ogmore by Sea, Wal,UK
26/D5 Ognon (riv.), Fr.
32/F3 Ognon (riv.), Fr.
36/B3 Ognon (riv.), Fr.
67/F3 Ogoamas (peak), Indo.
76/G6 Ogoja, Nga.
91/L3 Ogoki (res.), On,Can
91/L3 Ogoki (lake), On,Can
91/M3 Ogoki (riv.), On,Can
94/C1 Ogoki (riv.), On,Can
76/G8 Ogooué (riv.), Gabon
82/A1 Ogooué (riv.), Gabon
57/H7 Ogose, Japan
41/F4 Ogosta (riv.), Bul.
20/H4 Ogre, Lat.
42/E4 Ogre, Lat.
57/M9 Oguchi, Japan
33/L4 Ogulin, Cro.
40/B3 Ogulin, Cro.
76/F6 Ogun (riv.), Nga.
79/F5 Ogun (riv.), Nga.
79/F5 Ogun (state), Nga.
45/K5 Ogurchinskiy (isl.), Trkm.
51/H2 Ogurchinskiy (isl.), Trkm.
76/G2 Ohanet, Alg.
72/G8 O'Hares (cr.), Austl.
29/E2 Ohe (riv.), Ger.
31/E3 Ohey, Belg.
84/J6 Ohio (riv.), US
87/H4 Ohio (state), US
89/K3 Ohio (state), US
89/K4 Ohio (riv.), US
93/K3 Ohio (riv.), US
94/B4 Ohio (riv.), US
94/D3 Ohio (state), US
37/H2 Ohlstadt, Ger.
26/E3 Ohm (riv.), Ger.
23/F1 Oh Me Edge (hill), Eng,UK
27/H3 Ohře (riv.), Czh.
33/K1 Ohře (riv.), Czh.
26/F2 Ohre (riv.), Ger.
29/H3 Ohre (riv.), Ger.
39/G2 Ohrid (lake), Alb.
40/E5 Ohrid (lake), Alb.
39/G2 Ohrid, Macd.
39/G2 Ohrid (lake), Macd.
40/E5 Ohrid, Macd.
40/E5 Ohrid (lake), Macd.
54/D6 Oi (riv.), China
60/C2 Oi (riv.), China
63/G2 Oi (riv.), China
55/M4 Ōi (riv.), Japan
57/F3 Ōi (riv.), Japan
57/H7 Ōi, Japan
57/L9 Ōi (riv.), Japan
107/H3 Oiapoque, Braz.
107/H3 Oiapoque (riv.), Braz.
35/P10 Oieras, Port.
60/B2 Oiga, China
30/B3 Oignies, Fr.
36/B5 Oignin (riv.), Fr.
89/L3 Oil City, Pa,US
94/E3 Oil City, Pa,US
39/H3 Oinófita, Gre.
39/H3 Oinói, Gre.
28/C5 Oirschot, Neth.
19/S9 Oise (riv.), Fr.
19/T9 Oise (dept.), Fr.
26/B4 Oise (riv.), Fr.
30/B5 Oise (dept.), Fr.
30/B5 Oise (riv.), Fr.
32/E2 Oise (riv.), Fr.
30/C5 Oise à l'Aisne, Canal do (can.), Fr.
30/A4 Oisemont, Fr.
57/H7 Ōiso, Japan
28/C5 Oisterwijk, Neth.
30/C3 Oisy-le-Verger, Fr.
55/L5 Ōita, Japan
56/B4 Ōita, Japan
56/B4 Ōita (pref.), Japan
56/D4 Ōita (riv.), Japan
27/K3 Ojcowski Nat'l Park, Pol.
20/G2 Öjebyn, Swe.
42/D2 Öjebyn, Swe.
57/L10 Ōji, Japan
100/D2 Ojinaga, Mex.
93/F5 Ojinaga, Mex.
96/B4 Ojinaga, Mex
57/F2 Ojiya, Japan
100/E4 Ojocaliente, Mex.
100/B3 Ojo de Liebre (lag.), Mex.
103/G2 Ojo del Toro (peak), Cuba
109/C2 Ojos del Salado (peak), Arg.
105/C5 Ojos del Salado (peak), Chile
100/A2 Ojos Negros, Mex.
34/E2 Ojos Negros, Sp.
95/M7 Oka, Qu,Can
19/H3 Oka (riv.), Rus.
43/J4 Oka (riv.), Rus.
45/G1 Oka (riv.), Rus.
46/E4 Oka (riv.), Rus.
47/L4 Oka (riv.), Rus.
54/E1 Oka (riv.), Rus.
67/J5 Okaba, Indo.
82/C5 Okahandja, Namb.
95/M6 Oka Ind. Res., Qu,Can
87/K3 Okak (isl.), Nf,Can
90/C3 Okanagan (lake), BC,Can
86/D4 Okanagan (lake), BC,Can
90/D3 Okanagan Falls, BC,Can
82/B1 Okanda Nat'l Park, Gabon
90/D3 Okanogan (riv.), Wa,US
90/D3 Okanogan, Wa,US
53/K2 Okāra, Pak.
64/B2 Okāra, Pak.
46/F6 Okarem, Trkm.
52/F1 Okarem, Trkm.
82/C4 Okaukuejo, Namb.
82/D4 Okavango Delta (reg.), Bots.
56/B4 Ōkawa, Japan
47/P6 Okayama, Japan
55/L5 Okayama, Japan
56/C3 Okayama, Japan
56/C3 Okayama (pref.), Japan
55/M5 Okazaki, Japan
57/E3 Okazaki, Japan
57/N10 Okazaki, Japan
58/D4 Okch'ŏn, SKor.
104/A1 Okeechobee (lake), Fl,US
89/K6 Okeechobee (lake), Fl,US
97/H5 Okeechobee, Fl,US
57/H7 Okegawa, Japan
24/C5 Okehampton, Eng,UK
24/B5 Okement (riv.), Eng,UK
26/F3 Oker (riv.), Ger.
29/H4 Oker (riv.), Ger.
47/Q4 Okha, Rus.
39/J3 Ókhi (peak), Gre.
55/P2 Okhotsk (sea), Asia
47/Q4 Okhotsk (sea), Rus.
48/P4 Okhotsk (sea), Rus.
43/V6 Okhta (riv.), Rus.
47/P6 Oki (isls.), Japan
55/L4 Oki (isls.), Japan
56/C2 Oki (arch.), Japan
56/C2 Oki-Daisen Nat'l Park, Japan
80/B3 Okiep, SAfr.
82/C6 Okiep, SAfr.
48/M7 Okinawa (isls.), Japan
68/B2 Okinawa (isls.), Japan
68/C2 Okino-Tori-Shima (isl.), Japan
48/N7 Okino-Tori-Shima (Parece Vela) (isl.), Japan
63/G4 Okkan, Burma
58/D5 Okku, SKor.
88/G4 Oklahoma (state), US
93/H4 Oklahoma (state), US
89/G4 Oklahoma City (cap.), Ok,US
93/H4 Oklahoma City (cap.), Ok,US
96/D3 Oklahoma City (cap.), Ok,US
89/G4 Okmulgee, Ok,US
93/J4 Okmulgee, Ok,US
96/E3 Okmulgee, Ok,US
91/K5 Okoboji (lakes), Ia,US
97/F3 Okolona, Ms,US
90/E3 Okotoks, Ab,Can
74/E6 Okovango (riv.), Afr.
52/C4 Oko, Wādī (dry riv.), Sudan
20/D5 Oksbøl, Den.
26/E1 Oksbøl, Den.
20/E2 Oksskolten (peak), Nor.
46/F5 Oktyabr'sk, Kaz.
45/J1 Oktyabr'sk, Rus.
19/J3 Oktyabr'skiy, Rus.
43/M5 Oktyabr'skiy, Rus.
45/K1 Oktyabr'skiy, Rus.
46/F4 Oktyabr'skiy, Rus.
47/R4 Oktyabr'skiy, Rus.
55/K1 Oktyabr'skiy, Rus.
58/B4 Okuchi, Japan
42/G4 Okulovka, Rus.
55/M3 Okushiri (isl.), Japan
57/H7 Okutama, Japan
82/D5 Okwa (riv.), Bots.
20/N6 Ólafsfjördhur, Ice.
20/M7 Ólafsvík, Ice.
99/B3 Olalla, Wa,US
92/C3 Olancha, Ca,US
102/E3 Olanchito, Hon.
18/E3 Öland (isl.), Swe.
20/F4 Öland (isl.), Swe.
42/C4 Öland (isl.), Swe.
20/F4 Ölands södra udde (pt.), Swe.
33/G4 Olan, Pic d' (peak), Fr.
38/D2 Olanto (riv.), It.
73/B2 Olary, Austl.
92/F3 Olathe, Co,US
96/B2 Olathe, Co,US
93/J3 Olathe, Ks,US
96/E2 Olathe, Ks,US
109/D4 Olavarría, Arg.
27/J3 Oława, Pol.
29/F5 Olbach (riv.), Ger.
38/A2 Olbia, It.
26/F4 Olching, Ger.
33/J2 Olching, Ger.
37/H1 Olching, Ger.
95/S9 Olcott, NY,US
99/L11 Old (riv.), Ca,US
103/G1 Old Bahama (chan.), Bahm., Cuba
99/D3 Old Baldy (mtn.), Wa,US
73/E1 Old Bar, Austl.
25/G2 Old Bedford (can.), Eng,UK
22/A4 Oldcastle, Ire.
49/G8 Old City, Isr.
85/L2 Old Crow, Yk,Can
86/C2 Old Crow, Yk,Can
28/C4 Oldebroek, Neth.
28/C3 Oldemarkt, Neth.
26/E2 Oldenburg, Ger.
26/F1 Oldenburg, Ger.
29/F2 Oldenburg, Ger.
28/D4 Oldenzaal, Neth.
90/F4 Old Faithful (geyser), Wy,US
95/R9 Old Fort Niagara, NY,US
23/F4 Oldham, Eng,UK
85/H4 Old Harbor, Ak,US
22/A6 Oldleighlin, Ire.
90/E3 Oldman (riv.), Ab,Can
22/E3 Old Man of Coniston, The (mtn.), Eng,UK
99/Q15 Old Mill Creek, Il,US
25/F2 Old Nene (riv.), Eng,UK
29/F1 Oldoog (isl.), Ger.
28/B4 Old Rhine (riv.), Neth.
86/E3 Olds, Ab,Can
90/E3 Olds, Ab,Can
95/G2 Old Town, Me,US
19/M7 Old Windsor, Eng,UK
25/F4 Old Windsor, Eng,UK
91/G3 Old Wives (lake), Sk,Can
89/L3 Olean, NY,US
94/E3 Olean, NY,US
27/M1 Olecko, Pol.
34/B3 Oleiros, Port.
34/A1 Oleiros, Sp.
47/N4 Olekma (riv.), Rus.
99/B2 Olele (pt.), Wa,US
20/K1 Olenegorsk, Rus.
42/G1 Olenegorsk, Rus.
47/N2 Olenek (bay), Rus.
47/N2 Olenek (riv.), Rus.
48/L3 Olenëk (riv.), Rus.
32/C4 Oleron (isl.), Fr.
35/K6 Olesa de Montserrat, Sp.
27/J3 Oleśnica, Pol.
27/K3 Olesno, Pol.
29/E5 Olfen, Ger.
47/P5 Ol'ga, Rus.
46/J5 Ölgiy, Mong.
54/B2 Ölgiy, Mong.
34/B4 Olhão, Port.
33/L4 Olib (isl.), Cro.
38/A2 Oliena, It.
80/B2 Olifants (dry riv.), Namb.
80/B3 Olifants (riv.), SAfr.
80/L10 Olifants (riv.), SAfr.
80/E2 Olifantsrivier (riv.), SAfr.
80/Q12 Olifantsrivier (riv.), SAfr.
82/E5 Olifantsrivier (riv.), SAfr.
68/D4 Olimarao (atoll), Micr.
50/A3 Ólimbos, Gre.
39/H2 Ólimbos (Mount Olympus) (peak), Gre.
108/B2 Olímpia, Braz.
50/B2 Olimpos Beydağları Nat'l Park, Turk.
101/F5 Olinalá, Mex.
102/B2 Olinalá, Mex.
107/M5 Olinda, Braz.
35/E3 Oliva, Sp.
34/B3 Oliva de la Frontera, Sp.
34/A3 Olivais, Port.
108/C2 Oliveira, Braz.
34/B3 Olivenza, Sp.
90/D3 Oliver, BC,Can
32/D3 Olivet, Fr.
33/H3 Olivone, Swi.
37/E4 Olivone, Swi.
106/E8 Ollagüe (vol.), Bol.
19/S11 Ollainville, Fr.
35/E3 Ollería, Sp.
36/D5 Ollon, Swi.
62/C5 Ollūr, India
64/F3 Ollūr, India
34/C2 Olmedo, Sp.
25/F2 Olney, Eng,UK
94/B4 Olney, Il,US
97/F2 Olney, Il,US
98/J7 Olney, Md,US
101/F1 Olney, Tx,US
95/J1 Olomane (riv.), Qu,Can
27/J4 Olomouc, Czh.
46/B5 Olomouc, Czh.
42/G3 Olonets, Rus.
32/C3 Olonne-sur-Mer, Fr.
32/C5 Oloron-Sainte-Marie, Fr.
35/E1 Oloron-Sainte-Marie, Fr.
35/G1 Olot, Sp.
47/S3 Oloy (range), Rus.
29/E6 Olpe, Ger.
31/G1 Olpe, Ger.
29/F6 Olsberg, Ger.
41/K1 Ol'shanka, Ukr.
28/D4 Olst, Neth.
18/F3 Olsztyn, Pol.
27/L2 Olsztyn, Pol.
27/L2 Olsztyn (prov.), Pol.
42/D5 Olsztyn, Pol.
46/C4 Olsztyn, Pol.
27/L2 Olsztynek, Pol.
18/F4 Olt (riv.), Rom.
41/G3 Olt (co.), Rom.
41/G4 Olt (riv.), Rom.
44/C3 Olt (riv.), Rom.
33/G3 Olten, Swi.
36/D3 Olten, Swi.
41/H3 Olteniţa, Rom.
41/F3 Olteţ (riv.), Rom.
37/F6 Oltre il Colle, It.
45/G4 Oltu, Turk.
45/G4 Oltu (riv.), Turk.
50/E1 Oltu, Turk.
50/E1 Oltu (riv.), Turk.
61/J4 Oluan Pi (cape), Tai.
45/G4 Olur, Turk.
50/E1 Olur, Turk.
34/C4 Olvera, Sp.
35/H1 Olympe (mtn.), Fr.
39/G4 Olympia (ruins), Gre.
86/D4 Olympia (cap.), Wa,US
88/B2 Olympia (cap.), Wa,US
90/C4 Olympia (cap.), Wa,US
99/B3 Olympia (cap.), Wa,US
90/B4 Olympic (mts.), Wa,US
99/A2 Olympic (mts.), Wa,US
99/A1 Olympic Game Farm, Wa,US
99/A2 Olympic Nat'l For., Wa,US
90/B4 Olympic Nat'l Park, Wa,US
86/D4 Olympic Nat'l Park, Wa,US
88/B2 Olympic Nat'l Park, Wa,US
49/C2 Olympus (mtn.), Cyp.
50/C3 Olympus (mtn.), Cyp.
52/B2 Olympus (mtn.), Cyp.
90/C4 Olympus (peak), Wa,US
39/H2 Olympus, Mount (peak), Gre.
39/H2 Olympus, Mount (Óros Ólimbos) (peak), Gre.
39/H2 Olympus Nat'l Park, Gre.
47/S3 Olyutorskiy (bay), Rus.
43/K2 Oma (riv.), Rus.
57/E2 Ōmachi, Japan
57/F3 Omae-zaki (pt.), Japan
22/A2 Omagh, NI,UK
22/A2 Omagh (dist.), NI,UK
89/G3 Omaha, Ne,US
91/K5 Omaha, Ne,US
93/J2 Omaha, Ne,US
88/C2 Omak, Wa,US
90/D3 Omak, Wa,US
64/G3 Omalūr, India
48/E8 Oman
51/J5 Oman
53/G3 Oman
53/G4 Oman
77/R4 Oman
48/E7 Oman (gulf), Asia
53/G4 Oman (gulf), Asia
82/C5 Omaruru, Namb.
82/C4 Omatako (riv.), Namb.
106/D7 Omate, Peru
67/F5 Ombai (str.), Indo.
24/D2 Ombersley, Eng,UK
82/B4 Ombombo, Namb.
76/G8 Omboué, Gabon
82/A1 Omboué, Gabon
33/J5 Ombrone (riv.), It.
38/B1 Ombrone (riv.), It.
77/M4 Omdurman, Sudan
52/B5 Omdurman (Umm Durmān), Sudan
57/H7 Ōme, Japan
22/B3 Omeath, Ire.
33/H4 Omegna, It.
73/C3 Omeo, Austl.
50/B1 Ömerli (dam), Turk.
50/E2 Ömerli, Turk.
51/N7 Ömerli (res.), Turk.
102/E4 Ometepe (isl.), Nic.
102/B2 Ometepec, Mex.
52/C6 Om Hājer, Eth.
57/M9 Ōmi, Japan
57/M9 Ōmihachiman, Japan
38/E1 Omiš, Cro.
102/B2 Omitlán (riv.), Mex.
55/M4 Ōmiya, Japan
57/G2 Ōmiya, Japan
57/H7 Ōmiya, Japan
57/M10 Ōmiya, Japan
86/C3 Ommaney (cape), Ak,US
85/M4 Ommaney (cape), Ak,US
26/D2 Ommen, Neth.
28/D3 Ommen, Neth.
54/F2 Ömnödelger, Mong.
54/C2 Ömnögovĭ, Mong.
38/A2 Omodeo (lake), It.
48/D3 Omolon (riv.), Rus.
77/N6 Omo Nat'l Park, Eth.
74/F4 Omo Wenz (riv.), Eth.
77/N6 Omo Wenz (riv.), Eth.
46/H4 Omsk, Rus.
41/G3 Omul (peak), Rom.
44/C3 Omul, Vîrful (peak), Rom.
56/A4 Ōmura, Japan
41/H4 Omurtag, Bul.
55/L5 Ōmuta, Japan
56/B4 Ōmuta, Japan
43/M4 Omutninsk, Rus.
57/G1 Onagawa, Japan
93/J5 Onalaska, Tx,US
96/E4 Onalaska, Tx,US
34/D1 Oñate, Sp.
94/C2 Onaway, Mi,US
22/D3 Onchan, IM,UK
82/B4 Oncocúa, Ang.
35/E3 Onda, Sp.
82/C4 Ondangua, Namb.
27/L4 Ondava (riv.), Slvk.
82/C4 Ondjiva, Ang.
79/G5 Ondo (state), Nga.
47/M5 Öndörhaan, Mong.
54/G2 Öndörhaan, Mong.
54/C2 Öndorhangay, Mong.
18/G2 Onega, Rus.
18/G2 Onega (lake), Rus.
18/G2 Onega (riv.), Rus.
42/G3 Onega (lake), Rus.
42/H2 Onega (bay), Rus.
42/H2 Onega (pen.), Rus.
42/H3 Onega, Rus.
42/H3 Onega (riv.), Rus.
46/D3 Onega, Rus.
46/D3 Onega (lake), Rus.
46/D3 Onega (riv.), Rus.
86/D3 One Hundred Mile House, BC,Can
90/C3 One Hundred Mile House, BC,Can
94/F3 Oneida, NY,US
89/G3 O'Neill, Ne,US
91/J5 O'Neill, Ne,US
93/H2 O'Neill, Ne,US
94/F3 Oneonta, NY,US
36/C5 Onex, Swi.
54/E2 Ongiyn (riv.), Mong.
58/C4 Ongjin, NKor.
62/D4 Ongole, India
31/D3 Onhaye, Belg.
91/H4 Onida, SD,US
93/G1 Onida, SD,US
35/E3 Onil, Sp.
81/G8 Onilahy (riv.), Madg.
76/G6 Onitsha, Nga.
79/G5 Onitsha, Nga.
81/H7 Onive (riv.), Madg.
30/C3 Onnaing, Fr.
24/D2 Onny (riv.), Eng,UK
56/D3 Ono, Japan
56/E3 Ōno, Japan
57/K10 Ono, Japan
56/B4 Onoda, Japan
56/C3 Onomichi, Japan
54/F2 Onon (riv.), Mong.
54/G2 Onon, Mong.
47/M4 Onon (riv.), Rus.
54/G1 Onon (riv.), Rus.
68/G5 Onotoa (atoll), Kiri.
68/A7 Onslow, Austl.
70/B4 Onslow, Austl.
57/E3 Ontake-san (mtn.), Japan
91/L2 Ontario (prov.), Can
86/H3 Ontario (prov.), Can.
89/J1 Ontario (prov.), Can.
94/D1 Ontario (prov.), Can
99/G7 Ontario (prov.), Can.
95/R8 Ontario (lake), Can,US
94/E3 Ontario (lake), On,Can, NY,US
87/J4 Ontario (lake), Can,US
89/L3 Ontario (lake), On,Can, NY,US
98/C2 Ontario, Ca,US
86/E4 Ontario, Or,US
88/C3 Ontario, Or,US
90/D4 Ontario, Or,US
92/C1 Ontario, Or,US
84/K5 Ontario (lake), US, Can.
35/E3 Onteniente, Sp.
91/L4 Ontonagon, Mi,US
94/B2 Ontonagon, Mi,US
68/F5 Ontong Java (isl.), Sol.
58/D4 Onyang, SKor.
68/C7 Oodnadatta, Austl.
70/F5 Oodnadatta, Austl.
85/M5 Oona River, BC,Can
28/A6 Oostburg, Neth.
30/C1 Oostburg, Neth.
28/C4 Oostelijk Flevoland (polder), Neth.
26/B3 Oostende, Belg.
30/B1 Oostende (Ostend), Belg.
28/B5 Oosterhout, Neth.
26/B3 Oosterschelde (estuary), Neth.
28/A5 Oosterschelde (chan.), Neth.
28/A5 Oosterscheldedam (dam), Neth.
28/D3 Oosterwolde, Neth.
28/A7 Oosterzele, Belg.
30/C2 Oosterzele, Belg.
30/C1 Oostkamp, Belg.
28/C4 Oostvaardersplassen (lake), Neth.
26/C2 Oost-Vlieland, Neth.
28/C2 Oost-Vlieland, Neth.
28/B4 Oostzaan, Neth.
62/C5 Ootacamund, India
64/F3 Ootacamund, India
28/D4 Ootmarsum, Neth.
90/B2 Ootsa (lake), BC,Can
88/V12 Opaeula (stream), Hi,US
41/H4 Opaka, Bul.
77/K8 Opala, Zaire
82/D1 Opala, Zaire
27/J2 Opalenica, Pol.
33/L4 Opatija, Cro.
40/B3 Opatija, Cro.
27/L3 Opatów, Pol.
27/J4 Opava, Czh.
97/G3 Opelika, Al,US
89/H5 Opelousas, La,US
93/J5 Opelousas, La,US
96/E4 Opelousas, La,US
94/E2 Opeongo (lake), On,Can
28/C6 Opglabbeek, Belg.
31/E1 Opglabbeek, Belg.
101/H4 Opichén, Mex.
102/D1 Opichén, Mex.
31/G1 Opladen, Ger.
28/C5 Oploo, Neth.
28/B3 Opmeer, Neth.
20/J4 Opochka, Rus.
42/F4 Opochka, Rus.
27/L3 Opoczno, Pol.
44/B2 Opoczno, Pol.
100/C2 Opodepe, Mex.
27/J3 Opole, Pol.
27/J3 Opole (prov.), Pol.
44/A2 Opole, Pol.
27/L3 Opole Lubelskie, Pol.
40/E3 Opovo, Yugo.
97/G4 Opp, Al,US
20/D3 Oppdal, Nor.
36/E1 Oppenau, Ger.
20/D3 Oppland (co.), Nor.
90/D4 Opportunity, Wa,US
28/B7 Opwijk, Belg.
30/D2 Opwijk, Belg.
100/D3 Ora (riv.), Mex.
37/H5 Ora (Auer), It.
18/F4 Oradea, Rom.
40/E2 Oradea, Rom.
44/B3 Oradea, Rom.
39/G1 Orahovac, Yugo.
40/E4 Orahovac, Yugo.
40/C3 Orahovica, Cro.
62/C2 Orai, India
36/B4 Orain (riv.), Fr.
75/Q16 Oran, Alg.
75/Q16 Oran (wilaya), Alg.
76/E1 Oran, Alg.
55/K3 Ŏrang, NKor.

164

Orang – Padre

58/E2 Orang (riv.), NKor.
74/D7 Orange (riv.), Afr.
82/C6 Orange (riv.), Afr.
80/B3 Orange (riv.), Africa
68/D8 Orange, Austl.
71/H6 Orange, Austl.
73/D2 Orange, Austl.
32/F4 Orange, Fr.
107/H3 Orange (mts.), Sur.
98/C3 Orange, Ca,US
98/C3 Orange (co.), Ca,US
98/F5 Orange, NJ,US
89/H5 Orange, Tx,US
93/J5 Orange, Tx,US
96/E4 Orange, Tx,US
94/E4 Orange, Va,US
97/J2 Orange, Va,US
89/K5 Orangeburg, SC,US
97/H3 Orangeburg, SC,US
80/D3 Orange Free State (prov.), SAfr.
80/P13 Orange Free State (prov.), SAfr.
97/H4 Orange Park, Fl,US
94/D3 Orangeville, On,Can
101/H5 Orange Walk, Belz.
102/D2 Orange Walk, Belz.
78/A4 Orango (isl.), GBis.
27/G2 Oranienburg, Ger.
28/D3 Oranjekanaal (can.), Neth.
80/B3 Oranjemund, Namb.
82/C6 Oranjemund, Namb.
104/D4 Oranjestad, Aru.
106/D1 Oranjestad, Aru.
21/A4 Oranmore, Ire.
75/Q16 Oran, Sebkha d' (lake), Alg.
82/E5 Orapa, Bots.
49/F7 Or 'Aqiva, Isr.
41/F3 Orăştie, Rom.
40/E3 Oravița, Rom.
32/E5 Orb (riv.), Fr.
35/G1 Orb (riv.), Fr.
36/C4 Orbe, Swi.
36/C4 Orbe (riv.), Swi.
36/D1 Orbey, Fr.
34/C1 Órbigo (riv.), Sp.
71/H7 Orbost, Austl.
73/D3 Orbost, Austl.
34/D3 Orcera, Sp.
36/B3 Orchamps, Fr.
36/C3 Orchamps-Vennes, Fr.
99/F6 Orchard (lake), Mi,US
96/B2 Orchard City, Co,US
90/E4 Orchard Homes, Mt,US
99/F6 Orchard Lake Village, Mi,US
30/C3 Orchies, Fr.
33/G4 Orco (riv.), It.
32/F3 Or, Côte d' (uplands), Fr.
91/J5 Ord, Ne,US
93/H2 Ord, Ne,US
34/A1 Órdenes, Sp.
35/F1 Ordesa y Monte Perdido Nat'l Park, Sp.
54/F4 Ordos (des.), China
59/B3 Ordos (des.), China
44/F4 Ordu, Turk.
44/F4 Ordu (prov.), Turk.
46/D5 Ordu, Turk.
50/D1 Ordu, Turk.
50/D1 Ordu (prov.), Turk.
51/F2 Ordubad, Azer.
93/G3 Ordway, Co,US
96/C2 Ordway, Co,US
18/E3 Örebro, Swe.
20/E4 Örebro, Swe.
20/E4 Örebro (co.), Swe.
42/B4 Örebro, Swe.
42/B4 Örebro (co.), Swe.
46/B4 Örebro, Swe.
90/C4 Oregon (state), US
86/D4 Oregon (state), US
88/B3 Oregon (state), US
92/B2 Oregon (state), US
92/B2 Oregon Caves Nat'l Mon., Or,US
86/D4 Oregon City, Or,US
90/C4 Oregon City, Or,US
101/B1 Oregon Pipe Cactus Nat'l Mon., Az,US
18/G3 Orël, Rus.
44/F1 Orël, Rus.
46/D4 Orël, Rus.
44/E2 Orel' (riv.), Ukr.
34/C3 Orellana la Vieja, Sp.
44/E1 Orel Obl., Rus.
86/E4 Orem, Ut,US
88/D3 Orem, Ut,US
92/E2 Orem, Ut,US
19/J3 Orenburg, Rus.
45/K2 Orenburg, Rus.
46/F4 Orenburg, Rus.
45/K1 Orenburg Obl., Rus.
18/C4 Orense, Sp.
34/B1 Orense, Sp.
49/E2 Orentes (riv.), Asia
39/K2 Orestiás, Gre.
41/H5 Orestiás, Gre.
44/C4 Orestiás, Gre.
50/A1 Orestiás, Gre.
73/C4 Orford, Austl.
25/H2 Orford, Eng,UK
25/H2 Orford Ness (pt.), UK
92/D4 Organ Pipe Cactus Nat'l Mon., Az,US
34/D3 Orgaz, Sp.
19/S11 Orge (riv.), Fr.
36/B4 Orgelet, Fr.
19/R10 Orgeval, Fr.
41/J2 Orgeyev, Mol.
44/D3 Orgeyev, Mol.
38/A2 Orgosolo, It.
44/D5 Orhaneli, Turk.
41/J5 Orhangazi, Turk.
50/B1 Orhangazi, Turk.
54/F2 Orhon (riv.), Mong.
32/C5 Orhy, Pic d' (peak), Fr.
35/E1 Orhy, Pic d' (peak), Fr.
34/D4 Oria, Sp.
109/C6 Oriental (val.), Arg.
101/M7 Oriental, Mex.
103/H5 Oriental, Cordillera (range), Col.
106/D6 Oriental, Cordillera (range), SAm.
30/C4 Origny-Sainte-Benoîte, Fr.
35/E3 Orihuela, Sp.
87/J4 Orillia, On,Can
89/L3 Orillia, On,Can
94/E2 Orillia, On,Can
99/K11 Orinda, Ca,US
106/F2 Orinoco (riv.), Col., Ven.
105/C2 Orinoco (riv.), SAm.
105/C2 Orinoco (delta), Ven.
106/F2 Orinoco (delta), Ven.
38/E2 Oriolo, It.
99/F6 Orion (lake), Mi,US
62/D3 Orissa (state), India
38/A3 Oristano, It.
38/A3 Oristano (gulf), It.
20/H3 Orivesi, Fin.
42/E3 Orivesi, Fin.
107/G4 Oriximiná, Braz.
18/F5 Orizaba, Mex.
101/M8 Orizaba, Mex.
102/B2 Orizaba, Mex.
101/K6 Orizabita, Mex.
39/F1 Orjen (peak), Yugo.
40/D4 Orjen (peak), Yugo.
34/D4 Órjiva, Sp.
29/F6 Orke (riv.), Ger.
39/H3 Orkhomenós, Gre.
80/P13 Orkney, SAfr.
18/C3 Orkney (isls.), Sc,UK
100/E2 Orla, Tx,US
93/G5 Orla, Tx,US
96/C4 Orla, Tx,US
108/C2 Orlândia, Braz.
89/K6 Orlando, Fl,US
97/H4 Orlando, Fl,US
38/D3 Orlando, Capo d' (cape), It.
99/Q16 Orland Park, Il,US
32/D2 Orléanais (hist. reg.), Fr.
18/D4 Orléans, Fr.
32/D3 Orléans, Fr.
90/C5 Orleans, Ca,US
92/B2 Orleans, Ca,US
27/K4 Orlová, Czh.
19/T10 Orly, Fr.
19/T10 Orly (Paris) (int'l arpt.), Fr.
39/H2 Ormília, Gre.
97/H4 Ormond Beach, Fl,US
36/C4 Or, Mont d' (mtn.), Fr.
23/F4 Ormskirk, Eng,UK
32/F2 Ornain (riv.), Fr.
33/G3 Ornans, Fr.
36/C3 Ornans, Fr.
37/E6 Ornavasso, It.
26/C4 Orne (riv.), Fr.
31/F5 Orne (riv.), Fr.
32/C2 Orne (riv.), Fr.
32/F2 Orne (riv.), Fr.
20/E2 Ørnes, Nor.
42/B2 Ørnes, Nor.
27/L1 Orneta, Pol.
18/E2 Örnsköldsvik, Swe.
20/F3 Örnsköldsvik, Swe.
42/C3 Örnsköldsvik, Swe.
46/B3 Örnsköldsvik, Swe.
33/J3 Orobie (mts.), It.
37/F5 Orobie, Alpi (range), It.
76/E5 Orodara, Burk.
78/D4 Orodara, Burk.
35/E1 Oroel (peak), Sp.
90/D4 Orofino, Id,US
69/L6 Orohena (peak), FrPol.
69/X15 Orohena (peak), FrPol.
68/E4 Oroluk (atoll), Micr.
87/K4 Oromocto, NB,Can
95/H2 Oromocto, NB,Can
38/A1 Oro, Monte d' (mtn.), Fr.
69/H5 Orona (Hull) (atoll), Kiri.
36/C4 Oron-la-Ville, Swi.
95/G2 Orono, Me,US
50/D3 Orontes (riv.), Syria
34/C3 Oropesa, Sp.
55/J1 Oroqen Zizhiqi, China
67/F2 Oroquieta, Phil.
38/A2 Orosei, It.
38/A2 Orosei (gulf), It.
40/E2 Orosháza, Hun.
40/D2 Oroszlány, Hun.
90/D5 Orovada, Nv,US
92/C2 Orovada, Nv,US
100/C1 Oro Valley, Az,US
92/E4 Oro Valley, Az,US
92/B3 Oroville, Ca,US
88/C2 Oroville, Wa,US
90/D3 Oroville, Wa,US
19/P7 Orpington, Eng,UK
36/D3 Orpund, Swi.
23/F4 Orrell, Eng,UK
38/A3 Orroli, It.
19/T9 Orry-la-Ville, Fr.
30/B5 Orry-la-Ville, Fr.
20/E3 Orsa, Swe.
42/B3 Orsa, Swe.
19/S10 Orsay, Fr.
30/B6 Orsay, Fr.
19/Q7 Orsett, Eng,UK
18/G3 Orsha, Bela.
42/F5 Orsha, Bela.
44/D1 Orsha, Bela.
46/D4 Orsha, Bela.
19/J3 Orsk, Rus.
45/L2 Orsk, Rus.
46/F4 Orsk, Rus.
36/C4 Orsonnens, Swi.
40/F3 Orşova, Rom.
20/C3 Ørsta, Nor.
33/H4 Orta (lake), It.
50/C1 Orta, Turk.
50/B2 Ortaca, Turk.
44/E4 Ortaköy, Turk.
50/C1 Ortaköy, Turk.
50/D2 Ortaköy, Turk.
38/D2 Orta Nova, It.
40/B5 Orta Nova, It.
34/B1 Ortegal (cape), Sp.
32/C5 Orthez, Fr.
35/E1 Orthez, Fr.
37/H5 Ortigara, Monte (peak), It.
34/B1 Ortigueira, Sp.
99/C3 Orting, Wa,US
100/C2 Ortiz, Mex.
33/J3 Ortles (range), It.
37/G4 Ortles (peak), It.
37/G5 Ortles (mts.), It., Swi.
106/E6 Ortón (riv.), Bol.
55/H2 Orton (riv.), China
38/D1 Ortona, It.
40/B4 Ortona, It.
99/F6 Ortonville, Mi,US
91/J4 Ortonville, Mn,US
29/H3 Örtze (riv.), Ger.
46/E6 Orūmīyeh, Iran
51/F2 Orūmīyeh, Iran
52/E1 Orūmīyeh, Iran
106/E7 Oruro, Bol.
33/K5 Orvieto, It.
38/C1 Orvieto, It.
83/V Orville (coast), Ant.
25/H2 Orwell (riv.), Eng,UK
54/H2 Orxon (riv.), China
41/F4 Oryakhovo, Bul.
44/B4 Oryakhovo, Bul.
49/F7 Or Yehuda, Isr.
27/L2 Orzysz, Pol.
20/C3 Os, Nor.
103/F4 Osa (pen.), CR
106/B2 Osa (pen.), CR
43/M4 Osa, Rus.
93/J3 Osage Beach, Mo,US
96/E2 Osage Beach, Mo,US
55/M5 Ōsaka, Japan
56/D3 Ōsaka, Japan
56/D3 Ōsaka (pref.), Japan
57/L10 Ōsaka, Japan
57/L10 Ōsaka (bay), Japan
57/L10 Ōsaka (pref.), Japan
57/L10 Ōsaka Castle, Japan
55/K4 Osan, SKor.
58/D4 Osan, SKor.
107/J8 Osasco, Braz.
108/C2 Osasco, Braz.
109/G1 Osasco, Braz.
85/E3 Osborn (mt.), Ak,US
93/H3 Osborne, Ks,US
96/D2 Osborne, Ks,US
31/F4 Osburg, Ger.
93/K4 Osceola, Ar,US
94/B5 Osceola, Ar,US
97/F3 Osceola, Ar,US
26/F2 Oschersleben, Ger.
38/A2 Oschiri, It.
96/B3 Oscura (mts.), NM,US
29/G1 Osdorf, Ger.
46/H5 Osh, Kyr.
82/C4 Oshakati, Namb.
87/J4 Oshawa, On,Can
89/L3 Oshawa, On,Can
94/E3 Oshawa, On,Can
95/S8 Oshawa, On,Can
55/M3 Oshima (pen.), Japan
82/C4 Oshivelo, Namb.
91/H5 Oshkosh, Ne,US
86/H4 Oshkosh, Wi,US
89/J3 Oshkosh, Wi,US
91/L4 Oshkosh, Wi,US
94/B2 Oshkosh, Wi,US
42/E5 Oshmyany, Bela.
44/C1 Oshmyany, Bela.
51/F2 Oshnovīyeh, Iran
52/E1 Oshnovīyeh, Iran
76/F6 Oshogbo, Nga.
79/G5 Oshogbo, Nga.
82/C1 Oshwe, Zaire
18/E4 Osijek, Cro.
40/D3 Osijek, Cro.
33/K5 Osimo, It.
40/A4 Osimo, It.
40/E3 Osipaonica, Yugo.
44/D1 Osipovichi, Bela.
91/K5 Oskaloosa, Ia,US
93/J2 Oskaloosa, Ia,US
20/F4 Oskarshamn, Swe.
44/F2 Oskol (riv.), Rus., Ukr.
44/F2 Oskol (riv.), Ukr.
18/E3 Oslo (cap.), Nor.
20/D4 Oslo (cap.), Nor.
46/B4 Oslo (cap.), Nor.
53/L5 Osmānābād, India
62/C4 Osmānābād, India
44/E4 Osmancık, Turk.
50/C1 Osmancık, Turk.
41/K5 Osmaneli, Turk.
45/E1 Osmaniye, Turk.
50/D2 Osmaniye, Turk.
52/C1 Osmaniye, Turk.
20/J4 Os'mino, Rus.
18/D3 Osnabrück, Ger.
26/E2 Osnabrück, Ger.
29/F4 Osnabrück, Ger.
19/S9 Osny, Fr.
30/B5 Osny, Fr.
32/E2 Osny, Fr.
99/M11 Oso (mt.), Ca,US
37/E5 Osogna, Swi.
108/B4 Osório, Braz.
109/B5 Osorno, Chile
34/C1 Osorno, Sp.
90/D3 Osoyoos, BC,Can
71/H2 Osprey (reef), Austl.
72/B1 Osprey (reef), Austl.
26/C3 Oss, Neth.
28/C5 Oss, Neth.
71/H8 Ossa (peak), Austl.
73/C4 Ossa (peak), Austl.
39/H3 Ossa (mtn.), Gre.
34/B3 Ossa (range), Port.
79/G5 Osse (riv.), Nga.
32/D5 Osséja, Fr.
35/F1 Osséja, Fr.
23/G4 Ossett, Eng,UK
38/A2 Ossi, It.
98/G4 Ossining, NY,US
18/G3 Ostashkov, Rus.
42/G4 Ostashkov, Rus.
46/D4 Ostashkov, Rus.
29/E4 Ostbevern, Ger.
26/E2 Oste (riv.), Ger.
29/G1 Oste (riv.), Ger.
29/G1 Osten, Ger.
26/B3 Ostend (Oostende), Belg.
30/B1 Ostend (Oostende), Belg.
44/E1 Oster, Rus.
26/F2 Osterburg, Ger.
29/F4 Ostercappeln, Ger.
28/D1 Osterems (chan.), Neth.
20/E4 Östergötland (co.), Swe.
42/C4 Östergötland (co.), Swe.
26/G4 Osterhofen, Ger.
33/K2 Osterhofen, Ger.
26/E2 Osterholz-Scharmbeck, Ger.
29/F2 Osterholz-Scharmbeck, Ger.
29/H5 Osterode, Ger.
26/F3 Osterode am Harz, Ger.
18/E2 Östersund, Swe.
20/E3 Östersund, Swe.
42/B3 Östersund, Swe.
46/B3 Östersund, Swe.
29/H5 Osterwiek, Ger.
20/D4 Østfold (co.), Nor.
29/E2 Ostfriesland (reg.), Ger.
20/F3 Östhammar, Swe.
42/C3 Östhammar, Swe.
36/D1 Ostheim, Fr.
38/C2 Ostia Antica (ruins), It.
33/J4 Ostiglia, It.
102/E4 Ostional Nat'l Wild. Ref., CR
37/F2 Ostrach (riv.), Ger.
18/E4 Ostrava, Czh.
27/K4 Ostrava, Czh.
44/A2 Ostrava, Czh.
46/B5 Ostrava, Czh.
29/E2 Ostrhauderfehn, Ger.
30/C3 Ostricourt, Fr.
39/F1 Oštri Rt (cape), Yugo.
40/D4 Oštri Rt (cape), Yugo.
27/K2 Ostróda, Pol.
42/C5 Ostróda, Pol.
44/F2 Ostrogozhsk, Rus.
27/L2 Ostrołęka, Pol.
27/L2 Ostrołęka (prov.), Pol.
42/D5 Ostrołęka, Pol.
44/B1 Ostrołęka, Pol.
45/L1 Ostrolenka, Rus.
26/G3 Ostrov, Czh.
33/K1 Ostrov, Czh.
20/J4 Ostrov, Rus.
42/F4 Ostrov, Rus.
42/E5 Ostrovets, Bela.
27/L3 Ostrowiec Świętokrzyski, Pol.
44/B2 Ostrowiec Świętokrzyski, Pol.
27/L2 Ostrów Mazowiecka, Pol.
42/D5 Ostrów Mazowiecka, Pol.
44/B1 Ostrów Mazowiecka, Pol.
27/J3 Ostrów Wielkopolski, Pol.
44/A2 Ostrów Wielkopolski, Pol.
27/N2 Ostryna, Bela.
27/J3 Ostrzeszów, Pol.
27/G1 Ostseebad Göhren, Ger.
26/G1 Ostseebad Prerow, Ger.
29/H1 Oststeinbek, Ger.
102/C2 Ostuácan, Mex.
38/E2 Ostuni, It.
40/C5 Ostuni, It.
39/G2 Osum (riv.), Alb.
40/E5 Osum (riv.), Alb.
39/J1 Osŭm (riv.), Bul.
41/G4 Osŭm (riv.), Bul.
55/L5 Ōsumi (isls.), Japan
55/L5 Ōsumi (str.), Japan
56/B5 Ōsumi (arch.), Japan
56/B5 Ōsumi (pen.), Japan
56/B5 Ōsumi (str.), Japan
68/C1 Ōsumi (isls.), Japan
34/C4 Osuna, Sp.
108/B2 Osvaldo Cruz, Braz.
23/G3 Oswaldkirk, Eng,UK
23/F4 Oswaldtwistle, Eng,UK
99/P16 Oswego, Il,US
98/F6 Oswego (riv.), NJ,US
87/J4 Oswego, NY,US
89/L3 Oswego, NY,US
94/E3 Oswego, NY,US
23/E6 Oswestry, Eng,UK
27/K3 Oświęcim (Auschwitz), Pol.
55/M4 Ōta, Japan
56/C3 Ōta (riv.), Japan
56/F2 Ōta, Japan
56/C3 Ōtake, Japan
57/G3 Ōtaki, Japan
57/J7 Ōtaki, Japan
57/G2 Ōtakine-yama (mtn.), Japan
47/Q5 Otaru, Japan
27/G4 Otava (riv.), Czh.
33/K2 Otava (riv.), Czh.
82/C4 Otavi, Namb.
55/N4 Ōtawara, Japan
57/G2 Ōtawara, Japan
40/F3 Oțelu Roșu, Rom.
69/L6 Otepa, FrPol.
34/B1 Otero de Rey, Sp.
100/C3 Oteros (riv.), Mex.
54/D2 Otgon, Mong.
54/D2 Otgon Tenger (peak), Mong.
90/D4 Othello, Wa,US
19/U9 Othis, Fr.
30/B5 Othis, Fr.
39/F3 Othonoí (isl.), Gre.
79/F4 Oti (riv.), Gui.
100/D3 Otinapa, Mex.
71/R11 Otira, N.Z.
82/C5 Otjikango, Namb.
82/C5 Otjinene, Namb.
82/C5 Otjiwarongo, Namb.
82/B4 Otjokavare, Namb.
23/G4 Otley, Eng,UK
33/L4 Otočac, Cro.
40/B3 Otočac, Cro.
54/F4 Otog Qi, China
59/A3 Otog Qi, China
54/F4 Otog Qianqi, China
40/D3 Otok, Cro.
91/L3 Otoskwin (riv.), On,Can
57/N10 Otowa, Japan
18/D3 Otra (riv.), Nor.
20/C4 Otra (riv.), Nor.
46/A4 Otra (riv.), Nor.
45/J1 Otradnyy, Rus.
39/F2 Otranto (str.), Alb., It.
39/F2 Otranto, It.
27/J4 Otrokovice, Czh.
55/M5 Ōtsu, Japan
56/D3 Ōtsu, Japan
57/L9 Ōtsu, Japan
20/D3 Otta, Nor.
84/J4 Ottawa (isls.), Can.
84/K5 Ottawa (cap.), Can.
84/K5 Ottawa (riv.), Can.
87/H3 Ottawa (isls.), NW,Can
87/J4 Ottawa (cap.), Can.
89/L2 Ottawa (cap.), Can.
94/E2 Ottawa (riv.), On, Qu,Can
94/F2 Ottawa (cap.), Can.
89/M2 Ottawa (riv.), On, Qu,Can
95/M7 Ottawa (riv.), On, Qu,Can
89/J3 Ottawa, Il,US
91/L5 Ottawa, Il,US
93/K2 Ottawa, Il,US
94/B3 Ottawa, Il,US
89/G4 Ottawa, Ks,US
93/J3 Ottawa, Ks,US
96/E2 Ottawa, Ks,US
94/C3 Ottawa, Oh,US
24/C5 Otter (riv.), Eng,UK
31/G5 Otterbach, Ger.
31/G5 Otterberg, Ger.
23/F1 Otterburn, Eng,UK
29/F1 Otterndorf, Ger.
26/E2 Ottersberg, Ger.
29/G2 Ottersberg, Ger.
19/M7 Ottershaw, Eng,UK
24/C5 Ottery Saint Mary, Eng,UK
30/D2 Ottignies-Louvain-La-Neuve, Belg.
36/D2 Ottmarsheim, Fr.
37/G2 Ottobeuren, Ger.
26/F4 Ottobrunn, Ger.
33/J2 Ottobrunn, Ger.
80/P13 Ottosdal, SAfr.
98/E5 Ottsville, Pa,US
89/H3 Ottumwa, Ia,US
91/K5 Ottumwa, Ia,US
93/J2 Ottumwa, Ia,US
31/G5 Ottweiler, Ger.
101/L7 Otumba de Gómez Farías, Mex.
76/G6 Oturkpo, Nga.
106/C5 Otuzco, Peru
71/G7 Otway (cape), Austl.
73/B3 Otway (cape), Austl.
73/B3 Otway Nat'l Park, Austl.
27/L2 Otwock, Pol.
37/G4 Ötztal Alps (mts.), Aus., It.
33/J3 Ötztal Alps (mts.), Eur.
37/G3 Ötztaler Ache (riv.), Aus.
60/D4 Ou (riv.), Laos
65/C1 Ou (riv.), Laos
93/J4 Ouachita (riv.), Ar, La,US
93/J4 Ouachita (mts.), Ar, Ok,US
89/H5 Ouachita (riv.), Ar, La,US
89/H5 Ouachita (mts.), Ar, Ok,US
96/E3 Ouachita (mts.), Ok,US
76/C3 Ouadane, Mrta.
77/K6 Ouadda, CAfr.
77/J5 Ouaddaï (reg.), Chad
76/E5 Ouagadougou (cap.), Burk.
79/E3 Ouagadougou (cap.), Burk.
76/E5 Ouahigouya, Burk.
77/K6 Ouaka (riv.), CAfr.
76/D4 Oualâta, Mrta.
78/D2 Oualâta, Dhar (hills), Mrta.
76/F5 Ouallam, Niger
79/F3 Ouallam, Niger
77/K6 Ouanda Djallé, CAfr.
32/E3 Ouanne (riv.), Fr.
107/H3 Ouaqui, FrG.
76/C3 Ouarane (reg.), Mrta.
76/G1 Ouargla, Alg.
76/D1 Ouarzazate, Mor.
95/F1 Ouasiemsca (riv.), Qu,Can
75/S16 Ouassel, Nahr (riv.), Alg.
77/J6 Oubangui (riv.), CAfr.
79/E3 Oubritenga (prov.), Burk.
36/B3 Ouche (riv.), Fr.
57/L10 Ōuda, Japan
79/E3 Oudalan (prov.), Burk.
28/B5 Oud-Beijerland, Neth.
28/A5 Ouddorp, Neth.
28/D5 Oude IJssel (riv.), Neth.
30/C2 Oudenaarde, Belg.
28/B5 Oudenbosch, Neth.
30/B1 Oudenburg, Belg.
28/E2 Oude Pekela, Neth.
28/D2 Oude Westereems (chan.), Neth.
32/C3 Oudon (riv.), Fr.
80/C4 Oudtshoorn, SAfr.
82/D7 Oudtshoorn, SAfr.
28/B6 Oud-Turnhout, Belg.
74/B2 Oued Drâa (riv.), Mor.
78/E2 Oued el Hadjar (well), Mali
75/R16 Oued Rhiou, Alg.
76/D1 Oued Zem, Mor.
76/F6 Ouémé (riv.), Ben.
79/F4 Ouémé (riv.), Ben.
79/F5 Ouémé (prov.), Ben.
69/V13 Ouen (isl.), NCal.
75/W18 Ouenza, Alg.
75/M13 Ouerrha (riv.), Mor.
32/A2 Ouessant (isl.), Fr.
76/J7 Ouesso, Congo
79/H5 Ouest (prov.), Camr.
103/H1 Ouest (pt.), Haiti
103/H2 Ouest (pt.), Haiti
75/M13 Ouezzane, Mor.
76/D1 Ouezzane, Mor.
21/H7 Oughterard, Ire.
77/J6 Ouham (riv.), CAfr., Chad
30/C5 Ouichy-le-Château, Fr.
75/P13 Oujda, Mor.
76/E1 Oujda, Mor.
20/J2 Oulangan Nat'l Park, Fin.
42/F2 Oulangan Nat'l Park, Fin.
36/A6 Oullins, Fr.
73/A2 Oulnina (peak), Austl.
18/F2 Oulu, Fin.
20/H2 Oulu, Fin.
20/H2 Oulu (prov.), Fin.
42/E2 Oulu, Fin.
42/E2 Oulu (prov.), Fin.
46/C3 Oulu, Fin.
20/H2 Oulujärvi (lake), Fin.
18/F2 Oulujärvi (lake), Fin.
42/E2 Oulujärvi (lake), Fin.
75/V18 Oum El Bouaghi, Alg.
75/V18 Oum El Bouaghi (gov.), Alg.
76/D1 Oum er Rhia (riv.), Mor.
77/J5 Oum Hadjer, Chad
18/F2 Ounasjoki (riv.), Fin.
20/H2 Ounasjoki (riv.), Fin.
42/E2 Ounasjoki (riv.), Fin.
25/F2 Oundle, Eng,UK
77/K4 OuniangaKebir, Chad
31/E2 Oupeye, Belg.
31/E4 Our (riv.), Belg.
26/D3 Our (riv.), Eur.
33/G1 Our (riv.), Eur.
26/C5 Ource (riv.), Fr.
32/F3 Ource (riv.), Fr.
36/A2 Ource (riv.), Fr.
26/B4 Ourcq (riv.), Fr.
30/C5 Ourcq (riv.), Fr.
32/E2 Ourcq (riv.), Fr.
20/H1 Øure Anarjokka Nat'l Park, Nor.
42/E1 Øure Anarjokka Nat'l Park, Nor.
20/F1 Øure Dividal Nat'l Park, Nor.
42/C1 Øure Dividal Nat'l Park, Nor.
77/J3 Ouri, Chad
107/K5 Ouricuri, Braz.
107/J8 Ourinhos, Braz.
108/B2 Ourinhos, Braz.
109/C1 Ourinhos, Braz.
34/A4 Ourique, Port.
79/H3 Ourofané, Niger
108/C2 Ouro Fino, Braz.
81/F2 Ouro, Ponta do (pt.), Moz.
108/D2 Ouro Preto, Braz.
36/A4 Ouroux-sur-Saône, Fr.
26/C3 Ourthe (riv.), Belg.
31/E3 Ourthe (riv.), Belg.
31/E3 Ourthe Occidentale (riv.), Belg.
31/E3 Ourthe Oriental (riv.), Belg.
31/E3 Ourthe Oriental (riv.), Lux.
23/H4 Ouse (riv.), Eng,UK
25/G5 Ouse (riv.), Eng,UK
32/B3 Oust (riv.), Fr.
35/Q11 Outão, Port.
87/J4 Outaouais (riv.), Qu,Can
94/E2 Outaouais (riv.), Qu,Can
95/G1 Outardes (riv.), Qu,Can
95/G1 Outardes Quatre (res.), Qu,Can
78/D2 Outeid Arkas (well), Mali
21/A2 Outer Hebrides (isls.), Sc,UK
34/A1 Outes, Sp.
82/C5 Outjo, Namb.
86/F3 Outlook, Sk,Can
88/E1 Outlook, Sk,Can
90/G3 Outlook, Sk,Can
25/H5 Outreau, Fr.
30/A2 Outreau, Fr.
95/N6 Outremont, Qu,Can
69/V12 Ouvéa (isl.), NCal.
69/V12 Ouvéa (lag.), NCal.
32/F4 Ouvèze (riv.), Fr.
70/G7 Ouyen, Austl.
73/B2 Ouyen, Austl.
85/H4 Ouzinkie, Ak,US
44/F5 Ovacık, Turk.
50/C1 Ovacık, Turk.
33/H4 Ovada, It.
69/Y18 Ovalau (isl.), Fiji
109/B3 Ovalle, Chile
34/A2 Ovar, Port.
31/G2 Overath, Ger.
28/B5 Overflakkee (isl.), Neth.
20/D2 Overhalla, Nor.
42/A2 Overhalla, Nor.
30/D2 Overijse, Belg.
28/D3 Overijssel (prov.), Neth.
28/D4 Overijssels (can.), Neth.
20/G2 Överkalix, Swe.
42/D2 Överkalix, Swe.
93/J3 Overland Park, Ks,US
96/E2 Overland Park, Ks,US
98/K7 Overlea, Md,US
28/C6 Overpelt, Belg.
31/E1 Overpelt, Belg.
25/E1 Overseal, Eng,UK
25/H1 Overstrand, Eng,UK
25/E4 Overton, Eng,UK
23/F6 Overton, Wal,UK
92/D3 Overton, Nv,US
20/G2 Övertorneå, Swe.
42/D2 Övertorneå, Swe.
41/K2 Ovidiopol', Ukr.
18/C4 Oviedo, Sp.
34/C1 Oviedo, Sp.
22/B6 Ovoca, Ire.
20/C3 Øvre Årdal, Nor.
20/J1 Øvre Pasvik Nat'l Park, Nor.
42/F1 Øvre Pasvik Nat'l Park, Nor.
39/G3 Ovriá, Gre.
76/J8 Owando, Congo
82/C1 Owando, Congo
57/N9 Owariasahi, Japan
56/E3 Owase, Japan
98/F4 Owassa (lake), NJ,US
93/J3 Owasso, Ok,US
96/E2 Owasso, Ok,US
91/K4 Owatonna, Mn,US
93/J1 Owatonna, Mn,US
92/E3 Owego, NY,US
71/R11 Owen (peak), N.Z.
22/A2 Owenkillew (riv.), NI,UK
92/C3 Owens (riv.), Ca,US
89/J4 Owensboro, Ky,US
94/C4 Owensboro, Ky,US
97/G2 Owensboro, Ky,US
87/H4 Owen Sound, On,Can
89/K3 Owen Sound, On,Can
94/D2 Owen Sound, On,Can
76/G6 Owerri, Nga.
92/C2 Owhyee (mts.), Id,US
37/F2 Owingen, Ger.
98/K8 Owings, Md,US
98/K7 Owings Mills, Md,US
90/F4 Owl Creek (mts.), Wy,US
92/E2 Owl Creek (mts.), Wy,US
76/G6 Owo, Nga.
94/C3 Owosso, Mi,US
51/F3 Owrāmān, Iran
88/C3 Owyhee (riv.), US
92/C2 Owyhee (riv.), US
90/D5 Owyhee, Nv,US
92/C2 Owyhee, Nv,US
90/D5 Owyhee (riv.), Or,US
92/C2 Owyhee (lake), Or,US
90/D5 Owyhee, South Fork (riv.), Id, Nv,US
52/E1 Owzan (riv.), Iran
86/F4 Oxbow, Sk,Can
88/F2 Oxbow, Sk,Can
91/H3 Oxbow, Sk,Can
99/F6 Oxbow (lake), Mi,US
20/F4 Oxelösund, Swe.
42/C4 Oxelösund, Swe.
18/C3 Oxford, Eng,UK
25/E3 Oxford, Eng,UK
25/E3 Oxford (can.), Eng,UK
91/K2 Oxford (lake), Mb,Can
99/F6 Oxford, Mi,US
89/J5 Oxford, Ms,US
97/F3 Oxford, Ms,US
94/C4 Oxford, Oh,US
97/G2 Oxford, Oh,US
25/E3 Oxfordshire (co.), Eng,UK
19/M7 Oxhey, Eng,UK
101/H4 Oxkutzcab, Mex.
102/D1 Oxkutzcab, Mex.
72/E7 Oxley (cr.), Austl.
92/C4 Oxnard, Ca,US
98/J8 Oxon Hill Farm (park), Md,US
98/K8 Oxon Hill-Glassmanor, Md,US
19/M8 Oxshott, Eng,UK
19/N8 Oxted, Eng,UK
25/F4 Oxted, Eng,UK
57/E2 Oyabe, Japan
55/M4 Oyama, Japan
57/F2 Oyama, Japan
57/M10 Ōyamada, Japan
57/L10 Ōyamazaki, Japan
105/D2 Oyapock (riv.), Braz., FrG.
107/H3 Oyapock (riv.), FrG.
76/H7 Oyem, Gabon
90/F3 Oyen, Ab,Can
30/B2 Oye-Plage, Fr.
76/F6 Oyo, Nga.
79/F4 Oyo (state), Nga.
79/F5 Oyo, Nga.
56/B5 Ōyodo (riv.), Japan
57/L10 Ōyodo, Japan
36/B5 Oyonnax, Fr.
98/G5 Oyster Bay, NY,US
26/E2 Oyten, Ger.
29/G2 Oyten, Ger.
51/E2 Özalp, Turk.
32/D2 Ozanne (riv.), Fr.
96/E3 Ozark (mts.), Ar, Mo,US
96/E2 Ozark (plat.), Mo, Ok,US
93/J3 Ozark (plat.), US
97/G4 Ozark, Al,US
93/J4 Ozark, Ar,US
96/E3 Ozark, Ar,US
89/H4 Ozark (mts.), Ar, Mo,US
89/H4 Ozarks (lake), Mo,U
93/J3 Ozarks, Lake of the (lake), Mo,US
27/L4 Ózd, Hun.
40/E1 Ózd, Hun.
44/B2 Ózd, Hun.
47/S4 Ozernoy (cape), Rus
27/N2 Ozëry, Bela.
42/E5 Ozëry, Bela.
90/B3 Ozette (lake), Wa,U
44/F1 Ozherel'ye, Rus.
91/L3 Ozhiski (lake), On,C
38/A2 Ozieri, It.
27/K3 Ozimek, Pol.
50/C2 Özkonak, Turk.
19/U10 Ozoir-la-Ferrière, F
30/B6 Ozoir-la-Ferrière, F
101/E2 Ozona, Tx,US
93/G5 Ozona, Tx,US
96/C4 Ozona, Tx,US
27/K3 Ozorków, Pol.
19/U11 Ozouer-le-Voulgis, F
56/C4 Ōzu, Japan
101/F4 Ozuluama, Mex.
102/B1 Ozuluama, Mex.
101/L7 Ozumba de Alzate, Mex.
50/E1 Ozurgeti, Geo.

P

60/C5 Pa-an, Burma
63/G4 Pa-an, Burma
65/B2 Pa-an, Burma
26/F4 Paar (riv.), Ger.
33/J2 Paar (riv.), Ger.
37/H1 Paar (riv.), Ger.
80/B4 Paarl, SAfr.
80/L10 Paarl, SAfr.
82/C7 Paarl, SAfr.
88/U10 Paauilo, Hi,US
27/K3 Pabianice, Pol.
62/E3 Pābna, Bang.
42/E5 Pabradė, Lith.
106/F6 Pacaás Novos (mts
106/F6 Pacaás Novos Nat' Park, Braz.
107/H4 Pacajá (riv.), Braz.
106/F3 Pacaraima (mts.), Braz.
106/C5 Pacasmayo, Peru
38/C4 Paceco, It.
106/C6 Pachacamac, Peru
100/C2 Pacheco, Mex.
38/D4 Pachino, It.
62/C3 Pachmarhī, India
101/L6 Pachuca, Mex.
102/B1 Pachuca, Mex.
101/F4 Pachuca de Soto, Mex.
16/B4 Pacific (ocean)
68/* Pacific (ocean)
83/R Pacific (ocean)
48/N8 Pacific (ocean)
90/B3 Pacific (ranges), BC,Can
84/D5 Pacific (ocean)
105/A4 Pacific (ocean)
99/C3 Pacific, Wa,US
99/K11 Pacifica, Ca,US
86/D4 Pacific Rim Nat'l Park, BC,Can
66/D5 Pacinan (cape), Ind
66/D5 Pacitan, Indo.
35/P10 Paço de Arcos, Por
30/A5 Pacy-sur-Eure, Fr.
53/L2 Padam, India
66/B4 Padang, Indo.
66/B4 Padangpanjang, In
66/A3 Padangsidempuan, Indo.
19/N7 Paddington, Eng,UK
99/P14 Paddock Lake, Wi,
25/G4 Paddock Wood, Eng,UK
26/E3 Paderborn, Ger.
29/F5 Paderborn, Ger.
53/J3 Pad Īdan, Pak.
62/A2 Pad Īdan, Pak.
23/F4 Padiham, Eng,UK
106/F7 Padilla, Bol.
101/F3 Padilla, Mex.
40/E3 Padina, Yugo.
20/E2 Padjelanta Nat'l Park, Swe.
42/C2 Padjelanta Nat'l Park, Swe.
64/F4 Padmanābhapuram, India
33/J4 Padova (Padua), It.
101/F3 Padre (isl.), Tx,US
89/G6 Padre (isl.), Tx,US

165

Padre – Peal

96/D5 Padre (isl.), Tx,US
96/D5 Padre Island Nat'l Seashore, Tx,US
34/A1 Padrón, Sp.
80/D4 Padrone (cape), SAfr.
24/B5 Padstow, Eng,UK
18/E4 Padua, It.
33/J4 Padua (Padova), It.
89/J4 Paducah, Ky,US
94/B4 Paducah, Ky,US
97/F2 Paducah, Ky,US
93/G4 Paducah, Tx,US
96/C3 Paducah, Tx,US
34/D4 Padul, Sp.
38/D2 Padula, It.
55/K3 Paegam, NKor.
56/A2 Paektŏk-san (mtn.), SKor.
58/E4 Paektŏk-san (mtn.), SKor.
47/N5 Paektu-San (mtn.), NKor.
55/K3 Paektu-San (mtn.), NKor.
58/E2 Paektu-San (mtn.), NKor.
55/J4 Paengnyŏng (isl.), SKor.
58/C4 Paengnyŏng (isl.), SKor.
82/F5 Pafúri, Moz.
33/L4 Pag, Cro.
33/L4 Pag (isl.), Cro.
40/B3 Pag, Cro.
40/B3 Pag (isl.), Cro.
67/F2 Pagadian, Phil.
66/B4 Pagai Selatan (isl.), Indo.
66/A4 Pagai Utara (isl.), Indo.
60/B4 Pagan, Burma
63/F3 Pagan, Burma
68/D3 Pagan (isl.), NMar.
38/C1 Paganica, It.
88/D4 Page, Az,US
92/E3 Page, Az,US
27/L1 Pagėgiai, Lith.
60/A3 Pāgla, Bang.
31/F6 Pagny-dur-Moselle, Fr.
69/H6 Pago Pago (cap.), ASam.
69/T10 Pago Pago (cap.), ASam.
92/F3 Pagosa Springs, Co,US
96/B2 Pagosa Springs, Co,US
94/C1 Pagwachuan (riv.), On,Can
88/U11 Pahala, Hi,US
66/B3 Pahang (riv.), Malay.
103/F3 Páhara (lag.), Nic.
92/D3 Pahrump, Nv,US
101/L6 Pahuatlán de Valle, Mex.
92/C3 Pahute Mesa (upland), Nv,US
59/C5 Pai (lake), China
88/T10 Paia, Hi,US
39/L7 Paiania, Gre.
20/H4 Paide, Est.
42/E4 Paide, Est
24/C6 Paignton, Eng,UK
20/H3 Päijänne (lake), Fin.
42/E3 Päijänne (lake), Fin.
65/C3 Pailin, Camb.
88/T10 Pailolo (chan.), Hi,US
42/D3 Paimio, Fin.
94/D3 Painesville, Oh,US
24/C2 Painscastle, Wal,UK
91/J2 Paint (lake), Mb,Can
88/D4 Painted (des.), Az,US
92/E4 Painted (des.), Az,US
101/F2 Paint Rock, Tx,US
93/H5 Paint Rock, Tx,US
96/D4 Paint Rock, Tx,US
94/D4 Paintsville, Ky,US
97/H2 Paintsville, Ky,US
21/C3 Paisley, Sc,UK
62/C4 Paithan, India
20/G2 Pajala, Swe.
42/D2 Pajala, Swe.
67/K3 Pajęczno, Pol.
103/F4 Pajonal Abajo, Pan.
66/B3 Pakanbaru, Indo.
53/H3 Pak Ban, Laos
58/C3 Pakch'ŏn, NKor.
73/G6 Pakenham, Austl.
39/J5 Pákhnes (peak), Gre.
43/X9 Pakhra (riv.), Rus.
46/H6 Pakistan
48/F7 Pakistan
53/H3 Pakistan
62/A2 Pakistan
64/A2 Pakistan
40/B3 Paklenica Nat'l Park, Co.
33/L4 Paklenica Nat'l Park, Cro.
60/B4 Pakokku, Burma
63/G3 Pakokku, Burma
106/F3 Pakowki (lake), Ab,Can
53/K2 Pākpattan, Pak.
64/B2 Pākpattan, Pak.
63/H6 Pak Phanang, Thai.
40/C3 Pakrac, Cro.
42/D5 Pakruojis, Lith.
40/D2 Paks, Hun.
63/J4 Pakxe, Laos
65/D3 Pakxe, Laos
76/H6 Pala, Chad
35/N9 Palacio Real, Sp.
35/G2 Palafrugell, Sp.
38/D4 Palagonia, It.
38/E1 Palagruža (isls.), Cro.
40/C4 Palagruža (isls.), Cro.
61/F1 Palai, India
39/F3 Palaiokastritsa, Gre.
39/G3 Pálairos, Gre.
19/S10 Palaiseau, Fr.
62/D4 Pālakolla, India
39/H3 Palamás, Gre.
35/G2 Palamós, Sp.
47/R4 Palana, Rus.
42/D5 Palanga, Lith.
66/D4 Palangkaraya, Indo.
53/K4 Pālanpur, India
62/B3 Pālanpur, India
88/T10 Palaoa (pt.), Hi,US
82/E5 Palapye, Bots.
62/C5 Palar (riv.), India
60/A3 Palāsbāri, India
34/B1 Palas de Rey, Sp.
99/P15 Palatine, Il,US
89/K6 Palatka, Fl,US
97/H4 Palatka, Fl,US
54/A2 Palattsy, Kaz.
48/N9 Palau (terr.), US
68/C4 Palau (terr.), US
63/G5 Palaw, Burma
65/B3 Palaw, Burma
48/L9 Palawan (isl.), Phil.
67/E2 Palawan (chan.), Phil.
67/E2 Palawan (isl.), Phil.
68/A3 Palawan (isl.), Phil.
62/C6 Pālayankottai, India
64/F4 Pālayankottai, India
38/D4 Palazzolo Acreide, It.
20/H4 Paldiski, Est.
42/E4 Paldiski, Est.
76/G8 Palé, EqG.
67/F3 Paleleh, Indo.
66/B4 Palembang, Indo.
109/B5 Palena, Chile
34/C1 Palencia, Sp.
101/H5 Palenque, Mex.
102/D2 Palenque, Mex.
101/H5 Palenque Nat'l Park, Mex.
102/C2 Palenque Nat'l Park, Mex.
95/Q9 Palermo, On,Can
18/E5 Palermo, It.
38/C3 Palermo, It.
89/G5 Palestine, Tx,US
93/J5 Palestine, Tx,US
96/E4 Palestine, Tx,US
53/K5 Pālghar, India
64/F3 Pālghāt, India
56/A2 P'algong-san (mtn.), SKor.
58/D5 P'algong-san (mtn.), SKor.
58/E4 P'algong-san (mtn.), SKor.
108/B3 Palhoça, Braz.
53/K3 Pāli, India
62/B2 Pāli, India
40/D2 Palić, Yugo.
88/V13 Palikea (peak), Hi,US
39/H3 Palioúrion, Ákra (cape), Gre.
44/B5 Palioúrion, Ákra (cape), Gre.
31/E4 Paliseul, Belg.
53/K4 Pālitāna, India
62/B3 Pālitāna, India
20/G4 Palivere, Est.
42/D4 Palivere, Est.
101/G5 Palizada, Mex.
102/C2 Palizada, Mex.
40/C3 Paljenik (peak), Bosn.
64/G4 Palk (str.), India
62/C6 Palk (str.), India,SrL.
64/G4 Palk (bay), SrL.
64/G4 Palk (str.), SrL.
37/G4 Palla Bianca (Weisskugel) (mtn.), It.
73/D1 Pallamallawa, Austl.
72/B2 Pallarenda, Austl.
20/H1 Pallas-Ounastunturin Nat'l Park, Fin.
42/E1 Pallas-Ounastunturn Nat'l Park, Fin.
20/H1 Pallastunturi (peak), Fin.
42/E1 Pallastunturi (peak), Fin
71/S11 Palliser (cape), N.Z.
71/H3 Palm (isls.), Austl.
107/J6 Palma (riv.), Braz.
82/H3 Palma, Moz.
18/D5 Palma, Sp.
35/G3 Palma, Sp.
34/C4 Palma del Río, Sp.
38/C4 Palma di Montechiaro, It.
40/A3 Palmanova, It.
103/H4 Palmar (riv.), Ven.
107/L5 Palmares, Braz.
108/B3 Palmas, Braz.
74/B4 Palmas (cape), Libr.
76/D5 Palmas (cape), Libr.
78/D5 Palmas (cape), Libr.
103/H1 Palma Soriano, Cuba
97/H4 Palm Bay, Fl,US
72/H8 Palm Beach, Austl.
92/C4 Palmdale, Ca,US
108/B3 Palmeira, Braz.
74/K10 Palmeira, CpV.
107/L5 Palmeira dos Índios, Braz.
35/Q10 Palmela, Port.
83/V Palmer (arch.), Ant.
85/J3 Palmer, Ak,US
86/B2 Palmer, Ak,US
99/D3 Palmer, Wa,US
83/V Palmer Land (reg.), Ant.
72/C3 Palmerston (cape), Austl.
69/J6 Palmerston (atoll), CookIs.
71/R12 Palmerston, N.Z.
72/B2 Palmerston Nat'l Park, Austl.
71/S11 Palmerston North, N.Z.
98/E5 Palmerton, Pa,US
97/H5 Palmetto, Fl,US
97/H4 Palm Harbor, Fl,US
38/D3 Palmi, It.
72/B2 Palm I. Abor. Settlement, Austl.
103/F1 Palmillas (pt.), Cuba
101/F4 Palmillas, Mex.
106/C3 Palmira, Col.
108/B2 Palmital, Braz.
88/C5 Palm Springs, Ca,US
92/C4 Palm Springs, Ca,US
69/J4 Palmyra (isl.), PacUS
50/D3 Palmyra (ruins), Syria
52/C2 Palmyra (ruins), Syria
99/N14 Palmyra, Wi,US
62/E3 Palmyras (pt.), India
22/E2 Palnackie, Sc,UK
62/C5 Palni, India
64/F3 Palni, India
64/F3 Palni (hills), India
92/B3 Palo Alto, Ca,US
99/K12 Palo Alto, Ca,US
101/F3 Palo Alto Btld. Nat'l Hist. Site, Tx,US
100/C3 Palo Bola, Mex.
33/J4 Palon (peak), It.
101/F1 Palo Pinto, Tx,US
96/D3 Palo Pinto, Tx,US
35/E4 Palos, Cabo de (cape), Sp.
34/B4 Palos de la Frontera, Sp.
99/Q16 Palos Hills, Il,US
103/E4 Palo Verde Nat'l Park, CR
62/D2 Pālpa, Nepal
106/C6 Palpa, Peru
109/C1 Palpalá, Arg.
67/G4 Palpetu (cape), Indo.
20/H2 Paltamo, Fin.
42/E2 Paltamo, Fin.
68/A5 Palu, Indo.
44/F5 Palu, Turk.
50/D2 Palu, Turk.
66/C3 Pamangkat, Indo.
73/D3 Pambula, Austl.
32/D5 Pamiers, Fr.
35/F1 Pamiers, Fr.
46/H5 Pamir (reg.), Asia
46/H6 Pamir (riv.), Afg.,Taj.
88/F4 Pampa, Tx,US
93/G4 Pampa, Tx,US
96/C3 Pampa, Tx,US
105/C6 Pampas (plain), Arg.
109/D4 Pampas (plain), Arg.
34/B2 Pampilhosa da Serra, Port.
103/H5 Pamplona, Col.
106/D2 Pamplona, Col.
18/C4 Pamplona, Sp.
32/C5 Pamplona, Sp.
34/E1 Pamplona, Sp.
41/K5 Pamukova, Turk.
101/H4 Panabá, Mex.
102/D1 Panabá, Mex.
92/D3 Panaca, Nv,US
62/C6 Panadura, SrL.
39/J1 Panagyurishte, Bul.
41/G4 Panagyurishte, Bul.
66/B5 Panaitan (isl.), Indo.
53/K5 Panāji, India
62/B4 Panāji, India
103/F4 Panama
106/B2 Panama
84/J9 Panama
103/F4 Panama (can.), Pan.
103/G4 Panamá (bay), Pan.
103/G4 Panamá (cap.), Pan.
103/G4 Panama (gulf), Pan.
103/G4 Panama (isth.), Pan.
105/A2 Panama (can.), Pan.
105/B2 Panama (gulf), Pan.
106/B2 Panama (can.), Pan.
106/C2 Panamá (cap.), Pan.
106/C2 Panama (gulf), Pan.
106/C2 Panama (isth.), Pan.
84/K9 Panama (can.), Pan.
84/K9 Panama (gulf), Pan.
89/J5 Panama City, Fl,US
97/G4 Panama City, Fl,US
92/C3 Panamint (range), Ca,US
33/J4 Panaro (riv.), It.
48/M8 Panay (isl.), Phil.
67/F1 Panay (isl.), Phil.
68/B3 Panay (isl.), Phil.
92/C3 Pancake (range), Nv,US
40/E3 Pančevo, Yugo.
39/G1 Pančicev vrh (peak), Yugo.
40/E4 Pančicev vrh (peak), Yugo.
41/H3 Panciu, Rom.
81/F2 Panda, Moz.
64/E3 Pandalayini, India
82/E4 Pandamatenga, Bots.
109/B2 Pan de Azúcar Nat'l Park, Chile
53/L5 Pandharpur, India
62/C4 Pandharpur, India
60/A3 Pandu, India
63/F2 Pandu, India
18/F3 Panevėžys, Lith.
20/H5 Panevėžys, Lith.
42/E5 Panevėžys, Lith.
46/C4 Panevėžys, Lith.
46/J5 Panfilov, Kaz.
60/C4 Pang (riv.), Burma
65/B1 Pang (riv.), Burma
69/H7 Pangai, Tonga
39/J2 Pangaion (peak), Gre.
41/G5 Pangaion (peak), Gre.
74/F5 Pangani (riv.), Tanz.
82/G1 Pangani (riv.), Tanz.
25/G2 Pangbourne, Eng,UK
66/A3 Pangkalanberandan, Indo.
67/F4 Pangkalaseang (cape), Indo.
60/D4 Pang Kalom, Laos
66/C4 Pangkalpinang, Indo.
63/G3 Pang Long, Burma
87/K2 Pangnirtung, NW,Can
60/C3 Pangsau (pass), India
109/B4 Panguipulli, Chile
92/D3 Panguitch, Ut,US
67/F2 Pangutaran, Phil.
93/G4 Panhandle, Tx,US
96/C3 Panhandle, Tx,US
67/J4 Paniai (lake), Indo.
88/R10 Paniau (peak), Hi,US
68/F7 Panié (peak), NCal.
69/U12 Panié (peak), NCal.
53/L3 Pānīpat, India
62/C2 Pānīpat, India
53/K1 Panj (Pyandz) (riv.), Afg., Taj.
51/F3 Panjwīn, Iraq
52/E1 Panjwīn, Iraq
76/G6 Pankshin, Nga.
58/D4 P'anmunjŏm, NKor.
62/D3 Panna, India
72/F7 Pannikin (isl.), Austl.
49/C2 Pano Lefkara, Cyp.
50/C3 Pano Lefkara, Cyp.
50/C3 Pano Panayia, Cyp.
108/B2 Panorama, Braz.
64/G3 Panruti, India
55/K3 Panshi, China
23/E6 Pant, Eng,UK
25/G3 Pant (riv.), Eng,UK
107/G7 Pantanal (marsh), Braz.
76/H1 Pantellaria (isl.), Italy
18/E5 Pantelleria (isl.), It.
38/B4 Pantelleria, It.
38/B4 Pantelleria (isl.), It.
19/T10 Pantin, Fr.
34/B1 Pantón, Sp.
101/F4 Pánuco, Mex.
101/F4 Panuco (riv.), Mex.
102/B1 Pánuco, Mex.
102/B1 Pánuco (riv.), Mex.
60/D3 Panzhihua, China
63/H2 Panzhihua, China
102/D3 Panzós, Guat.
38/E3 Paola, It.
93/J3 Paola, Ks,US
96/E2 Paola, Ks,US
98/E5 Paoli, Pa,US
92/F3 Paonia, Co,US
96/B2 Paonia, Co,US
76/J6 Paoua, CAfr.
65/C3 Paoy Pet, Camb.
40/C2 Pápa, Hun.
102/E4 Papagayo (gulf), CR
88/U11 Papaikou, Hi,US
64/G3 Papanāsam, India
108/B3 Papanduva, Braz.
101/F4 Papantla, Mex.
102/B1 Papantla, Mex.
101/M6 Papantla de Olarte, Mex.
69/X15 Papara, FrPol.
69/L6 Papeete, FrPol.
69/X15 Papeete (cap.), FrPol.
29/F2 Papenburg, Ger.
28/B5 Papendrecht, Neth.
69/X15 Papenoo, FrPol.
69/X15 Papetoai, FrPol.
49/C2 Paphos, Cyp.
49/C2 Paphos (dist.), Cyp.
92/E5 Papigochic (riv.), Mex
91/J5 Papillion, Ne,US
93/H2 Papillion, Ne,US
39/G2 Papingut, Maj'e (peak), Alb.
67/H4 Papisoi (cape), Indo.
68/D5 Papua (gulf), PNG
67/J5 Papua New Guinea
68/D5 Papua New Guinea
70/E4 Papunya, Austl.
105/D3 Pará (riv.), Braz.
107/H4 Pará (riv.), Braz.
108/C1 Pará (riv.), Braz.
70/B4 Paraburdoo, Austl.
107/J7 Paracatu, Braz.
63/K4 Paracel (isls.)
48/L8 Paracel (isls.), China
61/F5 Paracel (isls.), China
48/N7 Parace Vela (Okino-Tori-Shima) (isl.), Japan
70/F6 Parachilna, Austl.
40/E4 Paraćin, Yugo.
44/B4 Paraćin, Yugo.
35/N8 Paracuellos, Sp.
108/C1 Pará de Minas, Braz.
62/E3 Paradip, India
90/F2 Paradise Hill, Sk,Can
107/J4 Paragominas, Braz.
89/H4 Paragould, Ar,US
93/K3 Paragould, Ar,US
94/B4 Paragould, Ar,US
97/F2 Paragould, Ar,US
106/F2 Paragua (riv.), Ven.
105/E4 Paraguaçu (riv.), Braz.
107/L6 Paraguaçu (riv.), Braz.
108/C2 Paraguaçu, Braz.
108/B2 Paraguaçu Paulista, Braz.
107/G6 Paraguai (riv.), Braz.
105/D5 Paraguai (riv.), SAm.
104/D5 Paraguaipoa, Ven.
106/D1 Paraguaná (pen.), Ven.
109/E2 Paraguarí, Par
105/D5 Paraguay
106/G8 Paraguay
109/E1 Paraguay
106/G8 Paraguay (riv.), Par.
109/E1 Paraguay (riv.), Par.
105/E5 Paraíba (riv.), Braz.
107/K8 Paraíba do Sul (riv.), Braz.
108/D2 Paraíba do Sul, Braz.
108/D2 Paraíba do Sul (riv.), Braz
103/F4 Paraíso, CR
101/G5 Paraíso, Mex.
102/C2 Paraíso, Mex.
107/J6 Paraíso do Norte de Goiás, Braz.
108/C2 Paraisópolis, Braz.
76/F6 Parakou, Ben.
79/F4 Parakou, Ben.
64/G4 Paramagudi, India
107/G2 Paramaribo (cap.), Sur.
103/G5 Paramillo Nat'l Park, Col.
106/C2 Paramillo Nat'l Park, Col.
107/K6 Paramirim (riv.), Braz.
39/G3 Paramithía, Gre.
47/R4 Paramushir (isl.), Rus.
48/Q5 Paramushir (isl.), Rus.
109/D3 Paraná, Arg.
109/D3 Parana (riv.), Arg.
107/J6 Paranã, Braz.
108/B2 Paraná (riv.), Braz.
108/B3 Paraná (state), Braz.
105/D5 Paraná (riv.), SAm.
107/H8 Paraná (riv.), SAm.
108/B3 Paranaguá, Braz.
108/B3 Paranaguá (bay), Braz.
109/G2 Paranaguá, Braz.
105/E3 Paranaíba (riv.), Braz.
107/H7 Paranaíba, Braz.
107/J7 Paranaíba (riv.), Braz.
108/B1 Paranaíba, Braz.
108/B1 Paranaíba (riv.), Braz.
108/C1 Paranaíba (riv.), Braz.
108/B2 Paranapanema (riv.), Braz.
109/F1 Paranapanema (riv.), Braz.
108/B3 Paranapiacaba (range), Braz.
109/G1 Paranapiacaba (mts.), Braz.
105/D4 Paranatinga (riv.), Braz.
107/H8 Paranavaí, Braz.
109/F1 Paranavai, Braz.
67/F2 Parang, Phil.
64/H4 Parangi (riv.), SrL.
108/C1 Paraopeba, Braz.
107/J8 Parapanema (riv.), Braz.
71/S11 Paraparaumu, N.Z.
106/F7 Parapeti (riv.), Bol.
108/C2 Parati, Braz.
19/T10 Paray-Vieille-Poste, Fr.
53/L4 Pārbati (riv.), India
53/L5 Parbhani, India
62/C4 Parbhani, India
26/F2 Parchim, Ger
76/H5 Parc National de Kalamaloué Nat'l Park, Camr.
82/E1 Parc National des Volcans Nat'l Park, Rwa.
27/M3 Parczew, Pol.
49/D3 Pardes Hanna, Isr.
50/C3 Pardes Hanna, Isr.
49/F7 Pardes Hanna-Karkur, Isr.
53/K4 Pārdi, India
62/B3 Pārdi, India
107/H8 Pardo (riv.), Braz.
107/J8 Pardo (riv.), Braz.
107/K7 Pardo (riv.), Braz.
108/C2 Pardo (riv.), Braz.
18/E3 Pardubice, Czh.
27/H3 Pardubice, Czh.
33/L1 Pardubice, Czh.
66/D5 Pare, Indo.
105/C4 Parecis (mts.), Braz.
106/F6 Parecis (mts.), Braz.
35/P10 Parede, Port.
34/C1 Paredes de Nava, Sp.
101/E3 Paredón, Mex.
102/C2 Paredón, Mex.
32/C4 Parempuyre, Fr.
94/E1 Parent (lake), Qu,Can
32/C4 Parentis-en-Born, Fr.
67/E4 Parepare, Indo.
35/L6 Parets del Vallès, Sp.
39/G3 Párga, Gre.
31/D6 Pargny-sur-Saulx, Fr.
43/V6 Pargolovo, Rus.
92/E3 Paria (riv.), Az, Ut,US
104/F5 Paria (gulf), Trin.,Ven.
106/F1 Paria (gulf), Trin., Ven.
105/C1 Paria (gulf), Ven.
106/F1 Paria (pen.), Ven.
106/F2 Pariaguán, Ven.
66/B4 Pariaman, Indo.
106/F3 Parima (mts.), Braz.
106/E7 Parinacota (peak), Bol.
73/B2 Paringa, Austl.
41/F3 Parîngu Mare (peak), Rom.
44/B3 Parîngu Mare, Vîrful (peak), Rom.
107/G4 Parintins, Braz.
18/D4 Paris (cap.), Fr
19/T10 Paris (cap.), Fr.
26/B4 Paris (cap.), Fr.
30/B6 Paris (cap.), Fr.
32/E2 Paris (cap.), Fr.
93/J4 Paris, Ar,US
96/E3 Paris, Ar,US
89/J4 Paris, Tn,US
94/B4 Paris, Tn,US
97/F2 Paris, Tn,US
89/G5 Paris, Tx,US
93/J4 Paris, Tx,US
96/E3 Paris, Tx,US
19/T9 Paris-Charles de Gaulle (int'l arpt.), Fr.
19/T10 Paris-Orly (int'l arpt.), Fr.
103/F4 Parita (bay), Pan.
92/F2 Park (range), Co,US
99/Q15 Park City, Il,US
92/D4 Parker, Az,US
93/F3 Parker, Co,US
96/B2 Parker, Co,US
101/F1 Parker, Tx,US
89/K4 Parkersburg, WV,US
94/D4 Parkersburg, WV,US
97/H2 Parkersburg, WV,US
71/H6 Parkes, Austl.
73/D2 Parkes, Austl.
25/H3 Parkeston, Eng,UK
91/L4 Park Falls, Wi,US
94/B2 Park Falls, Wi,US
22/B2 Parkgate, NI,UK
24/A5 Park Head (pt.), UK
25/E5 Parkhurst, Eng,UK
99/C3 Parkland, Wa,US
91/K4 Park Rapids, Mn,US
99/Q15 Park Ridge, Il,US
98/F4 Park Ridge, NJ,US
91/J3 Park River, ND,US
98/E6 Parkside, Pa,US
98/K7 Parkville, Md,US
99/L9 Parkway-Sacramento, Ca,US
34/D2 Parla, Sp.
35/N9 Parla, Sp.
62/D4 Parlakhemundi, India
53/L5 Parli, India
62/C4 Parli, India
18/E4 Parma, It.
33/J4 Parma, It.
94/D3 Parma, Oh,US
19/S9 Parmain, Fr.
30/B5 Parmain, Fr.
107/K4 Parnaíba, Braz.
107/K4 Parnaíba (riv.), Braz.
39/H3 Parnassós (peak), Gre.
39/H3 Parnassos Nat'l Park, Gre.
39/H3 Párnis (peak), Gre.
39/L6 Parnis (mt.), Gre.
44/B5 Párnis Óros Ethnikós Drimós (Mount Parnes Nat'l Park), Gre.
39/H4 Párnon (mts.), Gre.
18/F3 Pärnu, Est.
20/H4 Pärnu, Est.
42/E4 Pärnu, Est.
46/C4 Pärnu, Est.
62/E2 Paro, Bhu.
58/D3 P'aro-ho (lake), SKor.
26/B4 Paron, Fr.
32/E2 Paron, Fr.
71/G5 Paroo (riv.), Austl.
72/B4 Paroo (riv.), Austl.
73/C1 Paroo (riv.), Austl.
39/J4 Páros, Gre.
39/J4 Páros (isl.), Gre.
80/B4 Parow, SAfr.
80/L10 Parow, SAfr.
92/D3 Parowan, Ut,US
37/F4 Parpan, Swi.
108/D1 Parque Nacional da Serra do Cipo Nat'l Park, Braz.
108/B4 Parque Nacional de Aparados da Serra Nat'l Park, Braz.
109/F2 Parque Nacional de Aparados da Serra Nat'l Park, Braz.
108/C2 Parque Nacional de Itatiaia Nat'l Park, Braz.
107/L5 Parque Nacional de Paulo Afonso Nat'l Park, Braz.
108/B4 Parque Nacional de São Joaquim Nat'l Park, Braz.
107/K4 Parque Nacional de Sete Cidades Nat'l Park, Braz.
108/D2 Parque Nacional do Caparaó Nat'l Park, Braz.
109/D4 Parral, Chile
72/H8 Parramatta, Austl.
100/E3 Parras de la Fuente, Mex.
96/C5 Parras de la Fuente, Mex
24/D4 Parrett (riv.), Eng,UK
97/H3 Parris Island Marine Base, SC,US
103/E4 Parrita, CR
84/F2 Parry (chan.), Can.
84/F2 Parry (isls.), Can.
86/F1 Parry (chan.), NW,Can
87/H2 Parry (bay), NW,Can
87/R7 Parry (isls.), NW,Can
87/H4 Parry Sound, On,Can
89/K2 Parry Sound, On,Can
94/D2 Parry Sound, On,Can
26/F5 Parseierspitze (peak), Aus.
33/J3 Parseierspitze (peak), Aus.
37/G3 Parseierspitze (peak), Aus.
91/H4 Parshall, ND,US
98/F5 Parsippany, NJ,US
90/C2 Parsnip (riv.), BC,Can
93/J3 Parsons, Ks,US
96/E2 Parsons, Ks,US
42/C2 Pärtefjället (peak), Swe.
32/C3 Parthenay, Fr.
38/C3 Partinico, It
47/P5 Partizansk, Rus.
55/L3 Partizansk, Rus.
27/K4 Partizánske, Slvk.
94/D1 Partridge (riv.), On,Can
53/L5 Partūr, India
62/C4 Partūr, India
107/H4 Paru (riv.), Braz.
105/D3 Paru de Oeste (riv.), Braz.
107/G3 Paru do Oeste (riv.), Braz.
64/F3 Parūr, India
62/D4 Pārvathīpuram, India
23/G5 Parwich, Eng,UK
62/D1 Paryang, China
80/D2 Parys, SAfr.
80/P13 Parys, SAfr.
95/K1 Pasadena, Nf,Can
88/C5 Pasadena, Ca,US
92/C4 Pasadena, Ca,US
98/K7 Pasadena, Md,US
89/G6 Pasadena, Tx,US
93/J5 Pasadena, Tx,US
96/E4 Pasadena, Tx,US
106/C4 Pasaje, Ecu.
63/H4 Pa Sak (riv.), Thai.
65/C3 Pa Sak (riv.), Thai.
66/B3 Pasaman (peak), Indo.
51/F1 Pasanauri, Geo.
89/J5 Pascagoula, Ms,US
97/F4 Pascagoula, Ms,US
41/H2 Paşcani, Rom.
44/C3 Paşcani, Rom.
88/C2 Pasco, Wa,US
90/D4 Pasco, Wa,US
105/B4 Pasco, Cerro de, Peru
30/A3 Pas-de-Calais (dept.), Fr.
30/B3 Pas-en-Artois, Fr.
60/B2 Pāsighāt, India
63/G2 Pāsighāt, India
45/G5 Pasinler, Turk.
50/E2 Pasinler, Turk.
102/D2 Pasión, Río de la (riv.), Guat.
65/C5 Pasir Mas, Malay.
27/K1 Pasłęk, Pol.
42/C5 Pasłęk, Pol.
27/L2 Pasłęka (riv.), Pol.
33/L5 Pašman (isl.), Cro.
40/B4 Pašman (isl.), Cro.
53/H3 Pasni, Pak.
101/N8 Paso del Macho, Mex.
109/E2 Paso de Los Libres, Arg.
109/E3 Paso de los Toros, Uru.
101/F5 Paso de Ovejas, Mex.
101/N7 Paso de Ovejas, Mex
92/B4 Paso Robles (El Paso de Robles), Ca,US
64/C1 Pasrūr, Pak.
85/M3 Pass (peak), Yk,Can
98/F4 Passaic (co.), NJ,US
98/F5 Passaic, NJ,US
18/E4 Passau, Ger.
27/G4 Passau, Ger.
33/K2 Passau, Ger.
76/J3 Passe de Korizo (pass), Chad
30/C2 Passendale, Belg.
18/E5 Passero (pt.), It.
38/D4 Passero (pt.), It.
108/A3 Passo Fundo (res.), Braz.
109/F2 Passo Fundo, Braz.
79/E3 Passoré (prov.), Burk.
107/J8 Passos, Braz.
108/C2 Passos, Braz.
36/D3 Passwang (peak), Swi.
33/G4 Passy, Fr.
105/B3 Pastaza (riv.), Peru
86/F3 Pas, The, Mb,Can
106/C3 Pasto, Col.
85/F3 Pastol (bay), Ak,US
34/B1 Pastoriza, Sp.
66/D5 Pasuruan, Indo.
20/H4 Pasvalys, Lith.
42/E4 Pasvalys, Lith.
27/K5 Pásztó, Hun.
40/D2 Pásztó, Hun.
105/B7 Patagonia (reg.), Arg.
109/B6 Patagonia (reg.), Arg.
100/C2 Patagonia, Az,US
66/B4 Patah (peak), Indo.
53/K4 Pātan, India
62/B3 Pātan, India
107/G7 Patanal Matogrossense Nat'l Park, Braz.
98/K7 Patapsco (riv.), Md,US
98/G5 Patchogue, NY,US
24/D3 Patchway, Eng,UK
23/G3 Pateley Bridge, Eng,UK
35/E3 Paterna, Sp.
40/A2 Paternion, Aus.
38/D4 Paternò, It.
89/M3 Paterson, NJ,US
94/F3 Paterson, NJ,US
53/L2 Pathānkot, India
64/C1 Pathānkot, India
90/G5 Pathfinder (res.), Wy,US
63/G5 Pathiu, Thai.
66/A1 Pathiu, Thai.
66/D5 Pati, Indo.
106/C3 Patía, Col.
106/C3 Patía (riv.), Col.
53/L2 Patiāla, India
64/D2 Patiāla, India
67/F2 Patikul, Phil.
62/E2 Patna, India
22/D1 Patna, Sc,UK
67/F1 Patnongon, Phil.
51/E2 Patnos, Turk.
108/A3 Pato Branco, Braz.
109/F2 Pato Branco, Braz.
39/F2 Patos, Alb.
40/D5 Patos, Alb.
107/L5 Patos, Braz.
108/B4 Patos (lake), Braz.
109/E3 Patos (lake), Braz.
107/J7 Patos de Minas, Braz.
108/C1 Patos de Minas, Braz.
18/F5 Pátrai, Gre.
39/G3 Pátrai, Gre.
39/G3 Patrai (gulf), Gre.
23/H4 Patrington, Eng,UK
107/J7 Patrocínio, Braz.
108/C1 Patrocínio, Braz.
37/H3 Patscherkofel (peak), Aus.
63/H6 Pattani, Thai.
65/C5 Pattani, Thai.
66/B2 Pattani, Thai.
65/C3 Pattaya, Thai.
29/G4 Pattensen, Ger.
64/C2 Patti, India
38/D3 Patti, It.
42/E2 Pattijoki, Fin.
24/D1 Pattingham, Eng,UK
64/B2 Pattoki, Pak.
62/C5 Pattukkottai, India
64/G3 Pattukkottai, India
85/N4 Pattullo (mtn.), BC,Can
102/E3 Patuca (mts.), Hon.
103/E3 Patuca (pt.), Hon.
103/E3 Patuca (riv.), Hon.
98/K8 Patuxent (riv.), Md,US
98/K7 Patuxent Nat. Wild. Ref., Md,US
98/J7 Patuxent River St. Park, Md,US
101/E5 Pátzcuaro, Mex.
18/C4 Pau, Fr.
32/C5 Pau, Fr.
35/E1 Pau, Fr.
107/L7 Pau Brasil, Braz.
32/C4 Pauillac, Fr.
106/E5 Pauini (riv.), Braz.
60/B5 Pauksa (peak), Burma
103/E3 Paulaya (riv.), Hon.
98/F4 Paulins (kill), NJ,US
107/L5 Paulo Afonso, Braz.
98/E6 Paulsboro, NJ,US
93/H4 Pauls Valley, Ok,US
96/D3 Pauls Valley, Ok,US
24/D4 Paulton, Eng,UK
60/B5 Paungde, Burma
63/G4 Paungde, Burma
108/D1 Pavão, Braz.
52/E1 Pāveh, Iran
39/J1 Pavel Banya, Bul.
33/H4 Pavia, It
32/D5 Pavie, Fr.
35/F1 Pavie, Fr.
20/G4 Pāvilosta, Lat.
42/D4 Pāvilosta, Lat.
41/G4 Pavlikeni, Bul.
44/C4 Pavlikeni, Bul.
46/H4 Pavlodar, Kaz.
85/F4 Pavlof (vol.), Ak,US
44/E2 Pavlograd, Ukr.
42/J5 Pavlovo, Rus.
43/V7 Pavlovsk, Rus.
44/G2 Pavlovsk, Rus.
45/M1 Pavlovskiy, Kaz.
33/J4 Pavullo nel Frignano, It.
20/J4 Pavy, Rus.
66/D4 Pawan (riv.), Indo.
93/H3 Pawhuska, Ok,US
96/D2 Pawhuska, Ok,US
60/C4 Pawn (riv.), Burma
65/B2 Pawn (riv.), Burma
94/C3 Paw Paw, Mi,US
95/G3 Pawtucket, RI,US
39/F3 Paxoí (isl.), Gre.
39/G3 Paxoí (Yáios), Gre.
85/J3 Paxson, Ak,US
73/D2 Paxton, Austl.
66/B4 Payakumbuh, Indo.
36/C4 Payerne, Swi.
90/D5 Payette (riv.), Id,US
90/D4 Payette, Id,US
92/C1 Payette, Id,US
92/C1 Payette (riv.), Id,US
43/P1 Pay-Khoy (mts.), Rus.
46/G3 Pay-Khoy (mts.), Rus.
87/J3 Payne (lake), Qu,Can
73/C3 Paynesville, Austl.
109/E3 Paysandú, Uru.
32/D2 Pays de Caux (reg.), Fr.
19/T9 Pays de France (plain), Fr.
32/C3 Pays de la Loire (reg.), Fr.
92/E4 Payson, Az,US
92/E2 Payson, Ut,US
102/D3 Paz (riv.), ESal., Guat.
51/G4 Pāzanān, Iran
50/D1 Pazar, Turk.
50/D2 Pazarcık, Turk.
52/C1 Pazarcık, Turk.
39/J1 Pazardzhik, Bul.
41/G4 Pazardzhik, Bul.
44/C4 Pazardzhik, Bul.
44/D5 Pazaryeri, Turk.
33/K4 Pazin, Cro.
40/A3 Pazin, Cro.
108/A2 Peabiru, Braz.
90/D1 Peace (riv.), Ab, BC,Can
84/F4 Peace (riv.), Can.
86/E3 Peace (riv.), Ab,Can
56/C3 Peace Memorial Park, Japan
86/E3 Peace River, Ab,Can
90/D1 Peace River, Ab,Can
90/D3 Peachland, BC,Can
97/G3 Peachtree City, Ga,US
23/G5 Peak District Nat'l Park, Eng,UK
34/D4 Peal de Becerro, Sp.

166

Pearl – Pic de

88/W13 **Pearl** (har.), Hi,US
89/J5 **Pearl** (riv.), La, Ms,US
93/K4 **Pearl** (riv.), Ms,US
97/F3 **Pearl,** Ms,US
101/F2 **Pearl,** Tx,US
69/H2 **Pearl and Hermes** (reef), Hi.,US
99/G6 **Pearl Beach,** Mi,US
88/W13 **Pearl City,** Hi,US
61/G4 **Pearl River** (estuary), China, Hong Kong
98/F4 **Pearl River,** NY,US
101/F2 **Pearsall,** Tx,US
93/H5 **Pearsall,** Tx,US
96/D4 **Pearsall,** Tx,US
87/R7 **Peary** (chan.), NW,Can
93/H4 **Pease** (riv.), Tx,US
82/G4 **Pebane,** Moz.
25/E2 **Pebworth,** Eng,UK
39/G1 **Peć,** Yugo.
40/E4 **Peć,** Yugo.
37/E5 **Peccia,** Swi.
35/G1 **Pech de Guillaument** (mtn.), Fr.
20/J1 **Pechenga,** Rus.
19/J2 **Pechora,** Rus.
19/J2 **Pechora** (riv.), Rus.
43/M1 **Pechora** (bay), Rus.
43/M2 **Pechora** (riv.), Rus.
43/N2 **Pechora,** Rus.
46/F3 **Pechora,** Rus.
46/F3 **Pechora** (riv.), Rus.
93/G5 **Pecos** (riv.), NM, Tx,US
101/E2 **Pecos** (riv.), Tx.,NM,US
88/F5 **Pecos,** Tx,US
93/G5 **Pecos,** Tx,US
96/C4 **Pecos,** Tx,US
93/F4 **Pecos Nat'l Mon.,** NM,US
30/C2 **Pecq,** Belg.
30/C3 **Pecquencourt,** Fr.
18/E4 **Pécs,** Hun.
40/D2 **Pécs,** Hun.
103/F5 **Pedasí,** Pan.
71/H8 **Pedder** (lake), Austl.
73/C4 **Pedder** (lake), Austl.
103/E4 **Pedernal** (pt.), Nic.
103/J2 **Pedernales,** DRep.
104/D3 **Pedernales,** DRep.
100/D2 **Pedernales,** Mex.
101/F2 **Pedernales** (riv.), Tx,US
104/F5 **Pedernales,** Ven.
106/F2 **Pedernales,** Ven.
108/B2 **Pederneiras,** Braz.
98/C3 **Pedley,** Ca,US
107/K7 **Pedra Azul,** Braz.
74/K10 **Pedra Lume,** CpV.
104/D5 **Pedregal,** Ven.
35/F3 **Pedreguer,** Sp.
107/K5 **Pedreiras,** Braz.
100/E3 **Pedriceña,** Mex.
98/E6 **Pedricktown,** NJ,US
62/D6 **Pedro** (pt.), SrL.
101/H5 **Pedro Antonio Santos,** Mex.
102/D2 **Pedro Antonio Santos,** Mex.
85/H4 **Pedro Bay,** Ak,US
103/F1 **Pedro Betancourt,** Cuba
106/E3 **Pedro II,** Braz.
107/G8 **Pedro Juan Caballero,** Par.
109/E1 **Pedro Juan Caballero,** Par.
108/C1 **Pedro Leopoldo,** Braz.
109/D4 **Pedro Luro,** Arg.
101/F4 **Pedro Montoya,** Mex.
102/B1 **Pedro Montoya,** Mex.
108/A4 **Pedro Osório,** Braz.
72/F6 **Peel** (isl.), Austl.
86/G1 **Peel** (sound), NW,Can
95/G8 **Peel** (co.), On,Can
85/L2 **Peel** (riv.), Yk,Can
86/C2 **Peel** (riv.), Yk,Can
22/D3 **Peel,** IM,UK
23/F1 **Peel Fell** (mtn.), Eng,UK
28/C6 **Peer,** Belg.
31/E1 **Peer,** Belg.
71/R11 **Pegasus** (bay), NZ
26/F4 **Pegnitz,** Ger.
26/F4 **Pegnitz** (riv.), Ger.
33/J2 **Pegnitz,** Ger.
33/J2 **Pegnitz** (riv.), Ger.
35/E3 **Pego,** Sp.
23/G1 **Pegswood,** Eng,UK
60/B4 **Pegu** (mts.), Burma
60/C5 **Pegu,** Burma
60/C5 **Pegu** (riv.), Burma
63/G4 **Pegu,** Burma
63/G4 **Pegu** (div.), Burma
65/B2 **Pegu,** Burma
65/B2 **Pegu** (mts.), Burma
65/B2 **Pegu** (riv.), Burma
60/B5 **Pegu** (Bago) (div.), Burma
65/B2 **Pegu** (Bago) (div.), Burma
25/H4 **Pegwell** (bay), Eng,UK
39/K2 **Pehlivanköy,** Turk.
41/H5 **Pehlivanköy,** Turk.
109/D4 **Pehuajó,** Arg.
54/G4 **Peijiachuankou,** China
59/B3 **Peijiachuankou,** China
61/J4 **Peinanchu** (mtn.), Tai.
26/F2 **Peine,** Ger.
29/H4 **Peine,** Ger.
46/C4 **Peipus** (lake), Rus.,Est.
20/H4 **Peipus** (lake), Est.,Rus.
42/E4 **Peipus** (lake), Est., Rus.
18/F3 **Peipus** (lake), Rus.
37/H2 **Peissenburg,** Ger.
61/J4 **Peitawu** (peak), Tai.
37/G2 **Peiting,** Ger.
107/H6 **Peixe** (riv.), Braz.
108/B2 **Peixe** (riv.), Braz.
108/B3 **Peixe** (riv.), Braz.
59/D4 **Pei Xian,** China
108/C2 **Peixoto** (res.), Braz.
66/C5 **Pekalongan,** Indo.
66/B3 **Pekan,** Malay.
66/B3 **Pekan Nanas,** Malay.
43/Y9 **Pekhora** (riv.), Rus.
91/L5 **Pekin,** Il,US
93/K2 **Pekin,** Il,US
94/B3 **Pekin,** Il,US
38/C5 **Pelagie** (isls.), It.
76/H1 **Pelagie** (isls.), Italy
40/F3 **Peleaga, Vîrful** (peak), Rom.
44/B3 **Peleaga, Vîrful** (peak), Rom.
94/D3 **Pelee** (pt.), Can
87/H4 **Pelee** (pt.), On,Can
95/D3 **Pelee** (isl.), On,Can
104/F4 **Pelée** (mtn.), Mart.
95/R9 **Pelham,** On,Can
97/G3 **Pelham,** Al,US
27/H4 **Pelhřimov,** Czh.
33/L2 **Pelhřimov,** Czh.
90/E2 **Pelican** (mts.), Ab,Can
91/H2 **Pelican** (lake), Sk,Can
85/L4 **Pelican,** Ak,US
91/H2 **Pelican Narrows,** Sk,Can
78/A4 **Pelindã, Ponta de** (pt.), GBis.
39/G2 **Pelister** (peak), Macd.
40/E5 **Pelister** (peak), Macd.
39/G2 **Pelister Nat'l Park,** Macd.
40/E5 **Pelister Nat'l Park,** Macd.
40/C4 **Pelješac** (pen.), Cro.
38/E1 **Peljesec** (pen.), Cro.
39/H2 **Pélla,** Gre.
40/F5 **Pélla,** Gre.
40/F5 **Pélla** (ruins), Gre.
44/B4 **Pélla** (ruins), Gre.
99/P14 **Pell Lake,** Wi,US
20/H2 **Pello,** Swe.
42/E2 **Pello,** Swe.
86/H2 **Pelly** (bay), NW,Can
85/M3 **Pelly** (riv.), Yk,Can
86/C2 **Pelly** (riv.), Yk,Can
86/H2 **Pelly Bay,** NW,Can
85/L3 **Pelly Crossing,** Yk,Can
86/C2 **Pelly Crossing,** Yk,Can
39/G3 **Peloponnisos** (reg.), Gre.
38/D3 **Peloritani** (mts.), It.
108/A4 **Pelotas,** Braz.
108/B3 **Pelotas** (riv.), Braz.
109/F2 **Pelotas** (riv.), Braz.
109/F3 **Pelotas,** Braz.
27/K2 **Pelplin,** Pol.
67/F4 **Pemali** (cape), Indo.
67/F5 **Pemali** (cape), Indo.
66/A3 **Pematangsiantar,** Indo.
82/H3 **Pemba,** Moz.
75/G5 **Pemba** (isl.), Tanz.
82/H2 **Pemba** (isl.), Tanz.
90/C3 **Pemberton,** BC,Can
98/F6 **Pemberton,** NJ,US
90/E2 **Pembina** (riv.), Ab,Can
89/G2 **Pembina,** ND,US
91/J3 **Pembina,** ND,US
87/J4 **Pembroke,** On,Can
89/L2 **Pembroke,** On,Can
94/E2 **Pembroke,** On,Can
24/B3 **Pembroke,** Wal,UK
24/B3 **Pembroke Dock,** Wal,UK
24/A3 **Pembrokeshire Coast Nat'l Park,** UK
19/P8 **Pembury,** Eng,UK
25/G4 **Pembury,** Eng,UK
103/F4 **Peña Blanca** (mtn.), Pan.
34/A2 **Penafiel,** Port.
34/C2 **Peñafiel,** Sp.
34/D2 **Peñalara** (mtn.), Sp.
107/J4 **Penalva,** Braz.
34/B2 **Penamacor,** Port.
107/H8 **Penápolis,** Braz.
108/B2 **Penápolis,** Braz.
34/C2 **Peñaranda de Bracamonte,** Sp.
98/E5 **Pen Argyl,** Pa,US
35/E2 **Peñarroya** (mtn.), Sp.
34/C3 **Peñarroya-Pueblonuevo,** Sp.
24/C4 **Penarth,** Wal,UK
34/C1 **Peñas** (cape), Sp.
93/F4 **Peñasco** (dry riv.), NM,US
39/L6 **Pendelikón** (mt.), Gre.
78/C4 **Pendembu,** SLeo.
51/N7 **Pendik,** Turk.
79/F4 **Pendjari** (riv.), Ben., Burk.
76/F5 **Pendjari Nat'l Park,** Ben.
79/F4 **Pendjari Nat'l Park,** Ben.
23/F4 **Pendle** (hill), Eng,UK
86/E4 **Pendleton,** Or,US
88/C2 **Pendleton,** Or,US
90/D4 **Pendleton,** Or,US
90/D3 **Pend Oreille** (riv.), Id, Wa,US
90/D4 **Pend Oreille** (lake), Id,US
34/A2 **Peneda-Gerês Nat'l Park,** Port.
107/L6 **Penedo,** Braz.
24/C1 **Penegoes,** Wal,UK
94/E2 **Penetanguishene,** On,Can
53/L4 **Penganga** (riv.), India
62/C4 **Penganga** (riv.), India
19/N7 **Penge,** Eng,UK
61/H4 **Penghu** (isl.), Tai.
59/E3 **Penglai,** China
73/C4 **Penguin,** Austl.
60/D2 **Peng Xian,** China
108/B3 **Penha,** Braz.
90/E2 **Penhold,** Ab,Can
34/C4 **Penibético** (range), Sp.
34/A3 **Peniche,** Port.
104/F5 **Península de Paria Nat'l Park,** Ven.
35/F2 **Peñíscola,** Sp.
107/J5 **Penitente** (mts.), Braz.
101/E4 **Pénjamo,** Mex.
23/F6 **Penkridge,** Eng,UK
24/D1 **Penkridge,** Eng,UK
22/E5 **Penmaenmawr,** Wal,UK
32/A3 **Penmarch,** Fr.
32/A3 **Penmarc'h, Pointe de** (pt.), Fr.
38/D1 **Penna, Punta della** (cape), It.
40/B4 **Penna, Punta della** (cape), It.
38/C1 **Penne,** It.
40/C5 **Penne** (pt.), It.
62/C5 **Penner** (riv.), India
98/E5 **Penn Forest** (res.), Pa,US
94/E3 **Penn Hills,** Pa,US
33/G4 **Pennine Alps** (range), It., Swi.
36/D6 **Pennine Alps** (mts.), It., Swi.
23/F2 **Pennine Chain** (range), Eng,UK
33/K5 **Pennino** (peak), It.
98/E6 **Pennsauken,** NJ,US
98/E5 **Pennsburg,** Pa,US
98/E6 **Penns Grove,** NJ,US
87/H4 **Pennsylvania** (state), US
89/L3 **Pennsylvania** (state), US
94/E3 **Pennsylvania** (state), US
87/S7 **Penny** (str.), NW,Can
94/E3 **Penn Yan,** NY,US
98/E5 **Pennypack** (cr.), Pa,US
94/G2 **Penobscot** (riv.), Me,US
70/G7 **Penola,** Austl.
73/B3 **Penola,** Austl.
100/D3 **Peñón Blanco,** Mex.
70/E6 **Penong,** Austl.
103/F4 **Penonomé,** Pan.
22/E1 **Penpont,** Sc,UK
22/D5 **Penrhyn Mawr** (pt.), Wal,UK
22/D6 **Penrhyn Mawr** (pt.), Wal,UK
69/K5 **Penrhyn** (Tongareva) (atoll), Cookls.
72/G8 **Penrith,** Austl.
23/F2 **Penrith,** Eng,UK
24/A6 **Penryn,** Eng,UK
83/X **Pensacola** (mts.), Ant.
89/J5 **Pensacola,** Fl,US
97/G4 **Pensacola,** Fl,US
91/G3 **Pense,** Sk,Can
73/B3 **Penshurst,** Austl.
19/P8 **Penshurst,** Eng,UK
67/E3 **Pensiangan,** Malay.
24/B5 **Pensilva,** Eng,UK
98/J8 **Pentagon,** Va,US
68/F6 **Pentecost** (isl.), Van.
41/H3 **Penteleu** (peak), Rom.
44/C3 **Penteleu** (peak), Rom.
36/C4 **Penthalaz,** Swi.
86/E4 **Penticton,** BC,Can
88/C2 **Penticton,** BC,Can
90/D3 **Penticton,** BC,Can
24/B5 **Pentire** (pt.), UK
72/B3 **Pentland,** Austl.
24/C3 **Pentyrch,** Wal,UK
100/E2 **Penwell,** Tx,US
24/A6 **Penwith** (pen.), Eng,UK
23/E6 **Pen-y-Cae,** Wal,UK
23/F3 **Pen-y-Ghent** (mtn.), Eng,UK
22/E5 **Pen-y-Gogarth** (pt.), Wal,UK
24/C2 **Pen y Gurnos** (mtn.), Wal,UK
19/H3 **Penza,** Rus.
45/H1 **Penza,** Rus.
46/E4 **Penza,** Rus.
24/A6 **Penzance,** Eng,UK
45/G1 **Penza Obl.,** Rus.
26/F5 **Penzberg,** Ger.
33/J3 **Penzberg,** Ger.
37/H2 **Penzberg,** Ger.
47/S3 **Penzhina** (bay), Rus.
47/S3 **Penzhina** (riv.), Rus.
37/G1 **Penzing,** Ger.
26/G2 **Penzlin,** Ger.
89/J3 **Peoria,** Il,US
91/L5 **Peoria,** Il,US
93/K2 **Peoria,** Il,US
94/B3 **Peoria,** Il,US
101/E4 **Peotillos,** Mex.
103/F1 **Pepe** (cape), Cuba
88/U11 **Pepeekeo,** Hi,US
88/U11 **Pepeekeo** (pt.), Hi,US
78/B4 **Pepel,** SLeo.
31/E2 **Pepinster,** Belg.
40/D5 **Peqin,** Alb.
71/G2 **Pera** (head), Austl.
66/B4 **Perabumulih,** Indo.
35/M9 **Perales** (riv.), Sp.
34/E1 **Peralta,** Sp.
39/J5 **Pérama,** Gre.
64/G3 **Perambalūr,** India
87/K4 **Percé,** Qu,Can
89/P2 **Percé,** Qu,Can
95/H1 **Percé,** Qu,Can
36/C6 **Percée, Pointe** (peak), Fr.
32/D2 **Perche** (hills), Fr.
27/J4 **Perchtoldsdorf,** Aus.
70/C4 **Percival** (lakes), Austl.
71/J4 **Percy** (isls.), Austl.
72/C3 **Percy** (isls.), Austl.
80/Q13 **Perdekop,** SAfr.
39/G3 **Pérdhika,** Gre.
32/D5 **Perdido** (mtn.), Sp.
35/F1 **Perdido** (mtn.), Sp.
27/M4 **Perechin,** Ukr.
72/D4 **Peregian Beach,** Austl.
106/C3 **Pereira,** Col.
108/B2 **Pereira Barreto,** Braz.
35/F2 **Perelló,** Sp.
42/H5 **Peremyshl',** Rus.
27/H4 **Perg,** Aus.
109/D3 **Pergamino,** Arg.
50/A2 **Pergamum** (ruins), Turk.
37/H5 **Pergine Valsugana,** It.
33/K5 **Pergola,** It.
87/J3 **Péribonca** (riv.), Qu,Can
89/M2 **Péribonca** (riv.), Qu,Can
95/G1 **Péribonca** (lake), Qu,Can
95/G1 **Péribonca** (riv.), Qu,Can
103/F1 **Perico,** Cuba
100/D3 **Pericos,** Mex.
100/D4 **Pericos,** Mex.
18/D4 **Périgueux,** Fr.
32/D4 **Périgueux,** Fr.
106/D2 **Perijá** (mts.), Col., Ven.
103/H4 **Perijá, Sierra de** (range), Ven., Col.
52/D6 **Perim** (isl.), Yem.
65/C5 **Peringat,** Malay.
39/J3 **Peristéra** (isl.), Gre.
39/L6 **Peristéri,** Gre.
109/B6 **Perito Moreno,** Arg.
109/B6 **Perito Moreno Nat'l Park,** Arg.
62/C5 **Periyakulam,** India
64/F3 **Periyakulam,** India
64/F3 **Periyar** (riv.), India
64/F4 **Periyar Wild. Sanct.,** India
98/E5 **Perkasie,** Pa,US
98/E5 **Perkiomen** (cr.), Pa,US
31/F5 **Perl,** Ger.
103/F3 **Perlas** (lag.), Nic.
103/G4 **Perlas** (arch.), Pan.
103/F3 **Perlas, Punta** (pt.), Nic.
26/F2 **Perleberg,** Ger.
40/E3 **Perlez,** Yugo.
65/B5 **Perlis** (state), Malay.
19/J3 **Perm',** Rus.
43/N4 **Perm',** Rus.
46/F4 **Perm',** Rus.
43/M4 **Perm' Obl.,** Rus.
32/F4 **Pernes-les-Fontaines,** Fr.
18/F4 **Pernik,** Bul.
39/H1 **Pernik,** Bul.
40/F4 **Pernik,** Bul.
42/D3 **Perniö,** Fin.
26/B4 **Péronne,** Fr.
30/B4 **Péronne,** Fr.
32/E2 **Péronne,** Fr.
101/F5 **Perote,** Mex.
101/M7 **Perote,** Mex.
102/B2 **Perote,** Mex.
43/X9 **Perovo,** Rus.
18/D4 **Perpignan,** Fr.
32/E5 **Perpignan,** Fr.
35/G1 **Perpignan,** Fr.
30/A5 **Perriers-sur-Andelle,** Fr.
36/B4 **Perrigny,** Fr.
98/C3 **Perris,** Ca,US
98/C3 **Perris** (res.), Ca,US
103/G1 **Perros** (bay), Cuba
32/B2 **Perros-Guirec,** Fr.
95/N7 **Perrot** (isl.), Qu,Can
86/F2 **Perry** (riv.), NW,Can
89/K5 **Perry,** Fl,US
97/H4 **Perry,** Fl,US
97/H3 **Perry,** Ga,US
93/H3 **Perry,** Ok,US
96/D2 **Perry,** Ok,US
98/K7 **Perry Hall,** Md,US
93/G3 **Perryton,** Tx,US
96/C2 **Perryton,** Tx,US
85/G4 **Perryville,** Ak,US
93/K3 **Perryville,** Mo,US
94/B4 **Perryville,** Mo,US
97/F2 **Perryville,** Mo,US
19/S9 **Persan,** Fr.
26/B4 **Persan,** Fr.
30/B5 **Persan,** Fr.
32/E2 **Persan,** Paris
51/H4 **Persepolis** (ruins), Iran
52/F3 **Persepolis** (ruins), Iran
77/R2 **Persepolis** (ruins), Iran
24/D2 **Pershore,** Eng,UK
46/E7 **Persian** (gulf), Asia
48/D7 **Persian** (gulf), Asia
52/E3 **Persian** (gulf), Asia
77/Q2 **Persian** (gulf), Asia
50/D2 **Pertek,** Turk.
70/B6 **Perth,** Austl.
73/C4 **Perth,** Austl.
94/E2 **Perth,** On,Can
21/D2 **Perth,** Sc,UK
98/F5 **Perth Amboy,** NJ,US
52/C5 **Pertokar,** Eth.
32/F5 **Pertuis,** Fr.
35/H1 **Pertuis,** Fr.
32/C3 **Pertuis Breton** (inlet), Fr.
38/A2 **Pertusato** (cape), Fr.
105/B3 **Peru**
106/C5 **Peru**
91/L5 **Peru,** Il,US
93/K2 **Peru,** Il,US
94/B3 **Peru,** Il,US
94/C3 **Peru,** In,US
40/D4 **Perućačko** (lake), Bosn.
18/E4 **Perugia,** It.
33/K5 **Perugia,** It.
38/C1 **Perugia,** It.
108/C3 **Peruíbe,** Braz.
64/F3 **Perumpāvūr,** India
41/G4 **Perushtitsa,** Bul.
26/B3 **Péruwelz,** Belg.
30/C2 **Péruwelz,** Belg.
32/E1 **Péruwelz,** Belg.
50/E2 **Pervari,** Turk.
43/J5 **Pervomaysk,** Rus.
45/G1 **Pervomaysk,** Rus.
18/G4 **Pervomaysk,** Ukr.
41/K1 **Pervomaysk,** Ukr.
44/D2 **Pervomaysk,** Ukr.
46/D5 **Pervomaysk,** Ukr.
54/H1 **Pervomayskiy,** Rus.
43/N4 **Pervoural'sk,** Rus.
46/F4 **Pervoural'sk,** Rus.
31/D2 **Perwez,** Belg.
36/D3 **Péry,** Swi.
66/B4 **Pesagi** (peak), Indo.
33/K5 **Pesaro,** It.
61/H4 **Pescadore** (chan.), Tai.
18/E4 **Pescara,** It.
38/D1 **Pescara,** It.
40/B4 **Pescara,** It.
41/J1 **Peschanka,** Ukr.
45/J4 **Peschanyy, Mys** (cape), Kaz.
38/E2 **Peschici,** It.
36/C4 **Peseux,** Swi.
43/L2 **Pesha** (riv.), Rus.
53/K2 **Peshāwar,** Pak.
40/E5 **Peshkopi,** Alb.
39/J1 **Peshtera,** Bul.
41/G4 **Peshtera,** Bul.
91/M4 **Peshtigo,** Wi,US
94/B2 **Peshtigo** (riv.), Wi,US
94/C2 **Peshtigo,** Wi,US
44/F1 **Peski,** Rus.
36/B3 **Pesmes,** Fr.
34/B2 **Peso da Régua,** Port.
32/C4 **Pessac,** Fr.
32/D5 **Pessons, Pic dels** (peak), And.
35/F1 **Pessons, Pic dels** (peak), And.
27/K5 **Pest** (co.), Hun.
40/D2 **Pest** (co.), Hun.
43/X8 **Pestovkoye** (res.), Rus.
42/G4 **Pestovo,** Rus.
49/D3 **Petaḩ Tiqwa,** Isr.
49/F7 **Petaḩ Tiqwa,** Isr.
50/C3 **Petaḩ Tiqwa,** Isr.
97/F4 **Petal,** Ms,US
39/J4 **Petalión** (gulf), Gre.
39/M6 **Petalión** (gulf), Gre.
99/J10 **Petaluma,** Ca,US
99/J10 **Petaluma** (riv.), Ca,US
31/E4 **Pétange,** Lux.
104/E5 **Petare,** Ven.
106/E1 **Petare,** Ven.
39/G3 **Pétas,** Gre.
100/D3 **Petatlán** (riv.), Mex.
82/F3 **Petauke,** Zam.
94/E2 **Petawana** (riv.), On,Can
94/E2 **Petawawa,** On,Can
101/H5 **Petcacab,** Mex.
102/D2 **Petcacab,** Mex.
102/D2 **Peten Itzá** (lake), Guat.
91/L4 **Petenwell** (lake), Wi,US
70/F6 **Peterborough,** Austl.
87/J4 **Peterborough,** On,Can
89/L3 **Peterborough,** On,Can
94/E2 **Peterborough,** On,Can
25/F1 **Peterborough,** Eng,UK
21/E2 **Peterhead,** Sc,UK
83/T **Peter I** (isl.), Ant.
23/G2 **Peterlee,** Eng,UK
90/F1 **Peter Pond** (lake), Sk,Can
86/F3 **Peter Pond** (lake), Sk,Can
85/M4 **Petersburg,** Ak,US
86/C3 **Petersburg,** Ak,US
89/L4 **Petersburg,** Va,US
94/E4 **Petersburg,** Va,US
97/J2 **Petersburg,** Va,US
25/F5 **Petersfield,** Eng,UK
26/E2 **Petershagen,** Ger.
29/F4 **Petershagen,** Ger.
37/H1 **Petershausen,** Ger.
93/F3 **Peterson** (A.F.B.), Co,US
96/B2 **Peterson** (A.F.B.), Co,US
27/L4 **Petervására,** Hun.
38/E3 **Petilia Policastro,** It.
103/H2 **Pétionville,** Haiti
104/C3 **Pétionville,** Haiti
95/H2 **Petitcodiac,** NB,Can
103/H2 **Petite Rivière de l'Artibonite,** Haiti
31/F5 **Petite-Rosselle,** Fr.
103/H2 **Petit Goâve,** Haiti
30/C6 **Petit Marin** (riv.), Fr.
95/K1 **Petit Mécatina** (riv.), Qu,Can
87/K3 **Petit Mécatina** (riv.), Qu,Can
26/B4 **Petit Morin** (riv.), Fr.
32/E2 **Petit Morin** (riv.), Fr.
36/B4 **Petit-Noir,** Fr.
19/S9 **Petit Rosne** (riv.), Fr.
20/J3 **Petkeljärven Nat'l Park,** Fin.
42/F3 **Petkeljärven Nat'l Park,** Fin.
53/K4 **Petlād,** India
62/B3 **Petlād,** India
101/F5 **Petlalcingo,** Mex.
102/B2 **Petlalcingo,** Mex.
101/H4 **Peto,** Mex.
102/D1 **Peto,** Mex.
89/K2 **Petoskey,** Mi,US
94/C2 **Petoskey,** Mi,US
49/D4 **Petra** (ruins), Jor.
50/C4 **Petra** (ruins), Jor.
52/C2 **Petra** (ruins), Jor.
47/M2 **Petra** (isls.), Rus.
35/E3 **Petrel,** Sp.
38/C2 **Petrella** (peak), It.
39/H2 **Petrich,** Bul.
41/F5 **Petrich,** Bul.
44/B4 **Petrich,** Bul.
88/E4 **Petrified Forest Nat'l Park,** Az,US
92/E4 **Petrified Forest Nat'l Park,** Az,US
41/F3 **Petrila,** Rom.
20/J4 **Petrodvorets,** Rus.
42/F4 **Petrodvorets,** Rus.
43/U7 **Petrodvorets,** Rus.
43/V7 **Petrograd,** Rus.
39/H1 **Petrokhanski Prokhod** (pass), Bul.
41/F4 **Petrokhanski Prokhod** (pass), Bul.
43/W7 **Petrokrepost** (bay), Rus.
107/K5 **Petrolina,** Braz.
46/G4 **Petropavlovsk,** Kaz.
47/R4 **Petropavlovsk-Kamchatskiy,** Rus.
107/K8 **Petrópolis,** Braz.
108/D2 **Petrópolis,** Braz.
109/H1 **Petrópolis,** Braz.
41/F3 **Petroşani,** Rom.
44/B3 **Petroşani,** Rom.
40/D3 **Petrovaradin,** Yugo.
41/K2 **Petrovka,** Ukr.
45/H1 **Petrovsk,** Rus.
47/L4 **Petrovsk-Zabaykal'skiy,** Rus.
54/F1 **Petrovsk-Zabaykal'skiy,** Rus.
18/G2 **Petrozavodsk,** Rus.
42/G3 **Petrozavodsk,** Rus.
46/D3 **Petrozavodsk,** Rus.
23/F2 **Petterill** (riv.), Eng,UK
101/F2 **Pettus,** Tx,US
25/F5 **Petworth,** Eng,UK
40/A2 **Petzeck** (peak), Aus.
85/G4 **Peulik** (mt.), Ak,US
25/G5 **Pevensey,** Eng,UK
32/D1 **Pevensey,** Eng,UK
99/P13 **Pewaukee,** Wi,US
99/P13 **Pewaukee** (lake), Wi,US
25/E4 **Pewsey,** Eng,UK
51/G3 **Peyk,** Iran
32/C5 **Peyrehorade,** Fr.
43/K2 **Peza** (riv.), Rus.
32/E5 **Pézenas,** Fr.
35/G1 **Pézenas,** Fr.
37/G1 **Pfaffenhausen,** Ger.
26/F4 **Pfaffenhofen an der Ilm,** Ger.
33/J2 **Pfaffenhofen an der Ilm,** Ger.
37/G1 **Pfaffenhofen an der Roth,** Ger.
31/G6 **Pfaffenhoffen,** Fr.
37/E3 **Pfäffikon,** Swi.
36/D3 **Pfaffnau,** Swi.
37/E1 **Pfalzgrafenweiler,** Ger.
31/G5 **Pfälzwald** (for.), Ger.
29/G6 **Pfieffe** (riv.), Ger.
26/E4 **Pforzheim,** Ger.
33/H2 **Pforzheim,** Ger.
37/F1 **Pfronstetten,** Ger.
26/F5 **Pfronten,** Ger.
37/G2 **Pfronten,** Ger.
37/G4 **Pfroslkopf** (peak), Aus.
37/F2 **Pfullendorf,** Ger.
33/J3 **Pfunds,** Aus.
37/G4 **Pfunds,** Aus.
26/E4 **Pfungstadt,** Ger.
33/H2 **Pfungstadt,** Ger.
64/C2 **Phagwāra,** India
60/D4 **Phak** (riv.), Laos
65/C1 **Phak** (riv.), Laos
30/C2 **Phalempin,** Fr.
64/B1 **Phālia,** Pak.
53/K3 **Phalodi,** India
62/B2 **Phalodi,** India
31/G6 **Phalsbourg,** Fr.
60/C5 **Phan,** Thai.
63/H5 **Phanat Nikhom,** Thai.
65/C3 **Phanat Nikhom,** Thai.
63/H6 **Phangan** (isl.), Thai.
65/B4 **Phangan** (isl.), Thai.
66/B2 **Phangan** (isl.), Thai.
65/C3 **Phang Hoei** (range), Thai.
63/G6 **Phangnga,** Thai.
65/B4 **Phangnga,** Thai.
66/A2 **Phangnga,** Thai.
63/G6 **Phanom,** Thai.
66/A2 **Phanom,** Thai.
63/H5 **Phanom Dongrak** (mts.), Camb.,Thai.
65/C3 **Phanom Dongrak** (mts.), Camb., Thai.
63/J5 **Phan Rang,** Viet.
65/E4 **Phan Rang,** Viet.
66/C1 **Phan Rang,** Viet.
48/K8 **Phan Thiet,** Viet.
63/J5 **Phan Thiet,** Viet.
65/E4 **Phan Thiet,** Viet.
66/C1 **Phan Thiet,** Viet.
101/F3 **Pharr,** Tx,US
96/D5 **Pharr,** Tx,US
60/E4 **Phat Diem,** Viet.
63/H6 **Phatthalung,** Thai.
65/C5 **Phatthalung,** Thai.
66/B2 **Phatthalung,** Thai.
60/D5 **Phaya Fo** (peak), Thai.
65/C2 **Phaya Fo** (peak), Thai.
60/C5 **Phayao,** Thai.
63/G4 **Phayao,** Thai.
65/B2 **Phayao,** Thai.
97/G3 **Phenix City,** Al,US
80/C2 **Phepane** (dry riv.), SAfr.
63/G5 **Phet Buri,** Thai.
65/B3 **Phet Buri,** Thai.
63/H4 **Phetchabun,** Thai.
65/C2 **Phetchabun,** Thai.
63/J5 **Phiafai,** Laos
63/H4 **Phichai,** Thai.
63/H4 **Phichit,** Thai.
65/C2 **Phichit,** Thai.
97/F3 **Philadelphia,** Ms,US
89/L4 **Philadelphia,** Pa,US
94/F4 **Philadelphia,** Pa,US
98/E6 **Philadelphia,** Pa,US
98/E6 **Philadelphia** (int'l arpt.), Pa,US
52/B4 **Philae** (ruins), Egypt
91/H4 **Philip,** SD,US
93/G1 **Philip,** SD,US
30/D3 **Philippeville,** Belg.
94/D4 **Philippi,** WV,US
97/H2 **Philippi,** WV,US
68/B3 **Philippine** (sea)
48/M8 **Philippine** (sea)
48/M8 **Philippines**
61/H5 **Philippines**
67/F2 **Philippines**
68/B3 **Philippines**
90/E4 **Philipsburg,** Mt,US
28/B5 **Philipsdam** (dam), Neth.
22/A5 **Philipstown,** Ire.
64/C2 **Phillaur,** India
93/H3 **Phillipsburg,** Ks,US
96/D2 **Phillipsburg,** Ks,US
98/E5 **Phillipsburg,** NJ,US
65/C3 **Phimai** (ruins), Thai.
60/D5 **Phitsanulok,** Thai.
63/H4 **Phitsanulok,** Thai.
65/C2 **Phitsanulok,** Thai.
66/B1 **Phnom Penh** (Phnum Penh) (cap.), Camb.
63/H5 **Phnom Penh** (Phnum Penh) (cap.), Camb.
65/D4 **Phnom Penh** (Phnum Penh) (cap.), Camb.
63/H5 **Phnum Penh** (Phnom Penh) (cap.), Camb.
65/D4 **Phnum Penh** (Phnom Penh) (cap.), Camb.
66/B1 **Phnum Penh** (Phnom Penh) (cap.), Camb.
65/D3 **Phnum Tbeng Meanchey,** Camb.
63/H6 **Pho** (pt.), Thai.
65/C5 **Pho** (pt.), Thai.
66/B2 **Pho** (pt.), Thai.
69/H5 **Phoenix** (isls.), Kiri.
88/D5 **Phoenix** (cap.), Az,US
92/D4 **Phoenix** (cap.), Az,US
94/D4 **Phoenix** (peak), NC,US
97/H2 **Phoenix** (peak), NC,US
22/B5 **Phoenix Park,** Ire.
69/H5 **Phoenix** (Rawaki) (atoll), Kiri.
98/E5 **Phoenixville,** Pa,US
60/D4 **Phongsali,** Laos
63/H3 **Phongsali,** Laos
65/C1 **Phongsali,** Laos
60/D5 **Phou Bia** (peak), Laos
63/H4 **Phou Bia** (peak), Laos
65/C2 **Phou Bia** (peak), Laos
60/E5 **Phou Huatt** (peak), Viet.
63/H4 **Phou Huatt** (peak), Viet.
65/D2 **Phou Huatt** (peak), Viet.
60/D4 **Phou Loi** (peak), Laos
63/H3 **Phou Loi** (peak), Laos
65/C1 **Phou Loi** (peak), Laos
60/E5 **Phou Xai Lai Leng** (peak), Laos
63/H4 **Phou Xai Lai Leng** (peak), Laos
65/D2 **Phou Xai Lai Leng** (peak), Laos
60/D5 **Phrae,** Thai.
63/H4 **Phrae,** Thai.
65/C2 **Phrae,** Thai.
63/H5 **Phra Nakhon Si Ayutthaya,** Thai.
65/C3 **Phra Nakhon Si Ayutthaya,** Thai.
65/B4 **Phra Thong** (isl.), Thai.
65/C4 **Phsar Ream,** Camb.
63/J4 **Phuc Loi,** Viet.
65/D2 **Phuc Loi,** Viet.
60/E4 **Phuc Yen,** Viet.
63/J3 **Phuc Yen,** Viet.
60/D5 **Phu Hin Rong Kla Nat'l Park,** Thai.
65/C2 **Phu Hin Rong Kla Nat'l Park,** Thai.
63/J5 **Phu Hoi,** Viet.
65/E4 **Phu Hoi,** Viet.
66/C1 **Phu Hoi,** Viet.
63/G6 **Phuket,** Thai.
63/G6 **Phuket** (isl.), Thai.
65/B5 **Phuket,** Thai.
65/B5 **Phuket** (isl.), Thai.
66/A2 **Phuket,** Thai.
66/A2 **Phuket** (isl.), Thai.
60/D5 **Phu Kradung,** Thai.
60/D5 **Phu Kradung Nat'l Park,** Thai.
65/C2 **Phu Kradung Nat'l Park,** Thai.
62/D3 **Phulabāni,** India
64/B1 **Phularwan,** Pak.
65/D2 **Phu Loc,** Viet.
60/E4 **Phu Luong** (peak), Viet.
63/H3 **Phu Luong** (peak), Viet.
63/J3 **Phu Luong,** Viet.
65/D1 **Phu Luong,** Viet.
65/D1 **Phu Luong** (peak), Viet.
65/D1 **Phu Ly,** Viet.
65/D4 **Phumi Banam,** Cam
65/D3 **Phumi Chhlong,** Camb.
65/D4 **Phumi Chhuk,** Camb
65/C4 **Phumi Choan,** Camb
65/D3 **Phumi Kampong Putrea Chas,** Camb.
65/D3 **Phumi Kampong Trabek,** Camb.
63/H5 **Phumi Kouk Kduoch** Camb.
65/C3 **Phumi Kouk Kduoch** Camb.
65/D4 **Phumi Krek,** Camb.
65/D3 **Phumi Labang Siek,** Camb.
63/J5 **Phumi Mlu Prey,** Camb.
65/D3 **Phumi Mlu Prey,** Camb.
65/D3 **Phumi O Pou,** Camb
65/C3 **Phumi Phang,** Camb
65/D3 **Phumi Phsar,** Camb.
65/D3 **Phumi Phsa Romeas** Camb.
66/B1 **Phumi Phsa Romeas** Camb.
65/D3 **Phumi Prek Kak,** Camb.
65/D3 **Phumi Prek Preah,** Camb.
63/H5 **Phumi Samraong,** Camb.
65/C3 **Phumi Samraong,** Camb.
65/D3 **Phumi Spoe Tbong,** Camb.
66/C1 **Phumi Spoe Tbong,** Camb.
65/D3 **Phumi Sre Ta Chan,** Camb.
65/C3 **Phumi Ta Krei,** Cam
66/B1 **Phumi Ta Krei,** Cam
65/C3 **Phumi Thma Pok,** Camb.
65/C3 **Phumi Toek Sok,** Camb.
65/C4 **Phumi Veal Renh,** Camb.
65/E3 **Phu My,** Viet.
63/J5 **Phu Nhon,** Viet.
65/E3 **Phu Nhon,** Viet.
60/E5 **Phu Phan Nat'l Park** Thai.
65/D2 **Phu Phan Nat'l Park** Thai.
66/B1 **Phu Quoc** (isl.), Cam
63/H5 **Phu Quoc** (isl.), Viet.
65/C4 **Phu Quoc,** Viet.
65/C4 **Phu Quoc** (isl.), Viet.
65/D4 **Phu Rieng Sron,** Vie
60/D5 **Phu Rua Nat'l Park,** Thai.
65/C2 **Phu Rua Nat'l Park,** Thai.
60/E4 **Phu Tho,** Viet.
63/J3 **Phu Tho,** Viet.
65/D1 **Phu Tho,** Viet.
63/H4 **Phutthaisong,** Thai.
65/D2 **Phu Vang,** Viet.
54/H5 **Pi** (riv.), China
59/D4 **Pi** (riv.), China
61/H2 **Pi** (riv.), China
33/H4 **Piacenza,** It.
40/B5 **Piaggine,** It.
38/B1 **Piancastagnaio,** It.
38/A1 **Pianosa** (isl.), It.
27/L2 **Piaseczno,** Pol.
18/F4 **Piatra Neamţ,** Rom.
41/H2 **Piatra Neamţ,** Rom.
44/C3 **Piatra Neamţ,** Rom.
33/K3 **Piave** (riv.), It.
38/D4 **Piazza Armerina,** It.
37/F6 **Piazza Brembana,** It
37/G5 **Piazzi, Cima de'** (peak), It.
77/M6 **Pibor Post,** Sudan
94/C1 **Pic** (riv.), On,Can
106/E8 **Pica,** Chile
100/E2 **Picacho del Centinela** (peak), Mex.
93/G5 **Picacho del Centinela** (peak), M
96/C4 **Picacho del Centinela** (peak), M
19/T9 **Picardie** (reg.), Fr.
25/H6 **Picardie** (reg.), Fr.
26/B4 **Picardie** (reg.), Fr.
30/A4 **Picardie** (reg.), Fr.
32/E2 **Picardie** (reg.), Fr.
30/B4 **Picardy** (reg.), Fr.
98/F5 **Picatinny Arsenal,** NJ,US
97/F4 **Picayune,** Ms,US
38/E2 **Piccolo** (lag.), It.
76/D6 **Pic de Tibé** (peak), Gui.

02/D2 Pich, Mex.
106/F8 Pichanal, Arg.
09/D1 Pichanal, Arg.
02/C2 Pichucalco, Mex.
95/R8 Pickering, On,Can
23/H3 Pickering, Eng,UK
23/H3 Pickering, Vale of (val.), Eng,UK
91/L3 Pickle Lake, On,Can
72/B2 Picnic Bay, Austl.
35/S12 Pico (isl.), Azor.
107/K8 Pico da Bandeira (peak), Braz.
108/D2 Pico da Bandeira (peak), Braz.
106/E3 Pico da Neblina (peak), Braz.
106/F3 Pico da Neblina Nat'l Park, Braz.
108/C2 Pico das Agulhas Negras (peak), Braz.
107/K7 Pico de Itambé (peak), Braz.
108/D1 Pico de Itambé (peak), Braz.
01/M7 Pico de Orizaba Nat'l Park, Mex.
76/G7 Pico de Santa Isabel (peak), EqG.
100/E5 Pico de Tancítaro (peak), Mex.
76/B2 Pico de Teide (peak), Sp.
107/K5 Picos, Braz.
30/B4 Picquigny, Fr.
94/E3 Picton, On,Can
95/J2 Pictou, NS,Can
24/D5 Piddle (riv.), Eng,UK
62/D6 Pidurutagala (peak), SrL.
37/E5 Piedimulera, It.
33/G4 Piedmont (reg.), It.
36/E5 Piedmont (reg.), It.
99/K11 Piedmont, Ca,US
34/C3 Piedrabuena, Sp.
104/D5 Piedra Grande, Ven.
34/C2 Piedrahita, Sp.
106/D6 Piedras (riv.), Peru
101/E2 Piedras Negras, Mex.
101/N8 Piedras Negras, Mex.
88/F6 Piedras Negras, Mex.
96/C4 Piedras Negras, Mex.
27/K3 Piekary Śląskie, Pol.
80/B4 Piekenierskloof (pass), SAfr.
80/L10 Piekenierskloof (pass), SAfr.
20/H3 Pieksämäki, Fin.
42/E3 Pieksämäki, Fin.
20/J3 Pielinen (lake), Fin.
42/F3 Pielinen (lake), Fin.
27/L4 Pieniński Nat'l Park, Pol.
31/E5 Piennes, Fr.
27/H3 Pieńsk, Pol.
35/K6 Piera, Sp.
91/J5 Pierce, Ne,US
93/H2 Pierce, Ne,US
99/C3 Pierce (co.), Wa,US
90/F2 Pierceland, Sk,Can
04/G5 Pierre, US
86/F4 Pierre (cap.), SD,US
88/F3 Pierre (cap.), SD,US
91/H4 Pierre, SD,US
93/G1 Pierre, SD,US
36/B4 Pierre-de-Bresse, Fr.
19/T10 Pierrefitte-sur-Seine, Fr.
95/N7 Pierrefonds, Qu,Can
30/C5 Pierrefonds, Fr.
36/C3 Pierrefontaine-les-Varans, Fr.
32/F4 Pierrelatte, Fr.
19/S9 Pierrelaye, Fr.
30/A6 Pierres, Fr.
32/F5 Pierrevert, Fr.
35/H1 Pierrevert, Fr.
30/C5 Pierry, Fr.
27/J4 Piešťany, Slvk.
36/D3 Pieterlen, Swi.
81/E3 Pietermaritzburg, SAfr.
82/F6 Pietermaritzburg, SAfr.
82/E5 Pietersburg, SAfr.
38/D2 Pietramelara, It.
40/B5 Pietramelara, It.
40/B5 Pietramontecorvino, It.
81/E2 Piet Retief, SAfr.
82/F6 Piet Retief, SAfr.
41/G2 Pietrosul (peak), Rom.
44/C3 Pietrosul, Vîrful (peak), Rom.
37/E6 Pieve Vergonte, It.
90/E2 Pigeon (lake), Ab,Can
86/G4 Pigeon (riv.), On,Can, Mn,US
91/L3 Pigeon (riv.), Can., US
93/K3 Piggott, Ar,US
94/B4 Piggott, Ar,US
97/F2 Piggott, Ar,US
103/F1 Pigs (bay), Cuba
109/D4 Pigüé, Arg.
102/C3 Pijijiapan, Mex.
28/B4 Pijnacker, Neth.
102/E3 Pijol (peak), Hon.
88/D4 Pikelot (isl.), Micr.
88/E4 Pikes (peak), Co,US
93/F3 Pikes (peak), Co,US
96/B2 Pikes (peak), Co,US
98/K7 Pikesville, Md,US
80/B4 Piketberg, SAfr.
80/L10 Piketberg, SAfr.
89/K4 Pikeville, Ky,US
94/D4 Pikeville, Ky,US
97/H1 Pikeville, Ky,US
27/J2 Piła, Pol.
27/J2 Piła (prov.), Pol.
80/D2 Pilane, Bots.
80/P12 Pilanesberg (range), SAfr.
109/E2 Pilar, Par.
67/F1 Pilar, Phil.
36/E4 Pilatus (peak), Swi.
106/F8 Pilaya (riv.), Bol.
99/D1 Pilchuck (riv.), Wa,US
105/C5 Pilcomayo (riv.), SAm.
106/F8 Pilcomayo (riv.), SAm.
109/D1 Pilcomayo (riv.), SAm.
19/P7 Pilgrims Hatch, Eng,UK
25/G3 Pilgrims Hatch, Eng,UK
44/B2 Pilica (riv.), Pol.
39/H3 Pílion (peak), Gre.
44/B5 Pílion (peak), Gre.
40/D2 Pilis, Hun.
40/D2 Pilis (peak), Hun.
27/K5 Pilisvörösvár, Hun.
62/C2 Pilkhua, India
73/C4 Pillar (cape), Austl.
23/E2 Pillar (mtn.), Eng,UK
99/K12 Pillar (pt.), Ca,US
73/D1 Pilliga, Austl.
36/D5 Pillon, Col du (pass), Swi.
35/H1 Pilon du Roi (mtn.), Fr.
39/G4 Pílos, Gre.
94/C4 Pilot (peak), Tn,US
97/G2 Pilot (peak), Tn,US
85/G4 Pilot Point, Ak,US
85/F3 Pilot Station, Ak,US
27/G4 Pilsen, Czh.
33/K2 Pilsen (Plzeň), Czh.
37/H1 Pilsensee (lake), Ger.
20/G4 Piltene, Lat.
42/D4 Piltene, Lat.
92/E4 Pima, Az,US
53/K5 Pimpri-Chinchwad, India
62/B4 Pimpri-Chinchwad, India
103/G5 Piña (pt.), Pan.
35/G3 Pina, Sp.
100/B2 Pinacate, Cerro (mt.), Mex.
67/F1 Pinamalayan, Phil.
65/B5 Pinang (cape), Malay.
66/A2 Pinang (cape), Malay.
66/A2 Pinang (isl.), Malay.
50/D2 Pınarbaşı, Turk.
103/F1 Pinar del Río, Cuba
89/K7 Pinar del Río, Cuba
41/H5 Pınarhisar, Turk.
50/A1 Pınarhisar, Turk.
106/C4 Piñas, Ecu.
68/B3 Pinatubo (mt.), Phil.
86/G3 Pinawa, Mb,Can
89/G1 Pinawa, Mb,Can
91/K3 Pinawa, Mb,Can
23/H6 Pinchbeck, Eng,UK
86/E4 Pincher Creek, Ab,Can
90/E3 Pincher Creek, Ab,Can
94/D3 Pinconning, Mi,US
40/E2 Pincota, Rom.
95/N7 Pincourt, Qu,Can
27/L3 Pińczów, Pol.
108/C2 Pindamonhangaba, Braz.
107/J4 Pindaré (riv.), Braz.
107/J4 Pindaré-Mirim, Braz.
64/B1 Pind Dādan Khān, Pak.
53/K2 Pindi Gheb, Pak.
64/B1 Pindi Gheb, Pak.
39/G3 Pindos Nat'l Park, Gre.
39/G2 Pindus (mts.), Gre.
53/K4 Pindwāra, India
62/B3 Pindwāra, India
99/G6 Pine (riv.), Mi,US
97/F4 Pine (hills), Ms,US
91/G4 Pine (hills), Mt,US
98/F6 Pine Barrens (reg.), NJ,US
98/F6 Pine Beach, NJ,US
89/H5 Pine Bluff, Ar,US
93/J4 Pine Bluff, Ar,US
96/E3 Pine Bluff, Ar,US
91/G5 Pine Bluffs, Wy,US
93/F2 Pine Bluffs, Wy,US
68/C6 Pine Creek, Austl.
70/E2 Pine Creek, Austl.
98/G4 Pine Creek (pt.), Ct,US
35/G2 Pineda de Mar, Sp.
90/F5 Pinedale, Wy,US
92/E2 Pinedale, Wy,US
86/G3 Pine Falls, Mb,Can
89/G1 Pine Falls, Mb,Can
91/J3 Pine Falls, Mb,Can
42/J2 Pinega (riv.), Rus.
46/E3 Pinega (riv.), Rus.
98/F6 Pine Hill, NJ,US
91/L2 Pineimuta (riv.), On,Can
83/T Pine Island (bay), Ant.
94/A2 Pine Island, Mn,US
80/L10 Pinelands, SAfr.
86/F2 Pine Point, NW,Can
91/H5 Pine Ridge, SD,US
93/G2 Pine Ridge, SD,US
33/G4 Pinerolo, It.
99/G6 Pine, South Branch (riv.), Mi,US
81/E3 Pinetown, SAfr.
32/D4 Pineuilh, Fr.
60/C5 Ping (riv.), Thai.
63/G4 Ping (riv.), Thai.
65/B2 Ping (riv.), Thai.
60/D4 Pingbian Miaozu Zizhixian, China
63/H3 Pingbian Miaozu Zizhixian, China
61/E2 Pingchang, China
59/C3 Pingding, China
54/G5 Pingdingshan, China
59/C4 Pingdingshan, China
59/D3 Pingdu, China
68/F4 Pingelap (atoll), Micr.
70/B6 Pingelly, Austl.
59/D2 Pinggu, China
59/H6 Pinggu, China
63/J3 Pingguo, China
59/L9 Pinghu, China
59/C5 Pingjiang Guan (pass), China
61/G2 Pingjiang Guan (pass), China
54/F5 Pingjinpu, China
61/F3 Pingle, China
63/K3 Pingle, China
54/G4 Pinglu, China
59/B4 Pinglu, China
59/C3 Pinglu, China
63/K3 Pingnan, China
55/H3 Pingquan, China
59/D2 Pingquan, China
59/C3 Pingshan, China
59/C3 Pingshun, China
63/J2 Pingtang, China
61/J4 Pingtung, Tai.
59/C3 Pingxiang, China
60/E4 Pingxiang, China
61/G3 Pingxiang, China
63/K2 Pingxiang, China
65/D1 Pingxiang, China
59/C3 Pingxing Guan (pass), China
55/J4 Pingyang, China
54/G4 Pingyao, China
59/C3 Pingyao, China
55/H4 Pingyi, China
59/D4 Pingyi, China
59/D3 Pingyin, China
54/G5 Pingyu, China
59/C4 Pingyu, China
59/D3 Pingyuan, China
108/C2 Pinhal, Braz.
35/Q10 Pinhal Novo, Port.
108/B3 Pinhão, Braz.
107/J4 Pinheiro, Braz.
107/K7 Pinheiros, Braz.
108/D1 Pinheiros, Braz.
34/B2 Pinhel, Port.
39/G3 Piniós (riv.), Gre.
39/G4 Piniós (riv.), Gre.
40/C2 Pinkafeld, Aus.
28/C2 Pinkegat (chan.), Neth.
92/B3 Pinnacles Nat'l Mon., Ca,US
70/G7 Pinnaroo, Austl.
73/B2 Pinnaroo, Austl.
29/G1 Pinnau (riv.), Ger.
26/E2 Pinneberg, Ger.
29/G1 Pinneberg, Ger.
99/K10 Pinole, Ca,US
101/E4 Pinos, Mex.
92/C4 Pinos (peak), Ca,US
103/F1 Pinos (Juventad) (isl.), Cuba
35/E3 Pinoso, Sp.
34/D4 Pinos-Puente, Sp.
102/B2 Pinotepa Nacional, Mex.
67/E4 Pinrang, Indo.
68/F7 Pins (isl.), NCal.
69/V13 Pins (isl.), NCal.
68/F7 Pins, Ile des (isl.), NCal.
10/F3 Pinsk, Bela.
44/C1 Pinsk, Bela.
46/C4 Pinsk, Bela.
35/N9 Pinto, Sp.
37/G5 Pinzolo, It.
92/D3 Pioche, Nv,US
33/J5 Piombino, It.
38/B1 Piombino, It.
46/J2 Pioner (isl.), Rus.
42/D5 Pionerskiy, Rus.
27/L3 Pionki, Pol.
44/B2 Pionki, Pol.
106/F4 Piorini (riv.), Braz.
27/K3 Piotrków (prov.), Pol.
27/K3 Piotrków Trybunalski, Pol.
44/A2 Piotrków Trybunalski, Pol.
53/K3 Pīpār, India
62/B2 Pīpār, India
98/E5 Pipersville, Pa,US
92/D3 Pipe Spring Nat'l Mon., Az,US
91/L2 Pipestone (riv.), On,Can
86/G3 Pipestone (riv.), On,Can
91/H3 Pipestone (cr.), Mb, Sk,Can
91/J4 Pipestone, Mn,US
93/H1 Pipestone, Mn,US
91/J4 Pipestone Nat'l Mon., Mn,US
93/H1 Pipestone Nat'l Mon., Mn,US
53/K2 Piplān, Pak.
64/A1 Piplān, Pak.
87/J4 Pipmuacan (res.), Qu,Can
95/G1 Pipmuacan (res.), Qu,Can
94/C3 Piqua, Oh,US
107/H7 Piquiri (riv.), Braz.
108/A3 Piquiri (riv.), Braz.
108/B1 Piracanjuba, Braz.
107/J8 Piracicaba, Braz.
108/C2 Piracicaba, Braz.
109/G1 Piracicaba, Braz.
58/C2 Pirae-bong (mtn.), NKor.
108/B3 Piraí do Sul, Braz.
18/F5 Piraiévs, Gre.
39/H4 Piraiévs, Gre.
39/L7 Piraiévs, Gre.
44/B5 Piraiévs, Gre.
108/B2 Piraju, Braz.
108/B2 Pirajuí, Braz.
33/K4 Piran, Slov.
40/A3 Piran, Slov.
109/E2 Pirané, Arg.
108/D2 Piranga (riv.), Braz.
107/L5 Piranhas (riv.), Braz.
107/K7 Pirapora, Braz.
108/C1 Pirapora, Braz.
108/B2 Pirapòzinho, Braz.
108/C2 Pirássununga, Braz.
107/J7 Pires do Rio, Braz.
108/B1 Pires do Rio, Braz.
18/F5 Pírgos, Gre.
39/G4 Pírgos, Gre.
39/J5 Pírgos, Gre.
39/H2 Pirin (mts.), Bul.
39/H2 Pirin (peak), Bul.
41/F5 Pirin (mt.), Bul.
41/F5 Pirin (mts.), Bul.
44/B4 Pirin (peak), Bul.
39/H2 Pirin Nat'l Park, Bul.
41/F5 Pirin Nat'l Park, Bul.
107/K4 Piripiri, Braz.
64/B2 Pīr Mahal, Pak.
26/D4 Pirmasens, Ger.
31/G5 Pirmasens, Ger.
33/G2 Pirmasens, Ger.
27/G3 Pirna, Ger.
39/H1 Pirot, Yugo.
40/F4 Pirot, Yugo.
44/B4 Pirot, Yugo.
64/C1 Pir Panjal (range), India
103/G5 Pirre (mtn.), Pan.
44/E2 Piryatin, Ukr.
39/J3 Piryíon, Gre.
50/A2 Piryíon, Gre.
18/E4 Pisa, It.
33/J5 Pisa, It.
33/J4 Pisanino (peak), It.
67/E2 Pisau (cape), Malay.
106/D2 Pisba Nat'l Park, Col.
98/K8 Piscataway, Md,US
106/C5 Pisco, Peru
106/C6 Pisco (riv.), Peru
27/H4 Písek, Czh.
33/L2 Písek, Czh.
53/H3 Pīshīn, Iran
53/J2 Pishīn, Pak.
40/C3 Piškavica, Bosn.
37/G4 Pisoc, Piz (peak), Swi.
109/C2 Pissis (peak), Arg.
30/B4 Pissy, Fr.
99/P15 Pistakee (lake), Il,US
38/E2 Pisticci, It.
40/C5 Pisticci, It.
33/J5 Pistoia, It.
34/C1 Pisuerga (riv.), Sp.
27/L2 Pisz, Pol.
92/B2 Pit (riv.), Ca,US
106/C3 Pitalito, Col.
108/B3 Pitanga, Braz.
69/N7 Pitcairn (isl.), Pitc.
69/N7 Pitcairn Islands (terr.), U.K.
20/G2 Piteå, Swe.
42/D2 Piteå, Swe.
20/F2 Piteälv (riv.), Swe.
42/C2 Piteälv (riv.), Swe.
18/F4 Pitești, Rom.
41/G3 Pitești, Rom.
44/C3 Pitești, Rom.
39/K2 Píthion, Gre.
41/H5 Píthion, Gre.
50/A1 Píthion, Gre.
32/E2 Pithiviers, Fr.
30/D1 Pitigliano, It.
100/C2 Pitiquito, Mex.
85/F3 Pitkas Point, Ak,US
21/D2 Pitlochy, Sc,UK
98/E6 Pitman, NJ,US
40/C3 Pitomača, Cro.
30/A5 Pîtres, Fr.
80/D2 Pitsane, Bots.
80/N12 Pitsane, Bots.
72/H8 Pitt (lake), Austl.
103/F4 Pittier (mtn.), CR
99/L10 Pittsburg, Ca,US
89/H4 Pittsburg, Ks,US
93/J3 Pittsburg, Ks,US
96/E2 Pittsburg, Ks,US
93/J4 Pittsburg, Tx,US
96/E3 Pittsburg, Tx,US
84/K5 Pittsburgh, US
89/L3 Pittsburgh, Pa,US
94/E3 Pittsburgh, Pa,US
89/M3 Pittsfield, Ma,US
95/F3 Pittsfield, Ma,US
95/G2 Pittsfield, Me,US
94/F3 Pittston, Pa,US
72/C4 Pittsworth, Austl.
37/G3 Pitzbach (riv.), Aus.
107/J8 Piũí, Braz.
108/C2 Piũí, Braz.
106/B5 Piura, Peru
62/D2 Piuthān, Nepal
39/F1 Piva (riv.), Yugo.
103/H4 Pivijay, Col.
39/F1 Pivsko (lake), Yugo.
40/D4 Pivsko (lake), Yugo.
54/E5 Pi Xian, China
60/D2 Pi Xian, China
101/H5 Pixoyal, Mex.
102/D2 Pixoyal, Mex.
34/C4 Pizarra, Sp.
43/K4 Pizhma (riv.), Rus.
37/F4 Pizol (peak), Swi.
38/E3 Pizzo, It.
38/C1 Pizzuto (peak), It.
102/D2 Placentia (pt.), Belz.
95/L2 Placentia, Nf,Can
95/L2 Placentia (bay), Nf,Can
98/C3 Placentia, Ca,US
102/E2 Placer, Mex.
99/M9 Placer (co.), Ca,US
103/G1 Placetas, Cuba
39/J1 Plachkovtsi, Bul.
41/G4 Plachkovtsi, Bul.
36/D4 Plaffeien, Swi.
31/G3 Plaidt, Ger.
19/T9 Plailly, Fr.
30/B5 Plailly, Fr.
65/C3 Plai Mat (riv.), Thai.
36/C1 Plaine (riv.), Fr.
99/P16 Plainfield, Il,US
98/F5 Plainfield, NJ,US
49/G5 Plain of Esdraelon (plain), Isr.
60/D5 Plain of Jars, Laos
100/E1 Plains, Tx,US
93/G4 Plains, Tx,US
96/C3 Plains, Tx,US
94/A2 Plainview, Mn,US
88/F5 Plainview, Tx,US
93/G4 Plainview, Tx,US
96/C3 Plainview, Tx,US
93/H3 Plainville, Ks,US
96/D2 Plainville, Ks,US
19/R10 Plaisir, Fr.
67/E5 Plampang, Indo.
103/H1 Plana (cay), Bahm.
104/C2 Plana (cays), Bahm.
108/D1 Planalto do Brasil (plat.), Braz.
36/C2 Plancher-Bas, Fr.
36/C2 Plancher-les-Mines, Fr.
40/E3 Plandište, Yugo.
103/H4 Planeta Rica, Col.
37/F3 Planken, Lcht.
36/C5 Plan-les-Ouates, Swi.
99/N16 Plano, Il,US
101/F1 Plano, Tx,US
93/H4 Plano, Tx,US
96/D3 Plano, Tx,US
97/H5 Plantation, Fl,US
97/H4 Plant City, Fl,US
93/K5 Plaquemine, La,US
97/F4 Plaquemine, La,US
34/B2 Plasencia, Sp.
106/G4 Plast, Rus.
109/E4 Plata (est.), Arg.
38/C4 Platani (riv.), It.
105/D6 Plata, Río de la (estuary), Arg., Uru.
79/H4 Plateau (state), Nga.
30/D3 Plate Taile, Barrage de la (dam), Belg.
39/H2 Platí, Gre.
103/H4 Plato, Col.
106/D2 Plato, Col.
84/G5 Platte (riv.), US
93/J2 Platte (riv.), Mo,US
107/H5 Platte (riv.), Nb,US
89/G3 Platte (riv.), Ne,US
93/H2 Platte (riv.), Ne,US
91/J5 Platte, SD,US
93/H2 Platte, SD,US
91/L5 Platteville, Wi,US
93/K2 Platteville, Wi,US
94/D3 Platteville, Wi,US
26/G4 Plattling, Ger.
33/K2 Plattling, Ger.
87/J4 Plattsburgh, NY,US
89/M3 Plattsburgh, NY,US
94/F2 Plattsburgh, NY,US
26/G3 Plauen, Ger.
33/K1 Plauen, Ger.
39/F1 Plav, Yugo.
40/D4 Plav, Yugo.
37/G4 Plavna Dadaint, Piz (peak), Swi.
102/E3 Playa de los Muertos (ruins), Hon.
100/C2 Playa Noriega (lake), Mex.
92/E5 Playa Noriega (lake), Mex
106/B4 Playas, Ecu.
92/E5 Playas (lake), NM,US
101/G5 Playa Vicente, Mex.
102/C2 Playa Vicente, Mex.
63/J5 Play Cu (Pleiku), Viet.
65/E3 Play Cu (Pleiku), Viet.
107/J2 Playgreen (lake), Mb,Can
99/K11 Pleasant Hill, Ca,US
99/L11 Pleasanton, Ca,US
100/C1 Pleasanton, NM,US
88/G6 Pleasanton, Tx,US
93/H5 Pleasanton, Tx,US
96/D4 Pleasanton, Tx,US
99/Q14 Pleasant Prairie, Wi,US
101/E1 Pleasant Valley, Tx,US
98/G4 Pleasantville, NY,US
32/E4 Pléaux, Fr.
27/G4 Plechý (Plöckenstein) (peak), Czh.
63/J5 Plei Doch, Viet.
63/J5 Pleiku (Play Cu), Viet.
65/E3 Pleiku (Play Cu), Viet.
26/G3 Pleisse (riv.), Ger.
73/G5 Plenty (riv.), Austl.
71/S10 Plenty (bay), NZ
91/G3 Plentywood, Mt,US
32/B2 Plérin, Fr.
27/J3 Pleszew, Pol.
95/G1 Plétipi (lake), Qu,Can
29/E6 Plettenberg, Ger.
31/G1 Plettenberg, Ger.
18/F4 Pleven, Bul.
41/G4 Pleven, Bul.
44/C4 Pleven, Bul.
40/D1 Pliešovce, Slvk.
41/H4 Pliska, Bul.
40/B3 Plitvice Lakes Nat'l Park, Cro.
33/L4 Plitvička Jezera Nat'l Park, Cro.
39/F1 Pljevlja, Yugo.
40/D4 Pljevlja, Yugo.
36/D1 Plobsheim, Fr.
40/B4 Ploča, Rt (pt.), Yugo.
38/E1 Ploče, Cro.
40/C4 Ploče, Cro.
18/E3 Płock, Pol.
27/K2 Płock, Pol.
27/K2 Płock (prov.), Pol.
42/C5 Płock, Pol.
44/A1 Płock, Pol.
46/B4 Płock, Pol.
27/G4 Plöckenstein (Plechý) (peak), Ger.
40/C4 Pločno (peak), Bosn.
32/B3 Ploemeur, Fr.
18/F4 Ploiești, Rom.
41/H3 Ploiești, Rom.
44/C3 Ploiești, Rom.
46/C5 Ploiești, Rom.
39/K3 Plomárion, Gre.
44/C5 Plomárion, Gre.
50/A2 Plomárion, Gre.
31/E2 Plombières, Belg.
36/C2 Plombières-les-Bains, Fr.
36/A3 Plombières-lès-Dijon, Fr.
26/F1 Plön, Ger.
90/G2 Plonge (lake), Sk,Can
27/L2 Płońsk, Pol.
42/D5 Płońsk, Pol.
44/B1 Płońsk, Pol.
32/B3 Plouay, Fr.
27/H3 Ploučnice (riv.), Czh.
32/B2 Ploufragan, Fr.
32/A2 Plougastel-Daoulas, Fr.
32/B2 Plouguernével, Fr.
18/F4 Plovdiv, Bul.
39/J1 Plovdiv, Bul.
39/J2 Plovdiv (prov.), Bul.
41/G4 Plovdiv, Bul.
41/G5 Plovdiv (reg.), Bul.
44/C4 Plovdiv, Bul.
91/L4 Plover, Wi,US
94/B2 Plover, Wi,US
22/A2 Plumbridge, NI,UK
98/E5 Plumsteadville, Pa,US
20/G5 Plungė, Lith.
42/D5 Plungė, Lith.
104/F3 Plymouth (cap.), Monts.
18/C3 Plymouth, Eng,UK
24/B6 Plymouth, Eng,UK
24/B6 Plymouth (sound), Eng,UK
32/A1 Plymouth, Eng,UK
94/C3 Plymouth, In,US
97/J3 Plymouth, NC,US
95/G3 Plymouth, NH,US
94/C3 Plymouth, Wi,US
24/C2 Plynlimon (mtn.), UK
27/G4 Plzeň (Pilsen), Czh.
33/K2 Plzeň (Pilsen), Czh.
27/J2 Pniewy, Pol.
76/E5 Pô, Burk.
79/E4 Pô, Burk.
18/E4 Po (riv.), It.
33/J4 Po (riv.), It.
33/J4 Po (val.), It.
46/J5 Pobedy (peak), Kyr.
27/J2 Pobiedziska, Pol.
35/F1 Pobla de Segur, Sp.
93/K3 Pocahontas, Ar,US
97/F2 Pocahontas, Ar,US
84/F5 Pocatello, US
86/E4 Pocatello, Id,US
88/D3 Pocatello, Id,US
90/E5 Pocatello, Id,US
92/D2 Pocatello, Id,US
44/E1 Pochep, Rus.
44/E1 Pochinok, Rus.
58/D4 P'och'ŏn, SKor.
58/G6 P'och'ŏn, SKor.
102/B3 Pochutla, Mex.
27/G4 Pöcking, Ger.
33/K2 Pöcking, Ger.
37/H2 Pöcking, Ger.
68/E6 Pocklington (reef), PNG
23/H4 Pocklington, Eng,UK
93/J4 Pocola, Ok,US
96/E3 Pocola, Ok,US
107/G7 Poconé, Braz.
98/E4 Pocono (cr.), Pa,US
98/E4 Pocono (lake), Pa,US
98/E4 Pocono Lake, Pa,US
98/E4 Pocono Pines, Pa,US
107/J8 Poços de Caldas, Braz.
108/C2 Poços de Caldas, Braz.
109/G1 Poços de Caldas, Braz.
103/F4 Pocrí, Pan.
42/F4 Podberez'ye, Rus.
27/K3 Poddębice, Pol.
27/M3 Podlasie (reg.), Pol.
18/G3 Podol'sk, Rus.
42/H5 Podol'sk, Rus.
43/X9 Podol'sk, Rus.
44/F1 Podol'sk, Rus.
46/D4 Podol'sk, Rus.
78/B2 Podor, Sen.
42/G3 Podporozh'ye, Rus.
40/C3 Podravska Slatina, Cro.
39/G1 Podujevo, Yugo.
40/E4 Podujevo, Yugo.
33/J5 Poggibonsi, It.
39/G2 Pogradec, Alb.
40/E5 Pogradec, Alb.
85/F5 Pogromni (vol.), Ak,US
88/U11 Pohakuloa (mil. res.), Hi,US
55/K4 P'ohang, SKor.
56/A2 P'ohang, SKor.
58/E4 P'ohang, SKor.
55/K3 P'oha-ri, NKor.
98/E5 Pohatcong (cr.), NJ,US
95/G2 Pohénégamook, Can
20/G3 Pohjanmaa (reg.), Fin.
42/D3 Pohjanmaa (reg.), Fin.
68/E4 Pohnpei (isl.), Micr.
98/E5 Pohopoco (cr.), Pa,US
98/E5 Pohopoco Mtn. (ridge), Pa,US
83/H Poinsett (cape), Ant.
86/E2 Point (lake), NW,Can
93/K5 Point au Fer (isl.), La,US
97/F4 Point au Fer (isl.), La,US
85/M4 Point Baker, Ak,US
104/F3 Pointe-à-Pitre, Guad.
103/H2 Pointe à Raquette, Haiti
95/N6 Pointe-aux-Trembles, Qu,Can
95/N6 Pointe-Calumet, Qu,Can
95/N7 Pointe-Claire, Qu,Can
95/F2 Pointe-du-Lac, Qu,Can
99/H6 Point Edward, On,Can
82/B1 Pointe-Noire, Congo
104/F5 Point Fortin, Trin.
85/E2 Point Hope, Ak,US
85/F2 Point Lay, Ak,US
73/E1 Point Lookout (peak), Austl.
64/H4 Point Pedro, SrL.
94/D3 Point Pelee Nat'l Park, Can
99/G8 Point Pelee Nat'l Park, On,Can
98/F5 Point Pleasant, NJ,US
94/C4 Point Pleasant, Oh,US
97/G2 Point Pleasant, Oh,US
98/E5 Point Pleasant, Pa,US
94/D4 Point Pleasant, WV,US
97/H2 Point Pleasant, WV,US
33/G4 Poirino, It.
19/S10 Poissy, Fr.
18/D4 Poitiers, Fr.
32/D3 Poitiers, Fr.
32/C3 Poitou (hist. reg.), Fr.
32/C3 Poitou-Charentes (reg.), Fr.
30/A4 Poix-de-Picardie, Fr.
30/D4 Poix-Terron, Fr.
20/J3 Pojois-Karjala (prov.), Fin.
42/F3 Pojois-Karjala (prov.), Fin.
53/K3 Pokaran, India
62/B2 Pokaran, India
62/D2 Pokhara, Nepal
45/K1 Pokhvistnevo, Rus.
65/E4 Po Klong Garai Cham Towers, Viet.
77/L7 Poko, Zaire
27/H3 Polabská Nížina (val.), Czh.
33/L1 Polabská Nížina (reg.), Czh.
38/E1 Polače, Cro.
34/C1 Pola de Laviana, Sp.
34/C1 Pola de Lena, Sp.
34/C1 Pola de Siero, Sp.
44/A2 Pol'ana (peak), Slvk.
18/E3 Poland
27/K2 Poland
33/M1 Poland
42/D5 Poland
44/A2 Poland
46/D4 Poland
27/L3 Poľaniec, Pol.
43/P2 Polar Urals (mts.), Rus.
44/E5 Polatlı, Turk.
50/C2 Polatlı, Turk.
31/G3 Polch, Ger.
27/J2 Pol'czyn-Zdrój, Pol.
53/J1 Pol-e-Khomri, Afg.
83/E Pole of Inaccessibility, Ant.
25/E1 Polesworth, Eng,UK
40/E2 Polgár, Hun.
58/D5 Pŏlgyo, SKor.
39/J4 Políaigos (isl.), Gre.
38/D3 Policastro (gulf), It.
27/H2 Police, Pol.
38/E2 Policoro, It.
32/F3 Poligny, Fr.
36/B4 Poligny, Fr.
39/H2 Políkastron, Gre.
40/F5 Políkastron, Gre.
39/H2 Políkhni, Gre.
39/K3 Polikhnítos, Gre.
44/C5 Polikhnítos, Gre.
49/C2 Polis, Cyp.
50/C3 Polis, Cyp.
38/E3 Polistena, It.
39/H2 Políyiros, Gre.
44/B4 Políyiros, Gre.
33/L3 Polje, Slov.
40/B2 Polje, Slov.
27/J3 Polkowice, Pol.
38/D2 Polla, It.
40/B5 Polla, It.
64/F3 Pollāchi, India
35/G3 Pollensa, Sp.
102/D3 Polochic (riv.), Guat.
67/G2 Polomolok, Phil.
62/D6 Polonnaruwa, SrL.
64/H4 Polonnaruwa (dist.), SrL.
64/H5 Polonnaruwa, SrL.
44/C2 Polonnoye, Ukr.
18/F3 Polotsk, Bela.
42/F5 Polotsk, Bela.
46/C4 Polotsk, Bela.
24/B6 Polperro, Eng,UK
41/G4 Polski Trŭmbesh, Bul.
90/E4 Polson, Mt,US
18/G4 Poltava, Ukr.
44/E2 Poltava, Ukr.
46/D5 Poltava, Ukr.
44/E2 Poltava Obl., Ukr.
23/G4 Polvijärvi, Fin.
20/K1 Polyarnyy, Rus.
42/G1 Polyarnyy, Rus.
85/B2 Polyarnyy, Rus.
68/G6 Polynesia (reg.)
69/J3 Polynesia (reg.)
69/L7 Polynesia (reg.)
33/J5 Pomarance, It.
40/C5 Pomarico, It.
108/D2 Pomba (riv.), Braz.
107/L5 Pombal, Braz.
34/A3 Pombal, Port.
74/J9 Pombas, CpV.
27/H2 Pomerania (reg.), Pol.
27/H1 Pomeranian (bay), Ger., Pol.
108/B3 Pomerode, Braz.
22/B2 Pomeroy, NI,UK
90/D4 Pomeroy, Wa,US
68/E5 Pomio, PNG
98/C2 Pomona, Ca,US
82/C6 Pomona, Namb.
41/H4 Pomorie, Bul.
49/C2 Pomos (pt.), Cyp.
50/C3 Pomos (pt.), Cyp.
41/K1 Pomoshnaya, Ukr.
33/K4 Po, Mouths of the, It.
97/H5 Pompano Beach, Fl,US
38/D2 Pompei (ruins), It.
40/B5 Pompei (ruins), It.
108/C1 Pompeu, Braz.
31/F6 Pompey, Fr.
98/F4 Pompton Lakes, NJ,US
79/E4 Pô Nat'l Park, Burk.
89/G4 Ponca City, Ok,US
93/H3 Ponca City, Ok,US
96/D2 Ponca City, Ok,US
104/E3 Ponce, PR
94/E1 Poncheville (lake), Qu,Can
36/B5 Poncin, Fr.
87/J1 Pond (inlet), NW,Can
98/G4 Pond (pt.), Ct,US
62/B5 Pondicherry (terr.), India
62/C5 Pondicherry, India
62/C5 Pondicherry (terr.), India
62/D4 Pondicherry (terr.), India
64/E3 Pondicherry (terr.), India
64/G3 Pondicherry, India
64/G3 Pondicherry (terr.), India
87/J1 Pond Inlet, NW,Can
34/B1 Ponferrada, Sp.
58/D5 Pongdong, SKor.
56/A2 Ponghwa, SKor.
58/E4 Ponghwa, SKor.
81/E2 Pongolo (riv.), SAfr.
55/K4 Pongsan, NKor.
53/L2 Pongunagu, India
78/E4 Poni (prov.), Burk.
27/M3 Poniatowa, Pol.
64/G3 Ponnaiyar (riv.), India
64/E3 Ponnani, India
86/E3 Ponoka, Ab,Can
90/E2 Ponoka, Ab,Can
42/H2 Ponoy (riv.), Rus.
46/D3 Ponoy (riv.), Rus.
32/C4 Pons, Fr.
30/D3 Pont-à-Celles, Belg.
107/L7 Ponta da Baleia (pt.), Braz.
108/E1 Ponta da Baleia (pt.), Braz.
82/B4 Ponta da Marca (pt.), Ang.
35/S12 Ponta da Pico (mtn.), Azor.
82/B2 Ponta das Palmeirinhas (pt.), Ang.
35/T13 Ponta Delgada, Azor.
108/C3 Ponta do Camboriú (pt.), Braz.
82/B2 Ponta do Padrão (pt.), Ang.
35/U15 Ponta do Sol
108/B3 Ponta Grossa, Braz.
109/F2 Ponta Grossa, Braz.
108/E1 Pontal de Regência (pt.), Braz.
108/B1 Pontalina, Braz.
30/C2 Pont-à-Marcq, Fr.
20/D4 Pont-à-Mousson, Fr.
31/F6 Pont-à-Mousson, Fr.
32/G2 Pont-à-Mousson, Fr.
107/G8 Ponta Porã, Braz.
109/E1 Ponta Porã, Braz.
24/C3 Pontardawe, Wal,UK
24/B3 Pontardulais, Wal,UK
33/G3 Pontarlier, Fr.
36/C4 Pontarlier, Fr.
19/T10 Pontault-Combault, Fr.
30/B6 Pontault-Combault, Fr.
94/E1 Pontax (riv.), Qu,Can
19/U10 Pontcarré, Fr.
89/H5 Pontchartrain (lake), La,US
32/B3 Pontchâteau, Fr.
36/B5 Pont-d'Ain, Fr.
36/B6 Pont-de-Chéruy, Fr.
30/A5 Pont-de-l'Arche, Fr.
36/C3 Pont-de-Roide, Fr.
36/A5 Pont-de-Vaux, Fr.
36/A5 Pont-de-Veyle, Fr.
32/E4 Pont-du-Château, Fr.
40/B5 Pontecagnano, It.
37/G5 Ponte, Capo di, It.
38/C2 Pontecorvo, It.
34/A3 Ponte de Sor, Port.
37/G5 Ponte di Legno, It.
34/A2 Ponte do Lima, Port.
23/G4 Pontefract, Eng,UK
23/G1 Ponteland, Eng,UK
107/K8 Ponte Nova, Braz.
108/D2 Ponte Nova, Braz.
24/C2 Ponterwyd, Wal,UK
24/D1 Pontesbury, Eng,UK
106/G7 Pontes e Lacerda, Braz.
34/A1 Pontevedra, Sp.
91/L5 Pontiac, Il,US

168

Ponti – Provi

93/K2 Pontiac, Il,US
94/B3 Pontiac, Il,US
87/H4 Pontiac, Mi,US
89/K3 Pontiac, Mi,US
94/D3 Pontiac, Mi,US
99/F6 Pontiac, Mi,US
99/F6 Pontiac (lake), Mi,US
66/C4 Pontianak, Indo.
32/B2 Pontivy, Fr.
19/S9 Pontoise, Fr.
30/B5 Pontoise, Fr.
32/E2 Pontoise, Fr.
97/F3 Pontotoc, Ms,US
30/B5 Pontpoint, Fr.
33/H4 Pontremoli, It.
30/A3 Pont-Remy, Fr.
37/F5 Pontresina, Swi.
24/C2 Pontrhydfendigaid, Wal,UK
24/D3 Pontrilas, Eng,UK
30/B5 Pont-Sainte Maxence, Fr.
32/F4 Pont-Saint-Esprit, Fr.
24/B3 Pontyates, Wal,UK
24/C3 Pontyclun, Wal,UK
24/C3 Pont y Cymmer, Wal,UK
24/C3 Pontypool, Wal,UK
24/C3 Pontypridd, Wal,UK
38/C2 Ponza, It.
38/C2 Ponziane (isls.), It.
24/E5 Poole, Eng,UK
25/E5 Poole (bay), Eng,UK
32/C1 Poole, Eng,UK
53/K5 Poona, India
62/B4 Poona, India
105/C4 Poopó (lake), Bol.
106/E7 Poopó (lake), Bol.
20/G4 Pöösapää (pt.), Est.
42/D4 Pöösapää (pt.), Est.
98/H5 Poosepatuck Ind. Res., NY,US
60/B4 Popa (peak), Burma
106/C3 Popayán, Col.
30/B2 Poperinge, Belg.
100/C2 Popigochic (riv.), Mex.
70/G6 Popilta (lake), Austl.
73/B2 Popilta (lake), Austl.
73/B2 Popio (lake), Austl.
86/G3 Poplar (riv.), Mb,Can
91/K2 Poplar (riv.), Mb, On,Can
91/G3 Poplar (riv.), Mt,US
91/G3 Poplar, Mt,US
89/H4 Poplar Bluff, Mo,US
93/K3 Poplar Bluff, Mo,US
94/B4 Poplar Bluff, Mo,US
97/F2 Poplar Bluff, Mo,US
97/F4 Poplarville, Ms,US
76/J6 Popokabaka, Zaire
40/A4 Popoli, It.
68/D5 Popondetta, PNG
41/H4 Popovo, Bul.
44/C4 Popovo, Bul.
27/L4 Poprad, Slvk.
27/L4 Poprad (riv.), Slvk.
44/B2 Poprad, Slvk.
107/J6 Porangatu, Braz.
53/J4 Porbandar, India
62/A3 Porbandar, India
34/C4 Porcuna, Sp.
86/B2 Porcupine (riv.), Yk,Can, Ak,US
85/K2 Porcupine (riv.), Yk,Can, Ak,US
84/C3 Porcupine (riv.), US, Can.
72/B3 Porcupine Gorge Nat'l Park, Austl.
91/H2 Porcupine Plain, Sk,Can
33/K4 Pordenone, It.
41/G4 Pordim, Bul.
33/K4 Poreč, Cro.
40/A3 Poreč, Cro.
27/N2 Porech'ye, Bela.
42/E5 Porech'ye, Bela.
44/C1 Porech'ye, Bela.
45/H1 Poretskoye, Rus.
18/F2 Pori, Fin.
20/G3 Pori, Fin.
42/D3 Pori, Fin.
46/C3 Pori, Fin.
71/R11 Porirua, N.Z.
20/J4 Porkhov, Rus.
42/F4 Porkhov, Rus.
104/F5 Porlamar, Ven.
106/F1 Porlamar, Ven.
37/F5 Porlezza, It.
24/C4 Porlock, Eng,UK
72/A1 Pormpuraaw Abor. Land, Austl.
32/B3 Pornic, Fr.
47/Q5 Poronaysk, Rus.
55/N2 Poronaysk, Rus.
39/H4 Póros, Gre.
83/J Porpoise (bay), Ant.
36/D3 Porrentruy, Swi.
34/A1 Porriño, Sp.
20/H1 Porsangen (fjord), Nor.
20/D4 Porsgrunn, Nor.
44/D5 Porsuk (riv.), Turk.
50/B2 Porsuk (riv.), Turk.
106/F7 Portachuelo, Bol.
22/B3 Portadown, NI,UK
22/C3 Portaferry, NI,UK
94/C3 Portage, Mi,US
89/J3 Portage, Wi,US
91/L5 Portage, Wi,US
93/K2 Portage, Wi,US
94/B3 Portage, Wi,US
84/H5 Portage la Prairie, Can.
86/G4 Portage la Prairie, Mb,Can
89/G2 Portage la Prairie, Mb,Can
91/J3 Portage la Prairie, Mb,Can
86/D4 Port Alberni, BC,Can
88/B2 Port Alberni, BC,Can
90/B3 Port Alberni, BC,Can
73/C3 Port Albert, Austl.
34/B3 Portalegre, Port.
34/B3 Portalegre (dist.), Port.
88/F5 Portales, NM,US
93/G4 Portales, NM,US
96/C3 Portales, NM,US
85/M4 Port Alexander, Ak,US
80/D4 Port Alfred, SAfr.
90/B3 Port Alice, BC,Can
88/B2 Port Angeles, Wa,US
90/C3 Port Angeles, Wa,US
103/G2 Port Antonio, Jam.
22/A5 Portarlington, Ire.
89/H6 Port Arthur, Tx,US
93/J5 Port Arthur, Tx,US
96/E4 Port Arthur, Tx,US
95/K1 Port au Choix, Nf,Can
95/K1 Port au Choix Nat'l Hist. Park, Can
68/C8 Port Augusta, Austl.
70/F6 Port Augusta, Austl.
103/H2 Port-au-Prince (cap.), Haiti
104/C3 Port-au-Prince (cap.), Haiti
89/M8 Port-au-Prince (cap.), Haiti
22/C3 Portavogie, NI,UK
29/F4 Porta Westfalica, Ger.
32/C2 Portbail, Fr.
63/F5 Port Blair, India
99/B2 Port Blakely, Wa,US
93/J5 Port Bolivar, Tx,US
96/E4 Port Bolivar, Tx,US
32/E5 Portbou, Sp.
35/G1 Portbou, Sp.
76/E6 Port-Bouët, IvC.
78/E5 Port-Bouët, IvC.
87/K2 Port Burwell, Qu,Can
87/K3 Port-Cartier, Qu,Can
95/H1 Port-Cartier, Qu,Can
89/K6 Port Charlotte, Fl,US
97/H5 Port Charlotte, Fl,US
85/M5 Port Clements, BC,Can
94/D3 Port Clinton, Oh,US
95/R10 Port Colborne, On,Can
95/Q8 Port Credit, On,Can
95/S8 Port Darlington, On,Can
73/C4 Port Davey (har.), Austl.
103/H2 Port-de-Paix, Haiti
66/B3 Port Dickson, Malay.
99/B1 Port Discovery (bay), Wa,US
72/B2 Port Douglas, Austl.
85/M4 Port Edward, BC,Can
107/H4 Portel, Braz.
94/D2 Port Elgin, Can
80/D4 Port Elizabeth, SAfr.
82/E7 Port Elizabeth, SAfr.
22/D3 Port Erin, IM,UK
80/L10 Porterville, SAfr.
92/C3 Porterville, Ca,US
32/F4 Portes-lès-Valence, Fr.
103/J3 Portete (bay), Col.
76/B3 Port-Étienne, Mrta.
32/D5 Portet-sur-Garonne, Fr.
24/B3 Port Eynon (pt.), UK
24/B3 Port Eynon, Wal,UK
73/B3 Port Fairy, Austl.
99/B2 Port Gamble, Wa,US
99/B2 Port Gamble Ind. Res., Wa,US
76/G8 Port-Gentil, Gabon
82/A1 Port-Gentil, Gabon
21/C3 Port Glasgow, Sc,UK
22/B2 Portglenone, NI,UK
85/H4 Port Graham, Ak,US
24/C3 Porth, Wal,UK
76/G7 Port Harcourt, Nga.
79/G5 Port Harcourt, Nga.
86/D3 Port Hardy, BC,Can
90/B3 Port Hardy, BC,Can
95/J2 Port Hawkesbury, NS,Can
24/C4 Porthcawl, Wal,UK
68/A7 Port Hedland, Austl.
70/B4 Port Hedland, Austl.
85/G4 Port Heiden, Ak,US
24/A6 Porthleven, Eng,UK
22/D6 Porthmadog, Wal,UK
109/E7 Port Howard, Falk.
87/H4 Port Huron, Mi,US
89/K3 Port Huron, Mi,US
94/D3 Port Huron, Mi,US
99/H6 Port Huron, Mi,US
51/G2 Port Il'ich, Azer.
34/A4 Portimão, Port.
24/B5 Port Isaac, Eng,UK
24/B5 Port Isaac (bay), Eng,UK
32/A1 Port Isaac, Eng,UK
24/D4 Portishead, Eng,UK
70/D2 Port Keats, Austl.
99/G6 Port Lambton, On,Can
70/G7 Portland, Austl.
73/B3 Portland, Austl.
73/C4 Portland (cape), Austl.
73/D2 Portland, Austl.
103/G2 Portland (pt.), Jam.
24/D6 Portland (pt.), Eng,UK
85/N4 Portland (inlet), BC,Can, Ak,US
94/C3 Portland, In,US
87/J4 Portland, Me,US
89/M3 Portland, Me,US
95/G3 Portland, Me,US
86/D4 Portland, Or,US
88/B2 Portland, Or,US
90/C4 Portland, Or,US
94/C4 Portland, Tn,US
97/G2 Portland, Tn,US
101/F3 Portland, Tx,US
32/B1 Portland, Bill of (pt.), UK
24/D5 Portland, Isle of (pen.), Eng,UK
32/E5 Port-la-Nouvelle, Fr.
35/G1 Port-la-Nouvelle, Fr.
21/B4 Portlaoise, Ire.
101/F2 Port Lavaca, Tx,US
89/G6 Port Lavaca, Tx,US
93/H5 Port Lavaca, Tx,US
96/D4 Port Lavaca, Tx,US
68/C8 Port Lincoln, Austl.
70/F6 Port Lincoln, Austl.
85/H4 Port Lions, Ak,US
76/C6 Port Loko, SLeo.
78/B4 Port Loko, SLeo.
104/F3 Port-Louis, Guad.
81/S15 Port Louis (cap.), Mrts.
99/B2 Port Ludlow, Wa,US
73/B3 Port MacDonnell, Austl.
68/E8 Port Macquarie, Austl.
71/J6 Port Macquarie, Austl.
73/E1 Port Macquarie, Austl.
99/B2 Port Madison Ind. Res., Wa,US
103/G2 Port Maria, Jam.
22/B5 Portmarnock, Ire.
90/B3 Port McNeill, BC,Can
87/K4 Port-Menier, Qu,Can
95/H1 Port-Menier, Qu,Can
103/G2 Portmore, Jam.
68/D5 Port Moresby (cap.), PNG
95/G1 Portneuf (riv.), Qu,Can
80/B3 Port Nolloth, SAfr.
82/C6 Port Nolloth, SAfr.
38/A1 Porto (gulf), Fr.
18/C4 Porto, Port.
34/A2 Porto, Port.
34/A2 Porto (dist.), Port.
108/B4 Pôrto Alegre, Braz.
109/F3 Pôrto Alegre, Braz.
82/B3 Porto Amboim, Ang.
33/J5 Porto Azzurro, It.
108/B3 Pôrto Belo, Braz.
103/G4 Portobelo Nat'l Park, Pan.
38/D2 Portocannone, It.
37/E6 Porto Ceresio, It.
33/K5 Portocivitanova, It.
38/C1 Portocivitanova, It.
40/A4 Portocivitanova, It.
34/A3 Porto de Mós, Port.
38/C4 Porto Empedocle, It.
38/B1 Porto Ercole, It.
33/J5 Portoferraio, It.
38/B1 Portoferraio, It.
108/C2 Pôrto Ferreira, Braz.
104/F5 Port-of-Spain (cap.), Trin.
106/F1 Port-of-Spain (cap.), Trin.
33/K4 Porto Garibaldi, It.
33/K4 Portogruaro, It.
74/K10 Porto Inglês, CpV.
33/J4 Portomaggiore, It.
35/U15 Porto Moniz, Madr.
107/J6 Porto Nacional, Braz.
76/F6 Porto-Novo (cap.), Ben.
79/F5 Porto-Novo (cap.), Ben.
74/J9 Porto Novo, CpV.
64/G3 Portonovo, India
97/H4 Port Orange, Fl,US
99/B2 Port Orchard, Wa,US
38/C1 Porto San Giorgio, It.
40/A4 Porto Sant'Elpidio, It.
35/V14 Porto Santo (isl.)
38/B1 Porto Santo Stefano, It.
38/A2 Porto Torres, It.
108/B3 Pôrto União, Braz.
109/F2 Pôrto União, Braz.
37/E6 Porto Valtravaglia, It.
38/A2 Porto-Vecchio, Fr.
106/F5 Pôrto Velho, Braz.
106/B4 Portoviejo, Ecu.
22/C2 Portpatrick, Sc,UK
71/G7 Port Phillip (bay), Austl.
73/C3 Port Phillip (bay), Austl.
73/F6 Port Phillip (bay), Austl.
68/C8 Port Pirie, Austl.
70/F6 Port Pirie, Austl.
22/B1 Portrush, NI,UK
52/B2 Port Said, Egypt
77/M1 Port Said, Egypt
49/C4 Port Said (Būr Sa'īd), Egypt
50/C4 Port Said (Būr Sa'īd), Egypt
97/G4 Port Saint Joe, Fl,US
32/F5 Port-Saint-Louis-du-Rhône, Fr.
35/H1 Port-Saint-Louis-du-Rhône, Fr.
97/H5 Port Saint Lucie, Fl,US
22/D3 Port Saint Mary, IM,UK
25/E5 Portsea (isl.), Eng,UK
81/E3 Port Shepstone, SAfr.
82/F7 Port Shepstone, SAfr.
85/M4 Port Simpson, BC,Can
25/F5 Portslade by Sea, Eng,UK
104/F4 Portsmouth, Dom.
18/C3 Portsmouth, Eng,UK
25/E5 Portsmouth, Eng,UK
32/C1 Portsmouth, Eng,UK
87/J4 Portsmouth, NH,US
89/M3 Portsmouth, NH,US
95/G3 Portsmouth, NH,US
89/K4 Portsmouth, Oh,US
94/D4 Portsmouth, Oh,US
97/H2 Portsmouth, Oh,US
94/E4 Portsmouth, Va,US
97/J2 Portsmouth, Va,US
71/J6 Port Stephens (bay), Austl.
73/E2 Port Stephens (bay), Austl.
109/D7 Port Stephens, Falk.
22/B1 Portstewart, NI,UK
52/C5 Port Sudan, Sudan
77/N4 Port Sudan, Sudan
26/D5 Port-sur-Saône, Fr.
32/G3 Port-sur-Saône, Fr.
36/C2 Port-sur-Saône, Fr.
24/C3 Port Talbot, Wal,UK
90/C3 Port Townsend, Wa,US
18/B5 Portugal
34/A3 Portugal
32/B5 Portugalete, Sp.
34/D1 Portugalete, Sp.
21/A4 Portumna, Ire.
32/E5 Port-Vendres, Fr.
35/G1 Port-Vendres, Fr.
98/G5 Port Washington, NY,US
91/M5 Port Washington, Wi,US
93/L2 Port Washington, Wi,US
94/C3 Port Washington, Wi,US
66/B3 Port Weld, Malay.
22/D2 Port William, Sc,UK
109/B7 Porvenir, Chile
34/C3 Porzuna, Sp.
38/A2 Posada, It.
109/E2 Posadas, Arg.
34/C4 Posadas, Sp.
40/C3 Posavina (vall.), Bosn.
40/C3 Posavina (vall.), Cro.
37/G5 Poschiavo, Swi.
40/D5 Poshnjë, Alb.
53/G2 Posht-e Bādām, Iran
20/J2 Posio, Fin.
42/F2 Posio, Fin.
67/F4 Poso (lake), Indo.
45/G4 Posof, Turk.
51/E1 Posof, Turk.
55/K5 Posŏng, SKor.
58/D5 Posŏng, SKor.
58/D5 Posŏng (bay), SKor.
58/D5 Posŏng (riv.), SKor.
99/C2 Possession (pt.), Wa,US
99/C2 Possession (sound), Wa,US
101/E1 Post, Tx,US
93/G4 Post, Tx,US
96/C3 Post, Tx,US
37/H4 Postal (Burgstall), It.
42/E5 Postavy, Bela.
90/D4 Post Falls, Id,US
80/C3 Postmasburg, SAfr.
33/L4 Postojna, Slov.
40/B3 Postojna, Slov.
60/A2 Potala Palace, China
39/H5 Potamós, Gre.
80/D2 Potchefstroom, SAfr.
80/P13 Potchefstroom, SAfr.
93/J4 Poteau, Ok,US
96/E3 Poteau, Ok,US
18/E4 Potenza, It.
38/C1 Potenza (riv.), It.
38/D2 Potenza, It.
40/B5 Potenza, It.
34/C1 Potes, Sp.
90/D4 Potholes (res.), Wa,US
107/K5 Poti (riv.), Braz.
19/H4 Poti, Geo.
45/G4 Poti, Geo.
46/E5 Poti, Geo.
50/E1 Poti, Geo.
33/J5 Poti, Alpe di (peak), It.
76/H5 Potiskum, Nga.
94/E4 Potomac (riv.), Md, Va,US
98/J7 Potomac, Md,US
98/J7 Potomac (riv.), Md, Va,US
106/E7 Potosí, Bol.
88/F7 Potosí, Mex.
93/K3 Potosi, Mo,US
97/F2 Potosi, Mo,US
109/C2 Potrerillos, Chile
18/E3 Potsdam, Ger.
26/G2 Potsdam, Ger.
46/B4 Potsdam, Ger.
94/F2 Potsdam, NY,US
27/J5 Pottendorf, Aus.
33/M3 Pottendorf, Aus.
40/C2 Pottendorf, Aus.
19/N6 Potters Bar, Eng,UK
25/F3 Potters Bar, Eng,UK
25/F2 Potterspury, Eng,UK
25/F2 Potton, Eng,UK
94/F3 Pottstown, Pa,US
94/E3 Pottsville, Pa,US
62/D6 Pottuvil, SrL.
89/M3 Poughkeepsie, NY,US
94/F3 Poughkeepsie, NY,US
36/B3 Pouilley-les-Vignes, Fr.
22/B5 Poulaphouca (res.), Ire.
99/B2 Poulsbo, Wa,US
23/G5 Poulter (riv.), Eng,UK
23/F4 Poulton-le-Fylde, Eng,UK
58/D4 Poŭn, SKor.
33/G4 Pourri (mtn.), Fr.
31/E4 Pouru-Saint-Rémy, Fr.
107/J8 Pouso Alegre, Braz.
108/C2 Pouso Alegre, Braz.
109/G1 Pouso Alegre, Braz.
63/H5 Pouthisat, Camb.
63/H5 Pouthisat (riv.), Camb.
65/C3 Pouthisat, Camb.
65/C3 Pouthisat (riv.), Camb.
66/B1 Pouthisat (riv.), Camb.
32/C3 Pouzauges, Fr.
27/K4 Považská Bystrica, Slvk.
34/A2 Póvoa de Varzim, Port.
45/G2 Povorino, Rus.
55/L3 Povorotnyy, Mys (cape), Rus.
87/J2 Povungnituk, Qu,Can
87/J2 Povungnituk (riv.), Qu,Can
91/G4 Powder (riv.), Mt, Wy,US
88/E2 Powder (riv.), Mt, Wy,US
86/F4 Powder (riv.), Mt,Wy,US
92/E3 Powell (lake), Az, Ut,US
104/B1 Powell (pt.), Bahm.
88/E3 Powell, Wy,US
90/F4 Powell, Wy,US
92/E1 Powell, Wy,US
86/D4 Powell River, BC,Can
88/B2 Powell River, BC,Can
90/B3 Powell River, BC,Can
95/R9 Power (res.), NY,US
99/P14 Powers (lake), Wi,US
23/E6 Powys (co.), Wal,UK
24/C2 Powys (co.), Wal,UK
24/C1 Powys, Vale (vall.), Wal,UK
107/H7 Poxoréo, Braz.
59/C5 Poyang (lake), China
61/G2 Poyang (lake), China
23/F5 Poynton, Eng,UK
34/A1 Poyo, Sp.
27/J4 Poysdorf, Aus.
50/C2 Pozantı, Turk.
40/E3 Požarevac, Yugo.
44/B3 Požarevac, Yugo.
101/F4 Poza Rica, Mex.
101/M6 Poza Rica, Mex.
102/B1 Poza Rica, Mex.
40/E4 Požega, Yugo.
18/E3 Poznań, Pol.
27/J2 Poznań, Pol.
27/J2 Poznań (prov.), Pol.
44/A1 Poznań, Pol.
46/B4 Poznań, Pol.
34/D4 Pozo Alcón, Sp.
34/C3 Pozoblanco, Sp.
34/E3 Pozohondo, Sp.
35/N9 Pozuelo de Alarcón, Sp.
104/E5 Pozuelos, Ven.
38/D4 Pozzallo, It.
38/C1 Pozzoni (peak), It.
27/K2 Prabuty, Pol.
63/G5 Pracham Hiang (pt.), Thai.
65/B4 Pracham Hiang (pt.), Thai.
27/H4 Prachatice, Czh.
33/L2 Prachatice, Czh.
63/H5 Prachin Buri, Thai.
65/C3 Prachin Buri, Thai.
65/C3 Prachin Buri (riv.), Thai.
63/G5 Prachuap Khiri Khan, Thai.
65/B4 Prachuap Khiri Khan, Thai.
66/A1 Prachuap Khiri Khan, Thai.
37/G4 Prad am Stilfserjoch (Prato allo Stelvio), It.
27/J3 Praděd (peak), Czh.
32/E5 Prades, Fr.
35/G1 Prades, Fr.
107/L7 Prado, Braz.
108/E1 Prado, Braz.
98/C3 Prado (dam), Ca,US
34/C4 Prado del Rey, Sp.
98/C3 Prado Flood Control Basin, Ca,US
37/E4 Pragelpass (pass), Swi.
18/E3 Prague (cap.), Czh.
46/B4 Prague (cap.), Czh.
27/H3 Prague (Praha) (cap.), Czh.
33/L1 Prague (Praha) (cap.), Czh.
27/H3 Praha (reg.), Czh.
33/L1 Praha (reg.), Czh.
27/H3 Praha (Prague) (cap.), Czh.
33/L1 Praha (Prague) (cap.), Czh.
41/G3 Prahova (co.), Rom.
74/K11 Praia (cap.), CpV.
74/K11 Praia (int'l arpt.), CpV.
35/S12 Praia de Victória, Azor.
108/C3 Praia Grande, Braz.
88/F5 Prairie Dog Town Fk. (riv.), Ok, Tx,US
93/G4 Prairie Dog Town Fork (riv.), Ok, Tx,US
91/L5 Prairie du Chien, Wi,US
93/K2 Prairie du Chien, Wi,US
94/B3 Prairie du Chien, Wi,US
99/P15 Prairie Grove, Il,US
95/N6 Prairies (riv.), Qu,Can
91/J4 Prairies, Coteau des (upland), US
101/G2 Prairie View, Tx,US
96/E4 Prairie View, Tx,US
63/G5 Pran Buri (res.), Thai.
65/B3 Pran Buri (res.), Thai.
66/A1 Pran Buri (res.), Thai.
36/C5 Prangins, Swi.
62/D4 Prānhita (riv.), India
66/A3 Prapat, Indo.
63/H5 Prasat Preah Vihear, Camb.
65/D3 Prasat Preah Vihear, Camb.
27/K3 Praszka, Pol.
108/B1 Prata, Braz.
108/B1 Prata (riv.), Braz.
61/H4 Pratas (reef), China
61/H4 Pratas (Dongsha) (isl.), China
37/F4 Prätigau (val.), Swi.
33/J5 Prato, It.
37/G4 Prato allo Stelvio (Prad am Stilfserjoch), It.
38/C1 Pratola Peligna, It.
40/A4 Pratola Peligna, It.
37/E5 Prato (Leventina), Swi.
89/G4 Pratt, Ks,US
93/H3 Pratt, Ks,US
96/D2 Pratt, Ks,US
36/D2 Pratteln, Swi.
97/G3 Prattville, Al,US
36/B2 Prauthoy, Fr.
39/H1 Pravets, Bul.
41/F4 Pravets, Bul.
34/B1 Pravia, Sp.
24/C6 Prawle (pt.), UK
32/B1 Prawle (pt.), UK
100/D2 Praxedis G. Guerrero, Mex.
67/E5 Praya, Indo.
30/B5 Précy-sur-Oise, Fr.
33/J3 Predazzo, It.
41/G3 Predeal, Rom.
91/H3 Preeceville, Sk,Can
23/F6 Prees, Eng,UK
23/F4 Preesall, Eng,UK
26/F1 Preetz, Ger.
27/L1 Pregolya (riv.), Rus.
20/H4 Preiļi, Lat.
42/E4 Preiļi, Lat.
94/E1 Preissac (lake), On,Can
65/D4 Prek Pouthi, Camb.
37/F5 Premana, It.
26/B5 Prémery, Fr.
32/E3 Prémery, Fr.
35/L7 Premiá de Mar, Sp.
40/E5 Prenjas, Alb.
27/G2 Prenzlau, Ger.
27/J4 Přerov, Czh.
36/C6 Pré-Saint-Didier, It.
33/J3 Presanella (peak), It.
37/G5 Presanella, Cima (peak), It.
23/F5 Prescot, Eng,UK
94/F2 Prescott, On,Can
88/D5 Prescott, Az,US
92/D4 Prescott, Az,US
39/G1 Preševo, Yugo.
40/E4 Preševo, Yugo.
44/B4 Preševo, Yugo.
109/D2 Presidencia Roque Sáenz Peña, Arg.
107/K5 Presidente Dutra, Braz.
107/H8 Presidente Epitácio, Braz.
108/A2 Presidente Epitácio, Braz.
108/C1 Presidente Olegário, Braz.
107/H8 Presidente Prudente, Braz.
108/B2 Presidente Prudente, Braz.
109/F1 Presidente Prudente, Braz.
107/H8 Presidente Venceslau, Braz.
108/B2 Presidente Venceslau, Braz.
98/F6 Presidential Lake, NJ,US
100/D4 Presidio (riv.), Mex.
100/D2 Presidio, Tx,US
88/F6 Presidio, Tx,US
93/F5 Presidio, Tx,US
96/B4 Presidio, Tx,US
41/H4 Preslav, Bul.
19/U10 Presles-en-Brie, Fr.
30/B6 Presles-en-Brie, Fr.
37/G6 Presolana, Pizzo della (peak), It.
27/L4 Prešov, Slvk.
44/B2 Prešov, Slvk.
39/G2 Prespa (lake), Eur.
40/E5 Prespa (lake), Eur.
87/K4 Presque Isle, Me,US
89/N2 Presque Isle, Me,US
95/G2 Presque Isle, Me,US
23/E5 Prestatyn, Wal,UK
79/E5 Prestea, Gha.
24/D2 Presteigne, Wal,UK
27/G4 Přeštice, Czh.
33/K2 Přeštice, Czh.
73/G5 Preston, Austl.
23/F4 Preston, Eng,UK
24/D5 Preston, Eng,UK
90/F5 Preston, Id,US
92/E2 Preston, Id,US
99/D2 Preston, Wa,US
94/D4 Prestonsburg, Ky,US
97/H2 Prestonsburg, Ky,US
23/F4 Prestwich, Eng,UK
25/F3 Prestwood, Eng,UK
107/J6 Prêto (riv.), Braz.
80/E2 Pretoria (cap.), SAfr.
80/Q12 Pretoria (cap.), SAfr.
82/E6 Pretoria (cap.), SAfr.
29/F4 Preussisch Oldendorf, Ger.
33/L3 Prevalje, Slov.
40/B2 Prevalje, Slov.
39/G3 Préveza, Gre.
95/M6 Prévost, Qu,Can
47/M4 Priargunsk, Rus.
85/D4 Pribilof (isls.), Ak,US
40/D4 Priboj, Yugo.
27/H4 Příbram, Czh.
33/L2 Příbram, Czh.
88/D4 Price, Ut,US
92/E3 Price, Ut,US
92/E3 Price (riv.), Ut,US
97/F4 Prichard, Al,US
101/F2 Priddy, Tx,US
34/D2 Priego, Sp.
34/C4 Priego de Córdoba, Sp.
20/G5 Priekulė, Lith.
42/D5 Priekule, Lith.
27/M1 Prienai, Lith.
80/C3 Prieska, SAfr.
82/D6 Prieska, SAfr.
90/D3 Priest (lake), Id,US
90/D3 Priest River, Id,US
34/C1 Prieta (mtn.), Sp.
27/K4 Prievidza, Slvk.
26/F2 Prignitz (reg.), Ger.
40/C3 Prijedor, Bosn.
39/F1 Prijepolje, Yugo.
40/D4 Prijepolje, Yugo.
45/H3 Prikaspian (plain), Kaz., Rus.
45/H3 Prikaspian (plain), Rus.
46/E5 Prikaspian (plain), Kaz.,Rus.
45/H3 Prikumsk, Rus.
39/G2 Prilep, Macd.
40/E5 Prilep, Macd.
36/C4 Prilly, Swi.
18/G3 Priluki, Ukr.
44/E2 Priluki, Ukr.
46/D4 Priluki, Ukr.
38/C2 Prima Porta, It.
25/E1 Primethorpe, Eng,UK
51/G1 Primorsk, Azer.
20/J3 Primorsk, Rus.
27/L1 Primorsk, Rus.
42/F3 Primorsk, Rus.
45/H2 Primorsk, Rus.
47/P5 Primorsk Kray, Rus.
41/H4 Primorsko, Bul.
44/F3 Primorsko-Akhtarsk, Rus.
41/K3 Primorskoye, Ukr.
90/F2 Primrose (lake), Ab, Sk,Can
31/F5 Prims (riv.), Ger.
86/E1 Prince Albert (pen.), NW,Can
86/E1 Prince Albert (sound), NW,Can
86/F3 Prince Albert, Sk,Can
91/G2 Prince Albert, Sk,Can
80/C4 Prince Albert, SAfr.
91/G2 Prince Albert Nat'l Park, Ab, Sk,Can
86/F3 Prince Albert Nat'l Park, Ab,Sk,Can
86/D1 Prince Alfred (cape), NW,Can
87/Q7 Prince Alfred (cape), NW,Can
87/J2 Prince Charles (isl.), NW,Can
84/L5 Prince Edward (isl.), Can.
17/L8 Prince Edward (isls.), SAfr.
87/K4 Prince Edward Island (prov.), Can.
89/P2 Prince Edward Island (prov.), Can.
95/J2 Prince Edward Island (prov.), Can
95/J2 Prince Edward Island Nat'l Park, Can
86/D3 Prince George, BC,Can
90/C2 Prince George, BC,Can
98/K8 Prince Georges (co.), Md,US
87/R7 Prince Gustav Adolf (sea), NW,Can
83/C Prince Harold (coast), Ant.
86/G1 Prince Leopold (isl.), NW,Can
28/C2 Princenhof (lake), Neth.
70/G2 Prince of Wales (isl.), Austl.
84/G2 Prince of Wales (isl.), Can.
86/E1 Prince of Wales (str.), NW,Can
86/G1 Prince of Wales (isl.), NW,Can
87/R7 Prince of Wales (str.), NW,Can
85/M4 Prince of Wales (isl.), Ak,US
86/C3 Prince of Wales (isl.), Ak,US
83/C Prince Olav (coast), Ant.
84/E2 Prince Patrick (isl.), Can.
87/R7 Prince Patrick (isl.), NW,Can
86/G1 Prince Regent (inlet), NW,Can
85/M4 Prince Rupert, BC,Can
86/C3 Prince Rupert, BC,Can
25/F3 Princes Risborough, Eng,UK
83/A Princess Astrid (coast), Ant.
71/G2 Princess Charlotte (bay), Austl.
72/A1 Princess Charlotte (bay), Austl.
87/S6 Princess Margaret (range), NW,Can
83/Z Princess Martha (coast), Ant.
83/B Princess Ragnhild (coast), Ant.
90/A2 Princess Royal (isl. BC,Can
86/D3 Princess Royal (isl. BC,Can
90/C3 Princeton, BC,Can
91/L5 Princeton, Il,US
93/K2 Princeton, Il,US
94/B3 Princeton, Il,US
94/C4 Princeton, In,US
97/G2 Princeton, In,US
89/J4 Princeton, Ky,US
94/C4 Princeton, Ky,US
97/G2 Princeton, Ky,US
91/K4 Princeton, Mn,US
98/F5 Princeton, NJ,US
94/D4 Princeton, WV,US
97/H2 Princeton, WV,US
88/S9 Princeville, Hi,US
85/J3 Prince William (sound), Ak,US
86/B2 Prince William (sound), Ak,US
76/G7 Príncipe (isl.), SaoT
85/K3 Prindle (vol.), Ak,US
88/B3 Prineville, Or,US
90/C4 Prineville, Or,US
36/C6 Pringy, Fr.
28/B5 Prinsenbeek, Neth.
28/C2 Prinses Margriet (can.), Neth.
103/E3 Prinzapolka (riv.), Nic.
103/F3 Prinzapolka, Nic.
38/D4 Priolo di Gargallo,
34/A1 Prior (cape), Sp.
33/K5 Priore (peak), It.
46/J5 Priozernyy, Kaz.
20/J3 Priozersk, Rus.
42/F3 Priozersk, Rus.
44/C2 Pripet (marshes), Bela., Ukr.
46/C4 Pripyat (riv.), Bela.
18/F3 Pripyat (riv.), Bela., Ukr.
44/D2 Pripyat' (riv.), Bela., Ukr.
27/N3 Pripyat' (riv.), Ukr.
29/G1 Prisdorf, Ger.
51/G2 Prishib, Azer.
18/F4 Priština, Yugo.
39/G1 Priština, Yugo.
40/E4 Priština, Yugo.
37/G1 Prittriching, Ger.
26/G2 Pritzwalk, Ger.
32/F4 Privas, Fr.
45/H2 Privolzhskiy, Rus.
45/K1 Priyutovo, Rus.
39/G1 Prizren, Yugo.
40/E4 Prizren, Yugo.
40/C3 Prnjavor, Bosn.
40/D3 Prnjavor, Yugo.
39/H2 Probištip, Macd.
40/F5 Probištip, Macd.
66/D5 Probolinggo, Indo.
62/C5 Proddatūr, India
34/B3 Proença-a-Nova, Port.
101/M7 Profesor Rafael Ramírez, Mex.
31/D3 Profondeville, Belg
32/F1 Profondeville, Belg
101/E3 Progreso, Mex.
101/H4 Progreso, Mex.
102/D1 Progreso, Mex.
103/F4 Progreso, Pan.
101/K6 Progreso de Obreg Mex.
47/N5 Progress, Rus.
55/K2 Progress, Rus.
45/H4 Prokhladnyy, Rus.
46/J4 Prokop'yevsk, Rus.
39/G1 Prokuplje, Yugo.
40/E4 Prokuplje, Yugo.
44/B4 Prokuplje, Yugo.
60/B5 Prome, Burma
63/G4 Prome, Burma
108/B2 Promissão, Braz.
108/B2 Promissão (res.), Braz.
107/L6 Propriá, Braz.
38/A2 Propriano, Fr.
71/H4 Proserpine, Austl.
72/C3 Proserpine, Austl.
27/J2 Prosna (riv.), Pol.
39/H2 Prosotsáni, Gre.
41/F5 Prosotsáni, Gre.
85/L3 Prospector (mtn.), Yk,Can
22/B5 Prosperous, Ire.
27/J4 Prostějov, Czh.
72/C4 Proston, Austl.
27/L3 Prószowice, Pol.
41/H4 Provadiya, Bul.
32/F5 Provence (reg.), Fr.
33/G5 Provence (mts.), Fr.
33/G4 Provence-Alpes-Côte d'Azur (reg.), Fr.
35/H1 Provence-Alpes-Côte d'Azur (reg.), Fr.
87/J4 Providence (cap.), RI,US
89/M3 Providence (cap.), RI,US
95/G3 Providence (cap.), RI,US
106/F6 Providência (mts.), Braz.
103/F3 Providencia (isl.), C
103/H1 Providenciales (isl.), Trks.
104/C2 Providenciales (isl.), Trks.

169

Provi – Rabau

26/B4 **Provins**, Fr.
32/E2 **Provins**, Fr.
86/E4 **Provo**, Ut,US
92/E2 **Provo**, Ut,US
88/D3 **Provo**, Ut,US
35/T13 **Provoação**, Azor.
90/F2 **Provost**, Ab,Can
40/C4 **Prozor**, Bosn.
108/B3 **Prudentópolis**, Braz.
23/G2 **Prudhoe**, Eng,UK
84/C2 **Prudhoe** (bay), US
85/J1 **Prudhoe** (bay), Ak,US
85/J1 **Prudhoe Bay**, Ak,US
27/J3 **Prudnik**, Pol.
26/D3 **Prüm** (riv.), Ger.
31/F3 **Prüm** (riv.), Ger.
38/A2 **Prunelli-di-Fiumorbo**, Fr.
27/K1 **Pruszcz Gdański**, Pol.
27/L2 **Pruszków**, Pol.
18/F4 **Prut** (riv.), Eur.
44/C3 **Prut** (riv.), Eur.
46/C5 **Prut** (riv.), Eur.
41/J2 **Prut** (riv.), Mol., Rom.
44/C1 **Pruzhany**, Bela.
83/F **Prydz** (bay), Ant.
96/E2 **Pryor** (Creek), Ok,US
27/L2 **Przasnysz**, Pol.
27/H3 **Przemków**, Pol.
18/F4 **Przemyśl**, Pol.
27/M4 **Przemyśl**, Pol.
27/M4 **Przemyśl** (prov.), Pol.
44/B2 **Przemyśl**, Pol.
46/C5 **Przemyśl**, Pol.
27/M3 **Przeworsk**, Pol.
46/H5 **Przheval'sk**, Kyr.
42/C5 **Przylądek Rozewie** (cape), Pol.
27/L3 **Przysucha**, Pol.
39/H3 **Psakhná**, Gre.
39/J3 **Psará** (isl.), Gre.
39/G4 **Psárion**, Gre.
44/E2 **Psël** (riv.), Ukr.
20/J4 **Pskov** (lake), Est.,Rus.
42/F4 **Pskov** (lake), Est., Rus.
18/F3 **Pskov**, Rus.
20/J4 **Pskov**, Rus.
42/F4 **Pskov**, Rus.
46/C4 **Pskov**, Rus.
20/J4 **Pskov Obl.**, Rus.
42/F4 **Pskov Obl.**, Rus.
27/K4 **Pszczyna**, Pol.
39/G2 **Ptolemaís**, Gre.
40/E5 **Ptolemaís**, Gre.
33/L3 **Ptuj**, Slov.
40/B2 **Ptuj**, Slov.
65/C2 **Pua**, Thai.
60/E3 **Pu'an**, China
32/D5 **Puan**, SKor.
58/D5 **Puan**, SKor.
61/F4 **Pubei**, China
06/D5 **Pucallpa**, Peru
99/G7 **Puce**, On,Can
59/B4 **Pucheng**, China
37/H1 **Puchheim**, Ger.
50/D4 **Puch'on**, SKor.
58/F7 **Puch'on**, SKor.
41/G3 **Pucioasa**, Rom.
27/K1 **Puck**, Pol.
25/G3 **Puckeridge**, Eng,UK
02/D2 **Pucté**, Mex.
20/H2 **Pudasjärvi**, Fin.
42/E2 **Pudasjärvi**, Fin.
24/D5 **Puddletown**, Eng,UK
31/G2 **Puderbach**, Ger.
23/G4 **Pudsey**, Eng,UK
60/D3 **Pudu** (riv.), China
63/H2 **Pudu** (riv.), China
62/C5 **Pudukkottai**, India
64/C3 **Pudukkottai**, India
101/F5 **Puebla**, Mex.
101/F5 **Puebla** (state), Mex.
101/L8 **Puebla** (state), Mex.
02/B2 **Puebla**, Mex.
02/B2 **Puebla** (state), Mex.
84/H8 **Puebla**, Mex.
34/C3 **Puebla de Alcocer**, Sp.
34/D4 **Puebla de Don Fadrique**, Sp.
34/B3 **Puebla de la Calzada**, Sp.
34/A1 **Puebla del Caramiñal**, Sp.
34/B1 **Puebla de Sanabria**, Sp.
34/B1 **Puebla de Trives**, Sp.
101/L7 **Puebla de Zaragoza**, Mex.
03/H4 **Pueblito**, Col.
101/L8 **Pueblo** (state), Mex.
88/F4 **Pueblo**, Co,US
93/F3 **Pueblo**, Co,US
96/B2 **Pueblo**, Co,US
02/E3 **Pueblo Nuevo**, Nic.
02/D3 **Pueblo Nuevo Tiquisate**, Guat.
09/B3 **Puente Alto**, Chile
34/A1 **Puenteareas**, Sp.
34/A1 **Puente Caldelas**, Sp.
34/A1 **Puente-Ceso**, Sp.
01/K8 **Puente de Ixtla**, Mex.
34/A1 **Puentedeume**, Sp.
34/C4 **Puente-Genil**, Sp.
34/B1 **Puentes de García Rodríguez**, Sp.
8/R10 **Pueo** (pt.), Hi,US
60/D4 **Pu'er**, China
92/E4 **Puerco** (riv.), Az, NM,US
92/F4 **Puerco** (riv.), NM,US
09/B6 **Puerto Aisén**, Chile
03/F4 **Puerto Armuelles**, Pan.
06/C3 **Puerto Asís**, Col.
06/E2 **Puerto Ayacucho**, Ven.
02/D3 **Puerto Barrios**, Guat.
06/D6 **Puerto Bermúdez**, Peru
04/D5 **Puerto Cabello**, Ven.
06/E1 **Puerto Cabello**, Ven.
103/F3 **Puerto Cabezas**, Nic.
106/E2 **Puerto Carreño**, Col.
109/B5 **Puerto Cisnes**, Chile
103/F4 **Puerto Cortés**, CR
100/C3 **Puerto Cortés**, Mex.
104/D5 **Puerto Cumarebo**, Ven.
35/X16 **Puerto de la Cruz**, Canl.
100/B2 **Puerto de La Libertad**, Mex.
35/Y16 **Puerto del Rosario**, Canl.
34/A1 **Puerto del Son**, Sp.
109/C6 **Puerto Deseado**, Arg.
103/G4 **Puerto Escondido**, Col.
102/B3 **Puerto Escondido**, Mex.
109/F2 **Puerto Iguazú**, Arg.
106/E3 **Puerto Inírida**, Col.
104/E5 **Puerto La Cruz**, Ven.
106/F1 **Puerto La Cruz**, Ven.
106/D4 **Puerto Leguízamo**, Col.
103/F3 **Puerto Lempira**, Hon.
34/C3 **Puertollano**, Sp.
104/D5 **Puerto López**, Col.
34/E4 **Puerto Lumbreras**, Sp.
102/C3 **Puerto Madero**, Mex.
109/C5 **Puerto Madryn**, Arg.
106/E6 **Puerto Maldonado**, Peru
109/B5 **Puerto Montt**, Chile
102/E3 **Puerto Morazán**, Nic.
102/E1 **Puerto Morelos**, Mex.
109/B7 **Puerto Natales**, Chile
109/C7 **Puerto Nuevo**, Chile
103/G4 **Puerto Obaldía**, Pan.
103/G1 **Puerto Padre**, Cuba
100/B2 **Puerto Peñasco**, Mex.
104/E5 **Puerto Píritu**, Ven.
104/D3 **Puerto Plata**, DRep.
67/E2 **Puerto Princesa**, Phil.
34/B4 **Puerto Real**, Sp.
106/C3 **Puerto Rico**, Col.
104/E3 **Puerto Rico** (commonwealth), US
34/C4 **Puerto Serrano**, Sp.
106/G7 **Puerto Suárez**, Bol.
100/D4 **Puerto Vallarta**, Mex.
109/B5 **Puerto Varas**, Chile
103/E4 **Puerto Viejo**, CR
22/D5 **Puffin** (isl.), Wal,UK
45/J1 **Pugachev**, Rus.
90/C4 **Puget** (sound), Wa,US
86/D4 **Puget** (sound), Wa,US
88/B2 **Puget** (sound), Wa,US
99/C2 **Puget** (sound), Wa,US
38/E2 **Puglia** (reg.), It.
40/C5 **Puglia** (reg.), It.
32/D5 **Puigcerdà**, Sp.
35/F1 **Puigcerdà**, Sp.
32/E5 **Puigmal** (mtn.), Fr.
35/G1 **Puigmal** (mtn.), Fr.
35/G1 **Puigsacalm** (mtn.), Sp.
78/C5 **Pujehun**, SLeo.
60/D2 **Pujiang**, China
58/D2 **Pujŏn** (lake), NKor.
66/C5 **Pujut** (cape), Indo.
88/T10 **Pukalani**, Hi,US
58/F6 **Puk'ansan** (mt.), SKor.
58/D4 **Puk'an-san Nat'l Park**, SKor.
58/F6 **Puk'an-san Nat'l Park**, SKor.
69/J6 **Pukapuka** (isl.), Cookls.
69/M6 **Puka Puka** (atoll), FrPol.
69/M6 **Pukarua** (isl.), FrPol.
91/M3 **Pukaskwa Nat'l Park**, On,Can
87/H4 **Pukaskwa Nat'l Park**, On,Can
89/J2 **Pukaskwa Nat'l Park**, On,Can
94/C1 **Pukaskwa Nat'l Park**, On,Can
55/K4 **Pukch'ang**, NKor.
58/E2 **Pukch'ŏng**, NKor.
58/E2 **Pukdae** (riv.), NKor.
40/D4 **Pukë**, Alb.
58/D3 **Pukhan** (riv.), NKor., SKor.
58/D4 **Pukhan** (riv.), SKor.
58/G6 **Pukhan** (riv.), SKor.
88/T10 **Pukoo**, Hi,US
39/G1 **Pukovac**, Yugo.
40/E4 **Pukovac**, Yugo.
58/E2 **Pukp'ot'ae-san** (mtn.), NKor.
33/K4 **Pula**, Cro.
40/A3 **Pula**, Cro.
106/E8 **Pulacayo**, Bol.
58/A3 **Pulandian** (bay), China
67/F1 **Pulanduta** (pt.), Phil.
68/D4 **Pulap** (atoll), Micr.
89/J4 **Pulaski**, Tn,US
97/G3 **Pulaski**, Tn,US
94/D4 **Pulaski**, Va,US
67/J5 **Pulau** (riv.), Indo.
27/L3 **Puławy**, Pol.
44/B2 **Puławy**, Pol.
25/F5 **Pulborough**, Eng,UK
56/A3 **Pulguk-sa**, SKor.
58/E5 **Pulguk-sa**, SKor.
28/D7 **Pulheim**, Ger.
31/F2 **Pulheim**, Ger.
67/G3 **Pulisan** (cape), Indo.
64/F4 **Puliyangudi**, India
37/H1 **Pullach im Isartal**, Ger.
86/E4 **Pullman**, Wa,US
88/C2 **Pullman**, Wa,US
90/D4 **Pullman**, Wa,US
33/G3 **Pully**, Swi.
36/C5 **Pully**, Swi.
61/J5 **Pulog** (mt.), Phil.
27/G3 **Pulsnitz** (riv.), Ger.
27/L2 **Pułtusk**, Pol.
44/F5 **Pülümür**, Turk.
50/D2 **Pülümür**, Turk.
68/D4 **Puluwat** (atoll), Micr.
36/D2 **Pulversheim**, Fr.
24/C2 **Pumpsaint**, Wal,UK
63/F2 **Pumu** (pass), China
106/B4 **Puna** (isl.), Ecu.
69/X15 **Punaauia**, FrPol.
62/E2 **Punākha**, Bhu.
64/F4 **Punalūr**, India
106/E7 **Punata**, Bol.
53/K2 **Pūnch**, India
64/C1 **Pūnch**, India
64/C1 **Punch** (riv.), India
66/B3 **Punggai** (cape), Malay.
58/E4 **P'unggi**, SKor.
58/E2 **P'ungsan**, NKor.
82/F4 **Pungwe** (fall, falls), Zim.
77/L8 **Punia**, Zaire
82/E1 **Punia**, Zaire
64/C2 **Punjab** (state), India
53/K2 **Punjab** (plains), Pak.
62/B2 **Punjab** (prov.), Pak.
64/B2 **Punjab** (plain), Pak.
64/B2 **Punjab** (prov.), Pak.
64/G4 **Punkudutivu** (isl.), SrL.
106/D7 **Puno**, Peru
100/B3 **Punta Abreojos**, Mex.
102/E2 **Punta Allen**, Mex.
109/D4 **Punta Alta**, Arg.
109/B7 **Punta Arenas**, Chile
92/D5 **Punta Baja** (pt.), Mex
100/A2 **Punta Banda, Cabo** (cape), Mex.
104/D5 **Punta Cardón**, Ven.
92/C5 **Punta Colnett** (pt.), Mex
37/E5 **Punta d'Arbola** (Ofenhorn) (peak), It.
106/F2 **Punta de Mata**, Ven.
92/D5 **Punta Estrella** (pt.), Mex
102/D2 **Punta Gorda**, Belz.
103/F4 **Punta Gorda** (bay), Nic.
104/A1 **Punta Gorda**, Fl,US
97/H5 **Punta Gorda**, Fl,US
100/B2 **Punta Peñasco**, Mex.
88/D5 **Punta Peñasco**, Mex.
92/D5 **Punta Peñasco**, Mex.
92/D6 **Punta Prieta**, Mex
103/E4 **Puntarenas**, CR
34/B4 **Punta Umbría**, Sp.
81/S15 **Puodre d'Or**, Mrts.
88/S10 **Puolo** (pt.), Hi,US
59/C5 **Puqi**, China
61/G2 **Puqi**, China
106/D6 **Puquio**, Peru
46/H3 **Pur** (riv.), Rus.
106/C3 **Puracé** (vol.), Col.
106/C3 **Puracé Nat'l Park**, Col.
24/D5 **Purbeck, Isle of** (pen.), Eng,UK
93/H4 **Purcell**, Ok,US
96/D3 **Purcell**, Ok,US
37/G1 **Pürgen**, Ger.
33/L2 **Purgstall an der Erlauf**, Aus.
40/B1 **Purgstall an der Erlauf**, Aus.
62/D3 **Puri**, India
20/H4 **Purikari** (pt.), Est.
42/E4 **Purikari** (pt.), Est.
19/N8 **Purley**, Eng,UK
26/C2 **Purmerend**, Neth.
28/B3 **Purmerend**, Neth.
53/L5 **Pūrna** (riv.), India
62/C3 **Pūrna** (riv.), India
62/C4 **Pūrnia**, India
109/B5 **Purranque**, Chile
25/E3 **Purton**, Eng,UK
101/E4 **Puruándiro de Calderón**, Mex.
105/C3 **Purus** (riv.), Braz.
106/F4 **Purús** (riv.), Braz.
39/J1 **Pŭrvomay**, Bul.
41/G4 **Pŭrvomay**, Bul.
66/C5 **Purwokerto**, Indo.
55/K3 **Puryŏng**, NKor.
62/C4 **Pusad**, India
47/N6 **Pusan**, SKor.
55/K4 **Pusan**, SKor.
56/A3 **Pusan**, SKor.
58/E5 **Pusan**, SKor.
56/A3 **Pusan-jikhalsi** (prov.), SKor.
58/E5 **Pusan-Jikhalsi**, SKor.
66/A2 **Pusat Gayo** (mts.), Indo.
42/H5 **Pushchino**, Rus.
42/F4 **Pushkin**, Rus.
43/V7 **Pushkin**, Rus.
51/G2 **Pushkino**, Azer.
43/X9 **Pushkino**, Rus.
27/L5 **Püspökladány**, Hun.
40/E2 **Püspökladány**, Hun.
27/M4 **Pustomyty**, Ukr.
101/H5 **Pustunich**, Mex.
102/D2 **Pustunich**, Mex.
99/L9 **Putah** (cr.), Ca,US
63/G2 **Putao**, Burma
64/H4 **Puthukkudiyiruppu**, SrL.
41/G2 **Putila**, Ukr.
66/D4 **Puting** (cape), Indo.
102/B2 **Putla**, Mex.
46/K3 **Putorana** (mts.), Rus.
62/C6 **Puttalam**, SrL.
64/G4 **Puttalam**, SrL.
64/G4 **Puttalam** (dist.), SrL.
28/B6 **Putte**, Belg.
30/D1 **Putte**, Belg.
31/F5 **Puttelange-aux-Lacs**, Fr.
28/B5 **Putten** (isl.), Neth.
28/C4 **Putten**, Neth.
31/F5 **Püttlingen**, Ger.
78/C5 **Putu** (range), Libr.
105/B3 **Putumayo** (riv.), SAm.
106/D4 **Putumayo** (riv.), SAm.
66/D3 **Putussibau**, Indo.
88/U11 **Puuanahulu**, Hi,US
88/T10 **Puuiki**, Hi,US
88/T10 **Puu Kukui** (peak), Hi,US
88/V12 **Puu o Mahuka Heiau St. Mon.**, Hi,US
28/B6 **Puurs**, Belg.
30/D1 **Puurs**, Belg.
88/R10 **Puuwai**, Hi,US
63/H2 **Puwei**, China
59/B3 **Pu Xian**, China
90/C4 **Puyallup**, Wa,US
99/C3 **Puyallup**, Wa,US
99/C3 **Puyallup** (riv.), Wa,US
99/C3 **Puyallup Ind. Res.**, Wa,US
54/G4 **Puyang**, China
59/C4 **Puyang**, China
32/E4 **Puy de Barbier** (peak), Fr.
32/E4 **Puy de Sancy** (peak), Fr.
32/E5 **Puylaurens**, Fr.
35/G1 **Puylaurens**, Fr.
32/D5 **Puymorens, Col de** (pass), Fr.
35/F1 **Puymorens, Col de** (pass), Fr.
58/D4 **Puyŏ**, SKor.
35/E3 **Puzal**, Sp.
55/K4 **P'warwŏn**, NKor.
82/E2 **Pweto**, Zaire
22/D6 **Pwllheli**, Wal,UK
60/B5 **Pyamalaw** (riv.), Burma
46/G6 **Pyandzh** (riv.), Asia
53/K1 **Pyandz** (Panj) (riv.), Afg., Taj.
20/J2 **Pyaozero** (lake), Rus.
42/F2 **Pyaozero** (lake), Rus.
63/G4 **Pyapon**, Burma
46/J2 **Pyasina** (riv.), Rus.
45/G3 **Pyatigorsk**, Rus.
32/F4 **Pytara** (mtn.), Fr.
20/H3 **Pyhä-Häkin Nat'l Park**, Fin.
42/E3 **Pyhä-Häkin Nat'l Park**, Fin.
20/H3 **Pyhäjärvi**, Fin.
42/E3 **Pyhäjärvi**, Fin.
20/H2 **Pyhäntä**, Fin.
42/E2 **Pyhäntä**, Fin.
20/H2 **Pyhätunturi** (peak), Fin.
42/E2 **Pyhätunturi** (peak), Fin.
63/F3 **Pyingaing**, Burma
60/C5 **Pyinmana**, Burma
63/G4 **Pyinmana**, Burma
65/B2 **Pyinmana**, Burma
24/C3 **Pyle**, Wal,UK
58/C2 **P'yongan-Bukto** (prov.), NKor.
58/C3 **P'Yŏngan-Namdo** (prov.), NKor.
56/A2 **P'yŏngch'ang**, SKor.
58/E4 **P'yŏngch'ang**, SKor.
58/D3 **P'yŏnggang**, NKor.
58/E4 **P'yŏnghae**, SKor.
58/D3 **P'yŏngsan**, NKor.
58/C3 **P'yŏngsong**, NKor.
55/K4 **Pyŏngt'aek**, SKor.
58/D4 **Pyŏngt'aek**, SKor.
47/N6 **P'yŏngyang** (cap.), NKor.
55/K4 **P'yŏngyang** (cap.), NKor.
58/C3 **P'yŏngyang** (cap.), NKor.
58/C3 **P'Yŏngyang-Si**, NKor.
58/D5 **Pyŏnsanbando Nat'l Park**, SKor.
85/M4 **Pyramid** (mtn.), BC,Can
90/D5 **Pyramid** (lake), Nv,US
88/B3 **Pyramid** (lake), Nv,US
92/C3 **Pyramid** (lake), Nv,US
18/C4 **Pyrenees** (mts.), Eur.
32/C5 **Pyrenees** (mts.), Eur.
35/E1 **Pyrenees** (mts.), Eur.
32/C5 **Pyrénées Occidentales Nat'l Park**, Fr.
27/H2 **Pyrzyce**, Pol.
43/Q4 **Pyshma** (riv.), Rus.
20/H4 **Pytalovo**, Rus.
42/E4 **Pytalovo**, Rus.
60/C5 **Pyu**, Burma
63/G4 **Pyu**, Burma
65/B2 **Pyu**, Burma

Q

49/E4 **Qā'al Jafr** (salt pan), Jor.
50/D4 **Qā 'al Jafr** (area), Jor.
87/T7 **Qaanaaq**, Grld.
49/D3 **Qabalān**, WBnk.
49/G7 **Qabalān**, WBnk.
49/D3 **Qabāṭiyah**, WBnk.
49/G7 **Qabāṭiyah**, WBnk.
76/H1 **Qābis**, Tun.
52/E5 **Qabr Hūd**, Yem.
49/F7 **Qadima**, Isr.
64/A2 **Qādirpur Rān**, Pak.
51/H2 **Qā'emshahr**, Iran
52/F1 **Qā'emshahr**, Iran
53/G2 **Qā'en**, Iran
39/G1 **Qafa e Malit** (pass), Alb.
40/E4 **Qafa e Malit** (pass), Alb.
49/G7 **Qaffīn**, WBnk.
76/G1 **Qafṣah**, Tun.
55/J2 **Qagan** (lake), China
59/C2 **Qahar Youyi Qianqi**, China
54/C4 **Qaidam** (basin), China
52/B6 **Qala'an Naḥl**, Sudan
49/F7 **Qalansuwa**, Isr.
38/B4 **Qal'at Al Andalus**, Tun.
77/P4 **Qal at Bīshah**, SAr.
51/F2 **Qal'at Dizah**, Iraq
52/E1 **Qal'at Dizah**, Iraq
51/F4 **Qal'at Sukkar**, Iraq
49/B4 **Qallīn**, Egypt
49/D3 **Qalqīlyah**, WBnk.
49/F7 **Qalqīlyah**, WBnk.
49/B4 **Qalyūb**, Egypt
52/F5 **Qamar, Ghubbat al** (bay), Yem.
76/K1 **Qamīnis**, Libya
52/D3 **Qanā**, SAr.
49/G7 **Qanah, Wādī** (dry riv.), WBnk.
53/J2 **Qandahār**, Afg.
38/A4 **Qanṭarat Al Faḥṣ**, Tun.
52/D3 **Qārah**, SAr.
51/F2 **Qarāmqū** (riv.), Iran
75/W17 **Qar'at al Ashkal** (lake), Tun.
77/Q6 **Qardho**, Som.
51/G3 **Qareh Chāy** (riv.), Iran
52/E2 **Qareh Chāy** (riv.), Iran
45/H5 **Qareh Sū** (riv.), Iran
51/F2 **Qareh Sū** (riv.), Iran
39/G2 **Qarrit, Qaf'e** (pass), Alb.
38/B4 **Qarṭājannah** (ruins), Tun.
49/B5 **Qārūn, Birkat** (lake), Egypt
50/B4 **Qārūn, Birkat** (lake), Egypt
53/H3 **Qaṣr-e Qand**, Iran
51/F3 **Qaṣr-e-Shīrīn**, Iran
52/E2 **Qaṣr-e-Shīrīn**, Iran
50/A5 **Qaṣr Farāfirah**, Egypt
77/L2 **Qaṣr Farāfirah**, Egypt
38/B5 **Qaṣr Hallāl**, Tun.
52/D6 **Qa'ṭabah**, Yem.
49/E3 **Qaṭanā**, Syria
50/D3 **Qaṭanā**, Syria
48/E7 **Qatar**
52/F3 **Qatar**
77/Q2 **Qatar**
50/A4 **Qattara** (depr.), Egypt
77/L1 **Qattara** (depr.), Egypt
49/E2 **Qaṭṭīnah** (lake), Syria
52/C5 **Qawz Rajab**, Sudan
63/F2 **Qayü**, China
51/E3 **Qayyārah**, Iraq
52/D1 **Qayyārah**, Iraq
62/A2 **Qāzi Ahmad**, Pak.
46/F6 **Qazvīn**, Iran
48/D6 **Qazvīn**, Iran
51/G2 **Qazvīn**, Iran
52/F1 **Qazvīn**, Iran
49/F8 **Qedma**, Isr.
39/F2 **Qendrevica** (peak), Alb.
51/H5 **Qeshm** (isl.), Iran
53/G3 **Qeshm**, Iran
53/G3 **Qeshm** (isl.), Iran
77/S2 **Qeshm** (isl.), Iran
52/E1 **Qeydār**, Iran
52/E1 **Qezel** (riv.), Iran
51/F2 **Qezel Owzan** (riv.), Iran
63/J2 **Qi** (riv.), China
54/F5 **Qian** (riv.), China
58/B2 **Qian** (mts.), China
58/B2 **Qian** (peak), China
59/D4 **Qian** (riv.), China
59/D5 **Qian** (riv.), China
61/F2 **Qian** (riv.), China
61/H2 **Qian** (riv.), China
55/J3 **Qian'an**, China
59/D2 **Qian'an**, China
59/F1 **Qian'an**, China
59/C5 **Qianjiang**, China
61/G2 **Qianjiang**, China
61/H2 **Qianqiu** (pass), China
59/D5 **Qianqiu Guan** (pass), China
59/E2 **Qian Shan** (peak), China
55/H3 **Qianxi**, China
59/D2 **Qianxi**, China
59/J6 **Qianxi**, China
60/D3 **Qiaojia**, China
63/H2 **Qiaojia**, China
49/G8 **Qibyā**, WBnk.
55/J5 **Qidong**, China
59/E5 **Qidong**, China
59/L8 **Qidong**, China
61/J2 **Qidong**, China
63/K2 **Qidong**, China
61/F2 **Qifeng** (pass), China
59/B5 **Qifeng Guan** (pass), China
59/D3 **Qihe**, China
64/C1 **Qila Dīdār Singh**, Pak.
48/J6 **Qilian** (mts.), China
54/D4 **Qilian** (mts.), China
54/D4 **Qilian** (peak), China
49/G8 **Qilt, Wādī** (dry riv.), WBnk.
54/C4 **Qimantag** (mts.), China
59/D5 **Qimen**, China
61/H2 **Qimen**, China
54/G4 **Qin** (riv.), China
59/B4 **Qin** (mts.), China
59/C4 **Qin** (riv.), China
57/D3 **Qinā**, Egypt
77/M2 **Qinā**, Egypt
59/B5 **Qing** (riv.), China
61/F2 **Qing** (riv.), China
55/K2 **Qing'an**, China
55/J4 **Qingdao**, China
59/E3 **Qingdao**, China
54/H4 **Qingfeng**, China
59/C4 **Qingfeng**, China
55/K2 **Qinggang**, China
54/D4 **Qinghai** (lake), China
54/D4 **Qinghai** (mts.), China
60/B1 **Qinghai** (prov.), China
58/C2 **Qinghe**, China
59/C3 **Qinghe**, China
61/G2 **Qingjiang**, China
59/D2 **Qinglong**, China
65/E1 **Qingping**, China
59/E5 **Qingpu**, China
59/L8 **Qingpu**, China
61/J2 **Qingpu**, China
60/D2 **Qingshen**, China
61/F3 **Qingshui** (riv.), China
54/D5 **Qingshuihe**, China
59/B3 **Qingshuihe**, China
60/C3 **Qingshuilang** (mts.), China
59/D5 **Qingyang**, China
61/H2 **Qingyang**, China
61/G4 **Qingyuan** (mts.), China
61/H3 **Qingyuan**, China
63/K3 **Qingyuan**, China
59/D3 **Qingyun**, China
55/H4 **Qingzhou**, China
59/D3 **Qingzhou**, China
47/M6 **Qinhuangdao**, China
55/H4 **Qinhuangdao**, China
59/D3 **Qinhuangdao**, China
54/G4 **Qinshui**, China
59/C4 **Qinshui**, China
59/C4 **Qinyang**, China
59/C3 **Qinyuan**, China
61/F4 **Qinzhou**, China
63/J3 **Qinzhou**, China
65/E1 **Qinzhou**, China
63/K4 **Qionghai**, China
54/E5 **Qionglai**, China
54/E5 **Qionglai** (mts.), China
60/D2 **Qionglai**, China
60/D2 **Qionglai** (mts.), China
63/K4 **Qiongshan**, China
63/J4 **Qiongzhong**, China
65/E2 **Qiongzhong**, China
60/E1 **Qiqan** (pass), China
47/N5 **Qiqihar**, China
55/J2 **Qiqihar**, China
54/B3 **Qiquanhu**, China
49/D3 **Qiryat Ata**, Isr.
49/D3 **Qiryat Bialik**, Isr.
49/D4 **Qiryat Gat**, Isr.
49/F8 **Qiryat Gat**, Isr.
49/F8 **Qiryat Mal'akhi**, Isr.
49/D3 **Qiryat Shemona**, Isr.
50/C3 **Qiryat Shemona**, Isr.
52/C2 **Qiryat Shemona**, Isr.
49/D3 **Qiryat Yam**, Isr.
65/E1 **Qisha**, China
52/F5 **Qishn**, Yem.
46/J5 **Qitai**, China
54/B3 **Qitai**, China
47/P5 **Qitaihe**, China
55/L2 **Qitaihe**, China
61/G3 **Qitian** (mtn.), China
55/J4 **Qixia**, China
59/E3 **Qixia**, China
59/C4 **Qi Xian**, China
47/P5 **Qixing** (riv.), China
55/L2 **Qixing** (riv.), China
60/E3 **Qixing** (pass), China
46/F6 **Qom**, Iran
48/E6 **Qom**, Iran
51/G3 **Qom**, Iran
51/G3 **Qom** (riv.), Iran
52/F2 **Qom**, Iran
52/F2 **Qom** (riv.), Iran
62/E2 **Qomolangma** (Everest) (peak), China
52/F2 **Qomsheh**, Iran
53/J1 **Qondūz** (riv.), Afg.
60/A2 **Qonggyai**, China
63/F2 **Qonggyai**, China
51/F3 **Qorveh**, Iran
52/E1 **Qorveh**, Iran
51/J5 **Qoṭbābād**, Iran
53/G3 **Qoṭbābād**, Iran
51/F2 **Qoṭūr**, Iran
54/F5 **Qu** (riv.), China
61/E2 **Qu** (riv.), China
61/H2 **Qu** (riv.), China
95/F3 **Quabbin** (res.), Ma,US
25/F3 **Quainton**, Eng,UK
29/E3 **Quakenbrück**, Ger.
98/E5 **Quakertown**, Pa,US
73/B2 **Quambatook**, Austl.
54/H5 **Quan** (riv.), China
93/H4 **Quanah**, Tx,US
96/D3 **Quanah**, Tx,US
59/B4 **Quanbao Shan** (mtn.), China
63/J4 **Quang Ngai**, Viet.
65/E3 **Quang Ngai**, Viet.
65/D2 **Quang Trach**, Viet.
61/E5 **Quang Tri**, Viet.
63/J4 **Quang Tri**, Viet.
65/D2 **Quang Tri**, Viet.
59/D4 **Quanjiao**, China
24/C4 **Quantocks** (hills), Eng,UK
61/F3 **Quanzhou**, China
61/H3 **Quanzhou**, China
63/K2 **Quanzhou**, China
91/G3 **Qu'Appelle** (riv.), Ab, Sk,Can
91/G3 **Qu'Appelle** (dam), Can
88/E1 **Qu'Appelle** (riv.), Mb, Sk,Can
86/F3 **Qu'Appelle** (riv.), Sk,Can
91/H3 **Qu'Appelle**, Sk,Can
87/K2 **Quaqtaq**, Qu,Can
30/C3 **Quaregnon**, Belg.
66/E4 **Quarles** (mts.), Indo.
33/J5 **Quarrata**, It.
38/A3 **Quartu Sant'Elena**, It.
81/S15 **Quatre Bornes**, Mrts.
37/G4 **Quattervals** (peak), Swi.
38/A4 **Quballāt**, Tun.
75/W17 **Quballāt**, Tun.
46/F6 **Qūchān**, Iran
51/J2 **Qūchān**, Iran
53/G1 **Qūchān**, Iran
71/H7 **Queanbeyan**, Austl.
73/D2 **Queanbeyan**, Austl.
84/K5 **Québec**, Can.
87/J3 **Québec** (prov.), Can.
89/L2 **Québec** (prov.), Can.
95/G1 **Québec** (prov.), Can
87/J4 **Québec** (cap.), Qu,Can
89/M2 **Québec** (cap.), Qu,Can
95/G2 **Québec**, Qu,Can
101/M8 **Quecholac**, Mex.
24/D3 **Quedgeley**, Eng,UK
84/D4 **Queen Charlotte** (isls.), Can.
90/B3 **Queen Charlotte** (str.), BC,Can
85/M5 **Queen Charlotte**, BC,Can
85/M5 **Queen Charlotte** (isls.), BC,Can
86/C3 **Queen Charlotte** (isls.), BC,Can
86/C3 **Queen Charlotte** (sound), BC,Can
96/E3 **Queen City**, Tx,US
84/E2 **Queen Elizabeth** (isls.), Can.
87/R7 **Queen Elizabeth** (isls.), NW,Can
83/G **Queen Mary** (coast), Ant.
19/M7 **Queen Mary** (res.), Eng,UK
83/P **Queen Maud** (mts.), Ant.
86/F2 **Queen Maud** (gulf), NW,Can
83/Z **Queen Maud Land** (reg.), Ant.
70/D2 **Queens** (chan.), Austl.
98/G5 **Queens** (co.), NY,US
87/S7 **Queens** (chan.), NW,Can
22/E1 **Queensberry** (mtn.), Sc,UK
23/G4 **Queensbury**, Eng,UK
23/E5 **Queensferry**, Wal,UK
70/G4 **Queensland** (state), Austl.
72/B3 **Queensland** (state), Austl.
73/C1 **Queensland** (state), Austl.
95/R9 **Queenston**, On,Can
71/H8 **Queenstown**, Austl.
73/C4 **Queenstown**, Austl.
106/G2 **Queenstown**, Guy.
71/Q12 **Queenstown**, N.Z.
80/D3 **Queenstown**, SAfr.
82/E7 **Queenstown**, SAfr.
31/H5 **Queich** (riv.), Ger.
31/G5 **Queidersbach**, Ger.
107/H4 **Queimada**, Braz.
82/G4 **Quelimane**, Moz.
34/A3 **Queluz**, Port.
35/P10 **Queluz**, Port.
103/H1 **Quemado, Punta del** (pt.), Cuba
25/E3 **Quenington**, Eng,UK
103/E4 **Quepos**, CR
101/E4 **Querétaro**, Mex.
101/F4 **Querétaro** (state), Mex.
102/A1 **Querétaro**, Mex.
102/B1 **Querétaro** (state), Mex.
88/F7 **Querétaro**, Mex.
100/C2 **Querobabi**, Mex.
103/E4 **Quesada**, CR
34/D4 **Quesada**, Sp.
59/C4 **Queshan**, China
90/C2 **Quesnel** (lake), BC,Can
86/D3 **Quesnel**, BC,Can
86/D3 **Quesnel** (lake), BC,Can
90/C2 **Quesnel**, BC,Can
30/C2 **Quesnoy-sur-Deûle**, Fr.
65/E3 **Que Son**, Viet.
93/F3 **Questa**, NM,US
96/B2 **Questa**, NM,US
32/B3 **Questembert**, Fr.
36/B3 **Quetigny**, Fr.
53/J2 **Quetta**, Pak.
109/B5 **Queulat Nat'l Park**, Chile
106/C4 **Quevedo**, Ecu.
102/D3 **Quezaltenango**, Guat.
67/E2 **Quezon**, Phil.
68/A4 **Quezon**, Phil.
68/B3 **Quezon City**, Phil.
52/D3 **Qufār**, SAr.
54/H4 **Qufu**, China
59/D4 **Qufu**, China
82/B3 **Quibala**, Ang.
106/C2 **Quibdó**, Col.
32/B3 **Quiberon**, Fr.
32/B3 **Quiberon** (bay), Fr.
104/D5 **Quibor**, Ven.
82/B2 **Quiçama Nat'l Park**, Ang.
26/E2 **Quickborn**, Ger.
29/G1 **Quickborn**, Ger.
31/G5 **Quierschied**, Ger.
36/B3 **Quigney**, Fr.
92/D4 **Quijotoa**, Az,US
109/B5 **Quilán** (cape), Chile
99/B2 **Quilcene**, Wa,US
91/G2 **Quill** (lakes), Sk,Can
86/F3 **Quill** (lake), Sk,Can
106/D6 **Quillabamba**, Peru
106/E7 **Quillacollo**, Bol.
32/E5 **Quillan**, Fr.
35/G1 **Quillan**, Fr.
62/C6 **Quilon**, India
64/F4 **Quilon**, India
71/G5 **Quilpie**, Austl.
72/B4 **Quilpie**, Austl.
109/D2 **Quimilí**, Arg.
18/C4 **Quimper**, Fr.
32/A3 **Quimper**, Fr.
106/D6 **Quince Mil**, Peru
36/C2 **Quincey**, Fr.
97/G4 **Quincy**, Fl,US
89/H4 **Quincy**, Il,US
93/K3 **Quincy**, Il,US
94/B4 **Quincy**, Il,US
97/F2 **Quincy**, Il,US
95/G3 **Quincy**, Ma,US
90/D4 **Quincy**, Wa,US
19/T10 **Quincy-sous-Sénart**, Fr.
30/B6 **Quincy-Voisins**, Fr.
85/F4 **Quinhagak**, Ak,US
48/K8 **Qui Nhon**, Viet.
63/J5 **Qui Nhon**, Viet.
65/E3 **Qui Nhon**, Viet.
92/C2 **Quinn** (riv.), Nv,US
34/C3 **Quintana de la Serena**, Sp.
34/D3 **Quintanar de la Orden**, Sp.
34/E3 **Quintanar del Rey**, Sp.
101/H5 **Quintana Roo** (state), Mex.
102/D2 **Quintana Roo** (state), Mex.
89/J7 **Quintana Roo** (state), Mex.
35/E2 **Quinto**, Sp.
33/H3 **Quinto**, Swi.
37/E4 **Quinto**, Swi.
82/H3 **Quionga**, Moz.
82/H3 **Quirimba** (arch.), Moz.
73/D1 **Quirindi**, Austl.
107/H7 **Quirinópolis**, Braz.
108/B1 **Quirinópolis**, Braz.
104/F5 **Quiriquire**, Ven.
34/B1 **Quiroga**, Sp.
95/H2 **Quispamsis**, NB,Can
81/F2 **Quissico**, Moz.
82/F5 **Quissico**, Moz.
109/D2 **Quitilipi**, Arg.
97/H4 **Quitman**, Ga,US
97/F3 **Quitman**, Ms,US
93/J4 **Quitman**, Tx,US
96/E3 **Quitman**, Tx,US
106/C4 **Quito** (cap.), Ecu.
107/L4 **Quixadá**, Braz.
107/L5 **Quixeramobim**, Braz.
61/G3 **Qujiang**, China
63/K3 **Qujiang**, China
63/K3 **Qujie**, China
60/D3 **Qujing**, China
63/H2 **Qujing**, China
38/B4 **Qulaybīyah**, Tun.
54/C4 **Qumar** (riv.), China
86/G2 **Quoich** (riv.), NW,Can
22/C3 **Quoile** (riv.), NI,UK
80/B4 **Quoin** (pt.), SAfr.
80/L11 **Quoin** (pt.), SAfr.
82/C7 **Quoin** (pt.), SAfr.
70/F6 **Quorn**, Austl.
38/B4 **Qurānbālīyah**, Tun.
38/B4 **Qurbah**, Tun.
49/E2 **Qurnat as Sawdā'** (mtn.), Leb.
50/D3 **Qurnat as Sawdā'** (mtn.), Leb.
52/C2 **Qurnat as Sawdā'** (mtn.), Leb.
52/B3 **Qūṣ**, Egypt
63/F2 **Qusum**, China
38/B5 **Quṣūr As Saf**, Tun.
82/E7 **Quthing**, Les.
59/B4 **Quwo**, China
54/F4 **Quwu** (mts.), China
59/C3 **Quyang**, China
60/D4 **Quynh Nhai**, Viet.
63/H3 **Quynh Nhai**, Viet.
65/C1 **Quynh Nhai**, Viet.
59/C3 **Quzhou**, China
61/H2 **Quzhou**, China
40/D5 **Qyteti Stalin**, Alb.

R

33/L3 **Raab** (riv.), Aus.
40/B2 **Raab** (riv.), Aus.
27/H4 **Raabs an der Thaya**, Aus.
33/L2 **Raabs an der Thaya**, Aus.
72/G8 **Raaf-Richmond**, Austl.
20/H2 **Raahe**, Fin.
42/E2 **Raahe**, Fin.
28/D4 **Raalte**, Neth.
28/B5 **Raamsdonk**, Neth.
49/F7 **Ra'anana**, Isr.
87/S7 **Raanes** (pen.), NW,Can
77/P8 **Raas Jumbo**, Som.
33/L4 **Rab**, Cro.
33/L4 **Rab** (isl.), Cro.
40/B3 **Rab**, Cro.
40/B3 **Rab** (isl.), Cro.
40/C2 **Rába** (riv.), Hun.
33/M3 **Rábafüzes**, Hun.
33/M3 **Rábahidvég**, Hun.
52/B6 **Rabak**, Sudan
35/F1 **Rabastens**, Fr.
38/D5 **Rabat**, Malta
75/L13 **Rabat** (cap.), Mor.
76/D1 **Rabat** (cap.), Mor.
38/D4 **Rabat** (Victoria), Malta
68/E5 **Rabaul**, PNG

170

Rabbi – Reydo

33/K4 Rabbi (riv.), It.
52/C4 Rābigh, SAr.
74/K10 Rabil, CpV.
102/D3 Rabinal, Guat.
37/F4 Rabiusa (riv.), Swi.
27/K4 Rabka, Pol.
53/L5 Rabkavi, India
62/C4 Rabkavi, India
95/S8 Raby (pt.), On,Can
33/G4 Racconigi, It.
93/K5 Raccoon (pt.), La,US
97/F4 Raccoon (pt.), La,US
84/M5 Race (cape), Can.
87/L4 Race (cape), Nf,Can
63/J5 Rach Gia, Viet.
65/D4 Rach Gia, Viet.
65/D4 Rach Gia (bay), Viet.
66/C1 Rach Gia, Viet.
27/K3 Racibórz, Pol.
89/J3 Racine, Wi,US
91/M5 Racine, Wi,US
93/L2 Racine, Wi,US
94/C3 Racine, Wi,US
99/P14 Racine (co.), Wi,US
99/Q14 Racine, Wi,US
36/C3 Racine, Mont (peak), Swi.
40/D2 Ráckeve, Hun.
41/G2 Rădăuţi, Rom.
26/G4 Radbuza (riv.), Czh.
33/K2 Radbuza (riv.), Czh.
23/F4 Radcliffe, Eng,UK
23/G6 Radcliffe on Trent, Eng,UK
29/F4 Raddestorf, Ger.
40/A2 Radenthein, Aus.
29/E6 Radevormwald, Ger.
31/G1 Radevormwald, Ger.
94/D4 Radford, Va,US
97/H2 Radford, Va,US
53/K4 Rādhanpur, India
62/B3 Rādhanpur, India
90/G2 Radisson, Can
70/G6 Radium Hill, Austl.
73/B2 Radium Hill, Austl.
19/N6 Radlett, Eng,UK
25/F3 Radlett, Eng,UK
39/J1 Radnevo, Bul.
41/G4 Radnevo, Bul.
37/E2 Radolfzell, Ger.
18/F3 Radom, Pol.
27/L3 Radom, Pol.
27/L3 Radom (prov.), Pol.
44/B2 Radom, Pol.
46/C4 Radom, Pol.
39/H1 Radomir, Bul.
40/F4 Radomir, Bul.
27/K3 Radomsko, Pol.
44/A2 Radomsko, Pol.
39/H2 Radoviš, Macd.
40/F5 Radoviš, Macd.
33/L3 Radovljica, Slov.
40/B2 Radovljica, Slov.
33/K3 Radstadt, Aus.
24/D4 Radstock, Eng,UK
27/N1 Radun', Bela.
42/E5 Radun', Bela.
44/C1 Radun', Bela.
20/G5 Radviliškis, Lith.
42/D5 Radviliškis, Lith.
52/C4 Radwá, Jabal (mtn.), SAr.
24/C3 Radyr, Wal,UK
27/K2 Radziejów, Pol.
27/L2 Radzymin, Pol.
27/M3 Radzyń Podlaski, Pol.
44/B2 Radzyń Podlaski, Pol.
86/E2 Rae (riv.), NW,Can
87/H3 Rae (isth.), NW,Can
62/D2 Rāe Bareli, India
86/E2 Rae-Edzo, NW,Can
97/J3 Raeford, NC,US
31/F2 Raeren, Belg.
28/D5 Raesfeld, Ger.
70/C5 Raeside (lake), Austl.
58/A2 Raeyang (riv.), China
109/D3 Rafaela, Arg.
49/D4 Rafaḩ, Gaza
77/K7 Rafai, CAfr.
52/D3 Rafḩā', SAr.
77/P2 Rafḩā', SAr.
49/G7 Rafīdīyah, WBnk.
39/J3 Rafina, Gre.
39/M6 Rafina, Gre.
38/B4 Rafrāf, Tun.
51/J4 Rafsanjān, Iran
53/G2 Rafsanjān, Iran
90/E5 Raft (riv.), Id, Ut,US
92/D2 Raft (riv.), Id, Ut,US
37/E2 Rafz, Swi.
77/L6 Raga, Sudan
67/F2 Ragang (mt.), Phil.
22/A1 Raghtin More (mtn.), Ire.
24/D3 Raglan, Wal,UK
20/E2 Rago Nat'l Park, Nor.
42/B2 Rago Nat'l Park, Nor.
19/P8 Ragstone (range), Eng,UK
18/E5 Ragusa, It.
38/D4 Ragusa, It.
26/E2 Rahden, Ger.
29/F4 Rahden, Ger.
53/K3 Rahīmyār Khān, Pak.
62/B2 Rahīmyār Khān, Pak.
69/K6 Raiatea (isl.), FrPol.
62/C4 Raichūr, India
62/D3 Raigarh, India
98/C3 Railroad Canyon (res.), Ca,US
73/B2 Rainbow, Austl.
72/D4 Rainbow Beach, Austl.
92/E3 Rainbow Bridge Nat'l Mon., Ut,US
23/F4 Rainford, Eng,UK
19/P7 Rainham, Eng,UK
86/D4 Rainier (mt.), Wa,US
88/B2 Rainier (mt.), Wa,US
90/C4 Rainier (peak), Wa,US
67/G3 Rainis, Indo.
97/G3 Rainsville, Al,US
23/G5 Rainworth, Eng,UK
86/G4 Rainy (lake), On,Can
89/H2 Rainy (lake), On,Can
91/K3 Rainy (lake), Can., US
91/K3 Rainy (riv.), Can., US
94/A1 Rainy (lake), On,Can, Mn,US
86/G4 Rainy River, On,Can
89/H2 Rainy River, On,Can
91/K3 Rainy River, On,Can
94/A1 Rainy River, On,Can
48/H7 Raipur, India
62/D3 Raipur, India
52/C4 Ra'īs, SAr.
26/F1 Raisdorf, Ger.
99/E8 Raisin (riv.), Mi,US
20/G3 Raisio, Fin.
30/C3 Raismes, Fr.
69/L7 Raivavae (isl.), FrPol.
64/C2 Rāiwind, Pak.
66/A3 Raja (pt.), Indo.
62/D4 Rājahmundry, India
62/C5 Rājampet, India
66/D3 Rajang (riv.), Malay.
53/K3 Rājanpur, Pak.
62/B2 Rājanpur, Pak.
53/K2 Rājaori, India
62/C6 Rājapālaiyam, India
64/F4 Rājapālaiyam, India
53/K5 Rājāpur, India
62/B4 Rājāpur, India
62/B2 Rājasthān (state), India
53/K3 Rājawas, India
53/L3 Rājgarh, India
53/L4 Rājgarh, India
62/C3 Rājgarh, India
33/M2 Rajhrad, Czh.
27/J5 Rajka, Hun.
33/M3 Rajka, Hun.
40/C2 Rajka, Hun.
53/K4 Rājkot, India
62/B3 Rājkot, India
62/D3 Rāj-Nāndagaon, India
53/L2 Rājpura, India
64/D2 Rājpura, India
62/E3 Rājshāhi, Bang.
53/K4 Rājula, India
62/B3 Rājula, India
69/J5 Rakahanga (atoll), Cookls.
40/E1 Rakamaz, Hun.
53/K1 Rakaposhi (mtn.), Pak.
60/B5 Rakhine (state), Burma
63/F4 Rakhine (state), Burma
41/G1 Rakhov, Ukr.
53/H3 Rakhshān (riv.), Pak.
68/G6 Rakiraki, Fiji
82/D5 Rakops, Bots.
39/J1 Rakovski, Bul.
41/G4 Rakovski, Bul.
20/H4 Rakvere, Est.
42/E4 Rakvere, Est.
89/L4 Raleigh (cap.), NC,US
97/J3 Raleigh (cap.), NC,US
68/F4 Ralik Chain (arch.), Mrsh.
31/F4 Ralingen, Ger.
90/F3 Ralston, Ab,Can
103/E3 Rama, Nic.
52/D6 Ramādah, Yem.
107/K6 Ramalho (mts.), Braz.
49/D4 Rām Allāh, WBnk.
49/G8 Rām Allāh, WBnk.
64/G4 Rāmanāthapuram, India
64/G4 Ramanathaswamy Temple, India
53/K5 Ramas (cape), India
62/B4 Ramas (cape), India
49/D3 Ramat Gan, Isr.
49/F7 Ramat Gan, Isr.
49/F7 Ramat HaSharon, Isr.
80/D2 Ramatlabama, Bots.
36/C1 Rambervillers, Fr.
69/Z17 Rambi (isl.), Fiji
30/A6 Rambouillet, Fr.
24/B6 Rame (pt.), UK
62/E2 Rāmechhāp, Nepal
43/Y9 Ramenskoye, Rus.
62/C6 Rāmeshwaram, India
64/G4 Rāmeshwaram, India
51/G4 Rāmhormoz, Iran
52/E2 Rāmhormoz, Iran
49/D4 Ramla, Isr.
49/F8 Ramla, Isr.
50/C4 Ramla, Isr.
52/B2 Ramla, Isr.
52/D6 Ramlu (peak), Eth.
49/D5 Ramm, Jabal (mtn.), Jor.
50/C4 Ramm, Jabal (mtn.), Jor.
52/C3 Ramm, Jabal (mtn.), Jor.
49/G8 Rammūn, WBnk.
62/D3 Rāmnagar, India
36/C2 Ramonchamp, Fr.
49/D4 Ramon, Har (mtn.), Isr.
50/C4 Ramon, Har (mt.), Isr.
22/A4 Ramor, Lough (lake), Ire.
101/E3 Ramos Arizpe, Mex.
37/G4 Ramosch, Swi.
80/D2 Ramotswa, Bots.
85/H2 Rampart, Ak,US
53/L2 Rāmpur, India
62/B3 Rāmpur, India
64/D2 Rāmpur, India
60/B5 Ramree (isl.), Burma
63/F4 Ramree (isl.), Burma
52/F1 Ramsar (Sakht Sar), Iran
23/F4 Ramsbottom, Eng,UK
25/E4 Ramsbury, Eng,UK
37/E2 Ramsen, Swi.
94/D2 Ramsey (lake), On,Can
25/F2 Ramsey, Eng,UK
22/D3 Ramsey, IM,UK
22/D3 Ramsey (bay), IM,UK
24/A3 Ramsey (isl.), Wal,UK
25/H4 Ramsgate, Eng,UK
31/G5 Ramstein-Miesenbach, Ger.
68/D5 Ramu (riv.), PNG
20/H5 Ramygala, Lith.
62/E3 Rānāghāt, India
109/B3 Rancagua, Chile
32/B2 Rance (riv.), Fr.
32/E5 Rance (riv.), Fr.
35/G1 Rance (riv.), Fr.
108/B2 Rancharia, Braz.
90/G4 Ranchester, Wy,US
92/F1 Ranchester, Wy,US
62/E3 Rānchī, India
99/M9 Rancho Cordova, Ca,US
98/C2 Rancho Cucamonga, Ca,US
98/B3 Rancho Palos Verdes, Ca,US
109/D4 Rancul, Arg.
77/P5 Randa, Djib.
98/K7 Randallstown, Md,US
22/B2 Randalstown, NI,UK
38/D4 Randazzo, It.
80/P13 Randburg, SAfr.
37/E2 Randen, Hoher (peak), Ger.
20/D4 Randers, Den.
93/H5 Randolph (A.F.B.), Tx,US
96/D4 Randolph (A.F.B.), Tx,US
27/H2 Randow (riv.), Ger.
72/H8 Randwick, Austl.
20/G2 Råneå, Swe.
42/D2 Råneå, Swe.
63/H4 Rang (peak), Thai.
65/C2 Rang (peak), Thai.
60/B4 Rāngāmāti, Bang.
63/F3 Rāngāmāti, Bang.
64/G3 Ranganathaswamy Temple, India
67/E4 Rangasa (cape), Indo.
25/H6 Rang du Fliers, Fr.
30/A3 Rang-du-Fliers, Fr.
92/E2 Rangely, Co,US
101/F1 Ranger, Tx,US
93/H4 Ranger, Tx,US
96/D3 Ranger, Tx,US
60/A3 Rangia, India
71/R11 Rangiora, N.Z.
69/L6 Rangiroa (atoll), FrPol.
60/C5 Rangoon (div.), Burma
65/B2 Rangoon (div.), Burma
48/J8 Rangoon (Yangon) (cap.), Burma
60/C5 Rangoon (Yangon) (cap.), Burma
63/G4 Rangoon (Yangon) (cap.), Burma
65/B2 Rangoon (Yangon) (cap.), Burma
62/E2 Rangpur, Bang.
53/L6 Rānībennur, India
62/C5 Rānībennur, India
93/G5 Rankin, Tx,US
96/C4 Rankin, Tx,US
84/H3 Rankin Inlet, Can.
86/G2 Rankin Inlet, NW,Can
37/F3 Rankweil, Aus.
63/G6 Ranong, Thai.
65/B4 Ranong, Thai.
66/A2 Ranong, Thai.
26/D3 Ransbach-Baumbach, Ger.
31/G3 Ransbach-Baumbach, Ger.
95/S9 Ransomville, NY,US
28/B6 Ranst, Belg.
30/D1 Ranst, Belg.
67/F4 Rantekombola (peak), Indo.
30/B5 Rantigny, Fr.
49/G7 Rantīs, WBnk.
91/L5 Rantoul, Il,US
93/K2 Rantoul, Il,US
94/B3 Rantoul, Il,US
97/F1 Rantoul, Il,US
20/H2 Rantsila, Fin.
42/E2 Rantsila, Fin.
60/E5 Rao Co (peak), Laos
63/J4 Rao Co (peak), Laos
65/D2 Rao Co (peak), Laos
26/D4 Raon-L'Étape, Fr.
33/G2 Raon-L'Étape, Fr.
36/C1 Raon-l'Étape, Fr.
68/H7 Raoul (isl.), N.Z.
59/C3 Raoyang, China
69/L7 Rapa (isl.), FrPol.
86/F4 Rapid City, SD,US
88/F3 Rapid City, SD,US
91/H4 Rapid City, SD,US
94/E4 Rappahannock (riv.), Va,US
62/D2 Rapti (riv.), India
98/F5 Raritan (bay), NJ,NY,US
98/F5 Raritan (riv.), NJ,US
69/L6 Raroia (atoll), FrPol.
36/D5 Raron, Swi.
69/J7 Rarotonga (isl.), Cookls.
109/D5 Rasa (pt.), Arg.
38/A4 Ra's al Abyaḑ, Ar (cape), Tun.
50/E2 Ra's al 'Ayn, Syria
49/D2 Ra's al Basīt (pt.), Syria
48/E7 Ra's al Ḩadd (pt.), Oman
38/B4 Ra's Al Jabal, Tun.
51/G4 Ra's al Mish'āb (pt.), SAr.
77/J7 Ra's al Unūf, Libya
49/D5 Ra's An Naqb, Jor.
50/C4 Ra's An Naqb, Jor.
38/B4 Ra's aţ Ţīb (cape), Tun.
76/H1 Ra's aţ Ţīb (Cape Bon) (cape), Tun.
77/N3 Ra's Banās (pt.), Egypt
74/F3 Ras Dashen (peak), Eth.
77/N5 Ras Dashen (peak), Eth.
42/D5 Raseiniai, Lith.
75/Q16 Râs el Ma, Alg.
75/T16 Râs el Oued, Alg.
75/U18 Râs el Oued, Alg.
50/C4 Ras Gharib, Egypt
22/B2 Rasharkin, NI,UK
49/D3 Rāshayyā, Leb.
49/B4 Rashīd (Rosetta), Egypt
46/E6 Rasht, Iran
48/D6 Rasht, Iran
51/G2 Rasht, Iran
52/E1 Rasht, Iran
64/G3 Rāsipuram, India
39/G1 Raška, Yugo.
40/E4 Raška, Yugo.
53/K3 Rāsla, India
50/C5 Ra's Muḩammad (pt.), Egypt
77/M2 Ra's Muḩammad (pt.), Egypt
86/G2 Rasmussen (basin), NW,Can
35/P10 Raso (cape), Port.
70/C5 Rason (lake), Austl.
77/R2 Ra's Rakan (pt.), Qatar
45/G1 Rasskazovo, Rus.
26/E4 Rastatt, Ger.
31/H6 Rastatt, Ger.
33/H2 Rastatt, Ger.
26/E2 Rastede, Ger.
29/F2 Rastede, Ger.
85/B6 Rat (isls.), Ak,US
66/B5 Rata (cape), Indo.
53/K3 Ratangarh, India
62/B2 Ratangarh, India
63/G5 Rat Buri, Thai.
65/B3 Rat Buri, Thai.
62/C2 Rāth, India
22/B5 Rathangan, Ire.
91/K5 Rathbun (lake), Ia,US
22/B5 Rathcoole, Ire.
21/B4 Rathdowney, Ire.
22/B6 Rathdrum, Ire.
60/B4 Rathedaung, Burma
63/F3 Rathedaung, Burma
26/G2 Rathenow, Ger.
22/B3 Rathfriland, NI,UK
21/H7 Rathkeale, Ire.
22/B1 Rathlin (isl.), NI,UK
22/B1 Rathlin (sound), NI,UK
21/A4 Rathluirc, Ire.
21/H7 Rathmore, Ire.
22/B5 Rathmore, Ire.
22/B6 Rathnew, Ire.
22/B6 Rathvilly, Ire.
22/A5 Rathwire, Ire.
28/D6 Ratingen, Ger.
40/D3 Ratkovo, Yugo.
53/L4 Ratlām, India
62/C3 Ratlām, India
53/K5 Ratnāgiri, India
62/B4 Ratnāgiri, India
62/D6 Ratnapura, SrL.
27/N3 Ratno, Ukr.
22/B5 Ratoath, Ire.
88/F4 Raton, NM,US
93/F3 Raton, NM,US
96/B2 Raton, NM,US
20/E3 Rättvik, Swe.
42/B3 Rättvik, Swe.
26/F2 Ratzeburg, Ger.
66/B3 Raub, Malay.
20/P6 Raudhinúpur (pt.), Ice.
20/P6 Raufarhöfn, Ice.
20/D3 Raufoss, Nor.
108/D2 Raul Soares, Braz.
25/F2 Raunds, Eng,UK
71/S10 Raupehu (vol.), N.Z.
62/D3 Raurkela, India
42/F3 Rautjärvi, Fin.
38/C4 Ravanusa, It.
51/J4 Rāvar, Iran
53/G2 Rāvar, Iran
27/M3 Rava-Russkaya, Ukr.
28/C6 Ravels, Belg.
23/E3 Ravenglass, Eng,UK
33/K4 Ravenna, It.
26/E5 Ravensburg, Ger.
33/H3 Ravensburg, Ger.
37/F2 Ravensburg, Ger.
99/D3 Ravensdale, Wa,US
23/G5 Ravenshead, Eng,UK
71/H3 Ravenshoe, Austl.
72/B2 Ravenshoe, Austl.
70/C6 Ravensthorpe, Austl.
94/D4 Ravenswood, WV,US
97/H2 Ravenswood, WV,US
64/B2 Rāvi (riv.), India
53/K2 Rāvi (riv.), Pak.
64/B2 Rāvi (riv.), Pak.
35/G1 Raviège, Barrage de la (dam), Fr.
33/L3 Ravne na Koroškem, Slov.
40/B2 Ravne na Koroškem, Slov.
50/E3 Rāwah, Iraq
69/H5 Rawaki (Phoenix) (atoll), Kiri.
53/K2 Rāwalpindi, Pak.
64/B1 Rāwalpindi, Pak.
27/L3 Rawa Mazowiecka, Pol.
27/J3 Rawicz, Pol.
70/D6 Rawlinna, Austl.
86/F4 Rawlins, Wy,US
88/E3 Rawlins, Wy,US
90/G5 Rawlins, Wy,US
92/F2 Rawlins, Wy,US
23/G5 Rawmarsh, Eng,UK
109/C5 Rawson, Arg.
23/F4 Rawtenstall, Eng,UK
95/K2 Ray (cape), Can
87/L4 Ray (cape), Nf,Can
89/Q2 Ray (cape), Nf,Can
66/D4 Raya (peak), Indo.
62/C5 Rāyadrug, India
62/D4 Rāyagada, India
47/N5 Raychikhinsk, Rus.
55/K2 Raychikhinsk, Rus.
45/K1 Rayevskiy, Rus.
25/G3 Rayleigh, Eng,UK
86/E4 Raymond, Ab,Can
90/E3 Raymond, Ab,Can
88/B2 Raymond, Wa,US
90/C4 Raymond, Wa,US
99/P14 Raymond, Wi,US
101/F3 Raymondville, Tx,US
89/G6 Raymondville, Tx,US
96/D5 Raymondville, Tx,US
91/G3 Raymore, Sk,Can
101/F4 Rayón, Mex.
102/B1 Rayón, Mex.
101/E3 Rayones, Mex.
63/H5 Rayong, Thai.
65/C3 Rayong, Thai.
66/B1 Rayong, Thai.
101/E5 Rayón Nat'l Park, Mex.
102/A2 Rayón Nat'l Park, Mex.
52/E1 Razan, Iran
45/H4 Razdan, Arm.
51/F1 Razdan, Arm.
41/K2 Razdel'naya, Ukr.
41/J3 Razelm (lake), Rom.
39/K1 Razgrad (prov.), Bul.
41/H4 Razgrad, Bul.
41/H4 Razgrad (reg.), Bul.
44/C4 Razgrad, Bul.
39/H2 Razlog, Bul.
41/F5 Razlog, Bul.
32/A2 Raz, Pointe du (pt.), Fr.
32/C3 Ré (isl.), Fr.
24/D2 Rea (riv.), Eng,UK
18/C3 Reading, Eng,UK
25/F4 Reading, Eng,UK
89/L3 Reading, Pa,US
94/F3 Reading, Pa,US
106/E7 Real, Cordillera (range), Bol.
109/D4 Realicó, Arg.
37/E4 Realp, Swi.
63/H5 Reang Kesei, Camb.
65/C3 Reang Kesei, Camb.
66/B1 Reang Kesei, Camb.
69/M6 Reao (atoll), FrPol.
30/C6 Rebais, Fr.
70/C6 Rebecca (lake), Austl.
108/B3 Rebouças, Braz.
37/F3 Rebstein, Swi.
55/N2 Rebun (isl.), Japan
33/K5 Recanati, It.
40/A4 Recanati, It.
70/C6 Recherche (arch.), Austl.
31/F6 Réchicourt-le-Château, Fr.
44/D1 Rechitsa, Bela.
33/M3 Rechnitz, Aus.
36/D4 Rechthalten, Swi.
107/M5 Recife, Braz.
80/D4 Recife (cape), SAfr.
82/E7 Recife (cape), SAfr.
29/E4 Recke, Ger.
36/E5 Reckingen, Swi.
29/E5 Recklinghausen, Ger.
26/G2 Recknitz (riv.), Ger.
36/C3 Réclère, Swi.
65/B2 Reclining Buddha (Shwethalyaung) (ruins), Burma
109/E2 Reconquista, Arg.
36/D3 Reconvilier, Swi.
52/C4 Red (sea), Afr., Asia
74/F2 Red (sea), Afr., Asia
77/N3 Red (sea), Afr., Asia
48/C7 Red (sea), Asia
65/C1 Red (riv.), China
48/K7 Red (riv.), China, Viet.
63/H3 Red (riv.), China, Viet.
50/C5 Red (sea), Egypt, SAr.
22/B1 Red (bay), NI,UK
84/H5 Red (riv.), US
84/H6 Red (riv.), US
89/H5 Red (riv.), US
93/J5 Red (riv.), US
96/D2 Red (hills), Ks,US
86/G4 Red (lakes), Mn,US
89/H2 Red (lakes), Mn,US
27/K1 Reda, Pol.
31/E4 Redange-sur-Attert, Lux.
98/F5 Red Bank, NJ,US
93/G4 Red Bluff (lake), NM, Tx,US
88/B3 Red Bluff, Ca,US
90/C5 Red Bluff, Ca,US
92/B2 Red Bluff, Ca,US
25/F3 Redbourn, Eng,UK
19/P7 Redbridge (bor.), Eng,UK
23/G2 Redcar, Eng,UK
90/F3 Redcliff, Ab,Can
71/J5 Redcliffe, Austl.
72/F6 Redcliffe, Austl.
73/B2 Red Cliffs, Austl.
93/H2 Red Cloud, Ne,US
96/D1 Red Cloud, Ne,US
90/F3 Red Deer (riv.), Ab,Can
86/E3 Red Deer, Ab,Can
86/E3 Red Deer (riv.), Ab,Can
88/D1 Red Deer (riv.), Ab,Can
90/E2 Red Deer, Ab,Can
91/H2 Red Deer (lake), Mb,Can
86/F3 Red Deer (riv.), Sk,Can
91/H2 Red Deer (riv.), Mb, Sk,Can
85/G3 Red Devil, Ak,US
84/E5 Redding, US
86/D4 Redding, Ca,US
88/B3 Redding, Ca,US
90/C5 Redding, Ca,US
92/B2 Redding, Ca,US
25/E2 Redditch, Eng,UK
23/F1 Rede (riv.), Eng,UK
91/J4 Redfield, SD,US
99/F7 Redford, Mi,US
19/N8 Redhill, Eng,UK
25/F4 Redhill, Eng,UK
88/T10 Red Hill (peak), Hi,US
98/E5 Red Hill, Pa,US
60/E4 Red (Hong) (riv.), Viet.
65/D1 Red (Hong) (riv.), Viet.
37/G5 Re di Castello, Monte (peak), It.
95/K1 Red Indian (lake), Nf,Can
31/G6 Réding, Fr.
86/G3 Red Lake, On,Can
89/H1 Red Lake, On,Can
91/K3 Red Lake, On,Can
91/K3 Red Lake (riv.), Mn,US
86/G4 Red Lake (riv.), Mn,US
98/J7 Redland, Md,US
72/F7 Redland Bay, Austl.
98/C2 Redlands, Ca,US
90/F4 Red Lodge, Mt,US
88/B3 Redmond, Or,US
90/C4 Redmond, Or,US
99/C2 Redmond, Wa,US
93/G4 Red, North Fork (riv.), Ok, Tx,US
32/B3 Redon, Fr.
34/A1 Redondela, Sp.
34/B3 Redondo, Port.
99/C3 Redondo, Wa,US
98/B3 Redondo Beach, Ca,US
85/H3 Redoubt (vol.), Ak,US
91/J3 Red (Red R. of the North) (riv.), Mb,Can
86/G4 Red River of the North (riv.), US
91/K5 Red Rock (lake), Ia,US
93/J2 Red Rock (lake), Ia,US
91/J3 Red River of the North (riv.), US
24/A6 Redruth, Eng,UK
93/G4 Red, Salt Fork (riv.), Ok, Tx,US
52/C4 Red Sea (hills), Sudan
77/N3 Red Sea (hills), Sudan
86/D2 Redstone (riv.), NW,Can
91/K2 Red Sucker (lake), Mb,Can
91/H3 Redvers, Sk,Can
79/E4 Red Volta (riv.), Burk., Gui.
90/E2 Redwater, Ab,Can
90/C5 Redway, Ca,US
92/B2 Redway, Ca,US
86/G4 Red Wing, Mn,US
91/K4 Red Wing, Mn,US
92/F4 Red Wing, Mn,US
99/K12 Redwood City, Ca,US
91/K4 Redwood Falls, Mn,US
90/B5 Redwood Nat'l Park, Ca,US
86/D4 Redwood Nat'l Park, Ca,US
88/B3 Redwood Nat'l Park, Ca,US
92/A2 Redwood Nat'l Park, Ca,US
60/D4 Red (Yuan) (riv.), China
94/C3 Reed City, Mi,US
25/H1 Reedham, Eng,UK
92/C3 Reedley, Ca,US
91/L5 Reedsburg, Wi,US
94/B3 Reedsburg, Wi,US
90/B5 Reedsport, Or,US
73/B3 Reedy (cr.), Austl.
101/J5 Reef (pt.), Belz.
68/F6 Reef (isls.), Sol.
71/R11 Reefton, N.Z.
21/A4 Ree, Lough (lake), Ire.
25/H1 Reepham, Eng,UK
28/D5 Rees, Ger.
86/E5 Reese (riv.), Nv,US
88/C4 Reese (riv), Nv,US
92/C3 Reese (riv.), Nv,US
93/G4 Reese (A.F.B.), Tx,US
96/C3 Reese (A.F.B.), Tx,US
29/G2 Reessum, Ger.
28/D3 Reest (riv.), Neth.
23/G3 Reeth, Eng,UK
28/B4 Reeuwijk, Neth.
50/D2 Refahiye, Turk.
101/F2 Refugio, Tx,US
96/D4 Refugio, Tx,US
27/H2 Rega (riv.), Pol.
107/K5 Regeneração, Braz.
18/E4 Regensburg, Ger.
26/G4 Regensburg, Ger.
33/K2 Regensburg, Ger.
37/E3 Regensdorf, Swi.
26/G4 Regenstauf, Ger.
33/K2 Regenstauf, Ger.
72/H8 Regents Park, Austl.
19/N7 Regent's Park, Eng,UK
76/F2 Reggane, Alg.
28/D4 Regge (riv.), Neth.
18/E5 Reggio di Calabria, It.
38/D3 Reggio di Calabria, It.
33/J4 Reggio nell'Emilia, It.
41/G2 Reghin, Rom.
44/C3 Reghin, Rom.
86/F3 Regina (cap.), Sk,Can
88/F1 Regina (cap.), Sk,Can
91/G3 Regina (cap.), Sk,Can
107/H3 Régina, FrG.
92/F3 Regina, NM,US
96/B2 Regina, NM,US
91/G3 Regina Beach, Sk,Can
108/C3 Registro, Braz.
33/J2 Regnitz (riv.), Ger.
37/F5 Regoledo, It.
34/B3 Reguengosde Monsaraz, Port.
29/G4 Rehburg-Loccum, Ger.
31/F5 Rehlingen-Siersburg, Ger.
82/C5 Rehoboth, Namb.
31/E5 Réhon, Fr.
49/F8 Reḩovot, Isr.
36/D4 Reichenbach im Kandertal, Swi.
31/G5 Reichenbach-Steegen, Ger.
37/H1 Reichertshausen, Ger.
31/G2 Reichshof, Ger.
26/D4 Reichshoffen, Fr.
31/G6 Reichshoffen, Fr.
33/G2 Reichshoffen, Fr.
31/G6 Reichstett, Fr.
90/F3 Reid (lake), Sk,Can
36/D3 Reiden, Swi.
94/E4 Reidsville, NC,US
97/J2 Reidsville, NC,US
19/N8 Reigate, Eng,UK
25/F4 Reigate, Eng,UK
36/C5 Reignier, Fr.
18/D4 Reims, Fr.
26/C4 Reims, Fr.
30/D5 Reims, Fr.
32/F2 Reims, Fr.
30/D5 Reims, Cathédrale de, Fr.
105/B8 Reina Adelaida (arch.), Chile
109/A7 Reina Adelaida (isls.), Chile
36/D3 Reinach, Swi.
36/E3 Reinach, Swi.
29/H1 Reinbek, Ger.
84/G4 Reindeer (lake), Can.
91/J2 Reindeer (isl.), Mb,Can
91/H1 Reindeer (lake), Sk,Can
91/H1 Reindeer (riv.), Sk,Can
86/F3 Reindeer (lake), Mb,Sk,Can
34/C1 Reinosa, Sp.
31/F4 Reinsfeld, Ger.
31/F4 Reisdorf, Lux.
20/G1 Reisduoddarhal'di (peak), Nor.
28/D2 Reitdiep (riv.), Neth.
80/E2 Reitz, SAfr.
86/F2 Reliance, NW,Can
90/F5 Reliance, Wy,US
92/E2 Reliance, Wy,US
75/R16 Relizane, Alg.
75/R16 Relizane (wilaya), Alg.
76/F1 Relizane, Alg.
29/G1 Rellingen, Ger.
31/G2 Remagen, Ger.
107/K5 Remanso, Braz.
19/S11 Remarde (riv.), Fr.
66/D5 Rembang, Indo.
75/Q16 Remchi, Alg.
103/F4 Remedios, Pan.
31/F4 Remich, Lux.
31/E2 Remicourt, Belg.
107/H3 Rémire, FrG.
36/C1 Remiremont, Fr.
29/H4 Remlingen, Ger.
33/H2 Rems (riv.), Ger.
26/D3 Remscheid, Ger.
29/E6 Remscheid, Ger.
31/G1 Remscheid, Ger.
30/B5 Rémy, Fr.
54/F5 Ren (riv.), China
59/B5 Ren (riv.), China
61/F1 Ren (riv.), China
36/C3 Renan, Swi.
20/H4 Rencēni, Lat.
42/E4 Rencēni, Lat.
31/H6 Renchen, Ger.
36/E1 Renchen, Ger.
31/E3 Rendeux, Belg.
26/E1 Rendsburg, Ger.
33/G3 Renens, Swi.
36/C4 Renens, Swi.
87/J4 Renfrew, On,Can
89/L2 Renfrew, On,Can
94/E2 Renfrew, On,Can
66/B3 Rengam, Malay.
66/B4 Rengat, Indo.
31/G3 Rengsdorf, Ger.
63/K2 Renhua, China
60/E3 Renhuai, China
63/J2 Renhuai, China
41/J3 Reni, Ukr.
44/D3 Reni, Ukr.
28/C5 Renkum, Neth.
70/G6 Renmark, Austl.
73/B2 Renmark, Austl.
68/F6 Rennell (isl.), Sol.
31/H2 Rennerod, Ger.
18/C4 Rennes, Fr.
32/C2 Rennes, Fr.
33/J4 Reno (riv.), It.
86/E5 Reno, Nv,US
88/C4 Reno, Nv,US
92/C3 Reno, Nv,US
80/C3 Renoster (riv.), SAfr
80/D2 Renoster (riv.), SAfr
80/P13 Renoster (riv.), SAfr
54/H4 Renqiu, China
59/D3 Renqiu, China
94/C3 Rensselaer, In,US
32/C5 Rentería, Sp.
34/E1 Rentería, Sp.
90/C4 Renton, Wa,US
99/C3 Renton, Wa,US
30/D4 Renwez, Fr.
33/M3 Répcelak, Hun.
40/C2 Répcelak, Hun.
95/P6 Repentigny, Qu,Car
43/U6 Repino, Rus.
36/A5 Replonges, Fr.
23/G6 Repton, Eng,UK
90/D3 Republic, Wa,US
93/H2 Republican (riv.), K Ne,US
89/G3 Republican (riv.), K Ne,US
71/H4 Repulse (bay), Aust
72/C3 Repulse (bay), Aust
87/H2 Repulse Bay, NW,C
106/D4 Requena, Peru
35/E3 Requena, Sp.
44/F4 Reşadiye, Turk.
50/D1 Reşadiye, Turk.
37/G4 Reschen (Resia), It.
37/G4 Reschensee (Resia (lake), It.
39/G2 Resen, Macd.
40/E5 Resen, Macd.
108/C2 Resende, Braz.
34/B2 Resende, Port.
92/E4 Reserve, NM,US
37/G4 Resia, Passo di (pass), It.
37/G4 Resia (Reschensee (lake), It.
109/E2 Resistencia, Arg.
40/E3 Reşiţa, Rom.
44/B3 Reşiţa, Rom.
86/G1 Resolute, NW,Can
87/S7 Resolute, NW,Can
84/L3 Resolution (isl.), Ca
87/K2 Resolution (isl.), NW,Can
24/C3 Resolven, Wal,UK
34/C1 Respenda de la Pe Sp.
108/D1 Resplendor, Braz.
81/F2 Ressano Garcia, M
30/B4 Ressons-sur-Matz,
95/H2 Restigouche (riv.), NB,Can
91/H3 Reston, Mb,Can
98/J8 Reston, Va,US
99/C2 Restoration (pt.), Wa,US
27/L1 Reszel, Pol.
102/D3 Retalhuleu, Guat.
30/D4 Rethel, Fr.
29/G3 Rethem, Ger.
39/J5 Réthimnon, Gre.
28/C6 Retie, Belg.
31/E1 Retie, Belg.
40/F3 Retrezap Nat'l Par Rom.
44/B3 Retrezap Nat'l Par Rom.
27/K5 Rétság, Hun.
40/D2 Rétság, Hun.
37/G2 Rettenberg, Ger.
27/H4 Retz, Aus.
33/L2 Retz, Aus.
75/H7 Réunion (isl.), Fr.
81/R15 Réunion (dpcy.), F
35/F2 Reus, Sp.
28/C6 Reusel, Neth.
37/E3 Reuss (riv.), Swi.
37/E4 Reuss (riv.), Swi.
26/G2 Reuterstadt Stavenhagen, Ger.
26/E4 Reutlingen, Ger.
33/H2 Reutlingen, Ger.
37/F1 Reutlingen, Ger.
42/H5 Reutov, Rus.
43/X9 Reutov, Rus.
37/G3 Reutte, Aus.
49/F8 Revadim, Isr.
42/D4 Revda, Rus.
19/T10 Reveillon (riv.), Fr.
32/D5 Revel, Fr.
35/F1 Revel, Fr.
86/E3 Revelstoke, BC,Ca
88/C1 Revelstoke, BC,Ca
90/D3 Revelstoke, BC,Ca
101/F4 Reventadero, Mex
102/B1 Reventadero, Mex
72/H8 Revesby, Austl.
40/C2 Revfülöp, Hun.
31/D6 Revigny-sur-Orna Fr.
100/B5 Revillagigedo (isl Mex.
84/F8 Revillagigedo (isl Mex.
26/C4 Revin, Fr.
30/D4 Revin, Fr.
32/F2 Revin, Fr.
20/G1 Revsbotn (fjord), N
62/D3 Rewa, India
53/L3 Rewāri, India
62/C2 Rewāri, India
85/J3 Rex (mtn.), Ak,US
86/E4 Rexburg, Id,US
88/D3 Rexburg, Id,US
90/F5 Rexburg, Id,US
92/E2 Rexburg, Id,US
30/B2 Rexpoëde, Fr.
103/G4 Rey (isl.), Pan.
106/C2 Rey (isl.), Pan.
25/H2 Reydon, Eng,UK

106/E6 Reyes, Bol.
92/B3 Reyes (pt.), Ca,US
101/M6 Reyes de Vallarta, Mex.
49/E1 Reyhanlı, Turk.
50/D2 Reyhanlı, Turk.
52/C1 Reyhanlı, Turk.
18/A2 Reykjanestá (cape), Ice.
18/A2 Reykjavík (cap.), Ice.
20/N7 Reykjavík (cap.), Ice.
101/F3 Reynosa, Mex.
89/G6 Reynosa, Mex.
96/D5 Reynosa, Mex
36/B5 Reyssouze (riv.), Fr.
32/C3 Rezé, Fr.
18/F3 Rēzekne, Lat.
20/H4 Rēzekne, Lat.
42/E4 Rēzekne, Lat.
46/C4 Rēzekne, Lat.
33/H3 Rhaetian Alps (mts.), It., Swi.
37/F5 Rhaetian Alps (mts.), It., Swi.
37/F3 Rhätikon (mts.), Aus., Swi.
24/C2 Rhayader, Wal,UK
29/F5 Rheda-Wiedenbrück, Ger.
28/D5 Rhede, Ger.
29/E2 Rhede, Ger.
28/D5 Rheden, Neth.
25/F2 Rhee (Cam) (riv.), Eng,UK
33/G1 Rhein (riv.), Ger.
37/E2 Rheinau, Swi.
31/F2 Rheinbach, Ger.
28/D5 Rheinberg, Ger.
31/G2 Rheinbreitbach, Ger.
31/G3 Rheinbrohl, Ger.
26/D2 Rheine, Ger.
29/E4 Rheine, Ger.
37/E2 Rheinfall, Swi.
36/D2 Rheinfelden, Ger.
26/D3 Rhein (Rhine) (riv.), Ger.
28/D5 Rhein (Rhine) (riv.), Ger.
31/G2 Rhein (Rhine) (riv.), Ger.
37/F5 Rheinwaldhorn (peak), Swi.
76/E2 Rhemiles (well), Alg.
28/C5 Rhenen, Neth.
33/G2 Rhin (riv.), Fr.
36/D1 Rhinau, Fr
18/D3 Rhine (riv.), Eur.
26/D3 Rhine (riv.), Eur.
33/G1 Rhine (riv.), Eur.
36/D1 Rhine (riv.), Eur.
46/A4 Rhine (riv.), Eur.
29/E5 Rhine-Herne (can.), Ger.
89/J2 Rhinelander, Wi,US
91/L4 Rhinelander, Wi,US
94/B2 Rhinelander, Wi,US
20/D4 Rhineland-Palatinate (state), Ger.
31/F3 Rhineland-Palatinate (state), Ger.
33/G1 Rhineland-Palatinate (state), Ger.
28/D5 Rhine (Rhein) (riv.), Ger.
77/M7 Rhino Camp, Ugan.
75/R16 Rhiou (riv.), Alg.
31/D3 Rhisnes, Belg.
24/C1 Rhiw (riv.), Wal,UK
22/A5 Rhode, Ire.
87/J4 Rhode Island (state), US
89/M3 Rhode Island (state), US
95/G3 Rhode Island (state), US
18/F5 Rhodes (isl.), Gre.
50/A3 Rhodes (isl.), Gre.
50/B2 Rhodes (Ródhos), Gre.
39/H1 Rhodope (mts.), Bul.
41/F4 Rhodope (range), Bul.
101/F1 Rhome, Tx,US
24/C3 Rhondda, Wal,UK
18/D4 Rhône (riv.), Fr.
36/A6 Rhône (dept.), Fr.
32/F4 Rhône (riv.), Fr., Swi.
36/B6 Rhône (riv.), Fr., Swi.
37/E4 Rhone (glac.), Swi.
32/F4 Rhône-Alpes (reg.), Fr.
36/B5 Rhône-Alpes (reg.), Fr.
36/B3 Rhône au Rhin (can.), Fr.
36/D1 Rhône au Rhin (can.), Fr.
30/C3 Rhonelle (riv.), Fr.
23/E6 Rhosllanerchrugog, Wal,UK
24/B3 Rhossili, Wal,UK
22/E5 Rhuddlan, Wal,UK
21/B2 Rhum (isl.), Sc,UK
29/H5 Rhume (riv.), Ger.
75/V17 Rhumel (riv.), Alg.
24/C2 Rhyddhywel (mtn.), Wal,UK
24/B2 Rhydowen, Wal,UK
22/E5 Rhyl, Wal,UK
24/C3 Rhymney, Wal,UK
107/K6 Riacho de Santana, Braz.
98/C2 Rialto, Ca,US
34/A1 Rianjo, Sp.
34/C1 Riaño, Sp.
66/B3 Riau (isls.), Indo.
34/D2 Riaza, Sp.
34/A1 Ribadavia, Sp.
34/B1 Ribadeo, Sp.
34/C1 Ribadesella, Sp.
81/H8 Riban'i Manamby (mts.), Madg.
23/F4 Ribble (riv.), Eng,UK
23/F4 Ribblesdale (val.), Eng,UK
20/D5 Ribe, Den.
26/E1 Ribe, Den.
26/E1 Ribe (co.), Den.
36/D1 Ribeauvillé, Fr.
30/B4 Ribécourt-Dreslincourt, Fr.
108/B3 Ribeira (riv.), Braz.
74/J10 Ribeira Brava, CpV.
34/B2 Ribeira de Pena, Port.
107/L6 Ribeira do Pombal, Braz.
35/T13 Ribeira Grande, Azor.
74/J9 Ribeira Grande, CpV.
108/B2 Ribeirão do Pinha, Braz.
107/J8 Ribeirão Preto, Braz.
108/C2 Ribeirão Preto, Braz.
30/C4 Ribemont, Fr.
38/C4 Ribera, It.
106/E6 Riberalta, Bol.
26/G1 Ribnitz-Damgarten, Ger.
38/D2 Riccia, It.
40/B5 Riccia, It.
94/E2 Rice (lake), On,Can
86/G4 Rice Lake, Wi,US
89/H2 Rice Lake, Wi,US
91/L4 Rice Lake, Wi,US
94/B2 Rice Lake, Wi,US
86/C2 Richards (isl.), NW,Can
81/F3 Richard's Bay, SAfr.
82/F6 Richard's Bay, SAfr.
95/G2 Richardson (lakes), Me,US
98/E5 Richboro, Pa,US
28/C2 Richel (isl.), Neth.
95/P7 Richelieu, Qu,Can
95/P7 Richelieu (riv.), Qu,Can
88/D4 Richfield, Ut,US
92/D3 Richfield, Ut,US
22/B3 Richhill, NI,UK
86/E4 Richland, Wa,US
88/C2 Richland, Wa,US
90/D4 Richland, Wa,US
97/H3 Richland Balsam (peak), NC,US
91/L5 Richland Center, Wi,US
94/B3 Richland Center, Wi,US
93/H5 Richland Creek (res.), Tx,US
98/E5 Richlandtown, Pa,US
70/G4 Richmond, Austl.
72/A3 Richmond, Austl.
73/D2 Richmond, Austl.
90/C3 Richmond, Can
95/F2 Richmond, Can
80/C3 Richmond, SAfr.
23/G3 Richmond, Eng,UK
84/K6 Richmond, US
99/K11 Richmond, Ca,US
99/P15 Richmond, Il,US
89/K4 Richmond, In,US
94/C4 Richmond, In,US
97/G2 Richmond, In,US
89/K4 Richmond, Ky,US
94/C4 Richmond, Ky,US
97/G2 Richmond, Ky,US
99/G6 Richmond, Mi,US
98/F5 Richmond (co.), NY,US
96/E4 Richmond, Tx,US
89/L4 Richmond (cap.), Va,US
94/E4 Richmond, Va,US
97/J2 Richmond, Va,US
99/C2 Richmond Beach-Innis Arden, Wa,US
95/R8 Richmond Hill, On,Can
72/G8 Richmond-Raaf, Austl.
19/N7 Richmond upon Thames (bor.), Eng,UK
37/E3 Richterswil, Swi.
36/D2 Richwiller, Fr.
36/D2 Rickenbach, Ger.
19/M7 Rickmansworth, Eng,UK
25/F3 Rickmansworth, Eng,UK
34/E2 Ricla, Sp.
40/E1 Ricse, Hun.
52/D6 Ridā', Yem.
77/P5 Ridā', Yem.
28/B5 Ridderkerk, Neth.
94/E2 Rideau (lake), On,Can
88/C4 Ridgecrest, Ca,US
92/C4 Ridgecrest, Ca,US
23/G2 Riding Mill, Eng,UK
86/F3 Riding Mountain Nat'l Park, Mb,Can
91/H3 Riding Mtn. Nat'l Park, Mb,Can
88/F1 Riding Mtn. Nat'l Park, Mb,Can
98/E6 Ridley (cr.), Pa,US
29/F3 Riede, Ger.
27/G4 Ried im Innkreis, Aus.
33/K2 Ried im Innkreis, Aus.
36/D2 Riedisheim, Fr.
37/F1 Riedlingen, Ger.
31/F5 Riegelsberg, Ger.
98/E5 Riegelsville, Pa,US
37/H2 Riegsee (lake), Ger.
36/D2 Riehen, Swi.
31/E2 Riemst, Belg.
27/G3 Riesa, Ger.
31/G5 Rieschweiler-Mühlbach, Ger.
109/B7 Riesco (isl.), Chile
80/D3 Riet (riv.), SAfr.
80/L10 Riet (riv.), SAfr.
20/G5 Rietavas, Lith.
42/D5 Rietavas, Lith.
29/F5 Rietberg, Ger.
38/C1 Rieti, It.
23/G3 Rievaulx, Eng,UK
90/C4 Riffe (lake), Wa,US
92/F3 Rifle, Co,US
20/N6 Rifsnes (pt.), Ice.
42/D4 Riga (gulf), Est.,Lat.
20/G4 Riga (gulf), Est.,Lat.
18/F3 Riga (gulf), Est.,Lat.
18/F3 Riga (cap.), Lat.
20/H4 Riga (cap.), Lat.
46/C4 Riga (cap.), Lat.
46/C4 Riga (gulf), Est.,Lat.
20/H4 Rīga (Riga) (cap.), Lat.
42/E4 Rīga (Riga) (cap.), Lat.
42/E4 Riga (Rīga) (cap.), Lat.
90/F5 Rigby, Id,US
92/E2 Rigby, Id,US
53/H2 Rīgestan (reg.), Afg.
90/D4 Riggins, Id,US
36/D4 Riggisberg, Swi.
37/E3 Rigi (peak), Swi.
87/L3 Rigolet, Nf,Can
62/D3 Rihand Sāgar (res.), India
20/H3 Riihimäki, Fin.
42/E3 Riihimäki, Fin.
83/C Riiser-Larsen (pen.), Ant.
83/Y Riiser-Larsen Ice Shelf, Ant.
20/J2 Riisitunturin Nat'l Park, Fin.
42/F2 Riisitunturin Nat'l Park, Fin.
18/E4 Rijeka, Cro.
33/L4 Rijeka, Cro.
40/B3 Rijeka, Cro.
28/B4 Rijnsburg, Neth.
28/B5 Rijsbergen, Neth.
28/D4 Rijssen, Neth.
28/B4 Rijswijk, Neth.
69/M7 Rikitea, FrPol.
39/H1 Rila, Bul.
39/H1 Rila (mts.), Bul.
41/F4 Rila, Bul.
41/F4 Rila (mts.), Bul.
36/A6 Rillieux-la-Pape, Fr.
39/H1 Rilski Manastir, Bul.
69/K7 Rimatara (isl.), FrPol.
44/B2 Rimavská Sobota, Czh.
27/L4 Rimavská Sobota, Slvk.
40/E1 Rimavská Sobota, Slvk.
52/D3 Rīma, Wādi (dry riv.), SAr.
90/E2 Rimbey, Ab,Can
77/J5 Rimé (wadi), Chad
18/E4 Rimini, It.
33/K4 Rimini, It.
41/H3 Rîmnicu Sărat, Rom.
41/G3 Rîmnicu Vîlcea, Rom.
44/C3 Rîmnicu Vîlcea, Rom.
30/D4 Rimogne, Fr
87/K4 Rimouski, Qu,Can
89/N2 Rimouski, Qu,Can
95/G1 Rimouski, Qu,Can
36/D5 Rimpfischhorn (peak), Swi.
54/D1 Rinchinlhümbe, Mong.
103/F4 Rincón (pt.), Pan.
100/C1 Rincon (peak), Az,US
34/C4 Rincón de la Victoria, Sp.
103/E4 Rincón de la Vieja Nat'l Park, CR
100/E4 Rincón de Romos, Mex.
73/C4 Ringarooma, Austl.
22/C3 Ringboy (pt.), NI,UK
20/D3 Ringebu, Nor.
37/F4 Ringelspitz (peak), Swi.
20/D4 Ringkøbing, Den.
25/G5 Ringmer, Eng,UK
22/B1 Ringsend, NI,UK
26/F1 Ringsted, Den.
28/B4 Ringvaart (can.), Neth.
20/F1 Ringvassøy (isl.), Nor.
73/G5 Ringwood, Austl.
25/E5 Ringwood, Eng,UK
98/F4 Ringwood, NJ,US
39/J4 Rínia (isl.), Gre.
22/C2 Rinns, The (pen.), Sc,UK
29/G4 Rinteln, Ger.
30/A2 Rinxent, Fr.
106/C5 Río Abiseo Nat'l Park, Peru
108/B3 Rio Azul, Braz.
106/C4 Riobamba, Ecu.
102/B2 Río Blanco, Mex.
106/E5 Rio Branco, Braz.
108/B3 Rio Branco do Sul, Braz.
109/B5 Río Bueno, Chile
108/D2 Rio Casca, Braz.
103/G1 Río Cauto, Cuba
107/J8 Rio Claro, Braz.
108/C2 Rio Claro, Braz.
109/G1 Rio Claro, Braz.
104/F5 Rio Claro, Trin.
109/D4 Río Colorado, Arg.
109/D3 Río Cuarto, Arg.
107/K8 Rio de Janeiro, Braz.
108/D2 Rio de Janeiro, Braz.
108/D2 Rio de Janeiro (state), Braz.
109/H1 Rio de Janeiro, Braz.
90/B5 Rio Dell, Ca,US
92/A2 Rio Dell, Ca,US
108/B3 Rio do Sul, Braz.
109/G2 Rio do Sul, Braz.
102/D3 Río Dulce Nat'l Park, Guat.
35/Q10 Rio Frio, Port.
109/C7 Río Gallegos, Arg.
109/C7 Río Grande, Arg.
108/A5 Rio Grande, Braz.
109/F3 Rio Grande, Braz.
100/E4 Río Grande, Mex.
88/G6 Rio Grande (riv.), Mex., US
93/F5 Rio Grande (riv.), US
101/E2 Rio Grande (riv.), NM, Tx,US
101/F3 Rio Grande (plain), Tx,US
84/G7 Rio Grande (riv.), US, Mex.
101/F3 Rio Grande City, Tx,US
96/D5 Rio Grande City, Tx,US
108/A4 Rio Grande do Sul (state), Braz.
103/H4 Riohacha, Col.
106/D1 Riohacha, Col.
103/F4 Río Hato, Pan.
101/F3 Rio Hondo, Tx,US
106/C5 Rioja, Peru
106/F4 Rio Jaú Nat'l Park, Braz.
102/D1 Río Lagartos, Mex.
108/B1 Riolândia, Braz.
107/L5 Rio Largo, Braz.
32/E4 Riom, Fr.
34/A3 Rio Maior, Port.
109/B6 Río Mayo, Arg.
32/E4 Riom-ès-Montagne, Fr.
90/D3 Riondel, BC,Can
32/C5 Rion-des-Landes, Fr.
35/E1 Rion-des-Landes, Fr.
108/B3 Rio Negro, Braz.
103/H5 Rionegro, Col.
109/E3 Río Negro (res.), Uru.
38/D2 Rionero in Vulture, It.
108/C1 Rio Paranaíba, Braz.
108/A4 Rio Pardo, Braz.
109/E2 Río Pilcomayo Nat'l Park, Arg.
92/F4 Rio Rancho, NM,US
96/B3 Rio Rancho, NM,US
32/F3 Riorges, Fr.
34/B2 Ríos, Sp.
103/G5 Riosucio, Col.
109/D3 Río Tercero, Arg.
107/H7 Rio Verde, Braz.
108/B1 Rio Verde, Braz.
101/F4 Rioverde, Mex.
102/B1 Rioverde, Mex.
107/H7 Rio Verde de Mato Grosso, Braz.
99/L10 Rio Vista, Ca,US
36/C3 Rioz, Fr.
38/B1 Ripalti, Punta dei (pt.), It.
40/E3 Ripanj, Yugo.
19/M8 Ripley, Eng,UK
23/G5 Ripley, Eng,UK
97/F3 Ripley, Ms,US
93/K4 Ripley, Tn,US
94/B5 Ripley, Tn,US
97/F3 Ripley, Tn,US
35/G1 Ripoll, Sp.
35/L6 Ripoll (riv.), Sp.
35/L6 Ripollet, Sp.
23/G3 Ripon, Eng,UK
91/L5 Ripon, Wi,US
38/D4 Riposto, It.
23/G4 Ripponden, Eng,UK
24/C3 Risca, Wal,UK
55/N2 Rishiri (isl.), Japan
49/D4 Rishon LeẔiyyon, Isr.
49/F8 Rishon LeẔiyyon, Isr.
32/D2 Risle (riv.), Fr.
33/L4 Risnjak (peak), Cro.
40/B3 Risnjak (peak), Cro.
33/L4 Risnjak Nat'l Park, Cro.
40/B3 Risnjak Nat'l Park, Cro.
41/G3 Rîşnov, Rom.
93/J4 Rison, Ar,US
96/E3 Rison, Ar,US
20/D4 Risør, Nor.
19/T11 Ris-Orangis, Fr.
37/F1 Riss (riv.), Ger.
36/C5 Risse (riv.), Fr.
20/H4 Risti, Est.
42/E4 Risti, Est.
42/E3 Ristiina, Fin.
105/B2 Ritacuba (peak), Col.
106/D2 Ritacuba (peak), Col.
68/C2 Ritaiō (isl.), Japan
29/F2 Ritterhude, Ger.
57/L9 Rittō, Japan
90/D4 Ritzville, Wa,US
33/J4 Riva, It.
37/G6 Riva, It.
109/C3 Rivadavia, Arg.
109/D4 Rivadavia, Arg.
33/G4 Rivarolo Canavese, It.
102/E4 Rivas, Nic.
37/E6 Riva San Vitale, Swi.
53/G1 Rīvash, Iran
32/F4 Rive-de-Gier, Fr.
37/E5 Rivera, Swi.
109/E3 Rivera, Uru.
78/C5 River Cess, Libr.
88/M3 Riverhead, NY,US
95/F3 Riverhead, NY,US
71/H7 Riverina (reg.), Austl.
99/F7 River Rouge, Mi,US
90/B3 Rivers (inlet), BC,Can
91/H3 Rivers, Mb,Can
79/G5 Rivers (state), Nga.
80/C4 Riversdale, SAfr.
80/Q13 Riversdale, SAfr.
88/C5 Riverside, Ca,US
92/C4 Riverside, Ca,US
98/C3 Riverside, Ca,US
98/C3 Riverside (co.), Ca,US
72/G8 Riverstone, Austl.
21/A3 Riverstown, Ire.
91/J3 Riverton, Can
71/Q12 Riverton, N.Z.
86/F4 Riverton, Wy,US
88/E3 Riverton, Wy,US
90/F5 Riverton, Wy,US
92/E2 Riverton, Wy,US
95/H2 Riverview, NB,Can
99/F7 Riverview, Mi,US
99/Q15 Riverwoods, Il,US
30/A4 Rivery, Fr.
97/H5 Riviera Beach, Fl,US
98/K7 Riviera Beach, Md,US
87/K4 Rivière-du-Loup, Qu,Can
89/N2 Rivière-du-Loup, Qu,Can
95/G2 Rivière-du-Loup, Qu,Can
80/L11 Riviersonderendreeks (mts.), SAfr.
33/G4 Rivoli, It.
30/D2 Rixensart, Belg.
36/D2 Rixheim, Fr.
77/Q3 Riyadh (cap.), SAr.
52/E4 Riyadh (Ar Riyāḍ) (cap.), SAr.
49/E3 Rīyāq, Leb.
45/G4 Rize, Turk.
45/G4 Rize (prov.), Turk.
46/E5 Rize, Turk.
50/E1 Rize, Turk.
50/E1 Rize (prov.), Turk.
55/H4 Rizhao, China
59/D4 Rizhao, China
49/D2 Rizokarpasso, Cyp.
38/E3 Rizzuto (cape), It.
20/D4 Rjukan, Nor.
78/B2 Rkîz (lake), Mrta.
20/D3 Roa, Nor.
34/D2 Roa, Sp.
25/F2 Roade, Eng,UK
104/E3 Road Town, BVI
92/E3 Roan (plat.), Co,US
23/F1 Roan Fell (hill), Sc,UK
97/H2 Roan High (peak), NC,US
32/F3 Roanne, Fr.
97/G3 Roanoke, Al,US
89/L4 Roanoke, Va,US
94/E4 Roanoke, Va,US
94/E4 Roanoke (riv.), Va,US
97/J2 Roanoke, Va,US
89/L4 Roanoke Rapids, NC,US
94/E4 Roanoke Rapids, NC,US
97/J2 Roanoke Rapids, NC,US
102/E2 Roatán, Hon.
102/E2 Roatán (isl.), Hon.
53/G2 Robāţ-e Khān, Iran
53/G1 Robāţ-e Sang, Iran
51/G3 Robāţ Karīm, Iran
62/F1 Robāţ Karīm, Iran
73/C4 Robbins (isl.), Austl.
73/A3 Robe, Austl.
73/B1 Robe (peak), Austl.
21/A4 Robe (riv.), Ire.
36/B5 Robert (mtn.), Fr.
31/E6 Robert-Espagne, Fr.
101/E2 Robert Lee, Tx,US
96/C4 Robert Lee, Tx,US
85/E4 Roberts (mtn.), Ak,US
25/G5 Robertsbridge, Eng,UK
20/G2 Robertsfors, Swe.
42/D2 Robertsfors, Swe.
62/D3 Robertsganj, India
80/B4 Robertson, SAfr.
80/L10 Robertson, SAfr.
76/C6 Robertsport, Libr.
78/C5 Robertsport, Libr.
22/B5 Robertstown, Ire.
87/J4 Roberval, Qu,Can
89/M2 Roberval, Qu,Can
95/F1 Roberval, Qu,Can
23/H3 Robin Hood's Bay, Eng,UK
70/B5 Robinson (ranges), Austl.
94/C4 Robinson, Il,US
97/G2 Robinson, Il,US
99/C3 Robinson (pt.), Wa,US
105/B6 Robinson Crusoe (isl.), Chile
72/C4 Robinson Gorge Nat'l Park, Austl.
73/B2 Robinvale, Austl.
100/D1 Robledo (mtn.), NM,US
86/F3 Roblin, Mb,Can
91/H3 Roblin, Mb,Can
106/G7 Roboré, Bol.
90/D2 Robson (peak), Can
86/E3 Robson (mtn.), BC,Can
96/D5 Robstown, Tx,US
101/E1 Roby, Tx,US
93/G4 Roby, Tx,US
96/C3 Roby, Tx,US
35/P10 Roca (cape), Port.
34/A3 Roca, Cabo da (cape), Port.
32/D4 Rocamadour, Fr.
100/B5 Roca Partida (isl.), Mex.
101/G5 Roca Partida, Punta (pt.), Mex.
102/C2 Roca Partida, Punta (pt.), Mex.
107/M4 Rocas, Braz.
38/B1 Roccastrada, It.
33/G4 Rocciamelone (peak), It.
32/E5 Roc de France (mtn.), Fr.
35/G1 Roc de France (mtn.), Fr.
36/D1 Roc du Haut du Faite (mtn.), Fr.
109/F3 Rocha, Uru.
23/F4 Rochdale, Eng,UK
36/C5 Roche, Swi.
24/B6 Roche, Eng,UK
31/E3 Rochefort, Belg.
32/C4 Rochefort, Fr.
36/C3 Roche-lez-Beaupré, Fr.
35/J1 Roches Blanches (mtn.), Fr.
73/C3 Rochester, Austl.
25/G4 Rochester, Eng,UK
94/C3 Rochester, In,US
99/F6 Rochester, Mi,US
86/G4 Rochester, Mn,US
89/H3 Rochester, Mn,US
91/K4 Rochester, Mn,US
93/J1 Rochester, Mn,US
94/A2 Rochester, Mn,US
95/G3 Rochester, NH,US
87/J4 Rochester, NY,US
89/L3 Rochester, NY,US
94/E3 Rochester, NY,US
99/P14 Rochester, Wi,US
99/F6 Rochester Hills, Mi,US
25/G3 Rochford, Eng,UK
22/A5 Rochfortbridge, Ire.
91/L5 Rock (riv.), Il, Wi,US
93/K2 Rock (riv.), Il, Wi,US
94/B3 Rock (riv.), Il,US
89/J3 Rock (riv.), Il, Wi,US
90/C4 Rock (cr.), Or,US
22/A3 Rockcorry, Ire.
85/L3 Rock Creek, Yk,Can
78/B6 Rockdale, Austl.
99/P16 Rockdale, Il,US
83/R Rockefeller (plat.), Ant.
31/G4 Rockenhausen, Ger.
89/J3 Rockford, Il,US
91/L5 Rockford, Il,US
93/K2 Rockford, Il,US
94/B3 Rockford, Il,US
95/G2 Rock Forest, Qu,Can
91/G3 Rockglen, Sk,Can
68/E7 Rockhampton, Austl.
71/J4 Rockhampton, Austl.
72/C3 Rockhampton, Austl.
89/K5 Rock Hill, SC,US
97/H3 Rock Hill, SC,US
70/B6 Rockingham, Austl.
97/J3 Rockingham, NC,US
89/H3 Rock Island, Il,US
91/L5 Rock Island, Il,US
93/K2 Rock Island, Il,US
94/B3 Rock Island, Il,US
94/F2 Rockland, On,Can
89/N3 Rockland, Me,US
95/G2 Rockland, Me,US
98/F4 Rockland (co.), NY,US
70/G7 Rocklands (res.), Austl.
73/B3 Rocklands (res.), Austl.
97/H4 Rockledge, Fl,US
98/E5 Rockledge, Pa,US
101/F2 Rockport, Tx,US
96/D4 Rockport, Tx,US
84/G5 Rock Springs, US
101/E2 Rocksprings, Tx,US
93/G6 Rocksprings, Tx,US
96/C4 Rocksprings, Tx,US
86/F4 Rock Springs, Wy,US
88/E3 Rock Springs, Wy,US
90/F5 Rock Springs, Wy,US
92/E2 Rock Springs, Wy,US
73/C2 Rock, The, Austl.
94/E4 Rockville, Md,US
97/J2 Rockville, Md,US
98/J7 Rockville, Md,US
93/H4 Rockwall, Tx,US
96/D3 Rockwall, Tx,US
97/G3 Rockwood, Tn,US
101/F2 Rockwood, Tx,US
102/D2 Rocky (pt.), Belz.
90/D2 Rocky (mts.), Can., US
88/D2 Rocky (mts.), Can., US
84/F4 Rocky (mts.), NAm.
92/E2 Rocky (mts.), NAm
86/D2 Rocky (range), Can,US
94/D4 Rocky (peak), Ky,US
97/H2 Rocky (peak), Ky,US
73/C4 Rocky Cape Nat'l Park, Austl.
95/K1 Rocky Harbour, Nf,Can
94/D2 Rocky Island (lake), On,Can
89/L4 Rocky Mount, NC,US
97/J3 Rocky Mount, NC,US
94/E4 Rocky Mount, Va,US
97/J2 Rocky Mount, Va,US
86/E3 Rocky Mountain House, Ab,Can
90/E2 Rocky Mountain House, Ab,Can
93/F2 Rocky Mountain Nat'l Park, Co,US
88/E3 Rocky Mtn. Nat'l Park, Co,US
98/H5 Rocky Point, NY,US
30/D4 Rocroi, Fr.
31/G5 Rodalben, Ger.
20/D3 Rødberg, Nor.
26/F1 Rødbyhavn, Den.
95/K1 Roddickton, Nf,Can
26/E1 Rødding, Den.
23/F6 Roden (riv.), Eng,UK
24/D1 Roden (riv.), Eng,UK
100/D3 Rodeo, Mex.
99/K10 Rodeo, Ca,US
32/E4 Rodez, Fr.
39/H2 Rodholívos, Gre.
41/F5 Rodholívos, Gre.
50/B2 Ródhos (ruins), Gre.
50/B2 Ródhos (Rhodes), Gre.
26/G4 Roding, Ger.
33/K2 Roding, Ger.
19/P7 Roding (riv.), Eng,UK
29/F4 Rödinghausen, Ger.
39/E1 Rodoč, Bosn.
40/C4 Rodoč, Bosn.
39/F2 Rodonit, Kep i (cape), Alb.
40/D5 Rodonit, Kep i (cape), Alb.
22/B2 Roe (riv.), NI,UK
68/A7 Roebourne, Austl.
70/B4 Roebourne, Austl.
70/C3 Roebuck (bay), Austl.
37/H5 Roen (peak), It.
28/D6 Roer (riv.), Neth.
28/C6 Roermond, Neth.
31/E1 Roermond, Neth.
26/B3 Roeselare, Belg.
30/C2 Roeselare, Belg.
99/D2 Roesiger (lake), Wa,US
87/H2 Roes Welcome (sound), NW,Can
38/E1 Rogač, Cro.
44/D1 Rogachev, Bela.
20/C4 Rogaland (co.), Nor.
33/L3 Rogaška Slatina, Slov.
40/B2 Rogaška Slatina, Slov.
40/D4 Rogatica, Bosn.
89/H4 Rogers, Ar,US
93/J3 Rogers, Ar,US
96/E2 Rogers, Ar,US
94/D4 Rogers (peak), Va,US
97/H2 Rogers (peak), Va,US
94/D2 Rogers City, Mi,US
94/D4 Rogersville, Tn,US
97/H2 Rogersville, Tn,US
36/D3 Roggwil, Swi.
33/H5 Rogliano, Fr.
38/A1 Rogliano, Fr.
20/E2 Rognan, Nor.
42/B2 Rognan, Nor.
32/F2 Rognon (riv.), Fr.
36/B1 Rognon (riv.), Fr.
27/J2 Rogoźno, Pol.
92/B2 Rogue (riv.), Or,US
77/L6 Rohl (riv.), Sudan
27/J5 Rohrbach bei Mattersburg, Aus.
33/M3 Rohrbach bei Mattersburg, Aus.
40/C2 Rohrbach bei Mattersburg, Aus.
31/G5 Rohrbach-lès-Bitche, Fr.
53/J3 Rohri, Pak.
62/A2 Rohri, Pak.
37/H1 Röhrmoos, Ger.
63/H4 Roi Et, Thai.
65/C2 Roi Et, Thai.
30/C4 Roisel, Fr.
19/T10 Roissy, Fr.
19/T9 Roissy-en-France, Fr.
20/G4 Roja, Lat.
42/D4 Roja, Lat.
104/E3 Rojo (cape), PR
101/F4 Rojo, Cabo (cape), Mex.
102/B1 Rojo, Cabo (cape), Mex.
66/B3 Rokan (riv.), Indo.
72/A1 Rokeby-Croll Creek Nat'l Park, Austl.
78/C4 Rokel (riv.), SLeo.
20/H5 Rokiškis, Lith.
42/E5 Rokiškis, Lith.
57/L10 Rokkō-san (peak), Japan
36/B2 Rolampont, Fr.
108/B2 Rolândia, Braz.
28/D3 Rolde, Neth.
90/C2 Rolla, BC,Can
89/H4 Rolla, Mo,US
93/K3 Rolla, Mo,US
96/F2 Rolla, Mo,US
91/J3 Rolla, ND,US
33/G3 Rolle, Swi.
36/C5 Rolle, Swi.
99/B2 Rollingbay, Wa,US
99/P15 Rolling Meadows, Il,US
68/D7 Roma, Austl.
71/H5 Roma, Austl.
72/C4 Roma, Austl.
32/E4 Romagnat, Fr.
31/E5 Romagne-sous-Montfaucon, Fr.
97/J3 Romain (cape), SC,US
87/K3 Romaine (riv.), Qu,Can
95/J1 Romaine (riv.), Qu,Can
36/B2 Romaine (riv.), Fr.
41/F4 Roman, Bul.
41/H2 Roman, Rom.
44/C3 Roman, Rom.
67/G5 Romang (isl.), Indo.
67/G5 Romang (str.), Indo.
18/F4 Romania
27/M5 Romania
41/F3 Romania
44/C3 Romania
46/C5 Romania
103/G1 Romano (cay), Cuba
104/A1 Romano (cape), Fl,US
47/M4 Romanovka, Rus.
54/G1 Romanovka, Rus.
37/F2 Romanshorn, Swi.
32/F4 Romans-sur-Isère, Fr.
85/E3 Romanzof (cape), Ak,US
38/C2 Roma (Rome) (cap.), It.
26/D4 Rombas, Fr.
31/F5 Rombas, Fr.
32/G2 Rombas, Fr.
67/F1 Romblon, Phil.
18/E4 Rome (cap.), It.
89/J5 Rome, Ga,US
97/G3 Rome, Ga,US
87/J4 Rome, NY,US
89/L3 Rome, NY,US
94/F3 Rome, NY,US
99/N14 Rome, Wi,US
36/B4 Romenay, Fr.
99/F6 Romeo, Mi,US
99/P16 Romeoville, Il,US
38/C2 Rome (Roma) (cap.), It.
19/P7 Romford, Eng,UK
30/A5 Romilly-sur-Andelle, Fr.
26/B4 Romilly-sur-Seine, Fr.
32/E2 Romilly-sur-Seine, Fr.
28/D6 Rommerskirchen, Ger.
31/F1 Rommerskirchen, Ger.
25/G4 Romney Marsh (reg.), Eng,UK
44/E2 Romny, Ukr.
26/E1 Rømø (isl.), Den.
98/C3 Romoland, Ca,US
36/C4 Romont, Swi.
32/D3 Romorantin-Lanthenay, Fr.
25/E5 Romsey, Eng,UK
99/F7 Romulus, Mi,US
37/E3 Ron (riv.), Swi.
60/E5 Ron (cape), Viet.
63/J4 Ron (cape), Viet.
65/D2 Ron, Viet.
90/E4 Ronan, Mt,US
107/H6 Roncador (mts.), Braz.
36/C2 Ronchamp, Fr.
38/C1 Ronciglione, It.
30/C2 Roncq, Fr.
34/C4 Ronda, Sp.
20/D3 Rondane Nat'l Park, Nor.
107/H7 Rondonópolis, Braz.
61/F3 Rong (riv.), China
63/J2 Rong (riv.), China
61/F3 Rong'an, China
55/J4 Rongcheng, China
58/B4 Rongcheng, China
59/C3 Rongcheng, China
59/E3 Rongcheng, China
59/G7 Rongcheng, China
91/G2 Ronge (lake), Sk,Can
68/F3 Rongelap (atoll), Mrsh.
68/F3 Rongerik (atoll), Mrsh.
61/F3 Rongjiang, China
63/J2 Rongshui Miaozu Zizhixian, China
63/K3 Rong Xian, China
69/X15 Roniu (peak), FrPol.
20/E5 Rønne, Den.
27/H1 Rønne, Den.
20/E4 Ronneby, Swe.
83/U Ronne Entrance (inlet), Ant.
83/W Ronne Ice Shelf, Ant.
29/G4 Ronnenberg, Ger.
37/G2 Ronsberg, Ger
30/C2 Ronse, Belg.
107/H6 Ronuro (riv.), Braz.
80/P13 Roodepoort-Maraisburg, SAfr.
80/B2 Rooiberg (peak), Namb.
62/C2 Roorkee, India
26/C3 Roosendaal, Neth.
28/B5 Roosendaal, Neth.
83/N Roosevelt (isl.), Ant.
105/C4 Roosevelt (riv.), Braz.
106/F6 Roosevelt (riv.), Braz.
86/D3 Roosevelt (mtn.), BC,Can
92/E2 Roosevelt, Ut,US
85/L4 Root (mt.), Ak,US
99/Q14 Root (riv.), Wi,US
99/P14 Root, West Branch (riv.), Wi,US
34/D4 Roquetas de Mar, Sp.
34/D4 Roquetes, Sp.
105/C2 Roraima (peak), Guy.
106/F2 Roraima (peak), Guy.
107/F2 Roraima (peak), Guy.
81/E3 Rorke's Drift Battlesite, SAfr.
91/J3 Rorketon, Mb,Can
20/D3 Røros, Nor.
37/F3 Rorschach, Swi.
75/W17 Rosa (cape), Alg.
103/H1 Rosa (lake), Bahm.
104/C2 Rosa (lake), Bahm.
36/D5 Rosablanche (peak), Swi.
34/A2 Rosal, Sp.
100/D2 Rosales, Mex.
96/B4 Rosales, Mex
100/D4 Rosamorada, Mex.
37/G3 Rosanna (riv.), Aus.
100/C3 Rosa, Punta (pt.), Mex.
109/D3 Rosario, Arg.
107/K4 Rosário, Braz.
100/C3 Rosario, Mex.
100/D4 Rosario, Mex.
100/A2 Rosario de Arriba, Mex.
109/D2 Rosario de la Frontera, Arg.
109/F3 Rosário do Sul, Braz.
100/A1 Rosarito, Mex.
100/B2 Rosarito, Mex.
92/C4 Rosarito, Mex.
35/G1 Rosas (gulf), Sp.
106/C3 Rosa Zárate, Ecu.
29/H3 Rosche, Ger.
21/A4 Roscommon, Ire.
29/G6 Rosdorf, Ger.
69/J6 Rose (isl.), ASam.
85/M4 Rose (pt.), BC,Can
91/J3 Roseau (riv.), Can., US
104/F4 Roseau (cap.), Dom.

S

173

Saint – Salina

32/B2 **Saint-Brieuc** (bay), Fr.
95/P6 **Saint-Bruno** (co.), Qu,Can
95/P6 **Saint-Bruno-de-Montarville,** Qu,Can
32/D3 **Saint-Calais,** Fr.
95/M6 **Saint-Canut,** Qu,Can
94/E3 **Saint Catharines,** On,Can
95/R9 **Saint Catharines,** On,Can
104/F4 **Saint Catherine** (mtn.), Gren.
25/E5 **Saint Catherine's** (pt.), UK
25/E5 **Saint Catherine's** (hill), Eng,UK
32/D4 **Saint-Céré,** Fr.
36/C5 **Saint-Cergue,** Swi.
36/C5 **Saint-Cergues,** Fr.
32/F4 **Saint-Chamond,** Fr.
99/P16 **Saint Charles,** Il,US
94/E4 **Saint Charles,** Md,US
97/J2 **Saint Charles,** Md,US
89/H4 **Saint Charles,** Mo,US
93/K3 **Saint Charles,** Mo,US
94/B4 **Saint Charles,** Mo,US
97/F2 **Saint Charles,** Mo,US
32/E4 **Saint-Chély-d'Apcher,** Fr.
19/S11 **Saint-Chéron,** Fr.
104/D4 **Saint Christoffel** (peak), NAnt.
99/G7 **Saint Clair** (lake), On,Can, Mi,US
99/H6 **Saint Clair** (riv.), On,Can, Mi,US
94/D3 **Saint Clair,** Mi,US
99/G6 **Saint Clair** (co.), Mi,US
99/H6 **Saint Clair,** Mi,US
99/G7 **Saint Clair Beach,** On,Can
99/G6 **Saint Clair Shores,** Mi,US
32/F3 **Saint-Claude,** Fr.
36/B5 **Saint-Claude,** Fr.
24/B3 **Saint Clears,** Wal,UK
19/S10 **Saint-Cloud,** Fr.
30/B6 **Saint-Cloud,** Fr.
88/G4 **Saint Cloud,** Mn,US
89/H2 **Saint Cloud,** Mn,US
91/K4 **Saint Cloud,** Mn,US
24/B6 **Saint Columb Major,** Eng,UK
95/N7 **Saint-Constant,** Qu,Can
91/K4 **Saint Croix** (riv.), Mn, Wi,US
94/A2 **Saint Croix** (riv.), Mn, Wi,US
104/E3 **Saint Croix** (isl.), USVI
85/M3 **Saint Cyr** (mtn.), Yk,Can
19/S10 **Saint-Cyr-l'École,** Fr.
30/B6 **Saint-Cyr-l'École,** Fr.
19/S11 **Saint-Cyr-sous-Dourdan,** Fr.
100/C2 **Saint David,** Az,US
24/A3 **Saint David's Head** (pt.), Wal,UK
24/A3 **Saint David's,** Wal,UK
19/T10 **Saint-Denis,** Fr.
30/B6 **Saint-Denis,** Fr.
81/R15 **Saint-Denis,** Reun.
36/B6 **Saint-Denis-en-Bugey,** Fr.
36/A5 **Saint-Didier-sur-Saône,** Fr.
26/D4 **Saint-Dié,** Fr.
33/G2 **Saint-Dié,** Fr.
36/C1 **Saint-Dié,** Fr.
26/C4 **Saint-Dizier,** Fr.
32/F2 **Saint-Dizier,** Fr.
32/E3 **Saint-Doulchard,** Fr.
94/F2 **Sainte-Agathe-des-Monts,** Qu,Can
95/H1 **Sainte-Anne-des-Monts,** Qu,Can
95/N6 **Sainte-Anne-des-Plaines,** Qu,Can
36/C4 **Sainte-Croix,** Swi.
36/D1 **Sainte-Croix-aux-Mines,** Fr.
35/J1 **Sainte-Croix, Barrage de la** (dam), Fr.
95/N7 **Saint-Édouard-de-Napierville,** Qu,Can
95/G2 **Sainte-Foy,** Qu,Can
93/K3 **Sainte Genevieve,** Mo,US
94/B4 **Sainte Genevieve,** Mo,US
97/F2 **Sainte Genevieve,** Mo,US
19/T11 **Sainte-Geneviève-des-Bois,** Fr.
26/B4 **Sainte-Geneviève-des-Bois,** Fr.
30/B6 **Sainte-Geneviève-des-Bois,** Fr.
95/P6 **Sainte-Julie-de-Verchères,** Qu,Can
95/J2 **Saint Eleanors,** PE,Can
86/B2 **Saint Elias** (mts.), Yk,Can, Ak,US
85/K3 **Saint Elias** (mt.), Ak,US
85/K4 **Saint Elias** (cape), Ak,US
86/B2 **Saint Elias** (mt.), Ak,US
88/B3 **Saint Elias** (cape), Ak,US
85/K3 **Saint Elias** (mts.), Yk,Can, Ak,US
85/K3 **Saint Elias-Wrangell Nat'l Park and Prsv.,** Ak,US
32/E3 **Saint-Éloy-les-Mines,** Fr.
95/G2 **Sainte-Marie,** Can
104/F4 **Sainte-Marie,** Mart.
31/F5 **Sainte-Marie-aux-Chênes,** Fr.
36/D1 **Sainte-Marie-aux-Mines,** Fr.
81/J7 **Sainte Marie, Nosy** (isl.), Madg.
82/L10 **Sainte Marie, Nosy** (isl.), Madg.
95/N7 **Sainte-Martine,** Qu,Can
33/G5 **Sainte-Maxime,** Fr.
35/J1 **Sainte-Maxime,** Fr.
26/C4 **Sainte-Menehould,** Fr.
31/D5 **Sainte-Menehould,** Fr.
32/F2 **Sainte-Menehould,** Fr.
30/C5 **Sainte-Erme-Outre-et-Ramecourt,** Fr.
91/J3 **Sainte Rose du Lac,** Mb,Can
32/C4 **Saintes,** Fr.
95/M6 **Sainte-Scholastique,** Qu,Can
32/F4 **Sainte-Sigolène,** Fr.
95/N6 **Saint-Esprit,** Qu,Can
32/E5 **Saint-Estève,** Fr.
32/E5 **Saint-Estève,** Fr.
95/N6 **Sainte-Thérèse,** Qu,Can
95/N6 **Sainte-Thérèse-Ouest,** Qu,Can
18/D4 **Saint-Étienne,** Fr.
32/F4 **Saint-Étienne,** Fr.
30/A2 **Saint-Étienne-au-Mont,** Fr.
32/C5 **Saint-Étienne-de-Baïgorry,** Fr.
34/E1 **Saint-Étienne-de-Baïgorry,** Fr.
33/G4 **Saint-Étienne-de-Tinée,** Fr.
32/D2 **Saint-Étienne-du-Rouvray,** Fr.
36/C1 **Saint-Étienne-lès-Remiremont,** Fr.
32/F5 **Sainte-Tulle,** Fr.
35/H1 **Sainte-Tulle,** Fr.
95/N6 **Saint-Eustache,** Qu,Can
104/F3 **Saint Eustatius** (isl.), NAnt.
19/T11 **Saint-Fargeau-Ponthierry,** Fr.
95/F1 **Saint-Félicien,** Qu,Can
36/B6 **Saint-Felix,** Fr.
22/C3 **Saintfield,** NI,UK
26/B4 **Saint-Florentin,** Fr.
32/E2 **Saint-Florentin,** Fr.
32/E3 **Saint-Florent-sur-Cher,** Fr.
77/K6 **Saint-Floris Nat'l Park,** CAfr.
32/E4 **Saint-Flour,** Fr.
93/K4 **Saint Francis** (riv.), Ar, Mo,US
80/D4 **Saint Francis** (cape), SAfr.
93/G3 **Saint Francis,** Ks,US
96/C2 **Saint Francis,** Ks,US
99/Q14 **Saint Francis,** Wi,US
93/K5 **Saint Francisville,** La,US
97/F4 **Saint Francisville,** La,US
97/F2 **Saint Francois** (mts.), Mo,US
32/D5 **Saint-Gaudens,** Fr.
35/F1 **Saint-Gaudens,** Fr.
36/C5 **Saint-Genis-Pouilly,** Fr.
68/D7 **Saint George,** Austl.
71/H5 **Saint George,** Austl.
72/C5 **Saint George,** Austl.
95/H2 **Saint George,** NB,Can
87/L4 **Saint George** (cape), Nf,Can
95/K1 **Saint George** (cape), Nf,Can
85/E4 **Saint George,** Ak,US
85/E4 **Saint George** (isl.), Ak,US
90/B5 **Saint George** (pt.), Ca,US
92/A2 **Saint George** (pt.), Ca,US
97/H3 **Saint George,** SC,US
88/D4 **Saint George,** Ut,US
92/D3 **Saint George,** Ut,US
95/K1 **Saint George's** (bay), Nf,Can
95/J2 **Saint Georges** (bay), NS,Can
104/F4 **Saint George's** (cap.), Gren.
106/F1 **Saint George's** (cap.), Gren.
22/C6 **Saint George's** (chan.), Eur.
24/A3 **Saint George's** (chan.), Eur.
95/G2 **Saint-Georges,** Qu,Can
95/K1 **Saint George's,** Nf,Can
18/C3 **Saint George's** (chan.), Eur.
36/C2 **Saint-Germain,** Fr.
36/B4 **Saint-Germain-du-Bois,** Fr.
32/D2 **Saint-Germain-du-Corbéis,** Fr.
36/A4 **Saint-Germain-du-Plain,** Fr.
19/S10 **Saint-Germain-en-Laye,** Fr.
30/B6 **Saint-Germain-en-Laye,** Fr.
19/T11 **Saint-Germain-lès-Corbeil,** Fr.
19/U10 **Saint-Germain-sur-Morin,** Fr.
30/B6 **Saint-Germain-sur-Morin,** Fr.
30/A5 **Saint-Germer-de-Fly,** Fr.
36/C6 **Saint-Gervais-les-Bains,** Fr.
30/C3 **Saint-Ghislain,** Belg.
32/F5 **Saint-Gilles,** Fr.
35/H1 **Saint-Gilles,** Fr.
32/C3 **Saint-Gilles-Croix-de-Vie,** Fr.
36/C5 **Saint-Gingolph,** Swi.
32/D5 **Saint-Girons,** Fr.
35/F1 **Saint-Girons,** Fr.
30/C4 **Saint-Gobain,** Fr.
37/E4 **Saint Gotthard** (pass), Swi.
24/B3 **Saint Govan's Head** (pt.), Wal,UK
19/S10 **Saint-Gratien,** Fr.
80/B4 **Saint Helena** (bay), SAfr.
80/L10 **Saint Helena** (bay), SAfr.
82/C7 **Saint Helena** (bay), SAfr.
72/F6 **Saint Helena** (isl.), Austl.
74/B6 **Saint Helena** (isl.), U.K.
99/J9 **Saint Helena** (mt.), Ca,US
99/K9 **Saint Helena,** Ca,US
73/D4 **Saint Helens,** Austl.
73/D4 **Saint Helens** (pt.), Austl.
23/F5 **Saint Helens,** Eng,UK
90/C4 **Saint Helens,** Or,US
88/B2 **Saint Helens** (vol.), Wa,US
90/C4 **Saint Helens** (peak), Wa,US
32/B2 **Saint Helier,** Chl,UK
32/C3 **Saint-Herblain,** Fr.
95/M6 **Saint-Hermas,** Qu,Can
62/E3 **Sainthia,** India
36/C3 **Saint-Hippolyte,** Fr.
95/G1 **Saint-Honoré,** Can
26/C3 **Saint-Hubert,** Belg.
31/E3 **Saint-Hubert,** Belg.
32/F1 **Saint-Hubert,** Belg.
95/P7 **Saint-Hubert,** Qu,Can
95/F2 **Saint-Hyacinthe,** Qu,Can
91/M3 **Saint Ignace** (isl.), On,Can
94/C1 **Saint Ignace** (isl.), On,Can
94/C2 **Saint Ignace,** Mi,US
36/D3 **Saint-Imier,** Swi.
95/N7 **Saint-Isidore-de-Laprairie,** Qu,Can
72/H8 **Saint Ives,** Austl.
24/A6 **Saint Ives,** Eng,UK
24/A6 **Saint Ives** (bay), Eng,UK
25/F2 **Saint Ives,** Eng,UK
32/A1 **Saint Ives,** Eng,UK
95/P7 **Saint-Jacques-le-Mineur,** Qu,Can
86/C3 **Saint James** (cape), BC,Can
91/K5 **Saint James,** Mn,US
93/J2 **Saint James,** Mn,US
87/J4 **Saint-Jean** (lake), Qu,Can
95/G1 **Saint-Jean** (lake), Qu,Can
95/H1 **Saint-Jean** (riv.), Qu,Can
95/P7 **Saint-Jean** (co.), Qu,Can
32/C4 **Saint-Jean-d'Angély,** Fr.
32/D3 **Saint-Jean-de-la-Ruelle,** Fr.
30/B3 **Saint-Jean-de-Losne,** Fr.
32/C5 **Saint-Jean-de-Luz,** Fr.
34/E1 **Saint-Jean-de-Luz,** Fr.
89/M2 **Saint-Jean, Lac-** (lake), Qu,Can
95/G2 **Saint-Jean-Port-Joli,** Qu,Can
95/F2 **Saint-Jean-sur-Richelieu,** Qu,Can
95/P7 **Saint-Jean-sur-Richelieu,** Qu,Can
36/C5 **Saint-Jeoire,** Fr.
94/F2 **Saint-Jérôme,** Can
95/N6 **Saint-Jérôme,** Qu,Can
88/C2 **Saint Joe** (riv.), Id, Wa,US
90/D4 **Saint Joe** (riv.), Id,US
87/K4 **Saint John,** NB,Can
89/N2 **Saint John,** NB,Can
95/H2 **Saint John,** NB,Can
87/K4 **Saint John** (riv.), NB,Can, Me,US
32/B2 **Saint John,** Chl,UK
95/G2 **Saint John** (riv.), Me,US
95/H2 **Saint John** (riv.), NB,Can
104/E3 **Saint John** (isl.), USVI
104/F3 **Saint John's** (cap.), Anti.
22/C3 **Saint John's** (pt.), IM,UK
92/E4 **Saint Johns,** Az,US
89/K6 **Saint Johns** (riv.), Fl,US
95/F2 **Saint Johnsbury,** Vt,US
86/G3 **Saint Joseph** (lake), On,Can
91/L3 **Saint Joseph** (lake), On,Can
94/B1 **Saint Joseph** (lake), On,Can
94/C2 **Saint Joseph** (isl.), Mi,US
94/C3 **Saint Joseph** (riv.), Mi,US
89/H4 **Saint Joseph,** Mo,US
93/J3 **Saint Joseph,** Mo,US
96/E2 **Saint Joseph,** Mo,US
81/R15 **Saint-Joseph,** Reun.
32/E5 **Saint-Juéry,** Fr.
35/G1 **Saint-Juéry,** Fr.
36/B3 **Saint-Julien,** Fr.
36/C5 **Saint-Julien-en-Genevois,** Fr.
32/F2 **Saint-Julien-les-Villas,** Fr.
32/D4 **Saint-Junien,** Fr.
24/A6 **Saint Just,** Eng,UK
30/B5 **Saint-Just-en-Chaussée,** Fr.
24/A6 **Saint Just in Roseland,** Eng,UK
73/F5 **Saint Kilda,** Austl.
21/A2 **Saint Kilda** (isl.), Sc,UK
104/F3 **Saint Kitts** (isl.), StK.
84/L8 **Saint Kitts and Nevis**
104/E3 **Saint Kitts and Nevis**
95/P6 **Saint-Lambert,** Qu,Can
91/J3 **Saint Laurent,** Mb,Can
95/N6 **Saint-Laurent,** Qu,Can
30/B3 **Saint-Laurent-Blangy,** Fr.
32/E5 **Saint-Laurent-de-Cerdans,** Fr.
35/G1 **Saint-Laurent-de-Cerdans,** Fr.
107/H2 **Saint-Laurent du Maroni,** FrG.
36/B4 **Saint-Laurent-en-Grandvaux,** Fr.
32/C4 **Saint-Laurent-et-Benon,** Fr.
36/A5 **Saint-Laurent-sur-Saône,** Fr.
84/L5 **Saint Lawrence** (gulf), Can.
87/K4 **Saint Lawrence** (gulf), Can.
89/P2 **Saint Lawrence** (gulf), Can.
95/J1 **Saint Lawrence** (gulf), Can
95/L2 **Saint Lawrence,** Nf,Can
87/K4 **Saint Lawrence** (riv.), Can., US
95/G1 **Saint Lawrence** (riv.), Can., US
95/P6 **Saint Lawrence** (riv.), Can., US
89/N2 **Saint Lawrence** (riv.), Can., US
32/C1 **Saint Lawrence,** UK
84/A4 **Saint Lawrence** (isl.), US
47/U3 **Saint Lawrence** (isl.), Ak,US
85/D3 **Saint Lawrence** (isl.), Ak,US
84/K5 **Saint Lawrence** (riv.), US, Can.
94/E2 **Saint Lawrence Islands Nat'l Park,** Can
95/M7 **Saint-Lazare,** Qu,Can
31/E4 **Saint-Léger,** Belg.
30/A5 **Saint-Léger-du-Bourg-Denis,** Fr.
30/B3 **Saint-Léger-lès-Domart,** Fr.
73/G5 **Saint Leonard** (mt.), Austl.
95/N6 **Saint-Léonard,** Qu,Can
25/H5 **Saint-Léonard,** Fr.
30/A2 **Saint-Léonard,** Fr.
81/R15 **Saint-Leu,** Reun.
30/B5 **Saint-Leu-d'Esserent,** Fr.
19/S9 **Saint-Leu-la-Forêt,** Fr.
32/C2 **Saint-Lô,** Fr.
91/G2 **Saint Louis,** Can
95/N7 **Saint Louis** (lake), Qu,Can
36/D2 **Saint-Louis,** Fr.
81/R15 **Saint-Louis,** Reun.
76/B4 **Saint-Louis,** Sen.
78/A2 **Saint-Louis,** Sen.
78/B3 **Saint-Louis** (reg.), Sen.
94/A2 **Saint Louis** (riv.), Mn,US
89/H4 **Saint Louis,** Mo,US
93/K3 **Saint Louis,** Mo,US
94/B4 **Saint Louis,** Mo,US
97/F2 **Saint Louis,** Mo,US
95/N7 **Saint-Louis-de-Gonzague,** Qu,Can
95/H2 **Saint-Louis-de-Kent,** NB,Can
95/N6 **Saint-Louis-de-Terrebonne,** Qu,Can
103/H2 **Saint-Louis du Nord,** Haiti
26/D5 **Saint-Loup-sur-Semouse,** Fr.
33/G3 **Saint-Loup-sur-Semouse,** Fr.
36/C2 **Saint-Loup-sur-Semouse,** Fr.
30/A6 **Saint-Lubin-des-Joncherets,** Fr.
32/D2 **Saint-Lubin-des-Joncherets,** Fr.
95/P7 **Saint-Luc,** Qu,Can
104/F4 **Saint Lucia**
84/L8 **Saint Lucia**
104/F4 **Saint Lucia** (passg.), Mart.,StL.
81/F3 **Saint Lucia** (cape), SAfr.
82/F6 **Saint Lucia** (cape), SAfr.
81/F3 **Saint Lucia, Lake** (lag.), SAfr.
32/C3 **Saint-Maixent-l'École,** Fr.
91/J3 **Saint Malo,** Mb,Can
32/B2 **Saint-Malo,** Fr.
32/B2 **Saint-Malo** (gulf), Fr.
19/T10 **Saint-Mandé,** Fr.
32/F5 **Saint-Mandrier-sur-Mer,** Fr.
35/H1 **Saint-Mandrier-sur-Mer,** Fr.
95/P6 **Saint-Marc,** Qu,Can
103/H2 **Saint-Marc,** Haiti
30/A5 **Saint-Marcel,** Fr.
36/A4 **Saint-Marcel,** Fr.
103/H2 **Saint-Marc, Pointe de** (pt.), Haiti
19/U9 **Saint-Mard,** Fr.
30/B5 **Saint-Mard,** Fr.
25/H4 **Saint Margaret's at Cliffe,** Eng,UK
30/A1 **Saint Margaret's at Cliffe,** Eng,UK
90/D4 **Saint Maries,** Id,US
91/J3 **Saint Martin** (lake), Mb,Can
36/D5 **Saint-Martin,** Swi.
36/A5 **Saint-Martin-Belle-Roche,** Fr.
30/A2 **Saint-Martin-Boulogne,** Fr.
30/C6 **Saint-Martin-d'Ablois,** Fr.
32/F4 **Saint-Martin-d'Hères,** Fr.
19/T9 **Saint-Martin-du-Tertre,** Fr.
60/A4 **Saint Martins** (isl.), Bang.
104/F3 **Saint-Martin** (Saint Martin) (isl.), Guad.
104/F3 **Saint Martin** (Sint Maarten) (isl.), NAnt.
78/A3 **Saint Mary** (cape), Gam.
72/G8 **Saint Marys,** Austl.
73/D4 **Saint Marys,** Austl.
94/D3 **Saint Mary's,** Can
85/F3 **Saint Marys,** Ak,US
97/H4 **Saint Marys,** Ga,US
95/J2 **Saint Marys** (riv.), NS,Can
94/E3 **Saint Marys,** Pa,US
95/N7 **Saint-Mathieu,** Qu,Can
47/U3 **Saint Matthew** (isl.), Ak,US
85/D3 **Saint Matthew** (isl.), Ak,US
97/H3 **Saint Matthews,** SC,US
68/E5 **Saint Matthias** (isls.), PNG
19/T10 **Saint-Maur-des-Fossés,** Fr.
30/B6 **Saint-Maur-des-Fossés,** Fr.
87/J4 **Saint-Maurice** (riv.), Qu,Can
94/F1 **Saint-Maurice** (riv.), Qu,Can
36/C5 **Saint-Maurice,** Swi.
36/B6 **Saint-Maurice-de-Gourdans,** Fr.
24/A6 **Saint Mawes,** Eng,UK
31/F6 **Saint-Max,** Fr.
32/F5 **Saint-Maximin-la-Sainte-Baume,** Fr.
24/C3 **Saint Mellons,** Wal,UK
30/D6 **Saint-Memmie,** Fr.
32/F2 **Saint-Memmie,** Fr.
85/F3 **Saint Michael,** Ak,US
30/D4 **Saint-Michel,** Fr.
36/C1 **Saint-Michel-sur-Meurthe,** Fr.
19/S11 **Saint-Michel-sur-Orge,** Fr.
30/B6 **Saint-Michel-sur-Orge,** Fr.
26/C4 **Saint-Mihiel,** Fr.
31/E6 **Saint-Mihiel,** Fr.
32/F2 **Saint-Mihiel,** Fr.
37/F5 **Saint Moritz,** Swi.
33/H3 **Saint Moritz** (Sankt Moritz), Swi.
36/C1 **Saint-Nabord,** Fr.
18/C4 **Saint-Nazaire,** Fr.
32/B3 **Saint-Nazaire,** Fr.
25/F2 **Saint Neots,** Eng,UK
31/E2 **Saint-Nicolas,** Belg.
30/A4 **Saint-Nicolas-d'Aliermont,** Fr.
32/D2 **Saint-Nicolas-d'Aliermont,** Fr.
19/S10 **Saint-Nom-la-Bretèche,** Fr.
30/B2 **Saint-Omer,** Fr.
30/A4 **Saint-Omer-en-Chaussée,** Fr.
30/B3 **Saint-Ouen,** Fr.
19/S9 **Saint-Ouen-l'Aumône,** Fr.
95/G2 **Saint-Pamphile,** Qu,Can
95/G2 **Saint-Pascal,** Qu,Can
19/U9 **Saint-Pathus,** Fr.
90/F2 **Saint Paul,** Ab,Can
86/E3 **Saint Paul,** Ab,Can
17/N7 **Saint Paul** (isl.), Fr.
79/F5 **Saint Paul** (cape), Gha.
78/C5 **Saint Paul** (riv.), Libr.
81/R15 **Saint-Paul,** Reun.
85/D4 **Saint Paul,** Ak,US
85/E4 **Saint Paul** (isl.), Ak,US
76/C6 **Saint Paul** (riv.), Gui., Libr.
93/J3 **Saint Paul,** Ks,US
96/E2 **Saint Paul,** Ks,US
86/G4 **Saint Paul** (cap.), Mn,US
89/H3 **Saint Paul** (cap.), Mn,US
91/K4 **Saint Paul,** (cap.), Mn,US
94/A2 **Saint Paul,** (cap.), Mn,US
32/C5 **Saint-Paul-lès-Dax,** Fr.
72/B1 **Saint Pauls** (peak), Austl.
32/F4 **Saint-Paul-Trois-Châteaux,** Fr.
32/C5 **Saint-Pé-de-Bigorre,** Fr.
91/K4 **Saint Peter,** Mn,US
91/M3 **Saint Peter and Saint Paul,** (rocks), Braz.
32/B2 **Saint Peter Port,** Chl,UK
25/H4 **Saint Peter's,** Eng,UK
18/G3 **Saint Petersburg,** Rus.
46/D4 **Saint Petersburg,** Rus.
89/K6 **Saint Petersburg,** Fl,US
97/H5 **Saint Petersburg,** Fl,US
20/J4 **Saint Petersburg** (Leningrad), Rus.
42/F4 **Saint Petersburg** (Leningrad), Rus.
43/V7 **Saint Petersburg** (Leningrad), Rus.
20/J4 **Saint Petersburg Obl.,** Rus.
42/G3 **Saint Petersburg Obl.,** Rus.
95/P7 **Saint-Philippe-de-La Prairie,** Qu,Can
104/F4 **Saint-Pierre,** Mart.
81/R15 **Saint-Pierre,** Reun.
95/K2 **Saint-Pierre,** StP
95/K2 **Saint Pierre** (isl.), StP,Fr
84/M5 **Saint Pierre and Miquelon** (terr. coll.), Fr.
87/L4 **Saint Pierre and Miquelon** (terr. coll.), Fr.
95/K2 **Saint Pierre and Miquelon** (terr. coll.), Fr
32/D3 **Saint-Pierre-des-Corps,** Fr.
32/C4 **Saint-Pierre-d'Oleron,** Fr.
32/C5 **Saint-Pierre-du-Mont,** Fr.
19/T11 **Saint-Pierre-du-Perray,** Fr.
36/C5 **Saint-Pierre-en-Faucigny,** Fr.
91/J3 **Saint Pierre-Jolys,** Can
32/C2 **Saint-Pierre-sur-Dives,** Fr.
95/M6 **Saint-Placide,** Qu,Can
36/C4 **Saint-Point** (lake), Fr.
32/B2 **Saint-Pol-de-Léon,** Fr.
30/B1 **Saint-Pol-sur-Mer,** Fr.
30/B3 **Saint-Pol-sur-Ternoise,** Fr.
32/E5 **Saint-Pons** (mtn.), Fr.
35/G1 **Saint-Pons** (mtn.), Fr.
32/E3 **Saint-Pourçain-sur-Sioule,** Fr.
36/C5 **Saint-Prex,** Swi.
19/S9 **Saint-Prix,** Fr.
30/B5 **Saint-Prix,** Fr.
26/B4 **Saint-Quentin,** Fr.
30/C4 **Saint-Quentin,** Fr.
32/E2 **Saint-Quentin,** Fr.
30/C4 **Saint Quentin, Canal de** (can.), Fr.
30/A3 **Saint-Quentin-Lamotte-Croix-au-Bailly,** Fr.
36/B6 **Saint-Rambert-en-Bugey,** Fr.
33/G5 **Saint-Raphaël,** Fr.
35/J1 **Saint-Raphaël,** Fr.
95/N7 **Saint-Rémi,** Qu,Can
32/F5 **Saint-Rémy-de-Provence,** Fr.
19/S10 **Saint-Rémy-lès-Chevreuse,** Fr.
30/A6 **Saint-Rémy-sur-Avre,** Fr.
30/A3 **Saint-Riquier,** Fr.
95/N6 **Saint-Roch-de-l'Achigan,** Qu,Can
30/A4 **Saint-Saëns,** Fr.
32/B2 **Saint Sampson's,** Chl,UK
30/C3 **Saint-Saulve,** Fr.
36/C2 **Saint-Sauveur,** Fr.
95/M6 **Saint-Sauveur-des-Monts,** Qu,Can
32/C2 **Saint-Sauveur-le-Vicomte,** Fr.
32/C5 **Saint-Sever,** Fr.
35/E1 **Saint-Sever,** Fr.
97/H4 **Saint Simons** (isl.), Ga,US
97/H4 **Saint Simons Island,** Ga,US
19/U9 **Saint-Soupplets,** Fr.
87/K4 **Saint Stephen,** NB,Can
95/H2 **Saint Stephen,** NB,Can
24/B6 **Saint Stephen in Brannel,** Eng,UK
32/D5 **Saint-Sulpice,** Fr.
35/F1 **Saint-Sulpice,** Fr.
94/D3 **Saint Thomas,** On,Can
104/E3 **Saint Thomas** (isl.), USVI
95/M7 **Saint-Timothée,** Qu,Can
36/B5 **Saint-Trivier-de-Courtes,** Fr.
33/G5 **Saint-Tropez,** Fr.
35/J1 **Saint-Tropez,** Fr.
95/N7 **Saint-Urbain-Premier,** Qu,Can
36/D3 **Saint-Ursanne,** Swi.
32/D2 **Saint-Valéry-en-Caux,** Fr.
25/H6 **Saint Valéry sur Somme,** Fr.
30/A3 **Saint-Valéry-sur-Somme,** Fr.
32/F3 **Saint-Vallier,** Fr.
32/D3 **Saint-Vaury,** Fr.
30/B2 **Saint-Venant,** Fr.
70/F6 **Saint Vincent** (gulf), Austl.
73/C4 **Saint Vincent** (pt.), Austl.
104/F4 **Saint Vincent** (passg.), StL.,StV.
104/F4 **Saint Vincent** (isl.), StV.
84/L8 **Saint Vincent & the Grenadines**
104/F4 **Saint Vincent and the Grenadines**
106/F1 **Saint Vincent and the Grenadines**
32/C5 **Saint-Vincent-de-Tyrosse,** Fr.
34/E1 **Saint-Vincent-de-Tyrosse,** Fr.
36/B3 **Saint-Vit,** Fr.
26/D3 **Saint Vith,** Belg.
31/F3 **Saint Vith,** Belg.
33/G1 **Saint Vith,** Belg.
19/T11 **Saint-Vrain,** Fr.
90/F2 **Saint Walburg,** Sk,Can
19/T9 **Saint-Witz,** Fr.
32/D4 **Saint-Yrieix-la-Perche,** Fr.
62/D2 **Sāipal** (mtn.), Nepal
68/D3 **Saipan** (isl.), NMar.
57/F2 **Saitama** (pref.), Japan
57/H7 **Saitama** (pref.), Japan
56/B4 **Saito,** Japan
65/B3 **Sai Yok Nat'l Park,** Thai.
106/E7 **Sajama Nat'l Park,** Bol.
38/A4 **Sajānan,** Tun.
27/L4 **Sajószentpéter,** Hun.
40/E1 **Sajószentpéter,** Hun.
80/C3 **Sak** (riv.), SAfr.
57/H7 **Sakado,** Japan
57/J7 **Sakae,** Japan
57/M9 **Sakahogi,** Japan
55/M5 **Sakai,** Japan
56/E2 **Sakai,** Japan
57/F2 **Sakai,** Japan
57/H7 **Sakai** (riv.), Japan
57/L10 **Sakai,** Japan
56/C3 **Sakaide,** Japan
56/C3 **Sakaiminato,** Japan
52/D3 **Sakākah,** SAr.
77/P2 **Sakākah,** SAr.
91/H3 **Sakakawea** (lake), ND,US
87/J3 **Sakami** (lake), Qu,Can
81/H8 **Sakaraha,** Madg.
41/K5 **Sakarya** (prov.), Turk.
44/D4 **Sakarya** (prov.), Turk.
44/D4 **Sakarya** (riv.), Turk.
50/B1 **Sakarya** (prov.), Turk.
50/B2 **Sakarya** (str.), Turk.
47/P6 **Sakata,** Japan
55/M4 **Sakata,** Japan
56/C4 **Sakawa,** Japan
81/H7 **Sakay** (riv.), Madg.
60/A3 **Sakden,** Bhu.
81/H7 **Sakeny** (riv.), Madg.
47/Q4 **Sakhalin** (gulf), Rus.
47/Q4 **Sakhalin** (isl.), Rus.
48/P4 **Sakhalin** (isl.), Rus.
55/N1 **Sakhalin** (isl.), Rus.
47/Q4 **Sakhalin Obl.,** Rus.
55/N2 **Sakhalin-Zapadno** (mts.), Rus.
51/G2 **Sakht Sar,** Iran
52/F1 **Sakht Sar** (Ramsar), Iran
44/E3 **Saki,** Ukr.
27/M1 **Šakiai,** Lith.
42/D5 **Šakiai,** Lith.
48/M7 **Sakishima** (isls.), Japan
68/B2 **Sakishima** (isls.), Japan
45/L1 **Sakmara** (riv.), Rus.
60/E5 **Sakon Nakhon,** Thai.
63/H4 **Sakon Nakhon,** Thai.
65/D2 **Sakon Nakhon,** Thai.
53/J3 **Sakrand,** Pak.
62/A2 **Sakrand,** Pak.
82/D7 **Sakrivier,** SAfr.
46/G5 **Saksaul'skiy,** Kaz.
57/F2 **Saku,** Japan
57/J7 **Sakura,** Japan
57/L10 **Sakurai,** Japan
74/K10 **Sal** (isl.), CpV.
102/E3 **Sal** (pt.), Hon.
45/G3 **Sal** (riv.), Rus.
27/J4 **Šal'a,** Slvk.
20/F4 **Sala,** Swe.
42/C4 **Sala,** Swe.
38/D2 **Sala Consilina,** It.
40/B5 **Sala Consilina,** It.
100/A1 **Salada** (dry lake), Mex.
109/E2 **Saladas,** Arg.
105/C6 **Salado** (riv.), Arg.
109/C3 **Salado** (riv.), Arg.
109/D3 **Salado** (riv.), Arg.
109/E4 **Salado** (riv.), Arg.
103/G1 **Salado** (riv.), Cuba
101/F3 **Salado** (riv.), Mex.
92/F4 **Salado** (dry riv.), NM,US
105/C5 **Salado del Norte** (riv.), Arg
79/E4 **Salaga,** Gha.
51/E3 **Şalāḩ ad Dīn** (gov.), Iraq
67/G4 **Salahatu** (mtn.), Indo.
69/R9 **Sala'ilua,** WSam.
27/M5 **Sălaj** (co.), Rom.
40/F2 **Sălaj** (co.), Rom.
76/J5 **Salal,** Chad
52/F5 **Salālah,** Oman
102/D3 **Salamá,** Guat.
101/E4 **Salamanca,** Mex.
18/C4 **Salamanca,** Sp.
34/C2 **Salamanca,** Sp.
94/E3 **Salamanca,** NY,US
77/J6 **Salamat** (riv.), Chad
85/H3 **Salamatof,** Ak,US
74/K10 **Sal** (Amilcar Cabral) (int'l arpt.), CpV.
39/H3 **Salamis,** Gre.
39/L7 **Salamís,** Gre.
39/L7 **Salamís** (isl.), Gre.
44/B5 **Salamís,** Gre.
49/E2 **Salamīyah,** Syria
50/D3 **Salamīyah,** Syria
63/H3 **Sala Mok,** Laos
65/C1 **Sala Mok,** Laos
42/D4 **Salantai,** Lith.
63/H4 **Sala Pac Thu,** Laos
34/B1 **Salas,** Sp.
34/D1 **Salas de los Infantes,** Sp.
35/G1 **Salat** (riv.), Fr.
19/J3 **Salavat,** Rus.
45/K1 **Salavat,** Rus.
48/F4 **Salavat,** Rus.
68/B5 **Salayar** (isl.), Indo.
16/D7 **Sala y Gomez** (isls.), Chile
32/E3 **Salbris,** Fr.
104/D3 **Salcedo,** DRep.
32/E5 **Salces,** Fr.
35/G1 **Salces,** Fr.
27/N1 **Šalčininkai,** Lith.
42/E5 **Šalčininkai,** Lith.
44/C1 **Šalčininkai,** Lith.
24/C6 **Salcombe,** Eng,UK
34/C1 **Saldaña,** Sp.
80/B4 **Saldanha,** SAfr.
80/K10 **Saldanha,** SAfr.
80/K10 **Saldanhabaai** (bay), SAfr.
71/H7 **Sale,** Austl.
73/C3 **Sale,** Austl.
75/L13 **Salé,** Mor.
76/D1 **Salé,** Mor.
23/F5 **Sale,** Eng,UK
67/G3 **Salebabu** (isl.), Indo.
46/G3 **Salekhard,** Rus.
37/F2 **Salem,** Ger.
62/C5 **Salem,** India
64/G3 **Salem,** India
94/C4 **Salem,** In,US
97/G2 **Salem,** In,US
99/E7 **Salem,** Mi,US
93/K3 **Salem,** Mo,US
97/F2 **Salem,** Mo,US
95/G3 **Salem,** NH,US
86/D4 **Salem** (cap.), Or,US
88/B3 **Salem** (cap.), Or,US
90/C4 **Salem** (cap.), Or,US
94/D4 **Salem,** Va,US
97/H2 **Salem,** Va,US
38/C4 **Salemi,** It.
38/F2 **Salentina** (pen.), It.
18/E4 **Salerno,** It.
38/D2 **Salerno,** It.
38/D2 **Salerno** (gulf), It.
40/B5 **Salerno,** It.
40/B5 **Salerno** (gulf), It.
25/G3 **Sales** (pt.), UK
30/B4 **Saleux,** Fr.
49/D3 **Salfīt,** WBnk.
49/G7 **Salfīt,** WBnk.
23/F5 **Salford,** Eng,UK
45/H1 **Salgan,** Rus.
36/D5 **Salgesch,** Swi.
27/K4 **Salgótarján,** Hun.
40/D1 **Salgótarján,** Hun.
44/A2 **Salgótarján,** Hun.
107/L5 **Salgueiro,** Braz.
33/L5 **Sali,** Cro.
93/F3 **Salida,** Co,US
96/B2 **Salida,** Co,US
32/C5 **Salies-de-Béarn,** Fr
35/F1 **Salies-du-Salat,** Fr.
52/D5 **Şalīf,** Yem.
50/B2 **Salihli,** Turk.
82/F3 **Salima,** Malw.
77/L3 **Salīmah** (oasis), Sudan
34/B1 **Salime** (res.), Sp.
103/H1 **Salina** (pt.), Bahm.
104/C2 **Salina** (pt.), Bahm.
38/D3 **Salina** (isl.), It.
89/G4 **Salina,** Ks,US
93/H3 **Salina,** Ks,US
96/D2 **Salina,** Ks,US
92/E3 **Salina,** Ut,US
102/C2 **Salina Cruz,** Mex.
107/K7 **Salinas,** Braz.

Salin – Sanna

101/E4 Salinas, Mex.
88/B4 Salinas, Ca,US
92/B3 Salinas, Ca,US
92/B3 Salinas (riv.), Ca,US
35/G3 Salinas, Cabo de (cape), Sp.
93/F4 Salinas Nat'l Mon., NM,US
96/B3 Salinas Nat'l Mon., NM,US
38/D2 Saline (marsh), It.
93/J4 Saline (riv.), Ar,US
99/E7 Saline (riv.), Mi,US
107/J4 Salinópolis, Braz.
36/B4 Salins-les-Bains, Fr.
87/J2 Salisbury (isl.), NW,Can
24/D4 Salisbury (plain), Eng,UK
25/E4 Salisbury, Eng,UK
89/L4 Salisbury, Md,US
94/F4 Salisbury, Md,US
97/K2 Salisbury, Md,US
97/H3 Salisbury, NC,US
20/J2 Salla, Fin.
42/F2 Salla, Fin.
33/G4 Sallanches, Fr.
36/C6 Sallanches, Fr.
28/D4 Salland (reg.), Neth.
78/B4 Sallatouk (pt.), Gui.
30/B3 Sallaumines, Fr.
32/E1 Sallaumines, Fr.
35/F2 Sallent, Sp.
22/B5 Sallins, Ire.
93/J4 Sallisaw, Ok,US
96/E3 Sallisaw, Ok,US
52/C5 Sallūm, Sudan
62/D2 Sallyāna, Nepal
22/B5 Sally Gap (pass), Ire.
31/F3 Salm (riv.), Ger.
51/F3 Salmān Pāk, Iraq
51/F2 Salmās, Iran
20/G4 Salme, Est.
42/D4 Salme, Est.
90/C2 Salmon (riv.), BC,Can
90/D4 Salmon (riv.), Id,US
86/E4 Salmon, Id,US
86/E4 Salmon (riv.), Id,US
88/C2 Salmon (riv.), Id,US
88/D2 Salmon, Id,US
90/E4 Salmon, Id,US
92/C1 Salmon (riv.), Id,US
101/E2 Salmon (peak), Tx,US
86/E3 Salmon Arm, BC,Can
88/C1 Salmon Arm, BC,Can
90/D3 Salmon Arm, BC,Can
92/D2 Salmon Falls (riv.), Id, Nv,US
70/C6 Salmon Gums, Austl.
90/E4 Salmon River (mts.), Id,US
88/C2 Salmon River (mts.), Id,US
90/E4 Salmon, South Fork (riv.), Id,US
31/F4 Salmtal, Ger.
20/G3 Salo, Fin.
42/D3 Salo, Fin.
26/C4 Salon (riv.), Fr.
32/F3 Salon (riv.), Fr.
36/B2 Salon (riv.), Fr.
32/F5 Salon-de-Provence, Fr.
35/H1 Salon-de-Provence, Fr.
77/K8 Salonga Nat'l Park, Zaire
82/D1 Salonga Nat'l Park, Zaire
39/H3 Salonika (Thermaic) (gulf), Gre.
39/H2 Salonika (Thessaloníki), Gre.
40/E2 Salonta, Rom.
34/B3 Salor (riv.), Sp.
37/H5 Salorno (Salurn), It.
30/B4 Salouël, Fr.
78/B3 Saloum, Vallée du (wadi), Sen.
74/K10 Sal Rei, CpV.
35/G1 Salses, Fr.
19/H4 Sal'sk, Rus.
45/G3 Sal'sk, Rus.
46/E5 Sal'sk, Rus.
38/C4 Salso (riv.), It.
64/B1 Salt (range), Pak.
80/C3 Salt (riv.), SAfr.
103/J1 Salt (cay), Trks.
92/E4 Salt (riv.), Az,US
99/Q16 Salt (cr.), Il,US
100/D2 Salt (cr.), Tx,US
109/C1 Salta, Arg.
24/B6 Saltash, Eng,UK
32/A1 Saltash, Eng,UK
23/H2 Saltburn, Eng,UK
21/B4 Saltee (isls.), Ire.
20/E2 Saltfjorden (fjord), Nor.
42/B2 Saltfjorden (fjord), Nor.
24/D4 Saltford, Eng,UK
101/E3 Saltillo, Mex.
88/F6 Saltillo, Mex.
96/C5 Saltillo, Mex
86/E4 Salt Lake City (cap.), Ut,US
88/D3 Salt Lake City (cap.), Ut,US
90/F5 Salt Lake City (cap.), Ut,US
92/E2 Salt Lake City (cap.), Ut,US
108/C2 Salto, Braz.
38/C1 Salto (riv.), It.
109/E3 Salto, Uru.
101/G5 Salto de Agua, Mex.
102/C2 Salto de Agua, Mex.
109/F1 Salto del Guairá, Par.
88/C5 Salton Sea (lake), Ca,US
108/A3 Salto Santiago (res.), Braz.
42/D3 Saltvik, Fin.
62/D4 Sālūr, India
37/H5 Salurn (Salorno), It.
107/H2 Salut (isls.), FrG.
33/G4 Saluzzo, It.
107/L6 Salvador, Braz.
34/A3 Salvaterra de Magos, Port.
34/A1 Salvatierra de Miño, Sp.
60/C5 Salween (riv.), Asia
63/G4 Salween (riv.), Asia
65/B2 Salween (riv.), Asia
48/J8 Salween (riv.), Burma, China
54/D5 Salween (riv.), China
45/J5 Sal'yany, Azer.
51/G2 Sal'yany, Azer.
94/D4 Salyersville, Ky,US
97/H2 Salyersville, Ky,US
27/H5 Salza (riv.), Aus.
40/B2 Salza (riv.), Aus.
40/A2 Salzach (riv.), Aus.
26/G4 Salzach (riv.), Aus., Ger.
29/E4 Salzbergen, Ger.
18/E4 Salzburg, Aus.
26/G5 Salzburg, Aus.
27/G5 Salzburg (prov.), Aus.
33/K3 Salzburg, Aus.
33/K3 Salzburg (prov.), Aus.
40/A2 Salzburg, Aus.
40/A2 Salzburg (prov.), Aus.
26/F2 Salzgitter, Ger.
29/H4 Salzgitter, Ger.
29/H2 Salzhausen, Ger.
29/G4 Salzhemmendorf, Ger.
29/F5 Salzkotten, Ger.
26/F2 Salzwedel, Ger.
34/C1 Sama, Sp.
66/C4 Samak (cape), Indo.
67/F2 Samales (isls.), Phil.
62/D4 Sāmalkot, India
50/B4 Samālūt, Egypt
52/B3 Samālūt, Egypt
52/F2 Sāmān, Iran
104/C2 Samana (cay), Bahm.
104/D3 Samaná, DRep.
104/D3 Samaná (cape), DRep.
64/D2 Samāna, India
103/H1 Samana (Atwood) (cay), Bahm.
49/D1 Samandağı, Turk.
50/C2 Samandağı, Turk.
52/C1 Samandağı, Turk.
51/N7 Samandira, Turk.
49/B4 Samannūd, Egypt
49/D3 Samar, Jor.
48/M8 Samar (isl.), Phil.
68/B3 Samar (isl.), Phil.
19/J3 Samara, Rus.
45/J1 Samara, Rus.
45/K1 Samara (riv.), Rus.
46/F4 Samara, Rus.
68/E6 Samarai, PNG
45/J1 Samara Obl., Rus.
55/M2 Samarga (riv.), Rus.
49/G7 Samaria (reg.), WBnk.
49/G7 Samaria Nat'l Park, WBnk.
39/H5 Samarias Gorge Nat'l Park, Gre.
67/E4 Samarinda, Indo.
68/A5 Samarinda, Indo.
46/G6 Samarkand, Uzb.
51/E3 Sāmarrā', Iraq
52/D2 Sāmarrā', Iraq
53/K3 Samasata, Pak.
62/D3 Sambalpur, India
82/C2 Samba Lucala, Ang.
81/H7 Sambao (riv.), Madg.
66/D4 Sambar (cape), Indo.
66/C3 Sambas, Indo.
81/J6 Sambava, Madg.
27/M4 Sambor, Ukr.
44/B2 Sambor, Ukr.
65/D3 Sambor Prei Kuk (ruins), Camb.
26/C3 Sambre (riv.), Belg., Fr.
30/C3 Sambre (riv.), Belg.,Fr.
32/E1 Sambre (riv.), Belg., Fr.
30/C4 Sambre à l'Oise, Canal de (can.), Fr.
55/K4 Samch'ŏk, SKor.
56/A2 Samch'ŏk, SKor.
58/E4 Samch'ŏk, SKor.
58/E5 Samch'ŏnp'o, SKor.
82/G1 Same, Tanz.
37/F4 Samedan, Swi.
30/A2 Samer, Fr.
63/F3 Sami, Burma
39/G3 Sámi, Gre.
63/H5 Samit (cape), Camb.
65/C4 Samit (cape), Camb.
66/B1 Samit (cape), Camb.
63/H5 Samkos (peak), Camb.
65/C3 Samkos (peak), Camb.
66/B1 Samkos (peak), Camb.
99/C2 Sammamish (lake), Wa,US
56/A3 Samnangjin, SKor.
58/E5 Samnangjin, SKor.
37/G4 Samnaun, Swi.
33/L4 Samobor, Cro.
40/B3 Samobor, Cro.
36/C5 Samoëns, Fr.
39/H1 Samokov, Bul.
41/F4 Samokov, Bul.
44/B4 Samokov, Bul.
35/Q10 Samora (riv.), Port.
35/Q10 Samora Correia, Port.
50/A2 Sámos, Gre.
50/A2 Sámos (isl.), Gre.
39/J2 Samothráki, Gre.
39/J2 Samothráki (isl.), Gre.
41/G5 Samothráki, Gre.
41/G5 Samothráki (isl.), Gre.
35/E2 Samper de Calanda, Sp.
66/D4 Sampit, Indo.
66/D4 Sampit (riv.), Indo.
93/J5 Sam Rayburn (res.), Tx,US
60/D4 Sam Sao (mts.), Laos, Viet.
65/C1 Sam Sao (mts.), Laos, Viet.
72/E6 Samson (mtn.), Austl.
63/J4 Sam Son, Viet.
65/D2 Sam Son, Viet.
72/E6 Samsonvale (lake), Austl.
44/E4 Samsun (prov.), Turk.
44/F4 Samsun, Turk.
46/D5 Samsun, Turk.
50/C1 Samsun (prov.), Turk.
50/D1 Samsun, Turk.
38/A3 Samugheo, It.
63/H6 Samui (isl.), Thai.
65/B4 Samui (isl.), Thai.
66/B2 Samui (isl.), Thai.
57/H7 Samukawa, Japan
64/B2 Samundri, Pak.
45/J4 Samur (riv.), Azer., Rus.
46/E5 Samur (riv.), Azer., Rus.
65/C3 Samut Prakan, Thai.
63/H5 Samut Sakhon, Thai.
65/C3 Samut Sakhon, Thai.
63/H5 Samut Songkhram, Thai.
65/C3 Samut Songkhram, Thai.
60/A2 Samye Monastery, China
65/D3 San (riv.), Camb.
55/H5 San (riv.), China
76/E5 San, Mali
78/D3 San, Mali
18/F3 San (riv.), Pol.
27/M3 San (riv.), Pol.
44/B2 San (riv.), Pol.
40/C3 Sana (riv.), Bosn.
48/D8 San'a, Yem.
52/D5 Sanā', Yem.
77/Q4 Sanā', Yem.
77/P4 Sanaa (cap.), Yem.
52/D5 Sanaa (Sanā') (cap.), Yem.
34/A1 San Adrián, Cabo de (cape), Sp.
74/D4 Sanaga (riv.), Afr.
35/N8 San Agustín de Guadalix, Sp.
85/F5 Sanak (isl.), Ak,US
67/G4 Sanama (isl.), Indo.
105/B5 San Ambrosio (isl.), Chile
46/E6 Sanandaj, Iran
51/F3 Sanandaj, Iran
52/E1 Sanandaj, Iran
99/K11 San Andreas (lake), Ca,US
103/F3 San Andrés, Col.
103/F3 San Andrés (isl.), Col.
102/B1 San Andrés (lag.), Mex.
92/F4 San Andres (mts.), NM,US
96/B3 San Andres (mts.), NM,US
34/C1 San Andrés del Rabanedo, Sp.
101/G5 San Andrés Tuxtla, Mex.
102/C2 San Andrés Tuxtla, Mex.
108/B3 Sananduva, Braz.
88/F5 San Angelo, Tx,US
93/G5 San Angelo, Tx,US
96/C4 San Angelo, Tx,US
99/J11 San Anselmo, Ca,US
103/H4 San Antero, Col.
105/D6 San Antonio (cape), Arg.
109/E4 San Antonio (cape), Arg.
109/B3 San Antonio, Chile
100/C4 San Antonio, Mex.
92/F4 San Antonio, NM,US
96/B3 San Antonio, NM,US
98/C2 San Antonio (mt.), Ca,US
101/F2 San Antonio, Tx,US
101/F2 San Antonio (riv.), Tx,US
89/G6 San Antonio, Tx,US
93/H5 San Antonio, Tx,US
93/H5 San Antonio (riv.), Tx,US
96/D4 San Antonio, Tx,US
103/H5 San Antonio, Ven.
104/F5 San Antonio, Ven.
35/F3 San Antonio Abad, Sp.
103/E1 San Antonio, Cabo de (cape), Cuba
101/M8 San Antonio Cañada, Mex.
104/F5 San Antonio del Golfo, Ven.
109/D5 San Antonio Oeste, Arg.
100/B2 San Antonio, Punta (pt.), Mex.
52/D5 Şan'ā (Sanaa) (cap.), Yem.
77/P4 Şan'ā (Sanaa) (cap.), Yem.
100/D1 San Augustin (pass), NM,US
93/J5 San Augustine, Tx,US
96/E4 San Augustine, Tx,US
64/D2 Sanaur, India
53/L4 Sanāwad, India
62/C3 Sanāwad, India
38/D2 San Bartolomeo in Galdo, It.
40/B5 San Bartolomeo in Galdo, It.
33/K5 San Benedetto del Tronto, It.
38/C1 San Benedetto del Tronto, It.
40/A4 San Benedetto del Tronto, It.
100/C5 San Benedicto (isl.), Mex.
101/R10 San Bernardino (riv.), Mex.
98/C2 San Bernardino (mts.), Ca,US
88/C5 San Bernardino, Ca,US
92/C4 San Bernardino, Ca,US
101/L7 San Bernardino Contla, Mex.
109/B3 San Bernardo, Chile
103/H4 San Bernardo (pt.), Col.
100/C3 San Blas, Mex.
100/D4 San Blas, Mex.
100/E3 San Blas, Mex.
89/J6 San Blas (cape), Fl,US
97/G4 San Blas (cape), Fl,US
96/E3 San Bois (mts.), Ok,US
33/J4 San Bonifacio, It.
106/E6 San Borja, Bol.
95/S9 Sanborn, NY,US
100/B3 San Bruno, Mex.
99/K11 San Bruno, Ca,US
101/E3 San Buenaventura, Mex.
96/C5 San Buenaventura, Mex
33/K3 San Candido (Innichen), It.
109/B4 San Carlos, Chile
101/E2 San Carlos, Mex.
101/F3 San Carlos, Mex.
103/E4 San Carlos, Nic.
109/F3 San Carlos, Uru.
92/E4 San Carlos (lake), Az,US
99/K11 San Carlos, Ca,US
103/J4 San Carlos, Ven.
106/E2 San Carlos, Ven.
109/B5 San Carlos de Bariloche, Arg.
103/J4 San Carlos del Zulia, Ven.
106/D2 San Carlos del Zulia, Ven.
106/E3 San Carlos de Río Negro, Ven.
39/F2 San Cataldo, It.
40/D5 San Cataldo, It.
54/E5 Sancha, China
60/E3 Sancha (riv.), China
100/E4 Sánchez Román, Mex.
58/D5 Sanch'ŏng, SKor.
34/D3 San Clemente, Sp.
92/C4 San Clemente (isl.), Ca,US
109/D3 San Cristóbal, Arg.
103/F1 San Cristóbal, Cuba
104/D3 San Cristóbal, DRep.
102/E3 San Cristobal (vol.), Nic.
68/F6 San Cristobal (isl.), Sol.
100/B1 San Cristobal (cr.), Az,US
103/H5 San Cristóbal, Ven.
106/D2 San Cristóbal, Ven.
34/B1 San Cristóbal de Cea, Sp.
102/C2 San Cristóbal de las Casas, Mex.
103/G1 Sancti Spíritus, Cuba
90/F2 Sand (riv.), Ab,Can
20/C4 Sand, Nor.
80/D3 Sand (riv.), SAfr.
24/D4 Sand (pt.), Eng,UK
91/H5 Sand (hills), Ne,US
88/F3 Sand (mts.), Ne,US
93/G2 Sand (hills), Ne,US
58/D3 Sanda, Japan
57/L10 Sanda, Japan
22/C1 Sanda (isl.), Sc,UK
68/A4 Sandakan, Malay.
63/J5 Sandan, Camb.
65/D3 Sandan, Camb.
39/H2 Sandanski, Bul.
41/F5 Sandanski, Bul.
23/F5 Sandbach, Eng,UK
29/F2 Sande, Ger.
20/D4 Sandefjord, Nor.
83/Q Sanders (coast), Ant.
100/E2 Sanderson, Tx,US
93/G5 Sanderson, Tx,US
96/C4 Sanderson, Tx,US
97/H3 Sandersville, Ga,US
72/F6 Sandgate, Austl.
22/D2 Sandhead, Sc,UK
95/Q8 Sandhill, On,Can
25/F4 Sandhurst, Eng,UK
106/E6 Sandia, Peru
105/C8 San Diego (cape), Arg.
109/C7 San Diego (cape), Arg.
100/A1 San Diego, Ca,US
88/C5 San Diego, Ca,US
92/C4 San Diego, Ca,US
96/D5 San Diego, Tx,US
50/B2 Sandıklı, Turk.
38/D4 San Dimitri, Ras (pt.), Malta
67/E3 Sandkan, Malay.
20/C4 Sandnes, Nor.
20/E2 Sandnessjøen, Nor.
42/B2 Sandnessjøen, Nor.
82/D2 Sandoa, Zaire
27/L3 Sandomierz, Pol.
33/K4 San Donà di Piave, It.
40/E2 Sándorfalva, Hun.
78/B3 Sandougou (riv.), Gam., Sen.
60/B5 Sandoway, Burma
63/F4 Sandoway, Burma
25/E5 Sandown, Eng,UK
32/C1 Sandown, Eng,UK
85/F4 Sand Point, Ak,US
88/C2 Sandpoint, Id,US
90/D3 Sandpoint, Id,US
81/J7 Sandrakatsy, Madg.
73/F5 Sandringham, Austl.
25/G1 Sandringham, Eng,UK
85/M5 Sandspit, BC,Can
29/F2 Sandstedt, Ger.
61/E3 Sandu Shuizu Zizhixian, China
63/J2 Sandu Shuizu Zizhixian, China
94/D3 Sandusky, Mi,US
94/D3 Sandusky, Oh,US
20/D4 Sandvika, Nor.
20/F3 Sandviken, Swe.
42/C3 Sandviken, Swe.
31/F4 Sandweiler, Lux.
72/B2 Sandwich (cape), Austl.
25/H4 Sandwich, Eng,UK
71/J4 Sandy (cape), Austl.
72/D4 Sandy (cape), Austl.
91/K2 Sandy (lake), On,Can
86/G3 Sandy (lake), On,Can
25/F2 Sandy, Eng,UK
92/E2 Sandy, Ut,US
91/H2 Sandy Bay, Sk,Can
97/G3 Sandy Springs, Ga,US
31/E4 Sanem, Lux.
34/D2 San Esteban de Gormaz, Sp.
38/C2 San Felice Circeo, It.
109/B3 San Felipe, Chile
100/B2 San Felipe, Mex.
101/E4 San Felipe, Mex.
92/D5 San Felipe, Mex
104/D5 San Felipe, Ven.
106/E1 San Felipe, Ven.
101/E5 San Felipe del Progresso, Mex.
105/A5 San Félix (isl.), Chile
98/B2 San Fernando (valley), Ca,US
98/B2 San Fernando, Ca,US
109/B3 San Fernando, Chile
101/F3 San Fernando, Mex.
61/J5 San Fernando, Phil.
34/B4 San Fernando, Sp.
104/F5 San Fernando, Trin.
106/E2 San Fernando de Apure, Ven.
35/N9 San Fernando-de-Henares, Sp.
20/E3 Sånfjällets Nat'l Park, Swe.
42/B3 Sånfjällets Nat'l Park, Swe.
85/K3 Sanford (mt.), Ak,US
86/B2 Sanford (mt.), Ak,US
89/K6 Sanford, Fl,US
97/H4 Sanford, Fl,US
95/G3 Sanford, Me,US
97/J3 Sanford, NC,US
109/D3 San Francisco, Arg.
92/E4 San Francisco (riv.), Az, NM,US
102/D3 San Francisco, ESal.
100/B2 San Francisco, Mex.
102/E1 San Francisco, Mex.
86/D5 San Francisco, Ca,US
88/B4 San Francisco, Ca,US
92/B3 San Francisco, Ca,US
99/K11 San Francisco, Ca,US
99/K11 San Francisco (bay), Ca,US
99/K11 San Francisco (co.), Ca,US
104/D5 San Francisco, Ven.
99/K11 San Francisco Bay Nat'l Wild. Ref., Ca,US
102/E3 San Francisco de la Paz, Hon.
100/D3 San Francisco del Oro, Mex.
96/B5 San Francisco del Oro, Mex
104/D3 San Francisco de Macorís, DRep.
38/D3 San Fratello, It.
98/B2 San Gabriel, Ca,US
98/B2 San Gabriel (mts.), Ca,US
98/C2 San Gabriel (riv.), Ca,US
101/M8 San Gabriel Chilac, Mex.
100/B2 San Gabriel, Punta (pt.), Mex.
51/G1 Sangachaly, Azer.
53/K5 Sangamner, India
62/B4 Sangamner, India
93/K3 Sangamon (riv.), Il,US
94/B3 Sangamon (riv.), Il,US
53/H2 Sangān (mtn.), Afg.
25/H5 Sangatte, Fr.
30/A2 Sangatte, Fr.
32/D1 Sangatte, Fr.
106/C4 Sangay Nat'l Park, Ecu.
34/A1 Sangenjo, Sp.
103/G1 San Germán, Cuba
59/C2 Sanggan (riv.), China
66/D3 Sanggau, Indo.
58/B4 Sanggou (bay), China
74/D4 Sangha (riv.), Afr.
76/J7 Sangha (riv.), Congo
53/J3 Sanghar, Pak.
62/A2 Sanghar, Pak.
48/M9 Sangihe (isls.), Indo.
67/F3 Sangihe (isl.), Indo.
67/G3 Sangihe (isl.), Indo.
68/B4 Sangihe (isls.), Indo.
106/D2 San Gil, Col.
38/E2 San Giorgio Ionico, It.
38/C4 San Giovanni Gemini, It.
38/E3 San Giovanni in Fiore, It.
33/J4 San Giovanni in Persiceto, It.
40/B5 San Giovanni Rotondo, It.
54/D2 Sangiyn Dalay (lake), Mong.
55/K4 Sangju, SKor.
56/A2 Sangju, SKor.
58/E4 Sangju, SKor.
63/G4 Sangkhla, Thai.
67/E3 Sangkulirang, Indo.
64/B2 Sāngla, Pak.
53/K5 Sāngli, India
62/B4 Sāngli, India
76/H7 Sangmélima, Camr.
57/L10 Sangō, Japan
92/C4 San Gorgonio (peak), Ca,US
60/B3 Sangpang (mts.), Burma
93/F3 Sangre de Cristo (mts.), Co, NM,US
96/B2 Sangre de Cristo (mts.), Co,US
96/B2 Sangre de Cristo (mts.), NM,US
99/K12 San Gregorio, Ca,US
104/F5 Sangre Grande, Trin.
63/F2 Sangri, China
38/D2 Sangro (riv.), It.
40/A5 Sangro (riv.), It.
64/C2 Sangrūr, India
106/G6 Sangue (riv.), Braz.
32/C5 Sangüesa, Sp.
34/E1 Sangüesa, Sp.
79/E4 Sanguie (prov.), Burk.
59/D3 Sanhe, China
59/H7 Sanhe, China
100/B3 San Hipólito, Punta (pt.), Mex.
80/E3 Sani (pass), SAfr.
102/D2 San Ignacio, Belz.
106/E6 San Ignacio, Bol.
106/F7 San Ignacio, Bol.
100/B2 San Ignacio (riv.), Mex.
100/B3 San Ignacio, Mex.
100/D4 San Ignacio, Mex.
92/D5 San Ignacio (dry riv.), Mex
34/D2 San Ildefonso, Sp.
56/D3 San'in Kaigin Nat'l Park, Japan
76/D6 Saniquellie, Libr.
103/F4 San Isidro, CR
102/D2 San Isidro, Mex.
102/E3 San Isidro, Nic.
103/H4 San Jacinto, Col.
98/C3 San Jacinto (riv.), Ca,US
101/G2 San Jacinto (dam), Tx,US
35/E4 San Javier, Sp.
63/K3 Sanjia, China
55/M4 Sanjō, Japan
57/F2 Sanjō, Japan
106/F6 San Joaquín, Bol.
102/C2 San Joaquín, Mex.
92/B3 San Joaquin (val.), Ca,US
92/C3 San Joaquin (riv.), Ca,US
99/L10 San Joaquin (riv.), Ca,US
99/M11 San Joaquin (co.), Ca,US
105/C7 San Jorge (gulf), Arg.
109/C6 San Jorge (gulf), Arg.
103/H4 San Jorge (riv.), Col.
100/B2 San Jorge (bay), Mex.
92/D5 San Jorge (bay), Mex
102/E4 San Jorge, Nic.
35/F2 San Jorge (gulf), Sp.
101/H5 San Jose, Belz.
103/E4 San José (cap.), CR
106/B2 San José (cap.), CR
102/D3 San José, Guat.
100/C3 San José (isl.), Mex.
35/F3 San José, Sp.
86/D5 San Jose, Ca,US
88/B4 San Jose, Ca,US
92/B3 San Jose, Ca,US
99/L12 San Jose, Ca,US
103/H4 San José, Ven.
101/E3 San José de Aura, Mex.
67/F1 San Jose de Buenavista, Phil.
106/F7 San José de Chiquitos, Bol.
100/C2 San José de Gracia, Mex.
109/C3 San José de Jáchal, Arg.
100/C4 San José del Cabo, Mex.
106/D3 San José del Guaviare, Col.
102/E3 San José de los Remates, Nic.
109/E3 San José de Mayo, Uru.
100/C2 San José de Pimas, Mex.
101/E3 San José de Raíces, Mex.
104/D5 San José de Seque, Ven.
101/E4 San José Iturbide, Mex.
101/F5 San José Tenango, Mex.
109/C3 San Juan, Arg.
109/C3 San Juan (riv.), Arg.
109/D7 San Juan (cape), Arg.
103/E4 San Juan (riv.), CR, Nic.
104/D3 San Juan, DRep.
102/D3 San Juan (pt.), ESal.
104/E3 San Juan (cap.), PR
84/L8 San Juan (cap.), PR
92/E3 San Juan (riv.), US
88/E4 San Juan (mts.), Co,US
92/F3 San Juan (mts.), Co,US
96/B2 San Juan (mts.), Co,US
100/D1 San Juan, NM,US
96/A2 San Juan (basin), NM,US
109/E2 San Juan Bautista, Par.
35/E3 San Juan de Alicante, Sp.
34/B4 San Juan de Aznalfarache, Sp.
100/D5 San Juan de Lima, Punta (pt.), Mex.
103/F4 San Juan del Norte, Nic.
104/D5 San Juan de los Cayos, Ven.
106/E2 San Juan de los Morros, Ven.
100/C4 San Juan de los Planes, Mex.
100/B3 San Juanico, Punta (pt.), Mex.
101/M8 San Juan Ixcaquixtla, Mex.
101/M7 San Juan Ixtenco, Mex.
103/H4 San Juan Nepomuceno, Col.
101/F5 San Juan Quiotepec, Mex.
101/R9 San Juan Teotihuacan, Mex.
109/C6 San Julián, Arg.
109/D3 San Justo, Arg.
78/C4 Sankanbiriwa (peak), SLeo.
64/F4 Sankaranāyinarkovil, India
78/C4 Sankoroni (riv.), Gui., Mali
40/B2 Sankt Aegyd am Neuwalde, Aus.
33/L3 Sankt Andrä, Aus.
40/B2 Sankt Andrä, Aus.
29/H5 Sankt Andreasberg, Ger.
37/G3 Sankt Anton am Arlberg, Aus.
26/D3 Sankt Augustin, Ger.
31/G2 Sankt Augustin, Ger.
33/H3 Sankt Gallen, Swi.
37/F3 Sankt Gallen, Swi.
37/F3 Sankt Gallen (canton), Swi.
37/E1 Sankt Georgen im Schwarzwald, Ger.
37/G5 Sankt Gertraud (Santa Gertrude), It.
31/G3 Sankt Goar, Ger.
31/G3 Sankt Goarshausen, Ger.
26/D4 Sankt Ingbert, Ger.
31/G5 Sankt Ingbert, Ger.
37/H4 Sankt Jakob (San Giacomo), It.
33/K3 Sankt Johann im Pongau, Aus.
40/A2 Sankt Johann im Pongau, Aus.
33/K3 Sankt Johann in Tirol, Aus.
37/H4 Sankt Leonhard in Passeier (San Leonardo in Passiria), It.
37/H4 Sankt Martin in Passeier (San Martino in Passiria), It.
33/L3 Sankt Michael in Obersteiermark, Aus.
37/H5 Sankt Michael (San Michele), It.
33/H3 Sankt Moritz (Saint Moritz), Swi.
36/D5 Sankt Niklaus, Swi.
26/E1 Sankt Peter-Ording, Ger.
27/H4 Sankt Pölten, Aus.
33/L2 Sankt Pölten, Aus.
40/B1 Sankt Pölten, Aus.
36/D4 Sankt Stephan, Swi.
33/L3 Sankt Veit an der Glan, Aus.
40/B1 Sankt Veit an der Gölsen, Aus.
31/G5 Sankt Wendel, Ger.
33/G2 Sankt Wendel, Ger.
100/B3 San Lázaro, Cabo (cape), Mex.
99/K11 San Leandro, Ca,US
99/K11 San Leandro (res.), Ca,US
37/H4 San Leonardo in Passiria (Sankt Leonhard in Passeier), It.
106/E6 San Lorenzo, Bol.
106/B4 San Lorenzo (cape), Ecu.
106/C3 San Lorenzo, Ecu.
102/E3 San Lorenzo, Hon.
38/A3 San Lorenzo (cape), It.
100/D2 San Lorenzo, Mex.
100/D3 San Lorenzo (riv.), Mex.
102/E3 San Lorenzo, Nic.
99/K11 San Lorenzo, Ca,US
34/C2 San Lorenzo de El Escorial, Sp.
35/M8 San Lorenzo de El Escorial, Sp.
34/B4 Sanlúcar de Barrameda, Sp.
100/C4 San Lucas, Mex.
101/E5 San Lucas, Mex.
102/E3 San Lucas, Nic.
100/C4 San Lucas, Cabo (cape), Mex.
109/C3 San Luis, Arg.
103/H1 San Luis, Cuba
102/D2 San Luis, Guat.
96/B2 San Luis (val.), Co,U
104/D5 San Luis, Ven.
101/E4 San Luis de la Paz, Mex.
102/A1 San Luis de la Paz, Mex.
84/E6 San Luis Obispo, US
88/B4 San Luis Obispo, Ca,US
92/B4 San Luis Obispo, Ca,US
101/E4 San Luis Potosí, Me
101/E4 San Luis Potosí (state), Mex.
102/A1 San Luis Potosí (state), Mex.
88/F7 San Luis Potosí (state), Mex.
100/B1 San Luis Río Colorado, Mex.
88/D5 San Luis Río Colorado, Mex.
92/D4 San Luis Río Colorado, Mex
100/C1 San Manuel, Az,US
92/E4 San Manuel, Az,US
103/H4 San Marcos, Col.
106/C2 San Marcos, Col.
103/E4 San Marcos, CR
102/D3 San Marcos, Guat.
102/B2 San Marcos, Mex.
101/F2 San Marcos, Tx,US
89/G6 San Marcos, Tx,US
93/H5 San Marcos, Tx,US
96/D4 San Marcos, Tx,US
18/E4 San Marino
33/K5 San Marino
33/K5 San Marino (cap.), SMar.
109/C3 San Martín, Arg.
105/B7 San Martín (lake), Arg., Chile
106/F6 San Martín (riv.), Bo
101/L7 San Martín de las Pirámides, Mex.
109/B5 San Martín de los Andes, Arg.
34/C2 San Martín de Valdeiglesias, Sp.
38/A1 San Martino-di-Lota, Fr.
37/H4 San Martino in Passiria (Sankt Martin in Passeier), I
101/L7 San Martín Texmelucan, Mex.
79/E3 Sanmatenga (prov.), Burk.
35/F2 San Mateo, Sp.
88/B4 San Mateo, Ca,US
92/B3 San Mateo, Ca,US
99/K11 San Mateo, Ca,US
99/K12 San Mateo (co.), Ca,US
96/B3 San Mateo (mts.), NM,US
101/K7 San Mateo Atenco, Mex.
105/C7 San Matías (gulf), Arg.
109/D5 San Matías (gulf), Arg.
106/G7 San Matías, Bol.
101/L7 San Matías Tlalancaleca, Mex.
54/G5 Sanmenxia, China
59/B4 Sanmenxia, China
37/H5 San Michele (Sankt Michael), It.
106/F6 San Miguel (riv.), Bo
102/D3 San Miguel, ESal.
92/E5 San Miguel (riv.), Mex
96/C4 San Miguel, Mex
103/G4 San Miguel (gulf), Pan.
106/C5 San Miguel, Peru
101/E4 San Miguel de Allende, Mex.
109/C2 San Miguel de Tucumán, Arg.
101/L6 San Miguel Regla, Mex.
101/K8 San Miguel Totomaloya, Mex.
101/K7 San Miguel Zinacantepec, Mex.
61/H3 Sanming, China
57/L9 Sannan, Japan
52/B6 Sannār, Sudan
77/M5 Sannār, Sudan

175

Sanni – Sault

38/D2 **Sannicandro Garganico**, It.
40/B5 **Sannicandro Garganico**, It.
92/C4 **San Nicolas** (isl.), Ca,US
109/D3 **San Nicolás de los Arroyes**, Arg.
01/M7 **San Nicolás Terrenate**, Mex.
101/E4 **San Nicolás Tolentino**, Mex.
47/P2 **Sannikova** (str.), Rus.
19/S10 **Sannois**, Fr.
57/F2 **Sano**, Japan
27/M4 **Sanok**, Pol.
44/B2 **Sanok**, Pol.
103/H4 **San Onofre**, Col.
99/K10 **San Pablo** (bay), Ca,US
99/K11 **San Pablo**, Ca,US
99/K11 **San Pablo** (res.), Ca,US
100/D3 **San Pablo Balleza**, Mex.
99/K10 **San Pablo Bay Nat'l Wild. Ref.**, Ca,US
109/D1 **San Pedro**, Arg.
109/E3 **San Pedro**, Arg.
101/J5 **San Pedro**, Belz.
102/E2 **San Pedro**, Belz.
98/B3 **San Pedro** (bay), Ca,US
106/E8 **San Pedro** (vol.), Chile
109/C1 **San Pedro** (vol.), Chile
103/G1 **San Pedro** (riv.), Cuba
101/H5 **San Pedro** (riv.), Guat.
102/D2 **San Pedro** (riv.), Guat., Mex.
76/D7 **San Pédro**, IvC.
78/D5 **San Pédro**, IvC.
100/C4 **San Pedro**, Mex.
100/D3 **San Pedro** (riv.), Mex.
101/H5 **San Pedro** (riv.), Mex.
109/E1 **San Pedro**, Par.
34/B3 **San Pedro** (range), Sp.
100/C1 **San Pedro** (riv.), Az,US
92/E4 **San Pedro** (riv.), Az,US
102/D3 **San Pedro Carchá**, Guat.
100/E3 **San Pedro de las Colinas**, Mex.
96/C5 **San Pedro de las Colinas**, Mex
106/C5 **San Pedro de Lloc**, Peru
103/E3 **San Pedro de Lóvago**, Nic.
35/E4 **San Pedro del Pinatar**, Sp.
104/D3 **San Pedro de Macorís**, DRep.
100/B2 **San Pedro Martir** (mts.), Mex.
92/D5 **San Pedro Mártir** (range), Mex
102/D3 **San Pedro Sula**, Hon.
38/A3 **San Pietro** (isl.), It.
61/H2 **Sanqiao**, China
99/K11 **San Quentin**, Ca,US
22/E1 **Sanquhar**, Sc,UK
106/C3 **Sanquianga Nat'l Park**, Col.
100/B2 **San Quintín, Cabo** (cape), Mex.
109/C3 **San Rafael**, Arg.
101/H4 **San Rafael**, Mex.
102/D1 **San Rafael**, Mex.
99/J11 **San Rafael**, Ca,US
92/E3 **San Rafael** (riv.), Ut,US
103/J4 **San Rafael**, Ven.
104/D5 **San Rafael del Moján**, Ven.
106/D1 **San Rafael del Moján**, Ven.
103/E4 **San Ramón**, CR
102/D1 **San Ramón**, Mex.
99/L11 **San Ramon**, Ca,US
106/F8 **San Ramón de la Nueva Orán**, Arg.
109/D1 **San Ramón de la Nueva Orán**, Arg.
33/G5 **San Remo**, It.
104/D4 **San Román** (cape), Ven.
34/C4 **San Roque**, Sp.
34/E4 **San Roque**, Sp.
5/M12 **San Roque**, Sp.
101/F2 **San Saba** (riv.), Tx,US
93/H5 **San Saba**, Tx,US
93/H5 **San Saba** (riv.), Tx,US
96/D4 **San Saba**, Tx,US
104/C1 **San Salvador** (isl.), Bahm.
102/D3 **San Salvador** (cap.), ESal.
100/A2 **San Salvador**, Mex.
109/C1 **San Salvador de Jujuy**, Arg.
01/M7 **San Salvador el Seco**, Mex.
01/M8 **San Salvador Huixcolotla**, Mex.
89/M7 **San Salvador** (Watling I.) (isl.), Bahm.
38/D1 **San Salvo**, It.
40/B4 **San Salvo**, It.
18/C4 **San Sebastián**, Sp.
32/C5 **San Sebastián**, Sp.
34/E1 **San Sebastián**, Sp.
34/D2 **San Sebastián de los Reyes**, Sp.
35/N8 **San Sebastián de los Reyes**, Sp.
102/E3 **San Sebastián de Yali**, Nic.
33/J4 **San Sebastiano**, It.
38/D2 **San Severo**, It.
40/B5 **San Severo**, It.
61/F3 **Sansui**, China
63/J2 **Sansui**, China
54/F2 **Sant**, Mong.
106/E6 **Santa Ana**, Bol.
106/E7 **Santa Ana**, Bol.
102/D3 **Santa Ana**, ESal.
102/D3 **Santa Ana** (vol.), ESal.
102/E3 **Santa Ana**, Hon.
100/C2 **Santa Ana**, Mex.
92/E5 **Santa Ana**, Mex
92/C4 **Santa Ana**, Ca,US
98/C3 **Santa Ana**, Ca,US
98/C3 **Santa Ana** (mts.), Ca,US
98/C3 **Santa Ana** (riv.), Ca,US
104/D5 **Santa Ana**, Ven.
101/L7 **Santa Ana Chiautempan**, Mex.
101/F2 **Santa Anna**, Tx,US
108/D1 **Santa Bárbara**, Braz.
102/D3 **Santa Bárbara**, Hon.
100/D3 **Santa Bárbara**, Mex.
96/B5 **Santa Bárbara**, Mex
88/C5 **Santa Barbara**, Ca,US
92/C4 **Santa Barbara**, Ca,US
103/J4 **Santa Bárbara**, Ven.
106/E3 **Santa Bárbara**, Ven.
108/C2 **Santa Bárbara d'Oeste**, Braz.
103/F4 **Santa Catalina**, Pan.
88/C5 **Santa Catalina** (isl.), Ca,US
92/C4 **Santa Catalina** (gulf), Ca,US
92/C4 **Santa Catalina** (isl.), Ca,US
108/B3 **Santa Catarina** (isl.), Braz.
109/G2 **Santa Catarina** (isl.), Braz.
108/B3 **Santa Catarina** (state), Braz.
100/B2 **Santa Catarina**, Mex.
102/B2 **Santa Catarina Juquila**, Mex.
100/D3 **Santa Catarina Tepehuanes**, Mex.
108/B3 **Santa Cecília**, Braz.
101/Q9 **Santa Cecilia** (ruins), Mex.
103/G1 **Santa Clara**, Cuba
89/L7 **Santa Clara**, Cuba
100/E3 **Santa Clara**, Mex.
34/A4 **Santa Clara** (res.), Port.
99/L12 **Santa Clara**, Ca,US
99/L12 **Santa Clara** (co.), Ca,US
98/B2 **Santa Clara** (riv.), Ca,US
98/B2 **Santa Clarita**, Ca,US
35/G2 **Santa Coloma de Farners**, Sp.
35/L7 **Santa Coloma de Gramanet**, Sp.
34/A1 **Santa Comba**, Sp.
38/D2 **Santa Croce di Magliano**, It.
105/B8 **Santa Cruz** (riv.), Arg.
109/B7 **Santa Cruz** (riv.), Arg.
109/C7 **Santa Cruz**, Arg.
106/F7 **Santa Cruz**, Bol.
102/E4 **Santa Cruz**, CR
100/C2 **Santa Cruz**, Mex.
61/J5 **Santa Cruz**, Phil.
68/F6 **Santa Cruz** (isls.), Sol.
92/E5 **Santa Cruz** (dry riv.), Az,US
86/D5 **Santa Cruz**, Ca,US
88/B4 **Santa Cruz**, Ca,US
92/B3 **Santa Cruz**, Ca,US
92/C4 **Santa Cruz** (isl.), Ca,US
35/S12 **Santa Cruz da Graciosa**, Azor.
35/R12 **Santa Cruz das Flores**, Azor.
104/D5 **Santa Cruz de Bucaral**, Ven.
35/X16 **Santa Cruz de la Palma**, Canl.
34/D3 **Santa Cruz de la Zarza**, Sp.
102/D3 **Santa Cruz del Quiché**, Guat.
103/G1 **Santa Cruz del Sur**, Cuba
34/D3 **Santa Cruz de Mudela**, Sp.
35/X16 **Santa Cruz de Tenerife**, Canl.
76/B2 **Santa Cruz de Tenerife**, Sp.
108/B2 **Santa Cruz do Rio Pardo**, Braz.
109/F2 **Santa Cruz do Sul**, Braz.
102/D3 **Santa Cruz, Sierra de** (range), Guat.
102/B2 **Santa Cruz Zenzontepec**, Mex.
35/L7 **Sant Adrià de Besòs**, Sp.
102/E4 **Santa Elena** (bay), CR
102/E4 **Santa Elena** (cape), CR
102/E2 **Santa Elena**, Hon.
100/E3 **Santa Elena**, Mex.
101/E3 **Santa Elena**, Mex.
34/C4 **Santaella**, Sp.
34/A1 **Santa Eugenia de Ribeira**, Sp.
35/F3 **Santa Eulalia del Río**, Sp.
109/D3 **Santa Fé**, Arg.
103/F1 **Santa Fe**, Cuba
34/D4 **Santa Fé**, Sp.
88/E4 **Santa Fe** (cap.), NM,US
93/F4 **Santa Fe** (cap.), NM,US
96/B3 **Santa Fe** (cap.), NM,US
108/B2 **Santa Fe do Sul**, Braz.
38/D3 **Sant'Agata di Militello**, It.
37/G4 **Santa Gertrude** (Sankt Gertraud), It.
100/B2 **Santa Gertrudis**, Mex.
37/H5 **Santa Giustina** (lake), It.
107/H7 **Santa Helena de Goiás**, Braz.
108/B1 **Santa Helena de Goiás**, Braz.
107/J4 **Santa Inês**, Braz.
101/L7 **Santa Inés Zacatelco**, Mex.
102/D2 **Santa Isabel** (riv.), Guat.
100/C3 **Santa Isabel**, Mex.
68/E5 **Santa Isabel** (isl.), Sol.
101/F3 **Santa Juana**, Mex.
108/C1 **Santa Juliana**, Braz.
107/J4 **Santa Luzia**, Braz.
108/D1 **Santa Luzia**, Braz.
74/J10 **Santa Luzia** (isl.), CpV.
100/B3 **Santa Magdalena** (isl.), Mex.
100/B3 **Santa Margarita** (isl.), Mex.
35/T13 **Santa Maria** (isl.), Azor.
109/F2 **Santa Maria**, Braz.
74/K10 **Santa Maria**, CpV.
100/C3 **Santa María** (bay), Mex.
100/D2 **Santa María** (riv.), Mex.
101/L7 **Santa Mariá**, Mex.
102/A1 **Santa María** (riv.), Mex.
92/F5 **Santa Maria** (riv.), Mex.
88/B5 **Santa Maria**, Ca,US
92/B4 **Santa Maria**, Ca,US
81/F2 **Santa Maria, Cabo de** (cape), Moz.
34/B4 **Santa Maria, Cabo de** (cape), Port.
38/D2 **Santa Maria Capua Vetere**, It.
107/K6 **Santa Maria da Vitória**, Braz.
34/D1 **Santa María de Cayón**, Sp.
101/E4 **Santa María del Río**, Mex.
39/F3 **Santa Maria di Leuca** (cape), It.
108/D1 **Santa Maria do Suaçi**, Braz.
102/B3 **Santa María Huatulco**, Mex.
37/G4 **Santa Maria im Münstertal**, Swi.
37/E5 **Santa Maria Maggiore**, It.
103/H4 **Santa Marta**, Col.
106/D1 **Santa Marta**, Col.
103/H4 **Santa Marta, Sierra Nevada de** (range), Col.
98/B2 **Santa Monica**, Ca,US
98/B2 **Santa Monica** (mts.), Ca,US
98/B3 **Santa Monica** (bay), Ca,US
88/C5 **Santa Monica Mts. Nat'l Rec. Area**, Ca,US
35/V15 **Santana**, Madr.
107/K6 **Santana**, Braz.
35/P11 **Santana**, Port.
109/E3 **Santana do Livramento**, Braz.
103/H5 **Santander** (dept.), Col.
106/C3 **Santander**, Col.
18/C4 **Santander**, Sp.
34/D1 **Santander**, Sp.
101/F3 **Santander Jiménez**, Mex.
38/A3 **Sant'Antioco**, It.
38/A3 **Sant'Antioco** (isl.), It.
35/G3 **Santañy**, Sp.
34/B4 **Santa Olalla del Cala**, Sp.
98/A2 **Santa Paula**, Ca,US
35/E3 **Santa Pola**, Sp.
35/E3 **Santa Pola, Cabo de** (cape), Sp.
107/J4 **Santarém**, Braz.
18/C5 **Santarém**, Port.
34/A3 **Santarém**, Port.
34/A3 **Santarém** (dist.), Port.
35/Q10 **Santarem** (dist.), Port.
107/M5 **Santa Rita**, Braz.
101/E3 **Santa Rita**, Mex.
100/C1 **Santa Rita**, NM,US
108/C2 **Santa Rita do Sapucaí**, Braz.
106/F8 **Santa Rosa**, Arg.
109/C3 **Santa Rosa**, Arg.
109/D4 **Santa Rosa**, Arg.
109/F2 **Santa Rosa**, Braz.
106/C4 **Santa Rosa**, Ecu.
101/F4 **Santa Rosa**, Mex.
101/H5 **Santa Rosa**, Mex.
102/D2 **Santa Rosa**, Mex.
86/D5 **Santa Rosa**, Ca,US
88/B4 **Santa Rosa**, Ca,US
92/B3 **Santa Rosa**, Ca,US
92/B4 **Santa Rosa** (isl.), Ca,US
88/F5 **Santa Rosa**, NM,US
93/F4 **Santa Rosa**, NM,US
96/B3 **Santa Rosa**, NM,US
88/C3 **Santa Rosa** (mts.), Nv,US
92/C2 **Santa Rosa** (range), Nv,US
102/E3 **Santa Rosa de Aguán**, Hon.
102/D3 **Santa Rosa de Copán**, Hon.
108/C2 **Santa Rosa de Viterbo**, Braz.
100/B3 **Santa Rosalía**, Mex.
100/B2 **Santa Rosalía, Punta** (pt.), Mex.
102/E4 **Santa Rosa Nat'l Park**, CR
38/D2 **Sant'Arsenio**, It.
70/E4 **Santa Teresa**, Austl.
107/J6 **Santa Teresa** (riv.), Braz.
101/H5 **Santa Teresa**, Mex.
102/D2 **Santa Teresa**, Mex.
109/F3 **Santa Teresa Nat'l Park**, Uru.
107/H6 **Santa Teresinha**, Braz.
108/B1 **Santa Vitória**, Braz.
109/F3 **Santa Vitória do Palmar**, Braz.
35/L7 **Sant Boi de Llobregat**, Sp.
35/F2 **Sant Carles de la Ràpita**, Sp.
35/G2 **Sant Celoni**, Sp.
35/L6 **Sant Celoni**, Sp.
35/G2 **Sant Cugat del Vallès**, Sp.
35/L7 **Sant Cugat del Vallès**, Sp.
97/H3 **Santee** (dam), SC,US
100/E5 **San Telmo, Punta** (pt.), Mex.
33/J4 **Santerno** (riv.), It.
38/D3 **Sant'Eufemia** (gulf), It.
35/L7 **Sant Feliu**, Sp.
35/G2 **Sant Feliu de Guíxols**, Sp.
35/G2 **Sant Feliu de Llobregat**, Sp.
35/F1 **Sant Gervàs** (peak), Sp.
109/F2 **Santiago**, Braz.
109/B3 **Santiago** (cap.), Chile
104/D3 **Santiago**, DRep.
100/C4 **Santiago**, Mex.
101/E3 **Santiago**, Mex.
84/G7 **Santiago** (riv.), Mex.
103/F4 **Santiago**, Pan.
103/F4 **Santiago** (mtn.), Pan.
106/B2 **Santiago**, Pan.
106/B2 **Santiago** (mtn.), Pan.
61/J5 **Santiago**, Phil.
18/C4 **Santiago**, Sp.
98/C3 **Santiago** (peak), Ca,US
98/C3 **Santiago** (res.), Ca,US
100/E2 **Santiago** (peak), Tx,US
88/F5 **Santiago** (mts.), Tx,US
96/C4 **Santiago** (mts.), Tx,US
34/A1 **Santiago de Compostela**, Sp.
103/H1 **Santiago de Cuba**, Cuba
89/L7 **Santiago de Cuba**, Cuba
109/D2 **Santiago del Estero**, Arg.
34/A3 **Santiago do Cacém**, Port.
100/D4 **Santiago Ixcuintla**, Mex.
102/B2 **Santiago Jocotepec**, Mex.
102/B2 **Santiago Juxtlahuaca**, Mex.
101/M8 **Santiago Miahuatlán**, Mex.
100/D3 **Santiago Papasquiaro**, Mex.
101/G5 **Santiago Tuxtla**, Mex.
102/C2 **Santiago Tuxtla**, Mex.
33/H3 **Säntis** (peak), Swi.
37/F3 **Säntis** (peak), Swi.
34/D3 **Santisteban del Puerto**, Sp.
35/K6 **Sant Jeroni** (mtn.), Sp.
32/D5 **Sant Julià**, And.
35/F1 **Sant Julià**, And.
35/K6 **Sant Llorenc del Munt Nat'l Park**, Sp.
57/K9 **Santō**, Japan
57/M9 **Santō**, Japan
108/B2 **Santo Anastácio**, Braz.
107/J8 **Santo André**, Braz.
108/C2 **Santo André**, Braz.
109/G1 **Santo André**, Braz.
109/F2 **Santo Ângelo**, Braz.
74/J9 **Santo Antão** (isl.), CpV.
76/G7 **Santo António**, SaoT.
108/D2 **Santo Antônio de Pádua**, Braz.
103/F1 **Santo Domingo**, Cuba
104/D3 **Santo Domingo** (cap.), DRep.
89/N8 **Santo Domingo** (cap.), DRep.
100/B2 **Santo Domingo**, Mex.
101/E4 **Santo Domingo**, Mex.
32/B5 **Santo Domingo de la Calzada**, Sp.
34/D1 **Santo Domingo de la Calzada**, Sp.
106/C4 **Santo Domingo de los Colorados**, Ecu.
102/C2 **Santo Domingo Petapa**, Mex.
100/B3 **Santo Domingo, Punta** (pt.), Mex.
109/E3 **Santo Grande** (res.), Uru.
35/E3 **Santomera**, Sp.
32/B5 **Santoña**, Sp.
34/D1 **Santoña**, Sp.
39/J4 **Santorini** (Thíra), Gre.
107/J8 **Santos**, Braz.
108/C2 **Santos**, Braz.
109/G1 **Santos**, Braz.
108/D2 **Santos Dumont**, Braz.
102/B2 **Santos Reyes Nopala**, Mex.
100/A2 **Santo Tomás**, Mex.
100/D2 **Santo Tomás**, Mex.
106/D6 **Santo Tomás**, Peru
100/A2 **Santo Tomás, Punta** (pt.), Mex.
109/D3 **Santo Tomé**, Arg.
109/E2 **Santo Tomé**, Arg.
35/K7 **Sant Pere de Ribes**, Sp.
35/K7 **Sant Sadurní d'Anoia**, Sp.
32/B5 **Santurce-Antiguo**, Sp.
34/D1 **Santurce-Antiguo**, Sp.
35/K6 **Sant Vicenç de Castellet**, Sp.
35/L7 **Sant Vicenç dels Hort**, Sp.
49/G7 **Şanūr**, WBnk.
109/B6 **San Valentín** (peak), Chile
102/D3 **San Vicente**, ESal.
100/A2 **San Vicente**, Mex.
92/C5 **San Vicente**, Mex
34/B3 **San Vicente de Alcántara**, Sp.
106/C6 **San Vicente de Cañete**, Peru
35/E3 **San Vicente del Raspeig**, Sp.
33/K5 **San Vicino** (peak), It.
33/J5 **San Vincenzo**, It.
38/B1 **San Vincenzo**, It.
103/F4 **San Vito**, CR
38/C3 **San Vito** (cape), It.
61/F5 **Sanya**, China
63/J4 **Sanya**, China
65/E2 **Sanya**, China
108/C2 **São Bernardo do Campo**, Braz.
109/E2 **São Borja**, Braz.
107/J8 **São Carlos**, Braz.
108/C2 **São Carlos**, Braz.
109/G1 **São Carlos**, Braz.
108/B1 **São Domingos** (riv.), Braz.
107/H5 **São Félix do Xingu**, Braz.
108/D2 **São Fidélis**, Braz.
74/J11 **São Filipe**, CpV.
105/F3 **São Francisco** (riv.), Braz.
107/L5 **São Francisco** (riv.), Braz.
100/C1 **São Francisco** (riv.), Braz.
109/G2 **São Francisco** (isl.), Braz.
108/B3 **São Francisco do Sul**, Braz.
108/B4 **São Fransisco de Paula**, Braz.
109/F3 **São Gabriel**, Braz.
107/K7 **São Gabriel da Palha**, Braz.
108/D1 **São Gabriel da Palha**, Braz.
108/D2 **São Gonçalo**, Braz.
108/C1 **São Gonçalo do Abaeté**, Braz.
108/C2 **São Gonçalo do Sapucaí**, Braz.
108/C1 **São Gotardo**, Braz.
108/C2 **São Joachim da Barra**, Braz.
106/F5 **São João** (mts.), Braz.
107/K4 **São João**, Braz.
108/B3 **São João Batista**, Braz.
108/D2 **São João da Barra**, Braz.
108/C2 **São João da Boa Vista**, Braz.
34/A2 **São João da Madeira**, Port.
34/B2 **São João da Pesqueira**, Port.
35/P10 **São João das Lampas**, Port.
107/K8 **São João del Rei**, Braz.
108/C2 **São João del Rei**, Braz.
107/K5 **São João do Piauí**, Braz.
108/D1 **São João Evangelista**, Braz.
108/D2 **São João Nepomuceno**, Braz.
108/B4 **São Joaquim**, Braz.
35/S12 **São Jorge** (isl.), Azor.
108/B3 **São José**, Braz.
109/G2 **São José**, Braz.
108/A5 **São José do Norte**, Braz.
108/C2 **São José do Rio Pardo**, Braz.
107/J8 **São José do Rio Preto**, Braz.
108/B2 **São José do Rio Preto**, Braz.
107/J8 **São José dos Campos**, Braz.
108/C2 **São José dos Campos**, Braz.
109/G1 **São José dos Campos**, Braz.
108/B3 **São José dos Pinhais**, Braz.
108/B4 **São Leopoldo**, Braz.
107/G7 **São Lourenço** (riv.), Braz.
108/C2 **São Lourenço**, Braz.
35/Q10 **São Lourenço**, Port.
108/B4 **São Lourenço do Sul**, Braz.
82/C3 **São Lucas**, Ang.
107/K4 **São Luís**, Braz.
108/B2 **São Manoel**, Braz.
105/E3 **São Marcos** (bay), Braz.
107/K4 **São Marcos** (bay), Braz.
108/C1 **São Marcos** (riv.), Braz.
34/A3 **São Martinho do Porto**, Port.
107/L7 **São Mateus**, Braz.
108/D1 **São Mateus** (riv.), Braz.
108/E1 **São Mateus**, Braz.
108/B3 **São Mateus do Sul**, Braz.
35/T13 **São Miguel** (isl.), Azor.
108/C2 **São Miguel Arcanjo**, Braz.
104/D3 **Saona** (isl.), DRep.
26/C5 **Saône** (riv.), Fr.
32/F3 **Saône** (riv.), Fr.
36/A4 **Saône** (riv.), Fr.
36/A6 **Saône** (riv.), Fr.
36/C3 **Saône**, Fr.
36/B4 **Saône-et-Loire** (dept.), Fr.
74/J10 **São Nicolau** (isl.), CpV.
107/J8 **São Paulo**, Braz.
108/B2 **São Paulo** (state), Braz.
108/C2 **São Paulo**, Braz.
109/G1 **São Paulo**, Braz.
106/E4 **São Paulo de Olivença**, Braz.
108/D2 **São Pedro da Aldeia**, Braz.
34/A2 **São Pedro do Sul**, Port.
57/M9 **Saori**, Japan
105/F3 **São Roque, Cabo de** (cape), Braz.
35/S12 **São Roque do Pico**, Azor.
108/C2 **São Sebastião** (isl.), Braz.
74/F7 **São Sebastião** (pt.), Moz.
82/G5 **São Sebastião** (pt.), Moz.
108/C2 **São Sebastião do Paraíso**, Braz.
108/B1 **São Simão** (res.), Braz.
34/A4 **São Teotónio**, Port.
108/C2 **São Tiago**, Braz.
74/K10 **São Tiago** (isl.), CpV.
74/C4 **São Tomé** (cap.), SaoT.
76/G7 **São Tomé** (cap.), SaoT.
76/G7 **São Tomé** (isl.), SaoT.
74/C4 **São Tomé and Príncipe**
76/F7 **São Tomé and Príncipe**
105/E5 **São Tomé, Cabo de** (cape), Braz.
76/E1 **Saoura** (dry riv.), Alg.
108/C2 **São Vicente**, Braz.
74/J10 **São Vicente** (isl.), CpV.
18/C5 **São Vicente, Cabo de** (cape), Port.
34/A4 **São Vicente, Cabo de** (cape), Port.
63/H3 **Sa Pa**, Viet.
39/J2 **Sápai**, Gre.
41/G5 **Sápai**, Gre.
50/A1 **Sápai**, Gre.
41/K5 **Sapanca**, Turk.
39/H1 **Sapareva Banya**, Bul.
97/H4 **Sapelo** (isl.), Ga,US
50/B4 **Şaphane**, Turk.
39/G4 **Sapiéndza** (isl.), Gre.
36/D1 **Sapin Sec, Roche du** (mtn.), Fr.
58/D4 **Sapkyo**, SKor.
103/G5 **Sapo, Serraniía de** (range), Pan.
106/C5 **Saposoa**, Peru
26/D2 **Sappemeer**, Neth.
28/D2 **Sappemeer**, Neth.
72/B3 **Sapphire**, Austl.
47/Q5 **Sapporo**, Japan
55/N3 **Sapporo**, Japan
38/D2 **Sapri**, It.
46/E6 **Saqqez**, Iran
51/F2 **Saqqez**, Iran
52/E1 **Saqqez**, Iran
39/G1 **Šar** (mts.), Yugo.
40/E4 **Šar** (mts.), Yugo.
51/F2 **Sarāb**, Iran
52/E1 **Sarāb**, Iran
63/H5 **Sara Buri**, Thai.
65/C3 **Sara Buri**, Thai.
18/C4 **Saragossa**, Sp.
35/E2 **Saragossa**, Sp.
64/B1 **Sarāi Alamgir**, Pak.
18/E4 **Sarajevo** (cap.), Bosn.
40/D4 **Sarajevo** (cap.), Bosn.
97/F4 **Saraland**, Al,US
60/B3 **Saramati** (mtn.), India
66/D4 **Saran** (peak), Indo.
46/H5 **Saran'**, Kaz.
94/F2 **Saranac Lake**, NY,US
39/L6 **Sarandapótamos** (riv.), Gre.
39/G3 **Sarandë**, Alb.
53/L4 **Sārangpur**, India
62/C3 **Sārangpur**, India
19/H3 **Saransk**, Rus.
45/H1 **Saransk**, Rus.
46/E4 **Saransk**, Rus.
19/J3 **Sarapul**, Rus.
43/M4 **Sarapul**, Rus.
46/F4 **Sarapul**, Rus.
89/K6 **Sarasota**, Fl,US
97/H5 **Sarasota**, Fl,US
41/J2 **Sarata**, Ukr.
99/K12 **Saratoga**, Ca,US
90/G5 **Saratoga**, Wy,US
92/F2 **Saratoga**, Wy,US
94/F3 **Saratoga Springs**, NY,US
19/H3 **Saratov**, Rus.
45/H2 **Saratov**, Rus.
45/J1 **Saratov** (res.), Rus.
46/E4 **Saratov**, Rus.
45/H2 **Saratov Obl.**, Rus.
53/H3 **Sarāvān**, Iran
63/J4 **Saravan**, Laos
65/D3 **Saravan**, Laos
48/L9 **Sarawak** (state), Malay.
66/D3 **Sarawak** (reg.), Malay.
41/H5 **Saray**, Turk.
50/A1 **Saray**, Turk.
50/B2 **Sarayköy**, Turk.
50/C2 **Sarayönü**, Turk.
40/D2 **Sárbogárd**, Hun.
37/G5 **Sarca** (riv.), It.
19/T10 **Sarcelles**, Fr.
30/B6 **Sarcelles**, Fr.
62/D2 **Sarda** (riv.), India
38/A3 **Sardara**, It.
53/K3 **Sardārshahar**, India
62/B2 **Sardārshahar**, India
51/F2 **Sar Dasht**, Iran
52/E1 **Sar Dasht**, Iran
38/A2 **Sardegna** (reg.), It.
103/H4 **Sardinata**, Col.
33/G5 **Sardinaux, Cap de** (cape), Fr.
35/J1 **Sardinaux, Cap de** (cape), Fr.
18/D5 **Sardinia** (isl.), It.
38/A2 **Sardinia** (isl.), It.
93/K4 **Sardis** (lake), Ms,US
93/J4 **Sardis** (lake), Ok,US
20/F2 **Sareks Nat'l Park**, Swe.
42/C2 **Sareks Nat'l Park**, Swe.
20/F2 **Sarektjåkko** (peak), Swe.
67/E4 **Sarempaka** (peak), Indo.
37/H4 **Sarentino**, It.
37/F3 **Sargans**, Swi.
53/K2 **Sargodha**, Pak.
64/B1 **Sargodha**, Pak.
77/J6 **Sarh**, Chad
46/F6 **Sārī**, Iran
51/H2 **Sārī**, Iran
52/F1 **Sārī**, Iran
67/J4 **Saribi** (cape), Indo.
50/B1 **Sarıcakaya**, Turk.
38/A2 **Sari-di-Porto-Vecchio**, Fr.
68/D3 **Sarigan** (isl.), NMar.
50/B2 **Sarıgöl**, Turk.
45/G4 **Sarıkamış**, Turk.
50/E1 **Sarıkamış**, Turk.
44/E5 **Sarıkaya**, Turk.
50/C2 **Sarıkaya**, Turk.
50/C2 **Sarikaya** (prov.), Turk.
71/H4 **Sarina**, Austl.
72/C3 **Sarina**, Austl.
33/G3 **Sarine** (riv.), Swi.
36/D4 **Sarine** (riv.), Swi.
35/E2 **Sariñena**, Sp.
50/C2 **Sarıoğlan**, Turk.
77/K2 **Sarīr Kalanshiyū** (des.), Libya
77/J3 **Sarīr Tibasti** (des.), Libya
96/D5 **Sarita**, Tx,US
55/K4 **Sariwŏn**, NKor.
58/C3 **Sariwŏn**, NKor.
32/B2 **Sark** (isl.), Chl,UK
40/E2 **Sarkad**, Hun.
45/L4 **Sarkamyshskoye** (lake), Trkm., Uzb.
46/H5 **Sarkand**, Kaz.
50/B2 **Şarkîkaraağaç**, Turk.
44/F5 **Şarkışla**, Turk.
50/D2 **Şarkışla**, Turk.
41/H5 **Şarköy**, Turk.
44/C4 **Şarköy**, Turk.
50/A1 **Şarköy**, Turk.
32/D4 **Sarlat-La-Canéda**, Fr.
109/C6 **Sarmiento**, Arg.
33/K5 **Sarnano**, It.
33/H3 **Sarnen**, Swi.
36/E4 **Sarnen**, Swi.
87/H4 **Sarnia**, On,Can
94/D3 **Sarnia**, On,Can
99/H6 **Sarnia**, On,Can
44/C2 **Sarny**, Ukr.
39/I4 **Saronic** (gulf), Gre.
39/L7 **Saronic** (gulf), Gre.
39/K2 **Saros** (gulf), Turk.
41/H5 **Saros** (gulf), Turk.
44/C4 **Saros** (gulf), Turk.
27/L4 **Sárospatak**, Hun.
40/E1 **Sárospatak**, Hun.
31/G6 **Sarralbe**, Fr.
31/F6 **Sarre** (riv.), Fr.
26/D4 **Sarrebourg**, Fr.
31/G6 **Sarrebourg**, Fr.
33/G2 **Sarrebourg**, Fr.
26/D4 **Sarreguemines**, Fr.
33/G2 **Sarreguemines**, Fr.
31/G6 **Sarre-Union**, Fr.
34/B1 **Sarria**, Sp.
38/A3 **Sarroch**, It.
30/D6 **Sarry**, Fr.
29/G4 **Sarstedt**, Ger.
102/D3 **Sarstún** (riv.), Belz., Guat.
47/P3 **Sartang** (riv.), Rus.
38/B1 **Sarteano**, It.
38/A2 **Sartène**, Fr.
32/C3 **Sarthe** (riv.), Fr.
19/S10 **Sartrouville**, Fr.
30/B6 **Sartrouville**, Fr.
50/A2 **Saruhanlı**, Turk.
40/D2 **Sárvíz** (riv.), Hun.
46/H5 **Saryshagan**, Kaz.
46/G5 **Sarysu** (riv.), Kaz.
33/H4 **Sarzana**, It.
91/K3 **Sasaginnigak** (lake), Mb,Can
62/D3 **Sasaram**, India
57/L9 **Sasayama**, Japan
57/L9 **Sasayama** (riv.), Japan
55/K5 **Sasebo**, Japan
56/A4 **Sasebo**, Japan
86/F3 **Saskatchewan** (prov.), Can.
88/E1 **Saskatchewan** (prov.), Can.
90/G2 **Saskatchewan** (prov.), Can
90/F2 **Saskatchewan** (riv.), Can
90/F3 **Saskatchewan** (riv.), Can
84/G4 **Saskatchewan** (riv.), Can.
86/F3 **Saskatchewan** (riv.), Can
91/G2 **Saskatchewan** (riv.), Can
91/H2 **Saskatchewan, Sipanok Chan.** (riv.), Sk,Can
90/G2 **Saskatoon**, Sk,Can
86/F3 **Saskatoon**, Sk,Can
88/E1 **Saskatoon**, Sk,Can
103/E3 **Saslaya** (mtn.), Nic.
103/E3 **Saslaya Nat'l Park**, Nic.
80/P13 **Sasolburg**, SAfr.
19/H3 **Sasovo**, Rus.
45/G1 **Sasovo**, Rus.
46/E4 **Sasovo**, Rus.
76/D6 **Sassandra** (riv.), IvC.
78/D5 **Sassandra**, IvC.
78/D5 **Sassandra** (riv.), IvC.
18/D4 **Sassari**, It.
38/A2 **Sassari**, It.
29/F5 **Sassenberg**, Ger.
28/B4 **Sassenheim**, Neth.
27/G1 **Sassnitz**, Ger.
33/J4 **Sassuolo**, It.
35/E2 **Sástago**, Sp.
28/A6 **Sas Van Gent**, Neth.
30/C1 **Sas Van Gent**, Neth.
41/J3 **Sasyk** (lake), Ukr
55/L5 **Sata-misaki** (cape), Japan
56/B5 **Sata-misaki** (cape), Japan
53/K5 **Sātāra**, India
62/B4 **Sātāra**, India
68/F4 **Satawan** (atoll), Micr.
106/D6 **Satipo**, Peru
23/G2 **Satley**, Eng,UK
62/D3 **Satna**, India
27/L4 **Sátoraljaújhely**, Hun.
40/E1 **Sátoraljaújhely**, Hun.
46/G5 **Satpayev**, Kaz.
53/K4 **Satpura** (range), India
62/C3 **Satpura** (range), India
63/H5 **Sattahip**, Thai.
66/B1 **Sattahip**, Thai.
64/F4 **Sāttānkulam**, India
37/F3 **Satteins**, Aus.
64/F4 **Sāttūr**, India
63/H4 **Satuk**, Thai.
18/F4 **Satu Mare**, Rom.
27/M5 **Satu Mare**, Rom.
27/M5 **Satu Mare** (co.), Rom.
40/F2 **Satu Mare**, Rom.
40/F2 **Satu Mare** (co.), Rom.
44/B3 **Satu Mare**, Rom.
63/H6 **Satun**, Thai.
65/C5 **Satun**, Thai.
66/B2 **Satun**, Thai.
69/R9 **Satupaitea**, WSam.
64/F3 **Satyamangalam**, India
100/D2 **Saucillo**, Mex.
96/B4 **Saucillo**, Mex
20/N6 **Saudhárkrókur**, Ice.
48/D7 **Saudi Arabia**
49/E5 **Saudi Arabia**
50/E4 **Saudi Arabia**
52/D4 **Saudi Arabia**
77/Q3 **Saudi Arabia**
26/D4 **Sauer** (riv.), Fr.
29/F5 **Sauer** (riv.), Ger.
31/F4 **Sauer** (riv.), Ger., Lux.
37/H2 **Sauerlach**, Ger.
26/D3 **Sauerland** (reg.), Ger.
29/F6 **Sauerland** (reg.), Ger.
31/G1 **Sauerland** (reg.), Ger.
106/G6 **Sauêruiná** (riv.), Braz.
32/C4 **Saujon**, Fr.
91/K4 **Sauk** (riv.), Mn,US
91/K4 **Sauk Centre**, Mn,US
91/K4 **Sauk Rapids**, Mn,US
107/H3 **Saül**, FrG.
32/D3 **Sauldre** (riv.), Fr.
26/E4 **Saulgau**, Ger.
37/F1 **Saulgau**, Ger.
26/C5 **Saulieu**, Fr.
32/F3 **Saulieu**, Fr.
30/D5 **Sault-lès-Rethel**, Fr.
87/H4 **Sault Sainte Marie**, On,Can
89/K2 **Sault Sainte Marie**, On,Can

176

Sault – Settl

94/C2 **Sault Sainte Marie,** On,Can
87/H4 **Sault Sainte Marie,** Mi,US
89/K2 **Sault Sainte Marie,** Mi,US
94/C2 **Sault Ste. Marie,** Mi,US
26/C4 **Saulx** (riv.), Fr.
31/E6 **Saulx** (riv.), Fr.
32/F2 **Saulx** (riv.), Fr.
36/C2 **Saulx-de-Vesoul,** Fr.
36/C2 **Saulxures-sur-Moselotte,** Fr.
71/J4 **Saumarez** (reef), Austl.
72/D3 **Saumarez** (reefs), Austl.
32/C3 **Saumur,** Fr.
24/B3 **Saundersfoot,** Wal,UK
82/D2 **Saurimo,** Ang.
99/K11 **Sausalito,** Ca,US
19/S9 **Sausseron** (riv.), Fr.
103/G5 **Sautatá,** Col.
104/F4 **Sauteurs,** Gren.
40/C3 **Sava** (riv.), Cro.
33/L4 **Sava** (riv.), Cro., Slov.
18/E4 **Sava** (riv.), Eur.
102/E3 **Savá,** Hon.
38/E2 **Sava,** It.
40/C5 **Sava,** It.
73/C4 **Savage River,** Austl.
69/H6 **Savai'i** (isl.), WSam.
69/R9 **Savai'i** (isl.), WSam.
95/G1 **Savane** (riv.), Qu,Can
84/J6 **Savannah** (riv.), US
89/K5 **Savannah,** Ga,US
97/H3 **Savannah,** Ga,US
97/F3 **Savannah,** Tn,US
63/H4 **Savannaket,** Laos
65/D2 **Savannakhet,** Laos
103/G2 **Savanna la Mar,** Jam.
91/L3 **Savant** (lake), On,Can
94/B1 **Savant** (lake), On,Can
62/B4 **Sāvantvādi,** India
20/G3 **Sävar,** Swe.
42/D3 **Sävar,** Swe.
44/C5 **Savaştepe,** Turk.
50/A2 **Savaştepe,** Turk.
82/C4 **Savate,** Ang.
76/F6 **Savé,** Ben.
82/F5 **Save** (riv.), Moz.
74/F7 **Save** (riv.), Moz., Zim.
46/F6 **Sāveh,** Iran
51/G3 **Sāveh,** Iran
52/F1 **Sāveh,** Iran
41/H2 **Săveni,** Rom.
44/C3 **Săveni,** Rom.
32/D5 **Saverdun,** Fr.
35/F1 **Saverdun,** Fr.
26/D4 **Saverne,** Fr.
31/G6 **Saverne,** Fr.
33/G2 **Saverne,** Fr.
33/G3 **Savièse,** Swi.
33/G4 **Savigliano,** It.
33/K4 **Savignano sul Rubicone,** It.
19/T11 **Savigny-le-Temple,** Fr.
19/T10 **Savigny-sur-Orge,** Fr.
30/B6 **Savigny-sur-Orge,** Fr.
33/K5 **Savio** (riv.), It.
37/F4 **Savognin,** Swi.
36/C6 **Savoie** (dept.), Fr.
90/C3 **Savona,** BC,Can
33/H4 **Savona,** It.
20/J3 **Savonlinna,** Fin.
42/F3 **Savonlinna,** Fin.
85/D3 **Savoonga,** Ak,US
32/F4 **Savoy** (reg.), Fr.
36/C6 **Savoy Alps** (mts.), Fr.
45/G4 **Şavşat,** Turk.
50/E1 **Şavşat,** Turk.
20/E4 **Sävsjö,** Swe.
48/M10 **Savu** (sea), Indo.
67/F5 **Savu** (sea), Indo.
68/B5 **Savu** (sea), Indo.
68/G6 **Savusavu,** Fiji
66/B4 **Sawahlunto,** Indo.
77/N4 **Sawākin,** Sudan
60/C5 **Sawankhalok,** Thai.
63/G4 **Sawankhalok,** Thai.
65/B2 **Sawankhalok,** Thai.
57/G3 **Sawara,** Japan
57/F2 **Sawasaki-bana** (pt.), Japan
92/F3 **Sawatch** (range), Co,US
96/B2 **Sawatch** (range), Co,US
25/G3 **Sawbridgeworth,** Eng,UK
76/J2 **Sawdā** (mts.), Libya
52/D5 **Sawdā', Jabal** (mtn.), SAr.
77/L5 **Sawdirī,** Sudan
67/H4 **Saweba** (cape), Indo.
22/A2 **Sawel** (mtn.), NI,UK
50/B5 **Sawhāj,** Egypt
52/B3 **Sawhāj,** Egypt
77/M2 **Sawhāj,** Egypt
63/F6 **Sāwi,** India
52/G5 **Sawqirah, Ghubbat** (bay), Oman
53/G5 **Şawqirah, Ra's** (pt.), Oman
25/G2 **Sawston,** Eng,UK
73/E1 **Sawtell,** Austl.
90/E4 **Sawtooth** (range), Id,US
92/D1 **Sawtooth** (mts.), Id,US
67/F6 **Sawu** (isls.), Indo.
35/E3 **Sax,** Sp.
23/H5 **Saxilby,** Eng,UK
85/M4 **Saxman,** Ak,US
25/H2 **Saxmundham,** Eng,UK
26/A2 **Saxmundham,** Eng.,UK
36/D5 **Saxon,** Swi.
27/G3 **Saxony** (state), Ger.
33/K1 **Saxony** (state), Ger.
26/F3 **Saxony-Anhalt** (state), Ger.
29/H5 **Saxony-Anhalt** (state), Ger.
79/F3 **Say,** Niger
57/F3 **Sayama,** Japan
57/H7 **Sayama,** Japan
57/L10 **Sayama,** Japan
47/L4 **Sayansk,** Rus.
50/C3 **Şaydā,** Leb.
49/D3 **Şaydā** (Sidon), Leb.
52/F5 **Sayḩūt,** Yem.
77/R4 **Sayḩūt,** Yem.
101/H4 **Sayil** (ruins), Mex.
102/D1 **Sayil** (ruins), Mex.
31/G2 **Saynbach** (riv.), Ger.
47/M5 **Saynshand,** Mong.
48/L5 **Saynshand,** Mong.
54/G3 **Saynshand,** Mong.
89/F5 **Sayreville,** NJ,US
52/E5 **Saywūn,** Yem.
77/Q4 **Saywūn,** Yem.
39/F2 **Sazan** (isl.), Alb.
40/D5 **Sazan** (isl.), Alb.
33/L2 **Sázava** (riv.), Czh.
51/M6 **Sazli Dere** (riv.), Turk.
23/E3 **Scafell Pikes** (mtn.), Eng,UK
23/H3 **Scalby,** Eng,UK
38/D3 **Scalea,** It.
37/F5 **Scalino, Pizzo** (peak), It.
85/E3 **Scammon Bay,** Ak,US
99/B2 **Scandia,** Wa,US
37/J5 **Scandicci,** It.
95/R8 **Scarborough,** On,Can
23/H3 **Scarborough,** Eng,UK
26/B3 **Scarpe** (riv.), Belg., Fr.
30/B3 **Scarpe** (riv.), Fr.
21/A4 **Scarriff,** Ire.
98/G4 **Scarsdale,** NY,US
22/E1 **Scar Water** (riv.), Sc,UK
19/S10 **Sceaux,** Fr.
36/B2 **Scey-Saint-Albin,** Fr.
26/C3 **Schaerbeek,** Belg.
30/D2 **Schaerbeek,** Belg.
32/F1 **Schaerbeek,** Belg.
26/E5 **Schaffhausen,** Swi.
33/H3 **Schaffhausen,** Swi.
37/E2 **Schaffhausen,** Swi.
37/E2 **Schaffhausen** (canton), Swi.
37/H2 **Schäftlarn,** Ger.
26/C2 **Schagen,** Neth.
28/B3 **Schagen,** Neth.
28/C5 **Schaijk,** Neth.
29/E6 **Schalksmühle,** Ger.
31/G1 **Schalksmühle,** Ger.
73/C3 **Schanck** (cape), Austl.
36/D4 **Schangnau,** Swi.
37/F4 **Scharans,** Swi.
27/G4 **Schärding,** Aus.
33/K2 **Schärding,** Aus.
37/H2 **Scharfreiter** (peak), Aus.
29/F1 **Scharhorn** (isl.), Ger.
37/H3 **Scharnitz** (pass), Ger.
26/F1 **Schashagen,** Ger.
37/E3 **Schattdorf,** Swi.
37/E4 **Schattdorf,** Swi.
99/P15 **Schaumburg,** Il,US
28/D2 **Scheemda,** Neth.
37/F1 **Scheer,** Ger.
26/E2 **Scheessel,** Ger.
29/G2 **Scheessel,** Ger.
87/K3 **Schefferville,** Qu,Can
27/H4 **Scheibbs,** Aus.
37/F2 **Scheidegg,** Ger.
28/B6 **Schelde** (Scheldt) (riv.), Belg.
30/C2 **Schelde** (Scheldt) (riv.), Belg.
32/E1 **Scheldt** (riv.), Belg.
28/B6 **Scheldt** (Schelde) (riv.), Belg.
30/C2 **Scheldt** (Schelde) (riv.), Belg.
37/F1 **Schelklingen,** Ger.
92/D3 **Schell Creek** (range), Nv,US
29/H4 **Schellerten,** Ger.
99/K10 **Schellville,** Ca,US
87/J4 **Schenectady,** NY,US
89/M3 **Schenectady,** NY,US
97/F3 **Schenectady,** NY,US
29/G1 **Schenefeld,** Ger.
99/R16 **Schererville,** In,US
28/D5 **Schermbeck,** Ger.
28/C3 **Scherpenzeel,** Neth.
101/F2 **Schertz,** Tx,US
37/F2 **Scherzingen,** Swi.
37/F3 **Schesaplana** (peak), Aus.
37/H1 **Scheyern,** Ger.
26/C3 **Schiedam,** Neth.
28/B5 **Schiedam,** Neth.
29/G5 **Schieder-Schwalenberg,** Ger.
26/D2 **Schiermonnikoog** (isl.), Neth.
28/D2 **Schiermonnikoog,** Neth.
28/D2 **Schiermonnikoog** (isl.), Neth.
33/H3 **Schiers,** Swi.
37/F4 **Schiers,** Swi.
31/G5 **Schiffweiler,** Ger.
28/C5 **Schijndel,** Neth.
28/B6 **Schilde,** Belg.
30/D1 **Schilde,** Belg.
28/D2 **Schildmeer** (lake), Neth.
29/F1 **Schillighörn** (cape), Ger.
37/E1 **Schiltach,** Ger.
31/G6 **Schiltigheim,** Fr.
36/D1 **Schiltigheim,** Fr.
31/E2 **Schinnen,** Neth.
36/E3 **Schinznach-Dorf,** Swi.
28/D4 **Schipbeek** (riv.), Neth.
36/D1 **Schirmeck,** Fr.
39/G2 **Schkumbin** (riv.), Alb.
29/H4 **Schladen,** Ger.
40/A2 **Schladming,** Aus.
33/J3 **Schlanders** (Silandro), It.
37/G4 **Schlanders** (Silandro), It.
29/F5 **Schlangen,** Ger.
31/H3 **Schlangenbad,** Ger.
26/D3 **Schleiden,** Ger.
31/F2 **Schleiden,** Ger.
33/G1 **Schleiden,** Ger.
37/E2 **Schleitheim,** Swi.
26/E1 **Schleswig,** Ger.
26/E1 **Schleswig-Holstein** (state), Ger.
29/H1 **Schleswig-Holstein** (state), Ger.
26/E1 **Schleswig-Holsteinisches Wattenmeer Nat'l Park,** Ger.
36/D2 **Schliengen,** Ger.
37/E3 **Schlieren,** Swi.
29/F5 **Schloss Holte-Stukenbrock,** Ger.
29/G4 **Schloss Wilhelmstein,** Ger.
36/E2 **Schluchsee,** Ger.
36/D1 **Schlucht, Col de la** (pass), Fr.
26/E3 **Schlüchtern,** Ger.
33/H1 **Schlüchtern,** Ger.
37/G4 **Schluderns** (Sluderno), It.
26/F3 **Schmalkalden,** Ger.
33/J1 **Schmalkalden,** Ger.
29/F6 **Schmallenberg,** Ger.
31/H1 **Schmallenberg,** Ger.
37/F1 **Schmeich** (riv.), Ger.
37/F1 **Schmeie** (riv.), Ger.
31/F5 **Schmelz,** Ger.
36/D4 **Schmitten,** Swi.
98/E5 **Schnecksville,** Pa,US
26/D4 **Schneifel** (upland), Ger.
31/F3 **Schneifel** (plat.), Ger.
33/G1 **Schneifel** (plat.), Ger.
26/E2 **Schneverdingen,** Ger.
29/G2 **Schneverdingen,** Ger.
88/V12 **Schofield Barracks,** Hi,US
37/E1 **Schömberg,** Ger.
36/D2 **Schönau,** Ger.
37/H1 **Schondorf am Ammersee,** Ger.
26/F2 **Schönebeck,** Ger.
31/F3 **Schönecken,** Ger.
26/F5 **Schongau,** Ger.
37/G2 **Schongau,** Ger.
26/F2 **Schöningen,** Ger.
28/D3 **Schoonebeek,** Neth.
28/B5 **Schoonhoven,** Neth.
28/B3 **Schoorl,** Neth.
31/G4 **Schopfheim,** Ger.
36/D2 **Schopfheim,** Ger.
29/H4 **Schöppenstedt,** Ger.
29/E1 **Schortens,** Ger.
28/B6 **Schoten,** Belg.
30/D1 **Schoten,** Belg.
73/D4 **Schouten** (isl.), Austl.
68/C5 **Schouten** (isls.), Indo.
28/A5 **Schouwen** (isl.), Neth.
32/D5 **Schrader** (peak), Fr.
35/F1 **Schrader** (peak), Fr.
76/H3 **Şchrā Marzūq** (des.), Libya
26/E4 **Schramberg,** Ger.
33/H2 **Schramberg,** Ger.
37/E1 **Schramberg,** Ger.
37/H3 **Schrankogel** (peak), Aus.
36/E4 **Schreckhorn** (peak), Swi.
91/M3 **Schreiber,** On,Can
94/C1 **Schreiber,** On,Can
26/F4 **Schrobenhausen,** Ger.
80/B2 **Schroffenstein** (peak), Namb.
33/H3 **Schruns,** Aus.
37/F3 **Schruns,** Aus.
37/E3 **Schübelbach,** Swi.
26/E1 **Schuby,** Ger.
93/H5 **Schulenburg,** Tx,US
96/D4 **Schulenburg,** Tx,US
29/H4 **Schunter** (riv.), Ger.
36/E4 **Schüpfheim,** Swi.
37/F2 **Schussen** (riv.), Ger.
37/F1 **Schussenried,** Ger.
36/D1 **Schutter** (riv.), Ger.
36/D1 **Schutterwald,** Ger.
29/E4 **Schüttorf,** Ger.
98/E5 **Schuylkill** (riv.), Pa,US
26/F4 **Schwabach,** Ger.
33/J2 **Schwabach,** Ger.
37/H1 **Schwabhausen bei Dachau,** Ger.
26/E4 **Schwäbische Alb** (mts.), Ger.
33/H2 **Schwabische Alb** (range), Ger.
37/E1 **Schwäbische Alb** (uplands), Ger.
26/E4 **Schwäbisch Gmünd,** Ger.
26/E4 **Schwäbisch Hall,** Ger.
33/H2 **Schwäbisch Hall,** Ger.
37/G1 **Schwabmünchen,** Ger.
31/F5 **Schwalbach,** Ger.
26/E3 **Schwalm** (riv.), Ger.
29/G6 **Schwalm** (riv.), Ger.
28/D6 **Schwalmtal,** Ger.
31/F1 **Schwalmtal,** Ger.
37/F4 **Schwanden,** Swi.
26/G4 **Schwandorf im Bayern,** Ger.
33/K2 **Schwandorf im Bayern,** Ger.
66/D4 **Schwaner** (mts.), Indo.
29/F2 **Schwanewede,** Ger.
37/G2 **Schwangau,** Ger.
26/E2 **Schwarmstedt,** Ger.
29/G3 **Schwarmstedt,** Ger.
27/G3 **Schwartz Elster** (riv.), Ger.
80/B2 **Schwartzerberg** (peak), Namb.
40/A2 **Schwarzach im Pongau,** Aus.
26/F2 **Schwarzenbek,** Ger.
29/H2 **Schwarzenbek,** Ger.
31/F3 **Schwarzer Mann** (peak), Ger.
37/H3 **Schwarzhorn** (peak), Aus.
26/F5 **Schwaz,** Aus.
33/J3 **Schwaz,** Aus.
27/J4 **Schwechat,** Aus.
33/M2 **Schwechat,** Aus.
27/H2 **Schwedt,** Ger.
31/F4 **Schweich,** Ger.
31/G6 **Schweighouse-sur-Moder,** Fr.
26/F3 **Schweinfurt,** Ger.
33/J1 **Schweinfurt,** Ger.
29/E6 **Schwelm,** Ger.
37/F1 **Schwendi,** Ger.
98/E5 **Schwenksville,** Pa,US
18/E3 **Schwerin,** Ger.
26/F2 **Schwerin,** Ger.
46/B4 **Schwerin,** Ger.
26/F2 **Schweriner** (lake), Ger.
29/E6 **Schwerte,** Ger.
29/G1 **Schwinge** (riv.), Ger.
36/D2 **Schwörstadt,** Ger.
29/G5 **Schwülme** (riv.), Ger.
29/H4 **Schwülper,** Ger.
33/H3 **Schwyz,** Swi.
37/E3 **Schwyz,** Swi.
37/E3 **Schwyz** (canton), Swi.
38/C4 **Sciacca,** It.
38/D4 **Scicli,** It.
27/J3 **Ścinawa,** Pol.
33/G3 **Scionzier,** Fr.
36/C5 **Scionzier,** Fr.
98/E5 **Sciota,** Pa,US
94/D4 **Scioto** (riv.), Oh,US
91/G3 **Scobey,** Mt,US
25/G1 **Scolt** (pt.), UK
73/D2 **Scone,** Austl.
38/D4 **Scordia,** It.
23/G3 **Scotch Corner,** Eng,UK
83/W **Scotia** (sea), Ant.
18/C3 **Scotland,** UK
21/C2 **Scotland,** UK
22/A3 **Scotstown,** Ire.
83/L **Scott** (coast), Ant.
83/M **Scott,** Ant.
70/C2 **Scott** (reef), Austl.
86/D3 **Scott** (cape), BC,Can
86/F2 **Scott** (lake), NW,Can
87/R7 **Scott** (cape), NW,Can
93/G3 **Scott City,** Ks,US
96/C2 **Scott City,** Ks,US
86/F4 **Scottsbluff,** Ne,US
88/F3 **Scottsbluff,** Ne,US
91/H5 **Scottsbluff,** Ne,US
93/G2 **Scottsbluff,** Ne,US
93/F2 **Scotts Bluff Nat'l Mon.,** Ne,US
97/G3 **Scottsboro,** Al,US
94/C4 **Scottsburg,** In,US
97/G2 **Scottsburg,** In,US
73/C4 **Scottsdale,** Austl.
88/D5 **Scottsdale,** Az,US
92/E4 **Scottsdale,** Az,US
73/C4 **Scotts Peak** (dam), Austl.
94/C4 **Scottsville,** Ky,US
97/G2 **Scottsville,** Ky,US
94/C3 **Scottville,** Mi,US
89/L3 **Scranton,** Pa,US
94/F3 **Scranton,** Pa,US
23/H4 **Scunthorpe,** Eng,UK
37/G4 **Scuol,** Swi.
99/N14 **Scuppernong** (riv.), Wi,US
39/F1 **Scutari** (lake), Alb., Yugo.
40/D4 **Scutari** (lake), Alb., Yugo.
40/D4 **Scutari** (lake), Yugo.
89/K5 **Sea** (isls.), Ga,US
99/B2 **Seabeck,** Wa,US
99/B2 **Seabold,** Wa,US
25/G5 **Seaford,** Eng,UK
22/C3 **Seaforde,** NI,UK
72/C3 **Seaforth,** Austl.
100/E1 **Seagraves,** Tx,US
23/G2 **Seaham,** Eng,UK
87/H2 **Seahorse** (pt.), NW,Can
86/G3 **Seal** (riv.), Mb,Can
80/C4 **Seal** (cape), SAfr.
19/P8 **Seal,** Eng,UK
73/B2 **Sea Lake,** Austl.
98/B3 **Seal Beach,** Ca,US
23/H3 **Seamer,** Eng,UK
108/A3 **Seara,** Braz.
92/D4 **Searchlight,** Nv,US
89/H4 **Searcy,** Ar,US
93/K4 **Searcy,** Ar,US
96/F3 **Searcy,** Ar,US
22/E3 **Seascale,** Eng,UK
88/B2 **Seaside,** Or,US
90/C4 **Seaside,** Or,US
98/F6 **Seaside Heights,** NJ,US
98/F6 **Seaside Park,** NJ,US
99/C3 **SeaTac,** Wa,US
24/B6 **Seaton** (riv.), Eng,UK
24/C5 **Seaton,** Eng,UK
32/B1 **Seaton,** Eng,UK
23/G2 **Seaton Carew,** Eng,UK
23/G1 **Seaton Valley,** Eng,UK
86/D4 **Seattle,** Wa,US
88/B2 **Seattle,** Wa,US
90/C4 **Seattle,** Wa,US
99/C2 **Seattle,** Wa,US
99/C2 **Seattle Art Museum,** Wa,US
99/C2 **Seattle Ctr.,** Wa,US
102/E3 **Sébaco,** Nic.
75/T15 **Sebaou** (riv.), Alg.
97/H5 **Sebastian,** Fl,US
100/B2 **Sebastián Vizcaíno** (bay), Mex.
73/B3 **Sebastopol,** Austl.
66/D4 **Sebayan** (peak), Indo.
52/C5 **Sebderat,** Eth.
75/Q16 **Sebdou,** Alg.
41/K5 **Seben,** Turk.
41/F3 **Sebeş,** Rom.
44/B3 **Sebeş,** Rom.
44/F4 **Şebinkarahisar,** Turk.
50/D1 **Şebinkarahisar,** Turk.
40/F2 **Sebiş,** Rom.
27/H3 **Sebnitz,** Ger.
103/H4 **Seboruco,** Ven.
67/F2 **Seboto** (pt.), Phil.
75/M13 **Sebou** (riv.), Mor.
89/K6 **Sebring,** Fl,US
97/H5 **Sebring,** Fl,US
67/E4 **Sebuku** (isl.), Indo.
109/C4 **Seca** (plain), Arg.
33/J4 **Secchia** (riv.), It.
106/B5 **Sechura,** Peru
106/B5 **Sechura** (bay), Peru
106/B5 **Sechura** (des.), Peru
30/C2 **Seclin,** Fr.
100/C2 **Seco** (riv.), Mex.
92/E5 **Seco** (dry riv.), Mex
77/M3 **Second** (fall, falls), Sudan
80/Q13 **Secunda,** SAfr.
62/C4 **Secunderābād,** India
106/E7 **Securé** (riv.), Bol.
89/H4 **Sedalia,** Mo,US
93/J3 **Sedalia,** Mo,US
96/E2 **Sedalia,** Mo,US
26/C4 **Sedan,** Fr.
31/D4 **Sedan,** Fr.
32/F2 **Sedan,** Fr.
34/D1 **Sedano,** Sp.
65/B3 **Sedaung** (mtn.), Burma
23/F3 **Sedbergh,** Eng,UK
39/K2 **Seddülbahir,** Turk.
49/D4 **Sederot,** Isr.
23/G2 **Sedgefield,** Eng,UK
85/L2 **Sedgwick** (mtn.), Yk,Can
78/B3 **Sédhiou,** Sen.
27/H3 **Sedlo** (peak), Czh.
33/L1 **Sedlo** (peak), Czh.
88/D5 **Sedona,** Az,US
92/E4 **Sedona,** Az,US
49/F7 **Sedot Yam,** Isr.
75/V17 **Sedrata,** Alg.
27/L3 **Sędziszów,** Pol.
32/C2 **Sée** (riv.), Fr.
40/A2 **Seeboden,** Aus.
37/H3 **Seefeld in Tirol,** Aus.
37/G2 **Seeg,** Ger.
26/F2 **Seehausen,** Ger.
82/C6 **Seeheim,** Namb.
80/D3 **Seekooi** (riv.), SAfr.
27/H2 **Seelow,** Ger.
32/D2 **Sées,** Fr.
29/H5 **Seesen,** Ger.
29/G2 **Seeve** (riv.), Ger.
37/F4 **Seewis im Prättigau,** Swi.
44/E5 **Şefaatli,** Turk.
50/C2 **Şefaatli,** Turk.
51/G2 **Sefīd Rūd** (riv.), Iran
75/M14 **Sefrou,** Mor.
66/B3 **Segamat,** Malay.
41/F3 **Segarcea,** Rom.
38/C4 **Segesta** (ruins), It.
42/G3 **Segezha,** Rus.
35/E3 **Segorbe,** Sp.
76/D5 **Ségou,** Mali
78/D3 **Ségou,** Mali
78/D3 **Ségou** (reg.), Mali
34/C2 **Segovia,** Sp.
42/G3 **Segozero** (lake), Rus.
32/C3 **Segré,** Fr.
35/F2 **Segre** (riv.), Sp.
85/D5 **Seguam** (isl.), Ak,US
85/D5 **Seguam** (passg.), Ak,US
76/H3 **Séguédine,** Niger
76/D6 **Séguéla,** IvC.
78/D5 **Séguéla,** IvC.
101/F2 **Seguin,** Tx,US
89/G6 **Seguin,** Tx,US
93/H5 **Seguin,** Tx,US
96/D4 **Seguin,** Tx,US
34/D3 **Segura** (riv.), Sp.
82/D5 **Sehithwa,** Bots.
53/L4 **Sehore,** India
62/C3 **Sehore,** India
53/J3 **Sehwān,** Pak.
62/A2 **Sehwān,** Pak.
31/G4 **Seibersbach,** Ger.
40/B2 **Seiersberg,** Aus.
57/L10 **Seika,** Japan
36/B4 **Seille** (riv.), Fr.
93/H3 **Seiling,** Ok,US
96/D2 **Seiling,** Ok,US
26/D4 **Seille** (riv.), Fr.
31/F6 **Seille** (riv.), Fr.
32/F3 **Seille** (riv.), Fr.
20/G3 **Seinäjoki,** Fin.
42/D3 **Seinäjoki,** Fin.
91/L3 **Seine** (riv.), On,Can
86/G4 **Seine** (riv.), On,Can
18/D4 **Seine** (riv.), Fr.
19/S10 **Seine** (riv.), Fr.
26/B4 **Seine** (riv.), Fr.
30/A5 **Seine** (riv.), Fr.
32/C2 **Seine** (bay), Fr.
32/D2 **Seine** (riv.), Fr.
19/U10 **Seine-et-Marne** (dept.), Fr.
30/B5 **Seine-et-Marne** (dept.), Fr.
30/A4 **Seine-Maritime** (dept.), Fr.
19/T10 **Seine-Saint-Denis** (dept.), Fr.
30/B6 **Seine-St-Denis** (dept.), Fr.
20/G3 **Seitsemisen Nat'l Park,** Fin.
42/D3 **Seitsemisen Nat'l Park,** Fin.
57/M10 **Seiwa,** Japan
32/D5 **Seix,** Fr.
35/F1 **Seix,** Fr.
35/P10 **Seixal,** Port.
27/M1 **Sejny,** Pol.
42/D5 **Sejny,** Pol.
57/E3 **Seki,** Japan
57/M10 **Seki,** Japan
49/A1 **Seki** (riv.), Turk.
57/M9 **Sekigahara,** Japan
57/H6 **Sekiyado,** Japan
80/C2 **Sekoma,** Bots.
76/E7 **Sekondi,** Gha.
79/E5 **Sekondi,** Gha.
90/C4 **Selah,** Wa,US
63/H4 **Selaphum,** Thai.
38/A3 **Selargius,** It.
67/H5 **Selaru** (isl.), Indo.
66/D4 **Selatan** (cape), Indo.
85/F2 **Selawik,** Ak,US
85/F2 **Selawik** (lake), Ak,US
85/G2 **Selawik Nat'l Wild. Ref.,** Ak,US
67/F5 **Selayar** (isl.), Indo.
26/G3 **Selb,** Ger.
33/K1 **Selb,** Ger.
20/D3 **Selbu,** Nor.
23/G4 **Selby,** Eng,UK
91/H4 **Selby,** SD,US
98/K8 **Selby-on-the-Bay,** Md,US
33/K5 **Selci,** It.
50/A2 **Selçuk,** Turk.
85/H4 **Seldovia,** Ak,US
38/D2 **Sele** (riv.), It.
40/B5 **Sele** (riv.), It.
82/E5 **Selebi-Phikwe,** Bots.
47/P4 **Selemdzha** (riv.), Rus.
55/L1 **Selemdzha** (riv.), Rus.
40/D3 **Selenča,** Yugo.
50/B2 **Selendi,** Turk.
54/F1 **Selenga** (riv.), Rus.
54/E2 **Selenge,** Mong.
54/E2 **Selenge** (riv.), Mong.
47/L4 **Selenginsk,** Rus.
40/D5 **Selenicë,** Alb.
26/D4 **Sélestat,** Fr.
33/G2 **Sélestat,** Fr.
36/D1 **Sélestat,** Fr.
20/N7 **Selfoss,** Ice.
76/C4 **Sélibabi,** Mrta.
78/B3 **Sélibabi,** Mrta.
42/G4 **Seliger** (lake), Rus.
92/D4 **Seligman,** Az,US
50/A2 **Selimiye,** Turk.
38/C4 **Selinunte** (ruins), It.
90/D3 **Selkirk** (mts.), BC,Can
86/G3 **Selkirk,** Mb,Can
89/G1 **Selkirk,** Mb,Can
91/J3 **Selkirk,** Mb,Can
99/D3 **Selleck,** Wa,US
98/E5 **Sellersville,** Pa,US
36/B4 **Sellières,** Fr.
92/E5 **Sells,** Az,US
40/C3 **Sellye,** Hun.
24/E2 **Selly Oak,** Eng,UK
29/E5 **Selm,** Ger.
89/J5 **Selma,** Al,US
97/G3 **Selma,** Al,US
97/F3 **Selmer,** Tn,US
36/B2 **Selongey,** Fr.
85/M3 **Selous** (mtn.), Yk,Can
25/F5 **Selsey,** Eng,UK
32/C1 **Selsey Bill** (pt.), UK
25/F5 **Selsey Bill** (pt.), Eng,UK
29/G2 **Selsingen,** Ger.
31/H6 **Seltz,** Fr.
32/C2 **Sélune** (riv.), Fr.
105/L3 **Selvas** (for.), Braz.
106/E5 **Selvas** (reg.), Braz.
72/A3 **Selwyn** (mts.), Austl.
33/H2 **Selz** (riv.), Ger.
76/C2 **Semara,** WSah.
66/D5 **Semarang,** Indo.
51/F2 **Şemdinli,** Turk.
52/D1 **Şemdinli,** Turk.
32/D5 **Séméac,** Fr.
35/F1 **Séméac,** Fr.
43/K4 **Semenov,** Rus.
66/D5 **Semeru** (peak), Indo.
85/G4 **Semidi** (isls.), Ak,US
45/G1 **Semilovo,** Rus.
44/F2 **Semiluki,** Rus.
90/G5 **Seminoe** (res.), Wy,US
100/E1 **Seminole,** Tx,US
93/G4 **Seminole,** Tx,US
96/C3 **Seminole,** Tx,US
46/J4 **Semipalatinsk,** Kaz.
85/B5 **Semisopochnoi** (isl.), Ak,US
66/D4 **Semitau,** Indo.
46/F6 **Semnān,** Iran
51/H3 **Semnān,** Iran
51/H3 **Semnān** (gov.), Iran
52/F1 **Semnān,** Iran
32/C3 **Semnon** (riv.), Fr.
31/E4 **Semois** (riv.), Belg.
32/F2 **Semois** (riv.), Belg.
36/C2 **Semouse** (riv.), Fr.
36/B1 **Semoutiers,** Fr.
31/D4 **Semoy** (riv.), Fr.
36/E3 **Sempach,** Swi.
36/E3 **Sempacher See** (lake), Swi.
67/E3 **Semporna,** Malay.
36/C4 **Semsales,** Swi.
42/B2 **Semskefjellet** (peak), Nor.
63/H5 **Sen** (riv.), Camb.
65/D3 **Sen** (riv.), Camb.
63/H5 **Sena,** Thai.
65/C3 **Sena,** Thai.
52/C6 **Sen'afē,** Eth.
67/E2 **Senaja,** Malay.
82/D4 **Senanga,** Zam.
93/K4 **Senatobia,** Ms,US
97/F3 **Senatobia,** Ms,US
25/E2 **Sence** (riv.), Eng,UK
47/Q6 **Sendai,** Japan
55/N4 **Sendai,** Japan
56/B5 **Sendai,** Japan
56/B5 **Sendai** (riv.), Japan
56/D3 **Sendai** (riv.), Japan
57/G1 **Sendai,** Japan
57/G1 **Sendai** (bay), Japan
26/F4 **Senden,** Ger.
29/E5 **Senden,** Ger.
37/G1 **Senden,** Ger.
29/E5 **Sendenhorst,** Ger.
27/J4 **Senec,** Slvk.
30/D2 **Seneffe,** Belg.
74/A3 **Senegal**
76/C5 **Senegal**
78/B3 **Senegal**
74/A3 **Sénégal** (riv.), Afr.
76/B4 **Sénégal** (riv.), Afr.
78/B2 **Sénégal** (riv.), Afr.
80/D3 **Senekal,** SAfr.
94/C2 **Seney Nat'l Wild. Ref.,** Mi,US
43/X8 **Senezhkoye** (lake), Rus.
27/H3 **Senftenberg,** Ger.
108/B3 **Sengés,** Braz.
109/B6 **Senguerr** (riv.), Arg.
107/K6 **Senhor do Bonfim,** Braz.
27/J4 **Senica,** Slvk.
33/K5 **Senigallia,** It.
50/B2 **Senirkent,** Turk.
38/E2 **Senise,** It.
33/L4 **Senj,** Cro.
40/B3 **Senj,** Cro.
20/F1 **Senja** (isl.), Nor.
45/G4 **Şenkaya,** Turk.
50/E1 **Şenkaya,** Turk.
26/B4 **Senlis,** Fr.
30/B5 **Senlis,** Fr.
32/E2 **Senlis,** Paris
63/J5 **Senmonoron,** Camb.
66/C1 **Senmonoron,** Camb.
57/L10 **Sennan,** Japan
77/M5 **Sennar** (dam), Sudan
30/D2 **Senne** (riv.), Belg.
36/A4 **Sennecy-le-Grand,** Fr.
94/E1 **Senneterre,** Qu,Can
37/F3 **Sennwald,** Swi.
24/C3 **Sennybridge,** Wal,UK
79/F3 **Séno** (prov.), Burk.
40/D1 **Senohrad,** Slvk.
36/C1 **Senones,** Fr.
38/A3 **Senorbì,** It.
41/H4 **Senovo,** Bul.
26/B4 **Sens,** Fr.
32/E2 **Sens,** Fr.
102/D3 **Sensuntepeque,** ESal.
40/E3 **Senta,** Yugo.
82/E2 **Sentery,** Zaire
90/C2 **Sentinel** (peak), Can
68/E4 **Senyavin** (isls.), Micr.
36/E3 **Seon,** Swi.
62/C3 **Seoni,** India
62/C3 **Seonī Mālwā,** India
47/N6 **Seoul** (cap.), SKor.
58/G6 **Seoul** (prov.), SKor.
58/G7 **Seoul Grand Park,** SKor.
58/D4 **Seoul-Jikhalsi,** SKor.
55/K4 **Seoul** (Sŏul) (cap.), SKor.
58/D4 **Seoul** (Sŏul) (cap.), SKor.
58/F6 **Seoul** (Sŏul) (cap.), SKor.
108/D2 **Sepetiba** (bay), Braz.
68/D5 **Sepik** (riv.), PNG
27/J2 **Sępólno Krajeńskie,** Pol.
39/J1 **Septemvri,** Bul.
41/G4 **Septemvri,** Bul.
30/A6 **Septeuil,** Fr.
84/L4 **Sept-Îles,** Can.
87/K3 **Sept-Îles,** Qu,Can
95/H1 **Sept-Îles,** Qu,Can
34/B2 **Sequeros,** Sp.
99/A1 **Sequim** (bay), Wa,US
88/C4 **Sequoia Nat'l Park,** Ca,US
92/C3 **Sequoia Nat'l Park,** Ca,US
26/C3 **Seraing,** Belg.
31/E2 **Seraing,** Belg.
32/F1 **Seraing,** Belg.
36/B6 **Séran** (riv.), Fr.
66/C5 **Serang,** Indo.
66/C3 **Serasan** (str.), Indo., Malay.
39/G1 **Serbia** (reg.), Yugo.
39/G1 **Serbia** (rep.), Yugo.
40/E4 **Serbia** (rep.), Yugo.
45/H1 **Serdobsk,** Rus.
85/D2 **Serdtse-Kamen, Mys** (pt.), Rus.
44/F1 **Serednikovo,** Rus.
27/M1 **Seredžius,** Lith.
50/C2 **Şereflikoçhisar,** Tu
26/C5 **Serein** (riv.), Fr.
32/F3 **Serein** (riv.), Fr.
31/F5 **Serémange-Erzange,** Fr.
66/B3 **Seremban,** Malay.
82/F1 **Serengeti** (plain), Tanz.
77/M8 **Serengeti Nat'l Park,** Tanz.
82/F1 **Serengeti Nat'l Park,** Tanz.
82/F3 **Serenje,** Zam.
43/K5 **Sergach,** Rus.
46/J2 **Sergeya Kirova** (isls.), Rus.
18/G3 **Sergiyev Posad,** Ru
42/H4 **Sergiyev Posad,** Rus.
46/D4 **Sergiyev Posad,** Ru
66/D3 **Seria,** Bru.
33/H4 **Seriate,** It.
30/A5 **Sérifontaine,** Fr.
39/J4 **Sérifos,** Gre.
39/J4 **Sérifos** (isl.), Gre.
32/E5 **Sérignan,** Fr.
49/B1 **Serik,** Turk.
50/B2 **Serik,** Turk.
52/B1 **Serik,** Turk.
107/H5 **Seringa** (mts.), Braz.
31/D6 **Sermaize-les-Bains,** Fr.
67/G5 **Sermata** (isl.), Indo.
34/D4 **Serón,** Sp.
35/F2 **Serós,** Sp.
37/G5 **Serottini, Monte** (peak), It.
46/G4 **Serov,** Rus.
82/E5 **Serowe,** Bots.
34/B4 **Serpa,** Port.
38/A3 **Serpeddi** (peak), It.
70/D5 **Serpentine** (lakes), Austl.
73/C4 **Serpentine** (dam), Austl.
78/C3 **Serpent, Vallée du** (wadi), Mali
18/G3 **Serpukhov,** Rus.
42/H5 **Serpukhov,** Rus.
44/F1 **Serpukhov,** Rus.
46/D4 **Serpukhov,** Rus.
108/D2 **Serra,** Braz.
107/K8 **Serra da Bocaina Nat'l Park,** Braz.
108/C2 **Serra da Bocaina Nat'l Park,** Braz.
108/C2 **Serra da Canastra Nat'l Park,** Braz.
107/K5 **Serra da Capivara Nat'l Park,** Braz.
18/F4 **Sérrai,** Gre.
39/H2 **Sérrai,** Gre.
41/F5 **Sérrai,** Gre.
44/B4 **Sérrai,** Gre.
38/E3 **Serralta di San Vito** (peak), It.
38/A3 **Serramanna,** It.
106/E3 **Serranía de la Neblina Nat'l Park,** Ven.
103/G3 **Serranilla Bank** (reef), Col.
108/B1 **Serranópolis,** Braz.
38/E3 **Serra San Bruno,** It
38/A4 **Serrat** (cape), Tun.
75/W17 **Serrat** (cape), Tun.
107/L5 **Serra Talhada,** Bra
26/B4 **Serre** (riv.), Fr.
30/C4 **Serre** (riv.), Fr.
32/E2 **Serre** (riv.), Fr.
38/A3 **Serrenti,** It.
36/A3 **Serrigny,** Fr.
107/L6 **Serrinha,** Braz.
38/A3 **Sersale,** It.
34/A3 **Sertã,** Port.
108/C2 **Sertãozinho,** Braz.
49/C1 **Sertavul** (pass), Tu
50/C2 **Sertavul** (pass), Tu
54/C4 **Serteng** (mts.), Chir
66/D4 **Seruyan** (riv.), Indo
36/C2 **Servance,** Fr.
39/H2 **Sérvia,** Gre.
82/D4 **Sesheke,** Zam.
33/H4 **Sesia** (riv.), It.
34/A3 **Sesimbra,** Port.
35/P11 **Sesimbra,** Port.
32/B5 **Sestao,** Sp.
34/D1 **Sestao,** Sp.
33/J5 **Sesto Fiorentino,** It
33/H4 **Sesto San Giovann** It.
43/X8 **Sestra** (riv.), Rus.
43/U6 **Sestroretsk,** Rus.
43/V6 **Sestroretskiy Razli** (lake), Rus.
38/A3 **Sestu,** It.
37/G4 **Sesvenna, Piz** (pea It.
33/M4 **Sesvete,** Cro.
40/B3 **Sesvete,** Cro.
32/E5 **Sète,** Fr.
35/G1 **Sète,** Fr.
107/K7 **Sete Lagoas,** Braz.
108/C1 **Sete Lagoas,** Braz.
53/J3 **Sethārja,** Pak.
62/A2 **Sethārja,** Pak.
75/T15 **Sétif** (wilaya), Alg.
75/U17 **Sétif,** Alg.
75/U17 **Sétif** (wilaya), Alg.
76/G1 **Sétif,** Alg.
57/E3 **Seto,** Japan
57/N9 **Seto,** Japan
56/C3 **Seto-Naikai Nat'l Park,** Japan
56/C4 **Setonaikai Nat'l Park,** Japan
57/K10 **Seto-Naikai Nat'l Park,** Japan
33/G4 **Settimo Torinese,**
91/J2 **Setting** (lake), Mb,Can
23/F3 **Settle,** Eng,UK

)4/B1 **Settlement** (pt.), Bahm.
7/L10 **Settsu**, Japan
18/C5 **Setúbal**, Port.
34/A3 **Setúbal**, Port.
34/A3 **Setúbal** (dist.), Port.
5/Q10 **Setúbal**, Port.
5/Q10 **Setúbal** (dist.), Port.
5/Q11 **Setúbal** (bay), Port.
34/B4 **Setúbal** (bay), Sp.
32/C4 **Seudre** (riv.), Fr.
32/C4 **Seugne** (riv.), Fr.
31/K3 **Seul** (lake), On,Can
36/G3 **Seul** (lake), On,Can
34/A1 **Seul** (lake), On,Can
36/B4 **Seurre**, Fr.
37/E2 **Seuzach**, Swi.
45/H4 **Sevan** (lake), Arm.
46/E5 **Sevan** (lake), Arm.
51/F1 **Sevan**, Arm.
51/F1 **Sevan** (lake), Arm.
51/F1 **Sevan Nat'l Park**, Arm.
19/G4 **Sevastopol'**, Ukr.
14/E3 **Sevastopol'**, Ukr.
46/D5 **Sevastopol'**, Ukr.
37/F3 **Sevelen**, Swi.
23/H3 **Seven** (riv.), Eng,UK
21/A5 **Seven Heads** (pt.), Ire.
21/G7 **Seven Hogs** (isls.), Ire.
21/G7 **Seven Hogs** (pt.), Ire.
19/P8 **Sevenoaks**, Eng,UK
25/G4 **Sevenoaks**, Eng,UK
91/L2 **Severn** (riv.), On,Can
36/G3 **Severn** (riv.), On,Can
23/F6 **Severn** (riv.), Eng,UK
24/D3 **Severn** (riv.), Eng,UK
38/K7 **Severn**, Md,US
38/K7 **Severn** (riv.), Md,US
38/K7 **Severna Park**, Md,US
43/P3 **Severnaya Sos'va** (riv.), Rus.
48/K2 **Severnaya Zemlya** (isls.), Rus.
46/J2 **Severnaya Zemlya** (arch.), Rus.
24/C4 **Severn, Mouth of the** (est.), U. K.
43/Q2 **Severnyy**, Rus.
27/G3 **Severočeský** (reg.), Czh.
33/L1 **Severočeský** (reg.), Czh.
19/G4 **Severodonetsk**, Ukr.
44/F2 **Severodonetsk**, Ukr.
48/D5 **Severodonetsk**, Ukr.
48/G2 **Severodvinsk**, Rus.
42/H2 **Severodvinsk**, Rus.
46/D3 **Severodvinsk**, Rus.
47/R4 **Severo-Kuril'sk**, Rus.
3/M1 **Severomoravský** (reg.), Czh.
27/J4 **Severomoravský** (reg.), Slvk.
20/K1 **Severomorsk**, Rus.
42/G1 **Severomorsk**, Rus.
43/N3 **Severoural'sk**, Rus.
46/F3 **Severoural'sk**, Rus.
38/D4 **Sevier** (lake), Ut,US
48/D4 **Sevier** (riv.), Ut,US
32/D3 **Sevier** (des.), Ut,US
32/D3 **Sevier** (riv.), Ut,US
37/H3 **Sevierville**, Tn,US
73/G5 **Seville**, Austl.
32/C5 **Seville**, Sp.
34/C4 **Seville**, Sp.
39/J1 **Sevlievo**, Bul.
1/G4 **Sevlievo**, Bul.
33/L3 **Sevnica**, Slov.
40/B2 **Sevnica**, Slov.
40/D4 **Sevojno**, Yugo.
3/T10 **Sevran**, Fr.
3/S10 **Sèvres**, Fr.
76/C6 **Sewa** (riv.), SLeo.
78/C5 **Sewa** (riv.), SLeo.
85/E2 **Seward** (pen.), Ak,US
85/J3 **Seward**, Ak,US
36/D2 **Seward**, Ak,US
91/J5 **Seward**, Ne,US
93/H2 **Seward**, Ne,US
5/M5 **Sewell Inlet**, BC,Can
90/D2 **Sexsmith**, Ab,Can
1/H5 **Seybaplaya**, Mex.
2/D2 **Seybaplaya**, Mex.
5/V17 **Seybouse** (riv.), Alg.
5/H5 **Seychelles**
0/Q6 **Seydhisfjördhur**, Ice.
52/B2 **Seydişehir**, Turk.
49/D1 **Seyhan** (dam), Turk.
49/D1 **Seyhan** (riv.), Turk.
44/D5 **Seyitgazi**, Turk.
52/B2 **Seyitgazi**, Turk.
44/E2 **Seym** (riv.), Rus.
44/E2 **Seym** (riv.), Ukr.
1/H7 **Seymour**, Austl.
73/C3 **Seymour**, Austl.
93/H4 **Seymour**, Tx,US
96/D3 **Seymour**, Tx,US
46/C6 **Seynod**, Fr.
36/B6 **Seyssel**, Fr.
1/N6 **Şeytan** (riv.), Turk.
43/K4 **Sežana**, Slov.
0/A3 **Sežana**, Slov.
6/B4 **Sézanne**, Fr.
0/C6 **Sézanne**, Fr.
32/E2 **Sézanne**, Fr.
4/A3 **Sezimbra**, Port.
8/C2 **Sezze**, It.
1/G3 **Sfintu Gheorghe**, Rom.
4/C3 **Sfintu Gheorghe**, Rom.
/Q16 **Sfizef**, Alg.
8/C4 **'s-Graveland**, Neth.
8/B5 **'s-Gravendeel**, Neth.
6/C2 **'s-Gravenhage** (The Hague) (cap.), Neth.
8/B4 **'s-Gravenhage** (The Hague) (cap.), Neth.
9/C4 **Sha** (riv.), China
1/H3 **Sha** (riv.), China
59/B4 **Shaanxi** (prov.), China
61/F1 **Shaanxi** (prov.), China
77/P7 **Shabeelle** (riv.), Som.
41/J4 **Shabla**, Bul.
41/K2 **Shabo**, Ukr.
82/E1 **Shabunda**, Zaire
52/E5 **Shabwah**, Yem.
46/H6 **Shache**, China
83/M **Shackleton** (coast), Ant.
83/G **Shackleton Ice Shelf**, Ant.
51/G4 **Shādegān**, Iran
43/P4 **Shadrinsk**, Rus.
46/G4 **Shadrinsk**, Rus.
63/G2 **Shaduzup**, Burma
45/K1 **Shafranovo**, Rus.
100/D2 **Shafter**, Tx,US
93/F5 **Shafter**, Tx,US
96/B4 **Shafter**, Tx,US
24/D4 **Shaftesbury**, Eng,UK
41/K3 **Shagany** (lake), Ukr.
85/G3 **Shageluk**, Ak,US
64/D2 **Shāhābād**, India
62/A3 **Shāhbandar**, Pak.
51/J4 **Shahdād**, Iran
53/G2 **Shahdād**, Iran
53/J3 **Shāhdādkot**, Pak.
62/A2 **Shāhdādkot**, Pak.
53/J3 **Shāhdādpur**, Pak.
62/A2 **Shāhdādpur**, Pak.
62/D3 **Shahdol**, India
77/K1 **Shaḩḩāt**, Libya
62/C2 **Shāhjahānpur**, India
64/B2 **Shāh Kot**, Pak.
64/D1 **Shāhpur**, India
64/B1 **Shāhpur**, Pak.
53/K3 **Shāhpura**, India
62/A2 **Shāhpur Chākar**, Pak.
53/G2 **Shahr-e Bābak**, Iran
52/F2 **Shahr-e Kord**, Iran
46/E6 **Shāhrūd**, Iran
53/L4 **Shājāpur**, India
62/C3 **Shājāpur**, India
53/L2 **Shakargarh**, Pak.
64/C1 **Shakargarh**, Pak.
82/D4 **Shakawe**, Bots.
51/F2 **Shakhbuz**, Azer.
46/H5 **Shakhtinsk**, Kaz.
19/H4 **Shakhty**, Rus.
44/G3 **Shakhty**, Rus.
46/E5 **Shakhty**, Rus.
19/H3 **Shakhun'ya**, Rus.
43/K4 **Shakhun'ya**, Rus.
46/E4 **Shakhun'ya**, Rus.
85/F3 **Shaktoolik**, Ak,US
45/H4 **Shalbuzdag, Gora** (peak), Rus.
24/C5 **Shaldon**, Eng,UK
54/D5 **Shaluli** (mts.), China
60/C2 **Shaluli** (mts.), China
82/F2 **Shama** (riv.), Tanz.
49/C4 **Shamal Sīnā'** (gov.), Egypt
50/C4 **Shamal Sīnā'** (gov.), Egypt
91/M2 **Shamattawa** (riv.), On,Can
87/H3 **Shamattawa** (riv.), On,Can
53/L4 **Shāmgarh**, India
62/C3 **Shāmgarh**, India
51/J5 **Shamīl**, Iran
53/G3 **Shamīl**, Iran
51/F1 **Shamkhor**, Azer.
53/L3 **Shāmli**, India
62/C2 **Shāmli**, India
77/P2 **Shammar** (mts.), SAr.
50/E5 **Shammar, Jabal** (mts.), SAr.
52/D3 **Shammar, Jabal** (mts.), SAr.
94/E3 **Shamokin**, Pa,US
85/L3 **Shamrock** (mtn.), Yk,Can
93/G4 **Shamrock**, Tx,US
96/C3 **Shamrock**, Tx,US
82/F4 **Shamva**, Zim.
60/C4 **Shan** (plat.), Burma
60/C4 **Shan** (state), Burma
63/G3 **Shan** (plat.), Burma
63/G3 **Shan** (state), Burma
65/B1 **Shan** (plat.), Burma
65/B1 **Shan** (state), Burma
61/H3 **Shan** (pass), China
75/W18 **Sha'nabī, Jabal ash** (peak), Tun.
52/B5 **Shandī**, Sudan
77/M4 **Shandī**, Sudan
55/H4 **Shandong** (pen.), China
58/A4 **Shandong** (prov.), China
59/D3 **Shandong** (pen.), China
59/D3 **Shandong** (prov.), China
59/C4 **Shangcai**, China
54/H5 **Shangcheng**, China
59/C5 **Shangcheng**, China
61/G2 **Shangcheng**, China
61/G4 **Shangchuan** (isl.), China
54/G3 **Shangdu**, China
61/G3 **Shangdu**, China
55/J5 **Shanghai**, China
59/E5 **Shanghai**, China
59/E5 **Shanghai** (mun.), China
59/L8 **Shanghai**, China
59/L9 **Shanghai** (mun.), China
61/J2 **Shanghai**, China
61/J2 **Shanghai** (mun.), China
59/D3 **Shanghe**, China
63/J3 **Shanglin**, China
54/H5 **Shangqiu**, China
59/C4 **Shangqiu**, China
61/H2 **Shangrao**, China
59/C4 **Shangshui**, China
65/E1 **Shangsi**, China
54/G3 **Shangyi**, China
59/C2 **Shangyi**, China
61/G3 **Shangyou** (riv.), China
25/E5 **Shanklin**, Eng,UK
61/F3 **Shanmatang** (mtn.), China
63/K2 **Shanmen**, China
60/C3 **Shan-ngaw** (range), Burma
21/A4 **Shannon** (riv.), Ire.
54/C3 **Shanshan**, China
47/P4 **Shantar** (isls.), Rus.
48/N4 **Shantar** (isl.), Rus.
61/H4 **Shantou**, China
68/A2 **Shantou**, China
59/B3 **Shanxi** (prov.), China
54/G4 **Shanyin**, China
59/C3 **Shanyin**, China
61/F3 **Shaodong**, China
61/G3 **Shaoguan**, China
63/K3 **Shaoguan**, China
61/J2 **Shaoxing**, China
61/F3 **Shaoyang**, China
63/K2 **Shaoyang**, China
23/F2 **Shap**, Eng,UK
83/L **Shapeless** (peak), Ant.
42/F4 **Shapki**, Rus.
43/M2 **Shapkina** (riv.), Rus.
51/F2 **Shaqlāwah**, Iraq
77/Q2 **Shaqrā'**, SAr.
52/E6 **Shaqrā'**, Yem.
51/F2 **Sharafkhāneh**, Iran
53/G5 **Sharbatāt, Ra's ash** (pt.), Oman
54/D2 **Sharga**, Mong.
54/F2 **Sharingol**, Mong.
70/A5 **Shark** (bay), Austl.
104/A1 **Shark** (pt.), Fl,US
50/C5 **Sharm ash Shaykh**, Egypt
25/F2 **Sharnbrook**, Eng,UK
94/D3 **Sharon**, Pa,US
91/K2 **Sharpe** (lake), Mb,Can
91/J4 **Sharpe** (lake), SD,US
64/C2 **Sharqpur**, Pak.
19/H3 **Shar'ya**, Rus.
43/K4 **Shar'ya**, Rus.
46/E4 **Shar'ya**, Rus.
77/N6 **Shashemenē**, Eth.
59/C5 **Shashi**, China
61/G2 **Shashi**, China
90/C5 **Shasta** (lake), Ca,US
86/D4 **Shasta** (mt.), Ca,US
88/B3 **Shasta** (dam), Ca,US
88/B3 **Shasta** (mt.), Ca,US
90/C5 **Shasta** (dam), Ca,US
80/C6 **Shasta** (peak), Ca,US
92/B2 **Shasta** (dam), Ca,US
92/B2 **Shasta** (lake), Ca,US
92/B2 **Shasta** (peak), Ca,US
44/E1 **Shatalovo**, Rus.
27/M3 **Shatsky Nat'l Park**, Ukr.
44/B2 **Shatsky Nat'l Park**, Ukr.
51/F4 **Shatt al Arab** (riv.), Iran, Iraq
52/E2 **Shatt al Arab** (riv.), Iran,Iraq
74/C1 **Shatt al Jarīd** (depr.), Tun.
76/G1 **Shaṭṭ al Jarīd** (depr.), Tun.
93/H3 **Shattuck**, Ok,US
96/D2 **Shattuck**, Ok,US
86/F4 **Shaunavon**, Sk,Can
90/F3 **Shaunavon**, Sk,Can
25/E4 **Shaw**, Eng,UK
97/H3 **Shaw** (A.F.B.), SC,US
91/L4 **Shawano**, Wi,US
94/B2 **Shawano**, Wi,US
95/M6 **Shawbridge**, Qu,Can
23/F6 **Shawbury**, Eng,UK
24/D1 **Shawbury**, Eng,UK
87/J4 **Shawinigan**, Qu,Can
89/M2 **Shawinigan**, Qu,Can
95/F2 **Shawinigan**, Qu,Can
89/G4 **Shawnee**, Ok,US
93/H4 **Shawnee**, Ok,US
96/D3 **Shawnee**, Ok,US
51/E2 **Shaykhān**, Iraq
50/C3 **Shaykh, Jabal ash** (mtn.), Leb.
51/F3 **Shaykh Sa'd**, Iraq
52/E2 **Shaykh Sa'd**, Iraq
53/K1 **Shaymak**, Taj.
44/C1 **Shchara** (riv.), Bela.
44/F1 **Shchekino**, Rus.
43/X9 **Shchelkovo**, Rus.
43/X9 **Shcherbinka**, Rus.
44/F2 **Shchigry**, Rus.
27/N2 **Shchuchin**, Bela.
42/E5 **Shchuchin**, Bela.
44/C1 **Shchuchin**, Bela.
46/H4 **Shchuchinsk**, Kaz.
77/P6 **Shebelē Wenz** (riv.), Eth.
74/G4 **Shebelē Wenz, Wabē** (riv.), Eth., Som.
46/G6 **Sheberghān**, Afg.
53/J1 **Sheberghān**, Afg.
87/H4 **Sheboygan**, Wi,US
89/J3 **Sheboygan**, Wi,US
91/M5 **Sheboygan**, Wi,US
94/C3 **Sheboygan**, Wi,US
47/Q5 **Shebunino**, Rus.
95/H2 **Shediac**, NB,Can
22/A4 **Sheelin, Lough** (lake), Ire.
85/F2 **Sheep** (mtn.), Ak,US
28/D5 **'s Heerenberg**, Neth.
49/F7 **Shefayim**, Isr.
73/C4 **Sheffield**, Austl.
18/C3 **Sheffield**, Eng,UK
23/G6 **Sheffield**, Eng,UK
97/G3 **Sheffield**, Al,US
101/E2 **Sheffield**, Tx,US
25/F2 **Shefford**, Eng,UK
63/K2 **Shegangshi**, China
77/P6 **Shēh Husēn**, Eth.
109/B6 **Shehuen** (riv.), Arg.
59/B3 **Shejiaping**, China
94/C1 **Shekak** (riv.), On,Can
53/K2 **Shekhūpura**, Pak.
64/B2 **Shekhūpura**, Pak.
45/H4 **Sheki**, Azer.
51/F1 **Sheki**, Azer.
47/T2 **Shelagskiy** (cape), Rus.
95/H3 **Shelburne**, Can
94/C3 **Shelby**, Mi,US
93/K4 **Shelby**, Ms,US
97/F3 **Shelby**, Ms,US
86/E4 **Shelby**, Mt,US
88/D2 **Shelby**, Mt,US
90/F3 **Shelby**, Mt,US
97/H3 **Shelby**, NC,US
94/C4 **Shelbyville**, In,US
97/G2 **Shelbyville**, In,US
89/J4 **Shelbyville**, Tn,US
97/G3 **Shelbyville**, Tn,US
85/F3 **Sheldon Point**, Ak,US
47/R3 **Shelekhov** (gulf), Rus.
48/Q3 **Shelekhov** (gulf), Rus.
85/H4 **Shelikof** (str.), Ak,US
91/G2 **Shellbrook**, Sk,Can
91/L4 **Shell Lake**, Wi,US
94/B2 **Shell Lake**, Wi,US
25/G4 **Shell Ness** (pt.), UK
91/K5 **Shell Rock** (riv.), Ia,US
93/J2 **Shell Rock** (riv.), Ia,US
90/C4 **Shelton**, Wa,US
99/A3 **Shelton**, Wa,US
45/J4 **Shemakha**, Azer.
51/G1 **Shemakha**, Azer.
85/A5 **Shemya** (isl.), Ak,US
89/G3 **Shenandoah**, Ia,US
91/K5 **Shenandoah**, Ia,US
93/J2 **Shenandoah**, Ia,US
89/L4 **Shenandoah Nat'l Park**, Va,US
94/E4 **Shenandoah Nat'l Park**, Va,US
97/J2 **Shenandoah Nat'l Park**, Va,US
54/G4 **Shenchi**, China
59/C3 **Shenchi**, China
64/F4 **Shencottah**, India
78/B5 **Shenge** (pt.), SLeo.
40/D5 **Shëngjin**, Alb.
60/E3 **Shengjing** (pass), China
59/B5 **Shennongjia**, China
61/F2 **Shennongjia**, China
59/C4 **Shenqiu**, China
25/F1 **Shenstone**, Eng,UK
59/C3 **Shen Xian**, China
47/N5 **Shenyang**, China
55/J3 **Shenyang**, China
58/B2 **Shenyang**, China
59/E2 **Shenyang**, China
61/G4 **Shenzhen**, China
63/K3 **Shenzhen**, China
53/K3 **Sheoganj**, India
62/B2 **Sheoganj**, India
53/L3 **Sheopur**, India
62/C2 **Sheopur**, India
18/F3 **Shepetovka**, Ukr.
44/C2 **Shepetovka**, Ukr.
46/C4 **Shepetovka**, Ukr.
93/J5 **Shepherd**, Tx,US
96/E4 **Shepherd**, Tx,US
68/F6 **Shepherd** (isls.), Van.
93/H4 **Sheppard** (A.F.B.), Tx,US
96/D3 **Sheppard** (A.F.B.), Tx,US
71/H7 **Shepparton**, Austl.
25/G4 **Sheppey** (isl.), Eng,UK
23/G6 **Shepshed**, Eng,UK
25/E1 **Shepshed**, Eng,UK
24/D4 **Shepton Mallet**, Eng,UK
59/C4 **Sheqi**, China
87/H1 **Sherard** (cape), NW,Can
87/T7 **Sherard** (cape), NW,Can
24/D5 **Sherborne**, Eng,UK
78/B5 **Sherbro** (isl.), SLeo.
95/G2 **Sherbrooke**, Can
87/J4 **Sherbrooke**, Qu,Can
89/M2 **Sherbrooke**, Qu,Can
23/G2 **Sherburn**, Eng,UK
22/B4 **Shercock**, Ire.
79/H4 **Shere** (hill), Nga.
62/D3 **Sherghāti**, India
93/J4 **Sheridan**, Ar,US
96/E3 **Sheridan**, Ar,US
88/E3 **Sheridan**, Wy,US
90/G4 **Sheridan**, Wy,US
92/F1 **Sheridan**, Wy,US
25/H1 **Sheringham**, Eng,UK
89/G5 **Sherman**, Tx,US
93/H4 **Sherman**, Tx,US
96/D3 **Sherman**, Tx,US
64/F4 **Shertallai**, India
26/C3 **'s Hertogenbosch**, Neth.
28/C5 **'s-Hertogenbosch**, Neth.
98/G4 **Sherwood** (pt.), Ct,US
101/E2 **Sherwood**, Tx,US
86/E3 **Sherwood Park**, Ab,Can
90/E2 **Sherwood Park**, Ab,Can
18/C2 **Shetland** (isls.), Sc,UK
46/F5 **Shetpe**, Kaz.
64/G3 **Shevaroy** (hills), India
45/J4 **Shevchenko**, Kaz.
46/F5 **Shevchenko**, Kaz.
59/D5 **She Xian**, China
61/H2 **She Xian**, China
60/D1 **Sheyang** (riv.), China
59/E4 **Sheyang**, China
91/J4 **Sheyenne** (riv.), ND,US
86/G4 **Sheyenne** (riv.), ND,US
59/C4 **Shi** (riv.), China
99/E6 **Shiawassee** (riv.), Mi,US
52/E5 **Shibām**, Yem.
57/F2 **Shibata**, Japan
49/B4 **Shibīn al Kaum**, Egypt
50/B4 **Shibīn al Kaum**, Egypt
49/B4 **Shibīn al Qanāţir**, Egypt
91/L2 **Shibogama** (lake), On,Can
56/B5 **Shibushi** (bay), Japan
58/B3 **Shicheng** (isl.), China
61/H3 **Shicheng**, China
55/J4 **Shidao**, China
56/D3 **Shido**, Japan
24/D1 **Shifnal**, Eng,UK
56/E3 **Shiga** (pref.), Japan
57/L9 **Shiga**, Japan
57/M9 **Shiga** (pref.), Japan
57/M10 **Shigaraki**, Japan
59/C3 **Shigu Shan** (mtn.), China
39/F2 **Shijak**, Alb.
40/D5 **Shijak**, Alb.
54/G4 **Shijiazhuang**, China
59/C3 **Shijiazhuang**, China
61/H2 **Shijiu** (lake), China
53/J3 **Shikārpur**, Pak.
62/A2 **Shikārpur**, Pak.
57/M9 **Shikatsu**, Japan
57/H7 **Shiki**, Japan
47/P6 **Shikoku** (isl.), Japan
48/N6 **Shikoku** (isl.), Japan
55/L5 **Shikoku** (isl.), Japan
56/C4 **Shikoku** (isl.), Japan
56/C4 **Shikoku** (mts.), Japan
56/C4 **Shikoku** (prov.), Japan
55/P3 **Shikotan** (isl.), Rus.
23/G2 **Shildon**, Eng,UK
54/G5 **Shilipu**, China
47/M4 **Shilka**, Rus.
47/N4 **Shilka** (riv.), Rus.
48/L4 **Shilka** (riv.), Rus.
54/H1 **Shilka**, Rus.
55/H1 **Shilka** (riv.), Rus.
53/L2 **Shilla** (mtn.), India
22/B6 **Shillelagh**, Ire.
49/G7 **Shillo, Naḩal** (dry riv.), WBnk.
60/A3 **Shillong**, India
63/F2 **Shillong**, India
97/F3 **Shiloh Nat'l Mil. Park**, Tn,US
54/G4 **Shilou**, China
59/B3 **Shilou**, China
54/D2 **Shilüüstey**, Mong.
57/M10 **Shima** (pen.), Japan
56/B4 **Shimabara**, Japan
56/B4 **Shimabara** (bay), Japan
57/M10 **Shimagahara**, Japan
57/M10 **Shima-Ise Nat'l Park**, Japan
56/D3 **Shimamoto**, Japan
57/L10 **Shimamoto**, Japan
56/C3 **Shimane** (pref.), Japan
47/N4 **Shimanovsk**, Rus.
55/K1 **Shimanovsk**, Rus.
61/F4 **Shimao** (mtn.), China
57/M9 **Shimasahi**, Japan
77/Q5 **Shimber Berris** (peak), Som.
63/K2 **Shimenqiao**, China
61/H2 **Shimian**, China
55/M4 **Shimizu**, Japan
57/F3 **Shimizu**, Japan
57/F3 **Shimoda**, Japan
57/F2 **Shimodate**, Japan
53/L6 **Shimoga**, India
62/C5 **Shimoga**, India
57/L10 **Shimoichi**, Japan
56/A5 **Shimo-koshiki** (isl.), Japan
55/L5 **Shimonoseki**, Japan
56/B4 **Shimonoseki**, Japan
57/N9 **Shimoyama**, Japan
61/J2 **Shinaibeidong** (mtn.), China
55/M4 **Shinano** (riv.), Japan
57/F2 **Shinano** (riv.), Japan
53/H2 **Shindand**, Afg.
58/D4 **Shindo**, SKor.
58/F6 **Shindo**, SKor.
56/D4 **Shingū**, Japan
56/A3 **Shinhyŏn**, SKor.
56/C3 **Shinji** (lake), Japan
55/N4 **Shinjō**, Japan
57/L10 **Shinjō**, Japan
57/M9 **Shinkawa**, Japan
57/E2 **Shinminato**, Japan
57/M9 **Shinsei**, Japan
82/F1 **Shinyanga**, Tanz.
57/G1 **Shiogama**, Japan
55/M5 **Shio-no-misaki** (cape), Japan
56/D4 **Shio-no-misaki** (cape), Japan
57/G2 **Shioya-saki** (pt.), Japan
19/P8 **Shipbourne**, Eng,UK
39/J1 **Shipka**, Bul.
41/G4 **Shipka**, Bul.
23/G4 **Shipley**, Eng,UK
98/G4 **Shippan** (pt.), Ct,US
95/H2 **Shippegan**, NB,Can
57/M9 **Shippo**, Japan
88/E3 **Shiprock**, NM,US
92/E3 **Shiprock**, NM,US
96/A2 **Shiprock**, NM,US
25/E2 **Shipston on Stour**, Eng,UK
51/H4 **Shīr** (mtn.), Iran
52/F2 **Shīr** (mtn.), Iran
57/H8 **Shirahama**, Japan
57/G2 **Shirakawa**, Japan
56/E3 **Shirakawa-tōge** (pass), Japan
57/F2 **Shirane-san** (mtn.), Japan
57/F3 **Shirane-san** (mtn.), Japan
57/H6 **Shiraoka**, Japan
46/F7 **Shīrāz**, Iran
48/E7 **Shīrāz**, Iran
51/H4 **Shīrāz**, Iran
52/F3 **Shīrāz**, Iran
77/R2 **Shīrāz**, Iran
49/B4 **Shirbīn**, Egypt
23/G1 **Shiremoor**, Eng,UK
59/C5 **Shirjiu** (lake), China
57/J7 **Shiroi**, Japan
57/G2 **Shiroishi**, Japan
41/L2 **Shirokoye**, Ukr.
57/F2 **Shirone**, Japan
57/H7 **Shiroyama**, Japan
51/J2 **Shīrvān**, Iran
53/G1 **Shīrvān**, Iran
59/D2 **Shi San Ling**, China
85/F5 **Shishaldin** (vol.), Ak,US
54/D1 **Shishhid** (riv.), Mong.
85/E2 **Shishmaref**, Ak,US
59/C5 **Shishou**, China
61/G2 **Shishou**, China
57/J7 **Shisui**, Japan
51/E3 **Shithātha**, Iraq
60/D2 **Shiting** (riv.), China
54/F5 **Shituan**, China
39/K1 **Shivachevo**, Bul.
41/H4 **Shivachevo**, Bul.
53/L3 **Shivpurī**, India
62/C2 **Shivpurī**, India
63/K3 **Shixing**, China
54/G5 **Shiyan**, China
59/B4 **Shiyan**, China
61/F1 **Shiyan**, China
65/E1 **Shiyong**, China
60/D3 **Shizong**, China
54/F4 **Shizuishan**, China
55/N3 **Shizunai**, Japan
47/P6 **Shizuoka**, Japan
55/M5 **Shizuoka**, Japan
57/F3 **Shizuoka**, Japan
57/F3 **Shizuoka** (pref.), Japan
44/D1 **Shklov**, Bela.
18/E4 **Shkodër**, Alb.
39/F1 **Shkodër**, Alb.
40/D4 **Shkodër**, Alb.
39/G2 **Shkumbin** (riv.), Alb.
40/E5 **Shkumbin** (riv.), Alb.
85/C2 **Shmidta, Mys** (pt.), Rus.
73/D2 **Shoalhaven** (riv.), Austl.
91/H3 **Shoal Lake**, Can
72/C3 **Shoalwater** (bay), Austl.
72/C3 **Shoalwater Bay Mil. Trg. Area**, Austl.
56/C3 **Shōbara**, Japan
56/D3 **Shōdo** (isl.), Japan
25/G3 **Shoeburyness**, Eng,UK
53/L5 **Sholāpur**, India
62/C4 **Sholāpur**, India
49/G7 **Shomron** (ruins), WBnk.
57/M9 **Shonai** (riv.), Japan
57/J7 **Shōnan**, Japan
64/F3 **Shoranur**, India
62/C4 **Shorāpur**, India
25/F5 **Shoreham by Sea**, Eng,UK
99/P16 **Shorewood**, Il,US
99/Q13 **Shorewood**, Wi,US
53/K2 **Shorkot**, Pak.
64/B2 **Shorkot**, Pak.
72/F6 **Shorncliffe**, Austl.
97/G3 **Short** (peak), Tn,US
68/E5 **Shortland** (isl.), Sol.
25/E5 **Shorwell**, Eng,UK
92/C3 **Shoshone** (mts.), Nv,US
90/F4 **Shoshone** (riv.), Wy,US
92/E1 **Shoshone** (riv.), Wy,US
90/F5 **Shoshoni**, Wy,US
92/E2 **Shoshoni**, Wy,US
18/G3 **Shostka**, Ukr.
44/E2 **Shostka**, Ukr.
46/D4 **Shostka**, Ukr.
25/H3 **Shotley**, Eng,UK
23/G2 **Shotton**, Eng,UK
59/D4 **Shouguang**, China
59/D4 **Shou Xian**, China
59/C3 **Shouyang**, China
57/H7 **Shōwa**, Japan
88/D5 **Show Low**, Az,US
92/E4 **Show Low**, Az,US
44/D2 **Shpola**, Ukr.
64/G4 **Shree Meenakshi Temple**, India
89/H5 **Shreveport**, La,US
93/J4 **Shreveport**, La,US
96/E3 **Shreveport**, La,US
24/D1 **Shrewsbury**, Eng,UK
23/F6 **Shropshire** (co.), Eng,UK
24/D1 **Shropshire** (co.), Eng,UK
23/F5 **Shropshire Union** (can.), Eng,UK
23/F6 **Shropshire Union** (can.), Eng,UK
55/H4 **Shu** (riv.), China
59/D4 **Shu** (riv.), China
61/H2 **Shu** (riv.), China
60/D3 **Shuangbai**, China
63/H3 **Shuangbai**, China
47/N5 **Shuangcheng**, China
54/G5 **Shuangche**, China
59/E2 **Shuangliao**, China
63/K2 **Shuangpai**, China
55/K3 **Shuangyang**, China
47/P5 **Shuangyashan**, China
55/L2 **Shuangyashan**, China
46/F5 **Shubarkuduk**, Kaz.
49/B4 **Shubrā al Khaymah**, Egypt
50/B4 **Shubrā al Khaymah**, Egypt
52/B2 **Shubrā al Khaymah**, Egypt
49/B4 **Shubrā Khīt**, Egypt
55/H5 **Shucheng**, China
59/D5 **Shucheng**, China
61/H2 **Shucheng**, China
49/D4 **Shu'fāţ**, WBnk.
49/G8 **Shu'fāţ**, WBnk.
45/K1 **Shugurovo**, Rus.
60/D2 **Shuiluo** (riv.), China
59/D5 **Shuiyang** (riv.), China
53/K3 **Shujāābād**, Pak.
55/K3 **Shulan**, China
46/K5 **Shule** (riv.), China
54/D4 **Shule** (riv.), China
85/G4 **Shumagin** (isls.), Ak,US
41/H4 **Shumen**, Bul.
44/C4 **Shumen**, Bul.
43/K5 **Shumerlya**, Rus.
61/H3 **Shunchang**, China
85/G2 **Shungnak**, Ak,US
59/D2 **Shunyi**, China
59/H6 **Shunyi**, China
54/G4 **Shuo Xian**, China
59/C3 **Shuo Xian**, China
51/J4 **Shūr** (riv.), Iran
53/G2 **Shūr** (riv.), Iran
82/F4 **Shurugwi**, Zim.
51/G3 **Shūsh**, Iran
46/K4 **Shushenskoye**, Rus.
51/G3 **Shūshtar**, Iran
52/E2 **Shūshtar**, Iran
90/D3 **Shuswap** (lake), BC,Can
52/C6 **Shuwak**, Sudan
77/N5 **Shuwak**, Sudan
49/G7 **Shuwaykah**, WBnk.
42/J4 **Shuya**, Rus.
55/H5 **Shuyang**, China
59/D4 **Shuyang**, China
63/G4 **Shwebandaw**, Burma
60/B4 **Shwebo**, Burma
63/G3 **Shwebo**, Burma
65/A1 **Shwebo**, Burma
60/C5 **Shwegyin**, Burma
63/G4 **Shwegyin**, Burma
65/B2 **Shwegyin**, Burma
60/C4 **Shweli** (riv.), Burma
60/C5 **Shwemawdaw Pagoda**, Burma
65/B2 **Shwemawdaw Pagoda** (ruins), Burma
60/C5 **Shwethalyaung**, Burma
65/B2 **Shwethalyaung** (Reclining Buddha), Burma
53/L2 **Shyok** (riv.), India
53/H2 **Siāh** (mts.), Afg.
66/B3 **Siak** (riv.), Indo.
53/K2 **Siālkot**, Pak.
64/C1 **Siālkot**, Pak.
67/F2 **Siasi**, Phil.
67/F2 **Siaton** (pt.), Phil.
67/G3 **Siau** (isl.), Indo.
18/F3 **Šiauliai**, Lith.
20/G5 **Šiauliai**, Lith.
42/D5 **Šiauliai**, Lith.
46/C4 **Šiauliai**, Lith.
51/G1 **Siazan'**, Azer.
45/L1 **Sibay**, Rus.
33/L5 **Šibenik**, Cro.
40/B4 **Šibenik**, Cro.
46/K3 **Siberia** (reg.), Rus.
48/H3 **Siberia** (reg.), Rus.
48/J10 **Siberut** (isl.), Indo.
66/A4 **Siberut** (isl.), Indo.
53/J3 **Sibi**, Pak.
77/N7 **Sibiloi Nat'l Park**, Kenya
82/B1 **Sibiti**, Congo
18/F4 **Sibiu**, Rom.
41/G2 **Sibiu** (co.), Rom.
41/G3 **Sibiu**, Rom.
44/C3 **Sibiu**, Rom.
25/G3 **Sible Hedingham**, Eng,UK
66/A3 **Sibolga**, Indo.
60/B3 **Sibsāgar**, India
63/F2 **Sibsāgar**, India
67/F2 **Sibuco**, Phil.
67/F2 **Sibuko**, Phil.
77/J6 **Sibut**, CAfr.
67/F1 **Sibuyan** (isl.), Phil.
67/F1 **Sibuyan** (sea), Phil.
90/D3 **Sicamous**, BC,Can
61/J5 **Sicapoo** (mt.), Phil.
59/B5 **Sichuan** (prov.), China
60/D2 **Sichuan** (prov.), China
63/H2 **Sichuan** (prov.), China
35/H1 **Sicié** (cape), Fr.
38/C4 **Sicilia** (reg.), It.
18/E5 **Sicily** (isl.), It.
38/C3 **Sicily** (isl.), It.
38/B4 **Sicily** (isl.), It., Tun.
103/E3 **Sico** (riv.), Hon.
106/D6 **Sicuani**, Peru
40/D3 **Šid**, Yugo.
19/P7 **Sidcup**, Eng,UK
62/C4 **Siddipet**, India
38/E3 **Siderno Marina**, It.
108/B4 **Siderópolis**, Braz.
39/F3 **Sidhári**, Gre.
62/D3 **Sidhi**, India
39/H2 **Sidhirókastron**, Gre.
44/B4 **Sidhirókastron**, Gre.
53/K4 **Sidhpur**, India
62/B3 **Sidhpur**, India
75/S16 **Sidi Aïssa**, Alg.
75/Q16 **Sidi Bel-Abbes**, Alg.
75/Q16 **Sidi Bel-Abbes** (wilaya), Alg.
76/E1 **Sidi Bel-Abbes**, Alg.
38/A5 **Sīdī Bū Zayd** (gov.), Tun.
75/W18 **Sīdī Bū Zayd** (gov.), Tun.
76/C2 **Sidi Ifni**, Mor.
75/M13 **Sidi Kacem**, Mor.
38/B4 **Sīdī Nājī**, Tun.
49/B4 **Sīdī Sālim**, Egypt
38/B5 **Sīdī 'Umar Bū Ḩajalah**, Tun.
83/R **Sidley** (mtn.), Ant.
72/A1 **Sidmouth** (cape), Austl.
24/C5 **Sidmouth**, Eng,UK
90/C3 **Sidney**, Can
88/F2 **Sidney**, Mt,US
91/G4 **Sidney**, Mt,US
88/F3 **Sidney**, Ne,US
91/H5 **Sidney**, Ne,US
93/G2 **Sidney**, Ne,US
94/C3 **Sidney**, Oh,US
50/C3 **Sidon**, Leb.
52/C2 **Sidon**, Leb.
49/D3 **Sidon** (Şaydā), Leb.
74/D1 **Sidra** (gulf), Libya
76/J1 **Sidra** (gulf), Libya
29/F3 **Siede** (riv.), Ger.
27/L2 **Siedlce** (prov.), Pol.
27/M2 **Siedlce**, Pol.
44/B1 **Siedlce**, Pol.
31/G2 **Sieg** (riv.), Ger.
33/G1 **Sieg** (riv.), Ger.
31/G2 **Siegburg**, Ger.
26/E3 **Siegen**, Ger.
31/H2 **Siegen**, Ger.
33/H1 **Siegen**, Ger.
33/M3 **Siegendorf im Burgenland**, Aus.
27/M2 **Siemianówka** (lake), Pol.
27/M2 **Siemiatycze**, Pol.
44/B1 **Siemiatycze**, Pol.
65/D3 **Siempang**, Camb.
63/H5 **Siemreab**, Camb.
65/C3 **Siemreab**, Camb.
18/E4 **Siena**, It.
33/J5 **Siena**, It.
32/C2 **Sienne** (riv.), Fr.
27/K3 **Sieradz**, Pol.
27/K3 **Sieradz** (prov.), Pol.
44/A2 **Sieradz**, Pol.
27/J2 **Sieraków**, Pol.
36/D2 **Sierentz**, Fr.
31/F5 **Sierk-les-Bains**, Fr.
27/K2 **Sierpc**, Pol.
42/C5 **Sierpc**, Pol.
44/A1 **Sierpc**, Pol.
98/C3 **Sierra** (peak), Ca,US
100/D2 **Sierra Blanca**, Tx,US
93/F5 **Sierra Blanca**, Tx,US
96/D4 **Sierra Blanca**, Tx,US
34/B1 **Sierra de Coba de Serpe** (mtn.), Sp.
106/D3 **Sierra de la Macarena Nat'l Park**, Col.
93/G5 **Sierra del Carmen Nat'l Park**, Mex
96/C4 **Sierra del Carmen Nat'l Park**, Mex
100/B2 **Sierra de San Pedro Martir Nat'l Park**, Mex.
92/D5 **Sierra de San Pedro Mártir Nat'l Park**, Mex
109/C5 **Sierra Grande**, Arg.
74/A4 **Sierra-Leone**
76/C6 **Sierra Leone**
78/B4 **Sierra Leone**
76/C6 **Sierra Leone** (cape), SLeo.
78/B4 **Sierra Leone** (cape), SLeo.
84/G7 **Sierra Madre Occidental** (mts.), Mex.
84/G7 **Sierra Madre Oriental** (mts.), Mex.
100/E3 **Sierra Mojada**, Mex.
96/C5 **Sierra Mojada**, Mex
84/E6 **Sierra Nevada** (mts.), US
88/B4 **Sierra Nevada** (mts.), US
92/B3 **Sierra Nevada** (range), US
103/H4 **Sierra Nevada de Santa Marta Nat'l Park**, Col.
106/D1 **Sierra Nevada de Santa Marta Nat'l Park**, Col.
106/D2 **Sierra Nevada Nat'l Park**, Ven.
100/C2 **Sierra Vista**, Az,US
92/E5 **Sierra Vista**, Az,US
33/G3 **Sierre**, Swi.
36/D5 **Sierre**, Swi.
35/M8 **Siete** (peak), Sp.
109/B4 **Siete Tazas Nat'l Park**, Chile
39/J4 **Sífnos** (isl.), Gre.
75/Q16 **Sig**, Alg.
32/E5 **Sigean**, Fr.
35/G1 **Sigean**, Fr.
41/F2 **Sighetu Marmaţiei**, Rom.
44/B3 **Sighetu Marmaţiei**, Rom.
41/G2 **Sighişoara**, Rom.
23/F1 **Sighty Crag** (hill), Eng,UK
64/H5 **Sigiriya**, SrL.
75/T15 **Sigli** (cape), Alg.
66/A2 **Sigli**, Indo.

20/N6 **Siglufjördhur**, Ice.
26/E4 **Sigmaringen**, Ger.
33/H2 **Sigmaringen**, Ger.
37/F1 **Sigmaringen**, Ger.
37/F2 **Sigmarszell**, Ger.
36/D4 **Signau**, Swi.
30/D4 **Signy-l'Abbaye**, Fr.
30/D4 **Signy-le-Petit**, Fr.
36/D4 **Sigriswil**, Swi.
42/C4 **Sigtuna**, Swe.
102/E3 **Siguatepeque**, Hon.
34/D2 **Sigüenza**, Sp.
76/D5 **Siguiri**, Gui.
37/E3 **Sihl** (riv.), Swi.
37/E3 **Sihlsee** (lake), Swi.
101/H5 **Sihochac**, Mex.
102/D2 **Sihochac**, Mex.
59/D4 **Sihong**, China
62/D3 **Sihorā**, India
106/C5 **Sihuas**, Peru
20/H3 **Siilinjärvi**, Fin.
42/E3 **Siilinjärvi**, Fin.
49/G8 **Siʿīr**, WBnk.
46/E6 **Siirt**, Turk.
50/E2 **Siirt**, Turk.
50/E2 **Siirt** (prov.), Turk.
86/D3 **Sikanni Chief** (riv.), BC,Can
53/L3 **Sīkar**, India
62/C2 **Sīkar**, India
76/D5 **Sikasso**, Mali
78/D4 **Sikasso**, Mali
78/D4 **Sikasso** (reg.), Mali
63/G3 **Sikaw**, Burma
89/J4 **Sikeston**, Mo,US
93/K3 **Sikeston**, Mo,US
94/B4 **Sikeston**, Mo,US
97/F2 **Sikeston**, Mo,US
47/P5 **Sikhote-Alin'** (range), Rus.
48/N5 **Sikhote-Alin** (range), Rus.
55/M2 **Sikhote-Alin'** (mts.), Rus.
39/J4 **Síkinos**, Gre.
39/J4 **Síkinos** (isl.), Gre.
62/E2 **Sikkim** (state), India
40/D3 **Siklós**, Hun.
39/H3 **Sikoúrion**, Gre.
67/E2 **Sikuati**, Malay.
34/B1 **Sil** (riv.), Sp.
102/B2 **Silacayoapán**, Mex.
42/D5 **Šilalė**, Lith.
33/J3 **Silandro** (Schlanders), It.
37/G4 **Silandro** (Schlanders), It.
101/E4 **Silao**, Mex.
67/F1 **Silay**, Phil.
60/B3 **Silchar**, India
63/F3 **Silchar**, India
41/J5 **Şile**, Turk.
23/G6 **Sileby**, Eng,UK
25/E1 **Sileby**, Eng,UK
37/E4 **Silenen**, Swi.
27/H3 **Silesia** (reg.), Pol.
76/F3 **Silet**, Alg.
49/C1 **Silifke**, Turk.
50/C2 **Silifke**, Turk.
52/B1 **Silifke**, Turk.
62/E2 **Silīguri**, India
69/H6 **Silisili** (peak), WSam.
69/R9 **Silisili** (peak), WSam.
41/H3 **Silistra**, Bul.
44/C3 **Silistra**, Bul.
41/J5 **Silivri**, Turk.
44/D4 **Silivri**, Turk.
50/B1 **Silivri**, Turk.
20/D4 **Silkeborg**, Den.
23/G2 **Silksworth**, Eng,UK
37/H3 **Sill** (riv.), Aus.
35/E3 **Silla**, Sp.
20/H4 **Sillamäe**, Est.
42/E4 **Sillamäe**, Est.
64/B2 **Sillānwāli**, Pak.
56/A3 **Silla Tombs**, SKor.
58/E5 **Silla Tombs**, SKor.
34/A1 **Silleda**, Sp.
33/K3 **Sillian**, Aus.
23/E2 **Silloth**, Eng,UK
93/J3 **Siloam Springs**, Ar,US
96/E2 **Siloam Springs**, Ar,US
50/E2 **Silopi**, Turk.
52/D1 **Silopi**, Turk.
101/G2 **Silsbee**, Tx,US
93/J5 **Silsbee**, Tx,US
96/E4 **Silsbee**, Tx,US
23/G4 **Silsden**, Eng,UK
37/F5 **Silsersee** (lake), Swi.
102/C3 **Siltepec**, Mex.
76/J4 **Siltou** (well), Chad
27/L1 **Šilutė**, Lith.
42/D5 **Šilutė**, Lith.
50/E2 **Silvan**, Turk.
50/E2 **Silvan** (dam), Turk.
37/F5 **Silvaplana**, Swi.
62/B3 **Silvassa**, India
99/F7 **Silver** (cr.), Mi,US
90/D5 **Silver** (cr.), Or,US
92/B2 **Silver** (lake), Or,US
92/C2 **Silver** (riv.), Or,US
98/C3 **Silverado**, Ca,US
86/G4 **Silver Bay**, Mn,US
91/L4 **Silver Bay**, Mn,US
94/B2 **Silver Bay**, Mn,US
100/C1 **Silver City**, NM,US
88/E5 **Silver City**, NM,US
92/E4 **Silver City**, NM,US
85/L3 **Silver Creek**, Yk,Can
23/F3 **Silverdale**, Eng,UK
99/B2 **Silverdale**, Wa,US
99/P14 **Silver Lake**, Wi,US
99/C2 **Silver Lake-Fircrest**, Wa,US
98/J8 **Silver Spring**, Md,US
25/E2 **Silverstone**, Eng,UK
24/C5 **Silverton**, Eng,UK
92/F3 **Silverton**, Co,US
96/B2 **Silverton**, Co,US
90/C4 **Silverton**, Or,US
93/G4 **Silverton**, Tx,US
96/C3 **Silverton**, Tx,US
34/A4 **Silves**, Port.
38/D1 **Silvi**, It.
92/C2 **Silvies** (riv.), Or,US
37/G4 **Silvretta** (mts.), Aus., Swi.
38/A4 **Silyānah**, Tun.
38/A4 **Silyānah** (gov.), Tun.
75/W17 **Silyānah** (gov.), Tun.
37/G3 **Silz**, Aus.
66/D3 **Simanggang**, Malay.
60/D4 **Simao**, China
65/C1 **Simao**, China
94/E2 **Simard** (lake), Qu,Can
51/F3 **Şimareh** (riv.), Iran
50/B2 **Şimav**, Turk.
19/H3 **Simbirsk**, Rus.
43/L5 **Simbirsk**, Rus.
45/J1 **Simbirsk**, Rus.
46/E4 **Simbirsk**, Rus.
45/H1 **Simbirsk Obl.**, Rus.
87/J4 **Simcoe** (lake), On,Can
94/D3 **Simcoe**, On,Can
94/E2 **Simcoe** (lake), On,Can
77/N5 **Simēn** (mts.), Eth.
40/F3 **Simeria**, Rom.
48/J9 **Simeulue** (isl.), Indo.
66/A3 **Simeulue** (isl.), Indo.
19/G4 **Simferopol'**, Ukr.
44/E3 **Simferopol'**, Ukr.
46/D5 **Simferopol'**, Ukr.
50/A2 **Sími**, Gre.
37/G4 **Similaun** (peak), Aus.
33/J3 **Similaun** (peak), It.
59/E5 **Siming** (mtn.), China
61/J2 **Siming** (mtn.), China
103/H5 **Simití**, Col.
39/H2 **Simitli**, Bul.
41/F5 **Simitli**, Bul.
98/B2 **Simi Valley**, Ca,US
53/L2 **Simla**, India
64/D2 **Simla**, India
27/M5 **Şimleu Silvaniei**, Rom.
40/F2 **Şimleu Silvaniei**, Rom.
44/B3 **Şimleu Silvaniei**, Rom.
33/G3 **Simme** (riv.), Swi.
36/D4 **Simme** (riv.), Swi.
31/F2 **Simmerath**, Ger.
31/G4 **Simmerbach** (riv.), Ger.
31/G4 **Simmern**, Ger.
31/G4 **Simmertal**, Ger.
27/M1 **Simnas**, Lith.
58/C3 **Simni** (isl.), NKor.
20/H2 **Simo**, Fin.
42/E2 **Simo**, Fin.
102/C2 **Simojovel**, Mex.
90/D2 **Simonette** (riv.), Ab,Can
80/B4 **Simonstown**, SAfr.
80/L11 **Simonstown**, SAfr.
28/D1 **Simonszand** (isl.), Neth.
66/A3 **Simpang-kiri** (riv.), Indo.
31/E2 **Simpelveld**, Neth.
36/E5 **Simplon**, Swi.
36/E5 **Simplon** (tunnel), Swi.
36/E5 **Simplonpass** (pass), Swi.
70/F4 **Simpson** (des.), Austl.
86/G2 **Simpson** (riv.), NW,Can
86/H2 **Simpson** (pen.), NW,Can
20/E5 **Simrishamn**, Swe.
27/H1 **Simrishamn**, Swe.
67/E3 **Simunul**, Phil.
77/Q6 **Sinadhago**, Som.
52/B3 **Sinafir** (isl.), SAr.
77/M2 **Sinafir** (isl.), SAr.
49/C4 **Sinai** (pen.), Egypt
50/C4 **Sinai** (pen.), Egypt
52/B3 **Sinai** (pen.), Egypt
74/F2 **Sinai** (pen.), Egypt
77/M2 **Sinai** (pen.), Egypt
41/G3 **Sinaia**, Rom.
100/D3 **Sinaloa** (state), Mex.
100/C3 **Sinaloa de Leyva**, Mex.
33/J5 **Sinalunga**, It.
38/B1 **Sinalunga**, It.
44/E5 **Sincan**, Turk.
50/C2 **Sincan**, Turk.
103/H4 **Sincé**, Col.
103/H4 **Sincelejo**, Col.
106/C2 **Sincelejo**, Col.
30/C4 **Sinceny**, Fr.
58/C3 **Sinch'ŏn**, NKor.
90/G5 **Sinclair**, Wy,US
92/F2 **Sinclair**, Wy,US
62/C2 **Sind** (riv.), India
62/A2 **Sind** (prov.), Pak.
66/C5 **Sindangbarang**, Indo.
26/E4 **Sindelfingen**, Ger.
33/H2 **Sindelfingen**, Ger.
44/D5 **Sındırgı**, Turk.
50/B2 **Sındırgı**, Turk.
34/A4 **Sines**, Port.
34/A4 **Sines, Cabo de** (cape), Port.
76/D6 **Sinfra**, IvC.
78/D5 **Sinfra**, IvC.
48/K9 **Singapore**
66/B3 **Singapore**
66/B3 **Singapore** (cap.), Sing.
63/H5 **Sing Buri**, Thai.
65/C3 **Sing Buri**, Thai.
26/E5 **Singen**, Ger.
33/H3 **Singen**, Ger.
37/E2 **Singen**, Ger.
41/G2 **Singeorz-Băi**, Rom.
82/F1 **Singida**, Tanz.
54/B3 **Singim**, China
39/H2 **Singitic** (gulf), Gre.
67/F4 **Singkang**, Indo.
66/C3 **Singkawang**, Indo.
66/B4 **Singkep** (isl.), Indo.
71/J6 **Singleton**, Austl.
73/D2 **Singleton**, Austl.
79/F4 **Singou Rsv.**, Ben.
60/C4 **Singu**, Burma
65/B1 **Singu**, Burma
38/A2 **Siniscola**, It.
52/B6 **Sinjah**, Sudan
77/M5 **Sinjah**, Sudan
50/E2 **Sinjār**, Iraq
52/D1 **Sinjār**, Iraq
49/D3 **Sinjil**, WBnk.
49/G7 **Sinjil**, WBnk.
52/C5 **Sinkāt**, Sudan
30/C3 **Sin-le-Noble**, Fr.
26/E3 **Sinn** (riv.), Ger.
107/H2 **Sinnamary**, FrG.
58/D2 **Sinnam-dok-san** (mtn.), NKor.
53/K5 **Sinnar**, India
62/B4 **Sinnar**, India
38/E2 **Sinni** (riv.), It.
40/E2 **Sînnicolau Mare**, Rom.
49/B5 **Sinnūris**, Egypt
50/B4 **Sinnūris**, Egypt
52/B3 **Sinnūris**, Egypt
58/E4 **Sinnyŏng**, SKor.
78/C5 **Sino** (co.), Libr.
41/J3 **Sinoe** (lake), Rom.
107/G6 **Sinop**, Braz.
44/E4 **Sinop**, Turk.
44/E4 **Sinop** (prov.), Turk.
46/D5 **Sinop**, Turk.
50/C1 **Sinop**, Turk.
50/C1 **Sinop** (prov.), Turk.
50/C1 **Sinop** (pt.), Turk.
58/E2 **Sinp'o**, NKor.
55/K4 **Sint'aein**, SKor.
58/D5 **Sint'aein**, SKor.
66/D3 **Sintang**, Indo.
30/D2 **Sint-Genesius-Rode**, Belg.
28/B6 **Sint-Gillis-Waas**, Belg.
30/D1 **Sint-Gillis-Waas**, Belg.
28/B6 **Sint-Katelijne-Waver**, Belg.
30/D1 **Sint-Katelijne-Waver**, Belg.
28/A6 **Sint-Laureins**, Belg.
30/C1 **Sint-Laureins**, Belg.
104/F3 **Sint Maarten** (Saint Martin) (isl.), NAnt.
104/F3 **Sint Marten** (Saint Martin) (isl.), NAnt.
31/E2 **Sint-Martens-Voeren**, Belg.
28/C5 **Sint-Michielsgestel**, Neth.
26/C3 **Sint-Niklaas**, Belg.
28/B6 **Sint-Niklaas**, Belg.
30/D1 **Sint-Niklaas**, Belg.
28/C5 **Sint-Oedenrode**, Neth.
101/F2 **Sinton**, Tx,US
89/G6 **Sinton**, Tx,US
96/D4 **Sinton**, Tx,US
30/D2 **Sint-Pieters-Leeuw**, Belg.
34/A3 **Sintra**, Port.
35/P10 **Sintra**, Port.
35/P10 **Sintra** (mts.), Port.
31/E2 **Sint-Truiden**, Belg.
103/H4 **Sinú** (riv.), Col.
106/C2 **Sinu** (riv.), Col.
47/N5 **Sinŭiju**, NKor.
55/J3 **Sinŭiju**, NKor.
58/C2 **Sinŭiju**, NKor.
59/F2 **Sinŭiju**, NKor.
31/H6 **Sinzheim**, Ger.
31/G2 **Sinzig**, Ger.
40/D2 **Sió** (riv.), Hun.
67/F2 **Siocon**, Phil.
40/D2 **Siófok**, Hun.
82/D4 **Sioma Ngwezi Nat'l Park**, Zam.
33/G3 **Sion**, Swi.
36/D5 **Sion**, Swi.
32/E4 **Sioule** (riv.), Fr.
89/G3 **Sioux City**, Ia,US
91/J5 **Sioux City**, Ia,US
93/H2 **Sioux City**, Ia,US
86/G4 **Sioux Falls**, SD,US
89/G3 **Sioux Falls**, SD,US
91/J5 **Sioux Falls**, SD,US
93/H2 **Sioux Falls**, SD,US
86/G3 **Sioux Lookout**, On,Can
89/H1 **Sioux Lookout**, On,Can
91/L3 **Sioux Lookout**, On,Can
94/B1 **Sioux Lookout**, On,Can
38/E1 **Šipan** (isl.), Cro.
104/F5 **Siparia**, Trin.
55/J3 **Siping**, China
59/F2 **Siping**, China
91/J2 **Sipiwesk** (lake), Mb,Can
86/G3 **Sipiwesk** (lake), Mb,Can
83/Q **Siple** (coast), Ant.
83/R **Siple** (isl.), Ant.
66/A4 **Sipura** (isl.), Indo.
108/B2 **Siqueira Campos**, Braz.
100/D4 **Siqueros**, Mex.
103/E3 **Siquia** (riv.), Nic.
104/D5 **Siquisique**, Ven.
20/C4 **Sira** (riv.), Nor.
18/E5 **Siracusa**, It.
38/D4 **Siracusa** (Syracuse), It.
62/E3 **Sirājganj**, Bang.
90/C2 **Sir Alexander** (peak), Can
50/D1 **Şiran**, Turk.
70/F3 **Sir Edward Pellew Group** (isls.), Austl.
18/F4 **Siret** (riv.), Rom.
41/H2 **Siret**, Rom.
41/H3 **Siret** (riv.), Rom.
44/C3 **Siret** (riv.), Rom.
64/D2 **Sirhind**, India
51/J5 **Sīrīk**, Iran
53/G3 **Sīrīk**, Iran
66/D3 **Sirik** (cape), Malay.
60/D5 **Sirikit** (res.), Thai.
65/C2 **Sirikit** (res.), Thai.
49/G7 **Sīrīs**, WBnk.
63/H4 **Sirit** (res.), Thai.
85/B5 **Sirius** (pt.), Ak,US
86/D2 **Sir James MacBrien** (peak), NW,Can
51/H4 **Sīrjān**, Iran
53/G3 **Sīrjān**, Iran
73/D4 **Sir John** (cape), Austl.
64/G3 **Sirkali**, India
53/L3 **Sir Muttra**, India
37/F3 **Sirnach**, Swi.
50/E2 **Şırnak**, Turk.
52/D1 **Şırnak**, Turk.
53/K4 **Sirohi**, India
62/B3 **Sirohi**, India
62/C3 **Sironj**, India
39/J4 **Síros** (isl.), Gre.
41/H5 **Sırpsındığı**, Turk.
53/L3 **Sirsa**, India
62/C2 **Sirsa**, India
53/K6 **Sirsi**, India
62/B5 **Sirsi**, India
51/F3 **Sīrvān** (riv.), Iran
27/N1 **Širvintos**, Lith.
42/E5 **Širvintos**, Lith.
40/C3 **Sisak**, Cro.
63/H4 **Si Sa Ket**, Thai.
65/D3 **Sisaket**, Thai.
102/D1 **Sisal**, Mex.
65/B2 **Si Satchanalai** (ruins), Thai.
80/C2 **Sishen**, SAfr.
55/H4 **Sishui**, China
59/D4 **Sishui**, China
51/F2 **Sisian**, Arm.
37/E4 **Sisikon**, Swi.
91/H2 **Sisipuk** (lake), Mb, Sk,Can
63/H5 **Sisophon**, Camb.
65/C3 **Sisophon**, Camb.
36/D3 **Sissach**, Swi.
89/G2 **Sisseton**, SD,US
91/J4 **Sisseton**, SD,US
79/E4 **Sissili** (prov.), Burk.
30/C4 **Sissone**, Fr.
94/D4 **Sissonville**, WV,US
97/H2 **Sissonville**, WV,US
32/F4 **Sisteron**, Fr.
63/F3 **Sitākunda**, Bang.
81/E2 **Siteki**, Swaz.
35/F2 **Sitges**, Sp.
35/K7 **Sitges**, Sp.
39/H2 **Sithoniá** (pen.), Gre.
44/B4 **Sithoniá** (pen.), Gre.
39/K5 **Sitía**, Gre.
50/A3 **Sitía**, Gre.
54/C3 **Sitian**, China
85/M2 **Sitidgi** (lake), NW,Can
85/L4 **Sitka**, Ak,US
86/C3 **Sitka**, Ak,US
27/K4 **Sitno** (peak), Slvk.
40/D1 **Sitno** (peak), Slvk.
60/C5 **Sittang** (riv.), Burma
65/B2 **Sittang** (riv.), Burma
26/C3 **Sittard**, Neth.
28/C7 **Sittard**, Neth.
31/E2 **Sittard**, Neth.
29/G2 **Sittensen**, Ger.
37/F3 **Sitter** (riv.), Swi.
25/G4 **Sittingbourne**, Eng,UK
60/B4 **Sittwe** (Akyab), Burma
63/F3 **Sittwe** (Akyab), Burma
40/D3 **Sivac**, Yugo.
64/G4 **Sivaganga**, India
62/C6 **Sivakāsi**, India
64/F4 **Sivakāsi**, India
51/H4 **Sīvand**, Iran
52/F2 **Sīvand**, Iran
44/F5 **Sivas**, Turk.
44/F5 **Sivas** (prov.), Turk.
46/D6 **Sivas**, Turk.
50/D2 **Sivas**, Turk.
50/D2 **Sivas** (prov.), Turk.
50/D2 **Siverek**, Turk.
42/F4 **Siverskiy**, Rus.
36/C4 **Siviriez**, Swi.
44/D5 **Sivrihisar**, Turk.
50/B2 **Sivrihisar**, Turk.
30/D3 **Sivry-Rance**, Belg.
77/L2 **Sīwah**, Egypt
64/D2 **Siwālik** (range), India
62/D2 **Siwālik** (range), Nepal
62/D2 **Siwān**, India
99/Q15 **Six Flags Great America**, Il,US
55/H5 **Si Xian**, China
59/D4 **Si Xian**, China
22/A2 **Sixmilecross**, NI,UK
77/M4 **Sixth** (fall, falls), Sudan
74/F3 **Sixth Cataract** (falls), Sudan
85/K3 **Sixtymile**, Yk,Can
80/Q12 **Siyabuswa**, SAfr.
82/E6 **Siyabuswa**, SAfr.
55/H5 **Siyang**, China
59/D4 **Siyang**, China
54/F5 **Siyichang**, China
47/M5 **Siziwang**, China
54/G3 **Siziwang**, China
20/D5 **Sjælland** (isl.), Den.
39/G1 **Sjenica**, Yugo.
40/E4 **Sjenica**, Yugo.
20/M6 **Sjónfridh** (peak), Ice.
20/F1 **Sjøvegan**, Nor.
42/C1 **Sjøvegan**, Nor.
41/L2 **Skadovsk**, Ukr.
20/P7 **Skaftafell Nat'l Park**, Ice.
20/D4 **Skagen**, Den.
20/D4 **Skagens** (cape), Den.
18/D3 **Skagerrak** (str.), Eur.
20/D4 **Skagerrak** (str.), Eur.
46/A4 **Skagerrak** (str.), Eur
85/L4 **Skagway**, Ak,US
39/H4 **Skála**, Gre.
20/P6 **Skálfandafljót** (riv.), Ice.
27/J4 **Skalica**, Slvk.
33/K2 **Skalice** (riv.), Czh.
39/J3 **Skantzoura** (isl.), Gre.
20/E4 **Skaraborg** (co.), Swe.
27/L3 **Skarżysko-Kamienna**, Pol.
44/B2 **Skarżysko-Kamienna**, Pol.
42/D5 **Skaudvilė**, Lith.
27/K4 **Skawina**, Pol.
90/A2 **Skeena** (riv.), BC,Can
86/D3 **Skeena** (range), BC,Can
86/D3 **Skeena** (riv.), BC,Can
23/J5 **Skegness**, Eng,UK
18/F2 **Skellefteå**, Swe.
20/G2 **Skellefteå**, Swe.
42/D2 **Skellefteå**, Swe.
46/C3 **Skellefteå**, Swe.
18/E2 **Skellefteälv** (riv.), Swe.
20/F2 **Skellefteälv** (riv.), Swe.
42/C2 **Skellefteälv** (riv.), Swe.
20/G2 **Skelleftehamn**, Swe.
42/D2 **Skelleftehamn**, Swe.
23/G4 **Skelmanthorpe**, Eng,UK
23/F4 **Skelmersdale**, Eng,UK
23/H2 **Skelton**, Eng,UK
23/G2 **Skerne** (riv.), Eng,UK
22/B4 **Skerries**, Ire.
39/H3 **Skhimatárion**, Gre.
39/G4 **Skhiza** (isl.), Gre.
43/X9 **Skhodnya** (riv.), Rus.
39/H3 **Skíathos**, Gre.
44/B5 **Skíathos**, Gre.
93/H3 **Skiatook**, Ok,US
96/D2 **Skiatook**, Ok,US
21/H8 **Skibbereen**, Ire.
23/E2 **Skiddaw** (mtn.), Eng,UK
85/M5 **Skidegate**, BC,Can
27/N2 **Skidel'**, Bela.
42/E5 **Skidel'**, Bela.
44/C1 **Skidel'**, Bela.
39/H2 **Skídhra**, Gre.
40/F5 **Skídhra**, Gre.
18/D3 **Skien**, Nor.
20/D4 **Skien**, Nor.
46/A4 **Skien**, Nor.
27/K3 **Skierniewice** (prov.), Pol.
27/L3 **Skierniewice**, Pol.
75/V17 **Skikda**, Alg.
75/V17 **Skikda** (gov.), Alg.
76/G1 **Skikda**, Alg.
39/G4 **Skinári, Ákra** (cape), Gre.
23/H4 **Skipsea**, Eng,UK
23/F4 **Skipton**, Eng,UK
23/F3 **Skirfare** (riv.), Eng,UK
39/J3 **Skíros**, Gre.
39/J3 **Skíros** (isl.), Gre.
44/C5 **Skíros** (isl.), Gre.
20/D4 **Skjeberg**, Nor.
42/B2 **Skjelåtinden** (peak), Nor.
20/D5 **Skjern**, Den.
33/L3 **Škofja Loka**, Slov.
40/B2 **Škofja Loka**, Slov.
24/A3 **Skokholm** (isl.), Wal,UK
99/Q15 **Skokie**, Il,US
99/Q15 **Skokie** (riv.), Il,US
27/M4 **Skole**, Ukr.
43/X9 **Skolniki Park**, Rus.
24/A3 **Skomer** (isl.), Wal,UK
65/D3 **Skon**, Camb.
39/H3 **Skópelos**, Gre.
39/H3 **Skópelos** (isl.), Gre.
44/F1 **Skopin**, Rus.
18/F4 **Skopje** (cap.), Macd.
39/G2 **Skopje** (cap.), Macd.
40/E5 **Skopje** (cap.), Macd.
41/F5 **Skoútari**, Gre.
20/E4 **Skövde**, Swe.
47/N4 **Skovorodino**, Rus.
55/J1 **Skovorodino**, Rus.
89/N3 **Skowhegan**, Me,US
95/G2 **Skowhegan**, Me,US
42/E5 **Skrudaliena**, Lat.
85/L3 **Skukum** (mtn.), Yk,Can
21/H8 **Skull**, Ire.
93/K2 **Skunk** (riv.), Ia,US
94/A3 **Skunk** (riv.), Ia,US
27/G1 **Skurup**, Swe.
85/H3 **Skwentna**, Ak,US
27/H2 **Skwierzyna**, Pol.
21/B2 **Skye** (isl.), Sc,UK
99/D2 **Skykomish** (riv.), Wa,US
98/E4 **Skytop**, Pa,US
20/D5 **Slagelse**, Den.
23/F4 **Slaidburn**, Eng,UK
27/L4 **Slaná** (riv.), Slvk.
85/K3 **Slana**, Ak,US
22/B4 **Slane**, Ire.
22/B6 **Slaney** (riv.), Ire.
41/G3 **Slănic**, Rom.
41/H2 **Slănic-Moldova**, Rom.
20/J4 **Slantsy**, Rus.
42/F4 **Slantsy**, Rus.
41/G3 **Slatina**, Rom.
44/C3 **Slatina**, Rom.
98/E5 **Slatington**, Pa,US
101/E1 **Slaton**, Tx,US
84/F3 **Slave** (riv.), Can.
79/F5 **Slave Coast** (reg.), Afr.
86/E3 **Slave Lake**, Ab,Can
90/E2 **Slave Lake**, Ab,Can
46/H4 **Slavgorod**, Rus.
33/M2 **Slavkov u Brna**, Czh.
40/C3 **Slavonia** (reg.), Cro.
40/C3 **Slavonska Požega**, Cro.
40/D3 **Slavonski Brod**, Cro.
44/C2 **Slavuta**, Ukr.
41/G4 **Slavyanovo**, Bul.
44/F2 **Slavyansk**, Ukr.
44/F3 **Slavyansk-na-Kubani**, Rus.
27/J1 **Sławno**, Pol.
91/K5 **Slayton**, Mn,US
93/J2 **Slayton**, Mn,US
23/H6 **Sleaford**, Eng,UK
28/D3 **Sleen**, Neth.
87/H3 **Sleeper** (isls.), NW,Can
91/K4 **Sleepy Eye**, Mn,US
93/J1 **Sleepy Eye**, Mn,US
99/P15 **Sleepy Hollow**, Il,US
85/G3 **Sleetmute**, Ak,US
22/A4 **Sliabh na Caillighe** (mtn.), Ire.
27/K4 **Sliač**, Slvk.
89/J5 **Slidell**, La,US
97/F4 **Slidell**, La,US
20/D3 **Slidre**, Nor.
28/B5 **Sliedrecht**, Neth.
38/D5 **Sliema**, Malta
22/A3 **Slieve Beagh** (mtn.), NI,UK
22/C3 **Slieve Binnian** (mtn.), NI,UK
22/C3 **Slieve Croob** (mtn.), NI,UK
22/C3 **Slieve Donard** (mtn.), NI,UK
22/B3 **Slieve Gullion** (mtn.), NI,UK
22/A1 **Slieve Snaght** (mtn.), Ire.
18/C3 **Sligo**, Ire.
21/A3 **Sligo**, Ire.
21/A3 **Sligo** (bay), Ire.
20/F4 **Slite**, Swe.
42/C4 **Slite**, Swe.
18/F4 **Sliven**, Bul.
39/K1 **Sliven**, Bul.
41/H4 **Sliven**, Bul.
44/C4 **Sliven**, Bul.
39/H1 **Slivnitsa**, Bul.
40/F4 **Slivnitsa**, Bul.
95/S10 **Sloan**, NY,US
98/F4 **Sloatsburg**, NY,US
41/J2 **Slobodka**, Ukr.
43/L4 **Slobodskoy**, Rus.
41/J2 **Slobodzeya**, Mol.
41/H3 **Slobozia**, Rom.
28/D2 **Slochteren**, Neth.
42/E5 **Slonim**, Bela.
44/C1 **Slonim**, Bela.
28/C3 **Sloten**, Neth.
28/C3 **Slotermeer** (lake), Neth.
19/M7 **Slough**, Eng,UK
25/F4 **Slough**, Eng,UK
18/E4 **Slovakia**
27/K4 **Slovakia**
33/M2 **Slovakia**
40/D1 **Slovakia**
44/A2 **Slovakia**
46/B5 **Slovakia**
18/E4 **Slovenia**
33/L4 **Slovenia**
40/B3 **Slovenia**
33/L3 **Slovenj Gradec**, Slov.
40/B2 **Slovenj Gradec**, Slov.
33/L3 **Slovenska Bistrica**, Slov.
40/B2 **Slovenska Bistrica**, Slov.
27/K4 **Slovenska L'upča**, Slvk.
33/L3 **Slovenske Konjice**, Slov.
40/B2 **Slovenske Konjice**, Slov.
27/L4 **Slovenské Rudohorie** (mts.), Slvk.
27/J1 **Słowiński Nat'l Park**, Pol.
27/H2 **Słubice**, Pol.
44/C2 **Sluch'** (riv.), Ukr.
37/G4 **Sluderno** (Schluderns), It.
28/A6 **Sluis**, Neth.
30/C1 **Sluis**, Neth.
27/J2 **Słupca**, Pol.
27/J1 **Słupia** (riv.), Pol.
18/E3 **Słupsk**, Pol.
27/J1 **Słupsk**, Pol.
27/J1 **Słupsk** (prov.), Pol.
46/B4 **Słupsk**, Pol.
44/C1 **Slutsk**, Bela.
21/G7 **Slyne Head** (pt.), Ire.
47/L4 **Slyudyanka**, Rus.
54/E1 **Slyudyanka**, Rus.
19/N8 **Smallfield**, Eng,UK
25/F4 **Smallfield**, Eng,UK
84/L4 **Smallwood** (res.), Can.
87/K3 **Smallwood** (res.), Nf,Can
91/G2 **Smeaton**, Sk,Can
40/E3 **Smederevo**, Yugo.
44/B3 **Smederevo**, Yugo.
40/E3 **Smederevska Palanka**, Yugo.
20/E3 **Smedjebacken**, Swe.
42/B3 **Smedjebacken**, Swe.
44/D2 **Smela**, Ukr.
75/V17 **Smendou** (riv.), Alg.
27/J2 **Śmigiel**, Pol.
28/D3 **Smilde**, Neth.
20/H4 **Smiltene**, Lat.
42/E4 **Smiltene**, Lat.
47/Q5 **Smirnykh**, Rus.
83/V **Smith** (pen.), Ant.
90/B3 **Smith** (inlet), BC,Can
87/J2 **Smith** (isl.), NW,Can
90/F4 **Smith** (riv.), Mt,US
86/D3 **Smithers**, BC,Can
90/B2 **Smithers**, BC,Can
97/J3 **Smithfield**, NC,US
90/F5 **Smithfield**, Ut,US
92/E2 **Smithfield**, Ut,US
94/E4 **Smith Mtn.** (lake), Va,US
99/G6 **Smiths Creek**, Mi,US
94/E2 **Smiths Falls**, On,Can
71/H8 **Smithton**, Austl.
73/C4 **Smithton**, Austl.
95/Q9 **Smithville**, On,Can
93/J4 **Smithville**, Ok,US
96/E3 **Smithville**, Ok,US
73/E1 **Smoky** (cape), Austl.
90/D2 **Smoky** (riv.), Ab,Can
86/E3 **Smoky** (riv.), Ab,Can
93/H3 **Smoky** (hills), Ks,US
96/D2 **Smoky** (hills), Ks,US
70/E6 **Smoky Bay**, Austl.
88/F4 **Smoky Hill** (riv.), Ks,US
90/E2 **Smoky Lake**, Ab,Can
20/C3 **Smøla** (isl.), Nor.
18/G3 **Smolensk**, Rus.
42/G5 **Smolensk**, Rus.
44/E1 **Smolensk**, Rus.
46/D4 **Smolensk**, Rus.
42/F5 **Smolensk Obl.**, Rus.
44/D1 **Smolensk Obl.**, Rus.
44/D1 **Smolevichi**, Bela.
39/G2 **Smólikas** (peak), Gre.
39/J2 **Smolyan**, Bul.
41/G5 **Smolyan**, Bul.
44/C4 **Smolyan**, Bul.
94/D1 **Smooth Rock Falls**, On,Can
42/E5 **Smorgon'**, Bela.
44/C1 **Smorgon'**, Bela.
41/H4 **Smyadovo**, Bul.
83/U **Smyley** (isl.), Ant.
97/G3 **Smyrna**, Ga,US
22/D3 **Snaefell** (mtn.), IM,UK
85/M2 **Snake** (riv.), Yk,Can
86/C2 **Snake** (riv.), Yk,Can
90/D4 **Snake** (riv.), US
84/F5 **Snake** (riv.), US
86/E4 **Snake** (riv.), US
88/D3 **Snake** (riv.), US
92/C2 **Snake** (riv.), US
90/E5 **Snake River** (plain), Id,US
92/D2 **Snake River** (plain), Id,US
71/Q12 **Snares** (isls.), NZ
20/E2 **Snåsa**, Nor.
42/B2 **Snåsa**, Nor.
26/C2 **Sneek**, Neth.
28/C2 **Sneek**, Neth.
28/C2 **Sneekermeer** (lake), Neth.
80/B4 **Sneeuberg** (peak), SAfr.
80/D3 **Sneeuberg** (mts.), SAfr.
80/L11 **Sneeuwkop** (peak), SAfr.
95/Q8 **Snelgrove**, On,Can
25/G1 **Snettisham**, Eng,UK
27/H3 **Sněžka** (peak), Czh.
33/L4 **Snežnik** (peak), Yugo.
40/B3 **Snežnik** (peak), Yugo.
27/L2 **Śniardwy** (lake), Pol.
42/D5 **Śniardwy** (lake), Pol.
41/L2 **Snigirëvka**, Ukr.
25/G4 **Snodland**, Eng,UK
20/D3 **Snøhetta** (peak), Nor.
99/C2 **Snohomish**, Wa,US
99/C2 **Snohomish** (riv.), Wa,US
99/D2 **Snohomish** (co.), Wa,US
99/D2 **Snoqualmie**, Wa,US
99/D2 **Snoqualmie** (falls), Wa,US
99/D2 **Snoqualmie** (riv.), Wa,US
99/D2 **Snoqualmie Falls**, Wa,US
99/D3 **Snoqualmie, Middle Fork** (riv.), Wa,US
99/D3 **Snoqualmie-Mount Baker Nat'l For.**, Wa,US
99/D2 **Snoqualmie, North Fork** (riv.), Wa,US
99/D3 **Snoqualmie, South Fork** (riv.), Wa,US
20/E2 **Snøtind** (peak), Nor.
42/B2 **Snøtind** (peak), Nor.
22/D5 **Snowdon** (mtn.), Wal,UK
22/D5 **Snowdonia Nat'l Park**, Wal,UK
24/B1 **Snowdownia Nat'l Park**, Wal,UK
86/E2 **Snowdrift**, NW,Can
92/E4 **Snowflake**, Az,US
91/H2 **Snow Lake**, Mb,Can
73/D3 **Snowy** (riv.), Austl.
85/K2 **Snowy** (peak), Ak,US
73/D3 **Snowy River Nat'l Park**, Austl.
41/G1 **Snyatyn**, Ukr.
101/E1 **Snyder**, Tx,US
88/F5 **Snyder**, Tx,US
93/G4 **Snyder**, Tx,US
96/C3 **Snyder**, Tx,US
81/H7 **Soalala**, Madg.
81/J7 **Soanierana-Ivongo**, Madg.
23/G6 **Soar** (riv.), Eng,UK
25/E1 **Soar** (riv.), Eng,UK
81/H7 **Soavinandriana**, Madg.
58/D5 **Sobaek** (mts.), SKo
103/G4 **Soberania Nat'l Pa**, Pan.
27/H4 **Soběslav**, Czh.
33/L2 **Soběslav**, Czh.
67/K4 **Sobger** (riv.), Indo.
53/J3 **Sobhādero**, Pak.
62/A2 **Sobhādero**, Pak.
33/L1 **Sobotka**, Czh.
105/E3 **Sobradinho** (res.), Braz.
107/K6 **Sobradinho** (res.), Braz.
107/K4 **Sobral**, Braz.
37/G5 **Sobretta, Monte** (peak), It.
57/M9 **Sobue**, Japan
33/K3 **Soča** (riv.), Slov.
27/L2 **Sochaczew**, Pol.
42/D5 **Sochaczew**, Pol.
44/B1 **Sochaczew**, Pol.
19/G4 **Sochi**, Rus.
44/F4 **Sochi**, Rus.
46/D5 **Sochi**, Rus.
58/D4 **Sŏch'ŏn**, SKor.
69/K6 **Society** (isls.), FrPo
100/C5 **Socorro** (isl.), Mex.
88/E5 **Socorro**, NM,US
92/F4 **Socorro**, NM,US
96/B3 **Socorro**, NM,US
100/D2 **Socorro**, Tx,US
93/F5 **Socorro**, Tx,US
96/B4 **Socorro**, Tx,US
48/E8 **Socotra** (isl.), Yem.
63/J6 **Soc Trang**, Viet.
65/D4 **Soc Trang**, Viet.
66/C2 **Soc Trang**, Viet.
34/D3 **Socuéllamos**, Sp.
20/H2 **Sodankylä**, Fin.
42/E2 **Sodankylä**, Fin.
90/F5 **Soda Springs**, Id,U
92/E2 **Soda Springs**, Id,U
57/H7 **Sodegaura**, Japan
42/C3 **Söderfors**, Swe.
20/F3 **Söderhamn**, Swe.
42/C3 **Söderhamn**, Swe.
20/E4 **Södermanland** (co.), Swe.
42/C4 **Södermanland** (co.), Swe.
20/F4 **Södertälje**, Swe.
42/C4 **Södertälje**, Swe.
77/N6 **Sodo**, Eth.
29/F5 **Soest**, Ger.
28/C4 **Soest**, Neth.
26/D2 **Soeste** (riv.), Ger.
29/E3 **Soeste** (riv.), Ger.
39/H3 **Sofádhes**, Gre.
18/F4 **Sofia** (cap.), Bul.
81/J6 **Sofia** (riv.), Madg.
39/H1 **Sofia** (Sofiya) (cap.), Bul.
41/F4 **Sofia** (Sofiya) (cap.), Bul.
44/B4 **Sofia** (Sofiya) (cap.), Bul.
39/H1 **Sofiya** (prov.), Bul.
40/F4 **Sofiya** (reg.), Bul.
39/H1 **Sofiya** (Sofia) (cap.), Bul.
41/F4 **Sofiya** (Sofia) (cap.), Bul.
44/B4 **Sofiya** (Sofia) (cap.), Bul.
47/P4 **Sofiysk**, Rus.
20/J2 **Sofporog**, Rus.
106/D2 **Sogamoso**, Col.
29/E3 **Sögel**, Ger.
52/F2 **Şoghād**, Iran
20/B3 **Sognafjorden** (fjord), Nor.
20/C3 **Sogn og Fjordane** (co.), Nor.
76/J4 **Sogollé** (well), Cha
44/E4 **Soğuksu Milli Park**, Turk.
50/C1 **Soğuksu Nat'l Park**, Turk.
50/B2 **Söğüt**, Turk.
55/K5 **Sŏgwip'o**, SKor.
51/G3 **Soh**, Iran
25/G2 **Soham**, Eng,UK
31/G4 **Sohren**, Ger.
58/D3 **Sŏhŭng**, NKor.
30/D2 **Soignies**, Belg.
19/U11 **Soignolles-en-Brie**, Fr.
26/B4 **Soissons**, Fr.
30/C5 **Soissons**, Fr.
32/E2 **Soissons**, Fr.
19/T11 **Soisy-sur-Seine**, Fr.
56/C3 **Sōja**, Japan
53/K3 **Sojat**, India
62/B2 **Sojat**, India
58/C3 **Sŏjosŏn** (bay), NKo
45/J1 **Sok** (riv.), Rus.
65/C3 **Sok** (pt.), Thai.
57/H7 **Sōka**, Japan
27/N3 **Sokal'**, Ukr.
55/K4 **Sokch'o**, SKor.
58/E3 **Sokch'o**, SKor.
50/A2 **Söke**, Turk.
54/F1 **Sokhor** (peak), Rus
39/H2 **Sokhós**, Gre.
41/F5 **Sokhós**, Gre.
41/H1 **Sokiryany**, Ukr.
20/D3 **Sokna**, Nor.
40/E4 **Sokobanja**, Yugo.
76/F6 **Sokodé**, Togo
79/F4 **Sokodé**, Togo
42/J4 **Sokol**, Rus.
27/M2 **Sokółka**, Pol.
42/D5 **Sokółka**, Pol.
44/B1 **Sokółka**, Pol.
26/G3 **Sokolov**, Czh.
33/K1 **Sokolov**, Czh.
27/M2 **Sokołów Podlaski**, Pol.

4/B1 **Sokołów Podlaski,** Pol.
76/F5 **Sokoto** (plains), Nga.
76/F5 **Sokoto** (riv.), Nga.
6/G5 **Sokoto,** Nga.
9/G3 **Sokoto** (state), Nga.
9/G4 **Sokoto** (plains), Nga.
9/G4 **Sokoto** (riv.), Nga.
20/C4 **Sola,** Nor.
6/C2 **Solano** (pt.), Col.
9/L10 **Solano** (co.), Ca,US
7/H3 **Solbad Hall in Tirol,** Aus.
1/G2 **Solca,** Rom.
4/C4 **Sol, Costa del** (coast), Sp.
3/J3 **Sölden,** Aus.
7/H4 **Sölden,** Aus.
5/H3 **Soldotna,** Ak,US
8/B2 **Soledad** (canyon), Ca,US
3/H4 **Soledad,** Col.
6/D1 **Soledad,** Col.
1/N7 **Soledad de Doblado,** Mex.
8/A4 **Soledade,** Braz.
25/E5 **Solent** (chan.), Eng,UK
0/C3 **Solesmes,** Fr.
1/E4 **Soleuvre** (mtn.), Lux.
0/E2 **Solhan,** Turk.
18/F3 **Soligorsk,** Bela.
4/C1 **Soligorsk,** Bela.
6/C4 **Soligorsk,** Bela.
25/E2 **Solihull,** Eng,UK
19/J3 **Solikamsk,** Rus.
3/N4 **Solikamsk,** Rus.
46/F4 **Solikamsk,** Rus.
5/K2 **Sol'-Iletsk,** Rus.
26/D3 **Solingen,** Ger.
29/E6 **Solingen,** Ger.
1/G1 **Solingen,** Ger.
20/F3 **Sollefteå,** Swe.
2/C3 **Sollefteå,** Swe.
5/G3 **Sóller,** Sp.
26/F3 **Solling** (mts.), Ger.
29/G5 **Solling** (mts.), Ger.
20/D3 **Søln** (peak), Nor.
32/F3 **Solnan** (riv.), Fr.
6/B5 **Solnan** (riv.), Fr.
3/X8 **Solnechnogorsk,** Rus.
3/X9 **Solntsevo,** Rus.
6/D5 **Solo** (riv.), Indo.
6/B4 **Solok,** Indo.
2/D3 **Sololá,** Guat.
8/E5 **Solomon** (sea), PNG, Sol.
85/F3 **Solomon,** Ak,US
8/E6 **Solomon Islands**
45/L4 **Solonchak Goklenkui** (salt marsh), Trkm.
3/G3 **Solothurn,** Swi.
6/D3 **Solothurn,** Swi.
6/D3 **Solothurn** (canton), Swi.
41/F2 **Solotvina,** Ukr.
2/G2 **Solovetskiy** (isls.), Rus.
0/D3 **Solre-le-Château,** Fr.
35/F2 **Solsona,** Sp.
0/D2 **Solt,** Hun.
8/D1 **Šolta** (isl.), Cro.
0/B4 **Šolta** (isl.), Cro.
26/E2 **Soltau,** Ger.
9/G3 **Soltau,** Ger.
0/D2 **Soltvadkert,** Hun.
9/G2 **Solunska** (peak), Macd.
0/E5 **Solunska** (peak), Macd.
4/A3 **Solva** (riv.), Wal,UK
2/B4 **Solvang,** Ca,US
20/E4 **Sölvesborg,** Swe.
22/E2 **Solway Firth** (inlet), Eng,UK
2/E3 **Solwezi,** Zam.
7/G2 **Sōma,** Japan
4/C5 **Soma,** Turk.
0/A2 **Soma,** Turk.
0/C3 **Somain,** Fr.
5/G4 **Somalia**
7/Q6 **Somalia**
2/H1 **Somalia**
95/F1 **Somaqua** (riv.), Qu,Can
0/D3 **Sombor,** Cro.
9/H6 **Sombra,** On,Can
0/E4 **Sombrerete,** Mex.
8/B4 **Sombrio,** Braz.
3/G5 **Somercotes,** Eng,UK
8/C6 **Someren,** Neth.
0/G3 **Somero,** Fin.
2/D3 **Somero,** Fin.
0/E3 **Somers,** Mt,US
/Q14 **Somers,** Wi,US
4/H2 **Somerset** (isl.), Can.
6/G1 **Somerset** (isl.), NW,Can
4/D4 **Somerset** (co.), Eng,UK
0/F5 **Somerset** (co.), NJ,US
9/K4 **Somerset,** Ky,US
4/C4 **Somerset,** Ky,US
7/G2 **Somerset,** Ky,US
5/S9 **Somerset,** NY,US
3/C4 **Somerset-Burnie,** Austl.
0/D4 **Somerset East,** SAfr.
2/E7 **Somerset East,** SAfr.
0/B4 **Somerset West,** SAfr.
/L11 **Somerset West,** SAfr.
5/F2 **Somersham,** Eng,UK
5/G3 **Somersworth,** NH,US
4/D4 **Somerton,** Eng,UK
2/D4 **Somerton,** Az,US
8/F5 **Somerville,** NJ,US
3/H5 **Somerville** (lake), Tx,US
1/F2 **Someș** (riv.), Rom.
4/B3 **Someș** (riv.), Rom.
1/G2 **Someșul Mare** (riv.), Rom.
58/D5 **Sŏmjin** (riv.), SKor.
75/T15 **Sommam** (riv.), Alg.
26/B3 **Somme** (riv.), Fr.
30/A3 **Somme** (riv.), Fr.
30/B4 **Somme** (dept.), Fr.
30/D6 **Somme** (riv.), Fr.
32/D1 **Somme** (bay), Fr.
32/E1 **Somme** (riv.), Fr.
30/B4 **Somme, Canal de la** (can.), Fr.
31/E5 **Sommedieue,** Fr.
31/E3 **Somme-Leuze,** Belg.
30/D5 **Somme-Soude** (riv.), Fr.
36/A1 **Sommevoire,** Fr.
40/C2 **Somogy** (co.), Hun.
102/E3 **Somoto,** Nic.
25/F5 **Somptin,** Eng,UK
37/E4 **Somvix,** Swi.
58/C3 **Sŏnch'ŏn,** NKor.
37/G5 **Sondalo,** It.
20/D5 **Sønderborg,** Den.
80/L11 **Sonderend** (riv.), SAfr.
26/E1 **Sønderjylland** (co.), Den.
33/H3 **Sondrio,** It.
37/F5 **Sondrio,** It.
37/F5 **Sondrio** (prov.), It.
53/L3 **Sonepat,** India
62/C2 **Sonepat,** India
62/D3 **Sonepur,** India
63/J5 **Song Cau,** Viet.
65/E3 **Song Cau,** Viet.
65/D4 **Song Dinh,** Viet.
82/G3 **Songea,** Tanz.
47/N5 **Songhua** (riv.), China
48/M5 **Songhua** (riv.), China
55/K2 **Songhua** (riv.), China
59/F1 **Songhua** (riv.), China
58/D4 **Sŏnghwan,** SKor.
54/D2 **Songino,** Mong.
55/J5 **Songjiang,** China
59/E5 **Songjiang,** China
59/L8 **Songjiang,** China
56/A3 **Sŏngju,** SKor.
58/E5 **Sŏngju,** SKor.
63/H6 **Songkhla,** Thai.
65/C5 **Songkhla,** Thai.
66/B2 **Songkhla,** Thai.
60/D5 **Songkhram** (riv.), Thai.
63/H4 **Songkhram** (riv.), Thai.
65/C2 **Songkhram** (riv.), Thai.
55/J2 **Songling,** China
60/D4 **Song Ma,** Viet.
65/C1 **Song Ma,** Viet.
60/D3 **Songming,** China
63/H2 **Songming,** China
58/D4 **Sŏngnam,** SKor.
58/G7 **Sŏngnam,** SKor.
58/C3 **Songnim,** NKor.
82/F4 **Songo,** Moz.
82/B2 **Songololo,** Zaire
59/C4 **Song Shan** (peak), China
55/K4 **Songt'an,** SKor.
58/D4 **Songt'an,** SKor.
65/E2 **Songtao,** China
61/F2 **Songtao Miaozu Zizhixian,** China
55/K3 **Songwŏn,** NKor.
61/H3 **Songxi,** China
54/G5 **Song Xian,** China
59/C4 **Song Xian,** China
63/J2 **Songyan,** China
59/B5 **Songzi,** China
61/F2 **Songzi,** China
59/C5 **Songzi Guan** (pass), China
61/G2 **Songzi Guan** (pass), China
61/G2 **Songzi Hudu** (riv.), China
65/E3 **Son Ha,** Viet.
57/M10 **Soni,** Japan
47/M5 **Sonid Youqi,** China
54/G3 **Sonid Youqi,** China
47/M5 **Sonid Zuoqi,** China
54/G3 **Sonid Zuoqi,** China
60/D4 **Son La,** Viet.
65/C1 **Son La,** Viet.
53/J3 **Sonmiāni** (bay), Pak.
26/F3 **Sonneberg,** Ger.
33/J1 **Sonneberg,** Ger.
25/F4 **Sonning,** Eng,UK
37/H3 **Sonnjoch** (peak), Aus.
26/G5 **Sonntagshorn** (peak), Ger.
107/J5 **Sono** (riv.), Braz.
56/D3 **Sonobe,** Japan
57/L9 **Sonobe,** Japan
99/J10 **Sonoma** (co.), Ca,US
99/J10 **Sonoma** (cr.), Ca,US
99/J10 **Sonoma** (mts.), Ca,US
99/K10 **Sonoma,** Ca,US
100/C2 **Sonora** (riv.), Mex.
100/C2 **Sonora** (state), Mex.
88/D5 **Sonora** (state), Mex.
92/E5 **Sonora** (riv.), Mex
92/E5 **Sonora** (state), Mex
92/B3 **Sonora,** Ca,US
88/F5 **Sonora,** Tx,US
93/G5 **Sonora,** Tx,US
96/C4 **Sonora,** Tx,US
100/B2 **Sonoyta,** Mex.
100/B2 **Sonoyta** (riv.), Mex.
92/D5 **Sonoyta,** Mex
51/F3 **Sonqor,** Iran
52/E2 **Sonqor,** Iran
56/A2 **Sŏnsan,** SKor.
58/E4 **Sŏnsan,** SKor.
28/D5 **Sonsbeck,** Ger.
34/D3 **Sonseca,** Sp.
35/G3 **Son Servera,** Sp.
102/D3 **Sonsonate,** ESal.
68/C4 **Sonsorol** (isls.), Palau
40/D3 **Sonta,** Yugo.
60/E4 **Son Tay,** Viet.
65/D1 **Son Tay,** Viet.
37/G2 **Sontheim,** Ger.
26/F5 **Sonthofen,** Ger.
37/G2 **Sonthofen,** Ger.
29/G6 **Sontra,** Ger.
37/E5 **Sonvico,** Swi.
67/G3 **Sopi** (cape), Indo.
65/C1 **Sopka,** Laos
63/H3 **Sop Kai,** Laos
53/K2 **Sopore,** India
39/J1 **Sopot,** Bul.
41/G4 **Sopot,** Bul.
27/K1 **Sopot,** Pol.
18/E4 **Sopron,** Hun.
27/J5 **Sopron,** Hun.
33/M3 **Sopron,** Hun.
40/C2 **Sopron,** Hun.
24/D3 **Sôr** (riv.), Wal,UK
38/C2 **Sora,** It.
55/K4 **Sŏrak-san** (mtn.), SKor.
58/E3 **Sŏrak-san** (mtn.), SKor.
56/A1 **Sŏraksan Nat'l Park,** SKor.
58/E3 **Sŏraksan Nat'l Park,** SKor.
106/E7 **Sorata,** Bol.
34/D4 **Sorbas,** Sp.
31/E6 **Sorcy-Saint-Martin,** Fr.
89/M2 **Sorel,** Qu,Can
95/F2 **Sorel,** Qu,Can
73/C4 **Sorell-Midway Point,** Austl.
49/F8 **Soreq, Nabel** (dry riv.), Isr.
33/H4 **Soresina,** It.
32/F5 **Sorgues,** Fr.
44/E5 **Sorgun,** Turk.
50/C2 **Sorgun,** Turk.
34/D2 **Soria,** Sp.
66/A3 **Sorikmerapi** (peak), Indo.
45/K3 **Sor Karatuley** (salt pan), Kaz.
45/K3 **Sor Kaydak** (salt marsh), Kaz.
45/K3 **Sor Mertvyy Kultuk** (salt marsh), Kaz.
30/D4 **Sormonne** (riv.), Fr.
26/F1 **Sorø,** Den.
107/J8 **Sorocaba,** Braz.
108/C2 **Sorocaba,** Braz.
109/G1 **Sorocaba,** Braz.
45/K1 **Sorochinsk,** Rus.
41/J1 **Soroki,** Mol.
44/D2 **Soroki,** Mol.
68/D4 **Sorol** (atoll), Micr.
67/H4 **Sorong,** Indo.
68/C5 **Sorong,** Indo.
77/M7 **Soroti,** Ugan.
20/G1 **Sørøya** (isl.), Nor.
20/G1 **Sørøysundet** (chan.), Nor.
29/E6 **Sorpestausee** (res.), Ger.
34/A3 **Sorraia** (riv.), Port.
38/D2 **Sorrento,** It.
82/B5 **Sorris-Sorris,** Namb.
20/F2 **Sorsele,** Swe.
42/C2 **Sorsele,** Swe.
38/A2 **Sorso,** It.
35/F1 **Sort,** Sp.
20/J3 **Sortavala,** Rus.
42/F3 **Sortavala,** Rus.
20/G4 **Sõrve** (pt.), Est.
42/D4 **Sõrve** (pt.), Est.
58/D4 **Sosa,** SKor.
58/F7 **Sosa,** SKor.
58/D4 **Sŏsan,** SKor.
58/C4 **Sŏsan Haean Nat'l Park,** SKor.
34/E1 **Sos del Rey Católico,** Sp.
29/H5 **Söse** (riv.), Ger.
44/F1 **Sosna** (riv.), Rus.
43/M3 **Sosnogorsk,** Rus.
43/L4 **Sosnovka,** Rus.
20/J3 **Sosnovo,** Rus.
42/F3 **Sosnovo,** Rus.
47/M4 **Sosnovo-Ozerskoye,** Rus.
27/K3 **Sosnowiec,** Pol.
44/A2 **Sosnowiec,** Pol.
104/D3 **Sosúa,** DRep.
101/F4 **Soto la Marina,** Mex.
29/G2 **Sottrum,** Ger.
101/H4 **Sotuta,** Mex.
102/D1 **Sotuta,** Mex.
30/D6 **Soude** (riv.), Fr.
98/E5 **Souderton,** Pa,US
39/J5 **Soúdha,** Gre.
31/G6 **Souffelweyersheim,** Fr.
31/G6 **Soufflenheim,** Fr.
39/K2 **Souflíon,** Gre.
41/H5 **Souflíon,** Gre.
104/F3 **Soufrière** (peak), Guad.
104/F4 **Soufrière** (peak), StV.
32/D4 **Souillac,** Fr.
81/G15 **Souillac,** Mrts.
75/V17 **Souk Ahras,** Alg.
75/V17 **Souk Ahras** (gov.), Alg.
76/G1 **Souk Ahras,** Alg.
32/C4 **Soulac-sur-Mer,** Fr.
95/M7 **Soulanges** (co.), Qu,Can
55/K4 **Sŏul** (Seoul) (cap.), SKor.
58/D4 **Sŏul** (Seoul) (cap.), SKor.
36/D2 **Soultz-Haut-Rhin,** Fr.
31/G1 **Soultz-sous-Forets,** Fr.
79/E3 **Soum** (prov.), Burk.
31/E2 **Soumagne,** Belg.
20/E5 **Sound, The** (sound), Den., Swe.
26/B4 **Souppes-sur-Loing,** Fr.
32/E2 **Souppes-sur-Loing,** Fr.
80/E3 **Sources, Mont aux** (peak), Les.
107/J4 **Soure,** Braz.
34/A2 **Soure,** Port.
75/S15 **Sour El Ghozlane,** Alg.
91/H3 **Souris,** Mb,Can
95/J2 **Souris,** PE,Can
87/K4 **Souris,** PE,Can
86/F4 **Souris** (riv.), Can., US
91/H3 **Souris** (riv.), Can., US
88/F1 **Souris** (riv.), Can., US
78/E3 **Sourou** (prov.), Burk.
76/D2 **Sous** (wadi), Mor.
107/L5 **Sousa,** Braz.
34/B3 **Sousel,** Port.
32/C5 **Soustons,** Fr.
80/C3 **Sout** (dry riv.), SAfr.
80/M11 **Sout** (riv.), SAfr.
72/G8 **South** (cr.), Austl.
95/H2 **South** (mts.), NS,Can
87/H2 **South** (bay), NW,Can
71/Q11 **South** (isl.), N.Z.
71/Q12 **South** (cape), N.Z.
74/E7 **South Africa**
80/C3 **South Africa**
80/P12 **South Africa**
82/D6 **South Africa**
19/M7 **Southall,** Eng,UK
25/E2 **Southam,** Eng,UK
105/* **South America**
16/E6 **South America**
84/J3 **Southampton** (isl.), Can.
94/D2 **Southampton,** Can
87/H2 **Southampton** (cape), NW,Can
87/H2 **Southampton** (isl.), NW,Can
18/C3 **Southampton,** Eng,UK
25/E5 **Southampton,** Eng,UK
32/C1 **Southampton,** Eng,UK
25/E5 **Southampton Water** (inlet), Eng,UK
63/F5 **South Andaman** (isl.), India
97/H3 **South Augusta,** Ga,US
87/K3 **South Aulatsivik** (isl.), Nf,Can
70/E5 **South Australia** (state), Austl.
72/A4 **South Australia** (state), Austl.
73/A1 **South Australia** (state), Austl.
93/K4 **Southaven,** Ms,US
97/F3 **Southaven,** Ms,US
22/D3 **South Barrule** (mtn.), IM,UK
89/J3 **South Bend,** In,US
94/C3 **South Bend,** In,US
90/C4 **South Bend,** Wa,US
19/P8 **Southborough,** Eng,UK
25/G4 **Southborough,** Eng,UK
94/E4 **South Boston,** Va,US
97/J2 **South Boston,** Va,US
25/F5 **Southbourne,** Eng,UK
24/C6 **South Brent,** Eng,UK
95/F2 **South Burlington,** Vt,US
103/J1 **South Caicos** (isl.), Trks.
89/K5 **South Carolina** (state), US
97/H3 **South Carolina** (state), US
68/A3 **South China** (sea)
48/L8 **South China** (sea), Asia
61/G4 **South China** (sea), Asia
63/J6 **South China** (sea), Asia
66/D1 **South China** (sea), Asia
99/B2 **South Colby,** Wa,US
91/H4 **South Dakota** (state), US
86/F4 **South Dakota** (state), US
88/F3 **South Dakota** (state), US
93/G1 **South Dakota** (state), US
24/D5 **South Dorset Downs** (uplands), Eng,UK
25/F5 **South Downs** (hills), Eng,UK
32/C1 **South Downs** (hills), Eng,UK
71/H7 **South East** (pt.), Austl.
73/C3 **South East** (pt.), Austl.
103/H1 **Southeast** (pt.), Bahm.
104/C2 **Southeast** (pt.), Bahm.
80/D2 **South-East** (dist.), Bots.
103/G2 **Southeast** (pt.), Jam.
85/E3 **Southeast** (cape), Ak,US
99/P16 **South Elgin,** Il,US
23/G4 **South Elmsall,** Eng,UK
22/C1 **Southend,** Sc,UK
25/G3 **Southend on Sea,** Eng,UK
80/D2 **Southern** (dist.), Bots.
49/D4 **Southern** (dist.), Isr.
49/F8 **Southern** (dist.), Isr.
78/B5 **Southern** (prov.), SLeo.
71/Q11 **Southern Alps** (range), NZ
69/J6 **Southern Cook** (isls.), CookIs.
70/B6 **Southern Cross,** Austl.
86/G3 **Southern Indian** (lake), Mb,Can
97/J3 **Southern Pines,** NC,US
22/D1 **Southern Uplands** (mts.), Sc,UK
43/N5 **Southern Ural** (mts.), Rus.
25/G1 **Southery,** Eng,UK
73/C4 **South Esk** (riv.), Austl.
70/D3 **Southesk Tablelands** (plat.), Austl.
99/F7 **Southfield,** Mi,US
25/H4 **South Foreland** (pt.), UK
30/A1 **South Foreland** (pt.), Eng,UK
92/F3 **South Fork,** Co,US
96/B2 **South Fork,** Co,US
94/B4 **South Fulton,** Tn,US
97/F2 **South Fulton,** Tn,US
98/B3 **South Gate,** Ca,US
19/N7 **Southgate,** Eng,UK
99/F7 **Southgate,** Mi,US
83/X **South Georgia** (isl.), Ant.
24/C4 **South Glamorgan** (co.), Wal,UK
24/C6 **South Hams** (plain), Eng,UK
25/F5 **South Hayling,** UK
94/E4 **South Hill,** Va,US
97/J2 **South Hill,** Va,US
28/B5 **South Holland** (prov.), Neth.
99/Q16 **South Holland,** Il,US
19/N8 **South Holmwood,** Eng,UK
23/G4 **South Kirkby,** Eng,UK
47/N6 **South Korea**
48/M6 **South Korea**
55/K4 **South Korea**
56/A2 **South Korea**
58/D4 **South Korea**
92/C3 **South Lake Tahoe,** Ca,US
101/E1 **Southland,** Tx,US
91/J5 **South Loup** (riv.), Nb,US
82/F3 **South Luangwa Nat'l Park,** Zam.
99/E7 **South Lyon,** Mi,US
83/K **South Magnetic Pole,** Ant.
99/Q14 **South Milwaukee,** Wi,US
25/G3 **Southminster,** Eng,UK
24/C4 **South Molton,** Eng,UK
91/J2 **South Moose** (lake), Mb,Can
85/M5 **South Moresby Nat'l Park Rsv.,** BC,Can
86/C3 **South Moresby Nat'l Park Rsv.,** BC,Can
85/G4 **South Naknek,** Ak,US
23/G5 **South Normanton,** Eng,UK
19/P7 **South Ockenden,** Eng,UK
98/F5 **South Orange,** NJ,US
83/W **South Orkney** (isls.), Ant.
45/G4 **South Ossetian Aut. Obl.,** Geo.
51/E1 **South Ossetian Aut. Obl.,** Geo.
46/E5 **South Ossetian Aut. Oblast,** Geo.
19/M7 **South Oxhey,** Eng,UK
25/F3 **South Oxhey,** Eng,UK
68/G7 **South Pacific** (ocean)
24/D5 **South Petherton,** Eng,UK
72/E6 **South Pine** (riv.), Austl.
98/F5 **South Plainfield,** NJ,US
91/H5 **South Platte** (riv.), Co, Ne,US
88/F3 **South Platte** (riv.), Co, Ne,US
83/W **South Polar** (plat.), Ant.
83/A **South Pole,** Ant.
23/E4 **Southport,** Eng,UK
97/J3 **Southport,** NC,US
99/C3 **South Praire** (cr.), Wa,US
99/C3 **South Prairie,** Wa,US
99/F7 **South Rockwood,** Mi,US
83/Y **South Sandwich** (isls.), Ant.
99/K11 **South San Francisco,** Ca,US
86/E3 **South Saskatchewan** (riv.), Ab, Sk,Can
88/E1 **South Saskatchewan** (riv.), Sk,Can
83/W **South Shetland** (isls.), Ant.
23/G2 **South Shields,** Eng,UK
93/H2 **South Sioux City,** Ne,US
62/E3 **South Suburban,** India
71/R10 **South Taranaki** (bight), NZ
23/F2 **South Tyne** (riv.), Eng,UK
67/F2 **South Ubian,** Phil.
92/B2 **South Umpqua** (riv.), Or,US
19/N7 **Southwark** (bor.), Eng,UK
23/H5 **Southwell,** Eng,UK
71/H8 **South West** (cape), Austl.
73/C4 **South West** (cape), Austl.
104/B1 **Southwest** (pt.), Bahm.
104/C2 **Southwest** (pt.), Bahm.
73/C4 **South West Nat'l Park,** Austl.
73/E1 **South West Rocks,** Austl.
25/H2 **Southwold,** Eng,UK
26/A2 **Southwold,** Eng.,UK
25/G3 **South Woodham Ferrers,** Eng,UK
72/C4 **Southwood Nat'l Park,** Austl.
99/B2 **Southworth,** Wa,US
23/G5 **South Yorkshire** (co.), Eng,UK
34/B3 **Souzel,** Port.
41/G2 **Sovata,** Rom.
38/E3 **Soverato Marina,** It.
27/L1 **Sovetsk,** Rus.
42/D5 **Sovetsk,** Rus.
43/L4 **Sovetsk,** Rus.
47/Q5 **Sovetskaya Gavan',** Rus.
55/N2 **Sovetskaya Gavan',** Rus.
23/G4 **Sowerby Bridge,** Eng,UK
80/D2 **Soweto,** SAfr.
80/P13 **Soweto,** SAfr.
82/E6 **Soweto,** SAfr.
47/Q5 **Sōya-misaki** (cape), Japan
42/J2 **Soyana** (riv.), Rus.
56/A2 **Soyang** (lake), SKor.
58/D4 **Soyang** (lake), SKor.
32/D4 **Soyaux,** Fr.
36/D3 **Soyhières,** Swi.
83/E **Soyuz,** Ant.
44/D1 **Sozh** (riv.), Eur.
41/H4 **Sozopol,** Bul.
31/E3 **Spa,** Belg.
83/U **Spaatz** (isl.), Ant.
97/H4 **Spaceport USA,** Fl,US
99/D2 **Spada** (lake), Wa,US
37/E1 **Spaichingen,** Ger.
18/C4 **Spain**
32/B5 **Spain**
34/C2 **Spain**
76/E1 **Spain**
23/H6 **Spalding,** Eng,UK
99/C3 **Spanaway,** Wa,US
103/G2 **Spanish Town,** Jam.
37/E4 **Spannort** (peak), Swi.
40/B5 **Sparanise,** It.
86/E5 **Sparks,** Nv,US
88/C4 **Sparks,** Nv,US
92/C3 **Sparks,** Nv,US
99/G6 **Sparlingville,** Mi,US
94/D4 **Sparta,** NC,US
97/H2 **Sparta,** NC,US
98/F4 **Sparta,** NJ,US
94/C5 **Sparta,** Tn,US
97/G3 **Sparta,** Tn,US
91/L5 **Sparta,** Wi,US
94/B3 **Sparta,** Wi,US
89/K5 **Spartanburg,** SC,US
97/H3 **Spartanburg,** SC,US
39/H4 **Sparta** (Spárti), Gre.
34/C5 **Spartel** (cape), Mor.
75/M13 **Spartel** (cape), Mor
39/H4 **Spárti** (Sparta), Gre.
38/A3 **Spartivento** (cape), It.
38/E4 **Spartivento** (cape), It.
90/E3 **Sparwood,** BC,Can
44/E1 **Spas-Demensk,** Rus.
47/P5 **Spassk-Dal'niy,** Rus.
55/L3 **Spassk-Dal'niy,** Rus.
39/H5 **Spátha, Ákra** (cape), Gre.
88/F3 **Spearfish,** SD,US
91/H4 **Spearfish,** SD,US
93/G1 **Spearfish,** SD,US
37/F3 **Speer** (peak), Swi.
31/F4 **Speicher,** Ger.
37/F3 **Speicher,** Swi.
23/F5 **Speke,** Eng,UK
29/E4 **Spelle,** Ger.
86/G2 **Spence Bay,** NW,Can
68/C8 **Spencer** (gulf), Austl.
70/F6 **Spencer** (gulf), Austl.
70/F7 **Spencer** (cape), Austl.
85/E2 **Spencer** (pt.), Ak,US
86/G4 **Spencer,** Ia,US
89/G3 **Spencer,** Ia,US
91/K5 **Spencer,** Ia,US
93/J2 **Spencer,** Ia,US
29/F4 **Spenge,** Ger.
23/G2 **Spennymoor,** Eng,UK
39/H3 **Sperkhiás,** Gre.
39/H3 **Sperkhíos** (riv.), Gre.
22/A2 **Sperrin** (mts.), NI,UK
39/H4 **Spétsai,** Gre.
26/E4 **Speyer,** Ger.
33/H2 **Speyer,** Ger.
95/Q8 **Speyside,** On,Can
38/E3 **Spezzano Albanese,** It.
87/H2 **Spicer** (isl.), NW,Can
29/E1 **Spiekeroog** (isl.), Ger.
33/G3 **Spiez,** Swi.
36/D4 **Spiez,** Swi.
26/C3 **Spijkenisse,** Neth.
28/B5 **Spijkenisse,** Neth.
85/K2 **Spike** (mtn.), Ak,US
40/A2 **Spilimbergo,** It.
39/J5 **Spílion,** Gre.
23/J5 **Spilsby,** Eng,UK
38/A2 **Spina, Bruncu** (peak), It.
53/J2 **Spin Būldak,** Afg.
31/E5 **Spincourt,** Fr.
98/E5 **Spinnerstown,** Pa,US
90/D2 **Spirit River,** Ab,Can
90/G2 **Spiritwood,** Sk,Can
27/L4 **Spišská Nová Ves,** Slvk.
51/F1 **Spitak,** Arm.
25/E5 **Spithead** (chan.), Eng,UK
64/D1 **Spiti** (riv.), India
46/B2 **Spitsbergen** (isl.), Sval.
33/K3 **Spittal an der Drau,** Aus.
40/A2 **Spittal an der Drau,** Aus.
91/K2 **Split** (lake), Mb,Can
86/G3 **Split** (lake), Mb,Can
18/E4 **Split,** Cro.
40/C4 **Split,** Cro.
37/F4 **Splügen,** Swi.
37/F4 **Splügenpass** (pass), It.
90/D4 **Spokane** (riv.), Id, Wa,US
86/E4 **Spokane,** Wa,US
88/C2 **Spokane,** Wa,US
90/D4 **Spokane,** Wa,US
37/G5 **Spöl** (riv.), It.
33/K5 **Spoleto,** It.
38/C1 **Spoleto,** It.
93/K2 **Spoon** (riv.), Il,US
94/B3 **Spoon** (riv.), Il,US
89/H2 **Spooner,** Wi,US
91/L4 **Spooner,** Wi,US
94/B2 **Spooner,** Wi,US
91/K3 **Sprague,** Mb,Can
28/C5 **Sprang-Capelle,** Neth.
66/D2 **Spratly** (isls.)
27/H2 **Spree** (riv.), Ger.
31/G4 **Sprendlingen,** Ger.
33/K4 **Spresiano,** It.
31/E3 **Sprimont,** Belg.
93/J5 **Spring,** Tx,US
96/E4 **Spring,** Tx,US
80/D3 **Springbok,** SAfr.
82/C6 **Springbok,** SAfr.
98/E5 **Spring City,** Pa,US
95/K1 **Springdale,** Nf,Can
93/J3 **Springdale,** Ar,US
96/E2 **Springdale,** Ar,US
29/G4 **Springe,** Ger.
93/F3 **Springer,** NM,US
96/B2 **Springer,** NM,US
92/E4 **Springerville,** Az,US
93/G3 **Springfield,** Co,US
96/C2 **Springfield,** Co,US
89/J4 **Springfield** (cap.), Il,US
91/L6 **Springfield** (cap.), Il,US
93/K3 **Springfield** (cap.), Il,US
94/B4 **Springfield** (cap.), Il,US
97/F2 **Springfield** (cap.), Il,US
87/J4 **Springfield,** Ma,US
89/M3 **Springfield,** Ma,US
95/F3 **Springfield,** Ma,US
89/H4 **Springfield,** Mo,US
93/J3 **Springfield,** Mo,US
96/E2 **Springfield,** Mo,US
89/K4 **Springfield,** Oh,US
94/D4 **Springfield,** Oh,US
97/H2 **Springfield,** Oh,US
88/D4 **Springfield,** Or,US
88/B3 **Springfield,** Or,US
90/C4 **Springfield,** Or,US
94/C4 **Springfield,** Tn,US
97/G2 **Springfield,** Tn,US
98/J8 **Springfield,** Va,US
95/F3 **Springfield,** Vt,US
99/P15 **Spring Grove,** Il,US
95/H2 **Springhill,** NS,Can
93/J4 **Springhill,** La,US
96/E3 **Springhill,** La,US
80/E2 **Springs,** SAfr.
80/Q13 **Springs,** SAfr.
91/H3 **Springside,** Sk,Can
72/C4 **Springsure,** Austl.
73/G5 **Springvale** (nbrhd.), Austl.
91/K5 **Spring Valley,** Mn,US
93/J2 **Spring Valley,** Mn,US
94/A3 **Spring Valley,** Mn,US
98/F4 **Spring Valley,** NY,US
29/E6 **Sprockhövel,** Ger.
25/H1 **Sprowston,** Eng,UK
94/E4 **Spruce** (peak), WV,US
97/J2 **Spruce** (peak), WV,US
98/E5 **Spruce Run** (res.), NJ,US
28/B5 **Spui** (riv.), Neth.
23/J4 **Spurn Head** (pt.), Eng,UK
90/C3 **Squamish,** BC,Can
99/B3 **Squaxin I. Ind. Res.,** Wa,US
38/E3 **Squillace** (gulf), It.
39/F2 **Squinzano,** It.
40/D5 **Squinzano,** It.
40/D3 **Srbobran,** Yugo.
65/C4 **Sre Ambel,** Camb.
40/D3 **Srebrenica,** Bosn.
39/J1 **Sredna** (mts.), Bul.
41/G4 **Sredna** (mts.), Bul.
39/J1 **Srednogorie,** Bul.
41/G4 **Srednogorie,** Bul.
65/D3 **Sre Khtum,** Camb.
27/J2 **Śrem,** Pol.
44/A1 **Śrem,** Pol.
40/E3 **Sremčica,** Yugo.
40/D3 **Sremska Mitrovica,** Yugo.
65/C3 **Sreng** (riv.), Camb.
65/D3 **Sre Noy,** Camb.
65/D3 **Srepok** (riv.), Camb.
47/M4 **Sretensk,** Rus.
55/H1 **Sretensk,** Rus.
53/K3 **Sri Dungargarh,** India
53/K3 **Sri Gangānagar,** India
62/D4 **Srikākulam,** India
60/B5 **Sri Kshetra** (ruins), Burma
48/H9 **Sri Lanka**
62/D6 **Sri Lanka**
64/H4 **Sri Lanka**
53/K2 **Srīnagar,** India
64/G3 **Srīrangam,** India
64/F4 **Srīvaikuntam,** India
53/K5 **Srīvardhan,** India
62/B4 **Srīvardhan,** India
64/F4 **Srīvilliputtūr,** India
27/J3 **Środa Śląska,** Pol.
27/J2 **Środa Wielkopolska,** Pol.
72/A2 **Staaten** (riv.), Austl.
72/A2 **Staaten River Nat'l Park,** Austl.
20/H1 **Stabbursdalen Nat'l Park,** Nor.
28/B6 **Stabroek,** Belg.
26/E2 **Stade,** Ger.
29/G1 **Stade,** Ger.
30/C2 **Staden,** Belg.
26/D2 **Stadskanaal,** Neth.
28/D3 **Stadskanaal,** Neth.
37/G1 **Stadtbergen,** Ger.
29/G4 **Stadthagen,** Ger.
28/D5 **Stadtlohn,** Ger.
29/G5 **Stadtoldendorf,** Ger.
33/H3 **Stäfa,** Swi.
37/E3 **Stäfa,** Swi.
27/G1 **Staffanstorp,** Swe.
36/E3 **Staffelegg** (pass), Swi.
36/D2 **Staffelfelden,** Fr.
37/H2 **Staffelsee** (lake), Ger.
29/F3 **Staffhorst,** Ger.
23/F6 **Stafford,** Eng,UK
24/D2 **Stafford & Worcester** (can.), Eng,UK
23/F5 **Staffordshire** (co.), Eng,UK
24/D1 **Staffordshire** (co.), Eng,UK
38/B4 **Stagnone** (isls.), It.
23/G2 **Staindrop,** Eng,UK
109/B7 **Sta. Inés** (isl.), Chile
19/M7 **Staines,** Eng,UK
25/F4 **Staines,** Eng,UK
19/T10 **Stains,** Fr.
99/M12 **Stakes** (mt.), Ca,US
19/G4 **Stakhanov,** Ukr.
44/F2 **Stakhanov,** Ukr.
24/D5 **Stalbridge,** Eng,UK
36/D5 **Stalden,** Swi.
25/H1 **Stalham,** Eng,UK
26/A2 **Stalham,** Eng.,UK
87/S6 **Stallworthy** (cape), NW,Can
27/M3 **Stalowa Wola,** Pol.
44/B2 **Stalowa Wola,** Pol.
23/F5 **Stalybridge,** Eng,UK
39/J1 **Stamboliyski,** Bul.
41/G4 **Stamboliyski,** Bul.
71/G4 **Stamford,** Austl.
25/F1 **Stamford,** Eng,UK
94/F3 **Stamford,** Ct,US
98/G4 **Stamford,** Ct,US
101/F1 **Stamford,** Tx,US
23/H4 **Stamford Bridge,** Eng,UK
37/F5 **Stampa,** Swi.
80/B2 **Stampriet,** Namb.
82/C5 **Stampriet,** Namb.
20/E1 **Stamsund,** Nor.
42/B1 **Stamsund,** Nor.
22/B4 **Stamullin,** Ire.
80/E2 **Standerton,** SAfr.
80/Q13 **Standerton,** SAfr.
23/F4 **Standish-with-Langtree,** Eng,UK
25/G4 **Stanford le Hope,** Eng,UK
19/P6 **Stanford Rivers,** Eng,UK
20/D3 **Stange,** Nor.
81/E3 **Stanger,** SAfr.
23/F2 **Stanhope,** Eng,UK
40/D3 **Stanišić,** Yugo.
92/B3 **Stanislaus** (riv.), Ca,US
99/M12 **Stanislaus** (co.), Ca,US
39/H1 **Stanke Dimitrov,** Bul.
41/F4 **Stanke Dimitrov,** Bul.
44/B4 **Stanke Dimitrov,** Bul.
73/C4 **Stanley,** Austl.
73/C4 **Stanley** (peak), Austl.
95/H2 **Stanley,** Can
109/E7 **Stanley,** Falk.
62/C5 **Stanley** (res.), India
64/F3 **Stanley** (res.), India
23/G2 **Stanley,** Eng,UK
91/H3 **Stanley,** ND,US
74/E4 **Stanley** (falls), Zaire
77/L8 **Stanley** (fall, falls), Zaire
82/E1 **Stanley Falls,** Zaire
40/E4 **Stanovo,** Yugo.
47/N4 **Stanovoy** (range), Rus.
48/M4 **Stanovoy** (range), Rus.
33/H3 **Stans,** Swi.
37/E4 **Stans,** Swi.
19/P8 **Stansted,** Eng,UK
25/G3 **Stansted Mountfitchet,** Eng,UK
71/J5 **Stanthorpe,** Austl.
72/C5 **Stanthorpe,** Austl.
73/D1 **Stanthorpe,** Austl.
25/G2 **Stanton,** Eng,UK
98/C3 **Stanton,** Ca,US
94/D4 **Stanton,** Ky,US
97/H2 **Stanton,** Ky,US
101/E1 **Stanton,** Tx,US
93/G4 **Stanton,** Tx,US
96/C3 **Stanton,** Tx,US
19/M7 **Stanwell,** Eng,UK
26/D2 **Staphorst,** Neth.
28/D3 **Staphorst,** Neth.
23/G6 **Stapleford,** Eng,UK

180

Stapl – Sürüç

25/E4 **Stapleford**, Eng,UK
19/P7 **Stapleford Abbotts**, Eng,UK
25/G4 **Staplehurst**, Eng,UK
99/G7 **Staples**, On,Can
27/L3 **Stąporków**, Pol.
27/L3 **Starachowice**, Pol.
44/B2 **Starachowice**, Pol.
40/E3 **Stara Pazova**, Yugo.
40/F3 **Stara Planina** (mts.), Yugo.
18/G3 **Staraya Russa**, Rus.
42/F4 **Staraya Russa**, Rus.
46/D4 **Staraya Russa**, Rus.
27/N3 **Staraya Vyzhevka**, Ukr.
18/F4 **Stara Zagora**, Bul.
39/J1 **Stara Zagora**, Bul.
41/G4 **Stara Zagora**, Bul.
69/K5 **Starbuck** (isl.), Kiri.
72/B1 **Starcke Nat'l Park**, Austl.
27/H2 **Stargard Szczeciński**, Pol.
97/H4 **Starke**, Fl,US
89/J5 **Starkville**, Ms,US
97/F3 **Starkville**, Ms,US
37/H2 **Starnberg**, Ger.
37/H2 **Starnbergersee** (lake), Ger.
44/F3 **Staroderevyan-kovskaya**, Rus.
44/E1 **Starodub**, Rus.
27/K2 **Starogard Gdański**, Pol.
44/F3 **Staroshcher-binovskaya**, Rus.
24/C6 **Start** (pt.), UK
24/C6 **Start** (bay), Eng,UK
99/D2 **Startup**, Wa,US
45/G1 **Staryy Kistruss**, Rus.
19/G3 **Staryy Oskol'**, Rus.
44/F2 **Staryy Oskol'**, Rus.
46/D4 **Staryy Oskol'**, Rus.
45/J1 **Staryy Studenets**, Rus.
27/L3 **Staszów**, Pol.
99/B3 **State Capitol**, Wa,US
89/L3 **State College**, Pa,US
94/E3 **State College**, Pa,US
87/F5 **Staten** (isl.), NY,US
89/K5 **Statesboro**, Ga,US
97/H3 **Statesboro**, Ga,US
97/H3 **Statesville**, NC,US
26/E3 **Staufenberg**, Ger.
33/H1 **Staufenberg**, Ger.
36/D2 **Staufen im Breisgau**, Ger.
24/D3 **Staunton**, Eng,UK
89/L4 **Staunton**, Va,US
94/E4 **Staunton**, Va,US
97/J2 **Staunton**, Va,US
24/D2 **Staunton on Wye**, Eng,UK
37/G4 **Stausee Gepatsch** (lake), Aus.
18/D3 **Stavanger**, Nor.
20/C4 **Stavanger**, Nor.
46/A4 **Stavanger**, Nor.
23/F3 **Staveley**, Eng,UK
23/G5 **Staveley**, Eng,UK
31/E3 **Stavelot**, Belg.
28/C3 **Staveren**, Neth.
19/H4 **Stavropol'**, Rus.
45/G3 **Stavropol'**, Rus.
46/E5 **Stavropol'**, Rus.
45/G3 **Stavropol' Kray**, Rus.
39/H2 **Stavrós**, Gre.
41/F5 **Stavrós**, Gre.
73/B3 **Stawell**, Austl.
90/C4 **Stayton**, Or,US
99/L10 **Steamboat** (slough), Ca,US
88/E3 **Steamboat Springs**, Co,US
92/F2 **Steamboat Springs**, Co,US
85/F3 **Stebbins**, Ak,US
27/M4 **Stebnik**, Ukr.
37/E2 **Steckborn**, Swi.
29/H3 **Stederau** (riv.), Ger.
73/F5 **Steele** (cr.), Austl.
91/J4 **Steele**, ND,US
80/Q12 **Steelpoortrivier** (riv.), SAfr.
81/E2 **Steelpoortrivier** (riv.), SAfr.
28/B5 **Steenbergen**, Neth.
92/C2 **Steens** (mtn.), Or,US
87/J1 **Steensby** (inlet), NW,Can
30/B2 **Steenvoorde**, Fr.
26/D2 **Steenwijk**, Neth.
28/D3 **Steenwijk**, Neth.
70/A5 **Steep** (pt.), Austl.
91/G1 **Steephill** (lake), Sk,Can
24/C4 **Steep Holm** (isl.), Eng,UK
23/J5 **Steeping** (riv.), Eng,UK
85/J2 **Steese Nat'l Rec. Area**, Ak,US
86/F1 **Stefansson** (isl.), NW,Can
87/R7 **Stefansson** (isl.), NW,Can
33/G3 **Steffisburg**, Swi.
36/D4 **Steffisburg**, Swi.
36/D5 **Steg**, Swi.
26/G1 **Stege**, Den.
40/A2 **Steiermark** (prov.), Aus.
33/J2 **Steigerwald** (for.), Ger.
99/B3 **Steilacoom**, Wa,US
29/G3 **Steimbke**, Ger.
26/F4 **Stein**, Ger.
33/J2 **Stein**, Ger.
31/E2 **Stein**, Neth.
37/E2 **Steina** (riv.), Ger.
37/E2 **Stein am Rhein**, Swi.
89/G2 **Steinbach**, Mb,Can
91/J3 **Steinbach**, Mb,Can
31/G6 **Steinbourg**, Fr.
36/D2 **Steinen**, Ger.
29/F3 **Steinfeld**, Ger.
31/H5 **Steinfeld**, Ger.
31/E4 **Steinfort**, Lux.
37/G2 **Steingaden**, Ger.
29/F5 **Steinhagen**, Ger.
37/E3 **Steinhausen**, Swi.
37/F1 **Steinhausen an der Rottum**, Ger.
29/G5 **Steinheim**, Ger.
29/H3 **Steinhorst**, Ger.
29/G4 **Steinhuder Meer** (lake), Ger.
18/E2 **Steinkjer**, Nor.
20/D2 **Steinkjer**, Nor.
42/A2 **Steinkjer**, Nor.
46/B3 **Steinkjer**, Nor.
31/H5 **Steinweiler**, Ger.
28/B6 **Stekene**, Belg.
30/D1 **Stekene**, Belg.
37/F5 **Stella, Pizzo** (peak), It.
95/J2 **Stellarton**, NS,Can
29/H2 **Stelle**, Ger.
80/B4 **Stellenbosch**, SAfr.
80/L10 **Stellenbosch**, SAfr.
33/H5 **Stello** (mtn.), Fr.
33/J3 **Stelvio Nat'l Park**, It.
37/G5 **Stelvio Nat'l Park** , It.
37/G4 **Stelvio, Passo di** (pass), It.
95/H1 **Ste-Marguerite** (riv.), Qu,Can
31/E5 **Stenay**, Fr.
26/F2 **Stendal**, Ger.
39/J1 **Steneto Nat'l Park**, Bul.
41/G4 **Steneto Nat'l Park**, Bul.
20/D4 **Stenungsund**, Swe.
19/H5 **Stepanakert**, Azer.
45/H5 **Stepanakert**, Azer.
46/E6 **Stepanakert**, Azer.
51/F2 **Stepanakert**, Azer.
22/B5 **Stepaside**, Ire.
73/B1 **Stephens Creek**, Austl.
87/L4 **Stephenville**, Nf,Can
95/K1 **Stephenville**, Nf,Can
93/H4 **Stephenville**, Tx,US
96/D3 **Stephenville**, Tx,US
85/H3 **Sterling**, Ak,US
88/F3 **Sterling**, Co,US
93/G2 **Sterling**, Co,US
101/E2 **Sterling City**, Tx,US
93/G5 **Sterling City**, Tx,US
96/C4 **Sterling City**, Tx,US
99/F6 **Sterling Heights**, Mi,US
19/J3 **Sterlitamak**, Rus.
45/K1 **Sterlitamak**, Rus.
46/F4 **Sterlitamak**, Rus.
27/H4 **Sternstein** (peak), Aus.
33/J3 **Sterzing** (Vipiteno), It.
37/H4 **Sterzing** (Vipiteno), It.
27/J2 **Stęszew**, Pol.
86/E3 **Stettler**, Ab,Can
90/E2 **Stettler**, Ab,Can
94/D3 **Steubenville**, Oh,US
25/F3 **Stevenage**, Eng,UK
91/J2 **Stevenson** (lake), Mb,Can
85/H4 **Stevenson** (str.), Ak,US
86/H4 **Stevens Point**, Wi,US
89/J3 **Stevens Point**, Wi,US
91/L4 **Stevens Point**, Wi,US
94/B2 **Stevens Point**, Wi,US
85/J2 **Stevens Village**, Ak,US
90/E4 **Stevensville**, Mt,US
28/C3 **Stevinsluizen** (dam), Neth.
70/E2 **Stewart** (cape), Austl.
85/N4 **Stewart**, BC,Can
86/D3 **Stewart**, BC,Can
85/L3 **Stewart** (riv.), Yk,Can
86/C2 **Stewart** (riv.), Yk,Can
71/Q12 **Stewart** (isl.), NZ
85/L3 **Stewart Crossing**, Yk,Can
85/L3 **Stewart River**, Yk,Can
22/B2 **Stewartstown**, NI,UK
91/K5 **Stewartville**, Mn,US
93/J2 **Stewartville**, Mn,US
25/F5 **Steyning**, Eng,UK
27/H4 **Steyr**, Aus.
27/H5 **Steyr** (riv.), Aus.
33/L2 **Steyr**, Aus.
33/L3 **Steyr** (riv.), Aus.
40/B1 **Steyr**, Aus.
40/B2 **Steyr** (riv.), Aus.
99/D2 **Stickney** (mt.), Wa,US
26/C2 **Stiens**, Neth.
28/C2 **Stiens**, Neth.
93/J4 **Stigler**, Ok,US
96/E3 **Stigler**, Ok,US
85/M4 **Stikine** (riv.), BC,Can
86/D3 **Stikine** (riv.), BC,Can
80/P13 **Stilfontein**, SAfr.
39/H3 **Stilis**, Gre.
91/K4 **Stillwater**, Mn,US
94/A2 **Stillwater**, Mn,US
92/C3 **Stillwater** (range), Nv,US
89/G4 **Stillwater**, Ok,US
93/H3 **Stillwater**, Ok,US
96/D2 **Stillwater**, Ok,US
98/E4 **Stillwater** (lake), NY,US
38/E3 **Stilo, Punta** (cape), It.
93/J4 **Stilwell**, Ok,US
96/E3 **Stilwell**, Ok,US
39/G1 **Štimlje**, Yugo.
40/E4 **Štimlje**, Yugo.
22/D1 **Stinchar** (riv.), Sc,UK
93/G4 **Stinnett**, Tx,US
96/C3 **Stinnett**, Tx,US
39/H2 **Štip**, Macd.
40/F5 **Štip**, Macd.
44/B4 **Štip**, Macd.
31/F5 **Stiring-Wendel**, Fr.
21/D2 **Stirling**, Sc,UK
87/L4 **St. John's** (cap.), Nf,Can
95/L2 **St. John's** (cap.), Nf,Can.
84/M5 **St. John's** (cap.), Nf,Can.
20/D3 **Stjørdal**, Nor.
42/A3 **Stjørdal**, Nor.
37/F2 **Stockach**, Ger.
25/F4 **Stockbridge**, Eng,UK
27/J4 **Stockerau**, Aus.
33/M2 **Stockerau**, Aus.
40/C1 **Stockerau**, Aus.
98/E5 **Stockertown**, Pa,US
18/E3 **Stockholm** (cap.), Swe.
20/F4 **Stockholm** (cap.), Swe.
20/F4 **Stockholm** (co.), Swe.
42/C4 **Stockholm** (cap.), Swe.
42/C4 **Stockholm** (co.), Swe.
46/B4 **Stockholm** (cap.), Swe.
36/D4 **Stockhorn** (peak), Swi.
100/E2 **Stockon** (plat.), Tx,US
23/F5 **Stockport**, Eng,UK
23/F4 **Stocks** (res.), Eng,UK
23/G5 **Stocksbridge**, Eng,UK
88/B4 **Stockton**, Ca,US
92/B3 **Stockton**, Ca,US
99/M11 **Stockton**, Ca,US
93/G5 **Stockton** (plat.), Tx,US
96/C4 **Stockton** (plat.), Tx,US
23/G2 **Stockton-on-Tees**, Eng,UK
63/J5 **Stoeng Treng**, Camb.
65/D3 **Stoeng Treng**, Camb.
80/Q12 **Stoffberg**, SAfr.
24/B6 **Stoke** (pt.), Eng,UK
23/F5 **Stoke-on-Trent**, Eng,UK
73/B4 **Stokes** (pt.), Austl.
39/E1 **Stolac**, Bosn.
40/C4 **Stolac**, Bosn.
26/D3 **Stolberg**, Ger.
31/F2 **Stolberg**, Ger.
47/P2 **Stolbovoy** (isl.), Rus.
42/E5 **Stolbtsy**, Bela.
44/C1 **Stolbtsy**, Bela.
20/E3 **Stöllet**, Swe.
29/G3 **Stolzenau**, Ger.
80/K10 **Stompneuspunt** (pt.), SAfr.
39/E1 **Ston**, Cro.
40/C4 **Ston**, Cro.
23/F6 **Stone**, Eng,UK
60/D3 **Stone Forest**, China
70/G4 **Stonehenge**, Austl.
25/E4 **Stonehenge** (ruins), Eng,UK
24/D3 **Stonehouse**, Eng,UK
91/J3 **Stonewall**, Mb,Can
95/Q9 **Stoney Creek**, On,Can
99/G7 **Stoney Point**, On,Can
91/J2 **Stony** (pt.), Can
99/F6 **Stony** (cr.), Mi,US
98/G5 **Stony Brook**, NY,US
99/F6 **Stony Creek** (lake), Mi,US
91/J3 **Stony Mountain**, Mb,Can
98/G4 **Stony Point**, NY,US
85/G3 **Stony River**, Ak,US
46/K3 **Stony Tunguska** (riv.), Rus.
48/J3 **Stony Tunguska** (riv.), Rus.
94/D1 **Stooping** (riv.), On,Can
87/S7 **Stor** (isl.), NW,Can
29/G1 **Stör** (riv.), Ger.
20/F2 **Stora Sjöfallets Nat'l Park**, Swe.
42/C2 **Stora Sjöfallets Nat'l Park**, Swe.
20/F2 **Storavan** (lake), Swe.
42/C2 **Storavan** (lake), Swe.
26/F1 **Store Bælt** (chan.), Den.
20/C3 **Storebø**, Nor.
20/D3 **Støren**, Nor.
42/B3 **Storlien**, Swe.
71/H8 **Storm** (bay), Austl.
73/C4 **Storm** (bay), Austl.
89/G3 **Storm Lake**, Ia,US
91/K5 **Storm Lake**, Ia,US
93/J2 **Storm Lake**, Ia,US
22/C2 **Stormont**, NI,UK
41/G1 **Storozhinets**, Ukr.
25/F5 **Storrington**, Eng,UK
20/G1 **Storslett**, Nor.
20/F1 **Storsteinsfjellet** (peak), Nor.
42/C1 **Storsteinsfjellet** (peak), Nor.
26/F1 **Storstrøm** (co.), Den.
25/G3 **Stort** (riv.), Eng,UK
20/F2 **Storuman**, Swe.
90/G4 **Story**, Wy,US
92/F1 **Story**, Wy,US
25/F2 **Stotfold**, Eng,UK
37/G2 **Stötten**, Ger.
91/H3 **Stoughton**, Sk,Can
31/E3 **Stoumont**, Belg.
24/D5 **Stour** (riv.), Eng,UK
25/E2 **Stour** (riv.), Eng,UK
25/H3 **Stour** (riv.), Eng,UK
25/H4 **Stour** (riv.), Eng,UK
24/D2 **Stourbridge**, Eng,UK
24/D2 **Stourport on Severn**, Eng,UK
25/G2 **Stowmarket**, Eng,UK
25/E3 **Stow on the Wold**, Eng,UK
22/A2 **Strabane** (dist.), NI,UK
22/A5 **Stradbally**, Ire.
33/H4 **Stradella**, It.
28/D6 **Straelen**, Ger.
22/B5 **Straffan**, Ire.
73/C4 **Strahan**, Austl.
27/G4 **Strakonice**, Czh.
33/K2 **Strakonice**, Czh.
39/K1 **Straldzha**, Bul.
41/H4 **Straldzha**, Bul.
26/G1 **Stralsund**, Ger.
80/B4 **Strand**, SAfr.
80/L11 **Strand**, SAfr.
22/C3 **Strangford**, NI,UK
22/C3 **Strangford Lough** (inlet), NI,UK
42/C4 **Strängnäs**, Swe.
22/B1 **Stranocum**, NI,UK
22/C2 **Stranraer**, Sc,UK
91/G3 **Strasbourg**, Sk,Can
18/D4 **Strasbourg**, Fr.
26/D4 **Strasbourg**, Fr.
31/G6 **Strasbourg**, Fr.
33/G2 **Strasbourg**, Fr.
36/D1 **Strasbourg**, Fr.
31/F4 **Strassen**, Lux.
94/D3 **Stratford**, On,Can
71/R10 **Stratford**, N.Z.
98/G4 **Stratford**, Ct,US
98/G4 **Stratford** (pt.), Ct,US
98/E6 **Stratford**, NJ,US
93/G3 **Stratford**, Tx,US
96/C2 **Stratford**, Tx,US
25/E2 **Stratford upon Avon**, Eng,UK
73/A2 **Strathalbyn**, Austl.
22/D1 **Strathclyde** (reg.), Sc,UK
90/E3 **Strathmore**, Ab,Can
24/B5 **Stratton**, Eng,UK
26/G4 **Straubing**, Ger.
33/K2 **Straubing**, Ger.
20/M6 **Straumnes** (pt.), Ice.
27/G2 **Strausberg**, Ger.
101/F1 **Strawn**, Tx,US
41/G4 **Strazhitsa**, Bul.
70/E6 **Streaky** (bay), Austl.
68/C8 **Streaky Bay**, Austl.
70/E6 **Streaky Bay**, Austl.
99/P15 **Streamwood**, Il,US
19/N7 **Streatham**, Eng,UK
25/E3 **Streatley**, Eng,UK
91/L5 **Streator**, Il,US
93/K2 **Streator**, Il,US
94/B3 **Streator**, Il,US
27/G4 **Středočeská Žulová Vrchovina** (mts.), Czh.
33/L2 **Středočeská Žulová Vrchovina** (mts.), Czh.
27/H3 **Středočeský** (reg.), Czh.
33/L2 **Středočeský** (reg.), Czh.
27/K4 **Středoslovenský** (reg.), Slvk.
24/D4 **Street**, Eng,UK
95/Q8 **Streetsville**, On,Can
41/F3 **Strehaia**, Rom.
40/D2 **Strekov**, Slvk.
27/G3 **Střela** (riv.), Czh.
39/J1 **Strelcha**, Bul.
41/G4 **Strelcha**, Bul.
42/H2 **Strel'na** (riv.), Rus.
36/D3 **Strengelbach**, Swi.
23/F5 **Stretford**, Eng,UK
25/G2 **Stretham**, Eng,UK
26/E1 **Strib**, Den.
37/H5 **Strigno**, It.
28/B5 **Strijen**, Neth.
39/H2 **Strimón** (gulf), Gre.
41/F5 **Strimón** (gulf), Gre.
44/C4 **Strimón** (gulf), Gre.
39/H2 **Strimónas** (riv.), Gre.
109/D5 **Stroeder**, Arg.
39/G4 **Strofádhes** (isls.), Gre.
43/X9 **Strogino**, Rus.
31/G4 **Stromberg**, Ger.
38/D3 **Stromboli** (isl.), It.
20/D4 **Strømmen**, Nor.
20/D4 **Strömstad**, Swe.
20/E3 **Strömsund**, Swe.
42/B3 **Strömsund**, Swe.
37/E6 **Strona** (riv.), It.
38/E3 **Strongoli**, It.
27/J3 **Stronie Śląskie**, Pol.
33/M1 **Stronie Śląskie**, Pol.
24/D3 **Stroud**, Eng,UK
98/E5 **Stroudsburg**, Pa,US
39/G2 **Struga**, Macd.
40/E5 **Struga**, Macd.
80/C4 **Struisbaai** (bay), SAfr.
80/M11 **Struisbaai** (bay), SAfr.
22/A2 **Strule** (riv.), NI,UK
39/H1 **Struma** (riv.), Bul.
41/F5 **Struma** (riv.), Bul.
44/B4 **Struma** (riv.), Bul., Gre.
39/H2 **Struma** (riv.), Gre.
24/A2 **Strumble Head** (pt.), UK
39/H2 **Strumica**, Macd.
40/F5 **Strumica**, Macd.
44/B4 **Strumica**, Macd.
20/C3 **Stryn**, Nor.
27/J3 **Strzegom**, Pol.
27/H2 **Strzelce Krajeńskie**, Pol.
72/A5 **Strzelecki** (cr.), Austl.
73/B1 **Strzelecki** (cr.), Austl.
73/D4 **Strzelecki** (peak), Austl.
27/J3 **Strzelin**, Pol.
27/K2 **Strzelno**, Pol.
27/L4 **Strzyżów**, Pol.
90/B2 **Stuart** (lake), BC,Can
90/B2 **Stuart** (riv.), BC,Can
89/K6 **Stuart**, Fl,US
97/H5 **Stuart**, Fl,US
94/E4 **Stuarts Draft**, Va,US
26/G1 **Stubbekøbing**, Den.
27/G1 **Stubbenkammer** (pt.), Ger.
25/E5 **Studland**, Eng,UK
25/E2 **Studley**, Eng,UK
37/E2 **Stühlingen**, Ger.
27/J4 **Stupava**, Slvk.
33/M2 **Stupava**, Slvk.
42/H5 **Stupino**, Rus.
44/F1 **Stupino**, Rus.
91/J3 **Sturgeon** (bay), Mb,Can
91/L3 **Sturgeon** (lake), On,Can
94/B1 **Sturgeon** (lake), On,Can
94/D2 **Sturgeon** (riv.), On,Can
87/H4 **Sturgeon Bay**, Wi,US
89/J3 **Sturgeon Bay**, Wi,US
91/M4 **Sturgeon Bay**, Wi,US
94/C2 **Sturgeon Bay**, Wi,US
87/J4 **Sturgeon Falls**, On,Can
89/L2 **Sturgeon Falls**, On,Can
94/E2 **Sturgeon Falls**, On,Can
94/C3 **Sturgis**, Mi,US
88/F3 **Sturgis**, SD,US
91/H4 **Sturgis**, SD,US
93/G1 **Sturgis**, SD,US
24/D5 **Sturminster Newton**, Eng,UK
27/K5 **Stúrovo**, Slvk.
25/H4 **Sturry**, Eng,UK
70/G5 **Sturt** (des.), Austl.
72/A5 **Sturt** (des.), Austl.
73/B1 **Sturt** (des.), Austl.
73/B1 **Sturt** (peak), Austl.
99/Q14 **Sturtevant**, Wi,US
72/A5 **Sturt Nat'l Park**, Austl.
73/B1 **Sturt Nat'l Park**, Austl.
80/D4 **Stutterheim**, SAfr.
82/E7 **Stutterheim**, SAfr.
18/D4 **Stuttgart**, Ger.
26/E4 **Stuttgart**, Ger.
33/H2 **Stuttgart**, Ger.
93/K4 **Stuttgart**, Ar;US
96/F3 **Stuttgart**, Ar,US
20/M6 **Stykkishólmur**, Ice.
44/C2 **Styr** (riv.), Ukr.
27/H5 **Styria** (prov.), Aus.
33/L3 **Styria** (prov.), Aus.
40/B2 **Styria** (prov.), Aus.
108/D1 **Suaçui Grande** (riv.), Braz.
77/N4 **Suakin** (arch.), Sud.
100/C2 **Suaqui Grande**, Mex.
42/E5 **Subačius**, Lith.
66/C5 **Subang**, Indo.
61/F3 **Subao** (mtn.), China
38/C1 **Subasio** (peak), It.
75/W18 **Subayţilah**, Tun.
54/C4 **Subei**, China
66/C3 **Subi** (isl.), Indo.
18/E4 **Subotica**, Yugo.
40/D2 **Subotica**, Yugo.
41/G2 **Suceava** (co.), Rom.
41/H2 **Suceava**, Rom.
44/C3 **Suceava**, Rom.
27/L3 **Suchedniów**, Pol.
102/C2 **Suchilapan**, Mex.
21/A4 **Suck** (riv.), Ire.
106/E7 **Sucre** (cap.), Bol.
103/H4 **Sucre** (dept.), Col.
104/F5 **Sucre** (state), Ven.
106/G5 **Sucunduri** (riv.), Braz.
107/H7 **Sucuriú** (riv.), Braz.
108/B2 **Sucuriu** (riv.), Braz.
19/T10 **Sucy-en-Brie**, Fr.
42/H4 **Suda** (riv.), Rus.
52/B5 **Sudan**
74/E3 **Sudan**
77/L5 **Sudan**
74/C3 **Sudan** (reg.), Afr.
76/H5 **Sudan** (phys. reg.), Afr.
78/E3 **Sudan** (reg.), Afr.
87/H4 **Sudbury**, On,Can
89/K2 **Sudbury**, On,Can
94/D2 **Sudbury**, On,Can
25/G2 **Sudbury**, Eng,UK
74/F4 **Sudd** (swamp), Sudan
26/F2 **Sude** (riv.), Ger.
29/H2 **Sude** (riv.), Ger.
26/E1 **Süderbrarup**, Ger.
27/H3 **Sudeten** (mts.), Czh., Pol.
28/D5 **Südlohn**, Ger.
79/H5 **Sud-Ouest** (prov.), Camr.
74/E4 **Sue** (riv.), Sudan
77/L6 **Sue** (riv.), Sudan
35/E3 **Sueca**, Sp.
39/J1 **Sŭedinenie**, Bul.
41/G4 **Sŭedinenie**, Bul.
74/F1 **Suez** (can.), Egypt
49/C4 **Suez** (can.), Egypt
50/C4 **Suez** (can.), Egypt
52/B2 **Suez** (can.), Egypt
77/M1 **Suez** (can.), Egypt
49/C5 **Suez** (gulf), Egypt
50/C4 **Suez** (gulf), Egypt
52/B3 **Suez** (gulf), Egypt
74/F2 **Suez** (gulf), Egypt
77/M2 **Suez** (gulf), Egypt
52/B3 **Suez**, Egypt
77/M2 **Suez**, Egypt
49/C5 **Suez** (As Suways), Egypt
50/C4 **Suez** (As Suways), Egypt
49/D3 **Sūf**, Jor.
37/F4 **Sufers**, Swi.
98/F4 **Suffern**, NY,US
25/G2 **Suffolk** (co.), Eng,UK
98/H5 **Suffolk** (co.), NY,US
94/E4 **Suffolk**, Va,US
97/J2 **Suffolk**, Va,US
51/F2 **Şūfīān**, Iran
93/K2 **Sugar** (riv.), Il, Wi,US
99/P14 **Sugar** (cr.), Wi,US
99/P16 **Sugar Grove**, Il,US
93/J5 **Sugar Land**, Tx,US
96/E4 **Sugar Land**, Tx,US
71/J6 **Sugarloaf** (pt.), Austl.
24/C3 **Sugar Loaf** (mtn.), Wal,UK
97/H2 **Sugarloaf** (peak), Ky,US
50/C2 **Suğla** (lake), Turk.
47/M5 **Sühbaatar**, Mong.
48/L5 **Sühbaatar**, Mong.
54/F1 **Sühbaatar**, Mong.
26/F3 **Suhl**, Ger.
33/J1 **Suhl**, Ger.
29/H3 **Suhlendorf**, Ger.
50/B2 **Şuhut**, Turk.
65/B4 **Sui** (pt.), Thai.
107/H6 **Suia-Missu** (riv.), Braz.
55/L2 **Suibin**, China
63/K2 **Suichuan**, China
55/L3 **Suifenhe**, China
55/K2 **Suihua**, China
60/D2 **Suijiang**, China
63/H2 **Suijiang**, China
55/K2 **Suileng**, China
55/H5 **Suining**, China
59/D4 **Suining**, China
60/E2 **Suining**, China
54/G5 **Suiping**, China
59/C4 **Suiping**, China
26/C4 **Suippe** (riv.), Fr.
30/D5 **Suippe** (riv.), Fr.
32/F2 **Suippe** (riv.), Fr.
30/D5 **Suippes**, Fr.
21/B4 **Suir** (riv.), Ire.
99/K10 **Suisun** (bay), Ca,US
99/K10 **Suisun** (cr.), Ca,US
99/K10 **Suisun City**, Ca,US
57/L10 **Suita**, Japan
98/K8 **Suitland-Silver Hill**, Md,US
59/D4 **Suixi**, China
61/F4 **Suixi**, China
63/K3 **Suixi**, China
59/C4 **Sui Xian**, China
61/E3 **Suiyang**, China
63/J2 **Suiyang**, China
36/B2 **Suize** (riv.), Fr.
59/E2 **Suizhong**, China
54/G5 **Suizhou**, China
61/G2 **Suizhou**, China
53/K3 **Sūjāngarh**, India
62/B2 **Sūjāngarh**, India
66/C5 **Sukabumi**, Indo.
66/C4 **Sukadana**, Indo.
66/C4 **Sukadana** (bay), Indo.
57/G2 **Sukagawa**, Japan
67/E2 **Sukau**, Malay.
64/B2 **Sukheke**, Pak.
41/G4 **Sukhindol**, Bul.
44/E1 **Sukhinichi**, Rus.
42/J4 **Sukhona** (riv.), Rus.
46/E4 **Sukhona** (riv.), Rus.
60/C5 **Sukhothai**, Thai.
63/G4 **Sukhothai**, Thai.
65/B2 **Sukhothai**, Thai.
65/B2 **Sukhothai** (ruins), Thai.
19/H4 **Sukhumi**, Geo.
45/G4 **Sukhumi**, Geo.
46/E5 **Sukhumi**, Geo.
53/J3 **Sukkur**, Pak.
62/A2 **Sukkur**, Pak.
40/D2 **Sükösd**, Hun.
56/C4 **Sukumo**, Japan
61/G3 **Sul** (riv.), China
48/M10 **Sula** (isls.), Indo.
67/G4 **Sula** (isls.), Indo.
68/B5 **Sula** (isls.), Indo.
43/L2 **Sula** (riv.), Rus.
53/J3 **Sulaimān** (range), Pak.
50/C1 **Sulakyurt**, Turk.
67/E4 **Sulawesi** (Celebes) (isl.), Indo.
38/B4 **Sulaymān**, Tun.
22/D3 **Sulby** (riv.), IM,UK
27/H2 **Sulechów**, Pol.
27/H2 **Sulęcin**, Pol.
27/K3 **Sulejów**, Pol.
27/L2 **Sulejówek**, Pol.
37/F2 **Sulgen**, Swi.
41/J3 **Sulina**, Rom.
26/E2 **Sulingen**, Ger.
29/F3 **Sulingen**, Ger.
54/D4 **Sulin Gol** (riv.), China
20/F2 **Sulitjelma** (peak), Nor.
42/C2 **Sulitjelma** (peak), Nor.
106/B4 **Sullana**, Peru
90/F3 **Sullivan** (lake), Ab,Can
94/C4 **Sullivan**, In,US
97/G2 **Sullivan**, In,US
99/N13 **Sullivan**, Wi,US
94/E1 **Sullivan Mines**, Qu,Can
24/C4 **Sully**, Wal,UK
32/E3 **Sully-sur-Loire**, Fr.
38/C1 **Sulmona**, It.
40/A4 **Sulmona**, It.
93/J4 **Sulphur** (riv.), Ar, Tx,US
93/J5 **Sulphur**, La,US
96/E4 **Sulphur**, La,US
93/H4 **Sulphur**, Ok,US
96/D3 **Sulphur**, Ok,US
93/G4 **Sulphur Spring Draw** (creek), NM, Tx,US
93/J4 **Sulphur Springs**, Tx,US
96/E3 **Sulphur Springs**, Tx,US
99/D2 **Sultan**, Wa,US
99/D2 **Sultan** (cr.), Wa,US
50/B2 **Sultandağı**, Turk.
62/D2 **Sultānpur**, India
68/A4 **Sulu** (sea)
48/L9 **Sulu** (sea), Malay., Phil.
67/E2 **Sulu** (sea), Malay., Phil.
48/M9 **Sulu** (arch.), Phil.
67/F3 **Sulu** (arch.), Phil.
68/B4 **Sulu** (arch.), Phil.
44/E4 **Suluova**, Turk.
50/C1 **Suluova**, Turk.
77/K1 **Sulūq**, Libya
29/E6 **Sülz** (riv.), Ger.
31/G2 **Sülz** (riv.), Ger.
36/E2 **Sulz**, Swi.
37/E1 **Sulz am Neckar**, Ger.
31/G5 **Sulzbach**, Ger.
26/F4 **Sulzbach-Rosenberg**, Ger.
33/J2 **Sulzbach-Rosenberg**, Ger.
37/G2 **Sulzberg**, Ger.
83/P **Sulzberger** (bay), Ant.
83/Q **Sulzberger Ice Shelf**, Ant.
36/D2 **Sulzburg**, Ger.
37/F3 **Sulzfluh** (peak), Aus.
40/E3 **Šumadija** (reg.), Yugo.
106/D3 **Sumapaz Nat'l Park**, Col.
38/E1 **Sumartin**, Cro.
48/J9 **Sumatra** (isl.), Indo.
66/B4 **Sumatra** (isl.), Indo.
48/L11 **Sumba** (isl.), Indo.
66/E5 **Sumba** (isl.), Indo.
67/E5 **Sumba** (str.), Indo.
68/A6 **Sumba** (isl.), Indo.
45/L5 **Sumbar** (riv.), Trkm.
51/J2 **Sumbar** (riv.), Trkm.
48/L10 **Sumbawa** (isl.), Indo.
66/E5 **Sumbawa** (isl.), Indo.
68/A5 **Sumbawa** (isl.), Indo.
67/E5 **Sumbawa Besar**, Indo.
82/F2 **Sumbawanga**, Tanz.
82/B3 **Sumbe**, Ang.
47/L5 **Sümber**, Mong.
54/F2 **Sümber**, Mong.
85/M4 **Sumdum** (mt.), Ak,US
40/C2 **Sümeg**, Hun.
66/D5 **Sumenep**, Indo.
19/H4 **Sumgait**, Azer.
45/J4 **Sumgait**, Azer.
46/E5 **Sumgait**, Azer.
51/G1 **Sumgait**, Azer.
36/D3 **Sumiswald**, Swi.
23/G3 **Summer Bridge**, Eng,UK
90/D3 **Summerland**, BC,Can
95/J2 **Summerside**, PE,Can
94/D4 **Summersville**, WV,US
97/H2 **Summersville**, WV,US
97/G3 **Summerville**, Ga,US
97/H3 **Summerville**, SC,US
98/F5 **Summit**, NJ,US
99/C3 **Sumner**, Wa,US
56/D3 **Sumoto**, Japan
57/K10 **Sumoto**, Japan
27/J4 **Šumperk**, Czh.
33/M2 **Šumperk**, Czh.
89/K5 **Sumter**, SC,US
97/H3 **Sumter**, SC,US
18/G3 **Sumy**, Ukr.
44/E2 **Sumy**, Ukr.
46/D4 **Sumy**, Ukr.
44/E2 **Sumy Obl.**, Ukr.
60/B4 **Sun** (peak), Burma
90/E4 **Sun** (riv.), Mt,US
64/C2 **Sunām**, India
60/A3 **Sunāmganj**, Bang.
57/M9 **Sunami**, Japan
73/C3 **Sunbury**, Austl.
73/F5 **Sunbury**, Austl.
19/M7 **Sunbury**, Eng,UK
94/E3 **Sunbury**, Pa,US
25/F4 **Sunbury on Thames**, Eng,UK
58/D5 **Sunch'ang**, SKor.
58/C3 **Sunch'ŏn**, NKor.
55/K5 **Sunch'ŏn**, SKor.
58/D5 **Sunch'ŏn**, SKor.
80/P12 **Sun City**, SAfr.
92/D4 **Sun City**, Az,US
98/C3 **Sun City**, Ca,US
95/G3 **Suncook**, NH,US
48/J10 **Sunda** (isls.), Indo.
48/K10 **Sunda** (str.), Indo.
66/B5 **Sunda** (str.), Indo.
91/G4 **Sundance**, Wy,US
93/F1 **Sundance**, Wy,US
62/E3 **Sundarbans** (reg.), Bang., India
62/D3 **Sundargarh**, India
53/L2 **Sundarnagar**, India
64/D2 **Sundarnagar**, India
80/D4 **Sundays** (riv.), SAfr.
23/G2 **Sunderland**, Eng,UK
29/F6 **Sundern**, Ger.
36/D1 **Sundhouse**, Fr.
100/E1 **Sundown**, Tx,US
72/C5 **Sundown Nat'l Park**, Austl.
73/D1 **Sundown Nat'l Park**, Austl.
90/E3 **Sundre**, Ab,Can
20/D4 **Sunds**, Den.
18/E2 **Sundsvall**, Swe.
20/F3 **Sundsvall**, Swe.
42/C3 **Sundsvall**, Swe.
46/B3 **Sundsvall**, Swe.
63/H6 **Sungai Kolok**, Thai.
66/B2 **Sungai Kolok**, Thai.
66/B4 **Sungaipenuh**, Indo.
63/H6 **Sungai Petani**, Mal
66/B2 **Sungai Petani**, Ma
58/D5 **Sŭngju**, SKor.
39/K1 **Sungurlare**, Bul.
41/H4 **Sungurlare**, Bul.
44/E4 **Sungurlu**, Turk.
50/C1 **Sungurlu**, Turk.
59/C3 **Suning**, China
96/B4 **Sunland Park**, NM,
20/D3 **Sunndalsøra**, Nor.
20/E4 **Sunne**, Swe.
25/F4 **Sunninghill**, Eng,U
99/P15 **Sunnyside**, Il,US
88/B4 **Sunnyvale**, Ca,US
92/B3 **Sunnyvale**, Ca,US
99/K12 **Sunnyvale**, Ca,US
99/L11 **Sunol**, Ca,US
57/H8 **Su-no-saki** (cape), Japan
91/L5 **Sun Prairie**, Wi,US
93/K2 **Sun Prairie**, Wi,US
94/B3 **Sun Prairie**, Wi,US
98/F4 **Sunrise** (mtn.), NJ,
73/B2 **Sunset Country** (re Austl.
92/E4 **Sunset Crater Nat'l Mon.**, Az,US
73/F5 **Sunshine**, Austl.
47/P3 **Suntar-Khayata** (mts.), Rus.
29/G4 **Süntel** (mts.), Ger.
55/K2 **Sunwu**, China
76/E6 **Sunyani**, Gha.
79/E5 **Sunyani**, Gha.
82/F2 **Sunzu** (peak), Zam.
56/B4 **Suo** (sea), Japan
60/E4 **Suoi Rut**, Viet.
65/D1 **Suoi Rut**, Viet.
20/H3 **Suomenselkä** (reg. Fin.
42/E3 **Suomenselkä** (reg. Fin.
65/D4 **Suong**, Camb.
106/C6 **Supe**, Peru
84/J5 **Superior** (lake), Can.,US
86/H4 **Superior** (lake), Can,US
89/J2 **Superior** (lake), Can,US
90/L4 **Superior** (lake), Can,US
94/C2 **Superior** (lake), Can,US
92/E4 **Superior**, Az,US
88/D2 **Superior**, Mt,US
90/E4 **Superior**, Mt,US
86/G4 **Superior**, Wi,US
89/H2 **Superior**, Wi,US
91/K4 **Superior**, Wi,US
94/A2 **Superior**, Wi,US
94/B2 **Superior** (upland), Wi,US
63/H5 **Suphan Buri**, Thai.
65/C3 **Suphan Buri**, Thai.
67/J4 **Supiori** (isl.), Indo.
58/C2 **Sup'ung** (res.), Chir NKor.
58/C2 **Sup'ung** (dam), NK
59/F2 **Sup'ung** (dam), NK
52/D5 **Sūq 'Abs**, Yem.
51/F4 **Sūq ash Shuyūkh**, Iraq
52/E2 **Sūq ash Shuyūkh**, Iraq
49/E2 **Şuqaylabīyah**, Syr
50/D3 **Şuqaylabīyah**, Syr
55/H5 **Suqian**, China
59/D4 **Suqian**, China
99/B2 **Suquamish**, Wa,US
31/E4 **Sûr** (riv.), Belg.
88/B4 **Sur** (pt.), Ca,US
92/B3 **Sur** (pt.), Ca,US
43/K5 **Sura** (riv.), Rus.
45/H1 **Sura** (riv.), Rus.
66/D5 **Surabaya**, Indo.
62/D4 **Surada**, India
66/D5 **Surakarta**, Indo.
58/G6 **Suraksan** (mt.), SK
67/F2 **Surallah**, Phil.
64/G3 **Sūramangalam**, In
36/B5 **Suran** (riv.), Fr.
27/K4 **Šurany**, Slvk.
71/H5 **Surat**, Austl.
72/C4 **Surat**, Austl.
53/K4 **Surat**, India
62/B3 **Surat**, India
53/K3 **Suratgarh**, India
62/B2 **Suratgarh**, India
63/G6 **Surat Thani**, Thai.
65/B4 **Surat Thani**, Thai.
66/A2 **Surat Thani**, Thai.
31/G6 **Surbourg**, Fr.
40/E3 **Surčin**, Yugo.
39/H1 **Surdulica**, Yugo.
40/F4 **Surdulica**, Yugo.
44/B4 **Surdulica**, Yugo.
26/C4 **Sûre** (riv.), Belg., L
32/F2 **Sûre** (riv.), Belg., L
53/K4 **Surendranagar**, In
62/B3 **Surendranagar**, In
32/C3 **Surgères**, Fr.
46/H3 **Surgut**, Rus.
62/E3 **Sūri**, India
35/F2 **Súria**, Sp.
63/H5 **Surin**, Thai.
65/C3 **Surin**, Thai.
105/D2 **Suriname**
107/G3 **Suriname**
98/K8 **Surrattsville** (Clint Md,US
90/C3 **Surrey**, BC,Can
19/M8 **Surrey** (co.), Eng,U
25/F4 **Surrey** (co.), Eng,U
36/E3 **Sursee**, Swi.
45/H1 **Surskoye**, Rus.
76/J1 **Surt**, Libya
20/D3 **Sur-Trøndelag** (co Nor.
49/D3 **Şūr** (Tyre), Leb.
50/D2 **Sürüç**, Turk.
52/C1 **Sürüç**, Turk.

181
Surug – Tanna

57/F3 Suruga (bay), Japan
19/T9 Survilliers, Fr.
29/E3 Surwold, Ger.
38/B5 Sūsah, Tun.
38/B5 Sūsah (gov.), Tun.
75/X17 Sūsah (gov.), Tun.
75/X18 Sūsah, Tun.
76/H1 Sūsah, Tun.
56/C4 Susaki, Japan
51/G4 Sūsangerd, Iran
52/E2 Sūsangerd, Iran
88/B3 Susanville, Ca,US
90/C5 Susanville, Ca,US
92/B2 Susanville, Ca,US
44/F4 Suşehri, Turk.
50/D1 Suşehri, Turk.
54/G4 Sushui (riv.), China
59/B4 Sushui (riv.), China
27/G4 Sušice, Czh.
85/J3 Susitna (riv.), Ak,US
86/A2 Susitna (riv.), Ak,US
59/D5 Susong, China
61/H2 Susong, China
57/F3 Susono, Japan
94/E3 Susquehanna (riv.), Pa,US
94/E3 Susquehanna West Branch (riv.), Pa,US
95/H2 Sussex, NB,Can
98/F4 Sussex, NJ,US
98/F4 Sussex (co.), NJ,US
73/D2 Sussex Inlet, Austl.
25/F4 Sussex, Vale of (val.), Eng,UK
37/E4 Sustenhorn (peak), Swi.
37/E4 Sustenpass (pass), Swi.
28/C6 Susteren, Neth.
31/E1 Susteren, Neth.
47/Q3 Susuman, Rus.
44/D5 Susurluk, Turk.
50/B2 Susurluk, Turk.
27/K2 Susz, Pol.
50/B2 Sütçüler, Turk.
72/H9 Sutherland, Austl.
90/C5 Sutherlin, Or,US
92/B2 Sutherlin, Or,US
38/F1 Sutjeska Nat'l Park, Bosn.
40/D4 Sutjeska Nat'l Park, Bosn.
53/L2 Sutlej (riv.), India
64/B2 Sutlej (riv.), India, Pak.
53/K2 Sutlej (riv.), Pak.
39/K2 Sütlüce, Turk.
41/H5 Sütlüce, Turk.
99/L9 Sutter (co.), Ca,US
23/H6 Sutterton, Eng,UK
19/N7 Sutton, Eng,UK
19/N7 Sutton (bor.), Eng,UK
85/J3 Sutton, Ak,US
23/J6 Sutton Bridge, Eng,UK
25/G1 Sutton Bridge, Eng,UK
25/E1 Sutton Coldfield, Eng,UK
23/G5 Sutton in Ashfield, Eng,UK
23/J5 Sutton on Sea, Eng,UK
23/H5 Sutton on Trent, Eng,UK
80/D4 Suurberge (mts.), SAfr.
68/G6 Suva (cap.), Fiji
69/Y18 Suva (cap.), Fiji
41/H4 Suvorovo, Bul.
52/D6 Suwa, Eth.
57/F2 Suwa, Japan
27/M1 Suwałki, Pol.
27/M2 Suwałki (prov.), Pol.
42/D5 Suwałki, Pol.
69/J6 Suwarrow (atoll), Cookls.
49/D3 Şuwaylih, Jor.
58/D4 Suwŏn, SKor.
58/G7 Suwŏn, SKor.
36/D3 Suze (riv.), Swi.
55/H5 Suzhou, China
55/J5 Suzhou, China
59/D4 Suzhou, China
59/E5 Suzhou, China
59/L8 Suzhou, China
61/J2 Suzhou, China
58/C2 Suzi (riv.), China
57/E2 Suzu, Japan
57/E3 Suzuka, Japan
57/M10 Suzuka, Japan
57/M10 Suzuka (range), Japan
57/M10 Suzuka (riv.), Japan
55/M4 Suzu-misaki (cape), Japan
57/E2 Suzu-misaki (cape), Japan
33/J4 Suzzara, It.
46/C2 Svalbard (arch.), Nor.
27/M4 Svalyava, Ukr.
40/F1 Svalyava, Ukr.
27/H1 Svaneke, Den.
20/G2 Svanstein, Swe.
42/D2 Svanstein, Swe.
63/J5 Svay Rieng, Camb.
65/D4 Svay Rieng, Camb.
66/C1 Svay Rieng, Camb.
20/E4 Svealand (reg.), Swe.
27/G1 Svedala, Swe.
20/E3 Sveg, Swe.
42/B3 Sveg, Swe.
42/E5 Švenčionys, Lith.
20/D5 Svendborg, Den.
26/F1 Svendborg, Den.
87/S7 Svendsen (pen.), NW,Can
20/D4 Svenes, Nor.
20/E4 Svenljunga, Swe.
43/P4 Sverdlovsk (Yekaterinburg), Rus.
84/G2 Sverdrup (isls.), Can.
87/R7 Sverdrup (isls.), NW,Can
87/S7 Sverdrup (chan.), NW,Can
46/H2 Sverdrup (isl.), Rus.
47/P5 Svetlaya, Rus.
44/D1 Svetlogorsk, Bela.
27/L1 Svetlogorsk, Rus.
46/J3 Svetlogorsk, Rus.
45/G3 Svetlograd, Rus.
27/L1 Svetlyy, Rus.
45/M2 Svetlyy, Rus.
20/J3 Svetogorsk, Rus.
42/F3 Svetogorsk, Rus.
40/E4 Svetozarevo, Yugo.
44/B4 Svetozarevo, Yugo.
20/P7 Svíahnúkar (peak), Ice.
40/E3 Svilajnac, Yugo.
39/K2 Svilengrad, Bul.
41/H5 Svilengrad, Bul.
44/C4 Svilengrad, Bul.
50/A1 Svilengrad, Bul.
41/G4 Svishtov, Bul.
44/C4 Svishtov, Bul.
27/N2 Svisloch', Bela.
27/J4 Svitavy, Czh.
33/M2 Svitavy, Czh.
47/N4 Svobodnyy, Rus.
55/K1 Svobodnyy, Rus.
39/H1 Svoge, Bul.
41/F4 Svoge, Bul.
20/E1 Svolvær, Nor.
42/B1 Svolvær, Nor.
33/M2 Svratka (riv.), Czh.
40/F4 Svrljig, Yugo.
47/Q2 Svyatyy Nos (cape), Rus.
23/G6 Swadlincote, Eng,UK
25/E1 Swadlincote, Eng,UK
25/G1 Swaffham, Eng,UK
71/J4 Swain (reefs), Austl.
72/D3 Swain (reefs), Austl.
97/H3 Swainsboro, Ga,US
69/H5 Swains Island (atoll), ASam.
82/C2 Swa-Kibula, Zaire
82/B5 Swakopmund, Namb.
23/G3 Swale (riv.), Eng,UK
25/H4 Swalecliffe, Eng,UK
25/G4 Swale, The (chan.), Eng,UK
28/D6 Swalmen, Neth.
31/F1 Swalmen, Neth.
90/D2 Swan (hills), Ab,Can
86/E3 Swan (range), Ab,Can
103/F2 Swan (isls.), Hon.
91/H2 Swan (riv.), Mb, Sk,Can
99/F7 Swan (cr.), Mi,US
25/E5 Swanage, Eng,UK
32/C1 Swanage, Eng,UK
71/G7 Swan Hill, Austl.
73/B2 Swan Hill, Austl.
90/E2 Swan Hills, Ab,Can
19/P7 Swanley, Eng,UK
25/G4 Swanley Hextable, Eng,UK
99/F7 Swan, North Branch (cr.), Mi,US
73/A2 Swan Reach, Austl.
86/F3 Swan River, Mb,Can
88/F1 Swan River, Mb,Can
91/H2 Swan River, Mb,Can
19/P7 Swanscombe, Eng,UK
73/D4 Swansea, Austl.
18/C3 Swansea, Wal,UK
24/C3 Swansea, Wal,UK
24/C3 Swansea (bay), Wal,UK
98/E6 Swarthmore, Pa,US
80/D3 Swart Kei (riv.), SAfr.
80/P12 Swartruggens, SAfr.
98/F4 Swartswood (lake), NJ,US
99/E6 Swartz (cr.), Mi,US
27/J2 Swarzędz, Pol.
80/B2 Swarzrand (mts.), Namb.
22/B2 Swatragh, NI,UK
25/E5 Sway, Eng,UK
74/F7 Swaziland
81/E2 Swaziland
82/F6 Swaziland
18/E2 Sweden
20/E3 Sweden
27/G1 Sweden
42/B3 Sweden
98/E6 Swedesboro, NJ,US
90/C4 Sweet Home, Or,US
101/E1 Sweetwater, Tx,US
88/F5 Sweetwater, Tx,US
93/G4 Sweetwater, Tx,US
96/C3 Sweetwater, Tx,US
90/F5 Sweetwater (riv.), Wy,US
80/C4 Swellendam, SAfr.
27/J3 Świdnica, Pol.
27/M3 Świdnik, Pol.
44/B2 Świdnik, Pol.
27/H2 Świdwin, Pol.
27/J3 Świebodzice, Pol.
27/H2 Świebozin, Pol.
27/K2 Świecie, Pol.
86/F3 Swift Current, Sk,Can
88/E1 Swift Current, Sk,Can
73/C3 Swifts Creek, Austl.
25/E3 Swindon, Eng,UK
23/H6 Swineshead, Eng,UK
27/H2 Świnoujście, Pol.
23/G5 Swinton, Eng,UK
33/G3 Swiss (plat.), Swi.
38/D4 Swiss (plat.), Swi.
31/F2 Swist Bach (riv.), Ger.
18/D4 Switzerland
26/D5 Switzerland
32/H3 Switzerland
33/G3 Switzerland
36/D4 Switzerland
22/B5 Swords, Ire.
42/G3 Syamozero (lake), Rus.
42/G3 Syas'stroy, Rus.
27/J3 Syców, Pol.
68/E8 Sydney, Austl.
71/J6 Sydney, Austl.
72/H8 Sydney, Austl.
73/D2 Sydney, Austl.
84/L5 Sydney, Can.
87/K4 Sydney, NS,Can
89/P2 Sydney, NS,Can
95/J2 Sydney, NS,Can
69/H5 Sydney (Manra) (atoll), Kiri.
95/J2 Sydney Mines, NS,Can
26/E2 Syke, Ger.
29/F3 Syke, Ger.
98/K7 Sykesville, Md,US
19/J2 Syktyvkar, Rus.
43/L3 Syktyvkar, Rus.
46/F3 Syktyvkar, Rus.
89/J5 Sylacauga, Al,US
97/G3 Sylacauga, Al,US
20/E3 Sylarna (peak), Swe.
42/B3 Sylarna (peak), Swe.
60/A3 Sylhet, Bang.
63/F3 Sylhet, Bang.
26/E1 Sylt (isl.), Ger.
43/N4 Sylva (riv.), Rus.
94/D3 Sylvania, Oh,US
97/F6 Sylvan Lake, Mi,US
37/H2 Sylvenstein-Stausee (lake), Ger.
39/L6 Syntagma Square, Gre.
98/G5 Syosset, NY,US
83/C Syowa, Ant.
93/G3 Syracuse, Ks,US
96/C2 Syracuse, Ks,US
87/J4 Syracuse, NY,US
89/L3 Syracuse, NY,US
94/E3 Syracuse, NY,US
38/D4 Syracuse (Siracusa), It.
46/G5 Syrdar'ya (riv.), Asia
48/F5 Syrdar'ya (riv.), Asia
46/E6 Syria
88/B2 Syria
48/C6 Syria
49/E2 Syria
50/D3 Syria
52/C1 Syria
77/N1 Syria
63/G4 Syriam, Burma
77/N1 Syrian (des.), Asia
50/D3 Syrian (des.), Iraq, Jor.
52/C2 Syrian (des.), Syria, Jor.
20/H3 Sysmä, Fin.
42/E3 Sysmä, Fin.
43/L3 Sysola (riv.), Rus.
25/E1 Syston, Eng,UK
19/H3 Syzran', Rus.
45/J1 Syzran', Rus.
46/E4 Syzran', Rus.
27/L4 Szabolcs-Szatmár-Bereg (co.), Hun.
40/E1 Szabolcs-Szatmár-Bereg (co.), Hun.
27/J2 Szamotuły, Pol.
40/E2 Szarvas, Hun.
40/D2 Százhalombatta, Hun.
27/M3 Szczebrzeszyn, Pol.
18/E3 Szczecin, Pol.
27/H2 Szczecin, Pol.
27/H2 Szczecin (prov.), Pol.
46/B4 Szczecin, Pol.
27/J2 Szczecinek, Pol.
33/M1 Szczytna, Pol.
27/L2 Szczytno, Pol.
42/D5 Szczytno, Pol.
44/B1 Szczytno, Pol.
18/F4 Szeged, Hun.
40/E2 Szeged, Hun.
44/B3 Szeged, Hun.
40/E2 Szeghalom, Hun.
40/E2 Szegvár, Hun.
40/D2 Székesfehérvár, Hun.
40/D2 Szekszárd, Hun.
40/E1 Szendro, Hun.
27/K5 Szentendre, Hun.
40/D2 Szentendre, Hun.
40/E2 Szentes, Hun.
44/B3 Szentes, Hun.
40/C2 Szentlorinc, Hun.
27/L4 Szerencs, Hun.
40/E1 Szerencs, Hun.
27/M1 Szeskie (peak), Pol.
42/D5 Szeskie Wzgorza (peak), Pol.
40/C2 Szigetvár, Hun.
40/C2 Szil, Hun.
27/K5 Szirák, Hun.
40/D2 Szirák, Hun.
40/E2 Szolnok, Hun.
44/B3 Szolnok, Hun.
18/E4 Szombathely, Hun.
33/M3 Szombathely, Hun.
40/C2 Szombathely, Hun.
27/H3 Szprotawa, Pol.
27/K2 Sztum, Pol.
27/J2 Szubin, Pol.
27/L3 Szydłowiec, Pol.

T

104/F5 Tabaquite, Trin.
75/W17 Tabarqah, Tun.
46/F6 Tabas, Iran
51/J3 Tabas, Iran
53/G2 Tabas, Iran
103/F4 Tabasara, Serranía de (range), Pan.
100/E4 Tabasco, Mex.
101/G5 Tabasco (state), Mex.
102/C2 Tabasco (state), Mex.
107/K6 Tabatinga (mts.), Braz.
76/E2 Tabelbala, Alg.
86/E4 Taber, Ab,Can
88/D2 Taber, Ab,Can
90/E3 Taber, Ab,Can
35/E3 Tabernes de Valldigna, Sp.
68/F5 Tabiang, Kiri.
68/G5 Tabiteuea (atoll), Kiri.
67/F1 Tablas (isl.), Phil.
80/B4 Table (bay), SAfr.
80/L10 Table (bay), SAfr.
80/L10 Table (peak), SAfr.
34/B1 Taboada, Sp.
27/H4 Tábor, Czh.
33/L2 Tábor, Czh.
82/F2 Tabora, Tanz.
76/D7 Tabou, IvC.
78/D5 Tabou, IvC.
46/E6 Tabrīz, Iran
48/D6 Tabrīz, Iran
51/F2 Tabrīz, Iran
69/K4 Tabuaeran (Fanning) (atoll), Kiri.
61/J5 Tabuk, Phil.
50/D4 Tabūk, SAr.
52/C3 Tabūk, SAr.
77/N2 Tabūk, SAr.
38/A4 Ţaburbah, Tun.
38/A4 Tabursuq, Tun.
68/F6 Tabwemasana (mt.), Van.
102/C3 Tacaná (vol.), Mex.
103/G4 Tacarcuna (mtn.), Pan.
46/J5 Tacheng, China
61/J3 Tachia (riv.), Tai.
56/A4 Tachibana (bay), Japan
57/F3 Tachikawa, Japan
57/H7 Tachikawa, Japan
26/G4 Tachov, Czh.
33/K2 Tachov, Czh.
68/B3 Tacloban, Phil.
106/D7 Tacna, Peru
86/D4 Tacoma, Wa,US
88/B2 Tacoma, Wa,US
90/C4 Tacoma, Wa,US
99/C3 Tacoma, Wa,US
106/E7 Tacora (vol.), Chile
35/X16 Tacoronte, Canl.
101/G5 Tacotalpa, Mex.
102/C2 Tacotalpa, Mex.
109/E3 Tacuarembó, Uru.
100/C2 Tacupeto, Mex.
57/F2 Tadami (riv.), Japan
57/L10 Tadaoka, Japan
23/G4 Tadcaster, Eng,UK
76/F2 Tademaït (plat.), Alg.
62/D4 Tādepallegūdem, India
69/V12 Tadine, NCal.
25/E4 Tadley, Eng,UK
50/D3 Tadmur, Syria
52/C2 Tadmur, Syria
57/M9 Tado, Japan
58/C5 Tadohae Hasang Nat'l Park, SKor.
56/C3 Tadotsu, Japan
62/C5 Tādpatri, India
76/H2 Tadrart (mts.), Alg., Libya
19/N8 Tadworth, Eng,UK
58/D4 T'aean, SKor.
55/K4 T'aebaek (mts.), NKor., SKor.
58/D2 T'aebaek (mts.), NKor., SKor.
56/A2 T'aebaek (range), SKor.
58/E4 T'aebaek, SKor.
58/F7 Taebudo (isl.), SKor.
55/K4 Taech'ŏn, SKor.
58/D4 Taech'ŏn, SKor.
58/C4 Taech'ŏng (isl.), SKor.
58/D5 Taedŏk, SKor.
58/D3 Taedong (riv.), NKor.
55/K4 Taegang-got (pt.), NKor.
58/D3 Taegang-got (pt.), NKor.
47/N6 Taegu, SKor.
55/K4 Taegu, SKor.
56/A3 Taegu, SKor.
58/E5 Taegu, SKor.
56/A2 Taegu-jikhalsi (prov.), SKor.
58/E5 Taegu-Jikhalsi, SKor.
58/C5 Taehŭksan (isl.), SKor.
58/D5 T'aein, SKor.
47/N6 Taejŏn, SKor.
55/K4 Taejŏn, SKor.
58/D4 Taejŏn, SKor.
58/C2 Taeryŏng (riv.), NKor.
24/B3 Taf (riv.), Wal,UK
32/C5 Tafalla, Sp.
34/E1 Tafalla, Sp.
24/C3 Taff (riv.), Wal,UK
109/C2 Tafí Viejo, Arg.
63/H3 Ta Fou San, Laos
51/H4 Taft, Iran
52/F2 Taft, Iran
53/H3 Taftān (mtn.), Iran
57/M9 Taga, Japan
19/G4 Taganrog, Rus.
44/F3 Taganrog, Rus.
46/D5 Taganrog, Rus.
44/F3 Taganrog (gulf), Rus., Ukr.
78/C2 Tagant (reg.), Mrta.
51/J2 Tagarav (peak), Trkm.
53/G1 Tagarav (peak), Trkm.
56/B4 Tagawa, Japan
67/F2 Tagbilaran, Phil.
33/G5 Taggia, It.
76/E1 Taghit, Alg.
85/M3 Tagish, Yk,Can
33/K3 Tagliamento (riv.), It.
30/D5 Tagnon, Fr.
67/F2 Tagolo (pt.), Phil.
103/G1 Taguasco, Cuba
107/J7 Taguatinga, Braz.
61/J5 Tagudin, Phil.
68/E6 Tagula (isl.), PNG
43/P4 Tagun (riv.), Rus.
18/C5 Tagus (riv.), Port., Sp.
34/B3 Tagus (Tejo) (riv.), Port.
35/P10 Tagus (Tejo) (riv.), Port.
34/C3 Tagus (Tejo) (riv.), Sp.
34/D2 Tagus (Tejo) (riv.), Sp.
66/B3 Tahan (peak), Malay.
57/N10 Tahara, Japan
74/C2 Tahat (peak), Alg.
76/G3 Tahat (peak), Alg.
75/R16 Tahat, Oued et (riv.), Alg.
47/N4 Tahe, China
55/J1 Tahe, China
69/L6 Tahenea (atoll), FrPol.
45/G5 Tahir (pass), Turk.
50/E2 Tahir (pass), Turk.
69/L6 Tahiti (isl.), FrPol.
69/X15 Tahiti (isl.), FrPol.
89/H4 Tahlequah, Ok,US
93/J4 Tahlequah, Ok,US
96/E3 Tahlequah, Ok,US
73/D2 Tahmoor, Austl.
85/J3 Tahneta (pass), Ak,US
92/C3 Tahoe (lake), Ca, Nv,US
86/B4 Tahoe (lake), Ca,Nv,US
88/D4 Tahoe (lake), Ca,Nv,US
101/E1 Tahoka, Tx,US
93/G4 Tahoka, Tx,US
96/C3 Tahoka, Tx,US
76/G5 Tahoua, Niger
79/G3 Tahoua, Niger
79/G3 Tahoua (dept.), Niger
90/B3 Tahsis, BC,Can
50/B5 Taḩtā, Egypt
52/B3 Taḩtā, Egypt
77/M2 Taḩtā, Egypt
69/L6 Tahuata (isl.), FrPol.
67/G3 Tahulandang (isl.), Indo.
67/G3 Tahuna, Indo.
99/A3 Tahuya, Wa,US
99/B3 Tahuyo (riv.), Wa,US
55/J5 Tai (lake), China
59/D5 Tai (lake), China
59/L8 Tai (lake), China
61/H2 Tai (lake), China
55/H4 Tai'an, China
58/B2 Tai'an, China
59/D3 Tai'an, China
59/E2 Tai'an, China
69/X15 Taiarapu (pen.), FrPol.
54/F5 Taibai (peak), China
59/C3 Taibai Shan (mtn.), China
54/H3 Taibus Qi, China
59/E5 Taicang, China
59/L8 Taicang, China
61/J2 Taicang, China
48/M7 Taichung, Tai.
61/J3 Taichung, Tai.
68/B2 Taichung, Tai.
59/C3 Taigu, China
59/C3 Taihang (mts.), China
59/G7 Taihang (mts.), China
59/C4 Taihe, China
59/D5 Taihu, China
61/H2 Taihu, China
54/G5 Taikang, China
59/C4 Taikang, China
55/J2 Tailai, China
70/F7 Tailem Bend, Austl.
73/A2 Tailem Bend, Austl.
37/E1 Tailfingen, Ger.
57/L10 Taima, Japan
61/J4 Tainan, Tai.
68/B2 Tainan, Tai.
18/F5 Taínaron (cape), Gre.
39/H4 Taínaron, Ákra (cape), Gre.
76/D6 Taï Nat'l Park, IvC.
78/D5 Taï Nat'l Park, IvC.
69/L5 Taiohae, FrPol.
48/M7 Taipei, Tai.
61/J3 Taipei (cap.), Tai.
68/B2 Taipei (cap.), Tai.
55/J2 Taiping (peak), China
59/D5 Taiping, China
61/H2 Taiping, China
66/B3 Taiping, Malay.
56/C3 Taisha, Japan
61/G4 Taishan, China
57/L10 Taishi, Japan
61/H3 Taishun, China
30/D5 Taissy, Fr.
105/B7 Taitao (pen.), Chile
48/M7 Taiwan
61/J3 Taiwan
68/B2 Taiwan
61/H4 Taiwan (str.), China, Tai.
68/A2 Taiwan (str.), China, Tai.
48/L7 Taiwan (str.), China, Tai.
59/E4 Tai Xian, China
59/E4 Taixing, China
61/J1 Taixing, China
39/H4 Taiyetos (mts.), Gre.
54/G4 Taiyuan, China
59/C3 Taiyuan, China
55/H5 Taizhou, China
59/D4 Taizhou, China
59/E2 Taizi (riv.), China
52/D6 Ta'izz, Yem.
77/P5 Ta'izz, Yem.
66/C4 Tajam (peak), Indo.
76/H3 Tajarhī, Libya
46/H6 Tajikistan
48/F6 Tajikistan
53/K1 Tajikistan
57/F2 Tajima, Japan
57/E3 Tajimi, Japan
57/N9 Tajimi, Japan
57/L10 Tajiri, Japan
102/D3 Tajmulco (vol.), Guat.
34/C3 Tajo (riv.), Sp.
34/D2 Tajo (riv.), Sp.
51/G3 Tajrīsh, Iran
52/F1 Tajrīsh, Iran
34/D2 Tajuña (riv.), Sp.
60/C5 Tak, Thai.
63/G4 Tak, Thai.
65/B2 Tak, Thai.
57/G2 Takahagi, Japan
56/D3 Takahama, Japan
57/M10 Takahama, Japan
56/C3 Takahashi, Japan
56/C3 Takahashi (riv.), Japan
57/G2 Takahata, Japan
57/L10 Takaishi, Japan
55/L5 Takamatsu, Japan
56/D3 Takamatsu, Japan
57/M10 Takami-yama (peak), Japan
56/B4 Takanabe, Japan
55/M4 Takaoka, Japan
57/E2 Takaoka, Japan
68/G8 Takapuna, N.Z.
71/R10 Takapuna, N.Z.
57/L10 Takarazuka, Japan
69/L6 Takaroa (isl.), FrPol.
57/F2 Takasaki, Japan
57/M9 Takashima, Japan
57/L10 Takatori, Japan
56/D3 Takatsuki, Japan
57/E2 Takayama, Japan
55/M4 Takefu, Japan
56/E3 Takefu, Japan
56/C3 Takehara, Japan
51/G2 Tākestān, Iran
52/E1 Tākestān, Iran
56/B4 Taketa, Japan
57/M10 Taketoyo, Japan
63/H5 Takev, Camb.
65/D4 Takev, Camb.
66/B1 Takev, Camb.
53/L2 Takh, India
63/H4 Ta Khli, Thai.
46/G6 Takhta-Bazar, Trkm.
77/R2 Takht-e Jamshīd (Persepolis) (ruins), Iran
57/M10 Taki, Japan
86/E2 Takijuq (lake), NW,Can
55/N3 Takikawa, Japan
57/K10 Takino, Japan
90/B2 Takla (lake), BC,Can
48/H6 Takla Makan (des.), China
76/E7 Takoradi, Gha.
79/E5 Takoradi, Gha.
75/V17 Takouch (cape), Alg.
49/B4 Talā, Egypt
23/E5 Talacre, Wal,UK
64/B1 Talagang, Pak.
64/G4 Talaimannar, SrL.
53/K4 Talāja, India
62/B3 Talāja, India
76/G4 Talak (des.), Niger
79/G2 Talak (reg.), Niger
103/F4 Talamanca, Cordillera de (range), CR
37/F5 Talamona, It.
82/C2 Tala Mugongo, Ang.
67/G3 Taland (isls.), Indo.
66/B4 Talang (peak), Indo.
102/E3 Talanga, Hon.
31/F5 Talange, Fr.
26/C5 Talant, Fr.
32/F3 Talant, Fr.
36/A3 Talant, Fr.
106/B4 Talara, Peru
46/H5 Talas, Kyr.
50/C2 Talas, Turk.
76/G5 Talata Mafara, Nga.
48/M9 Talaud (isls.), Indo.
68/B4 Talaud (isls.), Indo.
34/C3 Talavera de la Reina, Sp.
34/B3 Talavera la Real, Sp.
62/D6 Talawakele, SrL.
77/M5 Talawdī, Sudan
63/G2 Talawgyi, Burma
100/C2 Talayotes, Mex.
34/C3 Talayuela, Sp.
73/D2 Talbingo, Austl.
70/D2 Talbot (cape), Austl.
109/B4 Talca, Chile
109/B4 Talcahuano, Chile
62/E3 Tālcher, India
46/H5 Taldy-Kurgan, Kaz.
32/C4 Talence, Fr.
36/C4 Talent (riv.), Swi.
52/E1 Tālesh, Iran
37/H4 Talfer (Talvera) (riv.), It.
46/H5 Talgar, Kaz.
24/C3 Talgarth, Wal,UK
67/F4 Taliabu (isl.), Indo.
51/E1 Talin, Arm.
77/M6 Tali Post, Sudan
67/E5 Taliwang, Indo.
85/H3 Talkeetna, Ak,US
86/A2 Talkeetna, Ak,US
49/B4 Talkhā, Egypt
52/F2 Tālkhūncheh, Iran
50/D2 Tall Abyaḑ, Syria
97/G3 Talladega, Al,US
50/E2 Tall 'Afar, Iraq
52/D1 Tall 'Afar, Iraq
22/B5 Tallaght, Ire.
89/K5 Tallahassee (cap.), Fl,US
97/G4 Tallahassee, (cap.), Fl,US
93/K4 Tallahatchie (riv.), Ms,US
73/C3 Tallangatta, Austl.
22/B4 Tallanstown, Ire.
49/G8 Tall 'Āsūr (Ba'al Hazor) (mtn.), WBnk.
98/E6 Talleyville, De,US
18/F3 Tallinn (cap.), Est.
20/H4 Tallinn (cap.), Est.
42/E4 Tallinn (cap.), Est.
46/C4 Tallinn (cap.), Est.
49/E2 Tall Kalakh, Syria
51/E2 Tall Kayf, Iraq
36/C6 Talloires, Fr.
97/H3 Tallulah (fall, falls), Ga,US
93/K4 Tallulah, La,US
97/F3 Tallulah, La,US
77/N5 Talo (peak), Eth.
53/K4 Taloda, India
62/B3 Taloda, India
53/J1 Tāloqān, Afg.
100/D4 Talpa, Mex.
109/B2 Taltal, Chile
86/E2 Taltson (riv.), NW,Can
65/C4 Talumphuk (pt.), Thai.
37/H4 Talvera (Talfer) (riv.), It.
53/L2 Talwāra, India
64/C2 Talwāra, India
57/H7 Tama, Japan
57/H7 Tama (riv.), Japan
57/H7 Tama-Chichibu Nat'l Park, Japan
57/H6 Tamagawa, Japan
57/M10 Tamaki, Japan
103/H4 Tamalameque, Col.
76/E6 Tamale, Gha.
79/E4 Tamale, Gha.
68/G5 Tamana (atoll), Kiri.
74/C2 Tamanghasset, Alg.
79/F1 Tamanghasset (wilaya), Alg.
76/G3 Tamanrasset, Alg.
63/G2 Tamanthi, Burma
94/F3 Tamaqua, Pa,US
24/B5 Tamar (riv.), Eng,UK
67/K5 Tamarike, Indo.
102/E4 Tamarindo Nat'l Wild. Ref., CR
35/F2 Tamarite de Litera, Sp.
37/E5 Tamaro, Monte (peak), Swi.
40/D2 Tamási, Hun.
106/E3 Tamatama, Ven.
101/F4 Tamaulipas (state), Mex.
102/B1 Tamaulipas (state), Mex.
89/G7 Tamaulipas (state), Mex.
100/D3 Tamazula, Mex.
100/E5 Tamazula, Mex.
101/F4 Tamazunchale, Mex.
102/B1 Tamazunchale, Mex.
57/L9 Tamba, Japan
57/L9 Tamba (hills), Japan
76/C5 Tambacounda, Sen.
78/B3 Tambacounda, Sen.
78/B3 Tambacounda (reg.), Sen.
66/C3 Tambelan (isls.), Indo.
67/E2 Tambisan, Malay.
72/B4 Tambo, Austl.
106/D6 Tambobamba, Peru
81/G7 Tambohorano, Madg.
37/F5 Tambo, Pizzo (peak), Swi.
67/E5 Tambora (peak), Indo.
73/C3 Tamboritha (peak), Austl.
19/H3 Tambov, Rus.
45/G1 Tambov, Rus.
46/E4 Tambov, Rus.
45/G1 Tambov Obl., Rus.
34/A1 Tambre (riv.), Sp.
77/L6 Tambura, Sudan
25/E1 Tame (riv.), Eng,UK
34/B2 Tâmega (riv.), Port.
76/G4 Tamgak (peak), Niger
79/H2 Tamgak (peak), Niger
78/B3 Tamgue, Massif du (reg.), Gui., Sen.
101/F4 Tamiahua, Mex.
102/B1 Tamiahua, Mex.
102/B1 Tamiahua (lag.), Mex.
62/C5 Tamil Nadu (state), India
64/F3 Tamil Nadu (state), India
49/B5 Ţāmiyah, Egypt
63/J4 Tam Ky, Viet.
65/E3 Tam Ky, Viet.
60/E5 Tam Le, Viet.
63/J4 Tam Le, Viet.
65/D2 Tam Le, Viet.
98/E5 Tammany (mt.), NJ,US
49/D3 Tammūn, WBnk.
49/G7 Tammūn, WBnk.
89/K6 Tampa, Fl,US
97/H5 Tampa, Fl,US
64/H4 Tampalakamam, SrL.
101/F4 Tampamolón Corona, Mex.
102/B1 Tampamolón Corona, Mex.
18/F2 Tampere, Fin.
20/G3 Tampere, Fin.
42/D3 Tampere, Fin.
46/C3 Tampere, Fin.
101/F4 Tampico, Mex.
102/B1 Tampico, Mex.
89/G7 Tampico, Mex.
101/F4 Tampico Alto, Mex.
102/B1 Tampico Alto, Mex.
81/J6 Tampon Ambohitra (peak), Madg.
66/A3 Tampulonanjing (peak), Indo.
33/K3 Tamsweg, Aus.
40/A2 Tamsweg, Aus.
101/F4 Tamuín, Mex.
102/B1 Tamuín, Mex.
102/B1 Tamuín (riv.), Mex.
60/A3 Tāmulpur, India
68/E8 Tamworth, Austl.
71/J6 Tamworth, Austl.
73/D1 Tamworth, Austl.
25/E1 Tamworth, Eng,UK
58/D5 Tamyang, SKor.
63/K3 Tan (riv.), China
74/F3 Tana (lake), Eth.
77/N5 Tana (lake), Eth.
46/C3 Tana (riv.), Nor.,Fin.
74/G5 Tana (riv.), Kenya
77/N8 Tana (riv.), Kenya
82/H1 Tana (riv.), Kenya
20/H1 Tana (riv.), Nor.
55/M5 Tanabe, Japan
56/D4 Tanabe, Japan
57/L10 Tanabe, Japan
108/B2 Tanabi, Braz.
85/K3 Tanacross, Ak,US
20/J1 Tanafjorden (fjord), Nor.
47/U4 Tanaga (isl.), Ak,US
85/C6 Tanaga (isl.), Ak,US
85/C6 Tanaga (vol.), Ak,US
38/D2 Tanagro (riv.), It.
57/G2 Tanagura, Japan
66/A4 Tanahbala (isl.), Indo.
67/K5 Tanahmerah, Indo.
63/H6 Tanah Merah, Malay.
65/C5 Tanah Merah, Malay.
66/B2 Tanah Merah, Malay.
70/E3 Tanami (des.), Austl.
63/J5 Tan An, Viet.
65/D4 Tan An, Viet.
66/C1 Tan An, Viet.
85/H2 Tanana, Ak,US
85/J3 Tanana (riv.), Ak,US
86/B2 Tanana (riv.), Ak,US
81/G8 Tanandava, Madg.
33/H4 Tanaro (riv.), It.
59/D4 Tancheng, China
55/K3 Tanch'ŏn, NKor.
58/E2 Tanch'ŏn, NKor.
62/C2 Tānda, India
62/D2 Tānda, India
78/D3 Tanda (lake), Mali
77/M5 Tandaltī, Sudan
41/H3 Ţăndărei, Rom.
53/L2 Tāndi, India
109/E4 Tandil, Arg.
64/B2 Tāndliānwāla, Pak.
53/J3 Tando Ādam, Pak.
62/A2 Tando Ādam, Pak.
53/J3 Tando Allāhyār, Pak.
62/A2 Tando Allāhyār, Pak.
53/J3 Tando Muhammad Khān, Pak.
62/A2 Tando Muhammad Khān, Pak.
70/G6 Tandou (lake), Austl.
73/B2 Tandou (lake), Austl.
22/B3 Tandragee, NI,UK
55/L5 Tanega (isl.), Japan
56/B5 Tanega (isl.), Japan
60/C5 Tanem (range), Burma, Thai.
65/B2 Tanem (range), Burma, Thai.
63/G4 Tanem (range), Thai.
74/B2 Tanezrouft (des.), Alg.
76/E3 Tanezrouft (des.), Alg., Mali
59/C3 Tang (riv.), China
59/C4 Tang (riv.), China
82/G2 Tanga, Tanz.
81/H8 Tangainony, Madg.
53/F1 Tangalī, Iran
74/E5 Tanganyika (lake), Afr.
82/F2 Tanganyika (lake), Afr.
107/G6 Tangará da Serra, Braz.
85/G1 Tangent (pt.), Ak,US
26/F2 Tangerhütte, Ger.
26/F2 Tangermünde, Ger.
34/C5 Tanger (Tangier), Mor.
75/M13 Tanger (Tangier), Mor.
76/D1 Tanger (Tangier), Mor.
59/C4 Tanghe, China
61/G1 Tanghe, China
34/C5 Tangier, Mor.
76/D1 Tangier, Mor.
75/M13 Tangier (Tanger), Mor.
58/D4 Tangjin, SKor.
99/B3 Tanglewilde-Thompson Place, Wa,US
47/M6 Tangshan, China
55/H4 Tangshan, China
59/D3 Tangshan, China
59/J7 Tangshan, China
61/F2 Tangyan (riv.), China
59/C4 Tangyin, China
55/K2 Tangyuan, China
60/C2 Taniantaweng (mts.), China
48/N10 Tanimbar (isls.), Indo.
67/H5 Tanimbar (isls.), Indo.
68/C5 Tanimbar (isls.), Indo.
36/C5 Taninges, Fr.
66/A3 Tanjungbalai, Indo.
48/K10 Tanjungkarang-Telukbetung, Indo.
66/C5 Tanjungkarang-Telukbetung, Indo.
66/C4 Tanjungpandan, Indo.
66/A3 Tanjungpura, Indo.
53/K2 Tānk, Pak.
64/A1 Tānk, Pak.
68/F6 Tanna (isl.), Van.

57/L9 **Tannan**, Japan
98/E4 **Tannersville**, Pa,US
54/C1 **Tannu-Ola** (mts.), Rus.
76/E6 **Tano** (riv.), Ghana
79/E5 **Tano** (riv.), Gui., IvC.
76/G5 **Tânout**, Niger
79/H3 **Tânout**, Niger
101/F4 **Tanquián**, Mex.
49/B4 **Ţanţā**, Egypt
50/B4 **Ţanţā**, Egypt
52/B2 **Ţanţā**, Egypt
77/M1 **Tantā**, Egypt
65/B2 **Tantabin**, Burma
98/J8 **Tantallon**, Md,US
76/C2 **Tan-Tan**, Mor.
101/F4 **Tantoyuca**, Mex.
62/D4 **Tanuku**, India
73/A2 **Tanunda**, Austl.
58/E4 **Tanyang**, SKor.
74/F5 **Tanzania**
77/M8 **Tanzania**
82/F2 **Tanzania**
57/H7 **Tanzawa-yama** (peak), Japan
54/E5 **Tao** (riv.), China
61/G3 **Tao** (riv.), China
65/B4 **Tao** (isl.), Thai.
55/J2 **Tao'er** (riv.), China
54/F4 **Taole**, China
55/J2 **Taonan**, China
38/D4 **Taormina**, It.
93/F3 **Taos**, NM,US
96/B2 **Taos**, NM,US
76/E3 **Taoudenni**, Mali
75/N13 **Taourirt**, Mor.
63/K2 **Taoyuan**, China
61/J3 **Taoyuan**, Tai.
20/H4 **Tapa**, Est.
42/E4 **Tapa**, Est.
102/C3 **Tapachula**, Mex.
105/D3 **Tapajós** (riv.), Braz.
107/G4 **Tapajós** (riv.), Braz.
100/E5 **Tapalpa**, Mex.
107/G3 **Tapanahoni** (riv.), Sur.
102/C2 **Tapantatepec**, Mex.
106/E5 **Tapauá** (riv.), Braz.
106/F5 **Tapauá**, Braz.
108/B4 **Tapejara**, Braz.
108/B4 **Tapes**, Braz.
78/C5 **Tapeta**, Libr.
34/B1 **Tapia de Casariego**, Sp.
60/C3 **Taping** (riv.), Burma
66/B3 **Tapis** (peak), Malay.
79/F3 **Tapoa** (prov.), Burk.
40/C2 **Tapolca**, Hun.
94/E4 **Tappahannock**, Va,US
97/J2 **Tappahannock**, Va,US
98/G4 **Tappan**, NY,US
98/G4 **Tappan Zee** (reach), NY,US
99/C3 **Tapps** (lake), Wa,US
53/K4 **Tāpti** (riv.), India
62/B3 **Tāpti** (riv.), India
63/G2 **Tapun**, India
52/C5 **Taqātu' Hayyā**, Sudan
108/B4 **Taquara**, Braz.
107/G7 **Taquari** (riv.), Braz.
108/B4 **Taquari**, Braz.
108/B2 **Taquaritinga**, Braz.
108/B2 **Taquarituba**, Braz.
72/C4 **Tara**, Austl.
40/D4 **Tara** (riv.), Bosn., Yugo.
46/H4 **Tara**, Rus.
39/F1 **Tara** (riv.), Yugo.
79/H4 **Taraba** (riv.), Nga.
49/D2 **Ţarābulus** (Tripoli), Leb.
50/C3 **Ţarābulus** (Tripoli), Leb.
76/H1 **Ţarābulus** (Tripoli) (cap.), Libya
22/B4 **Tara, Hill of** (hill), Ire.
67/E3 **Tarakan**, Indo.
68/A4 **Tarakan**, Indo.
41/K5 **Taraklı**, Turk.
73/D2 **Taralga**, Austl.
34/D2 **Tarancón**, Sp.
82/G1 **Tarangire Nat'l Park**, Tanz.
18/E4 **Taranto**, It.
18/E4 **Taranto** (gulf), It.
38/E2 **Taranto**, It.
38/E3 **Taranto** (gulf), It.
40/C5 **Taranto**, It.
40/C5 **Taranto** (gulf), It.
106/C5 **Tarapoto**, Peru
32/F4 **Tarare**, Fr.
32/F5 **Tarascon**, Fr.
35/H1 **Tarascon**, Fr.
32/D5 **Tarascon-sur-Ariège**, Fr.
35/F1 **Tarascon-sur-Ariège**, Fr.
106/D5 **Tarauacá**, Braz.
69/M7 **Taravai** (isl.), FrPol.
68/G4 **Tarawa** (atoll), Kiri.
34/E2 **Tarazona**, Sp.
34/E3 **Tarazona de la Mancha**, Sp.
53/K2 **Tarbela** (res.), Pak.
18/D4 **Tarbes**, Fr.
32/D5 **Tarbes**, Fr.
35/F1 **Tarbes**, Fr.
97/J3 **Tarboro**, NC,US
40/A2 **Tarcento**, It.
70/E6 **Tarcoola**, Austl.
73/C2 **Tarcutta**, Austl.
32/E3 **Tardes** (riv.), Fr.
35/E2 **Tardienta**, Sp.
32/D4 **Tardoire** (riv.), Fr.
55/M2 **Tardoki-Jani** (peak), Rus.
71/J6 **Taree**, Austl.
73/E1 **Taree**, Austl.
75/V18 **Tarf** (lake), Alg.
50/B4 **Ţarfā'** (dry riv.), Egypt
35/Y17 **Tarfaya**, Mor.
76/C2 **Tarfaya**, Mor.
22/D2 **Tarf Water** (riv.), Sc,UK
76/H1 **Tarhūnah**, Libya
77/R3 **Tarīf**, UAE
34/C4 **Tarifa**, Sp.
75/M12 **Tarifa**, Sp.
106/F8 **Tarija**, Bol.
67/J4 **Tariku** (riv.), Indo.
67/J4 **Tariku-taritatu** (plain), Indo.
46/J5 **Tarim** (basin), China
46/J5 **Tarim** (riv.), China
54/B4 **Tarim** (basin), China
52/E5 **Tarīm**, Yem.
53/J2 **Tarin** (riv.), Afg.
67/J4 **Taritatu** (riv.), Indo.
41/L3 **Tarkhankut** (cape), Ukr.
44/E3 **Tarkhankut, Mys** (cape), Ukr.
79/E5 **Tarkwa**, Gha.
106/C6 **Tarma**, Peru
29/G2 **Tarmstedt**, Ger.
32/D5 **Tarn** (riv.), Fr.
54/E2 **Tarna** (riv.), Mong.
53/J2 **Tarnak** (riv.), Afg.
27/L3 **Tarnobrzeg**, Pol.
27/L3 **Tarnobrzeg** (prov.), Pol.
44/B2 **Tarnobrzeg**, Pol.
18/F3 **Tarnów**, Pol.
27/L3 **Tarnów**, Pol.
27/L3 **Tarnów** (prov.), Pol.
44/B2 **Tarnów**, Pol.
64/C2 **Tarn Tāran**, India
33/J4 **Taro** (riv.), It.
61/J3 **Taroko Nat'l Park**, Tai.
51/H4 **Ţārom**, Iran
53/G3 **Ţārom**, Iran
72/C4 **Taroom**, Austl.
34/B2 **Tarouca**, Port.
76/D1 **Taroudannt**, Mor.
26/E1 **Tarp**, Ger.
40/F1 **Tarpa**, Hun.
89/K6 **Tarpon Springs**, Fl,US
97/H4 **Tarpon Springs**, Fl,US
23/F5 **Tarporley**, Eng,UK
38/B1 **Tarquinia**, It.
49/D4 **Tarqūmiyah**, WBnk.
49/G8 **Tarqūmiyah**, WBnk.
74/K10 **Tarrafal**, CpV.
18/D4 **Tarragona**, Sp.
35/F2 **Tarragona**, Sp.
73/C4 **Tarraleah**, Austl.
35/F2 **Tàrrega**, Sp.
98/G4 **Tarrytown**, NY,US
49/D1 **Tarsus**, Turk.
49/D1 **Tarsus** (riv.), Turk.
50/C2 **Tarsus**, Turk.
52/B1 **Tarsus**, Turk.
106/F8 **Tartagal**, Arg.
109/D1 **Tartagal**, Arg.
32/C5 **Tartas**, Fr.
35/E1 **Tartas**, Fr.
18/F3 **Tartu**, Est.
20/H4 **Tartu**, Est.
42/E4 **Tartu**, Est.
46/C4 **Tartu**, Est.
49/D2 **Ţarţūs**, Syria
49/D2 **Ţarţūs** (prov.), Syria
50/C3 **Ţarţūs**, Syria
50/C3 **Ţarţūs** (prov.), Syria
52/C2 **Ţarţūs**, Syria
57/M9 **Tarui**, Japan
56/B5 **Tarumizu**, Japan
42/H5 **Tarusa**, Rus.
65/B5 **Tarutao Nat'l Park**, Thai.
41/J2 **Tarutino**, Ukr.
54/D2 **Tarvagatay** (mts.), Mong.
23/F5 **Tarvin**, Eng,UK
36/D5 **Täsch**, Swi.
65/D3 **Ta Seng**, Camb.
54/B2 **Tashanta**, Rus.
46/F5 **Tashauz**, Trkm.
45/L4 **Tashauz Obl.**, Trkm.
63/F2 **Tashigang**, Bhu.
51/H4 **Tashk** (riv.), Iran
46/G5 **Tashkent** (cap.), Uzb.
84/P3 **Tasiilaq**, Grld.
66/C5 **Tasikmalaya**, Indo.
49/C1 **Taşkent**, Turk.
50/C2 **Taşkent**, Turk.
52/B1 **Taşkent**, Turk.
50/C1 **Taşköprü**, Turk.
45/G5 **Taşlıçay**, Turk.
51/E2 **Taşlıçay**, Turk.
71/R11 **Tasman** (bay), N.Z.
71/H8 **Tasman** (pen.), Austl.
73/C4 **Tasman** (pen.), Austl.
68/E8 **Tasman** (sea)
71/K7 **Tasman** (sea)
72/H9 **Tasman** (sea)
73/E3 **Tasman** (sea)
73/C4 **Tasman Head** (cape), Austl.
71/H8 **Tasmania** (state), Austl.
73/C4 **Tasmania** (state), Austl.
27/M5 **Tăşnad**, Rom.
40/F2 **Tăşnad**, Rom.
50/D1 **Taşova**, Turk.
101/K6 **Tasquillo**, Mex.
85/M5 **Tasu**, BC,Can
40/D2 **Tata**, Hun.
76/D2 **Tata**, Mor.
27/K5 **Tatabánya**, Hun.
40/D2 **Tatabánya**, Hun.
94/D2 **Tatachikapika** (riv.), On,Can
69/M6 **Tatakoto** (isl.), FrPol.
54/D4 **Tatalin** (riv.), China
98/E5 **Tatamy**, Pa,US
47/Q4 **Tatar** (str.), Rus.
48/P5 **Tatar** (str.), Rus.
55/N2 **Tatar** (str.), Rus.
43/L5 **Tatar Aut. Rep.**, Rus.
45/J1 **Tatar Aut. Rep.**, Rus.
41/J3 **Tatarbunary**, Ukr.
46/H4 **Tatarsk**, Rus.
76/H1 **Tatāwīn**, Tun.
57/E2 **Tate-yama** (mtn.), Japan
57/F3 **Tateyama**, Japan
57/H8 **Tateyama**, Japan
86/E2 **Tathlina** (lake), NW,Can
73/D3 **Tathra**, Austl.
78/B2 **Tatilt** (well), Mrta.
85/J3 **Tatitlek**, Ak,US
86/G3 **Tatnam** (cape), Mb,Can
79/H3 **Tatokou**, Niger
27/K4 **Tatranský Nat'l Park**, Slvk.
27/K4 **Tatrzański Nat'l Park**, Pol.
19/P8 **Tatsfield**, Eng,UK
25/G4 **Tatsfield**, Eng,UK
57/E3 **Tatsuno**, Japan
23/H5 **Tattershall**, Eng,UK
73/C3 **Tatura**, Austl.
50/E2 **Tatvan**, Turk.
107/K5 **Tauá**, Braz.
107/J8 **Taubaté**, Braz.
108/C2 **Taubaté**, Braz.
109/G1 **Taubaté**, Braz.
26/E4 **Tauber** (riv.), Ger.
26/E4 **Tauberbischofsheim**, Ger.
33/H2 **Tauberbischofsheim**, Ger.
26/G4 **Taufkirchen**, Ger.
33/K2 **Taufkirchen**, Ger.
26/E3 **Taufstein** (peak), Ger.
89/H4 **Taum Sauk** (mtn.), Mo,US
93/K3 **Taum Sauk** (peak), Mo,US
94/B4 **Taum Sauk** (peak), Mo,US
97/F2 **Taum Sauk** (peak), Mo,US
80/D2 **Taung**, SAfr.
60/B4 **Taungdwingyi**, Burma
63/G3 **Taungdwingyi**, Burma
60/C4 **Taunggyi**, Burma
63/G3 **Taunggyi**, Burma
65/B1 **Taunggyi**, Burma
60/B3 **Taungthonlon** (peak), Burma
60/B5 **Taungup**, Burma
60/B5 **Taungup** (pass), Burma
63/F4 **Taungup**, Burma
63/G4 **Taungzun**, Burma
53/K2 **Taunsa**, Pak.
64/A2 **Taunsa**, Pak.
95/S8 **Taunton**, On,Can
24/C4 **Taunton**, Eng,UK
95/G3 **Taunton**, Ma,US
26/E3 **Taunusstein**, Ger.
31/H3 **Taunusstein**, Ger.
33/H1 **Taunusstein**, Ger.
71/S10 **Taupo**, N.Z.
71/S10 **Taupo** (lake), N.Z.
27/M1 **Tauragė**, Lith.
42/D5 **Tauragė**, Lith.
68/G8 **Tauranga**, N.Z.
71/S10 **Tauranga**, N.Z.
32/D3 **Taurion** (riv.), Fr.
49/B1 **Taurus** (mts.), Turk.
50/C2 **Taurus** (mts.), Turk.
34/E2 **Tauste**, Sp.
32/C2 **Taute** (riv.), Fr.
69/X15 **Tautira**, FrPol.
68/E5 **Tauu** (isls.), PNG
51/F1 **Tauz**, Azer.
36/D3 **Tavannes**, Swi.
92/E3 **Tavaputs** (plat.), Ut,US
97/H4 **Tavares**, Fl,US
50/B2 **Tavas**, Turk.
32/F3 **Tavaux**, Fr.
36/B3 **Tavaux**, Fr.
43/Q4 **Tavda** (riv.), Rus.
46/G4 **Tavda**, Rus.
46/G4 **Tavda** (riv.), Rus.
25/H1 **Taverham**, Eng,UK
19/S9 **Taverny**, Fr.
30/B5 **Taverny**, Fr.
69/Z17 **Taveuni** (isl.), Fiji
34/B4 **Tavira**, Port.
24/B5 **Tavistock**, Eng,UK
63/G5 **Tavoy**, Burma
63/G5 **Tavoy** (pt.), Burma
65/B3 **Tavoy**, Burma
65/B3 **Tavoy** (pt.), Burma
55/L3 **Tavrichanka**, Rus.
44/D5 **Tavşanlı**, Turk.
50/B2 **Tavşanlı**, Turk.
24/B5 **Tavy** (riv.), Eng,UK
24/B4 **Taw** (riv.), Eng,UK
57/L10 **Tawaramoto**, Japan
89/K3 **Tawas City**, Mi,US
94/D2 **Tawas City**, Mi,US
67/E3 **Tawau**, Malay.
68/A4 **Tawau**, Malay.
24/C3 **Tawe** (riv.), Wal,UK
31/F4 **Tawern**, Ger.
64/C1 **Tāwi** (riv.), India
67/F2 **Tawi-tawi** (isl.), Phil.
52/C5 **Ţawkar**, Sudan
77/N4 **Ţawkar**, Sudan
51/F3 **Ţāwūq**, Iraq
76/G1 **Tawzar**, Tun.
101/F5 **Taxco**, Mex.
102/B2 **Taxco**, Mex.
101/K8 **Taxco de Alarcón**, Mex.
53/K2 **Taxila** (ruins), Pak.
64/B1 **Taxila**, Pak.
64/B1 **Taxila** (ruins), Pak.
53/L1 **Taxkorgan**, China
21/C2 **Tay** (lake), Sc,UK
21/D2 **Tay** (riv.), Sc,UK
106/C5 **Tayabamba**, Peru
102/D2 **Tayasal**, Guat.
20/K1 **Taybola**, Rus.
99/F7 **Taylor**, Mi,US
91/J5 **Taylor**, Ne,US
93/H2 **Taylor**, Ne,US
93/K3 **Taylorville**, Il,US
94/B4 **Taylorville**, Il,US
97/F2 **Taylorville**, Il,US
52/C3 **Taymā'**, SAr.
77/N2 **Taymā'**, SAr.
46/K2 **Taymyr** (pen.), Rus.
46/K2 **Taymyr** (riv.), Rus.
47/L2 **Taymyr** (isl.), Rus.
48/J2 **Taymyr** (pen.), Rus.
46/J2 **Taymyr Aut. Okr.**, Rus.
63/J5 **Tay Ninh**, Viet.
65/D4 **Tay Ninh**, Viet.
66/C1 **Tay Ninh**, Viet.
100/D3 **Tayoltita**, Mex.
103/H4 **Tayrona Nat'l Park**, Col.
46/K4 **Tayshet**, Rus.
67/E1 **Taytay**, Phil.
46/J3 **Taz** (riv.), Rus.
48/H3 **Taz** (riv.), Rus.
75/M13 **Taza**, Mor.
76/E1 **Taza**, Mor.
75/M13 **Tazekka** (peak), Mor.
94/D4 **Tazewell**, Tn,US
97/H2 **Tazewell**, Tn,US
94/D4 **Tazewell**, Va,US
97/H2 **Tazewell**, Va,US
77/K2 **Tāzirbū** (oasis), Libya
78/B4 **Tāzughrān**, Tun.
102/D3 **Tazumal** (ruins), ESal.
19/H4 **Tbilisi** (cap.), Geo.
45/H4 **Tbilisi** (cap.), Geo.
46/E5 **Tbilisi** (cap.), Geo.
51/F1 **Tbilisi** (cap.), Geo.
76/H8 **Tchibanga**, Gabon
82/B1 **Tchibanga**, Gabon
76/G4 **Tchin Tabaradene**, Niger
76/H6 **Tcholliré**, Camr.
27/K1 **Tczew**, Pol.
42/C5 **Tczew**, Pol.
106/E4 **Tea** (riv.), Braz.
100/D4 **Teacapán**, Mex.
101/F2 **Teague**, Tx,US
23/H5 **Tealby**, Eng,UK
71/Q12 **Te Anau**, N.Z.
71/Q12 **Te Anau** (lake), NZ
98/G5 **Teaneck**, NJ,US
40/B5 **Teano**, It.
101/G5 **Teapa**, Mex.
102/C2 **Teapa**, Mex.
71/S10 **Te Araroa**, N.Z.
39/G1 **Tearce**, Macd.
40/E4 **Tearce**, Macd.
71/S10 **Te Aroha**, N.Z.
71/S10 **Te Awamutu**, N.Z.
66/B4 **Tebak** (peak), Indo.
75/V18 **Tébessa** (gov.), Alg.
75/W18 **Tébessa**, Alg.
76/G1 **Tébessa**, Alg.
75/W18 **Tébessa** (mts.), Alg., Tun.
79/F2 **Tebesselamane** (well), Mali
109/E2 **Tebicuary** (riv.), Par.
66/A3 **Tebingtinggi**, Indo.
45/H4 **Tebulos-mta** (peak), Rus.
100/E5 **Tecalitlán**, Mex.
101/M8 **Tecamachalco**, Mex.
100/A1 **Tecate**, Mex.
92/C4 **Tecate**, Mex
32/E5 **Tech** (riv.), Fr.
35/G1 **Tech** (riv.), Fr.
41/J3 **Techirghiol**, Rom.
109/B5 **Tecka**, Arg.
101/H4 **Tecoh**, Mex.
101/F4 **Tecolutla**, Mex.
101/M6 **Tecolutla**, Mex.
102/B1 **Tecolutla** (riv.), Mex.
100/E5 **Tecomán**, Mex.
100/C2 **Tecoripa**, Mex.
101/K6 **Tecozautla**, Mex.
102/C2 **Tecpatán**, Mex.
100/D4 **Tecuala**, Mex.
88/E7 **Tecuala**, Mex.
41/H3 **Tecuci**, Rom.
44/C3 **Tecuci**, Rom.
99/G7 **Tecumseh**, On,Can
94/D3 **Tecumseh**, Mi,US
93/H2 **Tecumseh**, Ne,US
65/B2 **Tedodita Sakan**, Burma
46/G6 **Tedzhen**, Trkm.
46/G6 **Tedzhen** (riv.), Trkm.
53/H1 **Tedzhen**, Trkm.
23/G2 **Tees** (bay), Eng,UK
23/G2 **Tees** (riv.), Eng,UK
106/E4 **Tefé** (riv.), Braz.
106/F4 **Tefé**, Braz.
50/B2 **Tefenni**, Turk.
40/E4 **Teferič**, Yugo.
66/C5 **Tegal**, Indo.
28/D6 **Tegelen**, Neth.
26/F5 **Tegernsee**, Ger.
76/H2 **Tegherī** (well), Libya
22/E6 **Tegid, Llyn** (lake), Wal,UK
37/G5 **Teglio**, It.
79/H3 **Tégouma** (wadi), Niger
102/E3 **Tegucigalpa** (cap.), Hon.
86/G2 **Tehek** (lake), NW,Can
46/F6 **Tehrān** (cap.), Iran
48/E6 **Tehrān** (cap.), Iran
51/G3 **Tehrān** (gov.), Iran
51/G3 **Tehrān** (cap.), Iran
52/F1 **Tehrān** (cap.), Iran
101/F5 **Tehuacán**, Mex.
101/M8 **Tehuacán**, Mex.
102/B2 **Tehuacán**, Mex.
101/G5 **Tehuantepec** (isth.), Mex.
102/C2 **Tehuantepec** (isth.), Mex.
102/C2 **Tehuantepec** (riv.), Mex.
102/C3 **Tehuantepec** (gulf), Mex.
84/H8 **Tehuantepec** (gulf), Mex.
101/M8 **Tehuipango**, Mex.
35/X16 **Teide** (peak), Canl.
24/B2 **Teifi** (riv.), Wal,UK
24/B2 **Teifiside** (vall.), Wal,UK
77/L4 **Teiga** (plat.), Sudan
24/C5 **Teignmouth**, Eng,UK
32/B1 **Teignmouth**, Eng,UK
34/B3 **Tejo** (Tagus) (riv.), Port.
35/P10 **Tejo** (Tagus) (riv.), Port.
34/C3 **Tejo** (Tagus) (riv.), Sp.
34/D2 **Tejo** (Tagus) (riv.), Sp.
63/G2 **Teju**, India
91/J5 **Tekamah**, Ne,US
93/H2 **Tekamah**, Ne,US
71/R9 **Te Kao**, N.Z.
101/H4 **Tekax**, Mex.
102/D1 **Tekax**, Mex.
46/H5 **Tekeli**, Kaz.
46/J5 **Tekes** (riv.), China
52/C6 **Tekezē Wenz** (reg.), Eth.
77/N5 **Tekezē Wenz** (riv.), Eth., Sudan
41/H5 **Tekirdağ**, Turk.
44/C4 **Tekirdağ**, Turk.
50/A1 **Tekirdağ**, Turk.
50/A1 **Tekirdağ** (prov.), Turk.
101/H4 **Tekit**, Mex.
102/D1 **Tekit**, Mex.
62/D4 **Tekkali**, India
44/F4 **Tekke**, Turk.
50/D1 **Tekkeköy**, Turk.
50/E2 **Tekman**, Turk.
71/S10 **Te Kuiti**, N.Z.
62/D3 **Tel** (riv.), India
102/E3 **Tela**, Hon.
75/Q16 **Télagh**, Alg.
45/H4 **Telavi**, Geo.
51/F1 **Telavi**, Geo.
49/D3 **Tel Aviv** (dist.), Isr.
49/F7 **Tel Aviv** (dist.), Isr.
49/D3 **Tel Aviv-Yafo**, Isr.
49/F7 **Tel Aviv-Yafo**, Isr.
50/C3 **Tel Aviv-Yafo**, Isr.
52/B2 **Tel Aviv-Yafo**, Isr.
77/M1 **Tel Aviv-Yafo**, Isr.
35/X17 **Telde**, Canl.
78/E2 **Télé** (lake), Mali
101/F2 **Telegraph**, Tx,US
108/B3 **Telemaco Borba**, Braz.
109/F1 **Telemaco Borba**, Braz.
20/D4 **Telemark** (co.), Nor.
67/E3 **Telen** (riv.), Indo.
41/G4 **Teleorman** (co.), Rom.
76/G3 **Telertheba** (peak), Alg.
105/D3 **Teles Pires** (riv.), Braz.
107/G5 **Teles Pires** (riv.), Braz.
67/E4 **Telford**, Eng,UK

24/D1 **Telford**, Eng,UK
98/E5 **Telford**, Pa,US
33/J3 **Telfs**, Aus.
37/H3 **Telfs**, Aus.
29/E5 **Telgte**, Ger.
102/E3 **Telica**, Nic.
76/C5 **Télimélé**, Gui.
79/B4 **Télimélé**, Gui.
102/B2 **Telixtlahuaca**, Mex.
49/G8 **Tel Jericho Nat'l Park**, WBnk.
90/B2 **Telkwa**, BC,Can
75/Q16 **Tell Atlas** (mts.), Alg.
94/C4 **Tell City**, In,US
97/G2 **Tell City**, In,US
85/E2 **Teller**, Ak,US
62/C5 **Tellicherry**, India
64/E3 **Tellicherry**, India
31/E3 **Tellin**, Belg.
92/F3 **Telluride**, Co,US
96/B2 **Telluride**, Co,US
49/G6 **Tel Megiddo Nat'l Park**, Isr.
54/D2 **Telmen** (lake), Mong.
66/B3 **Telok Anson**, Malay.
101/F5 **Teloloapan**, Mex.
101/K8 **Teloloapan**, Mex.
102/B2 **Teloloapan**, Mex.
20/G5 **Telšiai**, Lith.
42/D5 **Telšiai**, Lith.
27/G2 **Teltow** (reg.), Ger.
76/E6 **Tema**, Gha.
79/E5 **Tema**, Gha.
94/D2 **Temagami** (lake), On,Can
80/E2 **Tembisa**, SAfr.
80/Q13 **Tembisa**, SAfr.
82/C2 **Tembo**, Zaire
24/D2 **Teme** (riv.), Eng,UK
39/H1 **Temelkovo**, Bul.
40/D3 **Temerin**, Yugo.
66/B3 **Temerloh**, Malay.
46/H4 **Temirtau**, Kaz.
95/F1 **Témiscamie** (riv.), Qu,Can
94/E2 **Témiscaming**, Qu,Can
54/E1 **Temnik** (riv.), Rus.
69/M7 **Temoe** (isl.), FrPol.
71/H6 **Temora**, Austl.
73/C2 **Temora**, Austl.
100/C3 **Temores**, Mex.
88/D5 **Tempe**, Az,US
92/E4 **Tempe**, Az,US
38/A2 **Tempio Pausania**, It.
89/G5 **Temple**, Tx,US
93/H5 **Temple**, Tx,US
96/D4 **Temple**, Tx,US
22/B2 **Templepatrick**, NI,UK
73/G5 **Templestowe**, Austl.
30/C2 **Templeuve**, Fr.
27/G2 **Templin**, Ger.
101/F4 **Tempoal**, Mex.
102/B1 **Tempoal** (riv.), Mex.
102/B1 **Tempoal de Sanchez**, Mex.
82/C3 **Tempué**, Ang.
44/F3 **Temryuk**, Rus.
28/B6 **Temse**, Belg.
30/D1 **Temse**, Belg.
109/B4 **Temuco**, Chile
71/R11 **Temuka**, N.Z.
101/H4 **Tenabó**, Mex.
102/D1 **Tenabó**, Mex.
85/L4 **Tenakee Springs**, Ak,US
76/D5 **Tena Kourou** (peak), Burk.
62/D4 **Tenāli**, India
101/F3 **Tenamaxtle**, Mex.
101/F5 **Tenancingo**, Mex.
102/B2 **Tenancingo**, Mex.
101/K8 **Tenancingo de Degollado**, Mex.
102/B2 **Tenango**, Mex.
101/K7 **Tenango de Arista**, Mex.
101/Q10 **Tenango de Arista**, Mex.
101/F5 **Tenango de Río Blanco**, Mex.
101/M8 **Tenango de Río Blanco**, Mex.
102/B2 **Tenango de Río Blanco**, Mex.
63/G5 **Tenasserim**, Burma
63/G5 **Tenasserim** (div.), Burma
65/B3 **Tenasserim**, Burma
65/B3 **Tenasserim** (range), Burma
66/A1 **Tenasserim**, Burma
65/B4 **Tenasserim** (Thanintharyi) (div.), Burma
36/B6 **Tenay**, Fr.
28/D2 **Ten Boer**, Neth.
24/D2 **Tenbury**, Eng,UK
24/B3 **Tenby**, Wal,UK
77/P5 **Tendaho**, Eth.
33/G6 **Tende**, Fr.
57/G1 **Tendō**, Japan
36/C4 **Tendre** (peak), Swi.
78/D3 **Ténenkou**, Mali
76/H4 **Ténéré** (des.), Niger
79/H2 **Ténéré** (des.), Niger
76/G3 **Ténéré du Tafassasset** (des.), Niger
79/H2 **Ténéré, 'Erg du** (des.), Niger
35/X16 **Tenerife** (isl.), Canl., Sp.
76/B2 **Tenerife** (isl.), Canl., Sp.
75/R15 **Ténès**, Alg.
35/L6 **Tenes** (riv.), Sp.
60/C4 **Teng** (riv.), Burma
63/G3 **Teng** (riv.), Burma
65/B1 **Teng** (riv.), Burma
60/C3 **Tengchong**, China
67/E4 **Tenggarong**, Indo.
54/E4 **Tengger** (des.), China
46/G5 **Tengiz** (lake), Kaz.
59/D4 **Teng Xian**, China
33/G4 **Tenibres** (peak), It.
106/F8 **Teniente Enciso Nat'l Park**, Par.
109/D1 **Teniente Enciso Nat'l Park**, Par.
36/D1 **Teningen**, Ger.
40/D3 **Tenja**, Cro.
64/F4 **Tenkāsi**, India
76/E5 **Tenkodogo**, Burk.
79/E4 **Tenkodogo**, Burk.
100/B1 **Tenmile** (cr.), Az,US
92/D4 **Tenmile** (creek), Az,US
68/C6 **Tennant Creek**, Austl.
70/E3 **Tennant Creek**, Austl.
94/B5 **Tennessee** (riv.), Ky, Tn,US
84/J6 **Tennessee** (riv.), US
89/J4 **Tennessee** (state), US
89/J5 **Tennessee** (riv.), US
93/K4 **Tennessee** (state), US
97/G3 **Tennessee** (state), US
31/E3 **Tenneville**, Belg.
20/H1 **Tenojoki** (riv.), Fin.
101/H5 **Tenosique**, Mex.
102/D2 **Tenosique**, Mex.
57/L10 **Tenri**, Japan
57/E3 **Tenryū**, Japan
57/E3 **Tenryū** (riv.), Japan
25/G4 **Tenterden**, Eng,UK
71/J5 **Tenterfield**, Austl.
73/D1 **Tenterfield**, Austl.
73/E1 **Tenterfield**, Austl.
65/B2 **Ten Thousand Buddhas, Cave of**, Burma
67/F3 **Tentolomatinan** (peak), Indo.
34/A1 **Teo**, Sp.
100/E4 **Teocaltiche**, Mex.
101/N7 **Teocelo**, Mex.
100/E4 **Teocuitatlán de Corona**, Mex.
108/A2 **Teodoro Sampaio**, Braz.
107/K7 **Teófilo Otoni**, Braz.
108/D1 **Teófilo Otoni**, Braz.
103/H4 **Teorama**, Col.
101/L7 **Teotihuacán** (ruins), Mex.
101/R9 **Teotihuacán** (ruins), Mex.
100/C2 **Tepache**, Mex.
100/E5 **Tepalcatepec**, Mex.
101/L8 **Tepalcingo**, Mex.
100/E4 **Tepatitlán**, Mex.
101/M7 **Tepatlaxco de Hidalgo**, Mex.
101/F5 **Tepeaca**, Mex.
101/M8 **Tepeaca**, Mex.
102/B2 **Tepeaca**, Mex.
101/F5 **Tepeapulco**, Mex.
101/L7 **Tepeapulco**, Mex.
102/B2 **Tepeapulco**, Mex.
100/E4 **Tepechitlán**, Mex.
101/K7 **Tepeji del Río**, Mex.
101/M8 **Tepexi de Rodríguez**, Mex.
100/E4 **Tepezalá**, Mex.
100/D4 **Tepic**, Mex.
26/G3 **Teplá** (riv.), Czh.
27/G3 **Teplice**, Czh.
100/B2 **Tepoca, Cabo** (cape), Mex.
69/L6 **Tepoto** (isl.), FrPol.
101/Q9 **Tepotzotlán**, Mex.
101/K8 **Tepoztlán**, Mex.
100/E4 **Tequila**, Mex.
35/G1 **Ter** (riv.), Sp.
76/F5 **Téra**, Niger
79/F3 **Téra**, Niger
34/B1 **Tera** (riv.), Sp.
28/B4 **Ter Aar**, Neth.
69/K4 **Teraina** (Washington) (atoll), Kiri.
33/K5 **Teramo**, It.
38/C1 **Teramo**, It.
40/A4 **Teramo**, It.
73/B3 **Terang**, Austl.
44/G5 **Tercan**, Turk.
50/E2 **Tercan**, Turk.
35/S12 **Terceira** (isl.), Azor.
41/K2 **Terderovsk** (bay), Ukr.
41/K2 **Terderovsk** (spit), Ukr.
45/H4 **Terek** (riv.), Rus.
107/K5 **Teresina**, Braz.
108/D2 **Teresópolis**, Braz.
27/M2 **Terespol**, Pol.
26/B4 **Tergnier**, Fr.
30/C4 **Tergnier**, Fr.
32/E2 **Tergnier**, Fr.
54/D4 **Tergun Daba** (mts.), China
28/B5 **Terheijden**, Neth.
42/G1 **Teriberskiy, Mys** (pt.), Rus.
28/C2 **Terkaplesterpoelen** (lake), Neth.
41/H5 **Terkirdağ** (prov.), Turk.
44/C4 **Terkirdağ** (prov.), Turk.
37/H4 **Terlano** (Terlan), It.
37/H4 **Terlan** (Terlango), It.
100/E2 **Terlingua**, Tx,US
37/H5 **Termeno** (Tramin), It.
46/G6 **Termez**, Uzb.
53/J1 **Termez**, Uzb.
38/C4 **Termini Imerese**, It.
101/H5 **Términos** (lag.), Mex.
102/D2 **Términos** (lag.), Mex.
90/C5 **Termo**, Ca,US
92/B2 **Termo**, Ca,US
38/D1 **Termoli**, It.
40/B4 **Termoli**, It.
22/B4 **Termonfeckin**, Ire.
28/E2 **Termunten**, Neth.
23/F6 **Tern** (riv.), Eng,UK
24/D1 **Tern** (riv.), Eng,UK
67/G3 **Ternate**, Indo.
68/B4 **Ternate**, Indo.
26/B3 **Terneuzen**, Neth.
28/A6 **Terneuzen**, Neth.
30/C1 **Terneuzen**, Neth.
47/P5 **Terney**, Rus.
38/C1 **Terni**, It.
32/F3 **Ternin** (riv.), Fr.
30/B3 **Ternoise** (riv.), Fr.
18/F4 **Ternopol'**, Ukr.
44/C2 **Ternopol'**, Ukr.
46/C5 **Ternopol'**, Ukr.
44/C2 **Ternopol' Obl.**, Ukr.
47/Q5 **Terpeniya** (bay), Rus.
47/Q5 **Terpeniya** (cape), Rus.
55/N2 **Terpeniya** (bay), Rus.
55/N2 **Terpeniya** (cape), Rus.
39/H2 **Terpní**, Gre.
41/F5 **Terpní**, Gre.
80/D3 **Terrace**, BC,Can
90/A2 **Terrace**, BC,Can
91/M3 **Terrace Bay**, On,Can
94/C1 **Terrace Bay**, On,Can
38/C2 **Terracina**, It.
95/Q8 **Terra Cotta**, On,Can
20/E2 **Terråk**, Nor.
42/B2 **Terråk**, Nor.
38/A3 **Terralba**, It.
87/L4 **Terra Nova Nat'l Park**, Nf,Can
95/L1 **Terra Nova Nat'l Park**, Nf,Can
35/G2 **Terrassa**, Sp.
35/L6 **Terrassa**, Sp.
32/D4 **Terrasson-la-Villedieu**, Fr.
95/N6 **Terrebonne**, Qu,Can
95/N6 **Terrebonne** (co.), Qu,Can
89/J4 **Terre Haute**, In,US
94/C4 **Terre Haute**, In,US
97/G2 **Terre Haute**, In,US
72/H8 **Terrey Hills**, Austl.
23/J6 **Terrington Saint Clement**, Eng,UK
25/G1 **Terrington Saint Clement**, Eng,UK
37/F4 **Terri, Piz** (peak), Swi.
91/G4 **Terry**, Mt,US
51/H2 **Tersakan**, Trkm.
53/G1 **Tersakan**, Trkm.
26/C2 **Terschelling** (isl.), Neth.
28/C2 **Terschelling** (isl.), Neth.
38/A3 **Tertenia**, It.
35/E2 **Teruel**, Sp.
63/G6 **Terutao** (isl.), Thai.
65/B5 **Terutao** (isl.), Thai.
66/A2 **Terutao** (isl.), Thai.
41/H4 **Tervel**, Bul.
44/C4 **Tervel**, Bul.
33/K3 **Terza grande** (peak) It.
33/K4 **Terzo d'Aquileia**
54/C1 **Tes**, Mong.
54/D2 **Tes**, Mong.
40/D3 **Tešanj**, Bosn.
32/D5 **Tescou** (riv.), Fr.
52/C5 **Teseney**, Eth.
37/H5 **Tesero**, It.
85/G1 **Teshekpuk** (lake), Ak,US
55/N3 **Teshio-dake** (mtn.), Japan
54/D2 **Tesiyn** (riv.), Mong.
54/C1 **Tes-Khem** (riv.), Rus.
40/C3 **Teslić**, Bosn.
86/C3 **Teslin** (lake), BC,Can
85/M3 **Teslin**, Yk,Can
86/C2 **Teslin**, Yk,Can
86/C2 **Teslin** (riv.), Yk,Can
76/F3 **Tessalit**, Mali
76/G5 **Tessaoua**, Niger
79/G3 **Tessaoua**, Niger
28/C6 **Tessenderlo**, Belg.
31/E1 **Tessenderlo**, Belg.
25/E4 **Test** (riv.), Eng,UK
40/C5 **Testa del Gargano** (pt.), It.
35/G1 **Têt** (riv.), Fr.
40/C2 **Tét**, Hun.
24/D3 **Tetbury**, Eng,UK
82/F4 **Tete**, Moz.
36/D1 **Tête de Faux** (peak), Fr.
33/G4 **Tête de l'Estrop** (peak), Fr.
36/C6 **Tête du Torraz** (peak) Fr.
101/L8 **Tetela del Volcán**, Mex.
101/M7 **Tetela de Ocampo**, Mex.
36/D5 **Tête Ronde** (peak), Swi.
39/J1 **Teteven**, Bul.
41/G4 **Teteven**, Bul.
23/H5 **Tetford**, Eng,UK
69/L6 **Tetiaroa** (isl.), FrPol.
69/X14 **Tetiaroa** (isl.), FrPol.
31/F5 **Teting-sur-Nied**, Fr.
85/K3 **Tetlin**, Ak,US
85/K3 **Tetlin Nat'l Wild. Ref.**, Ak,US
90/F4 **Teton** (riv.), Mt,US
34/C5 **Tétouan**, Mor.
75/M13 **Tétouan**, Mor.
76/D1 **Tétouan**, Mor.
39/G1 **Tetovo**, Macd.
40/E4 **Tetovo**, Macd.
37/F2 **Tettnang**, Ger.
35/N9 **Tetuan** (nbrhd.), Sp.
109/D1 **Teuco** (riv.), Arg.
37/F3 **Teufen**, Swi.
18/D5 **Teulada** (cape), It.
38/A3 **Teulada** (cape), It.
100/E4 **Teul de González Ortega**, Mex.
91/J3 **Teulon**, Mb,Can
102/E3 **Teupasenti**, Hon.
29/F4 **Teutoburger Wald** (for.), Ger.
33/K5 **Tevere** (Tiber) (riv.), It.
49/D3 **Teverya** (Tiberias), Isr.
52/C2 **Teverya** (Tiberias), Isr.
23/F1 **Teviot** (riv.), Sc,UK
71/J5 **Tewantin-Noosa**, Austl.
72/D4 **Tewantin-Noosa**, Austl.
24/D3 **Tewkesbury**, Eng,UK
93/J4 **Texarkana**, Ar,US
96/E3 **Texarkana**, Ar,US
89/H5 **Texarkana**, Tx,US
93/J4 **Texarkana**, Tx,US
96/E3 **Texarkana**, Tx,US
72/C5 **Texas**, Austl.
73/D1 **Texas**, Austl.
101/E2 **Texas** (state), US
88/G5 **Texas** (state), US
93/G4 **Texas** (state), US
96/C4 **Texas** (state), US
93/J5 **Texas City**, Tx,US
96/E4 **Texas City**, Tx,US
101/L7 **Texcoco de Mora**, Mex.
101/R9 **Texcoco de Mora**, Mex.
101/R9 **Texcoco, Lago del** (lake), Mex.
26/C2 **Texel** (isl.), Neth.
28/B2 **Texel** (isl.), Neth.
28/B3 **Texelstroom** (chan.), Neth.
93/G3 **Texhoma**, Ok,US
96/C2 **Texhoma**, Ok,US
93/H4 **Texoma** (lake), Ok, Tx,US
89/G5 **Texoma** (lake), Ok, Tx,US
42/J4 **Teykovo**, Rus.
33/K5 **Tezio** (peak), It.
101/F4 **Teziutlán**, Mex.
101/M7 **Teziutlán**, Mex.
102/B2 **Teziutlán**, Mex.
101/F5 **Tezoatlán**, Mex.
102/B2 **Tezoatlán**, Mex.
101/F5 **Tezonapa**, Mex.
101/N8 **Tezonapa**, Mex.
102/B2 **Tezonapa**, Mex.
101/L7 **Tezontepec**, Mex.
60/B3 **Tezpur**, India
63/F2 **Tezpur**, India
60/D4 **Tha** (riv.), Laos

65/C1 **Tha** (riv.), Laos
86/G2 **Tha-anne** (riv.), NW,Can
80/E3 **Thabana-Ntlenyana** (peak), Les.
82/E6 **Thabana-Ntlenyana** (peak), Les.
81/E2 **Thabankulu** (peak), SAfr.
80/D2 **Thabazimbi,** SAfr.
65/B3 **Tha Chin** (riv.), Thai.
65/B4 **Thaen** (pt.), Thai.
60/E4 **Thai Binh,** Viet.
63/J3 **Thai Binh,** Viet.
65/D1 **Thai Binh,** Viet.
48/J8 **Thailand**
60/D5 **Thailand**
63/H4 **Thailand**
65/C3 **Thailand**
66/A1 **Thailand**
48/K8 **Thailand** (gulf), Asia
63/H6 **Thailand** (gulf), Asia
65/C4 **Thailand** (gulf), Asia
66/B2 **Thailand** (gulf), Asia
60/E4 **Thai Nguyen,** Viet.
63/J3 **Thai Nguyen,** Viet.
65/D1 **Thai Nguyen,** Viet.
53/K2 **Thal,** Pak.
64/A1 **Thal,** Pak.
64/A2 **Thal** (des.), Pak.
65/C5 **Thaleban Nat'l Park,** Thai.
31/G5 **Thaleischweiler-Fröschen,** Ger.
27/G5 **Thalgau,** Aus.
33/K3 **Thalgau,** Aus.
37/E3 **Thalwil,** Swi.
63/H5 **Tha Mai,** Thai.
66/B1 **Tha Mai,** Thai.
52/E6 **Thamar, Jabal** (mtn.), Yem.
25/F3 **Thame,** Eng,UK
25/F3 **Thame** (riv.), Eng,UK
94/D3 **Thames** (riv.), On,Can
71/S10 **Thames,** N.Z.
19/P7 **Thames** (riv.), Eng,UK
25/G4 **Thames** (riv.), Eng,UK
19/P7 **Thames Barrier,** Eng,UK
53/K5 **Thāna,** India
62/B4 **Thāna,** India
53/L3 **Thāna Kasbā,** India
63/G4 **Thanbyuzayat,** Burma
25/H4 **Thanet, Isle of** (isl.), Eng,UK
63/J5 **Thang Duc,** Viet.
72/C4 **Thangool,** Austl.
60/E5 **Thanh Hoa,** Viet.
63/J4 **Thanh Hoa,** Viet.
65/D2 **Thanh Hoa,** Viet.
63/J4 **Thanh Lang Xa,** Viet.
63/J5 **Thanh Pho Ho Chi Minh** (Ho Chi Minh City), Viet.
63/J6 **Thanh Phu,** Viet.
65/D4 **Thanh Phu,** Viet.
66/C2 **Thanh Phu,** Viet.
65/D4 **Thanh Tri,** Viet.
65/B4 **Thanintharyi** (Tonasserim) (div.), Burma
62/C5 **Thanjavur,** India
64/G3 **Thanjavur,** India
36/D2 **Thann,** Fr.
37/G1 **Thannhausen,** Ger.
36/C1 **Thaon-les-Vosges,** Fr.
53/J3 **Thar** (des.), India, Pak.
62/B2 **Thar** (des.), India, Pak.
53/K4 **Tharād,** India
62/B3 **Tharād,** India
72/A5 **Thargomindah,** Austl.
60/B5 **Tharrawaddy,** Burma
63/G4 **Tharrawaddy,** Burma
39/J2 **Thásos,** Gre.
39/J2 **Thásos** (isl.), Gre.
41/G5 **Thásos,** Gre.
41/G5 **Thásos** (isl.), Gre.
44/C4 **Thásos** (isl.), Gre.
25/E4 **Thatcham,** Eng,UK
100/C1 **Thatcher,** Az,US
60/E4 **That Khe,** Viet.
65/D1 **That Khe,** Viet.
60/C5 **Thaton,** Burma
63/G4 **Thaton,** Burma
65/B2 **Thaton,** Burma
60/B3 **Thaungdut,** Burma
37/H3 **Thaur,** Aus.
63/H4 **Tha Uthen,** Thai.
60/D5 **Tha Wang Pha,** Thai.
63/H4 **Tha Wang Pha,** Thai.
25/G3 **Thaxted,** Eng,UK
27/H4 **Thaya** (riv.), Aus.
60/B5 **Thayetmyo,** Burma
63/G4 **Thayetmyo,** Burma
37/E2 **Thayngen,** Swi.
60/C4 **Thazi,** Burma
63/G3 **Thazi,** Burma
25/E4 **Theale,** Eng,UK
52/B3 **Thebes** (ruins), Egypt
77/M2 **Thebes** (ruins), Egypt
86/D4 **The Dalles,** Or,US
88/B2 **The Dalles,** Or,US
90/C4 **The Dalles,** Or,US
18/D3 **The Hague,** Neth.
46/A4 **The Hague** (cap.), Neth.
26/C2 **The Hague** (s'-Gravenhage) (cap.), Neth.
28/B4 **The Hague** (s'-Gravenhage) (cap.), Neth.
84/G3 **Thelon** (riv.), Can.
86/F2 **Thelon** (riv.), NW,Can
64/F4 **Theni-Allinagaram,** India
72/C4 **Theodore,** Austl.
91/H3 **Theodore,** Sk,Can
92/E4 **Theodore Roosevelt** (lake), Az,US
91/G4 **Theodore Roosevelt Nat'l Park,** ND,US
86/F4 **Theodore Roosevelt Nat'l Park,** ND,US
88/F2 **Theodore Roosevelt Nat'l Park,** ND,US
86/F3 **The Pas,** Mb,Can
91/H2 **The Pas,** Mb,Can
30/B5 **Thérain** (riv.), Fr.
32/D2 **Thérain** (riv.), Fr.
44/B4 **Thermaic** (gulf), Gre.
39/H2 **Thermaic** (Salonika) (gulf), Gre.
39/H2 **Thérmi,** Gre.
39/H3 **Thermopílai** (pass), Gre.
88/E3 **Thermopolis,** Wy,US
90/F5 **Thermopolis,** Wy,US
92/E2 **Thermopolis,** Wy,US
19/U9 **Thérouanne** (riv.), Fr.
39/G3 **Thesprotikón,** Gre.
94/D2 **Thessalon,** On,Can
18/F4 **Thessaloníki,** Gre.
40/F5 **Thessaloníki,** Gre.
44/B4 **Thessaloníki,** Gre.
39/H2 **Thessaloníki** (Salonika), Gre.
39/H3 **Thessaly** (reg.), Gre.
25/G2 **Thet** (riv.), Eng,UK
25/G2 **Thetford,** Eng,UK
87/J4 **Thetford Mines,** Qu,Can
89/M2 **Thetford Mines,** Qu,Can
95/G2 **Thetford Mines,** Qu,Can
31/E2 **Theux,** Belg.
19/T9 **Thève** (riv.), Fr.
93/J5 **The Woodlands,** Tx,US
96/E4 **The Woodlands,** Tx,US
19/P7 **Theydon Bois,** Eng,UK
19/T10 **Thiais,** Fr.
39/G3 **Thíamis** (riv.), Gre.
30/C3 **Thiant,** Fr.
31/E6 **Thiaucourt,** Fr.
93/K5 **Thibodaux,** La,US
97/F4 **Thibodaux,** La,US
89/G2 **Thief River Falls,** Mn,US
91/J3 **Thief River Falls,** Mn,US
36/C4 **Thielle** (riv.), Swi.
88/B3 **Thielsen** (mtn.), Or,US
90/C5 **Thielsen** (peak), Or,US
92/B2 **Thielsen** (peak), Or,US
65/D4 **Thien Ngon,** Viet.
32/E4 **Thiers,** Fr.
19/T9 **Thiers-sur-Thève,** Fr.
31/E5 **Thierville-sur-Meuse,** Fr.
76/B5 **Thiès,** Sen.
78/A3 **Thiès,** Sen.
78/A3 **Thiès** (reg.), Sen.
60/E4 **Thiet Tra,** Viet.
77/N8 **Thika,** Kenya
82/G1 **Thika,** Kenya
62/E2 **Thimphu** (cap.), Bhu.
20/N7 **Thingvellir Nat'l Park,** Ice.
69/V12 **Thio,** NCal.
26/D4 **Thionville,** Fr.
31/F5 **Thionville,** Fr.
33/G2 **Thionville,** Fr.
39/J4 **Thíra,** Gre.
39/J4 **Thíra** (isl.), Gre.
77/M4 **Third** (fall, falls), Sudan
74/F3 **Third Cataract** (falls), Sudan
99/P15 **Third Lake,** Il,US
23/E2 **Thirlmere** (lake), Eng,UK
23/G3 **Thirsk,** Eng,UK
36/C3 **Thise,** Fr.
20/D4 **Thisted,** Den.
20/P6 **Thistilfjördhur** (bay), Ice.
85/L3 **Thistle** (mtn.), Yk,Can
69/Z18 **Thithia** (isl.), Fiji
39/H3 **Thívai,** Gre.
44/B5 **Thívai,** Gre.
20/N7 **Thjórsa** (riv.), Ice.
63/F3 **Thlanship,** India
86/G2 **Thlewiaza** (riv.), NW,Can
60/C5 **Thoen,** Thai.
63/G4 **Thoen,** Thai.
63/J6 **Thoi Binh,** Viet.
65/D4 **Thoi Binh,** Viet.
66/C2 **Thoi Binh,** Viet.
36/A5 **Thoissey,** Fr.
28/B5 **Tholen,** Neth.
28/B5 **Tholen** (isl.), Neth.
31/G5 **Tholey,** Ger.
97/G3 **Thomaston,** Ga,US
97/G4 **Thomasville,** Al,US
89/K5 **Thomasville,** Ga,US
97/H4 **Thomasville,** Ga,US
97/H3 **Thomasville,** NC,US
71/G4 **Thompson** (riv.), Austl.
90/C3 **Thompson** (riv.), BC,Can
86/G3 **Thompson,** Mb,Can
91/J2 **Thompson,** Mb,Can
91/K5 **Thompson** (riv.), Ia,US
90/E4 **Thompson Falls,** Mt,US
90/D3 **Thompson, North** (riv.), BC,Can
99/B3 **Thompson Place-Tanglewilde,** Wa,US
86/E1 **Thomsen** (riv.), NW,Can
68/D7 **Thomson** (riv.), Austl.
72/A4 **Thomson** (riv.), Austl.
97/H3 **Thomson,** Ga,US
65/C3 **Thon Buri,** Thai.
63/J4 **Thon Cam Lo,** Viet.
65/B2 **Thongwa,** Burma
63/J5 **Thon Lac Nghiep,** Viet.
65/E4 **Thon Lac Nghiep,** Viet.
66/C1 **Thon Lac Nghiep,** Viet.
36/B1 **Thonnance-lès-Joinville,** Fr.
33/G3 **Thonon-les-Bains,** Fr.
36/C5 **Thonon-les-Bains,** Fr.
65/E4 **Thon Song Pha,** Viet.
66/C1 **Thon Song Pha,** Viet.
92/E4 **Thoreau,** NM,US
96/A3 **Thoreau,** NM,US
36/C6 **Thorens-Glières,** Fr.
90/E2 **Thorhild,** Ab,Can
19/U10 **Thorigny-sur-Marne,** Fr.
30/B6 **Thorigny-sur-Marne,** Fr.
20/N7 **Thorlákshöfn,** Ice.
99/Q16 **Thorn** (cr.), Il,US
23/G2 **Thornaby-on-Tees,** Eng,UK
24/D3 **Thornbury,** Eng,UK
23/H4 **Thorne,** Eng,UK
85/M4 **Thorne Bay,** Ak,US
95/R8 **Thornhill,** On,Can
22/E1 **Thornhill,** Sc,UK
23/G2 **Thornley,** Eng,UK
23/G3 **Thornthwaite,** Eng,UK
99/M10 **Thornton,** Ca,US
23/E4 **Thornton Cleveleys,** Eng,UK
23/H3 **Thornton Dale,** Eng,UK
95/R9 **Thorold,** On,Can
95/R9 **Thorold South,** On,Can
19/M7 **Thorpe,** Eng,UK
25/H3 **Thorpe le Soken,** Eng,UK
23/G2 **Thorpe Thewles,** Eng,UK
20/P6 **Thórshöfn,** Ice.
32/C3 **Thouars,** Fr.
32/C3 **Thouet** (riv.), Fr.
30/B5 **Thourotte,** Fr.
98/B2 **Thousand Oaks,** Ca,US
39/J2 **Thrace** (reg.), Gre.
41/G5 **Thrace** (reg.), Gre.
44/C4 **Thrace** (reg.), Gre.
39/J2 **Thracian** (sea), Gre.
41/G5 **Thracian** (sea), Gre.
44/C4 **Thracian** (sea), Turk.
99/E6 **Thread** (cr.), Mi,US
73/D3 **Thredbo Village,** Austl.
90/F4 **Three Forks,** Mt,US
85/L4 **Three Guardsmen** (mtn.), BC,Can
90/E3 **Three Hills,** Ab,Can
73/C4 **Three Hummock** (isl.), Austl.
68/G8 **Three Kings** (isls.), N.Z.
71/R9 **Three Kings** (isls.), NZ
65/B3 **Three Pagodas** (pass), Burma
76/E7 **Three Points** (cape), Gha.
79/E5 **Three Points** (cape), Gha.
94/C3 **Three Rivers,** Mi,US
70/B5 **Three Springs,** Austl.
101/F1 **Throckmorton,** Tx,US
93/H4 **Throckmorton,** Tx,US
96/D3 **Throckmorton,** Tx,US
70/C5 **Throssell** (lake), Austl.
24/B5 **Thrushel** (riv.), Eng,UK
24/D2 **Thruxton,** Eng,UK
65/D4 **Thu Dau Mot,** Viet.
66/C1 **Thu Dau Mot,** Viet.
65/D4 **Thu Duc,** Viet.
30/D3 **Thuin,** Belg.
32/E5 **Thuir,** Fr.
35/G1 **Thuir,** Fr.
87/T7 **Thule Air Base,** Grld.
33/G3 **Thun,** Swi.
36/D4 **Thun,** Swi.
86/H4 **Thunder Bay,** On,Can
89/J2 **Thunder Bay,** On,Can
91/L3 **Thunder Bay,** On,Can
94/B1 **Thunder Bay,** On,Can
33/G3 **Thuner See** (lake), Swi.
36/D4 **Thunersee** (lake), Swi.
60/D5 **Thung Salaeng Luang Nat'l Park,** Thai.
65/C2 **Thung Salaeng Luang Nat'l Park,** Thai.
33/H3 **Thur** (riv.), Swi.
37/E2 **Thur** (riv.), Swi.
37/F2 **Thurgau** (canton), Swi.
26/F3 **Thüringer Wald** (for.), Ger.
33/H1 **Thüringer Wald** (for.), Ger.
26/F3 **Thuringia** (state), Ger.
29/H6 **Thuringia** (state), Ger.
33/J1 **Thuringia** (state), Ger.
25/E2 **Thurlaston,** Eng,UK
70/G2 **Thursday Island,** Austl.
18/C3 **Thurso,** Sc,UK
83/T **Thurston** (isl.), Ant.
99/A3 **Thurston** (co.), Wa,US
33/H3 **Thusis,** Swi.
37/F4 **Thusis,** Swi.
83/S **Thwaites Iceberg Tongue,** Ant.
36/C5 **Thyez,** Fr.
82/G4 **Thyolo,** Malw.
106/E7 **Tiahuanco,** Bol.
85/M5 **Tian** (pt.), BC,Can
59/D4 **Tianchang,** China
61/E4 **Tiandeng,** China
63/J3 **Tiandeng,** China
63/J3 **Tian'e,** China
107/K4 **Tianguá,** Braz.
47/M6 **Tianjin,** China
55/H4 **Tianjin,** China
59/D3 **Tianjin,** China
59/D3 **Tianjin** (prov.), China
59/H7 **Tianjin,** China
59/H7 **Tianjin** (prov.), China
63/J3 **Tianlin,** China
54/G5 **Tianmen,** China
59/C5 **Tianmen,** China
61/G2 **Tianmen,** China
59/K9 **Tianmu** (mts.), China
46/H5 **Tian Shan** (range), Asia
48/H5 **Tian Shan** (mts.), China
54/F5 **Tianshui,** China
59/C5 **Tiantangzhai** (mtn.), China
61/G2 **Tiantangzhai** (mtn.), China
63/J3 **Tianyang,** China
59/C2 **Tianzhen,** China
61/F3 **Tianzhu,** China
63/J2 **Tianzhu,** China
75/R16 **Tiaret,** Alg.
75/R16 **Tiaret** (wilaya), Alg.
76/F1 **Tiaret,** Alg.
69/S9 **Tiavea,** WSam.
108/B3 **Tibagi,** Braz.
108/B2 **Tibaji** (riv.), Braz.
76/H6 **Tibati,** Camr.
23/F6 **Tibberton,** Eng,UK
24/D1 **Tibberton,** Eng,UK
78/C4 **Tibé, Pic de** (peak), Gui.
18/E4 **Tiber** (riv.), It.
33/K5 **Tiber** (riv.), It.
38/C1 **Tiber** (riv.), It.
49/D3 **Tiberias** (lake), Isr., Syria
49/D3 **Tiberias** (Teverya), Isr.
52/C2 **Tiberias** (Teverya), Isr.
74/D2 **Tibesti** (mts.), Chad
76/J3 **Tibesti** (mts.), Chad, Libya
48/H6 **Tibet** (aut. reg.), China
54/C5 **Tibet** (reg.), China
60/B2 **Tibet** (Xizang) Aut. Reg., China
62/E2 **Tibet** (Xizang) Aut. Reg., China
35/L7 **Tibidabo** (peak), Sp.
23/G5 **Tibshelf,** Eng,UK
103/H2 **Tiburon** (cape), Haiti
100/B2 **Tiburón** (isl.), Mex.
92/D5 **Tiburón** (isl.), Mex
103/G4 **Tiburón** (cape), Pan.
99/K11 **Tiburon,** Ca,US
25/G4 **Ticehurst,** Eng,UK
99/P14 **Tichigan** (lake), Wi,US
76/D4 **Tîchît,** Mrta.
78/C2 **Tîchît, Dhar** (hills), Mrta.
76/C3 **Tichla,** WSah.
33/H4 **Ticino** (riv.), It.
37/E5 **Ticino** (canton), Swi.
37/E5 **Ticino** (riv.), Swi.
23/G5 **Tickhill,** Eng,UK
41/F3 **Ţicleni,** Rom.
94/F3 **Ticonderoga,** NY,US
101/H4 **Ticul,** Mex.
102/D1 **Ticul,** Mex.
20/E4 **Tidaholm,** Swe.
63/F3 **Tiddim,** Burma
23/G5 **Tideswell,** Eng,UK
76/F2 **Tidikelt** (plain), Alg.
76/C4 **Tidjikdja,** Mrta.
78/C2 **Tidjikdja,** Mrta.
67/G3 **Tidore** (isl.), Indo.
78/A2 **Tidra** (isl.), Mrta.
35/X16 **Tiede Nat'l Park,** Canl.
37/F4 **Tiefencastel,** Swi.
28/C5 **Tiel,** Neth.
55/K2 **Tieli,** China
55/J3 **Tieling,** China
58/B1 **Tieling,** China
59/E2 **Tieling,** China
35/N9 **Tielmes,** Sp.
30/C1 **Tielt,** Belg.
31/D2 **Tielt-Winge,** Belg.
78/D4 **Tiemba** (riv.), IvC.
26/C3 **Tienen,** Belg.
31/D2 **Tienen,** Belg.
61/H3 **Tieniu** (pass), China
63/J4 **Tien Yen,** Viet.
65/D1 **Tien Yen,** Viet.
65/D2 **Tien Yen,** Viet.
72/C3 **Tieri,** Austl.
76/J3 **Tieroko** (peak), Chad
20/F3 **Tierp,** Swe.
42/C3 **Tierp,** Swe.
92/F3 **Tierra Amarilla,** NM,US
96/B2 **Tierra Amarilla,** NM,US
101/E4 **Tierra Blanca,** Mex.
101/F5 **Tierra Blanca,** Mex.
101/N8 **Tierra Blanca,** Mex.
102/A1 **Tierra Blanca,** Mex.
102/B2 **Tierra Blanca,** Mex.
109/C7 **Tierra del Fuego** (isl.), Arg.
105/B8 **Tierra del Fuego** (isl.), Arg., Chile
109/C7 **Tierra del Fuego Nat'l Park,** Arg.
106/C3 **Tierradentro,** Col.
101/E4 **Tierranueva,** Mex.
34/C2 **Tiétar** (riv.), Sp.
105/D5 **Tietê** (riv.), Braz.
107/J8 **Tietê** (riv.), Braz.
108/B2 **Tieté** (riv.), Braz.
76/C2 **Tifariti,** WSah.
94/D3 **Tiffin,** Oh,US
89/K5 **Tifton,** Ga,US
97/H4 **Tifton,** Ga,US
69/V12 **Tiga** (isl.), NCal.
76/H6 **Tignère,** Camr.
36/B6 **Tignieu-Jameyzieu,** Fr.
106/F2 **Tigre** (riv.), Ven.
48/D6 **Tigris** (riv.), Asia
77/Q1 **Tigris** (riv.), Asia
51/F4 **Tigris** (riv.), Iraq
52/E2 **Tigris** (riv.), Iraq
46/E6 **Tigris** (riv.), Iraq, Turk.
76/J4 **Tigui** (well), Chad
75/T15 **Tigzirt,** Alg.
101/F4 **Tihuatlán,** Mex.
102/B1 **Tihuatlán,** Mex.
20/J3 **Tiilikkajärven Nat'l Park,** Fin.
42/F3 **Tiilikkajärven Nat'l Park,** Fin.
78/B1 **Tijirît** (reg.), Mrta.
100/A1 **Tijuana,** Mex.
88/C5 **Tijuana,** Mex.
92/C4 **Tijuana,** Mex
108/B3 **Tijucas,** Braz.
108/B1 **Tijuco** (riv.), Braz.
102/D2 **Tikal** (ruins), Guat.
101/H5 **Tikal Nat'l Park,** Guat.
102/D2 **Tikal Nat'l Park,** Guat.
62/C3 **Tīkamgarh,** India
85/G3 **Tikchik** (lakes), Ak,US
69/L6 **Tikehau** (atoll), FrPol.
44/G3 **Tikhoretsk,** Rus.
18/G3 **Tikhvin,** Rus.
42/G4 **Tikhvin,** Rus.
46/D4 **Tikhvin,** Rus.
46/E6 **Tikrīt,** Iraq
51/E3 **Tikrīt,** Iraq
39/H2 **Tikveš** (lake), Macd.
40/F5 **Tikveš** (lake), Macd.
101/G5 **Tila,** Mex.
102/C2 **Tila,** Mex.
26/C3 **Tilburg,** Neth.
28/C5 **Tilburg,** Neth.
99/H7 **Tilbury,** On,Can
19/Q7 **Tilbury,** Eng,UK
25/G4 **Tilbury,** Eng,UK
73/B1 **Tilcha,** Austl.
96/D4 **Tilden,** Tx,US
60/B4 **Tilin,** Burma
63/F3 **Tilin,** Burma
23/H5 **Till** (riv.), Eng,UK
70/F5 **Tillabéry,** Niger
79/F3 **Tillabéry,** Niger
90/C4 **Tillamook,** Or,US
26/C5 **Tille** (riv.), Fr.
32/F3 **Tille** (riv.), Fr.
36/B3 **Tille** (riv.), Fr.
20/D4 **Tilst,** Den.
50/B5 **Ţimā,** Egypt
43/L2 **Timan** (ridge), Rus.
46/F3 **Timan** (ridge), Rus.
35/Y16 **Timanfaya Nat'l Park,** Canl.
71/R11 **Timaru,** N.Z.
44/F3 **Timashevsk,** Rus.
39/J5 **Timbákion,** Gre.
107/L5 **Timbaúba,** Braz.
78/C2 **Timbédra,** Mrta.
91/H4 **Timber Lake,** SD,US
108/B3 **Timbó,** Braz.
73/B3 **Timboon,** Austl.
74/B3 **Timbuktu,** Mali
78/E2 **Timbuktu,** Mali
67/H4 **Timbuni** (riv.), Indo.
39/G3 **Timfristós** (peak), Gre.
75/V18 **Timgad** (ruins), Alg.
76/G4 **Tîmia,** Niger
76/F2 **Timimoun,** Alg.
78/A2 **Timiris** (cape), Mrta.
40/E3 **Timiş** (co.), Rom.
40/E3 **Timiş** (riv.), Rom.
44/B3 **Timiş** (riv.), Rom.
18/F4 **Timişoara,** Rom.
40/E3 **Timişoara,** Rom.
44/B3 **Timişoara,** Rom.
79/G2 **Ti-m-Mershoï** (wadi), Niger
87/H4 **Timmins,** On,Can
89/K2 **Timmins,** On,Can
94/D1 **Timmins,** On,Can
91/L4 **Timms** (hill), Wi,US
94/B2 **Timms** (hill), Wi,US
107/K5 **Timon,** Braz.
98/K7 **Timonium,** Md,US
48/M10 **Timor** (isl.), Indo.
67/F5 **Timor** (isl.), Indo.
68/B5 **Timor** (isl.), Indo.
48/M11 **Timor** (sea)
68/B6 **Timor** (sea)
67/G5 **Timor** (sea)
70/D2 **Timor** (sea)
107/K7 **Timóteo,** Braz.
108/D1 **Timóteo,** Braz.
47/N4 **Timpton** (riv.), Rus.
20/F3 **Timrå,** Swe.
42/C3 **Timrå,** Swe.
80/E3 **Tina** (riv.), SAfr.
48/M9 **Tinaca** (pt.), Phil.
67/G2 **Tinaca** (pt.), Phil.
22/B6 **Tinahely,** Ire.
72/D4 **Tin Can Bay,** Austl.
62/C5 **Tindivanam,** India
76/D2 **Tindouf,** Alg.
34/D1 **Tineo,** Sp.
61/H3 **Ting** (riv.), China
72/F7 **Tingalpa** (cr.), Austl.
72/F7 **Tingalpa** (res.), Austl.
73/D3 **Tingaringy Nat'l Park,** Austl.
73/D1 **Tingha,** Austl.
76/H2 **Tinghert** (upland), Libya
78/C4 **Tingi** (mts.), Gui., SLeo.
85/F2 **Tingmerkpuk** (mtn.), Ak,US
106/C5 **Tingo María,** Peru
76/D5 **Tingréla,** IvC.
107/L6 **Tinharé,** Braz.
60/E5 **Tinh Gia,** Viet.
63/J4 **Tinh Gia,** Viet.
65/D2 **Tinh Gia,** Viet.
68/D3 **Tinian** (isl.), NMar.
98/E6 **Tinicum Nat'l Wild. Ref.,** Pa,US
93/H4 **Tinker** (A.F.B.), Ok,US
96/D3 **Tinker** (A.F.B.), Ok,US
78/C4 **Tinkisso** (riv.), Gui.
99/Q16 **Tinley Park,** Il,US
109/C2 **Tinogasta,** Arg.
39/J4 **Tínos,** Gre.
39/J4 **Tínos** (isl.), Gre.
30/C5 **Tinqueux,** Fr.
32/E2 **Tinqueux,** Fr.
76/G2 **Tinrhert** (plat.), Alg.
76/D1 **Tinrhir,** Mor.
60/B3 **Tinsukia,** India
63/G2 **Tinsukia,** India
24/B5 **Tintagel,** Eng,UK
24/B5 **Tintagel Head** (pt.), UK
24/D3 **Tintern Abbey,** Wal,UK
31/E4 **Tintigny,** Belg.
73/B2 **Tintinara,** Austl.
34/B4 **Tinto** (riv.), Sp.
23/G5 **Tintwistle,** Eng,UK
76/F4 **Ti-n-Zaouâten,** Alg.
91/H3 **Tioga,** ND,US
66/B3 **Tioman** (isl.), Malay.
37/G5 **Tione di Trento,** It.
75/R15 **Tipaza** (wilaya), Alg.
75/S15 **Tipaza,** Alg.
21/A4 **Tipperary,** Ire.
25/G3 **Tiptree,** Eng,UK
62/C5 **Tiptūr,** India
69/L6 **Tiputa,** FrPol.
107/J4 **Tiracambu** (mts.), Braz.
50/C5 **Tīrān** (isl.), SAr.
52/B3 **Tiran** (isl.), SAr.
77/M2 **Tīrān** (isl.), SAr.
18/E4 **Tiranë** (cap.), Alb.
39/F2 **Tiranë** (cap.), Alb.
40/D5 **Tiranë** (cap.), Alb.
33/J3 **Tirano,** It.
37/G5 **Tirano,** It.
18/F4 **Tiraspol',** Mol.
41/J2 **Tiraspol',** Mol.
44/D3 **Tiraspol',** Mol.
50/A2 **Tiro,** Turk.
44/F4 **Tirebolu,** Turk.
21/D2 **Tiree** (isl.), Sc,UK
79/F1 **Tirest** (well), Mali
41/G3 **Tîrgovişte,** Rom.
44/C3 **Tîrgovişte,** Rom.
41/H3 **Tîrgu Bujor,** Rom.
44/C3 **Tîrgu Bujor,** Rom.
41/F3 **Tîrgu Cărbuneşti,** Rom.
41/H2 **Tîrgu Frumos,** Rom.
44/C3 **Tîrgu Frumos,** Rom.
41/F3 **Tîrgu Jiu,** Rom.
44/B3 **Tîrgu Jiu,** Rom.
41/F2 **Tîrgu Lăpuş,** Rom.
44/B3 **Tîrgu Lăpuş,** Rom.
41/G2 **Tîrgu Mureş,** Rom.
44/C3 **Tîrgu Mureş,** Rom.
46/C5 **Tîrgu Mureş,** Rom.
41/H2 **Tîrgu Neamţ,** Rom.
41/H2 **Tîrgu Ocna,** Rom.
41/H3 **Tîrgu Secuiesc,** Rom.
44/C3 **Tîrgu Secuiesc,** Rom.
53/K1 **Tirich Mīr** (mtn.), Pak.
41/G2 **Tîrnava Mare** (riv.), Rom.
41/G2 **Tîrnava Mică** (riv.), Rom.
41/G2 **Tîrnăveni,** Rom.
39/H3 **Tírnavos,** Gre.
26/F5 **Tirol** (prov.), Aus.
33/J3 **Tirol** (prov.), Aus.
37/G3 **Tirol** (prov.), Aus.
108/C1 **Tiros,** Braz.
24/C1 **Tir Rhiwiog** (mtn.), UK
26/G4 **Tirschenreuth,** Ger.
33/K2 **Tirschenreuth,** Ger.
38/A2 **Tirso** (riv.), It.
62/C5 **Tiruchchendūr,** India
64/F3 **Tiruchchendūr,** India
62/C5 **Tiruchchirāppalli,** India
64/G3 **Tiruchchirāppalli,** India
62/C6 **Tiruchendūr,** India
64/G4 **Tiruchendūr,** India
64/F4 **Tirumangalam,** India
62/C6 **Tirunelveli,** India
64/F4 **Tirunelveli,** India
62/C5 **Tirupati,** India
62/C5 **Tiruppattūr,** India
64/G3 **Tiruppattūr,** India
62/C5 **Tiruppūr,** India
64/F3 **Tiruppūr,** India
62/C5 **Tirūr,** India
64/E3 **Tirūr,** India
64/G3 **Tirutturaippūndi,** India
64/F4 **Tiruvalla,** India
62/C5 **Tiruvannāmalai,** India
44/B2 **Tisa** (riv.), Eur.
27/M4 **Tisa** (riv.), Eur.
41/G1 **Tisa** (riv.), Eur.
24/D4 **Tisbury,** Eng,UK
86/F3 **Tisdale,** Sk,Can
91/G2 **Tisdale,** Sk,Can
93/H4 **Tishomingo,** Ok,US
96/D3 **Tishomingo,** Ok,US
75/R16 **Tissemsilt,** Alg.
75/R16 **Tissemsilt** (wilaya), Alg.
27/L4 **Tisza** (riv.), Hun.
40/E2 **Tisza** (riv.), Hun.
44/B3 **Tisza** (riv.), Hun.
40/E2 **Tiszaföldvár,** Hun.
40/E2 **Tiszafüred,** Hun.
40/E2 **Tiszakécske,** Hun.
40/E1 **Tiszalök,** Hun.
27/L5 **Tiszavasvári,** Hun.
40/E2 **Tiszavasvári,** Hun.
40/E3 **Titel,** Yugo.
105/C4 **Titicaca** (lake), Bol., Peru
106/E7 **Titicaca** (lake), Bol., Peru
36/E2 **Titisee Neustadt,** Ger.
62/D3 **Titlagarh,** India
33/H3 **Titlis** (peak), Swi.
37/E4 **Titlis** (peak), Swi.
38/D2 **Tito,** It.
18/E4 **Titograd,** Yugo.
39/F1 **Titograd,** Yugo.
40/D4 **Titograd,** Yugo.
40/D4 **Titovo Užice,** Yugo.
39/G2 **Titov Veles,** Macd.
40/E5 **Titov Veles,** Macd.
44/B4 **Titov Veles,** Macd.
39/G2 **Titov vrh** (peak), Macd.
40/E5 **Titov vrh** (peak), Macd.
19/P8 **Titsey,** Eng,UK
40/A1 **Tittmoning,** Ger.
41/G3 **Titu,** Rom.
89/K6 **Titusville,** Fl,US
97/H4 **Titusville,** Fl,US
78/A3 **Tivaouane,** Sen.
39/F1 **Tivat,** Yugo.
40/D4 **Tivat,** Yugo.
24/C5 **Tiverton,** Eng,UK
102/D1 **Tixkokob,** Mex.
101/L7 **Tizayuca,** Mex.
101/H4 **Tizimín,** Mex.
102/D1 **Tizimín,** Mex.
75/T15 **Tizi Ouzou,** Alg.
75/T15 **Tizi Ouzou** (wilaya), Alg.
53/L1 **Tiznap** (riv.), China
76/D2 **Tiznit,** Mor.
26/E1 **Tjæreborg,** Den.
28/C3 **Tjeukemeer** (lake), Neth.
101/M7 **Tlachichuca,** Mex.
102/B2 **Tlacolula,** Mex.
101/P8 **Tlacotalpan,** Mex.
101/R10 **Tláhuac,** Mex.
100/E3 **Tlahualilo de Zaragoza,** Mex.
96/C5 **Tlahualilo de Zaragoza,** Mex
101/K6 **Tlahuelilpa de Ocampo,** Mex.
100/E4 **Tlajomulco,** Mex.
101/N8 **Tlalixcoyan,** Mex.
101/R10 **Tlalmanalcó de Valásquez,** Mex.
101/K7 **Tlalnepantla,** Mex.
101/Q9 **Tlalnepantla,** Mex.
101/Q10 **Tlaloc** (mt.), Mex.
101/Q10 **Tlalpan,** Mex.
101/K8 **Tlaltizapan,** Mex.
102/B2 **Tlaltizapan,** Mex.
101/F5 **Tlapa,** Mex.
102/B2 **Tlapa,** Mex.
101/R10 **Tlapacoya** (ruins), Mex.
101/F5 **Tlapacoyan,** Mex.
101/M7 **Tlapacoyan,** Mex.
102/B2 **Tlapacoyan,** Mex.
101/E5 **Tlapehuala,** Mex.
100/E4 **Tlaquepaque,** Mex.
101/K8 **Tlaquiltenango,** Mex.
101/M7 **Tlatlauquitepec,** Mex.
101/E5 **Tlatlaya,** Mex.
102/A2 **Tlatlaya,** Mex.
101/F5 **Tlaxcala,** Mex.
101/F5 **Tlaxcala** (state), Mex.
101/L7 **Tlaxcala** (state), Mex.
102/B2 **Tlaxcala,** Mex.
102/B2 **Tlaxcala** (state), Mex.
101/L7 **Tlaxcala de Xicohténcatl,** Mex.
101/K6 **Tlaxcoapan,** Mex.
101/L7 **Tlaxco de Morelos,** Mex.
101/L8 **Tlayacapan,** Mex.
85/M5 **Tlell,** BC,Can
75/Q16 **Tlemcen,** Alg.
75/Q16 **Tlemcen** (wilaya), Alg.
76/E1 **Tlemcen,** Alg.
80/D2 **Tlokweng,** Bots.
76/J2 **Tmassah,** Libya
103/F4 **Toabré,** Pan.
41/G2 **Toaca** (peak), Rom.
75/G6 **Toamasina,** Madg.
81/J7 **Toamasina,** Madg.
81/J7 **Toamasina** (prov.), Madg.
99/B2 **Toandos** (pen.), Wa,US
69/L6 **Toau** (atoll), FrPol.
90/B3 **Toba** (inlet), BC,Can
54/D5 **Toba,** China
66/A3 **Toba** (lake), Indo.
57/E3 **Toba,** Japan
57/M10 **Toba,** Japan
104/F5 **Tobago** (isl.), Trin.
106/F1 **Tobago** (isl.), Trin.
53/J2 **Toba Kākar** (range), Pak.
34/E3 **Tobarra,** Sp.
64/B2 **Toba Tek Singh,** Pak.
21/A3 **Tobercurry,** Ire.
22/B2 **Tobermore,** NI,UK
107/L6 **Tobias Barreto,** Braz.
70/D4 **Tobin** (lake), Austl.
91/H2 **Tobin** (lake), Sk,Can
95/H2 **Tobique** (riv.), NB,Can
57/M9 **Tobishima,** Japan
45/M1 **Tobol** (riv.), Kaz.
46/G4 **Tobol** (riv.), Rus.,Kaz.
43/Q4 **Tobol** (riv.), Kaz., Rus.
48/F4 **Tobol** (riv.), Kaz., Rus.
46/G4 **Tobol'sk,** Rus.
77/K1 **Tobruk,** Libya
98/E4 **Tobyhanna,** Pa,US
98/E4 **Tobyhanna** (cr.), Pa,US
98/E4 **Tobyhanna** (lake), Pa,US
98/E4 **Tobyhanna St. Park,** Pa,US
43/L2 **Tobysh** (riv.), Rus.
107/J5 **Tocantinópolis,** Braz.
105/E3 **Tocantins** (riv.), Braz.
107/J4 **Tocantins** (riv.), Braz.
97/H3 **Toccoa,** Ga,US
33/H3 **Toce** (riv.), It.
37/E5 **Toce** (riv.), It.
57/F2 **Tochigi,** Japan
57/F2 **Tochigi** (pref.), Japan
101/L8 **Tochimilco,** Mex.
57/F2 **Tochio,** Japan
34/C4 **Tocina,** Sp.
106/D8 **Tocopilla,** Chile
109/B1 **Tocopilla,** Chile
103/G4 **Tocumen,** Pan.
106/C2 **Tocumen,** Pan.
73/C2 **Tocumwal,** Austl.
104/D5 **Tocuyito,** Ven.
106/E1 **Tocuyo** (riv.), Ven.
57/H7 **Toda,** Japan
62/C2 **Toda Bhīm,** India
25/F3 **Toddington,** Eng,UK
38/C1 **Todi,** It.
37/E4 **Tödi** (peak), Swi.
23/F4 **Todmorden,** Eng,UK
58/C5 **Todohas Haesang Nat'l Park,** SKor.
58/D5 **Todohas Haesang Nat'l Park,** SKor.
100/C4 **Todos Santos,** Mex.
36/E2 **Todtmoos,** Ger.
36/D2 **Todtnau,** Ger.
107/G3 **Toekomstig** (res.), Sur.
90/E2 **Tofield,** Ab,Can
20/E3 **Töfsingdalens Nat'l Park,** Swe.
42/B3 **Töfsingdalens Nat'l Park,** Swe.
69/H6 **Tofua** (isl.), Tonga
78/C2 **Togba** (well), Mrta.
37/F3 **Toggenburg** (val.), Swi.
22/B5 **Togher,** Ire.
85/F4 **Togiak,** Ak,US
85/G4 **Togiak Nat'l Wild. Ref.,** Ak,US
58/D2 **Togno** (riv.), NKor.
74/C4 **Togo**
76/F6 **Togo**
79/F4 **Togo**
57/N9 **Tōgō,** Japan
54/G3 **Togtoh,** China
59/B2 **Togtoh,** China
58/D5 **Tŏgyu-san Nat'l Park,** SKor.
92/E4 **Tohatchi,** NM,US
96/A3 **Tohatchi,** NM,US
98/E5 **Tohickon** (cr.), Pa,US
69/X15 **Tohivea** (peak), FrPol.
57/F2 **Tōhoku** (prov.), Japan
57/F3 **Toi,** Japan
57/M9 **Tōin,** Japan
92/C3 **Toiyabe** (range), Nv,US
56/C3 **Tojō,** Japan
57/L10 **Tōjō,** Japan
85/K3 **Tok,** Ak,US
86/B2 **Tok,** Ak,US
57/E3 **Tōkai,** Japan
57/M9 **Tōkai,** Japan
27/L4 **Tokaj,** Hun.
40/E1 **Tokaj,** Hun.
57/F2 **Tōkamachi,** Japan
68/B1 **Tokara** (isls.), Japan
44/F4 **Tokat,** Turk.
44/F4 **Tokat** (prov.), Turk.
46/D5 **Tokat,** Turk.
50/D1 **Tokat,** Turk.
50/D1 **Tokat** (prov.), Turk.
58/C4 **Tŏkchŏk** (arch.), SKor.
85/M4 **Tokeen,** Ak,US
69/H5 **Tokelau** (terr.), N.Z.
57/N9 **Toki,** Japan
57/N9 **Toki** (riv.), Japan
57/H6 **Tokigawa,** Japan
57/M10 **Tokoname,** Japan
68/G8 **Tokoroa,** N.Z.
71/S10 **Tokoroa,** N.Z.
57/F3 **Tokorozawa,** Japan
57/H7 **Tokorozawa,** Japan
55/K3 **Tŏksŏng,** NKor.
85/E3 **Toksook Bay,** Ak,US
54/B2 **Toksun,** China
55/L5 **Tokushima,** Japan
56/C4 **Tokushima** (pref.), Japan
56/D3 **Tokushima,** Japan
56/B3 **Tokuyama,** Japan
47/P6 **Tōkyō** (cap.), Japan
48/N6 **Tōkyō** (cap.), Japan
55/M4 **Tōkyō** (cap.), Japan
57/F3 **Tōkyō** (cap.), Japan
57/F3 **Tōkyō** (pref.), Japan
57/H7 **Tokyo** (bay), Japan
57/H7 **Tōkyō** (cap.), Japan
57/H7 **Tōkyō** (pref.), Japan
57/H7 **Tōkyō Disneyland,** Japan
102/E4 **Tola,** Nic.
75/G7 **Tôlanäro,** Madg.
45/K1 **Tolbazy,** Rus.
54/C2 **Tolbo,** Mong.
41/H4 **Tolbukhin,** Bul.
44/C4 **Tolbukhin,** Bul.

185

Tsets – Upper

47/L5 **Tsetserleg,** Mong.
54/E2 **Tsetserleg,** Mong.
80/C2 **Tshabong,** Bots.
82/D6 **Tshabong,** Bots.
82/D5 **Tshane,** Bots.
82/B1 **Tshela,** Zaire
82/D2 **Tshibwika,** Zaire
82/D2 **Tshikapa,** Zaire
74/E5 **Tshuapa** (riv.), Zaire
77/K8 **Tshuapa** (riv.), Zaire
82/D1 **Tshuapa** (riv.), Zaire
75/G6 **Tsiafajavona** (peak), Madg.
43/L2 **Tsil'ma** (riv.), Rus.
19/H4 **Tsimlyansk** (res.), Rus.
45/G2 **Tsimlyansk** (res.), Rus.
46/E5 **Tsimlyansk** (res.), Rus.
81/H9 **Tsiombe,** Madg.
81/H7 **Tsiribihina** (riv.), Madg.
81/H7 **Tsiroanomandidy,** Madg.
51/F1 **Tsiteli-Tskaro,** Geo.
80/C4 **Tsitsikamma Forest & Coastal Nat'l Park,** SAfr.
81/H9 **Tsivory,** Madg.
45/G4 **Tskhinvali,** Geo.
51/E1 **Tskhinvali,** Geo.
42/G4 **Tsna** (riv.), Rus.
45/G1 **Tsna** (riv.), Rus.
54/D2 **Tsogt,** Mong.
54/F3 **Tsogt-Ovoo,** Mong.
54/F3 **Tsogttsetsiy,** Mong.
54/F2 **Tsöh** (riv.), Mong.
80/D3 **Tsomo** (riv.), SAfr.
47/N6 **Tsu** (isl.), Japan
55/K5 **Tsu** (isl.), Japan
56/A3 **Tsu** (isls.), Japan
56/E3 **Tsu,** Japan
57/M10 **Tsu,** Japan
58/E5 **Tsu** (isl.), Japan
57/F2 **Tsubame,** Japan
56/E2 **Tsubata,** Japan
57/G2 **Tsuchiura,** Japan
57/M10 **Tsuchiyama,** Japan
55/M3 **Tsugaru** (str.), Japan
57/L10 **Tsuge,** Japan
57/M10 **Tsukigase,** Japan
57/H7 **Tsukui,** Japan
56/B4 **Tsukumi,** Japan
82/C4 **Tsumeb,** Namb.
57/K10 **Tsuna,** Japan
51/F1 **Tsurib,** Rus.
57/F3 **Tsuru,** Japan
56/E3 **Tsuruga,** Japan
57/H7 **Tsurugashima,** Japan
57/E2 **Tsurugi,** Japan
55/L5 **Tsurugi-san** (mtn.), Japan
56/D4 **Tsurugi-san** (mtn.), Japan
57/M9 **Tsushima,** Japan
55/L4 **Tsuyama,** Japan
56/D3 **Tsuyama,** Japan
41/L2 **Tsyurupinsk,** Ukr.
66/C5 **Tua** (cape), Indo.
34/B2 **Tua** (riv.), Port.
21/A4 **Tuam,** Ire.
69/L6 **Tuamotu** (arch.), FrPol.
59/B4 **Tuan** (riv.), China
66/A3 **Tuan** (pt.), Indo.
60/D4 **Tuan Giao,** Viet.
65/C1 **Tuan Giao,** Viet.
66/A3 **Tuangku** (isl.), Indo.
60/E5 **Tuan Thuong,** Viet.
65/D2 **Tuan Thuong,** Viet.
61/J5 **Tuao,** Phil.
44/F3 **Tuapse,** Rus.
61/J5 **Tuba,** Phil.
92/E3 **Tuba City,** Az,US
66/D5 **Tuban,** Indo.
52/D6 **Tuban** (riv.), Yem.
108/B4 **Tubarão,** Braz.
109/G2 **Tubarão,** Braz.
49/G7 **Ţūbās,** WBnk.
28/D4 **Tubbergen,** Neth.
26/E4 **Tübingen,** Ger.
33/H2 **Tübingen,** Ger.
37/F1 **Tübingen,** Ger.
30/D2 **Tubize,** Belg.
78/C5 **Tubmanburg,** Libr.
68/H6 **Tubou,** Fiji
77/K1 **Ţubruq** (Tobruk), Libya
69/K7 **Tubuaä** (isls.), FrPol.
69/K7 **Tubuaï** (isl.), FrPol.
103/G4 **Tubualá,** Pan.
100/C2 **Tubutama,** Mex.
104/D5 **Tucacas,** Ven.
27/J2 **Tuchola,** Pol.
27/L4 **Tuchów,** Pol.
31/E5 **Tucquegnieux,** Fr.
100/C1 **Tucson,** Az,US
88/D5 **Tucson,** Az,US
92/E4 **Tucson,** Az,US
88/F4 **Tucumcari,** NM,US
93/G4 **Tucumcari,** NM,US
96/C3 **Tucumcari,** NM,US
106/F2 **Tucupita,** Ven.
105/E3 **Tucuruí** (res.), Braz.
107/H4 **Tucuruí** (res.), Braz.
107/J4 **Tucuruí,** Braz.
34/E1 **Tudela,** Sp.
34/C2 **Tudela de Duero,** Sp.
19/P8 **Tudeley,** Eng,UK
32/E5 **Tude, Rochers de la** (mtn.), Fr.
35/G1 **Tude, Rochers de la** (mtn.), Fr.
37/H5 **Tuenno,** It.
50/D2 **Tufanbeyli,** Turk.
80/E3 **Tugela** (falls), SAfr.
81/E3 **Tugela** (riv.), SAfr.
67/F5 **Tukangbesi** (isls.), Indo.
49/B4 **Ţūkh,** Egypt
85/M2 **Tuktoyaktuk,** NW,Can
86/C2 **Tuktoyaktuk,** NW,Can
20/G4 **Tukums,** Lat.
42/D4 **Tukums,** Lat.
66/D4 **Tukung** (peak), Indo.
99/C3 **Tukwila,** Wa,US
101/F4 **Tula,** Mex.
101/K6 **Tula** (riv.), Mex.
19/G3 **Tula,** Rus.
44/F1 **Tula,** Rus.
46/D4 **Tula,** Rus.
101/K6 **Tula de Allende,** Mex.
99/C1 **Tulalip Bay,** Wa,US
99/C1 **Tulalip Ind. Res.,** Wa,US
101/F4 **Tula Nat'l Park,** Mex.
101/K6 **Tula Nat'l Park,** Mex.
102/B1 **Tula Nat'l Park,** Mex.
101/F4 **Tulancingo,** Mex.
101/L6 **Tulancingo,** Mex.
102/B1 **Tulancingo,** Mex.
44/F1 **Tula Obl.,** Rus.
92/C3 **Tulare,** Ca,US
100/D1 **Tularosa,** NM,US
93/F4 **Tularosa,** NM,US
93/F4 **Tularosa** (val.), NM,US
96/B3 **Tularosa,** NM,US
96/B3 **Tularosa** (val.), NM,US
80/L10 **Tulbagh,** SAfr.
106/C3 **Tulcán,** Ecu.
41/J3 **Tulcea,** Rom.
41/J3 **Tulcea** (co.), Rom.
44/D3 **Tulcea,** Rom.
99/L9 **Tule** (can.), Ca,US
93/G4 **Tulia,** Tx,US
96/C3 **Tulia,** Tx,US
85/E5 **Tulik** (vol.), Ak,US
68/E5 **Tulin** (isls.), PNG
49/D3 **Ţūlkarm,** WBnk.
49/G7 **Ţūlkarm,** WBnk.
50/C3 **Ţūlkarm,** WBnk.
97/G3 **Tullahoma,** Tn,US
73/C2 **Tullamore,** Austl.
32/D4 **Tulle,** Fr.
27/J4 **Tulln,** Aus.
40/C1 **Tulln,** Aus.
22/B6 **Tullow,** Ire.
72/B2 **Tully,** Austl.
42/G1 **Tuloma** (riv.), Rus.
46/D3 **Tuloma** (riv.), Rus.
89/G4 **Tulsa,** Ok,US
93/J3 **Tulsa,** Ok,US
96/E2 **Tulsa,** Ok,US
101/K7 **Tultepec,** Mex.
101/Q9 **Tultepec,** Mex.
106/C3 **Tuluá,** Col.
85/F3 **Tuluksak,** Ak,US
101/J4 **Tulum Nat'l Park,** Mex.
102/E1 **Tulum Nat'l Park,** Mex.
47/L4 **Tulun,** Rus.
103/E3 **Tuma** (riv.), Nic.
101/C2 **Tumacacori Nat'l Mon.,** Az,US
92/F5 **Tumacacori Nat'l Mon.,** Az,US
107/H3 **Tumac-Humac** (mts.), Braz.
106/C3 **Tumaco,** Col.
106/G2 **Tumatumari,** Guy.
77/J8 **Tumba** (lake), Zaire
82/C1 **Tumba** (lake), Zaire
101/G5 **Tumbalá,** Mex.
102/C2 **Tumbalá,** Mex.
73/D2 **Tumbarumba,** Austl.
106/B4 **Tumbes,** Peru
63/H5 **Tumbot** (peak), Camb.
65/C3 **Tumbot** (peak), Camb.
66/B1 **Tumbot** (peak), Camb.
70/F6 **Tumby Bay,** Austl.
59/B2 **Tumd Youqi,** China
59/B2 **Tumd Zuoqi,** China
47/N5 **Tumen,** China
55/K3 **Tumen,** China
58/E1 **Tumen** (riv.), China, NKor.
106/F2 **Tumeremo,** Ven.
62/C5 **Tumkūr,** India
55/M1 **Tumnin** (riv.), Rus.
63/H6 **Tumpat,** Malay.
65/C5 **Tumpat,** Malay.
66/B2 **Tumpat,** Malay.
67/F4 **Tumpu** (peak), Indo.
79/E4 **Tumu,** Gha.
71/H7 **Tumut,** Austl.
73/D2 **Tumut,** Austl.
99/B3 **Tumwater,** Wa,US
20/F3 **Tunadal,** Swe.
42/C3 **Tunadal,** Swe.
50/D2 **Tunceli,** Turk.
50/D2 **Tunceli** (prov.), Turk.
61/F5 **Tunchang,** China
63/K4 **Tunchang,** China
82/F2 **Tunduma,** Tanz.
82/G3 **Tunduru,** Tanz.
39/K1 **Tundzha** (riv.), Bul.
40/H4 **Tundzha** (riv.), Bul.
62/C4 **Tungabhadra** (res.), India
62/C4 **Tungabhadra** (riv.), India
73/C3 **Tungamah,** Austl.
58/C4 **Tŭngsan-got** (pt.), NKor.
86/D2 **Tungsten,** NW,Can
46/K3 **Tunguska, Lower** (riv.), Rus.
48/K3 **Tunguska, Stony** (riv.), Rus.
54/F2 **Tünhel,** Mong.
38/B4 **Tūnis** (cap.), Tun.
38/B4 **Tunis** (gov.), Tun.
38/B4 **Tunis** (gulf), Tun.
75/X17 **Tūnis** (cap.), Tun.
75/X17 **Tunis** (gulf), Tun.
76/H1 **Tūnis** (cap.), Tun.
38/A5 **Tunisia**
74/C1 **Tunisia**
75/W18 **Tunisia**
76/G1 **Tunisia**
106/D2 **Tunjá,** Col.
59/C3 **Tunliu,** China
85/F3 **Tuntutuliak,** Ak,US
87/K3 **Tunungayualuk** (isl.), Nf,Can
109/C3 **Tunuyán,** Arg.
54/E5 **Tuo** (riv.), China
60/E2 **Tuo** (riv.), China
63/J3 **Tuolu,** China
92/B3 **Tuolumne** (riv.), Ca,US
63/H4 **Tuong Duong,** Viet.
65/D2 **Tuong Duong,** Viet.
60/E3 **Tuoniang** (riv.), China
63/J3 **Tuoniang** (riv.), China
107/H8 **Tupã,** Braz.
108/B2 **Tupã,** Braz.
108/B1 **Tupaciguara,** Braz.
69/K6 **Tupai** (isl.), FrPol.
89/J5 **Tupelo,** Ms,US
97/F3 **Tupelo,** Ms,US
97/F3 **Tupelo Nat'l Bfld.,** Ms,US
101/G5 **Tupilco,** Mex.
102/C2 **Tupilco,** Mex.
108/B2 **Tupi Paulista,** Braz.
106/E8 **Tupiza,** Bol.
94/F2 **Tupper Lake,** NY,US
55/J2 **Tuquan,** China
62/F2 **Tura,** India
43/Q4 **Tura** (riv.), Rus.
46/G4 **Tura** (riv.), Rus.
47/L3 **Tura,** Rus.
77/P3 **Turabah,** SAr.
64/G3 **Turaiyūr,** India
46/K4 **Turan,** Rus.
54/C1 **Turan,** Rus.
55/L1 **Turana** (mts.), Rus.
71/S10 **Turangi,** N.Z.
46/G5 **Turan Lowland** (plain), Uzb.
52/C2 **Ţurayf,** SAr.
77/N1 **Ţurayf,** SAr.
103/H4 **Turbaco,** Col.
106/C1 **Turbaco,** Col.
53/H3 **Turbat,** Pak.
37/E3 **Turbenthal,** Swi.
103/H4 **Turbo,** Col.
106/C2 **Turbo,** Col.
36/D1 **Turckheim,** Fr.
41/F2 **Turda,** Rom.
44/B3 **Turda,** Rom.
69/M7 **Tureia** (atoll), FrPol.
27/K2 **Turek,** Pol.
44/A1 **Turek,** Pol.
46/G4 **Turgay Obl.,** Kaz.
94/E1 **Turgeon** (riv.), Qu,Can
41/H4 **Tŭrgovishte,** Bul.
44/C4 **Tŭrgovishte,** Bul.
44/C5 **Turgutlu,** Turk.
50/A2 **Turgutlu,** Turk.
44/F4 **Turhal,** Turk.
50/D1 **Turhal,** Turk.
20/H4 **Türi,** Est.
42/E4 **Türi,** Est.
35/F3 **Turia** (riv.), Sp.
107/J4 **Turiaçu,** Braz.
101/E5 **Turicato,** Mex.
18/D4 **Turin,** It.
33/G4 **Turin,** It.
47/L4 **Turka,** Rus.
27/M4 **Turka,** Ukr.
74/F4 **Turkana** (lake), Eth., Kenya
77/N7 **Turkana** (lake), Eth., Kenya
50/C1 **Türkeli,** Turk.
46/G5 **Turkestan,** Kaz.
40/E2 **Túrkeve,** Hun.
18/F4 **Turkey**
39/K2 **Turkey**
41/H5 **Turkey**
44/D4 **Turkey**
46/D6 **Turkey**
48/C6 **Turkey**
49/C1 **Turkey**
50/C2 **Turkey**
52/B1 **Turkey**
91/L5 **Turkey** (riv.), Ia,US
93/K2 **Turkey** (riv.), Ia,US
37/G1 **Türkheim,** Ger.
45/K5 **Turkmenistan**
46/F6 **Turkmenistan**
48/E6 **Turkmenistan**
51/H1 **Turkmenistan**
53/H1 **Turkmenistan**
50/D2 **Türkoğlu,** Turk.
104/D2 **Turks** (isls.), Trks.
84/K7 **Turks and Caicos Islands,** UK
103/H1 **Turks and Caicos** (isls.), UK
104/C2 **Turks and Caicos** (isls.), UK
89/M7 **Turks and Caicos** (isls.), UK
103/H1 **Turks and Caicos Islands,** UK
103/J1 **Turks Island** (passg.), Trks.
104/D2 **Turks Island** (passg.), Trks.
18/F2 **Turku,** Fin.
20/G3 **Turku,** Fin.
42/D3 **Turku** (Åbo), Fin.
46/C3 **Turku** (Åbo), Fin.
20/G3 **Turku Ja Pori** (prov.), Fin.
42/D3 **Turku Ja Pori** (prov.), Fin.
92/B3 **Turlock,** Ca,US
108/D1 **Turmalina,** Braz.
20/H5 **Turmantas,** Lith.
42/E5 **Turmantas,** Lith.
104/E5 **Turmero,** Ven.
22/D1 **Turnberry,** Sc,UK
100/C1 **Turnbull** (mt.), Az,US
102/E2 **Turneffe** (isls.), Belz.
98/E6 **Turnersville,** NJ,US
28/B6 **Turnhout,** Belg.
90/F1 **Turnor Lake,** Sk,Can
27/H3 **Turnov,** Czh.
33/L1 **Turnov,** Czh.
41/G4 **Turnu Măgurele,** Rom.
73/D3 **Tuross Head,** Austl.
46/J5 **Turpan,** China
54/B3 **Turpan,** China
103/G2 **Turquino** (peak), Cuba
78/B5 **Turtle** (isls.), SLeo.
90/F2 **Turtleford,** Sk,Can
23/F4 **Turton,** Eng,UK
46/J3 **Turukhansk,** Rus.
89/J5 **Tuscaloosa,** Al,US
97/G3 **Tuscaloosa,** Al,US
38/B1 **Tuscano** (arch.), It.
33/J5 **Tuscany** (reg.), It.
38/B1 **Tuscany** (reg.), It.
90/D5 **Tuscarora,** Nv,US
92/C2 **Tuscarora,** Nv,US
95/S9 **Tuscarora Ind. Res.,** NY,US
101/F1 **Tuscola,** Tx,US
43/X9 **Tushino,** Rus.
89/J5 **Tuskegee,** Al,US
97/G3 **Tuskegee,** Al,US
98/C3 **Tustin,** Ca,US
27/K3 **Tuszyn,** Pol.
51/E2 **Tutak,** Turk.
42/H4 **Tutayev,** Rus.
23/G6 **Tutbury,** Eng,UK
62/C6 **Tuticorin,** India
64/G4 **Tuticorin,** India
39/G1 **Tutin,** Yugo.
40/E4 **Tutin,** Yugo.
66/D3 **Tutong,** Bru.
41/H3 **Tutrakan,** Bul.
37/E2 **Tuttlingen,** Ger.
69/H6 **Tutuila** (isl.), ASam.
69/T10 **Tutuila** (isl.), ASam.
85/F2 **Tututalak** (mtn.), Ak,US
37/H2 **Tutzing,** Ger.
54/F2 **Tuul** (riv.), Mong.
20/H3 **Tuusula,** Fin.
42/E3 **Tuusula,** Fin.
46/K4 **Tuva Aut. Rep.,** Rus.
68/G5 **Tuvalu**
77/Q3 **Tuwayq** (mts.), SAr.
52/E4 **Ţuwayq, Jabal** (mts.), SAr.
23/H5 **Tuxford,** Eng,UK
100/D4 **Tuxpan,** Mex.
101/F4 **Tuxpan,** Mex.
101/F4 **Tuxpan** (riv.), Mex.
102/B1 **Tuxpan,** Mex.
102/B1 **Tuxpan** (riv.), Mex.
101/F5 **Tuxtepec,** Mex.
102/B2 **Tuxtepec,** Mex.
102/C2 **Tuxtla Gutiérrez,** Mex.
34/A1 **Túy,** Sp.
63/J5 **Tuy An,** Viet.
66/C1 **Tuy An,** Viet.
60/E5 **Tuyen Hoa,** Viet.
63/J4 **Tuyen Hoa,** Viet.
65/D2 **Tuyen Hoa,** Viet.
65/D1 **Tuyen Quang,** Viet.
63/J5 **Tuy Hoa,** Viet.
65/E3 **Tuy Hoa,** Viet.
66/C1 **Tuy Hoa,** Viet.
43/M5 **Tuymazy,** Rus.
45/K1 **Tuymazy,** Rus.
51/G3 **Tūysarkān,** Iran
52/E2 **Tūysarkān,** Iran
50/C2 **Tuz** (lake), Turk.
92/D4 **Tuzigoot Nat'l Mon.,** Az,US
51/F3 **Ţūz Khurmātū,** Iraq
52/D2 **Ţūz Khurmātū,** Iraq
40/D3 **Tuzla,** Bosn.
51/N7 **Tuzla,** Turk.
45/G4 **Tuzluca,** Turk.
51/E1 **Tuzluca,** Turk.
50/B2 **Tuzlukçu,** Turk.
41/K3 **Tuzly,** Ukr.
18/G3 **T'ver,** Rus.
42/G4 **T'ver,** Rus.
46/D4 **T'ver,** Rus.
42/G4 **T'ver Obl.,** Rus.
42/G4 **Tvertsa** (riv.), Rus.
39/J1 **Tvŭrditsa,** Bul.
41/G4 **Tvŭrditsa,** Bul.
44/C4 **Tvŭrditsa,** Bul.
27/J3 **Twardogóra,** Pol.
71/J5 **Tweed Heads,** Austl.
72/D5 **Tweed Heads,** Austl.
73/E1 **Tweed Heads,** Austl.
28/D4 **Twente** (can.), Neth.
28/D4 **Twente** (reg.), Neth.
95/Q9 **Twenty Mile** (riv.), On,Can
93/G5 **Twin Buttes** (res.), Tx,US
86/E4 **Twin Falls,** Id,US
88/D3 **Twin Falls,** Id,US
90/E5 **Twin Falls,** Id,US
92/D2 **Twin Falls,** Id,US
85/F4 **Twin Hills,** Ak,US
99/P14 **Twin Lakes,** Wi,US
29/G6 **Twiste** (riv.), Ger.
26/E2 **Twistringen,** Ger.
29/F3 **Twistringen,** Ger.
71/R11 **Twizel,** N.Z.
73/D3 **Twofold** (bay), Austl.
91/L4 **Two Harbors,** Mn,US
94/B2 **Two Harbors,** Mn,US
90/F2 **Two Hills,** Ab,Can
91/M4 **Two Rivers,** Wi,US
94/C2 **Two Rivers,** Wi,US
25/E1 **Twycross,** Eng,UK
25/F4 **Twyford,** Eng,UK
24/C1 **Twymyn** (riv.), Wal,UK
22/D2 **Twynholm,** Sc,UK
27/M4 **Tyachev,** Ukr.
41/F1 **Tyachev,** Ukr.
60/B4 **Tyao** (riv.), Burma, India
27/K3 **Tychy,** Pol.
44/A2 **Tychy,** Pol.
25/G1 **Tydd Saint Giles,** Eng,UK
94/E2 **Tyendinaga,** Can
47/N4 **Tygda,** Rus.
23/F4 **Tyldesley,** Eng,UK
89/G5 **Tyler,** Tx,US
93/J4 **Tyler,** Tx,US
96/E3 **Tyler,** Tx,US
47/Q4 **Tymovskoye,** Rus.
55/N1 **Tymovskoye,** Rus.
33/L2 **Týn,** Czh.
91/J5 **Tyndall,** SD,US
93/H2 **Tyndall,** SD,US
23/F2 **Tyne** (riv.), Eng,UK
23/G2 **Tyne & Wear** (co.), Eng,UK
23/G1 **Tynemouth,** Eng,UK
20/D3 **Tynset,** Nor.
85/H3 **Tyonek,** Ak,US
50/C3 **Tyre,** Leb.
52/C2 **Tyre,** Leb.
49/D3 **Tyre** (Şūr), Leb.
55/L2 **Tyrma** (riv.), Rus.
45/G4 **Tyrnyauz,** Rus.
73/B2 **Tyrrell** (cr.), Austl.
73/B2 **Tyrrell** (lake), Austl.
18/E4 **Tyrrhenian** (sea), Eur.
38/B3 **Tyrrhenian** (sea), It.
98/J8 **Tysons Corner,** Va,US
42/D5 **Tytuvénai,** Lith.
45/J3 **Tyub-Karagan** (pt.), Kaz.
45/J3 **Tyulen'i** (isls.), Kaz.
45/H3 **Tyuleniy** (isl.), Rus.
43/Q4 **Tyumen',** Rus.
46/G4 **Tyumen',** Rus.
43/Q4 **Tyumen' Obl.,** Rus.
24/B3 **Tywi** (riv.), Wal,UK
24/B1 **Tywyn,** Wal,UK
82/F5 **Tzaneen,** SAfr.
101/H4 **Tzucacab,** Mex.
102/D1 **Tzucacab,** Mex.

U

69/M5 **Ua Huka** (isl.), FrPol.
69/L5 **Ua Pou** (isl.), FrPol.
106/G4 **Uatumã** (riv.), Braz.
106/E3 **Uaupés** (riv.), Braz.
101/H5 **Uaxactún,** Guat.
102/D2 **Uaxactún** (ruins), Guat.
40/E3 **Ub,** Yugo.
107/K8 **Ubá,** Braz.
108/D2 **Ubá,** Braz.
31/F2 **Übach-Palenberg,** Ger.
43/Q5 **Ubagan** (riv.), Kaz.
74/D4 **Ubangi** (riv.), Afr.
77/J7 **Ubangi** (riv.), Zaire
107/L6 **Ubatã,** Braz.
108/C2 **Ubatuba,** Braz.
33/G4 **Ubaye** (riv.), Fr.
28/C5 **Ubbergen,** Neth.
56/B4 **Ube,** Japan
34/D3 **Úbeda,** Sp.
106/G7 **Uberaba** (lake), Bol.
107/J7 **Uberaba,** Braz.
108/C1 **Uberaba,** Braz.
31/F5 **Überherrn,** Ger.
107/J7 **Uberlândia,** Braz.
108/B1 **Uberlândia,** Braz.
37/F2 **Überlingen,** Ger.
37/F2 **Überlingersee** (lake), Ger.
67/J4 **Ubia** (peak), Indo.
81/F2 **Ubombo,** SAfr.
48/K8 **Ubon Ratchathani,** Thai.
63/H4 **Ubon Ratchathani,** Thai.
65/D3 **Ubon Ratchathani,** Thai.
34/C4 **Ubrique,** Sp.
77/L8 **Ubundu,** Zaire
82/E1 **Ubundu,** Zaire
105/B3 **Ucayali** (riv.), Peru
106/D5 **Ucayali** (riv.), Peru
26/C3 **Uccle,** Belg.
43/X8 **Ucha** (riv.), Rus.
19/J3 **Uchaly,** Rus.
43/N5 **Uchaly,** Rus.
46/F4 **Uchaly,** Rus.
43/X8 **Uchinskoye** (res.), Rus.
55/N3 **Uchiura** (bay), Japan
26/F2 **Uchte** (riv.), Ger.
29/F4 **Uchte,** Ger.
47/P4 **Uchur** (riv.), Rus.
31/F5 **Uckange,** Fr.
27/G2 **Uckermark** (reg.), Ger.
25/G5 **Uckfield,** Eng,UK
90/B3 **Ucluelet,** BC,Can
47/K4 **Uda** (riv.), Rus.
47/M4 **Uda** (riv.), Rus.
47/P4 **Uda** (riv.), Rus.
54/F1 **Uda** (riv.), Rus.
53/K4 **Udaipur,** India
62/B3 **Udaipur,** India
64/F3 **Udamalpet,** India
64/G4 **Udankudi,** India
18/E3 **Uddevalla,** Swe.
20/D4 **Uddevalla,** Swe.
46/B4 **Uddevalla,** Swe.
20/F2 **Uddjaure** (lake), Swe.
42/C2 **Uddjaure** (lake), Swe.
28/C5 **Uden,** Neth.
28/C5 **Udenhout,** Neth.
62/C4 **Udgīr,** India
53/L2 **Udhampur,** India
64/C1 **Udhampur,** India
18/E4 **Udine,** It.
33/K3 **Udine,** It.
40/A2 **Udine,** It.
62/B5 **Udipi,** India
43/L4 **Udmurt Aut. Rep.,** Rus.
60/D5 **Udon Thani,** Thai.
63/H4 **Udon Thani,** Thai.
65/C2 **Udon Thani,** Thai.
27/H2 **Ueckermünde,** Ger.
57/F2 **Ueda,** Japan
74/E4 **Uele** (riv.), Zaire
77/K7 **Uele** (riv.), Zaire
28/D4 **Uelsen,** Ger.
26/F2 **Uelzen,** Ger.
29/H3 **Uelzen,** Ger.
56/E3 **Ueno,** Japan
57/M10 **Ueno,** Japan
57/F3 **Uenohara,** Japan
57/H7 **Uenohara,** Japan
36/D4 **Uetendorf,** Swi.
29/G1 **Uetersen,** Ger.
29/H4 **Uetze,** Ger.
19/J3 **Ufa,** Rus.
43/M5 **Ufa,** Rus.
43/N5 **Ufa** (riv.), Rus.
46/F4 **Ufa,** Rus.
26/F4 **Uffenheim,** Ger.
37/H2 **Uffing,** Ger.
25/E3 **Uffington,** Eng,UK
74/F4 **Uganda**
77/M7 **Uganda**
82/F1 **Uganda**
39/F3 **Ugento,** It.
34/D4 **Ugíjar,** Sp.
33/G4 **Ugine,** Fr.
36/C6 **Ugine,** Fr.
55/N2 **Uglegorsk,** Rus.
42/H4 **Uglich,** Rus.
33/L4 **Ugljan** (isl.), Cro.
40/C2 **Ugod,** Hun.
42/G5 **Ugra** (riv.), Rus.
44/E1 **Ugra** (riv.), Rus.
54/F2 **Ugtaaltsaydam,** Mong.
39/J1 **Ugŭrchin,** Bul.
41/G4 **Ugŭrchin,** Bul.
27/J4 **Uherské Hradiště,** Czh.
27/G4 **Úhlava** (riv.), Czh.
33/K2 **Úhlava** (riv.), Czh.
82/C2 **Uíge,** Ang.
58/E4 **Ŭihŭng,** SKor.
58/D4 **Ŭijŏngbu,** SKor.
58/G6 **Ŭijŏngbu,** SKor.
58/C2 **Ŭiju,** NKor.
59/F2 **Ŭiju,** NKor.
45/K2 **Uil** (riv.), Kaz.
80/L11 **Uilkraal** (riv.), SAfr.
45/G4 **Uilpata, Gora** (peak), Rus.
92/E2 **Uinta** (mts.), Ut,US
56/A3 **Ŭiryŏng,** SKor.
58/E5 **Ŭiryŏng,** SKor.
55/K4 **Ŭisŏng,** SKor.
56/A2 **Ŭisŏng,** SKor.
58/E4 **Ŭisŏng,** SKor.
80/D4 **Uitenhage,** SAfr.
82/E7 **Uitenhage,** SAfr.
28/B3 **Uitgeest,** Neth.
28/B4 **Uithoorn,** Neth.
26/D2 **Uithuizen,** Neth.
28/D2 **Uithuizen,** Neth.
68/F4 **Ujae** (atoll), Mrsh.
68/F4 **Ujelang** (atoll), Mrsh.
27/L5 **Újfehértó,** Hun.
40/E2 **Újfehértó,** Hun.
57/L10 **Uji,** Japan
57/L10 **Uji** (riv.), Japan
57/L10 **Ujitawara,** Japan
53/L4 **Ujjain,** India
62/C3 **Ujjain,** India
67/E5 **Ujung Pandang,** Indo.
68/A5 **Ujung Pandang,** Indo.
63/F3 **Ukhiya,** Bang.
19/J2 **Ukhta,** Rus.
43/M3 **Ukhta,** Rus.
46/F3 **Ukhta,** Rus.
88/D4 **Ukiah,** Ca,US
92/B3 **Ukiah,** Ca,US
42/E5 **Ukmergė,** Lith.
18/F4 **Ukraine**
27/M4 **Ukraine**
41/K2 **Ukraine**
44/D2 **Ukraine**
46/D5 **Ukraine**
49/C2 **U.K. Sovereign Base Area** (poss.), Cyp.
50/B2 **Ula,** Turk.
47/L5 **Ulaanbaatar** (cap.), Mong.
54/F2 **Ulaanbaatar** (cap.), Mong.
46/K5 **Ulaangom,** Mong.
54/C2 **Ulaangom,** Mong.
54/B2 **Ulaanhus,** Mong.
54/F1 **Ulan-Burgasy** (mts.), Rus.
47/N5 **Ulanhot,** China
55/J2 **Ulanhot,** China
59/B2 **Ulansuhai** (salt lake), China
47/L4 **Ulan-Ude,** Rus.
54/F1 **Ulan-Ude,** Rus.
50/D2 **Ulaş,** Turk.
99/L10 **Ulatis** (cr.), Ca,US
82/G2 **Ulaya,** Tanz.
56/A2 **Ulchin,** SKor.
58/E4 **Ulchin,** SKor.
39/F2 **Ulcinj,** Yugo.
40/D5 **Ulcinj,** Yugo.
54/G2 **Uldz** (riv.), Mong.
55/H2 **Ulgain** (riv.), China
53/K5 **Ulhāsnagar,** India
62/B4 **Ulhāsnagar,** India
46/K5 **Uliastay,** Mong.
54/D2 **Uliastay,** Mong.
77/L8 **Ulindi** (riv.), Zaire
68/D3 **Ulithi** (atoll), Micr.
40/E3 **Uljma,** Yugo.
34/A1 **Ulla** (riv.), Sp.
73/D2 **Ulladulla,** Austl.
35/F2 **Ulldecona,** Sp.
20/F1 **Ullsfjorden** (fjord), Nor.
23/F2 **Ullswater** (lake), Eng,UK
55/L4 **Ullŭng** (isl.), SKor.
56/B2 **Ullŭng** (isl.), SKor.
26/E4 **Ulm,** Ger.
33/H2 **Ulm,** Ger.
37/F1 **Ulm,** Ger.
73/E1 **Ulmarra,** Austl.
31/F3 **Ulmen,** Ger.
37/E4 **Ulrichen,** Swi.
26/D2 **Ulrum,** Neth.
28/D2 **Ulrum,** Neth.
55/K4 **Ulsan,** SKor.
56/A3 **Ulsan,** SKor.
58/E5 **Ulsan,** SKor.
22/A3 **Ulster** (reg.), Ire.
22/A2 **Ulster American Folk Park,** NI,UK
102/E3 **Ulua** (riv.), Hon.
50/B2 **Uluborlu,** Turk.
50/B1 **Uludağ** (peak), Turk.
44/D4 **Uludağ, Tepe** (peak), Turk.
51/F2 **Uludoruk** (peak), Turk.
52/D1 **Uludoruk** (peak), Turk.
50/C2 **Ulukışla,** Turk.
102/D2 **Ulumal,** Mex.
54/B2 **Ulungur** (lake), China
54/B2 **Ulungur** (riv.), China
68/C7 **Uluru** (Ayers Rock) (peak), Austl.
70/E5 **Uluru** (Ayers Rock) (peak), Austl.
23/E3 **Ulverston,** Eng,UK
71/H8 **Ulverstone,** Austl.
73/C4 **Ulverstone,** Austl.
42/F4 **Ul'yanovka,** Rus.
43/V7 **Ul'yanovka,** Rus.
41/K1 **Ul'yanovka,** Ukr.
93/G3 **Ulysses,** Ks,US
96/C2 **Ulysses,** Ks,US
33/K4 **Umag,** Cro.
40/A3 **Umag,** Cro.
101/H4 **Umán,** Mex.
44/D2 **Uman',** Ukr.
62/D4 **Umarkot,** India
53/L2 **Umāsi La** (pass), India
33/K5 **Umbertide,** It.
68/D5 **Umboi** (isl.), PNG
37/G4 **Umbrailpass** (pass), Swi.
37/G4 **Umbrail, Piz** (peak), Swi.
33/K5 **Umbria** (reg.), It.
38/C1 **Umbria** (reg.), It.
33/K5 **Umbro-Marchigiano** (range), It.
46/B3 **Ume** (riv.), Swe.
18/F2 **Umeå,** Swe.
20/G3 **Umeå,** Swe.
42/D3 **Umeå,** Swe.
46/C3 **Umeå,** Swe.
18/E2 **Umeälv** (riv.), Swe.
20/F2 **Umeälv** (riv.), Swe.
42/C2 **Umeälv** (riv.), Swe.
81/E3 **Umfolozi** (riv.), SAfr.
81/E3 **Umgeni** (riv.), SAfr.
37/G3 **Umhausen,** Aus.
85/H2 **Umiat,** Ak,US
36/D1 **Umkirch,** Ger.
53/F4 **Umm as Samīm** (salt dep.), Oman
52/B5 **Umm Dhibbān,** Sudan
52/B5 **Umm Durmān** (Omdurman), Sudan
77/M4 **Umm Durmān** (Omdurman), Sudan
49/D3 **Umm el Fahm,** Isr.
49/G6 **Umm el Fahm,** Isr.
50/C3 **Umm el Fahm,** Isr.
37/F1 **Ummendorf,** Ger.
52/C3 **Umm Lajj,** SAr.
77/N2 **Umm Lajj,** SAr.
51/F4 **Umm Qaşr,** Iraq
77/M5 **Umm Ruwābah,** Sudan
47/V4 **Umnak** (isl.), Ak,US
85/E5 **Umnak** (isl.), Ak,US
85/E5 **Umnak** (passg.), Ak,US
90/C5 **Umpqua** (riv.), Or,US
86/D4 **Umpqua** (riv.), Or,US
88/B3 **Umpqua** (riv.), Or,US
92/B2 **Umpqua, North** (riv.), Or,US
92/B2 **Umpqua, South** (riv.), Or,US
58/D4 **Ŭmsŏng,** SKor.
80/E3 **Umtata,** SAfr.
82/E7 **Umtata,** SAfr.
109/F1 **Umuarama,** Braz.
39/K2 **Umurbey,** Turk.
80/E3 **Umzimvubu** (riv.), SAfr.
81/E3 **Umzinto,** SAfr.
40/B3 **Una** (riv.), Bosn.
33/L4 **Una** (riv.), Bosn., Cro.
53/K4 **Una,** India
71/R11 **Una** (peak), N.Z.
107/J7 **Unaí,** Braz.
85/F3 **Unalakleet,** Ak,US
47/V4 **Unalaska** (isl.), Ak,US
85/E5 **Unalaska,** Ak,US
85/E5 **Unalaska** (isl.), Ak,US
77/P2 **'Unayzah,** SAr.
50/D3 **'Unāzah, Jabal** (mtn.), SAr.
52/C2 **'Unāzah, Jabal** (mtn.), SAr.
35/E1 **Uncastillo,** Sp.
92/E3 **Uncompahgre** (plat.), Co,US
96/A2 **Uncompahgre** (plat.), Co,US
73/B2 **Underbool,** Austl.
91/H4 **Underwood,** ND,US
69/Z17 **Undu** (pt.), Fiji
44/E1 **Unecha,** Rus.
85/F4 **Unga** (isl.), Ak,US
82/H1 **Ungama** (bay), Kenya
73/C2 **Ungarie,** Austl.
84/L4 **Ungava** (bay), Can.
87/K3 **Ungava** (bay), Qu,Can
84/K3 **Ungava** (pen.), Can.
87/J2 **Ungava** (pen.), Can
41/H2 **Ungeny,** Mol.
44/C3 **Ungeny,** Mol.
55/L3 **Unggi,** NKor.
107/K4 **União,** Braz.
108/B3 **União da Vitória,** Braz.
107/L5 **União dos Palmares,** Braz.
47/V4 **Unimak** (isl.), Ak,US
85/E4 **Unimak** (isl.), Ak,US
85/E5 **Unimak** (passg.), Ak,US
106/F4 **Unini** (riv.), Braz.
93/K3 **Union,** Mo,US
94/B4 **Union,** Mo,US
97/F2 **Union,** Mo,US
98/F5 **Union,** NJ,US
90/D4 **Union,** Or,US
97/H3 **Union,** SC,US
99/K11 **Union City,** Ca,US
98/F5 **Union City,** NJ,US
94/B4 **Union City,** Tn,US
97/F2 **Union City,** Tn,US
103/F1 **Unión de Reyes,** Cuba
100/D5 **Unión de Tula,** Mex.
99/P14 **Union Grove,** Wi,US
102/C2 **Unión Hidalgo,** Mex.
97/G3 **Union Springs,** Al,US
94/E4 **Uniontown,** Pa,US
95/R8 **Unionville,** On,Can
91/K5 **Unionville,** Mo,US
93/J2 **Unionville,** Mo,US
48/E7 **United Arab Emirates**
51/H5 **United Arab Emirates**
52/F4 **United Arab Emirates**
77/R3 **United Arab Emirates**
18/C3 **United Kingdom**
21/* **United Kingdom**
26/A2 **United Kingdom**
30/A1 **United Kingdom**
46/A4 **United Kingdom**
56/A3 **United Nations Mem. Cem.,** SKor.
58/E5 **United Nations Mem. Cemetery,** SKor.
84/B2 **United States**
84/G5 **United States**
86/E4 **United States**
88/* **United States**
104/A1 **United States**
87/T6 **United States** (range), NW,Can
86/F3 **Unity,** Sk,Can
90/F2 **Unity,** Sk,Can
101/F2 **Universal City,** Tx,US
93/H5 **Universal City,** Tx,US
96/D4 **Universal City,** Tx,US
101/Q10 **University City,** Mex.
100/D1 **Univ. Park,** NM,US
53/K4 **Unjha,** India
62/B3 **Unjha,** India
55/K4 **Unjŏn,** NKor.
31/G2 **Unkel,** Ger.
29/E5 **Unna,** Ger.
62/D2 **Unnāo,** India
58/D3 **Ŭnsan-ŭp,** NKor.
26/F3 **Unstruct** (riv.), Ger.
29/H6 **Unstrut** (riv.), Ger.
37/E3 **Unterägeri,** Swi.
37/F2 **Unterargen** (riv.), Ger.
37/E3 **Unteriberg,** Swi.
36/E3 **Unterkulm,** Swi.
29/H3 **Unterlüss,** Ger.
37/H1 **Unterschleissheim,** Ger.
37/E2 **Untersee** (lake), Ger., Swi.
33/G3 **Unterseen,** Swi.
37/E2 **Untersiggenthal,** Swi.
37/G2 **Unterthingau,** Ger.
37/F4 **Untervaz,** Swi.
36/E4 **Unterwalden** (canton), Swi.
44/F4 **Ünye,** Turk.
50/D1 **Ünye,** Turk.
56/A4 **Unzen-Amakusa Nat'l Park,** Japan
56/B4 **Unzen-dake** (mtn.), Japan
43/K4 **Unzha** (riv.), Rus.
46/E4 **Unzha** (riv.), Rus.
57/E2 **Uozu,** Japan
103/E4 **Upala,** CR
106/F2 **Upata,** Ven.
82/E2 **Upemba** (lake), Zaire
82/E2 **Upemba Nat'l Park,** Zaire
87/L1 **Upernavik,** Grld.
80/C3 **Upington,** SAfr.
82/D6 **Upington,** SAfr.
98/E6 **Upland,** Pa,US
53/K4 **Upleta,** India
62/B3 **Upleta,** India
19/P7 **Upminster,** Eng,UK
88/U10 **Upolu** (pt.), Hi,US
69/H6 **Upolu** (isl.), WSam.
69/S9 **Upolu** (isl.), WSam.
92/C2 **Upper** (lake), Ca,US
89/J2 **Upper** (pen.), Mi,US
97/H1 **Upper Arlington,** Oh,US
90/D3 **Upper Arrow** (lake), BC,Can
27/G4 **Upper Austria** (prov.), Aus.
33/K2 **Upper Austria** (prov.), Aus.
40/A1 **Upper Austria** (prov.), Aus.
98/F6 **Upper Darby,** Pa,US
25/G5 **Upper Dicker,** Eng,UK
79/E4 **Upper East** (reg.), Gha.
37/F5 **Upper Engadine** (val.), Swi.
98/K7 **Upper Falls,** Md,US
71/S11 **Upper Hutt,** N.Z.
93/J2 **Upper Iowa** (riv.), Ia,US
90/C5 **Upper Klamath** (lake), Or,US

186

Upper – Verch

92/B2 Upper Klamath (lake), Or,US
22/B2 Upperlands, NI,UK
94/C2 Upper Peninsula (pen.), Mi,US
91/L5 Upper Peoria (lake), Il,US
91/K3 Upper Red (lake), Mn,US
99/F7 Upper Rouge (riv.), Mi,US
25/E3 Upper Thames (val.), Eng,UK
41/J2 Upper Trajan's Wall (ruins), Mol.
44/D3 Upper Trajan's Wall, Mol.
79/E4 Upper West (reg.), Gha.
25/F1 Uppingham, Eng,UK
18/E3 Uppsala, Swe.
20/F3 Uppsala (co.), Swe.
20/F4 Uppsala, Swe.
42/C3 Uppsala (co.), Swe.
42/C4 Uppsala, Swe.
46/B4 Uppsala, Swe.
85/D3 Upright (cape), Ak,US
72/B2 Upstart (bay), Austl.
72/B2 Upstart (cape), Austl.
91/G4 Upton, Wy,US
93/F1 Upton, Wy,US
24/D2 Upton upon Severn, Eng,UK
51/F4 Ur (ruins), Iraq
52/E2 Ur (ruins), Iraq
103/G4 Urabá (gulf), Col.
59/B2 Urad Qianqi, China
57/H7 Uraga (chan.), Japan
19/K2 Ural (mts.), Eur., Asia
45/J3 Ural (riv.), Kaz.
46/F5 Ural (riv.), Rus.,Kaz.
48/E5 Ural (riv.), Kaz., Rus.
43/N5 Ural (riv.), Rus.
45/K2 Ural (riv.), Rus.
46/F3 Ural (mts.), Rus.
48/F4 Ural (mts.), Rus.
73/D1 Uralla, Austl.
45/J2 Ural'sk, Kaz.
46/F4 Ural'sk, Kaz.
45/J2 Ural'sk Obl., Kaz.
73/C2 Urana, Austl.
86/F3 Uranium City, Sk,Can
106/F3 Uraricoera (riv.), Braz.
55/M4 Urawa, Japan
57/F3 Urawa, Japan
57/H7 Urawa, Japan
46/G3 Uray, Rus.
57/H7 Urayasu, Japan
94/B3 Urbana, Il,US
97/F1 Urbana, Il,US
98/J7 Urbana, Md,US
94/D3 Urbana, Oh,US
97/H1 Urbana, Oh,US
103/G1 Urbano Noris, Cuba
72/D5 Urbenville, Austl.
106/D6 Urcos, Peru
34/D3 Urda, Sp.
37/E3 Urdorf, Swi.
23/G3 Ure (riv.), Eng,UK
50/E1 Ureki, Geo.
100/C2 Ures, Mex.
92/E5 Ures, Mex
57/M10 Ureshino, Japan
50/D2 Urfa, Turk.
50/D2 Urfa (prov.), Turk.
52/C1 Urfa, Turk.
29/G6 Urft (riv.), Ger.
31/F3 Urft (riv.), Ger.
46/G5 Urgench, Uzb.
20/H1 Urho Kekkosen Nat'l Park, Fin.
42/E1 Urho Kekkosen Nat'l Park, Fin.
37/E4 Uri (canton), Swi.
103/H4 Uribia, Col.
106/F2 Urimáan, Ven.
36/C1 Uriménil, Fr.
100/D3 Urique (riv.), Mex.
37/E4 Uri-Rotstock (peak), Swi.
28/C3 Urk, Neth.
44/C5 Urla, Turk.
50/A2 Urla, Turk.
41/H3 Urlaţi, Rom.
64/C2 Urmar, India
55/L2 Urmi (riv.), Rus.
51/F2 Urmia (lake), Iran
52/D1 Urmia (lake), Iran
31/G3 Urmitz, Ger.
23/F5 Urmston, Eng,UK
37/F3 Urnäsch, Swi.
37/E4 Urnersee (lake), Swi.
39/G1 Uroševac, Yugo.
40/E4 Uroševac, Yugo.
22/E1 Urr Water (riv.), Sc,UK
101/N7 Ursulo Galván, Mex.
100/C3 Uruáchic, Mex.
107/J6 Uruaçu, Braz.
100/E5 Uruapan, Mex.
106/D6 Urubamba, Peru
106/D6 Urubamba (riv.), Peru
106/G4 Urubu (riv.), Braz.
107/J5 Uruçui (mts.), Braz.
107/J7 Urucuia (riv.), Braz.
109/E2 Uruguaiana, Braz.
105/D6 Uruguay
109/E3 Uruguay
108/A3 Uruguay (riv.), Braz.
105/D5 Uruguay (riv.), SAm.
109/E2 Uruguay (riv.), SAm.
104/D5 Urumaco, Ven.
46/J5 Ürümqi, China
54/B3 Ürümqi, China
73/E1 Urunga, Austl.
47/R5 Urup (isl.), Rus.
48/Q5 Urup (isl.), Rus.
40/B5 Ururi, It.
108/B4 Urussanga, Braz.
55/H1 Uryumkan (riv.), Rus.
45/G2 Uryupinsk, Rus.
41/H3 Urziceni, Rom.
44/C3 Urziceni, Rom.
19/R9 Us, Fr.
54/C1 Us (riv.), Rus.
56/B4 Usa, Japan
19/J2 Usa (riv.), Rus.
43/N2 Usa (riv.), Rus.
46/F3 Usa (riv.), Rus.
44/D5 Uşak, Turk.
50/B2 Uşak, Turk.
50/B2 Uşak (prov.), Turk.
82/C5 Usakos, Namb.
109/E7 Usborne (peak), Falk.
31/E4 Useldange, Lux.
52/C4 'Usfān, SAr.
20/J5 Ushachi, Bela.
56/B4 Ushibuka, Japan
57/J7 Ushiku, Japan
46/H5 Ushtobe, Kaz.
109/C7 Ushuaia, Arg.
62/C6 Usilampatti, India
64/F4 Usilampatti, India
19/H3 Usinsk, Rus.
46/E4 Usinsk, Rus.
24/D3 Usk, Wal,UK
24/D3 Usk (riv.), Wal,UK
41/J5 Üsküdar, Turk.
51/N6 Üsküdar, Turk.
29/G5 Uslar, Ger.
27/G4 Úslava (riv.), Czh.
44/F1 Usman', Rus.
98/K8 U.S. Naval Academy, Md,US
47/L4 Usol'ye-Sibirskoye, Rus.
54/E1 Usol'ye-Sibirskoye, Rus.
67/F1 Uson, Phil.
88/W13 U.S.S. Arizona Mem., Hi,US
32/E4 Ussel, Fr.
32/F3 Usses (riv.), Fr.
36/C5 Usses (riv.), Fr.
47/P5 Ussuri (riv.), Rus., China
55/L2 Ussuri (Wusuli) (riv.), China, Rus.
47/P5 Ussuriysk, Rus.
55/L3 Ussuriysk, Rus.
37/E3 Uster, Swi.
38/C3 Ustica, It.
38/C3 Ustica (isl.), It.
47/L4 Ust'-Ilimsk, Rus.
27/H3 Ústí nad Labem, Czh.
33/L1 Ústí nad Labem, Czh.
27/J1 Ustka, Pol.
47/S4 Ust'-Kamchatsk, Rus.
46/J5 Ust'-Kamenogorsk, Kaz.
47/L4 Ust'-Kut, Rus.
47/L4 Ust'-Ordynskiy, Rus.
54/E1 Ust'-Ordynskiy, Rus.
27/M4 Ustrzyki Dolne, Pol.
44/B2 Ustrzyki Dolne, Pol.
43/K3 Ust'ya (riv.), Rus.
48/E5 Ustyurt (plat.), Kaz.
45/K4 Ustyurt (plat.), Kaz., Uzb.
46/F5 Ustyurt (plat.), Kaz.,Uzb.
56/B4 Usuki, Japan
102/D3 Usulután, ESal.
102/C2 Usumacinta (riv.), Guat., Mex.
90/E5 Utah (state), US
86/E4 Utah (state), US
88/D4 Utah (state), US
92/E3 Utah (state), US
92/D2 Utah (lake), Ut,US
57/L10 Utano, Japan
20/H5 Utena, Lith.
42/E5 Utena, Lith.
63/H4 Uthai Thani, Thai.
65/C3 Uthai Thani, Thai.
99/F6 Utica, Mi,US
87/J4 Utica, NY,US
89/L3 Utica, NY,US
94/F3 Utica, NY,US
34/E3 Utiel, Sp.
91/K2 Utik (lake), Mb,Can
90/E2 Utikuma (lake), Ab,Can
102/E2 Utila (isl.), Hon.
68/G3 Utirik (atoll), Mrsh.
68/G5 Utiroa, Kiri.
62/D2 Utraula, India
18/D3 Utrecht, Neth.
26/C2 Utrecht, Neth.
28/C4 Utrecht, Neth.
28/C4 Utrecht (prov.), Neth.
34/C4 Utrera, Sp.
47/P6 Utsunomiya, Japan
55/M4 Utsunomiya, Japan
57/F2 Utsunomiya, Japan
64/F4 Uttamapālaiyam, India
60/D5 Uttaradit, Thai.
63/H4 Uttaradit, Thai.
65/C2 Uttaradit, Thai.
62/C2 Uttar Pradesh (state), India
64/D2 Uttar Pradesh (state), India
37/F1 Uttenweiler, Ger.
23/G6 Uttoxeter, Eng,UK
104/E3 Utuado, PR
68/F6 Utupua (isl.), Sol.
69/K6 Uturoa, FrPol.
36/D3 Utzenstorf, Swi.
54/G2 Uulbayan, Mong.
54/E1 Üür (riv.), Mong.
54/C1 Üüreg (lake), Mong.
54/C1 Uus (lake), Mong.
20/H3 Uusimaa (prov.), Fin.
42/E3 Uusimaa (prov.), Fin.
90/E3 Uva (riv.), Col.
101/F2 Uvalde, Tx,US
88/G6 Uvalde, Tx,US
93/H5 Uvalde, Tx,US
96/D4 Uvalde, Tx,US
46/E4 Uvals, Northern (upland), Rus.
45/G2 Uvarovo, Rus.
103/F4 Uvita (pt.), CR
55/L5 Uwajima, Japan
56/C4 Uwajima, Japan
77/L6 Uwayl, Sudan
67/K5 Uwimmerah (riv.), Indo.
19/M7 Uxbridge, Eng,UK
54/F4 Uxin Qi, China
59/B3 Uxin Qi, China
101/H4 Uxmal (ruins), Mex.
102/D1 Uxmal (ruins), Mex.
43/P5 Uy (riv.), Kaz., Rus.
54/E2 Uyanga, Mong.
54/C2 Üyench, Mong.
76/G6 Uyo, Nga.
60/B3 Uyu (riv.), Burma
106/E8 Uyuni, Bol.
49/F8 'Uza, Isr.
45/L4 Uzbekistan
46/G5 Uzbekistan
48/E5 Uzbekistan
32/D4 Uzerche, Fr.
32/F4 Uzès, Fr.
18/F4 Uzhgorod, Ukr.
27/M4 Uzhgorod, Ukr.
40/F1 Uzhgorod, Ukr.
44/B2 Uzhgorod, Ukr.
46/C5 Uzhgorod, Ukr.
27/M4 Uzhok (pass), Ukr.
44/F1 Uzlovaya, Rus.
37/E3 Uznach, Swi.
44/F5 Üzümlü, Turk.
50/D2 Üzümlü, Turk.
39/K2 Uzunköprü, Turk.
41/H5 Uzunköprü, Turk.
44/C4 Uzunköprü, Turk.
50/A1 Uzunköprü, Turk.
37/F3 Uzwil, Swi.

V

74/E7 Vaal (riv.), SAfr.
80/C3 Vaal (riv.), SAfr.
80/P13 Vaal (riv.), SAfr.
82/D6 Vaal (riv.), SAfr.
20/H2 Vaala, Fin.
80/E2 Vaaldam (res.), SAfr.
80/P13 Vaaldam (res.), SAfr.
31/F2 Vaals, Neth.
31/E2 Vaalsberg (hill), Neth.
32/F1 Vaalsberg (hill), Neth.
18/F2 Vaasa, Fin.
20/G3 Vaasa (prov.), Fin.
42/D3 Vaasa (prov.), Fin.
46/C3 Vaasa, Fin.
20/G3 Vaasa (Vasa), Fin.
42/D3 Vaasa (Vasa), Fin.
28/C4 Vaassen, Neth.
27/K5 Vác, Hun.
40/D2 Vác, Hun.
99/K10 Vaca (mt.), Ca,US
99/K10 Vaca (mts.), Ca,US
108/B4 Vacaria, Braz.
109/F2 Vacaria, Braz.
92/B3 Vacaville, Ca,US
99/L10 Vacaville, Ca,US
103/H2 Vache (isl.), Haiti
51/F1 Vachi, Rus.
87/J2 Vachon (riv.), Qu,Can
33/J5 Vada, It.
37/F4 Vadret, Piz (peak), Swi.
18/F1 Vadsø, Nor.
20/J1 Vadsø, Nor.
42/F1 Vadsø, Nor.
46/C2 Vadsø, Nor.
33/H3 Vaduz (cap.), Lcht.
37/F3 Vaduz (cap.), Lcht.
42/J3 Vaga (riv.), Rus.
33/L4 Vaganski vrh (peak), Cro.
40/B3 Vaganski vrh (peak), Cro.
43/R4 Vagay (riv.), Rus.
20/E4 Vaggeryd, Swe.
36/C1 Vagney, Fr.
34/A2 Vagos, Port.
27/J4 Váh (riv.), Slvk.
69/M6 Vahitahi (isl.), FrPol.
53/K5 Vaijāpur, India
64/F4 Vaikam, India
88/E4 Vail, Co,US
93/F3 Vail, Co,US
30/C5 Vailly-sur-Aisnes, Fr.
36/B1 Vair (riv.), Fr.
19/T10 Vaires-sur-Marne, Fr.
68/G5 Vaitupu (atoll), Tuv.
36/C2 Vaivre-et-Montoille, Fr.
44/F4 Vakfıkebir, Turk.
46/J3 Vakh (riv.), Rus.
53/K1 Vākhān (mts.), Afg.
53/J1 Vakhsh (riv.), Trkm.
40/D2 Vál, Hun.
36/D5 Valais (canton), Swi.
28/C5 Valburg, Neth.
109/C5 Valcheta, Arg.
36/C3 Valdahon, Fr.
42/G4 Valdai (hills), Rus.
31/F6 Val-de-Bide, Fr.
34/C3 Valdecañas (res.), Sp.
19/T10 Val-de-Marne (dept.), Fr.
30/B6 Val-de-Marne (dept.), Fr.
20/F4 Valdemarsvik, Swe.
42/C4 Valdemarsvik, Swe.
35/M8 Valdemorillo, Sp.
34/D3 Valdepeñas, Sp.
34/C2 Valderaduey (riv.), Sp.
34/C1 Valderas, Sp.
35/F2 Valderrobres, Sp.
105/C7 Valdés (pen.), Arg.
109/D5 Valdés (pen.), Arg.
34/C3 Valdeverdeja, Sp.
85/J3 Valdez, Ak,US
86/B2 Valdez, Ak,US
109/B4 Valdivia, Chile
36/C2 Valdoie, Fr.
19/S9 Val-d'Oise (dept.), Fr.
30/A5 Val-d'Oise (dept.), Fr.
87/J4 Val d'Or, Qu,Can
89/L2 Val d'Or, Qu,Can
94/E1 Val d'Or, Qu,Can
89/K5 Valdosta, Ga,US
97/H4 Valdosta, Ga,US
34/A1 Valdoviño, Sp.
51/E1 Vale, Geo.
90/D5 Vale, Or,US
92/C2 Vale, Or,US
27/M5 Valea lui Mihai, Rom.
86/E3 Valemount, BC,Can
90/D2 Valemount, BC,Can
107/L6 Valença, Braz.
108/D2 Valença, Braz.
109/H1 Valença, Braz.
34/A1 Valença, Port.
18/D4 Valence, Fr.
32/D4 Valence, Fr.
32/F4 Valence, Fr.
32/D5 Valence-sur-Baïse, Fr.
35/F1 Valence-sur-Baïse, Fr.
21/G8 Valencia (isl.), Ire.
18/C5 Valencia, Sp.
35/E3 Valencia, Sp.
35/E3 Valencia (aut. comm.), Sp.
35/F3 Valencia (gulf), Sp.
104/E5 Valencia, Ven.
106/E1 Valencia, Ven.
34/B3 Valencia de Alcántara, Sp.
34/C1 Valencia de Don Juan, Sp.
26/B3 Valenciennes, Fr.
30/C3 Valenciennes, Fr.
32/E1 Valenciennes, Fr.
37/F4 Valendas, Swi.
41/H3 Vălenii de Munte, Rom.
36/C3 Valentigney, Fr.
88/F3 Valentine, Ne,US
91/H5 Valentine, Ne,US
93/G2 Valentine, Ne,US
93/F5 Valentine, Tx,US
96/B4 Valentine, Tx,US
19/T10 Valenton, Fr.
33/H4 Valenza, It.
106/D2 Valera, Ven.
36/D1 Valff, Fr.
20/H4 Valga, Est.
42/E4 Valga, Est.
98/G4 Valhalla, NY,US
32/D5 Valier (mtn.), Fr.
35/F1 Valier (mtn.), Fr.
38/A2 Valinco (gulf), Fr.
40/D3 Valjevo, Yugo.
20/H4 Valka, Lat.
31/E2 Valkenburg, Neth.
28/C6 Valkenswaard, Neth.
27/N1 Valkininkai, Lith.
101/H4 Valladolid, Mex.
102/D1 Valladolid, Mex.
18/C4 Valladolid, Sp.
34/C2 Valladolid, Sp.
35/E3 Vall de Uxó, Sp.
99/L11 Valle (arroyo), Ca,US
35/N9 Vallecas (nbrhd.), Sp.
33/G5 Vallecrosia, It.
33/G4 Valle d'Aosta (reg.), It.
36/D6 Valle d'Aosta (reg.), It.
100/D3 Valle de Allende, Mex.
101/E5 Valle de Bravo, Mex.
100/A1 Valle de Guadalupe, Mex.
106/E2 Valle de la Pascua, Ven.
35/M8 Valle de los Caídos, Sp.
101/E4 Valle de Santiago, Mex.
100/D3 Valle de Zaragoza, Mex.
96/B5 Valle de Zaragoza, Mex
103/H4 Valledupar, Col.
106/D1 Valledupar, Col.
106/F7 Vallegrande, Bol.
35/X16 Vallehermoso, Canl.
101/F3 Valle Hermoso, Mex.
28/C4 Valleikanaal (can.), Neth.
92/B3 Vallejo, Ca,US
99/K10 Vallejo, Ca,US
109/B2 Vallenar, Chile
31/G3 Vallendar, Ger.
31/E5 Valleroy, Fr.
92/C5 Valle San Telmo, Mex
18/E5 Valletta (cap.), Malta
38/D5 Valletta (cap.), Malta
76/H1 Valletta (cap.), Malta
89/G2 Valley City, ND,US
91/J4 Valley City, ND,US
98/G4 Valley Cottage, NY,US
94/D2 Valley East, On,Can
95/M7 Valleyfield, Qu,Can
98/E5 Valley Forge Nat'l Hist. Park, Pa,US
101/F2 Valley Spring, Tx,US
98/G5 Valley Stream, NY,US
104/F3 Valley, The, Angu.
86/E3 Valleyview, Ab,Can
90/D2 Valleyview, Ab,Can
36/B4 Vallière (riv.), Fr.
38/D2 Vallo della Lucania, It.
40/B5 Vallo della Lucania, It.
36/C4 Vallorbe, Swi.
35/F2 Valls, Sp.
37/G3 Valluga (peak), Aus.
90/G3 Val Marie, Sk,Can
35/M8 Valmayor (res.), Sp.
29/F6 Valme (riv.), Ger.
20/H4 Valmiera, Lat.
42/E4 Valmiera, Lat.
19/S9 Valmondois, Fr.
32/C2 Valognes, Fr.
39/F2 Valona (bay), Alb.
40/D5 Valona (bay), Alb.
34/B2 Valpaços, Port.
62/C5 Vālpārai, India
64/F3 Vālpārai, India
109/B3 Valparaíso, Chile
100/E4 Valparaíso, Mex.
97/G4 Valparaiso, Fl,US
94/C3 Valparaiso, In,US
36/D6 Valpelline (riv.), It.
40/D3 Valpovo, Cro.
32/F4 Valréas, Fr.
67/F5 Vals (cape), Indo.
80/D2 Vals (riv.), SAfr.
53/K4 Valsād, India
62/B3 Valsād, India
101/L8 Valsaquillo (res.), Mex.
80/B4 Valsbaai (bay), SAfr.
80/L11 Valsbaai (bay), SAfr.
82/C7 Valsbaai (bay), SAfr.
36/B5 Valserine (riv.), Fr.
37/F4 Valserrhein (riv.), Swi.
32/F4 Vals-les-Bains, Fr.
37/F4 Vals Platz, Swi.
37/G4 Valsura (riv.), It.
37/F5 Valtellina (val.), It.
33/M2 Valtice, Czh.
44/F2 Valuyki, Rus.
35/X17 Valverde, Canl.
34/B4 Valverde del Camino, Sp.
20/G3 Vammala, Fin.
39/J5 Vámos, Gre.
27/K5 Vámosmikola, Hun.
40/E2 Vámospércs, Hun.
46/E6 Van, Turk.
46/E6 Van (lake), Turk.
51/E2 Van, Turk.
51/E2 Van (lake), Turk.
51/E2 Van (prov.), Turk.
69/L7 Vanavaro (isl.), FrPol.
93/J4 Van Buren, Ar,US
96/E3 Van Buren, Ar,US
95/H2 Van Buren, Me,US
93/K3 Van Buren, Mo,US
97/F2 Van Buren, Mo,US
93/H3 Vance (A.F.B.), Ok,US
96/D2 Vance (A.F.B.), Ok,US
101/E2 Vancourt, Tx,US
84/E5 Vancouver, BC,Can.
86/D4 Vancouver, BC,Can
88/B2 Vancouver, BC,Can
90/C3 Vancouver, BC,Can
84/D4 Vancouver (isl.), BC,Can
86/D4 Vancouver (isl.), BC,Can
88/A2 Vancouver (isl.), BC,Can
90/B3 Vancouver (isl.), BC,Can
86/D4 Vancouver, Wa,US
88/B2 Vancouver, Wa,US
90/C4 Vancouver, Wa,US
85/L3 Vancouver (mtn.), Yk,Can, Ak,US
83/L Vanda, Ant.
89/J4 Vandalia, Il,US
93/K3 Vandalia, Il,US
94/B4 Vandalia, Il,US
97/F2 Vandalia, Il,US
93/K3 Vandalia, Mo,US
97/F2 Vandalia, Mo,US
37/F3 Vandans, Aus.
92/B4 Vandenberg A.F.B., Ca,US
80/D2 Vanderbijl Park, SAfr.
80/P13 Vanderbijl Park, SAfr.
82/E6 Vanderbijl Park, SAfr.
86/D3 Vanderhoof, BC,Can
90/B2 Vanderhoof, BC,Can
70/F3 Vanderlin (isl.), Austl.
70/E2 Van Diemen (cape), Austl.
70/E2 Van Diemen (gulf), Austl.
26/D4 Vandoeuvre-lès-Nancy, Fr.
31/F6 Vandoeuvre-lès-Nancy, Fr.
27/M1 Vandžiogala, Lith.
101/E4 Vanegas, Mex.
18/E3 Vänern (lake), Swe.
20/E4 Vänern (lake), Swe.
46/B4 Vänern (lake), Swe.
20/E4 Vänersborg, Swe.
81/H8 Vangaindrano, Madg.
28/C2 Van Harinxmakanaal (can.), Neth.
65/D1 Van Hoa, Viet.
100/D2 Van Horn, Tx,US
88/F5 Van Horn, Tx,US
93/F5 Van Horn, Tx,US
96/B4 Van Horn, Tx,US
87/R7 Vanier (isl.), NW,Can
68/F6 Vanikoro (isl.), Sol.
36/D4 Vanil Noir (peak), Swi.
67/K4 Vanimo, PNG
68/D5 Vanimo, PNG
47/Q5 Vanino, Rus.
55/N2 Vanino, Rus.
20/F3 Vännäs, Swe.
42/C3 Vännäs, Swe.
32/E1 Vanne (riv.), Fr.
32/B3 Vannes, Fr.
63/J5 Van Ninh, Viet.
65/E3 Van Ninh, Viet.
66/C1 Van Ninh, Viet.
33/G4 Vanoise Nat'l Park, Fr.
80/E3 Vanreenenpas (pass), SAfr.
67/J4 Van Rees (mts.), Indo.
80/B3 Vanrhynsdorp, SAfr.
72/A2 Vanrook, Austl.
87/H2 Vansittart (isl.), NW,Can
20/H3 Vantaa, Fin.
42/E3 Vantaa, Fin.
68/G6 Vanua Levu (isl.), Fiji
69/Y17 Vanua Levu (isl.), Fiji
68/F6 Vanuatu
19/S10 Vanves, Fr.
94/C3 Van Wert, Oh,US
65/D1 Van Yen, Viet.
33/G5 Var (riv.), Fr.
103/F1 Varadero, Cuba
51/G3 Varāmīn, Iran
52/F1 Varāmīn, Iran
62/D2 Vārānasi, India
20/J1 Varangerfjorden (fjord), Nor.
20/J1 Varangerhalvøya (pen.), Nor.
31/F6 Varangéville, Fr.
38/D2 Varano (lake), It.
40/B5 Varano (lake), It.
33/M3 Varaždin, Cro.
40/C2 Varaždin, Cro.
33/H4 Varazze, It.
20/E4 Varberg, Swe.
39/G2 Vardar (riv.), Macd.
40/E5 Vardar (riv.), Macd.
26/E1 Varde, Den.
51/F1 Vardenis, Arm.
39/G3 Várdha, Gre.
20/J1 Vardø, Nor.
26/E2 Varel, Ger.
29/F2 Varel, Ger.
27/N1 Varėna, Lith.
42/E5 Varėna, Lith.
95/P6 Varennes, Qu,Can
30/A4 Varennes (riv.), Fr.
19/T10 Varennes-Jarcy, Fr.
32/E3 Varennes-Vauzelles, Fr.
40/D3 Vareš, Bosn.
33/H4 Varese, It.
37/E6 Varese (prov.), It.
107/J8 Varginha, Braz.
108/C2 Varginha, Braz.
20/C4 Varhaug, Nor.
39/H4 Vári, Gre.
39/L7 Vári, Gre.
32/D5 Varilhes, Fr.
20/H3 Varkaus, Fin.
42/E3 Varkaus, Fin.
64/F4 Varkkallai, India
20/E3 Värmland (co.), Swe.
18/F4 Varna, Bul.
39/K1 Varna (prov.), Bul.
41/H4 Varna, Bul.
41/H4 Varna (reg.), Bul.
44/C4 Varna, Bul.
45/M1 Varna, Rus.
20/E4 Värnamo, Swe.
36/B3 Varois-et-Chaignot, Fr.
40/C3 Varoška Rijeka, Bosn.
40/D2 Várpalota, Hun.
51/F1 Vartashen, Azer.
39/G4 Vartholomión, Gre.
50/E2 Varto, Turk.
22/B5 Vartry (res.), Ire.
22/B5 Vartry (riv.), Ire.
52/F2 Varzaneh, Iran
107/L5 Várzea Alegre, Braz.
108/C1 Várzea da Palma, Braz.
107/G7 Várzea Grande, Braz.
37/E5 Varzo, It.
42/H2 Varzuga (riv.), Rus.
40/C2 Vas (co.), Hun.
107/L5 Vasa Barris (riv.), Braz.
27/M4 Vásárosnamény, Hun.
42/D3 Vasa (Vaasa), Fin.
40/F2 Vaşcău, Rom.
43/K2 Vashka (riv.), Rus.
99/C3 Vashon, Wa,US
99/C3 Vashon (isl.), Wa,US
39/H2 Vasiliká, Gre.
44/D2 Vasil'kov, Ukr.
43/V7 Vasil'yevskiy (isl.), Rus.
41/H2 Vaslui, Rom.
41/H2 Vaslui (co.), Rom.
44/C3 Vaslui, Rom.
94/D3 Vassar, Mi,US
18/E3 Västerås, Swe.
20/F4 Västerås, Swe.
42/C4 Västerås, Swe.
46/B4 Västerås, Swe.
20/F2 Västerbotten (co.), Swe.
42/B2 Västerbotten (co.), Swe.
20/F4 Västerhaninge, Swe.
42/C4 Västerhaninge, Swe.
20/F3 Västernorrland (co.), Swe.
42/C3 Västernorrland (co.), Swe.
20/F4 Västervik, Swe.
42/C4 Västervik, Swe.
20/E3 Västmanland (co.), Swe.
42/C3 Västmanland (co.), Swe.
38/D1 Vasto, It.
40/B4 Vasto, It.
40/C2 Vasvár, Hun.
26/F4 Vaterstetten, Ger.
33/J2 Vaterstetten, Ger.
18/E4 Vatican City
38/C2 Vatican City
38/C2 Vatican City (cap.), VatC.
20/P7 Vatnajökull (glac.), Ice.
81/J7 Vatomandry, Madg.
41/G2 Vatra Dornei, Rom.
18/E3 Vättern (lake), Swe.
20/E4 Vättern (lake), Swe.
69/Y18 Vatukoula, Fiji
36/C4 Vaud (canton), Swi.
95/M7 Vaudreuil, Qu,Can
95/M7 Vaudreuil-sur-le-Lac, Qu,Can
95/Q8 Vaughan, On,Can
93/F4 Vaughn, NM,US
96/B3 Vaughn, NM,US
99/B3 Vaughn, Wa,US
36/C4 Vaulruz, Swi.
32/F4 Vaulx-en-Velin, Fr.
36/A6 Vaulx-en-Velin, Fr.
95/M7 Vaundreuil (co.), Qu,Can
105/B2 Vaupés (riv.), Col.
32/F5 Vauvert, Fr.
36/C2 Vauvillers, Fr.
26/C4 Vaux (riv.), Fr.
30/D4 Vaux (riv.), Fr.
32/F2 Vaux (riv.), Fr.
90/E3 Vauxhall, Ab,Can
19/R9 Vaux-sur-Seine, Fr.
31/E4 Vaux-sur-Sûre, Belg.
30/B3 Vaux-Vraucourt, Fr.
81/J7 Vavatenina, Madg.
69/H6 Vava'u Group (isls.), Tonga
64/H4 Vavuniya (dist.), SrL.
62/D6 Vavuniya, SrL.
64/H4 Vavuniya, SrL.
18/E3 Växjö, Swe.
20/E4 Växjö, Swe.
46/B4 Växjö, Swe.
19/J2 Vaygach (isl.), Rus.
46/F3 Vaygach (isl.), Rus.
108/C1 Vazante, Braz.
42/G5 Vazuza (res.), Rus.
36/D4 Vechigen, Swi.
28/B4 Vecht (riv.), Neth.
26/E2 Vechta, Ger.
29/F3 Vechta, Ger.
26/D2 Vechte (riv.), Ger.
29/E4 Vechte (riv.), Ger.
27/K5 Vecsés, Hun.
40/D2 Vecsés, Hun.
64/G3 Vedāranniyam, India
41/G3 Vedea (riv.), Rom.
34/A1 Vedra, Sp.
28/D2 Veendam, Neth.
26/C2 Veenendaal, Neth.
28/C4 Veenendaal, Neth.
28/A5 Veere, Neth.
28/A5 Veersedam (dam), Neth.
28/A5 Veerse Meer (res.), Neth.
20/D2 Vega (isl.), Nor.
85/B6 Vega (pt.), Ak,US
93/G4 Vega, Tx,US
96/C3 Vega, Tx,US
20/D2 Vegafjorden (fjord), Nor.
28/C5 Veghel, Neth.
39/G2 Vegorítis (lake), Gre.
40/E5 Vegorítis (lake), Gre.
90/E2 Vegreville, Ab,Can
20/H3 Vehkalahti, Fin.
42/E3 Vehkalahti, Fin.
32/D3 Veigné, Fr.
27/M1 Veisiejai, Lith.
27/H5 Veitsch, Aus.
40/B2 Veitsch, Aus.
34/C4 Vejer de la Frontera, Sp.
18/D3 Vejle, Den.
20/D5 Vejle, Den.
26/E1 Vejle, Den.
26/E1 Vejle (co.), Den.
31/E6 Velaines, Fr.
38/E1 Vela Luka, Cro.
40/C4 Vela Luka, Cro.
36/D6 Vélan, Monte (peak), It., Swi.
35/S12 Velas, Azor.
28/E6 Velbert, Ger.
80/B4 Velddrif, SAfr.
80/L10 Velddrif, SAfr.
82/C7 Velddrif, SAfr.
33/L3 Velden am Wörthersee, Aus.
26/C3 Veldhoven, Neth.
28/C6 Veldhoven, Neth.
28/D5 Velen, Ger.
33/L3 Velenje, Slov.
40/B2 Velenje, Slov.
39/G2 Velešta, Macd.
40/E5 Velešta, Macd.
39/H3 Velestínon, Gre.
34/D4 Vélez-Blanco, Sp.
75/M13 Vélez de la Gomera (isl.), Sp.
34/C4 Vélez-Málaga, Sp.
34/D4 Vélez-Rubio, Sp.
107/K7 Velhas (riv.), Braz.
108/C1 Velhas (riv.), Braz.
108/C1 Velhas (Araguari) (riv.), Braz.
33/M4 Velika Gorica, Cro.
40/C3 Velika Gorica, Cro.
33/L4 Velika Kladuša, Bosn.
40/B3 Velika Kladuša, Bosn.
40/E3 Velika Plana, Yugo.
20/J4 Velikaya (riv.), Rus.
42/F4 Velikaya (riv.), Rus.
47/T3 Velikaya (riv.), Rus.
27/M4 Velikiy Berëznyy, Ukr.
18/G3 Velikiye Luki, Rus.
42/F4 Velikiye Luki, Rus.
46/D4 Velikiye Luki, Rus.
19/H2 Velikiy Ustyug, Rus.
43/K3 Velikiy Ustyug, Rus.
46/E3 Velikiy Ustyug, Rus.
41/K2 Velikodolinskoye, Ukr.
45/G1 Velikodvorskiy, Rus
39/J1 Veliko Tŭrnovo, Bul.
41/G4 Veliko Tŭrnovo, Bul.
44/C4 Veliko Tŭrnovo, Bul.
39/J1 Velingrad, Bul.
41/G4 Velingrad, Bul.
44/C4 Velingrad, Bul.
42/F5 Velizh, Rus.
19/S10 Vélizy-Villacoublay, Fr.
33/M2 Vel'ke Leváre, Slvk.
27/J4 Velké Meziříčí, Czh.
33/M2 Velké Meziříčí, Czh.
27/K4 Vel'ký Krtíš, Slvk.
40/D1 Vel'ký Krtíš, Slvk.
64/G3 Vellār (riv.), India
38/C2 Velletri, It.
26/G1 Vellinge, Swe.
29/G6 Vellmar, Ger.
35/N8 Vellón (res.), Sp.
62/C5 Vellore, India
39/H4 Vélon, Gre.
42/J3 Vel'sk, Rus.
28/C4 Veluwe (reg.), Neth.
28/C4 Veluwemeer (lake), Neth.
28/C4 Veluwezoom Nat'l Park, Neth.
91/H3 Velva, ND,US
39/H2 Velvendós, Gre.
64/F3 Vembādi Shola (peak), India
64/F4 Vembanād (lake), India
40/D2 Vémend, Hun.
101/E4 Venado, Mex.
101/L6 Venados, Mex.
109/D3 Venado Tuerto, Arg.
38/D2 Venafro, It.
40/B5 Venafro, It.
108/A4 Venâncio Aires, Bra
33/G4 Venaria, It.
33/G5 Vence, Fr.
35/J1 Vence, Fr.
108/B2 Venceslau Brás, Braz.
34/A3 Vendas Novas, Port.
32/D3 Vendôme, Fr.
35/F2 Vendrell, Sp.
85/J2 Venetie, Ak,US
33/J4 Veneto (reg.), It.
37/H6 Veneto (reg.), It.
33/K4 Venezia (gulf), It.
33/K4 Venezia (Venice), It.
103/H4 Venezuela
104/E5 Venezuela
105/C2 Venezuela
106/E2 Venezuela
104/D5 Venezuela (gulf), Ver
105/B7 Venezuela (gulf), Ver
106/D1 Venezuela (gulf), Ver
53/K5 Vengurla, India
62/B4 Vengurla, India
85/G4 Veniaminof (vol.), Ak,US
18/E4 Venice, It.
89/K6 Venice, Fl,US
97/H5 Venice, Fl,US
33/K4 Venice (Venezia), It.
32/F4 Vénissieux, Fr.
62/C5 Venkatagiri, India
28/D6 Venlo, Neth.
20/C4 Vennesla, Nor.
36/C4 Venoge (riv.), Swi.
38/D2 Venosa, It.
40/B5 Venosa, It.
37/G4 Venosta (val.), It.
28/E5 Venray, Neth.
42/D4 Venta (riv.), Lat., Lith
20/G4 Venta (riv.), Lith.
34/C2 Venta de Baños, Sp.
106/E2 Ventauri (riv.), Ven.
80/P13 Ventersdorp, SAfr.
69/L6 Vent, Iles du (isls.), FrPol.
69/X15 Vent, Iles du (isls.), FrPol.
69/K6 Vent, Iles sous le (isls.), FrPol.
38/A2 Ventiseri, Fr.
25/E5 Ventnor, Eng,UK
32/C1 Ventnor, Eng,UK
18/F3 Ventspils, Lat.
20/G4 Ventspils, Lat.
42/D4 Ventspils, Lat.
46/C4 Ventspils, Lat.
88/C5 Ventura, Ca,US
92/C4 Ventura (San Buenaventura), Ca,U
33/J5 Venturina, It.
38/B1 Venturina, It.
69/X15 Vénus (pt.), FrPol.
102/C2 Venustiano Carranza, Mex.
101/E2 Venustiano Carranza (res.), Mex.
33/M3 Vép, Hun.
109/D2 Vera, Arg.
34/E4 Vera, Sp.
101/F5 Veracruz, Mex.
101/F5 Veracruz (state), Me
101/N7 Veracruz, Mex.
101/N7 Veracruz (state), Me
102/B2 Veracruz, Mex.
102/B2 Veracruz (state), Me
84/H8 Veracruz, Mex.
89/G7 Veracruz (state), Me
108/B4 Veranópolis, Braz.
53/K4 Verāval, India
62/B3 Verāval, India
33/H4 Verbania, It.
37/E6 Verbania, It.
30/B5 Verberie, Fr.
38/D3 Verbicaro, It.
33/H4 Vercelli, It.
36/E6 Vercelli (prov.), It.
36/C3 Vercel-Villedieu-le-Camp, Fr.
95/P6 Verchères, Qu,Can

187

Verch – Volko

95/P6 Verchères (co.), Qu,Can
20/D3 Verdal, Nor.
42/A3 Verdal, Nor.
108/B1 Verdão (riv.), Braz.
107/G6 Verde (riv.), Braz.
107/H7 Verde (riv.), Braz.
108/B1 Verde (riv.), Braz.
100/D3 Verde (riv.), Mex.
101/E4 Verde (riv.), Mex.
109/E1 Verde (riv.), Par.
74/A3 Verde (cape), Sen.
76/B5 Verde (cape), Sen.
92/E4 Verde (riv.), Az,US
34/B1 Verde, Costa (coast), Sp.
107/K7 Verde Grande (riv.), Braz.
26/E2 Verden, Ger.
29/G3 Verden, Ger.
39/G3 Verdhikoússa, Gre.
108/B1 Verdinho (riv.), Braz.
32/F5 Verdon (riv.), Fr.
95/N7 Verdun, Qu,Can
26/C4 Verdun-sur-Meuse, Fr.
31/E5 Verdun-sur-Meuse, Fr.
32/F2 Verdun-sur-Meuse, Fr.
80/D2 Vereeniging, SAfr.
80/P13 Vereeniging, SAfr.
82/E6 Vereeniging, SAfr.
37/H6 Verena, Monte (peak), It.
43/M4 Vereshchagino, Rus.
27/M4 Veretskiy Pereval (pass), Ukr.
78/B4 Verga (cape), Gui.
32/B5 Vergara, Sp.
34/D1 Vergara, Sp.
37/E5 Vergeletto, Swi.
95/F2 Vergennes, Vt,US
39/H2 Vergina (ruins), Gre.
40/F5 Vergina (ruins), Gre.
44/B4 Vergina (ruins), Gre.
37/F1 Verigenstadt, Ger.
34/B2 Verin, Sp.
108/B1 Veríssimo, Braz.
44/E1 Verkhnedneprovskiy, Rus.
42/F1 Verkhnetulomskiy (res.), Rus.
47/N3 Verkhoyansk (range), Rus.
47/P3 Verkhoyansk, Rus.
48/M2 Verkhoyansk (range), Rus.
29/F5 Verl, Ger.
30/C4 Vermand, Fr.
90/F2 Vermilion (riv.), Ab,Can
86/E3 Vermilion, Ab,Can
90/F2 Vermilion, Ab,Can
93/K2 Vermilion (riv.), Il,US
91/K4 Vermillion (range), Mn,US
86/G4 Vermillion, SD,US
89/G3 Vermillion, SD,US
91/J5 Vermillion, SD,US
93/H2 Vermillion, SD,US
87/J4 Vermont (state), US
89/M3 Vermont (state), US
95/F2 Vermont (state), US
88/E3 Vernal, Ut,US
92/E2 Vernal, Ut,US
36/D5 Vernayaz, Swi.
32/D2 Verneuil-sur-Avre, Fr.
19/R10 Verneuil-sur-Seine, Fr.
80/C3 Verneukpan (salt pan), SAfr.
36/C5 Vernier, Swi.
86/E3 Vernon, BC,Can
88/C1 Vernon, BC,Can
90/D3 Vernon, BC,Can
30/A5 Vernon, Fr.
32/D2 Vernon, Fr.
88/G5 Vernon, Tx,US
93/H4 Vernon, Tx,US
96/D3 Vernon, Tx,US
99/Q15 Vernon Hills, Il,US
98/F4 Vernon Valley, NJ,US
98/F4 Vernon Valley/Great Gorge & Action Park, NJ,US
19/R10 Vernouillet, Fr.
30/A6 Vernouillet, Fr.
31/F5 Verny, Fr.
89/K6 Vero Beach, Fl,US
97/H5 Vero Beach, Fl,US
39/H2 Véroia, Gre.
40/F5 Véroia, Gre.
18/E4 Verona, It.
33/J4 Verona, It.
36/C6 Verres, Pointe des (peak), Fr.
19/S10 Verrières-le-Buisson, Fr.
30/B6 Verrières-le-Buisson, Fr.
18/D4 Versailles, Fr.
19/S10 Versailles, Fr.
30/B6 Versailles, Fr.
32/E2 Versailles, Fr.
94/C4 Versailles, Ky,US
19/S10 Versailles, Chateau de, Fr.
44/E2 Verskla (riv.), Rus., Ukr.
46/D4 Verskla (riv.), Rus.,Ukr.
29/F4 Versmold, Ger.
36/C5 Versoix, Swi.
34/E1 Vert (riv.), Fr.
33/J3 Vertana (peak), It.
37/G4 Vertana, Cima (peak), It.
36/C6 Verte, Aiguille (peak), Fr.
19/T11 Vert-le-Grand, Fr.
19/T11 Vert-le-Petit, Fr.
32/C3 Vertou, Fr.
19/T11 Vert-Saint-Denis, Fr.
30/D6 Vertus, Fr.
31/E2 Verviers, Belg.
30/C4 Vervins, Fr.
25/E5 Verwood, Eng,UK
24/B6 Veryan (bay), Eng,UK
37/E5 Verzasca (riv.), Swi.
37/E5 Verzasca (Gerra), It.
30/D5 Verzenay, Fr.
33/G4 Verzuolo, It.
30/D5 Verzy, Fr.
38/A1 Vescovato, Fr.
32/F1 Vesdre (riv.), Belg.
31/F2 Vesdre (riv.), Ger.
41/K2 Veselinovo, Ukr.
45/G3 Veselyy (res.), Rus.
30/A6 Vesgre (riv.), Fr.
26/C4 Vesle (riv.), Fr.
30/D5 Vesle (riv.), Fr.
26/D5 Vesoul, Fr.
33/G3 Vesoul, Fr.
36/C2 Vesoul, Fr.
20/C4 Vest-Agder (co.), Nor.
18/E2 Vesterålen (isls.), Nor.
20/E1 Vesterålen (isls.), Nor.
18/E2 Vestfjorden (bay), Nor.
20/E2 Vestfjorden (fjord), Nor.
42/B2 Vestfjorden (fjord), Nor.
20/D4 Vestfold (co.), Nor.
18/A2 Vestmannaeyjar, Ice.
20/N7 Vestmannaeyjar, Ice.
26/F1 Vest-Sjælland (co.), Den.
20/E1 Vestvågøya (isl.), Nor.
38/D2 Vesuvius (mtn.), It.
40/C2 Veszprém, Hun.
40/C2 Veszprém (co.), Hun.
40/E2 Vészto, Hun.
80/D3 Vet (riv.), SAfr.
20/E4 Vetlanda, Swe.
43/K4 Vetluga (riv.), Rus.
46/E4 Vetluga (riv.), Rus.
41/H4 Vetovo, Bul.
38/C1 Vetralla, It.
36/C5 Vétraz, Fr.
33/K5 Vettore (peak), It.
32/D3 Veude (riv.), Fr.
30/B1 Veurne, Belg.
33/G3 Vevey, Swi.
36/C5 Vevey, Swi.
36/D5 Vex, Swi.
31/F2 Veybach (riv.), Ger.
36/B5 Veyle (riv.), Fr.
32/F4 Veynes, Fr.
36/C5 Veyrier, Swi.
36/C6 Veyrier-du-Lac, Fr.
36/C1 Vézelise, Fr.
32/D4 Vézère (riv.), Fr.
44/E4 Vezirköprü, Turk.
50/C1 Vezirköprü, Turk.
37/G5 Vezza d'Oglio, It.
106/E7 Viacha, Bol.
107/K4 Viana, Braz.
34/B1 Viana del Bollo, Sp.
34/B3 Viana do Alentejo, Port.
34/A2 Viana do Castelo, Port.
34/A2 Viana do Castelo (dist.), Port.
31/F4 Vianden, Lux.
28/C5 Vianen, Neth.
60/D5 Viangchan (Vientiane) (cap.), Laos
63/H4 Viangchan (Vientiane) (cap.), Laos
65/C2 Viangchan (Vientiane) (cap.), Laos
60/D4 Viangphoukha, Laos
63/H3 Viangphoukha, Laos
34/C4 Viar (riv.), Sp.
33/J5 Viareggio, It.
19/T9 Viarmes, Fr.
32/E4 Viaur (riv.), Fr.
20/D4 Viborg, Den.
38/E3 Vibo Valentia, It.
35/G2 Vic, Sp.
100/C3 Vicam, Mex.
34/D4 Vicar, Sp.
35/F1 Vic-en-Bigorre, Fr.
100/B2 Vicente Guerrero, Mex.
100/E4 Vicente Guerrero, Mex.
33/J4 Vicenza, It.
37/H6 Vicenza (state), It.
32/D5 Vic-Fezensac, Fr.
35/F1 Vic-Fezensac, Fr.
42/J4 Vichuga, Rus.
18/D4 Vichy, Fr.
32/E3 Vichy, Fr.
89/H5 Vicksburg, Ms,US
93/K4 Vicksburg, Ms,US
97/F3 Vicksburg, Ms,US
93/K4 Vicksburg Nat'l Mil. Park, Ms,US
97/F3 Vicksburg Nat'l Mil. Park, Ms,US
38/A1 Vico, Fr.
38/C1 Vico (lake), It.
40/B5 Vico del Gargano, It.
107/K8 Viçosa, Braz.
108/D2 Viçosa, Braz.
37/F5 Vicosoprano, Swi.
39/G3 Vicou Gorge Nat'l Park, Gre.
30/C5 Vic-sur-Aisne, Fr.
31/F6 Vic-sur-Seille, Fr.
70/F7 Victor Harbor, Austl.
74/F6 Victoria (lake), Afr.
77/M8 Victoria (lake), Afr.
82/F1 Victoria (lake), Afr.
109/D3 Victoria, Arg.
70/E3 Victoria (riv.), Austl.
70/G7 Victoria (state), Austl.
73/C3 Victoria (state), Austl.
102/D2 Victoria (peak), Belz.
60/B4 Victoria (peak), Burma
63/F3 Victoria (peak), Burma
84/F2 Victoria (isl.), Can.
90/C3 Victoria (cap.), BC,Can
86/D4 Victoria (cap.), BC,Can
88/B2 Victoria (cap.), BC,Can
86/E1 Victoria (isl.), NW,Can
86/F2 Victoria (str.), NW,Can
87/H7 Victoria (isl.), NW,Can
95/Q8 Victoria, On,Can
109/B4 Victoria, Chile
61/G4 Victoria (cap.), HK
63/K3 Victoria (cap.), HK
68/A2 Victoria (cap.), HK
102/E3 Victoria, Hon.
66/E2 Victoria, Malay.
67/E2 Victoria (peak), Phil.
41/G3 Victoria, Rom.
101/F2 Victoria, Tx,US
89/G6 Victoria, Tx,US
93/H5 Victoria, Tx,US
96/D4 Victoria, Tx,US
74/E6 Victoria (falls), Zam.
82/E4 Victoria (fall, falls), Zam.
83/L Victoria Land (reg.), Ant.
77/M7 Victoria Nile (riv.), Ugen.
70/E3 Victoria River Downs, Austl.
87/J4 Victoriaville, Qu,Can
95/G2 Victoriaville, Qu,Can
80/C3 Victoria West, SAfr.
109/C4 Victorica, Arg.
100/E4 Victor Rosales, Mex.
88/C5 Victorville, Ca,US
92/C4 Victorville, Ca,US
81/F3 Vidal (cape), SAfr.
89/K5 Vidalia, Ga,US
97/H3 Vidalia, Ga,US
93/K5 Vidalia, La,US
97/F4 Vidalia, La,US
108/B3 Videira, Braz.
41/G3 Videle, Rom.
34/B3 Vidigueira, Port.
40/F4 Vidin, Bul.
44/B4 Vidin, Bul.
62/C3 Vidisha, India
43/X9 Vidnoye, Rus.
93/J5 Vidor, Tx,US
96/E4 Vidor, Tx,US
32/E5 Vidourle (riv.), Fr.
32/C3 Vie (riv.), Fr.
109/D5 Viedma, Arg.
27/H4 Viehberg (peak), Aus.
34/C1 Vieja (mtn.), Sp.
100/D2 Vieja (peak), Tx,US
96/B4 Vieja (mts.), Tx,US
42/D4 Viekšniai, Lith.
32/D5 Viella, Sp.
35/F1 Viella, Sp.
31/E3 Vielsalm, Belg.
29/H5 Vienenburg, Ger.
18/E4 Vienna (cap.), Aus.
98/J8 Vienna, Va,US
94/D4 Vienna, WV,US
97/H2 Vienna, WV,US
27/J4 Vienna (Wien) (cap.), Aus.
33/M2 Vienna (Wien) (cap.), Aus.
40/C1 Vienna (Wien) (cap.), Aus.
32/D3 Vienne (riv.), Fr.
32/F4 Vienne, Fr.
60/D5 Vientiane (Viangchan) (cap.), Laos
63/H4 Vientiane (Viangchan) (cap.), Laos
65/C2 Vientiane (Viangchan) (cap.), Laos
104/E3 Vieques (isl.), PR
31/D6 Viere (riv.), Fr.
28/D5 Vierlingsbeek, Neth.
31/E4 Vierre (riv.), Fr.
28/D6 Viersen, Ger.
31/F1 Viersen, Ger.
33/H3 Vierwaldstätten See (lake), Swi.
37/E3 Vierwaldstättersee (Lucerne) (lake), Swi.
32/E3 Vierzon, Fr.
100/E3 Viesca, Mex.
38/E2 Vieste, It.
40/C5 Vieste, It.
48/K8 Vietnam
60/E5 Vietnam
63/J5 Vietnam
65/D2 Vietnam
66/C1 Vietnam
60/E4 Viet Tri, Viet.
63/J3 Viet Tri, Viet.
65/D1 Viet Tri, Viet.
32/C5 Vieux-Boucau-les-Bains, Fr.
36/C2 Vieux-Charmont, Fr.
30/C3 Vieux-Condé, Fr.
104/F4 Vieux Fort, StL.
36/D2 Vieux-Thann, Fr.
27/N1 Vievis, Lith.
36/C5 Vieze (riv.), Swi.
61/J5 Vigan, Phil.
68/B3 Vigan, Phil.
33/H4 Vigevano, It.
37/E6 Viggiù, It.
107/J4 Vigia, Braz.
38/C2 Viglio (peak), It.
30/B3 Vignacourt, Fr.
38/C1 Vignanello, It.
32/C5 Vignemale (mtn.), Fr.
35/E1 Vignemale (mtn.), Fr.
31/E6 Vigneulles-lès-Hattonchâtel, Fr.
19/T10 Vigneux-sur-Seine, Fr.
30/B6 Vigneux-sur-Seine, Fr.
33/J4 Vignola, It.
31/E6 Vignot, Fr.
18/C4 Vigo, Sp.
34/A1 Vigo, Sp.
31/F5 Vigy, Fr.
20/H2 Vihanti, Fin.
42/E2 Vihanti, Fin.
53/K2 Vihāri, Pak.
20/H3 Viitasaari, Fin.
42/E3 Viitasaari, Fin.
62/D4 Vijayawada, India
39/F2 Vijosë (riv.), Alb.
20/C3 Vik, Nor.
42/E2 Vikajärvi, Fin.
20/C4 Vikedal, Nor.
20/D4 Vikersund, Nor.
39/H2 Vikhren (peak), Bul.
41/F5 Vikhren (peak), Bul.
90/F2 Viking, Ab,Can
64/F4 Vikramasingapuram, India
68/F6 Vila (cap.), Van.
106/E4 Vila Bittencourt, Braz.
35/G2 Viladecans, Sp.
35/K7 Viladecans, Sp.
35/V14 Vila de Porto Santo
82/G4 Vila de Sena, Moz.
34/A4 Vila do Bispo, Port.
34/A2 Vila do Conde, Port.
35/T13 Vila do Porto, Azor.
35/K7 Vilafranca del Penedès, Sp.
34/A3 Vila Franca de Xira, Port.
35/Q10 Vila Franca de Xira, Port.
35/T13 Vila Franca do Campo, Azor.
32/B3 Vilaine (riv.), Fr.
20/H4 Viļaka, Lat.
42/E4 Viļaka, Lat.
81/H7 Vilanandro (cape), Madg.
82/G5 Vilanculos, Moz.
34/B2 Vila Nova de Fozcoa, Port.
34/A2 Vila Nova de Gaia, Port.
34/A4 Vila Nova de Milfontes, Port.
35/F2 Vilanova i la Geltrú, Sp.
35/K7 Vilanova i la Geltrù, Sp.
34/B2 Vila Pouca de Aguiar, Port.
34/B2 Vila Real, Port.
34/B2 Vila Real (dist.), Port.
34/B4 Vila Real de Santo António, Port.
34/B2 Vilar Formoso, Port.
107/K8 Vila Velha Argolas, Braz.
108/D2 Vila Velha Argolas, Braz.
34/B3 Vila Velha de Ródão, Port.
34/A2 Vila Verde, Port.
34/B3 Vila Viçosa, Port.
41/F3 Vilcea (co.), Rom.
34/D3 Vilches, Sp.
42/E5 Vileyka, Bela.
44/C1 Vileyka, Bela.
20/F2 Vilhelmina, Swe.
42/C2 Vilhelmina, Swe.
106/F6 Vilhena, Braz.
42/E5 Viliya (riv.), Bela.
20/H4 Viljandi, Est.
42/E4 Viljandi, Est.
80/P13 Viljoenskroon, SAfr.
27/M1 Vilkaviškis, Lith.
27/M1 Vilkija, Lith.
42/D5 Vilkija, Lith.
47/K2 Vil'kitsogo (str.), Rus.
37/F4 Villa, Swi.
104/D3 Villa Altagracia, DRep.
109/D2 Villa Ángela, Arg.
32/C5 Villaba, Sp.
34/E1 Villaba, Sp.
34/B1 Villablino, Sp.
106/E2 Villa Bruzual, Ven.
34/D3 Villacañas, Sp.
109/D3 Villa Carlos Paz, Arg.
34/D3 Villacarrillo, Sp.
33/K3 Villach, Aus.
40/A2 Villach, Aus.
100/C3 Villa Constitución, Mex.
34/C1 Villada, Sp.
100/E4 Villa de Cos, Mex.
34/A1 Villa de Cruces, Sp.
34/C4 Villa del Río, Sp.
34/C1 Villadiego, Sp.
109/C3 Villa Dolores, Arg.
37/E5 Villadossola, It.
35/E2 Villafamés, Sp.
102/C2 Villa Flores, Mex.
34/E1 Villafranca, Sp.
34/B1 Villafranca del Bierzo, Sp.
35/E2 Villafranca del Cid, Sp.
34/D3 Villafranca del los Caballeros, Sp.
34/B3 Villafranca de los Barros, Sp.
96/C5 Villa Frontera, Mex
34/A1 Villagarcía, Sp.
93/J5 Village Mills, Tx,US
96/E4 Village Mills, Tx,US
109/E4 Villa Gesell, Arg.
101/F3 Villagrán, Mex.
109/E3 Villaguay, Arg.
101/G5 Villahermosa, Mex.
102/C2 Villahermosa, Mex.
34/D3 Villahermosa, Sp.
100/C2 Villa Hidalgo, Mex.
100/D3 Villa Hidalgo, Mex.
103/J2 Villa Isabela, DRep.
104/D3 Villa Isabela, DRep.
103/J2 Villa Jaragua, DRep.
35/E3 Villajoyosa, Sp.
34/B1 Villalba, Sp.
34/B2 Villalcampo (res.), Sp.
101/E3 Villaldama, Mex.
96/C5 Villaldama, Mex
34/C1 Villalón de Campos, Sp.
34/C2 Villalpando, Sp.
109/D3 Villa María, Arg.
34/C4 Villamartín, Sp.
106/F8 Villa Montes, Bol.
37/H4 Villandro, Monte (peak), It.
103/H4 Villanueva, Col.
102/D3 Villa Nueva, Guat.
102/E3 Villanueva, Hon.
100/E4 Villanueva, Mex.
102/E3 Villanueva, Nic.
34/A1 Villanueva de Arosa, Sp.
34/C3 Villanueva de Córdoba, Sp.
34/D3 Villanueva del Arzobispo, Sp.
34/C3 Villanueva de la Serena, Sp.
34/D3 Villanueva de los Infantes, Sp.
34/B1 Villanueva de Oscos, Sp.
40/D3 Villány, Hun.
101/Q10 Villa Obregon, Mex.
98/C3 Villa Park, Ca,US
99/Q16 Villa Park, Il,US
32/B5 Villarcayo, Sp.
34/D1 Villarcayo, Sp.
35/E3 Villar del Arzobispo, Sp.
34/B2 Villardevós, Sp.
109/C4 Villa Regina, Arg.
103/H5 Villa Rosario, Col.
35/E3 Villarreal de los Infantes, Sp.
109/B4 Villarrica, Chile
109/E2 Villarrica, Par.
34/D3 Villarrobledo, Sp.
34/D3 Villarrubia de los Ojos, Sp.
36/B5 Villars-les-Dombes, Fr.
36/D4 Villars-sur-Glâne, Swi.
32/B5 Villasana de Mena, Sp.
34/D1 Villasana de Mena, Sp.
103/E3 Villa Sandino, Nic.
106/F7 Villa Serrano, Bol.
109/C2 Villa Unión, Arg.
100/D4 Villa Unión, Mex.
101/E2 Villa Unión, Mex.
34/C4 Villaverde del Río, Sp.
106/D3 Villavicencio, Col.
34/C1 Villaviciosa, Sp.
35/N9 Villaviciosa de Odon, Sp.
106/E8 Villazón, Bol.
109/C1 Villazón, Bol.
19/T10 Villecresnes, Fr.
19/S10 Ville-d'Avray, Fr.
32/E4 Villefranche-de-Rouergue, Fr.
32/F4 Villefranche-sur-Saône, Fr.
19/T10 Villejuif, Fr.
30/B6 Villejuif, Fr.
19/T10 Villemomble, Fr.
32/D5 Villemur-sur-Tarn, Fr.
35/F1 Villemur-sur-Tarn, Fr.
35/E3 Villena, Sp.
36/C5 Villeneuve, Swi.
26/B3 Villeneuve-d'Ascq, Fr.
30/C2 Villeneuve-d'Ascq, Fr.
19/S10 Villeneuve-la-Garenne, Fr.
19/U10 Villeneuve-le-Comte, Fr.
19/T10 Villeneuve-le-Roi, Fr.
32/F5 Villeneuve-lès-Avignon, Fr.
30/B6 Villeneuve-Saint-Georges, Fr.
30/C5 Villeneuve-Saint-Germain, Fr.
32/D4 Villeneuve-sur-Lot, Fr.
26/B4 Villeneuve-sur-Yonne, Fr.
32/E2 Villeneuve-sur-Yonne, Fr.
32/D5 Villeneuve-Tolosane, Fr.
35/F1 Villeneuve-Tolosane, Fr.
19/R10 Villennes-sur-Seine, Fr.
19/T10 Villeparisis, Fr.
30/B6 Villeparisis, Fr.
19/T10 Villepinte, Fr.
93/J5 Ville Platte, La,US
96/E4 Ville Platte, La,US
19/S10 Villepreux, Fr.
30/B4 Villers-Bocage, Fr.
30/B4 Villers-Bretonneux, Fr.
26/B4 Villers-Cotterêts, Fr.
30/C5 Villers-Cotterêts, Fr.
32/E2 Villers-Cotterêts, Fr.
36/C2 Villersexel, Fr.
31/E2 Villers-Le-Bouillet, Belg.
36/C3 Villers-le-Lac, Fr.
31/F6 Villers-lès-Nancy, Fr.
30/C3 Villers-Outreaux, Fr.
30/B5 Villers-Saint-Paul, Fr.
31/D4 Villers-Semeuse, Fr.
31/E5 Villerupt, Fr.
36/A6 Villeurbanne, Fr.
19/T10 Villevaudé, Fr.
80/Q13 Villiers, SAfr.
80/L10 Villiersdorp, SAfr.
31/D6 Villiers-en-Lieu, Fr.
19/T9 Villiers-le-Bel, Fr.
30/C6 Villiers-Saint-Georges, Fr.
19/T10 Villiers-sur-Marne, Fr.
36/B6 Villieu-Loyes-Mollon, Fr.
26/E4 Villingen-Schwenningen, Ger.
33/H2 Villingen-Schwenningen, Ger.
37/E1 Villingen-Schwenningen, Ger.
31/H3 Villmar, Ger.
62/C5 Villupuram, India
64/G3 Villupuram, India
18/F3 Vilnius (cap.), Lith.
27/N1 Vilnius (cap.), Lith.
42/E5 Vilnius (cap.), Lith.
46/C4 Vilnius (cap.), Lith.
20/H3 Vilppula, Fin.
42/E3 Vilppula, Fin.
37/G2 Vils, Aus.
26/F4 Vils (riv.), Ger.
26/G4 Vils (riv.), Ger.
33/K2 Vils (riv.), Ger.
26/G4 Vilsbiburg, Ger.
27/G4 Vilshofen, Ger.
33/K2 Vilshofen, Ger.
37/F3 Vilters, Swi.
30/D2 Vilvoorde, Belg.
47/M3 Vilyuy (range), Rus.
47/N3 Vilyuy (riv.), Rus.
48/L3 Vilyuy (riv.), Rus.
34/B1 Vimianzo, Sp.
20/E4 Vimmerby, Swe.
30/B3 Vimy, Fr.
76/H6 Vina (riv.), Camr.
109/B3 Viña del Mar, Chile
33/G5 Vinaigre (mtn.), Fr.
35/J1 Vinaigre (mtn.), Fr.
81/J6 Vinanivao, Madg.
35/F2 Vinaroz, Sp.
83/H8 Vincennes (bay), Ant.
19/T10 Vincennes, Fr.
19/U10 Vincennes (res.), Fr.
30/B6 Vincennes, Fr.
89/J4 Vincennes, In,US
94/C4 Vincennes, In,US
97/G2 Vincennes, In,US
98/F6 Vincentown, NJ,US
36/C1 Vincey, Fr.
26/F1 Vindeby, Den.
20/F2 Vindeln, Swe.
42/C2 Vindeln, Swe.
95/R9 Vineland, On,Can
89/L4 Vineland, NJ,US
94/F4 Vineland, NJ,US
95/R9 Vineland Station, On,Can
32/D3 Vineuil, Fr.
60/E5 Vinh, Viet.
63/J4 Vinh, Viet.
65/D2 Vinh, Viet.
34/B2 Vinhais, Port.
63/J5 Vinh Long, Viet.
65/D4 Vinh Long, Viet.
66/C1 Vinh Long, Viet.
61/E5 Vinh Moc, Tunnels of, Viet.
65/D2 Vinh Moc, Tunnels of, Viet.
65/D4 Vinh Quoi, Viet.
63/J5 Vinh Thanh, Viet.
65/E3 Vinh Thanh, Viet.
65/D1 Vinh Yen, Viet.
39/H2 Vinica, Macd.
40/F5 Vinica, Macd.
93/J3 Vinita, Ok,US
96/E2 Vinita, Ok,US
40/F3 Vinju Mare, Rom.
40/D3 Vinkovci, Cro.
31/G5 Vinningen, Ger.
18/F4 Vinnitsa, Ukr.
44/D2 Vinnitsa, Ukr.
46/C5 Vinnitsa, Ukr.
41/J1 Vinnitsa Obl., Ukr.
44/C2 Vinnitsa Obl., Ukr.
27/M4 Vinogradov, Ukr.
40/F1 Vinogradov, Ukr.
44/B2 Vinogradov, Ukr.
32/F5 Vinon-sur-Verdon, Fr.
35/H1 Vinon-sur-Verdon, Fr.
61/J5 Vintar, Phil.
98/F4 Viola, NY,US
73/C3 Violet Town, Austl.
19/R9 Viosne (riv.), Fr.
33/J3 Vipiteno (Sterzing), It.
37/H4 Vipiteno (Sterzing), It.
50/D2 Viranşehir, Turk.
52/C1 Viranşehir, Turk.
53/K5 Virār, India
62/B4 Virār, India
27/M1 Virbalis, Lith.
91/H3 Virden, Mb,Can
32/C2 Vire, Fr.
82/B4 Virei, Ang.
31/D3 Vireux-Wallerand, Fr.
109/C7 Virgenes (cape), Arg.
85/R9 Virgil, On,Can
84/L8 Virgin (isls.), NAm.
104/E3 Virgin (isls.), UK,US
92/D3 Virgin (riv.), US
104/E3 Virgin Gorda (isl.), BVI
22/A4 Virginia, Ire.
89/L4 Virginia (state), US
94/E5 Virginia (state), US
98/J8 Virginia (state), US
86/G4 Virginia, Mn,US
89/H2 Virginia, Mn,US
91/K4 Virginia, Mn,US
94/A2 Virginia, Mn,US
89/L4 Virginia Beach, Va,US
94/F4 Virginia Beach, Va,US
97/K2 Virginia Beach, Va,US
92/C3 Virginia City, Nv,US
19/M7 Virginia Water, Eng,UK
104/E3 Virgin Islands, UK
104/E3 Virgin Islands, US
104/E3 Virgin Islands Nat'l Park, USVI
36/B5 Viriat, Fr.
36/B6 Virieu-le-Grand, Fr.
65/D3 Virochey, Camb.
19/S10 Viroflay, Fr.
30/D3 Viroin (riv.), Belg.
93/K2 Viroqua, Wi,US
94/B3 Viroqua, Wi,US
40/C3 Virovitica, Cro.
31/E4 Virton, Belg.
20/G4 Virtsu, Est.
42/D4 Virtsu, Est.
62/C6 Virudunagar, India
64/F4 Virudunagar, India
19/T10 Viry-Châtillon, Fr.
30/B6 Viry-Châtillon, Fr.
38/D1 Vis (isl.), Cro.
40/B4 Vis (isl.), Cro.
40/C4 Vis, Cro.
62/D4 Visākhapatnam, India
88/C4 Visalia, Ca,US
92/C3 Visalia, Ca,US
67/F1 Visayan (sea), Phil.
29/F3 Visbek, Ger.
18/E3 Visby, Swe.
20/F4 Visby, Swe.
42/C4 Visby, Swe.
46/B4 Visby, Swe.
108/D2 Visconde do Rio Branco, Braz.
87/R7 Viscount Melville (sound), NW,Can
31/E2 Visé, Belg.
40/D4 Višegrad, Bosn.
18/C4 Viseu, Port.
34/B2 Viseu, Port.
34/B2 Viseu (dist.), Port.
41/G2 Vişeu de Sus, Rom.
43/L3 Vishera (riv.), Rus.
43/N3 Vishera (riv.), Rus.
80/L3 Vishoek, SAfr.
80/L11 Vishoek, SAfr.
53/K4 Visnagar, India
62/B3 Visnagar, India
40/D3 Višnjevac, Cro.
40/D4 Visoko, Bosn.
36/D5 Visp, Swi.
36/D5 Visperterminen, Swi.
29/G3 Visselhövede, Ger.
26/F1 Vissenbjerg, Den.
36/D5 Vissoie, Swi.
92/C4 Vista, Ca,US
39/J2 Vistonís (lake), Gre.
41/G5 Vistonís (lake), Gre.
18/E3 Vistula (riv.), Pol.
44/B2 Vistula (riv.), Pol.
46/C4 Vistula (riv.), Pol.
27/K2 Vistula (Wisła) (riv.), Pol.
39/J1 Vit (riv.), Bul.
41/G4 Vit (riv.), Bul.
91/J3 Vita, Mb,Can
33/J5 Vitalba (peak), It.
18/G3 Vitebsk, Bela.
42/F5 Vitebsk, Bela.
46/D4 Vitebsk, Bela.
42/E5 Vitebsk Obl., Bela.
44/D1 Vitebsk Obl., Bela.
38/C1 Viterbo, It.
40/C3 Vitez, Bosn.
65/D4 Vi Thanh, Viet.
34/B2 Vitigudino, Sp.
68/G6 Viti Levu (isl.), Fiji
69/Y18 Viti Levu (isl.), Fiji
47/M4 Vitim (plat.), Rus.
47/M4 Vitim (riv.), Rus.
48/L4 Vitim (riv.), Rus.
54/G1 Vitim (plat.), Rus.
54/G1 Vitim (riv.), Rus.
39/G1 Vitomirica, Yugo.
40/E4 Vitomirica, Yugo.
107/K8 Vitória, Braz.
108/D2 Vitória, Braz.
18/C4 Vitoria, Sp.
32/B5 Vitoria, Sp.
34/D1 Vitoria, Sp.
107/K6 Vitória da Conquista, Braz.
107/L5 Vitória de Santo Antão, Braz.
39/H1 Vitosha Nat'l Park, Bul.
41/F4 Vitosha Nat'l Park, Bul.
32/C2 Vitré, Fr.
36/B2 Vitrey-sur-Mance, Fr.
32/F5 Vitrolles, Fr.
30/B3 Vitry-en-Artois, Fr.
26/C4 Vitry-le-François, Fr.
30/D6 Vitry-le-François, Fr.
32/F2 Vitry-le-François, Fr.
19/T10 Vitry-sur-Seine, Fr.
30/B6 Vitry-sur-Seine, Fr.
20/G2 Vittangi, Swe.
42/D2 Vittangi, Swe.
36/C1 Vittel, Fr.
36/B1 Vittel, Fr.
38/D4 Vittoria, It.
33/K4 Vittorio Veneto, It.
32/F4 Vivarais (mts.), Fr.
34/B1 Vivero, Sp.
32/D3 Vivonne, Fr.
100/B3 Vizcaíno, Sierra de (mts.), Mex.
41/H5 Vize, Turk.
50/A1 Vize, Turk.
43/K2 Vizhas (riv.), Rus.
41/G1 Vizhnitsa, Ukr.
62/D4 Vizianagaram, India
26/C3 Vlaardingen, Neth.
28/B5 Vlaardingen, Neth.
40/F2 Vlădeasa (peak), Rom.
44/B3 Vlădeasa (peak), Rom.
19/H4 Vladikavkaz, Rus.
45/H4 Vladikavkaz, Rus.
46/E5 Vladikavkaz, Rus.
19/H3 Vladimir, Rus.
42/J4 Vladimir, Rus.
46/E4 Vladimir, Rus.
42/J5 Vladimir Obl., Rus.
27/N3 Vladimir-Volynskiy, Ukr.
44/C2 Vladimir-Volynskiy, Ukr.
47/P5 Vladivostok, Rus.
55/L3 Vladivostok, Rus.
26/D2 Vlagtwedde, Neth.
29/E2 Vlagtwedde, Neth.
41/G2 Vlăhiţa, Rom.
39/G1 Vlajna (peak), Yugo.
40/E4 Vlajna (peak), Yugo.
44/B4 Vlajna (peak), Yugo.
40/D3 Vlasenica, Bosn.
27/H4 Vlašim, Czh.
33/L2 Vlašim, Czh.
39/H1 Vlasotince, Yugo.
40/F4 Vlasotince, Yugo.
26/C2 Vlieland (isl.), Neth.
28/B2 Vlieland (isl.), Neth.
28/C2 Vliestroom (chan.), Neth.
28/C5 Vlijmen, Neth.
26/B3 Vlissingen, Neth.
28/A6 Vlissingen (Flushing), Neth.
18/E4 Vlorë, Alb.
39/F2 Vlorë, Alb.
40/D5 Vlorë, Alb.
29/F4 Vlotho, Ger.
27/H4 Vltava (riv.), Czh.
33/L1 Vltava (riv.), Czh.
101/F2 Voca, Tx,US
27/G4 Vöcklabruck, Aus.
33/K2 Vöcklabruck, Aus.
40/A1 Vöcklabruck, Aus.
33/L4 Vodice, Cro.
40/B3 Vodice, Cro.
42/H3 Vodlozero (lake), Rus.
20/D4 Vodskov, Den.
28/D5 Voerde, Ger.
33/H1 Vogelsberg (mts.), Ger.
33/H4 Voghera, It.
37/E5 Vogogna, It.
37/E5 Vogorno, Pizzo di (peak), Swi.
40/D4 Vogošća, Bosn.
26/F3 Vogtland (reg.), Ger.
33/J1 Vogtland (reg.), Ger.
69/U12 Voh, NCal.
33/K2 Vohenstrauss, Ger.
81/H8 Vohilava, Madg.
74/G7 Vohimena (cape), Madg.
81/H9 Vohimena (cape), Madg.
75/G7 Vohipeno, Madg.
81/H8 Vohipeno, Madg.
37/G1 Vöhringen, Ger.
82/G1 Voi, Kenya
31/E6 Void-Vacon, Fr.
99/C3 Voight (cr.), Wa,US
76/D6 Voinjama, Libr.
32/F4 Voiron, Fr.
32/D2 Voise (riv.), Fr.
87/K3 Voisey (bay), Nf,Can
30/B5 Voisne (riv.), Fr.
36/B4 Voiteur, Fr.
40/D5 Vojosë (riv.), Alb.
40/D3 Vojvodina (aut. prov.), Yugo.
31/F5 Völklingen, Ger.
37/H6 Volano, It.
103/F4 Volcán Barú Nat'l Park, Pan.
68/C2 Volcano (isls.), Japan
88/U11 Volcano, Hi,US
103/E4 Volcán Poás Nat'l Park, CR
20/C3 Volda, Nor.
28/C4 Volendam, Neth.
19/H4 Volga (riv.), Rus.
43/K4 Volga (riv.), Rus.
45/H3 Volga (riv.), Rus.
46/E5 Volga (riv.), Rus.
42/H3 Volga-Baltic Wtwy., Rus.
36/D1 Volgelsheim, Fr.
19/H4 Volgodonsk, Rus.
45/G3 Volgodonsk, Rus.
19/H4 Volgograd, Rus.
45/H2 Volgograd, Rus.
45/H2 Volgograd (res.), Rus.
46/E5 Volgograd, Rus.
45/G2 Volgograd Obl., Rus.
26/F4 Volkach, Ger.
28/B5 Volkerakdam (dam), Neth.
33/L3 Völkermarkt, Aus.
40/B2 Völkermarkt, Aus.
37/E3 Volketswil, Swi.
42/F4 Volkhov (riv.), Rus.
43/G4 Volkhov, Rus.
26/D4 Völklingen, Ger.
29/G6 Volkmarsen, Ger.
27/N2 Volkovysk, Bela.

188

Volko – Wawa

42/E5 **Volkovysk**, Bela.
44/C1 **Volkovysk**, Bela.
81/E2 **Volksrust**, SAfr.
82/E6 **Volksrust**, SAfr.
31/G5 **Volmunster**, Fr.
43/V7 **Volodarsky**, Rus.
18/G3 **Vologda**, Rus.
42/H4 **Vologda**, Rus.
46/D4 **Vologda**, Rus.
42/J3 **Vologda Obl.**, Rus.
26/D4 **Vologne** (riv.), Fr.
33/G2 **Vologne** (riv.), Fr.
36/C1 **Vologne** (riv.), Fr.
18/F5 **Vólos**, Gre.
39/H3 **Vólos**, Gre.
39/H3 **Volos** (gulf), Gre.
44/B5 **Vólos**, Gre.
27/M4 **Volovets**, Ukr.
42/E5 **Volozhin**, Bela.
44/C1 **Volozhin**, Bela.
33/J3 **Völs**, Aus.
37/H3 **Völs**, Aus.
19/H3 **Vol'sk**, Rus.
45/H1 **Vol'sk**, Rus.
46/E4 **Vol'sk**, Rus.
74/B4 **Volta** (lake), Gha.
74/C4 **Volta** (riv.), Gha.
79/E4 **Volta** (lake), Gha.
79/F5 **Volta** (reg.), Gha.
79/F5 **Volta** (riv.), Gha.
76/E6 **Volta** (lake), Ghana
76/F6 **Volta** (riv.), Ghana
107/K8 **Volta Redonda**, Braz.
108/C2 **Volta Redonda**, Braz.
109/H1 **Volta Redonda**, Braz.
33/J5 **Volterra**, It.
29/E4 **Voltlage**, Ger.
40/B5 **Volturino** (peak), It.
38/D2 **Volturno** (riv.), It.
75/M13 **Volubilis** (ruins), Mor.
39/H2 **Vólvi** (lake), Gre.
41/F5 **Vólvi** (lake), Gre.
44/C2 **Volyn Obl.**, Ukr.
27/M3 **Volyno Oblast**, Ukr.
43/L5 **Volzhsk**, Rus.
19/H4 **Volzhskiy**, Rus.
45/H2 **Volzhskiy**, Rus.
46/E5 **Volzhskiy**, Rus.
81/H8 **Vondrozo**, Madg.
85/H3 **Von Frank** (mtn.), Ak,US
39/G3 **Vónitsa**, Gre.
32/D3 **Vonne** (riv.), Fr.
28/B4 **Voorburg**, Neth.
28/B5 **Voorne** (isl.), Neth.
28/B4 **Voorschoten**, Neth.
28/D4 **Voorst**, Neth.
20/P6 **Vopnafjördhur**, Ice.
37/F4 **Vorab** (peak), Swi.
26/E5 **Vorarlberg** (prov.), Aus.
33/H3 **Vorarlberg** (prov.), Aus.
37/F3 **Vorarlberg** (prov.), Aus.
28/D4 **Vorden**, Neth.
33/H3 **Vorderrhein** (riv.), Swi.
37/E4 **Vorderrhein** (riv.), Swi.
40/D5 **Vorë**, Alb.
32/F4 **Voreppe**, Fr.
19/K2 **Vorkuta**, Rus.
43/Q2 **Vorkuta**, Rus.
46/G3 **Vorkuta**, Rus.
39/J5 **Vóroi**, Gre.
41/G1 **Vorokhta**, Ukr.
45/G1 **Vorona** (riv.), Rus.
19/G3 **Voronezh**, Rus.
44/F1 **Voronezh** (riv.), Rus.
44/F2 **Voronezh**, Rus.
46/D4 **Voronezh**, Rus.
45/G2 **Voronezh Obl.**, Rus.
27/N1 **Voronovo**, Bela.
42/G1 **Voron'ya** (riv.), Rus.
28/C6 **Vorst**, Belg.
31/E1 **Vorst**, Belg.
42/E4 **Võrts** (lake), Est.
20/H4 **Võru**, Est.
42/E4 **Võru**, Est.
43/Y8 **Vorya** (riv.), Rus.
26/D5 **Vosges** (mts.), Fr.
31/G6 **Vosges** (mts.), Fr.
33/G3 **Vosges** (mts.), Fr.
36/C1 **Vosges** (dept.), Fr.
36/C2 **Vosges** (mts.), Fr.
42/H5 **Voskresensk**, Rus.
44/F1 **Voskresensk**, Rus.
20/C3 **Voss**, Nor.
83/V **Vostock** (cape), Ant.
83/H **Vostok**, Ant.
69/K6 **Vostok** (isl.), Kiri.
19/J3 **Votkinsk**, Rus.
43/M4 **Votkinsk**, Rus.
43/M4 **Votkinsk** (res.), Rus.
46/F4 **Votkinsk**, Rus.
108/C2 **Votorantim**, Braz.
108/B2 **Votuporanga**, Braz.
34/B2 **Vouga** (riv.), Port.
36/B5 **Vouglans** (lake), Fr.
36/B5 **Vouglans, Barrage de** (dam), Fr.
36/C3 **Voujeaucourt**, Fr.
36/C5 **Vouvry**, Swi.
39/H5 **Voúxa, Ákra** (cape), Gre.
31/D5 **Vouziers**, Fr.
89/H2 **Voyageurs Nat'l Park**, Mn,US
91/K3 **Voyageurs Nat'l Park**, Mn,US
86/G4 **Voyageurs Nat'l Park**, Mn,US
94/A1 **Voyageurs Nat'l Park**, Mn,US
83/J **Voyeykov Ice Shelf**, Ant.
43/V7 **Voytolovka**, Rus.
43/M3 **Voy-Vozh**, Rus.
42/H3 **Vozhe** (lake), Rus.
41/K2 **Voznesensk**, Ukr.
44/D3 **Voznesensk**, Ukr.
41/K2 **Vradiyevka**, Ukr.
36/B1 **Vraine** (riv.), Fr.
41/H3 **Vrancea** (co.), Rom.
48/S2 **Vrangelya** (isl.), Rus.
39/G1 **Vranje**, Yugo.
40/E4 **Vranje**, Yugo.
44/B4 **Vranje**, Yugo.
39/H1 **Vranjska Banja**, Yugo.
40/F4 **Vranjska Banja**, Yugo.
27/L4 **Vranov nad Teplou**, Slvk.
39/G2 **Vrapčište**, Macd.
40/E5 **Vrapčište**, Macd.
39/H1 **Vratsa**, Bul.
41/F4 **Vratsa**, Bul.
44/B4 **Vratsa**, Bul.
40/C3 **Vrbas** (riv.), Bosn.
40/D3 **Vrbas**, Yugo.
80/E2 **Vrede**, SAfr.
80/P13 **Vredefort**, SAfr.
28/D4 **Vreden**, Ger.
80/B4 **Vredenburg**, SAfr.
80/K10 **Vredenburg**, SAfr.
82/C7 **Vredenburg**, SAfr.
80/B3 **Vredendal**, SAfr.
82/C7 **Vredendal**, SAfr.
31/D4 **Vresse-sur-Semois**, Belg.
33/L4 **Vrhnika**, Slov.
64/G3 **Vriddhāchalam**, India
28/D2 **Vries**, Neth.
28/D4 **Vriezenveen**, Neth.
26/B5 **Vrin** (riv.), Fr.
53/L3 **Vrindāban**, India
62/C2 **Vrindāban**, India
40/E4 **Vrnjačka Banja**, Yugo.
39/K3 **Vrondádhos**, Gre.
44/C5 **Vrondádhos**, Gre.
40/E3 **Vršac**, Yugo.
44/B3 **Vršac**, Yugo.
80/D2 **Vryburg**, SAfr.
82/D6 **Vryburg**, SAfr.
81/E2 **Vryheid**, SAfr.
82/F6 **Vryheid**, SAfr.
27/K4 **Vsetín**, Czh.
85/E5 **Vsevidof** (mt.), Ak,US
43/V6 **Vsevolozhsk**, Rus.
27/K4 **Vtáčnik** (peak), Slvk.
39/G1 **Vučitrn**, Yugo.
40/E4 **Vučitrn**, Yugo.
28/C5 **Vught**, Neth.
40/D3 **Vukovar**, Cro.
90/E3 **Vulcan**, Ab,Can
41/F3 **Vulcan**, Rom.
44/B3 **Vulcan**, Rom.
38/D3 **Vulcano** (isl.), It.
41/F4 **Vŭlchedrŭm**, Bul.
41/H4 **Vŭlchi Dol**, Bul.
38/B1 **Vulci** (ruins), It.
63/J4 **Vu Liet**, Viet.
65/D2 **Vu Liet**, Viet.
63/J5 **Vung Tau**, Viet.
65/D4 **Vung Tau**, Viet.
68/G7 **Vunisea**, Fiji
42/C2 **Vuoggatjålme**, Swe.
20/G2 **Vuollerim**, Swe.
42/D2 **Vuollerim**, Swe.
42/E1 **Vuotso**, Fin.
39/K1 **Vŭrbitsa**, Bul.
41/H4 **Vŭrbitsa**, Bul.
39/H1 **Vŭrshets**, Bul.
41/F4 **Vŭrshets**, Bul.
53/K4 **Vyāra**, India
62/B3 **Vyāra**, India
19/H3 **Vyatka**, Rus.
43/L4 **Vyatka**, Rus.
43/L4 **Vyatka** (riv.), Rus.
46/E4 **Vyatka**, Rus.
46/F4 **Vyatka** (riv.), Rus.
43/L4 **Vyatka Obl.**, Rus.
43/L4 **Vyatskiye Polyany**, Rus.
47/P5 **Vyazemskiy**, Rus.
55/L2 **Vyazemskiy**, Rus.
18/G3 **Vyaz'ma**, Rus.
42/G5 **Vyaz'ma**, Rus.
44/E1 **Vyaz'ma**, Rus.
46/D4 **Vyaz'ma**, Rus.
18/F2 **Vyborg**, Rus.
20/J3 **Vyborg**, Rus.
42/F3 **Vyborg**, Rus.
43/V7 **Vyborg**, Rus.
46/C3 **Vyborg**, Rus.
43/K3 **Vychegda** (riv.), Rus.
46/E3 **Vychegda** (riv.), Rus.
27/H3 **Východočeský** (reg.), Czh.
33/M2 **Vychodočeský** (reg.), Czh.
27/L4 **Východoslovenský** (reg.), Slvk.
42/G3 **Vygozero** (lake), Rus.
27/M4 **Vyhorlat** (peak), Slvk.
44/B2 **Vyhorlat** (peak), Slvk.
42/J5 **Vyksa**, Rus.
45/G1 **Vyksa**, Rus.
43/L3 **Vym'** (riv.), Rus.
42/F4 **Vyritsa**, Rus.
24/C1 **Vyrnwy** (riv.), Wal,UK
18/G3 **Vyshniy Volochek**, Rus.
42/G4 **Vyshniy Volochek**, Rus.
46/D4 **Vyshniy Volochek**, Rus.
27/J4 **Vyškov**, Czh.
33/M2 **Vyškov**, Czh.
40/D1 **Vyškovce nad Ipl'om**, Slvk.
41/L2 **Vysokopol'ye**, Ukr.
44/B1 **Vysokoye**, Bela.
18/G2 **Vytegra**, Rus.
46/D3 **Vytegra**, Rus.
45/G1 **Vyyezdnoye**, Rus.
47/Q5 **Vzmor'ye**, Rus.

W

76/E5 **Wa**, Gha.
79/E4 **Wa**, Gha.
37/G2 **Waal**, Ger.
26/C3 **Waal** (riv.), Neth.
28/C5 **Waal** (riv.), Neth.
28/C6 **Waalre**, Neth.
28/C5 **Waalwijk**, Neth.
28/A6 **Waarschoot**, Belg.
30/C1 **Waarschoot**, Belg.
90/E1 **Wabasca** (riv.), Ab,Can
86/E3 **Wabasca** (riv.), Ab,Can
90/E2 **Wabasca**, Ab,Can
94/C3 **Wabash**, In,US
94/C4 **Wabash** (riv.), Il, In,US
89/J4 **Wabash** (riv.), Il, In,US
94/C3 **Wabash** (riv.), Il, In,US
29/G6 **Wabern**, Ger.
91/K3 **Wabigoon** (lake), On,Can
91/J2 **Wabowden**, Mb,Can
27/K2 **Wąbrzeźno**, Pol.
59/D4 **Wabu** (lake), China
58/G6 **Wabu**, SKor.
57/L9 **Wachi**, Japan
28/A6 **Wachtebeke**, Belg.
30/C1 **Wachtebeke**, Belg.
28/D6 **Wachtendonk**, Ger.
31/H4 **Wackernheim**, Ger.
89/G5 **Waco**, Tx,US
93/H5 **Waco**, Tx,US
96/D4 **Waco**, Tx,US
91/K4 **Waconia**, Mn,US
57/J7 **Wada**, Japan
52/B6 **Wad al Ḩaddād**, Sudan
73/D3 **Wadbilliga Nat'l Park**, Austl.
76/J2 **Waddān**, Libya
26/C2 **Waddenzee** (sound), Neth.
28/C2 **Waddenzee** (sound), Neth.
90/B3 **Waddington** (peak), BC,Can
86/D3 **Waddington** (mtn.), BC,Can
23/F4 **Waddington**, Eng,UK
23/H5 **Waddington**, Eng,UK
28/B4 **Waddinxveen**, Neth.
72/D4 **Waddy** (pt.), Austl.
24/B5 **Wadebridge**, Eng,UK
86/F3 **Wadena**, Sk,Can
88/F1 **Wadena**, Sk,Can
91/H3 **Wadena**, Sk,Can
91/K4 **Wadena**, Mn,US
33/H3 **Wädenswil**, Swi.
37/E3 **Wädenswil**, Swi.
26/D4 **Wadern**, Ger.
31/F4 **Wadern**, Ger.
33/G2 **Wadern**, Ger.
29/F5 **Wadersloh**, Ger.
31/F5 **Wadgassen**, Ger.
52/B5 **Wad Ḩāmid**, Sudan
25/G4 **Wadhurst**, Eng,UK
49/D4 **Wādī As Sīr**, Jor.
38/A4 **Wādī Az Zarqā'**, Tun.
77/M3 **Wādī Ḩalfā'**, Sudan
49/D4 **Wādī Mūsá**, Jor.
98/H5 **Wading River**, NY,US
52/B6 **Wad Medanī**, Sudan
77/M5 **Wad Medanī**, Sudan
27/K4 **Wadowice**, Pol.
99/Q15 **Wadsworth**, Il,US
58/E5 **Waegwan**, SKor.
55/J4 **Wafangdian**, China
58/B3 **Wafangdian**, China
59/E3 **Wafangdian**, China
61/F1 **Wafangdian**, China
74/F4 **Wagagai** (peak), Ugan.
77/M7 **Wagagai** (peak), Ugan.
63/G4 **Wagaru**, Burma
26/E2 **Wagenfeld**, Ger.
29/F3 **Wagenfeld-Hasslingen**, Ger.
28/C5 **Wageningen**, Neth.
84/J3 **Wager** (bay), Can.
86/G2 **Wager** (bay), NW,Can
68/D8 **Wagga Wagga**, Austl.
71/H7 **Wagga Wagga**, Austl.
73/C2 **Wagga Wagga**, Austl.
70/B6 **Wagin**, Austl.
37/E3 **Wägitalersee** (lake), Swi.
33/L3 **Wagna**, Aus.
27/J2 **Wągrowiec**, Pol.
44/A1 **Wągrowiec**, Pol.
53/K2 **Wāh**, Pak.
67/G4 **Wahai**, Indo.
88/V12 **Wahiawa**, Hi,US
36/D4 **Wahlern**, Swi.
91/J5 **Wahoo**, Ne,US
93/H2 **Wahoo**, Ne,US
89/G2 **Wahpeton**, ND,US
91/J4 **Wahpeton**, ND,US
26/F2 **Wahrenholz**, Ger.
29/H3 **Wahrenholz**, Ger.
92/D3 **Wah Wah** (range), Ut,US
62/B4 **Wai**, India
88/S10 **Waialee**, Hi,US
88/V12 **Waialee**, Hi,US
88/S10 **Waialua**, Hi,US
88/V12 **Waialua**, Hi,US
88/V13 **Waianae**, Hi,US
59/D2 **Waibamiao**, China
26/G4 **Waidhaus**, Ger.
33/L2 **Waidhofen an der Thaya**, Aus.
27/H5 **Waidhofen an der Ybbs**, Aus.
33/L3 **Waidhofen an der Ybbs**, Aus.
40/B2 **Waidhofen an der Ybbs**, Aus.
67/H3 **Waigeo** (isl.), Indo.
68/C4 **Waigeo** (isl.), Indo.
67/E5 **Waikabubak**, Indo.
88/W12 **Waikane**, Hi,US
71/R11 **Waikari**, N.Z.
73/A2 **Waikerie**, Austl.
88/T10 **Waikiki**, Hi,US
88/U11 **Waikoloa Village**, Hi,US
88/T10 **Wailuku**, Hi,US
88/W13 **Waimanalo**, Hi,US
88/W13 **Waimanalo Beach**, Hi,US
71/R11 **Waimate**, N.Z.
88/S10 **Waimea**, Hi,US
88/V12 **Waimea** (falls), Hi,US
31/F3 **Waimes**, Belg.
95/R10 **Wainfleet**, On,Can
23/J5 **Wainfleet All Saints**, Eng,UK
62/C3 **Waingangā** (riv.), India
67/F5 **Waingapu**, Indo.
86/E3 **Wainwright**, Ab,Can
90/F2 **Wainwright**, Ab,Can
85/F1 **Wainwright**, Ak,US
88/S10 **Waipahu**, Hi,US
88/V13 **Waipahu**, Hi,US
88/U10 **Waipio**, Hi,US
88/V13 **Waipio Acres**, Hi,US
71/S11 **Waipukurau**, N.Z.
71/S10 **Wairoa**, N.Z.
71/R10 **Waitara**, N.Z.
71/R10 **Waitemata**, N.Z.
69/Z17 **Waiyevu**, Fiji
57/E2 **Wajima**, Japan
77/P7 **Wajir**, Kenya
67/G4 **Waka** (cape), Indo.
56/D3 **Wakasa**, Japan
56/D3 **Wakasa** (bay), Japan
91/G2 **Wakaw**, Sk,Can
47/P6 **Wakayama**, Japan
55/M5 **Wakayama**, Japan
56/D3 **Wakayama**, Japan
56/D4 **Wakayama** (pref.), Japan
57/L10 **Wakayama** (pref.), Japan
68/F3 **Wake** (isl.), PacUS
93/H3 **Wakeeney**, Ks,US
96/D2 **Wakeeney**, Ks,US
23/G4 **Wakefield**, Eng,UK
94/B2 **Wakefield**, Mi,US
60/B5 **Wakema**, Burma
63/G4 **Wakema**, Burma
56/D3 **Waki**, Japan
47/Q5 **Wakkanai**, Japan
55/N2 **Wakkanai**, Japan
57/H7 **Wakō**, Japan
73/C2 **Wakool**, Austl.
94/D1 **Wakwayowkastic** (riv.), On,Can
41/G3 **Walachia** (range), Rom.
41/G3 **Walachia** (reg.), Rom.
18/E3 **Wałbrzych**, Pol.
27/J3 **Wałbrzych**, Pol.
27/J3 **Wałbrzych** (prov.), Pol.
46/B4 **Wałbrzych**, Pol.
25/E4 **Walbury** (hill), Eng,UK
73/D1 **Walcha**, Austl.
37/H2 **Walchensee** (lake), Ger.
28/A5 **Walcheren** (isl.), Neth.
26/C3 **Walcourt**, Belg.
30/D3 **Walcourt**, Belg.
32/F1 **Walcourt**, Belg.
27/J2 **Wałcz**, Pol.
37/E3 **Wald**, Swi.
31/F4 **Waldbillig**, Lux.
31/G2 **Waldbreitbach**, Ger.
31/G2 **Waldbröl**, Ger.
37/F2 **Waldburg**, Ger.
29/G6 **Waldeck**, Ger.
93/F2 **Walden**, Co,US
36/D3 **Waldenburg**, Swi.
31/G3 **Waldesch**, Ger.
90/G2 **Waldheim**, Sk,Can
36/D2 **Waldighofen**, Fr.
26/D4 **Waldkirch**, Ger.
33/G2 **Waldkirch**, Ger.
36/D1 **Waldkirch**, Ger.
26/G4 **Waldmünchen**, Ger.
31/F4 **Waldrach**, Ger.
26/G4 **Waldsassen**, Ger.
37/E2 **Waldshut-Tiengen**, Ger.
27/H4 **Waldviertel** (reg.), Aus.
33/L2 **Waldviertel** (reg.), Aus.
67/F4 **Walea** (str.), Indo.
67/F4 **Waleabahi** (isl.), Indo.
37/F3 **Walensee** (lake), Swi.
37/F3 **Walenstadt**, Swi.
87/H2 **Wales** (isl.), NW,Can
24/B3 **Wales**, UK
18/C3 **Wales**, UK
85/E2 **Wales**, Ak,US
99/P13 **Wales**, Wi,US
31/F4 **Walferdange**, Lux.
71/H6 **Walgett**, Austl.
73/D1 **Walgett**, Austl.
83/T **Walgreen** (coast), Ant.
91/J3 **Walhalla**, ND,US
97/H3 **Walhalla**, SC,US
77/L8 **Walikale**, Zaire
82/E1 **Walikale**, Zaire
80/L11 **Walker** (bay), SAfr.
92/C3 **Walker** (lake), Nv,US
92/C3 **Walker** (riv.), Nv,US
71/H4 **Walkerston**, Austl.
72/C3 **Walkerston**, Austl.
94/D2 **Walkerton**, On,Can
90/E4 **Wallace**, Id,US
94/D3 **Wallaceburg**, On,Can
99/H6 **Wallaceburg**, On,Can
23/E5 **Wallasey**, Eng,UK
73/C2 **Walla Walla**, Austl.
86/E4 **Walla Walla**, Wa,US
88/C2 **Walla Walla**, Wa,US
90/D4 **Walla Walla**, Wa,US
99/F6 **Walled** (lake), Mi,US
58/G7 **Walled City**, SKor.
99/F6 **Walled Lake**, Mi,US
26/E2 **Wallenhorst**, Ger.
29/F4 **Wallenhorst**, Ger.
33/M3 **Wallern im Burgenland**, Aus.
30/C3 **Wallers**, Fr.
25/E3 **Wallingford**, Eng,UK
69/H6 **Wallis** (isls.), Wall.
68/G6 **Wallis & Futuna** (terr.), Fr.
37/E3 **Wallisellen**, Swi.
90/D4 **Wallowa** (mts.), Or,US
23/G2 **Wallsend**, Eng,UK
72/C4 **Wallumbilla**, Austl.
23/E3 **Walney, Isle of** (isl.), Eng,UK
92/E4 **Walnut Canyon Nat'l Mon.**, Az,US
99/K11 **Walnut Creek**, Ca,US
99/L10 **Walnut Grove**, Ca,US
98/E5 **Walnutport**, Pa,US
93/K3 **Walnut Ridge**, Ar,US
97/F2 **Walnut Ridge**, Ar,US
99/G6 **Walpole I. Ind. Res.**, On,Can
85/F4 **Walrus** (isls.), Ak,US
24/E1 **Walsall**, Eng,UK
88/F4 **Walsenburg**, Co,US
93/F3 **Walsenburg**, Co,US
96/B2 **Walsenburg**, Co,US
87/K2 **Walsingham** (cape), NW,Can
25/G1 **Walsingham**, Eng,UK
26/E2 **Walsrode**, Ger.
29/G3 **Walsrode**, Ger.
37/G2 **Waltenhofen**, Ger.
97/H3 **Walterboro**, SC,US
19/P6 **Waltham Abbey**, Eng,UK
19/N7 **Waltham Forest** (bor.), Eng,UK
25/G3 **Waltham Holy Cross**, Eng,UK
23/F4 **Walton-le-Dale**, Eng,UK
25/F4 **Walton on Thames**, Eng,UK
25/H3 **Walton on the Naze**, Eng,UK
29/E5 **Waltrop**, Ger.
82/B5 **Walvisbaai**, SAfr.
99/N14 **Walworth**, Wi,US
99/P14 **Walworth** (co.), Wi,US
37/F3 **Walzenhausen**, Swi.
82/C3 **Wama**, Ang.
76/G6 **Wamba**, Nga.
77/L7 **Wamba**, Zaire
28/C5 **Wamel**, Neth.
23/E2 **Wampool** (riv.), Eng,UK
90/G5 **Wamsutter**, Wy,US
92/F2 **Wamsutter**, Wy,US
59/D5 **Wan** (riv.), China
71/Q11 **Wanaka**, N.Z.
98/F4 **Wanaque**, NJ,US
98/F4 **Wanaque** (res.), NJ,US
55/L2 **Wanda** (mts.), China
60/C3 **Wanding**, China
63/G3 **Wanding**, China
58/D5 **Wando**, SKor.
72/C4 **Wandoan**, Austl.
19/N7 **Wandsworth** (bor.), Eng,UK
29/H6 **Wanfried**, Ger.
60/C5 **Wang** (riv.), Thai.
63/G4 **Wang** (riv.), Thai.
65/B2 **Wang** (riv.), Thai.
71/S10 **Wanganui**, N.Z.
71/H7 **Wangaratta**, Austl.
73/C3 **Wangaratta**, Austl.
59/C3 **Wangdu**, China
26/E5 **Wangen**, Ger.
33/H3 **Wangen**, Ger.
37/F2 **Wangen**, Ger.
36/D3 **Wangen an der Aare**, Swi.
36/D3 **Wangen bei Olten**, Swi.
29/E1 **Wangerooge** (isl.), Ger.
67/F6 **Wanggamet** (peak), Indo.
58/A2 **Wanghai** (peak), China
59/E2 **Wanghai Shan** (peak), China
63/G6 **Wang Hip** (peak), Thai.
65/B4 **Wang Hip** (peak), Thai.
37/E3 **Wängi**, Swi.
59/D5 **Wangjiang**, China
61/H2 **Wangjiang**, China
55/K2 **Wangkui**, China
65/E1 **Wangmao**, China
60/E3 **Wangmo**, China
59/E5 **Wangpan** (bay), China
59/L9 **Wangpan** (bay), China
61/J2 **Wangpan** (sea), China
55/K3 **Wangqing**, China
63/H4 **Wang Thong**, Thai.
63/G4 **Wān Hwè-ün**, Burma
67/F4 **Wani** (peak), Indo.
55/J4 **Wanjialing**, China
37/H2 **Wank** (peak), Ger.
63/K4 **Wanning**, China
57/M9 **Wanouchi**, Japan
59/C2 **Wanquan**, China
61/F5 **Wanquan** (riv.), China
59/B4 **Wanrong**, China
23/G1 **Wansbeck** (riv.), Eng,UK
19/P7 **Wanstead**, Eng,UK
25/E3 **Wantage**, Eng,UK
54/F5 **Wanxian**, China
61/F2 **Wanxian**, China
31/E2 **Wanze**, Belg.
94/C3 **Wapakoneta**, Oh,US
91/G2 **Wapawekka** (lake), Sk,Can
90/D2 **Wapiti** (riv.), Ab, BC,Can
67/J4 **Wapoga** (riv.), Indo.
93/K3 **Wappapello** (lake), Mo,US
91/K5 **Wapsipinicon** (riv.), Ia,US
93/J2 **Wapsipinicon** (riv.), Ia,US
94/A3 **Wapsipinicon** (riv.), Ia,US
57/H7 **Warabi**, Japan
62/C4 **Warangal**, India
73/C4 **Waratah**, Austl.
25/F2 **Warboys**, Eng,UK
26/E3 **Warburg**, Ger.
29/G6 **Warburg**, Ger.
70/F5 **Warburton** (cr.), Austl.
64/B2 **Warburton**, Pak.
31/F3 **Warche** (riv.), Belg.
71/R11 **Ward**, N.Z.
25/G4 **Warden** (pt.), UK
29/F2 **Wardenburg**, Ger.
62/C3 **Wardha**, India
23/F3 **Ward's Stone** (mtn.), Eng,UK
25/F3 **Ware**, Eng,UK
26/B3 **Waregem**, Belg.
30/C2 **Waregem**, Belg.
24/D5 **Wareham**, Eng,UK
31/E2 **Waremme**, Belg.
26/G2 **Waren**, Ger.
29/E5 **Warendorf**, Ger.
98/F6 **Waretown**, NJ,US
28/D2 **Warffum**, Neth.
25/F3 **Wargrave**, Eng,UK
73/D1 **Warialda**, Austl.
63/H4 **Warin Chamrap**, Thai.
65/D3 **Warin Chamrap**, Thai.
22/B3 **Waringstown**, NI,UK
23/F1 **Wark**, Eng,UK
27/L3 **Warka**, Pol.
71/R10 **Warkworth**, N.Z.
24/D2 **Warley**, Eng,UK
25/G3 **Warley**, Eng,UK
19/N8 **Warlingham**, Eng,UK
91/G2 **Warman**, Sk,Can
80/B3 **Warmbad**, Namb.
80/E2 **Warmbad**, SAfr.
29/G6 **Warmebach** (riv.), Ger.
29/H5 **Warme Bode** (riv.), Ger.
28/B3 **Warmenhuizen**, Neth.
30/D5 **Warmeriville**, Fr.
27/K1 **Warmia** (reg.), Pol.
24/D4 **Warminster**, Eng,UK
98/E5 **Warminster**, Pa,US
90/C5 **Warner** (mts.), Ca,US
92/B2 **Warner** (mts.), Ca,US
89/K5 **Warner Robins**, Ga,US
97/H3 **Warner Robins**, Ga,US
26/G2 **Warnow** (riv.), Ger.
28/D4 **Warnsveld**, Neth.
67/K5 **Waropko**, Indo.
70/E4 **Warrabri**, Austl.
70/F5 **Warrandirinna** (lake), Austl.
73/G5 **Warrandybe**, Austl.
68/D7 **Warrego** (riv.), Austl.
71/H5 **Warrego** (range), Austl.
71/H5 **Warrego** (riv.), Austl.
72/B4 **Warrego** (range), Austl.
72/B4 **Warrego** (riv.), Austl.
73/C1 **Warrego** (riv.), Austl.
71/H6 **Warren**, Austl.
73/C1 **Warren**, Austl.
85/M2 **Warren** (pt.), NW,Can
93/J4 **Warren**, Ar,US
96/E3 **Warren**, Ar,US
89/K3 **Warren**, Mi,US
94/D3 **Warren**, Mi,US
99/F6 **Warren**, Mi,US
91/J3 **Warren**, Mn,US
98/E4 **Warren** (co.), NJ,US
89/K3 **Warren**, Oh,US
94/D3 **Warren**, Oh,US
89/L3 **Warren**, Pa,US
94/E3 **Warren**, Pa,US
22/B3 **Warrenpoint**, NI,UK
93/J3 **Warrensburg**, Mo,US
96/E2 **Warrensburg**, Mo,US
80/D3 **Warrenton**, SAfr.
94/E4 **Warrenton**, Va,US
97/J2 **Warrenton**, Va,US
99/P16 **Warrenville**, Il,US
76/G6 **Warri**, Nga.
23/F5 **Warrington**, Eng,UK
97/G4 **Warrington**, Fl,US
70/G7 **Warrnambool**, Austl.
73/B3 **Warrnambool**, Austl.
91/K3 **Warroad**, Mn,US
73/D1 **Warrumbungle Nat'l Park**, Austl.
18/F3 **Warsaw** (cap.), Pol.
46/C4 **Warsaw** (cap.), Pol.
94/C3 **Warsaw**, In,US
93/J3 **Warsaw**, Mo,US
96/E2 **Warsaw**, Mo,US
27/L3 **Warsawa** (prov.), Pol.
27/L2 **Warsaw** (Warszawa) (cap.), Pol.
44/B1 **Warsaw** (Warszawa) (cap.), Pol.
27/H5 **Warscheneck** (peak), Aus.
40/B2 **Warscheneck** (peak), Aus.
23/G5 **Warslow**, Eng,UK
23/G5 **Warsop**, Eng,UK
29/F6 **Warstein**, Ger.
27/L2 **Warszawa** (Warsaw) (cap.), Pol.
44/B1 **Warszawa** (Warsaw) (cap.), Pol.
27/H2 **Warta** (riv.), Pol.
44/A1 **Warta** (riv.), Pol.
71/J5 **Warwick**, Austl.
72/D5 **Warwick**, Austl.
73/E1 **Warwick**, Austl.
25/E2 **Warwick**, Eng,UK
98/F4 **Warwick**, NY,US
95/G3 **Warwick**, RI,US
25/E2 **Warwickshire** (co.), Eng,UK
90/F5 **Wasatch** (range), Id, Ut,US
88/D4 **Wasatch** (range), Id,Ut,US
92/E2 **Wasatch** (range), Id,Ut,US
92/C4 **Wasco**, Ca,US
91/K4 **Waseca**, Mn,US
86/F1 **Washburn** (lake), NW,Can
23/G4 **Washburn** (riv.), Eng,UK
91/M3 **Washi** (lake), On,Can
23/H5 **Washingborough**, Eng,UK
23/G2 **Washington**, Eng,UK
90/C4 **Washington** (state), US
84/K6 **Washington** (cap.), US
86/D4 **Washington** (state), US
88/B2 **Washington** (state), US
89/L4 **Washington** (cap.), DC,US
94/E4 **Washington** (cap.), DC,US
97/J2 **Washington** (cap.), DC,US
98/J8 **Washington** (cap.), DC,US
91/L5 **Washington**, Il,US
93/K2 **Washington**, Il,US
94/B3 **Washington**, Il,US
94/C4 **Washington**, In,US
97/G2 **Washington**, In,US
97/J3 **Washington**, NC,US
89/M3 **Washington** (mt.), NH,US
95/G2 **Washington** (peak), NH,US
94/D3 **Washington**, Pa,US
99/C2 **Washington** (lake), Wa,US
94/C2 **Washington** (isl.), Wi,US
98/K7 **Washington-Baltimore** (int'l arpt.), Md,US
94/D4 **Washington Court House** (Washington), Oh,US
97/H2 **Washington Court House** (Washington), Oh,US
98/J8 **Washington National** (int'l arpt.), DC,US
69/K4 **Washington** (Teraina) (atoll), Kiri.
93/H4 **Washita** (riv.), Ok, Tx,US
99/E7 **Washtenaw** (co.), Mi,US
23/J6 **Wash, The** (bay), Eng,UK
25/G1 **Wash, The** (bay), Eng,UK
27/M2 **Wasilków**, Pol.
85/J3 **Wasilla**, Ak,US
86/B2 **Wasilla**, Ak,US
51/F3 **Wāsiţ** (gov.), Iraq
89/L1 **Waskaganish**, Qu,Can
94/E1 **Waskaganish** (Rupert House), Can
87/J3 **Waskaganish** (Rupert House), Qu,Can
85/G4 **Waskey** (mt.), Ak,US
103/F3 **Waspam**, Nic.
31/G6 **Wasselonne**, Fr.
37/E4 **Wassen**, Swi.
28/B4 **Wassenaar**, Neth.
28/D6 **Wassenberg**, Ger.
31/F1 **Wassenberg**, Ger.
31/F4 **Wasserbillig**, Lux.
37/G1 **Wasserburg**, Ger.
26/E3 **Wasserkuppe** (peak), Ger.
33/H1 **Wasserkuppe** (peak), Ger.
88/C4 **Wassuk** (range), Nv,US
36/A1 **Wassy**, Fr.
23/E3 **Wast Water** (lake), Eng,UK
94/E1 **Waswanipi** (lake), Qu,Can
67/E4 **Watampone**, Indo.
57/M10 **Watarai**, Japan
57/F2 **Watarase** (riv.), Japan
57/G1 **Watari**, Japan
24/C4 **Watchet**, Eng,UK
25/E3 **Watchfield**, Eng,UK
25/G2 **Waterbeach**, Eng,UK
89/M3 **Waterbury**, Ct,US
95/F3 **Waterbury**, Ct,US
95/Q9 **Waterdown**, On,Can
97/H3 **Wateree** (dam), SC,US
18/C3 **Waterford**, Ire.
21/B4 **Waterford**, Ire.
94/D3 **Waterford**, Mi,US
99/F6 **Waterford**, Mi,US
99/P14 **Waterford**, Wi,US
98/F6 **Waterford Works**, NJ,US
24/A6 **Watergate** (bay), Eng,UK
91/J2 **Waterhen** (lake), Mb,Can
90/F2 **Waterhen** (riv.), Sk,Can
30/D2 **Waterloo**, Belg.
32/F1 **Waterloo**, Belg.
94/D3 **Waterloo**, On,Can
89/H3 **Waterloo**, Ia,US
91/K5 **Waterloo**, Ia,US
93/J2 **Waterloo**, Ia,US
94/A3 **Waterloo**, Ia,US
93/K3 **Waterloo**, Il,US
94/B4 **Waterloo**, Il,US
97/F2 **Waterloo**, Il,US
30/D2 **Waterloo Battlesite** (1815), Belg.
25/E5 **Waterlooville**, Eng,UK
30/D2 **Watermael-Boitsfort**, Belg.
88/D2 **Waterton-Glacier Nat'l Park**, Ab,Can
90/E3 **Waterton Lakes Nat'l Park**, Ab,Can
86/E4 **Waterton Lakes Nat'l Park**, Ab, BC,Can
87/J4 **Watertown**, NY,US
89/L3 **Watertown**, NY,US
94/F3 **Watertown**, NY,US
86/G4 **Watertown**, SD,US
89/G3 **Watertown**, SD,US
91/J4 **Watertown**, SD,US
91/L5 **Watertown**, Wi,US
93/K2 **Watertown**, Wi,US
94/B3 **Watertown**, Wi,US
81/E2 **Waterval-Bo**, SAfr.
21/G8 **Waterville**, Ire.
95/G2 **Waterville**, Me,US
90/C4 **Waterville**, Wa,US
28/A6 **Watervliet**, Belg.
19/M7 **Watford**, Eng,UK
25/F3 **Watford**, Eng,UK
91/H4 **Watford City**, ND,US
23/G5 **Wath-upon-Dearne**, Eng,UK
104/C1 **Watling** (San Salvador) (isl.), Bahm.
25/F3 **Watlington**, Eng,UK
60/C5 **Wat Mahathat**, Thai.
65/B2 **Wat Mahathat**, Thai.
93/H4 **Watonga**, Ok,US
96/D3 **Watonga**, Ok,US
67/G3 **Watowato** (peak), Indo.
60/D5 **Wat Phra Si Ratana Mahathat**, Thai.
65/D3 **Wat Phu**, Laos
86/F3 **Watrous**, Sk,Can
88/E1 **Watrous**, Sk,Can
91/G3 **Watrous**, Sk,Can
77/L7 **Watsa**, Zaire
94/C3 **Watseka**, Il,US
86/D2 **Watson Lake**, Yk,Can
92/B3 **Watsonville**, Ca,US
30/B2 **Watten**, Fr.
31/H4 **Wattenheim**, Ger.
33/J3 **Wattens**, Aus.
30/C2 **Wattignies**, Fr.
25/G1 **Watton**, Eng,UK
30/C2 **Wattrelos**, Fr.
37/F3 **Wattwil**, Swi.
60/D5 **Wat Xieng Thong**, Laos
65/C2 **Wat Xieng Thong**, Laos
68/D5 **Wau**, PNG
73/E1 **Wauchope**, Austl.
97/H5 **Wauchula**, Fl,US
99/P15 **Wauconda**, Il,US
70/C4 **Waukarlycarly** (lake), Austl.
89/J3 **Waukegan**, Il,US
91/M5 **Waukegan**, Il,US
93/L2 **Waukegan**, Il,US
94/C3 **Waukegan**, Il,US
99/Q15 **Waukegan**, Il,US
89/J3 **Waukesha**, Wi,US
91/L5 **Waukesha**, Wi,US
94/B3 **Waukesha**, Wi,US
99/P13 **Waukesha**, Wi,US
99/P14 **Waukesha** (co.), Wi,US
99/B3 **Wauna**, Wa,US
24/C3 **Waun Fâch** (mtn.), Wal,UK
24/C1 **Waun Oer** (mtn.), UK
91/L4 **Waupaca**, Wi,US
94/B2 **Waupaca**, Wi,US
91/L5 **Waupun**, Wi,US
94/B3 **Waupun**, Wi,US
93/H4 **Waurika**, Ok,US
96/D3 **Waurika**, Ok,US
86/H4 **Wausau**, Wi,US
89/J3 **Wausau**, Wi,US
91/L4 **Wausau**, Wi,US
94/B2 **Wausau**, Wi,US
94/C3 **Wauseon**, Oh,US
99/P13 **Wauwatosa**, Wi,US
25/H2 **Waveney** (riv.), Eng,UK
23/E2 **Waver** (riv.), Eng,UK
72/A5 **Waverley Downs**, Austl.
73/G5 **Waverly**, Austl.
94/C4 **Waverly**, Tn,US
97/G2 **Waverly**, Tn,US
30/D2 **Wavre**, Belg.
30/B2 **Wavrin**, Fr.
77/L6 **Wāw**, Sudan
87/H4 **Wawa**, On,Can
89/K2 **Wawa**, On,Can

94/C2 **Wawa**, On,Can
76/F6 **Wawa**, Nga.
103/E3 **Wawa** (riv.), Nic.
94/E1 **Wawagosic** (riv.), Qu,Can
103/E3 **Wawasang** (mtn.), Nic.
101/F1 **Waxahachie**, Tx,US
93/H4 **Waxahachie**, Tx,US
96/D3 **Waxahachie**, Tx,US
31/F3 **Waxweiler**, Ger.
89/K5 **Waycross**, Ga,US
97/H4 **Waycross**, Ga,US
99/P16 **Wayne**, Il,US
99/F7 **Wayne**, Mi,US
99/F7 **Wayne** (co.), Mi,US
91/J5 **Wayne**, Ne,US
93/H2 **Wayne**, Ne,US
98/F5 **Wayne**, NJ,US
98/E5 **Wayne**, Pa,US
97/H3 **Waynesboro**, Ga,US
97/F4 **Waynesboro**, Ms,US
94/E4 **Waynesboro**, Pa,US
94/E4 **Waynesboro**, Va,US
97/J2 **Waynesboro**, Va,US
93/J3 **Waynesville**, Mo,US
96/E2 **Waynesville**, Mo,US
97/H3 **Waynesville**, NC,US
30/C3 **Waziers**, Fr.
64/C1 **Wazīrābād**, Pak.
57/L10 **Wazuka**, Japan
26/K2 **Wda** (riv.), Pol.
79/F3 **W du Niger Nat'l Park**, Afr.
76/F5 **W du Niger Nat'l Park**, Ben.
66/A2 **We** (isl.), Indo.
69/V12 **Wé**, NCal.
25/G4 **Weald, The** (grsld.), Eng,UK
23/G2 **Wear** (riv.), Eng,UK
23/F2 **Wear Head**, Eng,UK
93/H4 **Weatherford**, Ok,US
96/D3 **Weatherford**, Ok,US
101/F1 **Weatherford**, Tx,US
93/H4 **Weatherford**, Tx,US
96/D3 **Weatherford**, Tx,US
23/F5 **Weaver** (riv.), Eng,UK
90/C5 **Weaverville**, Ca,US
92/B2 **Weaverville**, Ca,US
93/G4 **Webb** (A.F.B.), Tx,US
96/C3 **Webb** (A.F.B.), Tx,US
91/J4 **Webster**, SD,US
91/K5 **Webster City**, Ia,US
93/J2 **Webster City**, Ia,US
77/M7 **Webuye**, Kenya
83/W **Weddell** (sea), Ant.
73/B3 **Wedderburn**, Austl.
73/C2 **Weddin Mountains Nat'l Park**, Austl.
26/E2 **Wedel**, Ger.
29/G1 **Wedel**, Ger.
29/G3 **Wedemark**, Ger.
24/D4 **Wedmore**, Eng,UK
24/D1 **Wednesbury**, Eng,UK
24/D1 **Wednesfield**, Eng,UK
90/C5 **Weed**, Ca,US
92/B2 **Weed**, Ca,US
25/E2 **Weedon Bec**, Eng,UK
97/H4 **Weeki Wachee Springs**, Fl,US
24/B5 **Week Saint Mary**, Eng,UK
28/D4 **Weerselo**, Neth.
28/C6 **Weert**, Neth.
31/E1 **Weert**, Neth.
37/F3 **Weesen**, Swi.
28/C4 **Weesp**, Neth.
73/D1 **Wee Waa**, Austl.
28/D6 **Wegberg**, Ger.
31/F1 **Wegberg**, Ger.
37/E3 **Weggis**, Swi.
27/L1 **Węgorzewo**, Pol.
27/M2 **Węgrów**, Pol.
44/B1 **Węgrów**, Pol.
27/G4 **Wegscheid**, Ger.
33/K2 **Wegscheid**, Ger.
37/E1 **Wehingen**, Ger.
36/D2 **Wehr**, Ger.
36/D2 **Wehra** (riv.), Ger.
29/G6 **Wehre** (riv.), Ger.
55/H4 **Wei** (riv.), China
55/H3 **Weichang**, China
26/G3 **Weida**, Ger.
33/K1 **Weida**, Ger.
26/G4 **Weiden**, Ger.
33/K2 **Weiden**, Ger.
31/H5 **Weidenthal**, Ger.
55/H4 **Weifang**, China
59/D3 **Weifang**, China
55/J4 **Weihai**, China
58/B4 **Weihai**, China
59/E3 **Weihai**, China
26/E3 **Weilburg**, Ger.
31/H3 **Weilburg**, Ger.
33/H1 **Weilburg**, Ger.
37/F2 **Weiler-Simmerberg**, Ger.
31/F2 **Weilerswist**, Ger.
26/F5 **Weilheim**, Ger.
33/J3 **Weilheim**, Ger.
37/H2 **Weilheim**, Ger.
26/F3 **Weimar**, Ger.
37/F2 **Weinfelden**, Swi.
26/E5 **Weingarten**, Ger.
33/H3 **Weingarten**, Ger.
37/F2 **Weingarten**, Ger.
26/E4 **Weinheim**, Ger.
27/J4 **Weinviertel** (reg.), Aus.
33/M2 **Weinviertel** (reg.), Aus.
89/K3 **Weirton**, WV,US
94/D3 **Weirton**, WV,US
90/D4 **Weiser** (riv.), Id,US
90/D4 **Weiser**, Id,US
92/C1 **Weiser**, Id,US
54/H5 **Weishan** (lake), China
59/D4 **Weishan**, China
59/D4 **Weishan** (lake), China
54/G5 **Weishi**, China
59/C4 **Weishi**, China
31/F4 **Weiskirchen**, Ger.
26/F3 **Weisse Elster** (riv.), Ger.
26/F4 **Weissenburg im Bayern**, Ger.
33/J2 **Weissenburg im Bayern**, Ger.
26/F3 **Weissenfels**, Ger.
37/G1 **Weissenhorn**, Ger.
36/D3 **Weissenstein** (mtn.), Swi.
31/G3 **Weissenthurm**, Ger.
31/F3 **Weisser Stein** (peak), Ger.
36/D5 **Weisshorn** (peak), Swi.
37/G4 **Weisskugel** (Palla Blanca) (peak), Aus., It.
33/G3 **Weissmies** (peak), Swi.
36/D5 **Weissmies** (peak), Swi.
27/H3 **Weisswasser**, Ger.
31/G2 **Weitefeld**, Ger.
27/H4 **Weitra**, Aus.
33/L2 **Weitra**, Aus.
63/G2 **Weixi**, China
59/C3 **Wei Xian**, China
63/J2 **Weixin**, China
54/E4 **Weiyuan**, China
60/D4 **Weiyuan** (riv.), China
33/L3 **Weiz**, Aus.
40/B2 **Weiz**, Aus.
61/F4 **Weizhou** (isl.), China
63/J3 **Weizhou** (isl.), China
27/K1 **Wejherowo**, Pol.
89/K4 **Welch**, WV,US
94/D4 **Welch**, WV,US
97/H2 **Welch**, WV,US
37/G1 **Welden**, Ger.
77/N5 **Weldiya**, Eth.
25/F2 **Weldon**, Eng,UK
77/M6 **Welel** (peak), Eth.
25/E4 **Welford**, Eng,UK
19/N6 **Welham Green**, Eng,UK
25/F3 **Welham Green**, Eng,UK
62/D6 **Weligama**, SrL.
31/E2 **Welkenraedt**, Belg.
80/D3 **Welkom**, SAfr.
82/E6 **Welkom**, SAfr.
95/R10 **Welland**, On,Can
95/R10 **Welland** (can.), On,Can
23/H6 **Welland** (riv.), Eng,UK
25/F1 **Welland** (riv.), Eng,UK
95/R10 **Wellandport**, On,Can
31/E2 **Wellen**, Belg.
70/F3 **Wellesley** (isls.), Austl.
31/E3 **Wellin**, Belg.
25/F2 **Wellingborough**, Eng,UK
71/H6 **Wellington**, Austl.
73/C3 **Wellington** (inlet), Austl.
73/D2 **Wellington**, Austl.
87/S7 **Wellington** (chan.), NW,Can
105/B7 **Wellington** (isl.), Chile
109/A6 **Wellington** (isl.), Chile
71/R11 **Wellington** (cap.), N.Z.
80/B4 **Wellington**, SAfr.
80/L10 **Wellington**, SAfr.
24/C5 **Wellington**, Eng,UK
24/D2 **Wellington**, Eng,UK
93/H3 **Wellington**, Ks,US
96/D2 **Wellington**, Ks,US
93/G4 **Wellington**, Tx,US
96/C3 **Wellington**, Tx,US
70/C5 **Wells** (lake), Austl.
90/C2 **Wells**, BC,Can
24/D4 **Wells**, Eng,UK
86/E4 **Wells**, Nv,US
88/D3 **Wells**, Nv,US
90/E5 **Wells**, Nv,US
92/D2 **Wells**, Nv,US
25/G1 **Wells next the Sea**, Eng,UK
94/D4 **Wellston**, Oh,US
97/H2 **Wellston**, Oh,US
100/B1 **Wellton**, Az,US
27/H4 **Wels**, Aus.
33/L2 **Wels**, Aus.
40/B1 **Wels**, Aus.
31/F4 **Welschbillig**, Ger.
37/H5 **Welshnofen** (Nova Levante), It.
24/C1 **Welshpool**, Wal,UK
29/E5 **Welver**, Ger.
25/F3 **Welwyn**, Eng,UK
25/F3 **Welwyn Garden City**, Eng,UK
23/F6 **Wem**, Eng,UK
82/F1 **Wembere** (riv.), Tanz.
90/D2 **Wembley**, Ab,Can
19/N7 **Wembley Stadium**, Eng,UK
24/B6 **Wembury**, Eng,UK
87/J3 **Wemindji**, Qu,Can
30/D2 **Wemmel**, Belg.
86/D4 **Wenatchee**, Wa,US
88/D2 **Wenatchee**, Wa,US
90/C4 **Wenatchee**, Wa,US
61/F5 **Wenchang**, China
63/K4 **Wenchang**, China
61/J3 **Wencheng**, China
76/E6 **Wenchi**, Gha.
79/E5 **Wenchi**, Gha.
29/H4 **Wendeburg**, Ger.
31/G2 **Wenden**, Ger.
55/J4 **Wendeng**, China
58/B4 **Wendeng**, China
59/E3 **Wendeng**, China
25/F3 **Wendover**, Eng,UK
90/E5 **Wendover**, Nv,US
92/D2 **Wendover**, Nv,US
24/A6 **Wendron**, Eng,UK
32/A1 **Wendron**, Eng,UK
63/K3 **Wengyuan**, China
24/D2 **Wenlock Edge** (ridge), Eng,UK
29/F6 **Wenne** (riv.), Ger.
29/G4 **Wennigsen**, Ger.
23/F3 **Wennington**, Eng,UK
98/E6 **Wenonah**, NJ,US
63/H3 **Wenshan**, China
59/D4 **Wenshang**, China
54/G4 **Wenshui**, China
59/C3 **Wenshui**, China
23/F3 **Wensleydale** (val.), Eng,UK
25/H1 **Wensum** (riv.), Eng,UK
23/G4 **Went** (riv.), Eng,UK
73/B2 **Wentworth**, Austl.
59/B4 **Wenxi**, China
59/C4 **Wen Xian**, China
61/J3 **Wenzhou**, China
68/B2 **Wenzhou**, China
53/L3 **Wer**, India
80/C2 **Werda**, Bots.
26/G3 **Werdau**, Ger.
33/K1 **Werdau**, Ger.
77/Q6 **Werdēr**, Eth.
29/E6 **Werdohl**, Ger.
28/B5 **Werkendam**, Neth.
29/E5 **Werl**, Ger.
29/E3 **Werlte**, Ger.
29/E6 **Wermelskirchen**, Ger.
31/G1 **Wermelskirchen**, Ger.
29/E5 **Werne an der Lippe**, Ger.
26/F4 **Werneck**, Ger.
29/H5 **Wernigerode**, Ger.
73/D2 **Werong** (peak), Austl.
26/E3 **Werra** (riv.), Ger.
29/G6 **Werra** (riv.), Ger.
33/H1 **Werra** (riv.), Ger.
26/E2 **Werre** (riv.), Ger.
29/F4 **Werre** (riv.), Ger.
73/E1 **Werrikimbe Nat'l Park**, Austl.
23/F5 **Werrington**, Eng,UK
73/D1 **Werris Creek**, Austl.
29/E5 **Werse** (riv.), Ger.
37/G1 **Wertach** (riv.), Ger.
26/E4 **Wertheim**, Ger.
33/H2 **Wertheim**, Ger.
98/H5 **Wertheim Nat'l Wild. Ref.**, NY,US
29/F4 **Werther**, Ger.
28/C3 **Wervershoof**, Neth.
30/C2 **Wervik**, Belg.
26/D3 **Wesel**, Ger.
28/D5 **Wesel**, Ger.
29/E5 **Wesel-Datteln-Kanal** (can.), Ger.
18/D3 **Weser** (riv.), Ger.
26/E2 **Weser** (riv.), Ger.
29/F2 **Weser** (riv.), Ger.
29/G4 **Wesergebirge** (ridge), Ger.
101/F3 **Weslaco**, Tx,US
96/D5 **Weslaco**, Tx,US
80/D2 **Wes-Rand**, SAfr.
80/P13 **Wes-Rand**, SAfr.
81/D2 **Wes-Rand**, SAfr.
82/E6 **Wes-Rand**, SAfr.
70/F2 **Wessel** (cape), Austl.
70/F2 **Wessel** (isls.), Austl.
26/E1 **Wesselburen**, Ger.
24/D4 **Wessex** (reg.), Eng,UK
91/J4 **Wessington Springs**, SD,US
93/H1 **Wessington Springs**, SD,US
71/G7 **West** (pt.), Austl.
73/C4 **West** (pt.), Austl.
101/F2 **West**, Tx,US
99/C2 **West** (pt.), Wa,US
94/B3 **West Allis**, Wi,US
99/P13 **West Allis**, Wi,US
97/H3 **West Augusta**, Ga,US
98/G5 **West Babylon**, NY,US
49/D3 **West Bank** (occ. zone)
49/G7 **West Bank** (occ. zone)
50/C3 **West Bank** (occ. zone)
52/C2 **West Bank** (occ. zone)
91/L5 **West Bend**, Wi,US
94/B3 **West Bend**, Wi,US
62/E3 **West Bengal** (state), India
25/G3 **West Bergholt**, Eng,UK
94/C2 **West Branch**, Mi,US
23/G6 **West Bridgford**, Eng,UK
25/E1 **West Bromwich**, Eng,UK
24/D4 **Westbury**, Eng,UK
98/G5 **Westbury**, NY,US
103/H1 **West Caicos** (isl.), Trks.
98/G4 **Westchester** (co.), NY,US
98/G4 **Westchester** (co. arpt.), NY,US
98/E6 **West Chester**, Pa,US
99/P16 **West Chicago**, Il,US
19/M8 **West Clandon**, Eng,UK
24/B3 **West Cleddau** (riv.), Wal,UK
97/H3 **West Columbia**, SC,US
23/G2 **West Cornforth**, Eng,UK
98/C2 **West Covina**, Ca,US
24/C5 **West Dart** (riv.), Eng,UK
28/A6 **Westdorpe**, Neth.
30/C1 **Westdorpe**, Neth.
18/F3 **West Dvina** (riv.), Eur.
96/B2 **West Elk** (mts.), Co,US
28/D3 **Westerbork**, Neth.
31/G2 **Westerburg**, Ger.
19/P8 **Westerham**, Eng,UK
37/G1 **Westerheim**, Ger.
29/E1 **Westerholt**, Ger.
29/E4 **Westerkappeln**, Ger.
20/D5 **Westerland**, Ger.
26/E1 **Westerland**, Ger.
28/B6 **Westerlo**, Belg.
31/D1 **Westerlo**, Belg.
49/A5 **Western** (des.), Egypt
77/L2 **Western** (des.), Egypt
79/E5 **Western** (reg.), Gha.
78/B4 **Western** (area), SLeo.
70/C4 **Western Australia** (state), Austl.
56/A3 **Western Channel** (str.), Japan, SKor.
58/E5 **Western Channel** (str.), Japan, SKor.
42/F5 **Western Dvina** (riv.), Bel., Rus.
46/C4 **Western Dvina** (riv.), Lat.,Rus.
53/K5 **Western Ghāts** (mts.), India
62/B4 **Western Ghats** (mts.), India
64/F3 **Western Ghats** (uplands), India
35/Y17 **Western Sahara**
74/A2 **Western Sahara**
76/B3 **Western Sahara**
69/H6 **Western Samoa**
69/R9 **Western Samoa**
46/K4 **Western Sayans** (mts.), Rus.
54/C1 **Western Sayans** (mts.), Rus.
28/A6 **Westerschelde** (chan.), Neth.
29/E2 **Westerstede**, Ger.
94/D3 **Westerville**, Oh,US
97/H1 **Westerville**, Oh,US
28/C5 **Westervoort**, Neth.
26/D3 **Westerwald** (for.), Ger.
31/G2 **Westerwald** (for.), Ger.
33/G1 **Westerwald** (reg.), Ger.
29/F4 **Westfalica, Porta** (pass), Ger.
105/C7 **West Falkland** (isl.), Falk.
109/D7 **West Falkland** (isl.), Falk.
91/J4 **West Fargo**, ND,US
68/D4 **West Fayu** (isl.), Micr.
30/B2 **West Flanders** (prov.), Belg.
93/K3 **West Frankfort**, Il,US
94/B4 **West Frankfort**, Il,US
97/F2 **West Frankfort**, Il,US
26/C2 **West Frisian** (isls.), Neth.
28/C2 **West Frisian** (isls.), Neth.
24/C3 **West Glamorgan** (co.), Wal,UK
23/H6 **West Glen** (riv.), Eng,UK
25/F1 **West Glen** (riv.), Eng,UK
19/P7 **West Ham**, Eng,UK
98/G4 **West Haverstraw**, NY,US
89/H5 **West Helena**, Ar,US
93/K4 **West Helena**, Ar,US
97/F3 **West Helena**, Ar,US
19/Q7 **West Horndon**, Eng,UK
19/M8 **West Horsley**, Eng,UK
23/F4 **Westhoughton**, Eng,UK
95/Q8 **West Humber** (riv.), On,Can
83/F **West Ice Shelf**, Ant.
103/G2 **West Indies** (isls.), NAm.
84/L7 **West Indies** (isls.), NAm.
71/J4 **West Islet** (isl.), Austl.
98/G5 **West Islip**, NY,US
92/E2 **West Jordan**, Ut,US
28/A5 **Westkapelle**, Neth.
19/P8 **West Kingsdown**, Eng,UK
23/E5 **West Kirby**, Eng,UK
99/F7 **Westland**, Mi,US
86/E3 **Westlock**, Ab,Can
90/E2 **Westlock**, Ab,Can
82/E3 **West Lunga Nat'l Park**, Zam.
22/A4 **Westmeath** (co.), Ire.
93/K4 **West Memphis**, Ar,US
97/F3 **West Memphis**, Ar,US
25/G3 **West Mersea**, UK
25/E2 **West Midlands** (co.), Eng,UK
98/F4 **West Milford**, NJ,US
98/B3 **Westminster**, Ca,US
94/E4 **Westminster**, Md,US
19/N7 **Westminster Abbey**, Eng,UK
19/N7 **Westminster, City of** (bor.), Eng,UK
99/Q16 **Westmont**, Il,US
98/E6 **Westmont** (Haddon), NJ,US
23/F3 **Westmoreland** (reg.), Eng,UK
95/N7 **Westmount**, Qu,Can
98/G4 **West Nyack**, NY,US
98/G4 **Weston**, Ct,US
93/J3 **Weston**, Mo,US
96/E2 **Weston**, Mo,US
94/D4 **Weston**, WV,US
97/H2 **Weston**, WV,US
80/P13 **Westonaria**, SAfr.
24/D4 **Weston super Mare**, Eng,UK
24/D4 **Weston Zoyland**, Eng,UK
98/F5 **West Orange**, NJ,US
104/A1 **West Palm Beach**, Fl,US
89/K6 **West Palm Beach**, Fl,US
97/H5 **West Palm Beach**, Fl,US
19/Q8 **West Peckham**, Eng,UK
97/G4 **West Pensacola**, Fl,US
93/K3 **West Plains**, Mo,US
96/F2 **West Plains**, Mo,US
97/F3 **West Point**, Ms,US
91/J5 **West Point**, Ne,US
93/H2 **West Point**, Ne,US
21/H7 **Westport**, Ire.
71/R11 **Westport**, N.Z.
98/G4 **Westport**, Ct,US
90/B2 **West Road** (riv.), BC,Can
99/L9 **West Sacramento**, Ca,US
95/S10 **West Seneca**, NY,US
46/H3 **West Siberian** (plain), Rus.
25/F4 **West Sussex** (co.), Eng,UK
26/C2 **West-Terschelling**, Neth.
28/C2 **West-Terschelling**, Neth.
19/P7 **West Thurrock**, Eng,UK
88/D3 **West Valley City**, Ut,US
92/E2 **West Valley City**, Ut,US
90/C3 **West Vancouver**, BC,Can
89/K4 **West Virginia** (state), US
94/D4 **West Virginia** (state), US
24/B4 **Westward Ho!**, Eng,UK
98/F5 **Westwood**, NJ,US
71/H6 **West Wyalong**, Austl.
73/C2 **West Wyalong**, Austl.
23/G4 **West Yorkshire** (co.), Eng,UK
96/B2 **Wet** (mts.), Co,US
48/M10 **Wetar** (isl.), Indo.
67/G5 **Wetar** (isl.), Indo.
67/G5 **Wetar** (str.), Indo.
68/B5 **Wetar** (isl.), Indo.
86/E3 **Wetaskiwin**, Ab,Can
90/E2 **Wetaskiwin**, Ab,Can
82/G2 **Wete**, Tanz.
94/E1 **Wetetnagami** (riv.), Qu,Can
23/F2 **Wetheral**, Eng,UK
23/G4 **Wetherby**, Eng,UK
70/G6 **Wetherell** (lake), Austl.
73/B2 **Wetherell** (lake), Austl.
29/E6 **Wetter**, Ger.
26/B3 **Wetteren**, Belg.
28/A7 **Wetteren**, Belg.
30/C1 **Wetteren**, Belg.
36/E4 **Wetterhorn** (peak), Swi.
37/E3 **Wettingen**, Swi.
29/E4 **Wettringen**, Ger.
37/E3 **Wetzikon**, Swi.
26/E3 **Wetzlar**, Ger.
33/H1 **Wetzlar**, Ger.
30/C2 **Wevelgem**, Belg.
68/D5 **Wewak**, PNG
93/H4 **Wewoka**, Ok,US
96/D3 **Wewoka**, Ok,US
22/B6 **Wexford** (co.), Ire.
21/B4 **Wexford**, Ire.
19/M8 **Wey** (riv.), Eng,UK
24/F4 **Wey** (riv.), Eng,UK
25/H1 **Weybourne**, Eng,UK
19/M7 **Weybridge**, Eng,UK
86/F4 **Weyburn**, Sk,Can
88/F2 **Weyburn**, Sk,Can
91/H3 **Weyburn**, Sk,Can
76/F3 **Weygand** (ruins), Alg.
29/H4 **Weyhausen**, Ger.
24/D5 **Weymouth**, Eng,UK
24/D5 **Weymouth** (bay), Eng,UK
32/B1 **Weymouth**, Eng,UK
71/S10 **Whakatane**, N.Z.
86/G2 **Whale Cove**, NW,Can
23/G5 **Whaley Bridge**, Eng,UK
23/F4 **Whalley**, Eng,UK
68/G8 **Whangarei**, N.Z.
71/R10 **Whangarei**, N.Z.
23/G3 **Wharfe** (riv.), Eng,UK
101/F2 **Wharton**, Tx,US
93/H5 **Wharton**, Tx,US
96/D4 **Wharton**, Tx,US
88/F3 **Wheatland**, Wy,US
91/G5 **Wheatland**, Wy,US
93/F2 **Wheatland**, Wy,US
99/H7 **Wheatley**, On,Can
25/E3 **Wheatley**, Eng,UK
94/B3 **Wheaton**, Il,US
99/P16 **Wheaton**, Il,US
24/D1 **Wheaton Aston**, Eng,UK
98/J7 **Wheaton-Glenmont**, Md,US
88/E4 **Wheeler** (peak), NM,US
93/F3 **Wheeler** (peak), NM,US
96/B2 **Wheeler** (peak), NM,US
92/D3 **Wheeler** (peak), Nv,US
88/V13 **Wheeler A.F.B.**, Hi,US
99/Q15 **Wheeling**, Il,US
89/K3 **Wheeling**, WV,US
94/D3 **Wheeling**, WV,US
23/F3 **Whernside** (mtn.), Eng,UK
23/G2 **Whickham**, Eng,UK
99/B1 **Whidbey** (isl.), Wa,US
90/C5 **Whiskeytown-Shasta-Trinity Nat'l Rec. Area**, Ca,US
92/B2 **Whiskeytown-Shasta-Trinity Nat'l Rec. Area**, Ca,US
93/B2 **Whiskeytown-Shasta-Trinity Nat'l Rec. Area**, Ca,US
23/G2 **Whitburn**, Eng,UK
94/E3 **Whitby**, On,Can
95/S8 **Whitby**, On,Can
23/H3 **Whitby**, Eng,UK
23/F6 **Whitchurch**, Eng,UK
25/E4 **Whitchurch**, Eng,UK
25/F3 **Whitchurch**, Eng,UK
24/C4 **Whitchurch**, Wal,UK
83/D **White** (isl.), Ant.
70/D4 **White** (lake), Austl.
87/L3 **White** (bay), Nf,Can
95/K1 **White** (bay), Nf,Can
94/C1 **White** (lake), On,Can
92/E2 **White** (riv.), Co, Ut,US
93/K4 **White** (riv.), La, Mo,US
91/H5 **White** (riv.), Ne, SD,US
18/G2 **White** (sea), Rus.
42/H2 **White** (sea), Rus.
46/D3 **White** (sea), Rus.
85/L4 **White** (pass), Ak,US
94/C4 **White** (riv.), In,US
93/J5 **White** (lake), La,US
99/F6 **White** (lake), Mi,US
92/D3 **White** (riv.), Nv,US
93/G4 **White** (riv.), Tx,US
94/D4 **White** (peak), Va,US
97/H2 **White** (peak), Va,US
99/D3 **White** (riv.), Wa,US
99/P14 **White** (riv.), Wi,US
95/K1 **White Bear** (riv.), Nf,Can
91/G3 **White City**, Sk,Can
73/B1 **White Cliffs**, Austl.
86/E3 **Whitecourt**, Ab,Can
90/E2 **Whitecourt**, Ab,Can
23/E1 **White Esk** (riv.), Sc,UK
91/K4 **Whiteface** (riv.), Mn,US
22/F4 **Whitefield**, Eng,UK
94/C2 **Whitefish** (bay), On,Can, Mi,US
88/D2 **Whitefish**, Mt,US
90/E3 **Whitefish**, Mt,US
85/L2 **Whitefish Station**, Yk,Can
24/B3 **Whiteford** (pt.), UK
91/G2 **White Fox**, Sk,Can
94/C3 **Whitehall**, Mi,US
90/E4 **Whitehall**, Mt,US
98/E5 **Whitehall** (Fullerton), Pa,US
22/E2 **Whitehaven**, Eng,UK
22/C2 **Whitehead**, NI,UK
85/L3 **Whitehorse** (cap.), Yk,Can
86/C2 **Whitehorse** (cap.), Yk,Can
25/E3 **Whitehorse** (hill), Eng,UK
98/K7 **White Marsh**, Md,US
85/F3 **White Mountain**, Ak,US
91/K3 **Whitemouth** (riv.), Mb,Can
85/J2 **White Mts. Nat'l Rec. Area**, Ak,US
74/F4 **White Nile** (riv.), Afr.
77/M5 **White Nile** (riv.), Sudan
98/K7 **White Oak**, Md,US
91/K3 **White Otter** (lake), On,Can
94/A1 **White Otter** (lake), On,Can
98/G4 **White Plains**, NY,US
87/H4 **White River**, On,Can
89/J2 **White River**, On,Can
94/C1 **White River**, On,Can
92/E4 **Whiteriver**, Az,US
96/B3 **White Rock**, NM,US
100/D1 **White Sands**, NM,US
92/F4 **White Sands**, NM,US
96/B3 **White Sands**, NM,US
101/D1 **White Sands Nat'l Mon.**, NM,US
92/F4 **White Sands Nat'l Mon.**, NM,US
96/B3 **White Sands Nat'l Mon.**, NM,US
100/D1 **Whites City**, NM,US
90/F4 **White Sulphur Springs**, Mt,US
94/D4 **White Sulphur Springs**, WV,US
97/H2 **White Sulphur Springs**, WV,US
97/J3 **Whiteville**, NC,US
74/B3 **White Volta** (riv.), Afr.
79/E4 **White Volta** (riv.), Burk., Gha.
76/E5 **White Volta** (riv.), Burk., Ghana
91/L3 **Whitewater** (lake), On,Can
98/E5 **Whitewater Kingdom/ Dorney Park**, Pa,US
99/D3 **White, West Fork** (riv.), Wa,US
91/H3 **Whitewood**, Sk,Can
22/D2 **Whithorn**, Sc,UK
99/R16 **Whiting**, In,US
24/B3 **Whitland**, Wal,UK
23/G1 **Whitley Bay**, Eng,UK
99/E7 **Whitmore Lake**, Mi,US
88/V12 **Whitmore Village**, Hi,US
88/C4 **Whitney** (mt.), Ca,US
92/C3 **Whitney** (peak), Ca,US
101/F2 **Whitney**, Tx,US
93/H4 **Whitney** (lake), Tx,US
24/B6 **Whitsand** (bay), Eng,UK
25/H4 **Whitstable**, Eng,UK
71/H4 **Whitsunday** (isl.), Austl.
72/C3 **Whitsunday I. Nat'l Park**, Austl.
99/E7 **Whittaker**, Mi,US
85/J3 **Whittier**, Ak,US
98/B3 **Whittier**, Ca,US
73/G5 **Whittlesea**, Austl.
25/F1 **Whittlesey**, Eng,UK
73/C2 **Whitton**, Austl.
23/G5 **Whitwell**, Eng,UK
23/F4 **Whitworth**, Eng,UK
86/F2 **Wholdaia** (lake), NW,Can
100/B1 **Why**, Az,US
68/C8 **Whyalla**, Austl.
70/F6 **Whyalla**, Austl.
60/C5 **Wiang Kosai Nat'l Park**, Thai.
65/B2 **Wiang Ko Sai Nat'l Park**, Thai.
94/D2 **Wiarton**, On,Can
79/E5 **Wiawso**, Gha.
28/A7 **Wichelen**, Belg.
30/C2 **Wichelen**, Belg.
89/G4 **Wichita**, Ks,US
93/H3 **Wichita**, Ks,US
96/D2 **Wichita**, Ks,US
93/H4 **Wichita** (mts.), Ok,US
96/D3 **Wichita** (mts.), Ok,US
93/H4 **Wichita** (riv.), Tx,US
84/H6 **Wichita Falls**, US
89/G5 **Wichita Falls**, Tx,US
93/H4 **Wichita Falls**, Tx,US
96/D3 **Wichita Falls**, Tx,US
88/D5 **Wickenburg**, Az,US
92/D4 **Wickenburg**, Az,US
25/G3 **Wickford**, Eng,UK
73/C3 **Wickham** (cape), Austl.
25/H2 **Wickham Market**, Eng,UK
22/B6 **Wicklow**, Ire.
22/B6 **Wicklow** (co.), Ire.
22/B6 **Wicklow** (mts.), Ire.
22/B5 **Wicklow Gap** (pass), Ire.
22/C6 **Wicklow Head** (pt.), Ire.
29/F4 **Wickriede** (riv.), Ger.
70/C6 **Widgiemooltha**, Austl.
37/F3 **Widnau**, Swi.
23/F5 **Widnes**, Eng,UK
27/J2 **Więcbork**, Pol.
31/G2 **Wied** (riv.), Ger.
33/G1 **Wied** (riv.), Ger.
29/G2 **Wiedau** (riv.), Ger.
29/F2 **Wiefelstede**, Ger.
29/F4 **Wiehengebirge** (ridge), Ger.
31/G2 **Wiehl**, Ger.
37/H2 **Wielenbach**, Ger.
27/L4 **Wieliczka**, Pol.
44/B2 **Wieliczka**, Pol.
30/C2 **Wielsbeke**, Belg.
27/K3 **Wieluń**, Pol.
27/J4 **Wien** (prov.), Aus.
33/M2 **Wien** (prov.), Aus.
40/C1 **Wien** (prov.), Aus.
27/J5 **Wiener Neustadt**, Aus.
33/M3 **Wiener Neustadt**, Aus.
40/C2 **Wiener Neustadt**, Aus.
27/J4 **Wien** (Vienna) (cap.), Aus.
33/M2 **Wien** (Vienna) (cap.), Aus.
40/C1 **Wien** (Vienna) (cap.), Aus.
33/L2 **Wienwald** (reg.), Aus.
27/M3 **Wieprz** (riv.), Pol.
44/B2 **Wieprz** (riv.), Pol.
28/D4 **Wierden**, Neth.
28/B3 **Wieringermeerpolder** (polder), Neth.
26/C2 **Wieringerwerf**, Neth.
28/C3 **Wieringerwerf**, Neth.
27/K3 **Wieruszów**, Pol.
18/D3 **Wiesbaden**, Ger.
26/E3 **Wiesbaden**, Ger.
31/H3 **Wiesbaden**, Ger.
33/H1 **Wiesbaden**, Ger.
33/G3 **Wiese** (riv.), Ger.
36/D2 **Wiese** (riv.), Ger.
46/H2 **Wiese** (isl.), Rus.
37/E2 **Wiesendangen**, Swi.
26/D2 **Wiesmoor**, Ger.
29/E2 **Wiesmoor**, Ger.
29/E3 **Wietmarschen**, Ger.
29/G3 **Wietze**, Ger.
29/G3 **Wietze** (riv.), Ger.
29/G3 **Wietzendorf**, Ger.
27/K1 **Wiezyca** (peak), Pol.
23/F4 **Wigan**, Eng,UK
97/F4 **Wiggins**, Ms,US
25/E5 **Wight** (isl.), Eng,UK
32/C1 **Wight** (isl.), Eng,UK
30/D3 **Wignehies**, Fr.
25/E1 **Wigston**, Eng,UK
23/E2 **Wigton**, Eng,UK
22/D2 **Wigtown**, Sc,UK
22/D2 **Wigtown** (bay), Sc,UK
28/C5 **Wijchen**, Neth.
28/D4 **Wijhe**, Neth.
28/C5 **Wijk bij Duurstede**, Neth.
52/C6 **Wik'ro**, Eth.
77/N5 **Wik'ro**, Eth.
37/F3 **Wil**, Swi.
93/H2 **Wilber**, Ne,US
72/G8 **Wilberforce**, Austl.
23/H4 **Wilberfoss**, Eng,UK
90/D4 **Wilbur**, Wa,US
93/J4 **Wilburton**, Ok,US
96/E3 **Wilburton**, Ok,US
70/G6 **Wilcannia**, Austl.
73/B1 **Wilcannia**, Austl.
37/E2 **Wilchingen**, Swi.
46/G1 **Wilczek** (isl.), Rus.
80/E4 **Wild Coast** (reg.), SAfr.
98/E5 **Wild Creek** (res.), Pa,US
36/D4 **Wilderswil**, Swi.
26/E2 **Wildeshausen**, Ger.
29/F3 **Wildeshausen**, Ger.
95/Q8 **Wildfield**, On,Can
37/G3 **Wildgrat** (peak), Aus.
37/F3 **Wildhaus**, Swi.
36/D5 **Wildhorn** (peak), Swi.
91/J4 **Wild Rice** (riv.), Mn,US
33/J3 **Wildspitze** (peak), Aus.
37/G4 **Wildspitze** (peak), Aus.
36/D5 **Wildstrubel** (peak), Swi.
98/K8 **Wild World**, Md,US
80/E2 **Wilge** (riv.), SAfr.
80/Q13 **Wilge** (riv.), SAfr.
68/D5 **Wilhelm** (peak), PNG
83/F **Wilhelm II** (coast), Ant.
107/G3 **Wilhelmina** (mts.), Sur.
28/C5 **Wilhelminakanaal** (can.), Neth.
29/G2 **Wilhelmsburg**, Ger.
26/E2 **Wilhelmshaven**, Ger.
29/F1 **Wilhelmshaven**, Ger.
89/L3 **Wilkes-Barre**, Pa,US
94/F3 **Wilkes-Barre**, Pa,US
94/D4 **Wilkesboro**, NC,US
97/H2 **Wilkesboro**, NC,US
83/J **Wilkes Land** (reg.), Ant.
99/C3 **Wilkeson**, Wa,US
86/F3 **Wilkie**, Sk,Can
90/F2 **Wilkie**, Sk,Can
83/V **Wilkins** (sound), Ant.
85/N4 **Will** (mtn.), BC,Can
99/P16 **Will** (co.), Il,US
90/C4 **Willamette** (riv.), Or,US
86/D4 **Willamette** (riv.), Or,US
73/C2 **Willandra Nat'l Park**, Austl.
90/B4 **Willapa** (bay), Wa,US
23/F5 **Willaston**, Eng,UK
73/B3 **Willaura**, Austl.
100/C1 **Willcox**, Az,US
92/E4 **Willcox**, Az,US
29/G5 **Willebadessen**, Ger.
28/B6 **Willebroek**, Belg.
30/D1 **Willebroek**, Belg.
104/D4 **Willemstad**, NAnt.
106/E1 **Willemstad**, NAnt.
28/B5 **Willemstad**, Neth.
19/N7 **Willesden**, Eng,UK
73/B3 **William** (peak), Austl.
92/D4 **Williams**, Az,US
99/N14 **Williams Bay**, Wi,US
94/C4 **Williamsburg**, Ky,US
97/G2 **Williamsburg**, Ky,US
89/L4 **Williamsburg**, Va,US
94/E4 **Williamsburg**, Va,US
97/J2 **Williamsburg**, Va,US
86/D3 **Williams Lake**, BC,Can
90/C2 **Williams Lake**, BC,Can
94/D4 **Williamson**, WV,US
97/H2 **Williamson**, WV,US
89/L3 **Williamsport**, Pa,US
94/E3 **Williamsport**, Pa,US
89/L4 **Williamston**, NC,US
97/J3 **Williamston**, NC,US
73/F5 **Williamstown**, Austl.
95/S10 **Williamsville**, NY,US
28/D6 **Willich**, Ger.
31/F1 **Willich**, Ger.
98/F5 **Willingboro**, NJ,US
29/F6 **Willingen**, Ger.
23/G2 **Willington**, Eng,UK
23/G6 **Willington**, Eng,UK
93/J5 **Willis**, Tx,US
96/E4 **Willis**, Tx,US
36/D3 **Willisau**, Swi.
71/J3 **Willis Islets** (isls.), Austl.
90/C2 **Williston** (lake), BC,Can
86/D3 **Williston** (lake), BC,Can
97/H4 **Williston**, Fl,US
86/F4 **Williston**, ND,US
88/F2 **Williston**, ND,US
91/H3 **Williston**, ND,US
24/C4 **Williton**, Eng,UK
92/B3 **Willits**, Ca,US
89/G2 **Willmar**, Mn,US
91/K4 **Willmar**, Mn,US
90/C2 **Willow** (riv.), BC,Can
85/H3 **Willow**, Ak,US

190

Willo – Xinzh

90/D4 Willow (cr.), Or,US
99/Q16 Willowbrook, Il,US
91/G3 Willow Bunch, Sk,Can
98/E5 Willow Grove, Pa,US
98/E5 Willow Grove Nav. Air Sta., Pa,US
80/C4 Willowmore, SAfr.
90/C2 Willow River, BC,Can
92/B3 Willows, Ca,US
73/D1 Willow Tree, Austl.
70/D4 Wills (lake), Austl.
36/D1 Willstätt, Ger.
99/Q15 Wilmette, Il,US
19/P7 Wilmington, Eng,UK
89/L4 Wilmington, De,US
94/F4 Wilmington, De,US
98/E6 Wilmington, De,US
89/L5 Wilmington, NC,US
97/J3 Wilmington, NC,US
94/D4 Wilmington, Oh,US
97/H2 Wilmington, Oh,US
97/H4 Wilmington Island, Ga,US
23/F5 Wilmslow, Eng,UK
26/E3 Wilnsdorf, Ger.
31/H2 Wilnsdorf, Ger.
33/H1 Wilnsdorf, Ger.
64/G4 Wilpattu Nat'l Park, SrL.
26/C3 Wilrijk, Belg.
28/B6 Wilrijk, Belg.
29/G2 Wilseder Berg (peak), Ger.
87/H2 Wilson (cape), NW,Can
98/B2 Wilson (mt.), Ca,US
97/J3 Wilson, NC,US
95/S9 Wilson, NY,US
98/E5 Wilson, Pa,US
71/H7 Wilsons Promontory (pen.), Austl.
73/C3 Wilsons Promontory Nat'l Park, Austl.
29/G2 Wilstedt, Ger.
29/G1 Wilster, Ger.
28/D3 Wilsum, Ger.
25/E4 Wilton, Eng,UK
99/M10 Wilton, Ca,US
98/G4 Wilton, Ct,US
25/E4 Wiltshire (co.), Eng,UK
31/E4 Wiltz, Lux.
68/B7 Wiluna, Austl.
70/C5 Wiluna, Austl.
19/N7 Wimbledon, Eng,UK
24/E5 Wimborne Minster, Eng,UK
32/C1 Wimborne Minster, Eng,UK
25/H5 Wimereux, Fr.
30/A2 Wimereux, Fr.
36/D4 Wimmis, Swi.
80/D3 Winburg, SAfr.
24/D4 Wincanton, Eng,UK
25/E3 Winchcombe, Eng,UK
25/G5 Winchelsea, Eng,UK
32/D1 Winchelsea, Eng,UK
25/E4 Winchester, Eng,UK
98/C3 Winchester, Ca,US
89/K4 Winchester, Ky,US
94/C4 Winchester, Ky,US
97/G2 Winchester, Ky,US
97/G3 Winchester, Tn,US
94/E4 Winchester, Va,US
97/J2 Winchester, Va,US
99/L12 Winchester Mystery House, Ca,US
100/D1 Wind (mtn.), NM,US
99/P14 Wind (lake), Wi,US
106/F5 Wind (riv.), Wy,US
86/F4 Wind (riv.), Wy,US
92/E2 Wind (riv.), Wy,US
37/G2 Windach (riv.), Ger.
91/G5 Wind Cave Nat'l Park, SD,US
88/F3 Wind Cave Nat'l Park, SD,US
93/G2 Wind Cave Nat'l Park, SD,US
97/H3 Winder, Ga,US
23/F3 Windermere, Eng,UK
23/F3 Windermere (lake), Eng,UK
31/G4 Windesheim, Ger.
98/E5 Wind Gap, Pa,US
82/C5 Windhoek (cap.), Namb.
99/P14 Wind Lake, Wi,US
91/K5 Windom, Mn,US
93/J2 Windom, Mn,US
70/G5 Windorah, Austl.
92/E4 Window Rock, Az,US
99/Q14 Wind Point, Wi,US
90/F5 Wind River (range), Wy,US
92/E2 Wind River (range), Wy,US
25/E3 Windrush (riv.), Eng,UK
72/G8 Windsor, Austl.
95/G2 Windsor, Qu,Can
95/H2 Windsor, NS,Can
95/L1 Windsor, Nf,Can
87/H4 Windsor, On,Can
89/K3 Windsor, On,Can
94/D3 Windsor, On,Can
99/F7 Windsor, On,Can
25/F4 Windsor, Eng,UK
103/H2 Windward (passg.), Cuba, Haiti
89/L8 Windward (passg.), Cuba, Haiti
84/K8 Windward (chan.), NAm.
104/F4 Windward (isls.), West Indies
90/D3 Winfield, Can
93/H3 Winfield, Ks,US
96/D2 Winfield, Ks,US
98/J7 Winfield, Md,US
25/F3 Wing, Eng,UK
23/G2 Wingate, Eng,UK
30/C1 Wingene, Belg.
95/R10 Winger, On,Can
73/E1 Wingham, Austl.
25/H4 Wingham, Eng,UK
70/C4 Winifred (lake), Austl.
91/M2 Winisk (lake), On,Can
91/M2 Winisk (riv.), On,Can
87/H3 Winisk, On,Can
87/H3 Winisk (riv.), On,Can
91/M2 Winisk, On,Can
86/G4 Winkler, Mb,Can
91/J3 Winkler, Mb,Can
79/E5 Winneba, Gha.
91/L5 Winnebago (lake), Wi,US
94/B3 Winnebago (lake), Wi,US
86/E4 Winnemucca, Nv,US
88/C3 Winnemucca, Nv,US
90/D5 Winnemucca, Nv,US
92/C2 Winnemucca, Nv,US
91/J5 Winner, SD,US
93/H2 Winner, SD,US
99/Q15 Winnetka, Il,US
90/F4 Winnett, Mt,US
93/J5 Winnfield, La,US
96/E4 Winnfield, La,US
31/G3 Winningen, Ger.
84/H4 Winnipeg (lake), Mb,Can.
91/J2 Winnipeg (lake), Mb,Can
86/G3 Winnipeg (lake), Mb,Can
89/G1 Winnipeg (lake), Mb,Can
86/G4 Winnipeg (cap.), Mb,Can
89/G2 Winnipeg (cap.), Mb,Can
91/J3 Winnipeg (cap.), Mb,Can
91/K3 Winnipeg (riv.), Mb, On,Can
91/J3 Winnipeg Beach, Mb,Can
84/G4 Winnipegosis (lake), Can.
91/H2 Winnipegosis (lake), Mb,Can
86/F3 Winnipegosis (lake), Mb,Can
89/F1 Winnipegosis (lake), Mb,Can
91/J3 Winnipegosis, Mb,Can
93/K4 Winnsboro, La,US
96/F3 Winnsboro, La,US
97/H3 Winnsboro, SC,US
31/G4 Winnweiler, Ger.
95/Q9 Winona, On,Can
86/G4 Winona, Mn,US
89/H3 Winona, Mn,US
91/L4 Winona, Mn,US
94/B2 Winona, Mn,US
26/D2 Winschoten, Neth.
28/E2 Winschoten, Neth.
24/D4 Winscombe, Eng,UK
23/F5 Winsford, Eng,UK
24/D4 Winsley, Eng,UK
25/F3 Winslow, Eng,UK
88/D4 Winslow, Az,US
92/E4 Winslow, Az,US
99/B2 Winslow, Wa,US
89/K4 Winston-Salem, NC,US
97/H2 Winston-Salem, NC,US
28/D2 Winsum, Neth.
29/F6 Winterberg, Ger.
80/D4 Winterberge (mts.), SAfr.
24/D3 Winterbourne, Eng,UK
97/H4 Winter Haven, Fl,US
37/F1 Winterlingen, Ger.
97/H4 Winter Park, Fl,US
99/L9 Winters, Ca,US
101/F2 Winters, Tx,US
37/F3 Winterstaude (peak), Aus.
28/D5 Winterswijk, Neth.
26/E5 Winterthur, Swi.
33/H3 Winterthur, Swi.
37/E2 Winterthur, Swi.
95/G2 Winthrop, Me,US
99/Q15 Winthrop Harbor, Il,US
70/G4 Winton, Austl.
72/A3 Winton, Austl.
63/G2 Wintong, India
31/H2 Wintzenheim, Fr.
26/F3 Wipper (riv.), Ger.
29/H2 Wipperau (riv.), Ger.
29/E6 Wipperfürth, Ger.
31/G1 Wipperfürth, Ger.
31/G3 Wirges, Ger.
23/G5 Wirksworth, Eng,UK
23/E5 Wirral (pen.), Eng,UK
25/G1 Wisbech, Eng,UK
36/D1 Wisches, Fr.
29/G1 Wischhafen, Ger.
91/L4 Wisconsin (state), US
86/G4 Wisconsin (state), US
89/H3 Wisconsin (state), US
93/K2 Wisconsin (state), US
94/B2 Wisconsin (state), US
99/P14 Wisconsin (state), US
91/L5 Wisconsin (riv.), Wi,US
86/G4 Wisconsin (riv.), Wi,US
93/K2 Wisconsin (riv.), Wi,US
94/B3 Wisconsin (riv.), Wi,US
91/L4 Wisconsin Rapids, Wi,US
94/B2 Wisconsin Rapids, Wi,US
85/H2 Wiseman, Ak,US
91/J4 Wishek, ND,US
27/K4 Wisła, Pol.
27/K1 Wiślany (lag.), Pol.
27/K2 Wisła (Vistula) (riv.), Pol.
27/L4 Wisłok (riv.), Pol.
27/L4 Wisłoka (riv.), Pol.
26/F2 Wismar, Ger.
25/H5 Wissant, Fr.
30/A2 Wissant, Fr.
31/G5 Wissembourg, Fr.
31/G2 Wissen, Ger.
25/G1 Wissey (riv.), Eng,UK
80/E2 Witbank, SAfr.
80/Q12 Witbank, SAfr.
80/A2 Witberg (peak), Namb.
23/H5 Witham (riv.), Eng,UK
25/G3 Witham, Eng,UK
24/C5 Witheridge, Eng,UK
23/J4 Withernsea, Eng,UK
85/J3 Witherspoon (mt.), Ak,US
23/F4 Withnell, Eng,UK
80/D3 Wit Kei (riv.), SAfr.
27/J2 Witkowo, Pol.
25/E3 Witney, Eng,UK
27/H2 Witnica, Pol.
82/C6 Witputz, Namb.
26/C4 Witry-lès-Reims, Fr.
30/D5 Witry-lès-Reims, Fr.
32/F2 Witry-lès-Reims, Fr.
36/D2 Wittelsheim, Fr.
31/E2 Witten, Neth.
29/E6 Witten, Ger.
37/F3 Wittenbach, Swi.
26/G3 Wittenberg, Ger.
26/F2 Wittenberge, Ger.
26/F2 Wittenburg, Ger.
26/D5 Wittenheim, Fr.
33/G3 Wittenheim, Fr.
36/D2 Wittenheim, Fr.
70/B4 Wittenoom, Austl.
25/F1 Wittering, Eng,UK
26/F2 Wittingen, Ger.
29/H3 Wittingen, Ger.
26/D4 Wittlich, Ger.
31/F4 Wittlich, Ger.
33/G2 Wittlich, Ger.
26/D2 Wittmund, Ger.
29/E1 Wittmund, Ger.
27/G1 Witton (pen.), Ger.
26/G2 Wittstock, Ger.
82/H1 Witu, Kenya
80/P12 Witwatersrand (reg.), SAfr.
29/G6 Witzenhausen, Ger.
24/C4 Wiveliscombe, Eng,UK
71/J5 Wivenhoe (lake), Austl.
25/G3 Wivenhoe, Eng,UK
99/E6 Wixom, Mi,US
107/G2 W.J. van Blommenstein (res.), Sur.
27/L2 Wkra (riv.), Pol.
42/D5 Wkra (riv.), Pol.
27/K1 Władysławowo, Pol.
27/K2 Włocławek, Pol.
27/K2 Włocławek (prov.), Pol.
44/A1 Włocławek, Pol.
27/K2 Włocławskie (lake), Pol.
27/M3 Włodawa, Pol.
27/K3 Włoszczowa, Pol.
22/D6 Wnion (riv.), Wal,UK
24/C1 Wnion (riv.), Wal,UK
25/F3 Woburn Abbey, Eng,UK
25/F2 Woburn Sands, Eng,UK
71/H7 Wodonga, Austl.
73/C3 Wodonga, Austl.
27/K4 Wodzisław Śląski, Pol.
28/B4 Woerden, Neth.
31/G6 Woerth, Fr.
28/C3 Wognum, Neth.
37/E3 Wohlen, Swi.
36/D4 Wohlen bei Bern, Swi.
26/D4 Woippy, Fr.
31/F5 Woippy, Fr.
33/G2 Woippy, Fr.
67/H5 Wokam (isl.), Indo.
55/K2 Woken (riv.), China
19/M8 Woking, Eng,UK
25/F4 Woking, Eng,UK
25/F4 Wokingham, Eng,UK
58/D5 Wŏlch'ul-san Nat'l Park, SKor.
95/S9 Wolcottsville, NY,US
27/K3 Wołczyn, Pol.
19/N8 Woldingham, Eng,UK
68/D4 Woleai (atoll), Micr.
85/H2 Wolf (mtn.), Ak,US
99/R16 Wolf (lake), In,US
94/B2 Wolf (riv.), Wi,US
37/E1 Wolfach, Ger.
37/E1 Wolfach (riv.), Ger.
85/F3 Wolf Creek (mtn.), Ak,US
90/E4 Wolf Creek, Mt,US
37/F2 Wolfegg, Ger.
26/G3 Wolfen, Ger.
26/F2 Wolfenbüttel, Ger.
29/H4 Wolfenbüttel, Ger.
29/G6 Wolfhagen, Ger.
88/E2 Wolf Point, Mt,US
91/G3 Wolf Point, Mt,US
37/H2 Wolfratshausen, Ger.
26/F2 Wolfsburg, Ger.
29/H4 Wolfsburg, Ger.
37/F3 Wolfurt, Aus.
27/G1 Wolgast, Ger.
36/E3 Wolhusen, Swi.
27/H2 Wolin, Pol.
27/H2 Woliński Nat'l Park, Pol.
27/J4 Wolkersdorf, Aus.
33/M2 Wolkersdorf, Aus.
86/E2 Wollaston (pen.), NW,Can
86/F3 Wollaston (lake), Sk,Can
109/C7 Wollaston (isl.), Chile
25/F2 Wollaston, Eng,UK
73/D2 Wollemi Nat'l Park, Austl.
37/E3 Wollerau, Swi.
68/E8 Wollongong, Austl.
71/J6 Wollongong, Austl.
73/D2 Wollongong, Austl.
31/G4 Wöllstein, Ger.
80/D2 Wolmaransstad, SAfr.
80/N13 Wolmaransstad, SAfr.
33/J3 Wolnzach, Ger.
76/C6 Wologizi (range), Libr.
27/L2 Wołomin, Pol.
44/B1 Wołomin, Pol.
27/J3 Wołów, Pol.
80/L10 Wolseley, SAfr.
23/G2 Wolsingham, Eng,UK
27/J2 Wolsztyn, Pol.
30/D2 Woluwé-Saint-Lambert, Belg.
26/D2 Wolvega, Neth.
28/D3 Wolvega, Neth.
24/D1 Wolverhampton, Eng,UK
99/F6 Wolverine Lake, Mi,US
25/F2 Wolverton, Eng,UK
94/D2 Woman (riv.), On,Can
24/D1 Wombourne, Eng,UK
23/G4 Wombwell, Eng,UK
72/C4 Wondai, Austl.
99/P15 Wonder (lake), Il,US
73/C1 Wongalarroo (lake), Austl.
58/D4 Wŏnju, SKor.
73/C3 Wonnangatta-Moroka Nat'l Park, Austl.
47/N6 Wŏnsan, NKor.
55/K4 Wŏnsan, NKor.
58/D3 Wŏnsan, NKor.
71/H7 Wonthaggi, Austl.
73/C3 Wonthaggi, Austl.
90/G3 Wood (peak), Can
91/H2 Wood (lake), Sk,Can
85/K3 Wood (mtn.), Yk,Can
98/J7 Woodbine, Md,US
95/Q8 Woodbridge, On,Can
25/H2 Woodbridge, Eng,UK
99/M10 Woodbridge, Ca,US
98/F5 Woodbridge, NJ,US
86/E2 Wood Buffalo Nat'l Park, Ab,Yk,Can
73/E1 Woodburn, Austl.
95/Q9 Woodburn, On,Can
22/C2 Woodburn, NI,UK
90/C4 Woodburn, Or,US
98/E6 Woodbury, NJ,US
99/Q16 Wood Dale, Il,US
73/E1 Woodenbong, Austl.
22/B6 Woodenbridge, Ire.
73/C3 Woodend, Austl.
72/D4 Woodgate, Austl.
72/D4 Woodgate Nat'l Park, Austl.
23/H5 Woodhall Spa, Eng,UK
99/F7 Woodhaven, Mi,US
92/B3 Woodland, Ca,US
99/L9 Woodland, Ca,US
93/F3 Woodland Park, Co,US
96/B2 Woodland Park, Co,US
68/E5 Woodlark (isl.), PNG
98/K7 Woodlawn, Md,US
25/F4 Woodley, Eng,UK
99/P16 Woodridge, Il,US
70/E5 Woodroffe (peak), Austl.
91/K3 Woods (lake), Can., US
99/D2 Woods (cr.), Wa,US
23/F6 Woodseaves, Eng,UK
99/K12 Woodside, Ca,US
86/G4 Woods, Lake of the (lake), Can., US
89/H2 Woods, Lake of the (lake), Can., US
84/H5 Woods, Lake of the (lake), Can., US
73/D2 Woodstock, Austl.
95/H2 Woodstock, NB,Can
87/K4 Woodstock, NB,Can
25/E3 Woodstock, Eng,UK
94/B3 Woodstock, Il,US
99/P15 Woodstock, Il,US
98/K7 Woodstock, Md,US
94/E4 Woodstock, Va,US
97/J2 Woodstock, Va,US
93/K5 Woodville, Ms,US
97/F4 Woodville, Ms,US
93/J5 Woodville, Tx,US
96/E4 Woodville, Tx,US
88/G4 Woodward, Ok,US
93/H3 Woodward, Ok,US
96/D2 Woodward, Ok,US
99/C2 Woodway, Wa,US
24/D5 Wool, Eng,UK
32/B1 Wool, Eng,UK
24/D4 Woolavington, Eng,UK
73/E1 Woolgoolga, Austl.
73/E1 Wooli, Austl.
23/G1 Woolsington, Eng,UK
73/A1 Wooltana, Austl.
19/P7 Woolwich, Eng,UK
68/C8 Woomera, Austl.
70/F6 Woomera, Austl.
93/H1 Woonsocket, SD,US
72/C4 Woorabinda Abor. Community, Austl.
23/F6 Woore, Eng,UK
94/D3 Wooster, Oh,US
25/E3 Wootton Basset, Eng,UK
36/D4 Worb, Swi.
80/B4 Worcester, SAfr.
80/L10 Worcester, SAfr.
82/C7 Worcester, SAfr.
24/D2 Worcester, Eng,UK
87/J4 Worcester, Ma,US
89/M3 Worcester, Ma,US
95/G3 Worcester, Ma,US
24/D2 Worcester & Birmingham (can.), Eng,UK
33/K3 Wörgl, Aus.
22/E2 Workington, Eng,UK
23/G5 Worksop, Eng,UK
28/C3 Workum, Neth.
86/F4 Worland, Wy,US
88/E3 Worland, Wy,US
90/G4 Worland, Wy,US
92/F1 Worland, Wy,US
16/* World
28/B4 Wormer, Neth.
30/B2 Wormhoudt, Fr.
19/N6 Wormley, Eng,UK
26/E4 Worms, Ger.
33/H2 Worms, Ger.
33/J2 Wörnitz (riv.), Ger.
29/F2 Worpswede, Ger.
31/H4 Wörrstadt, Ger.
23/G4 Worsbrough, Eng,UK
99/Q16 Worth, Il,US
101/F2 Wortham, Tx,US
31/H5 Wörth am Rhein, Ger.
25/F5 Worthing, Eng,UK
32/C1 Worthing, Eng,UK
91/K5 Worthington, Mn,US
93/J2 Worthington, Mn,US
37/H1 Wörthsee, Ger.
68/F3 Wotho (atoll), Mrsh.
68/G4 Wotje (atoll), Mrsh.
24/D3 Wotton under Edge, Eng,UK
28/C4 Woudenberg, Neth.
28/C5 Woudrichem, Neth.
103/F3 Wounta (lag.), Nic.
28/B5 Wouw, Neth.
67/F4 Wowoni (isl.), Indo.
23/H5 Wragby, Eng,UK
47/T2 Wrangel (isl.), Rus.
85/A5 Wrangell (cape), Ak,US
85/K3 Wrangell (mts.), Ak,US
85/M4 Wrangell, Ak,US
86/B2 Wrangell (mts.), Ak,US
86/C3 Wrangell, Ak,US
86/B2 Wrangell-Saint Elias Nat'l Park, Ak,US
85/K3 Wrangell-Saint Elias Nat'l Park & Prsv., Ak,US
23/J5 Wrangle, Eng,UK
18/C3 Wrath (cape), Sc,UK
93/G2 Wray, Co,US
19/M7 Wraysbury, Eng,UK
19/M7 Wraysbury (res.), Eng,UK
23/H6 Wreake (riv.), Eng,UK
71/K4 Wreck (reef), Austl.
80/B3 Wreck (pt.), SAfr.
24/D1 Wrekin, The (hill), Eng,UK
29/F1 Wremen, Ger.
23/F5 Wrenbury, Eng,UK
23/F5 Wrexham, Wal,UK
91/G5 Wright, Wy,US
93/F2 Wright, Wy,US
86/D2 Wrigley, NW,Can
25/G3 Writtle, Eng,UK
18/E3 Wrocław, Pol.
27/J3 Wrocław, Pol.
27/J3 Wrocław (prov.), Pol.
46/B4 Wrocław, Pol.
19/P8 Wrotham, Eng,UK
86/D1 Wrottesley (cape), NW,Can
87/Q7 Wrottesley (cape), NW,Can
24/D1 Wroxeter, Eng,UK
25/H1 Wroxham, Eng,UK
27/J2 Września, Pol.
44/A1 Września, Pol.
27/J3 Wschowa, Pol.
61/F3 Wu (riv.), China
61/G3 Wu (riv.), China
63/K2 Wu (riv.), China
59/C3 Wu'an, China
55/K3 Wuchang, China
59/C5 Wuchang, China
59/C5 Wuchang (lake), China
61/G2 Wuchang, China
59/D3 Wucheng, China
61/H3 Wuchiu (isl.), Tai.
59/B2 Wuchuan, China
55/K2 Wudalianchi, China
61/F1 Wudang (mtn.), China
61/F1 Wudang (mts.), China
59/B4 Wudang Shan (mtn.), China
59/D3 Wudi, China
59/B3 Wuding (riv.), China
70/F6 Wudinna, Austl.
61/F2 Wufeng, China
59/B5 Wufeng, China
61/G3 Wugong (mtn.), China
47/L6 Wuhai, China
54/F4 Wuhai, China
54/G5 Wuhan, China
59/C5 Wuhan, China
61/G2 Wuhan, China
55/H5 Wuhe, China
59/D4 Wuhe, China
55/H5 Wuhu, China
59/D5 Wuhu, China
61/H2 Wuhu, China
54/F3 Wujia (riv.), China
59/E5 Wujiang, China
59/L8 Wujiang, China
61/H2 Wujiang, China
61/J2 Wujiang, China
76/G6 Wukari, Nga.
63/G2 Wulang, China
28/E6 Wülfrath, Ger.
29/H5 Wulften, Ger.
54/F5 Wulian, China
55/H4 Wulian, China
59/D4 Wulian, China
60/D3 Wulian (mts.), China
60/D4 Wuliang (mts.), China
61/F2 Wuling (mts.), China
63/J2 Wulong, China
76/H6 Wum, Camr.
79/H5 Wum, Camr.
60/D3 Wumeng (mts.), China
29/F2 Wümme (riv.), Ger.
62/C3 Wūn, India
29/F5 Wünnenberg, Ger.
36/D4 Wünnewil, Swi.
26/E2 Wunstorf, Ger.
29/G4 Wunstorf, Ger.
92/E4 Wupatki Nat'l Mon., Az,US
28/E6 Wupper (riv.), Ger.
29/E6 Wupper (riv.), Ger.
31/G1 Wupper (riv.), Ger.
26/D3 Wuppertal, Ger.
29/E6 Wuppertal, Ger.
59/B3 Wuqi, China
59/C3 Wuqiang, China
59/D3 Wuqiao, China
28/D6 Würm (riv.), Ger.
31/F2 Würm (riv.), Ger.
37/H1 Würm (can.), Ger.
79/G3 Wurno, Nga.
31/F2 Würselen, Ger.
18/D4 Würzburg, Ger.
26/E4 Würzburg, Ger.
33/H2 Würzburg, Ger.
55/H5 Wushan (lake), China
61/G2 Wusheng (pass), China
59/C5 Wusheng Guan (pass), China
29/G6 Wüstegarten (peak), Ger.
55/L2 Wusuli (Ussuri) (riv.), China, Rus.
37/E2 Wutach (riv.), Ger.
54/G4 Wutai, China
54/G4 Wutai (peak), China
59/C3 Wutai, China
59/C3 Wutai Shan (peak), China
78/C4 Wuteve (peak), Libr.
37/E2 Wutöschingen, Ger.
28/B6 Wuustwezel, Belg.
54/E4 Wuwei, China
55/H5 Wuwei, China
59/D5 Wuwei, China
61/H2 Wuwei, China
55/J5 Wuxi, China
59/E5 Wuxi, China
59/L8 Wuxi, China
61/H2 Wuxi (riv.), China
61/J2 Wuxi, China
54/G4 Wuxiang, China
59/C3 Wuxiang, China
59/C5 Wuxue, China
61/G2 Wuxue, China
54/G5 Wuyang, China
59/C4 Wuyang, China
59/C3 Wuyi, China
61/H3 Wuyi (mts.), China
54/F3 Wuyuan, China
55/K2 Wuyur (riv.), China
54/G4 Wuzhai, China
59/B3 Wuzhai, China
59/C4 Wuzhi, China
61/F5 Wuzhi (mts.), China
61/F5 Wuzhi (peak), China
63/J4 Wuzhi (peak), China
65/E2 Wuzhi (mts.), China
65/E2 Wuzhi (peak), China
59/D2 Wuzhi Shan (peak), China
59/J6 Wuzhi Shan (peak), China
61/F4 Wuzhou, China
63/K3 Wuzhou, China
70/B6 Wyalkatchem, Austl.
99/F7 Wyandotte, Mi,US
99/F7 Wyandotte Nat'l Wild. Ref., Mi,US
73/D2 Wyangale (dam), Austl.
73/B3 Wycheproof, Austl.
98/F4 Wyckoff, NJ,US
24/D3 Wye (riv.), UK
73/D2 Wyee, Austl.
20/D5 Wyk, Ger.
26/E1 Wyk, Ger.
24/D4 Wylye (riv.), Eng,UK
23/G6 Wymeswold, Eng,UK
25/H1 Wymondham, Eng,UK
68/B6 Wyndham, Austl.
70/D3 Wyndham, Austl.
36/D3 Wynigen, Swi.
93/K4 Wynne, Ar,US
97/F3 Wynne, Ar,US
72/F6 Wynnum, Austl.
71/H8 Wynyard, Austl.
73/C4 Wynyard, Austl.
86/F3 Wynyard, Sk,Can
88/F1 Wynyard, Sk,Can
91/G3 Wynyard, Sk,Can
90/F5 Wyoming (state), US
86/F4 Wyoming (state), US
88/E3 Wyoming (state), US
92/E2 Wyoming (state), US
94/C3 Wyoming, Mi,US
90/F5 Wyoming (peak), Wy,US
92/E2 Wyoming (peak), Wy,US
92/E2 Wyoming (range), Wy,US
73/B2 Wyperfeld Nat'l Park, Austl.
23/F4 Wyre (riv.), Eng,UK
27/J2 Wyrzysk, Pol.
27/M2 Wysokie Mazowieckie, Pol.
27/L2 Wyszków, Pol.
42/D5 Wyszków, Pol.
94/D4 Wytheville, Va,US
97/H2 Wytheville, Va,US

X

65/D4 Xa Binh Long, Viet.
66/C1 Xa Binh Long, Viet.
54/D5 Xabyaisamba, China
102/B3 Xadani, Mex.
62/E2 Xaitongmoin, China
81/F2 Xai-Xai, Moz.
82/F6 Xai-Xai, Moz.
102/B2 Xalpatlahuac, Mex.
60/E4 Xam (riv.), Laos
65/D1 Xam Nua, Laos
65/D3 Xan (riv.), Viet.
28/D5 Xanten, Ger.
39/J2 Xánthi, Gre.
41/G5 Xánthi, Gre.
44/C4 Xánthi, Gre.
108/A3 Xanxerê, Braz.
77/Q7 Xarardheere, Som.
47/M5 Xar Moron (riv.), China
55/H3 Xar Moron (riv.), China
59/B2 Xar Moron (riv.), China
59/D2 Xar Moron (riv.), China
65/E4 Xa Song Luy, Viet.
66/C1 Xa Song Luy, Viet.
82/C3 Xassengue, Ang.
65/D3 Xa Tho Thanh, Viet.
107/J6 Xavantes (mts.), Braz.
108/B2 Xavantes (res.), Braz.
63/J5 Xa Vo Dat, Viet.
65/D4 Xa Vo Dat, Viet.
102/E2 Xcalak, Mex.
101/J4 X Can, Mex.
102/E1 X Can, Mex.
101/J4 Xel-há (ruins), Mex.
102/E1 Xel-há (ruins), Mex.
94/D4 Xenia, Oh,US
97/H2 Xenia, Oh,US
60/E5 Xeno, Laos
63/J4 Xeno, Laos
65/D2 Xeno, Laos
35/F2 Xerta, Sp.
26/D4 Xertigny, Fr.
36/C1 Xertigny, Fr.
48/L7 Xi (riv.), China
54/E3 Xi (riv.), China
54/F5 Xi (riv.), China
55/H5 Xi (riv.), China
58/A2 Xi (riv.), China
59/E2 Xi (lake), China
60/E2 Xi (riv.), China
61/F4 Xi (riv.), China
61/G2 Xi (riv.), China
63/K3 Xi (riv.), China
60/D3 Xiaguan, China
63/H2 Xiaguan, China
63/J3 Xiajia, China
59/C3 Xiajin, China
68/A2 Xiamen, China
59/B5 Xianfeng, China
61/F2 Xianfeng, China
61/G3 Xiang (riv.), China
54/G5 Xiangcheng, China
59/C4 Xiangcheng, China
60/C2 Xiangcheng, China
63/G2 Xiangcheng, China
54/G5 Xiangfan, China
59/C4 Xiangfan, China
61/G1 Xiangfan, China
54/G4 Xiangfen, China
59/B4 Xiangfen, China
59/D3 Xianghe, China
59/H7 Xianghe, China
61/G3 Xianghua (mtn.), China
60/D5 Xiang Khoang (plat.), Laos
60/D5 Xiangkhoang, Laos
63/H4 Xiangkhoang, Laos
65/C2 Xiang Khoang (plat.), Laos
65/C2 Xiangkhoang, Laos
60/D5 Xiang Ngeun, Laos
63/H4 Xiang Ngeun, Laos
59/B4 Xiangning, China
55/H5 Xiangshui, China
59/D4 Xiangshui, China
59/E4 Xiangshui, China
61/G2 Xiangtan, China
61/G3 Xiangtan, China
63/K2 Xiangtan, China
68/A2 Xiangtan, China
54/G4 Xiangyuan, China
59/C3 Xiangyuan, China
60/D3 Xiangyun, China
63/H2 Xiangyun, China
61/J2 Xianju, China
59/C5 Xianning, China
54/E5 Xianshui (riv.), China
60/D2 Xianshui (riv.), China
59/C5 Xiantao, China
61/G2 Xiantao, China
61/H2 Xianxia (mtn.), China
54/F5 Xianyang, China
59/C3 Xiao (riv.), China
60/D3 Xiao (riv.), China
61/F3 Xiao (riv.), China
63/H2 Xiao (riv.), China
63/K2 Xiao (riv.), China
55/J1 Xiaobole (peak), China
54/G5 Xiaogan, China
59/C5 Xiaogan, China
61/G2 Xiaogan, China
55/K2 Xiao Hinggang (mts.), China
61/G3 Xiaojiang, China
61/J3 Xiaojiang, China
60/D2 Xiaojin (riv.), China
61/G3 Xiaomei (pass), China
59/D3 Xiaoqing (riv.), China
59/L9 Xiaoshan, China
59/C3 Xiaowutai Shan (peak), China
59/D4 Xiao Xian, China
54/G4 Xiaoyi, China
59/B3 Xiaoyi, China
102/D2 Xiatil, Mex.
54/H5 Xiayi, China
59/D4 Xiayi, China
63/J2 Xiazichang, China
63/K2 Xibaxa (riv.), China
60/D3 Xichang, China
63/H2 Xichang, China
65/E1 Xichang, China
59/C4 Xicheng Shan (mtn.), China
63/H3 Xichou, China
54/G5 Xichuan, China
59/B4 Xichuan, China
101/F4 Xicohténcatl, Mex.
102/B1 Xicohténcatl, Mex.
101/F4 Xicotepec, Mex.
101/M6 Xicotepec, Mex.
102/B1 Xicotepec, Mex.
61/J2 Xidongting (mtn.), China
59/L8 Xidongting Shan (mtn.), China
59/C4 Xifei (riv.), China
54/F4 Xifeng, China
55/J3 Xifeng, China
59/F2 Xifeng, China
63/J2 Xifeng, China
62/E2 Xigazê, China
54/E5 Xihan (riv.), China
54/F4 Xihekou, China
59/B3 Xihekou, China
59/B3 Xihua, China
55/J3 Xiliao (riv.), China
59/E2 Xiliao (riv.), China
63/J3 Xilin, China
39/H3 Xilókastron, Gre.
60/C4 Ximeng Vazu Zizhixian, China
63/G3 Ximeng Vazu Zizhixian, China
65/B1 Ximeng Vazu Zizhixian, China
61/H2 Xin (riv.), China
59/C4 Xin'an, China
59/D5 Xin'an, China
61/H3 Xin'an, China
61/H3 Xinan, China
61/H2 Xin'anjang (res.), China
59/D5 Xin'anjiang (res.), China
81/F2 Xinavane, Moz.
55/H2 Xin Barag Zuoqi, China
58/C2 Xinbin, China
59/F2 Xinbin, China
61/F4 Xinbin, China
59/C4 Xincai, China
61/J2 Xinchang, China
59/C3 Xincheng, China
59/G7 Xincheng, China
61/G3 Xincheng, China
63/K3 Xindu, China
63/K3 Xinfeng, China
61/G4 Xinfengjiang (res.), China
61/F3 Xing'an, China
55/J3 Xingcheng, China
59/E2 Xingcheng, China
82/C2 Xinge, Ang.
55/H5 Xinghua, China
59/D4 Xinghua, China
55/L3 Xingkai (lake), China
59/D2 Xinglong, China
59/H6 Xinglong, China
61/F5 Xinglong, China
54/G5 Xingshan, China
59/B5 Xingshan, China
61/F2 Xingshan, China
54/G4 Xingtai, China
59/C3 Xingtai, China
105/D3 Xingu (riv.), Braz.
107/H4 Xingu (riv.), Braz.
59/C4 Xingyang, China
60/E3 Xingyi, China
59/C3 Xinhe, China
61/F3 Xinhuang Dongzu Zizhixian, China
54/E4 Xining, China
54/H4 Xinji, China
59/C3 Xinji, China
46/J5 Xinjiang (reg.), China
48/H5 Xinjiang (aut. reg.), China
59/B4 Xinjiang, China
55/J4 Xinjin, China
58/A3 Xinjin, China
59/E3 Xinjin, China
59/C3 Xinle, China
58/B2 Xinmin, China
59/E2 Xinmin, China
60/D3 Xinping Yizu, China
65/E1 Xinqiao, China
61/F3 Xinshao, China
55/H4 Xintai, China
59/D4 Xintai, China
54/G4 Xinxiang, China
59/C4 Xinxiang, China
54/G5 Xinyang, China
59/C4 Xinyang, China
61/G1 Xinyang, China
54/G5 Xinye, China
59/C4 Xinye, China
61/G1 Xinye, China
55/H5 Xinyi, China
63/K3 Xinyi, China
61/G3 Xinyu, China
59/C4 Xinzheng, China

59/C5 **Xinzhou**, China
61/F2 **Xinzhou**, China
61/F5 **Xinzhou**, China
61/G2 **Xinzhou**, China
65/E2 **Xinzhou**, China
59/D3 **Xiong Xian**, China
59/H7 **Xiong Xian**, China
59/C4 **Xiping**, China
54/E5 **Xiqing** (mts.), China
107/K6 **Xique-Xique**, Braz.
63/J2 **Xishui**, China
55/J5 **Xitang**, China
59/E5 **Xitang**, China
59/L9 **Xitang**, China
61/J2 **Xitang**, China
61/H2 **Xitianmu** (peak), China
59/D5 **Xitianmu Shan** (peak), China
59/K9 **Xitiao** (riv.), China
61/G2 **Xiu** (riv.), China
59/D5 **Xiuning**, China
61/H2 **Xiuning**, China
63/J2 **Xiuwen**, China
54/G4 **Xiuwu**, China
59/C4 **Xiuwu**, China
58/B2 **Xiuyan**, China
59/E2 **Xiuyan**, China
62/E2 **Xixabangma** (peak), China
60/D2 **Xixi** (riv.), China
54/G5 **Xixia**, China
59/B4 **Xixia**, China
60/E4 **Xiyang** (riv.), China
63/J3 **Xiyang** (riv.), China
60/B2 **Xizang** (Tibet) (aut. reg.), China
59/E3 **Xizhong** (isl.), China
102/D2 **Xmaben**, Mex.
101/F4 **Xochiatipan**, Mex.
102/B1 **Xochiatipan**, Mex.
101/K8 **Xochicalco** (ruins), Mex.
101/Q10 **Xochimilco**, Mex.
101/M8 **Xochitlán**, Mex.
54/C6 **Xoka**, China
63/F2 **Xoka**, China
61/H3 **Xu** (riv.), China
59/B5 **Xuan'en**, China
61/F2 **Xuan'en**, China
59/C2 **Xuanhua**, China
59/G6 **Xuanhua**, China
60/E3 **Xuanwei**, China
54/G5 **Xuchang**, China
59/C4 **Xuchang**, China
77/P7 **Xuddur** (Oddur), Som.
60/C3 **Xue** (mts.), China
59/E5 **Xuedou** (peak), China
61/J2 **Xuedou** (peak), China
54/D4 **Xugin Gol** (riv.), China
55/J3 **Xujiatun**, China
54/F5 **Xun** (riv.), China
55/K2 **Xun** (riv.), China
59/B4 **Xun** (riv.), China
61/F4 **Xun** (riv.), China
55/K2 **Xunke**, China
59/C4 **Xun Xian**, China
59/B4 **Xunyang**, China
59/L8 **Xupu**, China
61/F4 **Xuwen**, China
63/K3 **Xuwen**, China
59/D4 **Xuyi**, China
60/E2 **Xuyong**, China
55/H5 **Xuzhou**, China
59/D4 **Xuzhou**, China

Y

54/E6 **Ya'an**, China
60/D2 **Ya'an**, China
49/G7 **Ya'bad**, WBnk.
76/G7 **Yabassi**, Camr.
77/N7 **Yabēlo**, Eth.
39/J1 **Yablanitsa**, Bul.
41/G4 **Yablanitsa**, Bul.
47/M4 **Yablonovyy** (range), Rus.
48/L4 **Yablonovyy** (range), Rus.
54/F1 **Yablonovyy** (ridge), Rus.
54/F2 **Yablonovyy** (range), Rus.
49/G8 **Yabrūd**, WBnk.
104/E3 **Yabucoa**, PR
57/G2 **Yabuki**, Japan
60/E3 **Yachi** (riv.), China
57/J7 **Yachiyo**, Japan
57/K9 **Yachiyo**, Japan
109/B7 **Yacimiento Rio Turbio**, Arg.
108/A4 **Yacuí** (riv.), Braz.
106/F8 **Yacuiba**, Bol.
109/D1 **Yacuiba**, Bol.
62/C4 **Yādgīr**, India
57/L9 **Yagi**, Japan
100/D4 **Yago**, Mex.
41/K2 **Yagorlytsk** (gulf), Ukr.
76/J5 **Yagoua**, Camr.
54/D4 **Yagradagzê** (peak), China
102/E3 **Yaguale** (riv.), Hon.
103/J2 **Yague del Sur** (riv.), DRep.
57/N10 **Yahagi** (riv.), Japan
101/F4 **Yahualica**, Mex.
102/D1 **Yahualica**, Mex.
100/E4 **Yahualica de Gonzalez Gallo**, Mex.
50/C2 **Yahyalı**, Turk.
39/G3 **Yáios** (Paxoí), Gre.
57/F2 **Yaita**, Japan
57/F3 **Yaizu**, Japan
102/C2 **Yajalón**, Mex.
49/E1 **Yakacık**, Turk.
50/D2 **Yakacık**, Turk.
52/C1 **Yakacık**, Turk.
55/J2 **Yakeshi**, China
90/C4 **Yakima** (riv.), Wa,US
86/D4 **Yakima**, Wa,US
88/B2 **Yakima**, Wa,US
90/C4 **Yakima**, Wa,US
76/E5 **Yako**, Burk.
79/E3 **Yako**, Burk.
77/K7 **Yakoma**, Zaire
39/H1 **Yakoruda**, Bul.
41/F4 **Yakoruda**, Bul.
55/L5 **Yaku** (isl.), Japan
56/B5 **Yaku** (isl.), Japan
56/B5 **Yaku-Kirishima Nat'l Park**, Japan
57/K9 **Yakuno**, Japan
85/K4 **Yakutat** (bay), Ak,US
85/L4 **Yakutat**, Ak,US
86/B3 **Yakutat** (bay), Ak,US
86/C3 **Yakutat**, Ak,US
47/N3 **Yakut Aut. Rep.**, Rus.
47/N3 **Yakutsk**, Rus.
63/H6 **Yala**, Thai.
65/C5 **Yala**, Thai.
66/B2 **Yala**, Thai.
102/E1 **Yalahua** (lag.), Mex.
51/G1 **Yalama**, Azer.
102/D2 **Yalbac** (hills), Belz.
93/K4 **Yalobusha** (riv.), Ms,US
76/J6 **Yaloké**, CAfr.
48/K6 **Yalong** (riv.), China
54/E5 **Yalong** (riv.), China
60/D2 **Yalong** (riv.), China
63/H2 **Yalong** (riv.), China
41/J5 **Yalova**, Turk.
44/D4 **Yalova**, Turk.
50/B1 **Yalova**, Turk.
41/J3 **Yalpukh** (lake), Ukr.
72/A5 **Yalpunga**, Austl.
19/G4 **Yalta**, Ukr.
44/E3 **Yalta**, Ukr.
46/D5 **Yalta**, Ukr.
55/J2 **Yalu** (riv.), China
58/C2 **Yalu** (riv.), China
48/M5 **Yalu** (riv.), China, NKor.
55/J3 **Yalu** (riv.), China, NKor.
58/C2 **Yalu** (riv.), NKor.
47/N5 **Yalu** (riv.), NKor., China
50/B2 **Yalvaç**, Turk.
56/B4 **Yamaga**, Japan
47/P6 **Yamagata**, Japan
55/N4 **Yamagata**, Japan
57/F1 **Yamagata** (pref.), Japan
57/G1 **Yamagata**, Japan
55/L5 **Yamaguchi**, Japan
56/B3 **Yamaguchi**, Japan
56/B3 **Yamaguchi** (pref.), Japan
46/G2 **Yamal** (pen.), Rus.
48/F2 **Yamal** (pen.), Rus.
40/G3 **Yamal-Nenets Aut. Okr.**, Rus.
57/F3 **Yamanashi** (prof.), Japan
72/B2 **Yamanie** (falls), Austl.
72/D2 **Yamanie Falls Nat'l Park**, Austl.
48/F4 **Yamantau** (peak), Rus.
43/N5 **Yamantau, Gora** (peak), Rus.
57/N9 **Yamaoka**, Japan
57/L10 **Yamashiro**, Japan
55/M4 **Yamato**, Japan
57/F2 **Yamato**, Japan
57/H7 **Yamato**, Japan
57/L10 **Yamato** (riv.), Japan
57/L10 **Yamato-Kōriyama**, Japan
56/D3 **Yamatotakada**, Japan
57/L10 **Yamatotakada**, Japan
57/M10 **Yamazoe**, Japan
73/E1 **Yamba**, Austl.
77/L7 **Yambio**, Sudan
39/K1 **Yambol**, Bul.
41/H4 **Yambol**, Bul.
44/C4 **Yambol**, Bul.
67/H5 **Yamdena** (isls.), Indo.
60/C4 **Yamethin**, Burma
63/G3 **Yamethin**, Burma
65/B1 **Yamethin**, Burma
67/K4 **Yamin** (peak), Indo.
70/G5 **Yamma Yamma** (lake), Austl.
72/A4 **Yamma Yamma** (lake), Austl.
57/G1 **Yamoto**, Japan
76/D6 **Yamoussoukro** (cap.), IvC.
78/D5 **Yamoussoukro** (cap.), IvC.
92/F2 **Yampa** (riv.), Co,US
41/J1 **Yampol'**, Ukr.
53/L3 **Yamuna** (riv.), India
62/C2 **Yamuna** (riv.), India
64/D2 **Yamuna** (riv.), India
53/L2 **Yamunānagar**, India
64/D2 **Yamunānagar**, India
63/E2 **Yamzho Yumco** (lake), China
54/F4 **Yan** (riv.), China
59/B3 **Yan** (riv.), China
62/D6 **Yan** (riv.), SrL.
64/H4 **Yan** (riv.), SrL.
47/P3 **Yana** (riv.), Rus.
48/N3 **Yana** (riv.), Rus.
56/B4 **Yanagawa**, Japan
56/C4 **Yanai**, Japan
43/M4 **Yanaul**, Rus.
63/H2 **Yanbian**, China
52/C4 **Yanbu' al Baḩr**, SAr.
77/N3 **Yanbu' al Baḩr**, SAr.
55/J5 **Yancheng**, China
59/C4 **Yancheng**, China
59/E4 **Yancheng**, China
73/C2 **Yanco**, Austl.
69/T12 **Yandé** (isl.), NCal.
60/B5 **Yandoon**, Burma
63/G4 **Yandoon**, Burma
76/D5 **Yanfolila**, Mali
78/C4 **Yanfolila**, Mali
77/K7 **Yangambi**, Zaire
60/C3 **Yangbi** (riv.), China
63/G2 **Yangbi** (riv.), China
59/C4 **Yangcheng**, China
59/L8 **Yangcheng** (lake), China
61/H3 **Yangdang** (mts.), Laos
58/D3 **Yangdŏk**, NKor.
58/D2 **Yanggang-do** (prov.), NKor.
54/G3 **Yanggao**, China
59/C2 **Yanggao**, China
59/C3 **Yanggu**, China
55/K4 **Yanggu**, SKor.
58/D3 **Yanggu**, SKor.
61/F4 **Yangjiang**, China
63/K3 **Yangjiang**, China
58/A4 **Yangma** (isl.), China
61/F3 **Yangming** (peak), China
60/C5 **Yangon** (Rangoon) (cap.), Burma
63/G4 **Yangon** (Rangoon) (cap.), Burma
65/B2 **Yangon** (Rangoon) (cap.), Burma
58/D4 **Yangp'yŏng**, SKor.
54/G4 **Yangqu**, China
59/C3 **Yangqu**, China
54/G4 **Yangquan**, China
59/C3 **Yangquan**, China
58/E5 **Yangsan**, SKor.
63/K3 **Yangshan**, China
63/K3 **Yangshuo**, China
60/C3 **Yangtouyan**, China
55/D5 **Yangtze** (riv.), China
55/J5 **Yangtze** (riv.), China
59/L8 **Yangtze** (riv.), China
59/D5 **Yangtze** (Chang) (riv.), China
61/H2 **Yangtze** (Cheng) (riv.), China
60/D3 **Yangtze** (Jinsha) (riv.), China
77/P5 **Yangudi Rassa Nat'l Park**, Eth.
59/C5 **Yangxin**, China
59/D3 **Yangxin**, China
61/G2 **Yangxin**, China
63/J3 **Yangxu**, China
56/A1 **Yangyang**, SKor.
58/E3 **Yangyang**, SKor.
54/G3 **Yangyuan**, China
59/C2 **Yangyuan**, China
59/D4 **Yangzhong**, China
61/H1 **Yangzhong**, China
55/H5 **Yangzhou**, China
59/D4 **Yangzhou**, China
61/H1 **Yangzhou**, China
47/N5 **Yanji**, China
55/K3 **Yanji**, China
59/C4 **Yanjin**, China
60/E2 **Yanjin**, China
63/H2 **Yanjin**, China
54/D6 **Yanjing**, China
79/H4 **Yankari Game Rsv.**, Nga.
88/G4 **Yankton**, SD,US
89/G3 **Yankton**, SD,US
91/J5 **Yankton**, SD,US
93/H2 **Yankton**, SD,US
59/C4 **Yanling**, China
59/C3 **Yanmen Guan** (pass), China
59/D3 **Yanshan**, China
63/H3 **Yanshan**, China
59/C4 **Yanshi**, China
55/K2 **Yanshou**, China
47/N6 **Yantai**, China
55/J4 **Yantai**, China
59/E3 **Yantai**, China
27/K1 **Yantarnyy**, Rus.
42/C5 **Yantarnyy**, Rus.
60/E2 **Yanting**, China
59/C2 **Yantong Shan** (mtn.), China
73/G5 **Yan Yean** (res.), Austl.
60/D3 **Yanyuan**, China
63/H2 **Yanyuan**, China
59/D4 **Yanzhou**, China
56/D3 **Yao**, Japan
57/L10 **Yao**, Japan
63/H2 **Yao'an**, China
54/F4 **Yaodian**, China
59/B3 **Yaodian**, China
76/H7 **Yaoundé** (cap.), Camr.
68/C4 **Yap** (isls.), Micr.
106/E3 **Yapacana Nat'l Park**, Ven.
79/E4 **Yapei**, Gha.
67/J4 **Yapen** (isl.), Indo.
67/J4 **Yapen** (str.), Indo.
68/C5 **Yapen** (isl.), Indo.
98/H5 **Yaphank**, NY,US
50/C1 **Yapraklı**, Turk.
54/G5 **Yaqueling**, China
100/C2 **Yaqui** (riv.), Mex.
100/C3 **Yaqui**, Mex.
84/G7 **Yaqui** (riv.), Mex.
25/E5 **Yar** (riv.), Eng,UK
103/G1 **Yara**, Cuba
104/D5 **Yaracuy** (state), Ven.
50/C1 **Yaralıgöz** (peak), Turk.
44/E4 **Yaralıgöz Daği** (peak), Turk.
67/J4 **Yaramaniapuka** (mtn.), Indo.
43/K4 **Yaransk**, Rus.
43/B1 **Yardımcı** (pt.), Turk.
51/G2 **Yardymly**, Azer.
25/H1 **Yare** (riv.), Eng,UK
41/G1 **Yaremcha**, Ukr.
44/D3 **Yargora**, Mol.
57/E2 **Yari-ga-take** (mtn.), Japan
52/D6 **Yarīm**, Yem.
77/P5 **Yarīm**, Yem.
41/J5 **Yarımca**, Turk.
50/B1 **Yarımca**, Turk.
46/H6 **Yarkant** (riv.), China
53/L1 **Yarkant** (riv.), China
87/K4 **Yarmouth**, NS,Can
89/N3 **Yarmouth**, NS,Can
95/H3 **Yarmouth**, NS,Can
19/G3 **Yaroslavl'**, Rus.
42/H4 **Yaroslavl'**, Rus.
46/D4 **Yaroslavl'**, Rus.
42/H4 **Yaroslavl' Obl.**, Rus.
73/G5 **Yarra** (riv.), Austl.
73/G5 **Yarra Glen**, Austl.
73/C3 **Yarram**, Austl.
72/D4 **Yarraman**, Austl.
73/C3 **Yarrawonga**, Austl.
99/C2 **Yarrow Point**, Wa,US
46/K3 **Yartsevo**, Rus.
106/C2 **Yarumal**, Col.
63/G2 **Yarzhong**, China
69/Y17 **Yasawa** (isls.), Fiji
68/G6 **Yasawa Group** (isls.), Fiji
44/C1 **Yasel'da** (riv.), Bela.
52/E6 **Yashbum**, Yem.
76/F6 **Yashikera**, Nga.
57/H7 **Yashio**, Japan
57/K10 **Yashiro**, Japan
41/G1 **Yasinya**, Ukr.
45/L2 **Yasnyy**, Rus.
63/H4 **Yasothon**, Thai.
65/D3 **Yasothon**, Thai.
73/D2 **Yass**, Austl.
52/F4 **Yas, Sir Bani** (isl.), UAE
57/M10 **Yasu** (riv.), Japan
57/M9 **Yasu**, Japan
56/C3 **Yasugi**, Japan
52/F2 **Yāsūj**, Iran
50/D1 **Yasun** (pt.), Turk.
106/C4 **Yasuni Nat'l Park**, Ecu.
57/G2 **Yatabe**, Japan
50/B2 **Yatağan**, Turk.
24/D3 **Yate**, Eng,UK
25/F4 **Yateley**, Eng,UK
79/E3 **Yatenga** (prov.), Burk.
93/J3 **Yates Center**, Ks,US
96/E2 **Yates Center**, Ks,US
86/G2 **Yathkyed** (lake), NW,Can
57/M9 **Yatomi**, Japan
57/E2 **Yatsuo**, Japan
56/B4 **Yatsushiro**, Japan
49/D4 **Yaţţah**, WBnk.
50/C4 **Yaţţah**, WBnk.
24/D4 **Yatton**, Eng,UK
104/E3 **Yauco**, PR
101/K7 **Yautepec**, Mex.
43/X9 **Yauza** (riv.), Rus.
105/B3 **Yavarí** (riv.), Peru
100/C3 **Yavaros**, Mex.
62/C3 **Yavatmāl**, India
46/H2 **Yavay** (pen.), Rus.
102/C2 **Yaveo**, Mex.
103/G4 **Yaviza**, Pan.
49/F8 **Yavne**, Isr.
27/M4 **Yavorov**, Ukr.
50/D2 **Yavuzeli**, Turk.
57/J7 **Yawahara**, Japan
57/L10 **Yawata**, Japan
56/C4 **Yawatahama**, Japan
101/H4 **Yaxcabá**, Mex.
102/D1 **Yaxcabá**, Mex.
102/D2 **Yaxchilán** (ruins), Mex.
25/F2 **Yaxley**, Eng,UK
49/E2 **Yayladaği**, Turk.
50/D3 **Yayladaği**, Turk.
52/C1 **Yayladaği**, Turk.
50/E2 **Yayladere**, Turk.
46/F6 **Yazd**, Iran
48/E6 **Yazd**, Iran
51/H3 **Yazd** (gov.), Iran
51/H4 **Yazd**, Iran
53/F2 **Yazd**, Iran
93/K4 **Yazoo** (riv.), Ms,US
89/H5 **Yazoo City**, Ms,US
93/K4 **Yazoo City**, Ms,US
97/F3 **Yazoo City**, Ms,US
27/H4 **Ybbs** (riv.), Aus.
33/L2 **Ybbs**, Aus.
33/L2 **Ybbs** (riv.), Aus.
40/B1 **Ybbs** (riv.), Aus.
40/B1 **Ybbs an der Donau**, Aus.
27/H5 **Ybbsitz**, Aus.
40/B2 **Ybbsitz**, Aus.
32/C4 **Ychoux**, Fr.
63/G4 **Ye**, Burma
65/B3 **Ye**, Burma
23/G4 **Yeadon**, Eng,UK
24/B6 **Yealmpton**, Eng,UK
63/H5 **Yeay Sen** (cape), Camb.
65/C4 **Yeay Sen** (cape), Camb.
58/E4 **Yech'ŏn**, SKor.
35/E3 **Yecla**, Sp.
101/N7 **Yecuatla**, Mex.
41/K5 **Yedigöller Milli Park**, Turk.
44/D4 **Yedigöller Milli Park**, Turk.
50/B1 **Yedigöller Nat'l Park**, Turk.
51/M6 **Yedikule**, Turk.
44/C2 **Yedintsy**, Mol.
40/F5 **Yéfira**, Gre.
19/G3 **Yefremov**, Rus.
44/F1 **Yefremov**, Rus.
46/D4 **Yefremov**, Rus.
45/G3 **Yegorlak** (riv.), Rus.
101/M8 **Yehualtepec**, Mex.
49/F7 **Yehud**, Isr.
77/M7 **Yei**, Sudan
46/G4 **Yekaterinburg**, Rus.
43/P4 **Yekaterinburg Obl.**, Rus.
43/P4 **Yekaterinburg** (Sverdlovsk), Rus.
43/M5 **Yelabuga**, Rus.
45/G2 **Yelan'**, Rus.
72/C5 **Yelarbon**, Austl.
73/D1 **Yelarbon**, Austl.
19/G3 **Yelets**, Rus.
44/F1 **Yelets**, Rus.
46/D4 **Yelets**, Rus.
78/C3 **Yélimané**, Mali
47/Q4 **Yelizavety** (cape), Rus.
48/P4 **Yelizavety** (cape), Rus.
47/R4 **Yelizovo**, Rus.
75/R16 **Yellel**, Alg.
47/N6 **Yellow** (sea), Asia
48/M6 **Yellow** (sea), Asia
59/E4 **Yellow** (sea), Asia
55/J4 **Yellow** (sea), Asia
58/B4 **Yellow** (sea), Asia
91/G3 **Yellow Grass**, Sk,Can
47/L5 **Yellow** (Huang) (riv.), China
59/D3 **Yellow** (Huang) (riv.), China
84/F3 **Yellowknife**, Can.
86/E2 **Yellowknife** (cap.), NW,Can
86/E2 **Yellowknife** (riv.), NW,Can
84/G5 **Yellowstone** (riv.), Mt,US
86/F4 **Yellowstone** (riv.), Mt,US
91/G4 **Yellowstone** (riv.), Mt,US
88/E2 **Yellowstone** (riv.), Mt,US
90/F4 **Yellowstone** (lake), Wy,US
92/E1 **Yellowstone** (lake), Wy,US
90/F4 **Yellowstone Nat'l Park**, US
92/E1 **Yellowstone Nat'l Park**, US
86/E4 **Yellowstone Nat'l Park**, Wy,US
88/D3 **Yellowstone Nat'l Park**, Wy,US
96/E2 **Yellville**, Ar,US
44/E1 **Yel'nya**, Rus.
24/B6 **Yelverton**, Eng,UK
78/F5 **Yelwa**, Nga.
79/H4 **Yelwa**, Nga.
54/D4 **Yema** (riv.), China
48/D8 **Yemen**
52/E5 **Yemen**
77/Q5 **Yemen**
44/F2 **Yenakiyevo**, Ukr.
60/B4 **Yenangyaung**, Burma
63/F3 **Yenangyaung**, Burma
60/E4 **Yen Bai**, Viet.
65/D1 **Yen Bai**, Viet.
73/C2 **Yenda**, Austl.
76/E6 **Yendi**, Gha.
79/E4 **Yendi**, Gha.
63/G3 **Ye-ngan**, Burma
65/B1 **Ye-ngan**, Burma
41/L5 **Yeniçağa**, Turk.
41/H6 **Yenice**, Turk.
41/L5 **Yenice**, Turk.
44/E4 **Yenice**, Turk.
44/E1 **Yenice** (riv.), Turk.
49/D1 **Yenice**, Turk.
50/C2 **Yeniceoba**, Turk.
41/H5 **Yeniköy**, Turk.
51/M6 **Yeniköy**, Turk.
41/J5 **Yenişehir**, Turk.
44/D4 **Yenişehir**, Turk.
50/B1 **Yenişehir**, Turk.
46/J3 **Yenisey** (riv.), Rus.
48/H3 **Yenisey** (riv.), Rus.
54/C1 **Yenisey** (riv.), Rus.
46/K4 **Yeniseysk**, Rus.
60/E4 **Yen Minh**, Viet.
65/D1 **Yen Minh**, Viet.
70/C5 **Yeo** (lake), Austl.
24/D5 **Yeo** (riv.), Eng,UK
53/K4 **Yeola**, India
73/D2 **Yeoval**, Austl.
24/D5 **Yeovil**, Eng,UK
71/J4 **Yeppoon**, Austl.
72/C3 **Yeppoon**, Austl.
39/H3 **Yerakovoúni** (peak), Gre.
46/F5 **Yeraliyev**, Kaz.
100/E3 **Yerbanís**, Mex.
30/A4 **Yères** (riv.), Fr.
19/H4 **Yerevan** (cap.), Arm.
45/H4 **Yerevan** (cap.), Arm.
46/E5 **Yerevan** (cap.), Arm.
51/F1 **Yerevan** (cap.), Arm.
92/C3 **Yerington**, Nv,US
44/E5 **Yerköy**, Turk.
50/C2 **Yerköy**, Turk.
39/K2 **Yerlisu**, Turk.
41/H5 **Yerlisu**, Turk.
46/H4 **Yermak**, Kaz.
45/K1 **Yermekeyevo**, Rus.
46/H4 **Yermentau**, Kaz.
45/G1 **Yermish'**, Rus.
47/N4 **Yerofey Pavlovich**, Rus.
49/D4 **Yeroḩam**, Isr.
39/H4 **Yerolimín**, Gre.
32/D2 **Yerre** (riv.), Fr.
19/T10 **Yerres**, Fr.
19/U11 **Yerres** (riv.), Fr.
30/B6 **Yerres**, Fr.
30/C6 **Yerres** (riv.), Fr.
106/C6 **Yerupaja** (peak), Peru
49/D4 **Yerushalayim** (Jerusalem) (cap.), Isr.
77/N1 **Yerushalayim** (Jerusalem) (cap.), Isr.
60/B4 **Yesagyo**, Burma
63/G3 **Yesagyo**, Burma
58/D4 **Yesan**, SKor.
46/G4 **Yesil'**, Kaz.
50/C2 **Yeşilhisar**, Turk.
44/F4 **Yeşilırmak** (riv.), Turk.
49/E1 **Yeşilkent**, Turk.
50/D2 **Yeşilkent**, Turk.
50/B2 **Yeşilova**, Turk.
50/C2 **Yeşilova**, Turk.
49/F8 **Yesodot**, Isr.
58/D3 **Yesŏng** (riv.), NKor.
45/G3 **Yessentuki**, Rus.
34/D3 **Yeste**, Sp.
24/D5 **Yetminster**, Eng,UK
63/G3 **Ye-u**, Burma
32/B3 **Yeu** (isl.), Fr.
62/B3 **Yevla**, India
45/H4 **Yevlakh**, Azer.
51/F1 **Yevlakh**, Azer.
19/G4 **Yevpatoriya**, Ukr.
44/E3 **Yevpatoriya**, Ukr.
46/D5 **Yevpatoriya**, Ukr.
54/G5 **Ye Xian**, China
59/D3 **Ye Xian**, China
44/G3 **Yeya** (riv.), Rus.
19/G4 **Yeysk**, Rus.
44/F3 **Yeysk**, Rus.
32/C5 **Ygos-Saint-Saturnin**, Fr.
35/E1 **Ygos-Saint-Saturnin**, Fr.
54/G5 **Yi** (riv.), China
55/H4 **Yi** (riv.), China
59/C4 **Yi** (riv.), China
49/D2 **Yialousa**, Cyp.
39/H2 **Yiannitsá**, Gre.
40/F5 **Yiannitsá**, Gre.
44/B4 **Yiannitsá**, Gre.
39/H3 **Yiánnouli**, Gre.
39/J4 **Yíaros** (isl.), Gre.
60/E2 **Yibin**, China
54/G5 **Yichang**, China
59/B5 **Yichang**, China
61/F2 **Yichang**, China
54/G5 **Yicheng**, China
59/B4 **Yicheng**, China
59/C5 **Yicheng**, China
61/G2 **Yicheng**, China
54/G5 **Yichuan**, China
59/C4 **Yichuan**, China
47/N5 **Yichun**, China
55/K2 **Yichun**, China
61/G3 **Yichun**, China
63/K2 **Yichun**, China
54/D5 **Yidun**, China
63/K2 **Yifeng**, China
41/K5 **Yığılca**, Turk.
44/D4 **Yığılca**, Turk.
61/H3 **Yihuang**, China
55/K2 **Yilan**, China
50/D1 **Yıldız** (peak), Turk.
44/F5 **Yıldızeli**, Turk.
50/D2 **Yıldızeli**, Turk.
51/N6 **Yildiz Park**, Turk.
55/J1 **Yilehuli** (mts.), China
60/E3 **Yiliang**, China
63/H2 **Yiliang**, China
59/B4 **Yima**, China
60/D3 **Yimen**, China
63/H3 **Yimen**, China
55/J2 **Yimin** (riv.), China
47/L5 **Yin** (mts.), China
54/F3 **Yin** (mts.), China
55/H4 **Yinan**, China
60/D4 **Yinan**, China
54/F4 **Yinchuan**, China
70/C6 **Yindarlgooda** (lake), Austl.
54/H5 **Ying** (riv.), China
59/C4 **Ying** (riv.), China
54/G5 **Yingcheng**, China
59/C5 **Yingcheng**, China
61/G2 **Yingcheng**, China
63/K3 **Yingde**, China
47/N5 **Yingkou**, China
55/J3 **Yingkou**, China
58/B2 **Yingkou**, China
59/E2 **Yingkou**, China
65/E1 **Yingpan**, China
54/G5 **Yingshan**, China
59/C5 **Yingshan**, China
61/G2 **Yingshan**, China
59/D4 **Yingshang**, China
61/H1 **Yingshang**, China
61/H2 **Yingtan**, China
46/J5 **Yining**, China
61/J2 **Yinyang**, China
54/D5 **Yi'ong** (riv.), China
60/B2 **Yi'ong** (riv.), China
77/M6 **Yirol**, Sudan
61/F3 **Yishan**, China
55/H4 **Yishui**, China
59/D4 **Yishui**, China
39/H4 **Yíthion**, Gre.
59/F2 **Yitong** (riv.), China
54/C3 **Yiwu**, China
59/G7 **Yi Xian**, China
59/D5 **Yixing**, China
59/K8 **Yixing**, China
61/H2 **Yixing**, China
54/G5 **Yiyang**, China
59/C4 **Yiyang**, China
61/G2 **Yiyang**, China
63/K2 **Yiyang**, China
54/C6 **Yiyu**, India
59/D3 **Yiyuan**, China
63/K2 **Yizhang**, China
59/D4 **Yizheng**, China
61/H1 **Yizheng**, China
42/D4 **Ylakiai**, Lith.
22/E6 **Y Llethr** (mtn.), Wal,UK
20/G3 **Ylöjärvi**, Fin.
42/D3 **Ylöjärvi**, Fin.
93/H5 **Yoakum**, Tx,US
96/D4 **Yoakum**, Tx,US
58/D5 **Yŏch'ŏn**, SKor.
56/D3 **Yodo** (riv.), Japan
57/L10 **Yodo** (riv.), Japan
55/K4 **Yodŏk**, NKor.
47/P4 **Yoduma** (riv.), Rus.
76/J4 **Yogoum** (well), Chad
66/D5 **Yogyakarta**, Indo.
90/D3 **Yoho Nat'l Park**, BC,Can
86/E3 **Yoho Nat'l Park**, BC,Can
102/D3 **Yojoa** (lake), Hon.
58/D4 **Yŏju**, SKor.
76/J7 **Yokadouma**, Camr.
56/E3 **Yōkaichi**, Japan
57/M9 **Yōkaichi**, Japan
56/D3 **Yokawa**, Japan
57/L10 **Yokawa**, Japan
56/E3 **Yokkaichi**, Japan
57/M10 **Yokkaichi**, Japan
47/P6 **Yokohama**, Japan
55/M4 **Yokohama**, Japan
57/F3 **Yokohama**, Japan
57/H7 **Yokohama**, Japan
57/F3 **Yokosuka**, Japan
57/H7 **Yokosuka**, Japan
76/H6 **Yola**, Nga.
103/E4 **Yolaina, Serranías de** (range), Nic.
99/L9 **Yolo**, Ca,US
99/L9 **Yolo** (co.), Ca,US
60/D5 **Yom** (riv.), Thai.
63/H4 **Yom** (riv.), Thai.
65/C2 **Yom** (riv.), Thai.
76/H8 **Yombi**, Gabon
82/B1 **Yombi**, Gabon
55/J4 **Yŏmju**, NKor.
61/F4 **Yon** (riv.), China
32/C3 **Yon** (riv.), Fr.
55/L4 **Yonago**, Japan
56/C3 **Yonago**, Japan
55/N4 **Yonezawa**, Japan
57/G2 **Yonezawa**, Japan
58/D5 **Yŏngam**, SKor.
58/C3 **Yongamp'o**, NKor.
61/F3 **Yong'an** (pass), China
61/H3 **Yong'an**, China
55/K4 **Yŏngbyŏn**, NKor.
54/F4 **Yongchang**, China
59/D4 **Yongcheng**, China
56/A3 **Yŏngch'ŏn**, SKor.
58/E5 **Yŏngch'ŏn**, SKor.
63/G3 **Yongde**, China
47/M6 **Yongding** (riv.), China
54/H4 **Yongding** (riv.), China
59/H7 **Yongding** (riv.), China
55/K4 **Yŏngdŏk**, SKor.
56/A2 **Yŏngdŏk**, SKor.
58/E4 **Yŏngdŏk**, SKor.
58/D4 **Yŏngdong**, SKor.
58/F6 **Yongdungp'o**, SKor.
63/J3 **Yongfu**, China
58/D5 **Yŏnggwang**, SKor.
58/E4 **Yŏnghae**, SKor.
59/B3 **Yonghe**, China
50/D3 **Yŏnghŭng**, NKor.
58/D3 **Yŏnghŭng** (riv.), NKor.
59/B4 **Yongji**, China
58/F6 **Yŏngjong** (isl.), SKor.
55/K4 **Yŏngju**, SKor.
56/A2 **Yŏngju**, SKor.
58/E4 **Yŏngju**, SKor.
58/D4 **Yongmun-san** (mtn.), SKor.
59/C3 **Yongnian**, China
65/E1 **Yongning**, China
54/F4 **Yongping**, China
59/B3 **Yongping**, China
59/D3 **Yongqing**, China
59/H7 **Yongqing**, China
63/H2 **Yongren**, China
58/D5 **Yŏngsan** (riv.), SKor.
60/D2 **Yongshan**, China
63/H2 **Yongshan**, China
61/D3 **Yongsheng**, China
63/H2 **Yongsheng**, China
63/J2 **Yongshun**, China
55/K4 **Yŏngwŏl**, SKor.
56/A2 **Yŏngwŏl**, SKor.
58/E4 **Yŏngwŏl**, SKor.
63/K2 **Yongxin**, China
56/A2 **Yŏng-yang**, SKor.
58/E4 **Yŏng-yang**, SKor.
61/F3 **Yongzhou**, China
63/K2 **Yongzhou**, China
89/M3 **Yonkers**, NY,US
94/F3 **Yonkers**, NY,US
26/B5 **Yonne** (riv.), Fr.
32/E2 **Yonne** (riv.), Fr.
57/H7 **Yono**, Japan
55/K4 **Yŏnsan**, NKor.
98/C3 **Yorba Linda**, Ca,US
68/D6 **York** (cape), Austl.
70/B6 **York**, Austl.
70/C2 **York** (sound), Austl.
70/G2 **York** (cape), Austl.
95/Q8 **York** (co.), On,Can
95/R8 **York**, On,Can
95/H1 **York** (riv.), Qu,Can
23/G4 **York**, Eng,UK
97/F3 **York**, Al,US
91/J5 **York**, Ne,US
93/H2 **York**, Ne,US
89/L4 **York**, Pa,US
94/E4 **York**, Pa,US
97/H3 **York**, SC,US
94/E4 **York** (riv.), Va,US
70/F6 **Yorke** (pen.), Austl.
70/F7 **Yorketown**, Austl.
84/H4 **York Landing**, Can.
91/J1 **York Landing**, Mb,Can
23/G4 **York Minster**, Eng,UK
23/F3 **Yorkshire Dales Nat'l Park**, Eng,UK
23/H3 **Yorkshire Wolds** (grsld.), Eng,UK
86/F3 **Yorkton**, Sk,Can
88/F1 **Yorkton**, Sk,Can
91/H3 **Yorkton**, Sk,Can
101/F2 **Yorktown**, Tx,US
23/G3 **York, Vale of** (val.), Eng,UK
99/P16 **Yorkville**, Il,US
102/E3 **Yoro**, Hon.
57/F3 **Yōrō** (riv.), Japan
57/M9 **Yōrō**, Japan
57/M10 **Yoroi-zaki** (pt.), Japan
54/F2 **Yöröö**, Mong.
78/D3 **Yorosso**, Mali
23/F6 **Yorton**, Eng,UK
76/F6 **Yorubaland** (plat.), Nga.
79/F4 **Yorubaland** (plat.), Nga.
86/E5 **Yosemite Nat'l Park**, Ca,US
88/C4 **Yosemite Nat'l Park**, Ca,US
92/C3 **Yosemite Nat'l Park**, Ca,US
56/C4 **Yoshida**, Japan
56/D3 **Yoshii** (riv.), Japan
57/H7 **Yoshikawa**, Japan
56/D3 **Yoshimo** (riv.), Japan
57/L10 **Yoshino**, Japan
57/L10 **Yoshino** (riv.), Japan
56/E3 **Yoshino-Kumano Nat'l Park**, Japan
57/L10 **Yoshino-Kumano Nat'l Park**, Japan
19/H3 **Yoshkar-Ola**, Rus.
43/K4 **Yoshkar-Ola**, Rus.
46/E4 **Yoshkar-Ola**, Rus.
67/J5 **Yos Sudarso** (isl.), Indo.
55/K5 **Yŏsu**, SKor.
58/D5 **Yŏsu**, SKor.
55/N3 **Yōtei-san** (mtn.), Japan
57/J7 **Yotsukaidō**, Japan
61/E4 **You** (riv.), China
61/F2 **You** (riv.), China
61/G3 **You** (peak), China
21/B4 **Youghal**, Ire.
71/H6 **Young**, Austl.
73/D2 **Young**, Austl.
109/E3 **Young**, Uru.
99/C3 **Youngs** (lake), Wa,US
95/R9 **Youngstown**, NY,US
89/K3 **Youngstown**, Oh,US
94/D3 **Youngstown**, Oh,US
99/K10 **Yountville**, Ca,US
63/J2 **Youyang**, China
55/L2 **Youyi**, China
106/E2 **Yoví** (peak), Ven.
44/E5 **Yozgat**, Turk.
50/C2 **Yozgat**, Turk.
30/B2 **Ypres** (Ieper), Belg.
32/E1 **Ypres** (Ieper), Belg.
99/E7 **Ypsilanti**, Mi,US
22/D6 **Yr Eifl** (mtn.), Wal,UK
88/B3 **Yreka**, Ca,US
90/C5 **Yreka**, Ca,US
92/B2 **Yreka**, Ca,US
26/B3 **Yser** (riv.), Fr.
30/B2 **Yser** (riv.), Fr.
32/E1 **Yser** (riv.), Fr.
20/E5 **Ystad**, Swe.
27/G1 **Ystad**, Swe.
24/C3 **Ystalyfera**, Wal,UK
24/C3 **Ystradgynlais**, Wal,UK
24/C3 **Ystrad Mynach**, Wal,UK
24/C2 **Ystwyth** (riv.), Wal,UK
32/E4 **Ytrac**, Fr.
20/G2 **Ytterbyn**, Swe.
63/J3 **Yu** (riv.), China
61/J4 **Yü** (peak), Tai.
48/K7 **Yuan** (riv.), China
59/C5 **Yuan** (lake), China
61/F2 **Yuan** (riv.), China
61/G3 **Yuan** (riv.), China
63/H3 **Yuan** (riv.), China
59/B5 **Yuan'an**, China
61/F2 **Yuan'an**, China
61/F3 **Yuanbao** (mtn.), China
54/G4 **Yuanping**, China
59/C3 **Yuanping**, China
59/B4 **Yuanqu**, China
60/D4 **Yuan** (Red) (riv.), China
54/F5 **Yuanshan**, China
59/C3 **Yuanshi**, China
54/G4 **Yuanyang**, China
59/C4 **Yuanyang**, China
88/B4 **Yuba City**, Ca,US
92/B3 **Yuba City**, Ca,US
55/N3 **Yūbari**, Japan
98/C2 **Yucaipa**, Ca,US
89/J7 **Yucatan** (chan.), Cuba, Mex.
101/H4 **Yucatan** (state), Mex.
101/H5 **Yucatán** (pen.), Mex.
102/D1 **Yucatán** (state), Mex.
102/D2 **Yucatan** (pen.), Mex.
102/E1 **Yucatan** (chan.), Mex.
84/J7 **Yucatan** (pen.), Mex.
89/J7 **Yucatan** (state), Mex.
84/J7 **Yucatan** (chan.), Mex., Cuba
92/D4 **Yucca**, Az,US
59/C4 **Yucheng**, China
59/D3 **Yucheng**, China
54/G4 **Yuci**, China
59/C3 **Yuci**, China
61/G3 **Yudu**, China
60/E2 **Yuechi**, China
61/G2 **Yuelu** (mtn.), China
70/E4 **Yuendumu**, Austl.
61/J2 **Yueqing**, China
54/H5 **Yuexi**, China
59/D5 **Yuexi**, China
60/D2 **Yuexi** (riv.), China
61/H2 **Yuexi**, China
63/H2 **Yuexi**, China
61/G2 **Yueyang**, China
43/K3 **Yug** (riv.), Rus.
46/E4 **Yug** (riv.), Rus.
43/P1 **Yugorskiy** (pen.), Rus.
18/E4 **Yugoslavia**
39/F1 **Yugoslavia**
40/E3 **Yugoslavia**
44/B3 **Yugoslavia**
59/E5 **Yuhang**, China
61/G3 **Yuhua** (mtn.), China
61/J2 **Yuhuan**, China
57/F2 **Yūki**, Japan

192

Yukon – Żywie

85/F3 **Yukon** (riv.), Can,US
86/B2 **Yukon** (riv.), Can,US
84/B3 **Yukon** (riv.), Can,US
85/K2 **Yukon-Charley Rivers Nat'l Prsv.**, Ak,US
85/L3 **Yukon Crossing**, Yk,Can
85/F3 **Yukon Delta Nat'l Wild. Ref.**, Ak,US
85/J2 **Yukon Flats Nat'l Wild. Ref.**, Ak,US
85/L2 **Yukon Territory** (terr.), Can.
86/C2 **Yukon Territory** (terr.), Can.
51/F2 **Yüksekova**, Turk.
52/D1 **Yüksekova**, Turk.
56/B4 **Yukuhashi**, Japan
70/E5 **Yulara**, Austl.
72/C4 **Yuleba**, Austl.
59/B3 **Yulin** (riv.), China
61/F4 **Yulin**, China
63/J4 **Yulin**, China
63/K3 **Yulin**, China
65/E1 **Yulin**, China
65/E2 **Yulin**, China
61/H2 **Yuling** (pass), China
59/D5 **Yuling Guan** (pass), China
60/D3 **Yulongxue** (peak), China
100/B1 **Yuma**, Az,US
88/D5 **Yuma**, Az,US
92/D4 **Yuma**, Az,US
93/G2 **Yuma**, Co,US
77/L8 **Yumbi**, Zaire
82/E1 **Yumbi**, Zaire
106/C3 **Yumbo**, Col.
60/A2 **Yumbu Lhakang**, China
54/D4 **Yumen**, China
49/D1 **Yumurtalık**, Turk.
59/C5 **Yun** (riv.), China
61/G2 **Yun** (riv.), China
50/B2 **Yunak**, Turk.
59/B4 **Yuncheng**, China
59/C4 **Yuncheng**, China
59/C2 **Yungang Caves**, China
106/E7 **Yungas** (reg.), Bol.
61/F4 **Yunkai** (mts.), China
63/G2 **Yunlong**, China
60/D3 **Yunnan** (prov.), China
63/H3 **Yunnan** (prov.), China
65/C1 **Yunnan** (prov.), China
73/A2 **Yunta**, Austl.
59/D4 **Yuntai Shan** (peak), China
59/D2 **Yunwu Shan** (peak), China
54/G5 **Yunxi**, China
59/B4 **Yunxi**, China
54/G5 **Yun Xian**, China
59/B4 **Yun Xian**, China
60/D3 **Yun Xian**, China
63/H3 **Yun Xian**, China
59/D4 **Yunyan** (riv.), China
54/G4 **Yunyanzhen**, China
59/B3 **Yunyanzhen**, China
59/C3 **Yunzhong Shan** (mtn.), China
63/J2 **Yuping**, China
59/H7 **Yuqiao** (res.), China
56/D3 **Yura** (riv.), Japan
57/L9 **Yura** (riv.), Japan
42/E5 **Yuratishki**, Bela.
44/C1 **Yuratishki**, Bela.
46/J4 **Yurga**, Rus.
106/C5 **Yurimaguas**, Peru
43/N5 **Yuryuzan'** (riv.), Rus.
102/E3 **Yuscarán**, Hon.
61/J4 **Yushan Nat'l Park**, Tai.
59/C3 **Yushe**, China
55/K3 **Yushu**, China
58/D4 **Yusŏng**, SKor.
45/G4 **Yusufeli**, Turk.
50/E1 **Yusufeli**, Turk.
59/D4 **Yutai**, China
59/D3 **Yutian**, China
59/H7 **Yutian**, China
26/D4 **Yutz**, Fr.
31/F5 **Yutz**, Fr.
33/G2 **Yutz**, Fr.
54/G5 **Yu Xian**, China
59/C3 **Yu Xian**, China
59/C4 **Yu Xian**, China
61/J2 **Yuyao**, China
47/Q5 **Yuzhno-Sakhalinsk**, Rus.
55/N2 **Yuzhno-Sakhalinsk**, Rus.
41/K2 **Yuzhnyy Bug** (riv.), Ukr.
44/D2 **Yuzhnyy Bug** (riv.), Ukr.
46/C5 **Yuzhnyy Bug** (riv.), Ukr.
19/R10 **Yvelines** (dept.), Fr.
30/A6 **Yvelines** (dept.), Fr.
33/G3 **Yverdon**, Swi.
36/C4 **Yverdon**, Swi.
19/S10 **Yvette** (riv.), Fr.
30/B6 **Yvette** (riv.), Fr.
26/C3 **Yvoir**, Belg.
31/D3 **Yvoir**, Belg.
32/F1 **Yvoir**, Belg.
36/C4 **Yvonand**, Swi.
32/E3 **Yzeure**, Fr.

Z

54/D5 **Za** (riv.), China
60/C1 **Za** (riv.), China
75/N13 **Za** (riv.), Mor.
26/C2 **Zaandam**, Neth.
28/B4 **Zaandam**, Neth.
47/M5 **Zabaykal'sk**, Rus.
52/D6 **Zabīd**, Yem.
77/P5 **Zabīd**, Yem.
27/L2 **Ząbki**, Pol.
27/J3 **Ząbkowice Śląskie**, Pol.
39/F1 **Žabljak**, Yugo.
40/D4 **Žabljak**, Yugo.
53/H2 **Zābol**, Iran
27/J4 **Zábřeh**, Czh.
33/M2 **Zábřeh**, Czh.
18/E3 **Zabrze**, Pol.
27/K3 **Zabrze**, Pol.
44/A2 **Zabrze**, Pol.
46/B4 **Zabrze**, Pol.
102/D3 **Zacapa**, Guat.
101/M7 **Zacapoaxtla**, Mex.
101/E5 **Zacapú**, Mex.
100/E3 **Zacatecas** (state), Mex.
100/E4 **Zacatecas**, Mex.
88/F7 **Zacatecas**, Mex.
88/F7 **Zacatecas** (state), Mex.
102/D3 **Zacatecoluca**, ESal.
101/K8 **Zacatepec**, Mex.
102/C2 **Zacatepec**, Mex.
101/M7 **Zacatlán**, Mex.
93/K5 **Zachary**, La,US
97/F4 **Zachary**, La,US
101/F4 **Zacualtipán**, Mex.
102/B1 **Zacualtipán**, Mex.
102/D3 **Zaculeu**, Guat.
18/E4 **Zadar**, Cro.
33/L4 **Zadar**, Cro.
40/B3 **Zadar**, Cro.
65/B4 **Zadetkyi** (isl.), Burma
66/A2 **Zadetkyi** (isl.), Burma
54/D5 **Zadoi**, China
34/B3 **Zafra**, Sp.
27/H3 **Żagań**, Pol.
20/G4 **Žagarė**, Lith.
42/D4 **Žagarė**, Lith.
51/G3 **Zāgheh-ye Pā'īn**, Iran
38/A4 **Zaghwān** (gov.), Tun.
38/B4 **Zaghwān**, Tun.
75/W17 **Zaghwān** (gov.), Tun.
75/X17 **Zaghwān**, Tun.
39/H3 **Zagorá**, Gre.
33/L3 **Zagorjeob Savi**, Slov.
40/B2 **Zagorjeob Savi**, Slov.
18/E4 **Zagreb** (cap.), Cro.
33/M4 **Zagreb** (cap.), Cro.
40/C3 **Zagreb** (cap.), Cro.
46/F6 **Zagros** (mts.), Iran
51/F2 **Zagros** (mts.), Iran
52/E1 **Zagros** (mts.), Iran
48/F7 **Zāhedān**, Iran
53/H3 **Zāhedān**, Iran
62/C4 **Zahīrābād**, India
49/D3 **Zaḩlah**, Leb.
50/C3 **Zaḩlah**, Leb.
52/C2 **Zaḩlah**, Leb.
27/M4 **Záhony**, Hun.
40/F1 **Záhony**, Hun.
52/D5 **Zahrān**, SAr.
35/F2 **Zaidín**, Sp.
77/K7 **Zaire**
77/K7 **Zaire** (riv.), Congo, Zaire
74/E4 **Zaïre** (riv.), Congo, Zaire
74/E5 **Zaire** (Congo)
82/D1 **Zaire** (Congo)
40/F4 **Zaječar**, Yugo.
44/B4 **Zaječar**, Yugo.
47/L4 **Zakamensk**, Rus.
54/E1 **Zakamensk**, Rus.
51/F1 **Zakataly**, Azer.
39/G4 **Zakháro**, Gre.
51/E2 **Zākhū**, Iraq
52/D1 **Zākhū**, Iraq
39/G4 **Zákinthos**, Gre.
39/G4 **Zákinthos** (isl.), Gre.
27/K4 **Zakopane**, Pol.
77/J5 **Zakouma Nat'l Park**, Chad
39/J5 **Zakro** (ruins), Gre.
40/C2 **Zala** (co.), Hun.
40/C2 **Zala** (riv.), Hun.
40/C2 **Zalaegerszeg**, Hun.
34/C3 **Zalamea de la Serena**, Sp.
34/B4 **Zalamea la Real**, Sp.
55/J2 **Zalantun**, China
40/C2 **Zalaszentgrót**, Hun.
27/M5 **Zalău**, Rom.
40/F2 **Zalău**, Rom.
44/B3 **Zalău**, Rom.
33/L3 **Žalec**, Slov.
40/B2 **Žalec**, Slov.
77/P3 **Zalim**, SAr.
76/J2 **Zaltan** (well), Libya
28/C5 **Zaltbommel**, Neth.
60/B5 **Zalun**, Burma
63/G4 **Zalun**, Burma
57/H7 **Zama**, Japan
38/B5 **Zamālat As Sawāsī**, Tun.
74/F6 **Zambezi** (riv.), Afr.
82/F4 **Zambezi** (riv.), Afr.
82/D3 **Zambezi**, Zam.
74/E6 **Zambia**
82/E3 **Zambia**
67/F2 **Zamboanga City**, Phil.
68/B4 **Zamboanga City**, Phil.
27/M2 **Zambrów**, Pol.
42/D5 **Zambrów**, Pol.
44/B1 **Zambrów**, Pol.
35/P11 **Zambujal de Cima**, Port.
79/G3 **Zamfara** (riv.), Nga.
65/B3 **Zami** (riv.), Burma
65/D1 **Zamiao**, China
106/C4 **Zamora**, Ecu.
106/C4 **Zamora** (riv.), Ecu.
34/C2 **Zamora**, Sp.
100/E5 **Zamora de Hidalgo**, Mex.
27/M3 **Zamość**, Pol.
27/M3 **Zamość** (prov.), Pol.
44/B2 **Zamość**, Pol.
33/J3 **Zams**, Aus.
37/G3 **Zams**, Aus.
34/D3 **Záncara** (riv.), Sp.
28/A5 **Zandkreekdam** (dam), Neth.
28/B4 **Zandvoort**, Neth.
89/K4 **Zanesville**, Oh,US
94/D4 **Zanesville**, Oh,US
97/H2 **Zanesville**, Oh,US
59/C3 **Zanhuang**, China
46/E6 **Zanjān**, Iran
51/G2 **Zanjān**, Iran
51/G2 **Zanjān** (gov.), Iran
52/E1 **Zanjān**, Iran
92/E5 **Zanjón** (riv.), Mex
82/G2 **Zanzibar**, Tanz.
82/G2 **Zanzibar** (isl.), Tanz.
59/G3 **Zaoqiang**, China
57/G1 **Zaō-san** (mtn.), Japan
59/C4 **Zaoyang**, China
61/G1 **Zaoyang**, China
55/H5 **Zaozhuang**, China
59/D4 **Zaozhuang**, China
55/N2 **Zapadno-Sakhalin** (mts.), Rus.
26/G4 **Západočeský** (reg.), Czh.
33/K2 **Západočeský** (reg.), Czh.
27/J4 **Západoslovenský** (reg.), Slvk.
109/B4 **Zapala**, Arg.
106/E8 **Zapaleri** (peak), Arg.
109/C1 **Zapaleri** (peak), Arg.
103/F1 **Zapata** (pen.), Cuba
101/F3 **Zapata**, Tx,US
96/D5 **Zapata**, Tx,US
106/D2 **Zapatoca**, Col.
103/H4 **Zapatosa, Ciénaga de** (lake), Col.
20/J1 **Zapolyarnyy**, Rus.
42/F1 **Zapolyarnyy**, Rus.
19/G4 **Zaporozh'ye**, Ukr.
46/D5 **Zaporozh'ye**, Ukr.
44/E3 **Zaporozh'ye Obl.**, Ukr.
38/D2 **Zapponeta**, It.
33/L4 **Zaprešić**, Cro.
40/B3 **Zaprešić**, Cro.
44/F5 **Zara**, Turk.
50/D2 **Zara**, Turk.
103/H5 **Zaragoza**, Col.
106/D2 **Zaragoza**, Col.
101/E2 **Zaragoza**, Mex.
101/E4 **Zaragoza**, Mex.
101/M7 **Zaragoza**, Mex.
96/C4 **Zaragoza**, Mex
51/J4 **Zarand**, Iran
53/G2 **Zarand**, Iran
79/H4 **Zaranda** (hill), Nga.
20/H5 **Zarasai**, Lith.
42/E5 **Zarasai**, Lith.
109/E3 **Zárate**, Arg.
32/B5 **Zarauz**, Sp.
34/D1 **Zarauz**, Sp.
106/E2 **Zaraza**, Ven.
52/F2 **Zarch**, Iran
51/G3 **Zard** (mtn.), Iran
52/F2 **Zard** (mtn.), Iran
20/J2 **Zarechensk**, Rus.
51/H4 **Zargān**, Iran
52/F3 **Zargān**, Iran
76/G5 **Zaria**, Nga.
79/G4 **Zaria**, Nga.
53/H2 **Zarmast** (pass), Afg.
41/G3 **Zărneşti**, Rom.
44/C3 **Zărneşti**, Rom.
27/K4 **Žarnovica**, Slvk.
40/D1 **Žarnovica**, Slvk.
39/J5 **Zarós**, Gre.
51/F2 **Zarrīneh** (riv.), Iran
51/G3 **Zarrin Shahr**, Iran
27/J4 **Záruby** (peak), Slvk.
40/C1 **Záruby** (peak), Slvk.
27/H3 **Żary**, Pol.
34/B3 **Zarza la Mayor**, Sp.
34/A1 **Zas**, Sp.
20/H4 **Zasa**, Lat.
53/L2 **Zāskar** (range), India
64/D1 **Zāskar** (range), India
42/E5 **Zaslavl'**, Bela.
44/C1 **Zaslavl'**, Bela.
80/D3 **Zastron**, SAfr.
27/G3 **Žatec**, Czh.
33/K1 **Žatec**, Czh.
41/K2 **Zatoka**, Ukr.
49/F8 **Zavdi'el**, Isr.
30/D2 **Zaventem**, Belg.
41/H4 **Zavet**, Bul.
40/D3 **Zavidovići**, Bosn.
47/N4 **Zavitinsk**, Rus.
55/K1 **Zavitinsk**, Rus.
81/F2 **Závora** (pt.), Moz.
27/K3 **Zawadzkie**, Pol.
27/K3 **Zawiercie**, Pol.
44/A2 **Zawiercie**, Pol.
54/D6 **Zaya** (riv.), China
46/J5 **Zaysan**, Kaz.
46/J5 **Zaysan** (lake), Kaz.
48/H5 **Zaysan** (lake), Kaz.
54/A2 **Zaysan**, Kaz.
54/A2 **Zaysan** (lake), Kaz.
54/D6 **Zayü**, China
60/C2 **Zayü**, China
60/C2 **Zayü** (riv.), China
63/G2 **Zayü**, China
63/G2 **Zayü** (riv.), China
103/G1 **Zaza** (riv.), Cuba
104/D5 **Zazárida**, Ven.
27/H2 **Zbąszyń**, Pol.
27/H4 **Žďár nad Sázavou**, Czh.
33/L2 **Žďár nad Sázavou**, Czh.
27/K3 **Zduńska Wola**, Pol.
75/R16 **Zeddine** (riv.), Alg.
30/C1 **Zedelgem**, Belg.
26/B3 **Zeebrugge**, Belg.
73/C4 **Zeehan**, Austl.
28/A5 **Zeeland** (prov.), Neth.
28/C5 **Zeeland**, Neth.
94/C3 **Zeeland**, Mi,US
80/D2 **Zeerust**, SAfr.
80/P12 **Zeerust**, SAfr.
82/E6 **Zeerust**, SAfr.
28/C4 **Zeewolde**, Neth.
49/D3 **Zefat**, Isr.
52/C2 **Zefat**, Isr.
27/L2 **Zegrzyńskie** (lake), Pol.
27/G2 **Zehdenick**, Ger.
70/E4 **Zeil** (peak), Austl.
26/C2 **Zeist**, Neth.
28/C4 **Zeist**, Neth.
26/G3 **Zeitz**, Ger.
49/F8 **Zekharya**, Isr.
28/B6 **Zele**, Belg.
30/D1 **Zele**, Belg.
20/K2 **Zelenoborskiy**, Rus.
19/H3 **Zelenodol'sk**, Rus.
43/L5 **Zelenodol'sk**, Rus.
41/L2 **Zelenodol'sk**, Ukr.
20/J3 **Zelenogorsk**, Rus.
42/F3 **Zelenogorsk**, Rus.
43/U6 **Zelenogorsk**, Rus.
43/X8 **Zelenograd**, Rus.
27/L1 **Zelenogradsk**, Rus.
45/G3 **Zelenokumsk**, Rus.
28/D4 **Zelhem**, Neth.
31/G3 **Zell**, Ger.
36/D3 **Zell**, Swi.
37/E3 **Zell**, Swi.
36/E1 **Zell am Harmersbach**, Ger.
33/K3 **Zell am See**, Aus.
40/A2 **Zell am See**, Aus.
37/E2 **Zellersee** (lake), Ger.
36/D2 **Zell in Wiesental**, Ger.
27/K3 **Zelów**, Pol.
31/G4 **Zeltingen-Rachtig**, Ger.
40/B2 **Zeltweg**, Aus.
42/E5 **Zel'va**, Bela.
44/C1 **Zel'va**, Bela.
42/E5 **Želva**, Lith.
28/A6 **Zelzate**, Belg.
30/C1 **Zelzate**, Belg.
27/L1 **Žemaičiu Naumiestis**, Lith.
38/B4 **Zembra** (isls.), Tun.
39/H1 **Zemen**, Bul.
40/F4 **Zemen**, Bul.
77/L6 **Zemio**, CAfr.
31/F4 **Zemmer**, Ger.
75/R16 **Zemmora**, Alg.
101/N7 **Zempoala**, Mex.
101/Q10 **Zempoala** (mt.), Mex.
102/C2 **Zempoaltepec, Cerro** (mtn.), Mex.
28/B7 **Zemst**, Belg.
30/D2 **Zemst**, Belg.
90/C5 **Zenia**, Ca,US
92/B2 **Zenia**, Ca,US
40/C3 **Zenica**, Bosn.
99/C3 **Zenith**, Wa,US
33/J2 **Zenn** (riv.), Ger.
91/H2 **Zenon Park**, Sk,Can
56/C3 **Zentsūji**, Japan
40/D3 **Žepče**, Bosn.
75/S15 **Zeralda**, Alg.
75/L13 **Zerga** (lake), Mor.
36/D5 **Zermatt**, Swi.
37/G4 **Zernez**, Swi.
29/H2 **Zernien**, Ger.
44/G3 **Zernograd**, Rus.
40/E5 **Zerqan**, Alb.
51/E1 **Zestafoni**, Geo.
86/F1 **Zeta** (lake), NW,Can
60/A2 **Zêtang**, China
26/D2 **Zetel**, Ger.
29/E2 **Zetel**, Ger.
29/G2 **Zeven**, Ger.
28/D5 **Zevenaar**, Neth.
28/B5 **Zevenbergen**, Neth.
39/H4 **Zevgolatión**, Gre.
47/N4 **Zeya**, Rus.
47/N4 **Zeya** (res.), Rus.
47/N4 **Zeya** (riv.), Rus.
48/M4 **Zeya** (res.), Rus.
55/K1 **Zeya**, Rus.
55/K1 **Zeya** (res.), Rus.
55/K1 **Zeya** (riv.), Rus.
55/K1 **Zeya-Bureya** (plain), China
47/N4 **Zeya-Bureya** (plain), Rus.
50/A2 **Zeytindağ**, Turk.
34/A3 **Zêzere** (riv.), Port.
49/D2 **Zgharta**, Leb.
50/C3 **Zgharta**, Leb.
52/C2 **Zgharta**, Leb.
27/K3 **Zgierz**, Pol.
27/H3 **Zgorzelec**, Pol.
44/C1 **Zhabinka**, Bela.
65/E1 **Zhaixu**, China
55/K2 **Zhalantun**, China
54/G4 **Zhang** (riv.), China
59/B5 **Zhang** (riv.), China
61/F2 **Zhang** (riv.), China
61/G3 **Zhang** (riv.), China
59/C5 **Zhangdu** (lake), China
55/K3 **Zhangguangcai** (mts.), China
54/G3 **Zhanghei**, China
59/C2 **Zhanghei**, China
65/E1 **Zhanghuang**, China
47/M5 **Zhangjiakou**, China
54/G3 **Zhangjiakou**, China
59/C2 **Zhangjiakou**, China
59/D3 **Zhangqiu**, China
59/D3 **Zhangwei** (riv.), China
54/E4 **Zhangye**, China
61/H3 **Zhangzhou**, China
58/B3 **Zhangzi** (isl.), China
59/C3 **Zhangzi**, China
59/D3 **Zhanhua**, China
61/F4 **Zhanjiang**, China
63/K3 **Zhanjiang**, China
55/K2 **Zhaodong**, China
54/F5 **Zhaojiachang**, China
63/H2 **Zhaojue**, China
63/K3 **Zhaoping**, China
61/G4 **Zhaoqing**, China
63/K3 **Zhaoqing**, China
60/D3 **Zhaotong**, China
63/H2 **Zhaotong**, China
54/G4 **Zhao Xian**, China
59/C3 **Zhao Xian**, China
55/J4 **Zhaoyuan**, China
55/K2 **Zhaoyuan**, China
59/E3 **Zhaoyuan**, China
55/K2 **Zhaozhou**, China
63/G1 **Zhaxizê**, China
59/C4 **Zhecheng**, China
60/D2 **Zhedou** (pass), China
59/D5 **Zhejiang** (prov.), China
59/L9 **Zhejiang** (prov.), China
61/H2 **Zhejiang** (prov.), China
46/G2 **Zhelaniya** (cape), Rus.
27/L1 **Zheleznodorozhnyy**, Rus.
42/D5 **Zheleznodorozhnyy**, Rus.
43/L3 **Zheleznodorozhnyy**, Rus.
43/Y9 **Zheleznodorozhnyy**, Rus.
46/F3 **Zheleznodorozhnyy**, Rus.
18/G3 **Zheleznogorsk**, Rus.
44/E1 **Zheleznogorsk**, Rus.
46/D4 **Zheleznogorsk**, Rus.
47/L4 **Zheleznogorsk-Ilimskiy**, Rus.
61/J2 **Zhelin**, China
61/F3 **Zhenbao** (mtn.), China
60/E3 **Zhenfeng**, China
63/J2 **Zhenfeng Bouyeizu Miaozu Zizhixian**, China
59/C3 **Zhengding**, China
54/H3 **Zhenglan**, China
59/B4 **Zhengning**, China
54/G5 **Zhengyang**, China
59/C4 **Zhengyang**, China
61/G1 **Zhengyang**, China
54/G5 **Zhengzhou**, China
59/C4 **Zhengzhou**, China
55/H5 **Zhenjiang**, China
59/D4 **Zhenjiang**, China
61/H1 **Zhenjiang**, China
63/G3 **Zhenkang**, China
55/J2 **Zhenlai**, China
63/J2 **Zhenning Bouyeizu Miaozu Zizhixian**, China
54/F5 **Zhenping**, China
54/G5 **Zhenping**, China
59/C4 **Zhenping**, China
59/C4 **Zhentou** (riv.), China
59/B3 **Zhenwu Shan** (mtn.), China
63/H2 **Zhenxiong**, China
63/H3 **Zhenyuan**, China
54/G5 **Zhicheng**, China
59/B5 **Zhicheng**, China
61/F2 **Zhicheng**, China
45/J1 **Zhigulevsk**, Rus.
61/F3 **Zhijiag**, China
61/F2 **Zhijiang**, China
63/J2 **Zhijin**, China
42/D5 **Zhilino**, Rus.
45/J4 **Zhiloy** (isl.), Azer.
51/G1 **Zhiloy** (isl.), Azer.
18/F3 **Zhitomir**, Ukr.
44/D2 **Zhitomir**, Ukr.
46/C4 **Zhitomir**, Ukr.
44/C2 **Zhitomir Obl.**, Ukr.
44/D1 **Zhlobin**, Bela.
44/D2 **Zhmerinka**, Ukr.
53/J2 **Zhob**, Pak.
53/J2 **Zhob** (riv.), Pak.
42/F5 **Zhodino**, Bela.
44/D1 **Zhodino**, Bela.
47/R2 **Zhokhov** (isl.), Rus.
60/E2 **Zhongjiang**, China
59/B4 **Zhongnan Shan** (mtn.), China
61/G4 **Zhongshan**, China
63/K3 **Zhongshan**, China
61/F2 **Zhong Xian**, China
59/C5 **Zhongxiang**, China
61/G2 **Zhongxiang**, China
54/G4 **Zhongyang**, China
59/B3 **Zhongyang**, China
54/G5 **Zhoukou**, China
59/C4 **Zhoukou**, China
55/J5 **Zhoushan** (isls.), China
59/E5 **Zhoushan** (isls.), China
61/J2 **Zhoushan** (isl.), China
41/L2 **Zhovtnevoye**, Ukr.
44/E3 **Zhovtnevoye**, Ukr.
55/J4 **Zhuanghe**, China
58/B3 **Zhuanghe**, China
59/E3 **Zhuanghe**, China
55/H4 **Zhucheng**, China
59/D4 **Zhucheng**, China
61/G4 **Zhuhai**, China
63/K3 **Zhuhai**, China
61/J2 **Zhujia** (isl.), China
44/E1 **Zhukovka**, Rus.
42/H5 **Zhukovskiy**, Rus.
43/Y9 **Zhukovskiy**, Rus.
44/F1 **Zhukovskiy**, Rus.
54/G5 **Zhumadian**, China
59/C4 **Zhumadian**, China
54/H3 **Zhuolu**, China
59/C2 **Zhuolu**, China
59/G6 **Zhuolu**, China
54/H4 **Zhuo Xian**, China
59/G7 **Zhuo Xian**, China
59/C2 **Zhuozi**, China
54/G5 **Zhushan**, China
59/B4 **Zhushan**, China
61/F1 **Zhushan**, China
54/F5 **Zhuxi**, China
59/B4 **Zhuxi**, China
61/F1 **Zhuxi**, China
61/G3 **Zhuzhou**, China
63/K2 **Zhuzhou**, China
68/A2 **Zhuzhou**, China
54/D5 **Zi** (riv.), China
61/F3 **Zi** (riv.), China
55/H4 **Zibo**, China
59/D3 **Zibo**, China
60/B4 **Zibyu** (hills), Burma
27/J3 **Ziębice**, Pol.
27/H2 **Zielona Góra** (prov.), Pol.
27/H3 **Zielona Góra**, Pol.
37/G1 **Ziemetshausen**, Ger.
29/G6 **Zierenberg**, Ger.
28/A5 **Zierikzee**, Neth.
49/B4 **Ziftá**, Egypt
50/D1 **Zigana** (pass), Turk.
63/G4 **Zigon**, Burma
60/E2 **Zigong**, China
63/H2 **Zigong**, China
54/G5 **Zigui**, China
59/B5 **Zigui**, China
61/F2 **Zigui**, China
76/B5 **Ziguinchor**, Sen.
78/A3 **Ziguinchor**, Sen.
78/A3 **Ziguinchor** (reg.), Sen.
101/E5 **Zihuatanejo**, Mex.
59/G7 **Zijingguan**, China
59/B3 **Zijing Shan** (mtn.), China
49/F6 **Zikhron Ya'aqov**, Isr.
44/E4 **Zile**, Turk.
50/C1 **Zile**, Turk.
27/K4 **Žilina**, Slvk.
44/A2 **Žilina**, Slvk.
76/J2 **Zillah**, Libya
33/J3 **Ziller** (riv.), Aus.
36/D2 **Zillisheim**, Fr.
47/L4 **Zima**, Rus.
54/E1 **Zima**, Rus.
102/B2 **Zimatlán**, Mex.
82/F2 **Zimba**, Tanz.
82/E4 **Zimba**, Zam.
74/E6 **Zimbabwe**
82/E4 **Zimbabwe**
41/G4 **Zimnicea**, Rom.
44/C4 **Zimnicea**, Rom.
39/K1 **Zimnitsa**, Bul.
101/E5 **Zinapécuaro de Figueroa**, Mex.
82/F5 **Zinave Nat'l Park**, Moz.
76/G5 **Zinder**, Niger
79/H3 **Zinder**, Niger
79/H3 **Zinder** (dept.), Niger
52/E6 **Zinjibār**, Yem.
99/Q15 **Zion**, Il,US
88/D4 **Zion Nat'l Park**, Ut,US
92/D3 **Zion Nat'l Park**, Ut,US
101/E5 **Zirándaro**, Mex.
40/C2 **Zirc**, Hun.
33/L5 **Žirje** (isl.), Cro.
40/B4 **Žirje** (isl.), Cro.
33/J3 **Zirl**, Aus.
37/H3 **Zirl**, Aus.
63/F2 **Ziro**, India
40/D1 **Žitava** (riv.), Czech.
27/K5 **Žitava** (riv.), Slvk.
27/H3 **Zittau**, Ger.
40/D3 **Živinice**, Bosn.
59/B4 **Ziwu** (mtn.), China
61/G3 **Zixing**, China
63/K2 **Zixing**, China
59/D3 **Ziya** (riv.), China
59/H7 **Ziya** (riv.), China
61/F1 **Ziyang**, China
61/H3 **Ziyundong** (mtn.), China
60/E3 **Ziyun Miaozu Bouyeizu Zizhixian**, China
41/F2 **Zlatna**, Rom.
39/J2 **Zlatograd**, Bul.
41/G5 **Zlatograd**, Bul.
44/C4 **Zlatograd**, Bul.
39/G1 **Zlatorsko** (lake), Yugo.
40/E4 **Zlatorsko** (lake), Yugo.
43/N5 **Zlatoust**, Rus.
46/F4 **Zlatoust**, Rus.
18/E4 **Zlin**, Czh.
27/J4 **Zlin**, Czh.
27/J2 **Złocieniec**, Pol.
40/E3 **Zlot**, Yugo.
27/H3 **Złotoryja**, Pol.
27/J2 **Złotów**, Pol.
40/D3 **Žmajevo**, Yugo.
27/J3 **Żmigród**, Pol.
44/E2 **Znamenka**, Ukr.
27/L1 **Znamensk**, Rus.
27/J2 **Żnin**, Pol.
44/A1 **Żnin**, Pol.
27/J4 **Znojmo**, Czh.
33/M2 **Znojmo**, Czh.
101/Q10 **Zocálo**, Mex.
28/B6 **Zoersel**, Belg.
31/D1 **Zoersel**, Belg.
26/C2 **Zoetermeer**, Neth.
28/B4 **Zoetermeer**, Neth.
33/G3 **Zofingen**, Swi.
36/D3 **Zofingen**, Swi.
63/G2 **Zogang**, China
39/L7 **Zográfos**, Gre.
51/G4 **Zohreh** (riv.), Iran
52/F2 **Zohreh** (riv.), Iran
37/E3 **Zollikon**, Swi.
44/C2 **Zolochev**, Ukr.
44/E2 **Zolochëv**, Ukr.
44/E2 **Zolotonosha**, Ukr.
82/G4 **Zomba**, Malw.
24/B6 **Zone** (pt.), UK
101/N8 **Zongolica**, Mex.
41/K5 **Zonguldak**, Turk.
41/K5 **Zonguldak** (prov.), Turk.
44/D4 **Zonguldak**, Turk.
44/E4 **Zonguldak** (prov.), Turk.
50/B1 **Zonguldak**, Turk.
50/C1 **Zonguldak** (prov.), Turk.
63/F2 **Zongxoi**, China
59/D5 **Zongyang**, China
61/H2 **Zongyang**, China
28/C7 **Zonhoven**, Belg.
31/E2 **Zonhoven**, Belg.
30/B2 **Zonnebeke**, Belg.
38/A2 **Zonza**, Fr.
101/L7 **Zoquiapan y Anexas Nat'l Park**, Mex.
102/B2 **Zoquitlán**, Mex.
60/A4 **Zorarganj**, Bang.
29/H5 **Zorge** (riv.), Ger.
34/C3 **Zorita**, Sp.
26/D4 **Zorn** (riv.), Fr.
33/G2 **Zorn** (riv.), Fr.
31/G6 **Zorn** (riv.), Ger.
31/H4 **Zornheim**, Ger.
106/B4 **Zorritos**, Peru
30/C2 **Zottegem**, Belg.
79/F5 **Zou** (prov.), Ben.
76/J3 **Zouar**, Chad
76/C3 **Zouîrât**, Mrta.
79/E4 **Zoundwéogo** (prov.), Burk.
59/D3 **Zouping**, China
80/L10 **Zout** (riv.), SAfr.
59/D4 **Zou Xian**, China
40/E3 **Zrenjanin**, Yugo.
44/B3 **Zrenjanin**, Yugo.
34/D4 **Zubia**, Sp.
49/G6 **Zubūbā**, WBnk.
37/E5 **Zucchero, Monte** (peak), Swi.
37/H4 **Zuckerhütl** (peak), Aus.
33/H3 **Zug**, Swi.
37/E3 **Zug**, Swi.
37/E3 **Zug** (canton), Swi.
76/C3 **Zug**, WSah.
77/P5 **Zugar** (isl.), Yem.
45/G4 **Zugdidi**, Geo.
33/H3 **Zuger See** (lake), Sw
37/E3 **Zugersee** (lake), Swi.
26/F5 **Zugspitze** (peak), Ge
33/J3 **Zugspitze** (peak), Ge
37/G3 **Zugspitze** (peak), Ge
28/A6 **Zuidbeveland** (isl.), Neth.
28/C4 **Zuidelijk Flevoland** (polder), Neth.
28/D2 **Zuidhorn**, Neth.
28/D2 **Zuidlaardermeer** (lake), Neth.
28/D2 **Zuidlaren**, Neth.
28/C6 **Zuid-Willemsvaart** (can.), Belg.
28/D3 **Zuidwolde**, Neth.
30/C1 **Zuienkerke**, Belg.
34/C3 **Zújar** (res.), Sp.
34/C3 **Zújar** (riv.), Sp.
34/D4 **Zújar**, Sp.
103/H4 **Zulia** (riv.), Col., Ven.
103/H4 **Zulia** (state), Ven.
104/C5 **Zulia** (state), Ven.
31/F2 **Zülpich**, Ger.
30/C2 **Zulte**, Belg.
81/E2 **Zululand** (reg.), SAfr.
32/B5 **Zumárraga**, Sp.
34/D1 **Zumárraga**, Sp.
82/F4 **Zumbo**, Moz.
101/F5 **Zumpango de Ocampo**, Mex.
101/K7 **Zumpango de Ocampo**, Mex.
50/B2 **Zümrütkaya**, Turk.
28/B6 **Zundert**, Neth.
55/H3 **Zunhua**, China
59/D2 **Zunhua**, China
59/H6 **Zunhua**, China
92/E4 **Zuni** (dry riv.), Az, NM,US
92/E4 **Zuni**, NM,US
96/A3 **Zuni** (mts.), NM,US
61/E3 **Zunyi**, China
63/J2 **Zunyi**, China
61/E4 **Zuo** (riv.), China
63/J3 **Zuo** (riv.), China
65/D1 **Zuo Jiang** (riv.), China
54/F5 **Zuolongqou**, China
53/G2 **Zuoquan**, China
54/G4 **Zuoyun**, China
59/C3 **Zuoyun**, China
37/F4 **Zuoz**, Swi.
40/D3 **Županja**, Cro.
52/D6 **Zuqar, Jabal** (isl.), Yemen
39/G1 **Žur**, Yugo.
40/E4 **Žur**, Yugo.
51/F3 **Zurbāţīyah**, Iraq
52/E2 **Zurbāţīyah**, Iraq
18/D4 **Zürich**, Swi.
33/H3 **Zürich**, Swi.
37/E2 **Zürich** (canton), Swi.
37/E3 **Zürich**, Swi.
33/H3 **Zürichsee** (lake), Swi.
37/E3 **Zürichsee** (lake), Swi.
27/K2 **Żuromin**, Pol.
37/E2 **Zurzach**, Swi.
33/J2 **Zusam** (riv.), Ger.
37/G1 **Zusam** (riv.), Ger.
57/H7 **Zushi**, Japan
26/D2 **Zutphen**, Neth.
28/D4 **Zutphen**, Neth.
76/H1 **Zuwārah**, Libya
43/L4 **Zuyevka**, Rus.
40/D4 **Zvijesda Nat'l Park**, Yugo.
82/F5 **Zvishavane**, Zim.
27/K4 **Zvolen**, Slvk.
44/A2 **Zvolen**, Slvk.
40/D3 **Zvorničko** (lake), Yugo.
40/D3 **Zvornik**, Bosn.
32/D3 **Zwarte Meer** (lake), Neth.
28/D3 **Zwartsluis**, Neth.
76/D6 **Zwedru**, Libr.
31/G5 **Zweibrücken**, Ger.
33/G2 **Zweibrücken**, Ger.
36/D4 **Zweisimmen**, Swi.
29/G6 **Zwesten**, Ger.
30/C2 **Zwevegem**, Belg.
26/G3 **Zwickau**, Ger.
33/K1 **Zwickau**, Ger.
26/G3 **Zwickauer Mulde** (riv.), Ger.
28/B6 **Zwijndrecht**, Belg.
28/B5 **Zwijndrecht**, Neth.
29/F2 **Zwischenahn**, Ger.
29/F2 **Zwischenahner Me** (lake), Ger.
37/F3 **Zwischenwasser**, Aus.
27/L3 **Zwoleń**, Pol.
26/D2 **Zwolle**, Neth.
28/D4 **Zwolle**, Neth.
27/K2 **Żychlin**, Pol.
27/L2 **Żyrardów**, Pol.
46/J5 **Zyryanovsk**, Kaz.
54/B2 **Zyryanovsk**, Kaz.
45/J3 **Zyudev** (isl.), Rus.
27/K4 **Żywiec**, Pol.
44/A2 **Żywiec**, Pol.